WORLDCOMP'13
July 22-25, 2013
Las Vegas Nevada, USA
www.world-academy-of-science.org

PROCEEDINGS OF THE 2013 INTERNATIONAL CONFERENCE ON IMAGE PROCESSING, COMPUTER VISION, & PATTERN RECOGNITION

IPCV 2013

Volume I & II

Editors

Hamid R. Arabnia
Leonidas Deligiannidis, Joan Lu
Fernando G. Tinetti, Jane You

Associate Editors

George Jandieri
Gerald Schaefer, Ashu M. G. Solo
Vladimir Volkov

(An Imprint of Laxmi Publications Pvt. Ltd.)
An ISO 9001:2008 Company
BENGALURU • CHENNAI • COCHIN • GUWAHATI • HYDERABAD
JALANDHAR • KOLKATA • LUCKNOW • MUMBAI • RANCHI • NEW DELHI
BOSTON (USA) • ACCRA (GHANA) • NAIROBI (KENYA)

This set of volumes contains papers presented at The 2013 International Conference on Image Processing, Computer Vision, & Pattern Recognition (IPCV'13). Their inclusion in this publication does not necessarily constitute endorsements by editors or by the publisher.

Branches

	Branch	Telephone	
✆	Bengaluru	080-26 75 69 30	
✆	Chennai	044-24 34 47 26,	24 35 95 07
✆	Cochin	0484-237 70 04,	405 13 03
✆	Guwahati	0361-254 36 69,	251 38 81
✆	Hyderabad	040-27 55 53 83,	27 55 53 93
✆	Jalandhar	0181-222 12 72	
✆	Kolkata	033-22 27 43 84	
✆	Lucknow	0522-220 99 16	
✆	Mumbai	022-24 91 54 15,	24 92 78 69
✆	Ranchi	0651-220 44 64	

Published in India by

An ISO 9001:2008 Company
113, GOLDEN HOUSE, DARYAGANJ,
NEW DELHI - 110002, INDIA
Telephone : 91-11-4353 2500, 4353 2501
Fax : 91-11-2325 2572, 4353 2528
www.laxmipublications.com info@laxmipublications.com

C—
Printed at:

Foreword

It gives us great pleasure to introduce this collection of papers to be presented at the 2013 International Conference on Image Processing, Computer Vision, and Pattern Recognition (IPCV'13), July 22 through 25, 2013, at The New Tropicana Hotel, Las Vegas, USA.

An important mission of the World Congress in Computer Science, Computer Engineering, and Applied Computing (a federated congress to which this conference is affiliated with) includes *"Providing a unique platform for a diverse community of constituents composed of scholars, researchers, developers, educators, and practitioners. The Congress makes concerted effort to reach out to participants affiliated with diverse entities (such as: universities, institutions, corporations, government agencies, and research centers/labs) from all over the world. The congress also attempts to connect participants from institutions that have* ***teaching*** *as their main mission with those who are affiliated with institutions that have* ***research*** *as their main mission. The congress uses a quota system to achieve its institution and geography diversity objectives."* By any definition of diversity, this congress is among the most diverse scientific meeting in USA. We are proud to report that this federated congress has authors and participants from 82 different nations representing variety of personal and scientific experiences that arise from differences in culture and values. As can be seen (see below), the program committee of this conference as well as the program committee of all other tracks of the federated congress are as diverse as its authors and participants.

The program committee would like to thank all those who submitted papers for consideration. About 57% of the submissions were from outside the United States. Each submitted paper was peer-reviewed by two experts in the field for originality, significance, clarity, impact, and soundness. In cases of contradictory recommendations, a member of the conference program committee was charged to make the final decision; often, this involved seeking help from additional referees. In addition, papers whose authors included a member of the conference program committee were evaluated using the double-blinded review process. One exception to the above evaluation process was for papers that were submitted directly to chairs/organizers of pre-approved sessions/workshops; in these cases, the chairs/organizers were responsible for the evaluation of such submissions. The overall paper acceptance rate for regular papers was 30%; 12% of the remaining papers were accepted as poster papers (at the time of this writing, we had not yet received the acceptance rate for a few individual tracks.)

We are very grateful to the many colleagues who offered their services in organizing the conference. In particular, we would like to thank the members of the Program Committee of IPCV'13, members of the congress Steering Committee, and members of the committees of federated congress tracks that have topics within the scope of IPCV. Many individuals listed below, will be requested after the conference to provide their expertise and services for selecting papers for publication (extended versions) in journal special issues as well as for publication in a set of research books (to be prepared for publishers including: Springer, Elsevier, BMC, and others).

- *Dr. Alireza Abbasi; School of Engineering and Information Technology, University of New South Wales (UNSW), Canberra, Australia*
- *Dr. Selim Aissi (World Congress Steering Committee); formerly, Chief Strategist - Security, Intel Corp., USA; Senior Business Leader & Head of Global Enterprise Security Architecture, Visa Corporation, USA*
- *Prof. Babak Akhgar (World Congress Steering Committee); Fellow of the British Computer Society, CITP; Professor of Informatics; Co-Director of CENTRIC (Centre of Excellence in Terrorism, Resilience, Intelligence & organised Crime research), Sheffield Hallam University, Sheffield, UK*
- *Prof. Hussain Al-Asaad (PDPTA); Senior Member, IEEE; University of California at Davis, Davis, California, USA*
- *Dr. Fahad Al-Harby (EEE); The National Centre for Financial & Economic Information, Ministry of Finance, Riyadh, Saudi Arabia*
- *Prof. Nizar Al-Holou (World Congress Steering Committee); Professor and Chair, Electrical and Computer Engineering Department; Vice Chair, IEEE/SEM-Computer Chapter; University of Detroit Mercy, Detroit, Michigan, USA*
- *Dr. Haider M. AlSabbagh (ICAI); University of Basra, Iraq*

Mathematics and Statistics Department UMaine; Cooperating Professor School of Policy & International Affairs UMaine; University of Maine, Orono, Maine, USA

- *Prof. Gonzalo Pajares Martinsanz; Facultad de Informatica, Universidad Complutense de Madrid, Spain*
- *Dr. Sara Moein; Editorial Board, International Journal of Science and Technology; Faculty of Engineering, MultiMedia University, Malaysia*
- *Dr. Ali Mostafaeipour; Industrial Engineering Department, Yazd University, Iran*
- *Dr. Saurabh Mukherjee; Associate Professor, Department of Computer Science, Banasthali University, Banasthali, Rajasthan, India*
- *Dr. Josefa Mula (ICAI); Deputy/Sub Director, Degree programs in Educational Innovation and Quality in the Higher Polytechnic School of Alcoy; Polytechnic University of Valencia, Spain; Universitat Politecnica de Valencia, Spain*
- *Dr. Asoke Nath (EEE + FCS), Department of Computer Science, St. Xavier's College, India*
- *Prof. Noel De Palma (GCA + PDPTA); Associate Vice President for Research, Computer Science; Leader, ERODS Research, LIG Labs.; Board of Directors, OW2 Consortium; Department of Computer Science; University Joseph Fourier (UJF), Grenoble, France*
- *Prof. G. N. Pandey (World Congress Steering Committee); Vice-Chancellor, Arunachal University of Studies, Arunachal Pradesh, India; Adjunct Professor, Indian Institute of Information Technology, Allahabad, India*
- *Prof. James J. (Jong Hyuk) Park (World Congress Steering Committee); Professor of Computer Science and Engineering, Seoul National University of Science and Technology (SeoulTech), Korea; President, KITCS; President, FTRA; Editor-in-Chiefs: HCIS, JoC and IJITCC Journals*
- *Dr. Satish Penmatsa; Computer Science, University of Maryland - Eastern Shore, Maryland, USA*
- *Prof. Raul Poler (ICAI); Director, Research Centre on Production Management and Engineering, Polytechnic University of Valencia, Spain*
- *Prof. R. Ponalagusamy; Department of Mathematics, National Institute of Technology, Tiruchirappalli, India*
- *Prof. Junfeng Qu; Clayton State University, Morrow, Georgia, USA*
- *Prof. B. V. A. N. S. S. Prabhakar Rao (ICAI + SERP); School of Computing Science and Engineering, VIT University, Chennai Campus, India*
- *Dr. Gerald Schaefer (Session Chair, IPCV); Loughborough University, United Kingdom*
- *Dr. Liang Shi; Senior Researcher, McAfee, USA*
- *Dr. Zhefu Shi (PDPTA + MSV); Microsoft Corporation, Redmond, Washington, USA*
- *Dr. Kok Swee Sim; Faculty of Engineering and Technology, Jalan Ayer Keroh Lama, Melaka, Malaysia*
- *Ashu M. G. Solo, (Publicity Chair); Fellow of British Computer Society, Principal/R&D Engineer, Maverick Technologies America Inc., USA*
- *Dr. Jiao Tao (ICAI); Oracle USA, Redwood City, California, USA*
- *Prof. Fernando G. Tinetti (World Congress Steering Committee); School of Computer Science, Universidad Nacional de La Plata, La Plata, Argentina; Co-editor, Journal of CS & Technology (JCS&T)*
- *Dr. Predrag Tosic (World Congress Steering Committee); Microsoft, Washington, USA*
- *Dr. Vinay Vaidya; CTO and Vice President, Center for Research in Engineering Sciences and Technology (CREST), KPIT Cummins Infosystems Limited, Pune, India*
- *Prof. Vladimir Volkov (World Congress Steering Committee & Vice-Chair of IPCV); The Bonch-Bruevich State University of Telecommunications, Saint-Petersburg, Russia*
- *Prof. Patrick Wang; Fellow of IAPR, ISIBM, WASE; Zijiang Chair Professor, ECNU, Shanghai and NTUST, Taipei, Taiwan; Founding President and CEO, Wang Teknowlogy Lab.; MIT Research Consultant; Harvard University, Adj. Faculty, USA; Northeastern University, Boston, MA, USA*
- *Dr. Wei Wei (GCA + ICOMP + ICWN); School of Computer Science and Engineering, Xi'an University of Technology, Xi'an, P. R. China*
- *Prof. Jongwook Woo; Director, High-Performance Information Computing Center (HiPiC), Computer Information Systems Department, California State University, Los Angeles, California, USA*
- *Dr. Qiang Xu; Senior Lecturer, School of Science and Engineering, Teesside University, UK; UMIST (Institute of Science and Technology), The University of Manchester, UK; University of Huddersfield, UK*
- *Prof. Jane You; The Hong Kong Polytechnic University, Hong Kong*

As Sponsors-at-large, partners, and/or organizers each of the followings (separated by semicolons) provided help for at least one track of the World Congress: Aldebaran Robotics Inc., USA (http://www.aldebaran-robotics.com); Altera Corporation, USA (http://www.altera.com/); Computer Science Research, Education, and Applications Press (CSREA); Impulse Accelerated Technologies, Inc., USA (http://www.impulseaccelerated.com/); NVIDIA Corporation, USA (http://www.nvidia.com/object/about-nvidia.html); Parallella Community, Supercomputing for Everyone,

USA (http://forums.parallella.org/); Pico Computing, Inc., USA (http://picocomputing.com/); SemiWiki.com, The Semiconductor Wiki Project, USA (http://www.semiwiki.com/); Solarflare Communications, Inc., USA (http://www.solarflare.com/); Stream Computing, Performance Engineers, The Netherlands (http://streamcomputing.eu/); Taylor & Francis, UK (http://www.taylorandfrancis.com/); US Chapter of World Academy of Science (http://www.world-academy-of-science.org/) ; and WEBestSOL & Webest Solutions Ltd, UK (http://webestsol.com/). In addition, a number of university faculty members and their staff (names appear on the cover of the set of proceedings), several publishers of computer science and computer engineering books and journals, chapters and/or task forces of computer science associations/organizations from 5 countries, and developers of high-performance machines and systems provided significant help in organizing the conference as well as providing some resources. We are grateful to them all.

We express our gratitude to keynote, invited, and individual conference/tracks and tutorial speakers - the list of speakers appears on the conference web site. We would also like to thank the followings: UCMSS (Universal Conference Management Systems & Support, California, USA) for managing all aspects of the conference; Dr. Tim Field of APC for managing the printing of the proceedings; and the staff of the New Tropicana Hotel in Las Vegas for the professional service they provided. Last but not least, we would like to thank the Co-Editors and Associate Co-Editors of IPCV'13: Prof. Hamid R. Arabnia, Prof. Leonidas Deligiannidis, Prof. George Jandieri, Prof. Joan Lu, Prof. Gerald Schaefer, Ashu M. G. Solo, Prof. Fernando G. Tinetti, Prof. Vladimir Volkov, and Prof. Jane You.

We present the proceedings of IPCV'13.

Steering Committee, 2013
http://www.world-academy-of-science.org/

Contents

SESSION: STEREO, 3D, DEPTH ALGORITHMS, 3D Image Data Structures, AND APPLICATIONS

SESSION: SURVEILLANCE, SAFETY, SECURITY APPLICATIONS, AND RELATED METHODS AND SYSTEMS

SESSION: IMAGE CODING, COMPRESSION, WAVELETS, WATERMARKING, AND RELATED METHODS

SESSION: IMAGING SOFTWARE + SYSTEMS + CAMERA CALIBRATION

SESSION: BIOMETRICS: GAIT, IRIS, FINGERPRINT, ... + IDENTIFICATION + HANDWRITING ANALYSIS

SESSION: EDGE DETECTION AND ENHANCEMENT METHODS

SESSION: MEDICAL APPLICATIONS

SESSION: IMAGE RETRIEVAL AND IMAGE DATABASES

SESSION: IMAGING APPLICATIONS AND ALGORITHMS

SESSION: IMAGE RECONSTRUCTION AND RESTORATION

SESSION: IMAGE PROCESSING AND VISION ALGORITHMS

SESSION: FACE, GAZE, EXPRESSION RECOGNITION, DETECTION, TRACKING, OTHER RELATED METHODS

SESSION: SEGMENTATION ALGORITHMS AND APPLICATIONS

SESSION: TEXTURE ANALYSIS

SESSION: SIGNAL PROCESSING AND APPLICATIONS - INCLUDING, VOICE, MUSIC, AND OTHERS

SESSION: POSTERS AND SHORT PAPERS

SESSION: LATE BREAKING PAPERS: IMAGE PROCESSING AND COMPUTER VISION APPLICATIONS

SESSION: VISION AND IMAGING ALGORITHMS AND APPLICATIONS

SESSION

STEREO, 3D, DEPTH ALGORITHMS, 3D Image Data Structures, AND APPLICATIONS

Chair(s)

TBA

Reconfigurable Computing Architecture for Accurate Disparity Map Calculation in Real-Time Stereo Vision

P. Zicari, H. Lam, and A. George
NSF Center for High-Performance Reconfigurable Computing (CHREC)
Dept. of Electrical and Computer Engineering, University of Florida
Gainesville FL, USA 32611

Abstract - *This paper presents a novel hardware architecture using FPGA-based reconfigurable computing (RC) for accurate calculation of dense disparity maps in real-time, stereo-vision systems. Recent stereo-vision hardware solutions have proposed local-area approaches. Although parallelism can be easily exploited using local methods by replicating the window-based image elaborations, accuracy is limited because the disparity result is optimized by locally searching for the minimum value of a cost function. Global methods improve the quality of the stereo-vision disparity maps at the expense of increasing computational complexity, thus making real-time application not viable for conventional computing. This problem becomes even more evident when stereo vision is a single step integrated into a more complete image elaboration flow, where the depth maps are used for further detection, recognition, stereo reconstruction, or 3D enhancement processing. Our approach exploits a parallel and fully pipelined architecture to implement a global method for the calculation of dense disparity maps based on the dynamic programming optimization of the Hamming distance of the Census-transform cost function. The resulting stereo-vision core produces results that are significantly more accurate than existing hardware solutions using FPGAs that are based upon local approaches. The design was implemented and evaluated on an Altera Stratix-III E260 FPGA in a GiDEL PROCStar-III board. Tests were performed on 640×480 stereo images, with a Census transform window size = 3, correlation window size = 5, and disparity ranges of 30 and 50. Our hardware architecture achieved a speedup of about 319 and 512 respectively for the two disparity ranges, when compared to an optimized C++ implementation executed on a 2.26 GHz Xeon E5520 core. High accuracy in the output disparity map, together with high performance in terms of frames per second, make the proposed architecture an ideal solution for 3D robot-assisted medical systems, tracking, and autonomous navigation systems, where accuracy and speed constraints are very stringent.*

Keywords: Real-time stereo vision; dynamic programming; FPGA; reconfigurable computing

This work was supported in part by: the European Commission and the Calabria Region of Italy, through the European Social Fund, Regional Operational Program 2007/2013, Priority IV – Human Capital; and the I/UCRC Program of the National Science Foundation under Grant Nos. EEC-0642422 and IIP-1161022.

1 Introduction

Accurate and real-time 3D reconstruction from stereo vision is one of the most important research topics for improving computer-vision systems today and is essential in applications such as robotics, automated medical systems, video surveillance, object recognition, people tracking, obstacle detection, and autonomous navigation. Depth information in stereo vision is determined by processing the left and right images acquired by a stereo camera, which is composed of two calibrated cameras aligned at a baseline distance b. The stereo-matching problem consists of searching the correspondent points in the left and right images. A preprocessing operation, called rectification, simplifies the matching computation by aligning the acquired left and right stereo images so that the search can be executed on the horizontal scan lines. Fig. 1 shows an example of stereo matching in which the horizontal displacement D of the matched points, called disparity, is used to calculate the distance z of the real point in the scene from the stereo camera using Eq. 1, where f is the focal length.

$$z = \frac{b \times f}{D} \qquad (1)$$

Stereo-vision algorithms are widely recognized as extremely compute-expensive in the image-processing domain. Moreover, this complexity drastically increases when improving the quality of the depth maps. In the last several years, novel algorithmic improvements through software implementations has greatly extended the list of new entries in the Middlebury stereo evaluation table [1], which rates the different matching methods with respect to the accuracy of the disparity results over a set of benchmark stereo images: Tsukuba, Venus, Teddy, and Cones. These images, provided with ground-truth disparity maps, can be used as a common reference for fair comparisons. Although these algorithms can be implemented in a straightforward manner in software, their execution on CPUs is sequential, which does not always provide a viable solution for real-time applications with stringent performance requirements.

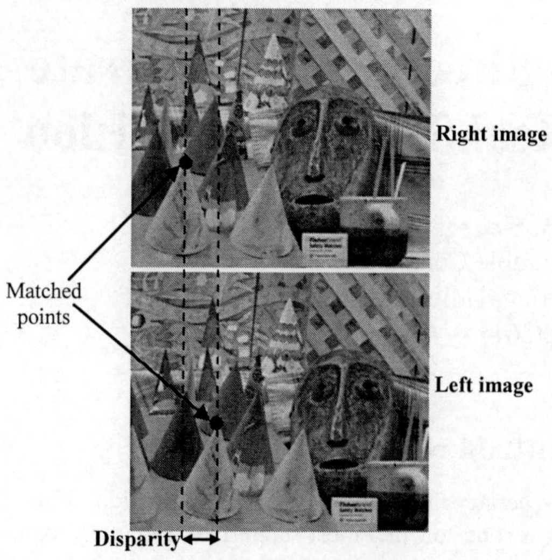

Fig. 1. The disparity of the matched points.

This paper presents a novel, FPGA-based hardware architecture for accurate calculation of dense disparity maps in real-time, stereo-vision systems. The elaboration flow design includes matching cost computation, cost aggregation, disparity calculation, and consistency-check validation. Unlike most recent stereo-vision hardware implementations, which are based solely upon local-area approaches [2-7], the proposed solution exploits a global method for the calculation of dense disparity maps based on the dynamic-programming optimization of the Hamming distance of the Census transform cost function. As a result, the parallel and fully pipelined architecture significantly improves the accuracy as compared to recent hardware solutions. Moreover, when compared to the more accurate stereo-matching approaches based on dynamic-programming methods running on CPUs and GPUs [9-14], the proposed stereo-vision architecture outperforms them by one to two orders of magnitude in speed. An implementation of the proposed architecture, running on an Altera Stratix-III EPSE260 FPGA, achieved speedups of about 319 and 512 for disparity ranges of 30 and 50, respectively, when compared to an optimized C++ baseline executed on a 2.26 GHz Xeon E5520 core.

The remainder of the paper is organized as follows. Section II presents the related works. Section III furnishes a detailed description of the approach and the design of the hardware stereo architecture. Section IV reports the experimental results and the comparisons against the most recent hardware and software solutions found in the literature. Finally, conclusions and directions for future research are given in Section V.

2 Related Works

In order to retrieve depth information, stereo-matching methods search for correspondences in a pair of right and left images acquired by a stereo camera. A detailed survey of the most recent methods for searching correspondences is presented in [15], where a classification in terms of matching cost, aggregation, and optimization functions is provided. In the plethora of methods present in the literature, local window-based algorithms have been preferred in recent hardware implementations [2-7] for the parallel execution of the repetitive operations on multiple windows. One of the first FPGA implementations of stereo systems is the reconfigurable PARTS engine [7], consisting of 16 Xilinx 4025 FPGAs, and 16 one-megabyte SRAMs. A frame rate of 42 frames per second (fps) was achieved when the Census algorithm was executed on 320×240 stereo images with a disparity range of 24 pixels. In [3], the Local Weighted Phase Correlation matching algorithm was implemented on four Virtex2000 FPGAs, where 256×360 disparity maps were calculated at a rate of 30 fps, with a disparity range of 20 pixels. In [5], a novel stereo-matching algorithm based on the Census transform of gradient images was proposed. The implemented version used a Stratix EP1S60 FPGA and a maximum of 60 fps was reached on a disparity range of 60 pixels. The FPGA stereo-vision system in [2] implemented the Census-based disparity matching over 640×480 stereo images. The disparity was computed by selecting the minimum winning cost over a disparity range of 64 pixels by using 11×11 Census transform windows and 15×15 correlation windows for the pixel aggregation. A frame rate of 230 fps was achieved when implemented on a Xilinx Xc4vlx200 FPGA. In [6], a fast and low-cost, stereo-vision system based upon SAD (Sum of Absolute Differences) was presented for real-time applications. A novel injective consistency check improves the efficiency by greatly reducing area usage with respect to the more common cross-checking methods which require the computation of both left and right disparity maps. In [8], a very different approach based on fuzzy logic was used to reach high frame rates and high accuracy in an Altera Stratix EP1S60 FPGA. Comparison of our proposed architecture with these hardware solutions will be given in Section IV.

Several software implementations of global methods have been presented in the literature, each achieving high-quality results but poor performance. Most global methods search for the optimum disparity distribution, which minimizes a specific global-energy function. Each selected disparity is not the result of a single independent decision as in the local methods, but is the result of a global decision that involves many disparity values considered together. Stereo matching based upon dynamic programming is a well-known class of global methods using scan-line optimization. Different approaches in using dynamic programming in stereo vision have been proposed in the literature [9-14]. The stereo-matching system in [14], rated highly in the Middlebury ranking [1], achieved very high accuracy due to the multi-direction scan-line optimization based on Hirschmüller's semi-global matching method, followed by several refinement steps systematically executed in order to correct the disparity errors in occluded and near-depth discontinuity regions. Unfortunately, the performance (about 10fps) was penalized by the high computational load in its CPU+GPU implementation. In [12], an adaptive aggregation step based upon the color and proximity weighting of the sum of absolute difference cost function was adopted in conjunction with a dynamic-programming scan-line optimization. Performances of 7.63 and 5.46 fps were achieved when 640×480 images are processed in the disparity ranges of 32 and 48 pixels, respectively, running on a 3GHz PC with an ATI Radeon XL1800 GPU. In [10], a system with a coarse–to-fine refinement approach was implemented on a 2.2 GHz AMD Athlon XP 2800+ CPU, achieving a frame rate of 12.3 fps when processing 640×480 stereo images in a disparity range of 50 pixels. In [13], the GPU-based Orthogonal Reliability-based Dynamic-Programming (GORDP) stereo system used two dynamic-programming passes with a local minimum searching process. Stereo images of 320×240 pixel sizes were processed at 10 fps for disparity ranges of 20 pixels. One of the most accurate dynamic-programming methods for stereo matching was proposed in [9], where a generalized ground control points (GGCP) scheme was introduced together with a two-pass optimization technique for reducing the inter-scan line inconsistency problem. Unfortunately, real-time is far from sustained by their Pentium IV 2.4GHz PC implementation, which calculates the disparity of the Tsukuba, Saw tooth, Venus and Map benchmark stereo images in 4.4, 11.8, 11.1 and 4.9 seconds, respectively. Comparison of our proposed architecture with these software solutions will also be given in Section IV.

3 Proposed Approach and Architecture

In order to evaluate the impact of using the dynamic-programming scan-line optimization when applied to the Hamming distance of Census transform cost functions, we performed an analysis over the Middlebury stereo-pair images. These benchmark images provide truth disparity maps as a reference for comparing the algorithmic results. As cited in [15], the percentage of bad pixels B is calculated as in Eq. 2 for the *non-occlusion*, *all* and *discontinuity* regions, where N is the total number of pixels, D and D_{truth} are the computed and the ground truth disparity values, respectively.

$$B = \frac{1}{N} \times \sum_{(x,y)\in \text{Region}} \left| D(x,y) - D_{truth}(x,y) \right| > 1 \qquad (2)$$

Fig. 2 shows the average percentage of bad pixels over the Tsukuba, Venus, Teddy, and Cones images, for the Census-Hamming, local-area approach and the proposed dynamic-programming approach. The cost function for both approaches uses an aggregation window size of 3×3, a correlation window size of 5×5, and consistency cross check is used to select the valid disparity values. The results show that the dynamic-programming optimization improves the quality of the output maps considerably in the *all* and *non-occluded* regions, while offering similar quality in the discontinuity regions. The average error over the benchmark stereo pairs is reduced by 51.74%, 48.04% and 1.77% for the *non-occlusion*, *all* and *discontinuity* cases, respectively. Note that abrupt changes of disparity inside discontinuity regions are not significantly improved by the applied global optimization method, since it is based on the minimization of an energy function aimed to smooth the depth discontinuity along the scan lines.

Our proposed architecture for dynamic programming in stereo vision is shown in Fig. 3. The datapath structure is fully pipelined and parallelized in order to enable a continuous input flow of left and right pair of pixels and output flow of disparity at each clock cycle. The left and right pixels of the acquired stereo images are serially inputted to the *Matching Cost Function* module for the Census transform and the Hamming distance calculation. The *Dynamic Programming* module searches for the optimum disparity path. Finally, the disparity in output is validated by the *Consistency Cross Check* module, which compares results of the left and right matching processes.

3.1 Matching Cost Function Module

The matching cost computation produces the Census transform over $Wc\times Wc$ windows, and then the Hamming distance of the Census vectors over $Wh\times Wh$ aggregation windows. According to [16], each element $CV(x,y,k)$ of the Census vector is the sign bit of the subtraction result between the generic $P(x+i,y+j)$ pixel and the central pixel $P(x,y)$ of the selected $Wc\times Wc$ window calculated as in Eq. 3, with $-(Wc-1)/2 \le i,j \le (Wc-1)/2$ and $k=(y+j-1)\times Wc+x+i$.

$$CV(x,y,k) = sign\,(P(x+i, y+j) - P(x,y)) \qquad (3)$$

The generic aggregated matching cost C, with respect to the disparity value z in the disparity range r, is calculated as in Eq. 4, by counting all the bit differences between the right CVR and the left CVL Census vectors in the selected $Wh\times Wh$ window. The matching cost based on the Hamming distance of Census transformed images is a non-parametric measure that is insensitive to differences in camera gains and bias [16].

$$C(x,y,z) = \sum_{i=-\frac{(Wh-1)}{2}}^{(Wh-1)/2} \sum_{j=-\frac{(Wh-1)}{2}}^{(Wh-1)/2} \sum_{k=1}^{Wc*Wc} [CVR(x+i, y+j, k) \oplus CVL(x+z+i, y+j, k)] \qquad (4)$$

The *Matching Cost Function* module consists of the *Census Transform* component and the *Hamming Distance* component. The high-level model designs of the two components are shown in Fig. 4 and Fig. 5, respectively. This module for the entire disparity range executes in parallel. Thus, two $C(x, y, 1{:}\ r)$ cost vectors are simultaneously computed for the left and right distinct processing flows at each clock cycle.

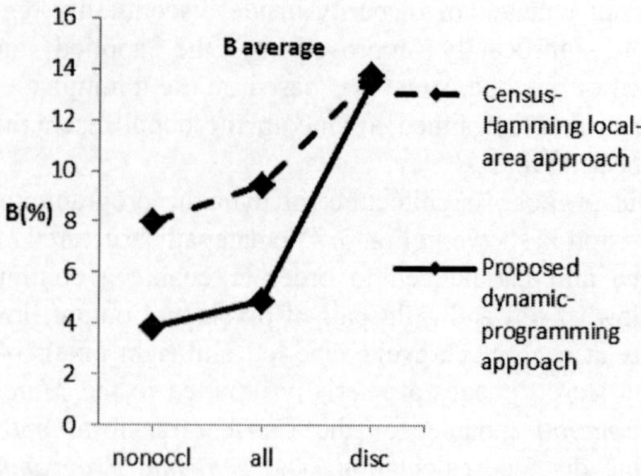

Fig. 2. The average percentage of bad pixels B over the benchmark Venus, Teddy, Cones and Tsukuba stereo images for the Census-Hamming, local-area approach and the proposed dynamic-programming approach.

In order to guarantee the parallel processing of the serially inputted $Nc\times Nr$ left and right images, two $Nc\times(Wc\text{-}1)+Wc$ pixel buffers (implemented as shift registers) are used. After a latency of $Nc\times(Wc\text{-}1)+Wc$ clock cycles, an entire $Wc\times Wc$ pixel window is inputted to the *Census Transform* component at each clock cycle. The sign bits outputted from the $n=Wc\times Wc$ parallel subtraction circuits of the *Census Transform* are then inputted into the *Census Buffer*, which uses $Nc\times(Wh\text{-}1)+r+Wh\text{-}1$ n-bit registers connected as shown in Fig. 5. After $Nc\times(Wh\text{-}1)+r+Wh\text{-}1$ clock cycles from the first Census vector input, one reference window and r candidate windows are outputted from each *Census Buffer* at each following clock cycle. The Hamming distance between a reference window and each candidate window is calculated in parallel by $2\times r$ *Hamming Distance (HD)* blocks. An *HD* block includes a bank of XOR-gates and a final tree of pipelined adders. Tree adders at the first level have multiple single-bit operands, while adders at the other levels have two operands, with the input precision incremented by one bit at each level.

3.2 Dynamic Programming Module

In our design, the *Dynamic Programming* module searches for the minimum cost path on the basis of a scan-line optimization. For each row, r different disparity paths are calculated by building the energy function matrix E and the matrix P of disparity paths. According to [15], each element $E(x,y,z)$ of the energy function matrix is calculated iteratively as shown in Eq. 5, with $1\leq x\leq Nc$, $1\leq y\leq Nr$ and $0\leq z<r$; $\delta(x,y,z)$, taking into account the depth discontinuity through the constant term λ as shown in Eq. 6.

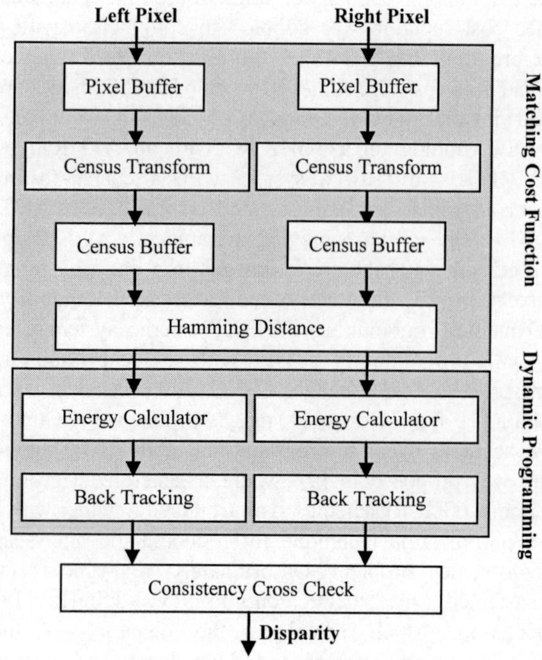

Fig. 3. Proposed Stereo-Vision Architecture.

$$E(x,y,z) = C(x,y,z) + \delta(x,y,z) \tag{5}$$

$$\delta(x,y,z) = \min\{\, C(x-1,y,z-1)+\lambda, C(x-1,y,z), C(x-1,y,z+1)+\lambda \} \tag{6}$$

According to [12], each element $P(x,y,z)$ is calculated as in Eq. 7 by selecting the minimum arguments calculated in Eq. 6 with respect to the index z.

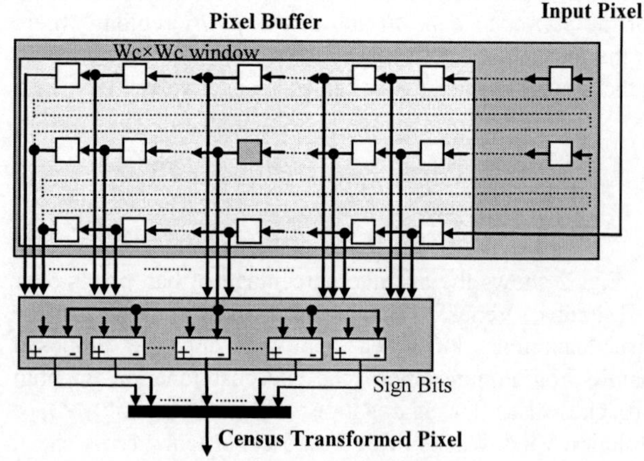

Fig. 4. Census Transform Component.

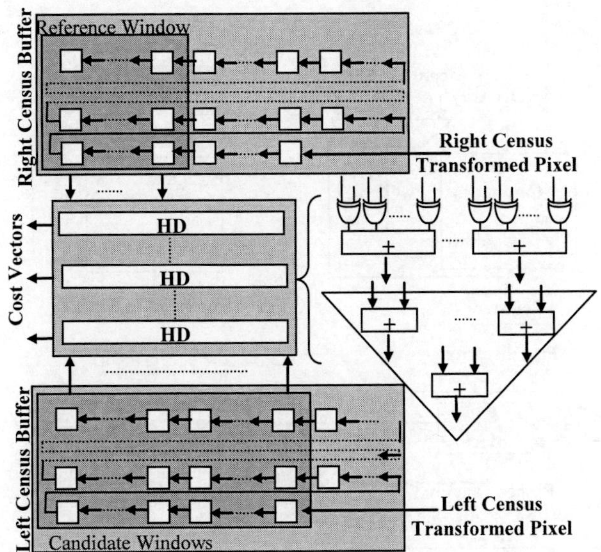

Fig. 5. Hamming Distance Component.

$$P(x,y,z)=\begin{cases} z-1 & \text{when } \delta(x,y,z)=C(x-1,y,z-1)+\lambda \\ z & \text{when } \delta(x,y,z)=C(x-1,y,z) \\ z+1 & \text{when } \delta(x,y,z)=C(x-1,y,z+1)+\lambda \end{cases} \quad (7)$$

The matrix P keeps track of all the possible r disparity paths for each row. The disparity map D is calculated as shown in Eq. 8. The last disparity in each scan line is the z position of the minimum energy value, while all the previous disparity values in each path are retrieved by back-tracking through the matrix P.

$$D(x,y)=\begin{cases} \arg(\min_{0\le z<r} E(x,y,z)) & \text{when } x=Nc \\ P(x+1,y,D(x+1,y)) & \text{when } 0<x<Nc \end{cases} \quad (8)$$

The design of the *Dynamic Programming* module is shown in Fig. 6. The optimal disparity path is calculated by iteratively processing the cost vector $c=C(x, y, 0{:}\ r-1)$ and the energy vector $e=E(x, y, 0{:}\ r-1)$ in a row-scanning order. At each clock cycle, a cost vector c is inputted to the *Dynamic Programming* module. The *EF Block* calculates the energy function as in Eq. 5. The *Disparity Path Storage Block* is used to store the r possible disparity paths. The *Min Tree Block* selects the best path which minimizes the energy function of the entire path, furnishing in the output the last disparity value. All of the previous disparity values in the optimum path are retrieved by the back-tracker *BT Block* in an inverted order. The disparity values are then queued in the *Disparity Storage Block* to be outputted in the right order by the forward tracker *FT Block*. As the energy of an entire path represents the energy accumulated in each single step, the energy function block is realized as a bank of r special accumulators as shown in Fig. 6. The aggregated matching costs are accumulated at each clock cycle. To take into account the depth discontinuity, the minimum value among the adjacent energy values is selected and appropriately corrected by the constant λ.

One of the main disadvantages of the dynamic-programming approach is the considerable amount of resources needed to store all of the possible disparity paths during the scan-line optimization. In fact, the optimum among all the disparity paths can be selected only at the end of the scan line after that the global energy is computed. If the optimization is performed on an entire image row, r paths of the row length need to be saved until the energy function for the entire row is calculated, thus requiring the storage of $Nc\times r$ disparity values. In our design, in order to reduce resource usage, instead of saving the disparity values, 2 bits of information are stored for tracking each s=+1, 0, –1 variation step with respect to the previous disparity value in the path, as shown in Eq. 9.

$$s(x,y,z)=\begin{cases} -1 & \text{if } \delta(x,y,z)=C(x-1,y,z-1)+\lambda \\ 0 & \text{if } \delta(x,y,z)=C(x-1,y,z) \\ +1 & \text{if } \delta(x,y,z)=C(x-1,y,z+1)+\lambda \end{cases} \quad (9)$$

The variation step s is calculated by the *Min* block inside the energy accumulator of the *EF Block*. In this way, after the *Min Tree Block* calculates the last disparity value of the path, all of the previous disparity values in the optimum path are back-tracked by the *BT Block*, by appropriately incrementing, disabling, or decrementing a counter register initially loaded with the last disparity value. The *BT Block* uses a multiplexer to select the next disparity step in the optimum path. After back-tracking, the disparity flow is inverted with respect to the left-to-right input order; thus a further step is required. The disparity variation steps of the optimum path are queued in the *Disparity Storage Block.* The *FT Block* then forward-tracks the disparity values starting from the first disparity value of the current row, outputted by the *BT Block* at the end of the back-tracking phase. The counter in the *FT Block* is controlled by the disparity variation step s outputted from the *Disparity Storage Block*. The *Disparity Path Storage Block* and the *Disparity Storage Block* are two shift-register bidirectional buffers storing the disparity steps in a LIFO (Last Input First Output) order. While the former stores all the possible paths into r stack lines, the latter stores only the optimum path in just one stack line. In order to use the same structure for contemporary pushing and pulling the disparity steps of two consecutive paths without stopping the pipelined processing flow, in each stack line the registers are interleaved by multiplexers. The select signals of the multiplexers are used to control the direction of the push-pull operation like a piston moving a cylinder back and forth in an engine. As the result of this design, the amount of resources for storage was reduced by 80% in the *Dynamic Programming* module, thus reducing by 60% the total amount of storage for the entire design.

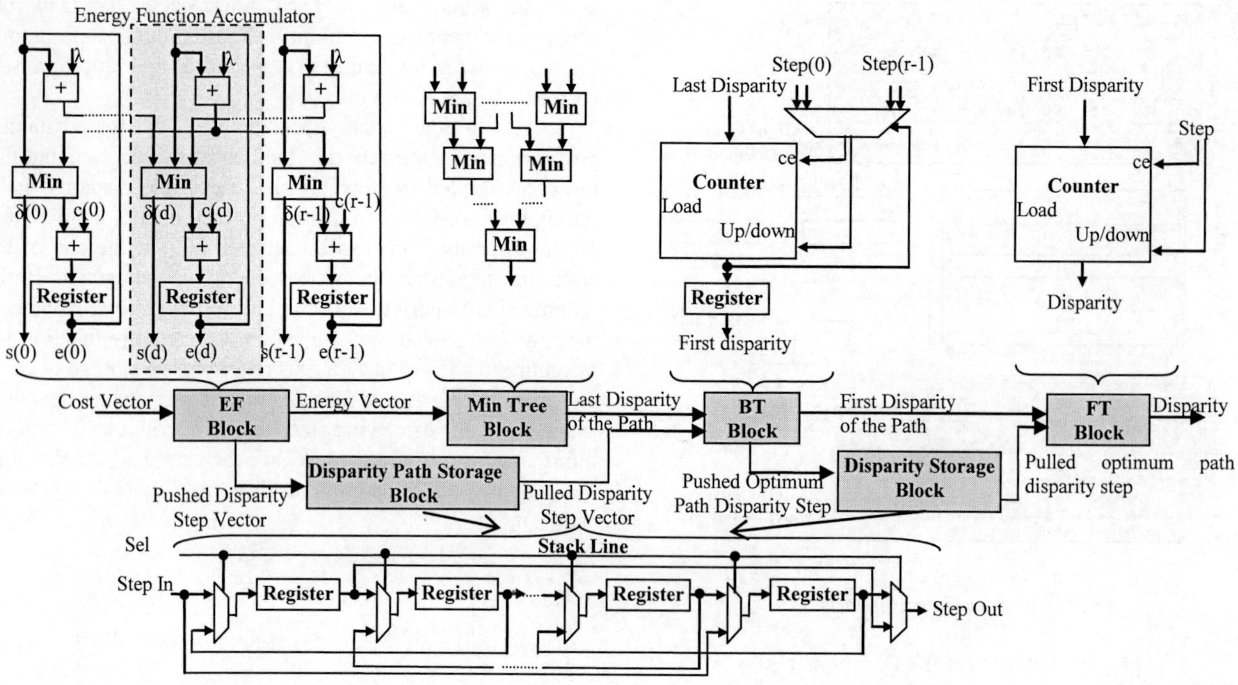

Fig. 6. Dynamic Programming Module.

3.3 Consistency Cross Check

Post-processing is adopted in order to reduce the matching errors that could be caused by occlusions and false matching. The cross check validates the consistency of the right and left results. The matching is considered valid by the cross check method when the right *Dr* and the left *Dl* disparity values satisfy the condition shown in Eq. 10. Only if this is the case, the disparity is flagged as a correct result.

$$Dr\,(x, y) = Dl\,(x + Dr\,(x, y), y) \tag{10}$$

The stereo-vision system executes the right and left matching processes in parallel. Thus, one right and one left disparity value are simultaneously ready at the output from the *Dynamic Programming* module at each clock cycle. As shown in Fig. 7, the disparity values are appropriately buffered in *r* registers, which are left-shifted at each clock cycle. A bank of *XNOR* logic gates inside the *Comparator* block are used to compare each right disparity with its matched left disparity, selected by a multiplexer. An active-high *valid* signal is outputted when the disparity passes the consistency check.

4 Experimental Results and Comparisons

In order to support different image-processing requirements and FPGA platforms, the proposed stereo-vision architecture for the disparity-map calculation was designed in VHDL as an IP core that can be parameterized in terms of image size, Census-transform size, aggregation-window size, and disparity range. Two versions of the proposed architecture have been implemented on an Altera Stratix-III E260 FPGA, the results of which are shown in the first row of Table I, calculating the disparity in the 30 and 50 pixel ranges, respectively. The Census transform is executed over 3×3 windows; the Hamming distance is calculated for aggregation windows of size 5×5; the input image size is 640×480 with 8-bit gray level pixels; and the depth discontinuity constant λ is fixed to 7. For the r=30 version, the complete circuit occupies 33,881 combinational ALUTs, 949 memory ALUTs, 101,802 dedicated logic registers, 102,288 total registers, and 493,683 total block-memory bits. For the r=50 version, it occupies 50,402 combinational ALUTs, 320 memory ALUTs, 157,005 dedicated logic registers, 157,491 total registers, and 505,355 total block-memory bits. The remainder of Table I is used to compare our solution with other works available in the literature. Comparison is made with both hardware solutions and CPU/GPU solutions.

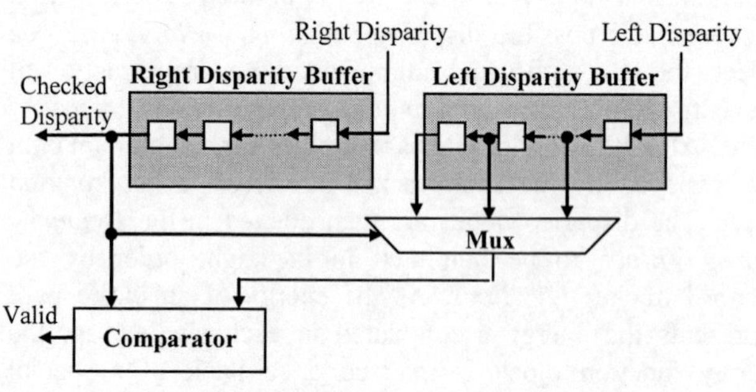

Fig. 7. Consistency Cross Check.

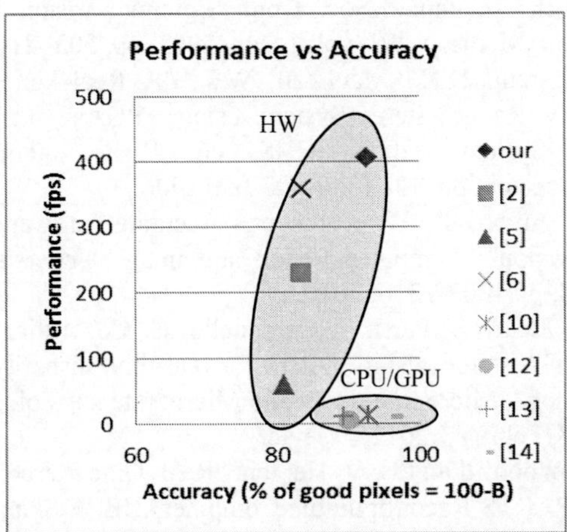

Fig. 8. Performance vs. Accuracy graph.

As shown in Table I, our solution significantly outperformed the cited hardware implementations [2, 5 and 6] in result quality, as indicated by the percentages of bad pixels of the validated disparity maps over Tsukuba, Venus, Teddy, and Cones stereo images in the last column. For the *non-occlusion* cases, the improvement ranges from 32% to 84%. For the *all* cases, the improvement ranges from 43% to 78%.

These results are expected because of our use of a global method for the calculation of dense disparity maps based upon the dynamic-programming optimization, as compared to the local-area approaches used by other hardware solutions. For the *discontinuity* cases, except for one result in [6] which is even better than the proposed one, the rest of the results show improvement from 16% to 63%. As noted previously, the improvement in this case is expected to be less because the abrupt changes of disparity inside discontinuity regions are not significantly improved by the applied global-optimization method since it is based on the minimization of an energy function aimed to smooth the depth discontinuity along the scan lines. The design was compiled and downloaded into a GiDEL PROCStar-III board for testing. As the proposed architecture exploits massive parallelism, an increase in the disparity range improves the speedup performance with respect to a software baseline implementation. Performance was measured with speedups of about 319 and 512, for the 30 and 50 disparity ranges respectively, as compared to optimized C++ code executed on a 2.26 GHz Xeon E5520 core. The maximum frame rate of 406 fps was achieved for both IP cores. Compared to the cited software implementations in the literature [10, 12, 13, 14, and 17], our proposed stereo-vision architecture outperformed them by one to two orders of magnitude in terms of frame rate.

TABLE I. COMPARISON OF PERFORMACE RESULTS

System	Image Size [Pixel]	Device	Disparity Range [Pixel]	Resources	Frame Rate [fps]	B [%] Tsukuba Nocc All Disc	Venus Nocc All Disc	Teddy Nocc All Disc	Cones Nocc All Disc
Our proposed stereo-vision architecture	640×480	FPGA Altera Stratix-III E260	30	33,881 Comb. ALUTs 949 Mem. ALUTs 101,802 Logic registers 102,288 Tot registers 493,683 Mem. Bits	406	4.39 5.21 15.54	2.41 2.96 13.81	5.13 6,54 15.76	3.30 4.75 8.63
			50	50,402 Comb. ALUTs 320 Mem. ALUTs 157,005 Logic registers 157,491 Tot registers 505,355 Mem. Bits					
[2]	640×480	FPGA Xilinx Xc4vlx200	64	12 DSP 322 18Kb-BRAM 51,191 Slices	230	9.79 11.56 20.29	3.59 5.27 36.82	12.50 21.50 30.57	7.34 17.58 21.01
[5]	750×400	FPGA Altera Stratix EP1S60	60	38,944 Logic Elements 557,056 Mem. Bits	60	22.7 23.7 26.2	15.1 15.9 25.3	13.9 20.7 29.0	5.96 12.7 15.5
[6]	640×480	FPGA Xilinx XC4VLX60	30	63 DSP 64 BRAM 12,974 Slices	358	9.99 10.64 12.88	11.42 12.28 16.61	17.19 19.38 25.75	17.12 20.18 23.61
	1280×720			63 DSP 128 BRAM 15,728 Slices	97				
[10]	640×480	CPU	32	AMD Athlon XP 2800+	15.2	n.a.* 4.12 n.a.*	n.a.* 10.10 n.a.*	n.a.* n.a.* n.a.*	n.a.* n.a.* n.a.*
			50		12.3				
[12]	640×480	CPU + GPU	32	3GHz PC + ATI Radeon XL1800	7.63	2.05 4.22 10.6	1.92 2.98 20.3	7.23 14.4 17.6	6.41 13.7 16.5
			48		5.46				
[13]	320×240	CPU + GPU	20	3 GHz P4 CPU 512 MB RAM ATI Radeon X800	10	1.34 3.36 7.10	2.73 3.81 10.1	9.03 16.8 18.4	13.1 20.1 20.1
[14]	512×384	CPU + GPU	60	Core2, 2.20GHz NVIDIA GeForce GTX 480	10	1.07 1.48 5.73	0.09 0.25 1.15	4.10 6.22 10.9	2.42 7.25 6.95
[17]	640×480	MIMD many-core architecture	48	Tilera TILEPro64	71.5	n.a.*			

* n.a. = not available

Compared to a CPU-only implementation [10] of a stereo-matching system based upon a coarse to fine approach of the dynamic programming on a 2.2 GHz AMD Athlon XP 2800+ CPU, our speedup in terms of fps is almost 33 times faster. Compared to an MIMD (Multiple Instruction, Multiple Data) many-core implementation [17], in which the disparity map calculation of the SSD (Sum of Squared Differences) correlation metric was executed on the Tilera TILEPro64 architecture, consisting of 64 32-bit processing cores, our speedup is almost 6 times faster. Compared to works that include CPU and GPU [12, 13, 14], our speedup ranges from about 40 to 74. In summary, a performance vs. accuracy graph of the systems reported in Table I is shown in Fig. 8, where performances are reported in terms of frames per second, and accuracy is the average of the percentage of good pixels calculated as (100-*B*) over the *Nocc*, *All* and *Disc* regions. As shown in this figure, our solution provides the highest speed performances while approaching the level of accuracy of the software CPU/GPU global-methods implementations.

5 Conclusions

This paper presents a novel hardware architecture using FPGA-based reconfigurable computing (RC) to calculate dense disparity maps by exploiting a global method based on the dynamic-programming optimization of the Hamming distance of the Census-transform cost function. Recent stereo-vision hardware solutions exploit parallelism by replicating the window-based image elaborations in local-area approaches, but accuracy is limited because the disparity result is optimized by locally searching for the minimum value of a cost function. Our proposed solution, based on global methods and a parallel and fully pipelined architecture, significantly improves the accuracy as compared to recent hardware solutions. Moreover, when compared to the more accurate stereo-matching approaches based on dynamic-programming methods executing on CPUs and GPUs, the proposed stereo-vision architecture outperforms them by one to two orders of magnitude in speed. As a result, our solution provides the best performance while approaching the level of accuracy of the software CPU/GPU global-methods implementations. High accuracy together with high performance make the proposed stereo-vision architecture an ideal solution for 3D robot-assisted medical systems, tracking, and autonomous navigation systems, where accuracy and speed constraints are very stringent.

6 References

[1] Middlebury Stereo-Vision page, available at http://vision.middlebury.edu/stereo/

[2] S. Jin, J. Cho, X. D. Pham, K. M. Lee, S. K. Park, M. Kim, and J. W. Jeon, "FPGA Design and Implementation of a Real-time Stereo Vision System", IEEE Trans. on Circuits and Systems for Video Technology, vol. 20, pp.15 – 26, 2010.

[3] A. Darabiha, J. Rose, and W. J. Maclean, "Video-rate stereo depth measurement on programmable hardware," in Proc. IEEE Comput. Soc. Conf. Comput. Vision Pattern Recognit., Madison, WI, vol. 1. Jun. 2003, pp. 203–210.

[4] Masrani, D.K.; MacLean, W.J.; "A Real-Time Large Disparity Range Stereo-System using FPGAs", Computer Vision Systems, 2006 ICVS '06. IEEE International Conference on, pp. 13- 13, 04-07 Jan. 2006.

[5] K. Ambrosch, W. Kubinger, "Accurate hardware-based stereo vision", Computer Vision and Image Understanding, Vol.114, pp.1303-1316, 2010.

[6] P. Zicari, S. Perri, P. Corsonello, G. Cocorullo, "Low-cost FPGA stereo vision system for real-time disparity maps calculation", Microprocessors and Microsystems, Vol. 36, pp. 281-288, February 2012, Elsevier.

[7] J. Woodfill and B. V. Herzen. "Real-Time Stereo Vision on the PARTS Reconfigurable Computer", IEEE Symposium on FPGAs for Custom Computing Machines, pp. 201–210, Napa Valley, CA, USA 1997.

[8] C. Georgoulas, I. Andreadis, "A real-time fuzzy hardware structure for disparity map computation", Journal of Real-Time Image Processing, DOI 10.1007/s11554-010-0157-6, 2010.

[9] J. C. Kim, K. M. Lee, B. T. Choi, and S. U. Lee., "A dense stereo matching using two-pass dynamic programming with generalized ground control points", Proceedings of Conference on Computer Vision and Pattern Recognition (CVPR), pp. 1075–1082, 2005.

[10] S. Forstmann, J. Ohya, Y. Kanou, A. Schmitt, and S. Thuering, "Real-time stereo by using dynamic programming", Proc. of CVPR Workshop on Real-time 3D Sensors and Their Use, 2004.

[11] M. Gong and Y.-H. Yang, "Near real-time reliable stereo matching using programmable graphics hardware", Proceedings of Conference on Computer Vision and Pattern Recognition (CVPR), pp. 924–931, 2005.

[12] L. Wang, M. Liao, M. Gong, R. Yang, D. Nister, "High-quality Real-time Stereo using Adaptive Cost Aggregation", 3D Data Processing, Visualization, and Transmission, Third International Symposium on, pp. 798 – 805, 14-16 June 2006.

[13] M. Gong and Y.H. Yang, "Real-Time Stereo Matching using Orthogonal Reliability-Based Dynamic Programming Algorithm," IEEE Trans. on Image Processing, Correspondence, Vol. 16, 2007, pp. 879-884.

[14] X. Mei, X. Sun, M. Zhou, S. Jiao, H. Wang and X. Zhang, "On Building an Accurate Stereo Matching System on Graphics Hardware", GPUCV'11: ICCV Workshop on GPU in Computer Vision Applications, 2011.

[15] D. Scharstein and R. Szeliski. "A taxonomy and evaluation of dense two-frame stereo correspondence algorithms", International Journal of Computer Vision, 47(1/2/3): 7-42, April-June 2002.

[16] R. Zabih, J. Woodfill. "A non-parametric approach to visual correspondence", IEEE Transaction on Pattern Analysis and Machine Intelligence, 1996.

[17] Safari, S.; Fijany, A.; Diotalevi, F.; Hosseini, F.; "Highly parallel and fast implementation of stereo vision algorithms on MIMD many-core Tilera architecture", Aerospace Conference, 2012 IEEE, pp.1-11, 3-10 March 2012.

Collision Prediction from Binocular Optical Flows

F. Mori[1], and N. Sugano[2]
[1]Brain Science Institute, Tamagawa University, Tokyo, Japan
[2]Faculty of Engineering, Tamagawa University, Tokyo, Japan

Abstract - *In the field of motion perception, the "aperture problem" exists in which the true motion direction of a point at a straight line edge on a retinal image cannot be determined by analysis of a local area only. Many straight line edges are found in a real environment. In this paper, we theoretically show that the aperture problem can be solved based on binocular apparent optical flows by the analysis of local area alone when objects and the observer (ego) move on a plane, but it is not solved completely when they move in an arbitrary 3D direction. The solution is applied to the prediction of collision location and collision time for objects and the observer moving on a horizontal plane which is an important function of human. A fairly precise real time solution can be obtained in a system composed of a stereo camera and a simple robot that is commercially available.*

Keywords: aperture problem, binocular apparent optical flows, collision prediction, analysis of local area

1 Introduction

Motion perception is one of the important visual functions for humans. Many straight line edges are observed in the environment. Due to the aperture problem, the true movement of a point at a straight line edge by analysis of the local area alone is unknown (see Fig. 1).

Three types of research have been conducted on the aperture problem: apparent motion influenced by a window frame, integration of local movements vertical to the edge orientation that is detected by a direction selective cell, and the inverse optics problem of local 3D motion. Wallach (1935)[1] reported that the true movement of a long line shown through a rectangular window is not observed, but apparent motion influenced by the window frame is observed. This type of research of the aperture problem was investigated by Shimojyo et al. (1989)[2], Anderson (1991)[3], and Wallach (1935)[1]. The second type of research is the integration process of the local apparent motion of multiple edges, as in the works of Adelson and Movshon (1982)[4], Nakayama (1983)[5], Horn and Schunk(1981)[6], Hildreth (1984)[7], Spies, Jahne and Barron(2002)[8], and Min and Sohn(2006)[9]. The third type of research is the integration process of the apparent optical flows (for example, the movement vertical to the edge orientation) of the left and right eyes, as shown by Lages and Heron (2010)[10] and Morgan and Castet (1977)[11].

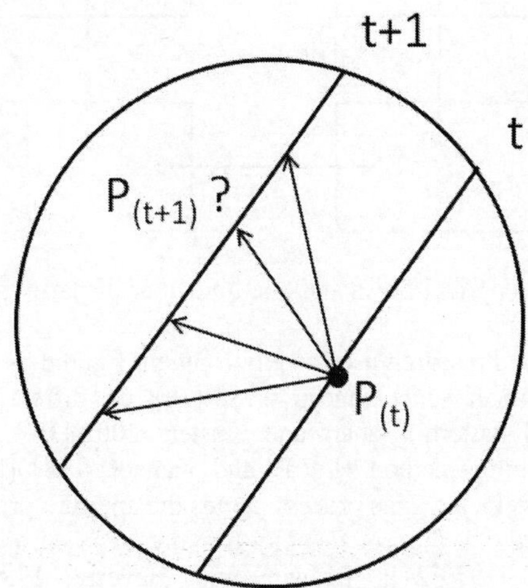

Fig. 1. The aperture problem.

Two types of depth motion detection systems may exist in the brain. Similar systems have been studied in the field of computer vision (Mori 1982)[12]. The first system consists of binocular disparity at time *t* and *t+1* and one optical flow system (see Fig. 2), as reported by, e.g., Gross and Tistarelli (1995)[13], Kagami et al. (1999)[14], Shimizu et al. (2004)[15]. In this type, the system which makes to match points in the space at time *t* to those at time *t+1* is included.

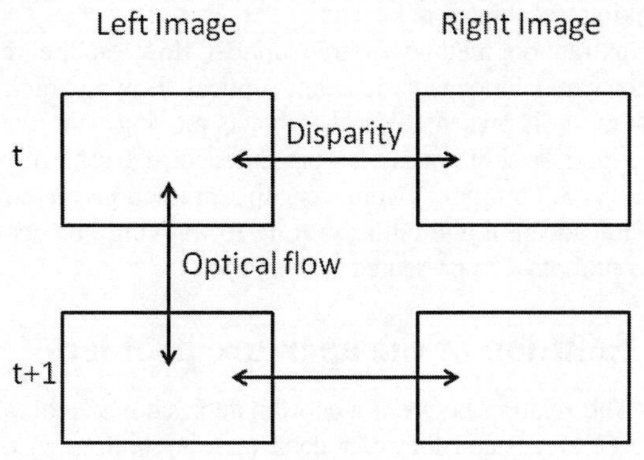

Fig. 2. Two binocular disparities and one optical flow system.

The second system consists of two optical flows and one binocular disparity system. In this system, one 2.5D sketch at time *t* and the two optical flows in the left and right eyes are used (see Fig. 3), e.g., Regan and Cynader (1982)[16], Toyama and Kozasa (1982)[17], Waxman and Duncan (1986)[18].

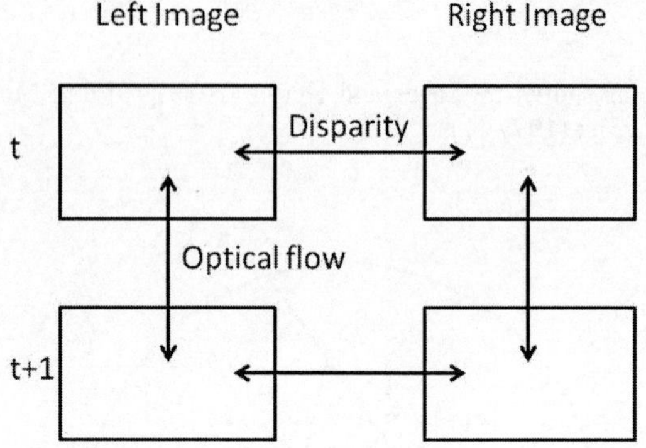

Fig. 3. Two optical flows and one binocular disparity system.

Conventional research used an environment figured by dense spots (Waxman and Duncan 1986)[18] or differentiable complicated pattern (Scharr and Kusters 2002)[19] or the block matching method (Lucas and Kanade 1981)[20] to obtain true velocity. This process avoids the aperture problem. It is assumed that the true velocity has already been obtained in Ullman 1979[21]; Reagan and Beverly 1985[22]; Kobayashi and Sugie 1984[23]; Mori 1985[24].

No general solution to the inverse optics problem of 3D motion perception exists, as mentioned in Lages and Heron (2010). Lages and Heron (2010) proposed two types of additive constraint to obtain any solution for arbitrary 3D motion: vector normal constraint and cyclopean average constraint. The first constraint is for the first type of depth motion detection system and the second constraint is for the second type of depth motion detection system. Lages and Heron(2012)'s constraints lead to such a wrong solution that an approaching vertical line must be perceived shrinking in the vertical direction although human does not perceives the shrinking phenomenon.

An extraction method of true optical flow on the retinal image from binocular apparent optical flows which are measurable, is presented for the objects moving on a plane in this paper. A solution is also presented in the case of some arbitrary 3D motion. Moreover, the prediction method of collision location and collision time for moving objects on a horizontal plane is presented in this paper.

2 Solution of the aperture problem

The relation between a coordinate system of real world space (*X, Y, Z*) and that of a coordinate system (*x, y*) of an image is shown in Fig. 4. It is also described by equation (1), where the projection plane is at distance 1, because the orbit form of the moving point on the projection plane is not affected by the focal distance, which therefore does not appear in the main equations of this paper. Cartesian space and perspective projection are postulated in the camera system.

$$(x, y) = \left(\frac{X}{Z}, \frac{Y}{Z}\right), \tag{1}$$

where *f* is set as $f = 1$ (If the image plane is further than 1, you must multiply it with the image distance).

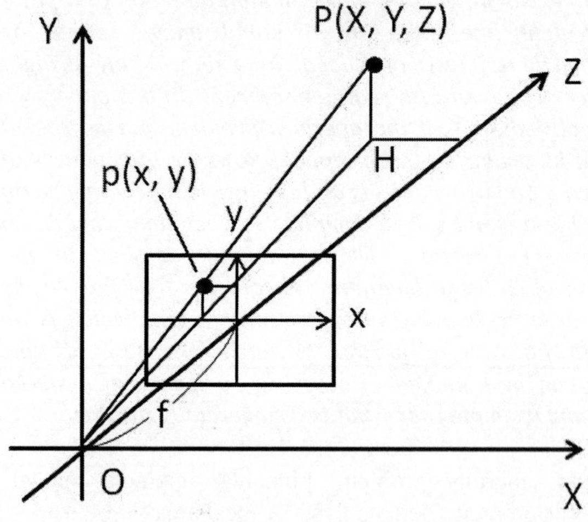

Fig. 4. The relation between real world space and the image coordinate systems.

The coordinate system of a stereo system is shown in Fig. 5. The optic axes of the right and left cameras are set in parallel.

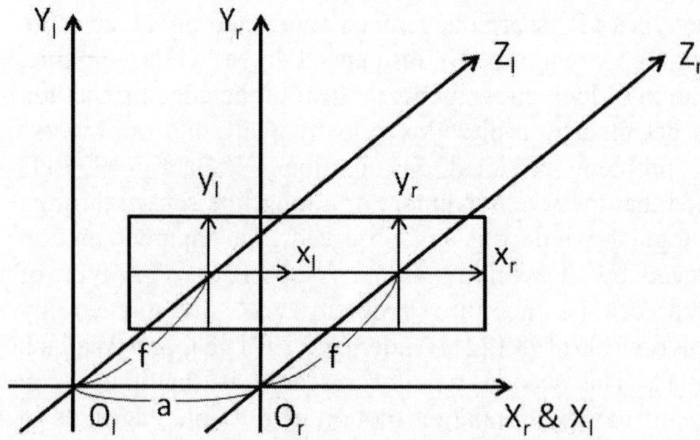

Fig. 5. Coordinate system of stereo camera (eye), where *a* is the camera distance (distance between the eyes) and subscripts l and r show the left camera and right camera, respectively.

The origin of the total stereo coordinate system is the lens center of the right eye.

The depth motion of each point on an object translated on a plane is represented as a motion on a horizontal plane whose height is fixed as Y_0 (a natural constraint). The simplified motion is shown in Fig. 6 (the precise 3D situation is shown in Fig. 8), where the point moves from $P(t)= P_0(X_0, Y_0, Z_0)$ to $P(t+1)=P(X, Y_0, Z)$ on the horizontal plane and the Y coordinates are omitted.

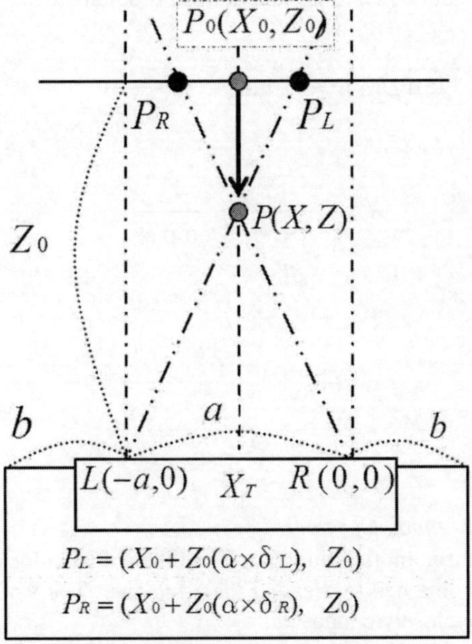

Fig. 6. Principle of collision prediction by a binocular velocity pair (Y coordinates are omitted).

$R(0, 0)$ and $L(-a, 0)$ in Fig. 6 show the Y_0 locations higher than the right eye camera and the left eye camera, respectively. P_L is a point of intersection between a straight line LP and a horizontal line including point P_0. The locations of P_L and P_R are $(X_0+Z_0* (\varepsilon*\delta_L),Y_0,Z_0)$ and $(X_0+Z_0* (\varepsilon*\delta_R),Y_0,Z_0)$, respectively. The parameter "ε" is equal to d/Z (a constant value), where d is one pixel length on the front parallel plane, and Z is the depth distance of the plane. The true x-component of movement on the left image is δ_L, and that on the right image is δ_R. We call (δ_L, δ_R) a binocular velocity pair. The coordinates X and Z of point $P(t)=P(X,Y_0,Z)$ are obtained from the coordinates of four points P_R, P_L, L and R when the binocular velocity pair (δ_L, δ_R) is obtained. This means that the 3D velocity $(X-X_0,0,Z-Z_0)$ is obtained. Therefore, the predicted collision location (X_T) and time (T) can easily be obtained as equations (2) and (3) when the true velocity pair is obtained.

$$X_T = a*\frac{\delta_R}{\delta_L - \delta_R} \tag{2}$$

$$T = \frac{a}{\varepsilon * Z_0 * (\delta_L - \delta_R)} \tag{3}$$

Unfortunately, in the case that $P(t)$ is on a straight line edge, the true binocular velocity pair (δ_L, δ_R) cannot be determined, but the apparent horizontal velocity pair (δ'_L, δ'_R) can be obtained precisely. (The discussion is the same for velocity pair (h_L, h_R), which is composed of vertical movement to the edge orientation.) The relation between (δ_L, δ_R) and (δ'_L, δ'_R) is shown in Fig. 7 and equation (4).

Equation (4) is obtained from three equations: $h=\delta'*\sin\theta$, $h=r*\sin(\beta-\theta)$, and $\delta=r*\cos\theta$, which are easily found in Fig. 7. In this figure, "h" is the distance between the straight lines at time (t) and at time $(t+1)$ on the projection plane, and "r" is the length of vector $P(t)P(t+1)$.

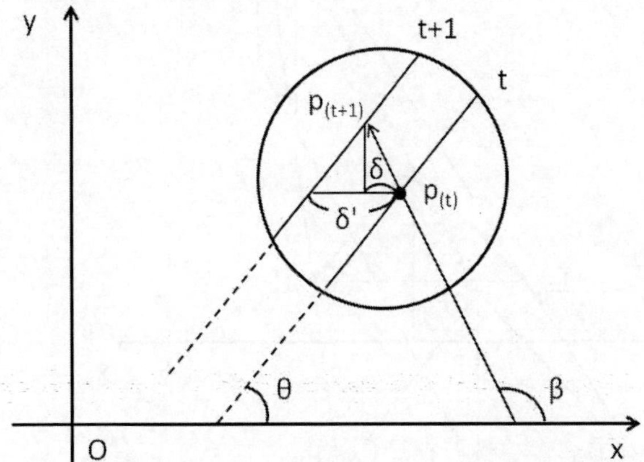

Fig. 7. Relation between true movement δ and apparent movement δ' ($\delta= \delta_L$ or δ_R , $\delta'= \delta'_L$ or δ'_R , $h = h_l$ or h_r , and $r = r_l$ or r_r).

$$\delta = \frac{\delta'}{1-\dfrac{\tan\beta}{\tan\theta}}, \tag{4}$$

where θ and β are the orientation of the straight line edge and the true moving direction of point P(t) on the image plane, respectively.

Equation (5) is obtained by substituting equation (4) for equation (2).

$$X_T = \frac{a}{\dfrac{\delta'_L}{\delta'_R} * \dfrac{1-\dfrac{\tan\beta_r}{\tan\theta_r}}{1-\dfrac{\tan\beta_l}{\tan\theta_l}} - 1} \tag{5}$$

To obtain equations including the three unknown parameters β_r, β_l, and X_T, the 3D trajectory of point $P(t)=P_0$ (X_0, Y_0, Z_0) up to the collision point $P_T=P(T)$ on the X-Y plane (ego) going through $P(t+1)=(X,Y,Z)$ and the two loci L_0L_T and R_0R_T of points L_0 and R_0 on the left and right images, corresponding to motion of the point $P(t)=P_0$ in the 3D space, are shown in Fig. 8. The actual motion of the point $P(t)$ on the straight line is just from $P(t)$ to $P(t+1)$. The x-coordinate X_T of collision location P_T is predicted from the small actual motion $P(t)P(t+1)$.

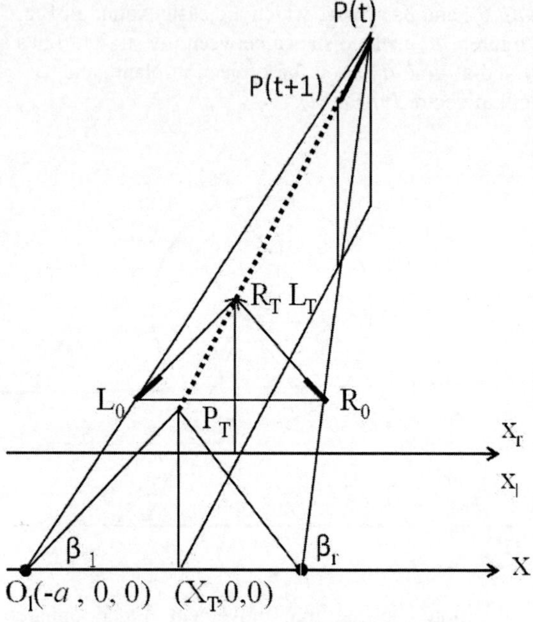

Fig. 8. Relation of collision location X_T and moving directions β_r and β_l on the images (P_T is the predicted collision point, and L_T and R_T are the intersections between the straight line P_0P_T and the image plane).

The coordinates of points R_0, L_0 , L_T and R_T on the image plane are shown in equation (6). The small solid thick lines marked at R_0 and L_0 are the actual motion on the image plane corresponding to the actual 3D motion P(t)P(t+1).

$$R_0 = \left(\frac{X_0}{Z_0}, \frac{Y_0}{Z_0}\right), L_0 = \left(\frac{X_0 + a}{Z_0}, \frac{Y_0}{Z_0}\right),$$

$$R_T = \left(X_T + \frac{(X_0 - X_T)}{Z_0}, Y_0\right),$$

$$L_T = \left(X_T + a + \frac{(X_0 - X_T)}{Z_0}, Y_0\right) \quad (6)$$

Equation (7) is directly obtained from equation (6) or the coordinates of the apices of the triangle O_lOP_T, because the triangle $L_0R_0R_T(L_T)$ and the triangle O_lOP_T are similar triangles. Thus, the three equations in equations (5) and (7) that include the three unknown parameters β_r, β_l, and X_T are obtained. Then, the solution of the aperture problem is obtained as equation (8) or equation (9), according to the situation. That is, when θ_r is equal to θ_l (the case that the long line is on a front parallel plane), equation (8) is obtained, and when θ_r is not equal to θ_l, equation (9) is obtained.

$$\tan\beta_r = \frac{Y_0}{X_T}, \tan\beta_l = \frac{Y_0}{X_T + a} \quad (7)$$

$$X_T = \frac{a}{\frac{\delta'_L}{\delta'_R} - 1} + \frac{Y_0}{\tan\theta} \quad (8)$$

$$X_T = \frac{a\delta'_R + Y_0\left(\frac{\delta'_L}{C_r} - \frac{\delta'_R}{C_l}\right)}{\delta'_L - \delta'_R}, \quad (9)$$

where $C_r = \tan\theta_r$, $C_l = \tan\theta_l$.

Both the true motion direction β and the collision location P_T are easily obtained by treating them together. The variables β and P_T are closely connected.

Next, the case in which objects move in an arbitrary 3D direction is considered, i.e., the Y coordinate of collision location Y_T is not equal to Y_0.

The generalized equations (10), (11), and (12) are easily obtained instead of equations (7), (8), and (9).

$$\tan\beta_r = \frac{Y_T}{X_T}, \tan\beta_l = \frac{Y_T}{X_T + a}, \quad (10)$$

$$X_T = \frac{a}{\frac{\delta'_L}{\delta'_R} - 1} + \frac{Y_T}{\tan\theta}, \quad (11)$$

$$X_T = \frac{a\delta'_R + Y_T\left(\frac{\delta'_L}{C_r} - \frac{\delta'_R}{C_l}\right)}{\delta'_L - \delta'_R}, \quad (12)$$

where $C_r = \tan\theta_r$ and $C_l = \tan\theta_l$.

These equations show that the aperture problem for arbitrary 3D motion cannot be solved completely, even with the addition of a third eye. However, we are able to know whether the dangerous line determined by equation (11) or (12) is far from the observer.

3 Collision prediction experiment

To see the effectiveness of the solution of the aperture problem and the collision prediction system mentioned in Section 2, collision prediction experiments were executed as follows. A low-speed radio-controlled car (53.5 ± 0.9 cm/s) and a high-speed car (146.9 ± 5.4 cm/s) with a long straight edge panel were set to run toward a simple stationary robot (Tokyo-seiki Co., Ltd, see Fig.9) with a stereo video camera (View Plus Co., Ltd).

Fig. 9. Stereo video camera and robot platform.

The prediction location and time were recorded in each frame. One of the records is shown in Fig. 10. The abscissa is the time, the left ordinate is the predicted collision time (shown by the solid lines) and the right ordinate is the predicted collision location (shown by the dotted lines). The upper two lines show the predicted collision time and location for the low-speed car and the lower two lines are those for the high-speed car. The dotted lower line shows that the predicted collision location is approximately 30 cm on the left from the right camera.

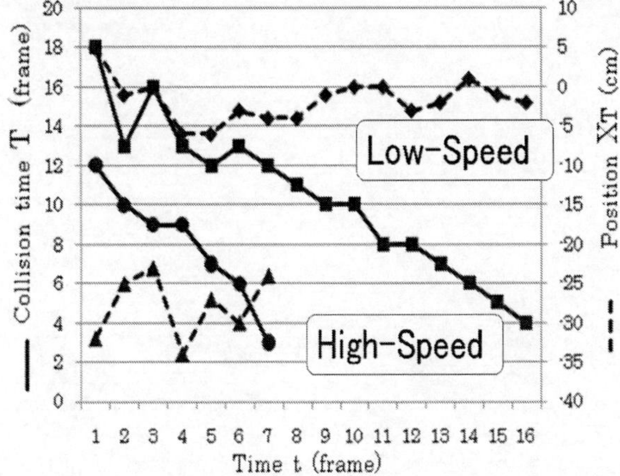

Fig. 10. Examples of $T(t)$ and $X_T(t)$.

The prediction of the collision time and location is done at each frame. The predicted location is approximately constant and the predicted time decreases at approximately a constant rate and predicts approximately a constant time.

These experiments were executed five times each. The mean times for the cars to travel from the start to the collision were 20.75 frames and 11.8 frames for the low-speed and the high-speed cars, respectively. We assumed these times as the correct prediction times. The means and the standard deviations of the error between the measured prediction time and the correct time were -0.28 frames (-0.042 s) and 1.87 frames (0.28 s) for collision of the low-speed car, and 1.26 frames (0.19 s) and 0.70 frames (0.11 s) for collisions of the high-speed cars. The means and the standard deviations of the error between the measured collision location and the predicted location were 1.8 cm (0.98 cm) for the low-speed car and 0.80 cm (1.06 cm) for the high-speed car.

The experimental results show that we can obtain fairly precise predictions even in a system composed of a stereo video camera and a simple robot that are commercially available.

4 Conclusions

In the field of motion perception, the "aperture problem" exists in which we cannot know the true motion direction of a point at a straight line edge on a retinal image by analysis of only a local area. In the present study, we theoretically showed that the problem can be solved based on binocular apparent optical flow. The true solution is obtained when objects and an observer (ego) move on a plane, but the aperture problem for arbitrary 3D motion cannot be solved completely, even with the addition of a third eye. However, we are able to know whether the dangerous line determined by equation (11) or (12) is far from the observer.

The experimental results show that we can obtain fairly precise predictions even in a system composed of a stereo video camera and a simple robot that are commercially available.

In the future, we hope to develop equipment that can be used in automobiles.

5 References

[1] Wallach H. "Uber visuell wahrgenommene Bewegungsrichtung"; Psychol. Forschung, Vol.20, 325-380, 1935.

[2] Shimojo S, Silverman GH, Nakayama K , "Occlusion and the solution to the aperture problem for motion". Vision Res. Vol.29, 619-626, 1989.

[3] Anderson BL, "Stereoscopic occlusion and the aperture problem for motion: a new solution". Vision Res.,Vol.39, 1273-1284, 1991.

[4] Adelson EH, Movshon JA, “Phenomenal coherence of moving visual patterns”. Nature, Vol. 300, 523-525, 1982.

[5] Nakayama K , “Biological image motion processing: A review”. Vision Res., Vol.25, 625-660, 1985.

[6] Horn BKP, Schunk BG, “Determining optical flow”. Artificial Intelligence, Vol.17, 185-203, 1981.

[7] Hildreth EC, “The computation of the velocity field”. Proc. R. Soc. Lond., Vol. B221, 189-220, 1984.

[8] Spies H, Jahne B and Barron J, “Range flow estimation”. Computer Vision and Image Understanding,Vol. 85, 209-231, 2002.

[9] Min D, Sohn K, “Edge-preserving simultaneous joint motion-disparity estimation”. ICPR’06:74-77, 2006.

[10] Lages M, Heron S, “On the inverse problem of binocular 3D motion perception”. PLoS Computational Biology Vol.6:e100-0999, 2010.

[11] Morgan M J, Castet E, “The aperture problem in stereopsis”. Vision Res. , Vol.37, 2737-2744, 1977.

[12] Mori T, “Visual motion perception”. Circulars of the Electro-technical Laboratory, No.207, 31-43, 1982.

[13] Gross E, Tistarelli M, “Active/dynamic stereo vision”. IEEE Trans. PAMI , Vol.PAMI-17, 868-879, 1995.

[14] Kagami S, Okada S, Inaba M, Inoue H, “Real time three dimensional optical flows generation system”. Proc. 17th meeting of Japanese Robotics, 29-30, 1999.

[15] Shimizu S, Yamamoto K, Wang C, Satou Y, Tanahashi H, Niwa Y, “Detection of moving object by mobile stereo omni-directional system”. EEJ Trans.,Vol. EIS124, 1288-1295, 2004.

[16] Regan D, Cynader M, “Neurons in cat visual cortex tuned to the direction of motion in depth: effect of stimulus speed”. Investigative Ophthalmology & Visual Science, Vol. 22, 535-550, 1982.

[17] Toyama K, Kozasa T, “Responses of Clare-bishop neurons to three dimensional movement of a light stimulus”. Vision Res. , Vol.22, 571-574, 1982.

[18] Waxman A M Duncan J H, “Binocular image flows: steps toward stereo-motion fusion”. IEEE Trans. PAMI, Vol.PAMI-8, 715-729, 1986.

[19] Scharr H, Kusters R, “A linear model for simultaneous estimation of 3D motion and depth”. WMVC2002:1-6, 2002.

[20] Lucas B D , Kanade T, “An iterative image registration technique with an application to stereo vision”. IJCAI’81:674-679, 1981.

[21] Ullman S, “The interpretation of structure from motion”. Proc. R. Soc. Lond. , Vol. B 203, :405-426, 1979.

[22] Regan D, Beverley KI, “How do we avoid confounding the direction we are looking and the direction we moving?”. Science, Vol. 5, 194-196, 1985.

[23] Kobayashi H, Sugie N, “Decomposition of spherically projected optical flow into translational and rotational components”. Nagoya University Technical Report, No.8403, 1984.

[24] Mori T, “An active method of extracting ego-motion parameters from optical flow”. Biological Cybernetics,Vol. 52, 405-407, 1985.

3D Active Shape Models Integrating Robust Edge Identification and Statistical Shape Models

Brent C. Munsell[1], **Martin Styner**[2,3], **Heather Hazlett**[3], **and Song Wang**[4]
[1]Department of Mathematics and Computer Science, Claflin University, Orangeburg, SC, USA
[2]Department of Computer Science, University of North Carolina, Chapel Hill, NC, USA
[3]Department of Psychiatry, University of North Carolina, Chapel Hill, NC, USA
[4]Department of Computer Science, University of South Carolina, Columbia, SC, USA

Abstract— *Based on the Point Distribution Model (PDM), Active Shape Model (ASM) is an iterative algorithm used to detect structures of interest from images. However, current ASM methods are sensitive to image noise that may trap the ASM to false edges and/or lead to a structure not within the shape space defined by the PDM. Such problems are particularly serious when segmenting 3D anatomical surface structures from 3D medical images. In this paper we propose two strategies to improve the performance of 3D ASM: (a) developing a robust edge-identification algorithm to reduce the risk of detecting false edges, and (b) integrating the edge-fitting error and statistical shape model defined by a PDM into a unified cost function. We apply the proposed ASM to the challenging tasks of detecting the left hippocampus and caudate surfaces from an subset of 3D pediatric MR images and compare its performance with a recently reported atlas-based method.*

Keywords: 3D Shape Modeling, 3D Active Shape Model, Unified Cost Function

1. Introduction

Image segmentation is a fundamental problem in medical image analysis. An accurate segmentation of the desired anatomical structures from medical images can aid clinical researchers or physicians in the diagnosis of diseased conditions, their possible prognosis, and the effective planning of surgical interventions. For example, given a patients history of epileptic seizures, segmentation of the hippocampus allows physicians to perform meaningful volumetric comparisons to that of a hippocampus affected with mesial temporal sclerosis (MTS). Evidence of an asymmetric MTS hippocampal volume assists physicians with the diagnosis of mesial temporal lobe epilepsy, and its possible treatments [9]. Segmentation of the hippocampus from medical images has also been investigated by clinical researchers in areas such as Alzheimer disease [10], [4], amnesic syndromes [12], and schizophrenia [3], [14], [13].

Active shape model (ASM) [2] is one of the widely used methods for medical image segmentation. The primary advantage of the ASM is its capability to detect structures with a desired shape, which is usually defined by a probabilistic Point Distribution Model (PDM). However, two significant limitations of the ASM can adversely affect its segmentation performance in practice. First, ASM is an iterative algorithm that deforms an initialized shape instance (in the form of boundaries in 2D and surfaces in 3D) to fit some identified image edges. Strong noise in many medical images usually introduce false edges that may trap the shape instance to incorrect locations. Techniques such as the construction of gray level active appearance models (AAM) for each point along the shape instance [1], [7], or statistical shape metrics based on inter-model landmark-based distances [11] have been used to address this limitation. However, the former requires high-quality training images which can be very expensive, while the later does not consider the wealth of information provided by the parameterized shape model. The second limitation is to ensure that the structure found by the ASM bears a shape defined within the shape space of the PDM. In the traditional ASM, this is usually achieved by directly rescaling the obtained shape back to the shape space independent of an image information.

In this paper we propose two strategies to address the limitations described above. Specifically, we propose a strategy to reduce the risk of noisy edges identification and a strategy to integrate the edge-fitting error and statistical shape model defined by a PDM into a unified cost function, which is of a quadratic form and its optimum can be efficiently calculated.

2. PDM, ASM and Problem Description

The statistical shape models used in active shape model (ASM) are called point distribution model (PDM) [2]. The PDM is usually constructed from a set of shape instances, e.g., a set of shape surfaces, say $S_1, S_2, \ldots, S_m$, in the 3D case. Specifically, n corresponded landmark points $\vec{v}_{ji} = (x_{ji}, y_{ji}, z_{ji}), i = 1, 2, \ldots, n$ are first identified from each shape surface S_j and this way, each shape surface S_j can be represented by these landmarks: a $3n$-dimensional vector $\vec{v}_j = (\vec{v}_{j1}, \vec{v}_{j2}, \ldots, \vec{v}_{jn})^t$. If these shape surfaces (and landmarks) have been normalized by removing the size, orientation, and location differences, a PDM is constructed as a multivariate Gaussian distribution $\mathcal{N}(\vec{\bar{v}}, D)$, where

$$\vec{\bar{v}} = \frac{1}{m}\sum_{j=1}^{m} \vec{v}_j \ , \quad D = \frac{1}{m-1}\sum_{j=1}^{m}(\vec{v}_j - \vec{\bar{v}})(\vec{v}_j - \vec{\bar{v}})^t. \ (1)$$

This probabilistic PDM models the shape-deformation space of the considered structure. Specifically, any valid landmark based shape instance $\vec{u}$, given $\mathcal{N}(\vec{\bar{v}}, D)$ can be written as

$$\vec{u} = \vec{\bar{v}} + \sum_{i=1}^{3n} b_i \vec{p}_i, \quad (2)$$

where $\vec{p}_i$ is the i-th eigenvector of D and b_i is the deformation along $\vec{p}_i$. In some prior literatures, $|b_i| \le 3\sqrt{\lambda_i}$, $i = 1, 2, \dots, 3n$ (λ_i is the eigenvalue along $\vec{p}_i$) is used as a criteria to decide whether $\vec{u}$ is a valid shape in the shape space defined by PDM $\mathcal{N}(\vec{\bar{v}}, D)$.

Given a PDM, ASM operates on a 3D image frame as follows: (a) Placing an initial estimate of the desired landmark-based shape surface $\vec{u} = (\vec{u}_1, \vec{u}_2, \dots, \vec{u}_n)$ in the image. This is achieved by applying an global transform $T(\vec{\bar{v}} : \vec{t}, s, \vec{\theta})$ to the PDM mean shape $\vec{\bar{v}}$, where $\vec{t}$, s, and $\vec{\theta}$ indicate the translation, scaling and rotation transform parameters respectively; (b) Searching along the normal directions for each of the n landmarks in $\vec{u}$, identifying strong image edges with high intensity-gradient magnitude; (c) Updating $\vec{u}$ to the ASM approximated shape $\vec{u}'$ by moving all the n landmarks to their corresponding identified edges while ensuring $\vec{u}'$ to be a valid shape in the PDM $\mathcal{N}(\vec{\bar{v}}, D)$; (d) Repeating (b) and (c) to further update the shape surface until convergence.

We can see that, in the above framework there are two major ASM operations which are edge identification and shape deformation. As shown in Fig. 1(a), edge identification is achieved by constructing a search profile along the normal direction of each landmark $\vec{u}_i$, where $i = 1, 2, \cdots, n$. Specifically, $2k+1$ locations are sampled along this profile and the magnitude of the voxel intensity gradient is calculated at each sampled location. The profile location with the strongest intensity-gradient magnitude α_i is then chosen as the identified edge point. This strongest edge point can then be written as $\vec{\hat{u}}_i = \vec{u}_i + \alpha_i \vec{n}_i$, where $\vec{n}_i$ is the unit normal vector at $\vec{u}_i$.

In shape deformation, we need to deform $\vec{u}$ to $\vec{u}'$, which updates both the global transform $T(\vec{\bar{v}} : \vec{t}, s, \vec{\theta})$ and the local-transform parameters $\vec{b} = (b_1, b_2, \dots, b_{3n})^t$ shown in Eq. (2). This shape deformation seeks a balance between two goals: (a) $\vec{u}'$ fits better to the identified edges $\vec{\hat{u}} = (\vec{\hat{u}}_1, \vec{\hat{u}}_2, \dots, \vec{\hat{u}}_n)^t$, and (b) $\vec{u}'$ still bears a valid shape in the PDM $\mathcal{N}(\vec{\bar{v}}, D)$. In some current 3D ASM implementations, the deformation from $\vec{u}$ to $\vec{u}'$ is simply achieved by modifying the identified edges $\vec{\hat{u}}$ to fit the given PDM: representing $\vec{\hat{u}}$ in the form of Eq. (2) and if any b_i is larger than $3\sqrt{\lambda_i}$ or smaller than $-3\sqrt{\lambda_i}$, b_i is re-scaled [2] to fit within the limits $3\sqrt{\lambda_i}$ or $-3\sqrt{\lambda_i}$ of the PDM shape space.

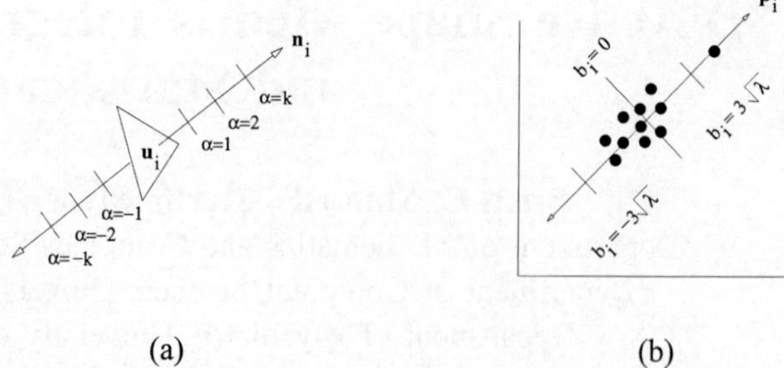

Fig. 1: An illustration of the edge identification and shape deformation in ASM. (a) Search for strong edges along the profile of landmark $\vec{u}_i$. The profile is uniformly sampled into $2k + 1$ points symmetric over $\vec{u}_i$ for calculating intensity-gradient magnitude. (b) A step of shape deformation by rescaling the parameter b_i that is out of the range $[-3\sqrt{\lambda_i}, 3\sqrt{\lambda_i}]$.

However, two problems exist in the above ASM algorithm. First, the strongest edge with the largest intensity gradient magnitude along the profile might not be the true edge of the desired structure. In practice, the strongest edges could be image noise or other neighboring structures. Previous research has shown that incorrect edge identification may result in very poor performance of the ASM [11]. Second, direct modification of $\vec{\hat{u}}$ for shape deformation may also result in poor ASM performance, especially when the identified edges $\vec{\hat{u}}$ contains much noise and the initial estimate of the shape surface is relatively far from the desired structure. In the worst case, such modification may keep the shape surface around the initial location without any further deformation. In the next section, we presented two strategies to address these two problems.

3. Proposed Method

3.1 Robust Edge Identification

Instead of independently detecting the strongest edge $\vec{\hat{u}}_i$ for each landmark $\vec{u}_i$ along the normal direction, we consider a *neighboring-consistency* property to improve the robustness of the edge identification: if two landmarks $\vec{u}_i$ and $\vec{u}_j$ are very close to each other, it is very likely that the detected edges $\vec{\hat{u}}_i$ and $\vec{\hat{u}}_j$ are close as well. In particular, the proposed edge-identification algorithm consists of three steps:

1) For each landmark $\vec{u}_i$, we find all its $m(i)$ neighboring landmarks defined on the triangular surface mesh of $\vec{u}$, as shown in Fig. 2(a). Let d_{ij} be the Euclidean distance between the landmark $\vec{u}_i$ and its j-th neighbor, where $i = 1, 2, \dots, n$ and $j = 1, 2, \dots, m(i)$. We can see that d_{ij} describes the spatial proximity from $\vec{u}_i$ to its neighbors. Later we will apply d_{ij} to weight the edge-identification consistency between $\vec{u}_i$ and its j-th neighbor.

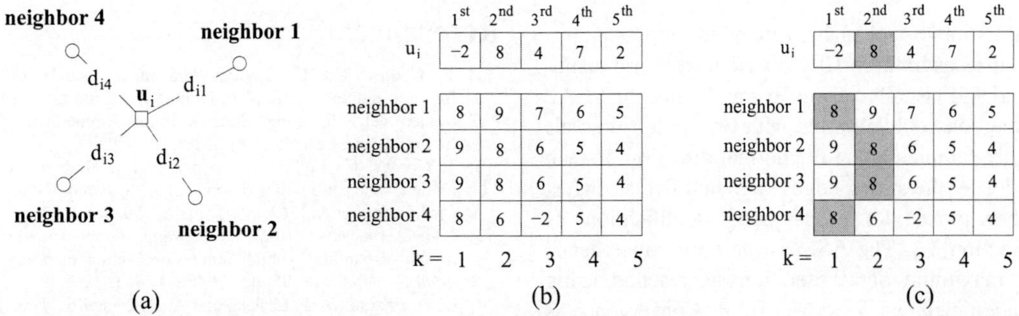

Fig. 2: An illustration of the robust edge identification algorithm. (a) Identify the neighbors of $\vec{u}_i$ and calculate the their distances. (b) The first five strongest edges identified for $\vec{u}_i$ and its five neighbors. The elements show the offset values of the identified edges along their respective profiles. (c) The optimal offset value $\alpha_i^* = 8$ minimizes the edge cost and we therefore choose $\hat{\vec{u}}_i = \vec{u}_i + 8\vec{n}_i$.

2) For landmark $\vec{u}_i$ and each of its neighboring landmarks, we construct a vector $\vec{e}$ that contains the locations of the first several strongest edges in a descending order. For example, $\vec{e}_i$ in Fig. 2(b) contains the first five strongest edges along the profile of $\vec{u}_i$, where $e_{i1} = -2$ indicates that the strongest edge is located at $\vec{u}_i - 2\vec{n}_i$ and $\vec{e}_{i5} = 2$ indicates that the fifth strongest edge is located at $\vec{u}_i + 2\vec{n}_i$. We further define a weight function to quantify the strength of each edge by its rank: the k-th strongest edge is simply set to have a weight of k in this paper.
3) Based on the information collected in the first two steps, the last step aims to more robustly determine the most likely edge $\hat{\vec{u}}_i$ for landmark $\vec{u}_i$. Specifically, we formulate the problem as identifying the optimal offset α_i^* along the normal direction that shows the best consistency for landmark $\vec{u}_i$ and all its neighbors. In short, for each offset value e_{ik}, we find the rank in j-th neighbor of $\vec{u}_i$ and denote this rank to be $r(i, j, k)$. The edge cost corresponding to the offset value e_{ik} is

$$\phi(e_{ik}) = k \sum_{j=1}^{m(i)} r(i, j, k) \cdot d_{ij}.$$

We finally choose α_i^* to be the offset value e_{ik} that minimizes the edge cost $\phi(e_{ik})$. Figure 2(c) gives an example of detecting the most likely edges for $\vec{u}_i$ by locating the offset that minimizes this new edge cost. We can see that, in this example, the most likely edge identified for $\vec{u}_i$ is different from the highest-ranked edge (the one with the largest intensity gradient magnitude) along the normal direction $\vec{n}_i$.

3.2 Shape Deformation Based on a Unified Cost Function

Each iteration of shape deformation aims to update the shape surface $\vec{u}$ to $\vec{u}'$ by minimizing the fitting error to the identified edges $\hat{\vec{u}}$ while keeping $\vec{u}'$ within the shape space of the given PDM. As discussed before, such deformation consists of updating both a global transform $T(\vec{t}, s, \vec{\theta})$ and a local transform described by parameters $\vec{b}$. For the global transform, we simply find the $T(\vec{t}, s, \vec{\theta})$ between the PDM mean shape vector $\bar{\vec{v}}$ and the identified edges $\hat{\vec{u}}$ [2]. For local transform, we find $\vec{u}'$ that minimizes a cost function

$$\sum_{i=1}^{n} \|\vec{u}_i' - \hat{\vec{u}}_i\|^2 + \beta(\vec{u}' - T(\bar{\vec{v}} : \vec{t}, s, \vec{\theta}))^t D_T^{-1} (\vec{u}' - T(\bar{\vec{v}} : \vec{t}, s, \vec{\theta}))$$

where $\vec{u}_i'$ is constrained to be along the normal direction of $T(\vec{u}_i : \vec{t}, s, \vec{\theta})$, i.e., the globally transformed version of $\vec{u}_i$. D_T^{-1} is the inverse of D_T which is the updated covariance matrix after the global transform, i.e. $D_T = T \cdot D \cdot T^t$. We can see that finding the optimal solution for local transform is a typical quadratic programming problem, which can be solved efficiently. In the above cost function, $\beta > 0$ is a coefficient that balances the contributions from the detected edges and the PDM.

4. Experiments

We applied the proposed ASM by segmenting the left hippocampus and caudate surfaces in MRI images from an pediatric autism study [6] from which we randomly selected a subset of 10 IR-prepped SPGR T1 weighted MRI brain scan images. The resolution of an image is $256 \times 256 \times 192$ with both the in-plane and inter-slice voxel spacing set at $1.0mm$. The hippocampus PDM was constructed using 42 adult hippocampus surfaces, each of which contains 642 identified corresponded landmarks. These corresponded landmarks are identified by using a minimum-description-length (MDL) implementation [8]. The caudate PDM was constructed using 85 caudate surfaces, each of which contains 742 corresponded landmarks. The corresponded caudate landmarks are identified by using the spherical-harmonic-descriptors (SPHARM) implementation [15].

The initial estimate and placement of the hippocampus and caudate surfaces in these 10 pediatric images are manually performed and visually verified using the Insight-SNAP software. Nine consecutive points with one voxel intervals were uniformly sampled along the normal direction of each landmark to locate the strong edges. The first five strongest edges are then picked for robust edge identification, as detailed in Section 3.1. The ASM is ran until convergence or when an maximum of 10 iterations is reached using an balance coefficient of $\beta = 5 \times 10^{-5}$. Convergence is achieved when both the global and local transform vary minimally.

We evaluate the segmentation results by comparing them with expertly segmented left hippocampus and caudate surfaces. The hippocampus was segmented using an semi-automatic method [16], and the caudate was segmented either via manual outlining, or semi-automatic geodesic curve evolution [17]. We measure their consistency using the Pearson correlation and dice coefficients [5]. The Pearson correlation coefficient c_P measures the volumetric correlation between manual and ASM segmentations on all 10 images, while the dice coefficient c_D assesses the structure similarity by measuring their volumetric overlap. The results are shown in Table-1. In this table, we also include the segmentation performance of the reported atlas-based method [5], which is based on 20 pediatric images from the same autistic study.

Although the performance of the atlas-based method is obtained from more images that the proposed method, we can see that the proposed ASM shows a comparable c_D performance to and better c_P performance than those of the atlas-based method. Fig. 3 shows the initially-placed shape surfaces and the ones segmented by the proposed ASM in the coronal, transverse and sagittal planes. Lastly, the proposed ASM does require an reasonable initial PDM placement but is not very sensitive.

5. Conclusion

In this paper, we presented two new strategies to address the limitations of the current 3D ASM methods. The preliminary study shows promising results: the proposed 3D ASM produces comparable or even better segmentation results than a recently reported atlas-based method. In the future, we plan to further investigate the sensitivity of the initial shape placement and apply the proposed ASM on segmenting other anatomic structures.

Acknowledgements

This work was funded in part by (a) NASA Curriculum Improvements Partnership Award for the Integration of Research (CIPAIR), and (b) by NSF-EIA-0312861.

References

[1] T. Cootes and C. Taylor, "Statistical models of appearance for computer vision," Technical Report, University of Manchester, Imaging Science and Biomedical Engineering, `http://www.wiau.man.ac.uk`, 1999.

[2] T. Cootes, C. Taylor, D. Cooper, and J. Graham, "Active shape models - their training and application," *Computer Vision and Image Understanding*, vol. 61, no. 1, pp. 38–59, Jan. 1995.

[3] J. G. Csernansky, S. Joshi, and L. Wang, "Hippocampal morphometry in schizo-phrenia by high dimensional brain mapping," *Proc Natl Acad Sci USA*, vol. 95, pp. 11 406–11 411, 1998.

[4] G. B. Frisoni, M. P. Laakso, and A. Beltramello, "Hippocampal and entorinhal cortex atrophy in frontotemporal dementia and alzheimers disease," *Neurology*, vol. 52, pp. 91–100, 1999.

[5] S. Gouttarda, M. Styner, S. Joshi, R. G. Smith, H. Cody, and G. Gerig, "Subcortical structure segmentation using probabilistic atlas priors," in *Proceedings of the SPIE Medical Imaging Conference*, 2007.

[6] H. C. Hazlett, M. D. Poe, G. Gerig, R. G. Smith, and J. Piven, "Cortical gray and white brain tissue volume in adolescents and adults with autism," *Biological Psychiatry*, vol. 59, pp. 1–96, 2006.

[7] T. Heimann, I. Wolf, , and H. P. Meinzer, "Active shape models for a fully automated 3d segmentation of the liver -an evaluation on clinical data," in *International Conference on Medical Image Computing and Computer Assisted Intervention*, vol. 2, 2006, pp. 41–48.

[8] T. Heimann, I. Wolf, T. Williams, and H.-P. Meinzer, "3d active shape models using gradient descent optimization of description length," in *Information Processing in Medical Imaging Conference*, 2005, pp. 566–577.

[9] R. E. Hogan, K. E. Mark, L. Wang, S. Joshi, M. I. Miller, and R. D. Bucholz, "Mesial temporal sclerosis and temporal lobe epilepsy: Mr imaging deformation-based segmentation of the hippocampus in five patients," *Radiology*, vol. 216, pp. 291–297, 2000.

[10] C. R. Jack, R. C. Petersen, and Y. Xu, "Rate of medial temporal lobe atrophy in typical aging and alzheimers disease," *Neurology*, vol. 51, pp. 993–999, 1998.

[11] K. Lekadir, R. Merrifield, and G. Z. Yang, "Outlier detection and handling for robust 3-d active shape models search," *IEEE Transactions on Medical Imaging*, vol. 26, pp. 212–222, 2007.

[12] G. A. Press, D. G. Amaral, and L. R. Squire, "Hippo-campal abnormalities in amnesic patients revealed by high-resolution magnetic resonance imaging," *Nature*, vol. 341, pp. 54–57, 1989.

[13] M. E. Shenton, G. Gerig, R. W. McCarley, G. Szekely, and R. Kikinis, "Amygdala - hippocampal shape differences in schizophrenia: the application of 3d shape models to volumetric mr data," *Psychiatry Research Neuroimaging*, vol. 115, pp. 15–35, 2002.

[14] M. E. Shenton, R. Kikinis, and F. A. Jolesz, "Abnormalities of the left temporal lobe and thought disorder in schizophrenia: a quantitative magnetic resonance imaging study," *New England Journal of Medicine*, vol. 327, pp. 604–612, 1992.

[15] M. Styner, J. A. Lieberman, R. K. McClure, D. R. Weingberger, D. W. Jones, and G. Gerig, "Morphometric analysis of lateral ventricles in schizophrenia and healthy controls regarding genetic and disease-specific factors," *Proceedings of the National Academy of Science*, vol. 102, pp. 4872–4877, 2005.

[16] M. Styner, S. C. Xu, M. El-Sayed, and G. Gering, "Correspondence evaluation in local shape analysis and structural subdivision," in *IEEE Symposium on Biomedical Imaging*, 2007.

[17] P. A. Yushkevich, J. Piven, H. C. Hazlett, R. S. Gimpel, S. Ho, J. C. Gee, and G. Gerig, "User guided 3d active contour segmentation of anatomical structures: Significantly improved efficiency and reliablility," *NeuroImage*, vol. 31, pp. 1116–1128, 2006.

Table 1: Segmentation performances of the proposed method and an atlas-based method compared against expertly segmented hippocampus and caudate data.

	Left Hippocampus		Left Caudate	
Segmentation Methods	c_P	c_D	c_P	c_D
Proposed ASM	0.7373	0.7792	0.8452	0.8318
Atlas-based Method [5]	0.1800	0.7500	0.7500	0.8400

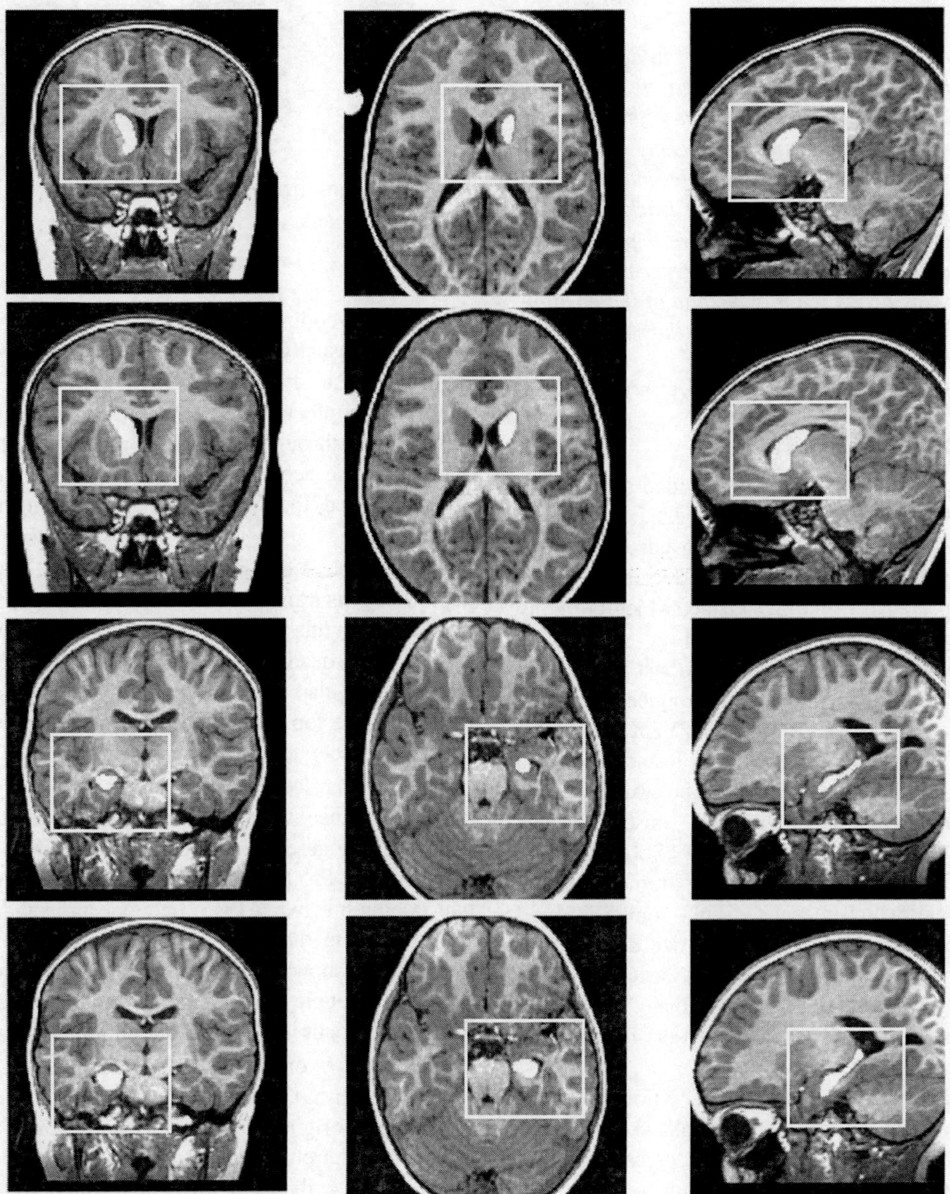

Fig. 3: Row 1: Initially placed left caudate. Row 2: Left caudate segmented by the proposed ASM. Row 3: Initially placed left hippocampus. Row 4: Left hippocampus segmented by the proposed ASM. Columns 1, 2 and 3 show the structures in the coronal, transverse, and sagittal planes respectfully.

Robust People Tracking Using A Light Coding Depth Sensor

Xun Changqing[1], **Yang Shuqiang**[2], **and Zhang Chunyuan**[1]
[1]College of Computer, National University of Defence Technology, ChangSha, China
[2]College of Electronic Science and Engineering, National University of Defence Technology, ChangSha, China

Abstract—*People tracking plays a key role in real-time automated surveillance system. Occlusion handling is facilitated by using depth sensors. However, when persons touch, it is still hard to identified them even in depth image. When someone have touched another, their heads usually keep distant from each other. And the shape of heads in top view is very stable. So we treat people tracking as multiple heads tracking in top view image, and present a directed semicircular template based multiple heads tracking method using a novel light coding depth sensor. We implement our method to run in real-time on PC. Our experiment shows our method can track heads reliably in spite of the position, pose of persons and the collision between them.*

Keywords: people tracking, depth sensor, video surveillance

1. Introduction

People tracking is a key component of video surveillance system. Traditional video surveillance system is built upon intensity cameras. Reliable people tracking has been found difficult by using conventional cameras. Because it relies on the object appearance in the 2D image, which is highly sensitive to lighting changes and occlusion.

Depth sensor gives the opportunity for robust and precise people tracking. Recently, companies introduced kinds of depth sensors: Deepsea G2 EVS[1] from TYZX, CamCube 3.0[2] from PMD, Kinect[3] from Microsoft and Xtion Pro Live[4] from ASUS. The first one is a stereo vision system, and the second is a Time-Of-Flight depth sensor. The last two are both designed based on PS1080[5][6] SoC developed by PrimeSense. The PS1080 SoC houses extremely parallel computational logic, which receives a light coding infrared pattern as an input, and produces a VGA-size depth image of the scene. The biggest advantage of Kinect and Xtion Pro Live is the cost. The price is less than 200 dollars. This makes cost acceptable to use depth sensors for common security application.

We use Xtion Pro Live in this paper. Xtion Pro Live is equipped with a RGB sensor and a light coding depth sensor. It has a 45 degrees vertical by 58 degrees horizontal field of view. Measuring range is 0.8m-3.5m. In fact, it still works over 3.5m, although the depth measurement accuracy slightly decreases. It provides 640×480 colour images and depth images at a frame rate of 30 FPS.

The main contribution of this paper is to present a directed semicircular template based multiple heads tracking method using a light coding depth sensor. When two persons touch, their heads usually keep distant. And the shape of heads in top view is steady as a spherical rigid body. Accordingly, we treat people tracking as multiple heads tracking, and track heads through a straightforward template matching approach. The accurate 3D positions of all people's heads are maintained, then we can get the positions and heights of them.

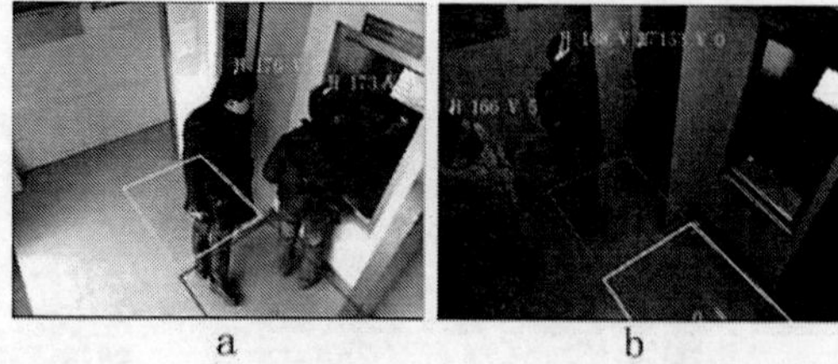

Fig. 1: Images from Xtion Pro Live in a business hall of self-service bank

Our method is comprised of two steps. First, the original depth image is transformed to top view image, which we call height map in this paper. Second, the background elimination and multiple heads tracking are applied to the height map. With height map generation, we don't need to install the camera at the top of the room and positions of objects are also more accurate.

The self-service banking hall is a perfect scenario for our surveillance system. Size of the room well suits the measuring range of the camera. Figure 1 shows two images from a Xtion Pro Live we installed in a self-service banking hall containing two ATMs. Left one is in the daytime and right one is in the night-time. Significant lighting changes happened as shown in the images. Overall aim of our project is to track people in real-time and analysis their behaviour. This paper focuses on the people tracking subsystem.

This paper is organized as follows. Some related work is reviewed later at this section. In section 2 we introduce how to transform original depth images to height maps. Then the directed semicircular template based multiple heads tracking method is described in section 3. Evaluation is discussed in section 4. Finally, we conclude this paper and outline future work.

Related work. People tracking has generated a vast literature. Many algorithms rely on binary blobs or regions extracted from single video [7][8]. Sometimes additional classification schemes based on colour, texture or other local image properties are used [10]. Methods using 2D appearance models of human beings have also been proposed [9].

It is straightforward to get 3D information by using multiple cameras. Mittal and Davis [13] propose a system that segments, detects, and tracks multiple people in a scene by using a wide-baseline setup of up to 16 synchronized cameras. In [14], individuals are tracked both in image planes and top view. Given two to four synchronized video streams taken at eye level and from different angles, Francois et el.[15] show that they can effectively combine a generative model with dynamic programming to accurately follow up to six individuals across thousands of frames in spite of significant occlusions and lighting changes.

TOF depth sensor is another kind of depth sensor using active light source. It measures the depth by detecting the phase shift between out-light and in-light. Salih et al.[16] describe a 3D head tracking algorithm which is based on recognition and correlation based weighted interpolation. Rudolf et al.[17] introduce a slicing algorithm for people tracking using TOF depth sensor.

Kinect and Xtion Pro Live offer promises for much more robust human computer communication. Most researchers focus on human pose recognition [18][19]. Jamie[19] takes an object recognition approach, designing an intermediate body parts representation that maps the difficult pose estimation problem into a simpler per pixel classification problem. NITE[5] from PrimeSense and Kinect SDK[3] from Microsoft both support skeleton tracking and simple multiple users tracking. Camera and person are horizontal for human body estimation. It is usually installed at height for surveillance. We take NITE for example to show the problems during people tracking. Figure 2-a and 2-b show that NITE confuses the user with background. When a person stands behind another and they touch, NITE cannot track them correctly as showed in Fig.2-c and 2-d.

2. Depth Image To Height Map Transformation

Transformation from depth images to height maps is comprised of three steps: depth image pre-processing, fast camera calibration and height map generation.

It is really not easy to do detailed experiments in a real self-service banking hall because of security issues. Instead we use our experimental room as shown in Fig.3. There is no essential difference between them for our method. Left is the colour image, and right is the corresponding floor plan. The camera is placed at the lower-left corner of the room. The room may be obstructed by tables, chairs or other furniture. We simply place a colour box for instance. A three dimensions right-handedness Cartesian coordinate system is established. The origin is the lower-left corner of the room. The Z-axis is perpendicular to the ground plane. The value of the Z coordinate is positive upward.

2.1 Depth Image Preprocessing

There are two steps needed to adjust the depth image captured by Xtion Pro Live. First, view points are different between colour images and depth images. It is easier to calibrate the RGB camera, because colour images are clear to locate calibration points pairs. Moreover, the operators of surveillance systems prefer colour image. So, we must set the view point of depth images to color images. OpenNI[5] which is another middleware developed by PrimeSense supports this function. Effect of view point setting is shown in Fig.4. Figure 4-a and 4-b are the detph images before and after view point setting respectively.

Second, Each pixel of the original depth image represents the Cartesian distance, in millimetres, from the camera plane to the nearest object at that particular x and y coordinate. What we need is to get the distance from the camera to the object. The difference is shown in Fig.5.

Distance can be calculated by Eq.(1). M and N represent the size of depth image, which are 640 and 480 respectively. fov_u and fov_v represent the field of view of depth sensor, which are 45 and 58 degrees for Xtion Pro Live. In order not to cause confusion, depth image preprocessed will still be called depth image later in this paper.

$$\begin{gathered} distance(u,v) = \frac{depth(u,v)}{\cos(\theta_u)\times\cos(\theta_v)} \\ \theta_u = (u-\frac{M}{2})\times\frac{fov_u}{M}, \theta_v = (v-\frac{N}{2})\times\frac{fov_v}{N} \end{gathered} \tag{1}$$

2.2 Fast Camera Calibration

Abdel-Azizh and Karara proposed the direct linear transformation (DLT)[20] method for camera calibration. DLT treats transformation from world coordinates to pixel coordinates as linear transformation as shown in Eq.(2). (x_w, y_w, z_w) represent world coordinates. (u, v) represent pixel coordinates. And m_{ij}s are elements of transformation matrix.More than 6 pairs of calibration points are needed to solve the transformation matrix. And it is hard to check validity of these data. As a consequence, Camera calibration with this method costs more than half an hour according to our experience.

$$z_c \begin{pmatrix} u \\ v \\ 1 \end{pmatrix} = \begin{pmatrix} m_{11} & m_{12} & m_{13} & m_{14} \\ m_{21} & m_{22} & m_{23} & m_{24} \\ m_{31} & m_{32} & m_{33} & m_{34} \end{pmatrix} \begin{pmatrix} x_w \\ y_w \\ z_w \\ 1 \end{pmatrix} \tag{2}$$

In order to simplify the process, we design a fast calibration method with only one special calibration points pair and the world coordinates of camera. The pixel coordinates of the special calibration points pair must be the centre of image. This method is based on three assumptions: (1), intrinsic

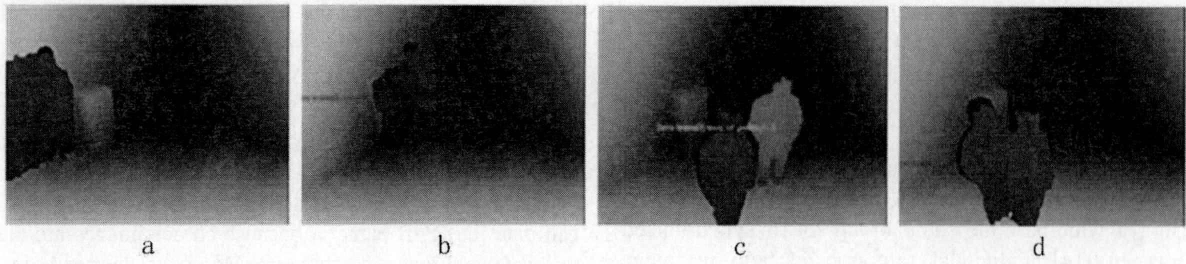

Fig. 2: Problems during NITE's user tracking

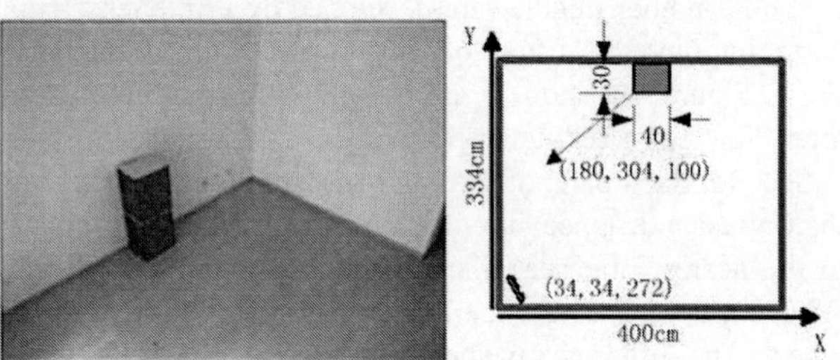

Fig. 3: Color image and floor plan of the experimental room

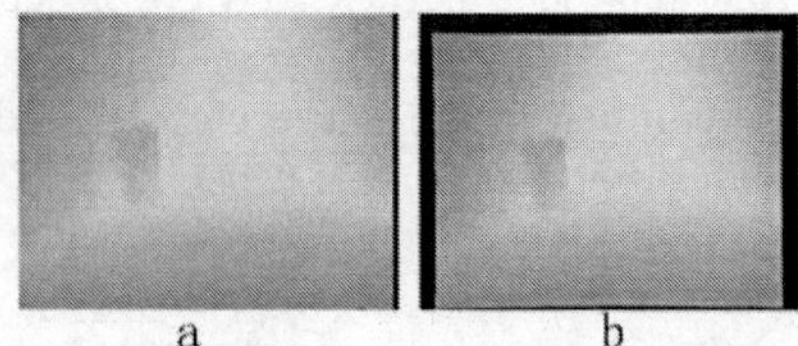

Fig. 4: View point setting for depth image

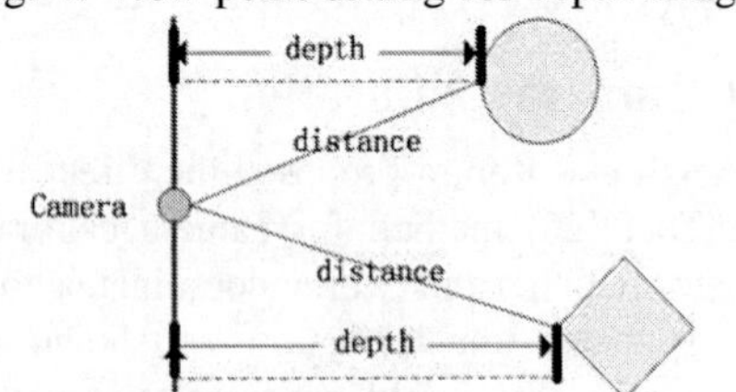

Fig. 5: Depth and distance

parameters of all Xtion Pro Live are identical, (2), the camera is horizontal, (3), the Cartesian coordinate system is right-handedness.

Given these assumptions, there are only two degrees of freedom of the camera as shown in Fig.6: horizontal rotation angle θ and vertical inclination angle φ. To make it simple, an assumption that the optical axis crosses the centre of the image is taken. So the equation of optical axis can be figured out with the world coordinates of the camera and a arbitrary real world point which is projected to the centre of image. Camera transformation matrix can be got within two minutes by combining the external parameters and the identical intrinsic parameters.

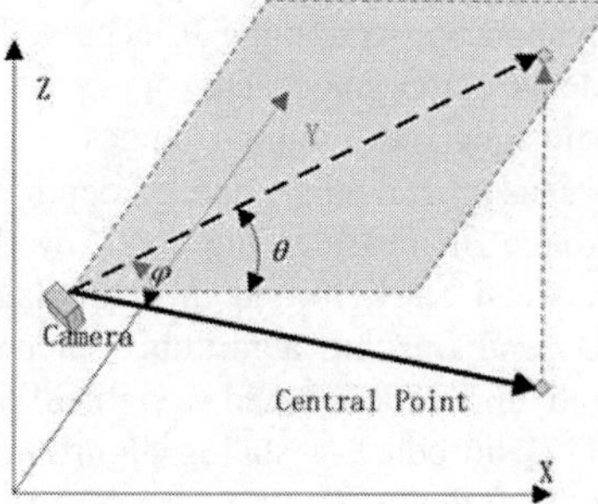

Fig. 6: Degrees of freedom of the camera

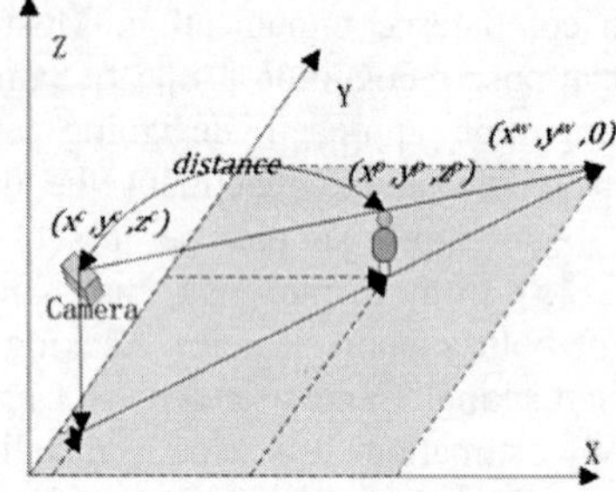

Fig. 7: The method to get the world coordinates of each pixel in depth image

2.3 Height Map Generation

Spatial resolution of the height map is 1cm per pixel. It is enough for common surveillance systems. Size depends on the room, and range of height is 0-255cm. Take our experimental room for example, height map is a 400×344 unsigned 8 bit integer matrix. Each element of the matrix represents the maximal height at that particular x and y coordinate.

Height map can be easily generated with camera transformation matrix and depth image. Figure 7 shows the method to get the world coordinates corresponding to each pixel in depth image. Given $z^w = 0$, for each (u, v), $(x^w, y^w, 0)$ is the solution to equation 2. (x^p, y^p, z^p) can be easily got with (x^c, y^c, z^c), $(x^w, y^w, 0)$ and distance. Height map can be generated though processing the whole depth image pixel by pixel.

Figure 8 shows the height map of our experiment room as

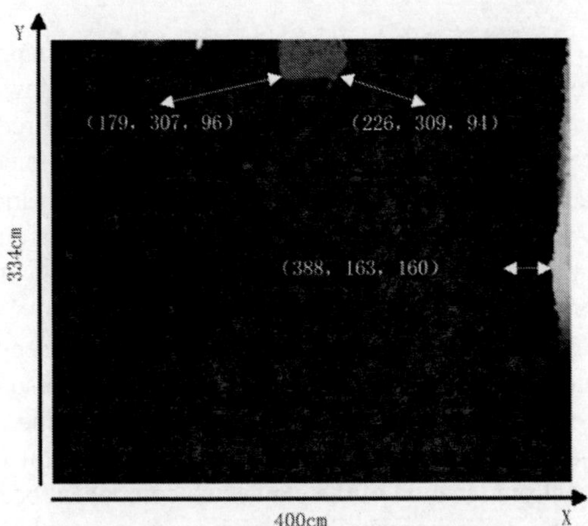

Fig. 8: Height map of our experimental room

a gray image. Gray scale of each pixel represents the height at the corresponding coordinates. Simple error analysis is done according to this height map. Coordinates of lower-left corner of the box are $(179, 307, 96)$, and the error are $(-1, +3, -4)$. Coordinates of lower-right corner are $(226, 309, 94)$, and the error are $(+6, +5, -6)$. The error are relatively small, because the box is near the camera. And error of the top wall are also small. Right wall is about 4 meters far from the camera. It is almost beyond the measuring range of the camera. As a result, x coordinate of the right wall is 12cm less.

3. Implementation of Multiple Heads Tracking Method

Implementation detail of our tracking method is presented in this section. The method is comprised of three parts. First, foreground segmentation is needed to eliminate the background such as floor, wall and the box. Second, directed semicircular template construction introduces what is the template and how to construct it for each head. Third, head tracking is responsible with updating status of every head overtime.

3.1 Foreground Segmentation

The height map we created in section 2 contains floor, wall and box. So we have to eliminate these things as background basically. It is very straightforward to obtain background model using height maps. An arbitrary height map without person at the scene can be the background model. In order to be stable, we use maximum of about 200 frames.

Foreground segmentation is easy based on this background model. For each pixel of height map, if its height is higher than background, it is a foreground pixel, otherwise it is a background pixel.

Fig. 9: Foreground segmentation example

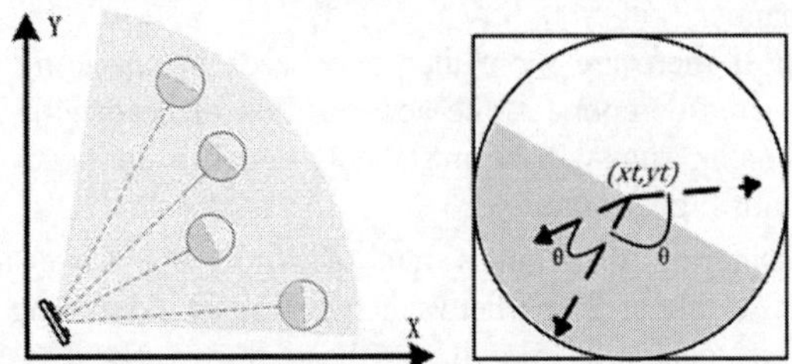

Fig. 10: Directed semicircular templates

Figure 9 shows a foreground segmentation example. Figure 9-a is the background model. Figure 9-b is the current depth image, and 9-c is the current foreground height map.

3.2 Directed Semicircular Template Construction

The simplest tracking can implemented based on connected component nearest-neighbour approach. But it cannot handle overlaps between targets. When two persons touch, collision occurs between the connected components arising from them in height map. It is difficult to detect the outline of them. When collision occurs, their heads still keep distant from each other. Moreover, head is a rigid body and usually at the top of human body. So we design a straightforward multiple heads tracking method based on shape template matching. With multiple heads tracking, we can get the position and height of everyone at the scene.

Shape is one of the most obvious characteristics of heads in height map. Light from the depth sensor can only illuminate the near side of the head. The sensor cannot measure the depth of the dark side of the head. Although a head is actually a sphere, it is a semicircle in height map.

Accordingly, we propose the conception of directed semicircular template and track every head through a straightforward template matching approach. Considering the size of heads, the radius of template is 10cm. Directions of semicircular templates for different targets are different. They are all oriented toward the camera, as shown in Fig.10.

3.3 Searching for new positions of heads

The key of tracking a head is to search the connected component nearest the head for its new position. For each head, its directed semicircular template is constructed first. And the foreground height map is convolved with this template. Intensities of the pixels are compared using the sum measure. Simply setting the position with the maximal sum in the connected component as the new position of head may lead to two problems:

1. In case of only one head in the connected component, the position with the maximal sum is the head mostly. But it is the shoulder or hand occasionally, especially when the person raises hands.
2. If there are more than two heads in one connected component, the new position of head with smaller sum will be mistakenly equal to the head with bigger sum.

Considering the frames rate of Xtion Pro Live, time interval is about 33ms between two frames. Assuming the speed of person is 5km/h, the head moves about 4.6cm between two frames. 4.6cm is much shorter than the distance from head to shoulder, and it is also much shorter than the distance between two heads. We take all positions with local maximal sum as candidates. The evaluation function of each candidates is designed as Eq.(3). Distance from starting position to new position is also be considered in the evaluation function. Considering the short distance from starting position to new position between two frames, we didn't predict the new position of head. We just use the position in last frame as the starting point for searching instead.

$$score^l = sum_{x^l y^l} - \sqrt{(x^l - x^t)(y^l - y^t)} \quad (3)$$

A head list being tracked is maintained by our tracker. If a connected component contains no head in the list, a new head will be added. The position of new head is initialized as the centroid location of the associated connected component. This simple method needs a precondition: persons entering the space separately. It means that the connected component of person entering the space newly is separated from others'.

4. Evaluation

In this section we describe the experiments performed to evaluate our method. Our method is implemented to run in real-time (that is 30fps) on a PC based on Intel Core i3 processor and 4GB RAM. Overall time of processing one frame is 20ms. Height map generation costs 14ms, and the rest costs 6ms. Height map generation needs a lot of CPU time, because it involves a great many of random memory access. 640×480 random access to 400×334 matrix is needed in our experiment.

Next we focus on the tracking robustness for single person and multiple persons.

4.1 Single Person

Figure 11 shows the tracking result for single person at different positions. For each position, there are three figures: left is the depth image, middle is the height map, and right zooms in the middle one. In right image, yellow spot represents the starting position of the head, and the red one represents the new position searched by our tracking method.

In fact, distance from starting position to new position is usually less than 4cm restricted by the speed of person and the frame rate of Xtion Pro Live. In our experiment, it is a little more than 4cm for strict testing.

Figure 11-a shows a person newly entering the space from the bottom of camera view. Right shoulder of the person can not be seen in the image. So in the height map, there are only the head and the left shoulder. Starting position is set to the centroid location of the connected component because the target is added newly. The position of red spot shows accurate result. Background elimination does not change the shape of heads as shown in Fig.11-e and 11-f.

Besides, tracking results for single person in different poses are listed in Fig.12. Shapes of heads in 12-d,12-e and 12-f are very clear. Positions of heads in 12-a,12-b and 12-c are far from the centroid location of connected components. The head is not the highest part of body in Fig.12-e. In order to show the advantage of our semicircular template, we use circular template for searching Fig.12-b. And the result position is at the left shoulder marked as a green spot.

When the person is near the camera such as Fig.11-a, or head up and down such as Fig.12-b and 12-c, shape of the head is close to circle. Otherwise, semicircle shaped heads are very clear.

As shown in the tracking results, our method can accurately track the head for single person at different positions or in different poses.

4.2 Multiple Persons

Tracking results for two persons when collision occurs between associated connected components are listed in Fig.13. It is emphasized that collision in height map means that they touch each other. Figure 13-a shows two persons stand side by side. Situation shown in Fig.13-b is the same to Fig.2-d. Result shows that the problem is overcome by our method. Figure 13-d shows an analysis of 13-b to discuss the robustness of our method. As long as the starting position of upper person is within the upper light gray region, and the starting position of lower person is within the lower dark gray region, both of them will be tracked correctly. Borderline between the light gray region and the dark gray region is very close to the real borderline of two persons. This implies that our method is very robust. Situation shown in Fig.13-c is a big challenge to our method. Because head of the person sitting down is much lower than the standing one's. Taking the distance from starting position to new position into account brings us correct tracking.

Figure 14 shows the tracking result for five persons. Persons in 14-a are sparse, and persons in 14-b are relatively

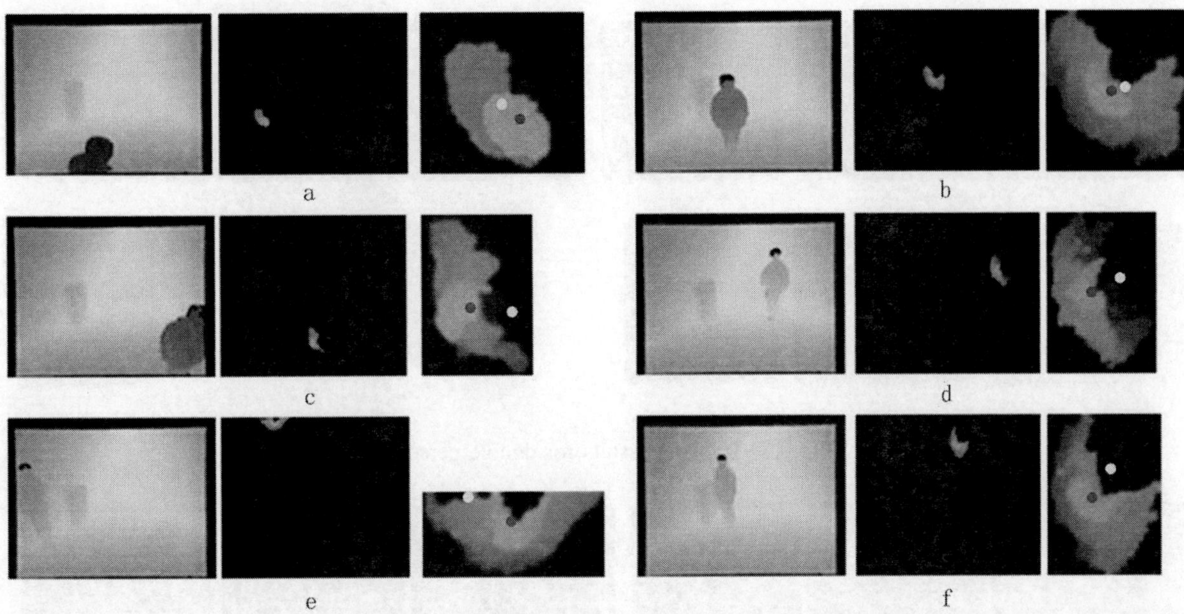

Fig. 11: Tracking results for single person at different positions

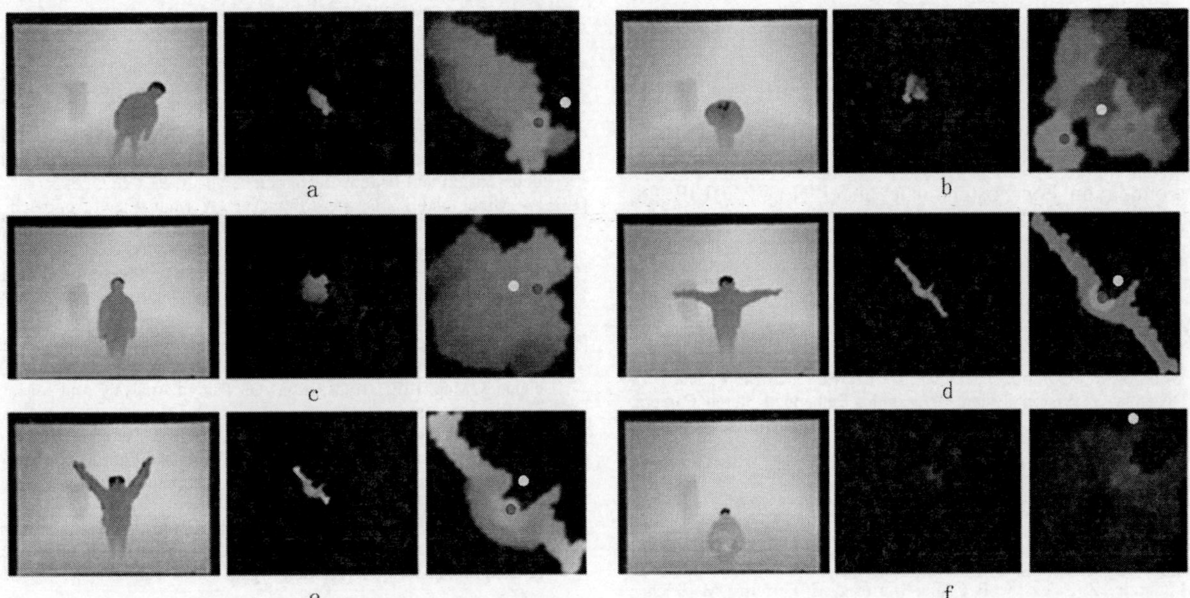

Fig. 12: Tracking results for single person in different poses

closer to each other. Results proved that our method is still work for more than two persons.

5. Conclusion

This paper presented a method for people tracking using a light coding depth sensor. We treat people tracking as multiple heads tracking, and propose a novel straightforward directed semicircular template matching based multiple heads tracking method. Experiments show our method can track heads reliably inspite of the position, pose of persons and the collision between them.

Acknowledgements

The authors gratefully acknowledge supports from National Nature Science Foundation of China under NSFC No.61033008, 60903041 and 61103080, Research Fund for

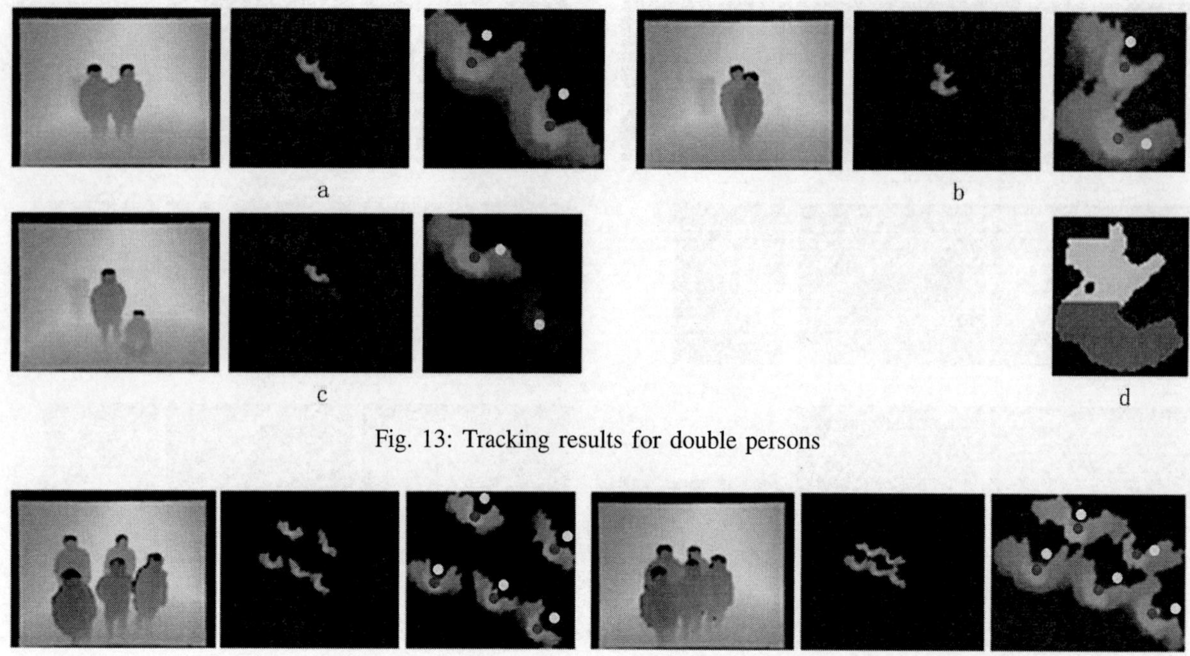

Fig. 13: Tracking results for double persons

Fig. 14: Tracking results for multiple persons

the Doctoral Program of Higher Education of China under SRFDP No.20104307110002, Hunan Provincial Innovation Foundation For Postgraduate under No.CX2010B028, Fund of Innovation in Graduate School of NUDT under No.B100603.

References

[1] Woodfill, J.I.; Gordon, G.; Jurasek, D.; Brown, T.; Buck, R., The Tyzx DeepSea G2 Vision System, ATaskable, Embedded Stereo Camera, Conference on Computer Vision and Pattern Recognition Workshop, 2006.

[2] http://www.pmdtec.com/products-services/pmdvisionr-cameras/pmdvisionr-camcube-30/.

[3] http://www.microsoft.com/en-us/kinectforwindows/.

[4] http://www.asus.com/Multimedia/Motion_Sensor/Xtion_PRO_LIVE/

[5] http://www.primesense.com/

[6] J Garcia, Z Zalevsky, P Garcia-Martinez, C Ferreira, M Teicher and Y Beiderman, Projection of speckle patterns for 3D sensing, EuroâĂŞAmerican Workshop on Information Optics, 2008.

[7] M. Isard, J. MacCormick, Bramble: A Bayesian Multiple-Blob Tracker, International Conference on Computer Vision, Vol. 2, 34-41, 2001.

[8] M. Han and W. Xu and H. Tao and Y.Gong, An Algorithm for Multiple Object Trajectory Tracking, IEEE Computer Society Conference on Computer Vision and Pattern Recognition, Vol. 1, 864-871, 2004.

[9] Nils T Siebel, Steve Maybank, Fusion of Multiple Tracking Algorithms for Robust People Tracking, European Conference on Computer Vision, 2002.

[10] R.T. Collins, Mean-Shift Blob Tracking through Scale Space, IEEE Computer Society Conference on Computer Vision and Pattern Recognition, Vol. 2, 234-240, 2003.

[11] D. Comaniciu, V. Ramesh, P. Meer, Real-Time Tracking of Non-Rigid Objects Using Mean Shift, IEEE Conference on Computer Vision and Pattern Recognition, Vol. 2, 142-149, 2000.

[12] K.Smith, D. Gatica Perez, J. M. Odobez, Using Particles to Track Varying Numbers of Interacting People, IEEE Conference on Computer Vision and Pattern Recognition, Vol. 1, 962-969, 2005.

[13] A. Mittal and L. Davis, M2tracker: A Multi-View Approach to Segmenting and Tracking People in a Cluttered Scene, International Journal of Computer Vision, Vol. 51, 189-203, 2003.

[14] J. Kang, I. Cohen, and G. Medioni, Tracking People in Crowded Scenes Across Multiple Cameras, Asian Conference Computer Vision, 2004.

[15] FrancÂÿois Fleuret, JeÂť roËĘme Berclaz, Richard Lengagne, and Pascal Fua, Multicamera People Tracking with a Probabilistic Occupancy Map, IEEE Transactions On Pattern Analysis And Machine Intelligence, Vol. 3, 2008.

[16] Salih Burak Gokturk, Carlo Tomasi, 3D Head Tracking Based on Recognition and Interpolation Using a Time-Of-Flight Depth Sensor, IEEE computer society conference on Computer vision and pattern recognition, 2004.

[17] Rudolf Tanner, Martin Studer, Adriano Zanoli, Andreas Hartmann, People Detection and Tracking with TOF Sensor, International Conference on Advanced Video and Signal Based Surveillance, 356-361, 2008.

[18] L. Bourdev and J. Malik. Poselets, Body part detectors trained using 3D human pose annotations, International Conference on Computer Vision, 1365-1372, 2009.

[19] Jamie Shotton, Andrew Fitzgibbon, Mat Cook, Toby Sharp, Mark Finocchio,Richard Moore, Alex Kipman, Andrew Blake, Real-Time Human Pose Recognition in Parts from Single Depth Images, IEEE computer society conference on Computer vision and pattern recognition, 1297-1304, 2011.

[20] Y.I.Adbel-Aziz, H.M. Karam, Direct linear transformation into object space coordinates in close-range photogrammetry, ASP Symp. Close Runge Photogrammetry, 1-19, 1971.

Enhanced Pre-conditioning Algorithm for the Accurate Alignment of 3D Range Scans

Shane Transue and Min-Hyung Choi
Department of Computer Science and Engineering
University of Colorado Denver
Denver, CO, United States

Abstract – *The process of accurately aligning 3D range scans to reconstruct a virtual model is a complex task in generic circumstances. Yet by exploiting the data characteristics common to many mobile 3D scanning devices, we propose a two phase alignment solution that improves the alignment provided by the iterative closest point (ICP) algorithm. Current approaches target how the ICP algorithm aligns two range scans based on modifying minimization functions, sampling functions, and point correspondence techniques. However, while these approaches have provided subtle improvements in the alignment process, the ICP algorithm is still incapable of aligning low resolution range scans with very little overlap. Based on our proposed algorithm, we are able to increase the accuracy of the alignment provided by the ICP algorithm by 40% on low resolution scan pairs and we demonstrate the versatility of this approach by accurately aligning a variety scan pairs with small overlap regions.*

Keywords: *3D scanning, range scan alignment, data filtering, object reconstruction, low-resolution scan alignment*

1 Introduction

The process of scanning physical objects to recreate virtual three dimensional models was once limited from widespread adoption due to costly hardware components and sophisticated reconstruction techniques required to produce a final model. However recent developments in mobile laser based scanning devices have eliminated these barriers in the domain of long range, low resolution object reconstruction. While there has been extensive research into the alignment of high resolution scans from devices with limited range, only a select few target the long range, low resolution scans that are associated with long range, laser based scanning devices. Based on these developments we propose an algorithm that aids existing alignment algorithms for the reconstruction of a virtual model given a very limited set of low resolution scans. We build on the extensive existing developments in range scan alignment algorithms to utilize the characteristics of low resolution laser based scanning devices to present improvements in exiting alignment techniques for datasets that exhibit these characteristics.

In this paper we provide a detailed process pipeline that culminates with a robust approach to providing highly accurate pair-wise alignments between range scans constructed with low resolution scanning devices. In Section 2 we present previous research in pair-wise scan alignment and we reflect on how our proposed approach works in cooperation with these existing developments. In Section 3 the characterizations of the targeted laser scanning devices are defined and a technical overview of the scanning process for these types of scanners is presented. Section 4 develops a set of robust range scan cleaning tools that allow for the automated and manual elimination of background data and outliers from collected scans. As a prerequisite for our proposed algorithm, Section 5 details an accurate initial alignment of all generated scans to provide a rough alignment that attempts to reconstruct the object's surface. Utilizing this approximate reconstruction we present our alignment algorithm that provides a highly accurate alignment between scans with very little overlap. Our proposed approach is extensively tested on a wide variety of datasets and it is demonstrated that our approach decreases the pair-wise alignment error provided by using a naïve alignment algorithm by approximately 40 percent.

2 Related Work

The process of performing a pair-wise alignment on a set of range scans is well studied and numerous alternative techniques have been proposed to improve the efficiency and accuracy of this process. Namely, the iterative closest point (ICP) algorithm proposed by Besl and McKay [1], has spurred the development of several variants that support additional approaches [2] to how their ICP algorithm is performed. These developments aim to improve the quality of the results obtained through this pair-wise alignment approach. These techniques target specific modular aspects of the ICP algorithm such as the error function, the form of sampling used, and alternative schemes for matching corresponding points between the overlap regions of the scans.

Torsello et al. [3] propose a method of selecting relevant points from individual scans with the intent of improving the alignment through feature based point selection as a variant of the sampling used for the ICP algorithm. The critical aspect of our development is that our method is algorithmically orthogonal to these developments that define on what basis the ICP algorithm provides an accurate alignment. Since this is the case, this improvement can be used in cooperation with our approach, thus providing an extended toolset for the process of rapidly aligning low resolution range scans, specifically those with minimal overlap regions.

Frank B. ter Harr and R.C. Veltkamp [4] propose a multi-view alignment scheme based on four scans which contain small overlap regions. However, this method does not target the low resolution scans obtained by most pan and tilt based time-of-flight (TOF) devices. Based on the complexities in this approach, alignment time is in the order of minutes for high resolution scans. In contrast, we are specifically targeting mobile devices and based on this requirement we present a series of algorithms that align similar high resolution scans in the order of milliseconds, thus making the alignment of lower resolution scans trivial. From this development we can than target mobile devices for the efficient alignment of low resolution scans.

A similar object reconstruction pipeline is proposed by Chatterjee et al. [5]. However, they rely on a high number of scans (~16) to reconstruct the surface of an object. In contrast, our objective is to minimize the total number of scans and we present an object reconstruction pipeline that facilitates this.

Unlike other approaches that rely on additional color information [6] in addition to distance measurements, we target TOF devices that only provide depth images to define an objects surface. By limiting our algorithms to perform only on depth information we target a larger range of TOF devices, specifically those without color or texture information.

Considering these prior developments, we propose that our algorithm can be utilized with any improvements of the ICP algorithm to increase the accuracy of our alignment. Our approach simply provides the consolidation of previous alignment techniques utilized by the ICP algorithm with an estimated selection of points contained in overlap regions. Based on these factors we improve the alignment provided by the ICP algorithm for scan pairs with small overlap regions.

By utilizing the ICP algorithm for a refined alignment, we extensively evaluate this proposed technique by statistically analyzing the root mean square deviation (RMSD) error produced by the naïve ICP alignment algorithm versus our proposed algorithm. This provides a well known basis upon which we can objectively evaluate the accuracy of the alignments performed by both algorithms for various datasets. Our evaluation is combined with some of the efficient variants of the ICP algorithm to provide robust and highly accurate alignment results. Specifically, the evaluation of our proposed algorithm utilizes uniform norm-space sampling and the point-to-plane variant proposed by Chen and Medioni [7] implemented by the Scanalyze package [8].

3 Scanning Device and Process

In this section the laser based scanning device and its data characteristics used in the development of our approach is declared and a detailed outline of the required scanning process is presented. The objective we propose is the reconstruction of a relatively large object such as a piece of furniture or a vehicle through the collection of range scans. This is performed with a laser based device around the object from various angles. In this context we refer to the reconstruction of the object as the process of collecting a set of scans from around the object and then aligning these consecutive scans to effectively model the object in 3D space. This process is accomplished through the use of a scanning device that is capable of measuring depth information at various locations on the target object's surface.

Specifically, we look at the use of a laser based TOF device to capture the surface information of a targeted object. The laser based TOF device is designed to construct a range scan through the use of two basic functions: tilt and pan. Using this basic functionality, the range scan captured by the TOF device is stored into a 2D array and is defined by five parameters: the position of the device P, n the number of tilt rows in the scan, m the number of columns, the pan range $(-\theta, \theta)$, and the tilt range $(-\phi, \phi)$. An abstract representation of the scan volume constructed by these parameters is illustrated in Figure 1. and each position in the 2D array corresponds to a single distance measurement between the scanner at position P and the surface of the target object.

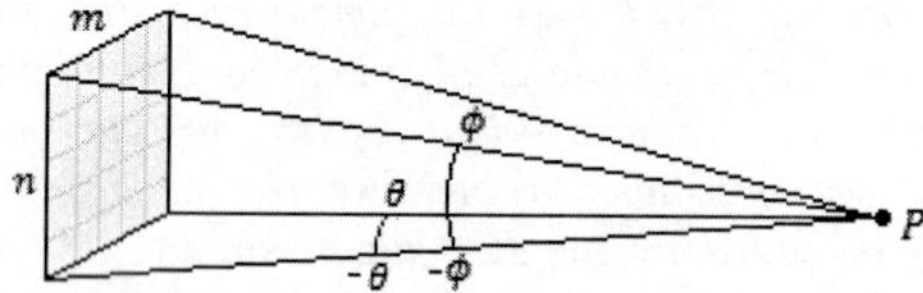

Figure 1. TOF Tilt-Pan Scanning Device

Utilizing this type of scanning device we construct the surface of the object, subject to the mobility limitations of the device. For the case of stationary tilt-pan laser scanners, this limits the movement of the device such that its position P moves coplanar to the ground around the object being scanned (specifically we utilized a tripod with adjustable tilt and elevation with a mounted TOF device). Given these constraints the surface of the object is defined by collecting a set of scans from various angles, counter-clockwise around the target object. Figure 2. illustrates this scanning procedure as seen from a top-down view:

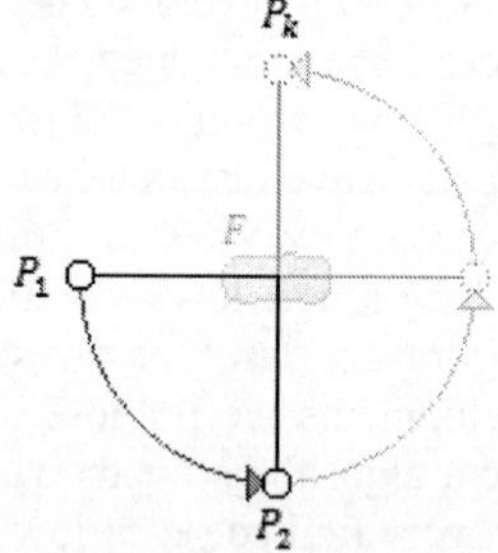

Figure 2. Tilt-Pan Device Scanning Procedure (Top-Down View)

Arbitrarily assigning some position as the starting position P_1, a set of scans is collected around the target object F. Each time a scan is captured, the device is moved to the next position where $P \in \{P_1, P_2, \ldots, P_k\}$ for k scans. Since position P_1 is the first scan we label this as scan as the 0° scan. For the next position (in Figure 2) at P_2 the scanner has been moved by 90° around the object. We label this scan as the 90° scan, and so on. This is continued for every scan performed around the object where $0° \leq angle \leq 360°$.

In our datasets, we consider two scan set sizes: 4 and 8. When we consider a scan set (also called a scan batch) of 4 scans this typically means that the scans were performed close to the following angles: $\{0, 90, 180, 270\}$ where the scanner was moved around the object by 90° after each scan. Similarly when we consider a scan batch with 8 scans, they are typically performed in 45° increments around the target object: $\{0, 45, 90, 135, 180, 225, 270, 315\}$. The angle value for each scan is provided by the user and used to apply the appropriate rotation to each scan during the reconstruction process. The user must estimate the approximate angle at which they are performing each scan. If the user is within ~10° of the actual angle, the construction is unaffected.

4 Automated Filtering and Painting

Scan data collected by a tilt and pan based TOF scanning device typically includes a lot of additional unnecessary information about the environment in which the target object resides. This background information is usually unintentionally included in the scan data and does not contribute to the surface definition of the object we are interested in reconstructing. Specifically, we identify any point that does not directly contribute to the definition of the surface of the target object as background information. The separation of these points from those that define the surface of the target object is handled through two phases (1) automated filtering and (2) manual data elimination painting.

Automated filters remove background information based on the TOF device parameters and the data collected from the device, and can be used to quickly eliminate a majority of the background information contained in a scan. Based on the characteristics of a tilt and pan TOF device, the following set of filters can be adopted: distance filters, signal strength filters, and filters based on the intervals for which the pan angle θ and tilt angle ϕ are valid. Providing these automated filters allows the target object to be easily cropped from its surrounding environment. This technique, however, does not address background information collected between complex surfaces as demonstrated in Figure 3. (center). Surfaces with complex material properties (such as transparency) cannot always be accurately removed with an automated process.

To address surfaces with complex material properties we provide a highly accurate data elimination painting tool. Based on the 3D to 2D projection of the individual points contained in the scan data, a radial painting tool can be used to carve out additional unnecessary data points. This allows for an extremely accurate representation of the objects surface to be extracted at the cost of manual intervention. However, based on the simplicity of the developed toolset, we illustrate the quality of a surface that can be extracted from a 90° scan of a vehicle using this manual technique after ~10 minutes of manual painting as shown in Figure 3. (right). This allows for the extraction of the target object which is required for the accuracy of the bounding volumes calculated in our proposed initial alignment algorithm that estimates the translations required to reconstruct the surface of the target object.

Figure 3. Unmodified Raw Data (left), Auto-Filtered Data (center), Manual Painting-Based Data Elimination (right).

5 Initial Alignment

When utilizing the ICP algorithm to perform a pair-wise alignment, a requirement of the algorithm is a rough initial guess alignment that provides an adequate starting position for each scan before their point distances are minimized. Thus, this process is a direct prerequisite for our highly accurate modified ICP algorithm. Again, we utilize the characteristics of the data provided by a pan and tilt TOF device. Specifically this allows us to consider a limited domain in which scans need to be properly aligned to reconstruct the surface of the target object. From Section 3, we note that the rotational value for each scan has been provided by the user within some error threshold. These rotations are applied to each scan to rotate them about the Y axis (the axis perpendicular to the ground upon which the scanning device sits). This provides the correct rotation for each scan as shown in Figure 5. (top row). However, a proper translation between each of the scans is required to accurately estimate an initial alignment that reconstructs the object's surface.

There are two aspects of this initial alignment scheme that dictate the quality of the alignment produced. First, the provided data must be properly rotated to match the scanning pattern performed around the object. Second, the point cloud data constructed from the scan information must not contain any outliers. Specifically, axis-aligned bounding boxes (AABB) are utilized to determine how much each scan must be shifted to accurately represent the objects surface. Therefore, the amount of error introduced by an outlier in the calculation of the AABB will significantly contribute to the misalignment of the scans in the batch; however, if both of these prerequisites can be fulfilled and a tilt and pan TOF device is used, an accurate estimation of the object's surface can be constructed efficiently.

In this section, we propose an efficient algorithm that determines the translations required to align two portions of a single surface contained in two consecutive scans. The idea behind this algorithm is that since we are utilizing a device that can only be moved around the target object in one plane, we can exploit that characteristic to provide a rough alignment of all scans in a batch with an efficient rough alignment algorithm. This rough alignment can then be used as a suitable initial alignment required by our proposed bounding volume assisted ICP algorithm.

Algorithm Description: Given a set of scans, each with an associated user provided angle that signifies the position of the scanner around the target object, rotate each scan about the Y axis and calculate the translation required to move each scan such that the surface contained in the scan's AABB is aligned with the previous scan in the batch.

From the provided scan batch we consider two scans at a time and define the user provided angle of the first scan as Θ and the angle of the second scan as Φ. We also define a Cartesian plane with four quadrants $(0-3)$. Since the scans AABBs reside in this plane, each of the four corners of each AABB correspond to the same quadrant labels. This scheme is used to determine how to shift one scans position to another based on their AABB extents.

We calculate the quadrant that has the highest percentage overlap based on Θ and Φ. This is illustrated in Figure 4. (left), where quadrant 0 has the highest percentage of overlap between the two scans. This indicates that scan two will be shifted to the first scan's position so that quadrant 0 of both AABBs coincide. This is illustrated in Figure 4. (center). This top-down view presents the AABBs of two individual scans before the initial alignment is performed. Since quadrant 0 has the highest amount of overlap for these two angles, it is selected and the AABB of scan two is shifted to the AABB of scan one (the upper right-hand corner).

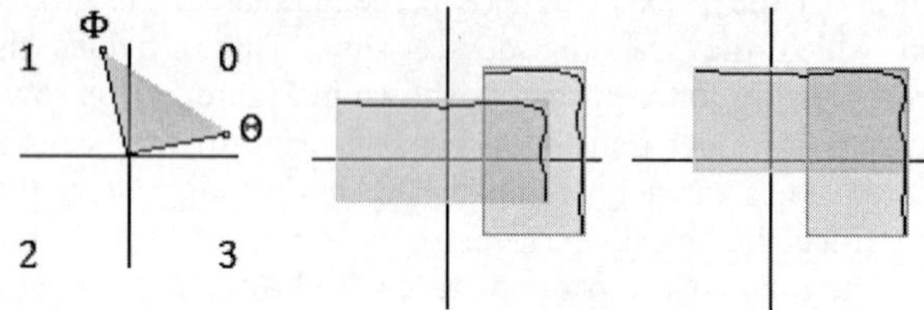

Figure 4. Quadrant Overlap for two Scans (left), initial scan positions (center), AABB aligned scans (right).

Input: A set of point clouds $P = \{P_1, \ldots, P_n\}$, A set of user provided angles A, where $|A| = |P|$, $0 \leq a_i \leq 360 \; \forall a \in A$, and a_i corresponds to p_i where $p_i \in P$.

Output: The modified set of point clouds P, where each scan is translated so that every scan approximates its appropriate portion of target object's surface.

<u>Algorithm: Pair-wise AABB Translational Alignment</u>

Sort P by angle $(p_1.angle \leq \cdots \leq p_n.angle)$
Translate each point cloud to its geometric centroid
For each pair of scans: $\{p_1, p_2\}, \{p_2, p_3\}, \ldots, \{p_{n-1}, p_n\}$
  $\theta = p_i.angle$
  $\phi = p_{i+1}.angle$
  // Calculate quadrant with highest overlap %
  $quad =$ HighestOverlap(θ, ϕ) // Figure 4. (left)
  $aabb_i = AABB(p_i)$
  $aabb_{i+1} = AABB(p_{i+1})$
  // Figure 4. (center, right) Translation t
  $t =$ Shift $aabb_{i+1}$ to $aabb_i$ based on the selected $quad$
  Apply t to point clouds $p_{i+1}, \ldots, p_n$

With the batch sorted by scan angle, each pair of scan angles are analyzed to determine what quadrant contains the highest overlap. Once the shift direction (quadrants $0-3$) is determined by this analysis, the AABBs of the two scans are calculated to determine the translation required to move $aabb_{i+1}$ to $aabb_i$.

The results of this algorithm are demonstrated through its application to various datasets and are illustrated in Figure 5. (bottom row). Three diverse scan batches are considered for the demonstration of this algorithm: the Stanford bunny model provided by the Stanford Scanning Repository [9], the Subaru Legacy dataset obtained from a pan and tilt TOF device, and a Toyota truck model constructed through the use of a virtual scanner developed to emulate the data collected from a pan and tilt TOF device.

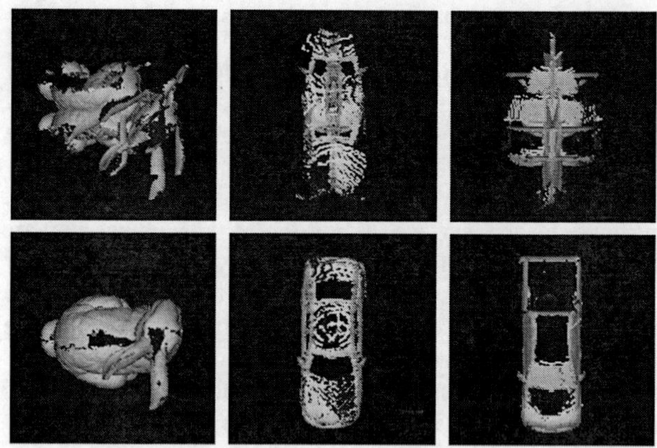

Figure 5. Initial Alignment performed on the Stanford Bunny (left), Subaru Legacy (center), and virtual Toyota Truck (right) datasets.

The results in Figure 5. (bottom row) demonstrate the accuracy of this approach. This is required by the bounding volume assisted ICP algorithm because it specifically targets overlap regions between scan pairs. Without this accurate initial alignment, our proposed method may not select the best overlap regions corresponding to each scan pair.

6 Bounding Volume Assisted ICP

In this section, we present an efficient way of improving the alignment between two scans that contain minimal overlap. Since we are utilizing a pan and tilt based TOF device to reconstruct a physical object, it is desirable to minimize the total number of scans required to accurately construct the entire surface of the object. However, limiting the number of scans performed dictates that between every scan pair, the overlap region is greatly reduced. This poses a challenge for the ICP algorithm, which operates under the assumption that there is a significant overlap region in common between both scans. Here we provide a method of extracting this overlap region and utilize the ICP algorithm to align the points that are contained in this volume. Therefore, the resulting alignment between the points in this volume will increase the accuracy of the alignment due to the high level of correspondence between the point sets.

In our alignment process, we aim to accurately calculate the overlap region shared between two scans. To do this, we utilize the accuracy of the initial alignment, provided in the previous section, to provide an efficient way of calculating this overlap region using bounding volumes. Since we are using a tilt and pan TOF device with limited mobility, we exploit this simplicity and use AABBs to represent the bounding volumes that will be used to calculate this overlap between scan pairs. This is performed by constructing AABBs for each scan and then calculating the AABB that represents their intersection. Once this intersection volume is defined, two sets of points are constructed (1) P_a, the points from the source scan that are contained in the intersection volume and (2) P_b the points from the target scan that are contained in the intersection volume. The ICP algorithm is then used to align these two point subsets from the original scans. Once the transformation is calculated by the ICP algorithm, it is simply applied to the source scan so that it is properly aligned to the target scan. This results in an improved alignment between the two scans with very little computational overhead, which is ideal for mobile scanning solutions.

Algorithm Description: Given a set of scans featuring a low percentage of pair-wise overlap, perform an ICP alignment between each pair of scans utilizing only the points that exist in their overlap region. The algorithm is provided in terms of abstract volumes.

Input: A set of point clouds $P = \{P_1, \ldots, P_n\}$
Output: The modified set of point clouds P, where each scan is aligned to the previous scan in the set.

Algorithm: Pair-wise AABB Assisted ICP Alignment

For each pair of scans: $\{p_1, p_2\}, \{p_2, p_3\}, \ldots, \{p_{n-1}, p_n\}$
$\quad v_i = Volume(p_i)$
$\quad v_{i+1} = Volume(p_{i+1})$
$\quad intersection = v_i \cap v_{i+1}$
$\quad$ // Collect the point subsets from each scan
$\quad$ For every point $p \in P_i$
$\quad\quad P_a += p$ iff $p \in intersection$
$\quad$ For every point $p \in P_{i+1}$
$\quad\quad P_b += p$ iff $p \in intersection$
$\quad$ // Perform the ICP algorithm between P_a and P_b
$\quad t = ICP(P_a, P_b)$
$\quad$ Apply t to P_{i+1}

In this algorithm, the intersection between the volumes associated with each scan is calculated, followed by the construction of two sets: P_a and P_b that will be used for the ICP alignment. The sets P_a and P_b contain points from the source and target scan respectively if and only if the points are contained in the intersection volume: $intersection$. The resulting transformation t is then applied to the source scan P_{i+1}. This is performed for each pair contained in the set, thus upon completion, when the ICP algorithm converges, the target object should be accurately reconstructed.

Figure 6. illustrates how this algorithm is applied to scan pairs during the alignment process. This illustration also demonstrates that based on our accurate initial alignment, we can determine the overlap areas that correspond to each scan.

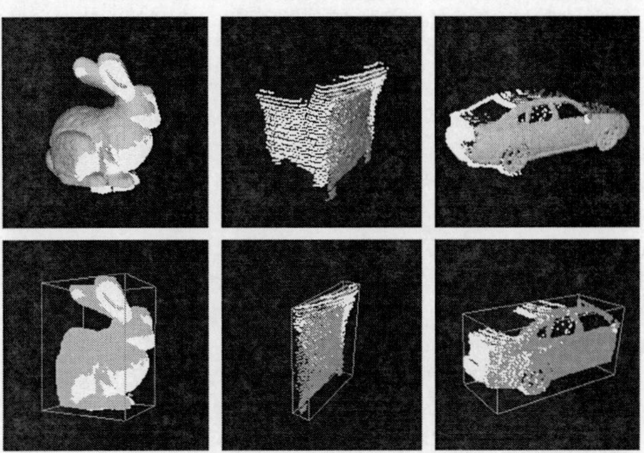

Figure 6. AABB Intersections between Scan Pairs for the Stanford Bunny (left), Chair (center), and Subaru Legacy (right) datasets.

The (top row) of Figure 6. displays two scans (where one is selected in white and the other is default gray), with an initial alignment performed. The (bottom row) of Figure 6. displays the intersection AABB calculated between the AABBs of each scan and the point sets P_a and P_b are shown in default gray and white respectively. These are the two point sets that are aligned using the ICP algorithm.

Based on this alignment scheme the overall alignment error between two scans with very little overlap is reduced thus allowing for a minimal number of scans (~4) to provide enough information to reconstruct an object. Figure 7. shows the results of this approach for the Stanford Bunny, the Subaru Legacy, Chair, and Virtual Toyota Truck scan sets.

Figure 7. Results of the AABB-Assisted ICP Alignment for all four datasets. Stanford Bunny (upper left), Subaru Legacy (upper right), Chair (lower left), and Virtual Truck (lower right).

7 Experimental Evaluation

In this section, it is shown that the proposed bounding volume assisted ICP algorithm yields better results for low overlap scan pairs in various datasets. These datasets are provided from three independent sources: the Stanford 3D Scanning Repository (Stanford Bunny), a pan and tilt based TOF device, and the virtual scanning device developed to emulate a pan and tilt TOF device (without distance measurement error). The application of the proposed algorithm to this diverse set of datasets illustrates the robust capabilities of the proposed algorithm in this domain. The ICP algorithm implementation from the Scanalyze package is utilized to perform all preceding tests. Specifically, from this implementation we utilize uniform normspace-sampling, with a point-to-plane minimization function.

For each test performed, we use the initial alignment algorithm provided in Section 5. to provide a starting position for each scan in a batch. This ensures that both our proposed algorithm and the ICP algorithm can rely on the same initial conditions prior to alignment. The limited set of parameters, modified depending on the overlap contained in each dataset for the ICP algorithm, are show below:

ICP Parameters
- Sampling Rate: 0.20
- Iterations: 10
- Minimization: Point-to-Plane
- Uniform Normspace Sampling
- Culling Percentage: Based on pair-wise overlap
  - 20 for scan batches containing 8 scans
  - 50 for scan batches containing 4 scans
- AABB Inflation*: 10%

* For datasets provided from a TOF scanning device that contain distance measurement errors we provide an artificial AABB inflation percentage for our proposed method to handle these erratic samples.

The results in Figure 8. and 9. illustrate the convergence of the two algorithms over the course of 10 iterations using the settings provided above for the Stanford Bunny and Legacy batches. Each of these batches contains four scans, each separated by 90°. The average RMSD collected over 10 repeated batch alignments is shown for the alignment between the 180° – 270° scans of both batches.

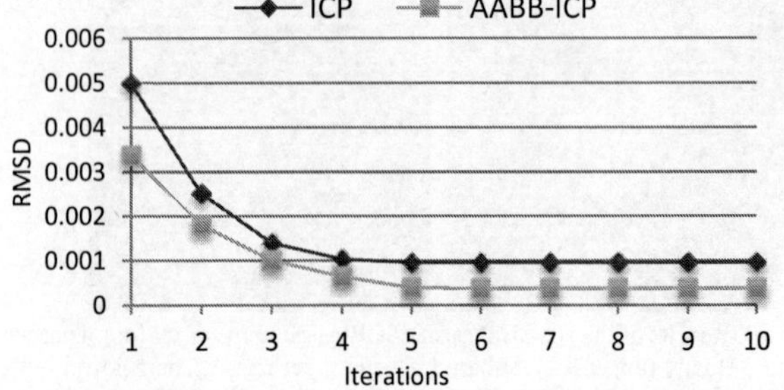

Figure 8. Stanford Bunny 180°-270° Scan Alignment RMSD

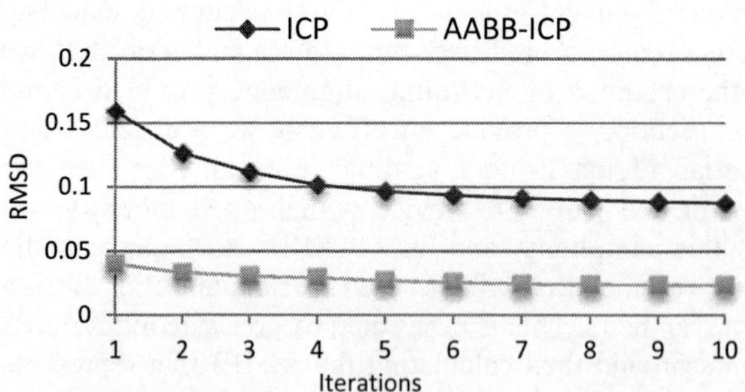

Figure 9. Subaru Legacy 180°-270° Scan Alignment RMSD

From these results, we observe that the AABB assisted ICP algorithm converges with a lower RMSD error than the unassisted ICP algorithm. We see a large discrepancy in RMSD error between the Stanford Bunny (Figure 8.) and Subaru Legacy (Figure 9.) datasets due to the vast resolution difference between these objects. However, both alignments improve upon the naïve ICP alignment by reducing the pair-wise RMSD, thus providing a more accurate alignment. We show this result is constant for all scan datasets by evaluating the RMSD error reduction percentage provided by the AABB-ICP algorithm over the naïve ICP algorithm for all available datasets.

Utilizing the same ICP settings and initial alignment as before, we evaluate the alignment performance between each algorithm for the datasets containing 8 scans. For these batches each scan pair is only separated by 45°. Figure 10. shows the percent decrease in RMSD for the AABB assisted algorithm versus the naïve ICP algorithm for these scans with approximately 50% overlap between each scan pair.

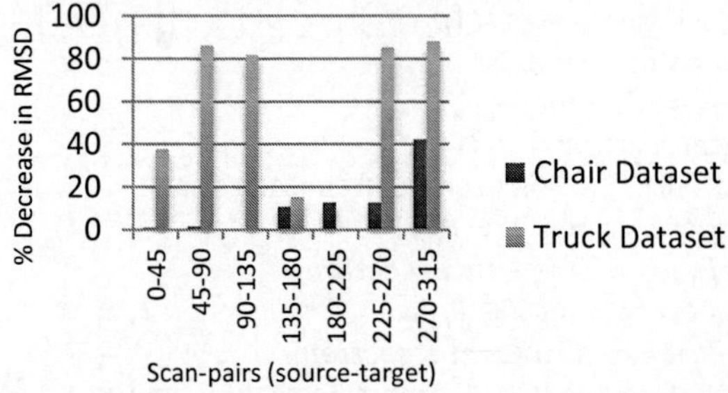

Figure 10. % Decrease in RMSD provided by the AABB assisted ICP algorithm [vs] the naïve ICP algorithm for batches with 8 scans.

While the proposed algorithm provides improvements in the alignment quality, the result varies dramatically due to the high overlap shared between each of these alignments. Since the scan pairs considered in these batches contain large overlap regions, the performance can degrade to that of the naïve ICP algorithm due to the large number of points selected for alignment from both scans.

Our approach, however, is specifically targeted at scan pairs with smaller overlap regions; therefore, we conduct the same test on the scan batches that only contain 4 scans. Each of the scans in these datasets are separated by 90° as stated before. This provides a very limited overlap region for each algorithm to use to find the proper correspondence between scan pairs. Figure 11. shows the results of this test.

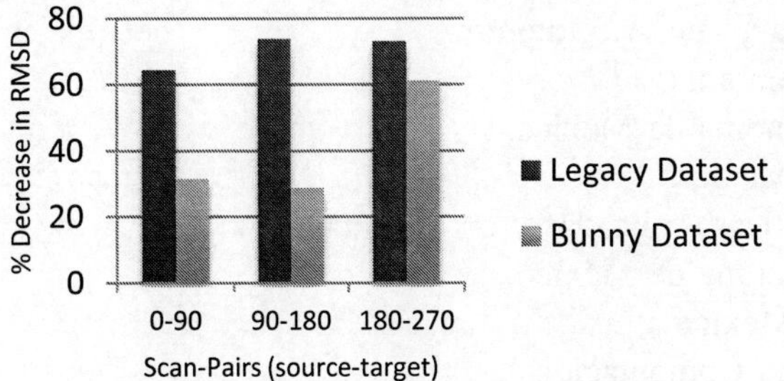

Figure 11. % Decrease in RMSD provided by the AABB assisted ICP algorithm [vs] the naïve ICP algorithm for batches with 4 scans.

The results we observe from the alignment of the scan batches containing 4 scans is that the AABB assisted ICP algorithm provides a consistent improvement in the accuracy of the alignment between scan pairs. Thus, this algorithm can be utilized to yield a better alignment than the naïve ICP algorithm.

8 Conclusion and Future Work

In this paper, we presented a two phase solution that improves the accuracy of the alignment provided by the ICP algorithm by approximately 40 percent. By exploiting the device characteristics common to most 3D scanning devices, including TOF devices, we have provided an extensive set of tools that can be utilized to ensure that the ICP algorithm converges, even for low resolution scan sets with small overlap regions. We also effectively illustrated that our approach can be utilized with existing variants of the ICP algorithm that improve the quality of the alignment between scan pairs as stated in Section 2. Sections 3 and 4 illustrated the process of collecting and editing scan data as the pre-processing steps required for our alignment algorithm. Sections 5 and 6 provided detailed descriptions of our two phase algorithm and formed a basis upon which we can evaluate this alignment approach. In Section 7, we presented two common ICP configurations that were effectively used to determine the decrease in RMSD provided by the second phase of our algorithm compared to using an ICP algorithm that tries to determine a correct alignment using all available points from both scans.

In our future work, we would like to address the requirement placed upon the user to provide the angle of each scan during the scanning process. By exploring the possibility of estimating the scanner position, we would like to remove this requirement by estimating this rotational value from the estimated scanner positions. We would also like to explore the possibilities of creating a fully automated filtering process to remove the manual editing requirement from our pre-processing as well. In this paper we think that we have contributed to the process of accelerating the adoption of mobile scanning devices and we would like to see these technologies made widely available for all purposes. We hope that by developing this two phase alignment algorithm we can simplify the process of reconstructing a physical object from range scan sets.

9 References

[1] Paul J. Besl, and Neil D. McKay. "A Method for Registration of 3-D Shapes". IEEE Transactions on Pattern Analysis and Machine Intelligence (PAMI), 14(2), pp. 239–256, 1992.

[2] Szymon Rusinkiewicz and Marc Levoy. "Efficient Variants of the ICP Algorithm". Proceedings of the International Conference on 3-D Digital Imaging and Modeling (3DIM), pp. 145–152, 2001.

[3] Torsello, A.; Rodola`, E.; Albarelli, A., "Sampling Relevant Points for Surface Registration," 3D Imaging, Modeling, Processing, Visualization and Transmission (3DIMPVT), 2011 International Conference on , vol., no., pp.290,295, 16-19 May 2011.

[4] ter Haar, F.B.; Veltkamp, R.C., "Automatic multiview quadruple alignment of unordered range scans," Shape Modeling and Applications, 2007. SMI '07. IEEE International Conference on, vol., no., pp.137,146, 13-15 June 2007.

[5] Avishek Chatterjee, Suraj Jain, and Venu Madhav Govindu. "A pipeline for building 3D models using depth cameras". ICVGIP '12 Proceedings of the Eighth Indian Conference on Computer Vision, Graphics and Image Processing. Article No. 38, 2012.

[6] Shen Yang, Yue Qi, Fei Hou, Xukun Shen, and Qinping Zhao. "A novel method based on color information for scanned data alignment". Proceedings of the 2008 ACM symposium on Virtual reality software and technology, pp. 201-204, 2008.

[7] Yang Chen, and Gerard Medioni. "Object Modeling by Registration of Multiple Range Images". International Journal of Image and Vision Computing, 10(3), pp. 145–155, 1992.

[8] Scanalyze: A System for Aligning and Merging Range Data. http://graphics.stanford.edu/software/scanalyze/

[9] Stanford 3D Scanning Repository http://www-graphics.stanford.edu/data/3Dscanrep/

Voxel-based object representation by means of edging trees

L. A. Martínez[1], **E. Bribiesca**[2], **and A. Guzmán**[3]
[1]Instituto de Astronomía,
Universidad Nacional Autónoma de México,
México, D. F., México
[2]Instituto de Investigaciones en Matemáticas Aplicadas y en Sistemas,
Universidad Nacional Autónoma de México,
México, D. F., México
[3]Centro de Investigación en Computación,
Instituto Politécnico Nacional,
México, D. F., México

Abstract—*A method is described for representing voxel-based objects (VBOs) by means of edging trees (EdTs). Given a VBO, an EdT is a tree which traces the borders of the object. The vertices of the EdT correspond to the vertices of the enclosing surface where some of them have been conveniently hidden in order to get a 1D representation. The computed EdT is represented by a base-five digit chain code descriptor suitably combined by means of parentheses. The EdT notation is invariant under rotation and translation, using this notation it is possible to obtain the mirror image of any VBO with ease. The EdT notation preserves the shape of VBOs. The proposed EdT notation is a good tool for storing of VBOs. Due to their features, EdTs can be considered as a 1D alternative to skeletons for representing VBOs.*

Keywords: Voxel-based objects, edging trees, chain coding, 3D tree representation

1. Introduction

Representation of voxel-based objects (VBOs) is an important topic in computer vision and pattern recognition; accordingly, getting means of representation that provide an object of lower dimension that can be used for analysis and recognition has attracted attention of many research groups. Several methods with different approaches have been proposed to get representations of this kind of objects. One of such representations consists of line-like that can be transformed into 1D representations [1], by means of chain codes, convenient for tasks related with pattern recognition.

Recently a new method to represent VBOs was proposed by Bribiesca *et. al.* [2]. In this representation a base-five digit chain code so-called 5OT that describes orthogonal direction changes of straight-line segments is used to define an enclosing tree (EcT) that traverses all the vertices of a VBO. The vertices of an EcT correspond to the vertices of the enclosing surface of the analyzed VBO. Although EcTs can be used for pattern recognition, they may over-represent a VBO specially on planar faces where convenient hidden vertices lead to a simplified tree without loss of information.

We are proposing a method for representing VBOs by means of edging trees (EdTs), as a first step in the development of an optimal representation based on the EcTs idea, which trace the borders of the object. The main aim of EdTs is to obtain a rough draft, as is the case of skeletons, of an object and representing it by means of the 5OT code. The EdT notation has several interesting properties such as to be invariant under rotation and translation, it is possible to obtain the mirror image of any VBO with ease. EdTs preserve the geometrical information of the underlying object and it can be recovered with ease from its EdT. In this connection, it should be noted that the 5OT chain code has shown be useful to represent 3D tree objects [3], to define a measure for shape dissimilarity of 3D curves [4] as well as to conduct compression efficiency studies of three-dimensional discrete curves [5], among other applications.

In order to offer a preliminary comparison, Figure 1 shows different representations for a given 3D object consisting of $11 \times 11 \times 11$ voxels (a): (b) is the skeleton obtained with the clasical prairie fire transformation [6], (c) is an EcT, and (d) the proposed EdT.

The paper is organized as follows. Section 2 presents the 5OT chain code and some preliminary definitions. Section 3 gives the method for generating EcTs. In Section 4, the definition of EdTs is presented, as well as some examples. Some properties of EdTs are given in Section 5.

2. The 5OT chain code

Before moving into the description of the 5OT chain code there are some preliminary concepts and remarks to be presented in this section. It is assumed that we will work only with VBOs. The length of each edge of voxels is considered equal to one, therefore the area of every face of each voxel is considered equal to one. There are three ways of connecting voxels: by edges, vertices, and faces. In the context of this

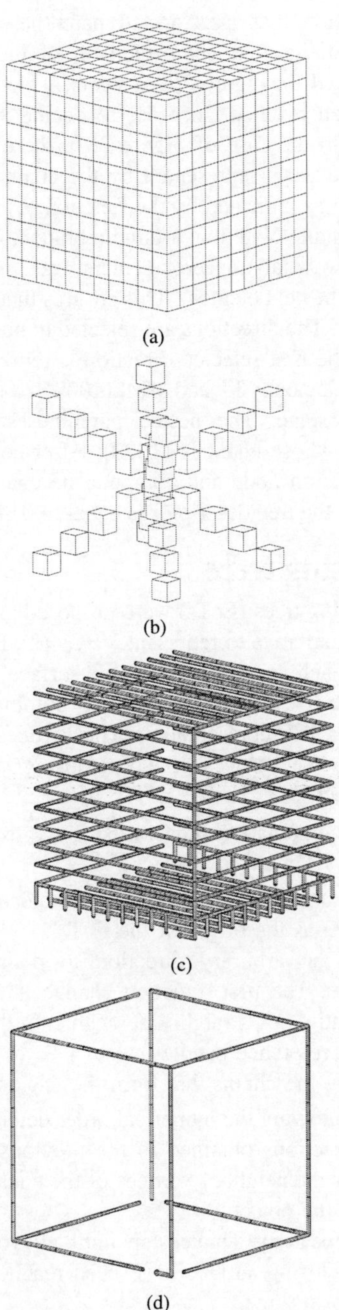

Fig. 1: Comparison of different representations of a given 3D voxel-based object (a): (b) is the praire fire skeleton, (c) is an enclosing tree and (d) an edging tree.

paper, we only consider face-connected voxels, i.e. voxels with six-connectivity. The area of the enclosing surface of an object composed of a finite number of voxels, corresponds to the sum of the areas of the voxels located on the visible faces of the solid. The chain descriptor of an object is defined by the computation of the chain elements using the nested-parentheses notation for trees. Following graph theory basic definitions, EcTs and EdTs describe trees of maximum degree six in three dimensions, this is due to the fact that EdTs only represent face-connected VBOs.

A chain a is an ordered sequence of n elements, and is represented by $a = a_1a_2a_3\ldots a_n = \{a_i : 1 \le i \le n\}$. An element $a_i \in \{0,1,2,3,4\}$ of a chain in the 5OT code indicates the orthogonal direction change of the contiguous straight-line segments of the 3D branch in that element position. Two contiguous straight-line segments of a branch define a direction change and two-direction changes define a chain element. If the consecutive sides of the reference angle have directions b and c as shown in Figure 2(b), and the side from the vertex to be labeled has direction d (from here on, by direction, we understand a vector of length 1), then the chain element is given by the following function:

$$\text{chain element}(b,c,d) = \begin{cases} 0 & \text{if } d = c, \\ 1 & \text{if } d = b \times c, \\ 2 & \text{if } d = b, \\ 3 & \text{if } d = -(b \times c), \\ 4 & \text{if } d = -b, \end{cases} \tag{1}$$

where $\times$ denotes the vector product in $\mathbb{R}^3$. The elements b and c constitute *the handle*.

Figure 2 summarizes the rules for labeling the vertices depending on the position of such an angle with respect to the preceding handle in the path. Figure 2(a) shows an example of a tree plotted over a VBO, and how function (1) is used to define its 5OT chain code descriptor. The dot indicates the initial tree vertex. Using the only five possible chain elements of Figure 2(b) given by function (1), a tree descriptor is constructed as new tree vertices are being discovered.

The procedure to find the tree descriptor is as follows:

1) Select an arbitrary end vertex of the tree as the origin. In Figure 2(c) the selected origin is represented by a sphere.
2) Compute the chain elements of the tree. Figure 2(c) shows that the first computed element of the chain corresponds to a "0" because the first straight-line segment follows the direction of the last segment. The second element corresponds to the chain element "1" and the handle is still the same as for the first chain element. Note that the dotted arrows indicate only

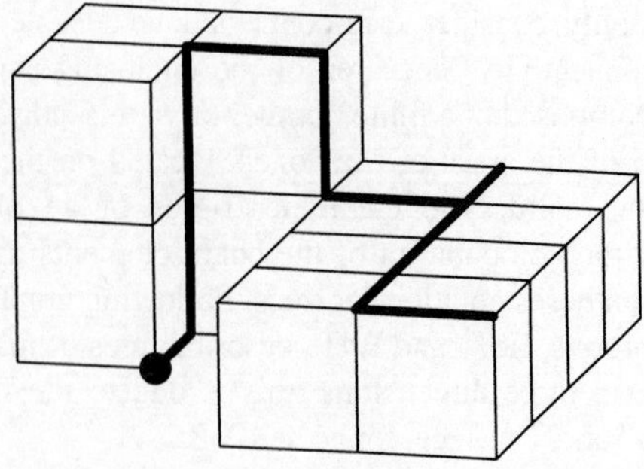

(a) An example of tree plotted over a voxel-based object.

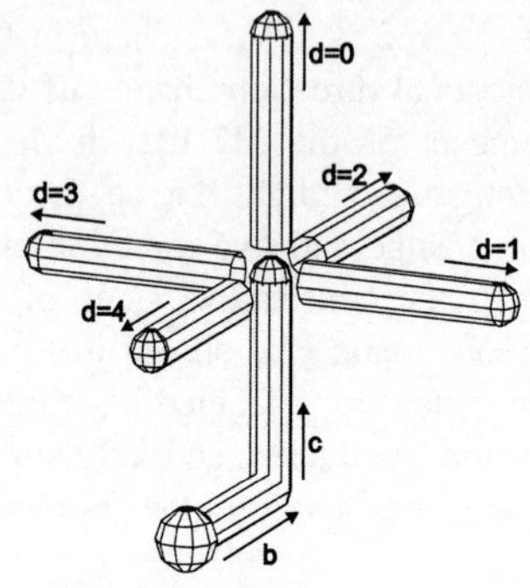

(b) Given the handle and vectors b and c, the five possible chain elements are shown.

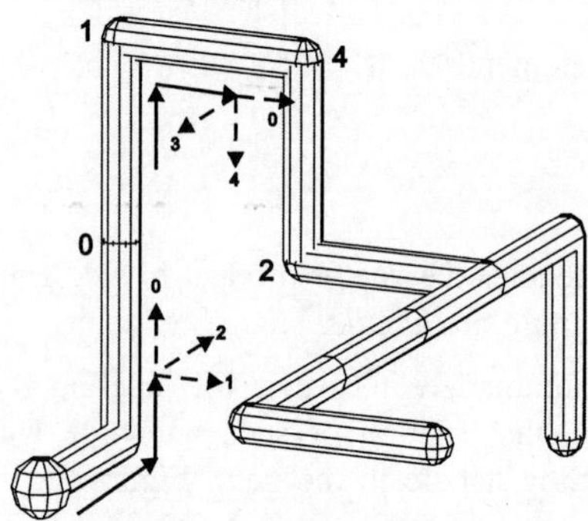

(c) The first four chain elements of an example of a tree and its corresponding partial descriptor: 0142.

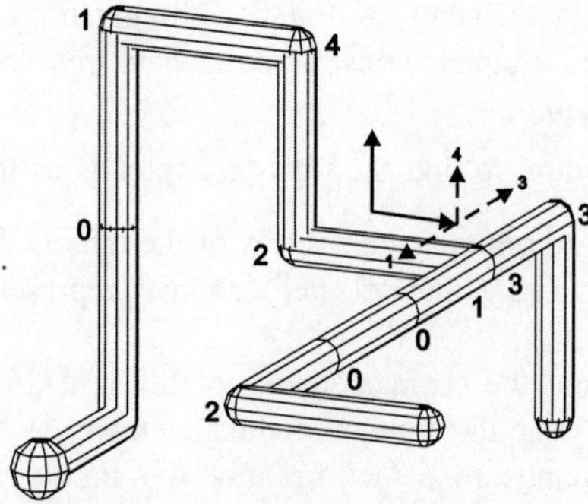

(d) The chain elements of the same tree and its complete tree descriptor: 0142(1002)(33).

Fig. 2: Example of a chain elements computation defined by function (1).

three of the five directions. At the end of this stage the chain is as follows: 0142.

3) It is a known fact that trees can be represented by a notation that uses nested parentheses. Using this notation the next chain element of the tree will be computed. In Figure 2(d) a vertex which is a junction has been reached. In order to decide what direction to go, in the case of Figure 2(d), there are only two possible ways represented by the chain elements "1" and "3" as indicated by the function (1) applied to the new handle. Note that around a branch, it is necessary to know what nonzero element was the last one to define the next element. This ensures that orientation is not lost. The directions are selected in numerical order. Thus, the first selected direction is represented by the chain element "1" and 0142(1002) is the descriptor at this stage. The nested parentheses describe the branch whose chain is (1002). After coming back to the junction node and compute the chain of the next branch, the tree descriptor is equal to 0142(1002)(33).

3. Enclosing trees

The enclosing trees (EcTs) were proposed as a 5OT chain code based alternative to represent VBOs [2]. EcTs are trees which cover each vertex of the visible surface of VBOs and provide a base-five digit strings suitably combined by means of parentheses 1D representation. The vertices of the EcTs correspond to the vertices of the enclosing surface of the analyzed object.

The EcTs computation process using the trees descriptor is as follows:

1) Select an arbitrary vertex of the enclosing surface of the VBO as the origin of the EcT.
2) Choose an arbitrary direction to define the chain elements. The first direction change is composed by two contiguous straight-line segments that will form the first reference handle.
3) Compute the chains that form the enclosing tree:
    a) Following the numerical order determined by the directions obtained in the previous step, search for the neighbor vertices of the enclosing surface of the object.
    b) Repeat the above step until all vertices of the enclosing surface have been reached by the enclosing tree.

Figure 3 illustrates the example of the smallest EcT that can be computed. This is the case for an object consisting of only one voxel. Figure 3(a) shows the original voxel, the initial vertex and the arbitrary direction chosen to conform the first handle to starting the EcT. Figure 3(b) displays the first junction node with the only two possible ways to continue the tree which coincide with chain elements "3" and "4". In this stage the tree descriptor is (3)(4). In the

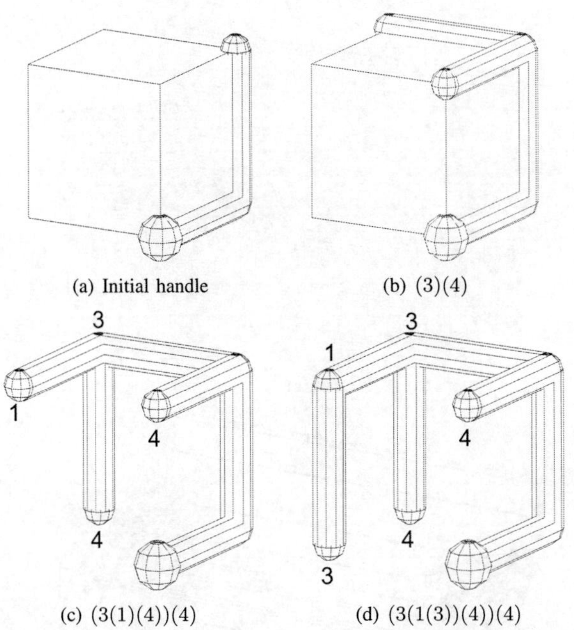

Fig. 3: Enclosing tree computation process for a voxel.

next stage, the processing restarts over the path indicated by the chain "3" because it is the lowest number. Figure 3(c) shows the neighbor vertices reached through the vertex that represents the chain element "3". Those vertices match with the chains "1" and "4". Thus the tree descriptor in this stage is (3(1)(4))(4). The tree descriptor cannot follow through the chain element "4" because all its neighbor vertices have been previously visited. Figure 3(d) shows the final stage of the EcT, and its tree descriptor is as follows: (3(1(3))(4))(4).

Figure 4 presents another example of EcT, in this case the underlying object is a pivoted lever. For a complete review of EcTs and their properties, see Ref. [2].

4. Edging trees

There are solids whose surfaces can be represented without going through all the vertices that make up those surfaces. In these cases, it can be considered that EcTs over-represent the VBO. Figure 1(c) shows an EcT and Figure 1(d) presents an EdT for a $11 \times 11 \times 11$ voxel VBO in which the EcT is considerably more complex than the EdT. The aim of EdTs is to cover VBOs traveling through their edge and represent it by means of a tree descriptor. The basic idea is to obtain a representation similar to a 1D *skeletal* representation via the 5OT chain code in which the planar faces of the 3D object have replaced by the border of the face. Figure 5 shows an example in which its EdT can be a more convenient representation than the corresponding EcT, especially for manufactured parts. Figure 7 presents another example of VBO and its respectie EdT. The chain descriptors of Figures 4, 5 and 7 were omited.

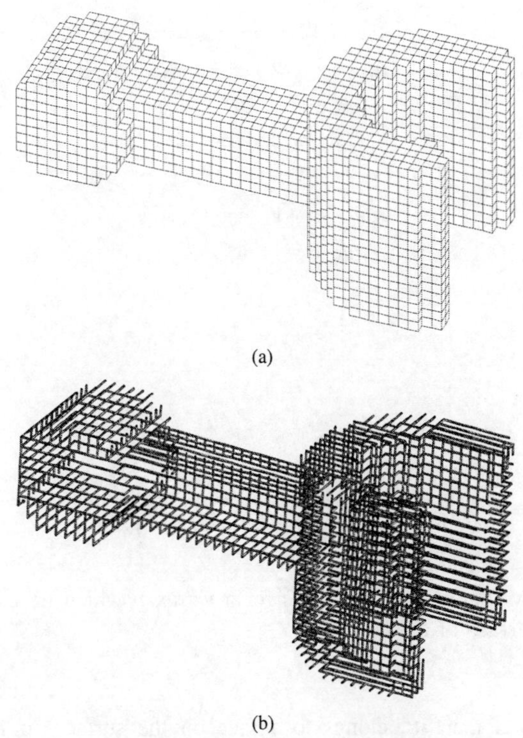

Fig. 4: A pivoted lever (a) with its computed enclosing tree (b).

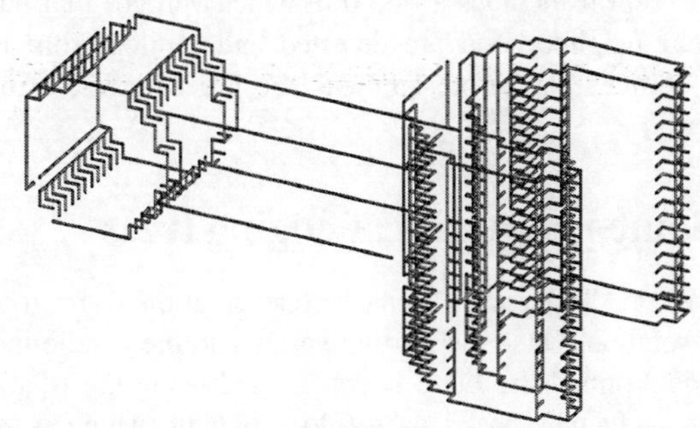

Fig. 5: Edging tree computed for the pivoted lever shown in Figure 4.

In order to compute an EdT it is necessary to omit some vertices in the computation process described in section 3. The candidates are those that have a planar neighborhood. The *xy-planar neighborhood* of v, denoted by $N_{xy}(v)$, is the set of 6 and 18-neighbors of v which lie on a plane parallel to the plane $z = 0$. $N_{xz}(v)$ and $N_{yz}(v)$ are the planar neighborhoods parallel to planes $y = 0$ and $x = 0$, respectively (see Figure 6(a) for an example of planar neighborhood). Figure 6(b) shows a planar neighborhood of v. Also it is a shown a vertex w which has no planar neighborhoods.

It should be noted that if a vertex has a planar neigh-

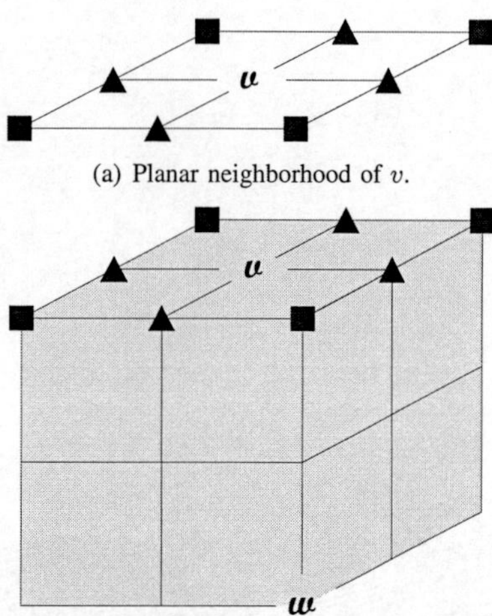

(a) Planar neighborhood of v.

(b) Planar neighborhood of w on a $2 \times 2 \times 2$ voxel-based object. The vertex w has no planar neighborhoods.

Fig. 6: Planar neighborhoods for a vertex v which lie over the surface of a VBO.

borhood then it belongs to a face on the surface of the VBO like v in Figure 6(b). Vertices that have no a planar neighborhood like w will constitute the border. Thus, the EdT computation process is the same as that used to compute EcTs except it includes a step 0 in which vertices that have a planar neighborhood are detected and omited from the VBO vertices list before applying the procedure described in section 3.

5. Some properties of edging trees

Given a VBO its EdT chain code notation is invariant under rotation. Once the starting vertex and the handle have been determined the EdTe is constructed using the relative direction changes based on the local handle which is not affected by a rotation of the underlying object [3].

Using the tree descriptor, the mirror image of any tree is obtained with ease. If a is a tree descriptor, its mirror descriptor can be obtained by replacing in a each occurrence of "1" by "3" and vice versa [3].

Given the descriptor of an EdT, the surface vertex list of the underlying 3D object can be recovered with the exception of those vertices omited because having planar neighborhoods. Due to the fact that the descriptor starts after the initial handle, the coordinates recovering will depend on the initial directions selected by the user in the first step of the process. Notice that every opening parenthesis "(" represents a tree node. The nested parentheses notation for trees used by the 5OT chain code corresponds to a pre-order *depth-first search* traversing [7], as a result the list shall have the same ordering.

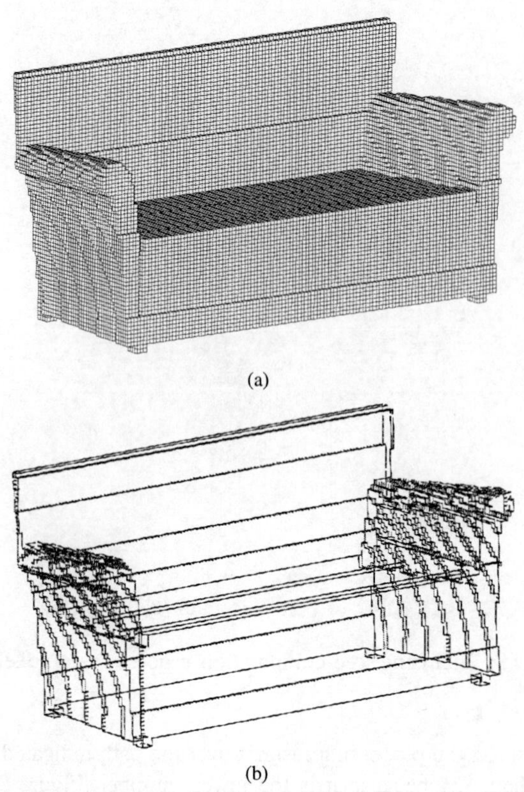

(a)

(b)

Fig. 7: Another example of VBO and its corresponding enclosing tree.

Whereas EcT notation may be used for lossless compression of VBOs because it preserves information and allows considerable data reduction [2]. EdTs can get a higher compression ratio. A priori is difficult to establish the reduction in the descriptor length when EdTs are used instead of EcTs due to the fact that the number of vertices to be deleted changes and varies according to the processed VBO. As a consequence of the selective deleting of surface vertices on planar faces, EdTs can reach every vertex in zones of VBOs that cannot be simplified. In fact, in the worst case when no vertices can be suppressed, EdTs are the same as EcTs.

6. Acknowledgments

L.A.M. acknowledges a DGAPA-UNAM grant and support from Instituto de Astronomía, Universidad Nacional Autónoma de México. This work is part of a doctoral dissertation under the direction of Prof. Bribiesca.

References

[1] A. Guzmán, "Canonical shape description for 3-d stick bodies", MCC Technical Report, Austin, TX. 78759, Tech. Rep. ACA-254-87, 1987.

[2] E. Bribiesca, A. Guzmán A and L. A. Martínez, "Enclosing trees", *Pattern Anal. Applic.*, vol. 15, pp. 1-17, 2012.

[3] E. Bribiesca, "A method for representing 3D tree objects using chain coding", *J. Visual Commun. Image Represent.*, vol. 19, pp. 184-198, 2008.
[4] E. Bribiesca and W. Aguilar, "A measure of shape dissimilarity for 3D curves", *Int. Journal of Contemp. Math. Sci.*, vol. 15, pp. 727-751, 2006.
[5] H. Sánchez-Cruz and E. Bribiesca, "Study if compression efficiency for three-dimensional discrete curves", *Opt. Eng.* . 47 (7), 077206, july 2008.
[6] R. O. Duda and P. Hart, *Pattern Classification and Scene Analysis*, Wiley, New York, 1973.
[7] D. Knuth, *The Art of Computer Programming*, Volume 1: *Fundamental Algorithms*, 3rd ed., Addison-Wesley, 1997.

On Real-Time LIDAR Data Segmentation and Classification

Dmitriy Korchev[1], Shinko Cheng[2], Yuri Owechko[1], and Kyungnam (Ken) Kim[1]
[1]Information Systems Sciences Lab., HRL Laboratories, LLC, Malibu, CA, USA
[2] Social, Google Inc., Mountain View, CA, USA

Abstract - *We present algorithms for fast segmentation and classification of sparse 3D point clouds from rotating LIDAR sensors used for real-time applications such as autonomous mobile systems. Such systems must continuously process large amounts of data with update rates as high as 10 frames per second which makes complexity and performance of the algorithms very critical. Our approach to the segmentation of large and sparse point clouds is efficient and accurate which frees system resources for implementing other more demanding tasks such as classification. Segmentation is the emphasis of this paper as a necessary important first step for subsequent classification and further processing. We propose methods for segmenting sparse point clouds from rotating LIDAR sensors such as the Velodyne HDL-64E using rectangular and radial grids. The main part of the segmentation is performed on small grid images instead of large point clouds which makes the process computationally fast, simple, and very efficient. The proposed algorithms do not require flat horizontal structure of the ground and they demonstrate stable performance in different urban conditions and scenes for detection of different street objects including pedestrians, cars, and bicyclists.*

Keywords: Real-Time LIDAR, 3D-Segmentation, 3D-Classification

1 Introduction

In this paper we address the problem of segmentation of large sparse LIDAR 3D point clouds in real time for subsequent classification. Advances in LADAR scanner technologies such as the Velodyne HDL-64E allow the development of experimental autonomous mobile systems described in [1,2]. Such systems contain a multi-beam rotating Velodyne LIDAR scanner mounted on top of a vehicle. The LIDAR sensor produces a continuous high data rate stream of 3D points, typically exceeding one million points per second. This stream of points is parsed into frames, where each frame corresponds to one complete rotation of the sensor; the frame rate is close to 10Hz. Each of the 64 lasers in the Velodyne sensor performs a circular scan of the environment, which results in a non-uniform spatial density of the scanned objects. The objects close to the sensor are represented with more dense point clouds vs. far objects that are represented with much sparser point clouds.

While progress has been made, researchers continue to look for new alternative algorithms for segmentation and classification. The goal of segmentation is to parse each separate distinct object in the point clouds for subsequent classification. The main challenges in this process are: high data rate, sparsity of the data, and non-uniform density of the scanned object data. The methods proposed in this paper extend to real-time applications the approach originally developed under DARPA URGENT contract [3,4] for automatic classification of urban objects in large static 3D point clouds collected by aerial and ground LIDARs.

2 Related Work

Efficient real-time object recognition is an important capability for autonomous robots and systems. This drives researchers to make these systems fast, efficient, and accurate. The relevant issues have been analyzed from different perspectives and approaches by various researchers to improve aspects of the system and shed more light on the problems that need to be solved. A number of papers were published in recent years that consider different aspects of real-time segmentation and classification of 3D point clouds [1,2-5-9]. The results presented in [1, 2] demonstrate systems that perform segmentation and classification in real or close to real time. Paper [5] shows good segmentation results using the convexity criterion with promising speed results for real time operation. Paper [6] considered using 3D models to improve classification performance but the overall speed of the system was not sufficient for real-time operations. The research in [7] focused on dense point clouds generated by a flash LIDAR which produces more uniformly dense scans of the objects, unlike spinning LIDARs such as the Velodyne HDL-64E. The approaches in [8] work on both dense and sparse point clouds with close to real-time performance. Another interesting approach to segmentation and classification is presented in [9], the results present Matlab implementation based timing which is promising for real-time operation. Computational complexity of the segmentation is the most significant limitation of the current methods mentioned above, especially for the future low cost embedded applications. The next two sections describe our 3D point cloud segmentation methods based on two different types of grids and a 3D classification algorithm adapted from DARPA URGENT program [4]. We then draw conclusions and compare our results with published results.

3 Segmentation

Our earlier 3D point cloud segmentation method [3, 4] developed under the DARPA URGENT program produced satisfactory segmentation results but it did not meet the real-time requirements that are imposed by the spinning multi-beam LIDARs such as the Velodyne HDL-64E. In this section we present novel methods for real-time segmentation of large sparse point clouds produced by spinning multi-beam LIDAR sensors, requiring processing rates of a million points per second and higher. The novelty of this algorithm is the projection of points onto rectangular or radial grids that allow maintaining point densities in each bin for LIDAR scanning sensors. Segmentation of objects and obstacles is performed by analyzing the minimum and maximum height maps (called Min and Max images) on these grids.

A typical autonomous driving system is based on a spinning multi-laser LIDAR such as the Velodyne HDL-64E which generates point clouds by an array of rotating lasers producing circular scan lines around the sensor. The Velodyne HDL-64E delivers a 360-degree horizontal field of view and 26.8 degree vertical field of view using 64 laser beams. This type of sensor can provide more than 1 million points per second, detecting all directions of environment around it. It has become a popular sensor for building and testing autonomous driving systems. A typical scan pattern of this kind of LIDAR as seen from above is shown in Figure 1. The vertical array of lasers rotates with a constant speed and produces a fixed number of scan lines (actually circles on the horizontal plane) per spin. That results in uneven spatial density of the scan lines, in particular, the scan line density decreases with the distance from the sensor. Since each scan line contains the same number of points, the density of the points within the scan lines also decreases with the distance from the sensor. These properties of the LIDAR lead to highly sparse point clouds at longer ranges compared to shorter ranges.

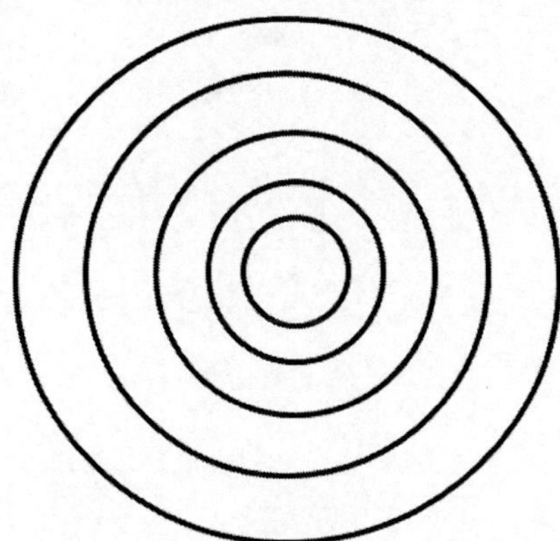

Figure 1 A typical Velodyne scan pattern shown in horizontal plane. Only five laser lines are shown.

We investigated the segmentation performance of two types of sampling grids: rectangular and radial. The initial processing of each grid is very similar. Every complete spin of the lasers produces a complete point cloud or frame of the scene. Each frame is projected into the grid along the z-axis, and is represented by minimum and maximum height maps called *Min image* and *Max image,* respectively. The Min and Max images have the same size defined by the type, size and parameters of the grid. A separate structure of the same size as the images is used to hold the associated points for each grid cell. This association is necessary to perform the reverse lookup to efficiently extract point cloud segments from these images. The processing of each grid is based on the general procedure shown in Figure 2.

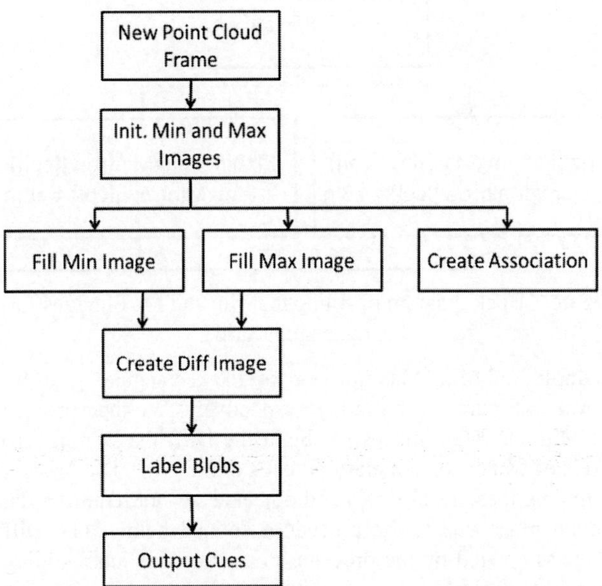

Figure 2 Block diagram of the grid processing of a single frame

The Min and Max images are 8-bit images representing 256 height gradations. Before processing a point cloud frame, all pixels of these images are set to 255 for the Min image and to 0 for the Max image.

3.1 Rectangular Grid

Let's define the max distance from the sensor as D_{max} and d as the lateral size of the grid cell. The dimensions of the Max and Min images in terms of rows H and columns W will be

$$W = H = \frac{2 \cdot D_{max}}{d} + 1.$$

Parameter h defines the vertical resolution of the grid. Typical values for the vertical and lateral resolutions for automotive applications are: $h = 10cm$, $d = 25 - 35cm$. The block diagram shown in Figure 3 describes the process of filling the

Min and Max images and associating the point with a grid-cell.

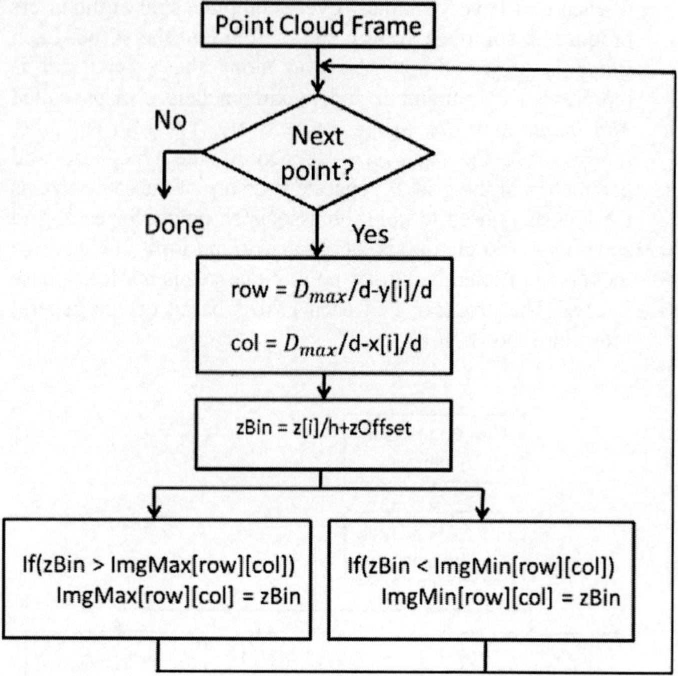

Figure 3 Bock diagram of filling the Min and Max images for the rectangular grid

Examples of Min, Max images for the rectangular grid are shown in Figure 4 (a) and (b), respectively. We then process the Min and Max images to obtain the Diff image, non-zero pixels of which contain elevated cells of the grid. The process of finding these locally elevated objects does not require a flat ground plane due to the procedure defined below. The Diff image is created by the procedure based on the small sliding windows of size MxM running in parallel in both Min and Max images. Typical size M for this window is from 1 to 5 for the grid cell sizes presented in this paper. The size of the window should be adjusted accordingly for different sizes of the grid cells to be able to capture local ground. The following steps describe the procedure of filling the Diff image:

1. For location of the window <i,j> find the min pixel value Pmin in the Min image.
2. Mark Diff image location <I,j> as 255 if abs(Pmin-Pmax(I,j) >= T and the cell is not empty
3. Move window to the next location.

The resulting Diff image is shown in Figure 4c. The Diff image is then processed with 8-connected component analysis that will label the blobs as shown in Figure 4d.

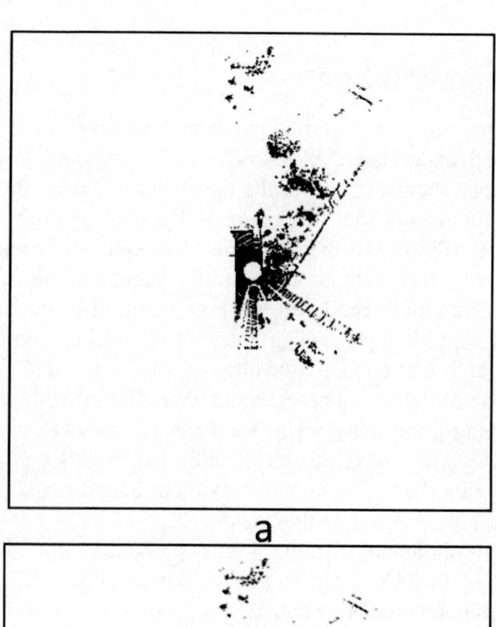

a

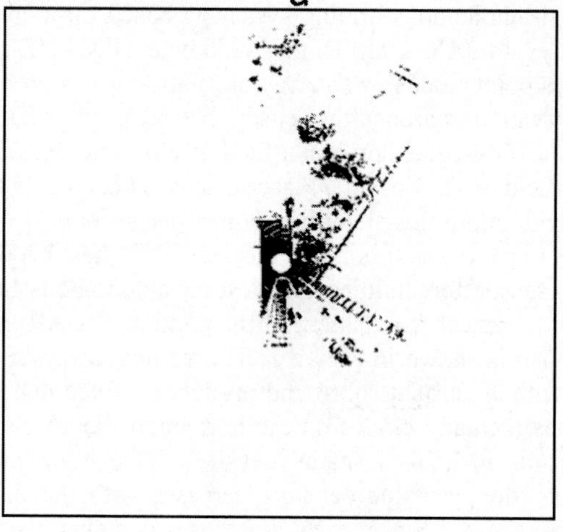

b

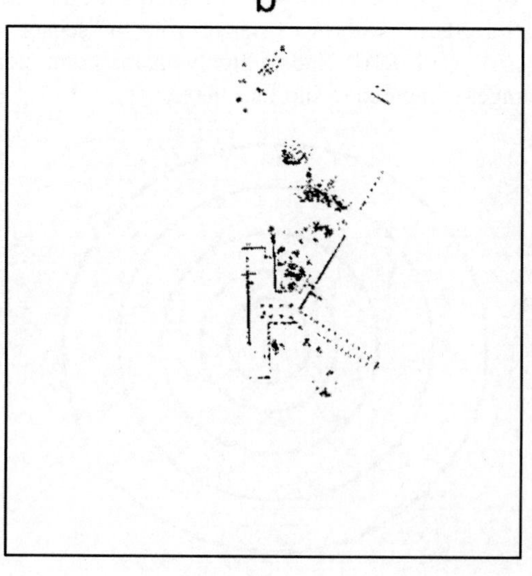

c

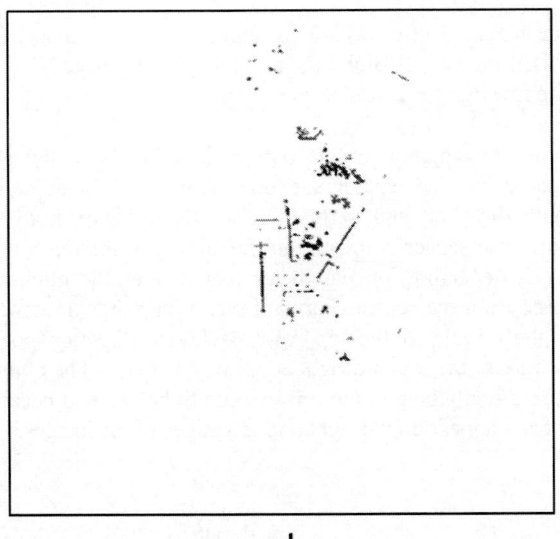

d

Figure 4 Rectangular grid: (a) - Min image, (b)- Max image, (c) - Diff image, (d) - Blob image. The sensor is located in the center of the image. Intensities of images (b) and (c) are inverted for better clarity.

The point cloud frame and the segmentation results based on the procedure described above for the rectangular grid are shown in Figure 5. Each segmented cue is colored with distinct random color. The ground points and points that do not belong to any other object are black.

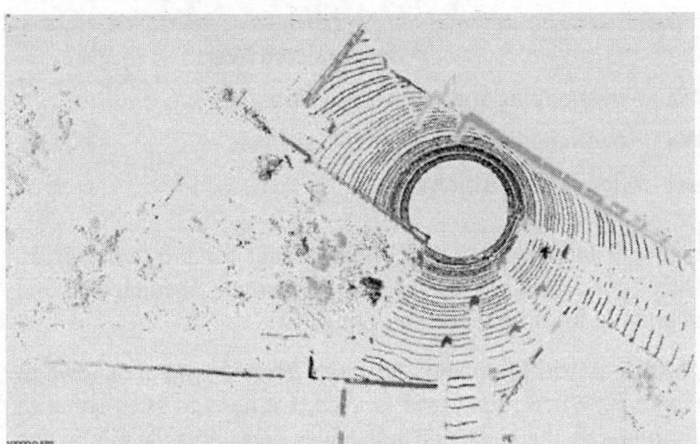

Figure 5 Segmentation results of our method with the rectangular grid, the connected segments are randomly colored; the ground points have black color. We can see that our method of segmentation handles different object correctly, including thin rail surrounding the patio.

We found that value of threshold $T=1$ produces good result for a variety of scenes and objects. After that, each blob is processed to generate the segmented point cloud. This process is accomplished by extracting the pixels that belong to the same blob and collecting the indices of the points in the original point cloud.

3.2 Radial Grid

A part of the radial grid is shown in Figure 6. This grid is better aligned with Velodyne scan pattern shown in Figure 1 and it produces less fragmentation of the segments.

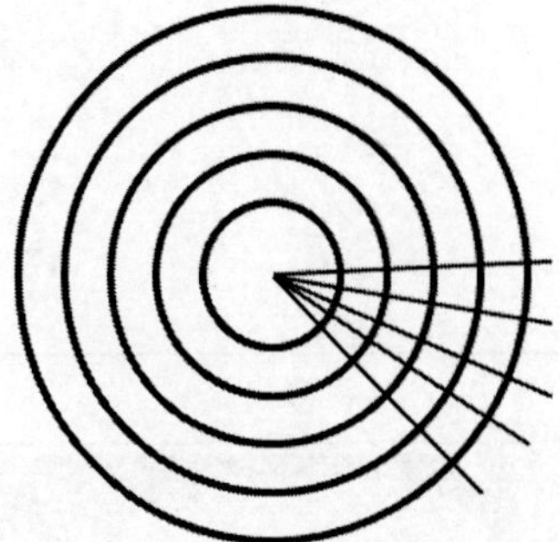

Figure 6 Fragment of radial grid on horizontal plane

The width W and height H of the Min and Max images are determined as

$W = 360/ResDeg$,

$H = (MaxRadius-MinRadius)/RangeRes$.

Where, *ResDeg is the* angular resolution and *RangeRes* is the range resolution. The block diagram of filling the Min and Max images for the radial grid is shown in Figure 7. The Diff and Blob images and the association of the points are created the same way as it was described for the rectangular grid.

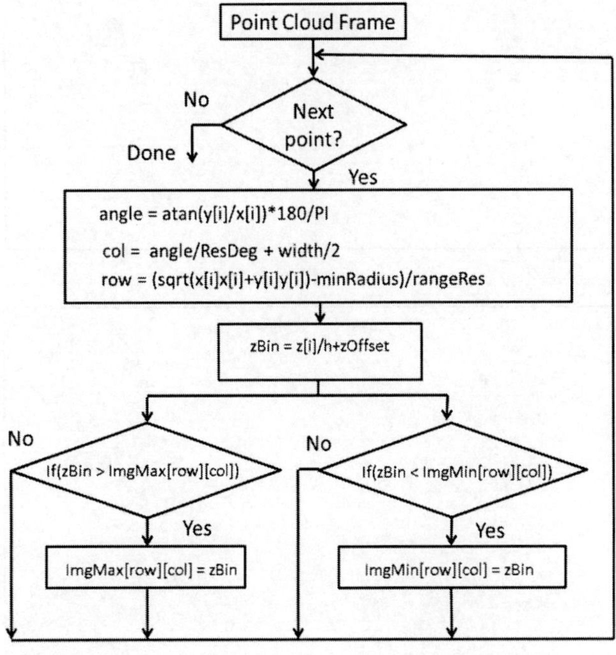

Figure 7 Block diagram of filling the Min and Max images for the radial grid

a

b

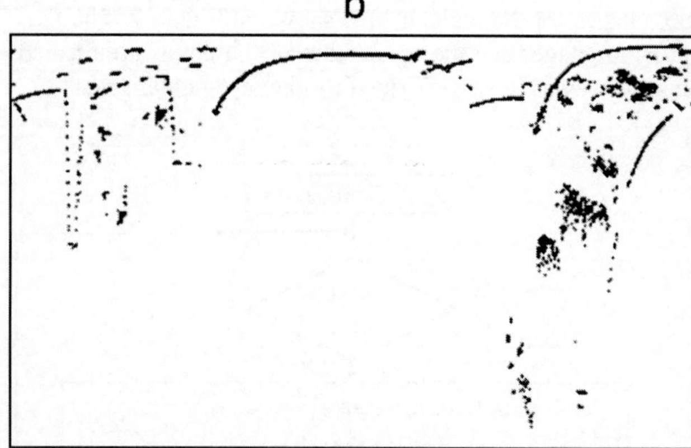

c

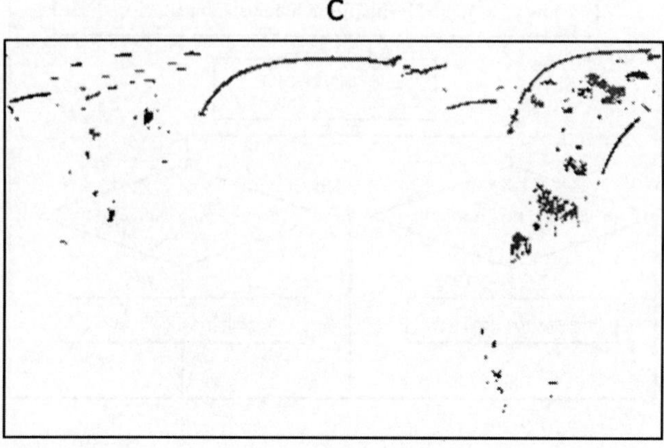

d

Figure 8 Radial grid: (a) - Min image, (b) - Max image, and (c) - Diff image, (d) Blob image. Intensities of images (b) and (c) are inverted for better clarity.

Overall segmentation of the data is less for the radial grid compared to the rectangular one. Horizontal axes define azimuth direction and vertical axis - the distance from the sensor. The sensor is located in the middle of the top row or above it depending on parameter that defines the minimum distance from the sensor. Forward direction points downward from the middle of the top row. Backward direction points downward at the left and right edges of the image. The objects that are directly behind the sensor need to be stitched because their parts appear on the right and left edges of the images.

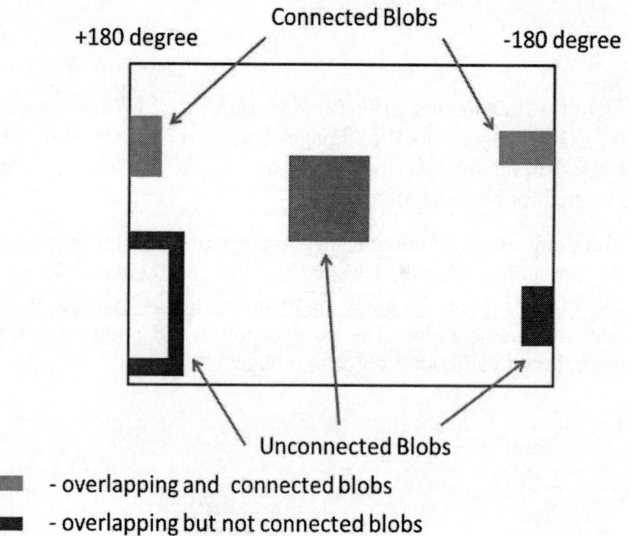

Figure 9 Demonstration of the stitching for the radial grids. Only "connected" blobs need to be merged, unconnected and internal blobs do not need merging.

The radial grid Min, Max, Diff and Blob images are shown in Figure 8. When radial grid is used, we need to stich some of the blobs at the right and left edges (see more details in the caption under Figure 8). These edges represent locations behind the sensor and are split by the line representing ±180 degree in azimuth. The blobs that need to be stitched are located on the left (col=0) and right (col=N-1) sides of the Blob image. Only objects that got cut by the ±180 degree azimuth need to be stitched. In the first step of the stitching process we select blobs that connect to the left and right edges of the image Figure 8 (d). After that we find the blobs that have overlapping vertical pixel coordinates for pixels belonging to the first and last columns, left and right of the image, correspondingly. These blobs are marked "connected" as it is shown in Figure 9 and they are merged into one blob representing a single object behind the sensor. This process is applied to all border blobs to correctly represent the objects located directly behind the sensor.

An example of a point cloud frame and segmentation with the radial grid is shown in Figure 10.

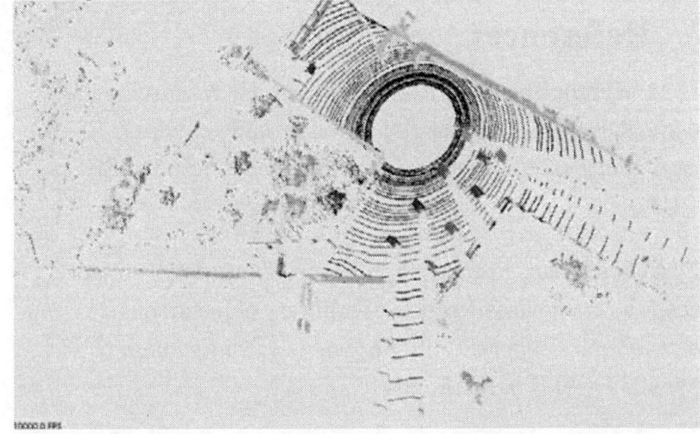

Figure 10 Segmentation results of our method with the radial grid, the connected segments are randomly colored; the ground points have black color. We can see that our method of segmentation handles different object correctly, including thin rail surrounding the patio.

The radial grid requires 20-30% fewer cells compared to the rectilinear one, which leads to faster processing speed. It also produces less fragmentation of the objects. An illustration of the fragmentation for a typical sequence of frames acquired while urban driving is shown in Figure 11. The chart shows that the average number of fragments is 12-13% fewer for the radial grid.

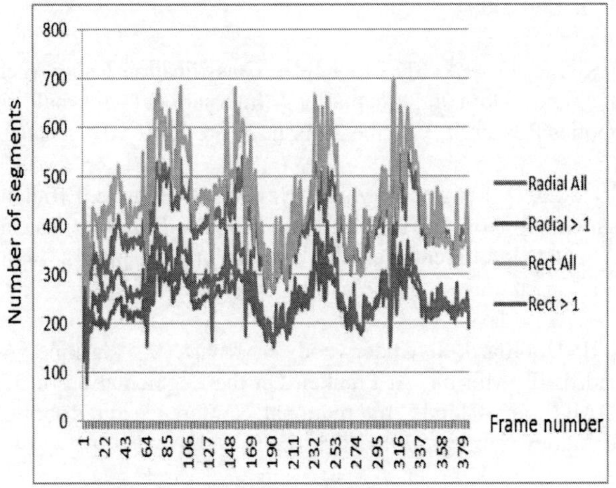

Figure 11 Charts showing number of fragments in each frame for a typical urban sequence for the radial and rectangular grids. Each type of grid has two charts: one for the total number of fragments in a frame and one for the number of fragments that are greater than one grid cell.

Table 1 Comparison of the fragmentation for rectangular and radial grids. The table shows that overall fragmentation of the segments for the radial grid 12-13% fewer than for the rectangular grid.

Blobs type	Average number of blobs
Radial (all blobs)	398.6
Radial (blobs bigger than 1 cell)	242.8
Rectangular (all blobs)	451.0
Rectangular (blobs bigger than 1cell)	271.8

4 Integration of 3D Segmentation with Classification

The block diagram of the segmentation/classification system we developed is shown in Figure 12. It consists of the Velodyne LIDAR, a converter from pcap format to XYZ point clouds, the 3D segmentation module described in the previous chapter, and the 3D classification module that is described below.

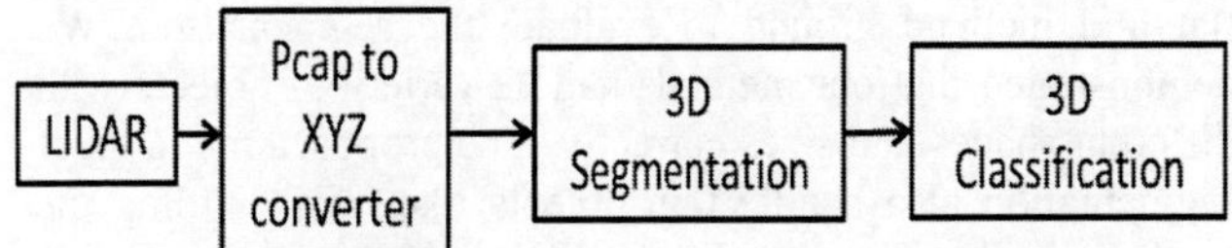

Figure 12 Block diagram of the developed system.

We used a modified 3D classifier [9] developed under the DARPA URGENT program for 17 urban objects. The core feature set for this classifier is based on size and rotation invariant volumetric features [3]. The classifier was developed to process dense point clouds acquired by aerial and ground LIDARs. More info and results for this classifier can be found in [3].

In our current work, we defined four classes which are the most relevant to autonomous mobile systems. These classes are: car, pedestrian, bicyclist, and background. We used 75 minimum points as the limit of the number of points in the cue as suggested in [2]. To validate the performance of the classifier we used the data set in [2] which contains significant numbers of labeled objects for car, pedestrian, bicyclist, and background. Overall performance of the classifier is presented in the table, Table 2. Each column in the table presents the result of the classifier trained on cues with minimum number of points 500, 250, 150, and 75. We used 5k examples for car, pedestrian, bicyclist, and 20k examples for background class. The table represents the performance of the classifiers on validation data sets that do not contain any training examples. The accuracy for pedestrian and bicyclist degrades about 5% with the reduction of minimum number of points in a cue from 500 to 75. The results suggest that the overall performance of the classifier achieved for these four classes is close to the state of the art results [2].

Table 2 Classification accuracy for car, pedestrian, bicyclist, and background. Each column represents classification accuracy for 500, 250, 150, and 75 minimum points in the cue.

Min number of points	500	250	150	75
Car		0.96	0.95	0.91
Pedestrian	0.93	0.91	0.9	0.88
Bicyclist	0.95	0.93	0.93	0.9
Background	0.98	0.98	0.98	0.97

5 Segmentation Results

The goal of segmentation and classification of 3D data is to achieve accurate performance and in real time which is the necessary part of an autonomous mobile system.

Due to unavailability of labeled data sets containing complete scans and difficulty of manual labeling of the data, we evaluated the performance of our system on our data qualitatively. The examples of the segmentations for rectangular and radial grids are presented in Figure 5 and Figure 10, respectively. We used different urban scenes with flat and inclined ground to evaluate the segmentation. We demonstrated that our methods handle variety of objects with different shapes and sizes correctly. The proposed methods of segmentation also handle thin objects like rails dividing the roads and sidewalks as well as roofs of the cars correctly; this importance was emphasized in [1]. Overall segmentation and classification results on Velodyne data were good with an acceptable amount of under and over segmentations. The time taken by the segmentation implemented on a single thread running on HP workstation Z400 was 30-40ms per frame depending on the grid parameters settings. We did not observe any significant fluctuations of processing time for different scenes and objects. This speed is more than enough to do the segmentation of Velodyne HDL-64E data in real time.

We also evaluated the performance of the 3D classifier on a labeled public data set from [2].The results of this evaluation show that the performance of our modified URGENT classifier is very close to other state of the art results.

6 Conclusions and Future Work

We developed a new 3D segmentation and classification framework that processes high volumes of LIDAR data in real time. The proposed segmentation algorithms can be applied to a variety of different applications and scenes; in particular, they can be used in autonomous mobile systems. We achieved good segmentation and classification quality and real-time performance of the system due to the novel approach to the segmentation of large sparse 3D point clouds. The core of the approach is based on processing of smaller images instead of large point cloud data. The methods proposed do not require a flat ground plane and they reliably handle a variety of complex urban environments and objects of interests.

Our future work will consist of integrating additional features such as tracking of 3D objects and fusion between LIDAR and EO sensors to improve overall system performance.

7 References

[1] M. Himmelsbach, F. Hundelshausen, H. Wuensche. Fast segmentation of 3D point clouds for ground vehicles. *Intelligent Vehicles Symposium (IV)* (pp. 560 - 565). IEEE, 2010

[2] A. Teichman, J Levinson, S.Thrun. Towards 3D object recognition via classification of arbitrary object tracks . *Internationa Conference on Robotics and Automation (ICRA)* (pp. 4034 - 4041). IEEE, 2011.

[3] Y. Owechko, S. Medasani, T. Korah. Automatic Recognition of Diverse 3-D Objects and Analysis of Large Urban Scenes Using Ground and Aerial LIDAR Sensors. Conference on Lasers and Electro-Optics. San Jose: Optical Society of America, 2010.

[4] T. Korah, S. Medasani, Y. Owechko. Strip Histogram Grid for efficient LIDAR segmentation from urban environments. *Conference on Computer Vision and Pattern Recognition Workshops, (CVPRW)* (pp. 74-81). IEEE, 2011.

[5] F. Moosmann, O. Pink, C. Stiller. Segmentation of 3D Lidar Data in non-flat Urban Environments using a Local Convexity Criterion. Intelligent Vehicles Symposium, pp.215-229, IEEE, 2009.

[6] K. Lai, D. Fox. 3D Laser Scan Classification Using Web Data and Domain Adaptation. International Journal of Robotics Research, Volume 29 Issue 8, pp. 1019-1037, 2010

[7] J. Aue, D. Langer, B. Muller-Bessler, B. Huhnke. Efficient Segmentation of 3D LIDAR Point Clouds Handling Partial Occlusion. Intelligent Vehicles Symposium IV, pp. 423-428, 2011

[8] B. Douillard, J. Underwood, N. Kuntz, V. Vlaskine, A. Quadros, P. Morton, A. Frenkel. On the Segmentation of 3D LIDAR Point Clouds. International Conference on Robotics and Automation, pp.2798-2805, IEEE, 2011.

[9] S.-M. Lee, J. J. Im, B.-H. Lee, A. Leonessa, A. Kurdila. A Real-Time Grid Map Generation and Object Classification for Ground-Based 3D LIDAR Data using Image Analysis Techniques. International Conference on Image Processing, ICIP, pp. 2253-2256, IEEE, 2010.

DENOISING TIME-OF-FLIGHT DEPTH MAPS USING TEMPORAL MEDIAN FILTER

[1] Fang-Yu Lin, [1,†]Yi-Leh Wu, [1]Wei-Chih Hung

[1]Department of Computer Science and Information Engineering
National Taiwan University of Science and Technology, Taiwan
[†]E-mail: ywu@csie.ntust.edu.tw

ABSTRACT

In many types of 3D cameras, The Time-of-Flight (TOF) cameras have the advantages of simplicity for use and lower price for general public. The TOF cameras can obtain depth maps at video speed. However, the TOF cameras suffer from low resolution and high random noise. In this paper, we propose methods to reduce the random noise in depth maps captured by the TOF cameras. For each point in the noisy TOF depth map, we substitute the depth value with the median depth value of its corresponding points in temporally consecutive depth maps captured by the TOF cameras. The proposed methods require only the depth data captured by the TOF cameras without any extra information, such as illumination, geometric shape, or complex parameters. Experiments results suggest that the proposed temporal denoising methods can effective reduce the noise in TOF depth maps for up to 44 percent.

Keywords *Time-of-Flight camera; 3D data, Median; Ranodm noise; Denoising;*

1. INTRODUCTION

Recently, 3D data has more common usages for general public and are more widespread for different domains; e.g., 3D model reconstruction [2, 14]. 3D models are popularly used in many kinds of fields. 3D models of real-world objects are reconstructed with 3D data, such as the depth information or the color information, are collected by 3D scanners. Not only for 3D models, 3D data is also employed for applications such as collision prevention, position determination, real-time object detection, etc. Nowadays, people are concerned about read-time response. The speed of operation and the accuracy of the 3D information always influence the performance of 3D applications.

There are many selections of 3D scanners. Depending on different hardware and scanning technologies, each 3D scanner comes with its own advantages, shortcomings, and costs. Some scanners can produce high quality data, but they are quite expensive and often require expert knowledge for using. Users of those kinds of scanners are limited. We conjecture that if 3D cameras are easy to use and less expensive that will produce more applications and usages.

The TOF camera [2, 3, 8, 13] is one of the 3D scanners which are easy-to-use and less expensive. The type of the TOF camera is active, which means the camera emits an extra energy to the subject, and then using the Time of Flight principle measures the data of 3D space by the projection of the energy. The TOF camera can obtain the 3D depth map of a scene at video rate by measuring the traveling time of the light pulses between the camera and the objects. Furthermore, for the general public, the TOF camera is not difficult to operate and with a lower cost compares to the 3D laser scanners. Even though, the TOF camera is now more popular to industrial purposes than commercial usages. With the price dramatically decreases, the TOF cameras becoming off-the-shelf products, such as webcams or personal digital cameras, would not be a dream.

Although, there are many advantages of the TOF camera, it still suffers from several limitations such as random noise and lower-resolution depth maps. Some researches endeavor to improve the low-resolution problem of TOF camera [3, 14, 15, 16, 17, 19] by using one single depth map with adjacent depth pixels or by combining several low resolution noisy depth images of a static model. The proposed methods have some disadvantages, such as complex parameters need or long executive time. Other researches enhance the resolution and improve the distortion of 3D data by combining image data and depth data [6, 7, 11]. They still suffer from artifacts and use extra information, such as the intensity edges or the geometric shapes.

In this paper, considering as the basic of any processes, we suppose that the less noise depth maps have, the more accurate the information of depth maps is for TOF applications. Therefore, we focus on reducing the random noise in the depth maps of the TOF camera. We denoise the TOF depth maps only with the information provided in the TOF depth maps without any extra data from other sensors. Besides, the denoised method does not need to calibrate any complex parameters. Through the denoised methods we proposed, the TOF depth maps have more accurate depth values when comparing to the ground truth. The execution time of the proposed system is also fast and does not influence the advantage of using the TOF cameras.

In the remaining part of this manuscript, we elaborate on the TOF datasets, the denoising methods, and the experiment results.

2. TOF DEPTH MAP DENOISING METHODS

We first give a brief introduction of the TOF datasets employed for the experiments. After the descriptions, we elaborate each procedure of the propoded TOF depth map denoising method.

2.1. TOF Datasets

Y. Cui et al. [18] provide the TOF datasets we used in the experiments. A MESA Swissranger SR4000 TOF camera [8] captured the original depth maps from subjects in the datasets by its LEDs in the front of camera emitting light pulses and the lens of camera gathering the reflection of light to its CMOS imaging sensor for measuring the distances. The TOF camera rotated around one subject and captured 600 depth map frames, as shown in Figure 1. The angle between the first frame and the last frame is 120° .

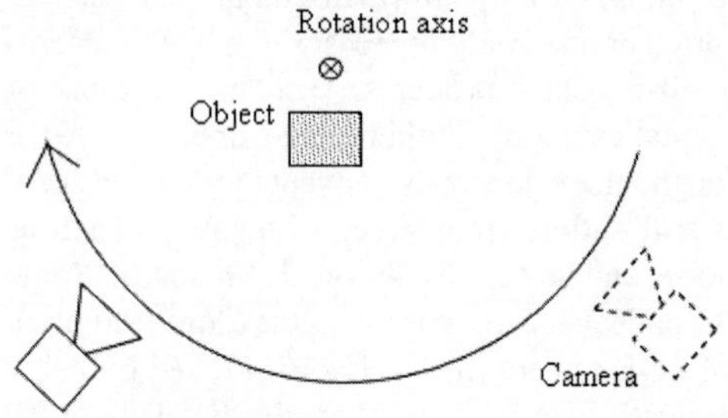

Figure 1: TOF Camera rotates around the rotation axis

An example of the original TOF depth map transfomed into a gray scale image is as shown in Figure 1.(a), where the depth values in the depth map are scaled to 0 to 255 gray values. The face in this image is severely corrupted by noisy pixels. Figure 1.(b) shows the 3D point cloud of the same TOF depth map in a 3D coordinate system. We observe that some points are very far from the surface of the 3D model and the outline of the model is indistinct. The TOF depth map suffering from these noising points would influence the accuracy of later processes. To reduce the noises in a TOF depth map, we modified the distorted depth values in a depth map which we treated as an X-Y plane with points and each point has its own depth value.

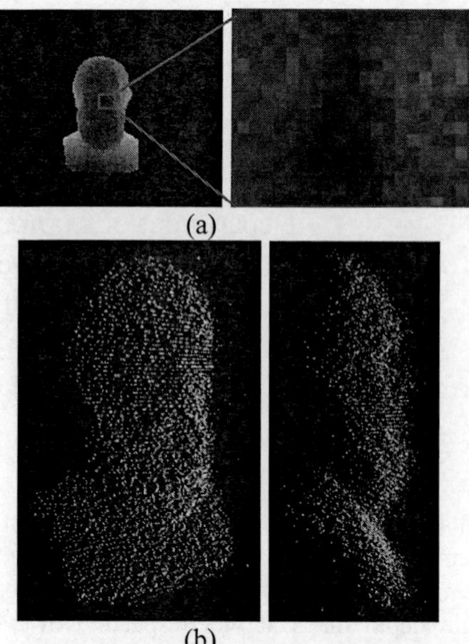

Figure 2: an example visualization of the depth values in a noisy TOF depth map

2.2. TOF Depth Map Denoising Processes

Median filter [1, 5] is one of the common smoothing methods for image denoising, which runs through the whole noise image pixel by pixel and replaces each pixel with the median value of the neighboring pixels. The number of the neighboring pixels involed is called "window". The median filter has good performance of denoising and preserving edges with a fixed window size. Instead of using spatially neighboring pixels of each pixel in the original TOF depth map, we propose to apply the median filter with points which are corresponding to the point to be modified in temporally adjacent TOF depth maps.

To obtain a denoised TOF depth map, firstly we selected a frame D_t, where t is the number of the depth map in time. We assume that D_t's preceding maps and succeeding maps were relevant to D_t. We then picked k consecutive depth maps, including the frame D_t, which k is the size of "window". The frame D_t is the middle one of these k depth maps in time. The (k-1)/2 preceding maps and the (k-1)/2 succeeding maps of the D_t are aligned to middle map D_t and find the corresponding points from the depth maps for each point in D_t. The depth value of each point of each map is represented as $D_t(x, y)$, where x is the x-coordinate and y is the y-coordinate of the point. Each point in the middle map has k corresponding depth values, including its own.

We compute the median of these k values which is the modified value of $D_t(x, y)$. We refer to the proposed TOF depth map denoising method, which includes the multi-map TOF depth maps denoising process with the TOF depth maps alignment process, as the Temporal-Median.

The flowchart which describes the procedures of the Temporal-Median is shown in Figure 3. First, k consecutive TOF depth maps with the middle one D_t are selected as input. Because of the rotation of camera, the same X-Y coordinate points in the k input TOF depth maps do not exactly indicate to the same position in the 3D scene represented by the TOF depth maps. By employing the TOF depth maps alignment process, each point in D_t would find k aligned depth points with k adjusted depth values separately in k TOF depth maps. After alignment, denoising process compute the proper values for each point in D_t with its own k aligning depth values and modify the depth value of each point in D_t. Finally, the Temporal-Median method outputs a denoised TOF depth map.

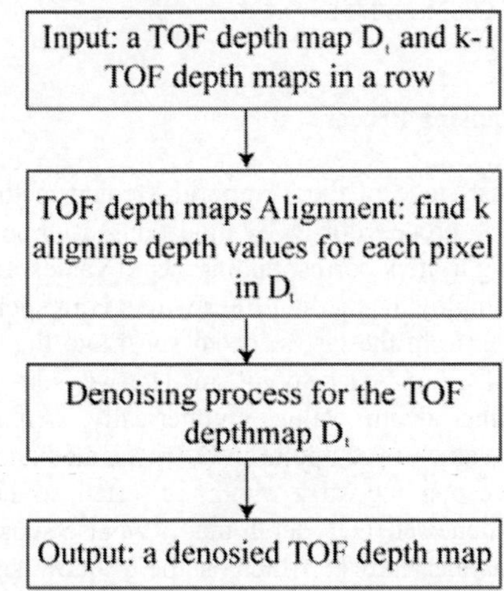

Figure 3: Flowchart of Temporal-Median.

2.3. TOF Depth Maps Alignment

In our TOF datasets, the TOF camera rotated around the object in the scene for 3D reconstruction purpose. This means that two points having the same X-Y coordinate in two TOF depth maps represents different position in the real 3D scene. Since the TOF camera did not move vertically when it rotated around the object, we only need to consider the X-Z coordinate offsets. Camera rotating around the rotation axis is equivalent to the object rotating around the axis in the converse wise. There are 600 TOF depth maps of frames in one dataset. The approximate angle of two frames is 2 degrees which is estimated with 120 degrees between the first frame and the last frame. Since that Dt is the middle map of its k corresponding depth maps, the X-Z coordinate of each depth point in preceding maps is adjusted by turning around with the specific rotation axis in clockwise direction and which in succeeding maps is adjusted by turning around with the same axis in counterclockwise direction.

The proposed TOF depth maps alignment process has two stages. The first stage is to estimate the specific rotation axis with three X-Z coordinates of the particular feature point captured separately from three of depth maps. Firstly, three X-Z coordinates of the particular feature point in three depth maps of frame A_1, B_1, C_1. (X_a, Z_a), (X_b, Z_b), and (X_c, Z_c) are separately represented the X-Z coordinate of the particular feature point a, b, c in depth maps of frame A_1, B_1, C_1. (X_p, Z_p) is the X-Z coordinate of a specific point p on the rotation axis L, and point a, b, and c separately forms a straight line with this specific point p which is on the rotation axis L. The angle of each straight line and the rotation axis L is 90 degree. The distance between two points of the X-Z plane can be found using the distance formula. The distance between point a, b, c and point p is represented as l_a, l_b, l_c, respectively. The distance from each point to the rotation axis L is the same in any frame so that $l_a = l_b = l_c$. Using $l_a = l_b$ and $l_b = l_c$, we can derive Equation 1,

$$\begin{cases}(X_a - X_r)^2 + (Z_a - Z_r)^2 = (X_b - X_r)^2 + (Z_b - Z_r)^2 \\ (X_b - X_r)^2 + (Z_b - Z_r)^2 = (X_c - X_r)^2 + (Z_c - Z_r)^2\end{cases}, \quad (1)$$

where X_r and Z_r are unknowns. According to Equation 1, a linear system is constituted as

$$\begin{bmatrix}-2X_a + 2X_b & -2Z_a + 2Z_b \\ -2X_b + 2X_c & -2Z_b + 2Z_c\end{bmatrix}\begin{bmatrix}X_r \\ Z_r\end{bmatrix} = \begin{bmatrix}-X_a^2 + X_b^2 - Z_a^2 + Z_b^2 \\ -X_b^2 + X_c^2 - Z_b^2 + Z_c^2\end{bmatrix} \quad (2)$$

The linear system in Euqation 2 is solved by linear algebra and thus the two unknowns, X_r and Z_r, are acquired, which is the X-Z coordinate of the specific point p on the rotation axis L. With the X-Z coordinate of point p and the characteristic of the rotation axis L which is perpendicular to X-Z plane, we can get the position of L in 3D space.

The second stage of the TOF depth maps alignment it to find the k corresponding depth values of the k corresponding points of each point in D_t with the specific rotation axis which is found from the first stage. Figure 4 shows the three steps of finding k corresponding depth values. To rotate adaptively, we transfer the rotation axis to the Y axis by translating the set of points of each depth map at first step. Second, as D_t is the middle depth map which does not need to rotate, the preceding maps of D_t turn around with the Y axis in clockwise direction and the succeeding maps of D_t turn around with the Y axis in counterclockwise direction. After rotation, we find the k corresponding depth values of k corresponding points in k calibrated TOF depth maps for each point in D_t.

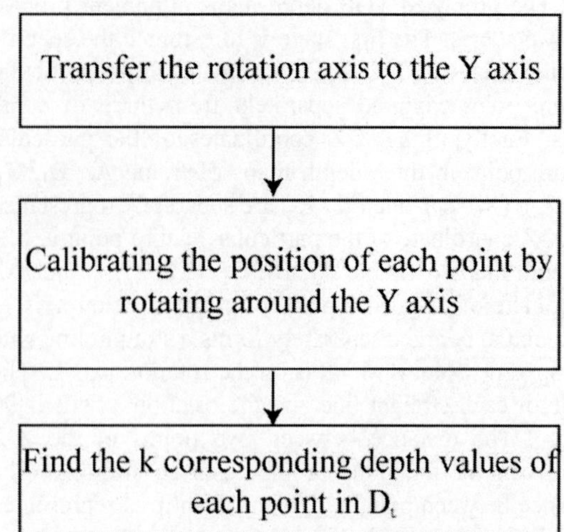

Figure 4: three steps in the second stage of the TOF depth maps alignment process

We then transfer the specific rotation axis L to the Y axis in each TOF depth maps, where p is a point on L and (X_p, Y_p, Z_p) is the coordinate of point p. For all points in k TOF depth maps, referring their 3D coordinates to a 1D matrix and adding the 1D matrix M = [$-X_p$, 0, $-Z_p$] to each 3D coordinate is to move the specific rotation axis to Y axis. If the original 3D coordinate of one point c is (X_c, Y_c, Z_c), after adding the matrix M, we have

$$[X_c', Y_c', Z_c'] = \lfloor X_c - X_p, Y_c, Z_c - Z_p \rfloor . \quad (3)$$

With all points in the k TOF depth maps adding matrix M, their rotation axis would be the Y axis.

Next, we calibrate the position of each point in the k TOF depth maps by rotation around the Y axis with its specific angle. The angle θ_i of TOF depth map D_i for rotation is determined by the difference between i and t, which is represented by Δ_i, where i is the frame number of map D_i and t is the frame number of the middle map D_t of k TOF depth maps. For all i which is included in window k, the angle θ_i is:

$$\theta_i = 0.2 \times \Delta_i . \quad (4)$$

If D_i is one of preceding maps of D_t, it turns around the Y axis in clockwise direction using rotation matrix. If D_i is one of the succeeding maps of D_t, it turns around the Y axis in counterclockwise direction. After the rotation process, we have k calibrated depth maps.

In the final step, we capture k corresponding depth values of each point in D_t with k calibrated depth maps. For each point t in D_t, we find the corresponding point p in each calibrated depth map D_i by measuring the minimum distance of each pair of points. In equation (5), cor(t, p), the corresponding point p in D_i of point t in D_t, is the point which has minimum distance between point t. Equation (6) measures dist(t, p) which is the distance between point p and point t, where X_t is the x-coordinate of point t, X_p is the x-coordinate of point p, Y_t is the y-coordinate of point t, and Y_p is the y-coordinate of point p. After this step, each point t in Dt has its k corresponding points. And the depth values of these k corresponding points is the k corresponding depth values of point t.

$$cor(t, p) = \min_{p \in D_i}(dist(t, p)) \quad (5)$$

$$dist(t, p) = \sqrt{(X_t - X_p)^2 + (Y_t - Y_p)^2} \quad (6)$$

2.4. Denoising Process

The last stage of the Temporal-Median method is the denoising process for D_t by modifying each point in D_t according to its k corresponding depth values. In this paper, we employ the median filter with k corresponding depth values from the last stage to substitute the depth values in D_t. For each point in D_t, we sort its k corresponding depth values numerically. And, we replace the value of each point in D_t by the median value of its k corresponding value which are sorted, so that we can have a denoised TOF depth map. We also substitute different number into k, which is the window size of median filter, to have good performance of denoising. The denoised depth maps produced by the proposed denoising process, with either window size nine or window size twenty five, have less noise and the outlines of the model are obviously clearer than the original frame.

In addition to median filter, we also experiment with other smoothing methods to replace the values of points in D_t. We refer to this method as the Temporal-Mean method. For each point in D_t, instead of the median number of its k corresponding depth values, we use the mean value of k corresponding depth values to replace the value of point in D_t.

3. EXPERIMENTS

We experiment with several TOF datasets [18] and compare the denoised results with ground truth models, which are provided from the opening online laser scanning models [18] captured by a Minolta Vivid 3D scanner. Some examples of the ground truth models are as shown in Figure 5.

Figure 5: Laser scanned data [18]

To evaluate the performance of the proposed Temporal-Media method and the Temporal-Mean method, the average difference of the depth values between the laser scanning data and noisy TOF depth map is employed. The original data captured by the TOF camera, compares with the average difference of depth values between the laser scanning data and denoised TOF depth maps produced by the proposed methods. In addition, we also try to deal with single TOF depth map by finding the respondent value of each point measured by Median filter or Smoothing method with an adjusted window size, which is the number of its nearest neighboring points in the same map. We also measure the average difference of depth values between the laser scanning data and the process data with the single TOF depth map.

The following results show the comparison of the average differences by different denoising procedures with the Head datasets. Figure 6 shows that denoising one example TOF depth map of Head dataset by Temporal-Median method with 9 window size and 25 window size. According to the figures of denoised results, the amount of points which are far from the model in Figure 6.(c) is less than in Figure 6.(b) and the outline of the models is clearer too.

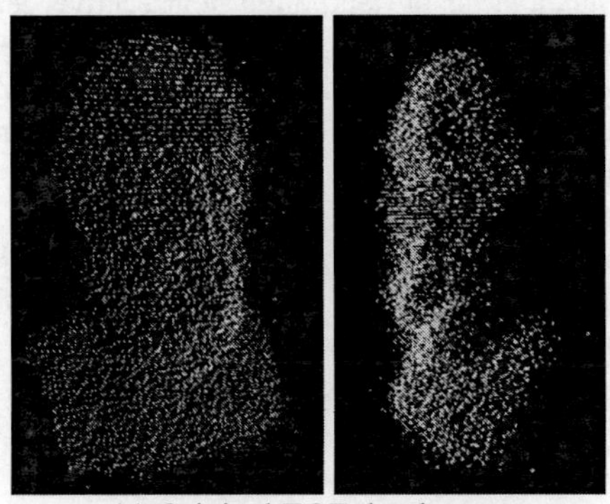

(a) Original TOF depth map

(b) Denoised result with 9 window size

(c) Denoised result with 25 window size

Figure 6: one example of Head dataset

We also try to denoise the original depth maps in Head datasets with single TOF depth map by computing the median value with 9 values and 25 values of nearest neighboring pixels. Figure 7.(a) is the denoised result, with window size 9, and Figure 7.(b) is denoised with window size 25. Comparing the denoised results of the Temporal-Median and the denoised results here, instead of clearer outline, with the bigger window size, the detail parts of the model in denoised results disappear and the outline of the model become blurred.

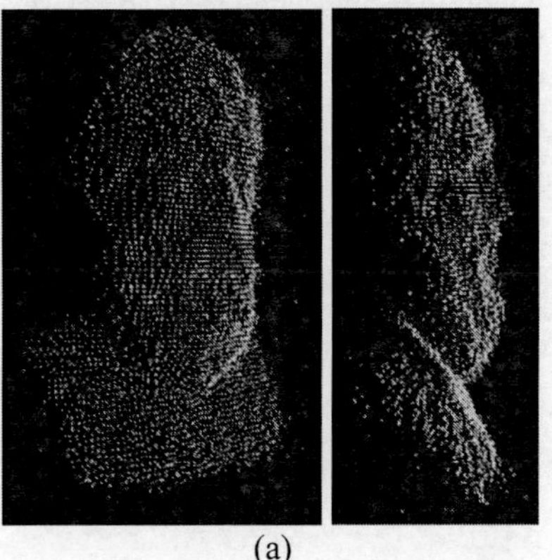

(a)

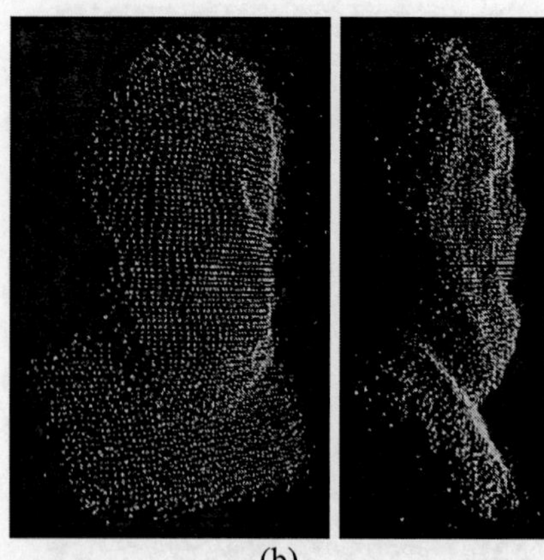

(b)

Figure 7: one denoised TOF depth map of Head dataset by single TOF depth map denoising method with different window sizes

Table 1 summarizes the denoised results with the Head dataset by different denoising methods and with two different window sizes. The average difference means that the average of depth value differences between the denoised depth map and the ground truth. And the improvement, which is compared with the original noisy TOF depth map and the denoised TOF depth map, indicate the deduction of the average differences in percentile. Table 1 show that denoising TOF depth maps with temporal consecutive depth maps result over 40% improvement. Denoising TOF depth map with spatially nearest neighboring points in one single depth map has only about 20% improvement. Table 1 also shows that when increasing the window size from 9 to 25, the Temporal-Median method produces additional 5% improvement. But with the spatial denoising methods, increasing the window size produces less than 1% improvement or even worse than with smaller window size.

Table 1: the average differences and the improvements of the denoised results with the Head dataset

Dataset / Window size / Denoising Method	Head Dataset			
	9 window size		25 window size	
	Average difference (cm)	Improvement	Average difference (cm)	Improvement
The original TOF Depth Map	0.83939	-	0.83939	-
Temporal-Median	0.51301	38.883%	0.46754	44.300%
Temporal-Mean	0.49234	41.345%	0.46648	44.426%
Spatial-Median	0.66829	20.384%	0.66477	20.803%
Spatial-Mean	0.65556	21.899%	0.66775	20.448%

4. CONCLUSION

3D information has widespread usages in common applications, not only for distance detection, but also for 3D model reconstruction. 3D models are often used in many kinds of domains, such as industrial design or game industry. TOF camera is one kind of ideal 3D scanners which are user-friendly and not so expensive gradually. Besides, TOF camera can obtain the 3D depth map of a scene at video rate. However, there are still some drawbacks of TOF camera. One of them that we are concerned about is the high random noise depth maps produced by the TOF cameras.

In this paper, we propose TOF depth maps denoising methods using temporally consecutive depth maps captured by the TOF camera. Experiments demonstrate that the proposed temporal denoising methods not only produce more accurate depth maps, but also have the advantage in speed.

In future work, the boundaries of the models in TOF depth maps have some space for improvement. We will also try to incorporate the proposed denoising process into the 3D reconstruction framework to enhance the accuracy of 3D model reconstruction,

Acknowledgments

This work was partially supported by the National Science Council, Taiwan, under the Grants No. NSC101-2221-E-011-141, NSC100-2221-E-011-121, and NSC101-2221-E-211-011.

REFERENCES

[1] A. K. Jain. "Fundamentals of Digital Image Processing". Prentice-Hall, New York, 1989.

[2] A. Kolb, E. Barth, R. Koch, and R. Larsen. "Time-of-Flight Sensors in Computer Graphics". Eurographics 2009.

[3] A. Rajagopalan, A. Bhavsar, F. Wallhoff, and G. Rigoll. "Resolution Enhancement of PMD Range Maps". Lecture Notes in Computer Science, 5096:304-313, 2008.

[4] C. Schaller. "Time-of-Flight – A New Modality for Radiotherapy". PhD Thesis , 2011.

[5] G. R. Arce. "Nonlinear Signal Processing: A Statistical Approach", Wiley:New Jersey, USA, 2005.

[6] J. Diebel and S. Thrun. "An application of markov random fields to range sensing". In Advances in Neural Information Processing Systems 18. Pages 291-298. 2006.

[7] J. Kopf, M. Cohen, D. Lischinski, and M. Uyttendaele. Joint bilateral upsampling. ACM TOG, 26(3), 2007.

[8] MESA Swissranger SR4000 TOF camera, http://www.mesa-imaging.ch/index.php.

[9] P. Henry, M. Krainin, E. Herbst, X. Ren, and D. Fox. RGB-D Mapping: Using Depth Cameras for Dense 3D Modeling of Indoor Environments. In Proc. of International Symposium on Experimental Robotics (ISER), 2010.

[10] P. S. Windyga. "Fast impulsive noise removal". IEEE Trans. On Image Processing, 10(1), 2001, pp. 173-179.

[11] Q. Yang, R. Yang, J. Davis, and D. Nister. Spatial-dapth super resolution for range images. In IEEE CVPR, 2007.

[12] R. C. Gonzalez and R. E. Woods. "Digital Image Processing". Addison-Wesley, New York, 1992.

[13] R. Lange. "3D time-of-flight distance measurement with custom solid-state image sensors in CMOS/CCD-technology", Dissertation, University of Siegen, 2000.

[14] S. Fuchs and S. May. "Calibration and registration for precise surface reconstruction with ToF cameras". Proceedings of the Dynamic 3D Imaging Workshop in Conjunction with DAGM (Dyn3D), VOL. I, 2007.

[15] S. Fuchs and G. Hizinger. "Extrinsic and Depth Calibration of TOF cameras". Proceedings of the IEEE Conference on Computer Vision and Pattern Recognition (CVPR), 2008.

[16] S. Schuon, C. Theobalt, J. Davis, and S. Thrun. "LidarBoost Depth Superresolution for ToF 3D Shape Scanning". Proceedings of the IEEE Conference on Computer Vision and Pattern Recognition (CVPR), 2009.

[17] S. Vaddadi, L. Zhang, H. Jin, and S. K. Nayar. "Multiple View Image Denoising". Proceedings of the IEEE Conference on Computer Vision and Pattern Recognition (CVPR), 2009.

[18] Y. Cui, S. Schuon, D. Chan, S. Thrun and C. Theobalt. TOF Datasets and Laser Scanning Datasets [Online], http://www.mpi-inf.mpg.de/~theobalt/tof/.

[19] Y. Cui, S. Schuon, D. Chan, S. Thrun and C. Theobalt. "3D Shape Scanning with a Time-of-Flight Camera". Proceedings of the IEEE Conference on Computer Vision and Pattern Recognition (CVPR), 2010.

View Synthesis Based on Depth Information and Graph Cuts for 3DTV

Anh Tu Tran, Koichi Harada
Graduate School of Engineering, Hiroshima University, Hiroshima, Japan

Abstract - *This paper presents a novel method that synthesizes a free-viewpoint based on multiple textures and depth maps in multi-view camera configuration. This method solves the cracks and holes problem due to sampling rate by performing an inverse warping to retrieve texture images. This step allows a simple and accurate re-sampling of synthetic pixel. To enforce the spatial consistency of color and remove the pixels wrapped incorrectly because of inaccuracy depth maps, we propose some processing steps. The warped depth and warped texture images are used to classify pixels as stable, unstable and disoccluded pixels. The stable pixels are used to create an initial new view by weighted interpolation. To refine the new view, Graph cuts is used to select the best candidates for each unstable pixel. Finally, the remaining disoccluded regions are filled by our inpainting method based on depth information and texture neighboring pixel value. Our experiment on several multi-view data sets is encouraging in both subjective and objective results.*

Keywords: View Synthesis; Depth Image Based Rendering (DIBR); Free-viewpoint TV; Graph Cuts

1. Introduction

Recently, 3D-TV application and system are rapidly growing. With the growing capability of capturing devices, multi-view capture system with dense or sparse camera array can be built with ease, Free-viewpoint television (FTV)[1] system has attracted increasing attentions. In FTV system, user can freely select the viewpoint of any dynamic real world seen. The chosen free-viewpoint can not only be selected from available multi-view camera views, but also any viewpoint between these cameras. This system requires a smart synthetic algorithm that allows free-viewpoint view rendering. To render a high quality image at arbitrary view point, one has to manage three main challenges as pointed out in [2]. First, empty pixels and holes due to sampling of the reference image have to be closed. Secondly, pixels at borders of high discontinuities cause contour artifacts. The third challenge involves inpainting disocclusions that remain after blending the projected images (these are invisible from any of the surrounding cameras). In [3] it is shown that one can obtain an improved rendering quality by using the geometry of the scene. When using depth information, a well-known technique for rendering is called Depth Image Based Rendering (DIBR), which involves the 3D-projection or 2D-warping from a viewpoint into another view.

In this paragraph, we describe briefly some recent research on free-viewpoint DIBR algorithm. In [2], author has developed a free-viewpoint rendering algorithm which is based on layered representation. For texture mapping, 3D meshes are created and the rendering is implemented on a Graphics Processing Unit (GPU). Although the results look good, the method is complex and requires a considerable amount of pre- and post-processing operations. This work is extended in [4] where the depth map is decomposed into three layers and these layers are warped separately. The warp results are obtained for each layer and merged. To deal with artifacts, they have introduced three post processing algorithms. In [5], a new viewpoint is rendered by some steps. First, the depth maps of the reference cameras are warped to the new viewpoint. Then the empty pixels are filled with a median filter. Afterwards, the depth maps are processed with a bilateral filter. Then, the textures are retrieved by performing an inverse warping from the projected depth maps back to the reference cameras. Ghost contours are removed by dilating the disocclusions. Finally, the texture images are blended and the remaining disocclusions are inpainted using the method proposed by Telea [6]. Although, the results look good, this method is remaining some issues such as not removing all holes by median filter, assigning a none-zero value for some pixels in disocclusion regions. This work is improving in [7] by introducing three enhancing techniques. First, re-sampling artifacts are filled in by a combination of median filtering and inverse warping. Second, contour artifacts are processed while omitting warping of edges at high discontinuities. Third, disocclusion regions are inpainted with depth information. The quality of this method is higher than the work in [5], but still having disadvantages. For example, they have to define the label of pixel at high discontinuities. The color consistency during blending is not verified to avoid jagged edges at straight line after blending. The work in [8] combines depth based hole filling and inpainting to restore the disoccluded pixels more accurately compared to inpainting method without using depth information. This method produces a notable blur and can be computationally inefficient when disoccluded region is larger in new view.

In this paper, we introduce a new free-viewpoint rendering algorithm from multiple color and depth images. First, the depth maps for the virtual views are created by warping the depth maps of reference cameras. We process the wrapped depth maps with median filter. Depth maps consist of smooth regions with sharp edges, so filtering with a median will not degrade the quality. Then, the textures are retrieved by performing an inverse warping from the warped depth maps to the reference cameras. This allows a simple and accurate re-sampling of synthetic pixel. After that, all warped depth and warped texture images are used to classify pixel as stable, unstable and disoccluded regions. An initial virtual view is created based on weighted interpolation of stable pixels. To refine the synthesis view, best candidates for unstable pixels are optimally selected by Graph cuts. By defining the types of pixels and using Graph cuts, the color is consistent and the incorrectly wrapped pixels because of inaccuracy depth maps are removed in the refined view. The remaining disoccluded pixels are inpainted by using depth and texture neighboring pixel values. Considering depth information for inpainting, blurring between foreground and background textures is reduced.

The rest of this paper is organized as follows: section 2 presents the proposed view synthesis algorithm; section 3 shows experimental results; and, finally, section 4 concludes this paper.

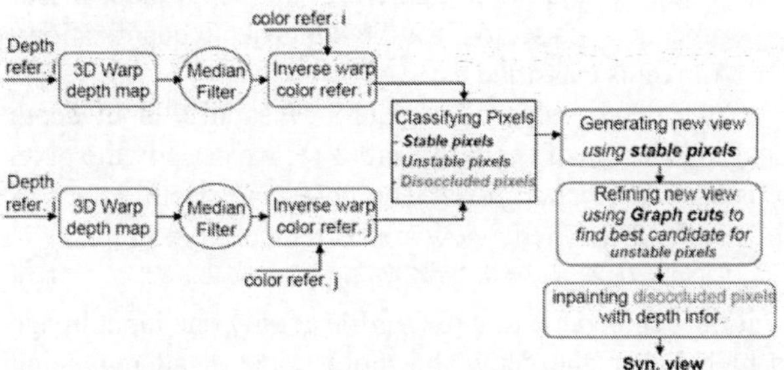

Fig. 1. Proposed view synthesis algorithm.

2. Proposed synthesis method

Our proposed method is shown in Fig. 1 and it consists of six steps. These steps are explained below.

2.1. 3D warping the depth maps

3D warping enables to synthesize a new view from the reference view as following.

Let $P_w = [X_w, Y_w, Z_w, 1]^T$ be the world point; $p_1 = [u_1, v_1, 1]^T$ and $p_2 = [u_2, v_2, 1]^T$ be its projection onto reference and synthetic image planes, respectively. P_w and p_1 , p_2 are related by the camera perspective projection (1) and (2).

$$\lambda_1 p_1 = K_1[R_1; -R_1T_1]P_w, \quad (1)$$

$$\lambda_2 p_2 = K_2[R_2; -R_2T_2]P_w, \quad (2)$$

where, K_i is an 3×3 upper triangular matrix representing the inner structure of the camera i and is called the intrinsic matrix. The 3×3 orthogonal matrix R_i represents the orientation and $3-vector$ T_i represents the position. The matrix $[R_i; -R_iT_i]$ is called the extrinsic matrix and it indicates the relationship between world coordinates and the camera coordinates.

Rearranging (1) we can derive 3D coordinate of the scene point P_w :

$$(X_w, Y_w, Z_w)^T = (K_1R_1)^{-1} \cdot (\lambda_1 p_1 + K_1R_1T_1). \quad (3)$$

Substituting (3) into (2) we obtain the synthetic pixel position p_2 :

$$\lambda_2 p_2 = K_2R_2(K_1R_1)^{-1} \cdot (\lambda_1 p_1 + K_1R_1T_1) - K_2R_2T_2. \quad (4)$$

Assuming that the world coordinate system is the same as the reference camera coordinate system and looks at along $Z-direction$, i.e., $T_1 = (0,0,0)$, $R_1 = I_{3x3}$ and $\lambda_1 = Z_w$, equation (4) can rewrite as following:

$$\lambda_2 p_2 = K_2R_2K_1^{-1} \cdot Z_w p_1 - K_2R_2T_2, \quad (5)$$

where Z_w is defined by the pixel value at coordinate point p_1 in the reference depth image.

Applying (5) for a point $p_1 = [u_1, v_1, 1]^T$ from the reference image we can calculate a point p_2 on the synthesis image. The problem that several points can be projected to the same point in virtual image is solved by using simple $z-buffering$ technique. Another issue of this process is that a pixel p_1 of reference view is not usually projected on to a point p_2 at integer pixel position. To obtain an integer pixel position, we map the sub-pixel p_2 to the nearest integer pixel $\hat{p}_2$ as follows equation:

$$\hat{p}_2 = (\hat{x}_2, \hat{x}_2, 1) = (\lfloor x_2 + 0.5 \rfloor, \lfloor y_2 + 0.5 \rfloor, 1). \quad (6)$$

In our method, only depth maps of reference cameras are projected to virtual image plane. The warping is specified by:

$$[Z_{syn}, \hat{p}_2] = 3D\_Warp(Z_{ref}, p_1), \quad (7)$$

where, Z_{ref} is depth map of a reference camera, $3D\_Warp$ is warping operation as above describing. The projected depth maps from two reference cameras for an arbitrary scene are shown in Fig. 2.

Fig. 2. The projected depth maps from two reference cameras (from the left side and from the right side)

2.2. Median filter the warped depth map

In this step, we consider the blank points that appeared

in projected depth map. The reasons for the appearance of these blank points are round off errors of the image coordinate by (6) and depth discontinuities. It can cause one pixel wide blank region to appear. This blank region can be filled by median filter with a window of 3×3 pixels. Depth maps consist of smooth regions with sharp edges, so filtering with a median will not degrade the quality.

This step can describe as:

$$Z_{syn\_filtered} = Median(Z_{syn}), \quad (8)$$

where, *Median* is a median filter with a window 3×3 pixels, $Z_{syn\_filtered}$ is output of median filter. The image in Fig. 2 can be processed by using median filter to obtained images in Fig. 3.

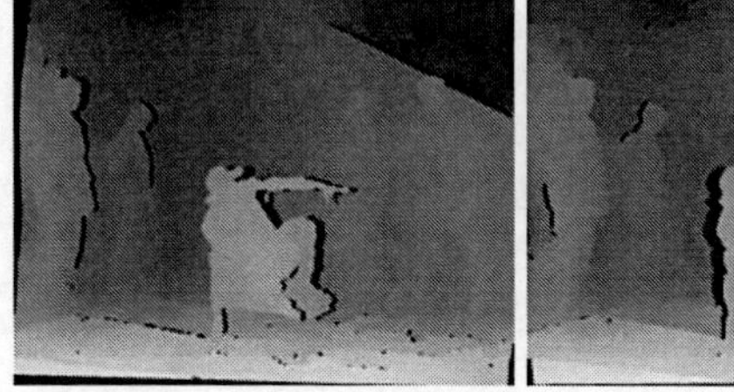
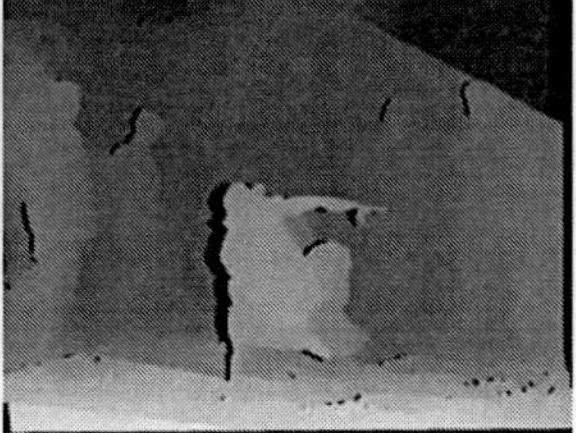

Fig. 3. Median filter depth maps

2.3. Retrieve texture image by inverse warping

In this step, the textures are retrieved by performing inverse warping from filtered projected depth maps back to the reference cameras.

For each pixel p_2 of the filtered projected depth image, a $3D$ world point $P_{2w} = (X_{2w}, Y_{2w}, Z_{2w})$ is calculated based on (3). Z_{2w} is defined by the depth value at coordinate p_2 in the filtered projected depth image. And then, the calculated $3D$ point P_{2w} is projected onto respective reference textures image by employing (5), such that color of the synthetic destination pixel p_2 is interpolated from the surrounding pixel p_1 in the reference color image. Fig. 4 illustrates the image rendering process using inverse warping.

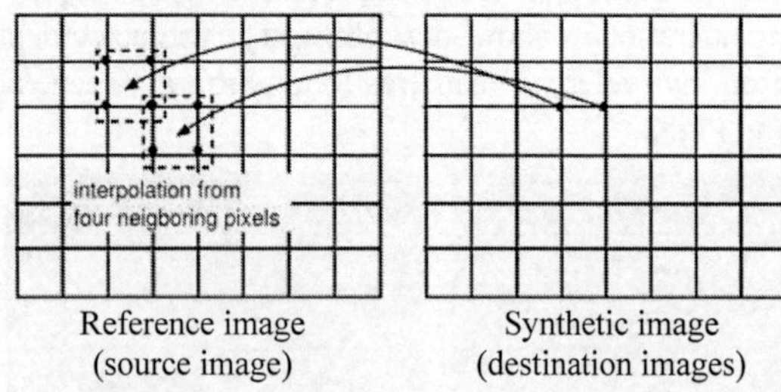

Fig. 4. Image synthesis process using inverse warping

This step can be specified by:

$$[I_{syn}, p_2] = 3D\_Warp^{-1}(Z_{syn\_filtered}, p_2). \quad (9)$$

The advantage of an inverse warping operation is that all pixels of the destination image are correctly defined and the color disoccluded pixels can be inferred by back projected $3D$ point P_{2w} onto multiple source image planes, covering all regions of video scene.

Fig. 5 shows the retrieved color images by inverse warping using depth maps in Fig. 3.

Fig. 5. Obtained color images by inverse warping

2.4. Pixel classification and initial new view creation

Formally, suppose that we have a set of N texture images $I = \{I_1, I_2, ..., I_N\}$ and N depth images $Z = \{Z_1, Z_2, ..., Z_N\}$. Let $I_m(p)$ and $Z_m(p)$ be the color and depth value at pixel p of $m-th$ image.

In this step, we describe the type of pixels in the synthetic view. We go through each pixel $p \in P$ of all N input images and classify as stable, unstable and disoccluded pixels. To detect the types of pixel, we set thresholds (depth threshold t_Z and color threshold t_C) and examine the color and depth values for pixel $p \in P$. For each color channel, the color threshold t_C is set to be 15. Depth threshold is the brightness in the depth map. In our experiments, t_Z is set to 5 for the 8 bits depth quantization.

A pixel is classified as:

+ if the depth value of a pixel $p \in P$ at all N input depth images is less than depth threshold t_Z, we classify the pixel p as the *disoccluded pixel.* The color and depth values of the pixel p at synthetic view are set temporally to zero.

$$I_{new}(p) = 0,\ Z_{new}(p) = 0,\quad if\ Z_k(p) \le t_Z,\ \forall k = 1,2,..,N. \quad (10)$$

+ if the depth value of a pixel $p \in P$ at only one input image is higher than the depth threshold t_Z and at all remaining $(N-1)$ images is less than t_Z, we classify the pixel p as the *stable pixel.* This is case the pixel p is visible in only one view. The values of the pixel p at synthetic view are just copied from the values of the pixel p in the visible view.

$$I_{new}(p) = I_k(p),\ Z_{new}(p) = Z_k(p),\\ if\ Z_k(p) > t_Z,\ Z_m(p) \le t_Z, \forall m = 1,2,..,N, m \ne k. \quad (11)$$

+ if the depth value of a pixel $p \in P$ is higher than the depth threshold t_Z in more than one view, we examine both the color and depth values of the pixel p to detect the types of pixel.

First step, for each view k, $k = 1,2,..,N$, we examine every pixel p. If the depth value of the pixel p is higher than the depth threshold t_Z, then we check other views j, $j = 1,2,..,N$, $j \ne k$. If the view j has both a depth value of the pixel p higher than the depth threshold t_Z and has color similarity at p of view j and k, $I_j(p)$ and $I_k(p)$ are called consistent color (the color similarity at pixel p of two input images j and k is defined based on the absolute color differences between $I_j(p)$ and $I_k(p)$ of R, G and B channels, $|I_j(p) - I_k(p)| < t_C$). We count the total number of view j, $j = 1,2,..,N$ having the consistent color with view k ($k = 1,2,..,N$, $j \neq k$) at pixel p. Assuming that for each view k, this total number is S_k, for $k = 1,2,..,N$ we have $S = \{S_1, S_2,..., S_N\}$.

Second step, we find the biggest number in $S = \{S_1, S_2,..., S_N\}$, assuming that the biggest number is M.

If $M \geq \lfloor N/2 + 0.5 \rfloor$, we classify the pixel p as the stable pixel. Otherwise, the pixel p is classified as the unstable pixel. The value of unstable pixel can set to be -1 so that they can be easily identified.

The color and depth values of stable pixel p at synthetic view are rendered by blending M pixels as following weighted interpolation:

$$I_{new}(p) = \left(\sum_{i=1}^{M} w_i * I_i(p)\right) \Big/ \sum_{i=1}^{M} w_i,\ Z_{new}(p) = \left(\sum_{i=1}^{M} w_i * Z_i(p)\right) \Big/ \sum_{i=1}^{M} w_i, \quad (12)$$

where, w_i is the weight factor assigned to view i, $I_i(p)$ and $Z_i(p)$ are color value and depth value of pixel p at view i. The weight assigned to each view should reflect its proximity with the view being synthesized. The views that are closer to the synthetic view should have a bigger weight. In general case, the weight w_i can be set based on baseline spacing. However, for more precise weighting, we use the angle distance determined by the point in $3D$ and camera positions as shown in Fig. 6. The weight factor w_i is calculated by

$$w_i = \begin{cases} e^{-c\alpha_i} & if\ \alpha_i < \pi/2 \\ 0 & otherwise, \end{cases} \quad (13)$$

where, i is view index, α_i is the angular distance of view I and w_i is weight for the view at that pixel. The constant c controls the fall off as the angular distance increases. Input views for which $\alpha_i \geq \pi/2$ are eliminated as they view the scene the other side. In practice, $c = 1$ or 2 has been found to work well.

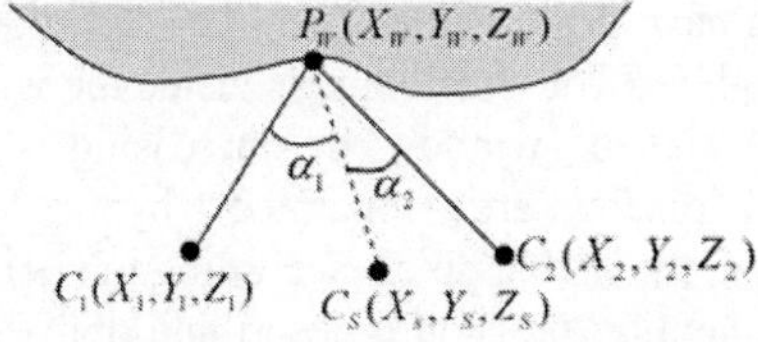

Fig. 6. Weighted interpolation based on angular distances

The new view is specified by

$$[I_{new}, Z_{new}] = InitialView(\{I_1, I_2,..., I_N\}, \{Z_1, Z_2,..., Z_N\}), \quad (14)$$

where, *InitialView* is the procedure of pixel classification and initial new view creation as above described.

Fig. 7 shows an example of a initial synthesized image with three types of pixels: stable, unstable and disoccluded pixels.

Fig. 7. An initial synthesized image with three types of pixels. (The white color pixels are unstable pixels, the red color pixels are disoccluded pixels and the remaining pixels are stable pixels).

2.5. Find the best candidate for unstable pixel by Graph Cuts

In this step, we focus on refining initial synthetic view with unstable pixels. Unstable pixels have multiple pixel candidates and we want to predict the best candidate that minimizes the energy function described in following part. We denote L as labeling space with $L = \{1,2,..,N\}$, representing the image index and let U be the set of unstable pixels. Let f_p be the label of unstable pixel p and $f_p \in L$. A labeling f is to assign a particular label f_p to a pixel $p \in U$. With this definition, our problem is to find the labeling f^* to fill the unstable region, such that the labeling f^* has minimum cost.

We define our energy function based on the Markov Random Fields (MRF) formulation:

$$E(f) = \sum_{p \in U} D_p(f_p) + \lambda \sum_{(p,q) \in N} V_{p,q}(f_p, f_q), \quad (15)$$

where, f is the labeling field; U is the set of unstable pixels, and N is the pixel's neighborhood system. $D_p(f_p)$ is called the data term, which defines the cost of assigning label f_p to pixel p. $V_{p,q}(f_p, f_q)$ denotes the smoothness term that evaluates the cost of disagreement between p and q which is assigned with f_p and f_q respectively. λ is a parameter to weigh the importance of these two terms.

Data term $D_p(f_p)$ is defined by

$$D_p(f_p) = \alpha Z_{f_p}(p) \sum_{q \in N_p} (1 - O_q) |I_{f_p}(p) - I_{new}(q)| + \beta \sum_{i=1}^{N} |I_{f_p}(p) - I_i(p)|, \quad (16)$$

where N_p is neighboring pixels of p. $Z_{f_p}(p)$ is the depth value of pixel p at candidate f_p. $I_{new}(q)$ and O_q (0 or 1) are the color value and disoccluded indicator of pixel q, respectively. α and β are weight factor. $I_i(p)$ is color value of pixel p at input image i. $|I_i(p)-I_j(q)|$ represents the sum of absolute color differences between $I_i(p)$ and $I_j(q)$ of R, G and B channels.

The first part of data term enforces the candidate pixel selected to agree with its neighbor pixels. And the neighboring pixel that is disocclusion does not influence the candidate selection process. It is also penalized less cost for the selecting a candidate pixel which has smaller depth value Z since the pixel with smallest depth value is closer to the camera and more likely defined the color of synthetic pixel p_2.

The second part of (16) is stationary cost, which is defined based on color similarity at pixel p of all the input images. If the pixel p has similar color at more input images, the stationary cost is smaller.

Smoothness term $V_{p,q}(f_p, f_q)$: measures the penalty of two neighboring pixel p and q with different labels and is defined as follow:

$$V_{p,q}(f_p, f_q) = \frac{\left\| I_{f_p}(p) - I_{f_q}(p) \right\| + \left\| I_{f_p}(q) - I_{f_q}(q) \right\|}{2}, \quad (17)$$

where, $\|*\|$ denotes the Euclidean distance in RGB color spaces. The smoothness term gives a higher cost if f_p and f_q do not match well. By incorporating such the smoothness term, we can achieve visually smooth in the synthetic image.

We apply graph cuts optimization that is public available in [9] to minimize our energy function $E(f)$. More detail about energy minimization with graph cuts can be found in [10, 11].

This step is specified by

$$I_{new}(U) = I_{f^*}, Z_{new}(U) = Z_{f^*}, \quad with\, f^* = \arg\min_f (E(f)), \quad (18)$$

The refinement of image in Fig. 7 by using graph cut to select the best candidate for unstable pixel is shown in Fig. 8.

Fig. 8. Refinement of initial synthesized image (image in Fig. 7) by using graph cut (the red color pixels are disoccluded pixels).

2.6. Inpainting disocclusion pixels based on the depth and color values of neighboring pixels

Until this step, only the disocclusion regions are remaining. To deal with these disoccluded pixels, many papers such as [5, 8] have developed algorithms based on the inpainting method proposed by Tela [6]. Inpainting is a process of reconstructing lost or corrupted parts of images using the values of neighborhood pixels. Although, these algorithms work sufficiently well, the resulting inpainted regions contain a notable blur because of the mixture background and foreground colors at the edge of disoccluded regions. In this paper, we develop a technique based on inpainting method with depth information. We assume that the disoccluded pixels belong only to background, and we employ depth information to select accurately background pixels at the edges of disoccluded regions so that the blur can be avoided. Our method consists of several steps as follow.

First, for reducing processing time we find the small disoccluded regions by defining a window with the size of 3×3 centered at p and counting the unstable pixel inside this window. If the number of visible pixels M inside this window is higher than 50%, then the disoccluded pixels is inpainted by a weighted interpolation from visible pixels, which is specified by

$$\begin{aligned} I_{new}(p_{occ}) &= \left(\sum_{i=1}^{M} d_i^{-1} * I_{new}(p_i) \right) \Big/ \sum_{i=1}^{M} d_i^{-1}, \\ Z_{new}(p_{occ}) &= \left(\sum_{i=1}^{M} d_i^{-1} * Z_{new}(p_i) \right) \Big/ \sum_{i=1}^{M} d_i^{-1}, \; \forall p_{occ} \in O, \end{aligned} \quad (19)$$

where, M is number of visible pixels inside the window. O is disoccluded region, and d_i is distance from disoccluded pixel p_{occ} to visible pixel p_i. $I_{new}(p_i)$ and $Z_{new}(p_i)$ are color and depth values of the visible pixel p_i.

Second, for each pixel p_o in remaining disoccluded regions we search in eight directions to find the pixel p_u which has the smallest depth value Z_{min} at the edge of disoccluded region and the distance d_u from this point to p_o. We define a window with the size of $(d_u+\Delta)\times(d_u+\Delta)$ centered at p_o (at first, $\Delta=0$), and we count the visible pixels which have depth value Z with $|Z-Z_{min}|\le 5$. If there are not enough 50% of visible pixels inside the window, we increase the size of window by increasing Δ. Finally, disoccluded pixels are inpainted by a weighted interpolation from visible pixels according to (19).

With inpainting procedure describing above, this step can summarized by

$$[I_{final}, Z_{final}] = \text{Inpaint}(I_{new}, Z_{new}). \quad (20)$$

3. Experimental results

We quantify the proposal method performance based on Peak Signal Noise Ratio (*PSNR*) and the structural similarity (SSIM) index between a reference image I_r and a synthetic image I_s. SSIM index is a method for measuring the similarity between two images [12]. The SSIM index value 1 is only reachable when two images are identical and the higher PSNR normally indicates that it is higher quality synthetic image. Before computing *PSNR* , the images are converted from RGB color space to YUV color space, and Y channel is used for calculation. Y channel is defined by

$$Y(i,j) = 0.299R(i,j) + 0.587G(i,j) + 0.114B(i,j). \quad (21)$$

The *PSNR* can be calculated by

$$PSNR = 10\log_{10}\left(\frac{255^2}{\frac{1}{w \cdot h}\sum_{i=0,j=0}^{w-1,h-1}\left\|Y_r(i,j) - Y_s(i,j)\right\|^2}\right), \quad (22)$$

where, w and h are the image width and height. Y_r and Y_s are the channels of reference image and synthetic image, respectively.

The proposed new view synthesis has tested on "Breakdancer" and "Ballet" sequence which are generated and distribution by Interactive Visual Group at Microsoft Research [13]. These datasets include a sequence of 100 images of 1024×768 pixels captured from 8 cameras with the calibration parameters. Fig. 9 shows the camera arrangement of these two sequences. Depth maps for each view are also provided. For more detail about these depth maps generation, please refer to [2].

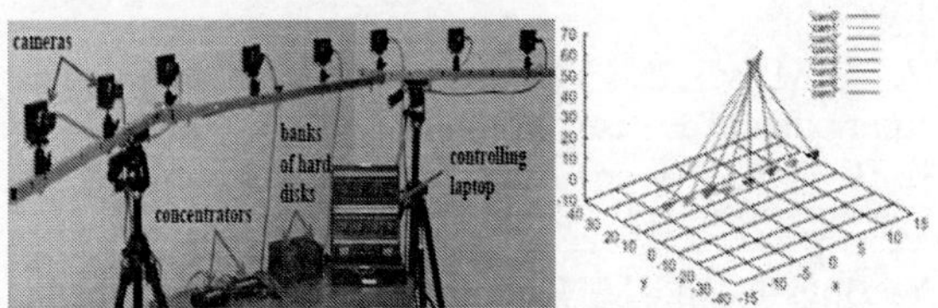

Fig. 9. A configuration of "Breakdancer" and "Ballet" sequences with 8 cameras [2].

In our paper, the synthetic view is set to be the same as the actual camera. View 3 and 5 are used with depth maps to synthesize view 4. Fig. 10 shows the example of view synthesis results. The experimental results show that the proposed method achieved on average over 33.7dB in PSNR and 0.92 index value in SSIM on the two sequence "Breakdancer "and "Ballet".

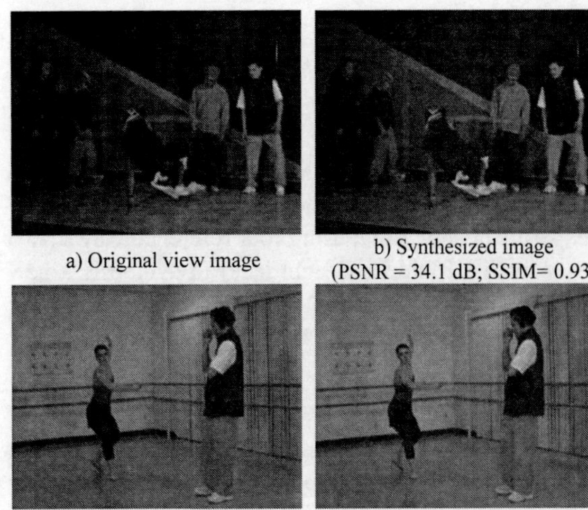

a) Original view image   b) Synthesized image (PSNR = 34.1 dB; SSIM= 0.93)

a) Original view image   b) Synthesized image (PSNR = 34.21dB; SSIM= 0.95)

Fig. 10. An example of the synthetic view.

Fig. 11 shows our PSNR and SSIM comparison with those of Sohl et al. [14] over 100 Frames for the "Breakdancer" and "Ballet" sequences.

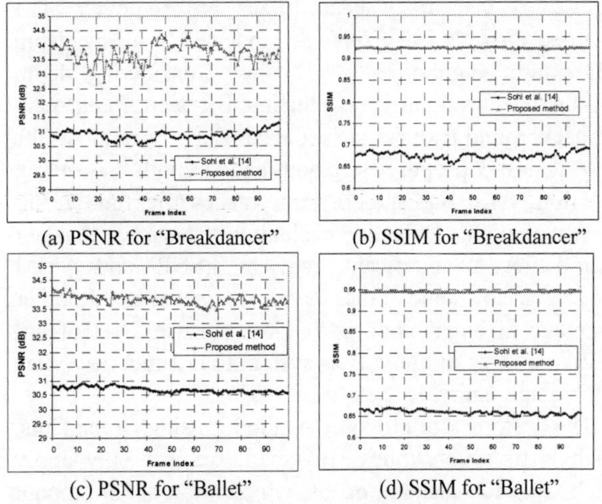

(a) PSNR for "Breakdancer" (b) SSIM for "Breakdancer"

(c) PSNR for "Ballet" (d) SSIM for "Ballet"

Fig. 11. PSNR and SSIM comparison for "Breakdancer" and "Ballet" sequences: (a) PSNR for "Breakdancer" (b) SSIM for "Breakdancer" (c) PSNR for "Ballet" (d) SSIM for "Ballet".

The measured synthetic qualities are compared with other methods and summarized in Table 1. From the results, the average PSNR of proposal is superior to that of other methods such as Mori et al [5], Sohl et al. [14] with a gain of 3.0dB. The structure similarity (SSIM) of our method is higher than that of Sohl et al. method.

Table 1. Exerimental results comparision.

Method	"Breakdancer"		"Ballet"	
	PSNR(dB)	*SSIM*	*PSNR(dB)*	*SSIM*
Sohl et al. [14]	30.8	0.68	30.7	0.66
Mori et al. [5]	30.0	Not Reported	31.5	Not Reported
Proposed method	**33.7**	**0.92**	**33.9**	**0.94**

Moreover, in multi-view configuration, we have N cameras which capture the scene at difference positions. For our experimental case, there are 8 cameras. Thus, instead of using only two neighbor views as above conventional methods, we can use more than two images to synthesize a new view. Our proposal can do this idea easily. Our experiment shows that using four reference views (two views on both left side and right side) to synthesis a new view, a higher PSNR (about $0.5 \div 1dB$) and SSIM are obtained than the case of using two reference views.

4. Conclusions

In this paper, we propose a novel synthesis method that enables to render a free-viewpoint from multiple existing cameras. The proposed method solves the main problems of depth based synthesis by performing pixel classification to generate an initial new view from stable pixels and using Graph cut to select the best candidate for unstable pixels. By defining the types of pixels and using Graph cuts, the color is consistent and the pixels wrapped incorrectly because of inaccuracy depth maps are removed. The remained disoccluded pixels are inpainted by using depth and texture neighboring pixel value. Considering depth information for inpainting, blurring between foreground and background textures are reduced. Experimental results show that the proposed method has strength in artifact reduction. Also our smooth term makes the final result visually smooth. Objective evaluation has shown that our method get a significant gain in PSNR and SSIM comparing to some other existing methods. Another advantage of our method is that we can use a set of un-rectified images in multi-view system to create a new view with higher quality.

The drawback of proposed method is using Graph Cuts, which is time consuming. However, we just only apply Graph Cuts for unstable pixels, which are a small amount of pixels comparing to whole image, so the time for Graph Cuts can be reduced.

The future work will focus on more improving synthesis quality with utilizing temporal information in successive video frames.

5. References

[1] M. Tanimoto, "Overview of FTV (free-viewpoint television)," presented at the Proceedings of the 2009 IEEE international conference on Multimedia and Expo, New York, NY, USA, 2009.

[2] C. L. Zitnick, S. B. Kang, M. Uyttendaele, S. Winder, and R. Szeliski, "High-quality video view interpolation using a layered representation," Acm Transactions on Graphics, vol. 23, pp. 600-608, Aug 2004.

[3] K. Pulli, M. Cohen, T. Duchamp, H. Hoppe, L. G. Shapiro, and W. Stuetzle, "View-base Rendering: Visualizing Real Objects from Scanned Range and Color Data," presented at the Proceedings of the Eurographics Workshop on Rendering Techniques '97, 1997.

[4] K. Muller, K. Dix, P. Merkle, P. Kauff, and T. Wiegand, "Intermediate view interpolation based on multiview video plus depth for advanced 3D video systems " in 15th IEEE International Conference on Image Processing (ICIP), 2008, pp. 2448 - 2451

[5] Y. Mori, N. Fukushima, T. Yendo, T. Fujii, and M. Tanimoto, "View generation with 3D warping using depth information for FTV," Signal Processing-Image Communication, vol. 24, pp. 65-72, Jan 2009.

[6] A. C. Telea, "An image inpainting technique based on the Fast Marching Method," Journal of Graphics Tools, vol. 9, pp. 25-36, 2004.

[7] S. Zinger, L. Do, and P. H. N. de With, "Free-viewpoint depth image based rendering," Journal of Visual Communication and Image Representation, vol. 21, pp. 533-541, Jul-Aug 2010.

[8] K.-J. Oh, S. Yea, and Y.-S. Ho, "Hole filling method using depth based in-painting for view synthesis in free viewpoint television and 3-D video" in Picture Coding Symposium, 2009.

[9] V. Kolmogorov and R. Zabih, "What Energy Functions Can Be Minimizedvia Graph Cuts?," IEEE Trans. Pattern Anal. Mach. Intell., vol. 26, pp. 147-159, 2004.

[10] Y. Boykov, O. Veksler, and R. Zabih, "Fast Approximate Energy Minimization via Graph Cuts," IEEE Trans. Pattern Anal. Mach. Intell., vol. 23, pp. 1222-1239, 2001.

[11] Y. Boykov and V. Kolmogorov, "An Experimental Comparison of Min-Cut/Max-Flow Algorithms for Energy Minimization in Vision," IEEE Trans. Pattern Anal. Mach. Intell., vol. 26, pp. 1124-1137, 2004.

[12] Z. Wang, A. C. Bovik, and H. R. Sheikh, "Image Quality Assessment: From Error Measurement to Structural Similarity," IEEE Trans. Image Processing, vol. 13, pp. 600-612, 2004.

[13] S. M. Rhee, Y. J. Yoon, I. K. Shin, Y. G. Kim, Y. J. Choi, and S. M. Choi, "Stereo Image Synthesis by View Morphing with Stereo Consistency," Applied Mathematics & Information Sciences, vol. 6, pp. 195-200, Jan 2012.

[14] M. Solh and G. AlRegib, "Hierarchical Hole-Filling For Depth-Based View Synthesis in FTV and 3D Video," IEEE Journal of Selected Topics in Signal Processing, vol. 6, pp. 495-504, Sep 2012.

Spatially Important Point Identification: A New Technique for Detail-Preserving Reduced-Complexity Representation of 3D Point Clouds

Rohit Sant[1], Ninad Kulkarni[1], Kratarth Goel[2], Salil Kapur[2] and Ainesh Bakshi[3]
[1]Department of EEE&I, BITS-Pilani K.K. Birla Goa Campus, Goa, India
[2]Department of CS/IS, BITS-Pilani K.K. Birla Goa Campus, Goa, India
[3]Department of Chemical Engineering, BITS-Pilani K.K. Birla Goa Campus, Goa, India

Abstract - *This paper describes a technique for reducing the inherent complexity of range data without discarding any essential information. Our technique implements this by searching for 'important' points in the range data and discarding intervening points, all of which may be regenerated to a good approximation by linear interpolation. The implementation uses a metric based on the 3D geometry of the scene to assign to each point an 'importance' value. We define Spatially Important Points, which are got by comparing this importance value with a customizable template and with importance values of its neighbours. The algorithm has been tested on various datasets and has been found to give, on an average, a 78% reduction in complexity while retaining almost all points of significance, as shown by reconstructing the dataset. Results have been tabulated at the end of the paper.*

Keywords: 3D, range data, terrain, compression, importance

1 Introduction

Optimal representation of the environment in terms of terrain maps has been a long-studied topic in mobile robotics. A long-standing debate exists on the benefits of either mapping technique, and the exclusive choice of either invariably results in a compromise [1], [2]. It is with this background and the subsequent motivation that we present our technique for data representation – we recognize the powerful nature of the geometric 3D model of the scene, and we work towards reducing its complexity while preserving that power. Since conventional downsampling causes an equal loss of useful information as that of redundancy, a specialized technique for reduction of complexity is needed.

We begin by detecting points essential to the representation of the terrain. This is done by comparing 'importance' values (defined in Section 3.2) of each point to those in its neighborhood, and also to a template. We define Spatially Important Points (SIPs) to be points of appreciable change in a terrain. Setting a threshold gives an output of SIPs for the scene. Our technique may be viewed as an importance based sorting algorithm; setting higher thresholds removes points in ascending order of importance. The scene may thus be represented in varying levels of detail based on the chosen value of the threshold, but the algorithm ensures that features absolutely essential to the representation of the terrain are retained for almost all realistic thresholds.

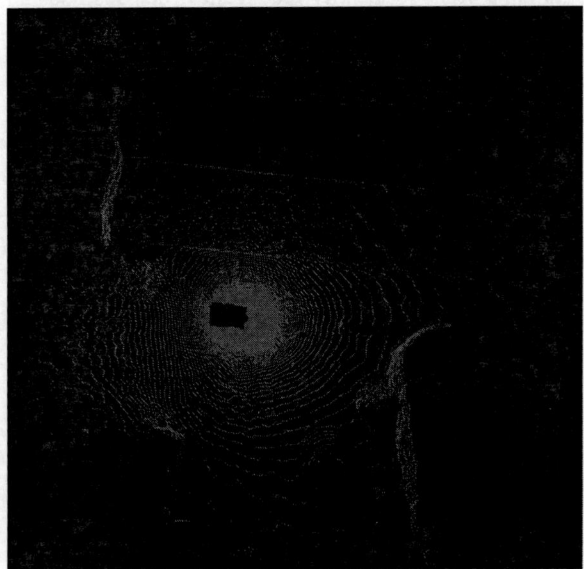

Figure 1. A sample point cloud displaying an outdoor scene. This point cloud, though it gives an accurate terrain representation, contains more than 100,000 points, making it unwieldy for easy storage and operation.

Put simply, the Spatially Important Point Representation (SIPR) of a scene results in a minimal representation with detail preservation. Its percentage retention of informative points (points which add to the information content of the scene) is far greater than that of redundant points. Detail-preserving, vastly compressed and easily reconstructable datasets result, which can be directly used in robotic applications like navigation, planning, mapping, locomotion.

The organization of the paper is as follows: Section (2) describes related work in this field, Section (3) describes, in detail, the working of our algorithm while the implementation is discussed in Section (4). Results are tabulated in Section (5) and Section (6) concludes the paper.

Note that in the +rest of this paper, the terms 'terrain', 'scene' and 'range data' are used interchangeably, with the understanding that they all imply a 3D range dataset..

2 Related Work

Reduced-complexity representation of 3D data is an implicit requirement for almost all research concerning 3D range data. Early work, for example that by Martin et al. [15] uses a median value to represent each 3D grid in an octree. Though this reduces complexity, it results in indiscriminate loss of detail. A variation on the same theme by Lee et al. [16] incorporates non-uniform grids, but the results still suffer due to the downsampling technique. A technique described in [14] uses multiple scans to identify redundancy, but this adds an unwanted restriction on the input and severely limits its usefulness in situations where multiple scans cannot be obtained. A notable implementation can be seen in [17], in which the authors approach this problem using curvature.

Since this is usually an interim step in a larger problem statement, most researchers do not bother with operating on raw data, preferring to use clustering [8], [9] usually with a k-nearest neighbors approach. In [10], a different technique involving plane detection to reduce complexity of range data has been described, but their requirement does not include the finer details in a point cloud.

Often geometric relations between points have been used in determining properties of the terrain. Labecki et al in [4] analyzed geometric configurations of a walking robot for terrain mapping. Schenker et al in [5] also use the geometric structure of scan-lines for terrain exploration. Most of the above research uses rudimentary metrics for actually detecting important points using range data, relying instead on powerful post-processing (Hough transforms [6]) and/or auxiliary peripherals for confirmation. A notable application of a similar technique is carried out by Khalifa et al [7], which uses a more refined scan-line based technique for CAD model acquisition from 3D range data. Our algorithm uses a more robust metric for determination of useful terrain points, and as a standalone tool gives a better output than current algorithms.

2.1 Our Contribution

Over the past 10-15 years, advances in high density point acquisition techniques have made datasets having the order 10^6 points commonplace in robotic navigation. This makes most of today's robotic applications like planning, mapping, and navigation computationally very expensive. Unlike [11], [15] and [16] which build upon more expensive constructs like meshes, grids, triangulations and /or expensive post-processing using ICP [14], we develop a completely new technique starting from basic geometry and build up on it. Our algorithm achieves better efficiency, due to its specialized nature. To the best of our knowledge, our algorithm for low-complexity range data representation does indeed provide a unique and useful solution for detail preserving reduction of point data – thus removing the final drawback of range data.

3 Algorithm Description

The structured nature of unprocessed range data can be effectively used to reduce the complexity of the representation without discarding essential information. We attempt to demonstrate the effectiveness of this approach through this algorithm.

3.1 Overview

Terrain data obtained from modern laser rangefinders follows a structure where points are scanned along a line of constant elevation. A Spatially Important Point (SIP), as defined by us, is a point where the terrain changes appreciably. A definition of this form has been made since all points which lie between two such consecutive constant-elevation SIPs can be replaced by a linear interpolation between the said SIPs, thus eliminating the need to store them explicitly. Spatially Important Point detection, as mentioned previously, is done by finding 'importance' values (defined in Section 3.2) of each point and then comparing with those of its neighbors. This stage involves minimal loss of actual detail. We therefore hypothesize that a representation of the terrain by its Spatially Important Points is a complete representation, from the point of view of robotic applications. The output of SIPR is still a point cloud consisting of raw points belonging to the original dataset, with no aberrations

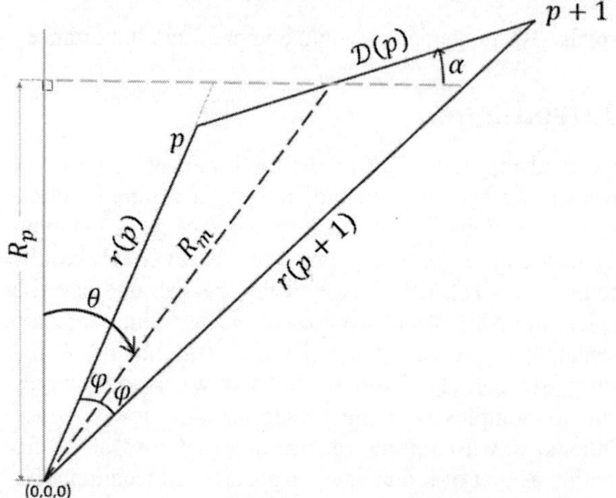

Figure 2. The schematic diagram for evaluating Spatially Important Points. A single segment from (p) to (p+1) is shown for purposes of clarity.

3.2 Importance Function

We define an importance function f for quantifying relevance of points. The requirement for this function is that it should provide a good indicator of the magnitude of change of the terrain from one point to the next.

Let $\mathbb{P}_i = \{p_{i1}, p_{i2}, \dots p_{in}\}$ be the ith constant-elevation scan line having n points. Then for each $\mathbb{P}_i$, points are treated pairwise, and the distances between adjacent points are stored in a set $\mathcal{D}_i$, where $\mathcal{D}_i(p_{ik})$ is the Euclidean distance between points p_{ik} and $p_{i(k-1)}$ (Figure 1). Further operations are done exclusively on $\mathcal{D}_i$. The function f is got by operating on $\mathcal{D}_i$ as follows:

$$f(p) = \frac{\mathcal{D}_i(p_{ik})}{g(r).h(\theta)} - \left|\overrightarrow{R_p}\right| \quad (1)$$

Where (Figure 2),

$$\left|\overrightarrow{R_p}\right| = \left|\overrightarrow{R_m}\right| \cos\theta \quad (2)$$

$$g(\vec{r}) = \left(1 + \frac{|\vec{r}(p_{i(k+1)})|}{|\vec{r}(p_{ik})|}\right) \quad (3)$$

$$h(\theta) = \frac{\tan\varphi.\sec^2\theta}{1+\tan\varphi.\tan\theta} \quad (4)$$

($\vec{r}(p_{ik})$ Is simply the radius vector of point p, and φ is half the constant angle subtended by each segment at the origin.)

3.2.1 Discussion

The defining characteristic of this function is that it identically equals zero for any consecutive point-pair on a flat terrain. Hence deviations of f from zero provide a good measure of the absolute change in the terrain. Comparisons with neighboring values of f is a good way of judging the relative change in the terrain.

The function $f(p_{ik})$ increases monotonically with decreasing α (Figure 1) and thus unambiguously gives a measure of deviation from local flatness.

The function $g(\vec{r})$ is a measure of the expected $\mathcal{D}_i(p_{ik})$ values for a flat terrain; the greater this function, the larger would be the expected value of $\mathcal{D}_i(p_{ik})$ for a flat terrain, since φ is constant everywhere. The ratio $\frac{\mathcal{D}_i(p_{ik})}{g(r)}$ would then describe the absolute deviation of a segment from flatness.

The function $h(\theta)$ arises out of the fact that for a flat terrain – our template for absolute comparison – $\mathcal{D}_i(p_{ik})$ and $g(\vec{r})$ values do not scale equally (φ is constant – a hardware constraint) with increasing θ.

3.3 Template

We choose a flat terrain as a basis for absolute comparison since it provides a practically desirable ideal in many cases.

For a hypothetical flat constant-elevation portion of the terrain at a given $\overrightarrow{R_p}$, each $\mathcal{D}_i(p_{ik})$ has a different value, since all of them subtend the same angle at the origin. However, the value of $f(p_{ik})$ for each $\mathcal{D}_i(p_{ik})$ is zero i.e. a constant. Thus the value of $\frac{\mathcal{D}_i(p_{ik})}{g(r).h(\theta)}$ for a flat terrain is equal to $\left|\overrightarrow{R_p}\right|$, and evaluating $f(p_{ik})$ merely measures the deviation of $\mathcal{D}_i(p_{ik})$ from a flat terrain.

An intricacy here is the choice of $\overrightarrow{R_p}$ – since the function f attains zero at an $\left|\overrightarrow{R_p}\right|$ equal to the perpendicular distance to a flat terrain constructed at the same place as each $\mathcal{D}_i(p_{ik})$, we have to choose $\overrightarrow{R_p}$ locally to ensure correct interpretation of the principle. We also assume the angle bisector to be invariant of the orientation of $\mathcal{D}_i(p_{ik})$, which is a reasonable assumption given the constant azimuth readings. As a result the angle bisector cosine is chosen as an appropriate $\overrightarrow{R_p}$.

It is worth mentioning that the algorithm can be used for very specialized detection purposes – any non-flat terrain can be compared against by merely calculating an f for that template and compare everything against this value.

3.4 Neighbor Comparison

Following this, we apply the threshold condition:

$$p_{ik} \in \mathbb{K} \; iff$$

$$\left(f(p_{ik}) - f(p_{i(k-1)}) \in \left((-\infty, -\mathcal{T}) \cup (\mathcal{T}, \infty)\right)\right)$$
$$or$$
$$\left(f(p_{i(k+1)}) - f(p_{ik}) \in \left((-\infty, -\mathcal{T}) \cup (\mathcal{T}, \infty)\right)\right) \quad (5)$$

Where

$\mathbb{K}$ is the set of Spatially Important Points
f is the importance function
p_{ik} is the point index in the original structured dataset
$\mathcal{T}$ is a constant threshold set as a decision boundary

3.4.1 Analysis

For a neighbor comparison, we impose the Spatially Important Point condition, which measures a difference of the deviations from flatness of adjacent points, thus establishing a measure for observing the trend in the terrain. A point is chosen as a Spatially Important Point if its deviation is sufficiently different from that of its neighbor.

4 Implementation

We deal with an input terrain represented as a point cloud in 3D. For the purposes of this research, we used the Canadian Planetary Emulation Terrain 3D Mapping Dataset [12]. Data is acquired through a laser rangefinder (LRF) with a constant 0.36° azimuthal separation (half of this angle is later referred to as φ) between consecutive readings at constant elevation. This data is represented as co-ordinates on a spherical (Range, Elevation, Azimuth) system [12]. We take advantage of the fact that this input data is structured, enabling us to traverse the dataset in lower time complexity as compared to an unstructured set.

Since the algorithm is run for all sets of constant-elevation data, all regularity (redundancy) is correctly identified (albeit in different iterations) and removed.

5 Results

The technique was tried on various sets of range data available through the Canadian Planetary Emulation Terrain 3D Mapping Dataset [12], the results of which are discussed below. One scene – Scene A (Figure 3) has been analyzed in this section, and a few more results have been displayed in Figures 4-7. All images are screenshots of point clouds viewed

Figure 3. The figure on the left indicates a piece of terrain and the figure on the right shows its SIPR (in red) superimposed on the dataset.

in the PCD viewer (part of Point Cloud Library [13]) or Meshlab [3]. The readers are requested to consult the full-color (electronic) version for maximum clarity.

5.1 Analysis of Scene A

This scene (Figure 3) comprises of a dense flat portion in the middle of the scene adjacent to which a fairly large rock is seen. A wall made of large, discrete rocks is seen in the background. A comparative picture of a section of the original dataset and its SIPR is shown here.

The full point cloud contains 105998 points, while the SIPR is built up of just 8722 points, resulting in a size reduction of nearly 92%. The complete boundary of the centered large rock is maintained, and every single junction between the discrete rocks in the wall is well identified by the SIP algorithm. Most of the discarded points belonged originally to the flat central portion seen in the middle of Figure 3, thus removing the (easily re-constructible) regularity present in the image. The code executes in 322ms for the above scene comprising of 44 scan lines and a total of 105998 points.

For the purposes of reconstruction, as described in the section below, such aggressive compression leads to less usable terrain, and an average compression of 75% is chosen.

5.2 Reconstruction – A measure of performance

We verify our claim – of our reduced point set being a good representation of the entire terrain – by reconstructing the terrain using a simple linear interpolation between our points. Figure 4 shows one such comparative result.

An alpha-shapes surface fitting is also done, in Figures 5 and 6. Features like trees, houses and contours between the house and the trees have been well reconstructed. We observe that the interpolation is done along the same scan lines as the original dataset – since SIPI operates on these scan lines for removing points, any other surface fit on the reconstructed points (splines, triangulations) too would generate much the same surfaces as the original.

This completes the motivation of this paper – we have shown that our Spatially Important Points, keeping merely 30% of the original dataset, manage to closely approximate the original dataset through a simple interpolation. Comparisons of alignment with the original dataset were done using Iterative Closest Point (ICP) and results have been reported in Table 1.

Figure 4. Reconstructed image of a point cloud on the left and the original image on the right

Figure 5. Alpha shapes for the original terrain

Figure 6. Alpha shape reconstruction for the terrain in Figure 4

5.3 Other Results

Figure 7 shows the variation of the alpha-shapes reconstruction with the number of retained data points. It is seen that at 27% retention, the reconstruction closely resembles the original terrain. Even at a 14% retention, the output is seen to be visually similar to the input.

These results were obtained on a machine with an Intel® Core i3-2310M processor (2.10 GHz) and 4 GB of RAM. The code

Figure 7. Alpha shape reconstruction for (L-R) (a)Original terrain (b) Reconstruction from 27% points and (c) Reconstruction from 14% points.

for executing this technique was written in C++ and compiled using version 4.4.3 of the GNU g++ compiler.

Table 1. Results of SIPI

Average data reduction (structured point clouds)	77.6%
Average runtime	314 ms
Average ICP Score of reconstructed terrain with original terrain	$1.162*10^{-3}$
Asymptotic Complexity	$O(n^2)$ (worst case)

6 Conclusion, Applications & Future Work

The Spatially Important Point Identification (SIPI) technique is a simple and fundamentally strong approach towards efficient representation of 3D data. It has been demonstrated that the Spatially Important Point Representation (SIPR) of a scene can successfully represent all defining characteristics present in the data using only, on an average, 22.4% of the complexity of the original data.

Some of the ideas highlighted in the paper are given here

1. Hypothesis of an efficient representation of range data which enhances detail while reducing redundancy
2. Adoption of a scan-lines based approach for identifying important points in a terrain
3. Definition and assignment of a unique ratio for gauging the importance of a point
4. Experiments done on terrain databases with favorable results as shown through reconstruction, with as much as 91.3% data reduction possible with no catastrophic loss of detail.

6.1 Future Work

We are implementing a dynamic-programming based planning algorithm on the basis of this data reduction technique. The current technique was developed with a view to integrating seamlessly with further robotic navigation techniques.

References

[1] Thrun, S., & Bucken, A. (1996). Integrating Grid-Based and Topological Maps for Mobile Robot Navigation. *The Thirteenth National Conference on Artificial Intelligence (AAAI'96)* (pp. 944-950). Portland: AAAI Press.

[2] Pfaff, P., Triebel, R., & Burgard, W. (2007). An Efficient Extension of Elevation Maps for Outdoor Terrain Mapping. *International Journal of Robotics Research*, 217-230.

[3] Cignoni, P., Corsini, M., Ranzuglia, G.: Meshlab: an open-source 3D mesh processing system. ERCIM News, 45–46 (2008)

[4] Łabęcki, P., Rosiński, D., & Skrzypczyński, P. (2011). Terrain Map Building for a Walking Robot Equipped with an Active 2D Range Sensor. *Journal of Automation, Mobile Robotics & Intelligent Systems*, 68-78.

[5] Schenker, P. S., & Sword, L. F. (1997). *Lightweight rovers for Mars science exploration and sample return.* Pasadena: California Institute of Technology.

[6] Borges, P., Zlot, R., Bosse, M., Nuske, S., & Tews, A. (2010). Vision-based Localization Using an Edge Map Extracted from 3D Laser Range Data. *International Conference on Robotics and Automation* (pp. 4902-4909). Anchorage,Alaska: IEEE.

[7] Khalifa, I., Moussa, M., & Kamel, M. (2003). Range image segmentation using local approximation of scan lines with application to CAD model acquisition. *Machine Vision and Applications*, 263-274.

[8] Zhao, Y., He, M., Zhao, H., Davoine, F., & Zha, H. (2012). Computing Object-based Saliency in Urban Scenes Using Laser Sensing. *International Conference on Robotics and Automation* (pp. 4436-4443). Saint Paul, Minnesota: IEEE.

[9] Zhao, H., Liu, Y., Zhu, X., Zhao, Y., & Zha, H. (2010). Scene Understanding in a Large Dynamic Environment through Laser-Based Sensing. *International Conference on Robotics and Automation, 2010* (pp. 127-133). Anchorage,Alaska: IEEE.

[10] Li, W., Wolberg, G., & Zokai, S. (2011). Lightweight 3D Modeling of Urban Buildings From Range Data. *2011 International Conference on 3D Imaging, Modeling, Processing, Visualization and Transmission* (pp. 124-131). Hangzhou: IEEE Computer Society.

[11] Moorthy, I., Millert, J. R., Hut, B., Berni, J. A., Zareo-Tejada, P. J., & Lit, Q. (2007). Extracting tree crown properties from ground-based scanning laser data. *IEEE International Geoscience and Remote Sensing Symposium* (pp. 2830-2832). Barcelona: IEEE.

[12] Tong, C., Gingras, D., Larose, K., Barfoot, T. D., & Dupuis, E. (2012). The Canadian Planetary Emulation Terrain 3D Mapping Dataset. *International Journal of Robotics Research (IJRR)*.

[13] Rusu, R. B., & Cousins, S. (2011). 3D is here: Point Cloud Library (PCL). *2011 IEEE International Conference on Robotics and Automation (ICRA)* (pp. 1-4). Shanghai: IEEE.

[14] Swadzba, A., Vollmer, A., Hanheide, M., & Wachsmuth, S. (2008). Reducing noise and redundancy in registered range data for planar surface extraction. *19th International Conference on Pattern Recognition, 2008* (pp. 1- 4). Tampa, FL: IEEE.

[15] R. R. Martin, I. A. Stroud and A. D. Marshall (1996). Data reduction for Reverse Engineering. RECCAD, Deliverable Document 1 COPERUNICUS project, No. 1068, Computer and Auto-mation Institute of Hungarian Academy of Science, Jan 1996

[16] K.H., Lee, H., Woo, & T., Suk (2001). Data Reduction Methods for Reverse Engineering. Int J Adv Manuf Technol, 735-743.Stanford University Computer Graphics Laboratory. (1994).

[17] Song, W., Cai, S., Yang, B., Cui, W., & Wang, Y. (2009). A Reduction Method of Three-Dimensional Point Cloud. 2nd International Conference on Biomedical Engineering and Informatics, 2009. (pp. 1-4). Tianjin: IEEE.

A dynamic background subtraction method for detecting walkers using mobile stereo-camera

Masaki Kasahara[1] **and Hiroshi Hanaizumi**[1]
[1]Hosei University Graduate School of Computer and Information Sciences, Tokyo, Japan

Abstract - *A method "Dynamic Background Subtraction" (DBS) was proposed for detecting walkers running out into the street using a stereo-camera. The method was based on the fact that front street scene extended from a point as the automobile moving. Analyzing the scene extensions, current scene was precisely predicted from the previous one. The difference between the two scenes indicated walkers' movements on a street in a video frame interval. The stereo-camera provided us depth information for the scene prediction and that for distance to walker. The proposed method was characterized by its simplicity in principle and high potentiality in easily realizing the system with low cost. In this paper, the principle and the procedures of the method were described. Some experimental results were also shown.*

Keywords: dynamic background subtraction; walker detection; mobile stereo-camera; scene prediction; depth image;

1 Introduction

Recently, number of traffic accidents between walkers and automobiles has been increasing, and main causes of the accidents were drivers looking aside and/or carelessness [1]. In order to prevent these accidents, an automated recognition system has been developed for detecting walkers running out into the street and for making alarm to driver or for stopping automobile [2]. A millimeter-wave radar system has already developed [3]. The radar system, however, was too expensive to spread.

In the scene recognition, walkers had various kinds of appearances in color as their clothes, skin, hair, and so on. Thus, walkers shape information was mainly used for their detection. Histogram of Gradient (HOG) or Support Vector Machine (SVM) [4]-[5] have used with template matching [6]-[7] for the walker detection in the mobile camera images. These methods, however, sometimes extracted background objects as walkers. In the point of view of accurate extraction of walkers, a background subtraction method had excellent performance in separating moving walkers from static background [8]-[9]. In case of mobile camera, the background subtraction method extracts background as moving objects because the background is not static. Thus, highly accurate methods with high cost performance have been required.

Here, we proposed a method for developing a one of those systems using mobile stereo camera. The basis of the method is the conventional background subtraction, but prediction images are used for the subtraction, i.e. the subtraction is performed between the current video scene and that predicted from the previous one. We call the method as Dynamic Background Subtraction (DBS). Distances among objects and automobile, which are given by a stereo camera, are needed for obtaining prediction image with high accuracy.

2 Principle and procedures

2.1 Infinite point

Suppose that a front view camera is mounted on an automobile moving in a straight line. We see that video scenes spread radially from a point. We call the point as Infinite Point. The point is not necessarily identical with the center of the video scene. Therefore, the infinite point should be determined by captured video images. The position of the point depends on camera direction setting. The Infinite Point is obtained from sequential video scenes in which some groups of corresponding points make some radial lines crossing the Infinite Point. Before the processing, image distortions caused by camera lenses are compensated by the camera calibration [10]-[11].

Figure 1 shows, for example, 4 groups of corresponding points in some sequential video scenes. As corresponding points in a group stand in a line passing the infinite point I, we can find the line using a least squares method so that sum of square of length of the perpendicular from points in the group to the line takes the minimum value S as

$$\left.\begin{aligned} S &= \min_{x,y} \sum_{j=1}^{M}\sum_{i=1}^{N}\left(\frac{a_j x_{ij} - y_{ij} + b_j}{\sqrt{a_j^2 + b_j^2}}\right)^2, \\ a_j &= \frac{\overline{y_j} - y}{\overline{x_j} - x}, \quad b_j = \frac{\overline{x_j}\, y - x\, \overline{y_j}}{\overline{x_j} - x}, \end{aligned}\right\} \quad (1)$$

where, x_{ij} and y_{ij} are coordinates of the i-th point in the j-th group, $\overline{x_j}$ and $\overline{y_j}$ gravity center of points in the j-th group, x and y coordinates of the infinite point. As least squares line always passes through the gravity center of the group, we put a candidate infinite point I' at the center of the image with initial lines passing through both I' and gravity center of each

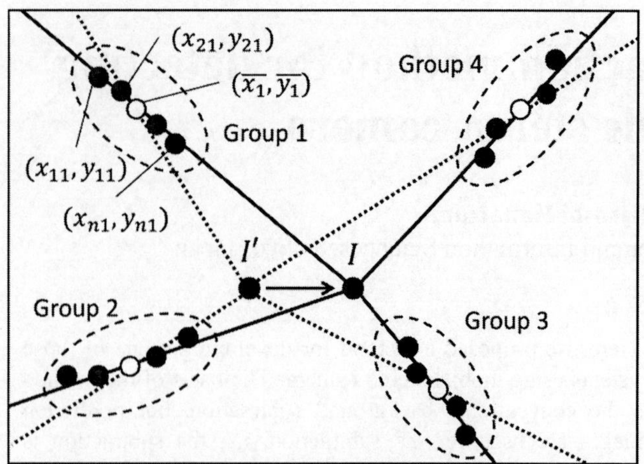

Fig. 1 Determination of the Infinite Point.

point group (dot lines in Fig.1). Then, we scan I' so that S takes the minimum. When S reaches to the minimum, I' is identical to the infinite point I as shown in Fig. 1.

2.2 Background extension

Mobile camera shows us background of front street scene extends from the infinite point as automobile moving. In order to predict current scene from the previous one precisely, we need to analyze the position change between the current and the previous images. Figure 2 shows geometry of the camera, current position of a background point W, and its previous position W_0. We observe W and W_0 as image points P and P_0, respectively. We assume that direction of camera movement is identical to its optical axis. So the infinite point is given as the cross point between the optical axis and the image. In order to predict the current scene from the previous one precisely, we need to know the ratio $\overrightarrow{IP}/\overrightarrow{IP_0}$ for all background points. In Fig.2, relation between the background point W_0 and the image point P_0 is described as

$$\left.\begin{aligned} \frac{\overrightarrow{IP_0}}{f} &= \frac{L}{Z}, \\ \frac{\overrightarrow{IP}}{f} &= \frac{L}{Z-\Delta Z}, \end{aligned}\right\} \quad (2)$$

where, ΔZ corresponds to movement of automobile, Z distance between camera and the background point. The extension rate k is derived from eq.(2) as

$$k = \frac{\overrightarrow{IP}}{\overrightarrow{IP_0}} = \frac{Z}{Z-\Delta Z} = \frac{Z}{Z-v\Delta t}, \quad (3)$$

where, v means the velocity of the automobile, Δt time interval for video frame rate. We see that the extension rate k depends on the distance Z and the velocity v. Figure 3 shows the extension rate for the combinations of distance Z and velocity v (we assume Δt =1/30 [s]). Figure 3 indicates that the extension rate k changes slowly in the far area, but rapidly in the near area. In the point of view of rough detection of objects, we can assume k is a constant, for example, in the

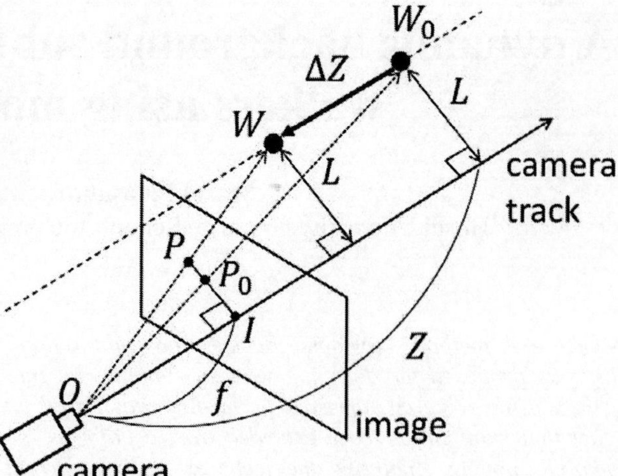

Fig. 2 Movement of background points.

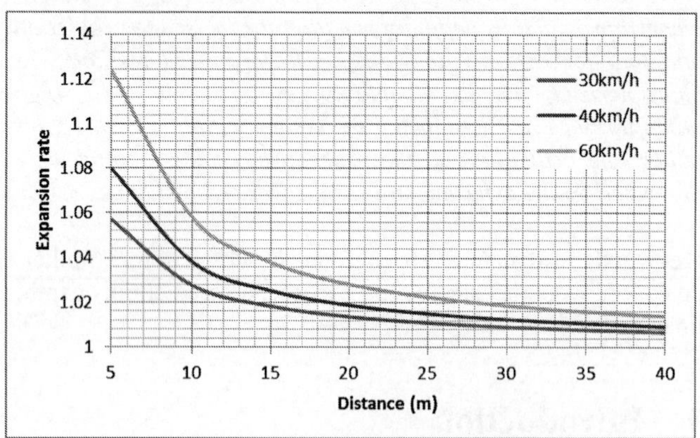

Fig. 3 Extension rate with distance Z.

range over 20m from the camera. Though the dynamic background subtraction gives us some noisy residuals, we can separate a larger object from the noisy residuals. But in the near region increase of k yields inseparable larger residuals. That is the reason why we introduce a stereo camera.

2.3 Depth map and scene prediction

In order to predict the position of a near object in the background from previous scene with high accuracy, distance between camera and the object is indispensable. Figure 4 shows schematic diagram of a stereo camera system. On the assumption that optical axes of left and right cameras are perfectly parallel, the distance Z between camera and an object in the background is obtained from parallax d as

$$Z = fc\frac{b}{d} = fc\frac{b}{x_l - x_r}, \quad (4)$$

where, x_l and x_r are the position of image point of the object, f focal length, b baseline and c a constant. A line-by-line block matching algorithm is used for finding the corresponding point pair of background objects. Using eqs.(2) and (4), the extension rate k is calculated as a function of the velocity of

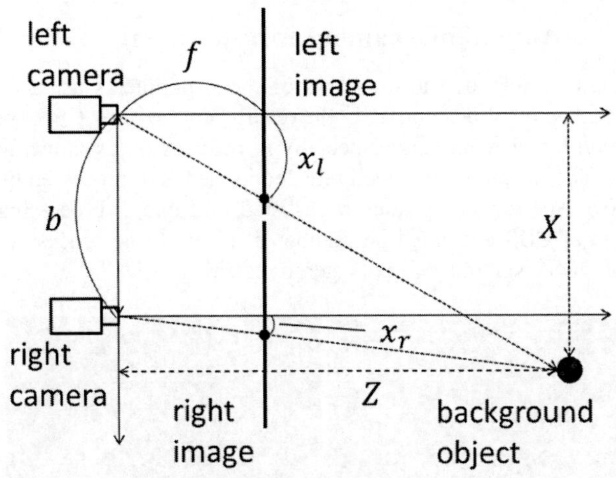

Fig. 4 A stereo camera system.

automobile v. Thus, we can predict the position of the point P from that of a point P_0 in the previous image (see Fig. 2).

2.4 Procedures of DBS

The procedures of our proposed method DBS are graphically shown in Figs. 5 (a)-(h). Firstly, we take stereo pair images as the previous scene as shown in (a) and (b). A block matching algorithm is applied to the images and depth map (c) is obtained. In the depth map, miss-matching areas, such as sky, are suppressed as noises by filling zeros. We can extract a range belt indicating assigned depth region as shown in (d). The range belt will be used for setting a special watch area.
The image (a) is extended by multiplying k calculated by using the depth map and the predicted scene (e) is obtained. The image (e) is the dynamic background we proposed. The predicted image is subtracted from the current video scene (f) (left image of stereo-pair). Residual image (g) indicates most of predicted background areas are removed by the subtraction almost the perfectly. Conventional background subtraction, i.e. subtraction image (a) from (f) gives us larger residual especially in a near field as shown in (h).

3 Experimental results

In order to evaluate the performance of the proposed method DBS, we applied DBS to 2 measured data sets. One was measurement using a rail camera and the other that of actual automobile camera. The rail camera was a hand-made device on which stereo camera smoothly moved with keeping the camera direction as shown Fig.6. The rail camera realized an ideal measurement without camera vibration. The stereo camera was attached to a tripod and fixed between front glass and passenger seat. In the measurement using the automobile camera, vibration of automobile in driving might affect the quality of video data. In both measurements, we used a stereo camera "FINEPIX REAL 3D" produced by FUJIFILM; circle in Fig.6 indicates the camera. The resolution of image was 640x480. The stereo camera had two lenses for stereo vision

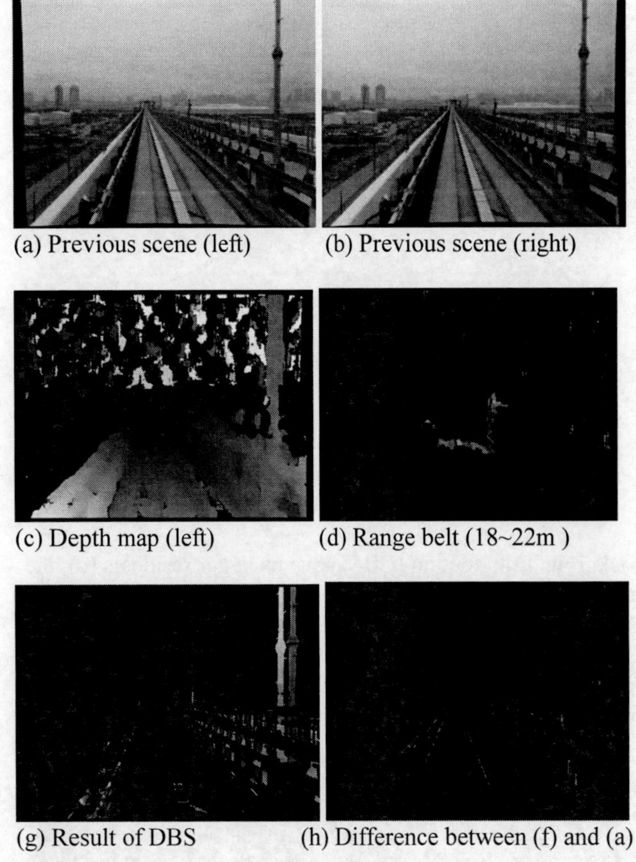

(a) Previous scene (left) (b) Previous scene (right)

(c) Depth map (left) (d) Range belt (18~22m)

(g) Result of DBS (h) Difference between (f) and (a)

Fig. 5 Graphical procedure of DBS

with base line of 75mm. The focal length was 18.9mm and frame rate was 30 fps. All of measured images were processed by a note PC (intel Core i5-2520M CPU, 2.50GHz).
The performance was evaluated by an index; remaining rate R_r as

$$R_r = \frac{M}{B}, \tag{5}$$

where, B was number of pixels in the background to be removed, M those of subtraction residuals. When the subtraction results fell down under a threshold, we regarded that the background was removed by the subtraction.

3.1 Rail camera measurement

Rail camera was set on a road and a man stood 20m away from the camera. The distance 20m was the safe braking distance of 40km/h automobile. The previous scene was taken. Assuming velocity of the automobile was 40km/h, we moved rail camera 37cm forward along the road and the man moved across the road 3.7cm correspondingly to walking speed 4km/h. Then we took the current scene. Figure 7 (a) shows the man on the road; ellipse in the scene indicates the man standing. The prediction image was shown in Fig.7 (b), where we filled zeros into stereo matching failure areas. Subtraction results were shown in (c) and (d). Though conventional

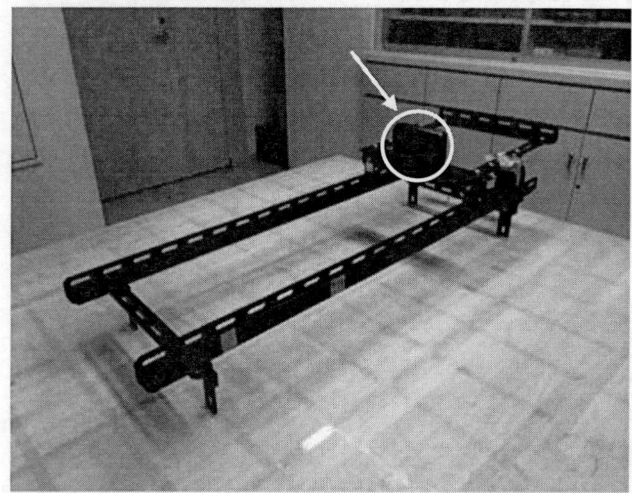

Fig.6 Rail camera.

background subtraction (CBS) gave us larger residuals (c), the proposed DBS gave fewer ones (d). The validity of DBS was confirmed. Table 1 indicates the quantitative performances of CBS and DBS. DBS had higher performance; one third remaining rate but DBS needed about 3 times longer processing time than CBS did.

(a) Current scene (left image)

(b) predicted background

(c)Subtraction without prediction

(d) with prediction

Fig.7 Experimental results by using a rail camera.

Table 1 Remaining rate and processing time for rail camera data

Method	Remaining rate [%]	Processing time [ms]
CBS	11.6	554
DBS	4.0	1776

3.2 Automobile camera measurement

Figures 8(a)-(d) shows results of the experiments using an actual automobile camera. In the results processed by CBS, we found larger remaining, especially in near region as shown in (c). The remaining was well reduced in the result processed by DBS. The remaining rates were listed in Table 2. Processing time of CBS depended on number of pixels to be processed, but DBS spent much time in stereo matching.

(a)Current scene (left image)

(b)background predicted

(c) result processed by CBS

(d) one by DBS

Fig. 8 Actual automobile camera results.

Table 2 Remaining rate and processing time of experiment in automobile

Method	Remaining rate [%]	Processing time [ms]
CBS	9.1	295
DBS	3.6	1866

Fig.9 shows another results processed by the proposed method. Oncoming automobile on opposite side was well detected (see white circle, right). Preceding automobile is also detected (white circle, left). According to those results of experiments, the propose method Dynamic Background Subtraction DBS reduced misdetection of background objects than conventional method CBS. However, the reduction of the subtraction residuals was insufficient. We considered that main cause of the insufficient performance was stereo matching problem.

Fig.9 Detection of moving target instead of walkers running into the street.

4 Conclusions

We proposed method DBS for dynamic background subtraction between sequential mobile video images to detect walkers running out to the street. We improved accuracy of the subtraction by using distance information from stereo-camera. In order to remove static background, we needed to predict a current scene from the previous one. Depth image obtained by a stereo camera enabled us to predict background dynamically with high accuracy.

To improve the performance in background reduction, to realize faster processing, to analyze system behavior in driving a curve and/or camera vibration due to bumpy road and to design a practical system are subjects for a future study.

5 References

[1] The Cabinet Office, "Traffic safety white paper ver.2012", vol.1, part.1, section.1, Nikkei printing, pp.18, Japan, 2013.

[2] T. Gandhi and M. M. Trivrdi, "Pedestrian collision avoidance systems: A survey of computer vision based recent studies", in *Proceedings of the IEEE Intelligent Transportation Systems Conference*, 2006, pp.976-981.

[3] M. Skutek, M. Mekhaiel, G. Wanielik, "A PreCrash System based on Radar for Automotive Applicaions", *Proc. IEEE*, Intelligent Vehicles Symposium, pp.37-41, June 20003.

[4] N. Dalal and B. Triggs, "Histograms of oriented gradients for human detection", *IEEE Computer Society Conference on Computer Vision and Pattern Recognition*, pp.886-893, 2005.

[5] A. Shashua, Y. Gdalyahu, and G. Hayun, "Pedestrian detection for driving assistance systems: Single-flame classification and system level performance", *Intelligent Vehicles Symposium, IEEE,* pp.1-7, 2004.

[6] D.M. Gavrila, "Pedestrian detection from a moving vehicle", Proc. European Conference on Computer Vision, pp.37-49, Dublin, Ireland, 2000.

[7] A. Broggi, M. Bertozzi, A. Fascioli, and M. Sechi, "Shape-based pedestrian detection", Proc. IEEE Intelligent Vehicles Symposium, pp.215-220, Dearbon, USA, 2000.

[8] S. Cheungm, C. Kamath, "Robust Background Subtraction with Foreground Validation for Urban Traffic Video", EURASIP Journal on Applied Signal Processing, Volume 2005, 1 January 2005.

[9] Massimo Piccardi, "Background subtraction techniques: a review", Proc. IEEE, 2004 IEEE International Comference on Systems, Man and Cybernetics, Vol. 4, pp.3099-3104, October 2004.

[10] J.g. Frayer and D.C. Brown, "Lens distortion for close-range photogrammetry", *Photogrammetric Engineering and Remote Sensing*, vol.52, pp.51-58, 1986

[11] Z.Zhang, "A flexible new technique for camera calibration", *IEEE transactions on Pattern Analysis and machine Intelligence*, vol.22, pp.1330-1334, 2000

[12] M. J. Black, P. Andan, "A framework for the robust estimation of optical flow", *Fourth International Conference on Computer Vision*, pp.231-236, May 1993

Performance Evaluation of Depth Map Upsampling on 3D Perception of Stereoscopic Images

Jong In Gil and Manbae Kim
Dept. of Computer and Communications Engineering, Kangwon National University
Chunchon, Republic of Korea
E-mail: manbae@kangwon.ac.kr

Abstract – *The depth map upsampling has gained much interest following the release of TOF camera and range sensors. Most of research works have focused on the comparison of an upsampled depth map and its original depth. A frequently used objective measurement is PSNR. Using this measurement, they examine the performance of their methods. In 3D stereoscopic field, the depth map plays an important role in the performance of 3D perception. The quality of the depth map is related to 3D perception and therefore it is important that investigate the mutual relation between the upsampled depth map and 3D perception. This important subject has often ignored by most of the depth map upsampling works. In this paper, we implement diverse upsampling methods and find the relation between 3D perception and objective measurement tools such as PSNR, sharpness degree, and blur metric. Experimental results demonstrate that edge PSNR map is important to 3D perception rather than sharpness degree or blur metric.*

Keywords: depth map, upsampling, 3D perception, objective measurement

1 Introduction

Following the significant advances in depth acquisition technologies over the last few years, high-performance active range sensors have been developed recently. They capture accurate per-pixel distance information of a real scene [1, 2] which is represented in the form of a depth map. It is often necessary to increase the spatial resolution of a low resolution (LR) depth map in order to obtain a high-resolution (HR) depth map. For this, diverse upsampling methods have been introduced. For instance, bi-linear and cubic interpolations [3] are common methods even though they produce noticeable blurring at the edges. To overcome this problem, a bilateral interpolation has been introduced [4]. As well, its variants such as joint bilateral filtering [5], distance transform-based upsampling [6], variance-based bilateral upsampling [7], and adaptive upsampling [8]. Among them, the joint bilateral upsampling and adaptive upsampling methods use both color data and depth map.

Most of depth map upsampling works have focused on the comparison of upsampled depth map and original depth map. One of objective measurement tools frequently used is PSNR (peak-to-signal noise). Using this measurement, they evaluate the performance of their methods. In 3D stereoscopic field, a depth map plays an important role in the performance of 3D perception. The quality of the depth map is related to 3D pereption and therefore it is of importance that we investigate the relation between the upsampled depth map and 3D perception. This important subject has often been ignored by most of research works on the depth map upsampling.

In this paper, we implement diverse upsamping methods and investigate the relation between 3D perception and objective measurement tools such as PSNR, *sharpness degree*, and *blur metric*. It is the main purpose of this paper to find the relation between such objective measurements and 3D stereoscopic images. DIBR (depth image based rendering) or 2D+Depth is used to generate a stereoscopic image.

Fig. 2 shows the overall framework that examines the relation between upsampling methods and 3D perception.

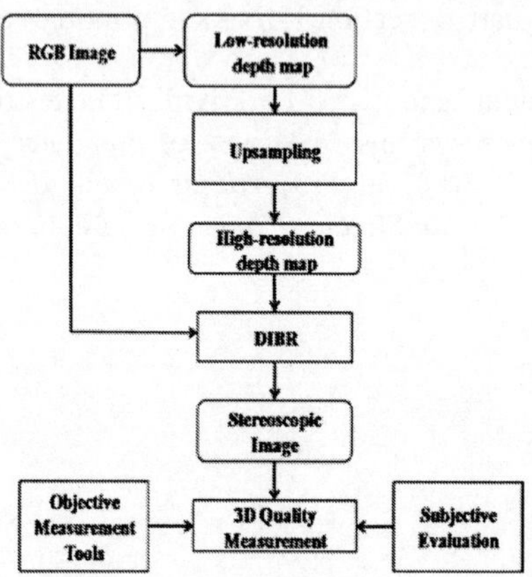

Fig. 1 shows the flow diagram for testing 3D quality of depth upsampling methods.

This paper is organized as follows: In the next section, we describe depth map upsampling methods that are used in our experiment. DIBR method is introduced in Section 3 followed by the experimental results of Section 4. Finally, we summarize our work in Section 5.

2 Upsampling Methods and Performance Measurement

2.1 Test Upsampling Methods

Until now, a varity of depth map upsampling algorithms have been introduced. Since it is difficult to investigage all methods, we have selected several methods that are expected to fulfill the goal of this work.

The *bilinear upsampling* (BLU) is widely used due to its simple implementation. Here, four neighboring pixels are weighted averaged using the Euclidian distance between them and its pixel to be interpolated. Eq. (1) shows the derivation process of the bilinear interpolation.

$$\begin{aligned} D_{X1} &= D_1 + l_x \cdot (D_2 - D_1) \\ D_{X2} &= D_3 + l_x \cdot (D_3 - D_4) \\ D_m &= D_{X1} + l_y \cdot (D_{X1} - D_{X2}) \end{aligned} \tag{1}$$

The *bicubic upsampling* (BCU) utilizes sixteen neighboring pixels as in Eq. (2)

$$f(x) = \begin{cases} (a+2)|x|^r - (a+3)|x|^2 + 1 & 0 \le |x| < 1 \\ a|x|^r - 5a|x|^2 + 8a|x| - 4a & 1 \le |x| < 2 \\ 0 & 2 \le |x| \end{cases} \tag{2}$$

The *bilateral upsampling* (BU) has been widly used for depth map upsampling [4]. Unlike the two previous interpolations, this upsampling preseves the edge, because the bilateral interpolation is an edge-preserving filter. The bilateral interpolation combines both a spatial filter and a range filter. More formally, given a low resolution (LR) depth $D^L{}_q$, a high resolution (HR) depth $D^H{}_p$ is computed by

$$D_p^H = \frac{\sum_{q \in S} w_q \cdot D_q^L}{\sum_{q \in S} w_q} \tag{3}$$

where p is an interpolated pixel and q is a reference pixel in S. S denotes the size of a filter. The weighting factor w_q is the multiplication of f and g.

$$w_q = f(\|p-q\|) \cdot g(D_p^H - D_q^L) \tag{4}$$

where f and g are the spatial and range weighting functions. For f and g, exponential functions are used as follows:

$$f(\|p-q\|) = \exp\left(\frac{-\|p-q\|^2}{2\sigma_a^2}\right) \tag{5}$$

$$g[D_p^H - D_q^L] = \exp\left(\frac{-[D_p^H - D_q^L]^2}{2\sigma_b^2}\right) \tag{6}$$

where $\|p-q\|$ is Ecluideean distance between pixels p and q.

Other upsampling methods that are based on the bilateral upsampling are a *joint bilateral upsampling* (JBU) [5], *variance-based upsampling* (VBU) [7], *distance transform-based upsampling* (DTBU) [6] and *adaptive bilateral upsampling* (ABU) [8]

The JBU utlizes both a color data and its low-resolution depth map, from which an upsampled depth map is reconstructed as follow s »

$$\begin{aligned} D_p &= \frac{1}{k_p} \sum_{q_\downarrow \in \Omega} D_{q_\downarrow} f(\|p_\downarrow - q_\downarrow\|) g(\|I_p - I_q\|) \\ g(\|I_p - I_q\|) &= \exp\left(\frac{-(\|I_p - I_q\|)^2}{2\sigma_a^2}\right) \end{aligned} \tag{7}$$

where I_p and I_q are grayscale value of p and q. f and g are defined in Eqs. (5) and (6).

Since the BU and JBU use a Gaussian function for the weighting function, the two variances σ_a and σ_b in f and g functions are needed. For this, a constant variance is often used. The VBU avoids the usage of the constant variance and uses a variance that is computed on each pixel block. The variance of local windows that contain inter-region edges are larger than that in homogenuous regions. In order to preseve detail or edge pixels that located near the center of the window, their neighborhood pixels should have small weight in the upsampling process. The variance of the local window replaces σ_b of Eq. (5) in the VBU.

Therefore an optimum variance σ_D can be incorporated into Eq. (7) and we obtain the following g function.

$$g(\|I_p - I_q\|) = \exp\left(\frac{-(\|I_p - I_q\|)^2}{2\sigma_D^2}\right) \tag{8}$$

The disadvantage of the JBF is that it is sensitive to homogenuous regions even though it performs well at edge pixels. Therfore, at non-edge pixels, the weighting function can be assigned a wrong variance. To solve this problem, an adaptive bilateral upsampling method (ABU) has been proposed, where a large weight is assigned to color image at edge pixels and a large weight is assigned to depth data at non-edge pixels [7]. Eq. (9) shows the formulae of the adaptive upsampling method.

$$D_p^h = \frac{1}{k_p} \sum_{q_l \in \omega} I_q^l f(\|p^l - q^l\|) [\alpha(\Delta) g(\|I_p^h - I_q^h\|) + (1-\alpha(\Delta)) h(\|D_p^l - D_q^l\|)] \tag{9}$$

The aforementioned methods have limitation in reducing blur at low-gradient edge regions. To overcome this, a *distance transform-based bilateral upsampling* (DTBU) have been proposed. Here, a range weighting function is controlled by the distance transform (DT) values [6]. Since the distance transform represents the distance between edges extracted from an image and all pixel positions in it [9], we can estimate whether a pixel belongs to a homogenous region or not. A DT map expresses the value of DT of an image. Before DT, *Canny* edge operator is used to extract a depth edge map E_D. For DT map generation, we perform DT on E_D in order to obtain DT map. Initially, edge pixels in E_D are set to zero, while non-edge pixels are assigned infinity value. Formally, based on *a-b* distance transform, the DT value $q^k(i, j)$ at iteration k is represented by

$$q^k(i,j) = \min\ [q^{k-1}(i-1,j-1)+b, q^{k-1}(i-1,j)+a, q^{k-1}(i-1,j+1)+b, \\ q^{k-1}(i,j-1)+a, q^{k-1}(i,j), q^{k-1}(i,j+1)+a, \\ q^{k-1}(i+1,j-1)+b, q^{k-1}(i+1,j)+a, q^{k-1}(i+1,j+1)+b] \quad (10)$$

where a and b define the strength of distance transform. b is empirically set to be a+1. A pixel near from its closest edge is assigned a small DT value. A pixel distant from the edge has a great DT value.

In the DTBU, a DT function e_{dt} is incorporated into function f as follows:

$$f(e_{dt}\cdot\|p-q\|) = \exp\left(\frac{-e_{dt}\cdot\|p-q\|^2}{2\sigma_a^2}\right) \quad (11)$$

e_{dt} is defined by

$$e_{dt} = \exp(-\tau) \quad (12)$$

τ is a distance transform value. Then, an upsampled pixel is computed by

$$D_{dt}^H = \frac{\sum_{q\in S}\omega_q\cdot D_q^L}{\sum_{q\in S}\omega_q} \quad (13)$$

where the weigting function w is computed by

$$\omega_q = f(e_{dt}\cdot\|p-q\|)\cdot g(|D_p^L - D_q^L|) \quad (14)$$

2.2 Performance Mesasurement Tools

For this, we firstly measure the objective performance measurements such as PSNR (peak-to-signal noise ratio), sharpness degree [10], and blur metric [11]. Sharpness or blur measurement are adopted to find whether they are related to 3D stereoscopic perception. On the contrary, PSNR is also used because it is a de-factor measurement among depth upsampling method comparison.

PSNR is defined by

$$PSNR = 10\cdot\log[\frac{\sum(D^h - D^U)^2}{255^2}] \quad (15)$$

where D_u is an upsampled depth map.

Sharpness degree is used to represent the extent of sharpness of the image and is defined by

$$\text{Sharpnees Degree} = \frac{1}{MN}\sum_{i=0}^{M-1}\sum_{j=0}^{N-1} G^2(x,y) \quad (16)$$

where

$$G(x,y) = D(x,y) - D(x\text{-}1,y) + D(x,y) - D(x,y\text{-}1)$$

Another tool for measureing blur attempts to measure the spread of the edges. First, we apply an edge detector (e.g. a Soble edge detector) to a grayscale image. We scan each row of the image For pixels corresponding to an edge location, the start and end positions of the edge are defined as the locations of the local extrema closest to the edge. The spread of the edge is then given by the distance between the end and start positions, and is identified as the local blur measure for this edge location. The global blur measure for the whole image is obtained by averaging the local depth values overal all edges found.

$$\text{Blur Metric} = \frac{\text{Sum of all edge widths}}{\text{No. of edges}} \quad (17)$$

3 Stereoscopic Image Generation

3.1 DIBR (Depth-based Image Rendering)

Given an RGB image and its upsampled depth map, a stereoscopic image can be made by DIBR(depth image-based rendering). Given a depth data D, the amount of shift (or disparity) d is computed by

$$d = \rho\times\left(1.0 - \frac{D_F}{255}\right) \quad (18)$$

where ρ is a maximum shift.

Then, we shift each pixel by d in the horizontal direction and make a left image I_L and a right image I_R as follows :

$$I_L(x-d,y) = I(x,y) \\ I_R(x+d,y) = I(x,y) \quad (19)$$

3.2 Subjective 3D Evaluation

We observed the stereoscopic images with a 3D monitor adopting DQCQS (Double Stimulus Continuous Quality Scale) subjective test [13]. At the first stage, original views were displayed to ten participants. Each participant watched an original stereoscopic image for 10 seconds and another stereoscopic image made by an upsampled depth map for the same period, and evaluated the effect of the 3D depth. For each image data, similar viewing was carried out in order to examine the 3D perception. Depth perception was then subjectively judged on a scale of 1 (no), 2 (mild), 3 (average), 4 (good) and 5 (excellent) in terms of 3D perception.

4 Performance Evaluation of Measurement Tools

To investigate the relationship of a measurement tool and 3D subjective evaluation, we use two different approaches, *cross correlation* and *linear regression*.

A) *Cross-correlation* : The cross-correlation is a measure of similarity of two random variables and is defined by

$$\rho = \frac{Cov(x,y)}{\sigma_x\sigma_y} = \frac{\frac{1}{N-1}\sum_{i=1}^{N}(x_i-\bar{x})(y_i-\bar{y})}{\sigma_x\sigma_y} \quad (20)$$

where y is 3D subjective grade and x is a measurement grade of PSNR, sharpness degree and blur metric. The lager |ρ| is, the greater the relation between x and y is.

B) *Linear regression*: Given K measurement data and N upsamping methods, the linear regression finds optimal coefficients minimizing a residual error. For instance, suppose that X_i is measurement data and Y is 3D grade. Then the residual is computed by

$$\varepsilon = \sum_{i=1}^{N} [y_i - (\alpha_1 x_i^1 + \alpha_2 x_i^2 + \ldots + \alpha_{K-1} x_i^{K-1} + \alpha_K x_i^K)]^2 \quad (21)$$

In the matrix form,

$$Y = X \cdot A$$

$$\begin{bmatrix} y_1 \\ y_2 \\ \cdot \\ \cdot \\ y_N \end{bmatrix} = \begin{bmatrix} x_1^1 & x_1^2 & \cdot & x_1^K \\ x_2^1 & x_2^2 & \cdot & x_2^K \\ x_3^1 & x_3^2 & \cdot & x_3^K \\ x_N^1 & x_2^2 & \cdot & x_N^K \end{bmatrix} \begin{bmatrix} \alpha_1 \\ \alpha_2 \\ \cdot \\ \cdot \\ \alpha_K \end{bmatrix} \quad (22)$$

From this, we have $\widetilde{A}$ an estimate of A that produces a minimum error of Eq. (21)

$$\widetilde{A} = (X^T X)^{-1} X^T Y \quad (23)$$

5 Experimental Results

As mentioned in the introduction, the aim of this work is to evaluate the peformance of depth map upsampling methods based 3D preception of a steroscopic image.

The performance of the seven methods is evaluated with the test depth maps, *aloe*, *bowling*, *cone*, *sawtooth*, *baby*, *woods*, *flowerpot*, *lampshade* from Middlebury stereo dataset [12]. Fig. 2 shows the test RGB and depth maps. In order to obtain low-resolution depth maps, we downsampled the original data. Then, we made high-resolution depth maps.

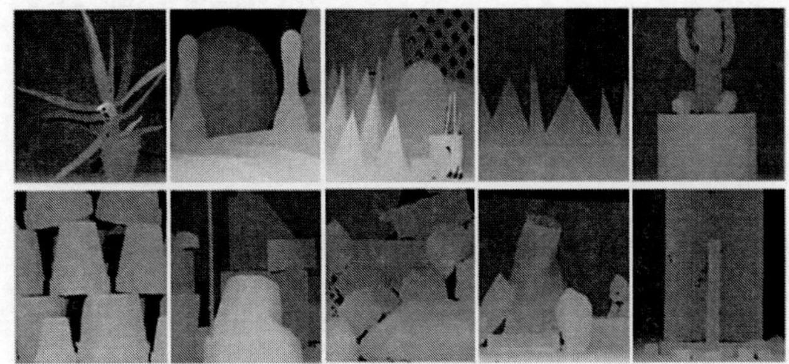

Fig. 2 Test RGB and depth maps provided by Middlebury [12]

Figs. 3~5 show the upsampled depth maps of the seven methods for *aloe*, *cone*, and *bowling*. The stereoscopic images are shown in Fig. 6.

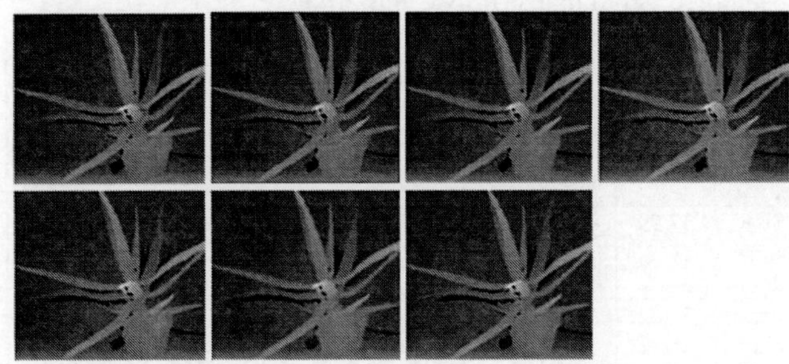

Fig. 3 Upsampled depth map of *aloe* obtained by BLU, BCU, BU, DTBU, JBF, ABU and VBU in the scan order.

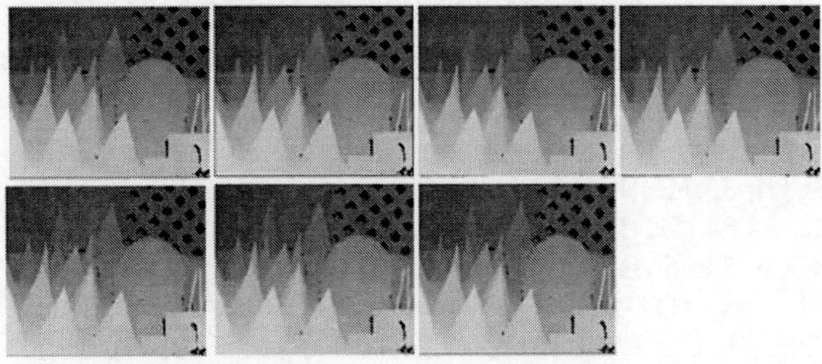

Fig. 4 Upsampled depth map of obtained by BLU, BCU, BU, DTBU, JBF, ABU and VBU in the scan order.

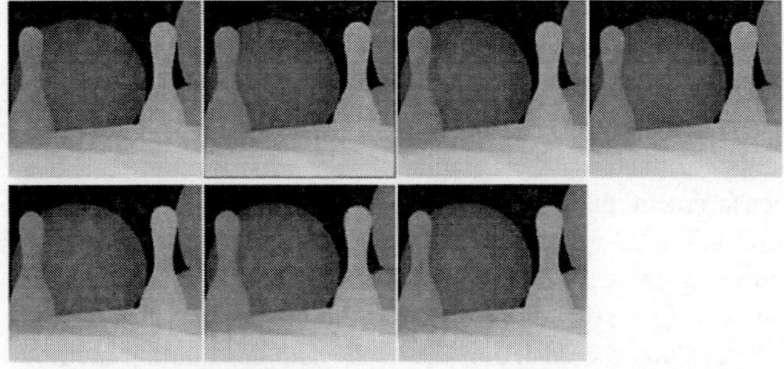

Fig. 5 Upsampled depth map of *bowling* obtained by BLU, BCU, BU, DTBU, JBF, ABU and VBU in the scan order.

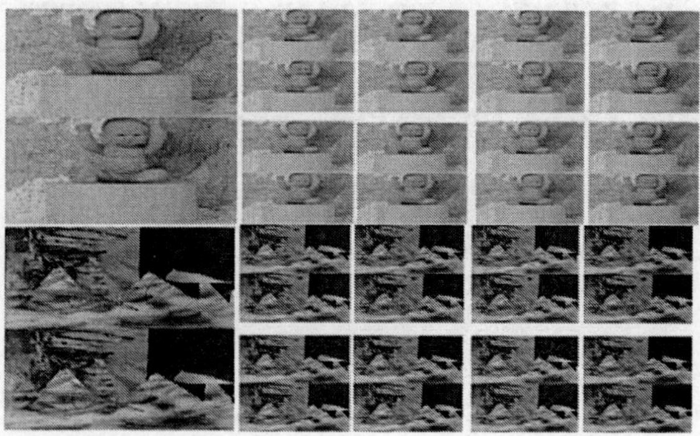

Fig. 6 Stereoscopic images in top-bottom format.

Table 1. Average measurement data and visual fatigue of upsampled depth maps (PSNR unit: dB)

Depth map	BLU	BCU	BU	JBF	VBU	ABU	DTBU
PSNR(image)	35.30	35.21	35.11	34.61	35.15	33.34	34.54
PSNR (edge)	24.34	24.27	24.36	23.54	24.08	21.27	23.81
PSNR (non-edge)	37.99	37.82	37.82	37.29	37.85	35.17	37.07
Sharpness Degree	51.02	54.33	54.33	62.54	41.48	113.88	87.63
Blur metric	10.27	12.42	12.42	12.31	12.28	87.63	12.10
Visual Fatigue	3.93	3.55	3.89	3.94	3.97	3.62	4.05

Table 1 compares the measurement data of the seven upsampling methods. The image PSNRs are 35.3 (BLU), 35.21 (BCU), 35.11 (BU), 34.61 (JBF), 35.15 (VBU), 33.34 (ABU) and 34.54 (DTBU). The edge PSNRs are 24.34 (BLU), 24.27 (BCU), 24.36 (BU), 23.54 (JBF), 24.08 (VBU), 21.27 (ABU) and 23.81 (DTBU). The non-edge PSNRs are 37.99 (BLU), 37.92 (BCU), 37.82 (BU), 37.29 (JBF), 37.85 (VBU), 35.17 (ABU) and 37.07 (DTBU). The average sharpness degrees are 51.02 (BLU), 54.33 (BCU), 54.33 (BU), 62.54 (JBF), 41.48 (VBU), 113.88 (ABU) and 87.63 (DTBU). The average BMs are 10.27 (BLU), 12.42 (BCU), 12.42 (BU), 12.31 (JBF), 12.28 (VBU), 87.63 (ABU) and 10.47 (DTBU). Finally, the visual fatigue values obtained by the subjective test are 3.93 (BLU), 3.55 (BCU), 3.89 (BU), 3.94 (JBF), 3.97 (VBU), 3.62 (ABU) and 4.05 (DTBU).

Fig. 7 shows the graph of the distribution of five measurement data and the visual fatigue grade. The cross correlation of each measurement tool and visual fatigue is shown in Table 2. The sharpness degree and blur metric have lowest values and edge PSNR has the largest one. This result indicates that the design of the depth map upsampling method should consider the improvement of edge PSNR. On the contrary either sharpness or blur is not an important factor in the depth map upsampling.

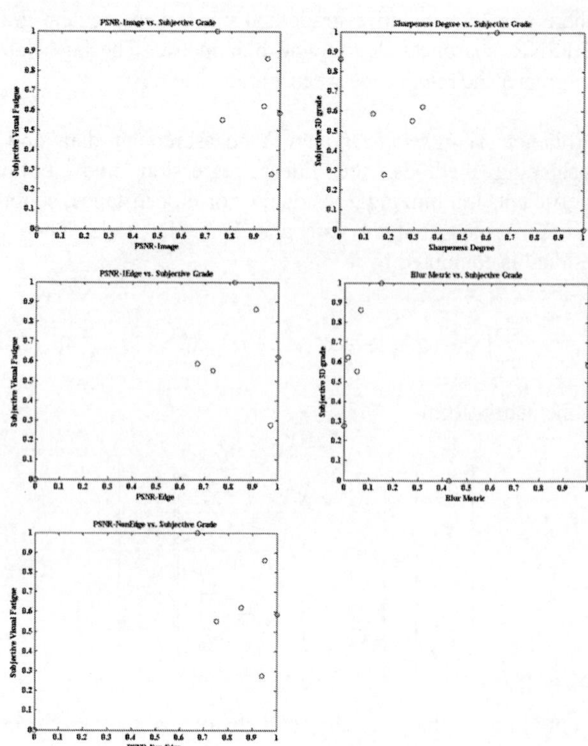

Fig. 7 The distribution of the five measurement data and visual fatigue.

Table 2. Cross correlation ρ between measurement data and visual fatigue

	PSNR (image)	PSNR (edge)	PSNR (non-edge)	Sharpness Degree	Blur metric
Visual Fatigue	0.6063	0.6405	0.5831	-0.4318	-0.1656

From the linear regression, the estimated coefficient is $\widetilde{A}$ = [-10.56, 6.98, 4.15, -0.75, 2.05]. This shows that the upsampling method needs to be designed satistfying $\widetilde{A}$.

$$\widetilde{\mathrm{A}} = \begin{bmatrix} \alpha_1 \\ \alpha_2 \\ \alpha_3 \\ \alpha_4 \\ \alpha_5 \end{bmatrix} = \begin{bmatrix} -10.56 \\ 6.98 \\ 4.15 \\ -0.75 \\ 2.05 \end{bmatrix} \quad (24)$$

6 Conclusions

In this paper, we have implemented diverse depth map methods and made steroscopic image with RGB image and upsampled depth maps. To find the relationship between 3D perception and upsamling methods, objective measurement tools such as PSNR, sharpness degree and blur metric were calculated. Also, the visua fatigue was graded for 3D perception of the stereoscopic images. The relation was mathematically expressed by the cross correlation as well as the linear regression method. Based on the experiment carried out in the subjective evaluation, we conclude that edge PSNR is a more important factor rather than blur and sharpness for

3D stereoscopic image. Futher the linear regress analysis found that an optimal upsampling method needs to be designed to satisfy the optimal coefficient values.

7 Acknowlegement

This work was supported in part by the IT R&D program of MKE/KCC/KEIT. [KI002058, Signal Processing Elements and their SoC Developments to Realize the Integrated Service System for Interactive Digital Holograms] and in part bby the MKE (The Ministry of Knowledge Economy)/KEIT, Korea under System and Semiconductor Application Promotion Project.

8 References

[1] G. J. Iddan and G. Yahav, "3D imaging in the studio and elsewhere," Proc. of Videometrics and Optical Methods for 3D Shape Measurements, San Jose, CA, USA, pp. 48-55, 2001.

[2] A. A. Dorrington, A. D. Payne, and M. J. Cree, "An evaluation of time-of-flight cameras for close range methodology applications," International Archives of Photogrammetry, Remote Sensing and Spatial Information Sciences, vol. XXXVIII, Part 5 Commission V Symposium, 2010.

[3] C. De Boor, "Bicubic spline interpolation," J. Math. and Phys., 41, 212-218, 1962.

[4] C. Tomasi and R. Manduchi, "Bilateral Filtering for Gray and Color Image," In Proc. IEEE Int. Conf. on Computer Vision, 836-846, 1998.

[5] J. Kopf, M. F. Cohen, D. Lischinski and M. Uyttendaele, "Joint bilateral upsampling," ACM Trans. on Graphics, vol. 26, no. 3, pp.1-6, 2007

[6] S. Jang, D. Lee, S. Kim, H. Choi, M. Kim, "Depth Map Upsampling with Improved Sharpness," Jounal of Broadcast Engineering, Vol. 17, No. 6, pp. 933-944, Nov. 2012.

[7] C. Pham, S. Ha, and J. Jeon, "A local variance-based bilateral filtering for artifact-free detail- and edge-preserving smoothing," PSIVT, Part II, LNCS 7088, pp. 60-70, 2011

[8] D. Yeo, E. Haq, J. Kim, M. Baig, H. Shin, "Adaptive Bilateral Filtering for Noise Removal in Depth Upsampling," SoC Design Conf., pp. 36-39, 2010.

[9] G. Borgefors, "Hierarchical chamfer matching: a parametric edge matching algorithm," IEEE Tran. Pattern Analysis Machine Intelligence, 10(6), pp. 849-865, 1988.

[10] C. Tsai, H. Liu, M. Tasi, "Design of a scan converter using the cubic convolution interpolation with canny edge detection, " 2011 International Conference on Electric Information and Control Engineering (ICEICE), pp. 5813-5816, Apr. 2011.

[11] P. Marziliano, F. Dufaux, S. Winkler, and T. Ebrahimi, "Perceptual blur and ringing metrics: application to JPEG2000," Int. Workshop on Multimedia Signal Processing, pp.403-408, Oct. 2008.

[12] D. Scharstein and R. Szeliski, "A taxonomy and evaluation of dense two-frame stereo correspondence algorithms," Int. J. of Computer Vision, vol. 47, no. 1-3, pp. 7-42, 2002

[13] E. Lee, H. Heo, and K. Park, "The comparative measurements of eyestrain caused by 2D and 3D displays," IEEE Trans. on Consumer Electronics, Vol. 56 , Issue 3, pp. 1677–1683, 2010

Relative Depth Estimation using a Rotating Camera System

Pallav Garg, Suresh Yerva and Krishnan Kutty
Centre for Research in Engineering Sciences and Technology (CREST)
KPIT Cummins Infosystems Ltd.
Pune, India
{Pallav.Garg, Suresh.Yerva and Krishnan.Kutty}@kpitcummins.com

***Abstract*— In the proposed method, the relative depth of the objects present in a 3D scene is calculated, using 2D images captured from a camera placed on a rotating platform. Unlike the conventional stereo imaging system, the proposed method captures multiple views of a 3D scene, each view taken at a different camera positions while on the rotating platform. The approach adapted calculates the disparity between the corresponding pixels present in both the views to get the relative depth of the objects. The relative depth of the objects can be calculated for the objects which are in common FOV (Field of View) of both the views captured. By virtue of the rotating platform, the proposed system is capable of creating a depth map in full 360 degree field of view unlike its traditional counterpart. The approach presented is a thereby also cost effective way for depth estimation since only one camera is being used.**

Keywords—stereo; image rectification; stereo matching; disparity; depth map

I. INTRODUCTION

Human beings tend to perceive depth by virtue of a powerful combination of a pair of eyes and a powerful neural network that estimates the depth based on the images captured on the retina by both the eyes. The same concept of stereo vision is employed in various robotic applications today- thanks to the active research happening in the field of Computer Vision. The research in computer vision started with simple analysis and interpretation of images and image data. Later, the development in the field of computer vision increased rapidly. The various developments in the field of computer vision include obstacle avoidance with stereo vision [1], automatic navigation, object recognition, pedestrian detection, medical imaging etc. Computer vision plays a vital role in automotive industry for driver assistance systems, which reduces the driver efforts. One of the important research areas in computer vision is stereo vision.

The existing stereo vision system comprises of two cameras placed at certain known distance to capture the two different views of a scene. The stereo vision system estimates the 3D point of the object in real world based on 2 images.

The following are some of the techniques used for calculating the depth of an object. The LASER (Light Amplification by Stimulated Emission of Radiation) Triangulation [2] projects LASER on an object and acquires the height profile using a camera. In [3], a known light pattern is projected on to an object. The depth information is calculated according to the distortion of the light pattern. Time of Flight (TOF) based Depth Sensor [4] synchronizes light source with image sensor in order to calculate distance based on the time between the pulse of light and the reflected light back onto the sensor. In the field of medical imaging, Optical Coherence Tomography (OCT) [5], uses infrared light to calculate depth information by measuring the reflections of light through the cross-section of the object. These are the some of the different technologies [6] to find the distance of an object from the source. Over the last decade, these techniques either got replaced or boosted up based on the performance of existing techniques. There are also some shortcomings of these methods. In the LASER triangulation method, the LASER sensor should be kept clean; else it may affect the accuracy of the system [7]. TOF based depth camera has low resolution which sometimes gives non homogeneous depth map, intensity based distance error and light interference effects [8]. These technologies are costly and take significant time to acquire data of an object. In order to optimize the cost and make the system work in various conditions, a rotating camera system is proposed.

Applications of scene reconstruction can be found not only in earth sciences but also in entertainment industry and in cultural heritage digital archival. The proposed system has common application in robotic vision, military (for spying), and to develop an autonomous vehicle. This system also finds applications where it can be used as a shape identifier, such as finding the shapes of bottle or coffee cup. It can also be used to enhance the accuracy of identification systems like facial recognition or other biometrics [6].

The rest of the paper is organized as follows: Section II describes our methodology; Section III shows the results and discussions; Section IV emphasis on concluding remarks thereafter appropriate references are provided.

II. METHODOLOGY

There are two approaches to obtain depth map of the scene. The first is a conventional approach, based on the camera calibration. This results in deriving the intrinsic and extrinsic parameters. This is followed by a process called Image Rectification (using intrinsic parameters), which aligns the row of both the views and further performing stereo matching to obtain depth information.

A camera transforms a point in the real world onto a point in 2D coordinate system. This transformation can be sub-divided into two transformations: *Extrinsic Transformation* projects real world coordinate into camera coordinate and *Intrinsic Transformation* projects camera coordinate into image coordinate system. Extrinsic Transformation is depicted as given below:

$$\begin{bmatrix} x \\ y \\ z \end{bmatrix} = R \begin{bmatrix} x_w \\ y_w \\ z_w \end{bmatrix} + T \quad (1)$$

(x_w, y_w, z_w) = Object world coordinate system

(x, y, z) = Camera 3D coordinate system

The parameters to be calibrated are *R* and *T,* where *R* is the (3 x 3) rotation matrix.

$$R = \begin{bmatrix} r_1 & r_2 & r_3 \\ r_4 & r_5 & r_6 \\ r_7 & r_8 & r_9 \end{bmatrix} \quad (2)$$

And T is the translation vector

$$T = \begin{bmatrix} T_x \\ T_y \\ T_z \end{bmatrix} \quad (3)$$

Intrinsic Transformation is depicted as given below:

$$s \begin{bmatrix} X \\ Y \\ 1 \end{bmatrix} = \begin{bmatrix} f_x & \gamma & O_x \\ 0 & f_y & O_y \\ 0 & 0 & 1 \end{bmatrix} \begin{bmatrix} x \\ y \\ z \end{bmatrix} \quad (4)$$

Where, s = scaling factor

$\begin{bmatrix} X \\ Y \\ 1 \end{bmatrix}$ = 2D-image coordinates

f_x, f_y = Horizontal and Vertical focal lengths of camera

O_x, O_y = Center of image

γ = Skew coefficient

[9, 10], describes in depth, the details of camera calibration with lens distortion. The second approach computes disparity without performing camera calibration i.e., without using exact intrinsic parameters for image rectification. This is an uncalibrated rectification approach, which is then followed by stereo matching. The second approach is presented in this paper.

Fig. 1 depicts the process flow in estimating the depth information.

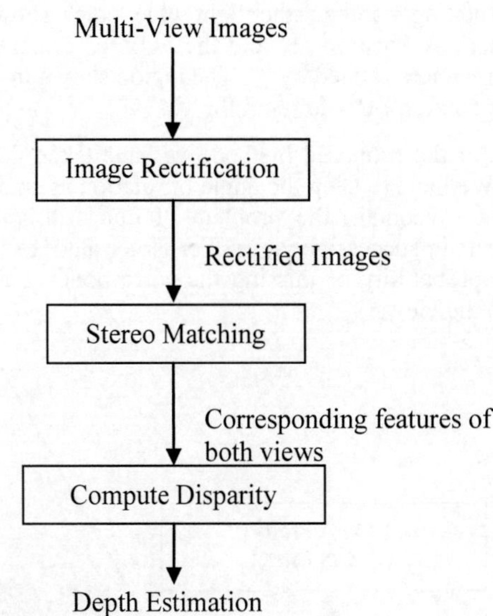

Fig. 1. Flow of Rotating Camera System

We have used the second approach since our set-up involves the use of a moving camera which in turn leads to the high calibration errors. Camera calibration is conventionally performed using images of a checker-board. However, due to the camera being placed on the rotating platform, many corners points of checker-board image are not captured simultaneously, in both views (at different camera position). This adds to the complexity for performing camera calibration. When the camera calibration was performed using image from the rotating platform, the 'pixel error' was 0.3167. This value is high when compared to the conventional stereo vision, when performed on normal stereo image pairs. [10] is used for the approximation of the pixel errors and distortion coefficient. Fig. 2 shows the error in detecting corners in various checker board images.

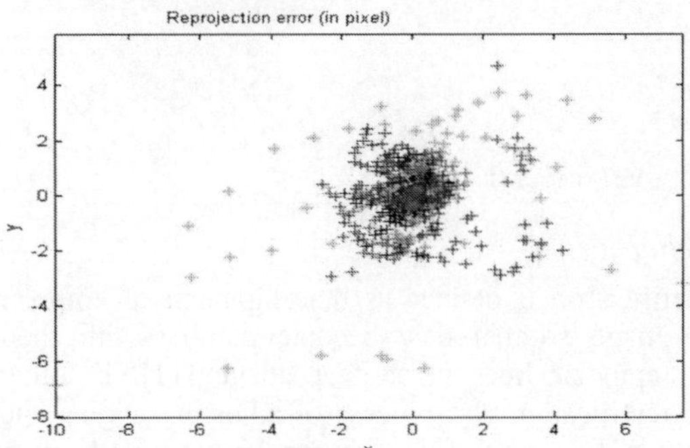

Fig. 2. Re-Projection Error Analysis

A. *Setup for Capturing Images at Different Camera Position*

In Fig.3, the setup for capturing images using the proposed rotating platform is depicted. Fig. 3 also illustrates the direction of rotating camera; the light blue color shows the FOV of camera at Position '1' and the FOV of camera at position '2' after camera rotated by θ°. The region shown in dark blue shows the common FOV for both the views.

For the proposed method, we have taken the images at θ = 5°. We have to keep the angle of rotation as small as possible in order to contain the problem of quick disappearance of the objects in successive views. For larger angles say θ > 10°, there is a probability of missing the corresponding feature points in both the views.

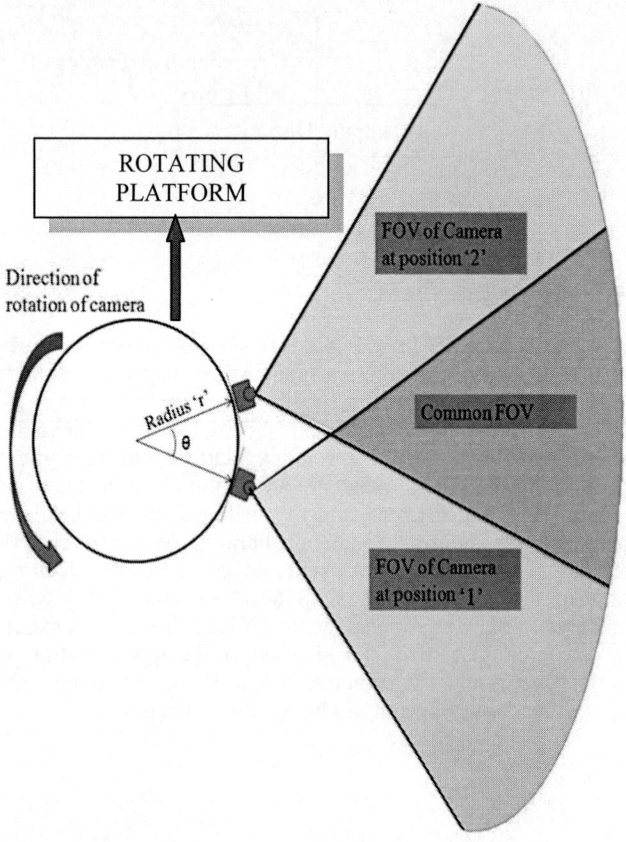

Fig. 3. Proposed setup to capture the Images

B. *Image Rectification*

Image Rectification is defined as the alignment of epipolar lines of one image so that they become parallel with their corresponding epipolar lines in another image [11]. In other words, image rectification is a process of adjusting angles and distances between the views of two images. Image Rectification results in row aligned and rectified images. Fig. 4 and Fig. 5 depict the epipolar lines before and after alignment respectively.

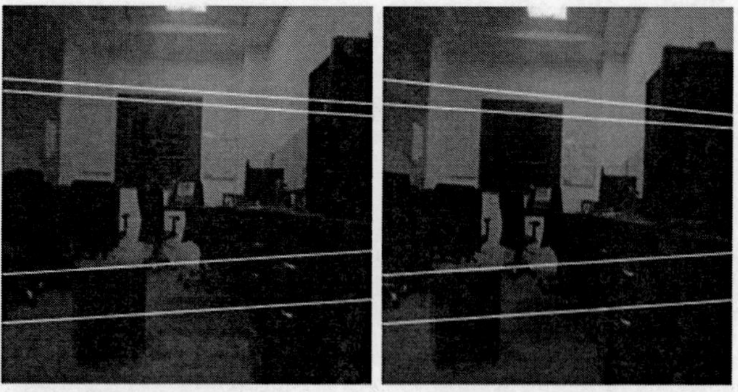

Fig. 4. Original Images showing corresponding epipolar lines in both image

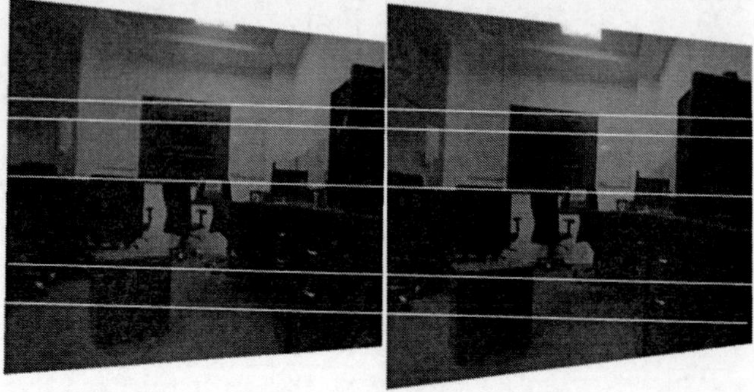

Fig. 5. Rectified Images showing epipolar lines

There are not many algorithms that perform image rectification without camera calibration. In this paper, we have adopted Fusiello and Luca Irsara's [12] approach, which performs image rectification without the need for calibrating the camera. This algorithm solves the problem of calculating camera projection matrices. This algorithm is best suited for rectifying images with two views. This method rotates the pair of projective images in order to make a pair of rectified images based on epipolar constraints. Other related algorithms that could also be used are Hartley's approach [13] which makes use of fundamental matrix to calculate rigid transformation; Isgro and Trucco's approach [14], which rectify images from feature points directly without calculating the fundamental matrix. There are few assumptions in our proposed approach. viz., intrinsic parameters are not known and corresponding points in both the views are available.

$$c_1^j \leftrightarrow c_2^j \tag{5}$$

Where, j is j^{th} correspondence of both the views of camera at position '1' and position '2'.

The fundamental matrix of the rectified image pair is considered to be a cross product of a vector, $u_1 = (1,0,0)$ and a skew symmetric matrix which has $a_{ik} = -a_{ki}$.

Here, 'i' denotes the row number in a matrix and 'k' denotes the column number in a matrix. Therefore, fundamental matrix [15] of rectified image pair would be

$$F = \begin{bmatrix} 0 & 0 & 0 \\ 0 & 0 & -1 \\ 0 & 1 & 0 \end{bmatrix} \quad (6)$$

The geometric re-projection error is calculated by Simpson's Error [16] which is a first order approximation of geometric error. The advantage of calculating Simpson's error is to have an idea of rectification results on different pair of images. The Sampson error for j^{th} correspondence is

$$E_S^j = \frac{\left(m_T^{j\,T} F m_l^j\right)^2}{\left\|[u_3]_x F m_l^j\right\|^2 + \left\|m_T^{j\,T} F [u_3]_x\right\|^2} \quad (7)$$

Where, $u_3 = (0,0,1)$

We take $E_S^j = 0$ i.e., for all corresponding points the error is reduced to zero. The rectifying transformations of both the views considered are,

$$H_1 = K_{n1} R_1 K_{o1}^{-1} \quad (8)$$

$$H_2 = K_{n2} R_2 K_{o2}^{-1} \quad (9)$$

Where, k_{oz} = Old Intrinsic Parameters (z = 1 and 2) and R_1, R_2 = Rotation matrices, are unknown. Therefore, K_{n1}, K_{n2} are kept randomly with a condition that vertical focal length and vertical principal point are same. And to get the old intrinsic parameters, calculation is made easier by taking skew coefficient as zero, principal points at the center of the image.

$$K_{o1} = K_{o2} = \begin{bmatrix} f & 0 & w/2 \\ 0 & f & h/2 \\ 0 & 0 & 1 \end{bmatrix} \quad (10)$$

Where 'f' indicates the focal length of camera, 'w' indicates the width of the image captured, 'h' indicates the height of the image.

The focal length is expected to vary in the interval given by,

$$[\tfrac{1}{3}(w+h), 3(w+h)] \quad (11)$$

C. Stereo Matching

The stereo matching is a process of matching features or finding corresponding points between two images of a scene which helps to compute disparity between the pixels.

The technique used here for correspondence matching is Block Matching [17]. Block matching is performed using SAD (Sum of Absolute Differences) algorithm [18]. SAD is a fast template matching algorithm, which is advantageous to be used for real time scenes. For block matching, n x n pixel block is taken around every pixel of the reference image. This block slides on the other view in a same row of pixel as images are rectified. The matching is done on the basis of SAD result. Suppose, we have two blocks to be compared namely 'X' *and* 'Y', SAD is performed with (12).

The block is matched to the reference block when the result of SAD is minimum. For example, take one reference matrix and perform SAD with other image matrices. The one which gives sum as minimum is a respective matched block. The SAD can be represented by (12).

$$\chi(X,Y) = \sum_{i=1}^{n}\sum_{j=1}^{n} |X(i,j) - Y(i,j)| \quad (12)$$

Where, 'χ' indicates the Sum of Absolute Differences to the matrix 'X' of one view and matrix 'Y' of another view.

D. Disparity

The disparity is defined as a displacement of the pixel when the pixels are matched in two different views. The calculation of disparity of the pixel is shown in the below fig. 6 and (13)

$$d = X_l - X_r \quad (13)$$

Where, d = disparity, X_l = Pixel in first view, X_r = Pixel in second view

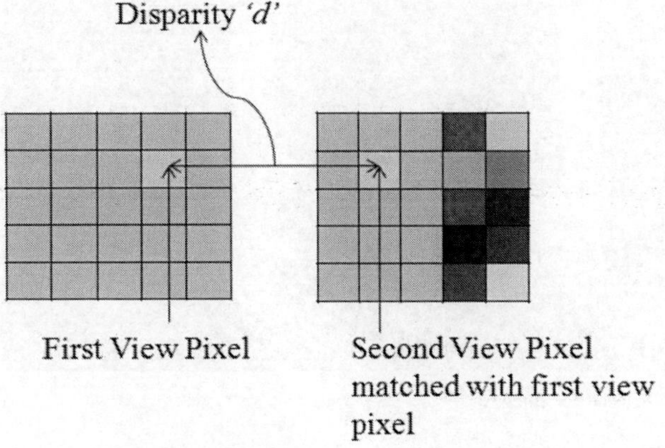

Fig. 6. Computation of Disparity

The relation between depth and disparity [19] is shown in (14). It can be inferred from (14) that higher the disparity between the pixels of an object, less will be the depth of that object.

$$Z = \frac{fT}{x^l - x^r} \quad (14)$$

Here, 'Z' indicates the depth of object from the camera; 'f' indicates the focal length of camera; 'T' indicates the distance between two fixed cameras; and $x^l - x^r$ = disparity between pixels.

III. Results And Discussions

The approach used in this paper is implemented on many set of rotated images taken in different environment. One pair of images is shown in Fig. 7. In this paper, the uncalibrated rectification is considered as compared to the conventional calibrated rectification. The uncalibrated rectification approach gives quite good results as compared to calibrated rectification results. Fig. 7 shows the original images captured at 5° rotation of camera along rotating platform.

Fig. 7. Original Images taken at 5° rotation of camera

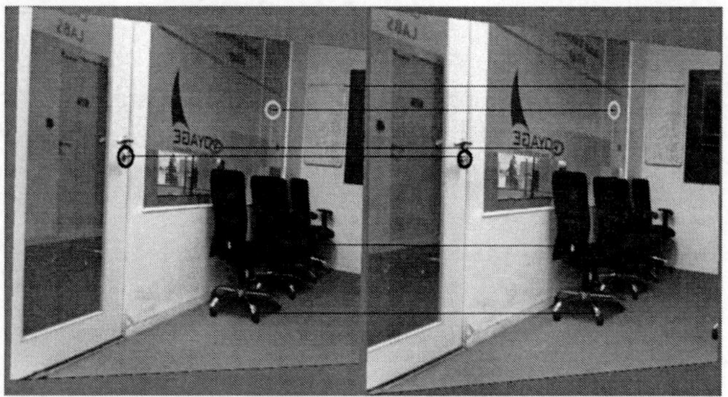

Fig. 8. Rectified Images

The rectified images corresponding to original images are shown in Fig. 8. The circles marked in Fig. 8 are some reference points taken to get the depth information of these marked points. Table I. shows the marked points, The door knob is represented by a black circle, 'V' point on side glass is represented by a red circle, and the upper corner of the side poster is represented by the light pink circle.

Table I shows the pixel positions from the rectified images and the corresponding disparity calculated with respect to the 'objects' marked with colored circles in Fig. 8. It can be noticed that the 'y' coordinate in first view is matched with the 'y' coordinate in second view. It clearly shows that the images are rectified and the disparity present is along 'x' direction only.

TABLE I. TABLE SHOWING DISPARITY BETWEEN MATCHED POINTS

	First View (x, y) in pixels	**Second View (x, y) in pixels**	**Disparity $d = X_l - X_r$**
Door Knob	(232,216)	(186,216)	46 pixels
'V' Point on Side Glass	(406,203)	(372,203)	34 pixels
Side Poster Upper Corner	(512,146)	(482,146)	30 pixels

With the calculation of disparity, the relative depth can be inferred as depth is inversely proportional to the disparity. Likewise, in given Fig. 7 and Fig. 8, the door knob is having highest disparity i.e., 46 pixels as compared to 'V' point on side glass which have 34 pixels and upper corner of side poster which have 30 pixels. From 14,

$$Z\ \alpha\ \frac{k}{d} \tag{15}$$

Where, 'k' indicates a constant value

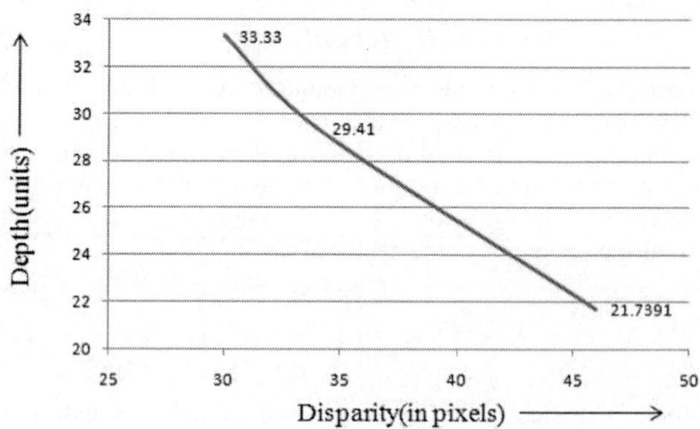

Fig. 9. Graph showing the relation between Disparity and Depth

In Fig. 9, the graph represents the depth corresponding to the disparity. It can be noticed that if disparity is decreasing or declining, the depth increases. Hence, it is clear that door knob is the closest point as depth comes to be the least according to the above relation i.e. and Side poster is the farthest point among other points taken in Fig. 8.

TABLE II. TABLE SHOWS OBJECT DISTANCE AND AVERAGE % ERROR

Objects Distance(in centimeters)	**% Error**
320	0.08125
415	4.40
532	7.70

Table II gives the average error at objects distance respectively.

Fig. 10 shows the average percentage error of the proposed system. The accuracy of the system depends on the quality of the camera and the rotation speed of the camera. For the proposed setup, the camera used is an off-the shelf web camera of VGA resolution (640 × 480).

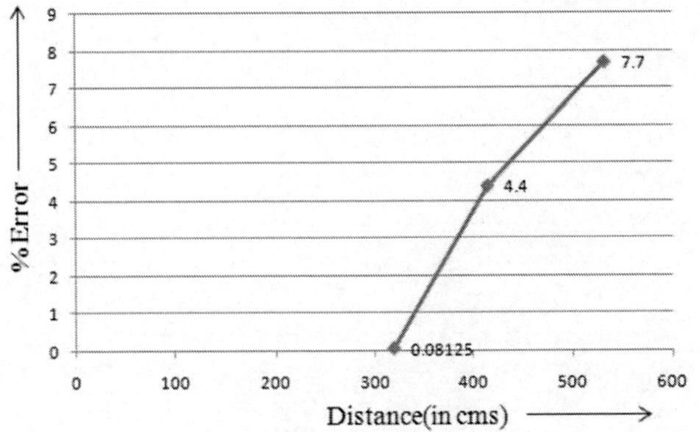

Fig. 10. Graph between Distance versus % Error

IV. CONCLUSION

The proposed single camera system on a rotating platform is a frugal method to estimate depth information a given object. The proposed system to find relative distance of the objects is theoretically and experimentally proven with the methodology adapted. It is difficult to find the depth of far objects as the disparity between the pixels of both views tends to move towards zero. The proposed stereo matching algorithm works better for images having noticeable pixel differences i.e., for the images with good texture, contrast etc. In future, we are planning to work more on the challenges faced. The major challenge of the system includes quick disappearance of the objects from the field of view of the camera as the camera is rotating. The future work includes estimating the absolute distance of an object from the axis of the rotating platform and to build a complete depth map of the environment around the camera set up.

REFERENCES

[1] G Steven Riddle, "Stereo Vision based Obstacle Avoidance," 2008/2009.

[2] Klancnik, Balik, Planinsic, "Obstacle Detection with Active LASER Triangulation," Advancement in Production Engineering & Management, pp. 79-90, 2007.

[3] J. Pages, J. Salvi, "Coded Light Projecttion Technique for 3D reconstruction," EDP Sciences, vol. 4 , 2005.

[4] S. Burak Gokturk, Hakan Yalcin, Cyrus Banji, "A Time-of-Flight Depth Sensor- System Description, Issues and Solutions," IEEE Computer Vision and Pattern Recognition Workshop, June 2004.

[5] Ian Y. Wong, Hideki Koizumi, Wico W. Lai, "Enhanced Depth Imaging Optical Coherence Tomography" Ophthalmic Surgery, LASERS & Imaging, vol. 42, No. 4, 2011.

[6] National Instruments, "3D Imaging with NI Lab VIEW," September 2012

[7] MTI Instruments Inc., "LASER Triangulation Systems".

[8] http://campar.in.tum.de/twiki/pub/Chair/TeachingSs11Kinect/2011-DSensors_LabCourse_Kinect.pdf

[9] Roger Y. Tsai, "A Versatile Camera Calibration Technique for High-Accuracy 3D Machine Vision Metrology Using Off-the-Shelf TV Cameras and Lenses," IEEE Journal of Robotics and Automation, vol. RA-3, No. 4, August 1987.

[10] Jean- Yves Bouguet, "Camera Calibration Toolbox for Matlab,".

[11] V. Srinivasa Rao, A. Satya Kalyan, "Comparative Study of Different Approaches for Efficient Rectification under General Motion," Indian Journal of Computer Science and Engineering, vol. 1, No. 4, pp. 251-257.

[12] Andrea Fusiello, Luca Irsara, "Quasi-Euclidean Uncalibrated Epipolar Rectification," IEEE International Conference on Pattern Recognition, 2008.

[13] Richard I. Hartley, "Theory and Practice of Projective Rectification," International Journal of Computer Vision, pp.115-127, 1999.

[14] Isgro, E. Trucco, "On Projective Rectification," IEEE conference on Image Processing and Analysis, vol. 1, pp. 42-46, July 1999.

[15] F. Isgro, E. Trucco, "Projective Rectification without Epipolar Geometry," IEEE Conference on Computer Vision and Pattern Recognition, pp. 94-99.

[16] R. Hartley, A. Zisserman, "Multiple View Geometry in Computer Vision," Cambridge University Press, 2nd ed., 2003.

[17] Kristian Ambrocsh, Wilfried Kubinger, Martin Humenburger, Andreas Steininger, "Flexible Hardware-Based Stereo Matching," EURASIP Journal on Embedded Systems, Article id. 386059, 2008.

[18] Nadir Nourain Dawoud, Brahim Belhaouari Samir, Josefina Janier, "Fast Template Matching Method Based Optimized Sum of Absolute Difference Algorithm for Face Localization," International Journal of Computer Applications, vol. 18, No. 8, March 2011.

[19] Gary Bradski, Adrian Kaehler, "Learning OpenCV," O'Reilly Media, Inc., 1st ed., September 2008.

SESSION

SURVEILLANCE, SAFETY, SECURITY APPLICATIONS, AND RELATED METHODS AND SYSTEMS

Chair(s)

TBA

A Secure ID Card based Authentication System using Watermarking

Peyman Rahmati[1], Thomas Tran[2], and Andy Adler[1]
[1]Dept. of Systems and Computer Eng., Carleton University, Ottawa, ON., Canada
[2]School of Electrical Eng. and Computer Science, University of Ottawa, Ottawa, ON., Canada

Abstract - *This paper shows a watermark-based approach to protect digital identity documents against a Print-Scan (PS) attack. We propose a secure ID card authentication system based on watermarking. For authentication purposes, a user/customer is asked to upload a scanned picture of a passport or ID card through the internet to fulfill a transaction online. To provide security in online ID card submission, we need to robustly encode personal information of ID card's holder into the card itself, and then extract the hidden information correctly in a decoder after the PS operation. The PS operation imposes several distortions, such as geometric, rotation, and histogram distortion, on the watermark location, which may cause the loss of information in the watermark. An online secure authentication system needs to first eliminate the distortion of the PS operation before decoding the hidden data. This study proposes five preprocessing blocks to remove the distortions of the PS operation: filtering, localization, binarization, undoing rotation, and cropping. Experimental results with 100 ID cards showed that the proposed online ID card authentication system has an average accuracy of 99% in detecting hidden information inside ID cards after the PS process. The innovations of this study are the implementation of an online watermark-based authentication system which uses a scanned ID card picture without any added frames around the watermark location, unlike previous systems.*

Keywords: Data hiding, geometric distortion, watermarking, and print-and-scan

1 Introduction

Copyright protection involves the authentication of the ownership and can be used to identify illegal copies. To detect reproduction of a digital product, a digital watermark created from information about the relationship between the product and its owner can be used. This information may be perceptible or imperceptible to the human senses. In 2009, Hirakawa and Iigima evaluated the effectiveness of using digital watermark technology for E-commerce website protection; and they reported a 60% reduction in the quantity of unauthorized content on E-commerce websites when protected by Digital watermarking technology [1]. In 2008, Sherekar et al. recommended that the watermarks for images in e-governance and e-commerce applications should be invisible for human eyes and robust for possible attacks, such as geometric attack, and compression attack (JPEG or other image compression formats) [2].

One of the most common attacks for watermarked multimedia products is Print-Scan (PS) process as the watermark can be degraded by the PS operation used once or several times [3]. The robustness of watermarking algorithm against PS attack for the online authentication system is a new, important challenge in multimedia communication security as well as E-commerce [4]. The progress in Print-Scan resilient watermarking will ease promoting watermark-based E-commerce and provide the ground for copyright tracking to prevent any illegally copying after selling a digital watermark product. This study proposes a watermark-based authentication system to be applied for an online, secure ID card submission. The proposed model in comparison with preceding models has five new preprocessing blocks in the decoder with the role of providing robustness for watermarking algorithm against PS distortions (figure 1).

The applications of the proposed online ID card based authentication system are where 1) a seller needs to check the identity of a buyer before successfully completing the trade through the internet and 2) an applicant needs to electronically submit his/her Passport/ ID card to a high security organization. For example, a company for authentication purposes may ask customers to upload a scanned picture of their watermarked Passport or watermarked ID card to continue a trade with them through the internet. The watermark extracted from the uploaded ID card image, which is already scanned from the hardcopy of the ID card, determines the genuineness of the hardcopy.

This paper is organized as follows: In the next section, we review related work and discuss their drawbacks; Section 3 is to explain the proposed ID card authentication method and also to detail the design of the five proposed preprocessing blocks in the decoder; Section 4 discusses the achieved experimental results; and finally conclusion is drawn in section 5.

2 Related works

In the print-scan resilient data hiding area, distortion parameters quantification due to print-scan operation is challenging. There are several papers that model Print-Scan

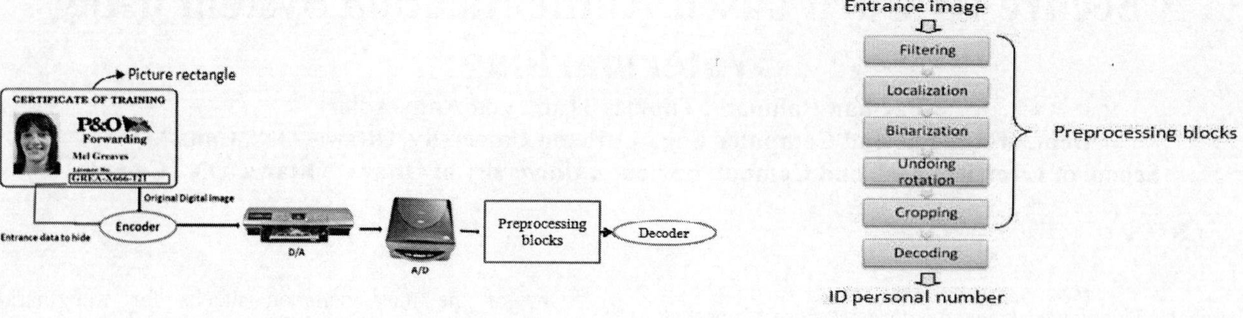

Fig. 1. Overall schematic of the proposed ID card based authentication system is presented in the left panel; and the sequence of applying the five proposed preprocessing blocks in the decoder to remove PS distortions is shown in the right panel.

distortions [5, 6]. The regained watermark from the inspected data is applied for authentication in different ways, such as localizing the occurred distortions [8-9] or recognizing the type of attacks performed [10].

The main challenge in online authentication system is to overcome the print-scan distortions, which is considered as a combination of different attacks [11]. Longjiang Yu [7] proposes a print-and-scan model so that his work is realized in the presence of an added rectangular frame around the watermark location. This rectangular frame around watermark location makes it easier to find the geometric distortion along the print-scan process, and to localize the watermark location. The main drawback of using a frame around the watermark location is that in various types of authentication applications either the presence of this frame is not allowed or not favorable. For example, it might not be allowed in important documents, such as passport, driving licence, and ID cards. Solanki et al. proposed a print-scan resilient data hiding algorithm analyzing halftone effect (intensity shift) occurred after print-and-scan operation for the sake of presenting a model of print-and-scan process [6]. The main drawback of their method is that halftone analyzing in PS operation is severely dependent to the hardware features of Printer and Scanner, which are variable from one commercial brand to another. This paper proposes a new online ID card authentication model which is different, compared with the preceding models [6, 7], in this way that it does not offer any added rectangular frame around the watermark location, and also there is no need to model halftone effect occurred after PS process.

3 Method

In this study, we used ID cards as the required document needed to be submitted through the internet for online authentication purposes. The proposed model establishes a linkage between the ID card holder's photo and his/her personal identification number, considered as the watermark. We use a simple block-based watermarking algorithm in spatial domain, and proposed five preprocessing blocks in the decoder to remove the PS distortions (figure 2). In the following, we will see the design of the proposed ID card based authentication system.

3.1 Encoder

In the first step of authentication system, we need to hide the personal information of user/customer into the original digital ID card image. We use block-based embedding due to its simplicity in implementation, providing low computing time for real time application. In this work, a simple block-based watermarking method using Hadamard patterns in spatial domain is introduced. The personal information, which is ID card personal number, is embedded into the ID card's holder photo place in the encoder. Two Hadamard patterns (f0 and f1) with small changes in their intensities, lower frequency than the frequency of the intensity changes in the original image, are applied to embed the data stream (ID card personal number) into the original image. First, the original image is divided into blocks with dimension of N×N and each bit of the data stream is assigned to each block. Then embedding procedure follows up this rule: if the bit of data stream assigned to a block is 0, f0 will add up to that block; if it is 1, f1 will add up to the block, see figure 2. The correlation between patterns (f0 and f1) and the blocks (B) is zero. Suppose that I is an original image with the dimensions N1×N2 which is divided into blocks, with the dimensions N×N. Since a bit of all desired data bits is embedded into each block, so, (N1.N2)/N2 bits can be hidden into the original image. Note that f0(k,l), f1(k,l) ; $0 \leq k, l \leq N-1$ are indicators of the Hadamard patterns, which has property of f0 = -f1, and B(k,l) indicates the blocks. We can write the binary bit (W(i, j)) to be hidden as follows:

$$W(i,j) \in \{0,1\}; \quad 0 \leq i \leq (N1/N)-1 \quad , \quad 0 \leq J \leq (N2/N)-1, \quad (1)$$

The embedding algorithm will start by converting the designed patterns to an image matrix. Therefore, the watermarked image is:

$$I_w(m,n)=I(m,n)+\lambda.f_w([m/N],[n/N])(m \text{ Mod } N, n \text{ Mod } N), \quad (2)$$

where $0 \leq m \leq N1-1$, $0 \leq n \leq N2-1$, IW (m, n) is the watermarked image, λ is Inductance Coefficient, [x] is the largest integer that is smaller or equal to x, and Mod is residue of an integer division. The above equation when f0 = -f1 can be shortened as:

$$I_w(m, n) = I(m, n) + \lambda.(2\ W([m/N],[n/N]) - 1).f\ (m \text{ Mod } N, n \text{ Mod } N) \quad (3)$$

Inductance Coefficient (λ) compromise between visual quality of the watermarked image and resistance of the used method against attacks. The bigger the Inductance Coefficient, the lower the quality of the watermarked image will be. In (3), if the bit in the binary watermark placed at the position (i, j) of the original image is zero, the block related to (i, j) from the original image will induce with the pattern f0, and reversely, if the bit at the position (i , j) is one, the block related to (i , j) from the original image will induce with the pattern f1. Finally, the security of the algorithm can obtain by a watermark key is fed to the encoder and decoder blocks.

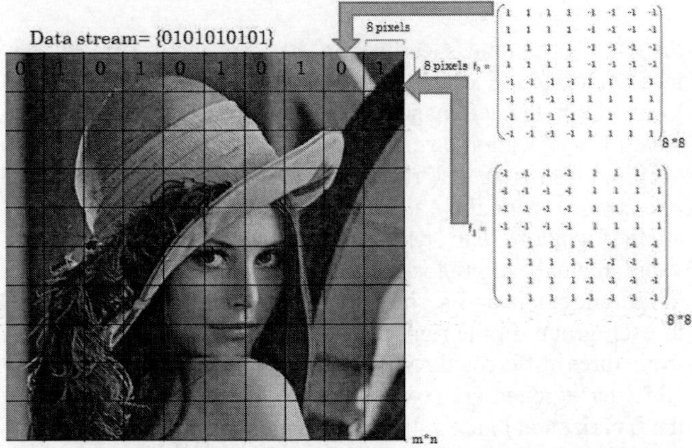

Fig. 2. Representing an example of embedding the data stream with 10 bits into Lena image using two Hadamard patterns (f0 and f1), which are low frequency and f0=-f1.

3.2 The Watermark localization in the decoder

The next step after embedding information in the encoder is decoding the information after attacking the authentication system by the PS operation. To provide robustness for PS distortions, five preprocessing blocks are proposed in the decoder. The right panel in figure 1 shows the name and the sequence of applying these preprocessing blocks in the decoder. As shown in the figure 1, the first block is named filtering block to remove the possible noise on the entrance image. Gaussian filter is used as a low pass filter to denoise the entrance image. Then, a localization block is proposed with the duty of estimating the location of watermark region (ID card's holder photo place). In this block an approximate watermark region is achieved and the remaining area out of this region is omitted. Whereas, we embed the information into a rectangular frame, belonging to the ID card holder's photo place, in the encoder, therefore, we should look for a rectangular frame (watermark region) in the decoder. To localize the rectangular watermark region, we put a rectangular mesh over the entrance image to the decoder, see the left panel in figure 3. The dimension of the rectangular elements inside the mesh can be calculated by having the maximum occurred rotation angle after PS operation. This maximum rotation angle (MRA) can be written by two parameters as MRA = $\theta_{max} = \theta_i + \theta_u$, where θ_i is maximum rotation angle created by the printer, and θ_u is maximum probable rotation angle that may occurs by user in the scanner. Now, the maximum dimension of the rectangular frame can be evaluated as:

$$\text{Height} \approx L.\cos(\theta_{max}) + W.\sin(\theta_{max}) + H0,$$

$$\text{Width} \approx W.\cos(\theta_{max}) + L.\sin(\theta_{max}) + W0, \quad (4)$$

where L is the approximate height of the ID card's holder photo place (watermark region), and W is the approximate width of watermark location. Both of these parameters are known by having "dots per inch" (dpi), which is adjustable in printer and scanner setting. H0, W0 are the additional parameters to qualify our approximation, selected by user. The left panel in figure 3 represents equation (4). After applying the mesh over the entrance image, the rectangular watermark region is achieved by the rule: The rectangular element inside the mesh with the biggest width in its histogram specification is the one has the watermark region inside. This rule comes from this fact that the watermark is embedded in the photo place of ID card's holder which has biggest width in its histogram compared with other regions of ID card. Note that, the output of the localization block is an estimate of the watermark region and we still need to have next blocks to get the exact watermark location.

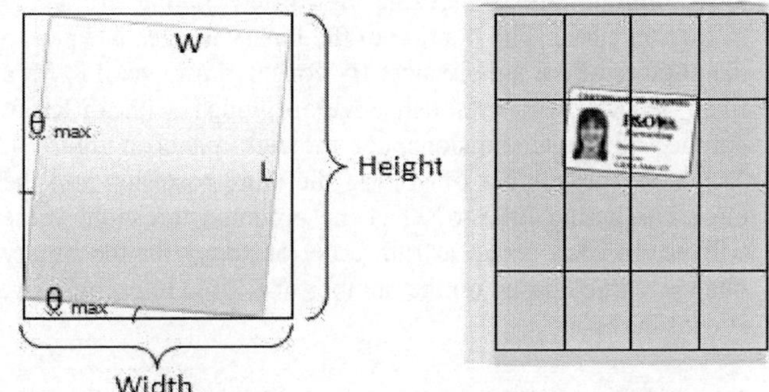

Fig. 3. A schematic to get a frame with the maximum dimension based on the maximum probable rotation angle θ max is shown in the left panel; the outline of how a rectangular grid is applied on the entrance image to localize the watermark location is represented in the right panel.

3.3 Binarization algorithm in the decoder

In the previous block an estimate of the watermark region, including regions without watermark, achieved. The binarization block, located after localization block, is proposed with the duty of discriminating the exact watermark location from the other region without any watermark inside. The proposed binarization method is based on the thresholding and tries to find the exact watermark location using histogram specification of the estimated watermark region, achieved from the localization block. The left panel in figure 4 shows the histogram specification of the estimated watermark region in localization block. The circular sign in this figure corresponds to the region without any watermark, which should be removed in this block. To remove the region without watermark, we need to use a threshold value to make a binary image from the entrance image. The first local minimum (star sign in figure 4) around the circular point can be the initial guess of threshold value to make a binary image. As it is shown in the right panel in figure 4, if we consider the star point as the threshold value, the earned binary image will not show our desired watermark region, a rectangular frame. However, we consider this point as our initial threshold value. Looking at the histograms depicted in figure 4, which belongs to the image in the right panel in figure 5(a) after print-scan operation, we can find out the existence of the gray levels shifting (halftone effect), appeared as several small peaks around the circular sign in figure 4. This is because of histogram distortion occurred after the print-scan operation.

A hierarchical algorithm to get the best threshold value, which discriminates exactly the watermark location from other regions, is proposed in this stage. We define parameter P over the histogram as start points for searching the threshold value as well as parameter D which indicates the distance of the search. Therefore, P-D is the last search point. We divide the distance D into K equal subdivision, and it is supposed that the bin with the least local minimum in each subdivision is our desired threshold value (figure 4). The local minima are achievable by differentiating from the histogram curve. The number of the binary images is equal to the number of our subdivision. By considering several K for a fixed D, we will establish several groups with different number of the subdivisions, see the right panel in figure 4. The more the number of groups, the more precision and the more computing time to select the optimum threshold value will be. In each group a truth criterion (d_{min}) for the binary images, earned based on the number of K used in each group, is considered as:

$$D_k = \sum_{m=1}^{M}[(V_{k,m} - V_{I,m})^2] \ ; \ d_{min} = min[D_k] \quad (5)$$

where D_k is vector distance, k=1,2,…,K, and K is the number of subdivisions used in each group, and VI is our ideal feature vector that includes M specified features and may be expressed as: VI = [VI,1 , VI,2 , … ,VI,M]T. As an example, the ideal feature vector can be chosen to include: The number of pixels in the watermark location, the perimeter of the watermark location, the aspect ratio of the watermark location, and the ratio of the number of pixels in the watermark location (black rectangle in figure 4(d)) to the number of pixels out of watermark location (white region in figure 4(d)). The binary image with the least distance criterion, dmin, in each group is considered as the output binary image in that group. The hierarchical process will be terminated in a group if the condition dmin<THD in that group is met, where THD is an arbitrary number selected by user. In the end, the output binary image of the group with the least dmin is selected as the final binary image. The right panel in figure 4 shows the experimental results of applying the proposed binarization block for different values of K. The higher the number of the subdivisions (K), the more the accuracy in estimating the watermark location (black region in figure 4 (d)) will be.

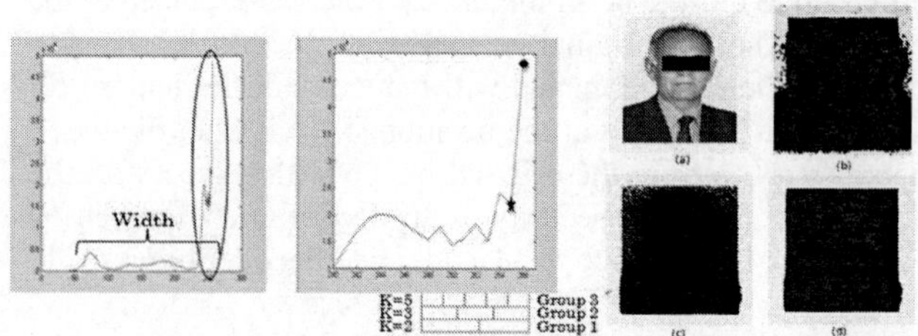

Fig. 4. Histogram specification of the output image of localization block, which is an estimated image of watermark location. In the left panel, the histogram of the estimated watermark location which has the biggest width. The occurred histogram distortion (halftone effect) after print-scan operation is marked by a black oval and also is magnified in another window. The star sign indicates the initial threshold value in binarization block, the circular sign indicates the end of search region, and K shows the number of the subdivisions in each group. In the right panel, three binary images earned from three different threshold values in an ID card with a white background are represented. (a) The entrance image to the binarization block with the histogram specification shown in the left panel. (b) The obtained binary image after applying the first local minimum (the star point) as initial threshold value. (c) Obtained binary image by choosing a Threshold value achieved in group 3 with 3 subdivisions (K=3, and D=10). (d) Obtained binary image in group 5 with 5 subdivisions, which is the best achieved binary image.

3.4 Undoing the rotation in the decoder

In this stage, we need to eliminate the occurred rotation angle on the obtained watermark location (black region in figure 4(d)) after print-scan operation. In this work, the method used for undoing rotation was Radon transform. The Radon transform is the projection of the image intensity on a radial line directed at a specific angle. We can estimate the rotation angle of the rectangular frame (watermark location) in the output image of binarization block using the following rule: the angle with the biggest projection value in its radon transform corresponds to the rotation angle of the rectangle frame. Applying the Radon transform, we can simply undo the rotation of the rectangle frame (watermark location), shown in black in figure 4 (d).

3.5 Cropping criterion

This phase of proposed authentication system is one of the most important units. This is because we need to crop the derotated image from the previous section at its optimum edges to achieve an accurate rectangular watermark location, where the personal information is hidden. Any mistake in estimating the optimum edges will result in the loss of hidden information inside the watermark location. The proposed algorithm to find the optimum edges uses two criterions: Average and Similarity criterion. We define two different regions: Non-transition region which is rows and columns with no intensity variation when we go from one row/column to its immediate adjacent row/column, and Transition region which is rows and columns with intensity variation when we go from one row/column to its immediate adjacent row/column, see figure 11. To reach to the optimum edges to crop the image, we need to first remove the non-transition region and then find the optimum edges within transition region. To remove the non-transition region, we define the average criterion (AVC) as follows:

$$AVC = |AV(i) - N_i| ; \qquad For\ rows$$

$$AVC = |AV(j) - N_i| ; \qquad For\ column \qquad (6)$$

where Ni is average of the gray levels of the most outer pixels of the rectangular watermark location, and AV(i) and AV(j) ; i=1,2,…,P ; j=1,2,…,Q are, respectively, the average of the pixels in each row and column in non-transition region. Also, P and Q are the number of rows and columns of the watermark location respectively. The rows and columns having AVC lower than T, a threshold value selected by user, have to be removed. By doing so, we would remove the rows and columns without any transition. This criterion is done in a small distance from the most outer edges of the rectangular watermark location, see figure 5(b). Note that, the existence of the region without any transition in Fig. 5(b) depends on the application and the value of rotation angle created by PS process. In cases with small applied rotation angle, we do not have any non-transition region. In the following, we need to choose the optimum edges within the transition region to crop the rectangular frame. To do so, we consider the homogeneity criterion for each one of rows or columns within the transition region. The homogeneity criterion (HMC) for rows and columns within the transition region is evaluated as:

$$HMC = \frac{VAR}{AVG} \qquad (7)$$

where VAR is the variance of gray levels of pixels in each row or column, and AVG is the average of the gray levels of the pixels in the same row or the column. It is supposed that the optimum edges within the transition region are located between two columns/rows with the highest similarity in intensity. Now, the similarity between the sequential rows/ columns can be evaluated by taking the difference between the homogeneity values of those rows/ columns. Therefore, the similarity criterion (SCR) can be written as:

$$SCR = |Hmc(i \pm 1) - Hmc(i)| ; \qquad For\ rows$$

$$SCC = |Hmc(j \pm 1) - Hmc(j)| ; \qquad For\ column \qquad (8)$$

Note that, the movement direction to compute the above equation is always from outer edges toward inner edges (see the direction of arrows in Figure 5). This difference (the similarity criterion) is the least amount at the optimum edges within the transition region. Therefore, we will consider a row or column as an optimum edge to crop the image if the SCR in that row or column is lower than a critical value CV, selected by user. We can write the cropping criterion (CRC) as follows:

$$CRC|_{i,j} = SCR|_{i,j} < CV \qquad (9)$$

Finally, we deliver the cropped rectangular frame to the next decoding block to extract the hidden data inside it.

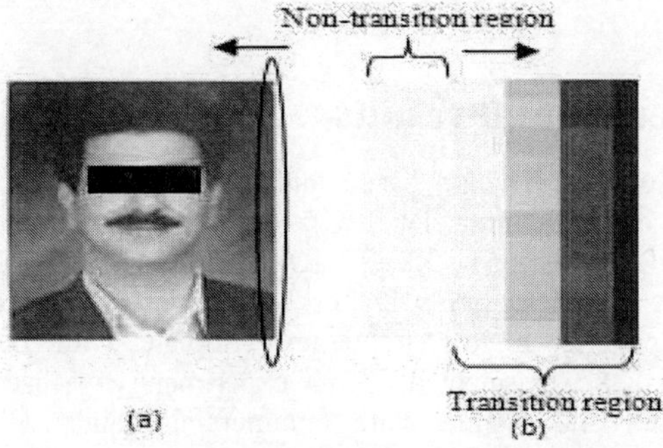

Fig. 5. Example of the transition and non-transition regions in a test image after print-scan operation. (a) Representing a derotated rectangular watermark location. (b) A close view of the black oval in figure 5(a) to represent the transition region, and non-transition region. (Note the direction of drawn arrows in figure 5(a) and figure 5(b)).

3.6 Decoding process

The final stage for the proposed authentication system is the decoding block. The decoding process is according to this property that the original image has a minimum similarity to the Hadamard patterns (f_0 and f_1), which are already used in the encoder. This means that correlation between the blocks (B) and Hadamard patterns is always zero, i.e. Corr(B, f_x)=0 where B is the blocks inside the original image in figure 4 and f_x can be either f0 or f1. A decision function for extracting a bit of the hidden data at the position (i, j) can be written as:

$$d(i,j) = Corr\left(B^{W}_{i,j}(k,l), f_1(k,l)\right) - Corr\left(B^{W}_{i,j}(k,l), f_0(k,l)\right) \qquad (10)$$

where $B^{w}_{i,j}(k,l)$ is the block in the watermarked image.

Since $B^{w}_{i,j}(k,l) = B_{i,j}(k,l) + \lambda . f_x(k,l)$,, and also Corr(B, f_x)=0; therefore, we can write:

$$d(i,j) = \lambda . Corr(f_1, f_x) - \lambda . Corr(f_0, f_x) = \begin{cases} +\lambda, & if \ x = 1 \\ -\lambda, & if \ x = 0 \end{cases} \quad (11)$$

where x is the unknown hidden bit in the block $B^{w}_{i,j}(k,l)$, and $Corr(X,W)$ is define as:

$$Corr(X,W) = \frac{\sum\sum(X-\overline{X}).(W-\overline{W})}{\sqrt{\left(\sqrt{(X-\overline{X})^2}.\sqrt{(W-\overline{W})^2}\right)}} \quad (12)$$

In the end, the decision function can be written as:

$$\widehat{W}(i,j) = sgn(d(i,j)) = \begin{cases} +1 & if \ x = 1 \\ -1 & if \ x = 0 \end{cases} \quad (13)$$

where $\hat{W}(i,j)$ is a bit of the binary hidden data at the position (i, j).

4 Experimental results

The proposed ID card based authentication algorithm was tested on a Pentium IV (PC), Intel 3.0 GHz, with Windows XP Professional, 3.0 GB RAM, in MATLAB 8.0 (Mathworks, Natwick, USA). After several testes on the Hadamard patterns a low frequency template with the dimension 8 × 8 was selected. In our experiments, we used typical printer and scanner with commercial brands: HP Photosmart 8450 and Canon L9950F, respectively. A database of 100 different ID cards with a wide range of possible colors, as background colors of the ID cards, was used. The original digital ID card image was printed with the resolution of 300 dpi, and then scanned with the resolution of 600 dpi. We embedded the ID card personal number, including 12 characters, inside the ID card's holder photo place in the encoder. The proposed ID card based authentication algorithm was applied to the whole of the database, including 100 ID cards, and an average accuracy criterion (ACC) was defines as:

$$ACC = 1 - \left(\frac{EB}{HB}\right) \quad (14)$$

where *EB* is the number of detected bits with error, and *HB* is the number of all hidden bits. The average accuracy criterion has been depicted as a diagram in Figure 6 for different parameters introduced in the proposed ID card based authentication system. As it is obvious from the drawn diagram, the more the number of subdivisions (*K*) in the binarization block, the higher the average accuracy of detecting the hidden data will be. In Figure 6, the average accuracy is increased from 80% to 86% when increasing the number of the used groups in binarization block from *K*=1 to *K*=2. In Figure 6, the ideal feature vector, *VI*, was applied to get the accuracy results with two features were: the number of pixels inside the watermark location, and the aspect ratio of the watermark location. Also in the case of applying four features to achieve the average accuracy in figure 6, the used features were the same ones mentioned in the binarization section. The threshold value (*THD)* was set to 0.05 and the number of the groups in binarization block was different between 3 and 5 over our database.

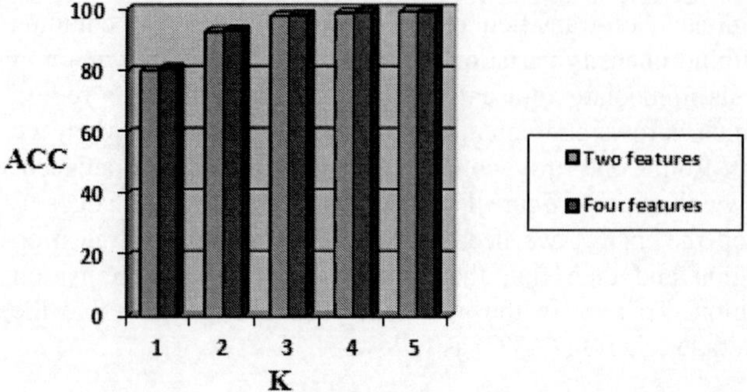

Fig. 6. Representing a diagram to compare the average accuracy criterion for different values of subdivision number (*K*), and also different number of used features. (Note that, the selected value for distance of search, *D*, was equal to 10).

Figure 7 shows several case studies selected from our database before watermarking (figure 7(a)) and after watermarking and PS operation (figure 7(b)).

Fig. 7. Experimental results of applying the proposed authentication system over five case studies selected form our database, including 100 ID cards. (a) The original image of ID card's holder before watermarking. (b) The Image of ID card's holder after watermarking and PS operation, including ID card's holder personal information. The background of the study cases is different from one case to the other.

5 Conclusion

This paper proposes an online secure ID card authentication system which uses scanned picture of customer's ID card as identity. Digital watermark technology embeds the user /customer's personal information into the digital content and makes it hard for criminals to abuse a content-based electronic business. In this work, the user/ customer takes the scan of hardcopy of his/her ID card and then uploads the scanned picture of ID card through the internet for authentication purposes to fulfill an online trade/transaction. The proposed authentication system extracts the watermark inside the ID card's holder photo place in the decoder and then checks it out with the ID card personal number. If the extracted watermark and the ID card personal number are the same, the identity of the user/ customer will be verified; otherwise, the identity will be denied. The main attack for the proposed authentication system is PS operation which imposes several distortions on the watermark location. To remove the PS distortions, five preprocessing blocks in the decoder are proposed. According to the experimental results, the proposed ID card authentication system has an average accuracy of 99% in finding correctly the hidden information into the 100 ID cards after PS operation. Unlike the preceding ID card authentication systems, the proposed authentication method does not need to add a rectangular frame around the watermark location, which makes it applicable for online passport based authentication system. Moreover, the proposed authentication method outperforms the preceding proposed authentication systems in this way that it does not need to model the PS distortion (halftone effect), which is *variable* for printers and scanners from one brand to another, to remove the PS distortion on the watermark location.

6 References

[1] Hirakawa, M., and Iijima, J. "Validating The Effectiveness of Using Digital Watermarking Technology for E-commerce Website Protection" The 9th Asian eBusiness Workshop, pp. 127-132, Japan, 2009.

[2] Role of Digital Watermark in E-governance and E-commerce" IJCSNS International Journal of Computer Science and Network Security, Vol. 8, No. 1, 2008.

[3] K. Solanki, U. Madhow, B. S. Manjunath, S. Chandrasekaran and I. El-Khalil, "'Print and scan' resilient data hiding in images," IEEE Trans. Information Forensics and Security. , vol. 1, no. 4, pp, 464– 478, Dec. 2006.

[4] Hyejoung Yoo, Kwangsoo Lee, Sangjin Lee, and Jongin Lim, "Off-Line Authentication Using Watermarks" Springer-Verlag Berlin Heidelberg, ICICS 2001, LNCS 2288, pp. 200–213, 2002.

[5] C. Y. Lin and S. F. Chang, "Distortion modeling and invariant extraction for digital image print-and-scan process," presented at the Int. Symp. Multimedia Information Processing Dec. 1999.

[6] K. Solanki, U. Madhow, B. S. Manjunath, and S. Chandrasekaran, "Estimating and undoing rotation for print-scan resilient data hiding," presented at the ICIP, Singapore, Oct. 2004.

[7] L.Yu, X. Niu and S. Sun, "Print-and-scan model and the watermarking countermeasure," in Image and Vision Computing., May 2005, vol 23, pp. 807- 817.

[8] R. B. Wolfgang and E.J. Delp, "Fragile watermarking using the VW2d watermark", Proceeding of the SPIE/IS&T International Conference on Security and Watermarking of Multimedia Contents, vol. 3657,pp. 204- 213,fan. 1999.

[9] J.Hu, j. Hunang, D.Hunang and Y. Q. Shi, "Image fragile watermarking based on fusion of multi-resolution tamper detection," IEE Electronic Letters, vol. 38, no. 24, pp 1512-1513, Nov. 2002.

[10]D. Kundur and D.Hatzinakos, "Digital watermarking for telltale temper-proofing and authentication," proceedings of the IEEE Special Issue on Identification and Protection of Multimedia Information, vol. 87, no. 7, pp. 1167-1180, July 1999.

[11]A. T. S. Ho, J. Shen, H. P. Tan, and J. Woon, "Security-printing authentication using digital watermarking," Electronic Imaging, vol. 13, no.1, Jan. 2003.

[12]Cox, J. Kilian, T. Leighton, and T. Shamoon, "Secure spread spectrum watermarking for multimedia," IEEE Trans. Image Process., vol. 6, pp. 1673–1687, Dec. 1997.

Smoke Detection in Video Surveillance Using Optical Flow and Green's Theorem

Melih Altun and Mehmet Celenk
School of Electrical Engineering and Computer Science
Stocker Center, Ohio University
Athens, OH 45701 USA
{ma231709, celenk}@ohio.edu
http://www.ohio.edu

Abstract - *Finding smoke in surveillance videos can be crucial in early detection of fire emergencies. Such early detections improve damage prevention and control by enabling the authorities to take the necessary precautionary steps. This paper describes a smoke detection technique developed for videos taken in visual band. The method makes use of optical flow and color filtering to detect smoke covered regions and the associated smoke sources. Next it extracts dynamic smoke features such as average upwards motion above the source and divergence around the source via Green's theorem. This determines whether the selected region contains smoke. In turn, the extracted dynamic characteristics of the smoke pattern greatly improve detection accuracy of the method and produce highly robust results as demonstrated in the experimental results.*

Keywords: Smoke detection, video surveillance, optical flow, Green's theorem

1 Introduction

This paper presents a smoke detection method based on video processing. Detection of smoke in videos is particularly useful in surveillance and automatic event detection applications.

Traditional smoke detectors measure certain chemicals and particles in the air. In small closed spaces these particles rapidly reach a high concentration so detectors can generate early warnings. However, they do not function as well in large spaces and they are simply not applicable to outdoor environments.

Video based fire and smoke detectors are known to overcome such difficulties by their remote sensing capabilities. Moreover, video based systems are also capable of obtaining information such as the exact location and the progress of fire.

Fire detection methods use visual and infrared (IR) cameras to find fire sources. They use color, shape and dynamic features such as flickering [1,2]. The disadvantage of both visual and IR methods is that they need direct visual of fire. In cases where fire is not directly seen or it is at an early phase where only smoke is visible, smoke detection systems provide an earlier response.

Smoke detection systems mainly use methods based on wavelet [3] information. [4] combines wavelet methods with Hidden Markov trees to account for the dynamic characteristics of smoke. Optical flow [5] and other dynamic features such as velocity histograms are also used [6]. [7,8] use color information and motion estimation methods for detecting smoke covered regions in a video frame. Although color information is vital for eliminating non-smoke objects, it is not sufficient for detection due to the presence of other objects with colors similar to smoke. Therefore, it is used in combination with other methods to reduce false detections. The idea behind our approach is similar to the method developed in [8]. However, instead of simple motion detection we use optical flow to model smoke behavior more precisely.

In this paper a smoke detection method based on optical flow and dynamic characteristics of smoke is described. Color filtering is also applied to reduce the possible smoke sources. After obtaining an optical flow vector field and determining a candidate smoke source, Green's theorem is applied around the selected source to test the divergent behavior of smoke. Moreover, since heat convection above the source causes the smoke to rise, average upward motion above the source is also calculated to improve the confidence of detection. The remainder of this paper is organized as follows: In section II the details of the smoke detection method is described. Experimental results are presented in section III. The last section contains conclusions.

2 Description of the Method

Color Filter: Smoke color can vary greatly from very dark to almost white shades. To select those gray levels and eliminate image segments with other colors we convert RGB values to HSL values and consider S value for selection. Since gray pixels have low saturation we take pixels with S values less than a certain threshold as a potential smoke pixel. As it is stated in [8], sometimes smoke can have a bluish tone. So, for pixels where blue value is higher than red and green we use a slightly higher saturation threshold to allow for bluish type of smoke. After selection of possible smoke pixels a Basic Sequential Algorithmic Scheme (BSAS) [9] clusters nearby smoke colored pixels together. However, most of these smoke colored clusters are usually stationary background areas. Using optical flow, which will be discussed in the next subsection, we are able to select dynamic regions and eliminate those stationary areas.

2.1 Optical Flow

To obtain the foreground objects in a video and accurately measure their motions optical flow is utilized. A fast and efficient optical flow method is essential for the real time requirements of detection. Our optical flow calculation is mostly parallel to the method proposed in [10]. First a spatiotemporal gradient of the video sequence *I(x,y,t)* is obtained. Then a 3D Gaussian filter is applied with linear convolution to smooth the gradient as in equations (1) and (2).

$$\nabla I(x,y,t) = \begin{bmatrix} \frac{\partial I(x,y,t)}{\partial x} & \frac{\partial I(x,y,t)}{\partial y} & \frac{\partial I(x,y,t)}{\partial t} \end{bmatrix}' \quad (1)$$

$$\overline{\nabla I}(x,y,t) = \nabla I(x,y,t) * H(x,y,t) \quad (2)$$

where H is the 3D Gaussian function and * is the convolution operation. Then the smoothed gradient vector is multiplied with its transpose to obtain the tensor matrix T.

$$T = \overline{\nabla I} \cdot \overline{\nabla I}' = \begin{bmatrix} t_1 & t_4 & t_5 \\ t_4 & t_2 & t_6 \\ t_5 & t_6 & t_3 \end{bmatrix} \quad (3)$$

Following the calculation of tensors, the velocity vectors are calculated using parameters t_1 through t_6, which are the elements of the symmetric tensor matrix.

$$v_x = \frac{t_6 t_4 - t_5 t_2}{t_1 t_2 - t_4^2} \quad \text{and} \quad v_y = \frac{t_5 t_4 - t_6 t_1}{t_1 t_2 - t_4^2} \quad (4)$$

Finally the velocity vectors for each pixel coordinate are smoothed by a 2D median filter [11] to obtain the final x and y component values of optical flow vector field. Optical flow for the sample frames given in Figure 1 can be seen in Figure 2.
Since we are interested in the motion of smoke and not the other objects, we mask our optical flow map with the smoke colored clusters found by our color filter. So we obtain a vector map showing only the motion of smoke colored foreground regions. And since these regions are clustered we can detect the appearance of a cluster and mark it as a smoke source. Green rectangle in Figure 3 and in other figures showing the detection results denotes the detected smoke source.

2.2 Application of Green's Theorem

After finding a potential smoke source with color filtering and obtaining the optical flow vector field with the methods described in previous subsections we are able to test the dynamic characteristics of smoke. The first dynamic characteristic we test is the divergent behavior of smoke around its source. One way to achieve this is to apply Green's Theorem. Green's Theorem states that outward flux of a vector field across a closed boundary is equal to the divergence of the vector field integrated over the region enclosed by the boundary. So if we define a simple closed curve, such as a small rectangle around the smoke source, a continuous positive outward flux across this rectangle indicates a divergent source within it.
We already have the horizontal and vertical components of the optical flow field. Divergence of the field is simply given by the equation 6.

$$\vec{V} = \vec{v_x} + \vec{v_y} = M\vec{i} + N\vec{j} \quad (5)$$

$$\nabla \cdot \vec{V} = \frac{\partial M}{\partial x} + \frac{\partial N}{\partial y} \quad (6)$$

General equation of Green's Theorem is given in equation 7.

$$\oint_C \vec{V} \cdot \vec{n}\, ds = \iint_R \left[\frac{\partial M}{\partial x} + \frac{\partial N}{\partial y}\right] dx\, dy \quad (7)$$

Here, $\vec{V}$ is the vector field, $\vec{n}$ is the normal to the closed curve C, s is an infinitesimal line segment over C and R is the region surrounded with C. We use the left side of this equation. Instead of calculating the divergence over the entire source region and summing it, we calculate the outward flux simply by taking the inner product of motion vectors and the normal vector over the rectangle surrounding the potential smoke source and sum the values. Divergent smoke sources are expected to produce positive results.

2.3 Average upwards motion above the source

Another dynamic characteristic of smoke is that it rises right above its source due to heat convection. We only consider the area above the source because as the smoke spreads away from the source it cools down and starts moving with the air currents in that environment. It even displays random Brownian motion if there is no dominant air current. However, its motion is predictable when it is close to the heat source. Therefore, we consider a rectangular region above the possible smoke source and examine the optical flow in this area. We take the average of vertical component of flow vectors in that region. If the result shows consistent upwards motion it is strong evidence that the possible source is an actual smoke source. Consistent upwards motion in conjunction with divergent behavior suggests that the selected cluster in the video frame is real smoke.

3 Experimental Results

For testing our smoke detection method we used sample videos from Bilkent University Signal and Image Processing Group [12] and Octec dataset from [13].
To demonstrate optical flow two consecutive frames are shown in Figure 1. Figure 2 shows the optical flow result in which, motions of rising smoke and running person are clearly seen. The result of smoke detection method is displayed in Figure 3

Figure 1: Consecutive frames from a sample video

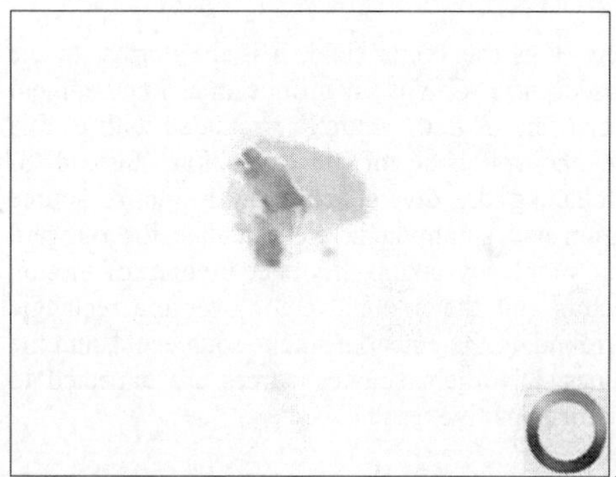

Figure 2: Optical flow results. Notice that hue represents direction as indicated by the circle on bottom right and saturation represents magnitude of the motion

Figure 3: Smoke detection result where smoke is marked by the red closed curve and smoke source is marked by the green rectangle.

In Figure 4 average of upwards optical flow vectors for the smoke source in Figure 1 is shown. Figure 5 displays the total outward flux around the smoke source in each frame of the video. Note that both average upwards motion and total outwards flux consistently maintain positive values and support our assertion.

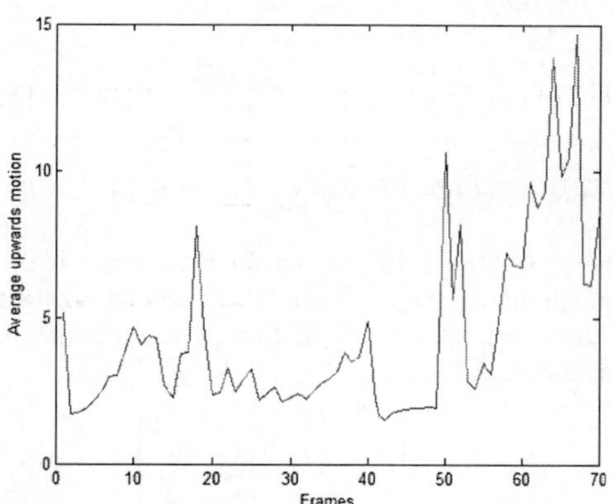

Figure 4: Average upwards motion above the smoke source for the video sequence given in Figure 1

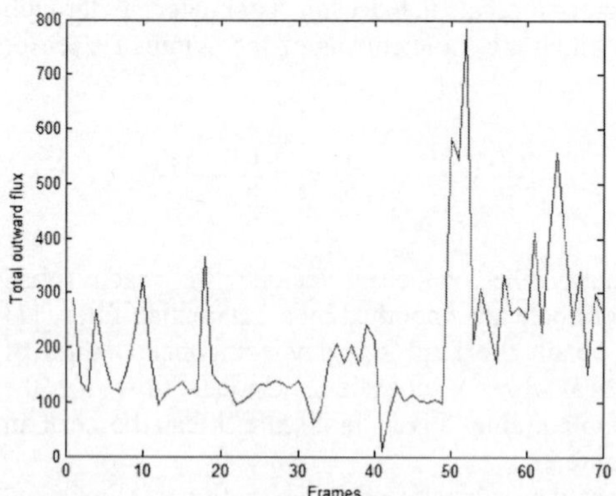

Figure 5: Total outward flux around the smoke source for the video sequence given in Figure 1. Notice the dip around frame #41. It corresponds to the time the person crosses in front of the smoke source and occludes it.

In order to measure our smoke detection rate, we also visually selected smoke covered areas in the video frames and established a ground truth. Then we compared the smoke regions detected by our algorithm to this ground truth. Figure 6 shows the rate of detection obtained by this comparison.

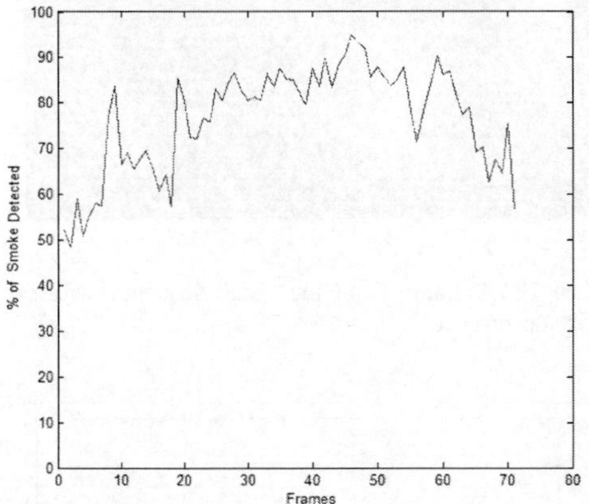

Figure 6: Rate of smoke detection for the first sample video sequence

Figure 7 shows another detection result from frame sequence with the appearance of smoke. Results of dynamic feature analysis are depicted in Figures 8 and 9. Again, average upwards motion and total outwards flux value remain consistently positive after smoke appears and source is detected. Detection ratio obtained by comparing smoke areas detected by our algorithm to ground truth also remains high as seen in Figure 10.

Figure 7: Smoke detection results for the Octec Dataset

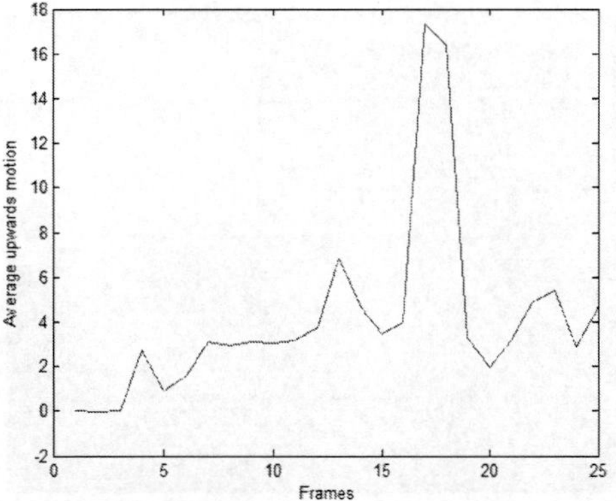

Figure 8: Average upwards motion above the smoke source for the video sequence given in Figure 7

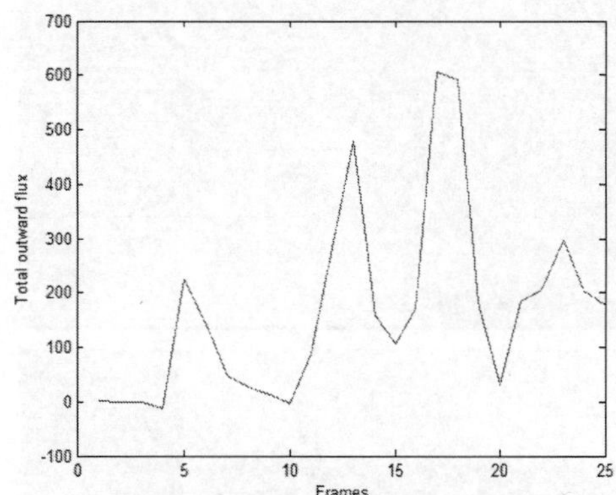

Figure 9: Total outward flux around the smoke source for the video sequence given in Figure 7

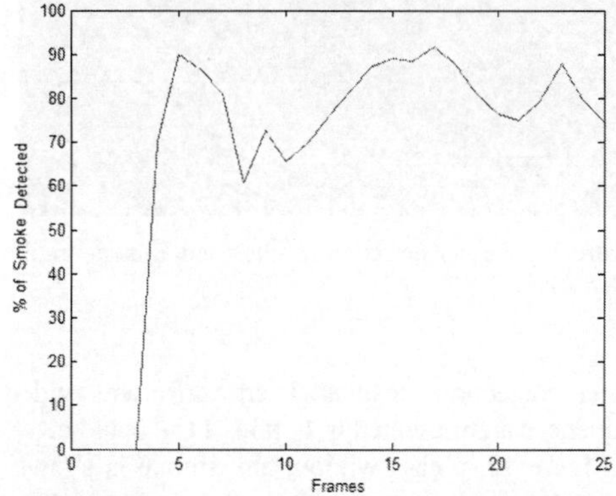

Figure 10: Rate of smoke detection for the second sample video sequence

Figure 11: Further detection results from Bilkent smoke video dataset

Other detection results from different video sequences are presented in Figures 11 a, b and c.

In Figure 12, a case without any smoke is shown. Even though an area on the left is selected as a possible source, total outwards flux and average upwards motion (Figures 13,14) show no signs of dynamic smoke behavior. Hence, there is no detection.

Figure 12: A frame from the video sequence with no smoke occurrence

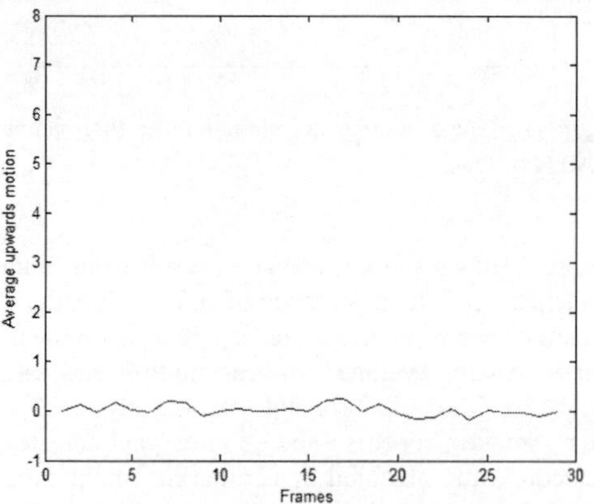

Figure 13: Average upwards motion above the detected source for the video sequence given in Figure 12

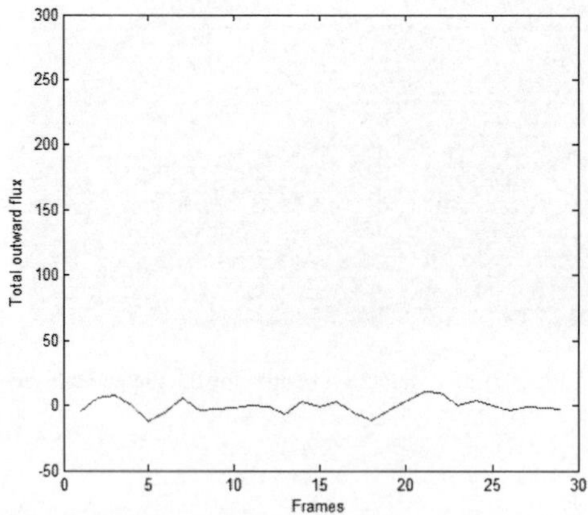

Figure 14: Total outward flux around the detected source for the video sequence given in Figure 12

4 Conclusion

In this paper we have presented a new method for detecting smoke with color filtering, optical flow and utilizing Green's Theorem. At first, by using a color filter possible smoke covered regions are found. Then, optical flow enables detection of motions in the video. Using the magnitude and the directionality of these motions, total outward flux and average upwards motion features are tested in order to confirm the presence of a divergent smoke source and a heat source in that selected region. Extracting these dynamic smoke features produces highly reliable results as it is demonstrated with the test cases.

5 References

[1] B.U. Toreyin, R.G. Cinbis, Y. Dedeoglu, A.E. Cetin, Fire detection in infrared video using wavelet analysis, Optical Engineering, vol. 46(6), pp. 67204-1 – 67204-9, 2007

[2] G. Marbach, M. Leopfe, T. Brupbacher, An image processing technique for fire detection in video images, Fire Safety Journal, vol. 41, pp 285-289, 2006

[3] B.U. Toreyin, Y. Dedeoglu, A.E. Cetin, Contour based smoke detection in video using wavelets, 14th European Signal Processing Conference EUSIPCO, 2006

[4] R.J. Ferrari, H. Zhang, C.R. Kube, Real-time detection of steam in video images. Pattern Recognition, vol. 40(3), pp. 1148-1159, 2007

[5] I. Kolesov, P. Karasev, A. Tannenbaum, E. Haber, Fire and smoke detection in video with optimal mass transport based optical flow and neural networks, 17th IEEE International Conference on Image Processing (ICIP), pp. 761-764, 2010

[6] J. Vicente, P. Guillemant, An image processing technique for automatically detecting forest fire, International Journal of Thermal Sciences, vol. 41(12), pp. 1113-1120, 2002

[7] D. Kim, Y. Wang. Smoke detection in video, IEEE WRI World Congress on Computer Science and Information Engineering, Vol. 5, pp. 759-763, 2009

[8] F. Yuan, A fast accumulative motion orientation model based on integral image for video smoke detection. Pattern Recognition Letters, vol. 29(7), pp. 925-932, 2008

[9] S. Theodoridis and K. Koutroumbas, Pattern Recognition, 4th ed. Elsevier, 2009.

[10] Z. Wei, D.J. Lee, B.E. Nelson, J.K. Archibald, and B.B. Edwards, FPGA-Based Embedded Motion Estimation Sensor, Int. Journal of Reconfigurable Computing, vol. 2008, no. 636145, p. 8, 2008.

[11] J. S. Lim, Two-Dimensional Signal and Image Processing, Prentice Hall, 1990

[12] Bilkent EE Signal Processing group, http://signal.ee.bilkent.edu.tr/

[13] D. Dwyer, Octec Limited, http://www.octec.co.uk/

A Walkthrough System to Display Video Corresponding to the Viewer's Face Orientation

T. Watanabe[1], C. Liu[2], and S. Shibusawa[2]
[1]Graduate School of Science and Engineering, Ibaraki University, Hitachi, Ibaraki, Japan
[2]Department of Computer and Information Sciences, Ibaraki University, Hitachi, Ibaraki, Japan

Abstract - *Walkthrough systems have hitherto been developed with the ability to produce a virtual display of a person's field of view. If the actual position and orientation of a person's face can be ascertained, then walkthrough images could be created to match this person's face direction, thereby recreating video corresponding to the view from this person's face direction. A possible application of this system is in store surveillance systems, where the direction in which someone is looking can be estimated to visualize what they are looking at in order to identify suspicious behavior. Therefore, we aim to produce a walkthrough system that uses image processing to acquire a person's position and face direction, and displays video corresponding to this person's face direction. In this system, multiple omnidirectional cameras are used to estimate the positions of people based on the bearings of moving bodies acquired by each camera. People's face orientations are estimated from the skin regions of their faces. We have created a system that uses a person's position and face orientation obtained in this way to provide an observer with walkthrough video corresponding to the person's face orientation. To evaluate this system, we conducted experiments on the accuracy of human positions and face orientations and the accuracy of the output video, and we confirmed that the system can display video images corresponding to a person's face direction.*

Keywords: face direction, walkthrough system, omni-directional camera, surveillance, skin area

1 Introduction

In recent years, surveillance systems have been used for purposes such as monitoring and recording the status of facilities. Due to improvements in surveillance technology and reductions in the price of sensor devices, it is now possible to use large numbers of sensors in surveillance systems. This has enabled the construction of systems that can monitor wide areas [1]. Situation recognition systems have also been studied for use in monitoring applications [2]. By learning the traffic lines of people acquired by this system, it is possible to predict the direction in which people will move based on their previous traffic lines. Recently, omnidirectional cameras [3],[4] have also been used in monitoring systems. These devices consist of a camera and a hyperboloidal mirror, and are capable of capturing an entire 360° field of view. With an omnidirectional camera, it is easy to provide wide coverage within which it is possible to track targets reliably.

Researchers have also been studying how to estimate the orientation of human faces [5],[6]. Most of these studies use the face orientation direction as the direction in which the person is interested. For example, in store surveillance applications, this technique can be used for marketing by identifying which product shelves the customers are looking at based on their face directions. It is also expected that the face direction can be used to identify suspicious behavior in surveillance applications. Normally, when people are committing crimes, they often look in different directions to the people around them, and their gaze point also changes in a different way. Someone who is about to commit a crime will often perform actions such as checking their surroundings, glancing at surveillance cameras and mirrors to search for blind spots, and loitering for prolonged periods [7],[8]. If video of the face direction can be displayed so that an observer can check for unusual behavior, this might be a useful way of preventing crimes before they take place.

Currently, studies are underway to identify abnormal behavior based on the traffic lines of people acquired from video images [9],[10]. In these studies, although it is possible to detect people who are acting strangely, it is not possible to figure out which way they are looking, or what they are looking at. For this reason, it is difficult for an observer to predict suspicious behavior based on positional information alone, such as traffic lines.

A number of walk-through systems have been developed that can produce a virtual representation of a person's field of view [11],[12]. So far, walk-through systems can only operate in virtual spaces. But if a person's actual position and face direction can be ascertained, then it should be possible to generate walkthrough video corresponding to this person's face direction.

In this study, we create a walk-through system that uses image processing to acquire a person's position and face direction, and display video corresponding to this person's face direction. This system first acquires a person's position and face direction as time-series data based on the video from multiple omnidirectional cameras. At the same time, a walkthrough space is constructed from the acquired video. The person's position and face direction are associated with a position and field of view inside this walkthrough space, and a walkthrough video oriented in this direction is output as a representation of this person's view. An observer can use this system to check the video corresponding to the face direction of the person being monitored. This gives the observer a better understanding of the objects and areas that the person is looking at, which aids in the identification of suspicious behavior.

To evaluate the system, we performed experiments to measure the face direction estimation accuracy, and to compare the system's video output with ordinary camera images captured from the same position with the same orientation. Our experiments showed that accurate estimation is possible in the central region covered by multiple cameras, but that the estimation accuracy declines at positions close to a camera and at positions that are distant from all the cameras. As for the estimation of face directions, it was found that accurate estimation is possible for people looking towards the camera, but the accuracy drops off for faces looking in the opposite direction. In the results of an experiment to compare the output of the system with the output of an ordinary camera, it was found that this system's output is similar to the camera image in the horizontal direction, and can display video of the face direction to some extent.

2 Related research

2.1 Monitoring systems

The number of cameras and other sensors used in monitoring systems has been increasing. This has also led to the construction of large-scale systems [1],[13]. Recently, monitoring systems have been constructed with the ability to make decisions differently in different situations through additional functions of situation recognition [2]. For example, the speed at which vehicles are judged to be driving dangerously can be changed by recognizing the distance between vehicles and the traffic levels for this time of day. In such a system, it is possible to predict the direction in which the target objects move and how they will behave.

However, these monitoring systems do not obtain face direction information, which would be useful for recognizing suspicious behavior. They also lack functions for specifically displaying video corresponding to the face direction of a surveillance target.

2.2 Face direction estimation

In previous studies to estimate the direction of human faces, face directions are mainly estimated either by a skin region method, or by a machine learning method. In the skin region method [14], the head position is identified in moving images obtained by a technique such as background subtraction, and an attempt is made to estimate the face direction from the skin regions identified as parts of the face. In machine learning methods [15], learning is performed by using images of different human heads in different orientations as input for machine learning, and by matching the current acquired frame to the machine learning results. There have also been many studies aimed at estimating the face direction of humans from the arrangement of parts of the face [16].

Another study, currently in progress, aims to estimate the actual gaze direction from detailed face images [17]. In this study, a person's position is acquired from multiple fixed cameras, and detailed face image data is then acquired by pointing a PTZ camera in this direction in order to estimate the person's field of sight. These methods require high-resolution face images, and thus have a smaller effective range and are less suited to surveillance applications.

2.3 Identifying suspicious behavior

Various sensors are used to identify suspicious behavior from behavior patterns [9]. In this study, a data set of human traffic lines obtained from devices such as cameras, GPS, and laser radars is used to detect people who are acting outside the normal range of human behavior patterns, and to classify behavior patterns. So far, no system has been able to reproduce video images in the direction of a person's face to allow an observer to check what the person is looking at.

3 Estimation of head position and face direction

3.1 Head position

Fig. 1(a) shows the appearance of an omnidirectional camera. An omnidirectional camera can capture images over an entire 360° field of view. It captures omnidirectional video images by using a camera to capture a view of its surroundings reflected in a hyperboloidal mirror. Fig. 1(b) shows the sort of image that can be captured with an omnidirectional camera.

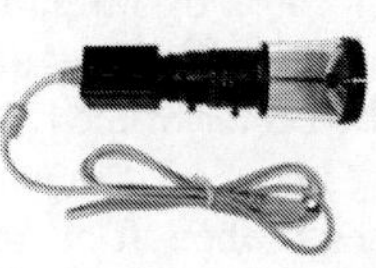

(a) Omnidirectional camera (b) Circular image captured by this camera

Figure 1. Omnidirectional camera

In this sort of omnidirectional image, the head of a person standing nearby will be positioned near the periphery of the image, as shown in Fig. 2. In this case, the head position can be estimated by using an image obtained by applying a distance transformation to the omnidirectional image. Distance transformation is a transformation to replace pixel values that have a value of 1 in a binary image with values corresponding to their distance from the closest pixel with a value of 0. In addition, the pixel value at the center of the head in a distance transform image is at least as large as some fixed value, that is, threshold value. It can therefore be assumed that the pixels furthest from the center of the image whose pixel value is greater than some fixed quantity correspond to the person's head. For example, Fig. 3(b) shows the image obtained from the distance transformation of Fig. 3(a). When the head position is obtained from this image, the results are as shown in Fig. 3(c).

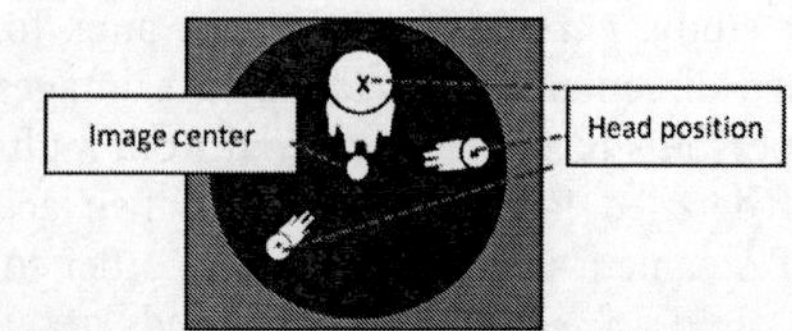

Figure 2. Head position in the omnidirectional image

(a) Motion extraction image (b) Distance transform image (c) Head position

Figure 3. Obtaining the head position from a distance transform image

3.2 Estimation of face direction

In an omnidirectional image containing a person, as shown in Fig. 4(a), we first find the following coordinates:

- Center of the head
- Center of the skin region of the head

This is shown in Fig. 4(b). Then, we find the vector from the central coordinates of the head in the omnidirectional image to the centroid coordinates of the skin region of the head. This is shown in Fig. 4(c). Since the face appears tilted as shown in Fig. 4(a) when using an omnidirectional camera, the transformation shown in Fig. 4(c) is used. In Fig. 4(c), r is the distance between the center of the image and the centroid of the skin region, R is the distance between the center of the image and the center of the head, θ is the difference between the angles subtended by the centroid of the skin region and the center of the head relative to the center of the image, and Φ is the angle used for estimation. This technique makes use of the characteristic that, when concentrating on parts of the head that are covered in hair and on the the skin region of the face, the skin region lies at under the center of the head when the face is pointing straight at the camera, and moves to the left and right when the head is turned to the left or right [19]. In this study, it is thought that the face direction can be estimated by associating this angle Φ with the actual angle of the face. It should be noted that this method is difficult to apply to people wearing masks or with close-cropped haircuts.

(a) Region of a person in an omnidirectional image

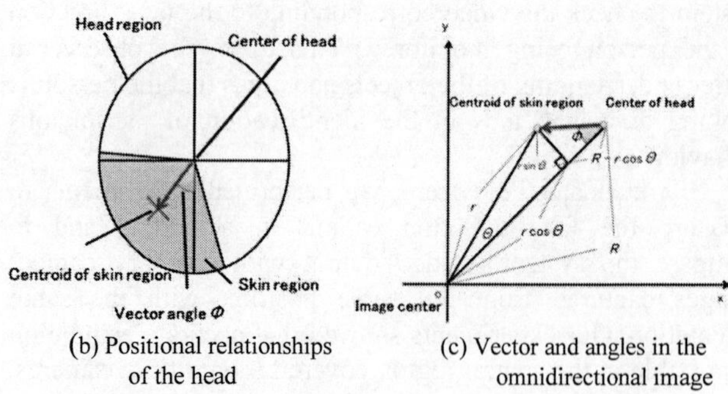

(b) Positional relationships of the head (c) Vector and angles in the omnidirectional image

Figure 4. Estimation of face direction from skin region and head position

4 Proposed system

4.1 System overview

Fig. 5 shows an overview of the system. From images obtained from the omnidirectional camera, the system creates an image close to the current view of the person being monitored. The system comprises a processing unit that estimates a person's position and performs face direction based on image processing of the camera output, and a walkthrough display unit. Video of the person's face direction is produced based on the person's position and face direction as acquired by the processing unit, which are converted into a walkthrough by the walkthrough display unit.

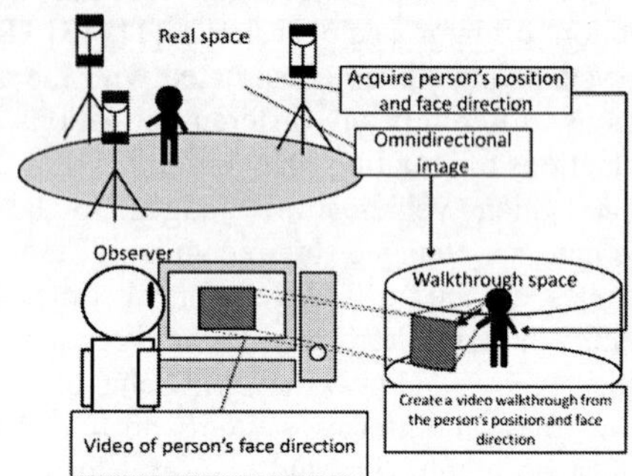

Figure 5. System overview

4.2 Estimating a person's position

A person's position is estimated from multiple omnidirectional camera images. Fig. 6 illustrates the position estimation method. First, as shown in Fig. 6(a), the person's outline is acquired from the region of movement obtained by background subtraction. This outline is scanned to determine the angular range of the region occupied by the moving object from the center of the image. Next, as shown in Fig. 6(b), the angular ranges of moving objects acquired by multiple omnidirectional cameras are displayed in a planar space, and the region where the angular ranges of all cameras overlap is acquired as the region where a person exists. The centroid of this region is taken to be the person's position. Fig. 6 shows how this is done.

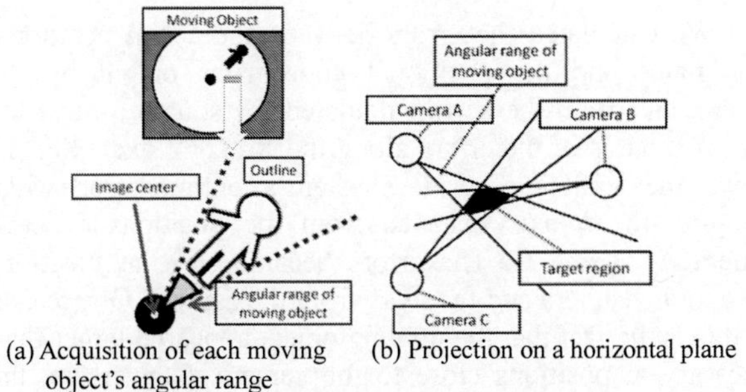

(a) Acquisition of each moving object's angular range (b) Projection on a horizontal plane

Figure 6. Acquiring a person's position

4.3 Estimation of face direction

The face direction is estimated according to the method of Section 3.2. First, background subtraction is used to extract a moving object. The head position of this moving body is then obtained from the method of Section 3.1. The skin region of the moving object is also extracted, and its centroid is calculated.

Fig. 7 shows the head position and the centroid of the skin region plotted on the moving object image. The circle indicates the head position, and the cross indicates the centroid of the skin region. Fig. 7 shows the results obtained for people facing in different directions: (a) straight towards the camera, (b) turned at 45°, (c) facing sideways, (d) facing directly away from the camera. Between images (a), (b) and (c), the angle Φ increases. In this way, the angle Φ in Fig. 4(b) can be obtained according to the method of Section 3.2. The face direction is estimated from the correspondence between this angle and face direction. In Fig. 4(d), the person is facing in the opposite direction to the camera so the face parts are not captured and the area of the skin region is very small. Therefore, a threshold value is set for the area of the skin region. A moving object that falls below this threshold is judged to be facing away from the camera. These processes are performed for all the moving object regions detected by background subtraction.

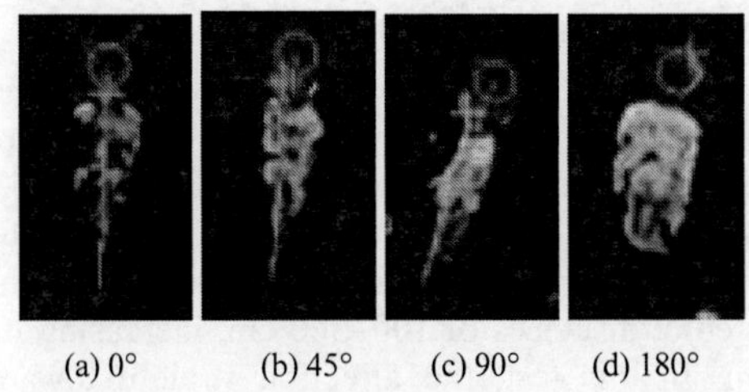

(a) 0° (b) 45° (c) 90° (d) 180°

Figure 7. Variation of angle with face direction

4.4 Correspondence between person's position and face direction

The people detected according to Section 4.3 are correlated with the results of face direction estimation for each camera. This process yields face direction information from a number of cameras for each person. These results are weighted and added together, and the result is treated as the final face direction. If there are n cameras within range, the weighting w_i of camera i is defined by the following formula:

$$w_i = \frac{S_i / M_i}{S_1 / M_1 + S_2 / M_2 + \cdots + S_n / M_n} \tag{1}$$

In (1), M_i and S_i represent the area of the entire moving object region and the area of the parts corresponding to the skin region in image from camera i. In the method of Section 3.2, the face direction is estimated with the highest accuracy when the face is oriented straight towards the camera. Therefore, greater weighting is applied to faces that are turned more towards the camera.

4.5 Creating the video walkthrough

A walkthrough space can be created relatively easily from the omnidirectional images. Fig. 8 shows an overview of a walkthrough based on an omnidirectional image. In this method, the circular image captured by the omnidirectional camera is first projected into a panoramic image. This image is associated with the walkthrough space, and its visible range is set. Movement of the walkthrough view and operations to move forwards and backwards are implemented by panning this range to the left and right and zooming in and out.

In the walkthrough system produced in this way, output video is produced using the positions and face directions of people obtained as described in Sections 4.3 and 4.4. First, the camera closest to the person's position in the walkthrough space is ascertained, and the video from this camera is used in the walkthrough. Next, the range of the image to be displayed in the walkthrough from this person's position and face direction is determined. This range is extracted from the video and displayed by enlarging or reducing it to match the window size.

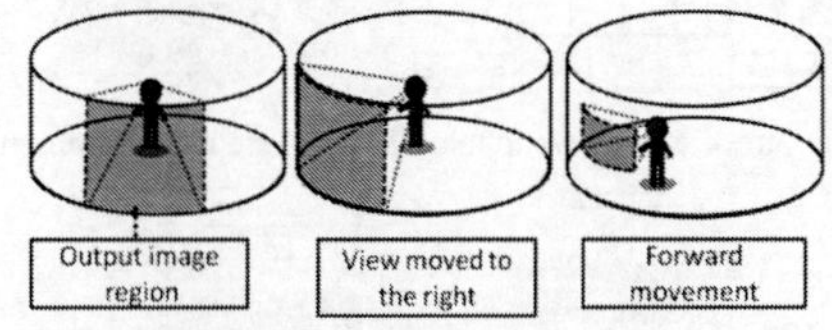

Figure 8. Walkthrough based on an omnidirectional image

5 System implementation

We implemented the system according to the design of Section 4. Fig. 9 shows the system in operation. The system displays separate windows for the video acquired from each camera, the results of background subtraction to extract moving objects, the head positions of these moving objects, the centroid positions of the facial skin regions, the coordinates and estimated face directions of people relative to the cameras, the traffic lines of these people, and the calculated walkthrough video.

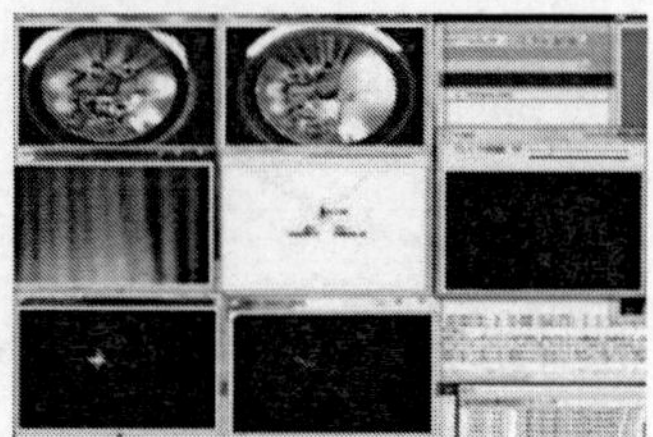

Figure 9. System operation screen

6 Evaluation experiments

To evaluate the created system, we performed the following three experiments.

- Evaluation of human position estimation accuracy and traffic line acquisition
- Evaluation of face direction estimation accuracy
- Comparison with actual images

6.1 Acquiring the positions and traffic lines of people

6.1.1 Experimental environment

The positions and traffic lines of people were acquired in the layout shown in Fig. 10(a). This test was performed using three cameras situated in the room shown in Fig. 10(b). In Fig. 10(a), people are assumed to be situated at each of the grid intersections, and the output coordinates of the system for each position are compared with the actual positional coordinates. Traffic lines are obtained by having people walk as shown by the dotted lines in Fig. 10(c) and (d).

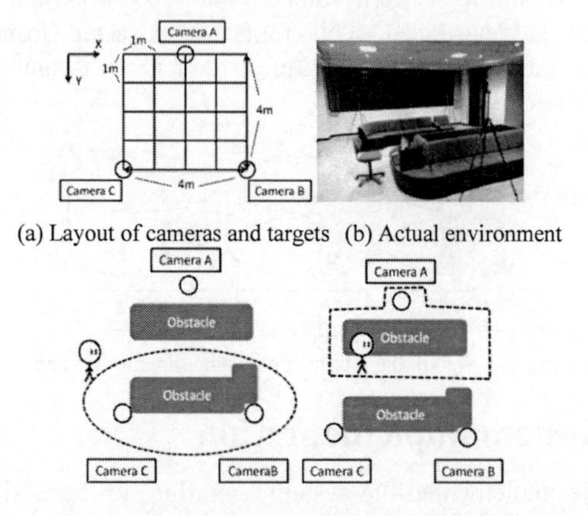

(a) Layout of cameras and targets (b) Actual environment

(c) Traffic line path 1 (d) Traffic line path 2

Figure 10. Experimental layout for acquiring the positions and traffic lines of people

6.1.2 Experimental results and discussion

Fig. 11 shows the results of using this system to acquire traffic lines. As this figure shows, it is possible to acquire traffic lines with a similar shape to the actual route. In Fig. 11(b), the break in the traffic line is thought to where the environment was unlit, or where the view was obscured by a camera tripod.

We calculated the errors between the actual positional coordinates and the positional coordinates output by the system, and from these we calculated the square root of the sum of squares of the errors along the X and Y axes. Fig. 12 shows the variation of the system's output error when changing the Y-axis distance from the positions of each camera A, B and C. The errors became large at positions close to the camera and far away from the camera. One reason for this is the fact that the moving object appeared larger than necessary at positions close to the camera. Conversely, the increased errors at locations far away from the camera are thought to be due to the inability to acquire a sufficient number of pixels over the moving object. For these reasons, the most accurate estimations were made at positions close to the center of the region surrounded by the cameras. To improve the precision of position estimation, it is necessary to extract only the region where a person's feet touch the floor on order to narrow down the person's position more accurately.

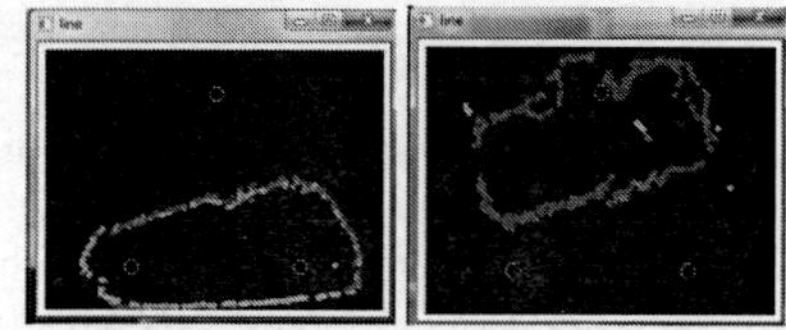

(a) Traffic lines on route 1 (b) Traffic lines on route 2

Figure 11. Acquired traffic lines

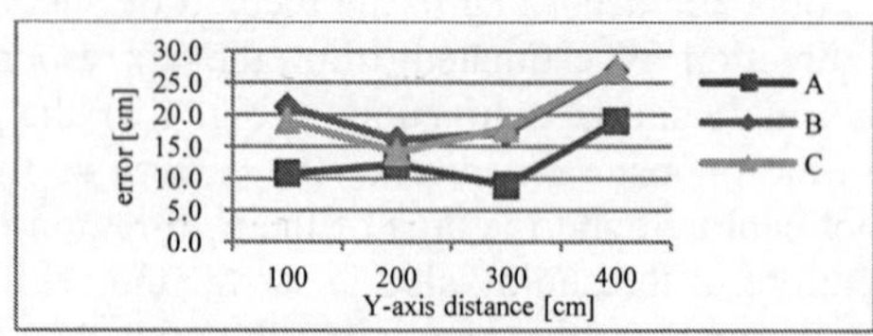

Figure 12. Error with distance from the camera

6.2 Estimation of face direction

6.2.1 Experimental environment

In the layout of Fig. 13, we estimated face directions using two cameras. In this experiment, the target person was first placed at a distance of 100 cm from the camera. At this position, the person's orientation was changed from 0 to 360° in 45° increments while estimating the face direction. This was repeated at distances of 100–500 cm, increasing in steps of 100 cm. In this test, the direction straight towards the camera was taken as 90°. The results were calculated from the average estimated value over 20 frames.

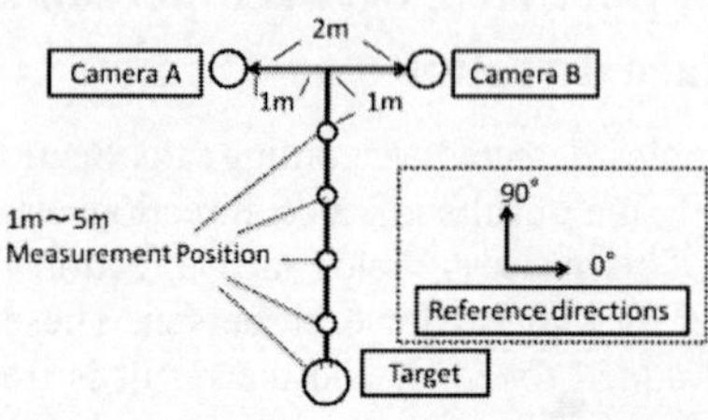

Figure 13. Layout of the face direction estimation experiment

6.2.2 Experimental results and discussion

Fig. 14 shows the target person's actual face direction and the errors of the system's output. In the overall test, the errors were small when the face direction was between 0 and 180°, but were large between 225 and 315°.

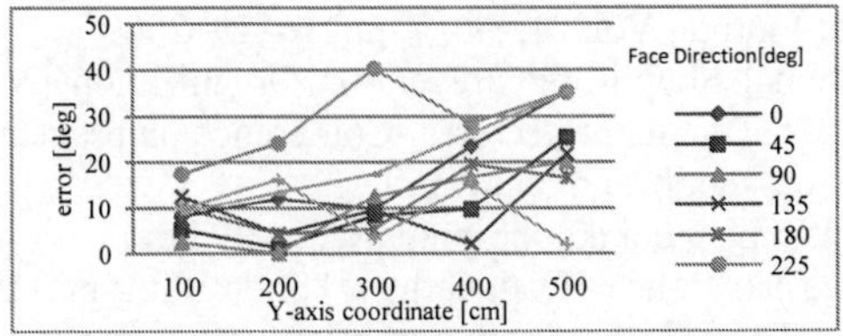

Figure 14. Errors in the estimation of face direction

Although there were errors in the results, we were able to estimate face directions to some extent. The errors were particularly small when the target was facing the camera. For face directions where there was a large number of face pixels in the image, the estimation accuracy was relatively high. There is also a tendency for the face direction estimation error to increase as the distance from the camera increases. This is because people occupy a smaller number of pixels as they move away from the camera, resulting in lower accuracy. Also, the lack of symmetry in the errors recorded at face directions of 0° and 180° is thought to be affected by the lighting direction in the test environment.

6.3 Comparison with photographic images

6.3.1 Experimental environment

To evaluate this system as a whole, we performed an experiment to compare the walkthrough video with pictures captured by an ordinary camera. The experiment was performed with four different layouts as shown in Fig. 15. In this experiment, we used two cameras installed 2 meters apart. First, a target object was placed in the test space. An ordinary camera was then used to photograph the target object from the person's location. We also saved the system's output video produced when oriented from this position in the direction of the target object. We then compared the saved images with the images captured by the ordinary camera.

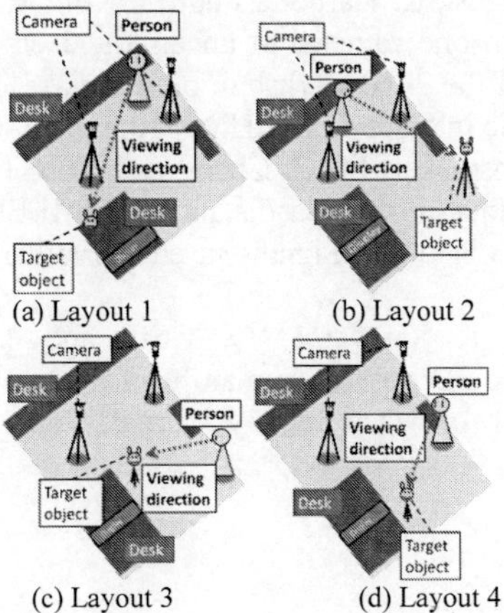

Figure 15. Experimental layouts for comparison with photographic images

6.3.2 Experimental results and discussion

Fig. 16(a) and (b) show the output of the system and an image taken with a camera in layout 1. Similarly, the results for layouts 2–4 are shown in Figs. 16(c) through (h) respectively. In Fig. 16, the position of the target object is enclosed by a circle. Also, Table 1 shows the pixel offset percentage between the photographic image and the system output at the target object. From the results of layouts 1 and 2, it can be seen that the image offset percentage is less than 10% in the X direction and less than 20% in the Y direction, and that in the horizontal plane it was possible to display video in the face direction. In layout 3, the target object was not captured and it was not possible to reproduce video in the face direction. Also, in layout 4, the offset in the Y direction of the image became larger.

In layout 3 as shown in Fig. 15(c), this system was unable to produce video in the face direction for a subject at an intermediate position with respect to the camera. To make it possible to do so, it would be necessary to increase the range over which video can be produced by increasing the number of cameras. Also, as shown in Figs. 16(g) and (h), this system produces large errors when reproducing directions that are tilted up or down. To improve the result, it would need to be capable of estimating the vertical component of the face direction.

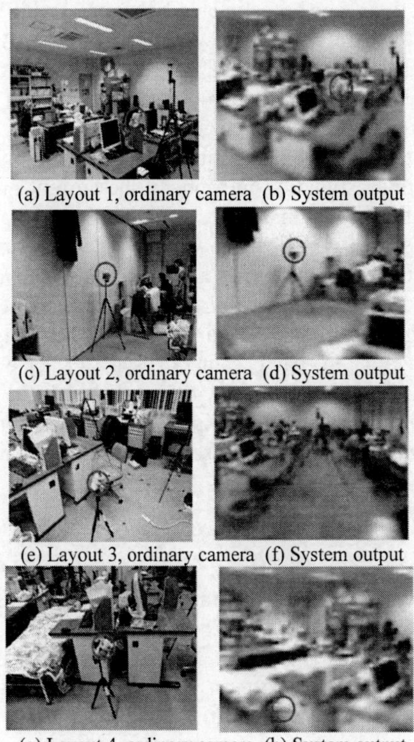

(a) Layout 1, ordinary camera (b) System output

(c) Layout 2, ordinary camera (d) System output

(e) Layout 3, ordinary camera (f) System output

(g) Layout 4, ordinary camera (h) System output

Figure 16. Results of comparison experiment

Table 1. Offset of system output from photographic image

	Offset of X coordinates[%]	Offset of Y coordinates[%]
Layout1	2	18
Layout2	8	12
Layout3	—	—
Layout4	16	37

7 Conclusions

In this study, we have produced and evaluated a walkthrough system that uses image processing to acquire a person's position and face direction, and displays video corresponding to this person's face direction. In this system, multiple omnidirectional cameras are used to determine a person's position based on regions of movement. The face direction is estimated from the head position and skin region. We have also produced a walk-through system that uses an omnidirectional image to create a walkthrough video in the person's face direction.

In evaluation experiments, we examined the system's accuracy in the estimation of human positions and face directions, and we compared the system's output with ordinary camera images captured from the same position and orientation. The positions of humans can be estimated accurately in regions surrounded by multiple cameras, but the accuracy decreases with increasing distance from the cameras. Face directions can be estimated accurately with low errors for faces that are pointing towards the camera. Also, in an experiment to compare camera images with the system output, we were able to acquire video close to the camera images in the system output for most positions.

In future studies, it will first be necessary to improve the face direction estimation method. In the current method, the face direction is estimated for each individual camera, but what is needed is a mechanism whereby the face direction can be estimated by the system as a whole. Specifically, it will be necessary to judge the face direction in three dimensions by associating 3D spatial coordinates with the image of the moving region in each camera used for face direction estimation. Furthermore, it will be necessary to introduce distributed processing on multiple PCs in order to reduce the processing load so that high-resolution images can be used.

8 References

[1] S. Kawabata, S. Hiura and K. Sato, "3D intruder detection system with uncalibrated multiple cameras," Trans. IEICE, Vol. J91-D, No. 1, pp. 110–119, 2008.

[2] B.T. Morris and M.M. Trivedi, "contextual activity visualization from long-term video observations," IEEE Intelligent Systems,Vol. 25, No.3, pp. 50–62, 2010.

[3] Y. Sato, Y. Yoneda, K. Hashimoto and Y. Shibata, "Face image tracking system for surveillance using an omnidirectional camera," IPSJ SIG Notes, Vol. 2007, No. 58, pp. 13–18, 2007.

[4] S. Morita, K. Yamazawa, M. Terazawa and N. Yokoya, "networked remote surveillance system using omnidirectional image sensors," Trans. IEICE, Vol. J88-D-II, No. 5, pp. 864–875, 2005.

[5] S. Minamitake, S. Takahashi, J. Tanaka, "A gaze information acquisition system for public large screens," Multimedia, Distributed, Cooperative and Mobile Symposium DICOMO 2008, CD-ROM, 2008.

[6] T. Kinebuchi, H. Arai, I. Miyagawa et al.: "A technique for measuring advert efficacy by image processing," NTT Technical Journal, Vol. 21, No. 7, pp. 16–19, 2009.

[7] National Shoplifting Prevention Organization (NSPO) Archive' 09, Tochigi prefecture, "Conference on preventative measures for shoplifting by juveniles," http://www.manboukikou.jp/html/archive09.html

[8] Nagasaki Police Headquarters, "Shoplifting prevention manual — Towards the creation of bright crime-free shops, " http://www.police.pref.nagasaki.jp/a60gaitai/a01higai/06shoplifting.pdf

[9] N. Suzuki, K. Hirasawa, K. Tanaka, Y. Kobayashi, Y. Sato and Y. Fujino, "Detection of abnormal behavior and patterns by human trajectories analysis," Trans. IEICE, Vol. J91-D, No. 6, pp.1550–1560, 2008.

[10] S. Kubota, M. Maruyama, T. Ikumi and M. Takahata, "Customer trajectory detection system using multiple omnidirectional cameras," Toshiba Review, Vol. 63, No. 10, pp. 44–47, 2008.

[11] S. Ikeda, T. Kunishima and K. Yokota, "Constructing virtual spaces based on panorama images," DBSJ Letters, Vol. 5, No. 1, pp.97-100, 2006.

[12] O. Saurer, F. Fraundorfer and M. Pollefeys, "OmniTour: Semi-automatic generation of interactive virtual tours from omnidirectional video," Proc. Int. Conf. on 3D Data Processing, Visualization and Transmission 3DPVT2010, 2010.

[13] C.H. Chen, Y. Yao, D. Page, B. Abidi, A. Koschan and M. Abidi, "Camera handoff and placement for automated tracking systems with multiple omnidirectional cameras," Computer Vision and Image Understanding, Vol. 114, No.2 , pp. 179–197, 2010.

[14] N. Robertson and I. Reid, "Estimating gaze direction from low-resolution faces in video," Proc. of European Conf on Computer Vision ECCV 2006, pp. 402–415, 2006.

[15] T. Vatahska, M. Bennewitz and S. Behnke, "Feature-based head pose estimation from images," 7th IEEE-RAS Int. Conf. on Humanoid Robots, pp. 330–335, 2007.

[16] S. Asteriadis, K. Karpouzis and S. Kollias, "Head pose estimation with one camera, in uncalibrated environments," Proceedings of the 2010 workshop on Eye gaze in intelligent human machine interaction EGIHMI '10, pp. 55–62, 2010.

[17] N. Krahnstoever, M. C. Chang and W. Ge, "Gaze and body pose estimation from a distance," 8th IEEE Int. Conf. on Advanced Video and Signal-Based Surveillance, pp. 11–16, 2011.

[18] H. Wu, T. Shioyama, Q. Chan and T. Shimada, "Estimating the 3D pose of human head from a single color image," Human Interface Society Journal, Vol. 1, No. 1, pp. 69–74, 1999.

SESSION

IMAGE CODING, COMPRESSION, WAVELETS, WATERMARKING, AND RELATED METHODS

Chair(s)

TBA

ρGBbBShift: Method for Introducing Perceptual Criteria to Region of Interest Coding

Jaime Moreno†, Christine Fernandez‡, and Salvador Saucedo†
†Superior School of Mechanical and Electrical Engineers, National Polytechnic Institute of Mexico, IPN Avenue, Lindavista, Mexico City, 07738, Mexico.
‡Signal, Image and Communications Department, University of Poitiers, Poitiers, 30179, France.
e-mail:jmorenoe@ipn.mx

Abstract— *This work describes a perceptual method (*ρGBbBShift*) for codding of Region of Interest (ROI) areas. It introduces perceptual criteria to the GBbBShift method when bitplanes of ROI and background areas are shifted. This additional feature is intended for balancing perceptual importance of some coefficients regardless their numerical importance. Perceptual criteria are applied using the CIWaM, which is a low-level computational model that reproduces color perception in the Human Visual System. Results show that there is no perceptual difference at ROI between the* MaxShift *method and* ρGBbBShift *and, at the same time, perceptual quality of the entire image is improved when using* ρGBbBShift*. Furthermore, when* ρGBbBShift *method is applied to* Hi-SET *coder and it is compared against* MaxShift *method applied to both the JPEG2000 standard and the* Hi-SET*, the images coded by the combination* ρGBbBShift-Hi-SET *get the best results when the overall perceptual image quality is estimated. The* ρGBbBShift *method is a generalized algorithm that can be applied to other Wavelet based image compression algorithms such as JPEG2000, SPIHT or SPECK.*

Keywords: Image Coding, JPEG2000, H*i*-SET, region of interest(ROI), bitplane coding, wavelet coding, maximum shift (MaxShift), bitplane-by-bitplane shift (BbBShift), generalized bitplane-by-bitplane shift (GBbBShift).

1. Introduction

1.1 JPEG2000 ROI Coding

Region of interest (ROI) image coding is a feature that modern image coders have, which allows to encode an specific region with better quality than the rest of the image or background (BG). ROI coding is one of the requirements in the JPEG2000 image coding standard [1], [2], which defines two ROI methods[3], [4]:

1) Based on general scaling [3]
2) Maximum shift (MaxShift) [4]

The general ROI scaling-based method scales coefficients in such a way that the bits associated with the ROI are shifted to higher bitplanes than the bitplanes associated with the background, as shown in Figure 1(b). It implies that during a embedded coding process, any background bitplane of the image is located after the most significant ROI bitplanes into the bitstream. But, in some cases, depending on the scaling value, φ, some bits of ROI are simultaneously encoded with BG. Therefore, this method allows to decode and refine the ROI before the rest of the image. No matter φ, it is posible to reconstruct with the entire bitstream a highest fidelity version of the whole image. Nevertheless, If the bitstream is terminated abruptly, the ROI will have a higher fidelity than BG.

The scaling-based method is implemented in five steps:

1) A wavelet transform of the original images is performed.
2) A ROI mask is defined, indicating the set of coefficients that are necessary for reaching a lossless ROI reconstruction, Figure 2.
3) Wavelet coefficients are quantized and stored in a sign magnitude representation, using the most significant part of the precision. It will allow to downscale BG coefficients.
4) A specified scaling value, $\tilde{\varphi}$, downscales the coefficients inside the BG.
5) The most significant bitplanes are progressively entropy encoded.

The input of ROI scaling-based method is the scaling value φ, while MaxShift method calculates it. Hence, the encoder defines from quantized coefficients this scaling value such that:

$$\varphi = \lceil \log_2 (\max \{\mathcal{M}_{BG}\} + 1) \rceil \tag{1}$$

where $\max \{\mathcal{M}_{BG}\}$ is the maximum coefficient in the BG. Thus, when ROI is scaled up φ bitplanes, the minimum coefficient belonging to ROI will be place one bitplane up of BG (Fig. 1(c)). Namely, 2^{φ} is the smallest integer that is greater than any coefficient in the BG. MaxShift method is shown in Figure 1(c). Bitplane mask (BP_{mask}) will be explained in section 2.2.

At the decoder side, the ROI and BG coefficients are simply identified by checking the coefficient magnitudes. All coefficients that are higher or equal than the φth bitplane belong to the ROI otherwise they are a part of BG. Hence, it is not important to transmit the shape information of the ROI or ROIs to the decoder. The ROI coefficients are scaled down

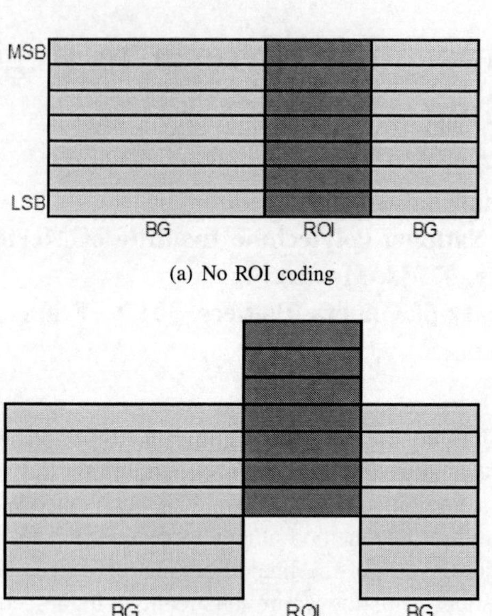

(a) No ROI coding

(b) Scaling Based Method

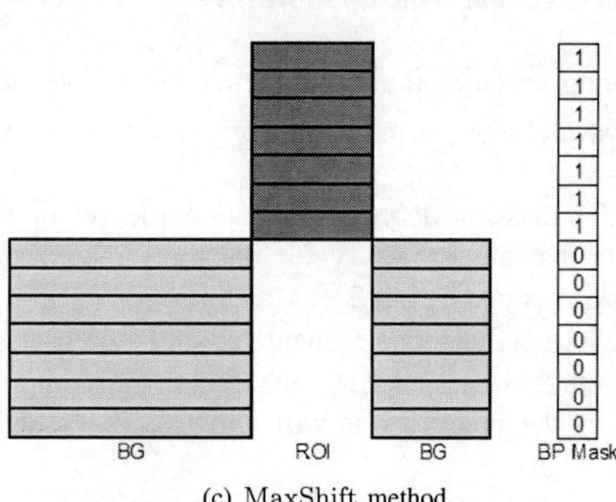

(c) MaxShift method

Fig. 1
JPEG2000 ROI CODING. (A) NO ROI CODING, (B) SCALING BASED ROI CODING METHOD ($\varphi = 3$) AND (C) MaxShift METHOD, $\varphi = 7$. BACKGROUND IS DENOTED AS BG, REGION OF INTEREST AS ROI AND BITPLANE MASK AS BP_{mask}. MSB IS THE MOST SIGNIFICANT BITPLANE AND LSB IS THE LEAST SIGNIFICANT BITPLANE.

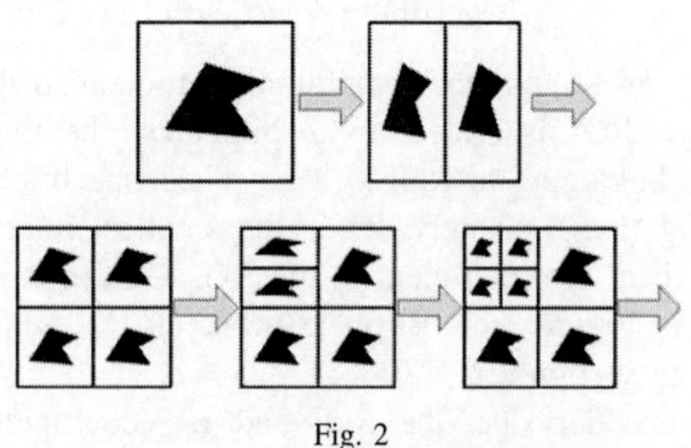

Fig. 2
ROI MASK GENERATION, WAVELET DOMAIN.

φ bitplanes before inverse wavelet transformation is applied.

1.2 Perceptual Coding

1.2.1 Chromatic Induction Wavelet Model

In order to generate an approximation to how every pixel is perceived from a certain distance taking into account the value of its neighboring pixels the Chromatic Induction Wavelet Model (CIWaM) is used. CIWaM attenuates the details that the human visual system is not able to perceive, enhances those that are perceptually relevant and produces an approximation of the image that the brain visual cortex perceives. CIWaM takes an input image $\mathcal{I}$ and decomposes it into a set of wavelet planes $\omega_{s,o}$ of different spatial scales s (i.e., spatial frequency ν) and spatial orientations o. It is described as

$$\mathcal{I} = \sum_{s=1}^{n} \sum_{o=v,h,dgl} \omega_{s,o} + c_n \ , \tag{2}$$

where n is the number of wavelet planes, c_n is the residual plane and o is the spatial orientation either *v*ertical, *h*orizontal or *d*ia*g*ona*l*. The perceptual image $\mathcal{I}_\rho$ is recovered by weighting these $\omega_{s,o}$ wavelet coefficients using the *extended Contrast Sensitivity Function* (e-CSF), which considers spatial surround information (denoted by r), visual frequency (ν related to spatial frequency by observation distance) and observation distance (d). Perceptual image $\mathcal{I}_\rho$ can be obtained by

$$\mathcal{I}_\rho = \sum_{s=1}^{n} \sum_{o=v,h,dgl} \alpha(\nu, r)\, \omega_{s,o} + c_n \ , \tag{3}$$

where $\alpha(\nu, r)$ is the e-CSF weighting function that tries to reproduce some perceptual properties of the HVS. The term $\alpha(\nu, r)\ \omega_{s,o} \equiv \omega_{s,o;\rho,d}$ can be considered the *perceptual wavelet coefficients* of image $\mathcal{I}$ when observed at distance d. For details on the CIWaM and the $\alpha(\nu, r)$ function, see [5].

1.2.2 Quantization

We employ the perceptual quantizer (ρSQ) either forward (F-ρSQ) and inverse (I-ρSQ), defined by Moreno and Otazu in [6]. Quantization is the only cause that introduces distortion into a compression process. Each transform sample at the perceptual image $\mathcal{I}_\rho$ (from Eq. 3) is mapped independently to a corresponding step size either Δ_s or Δ_n, thus $\mathcal{I}_\rho$ is associated with a specific interval on the real line. Then, the perceptually quantized coefficients $\mathcal{Q}$ (F-ρSQ), from a known viewing distance d, are calculated as follows:

$$\mathcal{Q} = \sum_{s=1}^{n} \sum_{o=v,h,d} sign(\omega_{s,o}) \left\lfloor \frac{|\alpha(\nu, r) \cdot \omega_{s,o}|}{\Delta_s} \right\rfloor + \left\lfloor \frac{c_n}{\Delta_n} \right\rfloor \tag{4}$$

The perceptual inverse quantizer (I-ρSQ) or the recovered $\widehat{\alpha}(\nu, r)$ introduces perceptual criteria to the classical Inverse

Scalar Quantizer and is given by:

$$\widehat{\mathcal{I}} = \begin{cases} \sum_{s=1}^{n} \sum_{o=v,h,d} sign(\widehat{\omega_{s,o}}) \frac{\Delta_s \cdot (|\widehat{\omega_s^o}| + \delta)}{\widehat{\alpha}(\nu, r)} & \\ + (|\widehat{c_n}| + \delta) \cdot \Delta_n \ , & |\widehat{\omega_{s,o}}| > 0 \\ 0, & \widehat{\omega_{s,o}} = 0 \end{cases} \quad (5)$$

2. Related Work

2.1 BbBShift

Wang and Bovik proposed the bitplane-by-bitplane shift (BbBShift) method in [7]. BbBShift shifts bitplanes on a bitplane-by-bitplane strategy. Figure 3(a) shows an illustration of the BbBShift method. BbBShift uses two parameters, φ_1 and φ_2, whose sum is equal to the number of bitplanes for representing any coefficient inside the image, indexing the top bitplane as bitplane 1. Summarizing, the BbBShift method encodes the first φ_1 bitplanes with ROI coefficients, then, BG and ROI bitplanes are alternately shifted, refining gradually both ROI and BG of the image (Fig. 3(a)). The encoding process of the BbBShift method is defined as:

1) For a given bitplane *bpl* with at least one ROI coefficient:
   - If $bpl \leq \varphi_1$, *bpl* is not shifted.
   - If $\varphi_1 < bpl \leq \varphi_1 + \varphi_2$, *bpl* is shifted down to $\varphi_1 + 2\,(bpl - \varphi_1)$
2) For a given bitplane *bpl* with at least one BG coefficient:
   - If $bpl \leq \varphi_2$, *bpl* is shifted down to $\varphi_1 + 2bpl - 1$
   - If $bpl > \varphi_2$, *bpl* is shifted down to $\varphi_1 + \varphi_2 + bpl$

2.2 GBbBShift

In practice, the quality refinement pattern of the ROI and BG used by BbBShift method is similar to the general scaling based method. Thus, when the image is encoded and this process is truncated in a specific point the quality of the ROI is high while there is no information of BG.

Hence, Wang and Bovik [8] modified BbBShift method and proposed the generalized bitplane-by-bitplane shift (GBbBShift) method, which introduces the option to improve visual quality either of ROI or BG or both. Figure 3(b) shows that with GBbBShift method it is posible to decode some bitplanes of BG after the decoding of same ROI bitplanes. It allows to improve the overall quality of the recovered image. This is posible gathering BG bitplanes. Thus, when the encoding process achieves the lowest bitplanes of ROI, the quality of BG could be good enough in order to portray an approximation of BG.

Therefore, the main feature of GBbBShift is to give the opportunity to arbitrary chose the order of bitplane decoding, grouping them in ROI bitplanes and BG bitplanes. This is posible using a binary bitplane mask or BP_{mask}, which contains one bit per each bitplane, that is, twice the amount of bitplanes of the original image. A ROI bitplane is represented by 1, while a BG bitplane by 0. For example, the BP_{mask} for MaxShift method in Figure 1(c) is 11111110000000, while for BbBShift in Figure 3(a) and GBbBShift in Figure 3(b) are 11101010101000 and 11100011110000, respectively.

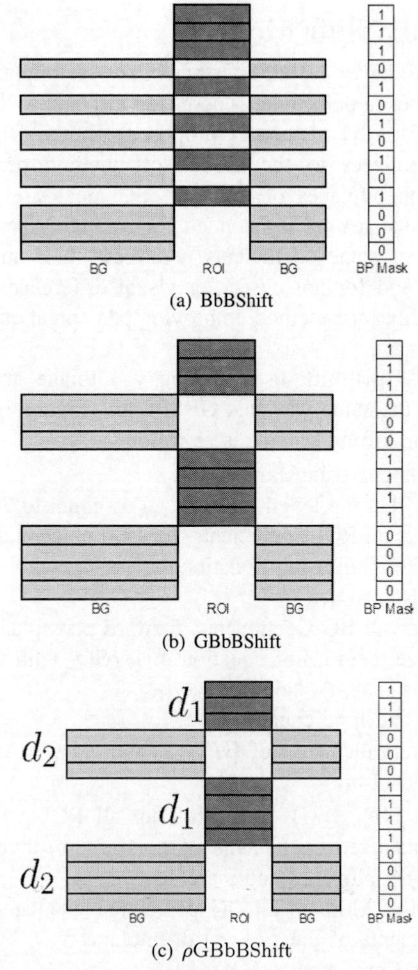

(a) BbBShift

(b) GBbBShift

(c) ρGBbBShift

Fig. 3

ROI CODING METHODS. (A) BBBSHIFT, $\varphi_1 = 3$ AND $\varphi_2 = 4$, (B) GBBBSHIFT AND (C)ρGBbBShift. BACKGROUND IS DENOTED AS BG (FOR ρGBbBShift METHOD IS PERCEPTUALLY QUANTIZED BY ρSQ AT d_2), REGION OF INTEREST AS ROI (FOR ρGBbBShift METHOD IS PERCEPTUALLY QUANTIZED AT d_1 BY ρSQ) AND BITPLANE MASK AS BP_{mask}.

At the encoder side, the BP_{mask} has the order of shifting both the ROI and BG bitplanes. Furthermore, BP_{mask} is encoded in the bitstream, while the scaling values φ or φ_1 and φ_2 from the MaxShift and BbBShift methods, respectively, have to be transmitted.

3. ρGBbBShift Method

In order to have several kinds of options for bitplane scaling techniques, a perceptual generalized bitplane-by-bitplane shift(ρGBbBShift) method is proposed. The ρGBbBShift method introduces to the GBbBShift method perceptual criteria when bitplanes of ROI and BG areas are shifted. This additional feature is intended for balancing perceptual importance of some coefficients regardless their numerical importance and for not observing visual difference at ROI regarding MaxShift method, improving perceptual quality of the entire image.

Thus, ρGBbBShift uses a binary bitplane mask or BP_{mask} in the same way that GBbBShift (Figure 3(c)). At the encoder, shifting scheme is as follows:

1) Calculate φ using Equation 1.
2) Verify that the length of BP_{mask} is equal to 2φ.
3)
   - For all ROI Coefficients, forward perceptual quantize them using Equation 4 (F-ρSQ) with viewing distance d_1.
   - For all BG Coefficients, forward perceptual quantize them using Equation 4 (F-ρSQ) with viewing distance d_2, being $d_2 \gg d_1$.
4) Let τ and η be equal to 0.
5) For every element i of BP_{mask}, starting with the least significant bit:
   - If $BP_{mask}(i) = 1$, Shift up all ROI perceptual quantized coefficients of the $(\varphi - \eta)$-th bitplane by τ bitplanes and increment η.
   - Else: Shift up all BG perceptual quantized coefficients of the $(\varphi - \tau)$-th bitplane by η bitplanes and increment τ.

At the decoder, shifting scheme is as follows:

1) Let $\varphi = \frac{length\ of\ BP_{mask}}{2}$ be calculated.
2) Let τ and η be equal to 0.
3) For every element i of BP_{mask}, starting with the least significant bit:
   - If $BP_{mask}(i) = 1$, Shift down all perceptual quantized coefficients by τ bitplanes, which pertain to the $(2\varphi - (\tau + \eta))$-th bitplane of the recovered image and increment η.
   - Else: Shift down all perceptual quantized coefficients by η bitplanes, which pertain to the $(2\varphi - (\tau + \eta))$-th bitplane of the recovered image and increment τ.
4) Let us denote as $c_{i,j}$ a given non-zero wavelet coefficient of the recovered image with 2φ bitplanes and $\overline{c}_{i,j}$ as a shifted down c obtained in the previous step, with φ bitplanes.
   - If $(c_{i,j}\ \&\ BP_{mask}) > 0$, inverse perceptual quantize $\overline{c}_{i,j}$ using Equation 5 (I-ρSQ) with d_1 as viewing distance.
   - If $(c_{i,j}\ \&\ BP_{mask}) = 0$, inverse perceptual quantize $\overline{c}_{i,j}$ using Equation 5 (I-ρSQ) with d_2 as viewing distance.

4. Experimental Results

The ρGBbBShift method, as the other methods presented here, can be applied to many image compression algorithms such as JPEG2000 or H*i*-SET[9]. We test our method applying it to H*i*-SET and the results are contrasted with MaxShift method in JPEG2000 and H*i*-SET. The setup parameters are $\varphi = 8$ for MaxShift and $BP_{mask} = 1111000110110000$, $d_1 = 5H$ and $d_2 = 50H$, where H is picture height (512 pixels) in a 19-inch LCD monitor, for ρGBbBShift. Also, we use the *JJ2000* implementation when an image is compressed by JPEG2000 standard[10].

4.1 H*i*-SET: Brief description of the coding algorithm

H*i*-SET considers three coding passes: Initialization, Sorting and Refinement[11].

1) **Initialization:**
   - Divide the original Image $\mathcal{I}_{org}(i,j)$ into four sets according to Hilbert Rules described in [9], i.e. from $(level)\mathcal{U}$ to $(level-1)\,\mathcal{LUUR}$.
   - Output $thr = \left\lfloor \log_2 \left(\max_{(i,j)} \{|\mathcal{I}_{org}(i,j)|\} \right) \right\rfloor$
   - Set the List of Significant Pixels (LSP) to empty.
2) **Sorting:**
   - Replace with the production rules only curves, which contain significant coefficients until reaching the fractal $level = 1$. If there is a significant coefficient, output the sign, 0 for positives and 0 for negatives.
3) **Refinement**
   - For each (i,j) at LSP, output the thr-th most significant bit of $|\mathcal{I}_{org}(i,j)|$.
   - Decrement thr and if $thr = 1$ go to step 2, otherwise a lossless compression would be reached.

4.2 Application in well-known Test Images

Figure 4 shows a comparison among methods MaxShift and GBbBShift applied to JPEG2000, in addition to, ρGBbBShift applied to H*i*-SET. The 24-bpp image *Barbara* is compressed at 0.5 bpp. It can be observed that without visual difference at ROI, the ρGBbBShift method provide better image quality at the BG than the general based methods defined in JPEG2000 Part II[1].In order to better qualify the performance of MaxShift, GBbBShift and ρGBbBShift methods, first, we compared these methods applied to the H*i*-SET coder and then, we compare MaxShift and ρGBbBShift methods applied to the JPEG2000 standard and H*i*-SET, respectively. We compress two different grayscale and color images of *Lenna* at different bit-rates. ROI area is a patch at the center of these images, whose size is 1/16 of the image. We employ the perceptual quality assessment proposed by Moreno and Otazu in [12], which weights the mainstream PSNR by means of a chromatic induction model (C_wPSNR).

Figs. 5(a) and 5(b) show the comparison among MaxShift(Blue Function), GBbBShift(Green Function) and ρGBbBShift(Red Function) methods applied to H*i*-SET coder. 512 × 512 pixel Image *Lenna* for gray-scale is employ for this experiment. These Figures also show that the ρGBbBShift method gets the better results both in PSNR(objective image quality, Fig. 5(a)) and C_wPSNR(subjective image quality, Fig. 5(b)) in contrast to MaxShift and GBbBShift methods. In addition, when MaxShift method applied to JPEG2000 coder and ρGBbBShift applied to H*i*-SET coder are compared, ρGBbBShift obtains less objective quality (Fig. 5(c)), but better subjective quality for gray-scale images (Fig. 5(d)).

Figure 6 shows a visual example, when image *Lenna* is compressed at 0.34 bpp by JPEG2000 and H*i*-SET. Thus, it can be observed that ρGBbBShift provides an important perceptual difference regarding the MaxShift method(Fig. 6(d)). Furthermore, Figs. 6(b) and 6(c) show the examples when MaxShift and GBbBShift methods, respectively, are applied to the H*i*-SET coder.

4.3 Application in other image compression fields

The usage of ROI coded images depends on an specific application, but in some fields such as manipulation and transmission of images is important to enhance the image quality of some areas and to reduce it in others[13], [14]. In Telemedicine or in Remote Sensing (RS) it is desirable to maintain the best quality of the ROI area, preserving relevant information of BG, namely the most perceptual frequencies. Figure 7 shows an example of the application of ROI in Remote Sensing. Image *2.1.05*, from *Volumen 2: aerials* of USC-SIPI image database 8 bits per pixel[15], is compressed at 0.42 bpp. MaxShift method spends all the bit-ratio for coding ROI, located at [159 260 384 460], while ρGBbBShift balances a perceptually lossless ROI area with an acceptable representation of the BG. Hence, the overall image quality measured by PSNR in Figure 7(a) is 16.06 dB, while in Figure 7(b) is 24.28 dB. When perceptual metrics assess the image quality of the ρGBbBShift coded image, for example, VIFP=0.4982, WSNR=24.8469 and C_wPSNR=27.07, while for MaxShift coded image VIFP=0.2368, WSNR=11.33 and C_wPSNR=16.72. Thus, for this example, both PSNR and these subjective metrics reflect important perceptual differences between ROI methods, being ρGBbBShift method better than MaxShift method.

5. Conclusions

A perceptual implementation of the Region of Interest, ρGBbBShift(), is proposed, which is a generalized method that can be applied to any wavelet-based compressor. We introduced ρGBbBShift method to the H*i*-SET coder and it visually improves the results obtained by previous methods like MaxShift and GBbBShift. Our experiments show that ρGBbBShift into H*i*-SET provides an important perceptual difference regarding the MaxShift method into JPEG2000, when it is applied to conventional images like *Lenna* or *Barbara*.

Acknowledgment

This work is supported by The National Polytechnic Institute of Mexico by means of a granted fund by the Committee of Operation and Promotion of Academic Activities (COFAA).

References

[1] M. Boliek, E. Majani, J. S. Houchin, J. Kasner, and M. Carlander, *Information Technology: JPEG2000 Image Coding System (Extensions)*, JPEG 2000 Part II final committee draft ed., ISO/IEC JTC 1/SC 29/WG 1, Dec. 2000.

[2] M. Boliek, C. Christopoulos, and E. Majani, *Information Technology: JPEG2000 Image Coding System*, JPEG 2000 Part I final committee draft version 1.0 ed., ISO/IEC JTC1/SC29 WG1, JPEG 2000, April 2000.

[3] D. S. Taubman and M. W. Marcellin, *JPEG2000: Image Compression Fundamentals, Standards and Practice*, ser. ISBN: 0-7923-7519-X. Kluwer Academic Publishers, 2002.

[4] E. Atsumi and N. Farvardin, "Lossy/lossless region-of-interest image coding based on set partitioning in hierarchical trees," in *International Conference on Image Processing*, vol. 1, oct 1998, pp. 87 –91 vol.1.

[5] X. Otazu, C. Párraga, and M. Vanrell, "Toward a unified chromatic induction model," *Journal of Vision*, vol. 10(12), no. 6, 2010.

[6] J. Moreno and X. Otazu, "Perceptual quantization using a chromatic induction model," July 2011, under review in IEEE Transactions on Image Processing.

[7] Z. Wang and A. C.Bovik, "Bitplane-by-bitplane shift (Bb BShift) - a suggestion for JPEG2000 region of interest image coding," *IEEE Signal Processing Letters*, vol. 9, no. 5, pp. 160 – 162, May 2002.

[8] Z. Wang, S. Banerjee, B. L. Evans, and A. C. Bovik, "Generalized bitplane-by-bitplane shift method for JPEG2000 ROI coding," *IEEE International Conference on Image Processing*, vol. 3, pp. 81–84, September 22-25 2002.

[9] J. Moreno and X. Otazu, "Image coder based on H*i*lbert Scaning of Embedded quadTrees: An introduction of H*i*-SET coder," *IEEE International Conference on Multimedia and Expo*, July 2011.

[10] C. Research, École Polytechnique Fédérale de Lausanne, and Ericsson. (2001) JJ2000 implementation in Java. Cannon Research, École Polytechnique Fédérale de Lausanne and Ericsson. [Online]. Available: http://jj2000.epfl.ch/

[11] J. Moreno and X. Otazu, "Image coder based on H*i*lbert Scaning of Embedded quadTrees," *IEEE Data Compression Conference*, p. 470, March 2011.

[12] ——, "Full-reference quality assessment using a chromatic induction model: Jpeg and jpeg2000," July 2011, under review in Journal of the Optical Society of America A.

[13] J. Bartrina-Rapesta, F. Auli-Llinas, J. Serra-Sagrista, A. Zabala-Torres, X. Pons-Fernandez, and J. Maso-Pau, "Region of interest coding applied to map overlapping in geographic information systems," in *IEEE International Geoscience and Remote Sensing Symposium*, 23-28 2007, pp. 5001 –5004.

[14] J. Gonzalez-Conejero, J. Serra-Sagrista, C. Rubies-Feijoo, and L. Donoso-Bach, "Encoding of images containing no-data regions within JPEG2000 framework," in *15th IEEE International Conference on Image Processing*, 12-15 2008, pp. 1057 –1060.

[15] S. I. P. I. of the University of Southern California. (1997) The USC-SIPI image database. Signal and Image Processing Institute of the University of Southern California. [Online]. Available: http://sipi.usc.edu/database/

(a) MaxShift in JPEG2000 coder, 0.5 bpp

(b) GBbBShift in JPEG2000 coder, 0.5 bpp

(c) ρGBbBShift in Hi-SET coder, 0.5 bpp

Fig. 4

512 × 640 PIXEL IMAGE *Barbara* WITH 24 BITS PER PIXEL. ROI IS A PATCH OF THE IMAGE LOCATED AT [341 280 442 442], WHOSE SIZE IS 1/16 OF THE IMAGE. DECODED IMAGES AT 0.5 BPP USING MaxShift METHOD IN JPEG2000 CODER((A) $\varphi = 8$), GBBBSHIFT METHOD IN JPEG2000 CODER ((B)BP_{mask} = 1111000110110000) AND ρGBbBShift METHOD IN Hi-SET CODER ((C)BP_{mask} = 1111000110110000).

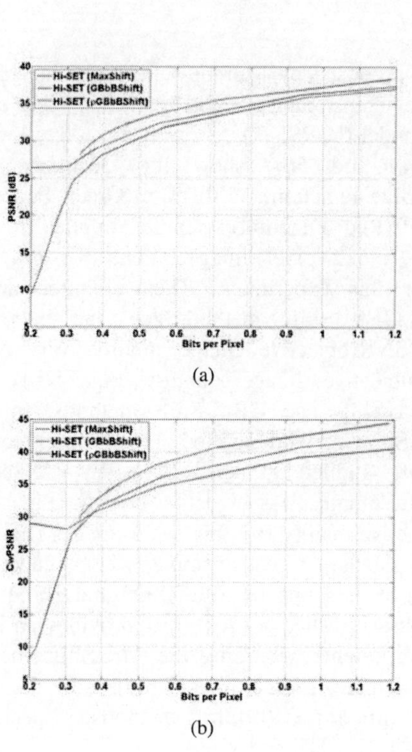

(a)

(b)

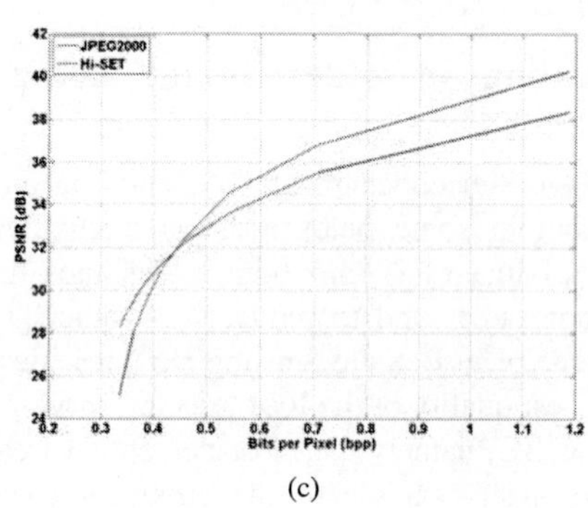

(c)

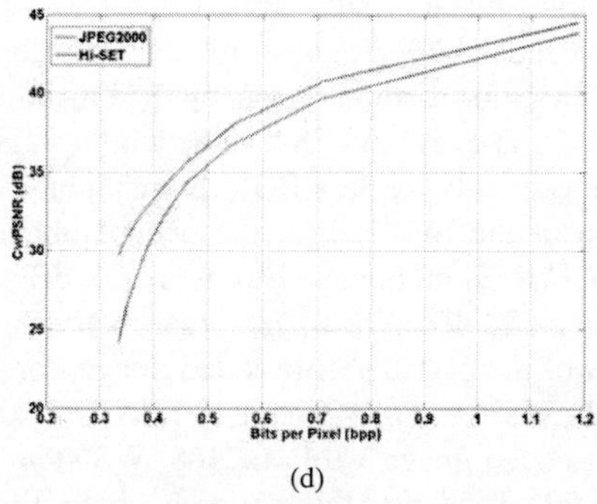

(d)

Fig. 5

(A-B) COMPARISON AMONG MaxShift(BLUE FUNCTION), GBBBSHIFT(GREEN FUNCTION) AND ρGBbBShift(RED FUNCTION) METHODS APPLIED TO Hi-SET CODER. (C-D) COMPARISON BETWEEN MaxShift METHOD APPLIED TO JPEG2000 CODER AND ρGBbBShift APPLIED TO Hi-SET CODER. 512 × 512 PIXEL IMAGE *Lenna* WITH 8 BITS PER PIXEL IS EMPLOYED FOR THIS EXPERIMENT. ROI IS A PATCH AT THE CENTER OF THE IMAGE, WHOSE SIZE IS 1/16 OF THE IMAGE. THE OVERALL IMAGE QUALITY OF DECODED IMAGES AT DIFFERENT BITS PER PIXEL ARE CONTRASTED BOTH (A AND C) OBJECTIVELY AND (B AND D)SUBJECTIVELY.

(a) MaxShift method in JPEG2000 coder, 0.34 bpp.

(b) MaxShift method in H*i*-SET coder, 0.34 bpp.

(c) GBbBShift method in H*i*-SET coder, 0.34 bpp.

(d) ρGBbBShift method in H*i*-SET coder, 0.34 bpp.

Fig. 6

512 × 512 PIXEL IMAGE *Lenna* FROM CMU IMAGE DATABASE WITH 8 BITS PER PIXEL. ROI IS A PATCH AT THE CENTER OF THE IMAGE, WHOSE SIZE IS 1/16 OF THE IMAGE. DECODED IMAGES AT 0.34 BPP USING $\varphi = 8$ FOR MaxShift METHOD (A) IN JPEG2000 CODER AND (B) IN H*i*-SET CODER, AND $BP_{mask} = 1111000110110000$ FOR (C) GBBBSHIFT AND (D) ρGBbBShift METHODS IN H*i*-SET CODER.

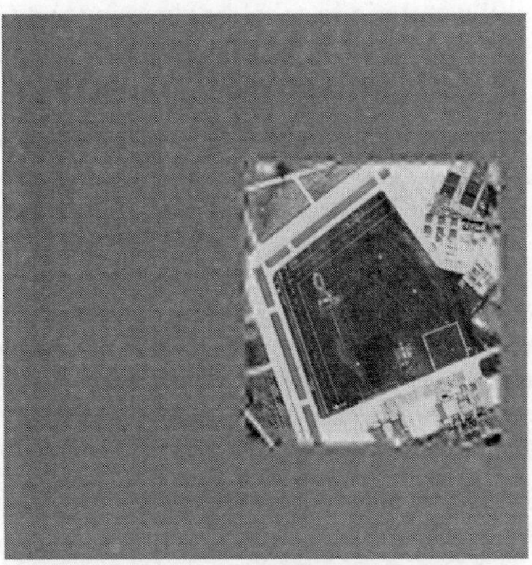

(a) MaxShift in JPEG2000 coder, 0.42 bpp

(b) ρGBbBShift method in H*i*-SET coder, 0.42 bpp

Fig. 7

EXAMPLE OF A REMOTE SENSING APPLICATION. 512 × 512 PIXEL IMAGE *2.1.05* FROM *Volumen 2: aerials* OF USC-SIPI IMAGE DATABASE AT 8 BITS PER PIXEL. ROI IS A PATCH WITH COORDINATES [159 260 384 460], WHOSE SIZE IS 225 × 200 PIXELS. DECODED IMAGES AT 0.42 BPP USING MaxShift METHOD ((A) $\varphi = 8$) IN JPEG2000 CODER AND ρGBbBShift METHOD ((B)$BP_{mask} = 1111000110110000$) IN H*i*-SET CODER.

Medical Image Compression Using Quad-tree Fractals and Segmentation

F.Khalili[1], **M. Celenk**[1], and **M. A. Akinlar**[2]
[1]School of Electrical Engineering and Computer Science, Ohio University, Athens, OH, USA
[2] Bilecik Seyh Edebali University, Bilecik, 11210, Turkey

Abstract - *In this paper, the possibility of using fractal compression on medical images is investigated. The utilized fractal method takes advantage of quad-tree partitioning and the results of fractal compression on x-ray images for different range size are presented. For making tradeoff between computational cost and compression accuracy, image segmentation is used and different range size assigned for each segments of image. The results show that applying larger range size for segments outside the region of interest reduce the computation time while the quality is still preserved.*

Keywords: Medical Image Compression, Fractal, Quad-tree, Compression ratio, NMSE

1 Introduction

It is the fact that medical images are acquired in digital format [1]. As most of these images are very large in size, storing and transferring them has been always an important issue. Although the cost of storage is falling drastically as the capacity per device increases, and the cost of transmission bandwidth is also falling; there remains a strong demand for medical image compression. Since the speed of computing is also increasing dramatically, the sophistication and complexity of compression schemes which are practical for use is increasing [2]. There are numerous ways of image compressions that can be categorized into two main groups; Lossless compression and Lossy compression.

Lossy compression provides greater compression rate, but the quality of the medical image reduces. On the other hand the lossless compression provides medical images of good quality but its compression rate is relatively low compared to the Lossy compression. In medical image we are in need of compression of the medical image at larger compression rate and also we need to preserve the quality of the medical image [3]. The redundancy and similarity among different regions of images makes compression feasible.

Fractal compression is kind of lossy compression uses the property of self-similarity of fractal objects. Exact self-similarity means that the fractal object is composed of scaled down copies of itself that are translated, stretched and rotated according to a transformation. Such a transformation is called affine transformation [4].

There are several works in image compression using fractal, each of which take advantage of different characteristics of an image or various known methods of fractal encoding. These methods are originated from the same ancestor by great number of similarities but some innovations in implementation [5][6][7][8][9].

In this work, the quad-tree partitioning fractal compression is utilized on two types of image. In the first experiment the original x-ray image is compressed by applying same range size for the entire image and in the second experiment a segmented x-ray image is compressed in a way that the range size is different in each segment. It is shown that applying different range size for different parts of one image, not only maintains its important information but also reduce the computation time. Remaining of the paper is organized as follow: section 2 gives more information about fractal compression, in section 3 the proposed algorithm is presented, the results of simulation are shown in section 4, and finally in section 5 the conclusion and future works are discussed.

2 Fractal Image Compression

Fractal encoding is a mathematical process used to encode any given image as a set of mathematical data that describes the fractal properties of the image. Fractal compression is very beneficial due to high Compression ratio, the decoding stage of the algorithm is independent of the reconstructed image and the reconstructed image is of good quality [10].

Fractal encoding relies on the fact that all objects contain information in the form of similar, repeating patterns called an attractor. Fractal encoding is largely used to convert the image into fractal codes. In the decoding it is just the reverse, in which a set of fractal codes are converted to image. The encoding process has intense computation, since large number of iterations is required to find the fractal patterns in an image.

The decoding process is much simpler as it interprets the fractal codes into the image. Fractal image compression is achieved either by using Iterated Function Systems (IFS) or by Partitioned Iterated Function Systems (PIFS).

The IFS uses contractive affine transformations which are combinations of three basic transformations; shear (enables rotation and reflection), translation (movement of a shape), and scaling/dilation (changing the size of a shape). A single transformation may be described by

$$w_i \begin{bmatrix} x \\ y \end{bmatrix} = \begin{bmatrix} a_i & b_i \\ c_i & d_i \end{bmatrix} \begin{bmatrix} x \\ y \end{bmatrix} + \begin{bmatrix} e_i \\ f_i \end{bmatrix} \quad (1)$$

The coefficients *a, d* determine the dilation, the coefficients *b, c* determine the shear, and *e, f* specify the translation.

The PIFS, which is a modified version of IFS, take advantage of 2 other parameters which are contrast and brightness. These two additional features give enough power to decode grayscale images from a description of the image consisting of the fractal operator. This transformation is described by

$$w_i \begin{bmatrix} x \\ y \\ z \end{bmatrix} = \begin{bmatrix} a_i & b_i & 0 \\ c_i & d_i & 0 \\ 0 & 0 & s_i \end{bmatrix} \begin{bmatrix} x \\ y \\ z \end{bmatrix} + \begin{bmatrix} e_i \\ f_i \\ o_i \end{bmatrix} \quad (2)$$

In which s_i specifies the contrast, o_i the brightness, and z variable is brightness function for given domain for each pair of x, y

$$z = f(x, y) \quad (3)$$

The partitioning scheme used to demarcate the range blocks is one of the most crucial elements of the fractal compression method. The fidelity and quality of the reconstructed image, the length and the structure of the fractal code, the shape of the transformations used to map domains into ranges and their descriptions in the fractal, code compression ratio, encoding time and all other important characteristics of the compression method are somehow influenced by the choice of the partitioning method [11]. There are plenty of partitioning methods among which quad-tree partitioning is selected for this work.

2.1 Quad-tree Partitioning

Partitioning the image in tree structure is the most popular partitioning mechanism. A quad-tree partitioning is a representation of an image as a tree in which each node corresponding to a square portion of the image contains four sub-nodes corresponding to the four quadrants of the square, the root of the tree being the initial image [12][13]. Fig. 1 shows the mechanism.

The squares at the nodes are compared with domains in the domain pool **D**, which are twice the range size. The pixels in the domain are averaged in groups of four so that the domain is reduced to the size of range and the affine transformation of the pixel values is found that minimizes the root mean square (RMS) difference between the transformed domain pixel values and the range pixel values. With a tolerance factor given for the rate or the quality, this method will break up into squares, thereby creating additional ranges with corresponding transformation codes and improving the reconstructed image quality until the desired rate or quality is obtained.

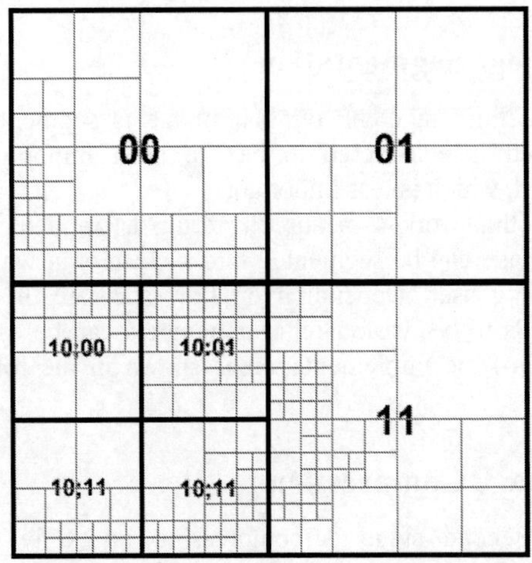

Fig. 1 Representation of Quad-tree mechanism

2.2 Decoding

Decoding process is done by iterating the set of transformations on an arbitrary initial image and the quad-tree partition is used to determine the range in the image. For each range block, the size of the domain block that maps to it, is shrunk by 2x2 pixel averaging. The pixel values of the shrunken domain block are then placed in the location in the range determined by the orientation information after scaling and offsetting. Computing all the range blocks constitutes one iteration. After several iterations, the decompressed image will be very close to the original image.

When the fractal image compression is compared to other methods used to compress different images, some of the main advantages and disadvantages can be summarized as follow:

Fractal compression advantages include; good mathematical encoding frame, resolution-free decoding, high compression ratio, and fast decompression. On the other hand, the same method suffers from slow encoding process [14].

3 Proposed Method

As it was mentioned in the previous section, fractal compression has got favourable characteristics that make it appropriate for compressing images with high compression ratio. But it should be taken in mind that for having decompressed image with acceptable degradation, the partitioning range size need to be very small. Applying small range size leads to increasing the computation time especially in encoding part which is undesirable.

In current method, the goal is using fractal compression by making less degradation on the decompressed image and reducing computation time. For doing so, the original image is partitioned into two segments, the background and the region of interest (ROI). For the background, whose information is not significant, the large range size can be used, while for the major part or the region of interest the small range size should apply to avoid loss of information.

3.1 Image Segmentation

In this stage the original image is segmented into ROI, which is considered to be the most important, and background, which is less important.

For this work k-means clustering is applied and the original image can be segmented into k clusters in which k is selectable by user. Depending on how accurate the output image needs to be, various cluster numbers can be assigned. The result of the implementation is shown in the following section.

3.2 Image Compression

The second stage is compressing image by taking advantage of fractal method. Here, quad-tree partitioning is applied and the domain size is considered two times the range size. In each part by rotating, flipping, and transposing the selected range we try to find the best similar part and find the parameters of affine transformation. After sweeping the whole image, the table of coefficients is produced and ready for the decompression algorithm. Despite the encoding which is complicated and time consuming, the decoding algorithm is straight forward and relatively fast.

4 Experimental Result

In this section, the implementation of the method is presented. The required codes are written in Matlab, by taking advantage of some pre-defined functions in image processing tool box.

This experiment consists of two parts, in the first part only the fractal compression is used and the results of different range size are presented. In the second part, which has two stages, firstly the image is segmented and then the fractal compression is applied.

4.1 Results of Fractal Compression

The following are the results of applying fractal image compression using quad-tree partitioning and different range size. As it is clear selecting smaller range size will produce better decompressed image with less noticeable artefacts which is more desirable. But at the same time making range size smaller needs more computation and the code will be very slow to produce the final coefficient results of the encoding part. To enhance this condition the second experiment is done.

Fig. 2 shows the results with 3 different range sizes for two sample x-ray images. To have a better sense of the resulting decompressed image quality, for each range size the Normalized Mean Square Error (NMSE) is also calculated. Moreover, the compression ratio needs to be calculated, the result of these calculations is shown in Table I. These results show that applying smaller range size leads to high quality decompressed image but low compression ratio.

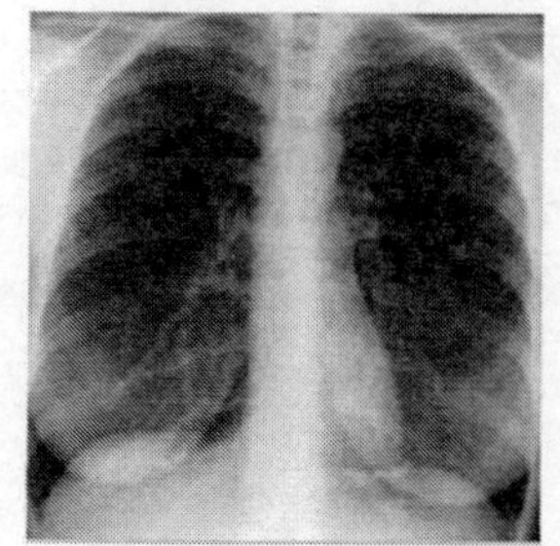
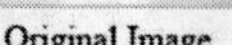
Original Image

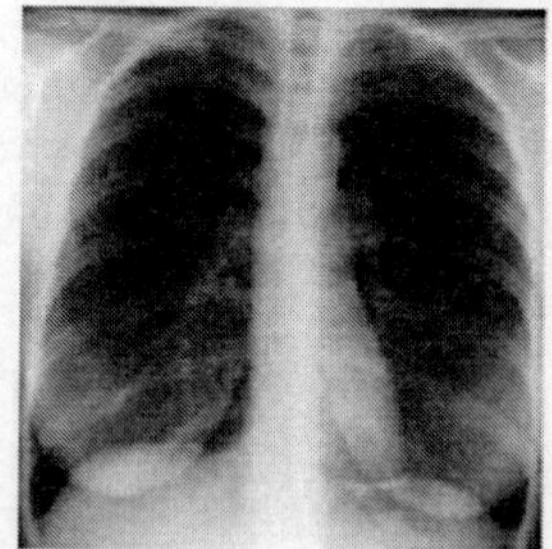
Decompressed Image with Range Size of 4

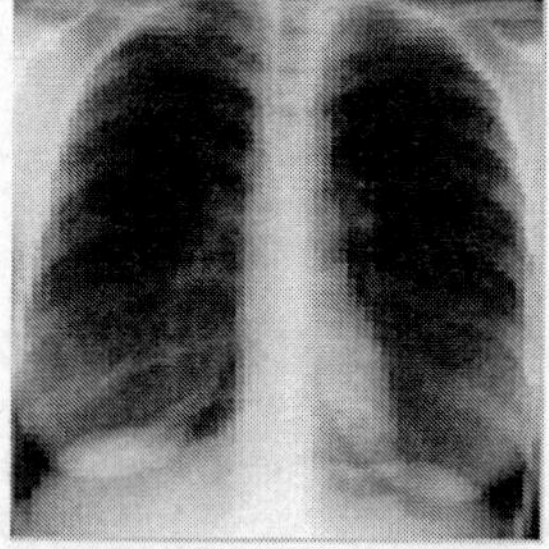
Decompressed Image with Range Size of 8

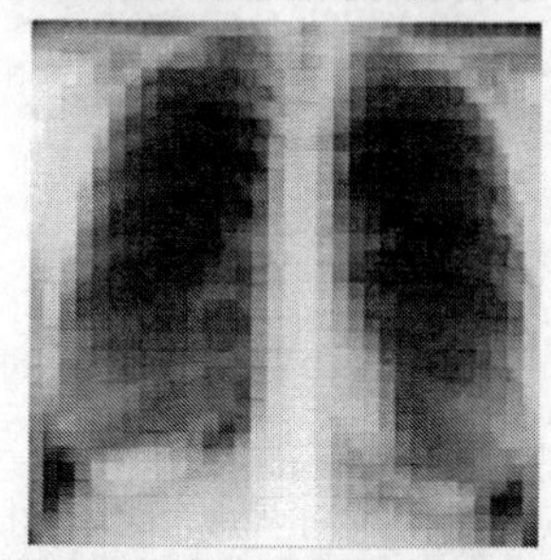
Decompressed Image with Range Size of 16

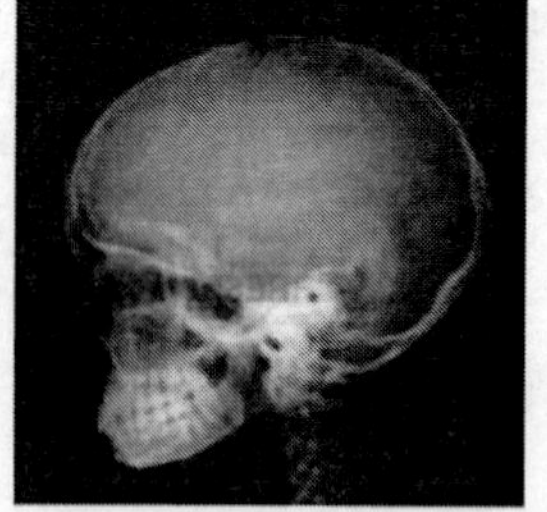
Original Image

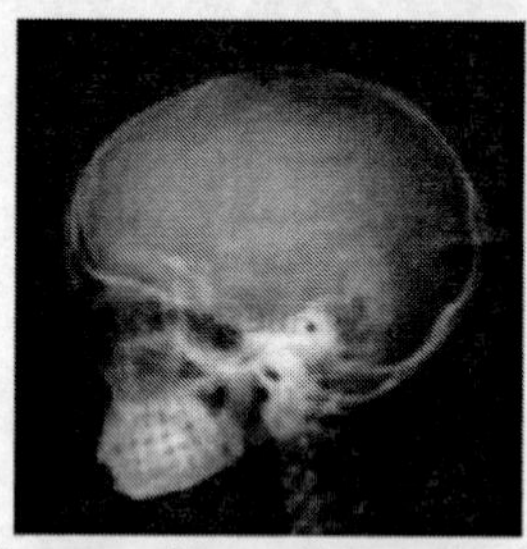
Decompressed Image with Range Size of 4

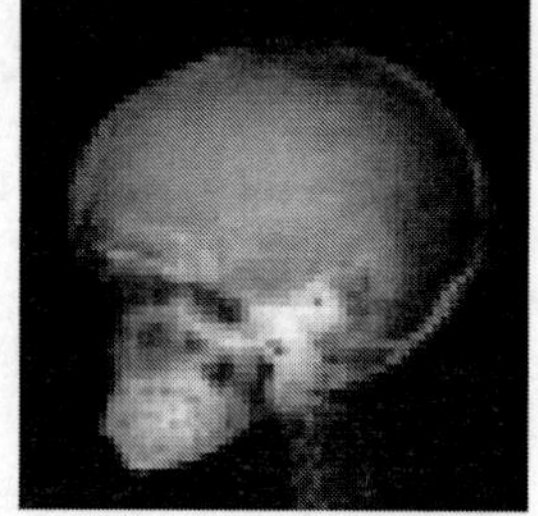
Decompressed Image with Range Size of 8

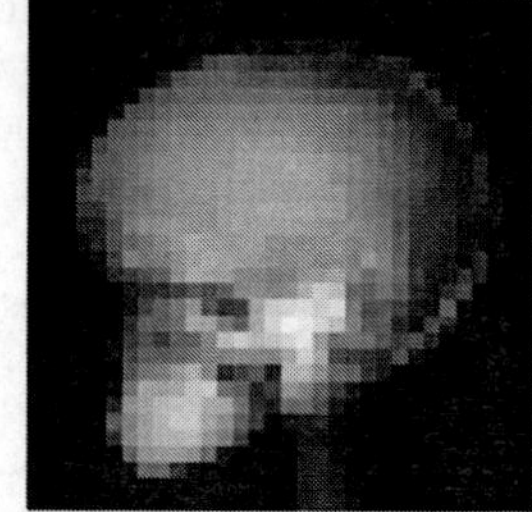
Decompressed Image with Range Size of 16

Fig. 2 Results of applying just Fractal Compression with different Range Size for two sample x-ray images

TABLE I
NORMALIZED MEAN SQUARE ERROR AND COMPRESSION RATIO FOR EACH RANGE SIZE AND TWO SAMPLE X-RAY IMAGE

Range Size	4	8	16
NMSE (chest x-ray)	1.53e-3%	5.56e-2%	3.9%
NMSE (head x-ray)	2.4e-3%	5.44e-2%	3.4%
Compression Ratio (chest x-ray)	3.2	12.8	51.2
Compression Ratio (head x-ray)	3.4	12.6	50.9

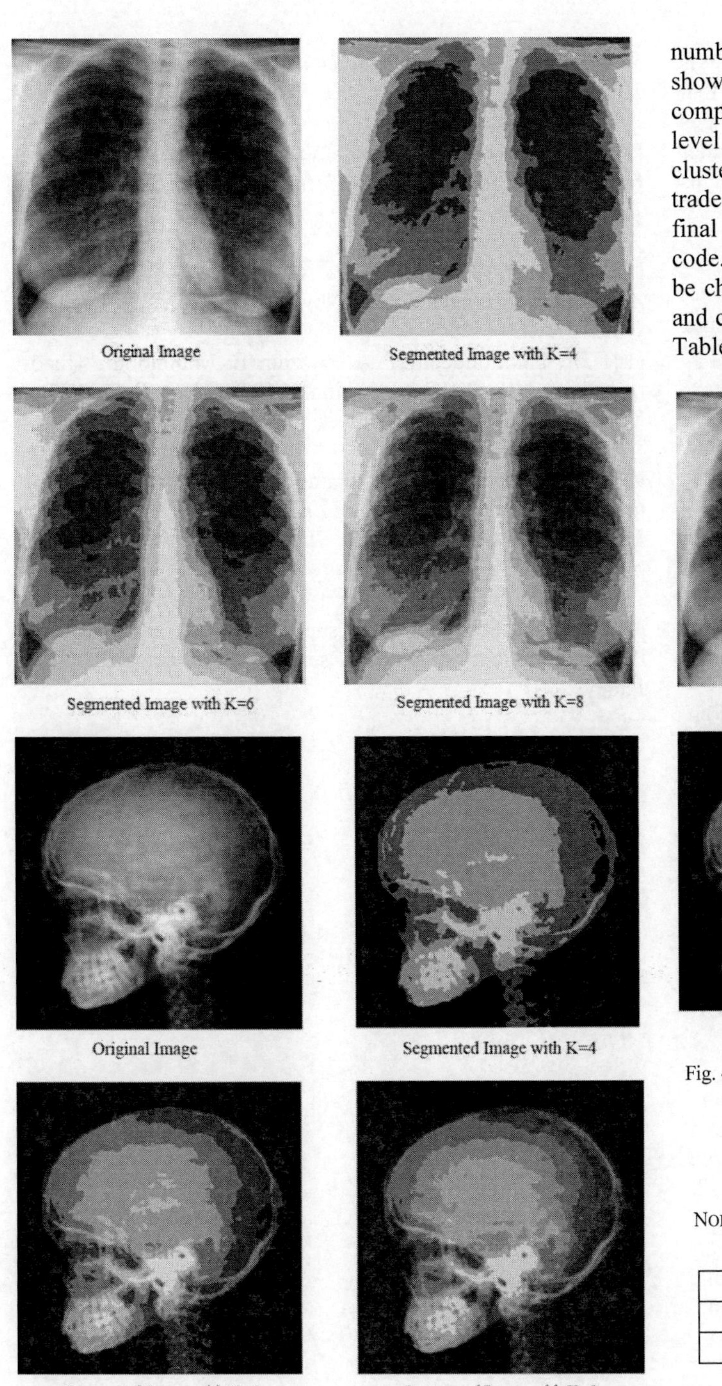

Fig. 3 Result of Segmentation with different clustering level for two sample x-ray image

4.2 Results of combining Segmentation and Fractals

In this experiment, the original image is firstly segmented to different clusters. Then for unimportant clusters (like background) large range size is applied and for the rest, which are assumed as ROI small range size is used. Fig. 3 shows the result image of the segmentation with different numbers of clusters and two sample x-ray images. Fig. 4 shows the final result of combining segmentation and compression for the two sample images. This result are for 6 level clustering and applying range size 8 for background cluster and 4 for ROI clusters. Needless to say that, there is a tradeoff between number of clusters, range size, quality of final decompressed image, and elapsed time for running the code. Based on the application, each of these parameters can be changed to achieve the best result. The calculated NMSE and compression ratio for sample experiment are presented in Table II.

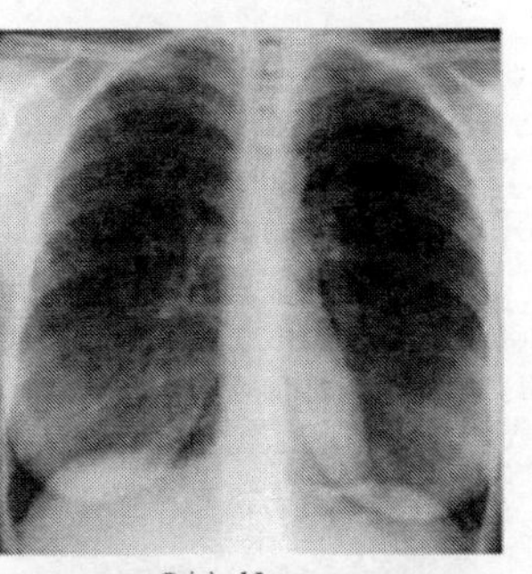

Original Image

Decompressed Image with K=6, Range Size of 4, 8

Original Image

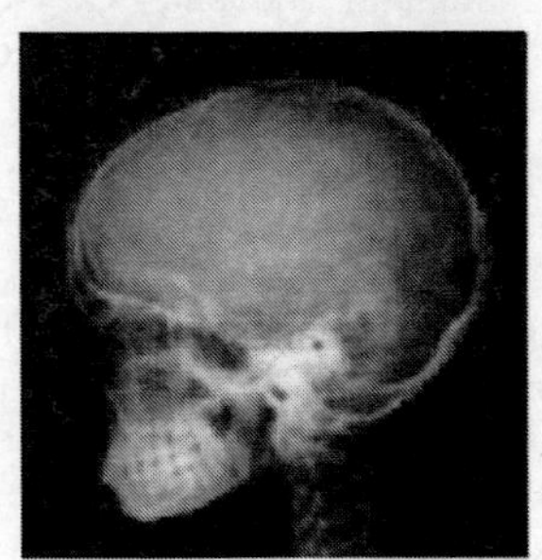

Decompressed Image with K=6, Range Size=4, 8

Fig. 4 Result of Combining Segmentation and Fractal Compression for two sample x-ray image

TABLE II
NORMALIZED MEAN SQUARE ERROR AND COMPRESSION RATIO FOR TWO SAMPLE X-RAY IMAGE BY APPLYING SEGMENTATION

x-ray sample	chest x-ray	head x-ray
NMSE	8.6e-3%	1.03e-2%
Compression Ratio	5.3	5.9

5 Conclusion

In this work, we try to compress medical x-ray image effectively by taking advantage of combining segmentation and Fractal compression. The results show that, when different range sizes are applied for different clusters, which are the output of segmentation, not only the computation time can be reduced, but the information of critical points in the image will preserve as well.

There are still some ways to improve the result of proposed method such as reducing blocky output in decompressed image. The exploited partitioning scheme is very likely the reason for this problem, it is believed that introducing a quad-map partitioning with overlapping ranges would be a better solution [15]. We can also apply other distributions to exploit self-similarity characteristic of images [16].

6 References

[1] Gloria Menegaz, "Trends in Medical Image Compression," *Current Medical Imaging Reviews,* 2006, pp. 1-21

[2] David A. Clunie, "Lossless Compression of Grayscale Medical Images - Effectiveness of Traditional and State of the Art Approaches," *Proc. SPIE*, Vol.3980, 2000, pp.74-84.

[3] S. Manimurugan, K. Porkumaran, "Fast and Efficient Secure Medical Image Compression Schemes," *European Journal of Scientific Research*, Vol.56 No.2, 2011, pp.139-150.

[4] Sumathi Poobal, G. Ravindran, "Arriving at an Optimum Value of Tolerance Factor for Compressing Medical Images," *International Journal of Biological and life sciences*, 2005, pp. 250-254.

[5] S. Bhavani, K. Thanushkodi, "A New Algorithm for Fractal Coding Using Self Organizing Map," *Journal of Computer Science 8 (6)*, 2012, pp.841-845

[6] Geoffrey M. Davis, "A Wavelet-Based Analysis of Fractal Image Compression," *IEEE TRANSACTIONS ON IMAGE PROCESSING*, 1997, pp.100-112

[7] Venkata Rama Prasad VADDELLA, Ramesh Babu INAMPUDI, "Fast Fractal Compression of Satellite and Medical Images Based on Domain-Range Entropy," *Journal of Applied Computer Science & Mathematics, no. 9 (4),* 2012, pp.21-26

[8] S. Bhavani, K. Thanushkodi, "A Novel Fractal Image Coding for Quasi-Lossless Medical Image Compression," *European Journal of Scientific Research*, Vol.70 No.1 (2012), pp. 88-97

[9] Hai Wang, "Fast Image Fractal Compression with Graph-Based Image Segmentation Algorithm," *International Journal of Graphics,* Vol. 1, No.1, November, 2010.

[10] Veenadevi.S.V.1 and A.G.Ananth, "Fractal Image Compression Using Quad tree Decomposition and Huffman Coding," *Signal & Image Processing: An International Journal (SIPIJ),* Vol.3, No.2, April 2012.

[11] Wojciech Walczak, "Fractal Compression of Medical Images," Master Thesis, Faculty of Computer Science and Management, Wrocław University of Technology, Poland, 2008.

[12] D.Saupe and S. Jacob, "Variance based quadtrees in fractal image compression", *Electronic Letters*, Vol.33, no.1, Jan1997, pp 46-48.

[13] Y.Fisher, *Fractal Image Compression: Theory and Application*, Springer Verlag, New York, 1995.

[14] Dr. Fakhiraldeen H. Ali Azzam E. Mahmood, "Quad-tree Fractal Image Compression," *Al-Rafidain Engineering,* Vol.14 No.4 2006, pp.82-98.

[15] Jacob Toft Pedersen, "Parallel fractal compression for medical imaging," *PARALLEL COMPUTING FOR MEDICAL IMAGING AND SIMULATION,* FALL 2010, pp.1-18.

[16] William Stallings, High speed Networks and Internets: Performance and quality of service, Prentice Hall, New Jersey, 2001

A Robust Color Image Watermarking Using Maximum Wavelet-Tree Difference Scheme

Chung-Yen Su[1] and Yen-Lin Chen[1]
[1]Department of Applied Electronics Technology,
National Taiwan Normal University, Taipei, Taiwan, R.O.C

Abstract - *Digital watermarking is a technique for copyright protection. In literature, many watermarking methods for gray images have been presented. Some of them are directly applied to the luminance component of a color image. A previous method applies to the difference between RGB components instead, and shows that the image quality can be improved. In this paper, we present a robust color image watermarking method to further improve the image quality. The proposed method is based on the maximum wavelet-tree difference scheme. Experimental results show the feasibility of the proposed method.*

Keywords: watermarking, wavelet-tree, robustness, discrete wavelet transform, copyright protection

1 Introduction

Nowadays, along with the multimedia technology to flourish, piracy also increases day by day. Therefore, copyright protection is getting more attention. Digital watermarking is such a technique, which embeds some information into a given media. In literature, many watermarking methods for gray images have been presented [1]-[6]. Especially, wavelet-tree based watermarking methods have been made great progress. Previous works show that the problem of gray image watermarking is how to quantize the wavelet trees to resist common image attacks, such as filtering, compression, cropping and noise. In [5], Run *et al.* proposed a more effective watermarking scheme than [1]-[4]. They embedded each watermark bit into the maximum and second maximum coefficients of a wavelet tree. In [6], Al-Otum and Samara presented a scheme to embed a binary watermark into wavelet-tree mutual differences between grouped coefficients of the wavelet-trees. In [7], the gray scale watermark is embedded into all the frequency-subbands of the image in each color component of YCbCr space. In [8][9], a binary watermark is embedded into the Y component while in [10] it is embedded three times separately in the YCbCr components of the image. Since the Y component of a color image is directly modified in these methods [7]-[10], the image quality will be degraded. To solve this problem, Al-Otum and Samara presented a method based on the selection of difference between the RGB components of a color image. In this study, we will present a method to further improve the image quality. The proposed method is mainly based on the maximum wavelet-tree difference scheme. The organization of this study is as follows. Section 2 briefly introduces the previous watermark scheme in [11]. Section 3 describes the proposed method. For completeness, the extraction algorithm is given in Section 4. Section 5 shows the experimental results to demonstrate the effectiveness of the proposed method. Finally, conclusions are given in Section 6.

2 Previous Watermark Embedding Scheme

We briefly introduce the algorithm in [11] as follows. We extract the R, G, and B components from a color RGB image. Then, we decompose each color component into the 4-layer subbands by using the 5/3 discrete wavelet transform (DWT). In each layer, the DWT produces four subbands. One is the low-pass band (LL) and the other three are the horizontal band (HL), the vertical band (LH), and the diagonal band (HH), respectively. The LL band is further decomposed into the next layer. We combine one coefficient in the LH4 (or HL4, HH4) band and four corresponding coefficients in the LH3 (or HL3, HH3) band and sixteen corresponding coefficients in the LH2 (or HL2, HH2) band to be a wavelet-tree, as shown in Fig. 1.

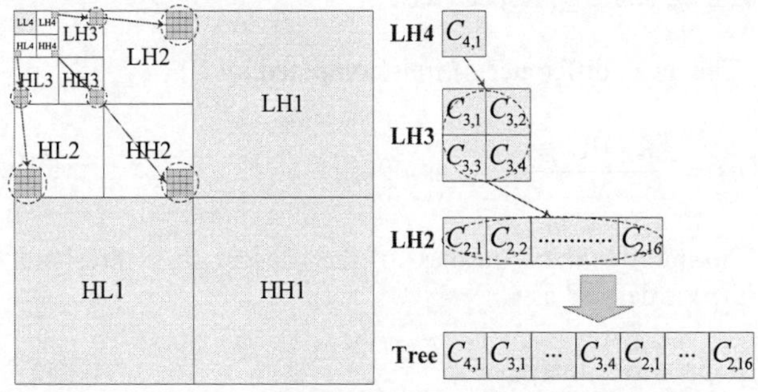

Fig. 1. The wavelet-tree scheme by 4-layer wavelet transform.

Next, we shuffle the order of the N-bit watermark with a seed by a pseudorandom number generator. After that, the N trees are formed respectively from R, G and B domains as T_R, T_G and T_B. Let d_{RG}, d_{GB} and d_{BR} denote the differences between corresponding trees in the same layers as

$$\begin{cases} d_{RG}(i,j) = T_R(i,j) - T_G(i,j) \\ d_{GB}(i,j) = T_G(i,j) - T_B(i,j) \\ d_{BR}(i,j) = T_B(i,j) - T_R(i,j) \end{cases} \quad (1)$$

where i and j denote the ith wavelet-tree and the jth coefficient in the ith wavelet-tree, respectively. Here, $i = 1 \sim N, j = 1 \sim 21$.

The sum of differences in the corresponding trees in the same layers is calculated by

$$\begin{cases} D_{RG}(i) = \sum_{j=1}^{21} d_{RG}(i,j) \\ D_{GB}(i) = \sum_{j=1}^{21} d_{GB}(i,j) \\ D_{BR}(i) = \sum_{j=1}^{21} d_{BR}(i,j) \end{cases} \quad (2)$$

where D_{RG}, D_{GB} and D_{BR} can be used to construct robust watermark selection scheme.

Since there are three sum-of-differences, it is possible to embed a watermark bit into one of them. The choice is depending on the least modification of the wavelet-tree coefficients to represent the watermark bit. We group all the differences into an array by the following order

$$D(i,p) = \left(D_{RG}(i), D_{GB}(i), D_{BR}(i)\right) \quad (3)$$

where p is a number of 1 to 3, which denotes the choice of D_{RG}, D_{GB}, and D_{BR}, respectively.

The mean difference $M(p)$ is computed by

$$M(p) = \frac{\sum_{i=1}^{N} D(i,p)}{N} \quad (4)$$

To improve the robustness of the watermark, a threshold $THR(p)$ is defined as

$$THR(p) = \alpha \times |M(p)| \quad (5)$$

where α is an embedding factor; $|\ \ |$ is the absolute value function.

Next, the embedding algorithm for each watermark bit is as follows.

Case 1: if the watermark bit is 1, define the $D^{old}(i)$ as the maximum value of the ith $D(i, p)$. Adjust the $D^{old}(i)$ if $D^{old}(i)$ is less than or equal to the positive $THR(p)$ by

$$T_R^{new}(i,j) = \begin{cases} T_R(i,j) + \frac{\left(THR(p) - D^{old}(i)\right)}{42}, if\ p = 1 \\ T_R(i,j) - \frac{\left(THR(p) - D^{old}(i)\right)}{42}, if\ p = 3 \end{cases}$$

$$T_G^{new}(i,j) = \begin{cases} T_G(i,j) - \frac{\left(THR(p) - D^{old}(i)\right)}{42}, if\ p = 1 \\ T_G(i,j) + \frac{\left(THR(p) - D^{old}(i)\right)}{42}, if\ p = 2 \end{cases}$$

$$T_B^{new}(i,j) = \begin{cases} T_B(i,j) - \frac{\left(THR(p) - D^{old}(i)\right)}{42}, if\ p = 2 \\ T_B(i,j) + \frac{\left(THR(p) - D^{old}(i)\right)}{42}, if\ p = 3 \end{cases} \quad (6)$$

Otherwise, the corresponding trees are kept intact. That is,

$$T_R^{new} = T_R, \quad T_G^{new} = T_G, \quad T_B^{new} = T_B \quad (7)$$

Case 2: if watermark bit is 0, define the $D^{old}(i)$ as the minimum value of the ith $D(i, p)$. Adjust the $D^{old}(i)$ if $D^{old}(i)$ is greater than or equal the negative $THR(p)$ by

$$T_R^{new}(i,j) = \begin{cases} T_R(i,j) - \frac{\left(D^{old}(i) - (-THR(p))\right)}{42}, if\ p = 1 \\ T_R(i,j) + \frac{\left(D^{old}(i) - (-THR(p))\right)}{42}, if\ p = 3 \end{cases}$$

$$T_G^{new}(i,j) = \begin{cases} T_G(i,j) + \frac{\left(D^{old}(i) - (-THR(p))\right)}{42}, if\ p = 1 \\ T_G(i,j) - \frac{\left(D^{old}(i) - (-THR(p))\right)}{42}, if\ p = 2 \end{cases}$$

$$T_B^{new}(i,j) = \begin{cases} T_B(i,j) + \frac{\left(D^{old}(i) - (-THR(p))\right)}{42}, if\ p = 2 \\ T_B(i,j) - \frac{\left(D^{old}(i) - (-THR(p))\right)}{42}, if\ p = 3 \end{cases} \quad (8)$$

Otherwise, the corresponding trees are kept intact as that in equation (7).

After all the watermark bits are embedded, a 4-layer inverse DWT is used to generate the watermarked image. Fig. 2 shows the flow chart of the aforementioned watermark embedding scheme.

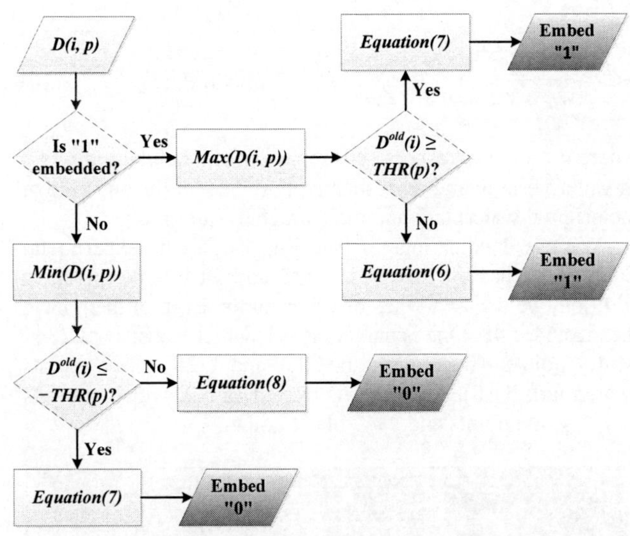

Fig. 2. The flow chart of the watermark embedding scheme.

3 Proposed Watermark Embedding Scheme

As the algorithm stated in Section 2, the value of $D^{old}(i)$ may be over adjusted, which leads to degraded image quality.

If watermark is 1

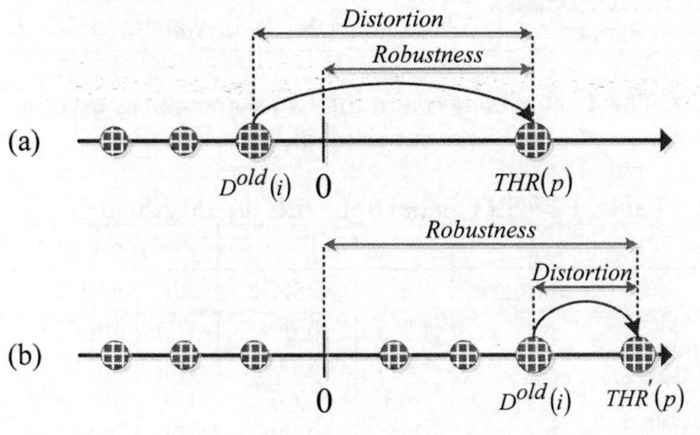

If watermark is 0

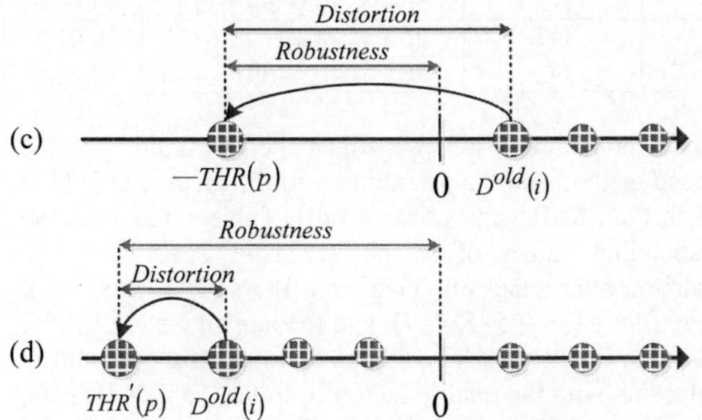

Fig. 3. Different watermark embedding schemes in [11] ((a) and (c)) and in the proposed scheme ((b) and (d)).

For example, the negative $D^{old}(i)$ in Fig. 3(a) will be adjusted to the positive $THR(p)$ when the watermark bit is 1. Another example is the positive $D^{old}(i)$ as shown in Fig. 3(c) will be adjusted to the negative $THR(p)$ when the watermark bit is 0. To solve this problem, we modify the equation (3), (5), (6) and (8) and define a positive threshold T. Specifically, we separately use the following four equations (9), (10), (11) and (12) to replace (3), (5), (6) and (8).

$$D'(i,p) = \left(D_{RG}(i), D_{GB}(i), D_{BR}(i), D_{GR}(i), D_{BG}(i), D_{RB}(i)\right) \tag{9}$$

where $D_{GR}(i) = -D_{RG}(i)$, $D_{BG}(i) = -D_{GB}(i)$, $D_{RB}(i) = -D_{BR}(i)$, and p can be the number of 4, 5, and 6 to represent the choice of D_{GR}, D_{BG}, and D_{RB}, respectively.

$$THR'(p) = \begin{cases} Max(M(p), T), & if\ watermark\ bit\ is\ 1 \\ Min(M(p), -T), & if\ watermark\ bit\ is\ 0 \end{cases} \tag{10}$$

where $Max(\ \ )$ is the maximum value function; $Min(\ \ )$ is the minimum value function.

$$T_R^{new}(i,j) = \begin{cases} T_R(i,j) + \dfrac{(THR'(p) - D^{old}(i))}{42}, & if\ p = 1,6 \\ T_R(i,j) - \dfrac{(THR'(p) - D^{old}(i))}{42}, & if\ p = 3,4 \end{cases}$$

$$T_G^{new}(i,j) = \begin{cases} T_G(i,j) - \dfrac{(THR'(p) - D^{old}(i))}{42}, & if\ p = 1,5 \\ T_G(i,j) + \dfrac{(THR'(p) - D^{old}(i))}{42}, & if\ p = 2,4 \end{cases}$$

$$T_B^{new}(i,j) = \begin{cases} T_B(i,j) - \dfrac{(THR'(p) - D^{old}(i))}{42}, & if\ p = 2,6 \\ T_B(i,j) + \dfrac{(THR'(p) - D^{old}(i))}{42}, & if\ p = 3,5 \end{cases} \tag{11}$$

$$T_R^{new}(i,j) = \begin{cases} T_R(i,j) - \dfrac{(D^{old}(i) - THR'(p))}{42}, & if\ p = 1,6 \\ T_R(i,j) + \dfrac{(D^{old}(i) - THR'(p))}{42}, & if\ p = 3,4 \end{cases}$$

$$T_G^{new}(i,j) = \begin{cases} T_G(i,j) + \dfrac{(D^{old}(i) - THR'(p))}{42}, & if\ p = 1,5 \\ T_G(i,j) - \dfrac{(D^{old}(i) - THR'(p))}{42}, & if\ p = 2,4 \end{cases}$$

$$T_B^{new}(i,j) = \begin{cases} T_B(i,j) + \dfrac{(D^{old}(i) - THR'(p))}{42}, & if\ p = 2,6 \\ T_B(i,j) - \dfrac{(D^{old}(i) - THR'(p))}{42}, & if\ p = 3,5 \end{cases} \tag{12}$$

The new embedding algorithm for each watermark bit is as follows. Case 1: if the watermark bit is 1, define the $D^{old}(i)$ as the maximum value of the *i*th $D'(i,p)$. Adjust the $D^{old}(i)$ if $D^{old}(i)$ is less than or equal to the $THR'(p)$ in (10) (see Fig. 3(b)). Case 2: if watermark bit is 0, define the $D^{old}(i)$ as the minimum value of the *i*th $D'(i,p)$. Adjust the $D^{old}(i)$ if $D^{old}(i)$ is greater than or equal to the $THR'(p)$ in (10) (see Fig. 3(d)).

With the proposed method, we not only can reduce the distortion of an image but also can increase the robustness of the embedded watermark. This improvement partly comes from the six sum-of-differences and partly comes from the positive threshold *T*. It is worth mentioning that the predefined positive threshold *T* can provide a tradeoff between the strength of the watermark and the quality of the watermarked image.

4 Watermark Extraction

We use the same algorithm as that in [11] to extract the watermark. For completeness, we briefly introduce the watermark extraction scheme herein. A watermarked image is decomposed into the 4-layer subbands by using the same DWT. Then, we generate T_R^{new} , T_G^{new} and T_B^{new} from the watermarked image and form $D^{new}(i, p)$ by using (9). To extract a watermark bit, we use the following equation

$$\text{Watermark bit} = \begin{cases} 1, & if\ D^{new}(i,p) \geq 0 \\ 0, & otherwise \end{cases} \quad (13)$$

where *i* is the *i*th wavelet tree; *p* is the position selection of the watermark bit from the embedding process.

Finally, we reshuffle the order of the *N*-bit watermark by a pseudorandom number generator with the same seed as that in the watermark embedding process to obtain the binary watermark image.

5 Experimental Results

We use the peak-signal to noise ratio (PSNR) and the normalized correlation coefficient (NC) to evaluate the image quality and the robustness of watermark. The PSNR of the color image is defined as below.

$$\text{PSNR} = 10\,log_{10}\frac{255^2}{\frac{1}{3}[MSE(R) + MSE(G) + MSE(B)]} \quad (14)$$

where MSE is the mean square error of the watermarked image and is defined as below.

$$\text{MSE} = \frac{1}{H \times W}\sum_{i=0}^{H-1}\sum_{j=0}^{W-1}[f(i,j) - f'(i,j)]^2 \quad (15)$$

where *H* and *W* respectively represent the height and width of the image, f and f' respectively represent the pixel value of the original image and the watermarked image. We define the NC as follows.

$$\text{NC} = \frac{1}{w_h \times w_w}\sum_{i=0}^{w_h-1}\sum_{j=0}^{w_w-1} w(i,j) \times w'(i,j) \quad (16)$$

where w_h and w_w respectively represent the height and width of watermark, w and w' respectively represent the bit value of the original watermark and the extracted watermark.

We use 4 color images (see Fig. 4) for the experiment. Each image has the size 512 × 512 and 24 bits per pixel. In addition, we use two types of watermarks. Both of them have the size 64 × 48. One is named as N1, which consists of 2347 white points (watermark bit 1) and 725 black points (watermark bit 0). The other is named as N2, which consists of 725 white points and 2347 black points.

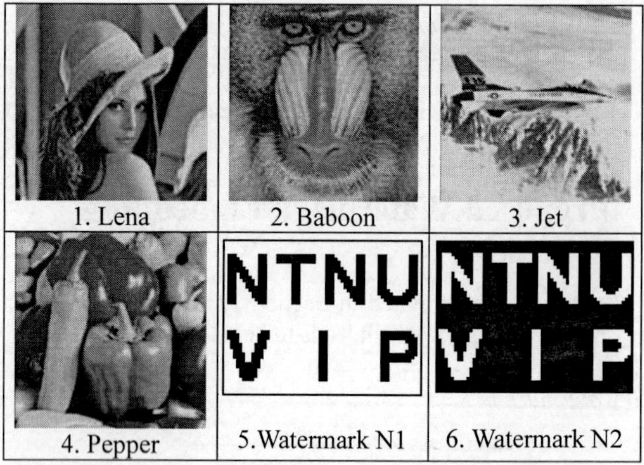

Fig. 4. The 4 color images and the two watermarks used in the experiment.

Table. 1 PSNR comparison with the threshold.

		[11]		Proposed	
Image	Watermark	α	PSNR	T	PSNR
Lena	N1	1165	40.0065	160	40.0275
	N2	1159	40.0041	160	40.0275
Baboon	N1	545	40.0097	199	40.0558
	N2	558	40.0066	199	40.0558
Jet	N1	30	40.2827	156	40.0427
	N2	30	40.0294	156	40.0427
Pepper	N1	26	40.1419	173	40.0220
	N2	26	40.3469	173	40.0220

For a fair comparison, we adjust the threshold *T* of the proposed method and the parameter α of the method in [11] to result in the PSNR values near 40 dB. Table 1 tabulates the corresponding values of α and *T*. Table 2 lists the NC comparison after attacks by Gaussian filters (3×3, 5×5, 7×7), average filters (3×3, 5×5, 7×7), and median filters (3×3, 5×5, 7×7). Table 3 lists the NC comparison after attacks by JPEG compression with the quality factor 10 to 90. Table 4 lists the NC comparison after attacks by the Gaussian noise with the variance 0.005, 0.01, 0.02, and 0.03, and the salt/pepper noise with the density 0.05, 0.1, 0.2 and 0.3.

Through the experiment, we found that the NC values of the proposed method are higher than those of the method in [11] at most of the cases of attacks except that case where the Baboon image is attacked by JPEG compression with the quality factor 10. Therefore, the proposed method is more robust than the method in [11] as expected. Note that the NC values of the proposed method for both watermarks are the same. This is because we use the maximum difference of the corresponding trees in the same layers to embed, which results in the chosen position will be the same for both types of watermarks.

Table 2. NC comparison for watermarked images by attacks of common signal filters.

Image	Method	W.	Null	Gauss. 3×3	Gauss. 5×5	Gauss. 7×7	Avg. 3×3	Avg. 5×5	Avg. 7×7	Med. 3×3	Med. 5×5	Med. 7×7
Lena	[11]	N1	1.0000	0.9843	0.9541	0.9147	0.9651	0.8323	0.7750	0.9498	0.8522	0.7893
		N2	1.0000	0.9866	0.9583	0.9215	0.9716	0.8492	0.7832	0.9495	0.8626	0.7945
	Pro.	N1	1.0000	0.9996	0.9944	0.9746	0.9964	0.8958	0.8134	0.9941	0.9111	0.8336
		N2	1.0000	0.9996	0.9944	0.9746	0.9964	0.8958	0.8134	0.9941	0.9111	0.8336
Baboon	[11]	N1	1.0000	0.9973	0.9661	0.9130	0.9778	0.7441	0.6679	0.9541	0.7307	0.6412
		N2	1.0000	0.9967	0.9667	0.9140	0.9820	0.7418	0.6595	0.9466	0.7246	0.6455
	Pro.	N1	1.0000	0.9973	0.9742	0.9280	0.9860	0.7500	0.6699	0.9648	0.7382	0.6569
		N2	1.0000	0.9973	0.9742	0.9280	0.9860	0.7500	0.6699	0.9648	0.7382	0.6569
Jet	[11]	N1	0.9990	0.9667	0.9371	0.9111	0.9446	0.8502	0.7805	0.9401	0.8697	0.8138
		N2	0.9993	0.9736	0.9414	0.9130	0.9527	0.8430	0.7796	0.9417	0.8746	0.8235
	Pro.	N1	1.0000	1.0000	0.9986	0.9899	0.9996	0.9222	0.8398	0.9977	0.9544	0.8736
		N2	1.0000	1.0000	0.9986	0.9899	0.9996	0.9222	0.8398	0.9977	0.9544	0.8736
Pepper	[11]	N1	1.0000	0.9996	0.9892	0.9661	0.9947	0.8841	0.8154	0.9873	0.9088	0.8417
		N2	1.0000	0.9986	0.9895	0.9641	0.9928	0.8883	0.8108	0.9905	0.9108	0.8388
	Pro.	N1	1.0000	1.0000	0.9973	0.9804	0.9993	0.9121	0.8313	0.9960	0.9267	0.8554
		N2	1.0000	1.0000	0.9973	0.9804	0.9993	0.9121	0.8313	0.9960	0.9267	0.8554

Table 3. NC comparison for watermarked images by attacks of JPEG compression.

Image	Method	W.	QF10	QF20	QF30	QF40	QF50	QF60	QF70	QF80	QF90
Lena	[11]	N1	0.6367	0.7024	0.7314	0.7594	0.7698	0.7799	0.7929	0.8245	0.8362
		N2	0.6308	0.7109	0.7483	0.7633	0.7799	0.7958	0.8079	0.8268	0.8463
	Pro.	N1	0.6738	0.7337	0.7737	0.8001	0.8147	0.8349	0.8466	0.8717	0.8854
		N2	0.6650	0.7333	0.7737	0.8001	0.8147	0.8349	0.8466	0.8717	0.8854
Baboon	[11]	N1	0.6132	0.6783	0.7125	0.7278	0.7496	0.7701	0.7936	0.8056	0.8626
		N2	0.6090	0.6699	0.7106	0.7275	0.7522	0.7669	0.7897	0.8147	0.8590
	Pro.	N1	0.6129	0.6884	0.7340	0.7587	0.7672	0.7825	0.8053	0.8186	0.8847
		N2	0.6087	0.6884	0.7340	0.7587	0.7672	0.7825	0.8053	0.8186	0.8847
Jet	[11]	N1	0.6347	0.6940	0.7200	0.7457	0.7760	0.7884	0.7985	0.8053	0.8359
		N2	0.5732	0.6888	0.7216	0.7535	0.7682	0.7874	0.8144	0.8092	0.8499
	Pro.	N1	0.6692	0.7272	0.7721	0.7962	0.8219	0.8522	0.8597	0.8782	0.9143
		N2	0.5960	0.7265	0.7721	0.7958	0.8219	0.8522	0.8597	0.8782	0.9143
Pepper	[11]	N1	0.6682	0.7447	0.7711	0.8017	0.8151	0.8206	0.8496	0.8554	0.8916
		N2	0.6695	0.7460	0.7734	0.7978	0.8229	0.8411	0.8473	0.8652	0.8919
	Pro.	N1	0.6930	0.7698	0.8004	0.8209	0.8401	0.8557	0.8707	0.8886	0.9114
		N2	0.6904	0.7701	0.8004	0.8209	0.8401	0.8557	0.8707	0.8886	0.9114

Table 4. NC comparison for watermarked images by attacks of Gaussian noise and salt/pepper noise.

Image	Method	W.	Gaussian Noise				Salt / Pepper Noise			
			Variance 0.005	Variance 0.01	Variance 0.02	Variance 0.03	Density 0.05	Density 0.1	Density 0.2	Density 0.3
Lena	[11]	N1	0.8365	0.7972	0.7347	0.7021	0.7548	0.6907	0.6383	0.5833
		N2	0.8457	0.7942	0.7343	0.7041	0.7581	0.6783	0.6331	0.5852
	Pro.	N1	0.9147	0.8632	0.7939	0.7320	0.8154	0.7324	0.6591	0.6051
		N2	0.9241	0.8583	0.7952	0.7298	0.8105	0.7366	0.6500	0.6113
Baboon	[11]	N1	0.9257	0.8753	0.8186	0.7597	0.8356	0.7558	0.6735	0.6243
		N2	0.9280	0.8697	0.7978	0.7646	0.8238	0.7617	0.6604	0.6422
	Pro.	N1	0.9433	0.8994	0.8444	0.8020	0.8619	0.7900	0.6878	0.6292
		N2	0.9514	0.9140	0.8395	0.7968	0.8629	0.7848	0.6940	0.6542
Jet	[11]	N1	0.8232	0.7802	0.7213	0.6871	0.7317	0.6725	0.6191	0.5888
		N2	0.8173	0.7877	0.7197	0.7067	0.7483	0.6940	0.6207	0.5878
	Pro.	N1	0.9140	0.8619	0.7796	0.7428	0.8020	0.7252	0.6448	0.6188
		N2	0.9121	0.8505	0.7783	0.7320	0.8089	0.7207	0.6481	0.5934
Pepper	[11]	N1	0.8964	0.8395	0.7675	0.7376	0.7942	0.7197	0.6292	0.6116
		N2	0.8889	0.8437	0.7731	0.7408	0.7945	0.7086	0.6542	0.6123
	Pro.	N1	0.9241	0.8798	0.8053	0.7506	0.8261	0.7438	0.6650	0.6292
		N2	0.9306	0.8671	0.8050	0.7688	0.8365	0.7366	0.6634	0.6282

6 Conclusion

In this paper, we proposed a robust watermarking algorithm for color images. The proposed algorithm includes a maximum difference selection of the wavelet-trees and an improved wavelet-tree embedding scheme. In addition, a positive threshold T is also proposed to make a balance between the image quality and the robustness of the watermark. Experimental results show that the proposed algorithm is feasible and it not only can produce higher image quality but also can produce more robust watermark than the previous methods.

7 References

[1] S.H. Wang and Y.P. Lin, "Wavelet tree quantization for copyright protection watermarking," *IEEE Transactions on Image Processing*, vol.13, pp. 154-165, 2004.

[2] B.K. Lien and W.H. Lin, "A watermarking method based on maximum distance wavelet tree quantization," in the *Proc. the 19th conference computer vision*, graphics and image processing, 2006.

[3] W.H. Lin, S.J. Horng, T.W. Kao, P.Z. Fan, C.L. Lee, and Y. Pan, "An efficient watermarking method based on significant difference of wavelet coefficient quantization," *IEEE Transactions on Multimedia*, vol.10, pp. 746-757, 2008.

[4] W.H. Lin, Y.R. Wang, and S.J. Horng, "A wavelet-tree-based watermarking method using distance vector of binary cluster," *Expert Systems with Applications*, vol.36, pp. 9869-9878, 2009.

[5] R.S. Run, S.J. Horng, W.H. Lin, T.W. Kao, and P. Fan, "An efficient wavelet-tree-based watermarking method," *Expert Systems with Applications*, vol.38, pp. 14357-14366, 2011.

[6] H. Al-Otum and N. Samara, "Adaptive blind wavelet-based watermarking technique using tree mutual differences," *Journal of Electronic Imaging*, vol.15, 043011, 2006.

[7] S. Rawat and B. Raman, "A new robust watermarking scheme for color images," in the *Proc. IEEE 2nd International Advance Computing Conference*, pp. 206-209, 2010.

[8] Q. Su, X. Liu, and W. Yang, "A watermarking algorithm for color image based on YIQ color space and integer wavelet transform," in the *Proc. International Conference on Image Analysis and Signal Processing*, pp. 70-73, 2009.

[9] S. Hongqin and L. Fangliamg, "A blind digital watermark technique for color image based on integer wavelet transform," in the *Proc. International Conference on Biomedical Engineering and Computer Science*, pp. 1-4, 2010.

[10] Y. Li, Y. Hao, and C. Wang, "A research on the robust digital watermark of color radar images," in the *Proc. IEEE International Conference on Information and Automation*, pp. 1091-1096, 2010.

[11] H. Al-Otum and N. Samara, "A robust blinds color image watermarking based on wavelet-tree bit host difference selection," *Signal Processing*, vol.90, pp. 2498-2512, 2010.

Informed Coded Modulation and Host Rejection Techniques for Color Inkjet Hardcopy Watermarking in the Spatial Domain

– Submitted to IPCV 2013 –

Joceli Mayer[1] and Steven J. Simske[2]
LPDS[1] - EEL - Federal University of Santa Catarina - UFSC - Brazil - CEP 88040-900 - P.O. box 476
HP[2] Print Production Automation Lab - Hewlett-Packard Labs - USA
E-mail: joceli.mayer@lpds.ufsc.br and steven.simske@hp.com

***Abstract*—This paper proposes improvements on the embedding and the detection watermarking techniques, aiming for improved color hardcopy watermarking using inkjet printers. We investigate informed coding along with a multibit spread spectrum modulation framework for watermarking color images to be deployed as printed media. The proposed approach aims to maximize the watermarking robustness with a modulation approach to achieve high payload with good transparency. At the encoding phase the impact of the color background on the detection metric is evaluated based on estimated color correlation and interference. This correlation is used to estimate and compare the robustness of sets of patterns which would be otherwise considered equivalent for modulating the same message. This allows a proper selection of sequences to be embedded for improved robustness. The detection is further improved by using a proposed whitening filter and a color rejection algorithm. Examples using real life images illustrate the performance enhancement achievable by employing the proposed approaches in color hardcopy watermarking systems.**

Keywords: Hardcopy color image watermarking, print-scan channel.

I. Introduction

Many office applications rely on a tight connection between physical and electronic documents. Physical (printed) images can be a token for the electronic document (or documents) it represents directly (or indirectly as part of a shared workflow). Hiding information in general color images to be printed can be used to embed side information or to save real estate on the label, document or packaging printed media. This hidden information is useful for location-based services, point-of-sale, security, counterfeit and piracy deterrence, content authentication, fingerprinting and more.

The characteristics of the color print-scan channel make information transmission using color printed media quite challenging [19]. This channel introduces many distortions into the color patterns transmitted along with the host interference image. Some of the challenging distortions are those originated from ink property variations such as spreading and mixing, from variations in the coated media properties, from the optical and mechanical disturbances at printing and scanning devices [1] and from scanning sensor responses.

Several techniques have been proposed for hardcopy watermarking over print-scan channels. The technique proposed in [15] conveys information by modulating the angle of oriented periodical sequences embedded into image spatial blocks, while dedicating one block to embed synchronism information. The approach deals only with luminance and does not considers either informed coding or the color channel properties. It achieves a resulting payload of 40 bits per page. The method in [16] modulates information into the luminance image phase spectrum with differential quantization index modulation. It exploits the printer resulting halftoning to estimate the rotation, and achieves a payload of hundreds of bits for monochromatic images. The method proposed in [17] relies on adaptive block embedding into DFT magnitude domain. Each block is classified into smooth or texture type and a different embedding method is applied to each block type. The Hough transform is used to detect the printed image boundaries for watermark synchronization. The approach is robust to the print-scan channel and to rotation, providing a total payload of 1024 bits with a bit error rate (BER) around 15% for monochromatic images. In [18] a circular template watermark is embedded into the the Fourier transform magnitude to facilitate inversion of rotation and scaling after the print-scan process. Another template watermark is embedded in spatial domain to invert translations. The message watermark is embedded into the wavelet domain. This technique achieves a payload of about 135 bits using the BCH error correction algorithm, resulting in a BER of 1.5%, it is also designed for monochromatic images. The approaches just described do not deal specifically with the color channel distortions, as they embed information only in the luminance channel. Thus, it is desirable to investigate new efficient strategies to address distortion in the color print channel.

Techniques that address color modulation for the print scan channel have been proposed in [7], [6]. The technique in [6] employs the Discrete Fourier Transform to embed information into the red component of the image, while the approach in [7] performs frequency domain informed embedding using halftoning modulation. However, halftoning modulation provides a very high capacity but requires to control the printer driver to bypass the printer processing and halftoning, which is reportedly difficult or requires re-halftoning [7], [9], [8]. Moreover, halftoning based techniques can not directly employ the informed coding based on the spatial color background as proposed in this paper.

This paper exploits the possibilities of space domain embedding in hardcopy color watermarking systems. Spatial domain embedding allows the optimization of informed coding following a "dirty paper" approach [2] by estimating the best embedding patterns for a given background image.

The use of a codebook of equivalent embedding patterns for the same message brings an innovative contribution to the field. Moreover, a color rejection algorithm can be used to mitigate host interference. These approaches are shown to lead to robustness to the distortions originated in the print-scan color channel. The proposed solution combines a color rejection algorithm and a whitening filter to reduce host interference and employs the HVS color system for detection by correlation in the frequency domain. Efficient embedding and detection approaches are proposed to address the massive processing required by hardcopy watermarking. It is conjectured that the proposed approaches can be selectively incorporated to existing hardcopy watermarking solutions to improve communication reliability over color print channel.

The paper is organized as follows. Section II-A describes an embedding technique based on a combinatorial direct sequence coding designed to improve transparency for a given payload. The proposed informed coding approach is described in Section II-B. This approach, named dirty paper coding in [2], facilitates the selection of the embedding patterns for a given message and a given host color image, increasing the robustness. Our approach provides an efficient modulation by inserting less patterns per message than competing modulation approaches, as discussed in Section II-C. The efficient detection approach is described in Section II-D and the color rejection algorithm is discussed in Section II-E. Section III describes experiments which illustrate the improvements achieved using the informed coding and color rejection approaches. Section IV concludes this paper.

II. Spatial Embedding for Color Hardcopy Watermarking

Spatial embedding for color hardcopy watermarking is composed of message coding, watermark embedding, message decoding and also post processing. This section discusses new approaches to improve the present state of the art in these steps. The entire process is illustrated in Fig. 2(a).

A. Multibit Embedding with Spread Spectrum Modulation

Most popular approaches to modulate a multi-bit watermarked message include basic M-ary modulation, quantization index modulation or direct sequence code division modulation. These are usually combined with time division modulation to achieve higher payload. Basic m-bit message modulation requires 2^m patterns [12] which, in turn, require an exponential number (2^m) of detections. Quantization index modulation schemes are highly sensitive to valumetric scaling, a type of distortion which is very strong in print-scan channels [11]. Direct sequence code division modulation requires the embedding of m patterns in the the host image and a number of detections proportional to m.

We propose to employ a multibit embedding with spread spectrum spatial modulation. A message dependent set of designed square dot color patterns is selected to be added (by substitution) to a host image and the resulting digital watermarked image is shown in Fig. 1(a). Moreover, some redundancy is allowed in the encoding to improve robustness, as explained in the following.

Consider m-bits of information to be conveyed by a digital color image I which is deployed as printed media. These m bits will be modulated by employing an additive spread spectrum modulation. To this end, a selected set of K dot patterns from a set of N available patterns, $P_i, i = 1, \ldots, N$ ($N \geq K$) is embedded into the color image. The choice of the K patterns set to be used, which is represented by a set of indexes, depends on the m bits to be modulated. Thus, there is a directed and reversible mapping between the m-bit message and the unordered set $S = \{k_1, k_2, \ldots, k_K\}$ of K pattern indexes, where $k_i \neq k_j$ for $i \neq j$. The resulting watermarked document I_w is:

$$I_w = I \oplus \sum_{i \in S} P_i \quad (1)$$

where the operation $\oplus$ represents a substitution embedding, instead of the traditional additive embedding as in [21]. The pixels of the image I are replaced by the pixels of the pattern whenever color pattern dots exist, as illustrated in Fig. 1(a). This approach provides a transparent embedding only for small size square dots and using inkjet printers. The inkjet printing process and the scanner optical blurring help to mix and hide the embedding dots as illustrated in Fig. 1(b), provided that the size is kept around 6x6 pixels in densities of 600 dpi/ppi for printing and scanning. For authentication applications, the transparency may not need to be high, as the goal is to validate some printed color document. However, the use of traditional 2D barcodes, as datamatrix, or modern color barcodes [20] may be too disturbing for most authentication applications.

The proposed substitutive approach is justified for color hardcopy watermarking by contrasting to additive embedding which require a great amount of energy and also results in lesser transparency considering the inkjet process properties. On the other hand, halftoning based approaches are more resilient to these effects but they require the control of the halftoning printer driver [7] which is hard in practice as manufactures do not allow halftoning control or substitution of the printer drivers.

For a given secret key ϕ, a set of N patterns is generated. These patterns consist of a certain number of small squared dots with a particular width. Each of the K patterns is generated with an unique color from the available primary printing cartridge or toner colors. Most inkjet printers uses the CMYK cartridge colors, thus usually we define $K = 4$. The same set of N patterns is generated at the decoder, which must know the secret key ϕ and the modulation parameters. To be able to implement an informed coding, we propose to add L alternative patterns for each of the N patterns in the database. This increases the total number of patterns to $N \times L$ and enables optimization. Given some metric emphasizing robustness, we can then search for the best set of embedding patterns. The price paid for this additional flexibility is the increase of the total number of required individual detections to decode the message to $N_D = N \times L$ as described in the next section.

B. Informed Coding and Pattern Selection

Consider the encoding process that maps an m-bit message to a set of K pattern indexes with a redundancy factor L to increase robustness. The proposed informed coding exploits the "dirty paper coding" principle [2] and is illustrated in Fig 2(a). By testing L color patterns for the same index k_i (given a background region), the embedder selects the set of K color patterns that maximizes the detection performance (robustness). To this end, the expected impact on detection quality for each set of L equivalent patterns must be estimated at the encoding side. The set of L patterns has equivalent patterns because each one in the set is associated to the same message, thus for a given message, any pattern of this set can be embedded in the image to enable the decoder to find the same message.

Hence, the choice of patterns depends on the neighboring colors in the host image. We have experimentally verified that some combinations of colors lead to better detection results than others. This is due to specific ink and coating properties of a given printer device, which affect color mixing and spreading. We exploit these findings to set the metric for selecting the best pattern for an embedding image region. This metric has been chosen to be the statistical correlation between a pair of images. One is the original pattern with some unique color and the other is the watermarked image (patterns and the interfering background) with the same pattern after printing and scanning. The combination that provides the highest correlation is chosen for each region. For example, the correlation estimates in Table I indicate that it is preferable to place magenta pattern dots over a cyan image background rather than a yellow background. This approach require training with the specific printing system to be used for generating the watermarked documents and images. All combinations of background color and patterns colors are printed and the resulting correlation metric is computed few times.

Each evaluation requires a new placement of the image in the scanbed to generate another scanning. The results are consistent for the same printer and scanner set, but if one of these devices is replaced a new training is required due to changes of the optics, mechanics, electronics or ink cartridge. These changes will affect the correlations considerably among different devices and even with a same device model. Table I shows that the results are consistent for 3 realizations and thus allow to predict which combinations are more robust before deciding which patterns to embed given the available alternative patterns. Moreover each pattern in this set uses only one color from the printing color system. This color may be cyan, magenta, yellow or black in a 4 colors printer. Thus, color halftoning is not an issue for our proposed approach.

Each embedding pattern in this set of patterns is limited to one color but the other patterns in the same set may have another colors. Moreover, each pattern (among L alternatives) is chosen based on the robustness to neighboring colors interference as described above. For instance, if $K = 4$ and the CMYK color printing system is used, each pattern will have a different color.

C. Payload, Robustness and Transparency

The information payload (m bits) achievable by the proposed modulation is determined by the number N_D of detections allowed (time complexity), the number N_R of embedding regions (time division modulation), the number K of color patterns per region, the total number N of patterns and the redundancy factor (L). For instance, using K patterns per region (not necessarily the same patterns for all regions) from a database of N patterns we can achieve a payload of $N_R \log_2(C_K^N)$ bits, where $C_K^N = N!/[K!(N-K)!]$. Therefore, the modulation parameters (K, N) are chosen such that:

$$N_R \log_2 \left(\frac{N!}{K!(N-K)!} \right) \geq m \qquad (2)$$

As an example, suppose we want to achieve a payload of $m = 800$ bits (100 bytes) embedding $K = 4$ color patterns per region, from a database with a total of $N = 50$ patterns. From (2) we determine the need to mark $N_R = 45$ regions, leading to 18 bits per region using the proposed modulation. This evaluation assumes that the database is created using single color patterns chosen from the primary printing colors to avoid color halftoning. We may decide to enforce redundancy by using $L = 3$, which will require $50 \times 3 = 150$ color pattern correlations to decode the message per image. The proposed correlation process is able to decode all the regions at same step, the computational complexity is proportional to the number of patterns N and redundancy L but does not depend on the number of regions N_R.

For this particular example with redundancy factor $L = 3$, other popular modulations would perform as follows:

- The **basic message coding** [12] requires one pattern per possible message. It would embed one pattern per region and would require 3×2^{18} correlations to detect the message. Thus, basic message coding is not practical for such a payload due to the computational requirements.
- The **direct sequence code division modulation** [13] would require embedding 18 patterns per region and $18 \times 3 = 54$ correlations to detect the message. This is a lower complexity than required by the proposed approach. However, this technique would require embedding much more patterns per region than embedded by our proposed encoding (4 patterns), which would result

in much lower transparency and lower robustness due to patterns cross-correlation.

- The **M-ary modulation** approach [10] could be designed for this case by splitting the payload (18 bits per region) into 4 codewords with lengths of 4, 4, 5 and 5 bits. Considering that each codeword would be encoded with basic message coding,[1] the resulting number of correlations would be $3 \times (2 \times 2^4 + 2 \times 2^5) = 288$, almost twice the number required by the proposed approach. This approach would embed 4 patterns per region as the proposed approach.

In conclusion, due to the reduced number of embedding patterns combined with small number of detections required, the proposed modulation provides a better tradeoff between transparency and computational complexity when compared to the alternative modulation options discussed and, due to the color rejection and dirty paper approach used, it also provides superior robustness properties. Notice that we are able to design a different set of parameters N, K, N_R and L for a given number m of embedding bits. The dot width and number of dots used in each pattern also affect the transparency and the robustness of the embedding. Each parameter combination will result in different transparency, decoding speed and robustness. We are aware that the spatial domain embedding is more visible than frequency domain methods. However, the embedding is still very transparent in the printed page, which is the media that will be distributed, when designed with small dots (around 6x6 pixels in 600 dpi/ppi) for inkjet printers. Inkjet printing process hides those dots quite well due to ink spreading and mixing, as illustrated in Fig. 1(b).

D. Pattern Detection and Message Decoding

The K color patterns embedded into the color image are assumed to be printed into paper and digitized using an image scanner before detection. The decoding system employs an efficient correlation scheme based on fast Fourier transform properties and on color rejection enabled by the proposed pattern generation protocol. The detection is based on the correlation between the observed watermarked image after the print-scan channel and the known patterns, which are locally generated with the help of a secret key ϕ. A correlation operation is performed for each pattern P_i in frequency domain using the fast Fourier transform.

The literature indicates that a major detection gain can be achieved by appropriate preprocessing of both the received image I_{wR} and the known patterns $P_i, i = 1, \ldots, L \times N$. Also, using a post-processing whitening filter mitigates the negative influence of the host signal on the correlation, thus improving the detection performance [4], [5]. We follow this approach by transforming both images to the HVS (Hue, Value and Saturation) color model, and then using a 3×3 mask $Log[m,n]$ filter (Laplacian of the Gaussian) to decorrelate the host signal. The experiments have shown that the LOG filter provides a better performance than using the matched filter approach which requires the estimation of the low pass filter effect in the channel. Other decorrelation approaches could be used, yet the log filter provides an elegant solution. It is well known that the detector performance severely degrades without decorrelation of the host image. This operation can be summarized as an average detection over the channels of the images (I_{wR} and P_i) represented in HVS color model:

$$C_i = \frac{1}{3} \sum_{k=H,V,S} IFFT(FFT(I_{wR_k}[m,n] * Log[m,n]) \times FFT(P_{i_k}[-m,-n] * Log[m,n])) \quad (3)$$

where $FFT(.)$ and $IFFT(.)$ denote, respectively, the fast 2D direct and inverse discrete Fourier transforms. The operator $*$ represents the 2D linear convolution which performs the whitening filtering with the $Log[m,n]$ filter mask. After $N \times L$ detections, the K indexes of patterns P_i corresponding to the highest correlations C_i are selected to compose the set of indexes S. With these indexes and the reverse map, we decode the message m.

For instance, consider the 4 CMYK colors and $K = 4$ and redundancy factor $L = 3$. $N \times L$ correlations are performed for each of the 4 colors and the index of the pattern with highest correlation peak value for each color is stored. The selected set of K indexes are associated by a look-up table to the message and the decoder will follow the same encoder assignment of message and indexes.

E. Color Rejection to Reduce Interference

We exploit the use of a unique color for each pattern to be detected by rejecting the pixels with any other color before computing the correlation in (3). For instance, suppose we decide to embed 4 patterns, each with one unique color from CMYK. Then, to detect the yellow pattern, we reject the other (CMK) colors generating the modified image I_{wR} before correlation. Consider an estimated color mean M_c of the printed and scanned color pattern, and a candidate color X_c, where colors are represented as vectors in RGB color model. The rejection occurs by computing the Euclidean distance:

$$d_E(X_c) = |X_c - M_c| > \tau \quad (4)$$

where τ is the distance threshold learned from experiments. Other distances can be used such as the Mahalanobis distance $d_M(X_c) = \sqrt{(X_c - M_c)^T Z^{-1} (X_c - M_c)}$, which takes in account the cross-correlation among colors. The Mahalanobis distance requires the estimation of the covariance matrix Z of the printed and scanned colors. Thus, distant colors can be rejected based on a distance from the mean M_c learned from the experiments. The parameters required in the distance metric need to be specifically estimated for the printer used to generate the document. As the rejection process is not perfect, the remaining image still has many residual interferences. The experiments show that a significant robustness improvement

[1] Direct sequence code division could be applied, with the corresponding savings in computational complexity. However, this would also be accompanied by much greater embedding distortion and resulting reduction in detection performance due to cross-correlation [13].

is achieved by employing the proposed informed coding modulation and post processing approaches.

III. Experiments

We illustrate the detection of a pattern embedded into a color image printed with a HPC4280 inkjet at 600 dpi and scanned at 600 ppi. We illustrate the performance with one image and one set of devices to validate the innovative algorithms proposed in this paper, naturally other experiments have been performed with other devices and images, resulting in similar performance. In these experiments we employed transparent patterns with dots of size 6x6 pixels. The number of dots is constrained to occupy at most 1% of the embedding region. The watermarked image, the scanned image and the resulting processed image by the $Log[m, n]$ filter in the HVS domain are illustrated in Figs. 1(a-b) and 2(b) respectively.

The resulting correlation performance using the approach proposed in Eq. (3) is illustrated in Fig. 3(a). The improvement in correlation due to the color rejection procedure is illustrated in Fig. 3(b) where we observe that the probability of false positive detection (indicated by the peaks around the main peak) is considerably reduced. We have repeated the experiments with different messages, and the gain of performance due to the rejection kept coherent for all tests. Due to the use of the proposed detection approach based on FFT we achieve a speedy correlation tests (which took few seconds each) even for huge images with size of 3200×2400 pixels.

We note that the pattern is almost invisible in the scanned image, Fig. 1(b), yet we achieved a very robust detection. To better appreciate the resulting transparency look at a printed (by an inkjet printer) watermarked image in A4 paper at 600 dpi. For the intended applications (where the user has access only to the printed and scanned image and not to the digital watermarked image), the generated printed and scanned watermarked image has almost invisible pattern dots, thus, without the secret generation key, it would be almost impossible to replicate the dot pattern aiming a fake authentication. Other combinations of dot sizes and dot frequencies (the amount of dots per pattern) has been extensively tested (4x4 size with higher frequency of dots and 8x8 size with lower frequency of dots). We found a good tradeoff between transparency and robustness using dot size of 6x6 pixels and 1% of occurrence when using inkjet printer and 600 dpi scanner. The size of the regions considerably affects the correlation as the number of regions is related to the payload and limited by the image size. For other combinations of region sizes, scanning and printing resolutions, the dot sizes and frequencies need to be determined by experimentation. These parameters are assumed known a priori by the decoder.

In our experiments with various inkjet printer and scanner devices, requiring a new training for each set of printer (HP4280, HP5580, HP3550) and scanner (HP5590, HPM1120, HP1005) used, we found that the same background has a different impact on the dot pattern depending on the color. The proposed informed color approach is shown in Fig. 2(a) and employs a set of databases with color patterns. This approach allows the selection of equivalent but different color patterns for the same message, aiming to optimize robustness. In Figs. 4(a) and 4(b) we illustrate the performance improvement in detection by properly choosing the color patterns for a given image host background. This choice is based on prior testing with devices to find the best combinations of color dot patterns and color backgrounds, as shown in Table I.

From the experiments and visual inspection we observed that certain combinations should be avoided due to the resulting lower correlation, such as using magenta or black dot patterns over yellow background. We infer that this phenomenon is caused by the different ink properties of each color cartridge and how the ink chemicals interact when mixed together. We provide an experiment where different backgrounds are chosen for a same cyan embedding pattern. We illustrate the images and resulting correlations after the print and scan channel for non recommended (Figs. 5(a) and 6(a)) and recommended backgrounds (Figs. 5(b) and 6(b)). Recommendation follows from our experiments with many color backgrounds and patterns, some of which are not included in Table I. Clearly, the correlation performance is superior when a proper combination of pattern color and background color is defined at embedding.

In order to validate the performance of the proposed techniques, it is sufficient to show the increased performance on correlation. To complete evaluate a given watermarking system, it would be interesting to provide experiments with bit error rate (BER). The probability of missing a pattern (which may convey many bits) of the proposed technique can be estimated by modeling the correlation metrics (peaks and non peaks) as two normal distributions and evaluating the false positive and false negative detection probabilities of the patterns[12]. In the experiments was found that the probability of missing a pattern is about to 10^{-10}. On the other hand, to estimate the BER is quite time consuming and in this case, not feasible. It requires about 10^{12} experiments of printing and scanning. Considering that each experiment takes about 6 minutes, it would take about 6^{12} hours. Considering the example for a payload of 800 bits, using 18 bits per regions with 45 regions, it would be necessary to detect 150 patterns, as explained in Section II-C. For this payload, it would result in an estimated probability of missing the entire message of $45(1-(1-10^{-10})^{150}) = 6.8^{-7}$. This estimation shows that the approaches provide a very robust watermarking with a considerably small probability of missing the transmitted message.

We verified that the robustness improvement achieved using redundancy does not increase linearly with L. This indicates a tradeoff between increases in computational complexity and in the redundancy factor L. Thus, some optimal finite L will exist for a given practical application. We noticed that small rotations and even small cropping under normal use do not invalidate the proper detection.

As we focus this research and the proposed techniques for authentication applications, we do not need and thus do not address rotation issues in this paper. A careful placement in the scanbed results in good detection performance as tests and experiments have confirmed, and this care is compatible with the authentication application: the user wants to keep the document authenticated. However, for other applications one may use the ideas in this paper, thus synchronization techniques proposed in the literature to deal with rotation can be included. Techniques include the use of Hough transform [17], synchronization blocks [15], synchronization signals in frequency domain [18] or exploiting printer halftoning [16]. The generated patterns are very hard to be detectable in the printed watermarked image without the knowledge of the generating key ϕ. This approach was not especially designed to be robust to malicious attacks aiming to erase the embedded patterns. Instead, we focus on authentication applications using a secure pattern generation to prevent an attacker from being able to create a valid set of patterns to authenticate a fake document or package. As the selection of the embedding patterns depends on the image and on the embedding message, an attacker would face a hard problem to estimate the patterns in order to deliver a substitution or an erasing attack.

IV. Conclusion

This work provides a framework to design color hardcopy watermarking systems by exploiting an informed coding approach and post-processing. The post-processing is based on a whitening filter and on color rejection when testing a color pattern. The proposed approaches are shown to be robust to the color inkjet print-scan channel. The performance improvements achieved using the proposed approaches are illustrated through experiments. The proposed framework allows the design of hardcopy color watermarking systems to be customized for various robustness and decoding speed tradeoffs by choosing proper embedding pattern parameters. Moreover, the transparency can be adjusted by changing the size of the pattern dots and their frequency of occurrence, as the inkjet printing process helps to hide the embedded patterns. As the number of pixels is considerably large for hardcopy watermarking, we propose modulation and detection approaches with low computational complexity. The proposed approaches can be employed for a variety of applications including authentication, fingerprinting and copyright protection of packages, images, documents and other printed media. The proposed approaches can be integrated in many existing hardcopy watermarking systems to improve transparency, robustness and payload.

(a) The digital watermarked image. (b) The printed and scanned watermarked image.

Fig. 1. (a) The digital watermarked image detail (with 1150×850 pixels, corresponding in a real size of 1.9 in $\times 1.4$ in) with a cyan pattern. The original image, scanned at 600 dpi, has 3200×2400 pixels. The digital domain is used only for embedding as the distribution media is the printed version where the embedding transparency is very high. (b) The printed and scanned watermarked image with a cyan pattern. Notice that the embedding dots are very transparent. Only this printed watermarked will be distributed, the digital version will not be available to the users for security reasons.

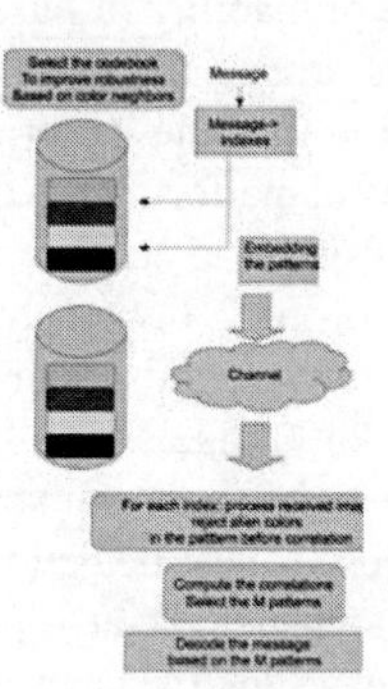

(a) Informed coding system. (b) Image processed for detection.

Fig. 2. (a) Informed coding system using the dirty paper approach based on a set of codebooks with color patterns. (b) The scanned watermarked image processed by the log filter in the HVS color model.

References

[1] P.V.K. Borges, Joceli Mayer, Ebroul Izquierdo, Robust and Transparent Color Modulation for Text Data Hiding, IEEE Transactions on Multimedia, Vol. 10, Num. 8, December, 2008.

[2] Max Henrique Machado Costa, Writing on Dirty Paper, IEEE Transactions on Information Theory, IT-29, 439-441, 1983.

[3] Martin Kutter, Performance Improvement of Spread Spectrum Based Image Watermarking Schemes Through M-ary Modulation, Proc. of the Workshop on Information Hiding, LNCS-1768, 1999.

[4] Hongseok Kim, Stochastic Model Based Audio Watermark and Whitening for Improved Detection, IEEE ICASSP, 2000.

[5] G. Depovere, T. Kalker, J.-P. Linnartz, Improved Watermark Detection Reliability Using Filtering Before Correlation, IEEE ICIP - International Conference on Image Processing, 1998.

[6] Guo, Chengqing Xu, Guoai Niu, Xinxin Yang, Yixian Li, Yang, A Color Image Watermarking Algorithm Resistant to Print-Scan, IEEE International Conference on Wireless Communications, Networking and Information Security (WCNIS), 2010.

[7] Basak Oztan and Gaurav Sharma, Multiplexed Clustered-Dot Halftone Watermarks Using Bi-Directional Phase Modulation and Detection, Proceedings of 2010 IEEE 17th International Conference on Image Processing, 2010.

[8] P. Bulan, G. Sharma, and V. Monga, Orientation Modulation for Data Hiding in Clustered-Dot Halftone Prints, IEEE Transactions on Image Processing, Vol. 19:8, 2010.

[9] Kacker, D.; Allebach, J.P. Joint Halftoning and Watermarking, IEEE Transactions on Signal Processing, Vol. 51:4, 2003.

[10] M. Kutter, Performance Improvements of Spread Spectrum Based Image Watemarking Schemes Through M-ary Modulation, Proceeding of the Third Information Hiding Workshop, pp. 245-260, Dresden, 1999.

[11] Qiao Li, Ingemar J. Cox, Using Perceptual Models to Improve Fidelity and Provide Resistance to Valumetric Scaling for Quantization Index Modulation Watermarking, IEEE Transactions on Information Forensics and Security, pp. 127 - 139, 2007.

[12] Mauro Barni, Franco Bartolini, Watermarking Systems Engineering, Marcel Dekker Inc., Signal Processing and Communication series, 2004.

[13] Joceli Mayer and José Carlos M. Bermudez, Improving Robustness of CDM Spread Spectrum Watermarking, IEEE ICASSP, 2007.

[14] Rafael C. Gonzalez and Richard E. Woods, Digital Image Processing,

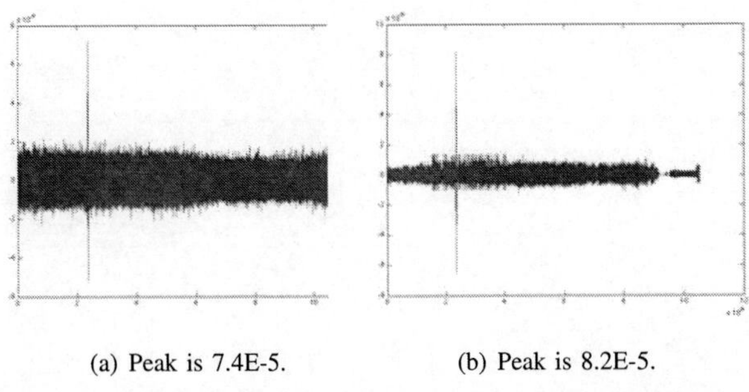

(a) Peak is 7.4E-5. (b) Peak is 8.2E-5.

Fig. 3. (a) The correlation performance **without color rejection**. Notice that the peak is at 7.4E-5 and the false positive peaks around 2E-5. (b) The correlation performance **with color rejection**. Notice that the peak is at 8.2E-5 and the false positive peaks around 1E-5. Superior detection performance using color rejection approach.

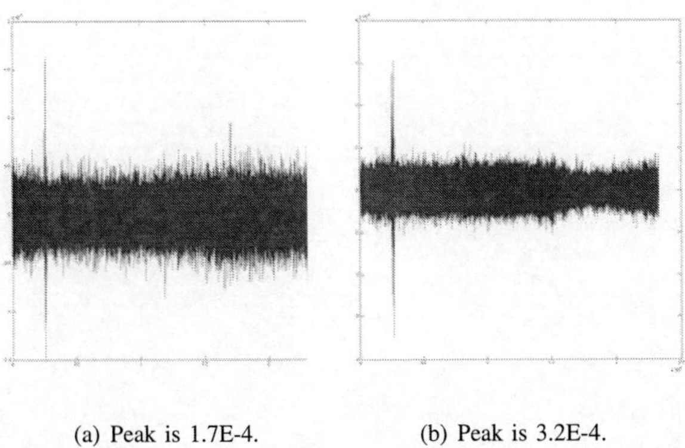

(a) Peak is 1.7E-4. (b) Peak is 3.2E-4.

Fig. 4. (a) Resulting correlation when choosing patterns while **disregarding the color background ink interference**. (b) Resulting correlation performance when **considering encoding the effects of color background** and selecting the best pattern available for the same message (informed coding). Performance improvement achieved by selecting patterns according to the background.

Prentice Hall, 2001.

[15] A. Keskinarkaus, A. Pramila, T. Seppänen, Image watermarking with a directed periodic pattern to embed multibit messages resilient to print-scan and compound attacks, the Journal of Systems and Software v. 83, pp. 1715-1725, 2010.

[16] Kaushal Solanki, Upamanyu Madhow, B. S. Manjunath, Shiv Chandrasekaran, and Ibrahim El-Khalil Print and Scan Resilient Data Hiding in Images, IEEE Trans. on Information Forensics and Security, Vol. 1, No. 4, Dec. 2006.

[17] Dajun He and Qibin Sun, A Practical Print-Scan Resilient Watermarking Scheme, IEEE International Conference on Image Processing-ICIP, 2005.

[18] Anu Pramila, Anja Keskinarkaus, and Tapio Seppänen, Multiple domain watermarking for print-scan and JPEG resilient data hiding, Proceedings of the 6th International Workshop on Digital Watermarking, IWDW, 2007.

[19] Alain Trémeau and Damien Muselet, Recent Trends in Color Image Watermarking, Journal of Imaging Science and Technology 53(1), 2009.

[20] Joceli Mayer, J.C.M. Bermudez, A.P. Legg, B. F. Uchôa-Filho, D. Mukherjee, A. said, R. Samadani and Steven Simske, Design of High Capacity 3D Print Codes with Visual Cues Aiming for Robustness to the PS Channel and External Distortions, IEEE Internacional Workshop Multimedia Signal Processing, 2009.

[21] Joceli Mayer and Steven J. Simske, Modulation in the HVS Domain for Hardcopy Watermarking of Color Documents, 8th International Conference on Signal Image Technology and Internet Based Systems, SITIS, 2012.

(a) **A non recommended** background. (b) **A recommended** background.

Fig. 5. (a) Embedding the cyan pattern over **a non recommended** color background. (b) Embedding the cyan pattern over **a recommended** color background.

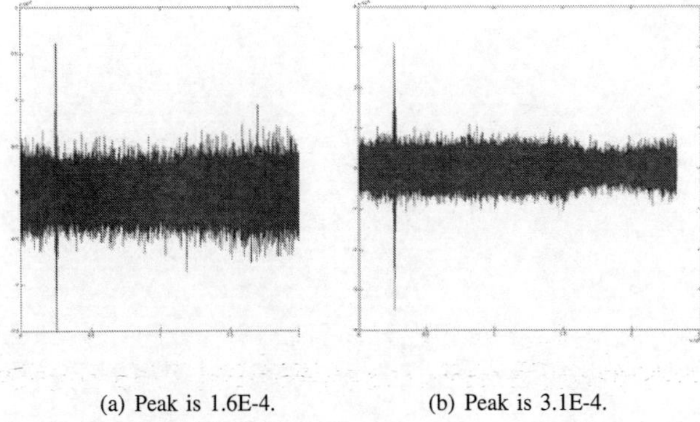

(a) Peak is 1.6E-4. (b) Peak is 3.1E-4.

Fig. 6. (a) Resulting correlation (peak is 1.6E-4) after embedding the cyan pattern over **a non recommended** color background. (b) Resulting correlation (peak is 3.1E-4) after embedding the cyan pattern over **a recommended** color background. The correlation performance is very superior when compared to non recommended background correlation.

TABLE I

RESULTING CORRELATION OF COLOR DOTS UNDER BASIC COLOR BACKGROUND INTERFERENCE. CORRELATION PERFORMANCE DEPENDS ON THE COMBINATION OF COLOR PATTERN AND BACKGROUND. THREE TESTS ARE SHOWN TO ASSURE THE CONSISTENCY OF RESULTS. NOTICE HOW THE MAGENTA AND THE BLACK INKS AFFECT DIFFERENTLY THE CORRELATION DEPENDING ON WHICH COLOR IS IN THE BACKGROUND.

Dot Color	Background	Corr 1	Corr 2	Corr 3
Cyan	Magenta	8.2E-4	8.6E-4	9.4E-4
Cyan	Yellow	3.7E-4	4.0E-4	3.1E-4
Cyan	Black	7.7E-4	10E-4	10E-4
Magenta	Cyan	5.4E-4	5.8E-4	5.E-4
Magenta	Yellow	2.1E-4	1.9E-4	2.0E-4
Magenta	**Black**	12E-4	14E-4	13E-4
Yellow	Cyan	7.8E-4	7.5E-4	7.8E-4
Yellow	Magenta	2.8E-4	2.7E-4	2.6E-4
Yellow	Black	6.6E-4	8.0E-4	4.5E-4
Black	Cyan	3.0E-4	2.6E-4	3.0E-4
Black	**Magenta**	2.8E-4	1.8E-4	2.2E-4
Black	Yellow	1.5E-4	1.3E-4	1.9E-4

SESSION

IMAGING SOFTWARE + SYSTEMS + CAMERA CALIBRATION

Chair(s)

TBA

Topological Detection of Chessboard Pattern for Camera Calibration

Gustavo Teodoro Laureano[1], **Maria Stela Veludo de Paiva**[1] and **Anderson Soares da Silva**[2]
[1]Department of Electrical Engineering, University of São Paulo (USP/EESC), São Carlos, São Paulo, Brazil
[2]Institute of Informatics, Federal University of Goiás (UFG), Goiás, Brazil

Abstract— *Most works on camera calibration are directed to the stage of parameter estimation, while the phase matching is not always addressed. Most of applications assume that the correspondences are established in advance or require user intervention. Since the automatic applications require that the entire pattern is detected, which is difficult in most cases. This work aims to identify patterns of camera calibration automatically where the pattern can not be fully detected. Therefore, a corner detection and a topological filter are presented. The correspondence is done using neighboring properties on a geometric mesh and the sub-pixel location is threshold independent. The results show that the algorithm provides a robust detection even when the pattern is partially occluded.*

Keywords: Camera Calibration, Chessboard Detection, Topological Detection

1. Introduction

The camera calibration aims to determine the geometric parameters of the image formation process [1]. This is a crucial step in computer vision applications especially when metric information about the scene is required. In these applications the camera is generally modeled with a set of intrinsic parameters (focal length, principal point, skew of axis) and your orientation is expressed by extrinsic parameters (rotation and translation). Both intrinsic and extrinsic parameters are estimated by linear or non-linear methods using known points in the real world and their projections in the image plane [2]. These points are presented as a calibration pattern with known geometry, usually a flat chessboard.

Many studies have given attention to the camera calibration area, most of them are dedicated to the parameters estimation phase and refinement location of the calibration points [3], [4], [5], [6]. Tsai [7] and Zhang [8] are examples of the most cited papers related to this area. They propose closed form solutions for the estimation of intrinsic and extrinsic parameters using 3D and 2D calibration patterns respectively. Hamayed [9] and Salvi et al. [10] present reviews about some related works.

Camera calibration is a much discussed topic but the lack of robust algorithms for features detection difficults the construction of automatic calibration process. Calibration pattern recognition is a hard task, where the lighting problems and high level of ambiguities are the principal challenges. For this reason, the algorithms often require user intervention for a reliable detection of the calibration points. The hand tuning of points is tedious, imprecise and require user skill [11].

Some tools for automatic camera calibration are available. The Bouguet MatLab Toolbox [12] implements a semi-automatic calibration process. The application asks the user to define four extreme points that represent the area where an algorithm searches for the calibration points, given the number of rows and columns of the pattern. The OpenCV library [13] is a very popular computer vision library that offers an automatic way to detect chessboard patterns in images by the *findChessboardCorners()* function. The method performs successive morphological operators until a number of black and white contours be identified, subsequently the corners of the contours make up the calibration point set. The pattern is recognized only if all rectangles are identified. In an online system this restriction causes a considerable loss of image frames, since is not always possible to detect all the chessboard rectangles.

Fiala and Shu [14] use an array of fiducial markers, each one with a unique self-identifying pattern. The described methodology is robust to noise and it is not necessary to identify the entire calibration pattern. In the other hand, the markers are complex and require a special algorithm to recognize them.

Escalera and Armingol [15] identify the calibration points as the intersections of lines. The methodology uses a combined analysis of two consecutive Hough transforms to filter the collinear points inside the pattern. The assumption that all points of interest are collinear makes this algorithm very sensitive to distortions, limiting its use only to cameras with low radial distortion.

The system named CAMcal [16] uses the Harris corner detection and a topological sort of squares within a geometric mesh. Harris corner detection is time consuming, sensible to noise, needs an empirical threshold to select interesting points and does not produce good results to the specific features of the chessboard image [17]. Furthermore, the system must to detect three circles to determine orientation of the pattern.

This work presents a system for automated detection of chessboard patterns for camera calibration. Initially a fast and specific x-shaped corner operator is performed to retrieve the interesting points. A geometric mesh is created from all the x-corners by Delaunay triangulation. A topological filter is proposed. Are taken as valid the triangles that match with the regularity of the pattern. The color and the neighborhood of the triangle are analyzed. Each remaining point defines a valid x-corner and a refinement location is performed locally.

The calibration process does not depend on full detection of the calibration pattern. When a minimum number of points is identified the calibration algorithm may be executed, in this case the Zhang's algorithm [8].

2. X-Corner Detector

The first stage of the algorithm is the features detection. Corners x-shaped are identified analyzing the alternations of high contrast in the neighborhood of each pixel.

Considering $V = \{\mathbf{p}_1, \mathbf{p}_2, \cdots, \mathbf{p}_n\}$ the neighborhood of a central pixel $\mathbf{p}_c$, defined by all the pixels in the border of a Breseham's circle [18], the number of alternations of high contrast is computed by the Equation 1.

$$N_{alt} = \sum_{i=1}^{n} \begin{cases} 1, & I(\mathbf{p}_i) > T_h \ \& \ I(\mathbf{p}_{i-1}) < T_l \\ 1, & I(\mathbf{p}_i) < T_l \ \& \ I(\mathbf{p}_{i-1}) > T_h \\ 0, & \text{otherwise} \end{cases} \quad (1)$$

where $\mathbf{p}_i \in V$, $I(\mathbf{p}_i)$ represents the pixel intensity of $\mathbf{p}_i$, T_l and T_h are the inferior and superior threshold respectively. Alternatively, both thresholds can be defined by: $T_l = m - gate$ and $T_h = m + gate$, with $m = \frac{1}{n}\sum_1^n I(\mathbf{p}_i)$.

The pixel $\mathbf{p}_c$ is classified as a x-corner if $N_{alt} = 4$ and $T_l < I(\mathbf{p}_c) < T_h$. For the Equation 1, if $i = 0$, $i - 1 = n$ is assumed. The Figure 1 shows the considered area by this detector.

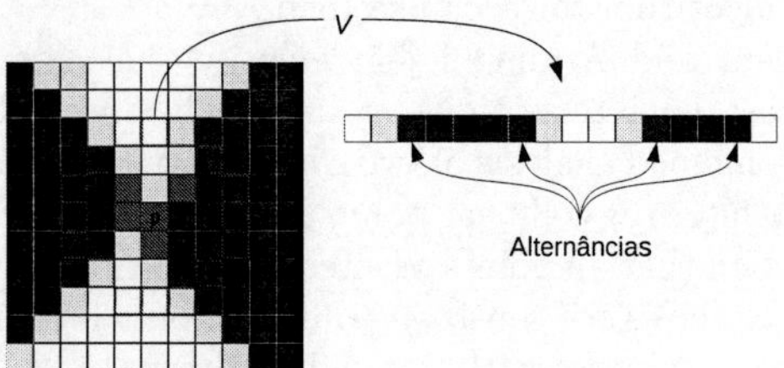

Fig. 1: Typical x-corner neighborhood.

The variable *gate* models the operator sensibility. Considering a previously blurred image, the number of alternations imposes large part of the restriction required for a proper classification. Thus the variable *gate* has little effect on the final result. In this work *gate* is defined with 10 empirically.

This detector can be seen as a specification of the proposed detector in Rosten and Drummond [19], which is considered high performance. Since only a small portion of the neighborhood of the pixel is analyzed, the computational cost of this operation is reduced. Another similar detectors can be found in Zhao et al. [17] and Sun et al. [20]. The Figure 2 shows a typical result of this detector over the original image.

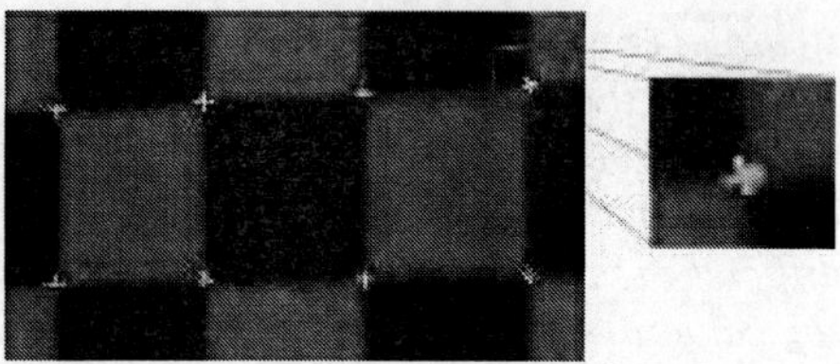

Fig. 2: X-corner operator response.

The formulation of this operator does not guarantee that only one pixel is classified as a x-corner in its neighborhood. To deal with this problem, the cost described by the Equation 2 is associated with each corner and a non-maximum suppression is performed [21].

$$max\left(\sum_{\mathbf{p}_i \in \ dark} |I(\mathbf{p}_i) - m|, \sum_{\mathbf{p}_i \in \ light} |I(\mathbf{p}_i) - m|\right) \quad (2)$$

The classes *dark* and *light* contains the dark and light pixels respectively. The right corner is the one with the highest associated cost.

3. Topological Filter

The identification of valid corners is an important step because not all x-corners present in the image belong to the calibration pattern. In this work, the identification of valid x-corners is made considering the regularity neighborhood of the chessboard image. This problem can be extended to the problem of creating geometric meshes in computer graphics. In a mesh composed of basic components such as triangles, vertices are connected according to their neighborhood [22].

The Delaunay triangulation is a classic problem in computational geometry. Given a set of points in a plane, the only valid triangulation is one where the circumcircle of each triangle contains no other vertex [23]. This feature ensures that the triangles are formed by the more closely vertexes. Guibas et al. [24] present an algorithm for incremental triangulation that that runs in time $O(n\ log(n))$.

With the creation of the mesh the neighborhood of each feature is defined. Figure 3 gives an example of this triangulation.

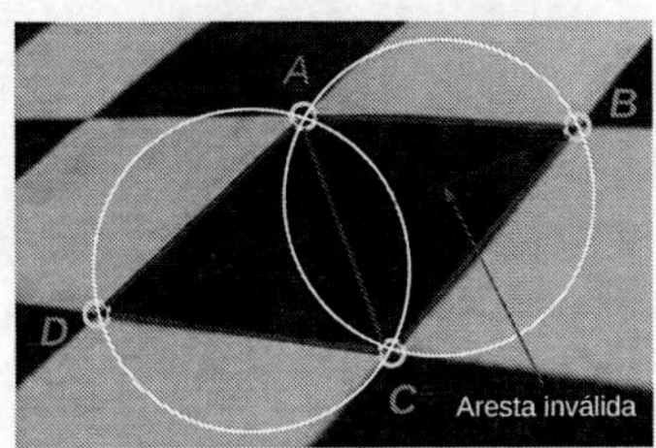

Fig. 3: Considering A, B, C and D four image corners, the valid triangulation if formed by the triangles $\Delta(A, B, C)$ and $\Delta(A, C, D)$.

Using the geometric mesh, the vertices and triangles are submitted to a topological filter to exclude those not satisfying the regularity of the pattern. The corners (or vertexes) share internal triangles of different colors in a regular manner. Each square of the chessboard pattern is represented by two triangles of the same color. Each triangle has no more than two neighboring triangles that form two squares with different colors alike. The internal vertexes have in common a maximum of eight triangles. Valid triangles have its interior filled with a single color.

Even after the projected image plane, the neighborhood relationship between the corners is still maintained. This restriction allows us to evaluate if the corners really belong to the calibration pattern. Thus, they are considered valid:

1) those triangles that do not have color transitions in your interior;
2) only those triangles that have a neighbor with the same color;
3) those triangles that have only two neighbors of the same color and different color triangle taken as a reference;

This filter is applied to the grid until there are no more invalid triangles. In the end, the vertices that do not form any triangle are also removed.

To avoid the use of thresholds in the comparison of colors, this filter uses a binarized version of the image. This is an important step in validating points. If binarization fails, noisy points can be identified and actual points can be disregarded. To minimize these effects this work uses adaptive binarization described in the work of Bradley and Roth [25]. This algorithm handles well with large variations in illumination and runs in linear time for any window size.

The binarization phase can be influenced by problems from the acquisition of images due to lighting variations and also by the fluctuation of the intensities of the pixels. In the regions near to the edges a range of values may be wrongly considered black or white pixels. This behavior can generate white triangles with black borders and black triangles with white edges. In practice, verification color transition is made in a region of the innermost triangle, ignoring the edges. Figure 4 shows the result of the topological filtering.

4. Point Correspondences

The next step of the algorithm associates each vertex to the real coordinates of the pattern. This is done by analyzing the relative position of each corner. First two neighboring triangles of the same color are arbitrarily selected: T_1 and T_2. Three vertices make up the triangle T_1, the origin of the coordinate system is defined by the vertex that has T_2 as its opposite triangle. For the remaining vertices are assigned the directions x and y of the Cartesian plane (Figure 5).

The propagation of coordinates consists in establishing the relative coordinates of the vertices neighbors. Given a triangle T whose vertices have already defined coordinates, where the origin is v_o, v_x and v_y are the vertices with the x and y directions respectively. T_v is defined as a neighbor triangle of T with a different color. If T_v and T are neighbors then they share an edge e and T_v has a opposite vertex to the T, called v_v. The coordinates of the opposite vertex needs to be determined, thus:

- If $v_x \in e$, then $v_v = [v_t^{(x)} \quad 2v_t^{(y)} - v_y^{(y)}]'$;
- If $v_y \in e$, then $v_v = [2v_t^{(x)} - v_y^{(x)} \quad v_t^{(y)}]'$;

It is understood by $v^{(\cdot)}$ the coordinate $(.)$ of vertex v. Similarly, T_{op} shares a border e_{op} with T_v, then $v_{op} = [v_h^{(x)} \quad v_v^{(y)}]'$, where v_h is the third vertex of T_v and v_{op} is the opposite vertex to e_{op}.

For each visited triangle, the vertexes coordinates of the current and opposite triangles are propagated. The algorithm performs recursively for each neighbor triangle to the pair T_v and T_{op}. It makes the algorithm $O(\frac{n}{2})$, where n is the number of triangles in the mesh.

5. Location Refinement

The use of the detector described in section 2 identifies the position of corners with low accuracy where the only information available is the position of discrete pixels. Since the quality of the calibration is directly dependent to the precision with which the position of features is found, there is a need for a technique refinement [1].

Traditional algorithms such as Harris and Stephens detector [26] and Shi and Tomasi [27], run throughout the image and use thresholds to select the features of interest. The sub-pixel precision is achieved by maximizing functions fitted to the square of the intensity profile of the local neighborhood of each pixel. The threshold has a direct impact on the quality of response of these

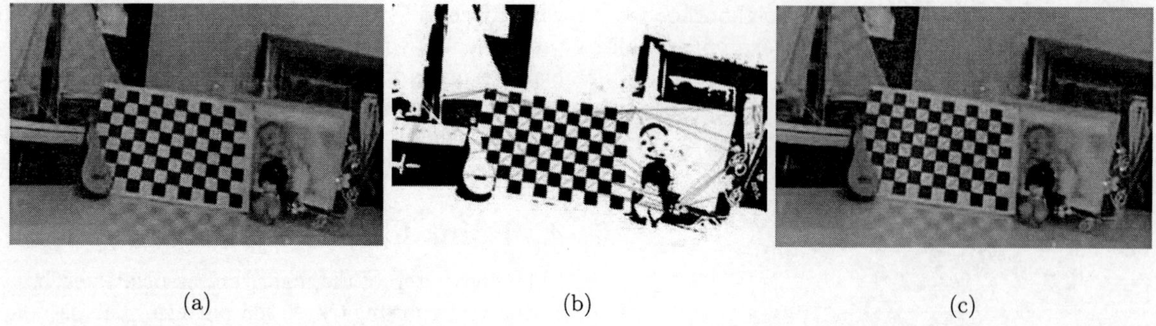

(a) (b) (c)

Fig. 4: Example of the detection and topological filter results. a) X-corners. b) Triangulation and binarized image. c) The valid triangles after the topological filter.

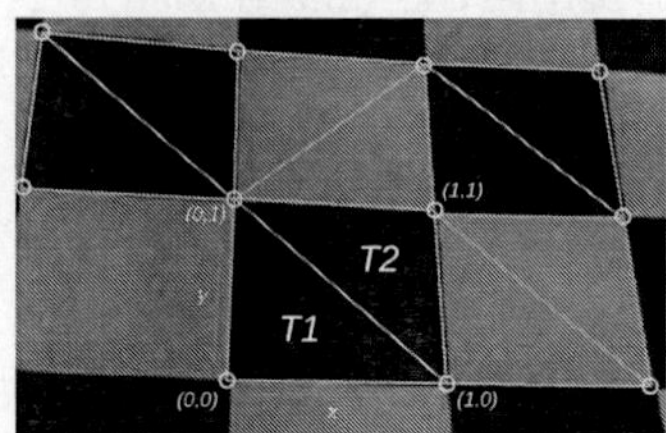

Fig. 5: The triangles $T1$ and $T2$ define the origin and the direction of coordinates.

detectors, so corners are usually classified as the N pixels with greater response to the operator.

Chen et al. [4] propose a new detector specially designed to fit corners of X-shape. Considering the neighborhood of a pixel as a surface, its Hessian matrix can be expressed as:

$$H = \begin{bmatrix} I_{xx} & I_{xy} \\ I_{xy} & I_{yy} \end{bmatrix} \tag{3}$$

where I_{xx}, I_{xy} and I_{yy} are the second partial derivatives of pixel $I(x, y)$. Thus, the x-corner detector is described as:

$$S = \lambda_1 \cdot \lambda_2 = I_{xx}I_{yy} - I_{xy}^2. \tag{4}$$

where, λ_1 and λ_2 are the eigenvalues of H.

In order to avoid unnecessary computation, this operator is only applied in regions defined by the valid vertices of triangle mesh. The x-corner can be detected by identifying the largest negative value of S and the refined coordinates $(x_0 + s, t + y_0)$ is given by:

$$s = \frac{I_yI_{xy} - I_xI_{yy}}{I_{xx}I_{yy} - I_{xy}^2}, \quad t = \frac{I_xI_{xy} - I_xI_{xx}}{I_{xx}I_{yy} - I_{xy}^2} \tag{5}$$

6. Experimental Results

In this section, the detector response is evaluated considering an image database and by means of experimental tests with two different cameras.

The image database is provided by the toolbox for MatLab prepared by Bouguet [12]. This database consists of 20 images of a chessboard calibration pattern, accounting 156 x-corners arranged as 12×13 matrix, being presented in different orientations. This set represents a common situation to most of systems where the pattern images are first captured and calibration is performed in an offline manner.

Figure 6 shows some examples of these images and Table 1 summarizes the results obtained for each one. The results are generated by applying the algorithm in each image and counting the number of corners identified. For Table 1, the vast majority of points is detected.

The mean accuracy of the algorithm is 85.38% however two images (Image 5 and 18) deserve attention by the low percentage of success. They represent situations where the calibration plane is very inclined to the camera. In this case it is expected that the corners are uncharacterized by high perspective distortion and lack of focus in the image. Another aspect to be considered is that the images in this database have low contrast, which complicates the identification of alternations of high contrast.

In general, the algorithm was able to find the most calibration points. If the two worst images are discarded, the accuracy of success rises to 90.88%, which reflects the efficiency of the methodology. The Figure 7 shows the worst and best results of the algorithm.

For the online experiments, we used two different cameras: (1) Philips Webcam SPC990NC e (2) Microsoft Webcam HD 5000. The calibration pattern used is formed by squares with 2.5cm of width and forms a matrix of 11 × 7 x-corners. For each camera, were tested 14 real images of the calibration pattern in various orientations and distances.

The algorithm runs on a sequence of captured frames. The amount of detected points, presented in the second and fourth column of Table 2 corresponds to the average of the points detected in 10 frames for each position of

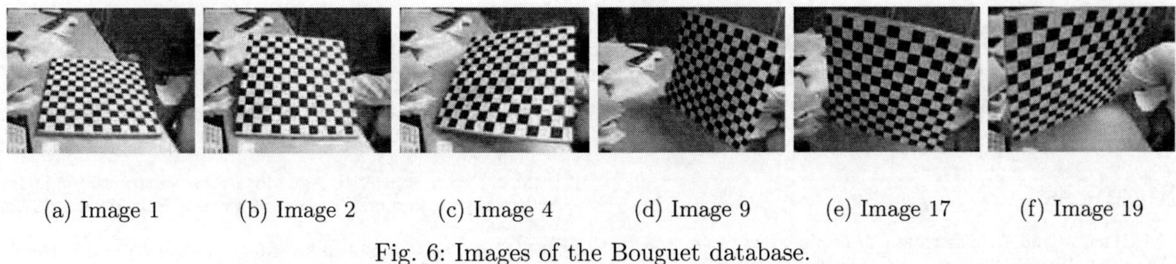

(a) Image 1 (b) Image 2 (c) Image 4 (d) Image 9 (e) Image 17 (f) Image 19

Fig. 6: Images of the Bouguet database.

Image	1	2	3	4	5	6	7	8	9	10
Corners	151	154	147	153	51	149	132	110	143	153
(%)	96.79	98.72	94.23	98.08	32.69	95.51	84.62	70.51	91.67	98.08
Image	11	12	13	14	15	16	17	18	19	20
Corners	152	155	156	138	121	154	155	61	111	118
(%)	97.44	99.36	100.00	88.46	77.56	98.72	99.36	39.10	71.15	75.64

Table 1: Results for the Bouguet database.

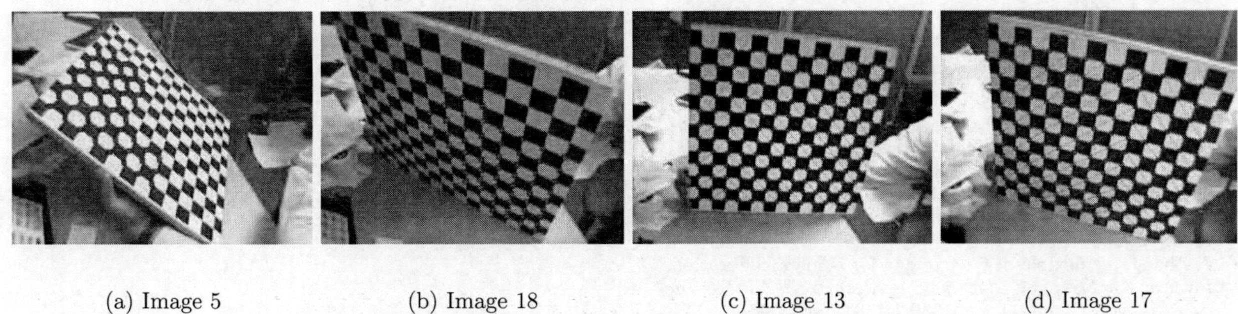

(a) Image 5 (b) Image 18 (c) Image 13 (d) Image 17

Fig. 7: Worst (Image 5 and 18) and best (Image 13 and 17) results in the Bouguet database.

	HD 5000		SPC900nc	
	x-corners	%	x-corners	%
Image 00	77	100	73	94.80
Image 01	77	100	77	100
Image 02	77	100	77	100
Image 03	73	94.80	76	98.70
Image 04	77	100	73	94.70
Image 05	77	100	77	100
Image 06	77	100	76	98.70
Image 07	77	100	77	100
Image 08	77	100	77	100
Image 09	77	100	76	98.70
Image 10	75	97.40	72	93.50
Image 11	70	90.90	76	98.70
Image 12	72	93.50	75	97.40
Image 13	70	90.90	77	100
Mean:		97.68		98.23

Table 2: Results for the online detection.

the calibration pattern.

The Figure 8 shows some of the images used in the second experiment. Once the pattern is completely visible, the algorithm has a high hit rate, while the missed corners tend to arise when there is a more accentuated inclination of the plane in relation to the camera. In these images no false positives were identified, which confirms the robustness of the filter used.

To illustrate the efficiency of the filter topological and propagation of coordinates, Figure 9 illustrates the result of the algorithm using complex backgrounds and partial occlusion of the pattern. The occluded corners do not interfere in the propagation of correct coordinates. Thus, it is possible to use the maximum of features identified for the estimation of camera parameters. The last column shows the reprojection plan calibration calculated from the detected points.

7. Conclusions

This work proposes a methodology for detecting calibration patterns. The experimental results show that it is possible to detect these patterns in a robust and automatic without the use of thresholds. Furthermore, a low computational cost is achieved, since the refinement of X-corners is directed to specific regions of the image. The filtering of topological corners-X allows handle cameras with radial distortion and high immunity to noise. A partial identification of the pattern allows the calibration process is considering giving maximum points detected. In conditions where few points are detected, most picture frames are utilized.

References

[1] R. I. Hartley and A. Zisserman, *Multiple View Geometry in Computer Vision*, 2nd ed. Cambridge University Press, ISBN: 0521540518, 2004.

[2] E. Trucco and A. Verri, *Introductory Techniques for 3-D Computer Vision.* Upper Saddle River, NJ, USA: Prentice Hall PTR, 1998.

[3] A. Dutta, A. Kar, and B. N. Chatterji, "A novel window-based corner detection algorithm for gray-scale images," in *Proceedings of the 2008 Sixth Indian Conference on Computer Vision, Graphics & Image Processing*, ser. ICVGIP '08. Washington, DC, USA: IEEE Computer Society, 2008, pp. 650–656.

[4] D. Chen and G. Zhang, "A new sub-pixel detector for x-corners in camera calibration targets." in *WSCG (Short Papers)'05*, 2005, pp. 97–100.

[5] X. Hu, P. Du, and Y. Zhou, "Automatic corner detection of chess board for medical endoscopy camera calibration," in *Proceedings of the 10th International Conference on Virtual Reality Continuum and Its Applications in Industry*, ser. VRCAI '11. New York, NY, USA: ACM, 2011, pp. 431–434.

[6] L. Krüger and C. Wöhler, "Accurate chequerboard corner localisation for camera calibration," *Pattern Recogn. Lett.*, vol. 32, no. 10, pp. 1428–1435, July 2011.

[7] R. Y. Tsai, "An efficient and accurate camera calibration technique for 3d machine vision," in *Proceedings of IEEE Conference on Computer Vision and Pattern Recognition*, 1986, pp. 364 – 374.

[8] Z. Zhang, "A flexible new technique for camera calibration," *Pattern Analysis and Machine Intelligence, IEEE Transactions on*, vol. 22, no. 11, pp. 1330 – 1334, nov 2000.

[9] E. Hemayed, "A survey of camera self-calibration," in *Proceedings. IEEE Conference on Advanced Video and Signal Based Surveillance, 2003.*, july 2003, pp. 351 – 357.

[10] J. Salvi, X. ArmanguÃĺ, and J. Batlle, "A comparative review of camera calibrating methods with accuracy evaluation," *Pattern Recognition*, vol. 35, no. 7, pp. 1617 – 1635, 2002.

[11] S. Bennett and J. Lasenby, "Chess - quick and robust detection of chess-board features," *CoRR*, vol. abs/1301.5491, 2013.

[12] J.-Y. Bouguet, "Camera calibration toolbox for matlab," http://www.vision.caltech.edu/bouguetj/calib_doc/.

[13] OpenCV, "Open source computer vision library," http://www.opencv.willowgarage.com/.

[14] M. Fiala and C. Shu, "Self-identifying patterns for plane-based camera calibration," *Machine Vision and Applications*, vol. 19, pp. 209–216, 2008, 10.1007/s00138-007-0093-z.

[15] A. de la Escalera and J. M. Armingol, "Automatic chessboard detection for intrinsic and extrinsic camera parameter calibration." *Sensors (Basel, Switzerland)*, vol. 10, no. 3, pp. 2027–44, Jan. 2010.

[16] C. Shu, A. Brunton, and M. Fiala, "A topological approach to finding grids in calibration patterns," *Machine Vision and Applications*, vol. 21, pp. 949–957, 2010, 10.1007/s00138-009-0202-2.

[17] F. Zhao, C. Wei, J. Wang, and J. Tang, "An automated x-corner detection algorithm(axda)," *JSW*, vol. 6, no. 5, pp. 791–797, 2011.

[18] J. Bresenham, "A linear algorithm for incremental digital display of circular arcs," *Commun. ACM*, vol. 20, no. 2, pp. 100–106, Feb. 1977.

[19] E. Rosten and T. Drummond, "Machine learning for high-speed corner detection," in *Proceedings of the 9th European conference on Computer Vision - Volume Part I*, ser. ECCV'06. Berlin, Heidelberg: Springer-Verlag, 2006, pp. 430–443.

[20] W. Sun, X. Yang, S. Xiao, and W. Hu, "Robust checkerboard recognition for efficient nonplanar geometry registration in projector-camera systems," in *Proceedings of the 5th ACM/IEEE International Workshop on Projector camera systems*, ser. PROCAMS '08. New York, NY, USA: ACM, 2008, pp. 2:1–2:7.

[21] M. S. Nixon and A. S. Aguado, *Feature Extraction and Image Processing*, 2nd ed. Academic Press ISBN: 978-0-12-372538-7, 2008.

[22] M. Bern and D. Eppstein, "Mesh generation and optimal triangulation," *Computing in Euclidean geometry*, vol. 1, no. 1, pp. 23–90, 1992.

[23] M. V. K. Mark De Berg, Otfried Cheong, *Computational Geometry: Algorithms and Applications*, 3rd ed. Springer-Verlag ISBN: 978-3-540-77973-5, 2008.

[24] L. Guibas, D. Knuth, and M. Sharir, "Randomized incremental construction of delaunay and voronoi diagrams," *Algorithmica*, vol. 7, pp. 381–413, 1992, 10.1007/BF01758770.

[25] D. Bradley and G. Roth, "Adaptive thresholding using the integral image." *Journal of Graphics Tools*, pp. 13–21, 2007.

[26] C. Harris and M. Stephens, "A combined corner and edge detector," in *Proceedings of the 4th Alvey Vision Conference*, 1988, pp. 147–151.

[27] J. Shi and C. Tomasi, "Good features to track," in *Computer Vision and Pattern Recognition, 1994. Proceedings CVPR '94., 1994 IEEE Computer Society Conference on*, jun 1994, pp. 593 -600.

Fig. 8: Example of images used in the second test. The left column shows all x-cornes and the triangulation. The right column shows the topological filter result.

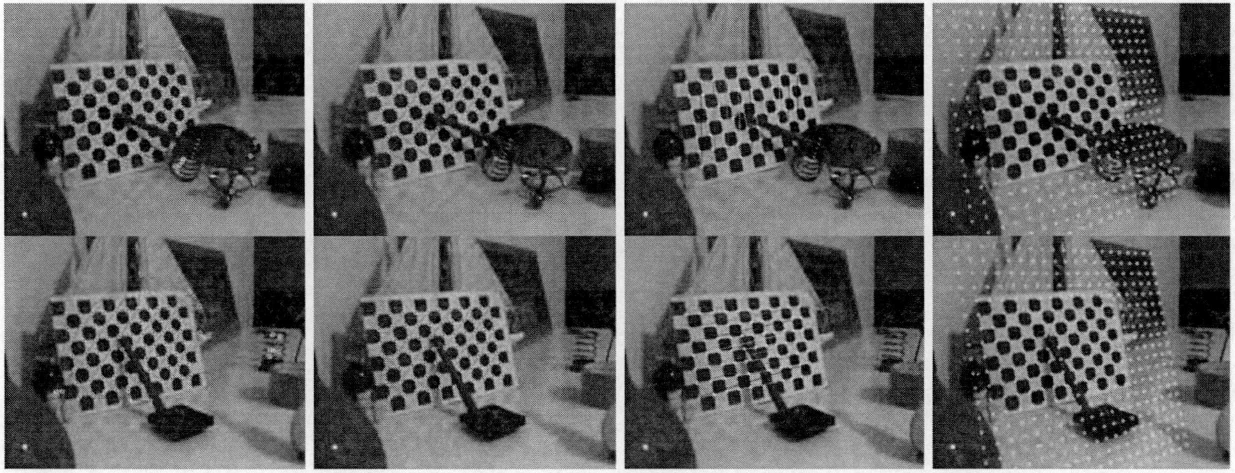

Fig. 9: Results with complex backgrounds and partial occlusion.

Image processing workflow middleware to archive high performance and usability

K. Iwata[1], **Y. Satoh**[1] **and I. Kojima**[1]
[1] National Institute of Advanced Industrial Science and Technology (AIST)
AIST Tsukuba Central 2, 1-1-1 Umezono, Tsukuba, Ibaraki 305-8568 Japan

Abstract - *We develop Lavatube as an image processing workflow middleware for efficient research and development. Lavatube is an object-oriented framework optimized for constructing a computer vision system, particularly a video and image processing system. Lavatube enables a description of a processing extension by combining various functional components. Since the data flow is easy to describe by graph-connecting icons on a GUI, a system can be created intuitively. For efficient and clearcut system construction, Lavatube provides functions for the dynamic generation of parameter setting dialog boxes and for perpetuation by XML. Lavatube can also be used cloud computing to process large amounts of data. Some actual image processing cases as examples are also introduced.*

Keywords: Image Processing, Middleware, Workflow, User Interface

1 Introduction

A computer vision system captures information from the external world as image data by using a camera and other devices, and analyzes the images on a computer for studying or measuring [1]. This kind of system is used as a major means of inspection, especially for semiconductors and electronic boards, because objects can be measured without contact. The range of applications, such as security, robot vision, medicine, welfare, and sports, has been growing even more in recent years.

A computer vision system that is expected to be applied so widely requires high-level knowledge and programming techniques for its design and adjustment. So, at a company or a university, what kind of abilities should be acquired to learn this system from the beginning? There is a lot of substantially important knowledge, such as statistics and geometry. In reality, however, he or she faces such problems as difficult programming for image acquisition from a camera or time-consuming analysis of a predecessor's program that requires great overhead.

Even an experienced person tends not to be commit-ted to programming because it requires a lot of time to construct a framework where arbitrary processing can be visualized and various parameters can be adjusted in real time. This consequently makes it necessary, yet sometimes impossible, to evaluate installed algorithms and set parameters satisfactorily.

To solve these problems, we developed Lavatube as a image processing middleware. Lavatube has the following advantages:

- A system can be constructed easily by graph connecting icons that express various functions on a graphical user interface (GUI), such as the one shown in figure 1.

- By arranging icons with the capturing function, a USB camera and various video files (AVI, MPEG, etc.) can be used as input. This realizes online and offline experiments using previously recorded videos on a single platform.

- Parameter setting dialog boxes can be generated dynamically and adjusted by viewing of the processing results online.

- Persistence by XML enables storage and reproduction of working environment.

- The framework operates at high speed with extremely small overhead. Since parallel flows are automatically threaded for parallel execution, this programming makes processing even faster than ordinary programming.

Fig.1 A GUI of Lavatube

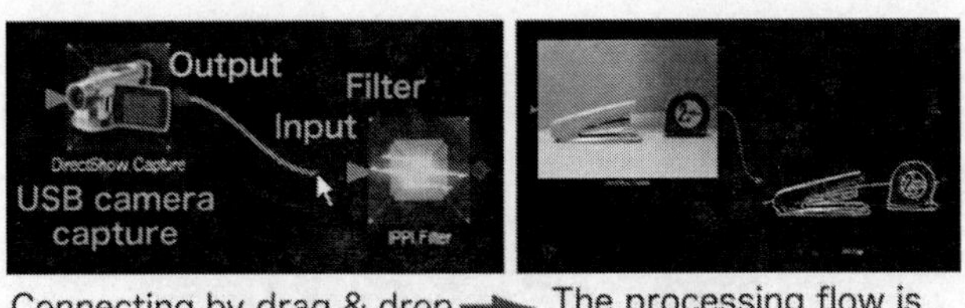

Fig.2 Description of data flow

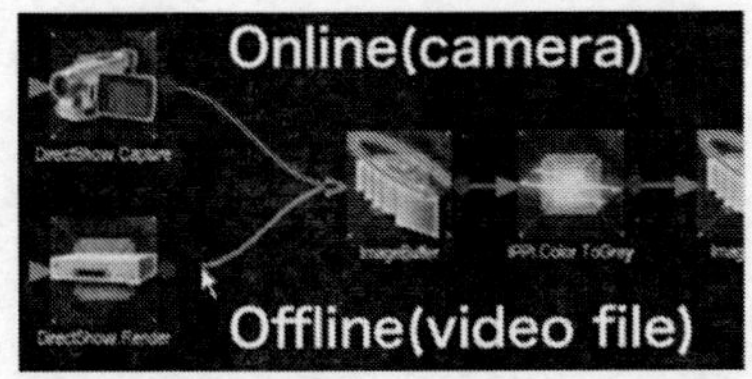

Fig.3 Switching online to offline environment.

Previously, the image processing environments, such as Khoros [2] and XITE [3] have been developed. More recently however, many visual programming environments for processing flows visually through this type of GUI have been available commercially. For example, MAX/MSP [4], which is mainly used by artists, is a visual programming environment extended from voice processing to video processing. Other marketed products include MATLAB/Simulink [5] for simulation and AVS/Express [6] for visualization. These are basically visual programming environments in which existing modules are combined to create a processing flow. If there are not enough modules, extension modules are created by using C or other languages. Since existing modules are not adequate for creating new algorithms, programmers need to create extension modules.

On the other hand, workflow systems have been developed to manage a business process [7] or scientific studies [8]. The workflow systems can be performed with the description of the cooperation of a variety of functions and services. However, these systems are not designed to be easy to use in image processing.

Lavatube was developed not as a visual programming environment via a GUI but rather as an object-oriented framework optimized for video and image processing. Lavatube is designed so that users can develop original function extensions easily by combining various functional components. These patches are compatible with GUIs, XML, and other support functions, and realize an efficient research and development environment, in which such functions are immediately available as a user interface, visualization, and perpetuation.

Over the past few years, large amounts of data are being accumulated. Recently, cloud computing has been attracting

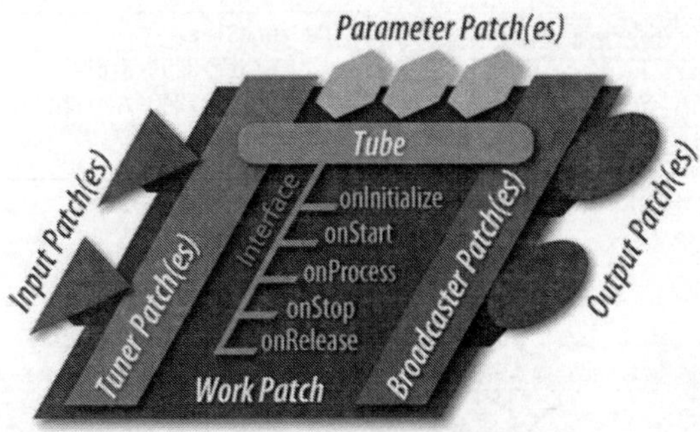

Fig.4 Structure of "work-patch"

attention as a useful infrastructure for the analysis of such data. We have developed a middleware to build a workflow of image processing on the cloud.

This paper outlines the Lavatube functions and introduces actual cases.

2 Outline

Lavatube is an object-oriented framework that sup-ports research on video and image processing, computer vision, and also trial application programming and tuning. The characteristic functions of Lavatube are de-scribed below.

2.1 Description of Data Flow by the GUI

In the GUI of Lavatube, each process (called a "work patch") is expressed as an icon. By connecting the input and output of each icon using a mouse, a data flow can be described very easily. Figure 2 shows an example of a data flow description. In this example, the image output from the USB camera is connected to the input of the contour detection filter.

This type of GUI makes it easy to partially modify and add processes. For example, online experiments and offline experiments can be easily realized in the same environment by switching the source of image input immediately to a camera or a video file, as shown in figure 3.

2.2 Extensibility

A program is described in small units called patches, and Lavatube operates by interpreting these patches automatically. As figure 4 shows, work-patches are created by combining patches of functions such as data I/O, parameters, and by describing a processing procedure on the object interface. Any user experienced in C++ programming can easily create work-patches of arbitrary functions.

At present, Lavatube has functions for image capturing from a USB camera, basic filtering, and arithmetic operations. The

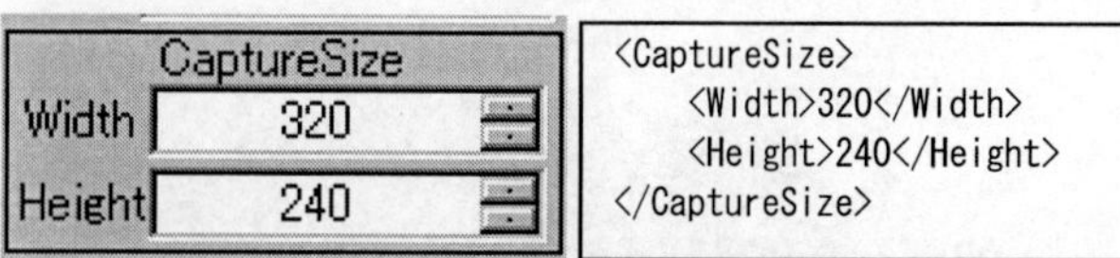

(a) Dialog (b) XML output

Fig.5 Parameter setup

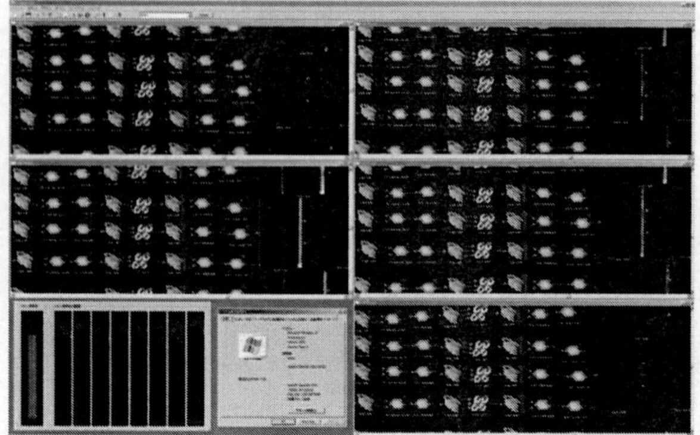

Fig.6 A parallel operation example

high extensibility allows for easy addition of functions to use other types of cameras.

2.3 Storage and Reproduction of Working Environment by XML

Lavatube can output a working environment including a data flow and parameters to an XML file for storage. The working environment can be completely re-produced by loading the XML files. As the system becomes complicated in ordinary programming, this processing becomes time-consuming and often causes a programming error. In Lavatube, each patch has a function that can be realized easily by separating the description. This function enables verification by reproducing the environment, as well as later additions or modifications of functions.

2.4 Parameter Setup via the GUI

Lavatube provides a GUI through which parameters can be adjusted easily. Since dialog boxes, such as figure 5(a), are created dynamically, programmers are free to use GUIs for additions or modifications without using a GUI builder or other software. The dialog boxes are automatically generated by describing any parameter in parameter function patches. Since parameter sets determined via the GUI are stored in an XML file, such as figure 5(b), a description of constant parameters can be separated from the source code to improve program maintainability.

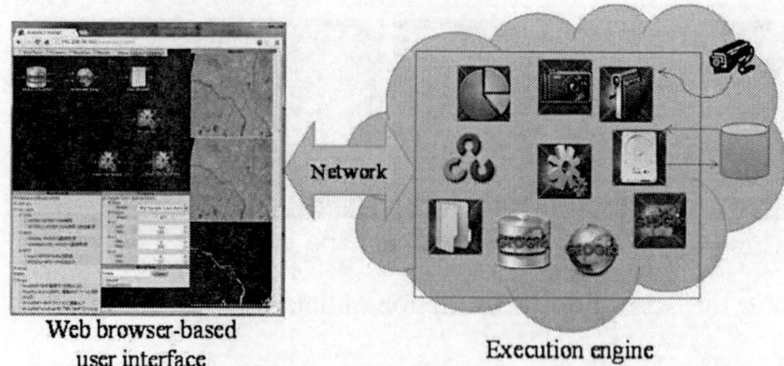

Fig.7 Cloud-based system for image processing workflow

2.5 Visualization of Operation Status

The real-time display of image data on a data flow allows the user to visually check the operation status sequentially for efficient parameter tuning and other tasks.

For real-time demonstration, Lavatube is designed to optimize the processing overhead and to operate the constructed system extremely quickly. The automatic parallel processing of tasks in each work patch is optimum for multi-core processors, which are becoming more widespread. Figure 6 shows a parallel operation example. In this figure, 25 tasks are operating on 8 cores PC.

3 Cloud-based system

The first version of Lavatube was an application for Windows. To take advantage of cloud computing, we developed Lavatube 2, which has a WEB-based user interface and cloud-based execution engine. The developed software, Lavatube 2, is divided into two parts: a user interface, Skylight, and an execution engine, Deepcave. The execution engine is located on the cloud and the user interface is provided from the Web browser. Figure 7 shows the configuration of Lavatube 2. This configuration has the following benefits. First, installation on a PC is not required, allowing the user to use Lavatube 2 independently of the equipment environment, including the performance of the PC and the operating system. Skylight is based on the latest HTML5 Web technology and allows the user to easily develop, with simple mouse operations in the Web browser window, a complex image analysis system consisting of programs to perform various processes and procedures. Data analysis by the execution engine Deepcave is performed by the cloud but not by the user's browser. This makes it possible to process massive amounts of data at high speed, making use of the computing capability of cloud computing.

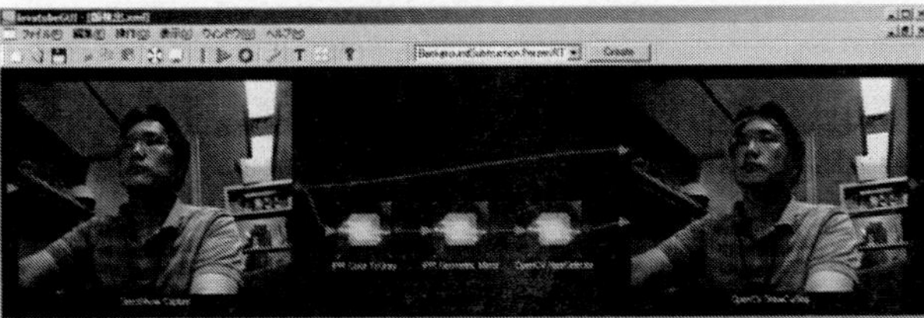

Fig.8 Face detection

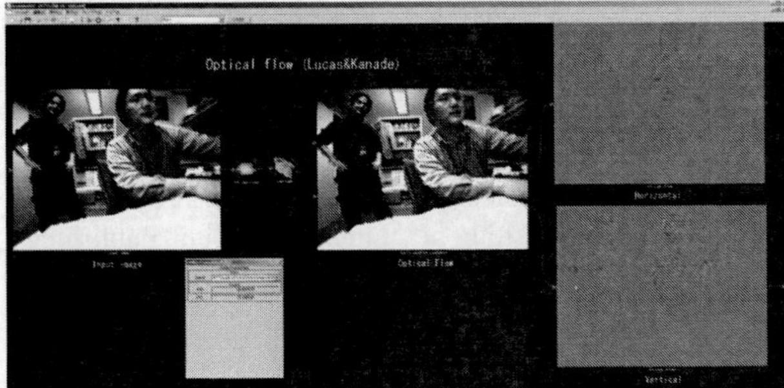

Fig.9 Optical flow estimation

4 Examples

4.1 Wrapping external libraries

By wrapping OpenCV and other external libraries as work patches, Lavatube can handle them easily. Figure 8 shows an example of detecting a human face by using the Viola-Jones face detector [9]. The left-side image is a work patch captured from a camera. According to the flow from there to the lower stage, color-to-gray image conversion and facial detection patches are connected. Since the facial detection patch outputs the position co-ordinates and dimensions of a face, it is connected to a work patch that draws a circle at the face position. This work patch is created to receive image and coordinate inputs.

Figure 9 shows an example of optical flow estimation by using the Lucas-Kanade method. Because optical flow estimation requires current image and previous image, a work-patch that buffers previous images is connected to an optical flow patch.

4.2 Satellite image processing

The user can perform a range of image processing tasks on obtained image data by using the built-in work patches in Lavatube 2. Figure 10 is an example of a change detection system of satellite images. Work-patches to support various services based on OGC [10] and access to geospatial information services. Figure 11 shows a schematic of the cooperation of geographic information processing be-tween Lavatube and OGC W*S services. OGC CS-W is a retrieval system for contents or services. CS-W responses contain the

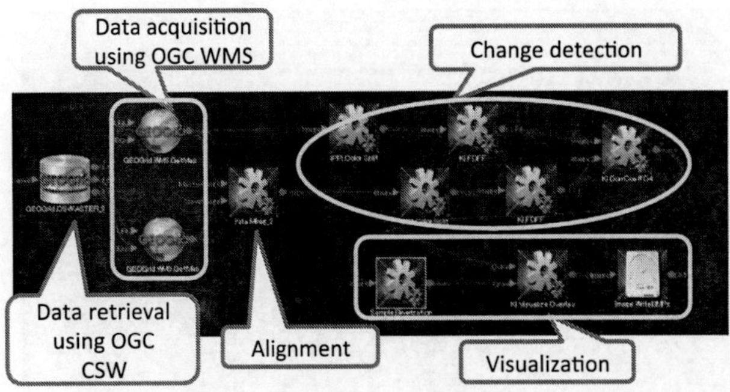

Fig.10 Change detection system of satellite image.

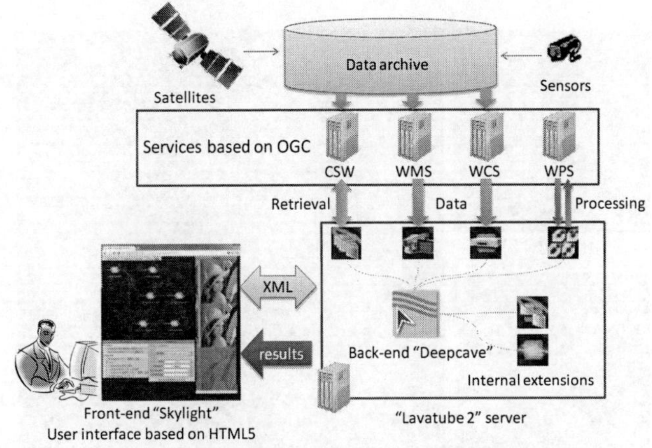

Fig.11 Integration of geoinformation processing between Lavatube and OGC W*S services

URLs of OGC WMS services. A WMS work patch request the map data of the obtained URL and the bounding box from the WMS service.

OGC CS-W is a retrieval system for contents or services. Figure 12 shows the retrieval of ASTER [11] data archive on GEO Grid [12]. A bounding box is specified using a Google Earth plug-in. A search query including the bounding box, dates and cloud covers is posted to a CS-W server, which lists the responses and presents them to the user.

Left of figure 13 shows data from June 2012 and June 2011 in the coastal area of northeast Japan. Right of figure 13 shows the result of change detection. The figure shows signs of change toward recovery one year after the Great East Japan Earthquake of 2011. The construction of this kind of change detection systems is not easy, because the satellite data exhibit variability in quality due to differences in vegetation and weather conditions. Thus, a change detection system requires trial and error experimentation using a combination of methods and parameters. Users can develop systems by trial and error using Lavatube 2.

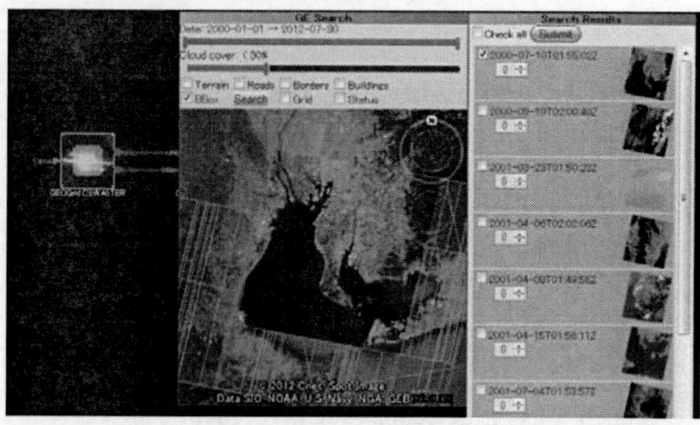

Fig.12 Satelite data retrival on the workflow system

Fig.13 Example of change detection

5 Conclusion

This paper outlines Lavatube as a workflow middleware to support trial programming and research for computer vision or image processing by a GUI and XML, and introduced some cases as examples. We are working on middleware that will provide a new infrastructure for geospatial information research.

Acknowlegedment

This work was supported in part by MEXT/JSPS KAKENHI 24700082.

References

[1] D. A. Forsyth and J. Ponce, Computer Vision: A Modern Approach, Prentice Hall, 2003

[2] K. Konstantinides and J. R. Rasure, The Khoros Software Development Environment for Image and Signal Processing, IEEE Trans. on Image Processing, Volume 3, Issue 3, pp.243–252, May 1994

[3] O. Milvang and T. Lonnestad. An Object Oriented Image Display System, Proc. of 11th ICPR, pp. 218-221, October 1992

[4] Max/MSP, http://www.cycling74.com

[5] MATLAB/Simulink, http://www.mathworks.com

[6] AVS/Express, http://www.avs.com

[7] Ko R.K.L., Stephen S. G., Lee E.W.: Business Process Management (BPM) Standards: A Survey. In: Business Process Management Journal, Emerald Group Publishing Limited. Vol. 15 Issue 5. ISSN 1463-7154, 2009.

[8] Ludäscher B., Altintas I., Berkley C., Higgins D., Jaeger-Frank E., Jones M., Lee E., Tao J., Zhao Y.: Scientific Workflow Management and the Kepler System. Special Issue: Workflow in Grid Systems. Concurrency and Computation: Practice & Experience 18(10): 1039-1065, 2006.

[9] P. Viola and M. Jones. Rapid Object Detection Using a Boosted Cascade of Simple Features, Proc. of CVPR2001, vol.1, pp.511-518, December 2001

[10] Open Geospatial Consortium (OGC), http://www.opengeospatial.org/

[11] Yamaguchi Y., Kahle B. A., Pniel M., Tsu H., Kawakami T.: Overview of Advanced Space-borne Thermal Emission and Reflection Radiometer (ASTER). IEEE Trans. Geosci. Remote Sens., Vol. 36, No. 4, pp. 1062-1071, 1998.

[12] Sekiguchi S., Tanaka Y., Kojima I., Yamamoto N., Yokoyama S., Tanimura Y., Nakamura R., Iwao K., Tsuchida S.: Design Principles and IT Overview of the GEO Grid. IEEE Systems Journal, Vol. 2, No. 3, pp. 374-389, 2008.

SESSION

BIOMETRICS: GAIT, IRIS, FINGERPRINT, ... + IDENTIFICATION + HANDWRITING ANALYSIS

Chair(s)

TBA

Conditional-Sorting Local Binary Pattern Based on Gait Energy Image for Human Identification

Chih-Hsien Hsia[1], Jen-Shiun Chiang[2], Yi-Jhe Dai[2], and Tien-An Lin[2]

[1] Department of Electrical Engineering
National Taiwan University of Science and Technology
Taipei, Taiwan
[2] Department of Electrical Engineering
Tamkang University
Tamsui, New Taipei City, Taiwan

Abstract — Gait recognition systems have recently attracted much interest from biometric researchers. This work proposes a new feature extraction method for gait representation and recognition. The new method is extended from the technique of Local Binary Pattern (LBP) by changing the sorting method of LBP according to the blend direction to create a new approach, Conditional-Sorting Local Binary Pattern (CS-LBP). After synchronizing and calibrating the gait sequence images, a cycle of images from the gait sequence can be captured to form a Gait Energy Image (GEI). We then apply the CS-LBP on GEI to derive different blend direction images and calculate the recognition ability for each blend direction image for feature selections. To solve the classification problem, the Euclidean distance and Nearest Neighbor (NN) approaches are used. With the experiments carried out on the CASIA-B gait database, our proposed gait representation has a very good recognition rate.

I. Introduction

Biometric identification techniques allow the identification of a person according to some geometric or behavioral traits that are uniquely associated with him or her. Commonly used biometrics includes face, iris, fingerprint, handwriting, palm shape, vena, and gait. An important limitation of most contemporary biometric identification systems is related to the fact that they require the cooperation of individual to be identified and some special capturing devices. Gait recognition is an emerging biometric technology which aims to identify individuals using their walking style. The apparent advantage of gait recognition in comparison to other biometrics is that it does not require the attention or cooperation of the observed subject. Gaits can thus be used in some situations when other biometrics might not be perceivable. Generally speaking, there are three steps in gait recognition: moving object tracking, gait feature extraction, and classification. Many proposed literatures [1]-[4] dedicate to the work of the second step. Gait recognition methods can be roughly classified into two major categories: model-based and appearance-based methods. The model-based methods [5]-[6] purpose to explicitly model the human body or motion, and the gait feature can be extracted by tracking the human body frame by frame. Generally, the feature extraction methods rely on the precise two-dimensional or three-dimensional model generation techniques to have a more accurate recognition result, and hence the calculation complexity of the model-based methods is relatively high [7]. The appearance-based methods for gait feature extraction use gait silhouettes directly without modeling the human body. Therefore, many gait recognition researchers made efforts on the appearance-based methods[8]-[9]. One of the most frequently used methods is

Gait Energy Image (GEI) [1], which represents the gait by using a single gray scale image obtained by averaging the silhouettes extracted over a complete gait cycle. This method is a really simple approach to get the complete gait information. In this research work we choose GEI as the based feature. Although there is wealth of information in GEI, how to extract useful features from GEI is worth developing [2]-[3]. The human movement is a progressive action; after the images are stacked into GEI, the result is an image with blend characteristics. Based on this factor, this research work proposes a new appearance-based method to extract these features. The new method is an extension from Local Binary Pattern (LBP). Here a new sorting method, Conditional-Sorting Local Binary Pattern (CS-LBP), is proposed, and in this approach the LBP is changed according to the direction of the blend. Based on the CASIA-B gait database [12], the experimental results of our proposed method demonstrate that it is very effective.

The rest of this paper is organized as follows. In Section II, related researches and GEI formation are described. Section III discusses the CS-LBP method and feature selection method. Section IV presents the experimental results and comparisons. Finally, Section V concludes this research work.

II. Feature Extraction and Related Works

After the preprocessing operation, we have to locate one cycle within the gait sequence, and use GEI to describe the human gait, and then we have to apply the CS-LBP method on GEI to extract more characteristic features from GEI. Because of the image resolution, techniques of Principal Component Analysis (PCA) and Linear Discriminant Analysis (LDA) are utilized to achieve better recognition results.

A. Human Gait Representation Using Gait Energy Image

After the gait period is estimated, the GEI can be computed from the calibrated and normalized silhouettes by the following equation:

$$G(x,y) = \frac{1}{N}\sum_{t=1}^{N} I(x,y,t) \tag{1}$$

where $G(x,y)$ denotes the GEI intensity at location (x,y), N the gait period, and $I(x,y,t)$ the normalized and calibrated silhouette at time t. GEI is a simple and effective method to describe the gait features [1], and it can keep static and dynamic information at the same time. One example of GEI extraction is shown in Fig. 1.

(a)

(b)

Fig. 1. Gait energy image extraction: (a) Gait sequences, (b) GEI.

B. Local Binary Pattern

LBP was proposed by Matti *et al.* [10], and it was widely used in many pattern recognition researches, such as face recognition and texture recognition [10]-[11]. LBP is an operator to describe the surrounding of a pixel by generating a bit-code from the binary derivatives of a pixel. Generally, LBP considers the 3×3 surrounding of a pixel and generates a binary 1 if the value of a neighboring pixel is larger than that of the center pixel, otherwise it will generate a binary 0. Then it connects every binary value along the clockwise or counterclockwise direction from one neighbor as the starting point, and it will generate an 8-bit binary code, which is the final value of the LBP. The LBP cannot effectively represent the image feature because it lacks a meaningful sorting method. Based on this factor, a new sorting method is proposed to solve this problem.

III. Conditional-Sorting Local Binary Pattern (CS-LBP)

A. Human Gait Recognition Using CS-LBP

The main task in gait recognition is the extraction of the appropriate and salient feature to effectively capture the gait characteristics. It is well known that human walking is a progressive movement; therefore, how to extract the progressive information is a critical issue. This work presents a modified LBP, Conditional Sorting-Local Binary Pattern (CS-LBP). The CS-LBP can be applied on GEI to extract many meaningful features. In the proposed approach, it first compares the surrounding neighbors with the middle pixel like the original LBP does. By dividing the neighbors into three blocks, high bit block, middle bit block, and low bit block, it then uses three graphics to represent each block (horizontal stripe, diagonal stripe, and vertical stripe). By this approach, eight sorting methods are defined for these three blocks as shown in Fig. 2. The horizontal stripe block corresponds to the most significant three bits of the 8-bit binary code (2^7, 2^6, 2^5), and the following equation can be used to find the final value:

$$\text{top(x)} = \begin{cases} 224, & \text{if x} = 3 \\ 192, & \text{if x} = 2 \\ 128, & \text{if x} = 1 \\ 0, & \text{otherwise} \end{cases} \quad (2)$$

where top(x) is the final value, and x is the number of 1 in this block. The diagonal stripe block corresponds to the middle two bits of the 8-bit binary code (2^4, 2^3), and the following equation can be used to find the final value:

$$\text{median(x)} = \begin{cases} 24, & \text{if x} = 3 \\ 16, & \text{if x} = 2 \\ 0, & \text{otherwise} \end{cases} \quad (3)$$

where median(x) is the final value, and x is the number of 1 in this block. The vertical stripe block corresponds to the least significant three bits of the 8-bit binary code (2^2, 2^1, 2^0), and the following equation can be used to find the final value:

$$\text{bottom(x)} = \begin{cases} 7, & \text{if x} = 3 \\ 3, & \text{if x} = 2 \\ 1, & \text{if x} = 1 \\ 0, & \text{otherwise} \end{cases} \quad (4)$$

where bottom(x) is the final value, and x is the number of 1 in this block. Finally, the following equation is to obtain the final value of CS-LBP:

$$Dv = \text{top(i)} + \text{median(j)} + \text{bottom(k)} \quad (5)$$

where Dv is the final value of CS-LBP. The sorting names are named to correspond the sorting method as shown in Fig. 2. The 8 sorting methods are: left-up (LU) sorting method, up (UP) sorting method, right-up (RU) sorting method, left (LE) sorting method, right (RI) sorting method, left-down (LD) sorting method, down (DO) sorting method, and right-down (RD) sorting method.

B. Feature Selection

Although there are eight images of the blend features after using CS-LBP, the critical issue is how to combine these blend features for better recognition. It has to find the blend features that can increase the distance between different objects and decrease the distance between same objects, just like the LDA concepts. The distance between the average images of each individual and average image of the total individuals is calculated as between-class distance, and the distance between the average images of each individual and images of each individual is calculated as the within-class distance. The between-class distance represents the distance of different individuals and the distance should be as large as possible, and the within-class distance represents the distance of the same individuals and the distance should be as small as possible. The recognition ability, proposed here, represents the between-class distance divided by the within-class distance, and the value should be as large as possible. The following equation is used to calculate the between-class distance:

$$BC_d = \sum \text{abs}\left|Avg_d(i,j) - Img_d^{obj_n}(i,j)\right| \quad (6)$$

where d is the direction of the blend feature, obj the individual number, n the stance of the individual, BC_d the between-class distance of direction d of the blend feature, and $Avg_d(i,j)$ the pixel located at (i,j) of direction d of the blend feature average image. $Img_d^{obj_n}(i,j)$ is the pixel located at (i, j) of direction d of the blend feature with numbers of obj individuals of n stance image. The following equation is to calculate the within-class distance:

$$WC_d = \sum \text{abs}\left|Avg_d^{obj}(i,j) - Img_d^{obj_n}(i,j)\right| \quad (7)$$

where WC_d is the within-class distance of direction d of the blend feature, and $Avg_d^{obj}(i,j)$ is the pixel located at (i, j) of direction d of the blend feature of numbers of obj individuals average image. The following equation is used to calculate the Recognition Ability (RA):

$$RA_d = BC_d / WC_d \quad (8)$$

The recognition ability, obtained from (8), of different directions of the blend features is shown in Fig. 3. In Fig. 3, the vertical axis is the recognition ability and the horizontal axis is different directions of the blend features. In this work, we select top four recognition ability directions of the blend features (DO, UP, RD, and LD) as our features, and use the following equation to fuse these features as the similarity distance:

$$S = \sum D_{dir}\,, dir = \mathrm{DO, UP, RD, LD} \tag{9}$$

where S is the similarity distance, dir the selected direction of the blend feature, and D_{dir} the similarity distance at direction dir.

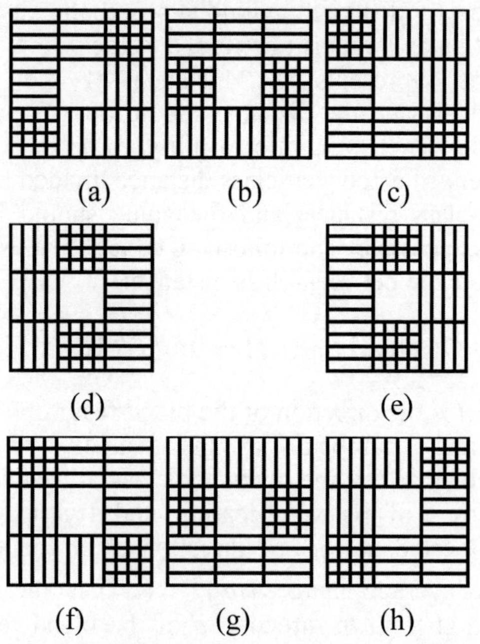

Fig. 2. The sorting methods of CS-LBP: (a) left-up (LU) sorting method, (b) up (UP) sorting method, (c) right-up (RU) sorting method, (d) left (LE) sorting method, (e) right (RI) sorting method, (f) left-down (LD) sorting method, (g) down (DO) sorting method, (h) right-down (RD) sorting method.

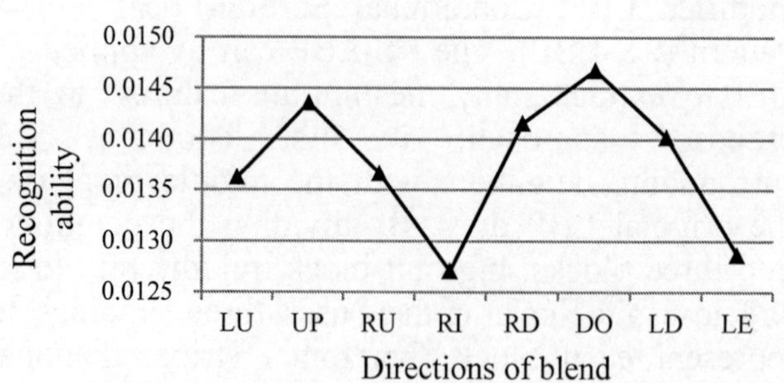

Fig. 3. The recognition ability of eight directions of the blend feature.

IV. Experimental Result

In the experiment, we would like to prove the robust of the proposed method and feature selection method. To verify our proposed method, this work has performed a number of experiments on the CASIA-B database [12]. There are 124 individuals and three variations in this database, namely view angle, clothing, and carrying conditions changes. For each individual there are ten gait sequences consisting of six normal gait sequences where the individual does not wear a bulky coat or carry a bag, two carrying-bag sequences and two wearing-coat sequences. The first four of the six normal gait sequences were used as the gallery set, and the rest of the normal gait sequences were used as the probe. The two carrying-bag gait sequences were used as the probe, and the two wearing-coat gait sequences were used as the probe.

A. Recognition with CS-LBP

We compared the proposed method with the original GEI method [1] and other improved GEI methods [2]-[4], and the recognition results are shown in Table 1. It shows from Table 1 that when the probe set is tested with the gallery set, all four methods yield pretty good recognition rates. However, with different covariate conditions, the recognition rates of all four methods are degraded. Nevertheless, our method can maintain stable recognition rates under different conditions. In the case of wearing-coat gait sequences, our CS-LBP outperforms the rest methods, and the CS-LBP can compete with other methods under carrying-bag gait sequences. The average recognition results, 82%, indicate that our CS-LBP method for gait recognition produces the best recognition results compared to all other methods as shown in Table 1.

TABLE 1. Performance with the CASIA-B database.

Methods	GEI + PCA + LDA [1]	SEIS + LDA [2]	AEI + PCA + LDA [3]	M_G^j + CDA [4]	This work
Normal	99%	99%	89%	100%	99%
Bag-carrying	44%	64%	75%	78%	75%
Coat-wearing	37%	72%	57%	44.0%	73%
Average recognitio n rate	60%	78%	74%	74%	82%

B. Feature Selection

In Section III, we proposed equation (8) to calculate and estimate the recognition ability for different directions of the blend features, and select the top four features for gait recognition according to the estimated recognition ability. Here we would like to evaluate different numbers of selecting features for gait recognition. After using equation (8) to estimate the recognition ability of different directions of the blend features, all eight directions are sorted according to the estimated recognition ability from high to low, and the direction with the highest recognition ability of the blend features is selected first as the gait features. Then, the second highest one, the third highest one, and all the way to all eight of them are selected. The actual recognition rate based on the selections is shown in Fig. 4. It shows that the recognition rate is the highest when the top four highest recognition abilities are chosen. The actual recognition rates are then compared with the recognition ability calculated by equation (8). Fig. 5 shows the comparison results, where the black line is the actual recognition rate and the block dotted line is the calculated recognition ability. The corresponding values are shown in Table 2. From Tables 2, the recognition ability, calculated by equation (8), closely matches the actual recognition rate for the top six features, and there are only two misses on the lowest two features. According to Table 2, the recognition ability difference between the last two features is only 0.002 (0.0129 and 0.0127) and the difference of the actual recognition rate between these two features is only 1.1% (57.4% and 58.5%). Therefore, our proposed approach is really robust.

TABLE 2. The values of the recognition rate and recognition ability.

Direction of blend feature	Recognition rate	Recognition ability
LU	63.2%	0.0136
UP	71.9%	0.0144
RU	65.9%	0.0137
RI	58.5%	0.0127
RD	70.6%	0.0142
DO	75.7%	0.0147
LD	69.1%	0.0140
LE	57.4%	0.0129

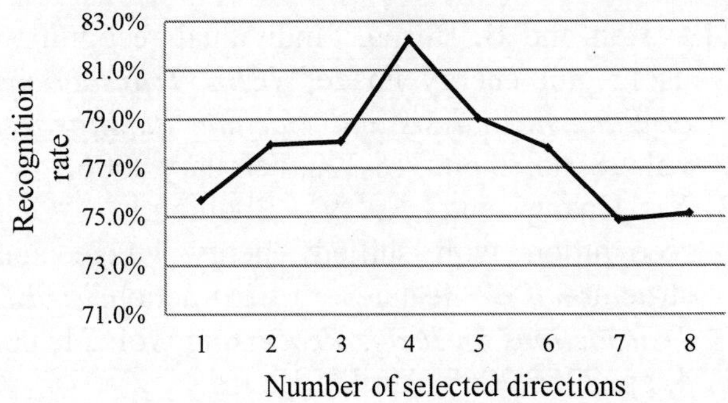

Fig. 4. The recognition rate of different number of selected directions.

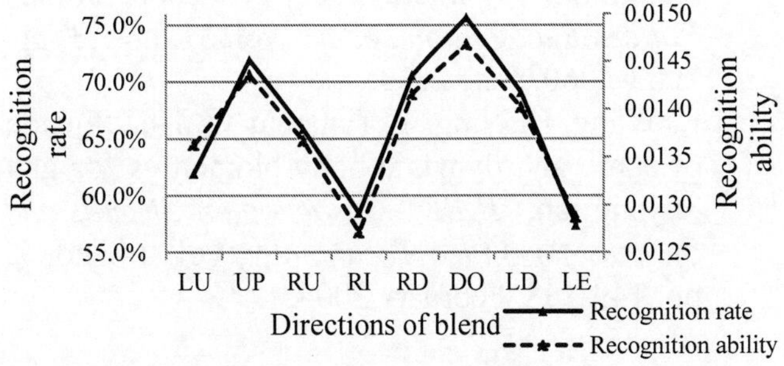

Fig. 5. Comparisons of the recognition rate and the recognition ability.

V. CONCLUSION

In this work, we propose a new method, Conditional-Sorting Local Binary Pattern (CS-LBP), which is extending from the local binary pattern to describe the gait feature. It is applied on Gait Energy Image (GEI) to extract more meaningful gait features. The CASIA-B database is used to evaluate the proposed method. The experiment results show that the proposed method can achieve better performance under appearance changes. Compared to recent literatures, the recognition rate of our method can achieve average recognition rate of 82% under different walking conditions.

Acknowledgement

This research is partially supported by National Science Council of Taiwan, ROC, under grant number: 101-2221-E-032-066-

References

[1] J. Han and B. Bhanu, "Individual recognition using gait energy image," *IEEE Transactions on Pattern Analysis and Machine Intelligence*, vol. 28, no. 2, pp. 316-322, February 2006.

[2] X. Huang and N. V. Boulgouris, "Gait recognition with shifted energy image and structural feature extraction," *IEEE Transactions on Image Processing*, vol. 21, no. 4, pp. 2256-2268, April 2012.

[3] E. Zhang, Y. Zhao, and W. Xiong, "Active energy image plus 2DLPP for gait recognition," *Signal Processing*, vol. 90, no. 7, pp. 2295-2302, July 2010.

[4] K. Bashir, T. Xiang, and S. Gong, "Gait recognition without subject cooperation," *Pattern Recognition Letters*, vol. 31, no. 13, pp. 2052-2060, June 2010.

[5] L. Wang, H. Ning, T. Tan, and W. Hu, "Fusion of static and dynamic body biometrics for gait recognition," *IEEE Transaction on Circuits and Systems for Video Technology*, vol. 14, no. 2, pp. 149-158, February 2004.

[6] I. Bouchrika and M. S. Nixon, "Model-based feature extraction for gait analysis and recognition," *Proceedings of Mirage: Computer Vision/Computer Graphics Collaboration Techniques*, pp. 150-160, May 2007.

[7] L. Wang, T. Tan, H. Ning, and W. Hu, "Silhouette analysis-based gait recognition for human identification," *IEEE Transactions on Pattern Analysis and Machine Intelligence*, vol. 25, no. 12, pp. 1505-1518, December 2003.

[8] D. Xu, S. Yan, D. Tao, L. Zhang, X. Li, and H. Zhang, "Human gait recognition with matrix representation," *IEEE Transactions on Circuits and Systems for Video Technology*, vol. 16, no. 7, pp. 896-903, July 2006.

[9] T. H. W. Lam and R. S. T. Lee, "A new representation for human gait recognition: motion silhouettes image (MSI)," *International Conference on Biometrics*, pp. 612–618, 2006.

[10] T. Ojala, M. Pietikainen, and T. Maenpaa, "Multiresolution gray-scale and rotation invariant texture classification with local binary patterns," *IEEE Transactions on Pattern Analysis and Machine Intelligence*, vol. 24, no. 7, pp. 971-987, Jul. 2002.

[11] Z. Guo, L. Zhang, and D. Zhang, "A completed modeling of local binary pattern operator for texture classification," *IEEE Transactions on Image Processing*, vol. 19, no. 6, pp. 1657-1663, June 2010.

[12] S. Yu, D. Tan, and T. Tan, "A framework for evaluating the effect of view angle, clothing and carrying condition on gait recognition," *Interenational Conference on Pattern Recognition*, vol. 4, pp.441-444, August 2006.

Iris texture feature extraction with orthogonal polynomials

R. Krishnamoorthy [1], G. Annapoorani [1] and Anil K. Kaushik[2]

1. Image Research and Information Science Laboratory, Department of Computer Science and Engineering, Bharathidasan Institute of Technology, Anna University, Tiruchirappalli – 620 024, India.

2. Department of Electronics and Information Technology, Ministry of Communication and Information Technology, New Delhi, India.

Abstract- *In this paper, a feature extraction technique with orthogonal polynomials based computational model to accurately extract local texture in iris images is presented. Initially, the normalized input iris image is subjected with the orthogonal polynomials model and the model coefficients are obtained. The model coefficients are subjected to statistical hypothesis testing with Hartley's test so as to extract the signal components due to texture in the iris images and simultaneously separating out the noise components. These model coefficients due to the orthogonal polynomials model, are utilized to represent the iris texture patterns along with their zonal positions, as the locations of the micro texture present in the image analysis is considered to be significant. The texture primitives thus extracted are represented with a decimal number and used for feature extraction.*

Keywords - Iris Biometrics, Orthogonal Polynomials, Hartley's statistical test, Texture feature Extraction.

1 Introduction

Biometric systems allow identification of human persons based on physiological or behavioral characteristics, such as voice, handprint, iris or facial characteristics. Iris Recognition is considered to be a high-confidence biometric identification system due to its robustness and unobtrusiveness, as opposed to most of the currently deployed systems, and makes it a good candidate to replace most of the security systems around. The feature extraction is a crucial step in an iris recognition system since the extracted features should be significant, compact, and fast to compute. In order to provide accurate recognition of individuals, the most discriminating information present in an iris pattern must be extracted. Only the significant features of the iris must be encoded so that comparisons between templates can be made fast. For the iris feature extraction, effective extraction of feature information such as texture from each iris category that represents the inherent characteristics of the iris is essential.

From the viewpoint of feature extraction, it is observed that there are six main approaches for iris representation: phase-based methods [1], texture analysis [2-16], zero-crossing representation [17-20], intensity variation analysis [21-22], fractal dimension analysis [23] and neural network [24]. Daugman [1] has utilized the use of 2-D Gabor wavelets to extract phase structure information of the iris. The advantages of the Daugman's approach are the speed of matching, easy handling of rotation and an interpretation of the matching as the result of a statistical test of independence. There are many categories of texture analysis methods that exist for identifying and manipulating the texture: Laplacian of Gaussian filters [2], Multi-channel Gabor filtering and the wavelet transform [3], Haar Wavelet transform [4], Multichannel Gabor filtering [5], Radial feature, circular feature, Fourier transform, and Circular-mellin filters [6], 1-D log polar Gabor wavelet [7], Multi-channel 2-D Gabor filter [8], Filter bank [9], Gabor filters and Wavelet maxima component [10], Laplacian of Gaussian (LoG) filters with many different scales [11], 1-D wavelet transform [12], Directional bi-orthogonal filters [13], spatial location of corner points [14], non-separable wavelet [15], and Daubchies wavelets [16]. The performance of an iris recognition system depends not only on the filter chosen, but also on the parameters of the filter. There are three categories of zero crossing representation such as One dimensional signal [17], discrete dyadic wavelet transform [18-19], and Discrete Cosine Transform (DCT) [20] that can be used to speed up the matching process. There are intensity variation analysis techniques such as Independent Component Analysis (ICA) [21], Dyadic wavelet [22] that can be used either as an alternative or supplement to wavelets for feature extraction. In [23], Chen and Yuan extracted unique iris features from iris images by using the fractal dimensions measure. The iris code representing the fractal dimension of the texture of an iris can then be used to recognize individuals. Liam et al. [24] have extracted the iris features with Self-Organization neural network.

Since the computational complexity of existing feature extraction methods is heavy and it could not be well suited to represent 2D singularities along edges or contours, a new iris feature extraction technique is presented in this paper. A low complexity integer orthogonal polynomials based framework is devised in this proposed work for feature extraction in iris images that represents the texture components.

2 Orthogonal Polynomials

In this section we describe the proposed orthogonal polynomials transform for analyzing the iris texture features. The orthogonal polynomials that have already been well established for iris localization [25] are extended in this proposed model to extract the iris local texture property. In the previous study [25], edge detection has been discussed along the boundary extraction for localizing the iris boundary points.

In this section the orthogonal polynomials model for analyzing the structure of an eye image is presented. In order to investigate the structure of iris from an eye image, a linear 2-D image formation system is considered around a cartesian coordinate separable, blurring, point spread operator in which the image I results in the superposition of the point source of impulse weighted by the value of the object f. Expressing the object function f in terms of derivatives of the image function I relative to its cartesian coordinates is very useful for analyzing the image. The point spread function $M(x, y)$ can be considered to be real valued function defined for $(x, y) \in X \times Y$, where X and Y are ordered subsets of real values. In case of gray-level image of size $(n \times m)$ where $X\ (rows)$ consists of a finite set, which for convenience can be labeled as $\{0, 1, \ldots, n-1\}$, the function $M(x, y)$ reduces to a sequence of functions.

$$M(i,t) = u_i(t), i, t = 0, 1, \ldots, n-1 \quad (1)$$

The linear two dimensional transformations can be defined by the point spread operator $M(x, y)(M(i,t) = u_i(t))$ as shown in equation (2).

$$\beta(\zeta,\eta) = \int_{x \in X}\int_{y \in Y} M(\zeta,x)\, M(\eta,y)\, I(x,y)\, dxdy \quad (2)$$

Considering both X and Y to be a finite set of values $\{0, 1, 2, \ldots, n-1\}$, equation (2) can be written in matrix notation as follows

$$|\beta'_{ij}| = (|M| \otimes |M|)^t\, |I| \quad (3)$$

where $\otimes$ is the outer product, $|\beta'_{ij}|$ are n^2 matrices arranged in the dictionary sequence, I is the image, $|\beta'_{ij}|$ are the coefficients of transformation and $|M|$ is

$$|M| = \begin{vmatrix} u_0(t_0)\ u_1(t_0) \cdots u_{n-1}(t_0) \\ u_0(t_1)\ u_1(t_1) \cdots u_{n-1}(t_1) \\ \vdots \\ u_0(t_{n-1})\ u_1(t_{n-1}) \cdots u_{n-1}(t_{n-1}) \end{vmatrix} \quad (4)$$

The set of orthogonal polynomials $u_0(t), u_1(t), \ldots, u_{n-1}(t)$ of degrees $\{0, 1, 2, \ldots, n-1\}$, respectively are considered. The generating formula for the polynomials is as follows

$$u_{i+1}(t) = (t - \mu)u_i(t) - b_i(n)u_{i-1}(t) \text{ for } i \geq 1, \quad (5)$$

$$u_1(t) = t - \mu, \text{ and } u_0(t) = 1,$$

where

$$b_i(n) = \frac{\langle u_i, u_i \rangle}{\langle u_{i-1}, u_{i-1} \rangle} = \frac{\sum_{t=1}^{n} u_i^2(t)}{\sum_{t=1}^{n} u_{i-1}^2(t)}$$

and

$$\mu = \frac{1}{n}\sum_{t=1}^{n} t.$$

Considering the range of values of t to be $t_i = i, i = 1, 2, 3, \ldots, n$, we get

$$b_i(n) = \frac{i^2(n^2 - i^2)}{4(4i^2 - 1)},$$

$$\mu = \frac{1}{n}\sum_{t=1}^{n} t = \frac{n+1}{2}$$

Next, point spread operator $|M|$ of different sizes are constructed from the above orthogonal polynomials as follows

$$|M| = \begin{vmatrix} u_0(t_0)\ u_1(t_0) \cdots u_{n-1}(t_0) \\ u_0(t_1)\ u_1(t_1) \cdots u_{n-1}(t_1) \\ \vdots \\ u_0(t_{n-1})\ u_1(t_{n-1}) \cdots u_{n-1}(t_{n-1}) \end{vmatrix} \quad (6)$$

for $n \geq 2$ and $t_i = i$.

For convenience of point spread operations, the elements of $|M|$ are scaled to make them integers.

These point spread operators are then utilized to characterize texture primitives in an iris image region.

3 Framework for iris texture characterization based on Orthogonal Polynomials

In this work, a frame work based on modeling the iris image for textureness is proposed. The texture information is modeled as feature descriptors and the resulting feature descriptors are used for discrimination as representative of the iris image. The feature descriptor constitutes the components of numerical characterization sequence. The proposed discriminative feature extraction approach is a direct and significant technique that varies from the conventional approaches and provides a comprehensive basis for the entire system design.

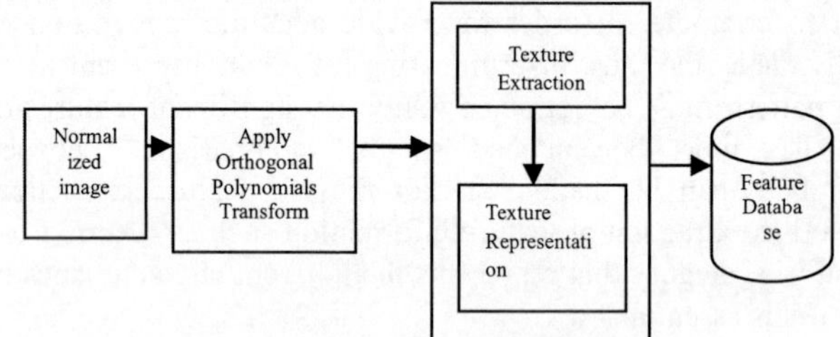

Figure .1: Proposed orthogonal polynomials based feature extraction technique

The proposed orthogonal polynomials based iris texture feature extraction technique is presented in *Figure 1*, wherein we design two schemes to:

i. Analyze orthogonal polynomial coefficients to extract the texture region.
ii. Design a texture descriptor to represent the texture present in the iris region.

3.1 Texture Characterization

Consider an $(n \times n)$ iris image region from the eye $I(x, y)$, where x and y are two spatial coordinates:

$$I(x, y) = g(x, y) + \eta(x, y) \tag{7}$$

In equation (7), $g(x, y)$ accounts for the spatial variation owing to texture and $\eta(x, y)$ is the spatial variation owing to additive noise. In order to measure the spatial variations owing to texture and noise separately, $I(x, y)$ is represented as shown in equation (8), that follows in terms of a set of uncorrelated basis spatial variations.

$$[I^n_{ij}] = \sum_{i=0}^{n-1} \sum_{j=0}^{n-1} \beta_{ij} [O^n_{ij}] \tag{8}$$

where $[I^n_{ij}]$ is $(n \times n)$ gray level image matrix, $[O^n_{ij}]$ accounts for the spatial, model variation and β_{ij} is $(i, j)^{th}$ coefficient of variation. β_{ij} is basically the effect of the variation accounted for by $[O^n_{ij}]$ over the image region $I(x, y)$. $[O^n_{ij}]$ is selected in such a manner that effects β_{ij} orthogonal to each other. Using the statistical design of experiments paradigm, we consider $I(x, y)$ to be the yields of the experiment with two factors x and y each at n different levels. Two types of spatial variations are considered. In one, spatial coordinate at a time is varying when the other remains constant. In the other, both the spatial coordinates vary jointly. The orthogonal effects due to the former kind of variation are called main effects, whereas the orthogonal effects due to the latter are called interaction effects. It has been observed experimentally that the spatial variation that causes the interaction effects are owing to micro texture present in the image region $[I^n_{ij}]$. The other spatial variations are owing to noise present in $[I^n_{ij}]$. Hence, the texture is characterized by the interaction effects. This is because, in presence of micro texture the two factors x and y do not operate independently rather the effect of one is dependent on different levels of the other. For computing orthogonal effects, the set of orthogonal polynomials has been used. $[O^n_{ij}]$s are $(n \times n)$ polynomial basis operators and β_{ij} are orthogonal effects due to spatial variations of gray levels present in the image region $[I^n_{ij}]$. The spatial variations are modeled by the polynomial basis operators $[O^n_{ij}]$. Various micro textured regions can then be characterized by estimating the orthogonal effects and their mean squares. The proposed methodology for texture detection is as follows:

Let the image under analysis be of size $(image\ width \times image\ height)$ and $[M]$ be the polynomial operator size of 3×3 and $[I]$ be a small region of size 3×3 extracted from the iris image. The orthogonal effects β_{ij} are computed as

$$[\beta_{ij}] = ([M]^t[M])^{-1}([M]^t[I][M])\ ([M]^t[M^t])^{-1} \tag{9}$$

and the mean square variances, $|Z^2_{ij}|$ corresponding to the orthogonal effects β_{ij} are computed as

$$[Z^2_{ij}] = ([M]^t[M])^{-1}([M]^t[I]\,[M])^2([M]^t[M])^{-1} \tag{10}$$

The value $Z_{ij}\,(=(Z^2_{ij})^{1/2})$ is described as the mean squared amplitude response of the operator $[o^3_{ij}]$. The set $A = \{Z^2_{01}, Z^2_{02}, Z^2_{10}, Z^2_{20}\}$ are the set of variances due to the main effects and the set $B = \{Z^2_{11}, Z^2_{12}, Z^2_{21}, Z^2_{22}\}$ are the set of variances due to the interaction effects. In this study, the presence of texture is characterized by proposing the Hartley's test among variances.

Based on the above computational model with orthogonal polynomials, a statistical test is proposed in the next subsection for separating out the texture features from the unwanted noise components.

3.1.1 A statistical procedure for separation of responses towards noise from the response towards signal (textures)

In the proposed orthogonal polynomials model, let ψ_s be the set of estimated variances corresponding to the mean squared amplitude responses towards signal and ψ_e be the set of estimated variances corresponding to the mean squared amplitude responses towards noise. The mean squared error variances are computed as the sum of those estimated variances in ψ_e which are basically estimates of the same noise variance η^2_0. In order to ensure that a set of $\chi^2 \sigma^2$ variates with known degrees of freedom are basically the estimates of the same noise variance, the following statistical procedure is used in this work.

We first compute the divergence among variance, in order to separate out the response from the responses towards noise, without any corrective factor as required in the Bartlett criteria [26]. It is observed that even using the corrective factor the D□ approximation is not altogether satisfactorily if some of the degrees of freedom, υ_i are 1, 2 or 3. Hence in this work, Hartley's approximation [27] has been adopted as it is more convenient and accurate. The D criterion for computing the divergence among variances is given by

$$D=\left(\upsilon \ln v_{av} - \sum_{i=1}^{k} \upsilon_i \ln(v_i)\right) \quad (11)$$

where v_i are the set of variances, υ_i are the degrees of freedom, υ is the total degree of freedom, and v_{av} is the average variance. The divergence values for various significance levels with different degrees of freedom are given by Hartley [27] and a portion of the table is shown in *Table 1*. It is also proved in [27] that the approximation is sufficiently accurate to allow the degrees of freedom □to drop to 2 and the approximation is still fair if some of the degrees of freedom are as small as 1. In this case, it is noted that a member passing the statistical test implies that it has significant contribution towards micro textures present in the iris image under analysis.

Table 1: Significant divergence (*D*) among variances for different degrees of freedom *k*

Degree of Freedom in denominator	5%	10%	20%	25%	50%
2	18.51	8.53	3.56	2.59	0.667
3	10.13	5.54	2.68	2.02	0.585
4	7.71	4.54	2.35	1.8	0.548

In this case, since each estimated variance is a $\chi^2\sigma^2$ variate with one degree of freedom, $\upsilon_1 = \upsilon_2 = \ldots, = \upsilon_k = 1$. If the computed value D is greater than the tabulated value then the divergence among the variances is significant i.e., they are not estimating the same noise variance. Those estimated variances in ψ_e for which the computed D value is not significant are called noise variances.

Finally, the mean square error variance $\overline{\eta_0^2}$ is computed as the sum of the estimated noise variances divided by their total degrees of freedom. After computing the error variance $\overline{\eta_0^2}$ the significance of the set ψ_s of estimated variances corresponding to the mean squared amplitude responses towards signal may be measured to select only the significant responses towards signal. Since $\frac{z_{ij}^2 \in \psi_s}{\eta_0^2}$ is distributed as the F distribution [28] with 1 and *m* degrees of freedom, where *m* be the number of Z_{ij}^2 taken from ψ_e to compute the error variance η_0^2, the *F*-test is conducted with each $Z_{ij}^2 \in \psi_s$ at the desired level of significance to determine whether this can be accounted for the signal compared to the noise present.

Table 2: *F* Distribution values, assuming the numerator has one degree of freedom

Values of k	2	3	4	5	6
5% points	5.99	7.81	9.49	11.07	12.59
10% points	4.61	6.25	7.78	9.24	10.65
20% points	3.22	4.64	5.99	7.29	8.56

Actually, the *F*-test is conducted to determine whether the null hypothesis that $Z_{ij}^2 \in \psi_s$ is the estimate of the same error variance $\overline{\eta_0^2}$ is unacceptable. The hypothesis is unacceptable if the tabulated value at the desired significance in the *F*-distribution table is less than the value computed for $\frac{Z_{ij}^2}{\eta_0^2}$. The portion of the *F*-distribution table which has relevance to this work is shown in *Table 2*.

Having described the statistical design of experiments for low level feature extraction process, the next task is to propose a texture representation based on this model and the same is presented in the next section.

3.2 Texture representation

With respect to the presence of texture in the image under analysis, the micro texture regions are represented properly to obtain a better local texture descriptor. A small region (3×3) is considered as a sample for performing the test. All the samples drawn from the image under analysis are included for the test as per the procedure stated in *Section 3*. The mean square error variance (*msv*) is computed as follows

$$msv=\frac{\left(\sum_{Z_{ij}^2\in V} Z_{ij}^2\right)}{\|V\|} \quad (12)$$

where $\|V\|$ is the cardinality of the set V. Each of the variances in $\{A+B-V\}$ is divided by the mean square variance error (*msv*) for computing the Signal-to-Noise Ratio. The strength of this signal compared to the noise present is measured by conducting the *F*-ratio test [29]. The fact that a member passing the test implies that it has significant contribution towards micro texture formation. If the contribution towards the presence of texture is not significant, it shall be assumed that the region may be noise or smooth. In case of significant contribution, the pixel in the original texture image whose zonal position corresponds to the zonal position of the variance term corresponding to the interaction effect is represented as 1; otherwise, it is represented as 0. The positions corresponding to the variance terms in V which are used for computing *msv* are represented as 0s. Then, the outcome of this test for measuring significance towards the micro texture is encoded as a binary string. The equivalent decimal number is obtained next in order to characterise the micro texture. The numerical characterization sequence is used as feature vector for further processing in iris recognition.

4 Experimental Results

The proposed feature extraction method for iris recognition has been experimented with all the 756 samples from standard CASIA V1.0 iris database [29]. Sample test images of size (340×280) with pixel values in the range $(0-255)$ are presented in *Figure 2*. In order to compensate the deformations in iris texture, the iris region is unwrapped to a rectangular normalization block with a fixed size of (360×45), and is presented in *Figure 3* for the original image shown in *Figure 2*. The normalized iris image is divided into $(n \times n)$ blocks of overlapping regions and the orthogonal polynomials based transformation is applied to extract the transformed coefficients β'_{ij} as described in *Section 2*. The variance Z^2 is computed from the transformed coefficients and the sets such as main effects (Set A), interaction effects (Set B) are obtained as described in *Section 3.1*. To test whether a given region belongs to a textured region, the Hartley's criteria are applied for testing the homogeneity among variances as described in *Section 3.1.1*. If all the mean square variances in B corresponding to all the interaction effects estimate the same variance, then one variance at a time is eliminated and the remaining variances are considered to check whether they are not estimating the same variances. In the worst case, at least two variances must be present so that they do not estimate the same variance. Otherwise, it is concluded that the region under consideration is not a textured region. That is, if the image region $[I]$ is tested for textureness, that is B to be more divergent and set A to be more convergent. Then, the image region $[I]$ under consideration may be concluded to be a textured region.

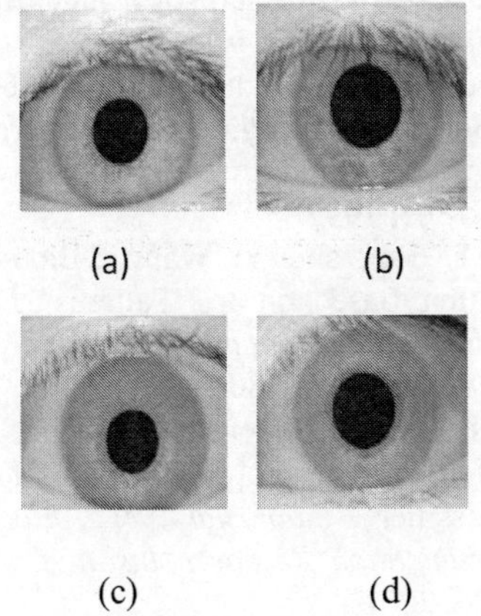

Figure: 2: Original sample test images considered for feature extraction

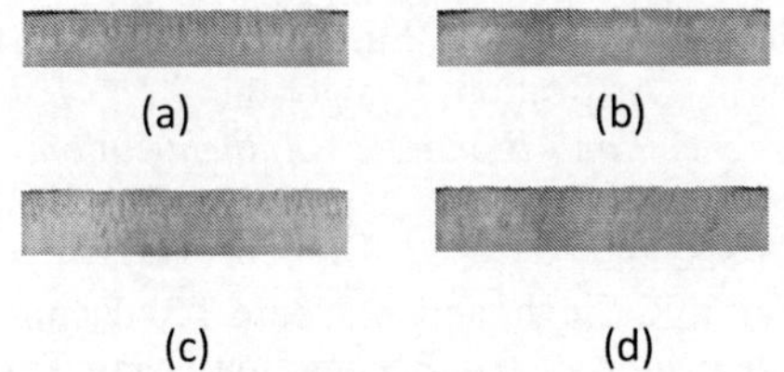

Figure 3: Rectangular normalization of the sample test images shown in Figure 2

Once, texture regions are identified, The F-ratio test is applied as described in *Section 3.2*. The outcome of the F-ratio test for measuring significance towards the micro texture is encoded as a binary string. The equivalent decimal number is obtained next in order to characterise the micro texture. The numerical characterization sequence is used as feature vector for further processing in iris recognition. The sample result of texture representation for the test image shown in *Figure 2* is presented in *Figure 4*.

During experimentation, the time taken to extract the texture features with the proposed technique is also obtained. The system used for this purpose is Intel (R) Core (TM) i7 CPU 965@3.20GHz system with 4.00GB RAM. The time consumed for the proposed feature extraction for each image is noted and is averaged for all the 756 CASIA iris images. The proposed technique takes an average of 32ms for texture feature extraction with a feature vector of 1800. This time consumption for feature extraction and the feature vector size of the proposed feature extraction technique are presented in *Table 3*. The performance of the proposed texture feature extraction is analyzed by comparing with other existing techniques. In this proposed work, four existing schemes viz. Daugman's method [1], Ma's method [22], Monro's method [20] and Vatsa's method [7] are considered. The Daugman's method [1] uses 2-D Gabor wavelets and results with a feature vector of dimension 2048. The time taken by this method for feature extraction is found to be 334ms. These results are also incorporated in *Table 3*. In the case of Ma's method [22], they constructed 1-Dimensional intensity signal and used particular class of wavelet with vector of position sequence of local sharp variations points as features and results with a feature vector of dimension 660. The time taken by this method for feature extraction is found to be 260ms. These results are also incorporated in *Table 3*. Monro [20] adopted DCT coefficient weighting factor in choosing the most discriminating bits and result with a feature vector of dimension 300. The time taken by this method for feature extraction is found to be 30ms. These results are also incorporated in *Table 3*. Vatsa [7] used a typical Daugman-style iris code as a texture features and Euler code as topological features and results with a feature vector of dimension 1684 (1680 textural features and 4 topological features). The time taken by this method for feature extraction is found to be 253ms. These results are also incorporated in *Table 3*.

4 12 3 4 36 4 3 4 72 4 7 12 4 7 8 16 4 1 4 219 4 1 13 4
8 4 44 36 5 36 44 12 76 36 255 3 36 12 4 36 12 36 72
219 36 32 72 36 4 12 36 1 4 36 1 36 8 36 32 8 36 12
36 5 36 44 36 16 36 12 72 36 12 5 36 8 5 36 32 12 36
12 36 72 12 ....

(a)

36 4 3 100 36 44 3 4 32 4 64 12 4 8 4 16 4 8 4 72 19 1
4 13 64 8 3 44 4 5 36 12 1 76 1 255 3 36 13 24 36 12
36 72 219 1 36 72 5 36 12 36 13 4 72 5 25 8 1 72 9 36
12 72 5 9 44 36 16 36 5 72 36 8 5 36 13 5 13 36 12 36
12 144 72 4 ....

(b)

144 4 3 4 36 4 3 4 160 4 9 12 4 1 4 212 4 64 4 192 4 9
13 4 8 4 144 36 152 36 32 36 72 36 255 3 36 32 4 36
12 36 136 219 36 9 72 36 144 12 36 212 4 36 144 36
8 36 72 32 36 12 36 5 36 44 36 16 36 200 72 36 136 5
36 212 5 36 144 200 36 12 36 72 4 ....

(c)

228 4 3 4 36 4 3 4 100 4 37 12 4 37 4 16 4 37 4 219 4
228 13 4 8 4 101 36 5 36 101 37 76 36 255 3 36 37 4
36 12 36 228 219 36 101 72 36 37 12 36 37 4 36 37
101 8 36 37 100 101 12 36 5 36 44 36 16 36 37 72 36
101 5 36 228 5 36 228 100 36 12 36 101 4
....

(d)

Figure 4: Texture Representation for the sample test images shown in Figure. 2

It is evident from *Table 3*, that the proposed orthogonal polynomials based feature extraction approach requires least amount of computations among all approaches except Monro's method. It is also evident from *Table 3*, that the feature vector size of proposed orthogonal polynomials based feature extraction is comparable with Daugman's method and Vatsa's method except Ma's method and Monro's method.

Table 3: Time taken for feature extraction with the proposed technique and feature vector size comparison with existing techniques

Method	Computation time (ms) for Feature Extraction	Feature vector size
Proposed System	32	1800
Daugman [1]	334	2048
Ma [24]	260	660
Monro [22]	30	300
Vatsa [9]	253	1684

It can be ascertained from *Table 3* that the performance improvement, due to the usage of orthogonal polynomials based feature vector, is significant. Hence, it is concluded that extracting the feature in the orthogonal polynomials domain is superior to extracting it in the original image domain. This method avoids that the features extracted from typically noisy regions can corrupt the biometric signature. It is concluded that the proposed iris feature extraction makes iris recognition system more robust than the various feature extraction methods.

5 Conclusion

The orthogonal polynomials based iris feature extraction framework that has been proposed in *Section 3* is implemented successfully for detection of textures in 2-D monochrome normalized iris images. The local image regions are represented by the proposed set of orthogonal polynomials and the spatial variation has been measured in terms of orthogonal effects. The orthogonal effects are divided into two subsets, namely, main and interaction effects. The interaction effects where both the spatial coordinates are varying jointly are due to the presence of texture. The main effects where the spatial coordinates are varying independently are due to the presence of Gaussian noise and can be considered as an estimate of the noise variance. The detected micro texture is then represented locally by measuring and combining the significance of the orthogonal effects. The local texture descriptor is computed for normalized iris image and stored as feature vector for further processing. Future work will include feature selection and iris classification strategy.

Acknowledgement

This work is sponsored by a grant from the Department of Information Technology of Ministry of Communication and Information Technology, New Delhi under Grant No. 12(12)/2008-ESD dated 06.01.2009.

REFERENCES:

[1] J. G. Daugman, "High Confidence Visual Recognition of persons by a test of statistical independence", *IEEE Transactions on Pattern Analysis and Machine Intelligence*, vol. 15, no. 11, pp. 1148-1161, 1993.

[2] R. P. Wildes, "Iris recognition: an emerging biometric technology", *Proceedings of the IEEE*, vol. 85, no. 9, pp. 1348–1363, 1997.

[3] Y. Zhu, T. Tan, and Y. Wang, "Biometric Personal Identification Based on Iris Patterns", *Proceedings of the 15th International Conference on Pattern Recognition*, vol. 2, pp. 805 - 808, 2000.

[4] S. Lim, K. Lee, O. Byeon, and T. Kim, "Efficient Iris Recognition through Improvement of Feature Vector and Classifier", *Journal of Electronics and Telecommunication Research Institute*, vol. 23, no. 2, pp. 61 – 70, 2001.

[5] L. Ma, T. Tan, Y. Wang and D. Zhang, "Personal Identification based on Iris Texture Analysis", *IEEE Transactions on Pattern Analysis and Machine Intelligence*, vol. 25, no. 12, pp. 1519-1533, 2003.

[6] B. Meena, M. Vasta, R. Singh, and P Gupta, "Iris based human verification algorithms", *International Conference on Biometric Authentication*, Springer Lecture Notes, vol. 3072, pp. 458-466, ISBN 3-540-22146-8, 2004.

[7] M. Vatsa, R. Singh, and A. Noore, "Reducing the False Rejection Rate of Iris Recognition Using Textural and Topological Features", *International Journal of Signal Processing*, vol. 2, no. 2, pp. 66-72, 2005.

[8] L. Yu, D. Zhang and K. Wang, "The relative distance of key point based iris recognition," Pattern Recognition, vol.40, pp.423-430, 2007.

[9] C. Park, J. Lee, S. Oh, Y. Song, D. Choi and K. Park" Iris Feature Extraction and Matching Based on

Multiscale and Directional Image Representation", *Springer Berlin / Heidelberg*, vol. 2695/2003, 2007.

[10] M. Nabti and A. Bouridane, "An effective and fast iris recognition based on a combined multiscale feature extraction technique", *International Conference on Pattern Recognition*, vol.41, pp. 808 – 879, 2008.

[11] L. Chenhong and L. Zhaoyang, "Local feature extraction for iris recognition with automatic scale selection," *Image and Vision Computing*, vol.26, pp.935-940, 2008.

[12] C. Chen, and C. Chu "High performance iris recognition based on 1-D Circular feature extraction and PSO-PNN classifier" *Expert Systems with Applications*, vol.36, pp. 10351–10356, 2009.

[13] A. Abhyankar, S. Schuckers, "Iris quality assessment and bi-orthogonal wavelet based encoding for recognition", *Pattern Recognition*, vol. 42, pp. 1878 – 1894, 2009.

[14] H. Mehrotra, G. S. Badrinath, B. Majhi, and P. Gupta, "An Efficient Dual Stage Approach for IRIS Feature Extraction using Interest Point Pairing", *IEEE Workshop on Computational Intelligence in Biometrics: Theory, Algorithms and Applications*, pp. 59-62, 2009.

[15] J. Huang, X. You, Y. Yuan, F. Yang and L. Lin, "Rotation invariant iris feature extraction using Gaussian Markov random fields with non-separable wavelet", *Neurocomputing: Bayesian Networks / Design and Application of Neural Networks and Intelligent Learning Systems (KES 2008 / Bio-inspired Computing: Theories and Applications*, vol. 73, no. 4-6, pp. 883-894, 2010.

[16] K. Roy, P. Bhattacharya and C. Y. Suen, "Towards non ideal iris recognition based on level set method, genetic algorithms and adaptive asymmetrical SVMs", *Engineering Applications of Artificial Intelligence*, vol. 24, no. 3, pp. 458-475, 2011.

[17] W. W. Boles and B. Boashash, "A Human Identification Technique Using Images of the Iris and Wavelet Transform", *IEEE Transactions on Signal Processing*, vol. 46, no. 4, pp. 1185-1188, 1998.

[18] C. Sanchez-Avila, and R. Sanchez-Reillo, "Multiscale Analysis for Iris Biometrics", *International Conference on Security Technology*, vol. 1, pp. 35-38, 2002.

[19] C. Sanchez-Avila, and R. Sanchez-Reillo, "Two different approaches for iris recognition using Gabor filters and multiscale zero-crossing representation", *Pattern Recognition*, vol. 38, pp. 231-240, 2005.

[20] D. M. Monro, S. Rakshit, and D. Zhang, "DCT-Based Iris Recognition", *IEEE Transactions on Pattern analysis and Machine Intelligence*, vol. 29, no. 4, pp. 586-595, 2007.

[21] Y. Huang, S. Weiluo, and E. Chen, "An Efficient Iris Recognition system", *International conference on Machine Learning and Cybernetics*, pp. 450-454, November 2002.

[22] L. Ma, T. Tan, Y. Wang and D. Zhang, "Efficient Iris Recognition by Characterizing Key Local Variations", *IEEE Transactions on Image Processing*, vol. 13, no. 6, pp. 739-750, 2004.

[23] W. Chen, and S. Yuan, "A Novel Personal Biometric Authentication Technique using Human Iris Based on Fractal Dimension features", *Proceedings of ICASSP*, vol.3, pp. 201-204, 2003.

[24] L. Liam, A. Chekima, L. Fan, and J. Dargham, "Iris recognition using self-organizing neural network", *IEEE Student Conference on Research and Developing Systems*, pp.169-172, 2002.

[25] R. Krishnamoorthi and G. Annapoorani, "A simple boundary extraction technique for irregular pupil localization with orthogonal polynomials", *Computer Vision and Image Understanding*, vol. 116, no. 2, pp. 262-273, 2012.

[26] L. Ganesan, and P. Bhattacharya, "Edge detection in untextured and textured images – A common computational framework", IEEE Transactions on Systems, Man, and Cybernatics, Part B, vol. 27, no. 5, pp. 823-834, 1997.

[27] H. O. Hartley, *Testing the Homogeneity of a set of variances*, Biometrika, vol. 31, pp. 249-255, 1940.

[28] R. A. Fisher and F. Yates, *Statistical Tables for Biological, Agricultural and Medical Research*, Oliver and Boyd, London, 1947.

[29] *http://www.biometris.idealtest.org*, Version 1.0, 2013.

Fingerprint grid enhancement on GPU

Raja Lehtihet[1], Wael El Oraiby[2], and Mohammed Benmohammed[3]

[1]Computer Science Departement, University of Constantine, Constantine, Algeria
[2]AIFU Ltd, Montreal, Quebec, Canada
[3]LIRE Laboratory, University of Constantine, Constantine, Algeria

Abstract— *This paper presents an optimized GPU (Graphics Processing Unit) implementation for fingerprint images enhancement using a Gabor filter-bank based algorithm. Given a batch of fingerprint images, we apply the Gabor filter bank and compute image variances of the convolution responses. We then select parts of these responses and compose the final enhanced batches. The algorithm exploits GPU parallelism by partitioning the data elements on the GPU parallel threads. The implementation was tested on different batch sizes and different image qualities from the FVC2004 DB2 database. We then compare the execution speed between the CPU and GPU. This comparison shows that the algorithm is by order of magnitudes faster on a GPU than the CPU.*

Keywords: biometrics, fingerprints, enhancement, Gabor filtering, GPGPU.

1. Introduction

fingerprint identification represents one of the most efficient and lowest cost detection systems in the biometric security market.

A fingerprint image presents a flow-like ridge structure. The structure of the ridges contains many local interesting characteristics such as islands, short ridges, enclosures, ridges endings and bifurcations. The ridge endings and bifurcations (called minutiae) are the most prominent identification characteristics.

A person is usually identified by an automated Fingerprint Identification Systems (AFIS) by matching his fingerprint minutiae-based signature with registered ones [14]. The result of such matching depends heavily on the quality of the input fingerprint image. However, the ridge structures and minutiae are not always well defined because of the presence of spurious features and discontinuities due to acquisition parameters and/or to reasons inherent to the fingerprint owner. Thus, fingerprint enhancement is a crucial step in a fingerprint identification process where an enhancement algorithm must retrieve and enhance the ridge structure for further minutiae extraction.

Several approaches for fingerprint image enhancement were proposed. they are often based on flow orientation and local ridge directional binarization [17]. In [13] frequency and orientation filters in the Fourier domain were designed. This method is computation intensive since it involves transformation to the frequency domain and multiple filtering. In [10] the properties of orientation and ridge frequency as parameters for a single Gabor filter were used and a short-time Fourier transform was proposed in [5].

Enhancing fingerprint images in real-time is a challenge given the computation time required in the process. With the current generation of programmable Graphics Processing Units (GPU), this is now possible since they currently have teraflops of floating point performance. General Purpose computing or programming on GPUs (GPGPU) was introduced as a parallel programming model for these devices, where developers decompose the problem into sub processing elements to exploit high level parallelism of the GPU.

Computer scientists and researchers are starting to use GPUs for running computational scientific applications. First, in [4], color image processing was mapped for GPU programming. In [1], Fast Fourier Transform (FFT) on GPU was computed giving faster execution time than on CPU. A set of frameworks for GPGPU processing are proposed such as: Image processing framework [12], the OpenVidia library [6], GPU accelerated generalized bi-dimensional distance transform [19], motion estimation [18], GPU4Vision for real-time optical flow [22] and total variation based image segmentation on GPU [21]. Now Cuda [15], DirectCompute [16] and OpenCL [8] are proposed as GPGPU programming APIs, allowing programmers to interface with the GPU directly to make massively parallel programs.

This paper presents a GPU implementation for enhancing batches of fingerprint images using a Gabor filter bank based algorithm in an accelerated execution time. The algorithm selects pixels corresponding to the maximum values of variances in the Gabor responses. The Gabor based enhancement of fingerprints has shown good results in works of [10], [9] and [3]. The algorithm scales very well on multiple core GPUs.

Experimental results with fingerprint images from the FVC2004 DB2 database [7] show that the execution of the algorithm gives enhanced images by order of magnitudes faster on the GPU in comparison to the CPU.

2. GPU Programming

In the GPGPU programming model, the CPU acts as a master controlling the GPU which acts as a slave. The GPU is composed of multiple cores and is designed to execute the same program called a kernel on different data elements simultaneously. These kernels are executed in threads divided across the multiple cores (see Figure 1). These threads are mapped relatively to the data elements, where each element is consumed in its own thread. For image processing algorithms such as filtering, that are designed to work on pixel blocks independently of previous steps, the GPGPU model is ideal. When a step is dependent on the previous one, the algorithm can be divided into multiple execution passes executed one after the other on the GPU as well.

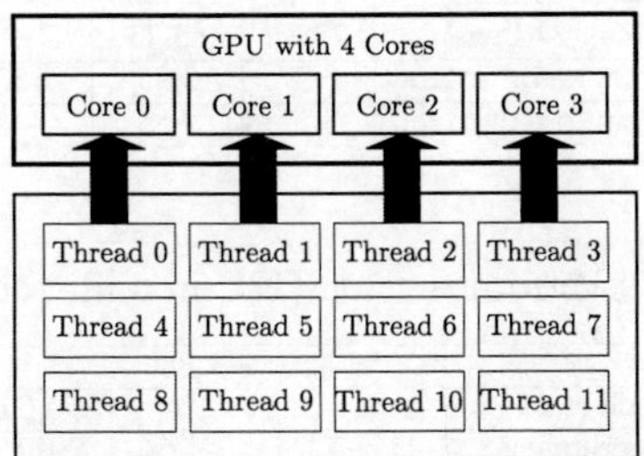

Fig. 1: Multi threaded program partitioned into blocks of threads.

In this direction, computing the FFT on GPU has been addressed successfully and efficiently with fast algorithms such as [2], [15], [20]. Most of these algorithms use butterfly algorithm [2] with multi-passes for different levels of the algorithm (where each level requires a pass).

3. Fingerprint enhancement

3.1 2-D Gabor wavelets

Let $G(x, y; \theta, \lambda)$ be the Gabor filter function centred at the origin with $1/\lambda$ as the spatial frequency and θ as the orientation. The response of a Gabor filter to an image is obtained by a 2D convolution operation, we can proceed by convoluting pixels of the image with an even symmetric filter [11] that can be constructed as follows:

$$g(x, y; \theta, \lambda) = exp\left(-\frac{1}{2}\left(\frac{x_\theta^2}{\sigma_G^2} + \frac{y_\theta^2}{\sigma_G^2}\right)\right)\cos(\frac{2\pi}{\lambda}x_\theta) \quad (1)$$

$$x_\theta = x\cos\theta + y\sin\theta \quad (2)$$

$$y_\theta = -x\sin\theta + y\cos\theta \quad (3)$$

Figure 2 shows one response of a Gabor filter: a filter with 45° of orientation, here we notice that high responses are located wherever there are ridges with the same orientation.

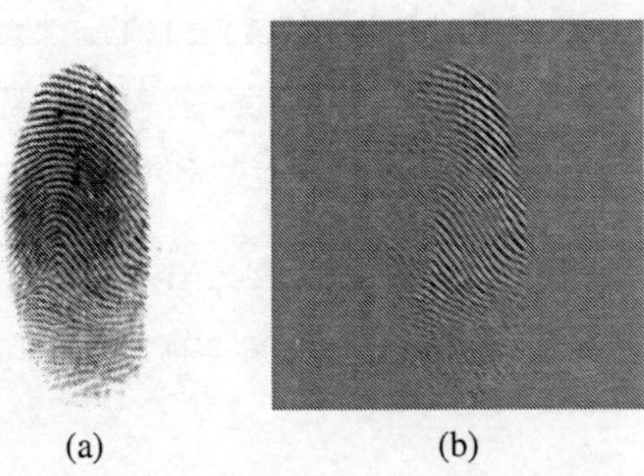

(a) (b)

Fig. 2: (a) Original fingerprint image. (b) Response for a Gabor filter of orientation $\theta = 45^\circ$

3.2 Gabor filter based enhancement algorithm

First we combine a set of $m = n^2$ 2D discreet fingerprint images with L-Gray levels into a tiled image I of $n \times n$ tiles. The image I is made of $W \times H$ pixels and $I(x, y)$ designates a pixel in this image (where W is the image width, H the image height, $0 \leq x < W$ and $0 \leq y < H$).

The proposed algorithm is composed of several stages as resumed in Figure 3:

- **Gabor filtering:** Apply a Gabor filter bank of 8 different orientations and 3 different frequencies to I. The result is made of 24 response images $\{R_0 \ldots R_{23}\}$ for every set.
- **Variance images computing:** Compute the local variance on the pixel neighbouring $b \times b$ of each Gabor response image of the 24 images resulting from the precedent filtering, this will give us 24 variance images, $\{V_0 \ldots V_{23}\}$.

$$V(x, y) = \frac{1}{b^2}\sum_{s=0}^{b-1}\sum_{t=0}^{b-1}(I(x - s, y - t) - \mu(x, y))^2 \quad (4)$$

where μ is the mean gray level of the $b \times b$ block:

$$\mu = \frac{1}{b^2}\sum_{s=0}^{b-1}\sum_{t=0}^{b-1} I(x - s, y - t) \quad (5)$$

The mean was computed using a two-passes filter (one for x and then for y). This leads to significant increase in speed and reduces the bottlenecks on the GPU significantly.

- **Best coefficient selection:** Let $T_i(x, y) = (R_i(x, y), V_i(x, y))$, be the tuple linking the pixel $R_i(x, y)$ with the variance value $V_i(x, y)$. We select the pixels with maximum local variance such that the final pixel $P(x, y) = \text{Arg}\max_{i\in[0,23]} T_i(x, y)$.
- **fingeprint binarization:** Binarize the image using a pixel values threshold.

4. Implementation

For the implementation we chose the following values: $b = 15$, $n \in \{2.04.0, 8.0\}$, $\sigma = 4$, $\lambda \in \{6.0, 8.0, 10.0\}$ and

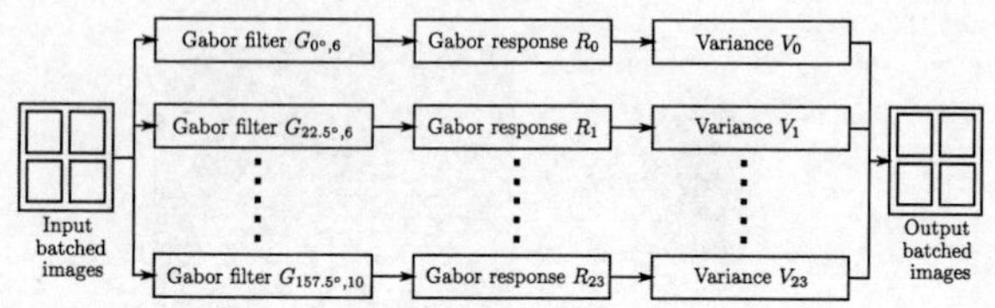

Fig. 3: Overview of the Gabor based enhancement algorithm.

$\theta \in \{0, 22.5, 45, 67.5, 90, 112.5, 135, 157.5\}$. Both λ and σ are empiric values since they provide best response to our image set. The orientations are chosen based on the work done in [9], [11] while the λ values were chosen related to fingerprint image resolutions. $\lambda = 8$ is the average value.

First the $n \times n$ target images are grouped into one image, then 24 Gabor bank images are constructed in the frequency domain. The resulting image is then transformed to frequency domain using FFT as well. We then multiply this image with all the 24 filters and store the results in 24 Gabor response images. These Gabor response images are then transformed back with inverse FFT to spatial domain. For each transformed Gabor response image we compute the variance using (4) in a different result image where the mean (5) was computed through FFT. Processing variance in this way is numerically more stable. Finally the pixels who have the maximum variance from the 24 Gabor response images are copied to the final image.

The CPU implementation was done in C language using FFTW in single precision, while the GPU version was coded in CUDA given its fast and stable implementation of FFT. On the GPU, the 24 Gabor filter banks are created in the frequency domain. These filters are noted G_i^F. The original image is converted to the frequency domain image I^F. The algorithm works in 4 passes, and for each pixel in every pass, a thread on the GPU is allocated. The memory needed for all operations is allocated before we enter the execution phase. This is needed to prevent overhead spent in data copy and resource synchronization between the GPU and the CPU.

Moreover, shared memory was used to compute variance. The speed increase is dramatic since it reduces GPU cores idling time waiting for memory fetches. There were between 12 to 16 speed increase using this approach on the current test configuration.

The 4 passes of the algorithm are as follows:

- **Pass 1:** Each gabor filter is multiplied with the frequency domain image, this will give a Gabor response image: $R_i^F = G_i^F \dot{I}^F$. Depending on the GPU power and memory, these multiplications can all be done simultaneously.
- **Pass 2:** R_i^F is converted back to spatial domain, giving R_i.
- **Pass 3:** The variance image V_i is computed from R_i.
- **Pass 4:** Once all variance images are done, the last step is to select pixels with highest variance.

Thus, the chosen pixel is the one for $P(x, y) = \text{Arg max}_{i \in [0,23]} T_i(x, y)$.

5. Experimental results

Table 1: Performance on GPU in milliseconds.

	GPU		
Batch size	4	16	64
Algorithm	151.3	413.09	1707.63
FFT/Multiplication (24 imgs)	99.17	257.08	1087.02
Variance(24 imgs)	19.68	77.28	348.24
ArgMax(24 imgs)	28.31	65.23	212.65
CPUMem to GPUMem	0.77	3.95	15.71
GPUMem to CPUMem	3.37	9.55	44.01

Table 2: Performance on CPU in milliseconds.

	CPU		
Batch size	4	16	64
Algorithm	1128.74	5025.56	20115.39
FFT/Multiplication (24 imgs)	1012.10	4467.28	17838.72
Variance(24 imgs)	31.92	228.4	970.54
ArgMax(24 imgs)	84.72	329.88	1306.13

We tested the implementations of the algorithm on an nvidia GeForce 560 Ti GPU with 192 cores running at 900Mhz and with 1024MB video memory. The test was also performed on an intel i7-2600K CPU at 3.40GHz and with 8GB of memory. The tests were performed on both Windows 7 and Ubuntu 12.04.

Results on GPU and CPU are shown in Tables 1 and 2. We applied the algorithm implementation on image batches from the FVC2004 DB2 database with batches of 4, 16 and 64 images. The graphical representations of these tables (as shown in Figure 4) show that for our fingerprint enhancement implementation, the GPU is at least 11 times more efficient than a CPU running at a significantly higher clock rate.

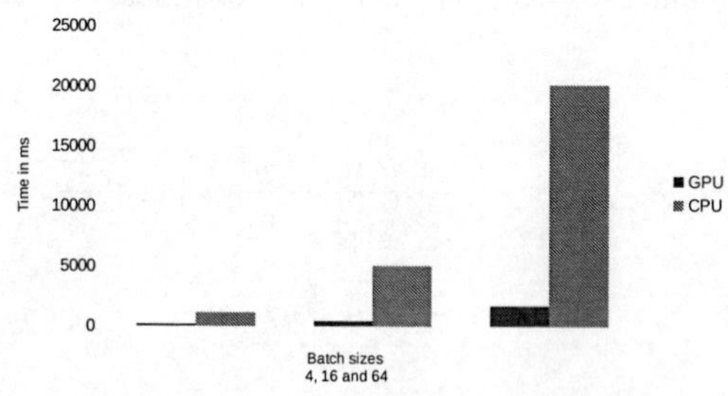

Fig. 4: GPU vs CPU performance

Figure 5 shows an example of the final result of the enhancement algorithm.

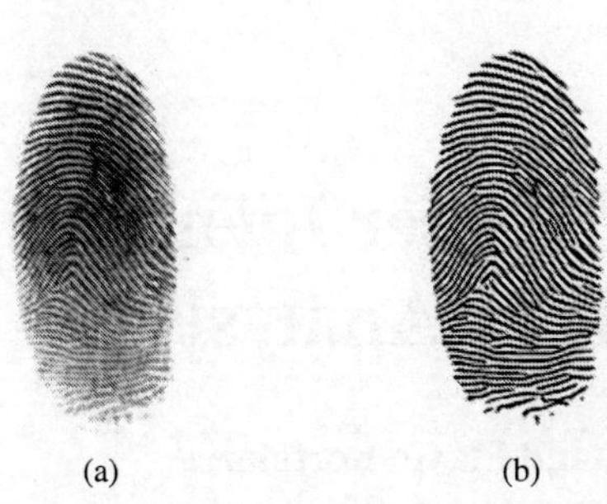

Fig. 5: (a) Original fingerprint image. (b) fingerprint image after Gabor enhancement application.

6. Conclusion

In this paper, we presented a study of the implementation on CPU and GPU of a fingerprint enhancement algorithm. The GPU implementation was done in an optimal way giving an accelerated time execution up to at least 11 times the CPU execution time. The used algorithm is based on a Gabor filter bank convolution and variance computing which are both costly on CPU.

Experimentations were realized on the FVC2004 fingerprint image database, as shown in the graphical representations of time execution values, the algorithm gives good enhancement results in an accelerated time execution.

Finally, the obtained results are encouraging to implement other costly fingerprint enhancement algorithms in a batched way in order to reduce processing time. Thus, future work will be oriented to process images using the big possibilities of GPGPU programmming.

References

[1] Edward Angel and Kenneth Moreland. Integrated image and graphics technologies. chapter Fourier processing in the graphics pipeline, pages 95–110. Kluwer Academic Publishers, Norwell, MA, USA, 2004.

[2] Eric Bainville. Opencl fast fourier transform. http://www.bealto.com/gpu-fft_dft.html, 2010.

[3] Sylvain Bernard, Nozha Boujemaa, David Vitale, and Claude Bricot. Fingerprint segmentation using the phase of multiscale gabor wavelets, 2002.

[4] Nabil Boukala, Jerome Da Rugna, and Universite Jean Monnet. Fast and accurate color image processing using 3d graphics cards. In *In Proceedings Vision, Modeling and Visualization*, 2003.

[5] Sharat Chikkerur, Chaohang Wu, and Venu Govindaraju. A systematic approach for feature extraction in fingerprint images. In *ICBA*, pages 344–350, 2004.

[6] James Fung and Steve Mann. Openvidia: parallel gpu computer vision. In *Proceedings of the 13th annual ACM international conference on Multimedia*, MULTIMEDIA '05, pages 849–852, New York, NY, USA, 2005. ACM.

[7] FVC2004. Fingerprint database. http://bias.csr.unibo.it/fvc2004/, 2004.

[8] Khronos group. Opencl khronos group. http://www.khronos.org/opencl/, 2011.

[9] Lin Hong, Anil K. Jain, Sharath Pankanti, and Ruud Bolle. Fingerprint enhancement. Technical Report MSU-CPS-96-45, Department of Computer Science, Michigan State University, East Lansing, Michigan, January 1996.

[10] Lin Hong, Yifei Wan, and Anil Jain. Fingerprint image enhancement: Algorithm and performance evaluation. *IEEE Transactions on Pattern Analysis and Machine Intelligence*, 20:777–789, 1998.

[11] Anil K. Jain, Salil Prabhakar, Lin Hong, and Sharath Pankanti. Filterbank-based fingerprint matching. *IEEE Transactions on Image Processing*, 9:846–859, 2000.

[12] Franck Jargstorff. A framework for image processing. In Randima Fernando, editor, *GPU Gems: Programming Techniques, Tips and Tricks for Real-Time Graphics*, pages 445–467. Addison Wesley, 2004.

[13] T. Kamei and M. Mizoguchi. Image filter design for fingerprint enhancement. *Computer Vision, International Symposium on*, 0:109, 1995.

[14] D. Maltoni, D. Maio, A. K. Jain, and S. Prabhakar. *Handbook of Fingerprint Recognition*. New York, 2003.

[15] Nvidia. Cuda presentation. http://www.nvidia.com/object/what_is_cuda_new.html, 2011.

[16] Nvidia. Direct compute. http://www.nvidia.com/object/cuda_directcompute.html, 2011.

[17] A. Ravishankar Rao. *A taxonomy for texture description and identification*. Springer-Verlag New York, Inc., New York, NY, USA, 1990.

[18] Robert Strzodka and Christoph Garbe. Real-time motion estimation and visualization on graphics cards. In *Proceedings of the conference on Visualization '04*, VIS '04, pages 545–552, Washington, DC, USA, 2004. IEEE Computer Society.

[19] Robert Strzodka and Alexandru Telea. Generalized Distance Transforms and skeletons in graphics hardware. In *Proceedings of EG/IEEE TCVG Symposium on Visualization (VisSym '04)*, pages 221–230, 2004.

[20] Thilaka Sumanaweera. Medical image reconstruction with the fft. In *GPU Gems 2: Programming Techniques for High-Performance Graphics and General-Purpose Computation (Gpu Gems)*. Addison Wesley, 2005.

[21] Manuel Werlberger, Thomas Pock, and Horst Bischof. Motion estimation with non-local total variation regularization. In *IEEE Computer Society Conference on Computer Vision and Pattern Recognition (CVPR)*, San Francisco, CA, USA, June 2010.

[22] Manuel Werlberger, Werner Trobin, Thomas Pock, Andreas Wedel, Daniel Cremers, and Horst Bischof. Anisotropic Huber-L1 optical flow. In *Proceedings of the British Machine Vision Conference (BMVC)*, London, UK, September 2009.

Multiple Graphometric Features for Writer Identification as part of Forensic Handwriting Analysis

Aline Maria M. M. Amaral[1,2], **Cinthia O. A. Freitas**[2], **and Flavio Bortolozzi**[1]
[1]Departament of Informatics, UniCesumar, Maringá, Paraná, Brazil
[2] Polytechnic School, Pontificia Universidade Católica do Paraná, Curitiba, Paraná, Brazil

Abstract - *This paper describes an approach to writer identification based on graphometric features. These features are used by Forensic Document Examiners (FDE) which realize their analysis observing and extracting from the questioned documents a set of important individualizing primitives. Thus, in this work we present a framework for offline writer identification which combine multiples graphometry features: relative placement habits, relative relationship between individual word heights and relative slant. This set of features is submitted to Support Vector Machine (SVM) classifier to realize the writer identification. Experiments with groups of writers gradually incremented were conducted to obtain the number of writers that stabilizes the accuracy of results. Finally the obtained results are promising when compared to the literature.*

Keywords: Handwriting recognition, forensic, writing, classification algorithms, image processing.

1 Introduction

According to Morris [1], the forensic handwriting identification is part of criminology and its analysis provides a great number of elements related to personnel writing. The crime of forgery was established in the sixteenth century and the FDE have a hard task since time. In this context, computer-based methods and techniques have been proposed to provide support for this task.

Usually, the forensic handwriting identification is performed by experts using optical device and/or chemicals methods. The manual features extraction process can provide doubts about the writer identification [2]. In addition, different examiners can extract the same features from a particular document in a different way. Then, the use of semi-automatic systems can be useful and helpful to the experts when the problem is to identify the forger's identity.

The identity of the forger must be established and it is necessary indicate the suspect demonstrating the handwriting characteristics used to do, utter or alter a false document, or offer the fraudulent document knowing its spurious nature.

In this context, different approaches have been presented in researches such as [3–11]. In works such as ours, an important aspect is the feature set used to reveal the individual characteristics in the handwriting. Figure 1 presents a classification, based on Sreeraj and Idicula [12], which groups the features according to their granularity. Features which consider information from the whole document are classified as Global, and features which consider information from a specific part of the document are classified as Local. Based on the input method of writing, automatic writer identification system has been classified as online and offline [12].

It is important to mention that only offline approaches are present in Figure 1 since online approaches are not included in the scope of this work.

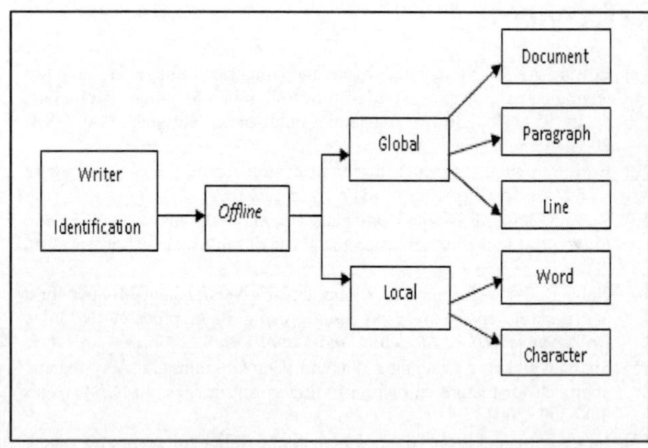

Figure 1. Classification Adapted from Sreeraj and Idicula [12]

Our work proposes a framework to writer identification, based on graphometric features that are used by experts during their analyses. These features were extracted from different levels, such as document, line and word; as showed in Figure 2.

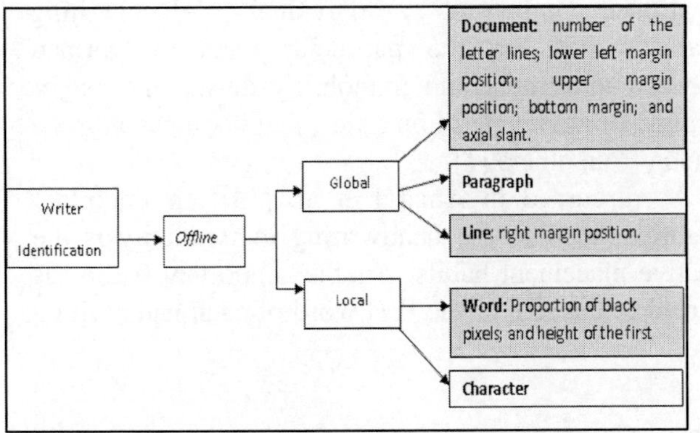

Figure 2. Feature set used in the framework proposed

It was observed that with 200 different writers (corresponding to 600 different letters – 3 letters from each writer) the identification rate of the framework was stabilized. These conditions have conducted to promising results. It is important to detach that the axial slant feature achieves, individually and in group, the best performance.

This paper is organized as follows. Section 2 presents the framework proposed for writer identification and some related works. Section 3 presents the Brazilian Forensic Letter Database. Section 4 discusses the experimental results and presents a brief discussion based on obtained results. Finally, Section 5 presents some considerations as well as points to future works.

2 Writer Identification Approaches

Based on Sreeraj and Idicula [12], as mentioned before, approaches related to the feature extraction for writer identification can be divided into: Global and Local. Different approaches for offline writer identification have been presented in the literature. Many of them use features extracted from the document image, such as the texture approaches [5, 8, 9] or codebook approaches [7, 11]. In our approach, we applied only graphometric features, those applied by the FDEs.

Table 1 presents a summary of related works that use graphometric features, including a brief description of the feature set and the performance achieved in experimental results.

Table 1. Summary of writer identification graphometry-based approaches

Class	Author	Feature	Number of writers	Classification methodology	Performance (%)
Local	Blankers et. al [4]	Shape of loops and lead-in strokes.	41	KNN	98
Local	Pervouchine and Leedham [6]	Features extracted from the characters: "d", "y" e "f" and the grapheme "th".	165	DistAl Algorithm	58
Local	Zois and Anastassopoulos [15]	Use of morphological operators to obtain the horizontal profile of the words.	50	Bayesian Naves/ Neural Network	95
Global	Hertel and Bunke [16]	Continuity of the stroke, closed regions, upper and lower edges.	50	KNN	90
Global	Schlapbach and Bunke [17]	Axial slant, height and slant of the text lines.	50	HMM	94.4
Global	Chen et. al [18]	Information regarding the contour of adjacent segments.	60	SVM	54.9
Global and Local	Luna et. al [10]	Left margin and right margin positions, percentage space of the separation between lines, axial slant, space between words, proportion of words and the words slant.	30	ALVOT algorithm	92
Global and Local	Amaral et. al [13]	Number of the letter lines, proportion of black pixels, right margin position, lower left margin position, upper margin position, bottom margin position, height of the first word.	20	SVM	80

Figure 3 summarizes our baseline system that is based on the paper presented by Amaral et al. [13] adding as a new feature the axial slant. This framework is composed by the following steps: Preprocessing, Feature Extraction and Classification. To conduct our experiments we use letters from 200 different writers (i=1…200) from Brazilian Forensic Letter Database [19].

During the first stage (training stage) it is necessary provide the model for each writer A_{ij} (i=1…200 and j=1..3) randomly selected from forensic database. Two letters from each writer was used in this stage. At second stage (testing stage), the framework compares a specific writer A_{ij} against the models established in the training stage applying the third letter of each writer.

2.1 Feature Extraction

Based on the feature set applied to writer identification process presented in [13] and adding a new feature, the framework feature set is composed by: relative placement habits (composed of primitives f_1,f_3,f_4,f_5,f_6), relative relationship between individual words height (composed of primitives f_2 and f_7) and axial slant (f_8). These features can be observed in Table 2.

Figures 4 and 5 present an overview of the extraction process considering the image of a forensic letter. The result of the extraction process is a vector containing 81 primitives. This vector is applied to SVM classifier [20] in the training and testing stages. As mentioned before, individual handwriting characteristics are the particular character formed between movement and immobility during the act of writing, or aggregate of qualities, that distinguishes one person from others [1].

As discussed in Amaral et al. [13], an important feature related to the handwriting individuality is the relative placement habits. Another important feature is related to the size of the first word of each handwriting line.

Table 2. Framework feature set

Group Feature	Feature
f_1 (1)	Number of lines in each forensic letter.
f_2 (2 -21)	Proportion of black pixels
f_3 (22 - 41)	Right margin position.
f_4 (42)	The lower left margin position
f_5 (43)	Upper margin position
f_6 (44)	Bottom margin position
f_7 (45 - 64)	Height of the first word
$f8$ (65 - 81)	Axial slant

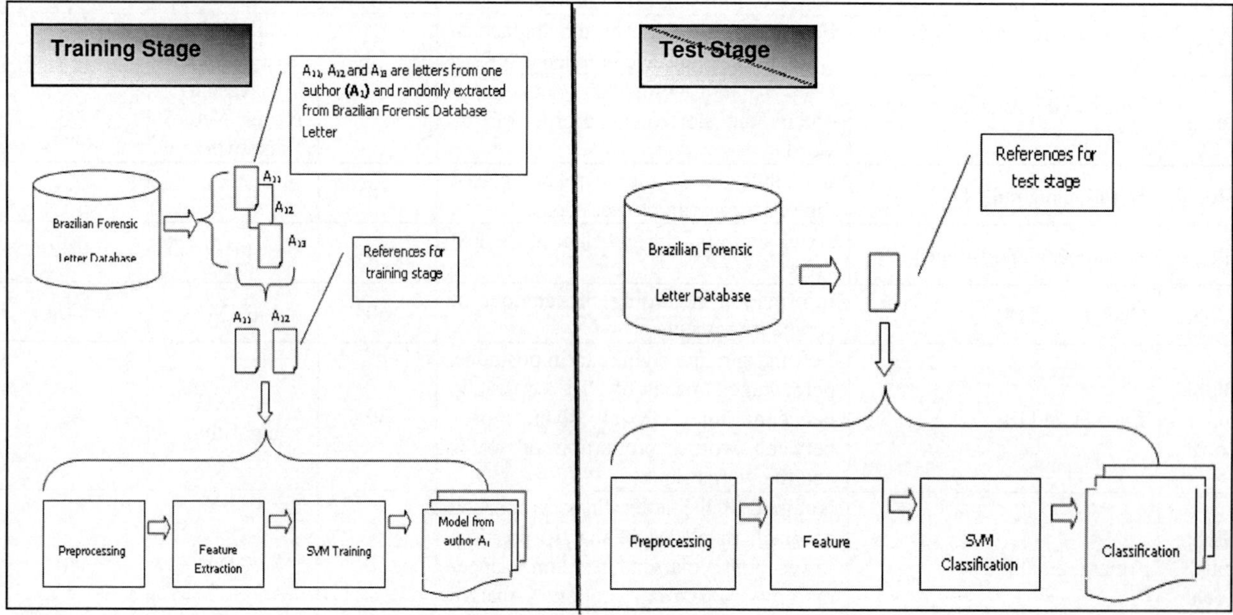

Figure 3. Method Proposed by Amaral et al.[13]

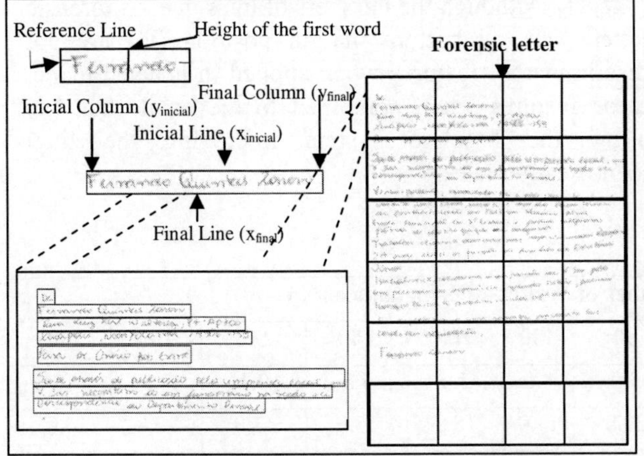

Figure 4 Overview of the feature extraction –

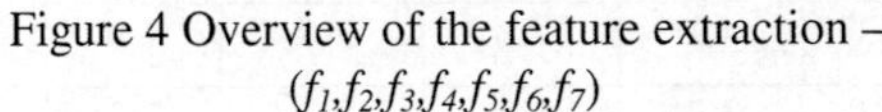
$(f_1,f_2,f_3,f_4,f_5,f_6,f_7)$

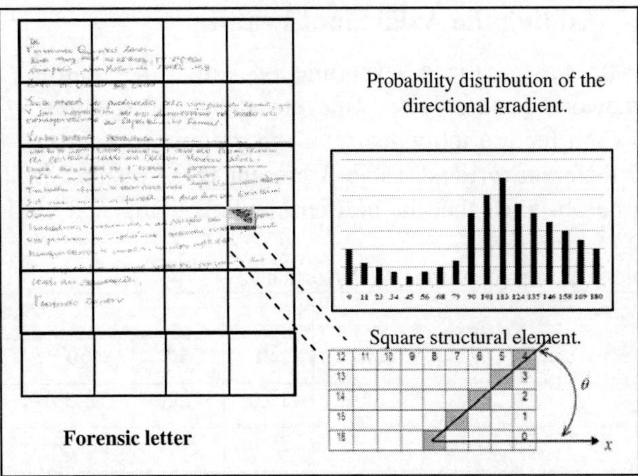

Figure 5 Overview of the feature extraction – (f_8)

The axial slant is a graphometry feature used by the FDEs and has been extensively used in approaches to automatic writer identification [10, 17]. This feature represents the general angle of the handwriting and has the best individually performance in the writer identification process proposed in this work, as demonstrated in Table 3. This important feature is explained better in the next Section

2.1.1 Axial Slant

In order to compute the axial slant feature, five segments are randomly selected from the segmented image (24 = 6 x 4). For each segment, its angle was computed [14]: all the directional gradients L (angles θ) are verified, starting from the central pixel in a square structural element (with 5 pixels, generating 17 directional gradient angles θ, Figure 5) and checking if the following pixels finished in the structural element extremities. This directional gradient vector is normalized by the probability distribution P(θ). The resulting histogram of each segment was added in the primitive vector submitted to the SVM classifier.

3 Brazilian Forensic Letter Database

A manuscript database is necessary for validating the efficiency of a writer identification framework. Thus, in order to ensure that the handwriting samples obtained from a writer having all the letters of the alphabet as well as numerals, accents, special symbols and punctuation symbols, standards forensic letters forms were proposed in the literature. London, Idaho, Egypt and CEDAR are some samples of forensic letters applied by the examiners to obtain the known writing of a specific person [1].

The forensic letters have been collected for several reasons. In their practice, document examiners frequently have to collect specimen of handwriting to make a professional examination. On the other hand, however, according to Freitas et al. [19], most work-related forensic letters found in the literature are devoted to English language, and thus they do not include characteristics from Brazilian Portuguese Language and Brazilian writers. In this context, these authors presented the Brazilian forensic letter database which was created to address the several particularities of the Portuguese Language.

Nowadays, this database contains 1800 letters being 3 letters from each one of 600 different writers.

4 Experimental Results

In this work two (2) groups of experiments were conducted. The first group aimed to evaluate the performance of the framework with the new feature added: axial slant, considering from 20 to 200 different writers. The second group of experiments was defined to observe the framework stabilization versus number of writers. All the experiments respect the same procedures. The next sections present the results of these experiments.

4.1 Adding the Axial Slant Feature

It was realized experiments with: the entire framework features set; some ensembles of features; and each feature individually; using groups from 20 to 200 different writers. Table 3 present these results. It can be observed that the best ensemble is composed of f_1&f_6&f_8. Although the numbers of lines in each forensic letter (*f1*) and bottom margin position (*f6*) are not discriminatory features when applied in isolated mode, these features when combined to the axial slant (f_8) allow the baseline system improving the final identification rate.

Table 3. Writer Identification Performance

Feature	Number of Writers/ Performance (%)									
	20	**40**	**60**	**80**	**100**	**120**	**140**	**160**	**180**	**200**
f_1	15.0	7.5.0	3.3	5.0	4.0	5.0	4.3	3.7	3.8	4.0
f_2	25.0	30.0	18.3	20.0	17.0	15.8	15.0	11.8	13.8	14.0
f_3	20.0	20.0	16.7	13.7	15.0	14.2	11.4	10.6	8.3	9.0
f_4	10.0	10.0	8.3	3.7	5.0	4.2	2.8	1.2	1.6	1.5
f_5	10.0	7.5	6.7	6.2	5.0	3.3	4.3	1.8	2.2	1.0
f_6	30.0	15.0	5.0	5.0	8.0	3.3	3.5	1.8	2.2	1.0
f_7	35.0	35.0	30.0	26.2	25.0	22.5	21.4	18.1	18.3	19.5
f_8	85.0	85.0	76.7	73.7	68.0	71.6	67.1	65	62.7	60.5
f_1 & f_8	85.0	87.0	76.7	78.7	76.0	71.7	71.4	68.7	68.8	67.5
f_6 & f_8	90.0	90.0	83.3	80.0	78.0	75.0	71.4	69.3	68.4	68.5
f_1 & f_6 & f_8	**93.0**	**92.0**	**89.5**	**83.7**	**80.0**	**78.3**	**77.1**	**75%**	**74.3**	**74.0**
f_1 & f_2 & f_3 & f_4 & f_5 & f_6 & f_7 - Amaral et al [13]	80.0	55.0	35.0	35.0	33.0	31.7	32.1	31.8	31.7	31.0
f_1 & f_2 & f_3 & f_4 & f_5 & f_6 & f_7& f_8	65.0	62.5	58.3	57.5	58.0	54.2	52.8	51.8	50.3	50.3

Table 4 presents a brief comparative between our best ensemble of features ***f1* & *f6* & *f8*** and others authors considering graphometry for writer identification. An important result observed is the accuracy maintenance of our experiments with an incremented number of writers Another important result is the performance obtained, individually and in group (see Table 3), by the feature axial slant. This kind of experimentation is very important to confirm all the principles of handwriting and how the axial slant can be more than a simple writer habit but demonstrated that everyone's writing has a particular overall slant as explained by Morris [1].

4.2 Number of Feature and the Stabilization of the Framework Performance

The second group of experiments aimed to obtain the number of writers which stabilizes the framework. In order to perform this task, writers randomly selected from the Brazilian Forensic Letter Database [19] were added in the group of users experimented in the framework, from 20 to 200 writers. The experiments were done with all the features and ensemble of features presented in Table 3, and the writer identification performance was computed, as can be seen in Table 3. Though, in the graphical visualization (Figure 6) only feature f_8 and the ensemble of features which present the best performance are presented.

It can be observed that gradually the relation between the number of writers and accuracy is stabilized, and with 200 writers the results are maintained. It is important note that applying 200 different writers it means to consider 400 letters in the training stage and 200 letters in the test stage, totaling 600 letters. Furthermore, the writer identification rate with the larger group (200 writers) was of 74%. When this result is compared with research such as [6] that uses sample with similar size (165 writers), our framework present best result.

Table 4. Comparison among recent studies

Author	Number of writers	Performance (%)
Zois and Anastassopoulos [15]	50	92.48
Hertel and Bunke [16]	50	90
Schlapbach and Bunke [17]	50	94.4
Pervouchine e Leedham [6]	165	58
Chen et al. [18]	60	54.9
Luna et al. [10]	30	92
Amaral et. al [16]	20	80
f1,f6,f8	20	93
f1,f6,f8	40	92
f1,f6,f8	60	89.5
f1,f6,f8	80	83.7
f1,f6,f8	100	80
f1,f6,f8	200	74

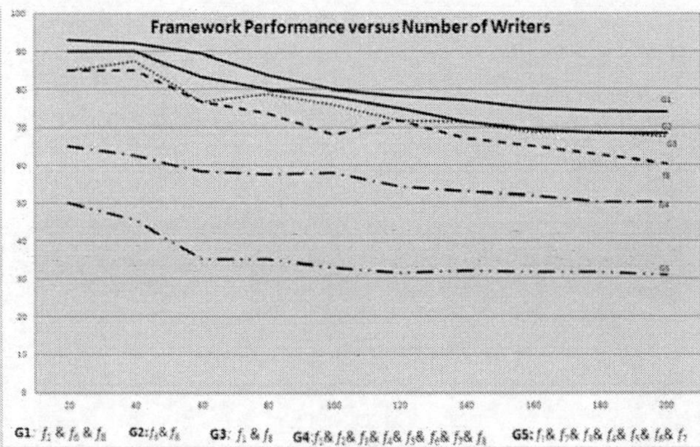

Figure 6. Overview about the performance versus the number of writers

5 Conclusion

In this paper we have discussed the efficiency of a graphometric feature set which can be applied to writer identification. Firstly, we have described the main features of graphometric and research related to them. Thereafter, we have demonstrated, based on experimental results, that these features achieved promising results for forensic handwriting analysis.

We observed that the set of features: number of lines in each forensic letter (f_1), bottom margin position (f_6) and axial slant (f_8); was capable to perform good identification rates with 20 to 200 different writers (all-against-all). Besides, experiments were conducted to establish the number of writers which stabilizes the framework performance, and with 200 different writers no gain or damage was perceived in the results. As future work, new features will be studied and will be included in our baseline system trying to improve our results and some tests with others classifiers will be prepared.

References

[1] R. N. Morris. “Forensic Handwriting Identification – fundamental concepts and principles”. Academic Press, 2000.

[2] R. Fernandez-de-Sevilla, F. Alonso-Fernandez, J. Fierrez, J. Ortega-Garcia. "Forensic writer identification using allographic features”. In: Proceedings of the 12th International Conference on Frontiers in Handwriting Recognition, pp.308-313, 2010.

[3] A. Bensefia, T. Paquet, L. Heutte. "A writer identification and verification system". Pattern Recognition Letters, Vol.26, n.13, pp.2080-2092, 2005.

[4] V. Blankers, R. Niels, L. Vuurpijl. "Writer identification by means of explainable features: shapes of loops and lead-in strokes". In: Proceedings of the 19th Belgian-Dutch Conference on Artificial Intelligence, pp.17-24, 2007.

[5] M. Bulacu, L. Schomaker, A. Brink, A. "Text-independent writer identification and verification on offline Arabic handwriting". In: Proceedings of the 9th Conference on Document Analysis and Recognition (ICDAR), 2007.

[6] V. Pervouchine, G. Leedham. "Extraction and analysis of forensic document examiner features used for writer identification". Pattern Recognition, Vol.40, pp.1004-1013, 2007.

[7] I. Siddiqi, N. Vincent. "Combining global and local features for writer identification". In: Proceedings of the 11th International Conference on Frontiers in Handwriting Recognition, pp. 48-53, 2008.

[8] Z. He, X. You, Y. Tang. "Writer identification of Chinese handrwriting documents using hidden Markov tree model". Pattern Recognition, Vol.41, pp.1295-1307, 2008.

[9] B. Helli, E. Moghaddam. "A text-independent Persian writer identification based on feature relation graph (FRG)". Pattern Recognition, Vol.43, pp.2199-2209, 2010.

[10] E. C. H. Luna, E. M. F. Riveron, S. G. Calderon. "A supervisoned algorihm with a new differentiated-weighting scheme for identifying the author of a handwritten text". Pattern Recognition Letters, Vol.32, pp. 1139-1144, 2011.

[11] L. Schomaker, K. Franke, M. Bulacu. “Using codebooks of fragmented connected-component contours in forensic and

historic writer identification". Pattern Recognition Letters, Vol. 28, pp.719–727, 2007.

[12] M. Sreejaj, S. M. Idicula. "A survey on writer identification schemas". International Journal of Computer Applications, Vol. 26, n. 2, pp.23-33, 2011.

[13] A. M. M. M. Amaral, C. O. A. Freitas, F. Bortolozzi. "The Graphometry applied to writer identification". In Proceedings of the 2012 International Conference on Image Processing, Computer Vision, and Pattern Recognition, Las Vegas, USA, vol.1, pp.10-16, 2012.

[14] M. Bulacu,L. Shomaker,L. Vuupirjl. "Writer Identification Using Edge-Based Directional Features". In Proceedings of 7th Int. Conf.on Document Analysis and Recognition (ICDAR 2003), IEEE Press, 2003, 937-941p

[15] E. Zois, V. Anastassopoulos. "Morphological Waveform coding for writer identification". Pattern Recognition, Vol. 33, n.3, pp. 385-398, 2000.

[16] C. Hertel, H. Bunke. "A set of novel features for writer identification". In: AVBPA'03 Proceedings of the 4th international conference on Audio- and video-based biometric person authentication, pp. 679-687, 2003.

[17] A. Schlapbach, H. Bunke. "Off-line Handwriting Identification Using HMM Based Recognizers". In: Proceedings of the Pattern Recognition, 17th International Conference on ICPR'04 , Vol.2, 2004.

[18] J. Chen, D. Lopresti, E. Kavallieratou. "The Impact of Ruling Lines on Writer Identification". In: 12th International Conference on Frontiers in Handwriting Recognition, 2010.

[19] C. O. A. Freitas, L. S. Oliveira; F. Bortolozzi, R. Sabourin. "Brazilian Forensic Letter Database". In: Proceedings of the 11th International Conference in Frontiers of Handwritten Recogntion, Montreal: IAPR e CENPARMI-Concordia University, Vol. 1, p. 64-69, 2008.

[20] V. Vapnik. "Estimation of Dependences based on empirical data". Nauka, Moscow, 1979. English translation: Springer Verlag, New York, 1982.

SESSION

EDGE DETECTION AND ENHANCEMENT METHODS

Chair(s)

TBA

Super-Resolution using Combination of Wavelet Transform and Interpolation Based Method

Tabinda Sarwar[1], **Dr. Fahim Arif**[1] **and Naveed Khattak**[1]
[1]National University of Sciences and Technology, Islamabad, Pakistan

Abstract - *Super-resolution is a technique of producing a high-resolution (HR) image from one or more low-resolution (LR) images. Classical interpolation based magnification techniques like nearest-neighbor, bilinear and bicubic interpolation results in a larger image along with undesirable artifacts like blurring, aliasing and ringing effects. So the aim of super-resolution is to provide a larger image with good quality (quality means an image with less undesirable artifacts). Previous super-resolution techniques are based on using multiple images and learning based methods but the idea here is to use a single image in the super-resolution process. Here we have used the combination of wavelet transform and interpolation based technique to achieve the super-resolution using a single image. First the edges of the image are enhanced using wavelet transform and then the magnification is done using an interpolation based method. A comparison of this algorithm with other technique is also done to provide the quantitative and qualitative result to prove the effectiveness of the methods.*

Keywords: Super-resolution, Magnification, Edge detection, Edge enhancement, Up-sampling

1 Introduction

Super-resolution (SR) produces a high-resolution (HR) image from one or more low-resolution (LR) images, which has become a popular research area due to fact that larger images are to be filled with such information which does not directly exist in the smaller images. The simple techniques for HR image production like pixel replication or linear interpolation are not satisfactory due to the creation of visual undesirable artifacts (blurring, ringing etc) though these produce good quantitative results [1]. The images captured by low resolution imaging devices produces low quality images (blur, distort, noisy) that can be improved in two ways: enhance the resolution of the imaging device or apply super-resolution methods to improve its quality [2]. SR is widely applied in image compression and transmission, medical image analysis, face recognition and image zoom [3]. SR techniques can be divided into three categories: Interpolation based methods, reconstruction based methods and learning based methods

Interpolation based methods (e.g. [4, 9, 10, 14, 16, 17, 18, 19, 21, 22, 23]) matches the LR images with the grid point of its HR images, after which non-uniform interpolation techniques are used to obtain the pixels of HR images. Post-processing (e.g. deconvolution) can also be used to enhance HR images clarity.

Reconstruction based methods (e.g. [7, 8, 11, 13, 15 24]) uses the pair relationship between LR images and HR images. Using this relationship, linear equations that connect the pixel values of HR and LR images are obtained. By solving these linear equations, HR images are obtained.

Learning based methods (e.g. [2, 3, 5, 20]) emphasizes on learning about the structure or content of images based on relevant prior knowledge, which helps in obtaining better results. Learning based methods are somewhat dependent on the training set hence it is only suitable for such images whose training set is available.

In this paper, we propose a method that uses the combination of wavelet transform and interpolation based method to achieve super-resolution. It is well known that in super-resolution or magnification process, the loss occurs in the high-frequency region that it across the edges. Our method tries to enhance the edges using the wavelet transform so that blurriness is reduced and then algorithm for magnification is proposed so that the undesirable artifacts (ringing or aliasing effect) are minimized.

Rest of the paper is arranged as follows: In section 2 states the proposed algorithm in detail that involves two basic steps: wavelet based edge boosting and interpolation based image magnification. Image magnification is further divided into three steps: expansion, edge detection and enhancement and filling the rest of the unknown pixels (referred here as holes) in comparison with the neighbor pixels. Section 3 presents the quantitative and qualitative results in comparison with other techniques and section 4 gives some concluding remarks on the method.

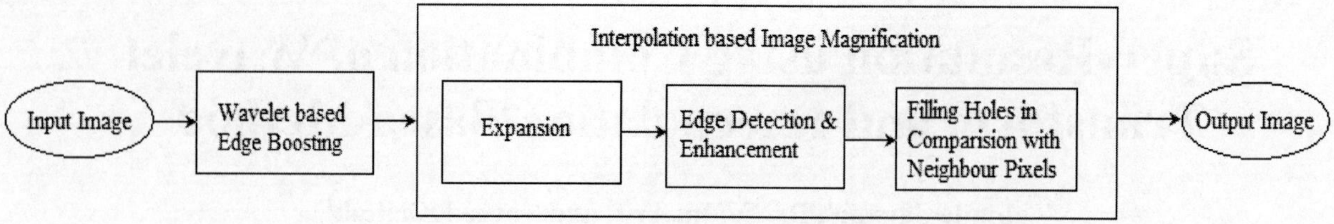

Figure 1: Flowchart of Proposed Method

2 Proposed Method

The proposed algorithm is shown diagrammatically in figure 1.

2.1 Wavelet based Edge Boosting

Wavelet transform decomposes the image into four sub-band images, namely, low-low (LL), low-high (HL), high-low (LH) and high-high (HH). Discrete Wavelet Transform (DWT) and Stationary Wavelet Transform (SWT) are two types of wavelet transform. Here we have used SWT as the sub-bands retain its size as compared to DWT, where in DWT the sub-bands size to down sampled. The three sub-bands (LL, HL and HH), represents the image edges so these are enhanced by multiplying with an appropriate threshold "Th". To calculate the value of threshold 'Th' CCC, PSNR and MSE (mentioned in section III) for 84 images were analyzed and appropriate value of 'Th' was selected. Table 1 outlines the value of "Th" that can be selected in the process.

Table 1: "Th" value for Wavelet based Edge Boosting

Image properties	Threshold value
Images with less edges (single face, animal image etc)	$2 \leq Th \leq 4$
Images with maximum edges (crowd, satellite images etc)	$1 < Th \leq 2$

The enhanced image "In" can be obtained using the inverse of SWT. This process is depicted in figure 2

2.2 Interpolation based Image Magnification

The edges of the input image are enhanced in the first step so that when the image is enlarged the blurriness is reduced. Here we have proposed a separate algorithm for image magnification instead of using any existing strategy because we want to avoid the ringing and aliasing effect.

2.2.1 Expansion

In this phase the HR image is produced from the enhanced image In(nxm) as Out(2n-1x2m-1). The mapping between the In and Out is done using equation 1

$$Out(2r-1,rc-1)=In(r,c) \quad (1)$$

Where r=1,2…..n and c=1,2,……m

Figure 3 shows the expansion and mapping process.

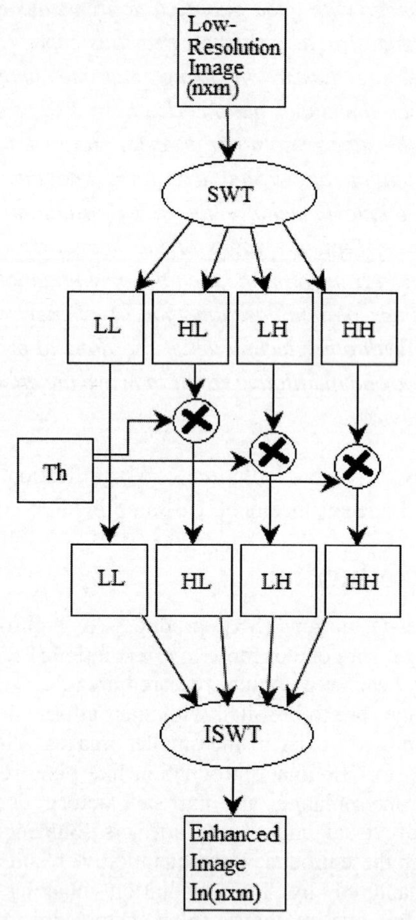

Figure 2: Block Diagram of Wavelet based Edge Boosting

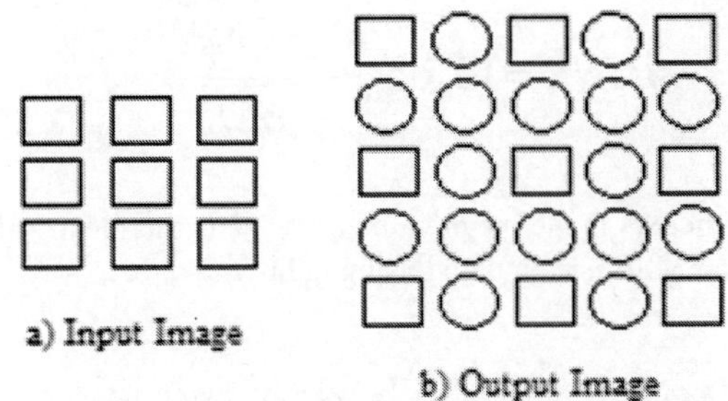

Figure 3: Expansion and Mapping of Input Image to Output Image

2.2.2 Edge Detection

At this stage, the edges in the enhanced input image are detected. Four types of edges are shown in figure 4.

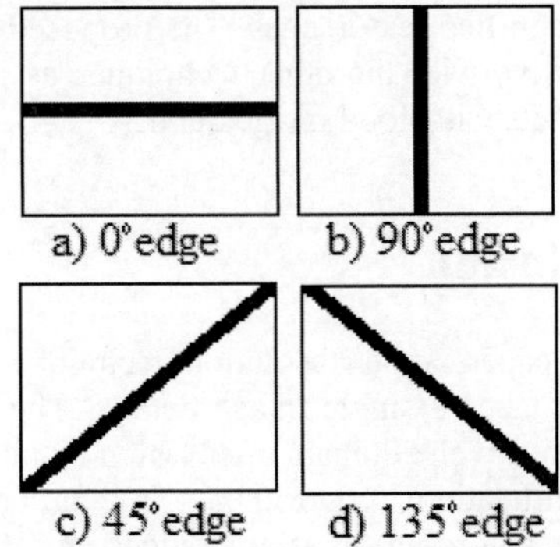

Figure 4: Four Types of Edge

For detecting the edge a threshold "T" is to be selected. There are 16 safe colors in 256 color RGB system [4]. So to calculate "T", median of 16 safe colors is calculated using the equation 2

$$M_d=(X_{n/2}+X_{n/2+1})/2 \quad (2a)$$
$$T=M_d \quad (2b)$$

Where n=16 and $X_1=0$, $X_2=1.....X_n=n-1$. After calculating "T" edge is detecting using equation 3, with reference to Out(x,y) which corresponds to an unknown pixel value

$$MAX=max[Out(x-1,y-1), Out(x-1,y+1), Out(x+1,y-1), Out(x+1,y+1) \quad (3a)$$
$$MIN=min[Out(x-1,y-1), Out(x-1,y+1), Out(x+1,y-1), Out(x+1,y+1)] \quad (3b)$$
$$|MAX-MIN|>T \quad (3c)$$

Where "max" and "min" selects the maximum and minimum intensity values from the given list respectively. This detects the existence of edge but it must be further categorize into one of the defined edges. To be classified as a 0° edge equation 4 must be satisfied.

$$Out(x-1,y-1)-Out(x-1,y+1)<T \;||\; Out(x+1,y-1)Out(x+1,y+1)<T \quad (4)$$

Similarly, 90°, 45° and 135° edge is classified using equation 5, 6 and 7 respectively.

$$Out(x-1,y-1)-Out(x+1,y-1)<T \;||\; Out(x-1,y+1)-Out(x+1,y+1)<T \quad (5)$$

$$Out(x-1,y-1)-Out(x-3,y+1)<T \;\&\&\; Out(x-3,y+1)-Out(x-1,y+1)<T \quad (6)$$

$$Out(x-3,y-1)-Out(x-1,y+1))<T \;\&\&\; Out(x-1,y+1))-Out(x-1,y-1)<T \quad (7)$$

2.2.3 Edge Enhancement

The edge enhancement technique used is different from other. Other techniques tend to find pixel "Q", shown in figure 5a, but in this technique "P1" and "P2", the pixels forming the edge are found first.

The value of "P1" and "P2" are calculated using the equation 8 after the classification of edge into one of the defined types because the intensity value of "T1", "T2" and "T3" depends on the type of edge.

$$P1=T1+T2/2 \quad (8a)$$

$$P2=T2+T3/2 \quad (8b)$$

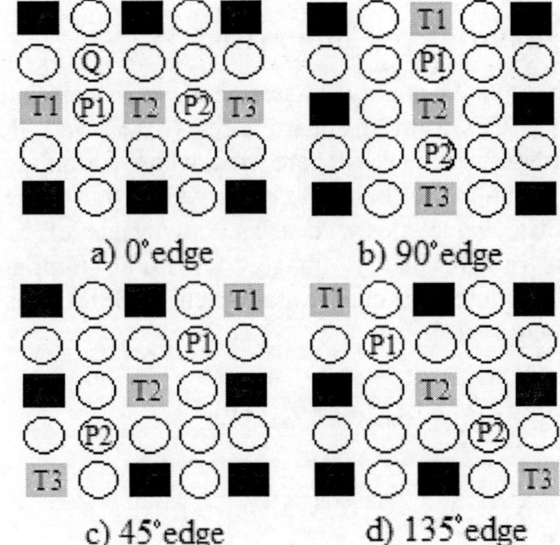

Figure 5: Edge Representation in Matrices

2.2.4 Fill the Holes in Comparison with Neighbor Pixels

The remaining unknown pixels are found iteratively using equation 2 from one of the neighbors relationship shown in figure 6(a or b). The reason for using median (equation 2) of neighbor pixels instead of average is that noise, extreme low or high value, are also averaged thus infecting the output pixels. But as median takes the midpoint of the values so in this way noise doesn't infect the pixels.

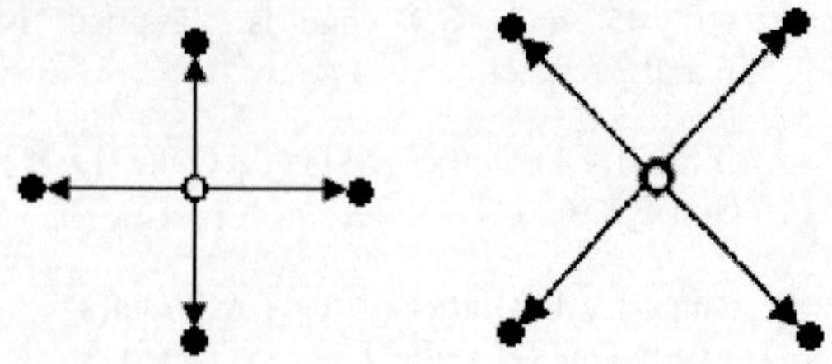

Figure 6: Pixel Neighborhood of Central Hole

3 Experimental Results

The proposed method was compared against bilinear (BL), bicubic (BC), cubic spline interpolation [14], DCC [17], DFDF [16], NEDI [22] and ICBI [9].

3.1 Qualitative Comparison

Figure 7 and 8 presents the visual comparison of the proposed techniques with other mentioned techniques. The "Th" value used in both figure is 4. It can clearly be seen that the edge are much sharper in the proposed methodology.

3.2 Quantitative Comparison

For image quality assessment cross-correlation coefficient (CCC), mean-square error (MSE) and Peak Signal-to-Noise ratio (PSNR) are used, whose formulas are given in equation 9, 10 and 11 respectively. High value of PSNR, CCC value closer to 1 and low value of MSE represents good quality image. Structural Similarity (SSIM) is not used for quality assessment as SSIM fails in blurred images [23].

$$CCC = \frac{\sum_m \sum_n (A_{mn} - \bar{A})(B_{mn} - \bar{B})}{\sqrt{\left(\sum_m \sum_n (A_{mn} - \bar{A})^2\right)\left(\sum_m \sum_n (B_{mn} - \bar{B})^2\right)}} \quad (9)$$

$$PSNR = 10\log_{10}\frac{(2^n - 1)^2}{\sqrt{MSE}} \quad (10)$$

Where $\bar{A}$ is the mean value of A, $\bar{B}$ is the mean value of B and MSE is calculated using (11).

$$MSE = \frac{1}{MN}\sum_{i=1}^{M}\sum_{j=1}^{N}(x(i,j) - y(i,j))^2 \quad (11)$$

For fairness of comparison study, we selected 84 images on which the mentioned methods were applied but due to the limited space only six images are used, which are shown in figure 9.

Table 2, 3 and 4 lists the CCC, PSNR (db) and MSE values of 2 times magnified test images. The proposed method is quite competitive with the other techniques as it provides consistent results with good image quality.

4 Conclusion

In this paper, super-resolution technique has been proposed that takes a single image details. The edges are boosted first in wavelet domain after which an interpolation based magnification algorithm is proposed. In magnification algorithm, first the edges are found and enhanced (edges are enhanced in a way that the unknown pixels that are a part of the edge, gets the value of the edge) after which the remaining unknown pixels (holes) are filled in correspondence with the neighborhood pixels. This method is applied to the grayscale images only. After the detail experimentation, this technique produces artifacts free HR image and its results (both quantitative and qualitative) are comparable with other well known techniques as mentioned in the paper.

This work can be extended in a way that instead of manually selecting the value of threshold (mentioned in section II), an algorithm can be devised that calculates the value of this threshold based on the input image

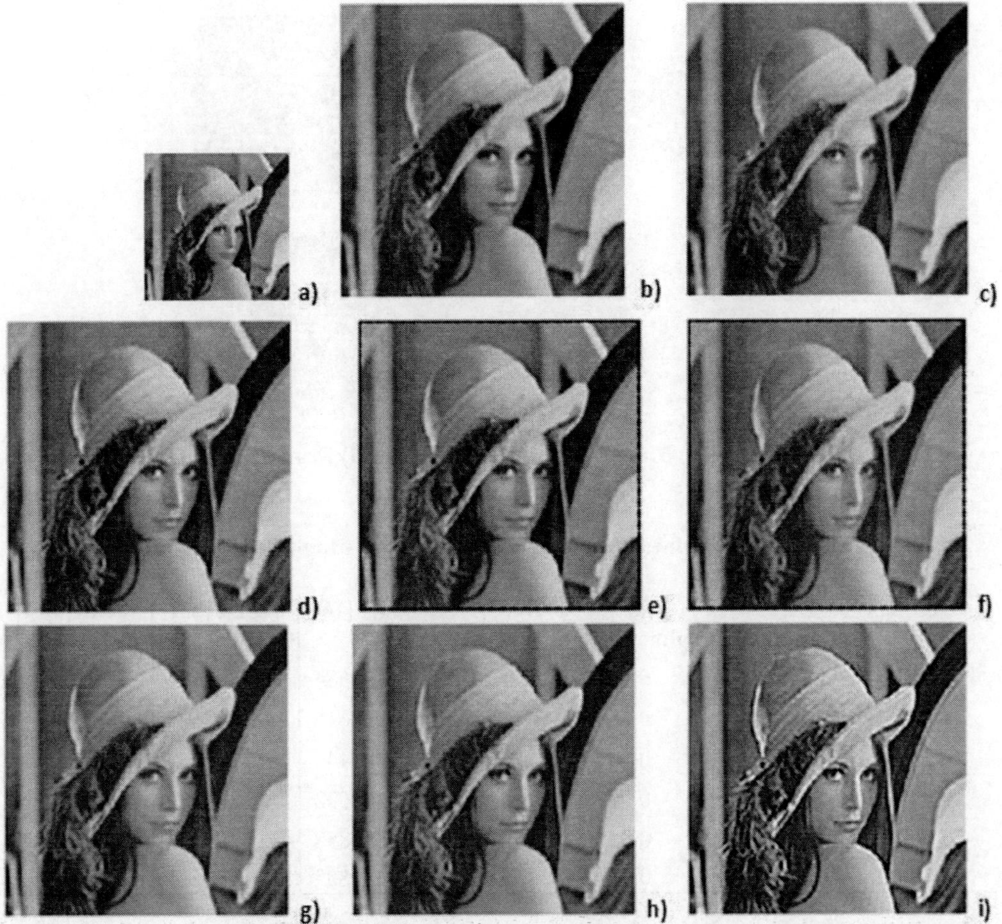

Figure 7: 2x Magnification Result Comparison a)Original LR Image b) Bilinear c) Bicubic d)Cubic Spline[14] e) DCC[1] f) DFDF[16] g) NEDI[22] h) ICBI[9] i) Proposed Method

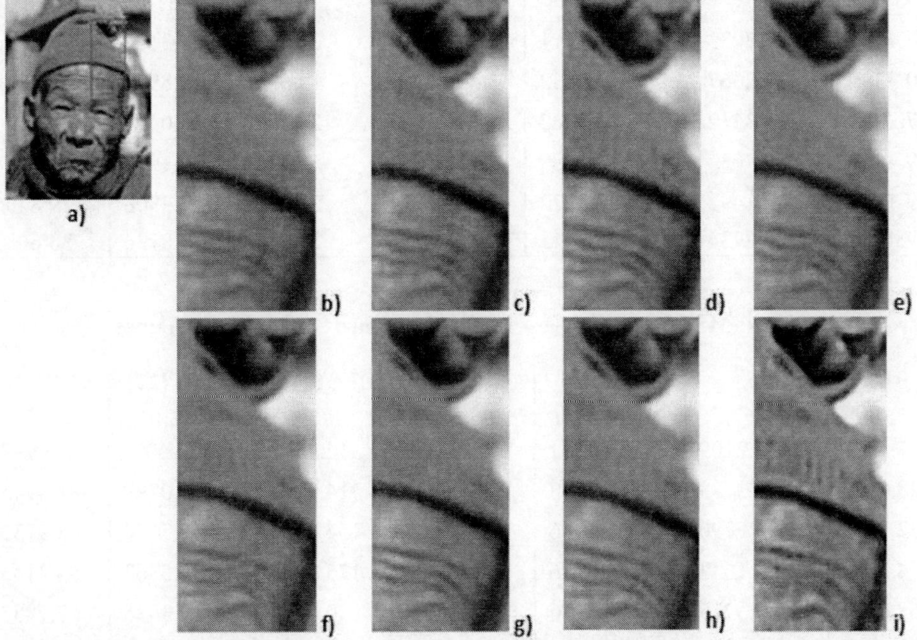

Figure 8: 2x Magnification Result Comparison a)Original LR Image b) Bilinear c) Bicubic d)Cubic Spline[14] e) DCC[1] f) DFDF[16] g) NEDI[22] h) ICBI[9] i) Proposed Method

Figure 9: Test Images a) Mouse b) Building c) Flower d) Frame e) Face f) Parrot

Table 2: CCC Values of Test Images in Figure 8 Magnified 2 Times

Image	BL	BC	Cubic Spline [14]	DCC[1]	DFDF[16]	NEDI [22]	ICBI[9]	Proposed Method
Mouse	0.9836	0.9843	0.9639	0.9643	0.9584	0.9654	0.9584	0.9865
Building	0.899	0.9046	0.8669	0.8595	0.8618	0.8685	0.9105	0.9116
Flower	0.9569	0.9658	0.9491	0.9475	0.9449	0.9042	0.9656	0.9658
Frame	0.9792	0.9802	0.9809	0.9503	0.9532	0.9552	0.9806	0.9809
Face	0.9924	0.993	0.9865	0.985	0.9858	0.9867	0.9928	0.9933
Parrot	0.9835	0.9863	0.9792	0.981	0.9809	0.981	0.9878	0.9881

Table 3: PSNR (db) Values of Test Images in Figure 8 magnified 2 Times

Image	BL	BC	Cubic Spline [14]	DCC[1]	DFDF[16]	NEDI [22]	ICBI[9]	Proposed Method
Mouse	27.4697	27.7033	24.1111	28.1896	23.1893	24.3102	27.8710	28.2870
Building	20.9383	21.2067	19.9832	20.3759	19.6218	19.8971	21.3304	21.6003
Flower	27.2883	28.3612	26.3007	26.1683	26.2870	26.0497	28.4720	28.5162
Frame	29.4651	29.7037	26.1488	24.8384	25.7268	26.1910	28.9058	29.7970
Face	29.7994	30.1492	27.3122	26.6811	27.0067	27.3968	29.8406	30.3094
Parrot	29.4470	30.2734	28.4843	28.3896	28.6546	28.8726	30.6682	30.8443

Table 4: MSE Values of Test Images in Figure 8 magnified 2 Times

Image	BL	BC	Cubic Spline [14]	DCC[1]	DFDF[16]	NEDI [22]	ICBI[9]	Proposed Method
Mouse	117.3565	111.2109	254.3151	258.4287	314.4502	242.9160	106.9997	97.2261
Building	528.0158	496.3733	581.1778	556.6331	714.9913	671.0799	482.4345	453.3664
Flower	122.3640	95.5790	153.6066	158.3602	154.0916	162.7454	93.9732	92.2273
Frame	74.1256	70.1633	159.0726	215.0986	175.3084	157.5362	84.3145	68.6716
Face	68.6334	63.3235	121.6916	140.7258	130.5614	119.3436	67.9853	61.0301
Parrot	74.4347	61.5370	92.9084	94.9553	89.3342	84.9609	56.1903	53.9572

5 Reference

[1] C. Sasi Varan, A. Jagan, Jaspreet Kaur, Divya Jyoti, Dr. D. S. Rao, Image Quality Assessment Techniques pn Spatial Domain, International Journal of Computer Science and Technology, volume 2, Issue 3, September 2011

[2] Shaofeng Chen, Hanjie Gong, Cuihua Li, Super-Resolution from a Single Image Based on Self-Similarity, International Conference on Computational and Information Science, 2011

[3] Huahua Chen, Baolin Jiang, Weiqiang Chen, Image Super-Resolution based on Patches Structure, 4th International Congress on Image and Signal Processing, 2011

[4] Muhammad Sajjad, Naveed Khattak and noman Jafri, Image Magnification Using Adaptive Interpolation by Pixel Level Data-Dependent Geometrical Shapes, International Journal of Computer Science and Engineering Volume 1 Number 2, 2007

[5] Jianhong Li and Xiaocui Peng, Single-Frame Image Super-Resolution through Gradient Learning, IEEE International Conference on Information Science and Technology, 2012

[6] He He and Wan-Chi Siu, Single Image Super-Resolution using Gaussian Process Regression, IEEE Computer Vision and Pattern Recognition Page no. 449-456, 2011.

[7] Yu-Wing Tai, Shuaicheng Liu, Micheal S. Brown, Stephen Lin, Super Resolution using Edge Prior and Single Image Detail Synthesis, IEEE Conference on Computer Vision and Pattern Recognition, 2010

[8] Wenze Shao, Zhihui Wei, Efficient Image Magnification and Applications to Super-Resolution Reconstruction, IEEE International Conference on Mechatronics and Automation, China, 2006

[9] Andrea Giachetti and Nicola Asuni, Fast Artifacts-Free Image Interpolation, Proceedings of British Machine Vision Conference, 2008

[10] Munib Arshad Chughtai and Naveed Khattak, An Edge Preserving Adaptive Anti-aliasing Zooming Algorithm with Diffused Interpolation, IEEE Proceedings of the 3rd Canadian Conference on Computer and Robot Vision, 2006

[11] Qi Shan, Zhaorang Li, Jiaya Jia, Chi-Keung Tang, Fast Image/Video Upsampling, ACM Transactions on Graphics, Volume 27, No. 5, Article 153, December 2008

[12] Hasan Demirel, Gholamreza Anbarjafari, Image Resolution Enhancement by Using Discrete and Stationary Wavelet Decomposition, IEEE Transaction on Image Processing, Volume 20. No. 5, May 2011

[13] Andrea Giachetti and Nicola Asuni, Real Time Artifact-Free Image Upscaling, IEEE Transactions on Image Processing, Volume 20, Issue 10, October 2011

[14] Jan Mihalik, Jozef Zavacky, Igor Kuba, Spline Interpolation of Image, Radioengineering, Volume 4, No. 1, 1995

[15] Dong Zhang and Cunxie Xie, A New Method for Super-resolution Reconstruction, Computational Engineering in Systems Applications, Volume 1 Page no. 65 – 67, October 2006

[16] Lei Zhang and Xiaolin Wu, An Edge Guided Image Interpolation Algorithm via Directional Filtering and Data Fusion, IEEE Image Processing, IET, Volume 15, Issue 8 Page 2226 - 2238, August 2006

[17] Dengwen Zhou, Xiaoliu Shen, Image Zooming Using Directional Cubic Convolution Interpolation, IEEE Image Processing, IET, Volume 6, Issue 6 Page 627 – 634, August 2012

[18] Ning Xu, Yeong-Taeg Kim, An Image Sharpening Algorith for High Magnification Zooming, IEEE International Conference on Consumer Electronics, Page no. 27-28, January 2010

[19] Huda Nawaz, Image Zooming Using Wavelet Transform, International Conference on System and Simulation in Engineering, Spain, December 2006

[20] Daniel Glasner, Shai Bagon, Michal Irani, Super-Resolution from a Single Image, IEEE 12th International Conference on Computer Vision, 2009

[21] Weizhong Su, Rabab K. Ward, An Edge-based Image Interpolation Approach Using Symmetric Biorthogonal Wavelets Transform, IEEE 8th Workshop on Multimedia Signal Processing, 2006

[22] Xin Li, Michael T. Orchard, New Edge-Directed Interpolation, IEEE Transactions on Image Processing, Volume 10, No. 10, October 2001

[23] Jinjun Wang, Yihong Gong, Fast Image Super-Resolution Using Connected-Component Enhancement, IEEE International Conference on Multimedia and Expo, 2008

[24] Bryan S. Morse, Duane Schwartzwald, Image Magnification Using Level-Set Reconstruction, IEEE Computer Society Conference on Computer Image Magnification Using Level-Set Reconstructionisision and Pattern Recognition, 2001

[25] R.C. Gonzalez and R.E. Woods, Digital Image Processing, Addison-Wesley, 1993

Efficient Edge-Forming Procedures for Real-Time Image Interpolation

Jamaris Moore[1], Yielin Um[2], and Seongjai Kim[3]
[1]Department of Mathematics and Statistics, Mississippi State University
Mississippi State, MS 39762-5921 USA Email: jdm570@msstate.edu
[2]Tabor Academy, 66 Spring Street, Marion, MA 02738 USA Email: yielin202@gmail.com
[3]Department of Mathematics and Statistics, Mississippi State University
Mississippi State, MS 39762-5921 USA Email: skim@math.msstate.edu (Contact Author)

Abstract—*This article is concerned with efficient edge-forming procedures for real-time image interpolation. Conventional linear interpolation methods are known to easily introduce interpolation artifacts such as aliasing distortions, image blur, and/or the checkerboard effect; but mostly on edges or fast-transition regions. Thus the resulting image can be further improved by applying an effective edge-forming procedure, as a post-process, without introducing a serious computational burden. The article investigates two different post-processing algorithms: a gradient-driven edge-directed weighting method and a curvature-driven interpolation method. The algorithms are compared in both interpolation quality and computational efficiency. The curvature-driven post-process has proved superior to the gradient-driven algorithm and efficient enough to be applicable for real-time image interpolation. Various numerical examples are presented to prove the claim.*

Keywords: Image interpolation, real-time processing, curvature interpolation method (CIM), edge-directed interpolation, inverse-distance weighting (IDW) method.

1. Introduction

Digital images are often to be resampled for various tasks such as image generation, compression, visualization, and zooming. Image resampling is necessary for every geometric transform of discrete images, except shifts over integer distances or rotations about multiples of 90 degrees. Image resampling consists of two basic steps: interpolation and evaluation (sampling). Image interpolation turns a discrete data into a continuous function and has been widely applied in image processing, computer vision, and communication [1], [2], [3].

There are various interpolation methods proposed in the literature. These methods are traditionally characterized by two kinds: linear and nonlinear ones. For linear methods, diverse interpolation kernels (polynomials) of finite size have been introduced as approximations of the *ideal* interpolation kernel (the sinc function) which is spatially unlimited; see [4], [1], [2], [5]. However, the linear methods perform the interpolation independently of the image content and therefore they may interpolate images crossing edges, which introduces artifacts such as aliasing distortions, image blur, and/or the checkerboard effect. Nonlinear interpolation methods have been suggested in order to reduce the artifacts of linear methods [6], [7], [8]. The major step in the nonlinear methods is to either fit the edges with some templates or predict edge information for the high resolution (HR) image from the low resolution (LR) one statistically. These edge-directed methods may result in sharper interpolated images, but they are computationally expensive and occasionally suffer from severe visual degradation (e.g., bumpy visual impression) in fine texture regions.

Recently, partial differential equation (PDE)-based methods have been introduced to constrain continuity of edges and reconstruct appropriate sharp edges through iterations [9], [10], [11], [12], beginning from an image interpolated by a conventional interpolation method. Most of these PDE-based interpolation methods reproduce sharp edges without checkerboard effects; however, they tend to weaken fine structures in the image, mostly because PDE-based diffusion processes cannot preserve fine structures in a desirable level.

In this article, we study efficient edge-forming procedures applicable for real-time image zooming. Note that the linear methods introduce their artifacts mostly on edges or fast-transition regions. Thus our idea is simple: (1) Magnify the image by using a simple and fast interpolation method such as the bilinear method and (2) apply a post-process only on edges in order to eliminate or significantly reduce the artifacts there. For the post-process, we will investigate two different algorithms: a gradient-driven edge-directed weighting method and a curvature-driven interpolation method such as the curvature interpolation method (CIM) [11].

Section 2 presents a brief review on the CIM. In Section 3, the two post-processing procedures are presented in detail. Section 4 gives numerical experiments for the post-processing procedures. Conclusions are drawn in Section 5.

2. Preliminaries

This section presents a brief review on curvature interpolation method (CIM). See review papers [1], [2], [5] for various linear interpolation methods.

The CIM for image zooming begins with a selection of a curvature-related term which measures curving of image surface appropriately. The PDE-based models that employ the (mean) curvature itself as the smoothing operator (e.g., the TV model [13]) are known to have a tendency to converge to a piecewise constant image. Such a phenomenon is called the *staircasing*. Thus the curvature would better be replaced by a curvature-related diffusion operator $\mathcal{K}$ which is more effective and convenient. In this article, we adopt the following gradient-weighted curvature

$$\mathcal{K}(u) = -|\nabla u|\, \nabla \cdot \Big(\frac{\nabla u}{|\nabla u|}\Big). \tag{1}$$

With an appropriate numerical realization, the above generalized curvature must be a measurement of curving of the image surface that holds desirable properties and is more convenient to handle than the mean curvature itself.

Let Ω and $\widetilde{\Omega}$ be the original LR image domain and its α-times magnified HR image domain, $\alpha > 1$, respectively; and $\widetilde{u}$ denote the HR image, the α-times magnification of an LR image u. Then we should have

$$u(\mathbf{x}) = \widetilde{u}(\widetilde{\mathbf{x}}), \quad \widetilde{\mathbf{x}} = \alpha \mathbf{x},$$

where $\mathbf{x} = (x, y)$ and $\widetilde{\mathbf{x}} = (\widetilde{x}, \widetilde{y})$ are the coordinates of the LR and HR images, respectively. Let $\nabla_{\mathbf{x}}$ and $\nabla_{\widetilde{\mathbf{x}}}$ be the gradient operators in the LR and HR coordinates. Since $\nabla_{\mathbf{x}} = \alpha \nabla_{\widetilde{\mathbf{x}}}$, the scaling factor between the gradient-weighted curvatures on Ω and $\widetilde{\Omega}$ becomes α^2. That is,

$$|\nabla_{\mathbf{x}} u|\, \nabla_{\mathbf{x}} \cdot \Big(\frac{\nabla_{\mathbf{x}} u}{|\nabla_{\mathbf{x}} u|}\Big) = \alpha^2\, |\nabla_{\widetilde{\mathbf{x}}} \widetilde{u}|\, \nabla_{\widetilde{\mathbf{x}}} \cdot \Big(\frac{\nabla_{\widetilde{\mathbf{x}}} \widetilde{u}}{|\nabla_{\widetilde{\mathbf{x}}} \widetilde{u}|}\Big). \tag{2}$$

Let $\widehat{\Omega}^0$ denote the set of pixel points in $\widetilde{\Omega}$ which can be expressed as $\alpha\mathbf{p}$, where $\mathbf{p}$ is a pixel point in Ω. Then the CIM [11] can be outlined as follows.

I. *Compute the generalized curvature of the given LR image* v^0*:*

$$\mathcal{K} = \mathcal{K}(v^0) \quad \text{on } \Omega. \tag{3}$$

II. *Interpolate* $\mathcal{K}$ *to obtain* $\widehat{\mathcal{K}}$ *on* $\widetilde{\Omega}$.

III. *Solve, for* u *on* $\widetilde{\Omega}$*, the following constrained problem*

$$\mathcal{K}(u) = \frac{1}{\alpha^2}\widehat{\mathcal{K}}, \quad u|_{\widehat{\Omega}^0} = v^0. \tag{4}$$

In the CIM, the generalized curvature measured from the original LR image is interpolated and incorporated as an explicit driving force for the *same* generalized curvature model defined on $\widetilde{\Omega}$. The driving force would help the model construct the HR image more effectively, enforcing the resulting image to satisfy the given curvature profile. It has been numerically verified [11] that the image construction of CIM is satisfactory except for a slight texture-oversmoothing; it produces images of clear and sharp edges. This article employs the CIM as an effective post-processing algorithm over edges.

The CIM sketched in (3)–(4) can be discretized effectively by employing the numerical schemes studied in [11]. A numerical realization of the CIM can be formulated as follows.

$$\begin{array}{ll}
\text{(i) } \textit{On } \Omega\textit{, evaluate the coefficient matrix } A & \\
\quad \textit{and the curvature } K \textit{ for given image } \mathbf{v}^0\textit{:} & \\
\quad\quad A\mathbf{v}^0 \approx \mathcal{K}(v^0), \quad K = A\mathbf{v}^0 & \\
\text{(ii) } \textit{Apply a linear method to zoom } A \textit{ and } K\textit{:} & \\
\quad\quad A \to \widehat{A}, \quad K \to \widehat{K} & \\
\text{(iii) } \textit{On the HR image domain } \widetilde{\Omega}\textit{, solve for } \mathbf{u}\textit{:} & \\
\quad\quad \widehat{A}\mathbf{u} = \dfrac{1}{\alpha^2}\widehat{K}, \quad \mathbf{u}|_{\widehat{\Omega}^0} = \mathbf{v}^0 &
\end{array} \tag{5}$$

Here the matrix $\widehat{A}$ is diagonally dominant and its main diagonal entries are all 4; see [11] for details. In order to solve (5.iii) efficiently, a Lagrange multiplier can be introduced to reformulate the problem as

$$\widehat{A}\mathbf{u} = \frac{1}{\alpha^2}\widehat{K} + \beta(\mathbf{v}^0 - \mathbf{u}), \tag{6}$$

or equivalently

$$(\widehat{A} + \beta I)\mathbf{u} = \frac{1}{\alpha^2}\widehat{K} + \beta\mathbf{v}^0, \tag{7}$$

where I denotes the identity matrix and β is the Lagrange multiplier which is positive on $\widehat{\Omega}^0$ and zero elsewhere. Now, (7) can be solved by a relaxation method such as the Richardson iterative method or the Jacobi iteration.

Note that the constraint in (5.iii) is barely operative for a non-integer magnification factor α. We may ignore the constraint (or equivalently, set $\beta \equiv 0$), particularly when the CIM is used as a post-process which updates the image values on fast-transition regions only.

3. Edge-Forming Methods

This section presents edge-forming interpolation methods to be utilized as post-processes. We will begin with general remarks on interpolation methods.

3.1 General remarks

Most interpolation methods (in particular, linear methods) bring up artifacts such as image blur and the checkerboard effect, when the image content shows fast-transition regions such as discontinuities and edges. Nonlinear interpolation methods have been suggested to reduce the artifacts of linear methods [6], [8]. However, these nonlinear methods are often computation-intensive and they can be one to two order more expensive than linear methods for 2D images. Furthermore, they may become ineffective in the estimation of the edge orientation for the class of edge models with fine scales, e.g., tightly packed edges that can be commonly found in the texture patterns [8].

In order to overcome the drawbacks of nonlinear methods and to accurately restore clear and sharp edges without introducing a high computational burden, we may develop effective post-processing methods to be applied on edges only. This section details two post-processing algorithms: a curvature-based procedure and a gradient-based method. Such post-processing algorithms need to detect discontinuities and edges in the image. Since they do not require a precise recognition of the edges, the edge detection can be simply carried out as follows.

- Compute the gradient magnitude of v^0, utilizing the Sobel difference operator:

$$G_m \approx |\nabla v^0|. \tag{8}$$

- Select a threshold T to determine edges E:

$$E = (G_m >= T), \tag{9}$$

where the comparison operation in the right side returns 1 at every pixel where the gradient magnitude is greater than or equal to T. In practice, the threshold T can be set slightly larger than (more specifically, twice) the arithmetic average of the gradient magnitude G_m.
- Interpolate E to get $\widetilde{E}$ on the HR domain $\widetilde{\Omega}$. The interpolation can be carried out by a simple interpolation method such as the bilinear method.

3.2 The CIM post-processing

An efficient edge-forming procedure can be formulated by applying the CIM on edges ($\widetilde{E} > 0$). This requires to apply (7) on edges to update image values. However, due to the involved interpolation operations in (5), the constructed surface may have image values different from those in the corresponding LR grid points. A natural remedy for this drawback is to update image values recursively by utilizing the difference between the LR image and the last updated image projected to the LR grid. In the following, $\check{\mathbf{u}}_{k-1}$ is the zoom-out of $\mathbf{u}_{k-1}$ defined on the LR grid and the subscript E denotes the edges in the indicated domain.

Initialize $\mathbf{u}_0 = 0$, on the HR image edges $\widetilde{\Omega}_E$
Select a tolerance $\tau > 0$
For $k = 1, 2, \cdots$
(i) Downsize $\mathbf{u}_{k-1}$ to get $\check{\mathbf{u}}_{k-1}$ on Ω_E
(ii) On LR image edges Ω_E, compute
$\mathbf{p}_k = \mathbf{v}^0 - \check{\mathbf{u}}_{k-1}$
(iii) Evaluate A and K for $\mathbf{p}_k$:
$K = A\mathbf{p}_k \approx \mathcal{K}(\mathbf{p}_k)$
(iv) Apply the bilinear method to zoom:
$A \to \widehat{A}, \quad K \to \widehat{K}$
(v) On $\widetilde{\Omega}$, solve for $\mathbf{w}_k$:
$\widehat{A}\mathbf{w}_k = \frac{1}{\alpha^2}\widehat{K}$
(vi) Update: $\mathbf{u}_k = \mathbf{u}_{k-1} + \mathbf{w}_k$
(vii) If $\|\mathbf{w}_k\|_\infty < \tau$, stop (10)

The algebraic system in (10.v) can be solved efficiently by the Richardson's iterative method: Set an initial solution $\mathbf{w}_{k,0}$ and find $\mathbf{w}_{k,m}$, $m = 1, 2, \cdots$, given by

$$\mathbf{w}_{k,m} = \mathbf{w}_{k,m-1} + r\left(\frac{1}{\alpha^2}\widehat{K} - \widehat{A}\mathbf{w}_{k,m-1}\right), \tag{11}$$

for some $r > 0$. The above iteration serves as the inner loop, while the iteration in (10) for updating $\mathbf{u}_k$ becomes the outer loop. The inner loop may start from an accurate initial value, for example, the bilinear interpolation of the misfit $\mathbf{p}_k$.

The values of the final image $\mathbf{u}_k$ are floating-point numbers and to be rounded to become the nearest integers for the 8-bit display and storage, which is called the quantization. Such a quantization process allows the image values to change by 0.5 in maximum. One may choose the tolerance $\tau = 0.5$, or slightly larger. It has been numerically verified that when $\tau = 1$, the outer iteration converges in 3–9 iterations, with the resulting image being barely different from the second iterate, for all examples we have tested. Thus two iterations in the outer loop will produce an accurate and reliable image.

Since the matrix $\widehat{A}$ is diagonally dominant and its main diagonal entries are all 4 [11], the inter iteration (11) converges for the algorithm parameter $r \leq 1/4$ and the convergence can be accelerated when the parameter is set cyclically.

It has been numerically verified that the global application of the procedure (10) results in images of a slightly better quality than when it is applied on edges only. However, the global application becomes a few times more expensive computationally, while the improvement in image quality is not so much impressive. With the strategy of edge detection presented in (8)–(9), the detected edges include 10–20% of pixels for most typical natural images. Thus the application of the CIM on edges only can improve efficiency a few times and result in images in similarly high interpolation qualities.

3.3 The gradient-driven weighting method

In this subsection, we will consider a gradient-driven edge-directed interpolation algorithm for fast-transition regions, which is a variant of the inverse-distance weighting (IDW) method [14]. The IDW method is one of the most popular interpolation algorithms particularly for arbitrarily spaced/scattered data. It is formulated as

$$u(\mathbf{x}) = \frac{\sum_k w(\mathbf{x}_k)u(\mathbf{x}_k)}{\sum_k w(\mathbf{x}_k)}, \quad w(\mathbf{x}_k) = \frac{1}{\|\mathbf{x} - \mathbf{x}_k\|^p}, \tag{12}$$

where $u(\mathbf{x})$ is the estimated value at location $\mathbf{x}$, $u(\mathbf{x}_k)$ is the image value at the point $\mathbf{x}_k$, $w(\mathbf{x}_k)$ denotes the weight for $\mathbf{x}_k$, $\|\cdot\|$ is the Euclidean norm, and p is an exponential number greater than or equal to 2. Here the summation takes place over a vicinity of $\mathbf{x}$, which often is a rectangular window centered at $\mathbf{x}$. The IDW interpolation method has

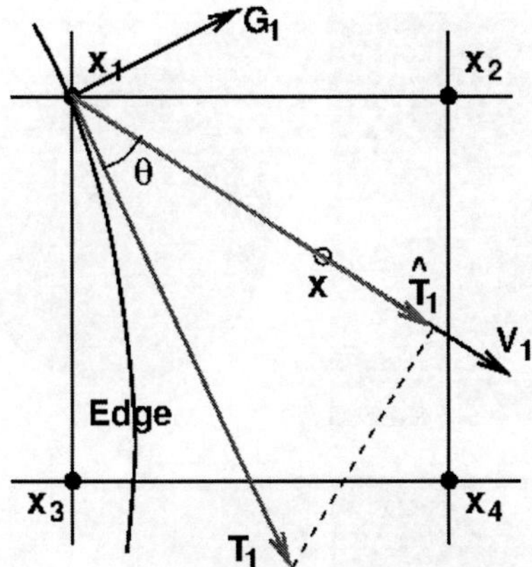

Fig. 1: Illustration of the edge-directed weighting scheme. The vector G_1 denotes the gradient at $\mathbf{x}_1$, i.e., $G_1 = G(\mathbf{x}_1)$.

been known to show serious ringing artifacts unless the window size is large enough.

In the following, we present a gradient-driven edge-directed IDW method which interpolates the image data as a weighted average of nearest four neighboring pixel values, utilizing edge-direction information on those four points. Let $G(\mathbf{x}_k) = (g_1(\mathbf{x}_k), g_2(\mathbf{x}_k))$ denote the evaluated gradient vector at the pixel point $\mathbf{x}_k$ in the LR image domain Ω.

For each pixel point $\mathbf{x} \in \widetilde{\Omega} \setminus \Omega^0$ where $\widetilde{E} > 0$

- (i) Recognize the four neighboring points in the LR image domain, $\{\mathbf{x}_k\} \subset \Omega^0$
- (ii) For each k, define the evaluation-direction vector: $V_k = \overrightarrow{\mathbf{x}_k\mathbf{x}}/\|\overrightarrow{\mathbf{x}_k\mathbf{x}}\|$
- (iii) define the unit tangential vector on $\{\mathbf{x}_k\}$: $T_k = T(\mathbf{x}_k) = (-g_{2,k}, g_{1,k})/\|(-g_{2,k}, g_{1,k})\|$
- (iv) compute the orthogonal projection of T_k to Span$\{V_k\}$: $\widehat{T_k} = \dfrac{T_k \cdot V_k}{V_k \cdot V_k} V_k = (T_k \cdot V_k)\, V_k$
- (v) and determine the weights: $w_k = \dfrac{\|\widehat{T_k}\|}{\|\mathbf{x} - \mathbf{x}_k\|^p}$
- (vi) Evaluate the image value: $u(\mathbf{x}) = \dfrac{\sum_k w_k u(\mathbf{x}_k)}{\sum_k w_k}$

(13)

Here $g_{i,k} = g_i(\mathbf{x}_k)$, $i = 1, 2$. The above algorithm deserves the following remarks.

- The edge-directed weighting scheme in (13) can be better illustrated as in Figure 1, where $\mathbf{x}$ is the evaluation point and V_1 denotes the evaluation-direction defined as in (13.ii) for the point $\mathbf{x}_1 \in \Omega^0$. Since the gradient is directing the fastest increasing direction of the function values, T_1 defined as in (13.iii) must be a unit vector tangent to the edge at $\mathbf{x}_1$.
- The length of $\widehat{T_1}$, the projection of T_1 to Span$\{V_1\}$, can be simplified as

$$\|\widehat{T_1}\| = \|(T_1 \cdot V_1)\, V_1\| = \cos\theta, \qquad (14)$$

where θ is the angle between the tangential direction of the edge (T_1) and the evaluation-direction (V_1). Thus the weight w_1 defined in (13.v) is a multiple of $\cos\theta$ and the weight in (12); it can be viewed as an edge-directed modification of the inverse-distance weight.

4. Numerical Experiments

The CIM (5) is easy to implement and has proved superior to linear interpolation methods for all synthetic and natural images we have tested. This section describes our numerical experiments. In order to investigate properties of the CIM post-processing (10) and the gradient-driven IDW method (13), sample images are downloaded from public domains as shown in Figure 2.

Below, CIM$_{E,m}$ and GIDW$_E$ denote respectively m iterations of the CIM and the gradient-driven edge-directed IDW method, applied on edges only, while Bilin indicates the bilinear method applied over the whole image domain. The inner iteration (11) is carried out with a cyclic choice of length 4; that is, the parameter r is cyclically assigned from the set $\{1/4, 1/5, 1/6, 1/7\}$. For GIDW$_E$, the gradient is evaluated from Sobel operators.

In Table 1, we present a PSNR analysis. The sample images in Figure 2 are first reduced (zoomed out) by a given factor ($\alpha = 2$ or 4), by applying the nearest neighbor interpolation method, to be used as the LR image. After magnifying the LR image by the same factor, the difference between the original image v^0 and the interpolated image u is measured by

$$\text{PSNR} = 10 \cdot \log_{10}\left(\frac{255^2}{\sum_{i,j}(v^0_{ij} - u_{ij})^2/(IJ)}\right) \text{ (dB)},$$

where the original image consists of $I \times J$ pixels. As one can see from the table, the PSNR values obtained by GIDW$_E$ post-processing are hardly better than those of the linear methods, while the CIM$_{E,2}$ has considerably improved the image quality in two iterations although it is applied on edges only.

One can improve the performance of the gradient-driven interpolation method (13) by employing more sophisticated strategies on the evaluation of the gradient and the selection of neighboring points for the evaluation of image values. When the Sobel gradient is further averaged by weighted box filters and 16 or 36 neighboring points are chosen for the evaluation of image values, the Bilin+GIDW$_E$ procedure shows better PSNR values than linear methods for most images shown in Figure 2. However, the resulting algorithm

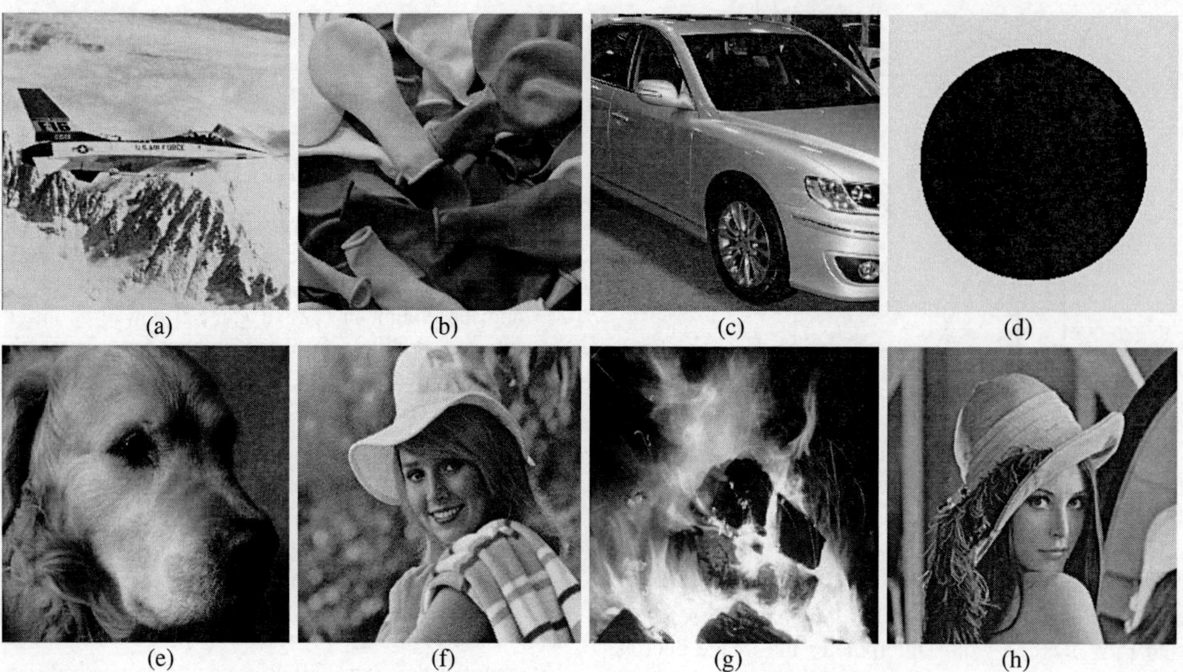

Fig. 2: Sample images: (a) Airplane, (b) Balloons, (c) Car, (d) Synthetic Disk, (e) Dog, (f) Elaine, (g) Fire, and (h) Lena. All are gray-scaled and of 256×256 pixels. The natural images are downloaded from public domains.

Table 1: PSNR analysis: magnification $\alpha = 2, 4$.

	$\alpha = 2$				$\alpha = 4$			
	Bilinear	Bicubic	Bilin+CIM$_{E,2}$	Bilin+GIDW$_E$	Bilinear	Bicubic	Bilin+CIM$_{E,2}$	Bilin+GIDW$_E$
Airplane	26.52	26.42	**26.71**	26.26	22.11	21.71	**22.23**	22.06
Balloons	32.32	32.63	**33.08**	32.17	27.12	27.22	**27.60**	27.07
Car	23.75	23.37	**23.94**	23.80	20.60	20.05	**20.73**	20.66
Disk	27.12	27.04	**27.90**	27.35	23.31	23.18	**24.05**	23.25
Dog	30.87	30.41	**30.93**	**30.93**	28.33	27.90	**28.40**	28.32
Elaine	30.01	29.81	**30.51**	29.89	25.92	25.86	**26.38**	25.94
Fire	31.03	31.15	**31.44**	30.85	25.96	25.82	**26.27**	25.90
Lena	30.20	30.54	**30.80**	29.89	24.53	24.29	**24.89**	24.57

is still inferior to Bilin+CIM$_{E,2}$ in both interpolation quality and computational efficiency, for most cases.

In order to further analyze performances of the methods, the Disk image is downsized by a relatively large factor of $\sqrt{44}\,(\approx 6.633)$ and magnified by the same factor, as shown in Figure 3. As one has expected, the bilinear method introduced a severe ringing artifact around edges. While GIDW$_E$ post-processing fails to reduce the artifact, the CIM$_{E,2}$ has cut down the oscillatory patterns significantly. Considering that the downsized image may involve certain ringing artifacts (it does indeed), the restored image by Bilin+CIM$_{E,2}$ shown in Figure 3(c) can be viewed as a very successful example.

Figure 4 depicts a numerical example for color image zooming. A part of Lena image in color (shoulder) is selected as in Figure 4(a) to be magnified by a factor of $\sqrt{23}\,(\approx 4.79583)$. The RGB components of the image are treated separately channel-by-channel. As one can see from Figures 4(b) and 4(c), the bilinear method and the bicubic method result in images in which ringing artifacts (checkerboard effects) are evident over edges. Figure 4(d) is the resulting image of the bilinear method post-processed by a single sweep of the CIM applied on edges. Traditional interpolation algorithms such as the bilinear and bicubic methods are known to easily involve artifacts such as image blur and checkerboard effects. The single iteration of the CIM post-processing has virtually eliminated the artifacts and produced a satisfactory image showing clear and sharp edges.

In order to examine efficiency of the CIM post-processing algorithm, the gray-scale Lena image in 256×256 pix-

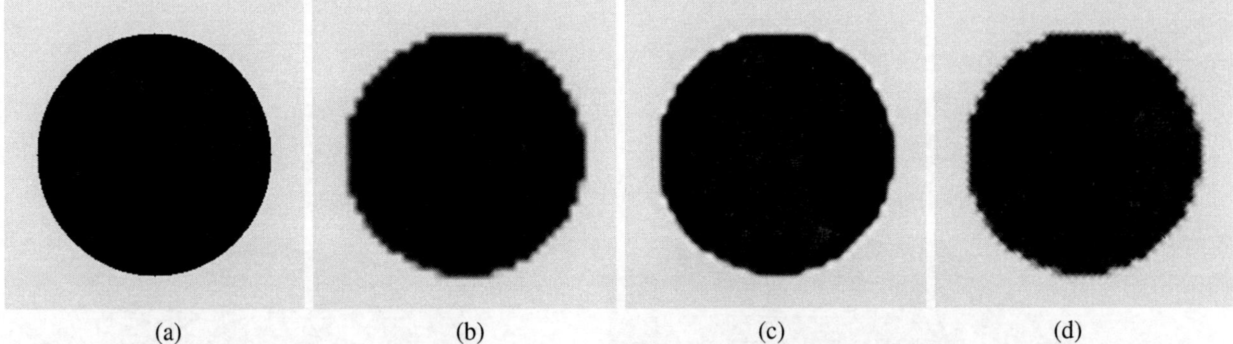

(a) (b) (c) (d)

Fig. 3: Disk: (a) The original Disk image and downsized-magnified images by a factor of $\sqrt{44}\,(\approx 6.633)$ by (b) the bilinear method, (c) Bilin+CIM$_{E,2}$, and (d) Bilin+GIDW$_E$.

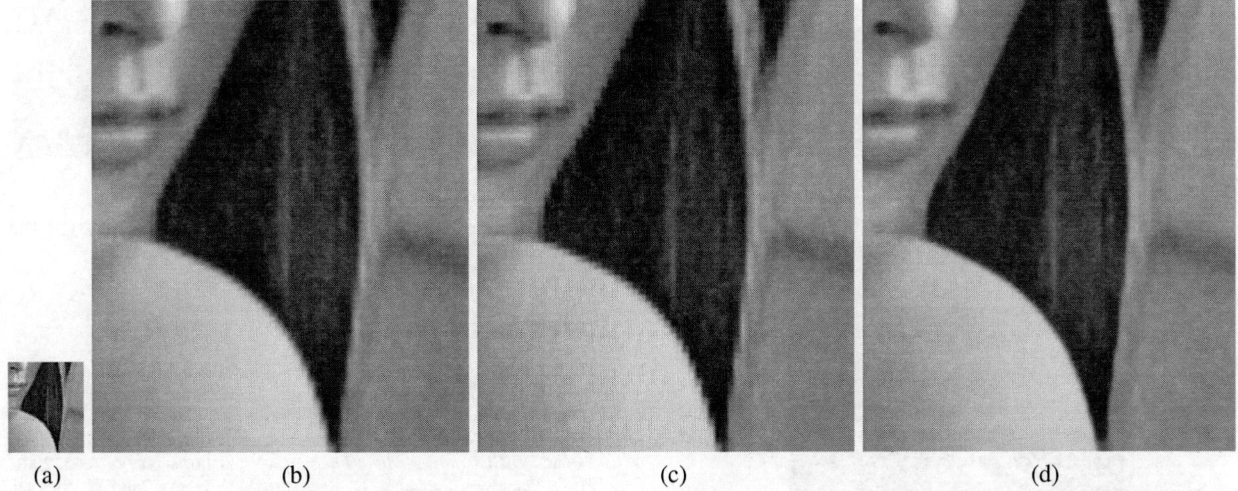

(a) (b) (c) (d)

Fig. 4: Lena shoulder: (a) The original color image in 60×70 pixels and zoomed images by a factor of $\sqrt{23}\,(\approx 4.79583)$ by (b) the bilinear method, (c) the bicubic method, and (d) Bilin+CIM$_{E,1}$.

els (shown in Figure 2(h)) is magnified by a factor of $1000/256 = 3.90625$; the resulting image includes a million pixels. For the example, the bilinear method and the bicubic method take 0.019 and 0.042 seconds, respectively, while Bilin+CIM$_{E,1}$ has finished the bilinear interpolation and updated 188,312 edge values in a total elapsed time of 0.130 seconds, on a Linux-operating 3.2 GHz laptop computer. Bilin+CIM$_{E,1}$ is a few times more expensive than the linear methods; however, it is efficient enough to produce a million-pixel image of clear and sharp edges in less than a seventh second on a laptop computer. Such an efficiency may not be achieved, unless the post-processing is applied on edges only and performed iteratively with cyclic parameters.

It is interesting to see if the CIM post-processing works for image zooming of large magnification factors. Figure 5 includes a numerical example for which the Apple image is magnified by a factor of $\sqrt{150}\,(\approx 12.247)$. As one can see from Figure 5(b), the bilinear method has introduced visible ringing artifacts to the resulting image. As for Figure 4, a single iteration of the CIM post-processing has again virtually eliminated the artifacts and resulted in a satisfactory image successfully. Figure 6 depicts the detected edges (fast-transition regions) of which nonzero pixel values count 353,028 that is approximately 16.0% of the total number of image values in high resolution (2,203,347).

5. Conclusions

Linear interpolation methods perform the interpolation independently of the image content and therefore they may interpolate images crossing edges, which can introduce serious interpolation artifacts. In order to eliminate or significantly reduce the artifacts on edges (or fast-transition regions), the article has introduced two edge-forming procedures applied as post-processes: a gradient-driven, edge-directed inverse-distance weighting (GIDW) method and a curvature-driven method, the curvature interpolation method (CIM). The procedures have been discussed in detail and compared with each other. The CIM has proved to be

(a) (b) (c)

Fig. 5: Apple: (a) The original image in 70×70 pixels and magnified images by a factor of $\sqrt{150}\,(\approx 12.247)$ by (b) the bilinear method and (c) Bilin+CIM$_{E,1}$.

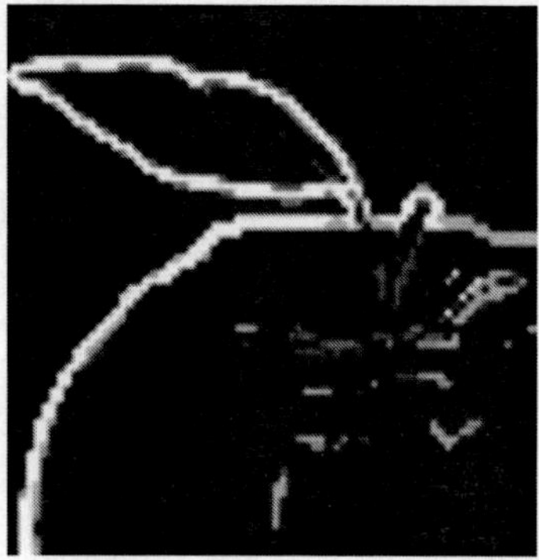

Fig. 6: Apple: The fast-transition regions, detected channel-by-channel by the schemes in (8)–(9) with the threshold T being twice the average of G_m.

superior to the GIDW method in both interpolation quality and computational efficiency. The curvature-driven method has also confirmed that it is efficient enough to be applicable for real-time image zooming, dealing with images in gray-scale or color equally efficiently for arbitrary magnification factors. Currently, the CIM is being applied for the surface reconstruction for arbitrarily spaced/scattered data and for more challenging image processing tasks including video processing.

Acknowledgment

S. Kim's work is supported in part by NSF grant DMS-1228337.

References

[1] T. Lehmann, C. Gönner, and K. Spitzer, "Survey: Interpolation methods in medical image processing," *IEEE Trans. Medical Imaging*, vol. 18, no. 11, pp. 1049–1075, 1999.

[2] ——, "Addendum: B-spline interpolation in medical image processing," *IEEE Trans. Medical Imaging*, vol. 20, no. 7, pp. 660–665, 2001.

[3] G. Penney, J. Schnabel, D. Rueckert, M. Viergever, and W. Niessen, "Registration-based interpolation," *IEEE Trans. Medical Imaging*, vol. 23, no. 7, pp. 922–926, 2004.

[4] R. Gonzalez and R. Woods, *Digital Image Processing, 2nd Ed.* Upper Saddle River, New Jersey: Prentice-Hall, Inc., 2002.

[5] P. Thévenaz, T. Blu, and M. Unser, "Interpolation revisited," *IEEE Trans. Medical Imaging*, vol. 19, no. 7, pp. 739–758, 2000.

[6] W. Carey, D. Chuang, and S. Hemami, "Regularity-preserving image interpolation," *IEEE Trans. Image Process.*, vol. 8, no. 9, pp. 1293–1297, 1999.

[7] Y. Cha and S. Kim, "The error-amended sharp edge (EASE) scheme for image zooming," *IEEE Trans. Image Process.*, vol. 16, no. 6, pp. 1496–1505, 2007.

[8] X. Li and M. Orchard, "New edge-directed interpolation," *IEEE Trans. Image Process.*, vol. 10, no. 10, pp. 1521–1527, 2001.

[9] Y. Cha and S. Kim, "Edge-forming methods for color image zooming," *IEEE Trans. Image Process.*, vol. 15, no. 8, pp. 2315–2323, 2006.

[10] ——, "Edge-forming methods for image zooming," *J. Math. Imaging and Vis.*, vol. 25, no. 3, pp. pp. 353–364, 2006.

[11] H. Kim, Y. Cha, and S. Kim, "Curvature interpolation method for image zooming," *IEEE Trans. Image Process.*, vol. 20, no. 7, pp. 1895–1903, 2011.

[12] F. Malgouyres and F. Guichard, "Edge direction preserving image zooming: A mathematical and numerical analysis," *SIAM J. Numer. Anal.*, vol. 39, pp. 1–37, 2001.

[13] L. Rudin, S. Osher, and E. Fatemi, "Nonlinear total variation based noise removal algorithms," *Physica D*, vol. 60, pp. 259–268, 1992.

[14] D. Shepard, "A two-dimensional interpolation function for irregularly-spaced data," in *Proceedings of the 1968 ACM National Conference*, 1968, pp. 517–524.

Automatic Navigation through a Single 2D Image using Vanishing Point

Geetha Kiran A[1], Murali S[2]
[1]Computer Science and Engineering, Malnad College of Engineering, Hassan, Karnataka, India
[2]Computer Science and Engineering, Maharaja Institute of Technology, Mysore, Karnataka, India

Abstract - *Image based navigation paradigms have recently emerged as an interesting alternative to conventional methods. This paper focuses on the problem of automatic navigation through Road scenes that mainly consist of single vanishing point. The algorithm infers frontier information directly from the image to navigate through Road images. The major cue to terminate the navigation is the vanishing point. The proposed algorithm has 3 major steps: First, the preprocessing techniques are applied to the given image to find the vanishing point. Second, compute the distance from the ground truth position to the vanishing point which is used as the termination point for navigation. Finally, create the navigation by cropping the image. Our approach is fully automatic, since it needs no human intervention. The approach finds applications, mainly in assisting autonomous cars, virtual walk through ancient time images and in forensics. Qualitative and quantitative experiments on nearly 150 Real-road images in different scenarios show that the proposed algorithm is more efficient and accurate.*

Keywords : canny edge detector, hough transform, vanishing point, termination point, video generation

1. Introduction

Navigation through a single 2D image is a challenging problem due to limited information from the input image. In Imaging devices, there is a trade-off between the images (snapshots) and video because of the limitation in storage capacity. Video clips need more storage space compared to images. This motivated to navigate through a single 2D image rather than storing video clips. Humans analyze variety of single image cues and act accordingly, unlike robots. The work is an attempt to make robots analyze similar to humans using single 2D image.

The task of generating video from photographs is receiving increased attention in many of the applications mainly with Road images. The application domain where the method can be applied are forensics and to assist autonomous cars by generating video from a single 2D image and assessing in advance - *how far there is a straight road*? If there is any suspected person or item in our path of journey, it could be detected prior and necessary action can be taken. We are addressing the key case where dimension of the real world object or measurement of object dimension in 2D plane is unknown. However navigation through a single image with the above constraints is very difficult because of the perspective view. Alternatively, navigation on a single image using proper ground known i.e., vanishing point could be easier. The work is carried out on outdoor images, mainly for Road scenes. We describe a unified framework for navigation through a single 2D image in lesser time. The input image may be easily acquired since no calibration target is needed or we can download Road images from internet.

This paper focuses on the automatic navigation through Road scenes that mainly consist of single vanishing point. Vanishing point is the major cue for obtaining the termination point for video generation. The approach can be used in a variety of applications, including forensics, virtual drive through the ancient images, to assist autonomous cars. It provides users with the important details available in the image while navigating.

The paper is organized as follows. In section 2 a review on the related works is highlighted. Section 3 gives description of finding the vanishing point from single view scene constraints and computing the distance from the ground truth position to the vanishing point. This is followed by the method of video generation in section 4. Implementation details are presented in section 5. Finally, some of the experimental results are presented in section 6.

2. Related Work

It is observed that some methods have been developed for detecting vanishing point on a single image, few which are directly relevant to the work are highlighted here. Techniques for estimating vanishing points can be roughly divided into two categories. One requiring the knowledge of the internal parameters of the camera and the other operates in an uncalibrated setting. A large literature exists on automatic detection of vanishing points, after Barnard [1] first introduced the use of the Gaussian Sphere as an accumulation space. He suggested that the unbounded space can be mapped into the bounded surface of the Gaussian sphere. Tuytelaars et. al. [2] mapped points into different bounded subspaces according to their coordinates. Rother [3] pointed out these methods could not preserve the original distances between lines and points. In this method, the intersections of all pairs of non-collinear lines are considered as accumulator cells instead of a parameter space. But these accumulator cells are difficult to index, searching for the maximal from the accumulator cells is slow. The simple calculation of a weighted mean of pairwise intersection is used by Caprile et. al.[4]. Researches [5-7] have used vanishing point as global constraint for road, they compute the texture orientation for each pixel and select the effective vote-points, then locate the vanishing point by using a voting procedure. Hui Kong et. al. [8-11] have proposed an adaptive soft voting scheme which is based upon a local voting region using high-confidence voters. However, there are some redundancies during the voting process and the accuracy on updating vanishing point. Murali S et. al. [12,13] have detected edges using canny edge detector and then the created edge is subjected to hough transform. The maximum votes of first N number of cells in the hough space is used for computing the vanishing point. We use the similar framework in [12-13] in our work to decide the vanishing point.

A very few Researchers have proposed different methods for navigation through a Single 2D image. Shuqiang jiang *et. al* [14] have proposed a method to automatically transform static images to dynamic video clips in mobile devices. Xian-sheng Hua *et. al* [15] developed a system named photo2video to convert a photographic series into a video by simulating camera motions. The camera motion pattern (both the key-frame sequencing scheme and trajectory/ speed control strategy) is selected for each photograph to generate a corresponding motion photograph clip. A region based method to generate a multiview video from a conventional 2-dimensional video using color information to segment an image has been proposed by Yun-Ki-Baek *et. al* [16]. Na-Eun Yang *et.al* [17] have proposed method to generate depth map using local depth hypothesis and grouped regions for 2D-to-3D conversion. The various methods of converting 2D to stereoscopic 3D images involves the fundamental, underlying principle of horizontal shifting of pixels to create a new image so that there are horizontal disparities between the original image and the new version. The extent of horizontal shift depends on the distance of the feature of an object to the stereoscopic camera that the pixel represents. It also depends on the inter-lens separation to determine the new image viewpoint.

The methods proposed by the authors for detecting vanishing points have made certain assumptions specific to the application. These artifacts are not of much importance in our work, this made us to propose a new method as proposed in [12,13], which decides the vanishing point in lesser time. Using the vanishing point, the distance from the ground truth position to the vanishing point could be computed. This helps in navigating through the single Road image.

3. Vanishing Point Detection

Images considered for modeling are perspective. In a perspective image, lines parallel in the world space appear to meet at a point called Vanishing point. Vanishing points provide a strong geometric cue for inferring information about 3 dimensional structure of a scene in almost all kinds of man-made environment. There are methods available for detecting vanishing points with known camera parameters and also with uncalibrated setting. The method described in this section requires no knowledge of the camera parameters and proceeds directly from geometric relationships. The steps involves detecting edges using canny edge technique to identify the straight lines depending upon the threshold fixed by the hough transform, compute the vanishing point using the intersection points of the lines. The above steps have been explained in the subsequent sections.

3.1 Line Determination

The given color image is converted to gray. Lines are edges of the objects and environment present in an image. These lines may or may not contribute to form the actual vanishing point. The existence of the lines are obtained by applying the canny edge detection algorithm. The versatility of the canny algorithm is to adapt to various parameters like the sizes of the Gaussian filter and the thresholds. This will allow it to be used in detecting edges of differing characteristics.

For an image as in Figure 1(a), after converting it to gray (Figure 1(b)), the edges are detected by applying Canny edge detection algorithm. A set of white pixels containing edges are obtained and the rest of the contents of the image are removed. A Canny edge detected image is shown in Figure 1(c). This image contains pixels contributing to straight lines and also other miscellaneous edges. Considering all these pixels of the edges contributing to the straight lines, Hough transformation is applied on the image. The result is shown in Figure 1(d).

(a)

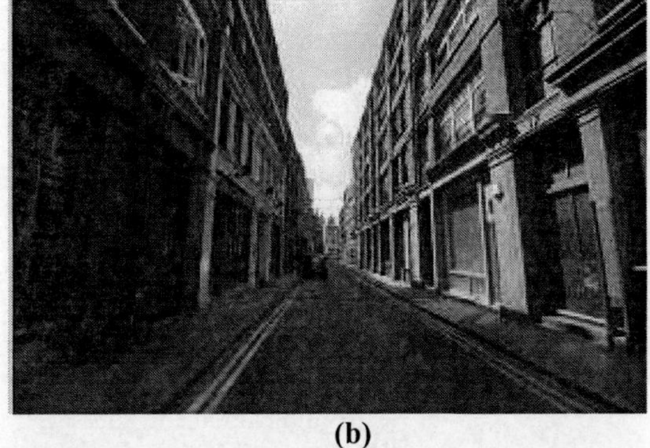
(b)

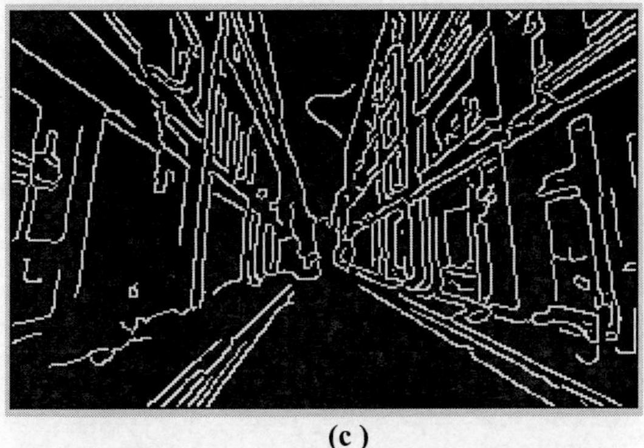
(c)

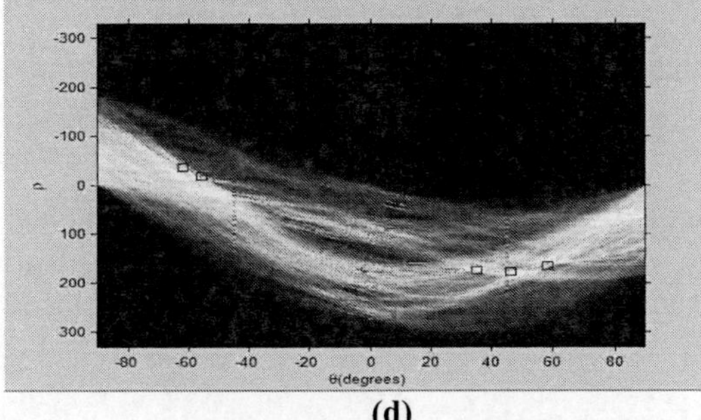

(d)

Figure 1. (a) Original Image (b) Gray Image (c) Edge detection (d) Hough transformation

As the outcome of the Hough transformation, a large number of straight lines are detected. These straight lines depend upon the threshold fixed up for the Hough transformation. Points belonging to the same straight line in the image plane have corresponding sinusoids which intersect in a single point in the polar space(Figure 1(d)). The need for calculating the number of straight lines is that there could be several straight lines in the image which intersects each other at different points in the image plane. In such case there arises a situation that more than one peak value in the polar space is obtained. Thus by selecting the number of peak values (in descending order of their votes) equal to the number of straight lines 'N' present in the image we restrict the unwanted lines which may not contribute to the real vanishing point. This reduces the computational complexity of vanishing point detection to only the number of straight lines contributing the possible vanishing point.

3.2 Intersection Point of any Two Lines

Lines drawn by Hough transformation are on edges of the object and environment in an image. These lines may or may not contribute to form the actual vanishing point. Depending upon the number of lines present in the image, the number of peaks in the Hough space is fixed up in a descending order of their occurrences. Each peak in the hough space signifies the existence of a longer edge in the image than any other points in the Hough space and hence a peak is formed. These peaks of the voted points of the hough space are calculated to find the intersection between two lines to calculate the vanishing point. Finding the intersection points for all combination of lines selecting two at a time, corresponding one (x,y) pair is obtained. The number of pairs of x and y values obtained for all combinations is given by the relation

$$Nc_2 = N!/((N-2)!*2!)$$

where N is the number of peaks selected. These (x,y) pairs are the probable vanishing points. All of them are within the vicinity of the actual vanishing point. We have taken the mean of the probable vanishing points (Figure 2(a)-blue color), since they are within the vicinity of the actual vanishing point. In our work vanishing point is used to find the distance from the ground truth position to the detected Vanishing point position. The distance obtained is used in the next section to facilitate the termination point for the navigation.

The distance of the Road identified could directly be used to decide the number of frames to be generated, generally 1:2 depends on the length and it can be varied with requirements.

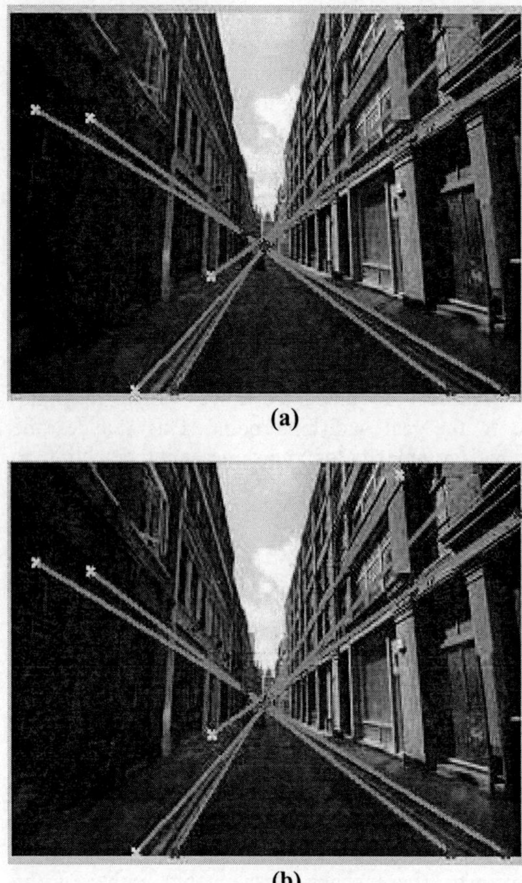

(a)

(b)

Figure 2. (a) Lines detected (white/green color), Probable vanishing points (black/blue color)
(b) Vanishing point (black/pink color)

4. Navigation through a Single Image

The information obtained from the previous section is used to navigate through a single Road image. The input for the navigation are - single 2D image, computed termination point based on the distance from the ground truth position to the detected vanishing point. Based on this strategy, the frames for navigation are generated by cropping the image based on the size of the image up to the computed distance. The input image is considered as the first frame and the image is cropped based on the size of the predefined rectangle. Then the cropped image is resized to the original image and stored in an array of images. An appropriate set of key-frames are determined for each image based on the distance computed by using vanishing point. The images obtained after cropping is given in Figure 3.

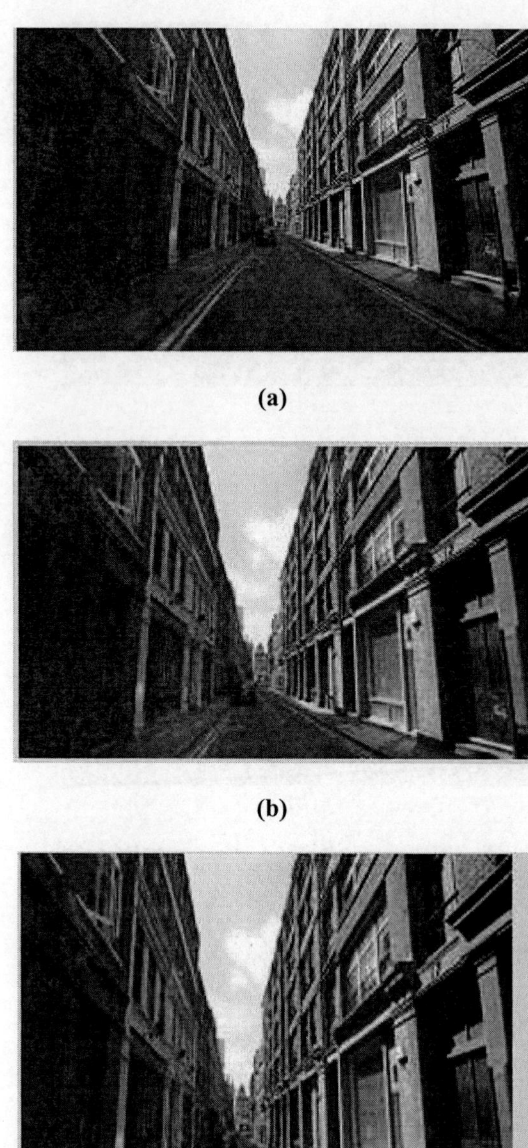

(a)

(b)

(c)

Figure 3. (a) 1st Frame (b) 40th Frame

(c) 80th Frame

Further navigation is based on the key frames stored in the array by writing the frames to the video file. This method provides vivid dynamic effect from global view to local details.

5. Implementation

Navigation through a single 2D Road image is a challenging task due to unknown z-coordinate. We have attempted to automatically navigate through a single 2D Road images based on geometric relationships. The navigation process is decomposed into two parts as follows:

- To find the distance from the ground truth position to the detected vanishing point.
- To navigate through a single Road image based on the determined path.

The entire *algorithm* of the proposed method to generate video is as below:

Step 1: Canny edge detector is applied to the normalized image which yields a binary image with only the edge information.

Step 2: The obtained image is then subjected to Hough transform.

Step 3: Select only the maximum votes of first N number of cells in the Hough space for further calculation.

Step 4: Calculate the intersection points for all combination of lines selecting two at a time. These are the probable vanishing points.

Step 5: Take the mean of the probable vanishing points.

Step 6: Find the distance from the ground truth position to the detected Vanishing point position.

Step 7: Crop the image based on the size of the image.

Step 8: Cropped image is resized to the original image and stored in an array of images.

Step 9: The steps 7 and 8 are repeated until the termination point as computed by using vanishing point.

6. Experimental Results

The algorithm is applied to a test set of nearly 150 images obtained from different real-road images in different scenarios that mainly consist of single vanishing point, we have observed that the results presented are indicative of the algorithm performance. The images used in the experimentation are downloaded from internet and few of them are self captured. The steps involves detecting edges using canny edge technique, to identify the straight lines, compute the vanishing point using the intersection points of the lines. All of them are within the vicinity of the actual vanishing point. Based on the ground truth position, we compute the distance from the ground truth position to the computed vanishing point. We also have evaluated the algorithm by manually detecting the distance from the ground truth value to the vanishing point and compared it with the distance generated by our method. Experimented images have an error distance not more than 8 pixels as shown in Chart 1.

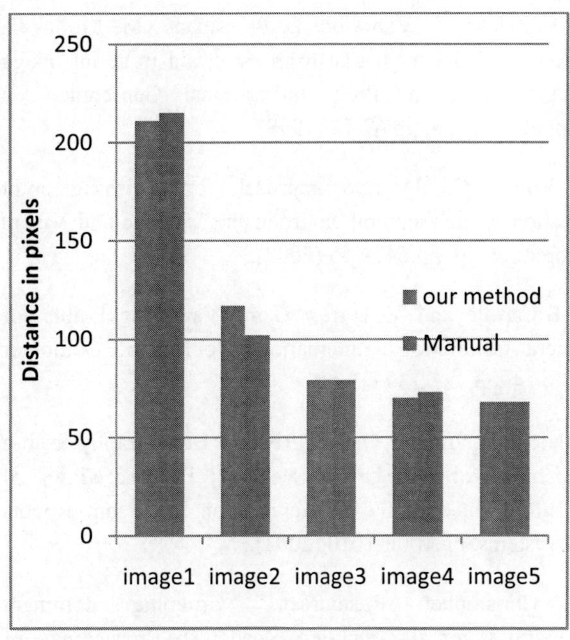

Chart 1.Comparison of vanishing point accuracy.

The first, intermediate and final frame generated by the method after finding the termination point is shown in Figure 4. We can observe the finer details in the intermediate and final frames that could be used in various applications including virtual walk through ancient time images, in forensics and in automated vehicle. The painting follows the geometric rules and also have color variations and therefore we can apply the methods developed here to have a virtual walk in the imaginary world.

7. Conclusion

An algorithm to navigate through a single 2D image is proposed and experimented for only Road Scenes. The work is experimented on nearly 150 images in difficult scenarios. This paper provides a solution to transform static single 2D image into video clips. It not only helps the users to enjoy the important details of the image but also provides a vivid viewing manner. The experimental results show that the algorithm is performing well on a number of outdoor scenes with Road. Further work may be extended to include investigating on more reliable Region Of Interest (ROI) detection techniques. Even finer details can be obtained from the key frames used in video generation. The work is done in view of assisting the automated vehicle at low cost.

References

[1] Barnard S T. "Interpreting perspective images"; Artificial Intelligence, 21, pp.435-462 (1983).

[2] Tuytelaars T, Van Gool L, Proesmans M, Moons T. "The cascaded Hough transform as an aid in aerial image interpretation"; In: Proc. International Conference on Computer Vision, pp.67-72 (1998).

[3] Rother C. "A new approach for vanishing point detection in architectural environments"; Image and Vision Computing 20, pp.647-655 (2002).

[4] B.Caprile and V Torre. "Using Vanishing Points for Camera Calibration"; International Journal of Computer Vision, 4, pp.127-139 (1990)

[5] Nicholas Simond, Patrick Rives. " Homography from a Vanishing Point in Urban Scences"; In Proceedings of IEEE/RSJ International Conference on Intelligent Robots and Systems, pp.1005-1010 (2003).

[6] Christopher Rasmussen, "Grouping dominant orientations for ill-structured Road"; In Proceedings of IEEE International Conference on Computer Vision and Pattern Recognition, pp.470-477 (2004).

[7] Christopher Rasmussen, Thommen Korah. "On-Vehicle and Aerial Texture analysis for vision-based desert Road"; In Proceedings of International Workshop on Computer Vision and Pattern Recognition, pp. 66-71(2005).

[8] Hui Kong, Jean-Yues Audibert, Jean Ponce. " Vanishing point detection for Road Detection"; In Proceeedings of IEEE Conference on Computer Vision and Pattern Recognition, pp.96-103(2009).

[9] Hui Kong, Jean-Yues Audibert. "Jean Ponce, General Road detection from a Single Image"; In Proceedings of IEEE Transactions on Image Processing, vol.19, no.8,pp.2211-2220(2010).

[10] M Nieto and L Salsgdo. "Real-time vanishing point estimation in Road sequences using adaptive steerable filter banks"; Advanced notes in Computer Science (2007).

[11] Christopher Rasmussen. " Texture-based Vanishing point voting for Road shape Estimation"; BMVC(2004).

[12] Avinash and Murali S. " A Voting scheme for Inverse Hough transform based Vanishing Point Determination"; In Proceedings of International Conference on Cognition and Recognition, Mysore, India(2005).

[13] Avinash and Murali S. " Mutiple Vanishing Point determination"; In Proceedings of IEEE International Conference on Computer Vision and Information Technology, Aurangabad, India(2007).

[14] Shuqiang Jiang and Huiying Liu and Zhao Zhao and ingming Huang and Wen Gao. " Generating video sequence from photo image for mobile screens by content analysis"; ICME, pp.1475-1478(2007).

[15] Xian-sheng Hua and Lie Lu and Hong-jiang Zhang. "Automatically Converting Photographic Series into Video"; 12th ACM International Conference on Multimedia,pp.708-715(2004).

[16] Yun-Ki Baek, Young-Ho Seo,Dong-Wook Kim and Ji-Sang Yoo. "Multiview Video Generation from 2-Dimensional video"; International Journal of Innovative Computing, Information and Control, Vol 8, Number 5(A), pp. 3135-3148 (2012).

[17] Na-Eun Yang, Ji Won Lee, Rae-Hong Park. " Depth Map Generation from a Single Image Using Local Depth Hypothesis"; 2012 IEEE ICCE ,pp.311-312,(2012).

Figure 4. (a) First Frame (b) Intermediate Frame (c) Last Frame

Implementation of SOBEL, PREWITT, ROBERTS Edge Detection on FPGA

F. Alim.Ferhat, L. Ait mohamed, O. Kerdjidj, K. Messaoudi, A. Boudjelal, S. Seddiki
Country Centre for Development of Advanced Technologies, Algiers, Algeria
{falim , laitmohamed, okerdjidj, kmessaoudi, aboudjelal, sseddiki}@CDTA.dz

Abstract - *The proposed work presents FPGA based architecture for Edge Detection using different operators of gradient: Sobel, Roberts, Prewitts. These different operators were chosen for its resistance to noise. Gray image is converted into file *.Coe format using MATLAB. The proposed gradient Edge Detection is modeled using Parallel Architecture and implemented in VHDL, then the result is reconverted by Matlab. This work is a first step in our chain of segmentation.*

Keywords: Gradient Operator, Edge Detection, Digital Image Processing, FPGA.

1 Introduction

FPGA has become an alternative for the implementation of algorithms that unique structure permitted the technology used in many applications, video surveillance and medical imaging. FPGA is an integrated circuit with a large scale that can be reprogrammed. The term "field programmable" refers to the ability to change the functioning of the device. Edge detection is one of the most in the processing of low-level image; the quality of detected contours has a very important role in the realization of complex automated computer vision/machine [1]. Many algorithms of edge detection are available in the literature and give different detection result on the same image input. Edge detection by Sobel operator is very used compared to the simple gradient operator because of its resistance to noise and facilitated its implementation. [2].

1.1 Diagram of the system of edge detection

The proposed work is represented as follows:

- Converting the image into a vector in a text file extension *.Coe using the tool MATLAB.
- Loading the file *. Coe in Rom FPGA.
- Detecting image contours with different operators of gradient Sobel, Robert, Prewitt in VHDL.
- Conversion by MATLAB of text file generated by the simulation tool ISE.

The synoptic is shown in Figure.1.

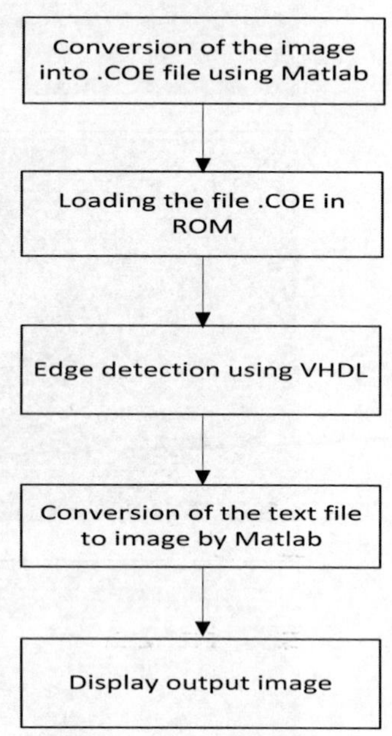

Fig 1: Synoptic of Edge detection system

2 EDGE DETECTION

Edge detection is a preliminary step in many applications of image analysis. The contours are indeed rich indices, as well as points of interest for any subsequent interpretation of the image. Contours in an image derived from:

- Discontinuities of reflectance function (texture, shadow)
- Depth discontinuities (object edges), the latter are characterized by discontinuities of the intensity function in the images.

The principle of edge detection is thus based on the study of the derivative of the intensity function from the image: the local extrema of the function gradient intensity and the zero crossings of the Laplacian. The difficulty resides in the presence of noise in the images.

2.1 Detection by gradient

This approach is based on research of image points with high gradient which corresponds to the points where the gradient magnitude is maximal. The gradient of an image I(x,y)is defined as the vector [3]

$$\vec{\nabla} I(x,y) = \frac{\partial I(x,y)}{\partial x}\vec{I}_x + \frac{\partial I(x,y)}{\partial y}\vec{I}_y. \qquad (1)$$

where: $\vec{I}_x$, $\vec{I}_y$ are a unit vector along X and Y and $\vec{\nabla}$ is the gradient is a vector which can be calculated in different ways.

In the discrete case, each component, calculated using a convolution gives the value of the gradient in any direction as shown in the following relationship:

$$\nabla_x = \frac{\partial I(x,y)}{\partial x} = I(x,y) * h_1(x,y).$$

$$\nabla_y = \frac{\partial I(x,y)}{\partial y} = I(x,y) * h_2(x,y). \qquad (2)$$

These operators can be applied to digital images "discrete case", the directional derivatives according to the horizontal and vertical directions to the site [i, j] are approximated by a simple finite differences:

$$\frac{\partial I}{\partial y} \approx \frac{\Delta I}{\Delta i} = I_i[i,j] = I[i+1,j] - I[i,j] \qquad (03)$$

$$\frac{\partial I}{\partial x} \approx \frac{\Delta I}{\Delta j} = I_j[i,j] = I[i,j+1] - I[i,j] \qquad (04)$$

The gradient magnitude is given by:

$$|\nabla I[i,j]| = \sqrt{I_j^2[i,j] + I_i^2[i,j]} \qquad (05)$$

$$|\nabla I[i,j]| \approx \max\{|I_j[i,j]|, |I_i[i,j]|\} \qquad (06)$$

$$|\nabla I[i,j]| = \frac{|I_j[i,j]| + |I_i[i,j]|}{2} \qquad (07)$$

The direction angle of the vector $\vec{\nabla} I$ at (x,y) is

$$\theta = Arc\tan\left(\frac{\nabla_y}{\nabla_x}\right) \qquad (08)$$

h1 is the convolution mask along x, and h2 the convolution mask along y.

There are various masks [4] of convolution, we give:

- Sobel operators:

$$h_1 = \begin{bmatrix} -1 & -2 & -1 \\ 0 & 0 & 0 \\ 1 & 2 & 1 \end{bmatrix} \qquad h_2 = \begin{bmatrix} -1 & 0 & 1 \\ -2 & 0 & 2 \\ -1 & 0 & 1 \end{bmatrix}$$

- Prewitt operators :

$$h_1 = \begin{bmatrix} -1 & -1 & -1 \\ 0 & 0 & 0 \\ 1 & 1 & 1 \end{bmatrix} \qquad h_2 = \begin{bmatrix} -1 & 0 & 1 \\ -1 & 0 & 1 \\ -1 & 0 & 1 \end{bmatrix}$$

- Roberts operators:

$$h_1 = \begin{bmatrix} 0 & 0 & 0 \\ -1 & 1 & 0 \\ 0 & 0 & 0 \end{bmatrix} \qquad h_2 = \begin{bmatrix} 0 & 0 & 0 \\ 0 & 1 & 0 \\ 0 & -1 & 0 \end{bmatrix}$$

3 Proposed Architecture of FPGA Implementation for Edge Detection

We used in this architecture a 3×3 convolution karnels processing 256 × 256 gray scale image.

The architecture is shown in Fig. 2.The system is divided into four modules: 3×3 pixel address generation, Memory ROM, convolution 3×3 structure and gradient operators. We have in this architecture 3 inputs and three outputs, we find a clock signal Clk, a reset signal and Sel_op signal for the selection of the gradients operators, Dout1, Dout2, Dout3 are the results of edge detection with different operators (Sobel, Robert, Prewitt].

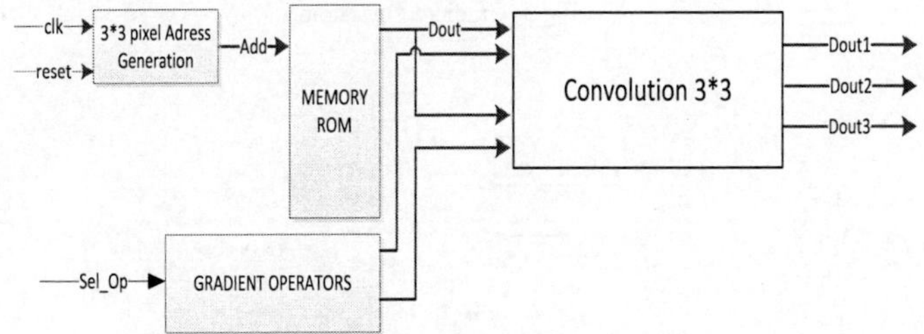

Fig 2: Architecture

The function and structure of each module are as follows:

- The structure of 3×3 pixel address generation module is shown in Fig.3. This module allows us to generate destine 9 addresses to the ROM for the operation of convolution Kernels [4] [5].

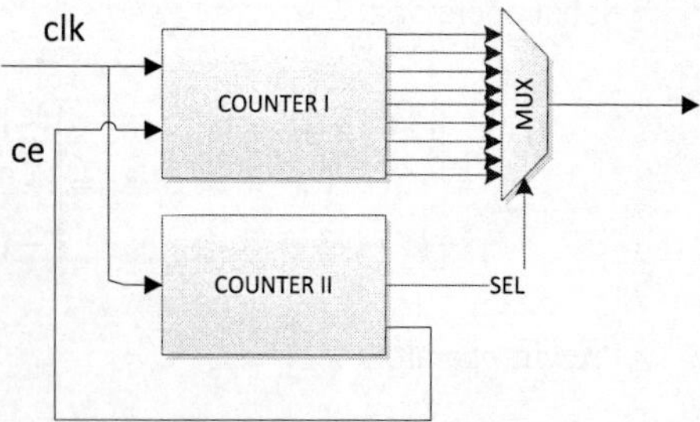

Fig 3: 3×3 Pixel Address Generation Module

- The structure of Memory ROM is shown in Fig.4: This module allows us to store the file *.Coe of image converted by Matlab.

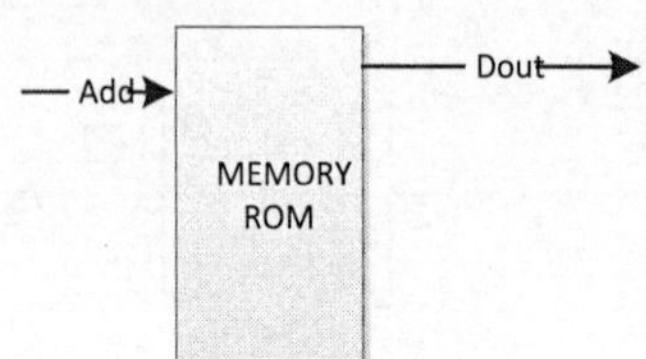

Fig 4: Memory ROM

- The structure of gradients operators is shown in Fig.5: This module permits to choose the coefficients of the different horizontal and vertical operators (Sobel, Prewitt, Roberts).

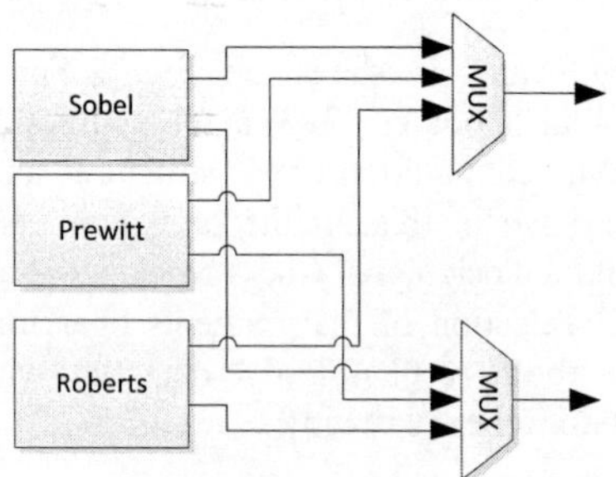

Fig 5: Gradient Operators

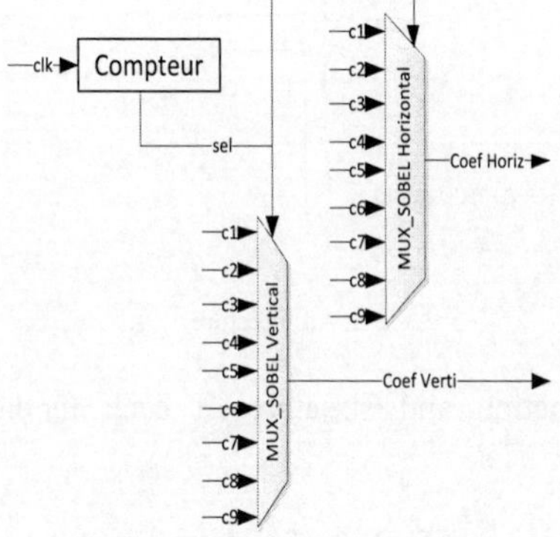

Fig 6: Unit generating the coefficients of the Sobel operator

- The structure of 3×3 convolution gradient is shown in Fig.7: This module done the convolution of pixels read by the ROM with the coefficients horizontal and vertical.

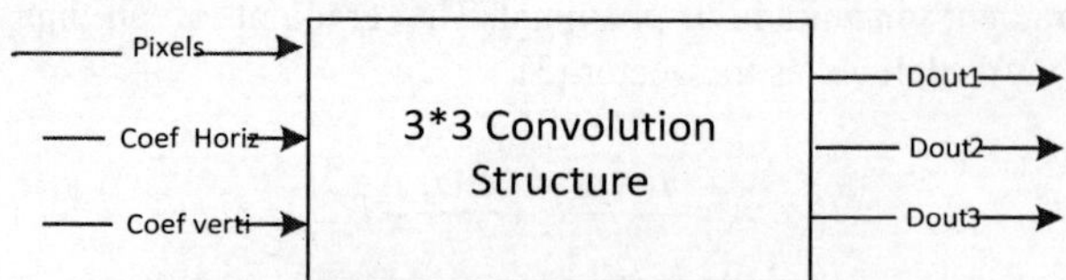

Fig 7: Convolution 3×3 Structure.

4 Experimental Results

All results for image edge detection in Matlab and its comparison in VHDL are represented in this section:

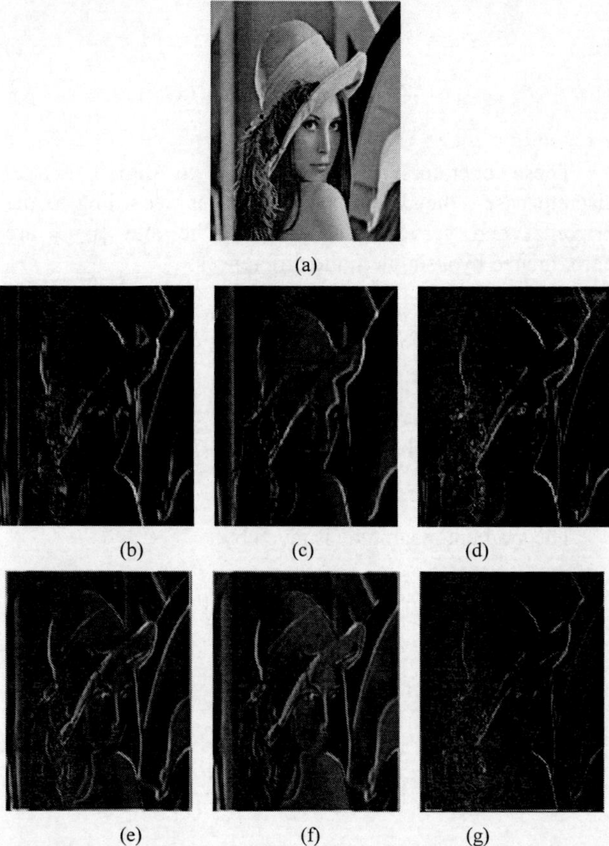

Fig 8: (a) original image, (b) Sobel Gradient using VHDL, (c) Prewitt Gradient using VHDL, (d) Roberts Gradient using VHDL, (e) Sobel Gradient Software, (f) Prewitt Gradient Software, (g) Roberts Gradient Software.

5 Synthesis

Synthesis consists in transforming the algorithms studied for a logic functions. It is done by the tool XST (Xilinx Synthesis Tool) integrated into ISE. We obtain a report that contains the occupancy rate (number of CLBs, SLICE, ...).

We implemented the proposed architecture on the circuit Virtex 4 device XC4VLX200 package FF1513. Resources used in the FPGA are given in Table 1.

TABLE I. RESOURCES OF PROPOSED ARCHITECTURE

Number of resources	Occupancy Rate
Number of Slices: 8653 out of 89088	9%
Number of Slice Flip Flops: 109 out of 178176	0%
Number of 4 input LUT: 17208 out of 178176	9%
Number of bonded IOBs: 61 out of 964	6%
Number of GCLKs: 1 out of 32	3%

6 Conclusion

The obtained results are simulated using ISE simulator. VHDL cannot use the standard image formats for that we converted her into binary file *.coe format using MATLAB. The binary file is applied as a vector, it is converted and displayed in MATLAB. The execution time of the entire program to edges detect of an image 256×256 is a few seconds. No operator is perfect for detecting contours. In practice, we obtain incomplete contours, there are pixels unnecessary gaps, errors in position and orientation of pixels contours. Everyone seems to have a preference for one method or another all depends on the application. Operator edge detection is only the first step in the chain of segmentation.

In order to improve speed and efficiency of edge detection a pre-filtering of the images is required. Linear filtering for noise with zero mean (Gaussian white noise, Gaussian filter). Non-linear filtering for impulse noise (median filter for example). Possible segmentation by watershed will give a better result .To improve the speed and efficiency pipeline and reconfigurable architecture can be further done in edge detection, also segmentation can be implemented on hardware using watershed or contour active methods .

7 Reference

[1] Raman Maini, Dr. Himanshu Aggarwal, “Study and Comparison of Various Image Edge Detection Techniques”, International Journal of Image Processing (IJIP), Volume (3)

[2] Tian Qiu, Yong Yan* FIEEE, Gang Lu SMIEEE, 2011. “A New Edge Detection Algorithm for Flame Image Processing”, IEEE.

[3] Maitine Bergounioux 2010 Quelques Méthodes de Filtrage en Traitement d'image

[4] Steve Kilts, Advanced FPGA Design: Architecture Implementation, and Optimization, John Tiley&Sons.

[5] Arrigo Benedetti, Andrea Prati, Nello Scarabottolo. “Image convolution on FPGAs: the implementation of a multi-FPGA FIFO structure”. Euromicro Conference, 1998.

SESSION

MEDICAL APPLICATIONS

Chair(s)

TBA

Automatic Ischemic Stroke Lesion Segmentation Using Single MR Modality and Gravitational Histogram Optimization Based Brain Segmentation

Nooshin Nabizadeh[1], Miroslav Kubat[2], Nigel John[3], Clinton Wright[4]
[1,2,3] Electrical and Computer Engineering Department, University Of Miami, Coral Gables, FL 33146, USA
[4]Evelyn F. McKnight Brain Institute, University of Miami, 1120 NW 14th Street, Miami, FL, 33136

Abstract— *In this paper the automatic and customized brain segmentation followed by a stroke lesion detection technique is presented applying single modality Magnetic Resonance Images (MRIs). A novel intensity-based segmentation technique called gravitational histogram optimization is developed for this purpose. By applying histogram gravitational optimization algorithm the brain can be segmented into discriminative area including stroke lesion. The mathematical descriptions as well as the convergence criteria of the developed algorithm are presented in detail. The application of the proposed algorithm in the segmentation of single Diffusion-Weighted Images (DWI) modality of healthy and lesion MR image slices for different number of segments is presented and the results are discussed. The segmented areas are then employed in automatic lesion slice detection and lesion extraction technique. The stroke lesion is extracted from the recognized lesion slice with acceptable accuracy.*

Index Terms—Brain segmentation, Stroke detection, Gravitational histogram optimization, MR imaging,

1. Introduction

Stroke or cerebrovascular space accident is the one of the most important causes of morbidity and mortality around the world [1]. Stroke is defined as a sudden development of a neurological deficit, and can be divided into two categories. The major category is ischemia, which comprises approximately 85%, in comparison to haemorrhage, which comprises 10% to 15% [2]. An accurate detection and diagnosis of ischemic lesion is extremely essential for clinical prognosis, treatment, and also stroke related research [3]. With limitations on access to stroke specialists and the need for timely diagnosis, an effective automatic stroke lesion detection algorithm is clinically useful and desirable.

In stroke diagnosis, Magnetic Resonsnce Imaging (MRI) (and specifically its Diffusion-Weighted Image modality (DWI)) is one of the strongest medical imaging techniques. MRI is a non-invasive procedure, which unlike other medical imaging techniques enables us to differentiate soft tissues.

Contact Author is Nooshin Nabizadeh, nzadeh@med.miami.edu

Another advantage of MRI is that it produces multiple images of the same tissue with different contrast mechanisms while applying different image acquisition protocols and parameters [4]. The pathophysiology of cerebral ischemia involves variation of brain water volume even in its earliest steps. Diffusion-Weighted Images (DWI)'s sensitivity to illustrate changes in tissue-free water content allows us to identify ischemic damage to the brain within one hour after onset [5]. Nevertheless, the random shape and location of infarct lesions make their segmentation a complex and difficult task. In confronting this challenge, manual segmentations have been widely employed but this is very time consuming, tedious, and subject to manual variation and subjective judgments. Another disadvantage of these interventions is their reliance upon subjective judgments, which raises the possibility that other observers will reach different conclusions about the presence or absence of lesions, or even that the same observer will reach different conclusions on separate occasions [2]. Thus there exits a clinical reason for the development of an automatic stroke lesion segmentation system.

Since collection of anatomical multi-spectral MR images is time and cost consuming, acquisition of just one anatomical MR modality is more practical in clinical conditions. In many situations such as ischemic stroke, due to patient condition severity and time importance, procurement of more than one MR modality is not feasible. Because of this, detecting and segmenting the stroke lesion based on single anatomical MR modality is necessary and important [6].

The majority of lesion segmentation methods employ multispectral MR images. That is because lesions usually have similar intensities to the normal tissues, and using multispectral MR images help to elucidate this problem. Applying multispectral MR images offers two difficulties [2]. First, acquiring such data is not always feasible. Second, available data suffer from not being consistent and aligned, thus registration is essential.

Most stroke lesion segmentation methods suffer from dependency on multi-parameter MRI data, or multi-scale classification, or knowing the number of tissue classes [7-10]. Moreover, usually the dependency on local or global registration of brain image to an anatomical atlas is a drawback of majority of studies [9, 11]. Furthermore, the detection of the slices including the lesion usually has been neglected. The effort presented here is motivated by the need to find a computationally light and fully automatic technique to detect the slice including lesion, and then segment ischemic stroke lesions using single-spectral MR Images. The DWI modality, which is the most useful modality for ischemic stroke diagnosis and prognosis, is employed here. The segmentation of the continuous spectrum of image intensity histogram into discrete segments is presented using a method called Histogram-based Gravitational Optimization Algorithm (HGOA). In this algorithm, convolving a rectangular window with brain histogram maximums, results in the generation of several clusters. Then applying three criteria and a gravitational optimization algorithm, the desired number of brain segments is achieved. Lower and upper cutoff boundaries of brain segments are then employed in the detection of the healthy and lesion slices. This also assists in the extraction of the location and area of the lesion strokes.

In Section III, the histogram-based gravitational optimization algorithm is explained. In Section IV, data acquisition and preprocessing are described. Results are discussed is Section V. Conclusion is addressed in Section VI.

2. Related Work

A number of studies have investigating lesion segmentation with respect to Multiple Sclerosis (MS), White Matter (WM) and tumor lesion segmentation but not stroke lesion segmentation. Parametric classifiers such as expectation maximization algorithm and non-parametric methods such as Parzen window and K-nearest neighbor are and the more frequently used methods in lesion classification [4, 12-14]. They can be categorized as statistical methods, which deals with the estimation of probability density functions. They are the most prevalent approaches in literature. In [15] a MS lesions segmentation method using a combined algorithm of parametric and non-parametric techniques is proposed.

Another group of lesion segmentation methods cover a wide range of Artificial Neural Networks (ANN), clustering methods, fuzzy sets, and their combinations [16-18]. The shortcomings of these methods are over-sensitivity to noise, the need for a suitable estimate of the number of layers and excessive training time [4].

There are some other studies employing multilevel thresholding and region growing techniques, which can be allocated into the data-driven methods category. These are the simplest approaches in that they only use the pixels intensities. This group accuracy is usually not very remarkable [19].

Some other methods concern volume estimation as deformable methods, which are the least prevalent group. Deformable techniques drawback is their need to match the MR images with an atlas, to locate the lesions [4].

The use of histograms for image segmentation has been adopted in many investigations. In [20], 2D histograms are employed to segment the brain images. In [21], brain MRI images are segmented using a fuzzy-clustering algorithm on the histogram. In [22], a fast automatic segmentation algorithm is proposed which is called random walk.

Very few studies work on ischemic stroke segmentation applying DWI sequence. In [11], ischemic lesion is segmented applying nonparametric density estimation based on mean shift algorithm and edge confidence map. In this study, applying a novel method called histogram-based gravitational optimization algorithm, the brain is segmented to four areas and stroke lesion is segmented using single modality (DWI) images.

3. Histogram Based Gravitational Optimization Algorithm

This algorithm can be separated into two parts as "histogram-based brain segmentation algorithm" and "gravitational optimization algorithm".

Histogram-based brain segmentation algorithm starts by building the image histogram. It is assumed that the local maximums of the histogram are potentially representative of various segments in the brain. Therefore, the number and the value of the histogram local maximums can be related to the number and the center value of segments, respectively. Since every pixel in the image must be assigned only to single segment, therefore, the distance from one local maximum to another one should be equally or proportionally divided between the two local maximums to cover the whole intensity range. If it is divided proportionally, then the local maximum value affects the width of each segment. Doing so, the brain can be segmented to the same number of its histogram's local maximums. However, if the desired number of brain segments is different from the total number of brain histogram's local maximums, histogram-based gravitational optimization algorithm helps to dynamically segment the brain into the required number of segments. For this purpose, it is necessary to define an optimization process in which the objective function is created from the histogram analysis. An optimization process is defined to minimize the difference between the calculated number of segments and the desired number of segments. The optimization process works based upon an iterative calculation of an objective function, which is created from histogram-based brain segmentation algorithm. In this study, a gravitational optimization algorithm, which is a recently developed algorithm, is employed.

3.1 Histogram Based Brain Segmentation Algorithm

The histogram-based brain segmentation algorithm can be described as following.

Step1: the image histogram is calculated.

Step2: for smoothing the histogram $H[n]$, local averaging technique is applied over the histogram using the equation (1).

$$\overline{H}[n_i] = \sum_{i}^{i+G} H[n_i] \Big/ G \quad (1)$$

where $H[n_i]$ is histogram distribution value of ith bin, G is the length of the averaging window and $\overline{H}[n_i]$ is local average value of the histogram. It is obvious the greater the G, the smother the averaged histogram will be. Also it shifts the histogram toward the higher intensities.

Step3: The local maximums of smoothed histogram are simply calculated by:

$$H_{max-Local}[n] = \bar{H}[n_i] | (\bar{H}[n_i] > \bar{H}[n_{(i+1)}]) \cap (\bar{H}[n_i] > \bar{H}[n_{(i-1)}]) \quad (2)$$

Step4: a rectangular window is convolved with the histogram local maxima calculated from step 3. It is assumed that the number and location of the local maxima of the histogram can be an indication of different segments in the brain image. Therefore, the key idea for brain image segmentation is to automatically grow a local maximum of the smoothed histogram toward its neighbor local maximum with respect to its amplitude, location, and anticipated number of brain segments. To do this, the convolution of $H_{max-Local}[n]$ and a rectangular window is employed to connect the local maximums that are in neighborhood. Let "W" be the length of a rectangular window, Win, and "M" be the length of $H_{max-Local}[n]$. Then $Y[n]$ is the vector of length $M + W - 1$ whose n^{th} element is calculated by:

$$Y[n] = Win[n] * H_{max}[n] = \sum_j Win[j] H_{max}[n-j] \quad (3)$$

$H_{max-Local}[n]$ is written as $H_{max}[n]$ for simplicity. The function $Y[n]$ potentially has several discriminative segments, which here are called clusters. The narrower window obviously produces higher number of clusters.

Step5: the lower and upper cutoff bondaries for all clusters are calculated using a threshold value. In order to have continuous and discriminative clusters, convolution of $H_{max-Local}[n]$ and a rectangular window Win is applied. The result is called $Y[n]$. Using a threshold value as Thr, controls the cutoff boundary and removes the values smaller than the threshold value in the distribution. Also it helps to increase the flexibility of optimization method. The cutoff boundaries of $Y[n]$ are calculated as:

$$X_{low}[n_i] = \{n | Y[n_{(i+1)}] > Thr \cap Y[n_{(i-1)}] < Thr\} \quad (4)$$

$$X_{high}[n_i] = \{n | Y[n_{(i-1)}] > Thr \cap Y[n_{(i+1)}] < Thr\} \quad (5)$$

The number of the clusters which are visible in histogram data is the same as the total number of lower or upper cutoff boundaries of the function $Y[n]$. The value of selected threshold has a great influence on the final number of clusters. For example the Thr_2 may only lead to one cluster and the choice of Thr_1 may lead to four clusters.

Step 6: the upper cutoff border of nth cluster is connected to the lower cutoff border of $(n+1)^{th}$ cluster proportionally to the clusters' amplitudes. The reason is to cover all intensity bins and fill up the gaps between $X_{high}[n_s]$ and $X_{low}[n_{(s+1)}]$. Also every pixel needs to be assigned to a single segment. In this step, upper cutoff border of one cluster proportionally reaches to the lower cutoff border of next one according to the following rule.

$$X_{up\_new}[s_n] = X_{low\_new}[s_{(n+1)}] = X_{up}(s_n) + \left(X_{low}(s_{n+1}) - X_{up}(s_n)\right) \times \frac{LM(s_n)}{LM(s_n) + LM(s_{n+1})} \quad (6)$$

where the s_n is the index of the nth cluster, $LM(s_n)$ is the local maximum amplitude of the cluster s_n , and $LM(s_{n+1})$ is the local maximum amplitude of the cluster s_{n+1}.

Step 7: After filling the gaps between the clusters, one specific intensity value is specified for each generated cluster. All intensity values fall between lower and upper cutoff borders of one cluster would be represented by one intensity value named $X_{center}(s_n)$. The intensity of the s_n^{th} cluster is defined as:

$$X_{center}(s_n) = \frac{X_{low\_new}(s_n) + X_{up\_new}(s_n)}{2} \quad (7)$$

Brain is segmented according to the number, intensity of the center, and the cutoff borders of generated clusters. In order to automate this process, an optimization process is applied to minimize difference between the calculated number of brain segments and the desired number of brain segments. The objective function is described as squared difference between the desired number of brain segments and the calculated number of brain segments. There are three variables that influence the objective function. These are the length of averaging window described in step two, the length of convolution window described in step four, and the threshold value described in step five.

In next part, the Gravitational optimization algorithm is explained. Figure 1 shows the diagram of histogram-based brain segmentation algorithm.

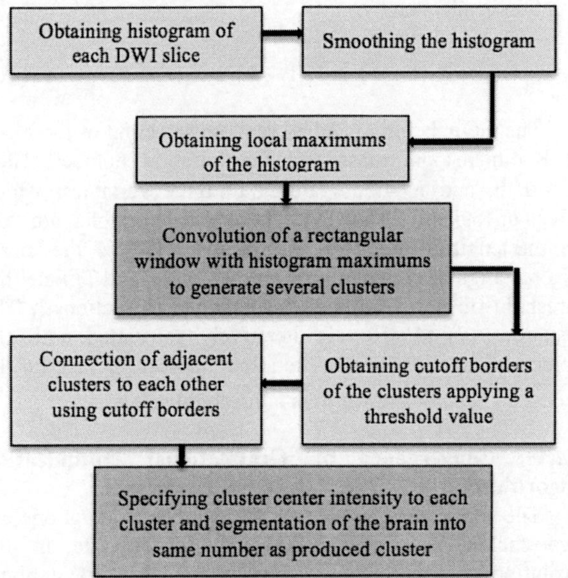

Fig. 1: Flowchart of the seven steps histogram-based brain segmentation

3.2 Gravitational Optimization Algorithm

The second part of the proposed algorithm is a gravitational optimization algorithm (GOA). In order to achieve the required number of the brain segments GOA is applied on the histogram-based brain segmentation algorithm, which plays the role of objective function. The objective function is defined as the squared difference between the desired number of segments and the calculated number of segments.

The GOA is launched by initializing an N set of K-dimensional mass randomly seeded over the K-dimensional searching space. [23]. In other words, for the K-dimensional search space, the ith mass, can be represented by an K-dimensional vector $X_i = [x_{i1}, x_{i2}, \dots, x_{ik}]^T$, and the velocity $\vec{V_i} = [v_{i1}, v_{i2}, \dots, v_{ik}]^T$. Therefore the total size of population is a (N×K) matrix. In GOA, the gravitational force on the ith object is calculated as:

$$\vec{F_i} = \sum_{j \neq i} \frac{g.\, m_i.\, m_j.\left(X_i(t) - X_j(t)\right)}{\left(\left(x_{i1} - x_{j1}\right)^2 + \cdots + \left(x_{ik} - x_{jk}\right)^2\right)^{2.5}} \quad (7)$$

Here, g is the gravity constant; m_i is defined by the value of the inverse objective function value, equation (8). In equation (8), ε is added to denominator to prevent dividing by zero.

$$m_i = \frac{1}{\text{ObjectiveFunctionValue}_i + \varepsilon} \quad (8)$$

Following the calculation of the gravitational force on the ith mass, by assuming a unit time length, the new speed of the object is calculated as:

$$\overrightarrow{V_i(t+1)} = \left(\vec{F_i}/m_i\right) + \overrightarrow{V_i(t)} \quad (9)$$

Having the speed of the system at t + 1 and the previous location of the ith mass at $X_i(t)$, the position in the next iteration is adjusted by:

$$X_i(t+1) = \overrightarrow{V_i(t+1)} + X_i(t) \quad (10)$$

The GOA is initialized by random selection of the N set of K-dimensional mass and the iteration number. Here $N = 100$, and $K = 3$, regarding to three variables, which affect on objective function. These three variables are "G" i.e. the length of the averaging window, "W" i.e. the length of a rectangular convolution window (Win), and Thr i.e. the threshold of cutoff borders as explained in section II. The equations (7) to (10) are iteratively calculated until the objective function or the iteration number is met or the $\overrightarrow{V_i(t+1)}$ becomes lower than a threshold value.

3.2.1 Convergence of Gravitational Optimization Algorithm

The initial population and the number of iterations are two factors that affect the convergence rate in the evolutionary optimization algorithms. In gravitational optimization algorithm the gravity constant, g, controls the acceleration rate of optimization. The higher value of g, the higher the acceleration rate will be.

In spite of all of these considerations, one may not see the objective value satisfaction since the convergence rate is also dependent to the nature of the objective function. For example, strictly speaking a second order function has only one local and global maximum. However, summing this function with a low value random function increases the number of local maximums or minimums. This idea is employed here to increase the chance of convergence. On the other word, the convergence of the optimization algorithm is not guaranteed but adding a low value random function I_u, with a growing rate g_r, to the preprocessed function I_f, during the optimization process increases the convergence chance. The size of I_u will be the same as function I_f as $M \times N$. The initial amplitude of the I_u is about one percent of I_f values. This leads to a random but slight movement of local maximums along the intensity vector. These movements increase the chance of optimization convergence. The whole process for image segmentation is summarized in figure 2.

4. Data Acquisition and Preprocessing

4.1 Image Acquisition

In all, 12 subjects (6 with stroke and 6 healthy, female = 5, mean age = 57.23, and standard deviation = 10.96, less than one months after stroke) were scanned in this study. All MR images were attained on a 3T Siemens Avanto scanner (Germany). High-resolution 3-D brain MRI images were acquired using a T1-weighted magnetization, with the following characteristics: repetition time (TR) = 6000 ms, echo time (TE) = 128 ms, inversion time = 2200 ms, one acquisition, flip angle = 90°, field of view (FOV) = 71 mm, 46 slices, voxel size = 1 mm × 1 mm × 1 mm, and in-plane matrix = 256 × 256. Prior to scanning, all participants gave written informed consent according to the guidelines of the University of Miami Institutional Review Board. Participants were not paid for participation.

The ground truth is prepared by labeling the ischemic stroke lesion by an expert. In this study the DWI sequences with stroke lesion are called LD; the DWI sequences without stroke lesion are called HD.

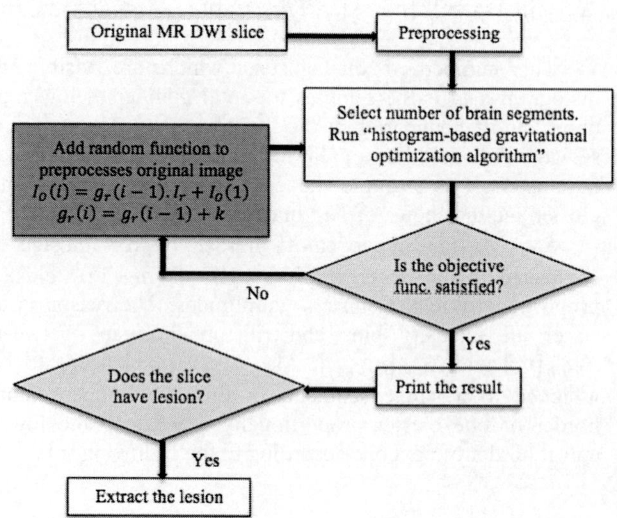

Fig. 2: Flowchart of the lesion detection

4.2 Noise Reduction and Normalization

Preprocessing includes background segmentation, noise reduction using low pass filter as Gaussian filter, and normalization. Gaussian Filter is a low-pass spatial frequency filter where all elements in this filter are weighted according to a Gaussian (Normal) distribution. Depending on the mean and the variance value, (μ, σ), in the Gaussian distribution, the convolution of this kernel with the image results in a smooth image [24]. Result of applying Gaussian filters with different variance value is represented in Fig. 3. By dividing the intensity values by the maximum intensity, normalized image is prepared.

4.3 Background Segmentation

Due to the prior knowledge of the background intensity values, it is necessary to exclude the back ground from the calculations wherever the histogram of the image is evaluated. The reason for doing this is that the background normally has much larger pixel number than brain ones.

5. Results

5.1 MRI Brain Segmentation

Original LD1 is represented in Fig. 3. The segmentation of LD1 into two, three and four levels is depicted in Fig. 4. Correspondingly, Fig. 5 displays the segmentation of LD1 into five, eight and twelve levels. It can be seen that after two levels of segmentation the stroke lesion appears in the segmented image. It can also be seen that in high levels of segmentation, some of the segments are visually indiscriminative; however, there is still a clear appearance of the stroke in the segmented image.

Figure 6 shows the original image of HD1 and its segmentation into three and four levels.

Figure 8(a) to 8(d), 9(a) to 9(d), respectively show the segmentation of LD1 for three and four level segmentation. Figures 8(a) and 9(a) correspond to image histogram after step 2. Figures 8(b) and 9(b) shows the local maximums of the histogram in step 3. Figures 8(c) and 9(c) show results of step 4. Figures 8(d) and 9(d) show the results of step 5 and 6. In all, red dots are initial lower and upper cutoff borders, which are result of step 5, and black dots are final lower and upper cutoff borders, which are result of step 6.

Figures 10 and 11 show the corresponding result as was explained for figures 8 and 9 respectively for HD1 slice.

5.2 Lesion Slice Detection

With comparison of position of cutoff borders, it is clear when brain is segmented into three or four segments, the last segment's width differs for healthy and lesion slices. After segmentation of the brain into L segment, L^{th} segment's width for lesion slices is much less than healthy ones. The following criterion is defined as first condition for lesion slice detection as:

$$\left[X_{up_{new}}(L) - X_{low_{new}}(L)\right] > q \qquad (11)$$

The equation of (11) is interpreted as if L^{th}segment's width is less than q, the slice is considered as lesion slice and vise verse as healthy one. Here, the q is selected as 1.8.

By comparison of figure 10(d) with 8(d), and 11(d) with 9(d), one can see the obvious differences in $(L-1)^{th}$ segment's initial and final lower and upper cutoff border movement in healthy and lesion slices. After segmentation of the brain into L segment, the following criterion is defined as second condition for lesion slice detection as:

$$\left[X_{up_{new}}(L-1) - X_{low_{new}}(L-1)\right] > (1+P).\left[X_{up_{old}}(L-1) - X_{low_{old}}(L-1)\right] \qquad (12)$$

The equation of (12) is interpreted as if the width of new cut off border is larger than $(1+P)$ times of the old cutoff borders. Here, the P is selected as 0.2; The implementation results show that for higher number of segmentation the movement of cut-off borders at segment $(L-1)$ is more discriminative than that of the lower number of segmentation. Therefore, for detection of the lesion slice the high number of segmentation is preferred. Foe example, brain is segmented to eight or twelve area. However, for lesion extraction from a detected lesion slice, the lower number of segmentation is more preferable since it covers wider areas around the stroke with a distributed intensity. For lesion extraction purpose, $L = 3$ and $L = 4$ is selected. All in all, for a complete stroke slide detection and lesion extraction two separate segmentation is needed. Initially the slice is segmented into a high number of segments (here 8) and the stroke slice is detected as to be a healthy or a lesion slice. If the slice was detected as a lesion slice, it is again segmented into three and four slices and the last segment is chosen as the stroke lesion. Here with considering logical OR between condition one and condition two, healthy and lesion slices are detected with $94.7 \pm 1.2\%$ accuracy.

5.3 Stroke Lesion Detection

After detection of healthy and the lesion slices, three and four area segmentation is implemented on the lesion slice. Because of high the intensity of stroke lesion, the stroke normally is positioned in the last segment and therefore with extracting the last segment, the stroke lesion can be extracted. Result of this step is depicted in Fig. 7. It is shown that the lesion extracted after segmenting the brain into four segments has smaller area than the labeled lesion, but include less false positives. Lesions extracted after brain segmentation into three segments have closer area to the labeled lesion but include more false positive. In the next step it is necessary to exclude false positive areas. With using the lesion results after segmenting the brain into three areas, the average overlap error is $16.39 \pm 2.3\%$, that is mainly because of false positive. With segmenting the brain into four areas, average overlap error is $21.6 \pm 1.9\%$, that is mostly because of smaller area of extracted lesion than labeled one. The total number of detected pixels, which do not have overlap with grand truth label divided by total number of grand truth pixels, is considered as error.

6. Conclusion

A new brain segmentation algorithm called histogram based gravitational optimization algorithm was proposed. The automatic brain segmentation into discrete segments was presented. The stroke slice detection and stroke extraction using single modality diffusion-weighted MR images with comparable and promising accuracy was implemented. Simplicity, low computational complexity, independency on multi-spectral MR images, multi-scale classification, and anatomical atlas registration are prominent advantages of this work. Furthermore, lesion slice detection is included before the lesion segmentation step. The algorithm is capable of detection and segmentation of small lesions ($< 1.5\ cm^3$).

The disadvantage of presented approach is the rate of false positives. It was demonstrated adding spatial information amends the capability of lesion segmentation methods and reduces false positive rates. For future work, applying anatomical atlas will be considered. Furthermore, more work will focus on evaluation of algorithm on other MRI modalities. Finally, additional focus on amending the current method to attain clinically worthwhile system in more general applications will be done. The potential outcome is remarkable for medical field and justifies further studies

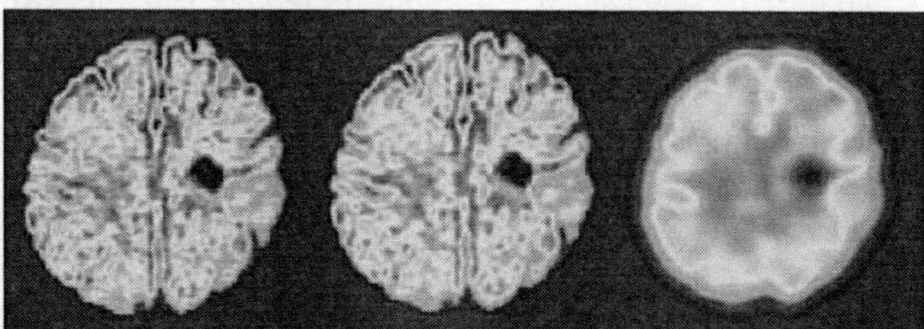

Fig. 3: Original DWI image with stroke lesion (first), the filtered DWI image (LD1) using Gaussian filter with $\sigma = 0.1$, (second), and with $\sigma = 4$ (third)

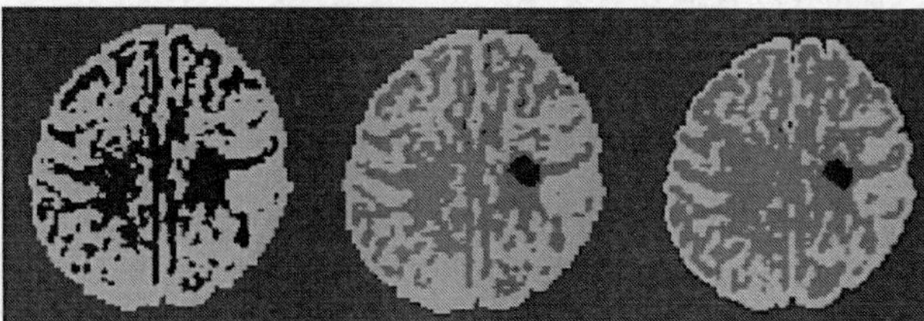

Fig. 4: Segmentation of the lesion DWI image (LD1) into two (first), three (second), and four (third) segments

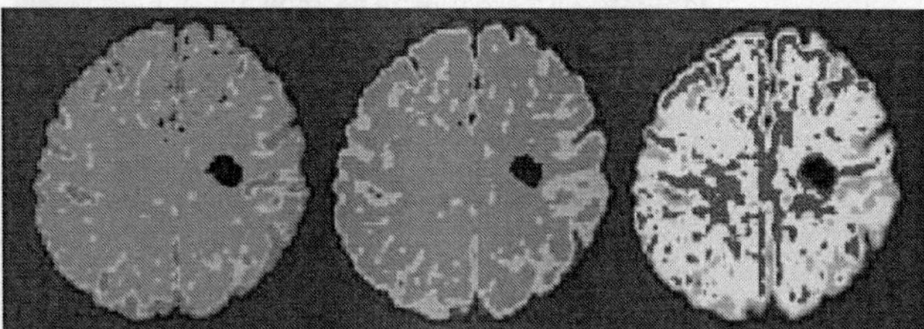

Fig. 5: Segmentation of the lesion DWI image (LD1) into five (first), eight (second), and twelve (third) segments after min-max filter

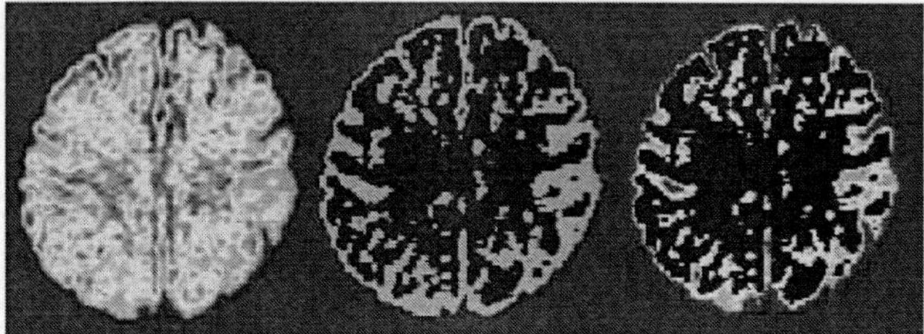

Fig. 6: Original healthy DWI image (first), its segmentation of the healthy three (second), and four (third) segments

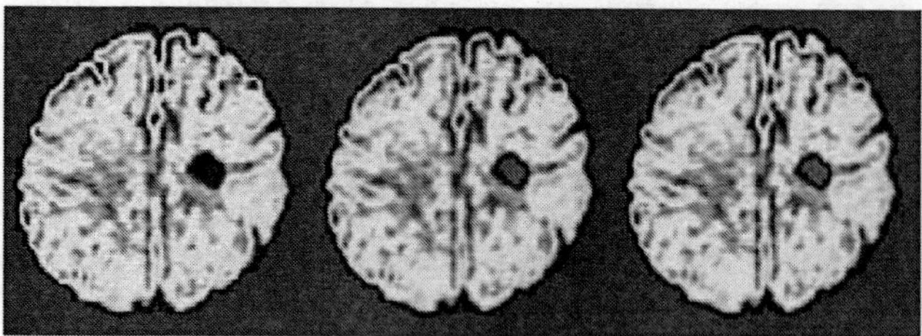

Fig. 7: Original DWI image with stroke lesion (first), stroke lesion extraction on LD1 after three levels of segmentation (second), after four levels of segmentation (third)

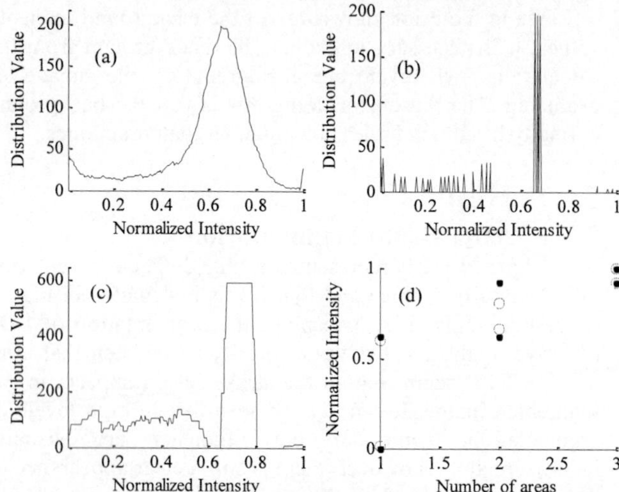

Fig. 8: The image histogram of LD1 after step 2 for 3 segmented areas (a), the local maximums of the histogram in step 3 (b), results of step 4 for three segments (c), and the results of step 5 and 6 (d)

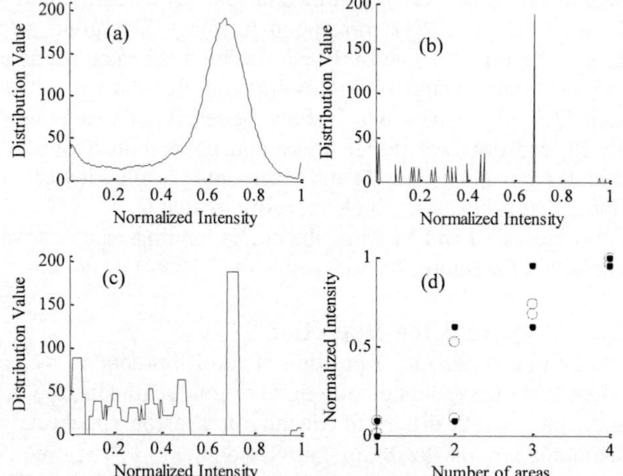

Fig. 9: The image histogram of LD1 after step 2 for 4 segmented areas (a), the local maximums of the histogram in step 3 (b), results of step 4 for four segments (c), and the results of step 5 and 6 (d)

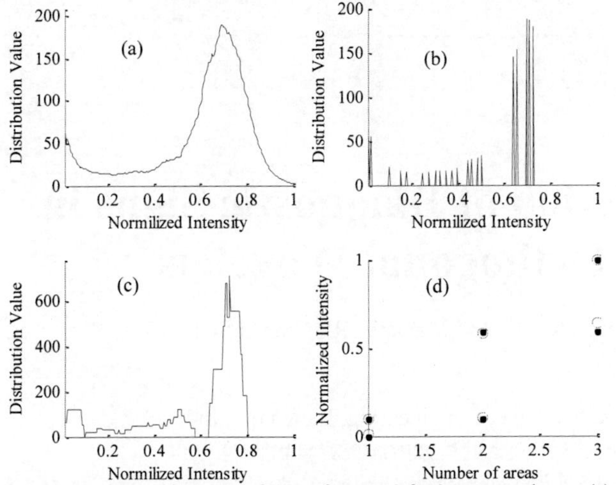

Fig. 10: The image histogram of HD1 after step 2 for 3 segmented areas (a), the local maximums of the histogram in step 3 (b), results of step 4 for three segments (c), and the results of step 5 and 6 (d)

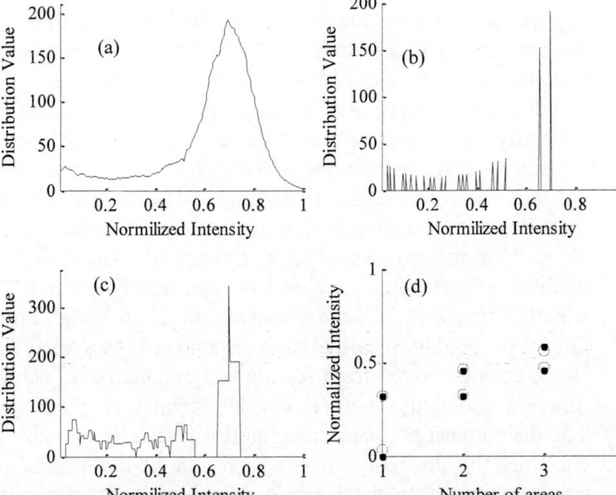

Fig. 11: The image histogram of HD1 after step 2 for 4 segmented areas (a), the local maximums of the histogram in step 3 (b), results of step 4 for four segments (c), and the results of step 5 and 6 (d)

7. References

[1] C L M. Sudlow et al. "Comparable studies of the incidence of stroke and its pathological types. Results from an international collaboration". Stroke 1997;28(3):491–9.

[2] Y.Kabir, M.Dojat, B.Scherrer, F.Forbes, C.Garbay, "Multimodal MRI segmentation of ischemic stroke lesions," Proceedings of the 29th Annual International Conference of the IEEE EMBS, August 2007.

[3] S. Shen, W. Sandham, M. Granat, and A. Sterr,"MRI Fuzzy Segmentation Of Brain Tissue Using Neighborhood Attraction With Neural-Network Optimization," IEEE Trans. Inf. Technol. Biomed., vol. 9, no. 3, pp. 459–467, Sep. 2005.

[4] Daryoush Mortazavi & Abbas Z. Kouzani & Hamid Soltanian-Zadeh, "Segmentation of multiple sclerosis lesions in MR images: a review," Springer 2011, Neuroradiology, DOI 10.1007/s00234-011-0886-7

[5] D. David et al., Magnetic Resonance Imaging, C.V. Mosby; 3rd edition (January 15, 1999)

[6] Shen S, Szameitat AJ, Sterr A, "Detection of infarct lesions from single MRI modality using inconsistency between voxel intensity and spatial location a 3-D automatic approach," IEEE Trans 2008

[7] M. A. Jacobs, S. Patel, P. Mitsias, H. Soltanian-Zadeh, D. J. Peck, and A. Ghanei, "Unsupervised segmentation of clinical stroke with multiparameter MRI," Proc. Intl. Soc. Mag. Reson. Med., vol. 8, p. 669, 2000.

[8] H. Soltanian-Zadeh, P. D. Mitsias, M. M. Khalighi, M. Lu, H. B. Ebadian, and J. R. Ewing, "Relationships among ISODATA, DWI, MTT, and T2 lesions in stroke," Proc. Intl. Soc. Mag. Reson. Med., vol. 11, p. 2245, 2003.

[9] Y. Han, E. Li, J. Tian, J. Chen, H. Wang, and J. Dai, "The application of diffusion – and perfusion – weighted magnetic resonance imaging in the diagnosis and therapy of acute cerebral infarction," Int. Jour. of Biomedical Imaging, vol. 2006, pp. 1–11, 2006.

[10] W. Li, J. Tian, E. Li, and J. Dai, "Robust unsupervised segmentation of infarct lesion from diffusion tensor MR images using multiscale statistical classification and partial volume voxel reclassification," Neuroimage, vol. 23, pp. 1507–1518, 2004.

[11] Nidiyare Hevia-Montiel, "Robust Nonparametric Segmentation of Infarct Lesion from Diffusion-Weighted MR Images," IEEE Conference, 2007

[12] P. Anbeek, K. L. Vincken, M. J. P. van Osch, R. H. C. Bisschops, and J. Van Der Grond, "Automatic segmentation of different-sized white matter lesions by voxel probability estimation," Med. Image Anal. vol. 8, pp. 205–215, 2004.

[13] S. Datta, B. R. Sajja, R. He, J. S. Wolinsky, R. K. Gupta, and P. A. Narayana, "Segmentation and quantification of black holes in multiple sclerosis," NeuroImage, vol. 29, pp. 467–474, 2006.

[14] K. Van Leemput, F. Maes, D. Vandermeulen, A. Colchester, and P. Suetens, "Automated segmentation of multiple sclerosis lesions by model outlier detection," IEEE Trans. Med. Imag., vol. 20, no. 8, pp. 677–688, Aug. 2001.

[15] Sajja BR, Datta S, He R, Mehta M, Gupta RK et al (2006) Unified approach for multiple sclerosis lesion segmentation on brain MRI. Ann Biomed Eng 34(1): 142–151

[16] Zijdenbos AP, Forghani R, Evans AC (2002) Automatic "pipeline" analysis of 3-D MRI data for clinical trials: application to multiple sclerosis. IEEE Trans Med Imag 21(10):1280–1291

[17] D. L. Pham and J. L. Prince, "Adaptive fuzzy segmentation of magnetic resonance images," IEEE Trans. Med. Imag., vol. 18, no. 9, pp. 737–752, Sep. 1999.

[18] S. Shen, W. Sandham, M. Granat, and A. Sterr,"MRI fuzzy segmentation of brain tissue using neighborhood attraction with neural-network optimization," IEEE Trans. Inf. Technol. Biomed., vol. 9, no. 3, pp. 459–467, Sep. 2005.

[19] Goldberg-Zimring D, Achiron A, Miron S, Faibel M, Azhari H (1998) Automated detection and characterization of multiple sclerosis lesions in brain MR images. J Magn Reson Imaging 16 (3): 311–318

[20] Nakib, A., Roman, S., Oulhadj, H., and Siarry, P., "Fast brain MRI segmentation based on two-dimensional survival exponential entropy and particle swarm optimization.," Proc. of IEEE Engineering in Medicine and Biology Society 1(2), 5563–5566 (2007).

[21] Dou, W., Ren, Y., Chen, Y., Ruan, S., Bloyet, D., and Constans, J.-M., "Histogram-based generation method of membership function for extracting features of brain tissues on MRI images," 2005.

[22] Jean-Philippe Morin, Christian Desrosiers, Luc Duong, "Image segmentation using random-walks on the histogram" Medical Imaging 2012: Image Processing, Proc. of SPIE Vol. 8314, 83140U

[23] Ying-Tung Hsiao, C. Chuang, J. Jiang, C. Chien, "A Novel Optimization Algorithm: Space Gravitational Optimization," IEEE International Conference On Systems, Man And Cybernetics, 2005

[24] Shapiro, L. G. & Stockman, G. C: "Computer Vision", page 137, 150. Prentence Hall, 2001

Image Enhancement for Detection of Diagnostic Signs in Mammograms using Bi-Orthogonal Wavelets

Amutha S[1], Ramesh Babu D.R[1], Ravi Shankar M[2], Radha Krishna A[3],Mamatha R[1], Vidhya Suman S[1]

[1]Department of Computer Science, Dayananda Sagar College of Engineering, Bangalore, India
[2]Department of Information Science, Dayananda Sagar College of Engineering, Bangalore, India
[3]Department of Radiology, Sagar Hospital, Bangalore, India

***Abstract**: Mammography is the primary method for early detection of abnormalities in the breast. However the diagnostic signs of breast diseases are difficult to detect because of the low-contrast and noisy nature of mammograms. This ensures the need for image enhancement to aid radiologists in interpretation. This paper presents an approach for enhancement of low contrast features in breast mammograms for accurate detection of diagnostic signs like mass and microcalcifications. Contrast of mammograms is enhanced by the use of mathematical morphology. Bi-orthogonal wavelet thresholding is applied for denoising. Identification of the suspicious region called the Region of interest (ROI) is performed based on homogenous pixel grouping and color quantization .The algorithm has been tested on a large number of mammograms from the database, Mammographic Image Analysis Society (MIAS). The performance of proposed algorithm is compared with other well-known algorithms like Visu shrink [19] and Bayes shrink, based on quantitative metrics and clinical evaluation. Our proposed algorithm seems to meaningfully improve the identification of ROI in the mammograms.*

Keywords –Mammograms, contrast enhancement, denoising, wavelet thresholding, Region of interest.

1 Introduction

Breast cancer is the second leading cause of death among women according to cancer facts & figures 2012[1]. Mammography has been recognized as a primary modality for breast tumor detection. However, some studies indicate that 10 – 25% of tumors are missed by radiologists [2,3]. Screening mammography has been recommended as the most effective method for early detection of breast cancer. The contrast of the images obtained with a low-dose X-ray machine is low. In the low-contrast images, it is difficult to discern the minute difference between the normal tissue and the malignant tissue which makes the interpretation [4]. Accurate detection and diagnosis of small, low contrast objects within the breast image often depends upon the quality of mammogram [5]. A clinically proven computer-aided diagnosis (CAD) system for breast cancer is very essential .Digital Image Processing techniques have been applied to improve the image quality for detection and further analysis of tumor. Conventional enhancement techniques such as contrast stretching and histogram equalization produce a feature contrast enhancement, but generally tend to proportionally increase noise [6]. Also they are single-scale spatial domain technologies which can only enhance the contrast of a finite range of sizes. To enhance, multi-resolution enhancement technologies based on the wavelet transform have been developed. Denoising of medical images using wavelets has been widely applied. The wavelet transform is the decomposition of an image into a family of functions called basis functions or wavelets [7]. Wavelets are derived from scaling and translation of a single function called the mother wavelet or analyzing function. The decomposition using integrated wavelets are flexible in choosing the discrete scales, which can fit the size of the abnormal area such as the size of the microcalcifications [8]. The major disadvantage of the method was that it required an empirical selection of appropriate thresholds for image denoising, as well as the specification of an appropriate size range for the structures to be enhanced. In the case of orthogonal wavelets, only one hierarchy of approximation spaces leads to a reconstruction and decomposition scheme. It depends on only two filters which are insufficient for perfect decomposition and reconstruction. Hence bi-orthogonal wavelets, which have two different scaling functions and two different wavelet functions with 4 filters result in a better decomposition and reconstruction were used. Bi-orthogonal allows for creating both orthogonal and symmetric wavelets [9]. It is well adapted for anisotropic elements, such as discontinuities along edges or curves in the image. The sub band images are invariant under translation and do not have aliasing [10]. Also alleviation of boundary effects via mirror extension of the signal is allowed. These characteristics avoid undesirable artifacts such as motion artifact, detector-associated artifacts, and software processing artifacts. Breast abnormalities like calcifications and masses in mammograms are characterized by the attributes such as size, shape, density, margin and contour of the breast. The edge pixels give significant information relevant to the above attributes. In practice, the high frequency components consists of edge information as well as noise. Therefore, edge information has to be enhanced while suppressing noise. Hence focus is on the preservation of edge information, which plays a role in diagnosis [11].Computer aided detection method were used to identify the masses in the image [17]. This technique did not require any human interruption during detection. It was based on region growing and GLCM Features. Mammographic mass detection using a mass template approach was applied previously. The pixels form the mammogram images were scanned in eight directions and region of interest was detected using various thresholds. Mass templates used to distinguish between true masses and non-masses depending on their morphologies [16]. Detection technique based on homogeneous block of size 8*8 was discussed in [15]. The drawback was, region size becomes big due to which subtle tumor was not visible. The organization of the paper is as follows. In Section 2, the proposed method for contrast enhancement and denoising of mammograms are presented in detail. Section 3 explains the steps for identification of suspicious region. Section 4 describes the experimental results and discussion followed by the conclusions in Section 5.

2 Wavelet Thresholding for Contrast Enhancement and Denoising

The proposed algorithm includes two modules. The image enhancement module followed by the detection of suspicious region (ROI) for cancer. Figure1 shows the algorithm for the contrast enhancement and denoising of mammograms.

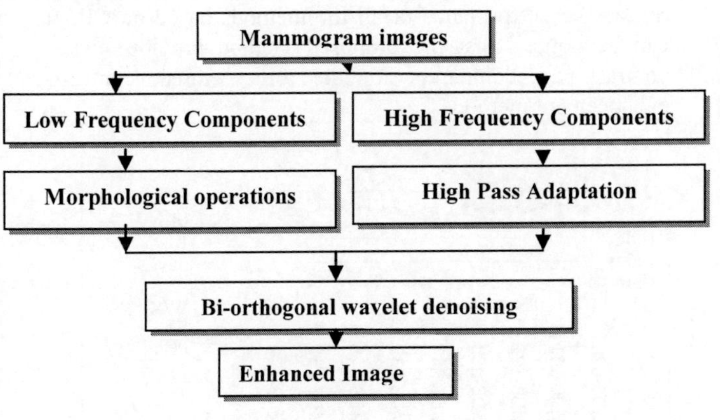

Figure 1. Block Diagram for Image Enhancement

The input mammogram was first splitted into low frequency and high frequency components using Gaussian low pass filter (GLPF). The contrast of the low frequency components $I_{lf}(x,y)$ was increased using modified mathematical morphological operations. Structuring element 'S' of disk shape with radius of 5 pixels was selected to emphasize on the disk-like features of the lesions.

$$M_o=I_{lf}(x,y)\circ S \quad (1)$$

M_o is the resulting image of the opening operation which involves erosion and dilation. Followed by the opening operation is the closing operation (□) of the low frequency components to preserve the background regions, which have the same shape of the structuring element resulting in M_c.

$$M_c=I_{lf}(x,y)\circ S \quad (2)$$

White top-hat opening was performed based on the equation (3). T_w is the resulting image of the above operation which contains the objects that were smaller than the structuring element and brighter than the surroundings.

$$T_w=I_{lf}(x,y)-M_s \quad (3)$$

The black top-hat closing was then performed to obtain the objects, which were smaller than the structuring element and darker than the surroundings. This was evaluated by the equation (4). T_b is the result of black top-hat closing operation.

$$T_b=M_c-I_{lf}(x,y) \quad (4)$$

To separate the foreground objects from the background, the difference between T_w and T_b were computed and added to the low frequency components resulting in the morphologically enhanced image $I_m(x,y)$.

$$I_m(x,y)=I_{lf}(x,y)+T_m-T_b \quad (5)$$

High pass adaptation technique was applied to the high frequency components $I_{hf}(x,y)$ to enhance the edges and suppress the noise. The threshold was calculated by evaluating the average of minimum and maximum pixel value in $I_{hf}(x,y)$. To exploit the fact that noisy pixels have higher intensities than the edge pixels, the pixel values below the threshold were considered to be the edge pixels and the pixels above the threshold were considered to be noisy pixels. The noise was suppressed and the edges were enhanced. Then morphologically enhanced low frequency components were added with the edge enhanced high frequency image to obtain the contrast enhanced image C(x,y). The contrast enhancement thus obtained was subjected to image denoising to remove artifacts. This was implemented using bi-orthogonal wavelets.

2.1 Bi-orthogonal Wavelet based Denoising

Bi-orthogonal wavelet was chosen to achieve denoising due to the advantages of using separate wavelets for decomposition and reconstruction [12]. Thresholding the detailed wavelet coefficients have to be performed to separate noise from edge information. We adopted a level dependent soft threshold because of the fact that the variance of the wavelet coefficients depend on the level in wavelet decomposition and is constant at each level [13]. The Threshold 'T' was calculated at each level based on the equation (6).

$$T = \frac{j}{2}\log 2\left(\max\left(d_j\right)\right) \qquad (6)$$

Here, j indicates the level and d_j is the wavelet coefficient value. The factor including the level information was halved to reduce the threshold value gradually and hence provide a better coverage of the span of the wavelet coefficients.

Two types of thresholding: hard and soft are used in practice. Soft-thresholding performs better than hard-thresholding as the latter applies a discontinuous function and causes artifacts in the recovered images. Soft thresholding eliminates the discontinuity that is inherent in hard thresholding. In soft thresholding coefficients below a threshold 'T' are attributed to noise and are set to zero. Coefficients above the threshold 'T' are modified by subtracting the threshold from the coefficients [14].

$F(x)= sign(x)(|x|-T)$ *if* $|x|-T$ *if* $|x|>T$ *else 0* (7)

3 Identification of Region of Interest (ROI)

The second module of the algorithm is the detection of suspicious region in the mammogram. Figure.2 shows the steps involved in detecting the ROI. We propose the detection based on grouping of homogeneous regions of size 4*4 and differentiating each region with color quantization technique. Each region describes the specific properties which helps in identifying the ROI.

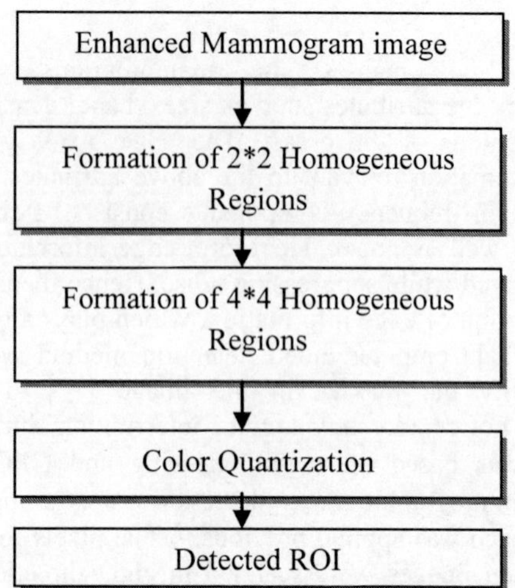

Figure 2. Block Diagram for ROI Detection

4 Experimental Results and Discussion

In order to measure the performance of the proposed algorithm, mammograms were selected from the Mammographic Image Analysis Society (MIAS) database. The experiment was composed of two parts. The first part was the objective measurement of the proposed method. The second part was the subjective analysis. In objective measurement, to measure the enhancement effectiveness quantitatively, performance measures Contrast Improvement Index (CII) and Edge Preservation Index (EPI) were defined, The contrast improvement index is defined by equation (8)

$$CII = \frac{C_{PROCESSED}}{C_{ORIGINAL}} \qquad (8)$$

The performance metrics CII and EPI were applied to the comparative methods: Visu shrink (VS), Sure shrink (SS), Bayes shrink (BS) and the proposed method. Figure 3. Shows the performance of all the methods based on CII. It can be noticed that the proposed method provides better contrast as compared to the other three contrast-enhancement methods

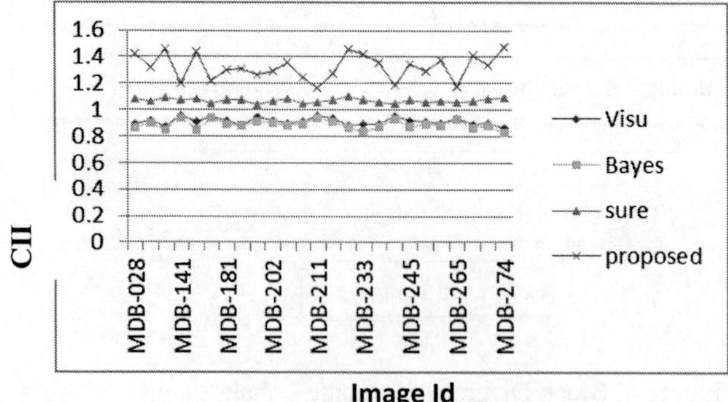

Figure 3. Performance on CII

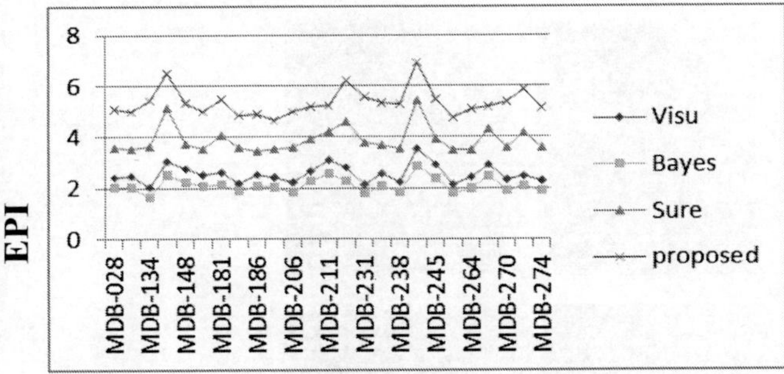

Figure.4.Performance based on EPI

The Edge Preservation Index is defined by equation (9)

$$EPI = \frac{\sum(|I_p(i,j) - I_p(i+1,j)| + |I_p(i,j) - I_p(i,j+1)|)}{\sum(|I_o(i,j) - I_o(i+1,j)| + |I_o(i,j) - I_o(i,j+1)|)} \quad (9)$$

Where I_o (i, j) is an original image pixel intensity value for the pixel location (x, y), I_p (i, j) is the processed image pixel intensity value for the pixel location (x, y). The greater value of EPI gives a much better indication of image quality.

The subjective analysis of the algorithm is described below

4.1 Radiological evaluation

The algorithm was subjected to radiological evaluation by a radiologist with 14 years of experience. The evaluation was conducted with five sets of images including the original images and results from the four contrast enhancement methods. The radiologist ranked the images with a rating of 1-5 indicating an ability to find the abnormalities. The original image rating was fixed as 3. A rating below 3 was considered as poor performance, while rating above 3 was considered as an improvement with respect to the original image. Figure 5. shows the rating done by the radiologist. The proposed method is showing better performance.

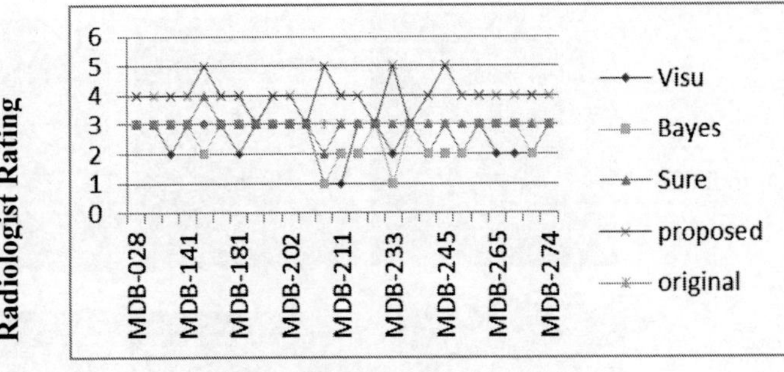

Figure.5. Radiologist Rating

4.2 *Receiver Operating Characteristics (ROC)*

The results of ROC analysis[18] are shown in figure 6. We randomized both benign and malignant images and given it to the radiologist. He marked the suspicious region for any findings. Based on the true positive and false positive values, the ROC graph was plotted. The area under the curve of the processed images is 0.9 and the area for the unprocessed images is 0.82. Greater the area depicts the good enhancement

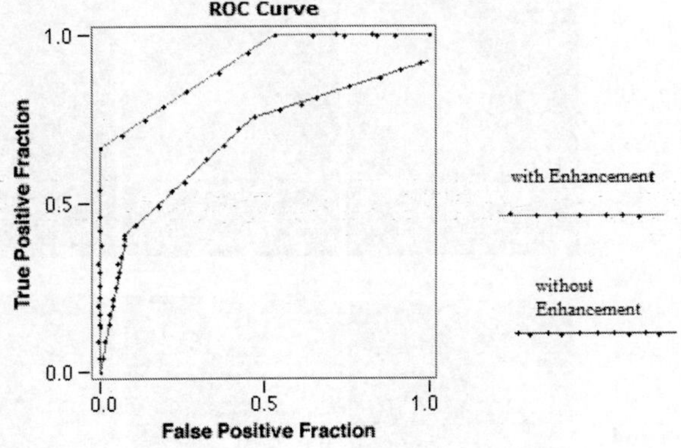

Figure.6. ROC curve

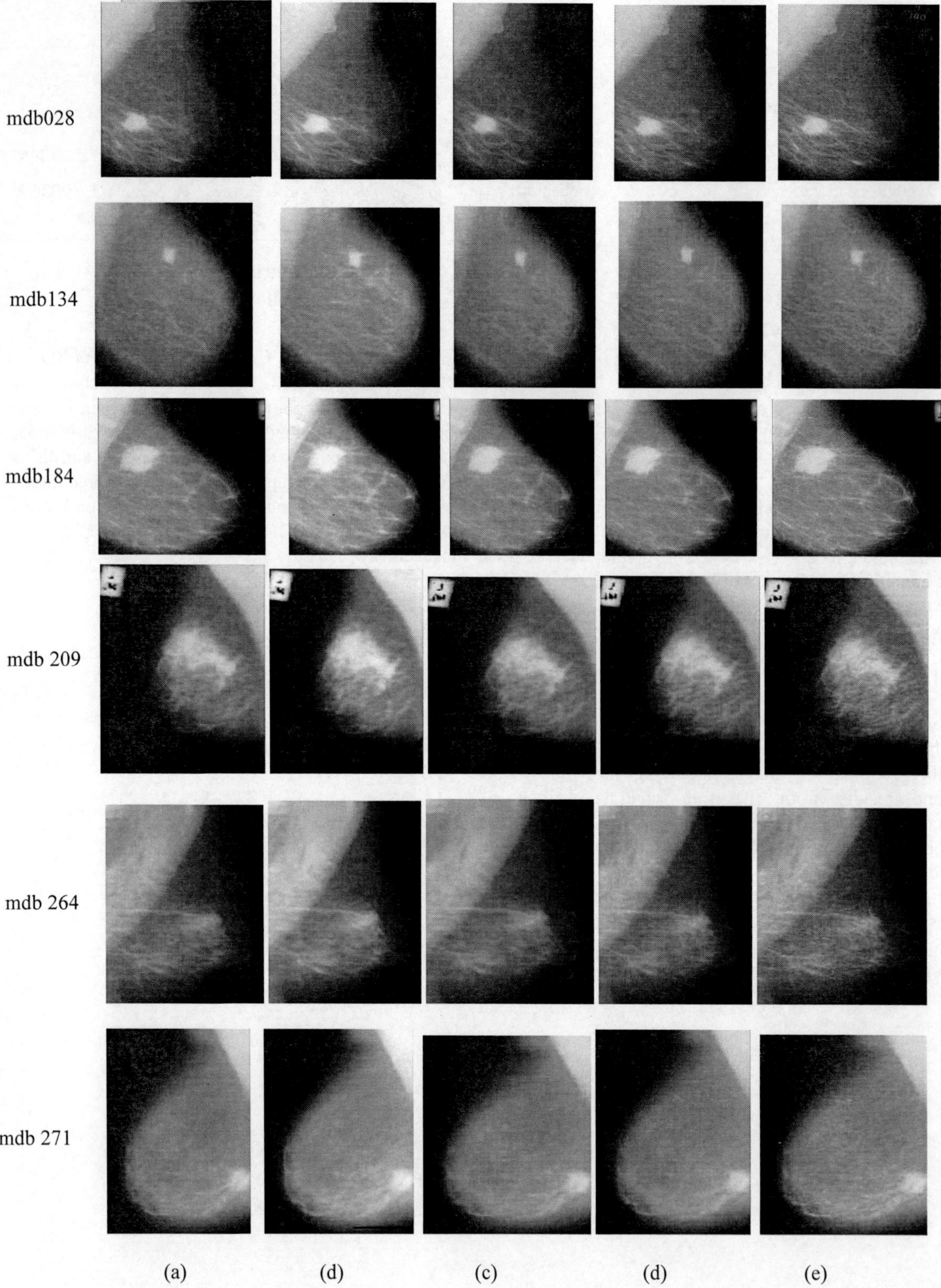

(a) (d) (c) (d) (e)

Figure.7. Enhanced Images:(a) original Image (b)Vishu shrink (c) Bayers shrink (d) Sure shrink (e) Proposed

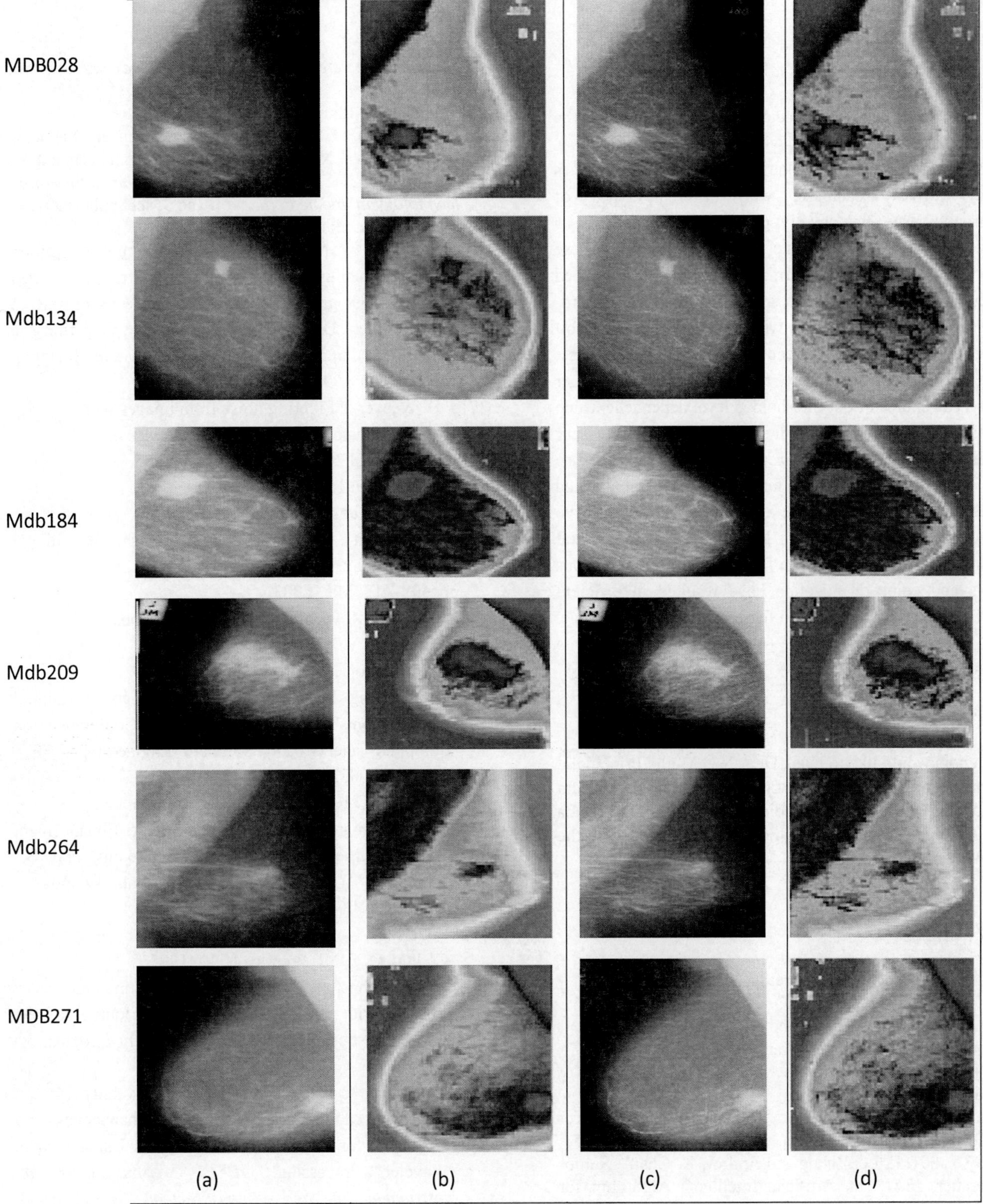

Figure.8. Detection of ROI: (a) original image (b) detection on original image (c) enhanced image (d) detection on enhanced image

5 Conclusion

In this paper, we have presented an algorithm to improve the contrast of the mammograms without enhancing the noise. 80 mammograms from the Mammographic Image Analysis Society (MIAS) database, with different types of background tissue such as fatty, glandular and dense breasts were obtained to evaluate the algorithm. These mammograms contain abnormalities like circumscribed masses, ill-defined masses, speculated masses, micro-calcifications and also images with no abnormality. The bi-orthogonal wavelet used for denoising provides linear phase, which is essential for image reconstruction with higher fidelity The choice of our threshold is level dependent which guarantees the preservation of fine details that are necessary for clinical evaluation. The ROC curve shows that the false positives per image have been fairly reduced. The enhanced images are free from the drawbacks of excessive enhancement wherein artifacts look like calcification and masking of existing lesion. The formations of homogeneous regions and color quantization have resulted in efficient identification of ROI. Although these results are acceptable, it is necessary to test the algorithm for real time mammograms.

Acknowledgment

The authors would like to thank Dr.A.N.N.Muthy,Principal, Dayananda Sagar College of Enigineering and Dr.Sairam Geethanath, HOD, dept. of Medical Electronics, Dayananda Sagar College of Engineering, India, for their support in the development of this work.

References

[1] American cancer Society Breast Cancer Facts & Figures 2011-2012.

[2] R. E. Bird, T. W. Wallace and B. C, Yankaskas, "Analysis of cancers missed at screening Mammography",*Radiology*, vol.184,pp,613–617, 1992

[3]Samuel K. Moore, "Better breat cancer detection", *IEEE* Spectrum, vol.38,Issue 5, pp. 50– 54, May 2001. [a]Lei Zheng and Andrew K. Chan*, Senior Member, *IEEE* an Artificial Intelligent Algorithm for Tumor Detection in Screening Mammogram *IEEE Transactions on medical imaging*, vol. 20,no. 7, July 2001

[4] Jinshan Tang, Xiaoming Liu, Qingling Sun. Adirect Image Contrast Enhancement Algorithm in the Wavelet Domain for Screening Mammograms. *IEEE Journal of Selected Topics in Signal Processing*. 3:74-80, 2009.

[5] Rangaraj M. Rangayyan, Liang Shen", Improvement of Sensitivity of Breast Cancer Diagnosis with Adaptive Neighborhood contrast enhancement of mammograms " *IEEE Transactions on information technology in biomedicine,* vol.1,no.3, september1997.

[6] E. D. Pisano, Shuquan Zong, B. M. Hemminger, M. Deluca, R. E. Johnston, K. Muller, M. P. Braeuning, and S. M. Pizer, Contrast Limited Adaptive Histogram Equalization Image Processing to Improve the Detection of Simulated Spiculations in Dense Mammograms.Journal of Digital Imaging, vol.11, no.4, 1998,pp.193-200.

[7] J. B. Weaver. " Filtering noise from images with wavelet transforms" *Magnetic Resonance in Medicine* vol 21, Issue 2, pages 288–295, October 1991.

[8] P. Heinlein et al. Integrated wavelets for enhancement of microcalcifications in digital mammography, *IEEE Trans. Med. Imag*., vol. 22, no. 3, pp. 402–413, Mar. 2003.

[9] Vetterli.M, Kovacevi'c. Wavelets and subband Coding. (NY, NJ: Prentice Hall), 1995.

[10] Walid Dabour. "Improve Wavelet Based Thresholding for Contrast Enhancement of Digital Mammograms". Proc. International Conference on Computer science and Software Engineering-*IEEE* . 948-951, 2008.

[11]Amutha.S, D.R Ramesh Babu, R.Ravishankar, Harish Kumar. "Mammographic Image Enhancement using Modified Mathematical Morphology and Bi-Orthogonal Wavelet". Proc. International symposium ITiME. 1: 548 – 553, 2011 China.

[12] Vetterli.M, Kovacevi'c. Wavelets and Subband Coding. (NY, NJ: Prentice Hall), 1995.

[13] Iain M. Johnstone. Wavelet threshold estimators for data with correlated noise, 1996. Journal of the Royal Statistical Society. Series B (Methodological) © 1997

[14] Mencattini A. Salmeri M Lojacono, University of Rome. Mammographic Images Enhancement and Denoising for Breast Cancer Detection Using Dyadic Wavelet Processing. *IEEE transactions on instrumentation and measurement*. 57:1422-1430, 2008.

[15] Indra Kantha maitra"Identification of Abnormal Masses in Digital Mammography Images"

[16] Korean J Radiol 2005, "Mammographic mass detection using a mass template"

[17] Meenalosini and Dr.J. Janet "Detection of Malignancy in Mammograms using Region Growing and GLCM Features"

[18] Eng J.ROC Analysis: Web-Based Calculator for ROC Curves.johns Hopkins university may 2006 . http://www.jrocfit.org

[19] Vijaya Kumar Gunturu, Ambalika Sharma "Contrast Enhancement of Mammographic Images Using Wavelet Transform" 978-1-4244-5540-9/10/ 2010 *IEEE*

Semi-Supervised Multi-Phase Image Segmentation and Application to Deep-Gray-Matter Segmentation in MRI Brain Images

Fuhua Chen[1], Hongyuan Wang[2]
[1]Dept. of Natural Science & Mathematics, West Liberty University, West Liberty, WV, USA
[2](Correspondence author) School of Information Science & Engineering
Changzhou University, Changzhou, Jiangsu, China

Abstract— *Unsupervised image segmentations are usually implemented without human interactions, but the segmentation is sometime incorrect for complicated images, especially when the features of different classes are very close. On the other hand, supervised image segmentation, utilizing the features obtained by machine-learning and then applying some classification algorithms to the features, can usually get much more satisfying results. But supervised methods, are usually time-consuming, and only efficient for a specific type of data for each method. By a trade-off, semi-supervised segmentation integrates the advantages of both supervised segmentation and unsupervised segmentation. In this paper, we proposed a semi-supervised multi-phase image segmentation framework which is motivated by image matting and central-gray-matter segmentation for magnetic resonance images (MRI). In our framework, an image is divided into two parts at the beginning, i.e., the known parts (labeled data) and the unknown parts (unlabeled data). The image segmentation is then to determine the unknown parts only. The class of a pixel in unknown part will be determined by not only its own features and the features of the known parts, but also its distance from the known parts. Experimental results demonstrate that our method outperforms unsupervised methods. Our method is also more efficient than supervised methods in the sense that there is no data required for training in order to obtain features for classification.*

Keywords: Semi-supervised segmentation, multiphase segmentation, MRI brain image segmentation, Deep gray matter segmentation

1. Introduction

Unsupervised methods explore the intrinsic data features to partition an image into regions with different statistics. The segmentation procedure can be implemented using some assigned algorithm automatically without human beings' interaction or interfering. Different from unsupervised segmentation, supervised image segmentation is a technique that classifies images using some assigned features for each class. These features usually obtained by machine learning due to the complexity of images. When image features are simple and able to be distinguished easily, supervised methods are not really necessary. However, when the image is much complicated, especially when the features of different classes are very close, unsupervised methods often fail to achieve a desired result. On the other hand, supervised image segmentation methods taking a learning procedure with a labeled training set to form a classifier, are likely to give a better result than unsupervised methods. However, marking the training set is very time-consuming.

The terms "supervised" or "unsupervised" comes from machine learning in computer vision. One typical example of unsupervised method is k-mean clustering. By only using image statistics, clustering algorithms partition an image in coherent groups without using labeled information. Most of the model-based segmentation methods belong to unsupervised methods. Many of them can still be viewed as an extension of clustering methods. Semi-supervised methods take a trade-off between supervised methods and unsupervised methods by inferring the classification from partially labeled data. The key difference between supervised learning and semi-supervised learning is that semi-supervised methods utilize the data features in both the labeled and unlabeled data points [2], while supervised learning only uses the features of labeled data. Hence, the main advantage of semi-supervised image segmentation methods is that they take advantage of the user markings to direct the segmentation, while minimizing the need for user labeling. There are several general approaches towards semi-supervised learning, but recent developments have mainly focused on graph-based methods [2] under discrete settings, probably because the graph-based representation naturally copes with nonlinear data manifolds. In this formulation, data are represented by nodes in a graph, and the edge weights are given by some measure of distance or affinity between the data. Then, the labels for the unlabeled points are found by propagating the labels of labeled points through the graph. Based on this methodology, a number of methods have been proposed [1], [6], [10], [11], [12]. Paper [13] gives a survey of literatures on semi-supervised learning. However, except for [6], these methods are all for general data classification, none of which are developed specifically for image segmentations, probably because of their discrete settings.

Although in some papers, authors didn't strictly distinguish semi-supervised methods and supervised methods, strictly supervised segmentation methods are actually quite different from semi-supervised segmentation methods. Generally speaking, the supervised segmentation sets up a learning machine before a segmentation is carried out. The learning process is performed at a large training set of the similar kind of data sets. Therefore, a strict supervised segmentation model is usually designed for a specific kind of images, such as cell segmentations, spine-segmentations, prostate segmentation, and so on. The learning procedure is usually carried out before the segmentation of such kind of images are performed. As soon as the learning procedure is finished, the features obtained can be used for segmentations of all such kind of images. Different from supervised segmentation, semi-supervised segmentation methods or interactive segmentation methods are carried out by interfering segmentation each time before an automatic segmentation procedure is performed.

Except for discrete settings, supervised image segmentation technique has also been embedded in continuous models. G. Gilboa and S. Osher [5] proposed a supervised segmentation model based on non-local information. N. Houhou et al. proposed a semi-supervised image segmentation method that relies on a non-local continuous version of the min-cut algorithm and labels or seeds provided by a user [6]. The segmentation process is performed via energy minimization. The proposed energy is composed of three terms. The first term defines labels or seed points assigned to objects that the user wants to identify. The second term carries out the diffusion of object and background labels and stops the diffusion when the interface between the object and the background is reached. The diffusion process is performed on a graph defined from image intensity patches. The graph of intensity patches is known to better deal with textures because this graph uses semi-local and non-local image information. The last term is the standard total variation (TV) term that regularizes the geometry of the interface.

Image matting is a 2-D interactive semi-supervised soft image segmentation technique for color images. In digital matting, a foreground element is extracted from an image by estimating a color and opacity for the foreground element at each pixel. The opacity value at each pixel is typically called its *alpha*, and the *opacity* image, taken as a whole, is referred to as the *alpha matte* (between 0 and 1) or *key*. Matting is used in order to composite the foreground element into a new scene. Matting and compositing were originally developed for film and video production. Some examples of image matting methods are Poisson Matting [9], Bayesian Matting [3] and Spectral Matting [8].

Formally, image matting methods take as input an image I, which is assumed to be a composite of a foreground image F and a background image B. The color of the i-th pixel

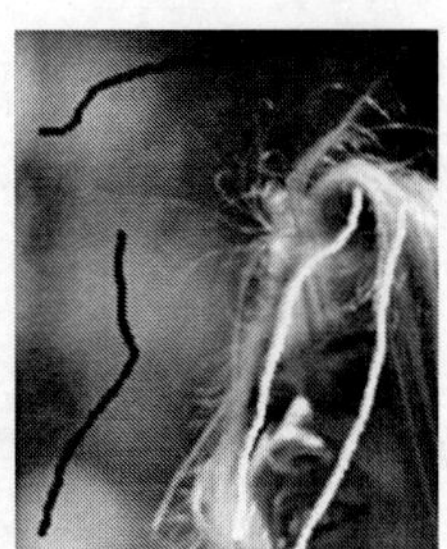

Fig. 1: Image matting.The black part drawn for background, the white part drawn for foreground, and other area for unknown part form a trimap.

is assumed to be a linear combination of the corresponding foreground and background colors,

$$I_i = \alpha_i F_i + (1 - \alpha_i) B_i \tag{1}$$

where α_i is the pixelą́rs foreground opacity. In natural image matting, all quantities on the right hand side of the equation are unknown. Obviously, this is a severely under-constrained problem, and user interaction is required to extract a good matte. Most recent methods expect the user to provide a trimap as a start. Such an example is shown in Figure 1. The trimap is a rough (typically hand-drawn) segmentation of the image into three regions: foreground (shown in white), background (shown in black) and unknown (shown in gray). Given the trimap, these methods usually solve for F, B, and α simultaneously. This is typically done by iterative nonlinear optimization, alternating the estimation of F and B with that of α. In practice, this means that for good results the unknown regions in the trimap must be as small as possible.

This paper is motivated by image matting and central-gray-matter segmentation for magnetic resonance (MR) brain images. It is a part of a large project "Biochemical Markers of Traumatic Brain Injury ą́s supported by NIH (National Institutes of Health) grant. In a MR brain image, the intensities of white matter are usually greater than the intensities of gray matter. However, in the central area, the intensities of gray matter (called deep gray matter or central gray matter) are very close to white matter. Even worse, the intensities of central gray matter are usually greater than the intensities of white matter located in outer layer of brain. Therefore, in order to precisely segment MR brain images, supervised or semi-supervised image segmentation methods must be used. Just like image matting, existing semi-supervised image segmentations are mostly developed for two-phase images. In this paper, we developed a new semi-supervised multi-phase image segmentation frame work based on the model developed in paper [4]. The following of this paper is organized as follows: Section 2 is an introduction to piecewise constant multi-phase soft segmentation model [4]. The model is then utilized to develop a semi-supervised framework in Section 3, followed by the implementation in Section 4. Section 5 shows some fundamental experimental results. At the end is a short conclusion.

2. Multi-phase Soft Segmentation Model

Given a source image $I(x)$, we assume the image contains N classes. Let $u_i(x)$ denote the i-th pattern and $p_i(x)$ be the i-th membership function. A piecewise smoothed soft Mumford-Shah model is defined as follow:

$$\begin{aligned} E(u;p) =& \sum_{i=1}^{N} \frac{1}{2} \int_{\Omega} (I(x) - u_i(x))^2 p_i(x) dx \\ &+ \sum_{i=1}^{N} \lambda \int_{\Omega} |\nabla u_i(x)| dx + \sum_{i=1}^{N} \mu \int_{\Omega} |\nabla p_i(x)| dx \end{aligned} \tag{2}$$

The iterations based on fast gradient-descent method are

$$\begin{cases} \dfrac{\partial E}{\partial u_i} = -\lambda div(\dfrac{\nabla u_i}{|\nabla u_i|}) + (u_i - I)p_i \\ \dfrac{\partial E}{\partial p_i} = -\mu div(\dfrac{\nabla p_i}{|\nabla p_i|}) + (u_i - I)^2 \end{cases} \tag{3}$$

The primal-dual form of (2) with respect to u is

$$\begin{aligned} \min_{u} \max_{|v| \le 1} E(u, v; p) =& \sum_{i=1}^{N} \frac{1}{2} \int_{\Omega} (I(x) - u_i(x))^2 p_i(x) dx \\ &+ \sum_{i=1}^{N} \lambda \int_{\Omega} u_i(x) div\ v_i dx \end{aligned} \tag{4}$$

The primal-dual form of (2) with respect to p is

$$\begin{aligned} \min_{p \in \Delta_{N-1}} \max_{|q| \le 1} E(u; p, q) =& \sum_{i=1}^{N} \frac{1}{2} \int_{\Omega} (I(x) - u_i(x))^2 p_i(x) dx \\ &+ \sum_{i=1}^{N} \lambda \int_{\Omega} p_i(x) div\ q_i dx \end{aligned} \tag{5}$$

The iteration on u and v is

$$\begin{cases} \dfrac{\partial u_i}{\partial t} = -\left[(u_i - I)p_i + \lambda div\ v_i\right] \\ \dfrac{\partial v_i}{\partial t} = -\lambda \nabla u_i \end{cases} \tag{6}$$

The iteration on p and q is

$$\begin{cases} \dfrac{\partial p_i}{\partial t} = -\left[(u_i - I)^2 + \mu div\ q_i\right] \\ \dfrac{\partial q_i}{\partial t} = -\mu \nabla p_i \end{cases} \tag{7}$$

3. From Unsupervised Segmentation to Semi-Supervised Segmentation

In an interactive semi-supervised image segmentation, an image is assumed to include two parts: the known part Ω_i, $i = 1, 2, ..., N$ and the unknown part Ω_U. Only the unknown part needs to be applied for segmentation. The above model is then to find segmentation only for the domain Ω_U, i.e., to minimize the following energy functional:

$$\begin{aligned} E(p) =& \sum_{i=1}^{N} \frac{1}{2} \int_{\Omega_U} (I(x) - u_i(x))^2 p_i(x) dx \\ &+ \sum_{i=1}^{N} \lambda \int_{\Omega_U} |\nabla u_i(x)| dx + \sum_{i=1}^{N} \mu \int_{\Omega_U} |\nabla p_i(x)| dx \end{aligned} \tag{8}$$

If we solve this problem still using previous procedures (6) and (7), then it is not a supervised segmentation since we didn't use any known information to instruct segmentation for the unknown area. The key point of our work is to update each pattern u_i based on the nearest point principle, i.e.,

$$u_i(x) = average\{u_i(y) |\ y = arg \min_{y} \{|x - y|, y \in \Omega_i\}\} \tag{9}$$

which is referred from the third step of Poisson Matting [9].

With initially given patterns $u_i(x)$ and under smoothness constraint of $p_i(x)$, the objective energy functional becomes

$$\begin{aligned} E(p) =& \sum_{i=1}^{N} \frac{1}{2} \int_{\Omega_U} (I(x) - u_i(x))^2 p_i(x) dx \\ &+ \sum_{i=1}^{N} \mu \int_{\Omega_U} |\nabla p_i(x)| dx \end{aligned} \tag{10}$$

where each $u_i(x)$ is determined by (9).

Considering that the close relation of points when they are near to each other and the loose relation when they are far away, we add a distance factor to the fitting term. The energy functional is therefore becomes

$$\begin{aligned} E(p) =& \sum_{i=1}^{N} \frac{1}{2} \int_{\Omega_U} (I(x) - u_i(x))^2 p_i(x) e^{\alpha d_i(x)} dx \\ &+ \sum_{i=1}^{N} \mu \int_{\Omega_U} |\nabla p_i(x)| dx \end{aligned} \tag{11}$$

where α is a parameter and $d_i(x)$ is the nearest distance from each pixel x to the i-th unknown area Ω_i. The factor $e^{\alpha d_i(x)}$ will force the influence to be ignored when the distance of a point x from a known area Ω_i is far away.

Correspondingly, we rewrite the energy with indication functions and replace the total variation by weighted total variation, we get the final energy functional

$$E(p) = \sum_{i=1}^{N} \int_{\Omega} (I(x) - u_i(x))^2 p_i(x) e^{\alpha d_i(x)} \chi_{\Omega_U}(x) dx + \sum_{i=1}^{N} \mu \int_{\Omega} |\nabla p_i(x)| g(\nabla \tilde{I}(x)) \chi_{\Omega_U}(x) dx \quad (12)$$

where $\tilde{I}$ is a smoothness of I and $g(x_1, x_2)$ is an edge function usually defined as $\frac{1}{1 + x_1^2 + x_2^2}$.

4. Solving Semi-Supervised Multi-phase Image Segmentation

The primal-dual form of (12) is

$$E(p) = \sum_{i=1}^{N} \int_{\Omega} (I(x) - u_i(x))^2 p_i(x) e^{\alpha d_i(x)} \chi_{\Omega_U}(x) dx + \sum_{i=1}^{N} \mu \sup_{q_i \in K} \int_{\Omega} p_i(x) div\ (g(\nabla \tilde{I}(x)) \chi_{\Omega_U}(x) q_i(x)) dx \quad (13)$$

where $K = \{\phi \in C_c^1(\Omega, R^2) : |\phi| \leq 1\}$.
So, the iteration on p and q are, respectively,

$$\begin{cases} \frac{\partial p_i}{\partial t} = -\left[(u_i - I)^2 e^{\alpha d_i(x)} \chi_{\Omega_U}(x) + \mu\ div\ (g(\nabla \tilde{I}(x)) \chi_{\Omega_U}(x) q_i(x))\right] \\ \frac{\partial q_i}{\partial t} = -\mu (\nabla p_i) g(\nabla \tilde{I}(x)) \chi_{\Omega_U}(x) \end{cases} \quad (14)$$

In our framework, the new memberships $p_i(x)$ obtained from above iterations are actually a temporary one. We still need to update the memberships based on the following rule: if $p_i(x) > 0.95$ and $I(x) \approx u_i(x)$ for some $1 \leq i \leq N$ and $x \in \Omega_U$, then put x to Ω_i^+. So, the known parts are updated by

$$\Omega_i = \Omega_i \cup \Omega_i^+. \quad (15)$$

Correspondingly, the unknown part is updated according to the following equation

$$\Omega_U = \Omega - \bigcup_{i=1}^{N} \Omega_i \quad (16)$$

We now describe the complete algorithm. Given an image I defined in a domain Ω, if the image contains N classes, then the complete algorithm for our semi-supervised multi-phase image segmentation is given as below.

1) **Initialization.**
   a) Initialize known parts Ω_i^0 using brush;
   b) Initialize unknown part by $\Omega_U^0 = \Omega - \bigcup_{i=1}^{N} \Omega_i^0$;
   c) Initialize memberships: For each $1 \leq i \leq N$ and $x \in \Omega_i^0$, set $p_i^0(x) = 1$ and $p_j^0(x) = 0$ for $j \neq i$; for $x \in \Omega_U^0$, set $p_i(x)$ randomly.
   d) Initialize patterns: For each $1 \leq i \leq N$ and $x \in \Omega_i^0$, set $u_i^0(x) = I(x)$; For any $x \in \Omega_U^0$, set $u_i^0(x)$ in terms of the nearest point principle as (9);
2) **Iterations.**
   a) Update memberships $p_i^k(x)$ by (14);
   b) Update known areas Ω_i^k by (15);
   c) Update unknown area Ω_U^k by (16);
   d) Update patterns $u_i^k(x)$ by (9);
3) **Termination** The iterations will be terminated if

$$\Omega_U = \emptyset$$

5. Experimental Results

We carried out several experiments to show the efficiency of our method. In Figure 2, we show how semi-supervised algorithm works differently from general unsupervised segmentation. The original image contains two objects with same intensities as shown in Figure 2(b). Suppose that only the left one is the object that we need to separate from the background. Under unsupervised segmentation methods, the segmentation of the foreground will be exactly the same as shown in Figure 2(b). However, if we circle a green mask as the seed for the background and circle a red mask as the seed for the foreground as shown in Figure 2(a), then the segmentation of the foreground is shown as in Figure 2(c), which is the desired one.

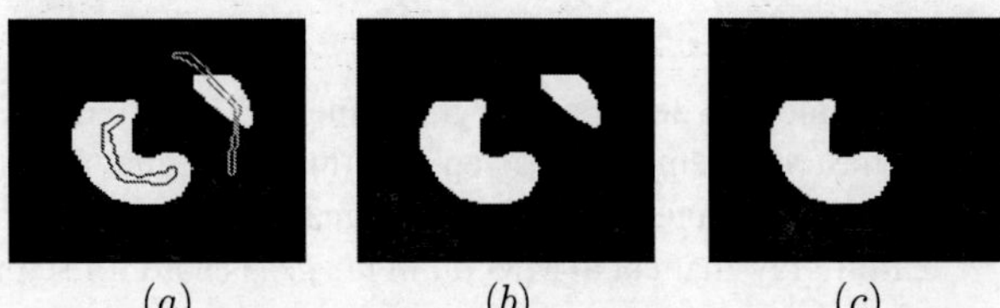

(a) (b) (c)

Fig. 2: Principle of semi-supervised segmentation: (a) Original image with masks. (b) Original image and unsupervised segmentation. (c) Supervised segmentation.

In Figure 3, we present a comparison of a flower segmentation using supervised segmentation and unsupervised segmentation. Note that the central part of the flower is same dark as the background. If we use unsupervised segmentation model, the central part of the flower will be classified as background (see the central part of (b1)). With semi-supervised method, the segmentation result is perfect (see the central part of (b2) and compare it with the central part of (b1)).

Figure 4 shows the shrinking procedure of the unknown area in the first 10 iterations in the flower segmentation, where dark areas are unknown areas, from where we can see how fast the iterations converge. For a 240×240 image, the iterations take around 8 seconds. However, if use the corresponding unsupervised method, the iterations will take around 68 seconds under same converge settings.

Fig. 3: Comparison between the segmentations using supervised method and unsupervised method: (a1) Original image. (a2) Original image with assigned class masks. (b1) and (c1) Unsupervised segmentation: (b1) is the pattern of background and (c1) is the pattern of foreground. (b2) and (c2) Supervised segmentation: (b2) is the pattern of background and (c2) is the pattern of foreground.

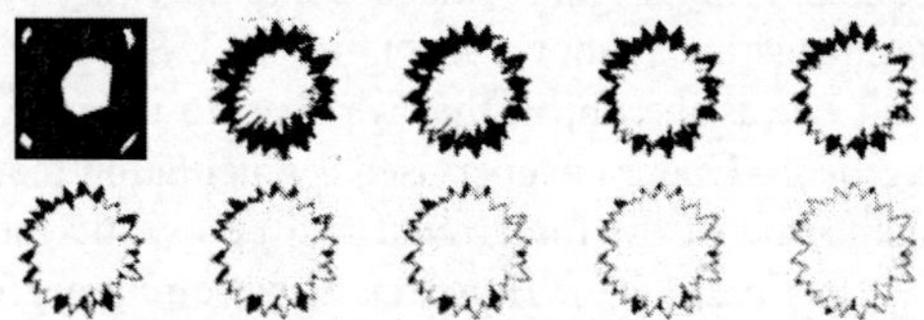

Fig. 4: Unknown area for the flower segmentation shrinks in the first ten iterations: converges very fast.

5.1 Application to deep-gray-matter segmentation of MRI brain images

The method developed in this paper is actually motivated by the requirement of deep-gray-matter segmentation in MRI brain images. The deep-gray-matter (sometimes called central-gray-matter) in MRI brain images is hard for segmentation due to its intensity much different from the general gray matter and very close to the intensity of white matter. We use the developed method to segment deep-gray-matter from MRI brain images and obtained ideal result.

In Figure 5, we show the comparison between unsupervised method and supervised method, as well as the comparison between using more known areas and using less known areas. We use an MR brain image as an example. It is well known that the central gray matter (or deep gray matter) has very similar intensities to the white matter's intensities. The first row is the segmentations with the unsupervised segmentation method; the second row is the segmentations with the supervised segmentation method but with less known area; the third row is the segmentations also with the supervised segmentation method but with more known area; and the last row is the segmentations obtained first with the unsupervised method and then fixed under experienced doctors' instructions. In the first row, (a1) is the original image, and (b1) through (d1) are the segmentations of cerebrospinal fluid (C.S.F), gray matter and white matter, respectively. In row 2, (a2) is the original image with less assigned class masks, and (b2) through (d2) are the segmentations of C.S.F, gray matter and white matter, respectively. In the third row, (a3) is the original image with more assigned class masks, and (b3) through (d3) are the segmentation of C.S.F, gray matter and white matter, respectively. In the last row, (a4) is the image with a mask drawn with hand by experienced doctors, and (b4) through (d4) are segmentations obtained with the unsupervised segmentation method and then fixed with the masks drawn in (4a).

From the results, we can easily see that supervised segmentation is always better than unsupervised segmentation, and supervised segmentation with more labeled area is better than the result with less labeled area. Figure 5(b4-d4) is the result obtained by unsupervised segmentation first and then fixed under the instruction of experienced doctors. So,(b4-d4) can serve as ground truth data. We can see that the supervised segmentation results (b3-d3) are very close to the ground truth. Meanwhile, with choosing some area from just SINGLE slice of the image, we can use supervised method to segment ALL slices of a 3-D MRI brain image very well. In this way, a lot of time can be saved.

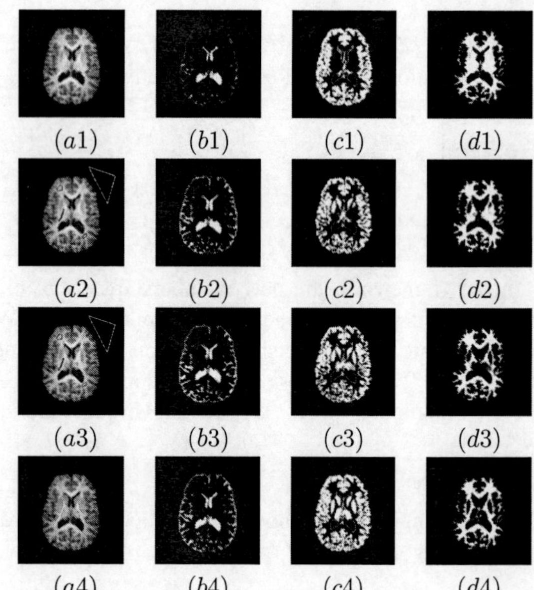

Fig. 5: Comparison between unsupervised method and supervised method, as well as the comparison between using more known areas and using less known areas.

6. Conclusion and future work

This work is motivated by MR brain image segmentations which is one part of our previous project. The project has been closed in the summer of 2012. It is well known that in the central area of a MR brain image, the intensities of gray matter is usually very close to the intensities of white matter. Sometimes (actually very often), the intensities of central gray matter is bigger than the intensities of white matter not located in the central part. If we only use unsupervised segmentation methods, we can't obtain the desired result.

The frame work of semi-supervised image segmentation discussed in this paper is still based on intensity. When the image contains some texture features, the frame work does not work very efficiently. In this case, feature-based model must be used in the frame work. Let $F : \Omega \subset R^n \rightarrow Z \subset R^m$ be a function which maps an n-dimensional image domain to a multi-dimensional (m-dimensional) space of contextual features Z. For each point $x \in \Omega$, $F(x)$ is a vector containing image statistics or features. Such features can encode contextual knowledge about the region of interest and its neighboring structures (e.g., size, shape, orientation, relationships to neighboring structures, etc.). Feature-based image segmentation is extensively used in texture segmentation and some medical image segmentation. Therefore, an immediate future work is to develop a feature-based semi-supervised multiphase image segmentation frame work. Please address any questions related to this paper to Hongyuan Wang by Email (`hywang@cczu.edu.cn`).

References

[1] M. Belkin, P. Niyogi, and V. Sindhwani, "On manifold regularization," *Proc. Intl. Workshop on Artificial Intelligence and Statistics*, Barbados, Jan. 2005.

[2] Olivier Chapelle, Bernhard Scholkopf, and Alexander Zien, (Eds.), *Semi-Supervised Learning*, MIT Press, 2006.

[3] Yung-Yu Chuang, Brian Curless, David H. Salesin, and Richard Szeliski, "A Bayesian approach to digital matting," *CVPR*, 2001.

[4] Fuhua Chen and Yunmei Chen, "A Stochastic Variational Model for Multi-phase Soft Segmentation with Bias correction," *Advanced Modeling and Optimization*, Vol. 12, No. 3, pp. 339-345, 2010.

[5] G. Gilboa and S. Osher, "Nonlocal linear image regularization and supervised segmentation," *UCLA cam report 06-47*, 2006

[6] N. Houhou, X. Bresson, A. Szlam, T. F. Chan, and J.-P. Thiram, "Semi-supervised segmentation based on nonlocal continuous min-cut," *Proc. of the Intl. Conf. on Scale Space and Variational Methods in Computer Vision*, LNCS 5567, Voss, Norway, June, 2009.

[7] S. Lee, "Efficient multistage approach for unsupervised image classification," *IEEE International Geoscience and Remote Sensing Symposium (IGARSS)*, Anchorage, AK, USA, pp. 1581–1584, 2004.

[8] A. Levin, A. Rav-Acha, and D. Lischinski, "Spectral Matting," *IEEE Trans. on PAMI*, Vol. 30, No. 10, pp. 1699–1712, 2008.

[9] Jian Sun, Jiaya Jia, Chi-Keung Tang, and Heung-Yeung Shum, "Poisson Matting," *ACM Trans. Graph.*, vol. 23, no. 3, pp. 315–321, 2004.

[10] Fei Wang, Jingdong Wang, Changshui Zhang, and Helen C. Shen, "Semi-supervised classification using linear neighborhood propagation," *Proc. IEEE Conf. on Computer Vision and Pattern Recognition*, New York, NY, USA, June, 2006.

[11] Dengyong Zhou, Olivier Bousquet, Thomas N. Lal, Jason Weston, and Bernhard Scholkopf, "Learning with local and global consistency," *Advances Neural Information Processing Systems*, Vancouver, BC, Canada, Dec. 2003.

[12] Xiaojin Zhu, Zoubin Ghahramani, and John Lafferty, "Semi-supervised learning with Gaussian fields and harmonic functions," *Proc. Intl. Conf. on Machine Learning*, Washington, D.C, USA, Aug. 2003.

[13] Xiaojin Zhu, "Semi-supervised learning literature survey," *Computer Sciences TR 1530*, University of WisconsinÍCMadison, 2008.

Cardiac Motion Reconstruction Using LKT Algorithm from 2D and 3D Echocardiography

Alice Gao[1], W. Li[2,3], C. Lin[2], M. Loomes[3], X. Gao[3]

[1] Barts and The London School of Medicine and Dentistry, Queen Mary, University of London, London E1 2AD, UK.
[2] Biomedical Engineering Institute, Fuzhou University, Fuzhou, Fujian 350002, China.
[3]School of Science and Technology, Middlesex University, London,NW4 4BT. UK.

Abstract- *The rhythm of the heart endows us with not only a life insurance but also a barometer indicating any potential abnormities. Hence the accurate measurement of heart motion has profound clinical benefit in assisting diagnostic decision making and yet remains a challenging issue to be confronted. Perceptibly, heart motion can be quantified manually from M-mode diagrams of echocardiographs which are created by way of sound waves while a patient undergoing scanning. Alternatively, the motion can be monitored automatically by post-image processing techniques analyzing B-mode video sequences. This paper explores the feasibility of the application of Lucas-Kanada-Tomasi algorithm towards the reconstruction of m-mode diagrams from 2D sequences and tissue velocity curves from 3D video clips for the left ventricle. Preliminary results reveals promising match between the post-processing findings and real-time scanning data and being in consistent agreement with the similar studies.*

Keywords: 2D and 3D echocardiographs, M-mode, B-mode, LKT algorithm, cardiac motion reconstruction

1. Introduction

Echocardiography has become an inseparable addition to the current array of advanced medical equipment, largely due to its competitive nature of being non-invasive, portable, inexpensive and easy to operate, leading to it being a ubiquitous imaging tool. More importantly, echocardiography displays the moving heart in real time, revealing the health status of the heart in vivo. One of the key indicators of potential heart-related diseases including ischemic is the function of heart motion, in which parameters such as directional moving curves, amplitude, velocity, and acceleration all play an important part.

In general, an echocardiography scanner has a built-in motion mode (i.e, m-mode) diagram depicting the moving patterns on a pre-defined line, in addition to the reconstruction of B-mode images (i.e., brightness sequenced images). In this way, an m-mode graph is rendered by using ultrasonic wave beams based on the principles frequency shift, the same way as to produce B-mode video images.

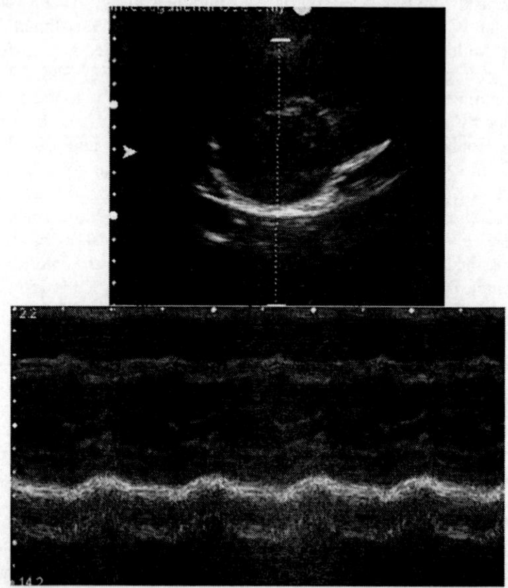

Figure 1. An m-mode diagram (bottom) acquired along the scanning line shown on the top image of left ventricle, which are acquired using Sonix Tablet.

Figure 1 demonstrates an example of m-mode waveform diagram (bottom) and a b-mode image (top) of a 2D echocardiograph. On an m-mode diagram, a number of measurements can be performed, including left ventricular dimensions (e.g., LVDd, LVDs, PWT, etc..), aortic root and left atrial dimensions (e.g., AO, LA) as well as a number of motion parameters, such as velocity (or slope).

In 3D/4D situations, tissue velocity curves can be constructed in real time, as illustrated in Figure 2. In this case, a tool of Tissue Velocity Imaging (TVI) needs to be in place which applies the principle of myocardial Doppler frequency shifts to quantify myocardial tissues motion (right graph) where the velocity curve refers to the point circled on the top left of the graph.

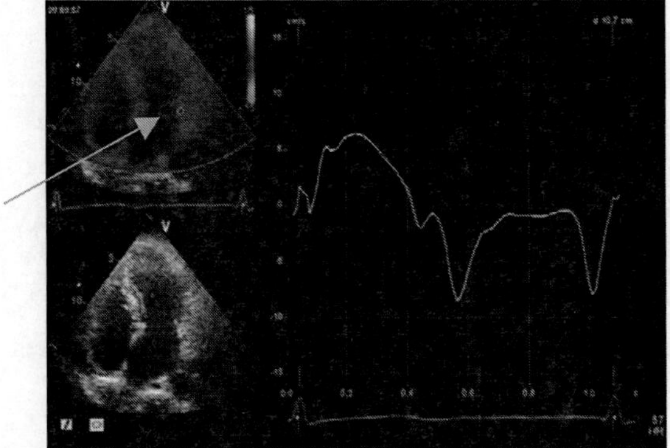

Figure 2. 3D/4D echocardiograph with tissue velocity curve (right) that correlates with the point circled in white on the top-left graph pointed by the arrow. These data are obtained from GE Vivid 7 scanner. The colour blue refers to the blood flow being away from the receiver whilst the red colour towards the transducer.

Ideally, any measurement related to the motion should be performed manually on a scanner in real time to reflect the up to date situation of the heart, which however at present is rarely feasible due to the compelling need of use of the scanner. Furthermore further investigations might be in need at a later stage necessitating the measurements on different direction lines. As a result, post processing on B-mode images have been actively researched in an attempt to re-build motion diagrams. Towards this end, the focus is shifted on to the study of optical flow that reflects velocities by using brightness patterns in an image [1, 2]. Capitalizing from the Lucas-Kanade algorithm, a number of promising optical flow techniques have been developed for evaluation of heart motions together with the verification techniques [3-5]. More recently, motion analysis of the heart has been deepened into biological (tissue) level by investigating myocardial motion [6]. Again, B-mode images constitute the starting point.

Optical flow works on the direct discovery of image motion at each pixel level based on brightness variations from spatio-temporal images. Although the approach can work on dense motion fields, it remains sensitive to the change of appearance resulting from the variations of brightness in images. Therefore it may be more suitable for video sequences with relative small motions.

On the other hand, an ultrasonic image can only generate a fan-shape view window depicting the characteristics of the heart being in a constant motion, suggesting that each image frame may always introduce new points/objects that are not present in the previous frame, leading to a wrong match of brightness-based points to a certain extent.

Furthermore, echocardiography are composed from 2D ultrasonic images that suffers from mixed outlines of gray level intensity and partial area occlusion with blurry edges, therefore the quality of the images are of generally low resolution. As a direct result, searching for the points with similar brightness or intensity values remains a challenge task while applying the optical flow technique, implying feature selections in an automatic way is very difficult. In this study, a slightly different approach is proposed, which classifies the motion patterns first and then tracks the feature points in a class which are defined by the user towards the reconstruction of M-mode diagrams and tissue velocity curves.

The overall aim of this work is to develop a system that circumvents some of the underlying problems inherent in the analysis of the dynamics of the heart by the application of Lucas-Kanade-Tomasi (LKT) motion tracking algorithm [7].

The original idea of the implementation of LKT intends to deal with the problem inherited from traditional image registration that is generally computationally costly. KLT makes efficient consideration of the spatial intensity information to direct the search towards the positions that can generate the best match. It therefore executes faster than traditional techniques by examining far fewer potential matches between the images. In this investigation, each video clip contains up to 2 seconds of duration of the information of a beating heart, arriving at around a hundred 2D frames with an average size of 650 x 400 pixels each, whereas 3D echocardiography is inherently volumetric. Initial feature points are selected manually or segmented on the first frame, which are then tracked using LKT approach on the following frames.

2. Methodology

2.1 Lucas-Kanade-Tomasi(KLT) algorithm

Since the seminal publication of Lucas-Kanade approach [3] on motion study using the optical flow technique, plethora algorithms are on the offer in providing solutions to solve two unknown parameters in one equation. As shown in Eq. (1) where optical flow is expressed from on frame (left) to the next frame (right) with the displacement $\vec{d} = (\xi, \eta)$ occuring at the point (x, y), (ξ, η) are the two unknowns.

$$I(x, y, t) = I(x + \xi, y + \eta, t + \tau) \quad (1)$$

Based on the Taylor expansion series, the following formula exists.

$$I(x + \xi, y + \eta, t + \tau) \approx I(x, y, t) + \frac{\partial I}{\partial x}\xi + \frac{\partial I}{\partial y}\eta + \frac{\partial I}{\partial t}\tau \quad (2)$$

which results in

$$\frac{\partial I}{\partial x}V_x + \frac{\partial I}{\partial y}V_y + \frac{\partial I}{\partial t} = 0 \quad (3)$$

Where V_x, V_y are the x *and* y components of the velocity or optical flow of *I(x, y, t)* and $\frac{\partial I}{\partial x}, \frac{\partial I}{\partial y}$ *and* $\frac{\partial I}{\partial t}$ are the derivatives of the image at (x, y, t) in the corresponding directions.

Again Eq. (3) has two unknowns that cannot be solved as such, a number of methods have since developed, which started with the popular Lucas-Kanade method [3]. It assumes that the flow is essentially constant in a local neighbourhood of the pixel under consideration, and that solves the basic optical flow equations for all the pixels in that neighbourhood, by the least squares criterion.

As an implementation, the LKT algorithm [7] considers the time as a brevity of duration. If images *I* and *J* are the two frames of a video clip, Eq.(1) is redefined as Eq. (4) by omitting the time variable.

$$J(\vec{x} + \vec{d}) = I(x + \xi, y + \eta, t + \tau) \quad (4)$$

$$J(\vec{x} + \vec{d}) = I(\vec{x}) + n \quad (5)$$

where n indicates noise. The displacement vector $\vec{d}$ is chosen so as to minimize the residue error defined by the double integral over the given window Ψ shown in Eq.(6).

$$\begin{aligned} \epsilon &= \int_\Psi [I(\vec{x}) - J(\vec{x} + \vec{d})]^2 \psi \, d\vec{x} \\ &= \int_\Psi [I(\vec{x}) - \vec{g} \cdot \vec{d} - J(\vec{x})]^2 \psi \, d\vec{x} \\ &= \int_\Psi [h - \vec{g} \cdot \vec{d}]^2 \psi \, d\vec{x} \end{aligned} \quad (6)$$

Where ψ is a weighting function that depends on the image intensity pattern, $J(\vec{x} + \vec{d}) = J(\vec{x}) + \vec{g} \cdot \vec{d}$ according to Taylor's series that is truncated to the linear term, $h = I(\vec{x}) - J(\vec{x})$, and image gradient $\vec{g} = (\frac{\partial I}{\partial x}, \frac{\partial I}{\partial y})$.

2.2 Point tracking

Minimising Eq.(6) gives Eq. (7).

$$\begin{aligned} \frac{d\epsilon}{d\vec{d}} &= \int_\Psi 2(h - \vec{g} \cdot \vec{d})\vec{g} \frac{d\vec{d}}{d\vec{x}} \psi \, d\vec{x} \\ &= \int_\Psi 2(h - \vec{g} \cdot \vec{d})\vec{g}\psi \, d\vec{d} = 0 \end{aligned} \quad (7)$$

Since $(\vec{g} \cdot \vec{d})\vec{g} = \vec{g} \cdot (\vec{g} \cdot \vec{d})^T = \vec{g} \cdot (\vec{g}^T \cdot \vec{d}^T) = (\vec{g} \cdot \vec{g}^T)\vec{d}^T$, the right hand side of Eq.(7) can be written as Eq.(8),

$$\int_\Psi \vec{g}\vec{g}^T \vec{d} \psi \, d\vec{d} = \int_\Psi h \vec{g} \psi \, d\vec{d} \quad (8)$$

Providing $\vec{d}$ remains constant within a window Ψ, Eq.(8) can be further processed as

$$G\vec{d} = \vec{e} \quad (9)$$

where G maintains as a symmetric 2 x 2 matrix

$$G = \int_\Psi \vec{g}\vec{g}^T \psi \, d\vec{d} \quad (10)$$

and

$$\vec{e} = \int_\Psi (I - J)\vec{g}\psi \, d\vec{d} \quad (11)$$

For every pair of adjacent frames, the matrix *G* can be worked out from one frame, by way of estimating the gradients and computing their second order moments. On the other hand, the vector $\vec{e}$ can be computed from the difference between the two frames, along with the gradient *G*. Therefore the displacement $\vec{d}$ can be solved in Eq. (9), which will lead to the location and thereafter tracking of the point of interest in the subsequent frames.

2.3. The complexity of cardiac motion

The heart has sustained a motion of rhythm that cannot be accounted for linearly. Even without the consideration of the artifact of respiration motion, the heart itself is in a state of constant contraction/expansion as well as shifting in response to the force generated by the movement of blood flows (e.g., by pumping out). Therefore the overall motion of the heart is a non-rigid body transformation, indicating that the displacement $\vec{d}$ in Eq. (8) does not retain constant when time progresses from t to $t + \tau$. As a direct result, in order to apply the LKT approach, each region has to maintain a motion with a relatively constant $\vec{d}$. Therefore classification of the heart structure should be performed first to ensure that within each class or sub-region, constant movement in a certain direction can be found, for example, aorta or left ventricle. In terms of the left ventricle, Figure 3 schematically illustrates a simplified motion diagram in an ideal situation.

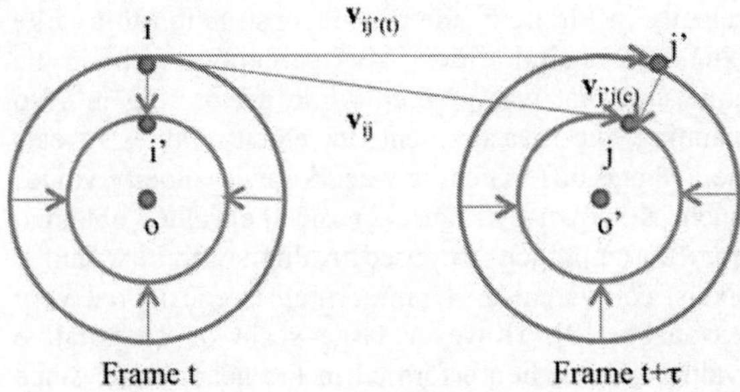

Figure 3. The simulation diagram displaying the ideal situation of left ventricle, where *i is an* arbitrary myocardial point of interest and *j* the corresponding one in the following frame.

For all the feature points in the left ventricle, the motion of the heart is the sum of translation (*t*) and contraction/expansion as presented in Eq. (12).

$$\vec{v}_{ij} = \vec{v}_{j'j(c)} + \vec{v}_{ij'(t)} \quad (12)$$

$$\iint \vec{v}_{ij} didj = \iint \vec{v}_{j'j(c)}\, didj + \iint \vec{v}_{ij'(t)}\, didj \quad (13)$$

$i.e.,$

$$\iint \vec{v}_{j'j(c)} = \iint (\vec{v}_{j'} - \vec{v}_{j})$$
$$= \iint (\vec{v}_{j'} - \vec{v}_{o'}) - \iint (\vec{v}_{j} - \vec{v}_{o'}) = 0 \quad (14)$$

As illustrated in Figure 3, in an ideal situation, the sum of the movement of contraction and expansion with reference to the ventricle centre, $v_{o'}$, for all the tissue points in the left ventricle, falls to zero.

Therefore the overall movement of the left ventricle is

$$\vec{v}_m = \iint \vec{v}_{ij'} didj \quad (15)$$

which represents the translation of the heart, i.e., the centre point $\vec{o}$ in the left frame can be treated as shifted $\vec{v}_m \times \tau$ units into $\vec{o}'$ on the following frame. In this way, the remaining contraction/expansion motion $\vec{v}_{j'j(c)}$ can be investigated separately by way of optical flow technique.

2.4 Reconstruction of M-mode diagrams

M-mode diagrams can be applied to analyze the motion patterns along a scanning line, as demonstrated in Figure 1. In a 2D form, the M-mode waveform can only be acquired in real time when the scanning line is defined. Since post image processing is complementary, necessitating the need of reconstruction of m-mode from the acquired video clips. In this study, after a line, $y=a\ x$, is assigned manually passing through the ventricle centre $\vec{o}$ = (0, 0), where a is a constant and the motion direction being along the line (i.e., contracting towards or expanding away from the centre), the points on the line are then tracked using Eq. (9), whereas the m-mode image is thereafter regenerated using Eq.(16) based on Eq. (12).

$$I_{m\text{-}mode}(t+\tau) = I_{i+1}(x + \xi, y) \quad (16)$$

Where ξ is the displacement compensating the translation movement expressed in Eq. (12), y representing all the points along the pre-defined line, $y = a\ x$.

2.5 Simulation of velocity curve

Due to the advances of imaging technology, tissue velocity imaging (TVI) tools are available in a number of 3D (= 4D with time) ultrasonic scanners, as illustrated in Figure 2. The speed value in TVI is calculated based on the movement of myocardium towards or away from the scanner transducer. In this investigation, the velocity of any pivot point is simulated using Eq. (17) that are figuratively explained in Figure 4, where v_x and v_y are obtained using Eq. (9), $\theta = atan(y_o/x_o)$, and $\phi = atan(v_y/v_x)$.

$$\vec{v}_l = \sqrt{|v_y|^2 + |v_x|^2} \times \cos(\phi - \theta) \quad (17)$$

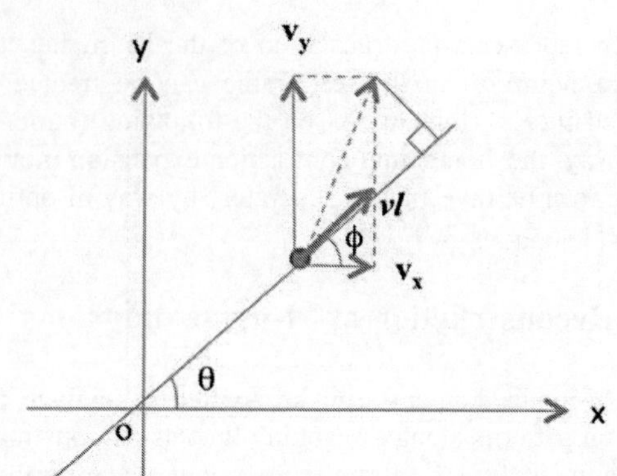

Figure 4. Illustration of the distribution of a velocity along each direction.

3. Results

The simulation is built on the Matlab program of KLT algorithm [9] and an in-house C++ program for motion analysis [8]. Figure 5 illustrates the M-mode regeneration for the image displayed in Figure 1.

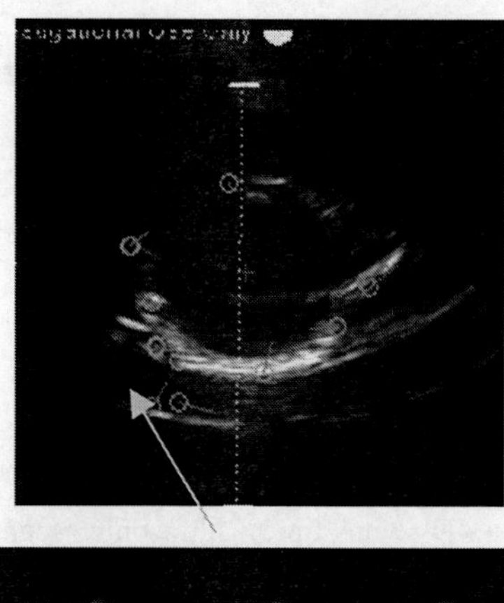

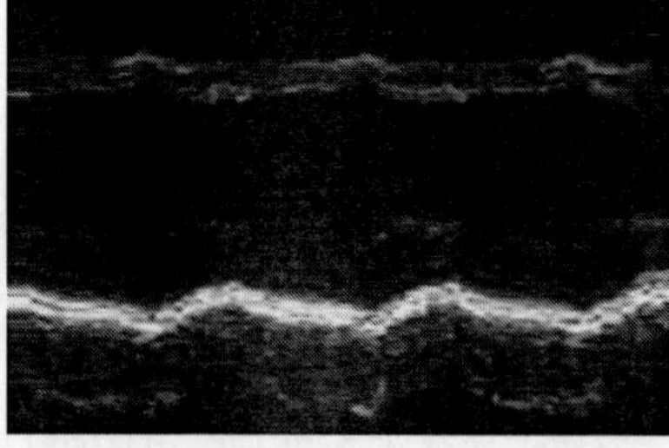

Figure 5. M-mode reconstruction (bottom) for the point near the scanning line as shown by the arrow on the top image, whereas the original m-mode graph is given in Figure 1.

With regard to tissue velocity estimation, Figure 6 demonstrates the re-creation of the velocity curve for the one displayed in Figure 2.

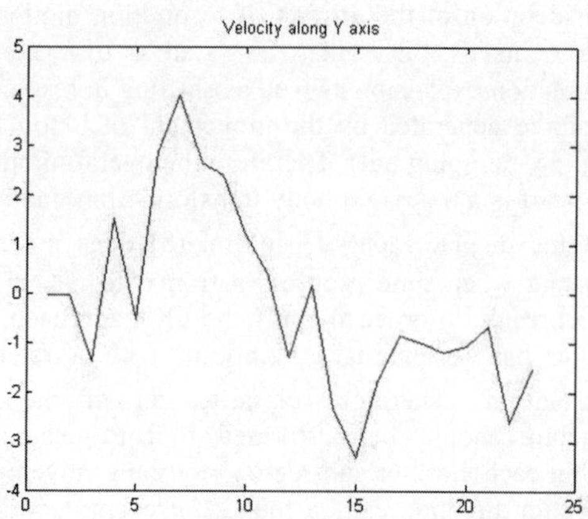

Figure 6. Tissue velocity regeneration using the approach in this study for 3D video image (shown in Figure 2).

Estimating from the appearance of waveform of the velocity in Figure 5, the post-reconstruction to a large extent, bears similarities. After calibration to be in the same unit that was applied while performing in vivo scanning, the measurement of velocity values reveals the average difference between known velocity values (such as shown in Figure 2) and the values obtained from the approach proposed in this study is within 4 pixels, equivalent to 4 mm, which is considered very reasonable [8]. However large scale of quantitative evaluation will be performed in the near future, since there are only ten sets of data are at deposit in this study.

When comparing m-mode waveforms between the original one (Figure 1) and the rendered one (as shown in Figure 5), the challenges lie on the detection of edges from which measuring the first order of derivative (i.e., velocity) of m-mode diagrams can be achieved, as demonstrated in Figure 7. Since the calculations account for the values of edges of m-mode diagrams, variations on edges can contribute to the comparisons, especially, when two images are generated in different ways, one based on the properties of ultrasound and one re-rendered according to the tracking of optical flow. All in all, the differences are within the range of 5 pixels, which again needs to be further exploited in the future.

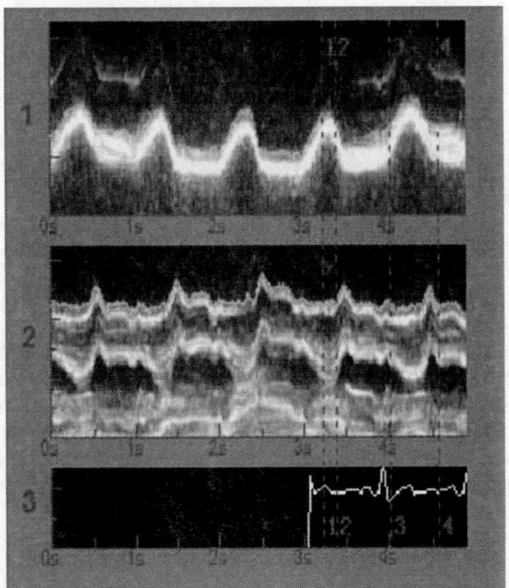

Figure 7. Simultaneous measurement of velocities from m-mode diagrams. Two different scanning lines from the same ventricle are illustrated here.

4. Discussion and Conclusion

Because of the convoluted nature of the heart motion, the application of existing popular motion detection methods remains far from a plug-in process, implying each sub-structure of the heart has to be dealt with individually, by taking into consideration of its specific characteristics.

With this in mind, the motion status of the left ventricle has been investigated in details in this study from both 2D and 3D video sequences and from both short axis (Figure 1) and long axis (Figure 2) parasternal views. Initial evaluation results have shown a very good match in the generation of M-mode diagrams and velocity curves. In 2D form where velocity data are not available, the motion curves can then be built on by using the first derivative of the edge of the M-mode images as illustrated in Figure 8, which can lead subsequent analysis of dynamics of the heart.

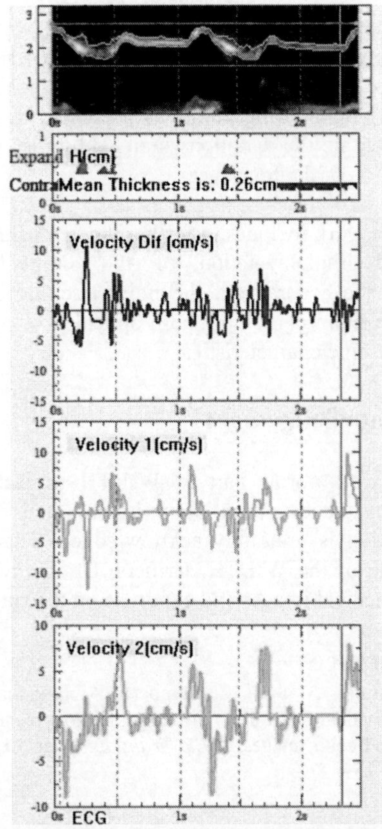

Figure 8. Velocity analysis from m-mode diagrams.

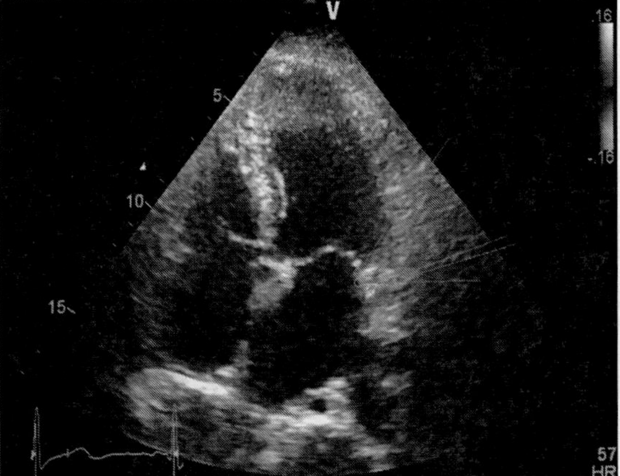

Figure 9. Four points are chosen to obtain the averaged velocity curve shown in Figure 6. The mark '+' indicates the ventricle centre.

With respect to the simulation of velocity curves from 3D video sequences, the evaluation tends to be a straightforward process providing the exact direction of the transducer is known. As it happens, the direction of the velocity shown in Figure 2 is always along the transducer, i.e, showing the colour blue while away from the transducer beams and red while towards them. Therefore averaged velocity is given in Figure 5 from the four neighbouring points as presented in Figure 8 to compensate the variations induced by the change of the position of the transducer.

Future work includes to further the evaluation of the proposed implementation of the simulation and improve the accuracy of the point tracking by using KLT algorithm combining both optical flow principles and ultrasonic characteristics.

5. Acknowledgement

This work forms part of WIDTH project that is funded by the European Commission. Their financial contribution is gratefully acknowledged. Thanks also go to one of the WIDTH partners, Dr. Lianyi Wang, for her medical images and expertise on the subject.

6. References

[1] P. Baraldi, A. Sarti, C. Lamberti, A. Prandini, and F. Sgallari, Evaluation of differential optical flow techniques on synthesized echo images, *IEEE Trans. Biomed. Eng.*, 1996, 43(3), pp. 259–272.

[2] D. Boukerroui, J.A. Noble, M. Brady, Velocity estimation in ultrasound images: a block matching approach, Inf Process Med Imagig. 2003 Jul;18:586-98.

[3] B. D. Lucas, and T. Kanade. “An Iterative Image Registration Technique with an Application to Stereo Vision”, *International Joint Conference on Artificial Intelligence*, 1981, pp. 674-679.

[4] D. Sun, S. Roth, and M.J. Black, "Secrets of Optical Flow Estimation and Their Principles", 2010, IEEE Int. Conf. on Comp. Vision & Pattern Recognition.

[5] B. Horn and B. Schunk, “Determining optical flow”, *Artif. Intell.*, 1981, 17, pp.185–203.

[6] M. Sühling , M. Arigovindan, C. Jansen , P. Hunziker, and M. Unser, Myocardial motion analysis from B-mode echocardiograms., *IEEE Trans Image Process*, 2005, 14(4), pp.525-36.

[7] J. Shi and C. Tomasi, “Good Features to Track”, IEEE *Conference on Computer Vision and Pattern Recognition*,1994, pp. 593-600.

[8] Q. Lin, W. Wu, L. Huang, Y. Lin, “An omnidirectional M-mode echocardiography system and its clinical application”, *Computerized Medical Imaging and Graphics*, 2006, 30, pp. 333–338.

[9] http://www.ces.clemson.edu/~stb/klt/, received on January 30, 2013.

Retinal Blood Vessel Detection Using Multiscale Line Filter and Phase Congruency

Baisheng Dai[1], **Wei Bu**[1,2], **Xiangqian Wu**[1], **Yalin Zheng**[3]
[1]School of Computer Science and Technology, Harbin Institute of Technology, Harbin, China
[2]Department of New Media, Harbin Institute of Technology, Harbin, China
[3]Department of Eye and Vision Science, University of Liverpool, Liverpool, UK

Abstract—*In this paper, a multiscale line filter is proposed which is integrated with phase congruency to detect the network of vessels in retinal images. The proposed line filter can reduces the influence of step edges compared with Gaussian matched filter, and the post process use the phase congruency demonstrated a substantial improvement in detecting vessels which have low contrast or minor width. The performance of the proposed method is evaluated on the publicly available databases DRIVE and STARE. The experimental results show that an effective and robust detection can be achieved.*

Keywords: retinal image, blood vessel, multiscale line filter, phase congruency

1. Introduction

Diabetic retinopathy (DR) is the commonest cause of blindness in the worldwide working-age population. The blood vessels is the most stable object in retinal fundus image which can reflect the state of the disease, and is also a landmark for localizing the optic nerve, fovea and lesions of DR [1]. Therefore, a reliable vessel detection is a prerequisite for subsequent retinal image analysis.

Blood vessels have some notable characteristics such as a Gaussian shape of cross-sectional grey-level profile, the vessels is piecewise linear and connected which formed a treelike structure, and the vasculature originates from the same location [2]. Many researchers have proposed a variety of techniques to detect vessels that generally fall into four categories. *Matched filter based*: The Gaussian matched filter first presented by Chaudhuri et al. employs a two-dimensional linear kernel that has a Gaussian cross-profile section and rotated into 12 different direction [3], and Zhang et al. propose a multiscale production of Gaussian matched filter to satisfy a wide range of vessel widths [4]. In [5] and [6] a mutliscale Gabor filter is applied to vessel detection; *Vessel model based*: Wang et al. proposed a vascular representation and segmentation algorithm based on a multiresoulution Hermite mode [7]. A "Ribbon of Twins" model presented by Al-Diri et al. uses a pair of contour to capture each vessel edge [8], while maintaining width consistency. Tsai et al. proposed a model based algorithm for locations of vascular structures branch and cross over in

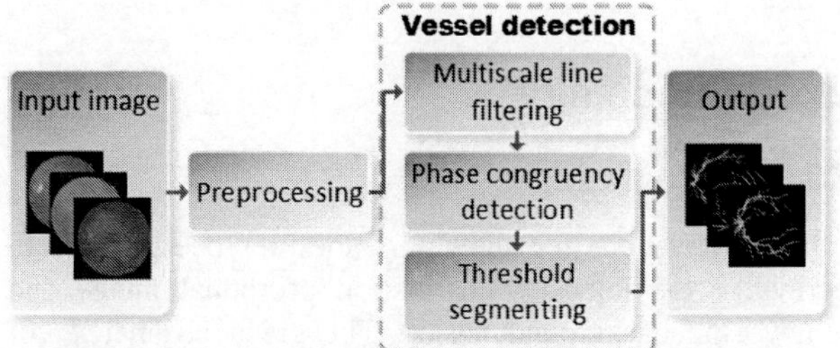

Fig. 1: The flowchart of the proposed vessel detection.

retinal images [9]; *Machine learning based*: Many method such as Fuzzy clustering [10], ANN [11], SVM [12] and other supervised or unsupervised techniques are frequently integrated with previous mentioned approaches for the final classification of positive vessel pixels; *Morphological processing based*: Morphological operators which is suitable for extracting linear shapes from background which can be very useful for vessel detection. Based on morphology method Zana et al. proposed an approach for the detection of vessel-like patterns in a noisy environment [13], and morphological reconstruction can be used to integrate segmentation fragment into a final vessel in [14]. Many published literature also use the morphological processing [15], [16] to roughly extract the vessel before lesions detection due to its simplicity and effectivity.

However, several challenges have emerged in the procedure of vessels detection from retinal images [1]. Blood vessels have a wide range of width, and there are many non vessels such as step edge will be introduced during the detection. Many proposed detection techniques are based on the grey-level and gradient information of retinal images, in case of the unideal or unsuitable lightness and low contrast condition, the difficulty of vessels extraction will be increased especially for the minor vessels. In addition, the border of optic disc and bright lesions in fundus image will also terribly influence the detection results of matched filters.

In this paper, a multiscale line filter extended from [17] and [18] is proposed for the enhancement of blood vessels in retinal image which focus on degrading the adverse impact caused by step edge, such as borders of optic disk, lesions and the field of view, and improve the ability of detecting the vessel has a high curvature. The proposed filter which composed of a dual first-order derivative of unscaled Gaussian with different standard deviation will also match real vessels in a better way. We then applied the measurement of phase congruency [19] to detect low contrast and minor vessels in the enhancement result of multiscale line filter. The flowchart of our vessel detection method is shown in Fig. 1. In the rest of the paper, the proposed methods are detailed in Section 2. The experimental results and performance evaluation are presented in Section 3, and followed by the conclusions in Section 4.

2. Methodology

2.1 Preprocessing

The motivations for applying some preprocessing are to normalize the intensity distribution of retinal image and remove the background nosies. The green channel I_g of retinal color image is used as the input cause which has the best contrast and saturation.

We first use the *shade correction* [20] to normalize the illumination of I_g. A median filter of size 40×40 is adopted to smooth I_g, and a estimate of background image I_{bg} is obtained. The illumination normalized image I_{sc} can be computed by

$$I_{sc} = I_g - I_{bg} \tag{1}$$

with

$$I_{bg} = I_g * f_m$$

where "$*$" is convolution operator and f_m is the median filter.

Next we employ a *edge-preserving smoothing* to remove background noises while preserving vessel edges. We expect to find a new image I_{eps} which is as close as possible to I_{sc}, meanwhile, is as smooth as possible everywhere except across the edge in I_{sc}. Hereby we use a weighted least squares optimization framework proposed in [21] to achieve the edge-preserving smoothing, the new image I_{eps} can be obtained by minimizing the following quadratic functional

$$\begin{aligned} F = \sum_q \Big(((I_{eps})_q - (I_{sc})_q)^2 \\ + \lambda \left(\alpha_x \left(\frac{\partial I_{eps}}{\partial x} \right)_q^2 + \alpha_y \left(\frac{\partial I_{eps}}{\partial y} \right)_q^2 \right) \Big) \end{aligned} \tag{2}$$

where q denotes the coordinate of a pixel. The goal of the first term is to minimize the distance between I_{eps} and I_{sc}, while the second term is to smooth I_{eps}. The parameters α_x and α_y are smoothness weights which depend on I_{sc}, while λ is used to balance the effects achieve by the two terms. An preprocessing example is shown in Fig. 2.

2.2 Multiscale line Filter

The Gaussian matched filter is a well-known method of vessel detection which estimate the gray-level profile of the cross section of the vessel by a Gaussian function [3], and the matched template can be rotated into different directions to detect the whole vessel network. However, the Gaussian matched filter responds not only to vessels but also to non-vessel edges [22], such as the border of optic disk, light lesions and the field of view as illustrated in the first row of Fig. 3. To overcome the sensitivity to non-vessel edges and improve the detection for the vessel has a high curvature, we extend the line filters proposed in [17] and [18] which are based on a nonlinear combination of linear filters.

Let $G_\sigma(x, y)$ denotes the unscaled Gaussian function $G_\sigma(x, y) = e^{-(x^2+y^2)/2\sigma^2}$, its first derivative $G'_\sigma(x, y)$ along x direction is an effective edge detector. We define edge detectors at scale i as

$$\begin{aligned} E_l^i(\mathbf{p}) = -G'_{\sigma_l^i}(x + w_l, \rho_l \times y), \ \forall \mathbf{p} \in N_l^i \\ E_r^i(\mathbf{p}) = G'_{\sigma_r^i}(x - w_r, \rho_r \times y), \ \forall \mathbf{p} \in N_r^i \end{aligned} \tag{3}$$

with

$$\begin{aligned} N_l^i = \{(x, y) \mid |x| \leq 3\sigma_l^i, |y| \leq L_l^i/2\} \\ N_r^i = \{(x, y) \mid |x| \leq 3\sigma_r^i, |y| \leq L_r^i/2\} \end{aligned}$$

where σ_l^i and σ_r^i are the standard deviation of unscaled Gaussian function. ρ controls the smoothness along the y direction, while L^i is the length of filters in y direction at that scale. D_l^i and D_r^i will detect the left and right edge of the vessel at location $x = \mp w$, and the distance between $x - w$ and $x + w$ can be used to estimate the width of vessel. The response of these two edge detector will be both positive for the line while one positive and one negative for the step edge.

To account for the multi-directions and tortuosity of vessel in retinal images, the rotation of D_l^i and D_r^i with angle α is then calculated by

$$E_l^{i,\alpha}(\mathbf{p}') = E_l^i(\mathbf{p}), \ E_r^{i,\alpha}(\mathbf{p}') = E_r^i(\mathbf{p}) \tag{4}$$

with

$$\begin{aligned} x' = x \cos \alpha + y \sin \alpha + \xi y'^2 \\ y' = y \cos \alpha - x \sin \alpha \end{aligned}$$

where the quadratic term $\xi y'^2$ is used to fix the bending of some vessels [23] and ξ describes the curvature of the vessel, as shown in Fig. 4 and Fig. 6.

The response of the new line filter at scale i convolved with the input image I_{eps} at location (u, v) can be expressed by

$$\mathcal{R}^i(u, v) = \prod_\xi \max_\alpha \left(\mathrm{Pos}(R_l^{i,\alpha}(u, v)) \cdot \mathrm{Pos}(R_r^{i,\alpha}(u, v)) \right) \tag{5}$$

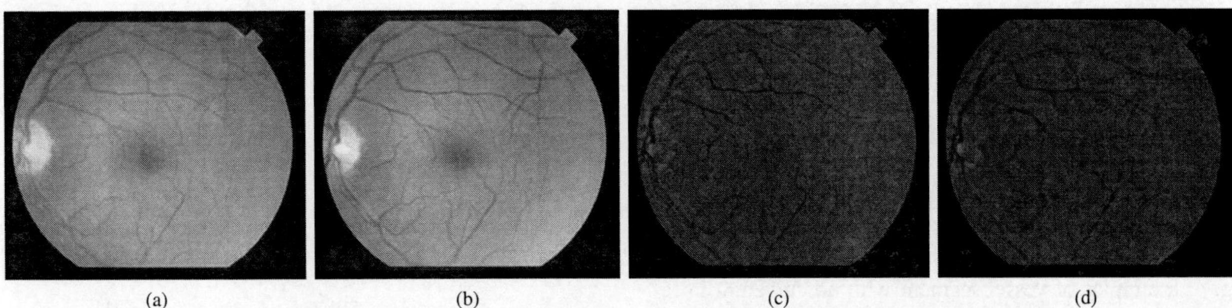

(a) (b) (c) (d)

Fig. 2: Illustration of preprocessing: (a) an original color retinal image, (b) the green channel of (a), (c) the shade corrected image and (d) the edge-preserving smoothed image.

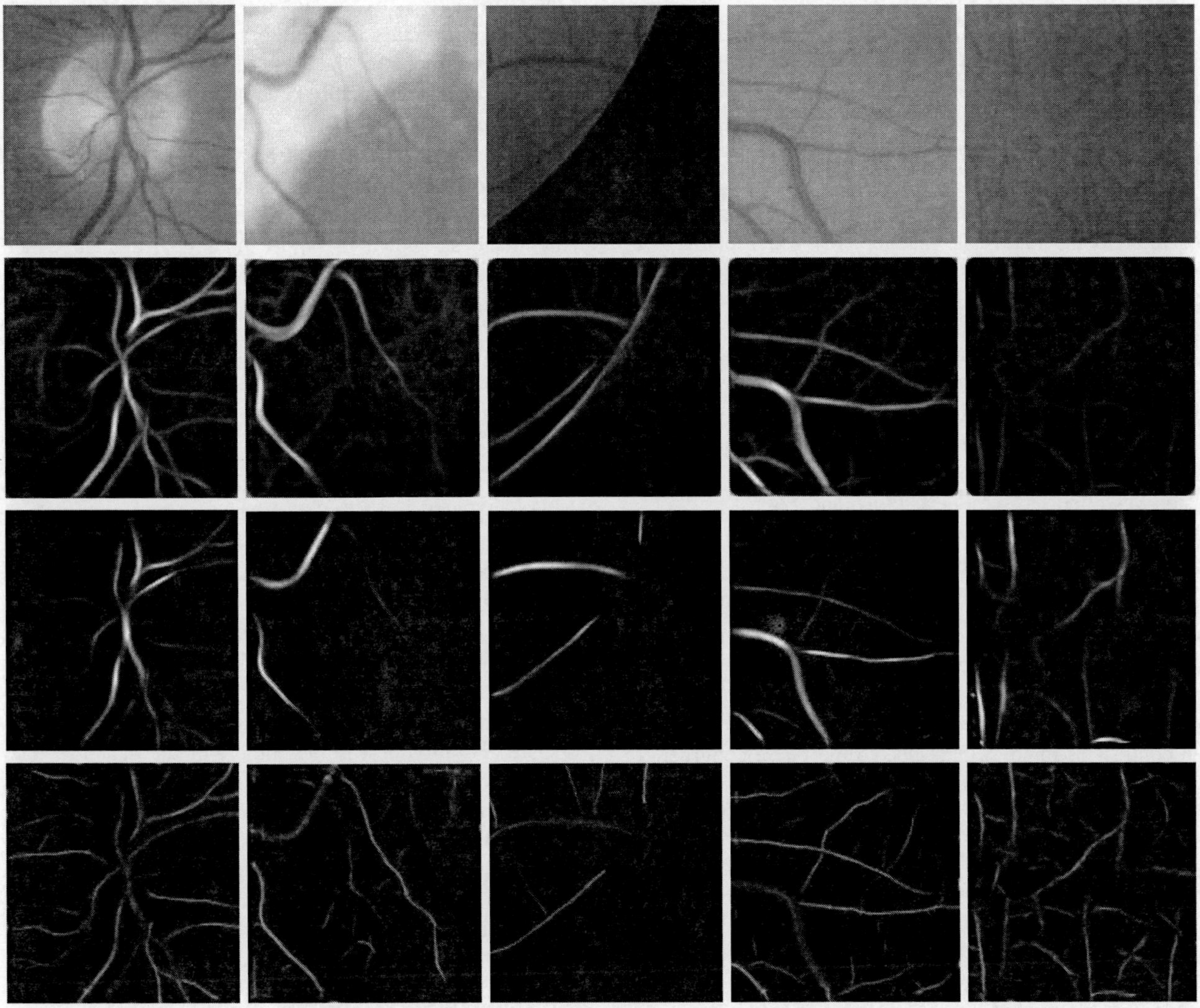

(a) optic disc (b) bright lesion (c) field of view (d) wide range (e) low contrast

Fig. 3: *First row*: unfavourable factors during the vessel detection. *Second row*: results of Gaussian matched filtering. *Third row*: results of the proposed line filter. *Fourth row*: the phase congruency of the third row. The edge steps are suppressed, and vessels which have low contrast and minor width are detected.

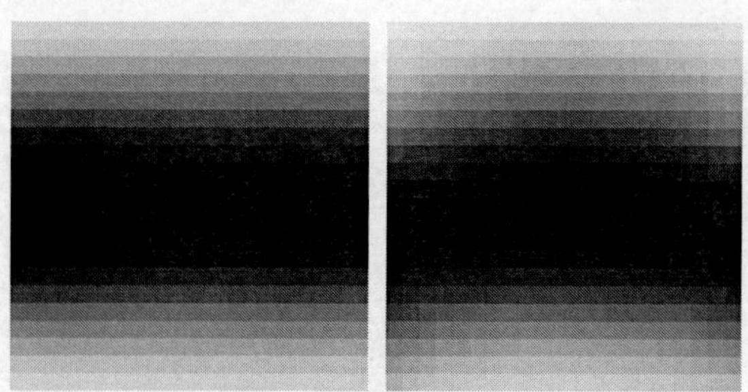

Fig. 4: Examples of vessel segment with no curvature in (a) and with some curvature in (b).

with

$$R_l^{i,\alpha}(u,v) = E_l^{i,\alpha}(u,v) * I_{eps}(u,v)$$
$$R_r^{i,\alpha}(u,v) = E_r^{i,\alpha}(u,v) * I_{eps}(u,v)$$
$$\text{Pos}(\psi) = \psi \cdot \Theta(\psi),\ \Theta(\psi) = \begin{cases} 1, & \psi > 0 \\ 0, & \text{else} \end{cases}$$

where $*$ is convolution operator, and we further extend the line filter to the multiscale manner [18] which can match vessels of various widths, and the final response is defined as the maximum of filter responses at all scales

$$\mathcal{R}(u,v) = \max_{1 \leq i \leq n} \mathcal{R}^i(u,v) \quad (6)$$

where n is the scale number.

The improved line filter can detect blood vessels with various widths and tortuosity, while suppressing the response to non-vessel edges, see Fig. 3, Fig. 6 and Fig. 7.

2.3 Phase Congruency

Phase congruency is a dimensionless quantity that is invariant to changes in image brightness [19]. If the maximum moment of phase congruency at a point is large then that point should be marked as a feature such as a line point, see Fig. 5. Therefore, it can be applied in vessel detection for the low contrast or minor width. Due to the phase congruency is also sensitive to image noise, herein we calculate it in the vessel enhanced image $I_v(x,y)$ which is processed by the proposed multiscale line filter.

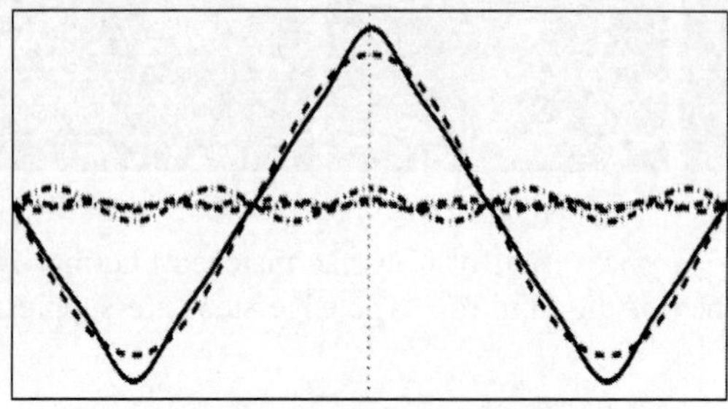

Fig. 5: The phase congruency of line feature.

Let $A_n(x,y)$ denotes the amplitude of $I_v(x,y)$ at a location (x,y) and $\phi_n(x,y)$ the phase angle, a measure of phase congruency developed by Kovesi [19] is

$$PC(x,y) = \frac{\sum_o \sum_n W(x,y) \lfloor A_{o,n}(x,y) \Delta\phi_{o,n}(x,y) - T \rfloor}{\sum_n A_{o,n}(x) + \varepsilon} \quad (7)$$

with

$$\Delta\phi_{o,n}(x,y) = \cos(\phi_{o,n}(x,y) - \bar{\phi}_o(x,y)) - |\sin(\phi_{o,n}(x,y) - \bar{\phi}_o(x,y))|$$

where o and n denotes the index over orientations and scales respectively, $\bar{\phi}_o(x,y)$ is the mean phase angle at orientation o, the term $W(x,y)$ is the sigmoid function used to weight a phase congruency, ε is added to avoid division by zero, T is a threshold to control the noise influence, the symbols $\lfloor\ \rfloor$ denote the enclosed quantity is equal to itself iff its value is positive, and zero otherwise.

In our paper the local frequency information is obtained via banks of log Gabor wavelets tuned to different spatial frequencies, and the phase congruency of vessel enhancement image as shown in Fig. 3 and Fig. 7, and on which the final vessel network is segmented by using hysteresis thresholding.

3. Experimental Results and Discussion

3.1 Materials

We have evaluated our approach on two publicly available databases DRIVE and STARE which were collected by Staal et al. [24] and Hoover et al. [25] respectively for testing the algorithm of vessel detection. The DRIVE database consists of 40 images captured by Canon CR5 3CCD camera with a 45° FOV which were digitized at 24-bits with a spatial resolution of 565×584 pixels and divided into a training set and a test set. The ground truths segmented manually for two sets and the mask images clearly marking the interior of FOV are also provides by the authors of the database. The STARE database consists of 20 images captured by TopCon TRV-50 fundus camera with a 35° FOV which were digitized at 24-bits with a spatial resolution of 700×605 pixels and in which there are 10 healthy fundus images and the other 10 unhealthy. The author of the database also provides ground truths for the performance evaluation of vessel detection.

3.2 Experimental Results

To compare the proposed approach with other retinal vessel detection algorithms, we use the sensitivity (SE), specificity (SP) and accuracy (ACC) as the performance measures. In general, there are four predict outcome in testing stage, such as true positive (TP), false positive (FP), true negative (TN) and false negative (FN). The sensitivity

Table 1: Performance measures of vessel detection for each test image on DRIVE database

No.	Sensitivity	Specificity	No.	Sensitivity	Specificity
1	0.7126	0.9660	11	0.6398	0.9752
2	0.7176	0.9655	12	0.6178	0.9779
3	0.6422	0.9598	13	0.6194	0.9794
4	0.5511	0.9908	14	0.7042	0.9672
5	0.5874	0.9899	15	0.7150	0.9712
6	0.6267	0.9780	16	0.7023	0.9756
7	0.6176	0.9807	17	0.6420	0.9798
8	0.5541	0.9854	18	0.7108	0.9731
9	0.6375	0.9786	19	0.7725	0.9673
10	0.6523	0.9784	20	0.6606	0.9779

Table 2: Performance comparison with different vessel detection methods on DRIVE database

Method	Accuracy	Sensitivity	Specificity
Second observer	0.9473	0.7761	0.9725
Chaudhuri [3]	0.8773	0.3357	N.A.
Amin [26]	0.9191	N.A	N.A.
Vlachos [27]	0.9285	0.7468	0.9551
Zhang [22]	0.9382	0.7120	0.9724
Staal [24]	0.9441	0.7193	0.9773
Mendonça [14]	0.9452	0.7344	0.9764
Proposed method	**0.9347**	**0.6542**	**0.9759**

and specificity can be written as:

$$SE = \frac{TP}{TP + FN} \tag{8}$$

$$SP = \frac{TN}{TN + FP} \tag{9}$$

and accuracy can be obtained from the following identity:

$$ACC = \frac{TP + TN}{TP + TN + FP + FN} \tag{10}$$

where SE is the proportion of pixels that are known to the vessel the approach detects positive for it, while SP the proportion of pixels are known to the non vessel the approach detects negative for it. The ACC represents the proportion of the total number of correctly classified pixels relative to the total number of pixels.

In our experiments $w = 1.5\sigma$ and our line detector are rotated into 12 direction, and we choose minor values of ξ to fix the bending of vessels since filters have small scales. The experimental results are demonstrated in Fig. 6 and Fig. 7, our proposed method can enhance the vessel with some curvature and detect the whole vessel network availably. The performance measures of each test image in DRIVE database are listed in Table 1, while Table 2 presents the performance of different methods on the DRIVE database. Our experimental results on the DRIVE database show that the proposed method performs better than the original Gaussian matched filter and the method in [26] which use the phase congruency measure directly. The results of each image in STARE database are shown in

Table 3: Performance measures of vessel detection for each image on STARE database

No.	Sensitivity	Specificity	No.	Sensitivity	Specificity
1	0.5562	0.9636	11	0.7411	09692
2	0.5263	0.9613	12	0.7424	0.9729
3	0.6398	0.9534	13	0.6498	0.9753
4	0.6050	0.9774	14	0.6567	0.9755
5	0.6323	0.9729	15	0.6597	0.9680
6	0.6266	0.9828	16	0.5955	0.9813
7	0.7200	0.9648	17	0.7287	0.9800
8	0.7238	0.9665	18	0.6226	0.9922
9	0.6878	0.9669	19	0.6664	0.9833
10	0.6452	0.9669	20	0.5825	0.9760

Table 4: Performance comparison with different vessel detection methods on STARE database

Method	Accuracy	Sensitivity	Specificity
Second observer	0.9348	0.8951	0.9384
Hoover [25]	0.9267	0.6751	0.9567
Fraz [28]	0.9367	0.6849	0.9710
Mendonça [14]	0.9440	0.6996	0.9730
Staal [24]	0.9516	0.6970	0.9810
Proposed method	**0.9392**	**0.6503**	**0.9722**

Table 3, and Table 4 compares the performance of different methods on the STARE database. Our experimental results on the STARE database show that the proposed method also achieves a competitive performance compare to the listed methods.

4. Conclusions

In this paper we propose a novel method for retinal blood vessel detection. The method is based on an multiscale line detector which integrated with the phase congruency. The performance of our method achieves competitive results compared to the existing solutions. However, our method yields a lower sensitivity that is mainly because of the width of vessel is not accurate and an high threshold value applied to reduce the noises introduce by the phase congruency. Our following work is devoted to overcome these problems by extracting the feature set of the vessel and training a optimal classifier to identify the vessel pixels and non vessel pixels. Meanwhile, the performance of vessel segmentation from images which have pathological changes will be improved in the future work.

Acknowledgment

This work was supported by the Natural Science Foundation of China (Grant No. 61073125), the Program for New Century Excellent Talents in University (Grant No. NCET-08-0155), the Fok Ying Tong Education Foundation (Grant No. 122035), and the Fundamental Research Funds for the Central Universities (Grant No. HIT. NSRIF. 2013091).

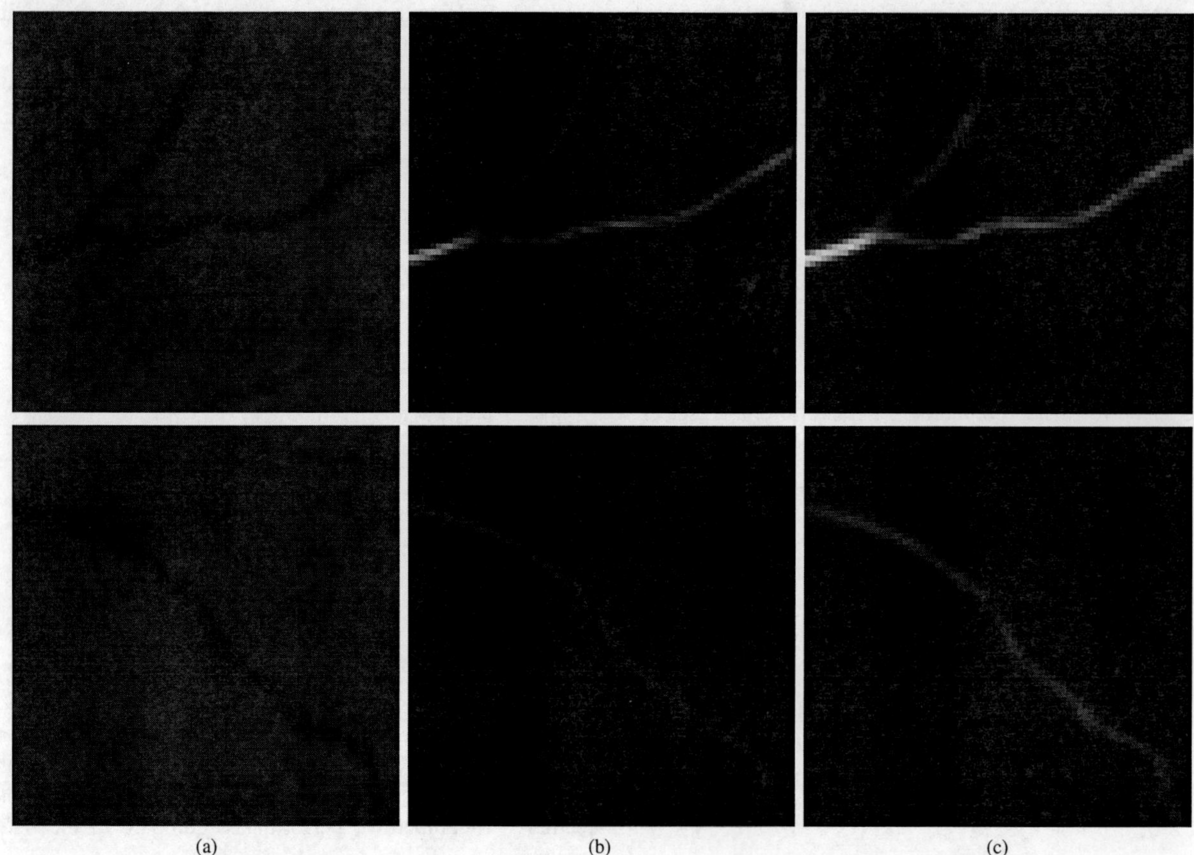

Fig. 6: The enhanced results of blood vessels with some tortuosity. (a) original vessel segment, (b) enhanced result without tortuosity fixed, (c) enhanced result with tortuosity fixed.

References

[1] M. Sofka and C. V. Stewart, "Retinal vessel centerline extraction using multiscale matched filters, confidence and edge measures," *IEEE TMI*, vol. 25, no. 12, pp. 1531–1546, 2006.

[2] B. Dhillonb, R. H. Eikelboomf, K. Yogesana, and I. J. Constablea, "Retinal image analysis: concepts, applications and potential," *Prog. Retin. Eye Res.*, vol. 25, pp. 99–127, 2006.

[3] S. Chaudhuri, S. Chatterjee, N. Katz, M. Nelson, and M. Goldbaum, "Detection of blood vessels in retinal images using two-dimensional matched filters," *IEEE TMI*, vol. 8, no. 3, pp. 263–269, 1989.

[4] B. Zhang, Q. Li, L. Zhang, J. You, and F. Karray, "Retinal vessel centerline extraction using multiscale matched filter and sparse representation-based classifier," in *ICMB'10*. Springer, 2010, pp. 181–190.

[5] Q. Li, J. You, L. Zhang, and P. Bhattacharya, "A multiscale approach to retinal vessel segmentation using gabor filters and scale multiplication," in *ICSMC'06*, vol. 4. IEEE, 2006, pp. 3521–3527.

[6] R. M. Rangayyan, F. J. Ayres, F. Oloumi, F. Oloumi, and P. Eshghzadeh-Zanjani, "Detection of blood vessels in the retina with multiscale gabor filters," *J. Electron. Imaging*, vol. 17, no. 2, pp. 023 018–023 018, 2008.

[7] L. Wang, A. Bhalerao, and R. Wilson, "Analysis of retinal vasculature using a multiresolution hermite model," *IEEE TMI*, vol. 26, no. 2, pp. 137–152, 2007.

[8] B. Al-Diri, A. Hunter, and D. Steel, "An active contour model for segmenting and measuring retinal vessels," *IEEE TMI*, vol. 28, no. 9, pp. 1488–1497, 2009.

[9] C.-L. Tsai, C. V. Stewart, H. L. Tanenbaum, and B. Roysam, "Model-based method for improving the accuracy and repeatability of estimating vascular bifurcations and crossovers from retinal fundus images," *IEEE TITB*, vol. 8, no. 2, pp. 122–130, 2004.

[10] A. Bhuiyan, B. Nath, J. Chua, and R. Kotagiri, "Blood vessel segmentation from color retinal images using unsupervised texture classification," in *ICIP'07*, vol. 5. IEEE, 2007, pp. V–521.

[11] C. Sinthanayothin, J. F. Boyce, H. L. Cook, and T. H. Williamson, "Automated localisation of the optic disc, fovea, and retinal blood vessels from digital colour fundus images," *Br. J. Ophthalmol.*, vol. 83, no. 8, pp. 902–910, 1999.

[12] E. Ricci and R. Perfetti, "Retinal blood vessel segmentation using line operators and support vector classification," *IEEE TMI*, vol. 26, no. 10, pp. 1357–1365, 2007.

[13] F. Zana and J.-C. Klein, "Segmentation of vessel-like patterns using mathematical morphology and curvature evaluation," *IEEE TIP*, vol. 10, no. 7, pp. 1010–1019, 2001.

[14] A. M. Mendonca and A. Campilho, "Segmentation of retinal blood vessels by combining the detection of centerlines and morphological reconstruction," *IEEE TMI*, vol. 25, no. 9, pp. 1200–1213, 2006.

[15] S. Ravishankar, A. Jain, and A. Mittal, "Automated feature extraction for early detection of diabetic retinopathy in fundus images," in *CVPR'09*. IEEE, 2009, pp. 210–217.

[16] A. D. Fleming, S. Philip, K. A. Goatman, J. A. Olson, and P. F. Sharp, "Automated microaneurysm detection using local contrast normalization and local vessel detection," *IEEE TMI*, vol. 25, no. 9, pp. 1223–1232, 2006.

[17] T. M. Koller, G. Gerig, G. Szekely, and D. Dettwiler, "Multiscale

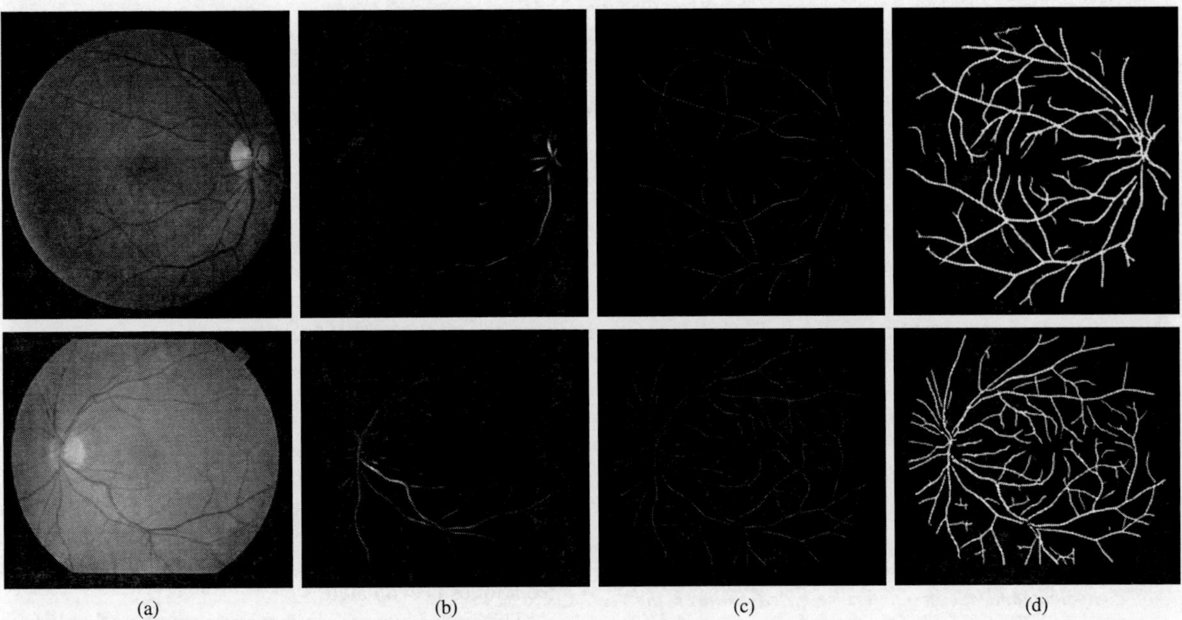

Fig. 7: Detection results for DRIVE and STARE database: (a) original color retinal images, (b) vessel enhancement images, (c) the phase congruency images of (b), (d) the final segmentation results.

detection of curvilinear structures in 2-d and 3-d image data," in *ICCV'95*. IEEE, 1995, pp. 864–869.

[18] Q. Li, L. Zhang, J. You, D. Zhang, and P. Bhattacharya, "Dark line detection with line width extraction," in *ICIP'08*. IEEE, 2008, pp. 621–624.

[19] P. Kovesi, "Image features from phase congruency," *Videre: Journal of Computer Vision Research*, vol. 1, no. 3, pp. 1–26, 1999.

[20] G. Øien and P. Osnes, "Diabetic retinopathy: Automatic detection of early symptoms from retinal images," in *Proc. Norwegian Sign. Proc. Sym.*, 1995.

[21] Z. Farbman *et al.*, "Edge-preserving decompositions for multi-scale tone and detail manipulation," *ACM TOG*, vol. 27, no. 3, Aug. 2008.

[22] B. Zhang, L. Zhang, L. Zhang, and F. Karray, "Retinal vessel extraction by matched filter with first-order derivative of gaussian," *Comput. Biol. Med.*, vol. 40, no. 4, pp. 438–445, 2010.

[23] M. Cree, D. Cornforth, and H. Jelinek, "Vessel segmentation and tracking using a two-dimensional model," *IVC New Zealand*, pp. 345–350, 2005.

[24] J. Staal, M. D. Abràmoff, M. Niemeijer, M. A. Viergever, and B. van Ginneken, "Ridge-based vessel segmentation in color images of the retina," *IEEE TMI*, vol. 23, no. 4, pp. 501–509, 2004.

[25] A. Hoover, V. Kouznetsova, and M. Goldbaum, "Locating blood vessels in retinal images by piecewise threshold probing of a matched filter response," *IEEE TMI*, vol. 19, no. 3, pp. 203–210, 2000.

[26] M. Amin and H. Yan, "Phase congruency based retinal vessel segmentation," in *ICMLC'09*, vol. 4. IEEE, 2009, pp. 2458–2462.

[27] M. Vlachos and E. Dermatas, "Multi-scale retinal vessel segmentation using line tracking," *Comput. Med. Imaging Graph.*, vol. 34, no. 3, pp. 213–227, 2010.

[28] M. Fraz, M. Javed, and A. Basit, "Retinal vessels extraction using bit planes," in *Proceedings of the Eighth IASTED International Conference*, vol. 630, no. 108, 2008, p. 18.

Efficacy of Gabor-Wavelet versus Statistical Features for Brain Tumor Classification in MRI: A Comparative Study

Nooshin Nabizadeh[1], Miroslav Kubat[2], Nigel John[3], Clinton Wright[4]
[1,2,3] Electrical and Computer Engineering Department, University Of Miami, Coral Gables, FL 33146, USA
[4]Neurology Department, Miller School of Medicine, University of Miami, 1120 NW 14th Street, Miami, FL, 33136

Abstract- *Automatic tumor segmentation can only be as successful as the feature extraction techniques it relies on. While many such techniques have been employed, it is still not quite clear which of feature extraction methods should be preferred. To help improve the situation, we present here the results of a study in which we compare the efficiency of using Gabor-wavelet features and statistical features, which are two main groups of competent and successful texture-based features in tumor segmentation. To be more specific, we experiment with three different segmentation techniques that employ Support Vector Machines (SVM), K-Nearest Neighbor classifiers (KNN), and the K-Means classifiers. The system that serves as our test-bed includes tumor slice detection, feature extraction, feature selection, and finally feature classification and comparison. The method implementation and the results are discussed.*

***Keywords*—**Tumor segmentation, Gabor-wavelet, Statistical feature, MR imaging,

1. Introduction

Medical imaging has a robust role in the diagnosis of the brain tumors in a reasonable time frame, which results in better controlling the diminishing the effects of the disease. Among the different techniques for identifying brain tumor, Magnetic Resonance Imaging (MRI) is the most widely used, and very prevalent [1]. This is because MRI is non-invasive (using no ionization rays), provides high resolution, and shows good contrast for various tissues [2].

In the majority of medical image diagnosis systems, separation of some specific cell and tissue from the rest of image content is needed [3]. This is regarded as segmentation, which is defined as the partitioning of the image into a set of relatively homogeneous regions, each of which can be tagged with a single label and possess similar properties [1]. Consequently, it is an important and crucial element in medical image processing, and effective research has been conducted in this field to develop computer-aided techniques with maximum possible accuracy. The success of tissue segmentation critically depends on the extraction of the most informative features [4]. This, however, can be a challenging task because the location, size, shape, and texture of a tumor is not constant.

Although texture-based features are pivotal in tumor segmentation field and many papers dealt with this issue, it is still not clear which feature extraction technique should be used and which are preferred. In this study, effectiveness and complexity of two main sets of well-established and proficient texture-based feature extraction techniques is evaluated.

The first group is Gabor-wavelet method that is known to be one of the most effective and commonly used feature extraction approaches thanks to its ability to yield optimized diverse resolution information in both time and frequency domains, which is very critical in MRI lesion segmentation. Furthermore, it can represent frequency locality, spatial locality, and orientation selectivity [5, 6].

The second group (we will call it *statistical features*) is based on applying beneficial and widespread texture-based feature extraction methods such as histogram analysis, Gray Level Co-occurrence Matrix (GLCM), Histogram of Oriented Gradient (HOG), and Grey Level Run Length Matrix (GLRLM) methods. These features take advantage of the relationship among image pixels or group of pixels. Furthermore, they estimate image properties related to first and second order statistics.

Although, Gabor-wavelet features and statistical features have been widely employed separately or in combination with each other in many different studies, their individual benefits and applicability have not been compared. This motivated the research reported in this paper to investigate the efficacy and capability of these features in tumor segmentation procedure.

2. Problem Statement And Performance Criteria

The Gabor-wavelet features and statistical features possess different abilities to give rise to accurate MRI lesion segmentation. We will quantify this ability using multistage algorithm and three commonly used performance criteria: sensitivity, specificity, and accuracy, defined by the following formulas.

$$Sensitivity = \frac{TP}{(TP + FN)} 100\% \qquad (5)$$

$$Specificity = \frac{TN}{(TN + FP)} 100\% \qquad (6)$$

$$Accuracy = \frac{(TP + TN)}{(TP + TN + FP + FN)} 100\% \quad (7)$$

where

$TP(True\ Positives) = correctly\ classified\ positive\ cases,$
$TN(True\ Negative) = correctly\ classified\ negative\ cases,$
$FN(False\ Negative) = incorrectly\ classified\ positive\ cases,$
$FP(False\ Positives) = incorrectly\ classified\ negative\ cases.$

The purposed multistage algorithm includes tumor slice detection, windowing, feature extraction, feature selection, and feature classification and comparison.

In the first step, using largest diameter, the midline of the brain is evolved. Based on brain midline, histogram asymmetry of left and right hemisphere is used for tumor slice detection. Subsequently, four window covers each brain hemisphere tissues. Two groups of features as Gabor-wavelet features and statistical features are then extracted from each window applying Gabor-wavelet transformation, histogram analysis, GLCM, GLRLM, and HOG methods. Followed by feature selection applying Principle Component Analysis (PCA), several classifiers methods as SVM, KNN, and K-Means classifiers are applied to classify the features. Final results are then compared using three performance criteria. The overall flow diagram of this work is shown in Fig. 1.

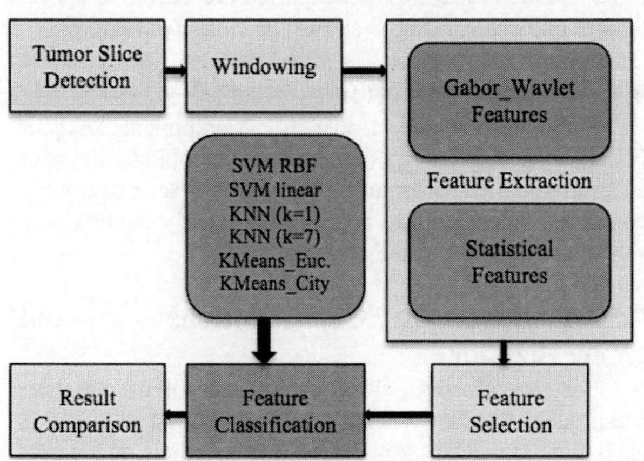

Fig. 1. Overall flow diagram of the system

3. Related Works

In this section, we first review relevant background information for feature extraction using Gabor-wavelet method and statistical techniques. In [7], Wavelet decomposition is first performed to remove noise from MR images. Afterward, Gabor-wavelets are used on Region of Interests (ROIs), which are manually selected from the tumor area, to extract the discriminant features, including tumor shape information. Afterward, SVM is used to segment the tumor shape to combine texture and shape information. Finally, linear discriminant analysis (LDA) is used to evaluate the performance of the Gabor texture features based on K-fold cross-validation experiments. In [8], beside Gabor-wavelet features, the intensity, symmetry, and shape related features were extracted from T1 and T2 weighted and T1 with gadolinium contrast agent. For extraction of symmetry and shape deformation features, registration to the specific template was used. Employing an AdaBoost classifier on the extracted features, the tumor region was finally segmented. In [9], a multi resolution approach using undecimated wavelet transform (UDWT) is applied on T1 andT2 images for noise removal. The UDWT approach produces four sub-bands, LL and LH and HL and HH, in full size. For feature extraction, Gabor-wavelet filters are then employed to the wavelet approximations (LL) at all levels to create the characteristic texture features such as entropy, second to fourth central moments and coefficient of variation. After feature extraction, K-means clustering produces the final tumor segmentation.

There are several studies that applied statistical features alone or in combination with other features. In [2], Gabor wavelets features, energy, entropy, contrast, and intensity mean, median, variance, standard deviation, correlation, and values of maximum and minimum intensity were obtained from three MR modalities including T1, T2_weighted and Proton Density (PD) images. After feature selection, a neural network was applied to classify the brain tissues to normal and abnormal classes automatically. The study concentrated on detecting the normal and abnormal slices. In [10], after manually tracing of ROIs, intensity characteristics (mean and variance), five shape features (circularity, irregularity, rectangularity, the entropy of radial length distribution of the boundary voxels, and the surface-to-volume ratio) and Gabor texture feature were extracted from T1, T1ce, T2, FLAIR, rCBV sequences. For feature classification, three pattern classification methods, SVM, KNN, and LDA, were applied. In [11], texture-based features including first-ordered and second-ordered statistical feature were extracted from brain MR images. In the second phase, ensemble base classifier was applied to classify brain images on the basis of these texture features. In [12], a tumor segmentation scheme based on the structural analysis on both tumorous and normal tissues was proposed. Firstly, three feature groups including intensity-based, symmetry-based and texture-based features are extracted from structural elements. Then applying Adaboost classification method, the structural elements were classified into normal tissues and abnormal tissues.

Extracting beneficial features is a challenging task. There are many different techniques available for feature extraction, but a comparative study is still missing in the tumor segmentation field. As it was shown, Gabor-wavelet features and statistical features are commonly used in the lesion segmentation area. However, comparison of their capability is essential, and it motivates us for this study. Statistical features include first-order histogram based features, histogram analysis features, GLRLM features, GLCM features, and HOG features. In the next section these feature extraction techniques are described briefly. Methodology is explained in Section 4. In Section 5, dataset and results are presented, and finally in Section 6, conclusion is discussed.

4. Methodology

The flow diagram of the proposed method is shown in Fig.1. The first step is tumor slice detection, which is followed by windowing. Subsequently, two main groups of features, Gabor-wavelet features and statistical features, are extracted from each window. After feature dimension reduction, several classifiers are used to distinguish between the features.

4.1 Tumor Slice Detection

The main idea in tumor slice detection is based on histogram asymmetry between the two brain hemispheres. In order to apply this idea, it is necessary to cut the MRI slice into right and left sub-slices or hemispheres. The brain separation into two hemispheres is achieved by finding the longest diameter as a brain midline. In order to find histogram asymmetry, histograms of each hemisphere is calculated. Lastly, with applying mutual information criterion and defining a threshold, the slice, which includes tumor, is recognized.

4.2 Windowing

From each selected tumor slice, four rectangular windows are extracted from each hemisphere, which covers brain tissues, as shown in Fig. 2. The location of windows change based on the size of the brain in each slice. Two groups of features as Gabor-wavelet features and statistical features are extracted using the described six methods.

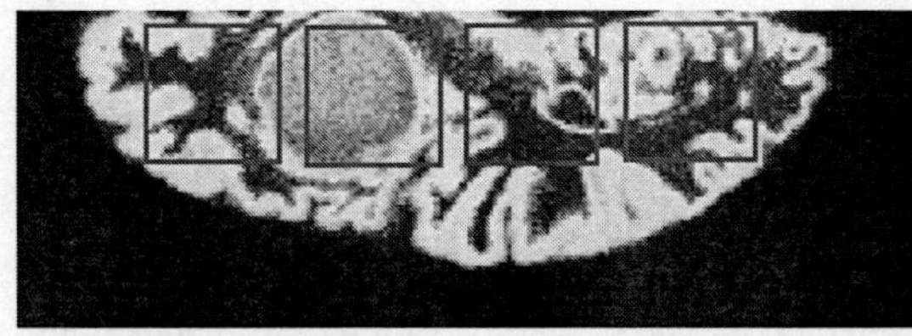

Fig. 2. One sample of windowing

4.3 Feature Aggregations

The Gabor-wavelet features and statistical features are extracted using Gabor-wavelet transform, GLCM, GLRLM, HOG, and histogram analysis methods.

Gabor-wavelet features are extracted by applying Gabor-wavelet kernels with five different scales, and eight orientations on 45×45 windows. Windows with different sizes were examined and 45×45 window attains better result. The length of Gabor feature vector is 81,000 with to 45×45 window size. For each window, for each Gabor wavelet kernel, the Gabor energy is calculated. The energy vector length for each window is forty; because of using Gabor filters in 8 orientations and 5 scales.

First-order histogram-based features are extracted as mean, variance, median, intensity energy and entropy, skewness and kurtosis [11].

GLCM features or Haralick features [13] are extracted by applying the angle $\theta = 0°, 45°, 90°$, and 135°. In each orientation, twenty features are derived. Totally, Eighty features are extracted by applying GLCM.

GLRLM features are calculated for 0, 45, 90 and 135 degrees [14]. Extracted features are Short Run Emphasis (SRE), Long Run Emphasis (LRE), Grey Level Distribution (GLD), Run length Distribution (RLD), and Run Percentage (RP) in four directions.

Histogram analysis features include four features, average intensity level, average contrast, smoothness and entropy [15].

HOG features measure the occurrences of gradient orientation in the regional areas of the image for the purpose of object detection [16, 17]. Using two scales and 8 orientations, eighty HOG feature values are extracted. One average feature is also added to this group. Totally eighty-one HOG features are used in this work.

Summation of seven first-order histogram based features, four histogram analysis features, twenty GLRLM features, eighty GLCM features, and eighty-one HOG features makes a statistical feature vector as a 192-dimentional vector. Fig. 3 shows the extracted features.

4.4 Feature Selection

For feature selection, Principle Component Analysis (PCA) is used. PCA is a mathematical technique that uses an orthogonal transformation to project a set of possibly correlated variables into a group of linearly uncorrelated variables called principle components [18].

4.5 Feature Classifications and Generalization

For classification, three supervised robust classifier techniques, Support Vector Machine (SVM) with radial basis function (RBF) kernel and linear kernels, K Nearest Neighborhood (KNN), and one unsupervised classifier method, k-means, are applied and the results are compared.

Hence the number of healthy windows are more than tumor windows, for preventing biased classification, same number of healthy windows and tumor windows are utilized for training the classifier methods.

Cross-validation method with 10 folds is used to validate the robustness of our model. Cross validation helps to prevent over-fitting.

5. Results

5.1. Materials And Labeling

In all, twenty simulated data of brain T1 weighted-MRI images were acquired from neuroimaging tools and resources (NITRC) [19, 20]. The data was generated using cross-platform simulation software called TumorSim. Each subject's MRI modality includes 181 slices.

For preparing class label for each window, if the tumor pixels cover more than half of the window, the label is designated as one. If the tumor pixels cover less than half of the window, the label is assigned as zero. This stance is called 50% tumor labeling.

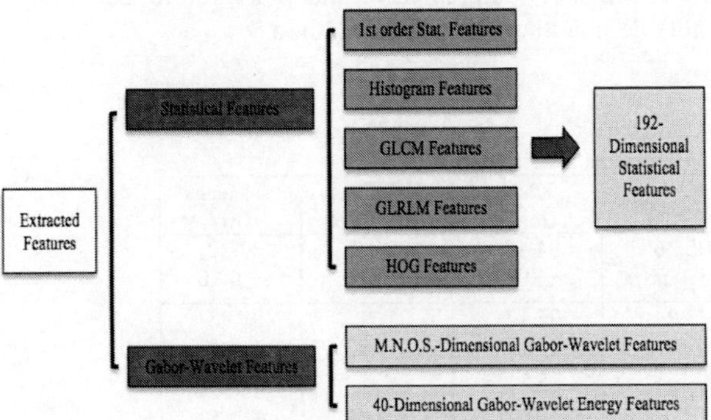

Fig. 3. Diagram of Extracted Features

5.2. Experimental Results

The proposed algorithm has been developed using MATLAB R2010a and is applied to T1 weighted MRI images of twenty subjects. Each subject has 181 T1 weighted slices. After detection of slices with tumor and then application of the windows, 3480 windows are available for investigation.

Then, Gabor-wavelet energy vector using 45×45 window-size and 50% tumor labeling is applied. The classification accuracy of different classifiers is presented in Fig. 4. As it is shown, SVM kernel linear kernel with $92.76 \pm 0.58\%$ and SVM kernel RBF with $93.89 \pm 0.67\%$ provide us with highest classification accuracy.

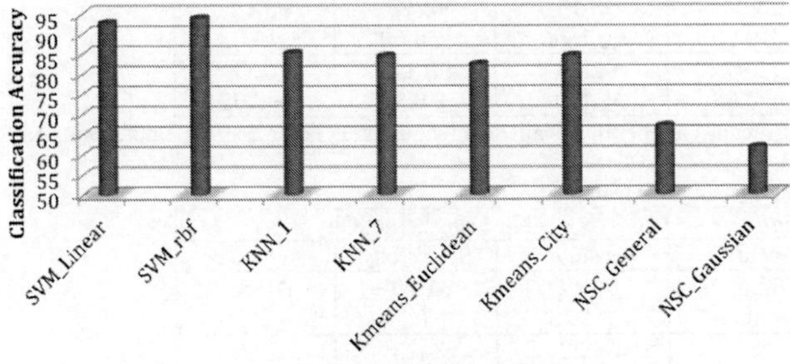

Fig. 4. Comparison of different classification methods using Gabor energy feature

The 192-dimensional statistical features vector is classified using supervised SVM kernel linear and RBF, and KNN classification methods for two different K (k=1, k=7). The classification accuracy of SVM and KNN are depicted in Fig. 5. With comparison of SVM and KNN, it is seen that with just 50 first Eigen vectors, PCA will converge. Classification accuracy of SVM kernel linear, SVM kernel RBF, KNN (k=1) and KNN (k=7) on 50 first Eigen vectors of statistical features are $97.87 \pm 0.51\%$, $96.93 \pm 0.48\%$, $91.97 \pm 0.62\%$, and $90.12 \pm 0.92\%$, respectively.

Subsequently, unsupervised K-means classification clusters statistical features vector into two groups of normal and tumors. Labels achieved from K-means clustering are then compared with the real labels, and the accuracy is calculated. Applying 50 first Eigen vectors of statistical features, K-Means kernel Euclidean clustering and the K-Means kernel Cityblock clustering accuracy are 82.66 ± 0.17 % and $84.52 \pm 0.13\%$, correspondingly.

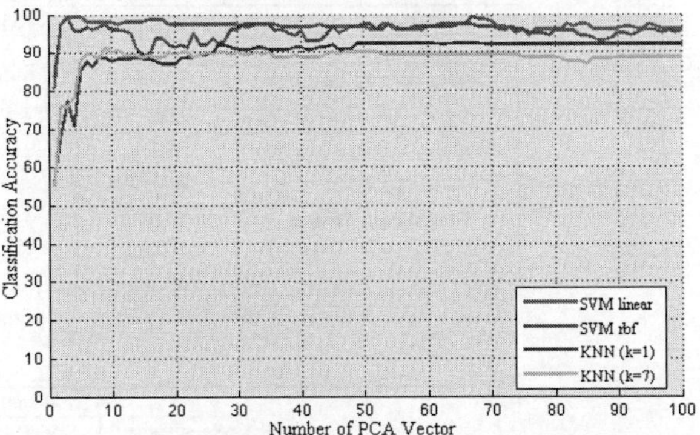

Fig. 5. Classification accuracy of SVM (kernel linear and RBF) and KNN (k=1 and k=7) based on different number of PCA Eigen vector, using statistical feature vector

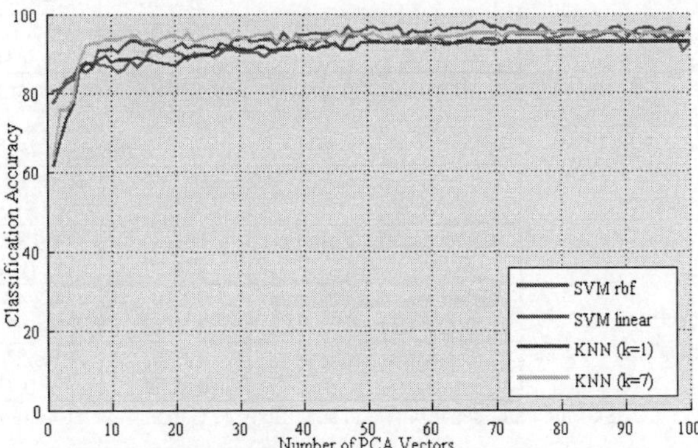

Fig. 6. Classification accuracy of SVM (kernel linear and RBF) and KNN (k=1 and k=7) based on different number of PCA Eigen vector, using Gabor feature vector

Applying PCA, 81,000-dimensional Gabor-wavelet features vector are classified using supervised SVM, KNN classification techniques. Classification accuracy of SVM kernel linear and RBF and KNN (k=1, k=7) are depicted in Fig. 6. With comparison of SVM and KNN, it is determined that with 50 Eigen vectors, the PCA converges. Classification accuracy of SVM kernel linear, SVM kernel RBF, KNN (k=1) and KNN (k=7) on 50 first

Eigen vectors of Gabor-wavelet features are 95.14 ± 0.69%, 96.58 ± 0.83%, 93.04 ± 0.9%, and 95.17 ± 1.03%, correspondingly.

The unsupervised K-means classification is applied to cluster Gabor-wavelet features vector into two groups of normal and tumors. The K-means cluster labels are compared with the real labels, and accuracy is calculated. Applying the first 50 Eigen vectors of Gabor-wavelet features, the accuracy of K-Means kernel Euclidean clustering and the K-Means kernel Cityblock clustering are 81.72 ± 0.52% and 82.93 ± 0.45%, respectively.

Table 1 shows that applying SVM kernel linear and RBF and k-means classifier, statistical features offers significantly higher accuracy than that of the Gabor features and Gabor energy features. Using KNN (k=1 and k=7), Gabor features leads to significantly higher accuracy than the other feature group. The highest classification accuracy occurs with SVM kernel linear and RBF, respectively, in statistical features classification. Classifier results are evaluated using sensitivity and specificity criteria as shown in Table 2 to 4, respectively [15].

It can be seen in Table 2 to 4, that sensitivity and specificity are also acceptable, verifying the two classes, tumor and healthy are well distinguished. These results indicate that statistical features in comparison with Gabor-wavelet features have the potential to be highly valuable in a tumor detection method.

Table 1. Classification Accuracy of three extracted feature groups*

	SVM Linear	SVM RBF	KNN (K=1)	KNN (K=7)	K-Means Euclidean	K-Means City
Gabor Energy Features	92.76 ± 0.58	93.89 ± 0.67	85.26 ± 0.53	84.48 ± 0.78	82.45 ± 0.26	84.22 ± 0.18
Gabor-wavelet Features	95.14 ± 0.69	96.58 ± 0.83	93.04 ± 0.90	95.17 ± 1.03	81.72 ± 0.52	82.93 ± 0.45
Statistical Features	97.87 ± 0.51	96.93 ± 0.48	91.97 ± 0.62	90.12 ± 0.92	82.66 ± 0.17	84.52 ± 0.13

*. Star indicates statistical feature accuracy is significantly higher than Gabor-wavelet feature and Gabor-energy feature using SVM, and K-Means Gabor-wavelet feature accuracy is significantly higher than statistical feature and Gabor-energy feature using KNN classifier

Table 2. Classification results using SVM*

	SVM kernel Linear			SVM kernel RBF		
	Sensitivity	Specificity	Accuracy	Sensitivity	Specificity	Accuracy
Gabor Energy Features	93.64 ± 2.02	92.07 ± 0.39	92.76 ± 0.58	95.49 ± 1.06	92.20 ± 0.43	93.89 ± 0.67
Gabor-wavelet Features	95.25 ± 1.86	94.18 ± 0.27	95.14 ± 0.69	96.81 ± 1.62	94.24 ± 0.31	96.58 ± 0.83
Statistical Features	97.46 ± 1.73	94.61 ± 0.18	97.87 ± 0.51	97.33 ± 1.38	96.51 ± 0.20	96.93 ± 0.48

*. Star indicates sensitivity and specificity of statistical features are significantly higher than Gabor-wavelet feature and Gabor-energy feature using SVM

Table 3. Classification results using KNN*

	KNN (K=1)			KNN (K=7)		
	Sensitivity	Specificity	Accuracy	Sensitivity	Specificity	Accuracy
Gabor Energy Features	86.21 ± 1.77	84.37 ± 0.96	85.26 ± 0.53	85.47 ± 1.30	82.64 ± 0.84	84.48 ± 0.78
Gabor-wavelet Features	93.39 ± 1.23	92.41 ± 0.71	93.04 ± 0.90	93.15 ± 1.43	92.47 ± 0.60	95.17 ± 1.03
Statistical Features	92.75 ± 1.54	90.28 ± 0.48	91.97 ± 0.62	92.69 ± 1.89	88.12 ± 0.57	90.12 ± 0.92

*. Star indicates sensitivity and specificity of Gabor-wavelet features are significantly higher than statistical feature and Gabor-energy feature using KNN

Table 4. Classification results using K-Means*

	K-Means kernel Euclidean			K-Means kernel City		
	Sensitivity	Specificity	Accuracy	Sensitivity	Specificity	Accuracy
Gabor Energy Features	84.22 ± 2.16	79.93 ± 1.13	82.45 ± 0.26	86.47 ± 1.25	81.18 ± 0.74	84.22 ± 0.18
Gabor-wavelet Features	82.71 ± 1.82	81.07 ± 0.97	81.72 ± 0.52	84.22 ± 1.58	81.13 ± 0.63	82.93 ± 0.45
Statistical Features	83.44 ± 1.76	80.33 ± 0.65	82.66 ± 0.17	85.27 ± 1.61	82.31 ± 0.51	84.52 ± 0.13

*. Star indicates sensitivity and specificity of statistical features are significantly higher than Gabor-wavelet feature and Gabor-energy feature using K-Means

6. Conclusions And Future Work

In this study, Gabor-wavelet features and statistical features are investigated for their capabilities and efficacy to discriminate healthy and tumor tissues.

Applying Gray Level Co-occurrence Matrix (GLCM), Grey Level Run Length Matrix (GLRLM), Histogram of Oriented Gradient (HOG), and Histogram Analysis (HA) method, several features are derived from T1-weighted brain images. Adding first-order histogram based features to the previous group, statistical features are elicited. Secondly, employing the Gabor-wavelet transform, Gabor-wavelet features and Gabor-wavelet energy features are captured.

For classification, three different techniques such as SVM with kernel RBF and linear, KNN (k=1, k=7), and K-Means with kernel Euclidean and Cityblock are compared. An integrated automated framework is implemented for tumor slice selection, slice windowing, feature extraction, feature ranking and comparison.

Results show statistical features offer higher accuracy than Gabor-wavelet energy features applying six classifier techniques. In addition, statistical features provide better accuracy than Gabor-wavelet features in using four out of six classifier techniques as SVM kernel linear, SVM kernel RBF, K-Means kernel Euclidean, and K-Means kernel Cityblock. Furthermore, statistical feature dimension is much less than Gabor-wavelet feature dimension (192 versus 81000). Although Gabor-wavelets are employed widely in computer vision and medical image processing due to their effective directional selectivity, they occupy lots of memory, are highly redundant and make the computation heavy and slow. The time estimation of steps are obtained for 20 patients on an Intel Xeon CPU X5472 at 3 GHz and with 64 GB of RAM. The time needed for slice detection is 12 min, Gabor-wavelet feature extraction is 15 min, statistical feature extraction is 22 min, statistical feature classification using PCA is 6 min, and Gabor-wavelet feature classification using PCA is 50 min.

In the future, we plan to extend our investigation into other MRI modalities like T2-weighted, FLAIR and proton density images. Further, adding other feature ranking and feature selection methods can offer wider scope of comparison.

7. Reference

[1] Ahmed Kharrat, Mohamed Ben Messaoud, "Detection Of Brain Tumor In Medical Images", 2009 International Conference On Signals, Circuits And Systems

[2] Amirehsan Lashkari, "A Neural Network Based Method For Brain Abnormality Detection In Mr Images Using Gabor Wavelets," International Journal Of Computer Applications (0975 – 8887) Volume 4 – No.7, July 2010

[3] M. Lee And W. Street "Dynamic Learning Of Shapes For Automatic Object Recognition," Proceedings Of The17th Workshop Machine Learning Of Spatial Knowledge, Stanford, Ca, Pp. 44-49, 2000.

[4] Shaheen Ahmed, Khan M. Iftekharuddin, And Arastoo Vossough, "Efficacy Of Texture, Shape, And Intensity Feature Fusion For Posterior-Fossa Tumor Segmentation In Mri," IEEE Transactions On Information Technology In Biomedicine, Vol. 15, No. 2, March 2011

[5] M. J. Lyons, Julien Budynek, Andre Plantey, Shigeru Akamatsu, "Classifying Facial Attributes Using A 2-D Gaborwavelet Representation And Discriminant Analysis" The 4th IEEE International Conference On Automatic Face And Gesture Recognition (Fg 2000), 26-30 March 2000, Grenoble, France.

[6] P. Yang, S. Shan, W. Gao, S. Z. Li, D. Zhang, "Face Recognition Using Ada-Boosted Gabor Features", The 6th IEEE International Conference On Automatic Face And Gesture Recognition (Fg2004), Seoul, Korea.

[7] Yi-Hui Liu, Manita Muftah, Tilak Das, Li Bai, Keith Robson, Dorothee Auer, "Classification Of Mr Tumor Images Based On Gabor Wavelet Analysis", Journal Of Medical And Biological Engineering, 2011, 32(1): 22-28

[8] Sahar Ghanavati, Junning Li, Ting Liu, Paul S. Babyn, Wendy Doda,Georgelampropoulos, "Automatic Brain Tumor Detection In Magnetic Resonance Images," IEEE-Isbi, 2012

[9] Gayatri Mirajkar, Balaji Barbadekar, "Automatic Segmentation Of Brain Tumors From Mr Images Using Undecimated Wavelet Transform And Gabor Wavelets," IEEE-Icecs 2010

[10] Evangelia I. Zacharaki, Sumei Wang, Sanjeev Chawla, Dong Soo Yoo, Ronald Wolf, Elias R. Melhem, And Christos Davatzikos, "Classification Of Brain Tumor Type And Grade Using Mri Texture And Shape In A Machine Learning Scheme," Magn Reson Med. 2009 December ; 62(6): 1609–1618.

[11] Qurat-Ul-Ain, Ghazanfar Latif, "Classification And Segmentation Of Brain Tumor Using Texture Analysis," Recent Advances In Artificial Intelligence, Knowledge Engineering And Data Bases

[12] Xiao Xuan, Qingmin Liao, "Statistical Structure Analysis In Mri Brain Tumor Segmentation," Fourth International Conference On Image And Graphics, IEEE 2007

[13] M R Haralick, "Textural Features for Image Classification," IEEE 1973

[14] M.M. Galloway, "Texture Analysis Using Grey Level Run Length," Computer Graphics Image Processing," 4: 172-179, [18]. June 1975.

[15] Wenan Chen, Rebecca Smith, Nooshin Nabizadeh, Kevin Ward, Charles Cockrell, Jonathan Ha, And Kayvan Najarian, "Texture Analysis Of Brain Ct Scans For Icp Prediction," Springer-Verlag Berlin Heidelberg, 2010

[16] Oswaldo Ludwig Junior, David Delgado, Valter Gonc ̧Alves, Urbano Nunes, "Trainable Classifier-Fusion Schemes: An Application To Pedestrian Detection," IEEE Conference On Intelligent Transportation System, 2009

[17] Dalal, N. And Triggs, B., Histograms Of Oriented Gradients For Human Detection, In IEEE Computer Society Conference On Computer Vision And Pattern Recognition, 2005, Pp. 886893.

[18] Chapter 1, "Principal Component Analysis," http://support.sas.com/publishing/pubcat/chaps/55129.pdf

[19] Marcel Prastawaa, Elizabeth Bullitt, Guido Gerig, "Simulation Of Brain Tumors In Mr Images For Evaluation Of Segmentation Efficacy," Med Image Anal. 2009 April ; 13(2): 297–311

[20] Http://Www.Nitrc.Org/Projects/Tumorsim

Remote respiratory sensing with an infrared camera using the Kinect™ infrared projector

Andrew Loblaw, Dr. John Nielsen, Dr. Michal Okoniewski and Mazhar Ali Lakhani
Department of Electrical & Computer Engineering, University of Calgary, Calgary, Alberta, Canada

Abstract— *The need for an inexpensive and portable remote respiratory monitor is in particular demand in a hospital setting as the respiratory rate provides early warning for cardiorespiratory arrest. This paper proposes an inexpensive infrared (IR) camera combined with the Microsoft Kinect™ IR projector as a low-cost module for accurate measurement of respiratory rate. The IR camera utilizes a background subtraction algorithm to obtain the respiratory information of a patient in a bed. Issues with ill-defined feature points for the background subtraction algorithm are overcome by using the Kinect™ IR projector. The IR camera can easily detect the subtle respiratory motion of a prone or side-sleeping patient, even under covers. The IR camera system is experimentally validated in a home scenario as well as with a respiratory mannequin at the Foothills hospital in Calgary.*

Keywords: CV Remote Sensing, Background Subtraction

1. Introduction

PATIENT'S in a hospital setting often require continuous monitoring of their vital signs as they are at a higher risk for mortality in which cardiorespiratory arrest is a common contributing factor. Early indication of a cardiorespiratory event are often indicated in the vital signs, specifically by an acceleration or slowing of the respiratory rate [1]. In a sleep apnea lab, an intensive care unit, or in an operating theater the respiratory rate of a patient is closely monitored. However, in a post-operative setting the respiratory rate of a patient is seldom monitored even though they are commonly administered narcotics for pain and are usually still under the influence of residual anaesthetic agents [2], [3]. A continuous respiratory monitoring method would offer the ability to recognize a cardiorespiratory event and intervene to prevent the event.

While there are many methods of continuous respiratory monitoring currently used in hospitals none of them are utilized for long term monitoring in the post-operative setting. The oronasal thermistor, the nasal pressure cannula, and the inductive plethysmography belt which are common in any sleep lab are cumbersome, and inconvenient. These instruments all require contact with the patient, a dedicated technician to set up, and may be prone to detachment from the patient. In addition, the need for contact with delicate or sensitive patients, such as burn victims, is infeasible. Many non-contact methods have been proposed, from microwave and millimeter-wave continuous wave (CW) Doppler radar [4], [5], [6] and ultra wideband (UWB) pulse [7], [8] to laser vibrometry [9], optical and infrared camera [10], [11], [12], and thermal cameras [13]. While microwaves and millimeter-waves have the potential to pass through bed sheets to measure respiration directly they lack spatial resolution and are therefore more prone to non-respiratory related interference. To obtain spatial information about a scene, cameras present themselves as the obvious alternative. A typical sleeping patient has very little visible light emitted on their person, so there are few well defined feature points making optical techniques infeasible. Thermal cameras are only able to measure exposed body parts, usually the neck and head, and are particularly expensive compared to CMOS camera technology. Infrared cameras can utilize active lighting that does not affect a sleeping subject. An infrared camera using active structured lighting [12] has demonstrated the ability to obtain geometric information. The downside to the technique presented in [12] is the need for pre-calibration to obtain the accurate physical profile.

Based on the previous development of respiratory sensing, a simplified respiratory sensing system using active structured lighting without the need for calibration is proposed. A background subtraction algorithm is applied to the raw infrared (IR) camera video to obtain a respiratory signal. Next, a respiratory classification and moving Fourier transform algorithm is applied to obtain the respiratory rate. The algorithms and techniques proposed in this paper are validated with several different experiments: two human subjects, male and female in a home setting covered by bed sheets; and a respiratory mannequin in a hospital setting covered by bed sheets.

2. Background Subtraction Algorithm

To detect the subtle motion of respiration a background subtraction algorithm is proposed. The Microsoft Kinect™ structured infrared light projector is used to provides feature points in the form of IR dots. A picture of the Kinect™ and the dot pattern is shown in fig. 1 and 2. A separate IR webcam is used to capture the data for processing. The overall setup is illustrated in fig. 3. As the subject inhales and exhales the projected IR dots will translate along the chest. The motion of the dots, which is enhanced for smaller projection angles (θ), can be detected by the separate IR camera. This exaggerated motion of the IR dots is the motivation for separating the IR camera and the projector.

Fig. 1: Microsoft Kinect™ device with the IR projector (left aperture) used for generating the feature points. The other Kinect™ features are not used.

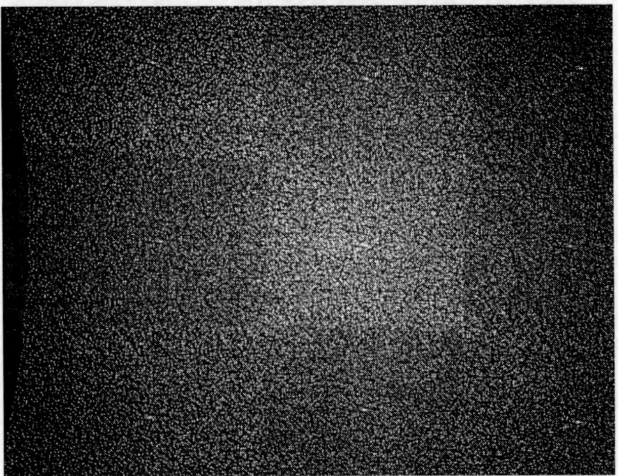

Fig. 2: Kinect™ IR projector pattern showing the ~30000 IR dots. Photo taken using the Kinect™ built-in IR camera while the Kinect™ is facing a smooth flat wall.

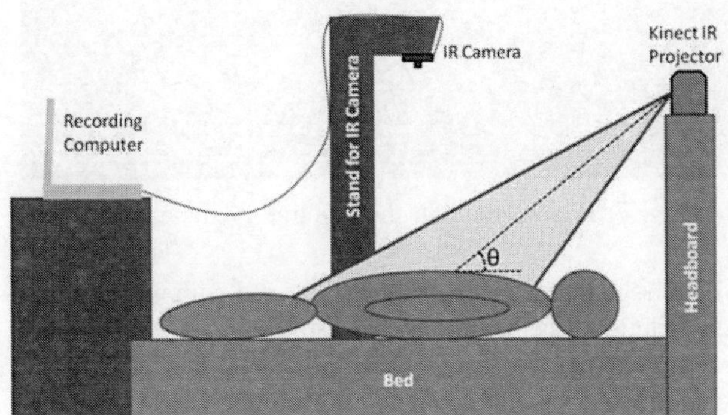

Fig. 3: IR Camera with Kinect™ measurement setup.

The first step in the background subtraction algorithm is a spatial pre-filter. A 5×5 Gaussian kernel is applied to each image in an effort to remove some of the environment and electronic noise. The kernel size of the Gaussian blur is chosen due to the physical nature of the IR feature points. The individual IR dots measure approximately 5 pixels squared, so the Gaussian kernel smooths out noise features without significant smearing of the IR dots.

The goal of the background subtraction algorithm is to classify all static scenery and non-respiratory related activity as part of the *background*. The *foreground* can be extracted as the difference between the source and the background video and will contain the respiratory motion. The background subtraction algorithm implements an infinite impulse response (IIR) filter operating separately on each individual pixel. Although the effective motion is a lateral translation of the dots during respiration the change in each individual pixel's intensity expresses this motion. Thus each individual pixel can be temporally filtered for its varying intensity. The combination of all of the pixels' motion yields the respiratory motion. The IIR filter impulse response is illustrated in fig. 4. A 0.1–1.5 Hz second order Butterworth band-stop filter is used in this paper. This filter bandwidth is chosen to prevent any possible respiratory frequencies (6-90 breaths per minute (BPM)) from being classified as *background*. A low pass filter could also have been used, although the band-stop filter provides the benefit of filtering out higher frequency noise and non-respiratory related motion.

After the background is computed using the IIR filter, it is a simple matter of computing the absolute value of a pixel-by-pixel image difference to generate the foreground. Once the foreground is established the respiratory motion is computed as the pixel-wise sum of all of the foreground pixels. The overall flow of the background subtraction algorithm is illustrated in fig. 5.

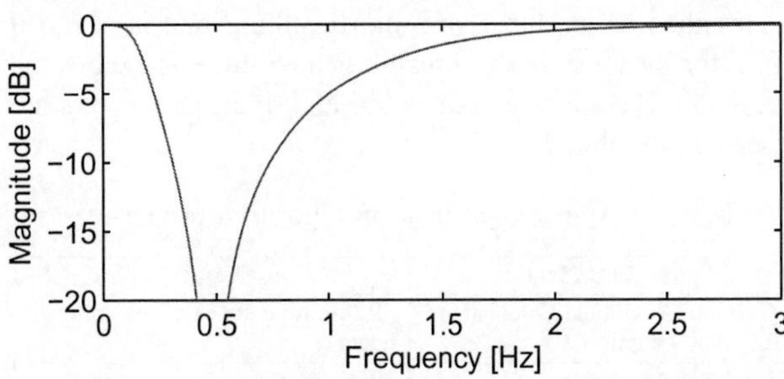

Fig. 4: Background subtraction algorithm IIR filter impulse response: 0.1–1.5 Hz 2nd order Butterworth band-stop filter.

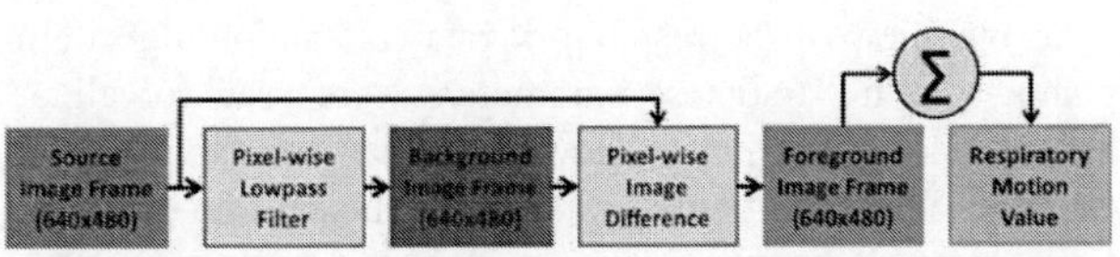

Fig. 5: Overview of the background subtraction algorithm used to obtain the respiratory motion waveform.

3. Respiratory Rate Computation Algorithm

In order to validate the background subtraction algorithm and obtain a useful metric from the respiratory motion, a respiratory rate computation algorithm is proposed. This algorithm takes the respiratory motion from the background subtraction algorithm as input and produces the respiratory rate as output.

The first step is to apply a 0.1–1.5 Hz second order Butterworth band-pass pre-filter to the respiratory signal. The pre-filter attenuates the low and high frequency noise and most importantly removes the large DC offset. Next a moving Fourier transform is computed. The peak frequency of the Fourier transform for each time step is selected as the respiratory rate. The parameters of the moving Fourier transform are described in table 1.

Table 1: Moving Fourier transform properties

Moving Fourier Transform	Value
Window Length	512 samples, ~17 seconds @30 FPS
Window Type	Hamming
Time steps between each Fourier transform	6 samples, 0.2 seconds @30 FPS

In order to detect periods where the patient may completely stop breathing entirely, an apnea classification algorithm is run in parallel with the moving Fourier transform. The apnea classification algorithm computes the average amplitude of the respiratory signal and determines the minimum baseline breathing amplitude required for *normal* breathing. If the amplitude of breathing falls below this threshold, it is classified as an apnea and the breathing rate is set to 0 BPM for as long as the breathing amplitude is below the threshold. The apnea classification algorithm parameters are described in table 2.

Table 2: Apnea classification algorithm properties

Apnea Classification	Value
Baseline Amplitude Calculation Window Length	Entire time series of respiratory data
Regional Amplitude Calculation Window Length	256 samples, ~8.5 seconds @30 FPS
Regional Amplitude Apnea Qualification	≤50% of the baseline breathing amplitude

An overview of the respiratory rate calculation algorithm is shown in fig. 6. These parameters were used for all of the results in this paper; however, they are flexible and variation of certain values can be beneficial. For example, if the patient's breathing rate is highly variable, a shorter Fourier transform time window may be advantageous since it would allow for faster tracking of the variable rate.

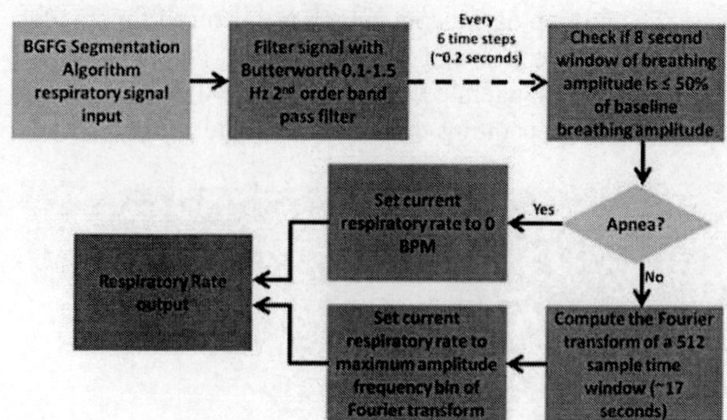

Fig. 6: Overview of the respiratory rate calculation algorithm used to obtain the respiratory rate

4. Results and Discussion

In the following demonstrations, the performance of the IR camera remote respiratory sensing system is shown and evaluated. The main metric is the accuracy of the respiratory rate computed by the respiratory rate calculation algorithm, although visual qualitative analysis of the respiratory signal computed by the background subtraction algorithm is also presented. The accuracy of the respiratory rate is evaluated by computing the root mean squared error (RMSE) between the measured and the known respiratory rate.

4.1 Mannequin Trials

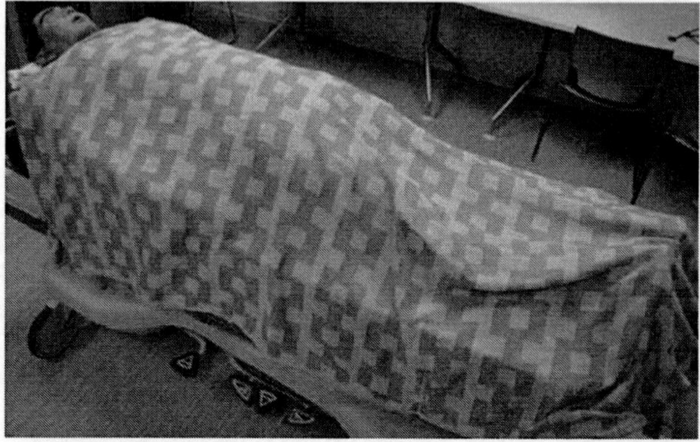

Fig. 7: Picture of Stan the respiratory mannequin.

The issue that is commonly encountered with most validation techniques is the difficulty in establishing a *ground truth* to compare against. Usually, the ground truth is established by employing a well known and trusted alternative measurement modality, such as a respiratory belt or a spirometer. This paper validates the system with measurements on a respiratory mannequin named Stan (Standard Man), pictured in fig. 7. Stan has the ability to very accurately control his respiratory rate so that no alternative measurement modality is needed. In addition, Stan has a highly consistent breathing depth which should be reflected in the processed IR output.

The IR camera background subtraction algorithm as well as the respiratory rate calculation algorithm are demonstrated on the mannequin in fig. 8→11. In each of these trials the mannequin's respiratory rate is different:

1) Fig. 8 shows the Mannequin breathing at 11 BPM.
2) Fig. 9 shows the Mannequin breathing at 15 BPM.
3) Fig. 10 shows the Mannequin breathing at 22 BPM.
4) Fig. 11 shows the Mannequin breathing at 40 BPM.

The individual respiratory events can be easily seen in figs. 8a, 9a, 10a, 11a. Interestingly, the mannequin has a different breathing behaviour than humans. Stan's breaths are sharp impulsive inhale-exhales rather than a sinusoidal inhale-exhale pattern more typical of human respiration. Another interesting characteristic of the mannequin's breathing is the additional periodic square-wave amplitude modulation which is detected by the background subtraction algorithm. This periodicity is most easily seen in figs. 10a and 11a. The detection of this periodicity demonstrates the ability of the IR system to detect subtle breathing mechanics.

The computed respiratory rate tracks the known respiratory rate quite accurately with a maximum average RMSE of 1.5 BPM. The results for all the mannequin trials are presented in table 3.

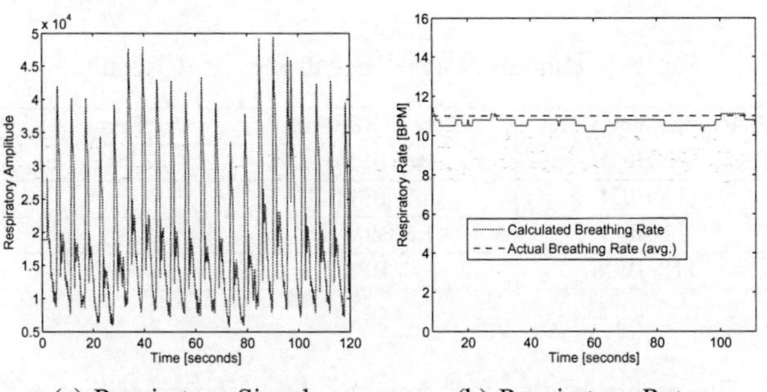

(a) Respiratory Signal (b) Respiratory Rate

Fig. 8: Two minute trial - mannequin breathing at 11 BPM. Each individual respiratory event is clearly visible.

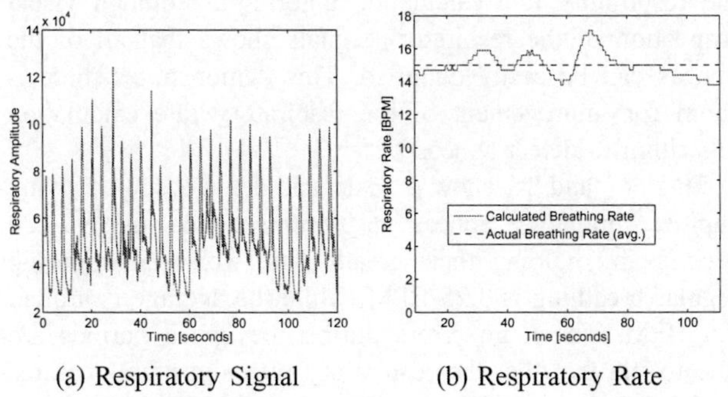

(a) Respiratory Signal (b) Respiratory Rate

Fig. 9: Two minute trial - mannequin breathing at 15 BPM.

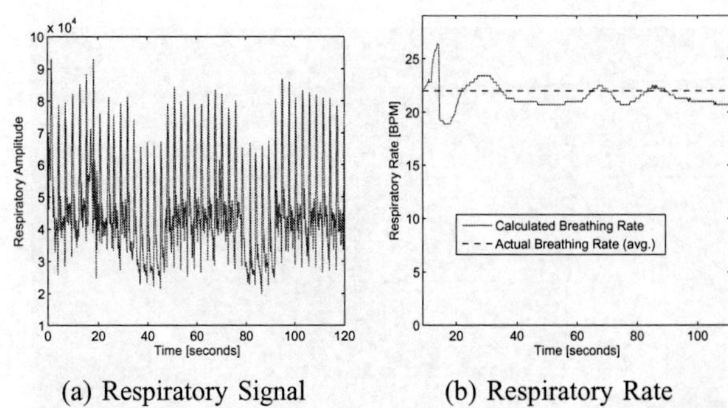

(a) Respiratory Signal (b) Respiratory Rate

Fig. 10: Two minute trial - mannequin breathing at 22 BPM.

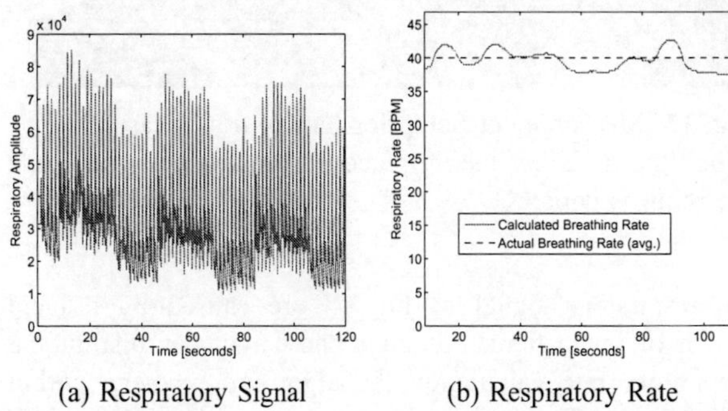

(a) Respiratory Signal (b) Respiratory Rate

Fig. 11: Two minute trial - mannequin breathing at 40 BPM.

Table 3: Mannequin Trial Results

Respiratory Rate	Error (BPM)	% Error
11 BPM	0.39 BPM	3.5%
15 BPM	0.71 BPM	4.7%
22 BPM	1.23 BPM	5.5%
40 BPM	1.55 BPM	3.9%

4.2 Human Trials

To demonstrate the performance of the system in a more realistic setting it is also tested on two different human subjects in several different trials. For all of the human trials the patient counted the total number of breaths over the entire trial or specific intervals to compute the average respiratory rate. This average respiratory rate is used as the ground truth for comparison, although there is expected to be some amount of variability in the breathing rate since their respiratory rate can vary breath to breath. The setup for the human subject trials is shown in fig. 12.

The background subtraction algorithm performs well to obtain the respiratory signal of both human subjects. The individual respiratory events can easily be seen in all of the trials. Contrary to the mannequin trials, the respiratory signals show a sinusoidal breathing pattern typical of human breathing and each inhale and exhale is detected separately. The respiratory rate calculation algorithm demonstrates the ability to ignore some amount of non-respiratory related interference as seen in fig. 13. The large disruptions in

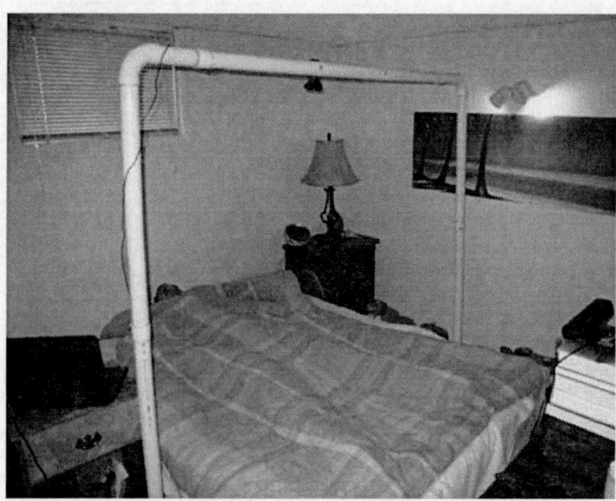

Fig. 12: Measurement Setup for human trial measurements. When the trials are taking place all lights are shut off and the room is darker.

the respiratory signal of fig. 15 are caused by a hand twitch of the patient. Although these twitches disrupt the respiratory rate calculation the algorithm recovers within ~10 seconds. These trials also demonstrate the ability of the IR camera background subtraction algorithm and respiratory rate calculation to accurately track the respiratory rate of a patient in both supine and side-sleeping postures.

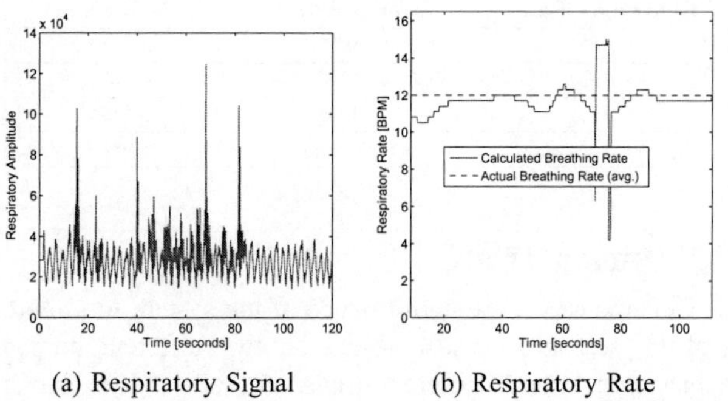

(a) Respiratory Signal (b) Respiratory Rate

Fig. 13: Female - supine, 24 breaths total = 12 BPM.

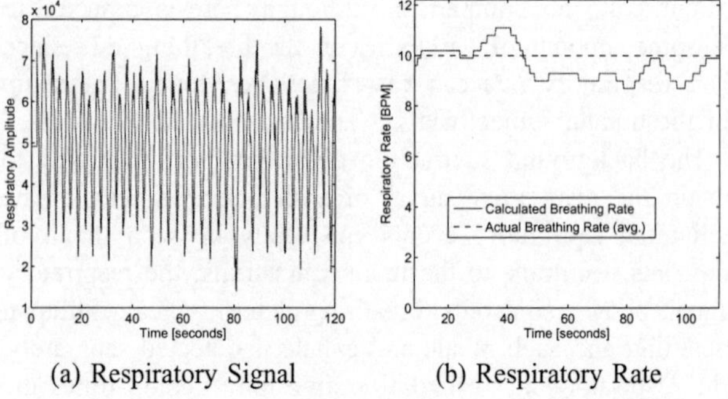

(a) Respiratory Signal (b) Respiratory Rate

Fig. 14: Male - supine, 20 breaths total = 10 BPM.

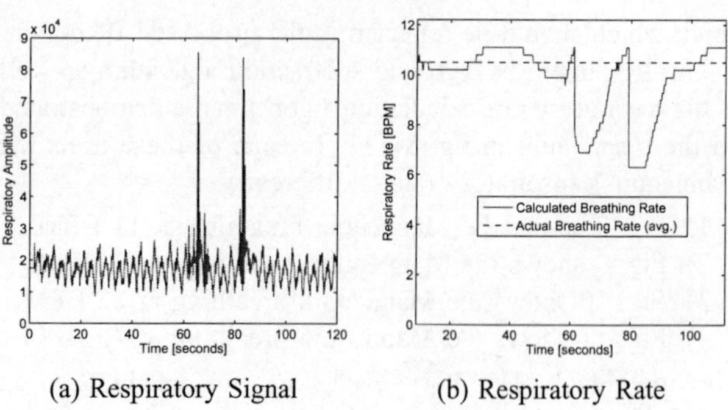

(a) Respiratory Signal (b) Respiratory Rate

Fig. 15: Female - side, 21 breaths total = 12 BPM.

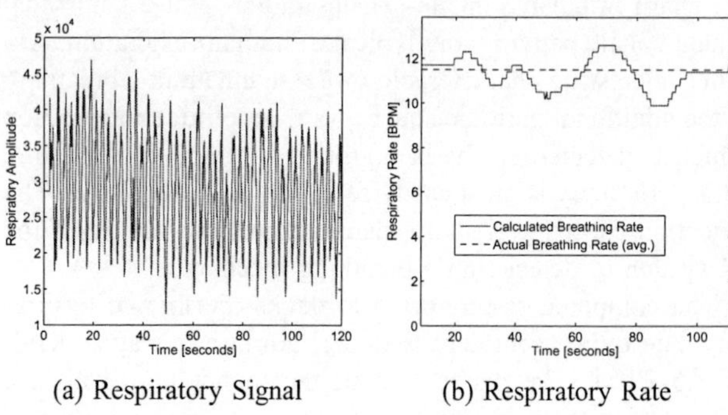

(a) Respiratory Signal (b) Respiratory Rate

Fig. 16: Male - side, 23 breaths total = 11.5 BPM.

Table 4: Human Normal Breathing Trial Results

Respiratory Rate	Error (BPM)	% Error
12 BPM	1.09 BPM	9.5%
10 BPM	0.73 BPM	4.7%
12 BPM	1.6 BPM	13.3%
11.5 BPM	0.72 BPM	6.3%

The ability of the background subtraction algorithm and respiratory rate calculation algorithm to detect apneas is presented in figs. 17→19. An apnea can be defined as a period where respiration decreases significantly for more than 10 seconds. All of the apneas are at least partially detected by the respiratory rate calculation algorithm, although visual inspection of the respiratory signals shows that all of the apneas can be easily qualified. This demonstrates there is room for improvement of the respiratory rate calculation algorithm to detect apneas faster.

Figs. 17 and 18 show a male and female subject lying supine, simulating apneas at 30-50 seconds and 90-100 seconds by holding their breath. The worst error during regular breathing is 3.25 BPM, while the average is around 1.5 BPM. The large errors during the apnea periods are due to the fact that the respiratory rate algorithm requires between 3-10 seconds to qualify the apnea.

The last trial, shown in fig. 19 is of a male subject lying supine. The subject counted the number of respirations in each 20 second interval and slowly decreased his breathing.

In the last 20 seconds of the trial the subject held his breath to simulate an apnea. While the patients respiration is decreasing, the respiratory rate is measured to less than 2 BPM of error. When the patient stops breathing, the apnea is detected within 3 seconds of starting.

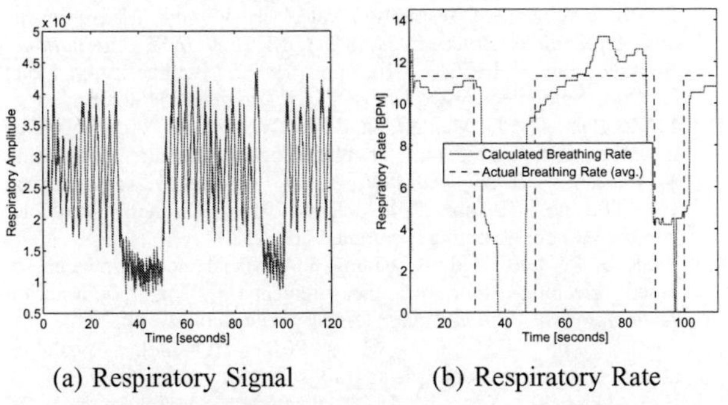

(a) Respiratory Signal (b) Respiratory Rate

Fig. 17: Female - supine, simulating an apnea between 30-50 seconds and 90-100 seconds. Average respiratory rate for periods of normal breathing = 11.33 BPM.

Table 5: RMSE in BPM between the measured and estimated respiratory rate for different respiratory rate regions of fig. 17.

Time	**8.5-30s**	**30-50s**	**50-90s**	**90-100s**	**100-111.5s**
Rate	**11.3 BPM**	**0 BPM**	**11.3 BPM**	**0 BPM**	**11.3 BPM**
Error	1.40	5.57	1.57	4.31	2.68
	12%	–	14%	–	24%

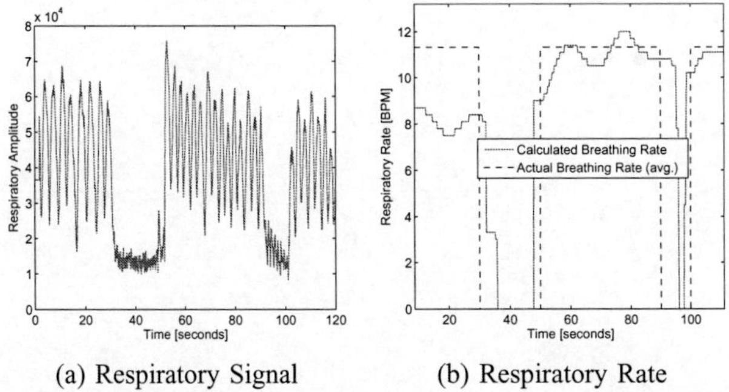

(a) Respiratory Signal (b) Respiratory Rate

Fig. 18: Male - supine, simulating an apnea between 30-50 seconds and 90-100 seconds. Average respiratory rate for periods of normal breathing = 11.33 BPM.

Table 6: RMSE in BPM between the measured and estimated respiratory rate for different respiratory rate regions of fig. 18.

Time	**8.5-30s**	**30-50s**	**50-90s**	**90-100s**	**100-111.5s**
Rate	**11.3 BPM**	**0 BPM**	**11.3 BPM**	**0 BPM**	**11.3 BPM**
Error	3.25	4.30	0.80	9.13	0.56
	29%	–	7.1%	–	5%

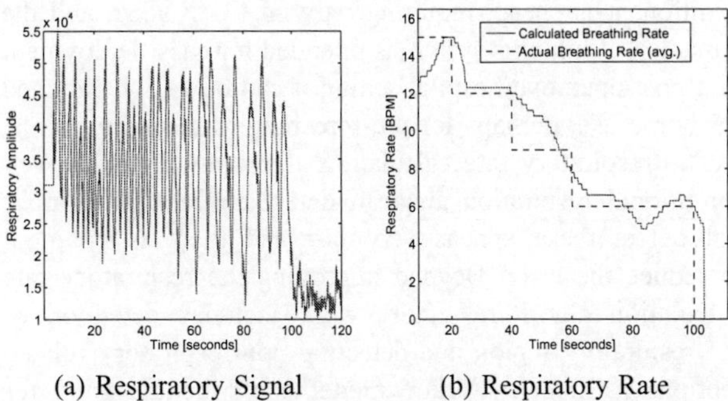

(a) Respiratory Signal (b) Respiratory Rate

Fig. 19: Male - supine, decreasing respiratory rate throughout trial until simulating an apnea from 100-120 seconds.

Table 7: RMSE in BPM between the measured and estimated respiratory rate for different respiratory rate regions of fig. 19.

Time	**8.5-20s**	**20-40s**	**40-60s**	**60-80s**	**80-100s**	**100-111.5s**
Rate	**15 BPM**	**12 BPM**	**9 BPM**	**6 BPM**	**6 BPM**	**0 BPM**
Error	1.47	1.19	1.82	0.79	0.64	2.98
	10%	10%	20%	13%	11%	–

5. Conclusion

The remote respiratory rate tracking system using an IR camera with the Microsoft Kinect™ IR projector has been successfully demonstrated. Several trials of a mannequin with varying respiratory rates were shown where the average error is less than 1.5 BPM. The system was also demonstrated on two human subjects for several different arrangements. Normal respiration is accurately detected with errors between 0.7 and 1.6 BPM. Scenarios in which the subjects simulate an apnea are also demonstrated and the system never fails to detect at least part of the apnea. The error measurements for the human subjects are somewhat misleading since the reference respiratory rate is really just the overall average. The time domain plots of the respiratory signal attest to the accuracy of the system as not a single breath was missed during normal operation. In terms of instantaneous breathing rate, the kernel of the system is

100% accurate. It is the respiratory rate calculation which gives the perception of inaccuracy. The system is capable of measuring subjects' respiratory rate in a variety of lighting conditions and the posture of the patient is not critical to obtaining an accurate measure of respiratory rate. The time domain results for the mannequin and human subjects demonstrate the ability of the system to differentiate between different breathing mechanics. The IR camera system requires no calibration and is very practical for sleeping patients since it does not emit or require visible light. In addition, it is cheap, requiring only an IR webcam and the Kinect™. While this system is intended for easy deployment in a post-operative hospital setting it can be easily designed for home use, perhaps for pre-screening of sleep apnea.

The respiratory rate calculation algorithm performs well for normal respiration and can detect apneas, but it does not detect these apneas very fast and there is potential to reduce the error. Beyond improving the respiratory rate calculation algorithm, future work includes detection of the respiratory region and detecting non-respiratory related motion. A hidden Markov model could be designed for classification of patient breathing states and postures for improved respiratory detection. Although not demonstrated in this paper, there is the potential for this technique to measure tidal volume if properly calibrated.

References

[1] M. DeVita, G. Smith, and S. Adam, ""Identifying the hospitalised patient in crisisâĂİ - A consensus conference on the afferent limb of Rapid Response Systems," *Resuscitation*, vol. 81, no. 4, pp. 375–82, Apr. 2010. [Online]. Available: http://www.ncbi.nlm.nih.gov/pubmed/20149516

[2] R. Robinson, C. Zwillich, E. Bixler, R. Cadieux, A. Kales, and D. White, "Effects of oral narcotics on sleep-disordered breathing in healthy adults." *CHEST* . . . , pp. 197–203, 1987. [Online]. Available: http://journal.publications.chestnet.org/article.aspx?articleid=1060018

[3] K. Pattinson, "Opioids and the control of respiration," *British journal of anaesthesia*, vol. 100, no. 6, pp. 747–58, June 2008. [Online]. Available: http://www.ncbi.nlm.nih.gov/pubmed/18456641

[4] A. Droitcour, O. Boric-Lubecke, V. Lubecke, J. Lin, and G. Kovacs, "Range correlation and I/Q performance benefits in single-chip silicon Doppler radars for noncontact cardiopulmonary monitoring," *Microwave Theory and Techniques, IEEE Transactions on*, vol. 52, no. 3, pp. 838–848, 2004. [Online]. Available: http://ieeexplore.ieee.org/xpls/abs_all.jsp?arnumber=1273725

[5] C. Li, J. Ling, J. Li, and J. Lin, "Accurate Doppler Radar Noncontact Vital Sign Detection Using the RELAX Algorithm," *Instrumentation and Measurement, IEEE Transactions on*, vol. 59, no. 3, pp. 687–695, Mar. 2010. [Online]. Available: http://ieeexplore.ieee.org/xpls/abs_all.jsp?arnumber=5247107

[6] I. Mikhelson, S. Bakhtiari, T. Elmer, and A. Sahakian, "Remote Sensing of Heart Rate and Patterns of Respiration on a Stationary Subject Using 94 GHz Millimeter Wave Interferometry," *Biomedical Engineering, IEEE Transactions on*, no. 99, pp. 1–7, Feb. 2011. [Online]. Available: http://ieeexplore.ieee.org/xpls/abs_all.jsp?arnumber=5709976

[7] I. Immoreev and T. Tao, "UWB radar for patient monitoring," *Aerospace and Electronic Systems Magazine, IEEE*, vol. 23, no. 11, pp. 11–18, Nov. 2008. [Online]. Available: http://ieeexplore.ieee.org/xpls/abs_all.jsp?arnumber=4693985

[8] J. Lai, Y. Xu, E. Gunawan, E. Chua, A. Maskooki, Y. Guan, K. Low, C. Soh, and C. Poh, "Wireless Sensing of Human Respiratory Parameters by Low-Power Ultrawideband Impulse Radio Radar," *Instrumentation and Measurement, IEEE Transactions on*, vol. 60, no. 99, pp. 1–11, 2011. [Online]. Available: http://ieeexplore.ieee.org/xpls/abs_all.jsp?arnumber=5618561

[9] L. Scalise, I. Ercoli, and P. Marchionni, "Optical method for measurement of respiration rate," in *Medical Measurements and Applications Proceedings (MeMeA), 2010 IEEE International Workshop on*. IEEE, 2010, pp. 19–22. [Online]. Available: http://ieeexplore.ieee.org/xpls/abs_all.jsp?arnumber=5480208

[10] M.-Z. Poh, D. J. McDuff, and R. W. Picard, "Advancements in noncontact, multiparameter physiological measurements using a webcam." *IEEE transactions on bio-medical engineering*, vol. 58, no. 1, pp. 7–11, Jan. 2011. [Online]. Available: http://www.ncbi.nlm.nih.gov/pubmed/20952328

[11] Y. Kuo, J. Lee, and P. Chung, "A visual context-awareness-based sleeping-respiration measurement system," *Information Technology in Biomedicine, IEEE Transactions on*, vol. 14, no. 2, pp. 255–265, Mar. 2010. [Online]. Available: http://ieeexplore.ieee.org/xpls/abs_all.jsp?arnumber=5325889

[12] H. Aoki, K. Koshiji, H. Nakamura, Y. Takemura, and M. Nakajima, "Study on respiration monitoring method using near-infrared multiple slit-lights projection," in *Micro-NanoMechatronics and Human Science, 2005 IEEE International Symposium on*. IEEE, 2005, pp. 291–296. [Online]. Available: http://ieeexplore.ieee.org/xpls/abs_all.jsp?arnumber=1590006

[13] M. Yang, Q. Liu, T. Turner, and Y. Wu, "Vital sign estimation from passive thermal video," *IEEE Computer Society Conference on Computer Vision and Pattern Recognition*, 2008. [Online]. Available: http://ieeexplore.ieee.org/xpls/abs_all.jsp?arnumber=4587826

Combining Anatomical Biomarkers with Neuropsychological Data for Multidimensional Classification of Alzheimer's Disease

Q. Zhou[1], M. Goryawala[1], M. Cabrerizo[1], J. Wang[1], W. Barker[2], R. Duara[2] and M. Adjouadi[1]
[1]Department of Electrical and Computing Engineering,
Florida International University, Miami, FL, USA
[2]Wien Center for Alzheimer's disease and Memory Disorders,
Mount Sinai Medical Center, Miami Beach, FL, USA

Abstract—*This study combines MRI data with neuropsychological Mini-Mental State Examination (MMSE) as a decisional space for Alzheimer's disease (AD). A new sorting/ranking method selects variables that make up the dimensions of an optimal decisional space. Specifically, 189 structural MRI scans with 60 AD patients and 129 cognitively normal controls (CN) obtained at Mount Sinai Medical Center were used for empirical evaluation. The results suggest that by using only the two volumetric measures, Right-Hippocampus and left inferior lateral ventricle, along with MMSE scores yielded an average accuracy of 92.3% (sensitivity: 82.8%; specificity: 96.7%). The study is consistent with the widely accepted notion of hippocampal atrophy and ventricular enlargement seen in AD patients. Moreover, the study through its inherent sorting and statistical ranking of the different variables provides a complete mapping of the significant subcortical brain regions which may act as important biomarkers in predicting AD.*

Keywords: Alzheimer's disease (AD); multi-dimensional classification; Mini-Mental State Examination (MMSE); neuropsychological test; brain atrophy

I. INTRODUCTION

Increased prevalence of Alzheimer's disease (AD) today is seen in the fact that there are 5.2 million people aged 65 and over suffering from AD in the US alone, which makes 1 out of every 8 of the American population aged 65 and over susceptible to the neurodegenerative disease and 1 out of every 2 among the population aged 85 and over[1]. Characterized as a neurodegenerative disease, AD is also thought to be the cause of the majority of dementia cases [2, 3]. Early and reliable diagnosis of AD through imaging and volumetric calculations is thus not only challenging, but remains essential in search of prospective treatments, especially when longitudinal studies become more meaningful in light of this optimal multidimensional decisional space.

To date, multiple modalities of biomarkers identifying AD have been found to be effective, including structural MRI [4-8], functional imaging modalities like Single-Photon Emission Computed Tomography (SPECT)[9], Positron Emission Tomography (PET) [8], as well as Central Spinal Fluid (CSF) [5, 8]. These biomarkers have been widely used to guide clinicians in delineating AD from cognitively normal controls. Moreover, combinations of two or more biomarkers have also been explored more recently to enhance the analysis and improve the results of the diagnosis [5-8, 10, 11]. For example, a combination of biomarkers of MRI and CSF is reported to yield a better accuracy than using either alone [5, 6, 8, 10]. In these studies, Yong et al. combined MRI and PET biomarkers [6]. Fejil et al. found that morphometric changes in AD and CSF biomarkers yield complementary information for identifying the prodromal stage of AD [10]. On the other hand, studies by Walhovd et al. and Daoqiang et al. reported that a combination of MRI, PET and CSF biomarkers yield most suitable and complementary indicators for the diagnosis of AD [7, 11].

In literature, there has been recent interest to combine neuropsychological test with medical imaging modalities. Among them, Ewers and his colleague combined the main MRI and CSF biomarkers with neuropsychological tests to predict conversion from mild cognitive impairment (MCI) to AD [12]. They determined that single-predictor models yielded comparable accuracies as multi-predictor models, with a prediction accuracy ranging from the mid-60s to a high of 68.5% when the entorhinal cortex is used as the single predictor. Gomar et al. investigated in a 2-year longitudinal study the usefulness of combining different variables drawn from a series of biomarkers with the inclusion of cognitive markers and risk factors to likewise predict conversion from MCI to AD [13]. Their findings suggest that cognitive markers at baseline are better suited as predictors for the conversion than are the temporal neurobiological markers.

Furthermore, they also suggest that sharp decline in functional ability is a better predictor for the conversion than the biomarkers. These findings add credence to the results obtained in this study, in that with the inclusion of neuropsychological data, accuracy in delineating AD from control is shown to increase to over 90%. It is noted that in both of these studies, which focus on more on the conversion from MCI to AD, the volumetric measures of the different brain regions were selected manually, and both studies relied on the ADNI (Alzheimer's disease Neuroimaging Initiative) public database. As such, the proposed study which provides an automated approach at ranking the neurobiological variables will augment and complement such findings, as reported in both of these studies, to reflect more globally patterns of structural and physiological abnormalities in their entirety[6], and with statistical context for a more meaningful choice of the different variables.

The Mini-Mental State Examination (MMSE) is a neuropsychological test that is most often administered to screen patients for cognitive impairment and dementia. This study demonstrates the merits of MMSE and extends its use to the screening of AD when used in conjunction with select volumetric variables. To the best of our knowledge of the literature, this study is the first that investigates the impact of combining MRI at baseline with Mini-Mental State Examination (MMSE) for the classification of AD and CN. Another important contribution this study makes is in the development of a fully automated feature extraction technique, which in its initial step associates equal weights to each of the measured volumes, and yet as its outcome is a ranking of the volumes that can be used as variables in a multidimensional decisional space for optimal classification.

II. Materials and Methods

The general structure of the proposed approach is illustrated in Figure 1, showing the main steps of the process from acquisition of the MRI scans, through the sorting and selection of select variables that will constitute the decisional space on which data is projected, and onto the classification process using in this case the well-established support vector machines (SVM). In the last step, the proposed approach is open to the use of other alternative classifications algorithms such as artificial neural networks, optimal discriminant analysis, and others. This study opted for SVM only for its implementation simplicity.

2.1 Subjects

All participants are patients of the Wien Center for Alzheimer's disease and Memory Disorders, Mount Sinai Medical Center, Miami Beach, FL, USA. A total of 189 subjects including 60 subjects with probable AD (range, 61 to 93 years old with an average of 79.5 ± 6.9 years; 34 female), 129 healthy controls (range, 60 to 100 years old with an average of 72.9 ± 6.4 years; 92 female) participated in this study as shown in Table 1.

Table 1: Participant demographics in this study

Diagnosis	NO. of Subjects	Age	Female/Male	MMSE [c]
CN [a]	129	72.9 ± 6.4	92 / 37	28.7 ± 1.4
AD [b]	60	79.5 ± 6.9	34 / 26	22.6 ± 3.4

Data Presented as mean ± S.D. where applicable
[a] CN: cognitively normal
[b] AD: Alzheimer's disease
[c] MMSE: Mini Mental State Examination

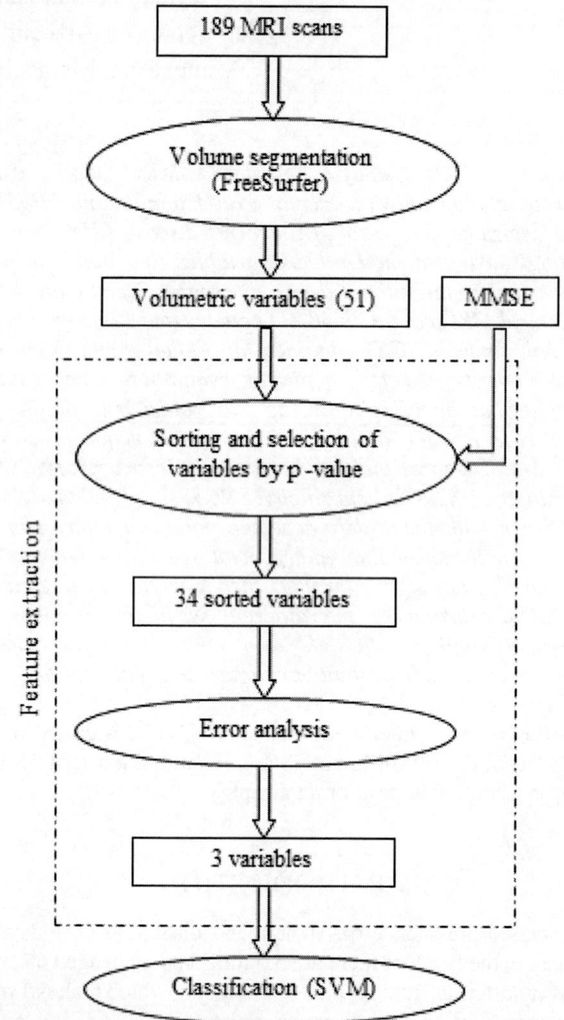

Figure 1: General structure of the classification approach

All subjects had: (1) a neurological and medical evaluation by a physician; (2) a full battery of neuropsychological tests [14], according to the National Alzheimer's Coordinating Center protocol (http://www.alz.washington.edu/), and the following additional tests: the Three-Trial Fold Object Memory Evaluation [15] and the Hopkins Verbal Learning Test[16]; as well as (3) a structural volumetrically acquired

MRI scan of the brain. The sum of boxes from the Clinical Dementia Rating Scale (CDR-sb) was used as the index of functional ability, and the MMSE was used as the index of cognitive ability.

The cognitive diagnosis was made by combining the physician's diagnosis and neuropsychological diagnosis, as described previously[17]. The etiological diagnosis was made by the examining physician. The diagnosis of cognitive normal (CN) required that the physician's diagnosis was CN and no cognitive test scores were ≥1.5 SD below age- and education-corrected means. A probable AD diagnosis required a dementia syndrome and National Institute of Neurological and Communicative Disorders and Stroke/Alzheimer's Disease and Related Disorders Association criteria for AD [18].

2.2 Imaging Protocol

MRI scans were acquired using a 1.5-T machine (Siemen's Symphony, Iselin, N.J., USA, or General Electric, HDX, Milwaukee, Wisc., USA) using a proprietary 3D-magnetization-prepared rapid-acquisition gradient echo or 3D spoiled gradient echo sequences. MRI scans were acquired in the coronal plane, and contiguous slices with thickness of ≤1.5 mm were reconstructed.

2.3 Image Analysis

Segmentation of brain regions is done by applying FreeSurfer pipeline (version 5.1.0) to the MRI scans to produce 55 volumetric variables, including 45 volumetric measures of white matter parcellation (e.g. Left-Lateral-Ventricle, Corpus Callosum Anterior, Right Hippocampus, etc.) and 10 morphometric statistics, for example, left hemisphere gray matter volume based on the pial surface (lhCortexVol). Of the 45 direct volumetric variables, 4 of them (Left White Matter Hypointensities, Right non White Matter Hypointensities, Left nonwhite Matter Hypointensities, and Right non White Matter Hypointensities) were excluded from further analysis since they were all characterized by zero values. Therefore, each MRI scan is converted to a vector of 51 elements and the whole data set is represented by a 189×51 matrix with each column representing a given variable and each row defining a given subject.

2.4 Support Vector Machine based Classifier

In this case, the classification between 129 CN subjects and 60 patients with probable AD is performed using a 2-fold cross validation process on the selected features in order to produce training and testing sets of approximately equal size. Each classification experiment using the selected combination of variables was run 50 timely and averaged to evaluate the performance in terms of accuracy, sensitivity, specificity and precision. For the 50 runs, the training set and testing set were randomly assigned while the number of CN and AD in each set were unchanged. The number of subjects used for the training and testing phases of the classifier is as shown in Table 2.

Table 2: Subject distribution of training set and testing set

Group	Total subjects	CN/AD
Training Set	94	64/15
Testing Set	95	65/15

Support vector machines (SVMs) are widely used in classification problems of all types, linear and nonlinear, and are shown to be effective as a classification tool for AD as well [19, 20]. The SVM as implemented in this study uses a sequential minimal optimization (SMO) scheme to implement a L1 soft-margin SVM classifier. SVM maps the original features via a kernel function to constructs a maximum margin classifier in a high dimensional feature space. The kernel function used in this study is Gaussian Radial Basis Function kernel (rbf) with a scaling factor (sigma) of 3.

2.5 Feature Extraction

AD patients suffer from cerebral atrophy, which can be distinguished from normal aging [4, 21]. However, different cerebral subcortical regions undergo different level of atrophy. It has been shown that hippocampal atrophy is more significant as disease progresses [22]. Also, hippocampus and entorhinal cortex volume changes are significant biomarkers for distinguishing between CN and AD as they suffer more atrophy than other areas [23]. Determination of the key atrophied/enlarged regions may thus serve as a key factor in distinguishing between the two groups namely CN and AD.

The initial objective of this study is to develop a rigorous blind feature selection technique not based on these prior assumptions by assigning equal weights to each and every determined volume. The goal is to thus extract through statistical context the features that are most appropriate for an optimal classification outcome under this equal-weight assignment. Various studies that made use of the ADNI open-source database have provided insights into the relevant areas of the brain which can offer discriminative or predictive properties.

This main objective of this study is to develop a methodology that generates a simple yet complete ranking system to identify the discriminative power of each of the determined brain volumes. It aims to take advantage of a relatively large database from a local medical center, the Wien Center for Alzheimer's disease and Memory Disorders, Mount Sinai Medical Center, to examine brain atrophy distribution of the AD patients based on statistical testing, which is the basis of the feature extraction method.

The feature extraction method combines the volumetric and the neuropsychological data for each subject to generate a 52-variable vector discriminator for each individual subject. The whole dataset matrix comprising of the 189 subjects with 52 elements each is divided into two groups, containing 129 cognitively normal patients (129×52), and 60 AD patients (60×52) respectively. Statistical comparison using a Student's T-test is carried out on each on the 52 variables to determine the significance of each variable towards the classification problem. Only those variables with a p-value lower than significance level (α) of 0.05 are selected. These significant variables are then sorted based on the p-values, which, in this case, is a good indicator of how significant is the mean difference between AD and CN groups for that variable.

In order for the T test to be conclusive, the normality assumption of all the variables is crucial. This can be ensured based on the central limit theorem, which states that, under certain conditions, if there is a sufficiently large number (>30) of independent random variables (with finite mean and variance), the mean of all the variables will be approximately normally distributed. In our case, all the volumetric measures and MMSE can thus be regarded as random variables due to the randomness of the individual differences. Since there are 60 subjects in the AD group and 129 in the CN group, it is safe to assume that the 52 variables as used in both categories satisfy the conditions imposed by the central limit theorem.

2.6 Error analysis based optimal variable set selection

The map of brain atrophy distribution provides an overall view of the discriminative power of each variable in identifying AD patients. Selection of the optimal variable set for the classification between the CN and AD patients is a form of dimensionality reduction problem. The dimensionality reduction issue in this study is performed using an extensive error analysis.

The key point of our proposed error analysis method is to find out the optimal set of top ranked variables that must be included in the classifier to yield the best classification performance in terms of accuracy, sensitivity, specificity and precision. To meet this objective, an incremental error analysis scheme is employed whereby an additional variable is introduced in the SVM classifier on each instance and the corresponding classifier statistics namely accuracy, sensitivity, specificity and precision are recorded to form a total of 34 cases for the 34 significant variables obtained by the feature extraction step. Or simply stated, case 1 corresponds to the classification results obtained when using only the highest ranked variable, case 2 corresponds to the same but when using the two top ranked variables, and so on so forth. All the 34 cases are executed following the same process outlined in section 2.4.

2.7 Validating the significance of MMSE in pattern classification by error analysis

In order to determine the significance of MMSE in classification, the error analysis was carried out by excluding MMSE and performing the SVM based classification only on image based volumetric measures. In this scenario, 33 cases corresponding respectively to cases 2-34 in the previous section were carried out in the absence of MMSE. For example, case 1 now contains only the second ranked variable, which corresponds to case 2 of the previous section and so on. The idea is to take out MMSE from all the 34 cases, since case 1 has only the MMSE, therefore, case 1 doesn't exist and case 2 is moved to case 1 in this section. A comparison of the two scenarios is presented in the results section to illustrate the significance in including neuropsychological data in the classification process.

III. Results

3.1 Volumetric brain atrophy ranking system

The 34 neurophysiological and volumetric variables which are estimated to be significant using the feature extraction step outlined in section 2.5 are given in Table 3. Based on a variable-by-variable comparison between the CN and AD groups, the T-test, at a significance level of 0.05, ranks the features as shown in Table 3.

Table 3: Rank of 34 selected variables based on statistical testing

Rank	Variables
1	MMSE
2	Right-Hippocampus
3	Left-Inferior-Lateral-Ventricle
4	Left-Hippocampus
5	Left-Amygdala
6	Right-Inferior-Lateral-Ventricle
7	Cortex-Volume
8	Left-Hemisphere-Cortex-Volume
9	Right-Hemisphere-Cortex-Volume
10	Total-Gray-Volume
11	3rd-Ventricle
12	Right-Amygdala
13	Right-choroid-plexus
14	Right-Lateral-Ventricle
15	Left-Lateral-Ventricle
16	Left-choroid-plexus
17	Corpus Callosum-Central
18	Corpus Callosum-Anterior
19	Corpus Callosum-Middle-Anterior
20	Right-Accumbens-area
21	Corpus Callosum-Posterior
22	Right-Thalamus-Proper
23	Corpus Callosum-Middle-Posterior
24	White-Matter-Hypo-Intensities
25	Left-Accumbens-area
26	Cerebral-Spinal-Fluid(CSF)
27	Right-Ventral-Diencephalon
28	Left-Thalamus-Proper
29	Non-White Matter-Hypo-Intensities
30	Subcortical-Gray Volume
31	Optic-Chiasm
32	5th-Ventricle
33	Right-Cerebellum-Cortex
34	Left-Putamen

The resultant ranking of the variables creates a map showing the regions of significant atrophy/enlargement in AD patients as compared to cognitively normal subjects. An important point to be noted is that even though MMSE is not an actual volumetric measure of atrophy, it is found to be one of the most important significant factors for classification.

From Table 3 it can be observed that MMSE ranks first followed by right hippocampus volume and left inferior lateral ventricle volume. A closer inspection of the results show that the top ranked significant volumetric measures, i.e. hippocampal atrophy [23, 24], ventricular enlargement[25, 26], cortical volume[23] and amygdala volume[24, 27], are all regions that have been proven to be effective predictors of AD or mild cognitive impairment (MCI). This observation is a strong indicator of the accuracy and usability of the ranking system developed in this study, as well as the error analysis which follows the feature extraction.

3.2 Optimal combination of variables based on the map of brain atrophy distribution and error analysis

The classification performance of accuracy for the 34 cases is plotted in Figure 2. This figure shows a clear trend of decline after case 3, where the first 3 variables (MMSE, right hippocampus volume and left inferior lateral ventricle volume) are considered. This optimal combination of variables (or optimal decisional space) yields a classification accuracy of 92.3%, a sensitivity of 82.8%, a specificity of 96.7%, and a precision of 92.2%. A summary of the results obtained for all cases is given in Table 4.

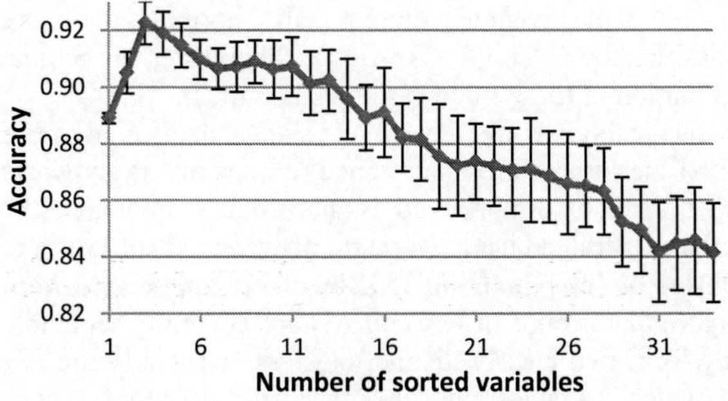

Figure 2: Performance of accuracy for all the 34 cases with C.I. defined in context indicated as error bar.

Table 4: Best Case Results

Significant Variables of Case 3 (Optimal Feature Set)	
MMSE	
Right hippocampus	
Left inferior lateral ventricle	
Classifier Statistics	
Accuracy	92.3% (range: 90.5 - 93.7%)
Sensitivity	82.8% (range: 78.3 - 86.7%)
Specificity	96.7% (range: 95.3 - 98.5%)
Precision	92.2% (range: 89.2 - 96.2%)

3.3 Significance of inclusion of the neurophysiological variable MMSE on the classification results

This section aims to highlight the merit of including MMSE in the classification process. The classification accuracy with and without MMSE are plotted in Figure 3 for all the 33 cases defined in section 2.7. Figure 3 shows the plot of the accuracy for both with MMSE and without MMSE, as a function of the number of variables included in the classifier. Trends similar to accuracy as shown in Figure 3 can be seen for sensitivity, specificity and precision of the classifier.

It can also be observed from Figure 3 that the difference of the two performance curves obtained with MMSE in the classifier and without is significant and consistent. Classification with MMSE has yielded an average increase of 7.28% (7.75% in case 3) on accuracy. On the other hand, without MMSE, the best classification performance achieved using the two highest ranked MRI volumes (right hippocampus and left inferior lateral ventricle) results in an accuracy of 85.1%, a sensitivity of 65.7%, a specificity of 94.1%, and a precision of 84.5%. These results clearly indicate that a combination of neuropsychological test (MMSE) and volumetric measures of MRI yields a much improved performance than when using either alone.

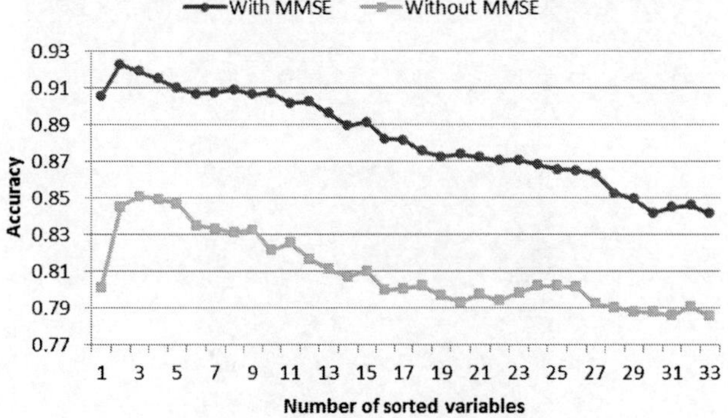

Figure 3: Comparison of accuracy between classification with MMSE and without MMSE for the corresponding 33 cases defined in section 2.7

IV. Discussion

The proposed feature selection technique suggests the significance of each variable obtained from MRI images and the neurophysiological test towards differentiation between CN and AD groups. The statistically significant volumetric measures are shown in Figure 4. Moreover, the error analysis, which is based on the rank derived in the feature selection step, identifies the optimal combination of variables that yield the best classification results. Therefore, the rank of variables is extremely important and is proven to be reliable. In this study, although the statistical test was performed using 129 normal controls and 60 AD patients for a total of 189 subjects, which is a relatively large number, randomly reducing this number to 100 or even to 50 did not alter the order of the top-ranked variables. This indicates that the optimal case which selects the top 3 ranked variables namely MMSE, right hippocampus volume and left inferior lateral ventricle volume is reliable, reproducible, and statistically meaningful even under a smaller subset of the data.

It can be argued that using only 34 combinations as suggested in this study may not be sufficient as there is a myriad of other combinations to be considered, all in the form of C_k^n (where n is all the 34 variables which then could be combined 2 at a time, 3 at time etc. for different values of k, yielding different multidimensional spaces). Such an exhaustive attempt at assessing all these combinations of the 34 variables is not only unyielding, but is rather unnecessary in light of the statistical meaningfulness which supports the proposed method of ranking these variables.

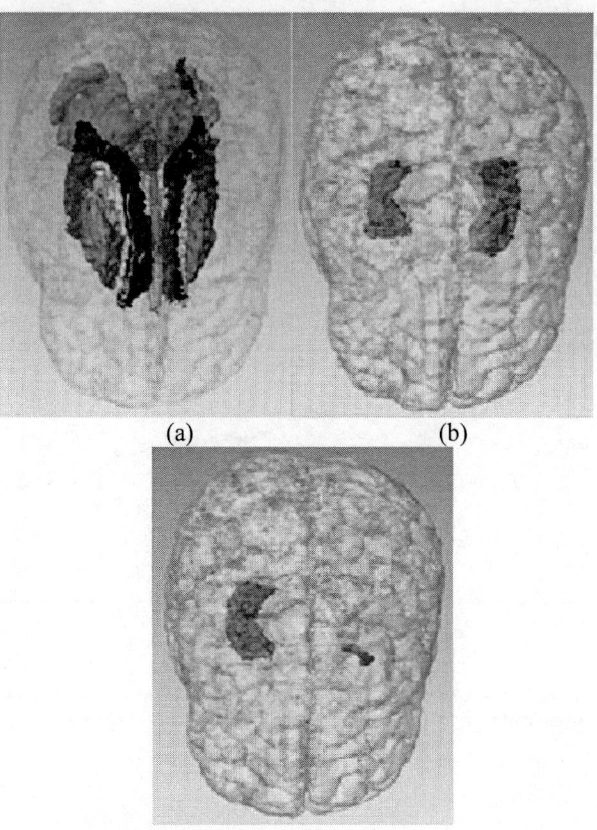

Figure 4: Representation of the statistically significant regions of brain atrophy/enlargement using different colors. a) All 34 variables except the morphometric variable i.e. total gray volume, b) The top 5 ranked variables, c) The variables ranked first and second in ranking system, namely right hippocampus and left inferior lateral ventricle

Also, as can be seen from Figure 2, there are situations where performance increases slightly as other lower-ranked variables are considered. In this case, inclusion of that variable does increase the classification performance and therefore should be considered as an added dimension in the decisional space. However, this could be due to the randomness of the subjects during the cross validation step of the SVM based classifier. A slightly more favorable distribution of subjects can yield a relatively improved result. Consequently, the random distribution of the subject data was the primary reason for averaging the results of a large number of randomized runs (50) of the program for each experiment.

To quantify if the increase of accuracy is significant, standard deviation of the 50 runs for each case is calculated to form a confidence interval (CI), which is defined as [mean ± S.D.] and shown in Figure 2 as the error bar indicates. The increase of accuracy is considered as significant only if its CI does not intersect with the CI of the preceding variable. Based on this assertion, the results in Figure 2 show that only the second and third highest-ranked variables, namely right hippocampus and left inferior lateral ventricle satisfy the aforementioned condition.

Also, the rank of the variable, especially lower-ranked variables, may suffer much variation from one dataset to another as they may intrinsically have close mean differences identified by the statistical T-test or close p values between the two groups (CN and AD). However as demonstrated earlier, even though ranking variability may be observed the positions of the top 5 ranked variables does not change. This indicates that the dataset consisting of 189 subjects used in the study is sufficiently large to secure the rank of the first 5 variables.

The result of this study shows that the three variables shown in Table 4 in combination yield the best classification performance and are the 3 principal components (or the three dimensions) in the decisional space on which the SVM-based classification is applied. If subjects have an abnormal distribution of the 3 components (i.e. an AD patient have a right hippocampus volume close to or even larger than the mean of that volume among all normal patients), misclassification could result. Therefore, accurate determination of these three variables is critical.

The projection of all the subjects on a decisional space based on these three aforementioned dimensions is shown in Figure 5, which as portrayed is an instance in which the classifier was trained using 94 randomly selected subjects and then tested on the remaining 95 subjects. It can be seen from this figure that groups of CN and AD are generally separable as they form two clearly distinct clusters, especially the CN group, which is a denser cluster. This clustering outcome adds further credence to the importance of these three dimensions (variables). Even though there are 4 misclassifications, shown as solid dots in Figure 5, the misclassifications can be justified due to the proximity of these data points as they are near the boundary separating the two clusters. These results indicate that our proposed method is efficient and accurate.

V. Conclusion

This study shows that, among all the volumetric measures from MRI scan, the right hippocampus and left inferior lateral ventricle volume contain the most discriminative information as they have the most statistically significant mean difference between the AD and CN groups based on 189 MRIs at baseline. We further showed that a combination of MRI measures and neuropsychological test score (MMSE) yield better diagnostic results (accuracy: 92.3%; sensitivity: 82.8%) than using either MRI (accuracy: 85.1%; sensitivity: 65.7%) or MMSE (accuracy: 88.9%; sensitivity: 73.3%) alone. The approach considered for selecting and then ranking MMSE and other MRI variables could be useful at augmenting other classification methods reported in the literature and could have broader impact in reevaluating the different variables as predictive measures of AD.

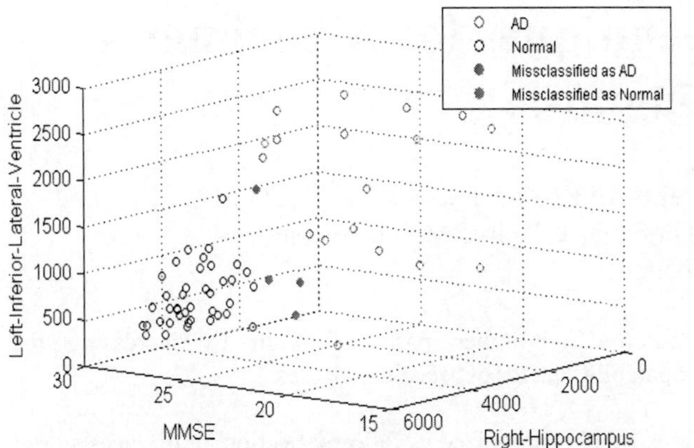

Figure 5: A typical case that displays the distribution of the subjects in the context of the first three principle variables. Out of the 95 subjects shown and used for testing the SVM classifier only 4 misclassifications are seen which are shown by solid dots.

A potential limit of this study would be a lack of study on MCI data to test the discriminative power of the proposed method to classify MCI from normal controls or AD from MCI. This could be done when MCI data are available to us. To our knowledge, our study is the first to combine MMSE with MRI measures based on a proposed map of regional brain atrophy. In addition, as Eric W. et al describe the concept of cost-benefits to assess the increased cost of combining biomarkers as the potential limitation[5], the proposed approach has the merit of low cost as it entails only an MRI scan and an MMSE score which is cognitive examination that usually every patient undergoes at the time of diagnosis. Thus, the proposed method can be used as an accurate, convenient, and low-cost tool to discriminate people with AD from cognitive normal people.

REFERENCE

[1] Alz.org, "2012 Alzheimer's disease facts and figures," *Alzheimer's & dementia : the journal of the Alzheimer's Association,* vol. 8, pp. 131-168, 2012.

[2] H. Braak and E. Braak, "Evolution of the neuropathology of Alzheimer's disease," *Acta Neurologica Scandinavica,* vol. 93, pp. 3-12, 1996.

[3] S. Duchesne, *et al.*, "MRI-based automated computer classification of probable AD versus normal controls," *Ieee Transactions on Medical Imaging,* vol. 27, pp. 509-520, Apr 2008.

[4] N. C. Fox and J. M. Schott, "Imaging cerebral atrophy: normal ageing to Alzheimer's disease," *Lancet,* vol. 363, pp. 392-4, Jan 31 2004.

[5] E. Westman, *et al.*, "Combining MRI and CSF measures for classification of Alzheimer's disease and prediction of mild cognitive impairment conversion," *Neuroimage,* vol. 62, pp. 229-38, Aug 1 2012.

[6] Y. Fan, *et al.*, "Structural and functional biomarkers of prodromal Alzheimer's disease: a high-dimensional pattern classification study," *Neuroimage,* vol. 41, pp. 277-85, Jun 2008.

[7] K. B. Walhovd, *et al.*, "Combining MR imaging, positron-emission tomography, and CSF biomarkers in the diagnosis and prognosis of Alzheimer disease," *AJNR Am J Neuroradiol,* vol. 31, pp. 347-54, Feb 2010.

[8] P. Vemuri, *et al.*, "MRI and CSF biomarkers in normal, MCI, and AD subjects: predicting future clinical change," *Neurology,* vol. 73, pp. 294-301, Jul 28 2009.

[9] K. A. Johnson, *et al.*, "Preclinical prediction of Alzheimer's disease using SPECT," *Neurology,* vol. 50, pp. 1563-1571, Jun 1998.

[10] A. M. Fjell, *et al.*, "CSF Biomarkers in Prediction of Cerebral and Clinical Change in Mild Cognitive Impairment and Alzheimer's Disease," *Journal of Neuroscience,* vol. 30, pp. 2088-2101, Feb 10 2010.

[11] D. Q. Zhang, *et al.*, "Multimodal classification of Alzheimer's disease and mild cognitive impairment," *Neuroimage,* vol. 55, pp. 856-867, Apr 1 2011.

[12] M. Ewers, *et al.*, "Prediction of conversion from mild cognitive impairment to Alzheimer's disease dementia based upon biomarkers and neuropsychological test performance," *Neurobiology of Aging,* vol. 33, pp. 1203-+, Jul 2012.

[13] J. J. Gomar, *et al.*, "Utility of Combinations of Biomarkers, Cognitive Markers, and Risk Factors to Predict Conversion From Mild Cognitive Impairment to Alzheimer Disease in Patients in the Alzheimer's Disease Neuroimaging Initiative," *Archives of General Psychiatry,* vol. 68, pp. 961-969, Sep 2011.

[14] R. Duara, *et al.*, "Reliability and Validity of an Algorithm for the Diagnosis of Normal Cognition, MCI and Dementia: Implications for Multi-Center Research Studies," *The American journal of geriatric psychiatry: official journal of the American Association for Geriatric Psychiatry,* vol. 18, p. 363, 2010.

[15] P. A. Fuld, *et al.*, "Object-Memory Evaluation for Prospective Detection of Dementia in Normal Functioning Elderly - Predictive and Normative Data," *Journal of Clinical and Experimental Neuropsychology,* vol. 12, pp. 520-528, Aug 1990.

[16] L. H. Lacritz, *et al.*, "Comparison of the hopkins verbal learning test-revised to the California verbal learning test in Alzheimer's disease," *Appl Neuropsychol,* vol. 8, pp. 180-4, 2001.

[17] D. A. Loewenstein, *et al.*, "Utility of a modified mini - mental state examination with extended delayed recall in screening for mild cognitive impairment and dementia among community dwelling elders," *International journal of geriatric psychiatry,* vol. 15, pp. 434-440, 2000.

[18] G. McKhann, *et al.*, "Clinical diagnosis of Alzheimer's disease: report of the NINCDS-ADRDA Work Group under the auspices of Department of Health and Human Services Task Force on Alzheimer's Disease," *Neurology,* vol. 34, pp. 939-44, Jul 1984.

[19] S. Kloppel, *et al.*, "Automatic classification of MR scans in Alzheimer's disease," *Brain,* vol. 131, pp. 681-9, Mar 2008.

[20] M. M. Lopez, *et al.*, "SVM-based CAD system for early detection of the Alzheimer's disease using kernel PCA and LDA," *Neuroscience Letters,* vol. 464, pp. 233-238, Oct 30 2009.

[21] B. H. Ridha, *et al.*, "Tracking atrophy progression in familial Alzheimer's disease: a serial MRI study," *Lancet Neurol,* vol. 5, pp. 828-34, Oct 2006.

[22] R. I. Scahill, *et al.*, "Mapping the evolution of regional atrophy in Alzheimer's disease: unbiased analysis of fluid-registered serial MRI," *Proc Natl Acad Sci U S A,* vol. 99, pp. 4703-7, Apr 2 2002.

[23] C. Pennanen, *et al.*, "Hippocampus and entorhinal cortex in mild cognitive impairment and early AD," *Neurobiol Aging,* vol. 25, pp. 303-10, Mar 2004.

[24] M. P. Laakso, *et al.*, "Volumes of hippocampus, amygdala and frontal lobes in the MRI-based diagnosis of early Alzheimer's disease: correlation with memory functions," *J Neural Transm Park Dis Dement Sect,* vol. 9, pp. 73-86, 1995.

[25] S. M. Nestor, *et al.*, "Ventricular enlargement as a possible measure of Alzheimer's disease progression validated using the Alzheimer's disease neuroimaging initiative database," *Brain,* vol. 131, pp. 2443-2454, September 1, 2008 2008.

[26] P. M. Thompson, *et al.*, "Mapping hippocampal and ventricular change in Alzheimer disease," *Neuroimage,* vol. 22, pp. 1754-66, Aug 2004.

[27] C. A. Cuenod, *et al.*, "Amygdala atrophy in Alzheimer's disease. An in vivo magnetic resonance imaging study," *Arch Neurol,* vol. 50, pp. 941-5, Sep 1993.

Automatic Thresholding Techniques for Alzheimer's Disease Diagnosis

Moumena Al-Bayati, and Ali El-Zaart
Department of Mathematics and Computer Science, Beirut Arab University
Beirut, Lebanon

Abstract - *Images has become an essential role in diagnosis the diseases especially the Magnetic Resonance Imaging(MRI). However, used(MRI)that diagnosis Alzheimer's disease is still remains a challenge, especially in the early stages, when the disease offers more chances to be treated. In this paper we present medical images diagnosis for Alzheimer's disease using different thresholding techniques. The used method is Otsu method ,because it is one of the most effective thresholding techniques for most real world images with regard to uniformity and shape measures. Our experiments will be as a test to determine which technique is effective in thresholding (extraction) atrophy neurons in the brain, and in the future these techniques can be very useful in detection other diseases .*

Keywords: Alzheimer disease(AD) , Magnetic Resonance Imaging (MRI),Segmentation ,Thresholding, Otsu method .

1 Introduction

Alzheimer's disease (AD) is a progressive neurologic disease of the brain that leads to irreversible loss of neurons [1,2]. It was first described by German neurologist Alois Alzheimer in 1906 and was named after him. (AD) symptoms are represented with difficulty in remembering recently events , irritability and aggression, mood swings, and language trouble [1]. Alzheimer disease occurs in old people. Approximately, 5-10% of people over 65 have the first signs of (AD)[3]. Computer-Aided-Diagnosis(CAD) techniques can help neurologists to discover the early stage of the disease, and (MRI) have been proved to be very useful in this task[5]. Commonly, Computer-Aided-Diagnosis(CAD)techniques use (MRI)to display valuable comparison between normal and abnormal neurons using the analysis of certain characteristics in a functional brain image, and determining the appearance of atrophied neurons[4,6]. Many (CAD)approaches appeared to diagnosis(AD) like (M.L´opez 2009) implement Eigenbrains and Bayesian Classification Rules. (J.Ramirez 2010) used partial least squares and random forest SPECT image classification. (F. Segovia 2012) used the ADNI database. (F.Martinez-Murica 2012)applied Mann–Whitney–Wilcoxon U-Test. In our experiments, we diagnose Alzheimer disease by implementing Otsu method ,which is an important non parametric method in medical image segmentation[8]. Its performance based on split the atrophied neurons from other parts of brain by increasing the separability factor between the classes.

This paper is organized as follows: Section2 introduces a brief description of segmentation and thresholding. Section3 has the formulas are used in thresholding. Section4 display Otsu method, and all the techniques related to it. Section 5 is about Evaluation Methods. We used in our experiments Gaussian distribution therefore we presented in Section 6. Experimental results are presented in Section 7. Finally, conclusions are drawn in Section 8.

2 Thresholding

Segmentation of brain region is a very complex work, because of the high interconnected , convoluted structure of the brain , and the various features of the images. The purpose of brain segmentation is to determine anatomical structures of the brain with respect to some input characteristics or expert knowledge[7]. Choosing the suitable segmentation methods between manual, semiautomatic ,and fully automatic based on gray level intensity ,quality of images, the required accuracy of the segmentation, and the number of regions to be segmented [7].

Automatic thresholding is a well-known and most effective tool in medical image segmentation. Its concept based on separate objects of interest in an image from the background depended on their gray level distribution [8,10]. As a previous work some researchers used thresholding in diagnosis (AD). Like Saxena [14] implements An automatic threshold-based scaling method for enhancing the usefulness of Tc-HMPAO SPECT in the diagnosis of Alzheimer's disease. However, all studies for diagnosis (AD) are still limited. Therefore, our aim in this paper is to put the scope on applying different thresholding techniques on (MRI) as a try to determine which one presents best detection of (AD).

3 Formulation

Suppose the pixels of an image be identified by L gray levels [0, 1,..., L-1]. The number of pixels in level i is identified by n_i, and the total number of pixels is identified by N=$n_0 + n_1 + \cdots + n_{L-1}$. The gray level histogram is normalized and regarded as the probability distribution function [9,10,11,12,13].

$$n=\sum_{i=0}^{L-1} n_i \quad (1)$$

Grey level histogram is normalized and regarded as a probability distribution:

$$h_i=\frac{n_i}{n} \quad (2)$$

The grey level of an image is [0... L-1].Where the grey level 0 is the darkest , and the grey level L-1 is the lightest.

The probability of occurrence of the two classes can be denoted as the following :

$$w_1(t)=\sum_{i=0}^{t} h(i) \quad w_2(t)=\sum_{i=t+1}^{L-1} h(i) \quad (3)$$

The mean and variance of the background and object are denoted respectively as the following:

$$\mu_1(t)=\sum_{i=0}^{t} i\,h(i), \sigma_1^2(t)=\sum_{i=0}^{t}(i-\mu_1(t))^2 h(i) \quad (4)$$

$$\mu_2(t)=\sum_{i=t+1}^{L-1} i\,h(i), \sigma_2^2(t)=\sum_{i=t+1}^{L-1}(i-\mu_2(t))^2 h(i) \quad (5)$$

4 Otsu Method

In 1979 Nobuyuki Otsu[9] presented his idea in extraction the object from the background by maximizing between class variance equivalent (minimizing within class variance). The following equations represent the within-class variance, and the between -class variance respectively.

$$\sigma_w^2(t)=\omega_1(t)\sigma_1^2(t)+\omega_2(t)\sigma_2^2(t) \quad (6)$$

$$\sigma_B^2(t)=\omega_1(t)(\mu_1(t)-\mu_T(t))^2+\omega_2(\mu_2(t)-\mu_T(t))^2 \quad (7)$$

The final form of between-class variance can also be denoted as the following :

$$\sigma_B^2(t)=\omega_1(t)\omega_2(t)(\mu_2(t)-\mu_1(t))^2 \quad (8)$$

The algorithm of Otsu method is as the following :

1) Compute the histogram.
2) Start from t=0....unitl 255 (all possible thresholds).
3) For each threshold:
   i. Update $\omega_i(t)$and $\mu_i(t)$.
   ii. Compute $\sigma_B^2(t)$.
4) Desired threshold is a threshold that maximums $\sigma_B^2(t)$.

The following techniques [10,11,12,13] are used to develop Otsu method.

4.1 Valley Emphasis Method

Hui-Fuang Ng [10] presents a revised method of Otsu method; this method succeeds in detection both large and small objects. It applies a new weight to ensure that the optimal threshold located at the deepest point between two peaks for (bimodal histogram), or at the bottom rim of a single peak for (unimodal histogram). In addition , it increases the variance between the classes as much as possible like in Otsu method.

The valley-emphasis equation is as in [10].

$$t_{opt}=\arg\max_{0\le t\le L-1}\{(1-h(t))(\omega_1(t)\mu_1^2(t)+\omega_2(t)\mu_2^2(t))\} \quad (9)$$

4.2 Neighborhood Valley Emphasis Method

Jiu-Lun Fan [11] improves the prior method (valley-emphasis method) by taking into account the neighborhood information (gray values) of the threshold point. It calculates between class variance σ_B^2 for both the threshold point and its neighborhood. Neighborhood valley emphasis method is suitable to choose optimal threshold for images with big diversity between object variance and background variance.

The sum of neighborhood gray level value $\bar{h}(i)$ is in Eq.(10) within the range n=2m+1 for gray level i , n represents the number of neighborhood that should be odd number.

If the image has one dimensional histogram h(i) ; the neighborhood gray value $\bar{h}(i)$ of the gray level i is denoted as the following :

$$\bar{h}(i)=[h(i-m)+...+h(i-1)+h(i)+h(i+1)+...+h(i+m)] \quad (10)$$

The neighborhood valley emphasis method is denoted as the following:

$$\xi(t)=(1-\bar{h}(t))((\omega_1(t)\mu_1^2(t)+\omega_2(t)\mu_2^2(t)) \quad (11)$$

The optimal threshold is in Eq. (12). The first part refers to the largest weight of the threshold and its neighborhood, while the second part refers to the maximum between class variance.

$$t_{opt}=\arg\max_{0\le t\le L-1}\{(1-\bar{h}(t))(\omega_1(t)\mu_1^2(t)+\omega_2(t)\mu_2^2(t))\} \quad (12)$$

4.3 Thresholding Based on Variance and Intensity Contrast

Yu Qiao [12] introduced a new formula to isolate small objects from difficult homogeneity background. The performance of this method based on the information of the weighted sum of both within-class variance and the intensity contrast at the same time.

The proposed formula is defined as the following:

$$J(\lambda,t)=(1-\lambda)\sigma_W(t)-\lambda|\mu_1(t)-\mu_2(t)| \quad (13)$$

In this method λ plays a central role. It is a weight that determines and balances the contribution of (within class variance , intensity contrast) in the formula. λ Values should be in interval [0, 1).

1) When $\lambda = 0$ the new formula based only on within class variance.
2) $\lambda =1$ the optimal threshold will be determined only by the intensity contrast .

In Eq. (13)$\mu_1(t)$, $\mu_2(t)$ are the mean intensities of the object and background. $\sigma_W(t)$Represents the square root of within-class variance. $\sigma_W(t)$is formulated from the following equation:

$$\sigma_w^2(t)=\omega_1(t)\ \sigma_1^2(t)+\omega_2(t)\sigma_2^2(t) \quad (14)$$

Where the first part represents the probability of occurrence and the standard deviation (variance) of the background, while the second part represents the probability of occurrence and the standard deviation (variance) of the object.

4.4 Variance Discrepancy Method

Zuoyong Li [13] introduces a new method to segment images have large variance discrepancy between the object and background. The new method takes into consideration both the class variance sum and variances discrepancy simultaneously. It is formulated as the following:

$$J(\alpha,t) = \alpha(\sigma_1^2(t)+\sigma_2^2(t)) + (1-\alpha)\sigma_D(t) \quad (15)$$

Where

$$\sigma_D(t)=\sigma_1(t)\sigma_2(t) \quad (16)$$

and, $\sigma_1^2(t)<=\sigma_D(t)<=\sigma_2^2(t)$ or $\sigma_2^2(t)<=\sigma_D(t)<=\sigma_1^2(t)$. $\sigma_D(t)$ Is a measurement of variance discrepancy of (object, background). $\sigma_1^2(t)$,$\sigma_2^2(t)$are the standard deviation(variances) of the two classes.

In this method α is an effective parameter; it balances the weight of class variance sum and variance discrepancy in the method. The values of α is within the range [0,1]. The smaller α , the larger weight of variance discrepancy in the method, and this means a limited effect of variance sum. On the contrary , if α is large , the method will be based on variance sum ,and the effect of variance discrepancy will be ignored.

5 Thresholding Evaluation Method

The quality of thresholding technique is a critical issue; it various depending on the type of the thresholding technique and the kind of image. In order to analyze the performance of the thresholding techniques, there are different evaluation methods used to measure their robustness and efficiency. In our study we used two evaluation methods Region Non-Uniformity (NU) and Inter–Region Contrast (GC) . Then, we compare the results of the five thresholding techniques to determine which technique is the best in determination the region of interest (object) from the background.

5.1 Region Non-Uniformity (NU)

This method measures the ability to distinguish between the background and object in the thresholded image. A good thresholded image should contain higher intra region uniformity, which is related to the similarity attribute about region element In the following NU Equation(17): $\sigma^2(t)$ denotes to the variance of the whole image, while $\sigma_0^2(t)$ denotes to the variance of the object (foreground). $w_0(t)$ denotes to the probability of occurrence of the object. NU equal to zero denotes to well thresholded image, but NU = 1 denotes to incorrect thresholded image [16].

$$\text{NU} = \frac{w_0(t)\ \sigma_0^2(t)}{\sigma^2(t)} \quad (17)$$

5.2 Inter –Region Contrast (GC)

This method is very important in measure the contrast degree in the thresholded image. A good thresholded image should have higher contrast across adjacent regions. In the following GC Equation(18) the object average gray-level is known as $\mu_o(t)$, and the background average gray–level is known as $\mu_b(t)$ [16].

$$GC = 1 - \frac{\mu_o(t)-\mu_b(t)}{\mu_o(t)+\mu_b(t)} \quad (18)$$

6 Gaussian Distribution

Gaussian distribution is a continuous probability distribution. Its form is concentrated in the center, then it decreases on either side taking a form as a bell shape. Each variable in (Gaussian distribution) has a symmetric distribution about its mean [15]. Gaussian distribution equation is defined as the following :

$$f(x,\mu,\sigma^2) = \frac{1}{\sigma\sqrt{2\pi}}\, e^{-\frac{(x-\mu)^2}{2\sigma^2}} \quad (19)$$

Where Π is approximately 3.14159 and *e* is approximately 2.71828.

The following figure displayed the form of Gaussian distribution.

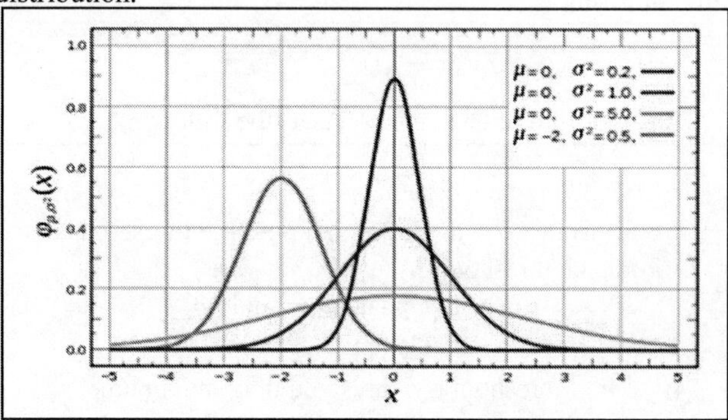

Figure 1 Gaussian Distribution.

In our experiments we used Gaussian distribution to represent our MRI for Alzheimer's disease for the following reasons:

1. It used for modeled symmetric data.
2. In Gaussian distribution and based on central limit theorem; the mean of a large number of random variables independently are distributed normally.
3. This type of distribution is very flexible analytically. Also, it is easy to apply mathematically.

7 Experimental Results

Commonly, Alzheimer's disease (AD) has four stages (pre–dementia, early , moderate, advanced). For diagnosis Alzheimer's disease the radiologist demonstrates that when the black region of the brain is larger than the white region; this indicates to advance stage of Alzheimer's Disease (AD). In other word, it refers to the shrink neurons size (white region). In our experiments the five techniques will detect if the disease in its beginning or advance stage, and for each thresholding method we evaluate its performance by using two evaluation methods (Region Non-Uniformity (NU)) and (Inter –Region Contrast (GC)). Actually, accurate thresholding of MR images plays a pivotal role in detection Alzheimer's Disease (AD).

The first image Fig.2(a) denotes to advance stage of Alzheimer's disease; in this image we will try to detect the disease by determining the best thresholded image. As seen in Fig.2 (b, c, d, e, f) the resultant thresholding images of the five thresholding methods detect the atrophy neurons from the background successfully. The optimal threshold for Otsu method T= 40, Valley Emphasis method T= 37, Neighborhood Valley Emphasis method T= 30, Variance and Intensity Contrast method T= 40, $\lambda = 0.05$, and Variance Discrepancy method T= 35, $\alpha = 0.9$. According to Table1 the smallest region non uniformity NU = 0.104404 is obtained from Otsu method and Variance and Intensity Contrast method, while the smallest inter region contrast GC= 0.446187 is get from neighborhood valley emphasis method.

In order to further compare the performance of the five thresholding techniques. We used another MR image for advance stage of Alzheimer's disease represent with Fig.3(a). In this image, we found the five thresholding methods isolate the atrophy neurons from the background successfully. Their optimal threshold values are as the following: Otsu method T=32. Valley Emphasis method T= 31. Neighborhood Valley Emphasis T= 31, Variance and Intensity Contrast method T=32, Variance Discrepancy method T=32. The smallest region non uniformity NU= 0.0912965 is get from Otsu method, Variance and Intensity Contrast method, and Variance Discrepancy method. On the other hand, the best inter region contrast GC= 0.56903 is introduced from neighborhood valley emphasis method.

It is known that diagnosis Alzheimer disease still remains a challenge task, especially in the first stages (pre–dementia, early, moderate), because the symptoms are very mild and can easily be confounded with effects of normal aging. In Fig.4(a) is MR image for early stage of Alzheimer disease. As shown in Fig.4 (b, c, d, e, f) the five thresholding techniques also extract the atrophy neurons from the background, but the best result is presented from Otsu method T= 44, and Variance and Intensity Contrast method T = 44, $\lambda = 0.25$. As shown in Table 1 the smallest region non uniformity NU= 0.0914579 is presented from Otsu method and Variance and Intensity Contrast method. On the other side, the best inter region contrast GC = 0.420276 is obtained from neighborhood valley emphasis method.

In Fig.5(a) the image indicate for moderate stage of Alzheimer's disease. The experimental results for this image show the superiority for Otsu method Fig.5(b) in separated the small atrophy neurons from the background with optimal threshold T = 42, and the smallest region non uniformity NU = 0.132943, while the smallest inter region contrast GC = 0.480673 is introduced from variance discrepancy method.

Table I. shows threshold values of five thresholding techniques (T, NU, GC, AV).

		Fig.2	Fig.3	Fig.4	Fig.5
Otsu	T	40	32	44	42
	NU	0.104404	0.0912965	0.0914579	0.132943
	GC	0.52922	0.576428	0.59251	0.553319
	AV	0.316812	0.333862	0.341984	0.343131
valley	T	37	31	34	36
	NU	0.139455	0.105855	0.22816	0.20129
	GC	0.506036	0.56903	0.49198	0.501847
	AV	0.322746	0.337442	0.36007	0.351569
Neighborhood valley	T	30	31	27	35
	NU	0.234735	0.105855	0.338629	0.210366
	GC	0.446187	0.56903	0.420276	0.494762
	AV	0.340461	0.337442	0.379452	0.352564
Variance and intensity contrast	T	40, λ= 0.05	32, λ =0.25	44, λ= 0	41, λ= 0.1
	NU	0.104404	0.0912965	0.0914579	0.144816
	GC	0.52922	0.576428	0.59251	0.543532
	AV	0.316812	0.333862	0.341984	0.344174
Variance discrepancy technique	T	35, α= 0.9	32, α= 0.4	32 α =1	33 α = 0.8
	NU	0.165087	0.0912965	0.259938	0.23084
	GC	0.487137	0.576428	0.467534	0.480673
	AV	0.326112	0.333862	0.363736	0.355757

8. Conclusion

In this work we introduce and test five automatic thresholding techniques based on between class variance. In each technique, we apply sequential search to select an optimal threshold value that determine and extract abnormal (atrophy) neurons from the background. The results ensure that the five thresholding techniques perform well in the advance stage of AD, but in early and moderate stages the best result are only get from Otsu method, and variance and intensity contrast method. They present the best accurate detection of (AD). Furthermore, evaluation of the resulting thresholded images shows that the Otsu method and variance and intensity contrast method yield best estimation of the optimal threshold by presenting the smallest values of region non uniformity and the smallest values of the average (combination of region non uniformity and inter region contrast) for all the thresholded images.

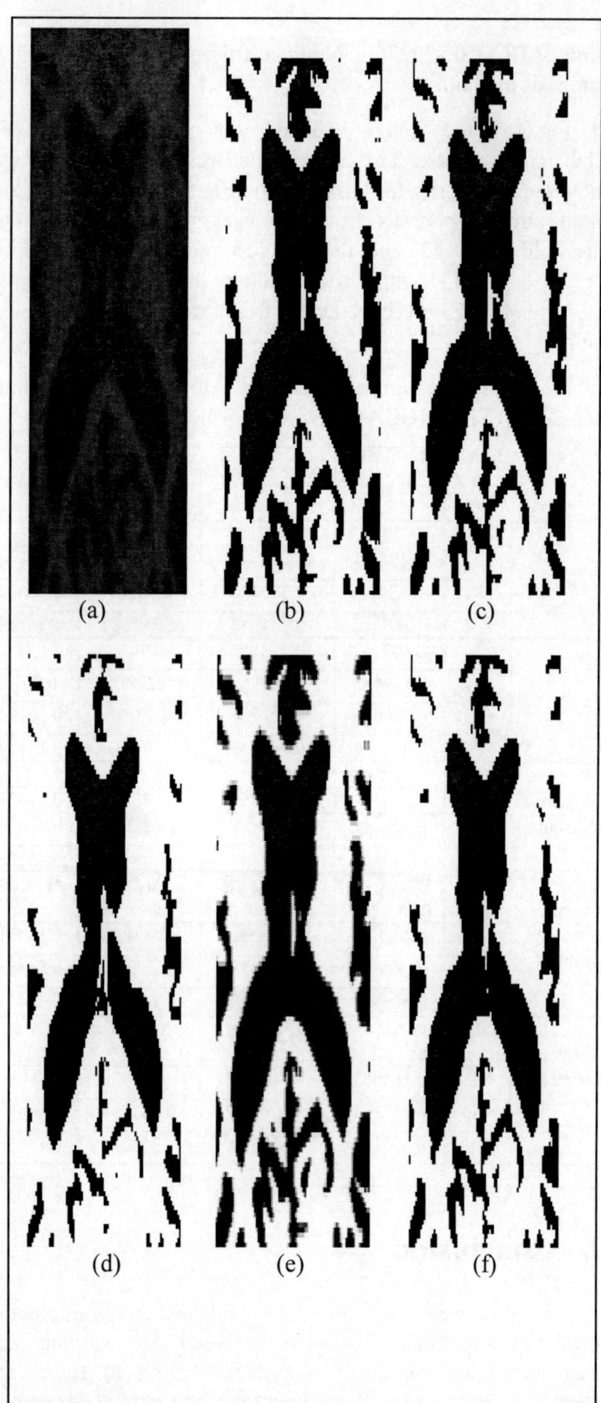

Figure 2 (a) Original image, (b) Otsu method T=40.(c) valley emphasis technique T=37.(d) Neighborhood valley emphasis T=30, (e) variance and intensity contrast T= 40, (f) variance discrepancy T=35.

Figure 3 (a) Original image, (b) Otsu method T =32.(c) Valley emphasis technique T =31.(d) Neighborhood valley emphasis T =31, (e) Variance and intensity contrast T =32, (f) Variance discrepancy T =32.

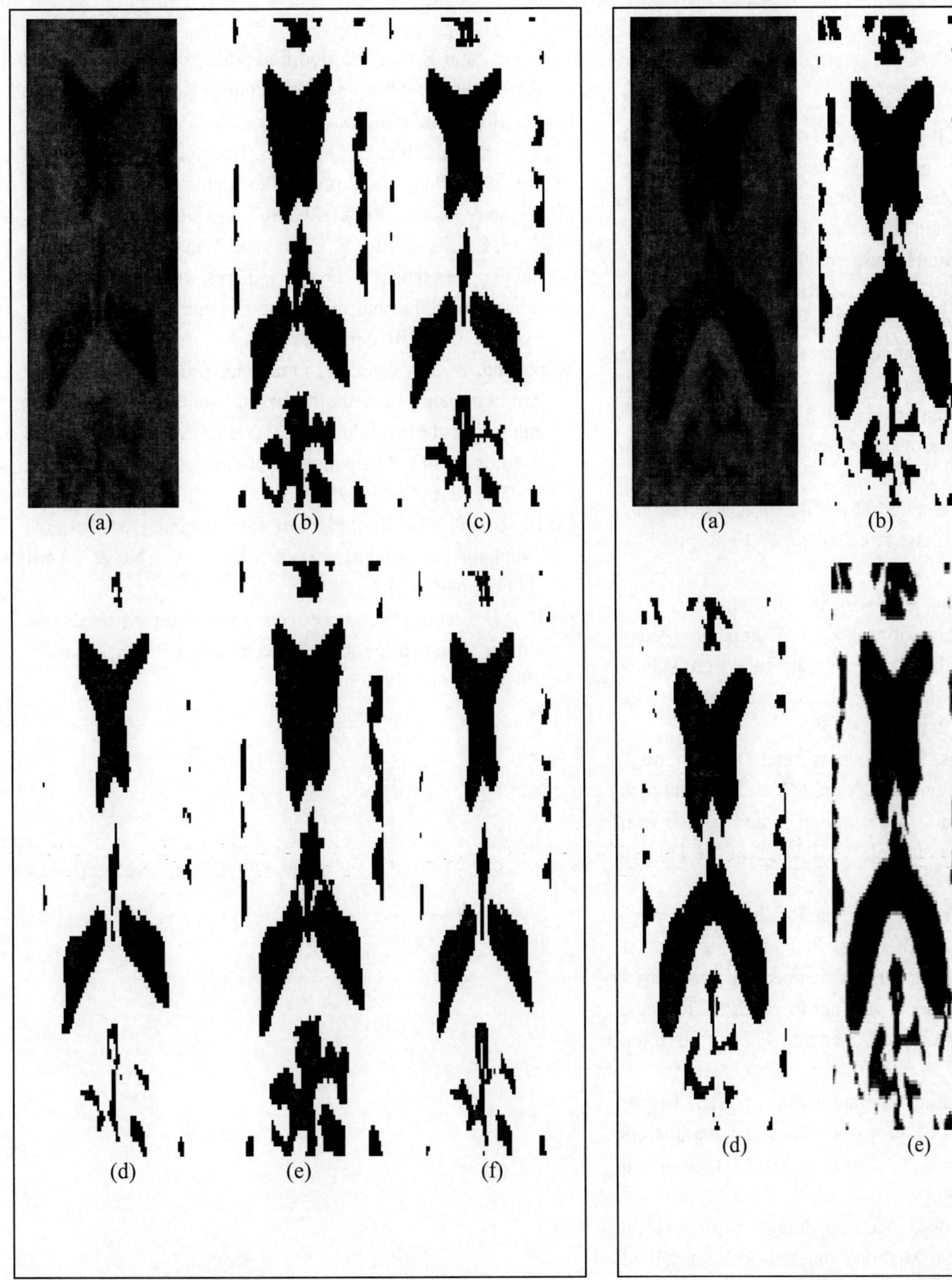

Figure 4 (a) Original image (b) Otsu method T=44. (c) Valley emphasis technique T=.34 (d)Neighborhood valley emphasis T=27, (e) Variance and intensity contrast T=44.(f) Variance discrepancy T=32.

Figure 5 (a) Original image, (b) Otsu method T= 42. (c) Valley emphasis technique T =36.(d) Neighborhood valley emphasis T=35, (e) Variance and intensity contrast T=41, (f) Variance discrepancy T=33.

9 References

[1] M. L´opez,_, J. Ram´ırez, J.M. G´orriz, I. ´Alvarez, D. Salas-Gonzalez F. Segovial, and C.G. Puntonet" Automatic System for Alzheimer's Disease Diagnosis Using Eigenbrains and Bayesian classification Rules" Springer-Verlag Berlin Heidelberg 2009, pp. 949–956.

[2] F. Segovia ,J.M. Go´ rriz , J.Ramı´ rez, D. Salas-Gonzalez , I .A´lvarez, M.Lo´ pez , R. Chaves "A comparative study of feature extraction methods for the diagnosis of Alzheimer's disease using the ADNI database" Neurocomputing 75 , 2012 , pp. 64–71.

[3] D.H. Small "The Role of the Amyloid Protein Precursor (APP) in Alzheimer's Disease: Does the Normal Function of APP Explain the Topography of Neurodegeneration " Neurochemical Research, Vol. 23, No. 5, 1998, pp. 795-806.

[4] F.J. Martinez-Murcia , J.M. Gorriz , J. Ramirez , C.G. Puntonet , D. Salas-Gonzalez " Computer Aided Diagnosis tool for Alzheimer's Disease based on Mann–Whitney–Wilcoxon U-Test", Expert Systems with Applications 39 ,2012, pp.9676–9685

[5] A . Worth, N Makris, V . Caviness., and D. Kennedy, " Neuroanatomical Segmentation in MRI: Technological Objectives" Pattern Recognition and Artificial Intelligence on Processing of MR Images of the Human Brain.

[6] J. Ramrez*, J.M. Górriz, F. Segovia, R. Chaves, D. Salas-Gonzalez, M. Lόpez, I. ɇlvarez, P. Padilla," Computer aided diagnosis system for the Alzheimer's disease based on partial least squares and random forest SPECT image classification" Neuroscience Letters 472 , 2010,pp. 99.103.

[7] H. Kekre and S Gharge," Segmentation of MRI Images Using Probability and Entropy as Statistical Parameters for Texture Analysis" Advances in Computational Sciences and Technology.

[8] C. Hima "An improved Medical Image Segmentation Algorithm Using Otsu Method" International Journal of Recent Trends in Engineering, Vol 2, No. 3, November 2009.

[9] N. Otsu, "A threshold Selection Method from Gray Level Histograms", IEEE Transactions on Systems, Man and Cybernetics, vol. SMC-9, no 1 , 1979, pp. 62–66.

[10]Hui -Fuang Ng "Automatic thresholding for Defect Detection" Pattern Recognition Letters, 27, 2006 , pp. 1644–1649.

[11]J. Fan, and B. Lei "A modified Valley-Emphasis Method for Automatic Thresholding", Pattern Recognition Letters 33, 2012, pp.703–708.

[12]Y. Qiaoa, Q. Hua, G. Qiana , S. Luob, and W. Nowinskia " Thresholding based on Variance and Intensity Contrast " Pattern Recognition , 40 ,2007,pp. 596 – 608 .

[13]Z. Li, C. Liu, G. Liu ,Y. Cheng , X. Yang ,and C. Zhao" A novel Statistical Image Thresholding Method", International Journal of Electronics and Communications , vol.64, Dec. 2010, pp.1137–1147.

[14]Saxena, P., Pavel, D. G., Quintana, J. C., & Horwitz, B" An automatic threshold based scaling method for enhancing the usefulness of Tc-HMPAO SPECT in the diagnosis of Alzheimer's disease", Springer, Vol. 1496,1998, pp. 623–630 .

[15]S. Stahl" The Evolution of the Normal Distribution", Mathematics Magazine, Vol.79, No .2, April 2006, pp.96-113.

[16]Y. J .Zhang, "A survey on Evaluation Methods for Image Segmentation", Pattern Recognition, Vol.29, No.8, August1996, pp.1335-133

An Efficient Model Based on Spatial Fuzzy Clustering and Region Growing for the Automated Detection of Masses in Mammograms

Hechmi Shili
MARS Research Group
Faculty of Sciences,
University of Monastir, Tunisia
Email: hechmi.shili@fsm.rnu.tn

Lotfi Ben Romdhane
MARS Research Group
High School of Sciences and
Technology, Hammam-Sousse,
University of Sousse

Bechir Ayeb
Faculty of Sciences,
University of Monastir, Tunisia

Abstract—**Breast cancer is the most common cancer in women worldwide. It is also the principle cause of death from cancer among women globally. In the last decade, digital mammography has come to be regarded as the gold standard for breast cancer diagnosis. However, detecting a subtle mass on a mammogram is a non-trivial task, as tumors present a large variety of borders and shapes with edges of low signal-to-noise ratio. This paper presents a computer aided diagnosis system that helps specialists detect breast masses in mammogram images. The first stage of the methodology aims to improve the mammogram image. Subsequently, we present our segmentation method in which we employ the spatial fuzzy c-means (SFCM) algorithm to place initial seeds for the growing process. To correct the over-segmentation, we merge similar regions by using the homogeneity criterion.**

Experimental results on MIAS and DDSM mammogram databases are very encouraging since our model exhibits a high performance in detecting masses compared to other proposals.
Keywords: mammogram segmentation; spatial fuzzy clustering; region growing and merging.

I. Introduction

Breast cancer is the most frequently diagnosed cancer and the major cause of deaths among women aged 30 and above. It is the most common form of cancer among women in both high- and low-resource setting countries. Presently, breast cancer constitutes a major public health issue globally, with over one million new cases diagnosed annually, resulting in over 400,000 annual deaths and about 4.4 million women living with the disease. It also affects one in eight women during their lifetimes [15]. Until now, there is no known way to prevent breast cancer but the earlier the cancer can be detected, the higher are the chances of survival for patients. Mammography is the most effective procedure for an early diagnosis of the anomalies which could mark a tumor, even if the detection of a tumor in a mammographic image is a difficult task due to the great number of non-pathological structures. Retrospective studies show that, in current breast cancer screenings, 10 - 25 % of the tumors are missed by the radiologists [3]. The causes of these false-negative screening examinations are not clear. The clinical significance of the early diagnosis and the difficulty of the diagnostic task have generated a tremendous interest in developing computer-aided detection (CAD) schemes for mammographic interpretations. CAD can be used to alert radiologists to locations of suspicious lesions and provides a second reading which has been found to reduce misdiagnosis. However, a well-trained computer program (which can screen a large volume of mammograms accurately and reproducibly) is needed in order for CAD to become practical in clinical settings. Such a program has yet to be developed.

Breast segmentation is the fundamental step in many CAD methods since its performance directly affects the performance of the subsequent processing steps in mammogram analysis. Unfortunately, detection of subtle mass on a mammogram is a difficult task which requires a dedicated strategy: shape and dimension of the masses are often irregular (see Figure (1)), the borders are ill-defined, thus making difficult the discrimination from parenchymas structures [3].

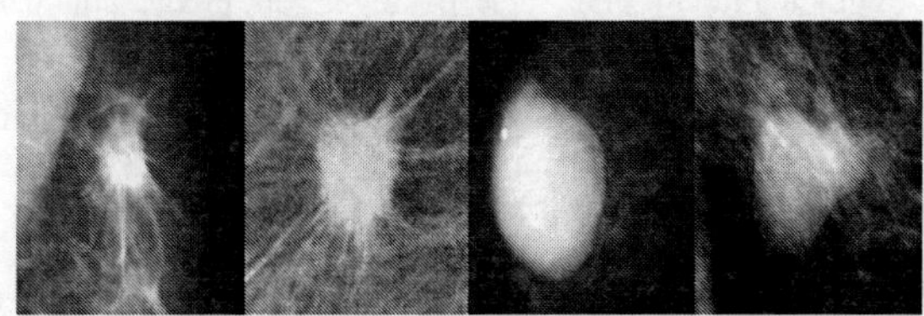

Fig. 1: Some examples of massive lesions selected from the database.

Depending on the adopted framework, existing methods for automatic mammogram segmentation can be classified into four approaches; namely, threshold techniques, boundary-based methods, region- based methods, and hybrid techniques which combine boundary and region criteria. Among region based segmentation methods, seeded region growing (SRG) is a frequently used segmentation method for the detection of breast abnormalities from digital mammograms [19], [10], [23]. The simplest approach to region growing is pixel aggregation where the process starts with a number of seed points and regions are grown from these seed points appending to each any neighbouring pixels which are similar to the seed point [1]. This method has the main advantages of being robust, rapid and free of tuning parameters. However, the SRG algorithm suffers from the problem of selection of initial seeds.

In this paper, we present a new idea for region growing by

pixel aggregation with a new automatic seed point selection method based on spatial fuzzy clustering. The rest of the paper is organized as follows. In Section II, we bring a literature review of the recently proposed methods for the breast segmentation. Next, in Section III we present our new method for detection of subtle mass on a mammogram; while section IV describes the experiments that have been conducted on benchmark data sets. Finally, Section V presents some concluding remarks.

II. Related work

Various segmentation techniques have been reported for mammography segmentation and which could be categorized with respect the adopted methodology. The main goal of this section is to present the basic principle of the most adopted model in each category; and by no way represents an exhaustive review of the existing literature. Survey techniques for mammography segmentation could be reached in the specialized literature [16], [5], [2].

Nunes et al. [14] proposed a methodology for the detection of masses that uses the K-means clustering algorithm and the template matching technique to segment the suspect regions. The methodology was tested with 650 mammographic images from the DDSM. The stage at which the suspect regions are segmented managed 603 masses in the sample, wich means 92.77% of the cases; and also selected 2076 non-masses. Then, geometry and texture measurements are extracted from each suspected region, and the texture is described through Simpsons diversity index. Finally, this information is submitted to an SVM to classify the suspect regions as masses or non-masses. The classification stage achieved an average accuracy of 83.94%, sensitivity of 83.24%, and 84.14% of specificity; with a rate of 0.55 false positives per image and 0.17 false negatives per image.

Another interesting technique is based on cellular neural networks (CNN). Sampaio et al. [21] proposed a new scheme for detection of masses in mammograms using CNN to segment the regions that might contain masses. These regions have their shapes analyzed through shape descriptors (eccentricity, circularity, density, circular disproportion and circular density) and their textures analyzed through geostatistic functions (Ripleys K function and Morans and Gearys indexes). Support vector machines are used to classify the candidate regions as masses or non-masses, with sensitivity of 80%, rates of 0.84 false positives per image and 0.2 false negatives per image, and an area under the ROC curve of 0.87.

Wirth et al. [25] proposed an active contour to segment the breast. The method obtains two preliminary regions using a convolution matrix to enhance the edges and a dual threshold obtained by different techniques. They obtain the control point for the snake with the comparison of the two regions. They evaluate the method over the MIAS database.

Recently, Rahmati et al. [17] proposed an algorithm for detection of suspicious masses in mammographic images that exhibits an accuracy of 86.85% for mass detection. The work used images coming from the DDSM database. The technique is based on a novel maximum likelihood active contour model using level sets (MLACMLS). The algorithm estimates the segmentation contour that best separates the lesion from the background using the Gamma distribution to model the intensity of both regions (foreground and background). The Gamma distribution parameters are estimated by the algorithm.

Rojas and Nandi [20] proposed statistical method to detect masses in mammograms using texture and shape features. Their study included 322 cases from the mini Mammogram Image Analysis Society (MIAS) database. According to the authors, this method has a better performance, with 80% of sensitivity [20].

Eltonsy et al. [8] showed a morphological model technique to detect the mass lesions in the mammogram images. The technique is based on the presence of concentric layers surrounding a focal area with suspicious morphological characteristics and low relative incidence in the breast region. The technique was implemented on 270 craniocaudal view cases from the DDSM and malignant masses were detected with 92%, 88%, and 81% sensitivity of 5.4, 2.4, and 0.6 false positive per image.

A region growing technique from a seed point has been applied to detect masses, but the drawback of this approach is that the result depends critically on the choice of seed point. To solve this problem, Zhang and Foo [26] divided the breast into small regions and the pixels with maximum grey value were taken as seed points, from which many candidate objects are grown using a modified region-growing technique. Following which false positive (FP) reduction using decision tree is applied to discard the normal tissue regions. A total of 40 mammograms from mammographic image analysis society (MIAS) are analyzed: 36 masses are correctly segmented by the proposed method, resulting in 90% true positive rate at 1.3 FPs per image.

One of the earliest approaches to segmentation of breast regions in mammograms was presented by Maitra et al. [11], who proposed a combination of techniques that incorporates seeded region growing with ASB algorithm to isolate normal and abnormal regions in the breast tissue. Their algorithm was tested on all mammograms from mini-MIAS mammogram database (322 mammograms).

Senthilkumar and Umamaheswari have proposed in [23] a new region growing algorithm for mammogram image segmentation to detect breast cancer. The authors used Harris corner detect theory [22] to auto find growing seeds and the seeded region growing rule for the development of regions. The methodology was tested with mammographic images from the mini-MIAS database, including circumscribed, spiculated, and ill-defined masses. According to the authors, this method performs well in breast cancer detection with comparatively small MAE (mean average error) of 0.45 and MSE (mean square error) of 11.91. The detection accuracy of this method is 93%.

III. Our Model

This section describes our methodology for mass detection in digital mammogram images. This methodology comprises the following stages: pre-processing, segmentation of regions of interest and post-processing. Hereafter, we will detail each step of our model.

A. First step: Pre-processing

Fuzzy set theory has been successfully applied to image processing and pattern recognition. It is believed that fuzzy set theory is a useful tool for handling the uncertainty associated with vagueness and/or imprecision [6]. Practically, we need to apply appropriate functions and measure the uncertainty as a quantitative justification of the results. The main idea of enhancement consists of four basic steps: Mammogram Normalization, Fuzzification; Applying a modification function; and defuzzification.

*1) **Mammogram Normalization**:* The mammograms are with different brightness and contrast due to the varying illumination. In order to reduce the variation and achieve computational consistency, the images are normalized. We map all mammograms into a fixed range of the intensities from I_{inf} to I_{sup} which represents the available range (For an 8-bit grayscale image this range would be [0,255]). The normalization equation would be as follows:

$$I'(x,y) = \mu\left(I(x,y)\right) + \lambda. \quad (1)$$

where

$$\mu = \frac{I_{inf} \times I_{max} - I_{sup} \times I_{min}}{I_{max} \times I_{min}}, \quad \lambda = \frac{I_{sup} - I_{inf}}{I_{max} - I_{min}} \quad (2)$$

$I(x,y)$ represents the value of original intensity level and $I'(x,y)$ represents the new intensity after the normalization process. I_{min} represents the minimum intensity value while I_{max} the maximum intensity value.

*2) **Fuzzification**:* The image fuzzification transforms the gray level of an image into values of membership function over [0..1]. The larger values of the membership represent the higher degrees of the belongings. That is, the membership value represents how closely an element resembles an ideal element. The shape of S-function [6] is commonly used for the representation of the degree of brightness or whiteness of pixels in the grey levels images.

$$\mu_X(x_{mn}) = \begin{cases} 0, & 0 \leq x_{mn} \leq a, \\ \frac{(x_{mn}-a)^2}{(b-a)(c-a)}, & a \leq x_{mn} \leq b, \\ 1 - \frac{(x_{mn}-c)^2}{(c-b)(c-a)}, & b \leq x_{mn} \leq c, \\ 1, & x_{mn} \geq c, \end{cases} \quad (3)$$

where a, b, and c are the parameters which determine the shape of the S-function. Notice that in this definition, b is not necessarily the midpoint of the interval $[a,c]$, and can be any point between a and c.

*3) **Membership Function Calculation**:* This process is needed to change the values of the membership functions resulting from the previous fuzzification process. The modified membership value $\mu'(x_{mn})$ using the transformed contrast $C'_{\mu(x_{mn})}$ [6]:

$$\mu'(x_{mn}) = \begin{cases} E_{\mu(x_{mn})} \frac{1-C'_{\mu(x_{mn})}}{1+C'_{\mu(x_{mn})}}, & \mu(x_{mn}) \leq E_{\mu(x_{mn})}, \\ E_{\mu(x_{mn})} \frac{1+C'_{\mu(x_{mn})}}{1-C'_{\mu(x_{mn})}}, & \mu(x_{mn}) > E_{\mu(x_{mn})}, \end{cases} \quad (4)$$

Where $E_{\mu(x_{mn})}$ is the mean edge value within a window on pixel (m,n) [6].

*4) **Defuzzification**:* After the values of fuzzy membership function are modified, the next step is to generate new gray level values. We have used gray-scale level defuzzification model defined as follows:

$$x'_{mn} = \begin{cases} L_{min}, & \mu(x_{mn}) = 0, \\ L_{min} + \left(\frac{L_{max}-L_{min}}{c-a}\right)\chi_1, & 0 < \mu'(x_{mn}) \leq \frac{b-a}{c-a}, \\ L_{max} - \left(\frac{L_{max}-L_{min}}{c-a}\right)\chi_2, & \frac{b-a}{c-a} < \mu'(x_{mn}) < 1, \\ L_{max}, & \mu(x_{mn}) = 1. \end{cases} \quad (5)$$

Where L_{min} et L_{max} are the maximum and minimum gray level, χ_1 and χ_2 given by:

$$\chi_1 = \sqrt{\mu'(x_{mn})(b-a)(c-a)} \quad (6)$$

$$\chi_2 = \sqrt{(1-\mu'(x_{mn})(b-a)(c-a))} \quad (7)$$

This defuzzification method maps a membership grade value [0, 1] to a crisp set [0,255] plane. Figure 2 shows the effect of the proposed method on a mammogram image. The image 2(a) is the original while 2(b) was enhanced using our method.

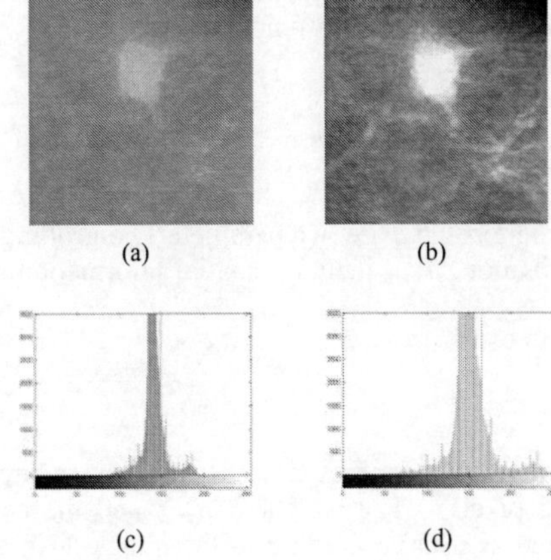

Fig. 2: a) Original Mammographic Image, b) Enhanced image by proposed method, c) The original Histogram, d) Histogram after enhancement.

B. Second step: Segmentation

1) Spatial Fuzzy Clustering: When applied to image segmentation, the fuzzy c-means (FCM) algorithm [4] assigns pixels to each category by using fuzzy memberships. Let X=(x_1, x_2,.,x_N) be an image with N pixels to be partitioned into C clusters, where x_i represents multispectral (features) data. The algorithm is an iterative optimization that minimizes the cost function defined as follows:

$$J = \sum_{n=1}^{N} \sum_{m=1}^{C} \mu_{mn}^{l} \|i_n - \nu_m\|^2 \quad (8)$$

where μ_{mn} represents the membership of pixel x_n in the i_m cluster; ν_m is the i_{th} cluster center; $\|.\|$ is a norm metric, and $l(>1)$ is a constant. The parameter l controls the fuzziness of the resultant segmentation. This function is subject to the following constraints:

$$\sum_{m=1}^{C} \mu_{mn} = 1; 0 \leq \mu_{mn} \leq 1; \sum_{m=1}^{C} \mu_{mn} > 0 \quad (9)$$

The membership functions μ_{mn} and the centroids ν_m are updated iteratively by [4]:

$$\mu_{mn} = \frac{\|i_n - \nu_m\|^{\frac{-2}{(l-1)}}}{\sum_{k=1}^{C} \|i_n - \nu_m\|^{\frac{-2}{(l-1)}}} \quad (10)$$

$$\nu_m = \frac{\sum_{n=1}^{N} \mu_{mn}^{l} i_n}{\sum_{n=1}^{N} \mu_{mn}^{l}} \quad (11)$$

One of the problems of standard FCM algorithms in image segmentation is the lack of spatial information. In fact, the pixels on an image are highly correlated; i.e. the pixels in the immediate neighborhood possess nearly the same feature data. To overcome this problem, Chuang et al. [7] proposed a spatial FCM in which spatial information can be incorporated into fuzzy membership functions using:

$$\mu_{mn} = \frac{\mu_{kn}^{p} h_{mn}^{q}}{\sum_{k=1}^{C} \mu_{kn}^{p} h_{mn}^{q}} \quad (12)$$

where p and q are two parameters controlling the respective contribution. h_{mn} includes spatial information by

$$h_{mn} = \sum_{k \in N_n} \mu_{nk} \quad (13)$$

where N_n denotes a local window centred around the image pixel n. The weighted μ_{mn} and the centroid ν_m are updated as usual according to Equations (10) and (11).

The SFCM algorithm performs a fuzzy partition of a given data set. The advantages of this method are its fairly robust behavior, its applicability to multichannel data and its ability of uncertainty data modeling [7]. However, the major disadvantage of the use of the SFCM algorithm is that it assumes a prior knowledge of the number of class c. However, in many practical situations such as mammograms, the appropriate number of classes is unknown; or even impossible to determine for some cases.

2) Modified Seed Based Region Growing: In general, region growing methods are sensitive to the initial seeds. Therefore selecting a good set of initial seeds is very important. As we know, seeds can't fall on noise points or edge points. The True seeds must be relevant to the meaningfull objects and be located at the homogeneity objects inner. In our method, unlike traditional SRG using pixels as initial seeds, we use regions which are the output of the SFCM algorithm discussed in section III-B1, as initial seeds of region growing algorithm (see Figure (3)).

$$A^T = \left\{ A_i^T \in A | \sum_{k=1}^{|A_i|} \frac{I(x_k)}{|A_i|} \geq t2 \right\}. \quad (14)$$

where

$$\begin{cases} A_i^T \bigcap A_j^T = \emptyset, \ \{A_i^T, A_j^T\} \in A^T \ and \ i \neq j, \\ A_i = (x_k)_{k \geq 1}, \\ I(x_k) \text{ is the intensity of a pixel } x_k, \end{cases} \quad (15)$$

In [13], the authors suggest that the following three criteria must be satisfied for automatic seed selection. First, the seed pixel must have high similarity to its neighbors. Second, seeds for different regions must be disconnected. Third, for an expected region, at least one seed must be generated in order to produce this region.

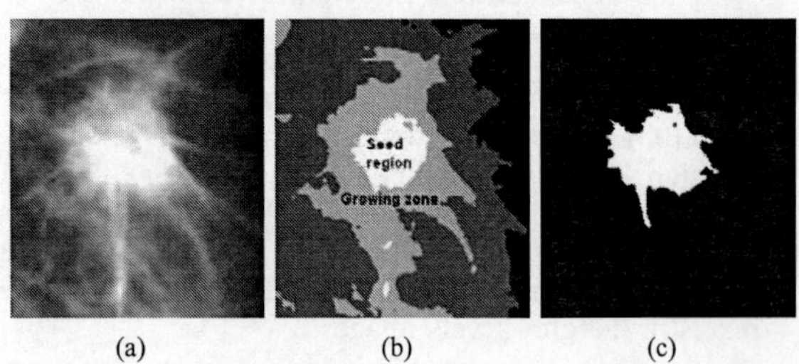

Fig. 3: The region-growing algorithm process explained (a) start of a growing region, (b) growing process after a few iterations.

The first condition is verified, since the use of the regions' centroids which must be representative of all the points in that cluster, by definition. The second condition is also assured by the choice the isolated regions (Figure (3)). As for the third condition, our approach can select more than the real number of seeds (which is the number of the isolated regions). For that, we have proposed the following merging step to overcome this possible problem.

The application of our method comprises a specification of the criteria used to terminate the recursive region grow process. In general, these criteria include region homogeneity, object contrast with respect to background, strength of the region boundary, size, conformity to desired texture features like texture, shape, color [12]. We used criteria mainly based on region homogeneity and region aggregation using intensity values and their gradient direction and magnitude [18]. This criterion is characterized by a cost function which exploits certain features of images around the seed. These cost function are verified for their match with the specified conditions of homogeneity criteria by comparing their value to be less than 1. If there is a match then the pixel under consideration is added to the growing region otherwise it is excluded. After being segmented into regions, an over segmentation could occur resulting in more regions than desired. For this, some regions need to be merged. This process is detailed subsequently.

C. Third step: Region Merging

The proposed region growing algorithm takes initials seeds from the output of the SFCM applied to original mammogram. However the SFCM Algorithm could not guarantee unique segmentation result and usually leads to over segmentation of images because initial cluster number C needs to be chosen in advance. To overcome this problem, we propose a procedure for merging regions based on the homogeneity criteria [12] defined as follows.

[Homogeneity] Given a region R, the homogeneity of R, denoted as $H(R)$, is computed by:

$$H(R) = \sum_{i=0}^{g_{max}} \sum_{j=0}^{g_{max}} [1 - (\frac{|(i-j)|}{g_{max}})^z] * C_{ij}. \qquad (16)$$

In equation (16), C_{ij} is the frequency of co-occurrence of the gray values i and j; z is weighting parameter; and g_{max} is the maximal gray level. Knauer et al. [12] used this definition of homogeneity to merge each two neighboring regions if the new combined region is homogeneous based on a fixed threshold whose value depends on the merged regions. Hence, we define a new function $f(R_i, R_j)$ between any two neighboring regions R_i and R_j as follows:

$$f(R_i, R_j) = \frac{\sqrt{size\,(R_i)} * H(R_i) + \sqrt{size\,(R_j)} * H(R_j)}{perimeter\,(R_i) + perimeter\,(R_j)}. \qquad (17)$$

where $H(.)$ is the homogeneity of a region; $size(.)$ is its size (number of pixels); and $perimeter(.)$ its perimeter (scope). Based on this function, two regions R_i and R_j are merged into a new region R if the following condition holds:

$$\frac{\sqrt{size\,(R)} * H(R)}{perimeter\,(R)} > f(R_i, R_j). \qquad (18)$$

Hence, using equation (18), similar regions are merged together in order to compensate the over-segmentation of the previous phase. Figure (6) illustrates this merging process: (a) centroids whose intensity is greater than the threshold (before growing); (b) result of the region growing.

In the next section, we will analyze experimentally our proposed model.

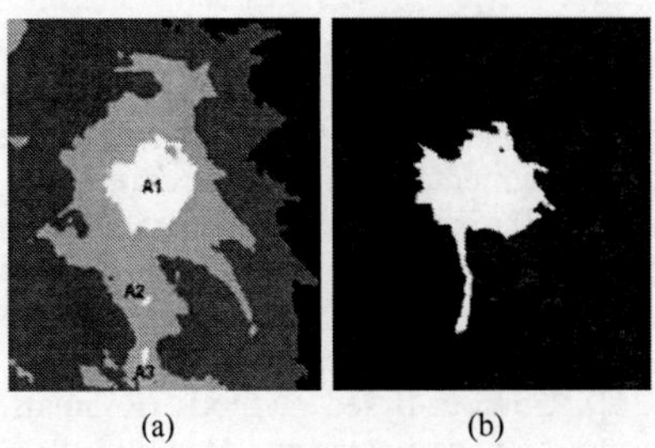

(a) (b)

Fig. 4: An example of our proposed region merging method.

IV. Experimentation

In this section, we will analyse experimentally our proposed model to well-known other proposals using standard mammogram databases. Experimental settings and results are described in the sequel.

A. Experimental settings

In order to test our method two public and widely known databases have been used: MIAS (Mammographic Image Analysis Society) database [24] and DDSM (Digital Database of Screening Mammographies) database [9]. Both are explained following:

MIAS includes 322 digital mammograms from 161 patients. Films were taken from the United Kingdom National Breast Screening Program; digitized to 50 micron pixel edge, and presented each pixel with an 8-bit word. The MIAS database provides annotations for each mammogram, and one of them is referred to the breast density. The images are labelled as: (i) fatty (106 images) if the breast is almost entirely fatty, (ii) glandular (104 images) if the breast contains some fibroglandular tissue, or (iii) dense (112 images) if the breast is extremely dense. Regarding DDSM, it consists of around 2600 cases. Each case has four views: Mediolateral oblique (MLO) and Craniocaudal (CC) views for the right and left breasts. This database provides for each mammogram additional information, including the density of the breast determined by an expert according to BIRADS categories. We use a set which consists of 400 Medio-Lateral Oblique mammograms from the right breast. Table I summarizes the composition of the database used.

TABLE I: Used benchmark databases

Database	MIAS	DDSM
BI-RADS I	128	100
BI-RADS II	80	100
BI-RADS III	70	100
BI-RADS IV	44	100
Total	322	400

The computer-segmented results were validated using the following standard criteria: sensitivity (SE), specificity (SP), accuracy (AC), average false positives per image (FPI), average false negatives per image (FNI), overlay index (Ov) and area under the ROC curve (AURC).

B. Comparative analysis

We will compare the results of our segmentation with the results of segmentation methods developed by other recent works. The choice of comparison methods is done to cover the main approaches for detection masses in mammograms: Model-based methods (Nunes et al. [14], Sampaio et al. [21]), Region-based methods (Eltonsy et al. [8], Zhang and Foo [26]), Contour-based methods (Rahmati et al. [17]) and Clustering methods (Rojas and Nandi [20]). Numerical results are summarized in Tables II and III.

Many of the cited works use sensitivity as a detection performance index. The proposed methodology yielded a higher sensitivity rate, with a mean of 84.52% for DDSM database and 86.44% for MIAS database. The specificity measure represents the probability that pixels are classified as truly not diseased (true-negative). Our model has a specifity of 85.55% and 83.54% on MIAS and DDSM databases, repectively. Accuracy represents the ratio of correctly classified pixels to the entire area of the ROI. Our model has accuracy of 83.75% for DDSM and 85.71% for MIAS. Through the comparison of false positives per image and false negatives per image, we can observe that our methodology achieved a very good performance. The area under the ROC curve (AURC) metric was only used by Sampaio et al. [21] with average rate 0.87. Our proposed yielded a higher mean area under the ROC curve rate of 0.88% for the DDSM and 0.90% for MIAS database.

The overlay index (Ov) indicates the average proportion of the size of the located areas related to the actual areas. If it is greater than one, this means that, on average, the located areas are larger than the original ones. If it is lower than 1, this means that, on average, the located areas are smaller than the original ones. Results show that the proposed methodology achieved better results than Sampaio et al. [21] method.

Comparing the results of both databases, performance obtained on MIAS are better than those on DDSM. This is related to the different breast tissue of the RoIs: as RoIs extracted from the DDSM database are denser than the RoIs extracted from the MIAS one.

Table IV summarizes the number of true-positive, true-negative, false-positive and false-negative masses. The results show that the reproducibility for the true-positive regions is substantially higher than that for the false-positive regions. For the true-positive mass regions, our model generated 263 masses from MIAS database, and 86.44% (51 of 59) of them were marked at the same locations. For the DDSM database, 84.52% (71 of 84) of masses were in the same locations for all 400 used mammograms. Table IV also shows the false-positive and false-negative rates for both databases does not exceed 16.45%. Table IV clearly demonstrates that our method produces, in general, more accurate segmentations than other techniques.

Figure (5) shows an example of mammogram segmentations results. Figure (5(a)) shows the original image, such as it is available at the DDSM. Using the method of Sampaio et al. [21], the segmentation stage failed to include the mass among the regions of interest (Figure (5)(b)). Regarding our method, it was able to correctly detect of the mass in a mammography image (Figure (5)(c)); as we can observe by the mark of the correct location of the mass, in yellow, in the original image. The efficiency of the proposed method compared with Rahmati et al. [17] method, is illustrated by another example, in Figure 6; which shows that our method gives a clearly better results. Our method reduces also the number of segmented regions and can successfully extract a clear boundary of the ROI. Some other segmentation results are given in Appendix *B*. Mammographic images was randomly selected from the DDSM and MIAS mammogram databases.

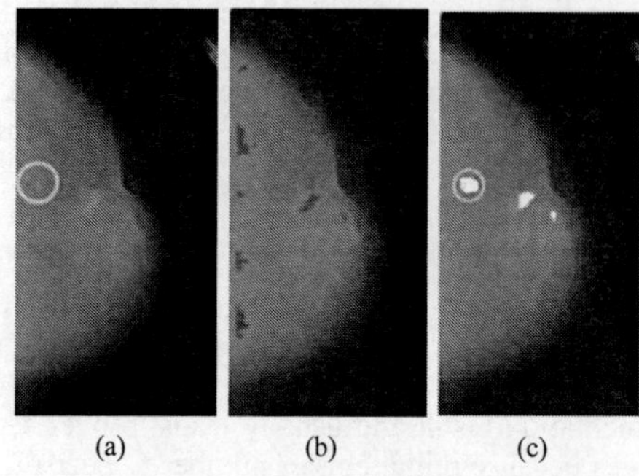

Fig. 5: Example of the detection for a mass in the DDSM database. (a) mammogram with a mass (Annotation contour given by the DDSM database). (b) Segmentation result by Sampaio et al. [21] method. (c) Segmentation by our method.

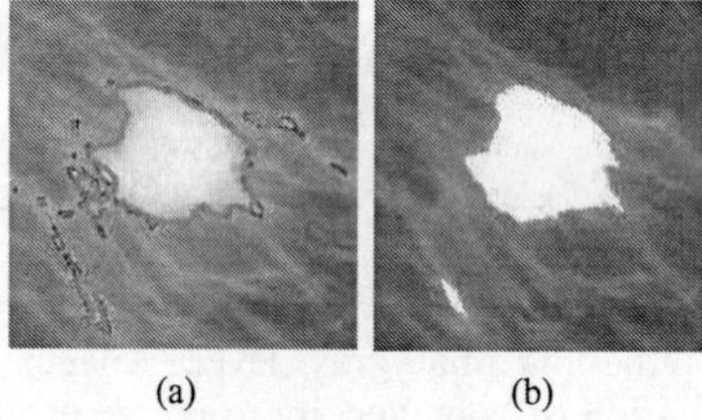

Fig. 6: ROI segmentation (MIAS-Mdb028 Mammogram) (a) Rahmati et al. [17] (b) our model.

As a summary to these simulations, we can say that our algorithm has acceptable performance compared to that obtained by the used comparison methods. Refining the system for false-positive reduction, and including a feature selection step are being considered for future work.

V. Conclusion

In this paper, we have developed a new method for the detection of abnormal masses in Mammograms. The proposed method uses the spatial fuzzy clustering to place initial seeds for the growing process, so selected initial seeds can provide more accurate segmentation of images. After the growing finishes, we proceed in our approach by merging some detected regions to overcome the over segmentation problem. Experimental results on the standard MIAS and DDSM databases are very encouraging and should stimulate future research. Refining the system for false-positive reduction, and including a feature selection step will be the focus of our immediate further work.

TABLE II: Comparison of methodologies for detection of masses using the MIAS database.

Scheme	SE (%)	SP (%)	AC (%)	FPI	FNI	AURC	Ov
Zhang and Foo [26]	90.00	-	-	1.30	0.10	-	-
A Rojas and A K Nandi [20]	80.00	-	-	0.32	-	-	-
Our Proposal	86.44	85.55	85.71	0.11	0.02	0.90	0.238

TABLE III: Comparison of methodologies for detection of masses using the DDSM database.

Scheme	SE (%)	SP (%)	AC (%)	FPI	FNI	AURC	Ov
Nunes et al. [14]	83.24	84.14	83.94	0.55	0.17	-	-
Eltonsy et al. [8]	81.00	-	-	0.60	-	-	-
Sampaio et al. [21]	80.00	85.68	84.62	0.84	0.20	0.87	0.325
Rahmati et al. [17]	82.34	-	86.85	-	-	-	-
Our Proposal	84.52	83.54	83.75	0.13	0.03	0.88	0.312

TABLE IV: Results of tests on the proposed methodology.

Database	Number of masses	True positive (%)	True Negative (%)	False Positive (%)	False Negative (%)
MIAS	59	51 (86.44)	225 (85.55)	38 (14.44)	8 (13.55)
DDSM	84	71 (84.52)	264 (83.54)	52 (16.45)	13 (15.47)

REFERENCES

[1] R. Adams and L. Bischof. Seeded region growing. *IEEE Transactions on Pattern Analysis and Machine Intelligence*, 16(6):641–647, 1994.

[2] S. K. Bandyopadhyay. Survey on segmentation methods for locating masses in a mammogram image. *International Journal of Computer Applications*, 9(11):25–28, November 2010.

[3] L. W. Bassett, R. H. Gold, and C. Kimme-Smith. History of the technical development of mammography. *Syllabus: A Categorical course in Physics RSNA*, 1994.

[4] J. C. Bezdek. Pattern recognition with fuzzy objective function algorithms. *Plenum Press*, 1981.

[5] H. D. Cheng, X. J. Shi, R. Min, L. M. Hu, X. P. Cai, and H. N. Du. Approaches for automated detection and classification of masses in mammograms. *Pattern Recognition*, 39(4):646–668, 2006.

[6] H. D. Cheng and H. J. Xu. A novel fuzzy logic approach to contrast enhancement. *Pattern Recognition*, 33 (5):809–819, 2000.

[7] K. S. Chuang, H. L. Tzeng, and S. Chen. Fuzzy c-means clustering with spatial information for image segmentation. *Comput Med Imaging Graph*, 30(1):9–15, 2006.

[8] N. H. Eltonsy, G. D. Tourassi, and A. S. Elmaghraby. A concentric morphology model for the detection of masses in mammography. *IEEE Trans. Med. Imag.*, 26(6):880–889, 2007.

[9] M. Heath, K. Bowyer, and D. Kopans. Current status of the digital database for screening mammography. *Digital Mammography, Kluwer Academic Publishers,*, pages 457–460., 1998.

[10] M. R. Hejazi and Y. S. Ho. Automated detection of tumors in mammograms using two segments for classification. *Lecturer Notes in Computer Science*, 3767:910–921, 2005.

[11] K. M. Indra, N. Sanjay, and S. K. Bandyopadhyay. Detection of abnormal masses using devide and conquer algorithm in digital mammogram. *International Journal of Emerging Sciences*, 1(4):767–786, 2011.

[12] U. Knauer and B. Meffert. Fast computation of region homogeneity with application in a surveillance task. *International Archives of Photogrammetry, Remote Sensing and Spatial Information Sciences*, 2010.

[13] S. Lai, X. Li, and W. Bischof. On techniques for detecting circumscribed masses in mammograms. *IEEE Trans. Med. Imag*, 8:377–386, 1989.

[14] A. P. Nunes, A. C. Silva, and A. C. de Paiva. Detection of masses in mammographic images using geometry, simpson's diversity index and svm. *Int. J. Signal Imaging Syst. Eng.*, 3(1):43–51, 2010.

[15] M. N. Okobia and C. H. Bunker. Estrogen metabolism and breast cancer risk: A review. *African Journal of Reproductive Health*, 10(1):13–25, 2006.

[16] A. Oliver, J. Freixenet, J. Marti, E. Prez, J. Pont, E. Denton, and R. Zwiggelaar. A review of automatic mass detection and segmentation in mammographic images. *Medical Image Analysis*, 14(2):87–110, 2010.

[17] P. Rahmati, A. Adler, and G. Hamarneh. Mammography segmentation with maximum likelihood active contours. *Medical Image Analysis*, 16(6):1167–1186, 2012.

[18] G. N. Harikrishna Rai and T. R. Gopalakrishnan Nair. Gradient based seeded region grow method for ct angiographic image segmentation. *CoRR*, abs/1001.3735, 2010.

[19] P. Regina and D. T. Klaus. Segmentation of medical images using adaptive region growing. *Medical Imaging 2001: Image Processing*, 4322:1337–1346, 2001.

[20] A. Rojas and A. Nandi. Detection of masses in mammograms via statistically based enhancement, multilevel-thresholding segmentation, and region selection. *Comput. Med. Imag. Graph.*, 32 (4):304 – 315, 2008.

[21] W. B. Sampaio, E. M. Diniz, A. C. Silva, A. C. Paiva, and M. Gattass. Detection of masses in mammogram images using cnn, geostatistic functions and svm. *Comput Biol Med*, 41(8):653–64, 2011.

[22] C. Schmid, R. Mohr, and C. Bauckhage. Evaluation of interest point detectors. *International Journal of Computer Vision*, 37:151–172, 2000.

[23] B. Senthilkumar and G. Umamaheswari. A new region growing segmentation algorithm for the detection of breast cancer. *International Journal of Computer Science and Communication*, 3(1):17–20, 2012.

[24] J. Suckling, J. Parker, D. Dance, S. Astley, I. Hutt, C. Boggis, I. Ricketts, E. Stamatakis, N. Cerneaz, S. Kok, P. Taylor, D. Betal, and J. Savage. The mammographic images analysis society digital mammogram database. *Experta Medica International Congress Series*, 1069:375–378, 1994.

[25] M. Wirth and A. Stapinski. Segmentation of the breast region in mammograms using snakes. In *Canadian Conference on Computer and Robot Vision*, pages 385–392, 2004.

[26] H. Zhang, S. W. Foo, S. M. Krishnan, and C. H. Thng. Automated breast masses segmentation in digitized mammograms. *IEEE International Workshop in Biomedical Circuits and System*, 2004.

SESSION

IMAGE RETRIEVAL AND IMAGE DATABASES

Chair(s)

TBA

Performance Evaluation of Different Query Sets on Expanded Diagnosed Dataset Using Content Based Image Retrieval in the Detection of Lung Nodules for Lung Cancer Diagnosis

Preeti Aggarwal,
UIET, Panjab University,
Chandigarh, India

Renu Vig,
UIET, Panjab University,
Chandigarh, India

H K Sardana
CSIO,
Chandigarh, India

Abstract:
In lung cancer computer-aided diagnosis (CAD) systems, having an accurate ground truth is critical and time consuming. In this study, we have explored Lung Image Database Consortium (LIDC) database containing pulmonary computed tomography (CT) scans, and we developed content-based image retrieval (CBIR) approach to exploit the limited amount of diagnostically labeled data in order to annotate unlabeled images with diagnoses. By applying this CBIR method iteratively and using pathologically confirmed cases, we expand the set of diagnosed data available for CAD systems from 17 nodules to 121 nodules. We evaluate the method using various combinations of lung nodule sets as queries and retrieves similar nodules from the diagnostically labeled dataset. Precision achieved in this study using Diagnosed dataset and computer-predicted malignancy data for undiagnosed query nodules indicate that CBIR expansion is an effective method for labeling undiagnosed images. Little knowledge of biopsy confirmed cases assist the physician's as second opinion.

Keywords: *Chest CT scan, computer-aided diagnosis, LIDC, cancer detection and diagnosis, biopsy.*

1. Introduction

Lung cancer is the leading cause of cancer death in the United States. Early detection and treatment of lung cancer is important in order to improve the five year survival rate of cancer patients. Medical imaging plays an important role in the early detection and treatment of cancer. It provides physicians with information essential for efficient and effective diagnosis of various diseases. In order to improve lung nodule detection, CAD is effective as a second opinion for radiologists in clinical settings [1]. A dataset with ground truth diagnosis information is essential for CAD systems in order to analyze new cases. The construction of a high-quality multimedia collection of cases is extremely time-consuming and expensive. It is often a bottleneck in studies on image-based CAD systems. The identification of the relevant cases, the consultation of the electronic health record (EHR) and picture archiving and communication systems (PACS) to gather the clinical parameters and the image series, the data entry as well as the database infrastructure and maintenance involve a large amount of work with a wide range of skills from medical knowledge to information technology (IT) expertise. To assess the high-quality of the data, several researchers and physicians have to be involved in the case selection process and the delineation of regions of interest (ROIs) to cope with the inter- and intra-observer variability, the latter being particularly important in radiology [2]. The agreement of the ethics committee has to be obtained before starting any investigations. Efforts for building a resource for the lung imaging research community are detailed in [3] [4]. In almost all the CAD studies, most authors created their own datasets with their own ground truth for evaluation. The use of different datasets makes the comparison of these CAD systems not feasible and therefore, there is an immediate need for reference datasets that can provide a common ground truth for the evaluation and validation of these systems.

The pulmonary CT scans used in this study were obtained from the LIDC [4], and we refer to the nodules in this dataset as the LIDC Nodule Dataset. Recently, diagnosis data for some of the nodules were released by the LIDC; however, because the diagnosis is available patient-wise not nodule-wise, only the diagnoses belonging to patients with a single nodule could be reliably matched with the nodules in the LIDC Nodule Dataset, resulting in 18 diagnosed nodules (eight benign, six malignant, three metastases and one unknown). The 17 nodules with known diagnoses comprise the initial Diagnosed Subset as one case with unknown diagnose cannot be considered as ground truth. Since the diagnoses in the LIDC Diagnosis Dataset are the closest thing to a ground truth available for the malignancy of the LIDC nodules, our goal is to expand the Diagnosed Subset by adding nodules similar to those already in the subset.

To identify these similar nodules and to predict their diagnoses, CBIR with classification is employed. The radiologist's annotation along with LIDC data is also considered as semantic rating to prepare the ground truth from LIDC data. Increasing the number of nodules for which a diagnostic ground truth is available is important for future CAD applications of the LIDC database. With the aid of similar images, radiologists' diagnoses of lung nodules in CT scans can be significantly improved [5]. Having diagnostic information for medical images is an important tool for datasets used in clinical CBIR [6]; however, any CAD system would benefit from a larger Diagnosed Subset as well as the semantic rating, since the increased variability in this set would result in more accurately predicted diagnoses for new patients.

1.1 State of the Art

Only a limited number of CAD studies have used a pathologically confirmed diagnostic ground truth, since there are few publically available databases with pathological annotations [7]. The results in these studies were validated with a pathological diagnostic ground truth; suggest that radiologists could benefit from the use of their proposed CAD system.

In CAD applications for which pathological diagnosis data is absent, determining a ground truth is more challenging. Even with LIDC data where biopsy confirmed cases are available still due to the variability in the opinion of four different radiologists made the LIDC data more complex and redundant. In exploring the relationship between content-based similarity and semantic-based similarity for LIDC images, Jabon et al. found that there is a high correlation between image features and radiologists' semantic ratings [8]. Despite this correlation, radiologist malignancy ratings cannot be considered a valid ground truth due to the variability among radiologists [7]. Though in this study, the malignancy rating is also considered for patients having multiple nodules by taking the mean of all the four radiologists rating.

McNitt-Gray *et al.* [9] [10] used nodule size, shape and co-occurrence texture features as nodule characteristics to design a linear discriminant analysis (LDA) classification system for malignant versus benign nodules. Armato *et al.* [11] used nodule appearance and shape to build an LDA classification system to classify pulmonary nodules into malignant versus benign classes. Takashima *et al.* [12] [13] used shape information to characterize malignant versus benign lesions in the lung. Samuel *et al.* [14] developed a system for lung nodule diagnosis using Fuzzy Logic. Matsuki *et al.* [15] also used both clinical information and sixteen features scored by radiologists to design an ANN for malignant versus benign classification.

Although the work cited above provides convincing evidence that a combination of image features can indirectly encode radiologists' knowledge about indicators of malignancy the precise mechanism by which this correspondence happens is unknown. To understand this mechanism, there is a need to explore several approaches for finding the relationships between the image features, radiologists' annotations and actual pathological report of those patients. A correlation between all these is required to prepare the ground truth of LIDC data. Also, in all these systems the major concern was to distinguish benign nodules from malignant one where as in the current study we have assigned a new class to the nodules metastases, which indicates that the nodule is malignant however the primary cancer is not lung cancer. The cancer has spread from other organ like neck, breast etc. to lung which can definitely further help the physicians in better understanding of cause and diagnosis for those patients.

In the current study, we adopted a semi-supervised approach for labeling undiagnosed nodules in the LIDC. CBIR is used to label nodules most similar to the query with respect to Euclidean distance of image features. By evaluating the method with a CAD application, we determined how to effectively expand the Diagnosed Subset with CBIR.

2. Materials and Methods

2.1 Lung Image Database Consortium (LIDC) Dataset; A Benchmark

The NIH LIDC has created a dataset to serve as an international research resource for development, training, and evaluation of CAD algorithms for detecting lung nodules on CT scans. The LIDC database, released in 2009, contains 399 pulmonary CT scans. Up to four radiologists analyzed each scan by identifying nodules and rating the malignancy of each nodule on a scale of 1-5. Eight other characteristics with their description are shown in Table 3. The boundaries provided in the XML files are already marked using manual as well as semi-automated methods [1] [5]. Both cancerous and non-cancerous regions appear with little distinction on CT scan image. For accurate detection of cancerous nodules, we need to differentiate the cancerous nodules from the noncancerous ones. The nine characteristics are presented in [16] are the common terms physicians consider for a nodule to be benign or malignant. To our best knowledge, this is the first use of the LIDC dataset for the purpose of validating and classifying lung nodule using biopsy report as well as the semantics attached.

2.2 Lung Nodule Detection and Selection of Slices

Lung nodules are volumetric and almost available in each slice of patient. It is used for nodule diagnosis as well as for monitoring tumor response to therapy. CT scan of chest is the better method to analyze these nodules for detection as well as for diagnosis. Due to multiple slices in CT, the physician has to see each and every slice for better understanding of each nodule, if present. This task is time consuming as well as not deterministic in any way. We presented a CAD system designed to ensure the nodules marked by different radiologists and consider only effective nodules which can lead to lung cancer, if any, present in the patient. This method can further lead to decrease in time needed to examine the patient's scan by a radiologist.

In this work, these marking are used for the nodule detection and segmentation from chest CT scan. For better results as well to prepare the ground truth the values of annotations are averaged for all the four radiologists. No automatic segmentation is considered as manual segmentation in medical imaging provides better results [17].

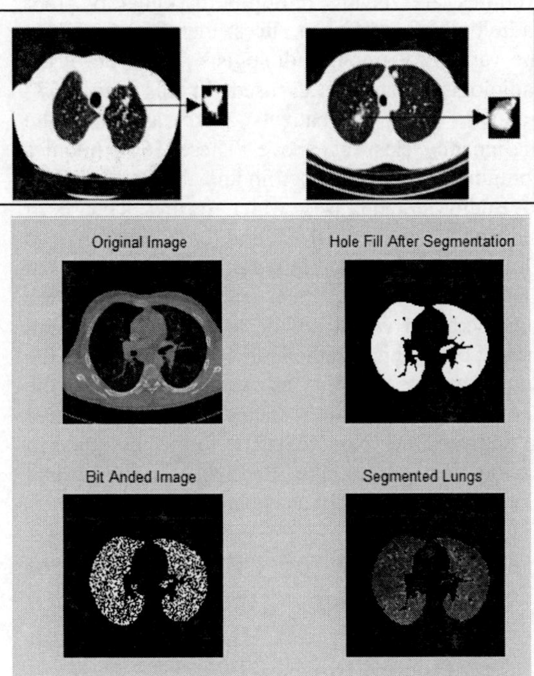

Figure1: Comparison of automated and radiologist segmentation

We have compared the results of manual segmentation with active contour segmentation, see Figure 1. For automatic segmentation, the method proposed in [18] by Armato is implemented. It is clear from the figure, in automatic segmentation some artifacts always persist as compared to manual segmentation. Each slice is read independently to identify its area marked by all the four radiologists and only those slices per nodule is considered to be in the database whose area is maximum [19].

2.3 Final Extracted Nodule Dataset

CT scan of 80 biopsy confirmed patients with solitary pulmonary nodules mostly less than 3 cm have been taken from. All the images are of size 512*512 and each having 16 bit resolution. All images are in DICOM (Digital Imaging and Communication in Medicine) format which is well known standard used in medical field. Each patient file is associated with an XML annotated file having details of nodule boundaries as well as physician's annotation is associated. Total of 1737 nodules are marked in 80 patients considering each slice of a patient having area greater than all those marked by four different radiologists. Out of 80 biopsy confirmed cases only 18 cases were available with single nodule. From these 18, only 17 cases were considered further to prepare the ground truth as diagnosis for one patient was unknown and this set will be referred to as the Diagnosed17. The classes assigned to these nodules were malignant, benign and metastases based on the diagnosis report available. Rest 62 patients were assigned the class based on the mean of malignancy rating provided by four different radiologists as no ground truth is available for these 62 patients with multiple nodules and this set will be referred as RadioMarked62. It contains 1677 nodules from 62 patients. 83 well known image features were extracted for each nodule based on texture, size, shape, and intensity [16]. The four feature extraction methods used to obtain these 83 features from the LIDC images were Haralick co-occurrence, GLDM, Gabor filters, and Intensity [16]. The number of nodules was reduced to 210 by removing nodules smaller than five-by-five pixels and multiple slices per nodules because features extracted from these smaller nodules are imprecise.
Four different "undiagnosed" query sets containing subsets of the LIDC Nodule Dataset were used, since neither computer-predicted nor radiologist-predicted malignancy ratings can be considered ground truth due to high variability between radiologists' ratings. Each of these query sets differed in diagnostic ground truth. The first query set (Rad210) used the radiologist-predicted malignancy, the second set (Comp210) used the computer-predicted malignancy, the third set (Comp_Rad_biopsy57) used only those nodules for which the radiologist, computer-predicted as well

as biopsy confirmed malignancies agreed and the fourth set used only those nodules form which the radiologist- and computer-predicted malignancies agreed. For each query set, nodules with unknown malignancies were removed, and the set was balanced to contain all the three classes i.e. benign, malignant and metastases. The radiologist-predicted and computer-predicted contained equal number of nodules i.e. 210 and radiologist-computer-biopsy-agreement query set contained 57, and Rad_Comp92 contained 92 nodules after all modifications.

3. Methods

3.1 Labeling of the Nodules

Nodules are labeled according to single nodule per patient and patients with multiple nodules. Following sections show the details:

3.1.1 Patients with Single Nodule

Out of 80, only 18 patient cases were having one nodule whereas 62 patients were having more than one nodule. The diagnostic report of LIDC data is patient-wise not nodule-wise. Due to this limitation, biopsy report is used only for 18 patients with one nodule to prepare the ground truth. Biopsy report for those patients has four classes identified as 0, 1, 2 and 3. The meaning of these terms is as described in following table, Table1:

Table1: Malignancy ratings and its meaning in LIDC dataset

Diagnosis	Diagnosis at patient level as per LIDC diagnosis report	Class assigned in this work	Description
0	Unknown	I	In-determined
1	Benign	B	Non-Cancerous
2	Malignant	M	Cancerous
3	Metastases	MT	Cancer is spreading from other organ to lung.

17 out of 18 biopsy confirmed cases were having the diagnosis as 1, 2 and 3 whereas only one patient was having the diagnosis as 0 which means unknown or indeterminate. This can decrease the classification results, so was not considered in this study. Consequently, 17 pathologically confirmed cases were assigned three classes malignant (M), benign (B) and metastases (MT). There are eight benign (B) nodules, six malignant (M) nodules and three metastases (MT) nodules present in the initial Diagnosed17 set.

3.1.2 Patients with Multiple Nodules

62 out of 80 biopsy confirmed cases with multiple nodules are assigned classes on the basis of radiologist's malignancy characteristics. The meaning and description of malignancy annotation feature of LIDC data is shown in Table1. Out of nine annotations only malignancy feature is used to assign the class to each nodule marked by radiologists as this is most promising feature to determine the malignancy of a nodule. Also, the other characteristics like margin, spiculation, and calcification are already involved in the medical definition of malignancy, so instead of considering all the nine only malignancy features is considered to assign the class as it approximately covers almost all the other features too. The method used to label each nodule is as follows

Nodules with malignancy rating >=3 assigned class Malignant (M) whereas
Nodules with malignancy rating <3 assigned class Benign (B)

Nodules are having multiple markings by four radiologists on different slices; therefore to reduce the variability among radiologists, the mean of the radiologists' ratings was used. In this way, 1677 nodules from 62 patients were assigned the malignancy class as above. These 1677 nodules contain multiple slices per nodule also and assigned to RadioMarked62 set, which further have been reduced to 210 and assigned to QueryNoduleSet210. If the same nodule appears in the multiple slices, then only those slices are considered in which nodule are having maximum area [19]. This method definitely reduces the database of nodules as well as makes the complexity of volumetric data simpler and effective to analyze.QueryNoduleSet210 further assigned to various categories like Rad210, Comp210 and Comp_Rad_biopsy210 as explained earlier.

3.2 Summary of CBIR Method of Expanding the Diagnosed Subset17; CBIR Expansion Occurs Iteratively.

As ground truth for only 17 patients were available, there is a need to expand the diagnostically labeled database. In the absence of diagnostic information, labels can be applied to unlabeled data using semi-supervised learning (SSL) approaches. In SSL, unlabeled data is exploited to improve learning when the dataset contains an insufficient amount of labeled data [20]. CBIR can be used as a machine learning process that trains a system to classify images as relevant or irrelevant to the query. Using available datasets and by evaluating the method with a CAD application, we determined how to effectively expand the Diagnosed17 with CBIR and assist the physicians in the final diagnosis. Each nodule in the QueryNoduleSet210 was then used as a query to retrieve the ten most similar images from the remaining nodules in the Diagnosed17 using CBIR with Euclidean distance. The query nodule was assigned predicted malignancy ratings based on the retrieved nodules (e.g., if the maximum retrieved nodules belong to class malignant then the query nodule was assigned the class M), Figure 2. The newly identified nodule was considered candidates for addition to the Diagnosed17.

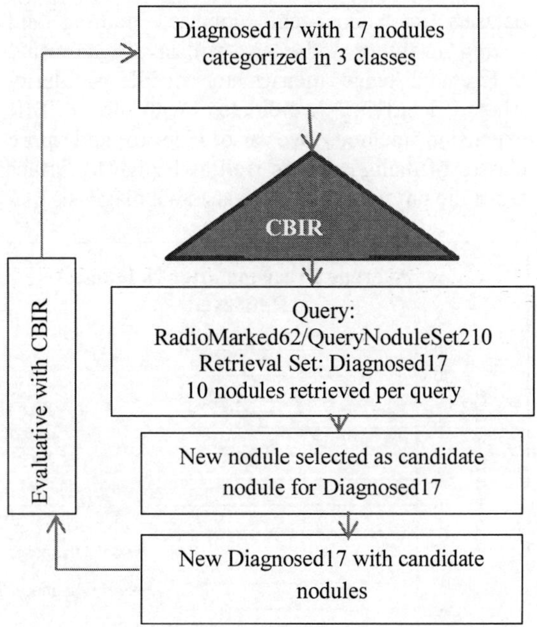

Figure2: Selection of candidate nodules using CBIR and Diagnosed17

3.3 Diagnosed Subset Evaluation

In the current study, we adopted a semi-supervised approach for labeling undiagnosed nodules in the LIDC. CBIR was used to label nodules most similar to the query with respect to Euclidean distance of image features. Nodules to be added to the Diagnosed17 were selected from the candidates described above. For verifying the addition of a candidate nodule in the Diagnosed17, a reverse mechanism is adopted. Diagnosed17 nodules acted as query and nodules to be retrieved are from QueryNoduleSet210, see Figure 2. The first three similar nodules are assigned the same malignancy as the query nodule if they were previously assigned as candidate nodules (i.e. if the query nodule is benign then the top three retrieved nodules are also assigned the class benign if previously are assigned as candidate nodule). Finally based on CBIR and CAD nodules are added in the Diagnosed17. With this mechanism Diagnosed17 in expanded to Diagnosed74, which means that now 74 nodules have the confirmed diagnosis and can be treated as LIDC ground truth. Predicted diagnosis with the pathologically-determined diagnosis, this process guarantees the accuracy of the CBIR-based diagnostic labeling.

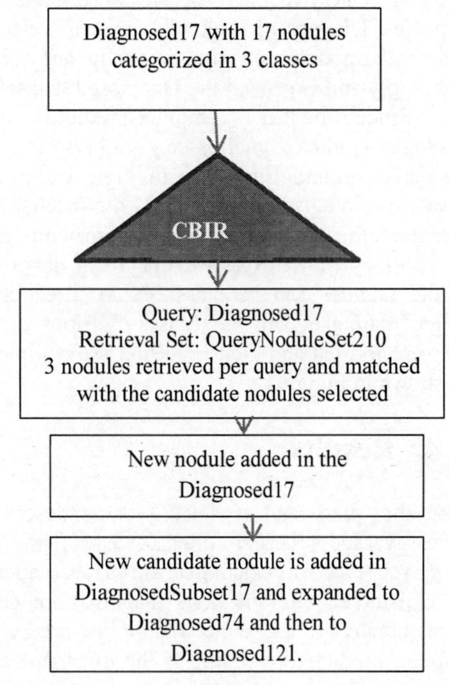

Figure3: Expansion of Diagnosed17 to Diagnosed74 and Diagnosed121

3.4 CBIR Mapping of Multiple Nodules Database with Single Nodule Database

An independent CBIR framework is implemented to increase the Diagnosed17 using CBIR from the QueryNoduleSet210. QueryNoduleSet210 is having multiple nodules per patient. 210 different nodules are present in this set. One by one each nodule is taken as query nodule and matched against Diagnosed17 using CBIR with Euclidean distance. As patient-wise diagnosis is available for QueryNoduleSet210, hence the top retrieved result is matched with this diagnosis. If top retrieved nodule class matches with the patient-wise diagnosis of query nodule then it is added in Diagnosed17 else discarded. With multiple iterations in this manner, Diagnosed17 is increased to Diagnosed121, see Figure 3. Predicted diagnosis with the pathologically-determined diagnosis, this process guarantees the accuracy of the CBIR-based diagnostic labeling.

3.5 Query and Retrieval Sets Concluded

In this CAD scenario, two ways process is implemented as discussed earlier. Once the nodules in Diagnosed17 were used as query and QueryNoduleSet210 was used for retrieving the nodules based on CBIR and Euclidean distance and expanded the ground truth to 74 nodules. Secondly, nodules in QueryNoduleSubset210 were treated as query and Diagnosed17 set was used to retrieve most similar nodules to assign the malignancy class accordingly and expanded the Diagnosed dataset to 121. Since neither computer-predicted nor radiologist-predicted malignancy ratings can be considered ground truth due to high variability between radiologists' ratings [7]. This mechanism guarantees the preparation of LIDC ground truth and accuracy of CBIR based diagnostic labeling. All the nodules can be classified in three class benign, malignant and metastases. Various query sets were formed and their precision are compared and shown in Figure.

4. Results

Using the query and retrieval sets as described above, average precision after 3, 5, 10, and 15 images retrieved was calculated. A retrieved nodule was considered relevant if its diagnosis matched the malignancy rating (either radiologist-predicted, computer-predicted, or both) of the query nodule. Initial precision values were obtained by using the 17 nodules in the initial Diagnosed17 as the retrieval set. Then, nodules were added to this set as described in sections 2.2 and 2.3. Precision was recalculated, and the nodule addition process was repeated iteratively using the new Diagnosed17. In each subsequent iteration, only the newly added nodules in the Diagnosed17 were used to identify new candidates. This process repeated until no candidate nodules were added to the Diagnosed17 following an iteration. Various experiments were setup for the validation of nodules examined.

Figure 4 shows that with five query sets and three retrieval sets Diagnosed17, Diagnosed74 and Diagnosed121, the precision increases respectively. Nodules in Comp_Rad_biopsy57 has provided the best precision i.e. 98% which is the best precision achieved in the history of medical CBIR with best of our knowledge.

5. Conclusion and Future Work

CBIR is an effective method for expanding the Diagnosed Subset by labeling nodules which do not have associated diagnoses. As LIDC is having lack of ground truth, CBIR techniques works tremendously better to prepare the ground truth. This method outperforms control expansion, yielding higher precision values when tested with a potential CAD application [17] that requires a diagnostically accurate ground truth. By increasing the size of the Diagnosed Subset from 17 to 74 and finally to 121 nodules, CBIR expansion provides greater variability in the retrieval set, resulting in retrieved nodules that are more similar to undiagnosed queries. The proposed CBIR expansion method can be applied to differentiate benign, malignant as well as metastases nodules. The third class metastases have not been introduced in the history of CBIR and medical imaging. An expanded set of diagnosed images is also useful for non-CBIR CAD systems, which require large datasets for robust and unbiased training and testing. In future studies, we will investigate using different distance metrics for nodule similarity when identifying candidates with the CBIR expansion method. We also plan to add more classes of malignancy as well as benign to further assist the physicians in more accurate diagnosis.

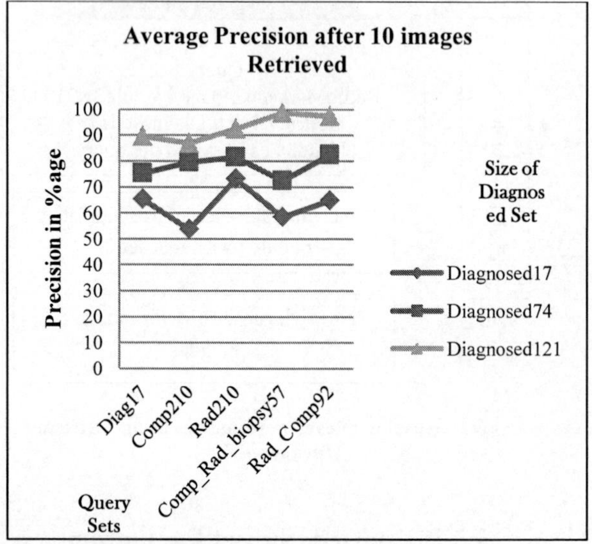

Figure4: Comparison of precision for different query sets at x-axis and different retrieval sets at y-axis.

References

[1] D. Wormanns, M. Fiebich, M. Saidi, S. Diederich, and W. Heindel, "Automatic detection of pulmonary nodules at spiral CT: clinical application of a computer-aided diagnosis system," European Radiology, vol. 12, pp. 1052-1057, 2002.

[2] A. Blum and T. Mitchell, "Combining Labelled and Unlabelled Data with Co-Training," Proceedings of the 11th Annual Conference on Computational Learning Theory (COLT '98), pp. 92-100, 1998.

[3] Armato SG, McLennan G, McNitt-Gray MF, Meyer CR, Yankelevitz D, Aberle DR, et al. Lung image database consortium: developing a resource for the medical imaging research community. Radiology 2004; 232(3):739–48.

[4] McNitt-Gray MF, Armato SG, Meyer CR, Reeves AP, McLennan G, Pais RC, et al. The lung image database consortium (LIDC) data collection process for nodule detection and annotation. Academic Radiology 2007;14(12):1464–74.

[5] Armato SG III, McLennan G, Bidaut L, McNitt-Gray MF, Meyer CR, Reeves AP, Zhao B, Aberle DR, Henschke CI, Hoffman EA, Kazerooni EA, MacMahon H, van Beek EJR, Yankelevitz D, et al.: The Lung Image Database Consortium (LIDC) and Image Database Resources Initiative (IDRI): A completed reference database of lung nodules on CT scans. Medical Physics; 38: 915–931, 2011.

[6] H. Müller and J. Kalpathy-Cramer, "Putting the Content Into Context: Features and Gaps in Image Retrieval," In J. Tan, New Technologies for Advancing Healthcare and Clinical Practices, IGI Global, Hershey PA, pp. 105-115, 2011.

[7] W. H. Horsthemke, D. S. Raicu, J. D. Furst, and S. G. Armato III, "Evaluation Challenges for Computer-Aided Diagnostic Characterization: Shape Disagreements in the Lung Image Database Consortium Pulmonary Nodule Dataset," In J. Tan, New Technologies for Advancing Healthcare and Clinical Practices, IGI Global, Hershey PA, pp. 18-43, 2011.

[8] S. A. Jabon, D. S. Raicu, and J. D. Furst, "Content-based versus semantic-based similarity retrieval: a LIDC case study," SPIE Medical Imaging Conference, Orlando, February 2009.

[9] McNitt-Gray, M.F.; Hart, E.M.; Wyckoff, N.; Sayre, J.W.; Goldin, J.G.; Aberle, D.R. A pattern classification approach to characterizing solitary pulmonary nodules imaged on high resolution CT: Preliminary results. Med. Phys. 1999, 26, 880–888.

[10] McNitt-Gray, M.F.; Wyckoff, N.; Sayre, J.W.; Goldin, J.G.; Aberle, D.R. The effects of co-occurrence matrix based texture parameters on the classification of solitary pulmonary nodules imaged on computed tomography. Comput. Med. Imaging Graph.1999, 23, 339–348.

[11] Armato, S.G., III; Altman, M.B.; Wilkie, J.; Sone, S.; Li, F.; Doi, K.; Roy, A.S. Automated lung nodule classification following automated nodule detection on CT: A serial approach. Med. Phys.2003, 30, 1188–1197.

[12] Takashima, S.; Sone, S.; Li, F.; Maruyama, Y.; Hasegawa, M.; Kadoya, M. Indeterminate solitary pulmonary nodules revealed at population-based CT screening of the lung: using first follow-up diagnostic CT to differentiate benign and malignant lesions. Am. J. Roentgenol. 2003, 180, 1255–1263.

[13] Takashima, S.; Sone, S.; Li, F.; Maruyama, Y.; Hasegawa, M.; Matsushita, T.; Takayama, F.; Kadoya, M. Small solitary pulmonary nodules (<1 cm) detected at population-based CT screening for lung cancer: reliable high-resolution CT features of benign lesions. Am. J. Roentgenol. 2003, 180, 955–964.

[14] Samuel, C.C.; Saravanan, V.; Vimala, D.M.R. Lung nodule diagnosis from CT images using fuzzy logic. In Proceedings of International Conference on Computational Intelligence and Multimedia Applications, Sivakasi, Tamilnadu, India, December 13−15, 2007; pp. 159–163.

[15] Matsuki, Y.; Nakamura, K.; Watanabe, H.; Aoki, T.; Nakata, H.; Katsuragawa, S.; Doi, K. Usefulness of an artificial neural network for differentiating benign from malignant pulmonary nodules on high-resolution CT: Evaluation with receiver operating characteristic analysis. Am. J.Roentgenol. 2002, 178, 657–663.

[16] Raicu, Daniela S; Varutbangkul, Ekarin; Furst, Jacob D, Modelling semantics from image data: opportunities from LIDC, International Journal of Biomedical Engineering and Technology, Volume 3, Numbers 1-2, 30 November 2009 , pp. 83-113(31)

[17] Anne-Marie Giuca, Kerry A. Seitz Jr., Jacob Furst, Daniela Raicu, Expanding diagnostically labeled datasets using content-based image retrieval, IEEE International Conference on Image Processing 2012, September 30 - October 3, Lake Buena Vista, Florida.

[18] S. G. Armato, F. Li, M. L. Giger, H. MacMahon, S. Sone, and K. Doi, "Lung cancer: performance of automated lung nodule detection applied to cancers missed in a CT screening program,"Radiology, vol. 225, no. 3, pp. 685–692, 2002.

[19] Preeti Aggarwal, Renu Vig, and H K Sardana, Largest Versus Smallest Nodules Marked by Different Radiologists in Chest CT Scans for Lung Cancer Detection, International conference on image engineering, ICIE-2013 organized by IAENG at Hong Kong. (In press).

[20] Z.-H. Zhou, "Learning with Unlabeled Data and Its Application to Image Retrieval," PRICAI'06 Proceedings of the 9th Pacific Rim International Conference on Artificial Intelligence, 2006.

Clustered microcalcification detection scheme for mammographic images

Matheus, B.[1]; Neto, J.[1]; Schiabel, H.[1]

Department of Electrical Engineering, University of São Paulo, São Carlos, São Paulo, Brazil

Abstract: *This paper describes a clustered microcalcification detection scheme for mammographic images improved from early designs by Chan et al (1) and Schiabel et al (2). This scheme includes a preprocessing segment in order to enhance the quality of the image without removing the smaller microcalcifications. The systems consist of a subtraction of a smoothed image from an image convoluted with a filter similar to a calcification in order to obtain an image with only the calcification-similar regions enhanced. The scheme was tested using DDSM (3) database (with a result of 89% sensitivity and 6.9 false positives per image) and INBreast (4) database (with a result of 89% sensitivity and 1.4 false positives per image).*

Keywords: Mammography, Mammographic CAD, Microcalcification detection, Image Analysis,

1. Introduction

In mammographic exams, calcifications are used as an indicator of malignancy. They are common in exams (around 50% of mammographic exams shows then), but when presented as clusters, there is 20 to 30% of chances of being a cancer signal (5). Unfortunately, although calcifications have a high density and opacity to X-rays, microcalcifications are smaller than 0.5 mm (6), having been found as small as 24μm (7). Due to its size the resulting contrast is low making them very hard to find. Another problem is that any noise can mask, or be mistaken for, a microcalcification.

In order to help the detection of microcalcifications this paper presents a microcalcification detection software. Unlike many other schemes for microcalcification detection (8) this one was designed to work with any type of image, considering different spatial and contrast resolutions, images from film-scanner systems and FFDM.

2. Materials and methods

The scheme described here was derived from a previous system from Schiabel et al (2). The flowchart in Figure 1 shows how it is structured.

Initially the system used a set of preprocessing methods before the detection. The first step crops the image to a rectangle close to the limits of the breast, removing a lot of background, tags and the white borders. This allows the system to work only in the breast area of the whole image, reducing the skew results of averages and border problems. This also reduces the size of the image to be processed (9).

If the digital image is yielded from a proper scanned mammographic film, a scanner correction is applied according to its characteristic curve (10). This process uses the digitizer characteristic curve to correct flaws on the image eventually caused by the digitization and to enhance the image quality as close as possible to a standard reference (10). This has been shown to reduce the false-positive rates of microcalcification detection. If the image is from a FFDM scanner this step is skipped.

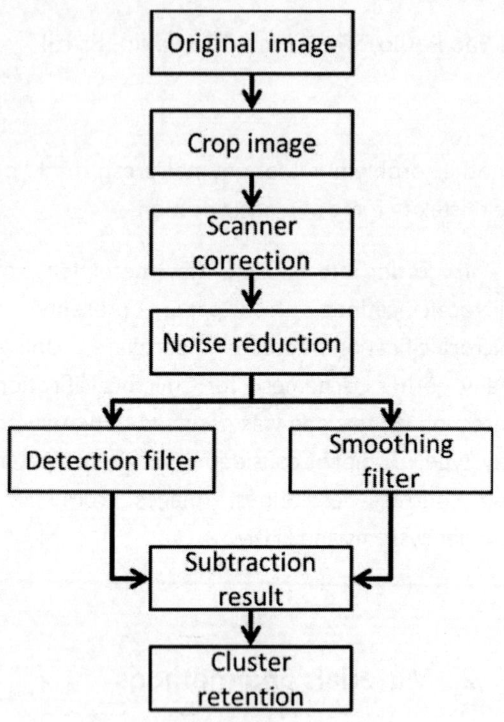

Figure 1: System flowchart

Also a noise reduction algorithm using an Ascomb transform (11) is applied in order to remove the noise with minimal effect on the signal. The resulting image has fewer artifacts that can be confused with a microcalcification, without affecting the overall system sensitivity.

As shown in Figure 1, the preprocessed image is copied and each copy is separately processed by two different filters. One is a detection filter and the other a smoothing filter, as described below.

A detection technique based on a filter derived from Chan et al (1) and modified by

This value was empirically selected in order to match the previous detection process (9) developed for images with 150µm.

Schiabel et al (2) starts with a convolution with a high pass filter used to enhance the calcifications. In this current technique, such a filter is changed to a function that can be scaled smoothly for different images sizes (Figure 2). This function is a Laplacian of a Gaussian function, also known as a Mexican hat function (1). It was chosen because of the visual similarities with the original filters when scaled down and the similarities with the microcalcifications being detected. The resulting filter is always used as a 35 by 35 square filter. The resulting image will be referred here as an enhanced image.

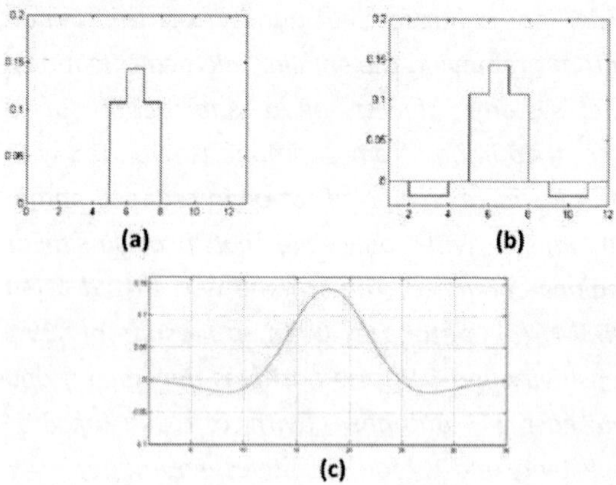

Figure 2: 2D cut of the center of the detection filter, (a) Chan (1), (b) Schiabel (2) and (c) New version

$$F(x,y) = \frac{2}{\left(\sqrt{3\sigma}\pi^{1/4}\right)\left(1-\frac{(x^2+y^2)}{\sigma^2}\right)e^{-\frac{(x^2+y^2)}{2\sigma^2}}} \quad (1)$$

Where σ is calculated based on image resolution (*R*) in microns, as shown in (2):

$$\sigma = \frac{240}{R} \quad (2)$$

Simultaneously the preprocessed image is smoothed using an average filter of size *S* also based on the image spatial resolution, as shown in (3). The result will be referred here as a smoothed image.

$$S = \frac{450}{R} \quad (3)$$

The final size value is forced to always be an odd integer; thus, the result is rounded and, if even, 1 is added. The size was chosen so that to remove the microcalcifications and to leave only the background tissue of the breast.

The smoothed image is, then, subtracted from the enhanced image, removing the background and leaving only the enhanced signal and some noise. The strongest remaining signal is, for the most part, the microcalcification. The scheme raises a histogram from the result and selects a percentage of the brightest points (meaning the most probable calcifications) as valid detections. This percentage defines the sensitivity of the scheme and a FROC curve was constructed to evaluate the best cost-benefit for this percentage. This percentage will be referred here as the *topmost* percentage. In tests with a set of 60 images the best result found was of a percentage of 0.08% (as shown in the results section). The positive results are marked as white in a binary image.

In order to eliminate false positives signals and random calcifications, since the focus is the cluster of microcalcifications, the algorithm removes isolated detections. The following steps are considered with this aim.

Firstly an area-point transformation (12) is used to turn all detected signals into points. Next a square of size T pixels ((4) is swept through the image. If there are 3 or more points inside the square a cluster is marked, otherwise the points in that region are ignored. The size of T was derived from tests by Schiabel et al (2). Remaining points represent clusters that are marked as positive results.

$$T = \frac{5000}{R} \quad (4)$$

Images used in our tests were acquired from 2 sources. The first set were 130 images from the DDSM Database (3), all scanned from mammographic films by using a Lumisys 200 digitizer (50µm of spatial resolution and 12-bits of contrast resolution). The second set was composed by 18 images from INBreast database (4), containing images from a MammoNovation Siemens FFDM (70µm of spatial resolution and 14-bits of contrast resolution).

3. Results

In order to evaluate the best topmost percentage to be used a FROC curve was determined using 60 images and a range from 0.03% to 0.15%, in 0.01% intervals. All images used for this test were from a Lumisys 200 laser scanner with a 50µm of spatial resolution from

the DDSM database (3). The result can be seen in

Figure .

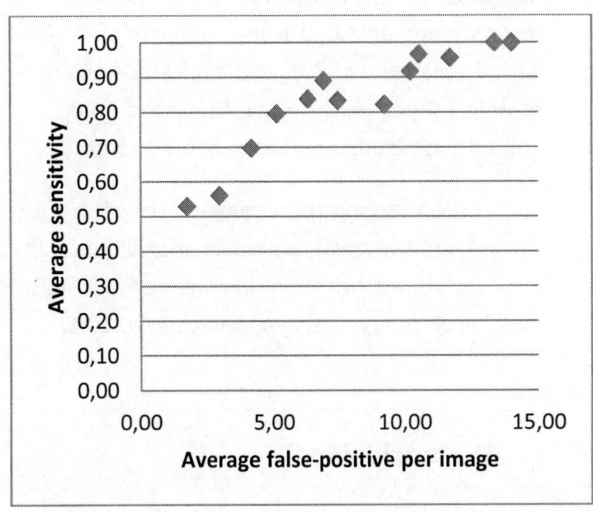

Figure 3: Evaluation of the system using FROC curve with DDSM database images

As shown in Fig. 3 the best cost–benefit value was found at 89% of sensitivity with 6.9 false-positives detections per image. This translates to a topmost percentage of 0.08% for detection after subtraction.

It is important to notice that the evaluation considered only the demarcation by the DDSM database for reference in order to check the accuracy in results. The DDSM database is known to have some problems in relation to its demarcations (4), especially considering the size and format of a region containing a cluster of microcalcifications.

One frequent problem for our scheme is the fact that several images from DDSM database show a lead sphere used to mark skin moles or scars for the visual exams. These spheres are placed by the technician against the skin of the patient before image acquisition to be used as reference for the radiologist. All these spheres have such a strong contrast that there is usually considered as a positive detection. Although radiologists ignore such marks, these points were considered here as false-positive cases in order to evaluate with the best possible accuracy the current proposed scheme.

When using the 18 images from INBreast database (4) with marked clusters, the best results were obtained using topmost of 0.10%, with a sensitivity of 89% and a false-positive rate of only 1.4 per image. Since the set of images is limited this results could have been skewed.

Considering the complete set of images (DDSM and INBreast), a global sensitivity of 92% was registered with an average of 6.9 false positive per image, using a topmost of 0.10%.

4. Conclusion

The results show that the system is capable of detecting clustered microcalcifications in film-scanner settings with a sensitivity of 89%, considering an average of 6.9 false positive detections per image.

When the system was used in FFDM images from INBreast database the results were remarkably better with 89% of sensitivity and only 1.4 false-positive per image. This is associated with a better demarcation given by the database images, including isolated microcalcifications, and also better images quality. Unfortunately the INBreast database has few images determined with clustered microcalcifications (only 18 images) and lacking access to bigger databases with FFDM images limits to test with this type of mammography image as well as a more significant statistical evaluation.

Considering the complete set of images (both DDSM and INBreast) the sensitivity result is 92% and 6.9 false positive per image. The sensitivity value is comparable with ImageChecker (8), a commercial system with a sensitivity of 91% according to its manual.

The number of false-positives per image, on the other hand, is very large. ImageChecker has only 1.5 false-positives per image according to its manual.

In the presented scheme, most of these false-positives are caused by noise and natural breast structures that the system detects as calcifications. The difference in results shown by the set of images from DDSM and INBreast seems to represent that the improved image quality from a FFDM system seems to improve significantly our scheme performance, which is a promising result in this field.

It is important to point out that while the ImageChecker software was designed to work with a specific system developed together, our system was designed to work with any image acquisition hardware with little or even no changes in the system. Also, when using images with less noise (like FFDM images), it has shown results comparable to the best ones.

Acknowledgments

To FAPESP for the financial support of this project and to Breast Research Group, INESC Porto, Portugal for the INBreast database images.

References

1. Chan HP, Doi K, Vyborny CJ, Schimidt RA, Metz CE, Lam KL, et al. Improvement in radiologists' detection of clustered microcalcifications on mammograms: the potential of computer-aided diagnosis. Investigative Radiology. 1990; 10(25): p. 1102-1110.

2. SCHIABEL H, NUNES F, AZEVEDO-MARQUES P, FRERE A. A computerized scheme for detection of clusters of microcalcifications by mammograms image processing. Medical Biological Engineering Computing. 1998; 35(2): p. 705.

3. Rose C, Turi D, Williams A, Wolstencroft K, Taylor C. Web services for the DDSM and digital mammography research. [Online].; 2003 [cited 2010. Available from: http://marathon.csee.usf.edu/~ddsm/search.html.

4. IC M, I A, I D, A C, MJ C, JS. C. INbreast: toward a full-field digital mammographic database. Academic radiology. 2012 Feb; 19(2): p. 236-48.

5. JM J, RR D, J L, R T. Image guided or needle localized open biopsy of. Journal of the American College of Surgeons. 1998 December; 6(187): p. 604-9.

6. American College of Radiology. American College of Radiology (ACR) Breast Imaging Reporting and Data System Atlas (BI-RADS® Atlas). ; 2003.

7. Imamura K, Ehara N, Inada Y, Kanemaki Y, Okamoto J, Maeda I, et al. Microcalcifications of Breast Tissue: Appearance on Synchrotron Radiation Imaging with 6-μm Resolution. American Journal of Roentgenology. 2008 April; 190(4).

8. HOLOGIC. ImageChecker Analog CAD. [Online].; 2012 [cited 2013 Mar 18. Available from: http://www.hologic.com/en/breast-screening/imagechecker/screen-film-cad-systems/.

9. SCHIABEL H, MENECHELLI RC. Automated characterization of secondary signals of breast cancer to compose a module from a CADx scheme. In 27th International Congress on Computer Assisted Radiology and Surgery (CARS2013); 2013; Germany.

10. Góes RdF, Sousa MAZ, Schiabel H. Automatic scanning software based on the characteristic curve of mammogram digitizers. Journal of Electronic Imaging. 2013 Jan - Mar; 1(22): p. 013024.

11. Romualdo LCS, Vieira MAC, Schiabel H, Mascarenhas NDA, Borges LR. Mammographic Image Denoising and Enhancement Using the Anscombe Transformation, Adaptive Wiener Filtering, and the Modulation Transfer Function. Journal of Digital Imaging. 2013 April; 26(2): p. 183-197.

12. NISHIKAWA RMea. Computer-Aided detection of clustered microcalcifications. In Proceeding of IEEE International Conference on Systems, Man and Cybernetics; 1992; Chicago: IEEE. p. 1375-1378.

Edge Based Shape Feature For Image Retrieval with Multiresolution Enhanced Orthogonal Polynomials Model

R.Krishnamoorthy[1], **S. Sathiya Devi**[1]
[1]Department of Computer Science and Engg., Bharathidasan Institute of Technology, Trichirappalli, Tamilnadu, India

Abstract - *In this paper, a new and simple edge based shape feature vector representation with multi resolution enhanced orthogonal polynomials model is proposed. In the proposed method, initially the orthogonal polynomials model coefficients are computed and reordered into multiresolution subband like structure. The edge map is extracted based on gradient and orientation of pixel values with the subband of the orthogonal polynomials model. Then the edge based shape feature such as autocorrelogram is computed utilizing the orientation and correlation between neighboring edges. The efficiency of the proposed feature vector extraction for image retrieval is experimented on the standard Corel Database images with the Canberra distance measure. The experimental result shows that the proposed edge based shape feature yields better retrieval rate compared with existing methods.*

Keywords: Orthogonal Polynomials, Edge, Edge oriented autocorrelogram, Shape, Image Retrieval, Multiresolution.

1 Introduction

With the advent of digital multimedia library, several applications such as entertainment, medicine, art and industry have effectively used this information. But searching, browsing and retrieving from this huge repository are difficult and require intelligent tools. Hence Content Based Image Retrieval (CBIR) addressed this problem by utilizing both the low level viz color, texture, edge and shape feature and high level content of the image. In CBIR, some types of similarity between images are computed using these image features extracted from them. Thus, users can search for images similar to query images quickly and effectively. Many image retrieval systems have been developed using all or some combination of these features such as color and shape, texture, color and shape etc. It includes Chabot [1], Photobook [2], QBIC [3], Virage [4], VisualSeek [5], MARS [6], Netra [7] and Excalibur [8]. The extensive literature and the state of art methods about content based image retrieval can be found in [9 - 14]. Among different visual characteristics such as texture, color and shape for the analysis of different types of images, search and retrieve the images by shape matching a portion of images is natural and efficient method. The shape based image retrieval is divided into (i) Segmentation based (ii) non-segmentation based methods. The segmentation based methods [15-17] detect the homogeneous regions of images and then compute the features with some region information like surface, contours and corners etc. The non-segmentation based methods extract shape features of an image and generate features without image segmentation [18-19] and the bases for these methods are edge. In this paper we introduce a new non-segmentation based shape feature extraction based on edge with orthogonal polynomials model.

This paper is organized as follows. In Section 2, detailed description on the orthogonal polynomials model is presented. The proposed edge based shape feature extraction with orthogonal polynomials coefficients is described in section 3. Section 4 discusses the performance evolution metric of the CBIR system. In section 5, we present the experiments and the results. Finally conclusion is presented in Section 6.

2 Orthogonal Polynomials Model

In this section we describe the proposed orthogonal polynomials model for analyzing the content of the image. The orthogonal polynomials that have already been well established for image coding [20 - 21], have been extended in this proposed CBIR system.

In order to analyze the content of an image for efficient proposal of CBIR system, a linear 2-D image formation system is considered around a Cartesian coordinate separable, blurring, point spread operator in which the image I results in the superposition of the point source of impulse weighted by the value of the object function f. Expressing the object function f in terms of derivatives of the image function I relative to its Cartesian coordinates is very useful for analyzing the low level features of the image. The point spread function M(x, y) can be considered to be real valued function defined for $(x, y) \in X \times Y$, where X and Y are ordered subsets of real values. In case of gray-level image of size (n X n) where X (rows) consists of a finite set, which for convenience can be labeled as {0, 1, …, n-1}, the function M(x, y) reduces to a sequence of functions.

$$M(i, t) = u_i(t), \quad i, t = 0, 1, \ldots, n-1 \qquad (1)$$

The linear two dimensional transformation can be defined by the point spread operator M(x, y)(M(i, t) = $u_i(t)$), as:

$$\beta'(\zeta,\eta) = \int_{x\in X}\int_{y\in Y} M(\zeta,x)\,M(\eta,y)\,I(x,y)\,dxdy \qquad (2)$$

Considering both X and Y to be a finite set of values {0, 1, 2, ... n −1}, equation (2) can be written in matrix notation as follows.

$$|\beta'_{ij}| = (|M|\otimes|M|)^t\,|I| \qquad (3)$$

where ⊗ is the outer product, $|\beta'_{ij}|$ are n^2 matrices arranged in the dictionary sequence, $|I|$ is the image , $|\beta'_{ij}|$ are the coefficients of transformation and the point spread operator |M| is

$$|M| = \begin{vmatrix} u_0(t_1) & u_1(t_1) & \cdots & u_{n-1}(t_1) \\ u_0(t_2) & u_1(t_2) & \cdots & u_{n-1}(t_2) \\ & & \vdots & \\ u_0(t_n) & u_1(t_n) & \cdots & u_{n-1}(t_n) \end{vmatrix} \qquad (4)$$

We consider the set of orthogonal polynomials $u_0(t)$, $u_1(t)$, …, $u_{n-1}(t)$ of degrees 0, 1, 2, …, n-1, respectively to construct the polynomial operators of different sizes from equation (4) for n ≥ 2 and t_i = i. The generating formula for the polynomials is as follows.

$u_{i+1}(t) = (t-\mu)u_i(t) - b_i(n)u_{i-1}(t)$ for $i \geq 1$, (5)

$u_1(t) = t-\mu$, and $u_0(t) = 1$,

where $b_i(n) = \dfrac{\langle u_i, u_i\rangle}{\langle u_{i-1}, u_{i-1}\rangle} = \dfrac{\sum_{t=1}^{n} u_i^2(t)}{\sum_{t=1}^{n} u_{i-1}^2(t)}$

and $\mu = \dfrac{1}{n}\sum_{t=1}^{n} t$

Considering the range of values of t to be $t_i = i$, $i = 1, 2, 3, \ldots n$, we get

$$b_i(n) = \frac{i^2(n^2-i^2)}{4(4i^2-1)}, \quad \mu = \frac{1}{n}\sum_{t=1}^{n} t = \frac{n+1}{2}$$

2.1. The Orthogonal Polynomial Basis

For the sake of computational simplicity, the finite Cartesian coordinate set X, Y is labeled as {1,2,3}. The point spread operator in equation (3) that defines the linear orthogonal transformation for image analysis can be obtained as $|M|\otimes|M|$, where $|M|$ can be computed and scaled from equation (4) as follows.

$$|M| = \begin{vmatrix} u_0(x_0) & u_1(x_0) & u_2(x_0) \\ u_0(x_1) & u_1(x_1) & u_2(x_1) \\ u_0(x_2) & u_1(x_2) & u_2(x_2) \end{vmatrix} = \begin{vmatrix} 1 & -1 & 1 \\ 1 & 0 & -2 \\ 1 & 1 & 1 \end{vmatrix} \qquad (6)$$

The set of polynomial operators O_{ij}^{n} (0 ≤ i, j ≤ n-1) can be computed as

$$O_{ij}^{n} = \hat{u}_i \otimes \hat{u}_j^{t}$$

where $\hat{u}_i$ is the (i + 1) st column vector of |M|.

For example, Polynomial basis operators of size (3 X 3) are

$$[O_{00}^3] = \begin{bmatrix} 1 & 1 & 1 \\ 1 & 1 & 1 \\ 1 & 1 & 1 \end{bmatrix}, [O_{01}^3] = \begin{bmatrix} -1 & 0 & 1 \\ -1 & 0 & 1 \\ -1 & 0 & 1 \end{bmatrix}, [O_{02}^3] = \begin{bmatrix} 1 & -2 & 1 \\ 1 & -2 & 1 \\ 1 & -2 & 1 \end{bmatrix}$$

$$[O_{10}^3] = \begin{bmatrix} -1 & -1 & -1 \\ 0 & 0 & 0 \\ 1 & 1 & 1 \end{bmatrix}, [O_{11}^3] = \begin{bmatrix} 1 & 0 & -1 \\ 0 & 0 & 0 \\ -1 & 0 & 1 \end{bmatrix}, [O_{12}^3] = \begin{bmatrix} -1 & 2 & -1 \\ 0 & 0 & 0 \\ 1 & -2 & 1 \end{bmatrix}$$

$$[O_{20}^3] = \begin{bmatrix} 1 & 1 & 1 \\ -2 & -2 & -2 \\ 1 & 1 & 1 \end{bmatrix}, [O_{21}^3] = \begin{bmatrix} -1 & 0 & 1 \\ 2 & 0 & -2 \\ -1 & 0 & 1 \end{bmatrix}, [O_{22}^3] = \begin{bmatrix} 1 & -2 & 1 \\ -2 & 4 & -2 \\ 1 & -2 & 1 \end{bmatrix}$$

It can be shown that a set of (n x n) (n ≥ 2) polynomial operators forms a basis, i.e. it is complete and linearly independent.

The following symmetric finite differences for estimating partial derivatives at (x, y) position of the gray level image I are analogous to the eight finite difference operators O_{ij} s excluding O_{00}

$$\frac{\partial I}{\partial y}\Big|_{x,y} = \sum_{i=-1}^{1}[I(x-i,y+1) - I(x-i,y-1)]$$

$$\frac{\partial I}{\partial x}\Big|_{x,y} = \sum_{i=-1}^{1}[I(x+1,y-i) - I(x-1,y-i)]$$

$$\frac{\partial^2 I}{\partial y^2}\Big|_{x,y} = \sum_{i=-1}^{1}[I(x-i,y-1) - 2I(x-i,y) + I(x-i,y+1)]$$

$$\frac{\partial^2 I}{\partial x^2}\Big|_{x,y} = \sum_{i=-1}^{1}[I(x-1,y-i)-2I(x,y-i)+I(x+1,y-i)]$$
(7)

and so on. We present the feature extraction process based on the transformed coefficients β' in the next section.

2.2 Multiresolution Reordering

Since subband representation of signals is of high use for low level image analysis, compactness and fast computation, we present a multiresolution representation of the orthogonal polynomials model coefficients in this subsection.

The orthogonal polynomials model coefficients β'_{ij} obtained from the previous sub section are reordered to provide image subbands in a multiresolution decomposition like structure. In this work, the model coefficients β'_{ij} are reordered into ($3\log_2 N+1$) multi resolution subbands for each *(N X N)* block. The following assumptions are made to reorder the proposed orthogonal polynomials based transformed coefficients β'_{ij} into the proposed multi resolution form. Let $2^{a-1} \le i < 2^a$ and $2^{b-1} \le j < 2^b$ where a and b are integers and i, $j \in$ *(N X N)* block. Let the model coefficient β'_{ij} be stored into a particular subband S_y, with y computed as

$$y = \begin{cases} 0 & \text{for } m = 0 \\ (m-1) + 2(a/m) + (b/m) & \text{otherwise} \end{cases} \quad (8)$$

where $m = \max(a, b)$. If the coefficient β'_{ij} from the block $B(z, w)$ belongs to S_y, the reordered location for β'_{ij} is then determined by the function presented in equation (9).

$$R = (2^{m-1}z + i - 2^{a-1}, 2^{m-1}w + j - 2^{b-1}) \quad (9)$$

Based on the equation (9) the orthogonal polynomials model coefficients are tuned to decompose into any level. These reordered coefficients possess the localization of both spatial and frequency characteristics of the image as in the case of wavelets. For illustration purpose, the one level decomposition of orthogonal polynomials model coefficients is presented in figure 2. In figure 2 an image of size (8 X 8) is considered and is divided into (2 X 2) sub blocks. The orthogonal polynomials model is applied to each sub block. The transformed coefficients β'_{00}, β'_{01}, β'_{10}, and β'_{11} are diagrammatically represented as @, x, 0 and + respectively as shown in figure 1(a). These coefficients are rearranged into four subbands namely S_1, S_2, S_3 and S_4 as shown in figure 2(b). Since the low frequency coefficient β'_{00} exhibits high energy compaction, these coefficients of all blocks are modeled into S_1 subband which posses the approximate image. The remaining high frequency coefficients β'_{01}, β'_{10}, and β'_{11} contain horizontal, vertical and diagonal information and these coefficients from all the blocks are modeled as S_2, S_3 and S_4 subbands as they hold detail information of the image. The use of this multiresolution decomposition of orthogonal polynomials coefficients is highlighted for extraction of edge information and the same is presented in the next section.

3 Proposed Edge Based Shape Feature Vector Extraction

In this section, we present the proposed shape feature extraction process based on orientation and gradient of edge points with orthogonal polynomials model coefficients β'. Since the low level features are best examined in micro level, the image under analysis is divided into blocks of size *(n X n)* where n is a power of 2 and $n \le M, N$ where M and N are the size of the image.

3.1 Edge based shape feature extraction

The shape features are extracted based on Edges. The Edge is a significant local changes in the image and are important feature for shape modeling. The proposed algorithm consists of three stages. (i) Edge point detection (or) Gradient and Orientation Computation (ii) Distance Set and (iii) Edge oriented auto correlogram construction.

3.1.1 Edge point detection (or) Gradient and Orientation Computation

It was shown in the section 2.1 that the β'_{ij} values are approximating the partial derivatives of various order of the image region. For example, O_{01} and O_{10} denotes first order differencing operation in y direction $(\frac{\partial}{\partial y})$ and x direction $(\frac{\partial}{\partial x})$ respectively. Then the gradient magnitude G and the edge orientation G_o can be calculated by considering the first order differences β'_{01} and β'_{10} as follows:

$$G = |\beta'_{01}| + |\beta'_{10}| \quad (10)$$

$$G_o = \tan^{-1}\frac{\beta'_{10}}{\beta'_{01}} \quad (11)$$

The polynomial operator, O_{01} and O_{10} are modeled to be gradient edge detectors because of their large value in regions having prominent edges and small values on nearly uniform edges. In order to obtain the edge points, the edge orientation is classified into four types. (i) horizontal (0^0 or 180^0), Vertical (90^0 or 270^0), Positive diagonal (45^0 or 225^0) and Negative Diagonal (135^0 or 315^0). Let the current pixel be (i, j) in the *(3 X 3)* neighborhood and its gradient value is *G (i, j)*. The following condition is satisfied if (i, j) be an edge.

(i) *G (i, j) > G (i-1, j) and G (i, j)> G (i+1, j)* when G_o = *'horizontal'*

(ii) *G (i, j) > G (i, j-1) and G (i, j)> G (i, j+1)* when G_o = *'vertical'*

(iii) *G (i, j) > G (i-1, j+1) and G (i, j)> G (i+1, j-1)* when G_o = *'positive diagonal'*

(iv) *G (i, j) > G (i-1, j-1) and G (i, j)> G (i+1, j+1)* when G_o = *'negative diagonal'*.

The real edges are then extracted by comparing with the given threshold value T and the orientation angle is also divided into *m* segments $G_1, G_2, \ldots, G_m$. Each segment is equal to 90^0.

3.2 Edge oriented auto correlogram construction

This step constructs the correlogram which is the correlation between edge orientation angle, edge point and distance set. The distance set D shows the distances from the current edge that is used in calculating correlation. In our algorithm we have chosen D = {1, 2} and *d* = 1. The edge oriented auto correlogram is a two dimensional array, consisting of *m* rows and *d* columns. The (*j, k*) element of this matrix ($1 \leq j \leq m$, k ε *D*) indicates the numbers of similar edges with orientation G_j, which are *k* pixel distance apart and is defined as

$$C_{u,v} = Pr\,(G(p_1) = u \wedge G(p_2) = v \,/\, |p1 - p2| = d) \qquad (12)$$

where (*u, v*) ε {*m*}, *d* ε {n}, p_1, p_2 are positions in *I*, and G_p is the orientation angle at position *p*. Then this matrix is used as feature vector for shape based image retrieval.

4 Similarity and Performance Measure

Having extracted the fusion texture features in the previous section, in this section our aim is to retrieve the relevant images from the database against the query image using the similarity measure since it is a key component of the content based image retrieval system. In the proposed retrieval scheme, the similarity between the query image and the images present in the database are calculated using the well known Canberra distance metric as shown in equation (12), as the same is reported to be the best among different distance metric [22].

$$d_C(x,y) = \sum_{i=1}^{d} \frac{|x_i - y_i|}{|x_i| + |y_i|} \qquad (13)$$

where x_i is a feature vector of query image Q, y_i is the feature vector of image I in the database and d is the size of the feature vector. In the above equation, the numerator signifies the difference and the denominator normalizes the difference. Thus the distance value will never exceed one whenever either of the feature components is zero and also reduces the scaling effect. The performance of the proposed method is measured in terms Average Retrieval Ratio (ARR) which is defined as follows.

$$ARR = \frac{1}{N} \sum_{i=1}^{N} \frac{m_i}{N} \qquad (14)$$

where *N* is the total number of similar images in one category and m_i is the number of retrieved relevant images.

The performance is also measured with popular measures viz precision and recall rate. Recall rate is the ratio of number of relevant images retrieved and the total number of relevant images in the collection and is represented as

$$Recall = \frac{\text{Number of retrieved relevant images}}{\text{Total number of relevant images in the collection}} \qquad (15)$$

The *precision rate* is the ratio of the number of relevant images retrieved and total number of images in the collection:

$$\text{Precision} = \frac{\text{Number of retrieved relevant images}}{\text{Total number of images in the collection}} \qquad (16)$$

5 Experiments and Results

The retrieval efficiency of the proposed edge based shape feature extraction with orthogonal polynomials model is experimented with the popular Corel [23] image database and the experimental results are presented in this section. We have considered five categories of images: Flowers, Dinosaurs, Buses, Elephants and Building and each class contain 40 images. The original images in each category are of color images and are converted into gray scale, each of size (128 X 128) with the pixel values in the range 0 -255. Some of the sample images are shown in the figure 1.

Figure 2. Sample Images from Corel Database

During experimentation, the image under analysis is divided into (2 x 2) non overlapping blocks and each block is subjected to the orthogonal polynomials model as described in section 2. The transformed coefficients are reordered into multi resolution like structure as described in section 2.3, for all the blocks in the image. The image is then decomposed into one level subband like structure and each subband is termed as S_1, S_2, S_3 and S_4. The S_2 and S_3 subband coefficients are used to compute gradient magnitude *G* as they posses the first order derivatives in horizontal and vertical directions. Then edge based shape feature is extracted in two steps. In the first step the edge gradient and orientation is computed based on the transformed coefficients β'_{01} and β'_{10} from each block in an overlapping manner with the equations (9) and (10) respectively. Then edge map is extracted based on the orientation direction and an appropriate threshold T. Then the 2 dimensional edge oriented auto corrologram matrix is constructed as described in section 3.1.2. The edge oriented auto correlogram matrix is termed as a feature vector for shape based image retrieval. Thus the two dimensional feature vector is indexed in the feature database.

A query image is then considered from any one category of database images and the feature extraction process is carried out as in the case of database images. Then the similarity measure is computed using the Canberra distance metric as presented in equation (13) for each pair of database and query images. The distances are then sorted in ascending order and the top 10 images are retrieved. For a sample query image shown in figure 3(a), the top 10 retrieval results by the proposed method are shown in Figure 3(b).

Figure 3. (a) Query image
(b) Retrieval of top 10 images with the proposed scheme corresponding to the query image (a).

It is apparent from figure 3 (b) that the proposed method retrieves perceptually similar images. We also measure the performance of the proposed method with Average Retrieval Ratio (ARR) as described in section 4. For this every image in the five image categories are considered as query image and the average recognition ratio is obtained. The obtained results are plotted as graph with the number of image categories in X axis and the percentage of retrieval in Y axis and the same is presented in figure 4. We can conclude from figure 4 that the proposed edge based shape feature extraction method can well represent the whole image and have more power to characterize the image. The average recognition rate of the proposed method is 82.54%. In order to evaluate the performance of the proposed method, it is compared with Haar based method and the result are also incorporated in the same figure 4. From the figure, it is inferred that, for some classes of images Haar based method also performs well with the proposed method.

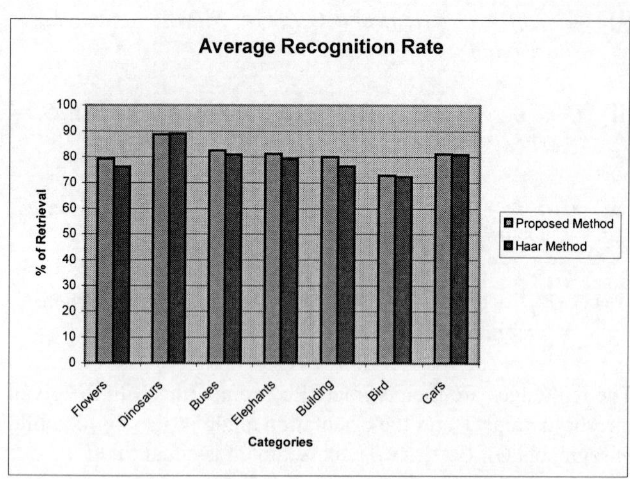

Figure 4. The average retrieval ratio of five image categories

Similarly, for the standard subset of Corel database, the well known measure called as average precision and recall is to be computed for the seven classes of images for the proposed and Haar based method. The obtained results are tabulated in the table 1. From the table it is inferred that the proposed method performs well than the Haar based method.

Table 1. Average Precision and recall rate of proposed and Harr based methods

	Average Recall	Average Precision
Proposed Method	0.80	0.64
Haar based Method	0.78	0.65

6 Conclusion

A new simple edge based shape feature with orthogonal polynomials model for image retrieval is presented in this paper. The orthogonal polynomials coefficients are reordered into multiresolution subband like structure and the edge map with orientation is directly extracted from the subband coefficients. Then the two dimensional edge oriented autocorrelogram feature is constructed from them. The proposed scheme is experimented with five categories of images. The proposed scheme yields better retrieval result than Haar based method.

References

[1] V.E. Ogle and M. Stonebraker, "Chabot: Retrieval from a Relational Database of Images", IEEE Computer, Vol. 28, no. 9, pp. 40 - 48, 1995.

[2] A. Pentland, R.W Picard and S. Sclaroff, "Photobook : Content Based Manipulation of Image Databases", International Journal of Computer Vision, Vol. 18, no.3, pp.233 - 254, 1996.

[3] M. Flickner. H. Sawhney, W. Niblack, J. Ashley, Q. Huang, B. Dom. M. Gorkani, J. Hafner, D. Lee, D. Petkovic, D. Steele, and P. Yanker, "Query by Image and Video Content: the QBIC System", IEEE Computer, Vol. 28, no. 9, pp. 23 - 32, 1995.

[4] J.R. Batch, C. Fuller, A. Gupta, A. Hampapur, B. Horowitz, B. Horowitz, R. Humphery, R. Jain and C.F. Shu, "The Virage Image Search Engine: An Open Framework for Image Management", In proc. SPIE Storage and Retrieval for Image and Video Databases IV, Vol. 2670, pp. 76 - 87, 1996.

[5] J.R Smith and S.F. Chang, "Querying by Color Region using the VisualSEEK Content Based Visual Query System", Intelligent Multimedia Information Retrieval, AAAI press, pp. 23 - 41, 1997.

[6] T.S. Huang, S. Mehrotra and K. Ramachandran, "Multimedia Analysis and Retrieval System (MARS) Project", In Proc of 33rd Annual Clinic on Library Application of Data Processing – Digital Image Access and Retrieval, 1996.

[7] W.Y Ma and B.S Manjunath, "Netra: A Toolbox for Navigating Large Image Databases", In Proc of IEEE International Conference on Image Processing (ICIP97), Vol. 1, pp. 568 - 571, 1997.

[8] J. Feder, "Towards Image Content-Based Retrieval for World-Wide-Web", Journal of Advanced Imaging, Vol. 11, no. 1, pp. 26 - 29, 1997.

[9] R. Datta, J. Li and J.Z. Wang, "Content Based Image Retrieval – Approaches and Trends of the New Age", Proceedings of the 7th ACM SIGMM International Workshop on Multimedia Information Retrieval MIR '05, ACM Press, pp. 253 - 262, 2005.

[10] Y. Rui, T.S. Huang, and S. F. Chang, "Image Retrieval: Current Techniques, Promising Directions and Open Issues", Journal of Visual Communication and Image Representation, Vol. 10, no. 4, pp. 39 - 62, 1999.

[11] A. Smeulders, M. Worring, S. Santini and A. Gupta, R. Jain, "Content Based Image Retrieval at the End of the Early Years", IEEE Transactions on Pattern Analysis and Machine Intelligence, Vol. 22, no. 12, pp.1349 - 1380, 2000.

[12] M. L. Kherfi , D. Ziou and A. Bernardi, "Image Retrieval From the World Wide Web: Issues, Techniques and Systems", ACM Computing Surveys, Vol. 36, no. 1, pp. 35 - 67, 2004.

[13] M. S. Lew, N. Sebe, C. Djeraba and R. Jain, "Content-Based Multimedia Information Retrieval: State of the Art and Challenges", ACM Transactions on Multimedia Computing, Communications and Applications, Vol. 2, no.1, pp.1-19, 2006.

[14] M. Kokare, B.N. Chatterji and P.K. Biswas, "A Survey on Current Content Based Image Retrieval Methods", IETE Journal of Research, Vol. 48, no.3&4, pp.261 - 271, 2002.

[15] S. Derretti, A. Del Bimbo and P. Pala, "Retrieval by Shape Similarity with Perceptual Distance and Effective Indexing", IEEE Transactions on Multimedia, Vol.2, no. 4, pp. 225 – 239, 2000.

[16] S. Abbasi and F. Mokhtarian, "Multi-View Object Representaion and Recognition through Curvature Scale Space", Proceedings of the Fifth Annual CSI International Conference, pp. 467 – 476, 2000.

[17] S. Abbasi, F. Mokhtarian and J. Kittler, "Curvature Scale Space in Shape Similarity Retrieval", Multimedia Systems, Vol. 7, no.6, pp.467 – 476, 1999.

[18] F. Mahmoudi, J. Shanbehzadeh and A.M. Eftekhari-Moghadam, "A Shape based Method for Content Based Image Retrieval", Proceedings of the Fifth Annual CSI International Conference, pp. 11 - 16, 2000.

[19] J. Shanbehzadeh, F. Mahmoudi, A. Sarafzadeh, A.M. Eftekhari-Moghadam and Z. Asarzadeh, " Image Indexing using Edge orientation Correlogram", Proceddings of the SPIE : Internet Imaging, Vol. 3964, pp. 102 – 108, 2000.

[20] R. Krishnamoorthi and P. Bhattacharyya, "A New Data Compression Scheme Using Orthogonal Polynomials", International Conference on Information, Communications and Signal Processing ICICS '97, Vol. 1, pp. 490 - 494, 1997.

[21] R. Krishnamoorthi, "Transform Coding of Monochrome Image with Statistical Design of Experiments Approach to Separate Noise", Pattern Recognition Letters, Vol. 28, No.7, pp. 771 - 777, 2007.

[22] M. Kokare, B.N. Chatterji and P.K. Biswas, "Comparison of Similarity Metrics for Texture Image Retrieval", IEEE proceedings on TENCON 2003, Conference on Convergent Technologies for Asia-Pacific Region, Vol. 2, pp. 571 - 575, 2003.

[23] WWW.COREL.COM

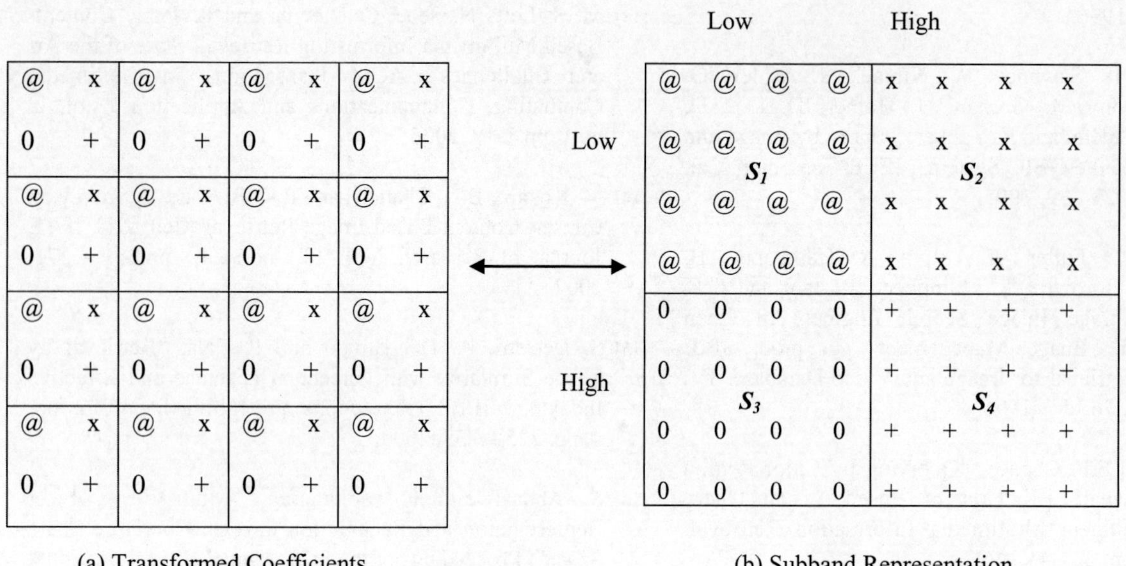

(a) Transformed Coefficients

(b) Subband Representation

Figure 1. Proposed one level decomposition of the orthogonal polynomials transformed coefficients

A SCALABLE INDEXING METHOD FOR SIFT FEATURES

[1]Wei-Chih Hung, [1, †] Yi-Leh Wu, [1]Tsung-Da Ho, [1]Kuan-Yuo Lin, and [2]Cheng-Yuan Tang
[1]Department of Computer Science and Information Engineering
National Taiwan University of Science and Technology, Taipei, Taiwan
[2]Department of Information Management, Huafan University, Taiwan
[†] E-mail: ywu@csie.ntust.edu.tw

ABSTRACT

This paper presents a method for the image recognition in a large database. The local invariant features and two-tier hashing are used so that the time complexity of image matching is not affected by the size of the image database. We propose a method to simplify the PCA-SIFT descriptor via binarization. The binarized PCA-SIFT keypoint descriptors still keep very high distinctiveness for the image matching process. Furthermore, the binarized PCA-SIFT keypoint descriptors can be indexed by two-tier hashing method very efficiently. Moreover, to reduce the time complexity of matching keypoint descriptors, minimal perfect hashing is applied to build a number of external hash tables. Through computation we can determine which external hash table is hit by the distinct keypoint descriptor without searching. The experiment result suggests that the proposed method can effectively keep the time complexity to O(1) irrespective to the number of images in the matching applications.

Keywords PCA-SIFT, Indexing, Minimal perfect hashing, External hash tables, Digital right management

1. INTRODUCTION

The image recognition methods serve as the foundations of applications such as similar image searching and copyrighted images detection. In the past few years a considerable number of studies have been made on the image retrieval problems [5, 6, 7]. The image retrieval methods consist of several technologies from different research domains such as machine learning, data mining and image process, etc. We limit discussions are constrained here by methods which are able to speed up the searching process in a large scale image database.

The SIFT (Scale-Invariant Feature Transform) is a robust feature extraction method for various 3D and 2D image applications. Lowe first proposed the SIFT algorithm in 2004 [1, 2]. The most important property of SIFT is that the SIFT descriptors are invariant under many image transformations (e.g., rotation, scaling, translation etc.) so that the SIFT algorithm is very effective for image retrieving. We can decide whether the pairs of images are of the same source with only very few pairs of keypoint descriptors matched (usually 3) from two given images. PCA-SIFT [3] was proposed to reduce the dimension of the SIFT descriptors to speed up keypoint descriptors matching. The Principal Components Analysis (PCA) [4] is a typically approach to reduce dimension. The PCA-SIFT algorithm reduces the 128-dimension SIFT descriptors to 36-dimension by using the Principal Components Analysis (PCA).

However the SIFT algorithm consider only grey level images, the CSIFT [8] proposed to include color invariant features. The color invariant features are discussed in detail in [9]. The number of detected keypoints increases with the number of added color invariant elements. The extra detected keypoints will encumber the performance of the retrieving process.

Regardless of the extraction methods, the keypoint descriptors of images are commonly in high dimension which leads to the problem of the curse of dimensionality. This dimensionality problem occurs when a bulk of keypoint descriptors are distributed over boundary of the feature space and are far away from the center of the feature space. To solve this problem, there are many multi-dimension access methods proposed [10]. But even some well-known multi-dimension indexing methods (e.g., the R-tree [11], the KD-tree [12] etc.) can usually reduce to lower dimension space (less than 10 dimensions). The LSH (Locality Sensitive Hashing) methods, proposed by Indyk and Motwani [13, 14], are the multi-dimension indexing methods. There are several other applications that use the LSH method to solve the k-NN (k Nearest Neighbors) queries [13]. Ke proposed to index the PCA-SIFT descriptors using the LSH to solve the sub-image near-duplicate and parts-based retrieval problem [15]. The general indexing structures using the LSH method can be found in [16]. Gong and Lazebnik proposed to minimize the quantization error using the iterative quantization (ITQ) method and the canonical correlation analysis (CCA) [19].

The general problem to solve is to match an image efficiently in a large image database. But the general indexing methods are not applicable in high-dimensional space. The main contributions are: first, we reduce the necessary number of keypoints in the image database and second, we propose a simple and efficient two-tier hashing structure while maintaining high retrieval accuracy.

In Section 2, we discuss the PCA-SIFT method. We present the proposed DRM system and the two-tier hashing system employed in this work in Section 3. Experimental results using 1 million image dataset are presented in Section 4. Finally, we conclude this work and discuss future research directions in Section 5.

2. PCA-SIFT

The detail of the PCA-SIFT can be found in [3]. The Principal Components Analysis (PCA) [4] is a common technology for reducing dimension. The first three stages of PCA-SIFT and SIFT are identical. To pre-build an eigenspace, the PCA-SIFT method performs the first three stages of SIFT from some images and 21,000 patches. The final stage of the PCA-SIFT method extracts a 41* 41 patch at the given scale of SIFT descriptors to estimate the principal components. The input vector contains 39*39*2 = 3042 elements which are produced by calculating the horizontal and the vertical gradient. The PCA is then applied to the covariance matrix of each vector and extracts the top n eigenvector as the projection matrix of PCA-SIFT. The normalized 3042-element gradient vectors are projected on low dimension space by using the eigenspace. Here we use n = 36 in the experiment to maintain high accuracy. We project the 128-dimensions SIFT descriptors onto the 36-dimensions PCA-SIFT descriptors. In [3], regardless of correctness or speed, it is shown that the PCA-SIFT method outperforms the SIFT method.

3. PROPOSED DRM SYSTEM

We propose a novel method for the Digital Right Management (DRM) to enhance the speed of image matching in a large image database. Fig. 1 shows the architecture of the proposed DRM method.

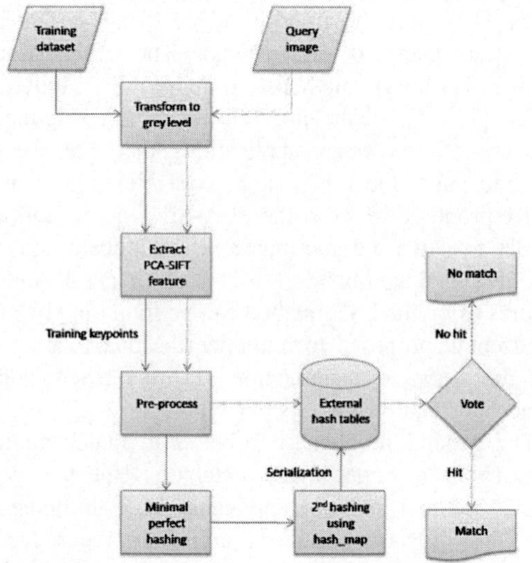

Fig. 1. The architecture of the proposed DRM system.

The proposed DRM method consists of three parts; the first part is the preprocessing, the second part is a two-tier hashing structure, and the final part is the method of matching a input query image.

3.1. Preprocessing Database

The dataset we used throughout this study is an image database with one million images from the Internet. First, all images are converted to the Portable Grey Map (PGM) format and then we extract the SIFT descriptors (128-dimension) from each converted image in the image database. Furthermore, each image is transformed to the PCA-SIFT descriptors (36-dimension). The keypoints are represented as vectors of values in the PCA-SIFT descriptors. To recognize which keypoint belongs to which image, each keypoint is assigned an image ID number. The preprocessing step helps to reduce the size of the keypoint database and to simplify the indexing structure.

3.2. Feature Reduction

Except from the reduction of the dimension of keypoints, it is also important to filter out unnecessary and distorted keypoints. The total number of keypoints extracted from the 1 million image dataset is 216,734,674. Ho [19] proposed methods to reduce the number of necessary keypoints by reserving only the robust keypoints with high geometric variances while keeping high retrieval accuracy, which is shown in Fig. 2. At first each image in the 1 million image dataset is rotated and scaled. There are four geometric transformations used: rotate 90 degrees, rotate 180 degrees, scale 2 times and scale 0.5 times. The keypoints extracted from the transformed images and the ones from the original images are compared. If the same keypoint pairs can be matched (with Euclidean distance less than 3000) from the transformed images and the original images it is considered that these keypoints are very robust against geometric variations. By keeping only the robust keypoints we can effectively reduce the size of the keypoint database. However, sometimes we can extract very few robust keypoints in some images, which makes the matching of those images difficult. Hence we set the constraint that for each image at least F keypoints will be kept in the keypoint database. The value of F is decided as shown in Equation (1). Let $\overline{X}$ is mean value of number of keypoints in training image,

$$\overline{X} = \frac{X_1 + X_2 ... + X_n}{n} = \frac{1}{n}\sum_{i=1}^{n} X_i$$

$$\sigma = \sqrt{\frac{1}{n}\sum_{i=1}^{n}(X_i - \overline{X})^2}$$

Where n is number of the training image and $\overline{X}$ is mean of the number of keypoints in all training images. For the Corel image dataset, $\overline{X}$ is 141 and σ is 90. Note that these values are decided after the keypoint reduction process. The F values for each training image are decided as below:

$$\begin{cases} If\ \bar{X}-\sigma <= R <= \bar{X}+\sigma & F = R \\ If\ R < \bar{X}-\sigma & F = R + offset \le \bar{X} \\ If\ R > \bar{X}+\sigma & F = \bar{X}+\sigma \end{cases} \quad (1)$$

In Equation (1), R is the number of keypoints in F_i as described in Fig. 2 The *offset* is the number of keypoints that are picking randomly from the original training images until $F = R + offset \le \bar{X}$. Through the adjusting mechanism, we keep the number of keypoints of each training image within range of $\bar{X}$ and one σ. If R is between $\bar{X}+\sigma$ and $\bar{X}-\sigma$, we set R as F. If R is more than $\bar{X}+\sigma$, we reduce number of keypoints in R until F is equal to $\bar{X}+\sigma$.

```
Input:
Tij: j-th keypoint in i-th training image.
Variables:
r90ik: k-th keypoint in i-th training image after rotates 90 degrees.
r180ik: k-th keypoint in i-th training image after rotates 180 degrees.
s2ik: k-th keypoint in i-th training image after scaling 2 times.
s05ik: k-th keypoint in i-th training image after scaling 0.5 times.
Fi: Reserve keypoints after reduced finally.
Procedure:
// Pi is number of keypoints in training image.
// Gik is number of keypoints in training image of different geometry
    For i = 1 → 1,000,000
        For j = 1 → Pi
            For k = 1 → Gik
                For s = 1 → 4
If Tij can find a match in r90, r180, s2 and s05 simultaneously
then   store Tij to Fi
```

Fig. 2. Keypoint reduction algorithm.

The number of training images in the experiment is 1,000,000 with total of 216,734,674 keypoints. After applying the proposed reduction process, we decrease the number of keypoint to 43,324,865, with the reduction rate of almost 80 percent. In the experiment section, we show experimental results that the proposed reduction process not only provides advantages in space and time but also without loosing retrieval accuracy.

3.3. Indexing Structure

We analyze the information about the training keypoints before selecting the proper indexing structure. The distribution of the keypoint values in each dimension of all training images is shown in Fig. 3. Note that the keypoints used here are before applying the reduction process discussed in Section 3.2. Fig. 3 shows the distribution of the 36-dimension PCA-SIFT descriptors of 216,734,674 keypoints with total number of descriptor values. From Fig. 3, we observe a highly skewed normal distribution with most of the descriptor values range from -1000 to 1000.

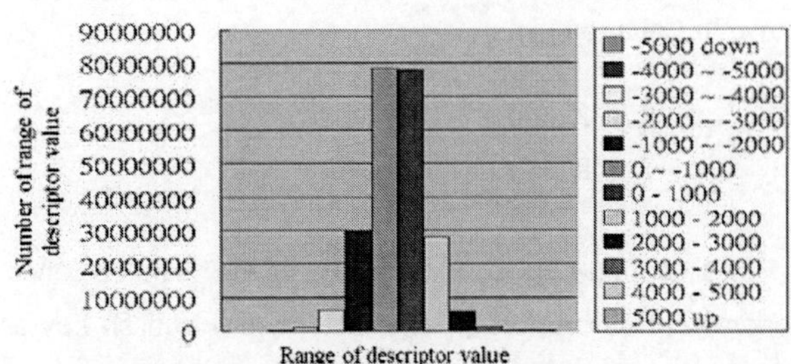

Fig. 3. Distribution of the PCA-SAFT descriptor values in the training set.

Two matcedh keypoint pairs with theirs corresponding descriptor values are both illustrated in Fig. 4. The top of diagram shows the Euclidean distance. The X-axis is the 36 dimensions (descriptor values) used in PCA-SIFT. The Y-axis is the descriptor value of each dimension. Note that if the Euclidean distance is less than 3000 which is considered a match in the PCA-SIFT [15]. From Fig. 4, we observe that a highly similar distribution of the descriptor values occurs between the training keypoints and the query ones if there is a match. When the Euclidean distance is low it is expected that the two lines are closed to each other. However when the Euclidean distance is closed to 3000 it is can still observed the same behavior shown in the bottom of Fig. 4. Fig. 4 shows very little discrepancy in comparing a pair of training and query keypoint if a match occurs.

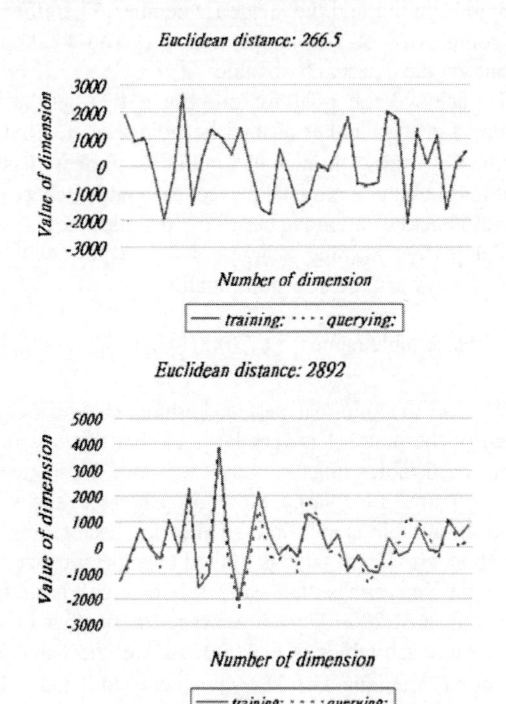

Fig. 4. Two distribution diagram of testing and training line.

We proposed to binarize the PCA-SIFT descriptors and use the binarized descriptors as the hashing keys based on the previous observations. The formula of the binarization is shown in Equation (2).

$$\begin{cases} If\ K_i \geq 0 & H_i = 1 \\ If\ K_i < 0 & H_i = 0 \end{cases}, i = 1 \sim 36 \quad (2)$$

In Equation (2), K_i is the value of the ith dimension in the keypoint descriptor. K_i is transformed into hash key as H_i. If $K_i \geq 0$, H_i is set to 1; otherwise is set to 0. Because the keypoint descriptors are 36-dimension the resulting hash keys consist of 36 digits of 1's and 0's with 2^{36} possible combinations.

At first we transform all the training images into grey level as the input images. Second, the SIFT descriptors are extracted from the training images and then are reduced the dimension of the descriptors by using the PCA. The keypoint reduction process as described in Fig. 2 is applied to keep only the robust keypoints. Finally, we binarize each keypoint to binary hash key using Equation (2) and store the key and image ID pairs into an external hash table built by two-tier hashing system.

3.4. Two-tier Hashing

After the preprocessing is completed, to speed up the image matching in a large set of keypoints we need to build an external hash table which records the relationship between an image keypoint and the image ID number. Therefore, the time complexity of the image matching can be kept as constant via the external hash table.

To achieve the goal we propose a two-tier hashing structure. Let the number of total keypoints be n. First, we run all keypoints through a minimal perfect hashing algorithm to obtain a minimal perfect hash table, where each keypoint generates a unique hash key, $0 \leq$ hash key $\leq n-1$. Minimal perfect hashing guarantees that n keys will map $0 \cdots n-1$ keys with no collisions at all.

$$\text{Hash table name} = \lfloor k / 2000 \rfloor, k \in \text{hash keys} \quad (3)$$

We use the minimal perfect hashing method because the size of the data set is very large so that the size of the external hash tables must be very large too. To reduce the access I/O time of a large external hash table, the whole external hash table is split into smaller sub hash tables, and each sub external hash table is limited to a specific size. The experiment determines that each sub external hash table contains at most 2000 keypoints hence the number of total sub external hash tables is $n / 2000$. As we know that each keypoint has a unique hash key value between 0 and n-1 via minimal perfect hashing, we can directly compute the input keypoint belongs to which external table. If the minimum perfect hash key of the input keypoint is k, the keypoint is stored in hash table numbered $k / 2000$.

The minimal perfect hashing can only create the relation between keypoint and hash key but no relation about image ID number. To record which keypoint belongs to which image ID number, we have to perform a second reverse hashing. The GNU C++ **hash_map** provides the functionality to store value pairs of (key, value). All hash keys of keypoints and their image ID numbers are together hashed into the **hash_map** structures. Finally the **hash_map** structures are serialized as external hash tables so that we can access the target external hash tables according to the conversion rule in Equation 3.

3.5. Two-tier Hashing

We now discuss how to query if an input image is in the database. Step 1, step 2 and step 3 in Fig. 1 are the same for querying images. From the query image, we extract the 36-dimension descriptor of each keypoint to a hash key by using Equation (2). We then use the hash keys in the query image to check if we can find a match in the hash table. If the hash key of query is found in the hash table, the returned value is the image ID number in that bucket.

The *No matched* result indicates that this bucket does not appear in the hash table and the *null* value is simply discarded. If matched, we then store each returned value (image ID number) into a matched list. To decide the final matched image we use simple voting with the largest number of the same image ID to decide the training image that matches with the query image. Note that the retrieval process needs no calculation of the Euclidean distance among keypoint, which is an important factor for efficiency and scalability. In addition, the accuracy of the retrieval process is very high. The detailed procedure of the retrieval process is depicted in Fig. 5.

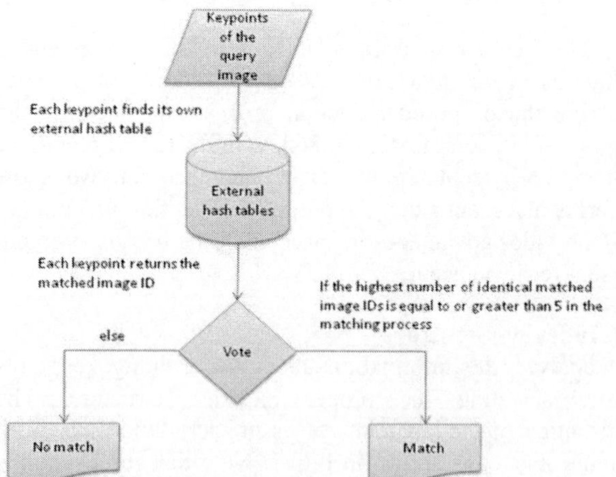

Fig. 5. Procedure for querying image.

4. EXPERIMENTS

The following experiments try to consolidate previous conjectures: The proposed indexing structure is indeed accurate, scalable and efficient.

4.1. Experimental Environment

The hardware environment for all experiments is as followings: INTEL CPU Q9550 2.83 GHz, 4G bytes DDR2 800 memory. The number of the image data set is 1,000,000, which is used as the training dataset. The two-tier hashing is the main indexing structure. The first hashing is minimal perfect hashing, and the second one is external hashing. The two-tier hashing do not support duplicate data therefore each image is unique in the dataset. Also note that all the experiment results in this section are measured by cold-start queries of the external hash tables to eliminate the potential influence of the caching mechanism.

Table 1. Total space for keypoints of different image dataset size.

Number of images	50,000	100,000	200,000	500,000	800,000	1,000,000
Size of image (pixel)	256*384 ~ 1024*768					
Disk space of external hash tables (MB)	37.9	72.4	139.9	363.2	551.3	738.4

Fig. 6 and Fig. 7 shows that the total size of external hash tables and the total number of keypoints both increase linearly as the size of training dataset increases.

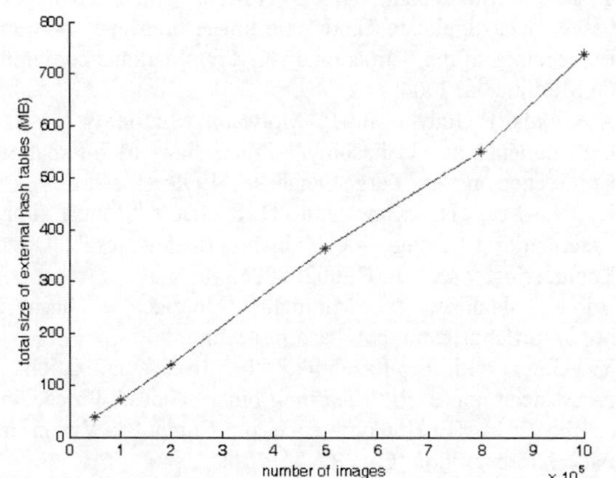

Fig. 6. The size of the external hash tables vs. the size of training dataset.

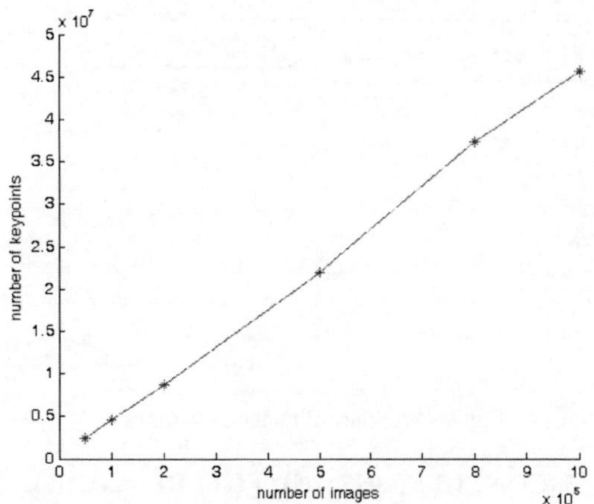

Fig. 7. The Number of keypoints vs. the size of training dataset.

4.2. Experimental Results

We now experiment the retrieval time with different sizes of the training database. Fig. 8 shows the matching time of 200 image retrievals in different training dataset sizes. We observe that the time complexity of retrieval time is O(1) to the size of the datasets. The retrieval time only depends on how many external hash tables have been accessed via equation (3). The main time cost is the I/O time to access the external hash tables. This result suggests that the size of dataset does not affect the retrieval time and the proposed two-tier hashing method is indeed scalable and efficient.

Fig. 9 shows the query accuracy of 200 image retrievals in different training dataset sizes. We observe that the accuracy of retrieval decrease very gradually as the database size increases, which is as we expected. However, even with database of millions of images, the proposed system still has accuracy higher than 98%. The result suggests that the proposed method is indeed quite accurate and can be applied to real-world DRM systems.

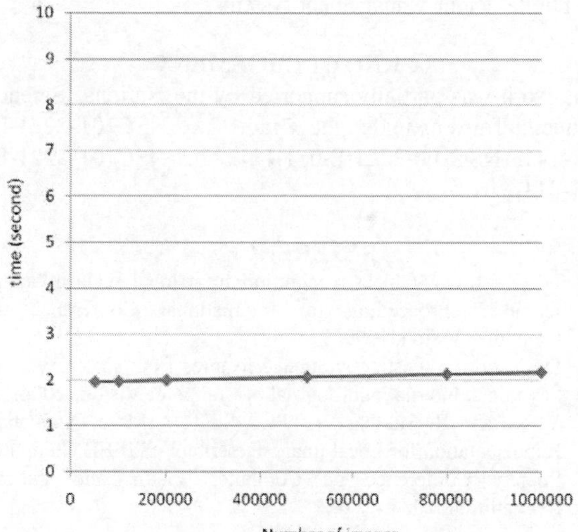

Fig. 8. Time cost of matching a query image.

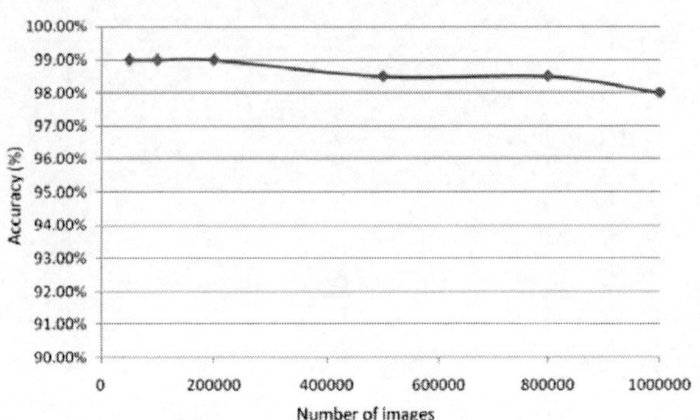

Fig. 9. Accuracy of matching images.

5. CONCLUSIONS AND FUTURE WORK

The Scale Invariant Feature Transform (SIFT) has been widely used in many 2D and 3D image matching allocations. However, the large number of local invariant keypoints extracted by the SIFT poses a scalability problem when the number of images to be matched increases. We propose a method to simplified the SIFT descriptor matching processing. First we adopt the PCA-SIFT method to reduce the dimension of each descriptor from 128 to 36. We show that the binarized SIFT descriptors still maintain very high distinctiveness for the image matching process in two-tier hashing structure. The binarized SIFT descriptors can be indexed by the proposed two-tier hashing system very efficiently. Most important of all, we successfully build the proposed system to reduce the time complexity of querying image to O(1) in a large database with high accuracy. The experiment results suggest that the proposed method can effectively alleviate the scalability problem in large scale image matching applications. One of future research directions is to develop more robust and less overhead external hash structures to further increase the descriptor matching efficiency. Other research directions are to apply the matching algorithms on real world applications such as the Digital Right Management systems.

ACKNOWLEDGEMENT

This work was partially supported by the National Science Council, Taiwan, under the Grants No. NSC101-2221-E-011-141, NSC100-2221-E-011-121, and NSC101-2221-E-211-011.

REFERENCES

[1] D. G. Lowe, "Object recognition from local scale-invariant features," Proceedings of International Conference on Computer Vision, 1999.

[2] D. G. Lowe, "Distinctive image features from scale-invariant keypoints. International Journal of Computer Vision, 2004.

[3] Y. Ke and R. Sukthankar, "PCA-SIFT: A More Distinctive Representation for Local Image Descriptors," IEEE Computer Society Conference on Computer Vision and Pattern Recognition, 2004.

[4] Y. Rui, T.S. Huang, and S. Chang, "Image Retrieval: Current Techniques, Promising Directions and Open Issues," Visual Comm. and Image Representation, vol. 10, no. 4, 1999.

[5] R. C. Veltkamp and M. Tanase, "Content-Based Image Retrieval Systems: A Survey," Technical Report UU-CS-2000-34, Dept. of Computing Science, Utrecht University, 2000.

[6] R. Datta , J. Li , and J. Z. Wang, "Content-based image retrieval: approaches and trends of the new age," Proceedings of the 7th ACM SIGMM international workshop on Multimedia information retrieval, 2005.

[7] A. E. Abdel-Hakim and A. A. Farag, "CSIFT: A SIFT descriptor with color invariant characteristics," IEEE Computer Society Conference on Computer Vision and Pattern Recognition, 2006.

[8] J.M. Geusebroek, R. van den Boomgaard, A.W.M. Smeulders, and H. Geerts. "Color Invariance," IEEE Trans. Pattern Analysis and Machine Intelligence," vol. 23, no. 12, 2001.

[9] E. A. Fox, L. S. Heath, Q. F. Chen, and A. M. Daoud, "Practical minimal perfect hash functions for large databases," Communications of the ACM, January 1992

[10] I.T. Jollife, "Principal Component Analysis," New York: Springer-Verlag, 1986.

[11] V. Gaede and O. Gunther, "Multidimensional Access Methods. ACM Computing Surveys," vol. 30, no. 2, 1998.

[12] J. L. Bentley, "Multidimensional binary search trees used for associative searching," Communications of the ACM, vol.18 no. 9, 1975.

[13] P. Indyk and R. Motwani, "Approximate nearest neighbors: towards removing the curse of dimensionality," Proceedings of the thirtieth annual ACM symposium on Theory of computing, 1998.

[14] Alex Andoni, "LSH Algorithm and Implementation (E2LSH)," http://web.mit.edu/andoni/www/LSH/index.html

[15] Y. Ke, R. Sukthankar, and L. Huston, "An efficient parts-based near-duplicate and sub-image retrieval system," Proceedings of the 12th annual ACM international conference on Multimedia, 2004.

[16] A. Gionis, P. Indyk, and R. Motwani, "Similarity search in high dimensions via hashing," Proceedings of International Conference on Very Large Databases, 1999.

[17] H. Y. Lee, H. Kim, and H.K. Lee, "Robust image watermarking using local invariant features," Optical Engineering, v.45 n.3, 037002, 2006.

[18] Bob Jenkins, "Minimal perfect hashing," http://burtleburtle.net/bob/hash/perfect.html

[19] Y. Gong and S. Lazebnik, "Iterative quantization: A procrustean approach to learning binary codes," Proceedings of the 2011 IEEE Conference on Computer Vision and Pattern Recognition (CVPR '11), 2011.

SESSION

IMAGING APPLICATIONS AND ALGORITHMS

Chair(s)

TBA

Object-Level Saliency Detection Combining the Contrast and Spatial Compactness Hypothesis

Chi Zhang[1], **Weiqiang Wang**[1, 2], **and Xiaoqian Liu**[1]
[1] School of Computer and Control Engineering, University of Chinese Academy of Sciences, Beijing, China
[2] Key Lab of intelligence information Processing, Institute of Computing Technology, CAS, Beijing, China

Abstract - *Object-level saliency detection is an important branch of visual saliency. Most previous methods are based on the contrast hypothesis which regards the regions presenting high contrast in a certain context as salient. Although the contrast hypothesis is valid in many cases, it can't handle some difficult cases, especially when the salient object is large. To make up for the deficiencies of contrast hypothesis, we incorporate a novel spatial compactness hypothesis which can effectively handle those tough cases. In addition, we propose a unified framework which integrates multiple saliency maps generated on different feature maps built on different hypotheses. Our algorithm can automatically select saliency maps of high quality according to the quality evaluation score defined in this paper. The experimental results demonstrate that each key component of our method contributes to the final performance and the full version of our method outperforms all state-of-the-art methods on the most popular dataset.*

Keywords: Saliency Detection, Salient Object Detection

1 Introduction

Human vision system is capable to effectively preselect the data of potential interest from a complex scene for further processing. The computer vision systems will be much more efficient if we endow them with such an excellent ability. To this end, a lot of efforts have been conducted on bottom-up saliency detection. In early years, saliency detection methods [1][2][3][4] are usually biologically inspired, they aim to produce consistent predictive fixations with human vision systems and the evaluation datasets are eye movement datasets which record the information of fixations. We call this category of saliency detection as fixation-level saliency detection. In recent years, a new trend that aims to uniformly highlight the whole salient object becomes popular because of its various applications in object based tasks, such as object recognition [5], image cropping [6], and content-aware image resizing [7], etc. This kind of work is evaluated on the datasets with salient objects manually labeled, so we call it as object-level saliency detection. In this paper, our research mainly focuses on the object-level saliency detection.

Due to the lack of high-level knowledge, every bottom-up detection method is established on some effective hypotheses inspired by the characteristics of salient objects or background. Among all hypotheses, the contrast hypothesis is the most widely used. It takes the region presenting high contrast in a local or global context as salient.

The contrast hypothesis is effective in most cases, because the salient object is usually distinct from its surroundings. So most existing object-level saliency detection methods, either explicitly or implicitly make use of this hypothesis. They usually implement it by measuring the difference between the current region and its surroundings in pixel-level [9], patch-level [10], super-pixel-level [12], the sliding window-level [18] or partial combination of them [11]. However, the contrast hypothesis is not omnipotent, because there are some tough cases it can't handle well. As shown in Fig.2, due to intrinsic flaw of the contrast hypothesis, the pure contrast hypothesis based methods (FT-CVPR09 [9], CA-CVPR10 [10] and RC-CVPR11 [12]) are usually fail to highlight the interior region of large salient object and the salient objects sharing similar appearance with the background, meanwhile, they can't suppress the highly textured background regions which also present high contrast. To cover the shortage of contrast hypothesis, we incorporate an effective spatial compactness hypothesis which believes that the salient regions should be spatially more compact than the background regions. In other words, a region is salient if its appearance-similar regions are nearby, and it is less salient if there are many appearance-similar regions far away from it. In this paper, we intuitively implement the spatial compactness hypothesis by computing the reciprocal of the sum of appearance weighted distances from the current region to all the other regions. It is fortunate that the spatial compactness can usually handle those tough cases described above. However, same like the contrast hypothesis, the spatial compactness hypothesis is not always valid because sometimes the background regions may be composed of some isolated regions which also show great spatial compactness or there are multiple similar salient objects far away from each other. At this moment, the contrast hypothesis is needed to make up for the deficiencies of the spatial compactness. So these two hypotheses could nicely complement each other and by combining the contrast hypothesis and spatial compactness hypothesis, our method is able to effectively handle most cases. Previous work which is the most relevant to ours is [14]. To our best knowledge, [14] is the first method that employs both contrast hypothesis and spatial compactness hypothesis, though it considers the spatial compactness hypothesis as one type of contrast hypothesis. It firstly over-segments the image into some super-pixels, and each super-pixel is represented by the mean color value of the pixels within the super-pixel in *Lab* space.

Then the color uniqueness (contrast) value and color distribution (spatial compactness) value of each super-pixel are computed. Finally, the color uniqueness values and color distribution values are combined and the saliency value is assigned to each super-pixel after a smoothing procedure. This method achieved improvement over the contrast hypothesis based state-of-the-art method [12]. However, in experiments, we find that the salient object sometimes presents salient only in individual color channels but not in the whole color space, so it is not wise to simply represent each super-pixel by the mean color value or only compute the contrast and spatial compactness values in the whole color space. In this paper, we compute the contrast and spatial compactness values not only in the whole color space but also in individual color channels. To fuse multiple saliency maps generated on different feature maps with different hypotheses into the final saliency map, we propose a unified framework that can automatically select saliency maps of high quality according to the quality evaluation score defined in this paper. The evaluation score is computed by combining three novel heuristic rules which are proposed according to the characteristics of salient object. What's more, it is convenient to add new features and hypotheses into this unified framework, e.g. we can easily generalize our method to video by incorporating some proprietary cues of video such as motion information.

2 The proposed method

2.1 Overview

The whole procedure of our method is listed as follows: firstly, the input image is converted into CIE *Lab* color space and split into uniform patches. The compact representations of patches in each color channel are obtained by PCA; then, the contrast saliency values and spatial compactness saliency values are computed for each color channel and the whole color space; next, the multiple saliency maps are refined by incorporating an image segmentation component. Finally, the quality score of each saliency map is computed and some saliency maps are selected and fused into the final saliency map. In the following, we will elaborate each step of our method.

2.2 Patch representation

For an input color image $\mathbf{I}$, we first convert its color space into CIE *Lab* and then partition it into some non-overlapping square patches size of $\mathrm{m} \times \mathrm{m}$ (we set m to 8 in our implementation). For each patch p_{ij} at row i and column j, $i = 1,2,\dots,M$, $j = 1,2,\dots,N$, it is represented as three vectors $\boldsymbol{v}_{ij}^c$, $c\epsilon\{L,a,b\}$, where $\boldsymbol{v}_{ij}^c$ is formed by concatenating the pixel values in patch p_{ij} on color channel c and the length of each vector is m^2. Correspondingly, image $\mathbf{I}$ is represented as three patch matrices $V^c = [\boldsymbol{v}_{ij}^c]_{M\times N}$, $c\epsilon\{L,a,b\}$. To eliminate the dimension with noises and make the following computation more efficient, we employ principal component analysis (PCA) to reduce the dimension of the patch representation and obtain the compact patch matrices $R^c = [\boldsymbol{r}_{ij}^c]_{M\times N}$, $\boldsymbol{r}_{ij}^c$ is the compact vector in low-dimensional space corresponding to $\boldsymbol{v}_{ij}^c$. In addition, the spatial position of patch p_{ij} is denoted by the vector $\boldsymbol{\rho}_{ij}$ in the following formulations.

2.3 Saliency maps generation

We introduce the details of how to generate saliency maps based on the contrast hypothesis and spatial compactness hypothesis in this subsection. It is interesting that the computation of both the contrast value and spatial compactness value can be formulated into a unified weighted linear combination form like the following formulation,

$$\sum_{s=1}^{M}\sum_{t=1}^{N} D_{st}\cdot W_{st} \tag{1}$$

where D_{st} is the main factor and W_{st} is the weight. The position dissimilarity between patches and appearance dissimilarity between patches alternately act as the main factor and weight. Concretely, for the contrast hypothesis, the appearance dissimilarity acts as the main factor, while the position dissimilarity is used to compute weight. They swap roles for the spatial compactness hypothesis. In this paper, the computation methods of those two kinds of dissimilarity are different. The appearance dissimilarity is measured by the Euclidean distance defined in Eqn. (2), while the position dissimilarity is computed via infinite norm distance defined in Eqn. (3),

$$D^{(r)}(\boldsymbol{r}_{ij}^c,\boldsymbol{r}_{st}^c) = ||\boldsymbol{r}_{ij}^c - \boldsymbol{r}_{st}^c||_2^2, \tag{2}$$

$$D^{(\rho)}(\boldsymbol{\rho}_{ij},\boldsymbol{\rho}_{st}) = ||\boldsymbol{\rho}_{ij} - \boldsymbol{\rho}_{st}||_\infty. \tag{3}$$

With the appearance dissimilarity in individual color channels, we can obtain the appearance dissimilarity in the whole color space easily by adding them together, namely, $D^{(r)}(r_{ij}^{Lab}, r_{st}^{Lab})=\sum_{c=\{L,a,b\}} D^{(r)}(r_{ij}^c, r_{st}^c)$. We add the whole color space *Lab* to the color channel set, namely, in the following, $c\epsilon\{L,a,b,Lab\}$. When position dissimilarity and appearance dissimilarity act as weights, both of them will be feed into a Gaussian function, which are respectively defined in Eqn. (4) and (5),

$$W^{(\rho)}(\boldsymbol{\rho}_{ij},\boldsymbol{\rho}_{st}) = \frac{1}{\Omega^{(\rho)}} exp\left(-\frac{D^{(\rho)}(\rho_{ij},\rho_{st})}{2\sigma^{(\rho)2}}\right), \tag{4}$$

$$W^{(r)}(\boldsymbol{r}_{ij}^c,\boldsymbol{r}_{st}^c) = \frac{1}{\Omega^{(r)}} \exp\left(-\frac{D^{(r)}(r_{ij}^c,r_{st}^c)}{2\sigma^{(r)2}}\right), \tag{5}$$

where $\Omega^{(p)}$ and $\Omega^{(r)}$ are the normalization factors to ensure $\sum_{s=1}^{M}\sum_{t=1}^{N} W^{(p)}(\rho_{ij},\rho_{st})$ and $\sum_{s=1}^{M}\sum_{t=1}^{N} W^{(r)}(r_{ij}^{c},r_{st}^{c})$ equal 1. And σ is an important factor that controls the influence of weights. The bigger the σ is, the smaller the influence of weights will be. So it is very important to choose an appropriate σ. Because $D^{(p)}(\rho_{ij},\rho_{st})$ and $D^{(r)}(r_{ij}^{c},r_{st}^{c})$ vary greatly with different images, it is difficult to select a fixed σ suiting all the images. So we employ adaptive $\sigma^{(p)}$ and $\sigma^{(r)}$ defined as,

$$\sigma^{(p)} = \hat{\sigma}^{(p)}\sqrt{max_{i,j,s,t}\, D^{(p)}(\boldsymbol{\rho}_{ij},\boldsymbol{\rho}_{st})}, \quad (6)$$

$$\sigma^{(r)} = \hat{\sigma}^{(r)}\sqrt{max_{i,j,s,t}\, D^{(r)}(\boldsymbol{r}_{ij}^{c},\boldsymbol{r}_{st}^{c})}, \quad (7)$$

in which, $\hat{\sigma}^{(p)}$ and $\hat{\sigma}^{(r)}$ are constant factors. We set both of them to 0.35 in this paper.

2.3.1 Contrast value computation

Similar to [14] [19], we obtain the contrast value by computing the sum of spatially weighted dissimilarities between the current patch and all other patches. Concretely, the contrast value $\Theta_{con}^{c}(p_{ij})$ of patch p_{ij} in color channel c is defined as,

$$\Theta_{con}^{c} = \sum_{s=1}^{M}\sum_{t=1}^{N} D^{(r)}(\boldsymbol{r}_{ij}^{c},\boldsymbol{r}_{st}^{c}) \cdot W^{(p)}(\boldsymbol{\rho}_{ij},\boldsymbol{\rho}_{st}), \quad (8)$$

where $D^{(r)}(\boldsymbol{r}_{ij}^{c},\boldsymbol{r}_{st}^{c})$ denotes the appearance dissimilarity between patch p_{ij} and p_{st} in color channel c defined in Eqn. (2) and $W^{(p)}(\boldsymbol{\rho}_{ij},\boldsymbol{\rho}_{st})$ is the position weight defined in (4).

2.3.2 Spatial compactness value computation

In this paper, the spatial compactness is defined as the reciprocal of the sum of appearance weighted position dissimilarities between the current patch and all the other patches. So the spatial compactness value $\Theta_{com}^{c}(p_{ij})$ of patch p_{ij} in color channel c is defined as,

$$\Theta_{com}^{c}(p_{ij}) = \left(\sum_{s=1}^{M}\sum_{t=1}^{N} D^{(p)}(\boldsymbol{\rho}_{ij},\boldsymbol{\rho}_{st})\, W^{(r)}(\boldsymbol{r}_{ij}^{c},\boldsymbol{r}_{st}^{c})\right)^{-1}, \quad (9)$$

where $D^{(p)}(\boldsymbol{\rho}_{ij},\boldsymbol{\rho}_{st})$ denotes the position dissimilarity between patch p_{ij} and p_{st} defined in Eqn. (3) and $W^{(p)}(\boldsymbol{\rho}_{ij},\boldsymbol{\rho}_{st})$ is the appearance weight defined in Eqn. (5).

2.3.3 Saliency value assignment

To reduce the impact of noise and improve the homogeneity of saliency map, we employ a weighted sum of the contrast values or spatial compactness values of the patches in a square neighborhood of the current patch as the saliency value defined as,

$$S_h^c(p_{ij}) = \sum_{s=i-k}^{i+k}\sum_{t=i-k}^{i+k} W^{(r)}(\boldsymbol{r}_{ij}^{c},\boldsymbol{r}_{st}^{c}) \cdot \Theta_h^c(p_{st}), \quad (10)$$

in which, c denotes the color channel, $c\epsilon\{L,a,b,Lab\}$ and h denotes the hypothesis we employ, $h\epsilon\{con,com\}$ and k controls the size of square neighborhood, in our method k=7. Finally, we normalize the obtained saliency maps to [0, 1] via a linear stretch defined as,

$$S_h^c(p_{ij}) = \frac{S_h^c(p_{ij}) - min_{i,j}(S_h^c(p_{ij}))}{max_{i,j}(S_h^c(p_{ij})) - min_{i,j}(S_h^c(p_{ij}))}. \quad (11)$$

By now, we obtain eight patch-level saliency maps generated on different color channel with different hypotheses. Based on these patch-level saliency maps, the pixel-level saliency maps can be easily obtained through assigning saliency value of the patch to the pixels within it. Then we get eight pixel-level saliency maps, they are $S_{con}^{L}(x,y)$, $S_{con}^{a}(x,y)$, $S_{con}^{b}(x,y)$, $S_{con}^{Lab}(x,y)$, $S_{com}^{L}(x,y)$, $S_{com}^{a}(x,y)$, $S_{com}^{b}(x,y)$, $S_{com}^{Lab}(x,y)$.

2.4 Saliency maps refinement

The obtained saliency maps are generated on the unit of patch, which may suffer from the blur of salient object boundary, because object boundaries may fall into different patches when an image is partitioned into the patches of the same size and shape without considering visual content. Therefore, these saliency maps may not achieve accurate saliency values near the object boundaries. So, we incorporate an image segmentation module to refine our saliency maps. The original image is over-segmented into a group of regions via the mean shift method implemented in the EDISON system [8], we set the min area of each region to 1000 in our implementation. Then the pixel-level saliency value $\overline{S_h^c}(x,y)$ in each region is given by the mean of pixel-level saliency values in it, i.e. ,

$$\overline{S_h^c}(x,y) = \frac{1}{|\Gamma|}\sum_{(\hat{x},\hat{y})\epsilon\Gamma} S_h^c(\hat{x},\hat{y}), \quad (12)$$

where Γ denotes the region which the pixel at location (x,y) belongs to, and $|\Gamma|$ is the total number of pixels in region Γ. The linear stretch normalization is performed to each refined saliency map $\overline{S_h^c}(x,y)$ as Eqn. (11).

2.5 Selection and fusion of saliency maps

The last but not least step is to fuse the multiple saliency maps obtained in preceding steps into the final saliency map. As shown in Fig.1, not all the obtained saliency maps are able to highlight the salient object uniformly and accurately, some saliency maps even mistakenly highlight the background regions. So it is not wise to fuse all those saliency maps into final result, the saliency maps of high quality should be picked out and those of poor quality should be discarded. Based on the above thoughts, we propose a fusion framework which can automatically pick out saliency maps of high quality according to the quality evaluation score defined in the following. In the framework, we first compute the evaluation score of each saliency map according to three

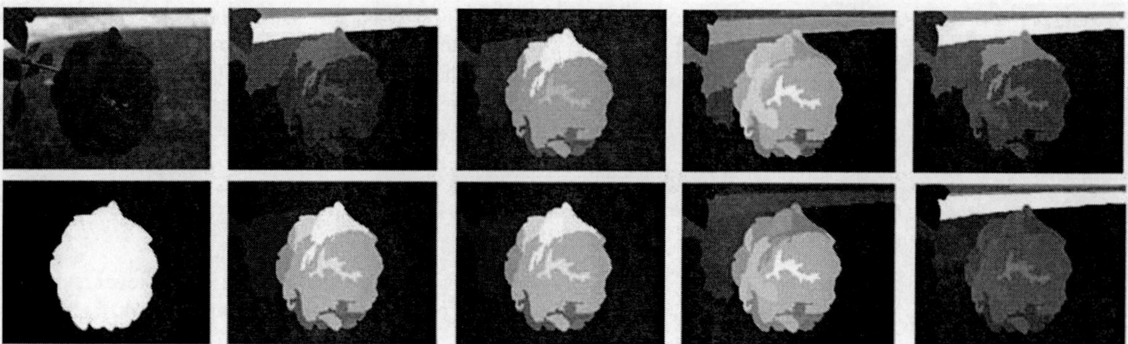

Figure 1. Refined saliency maps of each individual color channel and the whole color space built on both contrast hypothesis and spatial compactness hypothesis. In the first row from left to right: original image, $\bar{S}^{L}_{con}(x,y)$, $\bar{S}^{a}_{con}(x,y)$, $\bar{S}^{b}_{con}(x,y)$ and $\bar{S}^{Lab}_{con}(x,y)$. In the second row from left to right: ground-truth, $\bar{S}^{L}_{com}(x,y)$, $\bar{S}^{a}_{com}(x,y)$, $\bar{S}^{b}_{com}(x,y)$ and $\bar{S}^{Lab}_{com}(x,y)$. The evalutation scores of the first four saliency maps respectively are 1.83, 2.24, 1.79 and 1.68. The evalutation scores of the last four saliency maps respectively are 2.82, 2.82, 2.24 and 1.55. The selected saliency maps are $\bar{S}^{L}_{com}(x,y)$, $\bar{S}^{a}_{com}(x,y)$, $\bar{S}^{b}_{com}(x,y)$ and $\bar{S}^{a}_{con}(x,y)$.

novel heuristic rules we proposed. Then, the saliency map whose evaluation score is higher than a pre-defined threshold will be selected. Finally, we fuse those selected saliency maps in a linear weighted sum form, and the weight is the corresponding evaluation score.

2.5.1 Definition of the evaluation scores

According to the characteristics of salient object, we propose three novel heuristic rules to evaluate the quality of a saliency map, i.e., ratio of center-surround, distribution compactness and saliency variance. The final evaluation score is computed based on those three rules to measure the extent that how accurately and uniformly the saliency map highlights the salient object.

Based on the fact that salient objects usually lie near the center of an image and the finding that human eyes also tend to fixate on the center when viewing scenes [20], we choose the ratio of center-surround as one assessment rule. The ratio of center-surround is defined as the ratio of the sum of saliency values of the central region to that of the surrounding region, and in our implementation it is formulated as,

$$\psi_r(\overline{S^c_h}) = \frac{\sum_{x=(\frac{1}{2}-\frac{\sqrt{2}}{4})H}^{\left(\frac{1}{2}+\frac{\sqrt{2}}{4}\right)H} \sum_{y=(\frac{1}{2}-\frac{\sqrt{2}}{4})W}^{(\frac{1}{2}+\frac{\sqrt{2}}{4})W} \overline{S^c_h}(x,y)}{\sum_{x=1}^{H}\sum_{y=1}^{W}\overline{S^c_h}(x,y) - \sum_{x=(\frac{1}{2}-\frac{\sqrt{2}}{4})H}^{(\frac{1}{2}+\frac{\sqrt{2}}{4})H} \sum_{y=(\frac{1}{2}-\frac{\sqrt{2}}{4})W}^{(\frac{1}{2}+\frac{\sqrt{2}}{4})W} \overline{S^c_h}(x,y)}, \quad (13)$$

where W and H denote the width and height of the saliency map respectively. The high ratio of center-surround reflects high quality of a saliency map. However, salient objects don't always lie in the center of image, so we need other rules to enhance the reliability of the final evaluation score.

Because the salient objects are spatially compact as described by the spatial compactness hypothesis, in the saliency map of high quality the pixels with high saliency values should be spatially close as well. So we take the distribution compactness as the second assessment rule defined as,

$$\psi_d(\overline{S^c_h}) = \left(\frac{1}{D}\sum_{x=1}^{H}\sum_{y=1}^{W}\overline{S^c_h}(x,y)\cdot\left((x-\mu_x)^2 + (y-\mu_y)^2\right)\right)^{-1}, \quad (14)$$

$$D = \sum_{x=1}^{H}\sum_{y=1}^{W}\overline{S^c_h}(x,y), \quad (15)$$

$$\mu_x = \frac{1}{D}\sum_{x=1}^{H}\sum_{y=1}^{W}\overline{S^c_h}(x,y)\cdot x, \quad (16)$$

$$\mu_y = \frac{1}{D}\sum_{x=1}^{H}\sum_{y=1}^{W}\overline{S^c_h}(x,y)\cdot y, \quad (17)$$

where the D is the normalization factor, μ_x and μ_y denote the coordinates x and y of the gravity center, W and H are the width and height of the saliency map.

A lot of observations in the experiments show that the saliency map which is well consistent with the ground truth usually has a high pixel variance, so we employ the pixel variance of saliency map as the last assessment rule defined as,

$$\psi_v(\overline{S^c_h}) = \sum_{x=1}^{H}\sum_{y=1}^{W}(\overline{S^c_h}(x,y) - \Lambda)^2, \quad (18)$$

$$\Lambda = \frac{1}{H\cdot W}\sum_{x=1}^{H}\sum_{y=1}^{W}\overline{S^c_h}(x,y), \quad (19)$$

where Λ is the mean value of the saliency map.

With the above three assessment rules, we define the final quality evaluation score as,

$$\varphi(\overline{S^c_h}) = \frac{\psi_r(\overline{S^c_h})}{\gamma_r} + \frac{\psi_d(\overline{S^c_h})}{\gamma_d} + \frac{\psi_v(\overline{S^c_h})}{\gamma_v}, \quad (20)$$

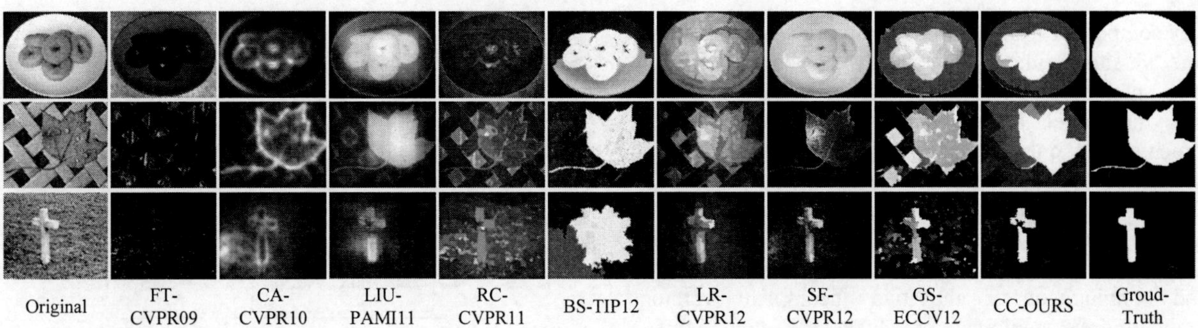

Figure 2. Three examples of qualitative comparison results between our method (CC-OURS) and other 8 state-of-the-art methods (FT-CVPR09 [9], CA-CVPR10 [10], LIU-PAMI11 [11], RC-CVPR11 [12], BS-TIP12 [13], LR-CVPR12 [14], SF-CVPR12 [15] and GS-ECCV12 [16]).

where Υ_r, Υ_d and Υ_v are the normalization factors, which are respectively the maximum of $\psi_r(\overline{S_h^c})$, $\psi_d(\overline{S_h^c})$ and $\psi_v(\overline{S_h^c})$, i.e.,

$$\Upsilon_r = max_{c\epsilon\{L,a,b,Lab\},h\epsilon\{con,com\}}\, \psi_r(\overline{S_h^c}), \quad (21)$$

$$\Upsilon_d = max_{c\epsilon\{L,a,b,Lab\},h\epsilon\{con,com\}}\, \psi_d(\overline{S_h^c}), \quad (22)$$

$$\Upsilon_v = max_{c\epsilon\{L,a,b,Lab\},h\epsilon\{con,com\}}\, \psi_v(\overline{S_h^c}). \quad (23)$$

2.5.2 Combination of saliency maps

After computing the quality evaluation score of each saliency map, we combine those selected saliency maps in a linear weighted sum form, which is formulated as,

$$\widehat{S_h^c}(x,y) = \sum_{\substack{c\epsilon\{L,a,b,Lab\},\\ h\epsilon\{con,com\}}} F\left(\varphi(\overline{S_h^c})\right)\cdot \overline{S_h^c}(x,y), \quad (24)$$

$$F\left(\varphi(\overline{S_h^c})\right) = \begin{cases} 0, & \varphi(\overline{S_h^c}) < T \\ \varphi(\overline{S_h^c}), & \varphi(\overline{S_h^c}) \geq T \end{cases}, \quad (25)$$

$$T = \frac{2}{3} \max_{c\epsilon\{L,a,b,Lab\},h\epsilon\{con,com\}} \varphi(\overline{S_h^c}), \quad (26)$$

where T is an adaptive threshold defined in Eqn. (26). The saliency map will be discarded, if its quality evaluation score is smaller than T. Finally, we normalize the final saliency map $\widehat{S_h^c}(x,y)$ as Eqn. (11). It is worth mentioning that, with the novel fusion framework, we can easily integrating new features and hypotheses into our method.

3 Experiments and results

We test our method on a publicly available dataset which contains 1000 images along with ground-truth (GT) in the form of human-labeled masks for salient objects provided by Achanta et al. [9]. We compare the proposed method (CC-OURS) with 8 state-of-the-art object-level saliency detection methods. We select these methods according to: popularity (FT-CVPR09 [9], CA-CVPR10 [10], LIU-PAMI11 [11] and RC-CVPR11 [12]) and recency (BS-TIP12 [13], LR-CVPR12 [14], SF-CVPR12 [15] and GS-ECCV12 [16]). The saliency maps of FT-CVPR09 [9] and RC-CVPR11 [12] are provided by [12]. The saliency maps of LIU-PAMI11 [11] are generated with the parameters reported in their paper using the code provided by the author. The saliency maps of other methods are obtained from the corresponding authors' homepages. In our experiments, both qualitative and quantitative comparisons are performed. Three examples of qualitative comparison results are shown in Fig.2. These three examples were selected as the most difficult stimuli by [17], because they represent three typical tough cases of the object-level saliency detection task, including large salient object, textured background and low contrast between salient object and background. It can be seen that our method consistently produces saliency maps close to ground-truth while the other methods don't perform well in at least one case. So our method is more robust than the rest 8 state-of-the-art methods and can handle the three tough cases well. In quantitative comparison, similar to [9], we employ the recall-precision curve to evaluate our method. With saliency value in the range [0,255], we binarize the saliency maps with varying thresholds from 0 to 255 and the recalls and precisions are obtained by comparing the binary results with the ground-truth. Concretely, the precision and recall under a certain threshold T are defined as,

$$Precision(T) = \frac{1}{N}\sum_{i=1}^{N}\frac{|B_i(T)\cap GT_i|}{|B_i(T)|}, \quad (27)$$

$$Recall(T) = \frac{1}{N}\sum_{i=1}^{N}\frac{|B_i(T)\cap GT_i|}{|GT_i|}, \quad (28)$$

where $B_i(T)$ is the binary mask under threshold T of the ith image, GT_i is the corresponding ground-truth and N is the number of test images. The recall-precision curves of 8 state-of-the-art methods and our method are shown in Fig.3 (a) (b). We can see that our method outperforms all the other 8 methods. Our method can predict the most salient regions accurately with a maximum precision about 0.96, meanwhile it keeps high precisions when the recalls are high (achieve a precision over 0.9 when the recall is 0.8 and a precision over 0.8 when the recall is 0.9). In addition, we also evaluate the incomplete versions of our method. Each of them eliminates one key component from the full version of our method. They are the version without contrast hypothesis, the version without spatial compactness hypothesis and the version without the novel fusion framework. The last one is implemented by only computing the contrast values and spatial compactness values in the whole color space and simply adding the saliency maps together without weights. The evaluation results are shown in Fig.3 (c). We can see that the proposed fusion framework play an important role in our method, relying on it the two incomplete versions respectively only employing one hypothesis both achieve satisfactory results. The results also show that compared with the version without spatial compactness hypothesis, the version without contrast hypothesis achieves higher precisions especially when the recalls are high. This is mainly because the spatial compactness hypothesis can usually highlight the whole salient object even when the salient object is large or doesn't present high contrast and suppress the background even if the background is textured while the contrast hypothesis isn't good at these tough cases. So the spatial compactness hypothesis is a nice complement to contrast hypothesis. By integrating all these three key components, the full version of our method achieves the optimal performance.

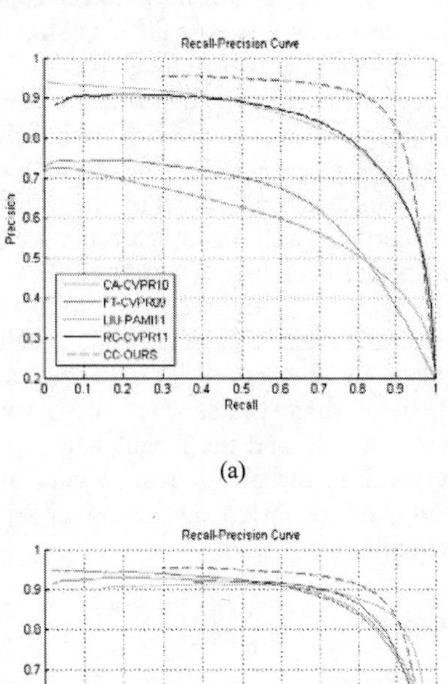

(a)

(b)

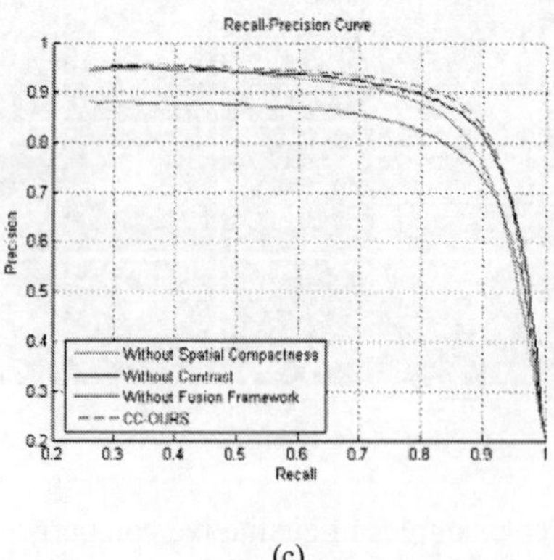

(c)

Figure 3. (a)(b) The recall-precision curves of 8 state-of-the-art methods and our method. (c) Evaluation of the methods without contrast hypothesis, without spatial compactness hypothesis, without thefusion framework and the full version of our method.

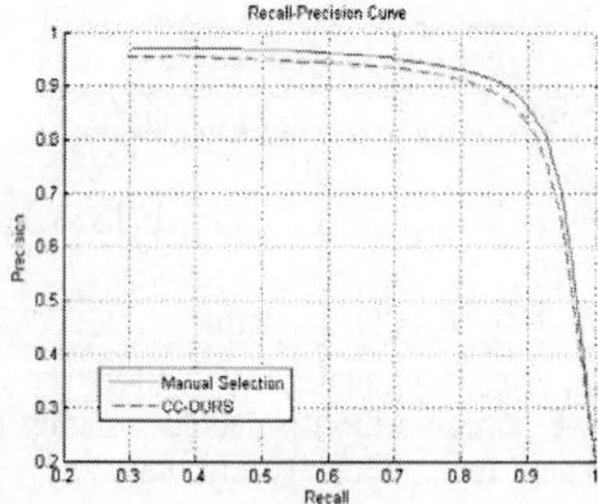

Figure 4. The recall-precision curves of the proposed method and the results generated by manually selecting the saliency maps of high quality in the fusion stage.

Figure 5. The failure cases of our method. The first column is the original image, the second column is the saliency map of our method, the third column is the ground-truth.

4 Conclusions

In this paper, we propose an object-level saliency detection method which integrates the popular contrast hypothesis and the effective spatial compactness hypothesis. The experimental results show that our method achieves satisfactory performance and outperforms all state-of-the-art methods in both qualitative and quantitative comparisons. In addition, we propose a fusion framework of multiple saliency maps that can automatically select saliency maps of high quality. The experimental results demonstrate that this fusion framework is very effective and plays an important role in our method. However, all though the proposed three assessment rules could help pick out the saliency maps of high quality accurately, as shown in Fig.4, there is still room for improvement comparing with manual selection. So we are supposed to find some new assessment rules to make the automatic selection more accurate. As shown in Fig.5, though the contrast hypothesis and spatial compactness hypothesis can handle most cases via cooperation, there are still some tough cases that neither of those two hypotheses can effectively deal with. So, to improve our method, we can incorporate some other effective hypotheses into our framework. As introduced before, we will try to make our method be utilized in video by incorporating some proprietary cues of video.

5 Acknowledgement

This work was supported by the National Natural Science Foundation of China under Grant No. 61175115, No. 61232013, No. 61271434.

6 References

[1] L. Itti, C. Koch, and E. Niebur, "A model of saliencybased visual attention for rapid scene analysis," TPAMI, vol. 20, no. 11, pp. 1254-1259, 1998.

[2] N.D.B. Bruce and J.K. Tsotsos, "Saliency based on information maximization," in NIPS, 2005.

[3] X. Hou and L. Zhang, "Saliency detection: A spectral residual approach," in CVPR, 2007, pp. 1–8.

[4] J. Harel, C. Koch, and P. Perona, "Graph-based visual saliency," in NIPS, 2006.

[5] U. Rutishauser, D. Walther, C. Koch, and P. Perona, "Is bottom-up attention useful for object recognition?," in CVPR, 2004.

[6] A. Santella, M. Agrawala, D. DeCarlo, D. Salesin, and M. Cohen, "Gaze-based interaction for semi-automatic photo cropping," in Proceedings of the SIGCHI conference on Human Factors, 2006.

[7] H. Wu, Y.S. Wang, K.C. Feng, T.T. Wong, T.Y. Lee, and P.A. Heng, "Resizing by symmetry-summarization," ACM Trans. Graph., vol. 29, no. 6, pp. 159:1–159:10, 2010.

[8] D. Comaniciu and P. Meer, "Mean shift: A robust approach toward feature space analysis," TPAMI, vol. 24, no. 5, pp. 603-619, 2002.

[9] R. Achanta, S. Hemami, F. Estrada, and Sabine Ssstrunk, "Frequency-tuned salient region detection," in CVPR, 2009.

[10] Stas Goferman, Lihi Zelnik-Manor, and Ayellet Tal, "Context-aware saliency detection," in CVPR, 2010.

[11] T. Liu, Z.J. Yuan, J. Sun, J.D. Wang, N.N. Zheng, X.O. Tang, and H.Y. Shum, "Learning to detect a salient object," TPAMI, vol. 33, no. 2, pp. 353-367, 2011.

[12] M.M. Cheng, G.X. Zhang, N.J. Mitra, X.L Huang, and S.M Hu, "Global contrast based salient region detection," in CVPR, 2011.

[13] Yulin Xie, Huchuan Lu, and Ming-Hsuan Yang,"Bayesian saliency via low and mid level cues," TIP, vol. 22 , no. 2, pp. 1689-1698, 2012.

[14] F. Perazzi, P. Krahenbul, Y. Pritch and A. Hornung, "Saliency filters: contrast based filtering for salient region detection," in: CVPR, 2012.

[15] X.H Shen and Y. Wu,"A unified approach to salient object detection via low rank matrix recovery," in CVPR, 2012.

[16] Y.C. Wei, F. Wen, W.J. Zhu, and J. Sun," Geodesic Saliency Using Background Priors," in ECCV, 2012.

[17] Ali Borji, Dicky N. Sihite, and Laurent Itti," Salient Object Detection: A Benchmark," in ECCV, 2012.

[18] Esa Rahtu, Juho Kannala, Mikko Salo, and Janne Heikkila, "Segmenting salient objects from images and videos," in ECCV, 2010.

[19] L.J. Duan, C.P Wu, J. Miao, L.Y. Qing and Y. Fu "Visual Saliency Detection by Spatially Weighted Dissimilarity," in CVPR, 2011.

[20] Benjamin W. Tatler, "The central fixation bias in scene viewing: Selecting an optimal viewing position independently of motor biases and image feature distributions," Journal of Vision, vol. 7, no. 14, pp. 1 – 17, 2007.

Vision-Based Localization and Text Chunking of Nutrition Fact Tables on Android Smartphones

Vladimir Kulyukin[1], Aliasgar Kutiyanawala[1], Tanwir Zaman[1], and Stephen Clyde[2]
[1]Department of Computer Science, Utah State University, Logan, UT, USA
[2]MDSC Corporation, Salt Lake City, UT, USA

Abstract—Proactive nutrition management is considered by many nutritionists and dieticians as a key factor in reducing and controlling cancer, diabetes, and other illnesses related to or caused by mismanaged diets. As more and more individuals manage their daily activities with smartphones, smartphones have the potential to become proactive diet management tools. While there are many vision-based mobile applications to process barcodes, there is a relative dearth of vision-based applications for extracting other useful nutrition information items from product packages, e.g., nutrition facts, caloric contens, and ingredients. In this paper, we present a vision-based algorithm to localize aligned nutrition fact tables (NFTs) present on many grocery product packages and to segment them into text chunks. The algorithm is a front end to a cloud-based nutrition management system we are currently developing. The algorithm captures frames in video mode from the smartphone's camera, localizes aligned NFTs via vertical and horizontal projections, and segments the NFTs into single- or multi-line text chunks. The algorithm is implemented on Android 2.3.6 and Android 4.2. Pilot NFT localization and text chunking experiments are presented and discussed.

Keywords—*computer vision; image processing; vision-based nutrition information extraction; nutrition management*

I. Introduction

According to the U.S. Department of Agriculture, U.S. residents have increased their caloric intake by 523 calories per day since 1970. A leading cause of mortality in men is prostate cancer. A leading cause of mortality in women is breast cancer. Mismanaged diets are estimated to account for 30-35 percent of cancer cases [1]. Approximately 47,000,000 U.S. residents have metabolic syndrome and diabetes. Diabetes in children appears to be closely related to increasing obesity levels. Many nutritionists and dieticians consider proactive nutrition management to be a key factor in reducing and controlling cancer, diabetes, and other illnesses related to or caused by mismanaged or inadequate diets.

Surveys conducted by the American Dietetic Association (http://www.eatright.org/) demonstrate that the role of television and printed media as sources of nutrition information has been steadily falling. In 2002, the credibility of television and magazines as sources of nutrition information were estimated at 14% and 25%, respectively. In contrast, the popularity of the Internet increased from 13% to 25% with a perceived credibility of 22% in the same time period. Since smartphones and other mobile devices have, for all practical purposes, become the most popular gateway to access the Internet on the go, they have the potential to become proactive diet management tools and improve public health.

Numerous web sites have been developed to track caloric intake (e.g., http://nutritiondata.self.com), to determine caloric contents and quantities in consumed food (e.g., http://www.calorieking.com), and to track food intake and exercise (e.g., http://www.fitday.com). Unfortunately, many such sites either lack mobile access or, if they provide it, require manual input of nutrition data. Manual input challenges on smartphones are well documented in the literatures (e.g., [2], [3]).

One smartphone sensor that can alleviate the problem of manual input is the camera. Currently, the smartphone cameras are used in many mobile applications to process barcodes. There are free public online barcode databases (e.g., http://www.upcdatabase.com/) that provide some product descriptions and issuing countries' names. Unfortunately, since production information is provided by volunteers who are assumed to periodically upload product details and to associate them with product IDs, almost no nutritional information is available and some of it may not be reliable. Some applications (e.g., http://redlaser.com) provide some nutritional information for a few popular products.

While there are many vision-based applications to process barcodes, there continues to be a relative dearth of vision-based applications for extracting other types of useful nutrition information from product packages such as nutrition facts, caloric contents, and ingredients. If successfully extracted, such information can be converted it into text or SQL via scalable optical character recognition (OCR) methods and submitted as queries to cloud-based sites and services.

Another problem and challenge for mobile computing is eyes-free access to nutrition information for visually impaired (VI), blind, and low vision smartphone users. One tool that is frequently mentioned in the literature for eyes-free access to print matter is the K-NFB reader (www.knfbreader.com). The K-NFB reader is a mobile OCR software tool for Nokia mobile phones. Given lower incomes of many VI and blind individuals, the cost of this technology ($2,500 per phone installation), quite possibly, puts it out of reach for many VI users. K-NFB users are required to learn to effectively align print matter with the camera, which may not be a problem for dedicated users but may dissuade others from adopting this technology. More importantly, K-NFB users are required to use small mobile phone keys for navigation and input. The speaker volume is too low for use in outdoors and noisy places such as shopping malls.

In a series of evaluation experiments conducted by the K-NFB system's developers and published at the company's web site, the system accurately identified simple black on white text but did not perform well on documents with color graphics and images, large signs, mixed and italic fonts. The current version of the system cannot read round containers such as cans or products with colored fonts and images and can read flat top boxes only if the text is plain black on white, which is a serious limitation for grocery products, because most of grocery product packages contain colorful images and variable fonts.

The Utah State University (USU) Computer Science Assistive Technology Laboratory (CSATL) is currently developing a mobile vision-based nutrition management system for smartphone users. The system will enable smartphone users to specify their dietary profiles securely on the web or in the cloud. When they go shopping, they will use their smartphones to extract nutrition information from product packages with their smartphones' cameras. The extracted information includes not only barcodes but also nutrition facts, such as calories, saturated fat, sugar content, cholesterol, sodium, potassium, carbohydrates, protein, and ingredients.

Our ultimate objective is to match the extracted information to the users' dietary profiles and to make dietary recommendations to effect behavior changes. For example, if a user is pre-diabetic, the system will estimate the amount of sugar from the extracted ingredients and will make specific recommendations to the user. The system, if the users so choose, will keep track of their long-term buying patterns and make recommendations on a daily, weekly or monthly basis. Dieticians will also be able to participate in and manage the system's data flow. For example, if a user exceeds his or her total amount of saturated fat permissible for the specified profile, the system will notify the user and, if the user's profile has appropriate permissions, the user's dietician.

In this paper, we present a vision-based algorithm to localize aligned NFTs and to segment them into single- or multi-line text chunks. The algorithm captures frames in video mode from the phone camera, localizes aligned NFTs via vertical and horizontal projections, and segments text chunks from localized NFTs. The latter part is referred to in this paper as text chunking. These segmented text chunks can subsequently be input into OCR engines. However, scalable mobile OCR is beyond the scope of this paper. The algorithm has been implemented and tested on the Android 2.3.6 and Android 4.2 platforms.

The remainder of our paper is organized as follows. Section 2 presents related work. Section 3 discusses the localization of aligned NFTs. Section 4 covers how single- or multi-line text chunks are segmented from localized NFTs. Section 5 discusses NFT localization and text chunking experiments. In Section 6, the experimental findings are discussed and several future work directions are outlined.

II. Related Work

Many current R&D efforts aim to utilize the power of mobile computing to improve proactive nutrition management. In [4], the research is presented that shows how such mobile applications can be designed for supporting lifestyle changes among individuals with type 2 diabetes and how these changes were perceived by a group of 12 patients during a 6-month period. In [5], an application is presented that contains a picture-based diabetes diary that records physical activity and photos taken with the phone camera of eaten foods. The smartphone is connected to a glucometer via Bluetooth to capture blood glucose values. A web-based, password-secured and encrypted short message service (SMS) is provided to users to send messages to their care providers to resolve daily problems and to send educational messages to users.

The presented NFT localization algorithm is based on vertical and horizontal projections used by numerous computer vision researchers for object localization. For example, in [6], projections are used to successfully detect and recognize Arabic characters. The presented text chunking algorithm also builds on and complements multiple projects in mobile computing and mobile computer vision that capitalize on the ever increasing processing capabilities of smartphone cameras. In [7], a system is presented for mobile OCR on mobile phones. In [8], an interactive system is presented for text recognition and translation.

III. NFT Localization

A. Vertical and Horizontal Projections

Images captured from the smartphone's video stream can be divided into foreground and background pixels. In general, foreground pixels are defined as content-bearing units in a domain-dependent manner. For example, content can be defined as black pixels, white pixels, pixels with specific luminosity levels, specific neighborhood connection patters (e.g., 4-connected, 8-connetected), etc. Background pixels are those that are not foreground.

Horizontal projection of an image (HP) is a sequence of foreground pixel counts for each row in an image. Vertical projection of an image (VP) is a sequence of foreground pixel counts for each column in an image. Figure 1 shows horizontal and vertical projections of a black and white image with three characters.

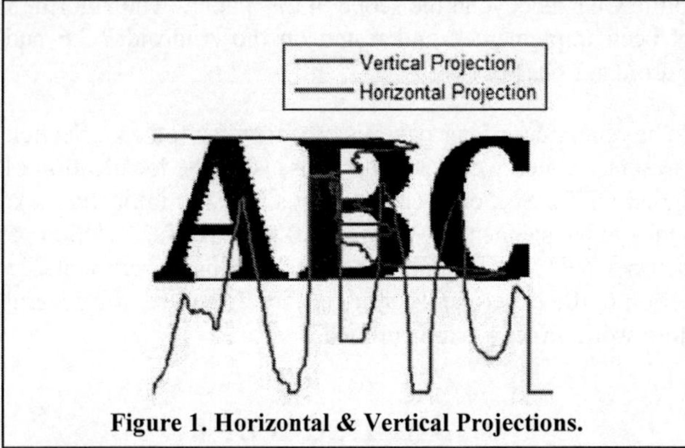

Figure 1. Horizontal & Vertical Projections.

Suppose there is an m x n image I where foreground pixels are black, i.e., $I(x,y)=0$, and the background pixels are white, i.e., $I(x,y)=255$. Then the horizontal projection of row y and the vertical projection of column x can defined as $f(y)$ and $g(x)$, respectively:

$$f(y)=\sum_{x=0}^{n-1}(255-I(x,y)); \qquad (1)$$
$$g(x)=\sum_{y=0}^{m-1}(255-I(x,y)).$$

For the discussion that follows it is important to keep in mind that the x axis in the image is the column dimension whereas the y axis is the row dimension. In other words, the vertical projections computed by $g(x)$ along the x axis are used in computing the vertical boundaries of NFTs while the horizontal projections computed by $f(y)$ along the y axis are used in computing the NFTs' horizontal boundaries.

B. Horizontal Line Filtering

In detecting NFT boundaries, three assumptions are currently made: 1) a NFT is present in the image; 2) the NFT present in the image is not cropped; and 3) the NFT is horizontally or vertically aligned. Figures 2 shows horizontally and vertically aligned NFTs. The detection of NFT boundaries proceeds in three stages. Firstly, the first approximation of vertical table boundaries is computed. Secondly, the vertical boundaries computed in the first stage are extended to the left and to the right. Thirdly, the upper and lower horizontal boundaries are computed.

The objective of the first stage is to detect the approximate location of the NFT along the horizontal axis $(x_s^{'}, x_e^{'})$. This approximation starts with the detection of horizontal lines in the image, which is accomplished with a horizontal line detection kernel (HLDK) that we developed in our previous research and described in our previous publications [9]. It should be noted that other line detection techniques (e.g., Hough transform [10]) can be used for this purpose. Our HLDK is designed to detect large horizontal lines in images to maximize computational efficiency. On rotated images, the kernel is used to detect vertical lines. The left image of Figure 3 gives the output of running the HLDK filter on the left image shown in Figure 2.

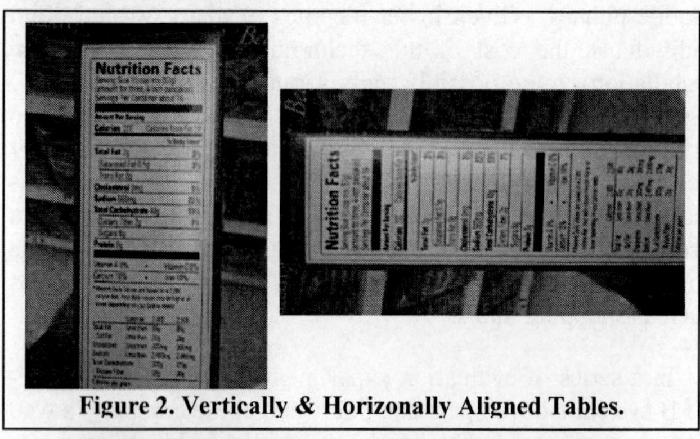

Figure 2. Vertically & Horizontally Aligned Tables.

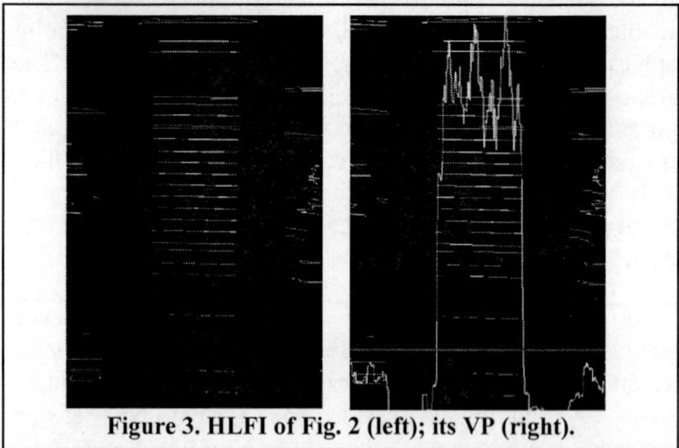

Figure 3. HLFI of Fig. 2 (left); its VP (right).

C. Detection of Vertical Boundaries

Let HLFI be a horizontally line filtered image, i.e., the image put through the HLDK filter or some other line detection filter. Let $VP(HLFI)$ be its vertical projection, i.e., the projections of white pixels computed by for each column of HLFI. The right image in Figure 2 shows the vertical projection of the HLFI on the left. Let θ_{VP} be a threshold, which in our application is set to the mean count of the white foreground pixels in columns. In Figure 3 (right), θ_{VP} is shown by a gray horizontal line in the lower part of the image. It can be observed that the foreground pixel counts in the columns of the image region with the NFT are greater than the threshold. Once the appropriate value of the threshold is selected, the vertical boundaries of an NFT are computed as follows:

$$x_l^{'}=\min\{c \mid g_x(c)\geq\theta_{VP}\}; \qquad (2)$$
$$x_r^{'}=\max\{c \mid g_x(c)\geq\theta_{VP} \;\&\; x_l^{'}\leq x_r^{'}\}.$$

The pairs of the left and right boundaries that are two close to each other, where 'too close' is defined as the percentage of the image width covered by the distance between the right and left boundaries. It has been experimentally found that the first approximation along the vertical boundaries are often conservative (i.e., text is cropped on both sides) and must be extended left, in the case of $x_l^{'}$, and right, in the case of $x_r^{'}$.

To put it differently, the left boundary is extended to the first column to the left of the current left boundary, for which the projection is at or above the threshold, whereas the right boundary is extended to the first column to the right of the current right boundary, for which the vertical projection is at or above the threshold. Figure 4 (left) shows the initial vertical boundaries (VBs) extended left and right.

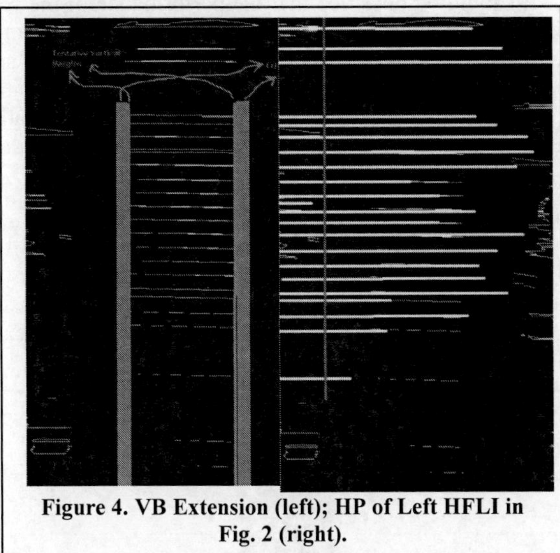

Figure 4. VB Extension (left); HP of Left HFLI in Fig. 2 (right).

D. Detection of Horizontal Boundaries

The computation of the horizontal boundaries of the NFT is confined to the image region vertically bounded by the extended vertical boundaries (x_l, x_r). Let $HP(HLFI)$ be the horizontal projection of the HLFI in Figure 2 (left) and let θ_{HP} be a threshold, which in our application is set to the mean count of the foreground pixels in rows, i.e., $\theta_{HP} = mean\{f(y) | f(y) > 0\}$. Figure 4 (right) shows the horizontal projection of the left HLFI in Figure 2. The gray vertical line in Figure 4 (right) shows θ_{HP}.

The horizontal boundaries of the NFT are computed in a manner similar to the computation of its vertical boundaries with one exception – they are not extended after the first approximation is computed. There is no need to extend the horizontal boundaries up and down, because the horizontal boundaries do not have as much impact on subsequent OCR of segmented text chunks as vertical boundaries. The horizontal boundaries are computed as follows:

$$r_u = \min\{r \mid f(r) \geq \theta_{HP}\}; \qquad (3)$$
$$r_l = \max\{r \mid f(r) \geq \theta_{HP} \,\&\, r \geq r_u\}.$$

Figure 5 (left) shows the nutrition table localized via vertical and horizontal projections and segmented from the left image in Figure 2.

IV. Text Chunking

A typical NFT includes text chunks with various caloric and ingredient information, e.g., "Total Fat 2g 3%." To optimize the performance of subsequent OCR, which is beyond the scope of this paper, these text chunks are segmented from localized NFTs. This approach is flexible in that segmented text chunks can be wirelessly transmitted to cloud servers for OCR. As can be seen in Figure 5 (left), text chunks are separated by black colored separators. Formally, text chunks are defined as text segments separated by horizontal black separator lines.

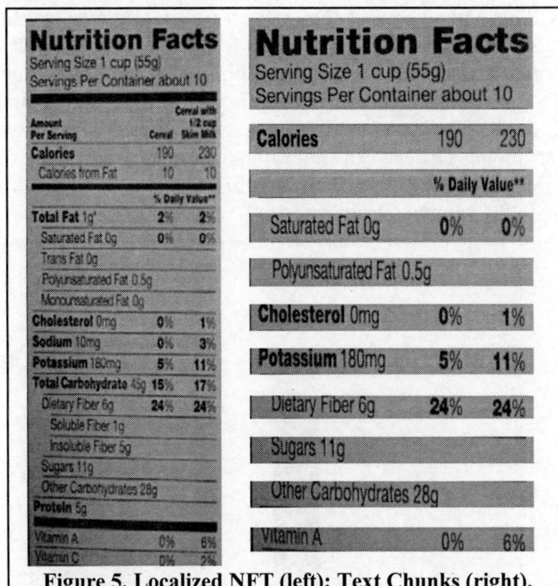

Figure 5. Localized NFT (left); Text Chunks (right).

Text chunking starts with the detection of these separator lines. Let N be a binarized image with a segmented NFT and let $p(i)$ denote the probability of image row i containing a black separator. If such probabilities are reliably computed, text chunks can be localized. Toward that end, let l_j be the length of the j-th consecutive run of black pixels in row i above a length threshold τ_l. If m be the total number of such runs, then $p(i)$ is computed as the geometric mean of $(l_0, l_1, ..., l_m)$. The geometric mean is more indicative of the central tendency of a set of numbers than the arithmetic mean. If θ is the mean value of all positive values of normalized by the maximum value of $p(i)$ for the entire image, the start and end coordinates, y_s and y_e, respectively, of every separator along the y axis can be computed by detecting consecutive rows for which the normalized values are above the threshold as follows:

$$y_s = i \mid p(i-1) \leq \theta \,\&\, p(i) > \theta; \qquad (4)$$
$$y_e = j \mid p(j+1) \leq \theta \,\&\, p(j) > \theta.$$

Once these coordinates are identified, the text chunks can be segmented from either the binarized or grayscale image, depending on the requirements of the subsequent of OCR. As can be seen from Figure 5 (right), some text chunks contain single text lines while others have multiple text lines.

V. Experiments

The NFT localization algorithm was implemented on Android 2.3.6 and Android 4.2. Forty five images were captured on a Google Nexus One (Android 2.3.6) in a local supermarket. The average running time of the algorithm is approximately one second per frame. All images were checked by a human judge to ensure that an NFT is present in the image, is not rotated, and is not cropped along any of its four sides. These images were then placed on a Google Nexus One smartphone (Android 2.3.6) and on a Galaxy Nexus (Android 4.2) smartphone with the installed application to obtain images with segmented NFTs and save them on the smartphones' SDK cards. The processed images were then analyzed by a human judge. On each original image, the four corners of an NFT were manually marked to obtain the ground truth to evaluate the segmentation process.

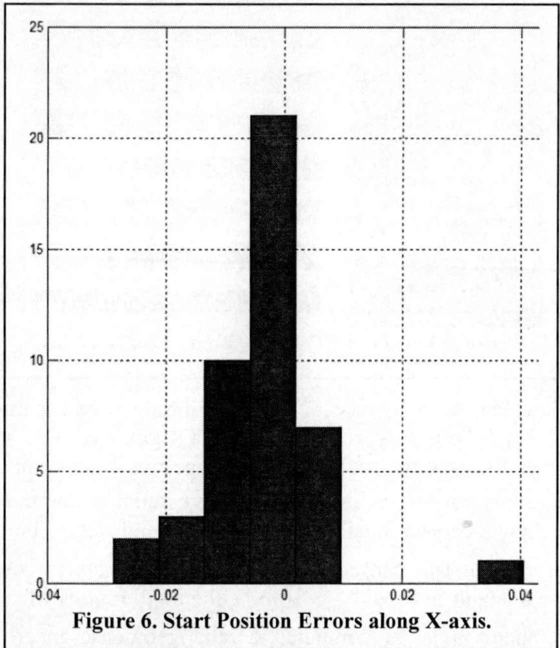

Figure 6. Start Position Errors along X-axis.

Figures 6 and 7 show the error histograms for the starting and ending positions of the segmented NFTs along the images' *x*-axis, respectively. In both figures, the *x*-axis encodes the error as a fraction of the NFT width while the *y*-axis encodes the number of images with a specific error value.

Figures 8 and 9 show the error histograms for the starting and ending positions of the segmented NFTs along the images' *y*-axis, respectively. In Figure 8 and 9, the *x*-axis encodes the error as a fraction of the NFT height. Positive errors occur in segmented images where segmented NFTs contain extra background pixels whereas negative errors occur when NFTs are cropped.

In general, positive errors are better for our purposes than negative ones because negative errors signal information loss that may result in subsequent OCR or image classification errors. It should be observed that the performance of the NFT localization algorithm has a mean error of 1% on the sample of images. There was one notable outlier, for which the start position on the *x*-axis error was 12.5% and the end position error on the *x*-axis was 14%. The same image was the outlier for the segmentation errors of the start and end positions along the *y*-axis.

Figure 10 shows the outlier image that caused the segmentation errors along both axes. It can be observed that the NFT in this image lacks a black colored bounding box that is usually present around nutrition fact tables. It is the absence of this box that caused the algorithm to fail to obtain the exact location of the NFT in the image.

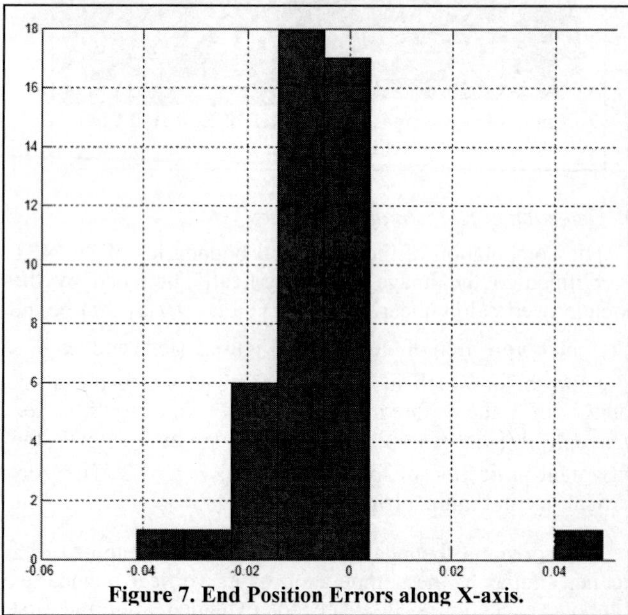

Figure 7. End Position Errors along X-axis.

The performance of the NFT localization algorithm along the *y*-axis has the mean errors of 5% and 7% for the start and end positions, respectively. Most errors, along both axes, are caused by NFTs that are not bounded by boxes, one of which is shown in Figure 10.

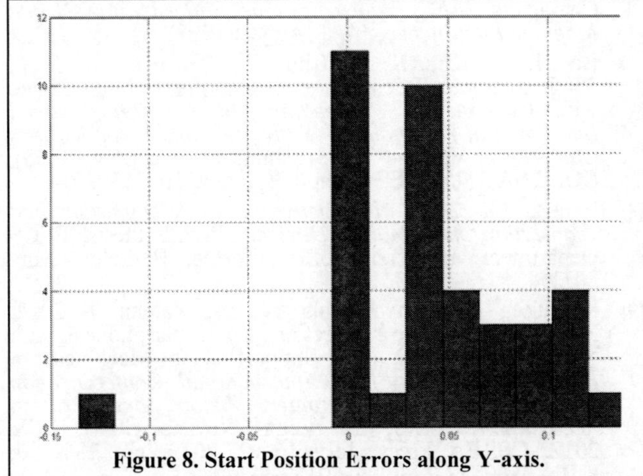

Figure 8. Start Position Errors along Y-axis.

The preliminary evaluation of the text segmentation algorithm was done on a set of 15 NFT images. A total of 303 text chunks (text segments between separator bars) were manually identified. Of these manually detected chunks, the algorithm detected 163, which gives a detection rate of 53.8%. The average running time of the text chunking algorithm is approximately half a second per localized NFT.

A statistical analysis of text chunk segmentation was executed. All text chunks readable by a human judge were considered as true positives. There were no true negatives insomuch as all text chunks had text. Text chunks which could not be read by a human judge were reckoned as false positives. False positives also included detection of separator bars between text chunks. Figure 11 contains a true positive example and two examples of false positives.

There were no false negatives in our sample of images, because all text chunks either contained some text or did not contain any text. The performance of the text chunking algorithm was evaluated via precision, recall, specificity and accuracy were calculated. The average values for these measures over the entire sample are given in Table 1.

VI. Discussion

The NFT localization algorithm had a mean error of 1% on the sample of NFT images. The average accuracy of the text chunking algorithm on the sample of images with localized NFTs is 85%. While we readily acknowledge that these results must be interpreted with caution due to small sample sizes, we believe that the approaches presented in the paper show promise as a front end vision-based nutrition information extraction module of a larger nutrition management system.

One limitation of the presented approach to NFT localization is that an image is assumed to contain a

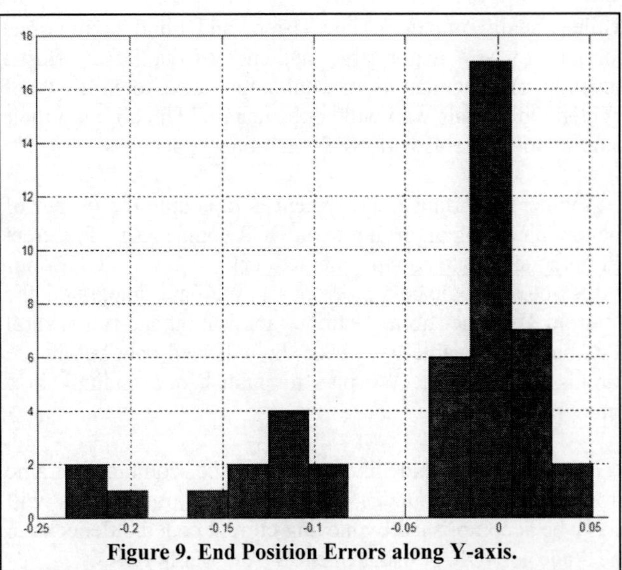

Figure 9. End Position Errors along Y-axis.

horizontally or vertically aligned NFT. We are currently working on relaxing this constraint to localize skewed NFTs in captured frames.

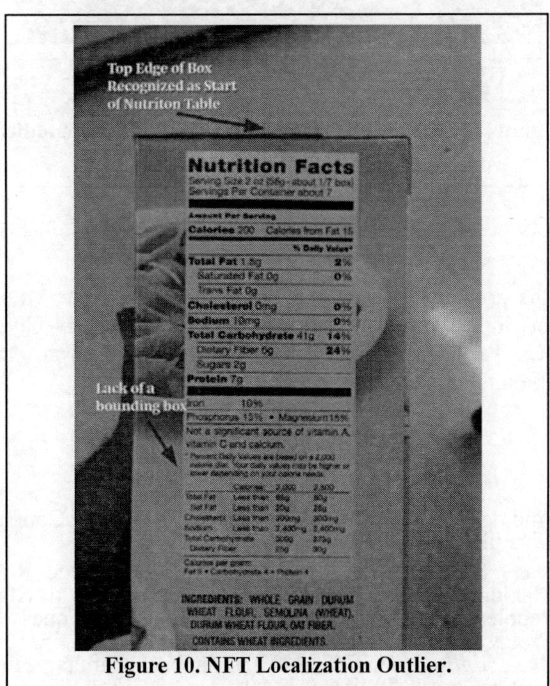

Figure 10. NFT Localization Outlier.

Table I. Average Recall, Precision, Specificity, Accuracy.

Precision	Recall	Specificity	Accuracy
0.70158	0.9308	0.88978	0.8502

The detection of skewed NFTs will make the system more accessible to users that require eyes-free access to visual information. However, it should be noted in passing that, while visually impaired, low vision, and blind populations continue to be a major target audience of our R&D efforts, nutrition management is of vital importance to millions of sighted individuals who will not have a problem aligning their smartphone cameras with NFTs on product packages.

Another important improvement is to couple the output of the text chunking algorithm to an OCR engine (e.g., Tesseract (http://code.google.com/p/tesseract-ocr) or OCRopus (https://code.google.com/p/ocropus)). We have integrated the Android Tesseract library into our application and run several tests but were unable to analyze the collected data before the submission deadline. We plan to publish our findings in a future publication.

Finally, we would like to bring the combined frame processing time to under one second per frame. This will likely be accomplished by moving current code bottlenecks to the Android NDK or using OpenCV Android libraries.

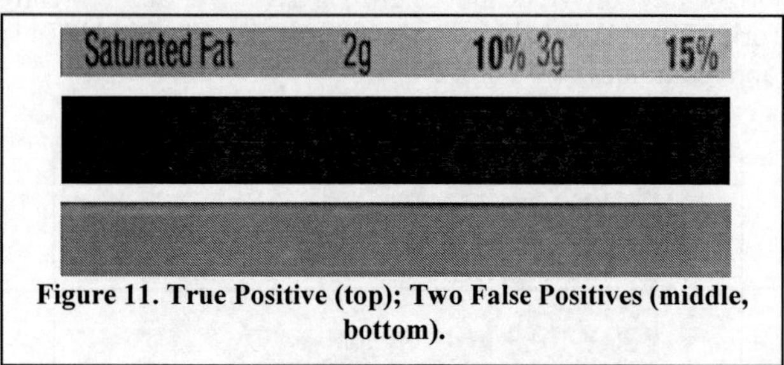

Figure 11. True Positive (top); Two False Positives (middle, bottom).

Acknowledgment

This project has been supported, in part, by the MDSC Corporation. We would like to thank Dr. Stephen Clyde, MDSC President, for supporting our research and championing our cause.

References

[1] Anding, R. *Nutrition Made Clear*. The Great Courses, Chantilly, VA, 2009.

[2] Kane S, Bigham J, Wobbrock J. (2008). Slide Rule: Making M obile Touch Screens Accessible to Blind People using Multi-Touch Interaction Techniques. In *Proceedings of 10-th Conference on Computers and Accessibility (ASSETS 2008)*, October, Halifax, Nova Scotia, Canada 2008; pp. 73-80.

[3] Kulyukin, V., Crandall, W., and Coster, D. (2011). Efficiency or Quality of Experience: A Laboratory Study of Three Eyes-Free Touchscreen Menu Browsing User Interfaces for Mobile Phones. *The Open Rehabilitation Journal*, Vol. 4, pp. 13-22, 2011, DOI: 10.2174/1874943701104010013.

[4] Årsand, E., Tatara, N., Østengen, G., and Hartvigsen, G. 2010. Mobile Phone-Based Self-Management Tools for Type 2 Diabetes: The Few Touch Application. *Journal of Diabetes Science and Technology*, 4, 2 (March 2010), pp. 328-336.

[5] Frøisland, D.H., Arsand E., and Skårderud F. 2010. Improving Diabetes Care for Young People with Type 1 Diabetes through Visual Learning on Mobile Phones: Mixed-methods Study. *J. Med. Internet Res.* 6, 14(4), (Aug 2012), published online; DOI= 10.2196/jmir.2155.

[6] Al-Yousefi, H., and Udpa, S. 1992. Recognition of Arabic Characters. *IEEE Transactions on Pattern Analysis and Machine Intelligence*, 14, 8 (August 1992), pp. 853-857.

[7] Bae, K. S., Kim, K. K., Chung, Y. G., and Yu, W. P. 2005. Character Recognition System for Cellular Phone with Camera. In *Proceedings of the 29th Annual International Computer Software and Applications Conference*, Volume 01, (Washington, DC, USA, 2005), COMPSAC '05, IEEE Computer Society, pp. 539-544.

[8] Hsueh, M. 2011. *Interactive Text Recognition and Translation on a Mobile Device*. Master's thesis, EECS Department, University of California, Berkeley, May 2011.

[9] Kulyukin, V., Kutiyanawala, A., and Zaman, T. 2012. Eyes-Free Barcode Detection on Smartphones with Niblack's Binarization and Support Vector Machines. In *Proceedings of the 16-th International Conference on Image Processing, Computer Vision, and Pattern Recognition*, Vol. 1, (Las Vegas, Nevada, USA), IPCV 2012, CSREA Press, July 16-19, 2012, pp. 284-290; ISBN: 1-60132-223-2, 1-60132-224-0.

[10] Duda, R. O. and P. E. Hart. 1972. Use of the Hough Transformation to Detect Lines and Curves in Pictures. *Comm. ACM*, Vol. 15, (January 1972), pp. 11-15.

Object Selection by Grouping of Straight Edge Segments in Digital Images

V. Volkov[1], R. Germer[2], A. Oneshko[1], D. Oralov[1]
[1]Department of Radioengineering, The Bonch-Bruevich State University of Telecommunications, Saint-Petersburg, Russia
[2]Institute of Technical Physics e.V., TU Berlin, Germany

Abstract – *A new method for finding geometric structures in digital images is proposed. An adaptive algorithm of straight line segments extraction is developed for manmade objects description in digital images. It uses an adjustment of oriented filter angle for precise extraction of line corresponding to real edge. Perceptual grouping approach is applied to these segments to obtain simple and complex structures of lines on the base of their crossings. Initial image is presented as a collection of closed structures with their locations and orientations. Applications to real aerial, satellite and radar images show a good ability to separate and select specific objects like buildings and other line-segment-rich structures.*

Keywords: object recognition, feature-based image matching, perceptual grouping, content-based image retrieval, building and road extraction

1 Introduction

Object extraction, selection and classification are most studied problems of image processing and computer vision. They have important applications for segmentation, visual tracking, image matching, image indexing and image retrieval [1-8].

Model-based approaches instead of view-based are generally used for manmade object recognition. Techniques of this kind analyze semantic information which is contained in object shape. The usual method is to extract contours and investigate their properties. Perceptual grouping is defined as the problem of aggregating primitive image features that project from a common structure in the visual scene [2]. Grouping of contours is a natural way to get these structures [4-6].

Our study relates to construction of structures for intermediate-level local description of objects in an image. It includes perceptual grouping of geometric primitives taking into account their intrinsic and relative properties [1,2,4,5,9-12].

There are many objects whose distinctive features are edges and geometrical relations between them. There are very important problems such as land use detection and classification, automatic building and road extraction, river and stream localization, landscape changes and change of object detection, image fusion and multi-image feature-based matching, which require the development and investigation of specific object models and feature descriptions with the use of straight line segments [11-24].

Though plenty of works were devoted to theoretical aspects of grouping problems there are not so much practically effective algorithms for manmade object selection in real images [3,15,17,19,20,23-27]. In addition it is often difficult to obtain performance characteristics for such algorithms, choose criteria and make comparative analysis.

2 Related work

Straight line segments play an important role in features description because almost all contours of real objects are locally straight [3,11-24].

These objects are buildings, bridges, roads, rivers, landscape boundaries and so on. There are many approaches of getting straight edge segments from an image. Most of them there interpreted in [10-14].

A new method proposed in [11,12] uses oriented filtering (slope line filter) and forming a gradient profile in the chosen direction. It has a very important advantage over other methods. It allows getting crossing points between extracted line segments. The second important property of this method is ordering of line segments with respect to the output of the slope line filter.

Idea of straight line grouping for features description seems was first theoretically developed in [9]. An image was interpreted as a collection of objects and relationships between these objects. At the first level points combines to get segments which can form ribbons, junctions and curves at higher levels. Grouping at each level is based on some geometric constraints such as continuity, parallelism, symmetry, overlapping, coincidence and others [1,9,10]. The information embedded in the graph is useful for a variety of tasks. Object recognition is often mapped into a graph matching problem.

In [23] authors develop new structural features called *consistent line clusters* that are useful in recognizing and locating man-made objects in images. An important question for content-based image retrieval is how to use the extracted segments to form more advanced features that can be used to recognize various objects.

Coordinates of straight line segments together with angles and magnitudes form the first level for object description [11,12]. Better extraction of straight line segments allows detection of corners and junctions of edges. We can further develop the known matching algorithms of [3,9] through the use of additional features. Some new ideas were discussed in [10], though without considering the sign of edge gradient.

Searching for related line pairs was implemented by comparing the relation of angles. In [3] a weighed matching measure model of straight lines which simultaneously use various linear features has been constructed and the values of weights of different features have been discussed. The method adopts a hierarchical straight line matching strategy, which uses the matching result of the first step as a restriction to reduce the searching range, and thus to finish the complete matching of the whole imagery. However, it has not overcome the incorrect matching caused by parallel straight lines.

Other descriptors, which are based on active contours, snakes, graph/trees, also including evaluation of the convex hull and the minimum bounding rectangle, have been proposed [10,17,20] (also see [12] for more citations).

3 Problem statement and method of solution

3.1 The problem statement and tasks

Our goal is to develop a practical algorithm for straight line segments grouping to select manmade objects in real imagery. These objects may have polygonal configuration, in most cases they are rectangular in shape.

We present a detailed description of the new method for straight line segments grouping to make structures which represent intermediate-level object description. We develop our method for straight edge segments extraction [11,12] because well-known detectors do not obtain surely localized edges and their intersections. New algorithm includes line angle adaptation loop to get precise estimate of edge orientation.

Straight line segments are ordered with respect to the mean gradient magnitudes of edges. Additional features are the orientation, intensity and width of the edge.

The problem is how to construct the object description on the basis of straight line segments and a set of low-level additional features. A novel method uses crossings in the ordered segments as the main property for grouping.

The next problem is a practical application and evaluation of this method to real aerial and satellite images for object extraction and recognition, and for image matching tasks.

3.2 Image processing structure and algorithm modifications

Image processing structure is shown in Fig.1. Pre-filtering and straight line segments extraction form a low-level description of an image content. A grey-level image X is obtained from registered initial image after some pre-filtering to smooth the initial image. Straight edge segment extraction algorithm was described in detail in [11,12]. In comparison with previous algorithm several improvements have been made to get better edge locations and to decrease the calculation time. Instead of rotating gradient images oriented filtering was obtained by the use of a bank of rectangular filter masks. Every mask has small width (about 3-5 pixels) and a length $lmask$. This length is a filter parameter which affected on the resulting lines ordering. It is also related to image sizes and determined edges which were extracted at the first steps.

Eight local gradients are calculated by the use of Sobel masks in corresponding sectors. Directional filter masks have different angles of orientation in these sectors with spacing of 6 degrees. The first extracted point has maximum value among all oriented filter outputs. Direction of this filter defines rough estimation of the first line orientation angle.

To obtain end points coordinates of the segment gradient profile along the obtained rough direction is formed which has to be averaged among several adjacent lines. In the top of Fig.2 gradient ridge is represented which has a small positive angle of orientation. Dashed line relates to the oriented filter mask which got maximum output filter value. It has horizontal direction which is a rough direction of the line. The corresponding gradient profile is described below. There is an angle error a between rough direction and the ridge slope. This error results in bad end points estimation which was a drawback of the previous algorithm.

In contrast to early version in the modified algorithm orientation angle of the line is adapted by maximizing the estimated length of the segment at this point. Oriented mask is rotated within the bounds of 6 degrees with the step of 0.5 degrees.

At every step a length of segment is calculated through the threshold circuit and the precise angle phi is set which corresponds to the maximum of the segment length. This procedure prevents fragmentation of lengthy lines in the image. The resulting profile is presented in the bottom of the Fig.2.

Threshold value $lengththresh$ is the other parameter of the algorithm which determines the resulting line lengths. All gradients inside the segment have to exceed the $lengthresh$. So high values of $lengthresh$ may cause line fragmentation. Too small values may result in connection of different lines in the same direction.

Number of lines $nlines$ is the last parameter which has to be chosen. It determines maximal number of extracted segments in the image.

In practice we may set additional threshold $gradthresh$ which restricts minimal gradient values for lines extraction. In this case exact number of lines may be less than $nlines$. The task of setting the value of $gradthresh$ relates to the problem of noisy lines cancellation.

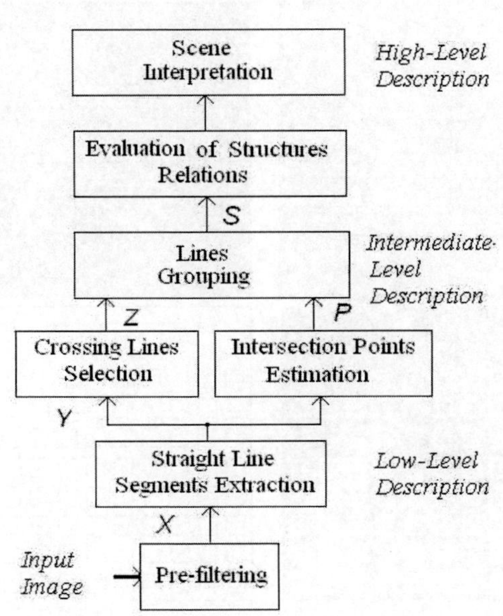

Fig.1. Image processing structure for object selection on the base of extracted straight line segments

At the beginning of processing the number *nlines* of extracted lines should be restricted by the use of some *a priori* information about number of objects in the image.

Together with coordinates of end points *coordinates* and the length of each line segment *length* the algorithm gives its angle *phi*, the maximal output of a directional filter *mfilter* and width of the ridge *width*. To calculate this width the second threshold value *widththresh* is needed. Algorithm forms several cross-sections of the ridge gradients and makes estimates of width which are averaged to form the resulting *width*.

All segments obtained are ordered with respect to the value *mfilter* of filter output.

The main operation for the next level of feature description is a detection of lines crossings. Every line may be crossed be several lines, and a final table Z contains rows with ordered numbers of all lines which cross (or adjoin) the chosen line. Corners and junctions are also included in this table. Crossing points coordinates P are geometrically calculated and may be also used for final structure description.

3.3 Lines grouping algorithms for object description and selection

The problem is to construct feature descriptors on the base of extracted ordered straight line segments for object recognition and image matching. A hierarchical set of features was developed in [11,12]. Here we present the detailed description and evaluation the performance of the method.

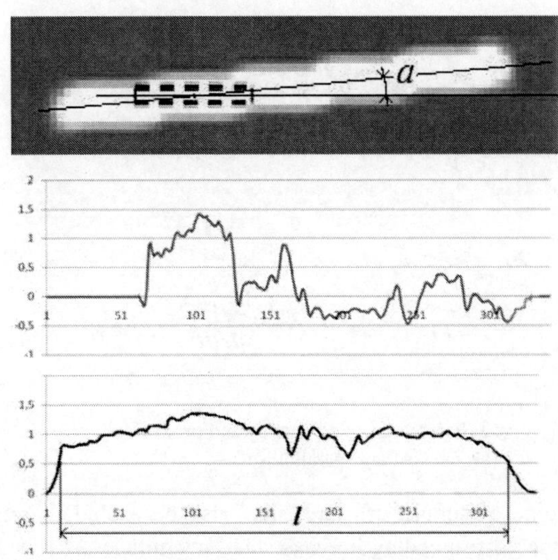

Fig.2. Gradient image of a ridge and gradient profiles of a segment along the rough and precise directions

At the intermediate level of description straight edge segments are grouped getting a simple structure for a given segment line. Here we define simple structure $C_k = \{L_k, L_m, L_n\}$ as a set of lines which may include up to two crossing lines for a given main line L_k, $k = 1, \ldots nlines$, $k < m < n$.

At the first step of grouping lines several restrictions may be applied to select the most interesting simple structures:

- contiguity describes touching or bordering of two lines; here a crossing of lines is a kind of contiguity;
- anti-parallelism of two lines which cross the main line means that they have absolute difference in orientations near 180 degrees; in practice we may define some angle *gamma* in degrees (the half of possible error) as a measure of anti-parallelism; anti-parallel lines are called APARS [14];
- proximity is being to or near; it can be evaluated by the distance d between lines;
- adjacency is being enough so as to touch; adjacent line results from road boarders extraction; it characterizes by the shift *delta* of one of anti-parallel line with respect to another.

These parameters are illustrated in Fig.3. It needs to normalized values d and *delta* with respect to minimal length of anti-parallel lines. Application of these restrictions results in selection of simple structures with desired properties among all possible structures.

Complex structure $S_k = \{C_k, C_m, C_n, C_p \ldots\}$ represents a collection of simple structures for a given line and for their crossing lines allows for mentioned restrictions.

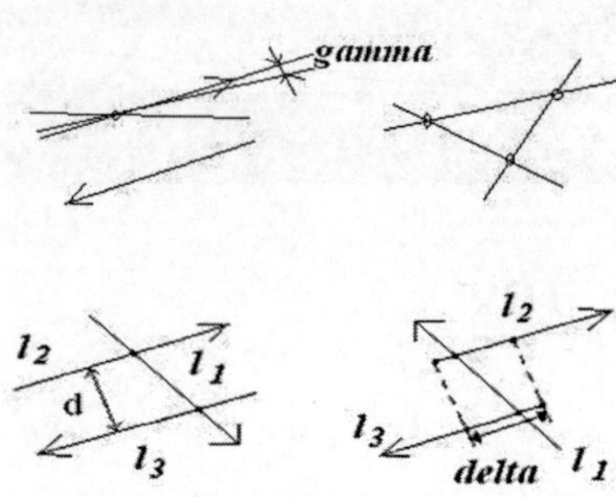

Fig. 3. Parameters of adjacency and proximity of anti-parallel lines

Some of simple structures may also be excluded from S_k if the corresponding line has small magnitude M_m with respect to the magnitude M_k of the main line. Resulting complex structure is used for object description along with properties of segments contained in this complex structure.

In this study compound objects with closed parallelogram structures are of primary interest. They may be considered as salient regions. Then a complex structure consists of two simple structures with mutual lines. This method can be generalized to form more complex collections of straight segments with corresponding descriptors.

4 Modelling of object detection, selection and localization

Consider a model of a noisy image which contains ten equal horizontal stripes, every stripe contain ten square objects of size 16x16 with Gaussian noise background (Fig.4, left top image). Signal-to-Noise ratio (SNR) is different in stripes. Its values vary from the top stripe to the bottom: 0,58; 1.16; 2.32; 3.49; 4.65; 5.81; 6.98; 8.14; 9,3; 11.6. The task is to detect and select square objects in the image.

Well-known Canny detector gives excellent extracted edge presentation (top right image in Fig.4) for object localization but it is difficult to test square shapes of the objects. It needs getting straight segments for solving the selection problem. The Hough transform can get straight line segments on the base of Canny edges. They are represented in the left bottom image in Fig.4. Few square objects may be extracted here even at high SNR.

One of modern algorithms is the Line Segment Detector [13] which obtains the presumed false alarms of noisy lines in the image. The result of lines extraction is shown in the right bottom image in Fig.5. The drawback of the LSD is the lack of crossing points but it is possible to construct closed objects by the use of lines fusion. By this way algorithm can detect and localize closed square objects but with low quality even at high SNR.

The proposed algorithm gives closed square objects as complex structures. Results of detection and localization are represented in the top of Fig.5.

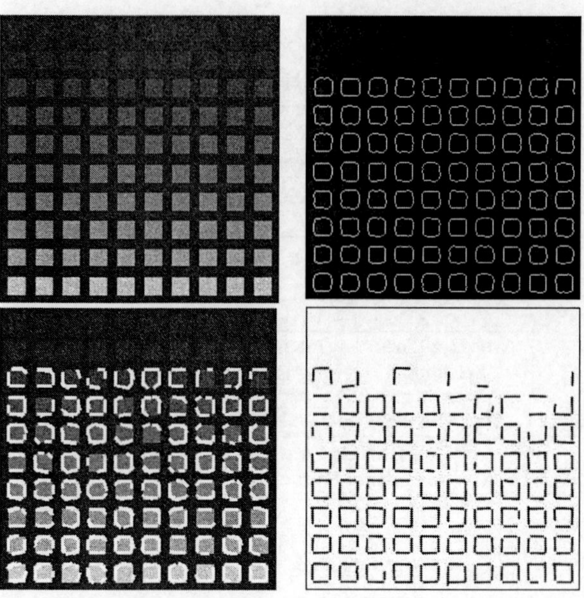

Fig. 4. Square objects detection in noisy model

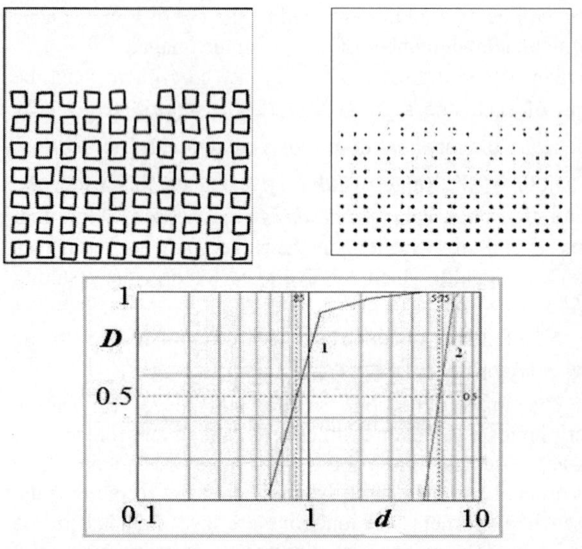

Fig. 5. Square object detection in comparison with the Harris corner detection

Parameters for detection were chosen to set rather weak restrictions on lines: $lmask = 16$, $gamma = 30$, $d = 0.1$, $delta = 0.1 - 10$. Threshold *gradthresh* was set so as to obtain not more than one noise line on the image. The value of *lengthresh* was chosen to get stable crossing points.

We can see good detection for SNR more than 3.5. Algorithm has better detection ability than LSD which cannot get closed structures even for high SNR.

Comparative analysis with Harris detector (right top picture) shows that the proposed algorithm can better detect crossing points. This is shown on the detection characteristic where curve 1 represents the proposed algorithm and curve 2 relates to Harris corner detector.

Consider another model of a noisy image which contains four stripes and different rectangular objects in each stripe (Fig.6).

Objects have different sizes in each stripe and SNR has increasing values 0.58, 1.16, 2.33 and 4.65 from top stripe to the bottom. The task is to select rectangular objects with different shapes, estimate their location and orientation parameters.

It is possible to control the selection process by varying the parameters $gamma$, d and $delta$. When we do not restrict the shape of objects algorithm extracts every rectangular object for SNR more than 1.16.

This is presented in Fig.6, where bottom images show location and orientation of the first two objects.

If minimal *delta* equals to 0.5 algorithm gives 6 objects in the centre. Reducing angle $gamma$ to 1 with *delta*=0.1-10, we get only well-shaped four objects (Fig.6).

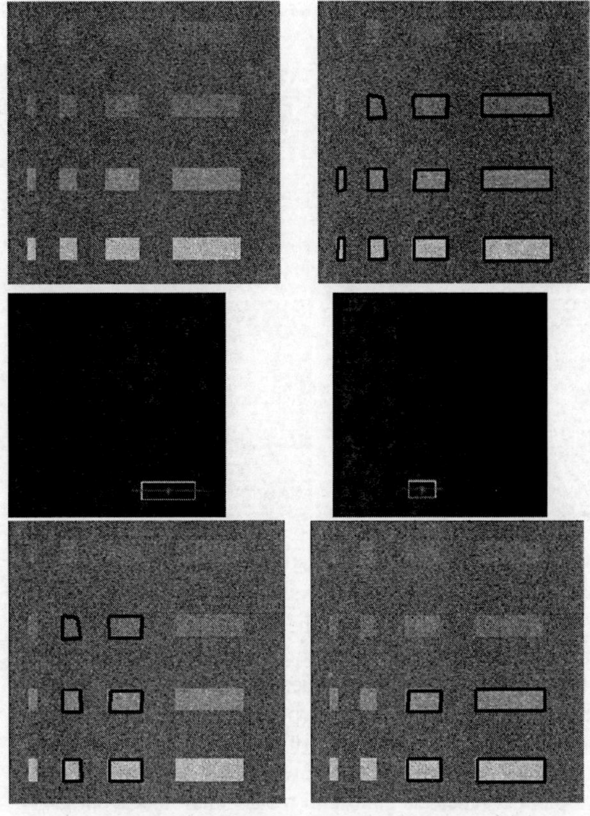

Fig. 6. Object shapes selection in noisy model

5 Experimental results for aerial, satellite and radar images

Original aerial and satellite images are shown at the top of Fig.7. They contain buildings which have straight edges. The aerial image (left-hand picture) has a better resolution than the satellite one (right-hand picture).

These pictures were investigated in [12] but closed structures have not been selected and localized. Here the processing was made more precisely. At the output we get 154 different closed structures in the left image and 107 structures in the right image. These structures represent whole objects and also different fragments of them and all have localization and orientation. We can initially distinguish ten objects which are the same in both images. Six of them can be extracted as a whole or partly.

Locations and orientations of the main object are shown on the bottom of Fig.7.

Another pair of images is represented in Fig.8. Aerial image on the left contains 187 closed structures and SAR radar image on the right side contains 190 structures for objects and their parts. Despite a poor quality of both images about a half of objects can be selected correctly.

The perspective investigations may relate to application of region-based methods of object extraction and recognition after previous segmentation is made by the use of lines grouping.

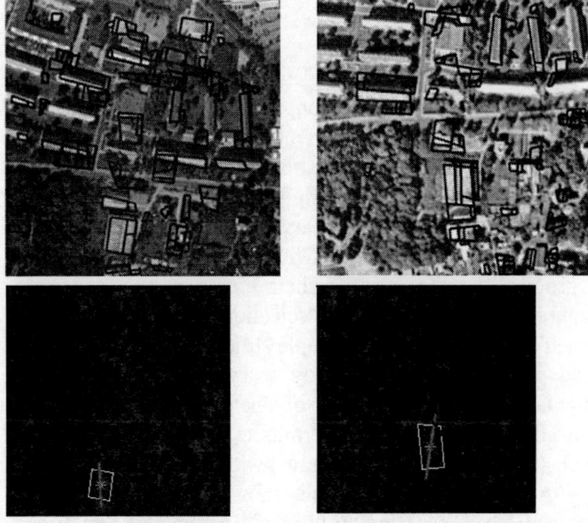

Fig. 7. Object selection in aerial and satellite images

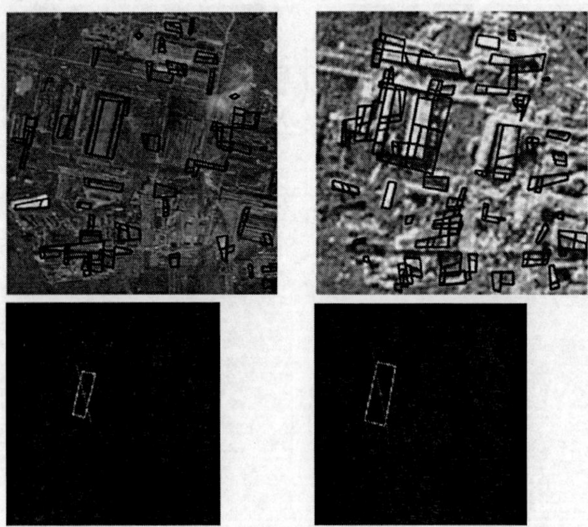

Fig. 8. Object selection in aerial and SAR radar images

Consider aerial image on the top of Fig.9 which is taken from [20] where active contour (snake) procedure was performed and the result is repeated in the second picture. Such a procedure needs initial points for successive object selection. The proposed algorithm works without initial setting and gives closed structures which are shown in the third picture. It selects almost all rectangular objects but gives several surplus structures. These structures do not relate to false or noisy objects but selection of useful objects needs additional analysis. Fourth picture in Fig.9 shows triangular structures on the image and fifth picture gets extracted roads.

6 Conclusions

The problem of object selection by the use of straight line segments extraction and grouping has been discussed. The method proposed includes several stages. At the first stage low-level description is obtained by the use of ordered list of straight line segments. Algorithm is improved by adaptation to decrease the errors of angle and length estimates. At the second stage crossing points of lines are calculated and lines are grouped on the base of their crossings to get simple structures. At the third stage selection is made subject to geometrical restrictions, and simple structures are joined to get closed complex structures. Only rectangular (or sometimes triangular) objects and parts of them were selected and localized here but algorithm permits to extract other types of objects (roads, polygonal structures) with little effort.

Analysis on noisy models shows the dependence of processing characteristics on the main parameters which can control the object selection process. Applications to real aerial, satellite and radar images show a good ability to separate and extract rectangular objects like buildings and other line-segment-rich structures. Most of objects are selected somehow or other and the following problem is how to improve grouping process.

7 References

[1] Q. Iqbal, J.K. Aggarwal. “Retrieval by classification of images containing large manmade objects using perceptual grouping”; Pattern Rec., 35, 1463—1479, 2002.

[2] V. Movahedi “Contour grouping”; Department of Computer Science and Engineering&Centre for Vision Research Qual. Exam- York University, 2009.

[3] G. Sohn, I.J. Dowman. “Extraction of buildings from high resolution satellite data”; In: Autom. Extract. of Man-Made Objects from Aerial and Space Images (III), Sweets&Zeitlinger, The Netherlands, 345—355, 2001.

[4] P. Srinivasan, L. Wang, J. Shi. “Grouping contours via a related image”; IEEE Conf. Computer Vision and Pattern Recognition (CVPR), 2010.

[5] V. Ferrari, L. Fevrier, C. Schmid. “Groups of adjacent contour segments for object detection”; IEEE Trans. V. PAMI-30, 36—51, 2008.

[6] Ch. Lu, L.J. Latecki, N. Adluru, X. Yang, H. Ling. “Shape guided contour grouping with particle filters”; ICCV, 2288—2295, 2009.

[7] V. Hedau, H. Arora, N. Ahuja. “Matching images under unstable segmentations”; Proc. 6th Euro Conf. on Comp. Vision, 551—563, 2008.

[8] J. Shao, R. Mohr, C. Fraser. “Multi-image matching using segment features”; Int. Arch. of Photogrammetry and Remote Sensing. Vol. XXXIII, Part B3. Amsterdam, 2000.

[9] R. Horaud, F. Veillon, T. Skordas. “Finding geometric and relational structures in an image”; First European Conf. Computer Vision, France April 23-27, 1990.

[10] S.K. Kim, H.S. Ranganah. “Efficient algorithms to extract geometric features of edge images”; Proc. IPCV’10, V. II, Las Vegas, Nevada, USA, 519—525, 2010.

[11] V. Volkov, R. Germer, A. Oneshko, D. Oralov. “Object description and extraction by the use of straight line segments in digital images”; Proc. IPCV’11, V. II, Las Vegas, Nevada, USA, 588—594, 2011.

[12] V. Volkov, R. Germer, A.Oneshko, D. Oralov. “Object description and finding of geometric structures on the base of extracted straight edge segments in digital images”; Proc. of the IPCV’12, V. II, P. 805—812, 2012

[13] R. Grompone von Gioi, J. Jakubovich, J-M. Morel, G. Randall. “LSD: A Line Segment Detector”; IEEE Trans., V. PAMI-32, N4, 722—732, 2010.

[14] G. Medioni, R. Nevatia. "Matching images using linear features"; IEEE Tr., V. PAMI-6, 675—685, 1984.

[15] Z. Fu, Z. Sun. "An algorithm of straight line features matching on aerial imagery"; Int. Arch. Phot. Rem. Sens. Spat. Inf. Sci., V. 37, Pt B3b, Beijing, 97—102, 2008.

[16] Y. Zhao, Y.Q. Chen. "Connected equi-length line segments for curve and structure matching"; J. Pattern Rec. and Artificial Intel. V. 18, 1019—1037, 2004.

[17] D.A. Lavigne, P. Saeedi, A. Dlugan, N. Goldstein, H. Zwick. "Automatic building detection and 3D shape recovery from single monocular electro-optic imagery"; SPIE Defence&Security Symp., Florida USA, 2007.

[18] E. Magli, G. Olmo, L.L. Presti. "On-board selection of relevant images: an application to linear feature recognition"; IP(10), No. 4, 543—553, 2001.

[19] E. Tretyak, O. Barinova, P. Kohli, V. Lempitsky. "Geometric image parsing in man-made environment"; Int. J. Comp. Vision, V. 67, 1—17, 2011.

[20] L.B. Theng. "Automatic building extraction from satellite imagery"; Engineering Letters, 13:3, Nov 2006.

[21] X. Jin, C.H. Davis. "Automated building extraction from high-resolution satellite imagery in urban areas using structural, contextual, and spectral information"; EURASIP J. on Applied Signal Processing, V. 14, 2196—2206, 2005.

[22] M. Ettarid, M. Rouchdi, L. Labouab. "Automatic extraction of buildings from high resolution satellite images"; ISPRS 2008, V. XXXVII, VIII, 61—65, 2008.

[23] Yi Li, L.G. Shapiro. "Consistent line clusters for building recognition in CBIR"; IPCR 2002.

[24] W. Jia, J. Zhang, J. Yang. "SAR image and optical image registration based on contour and similarity measures"; Proc. GSEM, 2009.

[25] P. Moreels, P. Perona. "Evaluation of features detectors and descriptors based on 3D Objects"; Int. J. of Computer Vision, V. 73, No. 3, 263—284, July 2007.

[26] Y. Song, X. Yuan, H. Xu. "A multi-temporal image registration method based on edge matching and maximum likelihood estimation sample consensus"; The Int. Arch. PRSSI Sci., V. XXXVII, Part B3b, Beijing, 61—66, 2008.

[27] R. Bergevin, J.-F. Bernier. "Detection of unexpected multi-part objects from segmented contour maps"; Pattern Recognition, V. 42, Issue 11, November 2009, 2403—2420.

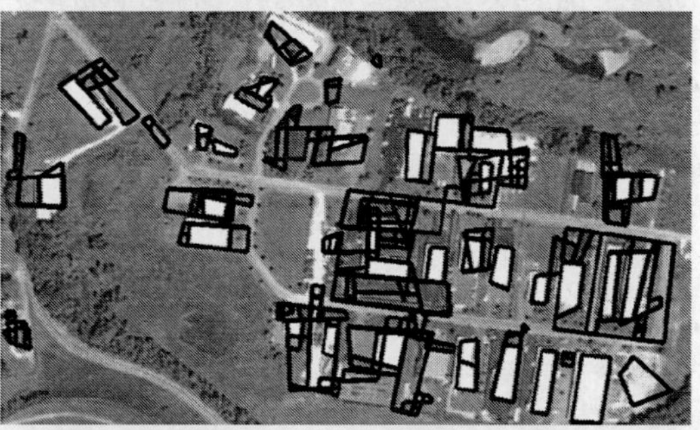

Fig. 9. Selection of different objects in aerial image

A Robust and Adaptive Image Inpainting Algorithm Based on a Novel Structure Sparsity

Zhidan Li, Hongjie He, Zhongke Yin, and Fan Chen
Sichuan Key Laboratory of Signal and Information Processing,
Southwest Jiaotong University, Chengdu, Sichuan, P.R. China

Abstract—*The existing patch sparsity based image inpainting algorithms have some problems in maintaining structure coherence and neighborhood consistence. To address the above problems, a robust and adaptive image inpainting algorithm based on a novel structure sparsity is proposed. The main improvement includes the following three aspects. Firstly, a novel structure sparsity function is defined according to the sparseness of the patch's nonzero similarities to its neighboring patches to encourage structure propagation preferentially. Secondly, the neighborhood consistence constraint factor is adaptively determined according to the target patch's structure sparsity value, which aims to reduce block effect and seam effect. Thirdly, to improve computational efficiency, the size of local search region is dynamically determined in accordance with the target patch's structure sparsity value. Experimental results demonstrate that the proposed algorithm can obtain more pleasurable vision results than that by other similar methods.*

Keywords: structure sparsity, image inpainting, adaptive, neighborhood consistence constraint

1. Introduction

With the rapid development of computer technology and multimedia technology in the recent years, image inpainting has become a hot research topic in the field of computer graphics and computer vision. Image inpainting, also known as image completion or image disocclusion, is a research area which uses known information to fill missing region under some rules, with the goal to achieve a visually plausible results. Image inpainting technique can be widely used in various areas, such as image coding and transmission, image and video editing.

Image inpainting methods can be roughly divided into two families: diffusion-based inpainting methods and exemplar-based inpainting methods. The former ones, where the missing area is filled by diffusing the image information from the source area into the missing area slowly, are based on the theory of partial differential equation[][1-5]. And they have acquired remarkable achievement for filling the non-textured or reversely smaller damaged area. However, because the diffusion-based approaches implicitly assume that the content of the missing region is smooth and nontextured, they are also inclined to bring in smooth effect in the textured area or large damaged region. Criminisi *et al.* [6, 7] proposed an exemplar-based inpainting algorithm which is suitable for repairing larger missing regions with different feature of structures and textures. In this approach, priority function and match criterion, which were adopted to determine filling order and find the most similar patch respectively, and firstly introduced into exemplar-based inpainting algorithm. The filling order and match criterion are two key issues of exemplar-based inpainting algorithms, and many researchers study on them to achieve more pleasurable repair results. Cheng et al. [8] amended the definition of priority function to obtain a more robust filling order. Wu [9] proposed a novel exemplar-based completion model which used a cross-isophote diffusion item to decide the filling order. Jemi [10] proposed to use DCT coefficients of exemplar to decide filling order and add the edge information into the match criterion to find the most similar patch. An exemplar-based inpainting based on local geometry was proposed in [11], where structure tensors were employed to define the priority and template matching. Wang [12] improved the exemplar-based inpainting algorithm by using D-S evidence theory to compute priority. Compared with the diffusion-based inpainting methods, the exemplar-based inpainting algorithms have got plausible results for inpainting the larger missing region. However, only the information of the patch located at fill-front was used to compute priority, and it is inadequate because the neighboring information was not considered. To solve the drawbacks, Zhang [13] proposed a novel priority scheme based upon the color distribution. Xu and Sun [14] proposed an inpainting algorithm based on patch sparsity. Patch sparsity was reflected in two aspects: firstly, structure sparsity function was defined to measure the sparseness of nonzero similarities of a patch with its neighboring patches, and it was used to compute priority function to get a more robust filling order; secondly, multiple candidate patches were selected to represent the target patch sparsely and then copy the sparse representation information to the target patch's missing region. Hesabi et al. [15] used structure sparsity and modified confidence term to compute priority to get a more robust filling order, but they still only used one candidate patch to fill missing region. However, Xu's algorithm still cannot well maintain structures coherence and textures consistence, because structure sparsity could not well measure confidence of a patch located at structure region, and neighborhood consistence constraint factor was fixed in different regions.

This paper proposes a robust and adaptive image inpainting algorithm to improve Xu's algorithm from three aspects: Firstly, a novel structure sparsity function is defined by measuring the confidence of a patch located at structure area instead of texture region. Secondly, the neighborhood consistence constraint factor is adaptively determined on the basis of target patch's structure sparsity value. Thirdly, local search region size is adaptively determined by target patch's structure sparsity value. Compared with Xu's algorithm, a novel structure sparsity function defined in this paper can better encourage the structure region to be filled preferentially; and because neighborhood consistence constraint factor changes with different neighboring features, the algorithm can obtain better guide information of sparse representation to maintain the consistence with neighboring information; also local search strategy can decrease computational complexity.

This paper is organized as follows. In Section 2, Xu's patch sparsity based image inpainting algorithm is briefly described. In Section 3, the details of the proposed image inpainting algorithm, including the novel structure sparsity, adaptive neighborhood consistent constraint and dynamic local search region are expound. The experimental results and comparisons with previous algorithms are presented in the Section 4. Finally, we conclude this work in Section 5.

2. Patch sparsity based algorithm

Xu and Sun proposed an image inpainting algorithm based on patch sparsity[14]. In this algorithm, structure sparsity was used to determine filling order. After target patch was selected, multiple candidate patches were found under sum of squared distance (SSD) criterion and were used to represent missing information sparsely. Then the sparse representation information was used to fill missing region. The procedures repeat until all missing pixels were filled. In the following, we briefly describe the structure sparsity and sparse representation.

2.1 Structure sparsity

Given an input image I, the missing region is denoted by Ω and its fill-front is $\delta\Omega$. The source region is indicated by $\Phi(=I-\Omega)$. Let Ψ_p be a square patch centered at the point $p \in \delta\Omega$, then structure sparsity $S(p)$ is defined as:

$$S(p) = \sqrt{\left[\sum_{k\in N_s(p)} \omega^2_{p,k}\right] \frac{|N_s(p)|}{|N(p)|}} \tag{1}$$

where $N(p)$ is a neighborhood window centered at p, which is set to be larger than the size of patch Ψ_p; $\omega_{p,k}$ measures the similarity between patch Ψ_p and its neighboring patch Ψ_k. The terms $N_s(p)$ and $\omega_{p,k}$ are defined as follows:

$$N_s(p) = \{\ k|k \in N(p) \quad and \quad \Psi_k \subset \Phi\ \} \tag{2}$$

$$\omega_{p,k} = \frac{1}{Z(p)} \exp\left(-\frac{d(\Psi_p, \Psi_k)}{25}\right) \tag{3}$$

where $d(\cdot,\cdot)$ measures the mean squared distance and $Z(p)$ is a normalization constant such that $\sum_{k\in N_s(p)} \omega_{p,k} = 1$.

2.2 Patch sparse representation

Let Ψ_p be the target patch, F and E be two matrices to extract already known and missing pixels of Ψ_p respectively, $\{\Psi_q\}_{q=1,\ldots,M}$ be the top M most similar patches, then Ψ_p is approximated by the linear combination of $\{\Psi_q\}_{q=1,\ldots,M}$, i.e.,

$$\Psi_t = \sum_{q=1}^{M} \alpha_q \Psi_q \tag{4}$$

Then the unknown pixels in patch Ψ_p are filled by the corresponding pixels in Ψ_t, i.e., $E\Psi_p = E\Psi_t$. The constraints for the linear combination in (4) include two aspects:

One is that the estimated patch Ψ_t should approximate the target patch Ψ_p over the already known pixels, i.e.,

$$\|F\Psi_t - F\Psi_p\|^2 \le \delta \tag{5}$$

The other is that newly filled pixels in the estimated patch Ψ_t should be consistent with the neighboring patches in appearance, i.e.,

$$\left\|\beta\left(E\Psi_t - E\sum_{k\in N_s(p)} \omega_{p,k}\Psi_k\right)\right\|^2 \le \delta \tag{6}$$

where $\omega_{p,k}$ is same as defined in (3), β balances the strength of the constraints in (5) and (6).

The combination coefficients $\vec{\alpha} = \{\alpha_1, \alpha_2, \cdots, \alpha_M\}$ are inferred by minimizing a constrained optimization problem in the framework of sparse representation. Then the linear combination coefficients $\vec{\alpha}$ can be inferred by optimizing the constrained optimization problem:

$$\arg\min\{\|\vec{\alpha}\|_0\} \ \text{s.t.} \|D\Psi_t - \Psi_T\|^2 < \delta \ \text{and} \ \sum_i^M \alpha_i = 1 \tag{7}$$

where $D = [\ F \quad \beta E\ ]^T$ and $\Psi_T = [\ F\Psi_p \quad \beta E \sum_{k\in N_s(p)} \omega_{p,k}\Psi_k\ ]^T$.

3. Proposed algorithm

To solve of the drawbacks of Xu's approach that structure coherence and texture consistence could not well be maintained, this paper proposed a robust and adaptive inpainting algorithm by introducing a novel structure sparsity function which is used to determine the filling order, neighborhood consistence constraint coefficients and local search region size. The details of our algorithm is expounded in the following.

3.1 Novel structure sparsity

From the definition of structure sparsity in Xu's algorithm, we can know that structure sparsity value is relate to the similarities between a patch and its neighboring known patches and the ratio between the numbers of known patches and the numbers of patches in the neighborhood (i.e. $|N_s(p)|/|N(p)|$). Suppose that a patch locates at structure part, but the numbers of known patches of its neighborhood is relative less, then structure sparsity value will be relative small and the structure patch will not be filled preferentially, which will result in the structures incoherence. Based on the consideration, a novel structure sparsity is proposed in this paper:

$$S(p) = \sqrt{\sum_{k\in N_s(p)} \omega_{p,k}^2} \tag{8}$$

where $\omega_{p,k}$ is same defined as (3). From the definition of novel structure sparsity, we can see that its value only relate to similarities. This definition is to avoid structure sparsity value being too small when a patch located at structure part with relative less surrounding known patches. Also we can learn that structure sparsity value increases with respect to the sparseness of patch's nonzero similarities to its neighboring patches. When a patch locates at structure part, it is saliently distributed within local region, therefore, it has higher structure sparsity value; while a patch locates at smooth part, it has many similar patches in the local neighborhood region, hence, it has smaller structure sparsity value. Under the guidance of structure sparsity, the patches located at structures(e.g., edges and corners) will have higher priority for patch inpainting compared with patches in texture or smooth regions. Since the similarity range is between 0 and 1, structure sparsity will also be in the range of 0 and 1. When a patch locates at smooth region, its structure sparsity value is close to zero hence it cannot lead to a robust filling order. In this paper we use the following transform to avoid structure sparsity value being too small, i.e.,

$$S(p) = \lambda S(p) + (1-\lambda) \tag{9}$$

where $0 < \lambda < 1$. In this paper λ is set to be 0.75.

3.2 Adaptive neighborhood consistent constraint

We still adopt the sparse representation of multiple candidate patches to fill missing information. Differing from Xu's approach where the neighborhood consistence constraint factor was fixed, we use a varied neighborhood consistence constraint factor. Image patch has different similarities to its neighboring patches, therefore the neighborhood consistence constraint will be different. Neighborhood consistence constraint can be reflected by factor β, then different neighborhood consistence constraint can be obtained for different region via adjusting factor β. When a patch locates at structure part, its structure sparsity value is relative large. Since the similarity between this patch and its neighborhood is relatively small, we should use relatively small neighborhood consistence constraint to maintain clarity of structure part. On the contrary, when a patch locates at smooth region, its structure sparsity value is relative small. Because the similarity between the patch and its neighborhood is relative large, we should apply relative large neighborhood consistence constraint to reduce block effect and seam effect. Therefore, we can vary the neighborhood consistence constraint with structure sparsity value. Based on the inversely proportional relationship between neighborhood consistence constraint and structure sparsity value, we adaptively determine the factor β according to:

$$\beta = 1/(\rho \cdot S(p)) \tag{10}$$

Because structure sparsity value varies between 0.25 and 1, and β should be in the range of [0,1], we multiply a factor ρ in the denominator. In this paper, ρ is set to be 6.

3.3 Dynamic local search region

The original global search in Xu's algorithm is time-consuming. To improve the performance from a efficiency prospective, we propose to adopt a local search method. From the definition of structure sparsity, we know that patch's location feature can be reflected by its structure sparsity value. The higher structure sparsity value is, the more likely that the patch locates at structure part and the smaller similarity between patch and its neighborhood is, and the search region size should be larger to find similar patch. The smaller structure sparsity value is, the more likely that a patch locates at smooth region, and the higher similarity between the patch and its neighborhood is, hence the local search region can be set smaller to decrease computational complexity rapidly. Here, we adaptively decide the local search region according to the target patch's structure sparsity value and the search region radius W is determined by

$$W = \begin{cases} \gamma \cdot S(p), & \text{if } \gamma \cdot S(p) > 30 \\ 30, & \text{others} \end{cases} \tag{11}$$

where γ is weight factor, in this paper γ is set to be 60.

3.4 Steps of the proposed algorithm

Let the degraded image indicated by I and missing region indicated by Ω, the steps of our painting algorithms are as follows.

Step 1: Compute priority. For any patch Ψ_p centered at p for point $p \in \delta\Omega$, the priority $P(p)$ is calculated by

$$P(p) = C(p)S(p) \tag{12}$$

where $S(p)$ is defined in (9) and $C(p)$ is the confidence term, defined as

$$C(p) = \sum_{q\in\Psi_p\cap\Phi} C(q) \Big/ |\Psi_p|. \tag{13}$$

Step 2: Search candidate patches. After priority values of all patch centered at fill-front are calculated, the patch with the biggest priority values is selected as the target patch Ψ_m. Then search the top M most similar patches in the local source region (its size is determined by equation (11)) under SSD criterion [6,7].

Step 3: Sparse representation. Use the M candidate patches to sparse representation the target patch Ψ_m. Before the sparse representation process, neighborhood consistence constraint coefficient is determined by target patch's structure sparsity value (i.e. equation (10)). Then linear coefficients are inferred by solving constrained optimization equation.

Step 4: Fill missing region. Copy sparse representation information Ψ_t to missing pixels of target patch Ψ_m.

Step 5: Updating confidence values. After the patch Ψ_m has been filled with new pixel values, the confidence $C(p)$ is updated in the area delimited by Ψ_m , as follows:

$$C(p) = C(m) \quad \forall p \in \Psi_m \cap \Omega \tag{14}$$

For each newly pixel on the fill-front, compute its patch priority.

Step 6: Repeat step 2-step 5 until all missing pixels are filled.

4. Experiment Results

In this section, we present simulation results of our approach on natural images, and compare the proposed approach with Xu's method [14] and Hesabi's method [15]. The algorithms are programmed using Matlab language and executed on a PC with Intel 2.5GHz CPU. In our approach the size of patch is set to $7*7$, the size of neighborhood (i.e., $N(p)$ around p in (1) is set to $25*25$, and the number of candidate patches M is set to 25.

4.1 Scratch and text removal

Figure 1 presents four examples for scratch and text removal. Peak signal-to-noise ratio (PSNR) between inpainted images and original images are measured for qualitative comparison and given in Table 1. As shown in Figure 1, the Xu's approach produces sharp inpainting results shown in the third column. However, due to the fact that the filling order is not enough robust and the neighborhood consistence constraint factor is fixed, some unpleasant visual discontinuities are introduced. For example, the structure incoherence appears within the red rectangle of Xu's result. Hesabi's approach produces less pleasant results because only the most similar patch is used to fill missing region. For example, the structure incoherence appears within the red rectangle of Hesabi's result in the second row of Figure 1, and the block effect and seam effect emerge within the red rectangle of Hesabi's result in the first row of Figure 1. For our proposed algorithm, not only the neighborhood can be maintained more consistent, but also the structure part can be kept more coherent. The reason is that in our algorithm, structure sparsity function is defined more reasonably, and the neighborhood consistence constraint factor is adaptively determined according to structure sparsity value, hence the guide information can be obtained more reasonable, which lead to more sharp and consistent repair results with the best PSNR values(presented in Table 1). The inpainting time of Xu's and our algorithm are present in Table 2. From Table 2, we can see that our method can reduce the compute time dramatically. Therefore, our algorithm not only improve the repair results, but also enhance computational efficiency.

Table 1: PSNR (dB) of image inpainting.

	Figure 1(a)	Figure 1(b)	Figure 1(c)	Figure 1(d)
Xu's method[14	35.01	33.13	35.07	29.33
Hesabi's method[15]	34.74	31.65	33.41	28.32
Our method	35.86	34.55	35.91	30.35

Table 2: Execution time (s) of image inpainting.

	Figure 1(a)	Figure 1(b)	Figure 1(c)	Figure 1(d)
Xu's method[14]	1116.3	750.6	1836.9	1549.8
Our method	172.1	132.2	249.9	232.9
Improved times	6.49	5.68	7.35	6.65

4.2 Object removal

We also use the proposed algorithm to recover the missing region after object removal. In the results of Xu's algorithm, the inpainted structures are not always consistent with the surrounding structures. For example the edge of bridge and wall cannot keep linear in the first and second example respectively. The Hesabi's algorithm uses modified priority function based on structure sparsity to determine filling order, so the results have less effect of structure incoherence, however, there are still some flaws in the results. For example, the unwanted structure appears within the red rectangle of Hesabi's result in the first row of Figure 2, and the structure incoherence appears within the black rectangle of Hesabi's result in the second row of Figure 2. As for the proposed algorithm, a novel structure sparsity is adopted and neighborhood consistence constraint is adaptively adjusted, therefore the structure coherence is well maintained and the inpainted patches are more consistent with the surrounding textures. In addition, our algorithm exhaust the less inpainting time, as shown in Table 3.

Table 3: Execution time (s) of image inpainting.

	Figure 2(a)	Figure 2(b)
Xu's method[14]	1858.1	1182.1
Our method	248.4	170.8
Improved times	7.48	6.92

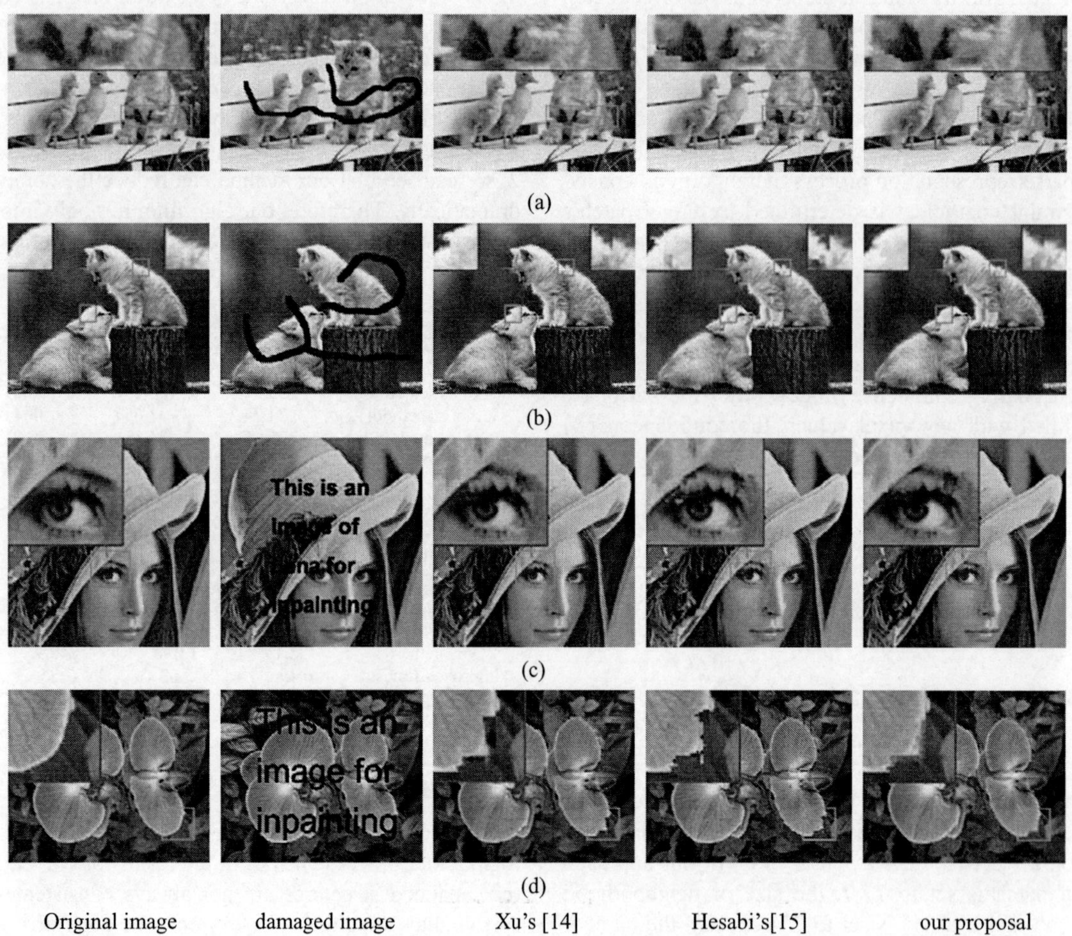

Figure 1: Comparison of inpainted images obtained with Xu's[14], Hesabi's[15] and our proposal.

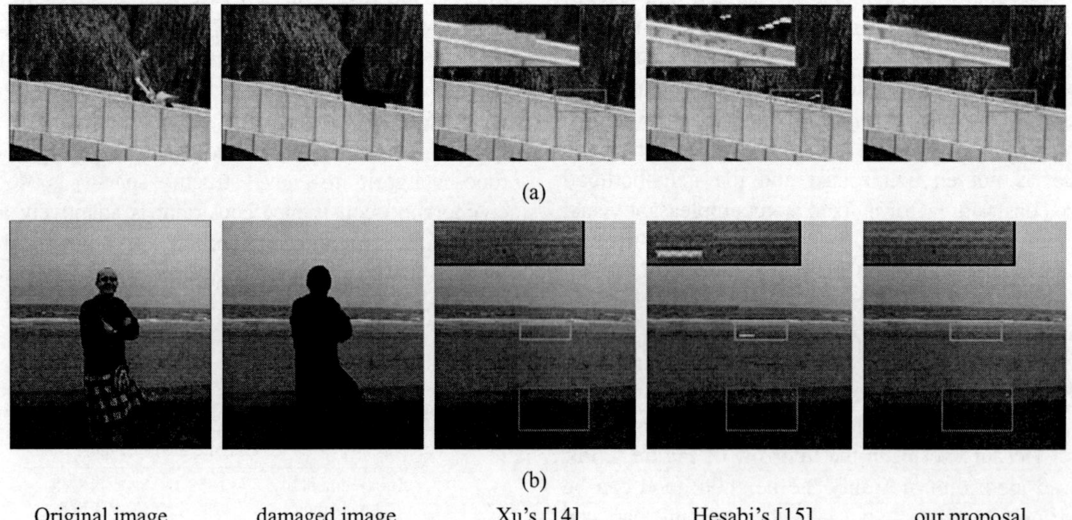

Figure 2: Comparison of inpainted images obtained with Xu's[14], Hesabi's[15] and our proposal.

5. Conclusion

This paper proposes a robust and adaptive image inpainting algorithm based on a novel structure sparsity. The major novelty of this work is that a novel structure sparsity, adaptive neighborhood consistence constraint and adaptive local search method are proposed. Experiments and comparisons have showed that the proposed exemplar-based algorithm can better infer the structures and textures of missing region, and produce sharp inpainting results consistent with the surrounding textures. In the future, we will further investigate the sparsity of natural images at multiple orientations, and apply it to image inpainting.

References

[1] M. Bertalmio, G. Sapiro, V. Caselles, and C. Ballester, "Image inpainting," in *Proc. ACM SIGGRAPH*, 2000, p.417-424.

[2] T. Chan, J. Shen, "Mathematical models for local nontexture inpaintings," *SIAM Journal on Applied Mathematics.*, vol. 62, pp. 1019-1043, 2001.

[3] T. Chan, J. Shen, "Nontexture inpainting by curvature-driven diffusions," *Journal of Visual Communication and Image Representation.*, vol. 12, pp. 436-449, 2001.

[4] J. Hahn, X. Tai, S. Borok, and A. Bruckstein, "Orientation-matching minimization for image denoising and inpainting," *International journal of computer vision.*, vol. 92, pp. 308-324, 2011.

[5] J. Miyoun, X. Bresson, T. Chan, and L. Vese, "Nonlocal mumford-shah regularizers for color image restoration," *IEEE Transactions on Image Processing.*, vol. 20, pp. 1583-1598, 2011.

[6] A. Criminisi, P. Perez, and K. Toyama, "Object removal by exemplar-based inpainting," in *IEEE Computer Society Conference on Computer Vision and Pattern Recognition*, 2003, p.721-728.

[7] A. Criminisi, P. Perez, and K. Toyama, "Region filling and object removal by exemplar-based image inpainting," *IEEE Transactions on Image Processing.*, vol. 12, pp. 1200-1212, 2004.

[8] W. Cheng, C. Hsieh, S. Lin, C. Wang, and J. Wu, "Robust algorithm for exemplar-based image inpainting," in *Prof. International Conference on Computer Graphics, Imaging and Vision.*", 2006, p.64-69.

[9] J. Wu, and Q.!Ruan, "Object removal by cross isophotes exemplar-based inpainting," in *Prof. 18th International Conference on Pattern Recognition.*, 2006, p.810-813.

[10] D. Jemi Florinabel, S.!Ebenezer Juliet, and V.!Sadasivam, "Combined frequency and spatial domain-based patch propagation for image completion," *Computers & Graphics*, vol. 35, pp. 1051-1062, 2011.

[11] O. Le Meur, J. Gautier, and C. Guillemot. "Examplar-based inpainting based on local geometry," in *Prof. IEEE International Conference on Image processing.*, 2011, p. 3401-3404.

[12] S. Wang, Y. Xu, and X. Yang, "Joint DS Evidence Theory and Priority Computation for Image Completion," *Recent Advances in Computer Science and Information Engineering.*, pp. 529-535, 2012.

[13] Q. Zhang and J. Lin, "Exemplar-based image inpainting using color distribution analysis," *Journal of Information Science and Engineering.*, vol. 28, pp. 641-654, 2012.

[14] Z. Xu and J. Sun, "Image inpainting by patch propagation using patch sparsity," emphIEEE Transactions on Image Processing., vol 19, pp. 1153-1165, 2010.

[15] S. Hesabi and N. Mahdavi-Amiri. "A modified patch propagation-based image inpainting using patch sparsity," in *Prof. International Symposium on Artificial Intelligence and Signal Processing.*, 2012, p.43-48.

LURID: A Heuristically Based System for Automated Image Safety Determination

Daniel S. Rosen[1]
[1]Director, Imaging Technology, GumGum, Inc., 12407 4th St., Suite 400, Santa Monica, CA, 90401

Abstract - *Much research has been devoted to the automatic detection of objectionable imagery. In those situations where image safety is directly tied to revenues, the minimization of false alarms rates is of primary importance. Skin detection algorithms that seek to classify images as being safe or unsafe based upon apriori skin content thresholds, have been found to have unacceptably high false alarm rates in classifying images as being objectionable. While improved trained classifiers have been introduced which provide good results, they require large training sets and great care must be exercised in the selection of the classification parameters in order to provide the best performance. LURID is a system that utilizes heuristics based on anthropometry to create a robust system for determining image safety with very low false alarm rates.*

Keywords: feature extraction; image safety; anthropometry; skin detection; heuristics

1 Introduction

GumGum is the world's largest in-image ad network. Our deep understanding of images allows us to pair advertisements with contextually relevant images. The result is an entirely new monetization stream for publishers and opportunity for marketers to place their marketing messages directly in-line with the content that users most actively engage with. GumGum's clients are sensitive not only to the topical content of the images they use, but whether those images are considered by the advertiser to be "safe". In addition, avenues for revenue generation utilizing image features, such as adding a moustache [1] to digital images are well known and it is likely that new ideas for monetization of features will be forthcoming. In order to be prepared, as much information as possible should be discovered and retained.

Determining image safety has concentrated on the detection of pornography through the use of support vector machine [2], [3], shape region techniques [4], pixel based detection [5]. While these techniques have been shown to be effective, they have been developed with a goal of detecting pornographic images and because this type of target imagery is deemed extremely unsafe, the probability of a Type 1 error is allowed to rise in order to provide the lowest possible Type 2 error. In addition, these techniques [6] are particularly tuned to these specific images; an approach which provides an almost universally accepted definition of image safety.

When dealing with in-image advertising, the definition of safe-vs.-unsafe must be broadened to include those images which are unacceptable to client advertisers or those images which might be deemed inappropriate due to specific marketed viewers. For example, an ad for children's toys might be deemed safe to serve to an image of a woman wearing a bikini bathing suit, but not an image of a woman wearing bra and panties. Similarly, an ad for a travel service to a Muslim country might be deemed unsafe to serve to an image of a woman with any skin exposure other than the face. In addition, these "thresholds of safety" might vary from one client to the next even within the same product target.

The previously cited techniques do not allow for simple and rapid definitions of safety and, in addition, systems that utilize them are not constructed to determine and retain anthropometric and feature data for possible further image data exploitation.

2 Approach

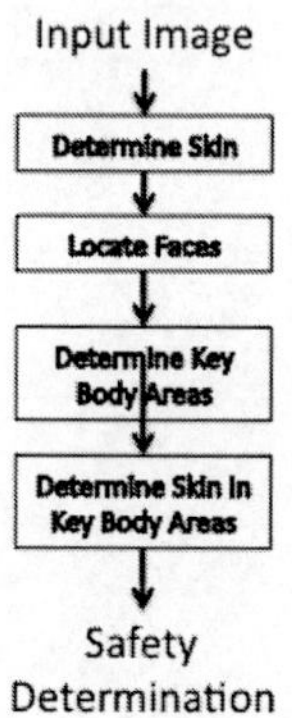

Figure 1.

LURID is constructed utilizing the logic shown in Figure 1.

2.1 Determine Skin

First, the entire target image T, with center (X_c, Y_c) is searched to find all pixels corresponding to skin. This skin detection is conducted utilizing the facial skin color model developed by Abdul Rahman, Wei and See [7]. As will be seen, this skin model, although targeted at the detection of faces performs extremely well in detecting body skin. This body area detection, while considered undesirable in the cited study is well suited for LURID.

The Abdul Rahman, Wei and See skin color model consists of 3 rules; Rule A, Rule B and Rule C which must all return TRUE for a given pixel in order for the pixel to be declared skin.

Two rules are defined to model skin in the RGB color space. One for skin under uniform daylight given as

$$(R > 95)\ AND\ (G > 40)\ AND\ (B > 20)\ AND\ (max\{R, G, B\} - min\{R, G, B\} > 15)\ AND\ (|R - G| > 15)\ AND\ (R > G)\ AND\ (R > B) \quad (1)$$

and the second for skin under flash or daylight lateral lighting given by

$$(R > 220)\ AND\ (G > 210)\ AND\ (B > 170)\ AND\ (|R - G| \leq 15)\ AND\ (R > B)\ AND\ (G > B) \quad (2)$$

A logical OR is then used to combine rule (1) and rule (2). This RGB rule is denoted as Rule A.

Next, 5 bounding rules enclosing the Cb-Cr color region were formulated as below:

$$Cr \leq 1.5862 \times Cb + 20 \quad (3)$$
$$Cr \geq 0.3448 \times Cb + 76.2069 \quad (4)$$
$$Cr \geq -4.5652 \times Cb + 234.5652 \quad (5)$$
$$Cr \leq -1.15 \times Cb + 301.75 \quad (6)$$
$$Cr \leq -2.2857 \times Cb + 432.85 \quad (7)$$

A logical AND is then used to combine rules (3) to (7). This CbCr rule is denoted as Rule B.

Finally, two cutoff levels are defined in the HSV color space as below:

$$H < 25 \quad (8)$$
$$H > 230 \quad (9)$$

A logical OR is then used to combine rules (8) and (9). This HSV rule is denoted as Rule C.

$$\text{Rule A:}\quad Equation(1) \cup Equation(2) \quad (10)$$
$$\text{Rule B:}\quad Equation(3) \cap Equation(4) \cap Equation(5) \cap Equation(6) \cap Equation(7) \quad (11)$$
$$\text{Rule C:}\quad Equation(8) \cup Equation(9) \quad (12)$$

Each pixel that fulfills Rule A, Rule B and Rule C is classified as a skin pixel,

$$Rule\ A \cap Rule\ B \cap Rule\ C \quad (13)$$

Figure 2. Skin Detection

Beyond the classification of each image pixel as "skin" or "not skin", no further processing is performed to segment the skin regions or to fill holes in regions (Figure 2), but skin related data statistics are gathered as follows.

The percentage, P, of skin pixels, in the image as a whole

$$P = \#skin\ pixels\ /\ total\ \#pixels \quad (14)$$

Given a pixel, $P_{j,k}$, at location x_k, y_j The spatial moment or order (m,n) is given by

$$M(m,n) = \sum_j \sum_k x_k^m\, y_j^n\, P_{j,k} \quad (15)$$

The center of mass of the skin area $C=(C_x, C_y)$ is calculated as

$$C_x = \frac{M(1,0)}{M(0,0)} \quad (16)$$
$$C_y = \frac{M(0,1)}{M(0,0)} \quad (16)$$

The area of the skin is defined as the zeroth spatial moment of the skin mass, M(0,0) and the skin pixel density, D, of the skin given by

$$D = \frac{P}{M(0,0)} \quad (17)$$

Finally, the convex hull of the skin pixels is calculated and a standard linear least squares fit to the convex hull is done to create a best-fit line to the skin area (Figure 3).

Figure 3.

Once these fundamental data have been generated, an early threshold is applied to determine if the percentage of skin in an image is too small to allow for a discernible human body or if the skin pixel density is so low that, again, no human form could exist. Through some trial and error, the lower bound of skin percentage for declaring that a human form might be possible was found to be 0.095 and a density value of 0.12 was found to be the lower bound on skin pixel density. If the target image is found to be below either of these values, the image is declared as safe due to it most likely being non-human, and no further processing is performed.

2.2 Locate Faces

If the percentage of skin and the skin density indicate a possible human form, a facial classifier such as defined by Viola and Jones [8] is utilized to detect all faces within the image. In particular a frontal face classifier [9] and a profile face classifier [10] are utilized to detect face candidates. In addition, all face detections must exceed a skin pixel threshold of 0.13 to be declared as a candidate face. As each face candidates is discovered, duplicate faces are removed. Removal is accomplished by a simple region-overlapping test. Given a set of n rectangular regions $R=\{R_1, R_2,\ldots R_n\}$, with rectangular region R_j having a center given by $(m_{j,x}, m_{j,y})$, width given by w_{rj} and height given by w_{hj}, and a candidate region R_c, we declare R_c to be a duplicate if

$$(M_{c,x}, M_{c,y}) \cap (M_{j,x}, M_{j,y}) \neq \varnothing \ \forall R_n \in R \qquad (18)$$

Frontal faces are detected first followed by profile faces as the probability of detection of faces in three-quarters profile by the frontal detector exceeds the probability of detection by the profile detector. This is due to the choice of detectors in each case and will change with the selection of other detectors. LURID does not depend on this ordering of detection.

Once the set of detected faces $\mathbf{F}=\{R_1, R_2, \ldots, R_m\}$, has been formed from the set of candidate facial regions R, a set of facial feature detectors [11] is utilized to determine the location of eyes, noses and mouths within each facial region, R_m (Figure 4).

Figure 4. Face and Facial Features

Each feature detector is run only against the image region contained within the facial region of interest, R_m.As each feature set $G=\{E_1, E_2,\ldots,E_j,N_1,N_2,\ldots,N_k,M_1,M_2,\ldots,M_m\}$, with eye region detections E_j, N_k, M_m ; $(j,k,m \in \mathbf{I})$, a set of heuristics based on anthropometric data is utilized to assemble complete faces, and rejecting false alarms for each feature. In particular, because of the various expressions which can be made with the human mouth, it is often confused for an eye by mouth detectors and vice-versa. It is known, for example, that a pair of eyes cannot be located below a nose or mouth except if a person is upside down, in which case a frontal face detector will not have made a detection. Similarly, anthropometric data from the United States Department of Defense [12] and [13], as well as fundamental anatomy, in the case of upright or tilted and/or rotated head positions rules out the location of the mouth at the top of the face, even in the presence of no other feature detections.

2.3 Determine Key Body Areas

The set of detected faces F is utilized to generate a set of probable search rectangles S, centered at $m^*=(m_{1,x}, m_{1,y})$ with width w_s, height h_s and rotation angle θ_s for body location (Figure 5).

Figure 5.

Again, anthropometric data creates a set of heuristics for these search rectangles as follows:
$\forall R \in F$, calculate Sj, centered at $s^*=(m_{j,x}, m_{j,y})$,
$w_s = w_{r1} \times 1.5$, $h_s = h_{r1} \times 2.0$, $a_s = 90$.

Determine the skin pixels utilizing equation (13) and determine the image moments of these pixels utilizing equation (15). Calculate the least squares linear fit to the convex hull and its angle β.

If $F=\{R_1\}$ *and* $(m_{1,x}, m_{1,y}) \approx (X_c, Y_c)$,
then $\theta_s = 90$, $w_s = w_{r1} \times 1.5$, $h_s = h_{r1} \times 3.0$ (H1)
If $F=\{R_1\}$ *and* $(m_{1,x}, m_{1,y}) \not\approx (X_c, Y_c)$ *and* $R_1 \cap C \neq \varnothing$,
$w_s = w_{r1} \times 1.5$, $h_s = h_{r1} \times 3.0$ *and*
calculate θ_s *as angle from* $(m_{1,x}, m_{1,y})$ *to* (C_x, C_y) (H2)
If $F=\{R_1\}$ *and* $(m_{1,x}, m_{1,y}) \not\approx (X_c, Y_c)$ *and* $R_1 \cap C = \varnothing$,
$w_s = w_{r1} \times 1.5$, $h_s = h_{r1} \times 3.0$, $\theta_s = \beta$. (H3)
If $F \neq \{R_1\}$, *then* $\forall R \in F$,
calculate Sj, *centered at* $(m_{j,x}, m_{j,y})$,
$w_s = w_{r1} \times 1.5$, $h_s = h_{r1} \times 2.0$, $\theta_s = \beta$. (H4)

Once the angle θ_s has been determined, three body area rectangles B_i are created, corresponding to the three key body areas (Figure 6). Specifically, B_1 = chest area, B_2 = midriff area and B_3 = crotch area. B_i is centered at $b^*=(b_{xi}, b_{yi})$, with height h_b, width w_b and rotation angle ρ_b. (b_{xi}, b_{yi}) is calculate as

$b_1{}^* = ((m^*\text{-}C)/\sqrt{m^2 + C^2}) \times (k \times (\sqrt{s^2 + C^2})$
where k= 95th percentile distance from face to chest (19)

$h_1{}^* = h_{rj} \times \gamma$
where γ = 95th percentile face height × a scale factor (20)

$w_1{}^* = w_{rj} \times \delta$
where δ = 95th percentile face width × a scale factor (21)

$\rho_1 = atan(m^*/C)$ (22)

$b_2{}^* = ((m^*\text{-}C)/\sqrt{m^2 + C^2}) \times (k \times (\sqrt{s^2 + C^2})$
where k= 95th percentile distance from face to midriff (23)

$h_2{}^* = h_{rj} \times \gamma$
where γ = 95th percentile face height × a scale factor (24)

$\rho_2 = \theta_s$ (25)

$w_2{}^* = w_{rj} \times \delta$
where δ = 95th percentile face width × a scale factor (26)

$b_3{}^* = ((m^*\text{-}C)/\sqrt{m^2 + C^2}) \times (k \times (\sqrt{s^2 + C^2})$
where k= 95th percentile distance from face to crotch (27)

$h_3{}^* = h_{rj} \times \gamma$
where γ = 95th percentile face height × a scale (28)

$w_3{}^* = w_{rj} \times \delta$
where δ = 95th percentile face width × a scale factor (29)

$\rho_3 = \theta_s$ (30)

Figure 6. Key Body Search Areas

2.4 Determine Safety

At each key body search area, the percentage of skin pixels (λ_i, i=1,2,3) is calculated using (13).

Safety is determined by a changeable set of heuristics that determine the state of clothing as shown in Table 1. The clothing state Δ is the logical AND of the key body areas:

$$\Delta = \lambda_1 \cap \lambda_2 \cap \lambda_3 \quad (31)$$

Clothing State	**% of skin in key body area**		
	Chest Area Skin	***Midriff Area Skin***	***Crotch Area Skin***
Clothed	< 0.10	< 0.01	< 0.01
Naked	> 0.70	> 0.70	> 0.70
Naked or very skimpy	> 0.85	> 0.4	< 0.4
Topless	> 0.85	< 0.4	< 0.4
Lowcut	$0.15 < \lambda_1 \leq 0.85$	< 0.10	Any
Bikini or bra/panties	> 0.10	>0.0	< 0.60
Bikini top or bra	> 0.10	0.0 (e.g. midriff not in image)	< 0.60
No pants or panties or "microbikini"	> 0.10	>0.0	> 0.67

Table 1. Safety Rules

Finally, LURID outputs all feature and image parameters determined to allow for downstream image data exploitation if desired.

3 Results and Further Work

A set of 11,621 random images from the Internet were inspected manually and classified as safe if clothing state= "clothed" or no human form, unknown if clothing state = "lowcut" or "bikini or bra/panties" or "bikini top or bra" and unsafe if clothing state = "Naked" or "Topless" or "naked or very skimpy" or "no pants or panties or microbikini" . 9483 were deemed safe, 202 were deemed unsafe and 1694 were deemed unknown.LURID correctly classified 9453 safe images as safe and classified 30 safe images as unsafe. LURID correctly classified 1581 images as unknown and classified 113 unknown images as unsafe. LURID correctly classified 192 unsafe images as unsafe, classified 10 unsafe images as safe. The most important statistic for LURID is the probability of false classification as an unsafe image. As can be seen, this initial test produced a probability of false unsafe = 1.3%

LURID has been shown to be an effective and flexible framework for determining image safety. It allows for a variable definition of safety and provides a significant amount of image-derived data to allow for future exploitation.

Moving forward, LURID will be expanded to include texture analysis to provide for a more accurate clothing estimate. In addition, an easy API and interface for defining safety as a function of key body areas will be added.

4 References

[1] facestache. (n.d.). *Facestache*. Retrieved March 1, 2013, from facestache.com: www.facestache.com

[2] Lin, Y.-C., Tseng, H.-W., & Fuh, C.-S. (2003). Pornography Detection Using Support Vector Machine. *16th IPPR Conference on Computer Vision, Graphics and Image Processing (CVGIP 2003)* (pp. 123-130). Kinmen, ROC: IPPR.

[3] Zhu, H., Zhou, S., Wang, J., & Yin, Z. (2007). An Algorithm of Pornographic Image Detection. *Proceedings of Fourth International Conference on Image and Graphics* (pp. 801-804). IEEE.

[4] Mofaddel, M. A., & Sadek, S. (2010). Adult Image Content Filtering: A Statisitcal Method Based on Multi-Color Skin Modeling. *IEEE International Symposium on Signal Processing and Information Technology* (pp. 366-370). IEEE.

[5] Kasaei, S. A. (2005). Pixel-Based Skin Detection for Pornography Filtering. *Iranian Journal of Electrical and Electronic Engineering , 1* (3).

[6] Fuangkhon, P., & Tanprasert, T. (2005). Nipple Detection for Obscene Pictures. *SSIP '05 Proceedings of the 5th WSEAS International conference on Signal, Speech and Image Processing* (pp. 242-247). WSEAS.

[7] bin Abdul Rahman, N. A., Wei, K. C., & John, S. (2007). *RGB-H-CbCr Skin Colour Model for Human Face Detection.* Multimedia University, Information Technology

[8] Viola, P., & Jones, M. (2001). Rapid Object Detection Using a Boosted Cascade of Simple Features. *IEEE Conference CVPR. 1*, pp. 511-518. IEEE.

[9] Lienhart, R. (n.d.). 20x20 gentle adaboost frontal face detector. *OpenCV* . Intel.

[10] Bradley, D. (n.d.). 20x20 profile face detector. *OpenCV* . Princeton University / Intel.

[11] Castrillon-Santana, M., Deniz-Suarez, O., Hernandez Tejera, M., & Guerra Artal, C. (2007). ENCARA2: Real-time Detection of Multiple Faces at Different Resolutions in Video Streams. *Journal of Visual Communication and Image Representation , 18* (2), 130-140.

[12] United States Department of Defense. (2012). Mil-STD 1472G.

[13] Bashour, M. (2005). *Is An Objective Measuring System for Facial Attractiveness Possible?* Dissertaion.com.

Indoor Navigation based on Fiducial Markers of Opportunity

Mazhar Ali Lakhani, John Nielsen, Gerard Lachapelle

Position Location and Navigation (PLAN) Group, University of Calgary,

2500 University Dr. NW, Calgary, Alberta, Canada, T2N 1N4 Calgary, Canada

malakhan@ucalgary.ca, nielsenj@ucalgary.ca, Gerard.Lachapelle@ucalgary.ca

Abstract— **Computer vision is becoming an important component of facilitating indoor positioning processing as applicable to a smart phone (SP). Typically such processing is in the form of ego-motion or identifying landmarks by correlating images from the SP camera via the inverse transform to pre-stored orthographic view images of the landmark. 3D ego-motion is difficult unless the feature points (fp) of opportunity are known to lie on a common plane. However, a coplanar subgroup of opportunistic fp's can be found in the form of building features such as windows, doors, wall frames, tiles, and markers that can be assumed to be rectangular are readily useable for estimating perspective transformations. With an assumed structure of the rectangle, a useful set of constraints emerges that facilitates the perspective mapping. In this paper SLAM processing is used, starting from a known marker and moving to observed rectangles of opportunity. The method of implementing the rectangular set of FP's into the SLAM algorithm is described.**

Index Terms— **Computer Vision (CV), Simultaneous Localization and Mapping (SLAM), smart phone (SP), fiducial markers (FM), fiducial marker of opportunity (FMO).**

1. INTRODUCTION

There is an obvious need to reliably extend the ability of accurately locating a smartphone for indoor environments. Traditional GPS methods which operate well outdoors are not reliable for indoor applications due to the weak signal which does not adequately penetrate indoor environments. As well there is the problem of the rather narrow bandwidth of GPS signaling which results in significant errors in multipath environments [1-2]. This is further contrasted with the higher accuracy demands for indoor positioning which is really only useful if the eventual positioning error is on the order of a meter or less. For this reason other observables that are applicable for facilitating indoor location are being considered such as using MEMS based gyros, accelerometers, magnetometers and most importantly computer vision (CV) based on using video output of the small camera built into every smart phone. Unfortunately CV applied to the general 3D vision processing as required for facilitating indoor location is highly computationally intensive, ill conditioned and complex. Hence simplifying assumptions are necessary to facilitate the required computation on a handset device. One successful simplification is that of implementing 2D ego-motion based on training the camera to look for fp's of opportunity on the floor or ceiling surface of the indoor environment. 2D ego-motion based on translation only at a reasonably constant height is computationally efficient and robust. It is certainly applicable to robotics where the camera can be held at a fixed height and the tilt of the camera is small. However, it is less applicable for the smart phone(SP) application where the user will invariably tilt the camera. Ego-motion that can accommodate the tilt is significantly more difficult as a full perspective processing is required. This increases the computational effort required as well as undermining the robustness of the location estimate as the processing is ill conditioned. To ameliorate the loss of robustness, it is necessary to use stereoscopic cameras or some form of pattern projection as is implemented into the Microsoft Kinect™. However, the additional hardware required in the smart phone to facilitate this is borderline prohibitive as the SP device form factor is so compact.

As it is desired to facilitate the ego-motion with a single web-cam quality camera it is necessary to implement the overall perspective processing such that the camera tilt issue can be accommodated. A method that has been researched and successfully implemented is that of recognizing templates or markers integrated into the floor surface. When these are observed in the camera's FOV, the points in the 2D geometry of the marker as observed in the cameras image plane can be related the known marker geometry providing a set of constraints from which the full perspective transformation can be evaluated. Hence if the indoor environment has a set of such markers integrated into the floor surface then a robust computationally efficient means of ego-motion can be realized that is implementable in the SP. Fiducial markers (FM)'s have been extensively used for localizing in both indoor and outdoor environments [3], especially for indoor navigation. For instance, [4] illustrates a method to enable navigation by assigning markers to location and then observing a short sequence of these markers. [5] is an example of using encrypted patterns from which the 3D position information can be decoded. This can be extended to markers on an arbitrary plane surface such that any combination of wall, ceiling or floor surfaces that have some innate geometric structure can be used for such processing.

In this paper we intend to further generalize the marker such that it can be a generic rectangle that is observed as a pseudo marker or template of opportunity. The structure of the rectangular geometric shape provides useful constraints from which the perspective transformation can be directly extracted. Buildings are full of simple geometric shapes with the rectangle being the most prevalent showing up in doorways, windows, wall frames, floor tiles, picture and poster frames and so forth. The photograph of a typical indoor building environment in Figure 1 is illustrative of the large number of rectangles that can be potentially used as coplanar subsets of fp's of opportunity that are vertices of rectangles. Of course there are geometric shapes that are not rectangles, notably triangles and trapezoidal shapes that can fool the ego-motion algorithm. However, such shapes occur far less frequent than the rectangle. The perspective transformation generated from non-rectangular shapes under the false pretense that they are rectangular will result in large outlier solutions that are identifiable by such algorithms as RANSAC such that they can be removed from the set of observable data.

The positioning method developed in this paper is based on the observation of a mix of isolated 2D markers that are known to the CV location algorithm combined with markers of opportunity that are only recognized by the algorithm to be potential rectangular shape. It is assumed that the known fiducial markers (FM) are rare relative to the plentiful FM's of opportunity consisting of observed and assumed rectangles. To simplify the development of the underlying SLAM processing, the known FM is initially observed such that the SLAM can extract a reasonably accurate estimate of the perspective transformation matrix. As the SP is moved, the camera image changes and an FM of opportunity (FMO) is in the camera FOV, along with the known FM. Based on the extracted perspective transformation of the first FM, the coordinates of the FMO are evaluated. The assumption of the set of vertex points extracted from the contoured image of the FMO is that it is a basic rectangular shape. This is tested by the constraints of the hypothesized rectangle (i.e. equal length sides and equal length diagonals). The perspective transformation is then transferred to this new FMO as the camera is moved and the original FM leaves the camera FOV. Then the next FMO is observed in the camera FOV, is tested based on the same hypothesized rectangular shape with the perspective transformation updated. As this procedure continues, there will be a random drift in the SLAM estimates as the errors with each new FMO processed will accumulate. To ameliorate this drift issue, it is necessary to assume that there are other observables available for the SP. This could be in the form of a known FM. It could also be that the SP gets an absolute location from a recognizable landmark or perhaps and RFID registration. Alternately it can use wireless signals and perhaps GPS which are inaccurate as pointed out earlier but do not suffer from accumulated trajectory estimation drift. The SLAM algorithm systematically appropriates the weighting of these disparate observables. However, the purpose of this paper is not the details of the SLAM algorithm but rather the perspective mapping of the sequence of known FM's and FMO's as input observables to the SLAM algorithm.

2. Methodology

2.1 The Underlying SLAM Algorithm

The underlying algorithm for determining the trajectory of the camera as it is moved by the user through the indoor environment is a modified version of SLAM. The generic SLAM algorithm accommodates disparate observations from a number of available sensor sources contained in the SP. It is assumed here that the SLAM can access to a map outlining the location of the known anchor FM's. However, these may be thinly distributed and not sufficient for ubiquitous location estimation of the SP. However, they provide justification for an initially known location of the SP. Note that the SLAM algorithm is more general in that it can accommodate arbitrary uncertainty as an initial belief map as to the location of the SP.

The SLAM variables typically consist of the location of observed fp's that could be known (anchor points) or fp's of opportunity that initially are of unknown location. In this application the perspective transformation of the FM's is included in the set of variables tracked by the SLAM algorithm. As the SP is moved, the camera trajectory is mapped out by the SLAM algorithm as an overall joint least squares estimate of the additional FMO location and perspective transformation variables. Occasionally when a FM of known location is observed, the SLAM recalculates the complete list of variables thus correcting for the drift in the estimation of the SP trajectory. As such the SLAM algorithm provides the best representation of the posterior probability of the set of state variables. As there are a large number of non-independent jointly distributed variables with a mix of Gaussian and non-Gaussian variables, it is necessary to use a fastSLAM version of SLAM.

Figure 1 Typical indoor environment indicating many possible rectangles that can be used as FMO's. The developed CV routine has preprocessed this image to outline one of these rectangles

2.2 Algorithm

An illustration of the overall algorithm is shown in Figure 2. Shown in Figure 2a is the camera first sees a known FM in the camera FOV. The perspective transformation is extracted from this geometry and known image of the FM. It is assumed that the SLAM algorithm is initialized in this known state. As the SLAM has a prior map of the known locations of the FM's, the SLAM begins with a location of the SP with small variance. In Figure 2b, the camera is moved along an unknown trajectory but the FM is contained in the FOV. Hence the initial segment of the SP trajectory is accurately calculated. As shown, an FMO which could be of variable information but not completely known to the SLAM is coincident in the camera FOV. As the SP location at this point is accurate, the perspective matrix of the new FMO can be estimated. The FMO is checked to verify that it indeed is a rectangular shape as described before. Note that the SP is assumed to move slowly relative to the frame rate of the camera such that multiple views of the simultaneous observation of the FM and FMO are obtained. SLAM accumulates the information regarding the state variables from all of these views building up an accurate estimate of the perspective transformation of the FMO as well as its absolute location. In Figure 2c, the camera has now moved such that only the FMO is in view. However, as the transformation matrix and location of the FMO are estimated, the SP trajectory can continue to be estimated. In Figure 2d, the SP trajectory evolves further to include the first FMO and an additional new FMO in the FOV. SLAM then proceeds to determine the perspective and location of the second FMO based on the first FMO. This process continues indefinitely until an FM of known location is recognized. At this point the overall location trajectory of the SP is recalculated.

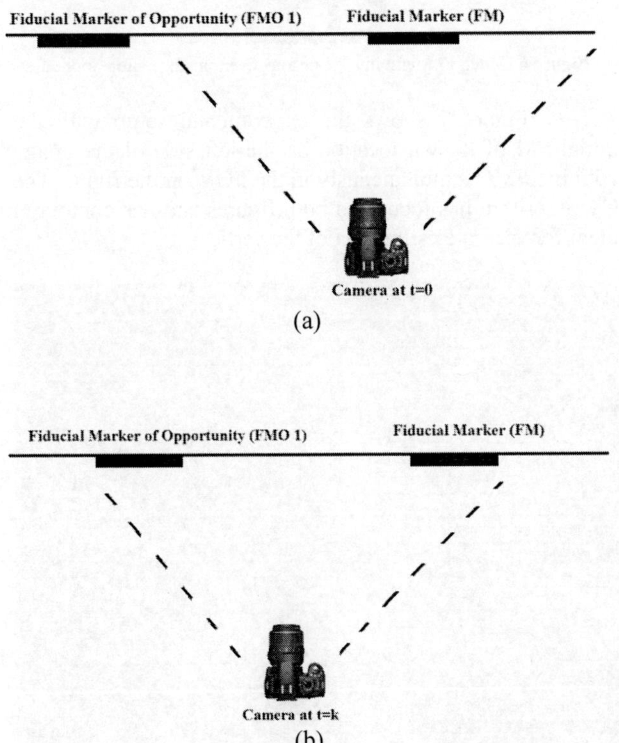

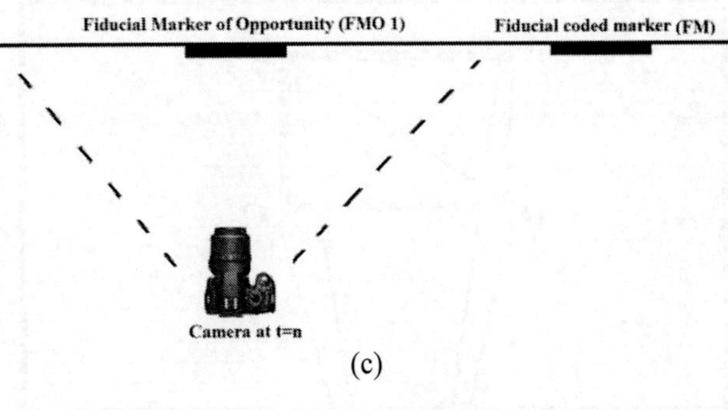

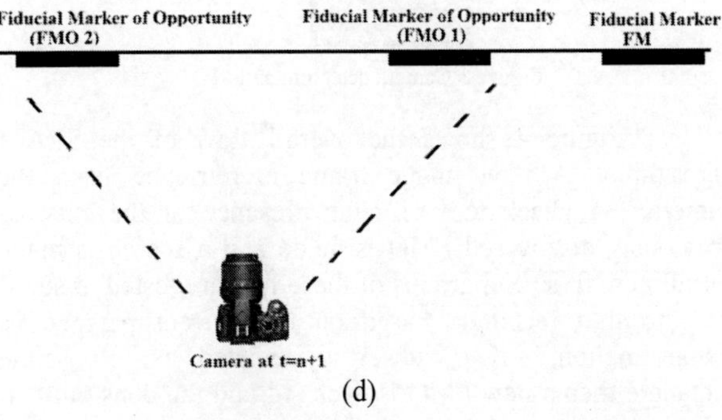

Figure 2 (a) camera at t=0 observing FM in the FOV. (b) Camera at t=k observing FM and FMO 1 in the FOV. (c) Camera at t=n observing only the FMO 1 in the FOV. (d) Camera at t=n+1 observing the FMO 1 and FMO 2 in the FOV.

Figure 3 illustrates the image of a rectangle FMO that is observed from some arbitrary perspective. Hence, in general it appears as a general quadrilateral. The initial assumption is that the FMO is on the same plane as the current world coordinate plane inferred from SLAM. Based on this assumption, the initial guess at the perspective transformation is set to that of the previous FMO. The constraints of the sides and diagonal as shown in Figure 3 are tested. If they are reasonably satisfied then the FMO is assumed to be a rectangle shape. The perspective matrix is then corrected by SLAM based on the constraint observation. Note that at this point SLAM has to account for the possible change in position and orientation of the camera as well as the uncertainty that the FMO is a true rectangle. It achieves this with statistical constraints and observations applied in the underlying Extended Kalman filter which is used in each particle of the fastSLAM algorithm.

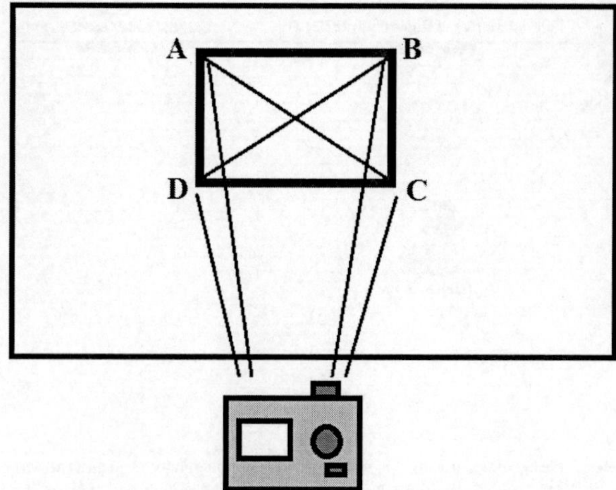

Figure 3 Camera detecting an FMO.

Figure 4 shows the overall flow of the SLAM algorithm. A new image frame is retrieved from the camera. A check to verify the presence of the existing previously discovered FMO is made and a search is made for all new fp's. Subgroups of these fp's are tested to see if they from a rectangle based on the current perspective transformation. If a subset is detected as a possible rectangle then a new FMO is declared and the constraints it generates are used as observables as input to the SLAM algorithm. The SLAM then runs the particle filter (PF) and in each particle the EKF is similar to the standard processing of fastSLAM.

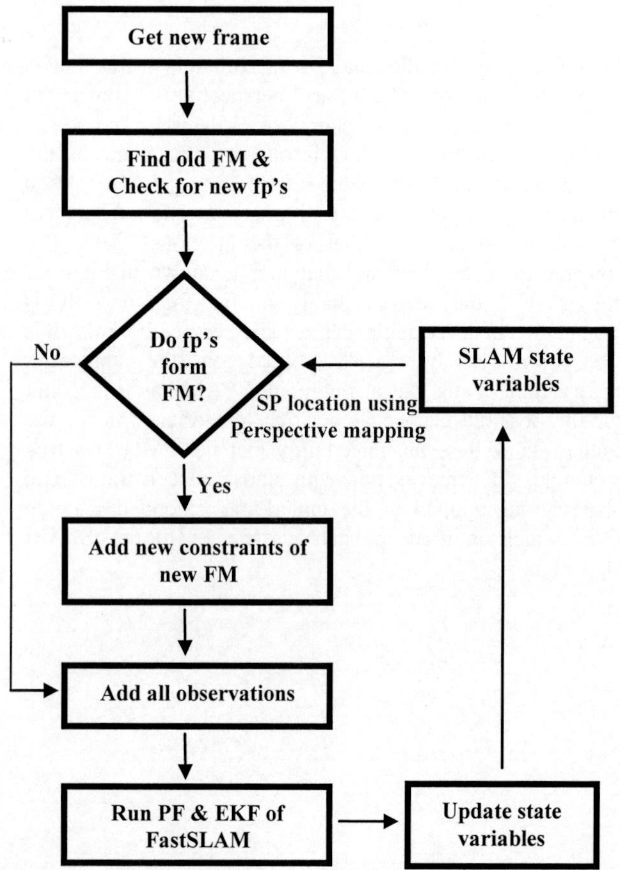

Figure 4 Overall SLAM algorithm

3. Experimental results of Algorithm

Figure 5 shows an example of the FM as it appears in the camera image plane. In this image, the CV algorithm has identified the FM and framed it with the assumed square shape such that the vertices can be extracted. The perspective transformation of the marker is then determined. As the initial map applied to SLAM gives the absolute location of the FM, the absolute location of the camera can be determined.

Figure 5 Image of the FM as it appears in the camera image plane that has been identified as a mapped FM and outlined for accurate estimation of the corner vertices.

Figure 6 shows the FM after the perspective transformation is applied as it appears in the world coordinate frame.

Figure 6 Coded FM with inverse perspective transformation applied

Figure 7 shows the experimental setup with the initial FM of known location on the left side of the image with the FMO simultaneously in the FOV on the right. The CV algorithm has identified both figures and has contoured them for accurate estimation of the vertices.

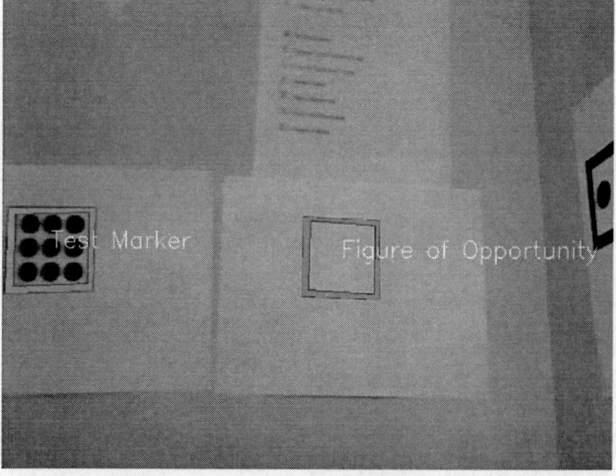

Figure 7 Image of the FM and FMO in the same FOV, as per set up 2b.

Figure 8 shows the FMO after the inverse perspective transformation has been applied showing the perspective of the rectangle as observed in the camera image coordinates restored back into the world coordinates. (The FM has been further translated which is equivalent to transforming the world reference system to coincide with the corner of the FMO.

Figure 8 Figure of opportunity as observed by the camera after performing inverse perspective transformation

Figure 9 shows the position of the camera relative to the defined world reference. The black dots represent the camera location estimation based on the successive perspective transformations that were done based on the known FM only. The red dots represent camera estimation based on the FMO of the unknown marker. These are based on the estimated perspective of the known initial FM. As noted, there is a small offset of several millimeters which is due to the estimate of the perspective transformation being slightly in error. The SLAM algorithm effectively smooths this trajectory as a best fit in the overall least squares sense. This is based on the assumptions of the motion of the camera itself which is generally expressed as a Markov model.

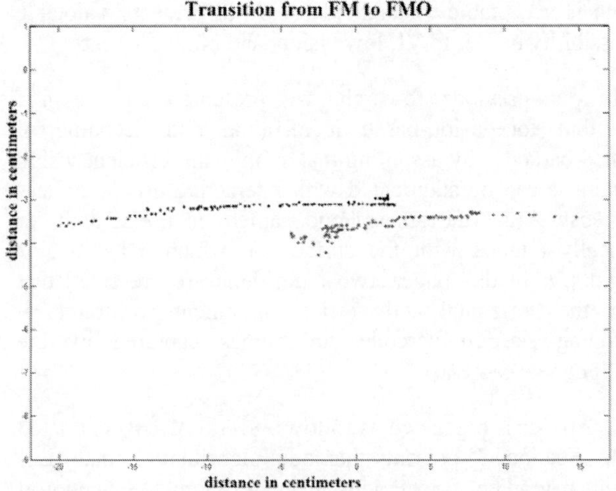

Figure.9. Camera moving from right to left as per figure 2 setup. The trajectory in red is calibrated with respect to the initial known FM while the trajectory in black is based on the FMO with initialization based on the first FM.

4. CONCLUSIONS

Accurate and robust indoor positioning is possible with a webcam quality camera that is typically found in a SP. In this paper, the use of a sequence of FM's and FMO's has been demonstrated to provide useful and sufficient input to a SLAM algorithm for estimating the location of the camera relative to the position of the FM's. The FMO's assumed are generic rectangle shapes that are ubiquitous throughout typical indoor environments. Currently effort is being expended on fitting the CV and SLAM algorithm into an SP with limited processing capability.

5. REFERENCES

[1] F. van Diggelen, "Indoor GPS theory and implementation:' Proc IEEE Position Locotion and Navigation Symp., pp. 240-247, April 2002

[2] M. lrsigler, B. Eisrfeller, "Comparison of multipath mitigation techniques with consideration of future signal structures," Proc. ION GPS/GNSS, pp. 2584-2592, Sept. 2003

[3] M. Fiala, "Designing Highly Reliable Fiducial Markers," IEEE Transactions on Pattern Analysis and Machine Intelligence, vol.32, no.7, pp.1317-1324, July 2010.

[4] S.S. Chawathe, "Marker-Based Localizing for Indoor Navigation," Intelligent Transportation Systems Conference, 2007. ITSC 2007. IEEE, vol., no., pp.885-890, Sept. 30 2007-Oct. 3 2007.

[5] T. Manabe, S. Yamashita, T. Hasegawa, "On the M-CubITS pedestrian navigation system," Intelligent Transportation Systems Conference, 2006. ITSC '06. IEEE , vol., no., pp.793-798, 17-20 Sept. 2006

[6] H. Lim, Y. S. Lee, "Real-time single camera SLAM using fiducial markers," ICCAS-SICE, 2009, vol., no., pp.177-182, 18-21 Aug. 2009.

[7] S. Thrun, D. Fox, W. Burgard, "Probabilistic Robotics", MIT press, 2005

[8] C. Golban, C. Mitran, S. Nedevschi, "A practical method for ego vehicle motion estimation from video," Intelligent Computer Communication and Processing, 2009. ICCP 2009. IEEE 5th International Conference on , vol., no., pp.87-94, 27-29 Aug. 2009.

Vision-Based Localization of Skewed UPC Barcodes on Smartphones

Vladimir Kulyukin and Tanwir Zaman
Department of Computer Science, Utah State University
Logan, Utah, United States of America

Abstract—Two algorithms are presented for vision-based localization of skewed UPC barcodes. The first algorithm localizes skewed barcodes in captured frames by computing dominant orientations of gradients (DOGs) of image segments and collecting smaller segments with similar dominant gradient orientations into larger connected components. The second algorithm localizes skewed barcodes by growing edge alignment trees (EATs) on binary images with detected edges. The DOG algorithm is implemented in Python 2.7.2 using the Python Image Library (PIL). The EAT algorithm is implemented on Android 2.3.6 with the Java OpenCV2.4 library. The performance of both algorithms was evaluated on a sample of 1,066 images of skewed UPC barcodes on bags, boxes, bottles, cans, books, and images with no barcodes. All images were taken on an Android 2.3.6 Google Nexus One smartphone.

Keywords—*computer vision; barcode localization; mobile computing; image gradients; skewed barcodes*

I. Introduction

The U.S. Department of Agriculture estimates that U.S. residents have increased their caloric intake by 523 calories per day since 1970 [1]. Mismanaged diets are estimated to account for 30-35 percent of cancer cases. A leading cause of mortality in men is prostate cancer. A leading cause of mortality in women is breast cancer. Approximately 47,000,000 U.S. residents have metabolic syndrome and diabetes. Diabetes in children appears to be closely related to increasing obesity levels. Many nutritionists and dieticians consider proactive nutrition management to be a key factor in reducing and controlling cancer, diabetes, and other illnesses related to or caused by mismanaged diets.

Surveys conducted by the American Dietetic Association (http://www.eatright.org/) demonstrate that the role of television and printed media as sources of nutrition information has been steadily falling. In 2002, the credibility of television as a source of nutrition information was estimated at 14%; the credibility of magazines were estimated at 25%. The popularity of the Internet increased from 13 to 25% with a perceived credibility of 22% in the same time period. Since smartphones and other mobile devices have, for all practical purposes, become the most popular gateway to access the Internet on the go, they can be used as nutrition management tools. As more and more users manage their daily activities with smartphones, smartphones are increasingly being used for proactive diet management. Numerous web sites have been developed to track calorie intake (e.g., http://nutritiondata.self.com), to determine caloric contents and quantities in consumed food (e.g., http://www.calorieking.com), and to track food intake and exercise (e.g., http://www.fitday.com).

There are free public online barcode databases (e.g., http://www.upcdatabase.com/) that provide some product descriptions and issuing countries' names. Unfortunately, since production information is provided by volunteers who are assumed to periodically upload product details and to associate them with product IDs, almost no nutritional information is available. Some applications (e.g., http://redlaser.com) provide some nutritional information for a few popular products.

Visually impaired (VI), low vision, and blind shoppers currently lack eyes-free access to nutritional information, some of which can be obtained by successfully locating and decoding package barcodes. While vision-based localization and decoding of barcodes is a well-known research program, VI and blind consumers have not greatly benefitted from recent advances. A common disadvantage of open source or commercial barcode readers is that they require that the smartphone camera is carefully aligned with a target barcode, which is acceptable for sighted users but presents a notable accessibility barrier to VI, low vision, and blind shoppers.

In our previous research, we presented an eyes-free algorithm for vision-based localization and decoding of aligned barcodes by assuming that simple and efficient vision techniques can be augmented with interactive user interfaces that ensure that the smartphone camera is horizontally or vertically aligned with the surface on which a barcode is sought [2]. In this paper, two algorithms are presented that relax the horizontal and vertical alignment constraint by localizing skewed barcodes in frames captured by the smartphone's camera.

Our paper is organized as follows. Section 2 covers related work. Section 3 presents barcode algorithm 1 that uses dominant gradient orientations in image segments. Section 4 presents barcode algorithm 2 that localizes skewed barcodes by growing edge alignment trees on binary images with detected edges. Section 5 presents our experiments. Section 6 discusses our results and outlines several directions for future work.

II. Related Work

Vision-based barcode localization on mobile phones is a well-known problem. Much research has been dedicated to developing and improve hardware such a laser readers to read the barcode. In [3] and [4], a computer vision algorithm is presented to guide a mobile phone user so that the user can center a target barcode in the camera frame via audio instructions. In [5], another vision-based algorithm is presented to detect barcodes on mobile phones. The algorithm is based on image analysis and pattern recognition method. A key assumption is that a barcode is present. In [6], an algorithm for scanning 1D barcodes is presented that is suitable for blurry and noisy low resolution images. The algorithm can detect barcodes only if they are slanted by less than 45 degrees. In [7], an automatic barcode detection and recognition algorithm is developed for multiple and rotation invariant barcode decoding. The proposed system is implemented and optimized on a DM6437 DSP EVM board, which is a special kind of embedded system. In [8-14], systems have been developed for scanning barcodes with mobile phones. However, these solutions have been developed for sighted users and may not be suitable for visually impaired (VI) individuals. We endorse this body of research and contribute to it two algorithms that localize skewed barcodes. Skewed barcode localization is necessary for eyes-free mobile barcode access, because visually impaired (VI), low vision, and blind individuals may not be capable of aligning smartphone cameras with target barcodes even in the presence of content-rich haptic and audio feedback.

III. Barcode Localization Algorithm I

A. Dominant Orientation of Gradients

Let I be an RGB image and let f be a linear relative luminance [7] function computed from a pixel's R, G, B components:

$$f(R,G,B) = 0.2126R + 0.7152G + 0.0722B. \quad (1)$$

The gradient of f and the gradient's orientation θ can then be computed as follows:

$$\nabla f = \left[\frac{\partial f}{\partial x}, \frac{\partial f}{\partial y}\right]; \theta = \tan^{-1}\left(\frac{\partial f}{\partial x} \Big/ \frac{\partial f}{\partial y}\right). \quad (2)$$

Let M be an n x n mask, $n > 0$, convolved with I. Let the dominant orientation of gradients of M, $DOG(M)$, be the most frequent discrete gradient orientation of all pixels covered by M. Let (c, r) be the column and row coordinates of the top left pixel of M. The regional orientation table of M, $RGOT(c, r)$, is a map of discrete gradient orientations to their frequencies in the region of I covered by M. The global gradient orientation table (GGOT) of I is a map of the top left coordinates of image regions covered by M to their RGOTs.

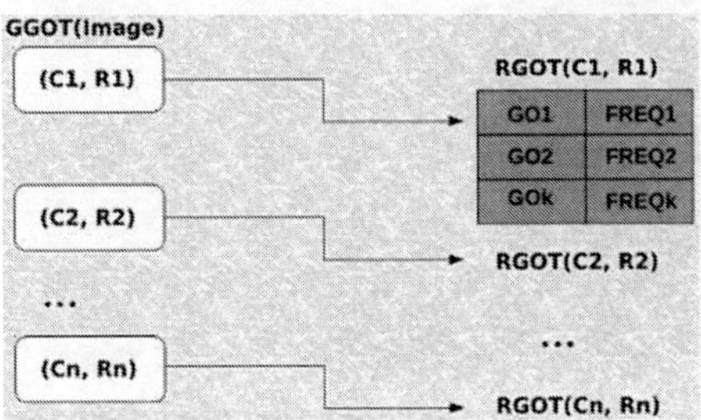

Figure 1. Global Gradient Orientation Table

Figure 1 shows the logical organization of an image's GGOT. In our implementation, both GGOTs and RGOTs are implemented as hash tables (i.e., Python dictionaries). A GGOT maps (c, r) integer tuples to RGOT hashes that, in turn, map discrete gradient orientations (*GO1*, *GO2*, …, *GOn* in Figure 1) to their frequencies (*FREQ1*, *FREQ2*, …, *FREQn* in Figure 1) in the corresponding image regions, i.e., the regions whose top left coordinates are specified by the corresponding (c, r) integer tuple and whose size is the size of M. Each RGOT is converted into the most frequent gradient orientation above a specific threshold. This number is the region's $DOG(M)$.

Figure 2. Skewed UPC-A Barcode

Consider an example of a skewed barcode in Figure 2. Figure 3 gives the DOGs for a *20* x *20* mask convolved with the image in Figure 2. Each green square is a *20* x *20* image region. The top number in the square is the region's *DOG*, in degrees, the bottom number is the frequency of that *DOG* in the region. For example, if the top number is 49 and the bottom number is 11, it means that in that region 11 pixels have a gradient orientation of 49^0. If no gradient orientation clears the frequency count threshold, both numbers are set to 0. Figure 4 displays the DOGs for a *50* x *50* mask. As the size of the mask increases, fewer image regions are expected to clear the DOG threshold if the latter is set as a ratio of pixels with specific gradient values over the entire number of region's pixels in the image.

Figure 3. GGOT for a *20* x *20* mask *M*

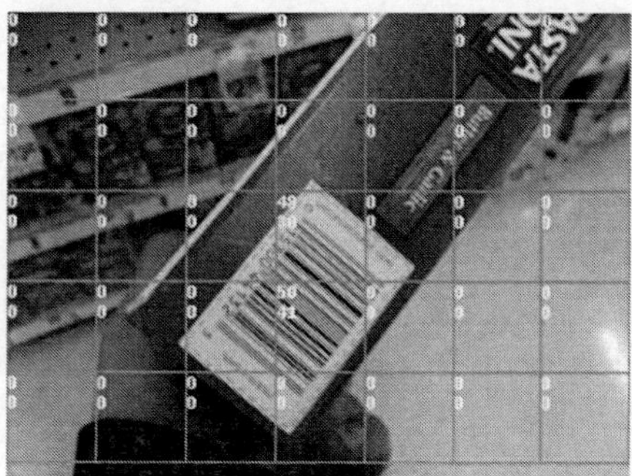

Figure 4. GGOT for a *50* x *50* mask *M*

Figure 5. D-neighborhood found in GGOT in Figure 3

Figure 6. Boxed D-neighborhood in Figure 5

B. DOG Neighborhoods

Suppose that an *n* x *n* mask *M* is convolved with an image. Let a an *RGOT 3-tuple* (c_k, r_k, DOG_k) be the DOG for the region of the image covered by *M* whose top left corner is at (c_k, r_k). A DOG neighborhood is a non-empty set of RGOT 3-tuples (c_k, r_k, DOG_k) such that for any 3-tuple (c_k, r_k, DOG_k) there exists at least one other 3-tuple (c_j, r_j, DOG_j) such that $(c_j, r_j, DOG_j) \neq (c_k, r_k, DOG_k)$ and $sim((c_j, r_j, DOG_j), (c_k, r_k, DOG_k)) = True$, where *sim* is a boolean similarity metric.

In our implementation, the similarity metric is true when the square regions specified by the top left coordinates, i.e., (c_k, r_k) and (c_j, r_j), and the mask size n are horizontal, vertical, or diagonal neighbors and the absolute difference of their DOGs does not exceed a small threshold.

The DOG neighborhoods (D-neighborhoods, for short) of an image are computed simultaneously with the computation of the image's GGOT. As each RGOT 3-tuple becomes available during the normal computation of RGOTs, it is placed into another hash table that keeps track of the neighborhoods. The computed D-neighborhoods are filtered by the ratio of the total area of their component RGOTs to the image area. Figure 5 shows a D-neighborhood, whose RGOTs are marked as blue rectangles, computed in parallel with the computation of the GGOT in Figure 3.

Detected D-neighborhoods are boxed by smallest rectangles that contain all of their RGOT 3-tuples, as shown in Figure 6, where the number in the center of the box denotes the neighborhood's DOG. Boxed D-neighborhoods are barcode region candidates. There can be multiple boxed D-neighborhoods detected in an image, especially if the D-neighborhood filter threshold is set too low. Figure 7 shows all boxed neighborhoods when the threshold is set to .01.

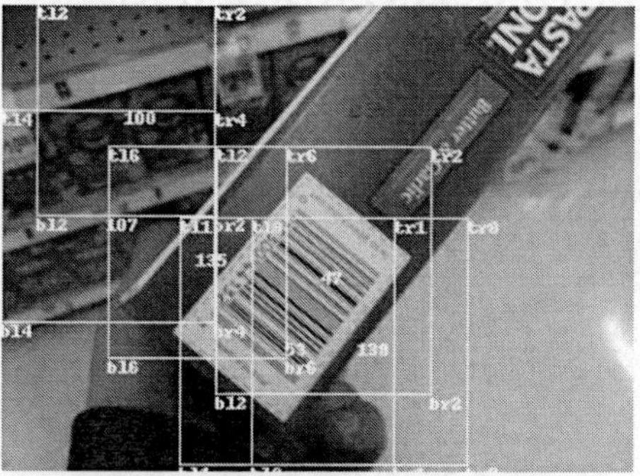

Figure 7. Multiple D-neighborhoods

Note that multiple D-neighborhoods in Figure 7 intersect over a skewed barcode. A D-neighborhood is a *complete* true positive if there is at least one straight line across all bars of a localized barcode. A *partial* true positive occurs if a straight line can be drawn across some, but not all, bars of a barcode. A false positive is a D-neighborhood with no barcode present. In Figure 7, the D-neighborhood whose DOG is 100, in the upper left corner of the image, is a false positive. False negatives occur when a boxed D-neighborhoods does not cover a barcode either completely or partially.

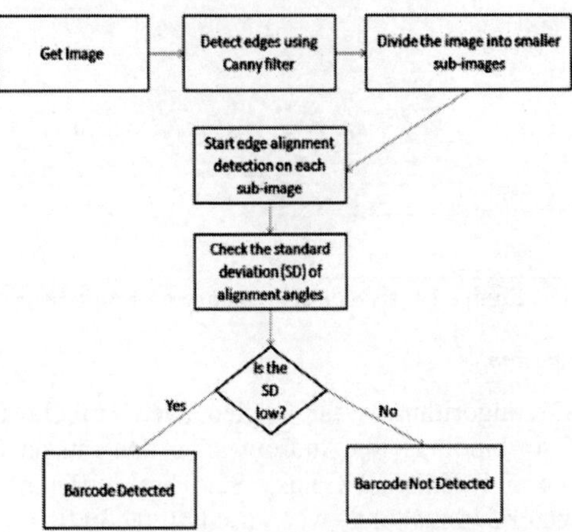

Figure 8. EAT Algorithm Flowchart

IV. Barcode Localization Algorithm II

A. Edge Alignment Trees

Figure 8 shows an overview of the barcode detection algorithm using edge alignment trees (EAT). The algorithm is based on the observation that barcodes characteristically exhibit closely spaced aligned edges with the same angle, which sets them apart from text and graphics. As the flowchart shows, a captured image is put throught a Canny edge detection filter to produce a binarized image. We chose the Canny because we experimentally found it to produced better barcode edges then the other two edge detection algorithms available in the standard OpenCV (opencv.org) distributions, e.g., watershed and flood fill.

The binarized image is next divided into smaller regions of interest (ROI) and scanned row by row and column by column. For each ROI, the edge alignment tree formation is started to detect the dominant skew angle of the edges. Figure 9 shows how EATs dynamically grow. The algorithm starts from the first row of each ROI and moves right column by column until the end of the row is reached. If a pixel's value is 255 (white), it is treated as a 1, marked as a root of an EAT, and stored in the list of nodes.

110100100001100000110
010010010000110000011
001001001000010000001
100100101100011000000
010010000010000110000

Figure 9. Growing EATs from Binarized Edges

$$\theta = \tan^{-1}\left(\frac{\text{current pixel's row} - \text{root's row}}{\text{root's column} - \text{current pixel's column}}\right) \quad (3)$$

If the current row is the ROI's first row, the node list contains the root nodes. Once all nodes in the current row are computed, the algorithm moves to the next row. In the next row (and all subsequent rows), whenever a white pixel (255) or 1 is found, it is checked against the current node list to see if any of the nodes can be the parent of this pixel. This is done by checking the angle between the root pixel and the current pixel using the formula shown in equation 3.

Specifically, if the angle is between 45° and 135°, the current pixel is added to the list of children of the found parent. This parent-child matching is repeated for all nodes in the current node list. If none of the nodes satisfies the parent condition, the orphan pixel becomes a root itself and is added to the node list.

These steps are executed for all rows in the ROI. Once all the EATs are grown, as shown in Figure 9, the dominant angle is computed for each EAT as the average of the angles between each parent and its children, all the way down to the leaves. For each ROI, the standard deviation of the angles is computed for all EATs. If the ROI's standard deviation is low (less than 5 in our current implementation), the ROI is a potential barcode region.

V. Experiments

The barcode localization performance of both algorithms was evaluated on a sample of 1,066 images of skewed UPC barcodes on bags, boxes, bottles, cans, books, and images with no barcodes. All images were taken on an Android 2.3.6 Google Nexus One phone. The outputs of both algorithms, boxed image regions, were evaluated by two human judges.

A. DOG Localization Experiments

The DOG algorithm is implemented in Python 2.7.2 using the Python Image Library (PIL). The mask sizes were tested from 5 x 5 up to 50 x 50 in increments of 5. For each mask size, five thresholds (.01, .02, .03, .04, and .05) were evaluated. The charts in Figures 10 – 14 summarize the performance analysis for the DOG algorithm for each product class. This algorithm is conservative in that the number of false positives is very low. The best mask size and thresholds for which DOG gave the best results are given in Table I. The algorithm gave the highest accuracy value of .85 for bags.

Table I. DOG Products, Mask Sizes, and Thresholds

Product	Mask Size	Threshold
Bag	20 x 20	0.02
Book	40 x 40	0.01
Bottle	40 x 40	0.02
Box	20 x 20	0.02
Can	20 x 20	0.01

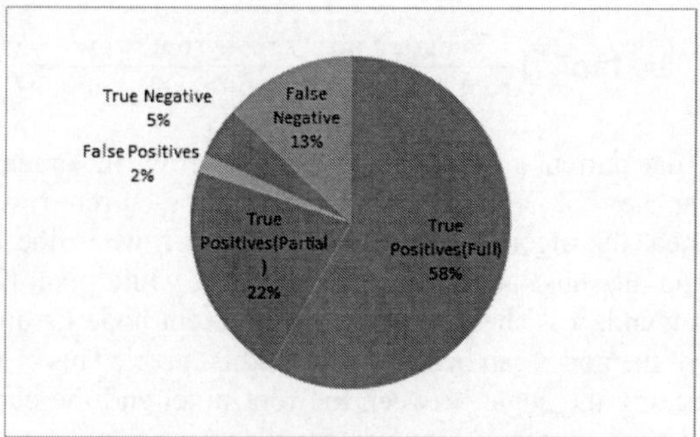

Figure 10. DOG Performance on Bags

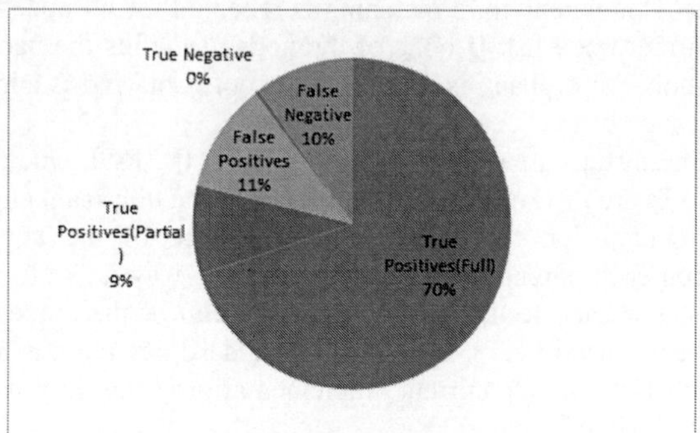

Figure 11. DOG Performance on Cans

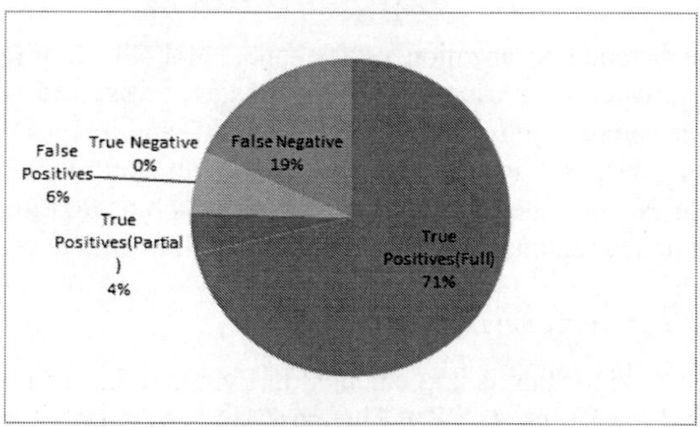

Figure 12. DOG Performance on Bottles

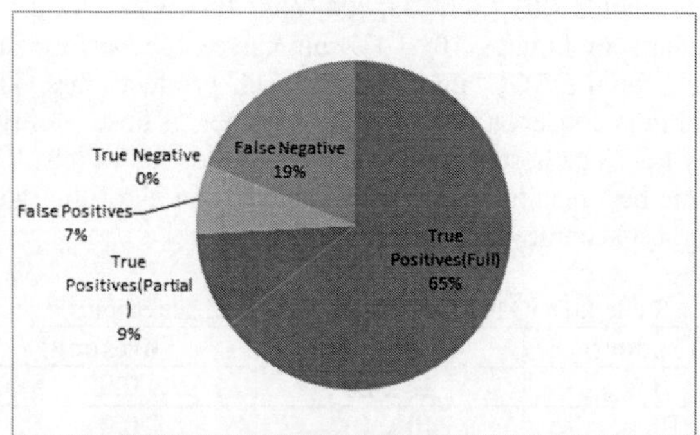

Figure 13. DOG Performance on Boxes

Tables II – VI give the statistics of the DOG barcode localization performance for each product category.

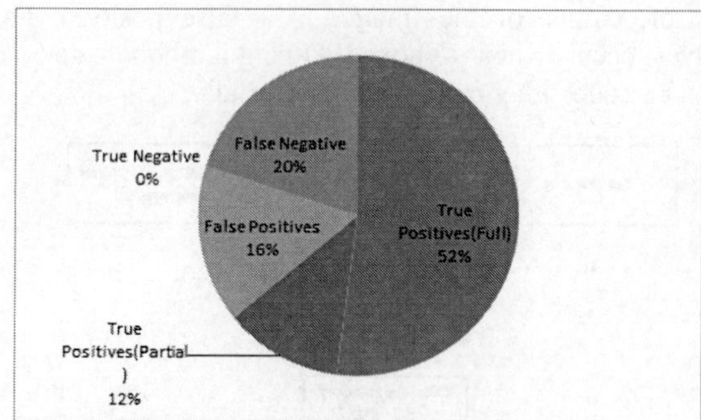

Figure 14. DOG Performance on Books

B. EAT Algorithm

The EAT algorithm was implemented in Java with OpenCV2.4 bindings for Android 2.3.6 and ran on Google Nexus One and Samsung Galaxy S2. Three different Canny edge detector's thresholds were used: (200,300), (300,400) and (400,500). Three different window sizes for the ROI calculations were evaluated: 10, 20 and 40.

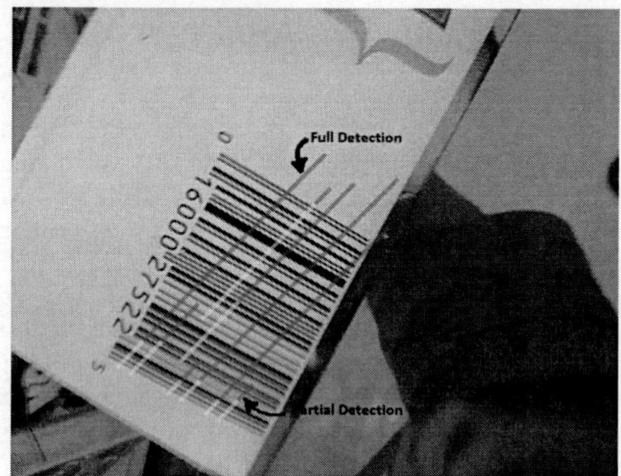

Figure 15. Complete & Partial Detections for EAT algorithm

Images where detected barcode regions had single lines crossing all bars of a real barcode were considered as complete true positives. Images where such lines covered some of the bars were reckoned as partial true positives. Figure 15 shows complete and partial true positives. Images where detected barcode regions did not have any barcodes were false positives. True negatives were identified as images with no barcodes where the algorithm did not detect anything. False negatives were the images where algorithms failed to detect a barcode.

The charts in Figures 16 - 19 summarize the performance of the EAT algorithm for each product category. The EAT algorithm gave best results for bags with a Canny threshold of (300,400). For bottles, boxes and cans it performed best with a Canny threshold of (400,500). The algorithm gave the most accurate results for window size of 10 for all categories of products. Out of all the product categories the algorithm gave the highest accuracy value of .8828 for boxes.

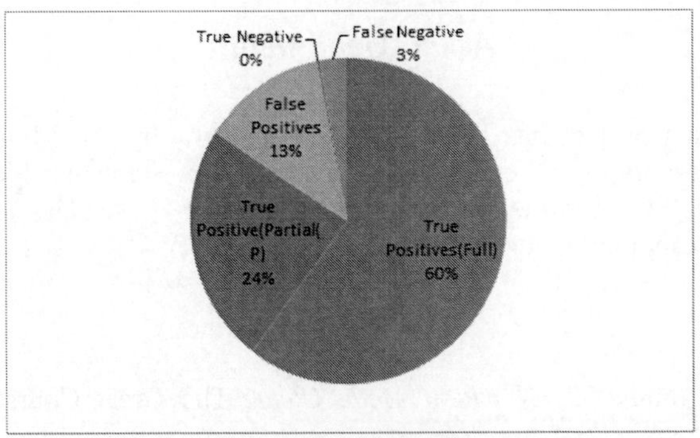

Figure 16. EAT Performance on Bags

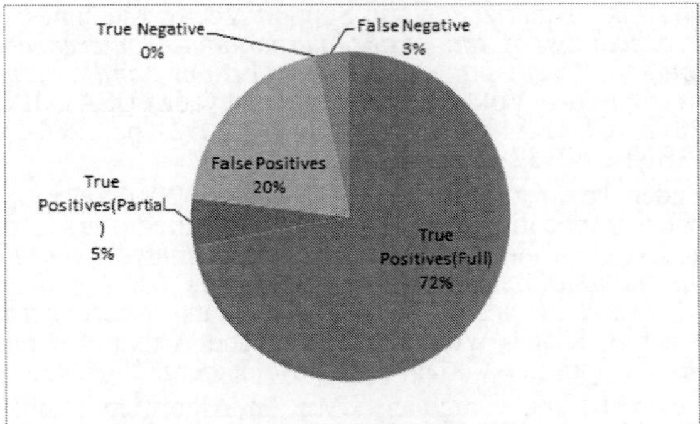

Figure 17. EAT Performance on Cans

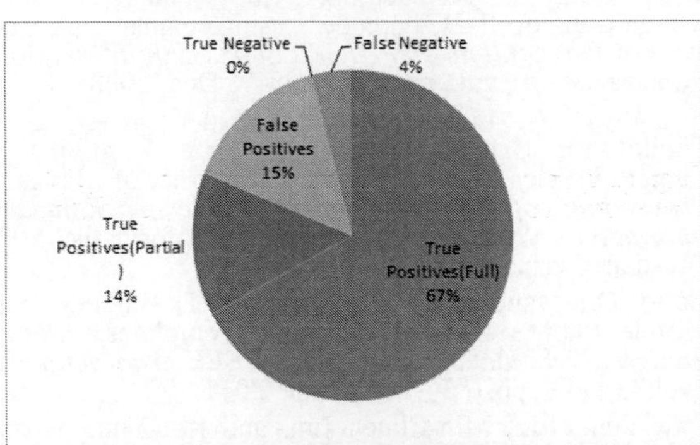

Figure 18. EAT Performance on Bottles

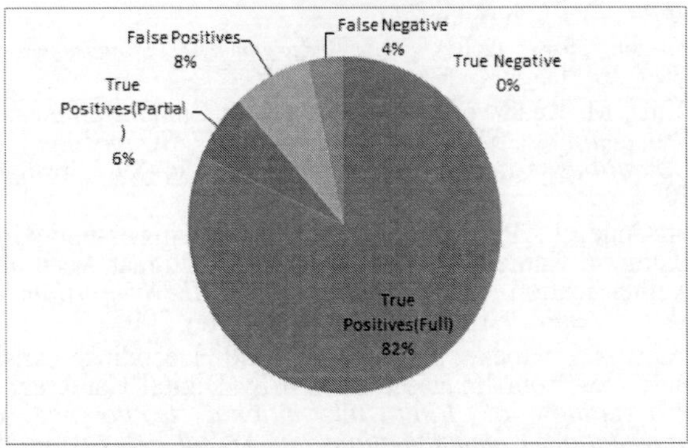

Figure 19. EAT Performance on Boxes

Tables VII - X show the precision, recall, specificity and accuracy averages for the four different categories of products.

The EAT algorithm performed well with images that were properly focused. It did not perform very well on out of focus or blurred images as shown in Figure 20.

Figure 20. A blurred image with a false positive.

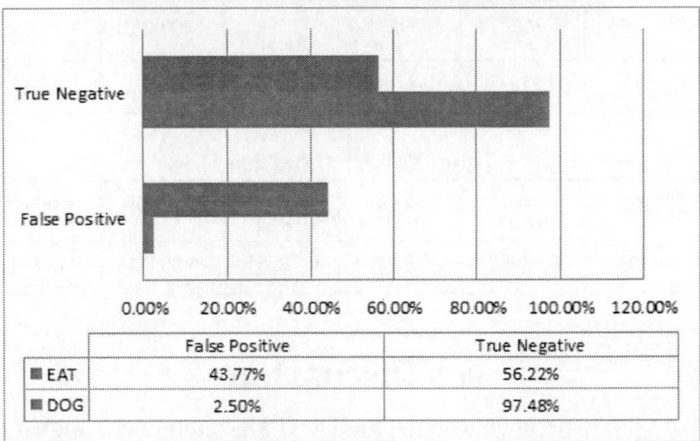

	False Positive	True Negative
EAT	43.77%	56.22%
DOG	2.50%	97.48%

Figure 21. Distribution of False Positives and True Negatives for EAT and DOG Algorithms

Table II. DOG Bag Data

Precision	Total Recall	Complete Recall	Partial Recall	Specificity	Accuracy
0.90896	0.48425	0.37954	0.30873	0.72141	0.46121

Table III. DOG Book Data

Precision	Total Recall	Complete Recall	Partial Recall	Specificity	Accuracy
0.88232	0.28699	0.25988	0.08062	0.0	0.27594

Table IV. DOG Bottle Data

Precision	Total Recall	Complete Recall	Partial Recall	Specificity	Accuracy
0.89031	0.55961	0.50903	0.23971	0.0	0.47493

Table V. DOG Box Data

Precision	Total Recall	Complete Recall	Partial Recall	Specificity	Accuracy
0.87369	0.52701	0.49681	0.24237	0.0	0.43242

Table VI. DOG Can Data

Precision	Total Recall	Complete Recall	Partial Recall	Specificity	Accuracy
0.93706	0.48894	0.46391	0.15826	0.51542	0.45702

Table VII. EAT Bag Data

Precision	Total Recall	Complete Recall	Partial Recall	Specificity	Accuracy
0.70158	0.9308	0.88978	0.8502	0.0125	0.66984

Table VIII. EAT Bottle Data

Precision	Total Recall	Complete Recall	Partial Recall	Specificity	Accuracy
0.76234	0.95345	0.93688	0.77586	0.00138	0.72496

Table IX. EAT Box Data

Precision	Total Recall	Complete Recall	Partial Recall	Specificity	Accuracy
0.76593	0.93631	0.91816	0.7197	0.0001	0.72697

Table X. EAT Can Data

Precision	Total Recall	Complete Recall	Partial Recall	Specificity	Accuracy
0.6903	0.93802	0.9198	0.72251	0.00351	0.66141

VI. Discussion

As the experiments show, the DOG algorithm has a higher precision (approximately 90%) than the EAT algorithm (approximately 70%). As shown in Figure 18, the DOG algorithm is better than the EAT algorithm in terms of true negatives (97% vs. 56%) and false positives (2.5% vs. 44%). On the other hand, the EAT algorithm is better than the DOG algorithm in terms of accuracy (approximately 40% vs. approximately 70%). The DOG algorithm appears to be better than the EAT algorithm on blurry images, but this has not been experimentally verified.

The choice of DOG vs. EAT is the choice between more vs. less conservative barcode region localizations. The DOG algorithm is preferable to the EAT algorithm when the objective is to minimize the percentage of false positives and to increase the percentage of true negatives. If, however, the objective is to maximize recall, either complete or partial, the EAT algorithm should be chosen.

An advantage of the EAT algorithm is that it has actually been implemented and tested on the Android platform whereas the DOG algorithm is currently implemented in Python 2.7.2. using the Python Image Library (PIL). We plan to port this DOG algorithm over to the Android platform in the near future and evaluate it on the same or similar sample of images. It should also be pointed out that the presented algorithms can run in the cloud if the data transmission rates are both inexpensive and efficient.

Acknowledgment

This project has been supported, in part, by the MDSC Corporation. We would like to thank Dr. Stephen Clyde, MDSC President, for supporting our research and championing our cause.

References

[1] Anding, R. *Nutrition Made Clear*. The Great Courses, Chantilly, VA, 2009.

[2] Kulyukin, V., Kutiyanawala, A., and Zaman, T. 2012. Eyes-Free Barcode Detection on Smartphones with Niblack's Binarization and Support Vector Machines. In *Proceedings of the 16-th International Conference on Image Processing, Computer Vision, and Pattern Recognition*, Vol. 1, (Las Vegas, Nevada, USA), IPCV 2012, CSREA Press, July 16-19, 2012, pp. 284-290; ISBN: 1-60132-223-2, 1-60132-224-0.

[3] Ender Tekin and James M. Coughlan. 2010. A mobile phone application enabling visually impaired users to find and read product barcodes. In *Proceedings of the 12th international conference on Computers helping people with special needs* (ICCHP'10), Klaus Miesenberger, Joachim Klaus, Wolfgang Zagler, and Arthur Karshmer (Eds.). Springer-Verlag, Berlin, Heidelberg, 290-295.

[4] Tekin, E. and Coughlan, J.M., An Algorithm Enabling Blind Users to Find and Read Barcodes. WACV09, 2009

[5] Wachenfeld, S.; Terlunen, S.; Xiaoyi Jiang; , "Robust recognition of 1-D barcodes using camera phones," *Pattern Recognition, 2008. ICPR 2008. 19th International Conference on* , vol., no., pp.1-4, 8-11 Dec. 2008.

[6] Adelmann R., Langheinrich M., Floerkemeier, C. A Toolkit for BarCode Recognition and Resolving on Camera Phones - Jump Starting the Internet of Things. In *Proceedings of the Workshop on Mobile and Embedded Information Systems* (MEIS'06) at Informatik 2006, Dresden, Germany, Oct 2006

[7] Gallo, O.; Manduchi, R.; , "Reading 1D Barcodes with Mobile Phones Using Deformable Templates," *Pattern Analysis and Machine Intelligence, IEEE Transactions on* , vol.33, no.9, pp.1834-1843, Sept. 2011

[8] Daw-Tung Lin, Min-Chueh Lin, and Kai-Yung Huang. 2011. Real-time automatic recognition of omnidirectional multiple barcodes and DSP implementation. *Mach. Vision Appl.* 22, 2 (March 2011)

[9] Poynton, Charles (2003). *Digital Video and HDTV: Algorithms and Interfaces*. Morgan Kaufmann. ISBN 1-55860-792-7.

[10] Rohs, M. Real-world Interaction with Camera-phones. In *Proceedings of 2nd International Symposium on Ubiquitous Computing Systems*, pp. 74–89, Springer, 2004.

[11] McCune, J., Perrig, A., Reiter, M. Seeing-is-believing: Using Camera Phones for Human-verifiable Authentication. In *Proceedings of IEEE Symposium on Security and Privacy*, pp. 110 – 124, May 2005.

[12] Chai, D., Hock, F. Locating and Decoding ean-13 Barcodes from Images Captured by Digital Cameras. In *Proceedings of Fifth International Conference on Information, Communications and Signal Processing*, pp. 1595–1599, Dec. 2005.

[13] Zxing, http://code.google.com/p/zxing/, retrieved May 19, 2011.

[14] Occipital, LLC. RedLaser, http://redlaser.com/.

Automated Industrial Inspection of Touch Panels Using Computer Vision

Hong-Dar Lin, Huan-Hua Tsai
Department of Industrial Engineering and Management, Chaoyang University of Technology, Taichung, 41349, Taiwan

Abstract – *Touch panels (TP) with advantages of water-proof, stain-proof, scratch-proof, fast response, are widely used in various electronic products built in touch technology functions. It is a difficult inspection task when defects embedded in surfaces of TPs with structural textures. This research proposes a Fourier transform based approach to inspect surface defects of TPs. When a TP image with four directional and periodic lines of texture is transformed to Fourier domain, four principal bands with high-energy frequency components crisscross at the center of Fourier spectrum. A multi-crisscross filter is designed to filter out the frequency components of the principal band regions. The filtered image is then transformed back to spatial domain. Finally, the restored image is segmented by a simple threshold method and defects are located. Experimental results show the proposed method achieves a high defect detection rate and a low false alarm rate on defect inspection of touch panels.*

Keywords: Industrial inspection; touch panels; surface defects; computer vision system; Fourier transform.

1 Introduction

Touch panels are common user interfaces which are widely used on computing devices such as personal computers, cashier machines, personal digital assistants, smart phones, etc. The most common touch panel technology is Resistive Touch Panel (RTP) but its poor durability and transparency enforce the market to shift to a new technology, Capacitive Touch Panel (CTP). Unlike RTP, the CTP requires a controller to compute and transform the touch signal to a simple data format for the system. The CTPs with advantages of water-proof, stain-proof, scratch-proof, fast response, etc., are widely used in various electronic products built in touch technology functions.

With the popularity of CTPs, inspection of surface defects has become a critical task for manufacturers who strive to improve product quality and production efficiency of touch panels. Surface defects affect not only the appearances of CTPs but also their functionality, efficiency and stability. The surfaces of CTPs are multi-layer structured and are classified as structural textures. It is a difficult inspection task when small defects embedded in the surfaces of structural textures. Small surface defects, frequently occurring in the manufacturing process of touch panels, cause much greater harms and impact when they appear in high-tech products than in industrial parts. Therefore, to survive in today's competitive market of high-tech products, manufacturers of touch panels simply cannot afford to ignore small surface defects.

Textures are generally classified into two types: structural textures and statistical textures [1]. Structural textures are those that are composed of repetitions of some basic texture primitives with a deterministic rule of displacement [2]. Statistical textures cannot be described with primitives and deterministic rules of displacement. The spatial distribution of gray levels in such textured images is rather stochastic [3]. In this research, we aim at the surface defect inspection for the specific CTP structural texture, called directional texture. A directional texture is a homogeneous texture that consists of an arrangement primarily of line structures appearing periodically on the surface [3]. Figure 1 shows the normal and defective images of CTP surfaces with directional textures. The directional textures reveal lattice shapes with lines in four directions (horizontal, vertical, and two diagonals). These background textures make the defect inspection tasks more difficult when small defects embedded in the surfaces of directional textures.

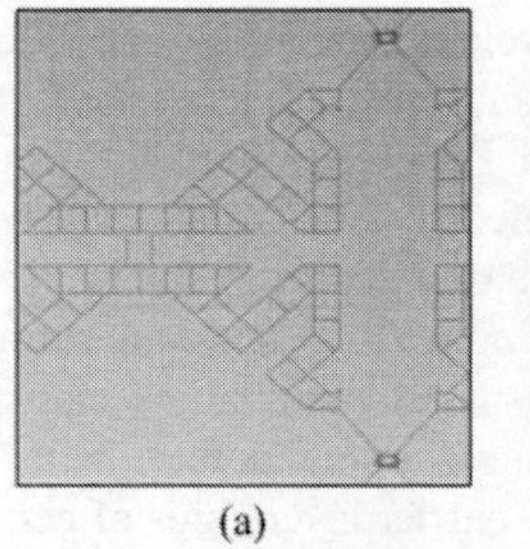
(a)

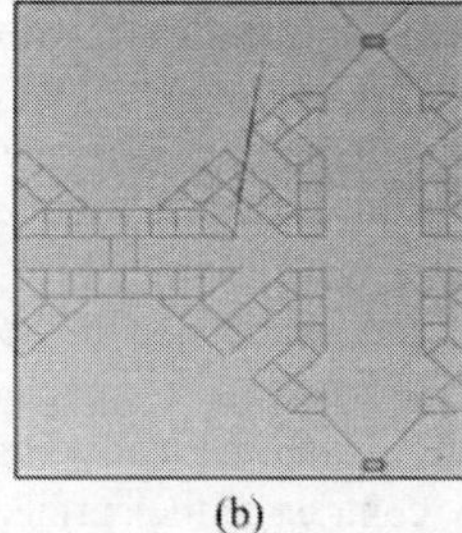
(b)

Figure 1. The CTP images with directional texture: (a) a normal image; (b) a defective image with scratch defect.

Currently, difficulties exist in precisely inspecting surface defects by machine vision systems because when product images are being captured, the area of a small defect could expand, shrink or even disappear due to uneven illumination of the environment, complex texture of the product surface, and so on. Therefore, we propose a Fourier transform based image restoration approach to overcome the difficulties of automated touch panel surface defect inspection.

2 Automated defect inspections

Automated inspection of surface flaws has become a critical task for manufacturers who strive to improve product quality and production efficiency [4, 5]. Flaw detection techniques, generally classified into the spatial domain and the frequency domain, compute a set of textural features in a sliding window and search for significant local deviations among the feature values. Latif-Amet *et al.* [6] presented wavelet theory and co-occurrence matrices for detection of defects encountered in textile images and classify each sub-window as defective or non-defective with a Mahalanobis distance. Cho *et al.* [7] applied the adaptive threshold technique and morphology method to detect defects from images of uniform fabrics for developing a real-time vision system. Perng *et al.* [8] used three extracted features of segmented fringe images and a control chart procedure to inspect optical defects in quasi-contact lenses.

Automated thresholding has also been widely used in the computer vision applications for automated optical inspection of defects [9]. The Otsu method [10] is one of the better threshold selection methods for general real world images with respect to uniformity and shape measures. This method selects threshold values that maximize the between-class variances of the histogram. The Otsu method is optimal for thresholding large objects from the background. It provides satisfactory results for thresholding an image with a histogram of bimodal distribution. Ng [11] revised the Otsu method for selecting optimal threshold values for both unimodal and bimodal distributions, and tested the performance of the revised method on common defect detection applications.

Fourier transform, wavelet transform and Gabor transform are common texture analysis techniques used in the frequency domain. Chan and Pang [12] used the Fourier transform to detect fabric defects. Tsai and Hsiao [13] proposed a wavelet transform based approach for inspecting local defects embedded in homogeneous textured surfaces. Lin [14] developed a wavelet-based multivariate statistical approach to automatically inspect ripple defects with low intensity contrast in the surface barrier layer chips of ceramic capacitors. Kumar and Pang [15] proposed supervised and unsupervised defect detection approaches for automated inspection of textile fabrics using Gabor wavelet features. Lin and Jiang [16] combined discrete cosine transform and grey relational analysis technique to inspect surface defects on encapsulations of light emitting diodes. Also, Lin [17] further developed a novel approach that applies discrete cosine transform decomposition and cumulative sum techniques for the detection of tiny defects on passive component chips.

Directional textures have homogeneous patterns and are commonly found on man-made objects, such as machined parts, fabric textiles, and electronic components. Tsai and Hsieh [3] proposed a global image restoration scheme using the Fourier transform and Hough transform for the automatic inspection of defects in directionally textured surfaces. Perng and Chen [2] developed a nonnegative matrix factorization based approach for automatically inspecting the defects in directional texture surfaces. As to inspecting defects of touch panels, Chen *et al.* [18] introduced an automated optical inspection system for analogical RTP. This system integrates mechanism, electrical control and machine vision, and applies digital image processing method to inspect defect of the RTP. The RTP has the texture of periodic spacers in spatial domain image and results in periodic dots in Fourier spectrum.

In this research, we explore the surface defect inspection of the popular CTP products. When a CTP image with four different directions of periodic lines in background texture is transformed to Fourier domain, at least four principal bands with high-energy frequencies crisscross at the center of Fourier spectrum image. It is difficult to precisely detect surface defects embedded in the complicated directional textures. Therefore, we present a global image restoration scheme using the Fourier transform and multi-crisscross filtering process for small surface defect detection on CTP images. This scheme does not need feature extraction and template matching processes.

3 Research method

This research proposes a Fourier Transform (FT) based multi-crisscross filtering approach to inspect surface defects of touch panels. When a touch panel image with four different directional line patterns of background texture is transformed to Fourier domain, four principal bands with high-energy frequencies crisscross at the center of Fourier spectrum image. A multi-crisscross filter is designed to filter out the frequencies of the areas of the four principal bands. The filtered image is then transformed back to the spatial domain. In the restored image, the homogeneous line regions in the original image will have an approximately uniform gray level, whereas the defective region will be clearly retained. Finally, the restored image is segmented by a simple threshold method and some features of the detected defects are extracted.

3.1 Fourier Transform

Fourier transform has the desirable properties of noise-immunity and enhancement of periodic features [1]. The Fourier domain characterizes the textured image in terms of frequency components. The periodically occurring features such as directional lines can be observed from the magnitude of frequency components. These global texture patterns are easily distinguishable as concentration of high-energy frequencies in the spectrum. Thus, the Fourier spectrum is ideally suited for describing the periodic structure in spatial domain images [1].

Let $f(x, y)$ be the gray level at coordinates (x, y). For a test image of size $M \times M$, the two-dimensional Discrete Fourier Transform (DFT) of $f(x, y)$ is given by

$$F(u,v) = \frac{1}{M^2}\sum_{x=0}^{M-1}\sum_{y=0}^{M-1} f(x,y)e^{-j2\pi(ux+vy/M)} . \quad (1)$$

where $j=\sqrt{-1}$, (u, v) is frequency variable and $u, v=0, 1, 2, \ldots, M-1$. The DFT is a complex function, i.e.

$$F(u,v) = R(u,v) + jI(u,v) \quad (2)$$

where $R(u, v)$ and $I(u, v)$ are the real and imaginary components of $F(u, v)$, i.e.

$$R(u,v) = \frac{1}{M^2}\sum_{x=0}^{M-1}\sum_{y=0}^{M-1} f(x,y)\cdot\cos\left[2\pi\left(ux+vy/M\right)\right] \quad (3)$$

$$I(u,v) = \frac{1}{M^2}\sum_{x=0}^{M-1}\sum_{y=0}^{M-1} f(x,y)\cdot\sin\left[2\pi\left(ux+vy/M\right)\right] \quad (4)$$

the Fourier spectrum $|F(u, v)|$ and power spectrum $P(u, v)$ are defined as

$$|F(u,v)| = [R^2(u,v)+I^2(u,v)]^{1/2} \quad (5)$$

$$P(u,v) = |F(u,v)|^2 = R^2(u,v)+I^2(u,v) \quad (6)$$

It is valuable to facilitate visual analysis of Fourier spectra. To show the spectrum as an intensity function scaled to 8-bit gray levels, $P(u, v)$ is converted by:

$$P(u,v) = \log(1+|F(u,v)|) \quad (7)$$

Therefore, the magnitude of the transform is centered on the origin of the Fourier domain image.

If we transform a vertical line in the spatial domain, it will appear a horizontal line in the Fourier domain. A line in the spatial domain image and its transformed counterpart in the Fourier domain image are orthogonal to each other. We rotate an original image by an angle and its corresponding frequency plane will be rotated by the same angle.

3.2 Fourier power spectrum

The directional properties of a gray-level image clearly correspond to high-energy frequency components, which are distributed along the straight bands in the Fourier domain image with directions orthogonal to their counterparts in the spatial domain image. When a touch panel image with four different directional lines of background texture is transformed to Fourier domain, four principal bands with high-energy frequency components crisscross at the center of Fourier spectrum image. Figures 2(a) and 2(b) show the power spectra of respective textured surfaces in Fig. 1(a) and 1(b), where brightness is proportional to the magnitude of $P(u, v)$. Note that the transform of periodic lines of the same orientation θ in the spatial domain image will result in high-energy frequency components distributed along a band with orientation (θ+90°) in the Fourier domain image. There are four bands in the FT spectrum of normal image and at least five bands in the defective spectrum images. It is clear that Fig. 2(b) has two more bands than that in Fig. 2(a). These extra bands resulted from the scratch defect in Fig. 1(b). Therefore, the line pattern information in the spatial domain image is highly concentrated on the high-energy frequency components distributed along the transformed bands in the Fourier domain image.

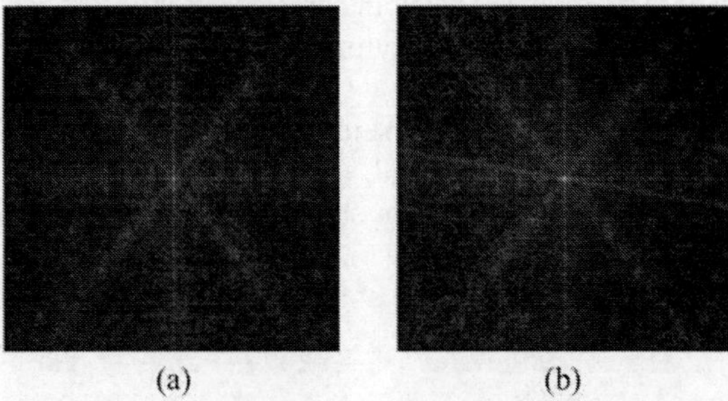

(a) (b)

Figure 2. The corresponding Fourier spectrum images of Fig. 1(a) and Fig. 1(b).

3.3 Fourier spectrum filtering

High-energy frequency components associated with periodical line patterns may appear around the principal bands in the Fourier domain image. To completely eliminate all homogeneous line patterns in the spatial domain image, not only the frequency components lying on the principal bands defined by θ_i but also those frequency components in the neighborhood of the principal bands must be removed from the Fourier domain image. The frequency components falling in the neighborhood of the principal bands in the Fourier domain image are virtually filtered by setting them to zero. Figure 3 shows two multi-crisscross filters with different cutting angles of the four principal bands: Fig. 3(a) using the rough cutting (45°-45°) method, Fig. 3(b) using the precise cutting (51°-39°) method. We will compare the defect detection performance of the proposed approaches with different cutting method later. After cutting the specific band regions, we take backward Fourier transform to get the filtered restored image in the spatial domain.

The filtering process and backward transform will remove all homogeneous and directional textures of the original image, and retains only defects in the restored image. In this research, we adopt a supervised defect inspection approach, i.e. non-defect samples of the textures of interest are given. Supervised approaches are common in machine vision applications and are more suitable for controlled circumstances in manufacturing. The only required parameter to the proposed precise cutting method is the orientations of the principal bands obtained from a set of non-defect samples.

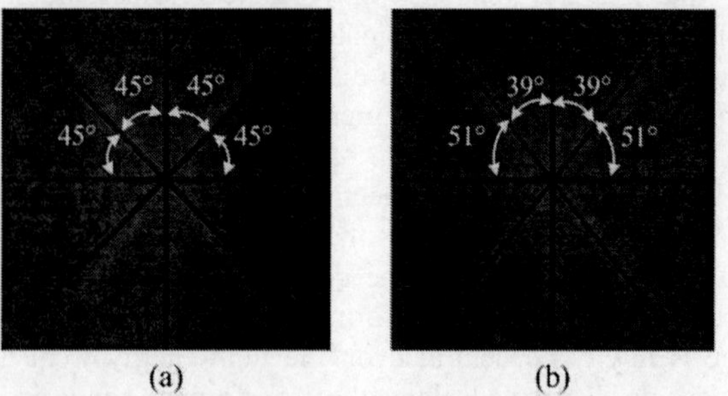

Figure 3. Two multi-crisscross filters with different cutting angles of four principal bands: (a) using the rough cutting (45°-45°) method, (b) using the precise cutting (51°-39°) method, both with cutting width 4 pixels.

The location of a single band filter can be determined by the direction angle of the band. According to general plane geometry, a single band region shown in Figure 4 comprises three parallel lines, centerline (L), upper and lower limit lines (L_U, L_L). The equation of the straight line L_U can be written as:

$$L_U : u\cos\phi + v\sin\phi = \rho \quad \text{or}$$

$$L_U : u\cos\left(\theta - \pi/2\right) + v\sin\left(\theta - \pi/2\right) = \rho$$

And can be further expressed as:

$$L_U : u\sin\theta - v\cos\theta = \rho$$

where the pixel coordinates (u, v) in the Fourier frequency domain of image size $M \times M$, the perpendicular distance ρ is from the central point $O(M/2, M/2)$ to the straight line L_U or L_L, the angle ϕ is the interior angle between the perpendicular line of straight line L_U and the horizontal u axis, and the angle θ is the exterior angle between the straight line L_U and the u axis.

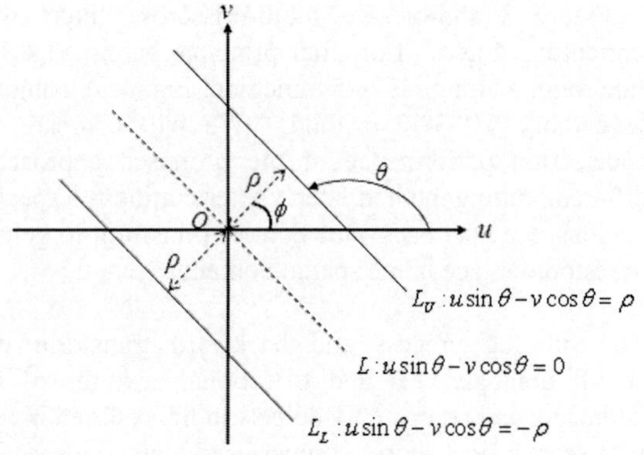

Figure 4. A single band filter with cutting angle θ and cutting width 2ρ.

Equations (8)-(10) define the whole region of a single band with cutting angle θ and cutting width 2ρ. The frequency components in this single band are high-energy and will be filtered out for removing the background texture.

$$L_U : u\sin\theta - v\cos\theta = \rho \tag{8}$$

$$L : u\sin\theta - v\cos\theta = 0 \tag{9}$$

$$L_L : u\sin\theta - v\cos\theta = -\rho \tag{10}$$

To specify the interior region of the band, the upper and lower limit lines are re-written as:

$$L_{U'} : u\sin\theta - v\cos\theta - \rho \le 0 \tag{11}$$

$$L_{L'} : u\sin\theta - v\cos\theta + \rho \ge 0 \tag{12}$$

that is $L_{U'} \cap L_{L'} = \{F(u, v) \mid F(u, v) \in L_{U'}$ and $F(u, v) \in L_{L'}\}$. The frequency components in this region will be set to zero and the others remain the same. This filtered image $F'(u, v)$ is expressed as:

$$F'(u,v) = \begin{cases} 0, & L_{U'} \cap L_{L'} \\ F(u,v), & \text{otherwise.} \end{cases} \tag{13}$$

When a touch panel image with four different directional line patterns of background texture is transformed to Fourier domain, four principal bands with high-energy frequencies crisscross at the center of Fourier spectrum image. The directional properties of a gray-level image clearly correspond to high-energy frequency components, which are distributed along the straight bands in the Fourier domain image with directions orthogonal to their corresponding line patterns in the spatial domain image. High-energy frequency components associated with periodical line patterns appear around the principal bands in the Fourier domain image. To significantly delete most of homogeneous line patterns in the spatial domain image, not only the frequency components occurring on the principal bands but also those frequency components in the neighborhood of the principal bands must be removed from the Fourier domain image. A multi-crisscross filter is designed to filter out the frequencies of the neighborhood regions of the four principal bands in Fourier domain.

3.4 Image reconstruction

After scanning all pixels (u, v) in the Fourier domain image, the filtered image is restored to the spatial domain using the inverse Fourier transform (IFT). That is,

$$f'(x,y) = \frac{1}{M^2} \sum_{u=0}^{M-1} \sum_{v=0}^{M-1} F'(u,v) e^{j2\pi(ux+vy/M)} \tag{14}$$

for x, y=0, 1, 2, …, M-1. The restored image $f'(x, y)$ will be approximately a uniform gray-level image if a non-defect surface image is tested.

The corresponding Fourier domain image shows that the periodic lines in the spatial domain image result in high-energy frequency components lying on the principal bands of different directions in the Fourier domain image. The filtered image illustrates the notches of the principal bands at four different directions. All frequency components $F(u, v)$ within the notch are set to zero. The restored image demonstrates that the transformed region associated with the periodic line pattern becomes an approximately uniform gray-level region and the non-periodic defects are retained in the restored image.

3.5 Defect detection

The restored image has uniform gray levels for pixels belonging to homogeneous line regions, but it also gives significantly different gray levels for pixels belonging to inhomogeneous defect areas. The intensity variation in homogeneous regions will be very small, whereas the gray-level variation in inhomogeneous areas will be large with respect to the entire restored image. Therefore, we can use a simple statistical principle to set up the control limits for distinguishing defects from periodic line patterns in the restored image. The upper and lower control limits (T_L, T_U) for intensity variation in the restored image are given by

$$T = \mu_{f'} \pm k\sigma_{f'} \tag{15}$$

where T is a threshold for segmenting defects from background, k is a control parameter, $\mu_{f'}$ and $\sigma_{f'}$ are the mean and standard deviation of the testing restored image of size $M \times M$.

The resulting binary image $B(x, y)$ for defect separation is

$$B(x,y) = \begin{cases} 255, & T_L \le f'(x,y) \le T_U \\ 0, & \text{otherwise.} \end{cases} \tag{16}$$

If a gray level value falls within the threshold T (in control) then intensity is set to 255 (white) as a background. Otherwise, intensity is set to 0 (black) as a part of defect (out of control).

If a pixel with the gray level falls within the control limits, the pixel is classified as a homogeneous element. Otherwise, it is classified as a defective element. As the defect size to be inspected are generally very small with respect to the entire surface image, $\mu_{f'}$ and $\sigma_{f'}$ can be computed directly from the restored image of a testing image to accommodate the variation of lighting in the inspection environment. All experimental samples demonstrated in this study are based on the $\mu_{f'}$ and $\sigma_{f'}$ from testing images, and the control constant k is set at different values.

The control limits are used to distinguish between homogeneous line patterns and defects in a filtered restored image. The upper and lower control limits of gray levels in a restored image are placed at a distance $k\sigma_{f'}$ from the mean $\mu_{f'}$. Figures 5 depicts the resulting binary images with two different control parameters of the restored images, where pixels with gray levels falling outside the control limits are represented by black intensity (defective regions), and the ones falling within the limits are represented by white intensity (homogeneous regions). Selecting a proper control parameter results in correctly discriminating defects from normal regions but an improper control parameter produces many erroneously detecting normal regions as defects. A smaller constant value k gives a tight control and may result in false alarms. A larger constant value k gives a loose control and may generate missing alarms.

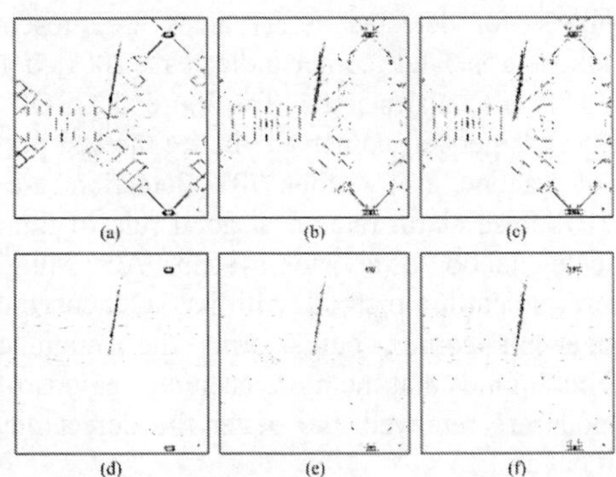

Figure 5. The resulting binary images with different control parameters using the precise cutting method; (a)-(c) the resulting binary image with k=3 for the defective image, respectively; (d)-(f) the corresponding resulting binary image with k=5.

4 Experiments and analyses

To evaluate performance of the proposed approach, experiments were conducted on real capacitive touch panels, provided by a touch panel manufacturing company. The CTP images (60) with thickness 0.78mm, of which 18 have no defects and 42 have various surface defects, were tested. All samples were randomly selected from manufacturing process of touch panels. Each image of the surface has a size of 256 x 256 pixels and a gray level of 8 bits. The surface defect detection algorithm is edited and executed on the seventh version of the Matlab software on a personal computer (Pentium-4 2.8 GHz and 1GB DDRII 667 Hz-RAM).

The performance evaluation indices, (1-α) and (1-β), are used to represent correct detection judgments; the higher the two indices, the more accurate the detection results.

Statistical type I error α suggests the probability of producing false alarms, i.e. detecting normal regions as flaws. Statistical type II error β implies the probability of producing missing alarms, which fail to alarm real flaws. We divide the area of normal region detected as flaws by the area of actual normal region to obtain type I error, and the area of undetected flaws by the area of actual flaws to obtain type II error. Therefore, the correct classification rate (CR) is defined as: $CR = (N_{cc} + N_{dd}) / N_{total}$ where N_{cc} is the pixel number of normal textures detected as normal areas, N_{dd} is the pixel number of flaws detected as defective regions, and N_{total} is the total pixel number of a testing image.

As the decision threshold value changes, so do its false alarm rate (α) and detection rate ($1\text{-}\beta$), both of which are used to describe the performance of a test according to hypothesis testing theory [19]. When various decision thresholds are used, their pairs of false alarm rates and detection rates are plotted as points on a Receiver Operating Characteristic (ROC) curve. The ROC curves of the two cutting methods, rough cutting and precise cutting methods both with cutting width 6 pixels, for detected defect areas are presented in Figure 6, whose upper-left corner indicates a 100% detection rate and a 0% false alarm rate. The more the ROC curve approaches the upper-left corner, the better the test performs. In industrial practice, a more than 90% detection rate and a less than 10% false alarm rate are a good rule of thumb for performance evaluation of a vision system. Accordingly, the proposed precise cutting method, with its ROC curve closest to the upper-left corner, outperforms the rough cutting method. This implies that the more accurate regions of band neighborhoods are removed, the better the defect detection results will have.

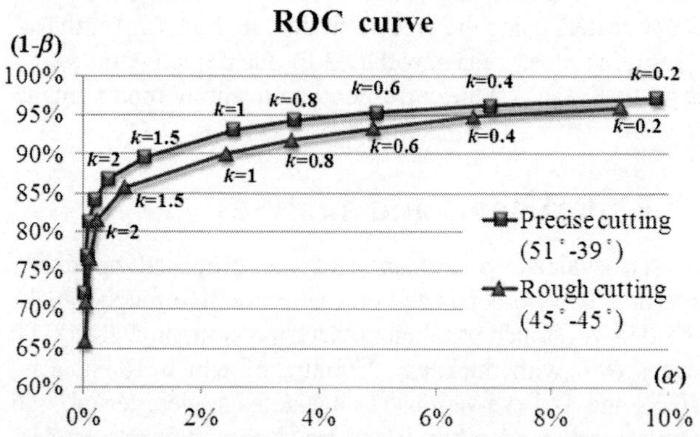

Figure 6. ROC curves of the precise cutting (51°-39°) method and the rough cutting (45°-45°) method with cutting width of 6 pixels, respectively.

High-energy frequency components associated with periodical line patterns may appear around the principal bands in the Fourier domain image. To completely delete all homogeneous line patterns in the spatial domain image, both of the frequency components on the principal bands and those frequency components in the neighborhood of the principal bands must be removed from the Fourier domain image. The cutting width determines the regions of the band neighborhoods will be filtered for high-energy frequency components. Figure 7 demonstrates the ROC curves of the proposed precise cutting (51°-39°) method with cutting widths of 3 and 6 pixels, respectively. It shows the defect detection performance of the precise cutting with 3 pixels is better than that of with 6 pixels. The precise cutting method with large cutting width (6 pixels) not only removes homogeneous line patterns but also local defects in the restored image and result in neglect small defects.

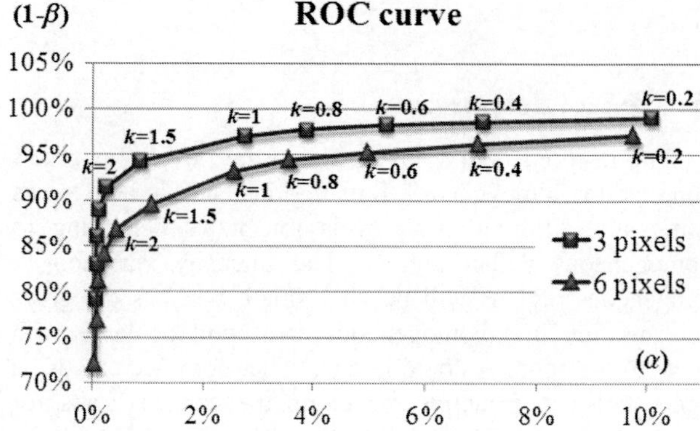

Figure 7. ROC curves of the precise cutting (51°-39°) method with cutting widths of 3 and 6 pixels.

5 Conclusions

In this study, we have presented a frequency filtering approach for automated inspection of surface defects in directional textures of touch panels. The line patterns of four directional textures in the spatial domain image can be easily removed by detecting four principal bands with high-energy frequency components crisscrossing at the center of Fourier spectrum image, setting them to zero by the multi-crisscross filter, and transforming back to a spatial domain image. In the filtered restored image of a textured surface, the periodic line region in the original image will have an approximately uniform gray level, whereas the defective region will be clearly retained. A simple statistical scheme is therefore used to set up the control limits for discriminating between defects and homogeneous line patterns. Experimental results show that the proposed method achieves a high 96.37% probability of correctly discriminating defects from normal regions and a low 5.62% probability of erroneously detecting normal regions as defects on structural textured surfaces of touch panels.

6 Acknowledgment

This work was partially supported by the National Science Council (NSC) of Taiwan, under Grant No. NSC 100-2221-E-324-009-MY2.

7 References

[1] R. C. Gonzalez and R. E. Woods, Digital Image Processing, Prentice Hall, New Jersey (2008).

[2] D. B. Perng and S. H. Chen, "Automatic surface inspection for directional textures using nonnegative matrix factorization," International Journal of Advanced Manufacturing Technology, 48, 671-689 (2010).

[3] D. M. Tsai and C. Y. Hsieh, "Automated surface inspection for directional textures," Image and Vision Computing, 18, 49-62 (1999).

[4] Y. S. P. Chiu and H. D. Lin, "A hybrid approach based on Hotelling statistics for automated visual inspection of display blemishes in LCD panels," Expert Systems With Applications, 36 (10), 12332-12339 (2009).

[5] E. N. Malamas, E. G. M. Petrakis, M. Zervakis, L. Petit and J. D. Legat, "A survey on industrial vision systems, applications and tools," Image and Vision Computing, 21, 171-188 (2003).

[6] A. Latif-Amet, A. Ertüzün and A. Ercil, "An efficient method for texture defect detection: sub-band domain co-occurrence matrices," Image and Vision Computing, 18, 543-553 (2000).

[7] C. S. Cho, B. M. Chung and M. J. Park, "Development of real-time vision-based fabric inspection system," IEEE Transactions on Industrial Electronics, 52, 1073-1079 (2005).

[8] D. B. Perng, W. C. Wang and S. H. Chen, "A novel quasi-contact lens auto-inspection system," Journal of the Chinese Institute of Industrial Engineers, 27, 260-269 (2010).

[9] M. Sezgin and B. Sankur, "Survey over image thresholding techniques and quantitative performance evaluation," Journal of Electronic Imaging, 13 (1), 146-156 (2004).

[10] N. Otsu, "A threshold selection method from gray level histogram," IEEE Transactions on Systems, Man and Cybernetics, 9, 62-66 (1979).

[11] H. F. Ng, "Automatic thresholding for defect detection," Pattern Recognition Letters, 27, 1644-1649 (2006).

[12] C. H. Chan and G. K. H. Pang, "Fabric defect detection by Fourier analysis," IEEE Transactions on Industry Applications, 36, 1267-1276 (2000).

[13] D. M. Tsai and B. Hsiao, "Automatic surface inspection using wavelet reconstruction," Pattern Recognition, 34, 1285-1305 (2001).

[14] H. D. Lin, "Automated visual inspection of ripple defects using wavelet characteristic based multivariate statistical approach," Image and Vision Computing, 25, 1785-1801 (2007).

[15] A. Kumar and K. H. Pang, "Defect detection in textured materials using Gabor filters," IEEE Transactions on Industry Applications, 38, 425-440 (2002).

[16] H. D. Lin and J. D. Jiang, "Applying discrete cosine transform and grey relational analysis to surface defect detection of LEDs," Journal of the Chinese Institute of Industrial Engineers, 24, 458-467 (2007).

[17] H. D. Lin, "Tiny surface defect inspection of electronic passive components using discrete cosine transform decomposition and cumulative sum techniques," Image and Vision Computing, 26, 603-621 (2008).

[18] Y. C. Chen, J. H. Yu, M. C. Xie and F. J. Shiou, "Automated optical inspection system for analogical resistance type touch panel," International Journal of the Physical Sciences, 6 (22), 5141-5152 (2011).

[19] D.C. Montgomery and G. C. Runger, Applied Statistics and Probability for Engineers, 2nd ed., New York: John Wiley & Sons, 296-304 (1999).

Automated change detection of multi-level icebergs near Mertz Glacier region using feature vector matching*

Zhen Liu[1], Ziying Zhao[2], Yida Fan[3], Dong Tian[4]
[1]Center of Information & Network Technology, Beijing Normal University, Beijing 100875, China; zliu@bnu.edu.cn
[2]National Institute of Education Science, Beijing 100088, China; zhaozy@nies.net.cn
[3]National Disaster Reduction Center of China, MCA, Beijing 100124, China; Fanyida@ndrcc.gov.cn
[4]Computer Network Information Center, CAS, Beijing 100190, China; tiandong@sccas.cn

Abstract - *It is valuable to study on spatio-temporal change of Antarctic icebergs' feature, such as shifting, melting and splitting, which play an important role in atmosphere, ocean current and climate change in Antarctic areas as well as the globe. This paper presents an approach to automatically detecting iceberg change and tracking iceberg based on feature vector matching. The matching consists of (i) using HAUSDORFF matching algorithm based on curvature extrema to identify the whole silhouette of iceberg, (ii) using local-feature-points matching based on SIFT algorithm to find the iceberg whose shape has changed dramatically due to collision or split. We used One-year ENVISAT/ASAR images to automatically track multi-level icebergs collapsed from Mertz Glacier and analyzed various features of icebergs, such as locations, shapes and area. The result suggests that icebergs from Mertz Glacier did not melt significantly while the loss of area due to collision is bigger than melt. All of medium and small-size icebergs have similar tracks which move counterclockwise along Antarctic ice sheet. The speed of movement is related to the size of iceberg, ocean current and the density of icebergs in this region.*

Keywords: Iceberg Tracking, Change Detection, Feature Vector Matching, Mertz Glacier

1 Introduction

In recent years, more and more research shows that iceberg change is closely related with atmospheric changes, changes in the oceans, geological changes, even the Earth's gravity change. Iceberg activities are affected by various marine environmental factors. Iceberg in the long-term drift process is affected constantly by wind, water washout and seawater thawing, which becomes smaller, until it disappears. But the study showed that the effects of wind and ocean currents are main factors, in which ocean currents affect about 75% of iceberg movement. Iceberg in the course of the campaign will affect the nearby sea temperature in turn affect changes in ocean currents and ocean currents change will affect the world's climate (Stefan, 2002). Iceberg is formed in the ice shelf disintegration. The observations of the past few decades show that a large area of the ice shelf disintegration has focused in the past global-warming 20 years. In addition to melting iceberg in the drift process, but also can occur secondary disintegration split event. Any increase in the number or increase in the amount of ice shelf melting iceberg, there may be through integration into large number of freshwater disrupt marine convective circulation. More and more study on multi-scale icebergs monitoring tracking and change analysis can have an important impact on polar change and global change.

This work was supported by the The National Basic Research Program of China (Grant No. 2012CB955501)

2 The bulk of research on iceberg tracking

The iceberg movement has a certain law, 90% of the icebergs are around Antarctica and polar ocean currents, floating along the Antarctic Circumpolar, and escape ultimately to the vicinity of the East Antarctic. There are also a small amount of an icebergs to escape in the other two Bay (Gill, 2001).Currently, National Snow and Ice Data Center (NSIDC) is tracking the giant Antarctic iceberg (length about over 18.5km) using a variety of satellite sensors. The update cycle is about 20 days (NIC, 2010). Microwave Earth Remote Sensing (MERS) Laboratory of Brigham Young University have analyzed the ten-year trajectory data of flat-topped iceberg in Antarctic from 1999 to 2009 using SeaWinds Scatterometer. The tracking cycle is 1 dyas while the length of the iceberg is about 5km above.The number of iceberg tracked by MERS, total of 250, is more than by NSIDC (Jarom, 2001). According to statistics, the average life expectancy of these giant icebergs is about 10 years(Stuart,2011).

Iceberg monitoring is basically done by artificial interpret using remote sensing image . Automated remote sensing image information extraction and change monitoring technology is not yet widely used in the polar regions of the iceberg monitoring. Due to the restrictions of the low efficiency of manual interpretation of factors, track and monitor these icebergs is limited to giant iceberg. Near the south pole, some of small-scale iceberg monitoring are implemented by ship-borne radar. But these monitoring information cannot be monitored in all regions of the iceberg of the Antarctic coastline. In fact, research on the distribution and activity patterns of small and medium-scale iceberg is a certain sense. Using an iceberg trajectory model, Gladstone et al(2002) found that small and medium-scale iceberg melt may be greater in some coastal areas than the difference between the amount of precipitation and evaporation. So melting of these icebergs may also play an important role in the ocean circulation.

The change detection of Antarctic ice is different from the traditional change detection, the result of which is changed or unchanged. Such as buildings and other man-made target detection, first of all we need register the different temporal images, and then determine where and which building is changed. In many studies on urban building change detection employing higher resolution aerial image, researchers use existent geo-database or CAD data as auxiliary to automatically register images, and then detect the building change (Mourad,2010; Liu,2010). Another example of change detection before and after the disaster, we also have to carry out the image matching to get corresponding comparison images, and then focuses on how to find changes in the disaster area(Zhu, 2011).Icebergs are constantly moving, change monitoring is on the tip of the tracking of a moving target detection problem, which does not focus on to judge the iceberg whether changes, but to track icebergs phase occurred in two is if not the same kind of changes, including changes in the move, rotate, melt. Iceberg tracking process is to search matched iceberg based on similarity within a certain range between different temporal images. The whole process is the object motion tracking, belonging to the technical field of image analysis and pattern recognition.

Silva and Bigg(2005) first used ERS-1 SAR image data to take advantage of the feature vector similarity matching method to achieve the automatic tracking and monitoring of the iceberg. The method uses the object-oriented thinking, combined with the feature vector matching method based on watershed image segmentation, target identification. The results showed that the effectiveness of the iceberg monitoring technologies is strong.

3 Algorithm Description

In this paper, it records iceberg outline of changes in different time through the establishment of monitoring the iceberg outline library. First, the contour of iceberg initial state will be recorded in the library. Then to contrast contour extraction results in the next time, the change will be updated to the iceberg outline library. The method of comparison is based on the matching of the feature vector. The process of the entire algorithm is shown in Fig. 1.

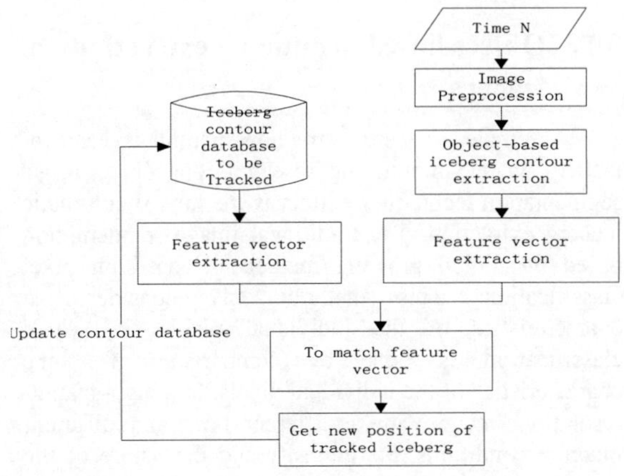

Fig. 1. Algorithm flowchart of Iceberg Tracking

The key technologies that need to be addressed in this method is feature extraction. Feature extraction results will affect the results of the different matching algorithms. The selection process of the feature vector is to select the feature from the target of interest which can best represent the object to match. Herein optional features include: the size, aspect ratio, similarity of shape (contour). An iceberg corresponds to a set of feature vectors. The iceberg tracking process is transformed into best matching between two different set of feature vectors. Traditionally, based on the ideas of the feature vector object matching method, the difference of the value of the corresponding feature between the two sets of feature vectors were calculated. Then for each feature vector given a certain weight, to concentrate all of the difference values and the weight multiplied with the vector sum of the representative of the degree of difference of the two objects. Calculate the degree of difference between all objects to be matched. Finally, select the object represented by the minimum differences within the effective range of the feature vector set as the match results.

For the tip of the match, a relatively large proportion of shape characteristics, area characteristics played constraints in the matching process. The year is divided into summer and winter seasons. Specific area of filter rules are defined as follows: If the iceberg area is A, search scales in the summer is from 0.25*A to 1.1*A. In the winter, search scale range is from 0.2*A to 1.15*A. The icebergs which similar to the shape but with too different area will be filtered through the area of screening rules. Then these icebergs will be applied to the matching method based on aspect ratio and shape similarity. This will be helpful to track iceberg more efficiently. Shape similarity calculation is the key step of this flow chart. This paper presents a HAUSDORFF matching algorithm based on Curvature Extrema to calculate the similarity between feature vectors. SIFT (Scale Invariable Feature Transformation) algorithm is also employed to iceberg matching, which can find the collapse of the iceberg object by the degree by the local features of an iceberg at different phases.

3.1 Object-based contour extraction of iceberg

Automated iceberg extraction method is basic of iceberg change monitoring research. The object-based segmentation techniques extract is the key of automatic iceberg extraction. The traditional image segmentation based on region growing method is based on pixel classification. This method only consider the characteristics of the individual pixels, in which classification is done by comparison of the characteristics of the individual pixels. In a high-spatial-resolution image with a different time and different imaging conditions, the intensity and the nature of the change for each pixel will not be identical. The misclassification often occur because of noise interference. The result of segmentation is relative fragmental. Within threshold, each calculation should read each pixel of the entire image, which results in the lower efficiency. In this study, the iceberg extraction method using object-based segmentation can get more accurate the iceberg profile (algorithm see Zhao et al., 2012)

3.2 Matching method based on Hausdorff distance of the curvature extrema of the iceberg contour

The main activities of the iceberg in the course of the campaign is drift, rotation, and melting. Occasionally soon, the movement speed of iceberg is so faster with rotation along with it drift process. The movement of the iceberg has become more difficult to track at different time. The characteristics of the shape is the key factors to detect icebergs drift, rotation, melting. Shown in Fig. 2, the icebergs will rotate in the drift process. The edge contour changes occur in varying degrees because of melting of iceberg. But the contour patterns of these icebergs still have a lot of similarities.

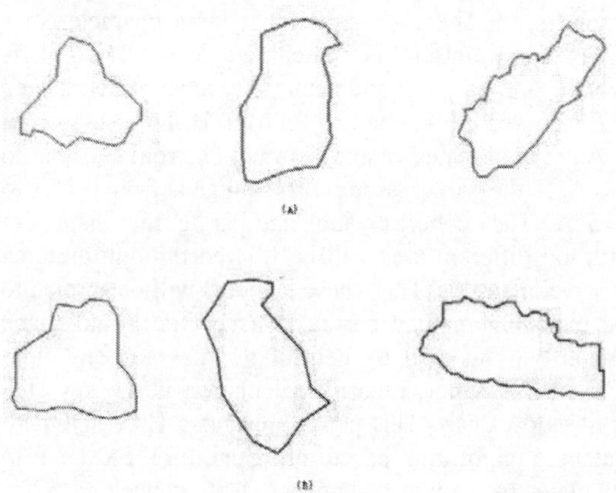

Fig. 2. Iceberg rotation, melting demonstration. (A) Contours of three selected icebergs in April11,2010; (B)Corresponding contours in April 27,2010.

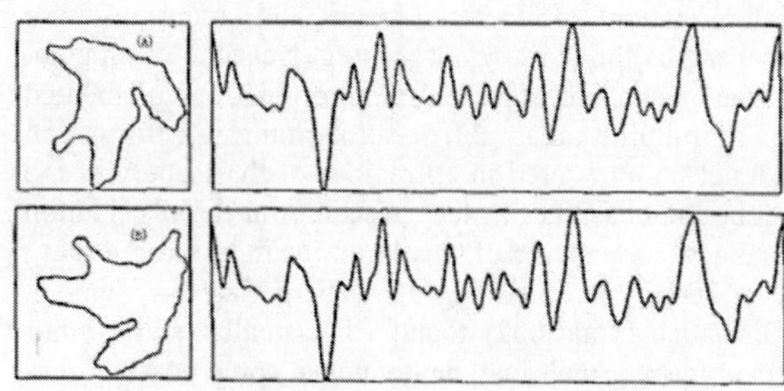

Fig. 3. Iceberg Contour at different time and corresponding curvature function

In this paper, the matching degree between curve extreme points of the curvature function of the iceberg outline is used as iceberg contour matching value. Shown in Fig. 3, A and B are the contour images of the iceberg at two different times while the right side is their corresponding curvature function. As can be seen from the figure, iceberg phase the rotation for the time profile of the A in B time, some edge area also occurs a certain degree of variation. But the two-time curvature function is very similar.

Extreme points of the curvature function of the iceberg contour curves compose the set of extreme points of each contour. The first point of each set is to take the collection of maximum curvature point. According to the order to take the extreme points remaining. Iceberg contour matching can convert a match between point sets. In this paper, matching approach based on Hausdorff distance (Christian,2011; David,2004) is employed to calculate the similarity between different collections of extreme points which is used as the similarity of iceberg contour matching. The entire process flow is shown in Fig. 4.

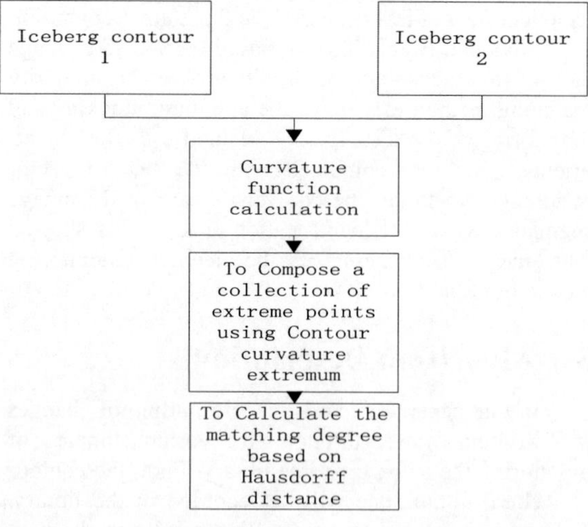

Fig. 4: Iceberg contour matching based Hausdorff distance of contour curvature extremum

3.3 Iceberg Matching Method Based on SIFT Algorithm

The iceberg will occur disintegration due to collision in the drift process. Matching based on area characteristics as well as global feature of contour is difficult to complete when icebergs occur disintegration. By summarizing, David (2004), based on the invariant feature detection technology methods proposed Scale Invariant Feature Transform algorithm(SIFT). SIFT , no limits of rotation and the position changing, can be achieved a partial match. This method helps to track fracture and collision of the iceberg.

SIFT feature vector generated in the two images, the Euclidean distance of eigenvectors of the key points is used as the basis of the feature point matching. Based on this method, can get matched feature point set between different-time iceberg contours. Figure 5 shows: (a) and (b) are the extracted iceberg contours at different time. (C) and (d) the feature vector is extracted using the SIFT algorithm. The matching result is shown in Figure 6. The experimental results show that the vector matching method based on SIFT feature points can effectively find the local matching features of different-time iceberg.

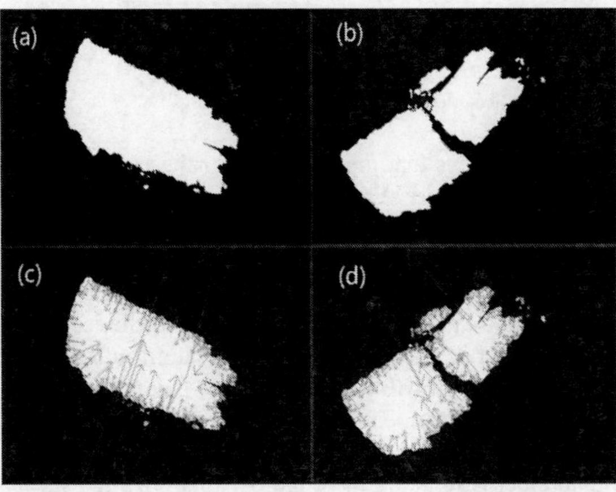

Fig.5. Case of SIFT Feature Vector Extraction from Iceberg

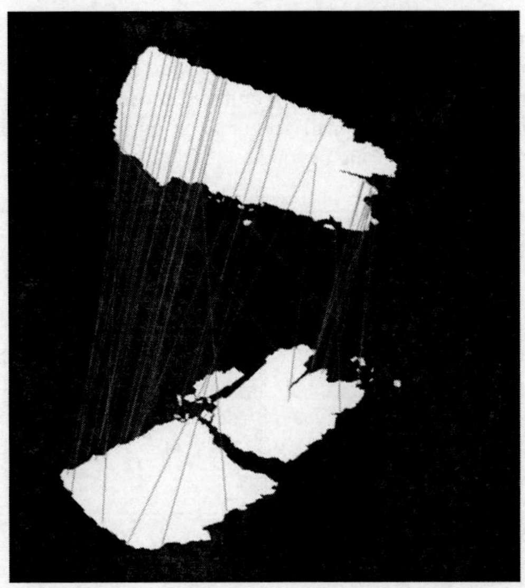

Fig.6. Case of Feature Point Matching Based SIFT for Iceberg

This paper presents a iceberg matching method based on SIFT feature vector matching. Based on the results of SIFT feature vector extraction , we can get the eigenvectors of the iceberg according to the location of feature points. Calculate the degree of match between the feature vector of each iceberg eigenvectors to be matched with the next time. Use the inclusion relations between matched Eigenvectors to determine if the new iceberg is a broken from a old one or merge from two icebergs.

4 Experiments

4.1 Study Area and Data

The Mertz Glacier region near the edge of the Antarctic ice sheet is the study area. Select Mertz iceberg as automatically change-monitoring and tracking objects. ASAR-WSM mode radar images from February, 2010 to 2010, December (about 1 year) were Selected as the data of this study which time resolution is 3-7 days while the spatial resolution 75M. Collided by C19 iceberg in February 2010, Mertz iceberg was separated from Mertz Glacier, which is 50 miles long and 20 miles wide. Mertz iceberg counterclockwise drift along the edge of the Antarctic ice shelves with the ocean circulation. In the drift of the process, it will melt and disintegrate, splitting out certain small icebergs.

4.2 Tracking Result of Mertz Iceberg

As shown in Fig. 7, with the different colors indicate different time location of the icebergs. We can get the iceberg trajectory in the past year, the change in shape, as well as decomposition circumstances. Ten days intervals, statistics the change of the total area of Mertz icebergs. The result indicates the area of Mertz iceberg show the general trend of declining which reduce the total area of about 75 square kilometers in the past one year. By one-year Monitoring, we found that a total of 53 sub iceberg generated by Mertz iceberg. 19 of them have continued to be monitored for more than half a year. But some small icebergs of them have melt, some drift monitoring beyond.

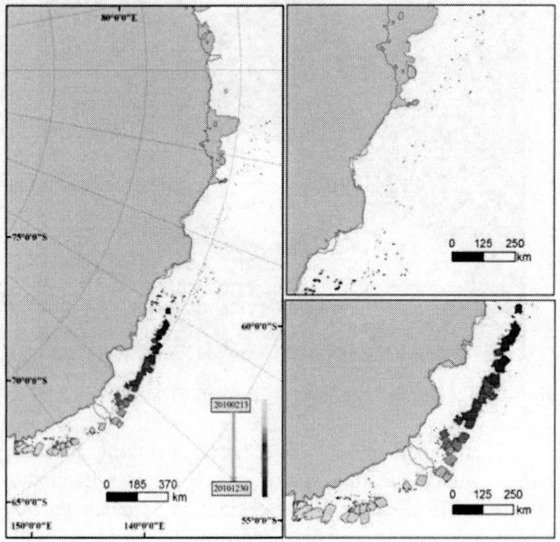

Fig.7. Time-Location Map of Mertz Iceberg

According to the area of iceberg, Mertz Icebergs were divided into groups of four different scales to be detected.

Level 1: 1800 Sq.km----100 Sq.km

Level 2: 100 Sq.km----20 Sq.km

Level 3: 20 Sq.km----5 Sq.km

Level 4: 5 Sq.km----1 Sq.km.

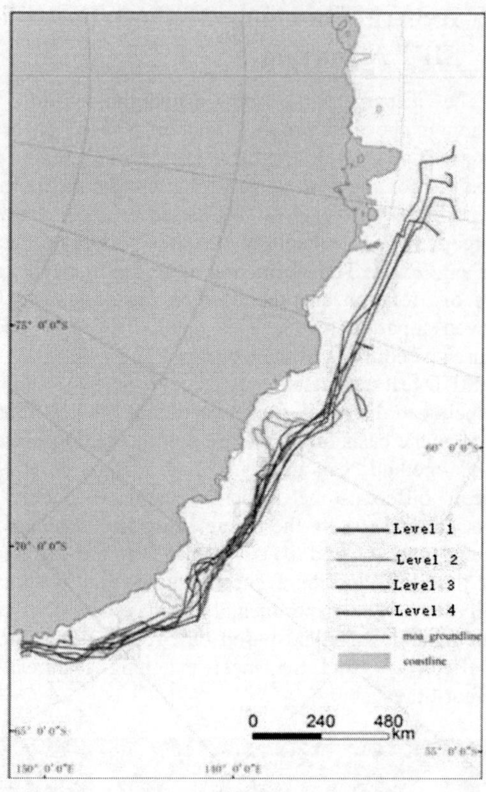

Fig.8. Trajectories of Four-scale Mertz Icebergs

Fig. 8 shows that the trajectory of these 4 different scales of the iceberg. From the result of tracking Mertz icebergs in the past year, we can draw the following conclusions:

1). In general, Mertz iceberg is appearing ablation. However, for each of the different scales of the iceberg, ablation trend is not obvious. Total ablation in summer and winter area growth close to the total balance.

2). The movement of the iceberg of all scales, mainly affected by the ocean currents. Trajectory counterclockwise along the edge of Antarctica ice sheet was basically consistent with the direction of the ocean circulation. Its velocity varies in the different regions.

3). The trajectory of iceberg with area of more than 5 square kilometers is similar. Scale of 5-20 km iceberg drift faster. Figure 16 shows the same-scale-iceberg trajectory is similar in the open ocean in the same time.

4). The iceberg drift along with the rotation. The collision is the main reason for changing the iceberg rotation direction.

5 Discussion

This paper presents a calculation method of iceberg contour matching degrees based the curvature-extremum Hausdorff distance, and the iceberg matching method based on vector matching using SIFT feature, which solve the overall matching of the iceberg, but also local matching of the iceberg caused by crushing or collision.

The paper Propose a method for automatically iceberg tracking and monitoring using continuous ASAR radar image data. The method has a certain robustness. Currently, automated Iceberg change detection is not mature enough. There is not specifically for the study about automatic change monitoring method for the polar icebergs. Monitoring is more about giant iceberg. In the future, we need to develop the small and medium-scale iceberg monitoring methods.

6 References

[1] Christian Knauer,Maarten Löffler,et al.The directed Hausdorff distance between imprecise point sets.Algorithms and Computation,2011,412 (32):4173-4186.

[2] Chunjiang Zhao,Wenkang Shi,Yong Deng.A new Hausdorff distance for image matching. Pattern Recognition Letters,2005,26 (5):581-586.

[3] David G.Lowe.Distinctive image features from scale-invariant keypoints. International Journal of Computer Vision,2004,60 (2) : 91-110.

[4] Gill R.Operational detection of sea ice edges and icebergs using SAR.Canadian Journal of Remote Sensing.2001, 27: 411-432.

[5] Gladstone R, Bigg G R.Satellite tracking of icebergs in the Weddell sea.Antarctic Science, 2002, 14: 278-287.

[6] Liu Z , Gong P, Shi PJ. Et.al (2010):Automated building change detection using UltraCamD images and existing CAD data, International Journal of Remote Sensing, 31:6, 1505-1517.

[7] Mourad Bouziani, Kalifa Goïta, et al.Automatic change detection of buildings in urban environment from very high spatial resolution images using existing geodatabase and prior knowledge.Journal of Photogrammetry and Remote Sensing, 2010, 65: 143153.

[8] NIC, update 2010.National Ice Center. http://www.natice.noaa.gov/.

[9] Stuart K M, Long D G.Tracking large tabular icebergs using the SeaWinds Ku-band microwave scatterometer.Deep-Sea Research II, 2011, 58 (11-12):1285-1300.

[10] Stefan R, Ocean circulation and climate during the past 120, 000 years.Nature, 2002, 419 : 207-214.

[11] Tchernia T, T F Jeannin. Circulation in Antarctic waters as revealed by iceberg tracks 1972-1983 [J] . Polar Record, 1984, 22 (138) : 263-269.

[12] Wua Jian-ming,Jing Zhongliang,et al.Study on an improved Hausdorff distance for multi-sensor image matching. Communications in Nonlinear Science and Numerical Simulation,2012,17 (2): 513-520.

[13] Zhao Z Y, Liu Z, Gong P. Automatic extraction of floating ice at Antarctic continental margin from remotely sensed imagery using Object-based segmentation.Science China Earth Science, 2012, 55(4):622-632.

[14] Zhu Hongping, Li Lin, et al.Damage detection method for shear buildings using the changes in the first mode shape slopes.Computers & Structures, 2011, 733-743.

A Multi-Stage Approach for Automatic Classification of Environmental Microorganisms

Chen Li, Kimiaki Shirahama,
Joanna Czajkowska, and Marcin Grzegorzek
Research Group for Pattern Recognition
University of Siegen, Germany
marcin.grzegorzek@uni-siegen.de

Fangshu Ma and Beihai Zhou
The Civil and Environment Engineering School
University of Science and Technology Beijing, China
zhoubeihai@sina.com

***Abstract*—Environmental Microorganisms (EMs) are currently recognised using molecular biology (DNA, RNA) or morphological methods. The first ones are very time-consuming and expensive. The second ones require a very experienced laboratory operator. To overcome these problems, we introduce an automatic classification method for EMs in the framework of content-based image analysis. In order to efficiently segment the EM structure, six segmentation approaches are tested. A Sobel edge detector based semi-automatic segmentation approach achieves the best evaluation performance on the testing data. To describe the shapes of EMs in microscopic images, we use Edge Histograms, Fourier Descriptors, extended Geometrical Features, as well as introduce Internal Structure Histograms. For classification, multi-class Support Vector Machine is applied to EMs represented by the above features. In order to quantitatively evaluate discriminative properties of features, we perform comprehensive experiments with a ground truth of manually segmented microscopic EM images. The classification result of 89.7% proves a high robustness of our method.**

Keywords—Environmental Microorganism Classification, Shape Features, Support Vector Machine, Microscopic Images, Image Segmentation

I. Introduction

Environmental microorganisms (EMs) and their species are very important indicators to evaluate environmental quality. For example, protozoa and metazoan are water quality indicator organisms in natural (rivers, lakes, oceans, etc.) and artificial water bodies (fish ponds, aeration tank, stabilisation ponds, etc.) [1]. However, it is a very complicated task to distinguish thousands of EMs from each other in the laboratory.

Molecular biology is an efficient way to distinguish EMs by DNA or RNA [2], [3], but it is time-consuming and very expensive. In the traditional morphological method, a microorganism is observed under a microscope and recognised manually based on its shape. It is much cheaper, but the training process remains very time-consuming. Furthermore, even very experienced operators are unable to distinguish thousands of EMs without taking into consideration additional sources of information like literature or searching on the Web.

In this paper we introduce a much cheaper and convenient classification method for EMs, in which their microscopic images are automatically analysed by computer algorithms [4], [5]. Our approach computationally simulates the morphological analysis, where environmental scientists investigated EMs by looking at their shapes. We first develop one manual and five semi-automatic segmentation approaches to obtain the shapes of EMs. The best segmentation results for the testing data is used in the subsequent processes. Then, EMs are described by shape features, Edge Histogram, Fourier Descriptors, Geometrical Features, and Internal Structure Histograms. Finally, Support Vector Machines are utilized to classify EMs represented by shape features. In order to quantitatively evaluate our approach, experiments are conducted using a ground truth of EMs that are segmented and annotated by hand.

The paper is structured as follows. Section II discusses related work. Segmentation algorithms and their comparison are described in Section III. In Section IV our shape-based feature extraction techniques are presented. Section V describes the classification phase of our framework. In Section VI experiments and results are described and discussed. Finally, Section VII closes our paper by conclusions.

II. Related Work

Many EMs are specific in form, some of them are even named according to their shapes. For example, the classification of protozoa is mainly based on the shape structure and mode of motion [6]. Although morphological taxonomy is not sufficient for determining the precise phylogenetic positions of environmental organisms, it plays an important role in, e.g., wastewater treatment and aquaculture management.

Classification of Microorganisms: To the best of our knowledge, there are no computer-based approaches in the literature towards solving the EMs classification problem that follow the morphological strategy. However, there is some related work towards classification of other types of microorganisms. For example, Riries et al. presented in [7] an approach for automatic classification of the tuberculosis bacteria. For this, the authors used seven geometrical characteristics and neural networks for classification. They performed the training phase based on 75 samples and used 25 samples for testing. In a very simplified scenario (two classes problem: tuberculosis, not tuberculosis) they achieved a classification rate of 100%. In [8] an approach for wastewater bacteria recognition based on microscopic image analysis was described. The authors used 11 geometrical characteristics and an improved neural

Chen is supported by the China Scholarship Council
Kimiaki is supported by the Japan Society for the Promotion of Science
Joanna is supported by the German Research Foundation within the Research Training Group 1564

network for classification. For experiments, two types of easily distinguishable wastewater bacteria were considered. With 387 training and 30 testing images a classification rate of 85.5% was achieved. Seokwon Yeom et al. worked on real-time 3D sensing, visualisation and recognition of dynamic biological microorganisms [9]. They extracted features by Gabor-based wavelets and perform classification by automated training vector selection. In their experiment, 100 trial samples were used as the reference, then 100 true-class and 100 false-class inputs were used to test the performance of the shape independent 3D recognition. A classification rate of around 80% was achieved. Das et al. used a statistical signal modelling techniques to distinguish seven kinds of water-borne microbial shapes, and a model was built on geometrical features based on the feature weighting and rotated coordinate system methods [10]. For each shape, the classifier was trained using 10 images, and tested by five images. The recognition result of the experiment was around 80% to 90%. Y.P. Ginoris et al. compared three classification methods on 22 classes of protozoa and metazoan [11]. In their experiment, geometrical features were used in feature extraction. Then, discriminant analysis, neural networks and decision trees were used for classification. Their data set contained about 1,500 training examples and 600 testing examples, and for 12 non-stalked classes, the recognition rate was about 80% to 90%, and for 10 stalked classes, that was about 50% to 70%.

Though all of the approaches described above obtained good classification rates (around 80% to 90%), each of them investigated only one single feature space (in the most of cases geometrical features). [10] and [11] considered a multi-class recognition problem, but other methods were limited to easily distinguishable two classes. In contrast to this, we investigate four different kinds of features which, considering all their concrete implementations, lead to 20 different feature spaces. Moreover, we take into account 10 different classes of microorganisms in our experiments.

Segmentation: There exist different algorithms used for segmentation, based on pixel intensity levels or image context [12], [13]. The primary intensity-based method is Otsu thresholding [14], whereas Sobel [15], Prewitt [16], Roberts [17], Laplacian of a Gaussian (LoG) [18], zero-crossing [19] and Canny edge detectors [20] analyse first- and second-order derivatives and the local gradients. Watershed algorithm [21] is used in distance, gradients or marker-controlled methods, which produce different segmentation results. As a pre- or post-processing techniques, different morphological operations are also applied [12], [13]. Among all of these algorithms, Canny detector seem to be the most robust method in the context of our approach. To evaluate the obtained image segmentation results we adopt different statistical measures described in literature [22].

Shape-Based Feature Extraction: Edge Histogram Descriptor defined within the MPEG-7 standard tracks five different categories of edges: vertical, horizontal, 45° diagonal, 135° antidiagonal and isotropic (non-edges) [23]. It produces a feature vector based on a concrete histogram construction method. Geometrical Features usually include perimeter, area, radii or extrema of axial lengths, seven invariant moments, etc. [8], [10], [11]. Internal Structure Angles (ISAs) are developed by the work of Michael Donoser et al. [24]. Each ISA is structured by every three sample points on the outline of a shape, and the shape could be described by the ISAs as a frame structure. It is a basis for our Internal Structure Histogram described in Section IV. Another very robust descriptor for shape contours is based on the Fourier transform [25]. However, with decreasing number of sample points its descriptive power for shape degrades.

Classification: Support Vector Machines (SVMs) are usually used as efficient classifiers for high-dimensional data [26]. The original SVM can only be used for two-class classification, so several multi-class SVM methods are developed as 1vs1, 1vsR, DAG methods, etc. [27].

III. SEGMENTATION

For extracting the shape features of EMs, we introduce a pre-processing segmentation step. Here, some microscopic EM images are characterised by low Contrast-to-Noise Ratios (CNR) and Signal-to-Noise Ratios (SNR), which make the segmentation difficult. To address this problem, we adopt and compare six segmentation approaches introduced in Section II. All the obtained segmentation results are presented in Fig. 1.

Manual Segmentation Method: To make the developed software more robust and to compare the obtained results with an expert delineation, a manual segmentation method is implemented based on mouse clicking operation. An obtained segmentation result is given in Fig. 1 C.

Semi-Automatic Segmentation Methods: The five segmentation results obtained using different semi-automatic procedures mentioned below are presented in Fig. 1 D-H. Their detailed description can be found in [12], [13].

Fig. 1 D shows the segmentation result of Otsu thresholding algorithm, performing histogram shape-based image analysis [14]. It assumes the bi-modal histogram of an image and calculates the optimum threshold for separating pixels into two classes, pixels belonging to the object and the background.

Fig. 1 E and F present the segmentation results obtained on the basis of Sobel and Canny edge detectors, respectively. Sobel and Canny detectors are both based on gradient theory, but adopt different approximation algorithms providing different detection results and visual effects. Assuming a 2D image function $f(x, y)$, the gradient is defined as

$$\nabla \mathbf{f} = (G_x, G_y)^{\mathrm{T}} = \left(\frac{\partial f}{\partial x}, \frac{\partial f}{\partial y}\right)^{\mathrm{T}}, \quad (1)$$

where the magnitude of the gradient vector is given by

$$\nabla f = \mathrm{mag}(\nabla \mathbf{f}) = (G_x^2 + G_y^2)^{\frac{1}{2}} = \left(\left(\frac{\partial f}{\partial x}\right)^2 + \left(\frac{\partial f}{\partial y}\right)^2\right)^{\frac{1}{2}}. \quad (2)$$

In order to simplify the computation, we approximate the magnitude formulas

$$\nabla f \approx G_x^2 + G_y^2, \quad (3)$$

$$\nabla f \approx |G_x| + |G_y|. \quad (4)$$

These two approximations still feature zero values in the areas of constant intensity and the values proportional to the degree

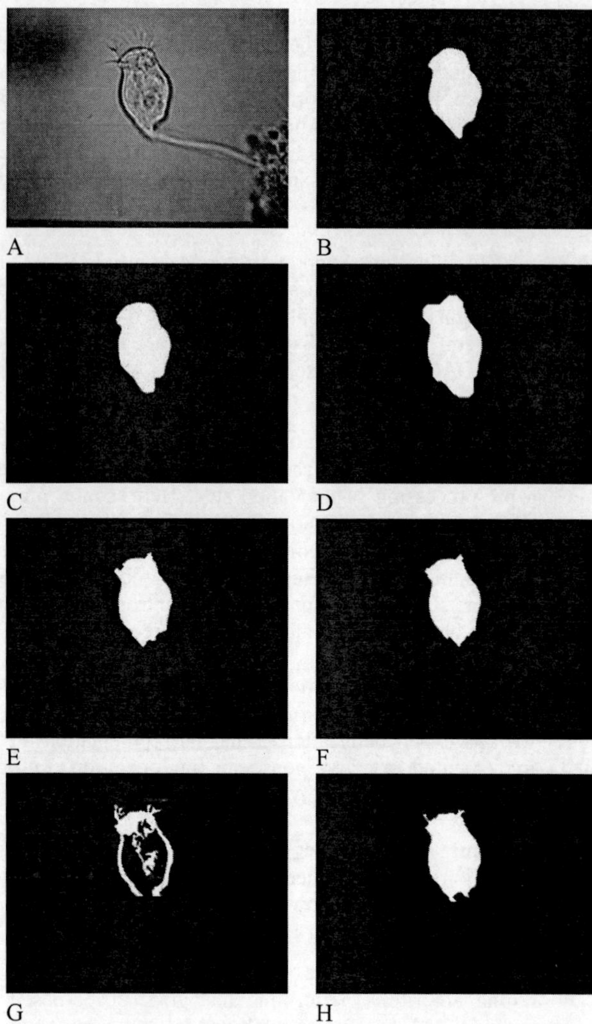

Fig. 1. Exemplary segmentation results. A: Original microscopic EM image; B: ground truth; C: manual segmentation result; D: Otsu thresholding algorithm; E: Sobel edge detector; F: Canny edge detector; G: watershed algorithm using marker-controlled method; H: an approach combining watershed transform, Canny detector and zero-crossing LoG algorithm.

of intensity changes in areas, where pixel values vary. Based on the mathematical background, we apply two-stages edge detection procedure. First, we find the regions where the magnitude of first derivative is greater than a specified threshold. Then, we find the regions where the second derivative has a zero-crossing [13]. The obtained experimental results proved, that the Canny edge detector is the most robust tool to solve our segmentation task.

Fig. 1 G visualises a segmentation result of watershed-based approach. In geography, a watershed is the ridge dividing the areas drained by different river systems. Similar to this, grey-scale image is perceived as a topological surface, with the values $f(x, y)$ interpreted as its heights [13]. In the implemented watershed transform the gradient computation theory introduced above is used.

The segmentation result in Fig. 1 H obtained by our method, which combines the advantage of watershed, Canny and zero-crossing algorithms. The watershed method provides good results in the segmentation of the outlines (see Fig. 1 G), whereas the Canny edge detector is effective for segmenting the main parts of the sample (see Fig. 1 F). The zero-crossing edge detector smooths the details [12], [13]. Therefore, we attempted to fuse these three methods to get better segmentation results. The segmentation process can be then summarised by three essential steps: the watershed-based segmentation of the outline, the main segmentation algorithm based on Canny edge detector and fusion of the previously obtained segmentation results by a zero-crossing edge detection procedure.

Comparison of Segmentation Results: Considering practical usage and statistical measure obtained using different segmentation procedures, the three most suitable EM microscopic image segmentation effects are given in Fig. 1 (E, F and H). Although our proposed approach provides the best segmentation in most of the cases, it requires at least 10 parameters and is not efficient for the complex structures. In such cases Sobel edge detector is used. Its advantages in comparison with Canny approach are visualised in Fig. 2. We can conclude that though Canny edge detector is very robust for detection of edges, it is too sensitive to the strong noise. The Sobel approach is less robust, however, more resistant to low SNR, and therefore, more sufficient for our task. Thus, we choose the Sobel edge detector-based segmentation technique as our image processing and analysis approach. As pre- and post-processing techniques we apply different mathematical morphology operators, like erosion, dilation, labelling, reconstruction, etc. The whole semi-automatic segmentation process is briefly sketched as: choosing the interested area in an image; computing the threshold of this area; using Sobel edge detector to detect the objective edges; performing morphological processing operations; selecting the interested object.

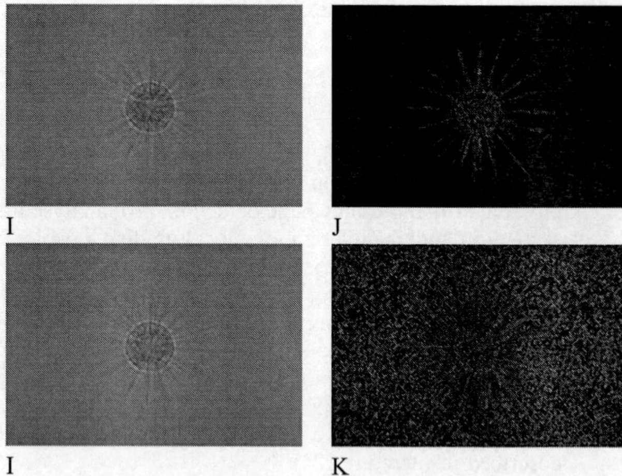

Fig. 2. Sobel Detector vs Canny Detector. I: original microscopic EM image; J: edges detected by Sobel detector; K: edges detected by Canny detector.

IV. Shape Features

For shape description, we use the Edge Histogram Descriptor and the Fourier Descriptor. Moreover, we significantly extend the Geometrical Features and introduce a completely new Internal Structure Histogram. The input for all feature extraction techniques listed above is a binary image distinguishing between the region of interest and the background.

Edge Histogram Descriptor: The Edge Histogram Descriptor (EHD) we use is based on connected components. First, we extract edges from the binary input image. Second, we count the number of pixels (edge length) in each edge (connected component). Finally, we create a histogram showing the distribution of edge lengths within the shape. For this, we use 13 bins (1-10 pixels, 11-20, 21-30, ..., 111-120, more than 120 pixels) which leads to a 13-dimensional feature space $\boldsymbol{h} = (h_1, \ldots, h_{13})^{\mathrm{T}}$.

Fourier Descriptor: The Fourier Descriptor (FD) starts with computing Euclidean distances $d_{t=0,1,\ldots,N-1}$ from the object centre to N points equidistantly distributed along its contour. Then, it performs the Discrete Fourier Transform on $d(t)$

$$a_{n=0,1,\ldots,N-1} = \frac{1}{N} \sum_{t=0}^{N-1} d_t \exp(\frac{-j2\pi nt}{N}) \quad . \tag{5}$$

In order to describe the shape, the acquired Fourier coefficients are normalised according to [25], so that they are rotation, scaling and start point invariant

$$\forall_{n\in\{0,1,\ldots,N-1\}}; \qquad b_n = \frac{a_n}{a_0} \quad . \tag{6}$$

In our experiments in Section VI, we use five different values of $N \in \{50, 100, 150, 200, 300\}$. The dimensionality of the resulting feature vector is equal to $N/2$, since the values of $\boldsymbol{b} = (b_0, \ldots, b_{N-1})^{\mathrm{T}}$ are symmetrically redundant ($\forall_{n=0,\ldots,N-1}$; $b_n = b_{N-1-n}$). These five feature spaces are named as $\boldsymbol{f}_1$ ($N/2 = 25$), $\boldsymbol{f}_2$ ($N/2 = 50$), $\boldsymbol{f}_3$ ($N/2 = 75$), $\boldsymbol{f}_4$ ($N/2 = 100$), $\boldsymbol{f}_5$ ($N/2 = 150$).

Geometrical Features: We analyse the following 13 geometrical characteristics: The perimeter (P) of a shape is the whole length of its outer edge or boundary. The area (A) of a shape is the squared amount of flat space or ground that this shape covers. The complex rate (C) describes a shape with the dependent relationship between P and A, and is computed as $C = P^2/4\pi A$. The longest axis (L) is the length of the long side of the bounding rectangle of a shape. The shortest axis (S) is the length of the short side of the bounding rectangle of a shape. The elongation (E) is the ratio of S and L with the value between $(0, 1]$, and is computed as $E = S/L$. Seven invariant moments ($I_1, \ldots, I_7$) proposed by Hu [28] are also used to describe the same shapes with the different transforms of zooming in, zooming out and revolve very robustly. By different combinations of these characteristics, we get the following seven geometrical feature (GF) spaces:

$\boldsymbol{g}_1 = (C, E)^{\mathrm{T}}$;
$\boldsymbol{g}_2 = (P, A, C)^{\mathrm{T}}$;
$\boldsymbol{g}_3 = (L, S, E)^{\mathrm{T}}$;
$\boldsymbol{g}_4 = (P, A, C, L, S, E)^{\mathrm{T}}$;
$\boldsymbol{g}_5 = (P, A, C, I_1, I_2, I_3, I_4, I_5, I_6, I_7)^{\mathrm{T}}$;
$\boldsymbol{g}_6 = (L, S, E, I_1, I_2, I_3, I_4, I_5, I_6, I_7)^{\mathrm{T}}$;
$\boldsymbol{g}_7 = (P, A, C, L, S, E, I_1, I_2, I_3, I_4, I_5, I_6, I_7)^{\mathrm{T}}$.

Each GF provides a feature space with different dimensionalities. For example, $\boldsymbol{g}_3$ represents a 3-dimensional feature space consisting of L, S and E, and $\boldsymbol{g}_5$ represents a 5-dimensional feature space consisting of P, A, C and seven invariant moments $T_1, \ldots, I_7$.

Internal Structure Histogram Descriptor: We extend the Internal Structure Angle (ISA) [24] descriptor and introduce the Internal Structure Histogram (ISH) in our work. As can be seen in Fig. 3, we take into account angles $\angle\alpha_{i,j}$ created using different shape points.

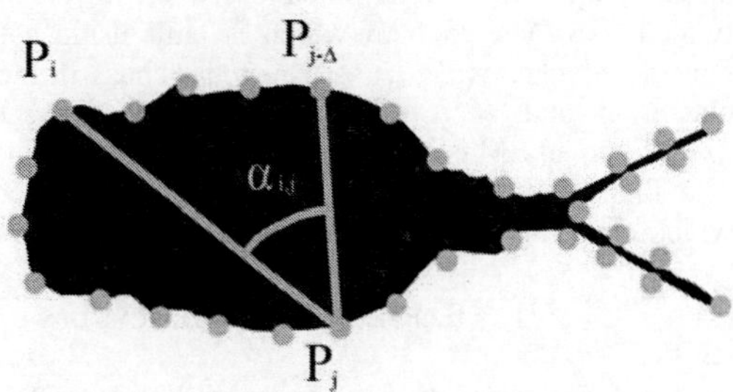

Fig. 3. An example of ISA

By considering all possible angles that can be achieved in this way, we build a histogram grouping the angle values into bins. For example, for following bins $[0°, 45°)$, $[45°, 90°)$, ..., $[315°, 360°)$ an 8-dimensional feature space for shape description is determined. However, the pure ISH feature can only describe the structure of a shape, but cannot distinguish different sizes. To overcome this, we combine the ISH features and geometrical features. By different amounts of sample points on the contour and concatenations with GFs, we get seven ISH feature spaces named as s_1, s_2, ..., s_7 (see TABLE I).

FSs	s_1	s_2	s_3	s_4	s_5	s_6	s_7
NoSSPs	50	100	100	100	100	100	100
GFs			g_2	g_3	g_4	g_4	g_4
NoHBs	40	40	40	40	40	20	10
Dim	40	40	43	43	46	26	16

TABLE I. ISH FEATURE SPACES USED IN OUR EXPERIMENTS. FSS - ISH FEATURE SPACES; NOSSPS - NUMBER OF SHAPE SAMPLE POINTS; GFS - GEOMETRICAL FEATURES USED FOR CONCATENATION; NOHBS - NUMBER OF HISTOGRAM BINS; DIM - DIMENSIONALITY OF RESULTING FEATURE SPACE.

V. Classification

Because of the high dimensionalities of feature spaces described in Section IV, we use a Support Vector Machine (SVM) for classification. Similarity-based classifiers like k-Nearest Neighbour or probability-based classifiers like Naive Bayes do not work well for high-dimensional feature vectors. Similarity-based classifiers fail for high-dimensional feature spaces, because usually many dimensions are irrelevant for measuring similarities. Probability-based classifiers need a large number of training examples to appropriately estimate probabilistic distributions in high-dimensional feature spaces which is not the case for our datasets (see Section VI).

For these reasons, we select an SVM which extracts a decision boundary between microscopic images of different classes based on the margin maximisation principle. Due to this principle, the generalisation error of the SVM is independent of the number of feature dimensions [26]. Furthermore, a complex (non-linear) decision boundary can be extracted using a non-linear SVM. In this process, microscopic images in a high-dimensional feature space are mapped into a higher-dimensional feature space using a kernel trick.

In our work, we adopt a multi-class Support Vector Machine (mSVM) using the one-against-one (1vs1) version. The class of an EM is determined based on a vote strategy of two-class SVMs, each of which is built using a pair of all considered classes $\{\omega_1, \omega_2, \ldots, \omega_K\}$. Thus, if there are K classes in total, $K(K-1)/2$ two-class classifiers have to be used. First, an EM is classified using all these two-class SVMs. The final classification result is determined by counting to which class the EM has been assigned most frequently.

VI. Experiments and Results

For experiments, we used two real datasets (DS1 and DS2) acquired in environmental laboratories of the University of Science and Technology Beijing. Both contain ten classes of environmental microorganisms ω_1, ω_2, ..., ω_{10}. Example images can be seen in Fig. 4.

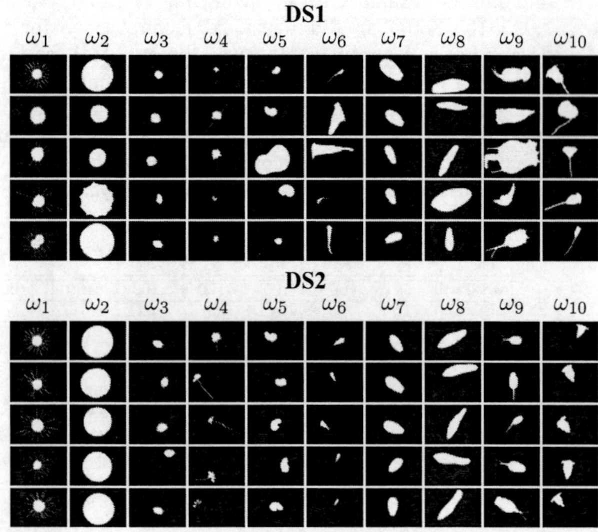

Fig. 4. DS1 and DS2 example images of all EM classes used for experiments.

Each class is represented by 20 microscopic images (altogether 200 images for DS1, and 200 images for DS2). However, conceptualising the first dataset DS1 we do not take into consideration the hierarchical structure of biological systematics for EMs. It means that in DS1, each class ω_k consists of different subclasses (subspecies). This leads to problems for some of the main classes (species). For instance, according to biological systematics, Rotifer (ω_9) is divided to more than 2200 subspecies with significantly different appearances. In DS1, ω_9 is represented by example microscopic images from six different subspecies. This makes it difficult to find invariant features describing this class. In contrast, in DS2 we consider microscopic images of EMs that belong to the same subclass (subspecies). Thus, it is expected that the classification on DS2 is more accurate than the one on DS1.

Feature and Classification: In our experiments, we randomly select 10 samples from each class as training examples, and use the left 10 as testing examples for classification. In order to increase statistical relevance, we repeat the selection process 10 times. As a result, 10 different sets of training and test datasets are obtained. Experiments are performed for all these datasets and mean recognition rates are considered for evaluation.

In Fig. 5, the classification results achieved for DS1 and DS2 with 20 different feature spaces (see Section IV) are compared to each other. As expected, for most feature spaces, better classification rates are obtained for DS2 than DS1. The reason for this is that in DS2 species (classes) are represented by examples from the same subspecies (subclass). Since the long-term objective of our research is a robust classification of subspecies, this problem will disappear in our future work (see Section VII). The best performance with an impressive classification rate of 89.7% is achieved for the g_4 feature space on the DS2 (see TABLE II).

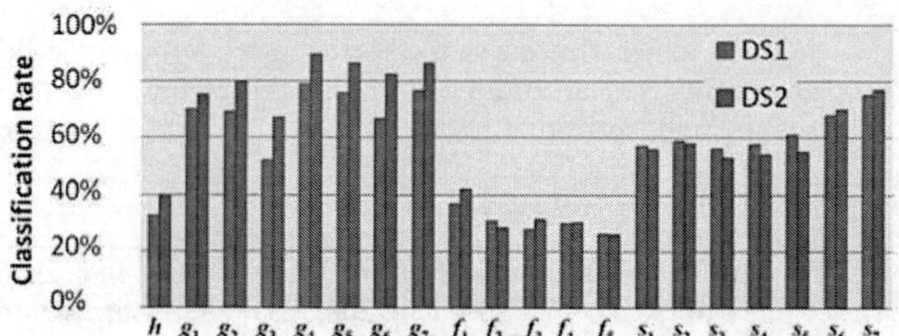

Fig. 5. Classification rates for DS1 and DS2 for different feature spaces.

	ω_1	ω_2	ω_3	ω_4	ω_5	ω_6	ω_7	ω_8	ω_9	ω_{10}	%
ω_1	**99**	0	0	1	0	0	0	0	0	0	99
ω_2	6	**90**	0	2	0	0	0	0	0	2	90
ω_3	0	0	**84**	6	2	2	0	0	0	6	84
ω_4	2	0	5	**93**	0	0	0	0	0	0	93
ω_5	0	0	4	0	**93**	3	0	0	0	0	93
ω_6	0	0	0	4	4	**92**	0	0	0	0	92
ω_7	1	0	0	2	0	0	**89**	0	0	8	89
ω_8	7	0	0	1	0	0	0	**89**	3	0	89
ω_9	2	0	0	4	0	0	0	2	**90**	2	90
ω_{10}	3	1	7	0	4	0	7	0	0	**78**	78
μ											**89.7**

TABLE II. Classification confusion matrix for the g_4 feature space on DS2. Classification rates are given in %.

We compare the four kinds of feature extraction methods introduced in Section IV (EHD, FD, GF, and ISH) by taking into consideration classification rates of their best performing feature spaces ($\boldsymbol{h}$, $\boldsymbol{f}_1$ $\boldsymbol{g}_4$, and s_7, respectively, see Fig. 6). Since EHD is meant for tracking of rather straight lines, $\boldsymbol{h}$ performs poorly in the task of EM classification. The classification rates for s_7 vary over different EM classes, because ISH is rather bad at describing shapes with large deformations. FD cannot describe robustly differences among shapes with similar sizes. Therefore, $\boldsymbol{f}_1$ can distinguish only one class from all others in a robust way. The most stable and best performing feature space turns out to be g_4. Obviously, it is able to express the relevant morphological information about EMs in a discriminative way. In TABLE III, we can find the best feature space for every separate class.

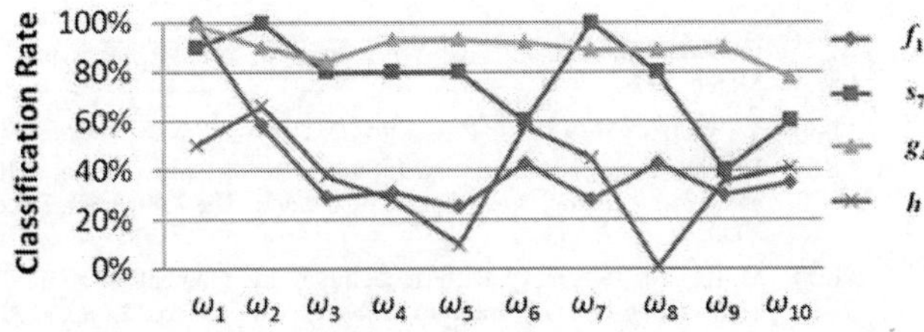

Fig. 6. Classification rates for selected feature spaces.

ω_1	ω_2	ω_3	ω_4	ω_5	ω_6	ω_7	ω_8	ω_9	ω_{10}
f_1	s_7	g_4	g_4	g_4	g_4	s_7	g_4	g_4	g_4
100	100	84	93	93	92	100	89	90	78

TABLE III. THE BEST FEATURE SPACES FOR DIFFERENT CLASSES. FIRST ROW: CLASSES; SECOND ROW: FEATURE SPACES; THIRD ROW: CLASSIFICATION RATES IN %.

Semi-Automatic Segmentation Evaluation: We evaluate our Sobel edge detector based segmentation method. A part of the 200 segmentation results and the corresponding ground truth on DS2 are both shown in Fig. 7. The presented examples prove the suitable segmentation results.

Semi-Automatic Segmentation Results

ω_1 ω_2 ω_3 ω_4 ω_5 ω_6 ω_7 ω_8 ω_9 ω_{10}

Ground Truth

ω_1 ω_2 ω_3 ω_4 ω_5 ω_6 ω_7 ω_8 ω_9 ω_{10}

Fig. 7. Semi-automatic segmentation results and ground truth on DS2.

To quantitatively evaluate the obtained results, we use four statistical measures, similarity, sensitivity, specificity and classification rate between the segmented images and the ground truth. Evaluation results by the first three measures are given in TABLE IV, and the result by last one can be found in TABLE V. Based on the TABLE IV and TABLE V, we can find that, though all of the first three measures prove good segmentation results, the last one indicates the low performance. This is because, our method is able to segment most of the meaningful areas of the objects, but it also loses some tiny but important details used in the feature extraction step. For example, from the visual evaluation in Fig. 7, ω_7 indicates very good segmentation results, but their perimeter feature values are much larger than the theoretical values. The reason is that the structure outlines are not as smooth as the ground truth, so that extracted features are disturbed and the classification rate is degraded to 5% (see TABLE V).

	ω_1	ω_2	ω_3	ω_4	ω_5	ω_6	ω_7	ω_8	ω_9	ω_{10}	Me
Si	97	99	100	99	99	100	99	97	99	99	99
Se	98	100	100	100	100	100	100	98	99	100	99
Sp	99	99	100	99	100	100	99	99	99	100	99

TABLE IV. EVALUATION OF SEMI-SEGMENTATION. SI: SIMILARITY; SE: SENSITIVITY; SP: SPECIFICITY; ME: MEAN VALUE. ALL THE VALUES ARE GIVEN IN %.

	ω_1	ω_2	ω_3	ω_4	ω_5	ω_6	ω_7	ω_8	ω_9	ω_{10}	%
ω_1	**14**	0	0	6	0	0	0	0	0	0	70
ω_2	2	**18**	0	2	0	0	0	0	0	2	90
ω_3	0	0	**20**	6	2	2	0	0	0	6	100
ω_4	0	0	3	**16**	0	1	0	0	0	0	80
ω_5	0	0	4	0	**11**	0	0	0	0	5	55
ω_6	0	0	0	11	0	**8**	0	0	1	0	40
ω_7	1	0	0	0	0	0	**1**	3	5	10	5
ω_8	3	0	0	1	0	0	0	**15**	2	0	75
ω_9	0	0	0	1	0	0	0	0	**19**	0	95
ω_{10}	4	0	0	0	5	0	0	0	1	**10**	50
μ											**66**

TABLE V. CLASSIFICATION CONFUSION MATRIX FOR SEMI-SEGMENTATION EVALUATION. THIS CLASSIFICATION PROCESS IS BASED ON g_4 FEATURE SPACE AND DS2 GROUND TRUTH. CLASSIFICATION RATES ARE GIVEN IN %.

VII. CONCLUSION

In this paper we described a method for automatic shape-based classification of EMs in microscopic images. Our main finding is that manual morphological recognition methods for EMs can be outperformed by automatic shape-based approaches working with microscopic images. An effective semi-automatic segmentation method was developed, and achieved good evaluation results of 99% similarity, 99% sensitivity and 99% specificity (see Section III). Furthermore, we showed that the most stable and best performing feature space turned out to the category of Geometrical Features (see Section IV). By representing the relevant morphological information about EMs with geometrical features, the classification rate of 89.7% has been obtained.

In the future, we will concentrate on the problem of subspecies (subclasses) recognition. The amount of classes to be considered will increase significantly. For this, we will have to improve our feature extraction techniques and apply more sophisticated classification schemes. Moreover, on the one hand, we will introduce semi-automatic and fully-automatic methods for segmentation of EMs in microscopic images. On the other hand, we will pay a much attention to segmenting, tracking and classifying moving EMs.

REFERENCES

[1] M. Martin-Cereceda, B. Perez-Uz, S. Serrano, and A. Guinea, "Dynamics of protozoan and metazoan communities in a full scale wastewater treatment plant by rotating biological contactors," *Microbiological Research*, vol. 156, no. 3, pp. 225–238, February 2001.

[2] D. Bernhard, D. D. Leipe, M. L. Sogin, and K. chlegel, "Phylogenetic relationships of the Nassulida within the phylum Ciliophora inferred from the complete small subunit rRNA gene sequences of Furgasonia blochmanni, Obertrumia georgiana, and Pseudomicrothorax dubius," *The Journal of Eukaryot Microbiol*, vol. 42, no. 2, pp. 126–131, March 1995.

[3] S. J. Greenwood, M. L. Sogin, and D. H. Lynn, "Phylogenetic relationships within the class Oligohymenophorea, phylum Ciliophora, inferred from the complete small subunit rRNA gene sequences of Colpidium campylum, Glaucoma chattoni, and Opisthonecta henneguyi," *Journal of molecular evolution*, vol. 33, no. 2, pp. 163–174, March 1991.

[4] R. Tadeusiewicz, "What does it means "automatic understanding of the images"?" in *IEEE International Workshop on Imaging Systems and Techniques*, Krakow, Poland, May 2007, pp. 1–3.

[5] R. Tadeusiewicz, *How intelligent should be system for image analysis?* Springer Verlag, Berlin, Heidelberg, New York, 2011, pp. V–X.

[6] Q. Zhou and S. Wang, *Microbiology of environmental engineering*. Beijing, China: Higher Education Press, 2008.

[7] R. Rulaningtyas, A. B. Suksmono, and T. L. Mengko, "Automatic classification of tuberculosis bacteria using neural network," in *Electrical Engineering and Informatics (ICEEI) 2011*, Bandung, Indonesia, July 2011, pp. 1–4.

[8] X. Li and C. Chen, "An improved BP neural network for wastewater bacteria recognition based on microscopic image analysis," *WSEAS Transactions on Computers*, vol. 8, no. 2, pp. 237–247, February 2011.

[9] S. Yeom, I. Moon, and B. Javidi, "Real-time 3-D sensing, nisualization and recognition of dynamic biological microorganisms," *Proceedings of the IEEE*, vol. 94, no. 3, pp. 550–566, March 2006.

[10] M. Dad, F. Butterworth, and R. Das, "Statistical signal modeling techniques for automated recognition of water-borne microbial shapes," in *Circuits and Systems 1996*, Ames, IA, August 1996, pp. 113–616.

[11] Y. Ginoris, A. Amaral, A. Nicolau, M. Coelho, and E. Ferreira, "Recognition of Protozoa and Metazoa using image analysis tools, discriminant analysis, neural networks and decision trees," *Analytica Chimica Acta*, vol. 595, no. 1-2, pp. 160–169, January 2007.

[12] R. C. Gonzalez and R. E. Woods, *Digital image processing third edition*. New Jersey, America: Pearson International Edition, 2008.

[13] R. C. Gonzalez, R. E. Woods, and S. L. Eddins, *Digital image processing using MATLAB processing*. Upper Saddle River, New Jersey, America: Pearson Education, Inc, 2004.

[14] N. Otsu, "A threshold selection method from gray-level histograms," *IEEE Trans. Sys., Man., Cyber*, vol. 9, no. 1, pp. 62–66, January 1979.

[15] N. Kazakova, M. Margala, and N. G. Durdle, "Sobel dege detection processor for a real-time volume rendering system," in *International Symposium on Circuits and Systems 2004*, May 2004, pp. 23–26.

[16] R. Maini and J.S.Sohal, "Performance evaluation of Prewitt edge detector for noisy images," *ICGST International Journal on Graphics, Vision and Image Processing*, vol. 6, no. 3, pp. 39–466, 2006.

[17] R. Jain, R. Kasturi, and B. G. Schunck, *Machine vision*. McGraw-Hill, Inc., 1995.

[18] F. Neycenssac, "Contrast enhancement using the Laplacian-of-a-Gaussian filter," *CVGIP: Graphical Models and Image Processing*, vol. 55, no. 6, pp. 447–463, 1993.

[19] J. J. Clark, "Authenticating edges produced by zero-crossing algorithms," *IEEE Transactions on Pattern Analysis and Machine Intelligence*, vol. 11, no. 1, pp. 43–58, January 1989.

[20] J. Canny, "A computational approach to edge detection," *IEEE Trans. Pattern Analysis and Machine Intelligence*, vol. PAMI-8, no. 6, pp. 679–698, November 1986.

[21] J. B. Roerdink and A. Meijster, "The watershed transform: definitions, algorithms and parallelization strategies," *Fundamenta Informaticae*, vol. 41, pp. 187–228, 2001.

[22] M. Grzegorzek, D. Paulus, M. Triersheid, and D. Papoutsis, "Teeth segmentation 3D dentition models for the virtual articulator," in *ICIP 2010*, Hongkong, China, September 2010, pp. 3609–3612.

[23] H. Frigui and P. Gader, "Detection and discrimination of land mines in ground-penetrating radar based on edge histogram descriptors and a possibilistic K-Nearest neighbor classifier," *Fuzzy Systems*, vol. 17, no. 1, pp. 185–199, February 2011.

[24] M. Donoser, H. Riemenschneider, and H. Bischof, "Efficient partial shape matching of outer contours ," in *Computer Vision ACCV 2009*, Xi'an, China, September 2009, pp. 281–292.

[25] D. Zhang and G. Lu, "A comparative study of curvature scale space and Fourier descriptors for shape-based image retrieval," *Journal of Visual Communication and Image Representation*, vol. 14, no. 1, pp. 39–57, March 2003.

[26] V. Vapnik, *Statistical learning theory*. Wiley-Interscience, 1998.

[27] J. C. Platt, N. Cristianini, and J. Shawe-Taylor, *Large margin DAGs for multiclass classification*. Denver, Colorado: The MIT Press, December 2000, pp. 547–553.

[28] M.-K. Hu, "Visual pattern recognition by moment invariants," *IRE Transactions on Information Theory*, vol. 8, no. 2, pp. 179–187, February 1962.

Photo-Sketch Recognition: Eigentransformation Method

M. A. A. Silva, G. Cámara-Chávez, D. Menotti
Computer Science Department, Federal University of Ouro Preto
Ouro Preto, MG, Brazil

Abstract—*Automatic systems for matching facial sketch images from the police mug shot database are very important for law enforcement agencies. These systems can help to locate or narrow down potential suspects. This paper deals the problem of face recognition through forensic sketches with focus on the eigentransformation method developed by Tang & Wang. This method is based on the Eigenface method. In this method a sketch is transformed into a photo using a global linear transformation, reducing significantly the difference between them, allowing an effective matching.*

Keywords: Face Recognition, Sketch Recognition, Eigenface, Eigentransformation.

1. Introduction

A new face recognition problem that has recently emerged is the association between sketches and photos. The consequence of this problem is the development of robust algorithms for security agencies. When a crime is observed by an eyewitness, often a verbal description of the features of the offender is employed by a police artist to draw a sketch of the suspect. Many criminals have been apprehended when identified by such sketches [1].

Automating this process helps the police to reduce the number of suspects, making the identification faster and less tiring. Besides making the search easier, this method can also help witnesses and designers to modify the design of sketch interactively [2].

The last two decades have witnessed tremendous advances in facial recognition. The research of Turk & Pentland [3], [4] has served as the foundation for the modern mechanisms of facial recognition [1].

However, due to the large difference between sketches and photos, in addition to the lack of knowledge about the psychological mechanisms of sketch generation, recognizing suspects through sketch becomes a much more difficult task than facial recognition [5].

Most of the researches in photo-sketch recognition in the last ten years have been developed by Tang and Wang [6], [7], [2], [5]. The first approaches developed by Tang and Wang (2002, 2003, 2004) [6], [7], [2] use global linear transformations, based on eigenface method [3], [4], to convert a photo into a sketch.

In [5], the authors propose a new method for photo-sketch synthesis and recognition based on a multiscale Markov random fields (MRF). They use a multi-scale MRF model to learn face structures at different scales. Local patches in different regions and structures are learned jointly. Another characteristic of this approach is that it can also synthesize face photos given sketches. The solution to the MRF was estimated using the belief propagation algorithm [8]. Solution patches are stitched together and form a synthetic photograph. The transformation of a photo into sketch (or the reverse) significantly reduces the difference between them. After the synthetic image generation, in principle, most of the algorithms for facial recognition may be applied directly.

Klare and Jain [1] proposed a Scale Invariant Feature Transform (SIFT) based local feature approach. The method consists in sampling the SIFT feature descriptors uniformly across all the sketch and photo images, then both are matched directly. The recognition proceeds by computing the distance of the SIFT representation between the sketch and photo, or using a dictionary composed by training pairs.

Most recent researches focus on identifying sketches that were drawn while a viewing a photograph of the person, this type of sketches are known as viewed sketches [7], [2], [9], [5], [1]. Unfortunately real-world scenarios only involve sketches that were drawn by interviewing a witness to gain a description of the suspect, known as forensic sketches. As we can see in Figure 1.

In [11], the authors presents a framework called LFDA where photo and sketch images are represented by descriptors SIFT and MLBP Multiscale Local Binary Patterns) features. Local feature-based discriminant analysis (LFDA) is used to compute the minimum distance matching between sketches and photos. Which creates a projection function based on vertical slices of sketches and photos. The LFDA attempts to maximize inter-class distances while the intra-class distances are minimized.

In this paper we evaluate with more details the eigentransformation method [2], varying the interocular distance, using five-fold cross-validation, and training and testing with "real" database, obtained from [10].

The paper is organized as follows. In Section 2 we briefly review the Eigentransformation method. The results of our experiments using this method can be found in Section 3. And the conclusions can be found in Section 4.

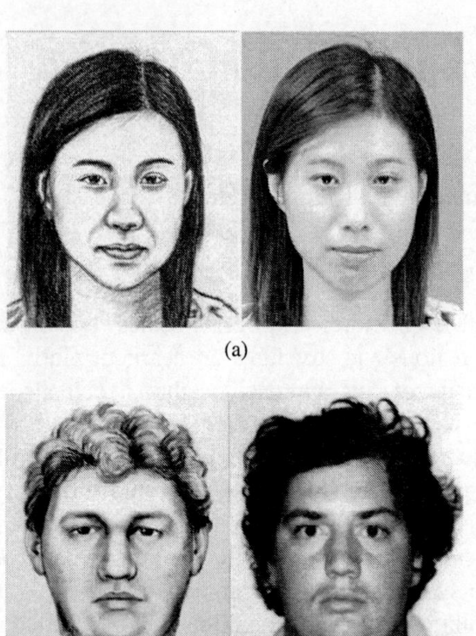

(a)

(b)

Fig. 1: Difference between sketch made by artist looking at the photo (a) and through the description of witnesses (b). Images from CUHK database[2] and *Forensic Art and Illustration*[10].

2. Eigentransformation

The Eigentransformation method is based on the eigenface method, developed by Turk and Pentland (1991) [3], [4], which is one of the classic methods for face recognition. Because of the structural similarity across all face images, there exists a strong correlation between them. The eigenface method takes advantage of this and produce a highly compressed representation of face images. Unfortunatey, this can not be extended to face photos and sketches. Direct application of the eigenface method for sketch-based face identification may not work. This occurs because the distance between a photo and a sketch is much larger than the distance between two photos of two different people. In order to overcome this problem, the authors developed a photo-sketch transformation to either project a sketch image into a photo space, or to project a photo image into a sketch subspace, see Figure 2.

First, create an eigenspace for photos and another for the sketches, using training pairs formed by their corresponding photos and sketches. Then, a new entering photo is projected in the photo space, and represented by a vector, where the coefficients represents the contribution of an existing face of the training samples. Thus, a new face can be approximately reconstructed from the training set and the coefficients of the projection of the photo space are used to build a sketch in the sketch face. An example can be seen in Figure 3.

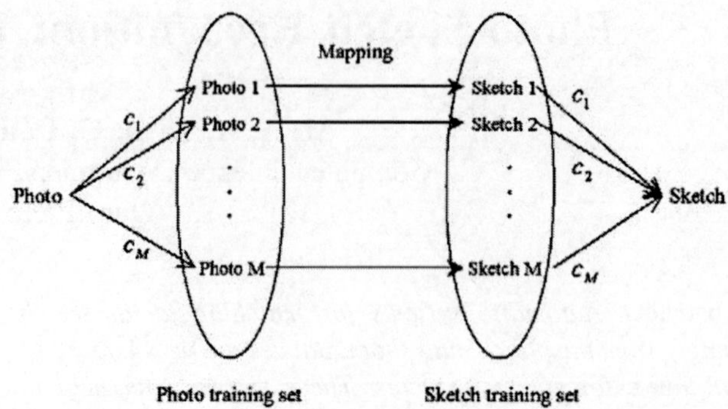

Fig. 2: Graphic representation of the projection method. Tang & Wang (2004) [2].

Fig. 3: Results of the synthesis of sketch from the projection method of coefficients of eigenspace.

Below is described the process of Tang & Wang's approach [2]:

$$\vec{m}_p = 1/M \sum_{i=1}^{M} \vec{Q}_i$$

$$\vec{P}_i = \vec{Q}_i - \vec{m}_p$$

$$A_p = [\vec{P}_1, \vec{P}_2, ..., \vec{P}_M]$$

$$W = A_p A_p^T$$

$$(A_p^T A_p) V_p = V_p \Lambda_p$$

$$(A_p A_p^T) A_p V_p = A_p V_p \Lambda_p$$

$$U_p = A_p V_p \Lambda_p^{-1/2}$$

$$\vec{b}_p = U_p^T \vec{P}_k$$

$$\vec{P}_r = U_p\vec{b}_p$$

With the vector $\vec{b}$ we can reconstruct the image in the same domain.

$$U_p = A_pV_p\Lambda_p^{-1/2}$$

$$\vec{P}_r = A_pV_p\Lambda_p^{-1/2}\vec{b}_p = A_p\vec{c}_p$$

With the vector $\vec{c}$ we can reconstruct the image from the contributions of the images of the training set. The proposed method, synthesize an image on another domain.

$$\vec{c}_p = V_p\Lambda_p^{-1/2}\vec{b}_p = [c_{p1}, c_{p2}, ..., c_{pM}]^T$$

$$\vec{P}_r = A_p\vec{c}_p = \sum_{i=1}^{M} c_{p_i}\vec{P}_i$$

Tang & Wang [2] method follows the next steps:

- Compute the average images $\vec{m}_p$ for the training set of photos and $\vec{m}_s$ for sketches.
- Compute the photo eigenspace U_p and sketch eigenspace U_s .
- Remove the photo mean $\vec{m}_p$ from the input photo image $\vec{Q}_k$ to get $\vec{P}_k = \vec{Q}_k - \vec{m}_p$.
- Project $\vec{P}_k$ in the eigenspace U_p to compute the eigenface weight vector $\vec{b}_p$.
- Found de contribution vector $\vec{c}_p = V_p\Lambda_p^{-1/2}\vec{b}_p$
- Reconstruct the pseudo-sketch by: $\vec{S}_r = A_s\vec{c}_p = \sum_{i=1}^{M} c_{p_i}\vec{S}_i$
- Finally, add back the average sketch: $\vec{T}_r = \vec{S}_r + \vec{m}_s$.

Then we can use the next metrics for recognition:

- $d_1 = ||\vec{c}_p - \vec{c}_s||$
  Direct distance
- $d_2 = ||\vec{b}_r - \vec{b}_s||$
  $\vec{b}_r$ is a pseudo-sketch
- $d_3 = ||\vec{b}_r - \vec{b}_p||$
  $\vec{b}_r$ is a pseudo-photo

3. Results and Discussion

In this section are shown the obtained results. We use Tang *et al.* data set, available in `http://mmlab.ie.cuhk.edu-.hk/facesketch.html`, composed by *viewed sketches* and *forensic sketches* from [10] composed by real sketches.

The implemention was done using the library OpenCV (Open Source Computer Vision Library) on the C++ language, since the methods require high computational performance.

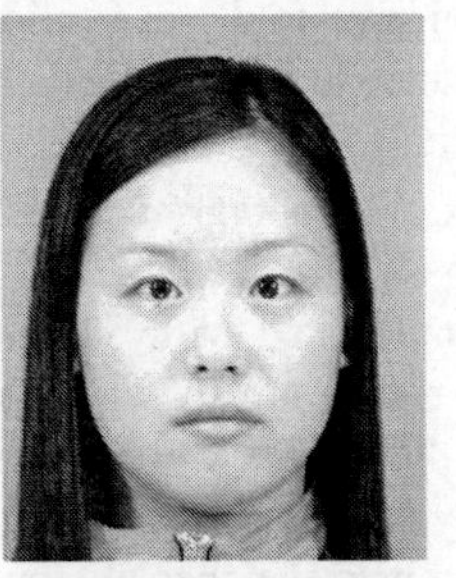
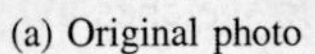

(a) Original photo

(b) Original sketch

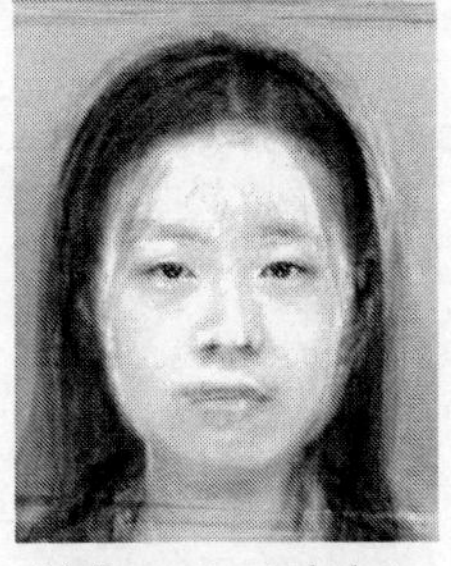

(c) Reconstructed photo

(d) Reconstructed sketch

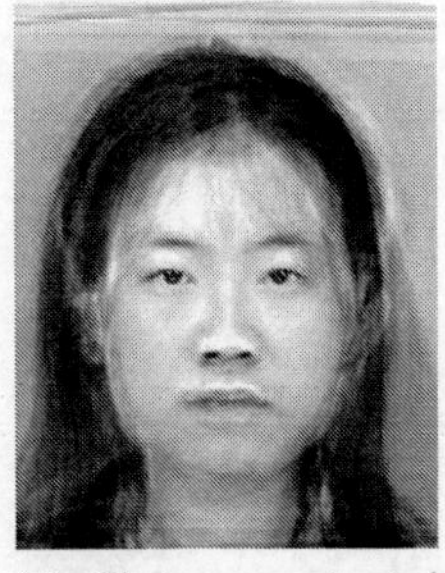

(e) Photo reconstructed from the sketch

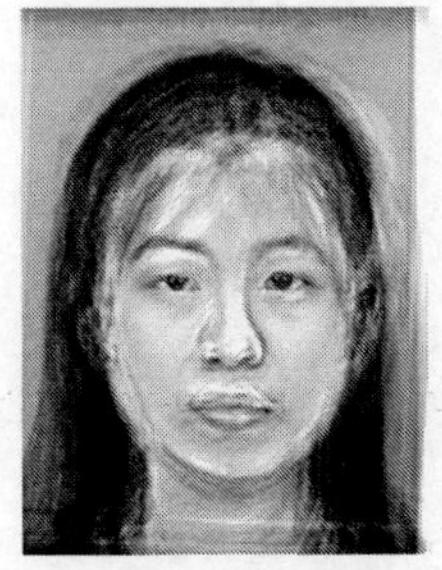

(f) Sketch reconstructed from the photo

Fig. 4: Results of reconstructions using the projections of the coefficients between eigenspaces.

In Figure 4 is presented the results of reconstructions of a photograph and a sketch.

The tests were done by changing the interocular distances. Different values were tested, the best results were achieved with 66 pixels of interocular distance, as we can see in Figures 5, 6 and 7. We keep the original window size of 200×250 pixels.

Table 1 and Figure 8 are shown the results obtained from the implementation of eigentransformation training and testing using the CUHK database [2]. The result from [2] is shown in the Table 2. In our experiments we observed that the variation in interocular distance modifies the results. The background reduction is the main factor to improve the results. Because background information acts as noise in this case, since the method uses global transformations. Then find a correct ratio to cropping is important.

We evaluate the method through five-fold cross-validation using 66 pixels of interocular distance in the CUHK database [2], the results are shown in Table 3.

We test the eigentransformation with real sketches, obtained from [10]. We trained with CUHK database(188 pairs of viewed sketches and photo) and tested with 58 pairs of forensic sketches and photos, the results are shown in Figure 9 and Table 4. We can see that the results were low, since the test database consisted of only 58 pairs. The ideal would be to have a training base with forensic sketches too, but this requires more sketches, which is a difficult task.

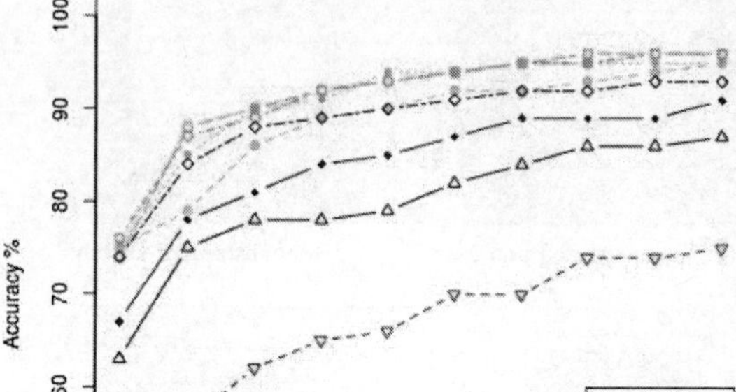

Fig. 5: Comparison of the results using distance method d_1.

Table 1: Results of the three methods of calculating the distance, running with the same database with 66 pixels of interocular distance.

Rank	1	2	3	4	5	6	7	8	9	10
d_1	76	87	89	92	93	94	95	95	96	96
d_2	84	93	96	97	98	98	99	99	99	100
d_3	71	78	83	84	85	88	90	90	91	91

Table 2: Results of the three methods of calculating the distance, shown in the original paper, running with CUHK database [2] (88 pairs for training and 100 pairs for testing.

Rank	1	2	3	4	5	6	7	8	9	10
d_1	20	49	59	65	69	73	75	76	81	82
d_2	71	78	81	84	88	90	94	94	95	96
d_3	57	70	77	79	83	84	85	86	87	88

Fig. 6: Comparison of the results using distance method d_2.

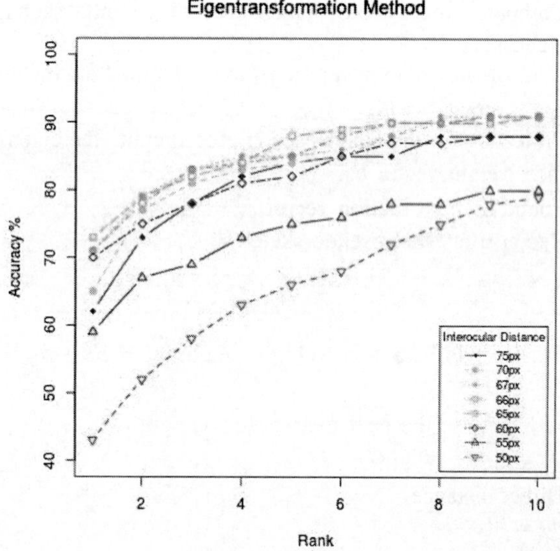

Fig. 7: Comparison of the results using distance method d_3.

4. Conclusions

The results demonstrated that how the images are cropped influences the method, since the method uses global transformation, then all information is computed. As we can see the method could have been explored to improve the results. We can not define if the method can be applied to forensic sketches, because is necessary a larger database for training and testing.

Table 3: Results of the three methods of calculating the distance, running with CUHK database [2] with five-fold cross-validation with 66 pixels of interocular distance.

Rank	1	2	3	4	5	6	7	8	9	10
d_1%	91.4±6.2	95.1±5.2	98.4±2.4	98.4±2.4	98.4±2.4	98.4±2.4	99.5±1.2	99.5±1.2	99.5±1.2	99.5±1.2
d_2%	93.5±2.4	98.4±2.4	98.4±2.4	98.4±2.4	98.4±2.4	98.4±2.4	98.4±2.4	98.4±2.4	98.4±2.4	99.5±1.2
d_3%	88.6±3.5	92.4±4	94.6±3.8	96.2±4.1	96.2±4.1	96.2±4.1	96.2±4.1	97.3±2.7	97.3±2.7	97.3±2.7

Table 4: Results of the three methods of calculating the distance, running with CUHK database [2] (188 pairs) for training and 58 pairs of photo and real sketch obtained from [10] for testing, both with 66 pixels of interocular distance.

Rank	1	2	3	4	5	6	7	8	9	10
d_1	3.4%	8.6%	10.3%	10.3%	12.1%	12.1%	17.2%	20.7%	20.7%	20.7%
d_2	1.7%	12.1%	17.2%	22.4%	24.1%	27.6%	34.5%	39.7%	43.1%	43.1%
d_3	5.2%	6.9%	8.6%	10.3%	17.2%	20.7%	22.4%	25.9%	25.9	27.6%

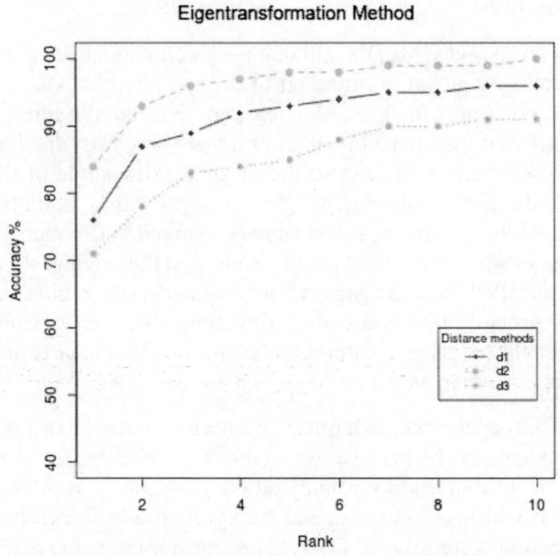

Fig. 8: Comparison of the three methods of distance with 66 pixels of interocular distance.

Fig. 9: Results of the method using the distance d_2. Training with CUHK database (188 pairs) and testing with 58 pairs of photo and real sketch.

References

[1] B. Klare and A. Jain, "Sketch to photo matching: A feature-based approach," *Proc. SPIE, Biometric Technology for Human Identification VII*, vol. 7667, pp. 766702–766702, 2010.

[2] X. Tang and X. Wang, "Face sketch recognition," *Circuits and Systems for Video Technology, IEEE Transactions on*, vol. 14, no. 1, pp. 50–57, 2004.

[3] M. Turk and A. Pentland, "Face recognition using eigenfaces," in *Computer Vision and Pattern Recognition, 1991. Proceedings CVPR'91., IEEE Computer Society Conference on.* IEEE, 1991, pp. 586–591.

[4] ——, "Eigenfaces for recognition," *Journal of cognitive neuroscience*, vol. 3, no. 1, pp. 71–86, 1991.

[5] X. Wang and X. Tang, "Face photo-sketch synthesis and recognition," *Pattern Analysis and Machine Intelligence, IEEE Transactions on*, vol. 31, no. 11, pp. 1955–1967, 2009.

[6] X. Tang and X. Wang, "Face photo recognition using sketch," in *Image Processing. 2002. Proceedings. 2002 International Conference on*, vol. 1. IEEE, 2002, pp. I–257.

[7] ——, "Face sketch synthesis and recognition," in *Computer Vision, 2003. Proceedings. Ninth IEEE International Conference on.* IEEE, 2003, pp. 687–694.

[8] J. Yedidia, W. Freeman, and Y. Weiss, "Generalized belief propagation," *Advances in neural information processing systems*, pp. 689–695, 2001.

[9] Q. Liu, X. Tang, H. Jin, H. Lu, and S. Ma, "A nonlinear approach for face sketch synthesis and recognition," in *Computer Vision and Pattern Recognition, 2005. CVPR 2005. IEEE Computer Society Conference on*, vol. 1. IEEE, 2005, pp. 1005–1010.

[10] K. T. Taylor, *Forensic art and illustration.* CRC Press, 2010.

[11] B. Klare, Z. Li, and A. Jain, "Matching forensic sketches to mug shot photos," *Pattern Analysis and Machine Intelligence, IEEE Transactions on*, vol. 33, no. 3, pp. 639–646, 2011.

Skew Estimation in Document Images Based on an Energy Minimization Framework

Youbao Tang[1], Xiangqian Wu[1], Wei Bu[2], and Hongyang Wang[3]
[1]School of Computer Science and Technology, Harbin Institute of Technology, Harbin, China
[2]Department of New Media, Harbin Institute of Technology, Harbin, China
[3]Honors School, Harbin Institute of Technology, Harbin, China

Abstract - *Skew estimation is important for document analysis and application. Most existing methods are proposed to deal with the document images consisting of words. In most cases, a complex document may include tables, irregular pictures and other non-text components. To address the challenging problem, this paper proposes a novel skew estimation approach based on an energy minimization framework for skewed scanning document images. In the proposed approach, the foreground pixel state information is computed at first. Then a new cost function that considers both background and foreground information for skew estimation is constructed by using state information. A coarse skew is yielded by employing line fitting technique. Then the coarse skew is refined by iteration so that the cost function gets minimum. The ICDAR2013 DISEC dataset is used to evaluate the proposed approach and the experimental results show its effectiveness.*

Keywords: Skew Estimation, Energy Minimization, Cost Function, Line Fitting, Foreground Pixel State Estimation

1 Introduction

With the increasing development of digital technology, the emergence of electronic documents is more and more popular in people's routine life due to their convenience and persistence. Such as using camera or scanner to record management and store historical documents, and so on. While acquiring electronic document images, a little skew is unavoidable. However, most of the document based systems (such as OCR, page layout analysis and character recognition, and so on) are sensitive to skew in document images. Thus, skew estimation becomes an important issue in the field of document image analysis and understanding [1]. To eliminate the skew, an alignment preprocessing is necessary during digitization procedure.

There are two different kinds of document images, handwritten document images (HDIs) and machine-printed document images (MPDIs). For handwritten document images, it's a hard work to detect their skew angles while the texts are written in an unconstrained condition. Compared with handwritten document images, machine-printed document images are regularly aligned. According to the content of MPDIs, they are categorized into simple MPDIs which only consist of pure texts and complex MPDIs which include tables, irregular pictures and other non-text components except texts. In recent years, extensive researches have been carried out on skew estimation for MPDIs. However, it is a still challenging problem to estimate the skew of complex MPDIs.

For complex MPDIs, although the contents of them are uncertain, the global information of them is obvious, such as: (i) The outermost foreground pixels can be fitted into lines in four different directions of MPDI and there is at least one line whose skew angle is close to the original skew angle of the MPDI. (ii) The length of gap region changes with rotating the MPDI while the size of rotated image is fixed and it can get maximum when the rotation angle is close to the original skew angle of MPDI, here the gap region is defined as the region has no foreground pixel in a certain direction. (iii) The variance between the numbers of foreground pixels in a certain direction can get maximum as (ii).

This paper proposes a novel approach that considers these information. To be precise, we convert the skew estimation problem into an energy minimization problem. A new cost function which considers global background and foreground information is constructed firstly. Then the minimization of the cost function yields the skew angle of MPDI. The proposed approach is summarized as a flow diagram showed in Figure 1.

The rest of this paper is organized as follows: Section 2 gives a brief introduction to some related work. Section 3 presents a description of the proposed approach in detail. Section 4 reports our experimental results. Finally, the conclusions are presented in Section 5.

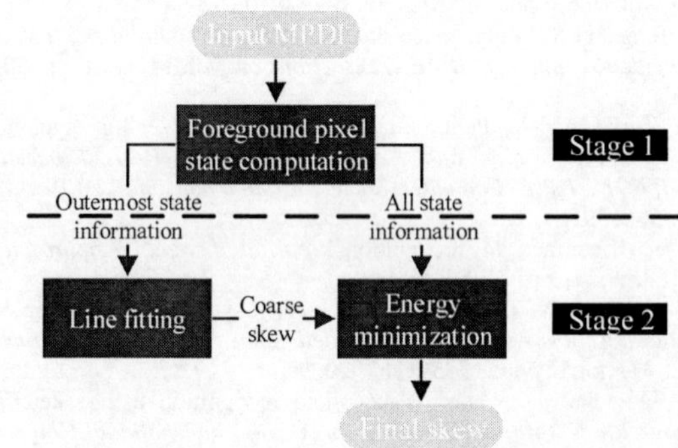

Figure 1: Flow diagram of the proposed approach.

2 Related work

Rezaei et al [2] surveys most existing methods of skew estimation. And they consider these methods can be roughly divided into eight categories: projection profile analysis [3-5], Hough transform [6, 7], nearest neighbor clustering [8], cross-correlation [9], piece-wise covering by parallelogram [10, 11], piece-wise painting algorithm [12], transition counts [13], and morphology [14, 15].

In this paper, we briefly summarize several methods published in recently. Singh et al [16] employ the Hough transform for skew estimation with a preprocessing stage which reduces the number of image pixels. Compared to traditional methods based on Hough transform, they address the speed and memory requirement problem to some extent.

Meng et al [17] exploit various types of visual cues of image extracted by Radon transform for skew estimation. A floating cascade is used to reject the outliers of visual cues by iterating. A bagging estimator is finally employed to combine the rest of visual cues on local image blocks.

Alaei et al [12] horizontally and vertically adopt the piece-wise painting algorithm on document image to obtain two painted images irrespective to the flow of writing and content. Linear regression and a proposed majority voting technique are utilized to find the best fitting line whose slope is the skew angle of the document image.

Fan et al [18] propose a Rectangular Active Contour Model (RAC Model) for content region detection and skew angle calculation by imposing a rectangular shape constraint on the zero-level set in Chan-Vese Model (C-V Model) according to the rectangular feature of content regions in document images.

Guan et al [19] develop a bilinear filtering model to extract the foreground regions and detect the edges in the document images without considering document layouts or contents. Then a dominant angle has been estimated as the skew angle of the document image based on the detected edges.

Most existing methods only adopt the foreground information or background information. However, the accuracy will be decreased by using one of them for skew estimation. This paper considers both global foreground and background information to improve the accuracy and proposes a novel skew estimation approach based on an energy minimization framework.

3 Methodology

The proposed approach consists of two stages: foreground pixel state computation and skew estimation based on energy minimization, as shown in Figure 1. In this section, these processes will be stated in detail.

3.1 Foreground pixel state computation

The proposed approach begins with the binarization of input document images. Since the background and foreground of MPDIs are easily split, a simple thresholding method is used for binarization.

After binarization, we compute the state information for each foreground pixel with the method described as follows. Given a binary document image I, a bounding box is defined as the boundary of I (seeing the yellow rectangle in Figure 2 (a)). Let $\mathbf{P}$ denote the set of foreground pixels and (W,H) denote the size of I. Then for $p \in \mathbf{P}$, assign a state $s_p = (x_p, y_p, w_p, h_p)$ to p as shown in Figure 2 (a), where (x_p, y_p) is the location of p in I, $w_p = W - x_p$, and $h_p = H - y_p$.

These states $\mathbf{S} = \{(x_p, y_p, w_p, h_p)\}_{p \in \mathbf{P}}$ will be used in line fitting and energy minimization to estimate the final skew angle of document images.

3.2 Skew estimation using energy minimization

This paper formulate the skew estimation problem as an energy minimization problem. The framework of energy minimization problem consists of two brief steps: cost function construction and the minimization of the cost function.

3.2.1 Cost function construction

1) Proposed cost function

To construct an appropriate cost function is important in energy minimization problem, because the cost function affects the optimal solution directly. Here, this paper presents a new cost function consisting of two terms. And its minimization considers global background and foreground information of document images.

Section 3.1 introduces the process of computing foreground pixel state information. We can observe the state information will be different while the bounding box is fixed and the document image is rotated around the center. Based on this observation, the skew estimation problem is formulated as

$$\hat{\mathbf{S}} = \arg\min_{S} E(\mathbf{S}) \tag{1}$$

where the cost function includes two terms, i.e.,

$$E(\mathbf{S}) = \omega E_B(\mathbf{S}) + (1-\omega) E_F(\mathbf{S}). \tag{2}$$

where ω is a constant. The first term $E_B(\mathbf{S})$ considers the global background information which is the length of gap region (LGR) in horizontal and vertical direction of document images. The second term $E_F(\mathbf{S})$ reflects the global foreground information which is the variance of the foreground pixel number (VFPN) in every row and column of document images.

2) Design of $E_B(\boldsymbol{S})$ and $E_F(\boldsymbol{S})$

The states $\mathbf{S}$ having large LGR and small VFPN is desirable, so the first term $E_B(\boldsymbol{S})$ is given by

$$E_B(\mathbf{S}) = e^{-(\varphi(\mathbf{S}) + \phi(\mathbf{S}))}, \tag{3}$$

and we set $\varphi(\cdot)$ and $\phi(\cdot)$ as below

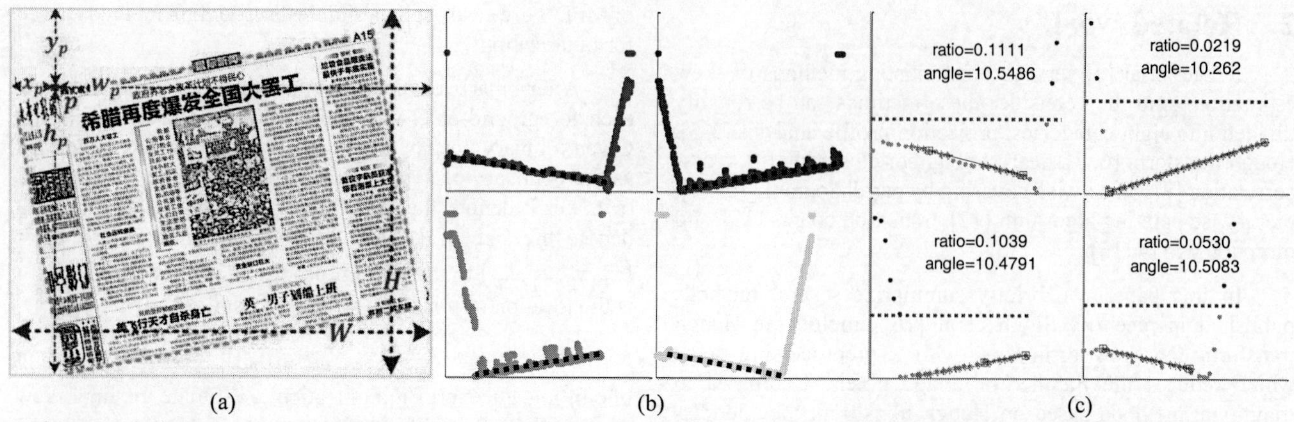

Figure 2: (a) gives an example of MPDI and the illustration of foreground pixel state information computation. The yellow rectangle is the bounding box of the MPDI. And the green dot lines are the fitting lines from four side of the MPDI. (b) plots the distances between the outermost states and fours sides of the bounding box from (a). The black dot lines show that these below points can be fitted as lines. (c) illustrates the line fitting procedure and gives the final fitting results from (b).

$$\varphi(\mathbf{S}) = \frac{1}{W}\sum_{i=1}^{W} Sgn(Y_i),\ \phi(\mathbf{S}) = \frac{1}{H}\sum_{j=1}^{H} Sgn(X_j)$$
$$Y_i = \{s_p \mid s_p \in \mathbf{S} \cap y_p \in s_p \cap y_p = i\} \quad (4)$$
$$X_j = \{s_p \mid s_p \in \mathbf{S} \cap x_p \in s_p \cap x_p = j\}$$

where $Sgn(\cdot)$ is a sign function formulated as

$$Sgn(A) = \begin{cases} 1, & A \neq \varnothing \\ 0, & A = \varnothing. \end{cases} \quad (5)$$

The second term $E_F(\boldsymbol{S})$ is given by

$$E_F(\mathbf{S}) = \delta(\mathbf{S}) + \lambda(\mathbf{S}), \quad (6)$$

and we set $\delta(\cdot)$ and $\lambda(\cdot)$ as below

$$\delta(\mathbf{S}) = \frac{1}{M_Y}\sqrt{\frac{1}{f(Y)}\sum_{k=1}^{f(Y)}\left(f(Y_k) - \bar{Y}\right)^2}$$
$$\bar{Y} = \frac{1}{f(Y)}\sum_{k=1}^{f(Y)} f(Y_k)$$
$$\lambda(\mathbf{S}) = \frac{1}{M_X}\sqrt{\frac{1}{f(X)}\sum_{k=1}^{f(X)}\left(f(X_k) - \bar{X}\right)^2} \quad (7)$$
$$\bar{X} = \frac{1}{f(X)}\sum_{k=1}^{f(X)} f(X_k),$$

where $Y = \bigcup_{i=1}^{W}(Y_i \cap Y_i \neq \emptyset)$, $X = \bigcup_{j=1}^{H}(X_j \cap X_j \neq \emptyset)$, $M_Y = \max\{f(Y_i)|Y_i \in Y\}$, $M_X = \max\{f(X_i)|X_i \in X\}$, and $f(\cdot)$ is a function to compute the number of elements in a set '·'.

There is one parameter ω in the proposed cost function. And it is determined by experiments conducted on training dataset.

3.2.2 Energy minimization

The minimization of the cost function is a hard and time-consuming work while the evaluation of $E(\mathbf{S})$ requires a number of operation (such as state rotation, variance computation and so on). Hence, we address this problem by developing an optimization technique described as follows: we use the outermost states to get a coarse solution at first, then iteratively refine this solution with all state to estimate the final skew.

1) Line fitting for coarse skew estimation

For the coarse solution, we exploit the line fitting technique stated as below. As shown in Figure 2 (a), a bounding box has four sides: top, bottom, left and right. For each side, such as top, we get a subset $TS \subset \mathbf{S}$ by

$$TS = \bigcup_{i=1}^{W} s_i$$
$$y_i \in s_i \cap y_i = \min\{y_p \mid y_p \in s_p \cap x_p \in s_p \cap x_p = i\}. \quad (8)$$

We plot a figure by using $x_p \in TS$ as x-coordinate and $y_p \in TS$ as y-coordinate, as shown in the top-left of Figure 2 (b). In the same way, we can get the rest of three subsets *BS*, *LS* and *RS*, corresponding to bottom, left and right of the bounding box, respectively. From Figure 2 (b), we observe that the bottom points of all figures can be fitted as lines, and the skew angles of some lines are close to the original skew angle of *I*. So in this paper, we use line fitting technique to obtain the coarse skew angles of document images.

Here, we take *TS* as an example to describe the process of line fitting in detail. To speed up the process of line fitting and get more accurate coarse skew estimation, we take sample from *TS* before line fitting. The *TS* is divided into *N* non-overlapping parts STS_i as below

$$TS = \bigcup_{i=1}^{N} STS_i$$
$$STS_i \cap STS_{j\neq i} = \varnothing \quad (9)$$
$$STS_i = \left\{s_p \mid x_p \in s_p \cap \frac{(i-1)\times W}{N} + 1 \leq x_p \leq \frac{i\times W}{N}\right\}.$$

In this work, we set $N = 32$. Then a subset *FTS* is constructed

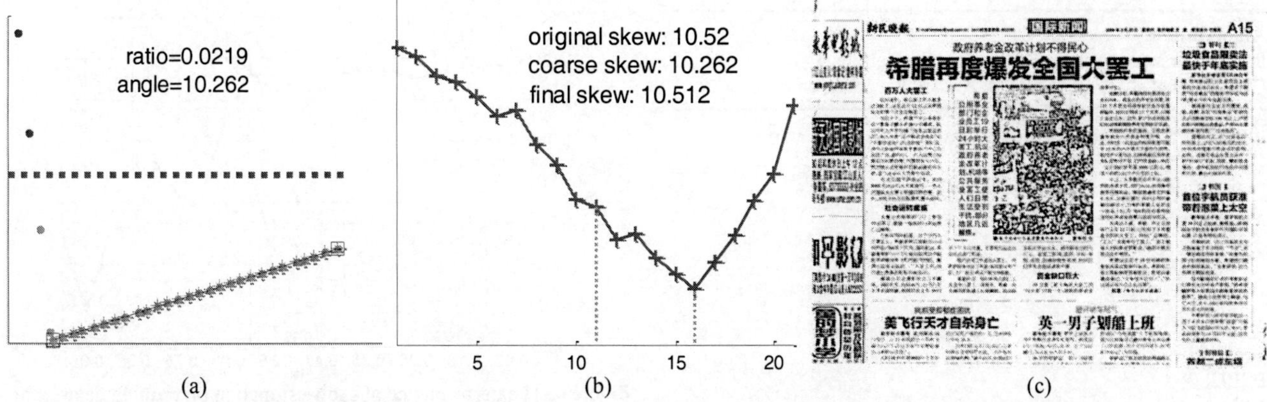

(a) (b) (c)

Figure 3: (a) shows the best-fitting line from Figure 2 (c) according to our criterion. So the coarse skew angle of Figure 2 (a) is 10.262, while the original skew angle is 10.52. (b) gives the iteration process of coarse skew refinement. *x*-coordinate is the iteration times and *y*-coordinate is $E(\mathbf{S})$ corresponding to iteration. The final skew angle is 10.512 while $E(\mathbf{S})$ gets minimum. (c) shows the skew correction result of Figure 2 (a).

by

$$FTS = \bigcup_{i=1}^{N} (s_i \cap s_i \in STS_i) \\ y_i \in s_i \cap y_i = \min\{y_p \mid y_p \in s_p \cap s_p \in STS_i\}. \tag{10}$$

Figure 2 (c) gives the sampling results of Figure 2 (b).

After doing the sampling operation, although most of outliers of states which is far away from desirable fitting line are removed, we need to further eliminate the outliers to obtain the valid states VTS (Seeing the states which below the red dot line in Figure 2 (c)) by

$$VTS = \left\{ s_p \mid s_p \in FTS \cap y_p \in s_p \cap y_p < \frac{H}{3} \right\} \tag{11}$$

Then we use the VTS to do line fitting with the behavior of exhaustive search. The purpose of exhaustive search is to find two states so that there will be more other states (Seeing the pink cross points in Figure 2 (c)) whose distances to the line that across these two states are less than a threshold *D*.

After obtaining four fitting lines (Seeing the green dot lines in Figure 2 (a) fitted by the pink cross points in Figure 2 (c)) from *TS*, *BS*, *LS* and *RS*, the next task is to find the best-fitting line. Let $\{l_t, l_b, l_l, l_r\}$ denote the fitting lines, and $\{LS_t, LS_b, LS_l, LS_r\}$ denote the line states (Seeing the pink cross points in Figure 2 (c)) which are close to the corresponding fitting lines. The lines whose line states number is less than a threshold *M* will not be considered in the following steps. For each line l_i, we calculate the sum of distances SD_i between all line states of LS_i and l_i. The ratio R_i is computed by

$$R_i = \frac{SD_i}{\left(f(LS_i)\right)^2}. \tag{12}$$

Then $\{R_t, R_b, R_l, R_r\}$ is adopted to get the best-fitting line which has the smallest R_i (Seeing the top-right of Figure 2 (c) and Figure 3 (a)). Finally, the slope of the best-fitting line is calculated as the coarse skew of the original document image.

During line fitting, there are two parameters (*D* and *M*) which decide the accuracy of coarse skew estimation. They are determined by experiments conducted on training dataset.

While all sides of a document image are irregular, the error deviation between the coarse skew and the original skew of the document image will be large. To handle this problem, we propose an algorithm which refines the coarse solution through an energy minimization procedure.

2) Minimization of the cost function

After line fitting, a coarse skew angle is yielded. The next work is to estimate a more accurate skew angle by employing all state information and the coarse skew angle. From a coarse skew angle θ of *I*, we iteratively refine the skew estimation based on the state rotation and cost $E(\mathbf{S})$ computation. In order to improve the computational efficiency, we directly rotate all states around the document image center, rather than rotate the image firstly then compute all foreground pixel state information. The rotation process is conducted as following operation

$$\mathbf{S}' = rotate(\mathbf{S}, \theta) \tag{13}$$

where $rotate(\cdot)$ is a function computing the rotation result $s_p{}'$of each state $s_p \in \mathbf{S}$ by

$$x_p{}' = \left(x_p - \frac{W}{2}\right)\cos\theta - \left(y_p - \frac{H}{2}\right)\sin\theta + \frac{W}{2} \\ y_p{}' = \left(x_p - \frac{W}{2}\right)\sin\theta + \left(y_p - \frac{H}{2}\right)\cos\theta + \frac{H}{2} \\ w_p{}' = W - x_p{}', \quad h_p{}' = H - y_p{}'. \tag{14}$$

During iteration, we fix the range of rotation about $[\theta - range, \theta + range]$ and set the angle step of rotation $step = 0.05$ and $range = 0.5$ through experiments conducted on training dataset. So the iteration times is $\boldsymbol{T} = 21$. After finishing all iteration, the final skew angle β is the rotation angle which gets $E(\mathbf{S}')$ minimum (Seeing Figure 3 (b)). Then the skew document image is corrected according to the final skew angle (Seeing Figure 3 (c)). Algorithm 1 describes the whole refinement process.

Algorithm 1:
Input: coarse skew angle θ, all states $\mathbf{S}$,iterations $\boldsymbol{T}$
Output: final skew angle β

<u>initialize</u> $t \leftarrow 0, \mathbf{S_0} \leftarrow \mathbf{S}, \theta_0 \leftarrow \theta, E_{min} \leftarrow E(\mathbf{S_0}), \beta \leftarrow \theta_0$
  <u>for</u> $t \leftarrow t+1$
    $\theta_t \leftarrow \theta_{t-1} + 0.05(t-1) - 0.5$
    $\mathbf{S}_t \leftarrow rotate(\mathbf{S}_{t-1}, \theta_t)$
    <u>if</u> $E(\mathbf{S}_t) < E_{min}$
      $E_{min} \leftarrow E(\mathbf{S}_t)$
      $\beta \leftarrow \theta_t$
    <u>end</u>
  <u>until</u> $t = \boldsymbol{T}$
<u>return</u> β
<u>end</u>

4 Experiments

4.1 Performance evaluation

4.1.1 Dataset

The ICDAR2013 DISEC dataset [20] is used to evaluate the performance of the proposed approach. The dataset consists of 200 document images, representative of most realistic cases. The document images contain figures, tables, diagrams, block diagrams, architectural plans, electrical circuits, while they are obtained from newspapers, scientific journals, museum guides, and so on. And the image documents are written in English, Chinese, Greek, and so on, while there are representative cases of various sizes of image documents, any kind of mixed content, vertical and horizontal writing, multisized fonts and multiple different number of columns in the same document.

We split this dataset into two parts. One containing 50 document images randomly selected is used for training, called training dataset. The other one including the rest 150 document images is used for test, called test dataset.

4.1.2 Evaluation criterion

The performance evaluation will be based on a well established technique for document skew estimation described as [20]. More specifically, the skew angle average error deviation (*AED*), the number of correct estimations (error deviation of less than 0.1°) (*NCE*) and the number of good estimations (error deviation of less than 0.2°) (*NGE*) will be taken into consideration.

4.2 Parameter optimization

We firstly determine these two parameters mentioned in line fitting: *D* and *M* with free searching method. This is done by sampling for the best performance of skew estimation on training dataset over $3 \leq D \leq 7$ at intervals of 0.5, $4 \leq M \leq 8$ at intervals of 1. The experimental results have best performance when *D*=5, *M*=5. And the largest error deviation is about 0.35°. So we set $range = 0.5$ in the refinement process.

Then the parameters step and ω of energy minimization will be determined respectively due to their independence. We

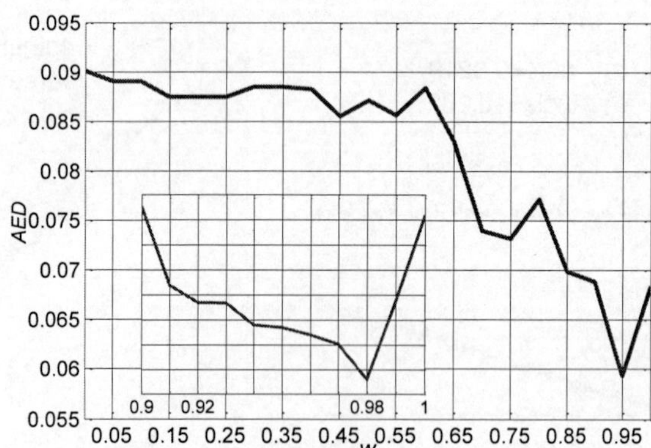

Figure 4: The performance of skew estimation on training dataset for testing ω when *step*=0.05.

test ω over $0 \leq \omega \leq 1$ at intervals of 0.05 on training dataset while we fix $step = 0.05$. The best experimental results can be obtained when $\omega = 0.95$. Then test ω over $0.9 \leq \omega \leq 1$ at intervals of 0.01. The *AED* gets minimum when $\omega = 0.98$, as shown in Figure 4. Then we fix $\omega = 0.98$ to test step with $step = \{0.01, 0.03, 0.05, 0.1\}$. Table 1 lists the experimental results. From Table 1, we can see when $step < 0.05$, the accuracy of skew estimation is good and stable, but the computational complexity is high. However, when $step = 0.1$, the results are contrary. Considering the trade-off, we finally set $step = 0.05$.

Table 1: The performance of skew estimation on training dataset (50 document images) for testing *step* when ω is set as $\omega = 0.98$.

step	*AED*(°)	*NCE*	*NGE*	Time (*s*)
0.01	0.0538	42	49	9.828
0.03	0.0547	41	49	3.428
0.05	0.0552	41	49	2.09
0.1	0.0604	39	48	1.068

All experiments are conducted in Visual Studio 2012 environment on the PC with i5-2430M (2.4 GHz) CPU and 2GB RAM. The computational time given in Table 1 and 2 is tested on a document image with size 1241×1870.

4.3 Experimental results

Using the parameters given in Section 4.2, we test the proposed approach on test dataset with different schemes. As mentioned above, there are two steps for skew estimation: coarse skew estimation (CS) and energy minimization (EM). Actually, these two steps are independent. Hence, they can be used to estimate skew alone, or CS can be replaced by other skew estimation methods. In this paper, we do CS before EM with considering the trade-off between speed and accuracy. To further improve speed, we can do 2:1 downsampling (DS) of the original document images. Table 2 presents the results of skew estimation with different schemes combination.

As shown in Table 2, the performance of skew estimation is the best by adopting the combination of CS and EM schemes, while the computational time is largest. We observe that the

Table 2: The performance of skew estimation on test dataset (150 document images) with different scheme combination.

Schemes	*AED*(°)	*NCE*	*NGE*	Time (*s*)
CS	0.0935	90	135	0.188
CS+EM	0.0542	134	146	2.09
CS+DS	0.1522	83	118	0.081
CS+EM+DS	0.0974	112	125	0.57

performance obviously decrease although much computational time is saved, when downsampling the document image before skew estimation. Because the document image will lose some important foreground pixel state information for skew estimation after downsampling. So different schemes can be adopted according to different applications or requirements.

Figure 5 lists some examples of skew estimation with our proposed approach.

5 Conclusions

In this paper, we propose a novel and efficient skew estimation approach for document images. We formulate the problem as an energy minimization problem. A new cost function which considers global background and foreground information is constructed and the line fitting technique is exploited to get a coarse skew angle. Then the minimization of the constructed cost function yields the final skew angle. The experimental results on ICDAR2013 DISEC dataset have shown that our approach accurately estimates the skew angle of document images with average error deviation 0.0542°.

6 Acknowledgements

This work was supported by the Natural Science Foundation of China (Grant No. 61073125), the Program for New Century Excellent Talents in University (Grant No. NCET-08-0155), the Fok Ying Tong Education Foundation (Grant No. 122035), and the Fundamental Research Funds for the Central Universities (Grant No. HIT. NSRIF. 2013091).

7 References

[1] G. Nagy, "Twenty years of document image analysis in PAMI," TPAMI, vol. 22, pp. 38-62, 2000.

[2] S. B. Rezaei, A. Sarrafzadeh, and J. Shanbehzadeh, "Skew Detection of Scanned Document Images," IMCECS, 2013.

[3] S. Li, Q. Shen, and J. Sun, "Skew detection using wavelet decomposition and projection profile analysis," PRL, vol. 28, pp. 555-562, 2007.

[4] J. Sadri and M. Cheriet, "A new approach for skew correction of documents based on particle swarm optimization," ICDAR, 2009, pp. 1066-1070.

[5] A. Papandreou and B. Gatos, "A Novel Skew Detection Technique Based on Vertical Projections," ICDAR, 2011, pp. 384-388.

[6] B. Epshtein, "Determining Document Skew Using Inter-line Spaces," ICDAR, 2011, pp. 27-31.

[7] D. Kumar, "Modified Approach of Hough Transform for Skew Detection and Correction in Documented Images," IJRCS, vol. 2, pp. 37-40, 2012.

[8] I. Konya, S. Eickeler, and C. Seibert, "Fast seamless skew and orientation detection in document images," ICPR, 2010, pp. 1924-1928.

[9] M. Chen and X. Ding, "A robust skew detection algorithm for grayscale document image," ICDAR, 1999, pp. 617-620.

[10] C.-H. Chou, S.-Y. Chu, and F. Chang, "Estimation of skew angles for scanned documents based on piecewise covering by parallelograms," PR, vol. 40, pp. 443-455, 2007.

[11] A. A. Mascaro, G. D. Cavalcanti, and C. A. Mello, "Fast and robust skew estimation of scanned documents through background area information," PRL, vol. 31, pp. 1403-1411, 2010.

[12] A. Alaei, U. Pal, P. Nagabhushan, and F. Kimura, "A Painting Based Technique for Skew Estimation of Scanned Documents," ICDAR, 2011, pp. 299-303.

[13] Y.-K. Chen and J.-F. Wang, "Skew detection and reconstruction based on maximization of variance of transition-counts," PR, vol. 33, pp. 195-208, 2000.

[14] A. Das and B. Chanda, "A fast algorithm for skew detection of document images using morphology," IJDAR, vol. 4, pp. 109-114, 2001.

[15] B. Dhandra, V. Malemath, H. Mallikarjun, and R. Hegadi, "Skew detection in Binary image documents based on Image Dilation and Region labeling Approach," ICPR, 2006, pp. 954-957.

[16] C. Singh, N. Bhatia, and A. Kaur, "Hough transform based fast skew detection and accurate skew correction methods," PR, vol. 41, pp. 3528-3546, 2008.

[17] G. Meng, C. Pan, N. Zheng, and C. Sun, "Skew estimation of document images using bagging," TIP, vol. 19, pp. 1837-1846, 2010.

[18] H. Fan, L. Zhu, and Y. Tang, "Skew detection in document images based on rectangular active contour," IJDAR, vol. 13, pp. 261-269, 2010.

[19] Y.-P. Guan, "Fast and robust skew estimation in document images through bilinear filtering model," IETIP, vol. 6, pp. 761-769, 2012.

[20] "ICDAR2013 DISEC Dataset," http://users.iit.demokritos.gr/~alexpap/DISEC13/resources.html.

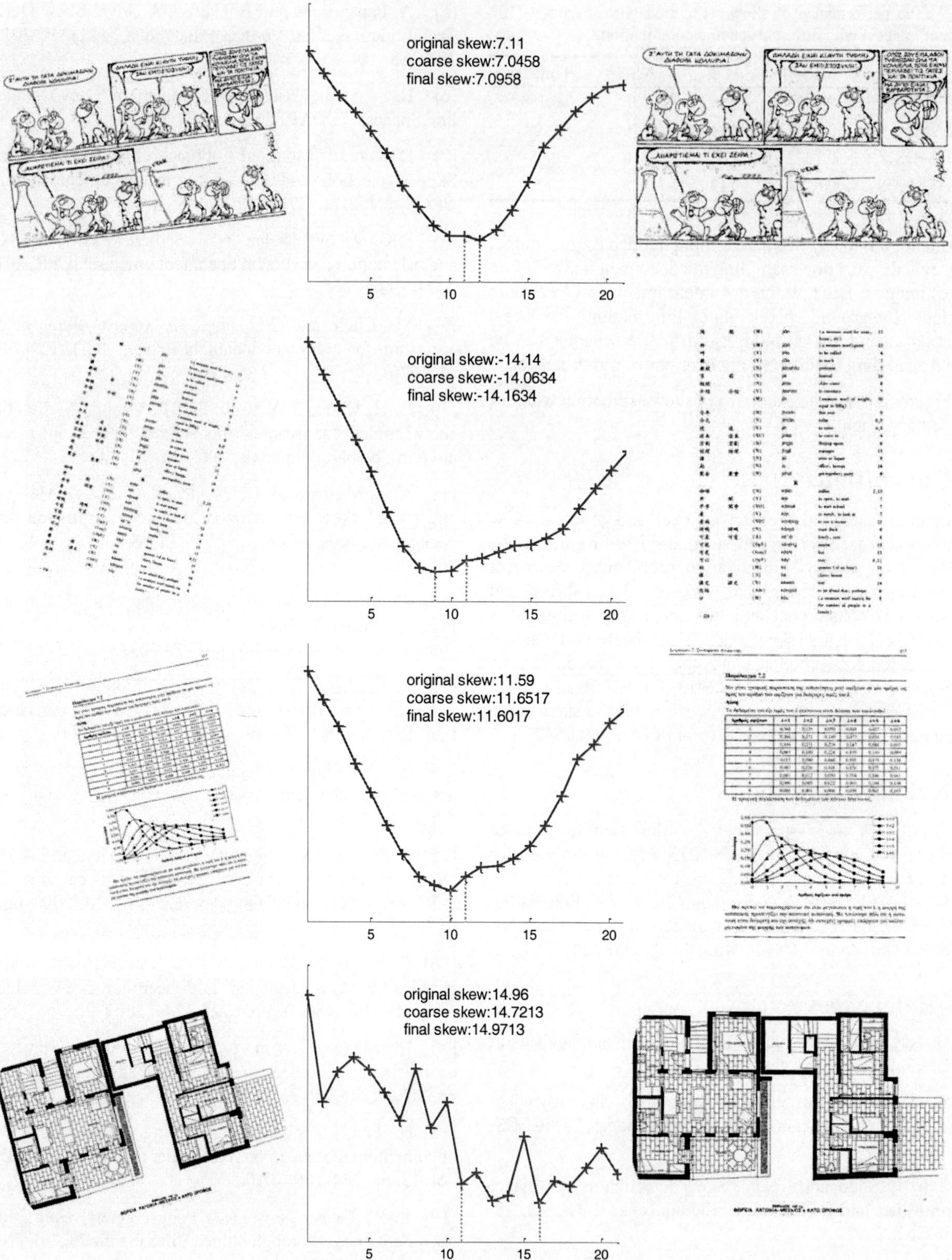

Figure 5: Four examples of skew estimation with the proposed approach. The first column gives the original document images. The second column gives the skew estimation results of the document images. The last column gives their corresponding skew correction results.

Traffic Sign Recognition Algorithm Based on Multi-Modal Representation and Multi-Object Tracking

Zixing Cai[1], Mingqin Gu[1, 2], and Baifan Chen[1]
[1]School of Information Science and Engineering, Central South University, Changsha, Hunan, China
[2]Science & Research Laboratories of mychery, Wuhu, Anhui, China

Abstract - *An algorithm for traffic sign recognition and tracking is proposed in this paper. Image segmentation based on color space conversion and shape classification based on signature feature are used to detect traffic signs in complex urban scenes. To improve recognition accuracy, a two-modal representation method is presented to classify the detected candidate regions for traffic sign. One modal utilizes 2D independent component analysis(2DICA) followed by dual-tree complex wavelet transform (DT-CWT), and the nearest neighbor classifier is employed later to classify the traffic sign images and reject the noise regions. The other modal is template matching based on intra pictograms of the traffic signs. The recognition results of the two representations are fused by some decision rules. A multiple-object tracking algorithm is used to track several traffic sign objects in the same scene. The experiment results show that the overall recognition rate of the proposed algorithm is more than 91%, and multiple objects of traffic signs are tracked steadily and effectively. It is proved that the proposed method is robust, effective, and accurate to classify and track the traffic signs.*

Keywords: Traffic sign recognition; DT-CWT; 2DICA; Intra pictogram; Multi-object tracking

1 Introduction

An important part of prospective vehicle is the perception system, which allows vehicles to perceive and comprehend their surroundings, including traffic signs. Traffic sign is to notify drivers about current state of driving environment and to give instant feedback for the critical circumstances. Automatic recognition and tracking of traffic signs are the essential task for regulating the traffic, guiding and warning drivers or pedestrians. Generally, this system can be divided into three parts: (1) Detection phase; (2) Recognition phase; (3) Tracking phase.

The detection phase can be divided into three categories (1) Some authors preferred to detect traffic sign edges in grayscale images, as they did not consider the color segmentation due to its sensitivity to various factors. A fast histogram of oriented gradient feature[1] is used to detect pedestrians and signs. Edge image can be obtained by edge detection methods such as Sobel[2] operator on grayscale image, and the candidate regions of traffic sign are searched later. Nevertheless, such methods mainly focus on shape analysis and are sensitive to noise. (2) the other approaches analyzes clustering and the intelligent feature to extract regions of interest(RoI). The features such as Haar, orientation correction[3] and the classifiers such as Adaboost are employed to detect traffic signs in the input image. However, these algorithms express a bias against the weak classifier families. A method of image representation and discriminative feature selection for road-sign recognition was adopted in [4]. Since it exhaustively search over the feature set, the training time grows with respect to the number of features. (3) Thirdly, the input image is segmented by distinctive colors of traffic sign, and then geometrical shapes of traffic sign are analyzed. The common color spaces are use in image preprocessing are RGB[5], HSI[6]etc. This approach achieves fine results for traffic signs detection and is adopted by majority of researchers, but it is very difficult to select appropriate thresholds for image segmentation.

After the initial detection for traffic sign, several RoIs are sent to classification stage. Typical classification method is template matching[7]. RoIs should be previously normalized in same size, and matched traffic sign templates in a collected database by cross correlation. The approach is vulnerable to imperfect traffic sign regions since the result of the normalized cross correlation is strongly dependent on the similarity of template and RoIs. The other commonly methods of classification are Neural Network. Lim King Hann *et al.*[8] applies principle component analysis(PCA) and Fisher's linear discriminant(FLD) to extract pictogram discriminant features, and proposes RBFNN(Radial Basis Function Neural Networks) based on Lyapunov stability theory to train and classify features. Neural networks can cope with large variances, however input data has to be normalized and the time complexity is high. The same drawback also exists in Support Vector Machine[9]. Other approaches develop special classification methods, Deng *et al.*[10] proposes a novel framework using the sparse model for traffic information representation and a classifier using the probability method for classification.

In tracking phase, the most common tracker adapted to the TSR problem is the Kalman filter[11] and its modifications. However, Meuter *et al.*[12] uses particle filter and Bayes algorithm to track traffic sign and fuse classification result. In this way, misinterpretations of the candidates can be reduced.

The above methods are either difficult to recognize the traffic sign in urban environments or have high computing complexity. This paper proposes a framework for recognizing and tracking the traffic signs for the intelligent vehicles in urban scenes.

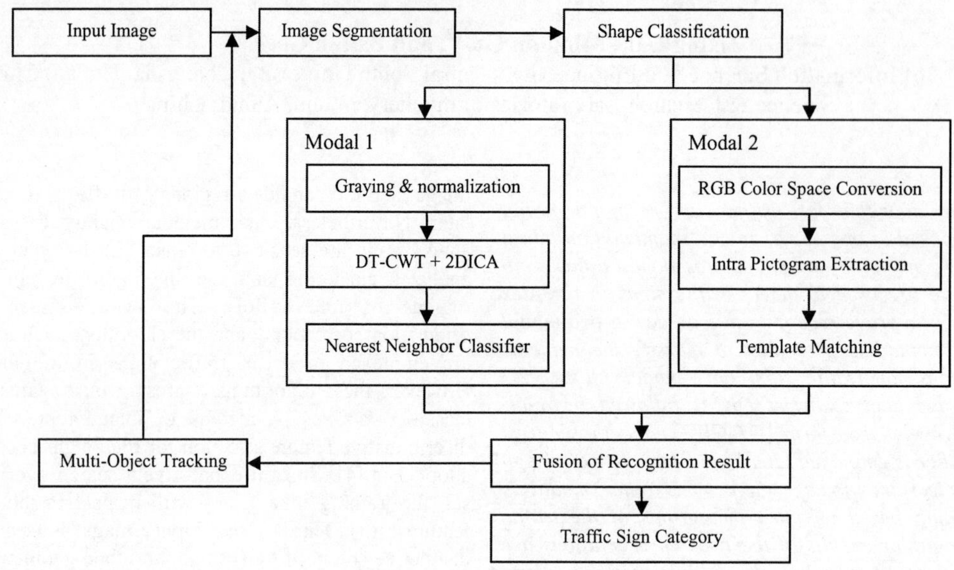

Figure 1. The Framework of Traffic Sign Recognition

2 Traffic Sign Detection

In China, traffic signs are designed in standardized geometrical shapes such as circle, octagon, triangle, rectangle, and square, with distinctive colors(such as red, blue, yellow). The traffic signs in urban and highway scenes carry abundantly useful information for drivers. The traffic sign regions are segmented from input image by the algorithm described in [13]. And the segmentation results are shown in figure 2.

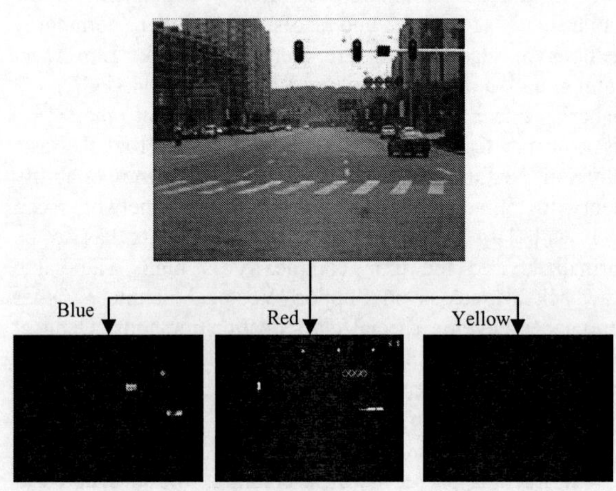

Figure 2. Color-based Image Segmentation

A template database of shapes(circle, triangle downward, octagon, rectangle, and equilateral triangle) is established for offline training. Each class includes 200 binary images.

In order to classify the traffic sign RoIs by shape, binary images are firstly normalized to 50×50 in size using the bilinear interpolation algorithm. Then the signatures of the RoIs are extracted by an algorithm designed in [13]. Due to discrepant number of boundary point in different shape, signature features varies in different RoIs and are unfit for shape classification directly. Therefore, the obtained shape feature needs to be expanded 360 by an interpolation algorithm before shape matching. After having obtained the shape features, a nearest neighbor classifier is used to distinguish shape of RoIs and to reserve appropriate RoIs as candidates of traffic signs. These color and binary images of candidates which are cropped from input and segmentation image, are denoted $CI_{i,c}$ and $BI_{i,c}$ respectively.

3 Traffic Sign Recognition

In order to improve recognition accuracy, A two-modal representation (DT-CWT+2D-ICA[14] and intra pictogram) is used to help to classify traffic signs. The classification results will be fused later.

3.1 DT-CWT+2DICA

DT-CWT is suitable for representation of traffic signs, due

to its directional advantage: less computation requirement, nearest shift and rotation invariance[15]. To obtain the same number of DT-CWT image features, the candidate images of traffic sign is converted into grayscale image from RGB color image, and normalized to 64×64 pixels in advance. Two trees are used for the rows of the image, and two trees for the columns in a quad-tree structure with a 4:1 redundancy[15]. The four quad-tree components of each DT-CWT coefficient are combined by simple arithmetic sum and differential operations to yield a pair of complex coefficients. This produces six directionally selective sub-bands for each scale of the two-dimensional DT-CWT at approximately $\pm 15^{\circ}$, $\pm 45^{\circ}$, and $\pm 75^{\circ}$.

Synthesis filters are used during the dual-tree complex wavelet transform to obtain $O_i, i = 1,\cdots,4$ represented synthesis filtering result of six direction selective sub-bands.

Feature matrix $\chi = (O_1,\cdots,O_4)^T$, each O_i has been normalized to unit variance before concatenation. To reduce the computational complexity, interlaced sampling method is employed to process feature matrix χ previously. Then a 2DICA algorithm described in [16] is used to reduce the dimension and eliminate the redundancy of traffic sign sample feature. The nearest neighbor classifier is adopted to sort category of traffic sign. The detailed process of algorithm is described in [14].

3.2 Intra pictogram extraction and matching

To extract the intra pictogram, the color image $CI_{i,c}$ and the binary image $BI_{i,c}$ of a candidate region are processed simultaneously.

For prohibition signs, speed limit signs and yield signs, the red border would affected to extract pictogram, since red pixels has approximate value with black in gray image. Then red border of candidate are set to 0 in advance. Assume the size of $BI_{i,c}$ was $row \times col$, and $IntraI$ is a zero image with same size of $BI_{i,c}$. Non-zero elements of each row in binary image $BI_{i,c}$ are found and denoted their ordinates as $y_k = \{y_{k,1}, y_{k,2},\cdots, y_{k,N}\}$, $k = 1,2,\cdots,row$, N is the number of non-zero elements. Let $D_{j-1} = y_{k,j} - y_{k,j-1}$, then the intra region is:

$$IntraI(k, y_{k,j-1} : y_{k,j}) = \begin{cases} 1, D_{j-1} > 0 \\ 0, otherwise \end{cases} \quad (6)$$

Then the region which has the maximum number of pixel is cropped from $CI_{i,c}$ and converted into gray image $G_{i,c}$. For warning, information or direction signs, $CI_{i,c}$ is only directly converted into grayscale image $G_{i,c}$ from RGB color space at preprocessing stage, since they are made up of 2 different representative colors generally.

Histogram that fell into 256 bins is the counted gray value of the intra region. Otsu's method is employed to automatically perform histogram shape-based image thresholding, and to obtain segmentation threshold $Level_{i,c}$. (x, y) is the coordinate of the inner pixel in candidate region. Since letters or pictograms of red and yellow traffic sign are generally black, whereas letters or pictograms of blue traffic sign are white. For the red and yellow traffic sign, $InB_{i,c}$ has

$$InB_{i,c}(x, y) = \begin{cases} 1, G_{i,c}(x, y) < Level_{i,c} \\ 0, otherwise \end{cases} \quad (7)$$

While, for blue traffic sign, $InB_{i,c}$ has

$$InB_{i,c}(x, y) = \begin{cases} 1, G_{i,c}(x, y) > Level_{i,c} \\ 0, otherwise \end{cases} \quad (8)$$

Erosion and dilation are used to eliminate noise pixels in binary image $InB_{i,c}$. The following steps perform pictograms extracting:

(1) If one row or column of $InB_{i,c}$ is all 0, it will be removed from $InB_{i,c}$.

(2) If $InB_{i,c}$ is empty or null, its output result will be labeled as 0, else, go to (3).

(3) Send $InB_{i,c}$ to the classifier of template matching, decide whether it belonged to any class of traffic signs or not, and label its corresponding result (class number or 0).

Denote the recognition results of three consecutive frames by DT-CWT+2DICA and intra pictogram + template matching are Dre, Ire respectively. If Dre equals to Ire, fusion result Out will be Dre, otherwise 0.

4 Multi-object traffic sign tracking

To track multiple traffic sign objects, a correspondence module is established to associate foreground candidates with objects that are already being tracked. A correspondence matrix C_m shows the association between the foreground regions extracted in current frame and the objects successfully be tracked in the previous frame. In the correspondence matrix C_m, the rows correspond to existing tracked objects in the previous frame and the columns to the foreground candidates in the current frame. The tracking information about the tracked objects is kept in a data structure named 'object database'. The information included: (1) Identity (ID); (2) Area; (3) Centroid; (3) Minimum Bounding Box; (4) Status; (5) Start Frame; (6) End Frame, where the Status could be A(Active), D(Disappear), E(Exit).

Suppose O_i^{t-1} represents the ith tracked object in $t-1$ frame where $i = 1,2,\cdots,M$, M denotes the number of the objects that already have being tracked in the previous frame. B_j^t denotes the j th candidate in the t th frame, $j = 1,2,\cdots,N$, N denotes the number of foreground candidates in the current frame. The distance between candidate B_j^t and object O_i^{t-1} can be determined as:

$$\left(D_x, D_y\right) = \left(\left|C_x^{O_i^{t-1}} - C_x^{B_j^t}\right|, \left|C_y^{O_i^{t-1}} - C_y^{B_j^t}\right|\right) \quad (9)$$

Where $\left(C_x, C_y\right)$ represented the respective centroid coordinate. The size of the correspondence matrix C_m is $M \times N$, and its elements' values can be defined as:

$$C_m[i,j] = \begin{cases} 1, D_x < \frac{W_{O_i^{t-1}} + W_{B_j^t}}{2} \cap D_y < \frac{H_{O_i^{t-1}} + H_{B_j^t}}{2} \cap S_W < T_W \cap S_H < T_H \cap S_{Area} < T_{Area} \\ 0, otherwise \end{cases}$$

Where $W_{O_i^{t-1}}$, $H_{O_i^{t-1}}$ represent the width and height of the tracked objects, and $W_{B_j^t}$, $H_{B_j^t}$ represent the width and height of the traffic sign candidate. The correspondence matrix contains binary values: '1' shows that there is an association between the corresponding object (O_i) and candidate (B_j). The analysis of correspondence matrix produced the following association cases:

(1) **Active Tracking:** A single candidate B_j in current frame is associated to a single object O_i in the previous frame, if all the candidates are isolated from each other, and not occluded. In such condition, the corresponding column and row in C_m have only one non-zero element. As soon as a candidate is declared as active tracking, the corresponding information in the database is updated.

(2) **Appearing or Reappearing:** If a column in C_m has all zero elements, the corresponding candidate B_j cannot be corresponded to any of the existing object. Thus, B_j should be a new region which is either caused by the entry of a new object or the reappearance of an existing object. If the candidate is from the boundary of the image, it is to be treated as a new object, or it might be an existing object. The appearance feature of the candidate B_j is matched against the objects having a 'Disappear' status in the database. If a match is found, the status of corresponding object will be replaced by 'Active', and object information will be updated in the database. However, if no match is found, the candidate is treated as a new object. If a candidate is detected as new object, its details should be added to the database and an 'Active' status is assigned to it.

(3) **Exit or Disappear:** If a row in C_m has all zero elements, it implies that the hypothesis of corresponding object O_i could not be supported by any of the foreground candidates. Thus, object O_i has either exited from the scene or disappeared for some time due to occlusion occurred by background objects. If the O_i is near the boundary, it is assumed to be at an existing status and its status is to be updated as 'Exit' in the database, otherwise it is assumed that the object O_i has disappeared for some time and its status is to be updated as 'Disappear'.

For each tracking object, the unscented Kalman filter(UKF) is utilized to predict the position and scale of object.

5 Experiment and Analysis

5.1 Experiments Data

To evaluate the traffic sign recognition algorithm, a JAI BB-141 mega-pixel camera equipped with a 12mm fixed lens of a 38.3×26.2 degree field of view(FOV) is mounted on the front of the car roof, facing straight ahead. Its resolution and frame rate are 1040×1392, 25fps respectively. Since the detection algorithm depends primarily on color, the gain and shutter speed are fixed to avoid over saturation of the traffic signs, particularly in the case of the mirror reflection on the smooth surface of the traffic signs. A database of sample images include 50 categories of the traffic sign is established. These samples are classified as prohibition signs, speed limit signs, obligation signs, stop signs, information signs, yield signs, and warnings by the meaning, and there are 200 samples in each category.

Experiments are performed using large-scale real-scene video record sequences which are collected from a moving intelligent vehicle in cluttered Chinese urban scenes. The sequence images vary in different weather such as sunny, cloudy, and in different illumination conditions e.g. adverse illumination, direct lighting. To test the robustness of the traffic sign recognition system, we drive the vehicle with the fore-mentioned configuration on the road of Changsha city at each of the three different times to emulate different conditions: in morning, at noon, at sunset. The recognition results include the experiment's time and date, the number and class of traffic signs that are stored in a text file.

5.2 Overall Performance

Table 1. Performance of Algorithm %

	1th group	2th group	3th group
Frame Number	2020	2356	3478
Detected Rate	97.27	95.46	97.07
DT-CWT+2DICA	96.78	95.82	95.82
Intra Pictogram Matching	95.88	97.15	95.64
Recognition Rate of Fusion	95.41	95.5	94.76
False Alarm Rate	0.15	0.08	0.17
Total	92.82	91.16	91.98

Figure 3 shows some results of the traffic sign recognition using the proposed algorithm. The detected traffic sign regions are enclosed by green boundaries and their recognition results are demonstrated with small standard pictures below the detected regions. At the same time, we can see that some regions which are similar as the traffic signs are successfully rejected by the color, shape and intra pictogram information of traffic signs. The false detection may be caused by a too long distance between the camera and the object, or dim surface of traffic sign and occlusion by other objects such as trees, signboard, buildings etc., or over-exposure or under-exposure of images, or quite slant viewing direction between the camera and the traffic sign.

To evaluate the overall performance of the algorithm, 3 groups of road scene videos captured in Changsha city were feed to the recognition system; tab. 1 illustrates their detection and recognition rate, shows that the overall recognition rate of proposed algorithm was up to 92.82% at the peak. Experiment result indicates that the proposed recognition method was robust, effective for classifying traffic signs. False positive cases were effectively reduced, because the color and shape of traffic signs have been considered in the detection stage. At the same time the false negative rate is slightly reduced due to the combination of the multiple representations of DT-CWT, 2DICA, intra pictogram, and template matching. However, the total recognition rate drop slightly.

Figure 3. Traffic Sign Detection and Recognition Results in Different Traffic Scenes and Road Conditions

Table 2. Performance comparison of different recognition algorithms %

Algorithm / Number	Template+2DICA	Gabor+2DICA	DT-CWT+PCA	DT-CWT +LPP	DT-CWT +2DPCA	the Proposed Algorithm
Red Sign: 15324	81.98	91.92	83.99	79.85	93.63	93.35
Blue Sign: 10357	86.15	91.65	84.59	82.46	91.93	93.42
Yellow Sign: 5639	83.82	92.16	85.45	80.35	91.43	91.56
Negative Sample: 3451	0.99	0.63	0.83	0.92	0.56	0.17

To evaluate the presented recognition algorithm, 31,320 images of traffic sign and negative sample are extracted from several traffic video sequences. These images are converted to Gray from RGB and normalized 64×64. For comparative analysis of different recognition algorithms, several separate experiments are performed here. Recognition results of the algorithms are displayed in Table 2. The results gave several conclusions. Firstly, the proposed algorithm, Gabor+2DICA and DT-CWT+2DPCA are of about the same recognition rate, but the recognition rate of proposed algorithm is more than Template+2DICA, DT-CWT+PCA, DT-CWT+LPP. Secondly, the error rate of the proposed algorithm is much lower than others algorithms. Then this algorithm is more suitable for traffic sign recognition.

5.3 Computational Time Analysis

The proposed algorithm is implemented using VC++.net. The hardware platform is a PC with a 2.5GHz Pentium(R) Dual-Core CPU and 3 Giga Bytes of RAM. The average computing time for the main steps are listed in table 3. It is obvious that the time consumption can be neglected. The overall average frame rate is up to 6.6fps and achieves nearly real-time performance in experiments.

Table 3. Computation Time Analysis

Step	Computation time(ms)
Image Acquisition	40
RoI Location	35
Shape Classification	13
DT-CWT+2DICA	26
Nearest Neighbor Classifier	22
Intra Pictogram Extraction	11
Template Matching	24
Recognition Result Fusion	—
Multi-Object Tracking	1
Total Computational Time	172

5.4 Traffic sign tracking

A video with two manually set traffic signs records in Changsha Railway College is used to test the performance of multi-object tracking. The initial information of objects is shown in Table 4.

Figure 4. Initializing position of multi-traffic signs

In Table 4, the first and the second value of the Minimum Bounding Box are the upper left coordinate of object region, and the third and the fourth are the width and height of external rectangular respectively. The number of items of the End Frame is set to 0 during the initialization. The tracked objects of traffic sign are boxed with cyan boundaries in fig. 4. The left sign is marked as the first object, and the right sign is marked as the second object.

The tracking result of the upper left coordinates; the width and the height of the two objects are showed in table 5. The red and black curves are the true position of traffic sign and the UKF tracking estimation results respectively. The UKF can effectively predict the changes of position and the scale of the traffic signs.

Table 4 Initializing tracking information of multi-traffic signs

Information	1st Object	2nd Object
ID	ID1	ID2
Area	1193	1795
Centroid	(192.83,341.25)	(942.53,355.84)
Minimum Bounding Box	(168,325,51,43)	(921,331,45,50)
Status	Active	Active
Start Frame	1	1
End Frame	0	0

Table 5 Tracking results of the 2 traffic sign objects

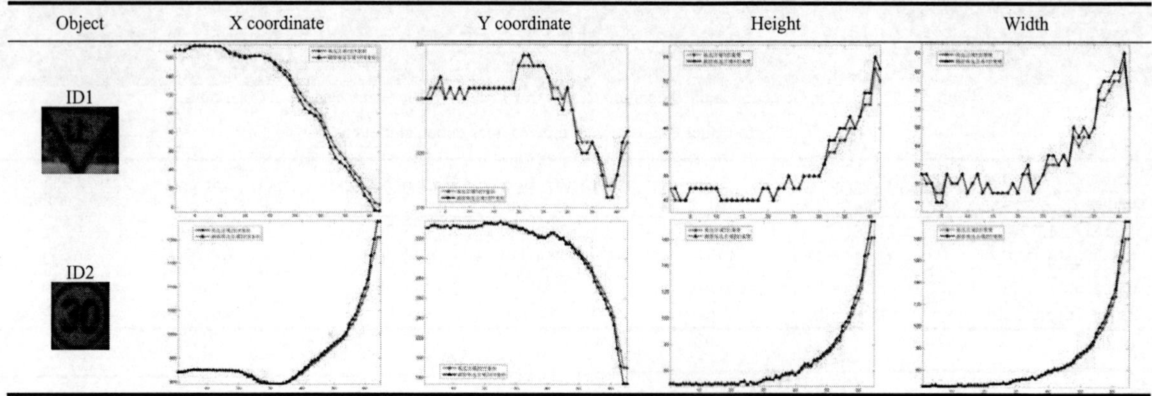

6 Conclusion

An algorithm for traffic sign recognition is introduced in this paper. In the detection stage, the color and shape of traffic signs are the main features for image segmentation and candidate region extraction. In the recognition stage, a two-modal representation is used to classify the detected candidate regions of traffic sign. One representation utilizes DT-CWT, 2DICA and the nearest neighbor classifier to classify traffic sign candidates and reject noise image. It can effectively represent and extract features from candidate region, eliminate feature's redundancy and fast classify traffic sign. The other representation is template matching using intra pictograms of traffic signs. It employs color and RoIs analysis to extract intra pictogram and matches intra pictogram of test image with the template database to recognize traffic signs. At the output stage, the results which are combination of the 2 previous results under some decision rules are output. Experimental results show that the overall recognition rate of the proposed algorithm is higher than 91%, the time of recognition is 172ms for a frame, and multiple objects of traffic signs could be tracked steadily and effectively.

However, there are still several challenges for the traffic sign detection: (1) A lot of Chinese characters exist in traffic signs, which provide abundant information to indicate road state for drivers; (2) the confusing signs like billboard on the road sides; (3) intelligent vehicles need to instantly obtain the traffic sign information at highway scene. How to overcome these challenges should be the main task in the future.

7 Acknowledgment

This work was supported in part by the National Natural Science Foundation of China under Grant 61175064, 90820302 and 60805027, Research Fund for the Doctoral Program of Higher Education under Grant 2001305330005, Academician Foundation of Hunan Province under Grant 2011FJ4043.

8 References

[1] Overett G., Petersson L., Andersson L., *et al.* "Boosting a heterogeneous pool of fast hog features for pedestrian and sign detection". In: IEEE Intelligent Vehicles Symposium, Xi'an, China. IEEE, Piscataway, USA, pp. 584–590, 2009.

[2] Nunn C., Kummert A., Muller-Schneiders S. "A two stage Detection Module for Traffic Signs". In: 2008 IEEE International Conference on Vehicular Electronics and Safety. Columbus, OH, USA. IEEE, Piscataway, USA, pp. 248–252, 2008.

[3] de la Escalera A., Moreno L. E.; Salichs M. A.; J. M. Armingol, "Road traffic sign detection and classification."

IEEE Transactions on Industrial Electronics, Vol.44, No.6, pp. 847–859, 1997.

[4] Ruta, Li Y., Liu X., "Towards real-time traffic sign recognition by class-specific discriminative features." In: Proceeding of the 18th British Machine Vision Conference. University of Warwick, UK. BMVA Press, UK, pp.399–408, 2007.

[5] Andrey V., Kang-Hyun J., "Automatic detection and recognition of traffic signs using geometric structure analysis." In: 2006 SICE-ICASE International Joint Conference. Busan, South Korea. IEEE, Piscataway, USA, pp. 1451–1456. 2006

[6] Nguwi Y., Kouzani A., "Automatic road sign recognition using neural networks." In: IEEE International Conference on Neural Networks, Vancouver, BC, Canada. IEEE, Piscataway, USA, pp.3955–3962. 2006.

[7] dela Escalera A., Armingol J. M., Pastor J. M., *et al*, "Visual sign information extraction and identification by deformable models for intelligent vehicles." IEEE Transactions on Intelligent Transportation Systems. Vol.5, No.2, pp.57–68. 2004.

[8] Lim King Hann, Seng Kah Phooi, Ang Li Minn. "Intra color-shape classification for traffic sign recognition." In: 2010 International Conference of Computer Symposium. Tainan, Taiwan. IEEE, Piscataway, USA, pp. 642-647, 2010.

[9] Maldonado-Bascón S., Lafuente-Arroyo S., Gil-Jiménez P., *et al.* "Road-sign detection and recognition based on support vector machines." IEEE Transactions on Intelligent Transportation System, Vol.8, No.2, pp.264–278. 2007.

[10] Deng Xiao, Wang Donghui, Cheng Lili, *et al*, "Traffic Sign Recognition Using Dictionary Learning Method." In: Proceedings 2010 Second WRI Global Congress on Intelligent Systems (GCIS). Wuhan, China. IEEE Computer Society, Los Alamitos, CA, USA, pp.372-375. 2010.

[11] Hoferlin B., Zimmermann K."Towards Reliable Traffic Sign Recognition". Intelligent Vehicles Symposium, pp.324-329. 2009.

[12] Meuter M., Muller-Schneiders S., Nunny C., *et al.* "Decision fusion and reasoning for traffic sign recognition". 13th International IEEE Conference on Intelligent Transportation Systems (ITSC). pp.324-329. 2010

[13] Gu Mingqin, Cai Zixing, He Fenfen, "Traffic sign recognition based on shape signature and gabor wavelet." CAAI Transactions on Intelligent Systems. Vol.6, No.6. pp.526-530. , 2011. (in Chinese).

[14] Cai Zi-Xing, Gu Ming-Qin. "Traffic Sign Recognition Algorithm Based on Shape Signature and Dual Tree-Complex Wavelet Transform". Journal of Central South University of Technology(English Edition). Vol. 20, No.4, pp.433-439. 2013.

[15] Selesnick W., Baraniuk R. G., Kingsbury N. C., "The dual-tree complex wavelet transform." Signal Processing Magazine, IEEE., Vol.22, No.6, pp.123-151, 2005.

[16] Hyvarinen A., Oja E., Independent component analysis: algorithms and applications. Neural networks. Vol.13, pp.4-5, pp.411-430, 2000.

An Embedded Pointing System for Lecture Rooms Installing Multiple Screen

Toshiaki Ukai, Takuro Kamamoto, Shinji Fukuma, Hideaki Okada, Shin-ichiro Mori
University of FUKUI,
Faculty of Engineering, Department of Information and Science
Bunkyou 3-9-1, Fukui-shi, Japan
ukai@sylph.fuis.u-fukui.ac.jp

Abstract - *This paper proposes the system which can detect a spot of a laser pointer which the lecturer uses and which can emphasize the spot on the sub-displays using FPGA as hardware. A lot of lecture rooms are installed a forward main-screen and several backward sub-displays. Under the environment, more effective teaching will be realized if the attention of students who watch the sub-displays is directed to the area where a lecturer wants them to pay. The contents of the emphasis are to overlay a cursor on the spot and to lower contrast at the area. As a result of this pointing system, we confirmed that this system could detect the spot of the laser pointer and emphasize the area of the spot.*

Keywords: multiple screen; point of interest; laser pointer; embedded system; FPGA

1 Introduction

Recently, many lecture rooms are gradually being renewed for distance learning and ICT based learning. Those rooms are provided a system which use a projector in order to present images or videos on a main-screen. Besides, they install an equipment which projects a lecturer's slide images and videos on not only main-screen but also sub-display placed at a backward lecture room. This paper calls this environment *the multi-screen environment*.

When the lecturers utilize the multi-screen environment, they connect their laptop computer terminal (PC) which the lecture slide images are in to a distributor. At the same time, the lecture slide images are shown on the sub-displays. Then, lecturers use a laser pointer to the main-screen so that they instruct the places where they want students to pay attention, the Point Of Interest (POI).

However the place of POI is indicated on the main-display, it is not transmitted to the sub-displays. In this situation, students who are watching the sub-displays cannot identify the place, and the lecturers are not able to indicate what they want to insist to those students. Effective lecture will not be conducted through this situation.

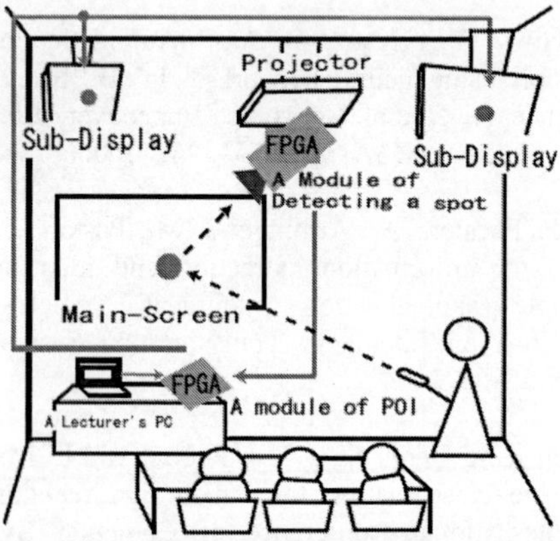

Fig.1. Proposed Pointing System

Although there are some marketed devices installing special function on laser pointer itself[4], it imposes a burden for the lecturers to prepare. Also, those special devices depend on the lecturers' PC environment such as Operating System (OS) and software.

This paper proposes a system design which can show the places of POI that the lecturers indicate by using a laser pointer to sub-displays (Fig.1). Simultaneously, this proposal aims not to make use of a special laser pointer or software depending on the lecturers' PC environment. It means a system that the lecturers do not need to prepare for using this system and that works when they just connect regular contacts. By not using software, but using FPGA as hardware, this system does not depend on OS of the lecturers' PC and ensures a real time process.

2 Overview of The Pointer System

This paper proposed pointing system which consists of a camera and FPGA (Field Programmable Logic Array) boards (Fig.2).

Fig.2. FPGA Boards and Camera

This system is composed two FPGAs (a module of detecting a spot and a module of processing POI). First FPGA will perform a detection of the spot, and second FPGA will perform a process of emphasis to a coordinates of the spot.

At the beginning, a composite video signal(Included a synchronous signal, a brightness signal, and a color signal) that was sent by a camera as NTSC(National Television System Committee) will be converted to a digital signal of ITU-656 format by an installed video decoder IC. Then, this digital signal will be processed through below order.

First, synchronous detection, and transformation from RGB color model to YCbCr color space are processed. Second processes are sampling of the spot, and an output after deciding a coordinates of the POI. Third, Putting a process of POI to the received coordinates. The first process is conducted by a system which was supplied by the vendors.

3 Pointer Detection

Fig.3 shows the block diagram of a module of the process which detects a spot, POI. Below is the detailed explanation of this module.

According to the function of a block which was supplied by the vendors, an analog video signal which the camera took is transformed to a value of RGB.

Second, a process of binarization is conducted in order that the identified spot will be '1'.

Third process calculates a coordinates of a spot based on binarized pixel data. Next are the explanations of each function in Fig.3.

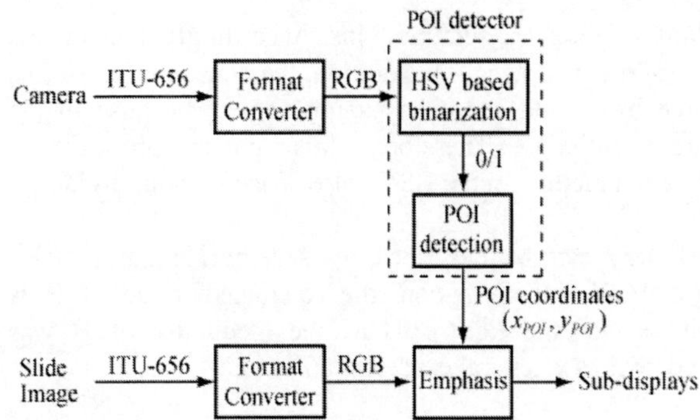

Fig.3. Block Diagram

3.1 Identifying Laser Pointer Spot

This system represents the received pixel data of RGB as HSV color space and identifies any color of the laser pointer.

The HSV color space is expressed by three components; Hue, Saturation, and Brightness (referred to as *H*, *S*, *V* respectively by using this model). We can identify every kinds of colors by setting the value of *H*. The convention from RGB to HSV color space is defined as

$$H' = \begin{cases} \dfrac{60(G-B)}{MAX-MIN}, & \text{if } MAX = R \\ \dfrac{60(B-R)}{MAX-MIN}+120, & \text{if } MAX = G \\ \dfrac{60(R-G)}{MAX-MIN}+240, & \text{if } MAX = B \end{cases}, \tag{1}$$

$$H = \begin{cases} H'+360, & \text{for } H'<0 \\ H', & \text{otherwise} \end{cases}, \tag{2}$$

$$S = \frac{MAX-MIN}{MAX}, \tag{3}$$

$$V = MAX, \tag{4}$$

where

$$MAX = \max\{\mathrm{R,G,B}\},\ MIN = \{\mathrm{R,G,B}\}$$

The binarization result is

$$b_{in} = \begin{cases} 1, & H_{low} < H < H_{high} \\ 0, & otherwise \end{cases}, \tag{5}$$

where H_{low} is the lower limit of hue and H_{high} is the higher one which are given by user.

Above transformation requires a division for calculating a value of H. When using a divider supplied as IP core, it needs 20 clocks and costs about 228ns at 87.5 MHz because of processing of two pixels per four clocks. In the ITU-656 standard, one pixel is sent per 74ns. Accordingly, the process has to follow the latency. In addition, the consumption of this resource by adding a divider cannot neglect because of the resource cutback. Therefore, this paper proposes a binarization method in the HSV color space without divider.

Eq.(5) can be described by several inequalities. By using a HSV transformation, the calculated value of H is substituted for the Eq.(6). Thus, the inequality of H was showed next as a general expression(7), (8).

$$H_{\text{low}} < \text{H} < H_{\text{high}}\,, \tag{6}$$

$$H_{\text{low}}\,\text{E} < 60\text{C} + \text{DE}, \tag{7}$$

$$60\text{C} + \text{DE} < H_{\text{high}}\,\text{E}, \tag{8}$$

where

$$C = \begin{cases} G-B, & \text{if } MAX = R \\ B-R, & \text{if } MAX = G \\ R-G, & \text{if } MAX = B \end{cases}, \tag{9}$$

$$D = \begin{cases} 360, & \text{if } MAX = R \\ 120, & \text{if } MAX = G \\ 240, & \text{if } MAX = B \end{cases}, \tag{10}$$

$$\text{E} = MAX - MIN, \tag{11}$$

If above inequalities(6), (7) are satisfied, then bin = 1 else bin = 0. When it directly calculates the formula from (9) to (11), computation of the maximum and minimum of R,G and B are needed. However, the maximum and minimum can be found by checking sign flags of subtraction G-B, B-R, and R-G. When the sign flags denote the sign flags of F_{RG}, F_{GB}, and F_{BR}, the relations of the sign flags, relation of the maximum and the minimum, *C*, and *E* are shown at TABLE1.

TABLE.1. Relation between Flags and Value

Sign flag F_{RG}	F_{GB}	F_{BR}	*MAX*	*MIN*	*C*	*E*
0	0	0	*R*	*R*	0	0
0	0	1	*R*	*B*	$G-B$	$-(B-R)$
0	1	0	*B*	*G*	$R-G$	$-(G-B)$
0	1	1	*R*	*G*	$G-B$	$R-G$
1	0	0	*G*	*R*	$B-R$	$-(R-G)$
1	0	1	*G*	*B*	$B-R$	$G-B$
1	1	0	*B*	*R*	$R-G$	$B-R$
1	1	1	*	*	*	*

*don't care

According to TABLE1, an absolute value of *E* has |G – B|, |B – R| or |R – G|, and the sign is decided by the flags. If the minus sign is put to *E*, the formula needs additional hardware, a complement circuit of two. Replacing E by $-E$, Eq. (7) and (8) are changed to

$$H_{\text{low}}(-\text{E}) < -60\text{C} + \text{D}(-\text{E}), \tag{7'}$$
$$-60\text{C} + \text{D}(-\text{E}) < H_{\text{high}}(-\text{E}), \tag{8'}$$

Besides, evaluation of the inequalities is implemented by a comparator. Consequently, if a comparator output is adequately chosen to a symbol of *E*, the calculation of two's complement of two is not needed. A logical function for finding the sign of *E* is

$$Sign = \bar{F}_{GB}\bar{F}_{BR} + \bar{F}_{RG}\bar{F}_{BR} + \bar{F}_{RG}\bar{F}_{GB}\,, \tag{12}$$

Thus, we can design a combinational logic circuit that it generates adequate *C*, *E*, and *D* through three sub, and their sign flag. Proposed binarized circuit can be implemented by three subtracters, four multipliers, and two comparators. In addition, we can identify narrower color by using the value of S and the value of V as an identification data.

3.2 Detecting Laser pointer Spot

The binary image, Bin from the *H* component, has many '1' pixel around the pointer spot because the laser is powerful and coherent light. Thus, it can expect that barycenter of the cluster will be position of the pointer spot. However, precise computation of the barycenter requires many resources such as large memory and divider, it is unfavorable for the embedded system.

This paper proposes a simple spot position detector suitable for the embedded system. Proposed detector has two 1-dimensional histograms, for horizontal and vertical direction, as shown in Fig. 4. They are assigned installed FPGA memory, namely Block RAM (BRAM). When a binary pixel is transmitted from previous binarization circuit in raster scan order, the detector updates each histogram whenever it receives a pixel. After all pixel are received, it estimates the coordinates of the spot from the intersection of peaks of histogram, as shown in Fig. 4. Note that if the distribution is unimodal then the peak is just maximum and BRAM is not required to compute the peak of vertical direction histogram.

4 Pointer Spot Emphasis

Fig.3 shows the block diagram of a module of the processing POI to sub-displays. Below is the detailed explanation of this module.

This module conducts the process of POI to the received slide image processing by the module of detecting the pointer spot. Based on the coordinates of the spot identified by the detecting block, this module overlays the slide image with several effects. The effects are preferred for directing students' attentions. Then, it outputs the result of the effects on the sub-displays while the lecturer direct the spot on the main-screen.

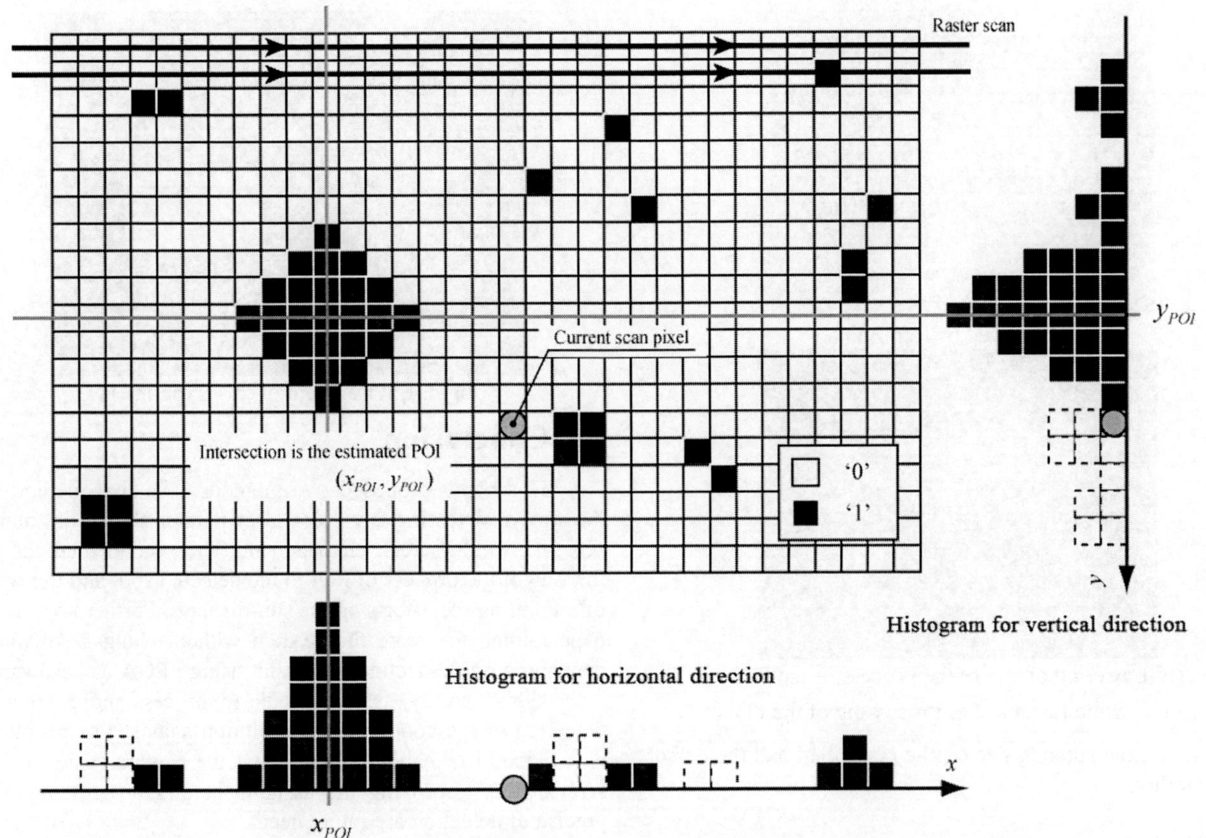

Fig.4. Histogram and Pointer Spot

Although this module receive the coordinates of the spot, the definition of the coordinates is not decided by this module. That is to say, the coordinates are not determined by this module so that this module cannot emphasize the POI to the coordinates.

Following ITU-656 format(Interlace, method, 30 fps, Valid pixels 720 × 485 pixels), two pixel data will be sent per four clock, and a scanning process of a line finishes after 1440 clocks by a raster scan.

Utilizing a number of clocks of the scanning process, a coordinate axis of the horizontal direction is defined as 0 to 720. Besides, vertical direction is defined 0 to 485 which is summed after counting each horizontal direction. Therefore, by using this specification, we determine the coordinates within this module. However there are blanking times in ITU-656 format(Fig. 5), we do not have to consider about blanking times due to this method.

By setting this method and counting up, we can identify the place of coordinates which are sent from former block and can emphasize the POI.

There are two contents for emphasizing the pointer spot. The one of effects is a method that overlays the slide image with a pointer cursor on the coordinates (x_{POI}, y_{POI}). The other

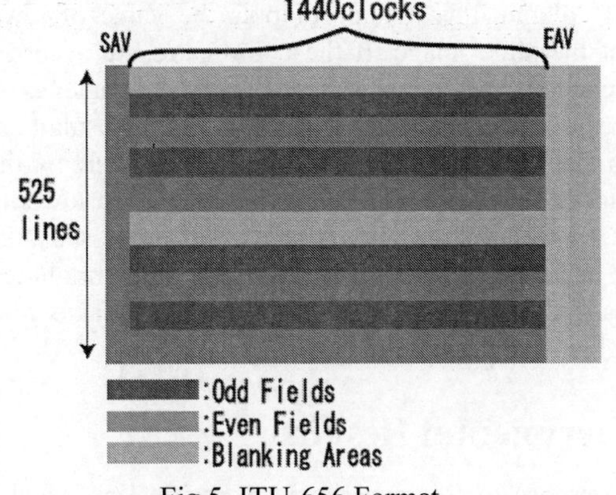

Fig.5. ITU-656 Format

is to lower the brightness of an out of area of POI so that the area can look bright. It can be performed by multiplying the brightness by 0.5.

The former method refers to the amount of counts of rows and columns. If the received coordinates are the same with an amount of counts of rows and columns, this module overlays any colors pointer cursor on the place. If this module overlaps a color to only the place of coordinates, the emphasized place is small and unclear so that the received coordinates is only one pixel. Therefore, if this starts overlapping several pixels' color from the place of received

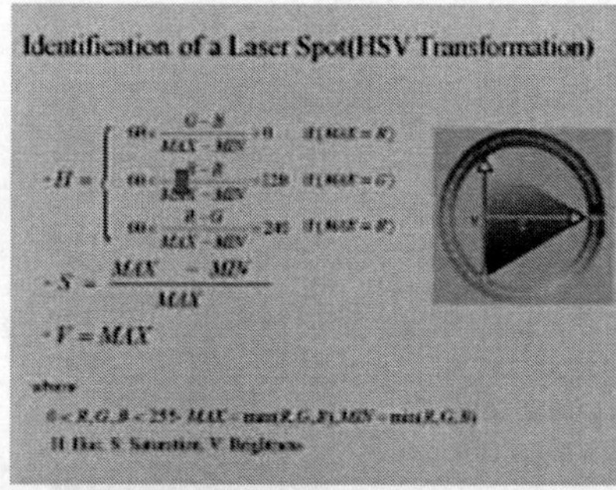

(a) Overlayed by Red Pointer

(b) Lowering of Out of the Process of the POI

Fig.6. Slide Images after Processing of the POI

coordinates, the cursor's size can be controlled and the cursor has visibility.

The latter method refers to only the counter of column. If the received coordinates of column is not accorded with the counter of column, this module outputs the value of lower contrast of the slide image. If the coordinates are accorded with the counter, this outputs the original slide image. As same with the former, the emphasized place is very small and unclear so that only one pixel will be received. Thereby, this can conduct stronger effect of POI to the area when lowering an out of contrast of the aiming area. The processed slide image can be achieved by lowering the value of the brightness of the image data of pixel data. Fig.6 are two images after processing the emphasis of the spot.

5 Experimental Results

The purpose of this experiment is verification whether this system can detect the spot of the laser pointer on the main-screen and whether it can emphasize the area of the spot. Under the environment(Fig.7), this system could detect the spot and emphasize the area. Fig.6(a) and (b) are the results of this experiment. However, this system could not clearly detect the spot when a distance between the main-screen and the camera is more than 2.0 m. This is because the camera does not directly receive a red light source but receives a reflected light once at the main-screen. Through the reason, the light intensity that the camera gets becomes weak. Besides, there is also a reason that the process of binarization is difficult because a size of the spot shown on the main-screen is small, and a detected range will be smaller.

Fig.7. Environment of this Experiment

6 Conclusion

This paper proposed two methods. The first method is the way of detecting any color laser pointer shown on main-screen in multi-screen environment. The second methods is the way of the process of POI to the detected spot and the way of outputting the effects on the sub-displays. Furthermore, this paper aimed to create this system without using a software depending on the lecturer's PC, but using FPGA as hardware.

Consequently, it is difficult to process more precise detection of the coordinates. A solution against this problem is a function of calibration to adapt the camera scale to the screen size. Improving the assignment and progressing the precise of detection are future needs.

7 Acknowledgement

This research was supported in part by JSPS KAKENHI Grants-in-Aid for Scientific Research (B) 25280042.

8 References

[1] Yoshihumi Oizumi, "An implement of Pointing system for distant learning" Master's thesis of Department of Information and Science of Graduate University of Fukui, March 2007

[2] Takuro Kamamoto, "Development and Implement of stereo mesurement system using FPGA", Bachelor's thesis of Department of Information and Science of University of Fukui, March 2012

[3] Atmark Techno "SUZAKU-V Hardware Manual" http://suzaku.atmark-techno.com/

[4] KOKUYO "LASER POINTER MOUSE" http://www.kokuyo-st.co.jp/stationery/lp/mouse/index01.html#ela_mgu91

Multi-Spectra Artificial Compound Eyes, Design, Fabrication and Applications

Yupei Yao, and Ruxu Du
Dept. of Mechanical and Automation Engineering, The Chinese University of Hong Kong, Hong Kong SAR, China

Abstract - *This paper introduces a Multi-Spectra Artificial Compound Eyes (MSACE) imaging system. It is made in two parts: First, multi-spectra filters are made by depositing pigment based photo-resist material on glass substrate. Second, a micro lens array (the artificial compound eye) is made by means of photolithography and thermal reflow. The resulting MSACE has a number of distinct features. First, it has an accurate lens profile. Second, it can catch different spectral information. Third, it is rather inexpensive to make. It is expected that the MSACE system will find many potential applications in the near future, such as endoscopic diagnosis and currency counterfeit checking.*

Keywords: Artificial Compound Eyes, micro lens array, thermal reflow, multi-spectra imaging

1 Introduction

It is well known that animals have different vision systems than human. First, many insects have compound eyes. It has very large view angle and is particularly effectively to see moving objects [1]. Second, animals have different viewing spectra. For example, bee's vision focuses on the color of the stamen and pistil of the flowers in ultraviolet [2], while snake sees infrared [3]. Inspired by these nature wonders, researchers around the world are avidly trying to develop multi-lens multi-spectrum imaging systems to see what human cannot see in naked eyes. For instance, Duparre and his team developed two apposition Artificial Compound Eyes (ACE) systems, one has planar structure [4] and the other has spherical structure [5]. The two systems have large field of view but their resolutions are low. Tanida and et al developed a planar ACE system with image reconstruction software [6]. Its reconstructed color image has higher resolution [7, 8]. Subsequently, they developed several applications, such as fingerprint capturing, multispectral imaging and color imaging [9]. Also, Lin and Tian [10] developed a 16 channel integrated narrow band-pass filter using etching technique, which can decompose an ordinary image into a number of images with specific spectral bands.

Our team has been working on ACE for several years [11 ~ 13]. In particularly, we developed a simple method to make ACE using the thermal reflow. The objective of this paper is to integrate the ACE with multi-spectrum filters to make a Multi-Spectrum Artificial Compound Eyes (MSACE) system. The rest of the paper is divided into three sections. Section 2 presents the fabrication procedure. Section 3 gives the testing results. Finally, Section 4 contains conclusions and future work.

2 Fabrication

It is known that the ACE can be made by a number of different methods. One is to use the traditional molding technology [14, 15]. First, a mold is made using ultra-precision lathe with diamond cutter. Then, using the mold and a precision injection molding machine, ACE can be made with materials such as PMMA. Figure 1 shows a sample ACE designed by us and made by Hong Kong Polytechnic University. This method is capable of making precision ACE in large quantities. Though, the mold is expensive and it requires additional steps to make MSACE.

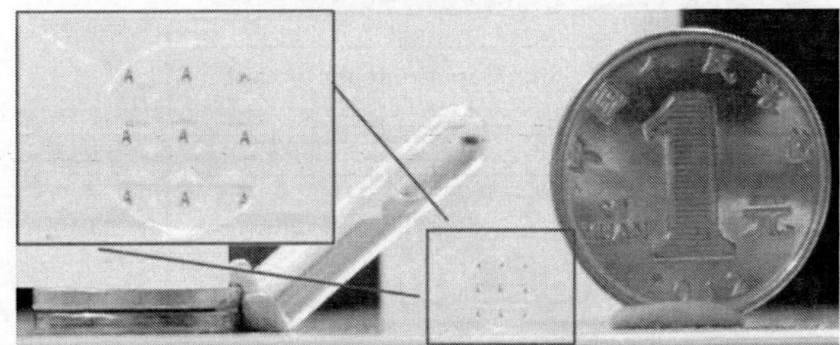

Figure 1: sample ACE made by conventional molding method

The other method is to use MEMS fabrication techniques, which was adopted in our early research [11 ~ 13]. It has a number of advantages, such as low fabrication cost, flexible, and most importantly, being capable of making MSACE. Therefore, this method is used in this paper. The MEMS fabrication method consists of two steps. First, a multi-spectrum filter is fabricated, and then, the ACE structure (a micro-lens array) on top of the multi-spectrum filter is fabricated. The details of the fabrication processes are presented below.

Figure 2 shows the fabrication process for making the multi-spectrum filter. It uses the pigment-dispersed method that is generally used in liquid crystal display fabrication [16]. The process consists of a number of repetitive steps:

Step 1: Clean the glass substrate using acetone and dehydrate the substrate in the oven;

Step 2: Spin-coat the pigment photoresist on the substrate (1st run: spin speed = 300 rpm, time = 20 s; 2nd run: spin speed = 600 rpm, time = 60 s, final thickness = 1 μm);

Step 3: Remove the residual solvent using pre-bake (temperature = 80 °C, time = 2 min);

Step 4: Expose the photoresist with UV light under the cover of the prepared mask (exposure dose = 150 mJ);

Step 5: Develop in the specific KOH developer (KOH:Water = 1:49, develop time = 40 s), by which one section of the filter is formed.

Step 6: Cure the photoresist completely using hard bake (temperature = 230 °C, time = 80 min).

This process gives one section of filter and is repeated for other color filters as shown in Figure 2. As shown in the figure, a total of four color sections are made including red, green, blue and red + green + blue, which is nearly black accepting only near-infrared to pass.

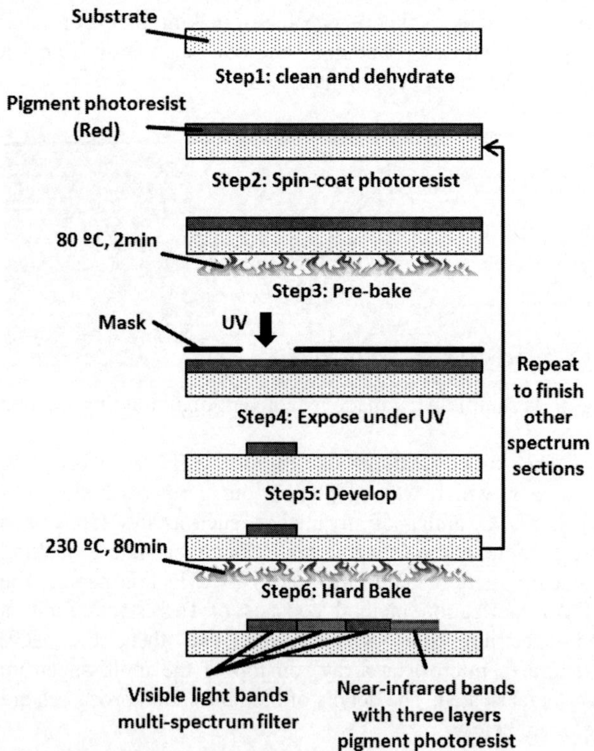

Figure 2: the fabrication process of the multi-spectrum filters

Figure 3 shows the fabrication process for making the artificial compound eyes(ACE) on the top of the multi-spectrum filters. The detailed steps are as follows:

Step 1: Spin-coat the photoresist (Model: AZ-4620, Manufacturer: Shipley, USA) on the substrate with the multi-spectrum filter (1st run: spin speed = 500 rpm, time = 20 s, 2nd run: spin speed = 2000 rpm, time = 60 s, 3rd run: spin speed = 3000 rpm, time = 1.2s);

Step 2: Pre-bake (temperature = 88 ℃, time = 10 min);

Step 3: Repeat Steps 1 and 2 so that the thickness of the photoresist reaches 20 ~ 25 μm;

Step 4: Expose the photoresist with UV light under the cover of the prepared mask (exposure dose = 250 mJ);

Step 5: Develop (time = 80 s);

Step 6: Conduct thermal reflow (temperature = 130 °C, time = 120 s), which will give the artificial compound eyes on the multi-spectrum filters.

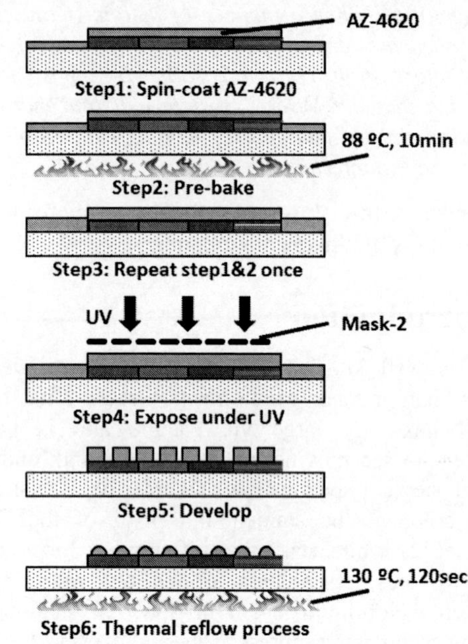

Figure 3: the fabrication processes of the ACE using thermal reflow

The aforementioned fabrication process shall be conducted in great care. In particularly, there are several important notes. First, because the exposing and developing steps are repeated for several times, any residual photoresist or moisture left on the substrate must be completed removed, as residual photoresist will cause uneven surface and moisture will cause bubbles.

Second, to compensate the effect of thermal reflow, the diameter of the lens on the mask should be slightly larger than that of the design. This is because the thermal reflow will melt a part of the material away. Based on our experience, for the lens of 750 μm in diameter, a margin of 2 ~ 3 μm will have the best result.

Last but not the least, controlling the temperature during the thermal reflow is very important. If the temperature is too high (above 140 °C) the mobility of the photoresist will increase causing the distortion of the shape of ACE. On the other hand, if the temperature is too low (under 120 °C), the mobility of the photoresist will be too low to form the ACE, which means the photoresist will solidify before forming the lens contour.

3 Fabrication Results

Using the aforementioned fabrication procedure, we have made a number of MSACE samples. Figure 4 shows a sample. It uses a simple design: the MSACE is made of four sections (red, blue, green and red + blue + green), and each section consists of 5 x 5 identical ACE. All ACE components are the same, 750 μm in diameter and 25 μm in height. From the figure, the MSACE patterns can be clearly seen.

Figure 4: A sample MSACE

Figure 5 shows center portion of the sample with an amplification of 5 times, it is taken under the background lighting while Figure 6 is taken under the normal lighting. From figure 5, with adjusting the focus of microscope to the bottom of the lens, it is seen that the lenses have sharp boundaries, and from figure 6, the uniform reflation of normal lighting indicates the lenses have smooth surface, proving that the aforementioned method is successful. It shall be pointed out that usually about 95% of the lenses are in good shape while the other 4 ~ 5% of the lenses are in bad shape. The bad lenses are randomly distributed in different places, they may be caused by many factors, such as the cleaning of the substrate, the contact between the substrate and the baker, the temperature distribution of the baker and etc. These problems may be resolved using better equipment.

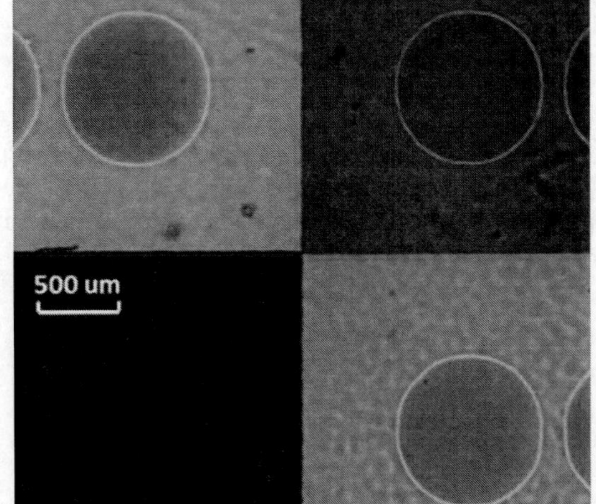

Figure 5: the center portion of the sample under background lighting with an amplification of 5 times

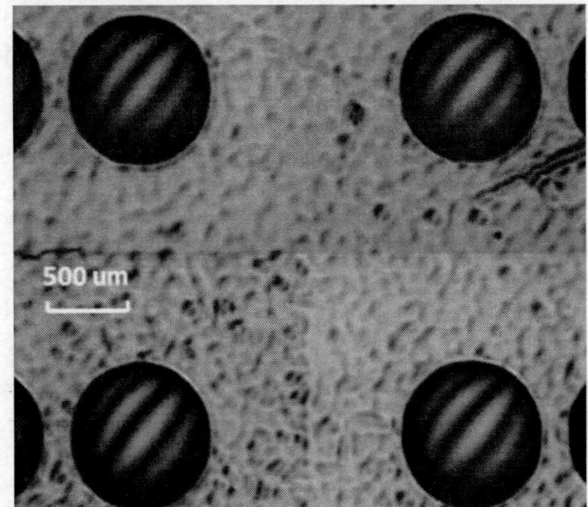

Figure 6: the center portion of the sample under normal lighting with an amplification of 5 times

Next, the contours of the lenses are carefully measured using a profiler (Model: Alpha-Step 500, Maker: Tencor Instruments Co., USA). It is found that the diameter of the lenses is about 760 to 780 μm, which is slightly larger than the cylinder before malting, while the height of the lenses is 4 ~ 6 μm smaller than the cylinder. Figure 7 compares the designed profile and the measured profile. From the figures, it is seen that the presented method is effective.

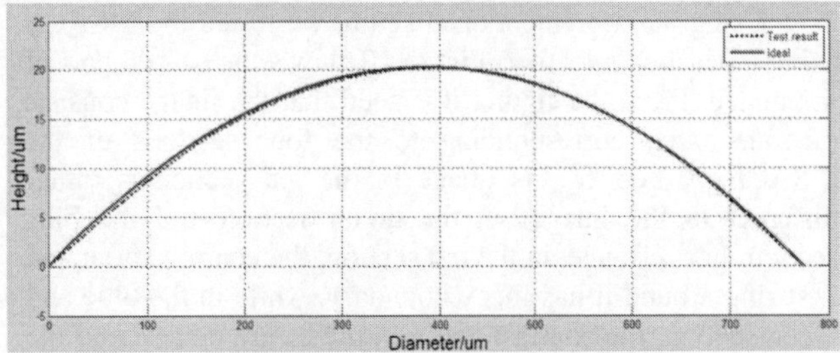

Figure 7: A comparison between the designed lens contour and the actual lens contour

Figure 8 shows the transmittance of the visible light through different sections of the MSACE measured by a spectrum analyzer (Model: U-3501, Manufacturer: HITACHI). Figure 8(a) shows the transmittance of the light in red, blue, and green sections respectively. Figure 8(b) shows the transmittance of the light in the red + blue + green section, which is equivalent to infrared. From the figure, the effects of the color filters can be clearly seen.

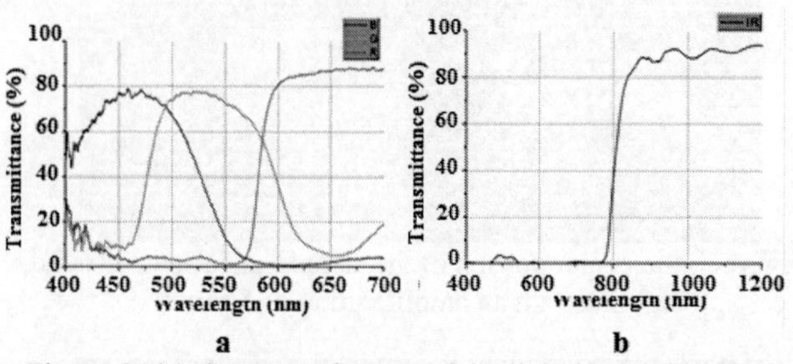

a b

Figure 8: (a) the transmittance of the light in red, blue and green sections respectively, (b) the transmittance of the light in red + blue + green section.

The fabricated MSACE can work with ordinary vision sensors. Figure 9 shows the setup with an industrial grade CCD sensor (Model: UC1000-C, Manufacturer: Acutance (BeiJing) Ltd.). The sensible band of the sensor ranges from 400 nm to 1200 nm.

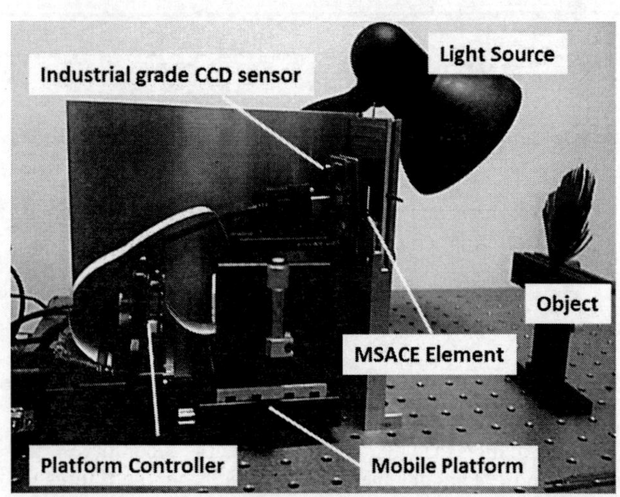

Figure 9: The experiment setup for testing the MSACE

Using the aforementioned setup, we tested the MSACE using a peacock's feather. Figure 10 shows the central part of the image. From the figure, it is seen that the image consists of four parts, corresponding to the four sections of the MSACE. Moreover, the image in the red section is rather different to the images in the green section and the blue section. For instance, in the red section, the centre pattern and first ring around it has fuzzy boundary, while in the blue and green section, the contrast between the centre pattern and the first ring is very clear; what's more, in the green section, there is a "highlighted" ring near the periphery of the feather pattern, while the same place is not so clear in either red or blue section. This will help to extract the hidden spectral patterns of the image. Though, the image in the red + green + blue section is too dark to be see, as the light source using in experiment provides little near infrared light.

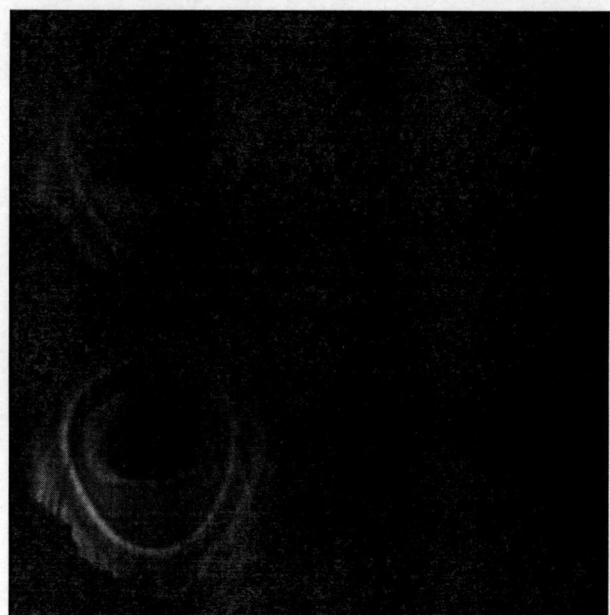

Figure 10: A sample imaging result of the MSACE

4 Conclusions and Future Work

This paper presents a novel Multi-Spectra Artificial Compound Eyes (MSACE) system. Based on the discussions above, following conclusions can be drawn:

(1). The MSACE is made in two parts: First, multi-spectra filters are made by means of depositing color pigment based photo-resists on glass substrate. Second, a micro lens array (the artificial compound eyes) is made by means of photolithography and thermal reflow.

(2) The MSACE system can effectively catch the hidden color patterns of an image.

(3) The MSACE is rather inexpensive and hence, can be used in many applications, such as medical diagnosis and currency counterfeit checking.

It shall be mentioned that the presented MSACE is still in its infancy. From the design point of view, for instance, the micro lens can be in different sizes and shapes, which gives the light field imaging. In addition, many more filters can be added covering more spectral bands. From the fabrication point of view, many improvements can be made, such as applying the heat source on top of the substrate for thermal reflow process other than using a hot plate under the substrate; and controlling the thermal reflow temperature and time.

5 Acknowledgement

The authors wish to thank Dr. S. Di and Mr. J. Jin of Guangzhou Chinese Academy of Sciences Institute of the Advanced Technology for helping to setup the imaging experiments.

6 References

[1] http://en.wikipedia.org/wiki/Eye.

[2] http://www.webexhibits.org/causesofcolor/17.html.

[3] http://en.wikipedia.org/wiki/Infrared_sensing_in_snakes

[4] J. Duparre, P. Dannberg, and et al, "Artificial Apposition Compound Eye Fabricated by Micro-Optics Technology," Applied Optics, Vol. 43, pp. 4303-4310, 2004.

[5] J. Duparre, D. Radtek and A. Tunnermann, "Spherical Artificial Compound Eye Captures Real Images," Proc. of SPIE; Paper No. 64660K-1-9, 2007.

[6] J. Tanida and et al, "Thin Observation Module by Bound Optics (TOMBO): Concept and Experimental Verification," Applied Optics; Vol. 40, pp. 1806-1813, 2001.

[7] R. Shogenji, Y. Kitamura, K. Yamada, S. Miyatake and J. Tanida, "Multispectral Imaging Using Compact Compound Optics," Optical Express, Vol. 12, pp.1643-1655, 2004.

[8] J. Tanida, R. Shogenji, and at el, "Color Imaging with an Integrated Compound Imaging system," Optical Express; Vol. 11, pp. 2109-2117, 2003.

[9] R. Shogenji, Y. Kitamura, K. Yamada, S. Miyatake and J. Tanida, "Bimodal Fingerprint Capturing System Based on Compound-Eye Imaging Module," Applied Optics; Vol. 43, pp. 1355-1359, 2004.

[10] B. Lin, and T. Y. Tian, "Study of Fabrication of 16 Channel Micro Integrated Filter," J. Infrared Millim. Waves, Vol. 25, No. 4, pp. 287-290 August, 2006.

[11] S. Di and R. Du, "The Controlling of Microlens Contour by Adjusting Developing Time in Thermal Reflow Method," International Symposium on Photoelectronic Detection and Imaging 2009, June 17-19, China.

[12] S. Di, H. Li and R. Du, "An Artificial Compound Eyes Imaging System Based on MEMS Technology," IEEE Robio 2009, Dec. 19 – 23, 2009, Guilin, China.

[13] S. Di, H. Lin and R. Du, "A Simple Method for Fabrication of Artificial Compound Eye," The 6th International Conference on Micro-Manufacturing (ICOMM 2011), March 7 – 10, 2011, Tokyo, Japan.

[14] B. K. Lee, D. S. Kim, and T. H. Kwon; "Replication of Microlens Arrays by Injection Molding," Microsystem Technologies, Volume 10, Issue 6-7, pp. 531-535, October 2004.

[15] Z. D. Popvic, R. A. Sprague and G. A. N. Connel, "Technique for Monolithic Fabrication of Microlens Arrays," Applied Optics, Vol. 27, No. 7, pp. 1281-1284, 1988.

[16] R. W. Sabnis, "Color Filter Technology for Liquid Crystal Displays," Displays, Vol. 20, pp. 119-129, 1999.

[17] G. Themelis, J. S. Yoo, and V. Ntziachristos, "Multispectral Imaging Using Multiple-Bandpass Filters," Optics Letters, Vol. 33, No. 9, 2008.

[18] B. E. Bayer, "Color Imaging Array," U.S. Patent 3,971,065, 1976.

[19] J. M. Eichenholz, N. Barnett, and et. al, "Real Time Megapixel Multispectral Bioimaging," Proc. of SPIE, Paper No. 7568, Jan. 2010.

[20] J. Y. Hardeberg, "Multispectral Color Image Capture Using a Liquid Crystal Tunable Filter," Optics Engineering, Vol. 41, No. 10, pp. 2532–2548, October 2002.

Computer Vision-based Object Recognition for the Visually Impaired Using Visual Tags

Rabia Jafri[1], Syed Abid Ali[2], and Hamid R. Arabnia[3]
[1]Department of Information Technology, King Saud University, Riyadh, Saudi Arabia
[2]ISM-TEC LLC, Wilmington, Delaware, U.S.A
[3]Department of Computer Science, University of Georgia, Athens, GA, U.S.A.

Abstract: *Recognizing generic objects in the surrounding environment is a major challenge for the visually impaired for which few assistive technological solutions have been devised to date. Nevertheless, in recent years, several computer vision-based strategies have emerged for this task which utilize visual tags affixed to objects for identification. These approaches are distinguished by their reliance on commercial off-the-shelf components and mobile technologies rendering them cost-effective, portable, intuitive and thus, compelling solutions to an urgent problem. The objective of this paper is to provide an overview of the state of the art in this area, highlighting the advantages offered by as well as the challenges faced by such systems, and to inspire and facilitate further exploration of this avenue of research.*

Keywords: visually impaired, assistive technologies, object recognition, computer vision, visual tags, review

1. Introduction

According to recent estimates by the World Health Organization (WHO), 285 million people worldwide are visually impaired [1]. Of these, 39 million are blind while 246 million have low vision. Without additional interventions, these numbers are predicted to significantly increase by the year 2020 [2]. Even though 80% of visual impairments are avoidable or curable, however, the unfortunate fact is that 90% of the visually impaired live in developing countries which do not have sufficient treatment and support options in place to deal with this disability. Moreover, 65% of the visually impaired are aged 50 years or older and this number is projected to increase [3]. Most commercial assistive products are beyond the financial reach of this population while many new-fangled technologies are hard, especially for the elderly, to grasp. These facts delineate an urgent need to develop solutions which are cost-effective, intuitive and make use of commonly available technologies. Computer vision-based techniques fit the bill perfectly: Generally, these methods do not require retrofitting the environment with special infrastructure or transmitters (unlike other technologies such as those that utilize RFID or infrared waves). Moreover, many of these solutions can be installed on mobile computing devices that the user already owns (e.g., cell phones and tablet computing devices) utilizing the built-in cameras and other pre-existing functions available therein. This also eliminates the need to carry around a separate gadget for recognizing objects. For solutions that do come with their own apparatus, the majority consist of lightweight equipment that the user can easily carry or wear. Also, unlike visual prosthetics devices, these systems are not dependent upon any part of the human vision system being intact.

A particular class of computer vision based approaches requires unique visual tags to be placed on all objects that need to be recognized. Rather than exploiting the object's physical features such as color, shape, texture, etc., these systems identify an object by capturing an image of the tag placed on it, extracting the tag and deciphering it.

Tag-based systems offer several advantages over their non-tag-based counterparts: Since the only piece of visual data that these systems extract, store and compare for each object is its tag, the computational power and storage space required for these systems is much less than that for non-tag-based systems which deal with much more detailed information, such as shape, size, color, etc., for each object. These solutions are also ideal for tasks that require differentiating among a group of objects which feel the same but have different visual encoding and contents, e.g., searching for a particular DVD in one's DVD collection, locating boxes during a move, or picking the right jelly jar from the refrigerator [4].The need for this differentiation becomes even more vital for the visually impaired when the contents of the object are hazardous, e.g., a tube of glue versus a tube of eye drops [5]. Moreover, many of these approaches do not require tags to be explicitly placed on store-bought products since these objects already have unique visual tags in the form of product barcodes. Furthermore, visual tags can be conveniently generated and printed out utilizing free online software thus, avoiding the hassle and cost involved in the purchase of non-visual tags such as RFID or infra-red ones.

Computer vision-based techniques that utilize visual tags to recognize objects have only recently begun to be employed in the domain of assistive technologies for the visually impaired; however, the results reported so far are very promising and clearly demonstrate the potential of such systems. A survey of such solutions has therefore, been undertaken in this paper. The objective is to provide an overview of the state of the art in this area, highlighting the advantages offered by as well as the challenges faced by such systems, and to inspire and facilitate further exploration of this avenue of research.

The rest of this paper is organized as follows: Section 2 describes other technologies that are currently being utilized for developing devices to assist the visually impaired in recognizing generic objects. Section 3 provides a review and analysis of computer vision-based object recognition solutions for the visually impaired that use visual tags. Section 4 concludes the paper with a discussion of issues related to these technologies and the identification of some directions for future research.

2. Related work

Non-visual tag-based computer vision approaches for the visually impaired perform object recognition based either on 3D model matching [6, 7] or on features extracted from 2D intensity images of objects. Approaches that adopt the latter strategy predominantly employ SIFT [8] and SURF [9] features for recognition since these descriptors have been shown to be invariant to image translation, scaling, and rotation, and are partially invariant to illumination changes and affine or 3D projection. Also SURF features can be computed very fast compared to other descriptors enabling real-time computation requirements to be met [9, 10] (See [11, 12] and [13-15] for examples of SIFT and SURF-based systems, respectively). However, since both SIFT and SURF do not take color information into account, some other strategies have opted to utilize color and edge detection for recognition [16, 17]. Another set of image-based approaches perform recognition by doing a raw translation of the image data into sound patterns [18] [19] or tactile stimulation on the tongue [20], torso [21, 22] or back [23]. However, these methods require a steep learning curve and it is not obvious how easy or intuitive it is for people to interpret these cues to form a mental representation of the visual scene.

Some other solutions have employed alternate sensing technologies, such as RFID [24, 25], sonar [26] and infrared [27] for this task, thus, avoiding some of the inherent drawbacks associated with image data-based strategies; however, these technologies suffer from limitations of their own., e.g., they all require special sensing equipment while infrared and RFID require specific tags; also, sonar and infrared are not very effective in indoors environments since such surroundings tend to be cluttered and the obstacles present therein may cause the reflected echoes to become distorted resulting in unreliable information being conveyed to the user.

3. Overview of computer vision-based object recognition approaches for the visually impaired which use visual tags

We now present an overview of some innovative computer vision-based systems developed in recent years to assist the visually impaired in recognizing generic objects by utilizing visual tags affixed to them. A summary and comparison of all the approaches discussed in this section is provided in Table 1.

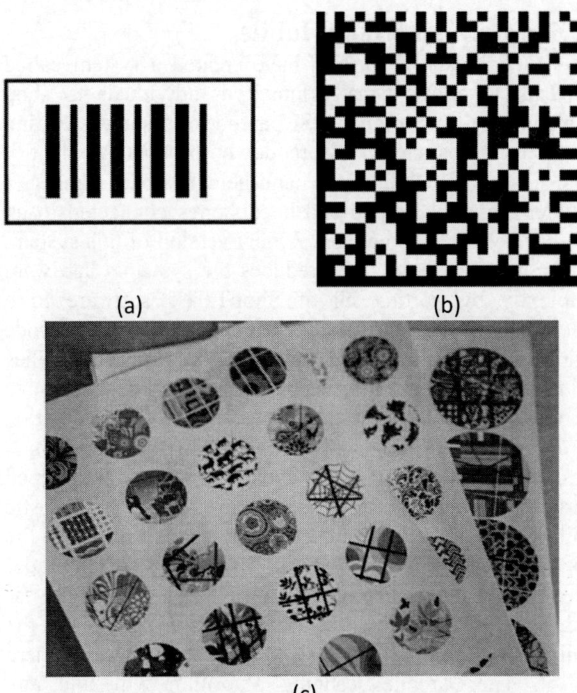

Figure 1. Visual tags for various tag-based systems: (a) Marker with 1D barcode (Badge3D[28]), (b) Semacode (Gude et al.[29]), (c) Printed vinyl stickers (LookTel[11] (©2011 IEEE))

3.1 Badge3D

Badge3D [28] is a relatively recent example of a tag-based system for the visually impaired that provides object recognition and obstacle detection capabilities. The tag in this case is a rectangular-shaped marker with a fixed, black band external boundary surrounding a single one dimensional barcode interior (Figure 1a). The system locates a tag in a captured image by detecting the outer black band using a Canny edge detector[29], extracts the barcode in its interior by applying various image processing techniques and identifies the object based on this barcode. This outer black band is also utilized for tracking the object and estimating its orientation relative to the camera.

The user wears a head-mounted video camera and sends queries to the system by speaking into a microphone while the system provides output to the user in the form of synthetic speech transmitted through headphones. When the user enters a new environment, the visual data from the video camera is used to determine which objects are in the user's surroundings based on their barcode tags. The user can query the system about a particular object and it can then guide him towards that object. Furthermore, untagged objects in the environment (which are considered obstacles in this case) can be detected by an ultrasound-based device mounted on the user's belt.

3.2 Shoptalk and ShopMobile

Nicholson et al. [30] have created a system called ShopTalk to allow visually impaired individuals to shop independently by scanning MSI barcodes on shelves to find product locations and UPC barcodes on products to identify them. This system utilizes a hand-held barcode scanner, a shoulder-mounted keypad and headphones connected to an ultra-portable OQO computer. A new version of this system, called ShopMobile [31, 32], reduces the system's hardware complexity by porting all of ShopTalk's software to a camera-equipped smartphone. The need for a barcode scanner is also obliterated since the system now relies exclusively on computer vision techniques to recognize barcodes (A detailed description of the barcode localization and decoding algorithm can be found in [33]). This system is still under development: it will consist of a camera-equipped smartphone enclosed in a hard case with two plastic stabilizers (≈ 10 cm long) inserted in to a small pocket at the back of the case (Figure 8). It will also have a screen reader and a screen magnifier as well as a wireless over-the-ear headpiece. In a supermarket aisle, the user will place the stabilizers on the lip of the shelf to align the phone's camera with it. The barcode scanning algorithm will find any barcodes in the camera images. If only a part of the barcode is visible, the system will ask the user to move the phone accordingly. Once the whole barcode is visible, it will be recognized and the product's identity would be transmitted to the user via the headpiece.

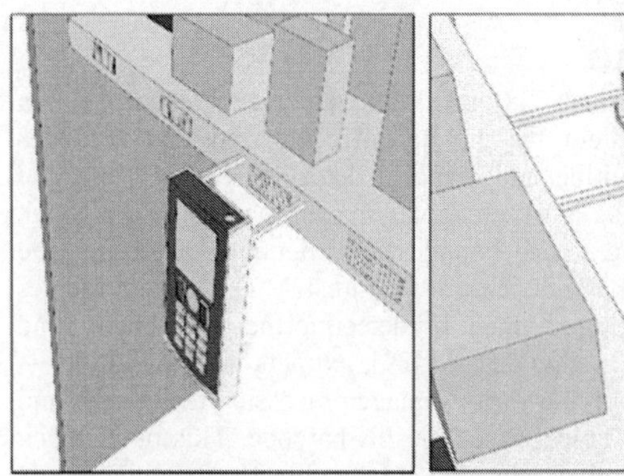

Figure 2. ShopMobile system consisting of a camera-equipped smart phone in a hard case with two plastic stabilizers [33]. (With kind permission of the Rehabilitation Engineering and Assistive Technology Society of North America (RESNA))

3.3 Trinetra

Lanigan et al. [5] have developed Trinetra, a system that assists the blind in identifying products in a grocery store. A product's barcode is scanned using a barcode scanning pencil and then sent via Bluetooth to a module on the user's mobile phone. This module checks a cache onboard the mobile phone and if a match for the product is not found, it communicates with a remote server which retrieves the product information either from a local cache or the online UPC database and sends it back to the mobile phone. A text-to-speech software on the phone converts the product information into speech which is relayed unobtrusively to the user via a Bluetooth headset. Their system's strength lies in that it is comprised entirely of commercial off-the-shelf (COTS) components and is thus, cost-effective and accessible.

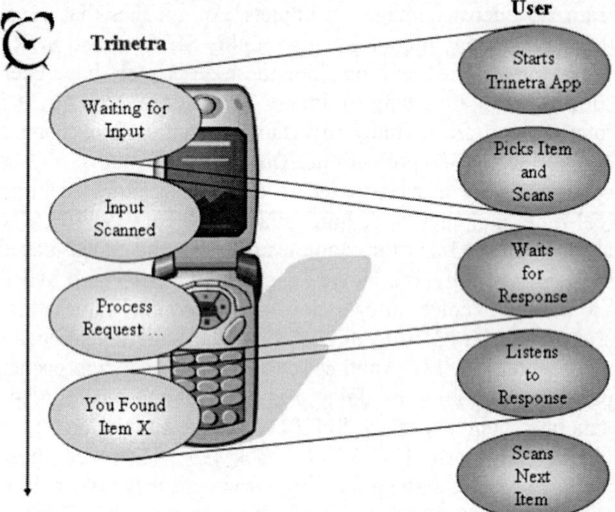

Figure 3. Mapping user actions to Trinetra [35]. (With kind permission of The Biological and Artificial Intelligence Foundation (BAIF))

3.4 Gude et al.'s approach

Gude et al. [34] have developed a prototype system for object recognition and navigation based on two-dimensional barcodes called Semacodes [35] (Figure 1b). The input to the system consists of video streams obtained through two video cameras, one embedded into the user's cane to detect tags placed on or near ground-level, and the other into the user's glasses to detect tags well above the ground-level. The Semacode reader may either be embedded into these cameras or it may be installed on a computer connected wirelessly to the cameras. The system provides output to the user via a tactile braille device mounted onto his cane. As the user walks around, video captured through the cameras is constantly processed and if any tags are

Table 1. Summary of computer vision-based object recognition approaches that use visual tags

Approach	Type of tag	Input device	Output device	User interface to enter queries/ preferences
Badge3D [28]	1D barcode with black rectangular boundary	Head-mounted video camera	Headphones	Microphone
ShopMobile [32, 33]	MSI and UPC barcodes	Smartphone camera	Wireless over-the-ear headpiece	Smartphone touchscreen
Trinetra [5]	UPC barcodes	Barcode scanning pencil	Bluetooth headset	Smartphone touchscreen
Gude et al. [29]	Semacodes	Head-mounted and cane-mounted video cameras	Cane-mounted tactile Braille device	-
Al-Khalifa [37]	QR codes	QR reader-equipped Mobile phone camera	Mobile phone speakers	-
LookTel [11]	1.5" or 3" round, re-stickable vinyl stickers with printed images	Smart phone camera	Open ear, sports-designed headset	Smartphone touchscreen
Tekin et al. [38]	UPC-A barcodes	Mobile phone video camera	Mobile phone speakers	-
TalkingTag™ LV (Low Vision) [40]	2D barcode	iPhone camera	iPhone speakers	iPhone touchscreen

detected, they are decoded by the software and the identity of the object is relayed to the user via the Braille device. Only a crude prototype of this system has been tested so far, which does not include the camera-embedded glasses. Furthermore, though they have suggested that the system can also be used for navigation purposes provided that the software is extended so that it also specifies the distance to the recognized objects, however, this capability has not been added to the system yet. Some preliminary tests showed that a camera embedded with a Semacode reader worked almost as well as a web camera connected to a laptop computer; this indicates the feasibility of utilizing cameras embedded with tag recognition software.

3.5 Al-Khalifa's approach

Al-Khalifa [36] proposes affixing QR codes (two-dimensional barcodes) to objects which can then be scanned using a mobile phone equipped with QR reader software. The reader decodes the barcode to a URL and directs the phone's browser to fetch an audio file containing a verbal description of the object from the internet which is then relayed to the user. The proposed system has not been implemented yet.

3.6 LookTel

A tagging option for object recognition is also included in LookTel [11] – a portable visual assistance system that allows a user to capture images of objects using a mobile device, such as a cellular phone, which are sent to a remote server where they are recognized based on the SIFT algorithm [8]. However, items with no clear distinguishing features (for example, clear glass jars or Tupperware containers) are not suitable for recognition by SIFT. These objects may be tagged with 1.5" or 3" round, re-stickable vinyl stickers with printed images produced by the developers for this purpose (Figure 1c). New tags with custom images may also be compiled by the users themselves. The system also affords navigation assistance: indoor locations can be added to the system as generic objects and the user can make his way through the environment by moving from one location to the other. Audio output is provided to the user via an open ear, sports-designed headset. A touch-based user interface has also been provided for the user to interact with the system. A major limitation of this system is that the recognition process is not fully automated since a sighted assistant has to help out with the training process.

3.7 Tekin et al.'s approach

Tekin et al. [37] have developed a mobile phone application that utilizes the phone's video camera to detect a UPC-A barcode in the scene in front of the user and then guides him to the detected barcode by providing audio feedback. The barcode digits are recognized using a Bayesian statistical approach and the resulting barcode is compared against a customizable user database as well as a manufacturers' database, which are stored on the phone, thus eliminating the need to access a remote server. If a match is found, product information is relayed to the user via the text-to-speech module on the phone. The application was tested on a Nokia N97 camera phone and suffered from the camera's erratic autofocus mechanism and the slow processing speed, problems which the developers assume would be ameliorated if the same application is run on newer generation devices such as the iPhone or Google Nexus One.

3.8 TalkingTag TM LV

We will wrap up our discussion about tag-based systems by mentioning a popular commercial product for recognizing visual tags available for iPhone [38] users: TalkingTag™ LV (Low Vision) [39] enables visually impaired people to label items with special coded stickers. Users can scan each sticker with their iPhone camera and record up to a one minute audio message identifying what is being labeled using the iPhone's VoiceOver feature. The message associated with a sticker can be erased and recorded over.

4. Conclusion

It should be noted that, despite their many merits, tag-based systems suffer from some inherent limitations: They require careful, a-priori selection of significant objects and the correct placement of tags on those objects and their use is restricted to surroundings where objects have been tagged. Also, if an area is heavily populated by tagged items, the user will be overwhelmed by receiving information about all those items simultaneously. Unlike RFID tags, visual tags have to be in line-of-sight of the camera, otherwise, they will not be detected. Furthermore, visual tags cannot be embedded in objects; the visibility of these tags may be unappealing from an aesthetic perspective. These approaches are also subject to the general difficulties faced by computer vision-based techniques in uncontrolled real-world environments due to imaging factors such as motion blur, image resolution, video noise, etc., as well as changes in conditions such as illumination, orientation and scale.

The above shortcomings notwithstanding, the systems described above, several of which are still proof-of-concept, have revealed the potential of utilizing visual tags for object recognition. These systems' universal reliance on commercial off-the-shelf components and mobile technology has rendered them cost-effective, portable, intuitive and thus, compelling solutions to an urgent problem. However, the following issues need to be addressed if these technologies are to be developed into practical solutions which can be used autonomously by the visually impaired: one major concern, which none of the above approaches explicitly addresses, is how to enable a user, who does not have the advantage of sight, to locate the visual tag and align it with the camera. The only exception is Al-Khalifa [36], who suggests putting a Braille marker on the QR code; this solution might work well for a limited number of objects but not, for instance, for general grocery items, unless product manufacturers start putting such markers on the barcodes. ShopMobile [31, 32] partially addresses this issue by providing stabilizers to align the phone's camera with the supermarket shelf while Tekin et al. [37] provide audio feedback to guide a user to a detected barcode; however, the assumption in both cases is that the barcode will be located on the front of the product which is not necessarily true. Also, though the prevalence of 1D and 2D barcodes as a means of identifying commercial products is not likely to diminish in the near future, however, the proliferation of other tags such as RFID tags, which do not suffer from the same limitations as visual tags (i.e., these are omnidirectional, can be embedded in objects, are reprogrammable, hold more product information, etc.) indicates the sagacity of augmenting visual tag-based systems with the capability to recognize these non-visual tags to produce a more robust solution capable of recognizing objects based on both kinds of tags. Some systems such as Trinetra [40] and BlindShopping [41] have already taken a step in this direction by incorporating RFID-based recognition modules into their systems.

Acknowledgements

The authors extend their appreciation to the Deanship of Scientific Research at King Saud University for partially funding the work through the research group project number RGP-VPP-157.

References

[1] D. Pascolini and S. P. Mariotti, "Global estimates of visual impairment: 2010," *British Journal Ophthalmology,* 2011.

[2] "Elimination of Avoidable Blindness Report by the Secretariat," World Health Organisation, Fifty-sixth World Health Assembly 2003.

[3] "Visual impairment and blindness: Fact sheet number 282. http://www.who.int/mediacentre/factsheets/fs282/en/," ed: WHO media center, 2012.

[4] A. Leibs, "Top 10 iPhone Apps for the Visually Impaired". Avaialable online: " http://assistivetechnology.about.com/od/ATCAT6/tp/Top-10-Iphone-Apps-For-The-Visually-Impaired.htm".

[5] P. E. Lanigan, A. M. Paulos, A. W. Williams, D. Rossi, and P. Narasimhan, "Trinetra: Assistive Technologies for Grocery Shopping for the Blind," *10th IEEE International Symposium on Wearable Computers,* pp. 147-148, Oct 11-14 2006.

[6] A. Hub, T. Hartter, and T. Ertl, "Interactive tracking of movable objects for the blind on the basis of environment models and perception-oriented object recognition methods," in *Proceedings of the 8th international ACM SIGACCESS conference on Computers and accessibility*, Portland, Oregon, USA, 2006, pp. 111-118.

[7] Y. Kawai and F. Tomita, "A Support System for Visually Impaired Persons to Understand Three-dimensional Visual Information Using Acoustic Interface," *Proceedings of the 16 th International Conference on Pattern Recognition (ICPR'02),* vol. 3, pp. 974-977, 2002.

[8] D. G. Lowe, "Object recognition from local scale-invariant features," *The Seventh IEEE International Conference on Computer Vision, 1999,* pp. 1150-1157 20-27 September 1999.

[9] H. Bay, A. Ess, T. Tuytelaars, and L. V. Gool, "Speeded-Up Robust Features (SURF)," *Comput. Vis. Image Underst.,* vol. 110, pp. 346-359, 2008.

[10] J. Bauer, N. S¨underhauf, and P. Protzel, "Comparing Several Implementations of Two Recently Published Feature Detectors," in *Proc. of the International Conference on Intelligent and Autonomous Systems*, Toulouse, France, 2007.

[11] J. Sudol, O. Dialameh, C. Blanchard, and T. Dorcey, "Looktel—A comprehensive platform for computer-aided visual assistance," in *IEEE Computer Society Conference on Computer Vision and Pattern Recognition Workshops (CVPRW)*, San Francisco, CA, 2010, pp. 73-80.

[12] B. Schauerte, M. Martinez, A. Constantinescu, and R. Stiefelhagen, "An Assistive Vision System for the Blind That Helps Find Lost Things," in *Computers Helping People with Special Needs*. vol. 7383, K. Miesenberger, A. Karshmer, P. Penaz, and W. Zagler, Eds., ed: Springer Berlin Heidelberg, 2012, pp. 566-572.

[13] R. Chincha and Y. Tian, "Finding objects for blind people based on SURF features," in *2011 IEEE International Conference on Bioinformatics and Biomedicine Workshops*, 2011, pp. 526-527.

[14] T. Winlock, E. Christiansen, and S. Belongie, "Toward real-time grocery detection for the visually impaired," in *Computer Vision Applications for the Visually Impaired (CVAVI)*, San Francisco, CA, 2010.

[15] J. Bigham, C. Jayant, A. Miller, B. White, and T. Yeh, "VizWiz::LocateIt - enabling blind people to locate objects in their environment," in *3rd Workshop on Computer Vision Applications for the Visually Impaired (CVAVI 10)*, San Francisco, California, 2010.

[16] W. Fink, M. Tarbell, J. Weiland, and M. Humayun, "DORA: Digital Object Recognition Audio–Assistant For The Visually Impaired," ed: NSF, 2004.

[17] R. Parlouar, F. Dramas, M. M.-J. Mace, and C. Jouffrais, "Assistive device for the blind based on object recognition: an application to identify currency bills," *Proceedings of the 11th international ACM SIGACCESS conference on Computers and accessibility,* pp. 227-228, 2009.

[18] B. D. C. Martinez, O. O. V. Villegas, V. G. C. Sanchez, H. D. J. O. Dominguez, and L. O. Maynez, "Visual perception substitution by the auditory sense," *Proceedings of the 2011 International Conference on Computational science and its Applications - Volume Part II,* pp. 522-533, 2011.

[19] R. Nagarajan, S. Yaacob, and G. Sainarayanan, "Role of object identification in sonification system for visually impaired," *Conference on Convergent Technologies for Asia-Pacific Region (TENCON 2003),* vol. 2, pp. 735-739, 15-17 October 2003.

[20] P. Bach-y-Rita, M. E. Tyler, and K. A. Kaczmarek, "Seeing with the brain," *International Journal of Human-Computer Interaction,* vol. 15, pp. 285–295, 2003.

[21] D. Dakopoulos, S. K. Boddhu, and N. Bourbakis, "A 2D Vibration Array as an Assistive Device for Visually Impaired," in *7th IEEE International Conference on Bioinformatics and Bioengineering, (BIBE 2007)*, Boston, MA, 2007, pp. 930- 937

[22] D. Dakopoulos, "TYFLOS: A wearable navigation prototype for blind and visually impaired; design, modelling and experimental results," Ph.D. Dissertation, Computer Science and Engineering, Wright State University, 2009.

[23] S. Akhter, J. Mirsalahuddin, F. B. Marquina, S. Islam, and S. Sareen, "A Smartphone-based Haptic Vision Substitution system for the blind," in *2011 IEEE 37th Annual Northeast Bioengineering Conference (NEBEC)*, Fairfax, VA, USA, 2011, pp. 1-2.

[24] M. Murad, A. Rehman, A. A. Shah, S. Ullah, M. Fahad, and K. M. Yahya, "RFAIDE – An RFID Based Navigation and Object Recognition Assistant for Visually Impaired People," in *7th International Conference on Emerging Technologies (ICET)*, Islamabad, Pakistan, 2011, pp. 1-4.

[25] M. A. Lawson, E. Y.-L. Do, J. R. Marston, and D. A. Ross, "Helping Hands versus ERSP Vision: Comparing object recognition technologies for the visually impaired," *HCI International 2011,* pp. 383-388, 9-14 July 2011.

[26] "Bay Advanced Technologies Ltd. (http://www.batforblind.co.nz/).".

[27] W. Crandall, J. Brabyn, B. L. Bentzen, and L. Myers, "Remote infrared signage evaluation for transit stations and intersections," *J Rehabil Res Dev.,* vol. 4, pp. 341-55, 1999.

[28] G. Iannizzotto, C. Costanzo, P. Lanzafame, and F. L. Rosa, "Badge3D for Visually Impaired," presented at the The 2005 IEEE Computer Society Conference on Computer Vision and Pattern Recognition (CVPR'05) - Workshops, 2005.

[29] J. F. Canny, "A computational approach to edge detection," in *Readings in computer vision: issues, problems, principles, and paradigms*, A. F. Martin and F. Oscar, Eds., ed: Morgan Kaufmann Publishers Inc., 1987, pp. 184-203.

[30] J. Nicholson, V. Kulyukin, and D. Coster, "ShopTalk: independent blind shopping through verbal route

directions and barcode scans," *The Open Rehabilitation Journal,* vol. 2, pp. 11-23, 2009.

[31] V. Kulyukin and A. Kutiyanawala, "Eyes-free barcode localization and decoding for visually impaired mobile phone users," *The 2010 International Conference on Image Processing, Computer Vision, and Pattern Recognition,* July 12-15 2010.

[32] V. Kulyukin and A. Kutiyanawala, "From ShopTalk to ShopMobile: vision-based barcode scanning with mobile phones for independent blind grocery shopping," *The 33-rd Annual Conference of the Rehabilitation Engineering and Assistive Technology Society of North America,* June 2010.

[33] A. Kutiyanawala and V. Kulyukin, "An Eyes-free vision-based UPC and MSI barcode localization and decoding algorithm for mobile phones," *Envision 2010,* 2010.

[34] R. Gude, M. Østerby, and S. Soltveit, "Blind Navigation and Object Recognition," Laboratory for Computational Stochastics, University of Aarhus, Denmark.

[35] "Semacode Corporation. http://semacode.com/about/."

[36] H. Al-Khalifa, "Utilizing QR code and mobile phones for blinds and visually impaired people," *Computers Helping People with Special Needs,* pp. 1065-1069, 2008.

[37] E. Tekin and J. M. Coughlan, "A mobile phone application enabling visually impaired users to find and read product barcodes," in *Proceedings of the 12th international conference on Computers helping people with special needs*, Vienna, Austria, 2010, pp. 290-295.

[38] "Apple Inc. http://www.apple.com/iphone/."

[39] "Perkins Products: TalkingTag LV multi-purpose voice labels. https://secure2.convio.net/psb/site/Ecommerce/352707661?VIEW_PRODUCT=true&product_id=6862&store_id=1101."

[40] P. E. Lanigan, A. M. Paulos, A. W. Williams, D. Rossi, and P. Narasimhan, "Trinetra: Assistive Technologies for Grocery Shopping for the Blind," *IEEE-BAIS Symposium on Research in Assistive Technologies,* April 2007.

[41] D. López-de-Ipiña, T. Lorido, and A. U. López, "Blindshopping: enabling accessible shopping for visually impaired people through mobile technologies," *Proceedings of the 9th International Conference on Toward Useful Services for Elderly and People with Disabilities: Smart homes and Health telematics,* pp. 266-270, 2011.

On Feature Extraction for Fingerprinting Grapevine Leaves

Dominik L. Michels
Institute of Computer Science II
University of Bonn
Germany
michels@uni-bonn.de

Sven A. Giesselbach, Thomas Werner, and Volker Steinhage
Institute of Computer Science III
University of Bonn
Germany
steinhag@cs.uni-bonn.de

Abstract—**Within the scope of CROP.SENSe.net, an interdisciplinary research network of Bonn University and the Jülich Research Centre, we work on a new model-based approach to the phenotyping of grapevine. Our algorithm performs a robust extraction of different features from a given leaf image, like specific points of the vein network, the vein network itself, and different distances respectively angles between special features. For that we present robust methods, like a template based method to extract the peduncle point, a detection strategy to determine end points of leaf veins, and a Gabor filter-based directional edge tracing procedure to extract the network. The extracted features are fed into a support vector machine in order to realize a full automatic sufficient variety identification.**

Keywords*—*Cultivar Classification, Feature Detection, Vein Extraction, Gabor Filters, Support Vector Machines

I. Introduction

Population growth, climate change, and the shortage of resources have caused an increased global interest of the agricultural community in intelligent farming methods. As a result, the integration of agricultural concepts and modern IT has paved the way for tremendous crop yield increases over the last decade. Dedicated robots for farm working, usually four-wheeled vehicles with robot manipulators, have been developed as part of the smart farming process. Equipped with recent satellite and sensor technologies they are able to autonomously navigate through vineyards, corn- or strawberry fields and at the same time take over the sowing and harvesting work of the agricultural laborer. Exhausted, depleted, and pesticide contaminated soils, on the other hand, reveal the disastrous consequences of the long-term use of classical monocrops and force modern agriculture more and more to embark on whole system approaches like sustainable agriculture, integrated farming, and permacultures, i.e. well-designed agriculturally productive ecosystems with the diversity, long-term stability, and synergistic properties of natural ecosystems. This poses new requirements for the autonomous harvesting vehicles: it is mandatory to furnish them with robust identification mechanisms that ensure a correct plant recognition by means of their phenotypic characteristics. Consequently, non-destructive approaches to the problem of computer aided analysis and screening of plant phenotypes have experienced a growing interest in the crop science community over the last decade. Matured computer vision techniques are employed for an automated plant recognition by means of the vein networks of their leaves which act as a unique classifier–a kind of fingerprint–for a specific cultivar.

In our contribution we tackle the challenging problem of extracting different features of vine leaves in order to classify them. The reason for focussing on vine leaves is that the perennial vinegrape is one of the oldest and most important crop plants in human history and the automated classification of cultivars of vinegrapes is still an important and challenging topic. The extracted data is used as a fingerprint for a certain cultivar and can thus be used as input for support vector machines to perform the final classification. We evaluate the robustness of our method on a test set consisting of vine leave images with different color patterns.

II. Related Work

Leaf feature extraction and cultivar classification is a well-established field in the computer vision and machine learning community. In this section we give a brief overview over the recent achievements.

In [1] the authors present a leaf vein extraction method based on the gray-scale morphology. An independent component analysis is used in [2] to realize a robust vein extraction method.

A leaf recognition algorithm based upon probabilistic neural networks is presented in [3]. Their approach allows for a robust plant classification. In contrast, the method described in [4] makes use of region-based features. A completely different approach is presented in [5] where the authors discuss an ant colony algorithm.

In contrast to these methods the authors of [6] aim to exploit knowledge from the position space on the first hand and extend it with information from the frequency domain in order to extract the different leaf veins. This is achieved on the firm basis of appropriate Gabor filters.

Our goal is to perform an automated classification of cultivars of vinegrapes. For that reason we have to extract different features, which can be seen as a fingerprint of specific cultivars. The specific contributions of the work presented here are as follows:

- Robust strategies to extract several cultivar specific features are developed.

- The influence of the different features on the classification rate is evaluated.
- An automated feature extraction and cultivar classification system for different grapevine cultivars is presented.
- The efficiency of our approach is demonstrated on a test set containing 30 images of vine leaves of different cultivars, specifically Müller-Thurgau, Muscat Blanc, Pinot Noir, Regent, and Riesling. The images show diverse characteristics like overlapping parts, handwritten labels, and severe discolorations, e.g. due to leaf diseases.

III. Problem Setting

To realize a successful classification of several grapevine leaves, we have to develop a collection of robust techniques in order to extract the needed features. Therefore, during the feature extraction procedures, we search for the peduncle point of the network, trace veins, determine end points, and measure lengths and angles. In this context, the following features are of interest:

(1) **Compactnesses**: The ratio of leaf border and area as defined in the formula given by B^2/A, in which B denotes the number of pixels at the border and A the number of pixels contained in the whole leaf including the border.
(2) **Exterior Angles**: The angles between the horizontal main vein and the other four veins.
(3) **Length Ratios**: The distances between the peduncle point and the vein end points in relation to the length of the corresponding main veins.
(4) **Vein Contours**: The contours of the main veins sampled with a chain code of length 10. The number of main veins, the so called veins of level zero, is always 5 in the case of the considered grapevine leaves, cf. Fig. (1).

The choice to take these specific features is well founded due to the fact, that these have become established phenotypic fingerprints recorded by the *International Plant Genetic Resources Institute*, cf. [7]. The extraction shall be performed automatically on an input image.

In our classification, the most challenging extraction procedure, is the detection of the vein contours. In this context, it is important to note that we exploit the fact that the phenotypical appearance of vine leaves always shows five level zero veins. These veins have a common start point–the so called peduncle point of the leaf as denoted above–and well-defined endpoints. The major problem we have to deal with is that the difference in the intensities of the level zero veins and their higher order branches is not large enough to prevent a standard vein detection algorithm from spuriously changing its tracing direction from the principal to a secondary direction at the branch-offs. Beside this level zero veins typically tend to become smaller with increasing distance from the peduncle point. As a consequence, it is difficult to distinguish between veins of different levels. This in turn promotes erroneous classifications of the vein levels. Because of that, we make use of an adaptive Gabor filter-based approach to overcome this problem.

IV. Robust Feature Extraction

In the following we briefly describe the extraction of the features specified above.

Fig. 1: Illustration of different level veins colored in blue (level 0), red (level 1), and yellow (level 2). A vein emanating from a level n vein is of level $n+1$.

The compactness is directly computed from the border, which is in the case of our test images easy to detect, because the background clearly differs from the leaf. Hence, our method just has to check the different intensities. Since we only use the lines between the peduncle point and the end points to determine the exterior angles and length ratios, this is trivial to compute after the detection of the specific points. Therefore, we go on with the description of a matching strategy and a radial search procedure in order to determine the feature points. After that, we give a brief overview over the contour extraction of the five main veins using a Gabor filter-based method.

A. Feature Point Detection

In order to determine the position of the peduncle point and the end points of the level zero veins we use some observations about the border of vine leafs. We divide each leaf in five areas called lobes. These lobes are defined such that every lobe contains exactly one of the five level zero veins. The end points of the level zero veins represent a local distance maximum of the border pixels of the corresponding lobe to the peduncle point of the leaf. A local distance minimum of the border pixels between two neighboring level zero veins to the peduncle point defines the border between two neighboring lobes. Each lobe is thus defined by two local minima and a local maximum of the border pixels.

Since the peduncle point is unknown at the start of the computation, we approximate it by calculating the barycenter of the leaf segment. Therefore, we preprocess the leaf segment by converting it into a binary image which separates background pixels from leaf pixels (threshold at minimum) and close small holes in the leaf-segment with a dilatation of the segment that does not affect the border pixels. After that, we extract the border pixels by applying an edge detecting algorithm.

Now we build our first hypothesis for the lobes. Therefore, we search for a global distance minimum from the border pixels to the barycenter. This point should separate two lobes. A vector is spanned from this position to the barycenter and rotated around it with an angle of 80°, which has been determined to be most precise for locating local minima by an evaluation over the whole dataset. In addition to the rotation angle a tolerance angle of 20° has been determined accordingly, which is used such that the next local minimum is searched from the previous local minimum in an area of rotating angle minus tolerance angle to rotating angle plus tolerance angle for the iterative detection of the remaining local minima. The leaf border between neighboring local minima is now examined for local maxima and represents the hypothesis for a level zero vein end point. Because the local maxima have a more distinct peculiarity, they are used to correct the local minima hypothesis. For that the local minimum between two neighboring local maxima is detected.

Now that we have created a first estimate for the local minima, maxima, the peduncle point and thus the lobes, we are able to determine a more precise approximation of the peduncle point. This is achieved by considering another property of the vine leaves: The angle between two hypothetical neighboring level zero veins is largest for the two level zero veins which enclose the peduncle point. Calculating the angles between the vectors from the barycenter to two neighboring local maxima hence allows us to order the local maxima clockwise and to determine the local maximum which represents the end point of the horizontal level zero vein. This vein can be used to orientate the leafs in the context of the vein extraction procedure. The exact position of the peduncle point is detected by using a template matching strategy. To find an appropriate template, the area around the peduncle point has been extracted of all images and all templates have been evaluated against each other in a way that the template has been chosen as best, which gives the best worst case performance. The template contains the peduncle point and the unique structure of the five level zero veins around it. For the template matching procedure the leaves are preprocessed with a Gaussian filter, histogram linearization and anisotropic filtering. This causes the level zero veins to be emphasized by dark pixels on the leaf structure, while the veins of higher level become more indistinct of the leaf surface, highlighting the unique features of the peduncle point. The area which is to be searched is bounded by a mean radius r with variance σ computed from the determined end point hypothesis around the barycenter and a vertical margin y orthogonal to the orientation of the vector from the peduncle point to the local maxima hypothesis for the horizontal level zero vein, cf. Fig. (2).

Radius and margin have been determined by measurements over the whole dataset. A bounding of rotation angles has been achieved by taking into account the mean average deviance of the orientation from the above mentioned vector to the horizontal level zero vein. The leaf image has also been scaled to fit the size of the leaf from which the template was taken under the assumption that the vein width is proportional to the leaf size. With these restrictions the template matching is finally being applied to determine the area of highest

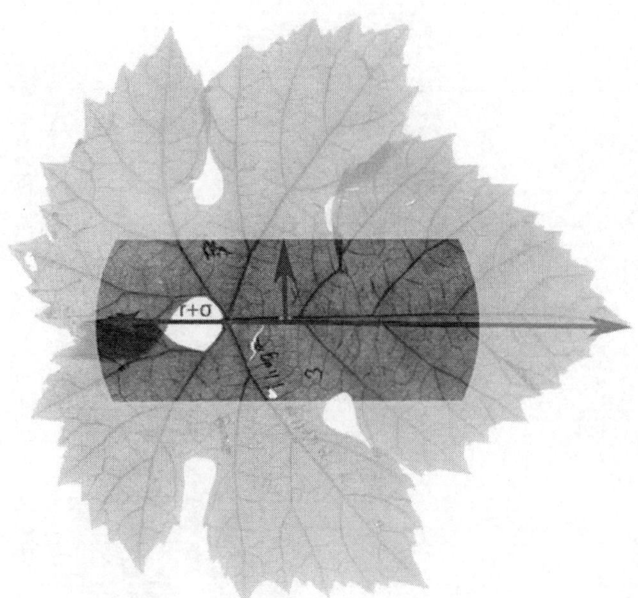

Fig. 2: Illustration of the area space limitation in order to reduce the costs of the template matching procedure.

correlation between the image and the template. This area should represent the area around the peduncle point which has to be the center of the area according to the template. In the case that the ex ante determined angles between two local maxima are not significantly large enough to determine a precise angle maximum and thus the horizontal level zero vein, a slightly different approach is used. In this case the image is preprocessed and scaled as described above. Since we do not know the horizontal vein, we rotate the leaf into the vector from the barycenter to each hypothetical local maximum once. For each orientation we restrict the area space as described above. The angle space is now chosen to be significantly smaller. This is illustrated in Fig. (3).

Template Matching is used to determine the orientation in which the correlation between the template and the image is the highest. The leaf should now be oriented in direction of the horizontal level zero vein because of the properties of the template and we can declare the associated local maximum as the one which belongs to the horizontal vein. After that the template matching procedure is used again but in the same way as described for the case where the horizontal vein is known to finally determine the peduncle point. Using our rotation based search to determine local minima, the hypothetical barycenter is better than from the hypothetical speduncle point since the local minima are arranged around the center of the leaf segment which is closer to the barycenter. Thus we use the first uncorrected hypothesis of local minima from the barycenter to create our final hypothesis about the local minima and maxima. Again the local maxima are searched between two neighboring local minima. But this time the maxima are measured as distance to the peduncle point instead of the barycenter. Then the local minima are corrected by calculating them as local

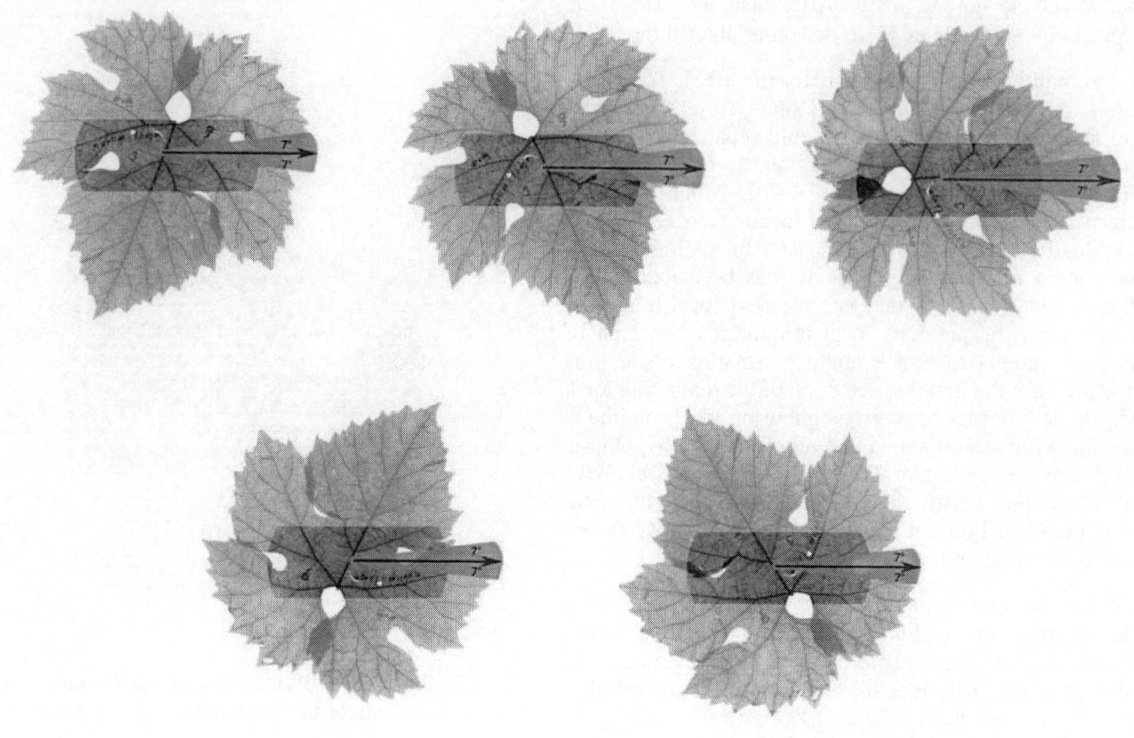

Fig. 3: Illustration of the reduced angle space. The leaf is rotated into the vector from the barycenter to each local maximum hypothesis once. A rotation tolerance angle of 7° has been determined to be most precise by an evaluation over the whole dataset.

minima from the peduncle point in between two neighboring local maxima. By using this technique, our method determ all needed feature points.

B. Vein Extraction

In order to overcome the aforementioned problems in the context of vein extraction, we make use of a Gabor filter-based approach as introduced and successfully applied in [6]. This allow us to exploit knowledge from the position space as well as from the frequency domain in order to extract the different leaf veins.

Appropriate transformations to the frequency domain allow us to study the frequency information of a time dependent phenomenon. In the one-dimensional, continuous case such a transformation is given by the well-known Fourier transform which maps the signal f in the time domain to the transformed version $\mathcal{F}[f]$ in the frequency domain. This transformation is represented by a scalar product in the functional space with the arguments f and a complex exponential with frequency ω. Hence, $\mathcal{F}[f](\omega)$ can be considered as the complex amplitude of the occurrence of the fundamental oscillation with frequency ω in the signal f. But there is no time domain information available in $\mathcal{F}[f]$. Since we are interested in a combination of time and frequency information, it is a common method to add a τ-shifted time domain window function g to the first argument of the scalar product in the sense of a multiplication with the signal f. Therefore, the resulting so called windowed or short-time Fourier transform

$$\mathcal{F}_g[f](\omega,\tau) = \int_{\mathbb{R}} f(t)\, g(t-\tau)\, \exp(-2\pi i \omega t)\, dt,$$

describes the frequency behavior of the signal f in the time domain neighborhood of τ. The transformation $\mathcal{G}[f] := \mathcal{F}_{g_\sigma}[f]$ with the Gaussian window function $g_\sigma(\cdot)$ with variance σ is known as the Gabor transformation of the signal f and shows how much of the signal f limited to $t \in [\tau-\sigma, \tau+\sigma]$ matches a given frequency.

We make use of the two-dimensional analogon: the Gabor filter G_θ with orientation θ, formally given by

$$G_\theta(\mathbf{x}) = \exp\left(-\frac{\hat{x}_1^2 + \gamma^2 \hat{x}_2^2}{2\sigma^2}\right) \cos\left(\frac{2\pi}{\lambda}\hat{x}_1 + \psi\right),$$

at the point $\mathbf{x} = (x_1, x_2)^\mathsf{T}$. The left factor describes a two-dimensional elliptic Gaussian in which the spatial aspect ratio γ denotes the ellipticity. The variance is given by σ and the direction is determined by the angle θ of the normal direction that influences the vector $\hat{\mathbf{x}} = \mathbf{R}_\theta \mathbf{x}$, in which $\mathbf{R}_\theta$ describes the two-dimensional mathematically negative rotation by the angle θ. The right factor is given by a cosine function with wavelength λ and phase shift ψ. G_θ is applied to an image F by using the two-dimensional convolution $F \otimes G_\theta$.

The main idea behind this approach is that for a given angle θ a θ-oriented vein of order zero will always dominate the Gabor filter response in contrast to the higher order veins

#	Feature	Poly 1	Poly 2	Poly 3	Poly 4	RBF	AVG
1	Compactnesses	0.50	0.47	0.47	0.40	0.40	0.45
2	Exterior Angles	0.47	0.53	0.43	0.50	0.40	0.47
3	Length Ratios	0.53	0.47	0.30	0.33	0.43	0.41
4	Vein Contours	0.47	0.60	0.50	0.47	0.30	0.47
1-4	Collectivity	0.70	0.67	**0.80**	0.73	0.37	0.66

TABLE I: Overview of the cross validation results by using different kernel functions, specifically polynomials 1-4 and a radial basis function.

that branch off. We exploit this fact by tracing the course of the veins on $F \otimes G_\theta$. This motivates the following algorithm: Starting at the peduncle point found by the procedure described above, the algorithm traces the course of the veins by comparing the intensity values. Only the red channel is used, since the contrast between the veins and the other parts of the leaf is significantly improved, because leaf pigments consist of the green chlorophyll and the different reddish-brown carotenes. During the tracing procedure the algorithm keeps track of the curvature of the vein. The curvature is defined as slope of the secant of the last five percent of the main vein with respect to the estimated total length of the detected vein. A simple heuristic is used to indicate when the algorithm is about to leave the exact course of the main vein: if the ratio of the difference of the current and the last curvature and that of the last three curvature differences is greater than ten percent the algorithm jumps back to the location where the curvature has changed and applies the Gabor filter to the red channel again. Since the Gabor filter is fed with the angle θ–computed from the curvature values–of the direction of the current subsection of the vein, it is guaranteed that all subsections of veins with this particular direction will be visible in the filter response while other directions are masked. Therefore, the course of the vein is traced on the filter response $F \otimes G_\theta$ and not on the original image. It should be clear that when the curvature and therefore the angle of the current subsection of the vein under consideration changes "too much" the filter response must be recomputed. The procedure is stopped when the border of the leaf is reached, which is easily detected because of the high contrast between the background and the leaf image.

The main veins typically become thinner as their distance from the peduncle point increases. The method accounts for this fact by adapting the wavelength and the variance parameters λ and σ of the Gabor filter through interpolation from the intensity values of the original image in the area where–based on the last curvature values–the next part of the vein is expected. In contrast to the wavelength and the variance, the influence of the spatial aspect ratio γ and the phase shift ψ can be regarded as global. Thus, we work with a constant aspect ratio and ignore the phase shift.

V. Evaluation and Results

Our feature extraction algorithm has been implemented in a vine leaf classification system written in Java. The different feature extraction procedures are carried out for the final classification of a given input leaf image. The test set consists of 30 images of vine leaves of different cultivars, specifically Müller-Thurgau, Muscat Blanc, Pinot Noir, Regent, and Riesling, which are taken in the context of the competence network for phenotyping science CROP.SENSe.net. Only in two case, the detection of the feature points fails because of a large shadow cast. Vein extraction fails in three cases, because of strong deformations and a large gap. The majority of complicating characteristics can be handled confidently, like overlapping parts and handwritten labels, and even distinct discolorations.

For the classification, the features are stored in a vector and fed into a support vector machine. Cross validations with different kernel functions are performed, whose results are shown in Tab. (I). It can clearly be seen, that the influence of the the different features is equally large. Hence we perform a second cross validation, in which we make use of all four features with equal weights. All in all we end up with a success rates of up to 80% in the case of a polynomial 3 kernel function for the whole classification.

In our implementation we embark on the WEKA SVM (cf. [8]). The classification of a single leaf took about 3 sec on a 3.20 GHz Intel Core i7-3930K, 32 GB RAM, under Microsoft Windows 7. The input images have been used in a downscaled resolution of 400×400 pixels, because there was no significant difference in the success rate compared to the larger scaled images.

A. Conclusion and Future Work

We have introduced robust extraction techniques for the detection of feature points and leaf veins. This was demonstrated on a set of grapevine leaves, at which the presented methods handled overlapping parts, handwritten labels, and discolorations. However, problems can still occur in the case of gaps. In addition a classification of different grapevine varieties was performed and works correct in up to 80% of all test cases. The classification system can be used efficiently, since a identification of a varieties can be carried out in 3 sec.

Our future work focuses on generalizing the presented approach to other cultivars with different phenotypical characteristics in the leaves to overcome the current restriction to vine leaves.

Acknowledgments.

Our sincere thanks are due to the many people who were involved in the competence network for phenotyping science CROP.SENSe.net. This project is funded by the German Federal Ministry of Education and Research (BMBF) within the scope of the competitive grants program Networks of excellence in agricultural and nutrition research (Funding code: 0315529) and from the European Union Funds for regional development (Funding code: z1011bc001a).

REFERENCES

[1] X. Zheng and X. Wang, "Leaf vein extraction based on gray-scale morphology," *International Journal of Image, Graphics and Signal Processing*, vol. 2, pp. 25–31, 2010.

[2] Y. Li, Z. Chi, and D. D. Feng, "Leaf vein extraction using independent component analysis," in *Systems, Man and Cybernetics, 2006. SMC '06. IEEE International Conference on*, vol. 5, 2006, pp. 3890–3894.

[3] S. Wu, F. Bao, E. Xu, Y.-X. Wang, Y.-F. Chang, and Q.-L. Xiang, "A leaf recognition algorithm for plant classification using probabilistic neural network," in *Signal Processing and Information Technology, 2007 IEEE International Symposium on*, dec. 2007, pp. 11 –16.

[4] C.-L. Lee and S.-Y. Chen, "Classification of leaf images," *International Journal of Imaging Systems and Technology*, vol. 16, no. 1, pp. 15–23, 2006. [Online]. Available: http://dx.doi.org/10.1002/ima.20063

[5] J. S. Cope, P. Remagnino, S. Barman, and P. Wilkin, "The extraction of venation from leaf images by evolved vein classifiers and ant colony algorithms," in *ACIVS (1)*, 2010, pp. 135–144.

[6] D. L. Michels and G. A. Sobottka, "A Gabor Filter-Based Approach to Leaf Vein Extraction and Cultivar Classification," in *Proceedings of the ICCSA 2013, Ho Chi Minh City, Vietnam published by Springer in Lecture Notes in Computer Science*, 2013.

[7] I. P. G. R. Institute, *Descriptors for Grapevine: (Vitis Spp.).*, ser. Descriptors IBPGRI. International Plant Genetic Resources Institute, 1997. [Online]. Available: http://books.google.de/books?id=FgyqPvwqErcC

[8] WEKA 3, "Data Mining with Open Source Machine Learning Software in Java." [Online]. Available: http://www.cs.waikato.ac.nz/~ml/weka/index.html

Improved Shadow Removal for Unstructured Road Detection

Ngouh Njikam Ahmed Salim, Xu Cheng, Degui Xiao
College of Information Science and Engineering, Hunan University, Changsha, P.R.China

Abstract - *One of the greatest challenges for vision-based road detection is the presence of shadows and other vehicles. It's particularly challenging to detect unstructured road when it has both shadowed and non shadowed area since the presence of shadows can cause hindrance and shape distortion of objects which may result in false detection of road. Shadows can also cause a significant problem in road detection since shadow boundaries may be incorrectly recognized or simply hinder the road detection process leading to a higher false rate detection. To tackle those issues, this paper introduces an effective road recognition system using an image processing method to eliminate or reduce considerably the presence of strong shadows for unstructured road detection. Our method's main novelties are the use of a simple and effective shadow detection and removal algorithm using bilateral filter combined with a model-based classifier. Shadows are detected using normalized difference index and subsequent thresholding based on Otsu's thresholding method. After the image-preprocessing step used for shadow removal, illumination invariant of road is estimated and a road probability map is calculated to determine whether or not each pixel belongs to road surface. Extensive experiments are carried out and the results show that our method effectively detect unstructured road areas while being robust to strong shadows and illumination variations. It's also important to note that the proposed algorithm does not depend on temporal restrictions and is invariant to road shape.*

Keywords: *Shadow detection, thresholding, road segmentation*

1 Introduction

Road detection is an important aspect of autonomous vehicle navigation system. For those autonomous vehicles to properly navigate on road, the roads must first be detected and the proper road and non-road area must be located for generating paths while avoiding any obstacles. Shadow detection and removal has also become an important research area in computer vision and image processing. This paper focuses on vision-based road detection, that is detecting the road surface ahead of the experimental vehicle using an onboard camera. In order to render our algorithm robust to the presence of illumination or strong shadows, an image preprocessing technique is first performed to eliminate the shadow. The presence of shadows can reduce a great deal the successful rate of road detection and extraction, therefore it is necessary to eliminate the shadow then restore the image before performing the task of road detection in an unstructured urban area. Several road detection systems have been developed so far to address the topic of unstructured road segmentation [1], [2], [3], [4], [5]. Those methods are mainly based on road model, road features and the combination of the fore mentioned both methods. The method based on road features uses texture information between the road region and the non-road region [6]. However, this kind of methods while having the advantage of being insensitive to road shapes, are very sensitive to illumination, strong shadows and are really time consuming. The detection systems based on road model usually detect road edges using gradient operators [7]. Those systems detect road edges quickly but have a stronger response to the change of road surface feature and shadow edges.

A simple and efficient algorithm for unstructured road detection using an improved shadow removal method is proposed in this paper. The paper addresses the problem of the presence of illumination or strong shadows and is structured in two main parts: the first part which is shadow detection and removal and the second part which describes the overall road segmentation process while avoiding the use of road shape feature as part of our algorithm. What's more, as a novelty, we propose the use of a simple shadow detection and removal method [8] as part of our road detection process to avoid the difficulties with noisy or cluttered road edges sometimes also caused by the presence of strong shadows. Prior to shadow removal process it first has to be detected. The shadow is first detected using Otsu's tresholding method in the Hue-Saturation-Value (HSV) color space then removed by using the mean and variance values of the non-shadow area around each shadow (buffer area). The proposed approach will exploit the properties of shadows in luminance and chromacity and will be applied in HSV color space.

2 Image preprocessing

This step is very important for road detection system because not only can it help reduce computational speed but also greatly improve the recognition rate of the road extraction process ahead of the vehicle by eliminating features like the presence of strong shadows that might hinder the results.

Fig.1. Unstructured Road images under different conditions [13].

2.1 Shadow detection

Firstly, we need to detect shadows prior to removing them; therefore shadow detection accuracy is crucial for a better shadow removal process. One of the first steps toward removing shadow in color images involves using the luminance and chromacity properties of shadows. The shadow detection process is performed using Otsu's tresholding algorithm in the HSV color space. HSV color space is somehow very sensitive to the brightness level of the image and it well describes the feature information of the shadow [9]. Since the input image containing shadows is in the RGB color space, a conversion from RGB to HSV space is therefore necessary. One of the reasons to process the image in the HSV space is that it's invariant to shadow. That is, it conveys the color characteristics of the image feature regardless of variations in scene illumination condition [10] and what's more, shadow detection methods based on HSV color space are more accurate than in the RBG color space. The relation between RGB space and HSV space is as follow:

$$V = \frac{1}{3}(R+G+B) \tag{1}$$

$$S = 1 - \frac{3\min(R,G,B)}{R+G+B} \tag{2}$$

$$H = \begin{cases} \theta & if\ B \leq G \\ 360^0 - \theta & if\ B \succ G \end{cases} \tag{3}$$

Where

$$\theta = \cos^{-1}\left\{ \frac{\frac{1}{2}[(R-G)+(R-B)}{\sqrt{(R-G)^2 + (R-B)(G-B)}} \right\}$$

After converting the image from RGB space to HSV space, the intensity component (V) and the hue component (H) are obtained. Both H and V components are used in extracting the shadowed area in color images. Secondly, the ratio image $(H+1)/(V+1)$ is obtained by applying the spectral ratio technique. The ratio image enhances the hue property of shadows with low luminance, that is, the grey value of the shadow region is larger than non-shadowed region. Thirdly, we apply the Otsu segmentation method over the histogram of the ratio image to determine the segmentation threshold for the ratio image. The Otsu's method finds an optimal threshold T, which maximizes

$$V(T) = \frac{(\bar{\mu}.w(T) - \mu(T))^2}{w(T).\mu(T)} \tag{4}$$

Where,

$w(T) = \sum_{i=0}^{T} p_i$, $\mu(T) = \sum_{i=T+1}^{255} p_i$, $\bar{\mu} = \sum_{i=0}^{255} ip_i$, and p_i is the probability of pixels with gray level i in the image.

After this step, the image is then segmented and the candidate shadow region image is obtained. The segmented image is firstly filtered by median filter for noise removal, then processed by morphological erosion and dilation techniques to get the shadow region. The image obtained after the tresholding will be a binary image where all shadow pixels are set to 1 and all non-shadow pixels are set to 0.

2.2 Shadow removal

Once the shadow detection has been performed, the image is divided into two parts, a shadowed region and a non-shadowed region. Let's denote I_s the binary image obtained earlier. In this paper we'll use the buffer area method developed in [8] for shadow removal. The buffer area is the area around the shadow and is used to compensate the shadow using the mean and variances of the shadow region. It's estimated using morphological operations on I_s. Firstly,

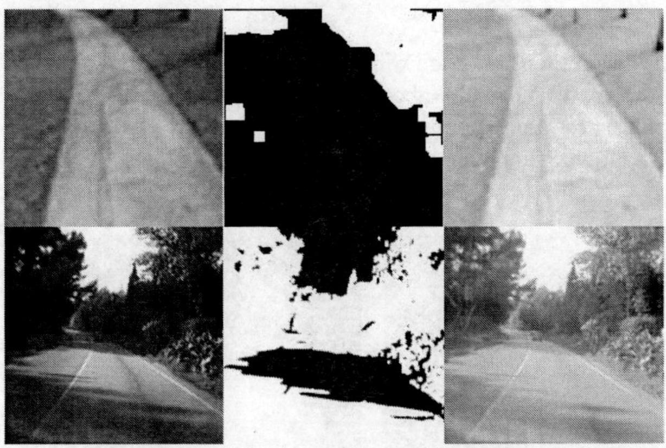
Fig.2 From left to right: input image, binary image showing shadows and shadow free image

shadows need to be classified based on the concept of connected components present on the binary image I_s. Each connected components correspond to a shadow and its elements are set to 1 while set to 0 otherwise. The following procedure determines all connected components in the binary image and terminates when $I_k = I_{k-1}$:

$$I_k = (I_{k-1} \oplus B) \cap I_s \quad k = 1,2,3... \qquad (5)$$

Where B is a suitable structuring element.

In the equation above, I_k contains all connected components of I_k and this process will create *m* sets of connected components representing *m* different shadows in the image.

Secondly, the buffer area of each shadow is computed using image subtraction operation and morphological dilation operation as follows:

$$I_{dilated,\,\mathrm{n}} = (I_{n-1} \oplus B_{square}) \qquad (6)$$

$$I_{buff,\,n} = (I_{dilated,\,n} - I_n) \qquad (7)$$

Where B_{square} is a square structuring element and $I_{buff,\,n}$ provides the location of the non-shadow points $n = 1,2,...,m$. These operations will expand the shadow boundaries.

Finally, the shadow removal image is obtained as follow:

$$I'_n(i,j) = \mu_{buff,n} + \frac{I_n(i,j) - \mu_n}{\sigma_{buff,n}} \sigma_n \quad n = 1,2,...,m \qquad (8)$$

Where $I'_n(i,j)$ is the compensated value of the shadow pixel; $\mu_{buff,n}$ and $\sigma_{buff,n}$ are the mean and variance of the pixels of image *I* at locations $I_{buff,\,n}$

3 Road detection algorithm

In this section, a road detection algorithm is devised for detecting unstructured roads which may have no lane markings on the road surface, degraded edges or road surfaces or strong shadow conditions which is solved by using the algorithm developed in the first section of this paper. It's also important to note that our road detection system is invariant to road shape. Several methods have been developed for unstructured road detection, they can mainly be classified into three groups [11]: one based on road features, another based on road model and the third one is the combination of the fore two methods. In this paper, after converting the original image back to RGB color space, we'll use color segmentation module based on Bayesian classifier where the probability distributions of the road and non-road pixels are approximated by histograms in a RGB space [1]. The classifier includes three stages which are the likelihood estimation, the filtering and decision. The resulting image is a binary image that defines which pixels are part of the road and which one are not. The road histogram is determined using the information of a fixed region of the image while the non-road histogram according to the classifier output.

3.1 Road histogram update

The road histogram is updated using a fixed set of pixels for each input image and the feedback from the road detection module. In order to do so, a temporal histogram of the pixels is obtained from the training area. Therefore, the road histogram is updated as:

$$H_r[r,g,b] = \alpha . H_r[r,g,b] + (1-\alpha) . H_t[r,g,b] \qquad (9)$$

Where H_r is the road histogram, H_t is the temporal histogram of the training area, and α is the weight of the memory of the road histogram

3.2 Classification using the bayesian theory

Bayesian classifier is used for color segmentation where the probability distributions of the road and non-road pixels are approximated by road histograms. The classifier includes three stages: likelihood estimation, the filtering and decision.

Likelihood-based classification: According to Bayesian decision theory, a classifier decision can be taken by comparing the quotient of both road and non-road likelihood with a decision threshold.

$$H_r \approx \{P(Color|Road)\} \quad (10)$$

$$H_n \approx \{P(Color|Non-road)\} \quad (11)$$

Where H_r and H_n which respectively represent the road and non-road histograms, are approximations of the probabilities of finding a RGB pixel in a road and non-road respectively.

The new image is therefore constructed by calculating the quotient of H_r and H_n for each pixel of the input image as follow:

$$S[i] = \frac{H_r[I_m(i)]}{H_n[I_m(i)]} \quad (12)$$

Filtering and Decision: This step uses the correlation between the probability quotient for a given pixel position. Temporal filtering is therefore applied to the probability quotient image to approximate this effect:

$$S_m[i] = \beta . S_m[i] + (1-\beta). S[i] \quad (13)$$

Given the fact that the probability that a pixel is part of the road depends not only on its color but also the color of its surrounding pixels, a median filter will thus be applied to the probability image to approximate this effect.

Finally, the final decision is taken by applying a decision threshold *T*:

$$B[i] = \begin{cases} 1 & S_m[i] \geq T \\ 0 & S_m[i] \prec T \end{cases} \quad (14)$$

4 Test results

Our road segmentation system has been tested in a variety of off-road scenarios under different illumination. The above method was tested in Matlab R2001b. Figure 1 above shows shadowed RBG road images and their corresponding binary image showing shadows. The shadows detected are shown in white color. The accuracy of shadow detection can be seen from the fact that roads are not detected as shadows. Figure 3 also shows shadow free road images and the resulting road segmentation images. It can be seen that our method has good robustness to the impact of shadow on the road due to the above shadow removal method. The results show the effectiveness of the proposed algorithm in de-shadowing and detecting unstructured roads.

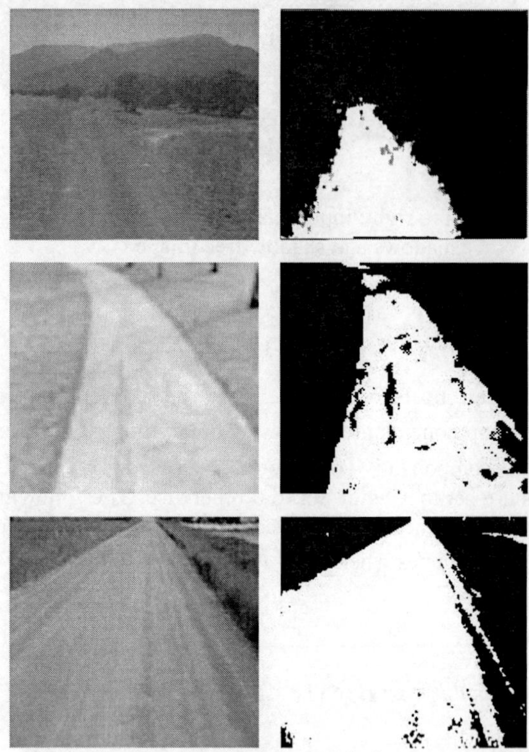

Fig.3. Shadow free images and their corresponding segmentation output.

Performance evaluation

In this section, we use recall and precision as the performance measures to evaluate the performance of the proposed road detection system. Quantitative evaluation are provided using three pixelwise measures namely precision, recall and effectiveness. Precison and recall are defined as:

$$recall = \frac{N_{success}}{N_{success} + N_{missing}} \times 100\% \quad (15)$$

$$precision = \frac{N_{success}}{N_{success} + N_{false}} \times 100\% \quad (16)$$

Where $N_{success}$ represents the number of successfully detected road from the detection process, $N_{missing}$ stands for the number of undetected road, and N_{false} represents the number of false alarms. The sum $N_{success} + N_{missing}$ is the total number of automatically generated ground truth data in the entire image sequences.

Low precision means that many background pixels are classified as road while low recall indicates failure to detect road surface. Equally weighting precision and recall, effectiveness is defined as follow:

$$F = \frac{2PR}{P+R} \tag{17}$$

Effectiveness represents the trade off using weighted harmonic mean between precision and recall.

5 Concluding remarks

In this paper, we have introduced a novel and efficient way for unstructured road detection based on a simple yet effective shadow detection and removal algorithm. First, the input image is converted to HSV space to detect shadows. Secondly, after the shadows are detected, they are removed by using the mean and variance value of the buffer area around each shadow. The said buffer area is estimated with the morphological operators. Finally, we also proposed a real-time visual-based road segmentation method based on the use of adaptive color histograms. The results show the robustness and effectiveness of the proposed method, it also shows that this system is a good approach to road detection for autonomous vehicle. Further studies will include other research fields such as pedestrian tracking, vehicle detection, road sign detection and so on to improve the completeness of our system., this can be a good approach for autonomous vehicle navigation system.

Acknowledgements

This work was partially supported by the National Natural Science Foundation of China under Grant No.61272062.

References

[1] F. Bernuy, J. Ruiz del Solar, I. Parra, and P. Vallejos, “Adaptive and Real-Time Unpaved Road Segmentation Using Color Histograms and Ransac,” Control and Automation (ICCA), 2011 9th IEEE International Conference on , vol., no., pp.136,141, 19-21 Dec. 2011.

[2] H. Kong , J.-Y. Audibert, J. Ponce, ”General Road Detection
From a Single Image”.Image Processing, IEEE Transactions on , vol.19, no.8, pp.2211-2220, Aug. 2010.

[3] Changbeom Oh; Jongin Son; Kwanghoon Sohn, "Illumination robust road detection using geometric information," *Intelligent Transportation Systems (ITSC), 2012 15th International IEEE Conference on* , vol., no., pp.1566,1571, 16-19 Sept. 2012 .

[4] Hsu, C.M.; Lian, F.L.; Lin, Y.C.; Huang, C.M.; Chang, Y.S., "Road detection based on region similarity analysis," *Automatic Control and Artificial Intelligence (ACAI 2012), International Conference on* , vol., no., pp.1775,1778, 3-5 March 2012.

[5] Chunzhao Guo; Mita, S.; McAllester, D., "Robust Road Detection and Tracking in Challenging Scenarios Based on Markov Random Fields With Unsupervised Learning," *Intelligent Transportation Systems, IEEE Transactions on* , vol.13, no.3, pp.1338,1354, Sept. 2012 .

[6] Crisman, J.D.; Thorpe, C.E., "SCARF: a color vision system that tracks roads and intersections," *Robotics and Automation, IEEE Transactions on* , vol.9, no.1, pp.49,58, Feb 1993.

[7] Yong Chen; Mingyi He; Yifan Zhang, "Robust lane detection based on gradient direction," *Industrial Electronics and Applications (ICIEA), 2011 6th IEEE Conference on* , vol., no., pp.1547,1552, 21-23 June 2011.

[8] Singh, Krishna Kant; Pal, Kirat; Nigam, M. J., " Shadow Detection and Removal from Remote Sensing Images Using NDI and Morphological Operators ,"*International Journal Of Computer Applications*, vol 42, no., p. 37, Mars 2012.

[9] Yu-jiao XiaHou; Sheng-rong Gong, "Adaptive Shadows Detection Algorithm Based on Gaussian Mixture Model," *Information Science and Engineering, 2008. ISISE '08. International Symposium on* , vol.1, no., pp.116,120, 20-22 Dec. 2008.

[10] Thomas M. Lillesand and Ralph W. Kiefer, *“Remote Sensing and Image Interpretation”*, Fourth Ed., John Wiley & Sons, 2000.

[11] Wang Xiaoyun; Wang Yongzhong; Wen Chenglin, "Robust lane detection based on gradient-pairs constraint," *Control Conference (CCC), 2011 30th Chinese* , vol., no., pp.3181,3185, 22-24 July 2011.

[12] Choi, H.-C., Park, J.-M., Choi, W.-S., Oh, S.-Y., “Vision-based fusion of robust lane tracking and forward vehicle detection in a real driving environment”, International Journal of Automotive Technology, 2012, 1229-9138.

[13] Qingji Gao; Qijun Luo; Sun Moli, "Rough Set based Unstructured Road Detection through Feature Learning," *Automation and Logistics, 2007 IEEE International Conference on* , vol., no., pp.101,106, 18-21 Aug. 2007.

Image Analysis For Fast Characterization of Uniformity Using Automated Image Capture

S. Panosyan*[1], A. Raheja[1], N. Pernalete[2], D. Still[3], A. Meyer[4]
[1]Department of Computer Science,
[2]Department of Electronics and Computer Engineering Technology
[3]Department of Plant Science,
*Graduate Student Researcher,
California State Polytechnic University, Pomona
[4]Ransom Seed Laboratory, Carpinteria, CA

Abstract — Over the past decade, numerous computer vision systems have been designed and developed to assist those responsible for performing seed examinations and testing [1-14]. With the vast number of plants and the multitude of shapes the seedling roots can take, a general system that measured interesting seed properties such as germination percentage and rate, seed quality, and seed vigor would be difficult to design. However, by narrowing their scope, vision systems can be designed to accurately measure these properties. Thus, the goals of this research are to automate the collection of seedling length measurements from images taken of different types of seedlings. The system should be robust enough to: a) measure different types of seedlings, b) provide length measurements for the seedling primary axis and, in future versions, simple secondary (lateral) roots, as well as c) imagery of the various processing stages for seedling researchers to examine.

Index Terms—**Image Processing and Analysis, Seed Agriculture Analysis, Seedling Analysis Automation, Uniformity, Seedling Length Measurement**

1. Introduction

Continual improvements in computer technology as well as the development of image processing and vision algorithms have made it possible to automate a great number of repetitive processes. Among these tedious processes is the automation of seed germination detection and measurement of seed vigor characteristics. Over the past decade and a half, numerous computer vision systems have been designed and developed to assist those responsible for performing seed examinations and testing [1-14]. With the vast number of agricultural plants and the multitude of shapes the seedling roots can take, it would be difficult to design a general system for classification and measurement of interesting seed properties such as germination percentage, germination rate, seed quality, and seed vigor. However, by considering a small subset of these plants, vision systems can be designed to accurately measure these properties.

By designing artificial intelligence systems to classify the metrics obtained from the image processing and vision components, effective vision systems are being developed to help automate the tedious tasks that expert technicians and seed nursery specialists must perform. Furthermore, by incorporating knowledge from experts within the horticultural biology and science fields, these systems can become more and more effective. In addition, previous research has shown that there are a multitude of different approaches that can be taken towards measuring the aforementioned characteristics [1-14].

Therefore, with these things in mind, the goals of this research are to automate the collection of seedling length measurements from images taken of different types of seedlings. The system should be robust enough to: a) measure different types of seedlings, such as lettuce and onion, b) provide length measurements for the seedling primary axis and, in future versions, simple secondary (lateral) roots, as well as c) imagery of the various processing stages for seedling researchers to examine.

The remainder of this paper is organized as follows. Section II will provide necessary background information on seedling biology and testing procedures. Section III will present an overview of the seedling length measurement algorithm as well as describe necessary image preprocessing steps. In Section IV, we will explain how to create of the Seedling Segment Graph from the Seedling Skeleton image, an important data structure for analyzing the seedling skeleton and determining the primary axis as well as secondary roots. Then, Section V will cover how to determine the number of seedlings in each seedling blob; an important step in handling seedling overlap correction. Section VI will detail how seedlings are built using the Seedling Segment Graph and information gathered from the steps described in Section V. As researchers need to know the length of seedlings in millimeters, Section VII will explain how the pixel to millimeter conversion ratio is calculated. In Section VIII, experimental results will be presented. Finally, Section IX will conclude the paper as well as provide future directions.

2. Background

This section will focus on explaining the biology of a seedling as well as one of the tests performed on seedlings. As terms used to refer to certain parts of seedlings will be used in later sections, this section focuses on identifying these terms. The following diagram labels the parts of the seedling, which may be referred to in the following sections, during various stages of growth.

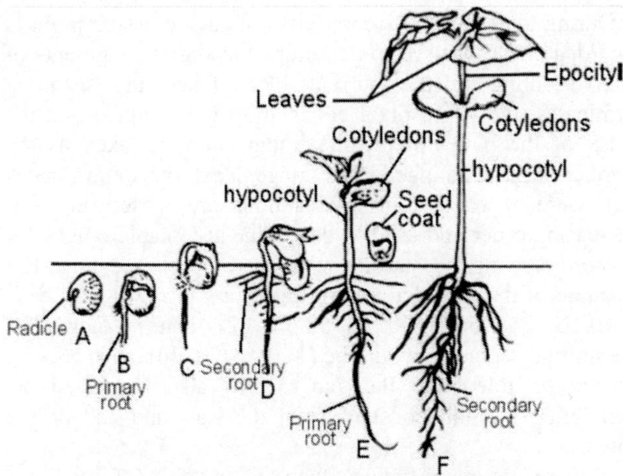

Figure 1. Seedling biology during all stages of growth.

Seed manufacturing company technicians as well as seedling nursery personnel devote inordinate amounts of time to measuring the viability and vigor of the seeds they produce, sell, and grow. These parties must do so because high quality seed production is a key feature of modern day agriculture [1]. There are several measures of seed quality which include seed vigor. As the computer vision system discussed in this paper will be used in computing seed vigor measurements, the following discussion will only touch on explaining seed vigor. Seed vigor is defined by ISTA as "the sum total of those properties of the seed which determine the level of activity and performance of the seed or seed lot during germination and seedling emergence" [1]. Though these tests differ between companies, they also portray valuable information about the viability of the seeds being tested. Once again, seeds are planted and a certain number of planted seeds are collected and examined at particular intervals defined by the Association of Official Seed Analysts (AOSA) vigor testing handbook and ISTA vigor testing handbook. For a test to be considered as a vigor test, it must meet some requirements:

1. Provide a more sensitive index of seed quality than standard germination testing
2. Provide a consistent ranking of seed lots in terms of potential performance
3. Be objective, rapid, simple, and economically practical
4. Be reproducible and interpretable

This figure conveys to the buyer the likelihood of the seeds becoming harvestable plants. Therefore, the accurate and rapid measurement of these properties greatly concern all parties involved. As such, the development of vision systems capable of extracting seed characteristics used to determine seed vigor are of great importance to the seed agriculture industry.

3. Algorithm Overview

Using the OpenCV computer vision library, the input image is first split into blue, green, and red component channel images. As the blue channel provides the clearest distinction between seedlings, the background, and measurement lines, it is used to create the seedling and measurement line binary images. These images are obtained by thresholding the blue channel image.

Next, the binary seedling image is smoothed to remove noise. The OpenCV Blobs Library is used to identify seedling blobs within the smoothed image. These blobs are then filtered based on width, height, and position to remove blobs that cannot belong to seedlings. The resulting filtered image is skeletonized using the Zhang-Suen skeletonization algorithm and blob labeling is performed once again on the seedling skeleton image to identify their sizes and locations.

From the seedling blob list generated by blob labeling, the median blob width and standard deviation are computed to help identify blobs that may contain multiple seedlings. These blobs are marked for further overlap detection and correction. For each seedling blob in the seedling blob list, a seedling segment graph and segment list are created that will later be used to reconstruct the seedling primary axis and determine the lateral secondary roots of the seedling. To ensure higher accuracy, each seedling blob is scanned to determine the number of seedlings it contains.

Using the information gathered during the scanning procedure, a starting and ending segment are picked for each potential seedling from the seedling segment list of the current blob being processed. Then, the seedling primary axis is created by generating a path from the starting to the ending segment using a breadth-first search on the seedling segment graph. Once the primary axis of each seedling in the blob is identified, the segment graph is traversed to search for potential lateral roots connected to each primary axis. After the search terminates, the current blob will now be completely separated into the correct number of seedlings, with each seedling containing information about its total length and lateral roots.

4. Creating The Seedling Segment Graph

To generate the seedling segment graph for a particular seedling blob, the algorithm starts by creating an empty vertex pixel queue (VPQ) as well as a Boolean array the size of the seedling blob that will be used to mark visited pixels (VPA). Then seedling skeleton image pixels falling within the area of the current blob are scanned from left to right and bottom to top until the bottommost pixel of the current blob is found. This pixel marks the beginning of the first seedling segment as well as the first vertex pixel in the graph. It is therefore added to the vertex pixel queue (VPQ) for further exploration. The algorithm then explores the connected components of the blob starting from this vertex pixel. As pixels are visited, they are marked in the visited pixels array (VPA) as well as added to the current seedling segment. For any pixel that connects to more than two other pixels, a vertex code is computed by taking a weighted sum of the eight-connected neighborhood as shown in the following figures.

64	32	16
128	Center	8
1	2	4

64	32	16
128	Center	8
1	2	4

Figure 2. Vertex Computation Kernel (left) and a vertex with code 73 (right).

If the vertex code is found in the following set, the vertex pixel marks the end of the current segment.

$$vertex_{code} \in \{21, 37, 41, 57, 69, 73, 74, 81, 82, 83, 84, 85, 138, 146, 147, 162, 164, 165, 168, 169, 170, 172, 228\}$$

In this case, an entry is added to the segment graph connecting the current segment and vertex pixel. The segment is also added to the segment list, which is just a list of all segments created and added to the graph. Next, the vertex pixel is added to the VPQ once for each unvisited neighboring pixel. The algorithm continues to create segments and add them to the graph in this manner until all pixels are explored and no vertex pixels remain in the VPQ. The following is an example of the seedling skeleton image and its corresponding seedling segment graph image.

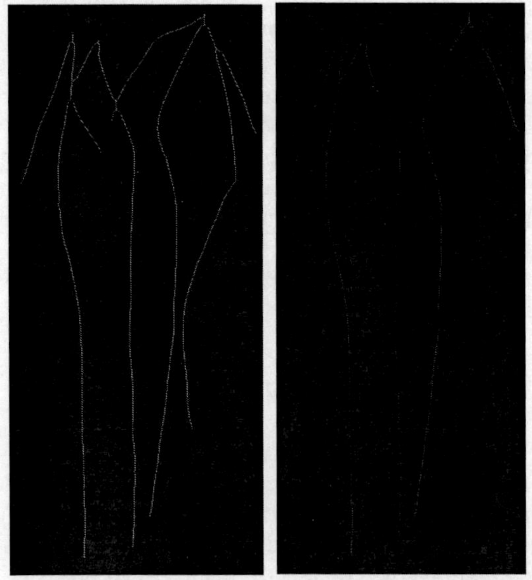

Figure 3. Seedling Skeleton Binary Image (left) and its Seedling Segment Graph Image (right). This is one example of a seedling blob containing multiple skeletons.

5. Counting the Seedlings in a Blob

During the overlap detection phase, the area of the seedling skeleton image containing the current blob being processed is scanned from the top left pixel to the bottom right pixel. An integer array is used to keep track of the number of incident white pixels encountered during a scan across the skeleton image. That is, if five white pixels are encountered during a particular scan, then the value in bin five is incremented by one. To provide enough sensitivity without rescanning the entire area of the blob again, the algorithm scans rows Y_SCAN_STEP pixels apart.

During the scan, the x coordinate of each crossing point is recorded and later used to determine the starting segments of each seedling in the current blob. Once the scanning terminates, the white pixel count array is examined and the index of the bin with the maximum count is taken as the number of the seedlings in this image. Next, the x coordinates that were recorded during scanning are sorted in non-decreasing order and used to determine acceptable ranges for x coordinate of the starting segment of each seedling. For example, if the recorded x coordinates are [1, 4, 4, 5, 6, 6, 7, 8, 10, 22, 23, 26, 28, 30, 56, 58, 60, 62], then the ranges for the starting segments would be (1 , 10), (22, 30), and (56, 62). For noise tolerance, the ranges are also expanded by subtracting a small constant from the start and end of the range.

If there are more ranges than the number of seedlings determined previously, the algorithm merges all ranges that overlap until the number of ranges equals the expected number of seedlings or no more ranges can be merged. The final list of ranges is used later on to determine the starting segment of the seedling roots.

6. Building The Seedlings

There are three stages to the seedling building algorithm. The first stage uses the seedling segment list built during seedling segment graph creation and list of ranges generated by the previous section to figure out likely pairings of starting and ending segments. Therefore, this stage is known as the Segment Pairing stage. The second takes the seedling segment graph and likely pairs and builds the seedling primary axis. Thus, the second stage is known as the Build Primary Axis stage. The final stage considers all segments connecting to the current seedling that are not part of the primary axis and selects the ones that are lateral roots. Section A below details the Segment Pairing stage. Then, Section B which explains the Building Seedling stage. Finally, Section C describes the how lateral roots are found and added to the seedling.

1. Segment Pairing Stage

As mentioned above, the segment pairing stage uses the x range and segment lists to determine likely starting and ending segment pairs for each seedling in the blob being processed. First, the segment list is sorted in decreasing order by looking at the starting Y coordinate of each segment. Next, a segment with the lowest possible starting Y coordinate is picked such that its X coordinate falls into one of the X ranges determined earlier. Once the best match for a particular X range is found, that range is removed from the list. In this case, the best segment is the segment with the largest starting Y coordinate that still falls into a particular X range.

Once the best starting segment is found for each range, a search now takes place to find the best ending segment for each starting segment. Each segment is considered by computing a fitness function and the segment with the lowest score is taken as the best fit for the current starting segment. The fitness function takes into consideration the X and Y proximity of the current segment to the starting segment, whether the current segment top endpoint is a terminal endpoint, and whether the current segment bottom endpoint is a terminal endpoint. It combines these factors in the following way:

$$fitness = w_{lower\ x\ distance} \times lower\ x\ distance + w_{upper\ x\ distance} \times upper\ x\ distance - w_{y\ distance} \times y\ distance$$

2. Building the Primary Axis

Now that the starting and ending segments for each seedling within the current blob have been determined, the algorithm uses the seedling segment graph and these paired segments to build the primary axis of each seedling. To do so, the algorithm traverses the segment graph beginning at the starting segment. At each step, the algorithm checks whether the current segment being considered is the ending segment. If so, it adds the segment to the seedling primary axis and terminates. Otherwise, the current segment is only added as a primary segment if the following criteria are met. First, the current segment must connect to other segments. This is because if the current segment is not the ending segment and is a terminal segment, it cannot possibly lead to the ending segment. Next, the algorithm checks whether the current segment endpoint not connected to the seedling primary axis grows towards the given ending segment. If these conditions are met, the current segment is added to the primary axis of the current seedling and all segments it connects to in the graph are examined. This process continues until the ending segment is reached.

3. Finding Lateral (Secondary) Roots

With the seedling primary axis constructed, the final stage of the seedling building algorithm examines all segments connecting to the primary axis that are not part of the primary axis. All segments that have one terminal endpoint are automatically added as lateral roots. Segments that grow downward from the primary axis of the seedling, but connect to another segment are explored to determine whether they contribute to a smaller lateral root network. The following figure shows the lateral root network highlighted in red and single lateral root in green.

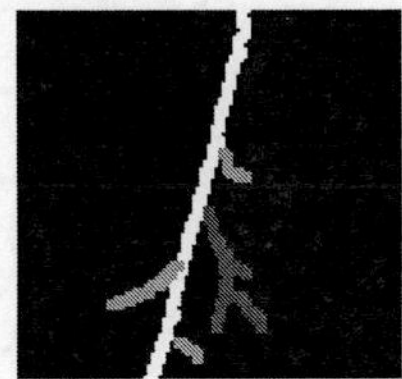

Figure 4. Examples of secondary roots and secondary root networks.

As it is non-trivial to determine when smaller secondary root networks have been encountered, this part of the algorithm is still in development.

7. Computing The Conversion Ratio

Since researchers are interested in measuring the length of each seedling in real world units (e.g. millimeters, centimeters) and not pixels, the algorithm also computes the pixels to millimeters conversion ratio. This is done by taking the blue channel image, thresholding it to obtain a binary image which only shows the measurement lines. The binary measurement line image is then analyzed using the Hough Line Transform. Once the lines are identified and filtered to leave the longest horizontal lines, the algorithm scans the resulting line image. By scanning the image vertically, all line crossings are recorded and the vertical distance between each line is computed. Then, to account for potential noise, the distance measurement that occurs the most is used as the conversion ratio. Now, since the distance between measurement lines is known to be 10 mm, the conversion ratio is simply 10 mm divided by the pixel distance.

8. Experimental Results

The seedling length computation algorithm was tested using images containing 20 to 25 seedlings on lined measurement paper. Two different types of seedlings were used in the experiments: lettuce and onion. In total, there were 6 images containing only lettuce seedlings and 5 images containing only onion seedlings. Results for each type of seedling will be discussed separately, with lettuce seedling results discussed first. As the input images are 3008 x 2000, the input and primary axis images are presented in multiple pieces in order to show more detail.

1. Lettuce Seedling Results

The following three images show the first 12 seedlings of one input image containing a total of 24 seedlings, the primary axes of these 12 seedlings, and a table containing the measurements computed by the algorithm as well as measurements provided by seed technicians from the laboratory of the data provider.

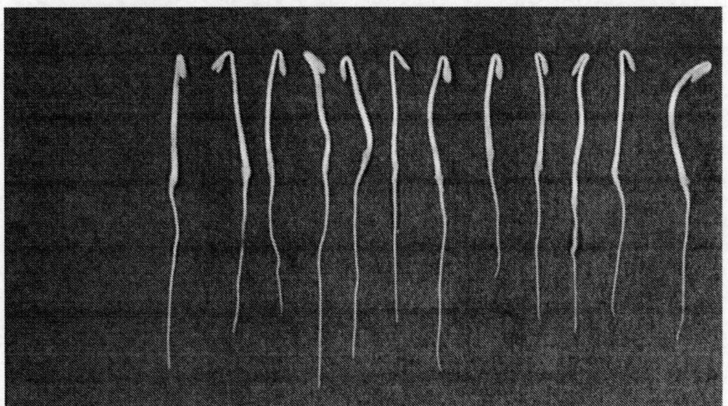

Figure 5. First 12 seedlings of one lettuce seedling input image

Figure 6. Primary axes for the 12 seedlings shown above. The second seedling in this image is split in two during the thresholding phase due to noise. One possible way to correct this error is to examine the size of all seedlings once the primary axes are determined. Then, using this information the algorithm can try to combine the smaller seedling primary axes with the larger one that is in close vertical proximity. Doing so will also make the algorithm more robust to noise and thresholding errors. However, as this correction mechanism is currently not implemented, the measurements in the table below reflect the larger, top half of the split seedling.

Seedling Number	*1*	*2*	*3*	*4*	*5*	*6*
Computed Length	48	30	40	51	47	42
Reference Length	50	45	40	50	45	40

Table 1. Measurements in millimeters for the first 6 seedlings in the input image presented above. Reference length is a rounded measurement, to the nearest 5 mm, given by the data provider.

Seedling Number	*7*	*8*	*9*	*10*	*11*	*12*
Computed Length	49	34	41	43	40	43
Reference Length	50	35	40	45	40	45

Table 2. Measurements in millimeters for the next 6 seedlings in the input image presented above.

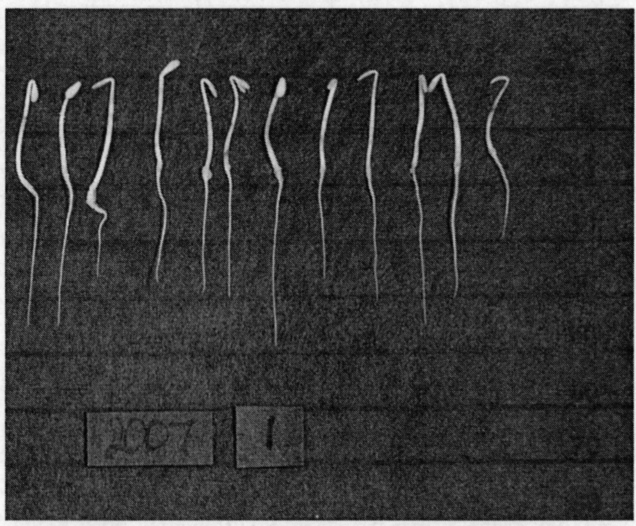

Figure 7. Last 12 seedlings of the same lettuce seedling input image.

Figure 8. Primary axes of the 12 seedlings in the previous image.

Seedling Number	*13*	*14*	*15*	*16*	*17*	*18*
Computed Length	45	45	36	37	39	40
Reference Length	45	45	35	35	40	40

Table 3. Measurements in millimeters for the next 6 seedlings in the input image presented above.

Seedling Number	*19*	*20*	*21*	*22*	*23*	*24*
Computed Length	49	36	40	45	40	30
Reference Length	50	35	40	45	40	30

Table 4. Measurements in millimeters for the last 6 seedlings in the input image presented above.

As the reference lengths are all rounded to the nearest 5 mm, rounding the computed lengths as well shows that the algorithm performs quite well in cases where seedlings do not overlap. This is the case for the input images shown above as well as for other input images provided that no seedlings get split during thresholding.

2. Onion Seedling Results

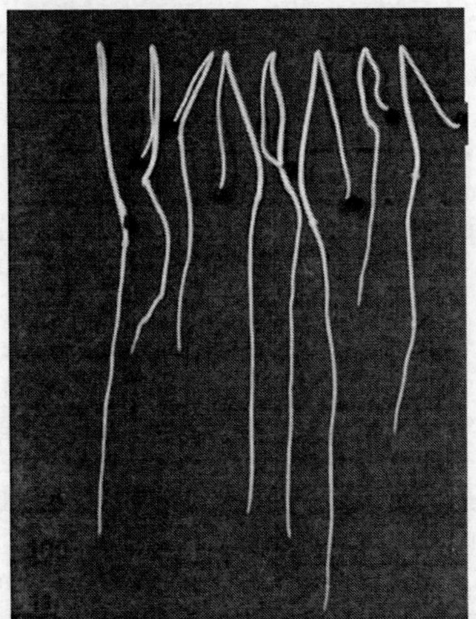

Figure 9. First 8 onion seedlings of one onion seedling input image.

Figure 10. Primary axes of seedlings presented in the previous image.

Seedling Number	*1*	*2*	*3*	*4*	*5*	*6*	*7*	*8*
Computed Length	95	59	59	90	95	109	60	74
Reference Length	95	60	60	90	95	110	60	75

Table 5. Primary axes and reference length measurements for previous 8 seedlings.

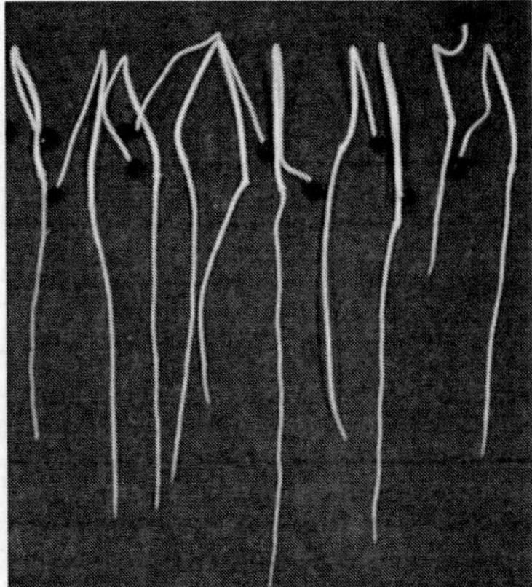

Figure 11. More onion seedlings taken from the same image as in Figure 10.

Figure 12. Correctly separated overlapping seedlings shown in different colors.

Seedling Number	*9*	*10*	*11*	*12*	*13*	*14*	*15*	*16*	*17*	*18*
Computed Length	67	79	77	75	60	90	66	83	39	69
Reference Length	65	80	80	75	60	90	65	85	40	70

Table 6. Primary axes and reference length measurements for the above 10 seedlings.

9. Conclusion

Despite the differences in growth patterns for lettuce and onion seedlings, the seedling length measurement algorithm is 99% accurate for non-overlap cases and 85% accurate in overlap cases. The difference is due to incorrect separation of overlapping seedlings in cases where two seedlings share a large portion of their primary axes. Further research is being done to discover a means for separating seedlings in such complex cases. In addition to the primary axis length, each seedling structure created by the algorithm also provides information regarding lateral roots.

Secondary roots provide agricultural researchers with valuable information regarding the growth of the developing plants nutrient networks [14]. That is because larger secondary roots and secondary root networks are responsible for the absorption of nutrients from the soil [1, 14]. Since seedling research experiments typically deal with thousands of seedlings, the ability to rapidly automate the collection of data regarding primary axis and secondary root growth is of great importance [14]. Furthermore, automation will allow researchers to spend more time analyzing the results of their experiments by eliminating the lengthy time required to perform these measurements by hand.

Thus, future directions of work will focus on accurately measuring the various segments that comprise these secondary root networks as well as improving the seedling overlap separation phase of the measurement algorithm.

10. AKNOWLEDGEMENTS

This work is supported by the Agricultural Research Initiative Grant number 12-04-199-11. Thanks to Aleta Meyr at Ransom Seed Lab for providing images of seedlings as well as describing general seedling testing processes.

11. References

[1] Dell'Aquila, A. (2006). Computerised seed imaging: a new tool to evaluate germination quality. Commun. Biometry Crop Sci. 1 (1), 20-31.

[2] Dell'Aquila, A. (2005). The use of image analysis to monitor the germination of seeds of broccoli and radish. Annals of Applied Biology. Vol. 146. pp. 545-550.

[3] Ducournau, S., Feutry,. A, Plainchault, P., Revollon, P., Vigouroux, B., Wagner, M.H. (2005). Using computer vision to monitor germination time course of sunflower (Heliantus annuus L.) seeds. Seed Sci. Technol. 33, 329–340.

[4] Dutt, M. (2004). Using Sequential Imagery to Evaluate Aspects of Seed Vigor and Germination." MS Thesis. Col. of Agriculture, U. of Kentucky.

[5] Geneve, R.L. and Kester, S.T. (2001). Evaluation of Seedling Size Following Germination Using Computer-aided Analysis of Digital Images from a Flat-bed Scanner. HortScience. 36(6), 1117-1120.

[6] Heijden, G. van der. (1999). Automatic determination of germination of seeds. Proc. of the World Seed Conference in Zurich, Netherlands.

[7] Howarth, M. S., Stanwood, P. C. (1993). Measurement of Seedling Growth Rate by Machine Vision. Transactions of the ASAE. Vol. 36 Issue 3 pp. 959-963.

[8] McCormac, A. C., Keefe, P. D. and Draper, S. R. (1990). Automated vigor testing of field vegetables using image analysis. Seed Science and Technology, 18, 103-112.

[9] Oakley, K. Kester, S.T., and Geneve, R.L. (2004). Computer-aided digital image analysis of seedling size and growth rate for assessing seed vigour in Impatiens. Journal of Seed Sci. & Technology. Vol 32. pp. 907-915.

[10] Sako, Y. (2000). Systems for seed vigor assessment and seed classification. M. S. Thesis, The Ohio State University, Columbus, OH.

[11] Steward, B. L., Shrestha, D. S. (2002). Automatic Corn Plant Population Measurement Using Machine Vision. Transactions of the ASAE. Vol. 46 Issue 2 pp. 559-565.

[12] Ureña, R., Rodriguez, F., Berenguel, M. (2001). A machine vision system for seeds germination quality evaluation using fuzzy logic. Computers and Electronics in Agriculture. Vol. 32. pp. 1-20.

[13] Xu, L., Fujimura, K., McDonald, M.B. (2007). Automatic separation of overlapping seedlings by network optimization. Journal of Seed Science and Technology. Vol. 35 Issue 2 pp. 337-350.

[14] Zambaux, K. et al. (2009). EZ-Rhizo: integrated software for the fast and accurate measurement of root system architecture. The Plant Journal.Vol. 57 pp. 945-956.

$\mathcal{NR}$PSNR: $\mathcal{N}$o-$\mathcal{R}$eference Peak Signal-to-Noise Ratio for JPEG2000

Jaime Moreno†, Salvador Saucedo†, and Beatriz Jaime†
†Superior School of Mechanical and Electrical Engineers, National Polytechnic Institute of Mexico, IPN Avenue, Lindavista, Mexico City, 07738, Mexico.

e-mail:jmorenoe@ipn.mx

Abstract— *The aim of this work is to define a no-referenced perceptual image quality estimator applying the perceptual concepts of the Chromatic Induction Model The approach consists in comparing the received image, presumably degraded, against the perceptual versions (different distances) of this image degraded by means of a Model of Chromatic Induction, which uses some of the human visual system properties. Also we compare our model with a original estimator in image quality assessment,* PSNR. *Results are highly correlated with the ones obtained by* PSNR *for image (99.32%* Lenna *and 96.95% for image* Baboon*), but this proposal does not need an original image or a reference one in order to give an estimation of the quality of the degraded image.*

Keywords*: Human Visual System, Contrast Sensitivity Function, Perceived Images, Wavelet Transform, Peak Signal-to-Noise Ratio, No-Reference Image Quality Assessment, JPEG2000.*

1. Introduction

The early years of the 21st century have witnessed a tremendous growth in the use of digital images as a means for representing and communicating information. A significant literature describing sophisticated theories, algorithms, and applications of digital image processing and communication has evolved.Aconsiderable percentage of this literature is devoted to methods for improving the appearance of images, or for maintaining the appearance of images that are processed. Nevertheless, the quality of digital images, processed or otherwise, is rarely perfect. Images are subject to distortions during acquisition, compression, transmission, processing, and reproduction. To maintain, control, and enhance the quality of images, it is important for image acquisition, management, communication, and processing systems to be able to identify and quantify image quality degradations. The development of effective automatic image quality assessment systems is a necessary goal for this purpose. Yet, until recently, the field of image quality assessment has remained in a nascent state, awaiting new models of human vision and of natural image structure and statistics before meaningful progress could be made.

Nowadays, Mean Squared Error (MSE) is still the most used quantitative performance metrics and several image quality measures are based on it, being Peak Signal-to-Noise Ratio (PSNR) the best example. But some authors like Wang and Bovik in [1], [2] consider that MSE is a poor algorithm, to be used in quality assessment systems. Therefore it is important to know what is the MSE and what is wrong with it, in order to propose new metrics that fulfills the properties of human visual system and keeps the favorable features that the MSE has.

In this way, let $f(i,j)$ and $\hat{f}(i,j)$ represent two images being compared and the size of them is the number of intensity samples or pixels. Being $f(i,j)$ the original reference image, which has to be considered with perfect quality, and $\hat{f}(i,j)$ a distorted version of $f(i,j)$, whose quality is being evaluated. Then, the MSE and the PSNR are, respectively, defined as:

$$MSE = \frac{1}{NM}\sum_{i=1}^{N}\sum_{j=1}^{M}\left[f(i,j) - \hat{f}(i,j)\right]^2 \quad (1)$$

and

$$PSNR = 10\log_{10}\left(\frac{\mathcal{G}_{max}{}^2}{MSE}\right) \quad (2)$$

where $\mathcal{G}_{max}$ is the maximum possible intensity value in $f(i,j)$ ($M\times N$ size). Thus, for gray-scale images that allocate 8 bits per pixel (bpp) $\mathcal{G}_{max} = 2^8 - 1 = 255$. For color images the PSNR is defined as in the Equation 2, whereas the color MSE is the mean among the individual MSE of each component.

An important task in image compression systems is to maximize the correlation among pixels, because the higher correlation at the preprocessing, the more efficient algorithm postprocessing. Thus, an efficient measure of image quality should take in to account the latter feature. In contrast to this, MSE does not need any positional information of the image, thus pixel arrangement is ordered as a one-dimensional vector.

Both MSE and PSNR are extensively employed in the image processing field, since these metrics have favorable properties, such as:

1) A convenient metrics for the purpose of algorithm optimization. For example in JPEG2000, MSE is used both in Optimal Rate Allocation [3], [4] and Region of interest [5], [4]. Therefore MSE can find solutions for these kind of problems, when is combined with the instruments of linear algebra, since it is differentiable.
2) By definition MSE is the difference signal between the two images being compared, giving a clear meaning of the overall error signal energy.

2. Image Quality Assessment

2.1 Full Reference (FR)

2.1.1 Bottom-Up Approaches

Psychological and physiological studies in the past century have gained us a tremendous amount of knowledge about the human visual system (HVS). Still, although much is known about the mechanisms of early, front-end vision, much more remains to be learned of the later visual pathways and the general higher level functions of the visual cortex. While the knowledge is far from complete, current models of visual information processing mechanisms have become sufficiently sophisticated that it is of interest to explore whether it is possible to deploy them to predict the performance of simple human visual behaviors, such as image quality evaluation.

Bottom up approaches to image quality assessment are those methods that attempt to simulate well modeled functionalities of the HVS, and integrate these in the design of quality assessment algorithms that, hopefully, perform similar to the HVS in the assessment of image quality. In this chapter we begin with a brief description of relevant aspects of the anatomy and psychophysical features of the HVS. This description will focus on those HVS features that contribute to current engineering implementations of perceptual image quality measures.

Most systems that attempt to incorporate knowledge about the HVS into the design of image quality measures use an error sensitivity framework, so that the errors between the distorted image and reference image are perceptually quantized according to HVS characteristics.

2.1.2 Top-Down Approaches

The bottom-up approaches to image quality assessment described in the last subsection (2.1.1) attempt to simulate the functional components in the human visual system that may be relevant to image quality assessment. The underlying goal is to build systems that work in the same way as the HVS, at least for image quality assessment tasks. By contrast, the top-down systems simulate the HVS in a different way. These systems treat the HVS as a black box, and only the input output relationship is of concern. A top-down image quality assessment system may operate in a manner quite different from that of the HVS, which is of little concern, provided that it successfully predicts the image quality assessment behavior of an average human observer.

One obvious approach to building such a top-down system is to formulate it as a supervised machine learning problem, as illustrated in Fig. 1. Here the HVS is treated as a black box whose inputŰoutput relationship is to be learned. The training data can be obtained by subjective experimentation, where a large number of test images are viewed and rated by human subjects. The goal is to train the system model so that the error between the desired output (subjective rating) and the model prediction is minimized. This is generally a regression or function approximation problem. Many techniques are available to attack these kinds of problems.

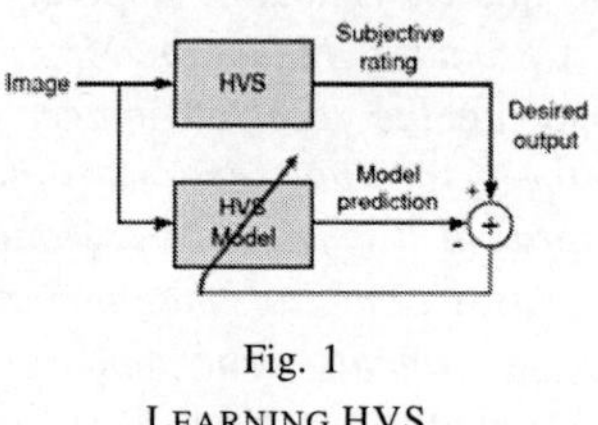

Fig. 1
LEARNING HVS.

Unfortunately, direct application of this method is problematic, since the dimension of the space of all images is the same as the number of pixels in the image. Furthermore, subjective testing is expensive and a typical extensive subjective experiment would be able to include only several hundred test imagesŮhardly an adequate coverage of the image space. Assigning only a single sample at each quadrant of a ten dimensional space requires a total of 1024 samples, and the dimension of the image space is in the order of thousands to millions. An excellent example of the problem of dimensionality.

2.2 No-Reference

No-reference (NR) image quality assessment is, perhaps, the most difficult (yet conceptually simple) problem in the field of image analysis. By some means, an objective model must evaluate the quality of any given real world image, without referring to an original high quality image. On the surface, this seems to be a mission impossible. How can the quality of an image be quantitatively judged without having a numerical model of what a good/bad quality image is supposed to look like? Yet, amazingly, this is quite an easy task for human observers. Humans can easily identify high quality images versus low quality images, and, furthermore, they are able to point out what is right and wrong about them without seeing the original. Moreover, humans tend to agree with each other to a pretty high extent. For example, without looking at the original image, probably every reader would agree that the noisy, blurry, and JPEG2000 compressed images in Fig. 2 have lower quality than the luminance shifted and contrast stretched images.

(a) Image *Baboon*

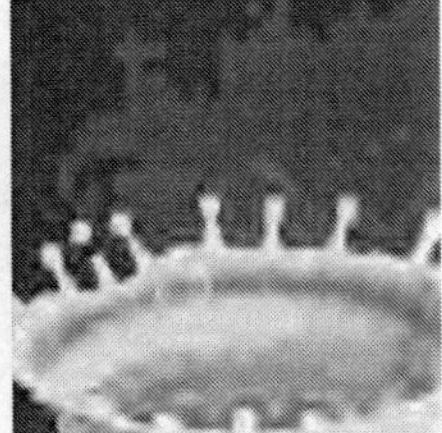

(b) Image *Splash*

Fig. 2
256×256 PATCHES (CROPPED FOR VISIBILITY) OF IMAGES *Baboon* AND *Splash* DISTORTED BY MEANS OF JPEG2000 COMPRESSION, ALTHOUGH BOTH IMAGES HAVE THE SAME OBJECTIVE QUALITY (PSNR=30DB), THEIR VISUAL QUALITY IS VERY DIFFERENT.

Before developing any algorithm for image quality assessment, a fundamental question that must be answered is what source of information can be used to evaluate the quality of images. Clearly, the human eyeŰbrain system is making use of a very substantial and effective pool of information about images in making subjective judgments of image quality.

Three types of knowledge may be employed in the design of image quality measures: knowledge about the original high quality image, knowledge about the distortion process, and knowledge about the human visual system (HVS). In FR quality assessment, the high quality original image is known a priori. In NR quality assessment, however, the original image is absent, yet one can still assume that there exists a high quality original image, of which the image being evaluated is a distorted representation. It is also reasonable to make a further assumption that such a conjectured original image belongs to the set of typical natural images.

It is important to realize that the cluster of natural images occupies an extremely tiny portion in the space of all possible images. This potentially provides a strong prior knowledge about what these images should look like. Such prior knowledge could be a precious source of information for the design of image quality measures. Models of such natural scenes attempt to describe the class of high quality original images statistically. Interestingly, it has been long conjectured in computational neuroscience that the HVS is highly adapted to the natural visual environment, and that, therefore, the modeling of natural scenes and the HVS are dual problems.

Knowledge about the possible distortion processes is another important information source that can be used for the development of NR image quality measures. For example, it is known that blur and noise are often introduced in image acquisition and display systems and reasonably accurate models are sometimes available to account for these distortions. Images compressed using block based algorithms such as JPEG often exhibit highly visible and undesirable blocking artifacts. Wavelet based image compression algorithms operating at low bit rates can blur images and produce ringing artifacts near discontinuities.

Of course, all of these types of distortions are application dependent. An application specific NR image quality assessment system is one that is specifically designed to handle a specific artifact type, and that is unlikely to be able to handle other types of distortions. The question arises, of course, whether an application specific NR system is truly reference free, since much information about the distorted image is assumed. However, nothing needs to be assumed about the original image, other than, perhaps models derived from natural scene statistics or other natural assumptions. Since the original images are otherwise unknown, we shall continue to refer to more directed problems such as these as application specific NR image quality assessment problems.

Of course, a more complex system that includes several modes of artifact handling might be constructed and that could be regarded as approaching general purpose NR image quality assessment. Before this can happen, however, the various components need to be designed. Fortunately, in many practical application environments, the distortion processes involved are known and fixed. The design of such application specific NR quality assessment systems appears to be much more approachable than the general, assumption free NR image quality assessment problem. Very little, if any, meaningful progress has been made on this latter problem.

Owing to a paucity of progress in other application specific areas, this work mainly focuses on NR image quality assessment methods, which are designed for assessing the quality of compressed images. In particular, attention is given to a spatial domain method and a frequency domain method for block based image compression, and a wavelet domain method for wavelet based image compression.

3. The $\mathcal{NR}$PSNR Algorithm

3.1 Chromatic Induction Wavelet Model

The *C*hromatic *I*nduction *Wa*velet *M*odel (CIWaM) [6] is a low-level perceptual model of the HVS. It estimates the image perceived by an observer at a distance d just by modeling the perceptual chromatic induction processes of the HVS. That is, given an image $\mathcal{I}$ and an observation distance d, CIWaM obtains an estimation of the perceptual image $\mathcal{I}_\rho$ that the observer perceives when observing $\mathcal{I}$ at distance d. CIWaM is based on just three important stimulus properties: spatial frequency, spatial orientation and surround contrast. This three properties allow to unify the chromatic assimilation and contrast phenomena, as well as some other perceptual processes such as saliency perceptual processes [7].

The CIWaM model takes an input image $\mathcal{I}$ and decomposes it into a set of wavelet planes $\omega_{s,o}$ of different spatial scales s (i.e., spatial frequency ν) and spatial orientations o. It is described as:

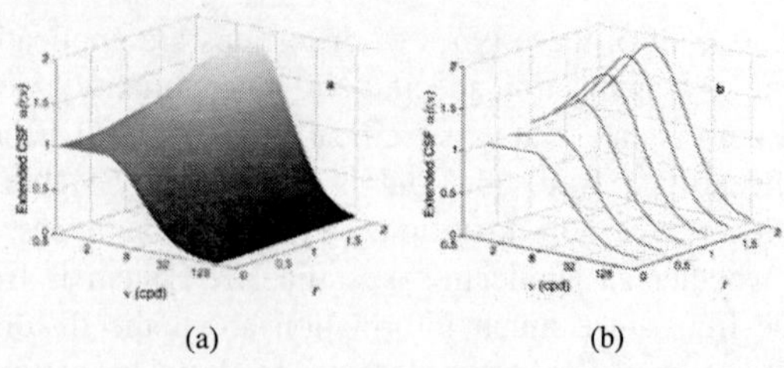

(a) (b)

Fig. 3
(A) GRAPHICAL REPRESENTATION OF THE E-CSF ($\alpha_{s,o,i}(r,\nu)$)) FOR THE LUMINANCE CHANNEL. (B) SOME PROFILES OF THE SAME SURFACE ALONG THE SPATIAL FREQUENCY (ν) AXIS FOR DIFFERENT CENTERŰSURROUND CONTRAST ENERGY RATIO VALUES (R). THE PSYCHOPHYSICALLY MEASURED CSF IS A PARTICULAR CASE OF THIS FAMILY OF CURVES (CONCRETELY FOR R = 1).

$$\mathcal{I} = \sum_{s=1}^{n} \sum_{o=v,h,dgl} \omega_{s,o} + c_n \;, \tag{3}$$

where n is the number of wavelet planes, c_n is the residual plane and o is the spatial orientation either *v*ertical, *h*orizontal or *d*ia*g*ona*l*.

The perceptual image $\mathcal{I}_\rho$ is recovered by weighting these $\omega_{s,o}$ wavelet coefficients using the *extended Contrast Sensitivity Function* (e-CSF, Fig. 3). The e-CSF is an extension of the psychophysical CSF [8] considering spatial surround information (denoted by r), visual frequency (denoted by ν, which is related to spatial frequency by observation distance) and observation distance (d). Perceptual image $\mathcal{I}_\rho$ can be obtained by

$$\mathcal{I}_\rho = \sum_{s=1}^{n} \sum_{o=v,h,dgl} \alpha(\nu,r)\, \omega_{s,o} + c_n \;, \tag{4}$$

where $\alpha(\nu,r)$ is the e-CSF weighting function that tries to reproduce some perceptual properties of the HVS. The term $\alpha(\nu,r)\ \omega_{s,o} \equiv \omega_{s,o;\rho,d}$ can be considered the *perceptual wavelet coefficients* of image $\mathcal{I}$ when observed at distance d and is written as:

$$\alpha(\nu,r) = z_{ctr} \cdot C_d(\dot{s}) + C_{min}(\dot{s}) \;. \tag{5}$$

This function has a shape similar to the e-CSF and the three terms that describe it are defined as:

z_{ctr} Non-linear function and estimation of the central feature contrast relative to its surround contrast, oscillating from zero to one, defined by:

$$z_{ctr} = \frac{\left[\frac{\sigma_{cen}}{\sigma_{sur}}\right]^2}{1+\left[\frac{\sigma_{cen}}{\sigma_{sur}}\right]^2} \tag{6}$$

being σ_{cen} and σ_{sur} the standard deviation of the wavelet coefficients in two concentric rings, which represent a center–surround interaction around each coefficient.

$C_d(\dot{s})$ Weighting function that approximates to the perceptual e-CSF, emulates some perceptual properties and is defined as a piecewise Gaussian function [8], such as:

$$C_d(\dot{s}) = \begin{cases} e^{-\frac{\dot{s}^2}{2\sigma_1^2}}, & \dot{s} = s - s_{thr} \le 0, \\ e^{-\frac{\dot{s}^2}{2\sigma_2^2}}, & \dot{s} = s - s_{thr} > 0. \end{cases} \tag{7}$$

$C_{min}(\dot{s})$ Term that avoids $\alpha(\nu,r)$ function to be zero and is defined by:

$$C_{min}(\dot{s}) = \begin{cases} \frac{1}{2}\, e^{-\frac{\dot{s}^2}{2\sigma_1^2}}, & \dot{s} = s - s_{thr} \le 0, \\ \frac{1}{2}, & \dot{s} = s - s_{thr} > 0. \end{cases} \tag{8}$$

taking $\sigma_1 = 2$ and $\sigma_2 = 2\sigma_1$. Both $C_{min}(\dot{s})$ and $C_d(\dot{s})$ depend on the factor s_{thr}, which is the scale associated to 4 cycles per degree when an image is observed from the distance d with a pixel size l_p and one visual degree, whose expression is defined by Equation 9. Where s_{thr} value is associated to the e-CSF maximum value.

$$s_{thr} = \log_2\left(\frac{d\tan(1^\circ)}{4\, l_p}\right) \tag{9}$$

(a) d=30 cm. (b) d=100 cm. (c) d=200 cm.

Fig. 4
(A) ORIGINAL COLOR IMAGE *Lenna* . (B)-(D) PERCEPTUAL IMAGES OBTAINED BY CIWAM AT DIFFERENT OBSERVATION DISTANCES d.

Fig. 4 shows three examples of CIWaM images of *Lenna*, calculated by Eq. 4 for a 19 inch monitor with 1280 pixels of horizontal resolution, at $d = \{30, 100, 200\}$ centimeters.

3.2 Basics

In the no-referenced image quality issue, there is only a distorted version $\hat{f}(i,j) = \Lambda[f(i,j)]$ that is compared with $f(i,j)$, being Λ a distortion model and the unknown original image $f(i,j)$ is considered a pattern Υ ([0,1;1,0]) like a chessboard (Figs. 5) with the same size of $\hat{f}(i,j)$. The difference between these two images depends on the features of the distortion model Λ. For example, blurring, contrast change, noise, JPEG blocking or JPEG2000 wavelet ringing.

In Fig. 2, the images *Babbon* and *Splash* are compressed by means of JPEG2000. These two images have the same

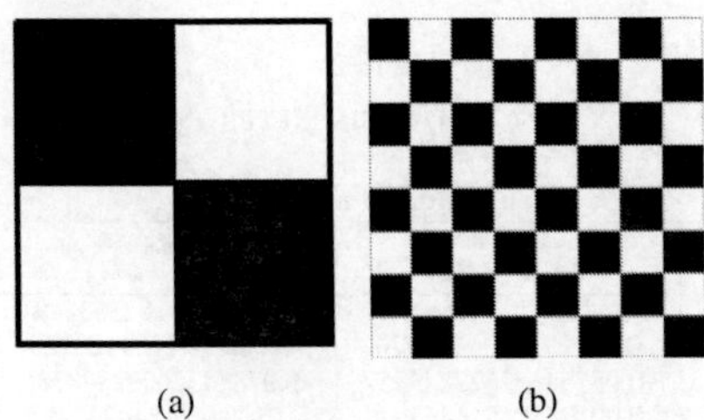

(a) (b)

Fig. 5

(A) PATTERN [0,1;1,0] OR Υ. (B) PATTERN Υ REPEATED SIXTEEN TIMES.

PSNR=30 dB when compared to their corresponding original image, that is, they have the same numerical degree of distortion (i.e. the same objective image quality PSNR). But, their subjective quality is clearly different, showing the image *Baboon* a better visual quality. Thus, for this example, PSNR and perceptual image quality has a small correlation. On the image *Baboon*, high spatial frequencies are dominant. A modification of these high spatial frequencies by Λ induces a high distortion, resulting a lower PSNR, even if the modification of these high frequencies are not perceived by the HVS. In contrast, on image *Splash*, mid and low frequencies are dominant. Modification of mid and low spatial frequencies also introduces a high distortion, but they are less perceived by the HVS. Therefore, correlation of PSNR against the opinion of an observer is small. Fig. 6 shows the diagonal high spatial frequencies of these two images, where there are more high frequencies in image *Baboon*.

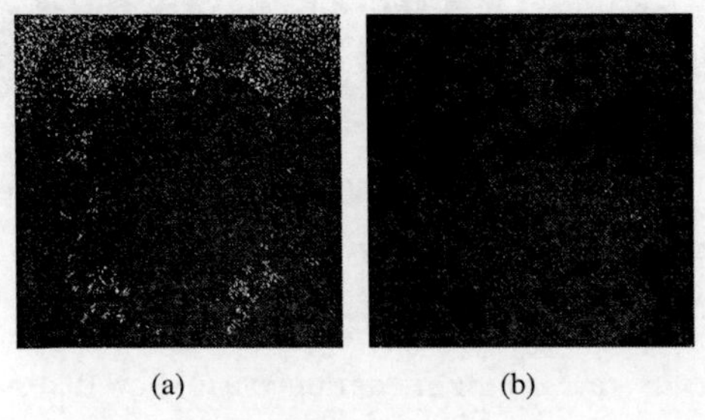

(a) (b)

Fig. 6

DIAGONAL SPATIAL ORIENTATION OF THE FIRST WAVELET PLANE OF IMAGES (A) *Baboon* AND (B)*Splash* DISTORTED BY JPEG2000 WITH PSNR=30DB.

If a set of distortions $\hat{f}_k(i,j) = \Lambda_k[f(i,j)]$ is generated and indexed by k (for example, let Λ be a blurring operator), the image quality of $\hat{f}_k(i,j)$ evolves while varying k, being k, for example, the degree of blurring. Hence, the evolution of $\hat{f}_k(i,j)$ depends on the characteristics of the original $f(i,j)$. Thus, when increasing k, if $f(i,j)$ contains many high spatial frequencies the PSNR rapidly decreases, but when low and mid frequencies predominated PSNR slowly decreases.

Similarly, the HVS is a system that induces a distortion on the observed image $\hat{f}(i,j)$, whose model is predicted by CIWaM. Hence, CIWaM is considered a HSV particular distortion model $\Lambda \equiv$ CIWaM that generates a perceptual image $\hat{f}_\rho(i,j) \equiv \mathcal{I}_\rho$ from an observed image $f(i,j) \equiv \mathcal{I}$, i.e $\mathcal{I}_\rho = CIWaM[\mathcal{I}]$. Therefore, a set of distortions is defined as $\Lambda_k \equiv \text{CIWaM}_d$, being d the observation distance. That is, a set of perceptual images is defined $\mathcal{I}_{\rho,d} = \text{CIWaM}_d[\mathcal{I}]$ which is considered a set of perceptual distortions of the hypothetical image $\mathcal{I}$.

When image $\hat{f}(i,j)$ is observed at distance $\bar{d}$ and this distance is reduced, the artifacts, if this possesses, are better perceived. In contrast, $\hat{f}(i,j)$ is observed from a far distance human eyes cannot perceive their artifacts, in consequence, the perceptual image quality of the distorted image is always high. The distance where the observer can perceive the best image quality of image $\hat{f}(i,j)$ is considered as the distance D.

3.3 Methodology

Let $f(i,j)$ and $\hat{f}(i,j)$ be an pattern image and a distorted image, respectively. $\mathcal{NR}$PSNR methodology is based on finding a distance D, where there is no perpetual difference between the wavelet energies of the images $f(i,j)$ and $\hat{f}(i,j)$, when an observer observe them at d centimeters of observation distance. So measuring the PSNR of $\hat{f}(i,j)$ at D will yield a fairer and No-reference perceptual evaluation of its image quality.

$\mathcal{NR}$PSNR algorithm is divided in five steps, which is summarized by the Figure 7 and described as follows:

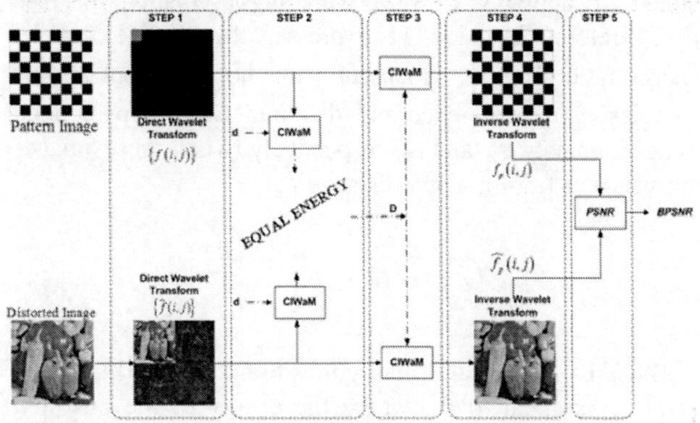

Fig. 7

METHODOLOGY FOR NO-REFERENCE PSNR WEIGHTING BY MEANS OF CIWAM. BOTH PATTERN AND DISTORTED IMAGES ARE WAVELET TRANSFORMED. THE DISTANCE D WHERE THE ENERGY OF PERCEPTUAL IMAGES OBTAINED BY CIWAM ARE EQUAL IS FOUND. THEN, PSNR OF PERCEPTUAL IMAGES AT D IS CALCULATED, OBTAINING THE $\mathcal{NR}$PSNR METRICS.

Step 1: Wavelet Transformation

Forward wavelet transform of images $f(i,j)$ and $\hat{f}(i,j)$ is performed using Eq. 3, obtaining the sets $\{\omega_{s,o}\}$ and $\{\hat{\omega}_{s,o}\}$, respectively. The employed analysis filter is the Daubechies 9-tap/7-tap filter (Table 1).

Table 1
9/7 ANALYSIS FILTER.

Analysis Filter		
i	Low-Pass Filter $h_L(i)$	High-Pass Filter $h_H(i)$
0	0.6029490182363579	1.115087052456994
±1	0.2668641184428723	-0.5912717631142470
±2	-0.07822326652898785	-0.05754352622849957
±3	-0.01686411844287495	0.09127176311424948
±4	0.02674875741080976	

Table 2
9/7 SYNTHESIS FILTER.

Synthesis Filter		
i	Low-Pass Filter $h_L(i)$	High-Pass Filter $h_H(i)$
0	1.115087052456994	0.6029490182363579
±1	0.5912717631142470	-0.2668641184428723
±2	-0.05754352622849957	-0.07822326652898785
±3	-0.09127176311424948	0.01686411844287495
±4		0.02674875741080976

Step 2: Distance D
The total energy measure or the *deviation signature*[9] $\bar{\varepsilon}$ is the absolute sum of the wavelet coefficient magnitudes, defined by [10]

$$\bar{\varepsilon} = \sum_{n=1}^{N} \sum_{m=1}^{M} |x(m,n)| \tag{10}$$

where $x(m,n)$ is the set of wavelet coefficients, whose energy is being calculated, being m and n the indexes of the coefficients. Basing on the traditional definition of a calorie, the units of $\bar{\varepsilon}$ are wavelet calories (wCal) and can also be defined by Eq. 10, since one wCal is the energy needed to increase the absolute magnitude of a wavelet coefficient by one scale.

From wavelet coefficients $\{\omega_{s,o}\}$ and $\{\hat{\omega}_{s,o}\}$ the corresponding perceptual wavelet coefficients $\left\{\omega_{s,o;\rho,\tilde{d}}\right\} = \alpha(\nu,r)\cdot\omega_{s,o}$ and $\left\{\hat{\omega}_{s,o;\rho,\tilde{d}}\right\} = \alpha(\nu,r)\cdot\hat{\omega}_{s,o}$ are obtained by applying CIWaM with an observation distance $\tilde{d}$. Therefore, Equation 11 expresses the relative wavelet energy ratio $\varepsilon\mathcal{R}\left(\tilde{d}\right)$, which compares how different are the energies of the reference and distorted CIWaM perceptual images, namely ε_ρ and $\widehat{\varepsilon}_\rho$ respectively, when these images are watched from a given distance $\tilde{d}$.

$$\varepsilon\mathcal{R}\left(\tilde{d}\right) = 10\cdot\left|\log_{10}\frac{\varepsilon_\rho\left(\tilde{d}\right)}{\widehat{\varepsilon}_\rho\left(\tilde{d}\right)}\right| \tag{11}$$

Thus, the main goal of this step is to find $\varepsilon\mathcal{R}(D)$, namely, at D ε_ρ is equal to $\widehat{\varepsilon}_\rho$, where the energy of the distorted images are the same than the energy of the pattern.

Step 3: Perceptual Images
Getting the perceptual images $\{f_p(i,j)\}$ and $\left\{\hat{f}_p(i,j)\right\}$ from the $\{f(i,j)\}$ and $\left\{\hat{f}(i,j)\right\}$ images watched at D centimeters, using Equation 4.

Step 4: Inverse Wavelet Transformation
Perform the Inverse Wavelet Transform of $\{\omega_{s,o;\rho,D}\}$ and $\{\hat{\omega}_{s,o;\rho,D}\}$, obtaining the perceptual images $f_{\rho(i,j),D}$ and $\hat{f}_{\rho(i,j),D}$, respectively. The synthesis filter in Table 2 is an inverse Daubechies 9-tap/7-tap filter.

Step 5: PSNR ***between perceptual images***
Calculate the PSNR between perceptual images $f_{\rho(i,j),D}$ and $\hat{f}_{\rho(i,j),D}$ using Eq. 2 in order to obtain the No-Reference CIWaM weighted PSNR i.e. the $\mathcal{NR}$PSNR.

4. Experimental Results

It is important to mention that $\mathcal{NR}$PSNR estimates the degradation, thus, the smaller the better. In this section, $\mathcal{NR}$PSNR performance is assessed by comparing the statistical significance of the images *Lenna* and *Baboon*, in addition to the Pearson correlation between $\mathcal{NR}$PSNR and PSNR data.

Figure 8 depicts three JPEG2000 distorted versions of the image *Lenna* with 0.05(Fig. 8(a)), 0.50 (Fig. 8(b)) and 1.00 (Fig. 8(c)) bits per pixel. PSNR estimates 23.41, 32.74 and 34.96 dB, respectively. While $\mathcal{NR}$PSNR computes 48.42, 36.56 and 35.95 dB, respectively. Thus, both PSNR and $\mathcal{NR}$PSNR estimate that image at 1.00 bpp has lower distortion.

(a) 0.05 bpp (b) 0.50 bpp (c) 1.00 bpp

Fig. 8
JPEG2000 DISTORTED VERSIONS OF COLOR IMAGE *Lenna* AT DIFFERENT BIT RATES EXPRESSED IN BITS PER PIXEL (BPP). (A) HIGH DISTORTION, (B) MEDIUM DISTORTION AND (C) LOW DISTORTION.

When this experiment is extended computing the JPEG2000 distorted versions from 0.05 bpp to 3.00bpp (increments of 0.05 bpp, depicted at Figure 9), we found that the correlation between PSNR and $\mathcal{NR}$PSNR is 99.32 %, namely for image *Lenna* for every 10,000 estimation $\mathcal{NR}$PSNR misses only in 68 assessments.

Figure 10 depicts three JPEG2000 distorted versions of the image *Baboon* with 0.05(Fig. 10(a)), 0.50 (Fig. 10(b)) and 1.00 (Fig. 10(c)) bits per pixel. PSNR estimates 18.55, 23.05 and 25.11 dB, respectively. While $\mathcal{NR}$PSNR computes 43.49, 30.07 and 28.71 dB, respectively. Thus, both PSNR and $\mathcal{NR}$PSNR estimate that image at 0.05 bpp has higher distortion.

When this experiment is extended computing the JPEG2000 distorted versions from 0.05 bpp to 3.00bpp

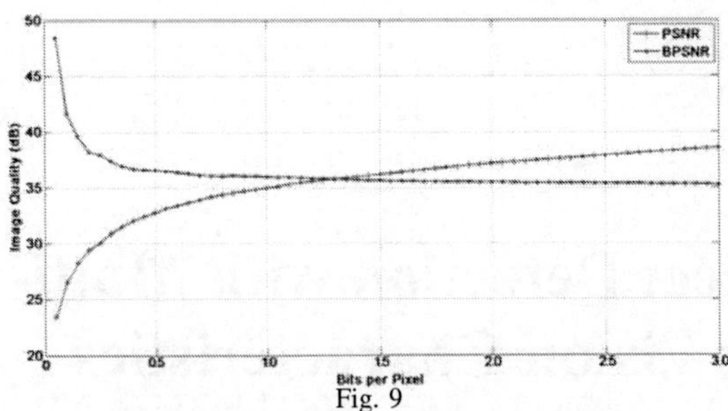

Fig. 9

COMPARISON OF PSNR AND $\mathcal{NR}$PSNR FOR THE JPEG2000 DISTORTED VERSIONS OF IMAGE *Lenna*.

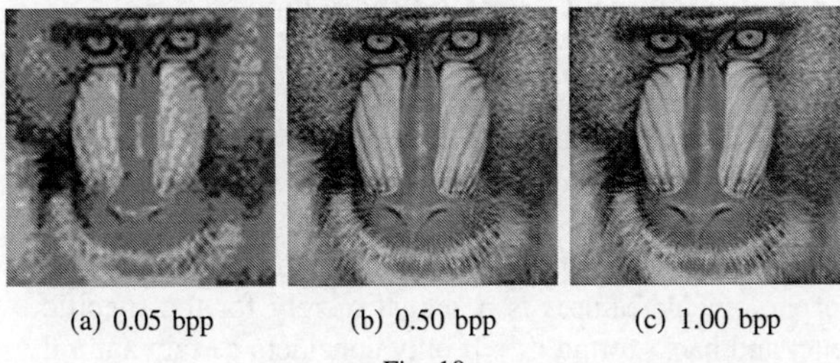

(a) 0.05 bpp (b) 0.50 bpp (c) 1.00 bpp

Fig. 10

JPEG2000 DISTORTED VERSIONS OF COLOR IMAGE *Baboon* AT DIFFERENT BIT RATES EXPRESSED IN BITS PER PIXEL (BPP). (A) HIGH DISTORTION, (B) MEDIUM DISTORTION AND (C) LOW DISTORTION.

(increments of 0.05 bpp, depicted at Figure 11), we found that the correlation between PSNR and $\mathcal{NR}$PSNR is 96.95 %, namely for image *Baboon* for every 10,000 estimation $\mathcal{NR}$PSNR misses only in 305 assessments.

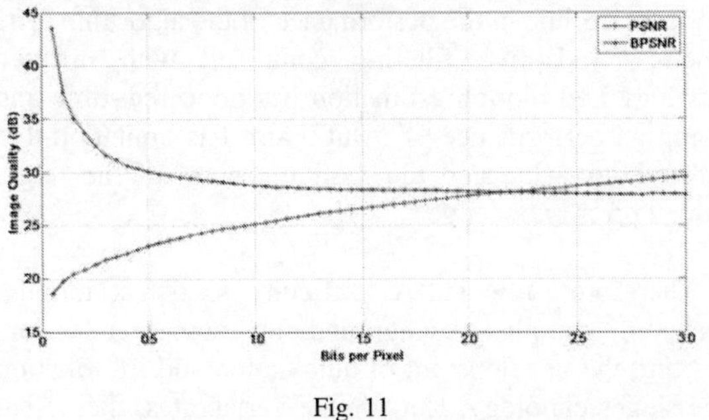

Fig. 11

COMPARISON OF PSNR AND $\mathcal{NR}$PSNR FOR THE JPEG2000 DISTORTED VERSIONS OF IMAGE *Baboon*.

5. Conclusions

$\mathcal{NR}$PSNR is a new metric for no-reference or blind image quality based on perceptual weighting of PSNR by using a perceptual low-level model of the Human Visual System (CIWaM model). The proposed $\mathcal{NR}$PSNR metrics is based on five steps.

The $\mathcal{NR}$PSNR assessment was tested in two well-known images, such as *Lenna* and *Baboon*. It is a well-correlated image quality method in these images for JPEG2000 distortions when compared to PSNR. Concretely, $\mathcal{NR}$PSNR correlates with PSNR, on the average in 98.13%.

It is possible to quantize a particular pixel while an algorithm of bit allocation is working, incorporating into embedded compression schemes such as EZW, SPIHT, JPEG2000 or H*i*-SET[11].

Acknowledgment

This work is supported by The National Polytechnic Institute of Mexico by means of a granted fund by the Committee of Operation and Promotion of Academic Activities (COFAA).

References

[1] Z. Wang and A. Bovik, "Mean squared error: Love it or leave it? a new look at signal fidelity measures," *Signal Processing Magazine, IEEE*, vol. 26, no. 1, pp. 98 –117, jan. 2009.

[2] Z. Wang and A. C. Bovik, *Modern Image Quality Assessment*, 1st ed. Morgan & Claypool Publishers: Synthesis Lectures on Image, Video, & Multimedia Processing, February 2006.

[3] F. Auli-Llinas and J. Serra-Sagrista, "Low complexity JPEG2000 rate control through reverse subband scanning order and coding passes concatenation," *IEEE Signal Processing Letters*, vol. 14, no. 4, pp. 251 –254, april 2007.

[4] D. S. Taubman and M. W. Marcellin, *JPEG2000: Image Compression Fundamentals, Standards and Practice*, ser. ISBN: 0-7923-7519-X. Kluwer Academic Publishers, 2002.

[5] J. Bartrina-Rapesta, F. Auli-Llinas, J. Serra-Sagrista, and J. Monteagudo-Pereira, "JPEG2000 Arbitrary ROI coding through rate-distortion optimization techniques," in *Data Compression Conference*, 25-27 2008, pp. 292 –301.

[6] X. Otazu, C. Párraga, and M. Vanrell, "Toward a unified chromatic induction model," *Journal of Vision*, vol. 10(12), no. 6, 2010.

[7] N. Murray, M. Vanrell, X. Otazu, and A. Parraga, "Saliency estimation using a non-parametric low-level vision model," in *Proceedings of IEEE Conference on Computer Vision and Pattern Recognition (CVPR'2011)*, 2010, pp. 433 –440.

[8] K. T. Mullen, "The contrast sensitivity of human colour vision to red-green and blue-yellow chromatic gratings." *The Journal of Physiology*, vol. 359, pp. 381–400, February 1985.

[9] G. van de Wouwer, P. Scheunders, and D. van Dyck, "Statistical texture characterization from discrete wavelet representations," *IEEE Transactions on Image Processing*, vol. 8, no. 4, pp. 592 –598, Apr. 1999.

[10] B. A. Wilson and M. A. Bayoumi, "A computational kernel for fast and efficient compressed-domain calculations of wavelet subband energies." *IEEE Transactions on Circuits and Systems II: Analog and Digital Signal Processing*, vol. 50, no. 7, pp. 389 – 392, July 2003.

[11] J. Moreno and X. Otazu, "Image coder based on H*i*lbert Scaning of Embedded quadTrees," *IEEE Data Compression Conference*, p. 470, March 2011.

A Bionic Method of Moving Object Detection with Multi-feature Fusion Based On Frog Vision Characteristics

Xiaogang Tang[1,2], Sun'an Wang[1], Hongyu Di[1], Litian Liu[2]
[1]School of mechanical Engineering, Xi'an Jiaotong University, Xi'an, Shaanxi, P.R. China
[2]Department of Information Equipment, Academy of Equipment, Beijing, P.R. China

Abstract - *In the complex natural background, the image features of moving objects usually change severely. And the kinematics and morphological features of dynamic target are unconspicuous due to the fast movement, unpredictable kinetic law and the accompanied scale transformation. The methods of motion detection based on one single morphological, statistics or kinetic features would not meet the requirements. Inspired by the visual characteristics of frog eye and the physiology characteristics of dynamic response of the retinal neural circuit, a spatial-temporal moving target recognition method based on the frog's vision is provided. This method introduces a biomimetic recognition algorithm of multi-feature fusion for dynamic target detection based on BP neural network. The experimental results show that the method achieves to inhibit the background information effectively and enhance the multidimensional moving target information through the mechanism of spatial and temporal characteristics and multi-feature fusion, which is better than the method based on single feature. The algorithm principle provides a biomimetic approach for motion detection.*

Keywords: Frog's vision characteristics, Complex natural background, Moving object detection, Multi-feature fusion, BP neural networks

1 Introduction

Moving object detection is one key technology of infrared tracking, precision-guided, air defense alerting, large field target detection and satellite remote sensing [1]. The effectiveness and real-time performance of the moving object detection algorithm will directly influences the precision and efficiency of the subsequent video servo and tracking. Moving object detection in complex natural background is much closer to practical application and thus attracts much attention. But due to the complicated background and unpredictable motion, the feature of dynamic target images is unstable. In addition, the target is usually of small size and accompanied with scale transformations like rotation, scaling, etc. Therefore, the moving object detection in complex background has always been a hot and difficult problem in the field of machine vision and image processing.

Moving object detection method based on morphological features is practical merely for the specific target and background [2-3]. It only considers certain natural attributes of the target. In complex backgrounds, the algorithm's robustness is insufficient. And when the target is micro compared to the background, the configuration of the target such as texture, color or shape is unconspicuous, making the effectiveness of that method limited. Another technique for moving object detection is based on the target and background statistical model. It has good performance in the simple background [4-6]. However, the statistical features of the target and the background are not stable in a dramatic changing environment, leading to a significant decline in the performance of the algorithm. The method of adaptive filtering combined with infrared technology and motion estimation has good real-time and recognition performance [7-9]. But it also has limitation that the threshold value and the motion feature of the target require a prior knowledge.

Therefore, it is still a difficulty to detect moving objects in complex background on computer vision, restricting the development of automation and information processing technology. But for the vertebrates, the visual behavior such as specific object detection, spatial location and motion tracking is an easy task. In the process of biological evolution, a variety of creatures developed a perfect tool for capturing the target, their vision systems, and provides an inspiration on the solution of the problem [10-11]. Frog has a relatively simple brain, and mainly relies on eye retinal neural for the target recognition. Besides, frog is sensitive to the dynamic targets of certain characters and is insensitive to static ones. At present, there is no unified model or fixed mechanism of frog vision on target identification. Most of the researches concentrate on the computer simulation of its specific features. According to frog eye sight is limited and its Predation depends on the target size, Zhi-ling Wang have proposed A Fuzzy Region Understanding Tactic for Object Tracking Based on Frog's Vision Characteristic [11], through filtering, maintain, merge method, the background interference was reduced and target texture, image contour features were highlighted gradually. Zhi-yong Li have presented a motion recognition method based on the bionic intelligence[12], moving target was determined through edge extraction and thermodynamic entropy threshold segmentation, and the algorithm had better effect. But none of the papers discussed the optic nerve mechanism of proposed method, and relatively narrowly focused the computer simulation of frog certain visual features.

This paper mainly focuses on the moving object detection in complex backgrounds. On the basis of summarizing the frog visual imaging features, the physiology characteristics of the frog retinal neural circuit and its response to dynamic target are induced. The impact factors of the frog visual neural circuit response to the target size, gray variance, shape characteristics and target motion feature are clarified. Then spatial-temporal recognition mechanism based on the frog's vision is come up with and a biomimetic recognition algorithm of multi-feature fusion for dynamic target is designed. This method combines the morphological and kinematic features of dynamic objects effectively and achieves the recognition of the moving objects in complex background through effectively inhibiting background information and enhancing dynamic target features in multi-dimension. The algorithm principle is simple and easy to implement, providing a biomimetic approach for motion detection.

2 Frog eyes features and bionic ideas

2.1 Features of frog eyes and physiological structure

Frog eye has a unique visual characteristics and physiological structure[13-14], which ensures the effectiveness of its predatory behavior in complex natural environment. The field of view of frog eye is limited, and it can only handle grayscale information, while it is sensitive to the rate of change of the gray-scale shading. Frog eye only has the ability to identify the specific size of the target, and it's more sensitive to the curved edge features of the target. Besides, the frog eye can only identify the moving target with the particular law of motion, but it fails to recognize static target. Frog eye is selective to the direction of motion of the dynamic target, which is more sensitive to the transverse crossing goal than the vertical crossing goal.

The unique visual characteristics of frog eyes rely on its unique physiological structure. The analysis of frog eye retinal nerve structure shows that the optic nerve fibers are divided into four major categories: darken detector, sustained contrast detector, convex edge detector and motion edge detector. The four types of nerve fibers achieve to recognize the target in grayscale images which has a specific size and a specific law of motion. R3, which is a basic physiological unit to compose the four kinds of nerve fibers, is one of the most important neurons of the frog retina, whose physiological characteristics determine the frog visual imaging characteristics and dynamic target recognition capabilities. Figure 1 is a simplified model of frog retinal ganglion cells R3[15]. Photoreceptors (Rec) convert light to membrane potential. Horizontal cells (H) reflect the environmental background brightness. Hyperpolarizing bipolar cells (HBC) and depolarizing bipolar cells (DBC) detect the instant changes of light on and light off, which means they can produce depolarization and hyperpolarization response to light stimulus. For motion stimulation, bipolar cells have a continuous output. ATH and ATD, two types of amacrine cells, are high-pass filter with a threshold, which respond to negative and positive changes of corresponding bipolar cells. The R3 cells can accept input of the ATD and ATH cells in all access roads within the receptive field. That means the increase in brightness stimulates R3 to response through ON channel, and the decrease in brightness stimulates R3 to response through OFF channel. Thus the R3 cells integrate the input of all channels in the space within the receptive field. The result shows that R3 cell is selective to size and speed of moving stimulation, because of its special structure and size. The receptive field size of the R3 cell determines the ability of neurons to detect stimulation. The difference of excitatory and inhibitory input synaptic delay and the time constant is an important basis to determine the moving type of the simulation.

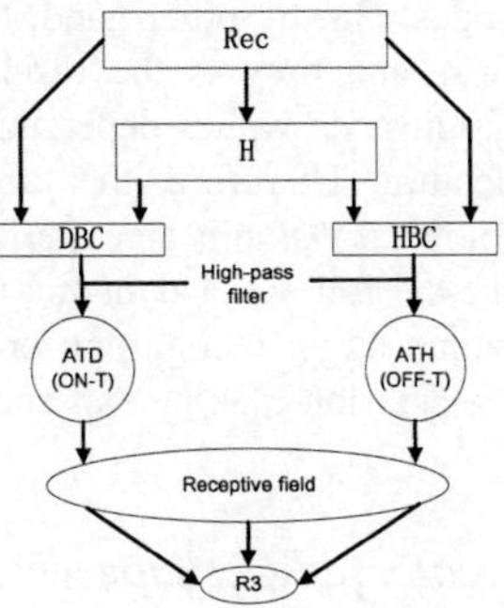

Figure 1. Overall structure of simplified R3 model

2.2 Bionic ideas of moving target detection

The above analysis shows that the physiological structure of the frog eye's R3 cell determines the spatial (the response characteristics to the stimulus of specific grayscale, edge and shape) and temporal (the response characteristics to the specific moving feature) characteristics of the moving target recognition. The moving target recognition process of frog eye is the result of multi-feature fusion. Based on the frog visual properties and biological identification mechanism, this paper constructs the bionic structure and identification mechanism of moving target recognition, which is shown in figure 2. The four bionic recognizers respectively identify the gray, gray change rate, shape and moving feature, and the single feature recognition results are weighted to input to the multi-feature fusion recognition neural network. The multi-feature fusion recognition result is input to frog brain to compare with the experience threshold of prey and predator and determine the target property and decide the follow action.

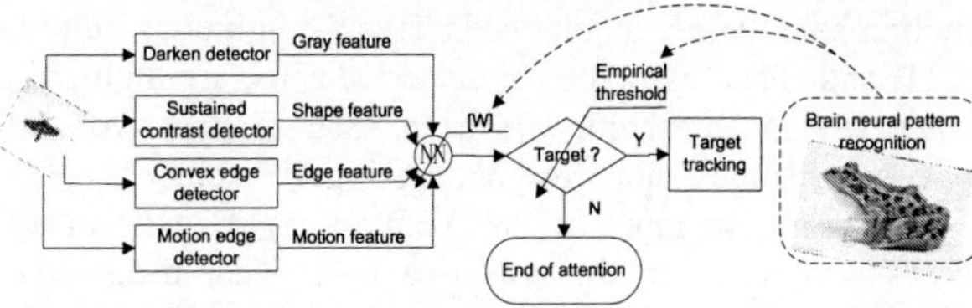

Figure 2. Moving target detection principle based on frog's vision characteristics

3 The Proposed Method

3.1 Model expression of dynamic target

From the bionic moving target recognition structure shown in figure 2, we can see that frog brain acts as a guide for the identification mechanism. On the one hand, frog brain should adjust the neural network weights to improve the accuracy of target recognition when the environment changes. On the other hand, the threshold to determine predators and prey is the result of long term learning and can adjust its values depending on the scene and the target feature. Therefore, the target recognition mechanism of biological vision is an experienced judgment process. We build the following dynamic target model to simulate the dynamic target recognition process based on the comprehensive decision-making experimental threshold. Dynamic target:

$$Object = [color, edge, shape, velocity] \quad (1)$$

In the expression, color stands for the color information of the object, and we choose the space chromaticity information using HIS model, namely $color = \{H : 0 \sim 255\}$. Edge stands for the edge information of the object, and we will take the gray space of edge feature expression, namely $edge = E_{m\times n} = (e_{ij})_{m\times n}, e_{ij} = \{0 \sim 1\};$. Shape is the shape information of the object, it obeys the particular shape feature that its expression is $f(x)$, $shape = S_{m\times n} = (s_{ij})_{m\times n}, s_{ij} = f(s_{ij});$. Velocity stands for the speed information of the object, which obeys the law of a particular motion that expression is $g(y)$, and is used for the recognition of movement style. which is $velocity = \{V : 0 \sim 1\}$. When $V \in g(y)$, $V = 1$, otherwise $V = 0$.

3.2 Bionic algorithm implementation

3.2.1 The bionic algorithm design

In order to achieve the bionic structure of moving target recognition and identification mechanism proposed in this paper, the bionic algorithm is to solve three major problems. (1) Rapid extraction method of dynamic spatial and temporal characteristics. (2) The mechanism of multi-feature fusion. (3) Dynamic threshold adjustment method. This paper uses chroma bandpass filter, edge detection based on Canny operator and shape detection based on Hough transform to realize the rapid extraction of the spatial feature of moving target. We use motion detection method based on optical flow to realize the rapid extraction of the temporal feature of moving target. Meanwhile, we also construct multi-input single-output three-layer neural network to realize the recognition mechanism of multi-feature fusion of moving target. In this paper, the objective determination threshold is set to a fixed value, and the dynamic adjust method of the threshold is to be studied in the future. The dynamic target recognition bionic algorithm is shown in figure 3.

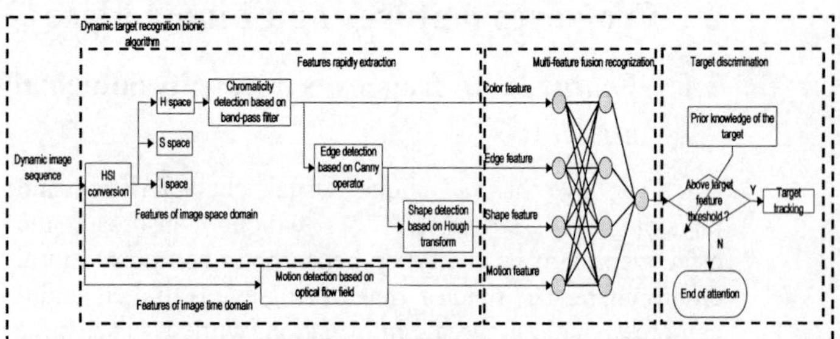

Figure 3. Dynamic target recognition bionic algorithm

3.2.2 Rapidly extraction method of moving target features

Dynamic sampling information model for target identification bionic platform is sequence images represented by RGB image model. If the image resolution is $M \times N$, to simulate the frog eye monochromatic visual features, the RGB image is transferred into a HIS image. Based on the prior knowledge, the band pass filter algorithm of H (chroma) information is designed and the target recognition of monochrome vision based on frog eye is realized. Chromaticity band pass filter is shown as follows:

$$h_{ij} = \begin{cases} 1, 当 H_{\min} \le H_{ij} \le H_{\max} \\ 0, 当 H_{ij} \le H_{\min} 或 H_{ij} \ge H_{\max} \end{cases} \quad (2)$$

h_{ij} is the filtering result of the point (i, j) in image matrix space through chromaticity band pass filter. H_{ij} is the chromaticity H component of the point (i, j) in image matrix space. $H_{\min}$ and $H_{\max}$ are the dynamic threshold ranges according to the prior knowledge, $i = 0,1 \cdots M-1$, $j = 0,1 \cdots N-1$.

To simulate the recognition feature of the frog eye for the particular shape of a target, a circular target is adopted for feature extraction in this paper. The basic thought to detect circle based on Hough transforms is to transfer the image spatial domain to the parameter space and use certain parameters which will satisfy most of the boundary points to describe the curves in the image. By setting the accumulator to accumulate, the point corresponding to the peak is the information needed. The principle of Hough transforms detecting the image spatial resolution of the curve is as follows. The general form of analytical curve parametric representation is:

$$f(x, a) = 0 \quad (3)$$

In the expression, x is a point on the curve (two-dimensional vector), and a is a point in the parameter space. For a circle, the radius is r, and the circle whose center coordinates is (a, b) can be represented in the parameter space as:

$$(x_i - a)^2 + (y_i - b)^2 = r^2 \quad (4)$$

At this time, the point $x = [x_i, y_i]^T$, $a = [a, b, r]^T$ is three dimensional in parameter space. For a circle in the image space, its radius is fixed and every point on the circumference of a circle forms a set of cone which has a equal r and different a, b. The points of the circle in image space which is an intersection of a bunch of cone mapping to the parameter space correspond to the center coordinates and the radius of the circle.

To simulate the recognition feature to the specific edge characteristics, this paper uses the edge detection method based on Canny operator, which has a high speed of extraction and is a mature method. The edge detection progress based on Canny operator is shown in Figure 4.

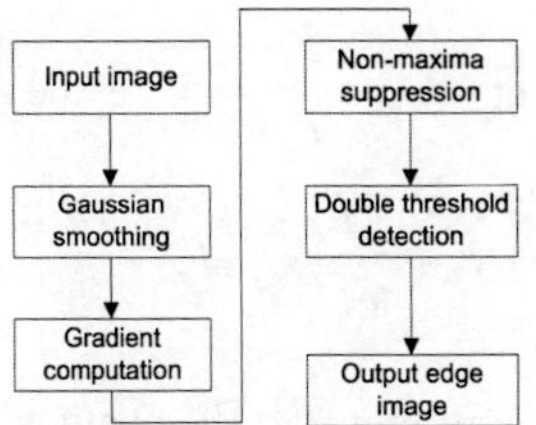

Figure 4. Edge detection based on Canny operator

Analysis of dynamic response of the frog visual characteristics and retinal nerve loop shows that moving target identification of the frog eye takes into account both the spatial characteristics (response characteristics to specific gray scale, shape, edge) and temporal characteristics (response characteristics to specific moving feature) of the moving target. The spatial-temporal identification mechanism makes full use of the morphological and kinematic characteristics of the target, which improves the effectiveness of target recognition.

Optical flow is the instantaneous speed of pixel movement which is projected onto the imaging plane by moving target. Optical flow field is the apparent change of the grayscale mode. Since the optical flow field contains the motion information of the image sequence, it is feasible to use the motion information of different elements to divide moving targets in image sequences.

In this paper, we adopt the gradient-based LK algorithm proposed by Lucas and Kanade[16]. Let $I(x,t)$ represents the gray value of the image at point x at the time t, and $v = (u, v)$ is the optical flow at this point. Obviously the grayscale values and the initial grayscale values of the image have the following relationship:

$$I(x,t) = I(x - vt, 0) \quad (5)$$

The image consistency assumptions:

$$\frac{dI(x,t)}{dt} = 0 \quad (6)$$

Coupled with the above Taylor expansion of formula (1), we get the following gradient constraint equation:

$$\nabla I(x,t) \cdot v + \frac{dI(x,t)}{dt} = 0 \quad (7)$$

Thus, we get: $v = -\frac{I_t}{I_x}$, where the I_t and I_x are defined as follows: $I_t = \frac{\partial I}{\partial t}\Big|_{x(t)}, I_x = \frac{\partial I}{\partial x}\Big|_t$.

Besides, by approximately calculating of the gradient constraint equation using the weighted least squares method, we can get the optimized optical flow field in each small interval Ω:

$$\sum_{X\in\Omega}[W(x)]^2 \cdot [\nabla I(x,t)\cdot v + \frac{dI(x,t)}{dt}]^2 \quad (8)$$

where $W(x)$ is the window function.

The recognition process of the motion feature based on the optical flow shows below:

Assuming the feature point in image A is $u = [u_x, u_y]^T$, motion estimation is to find the point:

$$v = u + d = [u_x + d_x \quad u_y + d_y]^T \quad (9)$$

In image B, where $d = [d_x \quad d_y]^T$, which is the displacement vector of feature point u. And v, which is approximately calculated by solving the gradient constraint equation using the weighted least squares method, is the optical flow field value of feature point u.

3.2.3 Strategy of multi-feature fusion

Because the external conditions and moving target changing have a bad influence, the moving target recognition method based on a single feature is limited. On the basis of the analysis of frog eye's recognition mechanism, this paper has designed a multi-feature fusion mechanism based on neural network. The fusion strategy takes full advantage of the spatial and temporal characteristics, and enhances multi-dimensional information of moving target. The strategy of multi-feature fusion based on neural network is shown in figure 5.

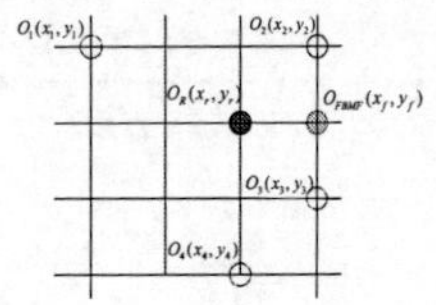

Figure 5. Multi-feature fusion recognition based on neural network

Where, $O_i(x_i, y_i), (i = 1,2,3,4)$ is the recognition result of the four rapid recognition method, which is to identify the central coordinate of the target. $O_R(x_r, y_r)$ is the real central coordinate of moving target, and $O_{FBMF}(x_f, y_f)$ is the objective central coordinate of multi-feature fusion recognition. And we have:

$$O_{FBMF} = \frac{\sum_{i=1}^{4} O_i * W_i}{\sum_{i=1}^{4} W_i} \quad (10)$$

Where $W_i(i = 1,2,3,4)$ is the nonlinear mapping matrix of the BP neural network input $O_i, (i = 1,2,3,4)$ and the output O_{FBMF}, whose value is determined by BP neural network weights matrix $w_{ij}^l(l = 1,2,3; i = 0,1\cdots k-1; j = 0,1\cdots n-1)$, and l is the layer ordinal number of the neural network, k is the number of neurons in each layer, n is the input number of a layer in the neural network. The BP model of 3 layers was used in the paper, and the function Sigmoid was chosen to be the activation function of neurons, which is:

$$f(x) = \frac{1}{1+e^{-x}} \quad (11)$$

The structure of BP neural network based on multi-feature fusion is shown in figure 6.

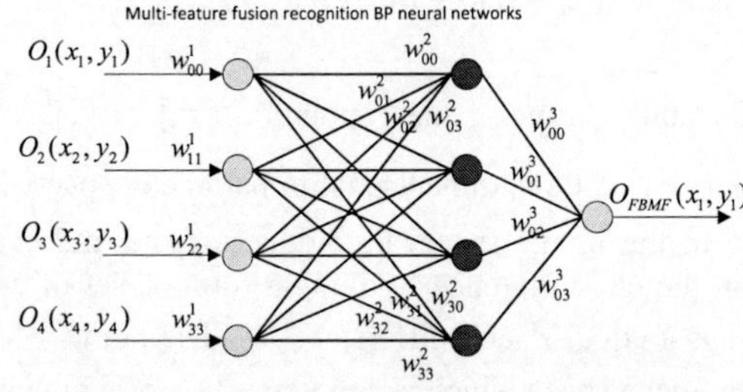

Figure 6. Multi-feature fusion recognition BP neural networks

The neural network was trained by inputting image sequences in which the central coordinate of the target had been calibrated in advance, so that the nonlinear mapping matrix $W_i(i = 1,2,3,4)$ was determined.

4 Moving object detection experimental results

In order to show the effectiveness of the algorithm, we conducted comparative experiments between a simple feature recognition and multi-feature fusion recognition in both simple and complex environment. In order to show the robustness of the algorithm, we conducted recognition experiments combining spatial and temporal characteristics together in strong similarity background interference and strong similarity target interference. The result is shown in Figure 10 to Figure 13.

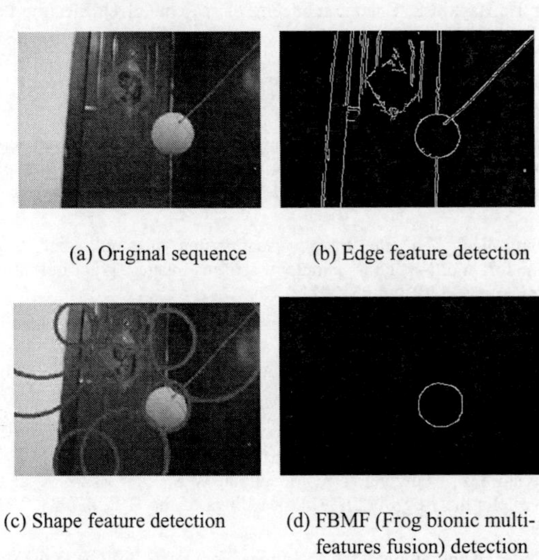

(a) Original sequence (b) Edge feature detection

(c) Shape feature detection (d) FBMF (Frog bionic multi-features fusion) detection

Figure 7. Recognition comparison experiment under simple background

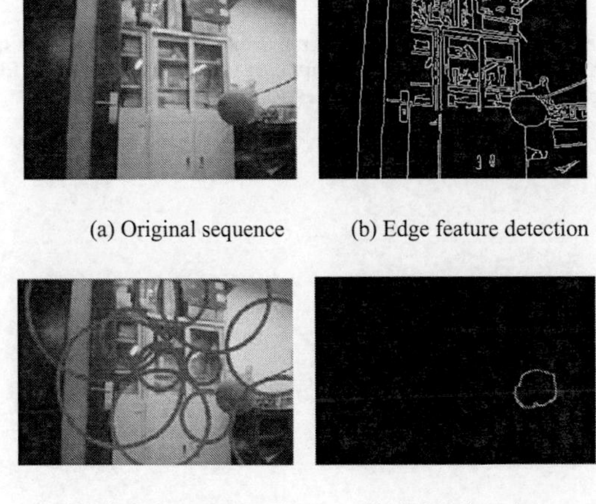

(a) Original sequence (b) Edge feature detection

(c) Shape feature detection (d) FBMF detection

Figure 8. Recognition comparison experiment under complex background

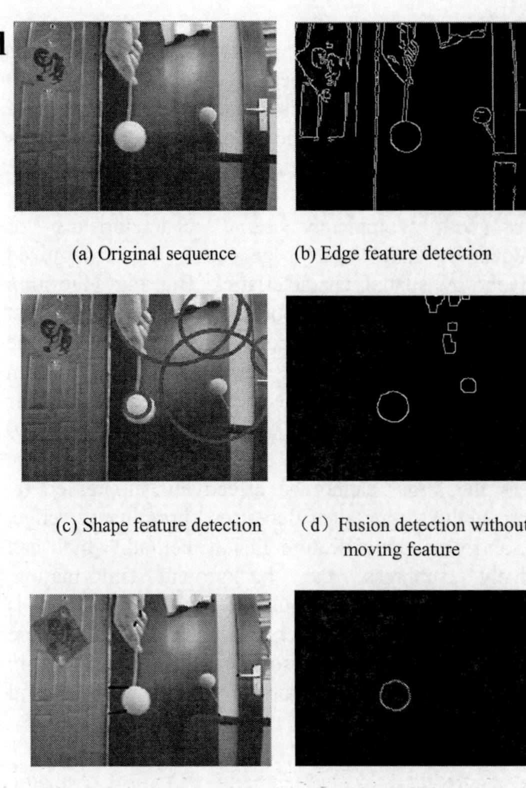

(a) Original sequence (b) Edge feature detection

(c) Shape feature detection (d) Fusion detection without moving feature

(e) Moving feature detection (f) FBMF detection

Figure 9. Experiment under strongly similar target interference

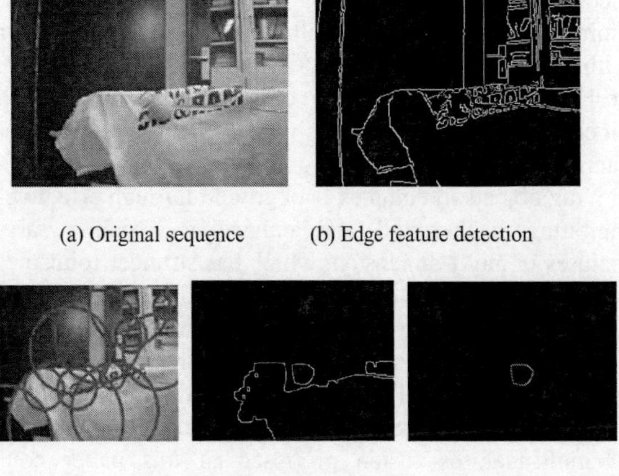

(a) Original sequence (b) Edge feature detection

(c) Shape feature detection (d) Fusion detection without moving feature (e) FBMF detection

Figure 10. Experiment under strongly similar background interference

The comparative experiments in Figure 7 and 8 shows that the recognition method based on the single morphological characteristics (for example only edge detection and shape feature detection) of the target is ineffective. The detection method of frog bionic multi-features fusion (FBMF), which enhances the target feature and suppresses the background in multiple dimensions, is effective. Figure 9 shows the experiment that was conducted under strongly similar target interference. Targets with completely same characteristics of chrominance, shape and edge can't be recognized effectively by spatial characteristics. But our algorithm combines the spatial and temporal characteristics of target so that the target feature has been enhanced. Thus, in the condition of strong similarity interference, the algorithm can detect moving target effectively. Experiment under strongly similar background interference in figure 10 shows that the wide range of background with the same color as the target cannot be effectively suppressed by filtering method. Our algorithm uses chrominance, edge, shape, and other multi-feature fusion method, which can effectively suppress the background information. Meanwhile, the moving feature recognition method is added to the algorithm, which made the detection more effective. The experimental results show that the algorithm based on bionic multi-feature fusion is robust and significant.

5 Conclusions

Based on frog's eyes visual characteristics, physiological structure and the dynamic responses of the retinal neural circuits, a spatial-temporal recognition mechanism based on the frog's vision is provided, and a biomimetic recognition algorithm based on neural network with multi-feature fusion for dynamic target detection is designed. The algorithm effectively combines the kinematic characteristics with the morphological characteristics of the moving target, and recognizes the moving objects in complex background through effectively inhibiting background and enhancing dynamic target features in multi-dimension, which has stronger robustness and effectiveness. Besides, this method make integrated use of filtering, edge extraction, image transformation and other image processing methods, which is easy to implement. Meanwhile, one point should be proposed that even the real frogs would be tricked by baits, so the method of multi-features fusion proposed in this paper could continue to improve. But the moving target recognition method that simulates the biological visual processing mechanisms provides a new approach for this kind of problem under the complex natural condition.

6 References

[1] Liu Yun-He, Si Xi-Cai, Jiao Shu-Hong etal. Study of detection algorithm for infrared small target[J]. Journal of Projectiles, Rockets, Missiles and Guidance, 28(1): 53-55,2008.

[2] PEN Jia-Xiong,ZHOU Wen-Lin. Infrared background suppression for segmenting and detecting small target[J]. Acta ELectronica Sinica, 27(12): 47-51, 1999.

[3] SUN Wei, XIA Liang-Zheng . Infrared target segmentation algorithm based on morphologic method[J]. Journal of Infrared and Millimeter Waves, 23 (3):233-236, 2004.

[4] Ling Jiangguo. Study on Robust Tracking and Recognition of Infrared Target [D]. Shanghai Jiaotong University.2007 .

[5] Wu Wei,Peng Jiaxiong. The feature of small target and its invariance analysis in infrared image sequence [J]. Journal of Huazhong University of Science and Technology, 30(3):83-85, 2002.

[6] Zhao Jiajia, etc. Infrared small target detection based on image sparse representation [J]. Journal of Infrared and Millimeter Waves, 30(2):156-166, 2011.

[7] Nan He,Haykin S. Chaotic modeling of sea clutter[K]. Electron.Lett, 28(22): 2076-2077, 2002.

[8] Yang L,Yang J,Yang K. Adaptive detection for infrared small target under sea-sky complex background[J]. Electron.Lett, 40(17):1083-1085.,2004.

[9] Yang Lei, Yang Jie, Zheng Zhong-Long. Detecting infrared small target based on adaptive local energy threshold under sea-sky complex background[J]. Journal of Infrared and Millimeter Waves, 25 (1):41-45, 2006.

[10] Huang Fengchen, etc. Insect visual system inspired small target detection for multi-spectral remotely sensed images [J]. Journal on Communications, 32(9):88-95, 2011.

[11]Wang Zhi-Ling,CHEN Zong-Hai.A Fuzzy Region Understanding Tactic for Object Tracking Based on Frog's Vision Characteristic[J].ACTA AUTOMATICA SINICA,35(8):1048-1054,2009.

[12]Zhi-yong Li,Zhen Jiang.A New Method of Motion Detection With Biological Intelligence[J].International Journal of Signal Processing,Image Process and Pattern Recognition,Vol.5,No.2:141-152,2012.

[13]Lettvian J Y, Maturana H R, Mcculloch W S, Pitts W H. What the frog's eye tells the frog's brain [J].Proceedings of the IRE, 47(11): 1940-1951, 1959.

[14]Ingle D. Disinhibition of tectal neurons by pretect allesions in the frog. Science, 180(84): 422-424, 1973.

[15]Jin Bo, etc. Physiological modeling of retinal neuronal circuit's response to moving stimuli[J]. Journal of Zhejiang University(Engineering Science),39(11):1713-1718,2005.

[16]LUCAS B.,KANADE T. An iterative image registration technique with an application to stereo Vision[C].Proc.of 7th International Joint Conference on Artificial Intelligence(IJCAI).674-679,1981.

Image inpainting scheme based discrete wavelet Transform

S.M. Elkaffas[1], **N.S. Khattab**[2], **and B. A. Youssef**[2]
[1] Arab Academy for Science, Technology & Maritime Transport, Alexandria, Egypt.
[2]City for Scientific Research and Technological Applications, Alexandria Egypt.

Abstract - This paper proposes a novel scheme for digital images inpainting based on discrete wavelet transform (DWT). Where the digital image is decomposed into four components and both structure and exemplar inpainting methods are individually applied on them to obtain the best arrangement with each component. Many cases if digital image have been used to verify the scheme. The aim of this research is to minimize the computation time without cause a big change in accuracy. Good inpainting results have been accomplished are obtained by testing the result of adding back the four sub images resulted from permutation method between these components. Experiments showed that the proposed scheme provides a better visual effect and less computation time.

Keywords: Image inpainting, Image reconstruction, Wavelet transform .

1 Introduction

The advancement in information technology, networking and communications make it easy to the users to transfer data, images and files. Editing image files may cause images to be destroyed or corrupted. Repairing damaged images is one of the main objectives of image processing that appears in image restoration and reconstruction of digital images. A new trend appears that simulates the work of professional restoration by replicating their techniques but-on digital images. The modification of images in a non-detectable way for the observer who does not know the original image is called *retouching* or *inpainting* [1]. The objective of inpainting is to reconstitute the corrupted or missing parts of the work, in order to make it more legible and to restore its unity. All what the user can do is only to specify the region to inpainted and not care how it will be filled or from where [1]. At present, mainly two classification techniques can be found in the literature related to digital image inpainting, Structure-based inpainting and texture-based inpainting [7, 8, 9, 10, 11]. Structure-based inpainting refers to the process of image inpainting which employs information around damaged region to estimate isophote from coarse to fine and diffuses information by diffusion mechanism. The most fundamental inpainting approach is the diffusion based approach in which the missing region is filled by diffusing image information from the known region into the missing region at the pixel level [1-3,12]. These algorithms are well founded on the theory of partial differential equation (PDE) and variational method filled in holes by continuously propagating the isophote (i.e., lines of equal gray values) into the missing region by [1].then further introduced Navier–Strokes equation in fluid dynamics into the task of inpainting[2]. In [3] proposed a variational framework based on total variation (TV) to recover the missing information. A curvature-driven diffusion equation was proposed to realize the connectivity principle which does not hold in the TV model[4]. A joint interpolation of isophote directions and gray-levels was also designed to incorporate the principle of continuity in a variational framework[5]. As PDE-based models have a good inpainting effect on the small-scale and non-texture damaged region such as the scratches, the creases and the spots and so on, but it is easy to cause the blurriness when they are used to inpaint relatively large damaged region.

The texture-based inpainting approaches propagates the image information from the known region into the missing region at the patch level, in which the texture is synthesized by sampling the best match patch from the known region[6] . In [6] an exemplar-based inpainting method based on the texture synthesis techniques proposed. The method fills in the inpainting domain gradually by copying from the most similar block in the image domain. Because sufficient information is considered in this method, it performs well on texture inpainting, even for large holes. But as for structure images, the direct block duplication from the image domain will cause block effect at image edges, and it can be detected easily by human eyes. Therefore, the exemplar-based inpainting approach performs poorly on inpainting gradient background image. Moreover, if the inpainting domain includes both texture and structure, the texture will disturb the inpainting process of the structure, which causes false edges in the repaired image [11]. Natural images are composed of structures and textures, in which the structures constitute the primal sketches of an image (e.g., the edges, corners, etc.) and the textures are image regions with homogenous patterns or feature statistics (including the flat patterns). Numerous approaches appears to overcome this problem by obtaining best combination of image inpainting, and texture synthesis by combining three developed components, image decomposition with inpainting and texture synthesis. This permits the simultaneous use of filling-in algorithms that are suited for different image characteristics that provide the best visual results. The total variation de-noising algorithm TV is used in decomposing image to structure and texture parts to be inpainted, respectively[7]. Another approach proposed a layered image inpainting scheme based on image decomposition by using discrete cosine transform (DCT)[8].

2 The Proposed Inpainting Scheme

In this section, the proposed inpainting algorithm used will be explained in details.

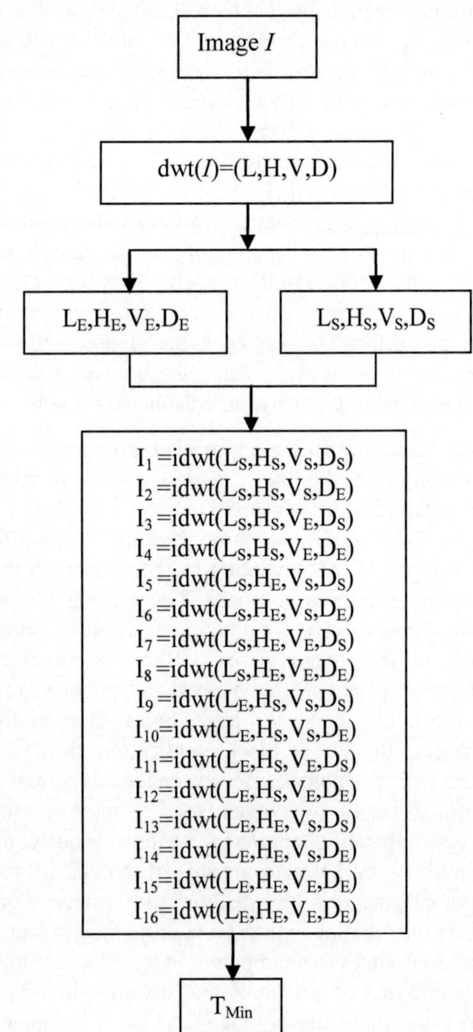

Figure 1: The proposed model

Where dwt is discrete wavelet transform, idwt is inverse discrete wavelet transform, (L,H,V,D) are the wavelet components, E means the image treated by exemplar inpainting, S means the image treated by structure inpainting and T_{Min} is minimum computing with good results.

The proposed algorithm, as shown in Figure (1), consists of the following phases:

Decompose the image using discrete wavelet transform that yields four components from the original image: Low (L) , High (H), Vertical (V) and Diagonal(D).

Then apply both PDE algorithm proposed by [1]inpainting algorithm and exemplar-based inpainting proposed in [6]on each components.

The four components is inpainted by both exemplar L_E,H_E,V_E,D_E and structure inpainting L_S,H_S,V_S,D_S

The components are then composed as inverse of DWT using permutation method between these components. This permutation results sixty output images.

The minimum computing time T_{Min} which is associated with good results is determined

2.1 Discrete Wavelets Transform

In this scheme, it is decided to choose Daubechies discrete wavelets transform. Although the Daubechies algorithm has a slightly higher computational overhead and is conceptually more complex, it can pick up the more detail that is missed by other wavelet algorithm. Daubechies discrete wavelets transform can be derived from mother wavelet

$$\Psi_{S,\tau}(t) = \frac{1}{\sqrt{S}}\Psi\left(\frac{t-\tau}{S}\right) \quad (1)$$

Where Ψ is wavelet function, t is wavelet function parameter, S is parameter scale and τ is parameter shift.

The Wavelet Transform for any discrete function $(f(t))$ can be expressed as the following

$$\gamma(S,\tau) = \int f(t)\ \Psi_{S,\tau}(t)\,dt \quad (2)$$

Where $f(t)$ is the image discrete data function and γ is coefficient of wavelet.

Also inverse wavelet Transform can be expressed as the following

$$f(t) = \int \gamma(S,\tau)\ \Psi_{S,\tau}(t)\,d\tau\,dS \quad (3)$$

2.2 Structure Image Inpainting

Structure image inpainting is an iterative process for repairing damaged images. The image holes are filled by propagating linear structure (isophote lines) into the region to be inpainted using PDE of physical heat flow, where the information propagate from the correct part of image to inpainted region in that image through its boundary.

Let image I, Ω stand for the region to be inpainted and $\delta\Omega$ for its boundary as in figure (2). The inpainting algorithm will be as follows:

$$\frac{\partial I}{\partial t} + R = 0 \quad (4)$$

$$R = \vec{N} \cdot \vec{\nabla}(\Delta I) \quad (5)$$

$$\vec{N} = \vec{\nabla}^T I \quad 6$$

Where the operators $\vec{\nabla}^T = \frac{\partial}{\partial y}\hat{x} - \frac{\partial}{\partial x}\hat{y}$,

$\vec{\nabla} = \frac{\partial}{\partial x}\hat{x} + \frac{\partial}{\partial y}\hat{y}$ and $\Delta = \frac{\partial^2}{\partial x^2} + \frac{\partial^2}{\partial y^2}$

The Equation 4 is discretized over the image domain as the flowing:

$$I_{i,j}^{n+1} = I_{i,j}^{n} + R_{i,j}^{n} \quad \forall (i,j) \in \Omega \quad (7)$$

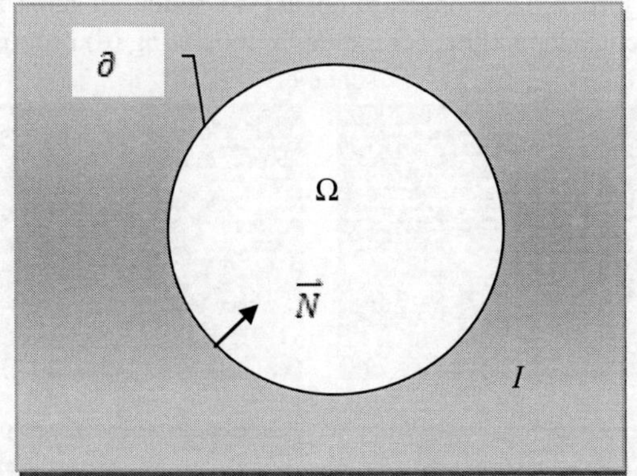

Figure 2: Propagation direction $\vec{N}$ as the normal to the signed distance to the boundary of the region to be inpainted.

2.3 Exemplar Inpainting

The exemplar based inpainting approach proposed by Criminisi [6], which is employed as a fundamental inpainting algorithm for texture synthesis in the proposed scheme. In image I the inpainted region Ω with boundary contour $\delta\Omega$ and the source region Φ clearly marked as shown in figure (3). The method can be summarized as follows:

At certain point $p \in \partial\Omega$ which is chosen according maximum priority Pp, a square patch ψ_p centered by p is constructed. This priority results from multiplication of data term D_p and confidence term C_p.

$$P_p = C_p . D_p \quad (8)$$

$$D_p = \frac{\left|\vec{\nabla}^{\perp} I_p . \vec{n}_p\right|}{\alpha} \quad (9)$$

$$C_p = \frac{\sum_{q \in \psi_p \cap \Omega} C_q}{\left|\psi_p\right|} \quad (10)$$

Where $\vec{\nabla}^{\perp} I_p$ is the isophote direction and $\vec{n}_p$ is a unit vector orthogonal to the front $\partial\Omega$ at the point p.

Comparing patch $\psi_p\big|_{with\,max\,P}$ is compared with all source patches ψ_q centered by $q \in \Phi$. ψ_q gets minimum distance $d(\Psi_p, \Psi_q)$ replaces ψ_p. Repeat until all points in the inpainting domain have been repaired.

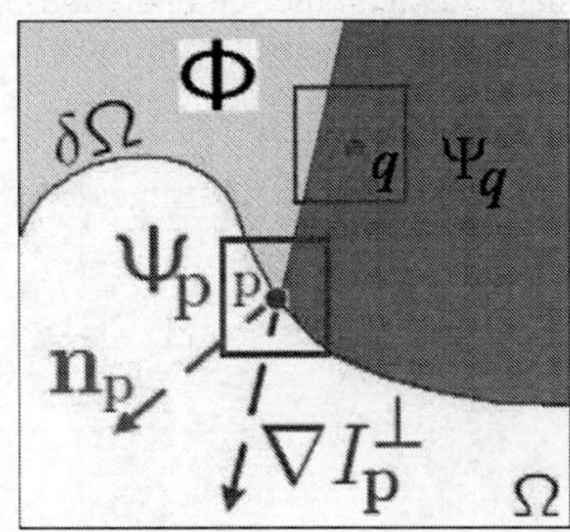

Figure 3: Notation diagram for Exemplar-based inpainting [11]. Given the patch ψ_p, $\vec{n}_p$ is the normal to the contour $\partial\Omega$ of the target region Ω and $\vec{\nabla}^{\perp} I_p$ is the isophote (direction and intensity) at point *p*. The source target is denoted with Φ

3 Experimental Results

The The proposed scheme was applied over wide variety of images to compare it with both the Structure and Exemplar inpainting which are individually applied. This scheme has been implemented using FORTRAN compiler and run using work station of due core CPU, two GHz processors and two Gb of RAM. Figure 4 shows an example of narrow cracks inpainting of gray level image where the scheme gives good results in less time. For this case the computation time has become 20.13 % of Structure inpainting and 3.52 % of Exemplar inpainting. Figure 5 indicates to remove small objects from color image. The image resulted from proposed scheme is better than that of structure inpainting whereas some shading appears. While Exemplar inpainting gives almost the same. Its computation time has become 90.16 % of Structure and 72.0% of Exemplar. Figure 6 states removing large objects from color image. The results have the characteristics that have been mentioned for Figure 5 while the computation time became 3.06 % of Structure and 82.35 % of Exemplar. Figure 7 depicts removing text from color image. The image resulted from proposed scheme; structure and Exemplar have the quality, while the computation time has become 66.78% of Structure and 3.22 % of Exemplar. The inpainted image of Figure 4 (d) and Figure 7 (d) are resulted from applying the structure inpainting on L wavelet component and the rest components may be treated by either structure or exemplar. The minimum computation is accomplished when then the exemplar inpainting over the all wavelet components. Figure 5 (d) and Figure 6 (d) are resulted from applying the Exemplar inpainting on the L wavelet component and the rest components may be treated by either structure or exemplar. But the minimum computation is accomplished when then the exemplar inpainting over the all wavelet components. Figure 8 shows a comparison between the proposed algorithm and other approaches where depicts the computation time versus different proposed cases of study.

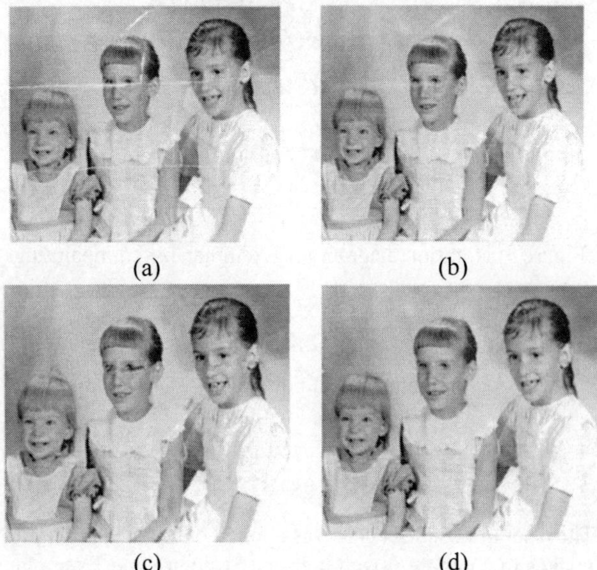

Figure 4: narrow cracks[1] (a) Original image. (b) Structure inpainting. (c) Exemplar inpainting. (d) proposed scheme.

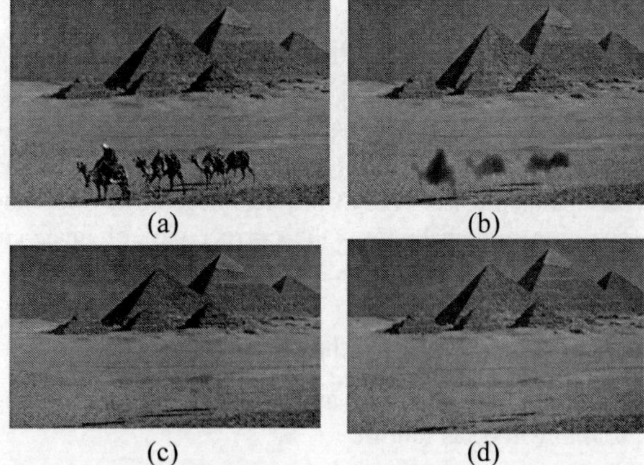

Figure 5: small object removal (a) Original image. (b) Structure inpainting. (c) Exemplar inpainting. (d) Proposed scheme.

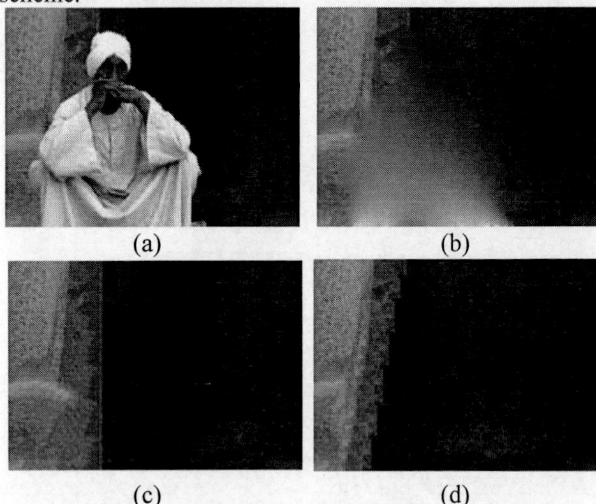

Figure 6: large object removal (a) Original image. (b) Structure inpainting. (c) Exemplar inpainting (d) proposed scheme.

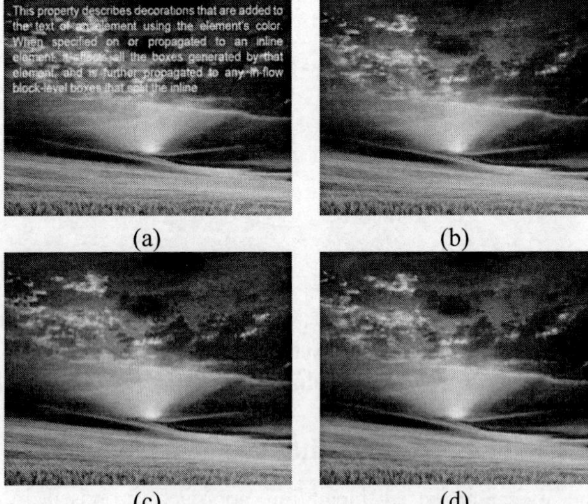

Figure 7: text removal (a) Original image. (b) Structure inpainting. (c) Exemplar inpainting. (d) Proposed scheme.

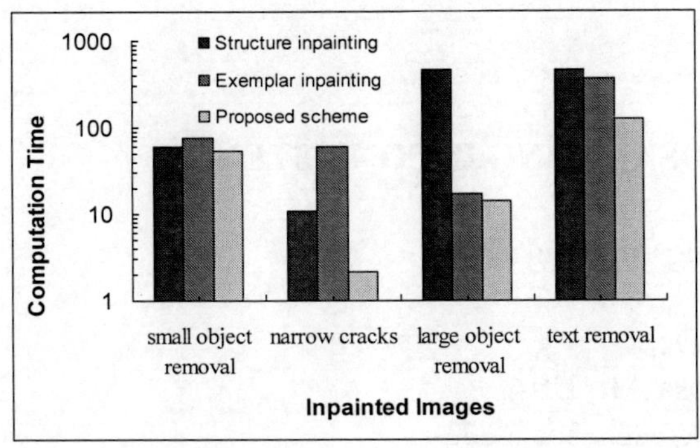

Figure 8: a comparison between the proposed schema and other approaches

4 Conclusions

This research presented an algorithm which is devoted to image inpainting. This algorithm relied on discrete wavelet transform. With applying the algorithm on variety of images to be inpainted processed which have a narrow cracks, small object removal, large object removal and text removal, the computation time has been minimized for the all cases and showed good accuracy which has evaluated visually for each case.

5 References

[1] M. Bertalmio, G. Sapiro, V. Caselles, and C. Ballester "Image Inpainting", in *Proc. SIGGRAPH*, pp. 417–424. , 2000

[2] M. Bertalmio, A. L. Bertozzi, and G. Sapiro "Navier–Strokes, Fluid Dynamics, And Image And Video Inpainting" in Proc. IEEE Computer Society Conf. Computer Vision and Pattern Recognition, pp. 417–424. , 2001

[3] T. Chan and J. Shen "Local Inpainting Models and TV Inpainting," SIAM J. Appl. Math., vol. 62, no. 3, pp. 1019–1043, 2001.

[4] T. Chan, J. Shen "Non-Texture Inpainting by Curvature-Driven Diffusions", J. Vis. Commun. Image Represent, vol. 4, no. 12, pp. 436–449, 2001.

[5] C. Bertalmio, M. Bertalmio, V. Caselles, G. Sapiro, and J. Verdera, "Filling-In By Joint Interpolation Of Vector Fields And Gray Levels," *IEEE Trans. Image Process.*, vol. 10, pp. 1200–1211, 2001.

[6] A. Criminisi, P. Perez and K. Toyama, "Object Removal by Exemplar-Based Inpainting", in .Proc. IEEE Computer Vision and Pattern Recognition, vol. 2, pp. 721-728, 2003.

[7] M. Bertalmio, L. Vese, G. Sapiro, S. Osher, "Simultaneous Structure And Texture Image Inpainting", IEEE Trans. Image Process. 12 (2003) 882–889.

[8] Kedar Shrestha, Qin Chuan, Wang Shuo-zhong ," Layered Image Inpainting Based On Image Decomposition"Journal of Shanghai University (English Edition), 2007, 11(6): 580–584 Digital Object Identifier(DOI):10.1007/s 11741-007-0611-2

[9] Aur´elie Bugeau, Marcelo Bertalmıo," Combining Texture Synthesis And Diffusion For Image Inpainting" VISAPP 2009, v 1 - 4 Jan 2011.

[10] Shutao Li, Ming Zhao," Image Inpainting With Salient Structure Completion And Texture Propagation",Pattern Recognition Letters 32 (2011) 1256–1266.

[11] Xiaowei Shao, Zhengkai Liu, Houqiang Li," An Image Inpainting Approach Based on the Poisson Equation", Proceedings of the Second International Conference on Document Image Analysis for Libraries (DIAL'06) 0-7695-2531-8/06 © 2006 IEEE

[12] B. A. Youssef , E.H. Atta "Digital Image Inpainting using Finite Volume approach and the Navier-Stokes Equations" Proc. of the 9th WSEAS Int. Conf. on Mathematical and Computational Methods in Science and Engineering, Trinidad and Tobago, November 5-7, 2007

IMAGE SPLICING DETECTION VIA DEMOSAICKING INCONSISTENCY

Zhonghai Deng, Jingyuan Zhang, Yuguang Zeng

Computer Science Dept.
Univ.of Alabama, Tuscaloosa AL, USA
zdeng@ua.edu;zhang@cs.ua.edu;yzeng3@ua.edu

ABSTRACT

Image splicing is to compose a new image from two or more images, and it is widely used for image forgery. Image splicing detection is a key problem in image forensics. However there are very few solutions to this problem. These solutions have a low detection accuracy, and most of them are not able to expose the spliced region. This paper proposes a novel image splicing detection method based on the assumption that images produced from different cameras use different demosaicking algorithms. The proposed method can effectively detect the spliced images, and expose their corresponding sliced region. Experiments show the proposed method has a high detection accuracy of 91.1% on Columbia Image Splicing Detection Evaluation Dataset. This paper also shows the procedure to detect the exposed region on a spliced image.

Index Terms— image forensics, splicing detection, demosaicking inconsistency

1. INTRODUCTION

In modern world, digital cameras and smart phones produce an enormous number of digital images. These images provide convincing evidence in all aspects. Meanwhile with the ease of the image manipulation tools, such as Photoshop and Gimp, digital images are more easily to be modified. Thus the phrase 'Seeing is believing' may no longer hold.

To make sure that an image is authentic, researchers propose two directions : active watermarking [1] and passive image forensics [2]. Watermarking actively requires embedding some message into images when they are generated or before they are distributed. However, this requires additional hardware, thus most imaging devices do not carry this function. Image forensics makes use of the characteristics of the imaging device and the properties of digital images to test whether images in question are authentic, in particular whether they have been manipulated. Among all the image manipulating operations, composing a new image from two or more images, referred to as 'image splicing', is a common operation.

Image forensics is still in its infancy. Although splicing detection is a key problem, not a lot of work has been done. Hsu and Chang [4] check the consistency of camera characteristics among different areas in an image, but they only received 70% precision. Chen *et al.* [5] extract features from the sharp transitions introduced by the spliced image part, their features mainly comes from the moments of wavelet characteristic functions and 2D phase congruence, but report only 80% around precision. Similarly, Shi *et al.* [6] extract features from moments of characteristic function of wavelet sub-band and Markov transition probabilities.

Most of existing methods use grayscale images or luminance components of color images, thus inevitably lose some information comparing to the color image. Further, based on benchmark database: 'Columbia Image Splicing Detection Evaluation Dataset' [?], blind detection precision [6, 7, 5] are not satisfying. Though Shi *et al.* [6] claims the 92% correctness, they use too many features, and what was worse, they cannot figure out the altered area if an image is spliced. Also, they do not use exactly the same image dataset.

In this paper, we propose a new blind and effective splicing detection approach based on the image demosaicking inconsistency. Due to the fact that at each image pixel, camera hardware can only generate one color value, and the other two are interpolated from their neighborhoods. We can imagine that different cameras would employ different interpolations algorithms, thus spliced parts could be recognized from the original part. Even two cameras employ the same interpolation algorithm by coincidence, their generated images would surfer different post-processing, which would disturbs the interpolations in two different degrees.

The rest of this paper is organized as follows. Section 2 briefly explains the basic interpolation process inside camera, and present our demosaicking estimation model. In section 3, we present our model find the interpolation relationship among pixels. And then, for each pixel, we calculate an error rate, which would be used to help determine whether this location is the spliced from other images. Section 4 presents two experiments in detail, identifying spliced image from untouched ones, and exposing the spliced area within an single image. Finally, conclusion and discussion are provided in Section 5.

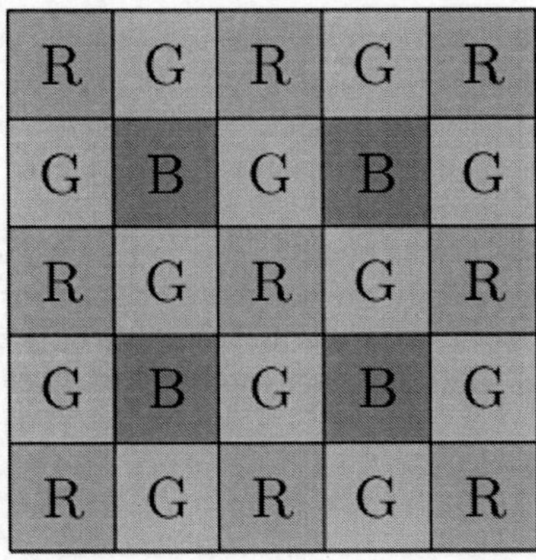

Fig. 1. Bayer Color Filter array

2. BACKGROUND

The key part of any digital camera is the sensor (CCD/CMOS), which transform light signals into electric ones. Because all these sensors are sensitive to the light energy, *i.e.*, they are blind to the color of lights, thus to generate a colorful image, most cameras employ a color filter array (*CFA*) overlaid on the sensor. On each sensor unit, CFA will allow only one color band to pass through, therefore, each sensor unit record only one color value. To build the full color image, the missing values are interpolated from the neighborhood available sensor readings. This interpolation process is often referred to as demosaicking, which is still an open problem, and is highly non-linear [8]. The most common CFA pattern is the Bayer color filter array, Fig 1. Nowadays most cameras employ the RGB color space, meaning that every position on an image has 3 color values: Red, Green, Blue. A Bayer filter mosaic is arranged in a square grid of photosensors, arranged in 50% green, 25% red and 25% blue square block, and two green values must lies diagonally.

With the simple interpolation algorithm, each color channel is interpolated independently, using neighboring values from the same channel. Simple example is nearest neighbor, bilinear and bicubic interpolation. Some sophisticated algorithms would perform the interpolation across color channel, for example, Green channels are interpolated alone, but Red and Blue channels are partially interpolated from Green value. Advanced algorithms would take all 3 neighboring values in consideration, and are adaptive to the local(global) characteristic of the image.

3. PROPOSED APPROACH

The underlying philosophy of the proposed method is quite simple: in an un-touched image, the whole image undergoes the same demosaicking process inside the camera. Thus if we estimate the demosaicking algorithm, the error rate should be approximately the same. For a manipulated image, the spliced part comes from different images, which undergoes different demosaikcing algorithm. Further, the spliced part, to fit into the original image, is often rotated, re-sized to fit the target location, which would makes the interpolation relationship different from original one. So, by checking the error rate on each pixel, we can determine whether the spliced parts.

3.1. Interpolation Estimation Model

For simplicity, we assume all the CFA patterns are in the '**RGGB**' form, column first. We use the quadratic form to approximate the demosaicking algorithm.

3.1.1. Region Selection

To avoid dealing with the border pixels, we ignore 6 pixels on on the left and right sides, the same for upper and lower border. Also, it is reasonable for us to assume that on smooth areas, horizontal neighbors and vertical pixels should have the same weight during interpolation. Thus, when considering interpolation area, we ignore the bordering areas with thickness of 5 pixels. For computational efficiency, we simplify the kernel interpolation filter in the shape of diamond with the vertical and horizontal lines as its diagonals. We know that most cameras would employ a edge sharping operation to make the edge sharper, and most sophisticated cameras would employ different demosaicking algorithm for smooth region and edges. Thus, to get a better approximation result, we only deal with the smooth region to find the interpolation model, though all the pixels on edges can only be used as the interpolation candidates.

3.2. Estimation Model

Although interpolations process inside camera is nonlinear, we still assume its linearity to simplify our process, but enhanced it to the quadratic model. We also assume that in all cameras, missing Green values are interpolated from a diamond form with radius of 5. Looking further into the diamond shape of the green channel, for any position whose green value is missing, its surrounding diamond area have 36 Green candidates, Fig 1. Taking into the symmetry into consideration, there are only 12 independent pixel candidates with flexible coefficients. Thus without loss of generality, we can treat pixels on the upper right part of the diamond as independent, Fig 2.

Also, as we consider the quadratic form of the interpolation model, we need consider the difference between two symmetric points, say a, b about the questioned location. In our model, we actually add the expression $(a - b) \Rightarrow ab$ into candidates. For simplicity, we consider only the green channel, and ignore the Red and Blue channel. From above analysis, for each candidate pixel p, assuming its independent points

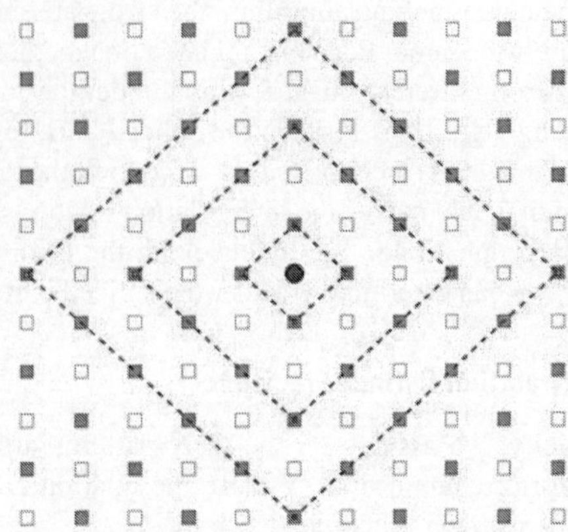

Fig. 2. Interpolation Candidates Model

x_i $i = 1, ..., 12$ on the upper right side, then the interpolation function in our model is :

$$F(p) = \sum_{i=1}^{12} \left(a_i * \sum S^2(x_i) + b_i * \sum S(x_i)\right) + \sum_{i=1}^{12} k_i * S0(k_i) + c \quad (1)$$

(2)

Where $S(x_i)$ is a function that returns pixels x_i' that are symmetric to x_i about origin or two diagonals, inclusive; $S0(x_i)$ returns pixels x_i' that are symmetric to x_i only about origin, none inclusive; and c is a constant.

For the pixels whose values are generated directly from sensor, their error should be zero, making them as black holes. So to facilitate our spliced region exposure, we use bicubic interpolation method to fill out these holes. Thus we can see that there are actually only 37 independent coefficients to be estimated from Equation 1.

3.3. Error Ratio Map

Given an image im, after above interpolation estimation, we got a map that shows the error our estimation for each pixel.

$$Err(im) = ||SG(im) - F(SGim))|| \quad (3)$$

And by considering the fact that with the same error at position (i, j), for example $Err(i, j) = 3.4$, for pixel with original value of 255 and original value of 0, means significant difference. We also take the estimation error rate into consideration.

$$ErrRatioMap(im) = ||SG(im) - F(SGim))||/SG(im) \quad (4)$$

Where $SG(:)$ is the function that extracts the smooth area on green channel, solely determined by the original image. Note that in the above process, the interpolation coefficients depends on the reverse image results, To describe the image error ratio map,we use the some common statistical metrics: maximum, mean, coefficients of variance, spread, skewness, kurtosis and Chi-square.

To avoid the divided by zeros case in Eqn. 4 and to cease turbulence, we simply exclude those points whose original value is only 0 or 1. Also, due to the fact that different images have different size, thus simply to normalize the error ratio map via

$$normalizedMap(im) = ErrRatioMap(im)*c/length(im) \quad (5)$$

Where c is a constant, assigned as 10000 in this experiment, and $lenght(im)$ is a function that returns the number of pixels in image im. Also, sequential backward feature selection is used to find the optimal feature set.

3.4. Classifier

In this experiment, we employ the LIBSVM [?] and use RBF kernel. Grid searching is used to find the best parameters from the classifier.

4. EXPERIMENTS

In our experiments, we apply the proposed method to solve two problems in image forensic : spliced image identification and exposing spliced area. To better justify the proposed method, we use the benchmark forensic database in experiments 4.1 and 4.3. As we focus on authentic/spliced image data, the only available public database comes from Columbia University [9], containing 183 authentic images from 4 cameras, and 180 spliced images. Note that different from common copy-move manipulation, whose forged parts come from the same target image; in image slicing forgery, forged part comes from a different source image.

4.1. Separate Spliced Image from Untouched Ones

In this experiment, we try to separate the spliced image from those untouched images. Its underlying theoretical basis comes from the assumption that, if an authentic image use the same demosaicking method, then the error ratio map should be smooth. On the other hand, as the source image tends to employ a different demosaicking method, even it happens to have undergone the same interpolation method, its post processing operations should be different. Therefore adding the spliced part would disturb the estimation error map. Further, these spliced image parts are very likely to have been rotated and re-sized, *etc.* Thus, it is reasonable to assume that the image error ratio map should have more turbulence than the authentic one. For simplicity, we merely use the histogram based features.

	Authentic	Spliced
Authentic	88.38%	11.63%
Spliced	9.20%	90.80%

Table 1. Confusion Matrix to identify the spliced image

4.2. Identification Performance

We run 10 times to get the average performance of the proposed method. The average performance could be seen at

Our overall classification rate is 89.59%, which outperforms their highest accuracy 87.55% in [9]. Due to the fact that the number of sliced image are a bit more than that of authentic image, the true positive (TP) rate slightly higher than the true negative (TN) rate.

4.3. Expose Spliced Area

Our method goes further to label the forged region for a sliced image. Since the spliced part have undergone different demosaicking algorithm from the original image, thus if we exclude the spliced parts and approximate the interpolation via the original part, we will received much better approximation result, *i.e.*, the interpolation residue would shrink significantly.

4.3.1. Region Labeling

Due to speed consideration, instead of considering all pixels in experiment 4.1, in this experiment we divide the image into 32-by-32 non-overlapping blocks. On each iteration, we label one block as the 'suspected' one, while its 8 neighborhoods are labeled as 'ambiguous', and ignored them when doing the regression.

For block (i, j), we calculate the interpolation coefficients using the rest pixels, say $imRest(:,:)$, and get a new estimation error map. Comparing the same part between the new error map with the one over the whole pixels, we could use their difference $Dif(i, j)$ to quantify the possibility the 'suspected' part could be a spliced part.

$$Dif(i,j) = |average(Err(imRest) - newErr(imRest))| \tag{6}$$

Where $Err()$ is the error map over the whole image, and $newErr()$ is the one that works only on the rest part of the image $imRest$, excluding the 'spliced' block and its neighborhoods. After the iteration, we use the block with largest difference, and check the $DifRatio$ to determine whether this part is large enough to make it a 'spliced' part.

$$DifRatio(i,j) = Dif(i,j)/mean(Err(im)) \tag{7}$$

4.3.2. Spliced Region Growing

Once we determined that the 'suspected' block is the 'spliced' part, we need expose the whole spliced region. Starting from the seeding block, we test the 4-way direct neighbor blocks, and determine which class (origninal/spliced) they belongs to. For simplicity, we still use the average of error map to determine the

$$classRatio(:,:) = mean(Err_{orig}(im))/mean(Err_{slic}(im)) \tag{8}$$

Where the $Err_{ori}(im)$ means the error map if treated as the original image, and similarly for $Err_{slic}(im)$. Note that after each iteration, so long as the spliced region has changed, we need recalculate the interpolation coefficients for both original and spliced image parts.

$$f(block_k) = \begin{cases} Original, & \text{if classRatio} > 1.5 \\ Spliced, & \text{if classRatio} < 0.667 \\ More\ discussion, & otherwise \end{cases} \tag{9}$$

In the case the $classRatio < 0.667$, we would divide the current questioned block into two equal sized parts, and check the belongings of each part. For example, in the case that the left part of the block is adjacent to spliced area, then the the block is divided into left and right part, both with the size 32-by-16. Similarly with the upper and lower adjacent case. If the questioned pars is adjacent to 'spliced' area on both left and upper side, then we choose the case that is discovered first.

By repeating the above step, we thus growing the spliced image into roughly the true sliced region. One example could be seen in figure 4.3.2.

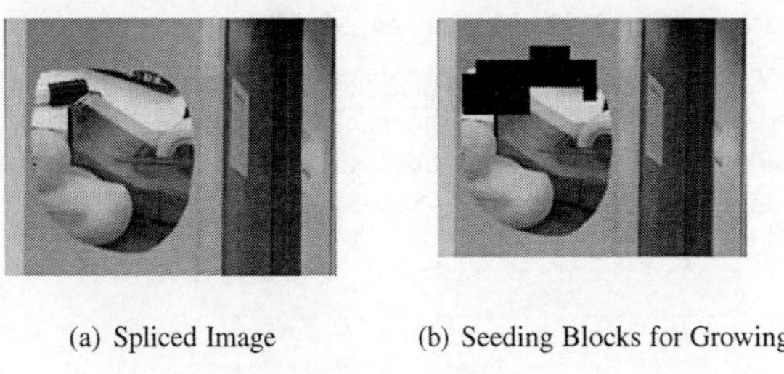

(a) Spliced Image (b) Seeding Blocks for Growing

Fig. 3. Starting growing block illustration

5. CONCLUSIONS

In this paper, based on the correlation of neighborhood demosaicking coefficients, we present a method for detection of spliced images. Experimental results show that our method delivers good performance for the detection. Our study also indicates that image complexity and splicing parts are important to evaluate the detection of splicing. Further, our method could also expose the copy-move detection within the same image part, undergoing the assumption that the the CFA pattern of spliced part do not fit the original part.

6. REFERENCES

[1] V.M. Potdar, S. Han, and E. Chang, “A survey of digital image watermarking techniques,” in *Proceedings of IEEE third international conference on industrial informatics, INDIN05*, 2005, pp. 709–16. 1

[2] Zhen Zhang, Yuan Ren, Xi-Jian Ping, Zhi-Yong He, and Shan-Zhong Zhang, “A survey on passive-blind image forgery by doctor method detection,” july 2008, vol. 6, pp. 3463 –3467. 1

[3] S. Bayram, H.T. Sencar, and N. Memon, “A survey of copy-move forgery detection techniques,” 2007.

[4] Y.F. Hsu and S.F. Chang, “Image splicing detection using camera response function consistency and automatic segmentation,” in *Multimedia and Expo, 2007 IEEE International Conference on*. IEEE, 2007, pp. 28–31. 1

[5] W. Chen, Y.Q. Shi, and W. Su, “Image splicing detection using 2-d phase congruency and statistical moments of characteristic function,” *Security, Steganography and Watermarking of Multimedia Contents IX, Proceeding. of SPIE, San Jose, CA, USA*, 2007. 1

[6] Yun Q. Shi, Chunhua Chen, and Wen Chen, “A natural image model approach to splicing detection,” in *MM&Sec ’07: Proceedings of the 9th workshop on Multimedia & security*, New York, NY, USA, 2007, pp. 51–62, ACM. 1

[7] T.T. Ng, S.F. Chang, and Q. Sun, “Blind detection of photomontage using higher order statistics,” in *Circuits and Systems, 2004. ISCAS’04. Proceedings of the 2004 International Symposium on*. IEEE, 2004, vol. 5, pp. V–688. 1

[8] BK Gunturk, J. Glotzbach, Y. Altunbasak, RW Schafer, and RM Mersereau, “Demosaicking: Color filter array interpolation in single chip digital cameras,” *IEEE Signal Processing Magazine*, vol. 22, no. 1, pp. 44–54, 2005. 2

[9] Y.-F. Hsu and S.-F. Chang, “Detecting image splicing using geometry invariants and camera characteristics consistency,” in *Proc. IEEE International Conference on Multimedia and Expo*, July 9–12, 2006, pp. 549–552. 3, 4

GPU and CPU Cooperative Accelerated Road Detection

Peng Xiong[1], Cheng Xu[1], Zheng Tian[1] and Tao Li[1]
[1]School of Computer and Communication, Hunan University
Changsha 410082, Hunan Province, China

Abstract - *In this paper, we propose a fast and robust unstructured road detection method that integrates GPU (Graphics Processing Unit) and CPU implementations. In order to ensure the robustness of the algorithm, BP (Back Propagation) Neural Network is employed to learn the color features from a set of sample of both road region and off-road region, and then to classify a newly pixel. And the B-spline curve model is employed to fit the boundaries of the lanes with the Least Square Method. To improve the real-time capability, the NVIDIA CUDA (Compute Unified Device Architecture) framework is used, and a GPU and CPU cooperative acceleration technique is proposed. Taking the advantages of these properties, the proposed implementation works out with high performance of detection in various environments. Meanwhile it is robust against noise, shadows and illumination variations. Moreover, it can performs about 10 times faster than a conventional implementation running on a CPU.*

Keywords: Neural Network, Road Detection, CUDA

1 Introduction

Road detection is one of the most important technologies in the vision-based intelligent navigation system, and is of high relevance for autonomous driving, road departure warning, and supporting driver-assistance systems such as vehicle and pedestrian detection [1]. A robust road detection algorithm should provide accurate road position and direction information for the navigation system [4]. However, conventional detection methods are of high computational costing, and cannot adapt to various environments. Therefore, it is a critical issue to search for a real-time and robust road detection approach, to improve the vision-based intelligent navigation system for a practical application.

Conventional unstructured road detection algorithms could be divided into two groups, the model-based and the feature-based.

The model-based method begins with the hypothesis of the road model, and then matches the road edge with the road model. A B-Spline based lane detection and tracking algorithm, proposed by Yue Wang et al. in [2], is a representative of this kind of methods. It can work without any cameras' parameters. Moreover, the algorithm is robust against noise, shadows, and illumination variations. Still, the result of such method is dependent on the hypothesis of the road model, so they cannot fit to the situation that the shape of road changes greatly.

The feature-based method divides the image into the road region and the off-road region based on the differences of gradient, color or texture between them. Compared with the model-based method, the feature-based method is not sensitive to the shape of the road. Hui Kong et al. have presented a method based on the texture feature of a single image in [3]. Another typical example of this kind of methods is an adaptive road detection algorithm based on BP neural network presented by Mike Foedisch et al. in [5]. The approach extracts the features of a number of road images and trains the neural network based on the feature vectors, and then computes the result of classification. It avoids manual annotation of images by taking advantage of the conforming structure in the road images, thus can adapt to various environments. But the algorithm still has the defect that it is not robust enough against to shadows. Moreover, in order to achieve real-time processing, it processes every other pixel in the image, which has reduced the processing accuracy. In conclusion, it is a huge challenge to meet the real-time constraints while ensuring the robustness for the high computational costing of feature-based methods.

In order to solve the disadvantages mentioned above, in this paper, we propose an approach based on BP Neural Network and B-spline curve, which takes the advantages of the model-based and the feature-based methods. Meanwhile we specifically construct a GPU and CPU cooperative acceleration technique to support real-time and high-performance detection.

In the rest of the article, we firstly introduce the B-spline curve and BP neural network in Section 2. Secondly, in Section 3, we present the detail of our algorithm. And then we present our GPU and CPU cooperative implementation in Section 4. Finally, we describe the experimental results in Section 5.

2 B-spline Curve and BP Neural Network

B-spline curve is a commonly used model in road detection, it is a linear combination of basis curves. Unlike other road model, a B-spline model has more advantages as local control that the degree of a B-spline curve is separated from the number of control points, and control flexibility that change the position of a control point without globally changing the shape of the whole curve [6].

However, as other model-based road detection methods, the result of B-spline curve model-based algorithm is dependent on the hypothesis of the road model. That is to say, this method is not robust enough against changing environment, such as when the road surface is not level, the method will make a big deviation.

Color appearance information has been widely used as the main cue for road detection, since color provides powerful information of the road to be detected in the absence of reliable shape information. In addition, color imposes less physical restrictions, leading to more versatile systems [7]. Therefore, we use neural network to segment road and off-road regions after learning the color features of the image. As a result, it overcomes B-spline curve's frangibility against the interference of the changing shapes of the road.

Neural network is a way to learn the nonlinearity at the same time as the linear discriminant. Such multilayer networks can provide the optimal solution to an arbitrary classification problem. The key power provided by such networks is that they admit fairly simple algorithms where the form of the nonlinearity can be learned from training data [8].

As a result, combing neural network with B-spline curve road model can take both advantages of these two methods. It can accurately divide the image into road region and off-road region, and then quickly fit the road boundary through the result of classification. This method is robust against shadows, illumination variations, and the changing road shapes.

3 The Road Detection Approach

Our algorithm mainly consists of five phases.

3.1 Classification

In the step, we classify every pixel using a BP Neural Network, which has been trained by samples of road region's and off-road region's color features.

The neural network presented consists of three layers, an input layer, a hidden layer, and an output layer. They are interconnected by links, which contain modifiable weights, between layers.

We convert the image to HSV (Hue, Saturation, Value) color space, and use H and S value as an input vector of the network. The input vector is presented to the input layer, each hidden unit performs the weighted sum of its inputs to form its net activation, the net activation can be written as:

$$net_j = \sum_{i=1}^{d} x_i \omega_{ji} + \omega_{j0} = \sum_{i=0}^{d} x_i \omega_{ji} = \boldsymbol{\omega}_j^t \mathbf{x} \qquad (1)$$

where the subscript i indexes units on the input layer, j for the hidden, ω_{ji} denotes the input-to-hidden layer weights at the hidden unit j. Each hidden unit emits an output that is a non-linear function of its activation: $y_j = f(net_j)$.

The net activation and emits of the output layer units net_k and z_k is computed similarly based on the hidden unit signals. Then we use z_k to classify the input pixel as road or off-road.

3.2 Block segment

Generally, the pixel in road and off-road region are continuous and similar, so we can divide the image into blocks, and then classify blocks by its four corner regions pixels. In actuality, the influence of noises can be reduced by the approach. The method is described as follows.

Suppose a pixel x belongs to either road area R or off-road area NR, that is $x \in \{R, NR\}$. And the corner region C belongs to road area or off-road area, which is represented as: $C \in \{R, NR\}$.The probabilities of a corner region belonging to the road area or off-road area can be computed as:

$$p(C \in R) = \sum if(x_i \in R)/N \qquad (2)$$

$$p(C \in NR) = \sum if(x_i \in NR)/N \qquad (3)$$

where N is the number of pixel in a corner.

If four corner regions in the block all belong to road area or off-road area, mark this block as road block or off-road block. The membership probability is defined as:

$$p(block \in R) = \sum p(C_i \in R)/4 \qquad (4)$$

$$p(block \in NR) = \sum p(C_i \in NR)/4 \qquad (5)$$

If some corner regions in a block belong to road area, while others belong to off-road area, mark the block as mixed block, and the membership probability $p(block \in MIX)$ is defined as the mean of the probabilities of four corners belong to the corresponding areas.

Now, the image can be regarded as a matrix of blocks, with each block marked as Road, Off-road or Mix. In some case, the blocks might be misjudged by the influence of noise. To deal with such error, we scan the blocks row by row. When we meet a Mix block, and the left block and the right block are marked as the same, then we test the probability of these three blocks. A block with a probability lower than a threshold will be reconfigured.

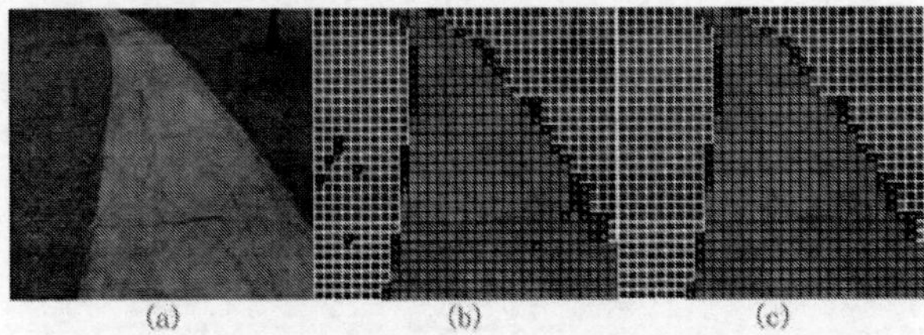

Fig. 1 Result of Classification

Fig. 1 shows the results of classification. (a) is the original image. (b) is the primary classifying result in which the thick-black blocks are mixed block. (c) shows the final result of classification which is modified by error fix based on the membership probability.

3.3 Edge Extraction

It can be sure that the current road boundaries exist only in the Mix blocks. Then we extract the road boundaries form these blocks using an approach as follows:

- *Scan the blocks from the bottom to the top. For each row, classify the midline pixels of Mix blocks from left to right. Take the continuous road pixels set in the scan line to be a candidate sub-segment line.*
- *Merge the close candidate road sub-segment line. Deal with all scan line's candidate road's sub-segment, and get the road line set.*
- *Finally, for the road segments on each scan line, extract the line segment's left and right boundary points, and then obtain the boundary points set of the road.*

3.4 Fitting

Due to its advantage of making the construction of curves with high stability, the B-spline curve is chosen as our road model. A cubic B-spline curve with $n+1$ control points $P_i(i=0,1,\cdots,n)$ can be expressed as:

$$C(u)=\sum_{i=0}^{n} P_i N_{i,4}(u) \tag{6}$$

where $N_{i,4}(u)$ is the base function [9], and the matrix format is:

$$C(u)=\left[u^3,u^2,u,1\right]\times\frac{1}{6}\begin{bmatrix}1&3&3&1\\3&6&3&0\\-3&0&3&0\\0&4&1&0\end{bmatrix}\times\begin{bmatrix}P_{i-1}\\P\\P_{i+1}\\P_{i+2}\end{bmatrix} \tag{7}$$

In practice, most roads have only one or two turning corners in an image, so, three control points to obtain B-spline curve model is robust enough for the navigation system. In our approach, we select the first and the last control points of the interpolation sequence $\left[P_1,P_2,\cdots,P_n\right]$ as the first interpolation point and the end interpolation point. Then, we use the Least Square Method to search the interpolation sequence $\left[P_2,P_3,\cdots,P_{n-1}\right]$ and select the optimized position of the second control point [4]. Making use of the accurate result of edge extraction, small numbers of points need to be searched for. As a result, the fitting process is very fast and robust.

3.5 Updating

To adapt to the changing environment, it is necessary to update the network weights. After the B-spline fitting phase, the image had been divided into road region and off-road region. Then we choose one block in road region and one block in the off-road region as samples for updating. In order to keep the network from the influence of noise, we agree on that the membership probability $p(block\in R)$ or $p(block\in NR)$ of the block chosen as sample is higher than a threshold.

Similar to the training phase of the network, the update rule for the hidden-to-output weights can be presented as follows:

$$\Delta\omega_{kj}=\eta\delta_k\frac{\partial net_k}{\partial\omega_{kj}}=\eta(t_k-z_k)f'(net_k)y_j \tag{8}$$

where η is the learning rate, δ_k is the sensitivity of unit k: $\delta_k=-\partial J/\partial net_k$.

The learning rule for the input-to-hidden weights is:

$$\Delta\omega_{ji}=\eta x_i\delta_j=\eta\left[\sum_{k=1}^{c}\omega_{kj}\delta_k\right]f'(net_k)x_i \tag{9}$$

where δ_j is defined as the sensitivity of unit j: $\delta_j\equiv f'(net_j)\sum_{k=1}^{c}\omega_{kj}\delta_k$.

4 GPU & CPU Cooperative Processing

In the classification phase, for every pixel, the net activation and emission of each unit in each layer need to be computed. It is clear that it needs much more computational cost with the heavy matrix computation. What's more, it is impossible for a general CPU implementation to handle in real time as the image size grows.

GPGPU (General-Purpose computation on GPUs) enables real-time processing for an algorithm requiring huge computational cost [10]. Thus, we present a CPU and GPU cooperative acceleration technique to support real-time road detection. In this section, we describe the detail of our GPU and CPU integrated implementation.

Our approach can be split into two parts: the host and the GPU processing.

On the CPU (host), the image is acquired and copied into GPU texture memory for fast access from the GPU. The weights of the neural network, which had been trained previously, are copied into GPU constant memory, in which the data could be accessed in only one GPU cycle in the ideal case. Since the weights of the neural network stay unchanged during the classification phase, such implementation could largely speed up the classification process though the constant memory cache.

On the GPU, the image pixels are classified into two classes, and the result of classification phase is sent to CPU.

Then in the edge extraction, the B-spline fitting and the network updating phase are finished on CPU. The block diagram can be expressed as Fig. 2.

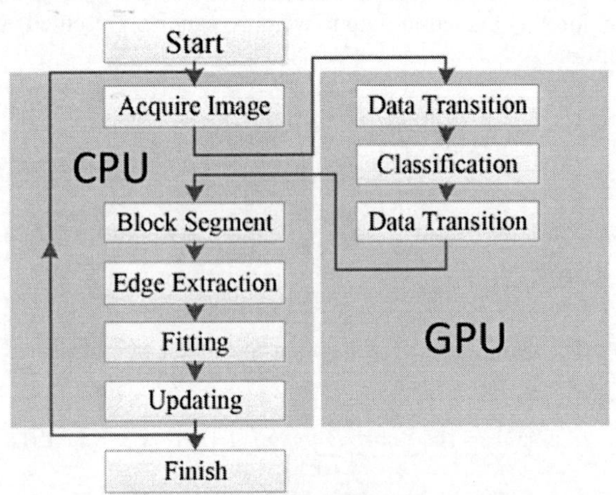

Fig. 2 The Algorithm Block Diagram

With the GPU-accelerated processing, the classification phase, which takes much computational cost, is accomplished by the GPU. Such a technique can speed up the processing course, but could be further promoted.

Since the edge extraction phase needs the result of classification which is produced by GPU, CPU has been waited in vain for the outcomes of GPU. On the other hand, while CPU starts with the edge extraction and fitting phase, GPU is in idle state. Due to the waiting process between CPU and GPU, both of them are not been fully used. Moreover, the transmission delay between CPU and GPU makes the situation worse for it deducing the benefits of GPU acceleration greatly. It can be described in Gantt chart in Fig. 3.

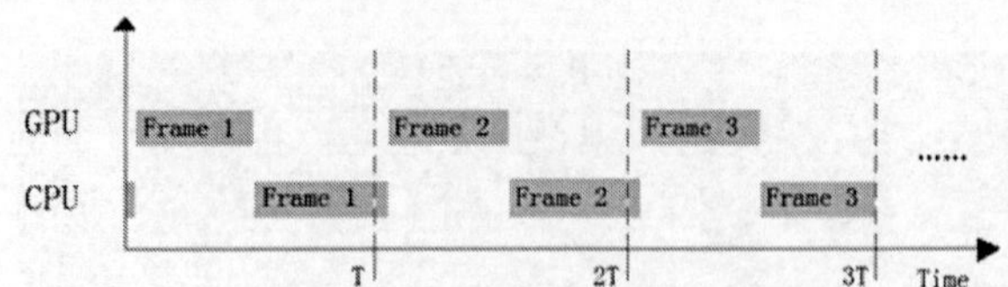

Fig. 3 Implementation with GPU-accelerated Processing

To deal with such problem, we present a GPU and CPU cooperative accelerated implementation, which is based on the basic idea of the pipeline. Such implementation can eliminate the waiting process, and further improve the processing speed. The detail of the technique is as follows:

An image is acquired on CPU and copied into GPU memory, and then GPU starts to process the image. While the classification process is accomplished, the result is sent to CPU. Then the CPU prepares the next frame, which is to be processed, and copy it into GPU memory. Then the edge extraction and following phase are processed on CPU, and the classification phase of next frame is processed on GPU in parallel. Such implementation could be described in Gantt chart in Fig. 4.

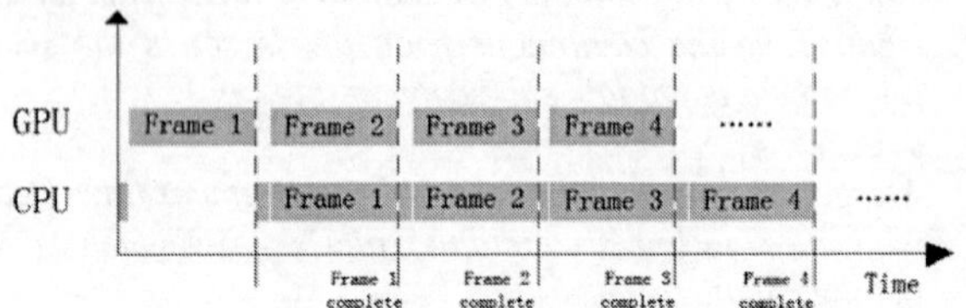

Fig. 4 GPU & CPU Cooperative Accelerated Processing

In practical application, different images generally take identical time cost on GPU, but the time consumption on CPU might vary depend on the complexity of the result of classification. The cooperative accelerated processing technique can maximize the use of both CPU and GPU, and efficiently reduce the waiting process. Moreover, such technique can conceal the delay of data transition between CPU and GPU and ultimately boost the peak performance. By using this technique, the propose implementation can performance in real time. The performance is presented in section 5.2.

5 Experiments

In this section, we will demonstrate the result of our algorithm performed on a personal computer equipped with NVIDIA GPUs. The proposed approach was realized using the lib of Open source Computer Vision library. We will show the efficiency and real-time capability of the proposed algorithm.

5.1 Effectiveness

In order to show the effectiveness of the proposed algorithm, we design two groups of experiments, one group is in the case of shadows and illumination variations while the other is with various environments. Due to the limitations of the experiment environment, we carry out a variety of simulation experiments on video images provided by the Vision and Automation System Center in Carnegie Mellon University instead of field tests. These sets of road pictures can be downloaded from http://vasc.ri.cmu.edu/idb/images/.

Fig. 5 demonstrates a part of results in our experiments. The first row shows the results of Group One where the experiments are carried out in the environment of shadows and illumination variations, and the second row is the results of Group Two where the experiments are carried out in different environments, such as snowy, rainy and fallen leaves. In the Fig. 5, (a) is a scene with shadows, the trees on the two sides project shadows on the road surface. (b) is a noon scene where there is great strong sunlight. (c) is a dusk scene where it is some kind of dark. (d) is a snow scene, the road surface is covered with snow. (e) is a scene after the rain, the boundaries between road and off-road regions are very fuzzy. (f) is a fall scene, both sides of the road is covered with fallen leaves. Clearly, our algorithm can accurately extract the boundary of the road. In scene (a), the road is covered by shadow, the block-classifying method used in our algorithm can exclude the interference of noise and accurately accomplish the fitting. In scene (e), it is difficult to distinguish between road and off-road regions even by eyes. However, our algorithm can still do perfect classification and accurately find the boundary of the road.

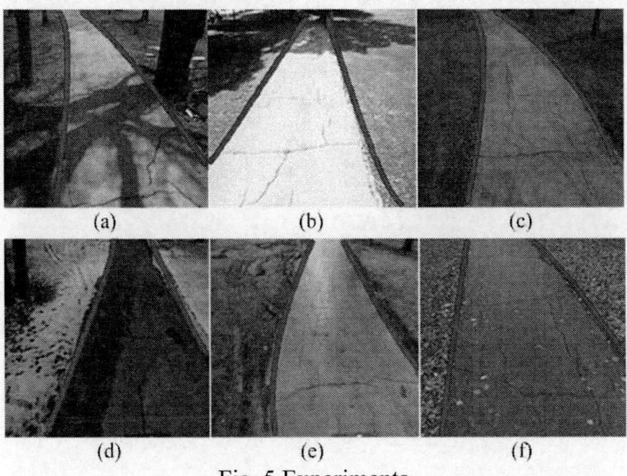

Fig. 5 Experiments

In order to evaluate the performance of our approach, we employ a pixel–wise measures from which three error measures are computed: quality, detection rate and detection accuracy [7], see Table 1 and Table 2. Five group of images advantage different environment are manually segmented to generate the ground-truth.

Table 1 Pixel–wise Measures Definition

Contingency Table		Ground-Truth	
		Off-Road	Road
Result	Off-Road	TN	FN
	Road	FP	TP

Table 2 Evaluation for the Performance of Detection Results

Pixel-wise measure	Definition
Q(Quality)	$\frac{TP}{TP+FP+FN}$
DR(Detection Rate)	$\frac{TP}{TP+FP}$
DA(Detection Accuracy)	$\frac{TP}{TP+FN}$

The performance of the proposed method is validated and compared to the algorithm based on kernel density estimation introduced in [4].

Our method can keep high and stable performance in various environments. Especially, our method is little interfered by shadows and illumination variations and the detection accuracy even reaches 98.4%, which we can clearly see from Table 3.

Table 3 Performance of Our Algorithm

	Kernel Density Estimation			Our method		
Shadows	Q	DR	DA	Q	DR	DA
Fall	0.747	0.909	0.784	0.967	0.982	0.984
After Rain	0.751	0.891	0.791	0.909	0.933	0.966
Snow	0.749	0.894	0.797	0.907	0.969	0.937
Night	0.689	0.824	0.782	0.774	0.903	0.81
Night	0.729	0.906	0.775	0.751	0.854	0.827

Only in the case of night that there is little difference between the hue and saturation of road and off-road regions, detection rate of our method might descend.

5.2 Real-time Capability

In order to demonstrate the effect of our acceleration technique, we design two group experiments.

We choose a video sequence which contains 35 images to run on two desktop for 30 times in each experiment. The average time consumption of each image is listed in Table 4.

Compare with Serial algorithm, the GPU-accelerated algorithm can reduce time consumption greatly. And through reducing the waiting process and transmission delay, our CPU and GPU cooperative acceleration technique could boost the performance further.

Table 4 Time Consumption Comparison

$\left({ms}/{frame} \right)$		Block size 8	Block size 16
Image size 256*240	Serial	74.2	24.2
	GPU- accelerated	16.5	10.6
	Our method	8.8	7.9
Image size 512*480	Serial	290.6	88.7
	GPU- accelerated	54.2	34.0
	Our method	29.4s	25.1

According to the effect of the cooperative processing on CPU and GPU, the speedup factor of our algorithm can reach 9.9, and can performs at most 1.88 times faster than a traditional GPU-accelerated implementation.

We also designed an experiment to compare the computational consumption of different image sizes and different GPUs, where the FLOPS (FLoating-point Operations Per Second) of GPU2 is two times than GPU1, to show the salability of our algorithm, see in Fig. 6.

On one hand, when the experiments are done on the same GPU, the computational consumption increases the same times as the image size. On the other hand, the computational cost descends by half as the computational capability ascends by 2 times in the condition that the image sizes are the same. As a result, our CPU and GPU cooperative technique can process more sophisticated and greater amount of data on more advanced GPU.

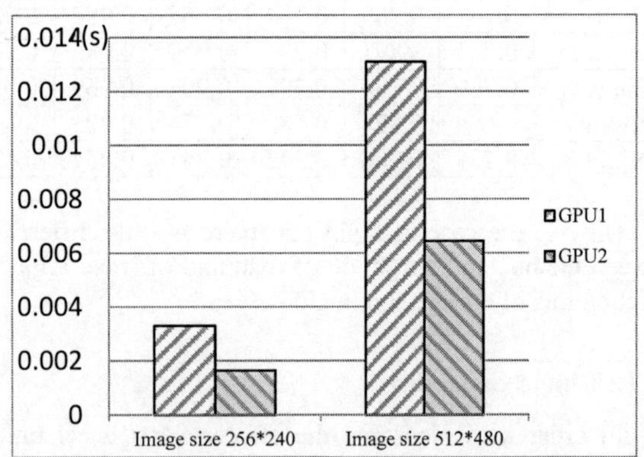

Fig. 6 GPU Computational Consumption

6 Conclusion

In this paper, we present a GPU and CPU cooperative accelerated road detection algorithm. The algorithm is robust against noise, shadows, and illumination variations. Meanwhile, the GPU & CPU cooperative parallel implementation makes sure that our method is real-time. The experiments verify that the algorithm is effective and real-time. Our cooperative technique can be used as reference for real-time system in intelligent navigation system.

7 Acknowledgements

This work is supported by National Natural Science Foundation of China under Grant No.61272062, Fundamental Research Funds for the Central Universities of Hunan University under Grant No.531107040421 and Hunan Provincial Innovation Foundation for Postgraduate (CX2011B138).

8 References

[1] J. M. Álvarez, A. M. Ĺopez, "Road detection based on illuminant invariance," IEEE Trans. ITS, Vol.12, No.1, pp. 184-193, March 2011.

[2] Y. Wang, E. K. Teoh, D. Shen, "Lane detection and tracking using b-snake," Image and Vision Computing, Vol.22, No.4, pp.269-280, April 2004.

[3] H. Kong, J. Y. Audibert, J. Ponce, "General road detection from a single image," IEEE Trans. IP, Vol.19, No.8, pp.2211-2220, August 2010.

[4] Z. Tian, C. Xu, X. Wang, Z. Yang, "Non-parametric model for robust road recognition," 10th ICSP, Beijing, China, pp.869-872, October 2010.

[5] M. Foedisch, A. Takeuchi, "Adaptive real-time road detection using neural networks," Proc. 7th IEEE Int. conf. on ITS, Washington DC, United States of America, pp.167-172, October 2004.

[6] H. Xu, X. Wang, H. Huang, K. Wu, Q. Fang, "A fast and stable lane detection method based on b-spline curve," IEEE 10th Int. Conf. on CAID &CD, Wenzhou, China, pp.1036-1040, November 2009.

[7] J. M. Alvarez, T. Gevers, A. M. Lopez. "3d scene priors for road detection," 10th IEEE Conf. on CVPR, San Francisco, United States of America, pp.57-64, June 2010.

[8] R. O. Duda, P. E. Hart, D. G. Stork, "Multilayer neural networks," in Pattern Classification (Second Edition), pp.282-347, John Wiley & Sons, New York, 2001.

[9] J. Sun, C. Yang, "Curves and surfaces," in Computer graphics, pp.284-289, Tsinghua University Press, Beijing, 1995.

[10] T. Machida, T. Naito, "Gpu & cpu cooperative accelerated pedestrian and vehicle detection," ICCV 2011 Workshops. Barcelona, United States of America, pp.506-513, November 2011.

A Monocular On-Road Vehicle Extraction Algorithm Utilizing Markov Random Field Model

Yuan Gao[1], Jing Li[1], Yixu Song[1], and Zehong Yang[1]
[1]Tsinghua National Laboratory for Information Science and Technology
State Key Laboratory on Intelligent Technology and Systems
Department of Computer Science and Technology, Tsinghua University, Beijing 100084, China

Abstract— *The detection of nearby vehicles from front-view road video sequence plays an important part in safety driving assistant systems. In this paper, we present a monocular vision-based vehicle extraction algorithm. We first propose a grid-based clustering method to generate an initial Object Map indicating the classified label distribution on pixels using color and locality cues in the current frame. Then a Markov Random Field (MRF) model is presented and trained using the Object Map to utilize the motion correlation between consecutive frames. The output is the extraction result of vehicles within the given frame. Our approach does not assume any physical models of the vehicle and is able to achieve stable results under unstructured urban road environment.*

Keywords: vehicle detection, Markov Random Field, grid clustering, Safety Driving Assist, road condition.

1. Introduction

Nowadays vehicles are becoming more intelligent by being equipped with safety driving assist systems. One of the key features for such systems is to detect nearby vehicles for the intelligent car to steer away from. On-road vehicle detection is thus a major subject and many reseach results have been developed. Among them, monocular vision-based method is an important branch. All methods discussed in this paper is thus within this scope. To acquire monocular vision, a camera is usually mounted near the windshield in the intelligent vehicle to capture the road condition videos in the hope of simulating the driver's perspective. Our driving assist system also adopts this framework.

The main approaches for vehicle detection among existing methods are feature-based. These approaches attempt to introduce various texture-based or shape-based features to train object models. For example, [1] uses Haar filters which are calculated by summing up pixel values under weighted rectangular regions inside the Region Of Interest (ROI). Then the Boosted Cascade [2] method is adopted to train the classifier. Only ROIs reaching a classification score above a chosen threshold are marked as objects. Similarly Edge Orientation Histogram (EOH) and Activation History Features (AHF) are chosen as features in [3], [4] respectively. [5] generates initial candidates using Horizontal Edge Filtering (HEF) on canny edge map. Bag-of-Features (BoF) with K-nearest neighbor algorithm is applied to verify those candidates. By the combination of both modules, it is able to retrieve final detection result of vehicles. Although these methods are successful, they are applied to static images without actually using all kinds of correlation between consecutive frames of driving surveillant videos. Thus they do not deal well when there are interventions like shadows or illumination changes.

Markov Random Field (MRF) is proposed in 1989 by Greig [6] for image segmentation purpose. Kamijo [7] uses a Spatio-Temporal Markov Random Field (SF-MRF) to track vehicles in low-angle and front-view images. The model considers not only spacial distribution but also time-axis correlation of pixels from consecutive frames. [8] presents a car tracker utilizing a Hidden Markov Model/Markov Random Field-based segmentation approach which is capable of classifying an image into three different categories: vehicles, shadows of vehicles and the background. However, these methods detect vehicles in traffic monitoring videos with an overhead view. Vehicles are relatively small and lined up in queues. Mostly only their roofs or fronts can be captured. Besides, in these videos, just the vehicles are moving while the background is static and can be extracted by averaging an image sequence for a certain period of time. All of these characteristics do not apply to our on-road scenarios.

In this paper, we present a novel vehicle extraction algorithm which is able to detect nearby vehicles from the front-view road videos. Our first assumption is that colors of the same objects are likely to be similar. So we generate an initial candidate map, as we call it the Object Map, using color and locality cues on the given frame, together with prior domain knowledge. See in Section 2. The Object Map serves as an input for the MRF model proposed later. Our next assumption is that the difference between two consecutive frames of the road video is subtle and that the detection result in the current frame has certain correlation with that of the previous frame. Therefore, we present a MRF model using time and motion correlation between multiple frames to obtain final target objects, aka neaby vehicles. As is described in Section 3. Section 4 conducts the experiments and evaluates our extraction algorithm. Finally, a discussion is presented in Section 5.

2. Initialization of Object Map

Based on our first assumption, color is a distinguishable feature for objects like sky, road, tree or vehicle in a urban road image. By clustering image pixels on their distribution over features like color and location, combined with prior domain knowledge on road environment, we could get a segmentation on different objects of the image from which initial vehicle candidate pixels will be extracted. These pixels are marked as target objects while the rest pixels of the image are labeled as background. Thus the labeling distribution of pixels in the current frame is referred to as an Object Map.

Clustering is a process of grouping objects with similar properties [9]. Existing approaches can be divided mainly into three categories (see [10]): 1) hierarchical methods like single-linkage, complete-linkage. 2) partitional ones like K-MEANS, ISODATA. 3) grid methods [11], which quantize the object space into a finite number of grids (hyper-rectangles) and then perform the required operations on the quantized space. The basic processing unit for 1) and 2) is pixel while for 3) depends on the number of cells in each dimension of quantized space. That's why 3) has faster processing time than 1) or 2) though at the cost of accuracy. Moreover, traditional grid clustering methods tend to combine high density neighbor grids together which turns out to be not so appropriate for road conditions. It would successfully cluster objects with lower significance but high density such as the sky or the road however do poorly for vehicles. So we propose an improved algorithm based on the hierarchical grid clustering method in [12] which addresses the priority of vehicles by:

- Redefining *grid distance* by taking color, density and etc. into account.
- Introducing *key grid* which has priority to be chosen when clustering.

We will first define some concepts before diving into the algorithm. The object space for our grid clustering algorithm has five dimensions. For a given pixel i, its feature vector $(h_i, s_i, v_i, x_i, y_i)$ composes of value of each channel in HSV space which implies the color cues, together with its horizontal and vertical positions in the image, which reflets its locality information. Hyper-rectangle Grid Set (GS) are generated by partitioning equally by extent E_k within each space k, more specifically (our image size is 320×240):

Space	Range	Grid Extent E_k	k
H	$[1, 180]$	6	1
S	$[0, 255]$	32	2
V	$[0, 255]$	32	3
X	$[1, 320]$	20	4
Y	$[1, 240]$	16	5

The *color distance* D_{color} between two grids g_1 and g_2 is defined as:

$$D_{color} = \lambda_H \Delta_H + \lambda_S \Delta_S \cdot \mathrm{MAX}_S + \lambda_V \Delta_V \cdot \mathrm{MAX}_V \quad (1)$$

$$\Delta_H = |h_{c_1} - h_{c_2}| \quad (2)$$

$$\Delta_S = |s_{c_1} - s_{c_2}| \quad (3)$$

$$\Delta_V = |v_{c_1} - v_{c_2}| \quad (4)$$

$$\mathrm{MAX}_S = \max(s_{c_1}, s_{c_2}) \quad (5)$$

$$\mathrm{MAX}_V = \max(v_{c_1}, v_{c_2}) \quad (6)$$

where c_1, c_2 are cluster centers of pixels within g_1, g_2 respectively. The density d_i of a grid g_i is defined as :

$$d_i = \frac{P_i}{V_i} \quad (7)$$

$$V_i = \prod_{k=1}^{5} E_k \quad (8)$$

where P_i is number of pixels in grid g_i and V_i is the grid's volume. The *location distance* $D_{loc}$for g_1 and g_2 is defined as:

$$D_{loc} = (x_{c_1} - x_{c_2})^2 (y_{c_1} - y_{c_2})^2 \quad (9)$$

Thus the *grid distance* D_{grid_same} for two grids g_1, g_2 with density d_1 and d_2 in same frame is defined as:

$$D_{grid\_same} = D_{color} \cdot D_{loc} \cdot d_1 \cdot d_2 \quad (10)$$

Grids that might present vehicles are called *key grids* and should be paid extra attention to while clustering. The prior domain knowledge is that empirically they tend to fall in the Region Of Interest (ROI) area in Fig. 1. So the criteria for selecting a key grid is defined as follows:

- Its center should fall in ROI.
- Its density should be greater than a certain threshold.

Fig. 1: An example of empirical ROI (the purple trapezoid).

The framework of our clustering algorithm is described in **Algorithm** 1, where T_{color}, $T_{density}$ are certain thresholds. SORT method in line 4 sorts set A according to the following comparsion rules:

- Key grids have higher priority than non-key grids.
- If both are key grids, grids with higher density wins.

NEIGHBOR method in line 6 and 29 generates a neighbor set for the given grid. Two grids are defined as neighbors if they are adjacent on one dimension and have same values for the rest four dimensions. By applying **Algorithm** 1, we first select eligible grids as set A with density larger than $T_{density}$ using GET_ACTIVE_GRIDS methods in line 2 and sort A using SORT function in descending order of priority described above. For each grid g_i in A we merge it with neighboring grids of similar color to form different clusters.

Algorithm 1 Framework of the improved clustering algorithm

```
1: procedure GRIDCLUSTER(GS)
2:     A ← GET_ACTIVE_GRIDS(GS)
3:     while A ≠ ∅ do
4:         SORT(A)
5:         g_i ← A[0]
6:         for each grid g_j ∈ NEIGHBOR(g_i) do
7:             if D_color (g_i, g_j) < T_color then
8:                 g_i = MERGE(g_i, g_j, A)
9:             end if
10:        end for
11:        A = A − {g_i}
12:        add g_i to result list
13:    end while
14:    return false
15: end procedure
16: procedure GET_ACTIVE_GRIDS(GS)
17:    A = ∅
18:    for each grid g_i ∈ GS do
19:        if density of g_i: d_i > T_density then
20:            A = A + {g_i}
21:        end if
22:    end for
23:    return A
24: end procedure
25: procedure MERGE(g_i, g_j, A)
26:    add all pixels of g_j to g_i
27:    update all parameters of g_i such as V_i, d_i and etc.
28:    A = A − g_j
29:    for each grid g_k ∈ NEIGHBOR(g_j) do
30:        unlink g_k with g_j
31:        link g_k with g_i
32:    end for
33:    return g_i
34: end procedure
```

An example of the result after clustering is shown in Fig.2. Only results with relatively big area are presented here. As we can see, several sets of grids are generated representing a certain type of an object, in this case, the sky, road, side lane and trees respectively. We then group overlapping grids into bigger grid and then add those within the ROI to the Merged Grid Set (MGS). Pixels in MGS are marked as initial vehicle candidates and comprise the Object Map for MRF model to use in the next step. Here we define the rectangle in XY-space containing all initial vehicle pixels to be the *key region* I_M of a given frame I. An example of the grouping process is shown in Fig.3. As we can see, scattered fragments are grouped together into the shape of the car, aka the target object.

3. Extracting Target Objects

In this section, we aim to integrate motion correlation between consecutive images along a time axis into the MRF model. We firstly generate a mapping of pixels for two successive frames to depict the motion cues and then propose the MRF model based on the Object Map and the mapping.

3.1 Generating Frame Mapping

The mapping is able to tell, for a pixel i' in the previous frame, whether there is a corresponding pixel i in the current frame such that the two pixels actually represent the same object. Given the mapping result, we are able to define a key region within a certain frame.

Similar to Equation (10), we first define the cross-frame grid distance D_{grid_diff} between g_1, g_2 as:

$$D_{grid\_diff} = D_{color} \cdot D_{loc} \cdot \max(\frac{d_1}{d_2}, \frac{d_2}{d_1}) \tag{11}$$

where d_1, d_2 represent the density of each grid. Thus for g in current frame, we search for a grid g' in the MGS of the previous frame with minimum D_{grid_diff}. If D_{grid_diff} is below a certain threshold, g' is considered as the matching grid for g. So we sort MGS in current frame first using the SORT method in **Algorithm 1**, find the matching grids in previous frame for top N grid, compute the average shift $(\Delta x, \Delta y)$ in XY space between the two sets of N grids, apply $(\Delta x, \Delta y)$ to each pixel i to get the corresponding pixel i' in the previous frame, and eliminate i' if the color difference between i and i' exceeds a certain threshold. By doing that, a pixel-to-pixel mapping between two successive frames is obtained.

3.2 Building MRF Models

For each pixel i in current frame I, we assign label l_i ($l_i \in \{-1, 1\}$) to it, $l_i = -1$ for the background and $l_i = 1$ for the target object. As suggested by previous work [13]:

1) Neighboring pixels are likely to have the same label.
2) Neighboring pixels with similar colors are more likely to have the same label.

Therefore we use a MRF prior on labels to model the above interactions:

$$I_M = \{i | i = 1, ..., M\} \tag{12}$$

$$p(l_i | i \in I_M) \propto \prod_{i \in I_M} \prod_{j \in N_i} \psi(l_i, l_j) \tag{13}$$

$$\psi(l_i, l_j) \equiv \exp\left(\lambda l_i l_j / (\alpha + d(i, j))\right) \tag{14}$$

where M is the number of pixels in key region I_M defined in Section 3.1. N_i is the 8 connected neighbors of pixel i.

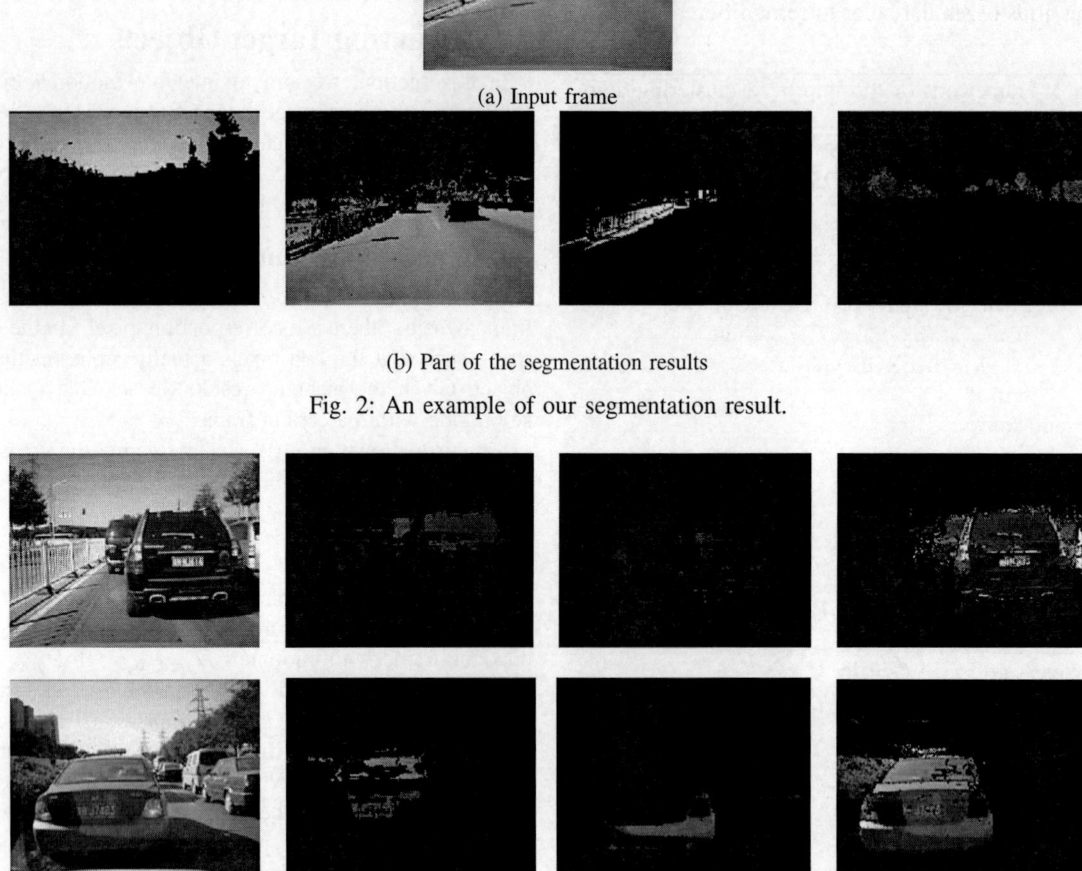

(a) Input frame

(b) Part of the segmentation results

Fig. 2: An example of our segmentation result.

(a) Original frame (b) Clustering results (c) The Object Map

Fig. 3: Examples of generating the Object Map.

$d(i,j)$ measures the color difference between pixel i and j and is similar to Equation (1). α, λ are parameters and should meet the following requirement:

$$\frac{\lambda}{\alpha} < 1, \lambda, \alpha > 0$$

From our previous conclusion, after mapping between two consecutive frames, motion cues are reliable for predicting the moving target objects. For pixel i in current frame, let f_i represent its feature. f_i is considered to be related with the following values:

1) l_i: label after pre-pocessing for pixel i of current frame.
2) $l_{i'}$: detected label for corresponding pixel i' in previous frame.
3) $f_{i'}$: detected feature for corresponding pixel i' in previous frame.
4) $d(i,i')$: color difference between i in current frame and its corresponding pixel i' in previous frame.

where i' is generated in Section 3.1. Therefore, we define:

$$f_i = \begin{cases} \lambda_1 l_i & \text{if } i' \text{ is invalid} \\ \lambda_1 l_i + \dfrac{\lambda_2 l_{i'} + \lambda_3 f_{i'}}{\alpha_1 + d(i,i')} & \text{else} \end{cases} \tag{15}$$

where $\lambda_1, \lambda_2, \lambda_3, \alpha_1$ are parameters, and:

$$\lambda_1 + \frac{\lambda_2 + \lambda_3}{\alpha_1} = 1$$

$$\lambda_1, \lambda_2, \lambda_3, \alpha_1 > 0$$

so that $f_i \in [-1, 1]$.

As defined in [14], the likelihood of frame I given a labeling $\{l_i | i \in I_M\}$ is:

$$p(I|\{l_i|i \in I_M\}) = \prod_{i \in I_M} p(f_i|l_i) \quad (16)$$

$$p(f_i|l_i) = \exp(f_i l_i) \quad (17)$$

With the above MRF prior and likelihood model, target object extraction in a given frame I comes down to finding the labeling that could maximize the following posterior:

$$\mathcal{L}(I) \equiv \frac{1}{Z} \prod_{i \in I_M} p(f_i|l_i) \prod_{i \in I_M} \prod_{j \in N_i} \psi(l_i, l_j) \quad (18)$$

where Z is the normalisation constant.

3.3 Optimization

The optimization problem of Equation (18) can be solved by graph cut algorithms [15], [16] or a loopy belief propogation method [17]. [14], [18] give detailed comparison between these algorithms. We adopt a similar graph cut algorithm based on [19] to obtain the optimized labeling distribution.

4. Experiments

We implemented our algorithm in C++ code and conducted the experiment on a 2.8GHz-CPU PC. The proposed algorithm is tested on video clips collected from Beijing urban roads with 25 fps frame rate under monocular vision. Each image frame is down sampled to size 320×240 (pixel$\times$pixel).

Examples of extraction results are given in Fig. 4. The two images in the left column are the original road condition frames. The target objects we aim to extract should be the red and black car respectively. We can see in the middle column that the Object Map would give a course range of the vehicles but with high noise. But after combining motion trends of previous frame using MRF model, pixels that belong to the background are deducted and pixels of target objects are correctly marked. More accurate extraction results are obtained as shown in the right column. Fig 5 shows the extraction results in continuous frames. As we can see, for those with clear target objects, our method achieves good detection results and is quite stable.

The algorithm would fail when continuous interference is involved, as shown in Fig. 6. The algorithm fail to seperate the taxi from the lawn area due to the color similarity (both green).

The proposed algorithm is experimented on 4000 frames and achieves a precision rate of 88.2%. Runtime of the algorithm would vary between 100ms/frame to 10s/frame due to different sizes of key regions in each frame. The average running time is 4.34s/frame for our data set.

5. Summary and Future Work

In this paper, we present a vehicle extraction algorithm for urban road environment under monocular vision. The approach is composed of an Object Map (OM) generation step utilizing color and locality cues and an object extraction step based on MRF model using the OM and motion cues. Our algorithm is now live on our driving assisting system and achieves good extraction results under complicated unstructured road conditions. It also sheds light upon using MRF method for solving tracking problems in driving surveillant scenarios.

There are several possible extensions for this work. The proposed algorithm could be tested on more diversed road conditions such as corners, unstable illumination and overlapping vehicles to evaluate more of its strength and limitation. As the input for MRF model, the OM quality largely influences the final extraction result. Thus the grouping of the grids can be improved by considering their texture or other implicit vison features. We intend to explore these directions in the future.

References

[1] M. Oren, C. Papageorgiou, P. Sinha, E. Osuna, and T. Poggio, "Pedestrian detection using wavelet templates," in *Computer Vision and Pattern Recognition, 1997. Proceedings., 1997 IEEE Computer Society Conference on.* IEEE, 1997, pp. 193–199.

[2] M. J. Jones and P. Viola, "Robust real-time object detection," in *Workshop on Statistical and Computational Theories of Vision*, 2001.

[3] K. Levi and Y. Weiss, "Learning object detection from a small number of examples: the importance of good features," in *Computer Vision and Pattern Recognition, 2004. CVPR 2004. Proceedings of the 2004 IEEE Computer Society Conference on*, vol. 2. IEEE, 2004, pp. II–53.

[4] M. Gressmann, G. Palm, and O. Lohlein, "Surround view pedestrian detection using heterogeneous classifier cascades," in *Intelligent Transportation Systems (ITSC), 2011 14th International IEEE Conference on.* IEEE, 2011, pp. 1317–1324.

[5] S. J. H. Pirzada, E. U. Haq, and H. Shin, "Single camera vehicle detection using edges and bag-of-features," in *Computer Science and Convergence.* Springer, 2012, pp. 135–143.

[6] D. Greig, B. Porteous, and A. H. Seheult, "Exact maximum a posteriori estimation for binary images," *Journal of the Royal Statistical Society. Series B (Methodological)*, pp. 271–279, 1989.

[7] S. Kamijo, K. Ikeuchi, and M. Sakauchi, "Vehicle tracking in low-angle and front-view images based on spatio-temporal markov random field model," in *8th World Congress on ITS, Sydney Oct*, 2001.

[8] J. Kato, T. Watanabe, S. Joga, Y. Liu, and H. Hase, "An hmm/mrf-based stochastic framework for robust vehicle tracking," *Intelligent Transportation Systems, IEEE Transactions on*, vol. 5, no. 3, pp. 142–154, 2004.

[9] S. A. Elavarasi, J. Akilandeswari, and B. Sathiyabhama, "A survey on partition clustering algorithms," *learning*, vol. 1, no. 1, 2011.

[10] R. Dubes and A. K. Jain, "Clustering methodologies in exploratory data analysis," *Advances in Computers*, vol. 19, no. 11, 1980.

[11] M. Ilango and V. Mohan, "A survey of grid based clustering algorithms," *International Journal of Engineering Science and Technology*, vol. 2, no. 8, pp. 3441–3446, 2010.

[12] E. Schikuta, "Grid-clustering: An efficient hierarchical clustering method for very large data sets," in *Pattern Recognition, 1996., Proceedings of the 13th International Conference on*, vol. 2. IEEE, 1996, pp. 101–105.

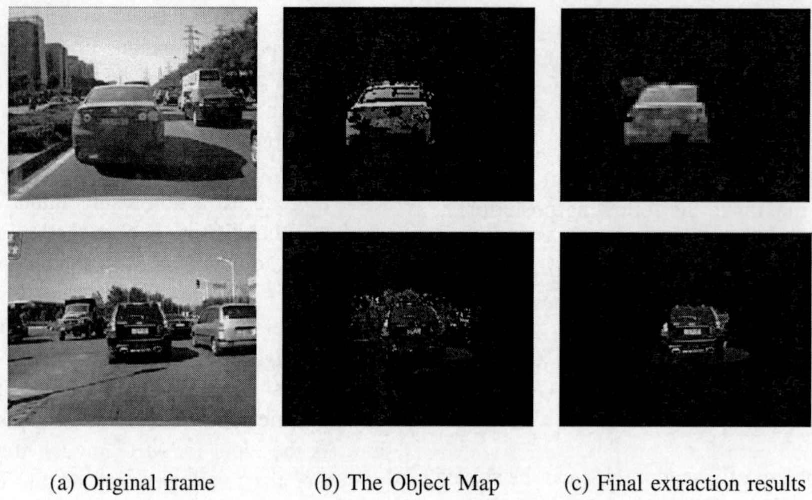

(a) Original frame (b) The Object Map (c) Final extraction results

Fig. 4: Examples of final extracted target object results.

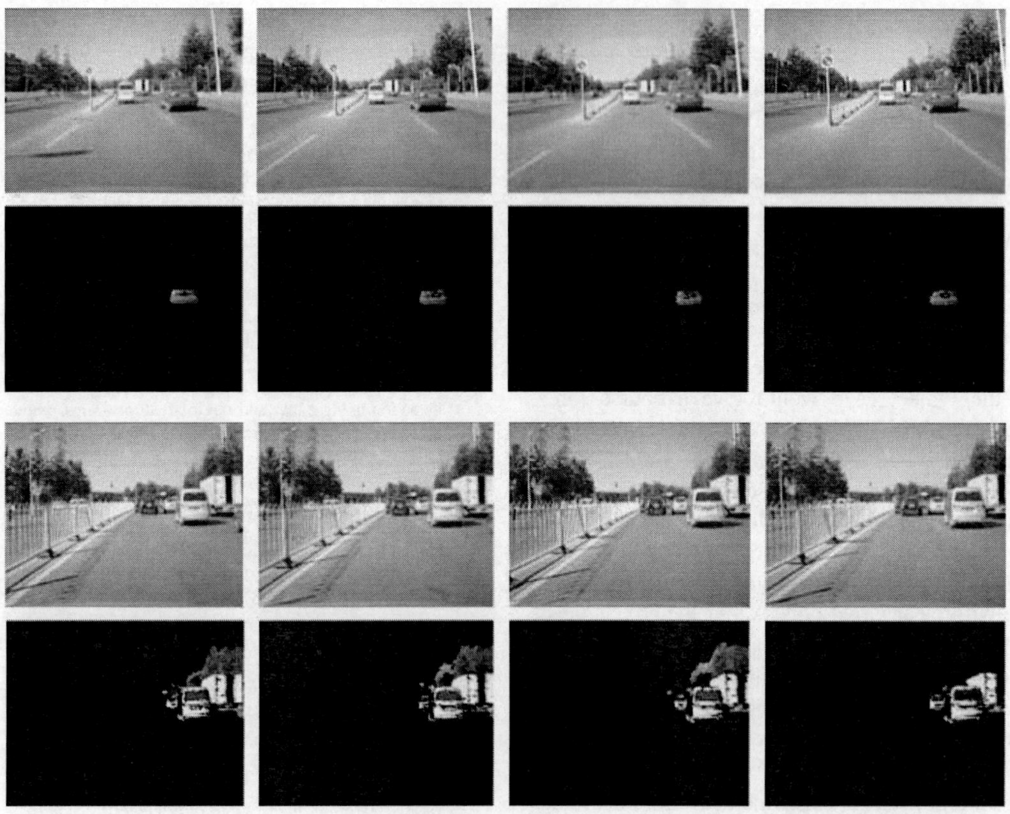

Fig. 5: Examples of final extracted target object results in consecutive frames.

Fig. 6: Examples of failed cases when continuous intervention is involved.

[13] F. Liu and M. Gleicher, "Learning color and locality cues for moving object detection and segmentation," in *Computer Vision and Pattern Recognition, 2009. CVPR 2009. IEEE Conference on*. IEEE, 2009, pp. 320–327.

[14] S. Mahamud, "Comparing belief propagation and graph cuts for novelty detection," in *Computer Vision and Pattern Recognition, 2006 IEEE Computer Society Conference on*, vol. 1. IEEE, 2006, pp. 1154–1159.

[15] Y. Boykov, O. Veksler, and R. Zabih, "Fast approximate energy minimization via graph cuts," *Pattern Analysis and Machine Intelligence, IEEE Transactions on*, vol. 23, no. 11, pp. 1222–1239, 2001.

[16] V. Kolmogorov and R. Zabin, "What energy functions can be minimized via graph cuts?" *Pattern Analysis and Machine Intelligence, IEEE Transactions on*, vol. 26, no. 2, pp. 147–159, 2004.

[17] J. S. Yedidia, W. T. Freeman, Y. Weiss, *et al.*, "Generalized belief propagation," *Advances in neural information processing systems*, pp. 689–695, 2001.

[18] R. Szeliski, R. Zabih, D. Scharstein, O. Veksler, V. Kolmogorov, A. Agarwala, M. Tappen, and C. Rother, "A comparative study of energy minimization methods for markov random fields," in *Computer Vision–ECCV 2006*. Springer, 2006, pp. 16–29.

[19] Y. Boykov and V. Kolmogorov, "An experimental comparison of min-cut/max-flow algorithms for energy minimization in vision," *Pattern Analysis and Machine Intelligence, IEEE Transactions on*, vol. 26, no. 9, pp. 1124–1137, 2004.

Establishment of the watershed image classified rule-set and feasibility assessment of its application

Cheng-Han Lin[1,*], Hsin-Kai Chuang[2] and Ming-Lang Lin[3], Wen-Chao Huang[4]

[1 2 3] Department of Civil Engineer, National Taiwan University, Taipei, Taiwan.

[4] Department of Civil Engineer, National Central University, Taoyuan, Taiwan.

[*]Corresponding author, E-mail address: r01521128@ntu.edu.tw (Cheng-Han Lin).

Abstract *Extreme weather events result in catastrophic disasters around the world recently. More commonly, these disasters occurred due to multiple reasons that coupled together. To develop disaster prevention strategies, application of satellite images can be effective because of its promptness and vast coverage area. This study established an image classified rule-set which used the object-based image analysis methodology. There are several surface features in the watershed image that were classified based on the proposed rule set, including main channels, secondary channels, sandbars, alluvial fans, landslides and place of the geotechnical damage. The study applied this rule-set in different watersheds and different-resolution satellite imagery, and assessed the feasibility by comparing in-situ data and calculating the error matrix. The results showed that the rule-set logic can be flexible in different watersheds and different images. The classification of the rule-set is reproducible and accurate. As this result we can apply the rule-set to disaster management and land use planning in the future work.*

Keywords: Watershed satellite image, Object-based image analysis, Rule-set, Geotechnical damage.

1. Introduction

More than 2,000 mm of cumulative rainfall was recorded during Typhoon Morakot, which happened on August 7 to 9 in 2009 in Taiwan. Typhoon Morakot caused severe damages in central and southern Taiwan. The long duration and high intensity rainfall caused serious damage such as landslides along river banks, the silted up of the channel, the debris dams and the basin flooding. These natural disasters have thus made field investigation difficult because of the interruption of main roads mountain roads. Limited by available man power, resorting to remote sensing techniques for disaster prevention is an urgent need.

In recent years the availability of the remote sensing technology has been continuously growing, the number of image band has increased, and image cost has been reduced. With high-resolution and multi-band satellite images, more ground information is able to be identified. Using remote sensing data and techniques for land surface change after natural disaster has gained increasing attentions (Gamanya et al., 2007; Hung, 2009; Huang, 2010; Chuang, 2012). Methodologically, most approaches are based on the analysis of object-based classification analysis. The application of object-based image analysis with high-resolution satellite image data has solved the existing survey in the problem of lack of space and timing, and the results also similar to artificial interpretation.

This research establishes a rule-set for classifying disaster-related surface features from watershed satellite image, and discusses the applicability of different resolution satellite images. Based on literature review, previous researches do not pay attention to the practicability of results derived from different image datasets. Therefore, the objective of this study is to identify disaster sites with high correctness using an object-based classification rule-set, and suggest the evaluation of suitability for different satellite image and different watershed.

2. Methods

2.1. Study area and Image data

The focus of this study was the Chenyoulan river watershed and the Lao-Nong river watershed in the central and southern Taiwan. The study site centered over lower stream in the Chenyoulan River and upper stream in the Lao-Nong River. During Typhoon Morakot, landslides, mudslides, floods and damaged public facilities occurred in these regions. The field investigations had highlighted the importance of watercourse alteration, surface features of flood plain area and artificial structures (Lin et. al., 2009; Chen et. al., 2009).

The satellite images which were used in this study were all acquired after Typhoon Morakot, comprising four multi-spectral bands and a panchromatic band. The detailed image information is shown as in Figure 2-1. In terms of satellite image identification, the spatial resolution is related to the identification of the surface feature and image bands provided extraction of spectral features. Revisit frequency expressed the period of time required when taking a photo to a given specific area.

	WorldView-2	QuickBird	Formosat-2
Swath width	16.4 km	16.5 km	24.0 km
Revisit Time	3.7 days	5.4 days	1.0 days
Spatial Resolution	Pan: 0.5 m MS: 2.0 m	Pan: 0.61 m MS: 2.40 m	Pan: 2.0 m MS: 8.0 m
Digitization	11 bits/ pixel	11 bits/ pixel	8 bits/ pixel
Image Bands	Pan, Red, Green, Blue, NIR1, Coastal Blue, Red-Edge, Yellow, NIR2	Pan, Red, Green, Blue, NIR1	Pan, Red, Green, Blue, NIR1

Fig. 2-1 Basic information of Satellite images. (From RiChi Technology Inc.).

Comparing individual differences of the images, although the spatial resolution of WorldView-2 is higher than those of QuickBird and Formosat-2, however, Formosat-2, which is a satellite system from Taiwan, is relatively convenience to use due to its price and timeliness.

2.2. Research procedures

The image classification in the first step is to segment the satellite image into the object segments. The second step is to assign the object segments into classes it belong. The research flow chart is shown in Figure 2-2.

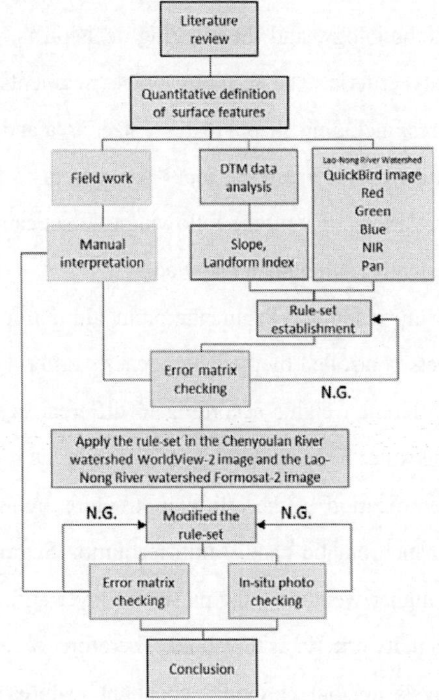

Fig. 2-2 Research flow chart

In addition to Blue, Green, Red, NIR and Pan layers used in this study, Slope and Landform Index which were produced by the high-resolution digital terrain model (DTM) were also added in the layers. The layer features in the classification was set on the basis of both spectral reflection and the topography relationship. Firstly, this study referred to the rule-set that was established by Lao-Nong river watershed QuickBird image (Chuang, 2012). Secondly, this rule-set was applied in the Chenyoulan river watershed WorldView-2 images and the Lao-Nong river watershed Formosat-2 image, respectively.

The feasibility is assessed by comparing with investigation photos and error matrices. In the conclusion section, the applicability and the subsequent application of the rules-set will be suggested. The main methodology of the study is described in the following sub-section.

2.3. Object-based image analysis

This study uses the object-based image analysis by the software eCognition, which has the segmentation algorithm of the Multi-resolution Segmentation. The procedure for the Multi-resolution Segmentation can be described as a region merging methodology, and the merging decision is based on heterogeneity criteria. The resulting object segments contain more features, including shape, texture, size, area and spectral value. These features are basic input parameters to build up the spatial relationship, and the following rule-set can be used more consistently with human knowledge.

The Multi-resolution Segmentation in addition to the size of the objects controlled by the heterogeneity criteria can also be given different weights according to different layers. For instance, the water body has strong reflection in the blue band, and the identification of the artificial structures require high resolution panchromatic band. Multi-resolution Segmentation can give a higher weight for the particular layer and compute the heterogeneity criteria as threshold. Therefore, object-based image analysis not only provides abundant features that are closer to human interpretation results, but also identifies boundary of the segment by choosing proper parameters such that it fits the surface feature.

2.4. Establishment of the rule-set

The rule-set is to integrate image analysis at every step from the segmentation to the classification, and to translate the human logic and expert knowledge into algorithms. In this study the hierarchy of the rule-set is divided into four stages sequentially. First of all, a large area of vegetation and shadow in the image are classified, and the segments that are not classified are moved into the next step. Finally the artificial structure, which is the smallest category, will be in classification (Fig. 2-3). The parameters are decided in the segmentation according to the spatial size of each category after the determination of the surface features and the hierarchy.

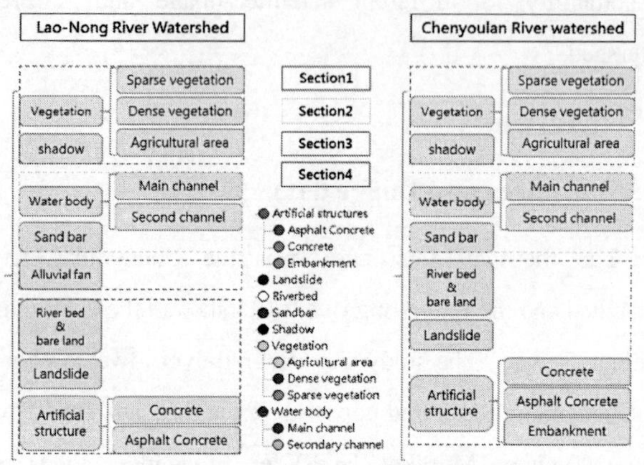

Fig. 2-3 Hierarchy of the classification rule-set section

Establishment of the rule set for the first time requires try and error to find the most efficient classification threshold. For example, the first stage is to find out the vegetation. According to common experiences in Remote Sensing, it has confirmed that the Normalized Difference Vegetation Index (NDVI) can be used to identify the vegetation area. Therefore, the "Assign Class" was selected for the vegetation classification. On the other hand, the fourth stage of the category is not easy to classify with single feature and threshold, therefore the "Nearest Neighbor", which performs selective sample training before executive supervised classification, was selected.

The result of the rule-set in Lao-Nong river watershed is shown in figure 2-4. Statistics of error matrix showed the Kappa value of 0.878 and the overall accuracy of 0.8489 in Baolai, and the Kappa value of 0.830 and the overall accuracy of 0.860 in Liouguei. This study visually presented the rule-set by using the decision tree. The tree structure and the flow component help application of the rule-set methodology for non-experts and the beginners (Fig. 2-5, 2-6).

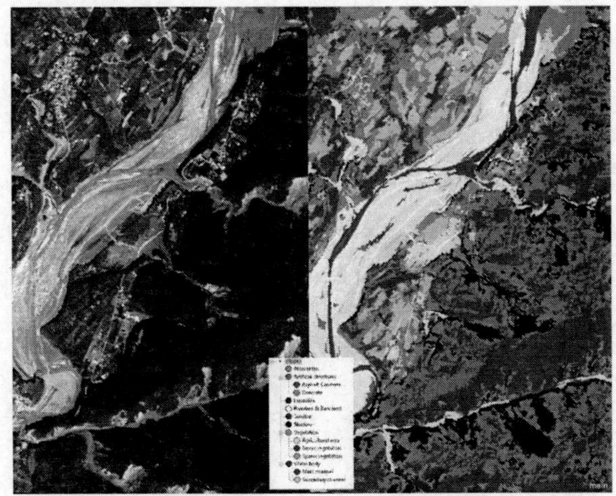

Fig. 2-4 Classification result in Baolai using the Lao-Nong river watershed QuickBird image

2.5. Feasibility assessment of its application

In this study there are two methodologies for checking the application of the rule-set. One was using the rule-set for the classification in the different watershed. It can be seen clearly that distinct land use between lower stream in the Chenyoulan River and upper stream in the Lao-Nong River. The other one evaluated the rule-set in the same watershed but different resolution satellite images. The spatial resolution of Formosat-2 image is relatively lower comparing to the QuickBird image. Formosat-2 only provides 2m panchromatic and 8m multispectral that cannot distinguish detailed surface features. With the resolution of the Formosat-2 image, the layers of Slope and Landform Index also produced by lower resolution DTM (40m).

The spectral distribution is influenced by both the satellite sensor and weather condition. Therefore it must modified classification algorithm in applied the rule-set in Chenyoulan river watershed. Adaption by adjusting the classification threshold and the Multi-resolution Segmentation parameters. Also, it is necessary to re-select the surface features because the land use in Chenyoulan river watershed is more complicated than in the Lao-Nong river watershed. For example the distribution of the agricultural area and the artificial structure are more abundant in Chenyoulan river watershed. Using the Landform Index layer to specify the domain is also helpful for the analysis, such as the case that the landslide is in steep slope and the high relative height, while the artificial structure is in the steep slope and the flat region.

Through the modification of the rule-set, it spent 10 hours in the WorldView-2 image analysis and only 70 minutes in the Formosat-2 image analysis. For both the WorldView-2 and Formosat-2 image classification results, Kappa value of the error matrix were all greater than 0.75. In the conclusion organizes the assessment results and made a description of the reflection.

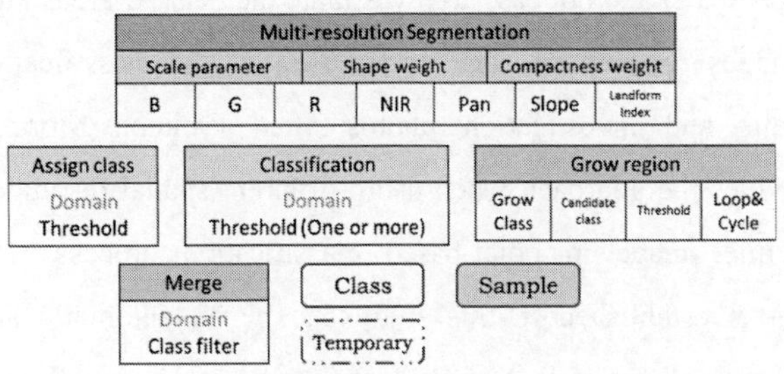

Fig. 2-5 Definition of the Rule-set tree component

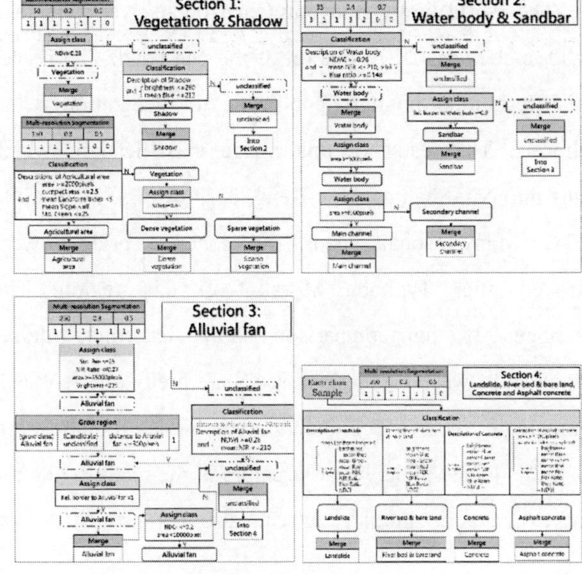

Fig. 2-6 Rule-set tree

3. Results and discussion

To evaluate the classification results, manual selection of ground true information and comparison with object-based image analysis results is a qualitative criterion. Calculating the error matrix can clearly determine the mutual confusion between the surface features. Based on its statistical parameters, it was observed that all classification results have overall accuracy up to 80%, and Kappa value greater than 75%. Joseph (2003) purposed that Kappa value up to 75% is an acceptable accuracy. However, higher misjudgment between the river bed and artificial structures occurred occasionally. This misjudgment was caused by the spatial site of the surface features, but more obviously it was caused by spectral reflection.

Usually the disaster triggered by extreme weather is in a larger scale, and not easy to investigate the disaster areas after damages were made. The comparison of the classification results and investigation photos after Typhoon Morakot provides the approach when using different spatial resolution satellite image in objet-based classification process. The rule-set established in this study can be an automatic and accurate disaster location identification tool in disaster mitigation planning.

The WorldView-2 image in Chenyoulan river watershed has 0.5 meters spatial resolution of the pan band. The higher spatial resolution is more applicable to recognition detail landforms. The result of this image classification, which zooms into Xin-Shan and Jun-Keng, is shown in Fig. 3-1 and Fig.3-2. Many asphalt roads and concrete bridges were destroyed after Typhoon Morakot in this region. The assessment of this comparison show that this rule-set distinguish between bridges and roads are pretty efficient, and for mountain roads, which is commonly hidden by the forest, can still be traced by its linear structure of the roads, while the villages and agricultural areas can also get its distribution range.

As for the application of the rule-set by using Lao-Nong river watershed but with different resolution image, Figure 3-3 can be seen that the spatial resolution influenced the object segments. The coarse object segments led to the results that the interpretation of the smaller landform in the Formosat-2 image is unable to comply with the surface features boundary, for example, bridges, roads and villages can only get its location. Considering large-scale disaster events, such as landslides, the alluvial fan caused by the mudslides, river channel accumulation, it is able to accurately evaluate disaster location, size and their possible impact ranges (Fig. 3-4). Even though the result does not guarantee perfect accuracy, it proved beneficial for the disaster prevention and planning of the post-disaster mitigation.

Fig. 3-1 Comparison of the Chenyoulan river watershed image with site photos in Xin-Shan (photos taken by Lin et. al., 2009)

Fig. 3-2 Comparison of the Chenyoulan river watershed image with site photos in Jun-Keng (photos taken by Lin et. al., 2009)

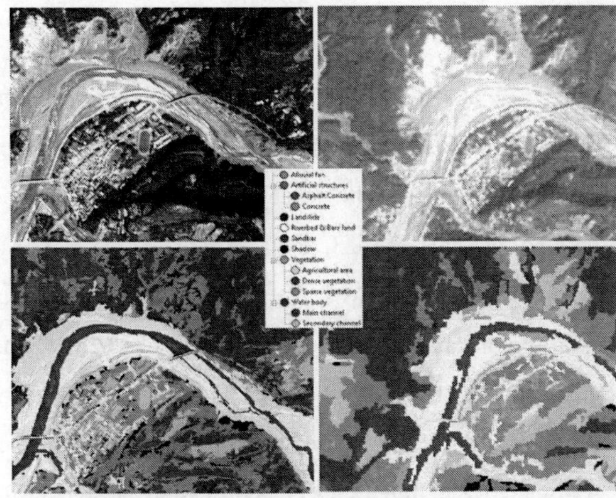

Fig. 3-3 Classification results in Baolai using different resolution image (left: QuickBird; right: Formosat-2)

Fig. 3-4 Comparison of the Lao-Nong river watershed image with site photos (photos taken by Chen et. al., 2009)

4. Conclusion

Most research approaches aim for the extraction of surface feature, such as landslide and artificial structures by focusing on a single satellite image. Even with high spatial resolution satellite images, such as QuickBird and WorldView-2, it is still incapable satisfying both aspects in classification accuracy and the program run time. This study applies the rule-set to watershed image classification by using QuickBird, WorldView-2 and Formosat-2 image data respectively. The result provides an automatic and applicable process of the watershed image classification, and demonstrates that the rule-set logicality is suitable to apply to different images and different watersheds. It is also proposed to modify the rule-set in this study, including the hierarchy from large to small spatial scale, determination of the scale parameter of the object-based segmentation, setting of layer weights, building the knowledge base of the classes, and selection of algorithms and threshold.

As error matrix is used to calculate the overall accuracy and the Kappa value with qualitative statistics. The feasibility was also assessed by comparing the classification result to the site photos. By using two methods for checking the accuracy, the watershed image classification rule-set was proved to be reproducible and applicable to non-experienced users. One important variable is different watershed region. The rule-set logic is flexible for adoption that surface features should be re-selected because the land use in different watershed is not the same. Another variable is different satellite image of a wide or narrow spectral distribution. Modification of the classification threshold or increase the other algorithms will be able to improve the classification accuracy. Using the rule-set for image analysis in the software eCognition, spend about 10 hours on a high-resolution image computing and only close to 70 minutes on Formosat-2 image. The enhancement of the proposed approach is the reduction of human errors, manual classification process and the reduction in processing time.

After the image classification by the software eCognition, the segments can output both shape file and Raster data. Those data can be used to estimate the land cover changes by using the software ERDAS Image or ArcGIS. The WorldView-2 and the QuickBird are both foreign commercial satellites. The images are too expensive and not prompt enough to response to the damages that happened here in Taiwan. Previous research of object-based image classification in Taiwan had used Formosat-2 multi-period image, and automated the analysis of landslide and artificial facilities (Huang, 2010). If the proposed approach is to apply to vast images more than two watersheds, we suggest to clip the satellite images by using the software ERDAS Image, or select the targeted surface features.

As is known form the literature (Chuang, 2012), the landform index layer combined with slope and relative elevation is used to describe the topography for the spatial relationship. Because the flat area around flood plain is with high priority in this study, the slope grading only simply divided into two grades. Future research can involve aspect and curvature as a data layer within the software eCognition, these parameters will result in effective interpretation for topology features. For establishing an object-based classification rule-set in the new location, the most rapid operation is through the high-resolution to low-resolution image, and the modification in the same watershed will be simpler than different watershed. Refer to the Figure 4-1. Subsequent application to establishment of rule-set, user can follow the real path, which is in the same location and from high-resolution to low-resolution.

Disasters caused by extreme weather events in the future must be discussed by the disaster historical perspective. Analysis of the land cover changes by using this methodology in each object segment is a priority in coupled-disaster assessment, land use change, environmental monitoring. Thus it is expected to avoid the recurrence of similar disasters in the future.

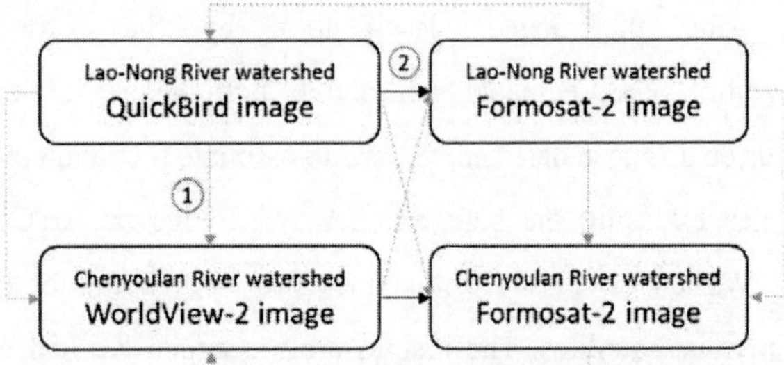

Fig. 4-1 Suggestion for establishing the rule-set (No.1 and No.2 are the assess methodology in this study)

5. Reference

[1] Baatz, M., A. SCHÄPE. "Multiresolution Segmentation: An optimization approach for high quality multi-scale image segmentation". Angewandte Geographische Informations-Verarbeitung, Vol. XII., 12–23, 2000.

[2] T.J. Chen, J.J. Wu, M.J. Weng, K.H. Xie, J.Z. Wang. "Slope failure of Lawnon basin induced by Typhoon Morakot". Sino-Geotechnics, Vol. 122, 13-20, 2009.

[3] Gamanya, R., Philippe De Maeyer, Morgan De Dapper. "An Automated Satellite Image Classification Design Using Object-Oriented Segmentation Algorithms- A Move towards Standardization". Expert System with Applications, Vol. 32(2), 616–624, 2007.

[4] H.K. Chuang. "Combining landform thematic layer and object-based image analysis to map the surface features of mountainous flood plain and surrounding areas". Master's dissertation, National Taiwan University, 2012.

[5] Joseph L. F., B. L., and M. C. P. "Statistical Methods for Rates and Proportions". 3rd Ed, 2003.

[6] J.Y. Lin, S.Q. Xu, P.H. Cai, S.C. Hui, C.Y. Lai, M.F. Lai, M.T. Yang, K.J. Shou, F.G. Huang, K.C. Chan, S.Y. Xu. "Slope disaster inducement in the Chenyoulan river watershed". Sino-Geotechnics, Vol. 122, 41-50, 2009.

[7] K.C. Hung. "Landslide detection using various features from multispectral imagery". Master's dissertation, National Cheng Kung University, 2009.

[8] National Science and Technology Center for Disaster Reduction. "Typhoon Morakot principal investigation plan: landslide (2)". Typhoon Morakot disaster investigation and analyzed, pp. 79-107, 2010.

[9] W.K. Huang. "Applying object-oriented analysis to segmentation and classification of landslide and artificial facilities with remote sensing images". Master's dissertation, National Taiwan University, 2010.

Greedy Approach for Low-Rank matrix recovery

A. Petukhov[1], **I. Kozlov**[2]
[1]Contact Author, Department of Mathematics, University of Georgia, Athens, GA 30602, USA, petukhov@math.uga.edu
[2]Algosoft Tech USA, Bishop, GA, USA, inna@algosoft-tech.com
IPCV'13

Abstract— *We describe the Simple Greedy Matrix Completion Algorithm providing an efficient method for restoration of low-rank matrices from incomplete corrupted entries.*

We provide numerical evidences that, even in the simplest implementation, the greedy approach may increase the recovery capability of existing algorithms significantly.

Keywords: Law-Rank Matrix Completion, Compressed Sensing, Image Inpainting, Motion Tracking, Face Recognition

1. Introduction

We consider a greedy strategy based algorithm for the recovery of the low-rank matrix from incomplete corrupted samples.

The problem of low-rank matrix completion is not new. However, it got a new impulse ([4], [2]) in connection with the development of the compressed sensing theory and algorithms and ideas to use the ℓ^1 minimization as a surrogate for the sparsest solution ([3], [6], [12]) .

This paper can be considered as a feasibility study for the methods inspired by ideas from both low-rank matrix completion and our compressed sensing oriented ℓ^1-greedy algorithm ([7], [10], [11]).

The problem is set as follows. It is required to restore (complete) the matrix $A \in \mathbb{R}^{m\times n}$ of rank r, $r < \min\{m, n\}$, given by its k entries, $k < nm$. The set of the given entries is $\Omega \subset \{1, \ldots, m\} \times \{1, \ldots, n\}$. $|\Omega|$ is the cardinality of Ω (which in our case is equal to k). We also introduce notation $d(\Omega)$ for the density of the set Ω, $d(\Omega) := |\Omega|/(nm)$. The complementary set $\bar{\Omega}$ is a set of erasures, $1 - d(\Omega)$ represents the density of erasures. The theoretical bounds for recoverability of the matrix depends not only on the density of the samples but also on the matrix A and on the 2D-geometry of Ω. The matrix consisting of only one non-zero entry is the simplest example of a rank 1 matrix which can be restored only if the value at the non-zero entry is known. Anyway, it turned out (cf. [2]) that under quite mild conditions random matrices of size $n \times n$ and rank r can be recovered from at most $O(rn^{1.2} \log n)$ entries as a matrix with the minimum of nuclear norm.

The popularity of that problem can be explained by an enormous number of applied problems which can be formulated in terms of matrix completion. Among many settings in different applied areas, we mention problems related to image processing. Image inpainting, including more particular image upsampling, face recognition technique, motion tracking and segmentation in video are most typical of those problems. While the problem of low-rank matrix completion is studied for a long time, the theory got a big push due to development of Compressed Sensing / Compressive Sampling (CS) technique. After some simplification, the CS data decoding goal can be reduced to solving underdetermined systems

$$A\mathbf{x} = \mathbf{y} + \mathbf{e}, \tag{1}$$

where $\mathbf{x} \in \mathbb{R}^n$ is a sparse vector of data "encoded" with the known to the decoder matrix $A \in \mathbb{R}^{m\times n}$, $m < n$; $\mathbf{y} \in \mathbb{R}^m$ is a vector of measurements (of $\mathbf{x}$) possibly corrupted by the vector $\mathbf{e} \in \mathbb{R}^n$. Here and bellow we assume that the sparse solution $\mathbf{x}$ exists and the vector of errors $\mathbf{e}$ is also sparse. The sparsity of $\mathbf{a} \in \mathbb{R}^N$ means that

$$|\mathbf{a}|_0 := |\{a_i \neq 0\}| < N.$$

The value $|\mathbf{a}|_0$ is called the Hamming weight of the vector $\mathbf{a}$. Since the problem of finding sparse solutions has non-polynomial complexity ([9]), the mainstream CS researches suggested to use to replace the minimization of $|\mathbf{x}|_0$ (or $|\mathbf{x}|_0$+$|\mathbf{e}|_0$) with the minimization of ℓ^1-norm. It turned out that that such approach based on convex optimization gives the optimal sparse solution at least when $|\mathbf{x}|_0$ is not very large (cf. [6], [3], [12] for the case $\mathbf{e} = \vec{0}$). Thus, in some special cases the original non-convex problem can be reduced to convex programming. In what follows, like for the notion for the Hamming weight, we use notation $|\cdot|_p$, $0 < p < \infty$, for element-wise (quasi-)norms of vectors and matrices. Say, for the matrix A, $|A|_p := \left(\sum_{i,j} |A_{ij}|^p\right)^{1/p}$. In particular, $|\cdot|_2$ is the Frobenius norm. The inner product of 2 matrices A and B is defined as $\langle A, B\rangle := \text{trace}(A^T B)$. Thus, $\langle A, A\rangle = |A|_2^2$. The notation $\|\cdot\|_p$ is reserved for the operator norms of matrices.

CS results inspired the authors of [2] and [4] on replacing the minimum rank condition leading to non-polynomial complexity with the minimization of the nuclear norm $\|A\|_* := \sum \sigma_i$ of the matrix A, where σ_i are singular values of A. To be more precise, the problem

$$\|A\|_* \to \min \text{ subject to } A_{ij} = M_{ij}, \quad (i,j) \in \Omega,$$

where $M_{i,j}$ are the known entries (measurements) of the matrix A, is considered as relaxation of the rank minimization problem above.

Many different settings giving a solution of the original problems have been studied for the last years. In most cases, the intention of those studies was to find the faster algorithms with the higher capability of the recovery. Typically, modifications of the problem leading to unconstrained optimization were introduced.

2. Basic Algorithm

For our experiments we need the algorithm providing convex minimization recovering low-rank matrices from incomplete corrupted samples. It is used as a basic constructive block in our algorithm. The problem of restoring a matrix from corrupted entries is less studied than the simpler matrix completion problem when the available entries are not corrupted at all or corrupted by noise with relatively low level magnitude. Anyway, there are a few computationally efficient algorithms solving that problem (e.g., [5], [8], [14]).

For our purposes, we selected the algorithm from [8] based on the method of Augmented Lagrange Multipliers (ALM) (e.g., [1]). Having corrupted samples, instead of finding the matrix with the sparsest set of singular values coinciding with the measurements on as large as possible set, the algorithm finds the minimum of the functional

$$L(A,E,Y,\mu) := \|A\|_* + \lambda|E|_1 + \langle Y,R\rangle + \frac{\mu}{2}|R|_2^2, \quad (2)$$

where $R = M - A - E$ is the residual of approximation of the measurements M of the estimate of the unknown matrix A and the estimate of the unknown matrix of errors E. The entries of the input matrix M on the $\bar{\Omega}$ are unknown. It is assumed that R vanishes on $\bar{\Omega}$ and does not contribute into the third and the forth terms as well as E does not contribute into the second term.

If it is known that the observed entries in M are not corrupted, the second term can be omitted. However, we assume that we never know whether the entries are corrupted. So, in what follows, we minimize the 4-term functional given in (2).

We will need the following notation

$$\mathcal{S}_\epsilon[x] := \begin{cases} x-\epsilon, & x > \epsilon, \\ x+\epsilon, & x < -\epsilon, \\ 0, & \text{otherwise;} \end{cases}$$

where x can be either a number or a vector or a matrix. For vectors and matrices the operator is applied entrywise. The operator $\mathcal{S}_\epsilon$ is called the shrinkage operator.

The minimization algorithm, as it is described in [8] and implemented in Matlab code, is as follows

Algorithm ALM.

Input. Observation matrix $M \in \mathbb{R}^{m\times n}$, defined on Ω, and $\lambda > 0$.

Initialization. $Y^0 = \frac{1}{\max\{\|M\|_2, \|M\|_\infty/\lambda\}} M$, $E^0 = 0$, $\mu_0 > 0$, $\rho > 1$, $k = 0$;

1. **while** not converged **do**
2. $(U,S,V) := \text{svd}(M - E^k + \mu^{-1}Y^k)$;
3. $A^{k+1} := U\mathcal{S}_{\mu_k^{-1}}[S]V^T$;
4. $E^{k+1} := \mathcal{S}_{\lambda\mu_k^{-1}}[M - A^{k+1} + \mu^{-1}Y^k]$;
5. $Y^{k+1} := Y^k + \mu_k(M - A^{k+1} - E^{k+1})$;
6. $\mu_{k+1} := \rho\mu_k$, $k := k+1$;
7. **end while**.

Output. A^{k+1}, E^{k+1}.

3. Our algorithm

Our modification of the algorithm above is inspired by significant success reached by applying greedy ideas to solving underdetermined systems ([7], [10], [11]). The general greedy strategy in optimization algorithms consists in sequential finding a simple suboptimal solutions giving some (incomplete) information about the optimal solution. A greedy algorithm picks up the most obvious features or elements of those solutions and gives them a privilege to be pivot for the next iteration of the suboptimal algorithm. Each iteration brings new pivot elements.

In the matrix recovery algorithm, the erasures from the set $\bar{\Omega}$ forms such group from the beginning. Whereas, the elements of Ω are just suspicious to be erroneous. If we have sufficient evidence that some element in Ω contains a random error independent of the content of other entries from Ω, that the decision to move this element to $\bar{\Omega}$ is quite justifiable. While the independence condition is not always accurate even in our experiments with artificially generated data, we use this strategy for estimation of the capability of the greedy ideas for matrix recovery.

Our greedy algorithm consists in iterating with updated (dilated) sets Ω_k. We will call it the Simple Greedy Matrix Completion Algorithm (SGMCA). Generally speaking , any matrix recovery algorithm, including SGMCA itself, which is able to fight the mixture of erasures and errors can be used as a basic block of SGMCA.

Formally, all our experiments can be described in the following way.

Algorithm SGMCA.

Input. M, Ω. **Initialization.** $\lambda > 1$, $\Omega_0 := \Omega$, $A^0 := M$, $E^0 := 0$, $0 < q_0, q_1 < 1$, $k = 0$.

1. Set $k := k+1$;
2. $A^k = ALM(M, \Omega_k)$;
3. **if** $k = 1$ **then** $T_1 = q_0 \max_{i,j}\{|A^1_{ij} - M_{ij}|$; **else** $T_k := q_1 T_{k-1}$;
4. $\Omega_{k+1} = \Omega_k \setminus \{(i,j) \mid |A^k_{ij} - M_{ij}| > T_k\}$;
5. **if** not converged **go to** 2.

4. Numerical Experiments

Since our intention was to conduct an algorithm feasibility study, the goal of this section is to give comparison with the output of recently published algorithms and with pure ALM (one iteration of the algorithm above with no update). The parameters in the basic algorithm are selected as $\mu_0 = 0.3/\|M\|_2$, $\rho = 1.1 + 0.5|\Omega|/(mn)$, $q_0 = 0.3$, $q_1 = 0.65$.

The parameter λ is defined by the combination of $d(\Omega)$ and the density of errors in Ω samples. The general trend can be characterized as follows: the higher error rate, the less value of λ has to be used. At the same time, too small value of λ may bring the increased level of the false alarm in identification of error locations. We will use the least values of λ in the cases when we have an additional mechanism for protection from the false alarm. One of such cases considered below is the case when the rank of the matrix A is known in advance. In what follows, we do not use fine tuning of λ. The same λ is used for big groups of our experiments. At the same time, tuning λ may bring significant increase of the algorithm efficiency. In this paper, we use values of λ in the range $0.02 \div 100$ (from the case of the known rank to the blind matrix completion).

For our experiments, we used Matlab implementation of ALM algorithm available at `http://perception.csl.illinois.edu /matrix-rank/home.html` We used the code for Matrix Completion via the inexact ALM Method with our adaptation to the input with errors.

In all our experiments with synthetic data, A are square $m \times n$, $m = n$, matrices of rank r obtained as $A = UV^T$, where $U, V \in \mathbb{R}^{n \times r}$. The matrices U and V consist of independent gaussian random values with zero expectation and the variance 1. The coordinates of erasures were selected randomly. The models of errors below were different for different experiments.

In the first experiment (Fig.1), we demonstrate advantage of the iterative SGMCA over ALM (one iteration of the same algorithm) for the matrix with fixed sizes $m \times n$, $m = n$, and the rank of matrices $r = 15$. We use the additive model of errors adding the random values from the standard normal distribution at the random available for reconstruction entries of the matrix A. The number of the corrupted entries is fixed in each experiment and does not exceed the value $|\Omega|$.

The solid curves on Fig. 1 correspond to SGMCA (up to 10 iterations) for n = 128, 512, 1024 (from the bottom to the top). The corresponding graphs for ALM algorithm are plotted with dashed curves.

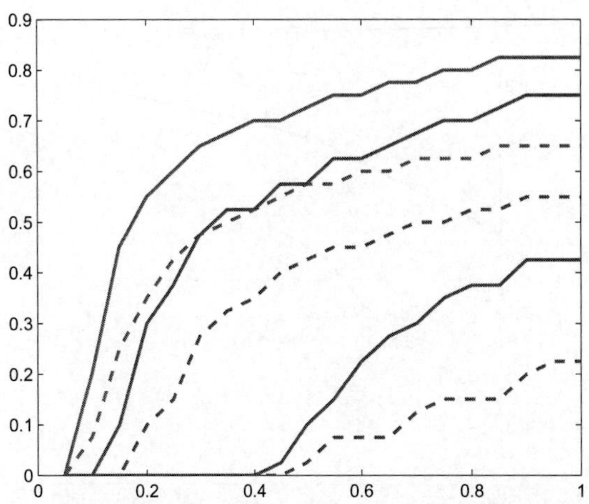

Fig.1. Greedy iterations vs. convex ALM optimization

The horizontal coordinate indicates the fraction of the matrix available for restoration (i.e., $d(\Omega)$), while the vertical coordinate is the fraction of randomly corrupted entries in Ω. The magnitude of the corruption is randomly set from the standard normal distribution. The curves define "phase transition" bounds. In our experiments, we run 10 trials. At the points of curves as well as under each curve all 10 attempts were accomplished with success, i.e., for the obtained estimate $\hat{A}$, $|A - \hat{A}|_2/|A|_2 < 10^{-3}$, whereas for the points above the curves, at least one attempt failed. This means that the regions under the curves are regions of "success".

The second experiment (Fig.2 and Fig.3) is devoted to comparison with the results from [5]. Unfortunately, we do not have full information about the error model. So we use the same additive model of errors as above. While all other parameters are taken from [5]. The matrix of rank 2 is constructed as above. Its size changes from 100 to 3000.

The experiment consists of 2 parts. The first plot (Fig.2) contains the curves for the fixed erasure rate 0.1, i.e, $d(\Omega) = 0.9$. However, the probability of errors in those entries varies. There are 3 graphs on Fig. 2. The solid line corresponds to 10 iterations of SGMCA, the dashed line corresponds to ALM, and the dotted curve corresponds to the result from [5]. The values defined by curves give the maximum error probability admitting successful correction by the corresponding algorithm. If we were aware of the error model from [5], the dashed and dotted curves have to coincide up to statistical discrepancy.

On the second plot (Fig.3) the error rate is fixed and equal to 0.1. The graphs show dependence of maximum possible rate of erasures from the size of matrix.

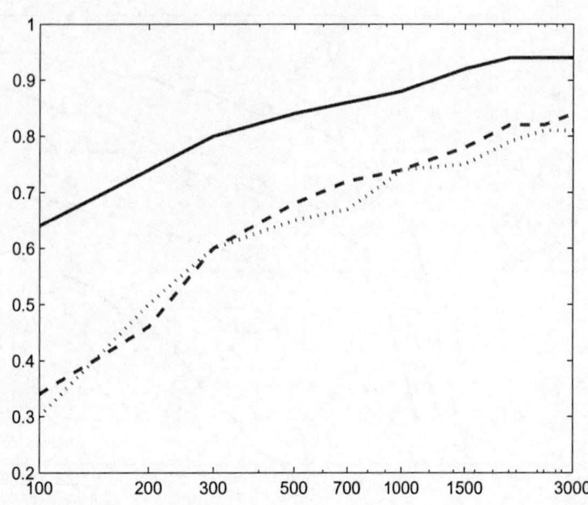

Fig.2. Admissible error rate for erasure rate 0.1.

The efficiency of the algorithms is defined by the distance of curve values on Fig. 2 and Fig. 3 to 1. On Fig. 2, this distance defines the fraction of uncorrupted entries among all available entries. Whereas that distance on Fig. 3 defines the fraction of entries available for the procedure of matrix completion among all uncorrupted entries. It is easy to see that, when the error rate is fixed, SGMCA curve is twice closer to 1 than ALM. Hence, SGMCA restores low rank matrices from only half of entries necessary for the ALM minimization. For the fixes erasure rate, the number of uncorrupted entries for SGMCA successful restoration can be only one third of that necessary for recovery with ALM.

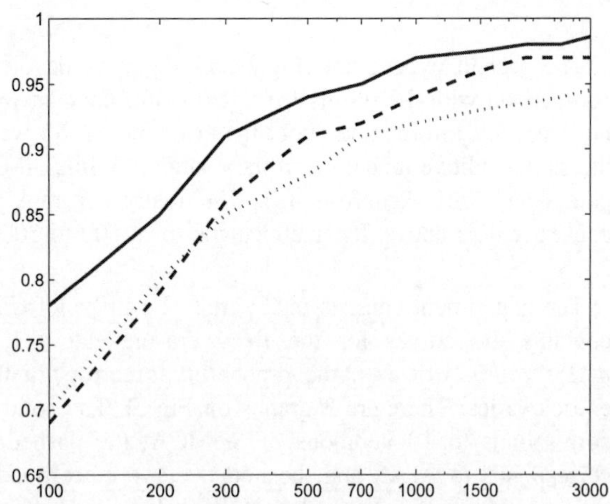

Fig.3. Admissible erasure rate for error rate 0.1.

The more precise value of the SGMCA graph at $m = 3000$ on Fig 3 is 0.986, i.e., having error probability 0.1, the matrix can be restored from 1.4% of random entries.

In our last experiment (Fig. 4–6), we compare the output of SGMCA with the results of RTRMC algorithm from [14] providing very impressive recovery. However, for such successful recovery it requires a priori knowledge of the rank of the matrix A. The ALM-based algorithm used as a basic algorithm in SGMCA does not require any knowledge about the rank while the rank knowledge is useful for it and can be incorporated. To provide equal opportunities for SGMCA and RTRMC we applied the internal fixation of the rank within the ALM procedure.

The results for ranks $r = 5, 15, 25$ are given on Fig. 4–6 correspondingly. The size of matrices is 512×512. The horizontal coordinate corresponds to $d(\Omega)$, whereas the the vertical coordinate is the probability of errors in the coefficients available for reconstruction. In most of cases, SGMCA outperforms RTRMC by 15–25% in the maximum admissible probability of errors. The reason why SGMCA loses on interval $[0, 0.175]$ on Fig.4 is the parameter $\lambda = 0.02$ which was fixed for all 3 experiments. Setting $\lambda = 0.2$ on that interval, we would get the overwhelming advantage of SGMCA. We emphasize that when the rank is known in advance, the optimal parameter λ can be computed for each $d(\Omega)$. This would not contradict the equal opportunity of the two algorithms. Thus, we can make conclusion that actually SGMCA outperforms RTRMC for all considered configurations of input data.

Optimal selection of λ is a reserve not used in our experiments.

The model of data in [14] is identical to the model described above. At the same time, the error model is different. The values of the corrupted entries are randomly uniformly distributed between minimum and maximum of uncorrupted values. In this case, the average magnitude of errors is significantly higher than in 2 models considered above. We also use that error model in our experiments presented on Fig. 4–6. So we satisfy all experiment conditions described in [14].

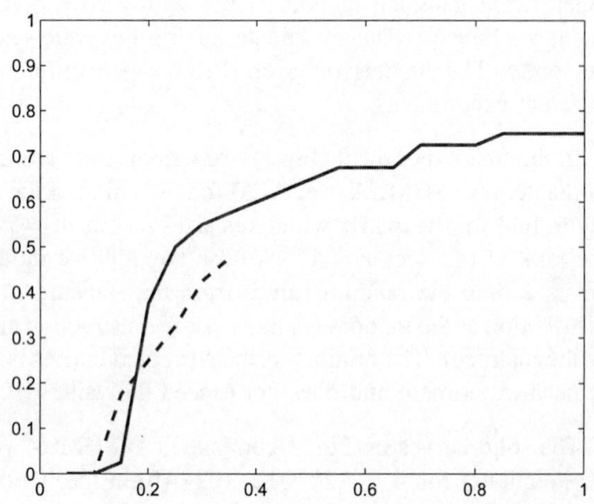

Fig.4. SGMCA vs. RTRMC. $r = 5$.

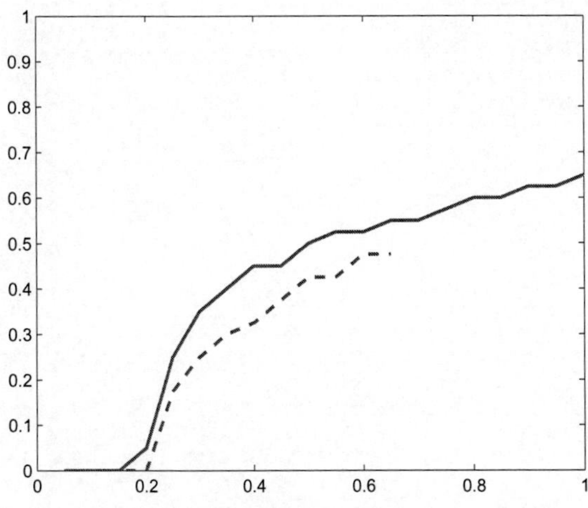

Fig.5. SGMCA vs. RTRMC. $r = 15$.

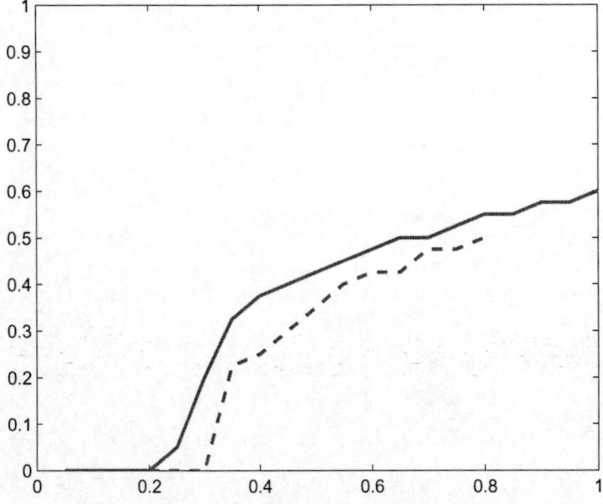

Fig.6. SGMCA vs. RTRMC. $r = 25$.

The dashed line corresponding to RTRMC is shorter than our solid line since we used the data directly from [14].

5. Future Studies

This study shows that even the simplest implementation of the greedy idea in the form of SGMCA outperforms the recent state-of-the-art algorithms significantly in the recovering ability for very incomplete measurements with high level of corruption. The results above show the feasibility of the idea, its perspectives and a high level of expectation.

Because of its iterative nature, the algorithm has to repeat the basic step a few times. We restricted the number of iterations by 10. However, in most of cases, 5 iterations provide necessary precision. Thus, SGMCA has obvious increase of algorithm computational cost in 5-10 times against the basic algorithm. Among possible directions for improvement, acceleration ways are needed to be considered.

One of possible ways is to do not wait for the completion of each iteration, updating Ω within internal iterations of the basic algorithm. In the simplest, but maybe in less efficient form, it can be done even with no intrusion into the basic algorithm. For instance, when the greedy step looks for coordinates of large errors, we do not need high precision output of the basic algorithm. So an update of the precision on each iteration from low to high may accelerate the algorithm for the data close to the limits of the potential recovering ability (phase transition points). However, it should be mentioned that this modification may slightly slow down the recovery of the data located far from the phase transition points. Other way for acceleration skipped by us in this paper is to use the estimate of A obtained on the previous iteration as a basic algorithm start point for the next iteration.

Now we discuss the ways for increasing the capability of SGMCA in the matrix recovery.

First of all, in our experiments, we practically did not use fine tuning of the weight λ. We used fixed λ for big range of the parameters of input data. Whereas, just by replacing the value 0.02 with the value 0.2, the results presented on Fig. 4–6 can be significantly improved for the high level of erasures (on the left side of the graphs). Indeed, when the rank of A and the model of errors is known, the optimal values of λ admitting the maximum density of error can be found in advance for any number of erasures and used in the recovery procedure.

When the rank is unknown or nature of possible corruption is unknown in advance, adaptive finding λ becomes a challenging problem. This problem has many common features with the problem of finding sparse solutions of underdetermined linear systems with corrupted input. In the mentioned problem, the weight λ is defined by the interaction between the sparsity of the possible solution and the error vector. In the problem of of matrix completion, the low rank plays a role of the solution sparsity in CS. So the methods (or at least principles) developed in CS can be applied to the matrix completion problem. In [11], we showed that the sparsity of the solution can be reliably estimated from the dynamic of change of the values $|\mathbf{x}|_{0.5}/|\mathbf{x}|_2$ and $|\mathbf{e}|_{0.5}/|\mathbf{e}|_2$ for the intermediate approximations $\mathbf{x}$ and $\mathbf{e}$ of the solution and errors. The same characteristic of the matrix A intermediate estimates probably can be used for the matrix completion procedure.

We also have to say that, generally speaking, for finding λ we do not need both the rank and the sparsity of errors estimates. Indeed, if we have the sparsity of errors, we can evaluate the potential maximum rank r admitting recovery with the given algorithm provided that λ is optimal. Then that optimal λ will also provide recovery of matrices with the rank less than r. Thus, the adaptive λ is one of quite realistic sources for increasing algorithm capability.

6. Conclusion

The paper presents a feasibility study for the Simple Greedy Matrix Completion algorithm. The considered algorithm is based on the ALM algorithm from [8]. While a problem of resistance of the matrix completion algorithms to discrete errors in data is not well studied yet., some recent development in this direction took place.

We gave numerical evidence that SGMCA outperforms recently developed algorithms of matrix completion from [5], [8], [14] significantly. We also discussed the ways for further increase of SGMCA efficiency.

References

[1] D. Bertsekas, Constrained Optimization and Lagrange Multiplier Method. Academic Press. 1982.

[2] E.J. Candès and B. Recht, Exact Matrix Completion via Convex Optimization, Comm. of the ACM, 55 (2012), # 6, 111–119

[3] E.J. Candès, T. Tao, Decoding by linear programming, IEEE Transactions on Information Theory, 51 (2005), 4203–4215.

[4] E.J. Candès, T. Tao,The Power of Convex Relaxation: Near-Optimal Matrix Completion, IEEE Transactions on Information Theory, 56 (2010), 2053–2080.

[5] Y. Chen, A. Jalali, S. Sanghavi and C. Caramanis, Low-rank matrix recovery from errors and erasures, IEEE International Symposium on Information Theory, Proceedings (ISIT), 2011, 2313–2317

[6] D. Donoho, Compressed Sensing, IEEE Trans. on Information Theory, 52 (2006), 1289–1306.

[7] I. Kozlov, A. Petukhov, Sparse Solutions for Underdetermined Systems of Linear Equations, chapter in Handbook of Geomathematics, Springer, 1243–1259, 2010.

[8] Z. Lin, M. Chen, Yi Ma The Augmented Lagrange Multiplier Method for Exact Recovery of Corrupted Low-Rank Matrices, Preprint, arXiv:1009.5055, 2010; revised 9 Mar 2011.

[9] B. K. Natarajan, Sparse approximate solution to linear systems, SIAM J. Comput., 24 (1995), 227–234.

[10] A. Petukhov, I. Kozlov, Fast Implementation of ℓ^1-greedy algorithm, Recent Advances in Harmonic Analysis and Applications, Springer, 2012, 317–326.

[11] A. Petukhov, I. Kozlov, Correcting Errors in Linear Measurements and Compressed Sensing of Multiple Sources, submitted to Applied Mathematics and Computation, 2012.

[12] M. Rudelson, R. Vershynin, Geometric approach to error correcting codes and reconstruction of signals, International Mathematical Research Notices 64 (2005), 4019–4041.

[13] J. Wright, A.Y. Yang, A. Ganesh, S.S. Sastry, and Yi Ma, Robust Face Recognition via Sparse Representation, Pattern Analysis and Machine Intelligence, IEEE Transactions on, 31 (2009), # 2, 210–227.

[14] M. Yan, Y. Yang, S. Osher, Exact Low-Rank Matrix Completion from Sparsely Corrupted Entries Via Adaptive Outlier Pursuit, J. Sci. Comput., January 2013.

ShareBook: An Application of Cross-Platform E-Book Viewer with Vector Graphic

Tseng-Yi Chen[1], Hsin-Wen Wei[2], Nien-I Hsu[1], Ying-Jie Chen[1], Wei-Kuan Shih[1]
[1]Department of Computer Science, National Tsing Hua University, Hsinchu, Taiwan
[2] Department of Information Management, Tamkang University, Taipei, Taiwan

Abstract - *Many handheld devices have been developed in the mobile industry. Most mobile devices in the market are carried Android operating system. Android also supports many other hardware components that increase mobile devices functionality. The operating system can be used for multimedia, touch screen, number of types of sensors and 2D/3D graphics. Due to open source license, many manufactures integrate their own production to Android system. Hence, this paper proposed a ShareBook software based on Android system. ShareBook integrates new types of sensor such as touch sensor, bending sensor and gyroscope to develop a flexible display platform with Android operating system. These sensors change user's operation in general smart mobile devices with Android. Flexible displays bring great difference in interaction behavior between system software and end user. However, there are some other problems in traditional E-Book application. Size of screen on mobile devices is the first problem. Hardware manufactures produce 4-5 inches display on their mobile phone production, the display size is at most 10.1 inches on pad production. Some people hardly read contents on small size screen. So, ShareBook can easily transfer e-book viewer to larger size display such as TV or LCD display when user can reach the larger size display in their environment. Second problem is application's performance efficiency. ShareBook integrates vector graphic library into Android and optimizes the performance of vector graphic library by Renderscript and GPGPU. ShareBook also combines cloud platform resource for image file transformation and storage resource extension.*

Keywords: Vector graphic, e-book, cloud, android apps.

1 Introduction

Smart mobile devices become the center of people's personal life and more ubiquitous. Android system occupies a considerable share of the market of smart handheld device. Android is a Linux-based operating system and is maintained as open source project by Google. Many programmers and manufactures are entering in to the system development due to open source. So, there are many applications and hardware devices which are developed based on Android operating system.

Today's advanced mobile devices are well integrated with the Internet and have far more functionality than mobile phones of the past. Some peoples use handheld devices to be personal multimedia device for playing music and movie through Internet. Some other people read books on mobile device. Hence, many software developers design applications of multimedia player and E-Book reader.

E-book became a popular application nowadays because of e-learning and paperless promotion. However, some open issues still need to improve for better user experience.

- *Small size display*: Many handheld devices equip with 4-5 inches display or at most 10.1 inches screen. However, user cannot change to large screen to view the content, if there are some larger display platforms around user current place. Users need to re-install the application and contents on larger display platform, if they want to switch to bigger display for comfortable viewing.

- *Performance efficiency*: E-Book applications spend a lot of time to process path calculation and drawing, if E-Book application is developed based on vector graphic library. Vector graphic library has a major strength for E-Book *application*. Vector graphic library avoid image distortion when user scales up the size of contents or images on E-Book application.

- *Resource limitation:* Users usually have many e-book contents and electronic comic books in their mobile devices. It is very inconvenient for user to manage their e-book content in small storage device. It occupies a large part of storage space in their device. Besides of storage limitation, processing image transformation is also a heavy load work on mobile device. Due to battery life, mobile devices try not to do a task with long processing time. Therefore, cloud platform help E-Book applications to solve the resource limitation problem.

In this paper, we develop ShareBook software on Android system. ShareBook combines new types of sensor with flexible display to create innovative mode of user interaction. ShareBook can easily switch the content view to larger display which is near to user. Larger size of display is more comfortable than small screen and user also can control the larger size of display by flexible display. Performance of ShareBook is also optimized by using GPGPU to improve vector graphic library and integrates with cloud computing resource.

The rest of this paper is organized as follows. Section II shows relate works of E-Book applications, vector graphic library, embedded GPGPU and cloud image file transformation processing. Section III presents our system architecture in the cloud service. In Section IV, we present our system execution result and benchmark. The brief conclusion is presented in Section V.

2 Related work

E-book application has been widely studied by research group and industry manufacture in recently. Some previous studies probe E-Book's applications [1, 2], security [3, 4], platform and standardization [5]. According to [5], we know that there are many different e-book file formats and each file format is not compatible with another e-book file format. Therefore, it is a important issue of uniform format for e-book application. Vector drawings can enlarge to any size without any loss in quality. Then, vector graphic is a free file format and it is also readable for any handheld devices and computers. So that, we can convert e-book file to xml descriptor of vector graphic. There are many libraries to support vector graphic reader in embedded platform [6] [7]. We integrate OpenVG [6] library with Android system and we also optimize it on our embedded platform.

In [8], they proposed some algorithms for converting file to vector graph format. They only deploy client server architecture to execute their algorithm. However, converting file format produce a huge workload when user need to transfer large amount of files. Our solution is a parallel implementation of the Autotrace that uses multi-VM and it achieves near-linear speedup on cloud computing platform.

Another advantage of cloud environment is the huge storage space [9]. We store our e-book file in cloud storage. After authorization, users can access their contents. If users are publishers, they can authorize their file to reader.

Besides cloud integration, ShareBook using embedded GPGPU to increase the performance of application. The embedded GPGPU is based on ARM Mali architecture. The Mali series of graphics processing units (GPUs) are semiconductor intellectual property cores produced by ARM Holdings. Mali-T604 supports Android Renderscript library. Renderscript [11] is a low-level API for intensive computation using heterogeneous computing. It allows developers to maximize the performance of their applications at the cost of writing a greater amount of more complex code. Some researches use it to optimize 3D graphics library [12] and multimedia development [13]. In ShareBook, Renderscript is used to optimize the performance of vector graphic library in Android system.

3 System architecture

As shown in Figure 1, there are three parts of our system: flexible display with vector graphic E-Book in end user, cloud platform for e-book file format transformation and content storage. Final part of system is near field communication. The near filed communication transfers data with smart TV or LCD displays which is equipped with NFC or Wi-Fi module.

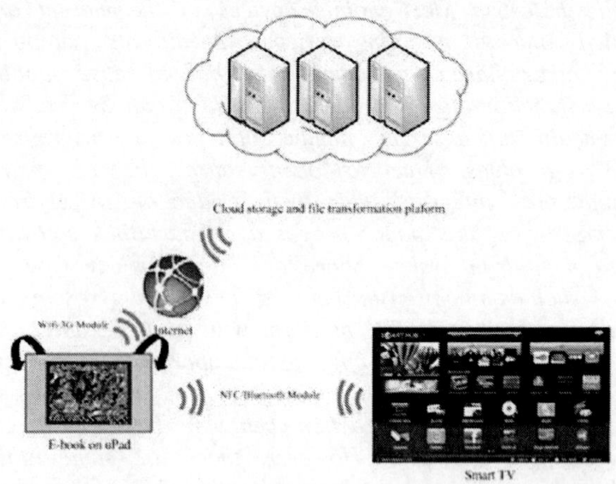

Fig. 1. System architecture

3.1 Flexible display with multiple sensor devices

The felxible display is still a propototype that simulate by bending sensor and plastic display. Our felxible display palform is integrated with friendlyarm mini 210 and combines with some new types of sensors into flexible display plaform. Sensors include touch sensor, bending sensor and gyroscope. Each sensor brings an innovative mode of user interaction in E-Book application. Touch sensor is placed on the back of flexible display. Touch sensor can recognize user's gesture and make the gesture to be a unique private key to login cloud platform for processing. Touch sensor in ShareBook is microchip mTouch platform. Figure 2 shows the concept of touch verification.

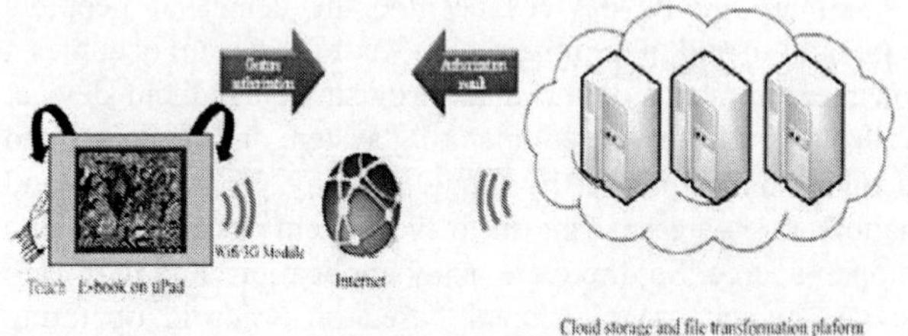

Fig. 2. Interaction mode of backboard touch sensor

Bending sensor let switching page be straightforward. User switches the page by bending different position sensor in flexible display. Figure 3 shows the concept of page switching in flexible display. User also can zoom in/out the view on flexible display through gyroscope.

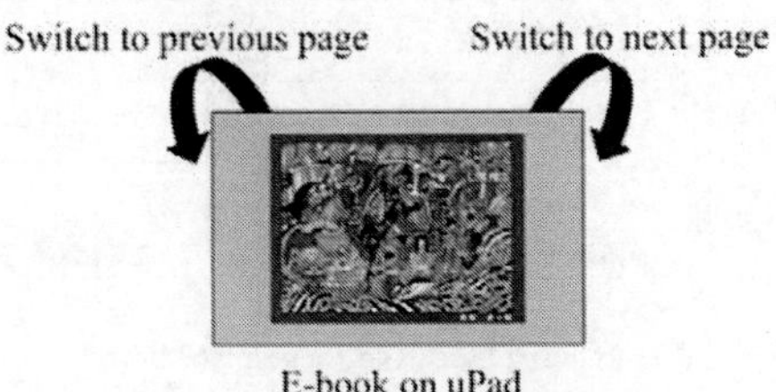

Fig. 3. Interaction mode of bending sensor

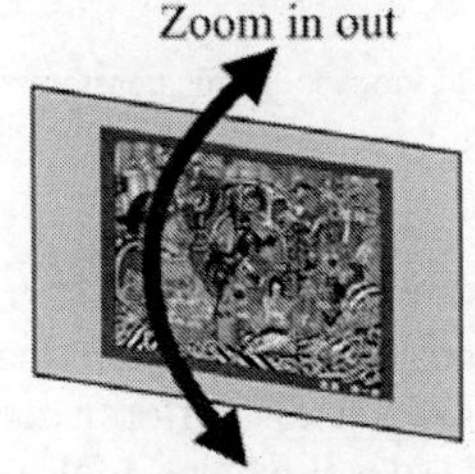

Fig. 4. Interaction mode of gyroscope

3.2 Optimize vector graphic library

ShareBook is developed based on vector graphic library. The vector graphic library fallows OpenVG standard for library implementation. OpenVG separates the procedures of drawing vector graphic to seven steps. We optimize the vector graphic library in step four on Android system by Renderscript. Triangulation is the main process in rasterization step. The time complexity is O(n3) in original algorithm. Renderscript reduce the significant time complexity of triangulation. Figure 5 shows modification flow of vector graphic library in ShareBook.

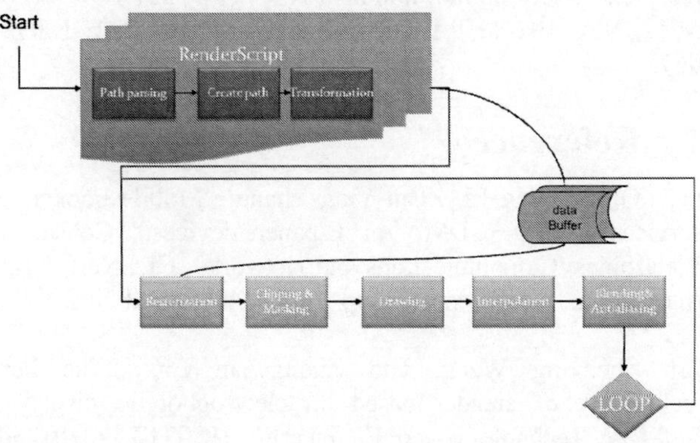

Fig. 5. Modification flow of vector graphic library with Renderscript

3.3 Cloud platform environment

This research work converts wide variety of image format to vector graphic descriptor in order to support more and more file format. However, file transformation procedure is a heavy workload process in embedded platform. For that reason, our solution takes advantage of cloud computing in order to enhance our computing power.

We deploy the Autotrace [5] code in cloud. Autotrace is software of file transformation. And we build up a domination machine to dispatch converting task to back end cloud platform. We parallelize the file format conversion task in group of images method. Our solution splits all images which are in e-book file to different group and the system assigns these group tasks to different computing virtual machine in cloud. We present our cloud solution in figure 6.

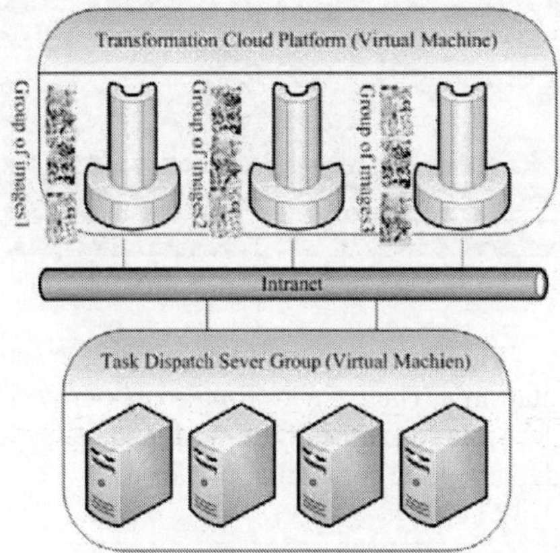

Fig. 6. Cloud parallel method

Users manage their contents through our web interface. Users can do some operation on management website, such as: uploading contents, downloading their contents and sharing their contents with copyright. We also put all contents which are uploaded by same user in single cloud storage. The placement method can increase data locality.

3.4 View switching

Flexible display equips a Bluetooth and Wi-Fi module. Hence, flexible display can connect to Internet or peer to peer network via network module. ShareBook design a matching mechanism for determines whether the view is switching to other display platform. First, ShareBook will send a packet to ask the size of display which can reach by near filed paring. The view is switched to other display platform, if the size of display is larger than flexible display platform. And user can control the larger display platform on flexible display platform via network communication.

4 System result

Flexible display equOur demo environment is described as follows: smart phone, pad and embedded development platform (FriendlyARM mini210), and private cloud computing platform. We show our execution result in figure 7 and performance result in figure 8.ipes a bluetooth and Wi-Fi module. Hence, flexible display can connect to Interenet or peer to peer network via netwrok module. ShareBook design a matching mechanism for determing whether the view is switching to other display platform. First, ShareBook will send a packet to ask the size of display which can reach by near filed paring. The veiw is swithed to other display platform, if the size of dispaly is larger than flexible display platform. And user can control the larger display platform on flexible display platform via network communication.

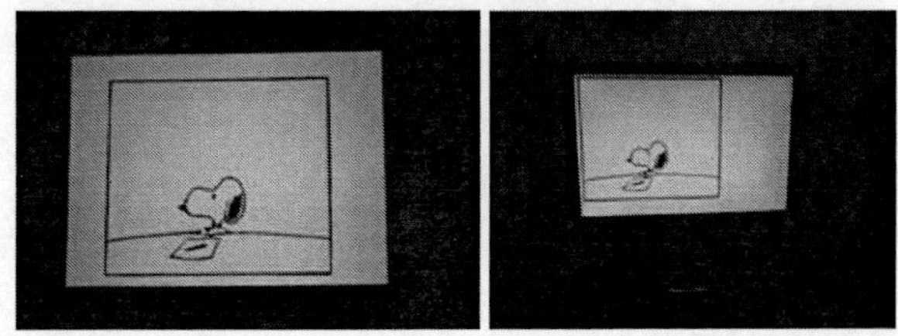

Fig. 7. Execution screen on FriendlyARM mini210

Figure 7 is the result of our system execution on embedded platform. Then, figure 8 presents our performance speedup. Our solution uses multi-VM and achieves near-linear speedup on cloud computing platforms.

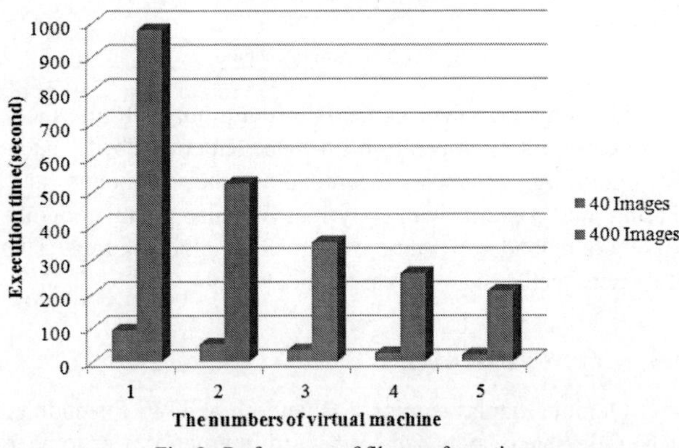

Fig. 8. Performance of file transformation

Figure 9 shows the performance speedup by optimization algorithm and we believe that ShareBook can get better performance after integrating Renderscript.

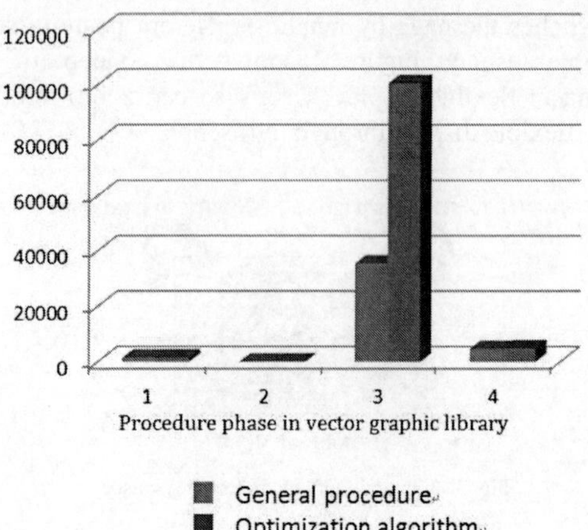

Fig. 9. Performance of file transformation

5 Conclusion

In this paper, we present an E-Book application, called ShareBook, which consider three factors that affect the user experience of display size, performance and resource limitation. The basic development tool of ShareBook is vector graphic library and we optimize the vector graphic library by replacing original triangulation algorithm with monotone triangulation and polygon partitioning. We also integrate new types of sensors into a flexible display. Every sensor brings an innovative mode of user interaction in E-Book application. Finally, ShareBook is also verified the cross-platform display function on flexible display and LCD monitor. In the future, ShareBook will be a popular application system.

6 Acknowledgement

We would like to thank the National Science Council of the Republic of China (Taiwan) for financial support of this research under contract numbers NSC 101-2221-E-007-128-MY2, NSC 101-2219-E-007-007 and NSC 101-2221-E-032-067.

7 Reference

[1] Qing-Cheng Li, Zhan-Ying Zhang, “Mobile bookstore services of TD-SCDMA in E-paper devices,” Consumer Electronics, Communications and Networks (CECNet), 2011 International Conference on, pp. 1406–1409, April 2011.

[2] Zhenxing Wang, and Zhongyuan Liu, “The key technology of ereader based on electrophoretic display”, Software Technology and Engineering (ICSTE), 2010 2nd International Conference on, pp.333–336, Oct. 2010.

[3] M. Lesk, “Reading: From Paper to Pixels,” in IEEE Security & Privacy, vol. 9, issue. 4, pp. 76–79, Aug. 2011.

[4] Zhiyong Zhang, "Security, trust and risk in Digital Rights Management ecosystem," High Performance Computing and Simulation (HPCS), 2010 International Conference on, pp. 498-503, July 2010.

[5] Kyong-Ho Lee, "Standardization aspects of eBook content formats", Computer Standards & Interfaces, vol. 24, issue 3, pp. 227-239, July 2002.

[6] Ferraiolo, J. "Scalable vector graphics (SVG) 1.0 specification". in Tech. rep., W3C Recommendation. Sep, 2010.

[7] Aekyung Oh, Hyunchan Sung, Hwanyong Lee, Kujin Kim and Nakhoon Baek, "Implementation of OpenVG 1.0 using OpenGL ES". In MobileHCI'07, 2007.

[8] Zhimao Guo, Shuigeng Zhou, Zhengchuan Xu, and Aoying Zhou. "G2ST: a novel method to transform GML to SVG". in ACM GIS'03, 2003

[9] Ann-Marie Horcher and Maxine Cohen. "Ebook Readers: An iPod for Your Books in the Cloud". In Communications in Computer and Information Science, Vol. No.174, pp 22-27, 2011.

[10] AutoTrace converts bitmap to vector graphic, http://autotrace.sourceforge.net/.

[11] Hervé Guihot, "RenderScript", Pro Android Apps Performance Optimization, pp 231-263, 2012

[12] Satya Komatineni, Dave MacLean, and Sayed Y. Hashimi. "Programming 3D Graphics with OpenGL". In Pro Android 3, pp. 623-629, 2011.

[13] Cheng-Liang Lin, Yi-Hsuan Huang, Huan-Yi Chen and Slo-Li Chu. "Content-aware smart remote control for Android-based TV". In Consumer Electronics (ICCE), 2012 IEEE International Conference on, pp. 678-679, Jan. 2012.

Exemplar-based Image Inpainting by Structured Sparse Representation

Wang Jiawen and Zhang Hongbin
College of Computer Science, Beijing University of Technology, Beijing, China

Abstract - *Image inpainting is a technique that aims to recovering missing or damaged regions of an image without any manual intervene. Conventional exemplar-based approaches suffer two major defects. One defect is that the inpainting quality heavily depends on the extent of self-similarity. If no similar samples exist in the already known region of the image, the missing region may be filled by irrelevant ones, which lead to an unexpected result. The other is that the process of finding the best-match sample is computationally intensive. In this paper, we introduce an exemplar-based image inpainting algorithm by exploiting structured sparse representation techniques to overcome the limitations mentioned above. The filling-in patch is estimated based on a composite dictionary instead of an exhausted search. The experimental results show that the proposed method achieves a good visual quality.*

Keywords: image inpainting, exemplar, structured sparse representation

1 Introduction

Image inpainting, a technique that aims to recovering a missing region or removing an object in an image, has drawn a considerable interest in recent years. Many works have been published to investigate this problem. In general, the approaches can be classified into diffusion-based [1-3] and exemplar-based [4-7]. In this paper, we focus on the latter.

Criminisi et al. [4] proposed a best-first filling algorithm which preferred patches along the image structure to be filled first. Wu [5] proposed a cross-isophotes exemplar-based inpainting algorithm, in which a cross-isophotes patch priority term was designed to determine the filling order. Wong [6] proposed a non-local means approach. The filling-in patch was estimated by a set of similar samples from the known region instead of a single one. Compared with diffusion-based inpainting algorithms, the exemplar-based ones can achieve more plausible results for large missing regions. Nevertheless, exemplar-based approaches suffer two major defects. One defect is that they heavily rely on the extent of self-similarity of images. Particularly, when no proper samples exist for filling in the missing region, an unexpected result may be produced. The other is that an exhausted search from the known region has to be performed to find the best-match sample, which is very high time-cost. Although some optimization algorithms can accelerate the search, it is still inefficient.

Sparse representation based image inpainting has been developed in recent years. Elad et al. [7] proposed an inpainting algorithm by separating the image into cartoon and texture layers, and sparsely represented these two layers using two incoherent dictionaries respectively. Mairal et al. [8] proposed a framework for color image restoration based on sparse representation by estimating filling-in information using a learned dictionary. The main benefit of sparse representation based algorithms is that the missing information can be estimated by dictionaries instead of an exhausted search. Assuming that the dictionary is abundant enough, the missing region can be recovered when the known region cannot provide enough information. However, [7, 8] represent images only considering sparsity. For natural images, there are latent structural relationships between dictionary atoms. It is necessary to give a better representation by exploiting structural features.

The main contribution of this paper is a novel approach of exemplar-based inpainting via structured sparse representation. The missing information is estimated under a structured sparsity regularization framework with a composite dictionary. Our approach can also be integrated into other inpainting schemes to achieve good visual quality.

2 Proposed Algorithm

The main procedures of the exemplar-based inpainting algorithm are composed of two parts: patch selection and patch inpainting. We mainly concentrate on inpainting the patch using structured sparse representation.

2.1 Patch Inpainting via Structured Sparse Representation

Let us consider an image patch $\mathbf{x} \in \mathbb{R}^m$, where m is the square of patch size. Assuming that it admits a sparse representation over a dictionary matrix $\mathbf{D} = \left[\mathbf{d}^1, ..., \mathbf{d}^K\right] \in \mathbb{R}^{m \times K}$, with K columns referred to as atoms, one can find a linear combination of atoms from $\mathbf{D}$ that is close to the patch $\mathbf{x}$. Under a square loss, this optimization problem can be written as

$$\{\hat{\boldsymbol{\alpha}}\} = \underset{\boldsymbol{\alpha}\in\mathbb{R}^K}{\arg\min} \frac{1}{2}\|\mathbf{x} - \mathbf{D}\boldsymbol{\alpha}\|_2^2 + \lambda \mathrm{N}(\boldsymbol{\alpha}) \quad (1)$$

Where $\boldsymbol{\alpha} \in \mathbb{R}^K$ is the representation coefficient vector of the patch $\mathbf{x}$. N is a regularization term, usually a norm, whose effect is controlled by the regularization parameter $\lambda > 0$. Then, the estimated patch can be computed as

$$\hat{\mathbf{x}} = \mathbf{D}\hat{\boldsymbol{\alpha}} \quad (2)$$

Due to the limitation of traditional sparsity norms, we use a structured sparsity-inducing norm instead, which takes a form as

$$N(\boldsymbol{\alpha}) = \sum_{g\in\mathcal{G}} \|\boldsymbol{\alpha}_g\|_2 \quad (3)$$

Where $\mathcal{G}$ is a set of groups. Eq. (2), known as a mixed ℓ_1/ℓ_2 norm, behaves like a ℓ_1 norm on the vector $\left(\|\alpha_g\|_2\right)_{g\in\mathcal{G}}$. Thus, N promotes sparsity between groups.

Given a tree structure $\mathcal{T}$ with n nodes indexed by j in $\{1,...,n\}$, the group set $\mathcal{G}$ is defined as follows:

$$\mathcal{G} \triangleq \{\mathrm{desc}(j), j \in \{1,...,n\}\} \quad (4)$$

Where $\mathrm{desc}(j) \subseteq \{1,...,n\}$ denotes the set of indices corresponding to the descendants of the node j (including j) in $\mathcal{T}$. When penalized by N defined in (3), some of the vectors $\boldsymbol{\alpha}_g$ are regularized to zero, i.e., coefficients corresponding to some complete sub-trees of $\mathcal{T}$ are set to zero. Such a setting indicates that if an atom is excluded from the representation, then atoms corresponding to its descendants in the tree should not be included either. Thus, a hierarchical structure is imposed on the dictionary atoms.

Due to the patch to be filled is partially known, we have to estimate it based on the already known part. Denoting by $\otimes$ the element-wise multiplication between two vectors, we aim to solving the following problem, which replaces (1):

$$\{\hat{\boldsymbol{\alpha}}\} = \underset{\boldsymbol{\alpha}\in\mathbb{R}^K}{\arg\min} \frac{1}{2}\|\mathbf{M} \otimes (\mathbf{x} - \mathbf{D}\boldsymbol{\alpha})\|_2^2 + \lambda \mathrm{N}(\boldsymbol{\alpha}) \quad (5)$$

Where $\mathbf{M}$ is a mask defined as

$$\mathbf{M}_{ij} = \begin{cases} 1, & p(i,j) \in \mathrm{I} - \Phi \\ 0, & p(i,j) \in \Omega \end{cases}$$

2.2 Implementation Details

The priority computation, which determines the filling order of the target region, is crucial to exemplar-based inpainting algorithms. In this paper, we use Criminisi's method to calculate the priority. For more details, see [4].

The dictionary can be chosen as a global or adaptive one. In most cases, the latter performs better than the former. In this paper, we choose to learn a structured dictionary, as described in [9], and use a composite dictionary, which consists of both the global and adaptive dictionary.

Sparse representation based methods usually treat color images in two manners, concatenating the RGB values into a single vector or performing in each channel separately. The former usually achieves better results, and produces less false colors and artifacts. Therefore, we choose the former way in our experiments.

3 Experiments

We test the proposed method on a variety of natural images and apply it to the applications of scratch/text removal and object removal. For comparison, we also run the same test images through two current exemplar-based inpainting algorithms [4, 6][1], which are most closely related to our work. The parameters are chosen as follows: the size of patch is set to 9×9. λ in Eq. (5) is set to 1.5. The adaptive dictionary with 512 atoms is learned from the source region of the image. The global dictionary is learned from our pre-specified image database, samples of which are shown in Fig. 1. Two metrics, Peak signal-to-noise ratio (PSNR) and Structure Similarity (SSIM), are used to measure performances in quantitative evaluation.

Table 1 presents the performances of three inpainting algorithms: the best-match method [4], the non-local means method [6] and our proposed method. It can be seen that our method shows an improvement in both PSNR and SSIM over the other two algorithms in most cases. The results for Fig. 2(a) and (b) indicate that our method outperform the other two for text removal. The reason is that images with imposed text have a small source region, which cannot provide enough information for filling and influences the inpainted results of the best-match method and the non-local means method. The small source region has a relatively slight effect on sparse representation based methods due to their abundant dictionaries. For Fig. 2(d), sufficient information in the source region makes the non-local means approach obtain the best result.

Table 2 shows the recovered result with damaged area of different percentage. From the first to the fifth rows are the degraded images with 4.7%, 9.9%, 16.8%, 25.7% and 36.4% damaged area, and the correspondent inpainted results of the best-match method [4], the non-local means method [6], and our proposed method. It shows that the non-local means method is slightly superior to our method when the damage percentage is lower than 5%. When the damage area is growing, our method can achieve better result that the other two with the available information becomes less and less.

[1] For objective comparison, all three methods use the same priority function proposed by Criminisi et al. [4].

Fig. 1. Samples from our image database.

(a) (b) (c) (d)

Fig. 2. Comparison for text and scratch removal. The first to fifth rows show the original images, the degraded images, the inpainted results of the best-match method [4], the non-local means method [6], and our method.

Table 1. PSNR/SSIM results for text and scratch removal.

Images	Best-match[4]	Non-local[6]	Our method
Fig. 2(a)	26.15/0.87	26.46/**0.88**	**27.45**/0.87
Fig. 2(b)	30.97/0.89	31.79/**0.90**	**32.58/0.90**
Fig. 2(c)	27.85/0.93	**29.34/0.94**	28.62/0.93
Fig. 2(d)	27.10/0.87	**28.13/0.88**	27.19/**0.88**
Mean	28.02/0.89	28.93/**0.90**	**28.96/0.90**

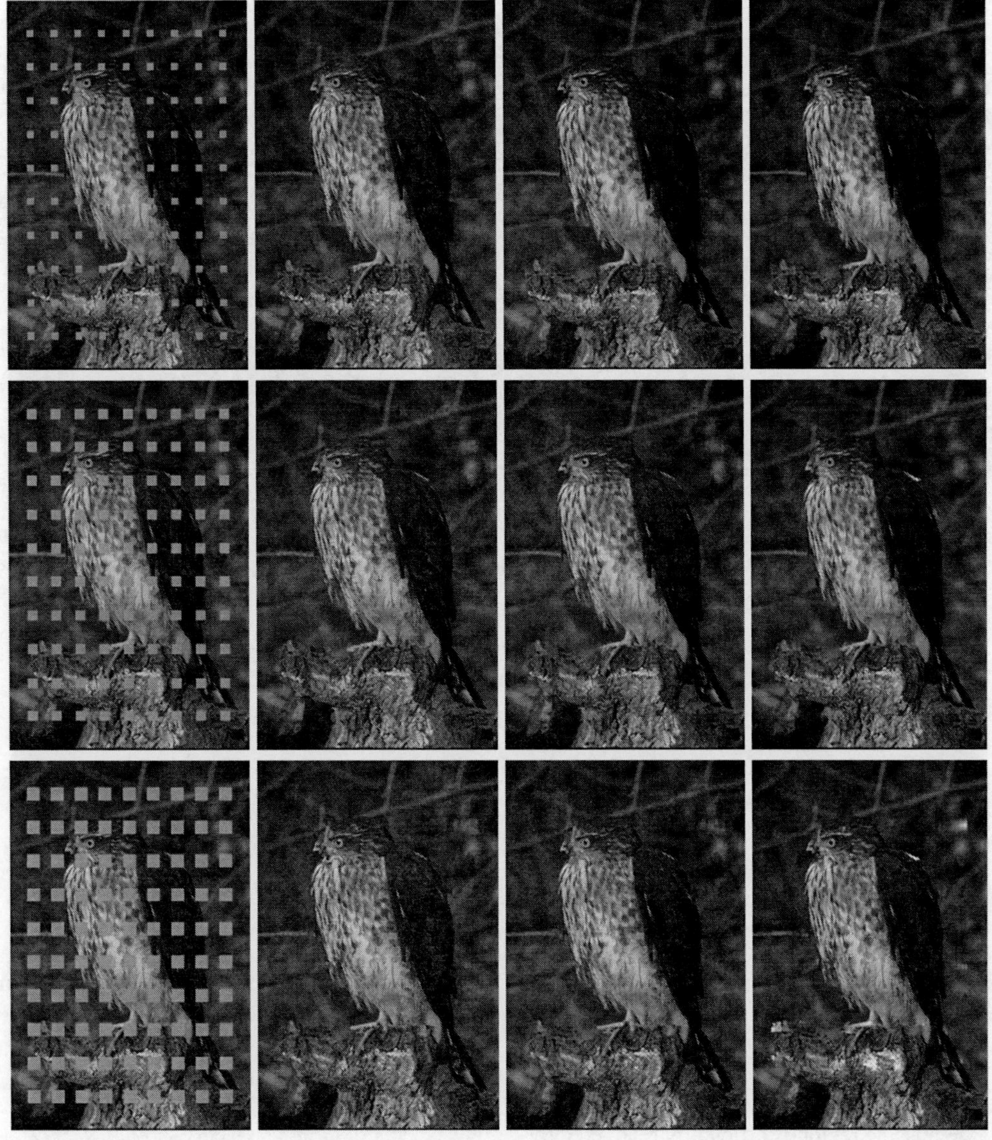

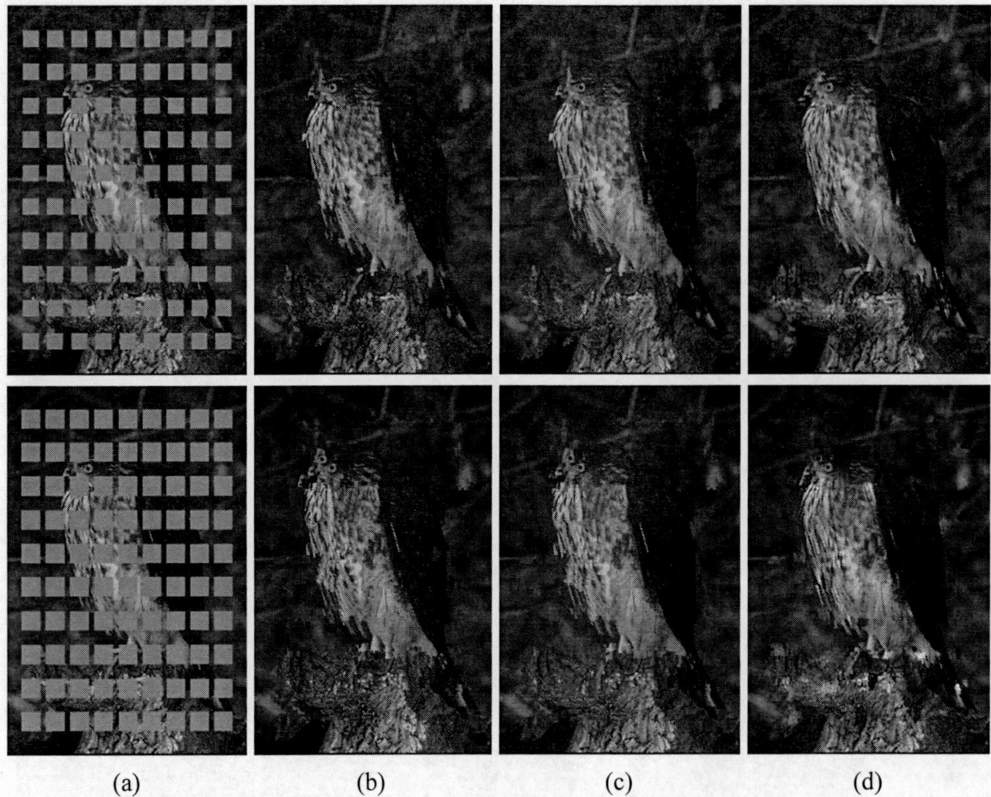

(a) (b) (c) (d)

Fig. 3. Comparison of inpainted results with different percentage of missing region. The first to fourth columns show the original images, the degraded images, the inpainted results of the best-match method [4], the non-local means method [6], and our method.

Table 2. PSNR/SSIM results for diffenent percentage of the missing region.

Missing Percentage	Best-match[4]	Non-local[6]	Our method
4.7%	33.41/0.95	**34.88/0.96**	34.62/**0.96**
9.9%	30.77/0.91	31.92/**0.92**	**32.08/0.92**
16.8%	28.52/0.85	29.26/**0.86**	**29.32/0.86**
25.7%	26.39/0.76	26.76/0.78	**27.57/0.79**
36.4%	24.59/0.66	25.21/0.69	**25.38/0.70**

Fig. 4 presents examples for object removal with a large missing region (14% missing). The first column is the removal of statue. It can be seen that the sky background and the contour of the stone are recovered very well by our method. The second column is the removal of person. It shows that the large missing region is efficiently recovered by the proposed method, which yields good visual quality.

4 Conclusions

This paper introduced a novel approach to exemplar-based inpainting using structured sparse representation. The filling-in information is computed based on dictionaries instead of an exhausted search, which can overcome the limitations of conventional exemplar-based methods. The experimental results show that the proposed method achieves a good visual quality. Future work includes investigating a better priority computation method, and inpainting from multiple images.

5 References

[1] Bertalmio, M., Sapiro, G., Caselles, V., Ballester, C.: Image Inpainting. Proc. SIGGRAPH. (2000) 417–424.

[2] Chan, T., Shen, J.: Local Inpainting Models and TV Inpainting. SIAM J. Appl. Math., Vol. 62. (2001) 1019–1043.

[3] Chan, T., Shen, J.: Non-texture Inpainting by Curvature-driven Diffusions. J. Vis. Com-mun. Image Represent., Vol. 4. (2001) 436–449.

[4] Criminisi, A., Perez, P., Toyama, K.: Object Removal by Exemplar Based Image Inpainting. Proc. Int. Conf. Comp. Vision. (2003) 721–728.

[5] Wu, J., Ruan, Q.: Object Removal by Cross Isophotes Exemplar-based Image Inpainting. Proc. Int. Conf. Pattern Recognition. (2006) 810–813.

[6] Wong, A., Orchard, J.: A Nonlocal-means Approach to Exemplar Based Inpainting. IEEE Int. Conf. Image Processing. (2008) 2600–2603.

[7] Elad, M., Starck, J. L., Querre, P., Donoho, D. L.: Simultaneous Cartoon and Texture Image Inpainting Using Morphological Component Analysis. Appl. Comput. Harmon. Anal., Vol. 19. (2005) 340–358.

[8] Mairal, J., Elad, M., Sapiro, G.: Sparse Representation for Color Image Restoration. IEEE Trans. Image Process., Vol. 17. (2008) 53–69.

[9] Wang, J.W., Zhang, H.B.: Structured Dictionary Learning using Composite Absolute Penalties. To appear.

Fig. 4. Examples of object removal.

Activity Recognition and Coordination Analysis of Two-Body Interactions Using Wearable Sensors

Ye Chen [a], Zhelong Wang [a], Hong Shang [b], Bo Zhu [c], Weijian Hu [b]

[a] School of Control Science and Engineering, Dalian University of Technology, Dalian, CHINA

E-mail: cy0004@163.com (Ye Chen)

[b] National Earthquake Response Support Service, Beijing, 100049, China

[c] College of Mechanical Science and Engineering, Jilin University, Jilin, CHINA

Abstract – **This paper describes the application for activity recognition of two-body interactions by using body sensor networks (BSN) and presents a model to give coordination analysis of their cooperation. A monitoring platform based on BSN is established and acceleration data is collected from wearable inertial sensors. Each individual's signal is divided into several segments, and then recognized corresponding to different stages of movements. The stages' synchronization between two people could be considered as the principal criteria to evaluate their cooperation quality. Several important performance parameters are also given to provide the necessary feedback for these activities in our system. A gait experiment of two-body interactions was performed on the sensor monitoring platform and the experimental results demonstrate the effectiveness of the proposed method.**

Keywords: Body sensor networks; Inertial sensors; Coordination; Two-body interactions

I. Introduction

Activities of two-body interactions widely exist in industrial production assembly, competitive sports and aerospace exploration, such as synchronized diving, double kayak, and two astronauts carrying out space mission. In such activities, they need cooperate to achieve goals. The coordination of their respective technical movements is important for improving the efficiency and quality in collaborative tasks. Therefore, it is necessary for us to establish an activity monitoring platform to recognize activities of two-body interactions.

Traditional human activity monitoring and recognition is based on visual information, however it might encounter some problems. Firstly, vision data are prone to the influence of environment factors, such as poor lighting conditions and occlusion of obstacles, which would reduce the accuracy of video recognition. Moreover, vision-based recognition just can present body movement gestures without human activity parameter information such as acceleration signal and ECG oxygen parameters. In addition, visual monitoring platform is expensive and inconvenient.

With the availability of low-cost sensors and the advancement in wireless sensor networks, researchers have made a lot of work on human activity monitoring by using body sensor networks (BSN), such as monitoring activities of daily living for the elderly or injured people [1-3]. The main contribution of this paper is to adopt BSN to monitor and recognize a class of activities of two-body interactions, which might give coordination analysis and provide the necessary feedback for these activities.

The organization of the paper is as follows: in section II, the related work is given. In section III, a detailed introduction of our proposed model and method is presented. In section IV, the hardware platform is introduced and an experiment is described. In section V, experimental results and coordination analysis are given to evaluate our system. Finally, concluding remarks are made in section VI.

II. Related Work

Researchers have made significant progress in the area of human activity recognition by using BSN in recent years, including human daily activity recognition [4-6], video games application [7], medical service [8], sports exercises monitoring and so on [9-11]. Existing work mainly focuses on recognizing single-user activities. Recognizing activities of two-body interactions using wearable sensors is more challenging. The main challenges are user interactions capture and modeling interacting processes, which need to measure and interpret sensor acceleration data from two people [12-13].

Our research mainly focuses on recognizing a class of activities of two-body interactions such as synchronized diving and double rowing, and then giving coordination analysis of these activities. The characteristics of this class of activities are distinctive in movement periodicity and cooperation synchronization. For example in double rowing (Fig. 1), each individual's technical movement consists of several actions and it is very important for them to perform synchronization in every action stage. There is a delicate balance between their cooperation.

Fig.1. Double rowing sports

In order to improve the proficiency in cooperative tasks between two subjects which is significant in many fields, the problem how to analyze their technical movements and evaluate their cooperation quality poses scientific challenges for us. In this paper, these problems will be considered and discussed.

In this paper, a monitoring platform based on BSN is established by us and acceleration signals are collected through sensor nodes. After acquiring sensor data, we divided the signals into several segments corresponding to each stage of technical movement. Then, we extract feature vectors from the segmented signals and recognize these movements. The matching of every technical movement between two subjects is the principal criteria for evaluating their cooperation quality. In addition, several important parameters are also given to provide the necessary feedback for our system.

III. PROPOSED MODEL AND RECOGNITION METHOD

Fig.2 shows the system architecture for the data analysis and activity recognition of two-body interactions. We establish a monitoring platform in our laboratory which could collect these data and stores them into a database.

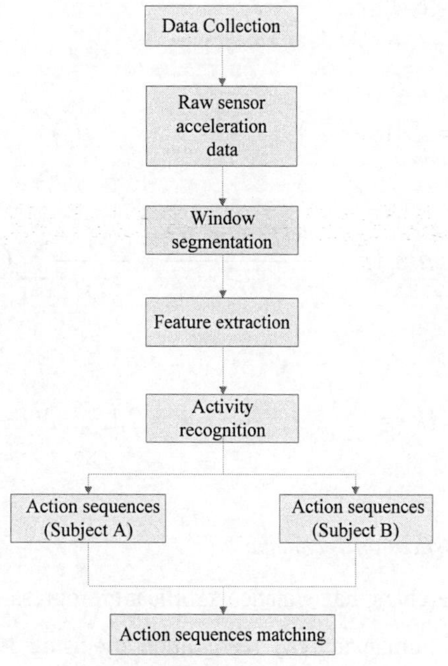

Fig.2. System architecture

A. Sensor data segmentation

Sensor data reflects an actor's behavior which could be collected on the monitoring platform. A key factor in continuous time activity recognition is how to divide the sensor data into different window sequences. Each window sequence corresponds to different ongoing actions. In this study, dynamic sensor data segmentation based on event-driven is used. We define several parameters to describe how the time window is manipulated. These parameters include start time, end time and window length.

B. Feature Extraction

After acquiring the signals which have been segmented as mentioned above, feature extraction is applied on the sensor data. The extracted features from each window are mean, variance, skewness and the peaks of the discrete Fourier transform (DFT). The usefulness of these features has been demonstrated in many prior studies [14-16]. All features are normalized into the interval [0,1]. These features are calculated as follows:

$$\mu_s = E\{s\} = \frac{1}{N_s}\sum_{i=1}^{N_s} s_i$$

$$\sigma^2 = E\{(s-\mu_s)^2\} = \frac{1}{N_s}\sum_{i=1}^{N_s}(s_i-\mu_s)^2$$

$$skewness(s) = \frac{E\{(s-\mu_s)^3\}}{\sigma^3} = \frac{1}{N_s\sigma^3}\sum_{i=1}^{N_s}(s_i-\mu_s)^3$$

$$S_{DFT}(k) = \sum_{i=0}^{N_s-1} s_i e^{-j2\pi ki/N_s}, k = 0,1,\ldots,N_s-1$$

C. Classfication Technique

Researchers have made significant progress in the area of human activity recognition by using BSN in recent years, and many classification methods have been used and compared [17]. Typical classifiers include decision tree, k-nearest neighbor (k-NN), support vector machines (SVMs), and artificial neural network (ANN). In addition, some state-space models such as Hidden Markov Model (HMM) and Dynamic Bayesian Network (DBN) have been used in human activity recognition. The classification technique used in this study is Radical Basis Function (RBF) neural network.

D. Action Sequences Matching

The work mentioned above could recognize every action style in a movement period. In the same time, the action sequences matching between two subjects could be considered as the principal criteria to analyze the activity synchronization of two-body interactions, which is an important factor for evaluating the quality of their cooperation performance.

E. Important Parameters

Several necessary parameters are proposed to further evaluate the cooperation quality between two subjects.

Let:

α : the start time for a time window.

ω : the length of a time window.

γ : the ratio of window length in a period time.

We can define a segmented window Ω_k with three important properties: α , ω and γ as shown in the expression $\Omega_k : (\alpha,\omega,\gamma)$, where ω is the time interval of each action stage, and γ is the ratio of ω in a period time. A detailed description will be explained in section V.

IV. Experimental Design

A. Experiment Platform

The experiment platform used in this study consisted of a collection node and a receive node which are shown in Fig.3.

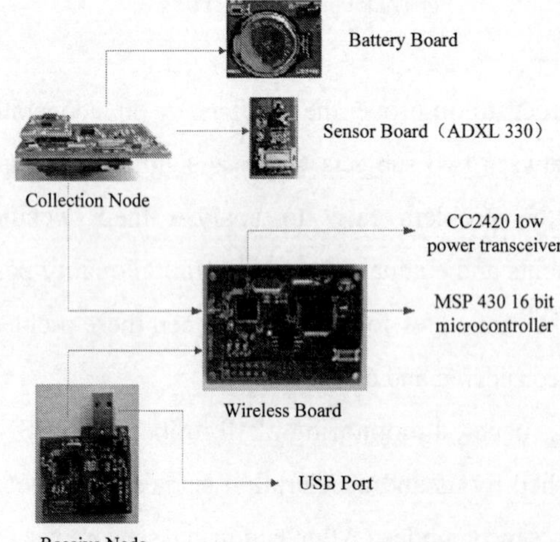

Fig.3. Configuration of the collection node and the receive node.

The collection node consisted of a sensor board, a wireless communication board and a battery board. The receive node consisted of a wireless communication board and a USB port. The sensor board included a tri-axial accelerometer (ADXL330) which could measure acceleration with a full-scale range of $\pm 3g$. The wireless communication board ran TinyOS system on a microcontroller (MSP430). Wireless communication between the collection node and the receive node was achieved through wireless transceiver chips (CC2420) with IEEE 802.15.4 protocol. The receiving frequency of acceleration signals was set to be 20Hz in this study with a minimal packet loss rate.

B. Data Collection

To validate the proposed system, we took a gait experiment for example. 8 volunteers (four males and four females, ages from 22 to 28) were invited to take part in the experiment. We performed the experiment in an open corridor which is no wireless interference with a region of $3.5m \times 40m$. In the experiment, each volunteer wore two sensor nodes on their feet ankle, as shown in Fig. 4. Every two volunteers formed a group and performed gait actions twice, walking about 15m's distance. The main purpose of this experiment is to test the gait coordination between two subjects. Before walking, a demonstration of basic process was given to each volunteer. The first part of experiment was performed to capture gait acceleration signal within the walking distance of 15m. Fig. 5 shows the gait action of two-body interactions in the experiment.

Fig.4. Subject wearing two sensor nodes.

Fig.5. Gait of two-body interactions

V. EXPERIMENTS RESULTS AND DISCUSSION

Fig. 6(a) and Fig. 6(b) show acceleration signals of two-body interactions collected by the BSN monitoring platform in the gait experiment. From these two signals, we hardly infer the quality of gait coordination between two subjects. Therefore, we divide every a periodical signal into four segments based on dynamic window. A detailed introduction could be demonstrated in the study [18]. After acquiring segmented signals, we recognize these four gait phases which are Foot Flat, Heel Off, Swing and Heel Strike. The phase sequence matching between two subjects is principal for two-body gait synchronization.

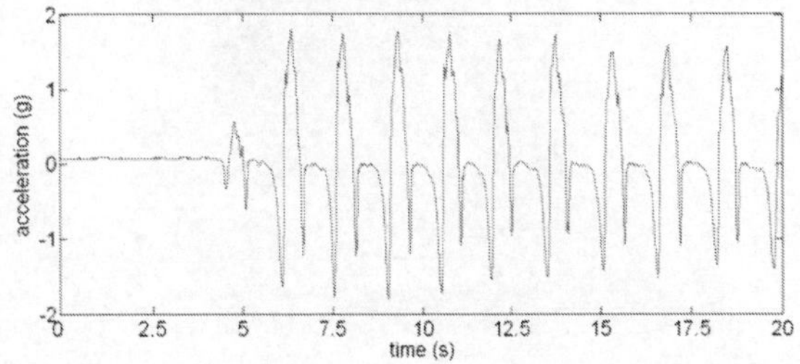

Fig.6. (a) Acceleration signal (subject A, left foot)

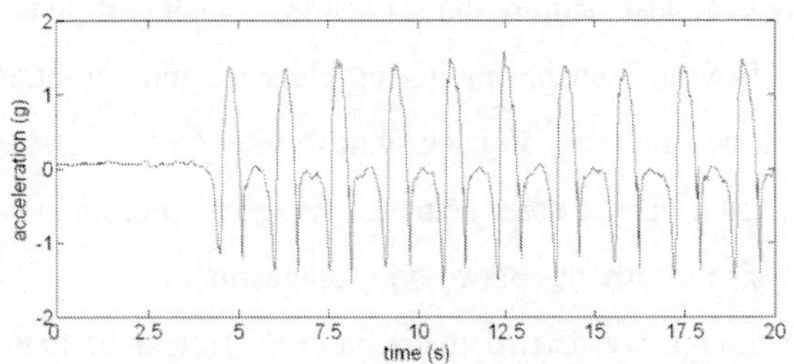

Fig.6. (b) Acceleration signal (subject B, left foot)

Fig. 7(a) and Fig. 7(b) show these four recognized gait phases and their percentages (γ) at the second gait, where two subjects' gait time interval are 1.46s and 1.42s. From Fig. 7(a) and (b), we can see that each gait phase between two subjects is matched, and has a similar percentage in a gait period, which show that a general synchronization for the second gait of two-body interactions.

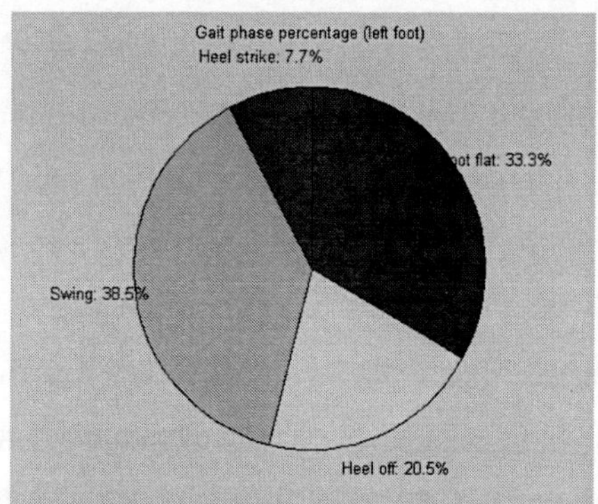

Fig.7. (a) Gait phase percentage (subject A, left foot)

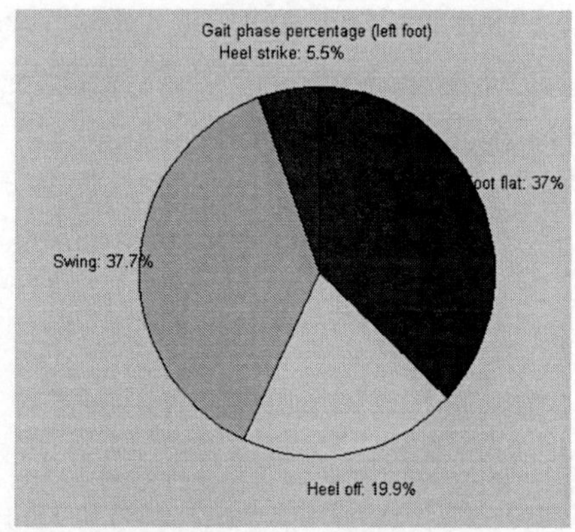

Fig.7. (b) Gait phase percentage (subject B, left foot)

We can also acquire the start time of each gait phase (α) from the sensor monitoring platform and compute the time interval of each gait phase (ω). These parameters may further help us give good coordination analysis for activities of two-body interaction.

Although we carried out a gait experiment of two-body interactions to illustrate the proposed method and the experimental analysis show that the approach could obtain a satisfactory result, it should be pointed out that this approach just is suitable for a class of activities of two-body interactions, such as synchronized diving, double kayak and double rowing. These interactive activities mentioned above have periodical movements, and every movement period consists of several different actions. Moreover, the coordination of every action between two subjects is necessary.

VI. CONCLUSION

In this paper, the recognition problem of activities of two-body interactions is proposed and discussed. The main contribution of this study is to monitor a class of interactive activities and evaluate their cooperation quality. A monitoring platform based on BSN is established and acceleration data is collected from wearable inertial sensors. We divide every signal into various segments corresponding to different stages of movements. Several important time parameters are also given to further analyze the coordination in their cooperation. A gait experiment of two-body interactions is analyzed on the monitoring platform, and experiment results demonstrate the effectiveness of the proposed method.

There are a number of limitations in this work. Although the datasets we collected in this paper contain some gait actions, more activities of two-body interactions such as double rowing and synchronized diving should be done in a practical scenario to further evaluate our proposed approach. Besides, we also plan to consider the problem of multi-user interactions in a more complex scenario in future work.

VII. ACKNOWLEDGMENT

This work was supported in part by the National Natural Science Foundation of China under Grant (61174027), Liaoning Higher-education Outstanding Young Scholar

Program (LJQ2012005), and National High Technology Research and Development Program (863 program) Project (2012AA041505) and by the sub-projects of National Science and Technology Major Project under Grant 2010ZX04007-011-5. We thank all volunteers that participated in the experiment for their help in data collection.

REFERENCES

[1] KING R C, ATALLAH L, WONG C, *et al.* Elderly Risk Assessment of Falls with BSN [C] // **Proceedings of 2010 International Conference on Body Sensor Networks**. Washington: IEEE Computer Society, 2010: 30-35.

[2] MCILWRAITH D, YANG G Z. Body sensor networks for sport, wellbeing and health [J]. **Sensor Networks**, 2009: 349–381.

[3] WANG Z L, JIANG M, ZHAO H Y, *et al.* A Pilot Study on Evaluating Recovery of the Post-Operative Based on Acceleration and sEMG [C] // **Proceedings of 2010 International Conference on Body Sensor Networks**. Washington: IEEE Computer Society, 2010: 3-8.

[4] ZHU C, SHENG W. Motion and location-based online human daily activity recognition [J]. **Pervasive and Mobile Computing,** 2011, **7**(2): 256-269.

[5] OSCAR D, ALFREDO J, MIGUEL A, *et al.* Centinela: a human activity recognition system based on acceleration and vital sign data [J]. **Pervasive and Mobile Computing,** 2012, **8**(5): 717-729.

[6] STROHRMANN C, ROSSI M, ARNRICH B, *et al.* A data-driven approach to kinematic analysis in running using wearable technology [C] // **The Ninth International Conference on Wearable and Implantable Body Sensor Networks**. 2012: 118-123.

[7] MORTAZAVI B, CHU K C, LI X, *et al.* Near-realistic motion video games with enforced activity [C] // **The Ninth International Conference on Wearable and Implantable Body Sensor Networks**. 2012: 28-33.

[8] PANTELOPOULOS A, BOURBAKIS N. A survey on wearable sensor-based systems for health monitoring and prognosis [J]. **Systems, Man, and Cybernetics, Part C: Applications and Reviews, IEEE Transactions on,** 2010, 40(1): 1-12.

[9] PANSIOT J, LO B, YANG G Z. Swimming stroke kinematic analysis with BSN [C] // **Body Sensor Networks (BSN), 2010 International Conference on.** IEEE. 2010: 153-158.

[10] GHASEMZADEH H, LOSEU V, GUENTERBERG E *et al.* Sport training using body sensor networks: a statistical approach to measure wrist rotation for golf swing [C] // **Proceedings of The Fourth International Conference on Body Area Networks. ICST.** 2009: 2-9.

[11] KING R, MCLLWRAITH D, LO B, *et al.* Body sensor networks for monitoring rowing technique [C] // **Wearable and Implantable Body Sensor Networks, BSN 2009. Sixth International Workshop on.** IEEE. 2009: 251-255.

[12] WANG L, GU T, TAO X P, *et al.* Recognizing multi-user activities using wearable sensors in a smart home [J]. **Pervasive and Mobile Computing,** 2011, 7(3): 287-298.

[13] GU T, WANG L, CHEN H H, *et al.* Recognizing multiuser activities using wireless body sensor networks [J]. **IEEE Transactions on Moblile Computing,** 2011, 10(11): 1618-1631.

[14] PREECE J S, GOULERMAS Y J, KENNEY P J L, *et al.* Activity identification using body-mounted sensors – a review of classification techniques [J]. **Physiological Measurement**, 2009, **30**: 1-33.

[15] SUN Z, MAO X, TIAN W, *et al.* Activity classification and dead reckoning for pedestrian navigation with wearable sensors [J]. **Measurement Science and Technology**, 2009, **20**(1): 1-10

[16] SINGLA G, COOK D, EDGECOMBE M S. Recognizing independent and joint activities among multiple residents in smart environments [J]. **Ambient Intelligence and Humanized Computing Journal**, 2010, 1(1):57-63

[17] RLTUN K, BARSHAN B, TUNCEL O. Comparative study on classifying human activities with miniature inertial and magnetic sensors [J]. **Pattern Recognition,** 2010, **43**(10): 3605-3620.

[18] WANG Z L, QIU S, CAO Z K, *et al.* Quantitative Assessment of Dual Gait Analysis Based on Inertial Sensors with Body Sensor Network [J]. **Sensor Review,** 2013, 33(1): 48-56.

Robust Detection of Copy-Move Forgery in Color Images

Nathalie Diane Wandji [1], **Sun Xingming** [2]

[1] School of Information Science and Engineering, Hunan University, Changsha, Hunan, P.R China

[2] Jiangsu Engineering Center of Network Monitoring, Nanjing University of Information Science and Technology, Nanjing, Jiangsu, P.R China

Abstract - *With rapid advances in digital image processing technology, there is a massive development of sophisticated tools and techniques for digital image forgery. Copy-move forgery is one of the techniques most commonly used. A part of an image is copied and pasted into the same image, in order to maliciously hide or clone an object or a region. In this paper, we propose a method that addresses this kind of fakery. Each component of the suspicious RGB image is used for feature extraction. Let Y be the Y-component of the corresponding YUV image. Then R, G, B and Y are splitted into fixed-size overlapping blocks, and characteristics are computed from each component. The 10-dimensional feature vectors made by concatenating the characteristic values of each component are then stored row wise in a matrix that will be lexicographically sorted to make similar image blocks neighbors. Duplicated image blocks are identified using Euclidean distance as similarity criterion. Experimental results showed that the proposed method can detect the duplicated regions even in case of slight JPEG compression, blur and noise addition.*

Keywords: Digital image forgery, Image forensics, Copy-move forgery.

1 Introduction

Powerful and easy to use digital cameras and image-editing software packages are becoming rampant. As a result, it has become relatively easy to manipulate digital images without leaving any visual clue, even for a novice. Recently, a lot of effort has been made to be able to decide on the authenticity and integrity of digital images, resulting into many approaches.

Generally, these approaches are divided into two main categories: the active methods on one hand and the passive/blind methods on the other hand. The use of active techniques such as digital signature and watermarking is limited, mainly by the requirement that certain information is embedded into the image during its creation since only few capturing devices on the market possess that feature. Unlike the watermark-based and signature-based methods; the passive approaches are concerned with determining the source and potential authenticity of an image without using any prior information. In this latter category, we will put our focus on one of the most commonly used tampering methods, namely the copy-move forgery. It proceeds by copying a part of an image and pasting it into another part of the same image, most of the time with the intention of deceiving people, or hiding/cloning an object. An example for this type of forgery can be seen in Fig.1, where the yellow hat is cloned.

(a)

(b)

Figure 1. Example of Copy-Move forgery (a) original image (b) tampered image

Several methods have been developed to provide solutions for detecting such forgery.

Jessica Fridrich et al. proposed a method using discrete cosine transform (DCT) of overlapping blocks and the lexicographical representation of the quantized DCT coefficients. Alin C. Popescu and Hany Farid [2] proposed a method based on the use of principal components analysis (PCA) to represent image blocks. A. N. Myna et al. [3] proposed a method using the idea of log-polar mapping and wavelet transforms. Hailing Huang et al. [4] used the SIFT algorithm to detect duplicated regions in the image. SIFT features were proven to be stable with respect to changes in illumination, rotation and scaling. Li Kang et al. [5] suggested to apply improved singular value decomposition to each image block to yield a reduced dimension representation and then lexicographically sort the feature matrix formed by the singular values. Their method was proven to be robust against noise distortion. Weiqi Luo et al. [6] presented a technique robust to various forms of post region duplication processing, including blurring, noise contamination and lossy compression. They represented each block by 7 intensity-based characteristics extracted from both the RGB color image and the YCbCr corresponding image. Sevinc Bayram et al. [7] proposed to first apply Fourier Mellin Transform (FMT) on the image blocks and then use the projection of the obtained log-polar values onto 1-D as feature vectors. W. Li et al. [8] analyzed the block artifact grids (BAG), caused by the blocking processing during JPEG compression assuming they usually mismatch when tampering with objects by copy–paste operations. G. Li et al. [9] proposed to decompose the image into four frequency sub-bands using DWT and represent each block by the singular vector obtained by applying Singular Value Decomposition (SVD) only on the low-frequency component to yield a dimension reduction. H.T Sencar et al. [10] presented a method based on the assumption average sharpness/blurriness value of the tampered area is expected to be different as compared to the non-tampered parts of the image. They estimated the sharpness/blurriness value of an image based on the regularity of its wavelet transform. J. Zhang et al. [11] started by applying DWT to the input image and then, computed the phase correlation to estimate the spatial offset between the copied region and the pasted region. Finally, they used the idea of pixel matching to locate the forged region. S. Khan et al. [12] proposed the use of DWT followed by the comparison of blocks extracted from the low frequency subband using Phase Correlation as similarity criterion. Their technique fails to detect duplicated regions with rotation or scaling.

In this paper, we propose an efficient and robust algorithm for detecting and locating Copy-Move forged regions within a color image.

2 Proposed Method

The detailed procedure proceeds as follows:

1. Read the suspicious RGB color image ***f*** of size $M \times N \times 3$ and convert it into YUV color space.
2. For each R, G, B and Y color component :
   2.1. Divide it into overlapping *bxb* blocks
   2.2. For each block of the Y component, compute its arithmetic average value *Ave_Y*.
   2.3. For each block of the R, G and B components, calculate 3 characteristics, namely the Average gray level (*Ave_g*); the average contrast (*Ave_c*) and the third moment (*Skew*) [13]. Let

$$\mu_n = \sum_{i=0}^{L-1} (z_i - m)^n \, p(z_i) \quad (1)$$

where z_i is a random variable representing intensity, $p(z_i)$ is the intensity-level histogram and L the number of possible levels. Then, the above characteristics are obtained by the following equations :

$$Ave\_g = \sum_{i=0}^{L-1} z_i \, p(z_i) \quad (2)$$

$$Ave\_c = \sqrt{\mu_2(z)} \quad (3)$$

$$Skew = \mu_3 = \sum_{i=0}^{L-1} (z_i - m)^3 \, p(z_i) \quad (4)$$

3. For each block of the color image, we therefore obtain a feature vector *V* of length *10*.

$$V = [Ave_Y, Ave_g{}^R, Ave_c{}^R, Skew^R, Ave_g{}^G, Ave_c{}^G, Skew^G, Ave_g{}^B, Ave_c{}^B, Skew^B] \quad (5)$$

4. Form a matrix **A** of dimensions ***(M-b+1)(N-b+1)*** rows and ***10*** columns and store the obtained features into rows of **A**.
5. Sort the matrix A lexicographically.
6. Set a threshold T_n controlling the amount of neighboring feature vectors to use for similarity check. For a given feature vector $A_p = (A_1^p, A_2^p, \dots, A_{10}^p)$, its neighbors are defined by $A_q = (A_1^q, A_2^q, \dots, A_{10}^q)$ where $q \in [k, l]$

$$k = \begin{cases} 1, & p < T_n \\ p - T_n, & otherwise \end{cases} \qquad l = \begin{cases} b^2, & p > b^2 - T_n \\ p + T_n, & otherwise \end{cases}$$

7. To evaluate similarity between image blocks, the Euclidian distance is exploited. The more similar the examined blocks are, the smaller the Euclidian distance ***d*** between their corresponding feature vectors is. If ***d*** is smaller than a pre-defined threshold T_{max}, the two blocks are considered as candidates for forgery and their respective positions $(x_i, y_i), (x_j, y_j)$ together with and the shift vector between them $[|x_i - x_j|, |y_i - y_j|]$ are stored.
8. Set a third threshold T_s . If the accumulative number of the corresponding shift vector is greater than T_s , the corresponding blocks are marked as suspicious.
9. Considering the fact that blocks close to each other in the input image might with a high probability have similar feature vectors, we conclude the regions are duplicated only if the actual euclidian distance between both regions is greater than a predefined threshold T_d.
10. Plot the blocks as copied and pasted regions on the gray-scaled image corresponding to the input image.

3 Experimental Results

Experiments are carried out on a computer with a configuration of CPU 2.7 GHz, RAM 2 G, Windows 7 32-bit Operating System, GIMP 2.6.12, and Matlab 7.12.0.635 (R2011a).

Original images are made available by authors in [14]. We scaled them to the size 267×200 and tampered with them as shown in Fig. 2. We tested different kinds of post processing such as noise addition, Gaussian blur and JPEG compression. The experimental results presented were all done with the same parameters, namely $b=16$ (block size); T_{max}=0.002; $T_d=2*b=32$; and $T_n= T_s$=b=16.

(a) (b)

Figure 2: (a) Original image (b) Tampered image

3.1 JPEG Compression

The whole forged image is compressed with a quality factor of 90.

3.2 Gaussian Blur

Gaussian blur with radius 3 is applied to to the whole forged image.

3.3 Additive Gaussian noise

Gaussian noise is added to the copied region with a standard deviation of 0.3 before pasting it.

4 Conclusions

With the rapid development of the image processing technology, there is a great need of a method that is able to detect digital image forgeries in general and copy-move forgeries in particular which is the most common forgery. In this paper, we consider the detection of such forgery in color images even when some post-processing operations such has Gaussian blur, Gaussian noise addition or JPEG compressed have been applied. Experimental results show that the proposed method was appropriate to some extent to identify and localize the forged region.

5 Acknowlegement

This work is supported by the NSFC (61232016, 61173141, 61173142, 61173136, 61103215, 61070196, 61070195, and 61073191), National Basic Research Program 973 (2011CB311808), 2011GK2009, GYHY201206033, 201301030, 2013DFG12860 and PAPD fund

6 References

[1] Jessica Fridrich, David Soukal and Jan Lukas. "Detection of copy–move forgery in digital images", in: Proceedings of Digital Forensic Research Work- shop, IEEE Computer Society, Cleveland, OH, USA, pp. 55–61, August 2003.

[2] Alin C. Popescu and Hany Farid. "Exposing digital forgeries by detecting duplicated image regions", Technical Report TR2004-515, Depart- ment of Computer Science, Dartmouth College, 2004.

[3] A.N. Myna, M.G. Venkateshmurthy and C.G. Patil. "Detection

of region duplication forgery in digital images using wavelets and log-polar mapping", in Proceedings of the International Conference on Computational Intelligence and Multimedia Applications (ICCIMA 2007), IEEE Computer Society, Washington, DC, USA, pp. 371–377, 2007.

[4] Hailing Huang, Weiqiang Guo, and Yu Zhang. "Detection of copy–move forgery in digital images using sift algorithm", in Proceedings of the 2008 IEEE Pacific-Asia Workshop on Computational Intelligence and Industrial Application (PACIIA '08), IEEE Computer Society, Washington, DC, USA, 2008, pp. 272–276.

[5] Weiqi Luo, Jiwu Huang and Guoping Qiu. "Robust Detection of Region-Duplication Forgery in Digital Images", In proceedings of the International Conference on Pattern Recognition, Washington, DC, pp. 746-749, 2006.

[6] Li Kang and Xiao-pin Cheng. "Copy-move forgery detection in digital image", 3rd International Congress on Image and Signal Processing (CISP), vol. 5, pp. 2419 – 2421, 2010.

[7] Sevinc Bayram, Taha Sencar and Nasir Memon. "An efficient and robust method for detecting copy-move forgery," In Procceedings of ICASSP, IEEE International Conference on Acoustics, Speech, and Signal Processing, 2009.

[8] Weihai Li, Yuan Yuan and Nenghai Yu. "Passive Detection of Doctored JPEG Image via Block Artifact Grid Extraction". Signal Processing, pp. 1821-1829, 2009.

[9] Guohui Li, Qiong Wu, Dan Tu, and ShaoJie Sun. "A Sorted Neighborhood Approach for Detecting Duplicated Regions in Image Forgeries based on DWT and SVD". in Proceedings of IEEE International Conference on Multimedia and Expo, Beijing China, pp. 1750-1753, July 2-5, 2007.

[10] Yagiz Sutcu, Baris Coskun, Husrev T. Sencar and Nasir Memon. "Tamper detection based on regularity of wavelet transform coefficients," In Proceedings of ICIP, International Conference on Image Processing, 2007.

[11] Qiumin Wu, Shuozhong Wang, and Xinpeng Zhang. "Detection of image region-duplication with rotation and scaling tolerance". In Proceedings of the Second International Conference on Computational Collective Intelligence (ICCCI) Part I, pp. 100 -108, November 2010.

[12] Jing Zhang, Zhanlei Feng and Yuting Su. "A New Approach for Detecting Copy-Move Forgery in Digital", in Procceedings of the 11th IEEE Singapore International Conference on Communication Systems, pp. 362–366, 2008.

[13] Rafael C. Gonzalez, Richard E. Woods and Steven L. Eddins. "Digital Image Processing using MATLAB", Second Edition, Pearson Publications, 2004.

[14] Amerini, L. Ballan, R. Caldelli, A. Del Bimbo, and G. Serra. "A sift-based forensic method for copy-move attack detection and transformation recovery", IEEE Transactions on Information Forensics and Security, vol. 6(3), pp. 1099 - 1110, 2011.

SESSION

IMAGE RECONSTRUCTION AND RESTORATION

Chair(s)

TBA

Binary Code Pattern Unwrapping Technique in Fringe Projection Method

R. Talebi, J. Johnson and A. Abdel-Dayem
Dept. of Mathematics and Computer Science, Laurentian University, Sudbury, Ontario, Canada

***Abstract*— Due to the growing need to produce three-dimensional data in various fields such as archaeology modeling, reverse engineering, quality control, industrial components, computer vision and virtual reality, and many other applications, the lack of a stable, economic, accurate, and flexible three-dimensional reconstruction system that is based on a factual academic investigation is recommended. As an answer to that demand, Fringe projection has emerged as a promising 3D reconstruction direction that combines low computational cost with both high precision and high resolution. In our previous work, an experimental study and implementation of a simple fringe projection system has been reported which was based on a multi wavelength unwrapping approach. In this paper we implemented a new method of phase unwrapping which is based on time analyses unwrapping approaches. Experimental results have shown that binary code pattern unwrapping method is a stable and reliable method that results in a high level of precision. At the cost of using more pictures the higher level of precision in the reconstructed 3-D model has been achieved. The level of preciseness in the resulting cloud point can be observed directly as a proof of the correctness of whole method.**

Three-dimensional reconstruction of small objects has been one of the most challenging problems over the last decade. Computer graphics researchers and photography professionals have been working on improving 3D reconstruction algorithms to fit the high demands of various real life applications. Medical sciences, animation industry, virtual reality, pattern recognition, tourism industry, and reverse engineering are common fields where 3D reconstruction of objects plays a vital role. Both lack of accuracy and high computational cost are the major challenges facing successful 3D reconstruction. It employs digital projection, structured light systems and phase analysis on fringed pictures. Research studies have shown that the system has acceptable performance, and moreover it is insensitive to ambient light.

***Keywords*—** Digital fringe projection, 3D reconstruction, phase unwrapping, phase shifting.

I. INTRODUCTION

In recent years there has been an increasing interest in 3D reconstruction of objects. Various methods and algorithms have been developed to fulfill the needs and demands in this particular area. Among these methods, the features and capabilities of digital sinusoidal pattern mapping method(fringe projection), was the subject to several studies. High flexibility, high speed, high accuracy and low cost, can be mentioned as the main characteristics of fringe projection method.

A structured light system such as fringe projection system is similar to a stereo technique as it only uses two devices for 3D shape measurement. However, fringe projection replaces one camera of a stereo system with a projector to project structured patterns, which are encoded through certain codification strategies. Then, the captured structured patterns are decoded. If the code-words (used to encode the structured pattern) are unique, the correspondence between the projector sensor and the camera sensor is uniquely identified, and 3D information can be calculated through triangulation. Generally, structured light systems use binary patterns, where only 0 and 1 s are used for codification. Binary patterns are easier to encode and decode, resulting in a considerable performance gain for the overall system. Three-dimensional measurement techniques are broadly classified into two categories; contact and non-contact approaches, refer to Fig. 1. We will limit our discussion to fringe projection as an effective non-contact approach.

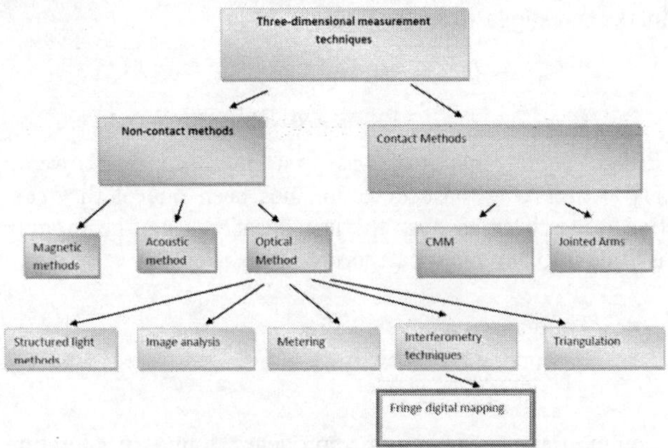

Fig. 1 Three dimensional reconstructed systems.[1]

The major stages of fringe projection method are;

- A sinusoidal pattern is projected over the surface of the object by using a projector, as illustrated in Fig. 2
- A digital camera is used to capture the pattern that has been assorted (phase modulated) by the topography of the object surface.
- The captured pattern is analyzed to extract relevant topographical information of the object (phase).
- A phase unwrapping algorithm is executed in order to unwrap the phase step
- A phase to height conversion method is used to materialized the 3-D dimension in every pixel

Phase modulation analysis uses the *arctan* function, which yields values in the range [-π,+π]. However, true phase values may extend over 2π range, resulting in discontinuities in the recovered phase. Phase unwrapping aims at finding the 2π coefficients, and consequently adding integral multiples of 2π at each pixel to remove such discontinuity.

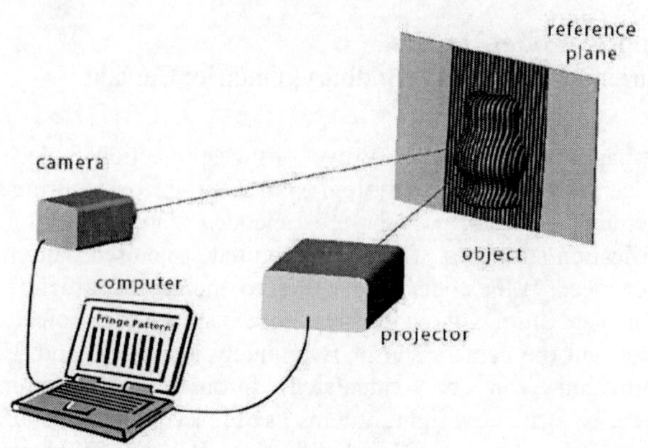

Fig. 2 Fringe projection arrangement [3]

The paper is organized as follows. Section II highlights previous research studies for fringe analysis. Then, Section III and Section IV present the fringe projection system set up and results, respectively. Finally, Section V offers concluding remarks and suggestions for future work.

II. PRIOR AND RELATED WORK

Fringe digital mapping was first proposed by Rowe *et al.*[1][2] in 1967. Phase detection has been one of the most active research areas over the last decade. It can be broadly classified into two main categories:

- Time-based analysis
- Frequency-based analysis

Common phase detection approaches found in literature were based on either Fourier transform [4] [5] [6] [7] [8] [9] [10], interpolated Fourier transform [11], continuous wavelet transform [12] [13] [14], two dimensional continues wavelet transform, discrete consign transform, neural network, phase locked loop, spatial phase detection, or phase transition [15].

Quan *et al.* [16] proposed the phase transition approach for small object measurement. In 2001, Berryman *et al.* [17] compared three different approaches (Fourier transform, phase transition, and spatial phase detection) on the reconstruction of a sphere using simulated data. Their experiments showed that in low noise conditions, phase transition produces the best results. With more than 10 % noise, using Fourier transform would be a good choice. However, on high noise levels spatial phase detection showed superior results.

Suutton *et al.* [18] proposed a phase detection scheme based on the use of Hilbert transform with Laplacian pyramid. The proposed scheme produces high precision level.

Gdeisat *et al.* [19] used two-dimensional continuous wavelet transform to eliminate the low component's frequency of the fringe. Then, Fourier transform was employed for phase detection. This method offers acceptable results; taking into consideration that it uses only one fringe.

III. FRINGE PATTERN ANALYSIS USING PHASE SHIFTING

The image of a projected pattern(sinusoidal patterns) can be written as the following commonly used standard formula :

$$g(x,y) = a(x,y) + b(x,y)\cos(2\pi f_0 x + \varphi(x,y)) \quad (1)$$

where, $a(x,y)$ is the background intensity, $b(x,y)$ is the amplitude modulation of fringes, f_0 is the spatial carrier frequency, $\varphi(x,y)$ is the phase modulation of fringes (the required phase distribution). Equation (5) contains three unknowns; $a(x,y)$, $b(x,y)$, and $\varphi(x,y)$. As a result, three independent equations are needed to eliminate $a(x,y)$ and $b(x,y)$. This goal can be achieved by using three identical fringe patters shifted by known amounts (2π/3 radians). This leads to the following three equations:

$$g_1(x,y) = a(x,y) + b(x,y)\cos(2\pi f_0 x + \varphi(x,y) - \tfrac{2}{3}\pi) \quad (2)$$

$$g_2(x,y) = a(x,y) + b(x,y)\cos(2\pi f_0 x + \varphi(x,y)) \quad (3)$$

$$g_3(x,y) = a(x,y) + b(x,y)\cos(2\pi f_0 x + \varphi(x,y) + \tfrac{2}{3}\pi) \quad (4)$$

Solving the above three equations, the phase $\varphi(x,y)$ can be obtained as:

$$\varpi(x,y) = \tan^{-1}\left[\!\left[\frac{\sqrt{3}(I_1 - I_3)}{2I_2 - I_1 - I_3}\right]\!\right] \quad (5)$$

IV. PHASE UNWRAPPING

There are many applications of digital image processing in industrial, medical and military that part of the procedure is dependent upon the phase extraction of input images. Magnetic Resonance Imaging (MRI), Synthetic Aperture Radar (SAR), fringe digital mapping, tomography, are spectroscopy, are just a few examples of the mentioned examples. These systems use longstanding or novel algorithm in phase extraction process. Even so, considering as a result of using the arc tan functions, the extracted phase contains 2p jumps. The extracted phase is totally useless, unless the phase be unwrapped. The procedure of determining these discontinuities on the wrapped phase, resolving them and achieving the unwrapped phase is called phase unwrapping. Phase unwrapping is one of the most active areas of research in image processing, and so many different algorithms and methods are provided as a solution to the phase unwrapping problem. Mathematical explanation of the phase unwrapping problem can be provided as follows:

$\Phi = \varphi + 2K\pi$

Where Φ is the unwrapped phase, φ is the ambiguity phase, and K is an integer number, which counts the number of coefficients of 2π.

Figure 2.17 illustrates a wrapped and unwrapped phase and their profiles accordingly.

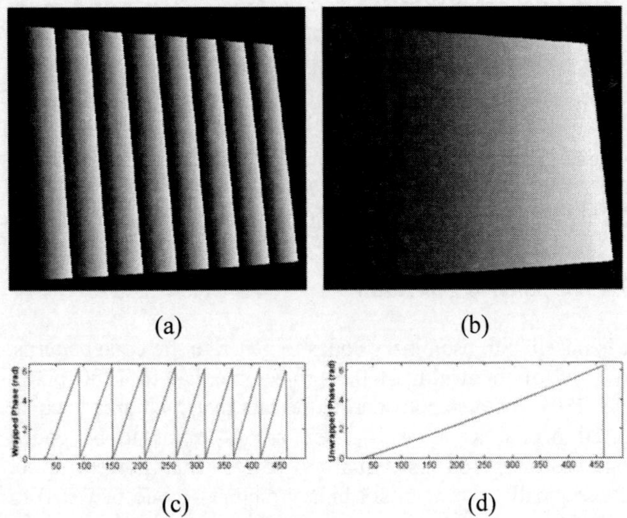

Figure 3 (a): Wrapped phase (b) Unwrapped phase (c) A profile of the wrapped phase (d) Profile of the unwrapped phase

There are three major solutions for solving the phase ambiguity or phase unwrapping :

- **spatial analyses :**

The main advantage in this method is that there is no need for additional helping patterns. In this method, all the pixels of wrapped phase will be processed and every two neighbor pixels that have sudden jump in their phase value, will be identified and $2\pi i$ coefficients will be added to the target pixels accordingly. This method is dramatically time consuming, and significantly inadequate facing complex objects and shadows.

- **Multi wavelength analyses:**

In this method, at least three additional fringe patterns with wavelength equal to the width of the projector should be obtained. In the next step $2\pi i$, coefficients will be calculated using these big wavelengths, and will be applied to the phase of the smaller wavelengths affording more precision. The main foible of this method is the considerable calculating error in the large wavelength phase. Consequently, The phase unwrapping results will not be precise. Considering the mentioned possible calculating errors these errors, They may be caused in using white shiny objects or high levels of contrast in projector light. The main advantage of this method is that it leads to greater precision at the expense of requiring only three additional patterns.

- **Time analyses :**

In this method binary code, patterns will be created according to each wavelength area and will be projected on the object such that the phase ambiguity can be calculated by using these code patterns. The only disadvantage in this method is that it needs more patterns, For instance, in our practical attempts, we used eight patterns to solve the phase ambiguity.

The Third method of these methods (Binary code patterns analyses)has been used in this paper. If the projector has 100 width pixels, then in each row, the fringe patterns will be repeated every 20 pixels. As a result, phase ambiguity of each pixel will be increased with the amount of 2π after each 20 pixels. In view of the above remark, if the phase ambiguity of each pixel is equal to $2k\pi i$ then, k values will be distributed in k = 0-1-2-3-4. where i is the $2k\pi$ coefficients.

V. PHASE TO HEIGHT CONVERSION

After phase unwrapping, height information of the measured object can be extracted. There are two common approaches to calculate depth information from the unwrapped phase map: relative coordinate calculation and absolute coordinate calculation. Absolute coordinate calculation is based on triangulation to estimate the absolute coordinate of every pixel in the world coordinate system. This approach requires precise knowledge about intrinsic and extrinsic parameters of both camera and projector. Thus, a system calibration step is essential. On the other hand, in the relative coordinate calculation approach, the depth of each pixel is calculated using a reference plane. A calibration process is not required. Moreover, the relative depth calculation approach is computationally less expensive compared to the absolute approach. Fig 4 shows a schematic diagram that illustrates the relative depth calculation approach. Points P and I are the perspective centers of the DLP projector and the CCD camera, respectively. The optical axes of the projector and the camera coincide at point O. After the system has been set up, a flat reference plane is measured first whose phase map is used as a reference for subsequent measurements. Then, the height of the object surface is measured relative to this reference plane.

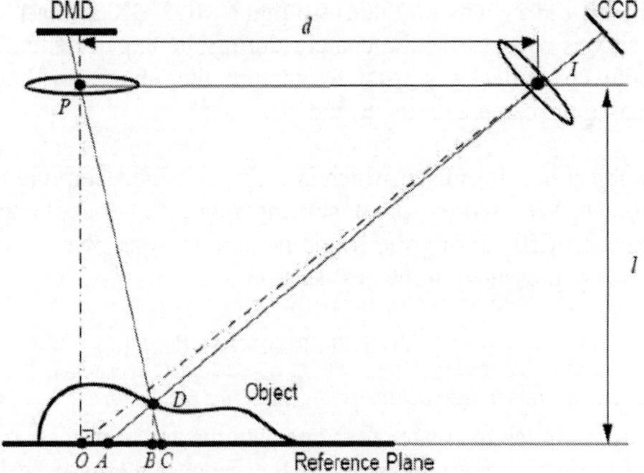

Figure 4 Schematic diagram of phase-to-height conversion using the relative depth calculation approach.

From the projector point of view, point D on the object surface has identical phase value as point C on the reference plane, i.e. $\varphi_D = \varphi_C$. On the other hand, from the CCD camera point of view, point D on the object surface and point A on the reference plane are imaged on the same pixel. By subtracting the reference phase map from the object phase map, we obtain the phase difference at this specific pixel:

$$\varphi_{AD} = \varphi_{AC} = \varphi_A - \varphi_C \tag{6}$$

Assume that points P and I are planned to be on the same axes with a distance l to the reference plane and a distance d between them, and that the reference plane is parallel to the device. Hence, the triangles PID and CAD in Fig. 4 are similar. Therefore:

$$\frac{d}{\overline{AC}} = \frac{l-\overline{DB}}{\overline{DB}} = \frac{l}{\overline{DB}} - 1 \tag{7}$$

where, d is the distance between the camera and the projector. Since d is much larger than AC for real measurement, this equation can be simplified as:

$$h(x,y) = \overline{DB} \cong \frac{1}{d}\overline{AC} = \frac{1}{d}\frac{\varphi_{AC}}{2\pi f} = K.\varphi_{AC} \tag{8}$$

where, f is the frequency of the projected fringes in the reference plane, K is a constant coefficient, and φ_{AC} is the phase containing the height information.

VI. System Setup

To conduct experiments to test viability of binary code patterns method presented in section [IV], we built a projection system with the configuration shown in Fig. 2. Our system is composed of a Casio XJ-A256 digital light processing unit (DLP), a PC with Intel Core i3 processor, and a Nikon D5100 DSLR camera. The DLP has the following technical specifications: 3000 ANSI lumens, 1800:1 contrast ratio, 16:10 aspect ratio, and a 1280x800 resolution. The DLP chip is 0.65-inch, and computer resolution is up to SXGA + (1600x1200). The camera has a resolution of 16.2 mega pixels and a kit sensor lens of 23.6x15.6 mm CMOS(DX format). A tripod was used to fix the camera during the experiments. A remote controller was used to capture the images without touching the camera on the tripod.

An object has been used which is a chalky white sculpture of a woman. We used the phase shifting approach (as explained in Section [III]) during the fringe pattern analysis phase. The results are presented in the next section.

VII. Experimental Results

A. Creating the fringe patterns

We used Matlab to create the fringe patterns and to process the images Fig. 5 present samples of the fringe patterns used in our experimentations.

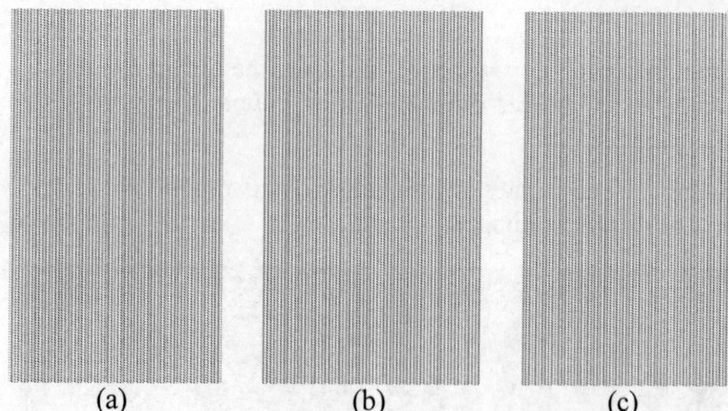

Figure 5 Fringe patterns with minimum gray value of 50 and maximum gray value of 200, maximum projector resolution 1280 -800, a wavelength of 20, and fringe transitions of: (a) -2π/3, (b) 2π/3, (c) zero.

B. Code patterns generating

It is possible to use binary codes to generate the code patterns. In view of the width of the projector equal to 1280 pixels (n=1280), and also considering the fact that each area is equal to 20 pixels, as a result; there are 64 areas to be coded (64=1280:20). 64 is equal to 2 to the power of 6. Consequently, we need six binary pictures (code patterns) to code 64 areas.

The code value will be a number between 0 to 63 which actually is the 2π coefficients in phase ambiguity and can be used to unwrap the phase. It is mandatory to create one black and one White binary patterns, in order to binarize the grey level pictures. Hence, a threshold value should be defined based on the grey values norms, and for each code if value is greater than the threshold, then it is going to change to one, otherwise it is going to change to zero. Therefore, the number of binary code patterns will be raised up to eight. Fig. 6 illustrates eight binary code patterns profiles, and Fig 7 illustrates the eight binary fringe patterns.

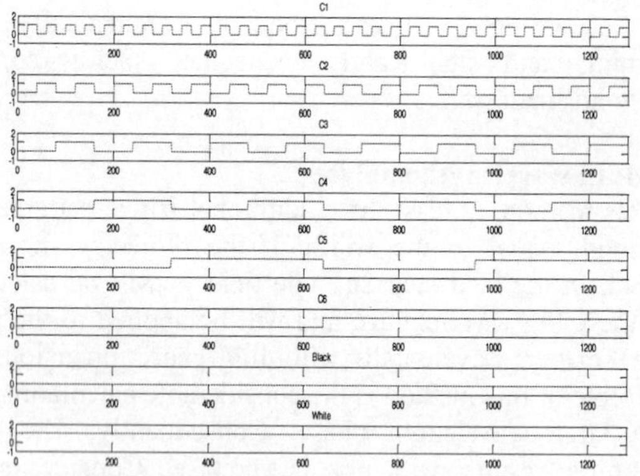

Figure 6 Binary codes patterns profiles

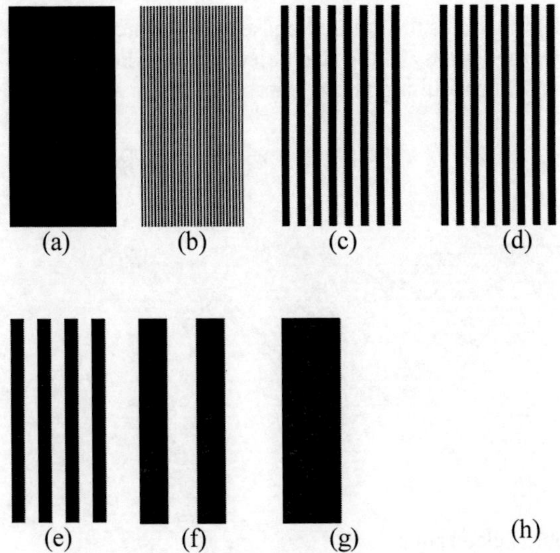

Figure 7 (a) Black pattern (b)-(g) Binary code patterns (h) White pattern

C. Three dimensional reconstruction

Three fringe patterns and eight code patterns were created and projected on the object and reference plane separately. Each one of the mentioned groups of eleven pictures was analyzed, and the phase map of each was calculated accordingly. Fig 8 and Fig. 9 present the projected patterns and binary code patterns on the object and reference plane respectively.

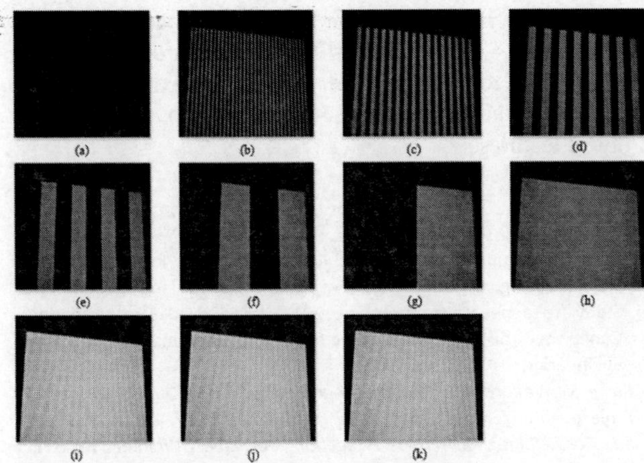

Figure 8 (a)-(h) Binary patterns projected on the reference plane (i)-(h) Fringe patterns projected on reference plane

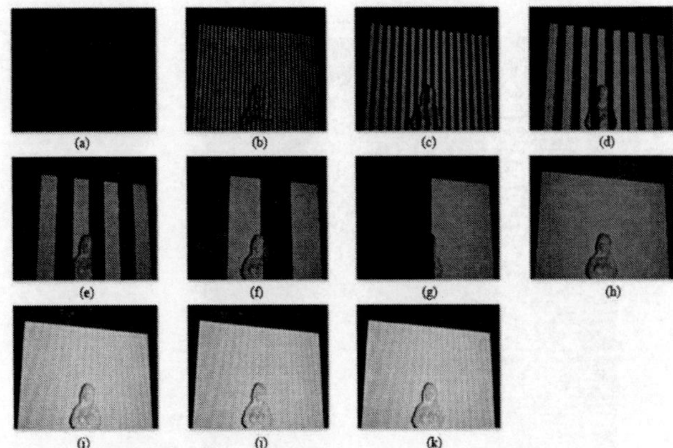

Figure 9 Binary patterns projected on the object (i)-(h) Fringe patterns projected on the object

Accordingly the object phase and reference plane phase can be achieved. Fig. 10 and Fig.11 present the reference plane phase and object phase.

Figure 10 Object phase

Figure 11 Reference plane phase

By subtracting the object phase from the reference phase the finalized phase map can be achieved. Fig 12 present the finalize phase map.

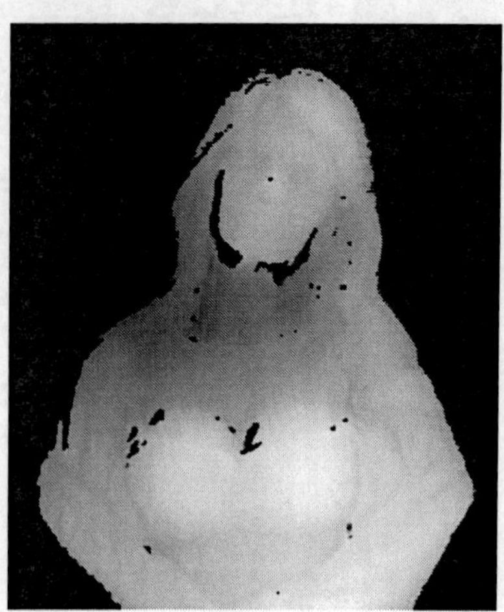

Figure 12 Object phase map

We used phase to height conversion as explained in section [V]. Following are the final results. The reader should observe that Fig 15 illustrates the cloud point of original object showing in Fig. 13

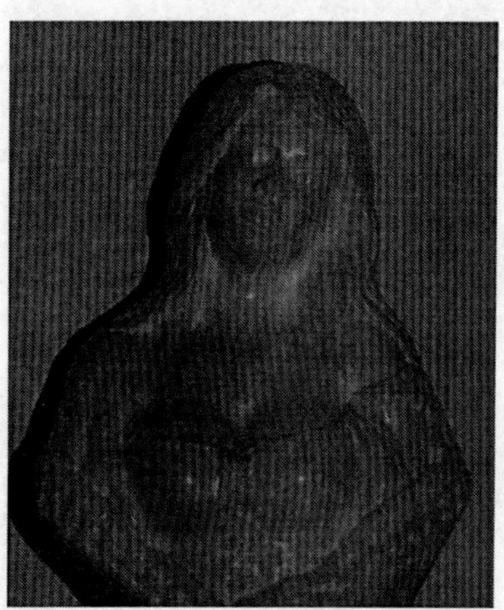

Figure 13 Object

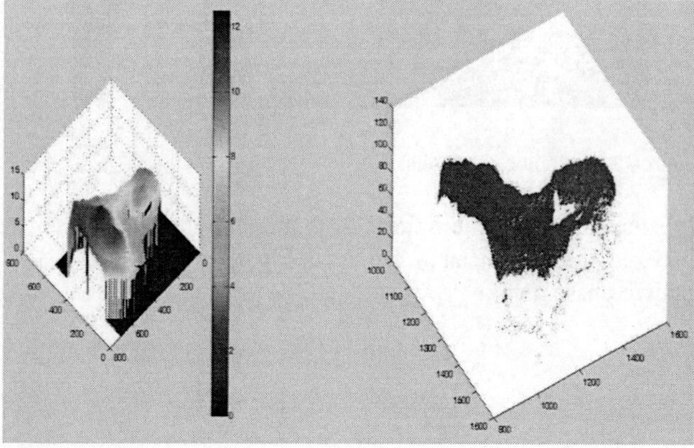

Figure 14 Phase map in color (left) and its corresponding cloud point (right)

Fig 14 (left) illustrates the colored phase map that helps us to compare the topography of the real object with the height distribution of the resulting phase map.

Figure 15 Object cloud point

III. Conclusion

Fringe projection is a powerful approach for 3D reconstruction of objects. In this paper, we developed a standalone implementation using one of the most advanced unwrapping algorithms in fringe projection method. Due to the fact that it uses greater number of pictures it has more level of accuracy compared with our previous method[1] that used spatial analysis for phase unwrapping. Experimental results demonstrated that using the new unwrapping algorithm captures more object details at the expense of using more pictures. In future, we plan to extend our experiments to consider other unwrapping methods in fringe projection analysis approaches. We aim at using sets of objects with various features like sudden changes in topography and more complexity in surface details to study the response of each approach to specific object features.

References:

[1] Reza Talebi,Amr Abdel-Dayem,Julia Johnson "3-D Reconstruction of Objects using Digital Fringe Projection: Survey and Experimental Study"(to appear Istanbul June 2013) ICCESSE 2013 : International Conference on Computer, Electrical, and Systems Sciences, and Engineering

[2] *Rowe SH,Welford WT. "Surface Topography Of Non-Optical Surfaces By Projected Interference Fringe, " Nature (London), 1967.*

[3] *S.S. Gorthi,P.Rastogi, "Fringe Projection Techniques: Whither We Are? ", Optics And Lasers In Engineering, 2010,48(2) 133-140.*

[4] *J.-F. Lin,X-Y. Su, "Two-Dimensional Fourier Transform Profilometry For The Automatic Measurement Of Three-Dimensional Object Shapes", Opt. Eng, 1995, 34 (11) 3297–3302.*

[5] *X. Su,W. Chen, "Fourier Transform Profilometry: A Review", Opt. Laser Eng, 2001, 35 (5) 263–284.*

[6] *F. Berryman,P. Pynsent, J. Cubillo, "The Effect Of Windowing In Fourier Transform Profilometry Applied To Noisy Images," Opt. Laser Eng, 2001, 41 (6) 815–825.*

[7] *M. A. Gdeisat,D. R. Burton, M. J. Lalor, "Eliminating The Zero Spectrum In Fourier Transform Profilometry Using A Two-Dimensional Continuous Wavelet Transform", Opt. Commun, 2006, 266 (2) 482–489.*

[8] *P. J. Tavares,M. A. Vaz, "Orthogonal Projection Technique For Resolution Enhancement Of The Fourier Transform Fringe Analysis Method, " Opt. Commun, 2006, 266 (2) 465–468.*

[9] S. Li, X. Su,W. Chen, L. Xiang, "Eliminating The Zero Spectrum In Fourier Transform Profilometry Using Empirical Mode Decomposition," J. Opt. Soc. Am, 2009, A 26 (5) 1195–1201.

[10] M. Dai,Y.Wang, "Fringe Extrapolation Technique Based On Fourier Transform For Interferogram Analysis With The Definition," Opt. Lett, 2009, 34 (7) 956–958.

[11] S. Vanlanduit,J. Vanherzeele, P. Guillaume, B. Cauberghe, P. Verboven, "Fourier Fringe Processing By Use Of An Interpolated Fourier-Transform Technique", Appl. Opt, 2004, 43 (27) 5206–5213.

[12] A. Dursun,S. Ozder, F. N. Ecevit, "Continuous Wavelet Transform Analysis Of Projected Fringe Patterns," Meas. Sci. Techn, 2004 15 (9) 1768–1772.

[13] J. Zhong,J. Weng, "Spatial Carrier-Fringe Pattern Analysis By Means Of Wavelet Transform: Wavelet Transform Profilometry," Appl. Opt, 2004 43 (26) 4993–4998.

[14] M. A. Gdeisat,D. R. Burton,M. J. Lalor, "Spatial Carrier Fringe Pattern Demodulation By Use Of A Two-Dimensional Continuous Wavelet Transform," Appl. Opt, 2006, 45 (34) 8722–8732.

[15] X. Su,G. Von Bally,D. Vukicevic, "Phase-Stepping Grating Profilometry: Utilization Of Intensity Modulation Analysis In Complex Objects Evaluation," Opt. Commun,1993, 98 (1-3) 141–150.

[16] Quan C,He XY, Wang CF, Tay CJ, Shang HM. "Shape Measurement Of Small Objects Using LCD Fringe Projection With Phase Shifting," Opt Commun 2001.

[17] F. Berryman,P. Pynsent,J. Cubillo, "A Theoretical Comparison Of Three Fringe Analysis Methods For Determining The Three-Dimensional Shape Of An Object In The Presence Of Noise," Opt. Laser Eng, 2003, 39 (1) 35–50.

[18] M. A. Sutton,W. Zhao, S. R. Mcneill, H.W. Schreier, Y. J. Chao, "Development And Assessment Of A Single-Image Fringe Projection Method For Dynamic Applications," Experimental Mechanics, 2001 41 (3) 205–217.

[19] M. A. Gdeisat,D. R. Burton, M. J. Lalor, "Eliminating The Zero Spectrum In Fourier Transform Profilometry Using A Two-Dimensional Continuous Wavelet Transform," Opt, Commun, 2006, 266 (2) 482–489.

[20] X. Su, W. "Chen,Fourier Transform Profilometry: A Review, " Opt. Laser Eng, 2001 35 (5) 263–284.

[21] Y. Tangy,W. Chen, X. Su, L. Xiang, "Neural Network Applied To Reconstruction Of Complex Objects Based On Fringe Projection," Opt. Commun, 2007 278 (2) 274–278.

Image Reconstruction for Arbitrarily Spaced Data Using Curvature Interpolation

William T. Cordell[1], Hakran Kim[2], Jeffrey L. Willers[3], and Seongjai Kim[4]
[1]Department of Mathematics and Statistics, Mississippi State University
Mississippi State, MS 39762-5921 USA Email: wc295@msstate.edu
[2] Department of Computational Engineering, Mississippi State University
Mississippi State, MS 39762 USA Email: hk246@msstate.edu
[3]USDA-ARS, Genetics and Precision Agriculture Research Unit
Mississippi State, MS 39762 USA Email: jeffrey.willers@ars.usda.gov
[4] Department of Mathematics and Statistics, Mississippi State University
Mississippi State, MS 39762-5921 USA Email: skim@math.msstate.edu (Contact Author)

Abstract— *The article is concerned with image reconstruction for arbitrarily spaced data using curvature interpolation. Image reconstruction is a challenging problem when no constraint is imposed on data locations. The problem is ill-posed and most numerical methods become overly expensive as the number of sample points increases. This article develops an effective partial differential equation (PDE)-based algorithm, called the recursive curvature interpolation method (R-CIM). The new method utilizes a curvature-related information which is estimated from an intermediate surface of the nonuniform data and plays a role of driving force for the reconstruction of a reliable image surface. The R-CIM is an interpolator, converges to a piecewise smooth image, possesses a minimum oscillatory behavior, and finishes all the computational tasks in $\mathcal{O}(N)$ operations, where N is the number of grid points. The new algorithm outperforms the inverse-distance weighting method, one of the most popular surface construction methods for scattered data.*

Keywords: Image reconstruction, scattered data, nonuniformly sampled data, curvature interpolation method (CIM), partial differential equation (PDE).

1. Introduction

Nonuniform sampling theory deals with the problem of defining the structure of sampling grids to convince a perfect recovery of functions that belong to prescribed function spaces. Most of the work is related to bandlimited function spaces [1], but some recent results have extended previous ideas for spline and wavelet spaces [2], [3].

Various interpolation methods of nonuniformly sampled data (or, arbitrarily spaced/scattered data) are widely applied to the fields of e.g. computer graphics and geosciences [4], [5]. The most cited are polynomial interpolation such as nearest-neighbor, linear, and cubic methods; these methods are easy to implement, but offer only low-quality results. Inverse-distance methods are also used, although they are computationally expensive and become impractical as the number of samples increases. A well-known interpolation model for arbitrarily spaced data is the method of thin-plate splines, which is based on radial basis functions [6]. However, the method is hard to be practical due to a high computational complexity. Since the solution must be found by solving a dense algebraic system, with the dimension being equal to the number of sample points, the problem becomes intractable even for mid-sized images. See [7], [8] for efforts for the reduction of computational complexity of the method. Various other methods have been proposed for the resampling of scattered data in terms of the approximation theory; see [9], [10], [11], [12], [13] for approximations in spline spaces and [14], [15] for those in wavelet spaces. For relevant works in computer graphics, see [16] and references therein.

In this article, the authors are interested in a novel PDE-based method for the image reconstruction of arbitrarily spaced data. The new method utilizes a curvature-related information which is estimated from an intermediate surface of the nonuniform data and plays a role of driving force for the construction of a reliable image surface. It is often the case that the constructed image surface does not contain all of the data values due to the estimated curvature. However, the error can be corrected by a recursive application of the curvature interpolation method: measure the misfit on the data points, construct an intermediate surface over the image domain based on the misfit values, estimate the corresponding curvature-related information, and build a correction surface to update the last iterate.

We will call the new algorithm the *recursive curvature interpolation method* (R-CIM) for the image reconstruction of arbitrarily spaced data. The R-CIM is an application of the curvature interpolation method (CIM) studied for image zooming [17]. It has been verified that the R-CIM shows a *minimum* oscillatory behavior, and yet it results in smooth images containing all the data values. Thus the R-CIM is an *interpolator*, while most of aforementioned methods employing spline/wavelet spaces are not interpolators but approximators. In addition to a recursive application of the CIM, our new method will incorporate 9-point schemes for the estimation of the curvature (Section 3.2), which would produce smoother correction surfaces than the conventional 5-point schemes.

The article is organized as follows. In Section 2, we present a brief review of the curvature interpolation method (CIM) studied for image zooming [17]. Section 2 describes in detail the R-CIM for image reconstruction of arbitrarily spaced data; a synthetic example is given to show the effectiveness of the new method. Section 4 contains numerical experiments for image reconstruction, dealing with natural images. In Section 5, we conclude our development and experiments.

2. Preliminaries

This section presents a brief review of the curvature interpolation method (CIM) studied for image zooming by Kim *et al.* [17].

Imaging zooming is a processing task to enlarge images by applying interpolation methods. The CIM is a partial differential equation (PDE)-based model; it begins with a selection of a curvature-related term which is measured from the low resolution (LR) image and interpolated to the high resolution (HR) image grid to be incorporated as a driving force for the construction of HR image. PDE-based models that employ the (mean) curvature itself as the smoothing operator (e.g., the TV model [18]) are known to have a tendency to converge to a piecewise constant image [19], [20]. Such a phenomenon is called the *staircasing*. Thus the curvature would better be replaced by a curvature-related diffusion operator $\mathcal{K}$ which is more effective and easier to handle. In [17], the authors adopted the following *gradient-weighted* (GW) curvature

$$\mathcal{K}(u) = -|\nabla u|\, \nabla \cdot \Big(\frac{\nabla u}{|\nabla u|}\Big), \tag{1}$$

of which the numerical realization could measure the degree of curving of the image surface holding desirable properties.

Let Ω and $\widetilde{\Omega}$ be the original LR image domain and its α-times magnified HR image domain, $\alpha > 1$, respectively; and $\widetilde{u}$ denote the HR image, the α-times magnification of an LR image u. Then we should have

$$u(\mathbf{x}) = \widetilde{u}(\widetilde{\mathbf{x}}), \quad \widetilde{\mathbf{x}} = \alpha \mathbf{x}, \tag{2}$$

where $\mathbf{x} = (x, y)$ and $\widetilde{\mathbf{x}} = (\widetilde{x}, \widetilde{y})$ are the coordinates of the LR and HR images, respectively. Since $\nabla_{\mathbf{x}} = \alpha \nabla_{\widetilde{\mathbf{x}}}$, the scaling factor between the GW curvatures on Ω and $\widetilde{\Omega}$ is α^2. That is,

$$|\nabla_{\mathbf{x}} u|\, \nabla_{\mathbf{x}} \cdot \Big(\frac{\nabla_{\mathbf{x}} u}{|\nabla_{\mathbf{x}} u|}\Big) = \alpha^2\, |\nabla_{\widetilde{\mathbf{x}}} \widetilde{u}|\, \nabla_{\widetilde{\mathbf{x}}} \cdot \Big(\frac{\nabla_{\widetilde{\mathbf{x}}} \widetilde{u}}{|\nabla_{\widetilde{\mathbf{x}}} \widetilde{u}|}\Big). \tag{3}$$

Now, let $\widehat{\Omega}^0$ denote the set of pixel points in $\widetilde{\Omega}$ which can be expressed as $\alpha\mathbf{p}$, where $\mathbf{p}$ is a pixel point in Ω. Then the CIM [17] can be outlined as follows.

I. *Compute the GW curvature of the given LR image v^0:*

$$\mathcal{K} = \mathcal{K}(v^0) \quad on\ \Omega. \tag{4}$$

II. *Interpolate $\mathcal{K}$ to obtain $\widehat{\mathcal{K}}$ on $\widetilde{\Omega}$.*

III. *Solve, for u on $\widetilde{\Omega}$, the following constrained problem*

$$\mathcal{K}(u) = \frac{1}{\alpha^2}\widehat{\mathcal{K}}, \quad u|_{\widehat{\Omega}^0} = v^0. \tag{5}$$

In the above algorithm, the GW curvature measured from the LR image is interpolated and incorporated as an explicit driving force for the same GW curvature model on $\widetilde{\Omega}$. The driving force would help the model construct the HR image more effectively, enforcing the resulting image to satisfy the given curvature profile. Such a curvature interpolation method turns out to produce HR images of little interpolation artifact [17].

3. The New Method: R-CIM

For image reconstruction of arbitrarily spaced data, let Ω^0 be the set of data pixels, where image values are initialized, that is v^0. Since Ω^0 is arbitrarily scattered, it would be better to construct an intermediate surface over the image domain Ω to obtain a useful curvature information, which is to be utilized as a driving force for the construction of an image surface. When the constructed surface does not contain all of the prescribed image values (v^0), the difference can be corrected by applying the procedure recursively. The following outlines the new algorithm; details will follow.

Initialize $\mathbf{u}_0 = 0$, on the image domain Ω
Select the tolerance $\tau > 0$
For $k = 1, 2, \cdots$

$$\left\{\begin{array}{ll}
\text{(i)} & \text{Compute the misfit on } \Omega^0\text{:} \\
 & \quad \mathbf{r}_{k-1} = \mathbf{v}^0 - \mathbf{u}_{k-1} \\
\text{(ii)} & \text{If } \|\mathbf{r}_{k-1}\|_\infty < \tau, \text{ stop} \\
\text{(iii)} & \text{Construct an intermediate surface } \phi_k\text{:} \\
 & \quad \left\{\begin{array}{ll} -\Delta\phi_k = 0, & \mathbf{x} \in \Omega \setminus \Omega^0 \\ \phi_k = \mathbf{r}_{k-1}, & \mathbf{x} \in \Omega^0 \\ \nabla\phi_k \cdot \mathbf{n} = 0, & \mathbf{x} \in \partial\Omega \end{array}\right. \\
\text{(iv)} & \text{Evaluate } A_k \text{ and } K_k \text{ from } \phi_k\text{:} \\
 & \quad K_k = A_k\phi_k \approx \mathcal{K}(\phi_k) \\
\text{(v)} & \text{Smoothen } K_k \text{ to get } \widetilde{K}_k \\
\text{(vi)} & \text{Construct a smooth, correction surface } \mathbf{w}_k\text{:} \\
 & \quad A_k \mathbf{w}_k = \widetilde{K}_k \\
\text{(vii)} & \text{Update :} \\
 & \quad \mathbf{u}_k = \mathbf{u}_{k-1} + \mathbf{w}_k
\end{array}\right. \tag{6}$$

Here $\mathbf{v}^0$ is the vector representation of the sampled data v^0, $\mathbf{r}_{k-1}$ denotes the misfit defined on the sample points Ω^0, ϕ_k is an intermediate surface, a solution of an interior value problem of the Poisson equation, $\mathbf{n}$ denotes the unit outward normal defined on the image boundary $\partial\Omega$, and $\|\cdot\|_\infty$ is the maximum norm. The equation $\nabla\phi_k \cdot \mathbf{n} = 0$ is called the no-flux condition.

A 9-point finite difference scheme will be introduced for both the curvature computation in Step (iv) and the surface reconstruction in Step (vi), which makes the correction surfaces $\mathbf{w}_k$ (and therefore the resulting image surface $\mathbf{u}_k$) smoother than that of the traditional 5-point scheme. Numerical schemes for Steps (iii)-(vi) will be discussed in detail in Sections 3.1-3.4 below.

We will call the algorithm (6) the *recursive curvature interpolation method* (R-CIM). Hereafter, we will omit the subscript k, for a simpler presentation, whenever no confusion is involved.

3.1 The intermediate surface ϕ

The construction of an intermediate surface ϕ is somewhat arbitrary. That is, there are many different ways to fulfill the task. In this article, we will adopt the Laplacian smoothing, due to its simplicity; it is easy to implement and results in a useful curvature information.

The diffusive PDE in (6.iii) can be discretized as follows.

$$\begin{aligned} 4\phi_{p,q} - \phi_{p,q-1} - \phi_{p-1,q} - \phi_{p+1,q} & \\ -\phi_{p,q+1} = 0, \quad \mathbf{x}_{p,q} \notin \Omega^0, & \end{aligned} \tag{7}$$

where $\phi_{p,q}$ denotes the value of ϕ at $\mathbf{x}_{p,q}$. Utilizing

$$\phi_{p,q} = \mathbf{r}_{k-1,p,q}, \quad \mathbf{x}_{p,q} \in \Omega^0, \tag{8}$$

and applying the no-flux condition along the boundary points, the associated algebraic system for the Laplacian smoothing can be formulated as

$$B\phi = \mathbf{g}_{k-1}, \tag{9}$$

where the source vector $\mathbf{g}_{k-1}$ has nontrivial values on only the rows corresponding to sample points. It is easy to see that the matrix B is nonsingular and the algebraic system can be solved with a reasonable efficiency by e.g. the successive over-relaxation (SOR) method, with a relaxation parameter ω appropriately chosen.

3.2 A 9-point scheme: Evaluation of A and K

The R-CIM in each iteration constructs a correction surface, representing the misfit which measures the difference between the scattered data and the last updated image. Thus it is necessary to make all the correction surfaces smooth enough in order to build up a smooth resulting image surface. This has motivated the authors to introduce 9-point difference schemes for both the curvature evaluation and for the construction of correction surfaces.

Let $\mathbf{x}' = (x', y')$ be the coordinates which are 45°-rotated counterclockwise from the standard coordinates $\mathbf{x} = (x, y)$.

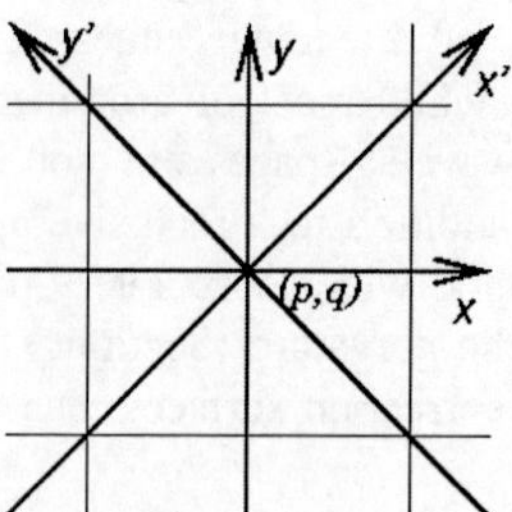

Fig. 1: The standard coordinates $\mathbf{x} = (x, y)$ and the 45°-rotated coordinates $\mathbf{x}' = (x', y')$ superposed on the vicinity of the pixel point (p, q).

See Figure 1. Then, as an alternative to (1), we may consider

$$\begin{aligned} \mathcal{K}(\phi) = & -|\nabla_{\mathbf{x}}\phi|_1 \left(\frac{\phi_x}{|\nabla_{\mathbf{x}}\phi|}\right)_x - |\nabla_{\mathbf{x}}\phi|_2 \left(\frac{\phi_y}{|\nabla_{\mathbf{x}}\phi|}\right)_y \\ & -|\nabla_{\mathbf{x}'}\phi|_1 \left(\frac{\phi_{x'}}{|\nabla_{\mathbf{x}'}\phi|}\right)_{x'} - |\nabla_{\mathbf{x}'}\phi|_2 \left(\frac{\phi_{y'}}{|\nabla_{\mathbf{x}'}\phi|}\right)_{y'}, \end{aligned} \tag{10}$$

where $|\nabla_{\mathbf{x}}\phi|_1$ and $|\nabla_{\mathbf{x}}\phi|_2$ are the same as $|\nabla_{\mathbf{x}}\phi|$, and $|\nabla_{\mathbf{x}'}\phi|_1$ and $|\nabla_{\mathbf{x}'}\phi|_2$ are the same as $|\nabla_{\mathbf{x}'}\phi|$; however, terms of different subscripts will be approximated in different ways.

Note that the curvature in (10) evaluates twice the conventional gradient-weighted curvature in (1). This does not require any modification in the R-CIM (6), because the matrix A will be correspondingly defined as in (6.iv) and utilized for the surface reconstruction in (6.vi).

For the (p, q)-th pixel of the intermediate image ϕ, we first compute the second-order difference approximations of $|\nabla\phi|$ at $\mathbf{x}_{p-1/2,q}\,(W)$, $\mathbf{x}_{p+1/2,q}\,(E)$, $\mathbf{x}_{p,q-1/2}\,(S)$, and $\mathbf{x}_{p,q+1/2}\,(N)$ and those of $|\nabla_{\mathbf{x}'}\phi|$ at $\mathbf{x}_{p-1/2,q-1/2}\,(SW)$, $\mathbf{x}_{p+1/2,q+1/2}\,(NE)$, $\mathbf{x}_{p+1/2,q-1/2}\,(SE)$, and $\mathbf{x}_{p-1/2,q+1/2}\,(NW)$:

$$\begin{aligned} d_{pq,W} &= [(\phi_{p,q} - \phi_{p-1,q})^2 + (\phi_{p-1,q+1} + \phi_{p,q+1} \\ &\qquad -\phi_{p-1,q-1} - \phi_{p,q-1})^2/16 + \varepsilon^2]^{1/2}, \\ d_{pq,E} &= d_{p+1,q,W}, \\ d_{pq,S} &= [(\phi_{p,q} - \phi_{p,q-1})^2 + (\phi_{p+1,q} + \phi_{p+1,q-1} \\ &\qquad -\phi_{p-1,q} - \phi_{p-1,q-1})^2/16 + \varepsilon^2]^{1/2}, \\ d_{pq,N} &= d_{p,q+1,S}, \\ d_{pq,SW} &= \left[\frac{(\phi_{p,q} - \phi_{p-1,q-1})^2}{2} + \frac{(\phi_{p-1,q} - \phi_{p,q-1})^2}{2} + \varepsilon^2\right]^{1/2}, \\ d_{pq,NE} &= d_{p+1,q+1,SW}, \\ d_{pq,SE} &= \left[\frac{(\phi_{p+1,q} - \phi_{p,q-1})^2}{2} + \frac{(\phi_{p,q} - \phi_{p+1,q-1})^2}{2} + \varepsilon^2\right]^{1/2}, \\ d_{pq,NW} &= d_{p-1,q+1,SE}, \end{aligned} \tag{11}$$

where $\varepsilon > 0$ is the regularization parameter introduced to prevent the differences from approaching zero. (We will set $\varepsilon = 0.1$ for all examples presented in this article.) Then, the directional curvature terms at $\mathbf{x}_{pq}$ can be approximated as

$$\begin{aligned}
\Big(\frac{\phi_x}{|\nabla\phi|}\Big)_x(\mathbf{x}_{pq}) &\approx \frac{1}{d_{pq,W}}\phi_{p-1,q} - \Big(\frac{1}{d_{pq,W}} + \frac{1}{d_{pq,E}}\Big)\phi_{pq} \\
&\quad + \frac{1}{d_{pq,E}}\phi_{p+1,q}, \\
\Big(\frac{\phi_y}{|\nabla\phi|}\Big)_y(\mathbf{x}_{pq}) &\approx \frac{1}{d_{pq,S}}\phi_{p,q-1} - \Big(\frac{1}{d_{pq,S}} + \frac{1}{d_{pq,N}}\Big)\phi_{pq} \\
&\quad + \frac{1}{d_{pq,N}}\phi_{p,q+1}, \\
\Big(\frac{\phi_{x'}}{|\nabla_{\mathbf{x}'}\phi|}\Big)_{x'}(\mathbf{x}_{pq}) &\approx \frac{1}{2}\Big[\frac{1}{d_{pq,SW}}\phi_{p-1,q-1} \\
&\quad - \Big(\frac{1}{d_{pq,SW}} + \frac{1}{d_{pq,NE}}\Big)\phi_{pq} + \frac{1}{d_{pq,NE}}\phi_{p+1,q+1}\Big], \\
\Big(\frac{\phi_{y'}}{|\nabla_{\mathbf{x}'}\phi|}\Big)_{y'}(\mathbf{x}_{pq}) &\approx \frac{1}{2}\Big[\frac{1}{d_{pq,SE}}\phi_{p+1,q-1} \\
&\quad - \Big(\frac{1}{d_{pq,SE}} + \frac{1}{d_{pq,NW}}\Big)\phi_{pq} + \frac{1}{d_{pq,NW}}\phi_{p-1,q+1}\Big].
\end{aligned} \tag{12}$$

Now, we discretize the gradient magnitudes as follows.

$$\begin{aligned}
|\nabla\phi|_1(\mathbf{x}_{pq}) &\approx \Big[\frac{1}{2}\Big(\frac{1}{d_{pq,W}} + \frac{1}{d_{pq,E}}\Big)\Big]^{-1}, \\
|\nabla\phi|_2(\mathbf{x}_{pq}) &\approx \Big[\frac{1}{2}\Big(\frac{1}{d_{pq,S}} + \frac{1}{d_{pq,N}}\Big)\Big]^{-1}, \\
|\nabla_{\mathbf{x}'}\phi|_1(\mathbf{x}_{pq}) &\approx \Big[\frac{1}{2}\Big(\frac{1}{d_{pq,SW}} + \frac{1}{d_{pq,NE}}\Big)\Big]^{-1}, \\
|\nabla_{\mathbf{x}'}\phi|_2(\mathbf{x}_{pq}) &\approx \Big[\frac{1}{2}\Big(\frac{1}{d_{pq,SE}} + \frac{1}{d_{pq,NW}}\Big)\Big]^{-1},
\end{aligned} \tag{13}$$

where the right-hand sides are harmonic averages of finite difference approximations of the gradient magnitudes in x-, y-, x'-, and y'-coordinate directions, respectively. Then, it follows from (10), (12), and (13) that

$$\begin{aligned}
\mathcal{K}(\phi)(\mathbf{x}_{pq}) \approx\; & 6\phi_{pq} - a_{pq,W}\,\phi_{p-1,q} - a_{pq,E}\,\phi_{p+1,q} \\
& - a_{pq,S}\,\phi_{p,q-1} - a_{pq,N}\,\phi_{p,q+1} \\
& - a_{pq,SW}\,\phi_{p-1,q-1} - a_{pq,NE}\,\phi_{p+1,q+1} \\
& - a_{pq,SE}\,\phi_{p+1,q-1} - a_{pq,NW}\,\phi_{p-1,q+1},
\end{aligned} \tag{14}$$

where

$$\begin{aligned}
a_{pq,W} &= \frac{2\,d_{pq,E}}{d_{pq,W} + d_{pq,E}}, & a_{pq,E} &= \frac{2\,d_{pq,W}}{d_{pq,W} + d_{pq,E}}, \\
a_{pq,S} &= \frac{2\,d_{pq,N}}{d_{pq,S} + d_{pq,N}}, & a_{pq,N} &= \frac{2\,d_{pq,S}}{d_{pq,S} + d_{pq,N}}, \\
a_{pq,SW} &= \frac{d_{pq,NE}}{d_{pq,SW} + d_{pq,NE}}, & a_{pq,NE} &= \frac{d_{pq,SW}}{d_{pq,SW} + d_{pq,NE}}, \\
a_{pq,SE} &= \frac{d_{pq,NW}}{d_{pq,SE} + d_{pq,NW}}, & a_{pq,NW} &= \frac{d_{pq,SE}}{d_{pq,SE} + d_{pq,NW}}.
\end{aligned}$$

Here it is easy to see that $a_{pq,W} + a_{pq,E} + a_{pq,S} + a_{pq,N} = 4$ and $a_{pq,SW} + a_{pq,NE} + a_{pq,SE} + a_{pq,NW} = 2$.

Let A denote the coefficient matrix of $\mathcal{K}$. Then, the GW curvature estimate K corresponding to the 9-point stencil can be expressed algebraically as

$$K = A\boldsymbol{\phi}, \tag{15}$$

where $\boldsymbol{\phi}$ is the vector representation of ϕ. It follows from (10) and (14) that the nonzero entries of A corresponding to $\mathbf{x}_{pq}$, in the stencil formulation, are

$$[A]_{pq} = \begin{bmatrix} -a_{pq,NW} & -a_{pq,N} & -a_{pq,NE} \\ -a_{pq,W} & 6 & -a_{pq,E} \\ -a_{pq,SW} & -a_{pq,S} & -a_{pq,SE} \end{bmatrix}. \tag{16}$$

Thus the sum of off-diagonal elements in a row of A is clearly -6 and therefore the Jacobi matrix of A defines a weighted averaging operator.

Note that the intermediate surface ϕ satisfies $\Delta\phi = 0$ except at the sample points. Thus the GW curvature vector K in (15) may have values large in modulus at sample points and small elsewhere. (The numerical schemes in (13) make the evaluated gradient magnitudes large at sample points.)

We will set the zero curvature, $K = 0$, along the image boundary for simplicity. For the evaluation of the coefficient matrix A at boundary points, the model should incorporate a boundary condition, which may affect the final outcome near the boundary. In this article, we will employ the Dirichlet boundary condition for the first pixel point $(0, 0)$ and the no-flux boundary condition for the other boundary points. The Dirichlet boundary condition makes the first row of the algebraic system strictly diagonally dominant, which in turn allows the coefficient matrix A to be nonsingular [21]. Thus (6.vi) can define the correction surface that satisfies the Dirichlet condition $w_{0,0} = \phi_{0,0}$.

3.3 Smoothing K

We adopt a simple 9-point averaging iteration for the smoothing operation: Let $K_0 = K$ and find K_m, $m = 1, 2, \cdots$, defined by

$$K_{m,p,q} = \frac{1}{9}\Big(\sum_{j=q-1}^{q+1}\sum_{i=p-1}^{p+1} K_{m-1,i,j}\Big), \tag{17}$$

for which the iteration stops either after certain number of iterations or when the relative change in L^∞-norm is less than a tolerance τ_s, i.e.,

$$\|K_m - K_{m-1}\|_\infty / \|K_m\|_\infty < \tau_s. \tag{18}$$

It has been observed from various numerical examples that the smoothed curvature $\widetilde{K}$ must be smooth enough to result in smooth correction surfaces (and the final smooth image). However, an oversmoothed curvature may slow down the convergence speed of the R-CIM iteration. When the curvature is smoothed reasonably, the R-CIM has converged in 3-6 iterations for all examples we have tested.

3.4 Construction of a smooth correction surface w

In each iteration of the R-CIM (6), the final nontrivial task is to construct a smooth correction surface $\mathbf{w}$ as the solution of (6.vi). Note that the curvature smoothing operator introduces tangible changes to the curvature only in the vicinity of sample points and therefore the solution $\mathbf{w}$ can be obtained correspondingly, incorporating changes of ϕ there. Thus, when the initial value of $\mathbf{w}$ is set ϕ, local relaxation methods such as the Jacobi method must converge in a few iterations.

3.5 A synthetic example

For a comparison purpose, we have also implemented the inverse-distance weighting (IDW) method [22], which is defined as

$$u(\mathbf{x}) = \frac{\sum_k w(\mathbf{x}_k)u(\mathbf{x}_k)}{\sum_k w(\mathbf{x}_k)}, \quad w(\mathbf{x}_k) = \frac{1}{\|\mathbf{x}-\mathbf{x}_k\|^p}, \quad (19)$$

where $u(\mathbf{x})$ is the estimated value at location $\mathbf{x}$, $u(\mathbf{x}_k)$ is the value at a neighboring sample point $\mathbf{x}_k$, $w(\mathbf{x}_k)$ denotes the weight for $\mathbf{x}_k$, $\|\cdot\|$ is the Euclidean norm, and p is an exponential number greater than or equal to 2. Here the summation takes place over a vicinity of $\mathbf{x}$, which often is a rectangular window centered at $\mathbf{x}$ and having a radius r. The IDW method is one of the most popular interpolation algorithms particularly for digital elevation modeling of point cloud data of geospatial survey acquired by the light detection and ranging (LiDAR) technology.

For the following example, the curvature is smoothed by 10 iterations of the smoothing operation (17) and the outer iteration of the R-CIM is stopped when $\|\mathbf{r}\|_\infty < \tau = 0.1$.

In Figure 2, we present a synthetic example of image reconstruction. Figure 2(a) shows a set of scattered data, of which the image domain contains 100×100 pixels and 20 random data points having values ranging between 0 and 255. As one can see from Figure 2(c), the R-CIM has constructed an image surface in four iterations, starting from the scattered data in Figure 2(a). Unlike the IDW method which has resulted in a nonsmooth surface as in Figure 2(b), the new method is able to produce a smooth surface everywhere including data points. The four iterations of the R-CIM took 0.237 seconds on a 2.6 GHz laptop computer, while the IDW method (with the search radius $r = 100$) finished the interpolation in 0.320 seconds. For this synthetic example, the R-CIM as an iterative algorithm is about 35% more efficient than the IDW method, a direction evaluation method.

4. Numerical Experiments

The R-CIM (6) has proved superior properties for the recovery of arbitrarily spaced image data. This section gives numerical examples to show effectiveness of the new image reconstruction method.

For all examples presented in this section, two iterations are applied for the smoothing operation (17) and the outer iteration of the R-CIM is stopped when $\|\mathbf{r}\|_\infty < \tau = 0.1$.

Figure 3 depicts (a) the Fruits image, (b) its randomly sampled data of 5% sampling rate, and reconstructed images by (c) the IDW with search radius of $r = 20$ and (d) the R-CIM in five iterations. As one can see from Figure 3(d), the R-CIM has reconstructed the image satisfactorily; the resulting image shows clear and sharp edges. Note that it is not blurry, although all correction surfaces are smooth. The IDW results in a much worse image, as shown in Figure 3(c), than the new method. For this example, the R-CIM converges in 5 iterations taking 1.43 CPU seconds of the 2.6 GHz laptop computer.

The computational cost for the example in Figure 3 measures only $6.03(= 1.43/0.237)$ times that of the tent-pole example in Figure 2, while the image size and the sample size become respectively 6.55 and 163.8 times larger. The R-CIM must be relatively more efficient for denser sample points; it may finished all the computational tasks in $\mathcal{O}(N)$ operations, where N is the number of grid points. It should be noticed that major components in the R-CIM simulation are the algebraic solvers for the construction of intermediate surfaces ϕ in (6.iii) and correction surfaces $\mathbf{w}$ in (6.vi). We are currently developing fast algebraic solvers for those tasks, in order for the R-CIM to be applicable for *real-time processing* of huge datasets, e.g., point cloud data of geospatial survey.

Figure 4 contains an image reconstruction result for the Lena image in color. The methods are applied channel-by-channel in the RGB format. As one can see from the figure, the IDW has produced an image of many artifacts as shown in Figure 4(c). On the other hand, the R-CIM again can construct a successful image of clear edges and of no significant artifacts (except for texture regions), although the sampling rate is just 8%. For this example, the R-CIM converges in four iterations. As the sampling rate increases, the first iterate of the R-CIM must become more accurate and the correction surfaces $\mathbf{w}_k$ in the second and later iterations ($k \geq 2$) should be a rapidly decreasing series in their magnitudes, which in turn makes the R-CIM converge faster.

5. Conclusions

This article has studied an innovative image reconstruction algorithm called the *recursive curvature interpolation method* (R-CIM), which is a PDE-based model and constructs smooth image surfaces for arbitrarily spaced data, incorporating a generalized curvature information as a driving force. Each iteration of the R-CIM consists of four steps: the computation of the misfit which is the difference between the data and the last undated image, the construction of an intermediate surface over the image domain, the estimation of smooth curvature information, and the construction of

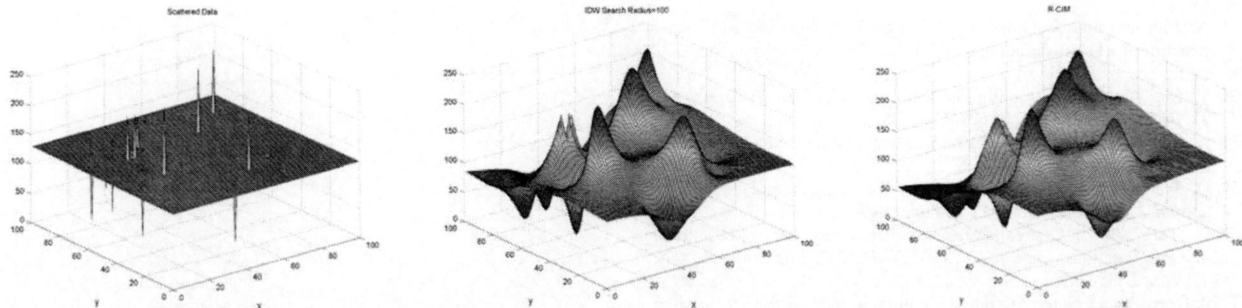

Fig. 2: A synthetic example of image reconstruction: (a) an arbitrarily spaced data in 100×100 pixels, and image surfaces constructed by (b) the IDW method with the search radius $r = 100$ and (c) the R-CIM converged in four iterations.

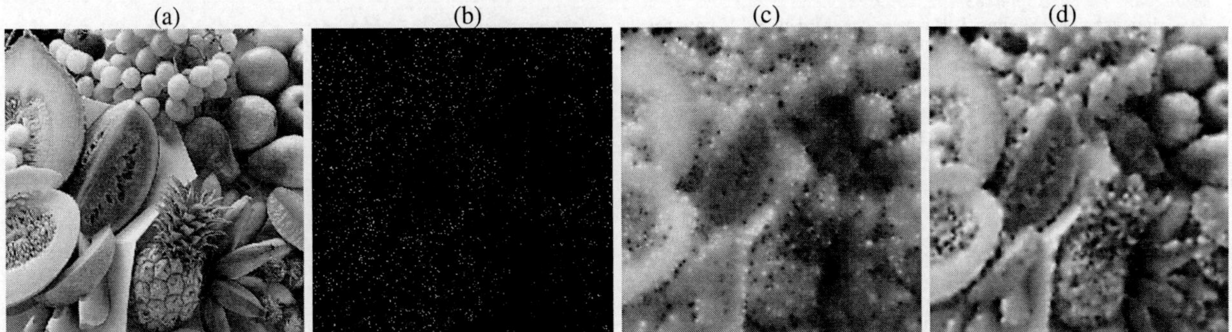

Fig. 3: Fruits: (a) The original image in 256×256 pixels, (b) a randomly sampled data (the sampling rate=5%), and reconstructed images by (c) the IDW with search radius of $r = 20$ and (d) the R-CIM in five iterations.

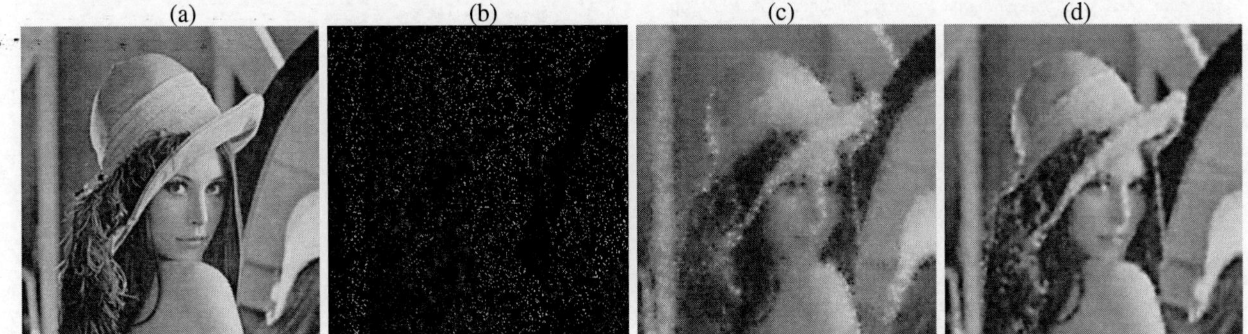

Fig. 4: Lena: (a) The original color image in 256×256 pixels, (b) a randomly sampled data (the sampling rate=8%), and reconstructed images by (c) the IDW with search radius of $r = 20$ and (d) the R-CIM in four iterations.

a smooth correction surface to update the last iterate. The iteration converges as the misfit diminishes and therefore the R-CIM is an interpolator. In order to reduce ringing artifacts, the R-CIM utilizes 9-point difference schemes for both the curvature evaluation and the image surface construction. Numerical schemes are presented in detail and numerical examples have been provided to show effectiveness of the R-CIM for image reconstruction of arbitrarily spaced data. It has been numerically verified that the R-CIM results in successful images of sharp edges, although the sampling rate is less than 10%; the suggested procedure outperforms the inverse-distance weighting method, one of most popular surface construction algorithms.

Acknowledgment

S. Kim's work is supported in part by NSF grant DMS-1228337.

References

[1] H. Feichtinger and K. Gröchenig, "Theory and practice of irregular sampling," in *Wavelet: Mathematics and Applications*, J. Benedetto and M. Frazier, Eds. Boca Raton, FL: CRC, 1994, pp. 305–363.

[2] A. Aldroubi and K. Gröchenig, "Non-uniform sampling and reconstruction in shift-invariant spaces," *SIAM Rev.*, vol. 43, pp. 585–620, 2001.

[3] Y. Liu, "Irregular sampling for spline wavelet," *IEEE Trans. Inf. Theory*, vol. 42, no. 2, pp. 623–627, 1996.

[4] A. Glassner, *Principles of Digital Image Synthesis*. San Mateo, CA: Morgan Kaufmann, 1995.

[5] D. Watson, *Contouring: A Guide to the Analysis and Display of Spatial Data*. New York: Pergamon, 1992.

[6] G. Turk and J. OB́rien, "Shape transformation using variational implicit functions," in *Proc. ACM SIGGRAPH*, Los Angeles, CA, 1999, pp. 335–342.

[7] F. Chen and D. Suter, "Using fast multipole method for accelerating the evaluation of splines," *IEEE Comput. Sci. Eng.*, vol. 5, no. 3, pp. 24–31, 1998.

[8] A. Faul and M. Powel, "Proof of convergence of an iterative technique for thin plate spline interpolation in two dimensions," *Adv. Comput. Math.*, vol. 11, no. 2, pp. 183–192, 1999.

[9] M. Arigovindan, M. Sühling, P. Hunziker, and M. Unser, "Variational image reconstruction from arbitrarily spaced samples: A fast multiresolution spline solution," *IEEE Trans. Image Process.*, vol. 14, no. 4, pp. 450–460, 2005.

[10] S. Lee, G. Wolberg, and S. Shin, "Scattered data interpolation with multilevel B-splines," *IEEE Trans. Vis. Comput. Graph.*, vol. 3, no. 3, pp. 228–244, 1997.

[11] R. Szeliski, "Fast surface interpolation using hierarchical basis functions," *IEEE Trans. Pattern Anal. Mach. Intell.*, vol. 12, no. 6, pp. 513–528, 1990.

[12] D. Terzopoulos, "The computation of visible-surface representation," *IEEE Trans. Pattern Anal. Mach. Intell.*, vol. 10, no. 4, pp. 417–438, 1988.

[13] C. Vázquez, E. Dubois, and J. Konrad, "Reconstruction of nonuniformly sampled images in spline spaces," *IEEE Trans. Image Process.*, vol. 14, no. 6, pp. 713–725, 2005.

[14] H. Choi and R. Baraniuk, "Interpolation and denoising of nonuniformly sampled data using wavelet-domain processing," in *Proc. IEEE Int. Conf. Acoustics Speech Signal Process.*, Phoenix, AZ, 1999, pp. 1645–1648.

[15] N. Nguyen and P. Milinfar, "A wavelet-based interpolation-restoration method for superresolution (wavelet superresolution)," *Circuits Syst. Signal Process.*, vol. 19, no. 4, pp. 321–338, 2000.

[16] A. Orzan, A. Bousseau, H. Winnemöller, P. Barla, J. Thollot, and D. Salesin, "Diffusion curves: A vector representation for smooth-shaded images," *ACM Trans. Graphics*, vol. 27, no. 3, p. Article 92, 2008.

[17] H. Kim, Y. Cha, and S. Kim, "Curvature interpolation method for image zooming," *IEEE Trans. Image Process.*, vol. 20, no. 7, pp. 1895–1903, 2011.

[18] L. Rudin, S. Osher, and E. Fatemi, "Nonlinear total variation based noise removal algorithms," *Physica D*, vol. 60, pp. 259–268, 1992.

[19] T. Chan and J. Shen, *Image Processing and Analysis*. Philadelphia: SIAM, 2005.

[20] A. Marquina and S. Osher, "Explicit algorithms for a new time dependent model based on level set motion for nonlinear deblurring and noise removal," *SIAM J. Sci. Comput.*, vol. 22, pp. 387–405, 2000.

[21] R. Varga, *Matrix Iterative Analysis*. Englewood Cliffs, NJ: Prentice-Hall, 1962.

[22] D. Shepard, "A two-dimensional interpolation function for irregularly-spaced data," in *Proceedings of the 1968 ACM National Conference*, 1968, pp. 517–524.

A Hybrid Regularization Algorithm for High Contrast Tomographic Image Reconstruction

Peyman Rahmati[1], Manuchehr Soleimani[2], and Andy Adler[1]
[1]Department of Systems and Computer Engineering, Carleton University, Ottawa, Ontario, Canada
[2]Department of Electronics & Electrical Engineering, University of Bath, UK

Abstract— *The common Level set based reconstruction method (LSRM) is applied to solve a piecewise constant inverse problem using one level set function and considers two different conductivity quantities for the background and the inclusion (two phases inclusion). The more the number of the piecewise constant conductivities in the medium, the higher the calculation effort of the LSRM, using multiple level set functions, will be. The assumption of piecewise constant conductivities (coefficients) is to discriminate between two regions with sharp conductivity interface; however, it may not be a realistic assumption when there are smooth conductivity gradients inside each region as well. In this paper, we propose a hybrid regularization method (HRM), which is a two steps solution, to solve ill-posed, nonlinear inverse problem with smooth conductivity transitions. The first step of this hybrid inversion framework plays the role of an initializing procedure for the second step, and acts in a similar way as a* source type *inversion method. In the first stage, the LSRM with one level set function is applied to determine the region of interest, which is defined as the region with sharpest interface. Then in the second stage, an inverse solver with penalty terms based on sum of absolute values (L1 norms), which are highly robust against measurement errors, is applied to reconstruct the conductivity changes inside the determined ROI. The generated forward solution in the final iteration of the level set is fed to the second stage where the L1 norms based penalty terms are minimized using primal-dual interior point method (PDIPM). The PDIPM has been shown to be effective in minimizing the L1 norms. The reconstructed images with the proposed HRM maintains the edge information as well as the smooth conductivity variations, a trait absent in all previously established level set based reconstruction method. The integration of the LSRM and the PDIPM can generate less noisy reconstructed images when comparing either with the reconstruction results of the PDIPM or with those of squared error based reconstruction methods, such as Gauss-Newton (GN) method. Our proposed HRM is tested on a circular 2D phantom with either sharp conductivity gradients (piecewise constant coefficients) or smooth conductivity transitions (smooth coefficients). We show that the proposed HRM maintains sharp edges and is robust against the measurement noise.*

Keywords: Inverse problem, tomographic image reconstruction, primal-dual interior point method, level set, sum of absolute values (L1 norms), and electrical impedance tomography

1. Introduction

Tomography has found widespread applications in many scientific fields, including physics, chemistry, astronomy, geophysics, and medicine. Tomographic image reconstruction is a visualization technique to produce a cross sectional image of the internal structures of an object. Different physical quantities are measured in different tomographic imaging modalities. For instance, X-ray CT measures the number of x-ray photons transmitted through the patient along individual projection lines and reconstructs the distribution of the linear attenuation coefficients in the desired cross sectional slice. To be able to easily differentiate between variant tissue types, high contrast image reconstruction is highly demanded in tomography. In this paper, we propose a novel high contrast image reconstruction algorithm to produce high quality reconstructed images. To show the implementation of the proposed reconstruction algorithm, we apply electrical impedance tomography (EIT).

EIT is a non-invasive tomographic imaging modality which reconstructs the internal conductivity distribution using the measurement of several difference voltages collected from the electrode pairs attached at the surface of the medium. Electrical current is injected into the medium and the resulting difference voltages at the surface of the medium is measured using several electrodes. The conductivity distribution is then estimated based on the measured voltages and medium geometry.

EIT image reconstruction is an ill-defined inverse problem. The possible number of surface measurements is limited creating a highly under-determined system with low spatial resolution. To address the instability of the EIT images, there are different regularization techniques to introduce priori information into the reconstruction algorithm. The traditional priori information is to have smooth conductivity gradients inside the medium. The assumption of smooth conductivity changes creates blurred reconstructed images. However, the physiologically meaningful reconstructed images are created when we consider sharp conductivity changes between organ boundaries. There are several reconstruction techniques to maintain sharp edges. Dai and Adler (2008) used a weighted identity matrix (LDM) for the regularization [2]. They assume piecewise smooth conductivity changes in the medium and use total variation (TV) technique to suppress the background fluctuations. Borsic (2010) compared the LDM technique and the Primal Dual-Interior Point Method (PDIPM) [1]. Borsic and Adler (2012) show the superiority of the L1 norm usage when comparing with L2 norm [3]. They use the L1 norm, on either the regularization or the data term of an inverse problem to produce higher quality reconstructed images when comparing with reconstructed images of applying L2 norm. We show the first application of level set based reconstruction method (LSRM) to produce clinically useful images by preserving the edges [4]. The LSRM is a nonlinear inversion scheme using L2 norm on the data and the regularization term. The implementation of the LSRM is based on the Gauss-Newton (GN) optimization approach to iteratively reduce a given cost functional, which is the norm of the difference between the simulated and measured data. In comparison to the voxel based reconstruction method (VBRM), the LSRM has the advantage of introducing the conductivity of background and that of inclusions as known priori information into the reconstruction algorithm, enabling it to preserve the edges and to provide sharp contrasts.

In this paper, we formulate a hybrid regularization method (HRM) containing the advantage of using the common LSRM in tracking propagating interfaces, preserving the edges, and that of using L1 norm in precisely reconstructing the conductivity variations inside the medium. We introduce the PDIPM solver into the level set based GN optimization algorithm (figure 1). We tested the proposed HRM using a circular 2D phantom under different test conditions: 1) without added noise. 2) with added zero-mean Gaussian noise (-60dB). 3) with noise (-60 dB) and data outliers (one measurement out of 208 for every EIT frame was missed). The 2D phantom is used in two different scenarios: 1) when there are sharp inclusions in the upper and lower regions of the phantom, 2) when there are smooth conductivity changes when traveling from the inclusion boundary towards the center of the inclusion. We compare the results of the proposed HRM with two the state of the art reconstruction algorithms (the PDIPM with L1 norms on the inverse problem terms and the GN approach)over the same simulated data and test condition.

2. Methodology

The idea of the HRM is similar to the idea of a *source-type* inverse scheme, where a nonlinear inverse problem is divided into two stand-alone subproblems and each subproblem is solved separately [6]. The advantage of *source-type* inverse method is its low sensitivity to the nonlinearity of the inverse problem. In the first stage of the proposed HRM, a *equivalent source* which fits the data (forward solution), with the assumption of known background and inclusion conductivity, is produced. The equivalent source is an approximation of the final inverse solution. Assuming the known background and inclusion conductivities, the LSRM is applied in the first stage of the HRM. The inverse solution of the LSRM is an approximation of the final solution and is defined as region of interest (ROI), the region with sharpest interface enclosing smooth conductivity transitions. In the second stage of the HRM, a PDIPM solver is applied to solve the second subproblem with smooth conductivity transitions defined over the achieved ROI from the first stage. In the second stage, PDIPM solver with penalty terms based on sum of absolute values (L1 norms), which are highly robust against measurement errors, is applied to reconstruct the smooth conductivity changes inside the determined ROI. The generated forward solution in the first stage, achieved in the final iteration of the level set, is fed to the second stage where the L1 norm based penalty terms are minimized using the PDIPM. The PDIPM has been shown to be effective in minimizing the L1 norms [3]. In the following, we introduce the applied LSRM. For details about the PDIPM framework, we refer the reader to [3].

The LSRM has been shown the capability of being suitable for reconstructing object with fast changes at its interface over time [5], [4]. The classic formulation of the LSRM assumes that the reconstructed image can take only two conductivity values: one for background with value σ_b and another one for inclusions with value σ_i. The regions which form the background and the inclusions are defined by a level set function (LSF), Ψ, which is a signed distance function to identify the unknown interface between the two high contrast regions. The value of the LSF is zero on the interface, negative inside the interface, and positive outside. A detailed study of the LSRM is shown in [4].

To begin with the HRM, we need to define an initial LSF, which may be a circle on level zero; and then deform this initial LSF using a predefined energy functional iteratively. Figure 1 represents the steps as k represents the iteration number. After defining the initial LSF, the mapping function Φ projects the LSF to a 2D mesh to be fed to difference solver block to calculate the system sensitivity matrix, Jacobian (J_k). To update the energy functional of the LSRM, ΔLSF_k, the element differential potential vectors, Δd_i is calculated. The initial LSF is then deformed by ΔLSF_k generating a new LSF. This new LSF is fed again to difference solver block for another iteration if the current iteration number (k) is not bigger than a maximum iteration number (K). According to the chain rule, the level set (LS) sensitivity matrix can be written as below:

$$Sensitivity = J_{LS} = \frac{\partial d}{\partial \Psi} = (\tfrac{\partial G}{\partial \Phi(\Psi)})(\tfrac{\partial \Phi(\Psi)}{\partial \Psi}) = (J_{GN})(M), \qquad (1)$$

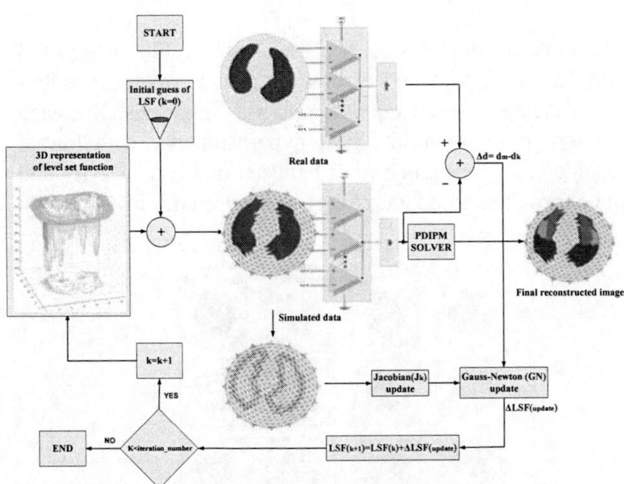

Fig. 1: The hybrid regularization technique using difference solver. Steps from top to down: LSF initial guess, inverse difference solver, PDIPM solver, Guass-Newton update, LSF displacement by the given update, and iteration number increment.

where $\frac{\partial G}{\partial \Phi(\Psi)}$ stands for the traditional GN sensitivity matrix (J_{GN}), and $\frac{\partial \Phi(\Psi)}{\partial \Psi} = M$ is the matrix representing the mapping function $(\Phi(\Psi))$. Then, the new GN update is [4]

$$\Psi_{k+1} = \Psi_k + \lambda \left[(J^T_{(LS,k)} J_{(LS,k)} + \alpha^2 L^T L)^{-1} \times (J^T_{(LS,k)}(d_{real} - d(\Psi_k))) - \left[\alpha^2 L^T L(\Psi_k - \Psi_{int}) \right] = \right.$$

$$\Psi_k + GN_{update} = LSF(k) + \Delta LSF, \quad (2)$$

where Ψ_{int} in the update term corresponds to the initial estimate of the LSF. The length parameter λ determines the magnitude of the LSF displacement, changing the shape of inclusion, in a given update. The higher the λ, the higher the LSF displacement will be. The effect of the regularization parameter α depends on the choice of the regularization operator L. As α increases, the smoother the final LSF tends to be.

In the second stage of the HRM, the forward solution of the LSRM, which is the differential potential vectors of the simulated data (equation (3) in the Appendix A), is fed to the PDIPM solver. The PDIPM iteratively minimizes the norms (L1 or L2 norms) on the data and the regularization terms of the inverse problem, see [3]. The inverse solution of the PDIPM is the smooth conductivity changes inside the ROI, defined by the final evolution of the level set function at final iteration K. Plugging the initial forward solution, measured from the achieved ROI from the first stage, into the PDIPM formulation, the convergence of the PDIPM happens rapidly.

3. Simulated data

We used 16 electrodes on one electrode plane with a circular finite element model. The adjacent current stimulation was considered for the evaluation of our simulation. Figure 2(a) shows the used 2D phantom to generate simulated data with 1024 elements. The phantom contains two sharp inclusions with the same conductivity located in the upper and the lower part of the mesh. The background conductivity value is 1 S/m and the inclusions have the conductivity of 0.9 S/m. The inverse problem used the mesh density of 576 elements, which was different than the mesh density of the forward problem (1024 elements). Figure 3(a) simulates the smooth conductivity changes in a circular, low conductive inclusion. The conductivity gradually decreases when traveling from the most outer band towards the inner. The most outer band has the highest conductivity of 0.9 S/m. The conductivity decreases smoothly with a small step size of 0.1 S/m as the distance to the center of the inclusion decreases. The most inner circle has the lowest conductivity of 0.4 S/m.

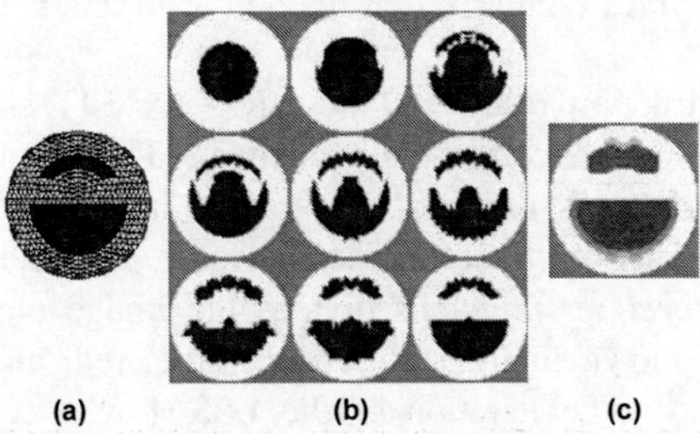

Fig. 2: The reconstructed image using the proposed hybrid regularization technique with difference solver. (a) The 2D phantom applied to generate the simulated data. (b) The reconstructed images of the level set based reconstruction method at every iteration. (c) The final reconstructed image using the proposed hybrid regularization method at iteration 9.

4. Results

The performance of the proposed HRM was assessed over three different test conditions: 1) original numerical phantom, 2) noisy phantom with an added zero mean Gaussian noise bringing the SNR to the typical value of 60 dB. 3) data outliers plus noise. Figure 2 shows the simulated result using the proposed hybrid regularization method. Figure 2(a) is the applied 2d phantom. The reconstructed image of the LSRM in each iteration is shown in figure 2(b). Figure 2(c) shows the final reconstructed image from the proposed HRM. The L1 norms on both the data term and the regularization term are applied to achieve the result presented in figure 2(c). The ROI is defined by the LSRM (the lower panel on the right corner in figure 2(b)) and the conductivity values inside the ROI are approximated using the PDIPM solver in figure 2(c). HRM image shows sharp edges at the interface as well as the conductivities inside the ROI, the region segmented by the level set technique. The reconstructed image by the proposed hybrid technique is very similar to the real phantom, with almost no artifacts at the electrode boundary. Figure 3 shows

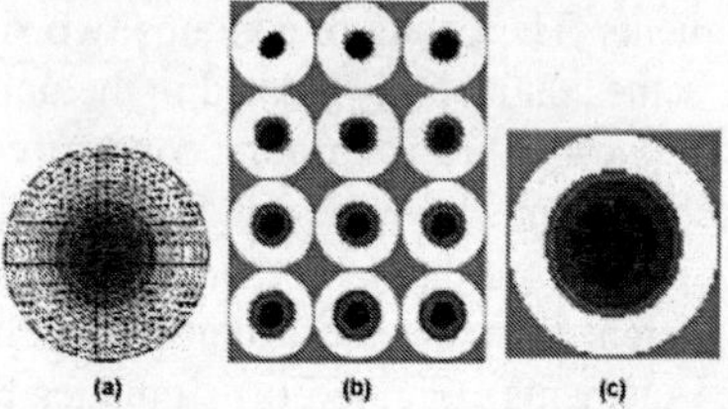

Fig. 3: The reconstructed image using the proposed hybrid regularization technique over EIT simulated data with smooth conductivity transitions. (a) The 2D phantom applied to simulate a low conductive inclusion with smooth conductivity changes. (b) The reconstructed images of the level set based reconstruction method with *two level set functions* at every iteration. (c) The final reconstructed image using the proposed hybrid regularization method at iteration 12.

the reconstruction results of the HRM for EIT simulated data with smooth conductivity changes. The conductivity values decrease as a function of radius in figure 3(a). In the upper panel on the left corner in figure 3(b), the LSRM with *two level set functions* divides the image plane into 4 regions, shown in light blue, dark blue, red, and white (background). The iteration of the LSRM with two level set functions are depicted in figure 3(b). The convergence is achieved after 12 iterations and the ROI is determined in the lower panel on the right corner in figure 3(b). Figure 3(c) shows the final reconstructed image of the HRM, which approximates the smooth conductivity changes inside the determined ROI. Figure 4 compares the HRM with two the state of the art EIT reconstruction methods ($PDIPM_{L2L2}$ and $PDIPM_{L1L1}$). In figure 4, a set of simulated results using PDIPM framework for L2 norm on the data mismatch term and the L2 norm on the regularization term (L2L2 problem) as well as for L1L1 problem under 3 different test conditions is represented. The row (a) is when there is no added noise to EIT simulated data. The row (b) is when we add zero-mean Gaussina noise (-60 dB) to EIT simulated data, and the row (c) is when there are both added noise and data outliers. As it can be seen in figure 4, there are acceptable reconstructed images when there is no noise (row (a)). However, the quality of the reconstructed images drops with the added noise (row(b)). The HRM results offer lower sensitivity to added noise (the last two panels in row (b)) when comparing with PDIPM results (the first two panels in row (b)). The reconstruction quality noticeably drops in row (c) for the PDIPM when there are data outliers and measurement noise. The HRM results are slightly less sensitive to added noise and data outliers, when comparing with the results of the PDIPM. The hyperparameter selection for all the results in figure 4 was based on trial and error over a wide range of values including very small quantities to very big ones. For each method in figure 4, the best hyperparameter with lowest residue error (mismatch term between real conductivity and the approximated conductivity) was selected.

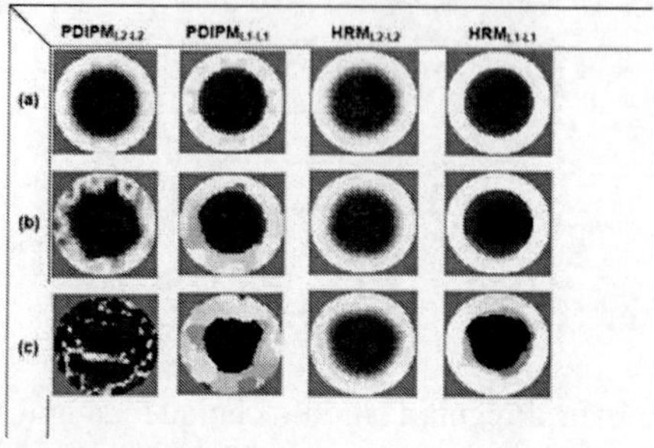

Fig. 4: EIT Reconstructed images for the 2D phantom in figure 3(a) using the proposed hybrid regularization technique as well as PDIPM algorithm with L2L2, or L1L1 norms under 3 different test conditions. (a) without any added noise to the simulated data. (b) with added zero-mean Gaussian noise (-60 dB). (c) with the presence of data outliers and noise.

5. Discussion and conclusion

We formulate a hybrid regularization method in difference mode to address the instability of the EIT reconstruction method. The concept of the proposed HRM is similar to the idea of a *source-type* inverse scheme, where a nonlinear inverse problem is divided into two stand-alone subproblems and each subproblem is solved separately. The proposed two step solution makes the final inverse solution of the HRM less sensitive to non-linearity of the problem, which is the notion of *source type* methods. In the first stage of the HRM, we approximate the inverse solution using the level set method and define a region of interest with sharpest interface, containing smooth conductivity transitions. Then in the second stage, the PDIPM solver is utilized to reconstruct the smooth conductivity changes inside the ROI. The main advantage of the proposed HRM is that it monitors both the smooth conductivity changes inside the inclusion as well as the big conductivity changes at the interface between the inclusion and the background (figure 3) with minimum amount of electrode artifacts at the medium boundary. The test studies based on Figure 4 show that PDIPM_{L2L2} is sensitive to the measurement noise as well as the data outliers (the first column of figure 4). The PDIPM_{L1L1} is better robust against the measurement noise (row (b) in figure 3). The HRM_{L2L2} is not severely affected by the measurement noise (row (b) in figure 4); however, is sensitive when there is both outliers and noise (row (c) in figure 4). The HRM_{L1L1} shows better performance in two scenarios: when there is no noise (row (a) in figure 4) , and with added zero-mean Gaussian noise (row (b) in figure 4).

6. Appendix A

The nonlinear error function with L2 norms over the data fidelity and the regularization terms can be written as follows:

$$e = \|y - F(\Psi(x))\|^2 + \|\Phi(\Psi(x)) - x_0\|^2, \quad (3)$$

where,

$$F(\Psi(x)) = G(\Phi(\Psi(x))), \quad (4)$$

function F maps electrical conductivity distribution $\Phi(\Psi(x))$ to the measured data, G is system matrix, and $\Psi(x)$ is the level set function. To minimize the nonlinear error function, we take the first derivative of the error function with respect to $\Psi(x)$:

$$\frac{de}{d\Psi(x)} = \frac{d}{d\Psi(x)}[(y - F(\Psi(x)))^t(y - F(\Psi(x))) + (\Phi(\Psi(x)) - x_0)^t R(\Phi(\Psi(x)) - x_0)] = \frac{d}{d\Psi(x)}[y^t y - 2y^t F(\Psi(x)) + F(\Psi(x))^t F(\Psi(x)) + (\Phi(\Psi(x)) - x_0)^t R(\Phi(\Psi(x)) - x_0)] = 0, \quad (5)$$

We define:

$$J_{LS} = \frac{\partial F(\Psi(x))}{\partial \Psi(x)} = (\frac{\partial G}{\partial \Phi(\Psi(x))})(\frac{\partial \Phi(\Psi(x))}{\partial \Psi(x)}) = (J)(M), \quad (6)$$

we indicate $F(\Psi(x)) = F$, $\Phi(\Psi(x)) = X$, thus:

$$\frac{de}{d\Psi(x)} = -2(JM)^t y + 2(JM)^t F(\Psi(x)) + 2M^t R(\Phi(\Psi(x)) - x_0) = 0,$$

$$\frac{de}{d\Psi(x)} = -M^t J^t y + M^t J^t F + M^t R(X - x_0) = 0,$$

$$M^t J^t F + M^t R(X - x_0) = M^t J^t y, \quad (7)$$

we have $F = G(X)$, therefore:

$$\begin{aligned} M^t J^t G(X) + M^t RX &= M^t J^t y + M^t R x_0, \\ J_{LS}^t G(X) + M^t RX &= J_{LS}^t y + M^t R x_0, \quad (8) \end{aligned}$$

The solution, X, of (8), which is a nonlinear equation, is successively approximated during the iterations of the level set function $\Psi(x)$. The simplest approach to estimate X is to apply the common GN solver in every iteration of the level set function. In this case, we can approximate that:

$$X = (J^t J + R)^{-1} J^t y, \quad (9)$$

where R is the Tikhonov regularization matrix. The final forward solution of the LSRM (equation (4)) is fed as initial forward solution to the second stage of the proposed HRM. In the second stage, the L1 norms of data fidelity and regularization terms of the inverse problem are minimized using PDIPM framework, see Borsic and Adler (2012) for the details.

References

[1] A. Borsic, B. Graham, A. Adler, and W. Lionheart, *In vivo impedance imaging with total variation regularization*,IEEE Trans. Med. Imaging, vol. 29, pp. 44âĂŞ54, 2010.

[2] T. Dai, and A. Adler, *Electrical impedance tomography reconstruction using l1 norms for data and image terms*, IEEE EMBC, pp. 2721âĂŞ2724, 2008.

[3] A. Borsic, and A. Adler *A primal dual - interior point framework for using the l1-norm or the l2-norm on the data and regularization terms of inverse problems*, Inverse Problems, 2012.

[4] _, M. Soleimani, S. Pulletz, I. Frerichs, and A. Adler, *Level Set based Reconstruction Algorithm for EIT Lung Images: First Clinical Results*, Journal of Physiological Measurement, vol 33 p 739, 2012.

[5] M. Soleimani, O. Dorn, and W. R. B. Lionheart, *A Narrow-Band Level Set Method Applied to EIT in Brain for Cryosurgery Monitoring*, IEEE Trans. Bio. Eng., vol 53, No 11, 2006.

[6] W. C. Chew, Y. M. Wang, G. Otto, D. Lesselier, and J. Ch. Bolomey, *On the inverse source method of solving inverse scattering problems*, Journal of Inverse Problems, vol 10, p 547,1994.

Iterative Refinement by Smooth Curvature Correction for PDE-based Image Restoration

Anup Gautam[1], Jihee Kim[2], Doeun Kwak[3], and Seongjai Kim[4]
[1]Department of Mathematics and Statistics, Mississippi State University
Mississippi State, MS 39762-5921 USA Email: ag769@msstate.edu
[2] 956-28 Daechi 2-dong, Gangnam-gu, Seoul, S. Korea Email: misskjh@hanmail.net
[3]F-4708 Samsung Tower Palace, Dogok 2-dong, Gangnam-gu
Seoul, S. Korea Email: kwakj16@gsiscommunity.kr
[4]Department of Mathematics and Statistics, Mississippi State University
Mississippi State, MS 39762-5921 USA Email: skim@math.msstate.edu (Contact Author)

Abstract— *This article studies iterative refinement algorithms for PDE-based image restoration models. In order to restore fine structures in the image, iterative refinement procedures employing an original idea by Bregman have been introduced in image restoration. However, the Bregman iterative procedure first recovers fine scales of the image and then restores the noise to converge to the observed noisy image; it must be stopped* manually *when the quality of the obtained image appears satisfactory. This article introduces an effective refinement procedure called the smooth curvature correction (SCC) model to overcome the drawback of the Bregman iteration. By incorporating the smoothed curvature of the previous iterate as a source term, the new model can successfully produce a convergent sequence of images having a better restoration quality than the best result of the Bregman procedure. Various numerical examples are given to confirm the claim and to show effectiveness of the SCC model.*

Keywords: Smooth curvature correction (SCC) model, iterative refinement, partial differential equation (PDE), image restoration, Bregman iteration.

1. Introduction

Mathematical techniques have become important components of image processing, as the field requires higher reliability and efficiency. During the last two decades or so, mathematical tools of partial differential equations (PDEs) and functional analysis have been successfully applied for various image processing tasks, particularly for image denoising and restoration [1], [2], [3], [4], [5], [6]. Those PDE-based models have allowed researchers and practitioners not only to introduce new, effective computational procedures but also to improve traditional algorithms in image restoration.

However, these PDE-based models tend to either converge to a piecewise constant image or introduce image blur (undesired dissipation), partially because the models are derived by minimizing a functional of the image gradient. As a consequence, the conventional PDE-based models may lose interesting image fine structures. In order to reduce the artifact, researchers have studied various mathematical and numerical techniques which either incorporate more effective constraint terms and iterative refinement [7], [3], [8] or minimize a functional of second derivatives of the image [9], [10]. These new mathematical models may preserve fine structures better than conventional ones; however, more advanced models and appropriate numerical procedures are yet to be developed.

Iterative refinement procedures have been introduced in image restoration [11], [8], employing an original idea of Bregman [12], in order to recover fine structures in the image. The Bregman iterative procedure tries to produce a sequence of images for the signal adjusted by all of the previous residuals. Thus, it recovers not only fine scales of the image but also the noise and reveals a strong tendency to converge to the observed noisy signal. For this reason the Bregman iterative procedure must be stopped *manually* when the quality of the obtained image appears satisfactory.

This article suggests an effective refinement procedure called the *smooth curvature correction* (SCC) model to overcome the drawback of the Bregman iteration. The SCC model computes new iterates incorporating the smoothed curvature of the last iterate. It has been numerically verified that the new model can successfully produce a convergent sequence of images having a better restoration quality than the best result of the Bregman procedure.

An outline of the paper is as follows. In the next section, we begin with a brief review of PDE-based image denoising models and then present the Bregman iterative refinement procedure, as preliminaries. Section 3 introduces the SCC model, a new iterative refinement procedure, as an alternative to the Bregman procedure. A numerical strategy is also considered in the same section in order to choose effective residual-driven constraint parameters. In Section 4, the new SCC model is compared with the Bregman procedure, with and without the residual-driven constraint parameters. Various numerical examples are presented to show effectiveness of the SCC model. Section 5 summarizes and concludes our experiments.

2. Preliminaries

In this section, we present a brief review of PDE-based image denoising models, followed by the Bregman iterative refinement.

2.1 PDE-based denoising models

Given an observed (noisy) image $f : \Omega \to \mathbb{R}$, where Ω is the image domain which is an open subset in $\mathbb{R}^2$, we consider the noise model of the form

$$f = u + g(u)\eta, \tag{1}$$

where u is the desired image and $g(u)\eta$ denotes the noise with η having a zero mean. For example, $g(u) = 1$ for Gaussian noise and $g(u) = \sqrt{u}$ for speckle noise in ultrasound images [13]. Then a common denoising technique is to minimize a functional of gradient:

$$u = \arg\min_u \Big\{ \int_\Omega \rho(|\nabla u|)\, d\mathbf{x} + \frac{\lambda}{2} \int_\Omega \Big(\frac{f-u}{g(u)}\Big)^2 d\mathbf{x} \Big\}, \tag{2}$$

where ρ is an increasing function (often, convex) and $\lambda \geq 0$ denotes the constraint parameter. It is often convenient to transform the minimization problem (2) into a differential equation, called the *Euler-Lagrange equation*, by applying the variational calculus [14]:

$$-\psi(u)\, \nabla \cdot \Big(\rho'(|\nabla u|) \frac{\nabla u}{|\nabla u|}\Big) = \lambda\, (f-u), \tag{3}$$

where

$$\psi(u) = \frac{g(u)^3}{g(u) + (f-u)g'(u)}.$$

For an edge-adaptive image denoising, it is required to hold $\rho'(s)/s \to 0$ as $s \to \infty$. For the speckle noise in ultrasound images, Krissian *et al.* [13] set $g(u) = \sqrt{u}$, which implies $\psi(u) = 2u^2/(f+u) \approx u$; the diffusion term becomes large at largely perturbed pixels (speckles) and therefore the resulting model can suppress speckles more effectively.

When $\rho(s) = s$ and $g(u) \equiv 1$, the model (3) becomes the total variation (TV) model [6]:

$$\kappa(u) = \lambda(f-u), \qquad \text{(TV)} \tag{4}$$

where $\kappa(u)$ is the negation of the *mean curvature* defined as

$$\kappa(u) = -\nabla \cdot \Big(\frac{\nabla u}{|\nabla u|}\Big). \tag{5}$$

It is often the case that the constraint parameter λ is set as a constant, as suggested by Rudin-Osher-Fatemi [6]. In order to find the parameter, the authors merely multiplied (4) by $(f-u)$ and averaged the resulting equation over the whole image domain Ω:

$$\lambda = \frac{1}{\sigma^2}\frac{1}{|\Omega|} \int_\Omega (f-u)\, \kappa(u)\, d\mathbf{x}, \tag{6}$$

where σ^2 is the noise variance

$$\sigma^2 = \frac{1}{|\Omega|} \int_\Omega (f-u)^2\, d\mathbf{x}. \tag{7}$$

(In [6], λ was evaluated after applying integration by parts on the right-side of (6), which could avoid approximations of second-derivatives.)

As another example of (3), the Perona-Malik (PM) model [5] can be obtained by setting $\rho(s) = \frac{1}{2}K^2 \ln(1 + s^2/K^2)$, for some $K > 0$, and $\lambda = 0$:

$$-\nabla \cdot (c(|\nabla u|)\, \nabla u) = 0, \qquad \text{(PM)} \tag{8}$$

where $c(s) = \rho'(s)/s = (1 + s^2/K^2)^{-1}$. Note that for the PM model, the function ρ is strictly convex for $s < K$ and strictly concave for $s > K$. (K is a threshold.) Thus the model can enhance image content of large gradient magnitudes such as edges and speckles; however, it will flatten regions of slow transitions.

Most of conventional PDE-based restoration models have shown either to converge to a piecewise constant image or to lose fine structures of the given image. Although these results are important for understanding of the current diffusion-like models, the resultant signals may not be desired in applications where the preservation of both slow transitions and fine structures is important.

The TV model tends to converge to a piecewise constant image. Such a phenomenon is called the *staircasing* effect. In order to suppress it, Marquina and Osher [3] suggested to multiply the stationary TV model by a factor of $|\nabla u|$:

$$|\nabla u|\, \kappa(u) = \lambda\, |\nabla u|\, (f-u). \qquad \text{(ITV)} \tag{9}$$

Since $|\nabla u|$ vanishes only on flat regions, its steady state is analytically the same as that of the TV model (4). We will call (9) the *improved TV* (ITV) model. Such a non-variational reformulation turns out to reduce the staircasing effect successfully; however, it is yet to be improved for a better preservation of fine structures.

The conventional PDE-based denoising models, including ones presented in this section, can be written in the following general form

$$\mathcal{L}(u) = \mathcal{C}(f-u), \tag{10}$$

where $\mathcal{L}$ is a diffusion (smoothing) operator and $\mathcal{C}$ denotes the constraint parameter.

2.2 Iterative refinement: Bregman iteration

In order to recover fine structures in the image, iterative refinement procedures employing an original idea by Bregman [12] have been introduced in image restoration and image zooming [11], [8]. The Bregman iterative refinement applied to the general denoising model (10) reads as follows: if u_1 is the solution of (10)

$$\mathcal{L}(u_1) = \mathcal{C}(f - u_1), \tag{11}$$

we denote the corresponding residual by r_1, i.e.,

$$r_1 = f - u_1.$$

Then we again solve the TV model with the signal replaced by $f + r_1$; the solution u_2 will satisfy

$$\mathcal{L}(u_2) = \mathcal{C}(f + r_1 - u_2), \tag{12}$$

and the new residual is defined as

$$r_2 = f + r_1 - u_2.$$

In general, the m-th iterate of Bregman iteration, u_m, is computed as the restoration for the signal $f + r_{m-1}$, i.e.,

$$\mathcal{L}(u_m) = \mathcal{C}(f + r_{m-1} - u_m), \quad m \geq 1, \tag{13}$$

where $r_0 = 0$, and the new residual is defined as

$$r_m = f + r_{m-1} - u_m. \tag{14}$$

As for other conventional PDE-based denoising models, each step of the Bregman iteration (13) may be parameterized by an artificial time t for a convenient numerical simulation. That is, u_m can be considered as an evolutionary function and the corresponding evolutionary equation can be obtained by adding $\frac{\partial u_m}{\partial t}$ on the left side of (13).

$$\frac{\partial u_m}{\partial t} + \mathcal{L}(u_m) = \mathcal{C}(f + r_{m-1} - u_m). \quad m \geq 1. \tag{15}$$

The explicit temporal discretization of (15) can be formulated as

$$u_m^n = u_m^{n-1} + \Delta t \left[-\mathcal{L}(u_m^{n-1}) + \mathcal{C}(f + r_{m-1} - u_m^{n-1}) \right], \tag{16}$$

where $u_m^0 = u_{m-1}$ and Δt denotes the temporal stepsize.

As indicated in [11], the Bregman iterative procedure first recovers fine scales of the image and then recovers the noise to converge to the observed noisy image f. For this reason the Bregman iterative procedure must be stopped *manually* when the quality of the obtained image appears satisfactory. Notice that the residuals r_m in (14) read

$$\begin{aligned} r_m &= (f - u_m) + r_{m-1} \\ &= (f - u_m) + (f - u_{m-1}) + r_{m-2} \\ &= \cdots = \sum_{i=1}^{m} (f - u_i). \end{aligned} \tag{17}$$

Thus the m-th iterate of Bregman iteration, u_m, is computed for the signal

$$f + r_{m-1} = f + \sum_{i=1}^{m-1} (f - u_i), \tag{18}$$

which is the original image f added by differences between each of the previous iterates and f. The additive amendment makes the constraint term accentuated, which in return forces the new iterate u_m become closer to f. One may try to modify the last term in (18) or the whole right side, by either normalizing or smoothing, in order to prevent the iterates u_m from recovering the noise from f. However, every trial has failed to improve image quality.

An research objective in this article is to develop PDE-based, iterative refinement denoising models which can restore images effectively and stop *automatically* satisfying the user-defined stopping criterion.

3. The New Iterative Refinement Model

3.1 The smooth curvature correction model

As an iterative refinement model for the basic restoration model of the form (10), we suggest the following. Given a noisy image f, set $v_0 = 0$ and find v_m by recursively solving

$$\mathcal{L}(v_m) = \mathcal{C}(f - v_m) + \mathcal{L}(v_{m-1}), \quad m \geq 1. \tag{19}$$

The new model deserves the following remarks.

1) The Bregman procedure (13) can be rewritten as

$$\mathcal{L}(u_m) = \mathcal{C}\, r_m = \mathcal{C}(f - u_m) + \mathcal{C}\, r_{m-1}.$$

When the problem is solved *exactly* in each iteration, we have $\mathcal{L}(u_m) = \mathcal{C}\, r_m$ for all $m \geq 1$. Thus the last term of the above equation, $\mathcal{C}\, r_{m-1}$, can be replaced by $\mathcal{L}(u_{m-1})$:

$$\mathcal{L}(u_m) = \mathcal{C}(f - u_m) + \mathcal{L}(u_{m-1}). \tag{20}$$

Since the first iterates of (13) and (19) are the same each other, i.e., $v_1 = u_1$, it follows from (19) and (20) that $v_m = u_m$ for all $m \geq 1$. In practice, however, it is often the case that each step in (13) is solved *approximately*, employing an iterative linearized solver (inner iteration) as in (16). Thus $\mathcal{L}(u_{m-1})$ becomes different from $\mathcal{C}\, r_{m-1}$ and therefore v_m differs from u_m.

2) It has been numerically verified that as m grows, the iterates of the new algorithm v_m shows a tendency of gaining the noise from the observed image f, but much weaker than the Bregman iterates. We have been able to stop the tendency of converging to f by slightly smoothing $\mathcal{L}(v_{m-1})$, the last term in (19); see numerical results shown in Section 4 below, more specifically, Table 2. In this article the iterative refinement (19) will be called the *smooth curvature correction* (SCC) model, when $\mathcal{L}(v_{m-1})$ is smoothed slightly by a smoothing method.

3) As for the Bregman iterative refinement, each step of the new denoising model (19) can be parameterized

by an artificial time t for a convenient numerical simulation.

$$\frac{\partial v_m}{\partial t} + \mathcal{L}(v_m) = \mathcal{C}(f - v_m) + \mathcal{L}(v_{m-1}), \quad m \geq 1. \tag{21}$$

Its equilibrium solution is a smooth, restored image of f with $\mathcal{L}(v_{m-1})$ incorporated as a source/correction term. It has been numerically verified that the curvature correction term allows the new iterate v_m to restore fine features more effectively. The explicit temporal discretization of (21) reads

$$\begin{aligned} v_m^n &= v_m^{n-1} + \Delta t \left[-\mathcal{L}(v_m^{n-1}) \right. \\ &\quad \left. + \mathcal{C}(f - v_m^{n-1}) + \mathcal{L}(v_{m-1}) \right], \end{aligned} \tag{22}$$

where $v_m^0 = v_{m-1}$ and Δt is the temporal stepsize.

3.2 Residual-driven variable constraint coefficients

The determination of the constraint parameter has been an interesting problem for PDE-based denoising models, of which the basic mechanism is diffusion. Thus the parameter $\mathcal{C}$ cannot be too large; it must be small enough to introduce a sufficient amount of diffusion. On the other hand, it should be large enough to keep the details in the image. However, in the literature the parameter has been chosen constant for most cases so that the resulting models can either smear out fine structures excessively or maintain an objectionable amount of noise into the restored image.

In order to overcome the difficulty, the parameter must be set variable, more precisely, *edge-adaptive*. Our strategy toward the objective is to

(a) initialize the parameter to be small, and
(b) allow the parameter grow wherever undesired dissipation is excessive, keeping it small elsewhere.

Note that the parameter would better be initialized small so that in the early stage of computation, the model (10) can remove the noise effectively and *equally* everywhere. Then, by letting the parameter grow, the model can return structural components (lost in the residual) back to the image.

An automatic and effective numerical method for the determination of the constraint coefficient $\mathcal{C}$, as a function of $(\mathbf{x}, t)$, can be formulated as follows.

1) *Select a desirable interval* $I_c = [c_0, c_1]$ *for which* $\mathcal{C}(\mathbf{x}, t) \in I_c$, *where* $c_0 \geq 0$ *is sufficiently small.*
2) *Initialize* $\mathcal{C}$ *as a constant:*

$$\mathcal{C}^0 = \mathcal{C}(\mathbf{x}, t = 0) = c_0. \tag{23}$$

3) *Set* $\mathcal{C}^1 = \mathcal{C}^0$ *and for* $n = 2, 3, \cdots$
   (3a) *Compute the absolute residual* $\mathcal{R}^{n-1}$ *and the correction vector* $\mathcal{H}^{n-1}$*:*

$$\begin{aligned} \mathcal{R}^{n-1} &= |f - u_m^{n-1}|, \\ \mathcal{H}^{n-1} &= \max\left(0, G_k(\mathcal{R}^{n-1}) - A_v(\mathcal{R}^{n-1})\right), \end{aligned} \tag{24}$$

   where G_k *is a localized Gaussian smoothing of radius* k *and* $A_v(\mathcal{R}^{n-1})$ *denotes the* L^2*-average of* $\mathcal{R}^{n-1}$.
   (3b) *Update:*

$$\mathcal{C}^n = \mathcal{C}^{n-1} + \xi^n \mathcal{H}^{n-1}, \tag{25}$$

   where ξ^n *is a scaling factor. For example, when the constraint coefficient is to be limited in a prescribed interval* $[c_0, c_1]$, *i.e.,* $\mathcal{C}(\mathbf{x}, t) \in [c_0, c_1]$ *for all* $(\mathbf{x}, t)$, *the scaling factor* ξ^n *can be chosen as*

$$\xi^n = \frac{1}{2^{n-1}} \cdot \frac{c_1 - c_0}{\|\mathcal{H}^{n-1}\|_\infty}, \quad n = 2, 3, \cdots. \tag{26}$$

Remark. The L^2-average of $\mathcal{R}^{n-1}$ is the standard deviation (SD) of the the residual, i.e.,

$$A_v(\mathcal{R}^{n-1}) = \left(\frac{1}{|\Omega|} \int_\Omega (f - u_m^{n-1})^2 \, d\mathbf{x} \right)^{1/2} =: \sigma^{n-1}.$$

The above procedure has been motivated from the observation that PDE-based denoising models tend to introduce a large numerical dissipation near fine structures such as edges and textures and the tendency in turn makes the residual have structural components there. Such structural components can be viewed as an indicator for an undesired dissipation. By adding the components to the constraint coefficient $\mathcal{C}$, we may reduce the undesired dissipation from the resulting image. We call the procedure the *residual-driven constraint* (RDC) parameterization.

4. Numerical Experiments

For comparison purposes, we consider the following four PDE-based restoration models, of which the last three are new models suggested to reduce drawbacks of the model $\mathcal{M}_1$.

($\mathcal{M}_1$) The Bregman iterative refinement (13), with $\mathcal{C}_m^n = \lambda |\nabla u_m^{n-1}|$ for a constant λ
($\mathcal{M}_2$) The Bregman iterative refinement (13), with RDC in (23)–(26)
($\mathcal{M}_3$) The SCC model (19), with $\mathcal{C}_m^n = \lambda |\nabla u_m^{n-1}|$ for a constant λ
($\mathcal{M}_4$) The SCC model (19), with RDC in (23)–(26)

Here the ITV model (9) is selected for the basic PDE-based restoration model, i.e.,

$$\mathcal{L}(u) = -|\nabla u| \, \kappa(u) = -|\nabla u| \, \nabla \cdot \left(\frac{\nabla u}{|\nabla u|} \right),$$

and $\mathcal{C}_m^n$ denotes the constraint parameter for the m-th refinement (outer) iteration and the n-th inner iteration. For the SCC model (19), the last term $\mathcal{L}(v_{m-1})$ is smoothed using the weighted box filter

$$\frac{1}{16} \begin{bmatrix} 1 & 2 & 1 \\ 2 & 4 & 2 \\ 1 & 2 & 1 \end{bmatrix}$$

Fig. 1: Sample images downloaded from public domains: (a) Balloons, (b) Dog, (c) Elaine, (d) House, (e) Lena, and (f) Swan. All are gray-scaled and of 256×256 pixels.

Fig. 2: Lena: (a) The noisy image of the noise PSNR=22.47 and the restored images by (b) $\mathcal{M}_1$ and (c) $\mathcal{M}_3$.

The models $\mathcal{M}_1$ and $\mathcal{M}_3$ perform differently depending somewhat strongly on the choice of the constant λ. We have found from various experiments that the constant λ can be chosen to make the maximum of $\mathcal{C}_m^n$ a constant for all $n \geq 1$, i.e.,

$$\|\mathcal{C}_m^n\|_\infty = \lambda \|\nabla u_m^{n-1}\|_\infty = \widehat{c}, \quad n \geq 1, \tag{27}$$

for some $\widehat{c} > 0$. Thus the constraint parameter for $\mathcal{M}_1$ and $\mathcal{M}_3$ can be found as follows: compute $|\nabla u_m^{n-1}|$ and scale it to make its maximum $\widehat{c}$. We select $\widehat{c} = 3$ for all examples presented in this article. (During the processing, all images are considered as discrete functions having real-values between 0 and 1, by scaling by a factor of 1/255. After processing, they are scaled back for the 8-bit display.)

Public domain images are downloaded, as shown in Figure 1, and then deteriorated by Gaussian noise. For the numerical schemes in (16) and (22), we choose $\Delta t = 0.2$ and the inner iteration is stopped when

$$\|u_m^n - u_m^{n-1}\|_\infty < 0.01$$

is satisfied or the maximum 50 iterations are performed. The outer iteration runs till the 1%–tolerance is satisfied:

$$\|u_m - u_{m-1}\|_\infty < 0.01.$$

Table 1 shows a PSNR analysis for the four models applied for the restoration of the sample images contaminated by Gaussian noise in two different levels. By PSNR, we mean the *peak signal-to-noise ratio* (PSNR) defined as

$$\text{PSNR} \equiv 10 \log_{10} \left(\frac{\sum_{ij} 255^2}{\sum_{ij} (g_{ij} - u_{ij})^2} \right) \text{dB},$$

where g denotes the original image and u is the restored image from a noisy image, f, which is a contamination of g by Gaussian noise. The floating point numbers in the table indicate the best PSNR values that the models can reach, the

Table 1: Best PSNR values. The numbers in parentheses denote the number of outer iterations for the models to obtain the best PSNR.

	f	$\mathcal{M}_1$	$\mathcal{M}_2$	$\mathcal{M}_3$	$\mathcal{M}_4$
Balloons	26.81	34.26(2)	33.45(1)	34.41(3)	33.21(2)
Dog	26.83	31.74(2)	31.78(2)	31.79(2)	31.81(2)
Elaine	26.49	31.27(2)	31.31(2)	31.28(3)	31.32(2)
House	26.63	33.41(2)	33.05(2)	33.37(4)	33.15(2)
Lena	27.11	32.50(2)	32.58(2)	32.62(4)	32.58(2)
Swan	25.98	32.29(2)	32.02(2)	32.27(3)	32.21(2)
Balloons	22.75	31.82(1)	30.94(1)	32.00(2)	31.20(2)
Dog	22.85	30.14(1)	30.06(1)	30.23(2)	30.07(2)
Elaine	23.43	29.76(1)	29.63(1)	30.02(2)	29.79(2)
House	22.74	30.88(2)	30.26(1)	30.89(3)	30.74(2)
Lena	22.47	29.59(1)	29.39(1)	29.80(2)	29.64(2)
Swan	23.31	30.78(1)	30.56(1)	30.91(2)	30.74(2)

Table 2: Convergence analysis for the Lena image.

	f	1	2	3	4	5	6
$\mathcal{M}_1$	27.11	30.62	**32.50**	32.30	31.73	30.96	30.55
$\mathcal{M}_2$	27.11	31.26	**32.58**	31.73	31.00	30.22	29.64
$\mathcal{M}_3$	27.11	30.62	32.10	32.61	**32.62**		
$\mathcal{M}_4$	27.11	31.26	**32.58**	32.57			
$\mathcal{M}_1$	22.47	**29.59**	29.40	27.52	26.62	26.17	25.46
$\mathcal{M}_2$	22.47	**29.39**	28.50	27.25	26.35	25.61	25.07
$\mathcal{M}_3$	22.47	29.59	**29.80**	29.78			
$\mathcal{M}_4$	22.47	29.39	**29.64**	29.58	29.58		

integers in parentheses denote the number of outer iterations for the models to obtain the best PSNR. The Bregman iterative refinement models ($\mathcal{M}_1$ and $\mathcal{M}_2$) have reached at the best image in one or two outer iterations for all images. Particularly, for the heavier noise (presented in the bottom part of the table), the Bregman refinement models show the best image after one outer iteration for all images except the House image. This implies that the Bregman models are hardly able to improve image quality through iterative refinement when the noise is relatively heavy. On the other hand, the SCC models ($\mathcal{M}_3$ and $\mathcal{M}_4$) have improved the image quality through iterative refinement. It is easy to see that the models $\mathcal{M}_3$ and $\mathcal{M}_4$ are superior respectively to $\mathcal{M}_1$ and $\mathcal{M}_2$. (Models $\mathcal{M}_1$ and $\mathcal{M}_3$ have the same first iterate and so do $\mathcal{M}_2$ and $\mathcal{M}_4$.)

The incorporation of RDC (Section 3.2) has promoted the PSNR values for only the Bregman model applied for the restoration of images from relatively low noise levels.

Table 2 exhibits a convergence analysis for the four denoising models. The Bregman refinement models ($\mathcal{M}_1$ and $\mathcal{M}_2$) are stopped in six outer iterations manually, while the SCC models ($\mathcal{M}_3$ and $\mathcal{M}_4$) have converged in three or four outer iterations. As one can see from the table, when the noise PSNR is 27.11, the Bregman refinement models get the highest PSNR for the second iterate; the PSNR decreases rapidly for later iterations, gaining the noise from the noisy image f. When the noise PSNR is 22.47, the Bregman models have failed to refine the resulting image; the PSNR decreases continuously from the beginning. On the other hand, the SCC models have converged in three or four iterations, although they reveal a weak tendency of catching up the noise from the given image. Model $\mathcal{M}_3$ has resulted in best images for most cases.

Figure 2 depicts the noisy image of Lena, having the noise PSNR=22.47, and the restored images by $\mathcal{M}_1$ and $\mathcal{M}_3$. As one can see from the figure, the SCC model has performed superior to the Bregman model. The resulting image obtained from the SCC model shows sharper and clearer edges than the best image of the Bregman procedure.

5. Conclusions

Partial differential equation (PDE)-based denoising models often lose important fine structures due to an excessive dissipation. In order to minimize such undesired dissipation, we have considered a new iterative refinement procedure called the *smooth curvature correction* (SCC) model, as an alternative to the Bregman iterative procedure. By incorporating the smoothed curvature of the previous iterate as a source/correction term, the new model has been able to produce a convergent sequence of images; the resulting image has preserved fine structures successfully and has shown a better restoration quality than the best image of the Bregman procedure. Various numerical examples have been presented to confirm the claim and to show effectiveness of the SCC model.

Acknowledgment

S. Kim's work is supported in part by the NSF grant DMS-1228337.

References

[1] T. Chan, S. Osher, and J. Shen, "The digital TV filter and nonlinear denoising," *IEEE Trans. Image Process.*, vol. 10, no. 2, pp. 231–241, 2001.

[2] S. Kim, "PDE-based image restoration: A hybrid model and color image denoising," *IEEE Trans. Image Processing*, vol. 15, no. 5, pp. 1163–1170, 2006.

[3] A. Marquina and S. Osher, "Explicit algorithms for a new time dependent model based on level set motion for nonlinear deblurring and noise removal," *SIAM J. Sci. Comput.*, vol. 22, pp. 387–405, 2000.

[4] M. Nitzberg and T. Shiota, "Nonlinear image filtering with edge and corner enhancement," *IEEE Trans. on Pattern Anal. Mach. Intell.*, vol. 14, pp. 826–833, 1992.

[5] P. Perona and J. Malik, "Scale-space and edge detection using anisotropic diffusion," *IEEE Trans. on Pattern Anal. Mach. Intell.*, vol. 12, pp. 629–639, 1990.

[6] L. Rudin, S. Osher, and E. Fatemi, "Nonlinear total variation based noise removal algorithms," *Physica D*, vol. 60, pp. 259–268, 1992.

[7] S. Kim and H. Lim, "A non-convex diffusion model for simultaneous image denoising and edge enhancement," *Electronic Journal of Differential Equations, Conference Special Issue*, vol. 15, pp. 175–192, 2007.

[8] S. Osher, M. Burger, D. Goldfarb, J. Xu, and W. Yin, "An iterative regularization method for total variation-based image restoration," *Multiscale Model. Simul.*, vol. 4, no. 2, pp. 460–489, 2005.

[9] S. Kim, "Image denoising by fourth-order PDEs," in *Proceedings of the Eighth IASTED International Conference on Signal and Image Processing*, 2006, pp. 249–254.

[10] M. Lysaker, A. Lundervold, and X.-C. Tai, "Noise removal using fourth-order partial differential equation with applications to medical magnetic resonance images in space and time," *IEEE Trans. Image Process.*, vol. 12, no. 12, pp. 1579–1590, 2003.

[11] A. Marquina and S. Osher, "Image super-resolution by TV-regularization and Bregman iteration," *J. Sci. Comput.*, vol. 37, pp. 367–382, 2008.

[12] L. Bregman, "The relaxation method of finding the common point of convex sets and its application to the solution of problems in convex programming," *USSR Computational Mathematics and Mathematical Physics*, vol. 7, no. 3, pp. 200–217, 1967.

[13] K. Krissian, R. Kikinis, C. F. Westin, and K. Vosburgh, "Speckle-constrained filtering of ultrasound images," in *IEEE Computer Vision and Pattern Recognition or CVPR*, 2005, pp. II: 547–552.

[14] R. Weinstock, *Calculus of Variations*. New York: Dover Pubilcations, Inc., 1974.

SESSION

IMAGE PROCESSING AND VISION ALGORITHMS

Chair(s)

TBA

Self-calibration of colormetric parameters in vision systems for autonomous mobile robots

António J. R. Neves[1], Alina Trifan[1], and Bernardo Cunha[1]
[1]ATRI, DETI / IEETA, University of Aveiro, 3810–193 Aveiro, Portugal

Abstract— *Vision is an extremely important sense for both humans and robots, providing detailed information about the environment. In the past few years, the use of digital cameras in robotic applications has been increasing significantly. The use of digital cameras as the main sensor allows the robot to take the relevant information from the surrounding environment and then take decisions. A robust vision system should be able to detect objects reliably and present an accurate representation of the world to higher-level processes, not only under ideal light conditions, but also under changing light intensity and color balance. In this paper, we propose an algorithm for the self-calibration of the most important parameters of digital cameras for robotic applications. The algorithm extracts statistical information from the acquired images, namely the intensity histogram, saturation histogram and information from a black and a white area of the image, to then estimate the colormetric parameters of the camera. We present experimental results obtained with several autonomous robotic platforms: two wheeled platforms, with different architectures of the vision system, a humanoid robots and an autonomous driving agent. The images acquired after calibration show good properties for further processing, independently of the initial configuration of the camera and the type and amount of light of the environment, both indoor and outdoor.*

Keywords: Robotic vision, digital cameras, image processing, camera calibration, colormetric parameters.

1. Introduction

In the past few years, the use of digital cameras in robotic applications has been increasing significantly. We can point out some areas of application of these robots, as the case of the industry, military, surveillance, service robots and we start also seeing vision systems in vehicles for assisted driving. The cameras are used as sensors that allow the robot to take the relevant information of the surrounding environment and then take decisions.

To extract information from the acquired image, such as shapes or colors, the camera calibration procedure is very important. If the parameters of the camera are wrongly calibrated, the image details are lost and it may become almost impossible to recognize anything based on shape or color (see for example Fig. 1).

Our experience, as well as the experience of all the researchers that work in the field of computer vision, show that the digital cameras fail regarding the quality of the images acquired under certain situations, even considering the most recent cameras (an example can be found in [1]. The algorithms developed for calibration of digital cameras assume some standard scenes under some type of light, which fails in certain environments. We did not find scientific references for these algorithms.

In this work, we show that the problem can be solved by adjusting the colormetric parameters of the camera in order to guarantee the correct colors of the objects, allowing the use of the same color classification independently of the light conditions (see for example the problem presented in [2]). This allows also a correct processing of the image if other features have to be extracted. We think that this paper presents an important contribution to the field of autonomous robotics.

We propose an algorithm to configure the most important colormetric parameters of the cameras, namely gain, exposure, gamma, white-balance, brightness, sharpness and saturation without human interaction, depending on the availability of these parameters in the digital camera that is being used. This approach differs from the well known problem of photometric camera calibration (a survey can be found in [3]), since we are not interested in obtaining the camera response values but only to configure its parameters according to some measures obtained from the acquired images in robotic applications. The self-calibration process for a single robot requires only few seconds, including the time necessary to interact with the application, which is considered fast in comparison to the several minutes needed for manual calibration by an expert user. Moreover, the developed algorithms can be used in the real-time by the robots while they are operating.

The work that we present in this paper was tested and is being used by several robotic platforms developed in the University of Aveiro, namely in the challenging environment of robotic soccer (where the goal is the development of multi-agent robotic teams), both with welled [4] and humanoid robots [5], and also in autonomous driving vehicles and a service robot [6]. These robots are presented in Fig. 2. In all these applications, the robots have to adjust, in a constrained time, their camera parameters according to the lighting conditions.

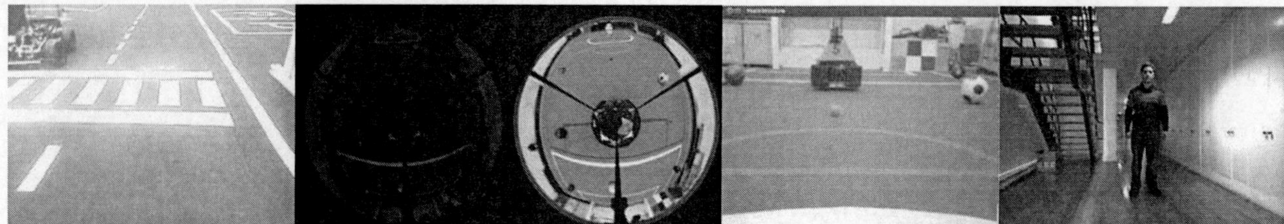

Fig. 1: Images acquired in different scenarios with different robots, using wrong colometric parameters in their digital cameras. From left to right, wrong value of gamma (high), exposure (low), saturation (high), gain (high), white-balance (high both in Blue and Red gains).

Fig. 2: Robotic platforms used in this work. From left to right, CAMBADA (RoboCup Middle Size league robotic soccer), NAO (RoboCup Standard Platform League soccer robot), CAMBADA@HOME (service robot for elderly and disabled people support - under test on RoboCup @HOME league) and autonomous driving.

This paper is structured in five sections, the first of them being this introduction. Section 2 provides an overview on the most important colormetric parameters of digital cameras and the properties on the image that are related to each one. Section 3 describes the proposed algorithm. In Section 4 the results and their discussion are presented. Finally, Section 5 concludes the paper.

2. Configuration of the camera parameters

The configuration of the parameters of digital cameras is crucial for object detection and has to be performed when environmental conditions change. The calibration procedure should be effective and fast. The proposed calibration algorithm processes the image acquired by the camera and computes several measurements that allow the calibration of the most important colormetric parameters of a digital camera, as presented in Fig. 3. Besides the referred parameters, the hardware related parameters gain and exposure are also taken into consideration.

Starting by some definitions, luminance is normally defined as a measurement of the photometric luminous intensity per unit area of light travelling in a given direction. Therefore, it is used to describe the amount of light that goes through, or is emitted from, a particular area, and falls within a given solid angle.

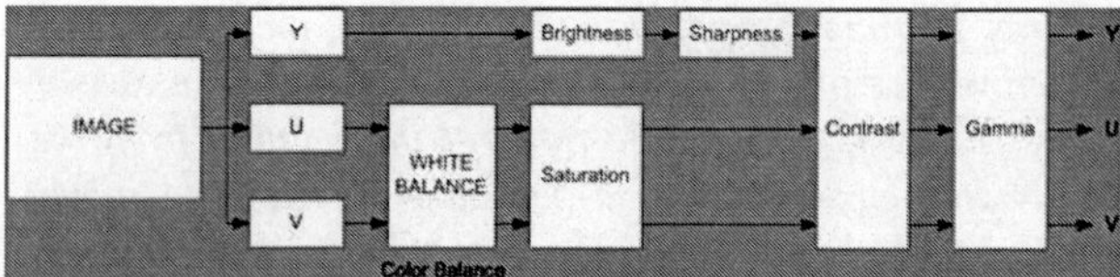

Fig. 3: A typical image processing pipeline (inside the image device) for a tri-stimulus system. This processing can be performed on the YUV or RGB components depending on the system. This should be understood as a mere example.

Chrominance is a numeral that describes the way a certain amount of light is distributed among the visible spectrum. Chrominance has no luminance information but is used together with it to describe a colored image defined, for instance, by an RGB triplet. Any RGB triplet in which the value of R=G=B has no chrominance information.

White balance is the global adjustment of the intensities of the colors (typically red, green, and blue primary colors). An important goal of this adjustment is to render specific colors – particularly neutral colors –correctly; hence, the general method is sometimes called gray balance, neutral balance, or white balance. This balance is required because of different color spectrum energy distribution depending on the illumination source. The proposed algorithm uses a white area as reference to calibrate this parameter. The idea is that the white region should be white – in the YUV color space this means that the average value of U and V should be 127.

The black and white regions can be defined manually beforehand to correspond to regions of the robots in the image or the algorithm can search in the image autonomously for white areas, after setting the camera to auto mode. In the case of the NAO robots, the robot stops and look to a defined position of its own body where these regions are. In the case of the wheeled robots, due to the use of a omnidirectional vision system [7], the own body is seen in the image and a white and black area was placed closed to the mirror. In case of the autonomous driving and service robots, an example of the white areas obtained from the images acquired by their vision systems can be found in Figs. 5 and 4.

The brightness parameter is basically a constant (or offset)

Fig. 4: From left to right, an example of an image acquired in auto mode by the camera the autonomous driving robot, the corresponding white areas obtained autonomously, and the corresponding black areas also obtained autonomously by the proposed algorithm.

that can be added (subtracted) from the luminance component of the image. It represents a measure of the average amount of light that is integrated over the image during the exposure time. If the brightness it too high, overexposure may occur which will white saturate part or the totality of the image. The proposed algorithm considers a black area in the image as reference to calibrate this parameter. In the CAMBADA and SPL robots, these areas are part of the robots and can be defined beforehand. In case of the autonomous driving and service robots, an example of the white areas obtained from the images acquired by their vision systems can be found in Figs. 5 and 4. The concept is that the black area should be black – in the RGB color space, this means that the average values of R, G and B should be close to zero in this region.

Fig. 5: From left to right, an example of an image acquired in auto mode by the camera the autonomous service robot, the corresponding white areas obtained autonomously, and the corresponding black areas also obtained autonomously by the proposed algorithm.

The saturation of a color is determined by a combination of light intensity that is acquired by a pixel and how much this light it is distributed across the spectrum of different wavelengths. Saturation is sometimes also defined as the amount of white that has been blended into a pure color. In the proposed algorithm, we consider the histogram of the Saturation (obtained in the HSV color space) and we force the MSV value of this histogram to 2.5, following the explanation above about the use of the MSV measure regarding the histogram of intensities, calibrating this parameter.

Sharpness is a measure of the energy frequency spatial distribution over the image. It basically allows the control of the cut-off frequency of a low pass spatial filter. This may be very useful if the image is afterward intended to be decimated, since it allows to prevent spatial aliases artifacts. We do not consider this parameter in the proposed calibration algorithm as in the referred applications of the robots we work with the resolution of the images acquired by the camera.

Gain, exposure, gamma and contrast are related and we use the information of the luminance of the image to calibrate them. The priority is to keep gamma out and the exposure to the minimum possible value to reduce noise in the image and the effect of the moving objects in the image. If the light conditions are very hard, the algorithm will calibrate the gamma and exposure time.

Gain is a constant factor that is applied to all the pixels in the image when the image is acquired. Exposure time is the time that the image sensor (CCD or CMOS) is exposed to the light. Gamma correction is the name of a nonlinear operation used to code and decode luminance or TGB tristimulus values. One of the most used definition of contrast is the difference in luminance along the 2D space that makes an object distinguishable. To calibrate all these parameters, it is used the histogram of luminance of the image and a statistical measure to balance the histogram of the acquired image, as presented next.

The histogram of the luminance of an image is a representation of the number of times that each intensity value appears in the image. Image histograms can indicate if the image is underexposed or overexposed. For a camera correctly calibrated, the distribution of the luminance histogram should be centered around 127 (for a 8 bits per pixel image). An underexposed image will have the histogram be leaning to the left, while an overexposed image will have the histogram leaning to the right (for an example see the Fig. 13)).

Statistical measures can be extracted from digital images to quantify the image quality [8], [9]. A number of typical measures used in the literature can be computed from the image gray level histogram. Based on the experiments presented in [10], in this work we used the mean sample value (MSV):

$$MSV = \frac{\sum_{j=0}^{4}(j+1)x_j}{\sum_{j=0}^{4}x_j},$$

where x_j is the sum of the gray values in region j of the histogram (in the proposed approach we divided the histogram into five regions). When the histogram values of an image are uniformly distributed in the possible values, then $MSV \approx 2.5$.

A graphical representation of the statistical measures extracted from the image acquired by the camera and its relation to the parameters to be calibrated on the camera is presented in Fig. 6.

3. Proposed algorithm

The algorithm configures the most important parameters, as referred above. For each one of these parameters, and

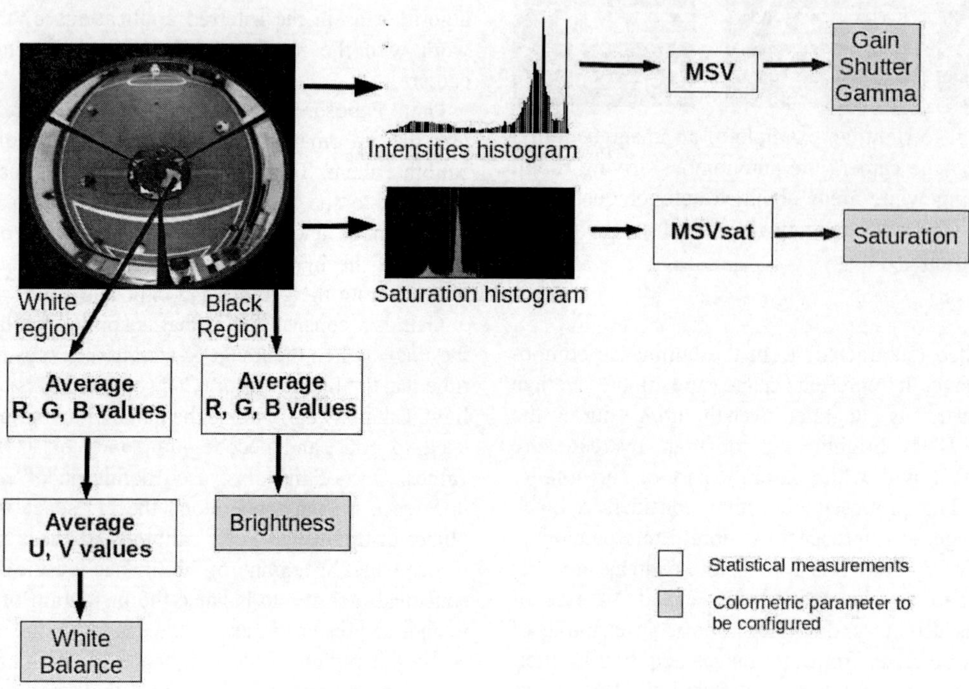

Fig. 6: A graphical representation of the statistical measures extracted from the image acquired by the camera and its relation to the parameters to be calibrated on the camera.

that are available on the camera, a PI controller was implemented. PI controllers are used instead of proportional controllers as they result in better control having no stationary error. The constants of the controller have been obtained experimentally for both cameras, guaranteeing the stability of the system and an acceptable time to reach the desired reference.

The algorithm presented next starts by the configuration of the parameters related to the luminance on the image, namely gain, exposure and gamma, by this order if necessary. To improve the quality of the image, i. e. to have the less noise as possible, the exposure should be as much as possible. On the other hand, the gamma should be the one that gives the best dynamic range for the intensity and we only want to change it is the gain and exposure alone cannot get good results.

When the image acquired have enough quality in terms of luminance, considering that the MSV for the histogram of intensities is between 2 and 3, the algorithm starts calibrating the other parameters, namely white-balance, saturation and brightness, according to the ideas expressed in the previous section. The algorithm stops when all the parameters have converged. This procedure solves the problem of the correlation that exists between the parameters.

```
do
  acquire image
  calculate the histogram and the MSV value of Luminance
  if MSV != 2.5
    if exposure and gain are in the limits
      apply the PI controller to adjust gamma
    else if gain is in the limit
      apply the PI controller to adjust exposure
    else
      apply the PI controller to adjust gain
    end
    set the camera with new gamma, exposure and gain values
  end
  if MSV > 2 && MSV < 3
    calculate the histogram and MSV value of saturation
    calculate average U and V values of a white area
    calculate average R, G and B values of a black area
    if MSVsat != 2.5
      apply the PI controller to adjust saturation
      set the camera with new saturation value
    end
  if U != 127 || V != 127
    apply the PI controller to adjust WB_BLUE
      apply the PI controller to adjust WB_RED
      set the camera with new white-balance parameters
    end
    if R != 0 || G != 0 || B != 0
      apply the PI controller to adjust brightness
      set the camera with new brightness value
    end
  end
while any parameter changed
```

4. Experimental results

To measure the performance of the proposed self calibration algorithm, experiments have been made in four robotic platforms: the CAMBADA robots (RoboCup Middle Size league robotic soccer robots) and NAO robots (RoboCup Standard Platform League soccer robot), in indoor scenarios, a wheeled service robot and an autonomous driving agent. In all the cases, the images acquired after the proposed autonomous colormetric calibration have good properties, both in terms of objective and subjective analysis.

The experiment that follows have been conducted using the cameras of the robots with different initial configurations inside a laboratory with both artificial and natural light sources. In Fig. 7, the experimental results are presented when the algorithm starts with the parameters of the camera set to lower value and Fig. 8 presents experiment results when the camera parameters are set to higher values. As it can seen, the configuration obtained after using the proposed algorithm is approximately the same, independently of the initial configuration of the camera.

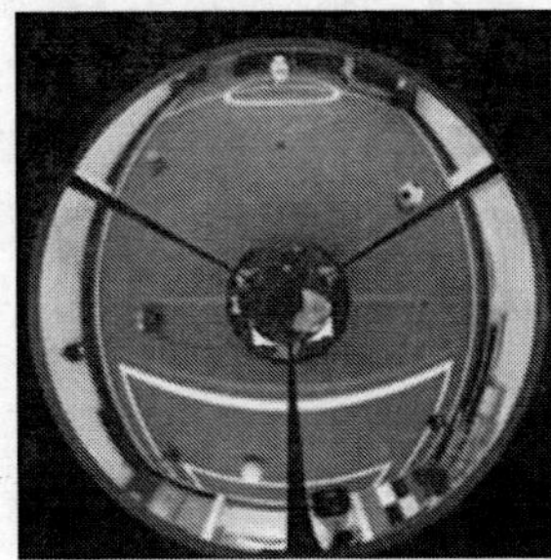

Fig. 7: Some experiments using the proposed automated calibration procedure. From left to right, an image captured with some of the parameters of the camera set to lower values, the corresponding image obtained after applying the proposed calibration procedure.

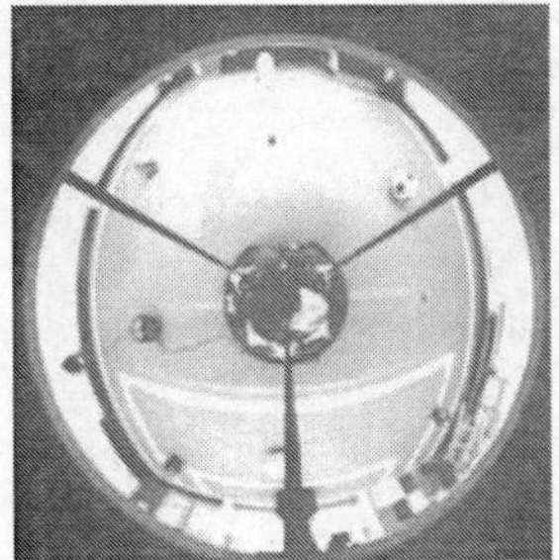
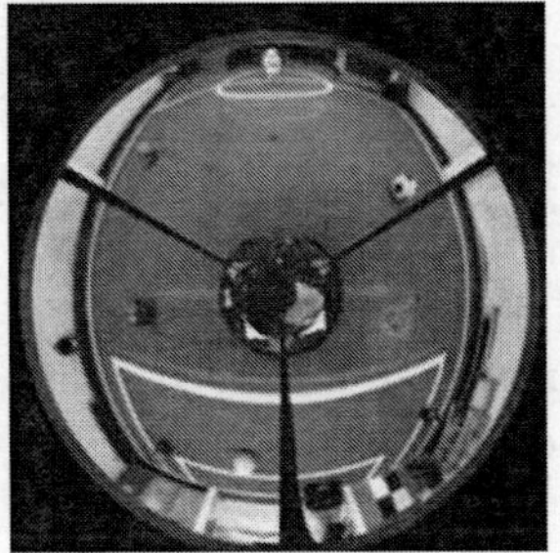

Fig. 8: Some experiments using the proposed automated calibration procedure. From left to right, an image captured with some of the parameters of the camera set to higher values and the corresponding image obtained after applying the proposed calibration procedure.

In Fig. 9 and 10 there are presented the variation of the camera parameters related to the experiment described above. As we can see, the convergence of the parameters is fast. It took less than 100 cycles to the camera converges to the correct parameters in order to obtain the images presented in Fig. 7 and Fig. 8. In this experiment, the camera was working at 30 fps that means a calibration time below 3 seconds. These are the worst case scenarios in calibration. Most of times, in practical use, the camera can start in auto mode and the algorithm applied after that. An example of this situation is presented in the video, where the lamps of the laboratory are switched on and off after the camera calibrated. In these situations, the camera converges in a reduced number of cycles.

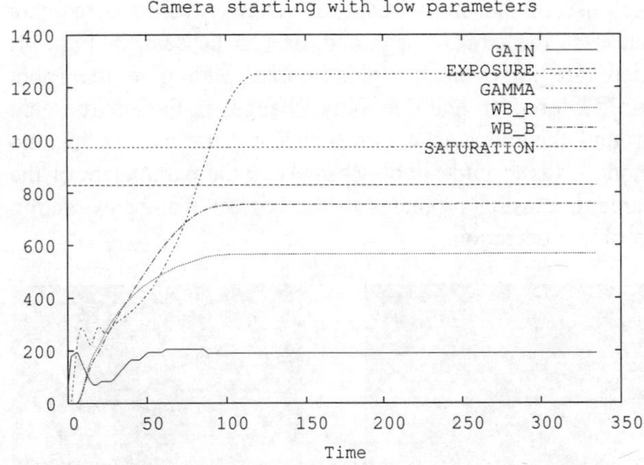

Fig. 9: A graphic showing the variation of the parameters of the camera when it started with higher values. We can see a fast convergence of the parameters.

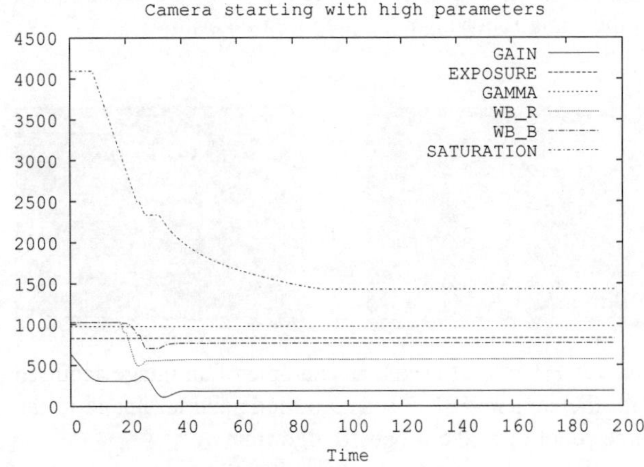

Fig. 10: A graphic showing the variation of the parameters of the camera when it started with higher values. We can see a fast convergence of the parameters.

In the NAO robot, we work with the cameras at 15 fps

due to the limitations on the processing capabilities, which leads to times close to 10 seconds. However, due the fact that the NAO robots do not have graphical interface with the user, the proposed algorithm is very useful to calibrate the two cameras of the robots.

In Fig. 11 we present an image acquired with the camera of a CAMBADA robot in auto mode and in Fig. 12 we present an image acquired with the camera of a NAO robot in auto mode. The results obtained using the camera with the parameters in auto mode are overexposed and the white balance is not correctly configured, both for the welled and NAO robots. The algorithms used by the digital cameras that are on the robots (we tested also some more models and the results are similar) is due several reasons explained next. In the case of the omnidirectional vision system, the camera analyzes the entire image and, as can be seen in Fig. 11, there are large black regions corresponding to the robot itself. Moreover, and due to the changes in the environment around the robot as it moves, leaving the camera in auto mode leads to undesirable changes in the parameters of the camera, causing problems to the correct feature extraction to object detection.

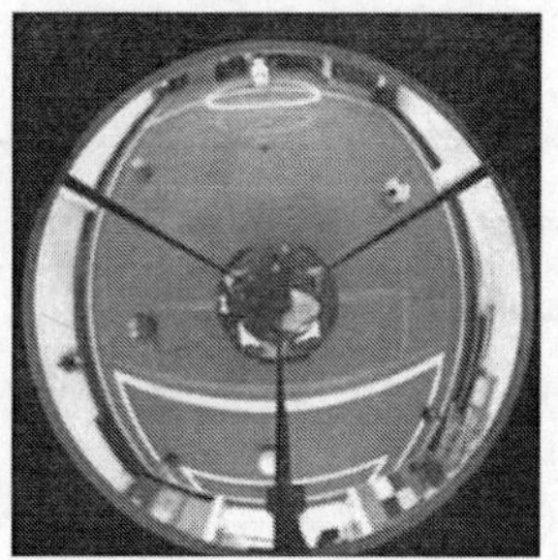

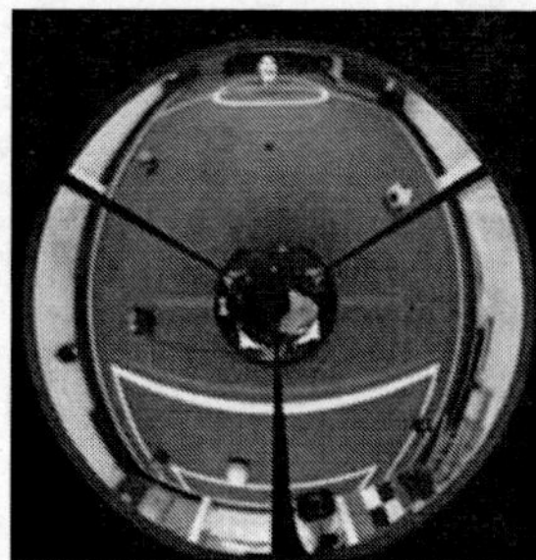

Fig. 11: From left to right, an example of an image acquired with the camera of the wheeled robot in auto mode, an image in the same robot after the proposed algorithm.

Fig. 12: From left to right, an example of an image acquired with the camera of NAO in auto mode and an image in the same robot after the proposed algorithm.

The good results of the automated calibration procedure can also be confirmed by the histograms presented in Fig. 14. The histogram of the image obtained after applying the proposed automated calibration procedure (Fig. 13) is centered near the intensity 127, which is a desirable property, as visually confirmed in Fig. 11. The histogram of the image acquired using the camera in auto mode (Fig. 13) shows that the image is overexposed, leading to the majority of the pixels to have saturated values.

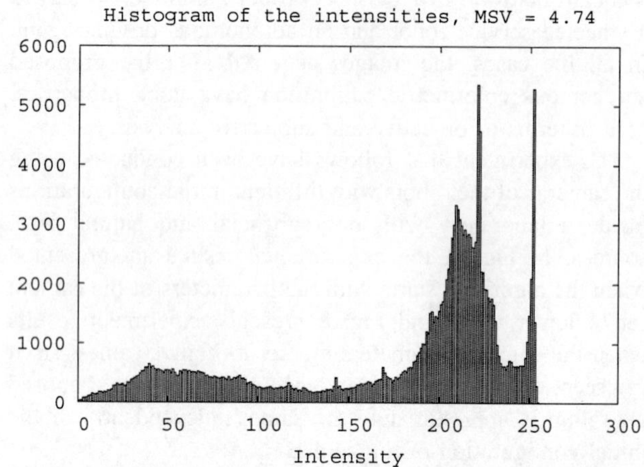

Fig. 13: The histogram of the intensities of the images presented in Fig. 11. This is the histogram of the image obtained with the camera parameters in auto mode.

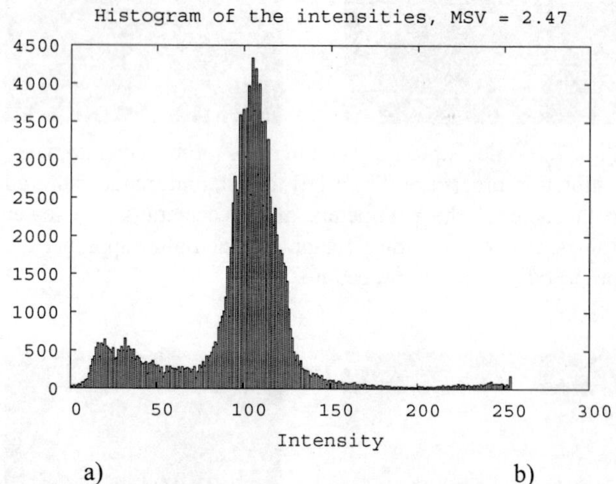

a) b)

Fig. 14: The histogram of the intensities of the images presented in Fig. 11. This is the histogram of the image obtained after applying the automated calibration procedure.

It is expected that robots can perform their tasks under natural lighting conditions and in an outdoor environment. This introduces new challenges. In outdoor environments, the illumination may change slowly during the day, due to the movement of the sun, but also may change quickly in short periods of time due to a partial and temporally varying covering of the sun by clouds. In this case, the robots have to adjust, in real-time, the camera parameters, in order to adapt to new lighting conditions.

The proposed algorithm was also tested outdoors, under natural light. Figure 15 shows that the algorithm works well even with different light conditions. It confirms that the algorithm can be used in non-controlled lighting conditions and under different environments.

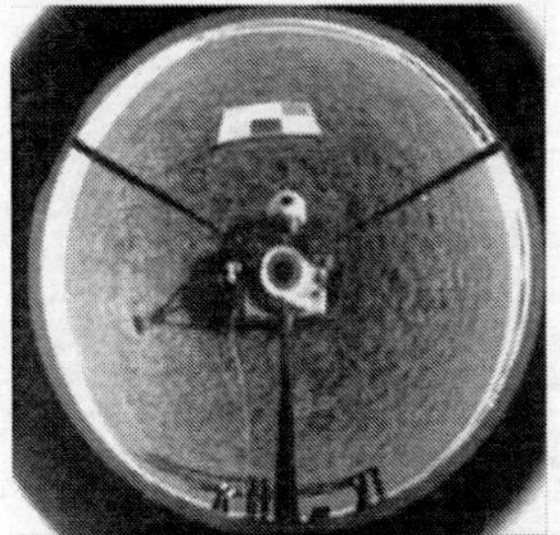

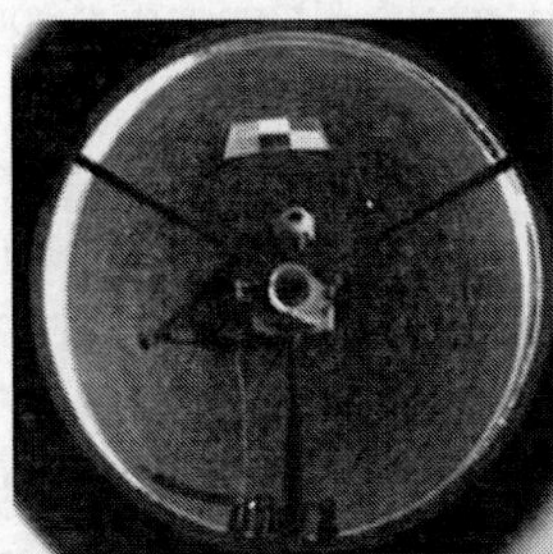

Fig. 15: On the left, an image acquired outdoors using the camera of a CAMBADA robot in auto mode. As it is possible to observe, the colors are washed out. That happens because the camera's auto-exposure algorithm tries to compensate the black around the mirror. On the right, the same image with the camera calibrated using the implemented algorithm. As can be seen, the colors and their contours are much more defined.

The algorithms developed by the industry for calibration of digital cameras assume some standard scenes under some type of light. However, besides the user manuals of the cameras tested, we did not find scientific references for these algorithms.

5. Conclusions

We propose an algorithm to autonomously configure the most important parameters of a digital camera. This procedure requires a few seconds to calibrate the colometric parameters of the digital cameras of the robots, independently of the initial parameters of the cameras, as well as the light conditions where the robots are being used. This is much faster than the manual calibration performed by an expert user, that even having as feedback the statistical measures extracted from the digital images that we propose in this paper needs several minutes to perform this operation.

The experimental results presented in this paper show that the algorithm converges independently of the initial configuration of the camera. These results allow the use of the same color ranges for each object of interest independently of the lighting conditions, improving the efficiency of the object detection algorithms .

The calibration algorithm proposed in this paper is also used in run-time in order to adjust the camera parameters during the use of the robots, accommodating some changes that can happen in the environment or in the light, without affect the performance of the vision algorithms.

As a future work, we would like to extend this work to more robotic applications in non-controlled environments, as well as to present more detailed results regarding its use in more models of digital cameras with different type of lens, that also affects the calibration of these parameters.

6. Acknowledgements

This work was developed in the Institute of Electronic and Telematic Engineering of University of Aveiro and was partially funded by FEDER through the Operational Program Competitiveness Factors - COMPETE and by National Funds through FCT - Foundation for Science and Technology in the context of the project FCOMP-01-0124-FEDER-022682 (FCT reference PEst-C/EEI/UI0127/2011).

References

[1] Y. Takahashi, W. Nowak, and T. Wisspeintner, "Adaptive recognition of color-coded objects in indoor and outdoor environments," in *RoboCup 2007: Robot Soccer World Cup XI*, ser. Lecture Notes in Artificial Intelligence. Springer, 2007.

[2] P. Heinemann, F. Sehnke, F. S., and A. Zell, "Towards a calibration-free robot: The act algorithm for automatic online color training," pp. 363–370, 2007.

[3] G. Krawczyk, M. Goesele, and H. Seidel, "Photometric calibration of high dynamic range cameras," Max-Planck-Institut für Informatik, Stuhlsatzenhausweg 85, 66123 Saarbrücken, Germany, Research Report MPI-I-2005-4-005, April 2005.

[4] A. Neves, J. Azevedo, N. L. B. Cunha, J. Silva, F. Santos, G. Corrente, D. A. Martins, N. Figueiredo, A. Pereira, L. Almeida, L. S. Lopes, and P. Pedreiras, *CAMBADA soccer team: from robot architecture to multiagent coordination*. I-Tech Education and Publishing, Vienna, Austria, In Vladan Papic (Ed.), Robot Soccer, 2010, ch. 2.

[5] A. Trifan, A. J. R. Neves, B. Cunha, and N. Lau, "A modular real-time vision system for humanoid robots," in *Proceedings of SPIE IS&T Electronic Imaging 2012*, January 2012.

[6] J. Cunha, A. J. R. Neves, J. L. Azevedo, B. Cunha, N. Lau, A. Pereira, and A. J. S. Teixeira, "A Mobile Robotic Platform for Elderly Care," in *AAL 2011 - 1st Int. Living Usability Lab Workshop on AAL Latest Solutions, Trends and Applications*, January 2011, pp. 36–45.

[7] A. J. R. Neves, A. J. Pinho, D. A. Martins, and B. Cunha, "An efficient omnidirectional vision system for soccer robots: from calibration to object detection," *Mechatronics*, vol. 21, no. 2, pp. 399–410, March 2011.

[8] M. V. Shirvaikar, "An optimal measure for camera focus and exposure," in *Proc. of the IEEE Southeastern Symposium on System Theory*, Atlanta, USA, March 2004.

[9] N. Nourani-Vatani and J. Roberts, "Automatic camera exposure control," in *Proc. of the 2007 Australasian Conference on Robotics and Automation*, Brisbane, Australia, December 2007.

[10] A. J. R. Neves, A. J. P. B. Cunha, and I. Pinheiro, "Autonomous configuration of parameters in robotic digital cameras," in *Proc. of the 4th Iberian Conference on Pattern Recognition and Image Analysis, IbPRIA-2009*, ser. Lecture Notes in Computer Science, vol. 5524. Póvoa do Varzim, Portugal: Springer, June 2009, pp. 80–87.

Fast and Robust Human Detection Method in Range Map of Complex Environment

Moon-soo Ra, Hoon Jo, and Whoi-Yul Kim
Department of Electronic Engineering, Hanyang University, Seoul, Korea

Abstract— *With increasing need of human-computer interfaces, pose estimation or gesture recognition has drawn a lot of attentions. Since humans are one of the subjects of human-computer interfaces, human detection is required as a preprocessing step for human-computer interaction system. In this paper, we propose a fast and robust human detection method by using a range map. Instead of finding exact shape of human in the range map, the proposed method uses static background modeling and labeling technique. The proposed method is robust against self-occlusions and can separate undesirably merged labels. The experiments show that the proposed method efficiently produces foreground regions within 10 ms. Due to its low complexity, the proposed method can be extended to restricted environments such as mobile or embedded systems.*

Keywords: Human detection, foreground detection, range map, pose variations, complex environment

1. Introduction

With the advancements in the range sensor techniques, small and inexpensive range sensors such as Kinect [1] and Creative Interactive Gesture Camera [2] become popular. Recently range sensors are widely used in many fields that require some kind of intelligence such as computer vision or robotic applications. With the growing need of natural user interfaces towards human computer interaction, pose estimation/action recognition have recently drawn a lot of attention, as being one of the most common applications using range sensors [3]. In such applications, foreground detection in the range map plays an important role as a preprocessing step. In general, since the objective of the foreground detection is to segment human from cluttered background, conventional approaches are focused on detecting the shape of human in the range map [4], [5], [6].

A method in [4] was designed for multiple oriented 2D elliptical filters (MO2DEFs) to detect non-facing human in the range map. Main role of MO2DEFs is encoding shape information of the human to several attributes with respect to orientations. Fujiyoshi [5], proposed a window-based human detection method using relational depth similarity features based on the range map. The method calculated a feature derived from a similarity of depth histograms that represent a relationship between two local regions. Xia et al. [6], proposed a model based approach which detects the human using a 2D head contour model and 3D head surface model. 2D chamfer distance matching is conducted to detect human candidates. These approaches tend to suffer from pose variations since the shape of the human is not well-defined in 2D projective space.

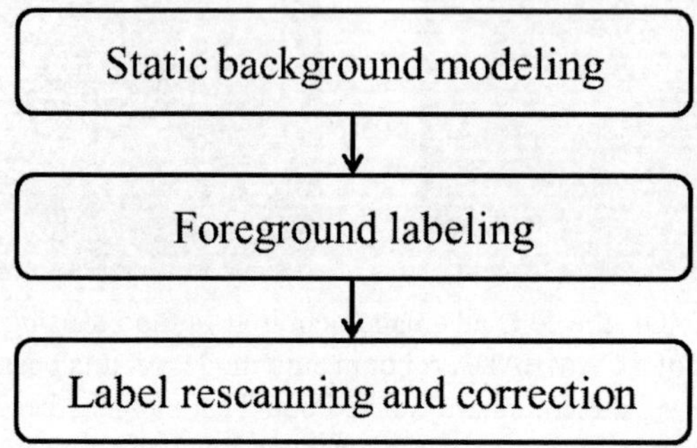

Fig. 1: Overall procedure of the proposed method.

In order to cope with such pose variations, a new method is proposed using static background modeling and labeling technique. In the proposed method's applications, moving objects in the scene are considered as human subjects. As illustrated in Fig. 1, the proposed method consists of three steps: static background modeling, foreground labeling, and label rescanning and correction. At first, static objects in the scene are modeled by Gaussian mixture model (GMM) [7] and floor modeling. Then foreground pixels that are in proximity in 3D space are grouped with the same label. Finally, obtained labels are rescanned and corrected to carry unique and consistent label for each object.

The rest of the paper is organized as follows. In section 2, steps of the proposed method are introduced. In section 3, experimental results are discussed. Then the conclusions are presented in section 4.

2. Foreground detection method

In this section, the details of algorithms for the proposed method are described. Since background modeling and foreground labeling have a conplementary relationship, both stages are explained in section 2.1. Corrections to be made by rescanning the labels are described in section 2.2.

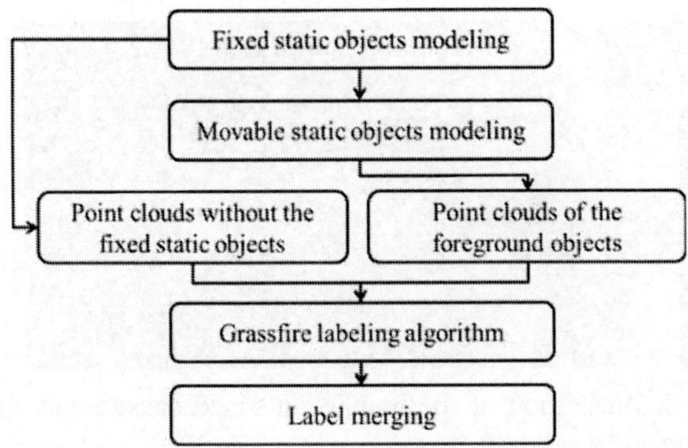

Fig. 2: Flowchart of static background modeling and foreground labeling stages.

2.1 Static background modeling and foreground labeling

The flowchart of the proposed algorithms is illustrated in Fig. 2. At first, static background modeling is described. Objective of static background modeling is to remove static objects from the range map. Typically, static objects in the scene are separated into two categories: fixed static objects and movable static objects. Fixed static objects include floor, ceil, or walls. Common property of the fixed static objects is that they can be modeled as planes. The other category is movable static objects which include objects such as chairs, tables, or any other furniture in the scene. Since the objects that fall into the second category have no common properties, they should be modeled pixel by pixel.

Fixed static objects are modeled first in the static background modeling step. In this paper, it is assumed that floor is the only fixed static object in the scene. Since the floor pixels in 2D projective space do not have a linear relationship, a floor model is made in a 3D real-world space. Many open Kinect libraries such as Kinect SDK [1] and OpenNI [8] provide a way to obtain real-world point clouds. The point clouds depend on the range map and camera parameters of Kinect.

This fixed static objects modeling algorithm utilizes a V-disparity map [9] to figure out linear structures in the scene. Among obtained 3D point clouds, only y and z coordinates are used to make the V-disparity map because the floor has a little variation in the x coordinate. After that, Hough transform [10] is applied on the V-disparity map to find the desired floor model. Fig. 3 shows the results of the fixed static object modeling step. Top-left image illustrates an accumulated V-disparity map. The result of Hough transform is illustrated in top-right image. Bottom-left shows a quantized range map. Right-bottom image represents an area being modeled as the floor. We denote a range map which has no fixed static objects as I_{FR}.

In the next step, GMM algorithm is applied on I_{FR} to model movable static objects. By using multimodal Gaus-

Fig. 3: Results of the fixed static objects modeling step.

sians, background modeling becomes robust against the slight movements of movable static objects. After removing both fixed and movable static objects, we can obtain a foreground range map I_{FG}.

One advantage of modeling these two categories of objects is that the proposed method can cope with a situation where the human is modeled as background in the movable static objects modeling step. This situation is denoted as human-contained background situation. In this situation, I_{FG} has too little information of finding a proper foreground of the human. On the other hand, I_{FR} has information of all movable static objects in the scene. Therefore, based on a little clue inside of I_{FG}, we recover shape information of the human from I_{FR}. In order to achieve this purpose, the grassfire labeling algorithm [11], in the proposed method, utilizes pixels in I_{FG} as seed points then process the algorithm on I_{FR}. In the labeling step, similarity between two pixels is computed as a 3D Euclidean distance.

Due to the similarity matric used in the labeling algorithm, some pixels which belong to the same object can have different labels. Those labels have to be merged before further processing. Since the point clouds belonging to the humans have low variations in x and z axis, such conditions can be easily detected by finding spatially adjacent labels in x-z plane. After the label merging algorithm, a unique label are assigned to each object.

2.2 Label rescanning and correction

This stage consists of two steps: rescanning and correction. The first step rescans the labels to assign a consistent label to each object. The second step detects undesirably merged labels and separate corresponding labels to several unique labels. Label rescanning and correction is efficiently implemented by using a union-find algorithm (disjoint-set data structure) [12].

A set of labels at time t is defined as $L_t = \{l_t^1, l_t^2, ..., l_t^n\}$. In the beginning of the rescanning step, label matching costs

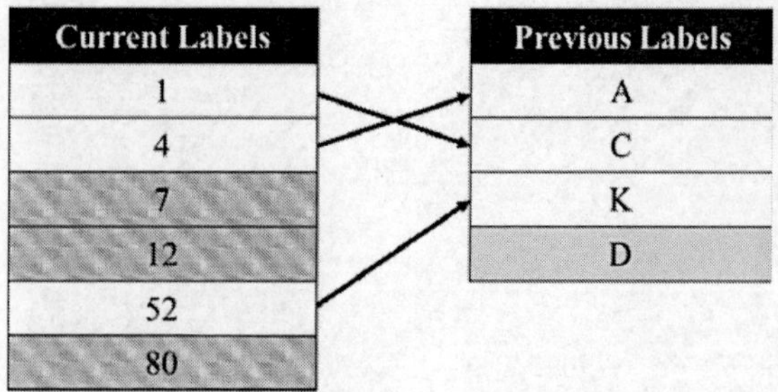

Fig. 4: Example of the label rescanning step.

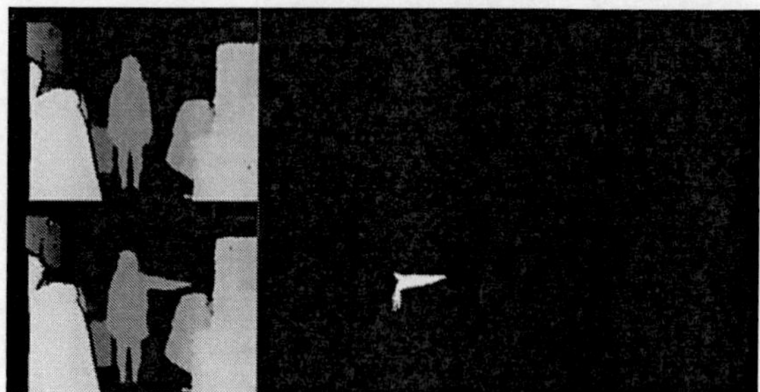

Fig. 5: Illustration of the human-contained background situation.

between L_t and L_{t-1} are calculated as:

$$d_{ij} = dist(com(l_t^i), com(l_{t-1}^j)), \tag{1}$$

where $com(l)$ estimates the center of mass of the points belonging to the label l and $dist(\mathbf{p}_1, \mathbf{p}_2)$ calculates the Euclidean distance between $\mathbf{p}_1$ and $\mathbf{p}_2$. For all pairs of distances with l_t^i, minimum matching index j^* is calculated as:

$$j^* = \underset{0 \leq j < N}{\operatorname{argmin}}(d_{ij}), \tag{2}$$

where N is a maximum number of labels in L_{t-1}. If d_{ij^*} has a value lower than the certain threshold, it indicates that l_t^i and $l_t^{j^*}$ are likely to belong to the same object. Therefore label index of l_t^i is replaced with the label index of $l_t^{j^*}$. Equation (2) is applied for all i to find all matching pairs of labels.

Subsequently, rescanning procedure is processed by using a list structure. For new observed labels, corresponding labels are inserted to the list. Matching pairs of labels are kept in the list and not-matching labels in a previous label space are removed from the list. The example of label rescanning step is illustrated in Fig. 4. In the figure, black lines represent matching pairs of labels. Dotted labels indicate new observed labels in the scene. A label shaded in gray represent the label which does no longer exists in the scene.

The label rescanning problem can be considered as a partitioning problem which keeps track of a set of elements partitioned into a number of disjoint sets. Union-find algorithm gives a solution for the problem. By utilizing a spaghetti stack based union-find algorithm, the proposed method takes $O(nlog(n))$ time for rescanning labels in consecutive frames.

One of the benefits of adopting union-find algorithm is that algorithm can easily find the undesirably merged labels. When two or more previous labels are matched with a single current label in the disjoint-set data structure, it means that two previous labels are undesirably merged to the current label. For every pixels $\mathbf{p}_m$ belong to the merged label l_t^m, we assign a new label l^{new} as:

$$l^{new} = \underset{l_{t-1}^j \in L_{t-1}^c}{\operatorname{argmin}} (dist(com(l_{t-1}^j), \mathbf{p}_m)), \tag{3}$$

where L_{t-1}^c is a set containing candidates of the new labels. After the correction step, new labels are assigned to the merged region.

3. Experimental results

After rescanning and correction is done, resulting labeled images are categorized and analyzed one by one. Furthermore, computational cost for the proposed method is measured to evaluate an efficiency of the method.

First case is the human-contained background situation which is illustrated in Fig. 5. Left-most column shows a quantized range map. Middle column contains visualized range maps of I_{FR} which has no information of fixed static objects. Right-most column shows labeled objects in the scene. As the human is modeled as background, the proposed method does not produce proper foreground regions (first row). After slight movements of the human, accurate foreground regions are recovered from information in I_{FR} (second row).

Second case is the self-occlusion problems. Some of self-occlusion cases are illustrated in Fig. 6. Left-most column shows a background removed range map. Middle column represents results of the labeling step. Right-most column shows corrected labeling results with the x-z plane projection. As human limbs have high degree of freedom, self-occlusions are often induced by them and become inevitable in HCI system, as showh in Fig. 6. The proposed method, by solving such problems, becomes robust against pose variations of the human.

Third case is separating undesirably merged labels. First and second rows of Fig. 7 illustrate undesirably merged labels where human-object or human-human are connected, respectively. First column shows a quantized range map. Second column illustrates labeling results without the labeling correction. Third column shows corrected labeling results of the proposed method. The proposed method separates undesirably merged labels very well, as can be seen in Fig. 7.

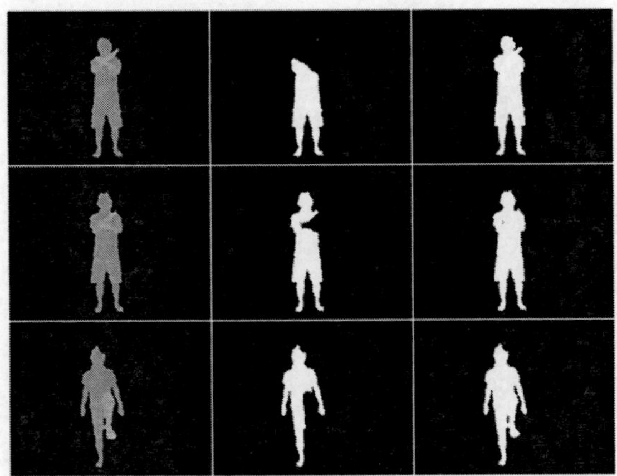

Fig. 6: Some of self-occlusion cases induced by human limbs.

In order to prove the efficiency of the proposed method, the time complexity of the method was evaluated. The evaluation was carried out on an Intel i5 3.3GHz computer with 4GB memory. A resolution of the input range map was 320×240. In this environment, the proposed method took 8.96 ms per frame. Due to the low computational complexity of the method, the proposed method can be easily extended to restricted environments such as mobile or embedded systems.

4. Conclusion

In this paper, a fast and robust human detection method in range map of complex environment is proposed. The proposed method is robust against self-occlusions and can separate undesirably merged labels. Moreover, the proposed method can cope with human-contained background situations. In common personal computer environment, the proposed method processed one frame range map within 10 ms. Due to efficiency and robustness of the method, the proposed method can be extended to mobile or embedded environments.

References

[1] Microsoft Corp. Redmon WA. Kinect for Xbox 360.

[2] Intel Corp. Santa Calra CA. Creative Interactive Gesture Camera.

[3] F. Karray, M. Alemzadeh, J. A. Saleh, and M. N. Arab, "Human-Computer Interaction: Overview on State of the Art," *International Journal on Smart Sensing and Intelligent Systems*, vol. 1, no. 1, pp. 137-159, 2008.

[4] S. H. Cho, T. Kim, D. Kim, "Pose Robust Human Detection in Depth Images Using Multiply-Oriented 2D Elliptical Filters," *International Journal of Pattern Recognition and Artificial Intelligence*, vol. 24, no. 5, pp. 691-717, 2010.

[5] S. Ikemura and H. Fujiyoshi, "Real-Time Human Detection using Relational Depth Similarity Features," *Asian Conference on Computer Vision*, vol. 6495, pp 25-38, 2011.

[6] L. Xia, C. C. Chen, and J. K. Agaarwal, "Human Detectio Using Depth Information by Kinect," *Workshop on Human Activity Understanding from 3D Data in conjunction with CVPR*, 2011.

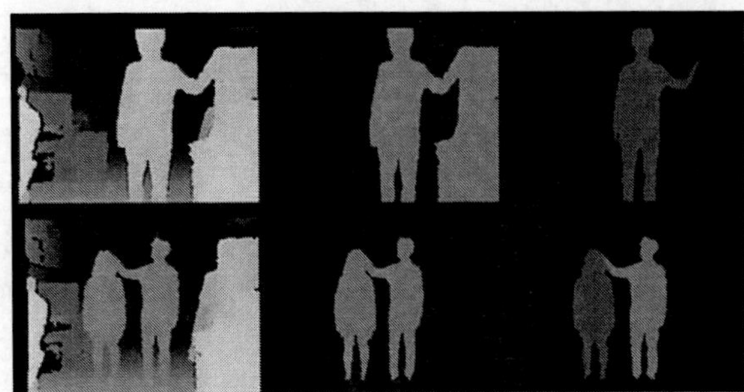

Fig. 7: Examples of the undesirably merged labels.

[7] C. Stauffer and W. E. L. Grimson, "Adaptive background mixture models for real-time tracking," *Computer Vision and Pattern Recognition*, 1998.

[8] http://www.openni.org

[9] R. Labayrade, D. Aubert, and J. P. Tarel, "Real Time Obstacle Detection in Stereovision on Non Flat Road Geometry Through "V-disparity" Representation," Intelligent Vehicle, 2002.

[10] L. G. Shapiro and G. Stockman, *Computer Vision*, Prentice Hall, 1st edition, 2001.

[11] R. C Gonzalez and R. E Woods, *Digital Image Processing*, Pearson Education, New Jersey, 2010.

[12] T. H. Cormen, C. E. Leiserson, R. L. Rivest, and C. Stein, *Introduction to Algorithms*, MIT Press and McGraw-Hill, 2nd edition, 2001.

Fingerspelling Alphabet Recognition Using A Two-level Hidden Markov Model

S. Lu, J. Picone, and S. Kong
Department of Electrical and Computer Engineering, Temple University, Philadelphia, PA, USA

Abstract - *Fingerspelling is widely used for communication amongst signers. Signer-independent (SI) recognition of the American Sign Language alphabet is a very challenging task due to factors such as the large number of similar gestures, hand orientation and cluttered background. We propose a novel framework that uses a two-level hidden Markov model (HMM) that can recognize each gesture as a sequence of sub-units and performs integrated segmentation and recognition. Features based on the Histogram of Oriented Gradient (HOG) method are used. The focus of this work is optimization of this configuration with respect to two parameters: the number of sub-units and the number of states in the HMMs. Moreover, we evaluated the system on signer-dependent (SD) and signer-independent (SI) tasks for the ASL Fingerspelling Dataset and achieved error rates of 2.0% and 46.8% respectively. The SI results improved the best previously published results by 18.2% absolute (28.0% relative).*

Keywords: American Sign Language, Fingerspelling, Hand Gesture Recognition, HOG, Hidden Markov Models

1 Introduction

Developing automated recognition of American Sign Language (ASL) is important since ASL is the primary mode of communication for most deaf people. In North America alone it is estimated that as many as *500,000* people use ASL as their primary language for communication [1]. ASL consists of approximately *6,000* words with unique signs. Additional words are spelled using fingerspelling [2] of alphabet signs. In a typical communication, *10%* to *15%* of the words are signed by fingerspelling of alphabet signs. Similar to written English, the one-handed Latin alphabet in ASL consists of *26* hand gestures. The objective of this paper is to design a recognition system that can classify *24* ASL alphabet signs from a static 2D image. We excluded *"J"* and *"Z"* because they are dynamic hand gestures. Recognition of dynamic gestures is the subject of future research that is a straightforward extension of the work presented here.

A popular approach to ASL gesture recognition is to use sensory gloves [3][4]. Advanced sensors, such as Microsoft's Kinect, have become popular in recent years because they provide alternate information such as depth that can be very useful for gesture recognition applications. Such systems typically achieve better performance than a simple 2D camera but are often costly, intrusive and/or inconvenient. Therefore, the focus of our work is to only use intensity information, which can be collected from any single 2D camera.

Feris et al. [5] used a multi-flash image capture system, and achieved a signer-dependent (SD) recognition error rate of 4% on a dataset consisting of 72 images from a single signer. Pugeault et al. [6] developed an approach that used Gabor features and random forests and evaluated it on a dataset that consisted of 5 sets of signs from 4 signers, 24 gestures per subject, and over 500 samples per gesture for each signer (a total of over 60,000 images). This dataset is known as the ASL Fingerspelling (ASL-FS) Dataset, and is the basis for the work presented here. Their best recognition error rate was 25%, achieved by combining both color and depth information. It is important to note, however, that this error rate was achieved using a closed-loop evaluation – the evaluation dataset contained the same five signers as the training set.

Munib et al. [2] proposed a fingerspelling recognition system based on a Hough transform and neural networks. On a dataset consisting of 15 signers and 20 signs per signer, they achieved an error rate of 20%. Vieriu et al. [7] developed a static hand gesture recognition system using the angle distribution of a hand contour and a simple left to right hidden Markov model (HMM), and achieved an error rate of 3.8% for an SD test. However, the database they used contained only 9 hand gestures with simple backgrounds.

Our proposed method, shown in Figure 1, is based on HMMs also, delivers an error rate that is 18.2% lower than [6] on the same data, and represents the best published results on the ASL dataset for both SD and signer-independent (SI) evaluations. Because the dataset is relatively small, we used a cross-validation approach to measure SI performance. Our system features an unsupervised training mode that only requires a label for the overall image. Detailed transcriptions of subsections of the images, such as finger segments, are not required.

Scale invariance and environment adaptation are desired properties for any practical fingerspelling recognition system. Typical solutions include normalization and/or a priori segmentation. Normalization often causes distortion of the original data and also changes the geometric structure of the hand gesture. A priori segmentation is sub-optimal and often fails in the presence of noisy backgrounds such as complex

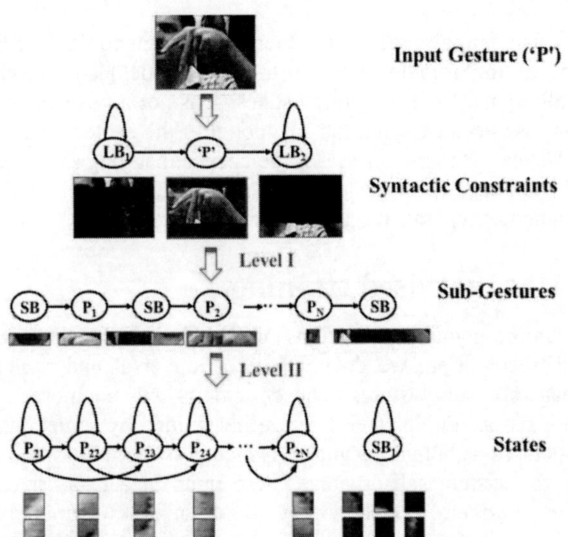

Figure 1: *A framework for fingerspelling that uses a two-level HMM architecture is shown.*

clutter. An HMM-based approach is attractive because it integrates the segmentation and recognition process, jointly optimizing both. However, the time-synchronous nature of the Markov model must be adjusted to deal with the 2D data presented by an image.

2 A two-level HMM architecture

A traditional HMM architecture typically involves three steps: (1) feature extraction, (2) parameter estimation via an iterative training process, and (3) recognition based on a Viterbi-style decoding [8]. In the architecture shown in Figure 1, each image is segmented into rectangular regions of $N \times N$ pixels, and an overlapping analysis window of $M \times M$ pixels is used to compute features. The image is scanned from left-to-right, top-to-bottom to facilitate real-time processing, as shown in Figure 2. The images in ASL-FS vary in size from *60x90* pixels to *170x130* pixels with the majority of the images approximately *80x100* pixels in dimension.

We ran an extensive series of baseline experiments on a subset of ASL-FS to optimize the frame and window sizes.

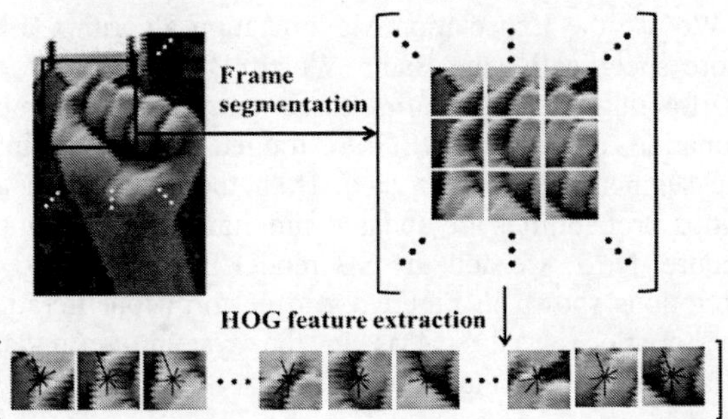

Figure 2: *A frame-based analysis was used to extract 9-dimensional HOG features.*

Selected results from these experiments are shown in Table 1. The best result was obtained with a combination of a frame size of *5* pixels and a window size of *30* pixels (referred to as *5/30*). The optimal number of states and model topology are related to these parameters. The *5/30* combination represents a good tradeoff between computational complexity, model complexity and recognition performance.

We selected Histogram of Oriented Gradient (HOG) features to use in our experiments [9][10] due to their popularity in imaging applications. To calculate HOG features, the image gradient magnitude, g, and angle, θ, for each pixel (u,v) are first calculated using a 1D filter and as shown below:

$$g(u,v) = \sqrt{g_x(u,v)^2 + g_y(u,v)^2} \tag{1}$$

$$\theta(u,v) = \arctan\frac{g_{y(u,v)}}{g_x(u,v)}. \tag{2}$$

For each frame, we compute a feature vector, f_i by quantizing the signed orientation into N orientation bins weighted by the gradient magnitude as defined by:

$$f_i = [f_i(n)]^T_{n\in[1,2,\ldots,N]} \tag{3}$$

$$f_i(n) = \sum_{(u,v)\in F_i} g(u,v)\delta[bin(u,v)-n]. \tag{4}$$

The function $bin(u,v)$ returns the index of the bin associated with the pixel (u,v). Parameter tuning experiments similar to those shown in Table 1 indicated that 9 bins were optimal, which is consistent with [10]. Since we used an overlapping analysis, we set each block to have only one cell when extracting HOG features.

These features were then used as input to the two-level HMM architecture shown in Figure 1. The top-level of the system applies syntactic constraints. This level serves two purposes. First, it restricts the system to output one hypothesis per image, which is consistent with the task definition – one sign is contained in each image. Any of the 24 signs can be output by the center node in the top-level HMM denoted "syntactic constraints" in Figure 1. This constraint avoids insertion errors by preventing multiple hypotheses per image.

Table 1. *A series of experiments were performed to optimize the value of the frame and window sizes.*

Frame (N)	Window (M)	% Overlap	% Error
5	20	75%	7.1%
5	30	83%	4.4%
10	20	50%	5.1%
10	30	67%	5.0%
10	60	83%	8.0%

Second, it implicitly performs segmentation of the image by forcing each frame of the image to be classified as either background, which we refer to as long background (LB), or gesture. LB can only occur immediately preceding or following a hypothesis of an alphabet sign. Images are modeled as having an arbitrary number of frames classified as background, followed by one alphabet sign, followed by an arbitrary number of frames again classified as background. Hence, this level implements a coarse segmentation of the image as part of the recognition process.

The second level, labeled "Sub-Gestures" in Figure 1, models each alphabet sign as a left-to-right HMM that alternates between a model denoted short background (SB) followed by a model corresponding to a sub-gesture (SG). This level models each sign as a sequence of sub-gestures. The optimal number of SG models for each sign will be addressed in the next section. The SB model allows for sections of the image between sub-gestures to be modeled as background (e.g., the space between two vertically raised fingers). The function of this level is to decompose each sign into a unique sequence of sub-gestures. Training of these models is performed in a completely unsupervised manner.

Each sub-gesture is implemented as a traditional left-to-right HMM with skip states. This model is known as a Bakis model [8] and has been used extensively in other HMM applications [11][12]. Performance is not extremely sensitive to the topology of this model, though in pilot experiments we obtained a slight decrease in error rate using skip states. The main virtue of the skip state model is that it allows the system to map fewer frames of data to the model, thereby reducing the minimum number of states required by the model.

Unlike many systems that recognize gestures as a whole, we model each alphabet sign with a sequence that typically consists of LB, SB and a sequence of SG models, as shown in Figure 3. The reason we have two different types of background models is that SB is more focused on small background regions within fingers or at image boundaries, while the LB model is used for modeling large background areas preceding or following the sign. The SB model is a single-state HMM with a self-transition. The LB model is 11 states and also allows each state to self-transition.

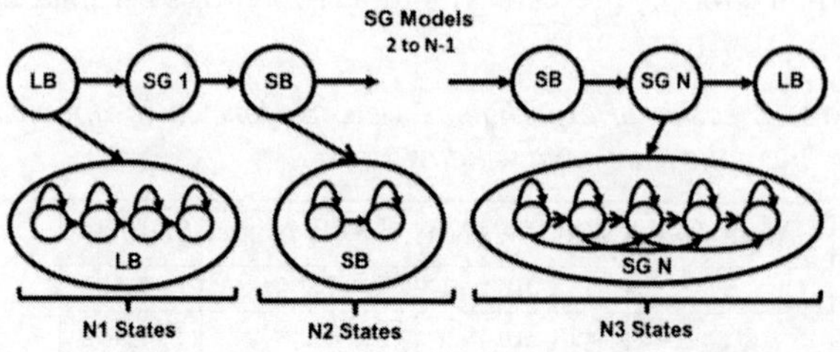

Figure 3: *Our HMM architecture uses a two-level approach that models an image as a combination of LB, SB and sub-gesture (SG) models.*

It is common practice in other applications to tie the SB model to the middle state of the LB model [13], which typically consists of only three states. It is not a wise choice in our case because tying the SB model to the center state of the 11-state LB model increases the chance that long stretches of a hand image will be mapped to LB. Therefore, LB and SB are trained as separate models in our experiments.

3 Unsupervised training

Unlike mature applications of HMMs in fields such as speech recognition, we do not have a universal underlying language for sub-gestures. The core units that compose an image such as an alphabet sign are not guided by something as structured as human language. Hence, it is highly desirable to let the system self-organize these units in a data-driven manner. Further, though supervised training is extremely effective, eliminating the need for transcribed training data significantly reduces the cost and development time of a pattern recognition system.

Therefore, we have implemented an unsupervised training process in which the LB, SB and SG models are learned without the need for any manual transcriptions other than the identity of the alphabet sign represented by the image. Each sample uses a generic transcript is "Start-LB, SG1, SB, SG2, ... , SGN, End-LB." Here, Start-LB refers to an LB model that must occur at the beginning of an image file. Both Start-LB and End-LB are tied, meaning they share the same HMM model.

Our training process follows procedures used extensively in speech recognition applications [11], and is based on the hidden Markov model toolkit, HTK [13]. We initialize our HMMs using a flat-start process in which all models are set to use a single Gaussian distribution with a mean and variance set to the global mean and variance computed across the whole training data [13]. The transition probabilities are manually initialized to favor a transition to the next state. For models with skip states, we initialize the self-transition, transition to the next state and the skip transition probabilities to be 0.1, 0.8 and 0.1, respectively. If there is no skip state, the self-transition and next state transition probabilities are set to 0.1 and 0.9.

We use the Expectation Maximization algorithm (EM), or more specifically, the Baum Welch (BW) algorithm, for HMM training. During the first three iterations of parameter reestimation, only LB and SG are trained so that we find a coarse segmentation of the data. Both the observation and transition probabilities are updated simultaneously within this procedure. Next, we add the SB model by introducing the transcriptions shown in Figure 3 and perform four iterations of reestimation. All HMMs in the system are updated simultaneously at each iteration.

Once we have a set of stable set of models that use a single Gaussian mixture model, we use a mixture-splitting approach to generate mixture models. At each stage, the algorithm repeatedly splits the mixture with the largest mixture weight into two mixture components [13]. This process is repeated until the required number of mixture components is obtained. We start with one mixture, and successively double the number of mixture components until we reach 16 mixture components. Four iterations of BW reestimation are run at each step of the process (e.g., after splitting 8 mixtures into 16 mixtures).

It is common practice in these types of HMM systems to use twice the number of mixture components for the LB and SB models as used in the SG models [14] to accommodate variation in background images. However, for ASL-FS, doubling the number of mixture components for LB and SB did not improve performance. Nevertheless, we followed this convention in our work here.

The decoding algorithm used for recognition is based on a Viterbi decoder [13] that utilizes a beam search algorithm. Pruning thresholds are set very high so that the decoder essentially only performs a dynamic programming-based pruning. The syntactic constraints are imposed using a nonprobabilistic model that constrains the output to one gesture per image and performs a forced-choice decision. Decoding one image typically requires *0.22* secs and *0.29* Mbytes of memory on a *2.67* GHz Pentium processor and is roughly $O(N_f \times N_s^2)$ in complexity, where N_f is the number of frames and N_s is the total number of states.

4 Experiments

Extensive tuning experiments were conducted to optimize the parameters of the system. Based on past experiences with other applications [14], we optimized these parameters on the SD task, for which performance was generally fairly high and relatively sensitive to changes in these parameter settings. Our experiments focused on optimizing the number of SG segments, states and mixture components. Since the data consists of at least 500 tokens per sign, the data for each sign for the SD task was partitioned into 10 randomly selected subsets. A cross-validation approach was used in which 9 subsets were selected for training and the remaining one was used for evaluation. We then rotated the sets so that each of the 10 partitions was used exactly once for evaluation.

The optimized parameter settings are shown in Table 3. The experiments for optimization of the frame size, window size and number of HOG bins were summarized in Section 2. The number of segments in each SG model was varied from 5 to 13, resulting in error rates that ranged from 10.9% to 9.9%. Optimal performance of 9.9% error was obtained with 11 sub-gesture segments.

Once the number of segments was fixed, we explored the optimal number of states for each sub-gesture model under the constraint that all models should have the same number of states (this is a reasonable approach based on previous experience [13]). We also varied the number of states for LB (from 3 to 21) and SB (from 1 to 9). The optimal number of states for SB, LB and SG were found to be 1, 11 and 21, respectively. Note that the SG models include skip states, so a sub-gesture model with 21 states requires a minimum of 10 frames to be hypothesized. An SB model of one state is fairly common in HMM systems. Its self-transition probability is 0.42, which means the average duration of an SB model is 1.7 frames. Similarly, the LB model's transition probability structure indicates that the average duration of LB model is 22.3 frames, which is slightly larger than the width of an image in frames.

Table 3. *A summary of the optimal parameter values for our two-level HMM system is shown.*

System Parameter	Value
Frame Size (pixels)	5
Window Size (pixels)	30
No. HOG Bins	9
No. Sub-gesture Segments	11
No. States Per Sub-gesture Model	21
No. States Long Background (LB)	11
No. States Short Background (SB)	1
No. Gaussian Mixtures (*SG* models)	16
No. Gaussian Mixtures (*LB/SB* models)	32

We explore optimization of the number of Gaussian mixtures for each state in Table 2. A significant reduction in error rate was achieved, and this is consistent with what we have seen in other applications. The mixture components for the SG models, not surprisingly, tend to model consistent variations in the data, such as lighting conditions. The mixture components for the LB model are close in weight, which implies the background was random and inconsistent.

Once the final system configuration was completed, we performed two sanity checks. First, we varied a number of parameters simultaneously to ensure that the final operating point was optimal. Since there is always a chance that parameter settings are coupled, we wanted to make sure our sequential optimization approach to optimization found at the very least a local optimum. Fortunately, we were able to verify that the operating point summarized in Table 3 was indeed optimal for this dataset.

Table 2. *A summary of performance as function of the number of mixture components for the SG models.*

No. Mixtures	Error Rate (%)
1	9.9
2	6.8
4	4.4
8	2.9
16	2.0

Second, we examined how performance varied as a function of the cross-validation set. Error rates for each set are shown in Figure 4 (labeled Set 1 to Set 5) as a function of the index of the cross-validation subset (for the 10 randomly chosen subsets for each set). We note that Set 4 always had a higher than average error rate. This is due to a larger degree of hand rotation as shown in Figure 5. The average error rate was 2.0%, which represents the best-published result on this task using only color information.

To remain consistent with previously published results, we also evaluated the system on a closed-loop test in which half of the data for a signer was used for training, while the remaining half was used for evaluation [6]. We refer this is as the "Shared" set in Table 4. The HMM system using only color information performs better than a color-only system and a system that uses both color and depth information.

To perform true open set evaluation, and yet maintain reasonable statistical significance, we also used a leave-one-out approach in which all but one of the signers was used for training and the remaining signer used for testing. We then rotated the set so that each signer was used exactly once as a test set. We refer to this as the "SI" set in Table 4. Our SI results with color only exceed the performance of the

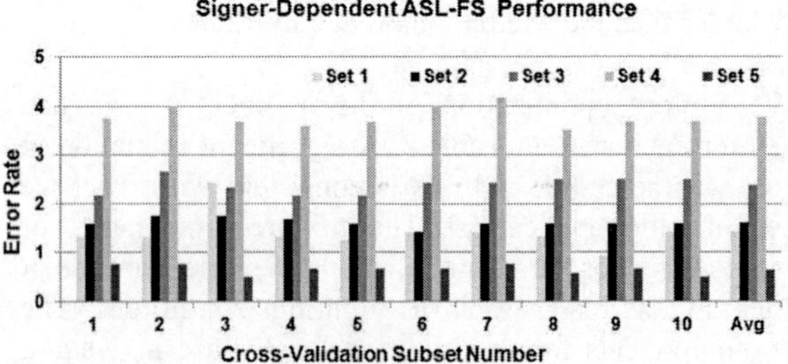

Figure 4: *SD results are shown as a function of the cross-validation set.*

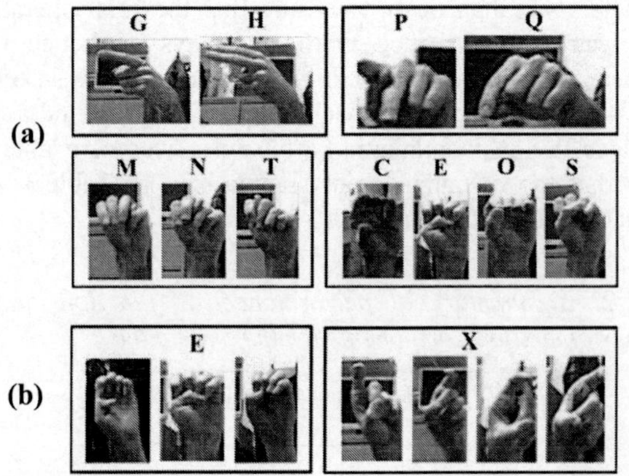

Figure 5: *Gestures with a high confusion error rate are shown in (a). Images with significant variations in background and hand rotation are shown in (b).*

Table 4. *Results for various training paradigms are shown for the ASL-FS dataset. Three tasks are included: signer-dependent (SD), multi-signer training in which the same subjects were used for training and evaluation (Shared), and signer-independent (SI).*

System	SD	Shared	SI
Pugeault (Color Only)	N/A	27.0%	65.0%
Pugeault (Color + Depth)	N/A	25.0%	53.0%
HMM (Color Only)	2.0%	7.8%	46.8%

color+depth system reported in [6] and represent the best-published results on an SI task for the ASL-FS dataset.

An analysis of the common error modalities indicated that a major contributor to the error rate was confusions between similar gestures. Examples of this are shown in Figure 5(a). Another factor that results in a large portion of the errors is signer variations, such as angle rotations and scale changes, as shown in Figure 5(b). These have a significant influence on the overall error rate and require more sophisticated sub-gesture models or rotation-independent features.

Finally, a major goal in this work was a system that could accurately segment the data inside the recognition loop. Segmentation is crucial to high performance recognition and must be done in an integrated fashion to be robust to background and lighting variations. We examined segmentations of some typical images as shown in Figure 6. Frames marked as LB are shown in yellow, are generally recognized well because they are constrained to occur at the beginning and end of an input image. However, the SB model, which is used to model small regions of background images, is not always correctly used. Lighting and changes in the background color seem to cause the SB model to incorrectly identify hand images. Additional work on segmentation is clearly needed.

5 Conclusions

In this paper, we have presented a two-level HMM-based ASL fingerspelling alphabet recognition system that trains gesture and background noise models automatically. Five essential parameters were tuned by cross-validation. Our best system configuration achieved a 2.0% error rate on an SD task, and a 46.8% error rate on an SI task. Both represent the best-published results on this data. An analysis of the confusion data suggests that gestures that are visually similar are, in fact, contributing most to the error rate. Hand rotations and scale changes are also challenges that need to be addressed.

As reliable detection by the SB model is crucial to a high performance system, we are currently developing new architectures that perform improved segmentation. Both supervised and unsupervised methods will be employed. Once that architecture definition is complete, we believe we

Figure 6: *Examples of segmentation results.*

will have a very stable platform from which we can experiment with better features and statistical models. We expect performance to be significantly better on the SI task.

Finally, all scripts, models, and data related to these experiments are available from our project web site: http://www.isip.piconepress.com/projects/asl_fs. The ASL-FS data is publicly available from [6].

6 Acknowledgements

This research was supported in part by the National Science Foundation through Major Research Instrumentation Grant No. CNS-09-58854. We also wish to thank Nicolas Pugeault and his colleagues for developing and releasing the ASL-FS Database.

7 References

[1] K. Li, K. Lothrop, E. Gill, and S. Lau, "A Web-Based Sign Language Translator Using 3D Video Processing," in *Proceedings of the International Conference on Network-Based Information Systems*, 2011, pp. 356–361.

[2] Q. Munib, M. Habeeb, B. Takruri, and H. Al-Malik, "American Sign Language (ASL) Recognition Based on Hough Transform and Neural Networks," *Expert Systems with Applications*, vol. 32, no. 1, pp. 24–37, Jan. 2007.

[3] J. M. Allen, P. K. Asselin, and R. Foulds, "American Sign Language Finger Spelling Recognition System," in *Proceedings of the IEEE Bioengineering Conference*, 2003, pp. 285–286.

[4] C. Oz and M. Leu, "American Sign Language Word Recognition with a Sensory Glove Using Artificial Neural Networks," *Engineering Applications of Artificial Intelligence*, vol. 24, no. 7, pp. 1204–1213, Oct. 2011.

[5] R. Feris, M. Turk, R. Raskar, K. Tan, and G. Ohashi, "Exploiting Depth Discontinuities for Vision-Based Fingerspelling Recognition," in *Proceedings of the IEEE Workshop on Real-time Vision for Human-Computer Interaction*, 2004, pp. 155–162.

[6] N. Pugeault and R. Bowden, "Spelling It Out: Real-time ASL Fingerspelling Recognition," in *Proceedings of the IEEE International Conference on Computer Vision Workshops*, 2011, pp. 1114–1119 (available at *http://info.ee.surrey.ac.uk/Personal/N.Pugeault/index.php?section=FingerSpellingDataset*).

[7] R.-L. Vieriu, B. Goras, and L. Goras, "On HMM Static Hand Gesture Recognition," in *Proceedings of International Symposium on Signals, Circuits and Systems*, 2011, pp. 1–4.

[8] L. Rabiner, "A Tutorial on Hidden Markov Models and Selected Applications in Speech Recognition," *Proceedings of the IEEE*, vol. 77, no. 2, pp. 257–286, 1989.

[9] M. B. Kaaniche and F. Bremond, "Tracking HOG Descriptors for Gesture Recognition," in *Proceedings of the Sixth IEEE International Conference on Advanced Video and Signal Based Surveillance*, 2009, pp. 140–145.

[10] N. Dalal and B. Triggs, "Histograms of Oriented Gradients for Human Detection," in *Proceedings of the IEEE Computer Society Conference on Computer Vision and Pattern Recognition*, 2005, vol. 1, pp. 886–893.

[11] J. Picone, "Continuous Speech Recognition Using Hidden Markov Models," *IEEE ASSP Magazine*, vol. 7, no. 3, pp. 26–41, Jul. 1990.

[12] M. Zimmermann and H. Bunke, "Hidden Markov Model Length Optimization for Handwriting Recognition Systems," in *Proceedings of the International Workshop on Frontiers in Handwriting Recognition*, 2001, pp. 369–374.

[13] S. Young, G. Evermann, M. Gales, T. Hain, D. Kershaw, X. Liu, G. Moore, J. Odell, D. Ollagson, D. Povey, V. Valtchev, and P. Woodland, *The HTK Book*, Cambridge, UK, 2006.

[14] I. Alphonso and J. Picone, "Network Training For Continuous Speech Recognition," in *Proceedings of the IEEE International Conference on Acoustics, Speech and Signal Processing*, 2004.

[15] J. Matoušek, D. Tihelka, and J. Psutka, "Automatic Segmentation for Czech Concatenative Speech Synthesis Using Statistical Approach with Boundary-specific Correction," in *Proceedings of the European Conference on Speech Communication and Technology*, 2003, pp. 301–304.

[16] Y. Kim and A. Conkie, "Automatic Segmentation Combining an HMM-based Approach and Spectral Boundary Correction," in *Proceedings of the International Conference on Spoken Language Processing*, 2002, pp. 145–148.

[17] V. Khachaturyan, "Handwritten Signature Verification Using Hidden Markov Models," in *Proceedings of the International Conference on Image Processing, Computer Vision, and Pattern Recognition*, 2012, pp. 347–350.

On Using Class-dependent Principle Component Analysis for Dissimilarity-Based Classifications

Sang-Woon Kim
Department of Computer Engineering, Myongji University, Yongin, 449-728 Korea

Abstract— *The aim of this paper* [1] *is to present an empirical evaluation on using class-dependent principle component analysis (PCA) for dissimilarity-based classifications (DBC) [18]. In DBC, the classification performance relies heavily on how well the dissimilarity space is constructed. In this paper, we study a way of constructing it in eigenspaces, spanned by the subset of principal eigenvectors, extracted from the training data set through the class-dependent PCA, instead of utilizing prototype selection methods and/or generalizing dissimilarity measures. In particular, we generate an eigenspace (i.e., a covariance matrix) per class, not for the entire data set, to compute distances in a vector space constructing a dissimilarity-based classifier. Our experimental results, obtained with well-known benchmark data and some UCI data sets, demonstrate that when the dimensionality of the eigenspaces has been appropriately selected, DBC, albeit not always, can be improved in terms of classification accuracies.*

Keywords: statistical pattern recognition, dissimilarity-based classification, class-dependent principle component analysis

1. Introduction

Dissimilarity-based classifications (DBC) [18] are a way of defining classifiers among the classes, where the process is not based on feature measurements of individual objects (a set of features), but rather on a suitable dissimilarity measure among the individual objects (pairwise object comparisons). The advantage of this methodology is that since it does not operate on the class-conditional distributions, the problems associated with feature spaces, such as the curse of dimensionality and the small sample size problem, can be avoided [13]. Another salient advantage of such a paradigm is that it can utilize expert knowledge when measuring (dis)similarities between the pairwise objects [4].

The problem with this strategy, however, is that we need to measure the inter-pattern dissimilarities for all the training data to ensure there is no zero distance between objects of different classes. Consequently, the classes do not overlap, and therefore, the lower error bound is zero. The major issues we encountered when designing DBCs are summarized as follows: (1) How can prototype subsets be selected (or created) from the training samples [13], [18], [19]? (2) How can the dissimilarities between object samples be measured [17], [18]? (3) How can classifiers be designed in the dissimilarity space [12], [18]?and (4) How can the dissimilarity space be embedded in the pseudo-Euclidean space [4]?

Several strategies have been used to explore these issues. Specifically, with regard to solving the first problem, various methods have been proposed in the literature [19] as a means of selecting a representation subset of data that is both compact and capable of representing the entire data set. In these methods, a training set, T, is pruned to yield a subset of representative prototypes, P, where, without loss of generality, $|P| \leq |T|$. However, it is difficult to find the optimal number of prototypes and, furthermore, selecting prototype stage may potentially lose useful information for discrimination. To avoid these problems, Riesen et al. [20] and Kim [11] prefer not to directly select the representative prototypes from the training samples; rather, they use a dimensionality reduction scheme after computing the dissimilarity matrix with the *entire* training samples.

On the other hand, subspace methods of pattern recognition [16] are a technique in which the object classes are not primarily defined as bounded regions in a feature space, but rather given in terms of eigenspaces defined by the basis vectors of the principal component analysis (PCA) [10]. However, unlike conventional PCA, an eigenspace can be generated per class, not for the entire data set, in order to maximize the discriminatory power of the subspace [21]. Because different classes may have different characteristics and hence the reliability of the estimated covariance matrices can be significantly different. However, as the objective of PCA is the best pattern reconstruction that may not be optimal for classification. In order to overcome this problem from the classification point of view, numerous strategies, including Probabilistic PCA [22], Rotational invariant l_1-norm PCA [3], [14], and Asymmetric PCA [8], [9], have been proposed in the literature. In particular, in [8], Jiang addressed the problem of applying PCA on the asymmetric classes and/or the unbalanced data. From this perspective, in this paper the training data set is partitioned into several subsets (i.e., one per class) and then performs PCA about each subset.

In DBC, on the other hand, the classification performance

[1]This work was supported by the National Research Foundation of Korea funded by the Korean Government (2012R1A1A2041661). The author is very grateful to Prof. Duin from the Delft University of Technology for the instructive discussions we had in Benicassim and his valuable comments.

relies heavily on how well the dissimilarity space, which is determined by the dissimilarity matrix, is constructed. Thus, to improve the classification performance, more robust dissimilarity matrices should be constructed. To achieve this goal, the prototype subset should be selected [19] and/or the dissimilarity could be generalized [17]. From this point of view, in this paper we perform DBC in eigenspaces spanned by the principal eigenvectors, expecting that the noise and outlier could be excluded from the dissimilarity representation, without the need to select prototypes or generalize the dissimilarity. Especially, we generate an eigenspace (i.e., a covariance matrix) per class, not for the entire data set.

The major goal of this paper is to demonstrate that the classification performance of DBC can be improved by measuring the dissimilarity in eigenspaces constructed with class-dependent PCA, not class-independent PCA that is usually employed in PCA-based applications. This goal can be achieved by appropriately projecting the data set on multiple eigenspaces, one per class, and effectively measuring the dissimilarity between the projected points. Experimental results, obtained with a well-known benchmark data and some UCI data sets, demonstrate that when the dimensionality of the eigenspaces has been appropriately selected, the DBC can be improved in terms of classification accuracies.

The remainder of the paper is organized as follows: In Section 2, after providing a brief introduction to DBC, we continuously present an explanation of the class-dependent PCA and that of the DBC in multiple eigenspaces. In Section 3, we present the experimental results obtained with the benchmark image data and UCI real-life data sets. Finally, in Section 4, we present our concluding remarks as well as some feature works that deserve further study.

2. Related Work

In this section, we briefly review dissimilarity-based classifications and distance measures in eigenspaces that are closely related to the present empirical study. The details of these methodologies can be found in the related literature, including [18] and [21].

2.1 Dissimilarity Representation [18]

A dissimilarity representation of a set of object samples, $T = \{\boldsymbol{x}_i\}_{i=1}^{n} \in \mathbb{R}^d$, is based on pairwise comparisons and is expressed, for example, as an $n \times m$ dissimilarity matrix, $D_{T,P}[\cdot,\cdot]$, where $P = \{\boldsymbol{p}_j\}_{j=1}^{m} \in \mathbb{R}^d$, a prototype set, is extracted from T, and the subscripts of D represent the set of elements on which the dissimilarities are evaluated. Thus, each entry, $D_{T,P}[i,j]$, corresponds to the dissimilarity between the pairs of objects, $\boldsymbol{x}_i$ and $\boldsymbol{p}_j$, where $\boldsymbol{x}_i \in T$ and $\boldsymbol{p}_j \in P$. Consequently, when given a distance measure between two vectors, $d(\cdot,\cdot)$, an object, $\boldsymbol{x}_i$, is represented as a column (or a row) vector, $\delta(\boldsymbol{x}_i, P)$, as follows:

$$\delta(\boldsymbol{x}_i, P) = [d(\boldsymbol{x}_i, \boldsymbol{p}_1), \cdots, d(\boldsymbol{x}_i, \boldsymbol{p}_m)], \; 1 \le i \le n. \quad (1)$$

Here, the dissimilarity matrix, $D_{T,P}[\cdot,\cdot]$, defines vectors in a *dissimilarity space* on which the d-dimensional object, $\boldsymbol{x}$, given in the input-feature space, is represented as an m-dimensional vector, $\delta(\boldsymbol{x}, P)$ or simply $\delta(\boldsymbol{x})$.

On the basis of what we explained briefly, an conventional algorithm for DBC is summarized in the following:

1. Select the prototype subset, P, from the training set, T, by using one of the prototype selection methods.

2. Using Eq. (1), compute the dissimilarity matrix, $D_{T,P}[\cdot,\cdot]$, in which each dissimilarity is computed on the basis of a distance metric.

3. For a test sample, $\boldsymbol{z}$, compute a dissimilarity vector, $\delta(\boldsymbol{z})$, by using the same measure used in Step 2.

4. Achieve the classification by invoking a classifier built in the dissimilarity space and operating it on the dissimilarity vector $\delta(\boldsymbol{z})$.

In the above algorithm, it can seen that the performance of DBC relies heavily on how well the dissimilarity space, which is determined by the dissimilarity matrix, is constructed. Thus, to improve the performance, we need to ensure that the dissimilarity matrix is well assembled.

2.2 Class-dependent PCA [21]

The data set, T, can be decomposed into subsets, T_i, $(i = 1, \cdots, c)$, as follows: $T = \bigcup_{i=1}^{c} T_i$, $T_i = \{\boldsymbol{x}_j\}_{j=1}^{n_i} \in \mathbb{R}^d$, with $n = \sum_{i=1}^{c} n_i$, $T_i \cap T_j = \phi, \forall i \neq j$. Our goal is to perform DBC in multiple eigenspaces constructed with this *training* data set, $\bigcup_{i=1}^{c} T_i$, and to classify a new sample into an appropriate class. More specifically, we generate an eigenspace for each class, i.e., class-dependent PCA, instead of a single eigenspace for the whole data (as is usually done in PCA-based methods). To achieve this, for each T_i, we first find eigenvectors and eigenvalues, $\boldsymbol{\mu}_k^{(i)}$ and $\lambda_k^{(i)}$, $(k = 1, \cdots, d)$, of the covariance matrix, Σ_i, using $\Sigma_i \boldsymbol{\mu}_k^{(i)} = \lambda_k^{(i)} \boldsymbol{\mu}_k^{(i)}$, and sort them in a decreasing order according to the corresponding eigenvalues, i.e., $\lambda_1^{(i)} \ge, \cdots, \ge \lambda_d^{(i)}$. Next, these eigenvectors are transposed and selected to form the row vectors of a transformation matrix, $A_i = \{\boldsymbol{\mu}_k^{(i)}\}_{k=1}^{q} \in \mathbb{R}^d$. We then project the data samples, $\boldsymbol{x}_j$, $(j = 1, \cdots, n_i)$, into c q-dimensional subspaces, called eigenspaces, spanned by the arranged principal eigenvectors, using a transformation formula for each subset (i.e., class/cluster) as follows [12]:

$$\boldsymbol{y}_j^{(i)} = A_i^T (\boldsymbol{x}_j - \boldsymbol{m}_i), \; 1 \le i \le c, \quad (2)$$

where $\boldsymbol{y}_j^{(i)}$ denotes the j-th q-dimensional vector generated in the i-th eigenspace, A_i^T is the transpose of A_i, and $\boldsymbol{m}_i = \frac{1}{n_i}\sum_{j=1}^{n_i} \boldsymbol{x}_j$, where $\boldsymbol{x}_j \in T_i$.

From Eq. (2), it can be seen that all the samples of classes are projected around the common center which is the origin of the q-dimensional space (refer to [21] for more details). Therefore, instead of $\boldsymbol{m}_i$, it is required to find a *reference* vector such that its direction and displacement from the origin provides maximum separable projections in the eigenspace. The reference vector, $\boldsymbol{m}_{ref}$, can be computed as a production of the maximum eigenvalue and the corresponding eigenvector, i.e., $\boldsymbol{m}_{ref} = \boldsymbol{\mu}_1 \lambda_1$, from $S_B \boldsymbol{\mu} = \lambda \boldsymbol{\mu}$, where $S_B = \sum_{i=1}^{c} n_i(\boldsymbol{m}_i - \boldsymbol{m})(\boldsymbol{m}_i - \boldsymbol{m})^T$; $\boldsymbol{m} = \frac{1}{c}\sum_{i=1}^{c} \boldsymbol{m}_i$; $\boldsymbol{\mu}$ and λ are eigenvectors and their corresponding eigenvalues, respectively.

As mentioned previously, PCA is applied separately to each subset T_i of the training data, where i runs from 1 to c, the number of classes. Hence, according to Eq. (2), there should be for each sample as many projections as classes. Among the c projections, a projection, $\boldsymbol{y}_j^{(i^*)}$, is selected as the final projection, $\boldsymbol{y}_j$, for example, using the k-nearest neighbor rule. That is, for a test sample, $\boldsymbol{z}$, out of the k-closest neighbors to $\boldsymbol{z}$, $\{\boldsymbol{x}_l\}_{l=1}^{k}$, we first identify the number k_i of the samples that belong to the class i, where $\sum_{i=1}^{c} k_i = k$. Then, we select $\boldsymbol{y}_j^{(i^*)}$ as $\boldsymbol{y}_j$, for which $k_i > k_l$, $\forall l \neq i$.

In order to provide an illustrative example for the reason why using the multiple eigenspaces of the class-dependent PCA, we consider two artificially generated 2-dimensional and 2-class data sets, named Simple and Highleyman [5], respectively. Here, the two classes of them are differently defined by two Gaussian distributions, $Gauss(\boldsymbol{m}_1^{(i)}, \boldsymbol{S}_1^{(i)})$ and $Gauss(\boldsymbol{m}_2^{(i)}, \boldsymbol{S}_2^{(i)})$, ($i$ = 1,2 for the two data sets), respectively [2], where

$$\boldsymbol{m}_1^{(1)} = \begin{bmatrix} 0 \\ 0 \end{bmatrix}, \; \boldsymbol{m}_2^{(1)} = \begin{bmatrix} 2 \\ 0 \end{bmatrix},$$

$$\boldsymbol{S}_1^{(1)} = \boldsymbol{S}_2^{(1)} = \begin{bmatrix} 1 & 0 \\ 0 & 1 \end{bmatrix},$$

and

$$\boldsymbol{m}_1^{(2)} = \begin{bmatrix} 1 \\ 1 \end{bmatrix}, \; \boldsymbol{m}_2^{(2)} = \begin{bmatrix} 2 \\ 0 \end{bmatrix},$$

$$\boldsymbol{S}_1^{(2)} = \begin{bmatrix} 1 & 0 \\ 0 & 0.25 \end{bmatrix}, \; \boldsymbol{S}_2^{(2)} = \begin{bmatrix} 0.01 & 0 \\ 0 & 4 \end{bmatrix}.$$

Then, the class priors are $P(1) = P(2) = \frac{1}{2}$. That is, both classes of Highleyman have different distributions for each class, while those of Simple are all Gaussian distributed with identity matrix as covariance matrix as shown in Fig. 1.

Fig. 2 shows Highleyman and its PCA projections in eigenspaces computed with the class-independent PCA and the class-dependent PCA methods. From the figures, it should be observed that the number of the overlapped points of Fig. 2 (b) is larger than that of Fig. 2 (c).

In order to compare discriminatory powers of two eigenspaces computed with the class-independent PCA and

[2]See *gendats* and *gendath* functions in [5] for more details.

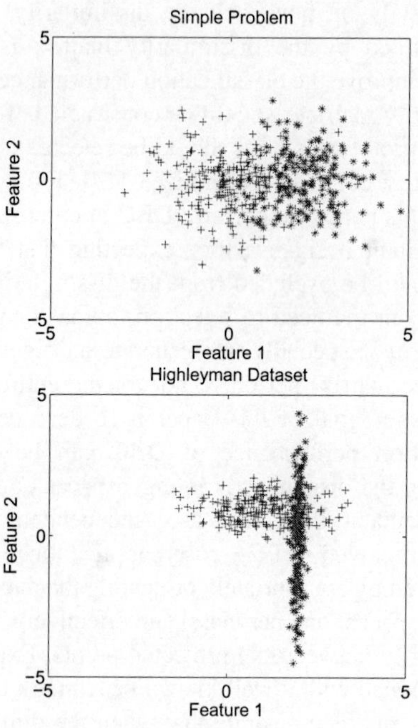

Fig. 1: Two artificial data sets: (a) top and (b) bottom; (a) Simple Problem and (b) Highleyman Dataset.

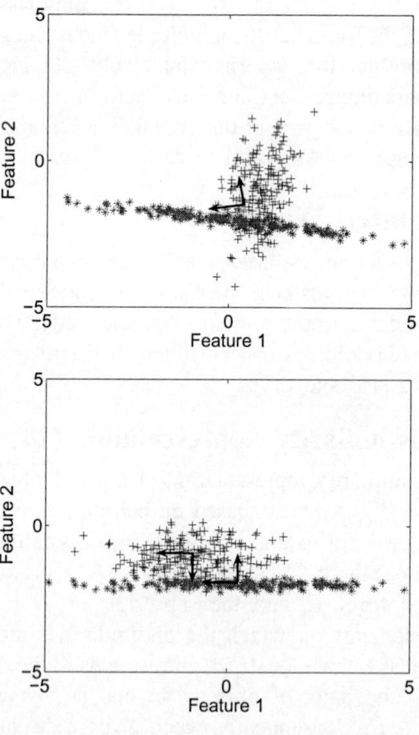

Fig. 2: PCA projections of Highleyman: (a) top and (b) bottom; (a) and (b) are obtained with the class-independent and the class-dependent PCA methods, respectively.

Table 1: Classification error rates (mean $\pm$ std) (%) obtained with two classifiers (*knnc* and *ldc*) in the two eigenspaces.

datasets	PCA	*knnc*	*ldc*
Simple	class-independent	27.20 $\pm$ 3.74	17.63 $\pm$ 3.25
	class-dependent	19.93 $\pm$ 3.41	19.93 $\pm$ 3.41
Highleyman	class-independent	12.03 $\pm$ 2.72	24.70 $\pm$ 3.87
	class-dependent	12.57 $\pm$ 2.67	12.57 $\pm$ 2.67

the class-dependent PCA methods, we carry out classifications on PCA projections of Simple and Highleyman in the subspaces and then obtain a result as summarized in Table 1. Here, the k-nearest neighbor classifier / the regularized normal density-based linear classifier (i.e., *knnc* / *ldc* [5]) and the *holdout* method are chosen.

From the result, the reader should observe that the discriminatory power in the eigenspaces of the class-dependent PCA is different from that of the class-independent PCA when the data have different distributions for each class.

2.3 DBC in Multiple Eigenspaces

The basic strategy of the proposed technique is to solve the classification problem by first mapping the input-feature space to eigenspaces using the class-dependent PCA, one for each class, and then performing a DBC in the eigenspaces. Therefore, the mean squared error between a feature vector, $\boldsymbol{x}$, and its projection, $\boldsymbol{y} = \widehat{\boldsymbol{x}}$, is: $\epsilon^2(q;\boldsymbol{\mu}_k) = E\left[||\boldsymbol{x} - \widehat{\boldsymbol{x}}||^2\right]$, where $E[\cdot]$ and $||\cdot||$ imply the expected value and the 2-norm, respectively. Here, since $||\widehat{\boldsymbol{x}}||^2 - 2\widehat{\boldsymbol{x}}^T\boldsymbol{x} = -\sum_{k=1}^{q}(\boldsymbol{\mu}_k^T\boldsymbol{x})^2 = -\sum_{k=1}^{q}(\boldsymbol{\mu}_k^T\boldsymbol{x}\boldsymbol{x}^T\boldsymbol{\mu}_k)$, we have an expression for ϵ^2 as follows:

$$\epsilon^2(q;\boldsymbol{\mu}_k) = E\left[||\boldsymbol{x}||^2\right] - \sum_{k=1}^{q}\boldsymbol{\mu}_k^T\Sigma\boldsymbol{\mu}_k, \qquad (3)$$

where $\Sigma = E\left[\boldsymbol{x}\boldsymbol{x}^T\right]$.

From Eq. (3), it can be seen that the larger value of the second term, $\sum_{k=1}^{q}\boldsymbol{\mu}_k^T\Sigma\boldsymbol{\mu}_k$, the smaller ϵ^2. That is, we can reduce the mean squared error, ϵ^2, when choosing appropriate basis vectors (eigenvectors) for each class. From this point of view, we employ the class-dependent PCA approach, instead of class-independent PCA that is usually done in PCA-based methods. The rationale of this strategy is presented in a later section together with experimental results. The proposed approach, which is referred to as an eigenspace DBC (EDBC), is summarized in the following:

1. Select the entire training set, $T = \bigcup_{i=1}^{c} T_i$, as the prototype subset, P.

2. For each subset T_i, after computing a transformation matrix A_i and a mean vector $\boldsymbol{m}_i$, transform the input-feature vectors $\boldsymbol{x}_j \in T_i$, $(j = 1, \cdots, n_i)$, into the c q-dimensional feature vectors $\boldsymbol{y}_j^{(i)}$ using Eq. (2).

3. Using Eq. (1), compute the dissimilarity matrix $D_{T,T}[\cdot,\cdot]$, in which each individual dissimilarity $d(\boldsymbol{x}_j, \boldsymbol{x}_k)$ is measured with $d(\boldsymbol{y}_j^{(i)}, \boldsymbol{y}_k^{(i)})$, where if $\boldsymbol{x}_j \in T_i$, then $\boldsymbol{y}_j^{(i)}$ and $\boldsymbol{y}_k^{(i)}$ belong to the same eigenspace generated with T_i, and $d(\cdot,\cdot)$ denotes a distance measure.

4. This step is the same as Step 3 in DBC.

5. This step is the same as Step 4 in DBC.

As in the case of DBC, almost all the processing CPU-time of EDBC is also consumed in computing the transformation matrix and the dissimilarity matrix. So, the difference in magnitude between the computational complexities of DBC and EDBC depends on the computational costs associated with the two matrices. More specifically, Step 1 requires $O(1)$ time in both algorithms. Then, in DBC, Step 2 of computing the $n \times n$ dissimilarity matrix requires $O(dn^2)$ time. On the other hand, the computation of that of EDBC needs $O(d^3 + cn^2 + dn^2)$ time in executing Steps 2 and 3. Here, the first and the second terms, d^3 and cn^2, are for computing the eigenvalue decomposition and the transformation matrix, respectively. Next, computing a test column vector, $\delta(\boldsymbol{z})$, requires $O(dn)$ time at Step 3 in DBC and $O(dn + 3dn)$ time at Step 4 in EDBC. Finally, in both algorithms, classification requires $O(\gamma)$ time, where γ is the time for classifying the test vector with a classifier designed in the dissimilarity space. From this analysis, it can be seen that the required time for EDBC is more sensitive to the number of samples n, the dimensionality d, and the number of classes c than that for DBC.

3. Experimental Results

The run-time characteristics of DBCs in eigenspaces spanned by the class-independent and class-dependent PCA methods are reported below. The results obtained with a well-known benchmark data are first presented and then followed by the results achieved with certain kinds of UCI data sets.

3.1 Experiment #1 (Benchmark data: Nist38)

The proposed approach has been tested and compared with conventional methods. As a baseline experiment, we first investigate the mean squared error, ϵ^2, with a normally distributed and well represented data, namely Nist38. The data set chosen from the NIST database [23] consists of two kinds of digits, 3 and 8, for a total of 1000 binary images. The size of each image is 32×32 pixels, for a total dimensionality of 1024 pixels. Fig. 3 shows the mean squared error values of Eq. (3) of ϵ^2 computed with the class-independent PCA and class-dependent PCA methods for the data set, where the values are represented by three lines, the dashed, solid, and dotted lines, in different colors. Also, the x-axis and the y-axis denote the selected dimensions and the ϵ^2 values, respectively.

From the picture shown in Fig. 3, it can be observed that there is a difference in the values between the class-independent PCA and class-dependent PCA (class-1 and

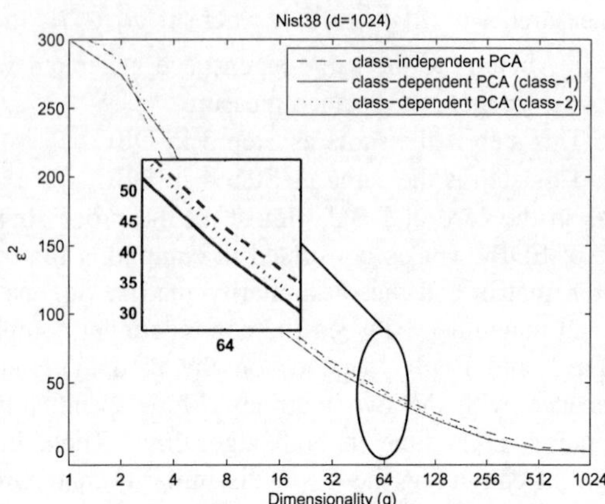

Fig. 3: Plot of the mean squared error values, ϵ^2 and ϵ_i^2, $(i = 1, 2)$, computed with the class-independent PCA and the class-dependent PCA methods for Nist38.

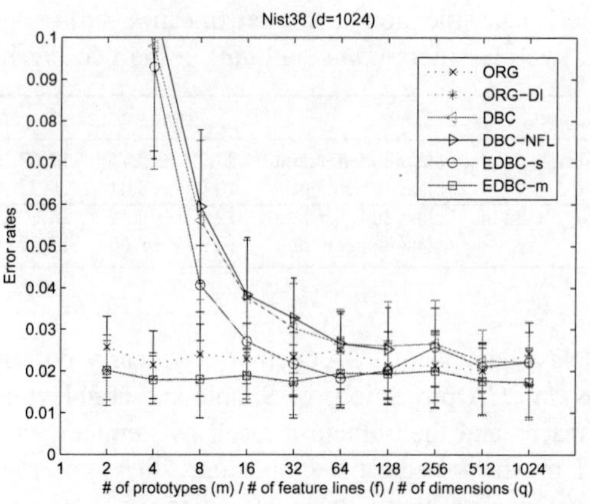

Fig. 4: Plot of the classification error rates obtained with NN classifiers designed with the six fashions: ORG, ORG-DI, DBC, EDBC-NFL, EDBC-s, and EDBC-m, for Nist38.

class-2) methods; the mean squared error values of the two class-dependent PCA methods are smaller than that of the class-independent PCA for a wide range of q, $(8 \leq q \leq 512)$; when $q = d$, the three values are consistent. For Nist38, the differences are marginal, which means that subspaces generated with eigenvectors can be further optimized by means of class-dependent PCA, rather than class-independent one. From this observation, we further experiment on classification accuracies of a classifier, namely the k-nearest neighbor classifier (NN, where k=1), designed in six fashions: ORG, ORG-DI, DBC, DBC-NFL, EDBC-s, and EDBC-m, which are summarized in the following:

First, two NNs of ORG and ORG-DI are designed in the original input-feature space, but different metrics. The former is the Euclidean distance (l_2 metric) based NN rule, while the latter is a maximum a posteriori (MAP) approach using a high order dissimilarity called dissimilarity increments (DI) [7]. In the interest of brevity, the details of the MAP-DI based NN rule are omitted here, but can be found in the related literature [1], [2].

Secondly, two NNs of DBC and DBC-NFL are all designed in the dissimilarity space. The former is that of the conventional DBC, but the latter is a generalized DBC by using the nearest feature lines (NFL) [15] as prototypes to enrich a given dissimilarity representation. In the interest of brevity, the details of DBC-NFL are also omitted here, but can be found in the literature, including [17].

Thirdly, two NNs of EDBC-s and EDBC-m are all of DBCs performed in eigenspaces. NN of EDBC-s is designed in the eigenspace generated with class-independent PCA (i.e., single eigenspace), while that of EDBC-m is designed in the eigenspace of class-dependent PCA - one per class (i.e., multiple eigenspaces). Here, in Eq. (2), $\boldsymbol{m}_i$ is replaced by the *reference* vector, $\boldsymbol{m}_{ref}$, as in [21].

The goal of this experiment is to show that classification accuracies of DBCs can be improved by utilizing the class-dependent PCA, without the need to select prototypes or generalize the dissimilarity. Therefore, ORG and DBC were included as a reference scheme, while ORG-DI and DBC-NFL were considered as state-of-the-art techniques of the two schemes. Also, in DBC (and DBC-NFL), a selection strategy of *RandomC* was used and the number of prototypes (and NFL), m (and f), was defined as: $m = min(q, n_i)$, where min is a function of finding the smallest component; q and n_i are the dimension of eigenspaces and the number of examples per class, respectively.

Fig. 4 shows a plot of the classification error rates (%) obtained with NNs designed in the six different fashions for Nist38, where the data set is randomly split into training sets and test sets at a ratio of 75%:25% (ratio typically used for training and test). Then, the training and test procedures are repeated 30 times and the results obtained are averaged. Also, note that, in DBC (and EDBC-s and EDBC-m), m (and q) increases from 2 to 1024, while, in DBC-NFL, the value of f is limited to 128 because the number of the nearest feature lines, which is given as $\sum_{i=1}^{c} f_i(f_i - 1)/2$, is too large, which leads to a *high*-dimensional dissimilarity space (for example, $d = 8128$ for $f_i = 128$). Finally, in ORG and ORG-DI, the dimension of the feature space remains constant as d.

The observations obtained from the plot shown in Fig. 4 are the followings. First of all, it should be pointed out that the estimated error rate, marked with a $\circ$ symbol, obtained with EDBC-s decreases *sharply* as the cardinality of q (and m) increases, while that of EDBC-m, marked with a $\square$ symbol, generally maintains a consistent height within the entire range of q, which means that, with regard to selecting the dimensionality of subspaces or the number

Table 2: Characteristics of the experimental data sets [6].

Name of datasets	# of samples per class (in total)	# of features	# of classes
Apect	40/40 (80)	44	2
Breast	444/239 (683)	9	2
Dermatology	112/61/72/49/52/20 (366)	34	6
Diabetes	500/268 (768)	8	2
Ecoli	143/77/52 (272)	7	3
Glass	70/76/17/13/9/29 (214)	9	6
Heart	160/137 (297)	13	2
Laryngeal1	81/132 (213)	16	2
Liver	145/200 (345)	6	2
Lung-cancer	9/13/10 (32)	56	3
Nist38	500/500 (1000)	1024	2
Yeast	463/429/244/163/51/ ··· 44/35/30/20/5 (1484)	8	10
vertebral C.3	60/150/100 (310)	6	3

of prototypes, the latter approach is more robust than the former is. Secondly, two error rates obtained with EDBC-s and EDBC-m are almost the same in the intermediate range of q, but, when $q = d$, classification accuracy of the latter is marginally better than that of the former as well as the others, such as ORG and DBC. (Here, the error rate of ORG-DI is almost the same as that of EDBC-m.)

Finally, it should be observed that two error rates of DBC and EDBC-s are the same when we select all of the eigenvectors as basis vectors of the eigenspace. This observation is coincident with the fact that, formally, Euclidean distances should not change after an eigenvalue decomposition that involves all eigenvectors, in which the space is just rotated. Consequently, the error rates of EDBC-s come to be the same as that of DBC, as shown in Fig. 4.

3.2 Experiment # 2 (UCI data)

To further investigate the advantage of using the proposed method, and, especially, to find out which kinds of significant data set are more suitable for the scheme, we repeated the above experiment # 1 with certain kinds of UCI data sets [6] as summarized in Table 2. Here, we chose four different numbers of classes of data: 2, 3, 6, and 10 classes. Moreover, the reader should observe that some data sets are class-imbalance problems, while other sets are small sample size problems.

Table 3 shows a numerical comparison of the averaged error rates and their standard deviations obtained with the NN classifiers built in the six methods, i.e., ORG, ORG-DI, DBC, DBC-NFL, EDBC-s, and EDBC-m, for the UCI data sets. Here, the experimental parameters shown in the second column, i.e., m (and f), q, and $\overline{\triangle\epsilon^2}$, are abbreviations for, respectively, the number of selected prototypes (and the number of nearest feature lines), the dimension of the eigenspaces, and the mean of the difference values of ϵ^2 given by Eq. (3), i.e., $\overline{\triangle\epsilon^2} = mean(\{{\epsilon_i}^2 - \epsilon^2\}_{i=1}^{c})$, where $mean$ is the mean value of the elements; ${\epsilon_i}^2$ and ϵ^2 are computed with the class-dependent and class-independent PCAs. In order to facilitate the comparison, for each row, the lowest error rate is bold-faced. In particular, the values highlighted with a * marker are the lowest ones among the four error rates of DBC and EDBC.

As shown in Fig. 4, the result in Table 3 shows again that EDBC-m generally obtains lower mean error than EDBC-s does. More specifically, consider first the values highlighted with a * marker, which are the lowest ones among the four error rates of two DBCs and two EDBCs. Among them, EDBC-m has most of the lowest error rates (for the whole data sets), except for a *low*-dimensional and class-imbalanced data set, such as Glass. Then, the bold-faced values are of the lowest error rate among the entire six methods, including ORG and ORG-DI. Thus, it should be pointed out that, for certain kinds of data sets, such as Dermatology, Laryngeal1, and Liver, the approach of DBC, to say nothing of EDBC, does not work satisfactorily.

From the comparison, the reader should observe that, for the two EDBCs performed in the eigenspaces of class-dependent and class-independent PCAs, the error rates of the latter EDBC are generally higher than those of the former when the dimensionality of the eigenspace is appropriately chosen. From the table, and as also reported in [11], we can clearly observe the possibility of improving classification performance of DBCs by utilizing PCA, especially class-dependent PCA, rather than class-independent one.

In review, it is not easy to find out which kinds of significant data set are more suitable for EDBC-m. However, in terms of classification accuracies, DBC performed in multiple eigenspaces seems to be more useful for certain kinds of data sets than the traditional DBC does. Especially, the experimental results obtained, as shown in Fig. 4 and Table 3, demonstrate that the class-dependent PCA scheme, albeit not always, works more efficiently with the well-balanced and *high*-dimensional data sets than it does with the class-imbalanced and *low*-dimensional ones.

4. Conclusions

In an effort to improve the classification performance of DBC, we studied a way of utilizing class-dependent PCA, rather than employing the methods of effectively selecting prototypes or generalizing the dissimilarity. To achieve this improvement of DBC, we first computed eigenvectors and eigenvalues of the training data, one for each class. Then, we performed DBC in the eigenspaces spanned by the subset of principal eigenvectors. The proposed scheme was tested on a well represented image data set and some UCI data sets, and the results obtained were compared with those of other methods, including two state-of-the-art techniques using DI (dissimilarity increments) and NFL (the nearest feature lines). Our experimental results demonstrate that the classification accuracies of DBC in eigenspaces were improved when the dimensionality of the eigenspaces is

Table 3: Classification error rates (mean ± std) (%) obtained with NNs built in the six fashions for the UCI data [6]. For each row, the lowest error rate is bold-faced. In particular, the values highlighted with a * marker are the lowest ones among the four error rates of DBC and EDBC.

Name of	Experimental parameters	Input-feature spaces		Dissimilarity spaces		Eigenspaces	
datasets	$m\ (f)\ /\ q\ /\ \overline{\triangle\epsilon^2}$	ORG	ORG-DI	DBC	DBC-NFL	EDBC-s	EDBC-m
Apect	30 / 32 / 2.6292e+003	33.83±10.40	27.00± 8.16	33.67± 9.19	32.33± 8.48	34.50± 8.34	***26.83**± 6.23
Breast	4 / 4 / 4.8352e+000	4.31± 1.13	2.96± 1.06	3.80± 1.31	38.78±10.58	3.39± 1.39	***2.65**± 1.16
Dermatology	15 / 32 / 0.0626e+000	**10.70**± 3.47	14.18± 3.14	27.00± 3.67	15.64± 3.42	25.09± 3.92	*13.52± 3.52
Diabetes	32 / 8 / 5.3173e-011	32.34± 2.82	29.58± 2.56	33.54± 2.56	32.53± 2.47	33.58± 2.79	***28.89**± 2.39
Ecoli	32 / 7 / 7.5681e-016	7.16± 2.36	4.48± 2.00	7.16± 2.61	7.26± 2.65	7.81± 2.47	***4.38**± 2.00
Glass	7 / 9 / 2.8319e-012	26.54± 5.04	36.09± 5.50	25.06± 4.45	25.83± 4.59	***24.74**± 4.48	33.53± 5.66
Heart	32 / 13 / 7.6138e-011	41.62± 4.96	35.95± 5.06	41.85± 5.47	41.35± 5.55	41.76± 5.23	***34.55**± 5.41
Laryngeal1	32 / 16 / 6.6958e-011	**22.01**± 5.50	25.16± 5.61	27.99± 6.13	23.14±11.67	27.92± 6.12	*23.84± 6.00
Liver	32 / 6 / 1.2173e-012	38.84± 3.81	**33.33**± 3.97	40.39± 4.47	39.73± 6.80	41.71± 4.73	*33.64± 3.85
Lung-cancer	7 / 32 / 1.8075e+001	51.43±12.78	48.10±16.98	53.33±15.44	50.48±14.88	50.95±12.82	***40.95**±19.76
Yeast	4 / 8 / 4.3566e-016	47.87± 1.74	44.38± 2.31	47.83± 2.47	47.90± 2.14	48.46± 2.33	***43.28**± 2.05
vertebral C.3	32 / 6 / 2.4493e-011	17.66± 2.63	18.27± 3.34	18.27± 3.56	17.62± 3.39	17.88± 3.23	***17.01**± 3.17

appropriately chosen. In particular, the experimental results demonstrate that, for the two DBCs in eigenspaces, performed in the single eigenspace for the whole data set and in the multiple eigenspaces, one per class, i.e., EDBC-s and EDBC-m, respectively, the error rates of the latter are generally lower than those of the former. Although we have shown that the classification accuracy of DBC can be improved by employing the class-dependent PCA approach, many tasks remain unchallenged. One of them is to theoretically further investigate the relationship between the improvement achieved in the multiple eigenspaces and the differences in the mean squared errors. An analysis of why using the multiple eigenspaces in DBC instead of selecting prototypes should also be performed in detail.

References

[1] Aidos, H. and Fred, A., "k-nearest neighbor classification using dissimilarity increments," In Campilho, A. and Kamel, M., editors, *Proc. of the 9th Int'l Conference on Image Analysis and Recognition (ICIAR 2012)*, pages 27–33, Aveiro, Portugal, June 2012. Springer-Verlag.

[2] Aidos, H. and Fred, A., "Statistical modeling of dissimilarity increments for d-dimensioanl data: Application in partitional clustering," *Pattern Recognition*, vol. 45, pp. 3061–3071, 2012.

[3] Ding, C., Zhou, D., He, X., and Zha, H., "R_1-PCA: Rotational invariant l_1-norm principal component analysis for robust subspace factorization," In *Proc. of the 23rd Intrnational Conference on Machine Learning (ICML 2006)*, Pittsburgh, PA, 2006.

[4] Duin, R. P. W., "Non-Euclidean problems in pattern recognition related to human expert knowledge," In *Proc. of ICEIS2010*, volume LNBIP-73, pages 15–28, Funchal, Madeira - Portugal, 2011. IEEE Computer Society Press.

[5] Duin, R. P. W., Juszczak, P., de Ridder, D., Paclík, P., Pękalska, E., and Tax, D. M. J., "PRTools 4: a Matlab Toolbox for Pattern Recognition," Delft University of Technology, The Netherlands, Technical Report, 2004. [Online]. Available: http://prtools.org/

[6] Frank, A. and Asuncion, A., "UCI Machine Learning Repository," University of California, School of Information and Computer Science, Irvine, CA, 2010. [Online]. Available: http://www.ics.uci.edu/~mlearn/MLRepository.html

[7] Fred, A. L. N. and Leitão, J. M. N. , "A new cluster isolation criterion based on dissimilarity increments," *IEEE Trans. Pattern Anal. and Machine Intell.*, vol. 25, no. 8, pp. 944–958, 2003.

[8] Jiang, X., "Asymmetric principle component and discriminant analyses for pattern classification," *IEEE Trans. Pattern Anal. and Machine Intell.*, vol. 31, no. 5, pp. 931–937, 2009.

[9] Jiang, X., "Linear subspace learning-based dimensionality reduction," *IEEE Signal Processing Magazine*, pp. 16–26, March 2011.

[10] Jolliffe, I. T., *Principle Component Analysis*. Springer-Verlag, New York, 2002.

[11] Kim, S. -W., "An empirical evaluation on dimensionality reduction schemes for dissimilarity-based classifications," *Pattern Recognition Letters*, vol. 32, no. 6, pp. 816–823, 2011.

[12] Kim, S.-W. and Duin, R.P.W., "Dissimilarity-based classifications in eigenspaces," In *Proc. of the 16th Iberoamerican Congress on Pattern Recognition (CIARP2011)*, volume LNCS-7042, pages 425–432, Pucón, Chile, 2011. Springer-Verlag.

[13] Kim, S. -W. and Oommen, B. J., "On using prototype reduction schemes to optimize dissimilarity-based classification," *Pattern Recognition*, vol. 40, pp. 2946–2957, 2007.

[14] Kwak, N., "Principle component analysis based on l_1 norm maximization," *IEEE Trans. Pattern Anal. and Machine Intell.*, vol. 30, no. 9, pp. 1672–1680, 2008.

[15] Li, S. Z. and Lu, J., "Face recognition using the nearest feature line method," *Neural Network*, vol. 10, no. 2, pp. 439–443, 1999.

[16] Oja, E., *Subspace Methods of Pattern Recognition*, Research Studies Press, England, 1983.

[17] Orozco-Alzate, M., Duin, R. P. W., and Castellanos-Dominguez, G., "A generalization of dissimilarity representations using feature lines and feature planes," *Pattern Recognition Letters*, vol. 30, pp. 242–254, 2009.

[18] Pękalska, E. and Duin, R. P. W., *The Dissimilarity Representation for Pattern Recognition: Foundations and Applications*, World Scientific Publishing, Singapore, 2005.

[19] Pękalska, E., Duin, R. P. W., and Paclík, P., "Prototype selection for dissimilarity-based classifiers," *Pattern Recognition*, vol. 39, pp. 189–208, 2006.

[20] Riesen, K., Kilchherr, V., and Bunke, H. , "Reducing the dimensionality of vector space embeddings of graphs," In *Proc. of the 5th Int. Conf. on Machine Learning and Data Mining*, pages 563–573, 2007.

[21] Sharma, A., Paliwal, K. K., and Onwubolu, G. C., "Class-dependent pca, mdc and lda: A combined classifier for pattern classification," *Pattern Recognition*, vol. 39, pp. 1215–1229, 2006.

[22] Tipping, M. E. and Bishop, C. M., "Probabilistic principle component analysis," *J. Royal Statistical Soc.: Series B (Statistical Methodology)*, vol. 61, no. 3, pp. 611–622, 1999.

[23] Wilson, C. L. and Garris, M. D., "Handprinted Character Database 3," National Institute of Standards and Technology, Gaithersburg, Maryland, Technical Report, 1992.

Image De-noising Using an Improved Bivariate Threshold Function in Tetrolet Domain

Yong-xin Zhang[1,2], Li Chen[1], and Jian Jia[3]
[1]School of Information Science and Technology, Northwest University, Xi'an , Shaan Xi, China
[2]School of Continuous Education, Luoyang Normal University, Luoyang, He Nan, China
[3]Department of Mathematics, Northwest University, Xi'an, Shaan Xi, China

Abstract *- The paper presents a new image denoising method based on an improved Bivariate Model (BM) in Tetrolet domain. This model fits the joint distribution of parent-child tetrolet coefficients with a Scale Variable Parameter Bivariate Model (SVPBM). Corresponding nonlinear threshold shrinkage functions are derived from SVPBM by using maximum a posteriori (MAP) estimator. To evaluate the performance of the proposed method, the algorithm is applied to images that are corrupted with additive Gaussian noise over a wide range of noise variance. Experimental results are compared with different denoising schemes. The experimental results indicate that the proposed method provides promising results and is advantageous both in terms of PSNR and in visual quality.*

Keywords: Image denoising; Tetrolet transform; Bivariate shrinkage; Noise variance;

1 Introduction

Image is an important way of access to information for people. But noises largely reduce the perceptual quality of images and may result in fatal errors [1]. Image denoising has been a fundamental problem in image processing. The wavelet transform is one of the most popular tools in image denosing due to its promising properties for singularity analysis and efficient computational complexity [2].

In the past decades, a fair amount ways and methods for image denoising are proposed by international and domestic academics [3-8]. VisuShrink [3] is the most popular approaches by setting all the coefficients smaller than the universal threshold and preserving or shrinking the rest, which was propsed by Donoho in 1994. But it may lose many of the details in over-smoothed image. Sureshrink [4] are proposed to overcome the weakness in 1995. Since then, wavelet denoising got very quick development in theory and technology area. Because of ability in preserving more useful image edge and details while removing noise, statistical approaches have drawn more and more attention of academics. According to the distribution features of wavelet coefficients, researchers exploit different types of dependencies between the wavelet coefficients to improve denoising further, a General Gauss Model (GGM) of wavelet coefficients is introduced by Grace Chang [5] in 2000. But the model only considers the intrascale dependencies between wavelet coefficients and ignores the interscale dependencies between wavelet coefficients. BM based on interscale dependencies between wavelet coefficients is introduced by Sendur [6,7] in 2002. The corresponding shrinkage functions are derived from the models using Bayesian estimation theory [8]. The denosing result of BM is superior to that of GGM. But in fact, the joint probability distribution function (PDF) of parent-child wavelet coefficient pairs in different scales is different. It is inaccurate to represent the PDF with the same BM. Some improved bivariate models is proposed by reference [9-18] to solve the problem. Applications of wavelets have been widely used in scientific and engineering fields , traditional wavelets perform well for representing point singularity. Recently, some researchers extend the ideas of bivariate shrinkage to the geometric wavelets shrinkage methods, e.g., curvelets [19], contourlets[20,21], directionlet[22] and shrinkage in high dimensional space [23]. Tetrolet Transform is a new adaptive Haar wavelet transform introduced by Jens Krommweh [24,25] in 2009. It has been applied to image processing [24]. But the image must be divided into blocks before Tetrolet Transform and the blocks are transformed separately. There are blocking artifacts and non-smoothness in the denoised image due to the non-smoothness of basic block functions. The blocking artifacts in denoised image increase with the noise variance. The de-noise capability of Tetrolete Tansform need to be improved and developed further. The paper focus on the Sendur's BM. The main idea is to extend the idea of BM to tetrolet domain and improve the denoising ability of Tetrolete Tansform.

The main contribution of this paper is that a new joint shrinkage function is given and a new method based on it in Tetrolet domain is proposed for image denoising. This function can estimate the present coefficient according to the dependencies between Tetrolet coefficients and their parents in detail. The basic idea was inspired by Sendur's Bivariate Shrinkage Theory (BST) and Jens Krommweh's Tetrolet Transform Theory.

The rest of the paper is organized as follows. In section 2, the basic idea of Tetrolet Transform will be briefly described. Section 3 will analyse the lack of BM and propose SVPBM function. Then, a novel method based on Tetrolet transform is presented for image denoising. In section 4, some computer simulations will be performed to evaluate the performance of the proposed method. Several experimental results will be presented and discussed. Finally, some concluding remark and future work are given in section 5.

2 Tetrolet Transform

As a Multiscale geometric analysis method, Tetrolet Transform can sparse represent image due to the non-redundance of basis functions. The image is divided into 4×4 blocks before Tetrolet Transform, then a tetromino partition in each block which is adapted to the image geometry in the block. Originally, tetrominoes were introduced by Golomb [26] in 1994, and they became popular through the famous computer game classic 'Tetris'. During Tetrolet Transform, tetrominoes are shapes made by connecting four equal-sized squares, each joined together with at least one other square along an edge. Disregarding rotations and reflections there are five different shapes, the so called free tetrominoes, see Fig.1. Larsson [27] verified that there are 117 solutions for disjoint covering of a 4×4 board with four tetrominoes in 1937. The tetrolet transform will choose the most appropriate one to fit the local structure in a 4×4 block of an image, and then apply the above template to the elements in the four tetrominoes.

Input image $a^0 = (a[i,j])_{i,j=0}^{N-1}, N = 2^J, J \in N$ is decomposed into r levels. The detailed steps are as follows:

(1) Divide the low-pass image a^{r-1} into 4×4 blocks $Q_{i,j}, i,j = 0,\cdots,N/4^r - 1$.

(2) Consider 117 admissible tetromino coverings $c = 1,\cdots,117$ for each block $Q_{i,j}$. A Haar Wavelet transform is performed on tetromino subsets $I_s^{(c)}, s = 0,1,2,3$. For each tilling, four low-pass coefficients and 12 high pass tetrolet coefficients can be obtained. Then, the covering c^* such that the l_1-norm of 12 tetrolet coefficients is minimal. The covering c^* can be chosen.

$$c^* = \arg\min_c \sum_{l=1}^{3} \| w_l^{r,(c)} \|_1 = \arg\min_c \sum_{l=1}^{3}\sum_{s=0}^{3} | w_l^{r,(c)}[s] | \qquad (1)$$

(3) For further scales of tetrolet decomposition, the low-pass coefficients and high-pass coefficients need to be rearranged of each block into a 2 × 2 block.

(4) Store the high-pass coefficients.

Fig. 1: The five free tetrominoes. O-I-T-S-L tetromino.

Repeat these steps, the input image can be decomposed into r levels .

3 Image Denoising Using BST

The BM proposed by Sendur is approximately able to produce similar plots as shown in Fig. 2. The distribution of Tetrolet coefficients is similar to the distribution of Wavelet coefficients. According to Tetrolet Transform's superiority in representing for geometric properties of directed structures in image, the paper extend the idea of BST from wavelet to Tetrolet Transform domain with some improvements. Fig. 2 shows the joint parent-child histogram of wavelet coefficients with different noise variance. Noise deviation in Fig. 2 (a) is 10 and in Fig. 2 (b) is 20. It is easy to see that the smaller noise variance, the narrower joint parent-child histogram of wavelet coefficients.

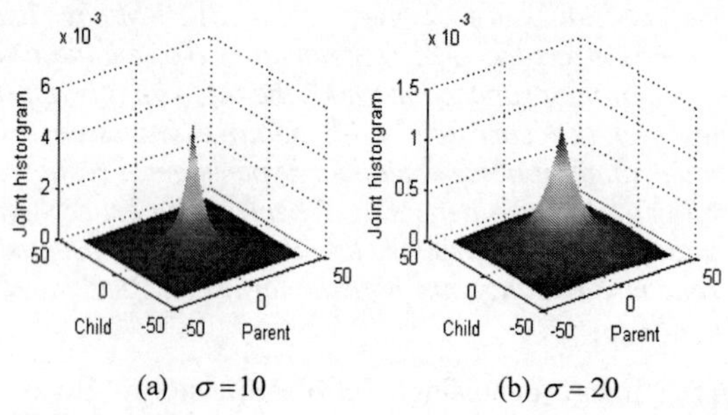

Fig. 2: Empirical joint parent-child histogram of tetrolet coefficients.

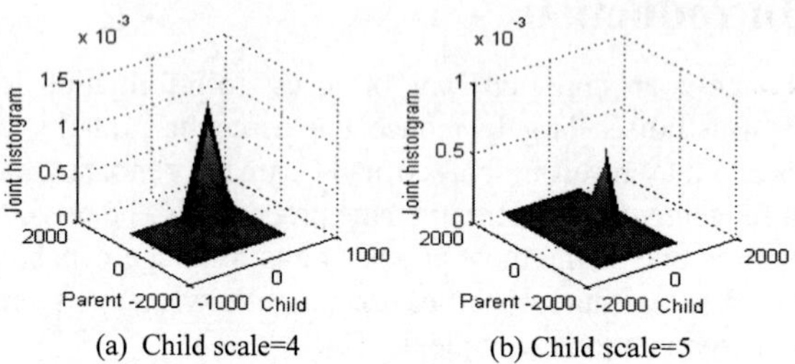

Fig. 3. Joint parent-child histogram of tetrolet coefficients of "Boat" image (512×512). (a) Child scale=4 , tetromino coverings $c = 16$; (b) Child scale=5 , tetromino coverings $c = 16$;

From Fig.3, it is easy to see that the joint parent-child histogram of tetrolet coefficients between scale 4 and 5 is different from that between 5 and 6. The BM assumes the variances of wavelet coefficients are the same for all scales, which conflicts with the fact that the variances of tetrolet coefficients of noisy images are quite different from scale to scale. The variances of tetrolet coefficients of natural images are quite different from subband to subband. So, it is inaccurate to model the tetrolet coefficients with BM. It should consider the influence of scale and subband on noise variance. In order to exactly describe joint distribution of tetrolet coefficients, the paper proposed SVPBM. In order to eliminate the influence of different scale and subband on joint distribution of tetrolet coefficients, the paper introduced scale parameters and control parameters .

SVPBM models the joint distribution of tetrolet coefficients with a circularly symmetric PDF. and are uncorrelated but not independent:

$$p_w(\omega) = \frac{(\varepsilon J)^2}{2\pi\sigma^2}\exp\left[-\frac{\varepsilon J}{\sigma}\sqrt{\omega_1^2+\omega_2^2}\right] \quad (2)$$

Let $f(\omega) = \log p_\omega(\omega)$, then

$$\hat{\omega}(y) = \arg\max_{\omega}[-\frac{(y_1-\omega_1)^2}{2\sigma_n^2} - \frac{(y_2-\omega_2)^2}{2\sigma_n^2} + f(\omega)] \quad (3)$$

This is equivalent to solving the following equations if $p_\omega(\omega)$ is assumed to be strictly convex and differentiable:

$$\frac{y_1-\hat{\omega}_1}{\sigma_n^2} + f_1(\hat{\omega}) = 0 \quad (4)$$

$$\frac{y_2-\hat{\omega}_2}{\sigma_n^2} + f_2(\hat{\omega}) = 0 \quad (5)$$

where f_1 and f_2 represent the derivate of $f(\omega)$ with respect to ω_1 and ω_2.

Solving the equation (4) and (5) by using .

$$f(\omega) = \log(\frac{(\varepsilon J)^2}{2\pi\sigma^2}) - \frac{\varepsilon J}{\sigma}\sqrt{\omega_1^2+\omega_2^2} \quad (6)$$

The joint bivariate shrinkage function can be written as:

$$\hat{\omega}_1 = \frac{(\sqrt{y_1^2+y_2^2} - \frac{\varepsilon J\sigma_n^2}{\sigma})_+}{\sqrt{y_1^2+y_2^2}} \cdot y_1 \cdot \quad (7)$$

where $\sigma_n^2 = median(|y_i|)/0.6745$ is noise variance, the estimator of standard deviation of true coefficient is

$$\sigma = \sqrt{\max(\hat{\sigma}_{y_1}^2 - \hat{\sigma}_n^2, 0)} = \sqrt{(\hat{\sigma}_{y_1}^2 - \hat{\sigma}_n^2)_+} \quad (8)$$

where $\hat{\sigma}_{y_1}^2 = \frac{1}{N}\sum_{y_{1i}\in N(k)} y_{1i}^2$.

From derivation above, it can be seen that joint bivariate shrinkage function doesn't consider the estimator of tetrolet coefficients at final scale. Image denoising using bivariate shrinkage function should consider the threshold processing on tetrolet coefficients at final scale. The paper proposes the image denoising method based on SVPBM function.

Specific steps are follows:

(1) Decompose the noisy image with Tetrolet Transform.

(2) Construct coefficient vector $y = (y_1, y_2)$ with high-pass coefficients at scale J and parent scale $J+1$. y_1 is the coefficient at the same position as y_2.

(3) Threshold process present coefficient y_1 with equation (7).

(4) Threshold process the high-pass coefficients at final scale.

(5) Tetrolet Transform are are inversed to get the denoised image.

4 Experimental Results

4.1 Experimental Setup

In order to evaluate the performance of the proposed method, the experiment is performed on a representative set of standard 8-bit grayscale images extracted from CVG-UGR database[28], such as Lena, Mandrill, Indians and Boat, each of size 512 × 512, corrupted by simulated additive Gaussian white noise with a standard deviation equal to 20, 30, 40, 50, 60. Several methods were used to filter the noisy image. The paper evaluated the performance of proposed method using the quality measure PSNR which is calculated as follows:

$$PSNR = 10 \times \log\left(\frac{255^2}{MSE}\right) \quad (9)$$

Here, the performance of proposed method is compared with different de-noising schemes that include Wavelet, Contourlet, Tetrolet.

4.2 Experimental Results

The comparison of PSNR obtained with these four denoising methods can be seen in Table 1 and Table 2. In Table 1, Tetrolet Transform's Tetromino coverings $c = 32$ and control parameters of SVPBM $\varepsilon = 2$. In Table 2, Tetrolet Transform's Tetromino coverings $c = 16$ and control parameters of SVPBM $\varepsilon = \sqrt{6}$.

As shown in Tables 1-2, the PSNR of the image denoised by the proposed method is obviously outperforms Wavelet, Contourlet and Tetrolet. It can be seen that PSNR obtained with the proposed method is enhanced 1.35 dB on average more than wavelet denoising methods. Compared with Contourlet method, PSNR obtained with the proposed method is still enhanced 1.3 dB on average. With the increase of noise variance, PSNR obtained with all these methods have a decrease trend, but PSNR obtained with the new method is still more than other PSNRs and proposed method has the best performance for all noise levels. A comparison of PSNR between proposed method and denoising method in tetrolet domain , is also made here. The proposed method gains over Tetrolet by about 1.0 dB on average. The paper attributes the better performance of proposed method to the better ability of the BM in matching the underlying distribution of the tetrolet coefficients. Further more, the better ability of Tetrolet Transform in image approximation and representing for geometric properties of directed structures in image is also very important.

Table 1 PSNR values (dB) obtained with "Man" and "Mandrill".

σ	Man			
	Wavelet	Contourlet	Tetrolet	Proposed
20	25.7546	25.5769	25.7030	**27.4844**
30	24.1934	24.0817	24.4327	**25.6884**
40	22.9875	23.0236	23.5060	**24.3261**
50	22.0687	22.2481	22.7213	**23.2261**
60	21.2985	21.6143	22.0638	**22.3498**
	Mandrill			
	Wavelet	Contourlet	Tetrolet	Proposed
20	22.1330	22.6849	22.1444	**23.4409**
30	20.9727	21.2713	21.4241	**22.2175**
40	20.1787	20.4313	20.8849	**21.3453**
50	19.6162	19.9062	20.4778	**20.6958**
60	19.1688	19.5200	20.1008	**20.1391**

Table 2 PSNR values (dB) obtained with "Lena" and "Boat"

σ	Lena			
	Wavelet	Contourlet	Tetrolet	Proposed
20	28.6716	28.5539	28.1448	**29.6102**
30	26.6407	26.8369	26.5903	**27.5168**
40	25.1928	25.5977	25.4855	**26.1235**
50	24.0550	24.5974	24.5626	**25.0012**
60	23.0555	23.7738	23.7807	**24.1137**
	Boat			
	Wavelet	Contourlet	Tetrolet	Proposed
20	27.1075	27.0783	26.8408	**28.2891**
30	25.2968	25.4103	25.4594	**26.3954**
40	23.9302	24.2963	24.4072	**25.0458**
50	22.9006	23.4197	23.6144	**24.0376**
60	22.0803	22.7301	22.8911	**23.1662**

From Table 1 and Table 2, it can be seen that the PSNR gap between proposed method and Wavelet descends from 1.35 to 0.95 dB. With the increase of noise variance, the PSNR gap between proposed method and Contourlet descends from 1.3 to 0.21 dB. The PSNR gap between proposed method and Tetrolet descends from 1.0 to 0.29 dB. It should be mentioned that the test images in Table 1 have strong localized linear singularity and the images in Table 2 have strong point singularities. So it can be seen that the proposed method has advantage in image with linear singularity over in image with point singularities.

For visual evaluation, two examples using standard "Man" and "Lena" are given in Fig.4 (a) and Fig.4 (b). As can be seen from Fig.4, the denoised image of the proposed has fewer artifacts and is clear than that of Wavelet, Contourlet and Tetrolet. There are still a little blocking artifacts in the denoised image when the noise deviation is large.

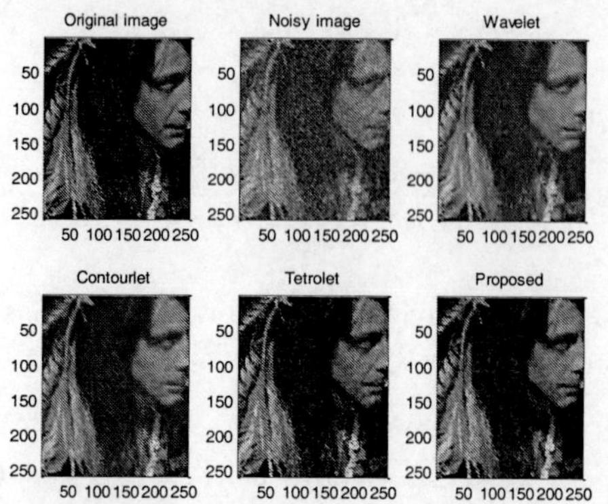

(a). Denoising results using different methods on "Man"

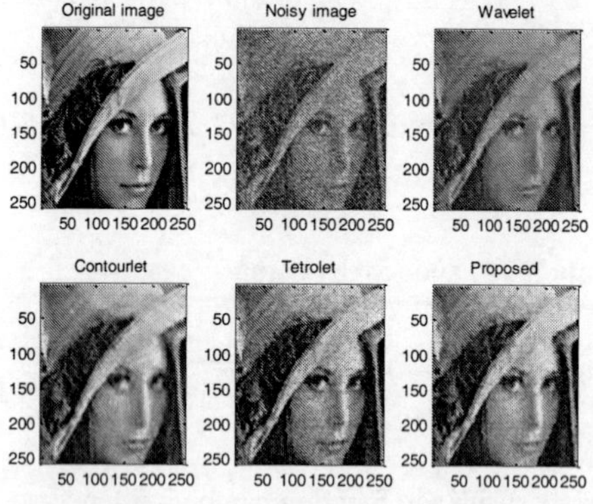

(b). Denoising results using different methods on "Lena"

Fig.4.Denoising results using different methods. Noisy image (a) noisy deviation $\sigma = 30$, tetromino coverings $c = 32$, control parameters $\varepsilon = 2$; (b) noisy deviation $\sigma = 40$, tetromino coverings $c = 16$, control parameters $\varepsilon = \sqrt{6}$.

5 Conclusion and future work

To improve the performance of Tetrolet in image denoising, the paper extends the ideas of bivariate shrinkage to Tetrolet Transform. The paper models the distribution of tetrolet coefficients with SVPBM and derives the scale bivariate shrinkage function according to the fact that the variances of tetrolet coefficients of noisy images are quite different from scale to scale. The SVPBM has better ability in fitting the distribution of tetrolet coefficients. A new improved image denoising method based on SVPBM is proposed. The paper compared the method with several other denoising schemes and the results showed that the proposed method is superior to Wavelet, Contourlet and Tetrolet both visually and in terms of PSNR.

It should be noted that the proposed method has advantage in image with linear singularity over in image with point singularities. But the image must be divided into 4×4 blocks before Tetrolet Transform and the blocks are transformed separately. It is not enough to improve the denoising performance only depend on improvement in tetrolet domain. It also should be considered combining the image denoising method both in frequency domain and space domain.

Acknowledgments

The work was supported by National Key Technology Science and Technique Support Program (No. 2013BAH49F03), Key Technologies R&D Program of Henan Province (No. 132102210515),Scientific Research Program Funded by Shaanxi Provincial Education Department (No. 2010JK865), Natural Science Basic Research Plan in Shaanxi Province of China (No. 2012JQ1012), Open Research Fund Program of Key Lab of Intelligent Perception and Image Understanding of Ministry of Education of China (Grant No. IPIU012011009). Many thanks to the various authors for providing their Matlab codes that are publicly available online at http://www.taco.poly.edu/WaveletSoftware/denoise2.html (BiShrink)

References

[1] Frank Lenzen; Florian Becker; Jan Lellmann; Stefania Petra; Christoph Schnörr .A class of quasi-variational inequalities for adaptive image denoising and decomposition [J]. Computational Optimization and Applications. 2013 , 54(2) :371-398.

[2] Talebi, H.;Zhu, X.;Milanfar, P.How to SAIF-ly Boost Denoising Performance[J]. Image Processing, IEEE Transactions on. 2013, 20(4) :1470-1485 .

[3] D.L. Donoho, I.M. Johnstone, Ideal spatial adaptation by wavelet shrinkage [J]. Biometrika.1994, 81 (3):425–455.

[4] Donoho D L. De-noising by soft-thresholding[J].IEEE Transactions on Information Theory, 1995, 41(3): 613-627.

[5] CHANG S G,YU B. Adaptive wavelet thresholding for image denoising and compression[J].IEEE Transactions On Image Processing,2000,9(9):1532-1546

[6] Sendur L and Selesnick I W. Bivariate shrinkage functions for wavelet-based denoising exploiting interscale dependency [J]. IEEE Trans. on Signal Proc, 2002, 50(11): 2744-2756.

[7] L. Sendur, I.W. Selesnick. Bivariate shrinkage with local variance estimation[J], IEEE Signal Process. Lett. 2002,9 (12) :438–441.

[8] Ho, J.;Hwang, W.-L.Wavelet Bayesian Network Image Denoising [J].Image Processing, IEEE Transactions on. 2013,22(4):1277-1290 .

[9] H. Rabbani, M. Vafadust, Image/video denoising based on a mixture of Laplace distributions with local parameters in multidimensional complex wavelet domain[J], Signal Process. 2008,88 :158–173.

[10] Rabbani,Hossein. Image denoising in steerable pyramid domain based on a local Laplace prior[J], Pattern Recognition. 2009, 42(9):2181–2193.

[11] PAN Jin-feng. Bivariate shrinkage denoising method based on variable parameter bivariate model[J].Journal of Computer Applications, 2010,30(7):1855-1858.

[12] Song feng Yin;Liangcai Cao;Yongshun Ling and Guofan Jin. Image denoising with anisotropic bivariate shrinkage[J]. Signal Processing,2011,91(8): 2078-2090.

[13] Chen, G.Zhu, W.-P. Xie, W. Wavelet-based image denoising using three scales of dependency[J]. Image Processing IET.2012,6(6): 756-760.

[14] Shuang Wang, Jiao Zhou, Jun Li, Biao Hou: SAR image despeckling method using bivariate shrinkage based on dual-tree complex wavelet. IGARSS 2012: 2117-2120.

[15] Mantosh Biswas;Hari Om.An Improved Image Denoising Method Based on Wavelet Thresholding[J].Journal of Biophysical Chemistry.2012,3(1) :109-116.

[16] K. K. V. Toh;N. A. Mat Isa.Locally adaptive bilateral clustering for universal image denoising Opto-Electronics Review[J].2012,20(4):347-361.

[17] Sandeep Palakkal;K.M.M. Prabhu.Poisson image denoising using fast discrete curvelet transform and wave atom [J].Signal Processing.2012,92(9) :2002-2017.

[18] Xiang-Yang Wang;Hong-Ying Yang;Zhong-Kai Fu. Edge structure preserving image denoising using OAGSM/NC statistical model [J].Digital Signal Processing. 2013,23(1): 200-212.

[19] Malar, E.;Kandaswamy, A.;Kirthana, S.S.;Nivedhitha, D.;Gauthaam, M. Curvelet image denoising of mammogram images[J]. International Journal of Medical Engineering and Informatics.2013,5(1):60-67.

[20] Jia Jian,Jiao Li-cheng, Xiang Hai-lin.Using Bivariate Threshold Function for Image Denoising in NSCT Domain[J].Journal of Electronics & Information Technology, 2009,31(3):532-536.

[21] Hatsuda, H. Robust Smoothing of Quantitative Genomic Data Using Second-Generation Wavelets and Bivariate Shrinkage[J]. Biomedical Engineering, IEEE Transactions on.2012,59(8): 2099-2102.

[22] Qingwei Gao; Yixiang Lu; Dong Sun; Zhan-Li Sun; Dexiang Zhang. Directionlet-based denoising of SAR images using a Cauchy model [J].Signal Processing. 2013, 93(5):1056-1063.

[23] Tan Shan. Ridgelet Bi-frame and multivariate statistical models of natural image [D]. [Ph.D. dissertation], Xidian University, 2007.

[24] Krommweh J. Tetrolet transform:a new adaptive Haar wavelet algorithm for sparse image representation[J]. Journal of Visual Communication and Image Representation, 2010, 21(4):364-374.

[25] J. Krommweh, J. Ma.Tetrolet shrinkage with anisotropic total variation minimization for image approximation, Signal Process. 2010,90(8): 2529-2539.

[26] S.W. Golomb, Polyominoes, Princeton University Press, 1994.

[27] B. Larsson, Problem 2623, in: Fairy Chess Review, 1937, 3(5) 51.

[28] CVG-UGR Image Database [EB/OL]. [2011-05-22]. http://decsai. ugr.es/cvg/dbimagenes/index.php.

Detecting Object Bending with Complex Polynomial Fitting

Hongjun Su and Hong Zhang*
Department of Computer Science and Information Technology
Armstrong Atlantic State University
Savannah, GA 31419 USA
E-mail: hongjun.su@cs.armstrong.edu, hong.zhang@armstrong.edu
**contact author*

Conference: IPCV'13
Keywords: Object bending, Image transformation, Conformal mapping, Least squares fitting

Abstract

Recognizing bending and curving patterns of objects in an image is useful in many practical image analysis and vision applications. We present a novel approach to the problem by detecting and modeling object bending using conformal mappings and complex polynomial least squares fitting, which also leads to a fully automatic method for correcting the bending.

1. Introduction

In many image processing and computer vision applications, bending and curving of flexible objects presents a challenge to their recognitions and analyses. Most pattern recognition techniques can usually accommodate transforms such as translation, rotation and scaling. However, more complex changes in geometric shapes of the objects such as non-linear bending and curving can significantly alter the extracted features and degrade the performance of recognition systems. For example, the problem of chromosome classification and karyotyping typically requires appropriate compensations for curved chromosomes ([1, 2]).

In this paper, we propose an approach to the automatic object bending detection problem. The field of complex numbers can be identified with the 2D Euclidean space. The analytic functions on complex numbers represent special mappings on the plane, known as conformal mappings. We use a conformal mapping as a model for an object bending. The conformal mapping and the associated analytic function is approximated using complex polynomial curve fitting.

Section 2 introduces conformal mappings and the method of least squares fitting with complex polynomials as an approximate model of conformal mappings. In Section 3, an algorithm is proposed for unbending an object in an image based on our bending model. Experimental results on artificially generated character images and discussions on practical issues related to the method are presented in Section 4.

2. Complex Polynomial Least Squares

A complex function $f:\mathbf{C}\rightarrow\mathbf{C}$ can be viewed as a transformation in $\mathbf{R}^2$. A complex analytic function represents a smooth transformation known as a conformal mapping, which preserves angles ([3]).

A polynomial with complex coefficients is a special case of analytic functions:

$$f(z)=\sum_{j=0}^{n}c_j z^j$$

$$c_j=a_j+ib_j,\quad j=0,1,\ldots,n$$

Since an analytic function has a power series expansion at any point in its domain, polynomials can be used to approximate a conformal mapping.

The curve fitting problem with complex polynomials is similar to the case with real polynomials. Given a set of complex points $(z_1,z_2,\ldots,z_m)$ and an associated target set of complex points $(w_1,w_2,\ldots,w_m)$, the objective of the least squares fitting is to find a complex polynomial $f(z)$ that minimizes the sum of squared residuals:

$$S = \frac{1}{2}\sum_{k=1}^{m}\left|f(z_k) - w_k\right|^2$$

To simply the notation, we define the following matrices:

$$Z = \begin{pmatrix} 1 & z_1 & \cdots & z_1^n \\ 1 & z_2 & \cdots & z_2^n \\ & & \cdots & \\ 1 & z_m & \cdots & z_m^n \end{pmatrix} \quad c = \begin{pmatrix} c_0 \\ c_1 \\ \vdots \\ c_n \end{pmatrix} \quad w = \begin{pmatrix} w_1 \\ w_2 \\ \vdots \\ w_m \end{pmatrix}$$

Then S can be written as

$$S = \frac{1}{2}\overline{(Zc - w)^T}(Zc - w)$$

By considering S as a function of the real variables a_j and setting the derivatives to 0, we have

$$\mathrm{Re}\left\{\overline{Z^T}(Zc - w)\right\} = 0$$

Similarly by taking the derivatives of S with respect to the real variables b_j and setting them to 0, we have

$$\mathrm{Re}\left\{\overline{Z^T}(Zc - w)i\right\} = 0$$

which is equivalent to

$$\mathrm{Im}\left\{\overline{Z^T}(Zc - w)\right\} = 0$$

Therefore, the least squares solution should satisfy the linear equation:

$$\overline{Z^T}(Zc - w) = 0$$

or

$$\overline{Z^T}Zc = \overline{Z^T}w$$

Another way to derive the equation is to consider w as a vector in the complex vector space $\mathbf{C}^m$, and the column space of Z as a subspace. The minimization of S is to minimize the distance from w to the subspace, which is attained at Pw, the perpendicular projection of w into the subspace ([4]). The equation above specifies the orthogonality between $w - Pw$ and the subspace.

3. An Algorithm

In order to apply the polynomial fitting, we need to obtain two sets of corresponding points $(z_1, z_2, \ldots, z_m)$ and $(w_1, w_2, \ldots, w_m)$ automatically. For simplicity, in this paper we make the assumption that the curved object in an image is approximately of a thin, linear shape. As illustrated in Figure 1, the object is ideally straight and in a vertical position. However, the object is flexible and only a bent version of the object is captured in the image.

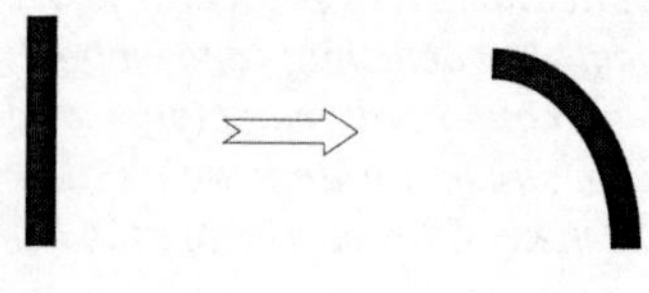

Figure 1. Object bending

The objective of the algorithm is to automatically detect this bending and to restore the original object from the observed image. The basic approach is to approximate this bending transformation by using a complex polynomial least squares fitting. The fitted polynomial represents a conformal mapping from the space of ideal object to the actual image space. A restored image can be created by mapping the coordinates in the ideal space to the image and interpolating the pixel values.

To extract the corresponding points associated with the bending, we use the medial axis (skeleton) of the object. The skeleton will condense the object to a curve, which provides a convenient representation of the bending. There are many available algorithms for finding skeletons ([5-11]).

The points on the skeleton are used as the vector $(w_1, w_2, \ldots, w_m)$. The corresponding $(z_1, z_2, \ldots, z_m)$ is taken from the points of a straight vertical line of the same length.

Following the construction of the complex polynomial $f(z)$ through the least squares fitting, a restored image can be computed based on the actual image and the mapping. For each pixel coordinates (x, y) in the ideal space, compute the mapped value $f(x+iy) = w = u + iv$ in the image space. Because the coordinates (u, v) may not have integer values, a bi-linear interpolation is performed on the pixel values of four neighboring coordinates of (u, v). The result is set as the pixel value of the restored image at (x, y).

4. Experimental Results and Discussions

To test the unbending algorithm, we generated some images using glyphs of standard fonts. The interiors of the characters are filled with grid lines, which will show the effects of the transformation. The results are shown in Figure 2.

The first column of Figure 2 contains the generated images of characters. The second column shows the detected skeletons. The third column has the restored images using the algorithm described in the previous section.

In all cases, polynomials of degree 4 are used for the least squares fitting. A morphological opening is applied to reduce the artifacts in the skeletons.

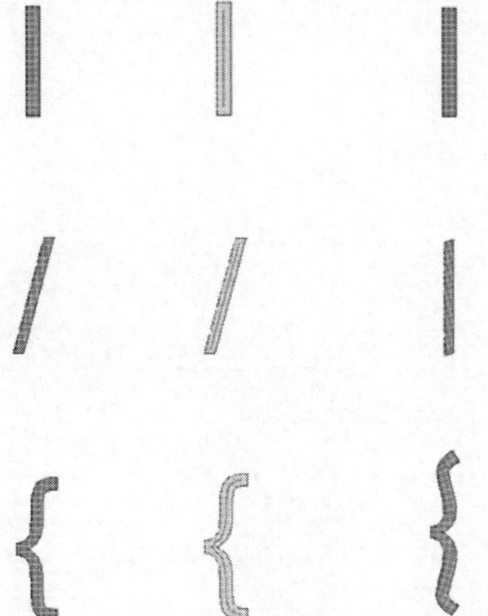

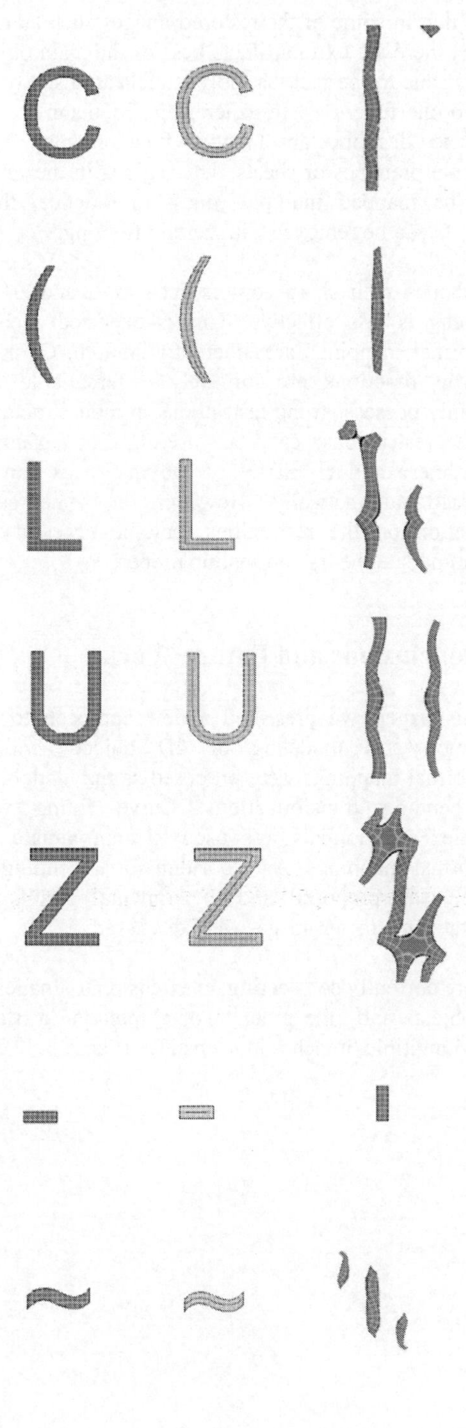

Figure 2. Unbending via conformal mappings

Note that in some of the restored images such as L, U and ~, there are extra artifacts besides the main object. This is due to the fact that polynomials are usually not one-to-one functions. In general, the Riemann surface used to describe an analytic function may have multiple branches or sheets. The regions in the image may be mapped multiple times. In practice, these artifacts can be removed with certain filtering.

On shapes with sharp corners such as L and Z, the mapping is less effective. This is expected because conformal mappings are inherently smooth. Complex analytic functions are infinitely differentiable and certainly possess strong restrictions in their structures. These restrictions can be useful. For example, smoothness and regularity of the mappings can be enforced automatically. However, in some cases relaxation on the restrictions may be necessary to accommodate the transformation properly.

5. Conclusions and Future Work

In this paper, we presented a new approach to the detection and modeling of 2D object bending. Conformal mappings were proposed as the models for the bending transformations. Curve fitting with complex polynomials was used to approximate the conformal mappings. An algorithm for unbending an object was proposed and experimental results on generated character images were discussed.

We are currently considering an extension to images of 3D objects and the problem of eliminating artifacts due to multiple branches in Riemann surfaces.

6. References

[1] J. Kao, J. Chuang, and T. Wang, "Chromosome classification based on the band profile similarity along approximate medial axis." Pattern Recognition, 41, 77-89, (2008).

[2] Z. Kou, L. Ji, and X. Zhang, "Karyotyping of comparative genomic hybridization human metaphases by using support vector machines," Cytometry, 47, 17-23, (2002).

[3] L. V. Ahlfors, Complex Analysis, McGraw-Hill, New York, (1979).

[4] P. R. Halmos, Finite-Dimensional Vector Spaces, Springer-Verlag, New York, (1974).

[5] H. Blum, "A transform for extracting new descriptors of shape," Symposium Models for Speech and Visual Form, Weiant Whaten-Dunn, ed., MIT Press, Cambridge, (1967)

[6] S. Zhang and K. S. Fu, "A thinning algorithm for discrete binary images," Proc. Inter. Conf. Computers and Applications, Beijing, China, 879-886, (1984).

[7] W. Choi, K. Lam and W. Siu, "Extraction of the Euclidean skeleton based on a connectivity criterion," Pattern Recognition, 36, 721-729, (2003).

[10] P. Morrison and J. Zou, "Skeletonization based on error reduction," Pattern Recoginition, 39, 1099-1109, (2006).

[11] J. Zou, H. Chang, and H. Yan, "Shape skeletonization by identifying discrete local symmetries," Pattern Rcognition, 34, 1895-1905, (2001).

Evaluation of color spaces for user-supervised color classification in robotic vision

Alina Trifan[1], António J. R. Neves[1], and Bernardo Cunha[1]
[1]ATRI, DETI / IEETA, University of Aveiro, 3810–193 Aveiro, Portugal

Abstract—*Autonomous robots are becoming an integrated part of our daily life. The use of a robot for substituting man power in different activities that might be too dangerous, repetitive or time consuming, has become a common procedure nowadays. Robotic soccer is a research branch that focuses on developing autonomous mobile robots, using the game of soccer as a testing platform. The soccer environment in RoboCup competitions is still more controlled than the one of the regular soccer games among human teams. For the vision system of the robotic soccer players, the colors of the objects of interest are still important clues for their detection. Thus, most of the research teams attending the robotic soccer competitions, use manual or user-supervised color classification procedures before each game, in order to guarantee an accurate object detection during the game. This paper intends to be an evaluation of the most common color spaces used in image processing applications that are based on color segmentation. The paper presents a graphical application used for testing both the performance of human users in the classification of different colors, under different color spaces, as well as the performance of user supervised algorithms for color classification. The results acquired prove that the color spaces which separate the luminance information from the chromatic one, mainly the YUV color space, provide a more accurate outcome.*

Keywords: Robotic vision, color classification, user-supervised algorithms, color image segmentation.

1. Introduction

The human brain can process all the visual information provided by the eyes in a short amount of time since it possesses 10^{10} neurons, out of which, some have over 10000 synapses with other neurons [1]. Looking at each neuron as a microprocessor and considering that these microprocessors are able to work in parallel, the human CPU cannot even be compared to any computer that has been invented so far. Thus, providing a visual sense similar to the human one, to a robot, is yet a far to be accomplished task. Because of this, most of the robotic platforms that are being developed nowadays and that need to process visual information about the surrounding world, perform in environments that are controlled up to a certain extent, depending on the practical application of the robot.

The RoboCup Federation [2] is an international initiative that focuses on the development of autonomous mobile robots and provides an environment for testing the developed robots, by means of different research competitions. The research lines involved in these types of competitions focus mostly on artificial intelligence, multi-agent systems and computer vision. The initiative is formed by several leagues, one of the most popular being the Soccer League. In this league, robots have to play soccer autonomously, without any human intervention. The league is then divided in subleagues, each of them involving different types of robots. The Middle Size League is formed by teams that build their one wheeled robots, of some standard dimensions. The Standard Platform League is attended by teams using a humanoid standard platform, that is, all teams use the same robots and their contributions focus on software developments. Finally, the Humanoid League fosters teams that build their own humanoid robots. The objective of the Soccer League is having by 2050 a team of fully autonomous humanoid robots, capable to play soccer against the most recent winner human team of the World Cup.

The goal of the league is still far from being achieved, since robots still play soccer in indoor environments, that are yet controlled, up to a certain extent. The controlling factor lays mostly on the fact that in most subleagues, all the objects of interest have distinctive, predefined colors. This is, the ball is orange in most of the subleagues, except for the Middle Size League, where the ball can have any saturated color. The soccer field is green, the goal posts can be yellow, blue or black and the lines of the field are white. In this type of scenarios, as well as in many industrial applications, the processing pipe of the visual information captured by a robot has as a first step, a color segmentation procedure. Especially in controlled environments, color can be an important clue for the detection of an object of interest. The color segmentation procedures imply the definition of color ranges for all the colors of interest of the application. Defining color ranges can be done by a human user, as an offline procedure, prior to the performance of the robot [3], [4] or it can be done online, by using semi-automatic algorithms [5], [6], [7]. The representation of the colors in digital format depends on the color space chosen and so far in literature there is not a clear, unanimous choice for a certain color space that might be the most appropriate.

In this paper we present the results of a study on the use

of color spaces in robotic vision, in order to understand if there is a more appropriate one to be used in these kind of applications. We intend our paper to be a contribution for the robotic soccer community but it is not limited to this. A tool for defining color ranges, both by an user and by a semi-automatic algorithm of region growing, under different color spaces, has been developed and the acquired results are presented. The results obtained facilitate the choice of a color space when implementing a vision system for robotic soccer players and its application can be extended to any computer vision procedure that implies color segmentation or classification.

This paper is structured in five sections, the first of them being this introduction. Section 2 provides an overview on the color spaces that have been included in the testing platform. Section 3 describes the features of the graphical tool that has been developed and the algorithms that have been implemented for the supervised color classification. In Section 4 the results and their discussion are presented. Finally, Section 5 concludes the paper.

2. Color Spaces

For the purpose of this study, five different color spaces were studied [8]. A color space is a mathematical model for defining and representing a color. The conversions between these five color spaces are based on linear mathematic equations [9], [10] (Subsection 2.1). Each of the color space has emerged at some moment in the history due to the necessity of rendering images on different devices or with different infrastructures. The study that the authors are proposing, aims at finding the most appropriate color space for robotic applications.

The RGB color space [11], [12] is the foundation of much visual technology, being used mostly for the sensing, representation, and display of images in electronic systems, such as televisions and computers, though it has also been used in conventional photography [13]. An RGB color space is an additive color space, defined by the three chromaticities of the red, green, and blue. To form a color with RGB, three colored light beams (one red, one green, and one blue) must be superimposed (Fig. 1). Each of the three beams is called a component of that color, and each of them can have an arbitrary intensity, from fully off to fully on, in the mixture. The RGB color space is not visually uniform and not very intuitive for a user to use it, as humans do not perceive color as the superimposition of the three primary colors.

The HSV color space is a related representation of points in an RGB color space, which attempts to describe perceptual color relationships more accurately than RGB [13], [14]. HSV stands for hue, saturation, value and it describes colors as points in a cone. The HSV color space is mathematically cylindrical (Fig. 2), but it can be thought of conceptually as an inverted cone of colors (with a black point at the bottom, and fully–saturated colors around a circle at the top). Because HSV is a simple transformation of device-dependent RGB, the color defined by the (h, s, v) triplet depends on the particular color of red, green, and blue "primaries" used.

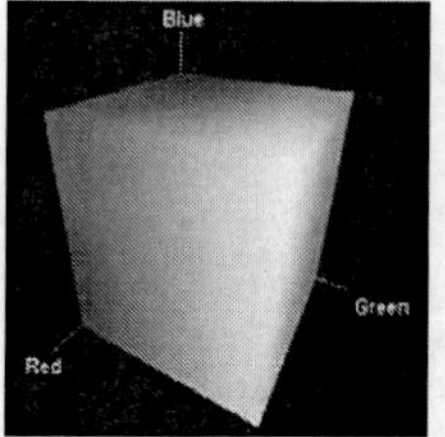

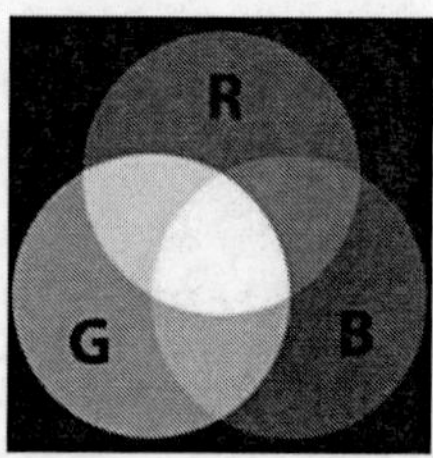

Fig. 1: On the left, the RGB cube and on the right, an example of an additive color mixing: adding red to green yields yellow, adding all three primary colors together yields white.

The central axis of the cone ranges from black at the bottom to white at the top, with neutral colors between them, where angle around the axis corresponds to "hue", distance from the axis corresponds to "saturation", and distance along the axis corresponds to "value". The hue represents the percentage of color blend, the saturation is the strength of the color and the value is the brilliance or brightness of the color [12]. Varying H corresponds to traversing the color circle. Decreasing S (desaturation) corresponds to increasing whiteness, and decreasing V (devaluation) corresponds to increasing blackness [12].

This color model is based on how colors are organized and conceptualized in human vision in terms of hue, lightness, and chroma, as well as on traditional color mixing methods which involve mixing brightly colored pigments with black or white to achieve lighter, darker, or less colorful colors [12]. For these reasons, the HSV color space is considered the most intuitive for human users to use it.

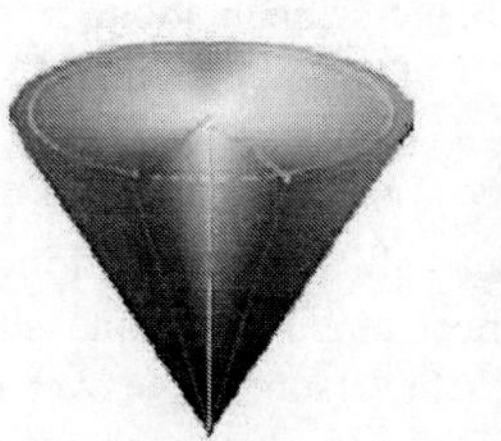

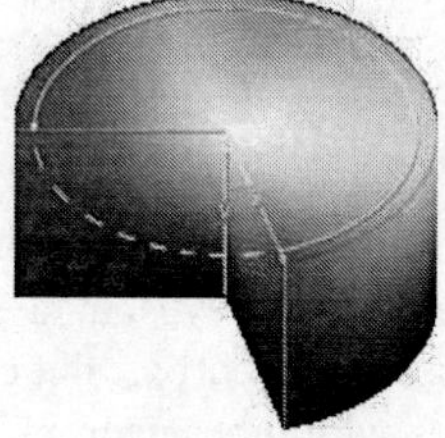

Fig. 2: The conical and cylindrical representations of the HSV color space.

The HSL color space is similar to the HSV one, the definition of hue and saturation, being the same as for the HSV color space [8]. The "value" component is replaced by "lightness" and the main difference is the fact that the value, or the brightness of a pure color is considered to be the brightness of white, whereas the lightness of a pure color is the lightness of medium gray. The geometrical representation of the HSL color space is a double cone or double hexcone [12] (Fig. 3). Although the HSL color space is used interchangeably with HSV in many texts, it was originally used to describe another (distinct) color space. Hue and Saturation are defined as for the HSV color space, but lightness quantifies the energy in a color rather than its non-blackness.

The HSI color space is yet another variation from the HSV color space [10]. The H and S components have the same meaning as for the HSV color space, while I stands for intensity and is the simple average of the three components of the RGB color space. The advantage is that this representation preserves angles and distances from the RGB cube.

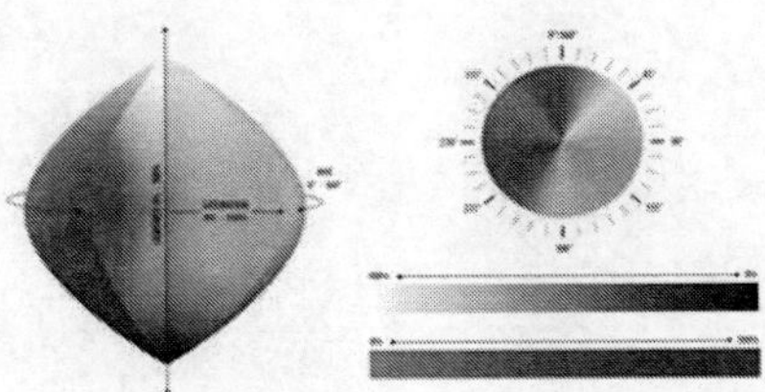

Fig. 3: The geometrical representation of the HSL color space.

In the YUV color space [10], [8], the color is represented in terms of a luminance component (Y stands for luma) and two chrominance, or color, components (U and V) (Fig. 4). This color space appeared as a necessity of introducing color television using a black and white infrastructure and encodes a color image also taking the human perception into consideration, that is, separating the luminance information from the color information.

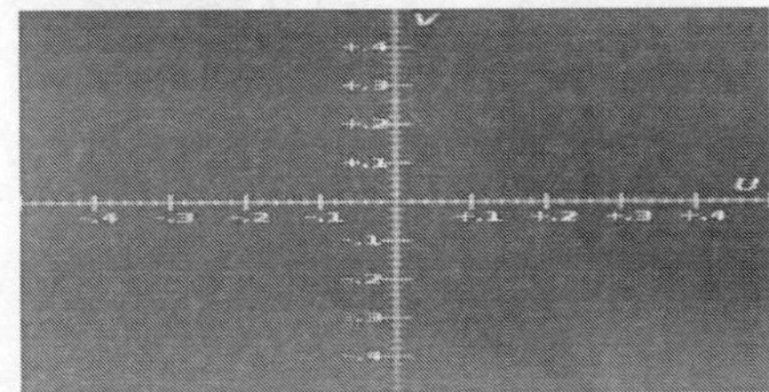

Fig. 4: Geometrical representation of U-V color plane, when Y = 0.5.

2.1 Conversions between color spaces

Conversions from one color space to another are based on mathematic expressions that are presented as follows. For the practical implementation of our application, the images used had been acquired in RGB and they have been converted to different color spaces, based on the formulas found in [10]. In all these cases, we consider the R, G and B components with values from 0 to 255.

- RGB to HSV:

$$V = \max(R, G, B)$$

$$S = \begin{cases} \frac{V - \min R,G,B}{V} & if\ V \neq 0 \\ 0 & otherwise \end{cases}$$

$$H = \begin{cases} 60(G-B)/S & if\ V = R \\ 120 + 60(B-R)/S & if\ V = G \\ 240 + 60(R-G)/S & if\ V = B \end{cases}$$

- RGB to HSL:

$$V_{max} = \max(R, G, B)$$
$$V_{min} = \min(R, G, B)$$

$$L = \frac{V_{max} + V_{min}}{2}$$

$$S = \begin{cases} \frac{V_{max}-V_{min}}{V_{max}+V_{min}} & if\ L < 0.5 \\ \frac{V_{max}-V_{min}}{2-(V_{max}+V_{min})} & L \geq 0.5 \end{cases}$$

$$H = \begin{cases} 60(G-B)/S & if\ V_{max} = R \\ 120 + 60(B-R)/S & if\ V_{max} = G \\ 240 + 60(R-G)/S & if\ V_{max} = B \end{cases}$$

- RGB to HSI

$$V_{max} = \max(R, G, B)$$
$$V_{min} = \min(R, G, B)$$

$$I = \frac{R+G+B}{3}$$

$$S = \begin{cases} \frac{V_{max}-V_{min}}{V_{max}+V_{min}} & if\ L < 0.5 \\ \frac{V_{max}-V_{min}}{2-(V_{max}+V_{min})} & L \geq 0.5 \end{cases}$$

$$H = \begin{cases} 60(G-B)/S & if\ V_{max} = R \\ 120 + 60(B-R)/S & if\ V_{max} = G \\ 240 + 60(R-G)/S & if\ V_{max} = B \end{cases}$$

- RGB to YUV
  $Y = K_r R + (1 - K_r - K_b)G + K_b B$
  $U = 0.5(B - Y)/(1 - K_b)$
  $V = 0.5(R - Y)/(1 - K_r)$
- Constants K_b and K_r depend on the RGB color space that is used.

3. The Color Spaces Tool

In order to obtain experimental results, a graphical user interface tool has been developed. The tool has two distinctive applications. First, it can be used for the manual classification of several colors, under the five color spaces (Fig. 5). Using sliders, users can manually determine the ranges for each one of the following colors: red, blue, green, yellow, orange, white and black.

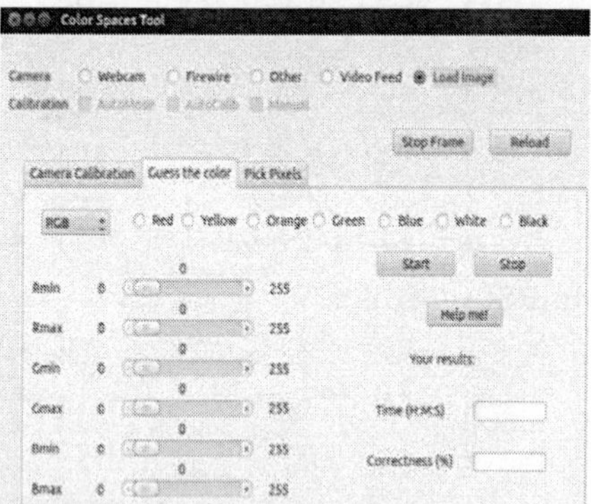

Fig. 5: Illustration of the feature of the Color Spaces Tool allowing manual classification of colors.

This feature works as follows: the user chooses an image that wants to classify, called *TrialImageX*, where X is a number identifying the chosen image. The set of trial images contains several images that have different degrees of difficulty in what concerns the color classification. That is, some of the images contain simple colored objects, without any shadows and without being affected by much noise (Fig. 6(a)). The color ranges of these objects are very close to the color ranges established in the literature, which makes the classification easier. The trial images set contains also images that might be more difficult to classify since they contain objects whose colors are affected by the illumination (Fig. 6(b)). When gathering results about this part of the study, each user has been advised to try the classification of at least one simple image and of one more complex image.

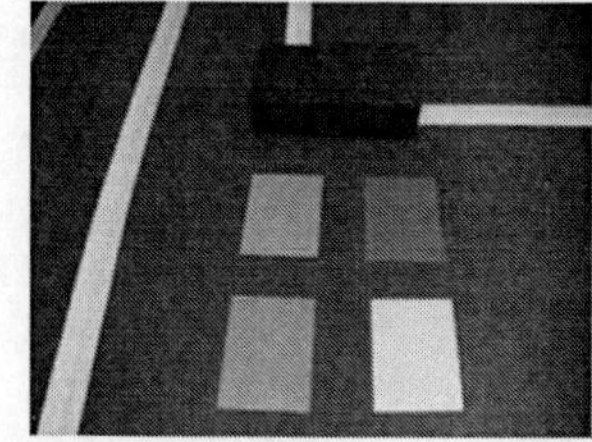

Fig. 6: On the left, an example of a simple image used for testing manual color classification. On the right, a more complex image that contains color gradients, shadows and objects with more details.

When choosing the *TrialImageX*, the *GroundTruthX* image is also loaded and will be further used for generating the results of the classification. The *ground truth* image is an image that has been already classified by an experienced user(Fig. 7). This image is considered to have the correct color ranges for all the colors and will be used for computing the correctness of the classification of each user. The correctness is calculated by direct comparison, pixel by pixel, of the images *GroundTruthX* and *TrialImageX*, when the user concludes the classification. In terms of results, the users are asked to record their correctness as well as their performance time, for each of the color spaces. The performance time is calculated by the graphical tool from the moment in which the user started the classification until the moment that he decided that his classification is correct, thus requesting it to be compared with the ground truth. At the end of all the trials, the users are asked to fill in a questionnaire that will be presented in Section 4.

Fig. 7: On the left, one of the images used as ground truth validation. On the right, the color classification performed by an user.

For the second part of the evaluation method, we have tested two different implementations of a region growing segmentation algorithm [10], [15]. The user chooses a trial image from the same set that was already presented and the correctness of the performance of the algorithm is calculated, as before, by direct comparison to the corresponding ground truth image. This feature of the Color Spaces Tool is illustrated in Fig. 8.

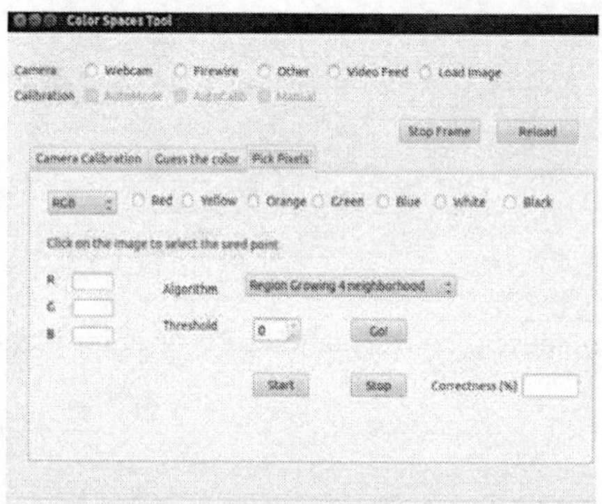

Fig. 8: Illustration of the feature of the Color Spaces Tool allowing supervised classification of the colors.

One approach was using the region growing algorithms provided by the OpenCV library [9]. The user has to choose a starting point(seed point) for each of the colors that he or she wants to classify and the algorithm will return all the pixels in the image that have the same color, +/- a predefined threshold, based on the following simple

mathematic relation:
$src(sP.x, sP.y)_r$ - infThresh $<=$ $src(x, y)_r$ $<=$ $src(sP.x, sP.y)_r$ + supThresh
$src(sP.x, sP.y)_g$ - infThresh $<=$ $src(x, y)_g$ $<=$ $src(sP.x, sP.y)_g$ + supThresh
$src(sP.x, sP.y)_b$ - infThresh $<=$ $src(x, y)_b$ $<=$ $src(sP.x, sP.y)_b$ + supThresh,

where *sP* represents the seed point, *infThresh* is the value of the threshold to be used when calculating the minimum value of the color range and *supThresh* is the value of the threshold to be used when calculating the maximum value of the color range for the classification of a pixel. In this example the algorithm is presented for (r, g, b) values of the pixels but it was used in the same manner for the triplets describing the value of a pixel in all the mentioned color spaces.

Starting from the seeding point and based on the values of the threshold introduced by the user, the algorithm will search the neighbor pixels (both 4-neighbor and 8-neighbor implementations are being tested). If the color of a neighbor pixel is in the range $[(color_{seedPoint} - infThresh), (color_{seedPoint} + supThresh)]$, the neighbor is classified as having the same color as the seed point and it is also marked as the new seed point for the following iteration. The algorithm stops when there are no more pixels to be classified.

The second approach was implementing a region growing algorithm from scratch, by the authors. The logic behind the algorithm is the same as previously described, with a small twist. Starting from the seed point, the 4-neighbors or the 8-neighbors pixel values are checked and if a neighbor's value is in the vicinity of the seed point's value (+/- a threshold), the pixel is marked as visited and is considered to be the new seed point for repeating the algorithm. The small twist for this algorithm is that the threshold value has to be the same for all of the three components that give the value of a pixel in each of the color spaces.

The presented tool can also accept video feed and configure color ranges based on direct images captured by the vision system of different robots, and can save the color ranges to a configuration file to be used in the further performance of the robot. Also, it allows manual calibration of the colormetric parameter of the camera that provides the video feed, in order to insure a proper image acquisition.

4. Results and Comments

In this section, the results obtained so far with the Color Spaces Tool will be presented and commented.

The tool has been developed for the study of color spaces when performing manual color classification, as well as for studying the same color spaces when using semi-automatic color segmentation algorithms, or what the authors call supervised color classification. For the manual classification of the color ranges, the results are presented in Table 1. A number of 15 subjects have been tested and the surprising result was that most of them had the best performance in the YUV color space, both in terms of correctness and performance time. This result is remarkable considering that in literature the idea that the HSV color space is more intuitive to humans is promoted [16].

	RBG	HSV	HSL	HSI	YUV
Average Time	5min 33s	4min 19s	4min 34s	4min 49s	4min 13s
Correctness	72%	92%	89%	85%	95%

Table 1: Table with the results obtained with the Color Spaces Tool for manual color classification.

Just like the HSV color space, in which the users actually have similar performance as in the YUV color space, the latter separates the color information into luminance and chromaticity. These characteristics make it indeed more intuitive to humans, considering it is similar to the way we perceive colors. This result is very important because most of digital cameras nowadays acquire images in the YUV color space and being able to perform the color classification in the same color space, would save important processing time that is spent in converting the YUV images to a different color space.

At the end of the trials, the subjects were also asked to fill in a questionnaire that would help the authors understand if there is any preferred or easier to use color space. The results show so far that the users preferred YUV, HSV and HSL color spaces,in this order, while RGB and HSI were more difficult to handle. All of them considered the "primary colors", red, green and blue easier to be classified.

Table 2 presents the results in terms of correctness of the classification:

	RBG	HSV	HSL	HSI	YUV
OpenCV-4n	87%	90%	85%	72%	92%
OpenCV-8n	90%	90%	87%	77%	93%
RG-4n	80%	75%	70%	63%	85%
RG-8n	82%	78%	71%	63%	90%

Table 2: Table showing the correctness of the region growing algorithms for all the color spaces.

These results show once again that the color classification algorithm performs better in the YUV color space. Moreover, in terms of implementation logic, the results prove to be more accurate when the supervising user has the possibility of choosing different threshold values for the three components of a color, for the color classification algorithm.

As stated before, each user was asked to fill in a questionnaire concerning his interaction with the Color Spaces Tool. The questions asked are presented as follows, as well as the averaged responses of the users.

• *Are you working in the area of computer vision/image processing?*

The first question was relevant for the authors of the applications in order to establish a connection between the performance time of each user and its background in a related field. The subjects were mainly non experienced users, only 20% of them have had some experience in this field. The users that were familiar to these issues, performed slightly faster (in average, 30 seconds faster).

- *The notion of color spaces was familiar to you at the beginning of this test?*

All users replied that they were aware of the definition of a color space. However, most of them were not familiar with the characteristics of each color space. The tool has a "Help me!" button which allows the user to choose a color space and the geometrical representation of the color spaces will be displayed in a separate window, similar to the ones presented in Section 2

- *Do you think that some of the color spaces were more intuitive to use, than the others? If yes, which ones were easier to use?*

65% of the users' first choice was YUV, followed by HSL. In opposition to this, RGB was the more difficult one for all the users.

- *Do you think that some of the colors that you had to classify were more intuitive to classify than others? If yes, which ones?*

85% of the users answered that white, black and the RGB primary colors were easier to classify that the rest.

5. Conclusions and Future Work

The major issue that this study addresses is the influence of a color space in the process of color classification. For this purpose, the amount of time spent by a human user for classifying colors under different color spaces, as well as number of pixels correctly classified both manually or automatically, under the same color spaces have been recorded and the results obtained have been presented. The results that we have presented show that, contrary to common belief, human users perform better when working in the YUV color space.

6. Acknowledgements

This work was developed in the Institute of Electronic and Telematic Engineering of University of Aveiro and was partially funded by FEDER through the Operational Program Competitiveness Factors - COMPETE and by National Funds through FCT - Foundation for Science and Technology in the context of the project FCOMP-01-0124-FEDER-022682 (FCT reference PEst-C/EEI/UI0127/2011).

References

[1] E. R. Davies. *Machine Vision - Theory, Algorithms, Practicalities*. Elsevier, 3 edition, 2005.

[2] RoboCup Federation. http://www.robocup.org. Last visited - November, 2012.

[3] A. Trifan, A.J.R. Neves, N. Lau, and B. Cunha. A modular real-time vision system for humanoid robots. In *Proceedings of IS&T/SPIE Electronic Imaging 2012*, (in press, 2012).

[4] A. Neves, J. Azevedo, N. Lau B. Cunha, J. Silva, F. Santos, G. Corrente, D. A. Martins, N. Figueiredo, A. Pereira, L. Almeida, L. S. Lopes, and P. Pedreiras. *CAMBADA soccer team: from robot architecture to multiagent coordination*, chapter 2. I-Tech Education and Publishing, Vienna, Austria, In Vladan Papic (Ed.), Robot Soccer, 2010.

[5] S. Barrett, K. Genter, M. Hausknecht, T. Hester, P. Khandelwal, J. Lee, A. Tian, M. Quinlan, M. Sridharan, and P. Stone. TT-UT Austin Villa Team Description. RoboCup 2011, Istanbul, Turkey, 2011.

[6] leader@austrian kangaroos.com. Austrian Kangaroos Team Description. RoboCup 2011, Istanbul, Turkey, 2011.

[7] T. Rofer, T. Laue, C. Graf, T. Kastner, A. Fabisch, and C. Thedieck. B-Human Team Description. RoboCup 2011, Istanbul, Turkey, 2011.

[8] G.D. Hastings and A. Rubin. Colour spaces - a review of historic and modern colour models. *The South African Optometrist*, 71:133–143, 2012.

[9] OpenCV Computer Vision Library. http://docs.opencv.org. Last visited - November, 2012.

[10] Rafael C. Gonzalez and Richard E. Woods. *Digital Image Processing*. Addison-Wesley Longman Publishing Co., 2 edition, 2001.

[11] G.W. Meyer and D.P. Greenberg. Perceptual color spaces for computer graphics. *Computer Graphics*, 14:254–261, 2012.

[12] George H. Joblove and Donald Greenberg. Color spaces for computer graphics. In *Proceedings of the 5th annual conference on Computer Graphics and Interactive Techniques*, pages 20–25, 1978.

[13] T. Acharya and A. Ray. *Image Processing: Principles and Applications*. Wiley New York, 2005.

[14] P. M. R. Caleiro, A. J. R. Neves, and A. J. Pinho. Color-spaces and color segmentation for real-time object recognition in robotic applications. *Revista do DETUA*, 4(8):940–945, June 2007.

[15] M. Petrou and P. Bosdogianni. *Image Processing the Fundamentals*. Wiley, 2004.

[16] M. Tkalcic and J. F. Tasic. Color spaces - perceptual, historical and application background. *The IEEE Region 8 EUROCON 2003*, 1:304–308, 2003.

BINS: Blackboard-based Intelligent Navigation System for Multiple Sensory Data Integration

Jun Jo[1], Yukito Tsunoda[1], Tommi Sullivan[1], Michael Lennon[1], and Timothy Jo[2]
[1]School of Information and Communication Technology, Griffith University, Australia
[2]All Saints Anglican College, Australia
j.jo@griffith.edu.au

Yong-Sik Chun[3]
[3]Satellite Information Research Centre
Korea Aerospace Research Institute
sik@kari.re.kr

***Abstract*— An Intelligent Navigation System is equipped with various types of sensors to perceive and react to its environmental situations. The data types produced from these sensors are varied and easily complicate the integration and analysis of the data.**

This paper introduces a blackboard-based cooperative system for the sensor data to be plotted, analysed and integrated. The situation analysis process employs two mechanisms to improve the efficiency of the system: multi-layered analysis and minimising regions of analysis. A case study was implemented for road boundary detection using a camera and a Lidar scanner. The result from the implementation demonstrated its promising aspect.

***Index Terms*— intelligent navigation system, sensor data analysis, data integration, segmentation, region of interest, Lidar scanner**

I. Introduction

A robot or an autonomous vehicle equipped with an intelligent navigation system (INS), usually integrates many different sensors, control modules and actuators. A device with an INS can travel to a destination along a path safely and efficiently, avoiding unnecessary accidents. An INS is designed to implement various functions including planning of the shortest route, detecting road boundaries and lane-marks, avoiding obstacles as well as motion planning and execution. There are a various range of sensor types for an INS to perceive and react to its environmental situations. An INS is usually equipped with many such sensors that quickly become intricate to handle. Sensors may operate independently or cooperatively with other sensors depending on the size of coverage or type of the duty. The data types produced from the range of sensors are varied and easily complicate the integration and analysis of the data. Many parameters, algorithms and often high-level reasoning are involved in the process. A single sensor alone may not be able to detect sufficient reliable information. For example, it is difficult to analyse road images captured by one camera alone, especially when taken during the night or as it passes the shadow of a tree. Data obtained from a laser scanner often includes many noises, especially when it scans visually complex objects, such as trees or grasses. To solve these problems, the combination of both camera and laser scanner can constructively interact, hence enhancing the sensing performance. However, the integration of heterogeneous types of data is challenging.

Much research has produced a number of methods regarding the integration of the various types of sensor data [1-3]. However most of these methods are problem specific and therefore not suitable for the more complex or diverse range of situations. Integrating such complicated data types needs a general and robust platform for various situations.

This research particularly focuses on how sensor data is integrated and shared for many functions in the INS. This paper introduces a blackboard-based cooperative system for various types of raw and analysed sensor data to be plotted and integrated. The controller gains and utilises information regarding the environment from the shared blackboard. This method makes the process very efficient as each resource can be used multiple times, for various tasks. Although all the sensor data is plotted in the blackboard, only the parts of interest are analysed, depending on the need. For example, only a small part of a whole image is required to be analysed in the detection of road boundaries. To implement the concept, a Light Detection and Ranging (Lidar) sensor and a camera sensor is used. The sensors capture the local environment, which, in this case, is the road situation in front of the vehicle. The data is then processed, plotted in the blackboard and used for a number of analysis tasks. For the experiment, a miniature vehicle was built and used. The vehicle is equipped with a laptop computer and three perception sensors: a Lidar, a camera and a GPS.

II. Blackboard-based Intelligent Navigation System (BINS)

The INS in this research is composed of four major units: the Central Control Unit (CCU), the Situation Analysis Unit (SAU), the Actuation Unit (AU) and the Blackboard Unit (BU), Figure 1. The CCU is the core of the whole system. It comprehends all situations, inside and outside the vehicle, by referring to the BU, making decisions and sending appropriate instructions, such as the new speed of a motor to the AU. In each cycle of the process, the CCU generates a new set of waypoints, which contain an information set of the required speed and direction of the vehicle, considering obstacles (as well as its movements) around the vehicle, road lane-marks or boundaries, the current vehicle speed, the distance to the next turn as well as the shape of the road. If any emergency situation occurs during the process, the CCU generates and deploys a risk management procedure to the AU so that the vehicle will avoid or mitigate the situation.

The BU is a place of information sharing for tasks hosted in the SAU. When a sensor generates data, it will plot the data in the BU. The task modules in the SAU will use the data in order to analyse various situations.

The SAU accesses all the sensory information in the BU for situation analysis. It also updates the data in the BU so that other analysis tasks may refer to the updated data. The analysed data is sent to the CCU for further context analysis.

The CCU runs a reasoning process, in order to generate instructions for the actuators in the AU. The AU consists of various actuators, such as electric motors, linear actuators and muscle wires. It implements physical movements as instructed by the CCU. The instructions for the AU include forward (angle, speed), backward (angle, speed), turn (left/right, speed) and stop (distance).

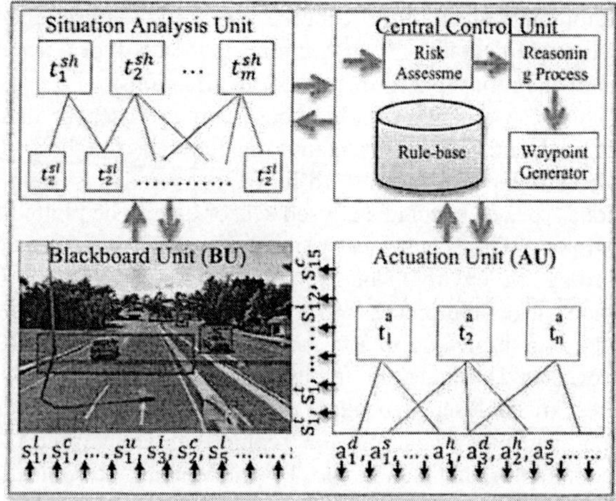

Fig. 1. The Blackboard-based INS, including four major units: the Controller Unit, the Situation Analysis Unit, the Actuation Unit and the Blackboard Unit.

III. Multilayered Situation Analysis

In this research, the analysis tasks use an efficient mechanism of Region of Interest (ROI) and Line of Interest (LOI), Figure 2. ROIs and LOIs are the specific areas related to the analysis tasks. Instead of processing data of the whole environment in every update, the analysis tasks are implemented within such limited areas, reducing the computational burden significantly. An ROI is a rectangular area containing information related to an analysis task. An LOI is similar to ROI but is used when the target area is narrow and positioned across a wide or long range. Some examples of ROIs and LOIs are:

$$ROI^c = \{ROI^c_1, ROI^c_2, \dots ROI^c_l\}$$

// ROI^c_i is an ROI in a camera image

$$ROI^i = \{ROI^i_1, ROI^i_2, \dots ROI^i_m\}$$

// ROI^i_i is an ROI in an infrared image

$$LOI^c = \{LOI^c_1, LOI^c_2, \dots LOI^c_n\}$$

// LOI^c_i is an LOI in a camera image

$$LOI^u = \{LOI^u_1, LOI^u_2, \dots LOI^u_o\}$$

// LOI^u_i is an LOI of Ultrasonic data

$$LOI^l = \{LOI^l_1, LOI^l_2, \dots LOI^l_p\}$$

// LOI^c_k is an LOI of Lidar scanned data

Figure 2 illustrates the BU where the captured sensor data is plotted. The area within the large rectangle, ROI^c_1, is associated with the lane-mark detection task. The other two rectangles, ROI^c_2 andROI^c_3, together with ROI^c_1 are used by the obstacle detection task. The ROIs are movable, and detect and follow any moving objects. The length and direction of the yellow arrow in front of each vehicle denote its velocity. The Lidar sensor measures the distance to the target surface, LOI^l_1. The GPS sensor provides the information of the current location, the current speed, the position of the next turn as well as the distance to the final destination. Based on all the information in the BU, the SAU analyses the situation and the CCU calculates and generates the waypoints, which are shown in green in the figure. Each waypoint contains the information about the expected speed and direction when the vehicle passes it. The SAU adopts a task-based multilayer architecture for integrating and analysing multiple types of sensory information. In this unit, the data, which was perceived by the sensor array and recorded in the BU, is utilised by one or more number of tasks. Often data captured by a single sensor is used for two or more tasks. For example, a camera image may be used for detecting lane-marks, road boundaries and obstacles. On the other hand, a single task often needs multiple types of sensor data, for example the road boundary detection task may integrate and use the data from both a Lidar and a camera.

Fig. 2. A visual display of an example in the BU. The image contains three ROIs (blue boxes) and an LOI (red line). The green dots represent waypoints between the current position and the next turn. The yellow arrows represent the velocity vectors of moving objects.

The analysis tasks, t^s , are classified into two groups: low-level and high-level. The low-level analysis tasks, t^{sl}, are context independent algorithms. Some examples of the low-level tasks are image segmentation algorithms, line extraction algorithms and Kalman-filter. The high-level analysis tasks, t^{sh}, are context specific and usually incorporate multiple low-level algorithms. Some examples of high-level tasks are road boundary detection, lane-mark detection and obstacle detection.

$$t^{s} = \{t^{sl}, t^{sh}\}$$

Figure 3 shows the relationships between the two-layered tasks in the SAU. Each high-level task deals with one or more number of low-level tasks. A low-level task is associated with a number of ROIs and LOIs. For example, the road boundary detection task, t^{sh}_{rbd}, obtains information from two low-level tasks: the breakpoint detection task, t^{sl}_{bpd} and the corner-point detection task, t^{sl}_{cpd}, The low-level tasks are then linked to a number of ROIs and LOIs.

$$t^{sh}_{rbd} = \{t^{sl}_{bpd}, t^{sl}_{cpd}\}$$
$$t^{sl}_{bpd} = [LOI^{c}_{1}, LOI^{l}_{1}]$$
$$t^{sl}_{cpd} = [ROI^{c}_{1}, LOI^{l}_{1}]$$

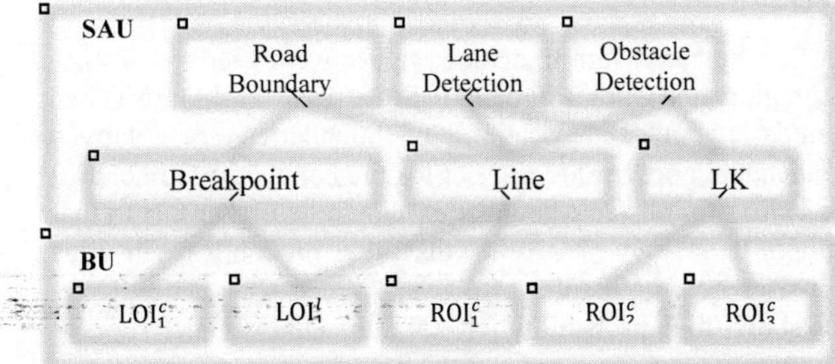

Fig. 3. An example of the Situation Analysis Unit with high-level and low-level tasks

IV. CASE STUDIES

This section introduces an example of the situation analysis tasks for road boundary detection using a Lidar sensor and a camera. This study manipulates two types of raw data: distance arrays scanned by a Lidar sensor and colour value arrays generated by a camera.

A. The low-level segmentation tasks

The low-level tasks in the SAU are basic algorithms that are context independent. The results of these tasks are used by one or more high-level as well as other low-level tasks. Four low-level tasks were used for this study: breakpoint detection, corner point detection, likelihood estimation, and Mean-shift segmentation.

The process begins with the tasks that segment a measured range data into a number of small groups and extract distinct features. This research implements the segmentation process by considering the differences of distances and movement patterns among the scanned points [4]. The road used for this case study consisted of a concrete texture surrounded by grass, mulch and shrubbery, figure 4.

A Lidar measures the distance to the object based on the Time of Flight (TOF) notion and the speed of light. The general form of raw data measured by a Lidar is represented in Cartesian coordinate system as below:

$$P = \{p_1, \ldots, p_N\}$$
$$p_i(x_i, y_i) = (\cos(r_i\ \varphi_i), \sin(r_i\ \varphi_i))$$

Fig. 4. The test road. The green line shows the scan points of Lidar, LOI^{l}_{1}

Where, P is a set of points and (r_i, φ_i) is the polar coordinates of the i-th scan point [5][6]. The measured data from a Lidar usually contains many noises and needs some filtering process in order to obtain a usable data set. Figure 5 illustrates the Lidar scanned data showing a road segment with many noises from the grass and mulches in figure 4.

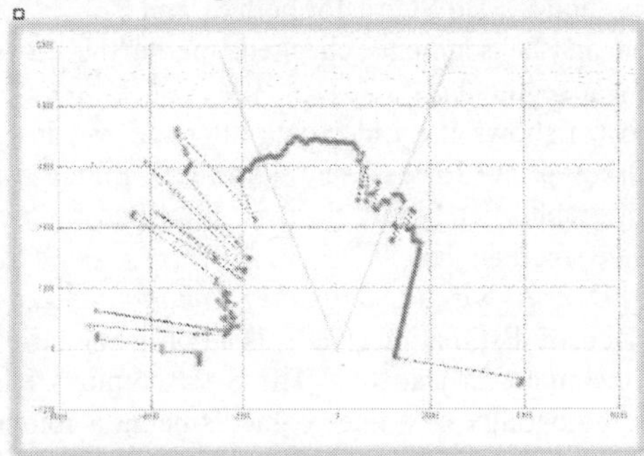

Fig. 5. The unprocessed Lidar data scanned from the test road. The two yellow lines define the camera scope.

1) Breakpoint Detection, t^{sl}_{bpd}, using Distance-based Segmentation

This segmentation task groups scanned points by examining the distance between two consecutive points. A breakpoint refers to a scanned point that indicates a presence of discontinuity between adjacent point segments [5]. The general form of the Point Distance-Based Segmentation (PDBS) techniques is shown below:

$$\text{if } D(p_i, p_{i+1}) > D_{max}, \quad p_{i+1} \in S_{j+1}$$
$$\text{else } p_i \,\&\, p_{i+1} \in S_j$$

$D(p_i, p_{i+1})$ is the Euclidean distance between two consecutive points p_i and p_{i+1}; D_{max} is the threshold; S_j and S_{j+1} are point segments [7]. This approach compares the distance between the adjacent points p_i and p_{i+1}. If the distance is greater than the threshold D_{max}, the two points p_i and p_{i+1} are regarded as different segments. Although this simple and intuitive approach has been widely used to solve clustering problems [8], the difficulty of tuning the threshold D_{max} is the major issue for the PDBS. This research employs the Adaptive Breakpoint Detector (ABD) which is a segmentation algorithm utilising an adaptive threshold [5].

2) Corner Point Detection, t^{sl}_{cpd}, using Iterative End Point Fit

Corners play important roles in feature extraction from images. The principle of Iterative End Point Fit (IEPF) is to search for a breaking point of a segment, or a corner point, which occurs at the maximum perpendicular distance to a line. The process starts by connecting the first and last data points of a segment via a straight line. IEPF is one of the most simple and popular algorithms for line extraction based on Split and Merge [4][9]. The following describes the steps of the Split and Merge procedure.

a) Fit a line l to a set of points S $[p_1, \ldots, p_i]$
b) Detect the point p_m, which has the maximum distance to l.
c) If the distance between p_m and l is smaller than the threshold, go to Step 1.
d) Otherwise, regard p_m as a breakpoint, and split S at p_m into S_1 and S_2. Do Step 1 for both S_1 and S_2.
e) When all the segments checked, merge the close and collinear segments.

Figure 6 (a) shows the Lidar data after the two low-level tasks: ABD-based and IEPF-based algorithms. Figure 6 (b) is the resultant graph after Figure 6 (a) is simplified by merging lines that have small angles.

3) Kernel Density-based Likelihood Estimation, t^{sl}_{kde}.

Kernel Density Estimation (KDE) is a non-parametric data-smoothing technique in statistics. The SAU employs KDE to estimate the probability of a line segments being a component of a certain object (i.e. tree, grass, road, etc.) through the identification of relevant features in each respective case. The likelihood of an object can be represented using summation of normal distributions of each breakpoint $b_i(x)$ at x coordinates:

$$\hat{f}_h(x) = \frac{1}{nh}\sum_{i=1}^{m} K\left(\frac{x - b_i(x)}{h}\right)$$

For the density at each break point, we use the Gaussian kernel f(x) as:

$$f(x) = \frac{1}{\sqrt{2\pi}} e^{-\frac{x^2}{2}}$$

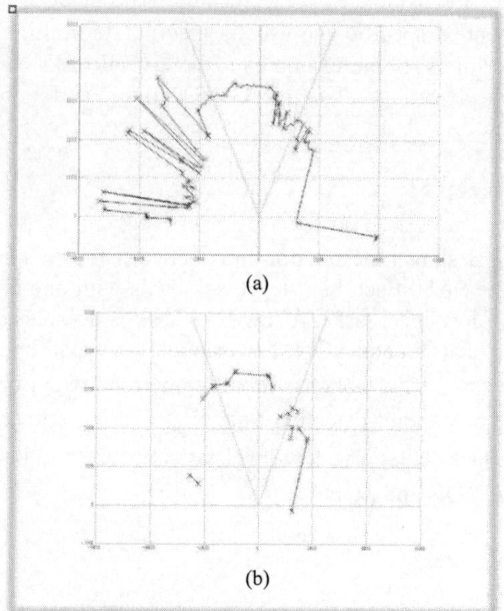

Fig. 6. (a) The Lidar scanned data. The red crosses show the breakpoints detected by ABD, and the green crosses by IEPF. (b) after the line segments are simplified.

For the bandwidth h, distinct values were used for obstacle estimation and curb estimation. Since road curbs are salient boundaries and the locations of boundaries are relatively predictable, a low value was set for the bandwidth. In contrast, the values for obstacle boundaries should be higher due to their ambiguity. Figure 7 shows that the probability, in blue, increases near both sides of a road surface whereas the green line shows high probability for other objects.

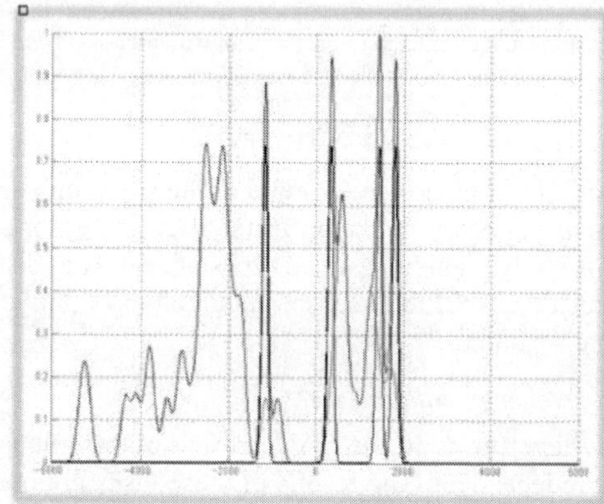

Fig. 7. The likelihood estimated Lidar data. The green line shows where obstacles are likely to be, and the blue line for boundaries. The red colour represents the sum of the green and red lines.

4) Mean-Shift Algorithm, t^{sl}_{msa}

Mean shift is a procedure for locating the local maxima of the probability density function given by discrete data samples. The algorithm repeats the same procedure finding a centroid of the data set, until convergence occurs. Figure 8 is an outcome of the Mean-Shift algorithm when applied to an ROI in the test road image.

Fig. 8. An ROI within the camera image chosen for Mean-Shift Segmentation. Colours are segmented using the Mean-Shift Segmentation Algorithm.

B. High-level Task Processing, t_{rbd}^{sh}

High-level tasks in SAU are context specific. They associate with one or more low-level tasks. Road boundary detection is chosen as an example in this research. This task executes and integrates the low-level tasks listed in the previous section. Some of these low-level tasks may be reused for other high-level tasks such as lane-mark detection, t_{lmd}^{sh}.

$t_{rbd}^{sh} = \{t_{bpd}^{sl}, t_{cpd}^{sl}, t_{msa}^{sl}, t_{kde}^{sl}\}$

The t_{rbd}^{sh} task begins with the line extraction and merging process, running breakpoint detection, t_{bpd}^{sl}, and corner point detection, t_{cpd}^{sl}. The results of the operations are translated to the probability of a road boundaries occurrence using the t_{kde}^{sl} task.

```
B = t_bpd^sl
// ABD creates a breakpoint for each segment. B is a break
   point set.
For i = 1 : numOfPoints-1

    S = (b_i + 1, ... b_{i+1})    // Define a segment, S,
                                     containing all the points.
    C = t_cpd^sl                  // IEPF(S) detects corner
                                     points, C, in each S.
    update(B, C)                  // Add the detected corner
                                     points in the set B
End
```

The Mean-shift algorithm, t_{msa}^{sl}, on an ROI^c, runs and classifies textures. Figure 9 shows the result of the applied algorithm along with the probability graph.

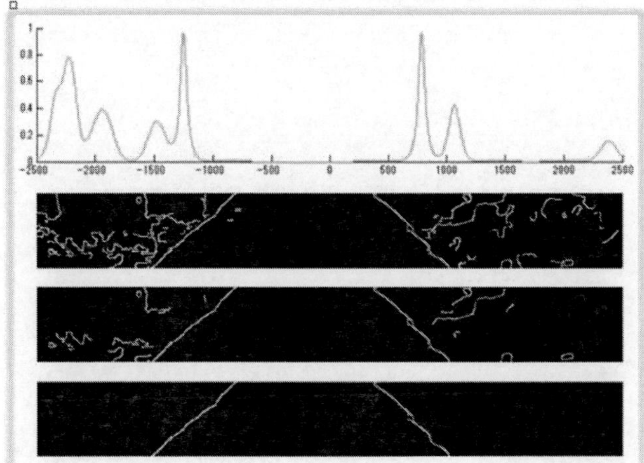

Fig. 9. The estimated likelihood result of the ROI. The edges of the ROI^c were obtained over different contrast settings by Mean-shift Segmentation.

Figure 10 shows the result produced by the integration of low-level tasks using the two types of sensor data: camera and Lidar. The graph clearly demonstrates the distinction of road boundaries (green) from other noises.

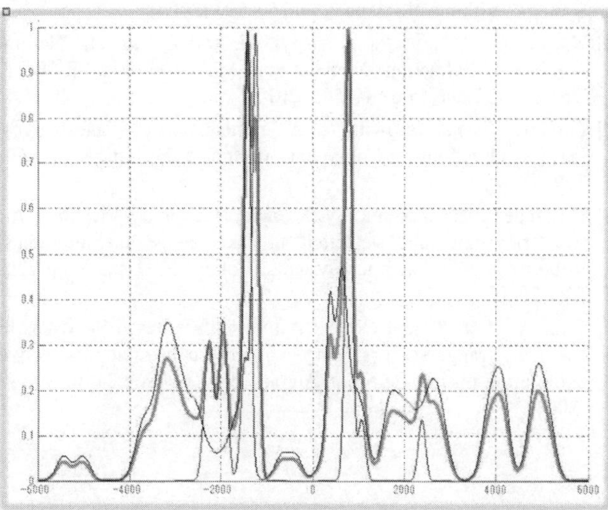

Fig. 10. The final result (the green line) of the road boundary detection task from the integration of a number of low-level tasks on two types of sensor data: line extraction and merging on the Lidar data (blue), the Mean-shift segmentation applied to the camera image (red).

V. Conclusion

This research proposed a Blackboard-based Intelligent Navigation System, BINS. The BINS presents a number of distinctive features including information plotting and sharing in the BU, two-levels of task management, and efficient analysis using ROIs and LOIs. For the case study, road boundary detection was implemented using two sensor types, a camera and a Lidar scanner. The target areas within the environment were reduced through the use of ROIs and LOIs. The results of low-level tasks – such as breakpoint detection, corner point detection, Kernel Density Estimation and Mean-shift algorithm – were integrated during the high-level task process. Although the performance of BINS was not one of the key points of this paper, the outcome, as shown on figure 10, demonstrated the efficiency and usefulness of the proposed concepts.

VI. References

[1] How, J.P., Bethke, B., Frank, A., Dale, D. and Vian, J.: Real-Time Indoor Autonomous Vehicle Test Environment, IEEE CONTROL SYSTEMS MAGAZINE, pp 51- 64 (2008)

[2] Subramaniana, V., Burksa, T.F. and Arroyob A.A.: Development of machine vision and laser radar based autonomous vehicle guidance systems for citrus grove navigation, Computers and Electronics in Agriculture, Elservier, Volume 53, Issue 2, pp 130-143 (2006)

[3] Sun, J., Wu, Z. and Pan, G.: Context-aware smart vehicle: from model to prototype, Journal of Zhejiang University SCIENCE A, volume 10 Issue 7 pp 1049-1059 (2009)

[4] Premebida, C. and Nunes, U.: Segmentation and Geometric Primitives Extraction from 2D Laser Range Data for Mobile Robot Applications, Robótica 2005, pp 17-25 (2005)

[5] Borges, G.A. and Aldon, M.: Line Extraction in 2D Range Images for Mobile Robotics, Journal of Intelligent and Robotic Systems, Volume 40, Issue 3, pp 267-297 (2004)

[6] Xiaowei,F., Minglun, F., Yongyi, H. and Qiong, H.: Natural Landmark Extraction Method for Mobile Robot, ROBOT, Volume 32 Issue 4 pp 540-546 (2010)

[7] Pavlidis, T. and Horowitz, S.L.: Segmentation of Plane Curves. IEEE Transactions on Computers, Volume c-23, Issue 8, pp 860-869 (1974)

[8] Fernández, C., Moreno, V., Curto, B.J. and Vicente, A.: Clustering and line detection in laser range measurements, Robotics and Autonomous Systems, Volume 58, Issue 5, pp 720-726 (2010)

[9] Choi, Y., Lee, T. and Oh, S.: A line feature based SLAM with low grade range sensors using geometric constraints and active exploration for mobile robot, Auton Robot Volume 24, pp 13–27 (2008)

A Probabilistic Mixture Approach to Automatic Ellipse Detection

Lei Huang, Jinwen Ma
Department of Information Science, School of Mathematical Sciences
Peking University, Beijing, 100871, China
Emails: hleicug@gmail.com and jwma@math.pku.edu.cn

Abstract—**Ellipse detection from a digital image, especially with a complicated background, is still a very challenging problem in image analysis and understanding, and its difficulty relies on how to effectively model these ellipses from edge pixels and locate them automatically. In this paper, we propose a probabilistic mixture model for the probable ellipses in the image and implement a Bayesian Ying-Yang (BYY) harmony learning algorithm to learn the parameters of the mixture with automatic model selection so that the correct number of ellipses can be detected and located in an automatic way. Various simulation experiments demonstrate better and robust performance by compared with the current state-of-the-art ellipse detection methods. Moreover, it is successfully applied to the elliptical shape detection in complex real-world images and the fetal abdominal segmentation in ultrasound images.**

Keywords: Ellipse detection, Finite mixture, Bayesian Ying-Yang (BYY) harmony learning, Object detection.

I. Introduction

Ellipse detection, i.e., detecting ellipses from a digital image, is an important and challenging task in image analysis and understanding, computer vision, and pattern recognition. Actually, it is key to many practical applications such as cell segmentation [1] and fetal abdominal segmentation in ultrasound images [2]. So far, there have been a variety of ellipse detection methods which can be typically divided into three categories: voting based approaches, objective function based methods, and the edge-following or arc fragments based methods.

As a typical voting based algorithm, the Hough transform (HT) method [3] might be the eldest and widely used approach to ellipse detection. However, it suffered from a great deal of computation and large storage requirements. In order to reduce its complexity, Randomized Hough Transform (RHT) [4] was suggested. The extensions of RHT were further developed to select more representative edge pixels for the increase of the detection accuracy. However, these sampling based HT algorithms probably leave some actual ellipses undetected, and their detection accuracy relies on the sampled pixels in a great extent. Moreover, as the quantization error cannot be avoidable, the HT based methods may select more false peaks that lead to a larger number of detected ellipses.

As for the objective function based methods, the Genetic Algorithm (GA) based approach [5] is a representative example, which actually transforms the ellipse detection task into a multi-objective optimization problem. To achieve a high accuracy of ellipse detection, a fitness evaluation mechanism was further suggested for the GA based approaches, but it is still a difficult problem to implement such a mechanism. Moreover, it is time-consuming to search for a global maximum of the fitness function in the state space and there is also a risk that the solution may be just a local optimum.

Obviously, those two kinds of ellipse detection approaches mainly focus on all the edge pixels together, ignoring the arc fragments of connected edge pixels, which may provide more accurate and complete geometrical information. In fact, the edge-following based algorithms tries to exploit these arcs, leaving the unrelated discrete edge pixels disregarded, so they are more robust to the scattered noise. For example, Mai et al. [6] proposed a typical edge-following approach as follows. Firstly, line segments from the edge pixels are extracted and linked together to form arc segments in light of their connectivity and curvature conditions. Next, the arc segments are grouped or clustered according to the consistence of an ellipse. Finally, the ellipses are detected by fitting the arc segments of each group together. Actually, a similar ellipse detection approach was also suggested in [7].

However, this grouping strategy of arc fragments reckons without the global shape information provided collectively by those arc fragments belong to the same ellipse. In order to improve this weakness, Chia et al. [8] proposed an ellipse detector by using a repeatedly splitting and merging mechanism. Actually, the hypothetical ellipses are firstly generated by fitting the groups of arc segments and then their confidence values of goodness are evaluated. Further, a feedback loop is used to drop the low confidence ellipses and to regenerate a new set of hypothetical ellipses by re-combining the elliptical arcs from different groups. Until the confidence values of goodness of all the ellipses exceed a given threshold, i.e., no low confidence ellipses exist, the final hypothetical ellipses are accepted as the actual or detected ellipses in the image. Prasad et al. [9] also generated a enough number of hypothetical ellipses and utilized a hybrid criterion to select the true positive ellipses. However, the used hybrid criterion suffered problems since it was based on some local heuristic strategies and could not be robust to the noise. Actually, it is still challenging to correctly collect the actual edge pixels of a true ellipse when there exist some outliers as well as a cluttering of the edge pixels.

In this paper, we follow the edge-following paradigm and propose a novel probabilistic mixture model with its components being able to fit the actual ellipses adaptively and automatically via a BYY harmony learning algorithm. In addition, we implement an edge-following strategy to set the parameter initialization of the BYY harmony learning algorithm. Simulation experiments demonstrate that the proposed probabilistic mixture approach is able to detect actual ellipses automatically under the scenarios of image cluttering, partial occlusion as well as salt-and-pepper noise. Moreover, it is successfully applied to the elliptical shape detection in complex real-world images and the fetal abdominal segmentation in ultrasound images.

The remainder of this paper is organized as follows. In Section 2, we present the probabilistic mixture model for multi-ellipse detection and derive its BYY harmony learning algorithm for parameter estimation and automatic model selection. Section 3 conducts various experiments on synthetic, complex real images and ultrasound images to demonstrate the efficiency of our proposed approach. In Section 4, we give a brief conclusion.

II. BYY HARMONY LEARNING FOR ELLIPSE DETECTION

A. Finite Mixture Model for Multi-ellipse Cases

As is known, the parameters of a single ellipse consists of the length of semi-major axis a, the length of semi-minor axis b, the inclination φ and the center (x_0, y_0). That is, a five element vector $(a, b, x_0, y_0, \varphi)$ can determine an ellipse uniquely. In particular, the equation of an ellipse with the above five parameters can be stated as:

$$\begin{pmatrix} x - x_0 \\ y - y_0 \end{pmatrix} = \begin{pmatrix} cos\varphi & -sin\varphi \\ sin\varphi & cos\varphi \end{pmatrix} \begin{pmatrix} a & 0 \\ 0 & b \end{pmatrix} \begin{pmatrix} cos\theta \\ sin\theta \end{pmatrix}, \tag{1}$$

where $\theta \in [0, 2\pi]$, is a free parameter. Eliminating θ from Eq.(1) and setting

$$\Phi = (cos\varphi, -sin\varphi; sin\varphi, cos\varphi), \tag{2}$$

and

$$D = (1/a^2, 0; 0, 1/b^2), \tag{3}$$

we obtain

$$(\mathbf{x} - \mathbf{x}_0)^T \mathbf{A} (\mathbf{x} - \mathbf{x}_0) = 1, \tag{4}$$

where

$$\mathbf{A} = \Phi^T D \Phi, \tag{5}$$

$$\mathbf{x} = (x, y), \tag{6}$$

$$\mathbf{x}_0 = (x_0, y_0). \tag{7}$$

However, the samples always contain some noises, i.e., they don't locate on the ellipse rightly. Suppose that a sample point $\mathbf{x}_t = (x_t, y_t)$ satisfies the following equation:

$$(\mathbf{x}_t - \mathbf{x}_0)^T \mathbf{A} (\mathbf{x}_t - \mathbf{x}_0) = r^2, \tag{8}$$

where r is a random variable that follows a normal distribution denoted by $r \sim N(1, \sigma^2)$. In fact,

$$r = (d_r + d)/d, \tag{9}$$

where d_r, as showed in Fig.1, is the distance between $\mathbf{x}_t$ and $\mathbf{x}$, d is the distance between $\mathbf{x}$ and the center $\mathbf{x}_0$.

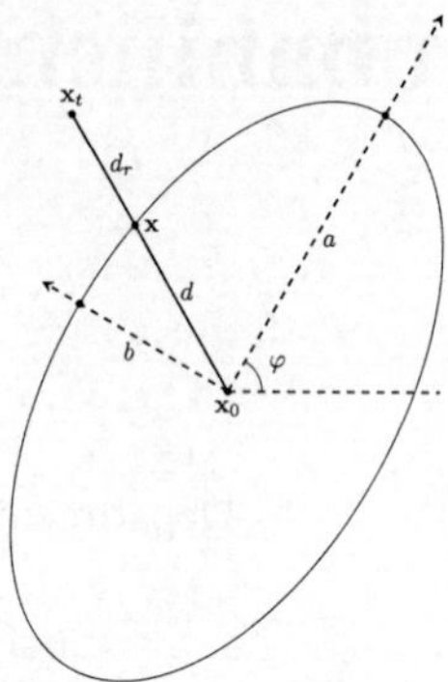

Fig. 1: The distance between a sample $\mathbf{x}_t$ and an ellipse.

We refer to r as the radial distance ratio. It is reasonable to assume that the error of a sample to the original ellipse is approximately proportional to $r - 1$ [10]. Further, we assume that the parameter θ to be a random variable that is subject to a uniform distribution in the interval $[0, 2\pi]$, denoted by $\theta \sim U[0, 2\pi]$. r and θ are independent, and thus the joint probability density function (pdf) of r and θ can be written as follows.

$$f(r, \theta|\psi) = \frac{1}{2\pi\sqrt{2\pi}\sigma} \exp\left(-\frac{(r-1)^2}{2\sigma^2}\right). \tag{10}$$

Considering the transformation between(r, θ) and (x_t, y_t) from Eq.(4), we can easily figure out that the determinant of Jacobian of the transformation is $1/(ab\sqrt{x_t^2 + y_t^2})$. Therefore, the joint pdf of x_t and y_t can be given by

$$q(x_t, y_t|\psi) = \frac{1}{2\pi\sqrt{2\pi}ab\sqrt{x_t^2 + y_t^2}\sigma} \exp\left(-\frac{(\sqrt{x_t^2 + y_t^2} - 1)^2}{2\sigma^2}\right), \tag{11}$$

where the parameters $\psi = (a, b, x_0, y_0, \varphi, \sigma)$. For multi-ellipse detection, we can utilize the following finite mixture model:

$$q(x_t, y_t|\Psi_k) = \sum_{j=1}^{k} \alpha_j q(x_t, y_t|\psi_j), \tag{12}$$

where $\Psi_k = (\psi_1, \cdots, \psi_k)$, and α_j is the mixing proportions with $\sum_{j=1}^{k} \alpha_j = 1$. So, by solving the above finite mixture model, we fit the samples (edge data) to the (hypothetical) ellipses.

B. BYY Harmony Learning for the Finite Mixture Model

For the finite mixture modeling, a BYY harmony learning approach (e.g,[11],[12],[13]) has been developed to make model selection automatically during parameter learning. In fact, given a sample data set $\mathcal{S} = \{\mathbf{x}_t\}_{t=1}^{N}$ from the above finite probabilistic mixture given in Eq.(12), its BYY harmony learning can be implemented by maximizing the following harmony function:

$$J(\Theta_k) = \frac{1}{N} \sum_{t=1}^{N} \sum_{j=1}^{k} \frac{\alpha_j q(x_t, y_t|\psi_j)}{q(x_t, y_t|\Psi_k)} \ln\left(\alpha_j q(x_t, y_t|\psi_j)\right). \tag{13}$$

For clarity, we denote:

$$p(j|x_t, y_t) = \frac{\alpha_j q(x_t, y_t|\psi_j)}{q(x_t, y_t|\Psi_k)} \tag{14}$$

To avoid the overfitting phenomenon, we add a penalty to $J(\Theta_k)$, that is,

$$L_\lambda(\Theta_k) = J(\Theta_k) - \lambda \frac{1}{N}\sum_{t=1}^{N}\sum_{j=1}^{k} p(j|x_t, y_t)\ln p(j|x_t, y_t). \tag{15}$$

We adopt the same BYY learning system and strategy as [13] to maximize $L_\lambda(\Theta_k)$. Dividing the parameters into two groups: Θ_1 and Θ_2, where $\Theta_1 = \{p(j|x_t, y_t), t = 1, \cdots, N, j = 1, \cdots, k\}$ and $\Theta_2 = \{a_j, b_j, x_{0j}, y_{0j}, \varphi_j, \sigma_j, \alpha_j\}_{j=1}^k$. Then, we obtain:

$$\max_{\Theta_k} L_\lambda(\Theta_k) = \max_{\Theta_1,\Theta_2} L_\lambda(\Theta_k) = \max_{\Theta_1,\Theta_2} L_\lambda(\Theta_1, \Theta_2), \tag{16}$$

which can be implemented through an alternative maximization iterative procedure [13]:
Step 1: Fix $\Theta_2 = \Theta_2^{old}$, get $\Theta_1^{new} = \text{argmax}_{\Theta_1} L_\lambda(\Theta_1, \Theta_2)$.
Step 2: Fix $\Theta_1 = \Theta_1^{old}$, get $\Theta_2^{new} = \text{argmax}_{\Theta_2} L_\lambda(\Theta_2, \Theta_2)$.
Firstly, we fix Θ_2 and solve the maximum of Θ_1. Since $\sum_{j=1}^{k} p(j|x_t, y_t) = 1$, we introduce N Lagrange multipliers $\beta_1, \cdots, \beta_N$ to construct the following Lagrange function:

$$L_1 = L_\lambda(\Theta_k) + \sum_{t=1}^{N}\beta_t\left(\sum_{j=1}^{k} p(j|x_t, y_t) - 1\right). \tag{17}$$

Letting the derivatives of L_1 w.r.t all β_t and $p(j|x_t, y_t)$ be zeros, we obtain the following solution of Θ_1:

$$p(j|x_t, y_t) = \frac{(\alpha_j q(x_t, y_t|\psi_j))^{1/\lambda}}{\sum_{i=1}^{k}(\alpha_j q(x_t, y_t|\psi_j))^{1/\lambda}}. \tag{18}$$

Secondly, fix Θ_1 and solve the maximum of Θ_2. Since $\sum_{j=1}^{k}\alpha_j = 1$, we introduce a Lagrange multiplier β to construct the following Lagrange function:

$$L_2 = L_\lambda(\Theta_k) + \beta\left(1 - \sum_{j=1}^{k}\alpha_j\right). \tag{19}$$

Letting the derivatives of L_2 w.r.t $\alpha_j, \beta, \sigma_j$ to be zeros, we have

$$\alpha_j = \frac{1}{N}\sum_{t=1}^{N} p(j|x_t, y_t) \tag{20}$$

$$\sigma_j^2 = \frac{\sum_{t=1}^{N} p(j|x_t, y_t)(r_{j_t} - 1)^2}{\sum_{t=1}^{N} p(j|x_t, y_t)}, \tag{21}$$

where r_{j_t} denote the radial distance ratio of t-th sample that belongs to j-th ellipse. Letting the derivatives of L_2 w.r.t the ellipse parameters $a_j, b_j, x_{0_j}, y_{0_j}, \varphi_j$ to be zeros, we obtain five non-linear equations. The analytic solutions of x_{0_j},y_{0_j},a_j,b_j and φ_j can not be gotten from these equations. However, we can resort to some stable numerical approaches to solve these nonlinear equations iteratively. Here, we utilize the trust region dogleg algorithm [14] to solve the five non-linear equations to update parameters $\{a_j, b_j, x_{0j}, y_{0j}, \varphi_j\}_{j=1}^k$.

From above derivations, we have established an alternative optimization approach to maximizing $L_\lambda(\Theta_k)$. Actually, during the learning process, some mixing proportions may be very small. In order to accelerate the convergence of the algorithm, a component with a mixing proportion being lower than an annihilation threshold δ will be cancelled directly. However, the initial numbers of ellipse k should set to be larger than the true numbers k^*. But this is easy to achieve for the number of the elliptical arcs is always larger than the number of existing ellipses.

C. Proposed Approach to Automatic Ellipse Detection

Given a set of ellipse edge data (black pixels) $\mathcal{E} = \{\mathbf{x}_t = (x_t, y_t)\}_{t=1}^N$ from an edge image (i.e., black or edge pixels of the image), we assume that these edge pixels are subject to the finite mixture distribution given by Eq.(12). Then, we can implement the BYY harmony learning algorithm to determine the number of components and to estimate the parameters as well in the mixture from the given data. If we get k^* ellipses with the parameters respectively denoted by $\{a_j, b_j, x_{0j}, y_{0j}, \varphi_j\}$, we can then locate the k^* ellipses accurately and solely in the image. Hence, detecting the ellipses in an edge image is equal to the BYY harmony learning on this finite mixture. However, for detecting complicated ellipses especially when the ellipses are occluded and overlapped, we need to set an appropriate initialization for the parameters in the BYY harmony learning algorithm. Moreover, the edge map of the real image may contain ceratin pixels that do not fit any elliptical shape at all. In order to eliminate the adverse impact of these pixels, which can be considered as noises in fitting the finite mixture model to the edge pixels, we need to remove them from an edge image to obtain the valid ellipse edge pixels and the finite mixture model will only build on the valid ellipse edge pixels. Taking the above two points into consideration, we adopt the following three steps to pre-processing the edge image. From the first two steps,we obtain the valid elliptical edge pixels(i.e.,$\mathcal{E}$). After these three steps,we obtain an initial guess of the parameters for the mixture model.

1) Contour Fragments Extraction: The contour fragments extraction process aims at breaking an edge image into curve fragments. We implement the Kovesi's scheme [15] to extract the connected edge contours. Here, the edge contours owning less than 5 pixels will be discarded directly for they are probably generated by the noise. As ellipse arcs should contains only smooth and convex curves, we can break the edge contours at the sharp turning points (corner points) and inflection points if they have these points. Due to the noises or errors generated by the edge detection method, some false corner or inflection points may exist in the edge contours. Actually, we can implement the curvature based approach [16] to find the the corner and inflection points and break the edge contours at them. After this breaking process, we obtain the smooth contour fragments.

2) Valid Elliptical-arcs Recognition: The valid elliptical-arcs identification process aims at recognizing the valid elliptical-arcs from those curve fragments F_i. For this purpose, we implement the direct least square fitting algorithm [17] to fit each curve fragment F_i into its corresponding ellipse E_i. Let N_i denote the number of the edge pixels of F_i, we use the following measure to evaluate whether a curve fragment should identify to be a valid elliptical arc:

$$\text{Valid}(F_i, E_i) = \frac{\sum_{\forall \mathbf{x} \in F_i} I(\mathbf{x}, E_i)}{N_i}, \tag{22}$$

where $I(\cdot)$ is just the membership function of an edge pixel for the ellipse given by

$$I(\mathbf{x}, E_i) = \begin{cases} 1 & \text{if } d(\mathbf{x}, E_i) <= d_1; \\ 0 & \text{otherwise,} \end{cases} \tag{23}$$

where $d(\cdot)$ denotes the radial distance from an edge pixel to the ellipse, i.e.,

$$d(\mathbf{x}, E_i) = |\,(\mathbf{x} - \mathbf{x}_{0_i})^T \mathbf{A}_i (\mathbf{x} - \mathbf{x}_{0_i}) - 1|. \tag{24}$$

Clearly, Valid$(\cdot)$ reflects how much percentage of the edge pixels of the curve fragment locate at or near to the fitted ellipse, that is, the greater number of such pixels, the higher value of Valid$(\cdot)$. When Valid$(\cdot)$ is low enough, that is, the most of the points in the curve fragment are not fitted or close to the ellipse, it is nature that this curve fragment does not own an elliptical shape. Moreover, the value of $d(\cdot)$ will be small if an edge pixel lies around the ellipse boundary. If an edge pixel coincides or lies on the ellipse, the value of $d(\cdot)$ will be 0. In view of the above points, our method is reasonable and effective to determine whether a curve fragment has an elliptical shape.A curve fragment F_i is identified to be a valid elliptical arc if Valid(F_i, E_i) is larger than a threshold τ.

3) Valid Elliptical-arcs Grouping and Fitting: After obtaining the valid elliptical-arcs, we need to group them for different probable ellipses. Here, we adopt a pair-wise grouping strategy. Suppose that all the valid ellipse-arcs are given by $\{\overline{F}_i\}_{t=1}^{N}$. Specifically, let $\overline{F}_1 = (c_1^1, c_2^1, \cdots, c_{n_1}^1)$ and $\overline{F}_2 = (c_1^2, c_2^2, \cdots, c_{n_2}^2)$. That is, $\overline{F}_1$ has n_1 connected edge points, while $\overline{F}_2$ has n_2 connected edge points. We firstly compute the distance between $\overline{F}_1$ and $\overline{F}_2$, where the distance is defined as the smallest one of the four Euclidean distances between the end points of the two arcs. If the distance is higher than a threshold d_0, we do not group them. Otherwise, if the distance is no higher than d_0, we further fit $\overline{F}_1$ to $\overline{E}_1$, fit $\overline{F}_2$ to $\overline{E}_2$ and fit these (n_1+n_2) points into an ellipse $\overline{E}_m$. We group $\overline{F}_1$ and $\overline{F}_2$ to $\overline{F}_m$ if the following conditions are satisfied.

$$\begin{aligned} \text{Valid}(\overline{F}_1, \overline{E}_m) &\geq r_0, \\ \text{Valid}(\overline{F}_2, \overline{E}_m) &\geq r_0. \end{aligned} \tag{25}$$

Continuing the pair-wise grouping until the arcs which belong to the same ellipse with $\overline{F}_1$ are all merged into a single elliptical arc. Then recursively repeat the above steps by grouping the rest arcs to finish the grouping process. In this way, the arcs will be divided into a number of groups. The parameters of the ellipses fitted from the grouped elliptical arcs will be used as the initial parameters for the BYY harmony learning algorithm and can be denoted as $\{a_j^{(0)}, b_j^{(0)}, x_{0j}^{(0)}, y_{0j}^{(0)}, \varphi_j^{(0)}\}_{j=1}^{k}$.

Then,the initial value of $\{\sigma_j^{(0)}\}_{j=1}^{k}$ can be computed by

$$\sigma_j^{(0)} = \frac{\sum_{\forall \mathbf{x} \in G_j} d(\mathbf{x}, E_j)}{N_j}, \tag{26}$$

where G_j denotes the j-th grouped elliptical arcs. The initial value of $\{\alpha_j^{(0)}\}_{j=1}^{k}$ are set equal to $\frac{1}{k}$. Finally, we summarize our algorithm as follows.

Step 1. Extract the fragments of the input edge image and recognize the valid elliptical arcs from these fragments.

Step 2. Group the elliptical arcs and fit all the edge pixels of the elliptical arcs in each group separately to obtain all the initial parameters $\Theta_2 = \{a_j^{(0)}, b_j^{(0)}, x_{0j}^{(0)}, y_{0j}^{(0)}, \varphi_j^{(0)}, \sigma_j^{(0)}, \alpha_j^{(0)}\}_{j=1}^{k}$ of the possible ellipses. As an ellipse contour is always broken into several elliptical arcs and when r_0 is set properly, k will be larger than k^*, i.e., the true number of ellipses in the image.

Step 3. Update the mixture variables and parameters $p(j|x_t, y_t)$, α_j, σ_j, by Eq.(18),(20)and(21), respectively. Moreover, update $\{a_j, b_j, x_{0j}, y_{0j}, \varphi_j\}_{j=1}^{k}$ by solving the five nonlinear equations using the Trust region dogleg method.

Step 4. Delete the j-th component or corresponding elliptical parameters if $\alpha_j < \delta$.

Step 5. Repeat Steps 3& 4) until $|L(\Theta_k^{new}) - L(\Theta_k^{old})| \leq \varepsilon$. Output the current Θ_k.

In summary, for the purpose of ellipse detection from the arcs in an edge image, we propose a finite probabilistic mixture model on the edge pixels. Then, the ellipses detection becomes the problem of estimating the parameters in the finite mixture with automatic model selection. We implement a BYY harmony learning algorithm to make model selection automatically during the parameter learning on the finite mixtures. To make an initial guess of the parameters, we extract the valid elliptical-arcs and further group them and the initial parameters is finally obtained by fitting a probable ellipse to the valid elliptical-arcs in each group.

III. Experimental Results

A. Comparison Criterion

Supposing that there are T_n actual ellipses in the image, d_n is the number of detected ellipses, d_{rn} is the number of true positive ellipses among the detected ones[1], the Detection Precision (DP) is computed by

$$DP = \frac{d_{rn}}{d_n}. \tag{27}$$

And the Ellipse Recall (ER) is computed by

$$Recall = \frac{d_{rn}}{T_n}. \tag{28}$$

With the above two indexes, the F-measure is computed by

$$F - measure = \frac{2 * DP * ER}{DP + ER}. \tag{29}$$

[1]Note that if the overlap ratio between a detected ellipse and an actual or true ellipse is larger than 0.95, the detected ellipse is considered as a true positive ellipse.

In terms of F-measure, we can compare our proposed algorithm (referred to as PM-BYY) with four current state-of-the-art ellipse detection methods including the multi-population genetic algorithm (referred to as MPG) [5], the hierarchical edge-following approach (referred to as HEF) [6], the fast and robust ellipse extraction method (referred to as FREE) [7], and the edge curvature and convexity based method (referred to as ECCB) [9]. We use the control parameters of these four methods suggested in literature.

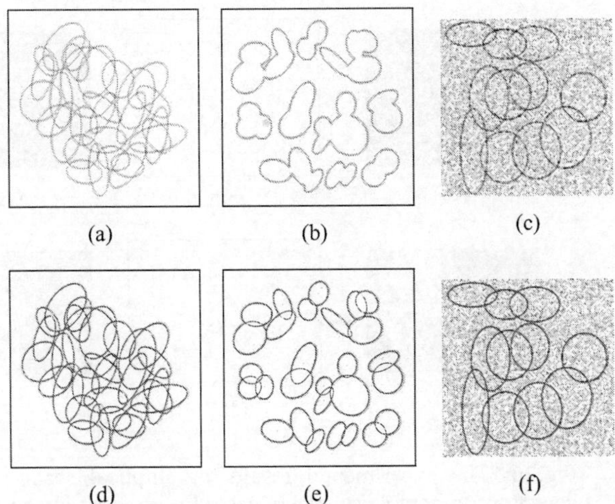

Fig. 2: The ellipse detection results of the proposed algorithm on synthetic images. (a). The test image of twenty-nine highly overlapping ellipses. (b). The test image of twenty-eight partial occluded ellipses. (c). The test image with added salt-and-pepper noise where the noise level is 24%. (d). The ellipse detection result on image(a). (e). The ellipse detection result on image(b). (f). The ellipse detection result on image(c).

B. Discussion on the Control Parameters

To recognize the valid elliptical-arcs from the image, we set $\tau = 0.4$. This value will allow some outliers contained curve fragments to be valid elliptical-arcs. To stop the algorithm, we let $\varepsilon = 10^{-4}$. To accelerate the convergence of our proposed algorithm, we set $\delta = 0.015$. For the images with some rather small ellipses, δ should set to be smaller. The threshold d_1 for valid elliptical-arcs identification is fixed to be 0.08. The threshold r_0 for grouping condition is fixed to be 0.9 for synthetic images. For real images and ultrasound images, the value of r_0 can vary in the range [0.45,0.80]. The value of d_0 can be given in the range [40, 90] according to the size of the images. The suitable range of the penalty coefficient λ is [0.1,0.5]. Actually, the performance of our proposed algorithm will not be deteriorated if λ is within this range.

C. On the Synthetic images

In order to test our proposed algorithm (i.e., PM-BYY), we generate 5 complicated images that contains 17, 20, 23, 26 and 29 overlapping ellipses, respectively. As shown in Fig. 2(a), it is the image that contains 29 highly overlapping ellipses. Even in such a complicated case, our proposed algorithm can detect the actual ellipses correctly, which is shown in Fig. 2(d). In fact, our proposed algorithm works well on each of the five synthetic images. Moreover, the comparison results of our proposed algorithm with the four contrastive methods are shown in Fig.3 in terms of F-measure. It is clear that our proposed algorithm gets better results than the four contrastive methods. With the number of overlapping ellipses increasing, our proposed algorithm can keep a good and stable performance, while all the four contrastive methods deteriorate quickly. Specifically, MPE cannot detect any true positive ellipse when the number of overlapping ellipses has increased to 29. ECCB may obtain high precision results, but with many actual ellipses undetected. HEF tends to generate many false positive ellipses as the number of the ellipses increases. As a matter of fact, the F-measures of the four contrastive methods are all below 0.4 on the image with 29 overlapping ellipses.

In real images, the edge contours of a ellipse may be broken into many disconnected edge fragments. For these cases, we test the proposed algorithm on 5 synthetic images that contain 12, 16, 20, 24, and 28 partial occluded ellipses, respectively. Actually, these images are generated by the same method used in [8]. Fig.2(b) gives the image that contains 28 partial occluded ellipses. The comparison results of the proposed algorithm with the four contrastive methods are shown in Fig.4 in terms of F-measure. It is clear that the proposed algorithm also outperforms the contrastive methods in such a more complicated situation.

Furthermore, we can add the salt-and-pepper noise to a synthetic image with noise level to be 12%,16%,20%,24%, and 28%, respectively. Fig.2(c) shows the image with such a noise of the level 24%. We compare the proposed algorithm with the four contrastive methods on these corrupted images and the comparison results are shown in Fig.5. It can be found that ECCB always fails on ellipse detection when the noise level is higher than 12%. MPE is also sensitive to the noise. Actually, if the noise level is over 12%, all the detected ellipses are incorrect. The detection performances of HEF and FREE deteriorate quickly as the edge corruption level becomes higher.

As a result, the experimental results have demonstrated that our proposed algorithm outperforms the four contrastive methods in terms of F-measure under the scenarios of highly overlapping, partial occlusion, and high noise.

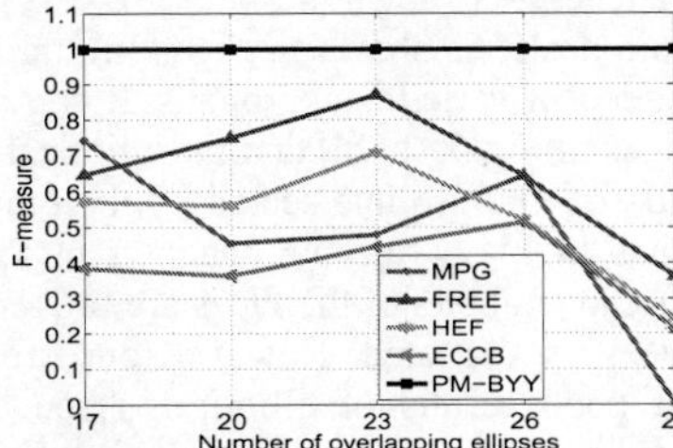

Fig. 3: The comparison results of the proposed algorithm with the four contrastive methods on the synthetic images which contains overlapping ellipses, where F-measure is sketched against the number of the ellipses in the image.

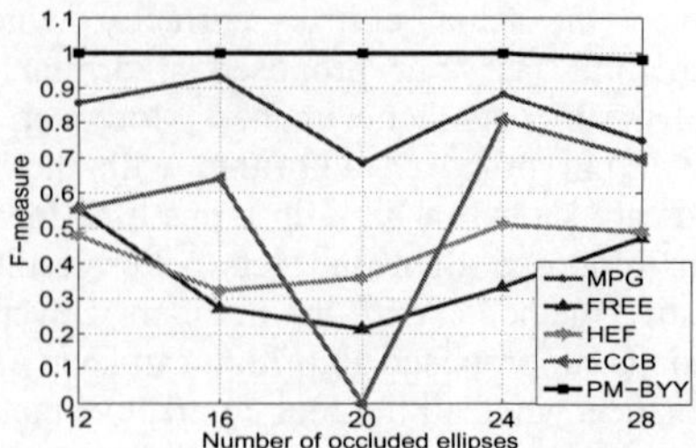

Fig. 4: The comparison results of the proposed algorithm with the four contrastive methods on the synthetic images which contains partial occluded ellipses, where F-measure is sketched against the number of the ellipses in the image.

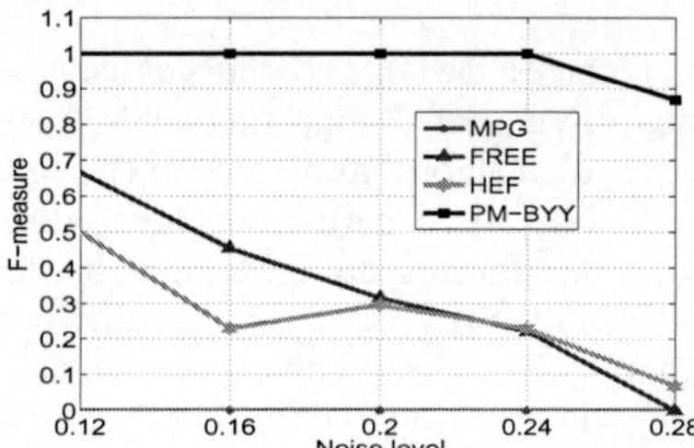

Fig. 5: The comparison results of the proposed algorithm with the three contrastive methods on the synthetic images with added noise, where F-measure is sketched against the noise level.ECCB is failed in implementation due to the corruption of the edge map.

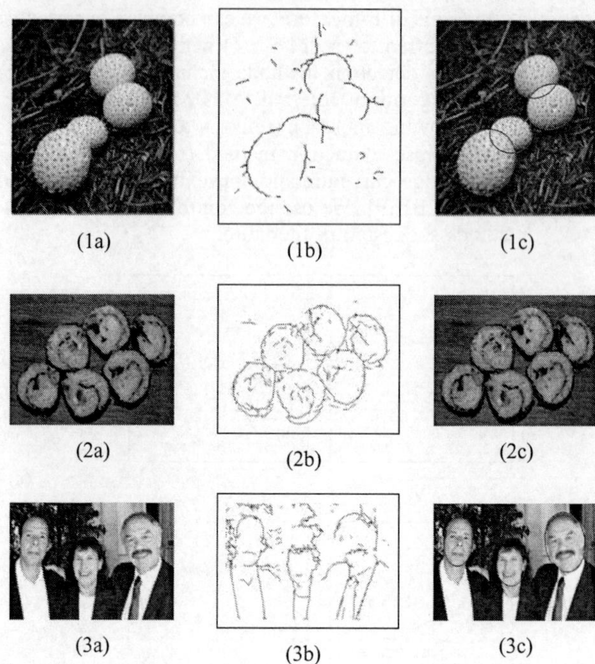

Fig. 6: The experimental results of elliptical shape object detection on complex real images. (1a-3a). Test images, (1b-3b). Edge maps of (1a-3a), and (1c-3c). The whole or partial ellipses detected by the proposed algorithm.

D. Elliptical Shape Object Detection in Complex Real Images

We further apply the proposed algorithm to detecting elliptical shape objects in complex real images, which is considered as a great challenge in pattern recognition and computer vision. Usually, the elliptical contours are corrupted by complex backgrounds. Fig.6 shows certain elliptical shape object detection results of our proposed algorithm on three complex real images. Here, to extract the edge pixels from each image, we firstly obtain the phase congruency strength map using the method proposed by Kovesi in [18]. We further threshold the phase congruency image to obtain the edge image. As shown in Fig.6(1a), four mushrooms are imbedded in dry branches. As shown in Fig.6(2a), six pieces of sushi are placed on a desk. As shown in Fig.6(3a), three elliptical faces are imbedded in varied backgrounds. It can be seen from the edge images in Fig.6(1b-2b) that the elliptical counters contain many outliers, and are intersected by the other features (such as branches in Fig.6(1a), and shadows in Fig.6(2a)). As for Fig.6(3b), the counters of the faces are broken into fragments, which are very cluttered. However, our proposed algorithm obtains a good results of elliptical shape object detection, which can be observed from Fig.6(1c-3c). On the other hand, the contrastive methods have poor detection performances on these images. Actually, for Fig.6(1a), most of the contrastive methods can detect only one ellipse from the four. As for Fig.6(2a)and (3a), all the four contrastive methods always fail to detect any actual ellipse. Therefore, our proposed algorithm can be successfully applied to the elliptical shape objects detection.

E. Fetal Abdominal Segmentation in Ultrasound Images

We finally apply the proposed algorithm to the fetal abdominal segmentation in ultrasound images. Actually, effective monitoring of fetal growth is very important to prenatal care [2]. Fetal abdominal circumference (AC) is well correlated with fetal growth and is an effective index for birth weight estimation [19]. In fact, fetal abdominal segmentation in an ultrasound image provides us an useful way to measure the AC. We apply the proposed algorithm to detecting the ellipse that fits to the abdominal contour. To extract the fetal abdominal contour, we firstly extract the region-of-interest (ROI) that encloses the target area. Then, we apply a local phase based method [20] to the ROI to obtain the phase symmetry map. Finally, the edge map is obtained by thresholding the phase symmetry map. Fig.7 outlines the implementation processes of our proposed algorithm. Specifically, Fig.7(e) shows the segmentation results of Fig.7(a). Fig.7(f) shows the manual segmentation results of Fig.7(a). The overlap ratio between the ground truth and the detected ellipse is as high as 96%. Therefore, this application result has also evaluated the effectiveness of the proposed algorithm for detecting the ellipse from very noisy contours.

IV. Conclusions

We have developed a novel automatic ellipses detection algorithm via the BYY harmony learning of a probabilistic

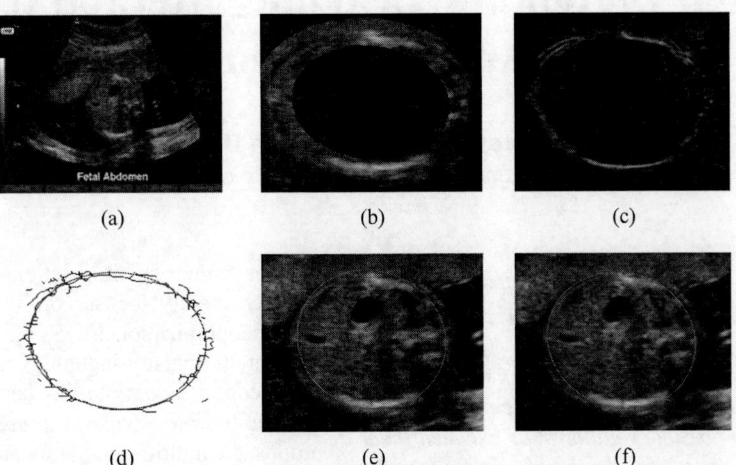

Fig. 7: The experimental results of fetal abdominal segmentation from an ultrasound image. (a). Test image, (b). The elliptical region of interest (ROI), (c). The phase symmetry map of (b), (d). The binary map of (c),(e). The segmentation result, (f). The manual segmentation result.

mixture of finite components to fit the actual ellipses adaptively and automatically. By considering the potential existence of the outliers in the elliptical-arcs, the probabilistic mixture model sets up a powerful framework to clustering the edge pixels of the existing ellipses. Meanwhile, the established BYY harmony learning algorithm for the mixture model leads to a good parameter estimation with automatic model selection. These two strategies enable the proposed algorithm robust and efficient for ellipse detection. Detailed evaluation of the proposed algorithm is performed on various kind of synthetic images. It has been demonstrated by the experiments that the proposed algorithm achieves better results than four current state-of-the-art methods in terms of F-measure, especially when the test images are complicated. Moreover, our proposed algorithm is successfully applied to the elliptical shape objection detection in complex real images and the fetal abdominal segmentation in ultrasound images.

Acknowledgment

This work was supported by the Natural Science Foundation of China for Grant 61171138.

References

[1] X. Bai, C. Sun, and F. Zhou, "Splitting touching cells based on concave points and ellipse fitting," *Pattern Recognition*, vol. 42, no. 11, pp. 2434–2446, 2009.

[2] J. Yu, Y. Wang, P. Chen, and Y. Shen, "Fetal abdominal contour extraction and measurement in ultrasound images," *Ultrasound in Medicine and Biology*, vol. 34, no. 2, pp. 169 – 182, 2008.

[3] R. Duda and P. Hart, "Use of the hough transformation to detect lines and curves in pictures," *Communications of the ACM*, vol. 15, no. 1, pp. 11–15, 1972.

[4] L. Xu, E. Oja, and P. Kultanen, "A new curve detection method: randomized hough transform (rht)," *Pattern Recognition Letters*, vol. 11, no. 5, pp. 331–338, 1990.

[5] J. Yao, N. Kharma, and P. Grogono, "A multi-population genetic algorithm for robust and fast ellipse detection," *Pattern Analysis and Application*, vol. 8, no. 1, pp. 149–162, 2005.

[6] F. Mai, Y. Hung, H. Zhong, and W. Sze, "A hierarchical approach for fast and robust ellipse extraction," *Pattern Recognition*, vol. 41, no. 8, pp. 2512–2524, 2008.

[7] E. Kim, M. Haseyama, and H. Kitajima, "Fast and robust ellipse extraction from complicated images," in *Proceedings of IEEE International Conference on Information Technology and Applications*, 2002, pp. 357–362.

[8] A. Chia, S. Rahardja, D. Rajan, and M. Leung, "A split and merge based ellipse detector with self-correcting capability," *IEEE Transactions On Iamge Processing*, vol. 20, no. 7, pp. 1991–2006, 2011.

[9] D. Prasad, M. Leung, and S. Cho, "Edge curvature and convexity based ellipse detection method," *Pattern Recognition*, vol. 45, no. 9, pp. 3204–3221, 2012.

[10] F. Bookstein, "Fitting conic sections to scatted data," *Computer Graphics and Image Processing*, vol. 9, no. 1, pp. 56–71, 1979.

[11] J. Ma, T. Wang, and L. Xu, "A gradient byy harmony learning rule on gaussian mixture with automated model selection," *Neurocomputing*, vol. 56, pp. 481–487, 2004.

[12] J. Ma and L. Wang, "Byy harmony learning on finite mixture: adaptive gradient implementation and a floating rpcl mechanism," *Neural Processing Letters*, vol. 24, no. 1, pp. 19–40, 2006.

[13] J. Ma and J. Liu, "The byy annealing learning algorithm for gaussian mixture with automated model selection," *Pattern Recognition*, vol. 40, no. 7, pp. 2029–2037, 2007.

[14] J. Nocedal and S. J. Wright, *Numerical Optimization*, 2nd ed. Springer, 2006.

[15] P. Kovesi, 2006, <http://www.csse.uwa.edu.au/∼pk/research/matlabfns/>.

[16] N. Y. X.C. He, "Corner detector based on global and local curvature properties," *Optical Engineering*, vol. 47, no. 5, pp. 057008-1–057008-12, 2008.

[17] A. Fitzgibbon, M. Pilu, and R. Fisher, "Direct least square fitting of ellipses," *IEEE Transactions on Pattern Analysis Machine Intelligence*, vol. 21, no. 5, pp. 476–480, 1999.

[18] P. Kovesi, "Phase congruency detects corners and edges," in *in The Australian Pattern Recognition Society Conference: DICTA 2003*, 2003, pp. 309–318.

[19] W. D. Campbell S, "Ultrasonic measurement of the fetal abdomen circumference in the estimation of fetal weight," *Br J Obstet Gynaecol*, no. 82, pp. 689–697, 1975.

[20] P. Kovesi, "Symmetry and asymmetry from local phase," in *Tenth Australian Joint Converence on Artificial Intelligence*, 1997, pp. 185–190.

A Structured Dictionary Learning Method for Multi-scale Sparse Representation

Wang Jiawen and Zhang Hongbin
College of Computer Science, Beijing University of Technology, Beijing, China

Abstract - *In this paper, we address the problem of learning multi-scale sparse representations of natural images using structured dictionaries. Dictionaries learned by traditional algorithms have two major limitations: lack of structure and fixed size. These methods treat atoms independently from each other, and do not exploit possible relationships between them. Fixed size of atoms restricts the flexibility of representing natural images, which usually consist of complicated structure and texture. We put forward a novel approach to learn a dictionary by performing structured sparse coding under a multi-scale binary tree model of patches. Atoms of different sizes are laid out in a grouped or hierarchical fashion, which can be fully exploited by structured sparsity regularization techniques. Experiments show that both quantitative and qualitative improvements are achieved for restoration tasks. It is worth noting that our approach can be easily integrated into existing sparse representation-based applications in image processing.*

Keywords: Sparse representation, multi-scale, dictionary learning, denoising

1 Introduction

The underlying representations of many real-world data sets are often sparse. Describing a signal as a sparse linear combination of atoms selected from a redundant dictionary has become a popular model in many fields, including signal processing, machine learning and statistics. How to choose a dictionary to sparsify the signal is crucial to the success of this model. In general, there are two ways of choosing a proper dictionary: using a pre-specified set of basis functions, such as wavelets, curvelets, contourlets, wedgelets, bandlets and steerable wavelets, or learning from a set of training examples. In this paper, we focus on the latter.

Dictionary learning, initially introduced by Olshausen and Field [1], has drawn considerable interest in recent years. A series of related studies have been published to address this problem, such as Method of Optimal Directions (MOD), K-SVD [2], notably leading to state-of-the-art algorithms for many applications in image processing [3]. However, dictionaries obtained by all these methods suffer from two major defects: no structure and fix-sized atoms. We call these traditional approaches. In many cases, the structure of the problem, such as the spatial distribution of pixels in an image, induces some latent relationships between atoms. Latest research mainly focuses on structured sparse representation and its optimization [4, 5, 6]. Atoms are regularized using structured sparsity-inducing norms. To the best of our knowledge, seldom studies concern on learning dictionaries for multi-scale sparse representation. Mairal, et al., [7] proposed a multi-scale dictionary learning algorithm based on a quad-tree decomposition. However, they perform sparse coding using OMP, which cannot fully exploit the structure of the tree model. We observe that different natural images prefer different sizes of atoms for optimal performance, e.g., a smooth image may prefer a larger size, and a texture image may prefer a smaller one. Also, natural images are so complicated that only one size cannot efficiently capture image features. Therefore, it is natural to demand a multi-scale dictionary for a better representation.

The main contribution of this paper is proposing a novel approach to learn structured dictionaries for multi-scale sparse representation. Under the structured sparsity regularization framework, atoms are laid out in a grouped or hierarchical fashion. Dictionaries learned under the binary tree model with multiple sizes of atoms can strengthen the ability of representing natural images. We also employ sequential dictionary updating technique from [2] to accelerate convergence.

2 Structured Sparsity

Before describing our proposed method, it is necessary to provide a brief overview of the concepts of regularization using the structured sparsity-inducing norm. And see how such a norm can impose structure relationships on atoms.

Let us consider a signal $\mathbf{x} \in \mathbb{R}^m$. Assuming that it admits a sparse representation over a dictionary matrix $\mathbf{D} = \left[\mathbf{d}^1, \dots, \mathbf{d}^K\right] \in \mathbb{R}^{m \times K}$, with K columns referred to as atoms, one can find a linear combination of atoms from $\mathbf{D}$ that is close to the signal $\mathbf{x}$. Under a square loss, this optimization problem can be written as:

$$\min_{\boldsymbol{\alpha} \in \mathbb{R}^K} \frac{1}{2} \|\mathbf{x} - \mathbf{D}\boldsymbol{\alpha}\|_2^2 + \lambda \Omega(\boldsymbol{\alpha}) \quad (1)$$

Where $\boldsymbol{\alpha} \in \mathbb{R}^K$ is the representation coefficient vector of the signal $\mathbf{x}$. Ω is a regularization term, usually a norm, whose effect is controlled by the regularization parameter $\lambda > 0$.

When Ω is the ℓ_1 norm, Eq. (1) is the classic ℓ_1 regularization, often referred to as Lasso. Note that overcomplete dictionaries with $K > m$ are allowed.

2.1 Group Sparsity

In practical applications, one often knows a structure on the coefficient vector $\boldsymbol{\alpha}$ in addition to sparsity. Assuming that $\boldsymbol{\alpha}$ is partitioned into several groups. It is then natural to select or remove simultaneously all the variables in the same group, i.e., set variables in the same group zero or nonzero, as illustrated in Fig. 1. A regularization norm exploiting explicitly this group structure can be shown to improve the prediction performance and interpretability of the learned models [4]. Such a norm takes a form:

$$\Omega(\boldsymbol{\alpha}) = \sum_{g \in \mathcal{G}} w_g \left\| \alpha_g \right\|_q \tag{2}$$

Where $\mathcal{G}$ is a partition of $\{1,\dots,K\}$, and w_g denotes the weight for the g group. Without loss of generality, w_g is usually set to 1. Eq. (2), known as a mixed ℓ_1/ℓ_q norm, behaves like a ℓ_1 norm on the vector $\left(\left\| \alpha_g \right\|_q \right)_{g \in \mathcal{G}}$. Thus, Ω promote sparsity between groups. We choose $q = 2$ or ∞ in most cases.

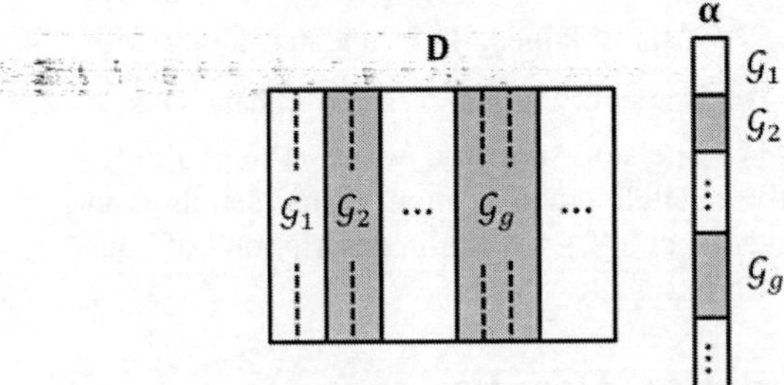

Fig. 1. Illustration of group sparse coding. The coefficient vector $\boldsymbol{\alpha}$ is partitioned into groups. Some of them with gray color are set to zero, thus the corresponding atoms with gray color in **D** are removed.

2.2 Hierarchical Sparsity

In order to better explore structured relationships between atoms, latest research focuses on the situations that groups in $\mathcal{G}$ is overlapped [5, 6], which means a given coefficient could belong to different groups. Given a tree structure $\mathcal{T}$ with p nodes indexed by j in $\{1,\dots,p\}$, we want to embed coefficients into $\mathcal{T}$, obeying the following rule:

$$\alpha_j = 0 \Rightarrow \alpha_k = 0, \forall k \in \operatorname{desc}(j) \tag{3}$$

Where $\operatorname{desc}(j) \subseteq \{1,\dots,p\}$ denotes the set of indices corresponding to the descendants of the node j (including j) in $\mathcal{T}$. Eq. (3) indicates that if a dictionary atom is not involved in the decomposition, then its descendants in the tree should not be included either. To achieve this, group set $\mathcal{G}$ is defined as follows:

$$\mathcal{G} \triangleq \{\operatorname{desc}(j), j \in \{1,\dots,p\}\} \tag{4}$$

When penalized by Ω defined in (2) on the above group set, some of the vectors α_g are regularized to zero, as illustrated in Fig. 2. Therefore, hierarchical sparsity can be achieved by the norm (2) with overlapped groups.

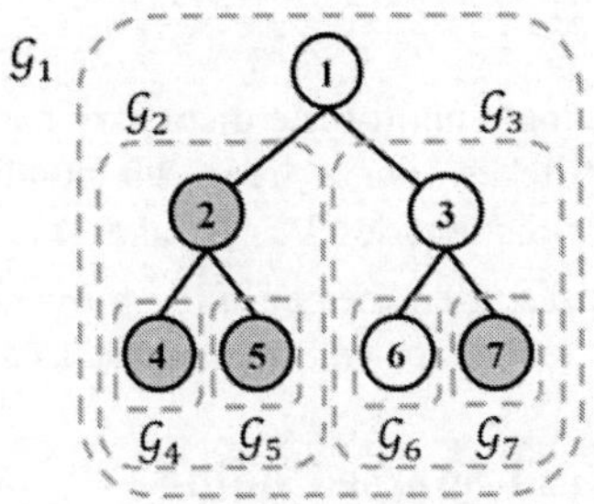

Fig. 2. Illustration of the tree-structured set of groups $\mathcal{G}$ (dashed contours in gray), corresponding to a tree $\mathcal{T}$ with $p = 7$ nodes represented by black circles. Group {2 4 5}, {4}, {5} and {7} are set to zero, so that the corresponding nodes with gray color are removed.

3 Proposed Algorithm

This section presents our novel dictionary learning algorithm for multi-scale sparse representation by performing structured sparse coding under the binary tree model. In general, dictionary learning consists of sparse coding and dictionary updating. We divide it into two parts, and describe them, respectively.

3.1 Multi-scale Dictionary Model

We aim to use atoms of different sizes simultaneously for sparse representation. In our multi-scale framework, we put forward a binary tree model of patches. As depicted by Fig. 3, a large root patch of size m pixels is divided along the tree into sub-patches of sizes $m_s = m/2^s$, where $s = 0,\dots,N-1$, N is the number of scales.

In many cases, especially for image processing tasks, dictionary atoms are built by converting image patches into vectors. Different scales of patches are corresponding to different sizes of atoms. Denote by $\mathcal{BT}$ a binary tree with scales $N = 3$. Supposing that $\mathbf{D}_0$, which is built on patches of scale $s = 0$, consists of K atoms with size m pixels. For

$s=1$, the number of atoms in $\mathbf{D}_1$ is $2K$, and $m_1 = m/2$. For $s=2$, $\mathbf{D}_2 = 4K$, and $m_1 = m/4$. Then, we obtain the overall dictionary $\mathbf{D}$ by merging dictionaries of each scale $\mathbf{D}_s$, where $0 \le s \le 2$, into a large one contained $7K$ atoms of three different sizes. Note that $\mathcal{BT}$ can be changed depending on specific applications.

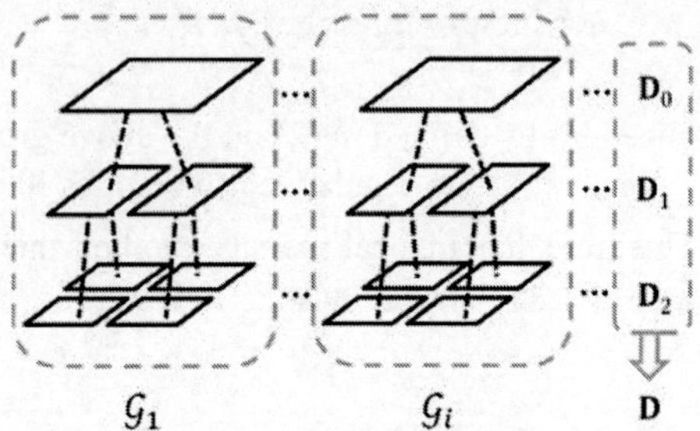

Fig. 3. Constructing a multi-scale dictionary based on binary tree model of patches. For a tree with number of scales $N=3$, three sub-dictionaries $\mathbf{D}_0$, $\mathbf{D}_1$ and $\mathbf{D}_2$ are built with different atom sizes, then merged into an overall dictionary $\mathbf{D}$. Each binary tree of a patch is considered as a group.

3.2 Structured Sparse Coding

We propose two schemes to perform sparse coding in grouped and hierarchical fashion respectively. Let us consider an atom $\mathbf{d}_i$ of scale 0, where $1 \le i \le K$, a group $\mathcal{G}_i$ is built by assembling $\mathbf{d}_i$ and all its corresponding sub-atoms in $\mathcal{BT}$, as illustrated in Fig. 3. Then, group sparse coding is performed based on the following assumption:

Assumption 1. If any atom in $\mathcal{G}_i$ is involved in the decomposition, then all its group members are inclined to be chosen.

Assumption 1 indicates that atoms in $\mathcal{G}_i$ should be selected or removed simultaneously. This is intuitive because atoms in the same tree are highly correlated. This grouped relationship can be achieved by regularizing coefficient vector with the group sparsity norm, as described in section 2.1. Defining the group set $\mathcal{G}^1$ as $\mathcal{G}^1 \triangleq \{\mathcal{G}_i, 1 \le i \le K\}$, where K is the number of atoms at scale 0, group sparse coding can be performed by solving such a regularized problem:

$$\min_{\boldsymbol{\alpha}} \frac{1}{2}\|\mathbf{x} - \mathbf{D}\boldsymbol{\alpha}\|_2^2 + \lambda \sum_{g \in \mathcal{G}^1} \|\alpha_g\|_2 \quad (5)$$

Note that each group $\mathcal{G}_i$ is a binary tree, which has a hierarchical nature. It is natural to combine hierarchical sparse coding with the binary tree model, based on the assumption as follows:

Assumption 2. If the atom $\mathbf{d}_i$ is not involved in the decomposition, then its sub-atoms in $\mathcal{G}_i$ should be removed.

An atom can be viewed as a linear combination of its sub-atoms. Therefore, if an atom does not participate in the decomposition, then there is no need considering its sub-atoms. Such a tree-structured relationship can be achieved by regularizing with the hierarchical sparsity norm, as described in section 2.2. Given a binary tree $\mathcal{BT}$ with p nodes indexed by j in $\{1,\ldots,p\}$, for each group $\mathcal{G}_i$, its corresponding group set $\mathcal{G}_i^2$ is built following (4). Then group set $\mathcal{G}^2$ is obtained by $\mathcal{G}^2 = \bigcup_i \mathcal{G}_i^2$. Hierarchical sparse coding can be performed by solving such a regularized problem:

$$\min_{\boldsymbol{\alpha}} \frac{1}{2}\|\mathbf{x} - \mathbf{D}\boldsymbol{\alpha}\|_2^2 + \lambda \sum_{g \in \mathcal{G}^2} \|\alpha_g\|_2 \quad (6)$$

Note that both objective function (5) and (6) are non-smooth, we employ [8] to solve them. For practical realization, we treat each atom the same size by padding with zeros for atoms of smaller sizes.

3.3 Sequential Dictionary Updating

Denote by $\mathbf{X} = [\mathbf{x}_1,\ldots,\mathbf{x}_n] \in \mathbb{R}^{m \times n}$ a set of n examples. Once decomposition coefficients matrix $\mathbf{A} = [\boldsymbol{\alpha}_1,\ldots,\boldsymbol{\alpha}_n] \in \mathbb{R}^{K \times n}$ is obtained, $\mathbf{D}$ is updated along with it, so that $\mathbf{x}_i \approx \mathbf{D}\boldsymbol{\alpha}_i$ for every signal $\mathbf{x}_i$. We update $\mathbf{D}$ in a sequential way, i.e., one atom at a time, which is similar to K-SVD, but with a slight modification. This setting can accelerate convergence [2]. A full description of our algorithm is shown in Fig. 4.

4 Experimental Results

We integrate our methods into the framework of image denoising based on sparse representation [3], and compare the results with ℓ_1 regularization method in two aspects: multi-scale vs. single-scale, non-structured vs. structured.

Due to space limitation, we only list PSNR results with 12×12 patch size, number of scales $N=3$ and noise level $\sigma = 25$ for four standard test images, as shown in Table 1, where G, H, sgl, mul represent group, hierarchical, single and multi-scale, respectively. It can be shown from Table 1 that our proposed algorithms, G-mul and H-mul, outperform traditional algorithm ℓ_1-sgl with an improvement in PSNR about 0.3~0.6 dB. In general, multi-scale methods achieve better performances than single-scale methods. Especially for images containing many textures, such as boat and pirate, the improvement in PSNR is about 0.6 dB. This shows that our multi-scale methods can strengthen the ability of representing natural images. Fig. 5 and Fig. 6 show comparison of denoising results obtained by ℓ_1-sgl and H-mul. It can be seen that some fine textures, e.g. fence and scratches, are recovered very well by our method, as marked by white rectangles. Note that in the experiment, we only use dictionaries with three scales. It shows great potential in representing natural images by our multi-scale dictionaries.

Initialization: Set the multi-scale dictionary $\mathbf{D}^{(0)}$ with ℓ_2 normalized columns.

Loop: Repeat J times

- Structured sparse coding: compute the coefficient vector $\boldsymbol{\alpha}_i$ for each signal $\mathbf{x}_i$, by solving

$$\min_{\boldsymbol{\alpha}_i} \frac{1}{2}\|\mathbf{x}_i - \mathbf{D}\boldsymbol{\alpha}_i\|_2^2 + \lambda\Omega(\boldsymbol{\alpha}_i)$$

- Sequential dictionary updating: for each atom $\mathbf{d}_i$ of each scale in $\mathbf{D}^{(J-1)}$, update it by
  - Select the set of signals that use this atom

$$w_i = \{j \mid 1 \le j \le n, \boldsymbol{\alpha}_i^T(j) \ne 0\}$$

  - Compute the overall representation error matrix $\mathbf{E}_i$ by

$$\mathbf{E}_i = \mathbf{X} - \mathbf{DA} + \mathbf{d}_i\boldsymbol{\alpha}_i^T$$

  - Restrict $\mathbf{E}_i$ by choosing only the columns corresponding to w_i.
  - Update $\mathbf{d}_i$ and $\boldsymbol{\alpha}_i^T(j)$, $j \in w_i$ using SVD decomposition

$$(\mathbf{d}_i, \boldsymbol{\alpha}_i^T(j)) = \arg\min \left\|\mathbf{R}_i(\mathbf{E}_i - \mathbf{d}\boldsymbol{\alpha}^T)\right\|_F^2$$

Where $\mathbf{R}_i$ is a binary matrix which extracts the corresponding part for $\mathbf{d}_i$, $\|\bullet\|_F$ is the Frobenius norm.

Fig. 4. The full description of our proposed algorithm.

Table 1. PSNR results of algorithms (dB), $\sigma = 25$

methods	barbara	boat	lena	pirate
ℓ_1-sgl	29.12	28.70	30.91	28.44
G-sgl	29.16	28.78	30.96	28.54
H-sgl	29.23	28.71	30.92	28.46
ℓ_1-mul	29.38	29.26	31.27	28.99
G-mul	29.46	**29.35**	**31.38**	29.02
H-mul	**29.55**	29.31	31.35	**29.09**

5 Conclusions

This paper introduced a novel approach to learn multi-scale sparse representation with structured dictionaries. By performing structured sparse coding under the multi-scale binary tree model, we can obtain a multi-scaled and structured dictionary, which is more powerful than the traditional dictionary. Experimental results show the effectiveness of our method for restoration tasks. Future work includes investigating alternative techniques to accelerate the structured sparse coding progress.

6 References

[1] B.A. Olshausen and D.J. Field, “Emergence of Simple-cell Receptive Field Properties by Learning a Sparse Code for Natural Images,” Nature 381, pp. 607-609, 1996.

[2] M. Aharon, M. Elad, and A.M. Bruckstein, “K-SVD: An Algorithm for Designing of Overcomplete Dictionaries for Sparse Representation,” IEEE Trans. on Signal Processing, vol. 54, no. 11, pp. 4311-4322, November 2006.

[3] M. Elad, M. Aharon, “Image Denoising Via Sparse and Redundant Representations Over Learned Dictionaries,” IEEE Trans. on Image Processing, vol. 15, no. 12, pp. 3736-3745, December 2006.

[4] M. Yuan, Y. Lin, “Model Selection and Estimation in Regression with Grouped Variables,” Journal of The Royal Statistical Society Series B, vol. 68, pp. 49-67, 2006.

[5] P. Zhao, G. Rocha, B. Yu, “The Composite Absolute Penalties Family for Grouped and Hierarchical Variable Selection,” Annals of Statistics, vol. 37, no. 6A, pp. 3468-3497, 2009.

[6] R. Jenatton, J. Mairal, G. Obozinski, F. Bach, “Proximal Methods for Hierarchical Sparse Coding,” Journal of Machine Learning Research, vol. 12, pp. 2297-2334, 2011.

[7] J. Mairal, G. Sapiro, and M. Elad, “Learning Multiscale Sparse Representations for Image and Video Restoration,” SIAM Multiscale Modeling and Simulation, vol. 7, no. 1, pp. 214-241, April 2008.

[8] J. Liu, S. Ji, and J. Ye. “SLEP: Sparse Learning with Efficient Projections,” Arizona State University, 2009.

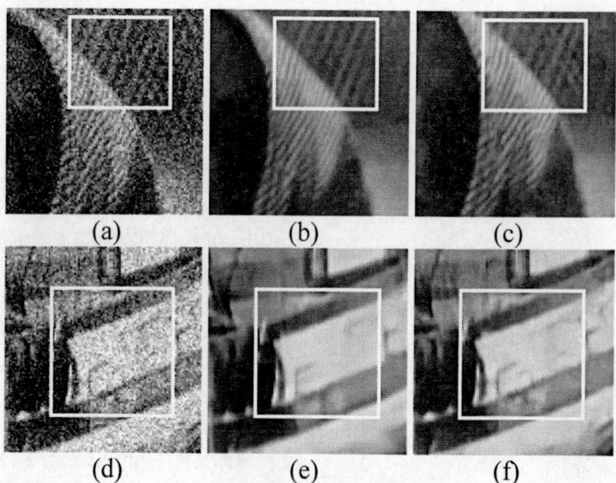

Fig. 5. Comparison of local details for denoised images. (a, d) noisy images from barbara and boat; (b, e) Results obtained by ℓ_1-sgl; (c, f) Results obtained by H-mul.

Fig. 6. Comparison of denoised images from lena and boat. (a, c) Results obtained by ℓ_1-sgl; (b, d) Results obtained by H-mul.

A Mathematical model for the determination of distance of an object in a 2D image

Deepu R[1], Murali S[2],Vikram Raju[3]
Maharaja Institute of Technology Mysore, Karnataka, India
rdeepusingh@mitmysore.in[1], murali@mitmysore.in[2], vikramraju17@gmail.com[3]

Abstract-*Distance measurement in real world has always been one of the challenging tasks to be performed in the field of computer vision. Photographic images are two dimensional depiction of three-dimensional real space. Various methods have been developed, researched and improvised over the years depending on the focus of the object, defocus of the background, the vanishing point of an image and other information derived from images. The impact of various features of the camera are also considered when the above problem is under study like, focal length of the camera, ISO levels, white balance, resolution etc. The effect of the resolution of an object in an image, its actual size, the focal length of the camera, the camera resolution, all contribute in determining the distance between the camera and the object. In this paper we have proposed a model for the relationship between the resolution of an object of interest and the distance from the camera as a growth series. Relationship between the resolution of an object of interest and focal length is also expressed as a growth series model. The object of interest is segmented out and its pixels account to its resolution, which is standardized and used to determine either the distance or the focal length of the camera or the vice versa. This model, thus, very easily helps in tracking the object using a camera with minimal error rate, provided the image is along the optical axis of the camera.*

Keywords: Resolution, Focal Length, Camera and object distance, growth series, Pixels per inch, Geometric Progression.

1 Introduction

The knowledge about the distance of an object in an image has its applications in many fields of science and technology and research, like, human motion estimation, web conferencing, gaming industry, surveillance, security systems, robotics, medical systems and imaging. Etc. The major factors in a photo that cannot be changed once the photo has been clicked are Aperture of the lens, focal length, number of pixels or resolution and shutter speed. A method which allows refocusing is a potential powerful tool for digital image editing. Once the depth map has been obtained, one can de-blur the image in order to acquire an all focus image or blur the image even more to create certain visual effects [1]. The depth map can also apply to the task such as automatic scene segmentation, post exposure refocusing and re-rendering of the scene from an alternative view point. By analyzing the depth of field, the coarse depth map of scene can be recovered [2]. Depth from defocus and depth from focus are the two methods to estimate the 3D geometry of the scene by exploiting image focus [3]. In adaptive depth from focus, depth estimation method for images in narrow depth of field setting, the segments produced by mean shift segmentation as windows to analyze the focus measure and employ a hierarchical Markov Random Field to infer from the depth map [4]. Ina non-linear approach, the precise sparse depth map extraction, the noisy focus measurements are replaced with estimated values, which in turn helps to accurately compute 3D shapes while preserving edges of objects [5].In paper [6],authors have proposed a real-time method which can measure distance using a modified camera. The camera's image sensor is inclined by a certain angle. Thus, the image projected on the sensor is defocused differently at different areas. The area where the image is focused best is just at projection plane. The position of the projection plane can be obtained after finding out this area. The distance between the projection plane and the lens of the camera is image distance. Object distance can be obtained by applying image distance to lens formula.

Although the results of the above methods are very promising, it is computationally expensive to employ Markov Random Fields or any of the procedures given in above papers. In real world applications it is necessary to provide real-time computations. By studying the model or rate at which features change in an image like size, distance, pixels of an object, focal length, give us a better approximation and a simpler computationally efficient method to determine the relationship among them.

The resolution of an image or the number of pixels of an image is a constant, which depends on the camera. Once an image is captured, its focal length is also constant. When an image is captured by a camera, the distance of the image from the camera or the viewer, thus can be determined using the above variables. The resolution also directly depends on the focal length, since it has a proportional relationship with the image size. The camera, like the human eye, works on perspective vision, where, the change in image size with variation of Focal Length and Distance is not linear. To study the relationship among the above, the following methodology is proposed.

2 Method

With an objective of designing a robust model, sequence of images at different distances D from the object and for different focal lengths are taken along the optical axis. Every image is of size $iX\,j$ and it is acquired for objects of various shapes and sizes. The total number of pixels P, in the image is thus given by

$$P = ij \qquad (1)$$

The set of the pixels in an object P_o, is a subset of P. The image is converted to grey scale using a basic thresholding algorithm to obtain the object of interest and the number of pixels in the object is obtained. This becomes the set of pixels in an object, and stored in a set P_o. The behavior of the relationship between the distance with respect to the resolution factor R_f and that of the focal length and the resolution factor is sought.

To determine the resolution factor, first, the Resolution per Inch, R_{In}, of the object is determined. It is then multiplied by the resolution of the camera and later natural log is taken to scale down the data. This is so done in order to standardize the factor arising due to the resolution of the images and of the objects in them, thus making the method applicable to any kind of camera and of any resolution. In a way, it makes the method independent of the resolution itself.

$$R_f = \ln{(R_{In}P)} \qquad (2)$$

Figure1 shows the variation of size of the image with the changes in distance from the camera.

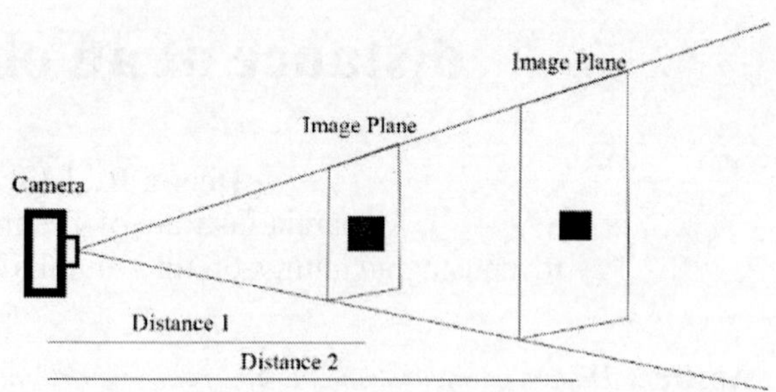

Figure 1: Experimental setup varying distance from camera to objects.

Once the images are captured, the background is segmented, to get only the pixels of the object of interest. Image preprocessing is necessary at times, when noise is found in the images, when the automatic thresholding algorithm fails to extract the object clearly. Manual image cleaning was used to remove unwanted noise in the image. This can be avoided using a better efficient object extraction algorithm

The image segmentation and cleaning was carried out using MATLAB. To build the mathematical model, IBM SPSS was used.

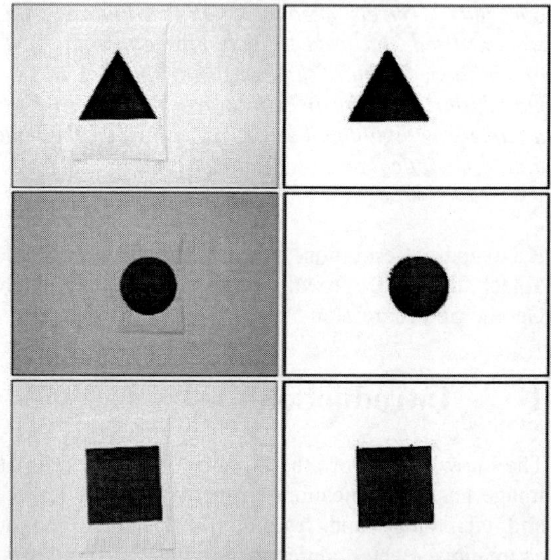

Figure 2: Test Images (left) and Objects extracted from the image (right)

3 Results

The results can be analyzed in two folds, one model with resolution factor and distance of object in an image and the other with resolution factor and the focal length of the camera. Following results were tabulated for 3 different objects. Table 1 gives the difference between expected distance and obtained distance for circle object where as Table2 and Tables3 specify the same for square and triangle objects. We can also note that there is a relationship between pixels in an object to distance which is expressed by our model.

Table 1: Observed results for circle object of area 39.88 sq.in

Expected distance	Pixels in object	R_f	Constant A	Constant B	Calculated Result
120	25607	22.58640744	15.727	-0.485	118.2253313
110	30708	22.7680645	15.727	-0.485	108.2548884
100	36665	22.94536431	15.727	-0.485	99.33503302
90	46317	23.17905075	15.727	-0.485	88.69117431
80	59011	23.42126556	15.727	-0.485	78.86095732
70	77981	23.7000069	15.727	-0.485	68.88900971
60	110277	24.04653707	15.727	-0.485	58.23167902
50	161026	24.42510753	15.727	-0.485	48.46407716
40	260089	24.90456557	15.727	-0.485	38.40876536
30	481634	25.52072618	15.727	-0.485	28.48699885

Table 2: Observed results square object of area 41.69 sq.in

Expected distance	Pixels in object	R_f	Constant A	Constant B	Calculated Result
120	27117	22.5994143	15.727	-0.485	117.4818745
110	32619	22.78414841	15.727	-0.485	107.4137309
100	39329	22.97098676	15.727	-0.485	98.10824601
90	48855	23.18811019	15.727	-0.485	88.30233539
80	61989	23.42606522	15.727	-0.485	78.67759046
70	82176	23.70811676	15.727	-0.485	68.61858205
60	113256	24.02890421	15.727	-0.485	58.73180823
50	166859	24.41640261	15.727	-0.485	48.66911954
40	269075	24.89424362	15.727	-0.485	38.60152738
30	542148	25.59479249	15.727	-0.485	27.48184598

Table 3: Observed results triangle object of area 20 sq.in

Expected distance	Pixels in object	Rf	Constant A	Constant B	Calculated Result
120	12813	22.58444482	15.727	-0.485	118.33792
110	15606	22.78164	15.727	-0.485	107.5444877
100	19084	22.98283483	15.727	-0.485	97.54610201
90	23795	23.20346002	15.727	-0.485	87.64739511
80	30152	23.4402358	15.727	-0.485	78.13871446
70	39964	23.72196359	15.727	-0.485	68.15930311
60	55254	24.04592528	15.727	-0.485	58.2489601
50	82014	24.44087451	15.727	-0.485	48.09488662
40	135268	24.94124254	15.727	-0.485	37.73157847

Part I: Resolution Factor and Distance

The distance is considered as the dependent variable in the analysis of the model and the resolution factor is taken as the independent variable. In each case of the focal length the model is tested.

Table 4: Model Summary and Parameter Estimates for Distance and Resolution Factor for a focal length of 18mm.

Dependent Variable: Distance							
Equation	Model Summary					Parameter Estimates	
	R Square	F	df1	df2	Sig.	Constant	b1
Growth	.999	40987.115	1	28	.000	15.727	-.485

The R Square value shows a 99.9% significance to the model, which is a good fit for the data set observed.

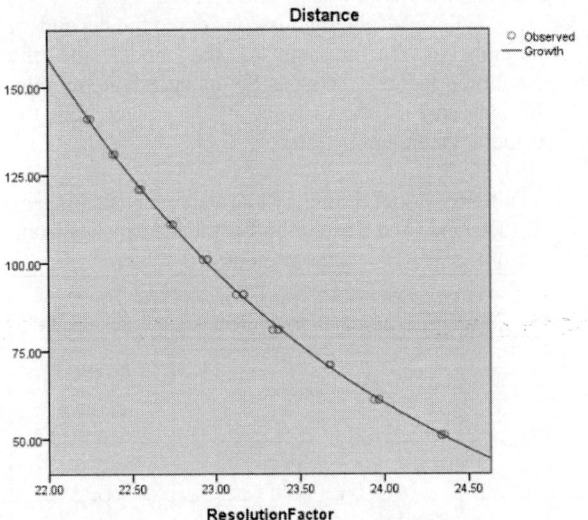

Figure 3: The growth series of distance and resolution factor of object in image

The model agrees completely with the growth series and gives us the following equation to determine the distance of the object from the camera:

$$D = e^{A+BR_f} \qquad (3)$$

Where, D is the distance of the object from the camera, A and B are constants in the growth series, which are determined by a geometric series, and R_f is the resolution factor. The r in the geometric ratio is 1.01.The geometric series gives the values of the constants from the above equation.

Table 5: The geometric series to determine the constants of the growth series model.

Focal Length	A	B
18mm	15.727	-0.485
24mm	15.727r	-0.485r
30mm	$15.727r^2$	$-0.485r^2$
36mm	$15.727r^3$	$-0.485r^3$
42mm	$15.727r^4$	$-0.485r^4$
48mm	$15.727r^5$	$-0.485r^5$
54mm	$15.727r^6$	$-0.485r^6$
60mm	$15.727r^7$	$-0.485r^7$
66mm	$15.727r^8$	$-0.485r^8$

The model was tested on random image samples, which agreed with the growth series model, with very minimal error. The error in determining the distance was in the range of 0.5-1 percent.

Part II: Resolution Factor and Focal Length

The focal length is considered the dependent variable in the analysis of the model and the resolution factor is taken as the independent variable. In each case of the distance of the object from the camera, the model is tested.

Table 6: Model Summary and Parameter Estimates for Distance and Resolution Factor at 51 inches from the camera.

Dependent Variable: Focal Length							
Equation	**Model Summary**					**Parameter Estimates**	
	R Square	**F**	**df1**	**df2**	**Sig.**	**Constant**	**b1**
Growth	.991	2899.688	1	25	.000	-10.342	0.543

The R Square value shows a 99.1% significance to the model, which is a good fit for the data set observed.

The model agrees completely with the growth series and gives us the following equation to determine the focal length:

$$F = e^{A+BR_f} \quad (4)$$

Where, F is the focal length of the camera, A and B are constants in the growth series, which are determined by a geometric series, and R_f is the resolution factor. The r in the geometric ratio is 1.01.

The geometric series gives the values of the constants from the above equation.

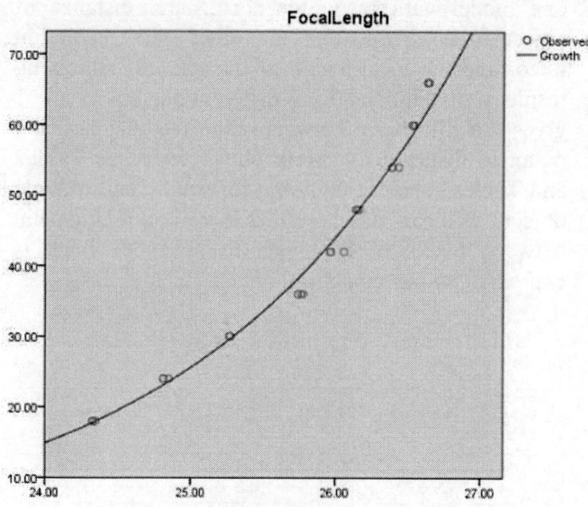

Figure 4: The growth series of focal length and resolution factor of object in an image

The model was tested on random image samples, which agreed with the growth series model, with very minimal error. The error in determining the distance was in the range of 1-2 percent.

Table 7: The geometric series to determine the constants of the growth series model.

Distance	A	B
51in	-10.342	0.543
61in	-10.342r	0.543r
71in	$-10.342r^2$	$0.543r^2$
81in	$-10.342r^3$	$0.543r^3$
91in	$-10.342r^4$	$0.543r^4$
101in	$-10.342r^5$	$0.543r^5$
111in	$-10.342r^6$	$0.543r^6$
121in	$-10.342r^7$	$0.543r^7$
131in	$-10.342r^8$	$0.543r^8$
141in	$-10.342r^9$	$0.543r^9$

4 Applications

The model finds its use in many applications like obstacle detection in robotics, detection of road humps, navigation systems for the blind, unknown territory exploration, 3D game development are a few to name.

5 Future Work

The distance of the object from the camera and focal length model is applicable only when the object is head-on or in the line of the optical axis of the camera. Future work can be done on studying the effect of resolution and distance for images not in the axis of the camera, considering the evolution of perspective vision of an image. It can also be used to create 3D scenes by determining the distance from the camera and rebuilding another scene with the same distance.

6 Conclusions

The model shows promising enhancement on further development and an efficient model to determine the distance of an object in an image from the camera making use of the data in the resolution of an image, which cannot change once an image is taken. Building the model for varied focal lengths enables the model to work with cameras of any focal length. The obtained growth series enables to work with distance and focal length. With knowing one of the two, the other can be calculated and be easily modeled in the system. Computationally the calculation of the growth series works efficiently than the iterative approach.

7 Acknowledgements

The work presented in this paper was supported by VTU research grants (Ref. No. VTU/ Aca./2009-10/A-9/13551). We thank Visvesvaraya Technological University, Belgaum for this.

8 References

[1] Potmesil, M., and Chakravarty, I., 1981. A lens and aperture camera model for synthetic image generation.In proc. Siggraph, 297-305.

[2] Pentland, A. P., 1987. A new sense for depth of field.IEEE Trans. Pattern anal. Mach. Intell. 9, 4, 523-531.

[3] Hasinoff S. W., Kutulakos K. N., A layer-based restoration framework for variable-aperture photography, F, 2007 [C], IEEE.

[4] Bing-Zhong Jing, Daniel S. Yeung, 2011. Recovering depth from images using adaptive depth from focus. IEEE 978-1-4673-1487-9/12, 1205-1211.

[5] Muhammad Tariq Mahmood, Ikhyun Lee, Wook-Jin Choi, Tae-Sun Choi, 2012. A non-linear approach for depth from focus for digital cameras. IEEE 978-1-4244-8712-7/11, 187-188.

[6] Liu Xiaoming, Qin Tian, Chen Wanchen, Yin Xingliang, 2009. Real Time Distance Measurment Using a Modified Camera.IEEE 978-1-4244-2787-1/09.

SESSION

VIDEO PROCESSING, ANALYSIS AND APPLICATIONS + ANIMATION

Chair(s)

TBA

Video Object Segmentation Using Spatio-Temporal Information and Marked-Watershed Operation

Qingqing Fu[1,2] and Mehmet Celenk[2]
[1]College of Electronics and Information Engineering,
Yangtze University, Jingzhou, Hubei 434023, China
[2]School of Electrical Engineering and Computer Science,
Stocker Center, Ohio University, Athens, OH 45701, USA

Abstract - *In this paper, we propose a video object segmentation algorithm based on spatio-temporal information and marked-watershed for extracting the moving objects from a video sequence. The algorithm begins with difference image between two adjacent frames and, using the Canny operator on the difference image, determines the initial edge mask for the object in motion. Morphological techniques are applied to the initial edge mask to obtain initial temporal segmentation mask of the moving object and binary marker image of the foreground and background subject to the watershed thresholding. The markers are used to modify multi-scale morphological gradient image of current frame. Finally, the watershed algorithm is performed on the modified gradients to locate the non-stationary objects accurately in the spatial domain of motion frames. Simulation results show that the proposed technique can overcome the shortcoming of over-segmentation of the watershed algorithm and can efficiently segment and extract meaningful motion objects with slow or fast moving from the video sequence with complex background with low computational complexity.*

Keywords: video object segmentation, marked-watershed algorithm, morphological operators, computational complexity

1 Introduction

Video object segmentation involves extracting objects in motion from video frame sequences and plays an important role in digital video processing, data compression, and visual pattern recognition. It is one of the most important operations for the video coding standard MPEG-4 [1], and is widely used in many fields such as video surveillance, machine vision, intelligent transportation system, military, etc. Hence, video segmentation technique has great significance both in theoretical research and practical application. Although this field has experienced significant growth and progress, it is still a challenging problem in the field of video processing technique [2].

Over the last few decades, many researchers have proposed a lot of video moving object segmentation techniques and algorithms [3-20], each of which has its own characteristics and special applications. The algorithm presented in [3-5] makes use of the frame difference. The technique in [6] relies on the use of optical flow field. The background modeling method is employed for video segmentation in [7-9]. These algorithms take advantage of the time-domain information to obtain change detection mask, and then the post-processing is utilized on the mask to obtain a video object template. Although the efficiency of these algorithms is high, the target information can not be obtained accurately. In recent years, many segmentation schemes based on temporal and spatial information have been proposed [10-20], which take into account the spatio-temporal relationship and yield better segmentation results. As a spatial segmentation algorithm with high performance, watershed segmentation methodology is incorporated into the video segmentation techniques based on the spatio-temporal information [10-18]. However, the watershed algorithm is particularly sensitive to noise, usually leads to over-segmentation. In [21], the segmentation is applied to the simplified image to reduce the influence of noise while preserving edge information. There is still a considerable number of dark noisy points and profiles in the simplified image. In [14, 17], the motion parameters estimated to merge the regions with coherent motions on the basis of watershed segmentation results. The region merging is carried out according to the similarity of the mean and standard deviation after the watershed segmentation in [12]. The technique in [15, 18] utilizes the Markov random field model for analysis and processing following the initial watershed segmentation. The watershed transformation usage in the mentioned literature is only confined in spatial partition followed by region merging which is time-consuming calculation. The over-segmentation still appears in some of these algorithms [14].

In this paper, by combining the temporal and spatial information, we propose video object segmentation algorithm based on spatio-temporal information and marked-watershed operation. In the proposed method, initial temporal segmentation mask is firstly obtained in the time-domain and morphological techniques are applied to initial temporal segmentation mask of the moving target to obtain the foreground and background markers for the watershed algorithm. This is utilized for guiding watershed segmentation in spatial image domain to obtain an accurate video object boundary. In turn, the overall approach effectively overcomes the problem of over-segmentation and avoids computationally expensive region merging process. As demonstrated in the experimental result section, the proposed method can segment and extract contextually important and semantically meaningful object with fast and slow motion in video sequences with low computational complexity.

2 Overview of the proposed approach

Block diagram of the proposed algorithm is depicted in Fig. 1. The input is video frames and the output is the extracted moving objects. Our video segmentation algorithm starts with generating the difference image between the two adjacent frames. Because the frame difference image contains all the inter-frame change information with noise, the edge map of frame difference image is obtained by the Canny operator which has relatively high accuracy in locating edges and strong ability in restraining the false edges. Morphological techniques are then applied to the resultant edge map to obtain initial temporal segmentation mask of the moving target along with the foreground and background markers for the watershed algorithm. In spatial segmentation, to overcome the problem of over-segmentation which are caused by noise or quantization error, multi-scale morphological gradient operator [14] with strong ability in suppressing noise is applied to the current frame image firstly to create the gradient image. It is then modified by the previously obtained foreground and background markers, at last, watershed segmentation is performed on the modified gradient image in order to extract the moving objects. This means that the spatial segmentation is guided by the temporal segmentation results.

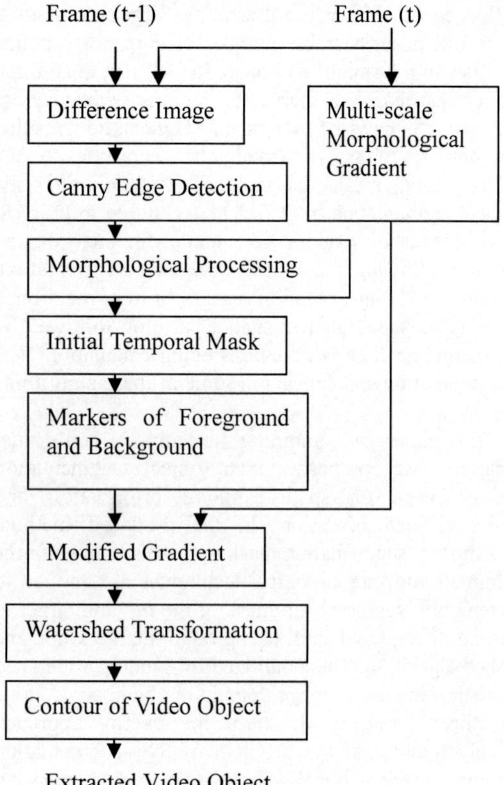

Fig.1 Block diagram of the proposed algorithm

3 Temporal segmentation

Change detection based on inter-frame difference is one of the most feasible image segmentation algorithm [3-5]. Temporal segmentation in the proposed technique consists of two steps: The first step involves finding the frame difference image between the two adjacent frames and then applying the Canny operator to detect the edge information of the moving object. The second step makes use of morphological post-processing technique on the edge map so as to generate initial mask of the video object.

3.1 Edge detection of moving object

Let f_t denote the image of the current frame and f_{t-1} represent the image of the previous frame. The edge of the inter-frame difference image DE_t is defined as

$$DE_t = canny(|f_{t-1} - f_t|) \quad (1)$$

Equation (1) indicates that the difference image edge map DE_t is obtained by the Canny operator. According to the standards based on the signal-to-noise ratio, the positioning accuracy and single-edge, the Canny edge detection operator based on optimization algorithm is proposed by John F. Canny in 1986 [22], which is simple high performance operator, has been more widely used in practice. Its edge detection operation can be described as follows: 1) The input image is smoothed using a Gaussian low-pass filter with a standard deviation σ to reduce the influence of noise. 2) The local gradient (magnitude and direction) is computed using a gradient operator for each point in the smoothed image. 3)Appling the non-maximum value suppression (non-local maximum is set to 0) to the gradient magnitude to thin the edge. 4) The ridge pixels are then thresholded using high and low double thresholds to detect and link edges. As a result, a map of clear and thinned edges is reached for further utilization.

3.2 Morphological process

Due to the influence of background complexity and illumination, the noise in edge map can not be completely eliminated even if the canny operator is used. Here, we adopt the morphological techniques to deal with this problem. The most basic operation is the dilation and erosion in morphological image processing. Suppose that A, B be sets in Z^2, ϕ be the empty set, B as structuring elements, $\hat{B}$ denote the reflection of set B. The translation of set B by point $z = (z_1, z_2)$ is denoted by $(B)_Z$, the dilation of A by B, denoted $A \oplus B$, is defined as [22]

$$A \oplus B = \{z \mid (\hat{B})_Z \cap A \neq \Phi\} \quad (2)$$

As can be seen from the equation (2), the dilation process is to obtain the reflection of B about its origin and shifting this reflection by z, the dilation of A by B then is the set of all displacements, z, such that $\hat{B}$ and A overlap by at least one element. The dilation is to merge all of the background points connected with the object into the object so that the boundary can expand to the external.

Erosion operation eliminates boundary point(s) in such a way that the boundary can shrink to the internal shape. In this way, it is used to discard small size objects which are not contextually meaningful and semantically important. Corrosion of A by B, denoted $A\Theta B$, is defined as [22]

$$A\Theta B = \{z \mid (B)_Z \cap A^C \neq \Phi\} \tag{3}$$

where A^C is the complement of set A, from the above formula (3), the corrosion of A by B then is the set of all displacements, z, $(B)_Z$ and A^C overlap by at least one element.

According to the above described morphological processing framework, the dilation operator is firstly used on the edge map of the frame difference image and makes the edges of object lengthening and thickening. Thus it can fill in space of the object. Then the holes are treated in the same way. The MatLab function 'bwareaopen' is employed to remove all the connected components that have fewer than a certain number of pixels so as to eliminate the background noise. At last, the overall outline of the object is recovered using erosion operator. Hence, we can get initial binary mask of the moving object. In the above mentioned dilation and corrosion operator, a flat, disk-shaped structuring element is selected, which can eliminate dependence of the gradient edge on the edge direction.

4 Spatial segmentation

We only obtain coarse area through temporal segmentation due to the complexity of the motion information. Spatial segmentation is needed to get more accurate object boundary. Watershed algorithm proposed by Vincent based on immersion simulation [23] is known to be a fast segmentation method of the mathematical morphology in the field of image segmentation. An image is often interpreted as geographical surfaces and its gray level is regarded as altitude, as shown in Figure.2. A local minimum corresponds to the valley, whereas the maximum corresponds to the peak. Water will overflow upward from each local minimum and different local area will be gradually filled with water. As the water continues to rise, the rising water in various regions is about to merge. If a dam is built at the meeting place to prevent the merging, then the topography is divided into different regions, which are called the catchment basins. At the end of this immersion procedure, each minimum is completely surrounded by dams, the edge of the region where dam is built called watershed. Hence, watershed segmentation is to find catchment basins and watershed ridge lines.

Watershed algorithm is usually performed on the gradient image [22]. Conventional gradient operators generally produce many local minima results in over-segmentation, which is caused by noise or quantization error. To alleviate this problem, also because morphological gradient makes grayscale of the input image jump change more dramatical, compared with the obtained gradient image using spatial template, morphological gradient image by symmetrical structuring elements has less dependence on edge direction. In this paper, the multi-scale morphological gradient algorithm proposed by Wang in [14] is applied to the current video frame, and foreground and background markers are used to control watershed segmentation to achieve better spatial segmentation.

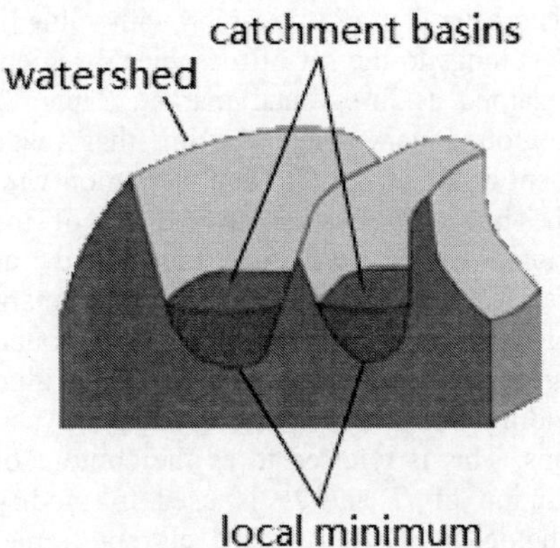

Fig.2 Three-dimensional model of watershed transform

4.1 Multi-scale morphological gradient

Simple single-scale morphological gradient operator is defined as

$$G(f) = f \oplus B - f\Theta B \tag{4}$$

where f denotes the input gray scale image and B the structuring element, $\oplus$ and Θ ,respectively, denote morphological dilation and erosion operations mentioned in Section 3.2. Its performance depends on the size of the structuring element B. if B is large, it will cause the overlap between the edges which may leads to the gradient maxima not coinciding with edges. However, if the structuring elements is too small, this gradient operator has a high spatial resolution and produces a low output value for ramp edges. The multi-scale morphological gradient operator is described as[14]

$$MG(f) = \frac{1}{3}\sum_{i=1}^{3}[((f \oplus B_i) - (f\Theta B_i))\Theta B_{i-1}] \tag{5}$$

where B_i is a group of disk-shaped structuring element, and its radius is $2i+1, 0 \leq i \leq 3$. In this definition, the multi-scale morphological gradient has respective advantages of both large and small structuring elements. It is more robust to noise and edge interaction due to the averaging operation used in the algorithm. It effectively enhances blurred edges and reduces the number of the irrelevant local minima.

4.2 Marker extraction

Marking the object in the watershed transformation plays an important role in the control of the over-segmentation. Markers are connected component belonging to an image. If we can find a marker set of the foreground completely included in the objects of interest, and a marker set of the background completely included in the region of background, we can use these markers to modify the gradient image so that the local minimum area appears only in the marked location.

After using the erosion operator with the size of *r1* and *r2* on the initial binary mask of the moving object mentioned in Section III.B, we can obtain binary image *f1* and *f2*, where *r1* is greater than *r2*, the region with value of 1 in the image *f1* belongs to the set of the objects region, which will be regarded as foreground marker. Thus, *f1* represents the foreground mark image. Assume that image *fb* is the complement of the image *f2*. Then the region with value of 1 in the image *fb* belongs to the set of the background region, which will be considered as background marker. Thus, *fb* denotes the background mark image. The area between the foreground and background marker is contour region, in which watershed algorithm can find the dividing line between the foreground and background regions. This is referred to as the contour of the object. The union of *f1* and *fb* is used to modify multi-scale morphological gradient of the current frame. Here, we denote the *Gmark* as the modified gradient image, the MatLab function *'imimposemin '* is used to find the minima imposition so as to make the local minimum area only appears in the marked position. Implementation syntax of this function is shown as

$$Gmark = imimposemin\ (MG(f), f1 \mid fb) \quad (6)$$

where *MG(f)* is the multi-scale morphological gradient of current image. At last, watershed segmentation algorithm will perform on *Gmark* and the MatLab function *'watershed'* is employed to get watershed ridge line which is also called the ideal video object contour. Implementation of this function is described as in (7), where *contour* denotes watershed ridge line.

$$contour = wartershed\ (Gmark) \quad (7)$$

Marker process is applied to traditional watershed algorithm, and over-segmentation phenomenon does not appear during the segmentation phase. There is no need to conduct region merging. In this way, the computational complexity is reduced, respectively.

5 Experimental results

The algorithm proposed in this paper for video segmentation is implemented using the MatLab software of version R2008a. The selected test sequences are the standard video sequences called *Akiyo* and *hall_monitor* in the filed of the image segmentation, and compared with the results of the watershed algorithm directly used on gradient image. The segmentation process of sequence *Akiyo* is illustrated in Figure.3. The sequence *Akiyo* is a typical of head and shoulders sequence exhibits slow and small amplitude motion over the stationary background but more complex textures. Figure.3 (a) is the original frame 15. Figure.3 (b) is the edge image resulting from the Canny operator on the frame difference between the frame 15 and its adjacent image. As we can see in Figure.3 (b), there still exists some background noise. Figure.3 (c) shows the result of initial temporal mask after morphological processing on the Figure.3 (b). Figure.3 (d) is the result directly using the watershed transform on the gradient image of the current frame. Notice that over-segmentation problem is considerably serious for the object extraction. Figure.3 (e) displays contour image after executing watershed transform on the modified gradient image. The extracted video motion object is shown in Figure.3 (f). Figure.4 (a-f) is the segmentation results of applying the proposed algorithm to *hall_monitor* video sequence, the sequence exhibits rapid and great deformable motion over the stationary background but more complex textures. It exhibits illumination effect and the resulting visualization. From the segmentation results of the above two video sequences we can see that the new algorithm captures foreground and background markers through the temporal segmentation information and markers are used to control the spatial segmentation. It effectively overcome the problem of over-segmentation. Further, it can segment and extract meaningful object with fast and slow motion in video sequences.

(a) original frame 15

(b) edge image of frame difference

(c) initial temporal mask

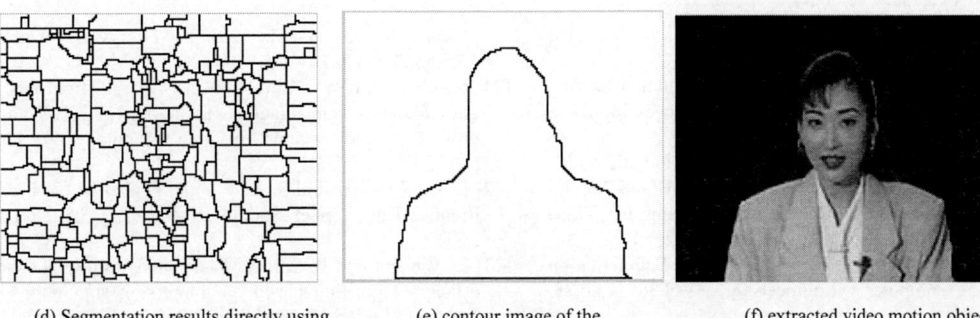

(d) Segmentation results directly using the watershed on the gradient image (e) contour image of the marked-watershed transformation (f) extracted video motion object

Fig.3 Segmentation results for the video sequence *Akiyo*

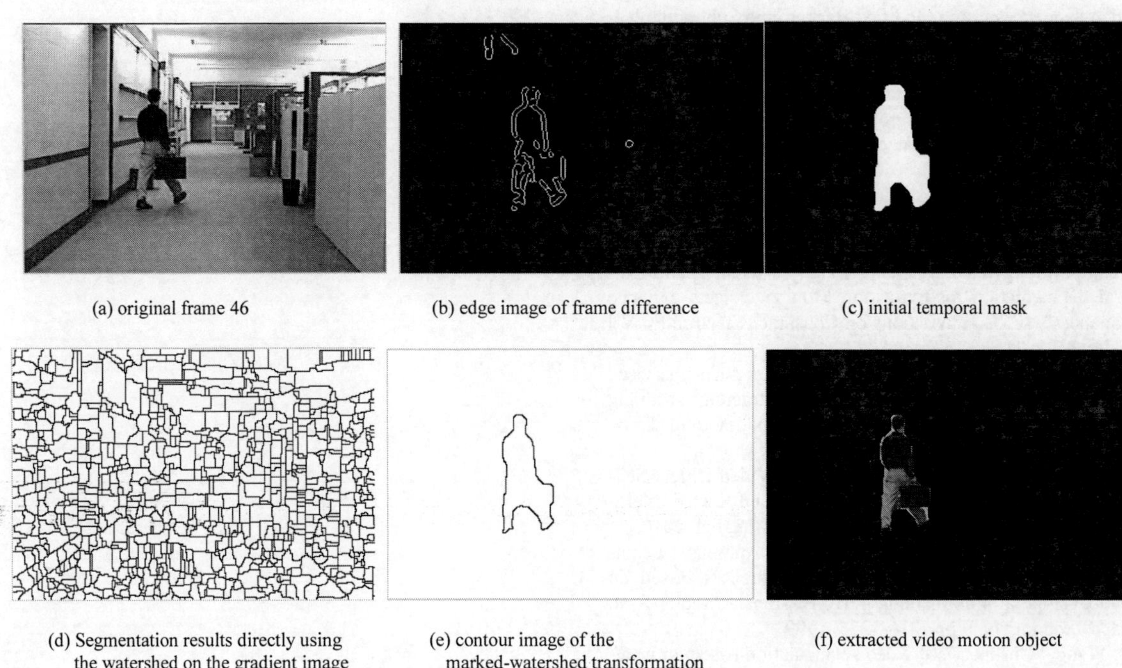

(a) original frame 46 (b) edge image of frame difference (c) initial temporal mask

(d) Segmentation results directly using the watershed on the gradient image (e) contour image of the marked-watershed transformation (f) extracted video motion object

Fig.4 Segmentation results for the video sequence *hall_monitor*

6 Conclusions

In this paper, a video object segmentation algorithm based on temporal and spatial information is proposed which makes use of the marked-watershed procedure. During the temporal segmentation phase, the Canny operator is employed to detect the edges of frame difference between the two adjacent frames. Initial temporal segmentation mask is obtained through morphological processing. Erosion operation is chosen to work on the temporal segmentation mask to extract foreground and background markers for watershed algorithm. In the spatial segmentation phase, multi-scale morphological gradient operator with strong ability in suppressing noise is applied to the current frame image to produce the gradient image, which is then modified by the foreground and background markers. At last, watershed segmentation is performed on the modified gradient image. The proposed technique can efficiently segment and extract meaningful motion objects with slow or fast moving from the video sequence with stationary background of complex textures. It is least influenced by the noise and illumination variation. It overcomes the over-segmentation of the watershed algorithm and avoids region merging process in order to reduce the computational complexity. The proposed technique involves several parameters such as the high and low thresholds in the Canny operator and the size of the structuring element which are empirically set in the simulations. The future extension of this work is toward automatic determination of the parameters used in this technique and detection of multiple objects in motion.

7 References

[1] Sikora T, "The MPEG-4 video standard verification model", IEEE Transactions on Circuits System for Video Technology, Vol.7,19~31,1997.

[2] King Ngi Ngan, Hongliang Li ,"Video segmentation and its

applications" [electronic resource] , New York : Springer, c2011.

[3] Neri, A, Colonnese, S, Russo, G,Talone, P, " Automati moving object and background separation", Signal Processing,APR, Vol.66,no.2, p.219-p232,1998.

[4] Changick Kim,,Jen-Neng Hwang," Fast and Automatic Video Object Segmentation and Tracking for Content-Based Application ",IEEE Transactions on Circuits & Systems for Video Technology, Vol. 12, Issue 2, p.122-129,Feb2002.

[5] HU Xue-gang, HU Wen-tao,"New Video Image Segmentation Algorithm", Computer Engineering, Vol.36 ,no.23, p.217-219,2012.

[6] Barron J,Fleet D,Beauchemin S,"Performance of optical flow techniques", International Computer Vision, vol.12,no.1, p.42-77,1994.

[7] Chinchkhede, D. W.; Uke, N. J," Image Segmentation in Video Sequences Using Modified Background Subtraction", International Journal of Computer Science & Information Technology, Vol. 4, Issue 1, p.93-104, Feb2012.

[8] Luís F.,Teixeira, Jaime S, Cardoso, Luís Corte-Real," Object Segmentation Using Background Modelling and Cascaded Change Detection", Journal of Multimedia, Vol 2, No 5,p. 55-65, Sep 2007.

[9] Lee D S. "Effective Gaussian mixture learning for video background subtraction," IEEE Trans. on PAMI, vol.27, p.827-832, 2005.

[10] Renjie Li,Songyu Yu, Xiaokang Yang," Efficient Spatio-temporal Segmentation for Extracting Moving Objects in video Sequences", IEEE Transactions on Consumer Electronics, Vol. 53, Issue 3, p.1161-1167, Aug2007.

[11] LI Ren-jie, YU Song-yu, WANG Xiang-wen ,"Unsupervised Spatio-Temporal Segmentation for Extracting Moving Objects in Video Sequences",J. Shanghai Jiaotong Univ. (Sci.),Vol. 14,no.2,p. 154-161, 2009.

[12] Deng Qinglin,Liu Haihua,Wu Liangjian,"Video Object Segmentation Algorithm Based on Watershed and Region Merging"Modern Scientific Instruments,no.1,p.34-38, Feb 2010.

[13] Kim M,Choi J G. A VOP Generation Tool: Automatic Segmentation of Moving Objects in Image Sequences Based on Spatio-Temporal Information[J]. IEEE Trans. Circuits Syst. Video Technol,vol. 9,pp.1216-1226. 1999.

[14] D. Wang, "Unsupervised video segmentation based on watersheds and temporal tracking", IEEE Transactions on Circuits and Systems for Video Technology, vol. 8, pp.539 -546 , 1998.

[15] Yaakov Tsaig and Amir Averbuch, " Automatic Segmentation of Moving Objects in Video Sequences: A Region Labeling Approach, " IEEE Trans. Circuits and Systems for Video Technology, vol.12, no.7, pp.597-611,Jul. 2002.

[16] Xu Haifeng ,Akmal A Y,Mansur R K." Automatic moving object extraction for content-based applications", IEEE Trans on Circuits and Systems for Video Technology, vol.14, no.6 ,p.796- 812,2004.

[17] K Ganesan, S Jalla ,"Video Object Extraction Based on a Comparative Study of Efficient Edge Detection Technique ",International Arab Journal of Information Technology (IAJIT), Vol. 6, Issue 2, p.107-115, Apr2009.

[18] Patras I, Hendriks E A, Lagendijk R L. Video segmentation by MAP labeling of watershed segments,IEEE Trans Pattern Anal Machine Intell, vol.23,p.326-332,2001.

[19] Mezaris,V,Kompatsiaris,I.Strintzis, M.G ,"Video object segmentation using Bayes-based temporal tracking and trajectory-based region merging", IEEE Transactions on Circuits and Systems for Video Technology,Vol.14, Issue 6, p.782 -795,2004.

[20] Jin Wang, ZhaoHui Li,DongMei Li,Hui Sun , "A spatio-temporal video segmentation method based on edge information ",2011International Conference on Energy Systems and Electrical Power (ESEP 2011), Energy Procedia, vol. 13,p.5508-5515 ,2011.

[21] Gao Hai ,Siu Wan2Chi ,Hou Chao2Huan," Improved techniques for automatic image segmentation", IEEE Transactions on Circuits and Systems for video technology, Vol.11 ,no.12, p. 1273 - 1280 ,2001.

[22] R. C. Gonzalez and R. E. Woods, Digital Image Processing, Prentice-Hall, Upper Saddle River, NJ, USA, 2nd edition, 2002.

[23] L. Vincent and P. Soille, "Watersheds in digital spaces: An efficient algorithm based on immersion simulations," IEEE Trans. on Pattern Analysis and Machine Intelligence, vol. 13, pp. 583–598, 1991.

A Control Cross-Sections Method for Character Deformation

A. A. Bukatov[1], E. E. Gridchina[2], D. A. Zastavnoy[2], and B. A. Zastavnoy[1]
[1]SFU Computer Center, Southern Federal University, Rostov-on-Don, Russia
[2]Informatics and Computational Experiment Department, Southern Federal University, Rostov-on-Don, Russia

Abstract— *The traditional skinning technique used extensively in game development due to its simplicity is notorious for its undesired artifacts. Some of the methods developed provide full control over animation while being highly labor-intensive. A new example-based method for character animation is described. Based on linear blend skinning (LBS) the method extends the concept of Pose Space Deformation (PSD) technique. The character model is realized as a set of sections, and control cross-sections are defined. To avoid LBS defects, sample control sections are used, with the vertices positions not belonging to the control sections calculated using Catmull-Rom splines with chord-length parameterization.*

Keywords: skinning; example-based methods; cross-sections.

1 Introduction

Skeletal animation and human-like character skinning have been studied extensively in recent years [1], [2], since traditionally used skinning techniques are characterized by well-known shortcomings [3]. In spite of many new techniques appearing the standard skeletal animation algorithm — linear blend skinning (LBS) — is still widely used due to its simplicity and versatility. It is also referred to as skeletal subspace deformation, vertex blending and enveloping. Combining traditional LBS with blending, Pose Space Deformation (PSD) [4] is considered a welcome addition to LBS. Although labor-intensive PSD is also widely used as it allows the artist to obtain desired realistic deformations [5]. In this paper a technique for adjusting LBS deformations is presented, the latter based on using control cross-sections. 2-dimensional character models are considered, though the technique can be extended for 3-dimensional cases.

1.1 Notation

Scalar quantities are written in italics, as in w, and vectors are denoted as $\vec{v}$. Matrices will be denoted by uppercase letters, as in A. A^{-1} denotes the inverse of A. Bold uppercase letters, as in $\boldsymbol{S}$, denote character skeleton. Skeleton configurations are denoted as $\{B_i\}$.

2 2-dimensional LBS-model

Let polygon P be a 2D character model. Let V_P be the set of all the vertices of P. Let $\boldsymbol{S} = \{\vec{b_i}\}$ be a skeleton, i.e. a hierarchy of bones. Every bone $\vec{b_i}$ is assigned a coordinate system and a 2D transformation (translation, rotation and scaling), stored as a 3×3 matrix W_i. The transformation of a child node of the hierarchy inherits its parent node transformation. Every vertex $\vec{v} \in V_P$ is associated with a set of weights $\{w_i\}$, $\sum_i w_i = 1$, where w_i denotes the weight of the bone $\vec{b_i}$. Weight w_i defines the extent to which the vertex position is influenced by the bone $\vec{b_i}$. Let $\{B_i\}$ be the skeleton configuration in the bind pose. The skeleton being in an arbitrary pose $\{W_i\}$, the transformed position of vertex $\vec{v}'$ is calculated according to the formulae

$$\vec{v}' = LBS(\vec{v}) = \sum_i w_i W_i B_i^{-1} \vec{v} \quad (1)$$

Being computationally efficient and versatile, LBS has some undesired artifacts, such as volume loss. One of the defects, the so-called "collapsing elbow", results in ruining the natural look of the character (see Fig. 1).

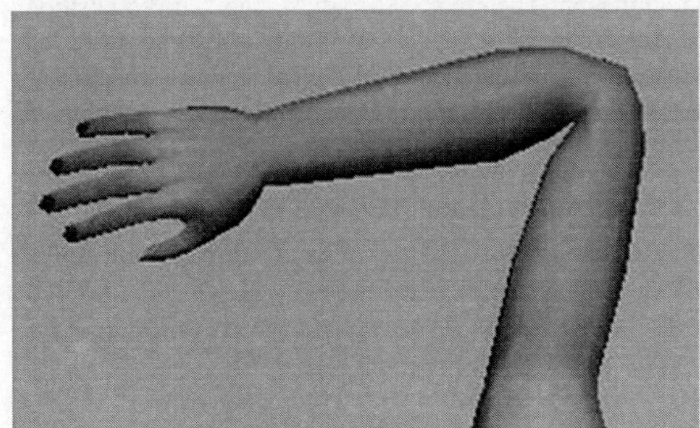

Fig. 1: Arm model bent using LBS.

3 Control cross-sections method

To make the character look realistic an additional transformation is required in order to improve the position of the vertices deformed inadequately. For that purpose we propose the control cross-sections method (CSM). Belonging to the example-based group, the technique uses control cross-sections data to adjust the standard LBS deformations of the model.

3.1 Model control section

Model section s_{ij} is defined as a pair of vertices $<\vec{v_i}, \vec{v_j}>$, $i \neq j$, $\vec{v_i}, \vec{v_j} \in V_P$. For rigged models (i.e. for the models with skeleton $S = \{\vec{b_i}\}$ and assigned weights) the cross-section is understood as section s_{ij} in the bind pose such that $\exists \vec{b_k}, \vec{b_l} \in B \mid (\vec{v_i}\vec{v_j}, \vec{b_k}\vec{b_l}) = 0$; $\vec{b_k}$ is a child node of $\vec{b_l}$ in the hierarchy of the skeleton S. Further on only cross-sections are considered. It should also be noted that in the case of a 3D model a section can be understood as a set of model vertices not necessarily forming a "section" in the traditional sense (vertices need not be coplanar). For certain chatacter poses characterized by undesired artifacts, sample positions of some sections vertices are defined, those sections belonging to troublesome areas of the model. Such sections are referred to as *control sections*. To adjust LBS deformations, pairs $<X^i, S^i>$ are used assuming that X^i is a skeleton configuration and S^i is a set of control sections. The set of control sections also includes all the sections with vertices associated with only one bone, i.e. $\exists \vec{b_k} \in S \mid w_k = 1$.

3.2 Keyframe animation

When animating a character, key frame animation is a traditional technique to use. For every key frame the animator defines a pose for the character, all the in-between poses of the skeleton are calculated automatically using interpolation methods. According to the traditional skeletal animation, model vertices positions are recalculated for every frame of the animation. Therefore CSM adjusts the vertices position for every frame. The vertices of the control sections are the first to be processed. Based on the recalculated position of the control sections vertices, the other vertices position is calculated.

3.3 Control sections vertices recalculation

Let us assume that $\vec{v} \in s \in S^i$ is a vertex position in the sample control section in the pose X^i, $\vec{v_0}$ is vertex position in the bind pose B. Then displacement $\vec{d_j}$ in the $\vec{b_j}$ local coordinate system is calculated as follows:

$$\vec{d_j} = LBS^{-1}(\vec{v}, \vec{b_j})B_j^{-1}\vec{v_0}. \quad (2)$$

If the current pose $X = X^i$, the current position of the control section vertex $\vec{v}$ is calculated as:

$$\vec{v'} = LBS(\vec{v}, \vec{d}) = \sum_j w_j W_j(B_j^{-1}\vec{v} + \vec{d_j}). \quad (3)$$

In-betweens of the control sections vertices are calculated likewise with PSD.

3.4 Other vertices recalculation

If a vertex does not belong to any of the control sections, recalculating its position is based on its current LBS position and its nearest control sections position. To avoid LBS artifacts, the LBS vertex position is adjusted using cubic Catmull-Rom splines [6] so that it corresponds to the position of the control sections vertices.

3.4.1 Catmull-Rom splines

Using interpolation, C^1-continuity and local control, Catmull-Rom splines are an adequate way to solve the task. The C^1-continuity of the spline provides a smooth natural look of the character, with the spline remaining flexible. Also the spline interpolates its control points giving direct control over the points of the curve. With local control the spline has every control vertex provide a slight impact on the overall look, and preserving the model details. Therefore Catmull-Rom splines allow the achievement of realistic deformation of traditionally difficult areas of character models, e.g. the elbow.

3.4.2 Spline parameterization

The shape of the curve the Catmull-Rom spline gives depends heavily on the parameterization defined [7]. Choosing a spline parameterization for our method we considered three types:

- uniform parameterization;
- chord-length parameterization;
- centripetal parameterization.

Uniform parameterization is considered the most popular choice for Catmull-Rom splines, though for curves with segments of different length this parameterization often leads to artifacts such as self-intersections within short curve segments [7], which is unacceptable in the animation of a character (see Fig. 2a). Cusps and intersections are also possible when using chord-length parameterization, the curve "overshoots" within longer curve segments (see Fig. 2b). Centripetal parameterization is the only not to generate such artifacts. Moreover, among these parameterizations the centripetal version appears to produce a curve that is closer to the control polygon than the others (see Fig. 2c).

Despite the fact that it is mathematically proven that centripetal parameterization lacks traditionally undesired features such as cusps and intersections within a segment [7], the CSM uses chord-length parameterization. Our reasoning behind this preference differs from the standard one as CSM deals with character models. Firstly, the curvature of the relatively long curve segments is larger in comparison with the results of the other parameterizations considered, and it tends to remain small within shorter curve segments. It helps achieve a more realistic look of the character, as human-like models will not lose much volume when animated. Secondly, according to [8] chord-length parameterization is considered the best as it provides a very well-conditioned linear system of equations compared to other parameterization types. So if $\vec{p_i}$, $\vec{p}_{i+1}$ are spline control points the parameterization $t_{i+1} = t_i + \mid \vec{p}_{i+1} - \vec{p_i} \mid$ is used.

The Catmull-Rom curve segment shape depends on four neighboring data points: $\vec{p}_{i-2}$, $\vec{p}_{i-1}$, $\vec{p}_{i+1}$, $\vec{p}_{i+2}$. The set of recalculated control sections vertices is denoted as $V_C = \{\vec{v}_{j_k}\}_k \mid j_{k_1} < j_{k_2}, k_1 < k_2, V_C \subset V_P$. It is necessary

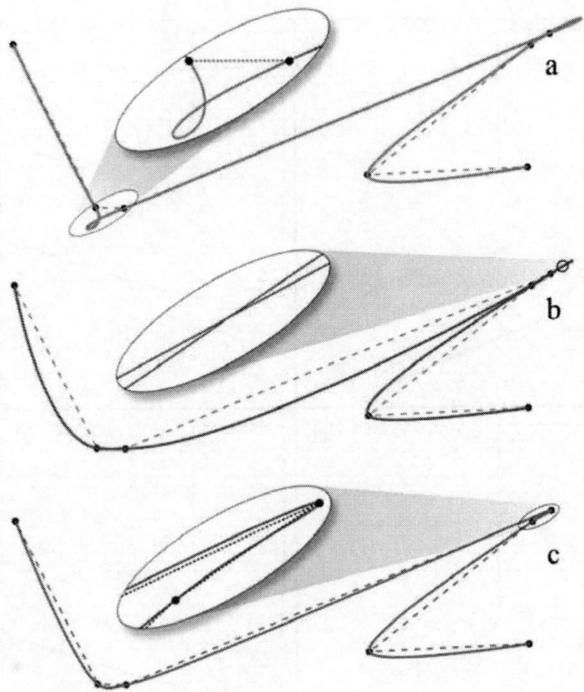

Fig. 2: Catmull-Rom splines with uniform (a), chord-length (b) and centripetal parameterization (c) (courtesy of [7]).

to calculate the position for all the vertices between neighboring control vertices $\vec{v}_{j_n}, \vec{v}_{j_{n+1}} \in V_C \mid, j_{n+1} \neq j_n + 1$. In this case $\vec{p}_{i-1} = \vec{v}_{j_n}, \vec{p}_{i+1} = \vec{v}_{j_{n+1}}$, while the choice of control vertices $\vec{p}_{i-2}, \vec{p}_{i+2}$ is not as easily defined. As a rule, $\vec{p}_{i-2} = \vec{v}_{j_{n-1}}, \vec{p}_{i+2} = \vec{v}_{j_{n+2}}$, but some of the model vertices can be special cases, e.g. vertices of extreme sections when a part of a model is processed. Both vertices of such a section must not be spline control points, as it will produce undesired artifacts. Given $\vec{p}_{i+1}$ is a special case vertex, i.e. the model lacks $\vec{p}_{i+2}$, an additional control vertex is constructed with the reflection method: $\vec{p}_{i+2} = \vec{p}_{i+1} + (\vec{p}_{i+1} - \vec{p}_{i-1})$.

4 Setting control cross-section

A control section can be set in several ways:

- manually by setting the vertices position of the control section for skeletal configuration of every sample pair;
- on the base of existing sample shapes, defining only the set of vertices of the control section (provided all the sample shapes have the same topology, control sections vertices position can be extracted automatically from every shape);
- connecting a control section shape to a bone rotation (it could allow for creating muscle bulging effect).

5 Discussion

On one hand, based on LBS, CSM remains versatile. On the other hand, the proposed method allows for realistic deformation, by adjusting undesired LBS artifacts with the use of sample sections. In the general case CSM gives less control over animation than PSD. Nevertheless, if the character model topology allows it is possible to define all the sections of the model as control ones in order for the CSM to perform like PSD. Therefore CSM can be considered a type of PSD generalization. In comparison with PSD, CSM needs less input sample data, and appears less labor-intensive. The animator need not construct samples of the whole character; it is enough to define control sections for problematic pieces of the model. Moreover, CSM allows using fewer <pose, control sections set> pairs due to the calculation in the local coordinate system of the bones and the use of splines for non-control vertices.

6 Control section method demonstrational usage example

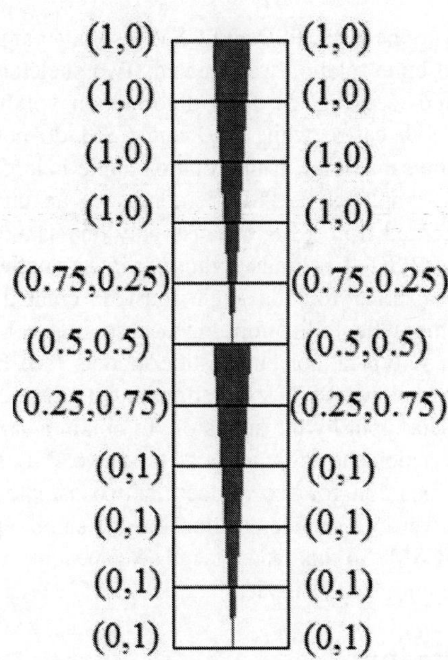

Fig. 3: Cylindrical model with a two bones skeleton. The bones' weights are written in brackets: left number denotes the parent bone weight of a vertice, right number denotes the child bone weight of a vertice.

A flat cylinder model (a simplified "hand" model) with rigging (see Fig. 3) is used as a demonstrational example of the proposed method. Vertices lying in the bending area are sure to be the most troublesome. So the section whose vertices are $(0.5, 0.5)$-weighted is chosen as the only control section. Then <pose, control sections set> pairs are defined. For the model under consideration, only one pair is defined using the existing PSD shape of the model (see Fig. 4).

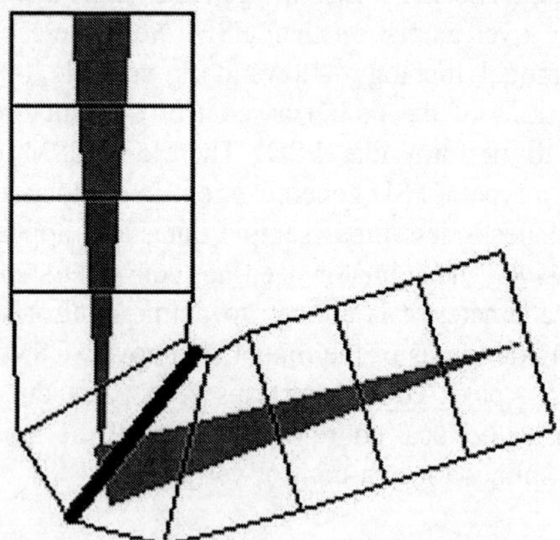

Fig. 4: Defining the <pose, control sections set> pair (control section in bold).

To compare the LBS, PSD and CSM results an animation with a child bone rotation was created. Two skeleton poses are compared (see Fig. 5). LBS deformation volume loss is seen in both cases, while PSD and CSM do not show defects of the same kind. If the rotation angle is larger than that of the sample pose, PSD demonstrates an undesired artifact, inherited from LBS, because only one sample pose is defined for PSD. To eliminate those artifacts another PSD shape with a larger rotation angle must be created. CSM will show more flexibility forming a cusp in the bending area, which is typical for human-like models (see Fig. 6). Hence CSM allows PSD level animation to be achieved using less data input by the animator. To obtain a satisfying level of animation the PSD needs at least two PSD shapes, i.e. sample position for six vertices in two sample poses, while a two vertices sample position for one sample pose is enough for CSM. So this model takes six times less vertices data for the animator to input.

7 Conclusions

The proposed control cross-sections method (CSM) for character animation is an example-based method, adjusting LBS results and generalizing PSD ideas. The original term of control cross-section is introduced. Control cross-sections allow for avoiding the undesired artifacts of underlying LBS transformations. Unlike PSD the method proposed assumes the storage of control sections samples for only troublesome vertices of the character. CSM tends to reduce the labor-intensity of the animator's work. Due to its greater flexibility CSM provides PSD quality animation using less data input by the animator.

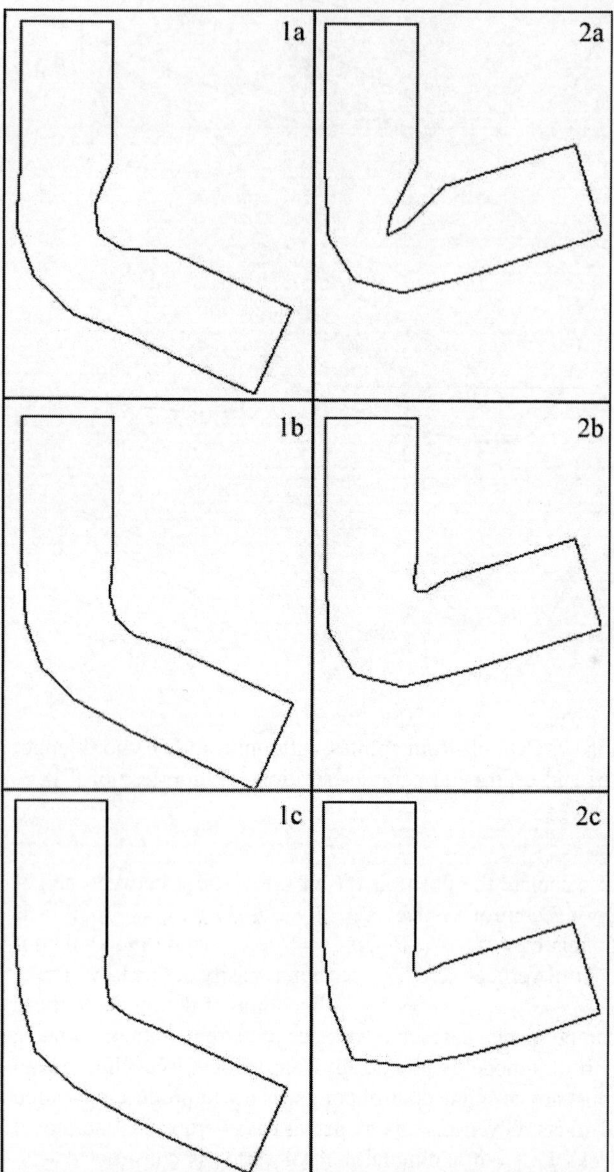

Fig. 5: Frames from child bone rotation animation. 1a, 2a — LBS; 1b, 2b — PSD; 1c, 2c — CSM.

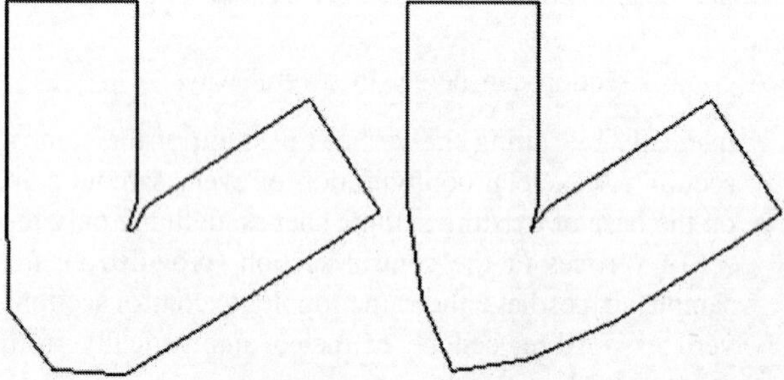

Fig. 6: Animation frame with the rotation angle greater than the sample rotation angle. Left — PSD; right — CSM.

References

[1] I. Z. Frey and I. Herzeg, "Spherical skinning with dual quaternions and qtangents," in *ACM SIGGRAPH 2011 Talks (SIGGRAPH '11)*, New York: ACM, 2011, p. 11.

[2] A. A. Vasilakis and I. Fudos, "GPU rigid skinning based on a refined skeletonization method," *Comp. Anim. and Virt. W.*, vol. 22, pp. 27–46, Jan. 2011.

[3] A. A. Bukatov, E. E. Gridchina, and D. A. Zastavnoy, "Skeletal animation techniques for deforming polygonal surface of 3D models," *Inzhenerny Vestnik Dona*, vol. 3, pp. 59–74, 2012. [Online]. Available: http://www.ivdon.ru/uploads/article/pdf/2012_3_11.pdf_897.pdf

[4] J. P. Lewis, M. Cordner, and N. Fong, "Pose space deformation: a unified approach to shape interpolation and skeleton driven deformation," in *Proceedings of the 27th Annual Conference on Computer Graphics and Interactive Techniques*, New York: ACM Press/Addison-Wesley Publishing, 2000, pp. 165–172.

[5] G. S. Lee and F. Hanner, "Practical experiences with pose space deformation," in *ACM SIGGRAPH ASIA 2009 Sketches*, New York: ACM, 2009, p. 43.

[6] E. Catmull and R. Rom, "A class of local interpolating splines," in*Computer Aided Geometric Design*, New York: Academic Press, 1974, pp. 317–326.

[7] C. Yuksel, S. Schaefer, and J. Keyser, "On the parameterization of Catmull-Rom curves," in *ACM Joint Conference on Geometric and Physical Modeling (SPM '09)*, New York: ACM, 2009, pp. 47–53.

[8] E. B. Kuznetsov, A. Yu. Yakimovich, "The best parameterization for curve and surface approximation," *Zhurnal Vychislitel'noy Matematiky i Matematicheskoy Fiziky*, vol. 5, pp 760–744, 2005.

Detecting Handwritten Annotation by Synchronization of Lecture Slides and Videos

J.-L. Kao [1], S.-Y. Chen [1], and D.-J. Duh [2]

[1] Department of Computer Science and Engineering, Yuan Ze University, Chungli, Taoyuan, Taiwan

[2] Department of Computer Science and Information Engineering, Chien Hsin University of Science and Technology, Chungli, Taoyuan, Taiwan

Abstract - *Pervasiveness of streaming media and the Internet have led to the widespread popularity of e-Learning, necessitating an effective means of retrieving lecture videos conveniently. Teachers usually illustrate major pedagogical concepts by taking a considerable amount of time in explanation with handwritten annotations. This study presents a handwritten annotation detection method for e-Learning video streams to facilitate retrieval of annotated slides and increase students' learning efficiency. Although many visual content-based retrieval methods have been proposed for lecture videos in terms of slide, topic, and text, few are specifically designed for handwritten annotations. Moreover, most existing annotation retrieval methods are developed for chalkboard presentation rather than electronic slides. Therefore, the objective of this study is to develop a simple yet effective annotation detection method for lecture videos using slide presentation. The proposed method consists of three stages, slide keyframe extraction, slide/video synchronization, and handwritten annotation detection. Experimental results demonstrate the feasibility of the proposed method.*

Keywords: Slide-video synchronization, Handwritten annotation, Lecture videos, SFIT matching, e-Learning.

1 Introduction

The e-Learning environments for educational purposes are extensively constructed to record class scenarios in a video stream format. Although distance learning students can review course content by watching an e-Learning video stream, a considerable amount of time is spent in watching e-Learning video streams to identify the important parts, ultimately degrading the incentive of learning. Major concepts are often demonstrated by teachers with handwritten annotations. Therefore, detecting handwritten annotations from e-Learning video streaming can help students to focus on the important parts (i.e., annotated slides), subsequently increasing their learning efficiency.

Many research issues emerge [1–3] to retrieve lecture videos conveniently. According to the narrative forms used by instructors, the presentations recorded in lecture videos can be electronic slides [4–14], chalkboard [15, 16], or mix of whiteboard and electronic slides [17]. In terms of indexing strategies, the visual content retrieval for e-learning lectures can be divided into four categories, slide [4–11], topic [10–12], printed text [10–14], handwritten annotation [15-17] or a hybrid [10–14]. However, most handwritten annotation retrieval methods were proposed for chalkboard [15, 16] or mix of whiteboard and electronic slides [17]. This study proposed a method to detect handwritten annotation in electronic slides without off-line calibration procedure that records the geometric and photometric transfer between the projector and the camera in a look-up table as in Ref. [17].

The proposed method consists of three stages, slide keyframe extraction, slide/video synchronization, and handwritten annotation detection. Shot boundaries are detected to resample a video stream in a set of keyframes. Non-slide keyframes are then excluded based on slide characteristics. SIFT (Scale Invariant Feature Transformation) matching is used to synchronize lecture slides and videos. Slide images can then be back-projected into the video through homographic transformation. Finally, handwritten annotations are detected using binarization difference. Experimental results demonstrate the feasibility of the proposed method. The rest of this paper is organized as follows. Section 2 introduces slide keyframe extraction. Sections 3 and 4 describe slide-video synchronization and handwritten annotation detection, respectively. Section 5 gives experimental results. Finally, Section 6 concludes this study and proposes future works.

2 Slide keyframe extraction

Slide keyframe extraction includes three steps, illumination equatization, transition detection and slide keyframe detection. The former two steps are based on our previous work [18]. Only the step of slide keyframe detection is proposed in this study.

A lecture video contains different scenes. The camera takes the speaker, slide which has been reported, or the handwritings on the slides. According to the appearance of slide, the scenes can be divided into three categories, full, small, and no slides. Only the slide keyframes including full or small slides are processed by the proposed method. The non-slide keyframes will be excluded before performing slide-video synchronization. Because the background in non-slide keyframe is more complicated than that in slides keyframes, the histograms of projection in binary images are different between slides and non-slides (Figure 1). This observation is the key concept to separate slide and non-slide in this study.

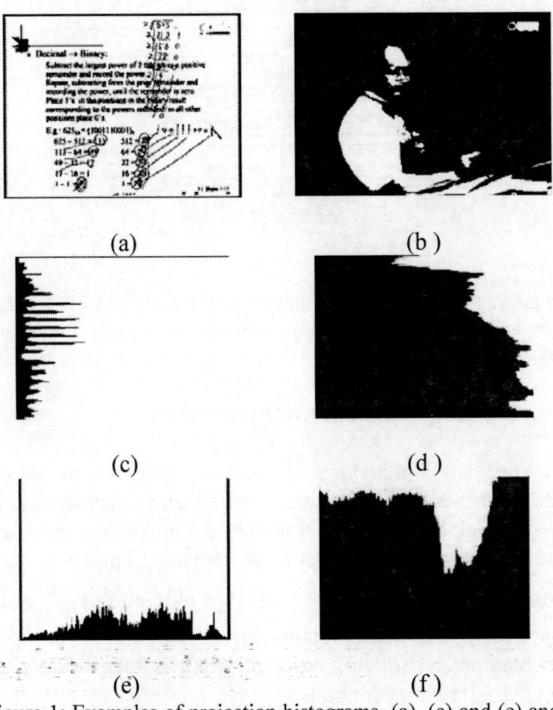

Figure 1: Examples of projection histograms. (a), (c) and (e) and (b), (d) and (f) denote the binary images, x and y projections for slide and non-slide keyframes, respectively.

Two-means algorithm is generally adopted for binarizatin. The maximum and minimum gray values for each keyframe are obtained as the initial values of the two-means algorithm. The two-means classifier then divides gray values for each keyframe into two parts, white and black parts. The former is considered as background, i.e. slide background; and the latter is foreground, i.e., slide content including handwritten annotation. Let the binarization result of keyframe $KF(x,y)$ be $B(x,y)$. Each pixel of binary image is then projected into x-axis and y-axis, yielding two 1D histograms, $p^h(y)=\sum_{x=1}^{W} B(x,y)$ $p^v(x)=\sum_{y=1}^{H} B(x,y)$, where W and H denote the width and height of a keyframe image and are set to 320 and 240 in this study. Figure 1 presents examples of projection histograms and reveals that the curve of projection for non-slide image is more complicated and diversity. The characteristics are used for slide detection. The detection rule is then defined using the following equation

$$Slide(KF(x,y)) = \begin{cases} \text{TRUE} & \text{if } LR \geq TH_l \text{ and } SN \leq TH_n \\ \text{FALSE} & \text{otherwise} \end{cases} \quad (1)$$

$$LR = \frac{1}{W+H}\left[\sum_{y=1}^{H} s(p_h(y)-TH_p) + \sum_{x=1}^{W} s(p_v(x)-TH_p)\right]$$

$$SN = \sum_{y=1}^{H-1} s(p_h(y+1)-p_h(y)-TH_q) + \sum_{x=1}^{W-1} s(p_v(x+1)-p_v(x)-TH_q)$$

$$s(x) = \begin{cases} 1 & x \geq 1 \\ 0 & \text{otherwise} \end{cases}$$

where the threshold values TH_l, TH_n, TH_p, and TH_q, are set empirically to 0.4, 0.6, 70, 70, respectively in this study.

3 Slide-video synchronization

SIFT (Scale Invariant Feature Transformation) matching is used to synchronize lecture slides and videos. Slide images can then be projected into the video through homographic transformation.

3.1 SIFT Matching

The SIFT key-points [19] are used for matching between slide keyframes and electronic slides. Each key-point is associated with a descriptor of 128-element vector. This study generates key-points from images offline by using a publicly available SIFT-key-point detector [20]. The feature similarity between two key-points can then be measured by the Euclidean distance of the key-point descriptor vectors of 128 dimensions. The match (or correspondence) of a key-point in electronic slide is defined as the nearest neighbor (NN) among all of the key-points in the slide keyframe. To accept a point match as valid, false matches are discarded on based of the relationship between the NN and the second NN, as suggested by Lowe [19]. Restated, let P_e and P_k be two key-points from electronic slide image ES and slide keyframe KS, respectively, with P_e being the NN of P_k in the feature space. Then, P_e is considered a valid match to P_k only if

$$\frac{d(f_S(P_e), f_S(P_k))}{d(f_S(P'_e), f_S(P_k))} \leq TH_m \quad (2)$$

where $d(\cdot,\cdot)$ denotes the Euclidean distance between two descriptor vectors and $f_S(P)$ is the SIFT descriptor vector of a key-point P. The point P'_e is the second nearest key-point of P_k in image *ES*. For each slide keyframe, the electronic slide having the largest number of valid SIFT matching pairs is selected as the corresponding slide to which the keyframe is matched.

However, those pairs satisfying Eq. (2) may not be mutually consistent. This study uses three constraints to prune inconsistent pairs (Figure 2(a)) to obtain the final consist matching pairs (Figure 2(b)). The three constraints are in terms of majority distance, scale and tendency, respectively. Assume that there are *N* matching pairs satisfy Eq. (2). Let a line segment $L_{e,k}^{(i)}$ with endpoints $P_e^{(i)}$ at electronic slide *ES* and $P_k^{(i)}$ at slide keyframe *KS*, and the respective matching pairs $(P_e^{(i)}, P_k^{(i)})$ has the length $l_{e,k}^{(i)}$ and the orientation $\theta_{e,k}^{(i)}$ with respect the *x*-axis. Find the mean values and standard deviations of all matching pairs for length $l_{e,k}^{(i)}$ as l_m and l_d, respectively. The same is for orientation $\theta_{e,k}^{(i)}$ to obtain θ_m and θ_d. In addition, let $(P_e^{(i)}, P_k^{(i)})$ and $(P_e^{(j)}, P_k^{(j)})$ be any two matching pairs among the *N* matching pairs, and define the ratio of the length of $(P_e^{(i)}, P_e^{(j)})$ to that of $(P_k^{(i)}, P_k^{(j)})$ as $R_{e,k}^{(i,j)}$. The majority scale, i.e., the mode of all the $R_{e,k}^{(i,j)}$ can be obtained as R_m. The three constraints are the defined in cascaded sequence as the following equations.

$$S_1 = \left\{ (P_e^{(i)}, P_k^{(i)}) \middle| l_m - l_d \le l_{e,k}^{(i)} \le l_m + l_d, 1 \le i \le N \right\}$$
$$S_2 = \left\{ (P_e^{(i)}, P_k^{(i)}) \middle| \begin{array}{l} R_{e,k}^{(i,j)} = R_m, \\ \exists (P_e^{(j)}, P_k^{(j)}) \in S_1, (P_e^{(i)}, P_k^{(i)}) \in S_1 \end{array} \right\} \quad (3)$$
$$S_3 = \left\{ (P_e^{(i)}, P_k^{(i)}) \middle| \begin{array}{l} \theta_m - \theta_d \le \theta_{e,k}^{(i)} \le \theta_m + \theta_d, \\ (P_e^{(i)}, P_k^{(i)}) \in S_2 \end{array} \right\}$$

Those matching pairs satisfying the three constraints are considered consistent matching pairs and used for homographic transformation. Figure 2 presents an example of matching between a slide keyframe and the corresponding lecture slide.

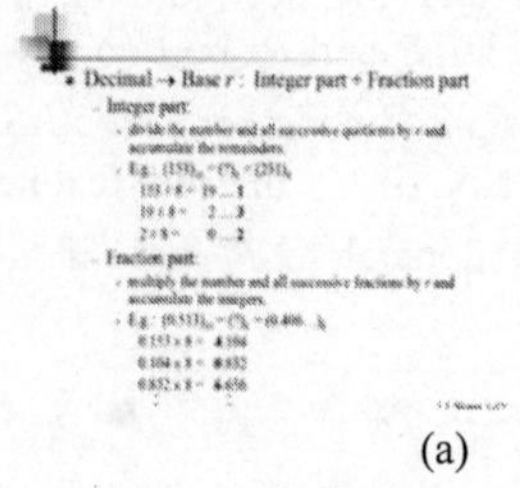
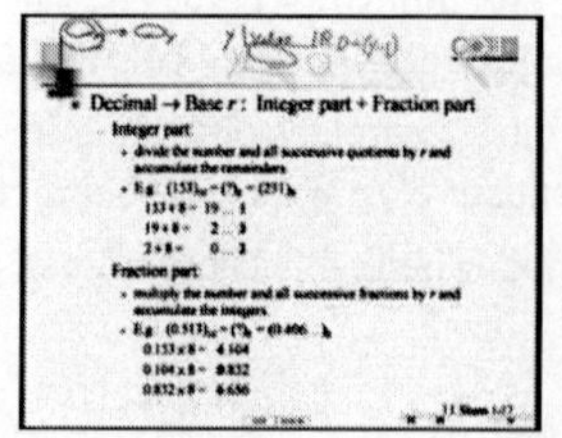

(a)

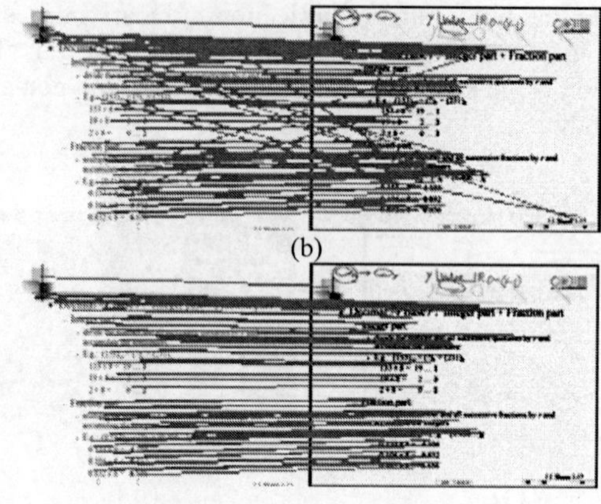

(b)

(c)

Figure 2: Example of SIFT matching. (a) A pair of electronic slide and slide keyframe; (b) matching pairs; (c) consistent matching pairs.

3.2 Homographic transformation

After SIFT matching is used to synchronize lecture slides and videos, slide images can be then projected into the video through homographic transformation. Assume that there are *m* consistent matching pairs, $(P_e^{(i)}, P_k^{(i)}) \in S_3$, and let the (*x*, *y*) coordinates of $P_e^{(i)}$ and $P_k^{(i)}$ be $(x_e^{(i)}, y_e^{(i)})$ and $(x_k^{(i)}, y_k^{(i)})$, respectively, the homographic transformation in terms of eight parameters, (*a*, *b*, *c*, *d*, *e*, *f*, *g*, *h*), is then defined by using the following equations.

$$x_k^{(i)} = \frac{a x_e^{(i)} + b y_e^{(i)} + c}{g x_e^{(i)} + h y_e^{(i)} + 1}, \; y_k^{(i)} = \frac{d x_e^{(i)} + e y_e^{(i)} + f}{g x_e^{(i)} + h y_e^{(i)} + 1} \quad (4)$$

and solved using the following equations

$$\begin{bmatrix} x_e^{(1)} & y_e^{(1)} & 1 & 0 & 0 & 0 & -x_k^{(1)}x_e^{(1)} & -x_k^{(1)}y_e^{(1)} \\ 0 & 0 & 0 & x_e^{(1)} & y_e^{(1)} & 1 & -y_k^{(1)}x_e^{(1)} & -y_k^{(1)}y_e^{(1)} \\ x_e^{(2)} & y_e^{(2)} & 1 & 0 & 0 & 0 & -x_k^{(2)}x_e^{(2)} & -x_k^{(2)}y_e^{(2)} \\ 0 & 0 & 0 & x_e^{(2)} & y_e^{(2)} & 1 & -y_k^{(2)}x_e^{(2)} & -y_k^{(2)}y_e^{(2)} \\ \vdots & \vdots & \vdots & \vdots & \vdots & \vdots & \vdots & \vdots \\ \vdots & \vdots & \vdots & \vdots & \vdots & \vdots & \vdots & \vdots \\ x_e^{(n)} & y_e^{(n)} & 1 & 0 & 0 & 0 & -x_k^{(n)}x_e^{(n)} & -x_k^{(n)}y_e^{(n)} \\ 0 & 0 & 0 & x_e^{(n)} & y_e^{(n)} & 1 & -y_k^{(n)}x_e^{(n)} & -y_k^{(n)}y_e^{(n)} \end{bmatrix} \begin{bmatrix} a \\ b \\ c \\ d \\ e \\ f \\ g \\ h \end{bmatrix} = \begin{bmatrix} x_k^{(1)} \\ y_k^{(1)} \\ x_k^{(2)} \\ y_k^{(2)} \\ \vdots \\ \vdots \\ x_k^{(n)} \\ y_k^{(n)} \end{bmatrix} \quad (5)$$

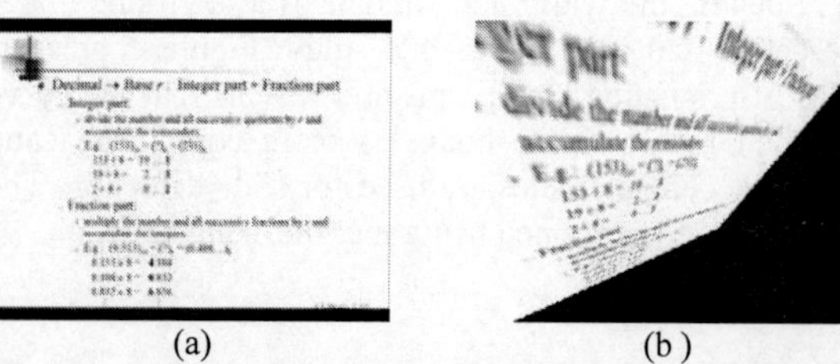

(a) (b)

Figure 3: Example of homographic transformation. (a) Results based on incorrect matching pairs of Figure 2(b); (b) transform results based on consistent matching pairs of Figure 2(c).

4 Handwritten annotation detection

This section describes how to detect handwritten annotations using binarization difference. Figure 4 presents the flowchart of handwritten annotation detection.

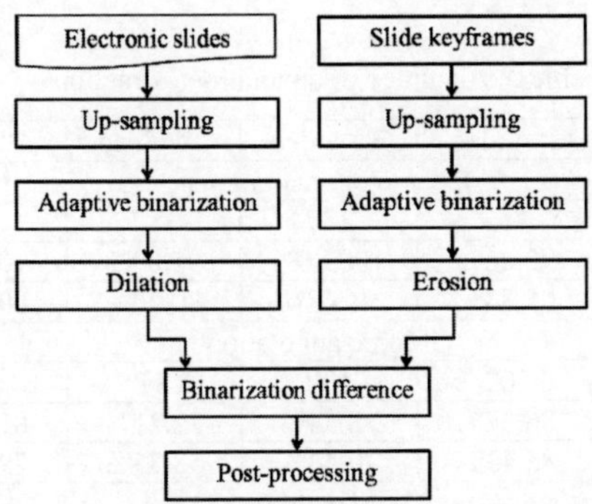

Figure 4: Flowchart of handwritten annotation detection.

Since lecture videos are generally compressed into a low resolution form for reducing transmission bandwidth cost, slide keyframes should be up-sampled into a higher resolution quality to facilitate subsequent handwritten annotation extraction. Bilinear interpolation is used in this study for up-sampling. The same procedure is applied to electronic slides. Therefore, adaptive binarization is first applied to electronic slides and slide keyframes, followed by the correlation analysis on slide-video synchronization.

Two-means algorithm is generally adopted for binarization. However, this algorithm cannot handle non-uniform illumination problems that are typically encountered in lecture videos. This study used an adaptive method based on the two-means algorithm to select the proper threshold. Each electronic slide *ES* and the matched slide keyframe *KS* are first divided into small patches, 20×20 in this study. The localized two-means classifier is then applied to each patch individually. The maximum and minimum gray values for each patch are calculated as the initial values of the two-means algorithm. The two-means classifier then divides gray values for each patch into two parts. Following clustering, all of the patches are binarized individually.

After adaptive binarization is applied to *ES* and *KS*, let the darker part of *ES* and *KS* be $F_{es}(x,y)$ and $F_{ks}(x,y)$. The morphological processing with structuring element of 7×7 block is then applied to $F_{es}(x,y)$ and $F_{ks}(x,y)$ with respective dilation and erosion operator to obtain $F'_{es}(x,y)$ and $F'_{ks}(x,y)$, respectively.

The resulting handwritten annotation, $C(x,y)$, is then defined as the difference part of $F'_{es}(x,y)$ and $F'_{ks}(x,y)$, i.e., all the elements in $F'_{ks}(x,y)$ but not in $F'_{es}(x,y)$, using the following equation.

$$C(x,y) = F'_{ks}(x,y) \wedge \neg F'_{es}(x,y) \qquad (6)$$

where $\neg$ and $\wedge$ denotes the logical NOT and AND operators, respectively. Morphological dilation operator with structuring element of 7×7 block is then applied to $C(x,y)$ to obtain more compact annotations $C'(x,y)$. Finally, the elements in $C'(x,y)$ with size small than TH_s are considered noises and removed. The threshold value of TH_s is set to 25. Figure 5 presents an example of handwritten annotation detection.

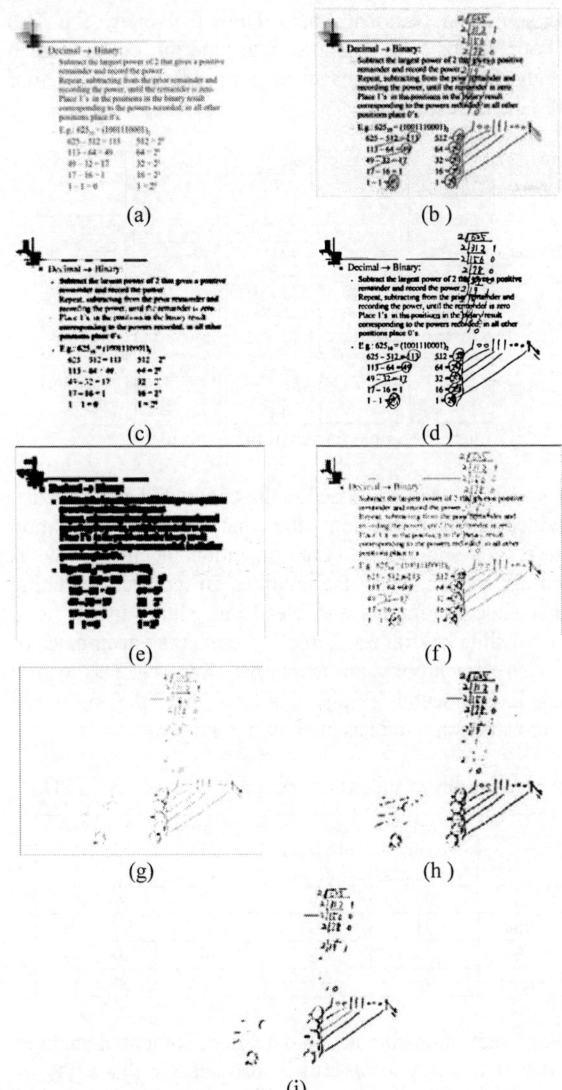

Figure 5: An example of handwritten annotation detection. (a) Original electronic slide image; (b) original corresponding slide keyframe; (c) and (d) binarization results of up-sampling results of (a) and (b); (e) dilation result of (c); (f) erosion result of (d); (g) difference result of (e) and (f); (h) dilation result of (g); (i) noise removal of (h).

5 Experimental results

The proposed method was implemented on a GIGABYTE motherboard with a quad 2.67 GHz core Intel Q8400 CPU and 4 Gigabytes DDR2 SDRAM. The operating system is Microsoft Windows 7 professional version. The program is developed in the C++ language with an open source OpenCV library and compiled under Microsoft Visual Studio 2010. The lecture videos were collected from the open course source in National Chaio Tung University (NCTU) [21]. Four videos with simple background are considered in this study. Figure 6 presents some sample frames of the four lecture videos, respectively.

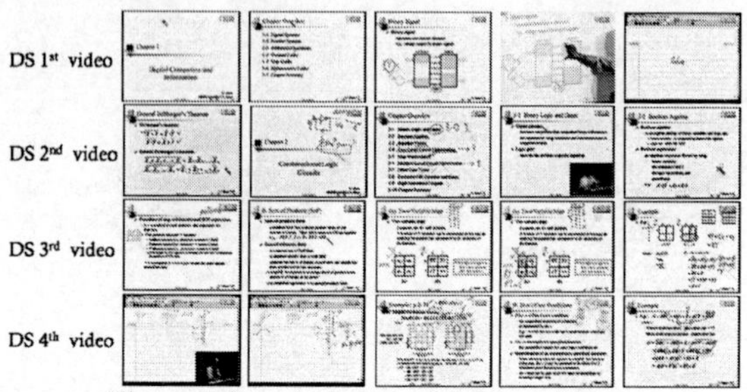

Figure 6: Sample frames of the four videos.

Two issues were addressed in the conducted experiments: slide-video synchronization and handwritten annotation detection. For slide-video synchronization, accuracy rate is defined as the ratio of the number of correct matching between slide keyframes and electronic slides to the total number of slide keyframes. Table 1 presents the accuracies of slide-video synchronization over the four NCTU lecture videos. Experimental results indicate that the proposed synchronization method has high alignment power.

Table 1: Accuracy of slide keyframe synchronization in NTCU.

	Number of slide keyframes	Number of correct matching	Number of slides	Matching accuracy
1st video	93	89	19	96.73%
2nd video	71	69	29	97.18 %
3rd video	53	52	26	98.11%
4th video	94	81	33	86.17%

For handwritten annotation detection, content element as defined by Choudary *et al.* [16] is also used in this study. A character is defined as a content element for text; a stroke is defined as a content element for figures and drawings. Figure 7 shows examples of content elements in the detected content of lecture videos. The detection accuracy refers to the ratio of the number of content elements detected accurately to the total number of ground truth, *i.e.* the number of authentic content elements. Notably, both the numbers of elements detected correctly and ground truth are counted manually. Table 2 lists the average accuracy over the four NCTU videos. Figure 5 illustrates an example of annotation detection.

(a) (b)
Figure 7: Examples of content elements. (a) Characters; (b) graphics.

Table 2: Accuracy of annotation extraction.

	1st video	2nd video	3rd video	4th video
Character annotations				
Number	155	137	117	71
Precision	92.26%	100.00%	91.09%	90.14%
Recall	95.33%	94.48%	80.70%	69.57%
Graphic annotation				
Number	102	192	84	105
Precision	86.27%	88.54%	72.21%	81.02%
Recall	85.43%	79.44%	58.75%	79.29%
Total				
Precision	91.30%	85.52%	74.12%	85.58%
Recall	89.89%	93.31%	84.40%	74.43%

6 Conclusions and future works

A slide keyframe extraction is first proposed to exclude non-slide background frames and to extract slide keyframes from lecture videos. The alignment of electronic slides and slide keyframes of lecture video is then proposed to achieve slide-video synchronization. Finally, handwritten annotations are detected based on the synchronization information. Various experimental results confirm the proposed method.

Future works can be directed to the following topics. First, the proposed handwritten annotation detection can be used for subsequent quality enhancement of lecture videos. Second, the proposed handwritten annotation detection can be extended to handle more complicated scenarios. Finally, the proposed handwritten annotation detection can be extended to resolve annotation recognition problem.

7 References

[1] T. Liu and J. R. Kender. Lecture videos for e-learning: Current research and challenges," in *Proc. IEEE Int'l Symp. Multimedia Software Engineering*, 574–578, 2004.

[2] B. Erol and Y. Li, "An overview of technologies for e-meeting and e-lecture," in *Proc. IEEE Int'l Conf. Multimedia Expro*, 6–14, 2005.

[3] A. Efrat, A. Amir, K. Barnard, and Q. Fan, "Cross-modality indexing, browsing and search of distance learning media on the web in eBook," *Internet Multimedia Search and Mining*, edited by X.-S. Hua, M. Worring, and T.-S. Chua, 1–14.

[4] Q. Fang, A. Amir, K. Barnard, R. Swaminathan, and A. Efrat, "Robust spatiotemporal matching of electronic slides to presentation videos," *IEEE Trans. Image Processing*, 20(8):315–2328, 2011.

[5] X. Wang and M. Kankanhalli, “Robust alignment of presentation videos with slides,” in *Proc. Pacific Rim Conf. Multimedia*, 311–322, 2009.

[6] X. Wang, S. Ramanathan, and M. Kankanhalli, “A robust framework for aligning lecture slides with video,” in *Proc. IEEE Int'l Conf. Image Processing*, 249–252, 2009.

[7] G. Gigonzac, P. Pitie, and A. Kokaram, “Electronic slide matching and enhancement of a lecture video,” in *Proc. Eur. Conf. Visual Media production*, 1–7, 2007.

[8] A. Mavlankar, P. Agrawal, D. Pang, S. Halawa, N.M. Cheung, and B. Girod, “An interactive region-of-interest video streaming system for online lecture viewing,” in *Proc. IEEE Int'l Packet Video Workshop*, 64–71, 2010.

[9] A. Behera, D. Lalanne, and R. Ingold, “DocMIR: An automatic document-based indexing system for meeting retrieval,” *Multimedia Tools and Applications*, 37(2) 135–167, 2008.

[10] F. Wang, C.W. Ngo, and T.C. Pong, “Structuring low-quality videotaped lectures for cross-reference browsing by video text analysis,” *Pattern Recognition,* 41(10): 3257–3269, 2008.

[11] T. F. Syeda-Mahmood, “Indexing for topics in videos using foils,” in *Proc. IEEE Conf. Computer Vision and Pattern Recognition*, 312–319, 2000.

[12] A. Mittal, P. V. Krishnan, and E. Altman, “Content classification and context-based retrieval system for e-learning,” *Educational Technology & Society*, 9(1): 276–291, 2006.

[13] A. Zandifar, R. Duraiswami, and L. S. Davis, “A video-based framework for the analysis of presentation/posters,” *Int'l J. Document Analysis and Recognition*, 7(2–3): 178–187, 2005.

[14] A. S. Imran, L. Rahadianti, F. A. Cheikh, S. Y. Yayilgan, “Semantic tags for lecture videos,” in *Proc. IEEE Int'l Conf. Semantic Computing*, 117–120, 2012.

[15] A. S. Imran, S. Chanda, F. A. Cheikh, K. Franke, and U. Pal, “Cursive Handwritten segmentation and recognition for instructional videos,” in *Proc. Int'l Conf. Signal Image Technology and Internet Based Systems*, 155–160, 2012.

[16] C. Choudary and T. Lie, “Summarization of visual content in instructional videos,” *IEEE Trans. Multimedia*, 9(7): 1443–1455, 2007.

[17] M. Liao, R. Yang, and Z. Zhang, “Robust and accurate visual echo cancelation in a full-duplex projector-camera,” *IEEE Trans. Pattern Recognition and Machine Intelligence*, 30(10): 1831–1840, 2008.

[18] C.-Y. Shiao and S.-Y. Chen, “Text extraction for lecture videos,” in *Proc. IPPR Conf. Computer Vision, Graphics and Image Processing*, 108, 2011

[19] D. G. Lowe, “Distinctive image features from scale-invariant keypoints,” *Int'l J. of Computer Vision,* 60(2): 91–110, 2004.

[20] Rob Hess, “SIFT Library” [Online]. Available http://blogs.oregonstate.edu/hess/code/sift/.

[21] Open course source in National Chaio Tung University, http://ocw.nctu.edu.tw/riki_detail.php?pgid=170&cgid=12.

Acknowledgments

The authors would like to thank Prof. Chung-Ping Chung and Open Course Ware of National Chiao Tung University for providing lecture videos and slides. This work was partially supported by National Science Council of Taiwan (NSC-101-2221-E-155-060)

Improved Strategy for TZSearch Algorithm

Shan Wang*[1], Siqi Sun[1], Wenfeng Shen[1], Weimin Xu[1] and Yanheng Zheng[1]
[1]School of Computer Engineering and Science, Shanghai University, Shanghai, China

Abstract - *TZSearch algorithm is a fast search algorithm which is adopted in multiview video coding. In this paper, improved methods for TZSearch algorithm are proposed. The octagon-based search pattern is used to replace the 8-point diamond search pattern (or 8-point square search pattern) in the initial search step of TZSearch algorithm. In addition, a threshold is set up to terminate the initial search in advance. These improvements reduce the number of search points substantially and speed up the encoding process of multiview video. The experimental results show that, in various testing sequences, the runtime of TZSearch algorithm and the total encoding time reduce about 80% and 40% separately, which are dramatic in comparison with the approximately unchanged PSNR and bitrate.*

Keywords: multiview video coding (MVC), motion estimation, TZSearch algorithm, octagon-based search pattern

1. Introduction

Traditional video presents a two-dimensional image which is taken by one camera, while multiview video contains a number of two-dimensional images which are taken by several cameras from different places in the same scene from which people can feel the depths of the objects in the scene [1]. Multiview video can be extensively used in numerous fields, such as entertainment, industrial control and teleeducation [2]. Since the entire data of multiview video is more than twice the data of traditional video, it is important to encode multiview video to compress the tremendous data [2]. The encoding solution of multiview video is proposed in the extended standard of H.264/AVC [3]. JMVC [4,5], the corresponding test model, exploits the temporal and spatial information of images to implement motion estimation in encoding multiview video. To reduce the bitrate while maintaining the PSNR of multiview video, motion estimation occupies a large amount of time consuming while encoding multiview video. According to the researches in several references, motion estimation consumes 80% of the total encoding time when encoding video including 5 points of view [6,7].

TZSearch algorithm is one of the fast search algorithms in motion estimation of JMVC which reduces the encoding time while maintaining PSNR and bitrate approximately unchanged. In spite of this, the encoding time is far from the demand of real time multiview video coding. There is a requirement to further speed up the encoding while keeping PSNR and bitrate in an appropriate range. The existing improvements of TZSearch algorithm are choosing different search pattern and setting threshold to terminate search ahead of time [8,9]. To decrease encoding time and get a well performance of both PSNR and bitrate, improved methods for TZSearch algorithm are proposed in this paper, which incorporate a modified octagon-based search pattern and a threshold. The remainder of the paper is organized as follows. In section 2, original TZSearch algorithm will be introduced. Section 3 describes the improved methods for TZSearch algorithm. Experimental results are presented of the original and the improved TZSearch algorithm in section 4 followed by conclusion in section 5.

* Corresponding author
Email address: sanbid@hotmail.com

2. Analysis of TZSearch algorithm

TZSearch Algorithm is a mixture search algorithm with good encoding performance but time consuming. The procedure of TZSearch algorithm can be described as follows:

Step 1: At the beginning, a start point should be determined as the search center of next step. It calculates the SAD (Sum of Absolute Difference) of five points with different predicted motion vector (zero, median, left, up and upper right) in the reference frame. The start point is the one with the minimum SAD.

Step 2: In the initial search, the 8-point diamond search pattern or the 8-point square search pattern is used to search the window in the reference frame with different stride lengths. If the search range is 64, the stride length ranges from 1 to 64, in multiples of 2. The point with the smallest SAD is the center of further refined search and the stride length of the center point is stored as the shortest distance.

Step 3: If the shortest distance is 1, the 2-point search pattern is used to calculate SAD of two points near the center and the shortest distance is set 0. If the shortest distance is greater than the parameter 'iRaster', the raster search pattern is employed to find the point with the smallest SAD as the center of next step. The stride length of raster search, iRaster, is stored in the shortest distance.

Step 4: If the shortest distance is greater than 0, the raster refinement or the star refinement is implemented until it is 0. Both of these refinements include 8-point diamond search pattern, 8-point square search pattern and 2-point search pattern. When the shortest distance is 0, the center point is the optimal point and the search algorithm is finished.

3. Improved strategy

3.1 Directional center-biased characteristic

The statistical results of experiments show that motion estimation is center-biased [10,11], which means that the probability distribution of the optimal point declines around the center in the search window. The statistic of 18 standard video sequences [11] shows the average probability distribution of motion vector which is presented in Table 1. In this table, the horizontal and vertical numbers are the absolute distance from the center point to the searching points. It can be concluded that 58.05% of motion vectors are just in the center of the search window (i.e. A in Fig. 1) and 76.57% of motion vectors are in the cross center (i.e. A+B in Fig. 1). According to the statistic of motion vectors, it is in favor of adopting appropriate search pattern to search points around the center of the search window to improve the speed and precision of the search. In addition, it is obviously that the motion vector distributes in horizontal and vertical directions more than other directions which is also proved in paper [12]. Therefore, the directional distribution of motion vectors should be taken advantage of to reduce the redundancy of the search. The above-mentioned characteristic is the foundation of the proposed improvements for TZSearch algorithm in this paper.

Table 1 Average probability distribution of motion vector [11]

Radius	0	1	2	3	4	5
0	0.5805	0.1280	0.0591	0.0170	0.0072	0.0054
1	0.0572	0.0242	0.0092	0.0051	0.0041	0.0029
2	0.0067	0.0062	0.0034	0.0031	0.0017	0.0011
3	0.0031	0.0029	0.0019	0.0022	0.0012	0.0009
4	0.0022	0.0018	0.0014	0.0012	0.0010	0.0006
5	0.0012	0.0016	0.0009	0.0011	0.0007	0.0005

E	E	C	E	E
E	D	B	D	E
C	B	A	B	C
E	D	B	D	E
E	E	C	E	E

A: 58.05%
B: 18.52%
C: 6.58%
D: 2.42%
E: 1.88%

Fig. 1 Total probability of motion vector at the same distance to the center

3.2 Improvements for TZSearch algorithm with octagon-based search pattern

In the motion estimation, the performance of search algorithm is impacted by the shape of the search pattern. Ideally, a circle-shaped pattern is the most appropriate search pattern, for the symmetrical distribution characteristic which includes the minimum number of search points and the lowest matching error. On the basis of the theory, the octagon-based search pattern [13] is used to replace the 8-point diamond pattern or 8-point square pattern in the initial search step of TZSearch algorithm. The octagon-based search pattern, which is illustrated in Fig. 2, consists of a rood pattern and an octagon pattern around the center approximating a circle. In the improved method, the rood pattern is used to determine the direction of the search. If the center is not the optimal point when searching the five points in the rood pattern, the direction from the center to the optimal point will be used in the following search. The process will be repeated until the optimal point is in the center, and the stride length of the loop should not be greater than the parameter 'iRaster', exactly as paper [9], setting a threshold to terminate the initial search in advance.

The improved process of the initial search step is as follows:

(1) Search the five points in the rood pattern while the stride length is 1. If the optimal point is the center (i.e. Point 1 in Fig. 2), the initial search is finished.

(2) If the optimal point is on the top, bottom, left or right of the center, search four points in the octagon pattern which are chosen according to the direction from the center to the optimal point. For example, if the optimal point is Point 2 in Fig. 2, search Point 6,7,8 and 9 in the octagon pattern.

(3) Multiply the stride length by 2 and repeat the above-mentioned two processes. The initial search step is finished until the stride length is greater than the parameter 'iRaster'.

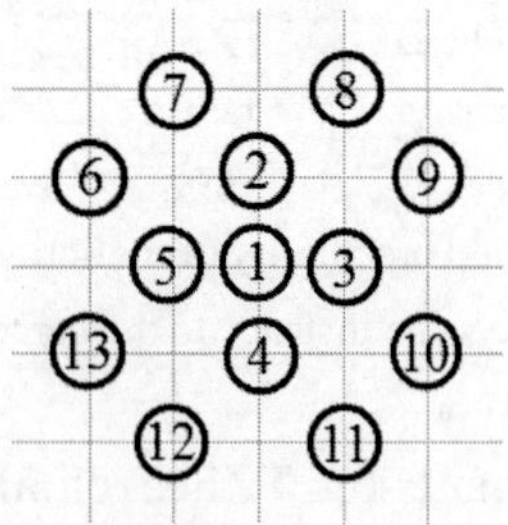

Fig. 2 Octagon-based search pattern

In the initial search step of the original TZSearch algorithm, the number of the search points can be calculated as follow (n represents search round):

$$M = 1 + 4 + 8 * (n - 1)$$

Because 58.05% of motion vectors are in the center, the number of the search points of the improved method in this paper can be calculated as follow:

$$N = 1 + \left(4 + 4 * (1 - 0.5805)\right) * n$$

The speed improvement rate (SIR) is:

$$SIR(\%) = \frac{M - N}{M} * 100\% \quad = (2.322 * n - 4) * 100\%$$

When the parameter 'iRaster' is 5, the search round is 3 (ceiling of ($\sqrt{5}$ + 1)), and the SIR is 14.12%, which means that in a 5*5 search window, 14.12 percent of the search points can be reduced which drastically speeds up the encoding.

4. Experiment results

The experiments validate the proposed improved TZSearch algorithm on the reference software JMVC8.5, running on Win 7 64-bit operating system, Intel Core i7 920@2.67 GHz, 6 GB RAM, using the standard testing sequences, ballroom, exit and vassar which are provided by MERL [14]. The parameter 'QP' adopts 24, 28, 32 and 36 separately, 'searchrange' is 64, 'GOP' is 12 and the threshold 'iRaster' is 5. All of the sequences are 25 fps and 640 * 480 frame size. Each sequence is encoded of 8 views while each view contains 100 frames. The PSNR in the experiments is calculated by the formula: PSNR = (Y-PSNR * 4 + U-PSNR + V-PSNR) / 4. The values of PSNR, bitrate, runtime and total encoding are the average of 8 views which are presented in Table 2, and the RD curves of the three sequences are illustrated in Fig. 3.

The three standard testing sequences, ballroom, exit and vassar are belong to different kinds of movement sequences. In ballroom, the movement of the background is slow while the movement of the foreground is moderate. The backgrounds of exit and vassar are both static while the foregrounds are moderate movement and rapid movement separately. In the results, it can be obviously seen that the runtime of the improved TZSearch algorithm is drastically reduced 80% and the total encoding time decreases almost 40% while the PSNR and the bitrate are approximately unchanged compared with the original TZSearch algorithm in different kinds of movement sequences.

Table 2 Comparison between the original and improved TZSearch algorithm

Sequence	QP	PSNR(dB)			Bitrate(kbps)			Runtime(sec)			Total Encoding Time(sec)		
		TZS	TZS'	ΔP	TZS	TZS'	ΔR(%)	TZS	TZS'	ΔT(%)	TZS	TZS'	ΔT(%)
ballroom	24	39.44	39.43	-0.01	1146.37	1153.46	0.62%	2555.16	605.37	-76.31%	40097	24351	-39.27%
	28	37.73	37.71	-0.02	665.51	671.57	0.91%	2431.65	543.06	-77.67%	38470	23199	-39.70%
	32	35.90	35.87	-0.02	398.39	403.74	1.34%	2299.33	474.01	-79.38%	36916	22112	-40.10%
	36	34.04	34.00	-0.04	247.21	252.07	1.97%	2146.37	397.57	-81.48%	35220	20955	-40.50%
Exit	24	40.67	40.65	-0.01	569.50	573.34	0.67%	2322.64	503.41	-78.33%	37560	22804	-39.29%
	28	39.46	39.45	-0.02	298.39	301.93	1.19%	2173.98	441.26	-79.70%	35607	21533	-39.53%
	32	38.09	38.06	-0.03	177.17	180.40	1.82%	2042.31	377.77	-81.50%	34096	20537	-39.77%
	36	36.46	36.43	-0.04	113.43	115.63	1.94%	1912.51	307.12	-83.94%	32653	19521	-40.22%
vassar	24	39.34	39.34	0.00	665.38	667.07	0.25%	1761.35	311.95	-82.29%	33092	21394	-35.35%
	28	38.07	38.07	0.00	297.12	299.97	0.96%	1597.82	267.28	-83.27%	30862	20143	-34.73%
	32	36.76	36.75	-0.01	147.23	149.03	1.23%	1457.35	229.11	-84.28%	29222	19288	-33.99%
	36	35.31	35.29	-0.02	77.74	78.82	1.39%	1331.31	196.19	-85.26%	27836	18638	-33.04%

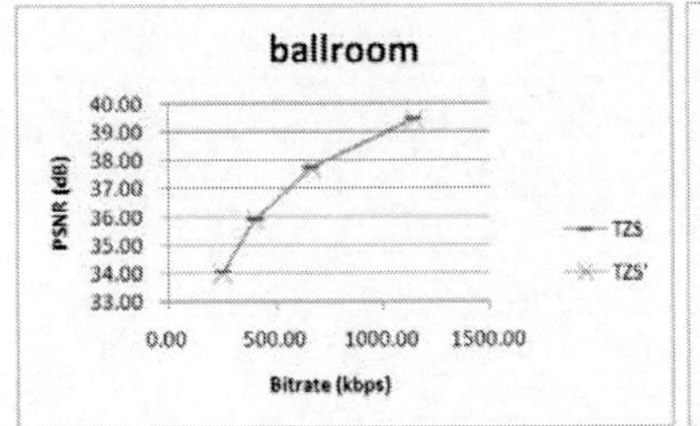

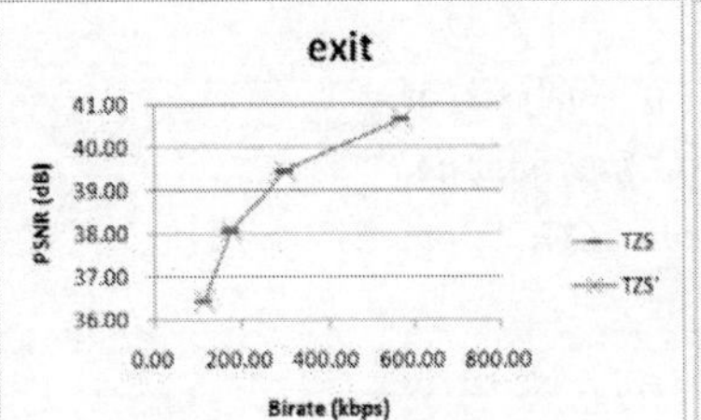

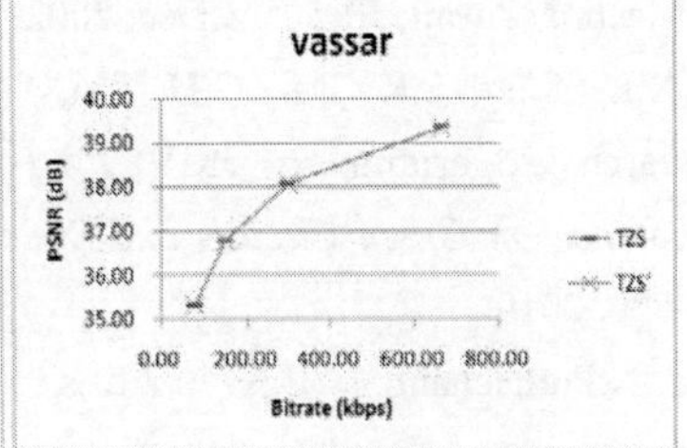

Fig. 3 RD curves of ballroom, exit and vassar

5. Conclusion

In this paper, improved methods for TZSearch algorithm are proposed to reduce the encoding time of multiview video while maintaining PSNR and bitrate. The octagon-based search pattern is adopted in the initial search step which increases the accuracy of predicting motion vector according to the directional center-biased characteristic. In addition, a threshold is set to terminate the initial search in advance. These improvements dramatically reduce the number of the search points and speed up the multiview video coding. The experimental results demonstrate that the encoding time is drastically reduced while the PSNR and the bitrate are approximately unchanged, which benefits the realization of the real time multiview video coding. Further research will be reducing the encoding time of the refinement search step of TZSearch algorithm while both PSNR and bitrate are negligible impaired.

6. Acknowledgment

This study was supported by National High-tech R&D Program of China (Grant NO. 2009AA012201), the Shanghai Leading Academic Discipline Project (Project No.J50103), and the Innovation Project of Shanghai University.

7. References

[1] A. Vetro, T. Wiegand, G.J. Sullivan, "Overview of the Stereo and Multiview Video Coding Extensions of the H.264/MPEG-4 AVC Standard," *Proceeding of IEEE SPECIAL ISSUE: 3-D Media and Displays*, vol. 99, no. 4, pp. 626-642, Apr. 2011.

[2] Y.S. Ho, K.J. Oh, "Overview of Multi-view Video Coding," *IWSSIP and EC-SIPMCS-Proc. 14th Int. Workshop on Systems, Signals and Image Processing and 6th EURASIP Conf. Focused on Speech and Image Processing, Multimedia Communications and Services*, pp. 5-12, 2007.

[3] G.J. Sullivan, T. Wiegand, H. Schwarz, "Editors' draft revision to ITU-T Rec. H.264 | ISO/IEC 14496-10 Advanced Video Coding – in preparation for ITU-T SG 16 AAP Consent," JVT-AD007, 30th Meeting: Geneva, CH, 29 Jan. – 3 Feb. 2009.

[4] H. Schwarz, T. Hinz and K. Suehring, JMVC software model Version 8.5, Mar. 2011.

[5] JVT of ISO/IEC MPEG, ITU-T VCEG, MVC software Reference Manual-JMVC 8.5, Mar. 2011.

[6] X.Z. Xu, Y. He, "Improvements on Fast Motion Estimation Strategy for H.264/AVC," *IEEE Transactions on Circuits and Systems for Video Technology*, vol. 18, no. 3, pp. 285-293, Mar. 2008.

[7] Z.B. Chen, P. Zhou, Y. He, "Fast Integer Pel and Fractional Pel Motion Estimation for JVT," JVT-F017, 6th Meeting: Awaji, JP, 5 - 13 Dec. 2002.

[8] X.L. Tang, S.K. Dai, C.H. Cai, "An Analysis of TZSearch Algorithm in JMVC," *1st International Conference on Green Circuits and Systems ICGCS*, pp. 516-520, 2010.

[9] N.Purnachand, L.N. Alves, A. Navarro, "Improvements to TZ search motion estimation algorithm for multiview video coding," *19th International Conference on Systems, Signals and Image Processing IWSSIP*, pp. 388-391, 2012.

[10] C.W. Lam, L.M. Po, C.H. Cheung, "A new cross-diamond search algorithm for fast block matching motion estimation," *Proceedings of International Conference on Neural Networks and Signal Processing ICNNSP*, vol. 2, pp. 1262-1265, 2003.

[11] H.J. Jia, L. Zhang, "Directional diamond search pattern for fast block motion estimation," *Electronics Letters*, vol. 39, no. 22, pp. 1581-1583, Nov. 2003.

[12] Y. Nie, K.K. Ma, "Adaptive rood pattern search for fast block-matching motion estimation," *IEEE Transactions on Image Processing*, vol. 11, no. 12, pp. 1442-1449, Dec. 2002.

[13] L.P. Chau, C. Zhu, "A fast octagon-based search algorithm for motion estimation," Signal Processing, vol. 83, no. 3, pp. 671-675, 2003.

[14] MERL, http://www.merl.com /pub /avetro /mvctestseq/orig-yuv /, 2009-7-10.

Robust Super-resolution for UAS Video Data

Qiang He [1]
[1]*Department of Mathematics, Computer and Information Sciences*
Mississippi Valley State University
Itta Bena, MS 38941
E-MAIL: qianghe@mvsu.edu

Chee-Hung Henry Chu[2] and Aldo Camargo[3]
[2]*The Center for Advanced Computer Studies*
University of Louisiana at Lafayette
Lafayette, LA 70504-4330
[3]*Research and Development at I+T, Lima 39*
Lima, Peru

***Abstract*—The Unmanned Aircraft Systems (UAS) have been widely applied for reconnaissance and surveillance by exploiting the information collected from the digital imaging payload. However, the analysis of real surveillance video is limited from time to time because of the constraints of imaging equipment, winds buffeting the vehicle, less than ideal atmospheric conditions, etc. As a consequence, the super-resolution (SR) on low-resolution (LR) UAS surveillance video frames, becomes a critical requirement for UAS video processing and an important pre-step for further effective image understanding. In this paper we develop a novel robust super-resolution framework which does not require the construction of sparse matrices. The proposed method implements image operations in the spatial domain and applies an iterative process to construct super-resolution images from the overlapping UAS surveillance video frames. Our method adopts the sum of forward-projection fitting errors (from SR images to LR images) and backward-projection fitting errors (from LR images to SR images) as the optimization measure. The proposed algorithm has been tested on two sets of real UAS video data and its performance is compared with those from other SR algorithms. The experimental outcomes show the good performance of the proposed algorithm in comparison with other algorithms.**

***Keywords*—Unmanned Aircraft System (UAS); iterative process; super-resolution; robust estimation**

I. INTRODUCTION

An Unmanned Aircraft System (UAS) [1] is an aircraft or ground station that can be either remote controlled manually or is capable of flying autonomously under the guidance of pre-programmed GPS waypoint flight plans or more complex onboard intelligent systems. The UAS aircrafts have recently found extensive applications in military reconnaissance and surveillance, homeland security, precision agriculture, wildlife conservation, fire monitoring and analysis, and other different kinds of aids during disasters. The different UAS missions can be conducted with surveillance videos captured by a UAS digital imaging payload over the interest areas. However, the data analysis of UAS videos is frequently limited by motion blurring, resulting from the frame-to-frame movement induced by aircraft rolling, the constraints of imaging equipment, winds buffeting the vehicle, less than ideal atmospheric conditions, the noise inherent within the image sensors, etc. As a consequence, the super-resolution (SR) on low-resolution (LR) UAS surveillance video frames, becomes a critical requirement for UAS video processing and an important pre-step for further effective image understanding.

Super-resolution image reconstruction is a technique to reconstruct a highly resolved image of a scene from one single or a series of low-resolution overlapping images based on image registration between different image frames [7,17]. By fusing several low-resolution images together, we can restore high-resolution image and thus improve imaging system performance. Four major applications for super-resolution image reconstruction are listed as follows.

1. *Automatic target recognition*: For a series of low-resolution images taken by a small Unmanned Aircraft System (UAS) flown through an interesting area, we need to perform super-resolution restoration technique to enhance image quality and automatically recognize interesting objects.
2. *Medical imaging*: In medical imaging, if several images taken for the same area are blurred because of imaging acquisition limitation, we can recover and improve the image quality through super-resolution.
3. *Remote sensing*: Remote sensing is to observe earth and predict weather based on the stand-off collected image data. We can gather information on a given object or area by increasing image resolution.
4. *Environmental monitoring*: Related to remote sensing, environmental monitoring is to determining if an event is unusual or extreme, and to developing appropriate experimental design based on monitoring data. The super-resolution can be applied to analyze monitoring data.

The super-resolution image reconstruction can be realized from single image frame [25] or from multiple image frames [2,5,8,9,10,21,22,23]. In general, the multiple-frame super-resolution image reconstruction is much useful since multiple frames provide much more information for image restoration than single frame. The super-resolution image reconstruction algorithms can be divided into two categories: super-resolution from frequency domain [22,24] and super-resolution from space domain [4,6,11,13,27] according to the between-frame motion estimation from frequency domain or from space domain.

The frequency-domain super-resolution assumes that between-frame motion is global. Hence, we can register a sequence of images through phase difference in frequency domain. The phase shift can be computed by correlation. The frequency-domain technique is effective in making use of low-frequency parts to register a set of images with aliasing artifacts inside. Aliasing artifacts result from high-frequency and cannot be handled in space domain. However, frequency domain approaches are very sensitive to motion errors. For space-domain super-resolution technique, the between-frame image registration is computed from the feature corres-pondences in space domain. The motion models can be global for the whole image or local for a set of corresponding feature vectors [3]. Zomet et al. [27] developed a robust super-resolution method. The approach uses median filter in the sequence of image gradients to iteratively update super-resolution results. It is robust to outliers but computationally expensive. Keren et al. [13] developed an algorithm using Taylor expansion on motion model extension and then simplified parameter computation. Irani et al. [11] applied local motion models in spatial space and computed between-frame multiple different motions through optical flow.

This paper proceeds as follows. Section 2 describes the modeling of super-resolution image reconstruction, including the basic modeling of general super-resolution image reconstruction and our proposed super-resolution algorithm. The experimental results are given in Section 3. We draw a conclusion for this paper in Section 4.

II. Modeling of Super-resolution Image Reconstruction

2.1 Basic Modeling of SR Image Reconstruction

Following the descriptions in [5,8], we extend the images column-wise and represent them in column vectors. We set up the linear relationship between original high resolution image $\vec{X}$ and each measured low resolution image $\vec{Y}_k$ through matrix representation. Given a sequence of low resolution images $i_1, i_2, \cdots, i_n$ (where n is the number of images), then the relationship between low resolved image $\vec{Y}_k$ and high resolved image $\vec{X}$ can be formulated with a linear system as

$$\vec{Y}_k = D_k C_k F_k \vec{X} + \vec{E}_k \text{ , for } k = 1, \cdots n \tag{1}$$

where $\vec{X}$ is the vector representation for the original highly resolved image, $\vec{Y}_k$ is the vector representation for each measured low-resolution image, $\vec{E}_k$ is the Gaussian white noise vector for measured low-resolution image i_k, F_k is the geometric warping matrix, C_k is the blurring matrix, D_k is the down-sampling matrix. Assume the original highly resolved image has dimension $p \times p$ and every low-resolution image has dimension $q \times q$. Therefore, $\vec{X}$ is a $p^2 \times 1$ vector and $\vec{Y}_k$ is a $q^2 \times 1$ vector. In general, $q \ll p$. So equation (1) is underdetermined. If we group all n equations together, we can generate an overdetermined linear system

$$\begin{bmatrix} \vec{Y}_1 \\ \vdots \\ \vec{Y}_n \end{bmatrix} = \begin{bmatrix} D_1 C_1 F_1 \\ \vdots \\ D_n C_n F_n \end{bmatrix} \vec{X} + \begin{bmatrix} \vec{E}_1 \\ \vdots \\ \vec{E}_n \end{bmatrix} . \tag{2}$$

Equivalently,

$$\mathbf{Y} = \begin{bmatrix} \mathbf{H}_1 \\ \vdots \\ \mathbf{H}_n \end{bmatrix} \vec{X} + \mathbf{E} = \mathbf{H}\vec{X} + \mathbf{E} \tag{3}$$

where

$$\mathbf{Y} = \begin{bmatrix} \vec{Y}_1 \\ \vdots \\ \vec{Y}_n \end{bmatrix}, \ \mathbf{E} = \begin{bmatrix} \vec{E}_1 \\ \vdots \\ \vec{E}_n \end{bmatrix},$$

$$\mathbf{H} = \begin{bmatrix} D_1 C_1 F_1 \\ \vdots \\ D_n C_n F_n \end{bmatrix} = \begin{bmatrix} \mathbf{H}_1 \\ \vdots \\ \mathbf{H}_n \end{bmatrix} \text{ with } \mathbf{H}_i = D_i C_i F_i$$

($i = 1, \ \cdots, \ n$).

There are three typical methods to solve this linear system [5], that is, (1) maximum likelihood (ML) estimator, (2) maximum a posteriori (MAP) probability estimator, and (3) projection onto convex sets (POCS).

2.2 Robust SR Image Reconstruction

Different from the above methods and the close work to ours, Zomet et al. [27] developed a robust super-resolution method. The approach uses median filter in the sequence of image gradients to iteratively update super-resolution results. From equation (1), the total error for super-resolution restoration in 2-norm can be represented as

$$L_2(\vec{X}) = \frac{1}{2}\sum_{k=1}^{n}\left\|\vec{Y}_k - D_k C_k F_k \vec{X}\right\|_2^2 = \frac{1}{2}\sum_{k=1}^{n}\left\|\vec{Y}_k - \mathbf{H}_k \vec{X}\right\|_2^2 . \quad (4)$$

Differentiating $L_2(\vec{X})$ with respect to $\vec{X}$, we have the gradient $\nabla L_2(\vec{X})$ of $L_2(\vec{X})$ as the sum of derivatives over input images

$$\nabla L_2(\vec{X}) = \sum_{k=1}^{n} F_k^T C_k^T D_k^T \left(D_k C_k F_k \vec{X} - \vec{Y}_k\right) = \sum_{k=1}^{n} \mathbf{H}_k^T\left(\mathbf{H}_k \vec{X} - \vec{Y}_k\right). \quad (5)$$

Where T denotes the transpose of a matrix.

Then we can perform the gradient-based iterative process to reach the minimum value of $L_2(\vec{X})$.

$$\vec{X}^{t+1} = \vec{X}^t + \lambda \nabla L_2(\vec{X}) \quad (6)$$

where λ is a scalar to define the step size of each iteration in the direction of gradient $\nabla L_2(\vec{X})$.

Instead of the summation of gradients over input images, Zomet [27] calculated n times of a scaled pixel-wise median of the gradient sequence in $\nabla L_2(\vec{X})$. That is,

$$\begin{aligned}\vec{X}^{t+1} &= \vec{X}^t + \lambda \cdot n \cdot median\{F_1^T C_1^T D_1^T \left(D_1 C_1 F_1 \vec{X}^t - \vec{Y}_1\right), \\ &\quad \cdots, F_n^T C_n^T D_n^T \left(D_n C_n F_n \vec{X}^t - \vec{Y}_n\right)\} \\ &= \vec{X}^t + \lambda \cdot n \cdot median\{\mathbf{H}_1^T\left(\mathbf{H}_1 \vec{X}^t - \vec{Y}_1\right), \cdots, \mathbf{H}_n^T\left(\mathbf{H}_n \vec{X}^t - \vec{Y}_n\right)\}\end{aligned} \quad (7)$$

where t is the iteration step number.

On one side, the median can approximate the mean quite well in a symmetric probabilistic distribution if enough samples are available. On the other side, the median can avoid the distant outliers, which is more robust than the mean.

Equation (4) is the fitting errors in the forward-projection from high-resolution (HR) images to low-resolution (LR) images. There is another fitting errors in the back-projection from low-resolution (LR) images to high-resolution (HR) images. Instead of only using the fitting errors in the forward-projection from high-resolution (HR) images to low-resolution (LR) images, we here use the sum of these two fitting errors. The fitting errors in the back-projection from low-resolution (LR) images to high-resolution (HR) images are computed from Equation (3). Since the Equation (3), $\mathbf{Y} = \mathbf{H}\vec{X} + \mathbf{E}$, is an overdetermined linear system, that is, the matrix $\mathbf{H}$ has more rows than columns and its size is $(nq^2) \times p^2$. Conducting the Singular Value Decomposition (SVD) on $\mathbf{H}$, we obtain

$$\mathbf{H} = U \Sigma V^T \quad (8)$$

Where matrix U is a $(nq^2) \times (nq^2)$ unitary matrix, the matrix Σ is a $(nq^2) \times p^2$ diagonal matrix with nonnegative real numbers on the diagonal and the nonzero values are called singular values, and matrix V is a $p^2 \times p^2$ unitary matrix. Then the pseudo-inverse $\mathbf{H}^+$ of $\mathbf{H}$ is

$$\mathbf{H}^+ = V \Sigma^+ U^T \quad (9)$$

Where Σ^+ is the transpose of Σ, but with the reciprocals of nonzero singular values on the disgonal. Then we have

$$\mathbf{H}^+ \mathbf{H} = V \Sigma^+ U^T U \Sigma V^T = \mathbf{I} \quad (10)$$

Where $\mathbf{I}$ is the identity matrix with size $p^2 \times p^2$.

Multiply the pseudo-inverse $\mathbf{H}^+$ of $\mathbf{H}$ on two side of the equation (3), we have the projection from low-resolution (LR) images to high-resolution (HR) images

$$\vec{X} = \mathbf{H}^+ \mathbf{Y} + \mathbf{E}' \quad (11)$$

Where $\mathbf{H}^+$ is the pseudo-inverse of $\mathbf{H}$ and $\mathbf{E}' = \mathbf{H}^+ \mathbf{E}$ is the corresponding Gaussian white noise vector.

The sum of fitting errors in the forward-projection from high-resolution (HR) images to low-resolution (LR) images and the back-projection from low-resolution (LR) images to high-resolution (HR) images will be adopted as the optimization measure for the overdetermined linear system

$$L_2'(\vec{X}) = \frac{1}{2}\sum_{k=1}^{n}\left\|\mathbf{H}_k \vec{X} - \vec{Y}_k\right\|_2^2 + \frac{1}{2}\left\|\vec{X} - \mathbf{H}^+ \mathbf{Y}\right\|_2^2 . \quad (12)$$

In practice, we can approximate the fitting error

$$\frac{1}{2}\left\|\vec{X} - \mathbf{H}^+ \mathbf{Y}\right\|_2^2 \approx \frac{1}{2}\sum_{k=1}^{n}\left\|\vec{X} - \mathbf{upsample}(\vec{Y}_k)\right\|_2^2 . \quad (13)$$

Where $\mathbf{upsample}(.)$ is the up-sampling operation on low-resolution images.

Then the optimization measure becomes as

$$L_2'(\vec{X}) = \frac{1}{2}\sum_{k=1}^{n}\left\|\mathbf{H}_k\vec{X} - \vec{Y}_k\right\|_2^2 + \frac{1}{2}\sum_{k=1}^{n}\left\|\vec{X} - \mathbf{upsample}(\vec{Y}_k)\right\|_2^2 \tag{14}$$

Take the differentiation on $L_2'(\vec{X})$, we have

$$\begin{aligned}\nabla L_2'(\vec{X}) &= \sum_{k=1}^{n}\left[\mathbf{H}_k^T\left(\mathbf{H}_k\vec{X} - \vec{Y}_k\right)\right] + \sum_{k=1}^{n}\left[\vec{X} - \mathbf{upsample}(\vec{Y}_k)\right] \\ &= \sum_{k=1}^{n}\left\{\mathbf{H}_k^T\left(\mathbf{H}_k\vec{X} - \vec{Y}_k\right)\right] + \left[\vec{X} - \mathbf{upsample}(\vec{Y}_k)\right]\right\}\end{aligned} \tag{15}$$

Instead of the summation of gradients over input images, we calculated n times of the median for the gradient sequence of $\nabla L_2(\vec{X})$. That is,

$$\begin{aligned}\vec{X}^{t+1} = \vec{X}^t + \lambda \cdot n \cdot median\Big\{&\left[\mathbf{H}_1^T\left(\mathbf{H}_1\vec{X}^t - \vec{Y}_1\right)\right] + \\ &\left[\vec{X}^t - \mathbf{upsample}(\vec{Y}_1)\right], \cdots, \\ &\left[\mathbf{H}_n^T\left(\mathbf{H}_n\vec{X}^t - \vec{Y}_n\right)\right] + \left[\vec{X}^t - \mathbf{upsample}(\vec{Y}_n)\right]\Big\}\end{aligned} \tag{16}$$

2.3 Motion Estimation

As required in most super-resolution approaches, the very important step is image registration between additional frames and the reference frame. Here we apply the sub-pixel motion estimation [13,19] to estimate between-frame motion. If the between-frames motions are determined mostly by translation and rotation (that is, the affine model), then the Keren motion estimation [13] presents a good performance. The motions between images taken from an aircraft or a satellite can be well approximated with this model.

In mathematical representation, the Keren motion model can be formulated as

$$\begin{pmatrix} x' \\ y' \end{pmatrix} = s\begin{pmatrix} \cos(\theta) & -\sin(\theta) \\ \sin(\theta) & \cos(\theta) \end{pmatrix}\begin{pmatrix} x \\ y \end{pmatrix} + \begin{pmatrix} a \\ b \end{pmatrix} \tag{17}$$

where θ is the rotation angle, and a and b are translations along directions x and y, respectively. s is the scaling factor. x$'$ and y' are registered coordinates of x and y in the reference coordinate system.

III. EXPERIMENTAL RESULTS

The algorithm is tested on two sets of real data. The real video data were captured by an experimental small Unmanned Aircraft Systems (UASs) operated by Lockheed Martin Corporation flying a custom-built electro-optical (EO) and uncooled thermal infrared (IR) imager. The time series of images are extracted from the UAS videos with low-resolution 60 x 80.

In comparison with five well-known super-resolution algorithms on real UAS video tests, namely the robust super-resolution algorithm [27], bi-cubic interpolation, projection onto convex sets (POCS) [20], the Papoulis-Gerchberg algorithm [9,16], and the iterated back projection algorithm [10], our presented algorithm proved to give both strong efficiency and robustness as well as good visual performance. For low resolution 60 by 80 image sequences with five frames in every image sequence, the super-resolution restoration with scaling factors 2 and 4 can be implemented very efficiently (approximately real-time processing). In addition, it presents very good visual performance. Our algorithm was developed using MATLAB and was performed in nearly real time. We implemented our algorithm on a Dell Optiplex 960 workstation with an Intel Core 2 Duo CPU running at 3.32 GHz and 3.33 GHz and a 3.25 GB RAM. If we ported the algorithm into the C programming language, the algorithm would execute much more quickly.

Test data taken from small UAS aircraft are highly susceptible to vibration and sensor pointing movements. Therefore, the super-resolution image reconstruction is necessary for further image understanding tasks. The experimental results for the first data set are given in Figure 1 and 2. The experimental results for the second data set are displayed in Figures 3 and 4. In comparison with the experimental outcomes from other algorithms, our proposed algorithm provides the best visual performance. There are obvious artifacts in the constructed SR images from other SR reconstruction algorithms, in particular, from the iterated back projection algorithm, the Papoulis Gerchberg algorithm, and the robust super-resolution algorithm. However, the influence of artifacts is considerably reduced in our proposed algorithm.

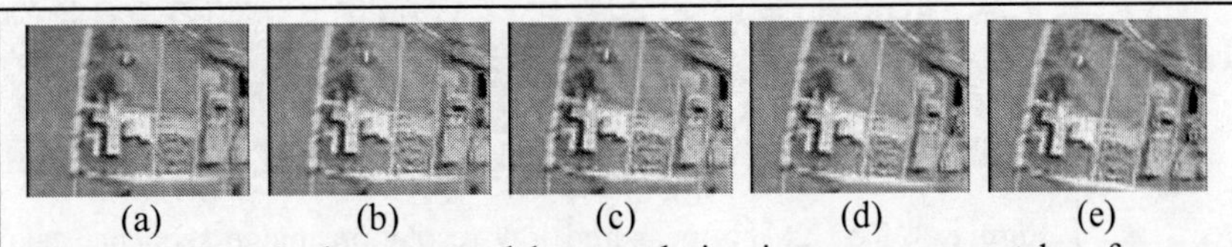

(a) (b) (c) (d) (e)

Figure 1. Test 1: the measured low resolution image sequence taken from an UAS. (a), (b), (c), (d), and (e) are five typical images. The resolution is 60 by 80.

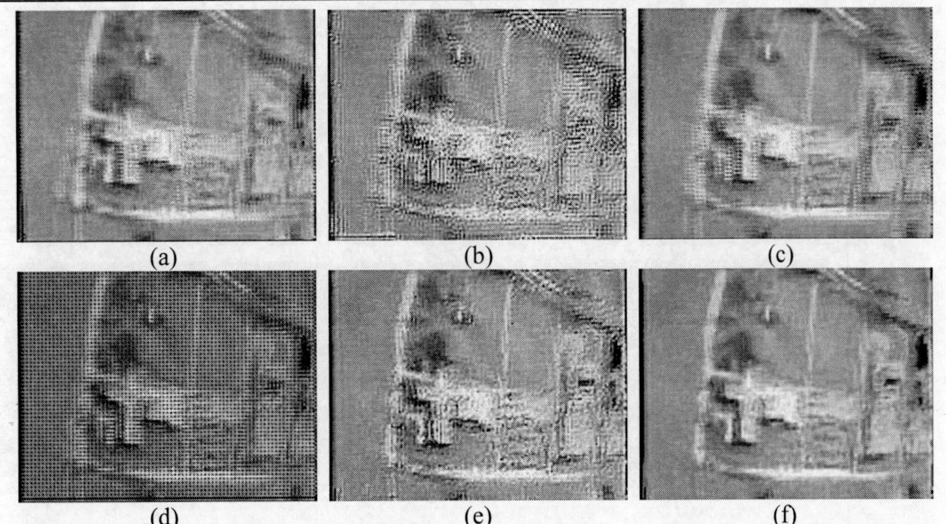

(a) (b) (c)

(d) (e) (f)

Figure 2. Test 1: super resolved images with factor 2. (a) is the super-resolved image through bicubic interpolation. (b) is the super-resolved image through iterated back projection algorithm. (c) is the super-resolved image through Projection On Convex Sets(POCS) algorithm. (d) is the super-resolved image through Papoulis Gerchberg algorithm. (e) is the super-resolved image through robust super-resolution algorithm. (f) is the super-resolved image through our method.

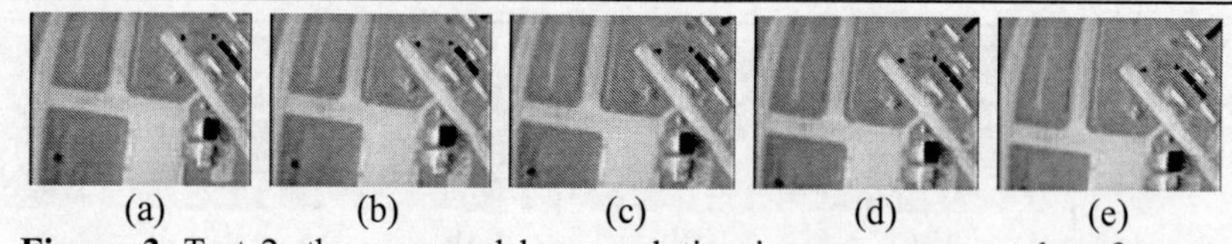

(a) (b) (c) (d) (e)

Figure 3. Test 2: the measured low resolution image sequence taken from an UAS. (a), (b), (c), (d), and (e) are five typical images. The resolution is 60 by 80.

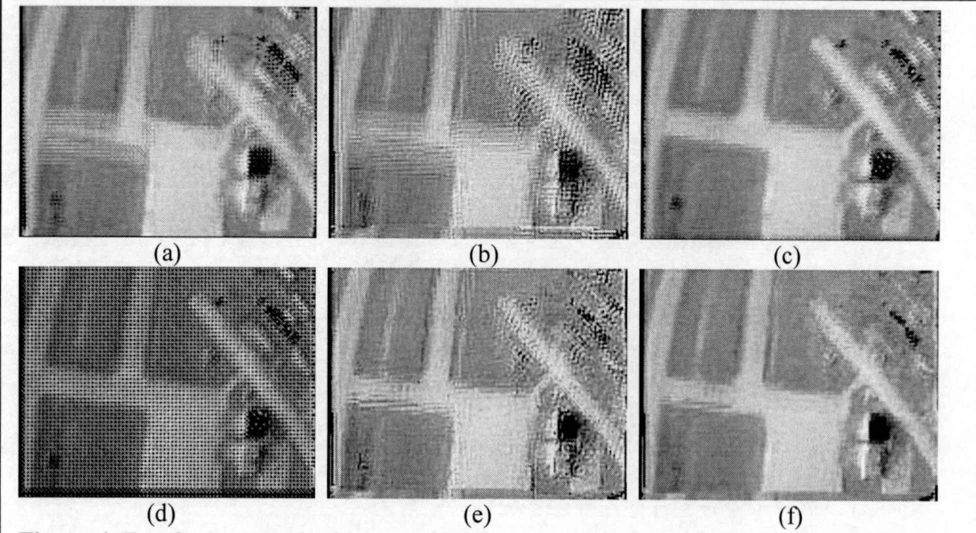

(a) (b) (c)

(d) (e) (f)

Figure 4. Test 2: super resolved images with factor 2. (a) is the super-resolved image through bicubic interpolation. (b) is the super-resolved image through iterated back projection algorithm. (c) is the super-resolved image through Projection On Convex Sets(POCS) algorithm. (d) is the super-resolved image through Papoulis Gerchberg algorithm. (e) is the super-resolved image through robust super-resolution algorithm. (f) is the super-resolved image through our method.

IV. CONCLUSION

Here we present an efficient and robust super-resolution restoration method. In comparison with other popular super-resolution restoration approaches, our algorithm not only is robust, but also present good visual performance. We will explore the quantity analysis on the algorithm efficiency and performance in the future work. Synthetic data may be applied in the future tests since it is hard for us to obtain ground truth outcome for the real test data. In addition, we plan to try other motion model like planar homography and see whether we can obtain better performance.

REFERENCES

[1] R. K. Barnhart, S. B. Hottman, D. M. Marshall, and E. Shappee. Introduction to Unmanned Aircraft Systems. CRC Press, 1 edition, October 25, 2011.

[2] S. Borman and R. Stevenson. Spatial resolution enhancement of low-resolution image sequences - a comprehensive review with directions for future research. University of Notre Dame, Tech. Rep., 1998.

[3] D. Capel and A. Zisserman. Computer vision applied to super resolution. *IEEE Signal Processing Magazine*, vol. 20, no. 3, pp. 75–86, May 2003.

[4] M. C. Chiang and T. E. Boulte. Efficient super-resolution via image warping. *Image Vis. Comput.*, vol. 18, no. 10, pp. 761–771, July 2000.

[5] M. Elad and A. Feuer. Restoration of single super-resolution image from several blurred, noisy and down-sampled measured images. *IEEE Trans. Image Processing*, vol. 6, pp. 1646–1658, Dec. 1997.

[6] M. Elad and Y. Hel-Or. A fast super-resolution reconstruction algorithm for pure translational motion and common space invariant blur. *IEEE Trans. Image Processing*, vol. 10, pp. 1187–1193, Aug. 2001.

[7] S. Farsiu, D. Robinson, M. Elad, and P. Milanfar. Advances and Challenges in Super-Resolution. *International Journal of Imaging Systems and Technology*, Special Issue on High Resolution Image Reconstruction, vol. 14, no. 2, pp. 47-57, August 2004.

[8] S. Farsiu, D. Robinson, M. Elad, and P. Milanfar. Fast and Robust Multi-frame Super-resolution. *IEEE Transactions on Image Processing,* vol. 13, no. 10, pp. 1327-1344, October 2004.

[9] R.W. Gerchberg. Super-resolution through error energy reduction. *Optica Acta* 21(9), pp. 709-720, 1974.

[10] M. Irani and S. Peleg. Super Resolution From Image Sequences. *International Conference on Pattern Recognition*, 2:115--120, June 1990.

[11] M. Irani, B. Rousso, and S. Peleg. Computing occluding and transparent motions. *International Journal of Computer Vision*, vol. 12, no. 1, pp. 5–16, February 1994.

[12] M. Irani and S. Peleg. Improving resolution by image registration. *CVGIP: Graph. Models Image Processing*, vol. 53, pp. 231–239, 1991.

[13] D. Keren, S. Peleg, and R. Brada. Image sequence enhancement using sub-pixel displacements. In *Proceedings of IEEE Computer Society Conference on Computer Vision and Pattern Recognition (CVPR '88)*, pp. 742–746, Ann Arbor, Mich, USA, June 1988.

[14] R. L. Lagendijk and J. Biemond. *Iterative Identification and Restoration of Images*. Boston, MA: Kluwer, 1991.

[15] N. Nguyen, P. Milanfar, and G. H. Golub. A computationally efficient image superresolution algorithm. *IEEE Trans. Image Processing*, vol. 10, pp. 573–583, Apr. 2001.

[16] A. Papoulis. A New Algorithm in Spectral Analysis and Band-Limited Extrapolation. *IEEE Transactions on Circuits and Systems* 22(9), pp. 735-742, 1975.

[17] S. C. Park, M. K. Park, and M. G. Kang. Super-resolution image reconstruction: A technical overview. *IEEE Signal Processing Magazine*, vol. 20, no. 3, pp. 21–36, May 2003.

[18] S. Peleg, D. Keren, and L. Schweitzer. Improving image resolution using subpixel motion. *CVGIP: Graph. Models Image Processing,* vol. 54, pp. 181–186, Mar. 1992.

[19] R. R. Schultz, L. Meng, and R. L. Stevenson. Subpixel motion estimation for super-resolution image sequence enhancement. *Journal of Visual Communication and Image Representation*, vol. 9, no. 1, pp. 38–50, 1998.

[20] H. Stark and P. Oskoui. High-resolution image recovery from image-plane arrays using convex projections. *Journal of the Optical Society of America, Series A*, vol. 6, pp. 1715-1726, Nov., 1989.

[21] H. S. Stone, M. T. Orchard, E.-C. Chang, and S. A. Martucci. A fast direct Fourier-based algorithm for sub-pixel registration of images. *IEEE Transactions on Geoscience and Remote Sensing*, vol. 39, no. 10, pp. 2235–2243, October 2001.

[22] R. Y. Tsai and T. S. Huang. Multiframe image restoration and registration. In *Advances in Computer Vision and Image Processing*, vol. 1, chapter 7, pp. 317–339, JAI Press, Greenwich, Conn, USA, 1984.

[23] H. Ur and D. Gross. Improved resolution from sub-pixel shifted pictures. *CVGIP: Graph. Models Image Processing*, vol. 54, no. 181–186, Mar. 1992.

[24] P. Vandewalle, S. Susstrunk,and M. Vetterli. A Frequency Domain Approach to Registration of Aliased Images with Application to Super-Resolution. EURASIP Journal on Applied Signal Processing Volume 2006, Article ID 71459, Pages 1–14.

[25] J. Yang, J.Wright, T. Huang, and Y. Ma. Image Super-resolution via Sparse Representation. IEEE Transactions on Image Processing (TIP), pp. 2861-2873, vol. 19, issue 11, May, 2010.

[26] B. Zitova and J. Flusser. Image registration methods: a survey. *Image and Vision Computing*, vol. 21, no. 11, pp. 977–1000, 2003.

[27] A. Zomet, A. Rav-Acha, and S. Peleg. Robust superresolution. In *Proceedings of IEEE Computer Society Conferenceon Computer Vision and Pattern Recognition (CVPR '01)*, vol. 1, pp. 645–650, Kauai, Hawaii, USA, December 2001.

Mathematical Recognition Problems of Particle Flow Characteristics by Video Sequence Images

Alexander P. Buslaev[1], **Andrew V. Provorov**[2], **Marina V. Yashina**[2]
[1]Department of Mathematics, Moscow State Automobile and Road Tech. University, Russia
[2]Department of Mathematical Cybernetics, Moscow Tech. University of Communications and Informatics, Russia

Abstract— *The paper is devoted to recognition methods of similar moving particles combined in laminar flow. It is important to obtain data about intensity, velocity and density changes of visible traffic flow areas on image. Video stream from the camera with a fixed angle is received. Algorithms allows to determine the semantics of the image is proposed.*

In this paper the problem of optimal placement of virtual detectors, definition of flow characteristics and automatic control of flow behavior at the crossroads is considered.

We present an effective algorithm for the solution of these problems.

Keywords: image processing, virtual detectors, multidimensional signal, laminar flow, variation of function, flow characteristics

1. Introduction

We have a sequence of video frames, that were made by using usual cameras with frequency about 25 frames per second. Camera has constant angle and can fix certain particles movement. Particles are identified by eye, their movements can be described by laminar flows.

Laminar flow is a stream of particles without mixing and ripple.

In this case, there are no abrupt changes in the rate, regarded as a vector, either in magnitude or direction. In contrast to laminar flow, turbulent flow involves disordered unsteady flow with vigorous stirring. The classical model of the flow is the Navier-Stokes equations with Reynolds R_e parameter, transition through which corresponds as a model of transition from laminar to turbulent flow.

Laminar flow properties is used to create algorithms for image processing and recognition. These methods can be applied, for example, into intelligent processing of video streams of pedestrians, shoal of fishes, vehicles, cells under a microscope (Fig.1, 2), etc.

Most easily to get video of traffic flows, so we will use this type of particles to illustrate the algorithms of video-processing.

2. Image Depth

The basic notion of semantic image analysis is the depth. Fig.3 (a) shows a laminar flow of vehicles on frontal view

(a) (b)

Fig. 1: Laminar flow of pedestrians (a) and fishes (b)

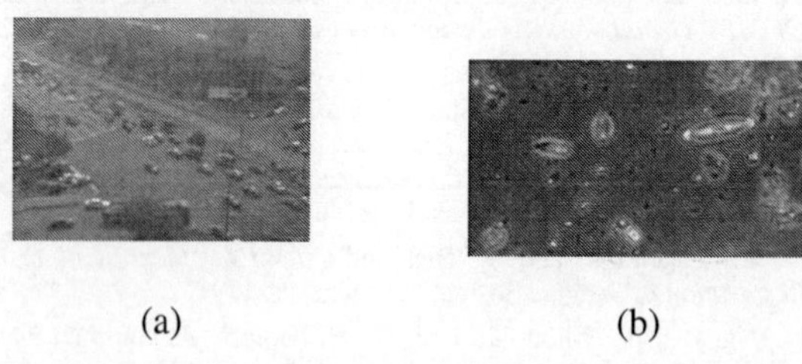

(a) (b)

Fig. 2: Laminar flow of vehicles (a) and biological cells (b)

from the top. This image has constant depth, so processing using the uniform partition Fig.3 (b).

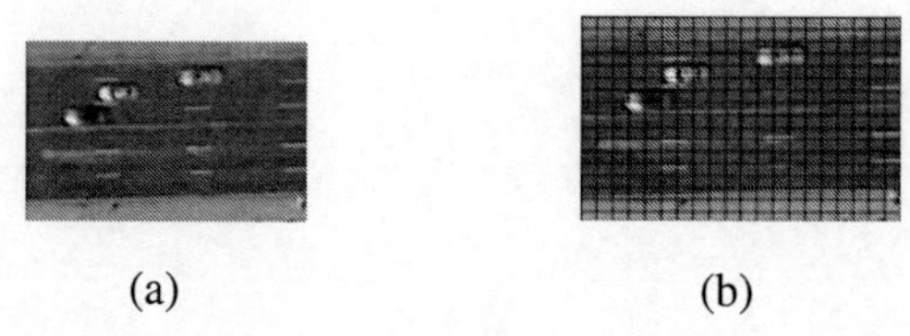

(a) (b)

Fig. 3: Constant depth

Using methods of virtual detectors [5, 6] for video of laminar traffic flow (Fig.4) we get a signal of color intensity.

3. Grid partition for image with nonconstant depth

Flow characteristics performed by video sequence from the fixed angle in the case of nonconstant image depth (Fig.4). The image, obtained by the decomposition of the

Fig. 4: Video of laminar flow with virtual detector

grid, is imposed on the frames, parameters of which correspond to an equal-area. Average intensity of the color in each cell is fixed.

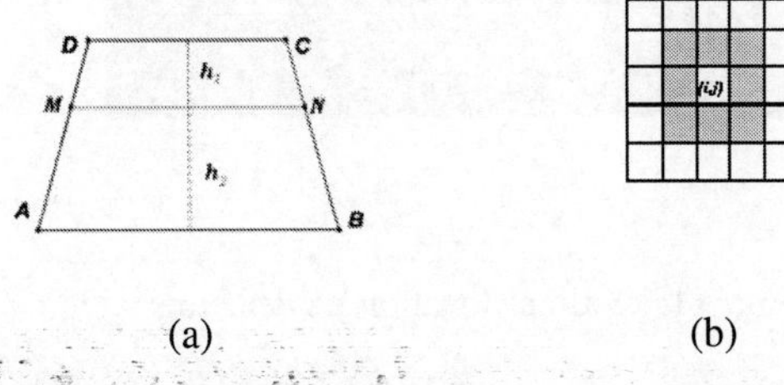

(a) (b)

Fig. 5: Trapezoid (a) and close cells of partition (b)

The method of partition consists of the following. Let q be a ratio of the top to the bottom base of the trapezoid, Fig.5 (a).

$$aq^n = b, q = \left(\frac{b}{a}\right)^{\frac{1}{n}} \quad (1)$$

Then

$$H = h_1 + h_2 + \ldots + h_n = h_1 + qh_1 + \ldots + q^n h_1 \quad (2)$$

and,

$$h_1 = \frac{1 - q^n}{1 - q} H \quad (3)$$

So the vertical coordinates of the trapezoids (Fig.5) are found from

$$y_{k+1} = y_k - h_1 q^k, \; k = 0, \ldots, n-1. \quad (4)$$

That we get a field of virtual detectors, Fig.6.

4. Multidimensional signal from field of detectors

If (i, j) is number of grid cell (Fig.5, b), we fix the average value of color intensity on the cell f_{ij}. For each i and j the variation of function is calculated:

Fig. 6: Grid partition with variable depth

Fig. 7: Two detectors

$$Var_0^N(f_{i,j}) = \sum_{k=0}^{N} |f_{i,j}(k+1) - f_{i,j}(k)|. \quad (5)$$

Then we get mapping of grey scale:

$$[\min_{i,j}\{Var_0^N(f_{i,j})\}, \max_{i,j}\{Var_0^N(f_{i,j})\}] \to [0, 255] \quad (6)$$

Thus, we get a signal from any detectors on the field. Consider some of cells on the grid partition on image with various depth, these detectors denote A and B (fig.7). Fig.8. shows the signals from detector A (a) and detector B (b) respectively.

If signal from virtual detector is about to constant, we determine it as a noise (Fig.9). Field of detectors generate *the multidimensional signal of the video sequence.*

5. Recovery of trajectory bundles and estimation of flow intensity and density

The algorithms of video analysis for density and intensity evaluations of laminar flow are developed. Every noticeable peak of signal is equal to fix one of particles.

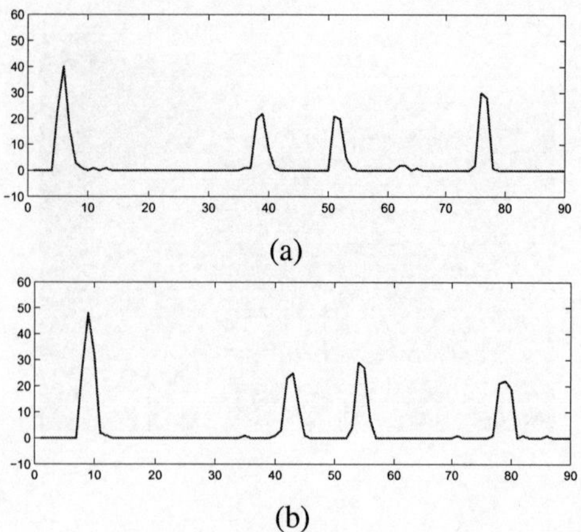

Fig. 8: Signal from virtual detector A (a) and B (b)

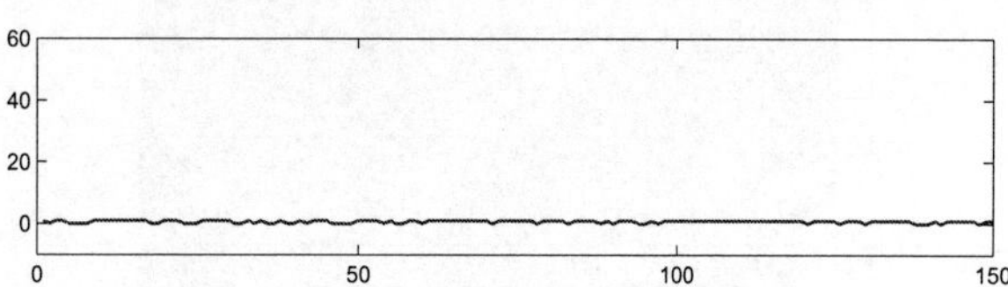

Fig. 9: Noise signal from the detector

So let function $U(t,x,y)$ be a value of color intensity on the field of detectors.

$$\frac{dU}{dt} = U((k+1)\Delta t, x, y) - U(k\Delta t, x, y) = \Delta U_t(t, x, y)$$

Let consider the second difference

$$\Delta_t^2 U = U((k+2)\Delta t, x, y) - 2U((k+1)\Delta t, x, y) + U(k\Delta t, x, y) \quad (7)$$

(a) (b)

Fig. 10: Laminar flow of vehicles (a) and bundle of trajektories (b)

$$\Longrightarrow$$

$$U(t+1, x, y) = \Delta^1 U + \Delta^0 U \quad (8)$$

$$U(t+2, x, y) = \Delta^2 U + \Delta^1 U + \Delta^0 U \quad (9)$$

By changing the parameters of the trapezoid: number sensors on the horizontal and vertical vertices of the trapezoid, we can achieve the high accuracy of evaluation, carry out various flows video and a lot of points of view.

Fig. 11: Optimal location of detectots

The procedure for the cluster through successive detectors determines the trajectory of the cluster.

6. Optimal placement of detectors

Analyzing the trajectory we solve the problem of optimal placement of detectors.

For identifying moving cluster joined to nearby cells width signs of movement.

Recognition parameters determine recognition quality. We carried out empirical estimations in the fields of bundles detection, lanes detection and road network recovery.

This method can be used for research of the changeable modes of flow. For example the flows on the crossroads we can estimate the mode time by video.

Analyzed specially constructed field of virtual detectors is a discrete function of two variables. Formulated algorithmically accurate decision rules that allow automatically to recover the network, the carriers of these flows and determine the behavior of flows. In particular, the most important problem is to recovery the matrix of flows mixing in the nodes of a planar graph as a function of time (Fig.12).

This information is necessary for an adequate model of the flow dynamics in complex physical networks with saturation and prevent congestion and also for the automatic identification of sources and sinks of flows on these networks.

(a) (b)

Fig. 12: Flows on crossroads

7. Conclusion & Future work

Experimental studies are conducted on the basis of the mobile laboratory of its own design, equipped with a special system of monitoring and processing on the computer and smartphones using the SSSR-traffic system [10].

The considered approach allows to quantify the measure mixing area of turbulence for different configurations of the flow support and optimize the movement by on-line control.

As next goal we investigate a transition from a laminar flow to a turbulent one. This process for traffic flow is reflected in lane change of vehicles. In the further we plan to apply the algorithms using the field detectors for the estimation of number of lane change of vehicles by video sequence images.

References

[1] R. O. Duda, P. E Hart. *Pattern Classification and Scene Analysis.* John Wiley & Sons, Inc., 1973.

[2] G.Bradski, A.Kaehler. *Learning OpenCV*, O'Really Media, Inc. (2008).

[3] Vehicular Networks. From Theory to Practice. Edited by Stephan Oariu and Michele C.Weigle. Chapman and Hall/CRC, 2009, – 472.

[4] R. Cucchiara, M. Piccardi, P. Mello. Image analysis and rule-based reasoning for a traffic monitoring system. IEEE Transactions on Intelligent Transportation Systems - TITS , vol. 1, no. 2, pp. 119-130, 2000. DOI: 10.1109/6979.880969

[5] A. P. Buslaev, M. V. Yashina. Virtual detectors, transformation and application to pattern recognition problems. In proc.: computational and mathematical methods in science and engineering (CMMSE2010), Eds. J.Vigo-Aguiar, Vol.1 (2010), p.213-217.

[6] A. P. Buslaev, M. V. Yashina, I. S. Kotovich. On problems of intelligent monitoring for traffic. Logic Journal of the IGPL/ //Neuro-symbolic algorithms and models for bio-inspired systems. (2011), v. 19(2), 384-394.

[7] Buslaev A.P., Dorgan V.V., Prikhodko V.M., Travkin V.Ur., Yashina M.V., *Image recognition and monitoring of road pavement, traffic flows and movement safety factors*, Vestnik MADI(STU), No 4, (2005) 102–109 (In Russian)

[8] A. P. Buslaev, A. V. Provorov, M. V. Yashina. Traffic and distributed information-calculated networks. Problems and solutions. Part 1-2. Traffic and positioning. – M., Techpoligrafcentr, 2011, – 263 p.

[9] Herman, R., Montroll, E.W., Potts, R.B., Rothery, R.W., 1959. Traffic dynamics: analysis of stability in car-following. Operations Research 7 (1), 86–106.

[10] A.V. Provorov. On algorithms and software for traffic intelligent systems using SSSR mobile devices system. *Proc. of 12th International Conference on Computational and Mathematical Methods in Science and Engineering*, 2012.

Scale-Accurate 3D Vehicle Point Cloud Extraction from Single-Camera Traffic Video

Jędrzej Kowalczuk, Eric T. Psota, and Lance C. Pérez
Department of Electrical Engineering, University of Nebraska, Lincoln, NE, U.S.A.

Abstract—*Reliable data extraction is essential to achieving a high-level understanding of the processes ongoing in the traffic environment. The ability to extract 3D structural properties of vehicles enables advanced traffic analysis such as vehicle classification and the detection of traffic rule violations, accidents, and near-collisions. A novel method is presented for extracting 3D structural properties of moving vehicles using a single camera. This method operates by tracking features of the vehicle as it travels through the camera's field of view. Two-frame structure from motion is then used to extract a 3D point cloud representing the structure of the vehicle. In addition, a robust pose estimation algorithm is given for relating the geometry of the street surface to the position of the camera with minimal user interaction. It is shown that the resulting 3D point cloud can be used to accurately approximate the dimensions of vehicles to within a half foot of their true dimensions.*

Keywords: Traffic camera, 3D reconstruction, structure from motion, pose estimation, bundle adjustment.

1. Introduction

Image processing is often used to detect low-level traffic events. These low-level events include vehicle velocity and traffic flow rate estimation by counting cars that enter and exit the camera's field of view. Methods for low-level traffic event detection typically rely on some form of background subtraction and frame-to-frame tracking of binary connected components. While basic traffic data can be extracted from a 2D projection of the video frames to the street plane, extracting information regarding the 3D structure of vehicles is a much more challenging problem to computer vision researchers.

Within the intelligent transport systems (ITS) research field, a large volume of research has been focused on automated event detection and data extraction from traffic video [1]. As the cost of video-capture hardware continues to decrease, there has been an increased number of traffic video monitoring systems deployed for both red light enforcement and traffic flow analysis. These systems, combined with the decreasing cost and increasing capacity of digital storage, have made it possible to obtain an abundance of traffic video. However, analysis and understanding of traffic behaviors create a need for reliable data extraction from traffic video, which preferably requires minimal user interaction. Examples of data that are commonly extracted from traffic video include traffic flow rate, vehicle velocities, traffic violations, and the presence of roadway debris.

To address the need for automated high-level data extraction towards sophisticated traffic video analysis, a novel method is presented for recovering scale-accurate structural properties of moving vehicles in the form of 3D point clouds. This method integrates the constraints governing vehicular motion into the process of structure recovery and motion estimation from single-camera traffic video. It is expected that the proposed method will lead to more robust traffic video analysis, a better understanding of traffic behavior, and improved driver safety.

2. Background

A variety of methods exist for extracting data from traffic video. These methods are thoroughly reviewed in the excellent survey paper by Buch et al. [1]. Most often, traffic video is processed using a common series of stages, arguably the most important of which is background subtraction used to isolate moving vehicles from a relatively stable environment. Several factors make background subtraction a challenging task including the slowly varying angle of sunlight, cloud movement, shadows created by vehicles, non-rigid objects (e.g., foliage), image sensor noise, and photometric variations [1], [2], [3]. Methods that have been shown to be effective for estimating background include the approximation of slowly varying pixel-level Gaussian intensity distributions [4], and the detection and removal of shadows [5].

Given traffic video captured from a small angle of incidence with respect to the street plane, detecting the presence of vehicles and estimating their velocities is a relatively straightforward task once foreground and background have been separated. In contrast, urban environments are more difficult to analyze since their associated traffic video is typically obtained from a larger angle of incidence [1]. In addition, tasks such as automatic classification of vehicles, detection of illegal turns, lane changes, and accidents are difficult to achieve using vision-based traffic analysis. Many approaches to performing vehicle classification use precomputed 3D models of the vehicle types they are trying to identify [6]. The most common approach is to orient a projection of the 3D model in the scene in such a way that it accurately matches the silhouette provided by background subtraction. Along this line, simple wireframe approximations of automobile types have recently been proposed to simultaneously identify vehicle type and 3D pose from single-camera video [7].

One significant limitation of the model-based vehicle classification schemes is that they rely on precomputed 3D models and exhaustive orientation search in order to fit the model to

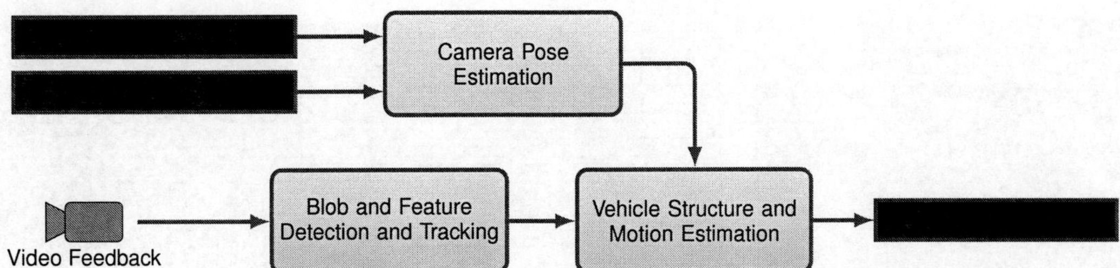

Fig. 1: The proposed traffic video processing pipeline.

the vehicle extracted from the video sequence. The method presented in [8] addresses this limitation by incorporating unsupervised learning in order to adapt basic vehicle templates to specific vehicle models from video sequences. It has been suggested that stereo video can be used to improve vehicle classification due to the fact that stereo video processing enables 3D structure recovery [1]. Results given in [9] demonstrate that reliable vehicle classification can be achieved using a stereo vision-based feature extraction method for computing 3D properties of vehicles. The primary advantage of stereo video lies in the fact that 3D structure can be computed at a single instant in time and that structural data can be fit to known models using common 3D-to-3D registration techniques, such as the orthogonal Procrustes algorithm [10] and iterative closest point [11].

3. Method

The proposed method assumes that the camera has been calibrated, i.e., internal camera parameters (focal length and principal point offset) are known prior to processing of video feedback. It is also assumed that the user has defined a plane of known geometry within the view of the camera associated with the surface of the street. These two inputs are necessary to recover the relative position and orientation (pose) of the camera with respect to the street. After recovering the pose of the camera, a sequence of operations including blob detection and tracking followed by feature detection and matching, and two-frame structure and motion estimation with bundle adjustment are performed to extract a scale-accurate 3D point cloud representing the sparse structure of each vehicle moving through the field of view. The complete traffic video processing pipeline is shown in Figure 1. In the following, the processing pipeline and its stages are described in detail.

3.1 Camera Pose Estimation

Knowledge of a precise mapping between the camera coordinate system and the world coordinate system is essential for reliable recovery of 3D structure of vehicles within the view of the camera. This mapping is used to resolve the scale ambiguity inherent in single camera structure from motion, under the assumption that vehicle motion occurs along the street plane and the camera position and orientation are fixed.

To obtain the mapping from world to camera coordinates, the user must first select a set of four coplanar street points with known world coordinates, as illustrated in Figure 2(a). Using the four street plane coordinates and their corresponding image points, it is possible to accurately approximate the pose of the camera relative to the street plane, where the orientation of the camera is represented by a 3×3 rotation matrix $\boldsymbol{R}$ and its position is represented by a 3D vector $\boldsymbol{C}$. The pose is derived using an extension of the perspective 4-point algorithm introduced in [12].

Given the internal camera calibration matrix $\boldsymbol{K}$, the homogeneous image points $\boldsymbol{x} = [x, y, 1]^{\mathsf{T}}$, and their corresponding locations on the street plane $\boldsymbol{X} = [X, Y, 0, 1]^{\mathsf{T}}$ (under the assumption that the street plane lies on the XY-plane with $Z = 0$), the mapping from world coordinates to image points is given by

$$\boldsymbol{x} \cong \boldsymbol{K}[\boldsymbol{R} \mid -\boldsymbol{RC}]\boldsymbol{X} = \boldsymbol{K}[\boldsymbol{r}_1\ \boldsymbol{r}_2 \mid -\boldsymbol{RC}]\overline{\boldsymbol{X}} \quad (1)$$

where $\boldsymbol{R}$ is the rotation matrix with columns $\boldsymbol{r}_1$, $\boldsymbol{r}_2$, $\boldsymbol{r}_3$ representing the orientation of the camera, vector $\boldsymbol{C}$ holds the 3D coordinate of the camera center, and $\overline{\boldsymbol{X}} = [X, Y, 1]^{\mathsf{T}}$ is the world coordinate vector with Z removed. Left-multiplying both sides of Equation (1) by $\boldsymbol{K}^{-1}$ results in

$$\boldsymbol{K}^{-1}\boldsymbol{x} = [\boldsymbol{r}_1\ \boldsymbol{r}_2 \mid -\boldsymbol{RC}]\overline{\boldsymbol{X}} \quad (2)$$

where the 3×3 transformation matrix $\boldsymbol{T} = [\boldsymbol{r}_1\ \boldsymbol{r}_2 \mid -\boldsymbol{RC}]$ can be solved for using the DLT algorithm (Algorithm 4.1 in [13]). Under ideal conditions, the first two columns $\boldsymbol{r}_1$ and $\boldsymbol{r}_2$ should both have unit norm and be orthogonal to each other. However, since the method given in [12] does not guarantee that $\boldsymbol{T}$ will maintain these properties under realistic conditions, a valid orthogonal rotation matrix $\boldsymbol{R}$ can be constructed using

$$\begin{aligned} \boldsymbol{T} &\leftarrow \frac{\boldsymbol{T}}{||\boldsymbol{r}_1||} && (3) \\ \boldsymbol{r}_3 &= \frac{\boldsymbol{r}_1 \times \boldsymbol{r}_2}{||\boldsymbol{r}_1 \times \boldsymbol{r}_2||} && (4) \\ \boldsymbol{r}_2 &= \boldsymbol{r}_3 \times \boldsymbol{r}_1 && (5) \\ \boldsymbol{R} &= [\boldsymbol{r}_1\ \boldsymbol{r}_2\ \boldsymbol{r}_3], && (6) \end{aligned}$$

and the associated camera center can then be computed as $\boldsymbol{C} = -\boldsymbol{R}^{\mathsf{T}}\boldsymbol{r}_3$. Due to point selection error and image coordinate quantization, the pose parameters obtained using this method require further refinement.

The initial pose estimate is refined using the Levenberg-Marquardt algorithm to find $\boldsymbol{R}$ and $\boldsymbol{C}$ that minimize the reprojection error from $\boldsymbol{X}$ to $\boldsymbol{x}$. The algorithm requires the Jacobian matrix relating the output $\boldsymbol{x}$ to the input $\boldsymbol{X}$ with respect to the

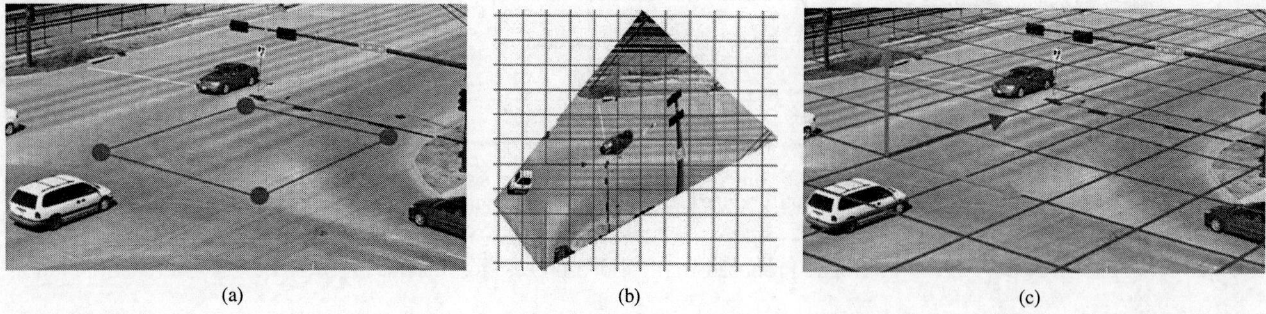

(a) (b) (c)

Fig. 2: The street plane is identified by having the user select four coplanar points located on the surface of the street (a). These points can be used to derive an image warping transformation that can be used to easily convert image points on the street to world coordinates (b). An illustration of the world coordinate system as viewed by the camera is given in (c).

unknown pose parameters. Rather than evaluating the Jacobian directly, the projection process is decomposed into a series of steps such that the Jacobian can be computed by back-propagating and chaining the intermediate derivatives [14].

To handle linearization of the 3D rotation, an incremental rotation matrix

$$\Delta\boldsymbol{R}(\boldsymbol{v}) = \begin{bmatrix} 1 & -v_z & v_y \\ v_z & 1 & -v_x \\ -v_y & v_x & 1 \end{bmatrix} \quad (7)$$

is defined where $\boldsymbol{v} = (v_x, v_y, v_z)$ is a minimal rotation vector, such that the direction of $\boldsymbol{v}$ specifies the axis and its magnitude specifies the angle of rotation. Note that the definition of $\Delta\boldsymbol{R}(\boldsymbol{v})$ in Equation (7) is only valid for small rotations. In this implementation $\Delta\boldsymbol{R}(\boldsymbol{v})$ is allowable since an incremental update to the initially estimated rotation matrix given in Equation (6) is sought. Using this definition of incremental rotation, projection is decomposed into

$$\begin{aligned} \boldsymbol{X}_C &= \boldsymbol{X} - \boldsymbol{C} && (8) \\ \boldsymbol{X}_R &= \boldsymbol{R}\boldsymbol{X}_C && (9) \\ \boldsymbol{X}_v &= \Delta\boldsymbol{R}(\boldsymbol{v})\boldsymbol{X}_R && (10) \\ \hat{\boldsymbol{X}} &= [X_v/Z_v, Y_v/Z_v, 1]^{\mathsf{T}}, && (11) \end{aligned}$$

where $\hat{\boldsymbol{X}} = \boldsymbol{K}^{-1}\boldsymbol{x}$ since the internal camera parameters are fixed and do not affect minimization. The stages of projection along with the associated partial derivatives are shown in Figure 3. Combining the partial derivatives associated with the stages shown in Figure 3 leads to the formulation of the Jacobian

$$\begin{aligned} \frac{\partial \hat{\boldsymbol{X}}}{\partial(\boldsymbol{C}, \boldsymbol{v})} &= \left[\frac{\partial \hat{\boldsymbol{X}}}{\partial \boldsymbol{C}} \;\middle|\; \frac{\partial \hat{\boldsymbol{X}}}{\partial \boldsymbol{v}} \right] \\ &= \left[\frac{\partial \hat{\boldsymbol{X}}}{\partial \boldsymbol{X}_v} \frac{\partial \boldsymbol{X}_v}{\partial \boldsymbol{X}_R} \frac{\partial \boldsymbol{X}_R}{\partial \boldsymbol{X}_C} \frac{\partial \boldsymbol{X}_C}{\partial \boldsymbol{C}} \;\middle|\; \frac{\partial \hat{\boldsymbol{X}}}{\partial \boldsymbol{X}_v} \frac{\partial \boldsymbol{X}_v}{\partial \boldsymbol{v}} \right], \quad (12) \end{aligned}$$

which is used for updating the pose parameters in the Levenberg-Marquardt algorithm. Note that, to allow for large rotation adjustments, the camera rotation matrix is recalculated using $\boldsymbol{R} \leftarrow \Delta\boldsymbol{R}(\boldsymbol{v})\boldsymbol{R}$ after each iteration of minimization. Orthogonality of the rotation matrix is then forced and $\boldsymbol{v}$ is set to zero prior to the next iteration.

In addition to determining the camera pose, a planar homography transformation $\boldsymbol{H}$, such that $\boldsymbol{X} = \boldsymbol{H}\boldsymbol{x}$, is derived from the four user-defined image points. This homography allows for the recovery of 3D world coordinates of image points located on the street surface, as illustrated in Figures 2(b) and 2(c). Later on, when generating vehicle point clouds, this transformation is used to remove scale ambiguity associated with single-camera structure from motion.

3.2 Blob and Feature Detection and Tracking

The vehicles are identified in the video using adaptive background subtraction, where pixel intensity distributions (approximated as Gaussians) are estimated independently for every pixel location. This method is known to mitigate the effects of camera shake and other persistent intensity variations within the scene [4]. Foreground pixels are defined as those with distance from the mean value that is greater than some multiple of the variance. The output of adaptive background subtraction is a binary image where foreground objects are assigned a value of 1 and the background is set to 0. A sample frame of the video sequence and the corresponding mean image are given in Figures 4(a) and 4(b).

The binary image obtained through background subtraction is subjected to median filtering and morphological closing (dilation followed by erosion), which are necessary to eliminate noise artifacts resulting from thresholding and to fill gaps in the image objects. Once the filtering is complete, standard 4-connected neighborhoods of the binary image are examined in order to identify, label, and characterize blobs that correspond to vehicles. For each of the blobs, a set of key properties is recovered, which include area, bounding box, centroid, and blob shape in the form of a binary mask. Smaller blobs are excluded from further analysis, since they are due to noise or do not represent vehicles. An example of blob detection is shown in Figure 4(c).

To allow for vehicle tracking, the system maintains a list of vehicles present in the current view and updates this information as new frames become available. Correspondences of blob centroids are recovered between successive frames through

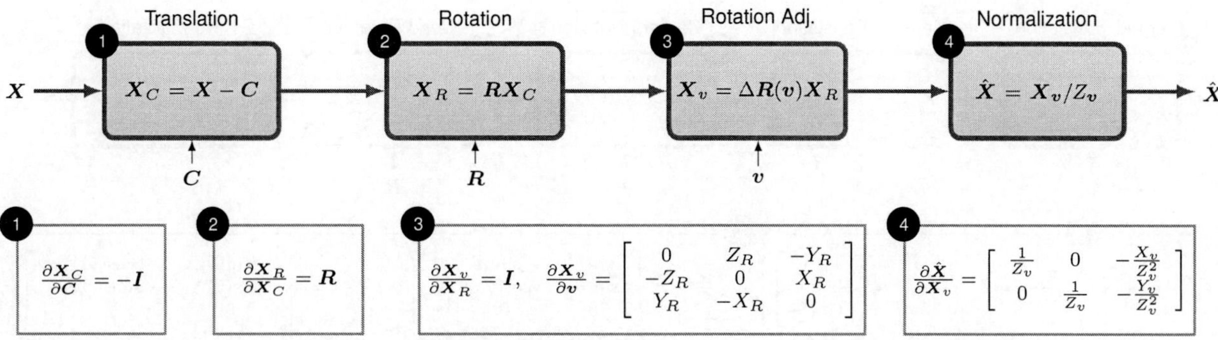

Fig. 3: Decomposition of the projection process for camera pose refinement using the Levenberg-Marquardt algorithm. The reprojection error is minimized with respect to the camera center C and rotation adjustment $\Delta R(v)$.

(a) Sample Frame

(b) Mean Image

(c) Vehicle Detection

(d) Vehicle Tracking

Fig. 4: The vehicles are identified in the image using a combination of adaptive background subtraction and blob detection. The vehicles are then tracked using the assumption of small frame-to-frame movement.

geometrically constrained nearest neighbor matching, leading to the recovery of frame-to-frame motion vectors associated with particular vehicles. In case a match cannot be established for a given blob centroid, the corresponding vehicle is either entering or exiting the view, which is handled appropriately. An illustration of vehicle tracking is given in Figure 4(d).

In addition to vehicle tracking, features are detected and matched as the vehicle moves through the scene. This feature detection and matching is necessary for computing the 3D point cloud of the vehicle. The SURF feature detection method is used to detect features and assign feature descriptors since it is invariant to changes in intensity, scale, and rotation, and handles small affine distortions [15]. Features are matched using a nearest neighbor distance ratio threshold of 0.6 and consistency is enforced to identify pairs of uniquely matched features. The results of feature matching between two views of the same vehicle is shown in Figure 5.

Fig. 5: A set of consistent matches obtained using SURF with a nearest neighbor distance ratio (NNDR) threshold of 0.6

3.3 Vehicle Structure and Motion Estimation

The movement of the vehicle through the scene can be interpreted in two ways: displacement of the vehicle with a fixed camera, or displacement of the camera with a fixed vehicle. The proposed method aims to recover the displacement of the camera under the assumption that the vehicle is fixed. The planar nature of vehicle motion constrains the relative movement of the camera between views, in that the camera center is translated along the XY-plane and rotated around the Z-axis of the world coordinate system. Therefore, relative camera motion in the world coordinate system is parameterized

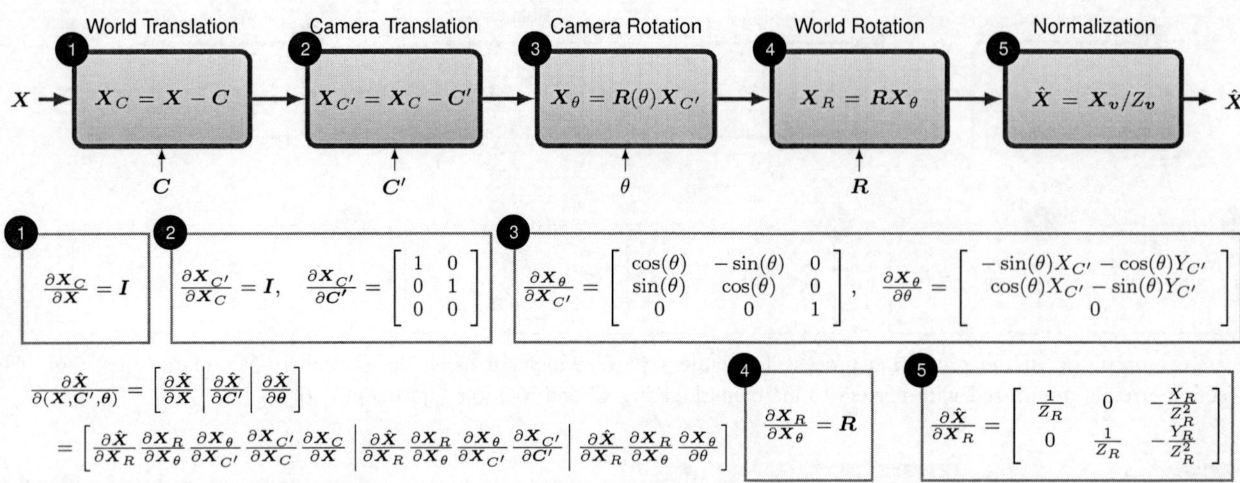

Fig. 6: Decomposition of the projection process for two-frame bundle adjustment using the Levenberg-Marquardt algorithm. The camera translation C' and camera rotation $R(\theta)$ represent the relative movement of the camera assuming the vehicle position is fixed. The parameters C' and $R(\theta)$ are set to zero and identity, respectively, in one view and optimized for the other view with respect to reprojection error. Note that the 3D points X are also adjusted along with rotation and translation between views.

by the displacement vector $C' = [c'_x, c'_y, 0]^\mathsf{T}$ and the rotation

$$R(\theta) = \begin{bmatrix} \cos(\theta) & -\sin(\theta) & 0 \\ \sin(\theta) & \cos(\theta) & 0 \\ 0 & 0 & 1 \end{bmatrix}, \quad (13)$$

where θ defines the angle of rotation around the Z-axis.

With a set of matched vehicle feature points between two views, bundle adjustment is used to estimate the relative motion of the camera and the 3D points corresponding to features. Analogously to the pose estimation method described in Section 3.1, motion parameters are acquired through non-linear optimization using the Levenberg-Marquardt algorithm to minimize the reprojection error of 3D structure coordinates to 2D image points. Whereas pose estimation minimizes reprojection error in a single view, bundle adjustment aggregates the reprojection error in a pair of views while simultaneously adjusting the 3D structure coordinates. The decomposition of the projection process is given in Figure 6.

In order to eliminate outliers from the set of feature matches, RANSAC [16] is applied. At each iteration of RANSAC, a sampling of eight features is randomly chosen to estimate C' and $R(\theta)$. Using the estimated camera motion parameters, 3D vehicle coordinates are triangulated (Equation 7.4 in [14]) from the entire set of feature matches. The 3D coordinates are then projected into both views and outliers are identified as those that exceed an empirically chosen reprojection error. Next, the chosen set of inliers is processed by bundle adjustment to derive the final structure and motion parameters.

4. Results

To evaluate the accuracy of the proposed method, four sample vehicles with different body types (sedan, van, SUV, and a pickup truck) were processed to extract 3D point clouds. The four vehicles with their features in both views are

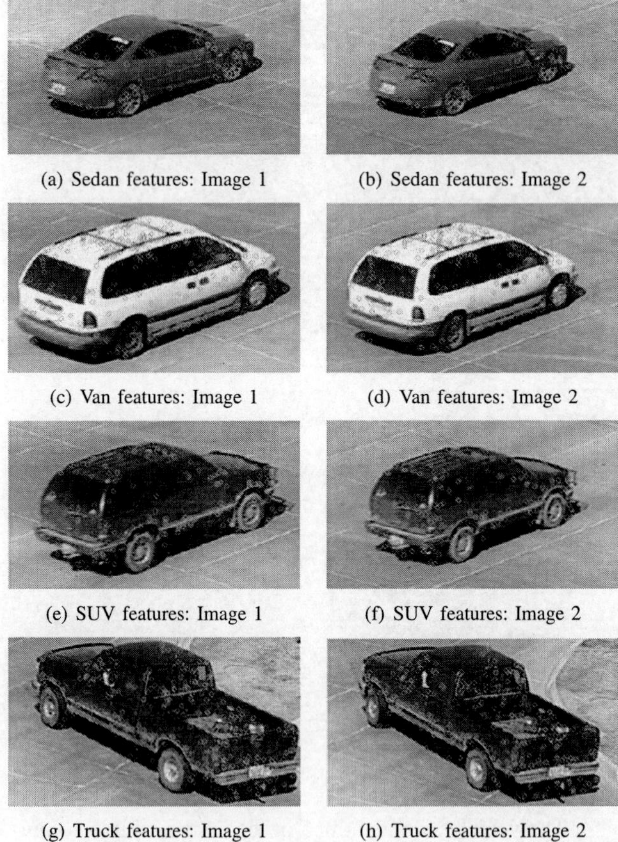

(a) Sedan features: Image 1 (b) Sedan features: Image 2

(c) Van features: Image 1 (d) Van features: Image 2

(e) SUV features: Image 1 (f) SUV features: Image 2

(g) Truck features: Image 1 (h) Truck features: Image 2

Fig. 7: Vehicles used to verify the accuracy of the proposed method along with the features that were identified in each of the frames.

shown in Figure 7. The accuracy of the method is evaluated by comparing vehicle dimensions manually extracted from the 3D points clouds with the actual dimensions. Figure 8 demonstrates the extraction of vehicle dimensions from the 3D point cloud corresponding to the van.

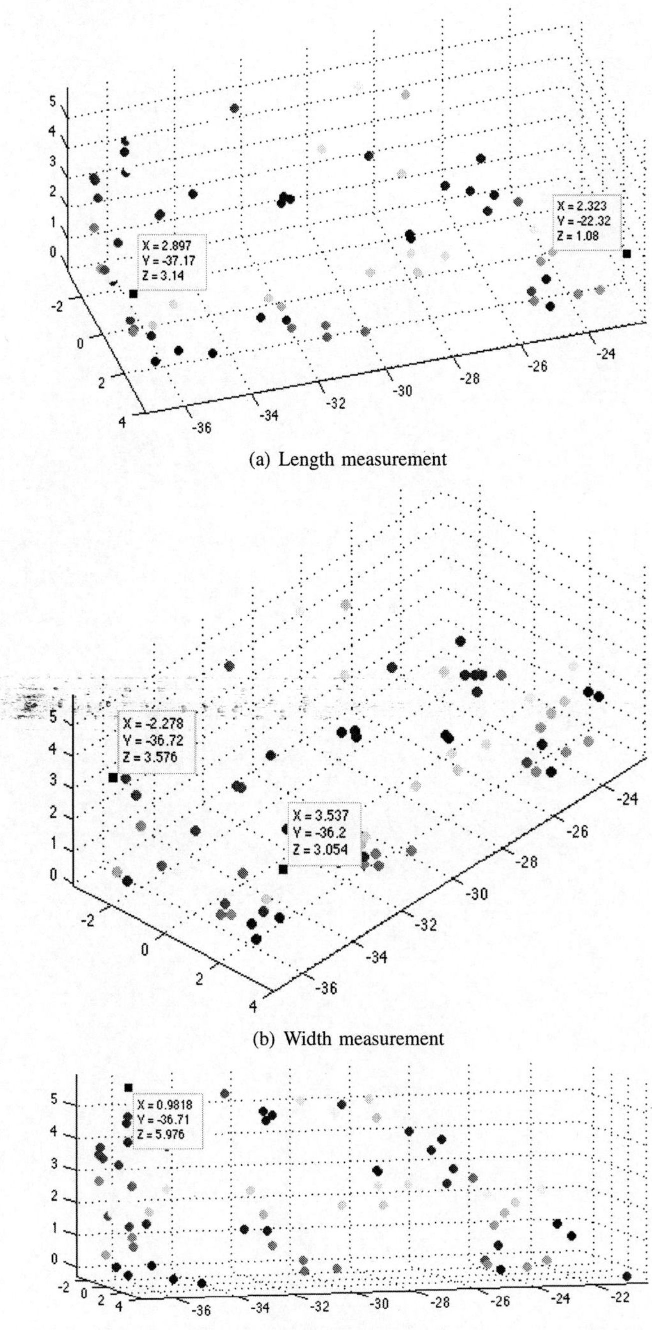

(a) Length measurement

(b) Width measurement

(c) Height measurement

Fig. 8: Point cloud of a van obtained using the proposed method along with measurement points used to obtain the length, width, and height of the van. Note that the height measurement requires only one sample since the vehicle lies on the plane at $Z = 0$.

Table 1: Dimensions of various vehicles recovered using the proposed method along with their actual dimensions and the corresponding average absolute measurement errors.

	Actual dimensions			Extracted dimensions			
Vehicle	L x W x H (ft)			L x W x H (ft)			Avg. error
Sedan	15.42	5.80	4.35	15.33	6.15	3.88	0.30
Van	15.48	5.71	6.42	15.00	5.86	5.98	0.36
SUV	15.10	5.65	5.57	15.07	5.19	5.33	0.24
Truck	19.61	6.58	6.17	20.08	6.87	5.94	0.33

A comparison between actual vehicle dimensions and those extracted using the proposed method is given in Table 1. The results show that the method is capable of recovering the dimensions of vehicles with average absolute measurement error of less than 0.36 feet. In addition, the maximum error in a single dimension is 0.48 feet.

The availability of sparse, accurate 3D point clouds creates the opportunity to recover precise vehicle trajectories, which also enables high-level detection of events such as lane changes, traffic violations, accidents, and near-collisions. The points can also be used to accelerate model fitting for automated vehicle classification. Altogether, the resulting enhancements to traffic data collection are expected to help identify abnormal and unsafe driver behaviors, which is important to improving intersection safety.

5. Conclusion

A method has been presented for obtaining scale-accurate 3D point cloud representations of vehicles from a single traffic camera. With only two inputs provided by the user - internal camera calibration and four user-defined street surface points with known dimensions - the six-dimensional pose of the camera relative to the street plane can be reliably estimated prior to 3D point cloud extraction. As vehicles pass through the camera's field of view, blob detection and tracking is used to separate the vehicles from the background, and two sufficiently different perspectives of the vehicle are obtained. Correspondences between the two views are acquired using SURF feature detection and matching. The correspondences are then processed using two-frame structure from motion with bundle adjustment to estimate the 3D point cloud coordinates along with the motion of the vehicle under the assumption of translation on the XY-plane and rotation around the Z-axis in the world coordinate system. Outliers in the 3D point cloud are further eliminated using RANSAC to minimize the reprojection error of triangulated feature matches.

Results demonstrate that the proposed method is capable of accurately obtaining structural properties of passing vehicles. It has been demonstrated that vehicle length, width, and height can be recovered with an average error within 0.36 feet when compared to their actual values. For added robustness to varying environmental conditions, methods for efficient detection and removal of shadows from the images after background subtraction should be integrated with the proposed method. Moreover, incorporating additional views into the structure recovery process is expected to improve the accuracy of the resulting point clouds. Alternative geometric primitives, including lines and image segments, may be identified and matched between views in order to obtain more detailed vehicle models. This method also lends itself well to dense reconstruction techniques like stereo matching, allowing for robust model-fitting for the purpose of vehicle classification.

References

[1] N. Buch, S. Velastin, and J. Orwell, "A review of computer vision techniques for the analysis of urban traffic," *Intelligent Transportation Systems, IEEE Transactions on*, vol. 12, no. 3, pp. 920–939, 2011.

[2] Y. Zhang, P. Shi, E. Jones, and Q. Zhu, "Robust background image generation and vehicle 3d detection and tracking," in *Intelligent Transportation Systems, 2004. Proceedings. The 7th International IEEE Conference on*, pp. 12–16, 2004.

[3] P. Shi, E. G. Jones, and Q. Zhu, "Median model for background subtraction in intelligent transportation system," in *Proc. SPIE 5298, Image Processing: Algorithms and Systems III*, pp. 168–176, 2004.

[4] B. Morris and M. Trivedi, "Robust classification and tracking of vehicles in traffic video streams," in *Intelligent Transportation Systems Conference, 2006. ITSC '06. IEEE*, pp. 1078–1083, 2006.

[5] B. Johansson, J. Wiklund, P. Forssén, and G. Granlund, "Combining shadow detection and simulation for estimation of vehicle size and position," *Pattern Recognition Letters*, vol. 30, no. 8, pp. 751 – 759, 2009.

[6] Z. Chen, T. Ellis, and S. Velastin, "Vehicle type categorization: A comparison of classification schemes," in *Intelligent Transportation Systems (ITSC), 2011 14th International IEEE Conference on*, pp. 74–79, 2011.

[7] Y. Zheng and S. Peng, "Model based vehicle localization for urban traffic surveillance using image gradient based matching," in *Intelligent Transportation Systems (ITSC), 2012 15th International IEEE Conference on*, pp. 945–950, 2012.

[8] N. Ghosh and B. Bhanu, "Incremental unsupervised three-dimensional vehicle model learning from video," *Intelligent Transportation Systems, IEEE Transactions on*, vol. 11, no. 2, pp. 423–440, 2010.

[9] Q. Houben, J. C. T. Diaz, N. Warzée, O. Debeir, and J. Czyz, "Multi-feature stereo vision system for road traffic analysis," in *International Conference on Computer Vision Theory and Applications*, vol. 2, 2009.

[10] P. Sch onemann, "A generalized solution of the orthogonal Procrustes problem," *Psychometrika*, vol. 31, no. 1, pp. 1–10, 1966.

[11] P. Besl and N. D. McKay, "A method for registration of 3-d shapes," *Pattern Analysis and Machine Intelligence, IEEE Transactions on*, vol. 14, no. 2, pp. 239–256, 1992.

[12] Y. Yang, Q. Cao, C. Lo, and Z. Zhang, "Pose estimation based on four coplanar point correspondences," in *Fuzzy Systems and Knowledge Discovery, 2009. FSKD '09. Sixth International Conference on*, vol. 5, pp. 410–414, 2009.

[13] R. I. Hartley and A. Zisserman, *Multiple View Geometry in Computer Vision*. Cambridge University Press, 2nd ed., 2003.

[14] R. Szeliski, *Computer Vision: Algorithms and Applications.* Texts in Computer Vision, 2011.

[15] H. Bay, A. Ess, T. Tuytelaars, and L. V. Gool, "Speeded-up robust features (surf)," *Computer Vision and Image Understanding*, vol. 110, no. 3, pp. 346 – 359, 2008. Similarity Matching in Computer Vision and Multimedia.

[16] M. A. Fischler and R. C. Bolles, "Random sample consensus: a paradigm for model fitting with applications to image analysis and automated cartography," *Commun. ACM*, vol. 24, no. 6, pp. 381–395, 1981.

A decomposition method for non-rigid structure from motion with orthographic cameras

X. B. Zhang **A. W. K. Tang** **Y. S. Hung**
Department of Electrical and Electronic Engineering, The University of Hong Kong
Postal address: Room 501, CYC Building, The University of Hong Kong, Hong Kong

Abstract

In this paper, we propose a new approach to non-rigid structure from motion based on the trajectory basis method by decomposing the problem into two sub-problems. The existing trajectory basis method requires the number of trajectory basis vectors to be specified beforehand, and then camera motion and the non-rigid structure are recovered simultaneously. However, we observe that the camera motion can be derived from a mean shape without recovering the non-rigid structure. Hence, the camera motion can be recovered as a sub-problem to optimize an error indicator without a full recovery of the non-rigid structure or the need to pre-define the number of basis required for describing the non-rigid structure. With the camera motion recovered, the non-rigid structure can then be solved in a second sub-problem together with the determination of the basis number by minimizing another error indicator. The solutions to these two sub-problems can be combined to solve the non-rigid structure from motion problem in an automatic manner, without any need to pre-define the number of basis vectors. Experiments show that the proposed method improves the reconstruction quality of both the non-rigid structure and camera motion.

Keywords: non-rigid structure, orthographic camera, structure from motion, automatic recovery

1. Introduction

Structure from motion is one of the most important problems in computer vision. For a 3D structure projected to a set of cameras, the structure from motion problem is to recover the structure in 3D from the 2D image projections [1]. Traditionally, 3D structures are assumed to be rigid and stationary. Such an assumption incurs a rank-3 (rank-4 in perspective camera case) condition on image measurements. With such a condition, various methods have been proposed [2, 3], most of which are based on rank constrained factorization [4, 5].

In recent years, more and more attention is paid to the non-rigid structure from motion problem [6-8], where the 3D structure is allowed to move and deform. Based on an assumption that the deformation of a non-rigid structure can be modeled by a linear combination of a set of rigid shapes, the traditional factorization approach for rigid structure reconstruction has been extended to handle non-rigid structure recovery [9, 10]. As the non-rigid structure is represented as a linear combination of a shape basis, the method is referred to as the shape basis method in literature.

Then, Akhter et al. developed a trajectory basis method for non-rigid structure representation [11], which, as shown by the authors, is dual to the shape basis method. By tracking trajectories of corresponding points of a non-rigid structure and modeling them using a DCT (Discrete Cosine Transform) basis, the trajectory basis method recovers the structure in 3D space using not only the rank constraint, but also an implicit "smooth deforming trajectory" constraint. The introduction and enforcement of the "smooth deforming trajectory" constraint effectively prevents meaningless solutions and significantly reduce the gap between recovered structure and original structure. Despite so, the trajectory basis method has two persisting problems inherited from shape basis method:

a. the number of basis for non-rigid structure representation, which is normally unknown in advance, has to be pre-defined
b. there is no criteria for quality evaluation of the recovered structure and camera motion

In this paper, we proposed a new method based on trajectory basis representation that solves both of these two problems. By disassociating camera motion recovery with structure recovery and proposing a criterion for quality evaluation, we are able to obtain better solutions for camera matrices. At the same time, a criterion reflecting the error of fitting a non-rigid structure using trajectory basis representation with different number of basis is proposed, leading to a method for automatic determination of the best basis number for non-rigid structure representation.

The rest of the paper is organized as follows: In Section 2, some preliminaries about trajectory basis method are introduced, together with notations used in this paper. In Section 3, the non-rigid structure from motion problem with orthographic cameras is reformulated and a new method is proposed. In Section 4, experimental evaluations are presented, including comparisons with existing algorithms. Some concluding remarks are given in Section 5.

2. Trajectory basis for non-rigid structure from motion

2.1. Non-rigid structure from motion

Let $\{x_{ij} \in R^{2\times1} \mid i = 1,2,\cdots,F, j = 1,2,\cdots,N\}$ be the orthographic projections of N 3D points $\{X_{ij} \in R^{3\times1}\}$ projected to F frames of a moving camera. Then

$$x_{ij} = \mathrm{R}_i X_{ij} \quad (1)$$

where $\mathrm{R_i} \in \mathrm{R}^{2\times3}$ is the camera matrix associated with the ith frame. It follows that

$$\mathrm{W} = \begin{bmatrix} x_{11} & \cdots & x_{1N} \\ \vdots & \ddots & \vdots \\ x_{F1} & \cdots & x_{FN} \end{bmatrix} = \begin{bmatrix} \mathrm{R_1X_1} \\ \vdots \\ \mathrm{R}_F\mathrm{X}_F \end{bmatrix} \quad (2)$$

where $\mathrm{X}_i = [X_{i1}, X_{i2}, \cdots, X_{iN}] \in R^{3\times N}$ is called structure matrix and W is called measurement matrix.

The structure from motion problem refers to the problem of recovering camera matrix R_i and structure matrices X_i given the measurement matrix W.

For a rigid stationary object, the structure matrices X_i are equal across all frames. Thus a rank-3 constraint can be enforced in the measurement matrix, which is the basis for all factorization based algorithms for solving the rigid structure from motion problem.

For a non-rigid object, the rank-3 constraint does not hold anymore. Thus other constraints are necessary in order to make the problem solvable. A common assumption made is that the structure deformation can be modeled by a linear combination of a fixed set of K shape basis $\mathrm{B}_k \in R^{3\times N}$ $(k = 1,2,\cdots,K)$. Formally, the assumption can be written as

$$X_{ij} = \sum_{k=1}^{K} c_{ik} B_{kj}, \qquad i = 1,2,\cdots,F, j = 1,2,\cdots,N \quad (3)$$

where $\mathrm{B}_k = [B_{k1}, B_{k2}, \cdots, B_{kN}]$ and c_{ik} is the coefficient of the ith frame at the kth shape basis.

Such an assumption imposes a rank-$3K$ constraint on the measurement matrix and thus makes it possible to extend the factorization approach from rigid structure to non-rigid structure recovery.

2.2. Trajectory basis for non-rigid structure representation

Trajectory basis representation can be regarded as the dual of the shape basis representation by taking c_{ik} in equation (3) as the kth trajectory basis entry at the ith frame and B_{kj} as a corresponding vector of weighting coefficients. The trajectory basis method has been demonstrated to be more stable in non-rigid structure recovery by restricting the recovered non-rigid structure to be smoothly deforming in consecutive frames. Moreover, the trajectory basis is pre-defined and is independent of the non-rigid structure dataset, thus reducing the parameters to be solved in the optimization problem.

With trajectory basis method, the measurement matrix in equation (2) can be rewritten as

$$\mathrm{W} = \begin{bmatrix} \mathrm{R}_1 & \cdots & 0 \\ \vdots & \ddots & \vdots \\ 0 & \cdots & \mathrm{R}_F \end{bmatrix} \begin{bmatrix} c_{11}\mathrm{I}_3 & \cdots & c_{1K}\mathrm{I}_3 \\ \vdots & \ddots & \vdots \\ c_{F1}\mathrm{I}_3 & \cdots & c_{FK}\mathrm{I}_3 \end{bmatrix} \begin{bmatrix} B_{11} & \cdots & B_{1N} \\ \vdots & \ddots & \vdots \\ B_{K1} & \cdots & B_{KN} \end{bmatrix} \quad (4)$$

$$= \begin{bmatrix} c_1 \otimes \mathrm{R}_1 \\ \vdots \\ c_F \otimes \mathrm{R}_F \end{bmatrix} \begin{bmatrix} \mathrm{B}_1 \\ \vdots \\ \mathrm{B}_K \end{bmatrix} \quad (5)$$

$$= \mathrm{MB} \quad (6)$$

where $c_i = [c_{i1}, c_{i2}, \cdots, c_{iK}] \in R^{1\times K}$ is a row vector consisted of trajectory basis entries of the ith frame, $\mathrm{M} \in R^{2F\times 3K}$ represents a scaled motion matrix and $\mathrm{B} \in R^{3K\times N}$ is a coefficient matrix.

3. Non-rigid structure and motion recovery

3.1. Problem decomposition

Equation (6) suggests that the measurement matrix of a non-rigid structure with orthographic cameras is subject to a rank-$3K$ constraint, and thus both structure and camera matrices can be obtained using a factorization method similar to that for rigid structure reconstruction. The idea can be summarized with the following equations.

$$\mathrm{W} = \widehat{\mathrm{M}}\,\widehat{\mathrm{B}} \quad (7)$$

$$= \widehat{\mathrm{M}}\,\mathrm{GG}^{-1}\,\widehat{\mathrm{B}} \quad (8)$$

where W is first factorized into rank 3K matrices $\widehat{\mathrm{M}}$ and $\widehat{\mathrm{B}}$ in a projective space, and then a metric upgrade is performed by finding $\mathrm{G} \in R^{3K\times 3K}$ that satisfies

$$\widehat{\mathrm{M}}_i\mathrm{G} = c_i \otimes \widehat{\mathrm{R}}_i, i = 1,2,\cdots,F \quad (9)$$

where $\widehat{\mathrm{R}}_i \in R^{2\times3}$ represents recovered camera matrix of the ith frame with row-orthonormal properties.

An inherent problem with the above method is that the number of basis required for non-rigid structure description needs to be specified beforehand. Notice however that the camera matrices in (4) are independent of the structure model in 3D space. It may be possible to recover camera matrices without the recovery of non-rigid structure. Also, the recovery of 3D structure is independent of the method used for camera motion recovery. As long as camera matrices are given, structure in 3D space can be recovered optimally from 2D measurements under the trajectory basis model.

Hence, we propose to decompose the non-rigid structure

from motion problem into two sub-problems. The first one is to recover camera motion, and the second problem is to recover the structure in 3D space when camera motion is already known.

The benefit of the problem decomposition is that optimal solutions can be obtained in both of these two sub-problems. Furthermore, both sub-problems can be solved in an automatic manner with the help of error indicators that may not be available when solving the two sub-problems as a whole.

3.2. Recovery of camera projection matrices

If the trajectory basis in (4) is generated using DCT, the first basis vector is given by $[c_{11}, c_{21}, \cdots, c_{F1}]^T = \frac{1}{\sqrt{F}}[1,1,\cdots,1]^T$. Hence we may rewrite (5) as:

$$W = \begin{bmatrix} R_1 \\ \vdots \\ R_F \end{bmatrix} \frac{B_1}{\sqrt{F}} + \begin{bmatrix} c_{1,2\cdots K} \otimes R_1 \\ \vdots \\ c_{F,2\cdots K} \otimes R_F \end{bmatrix} \begin{bmatrix} B_2 \\ \vdots \\ B_K \end{bmatrix} \tag{10}$$

$$= RS + D \tag{11}$$

where $c_{i,2\cdots K} = [c_{i2}, c_{i3}, \cdots, c_{iK}]$, R consists of the stacked rotation matrices, and S and D are defined in an obvious manner.

We may interpret (11) as decomposing W into two components: (i) the projection of a mean shape S with orthographic camera matrices in R, and (ii) the projection of deformations D of the non-rigid structure. Furthermore, we note that the camera matrices can be recovered from the first component (i) alone if W is decomposed as in (11). In view of (11), we propose to recover the camera matrices by a partial upgrade of only the mean shape component of the non-rigid structure, by writing (7) – (9) as:

$$W = \widehat{M}\,\widehat{B} \tag{12}$$

$$= \widehat{M}[G_{13} \quad G_{4K}][G_{13} \quad G_{4K}]^{-1}\widehat{B} \tag{13}$$

$$= [\widehat{M}G_{13} \quad \widehat{M}G_{4K}]\begin{bmatrix} \widehat{S} \\ \widehat{V} \end{bmatrix} \tag{14}$$

$$= [\widehat{R} \quad \widehat{M}G_{4K}]\begin{bmatrix} \widehat{S} \\ \widehat{V} \end{bmatrix} \tag{15}$$

$$= \widehat{R}\widehat{S} + \widehat{M}G_{4K}\widehat{V} \tag{16}$$

subject to

$$\widehat{M}_i G_{13} G_{13}^T \widehat{M}_i^T = I_2, \qquad i = 1,2,\cdots,F \tag{17}$$

where W is factorized into two rank-K matrices $\widehat{M} \in R^{2F\times K}$ and $\widehat{B} \in R^{K\times N}$, $G_{13} \in R^{K\times 3}$ and $G_{4K} \in R^{K\times(K-3)}$ are the 1st-3rd columns and 4th - Kth columns of an upgrade matrix, respectively, $\widehat{R} \in R^{2F\times 3}$ is the recovered stacked camera matrix, $\widehat{S} \in R^{3\times N}$ is mean shape of the 3D structure, and $\widehat{V} \in R^{(K-3)\times N}$ is a matrix spanning the deformation space of the non-rigid structure.

Equation (16) suggests that camera matrices with non-rigid structure projections can be obtained by a rank-K factorization followed by applying a metric upgrading matrix $G_{13} \in R^{K\times 3}$ which is subject to a non-linear constraint stated in equation (17). An algorithm to solve for camera matrices is described in Table 1.

Table 1: Algorithm for camera motion recovery

<u>Objective</u>

Given a set of image measurements of a non-rigid structure projected by orthographic cameras and a factorization rank K, compute a set of rotation matrices that enforce condition (17).

<u>Algorithm 1</u>

Camera motion recovery

1. Factorize measurement matrix with equation (12).
2. Find a triple column metric upgrading matrix G_{13} that satisfying equation (17).
3. Output stacked rotation matrices $\widehat{R} = \widehat{M}G_{13}$

At a given factorization rank, Algorithm 1 looks for a set of rotation matrices satisfying the orthonormality constraint stated in (17) which is shown to be sufficient to recover camera projection matrices [12]. As factorization rank in (12) is unknown, it is necessary to identify the best factorization rank for each dataset. To achieve such a goal, we propose to employ 2D reprojection error as an error indicator at different factorization rank, as described in the next subsection.

3.3. Error indicator using 2D reprojection error

Using different factorization rank in (12) results in different level of approximation to the non-rigid structure. The approximation of non-rigid structure leads to errors in the mean shape, and thus affects the error of recovered camera matrices. Hence it is necessary to have an indicator reflecting the quality of recovered camera matrices at different factorization rank. Noting that the error of recovered camera matrices based on (16) is correlated to the reprojection error evaluated with a full projection model shown in (5), we propose to take the difference norm of equation (5) as an error indicator for recovered projection matrices. The key problem of evaluating the difference norm of equation (5) is that the coefficient matrix $\widehat{B}$ is unknown. Here we use a coarse to fine approach for obtaining the coefficient matrix. Let $\boldsymbol{c}^k \in R^{F\times 1}$ be the kth trajectory basis vector, and

$$K_m = \lfloor \text{rank}(W)/3 \rfloor \tag{18}$$

be the maximum number of basis that can be chosen for current non-rigid structure description where $\lfloor a \rfloor$ means the maximum integer $\leq a$. The coefficient matrix $\widehat{B}$ can be obtained by iteratively solving the following problem:

$$\widehat{B}_k = \arg\min_{\widehat{B}_k} \left\| W_r^k - [diag(\boldsymbol{c}^k) \otimes I_2]\widehat{R}\widehat{B}_k \right\|^2 \qquad k = 1,2,\cdots,K_m \tag{19}$$

where

$$W_r^1 = W \tag{20}$$

$$W_r^{k+1} = W_r^k - [diag(\boldsymbol{c}^k) \otimes I_2]\widehat{R}\widehat{B}_k \qquad k = 1,2,\cdots,K_m - 1 \tag{21}$$

Thus error indicator for recovered camera matrices using 2D reprojection error can be defined as

$$e = \sum_{i=1}^{F} \|W_i - [c_i \otimes \widehat{R}_i]\widehat{B}\|^2 \quad (22)$$

Although the correct number of basis remains unknown, we add basis vectors one by one and solve for optimal coefficients for each newly added basis vector until the maximum number of basis allowed is reached. This procedure has the effect of avoiding over-fitting caused by unnecessary basis vectors because the optimization of equation (19) would not disturb the trajectory coefficients that have already been recovered using a smaller number of basis vectors. Hence, e is defined without the need to specify the number of basis, and is an indicator of the quality of the camera matrices alone.

3.4. Cross validation for automatic basis number decision

Given rotation matrices, the problem of non-rigid structure recovery using a trajectory basis model is to find suitable coefficient matrix $\widehat{B}$ that solves the following problem:

$$\min_{\widehat{B}} \sum_{i=1}^{F} \|W_i - [c_i \otimes \widehat{R}_i]\widehat{B}\|^2 \quad (23)$$

The key issue in solving the above problem is that the number of basis K_b for the non-rigid structure description is unknown. As long as K_b is defined, the above problem can be solved with standard least square techniques. In order to decide the best number of basis for the non-rigid structure representation, it is necessary to have an error indicator signifying the quality of recovered non-rigid structure at different number of basis.

Similar to [13], we use cross validation score as an error indicator. The idea is to partition the image measurements of each frame into training data and testing data. While the collection of training data is used to recover the non-rigid structure; that of testing data is used to quantify how well the recovered non-rigid structure is by evaluating the distance between testing data measurements and testing data reprojections. The cross validation score is taken to be the average distance of several such partitions. An algorithm for automatic basis number decision is given in Table 2.

Table 2: Algorithm for automatic basis number decision

Objective

Given a set of image measurements of a non-rigid structure and a set of camera matrices, compute a suitable number of trajectory basis such that its cross validation score is the smallest.

Algorithm 2

Automatic bases number decision

1. Randomly partition measurements of each frame into training data and testing data for K_p times.
2. For $k = 2 : K_m$
   a) Define trajectory basis matrix c with k basis vectors.
   b) For each partitioned dataset, solving for coefficient matrix $\widehat{B}$ in (23) with the collection of training data.
   c) Obtain non-rigid structure using recovered coefficients and defined trajectory basis.
   d) Reproject the recovered non-rigid structure onto images; evaluate the distance between measurements of testing data and reprojections of testing data.
   e) Average the distance over K_p trials and record it as cross validation score s.
3. Find the smallest cross validation score s and output its corresponding basis number.

Table 3: Algorithm for non-rigid structure recovery

Objective

Given a set of image measurements of a non-rigid structure projected by orthographic cameras, reconstruct the non-rigid structure in 3D space.

Algorithm 3

Non-rigid structure recovery

1. For $k = 3 : \text{rank}(W)$
   a) Seek for rotation matrices $\widehat{R}_k$ using Algorithm 1 with rank-k factorization.
   b) Evaluate the 2D reprojection error e using equation (22) with rotation matrices $\widehat{R}_k$.
2. Select rotation matrices $\widehat{R}$ with smallest 2D reprojection error e.
3. Find the optimal basis number K_b using Algorithm 2 with recovered rotation matrices $\widehat{R}$.
4. Define trajectory basis matrix c_b with K_b basis vectors for non-rigid structure description.
5. Solve for optimal coefficients $\widehat{B}$ by solving (23) with camera matrices $\widehat{R}$ and trajectory basis matrix c_b.
6. Evaluate equation (3) with c_b and $\widehat{B}$, and obtain the non-rigid structure in 3D space.

3.5. Algorithm for non-rigid structure recovery

The solutions to the two sub-problems, namely Algorithms 1 and 2, can now be combined to recover the non-rigid structure using trajectory basis representation in an automatic manner. An overview of the algorithm for non-rigid structure recovery is given in Table 3.

4. Experimental results

The proposed method is evaluated with both synthetic images of non-rigid structures and images of deforming structures in the real world. Comparisons with existing trajectory basis method are also made in this section.

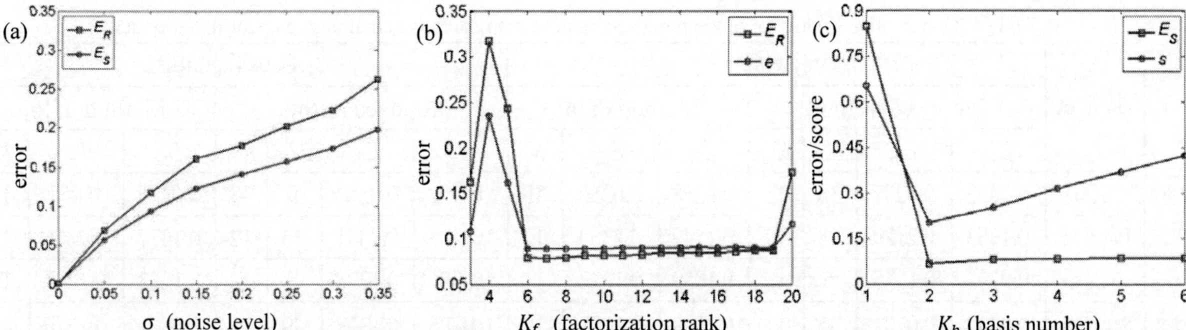

Figure 1: Algorithm performance evaluation with synthetic data. (a) Algorithm performance with regard to noise contamination of measurement matrix. (b) Correlation between the error of rotation matrices and the 2D reprojection error evaluated using equation (22). (c) Correlation between structure error and cross validation score.

4.1. Performance on synthetic non-rigid structure

A total of 20 points are randomly generated in a $1.0 \times 1.0 \times 1.0$ cube in 3D space. The points are allowed to move in such a way that their locations are defined by equation (3) using trajectory basis model with $K = 2$. Around those points, 36 randomly positioned orthographic cameras are pointing at them, producing 36 images of size 1.0×1.0. Each image contains a set of measurements of the non-rigid structure. Those measurements are stacked together forming a noise-free measurement matrix. Different levels of Gaussian noise (standard deviation σ ranging from 0 to 0.35) are added to the measurement matrix, which is then used for motion and structure recovery.

Let R_i and $\hat{\mathrm{R}}_i$ be the ground truth and recovered camera matrix of the ith image frame, respectively, and S_i and $\hat{\mathrm{S}}_i$ be ground truth structure and recovered structure at the ith frame, respectively. We define the rotation matrix error E_{R} and structure error E_{S} as

$$E_{\mathrm{R}} = \min_{R} \sqrt{\frac{1}{F}\sum_{i=1}^{F}\|\mathrm{R}_i - \hat{\mathrm{R}}_i R\|^2} \quad (24)$$

$$E_{\mathrm{S}} = \min_{R} \sqrt{\frac{1}{F \cdot N}\sum_{i=1}^{F}\|\mathrm{S}_i - R\hat{\mathrm{S}}_i\|^2} \quad (25)$$

where R is a 3×3 matrix aligning recovered camera (or structure) matrices with ground truth.

Figure 1(a) shows the proposed algorithm's performance with regard to noise. At each noise level, a total of 30 trials are performed, and their average errors are plotted in Figure 1(a). It shows that both camera matrix error and structure error increase almost linearly with regard to noise contamination in the measurement matrix, indicating the structure and motion can be recovered robustly.

The camera matrix error recovered using Gaussian noise (σ=0.05) contaminated measurement matrix at different factorization rank is shown in Figure 1(b) in blue squares, together with 2D reprojection error shown in green circles. The correlation between 2D reprojection error and camera matrix error is evident, and thus the best factorization rank can be identified using 2D reprojection error, in case of real images where the camera error is unknown. In this example, as the measurements are generated exactly using equation (5), it is expected that the best factorization rank is $3K$.

For a given set of camera matrices (recovered from $\sigma = 0.05$ Gaussian noise contaminated measurements with factorization rank $K_f = 6$), the structure error for different number of trajectory basis vectors is shown in Figure 1(c). Also shown in the figure is the cross validation score which indicates the quality of recovered non-rigid structures. It can be seen that cross validation score correlates with structure error well and thus is a good indicator of the quality of recovered non-rigid structure.

4.2. Real non-rigid structure

The proposed algorithm is also quantitatively evaluated with images of deforming object in the real world. Datasets containing real world object deformations are obtained from the project website of Akhter et al. [14]. In each dataset, a sequence of synthetic orthographic cameras are rotating 5 degrees per frame around the z-axis, pointing to the object and generating image measurements. In our experiments, noises are added in such a way that the standard deviation of Gaussian noise is 5% of the standard deviation of measurement matrix. And, in order to make error comparison more meaningful, non-rigid structure is centroid removed and normalized with standard deviation being equal to 1 before evaluating structure error using equation (25).

Table 4 shows a quantitative comparison with existing trajectory basis method [6] whose code is provided by the authors at their project website [14]. Both recovered

Table 4: Quantitative evaluation of the proposed method with datasets containing real world deformations

Dataset	noise free							5% Gaussian noise						
	Proposed method				Method of [6]			Proposed method				Method of [6]		
	E_R	E_S	K_f	K_b	E_R	E_S	K	E_R	E_S	K_f	K_b	E_R	E_S	K
Drink	0.0052	0.0247	33	13	0.0058	0.0250	13	0.0292	0.0544	9	13	0.0335	0.053	13
PickUp	0.1363	0.2129	13	10	0.1549	0.2369	12	0.1465	0.2331	35	12	0.1477	0.2315	12
Yoga	0.0792	0.1125	5	10	0.1059	0.1622	11	0.0796	0.1238	5	8	0.1263	0.1801	11
Stretch	0.0487	0.0702	37	11	0.0549	0.1088	12	0.0785	0.1317	39	11	0.0861	0.1516	12

Figure 2: Reconstructed Yoga structures using 5% Gaussian noise contaminated image measurements. The upper row is the structure obtained by the proposed decomposition method, and the lower row is structure obtained by method of [6].

rotation matrices and recovered structure are compared with ground truth, and the errors are evaluated using equation (24) and (25). Also, in Table 4 we show the factorization rank K_f and basis number K_b that are generated by the proposed method; whereas the basis number K for the method of [6] is suggested by the authors (with the same basis number chosen in noisy case).

An example of recovered non-rigid structure (shown in grey circles) using noise contaminated Yoga dataset is shown in Figure 2, with ground truth structure (shown in black dots) superimposed. The upper row of Figure 2 is the structure recovered using the proposed decomposition method, and the lower row is the structure recovered using the method of [6].

5. Conclusions

In this paper, we proposed a new method to recover camera motion and non-rigid structure with a trajectory basis representation for the non-rigid structure. By decomposing the problem into two sub-problems and solving for optimal solution to each sub-problem, the method first recovers camera motion without the need to pre-define the basis number. Then, with recovered camera motion, the method finds the best number of basis that should be used for non-rigid structure representation. Hence, the proposed method leads to a completely automatic algorithm for non-rigid structure reconstruction. Experiments demonstrate that the method improves the reconstruction quality of both the non-rigid structure and the camera motion.

Acknowledgements

The work described in this paper was supported by a grant from the Research Grants Council (project no. HKU 712911E) of the Hong Kong Special Administrative Region, China and CRCG of the University of Hong Kong.

References

[1] R. I. Hartley and A. Zisserman, *Multiple view geometry in computer vision*, 2nd ed.: Cambridge University Press, 2004.

[2] Y. S. Hung and W. K. Tang, "Projective reconstruction from multiple views with minimization of 2D reprojection error," *International Journal of Computer Vision,* vol. 66, pp. 305-317, 2006.

[3] P. Sturm and B. Triggs, "A factorization based algorithm for multi-image projective structure and motion," in *European Conference on Computer Vision*, 1996, pp. 709-720.

[4] C. Tomasi and T. Kanade, "Shape and motion from image streams under orthography: a factorization method," *International Journal of Computer Vision,* vol. 9, pp. 137-154, 1992.

[5] B. Triggs, "Factorization methods for projective structure and motion," in *Computer Vision and Pattern Recognition*, 1996, pp. 845-851.

[6] I. Akhter, Y. Sheikh, S. Khan, and T. Kanade, "Trajectory space: a dual representation for nonrigid structure from motion," *IEEE Transactions on Pattern Analysis and Machine Intelligence,* vol. 33, pp. 1442-1456, 2011.

[7] M. Brand and R. Bhotika, "Flexible flow for 3D nonrigid tracking and shape recovery," in *Computer Vision and Pattern Recognition*, 2001, pp. I-315-I-322 vol.1.

[8] J. Xiao, J. Chai, and T. Kanade, "A closed-form solution to non-rigid shape and motion recovery," *International Journal of Computer Vision,* vol. 67, pp. 233-246, 2006.

[9] M. Brand, "A direct method for 3D factorization of nonrigid motion observed in 2D," in *Computer Vision and Pattern Recognition*, 2005, pp. 122-128 vol. 2.
[10] R. Hartley and R. Vidal, "Perspective nonrigid shape and motion recovery," in *European Conference on Computer Vision*, Marseille, France, 2008, pp. 276-289.
[11] I. Akhter, Y. Sheikh, S. Khan, and T. Kanade, "Nonrigid structure from motion in trajectory space," in *Neural Information Processing Systems*, 2008.
[12] I. Akhter, Y. Sheikh, and S. Khan, "In defense of orthonormality constraints for nonrigid structure from motion," in *Computer Vision and Pattern Recognition*, 2009, pp. 1534-1541.
[13] A. Bartoli, V. Gay-Bellile, U. Castellani, J. Peyras, S. Olsen, and P. Sayd, "Coarse to fine low rank structure from motion," in *Computer Vision and Pattern Recognition*, 2008, pp. 1-8.
[14] http://cvlab.lums.edu.pk/nrsfm/

SESSION

FACE, GAZE, EXPRESSION RECOGNITION, DETECTION, TRACKING, OTHER RELATED METHODS

Chair(s)

TBA

Rough-Fuzzy system-based real-time face tracking

A. Petrosino[1], **G. Salvi**[2]
[1]Department of Applied Science, University of Naples "Parthenope", Naples, Italy
[2]Department of Economics Studies, University of Naples "Parthenope", Naples, Italy

Abstract—*Automatic detection and tracking of human faces in video sequences are considered fundamental in many applications, such as face recognition, video surveillance and human-computer interface. In this study, we propose a technique for real-time robust facial tracking in human facial videos based on a new algorithm for face detection in color images. As a part of face tracking, the Kalman filter algorithm is used to predict the next face detection window and smooth the tracking trajectory. Experiments on the five benchmark databases demonstrate the ability of the proposed algorithm in detecting and tracking faces in difficult conditions.*

1. Introduction

Visual location and tracking of objects of interest, particularly, human faces in video sequences, is a critical task and an active field in computer vision applications that involves interaction with the human face by using surveillance, human-computer interface, biometrics, etc. As the face is a deformable target and its appearance easily changes because of the face-camera pose, sudden changes in illumination and complex background, tracking it is very difficult. Common methods of face detection include skin color [1], [2], boosting [3], [4], neural networks (NNs) [5], support vector machines (SVMs) [6], [7] and template matching [8].

The results of the skin-color based method are strongly influenced by sudden changes in lighting and the method often fails to detect people with different skin colors. In many cases, the results of the boosting, SVMs, and in particular, the NN methods suffer from the disadvantage of being strongly linked to the set of images selected for learning. For this type of approach, as face characteristics are implicitly derived from a window, a large number of face and non-face training examples are required to train a well-performed detector. The correlations between an input image and the stored patterns are computed for detection; thus, they appear sensitive to variations of both pose and orientation.

The main purpose of face detection is to localize and extract with certainty a subset of pixels which satisfy some specific criteria like chromatic or textural homogeneity, the face region, from the background also to hard variations of scene conditions, such as the presence of a complex background and uncontrolled illumination. Rough set theory offers a novel approach to manage uncertainty that has been used for the discovery of data dependencies, importance of features, patterns in sample data, feature space dimensionality reduction, and the classification of objects. We specifically propose to adopt rough fuzzy sets together with on-line learning [9].

The hybrid notion of rough fuzzy sets comes from the combination of two models of uncertainty like coarseness by handling rough sets [10] and vagueness by handling fuzzy sets [11]. In particular the rough sets defines the contour or uniform regions in the image that appear like fuzzy sets and their comparison or combination generates more or less uniform partitions of the image. Rough fuzzy sets, and in particular C-sets firstly introduced by Caianiello [12], are able to capture these aspects together, extracting different kinds of knowledge in data.

Based on these considerations, we report a real-time face tracking system based on rough fuzzy sets and on-line learning by NN [9], able to detect skin regions in the input image at hand and thus independently from what previously seen. The extracted features at different scales by rough fuzzy sets are clustered from a unsupervised NN by minimizing the fuzziness of the output layer. The face detection method, named multi scale rough neural network (MS-RNN), has been applied to real-time face tracking using Kalman filtering algorithm [13], this filter is used to predict the next face detection window and smooth the tracking trajectory.

2. Theoretical background

The definition of rough fuzzy sets we propose to adopt here takes inspiration, as firstly made in [14], from the notion of composite sets [12], [15]. A *composite set* or C-set is a triple $C = (\chi, m, M)$ (where $\chi = \{X_1, \ldots, X_p\}$ is a partition of X in p disjoint subsets $X_1, \ldots, X_p$, while m and M are mappings of kind $X \rightarrow [0,1]$ such that $\forall x \in X, m(x) = \sum m_i \mu_{X_i}(x)$ and $M(x) = \sum M_i \mu_{X_i}(x)$ where

$$m_i = \inf\{f(x)|x \in X_i\} \quad (1)$$
$$M_i = \sup\{f(x)|x \in X_i\} \quad (2)$$

for each choice of function $f : X \rightarrow [0,1]$. χ and f uniquely define a composite set. Based on these assumptions we may formulate the following definition of rough fuzzy set:

1) If f is the membership function μ_F and the partition χ is made with respect to a relation R, i.e. $\chi = X/R$, a fuzzy set F gets two approximations $R^-(F)$ and $R_-(F)$, which are again fuzzy sets with membership functions defined as Eqs. (1) and (2), i.e. $m_i = \mu_{R_-(F)}$ and $M_i = \mu_{R^-(F)}$. The couple of sets $(R^-(F), R_-(F))$ is a *rough fuzzy set.*
2) Let $C = (\chi, m, M)$ and $C' = (\chi', m', M')$ two rough fuzzy sets related, respectively, to partitions $\chi = (X_1, \ldots, X_s)$ and $\chi' = (X'_1, \ldots, X'_s)$ with $m(m')$ and $M(M')$ indicating the measures expressed in Eqs. (1) and (2). The *product* between two C-sets C and C', denoted by $\otimes$, is defined as a new rough fuzzy set $C'' = C \otimes C' = (\chi'', m'', M'')$ where χ'' is a new partition whose elements are $X''_{i,j} = X_i \cap X'_j$ and m'' and M'' are obtained by

$$m''_{i,j} = \sup\{m_i, m'_j\}, \quad M''_{i,j} = \inf\{M_i, M'_j\}$$

As shown in [15], recursive application of the previous operation provides a refinement of the original sets, thus realizing a powerful tool for measurement and a basic signal processing technique.

3. Face detection method

The overall algorithm for face detection is given as flow chart in Fig. 1 where the input to the algorithm is an RGB image. The algorithm first transforms red, green end blue color component in CIE*Lab* color space. The luminance component L and the chrominance components a are used to create the skin map at each pixel (x, y) as follows:

$$SM(x, y) = SM_L(x, y) \cap SM_a(x, y)$$

where $SM_L(x, y)$ and $SM_a(x, y)$ are obtained as the output of a specialized NN incurred from the integration of the rough fuzzy set based scale space transform and neural clustering, and separately applied to the L component image and a component image, as depicted in Fig. 1. Finally, the skin map SM is fed as input to an algorithm for the detection of elliptical objects, as an extension of the technique reported in [16].

The smooth shape and curve of a face, in some cases, may be varied considerably the intensity of the light reflected from it. The chromaticity components, instead, remain relatively unchanged and it can be used to detect skin regions. For this reason, to separate the skin from the non-skin regions, we analyze only the chromaticity distribution of an image, in particular, those relating to the chromaticity component a regardless of the lightness component. After detection of the skin regions, the luminance component of the colors is used to capture the details of the face (eyes, nose, lips, eyebrows, beard, etc.).

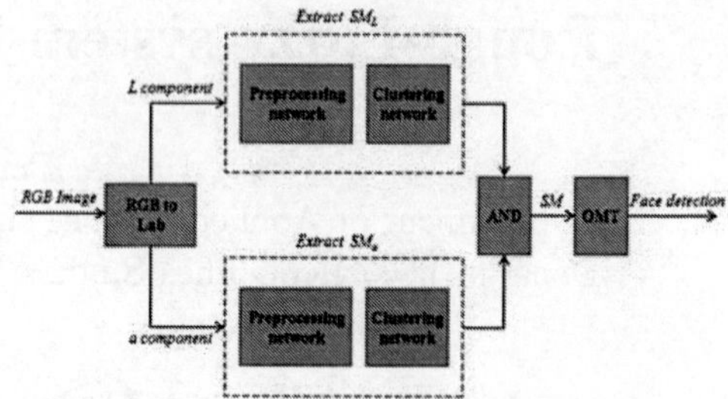

Fig. 1: Overall face detection method

3.1 The proposed multi-scale method

The multi-scale construction follows that of a fuzzy neural network [17], [18]. Specifically, it consists into two pyramidal-layered networks with fixed weights, each looking upon an $2^n \times 2^n$ image. By fixing the initial dimension of ***CRC*** (***C***andidate ***R***egion to be ***C***ategorized), each pyramidal network is constituted by $n - R$ multiresolution levels. Each processing element (i, j) at the $r - th$ level of the first pyramid (respectively second pyramid) computes the minimum value (respectively maximum value) over a $2w \times 2w$ area at the $(r-1) - th$ level. The pyramidal structures are computed in a top-down manner, firstly analyzing regions as large as possible and then proceeding by splitting regions turned out to be not of interest. The mechanism of splitting operates as follows. If we suppose to be at the $r - th$ level of both pyramid-networks and analyze a region $w \times w$ which is the intersection of four $2w \times 2w$ regions, the minimum and maximum values computed inside are denoted by $m_{s,t}$ and $M_{s,t}$, $s = i, \ldots, i + w, t = j, \ldots, j + w$. The combination of the minima and maxima values is made up at the output layer, i.e.

$$c^1_{i,j} = \min_{s,t}[M_{s,t}] \qquad c^2_{i,j} = \max_{s,t}[m_{s,t}]$$

If $c^1_{i,j}$ and $c^2_{i,j}$ satisfy a specific constraint, the region under consideration is seen as ***RC*** (***R***egion to be ***C***ategorize) and the values are retained as elementary features of such a region. Otherwise, the region is divided in four sub-regions each of dimension equal to $w/2$. The preprocessing subnetwork is applied again to the newly defined regions. The fuzzy intersections computed by the preprocessing subnetwork are fed to a clustering subnetwork which is described in the following.

3.2 Clustering subnetwork

Each node in the clustering subnetwork receives, as shown in Fig. 2, two input values from each corresponding neuron at the previous layer. In particular, at each iteration, a learning step is applied to the clustering subnetwork according to the minimization of a *Fuzzines Index* (FI), applying, and somewhere extending, the learning mechanism proposed in [19].

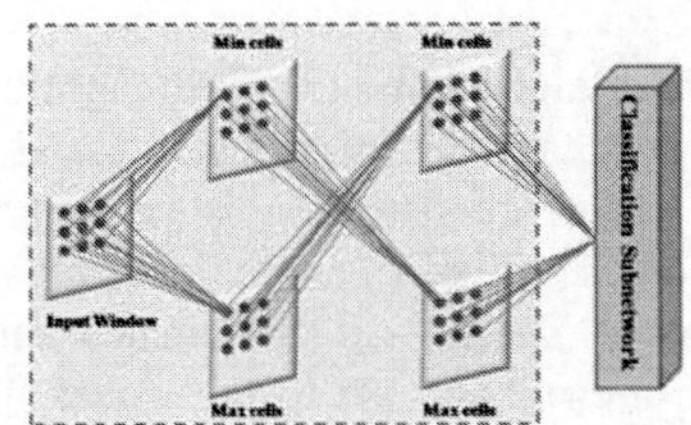

Fig. 2: The preprocessing networks.

The output of a node j is then obtained as

$$o_j = f(I_j);\; I_j = g(\underline{O}_i, \underline{W}_{ji})$$

where $\underline{O}_i = (o_i^{2,1}, o_i^{2,2})$ and $\underline{W}_{ji} = (w_{j,i}^1, w_{j,i}^2)$ where $w_{j,i}^q$ indicates the connection weight between the jth node of the output layer and the ith node of the previous layer in the qth cell-plane, $q = 1, 2$. Each sum is intended over all nodes i in the neighborhood of the jth node at the upper hidden layer. f (the *membership function*) can be sigmoidal, hyperbolic, Gaussian, Gaborian, etc. with the accordance that if o_j takes the value 0.5, a small quantity (usually 0.001) is added; this reflects into dropping out instability conditions. g is a similarity function, e.g. correlation, Minkowsky distance, etc. To retain the value of each output node o_j in [0, 1], we apply the following mapping to each input image pixel g

$$g' = \frac{g - g_{min}}{g_{max} - g_{min}}$$

where g_{min} and g_{max} are the lowest and highest gray levels in the image.

The subnetwork has to self-organize by minimizing the fuzziness of the output layer. Since the membership function is chosen to be sigmoidal, minimizing the fuzziness is equivalent to minimizing the distances between corresponding pixel values in both cell-planes at the upper hidden layer. Since random initialization acts as noise, all the weights are initially set to unity. The adjustment of weights is done using the gradient descent search, i.e. the incremental change $\Delta w_{j,i}^l, l = 1, 2$, is taken as proportional to the sum of the negative gradient $-\eta \frac{\partial E}{\partial o_i} f'(I_i) o_j$. The adjustment rule is then the following:

$$w_{j,i}^l = w_{j,i}^l + \eta \Delta w_{j,i}^l$$

Specifically, we adopted the Linear Index of Fuzziness, whose updating rules look as follows, where E indicates the energy-fuzziness of our method and $n = M \times N$.

Linear Index of Fuzziness (LIF) learning:

$$\Delta w_{j,i}^1 = \begin{cases} -\eta_{LIF}(1 - o_j) o_j o_i^{2,2} & \text{if } 0 \leq o_j \leq 0.5 \\ \eta_{LIF}(1 - o_j) o_j o_i^{2,2} & \text{if } 0.5 < o_j \leq 1 \end{cases}$$

$$\Delta w_{j,i}^2 = \begin{cases} -\eta_{LIF}(1 - o_j) o_j o_i^{2,1} & \text{if } 0 \leq o_j \leq 0.5 \\ \eta_{LIF}(1 - o_j) o_j o_i^{2,1} & \text{if } 0.5 < o_j \leq 1 \end{cases}$$

where $\eta_{LIF} = \eta \times 2/n$.

The previous rules hold also for the determination of an exact threshold value, θ, adopted for divide the image in skin regions e non skin regions, when convergence is reached. According to the properties of fuzziness the initial threshold is set to be 0.5; this value allows to determine an hard decision from an unstable condition to a stable one.

As said before, the updating of weights is continued until the network stabilizes. The method is said *stable* (the learning stops) when

$$E(t+1) \leq E(t) \qquad and \qquad |O(t+1) - O(t)| \leq \gamma$$

where $E(t)$ is the method fuzziness computed at the tth iteration, γ is a prefixed very small positive quantity and $O(t) = \sum_{j:o_j \geq 0.5} o_j$. After convergence, the pixels j with $o_j > \theta$ are considered to constitute the skin map of the image; they are set to take value 255, in contrast with the remaining which will constitute the background (value 0).

4. Skin map segmentation

We transformed the image model into CEI*Lab*, and normalized the luminance component L and the chrominance components a in the range of $[0, 255]$. To realize multi-class image segmentation, the ***CRC*** must satisfy a homogeneity constraint, i.e. the difference between $c_{i,j}^1$ and $c_{i,j}^2$ must be less than or equal to a prefixed threshold. In such a case, the region is seen as uniform and becomes ***RC*** otherwise, the ***CRC*** is split into four newly defined ***CRC***, letting w be $w/2$. The parameters of the preprocessing sub-network have been set to the following values:

- $w_0 = 8,\; w_t = w_{t-1/2}$ (t denotes iteration)
- $\theta = 50$

The output of the preprocessing sub-network normalized in the $[0, 1]$ range is fed to a clustering subnetwork. The parameters of the clustering subnetwork have been set to the following values:

- $\eta = 0.2$ (learning rate)
- $\gamma = 0.001$ (convergence rate)

The reason for these choices resides in a most successful skin detection system, both for detecting skin and suppressing noise, while requiring the minimum amount of computation or, equivalently, minimum number of iterations to converge.

5. Face detection

Face detection is achieved by detecting elliptical regions in the skin map by properly modifying the *Orientation Matching* (OM) technique reported in [16]. The technique detects circular objects of radius in the interval $[r_m, r_M]$, computing the OM transform of the input image and taking the peaks of the transform, which correspond to the centers of the circular patterns.

To customize the technique for handling our problem of detecting elliptical pattern in the skin map, we performed a statistical analysis on 500 images taken from the databases used to test the method to find a proper ratio between major and minor semi-axis of ellipses around faces. We statistically found this ratio as 0.75.

Let a and b represent the semi-major axis and semi-minor axis, respectively. We modified the OM transform to find all the ellipses in the image with $b = 0.75 \times a$. Specifically, we aimed to detect elliptical objects of semi-major axis in the interval $[a_m, a_M]$. Let us consider $E_{a_m}^{a_M}(0,0)$ as the ellipses of the semi-major axis a_m and a_M with center in the origin:

$$E_{a_m}^{a_M}(0,0) = \{(x,y) \in \Re^2 : a_m^2 \leq \frac{16}{9}x^2 + y^2 \leq a_M^2\}$$

The function $\phi^*(x,y)$, defined over $E_{a_m}^{a_M}(0,0)$, represents the orientation of the gradient of an ideal ellipse with the center in the origin of the semi-major axis a and semi-minor axes $b = 0.75 \times a$ or, equivalently, as the solution of

$$\cos\phi^*(x,y) = -\frac{4}{3}\frac{x}{a} \qquad \sin\phi^*(x,y) = -\frac{y}{a}$$

with $(x,y) \in E_{a_m}^{a_M}(0,0)$. Given an image $I(x,y)$ and a set $\phi(x,y)$ satisfy the method:

$$\cos\phi = I_x/(I_x^2 + I_y^2)^{1/2} \qquad \sin\phi = I_y/(I_x^2 + I_y^2)^{1/2}$$

the OM transform can be obtained as follows:

$$OM(u,v) = \frac{4}{5\pi\sqrt{2}(a_M - a_m)} \times$$

$$\int\int_{E_{a_m}^{a_M}} \frac{\cos(\phi^*(x-u, y-v) - \phi(x-y))}{a} dxdy$$

where the perimeter of the ellipse is given by

$$C = 4\int_0^{\pi/2} \sqrt{a^2\sin^2\phi + b^2\cos^2\phi d\phi} \approx$$

$$\pi\sqrt{2(a^2+b^2)} = (Since\ b = 0.75 \times a) = \frac{4}{5\pi\sqrt{2}a}$$

This approximation will be within about 5% of the true value; thus, a is not more than three times longer than b (in other words, the ellipse is not very "squashed").

6. Face tracking

The use of our MS-RNN method for face tracking relies on the fact that the skin color is invariant to face orientation and is insensitive to partial occlusion. Also, our system proved insensitive to variations of scene conditions, such as the presence of a complex background and uncontrolled illumination. Based on these considerations, we applied the MS-RNN method at any frames of video sequences and the Kalman filter algorithm [13]. Kalman filtering helps to predict the next face detection window and smooth the tracking trajectory. Face detection is performed within a predicted window instead of an entire image region to reduce computation costs. The $x - y$ coordinates and height of the face region are initially set to the values given by the face detection process, while the velocity values of the state vector are set to 1. The face motion model used in our tracking method can be defined by the following set of space-state equations:

$$\begin{aligned} \mathbf{x}_{k+1} &= \Phi\mathbf{x}_k + \mathbf{w}_k \\ \mathbf{z}_{k+1} &= \mathbf{H}\mathbf{x}_{k+1} + \mathbf{v}_k \end{aligned}$$

where $\mathbf{x}_k$ represents the state vector at the time k, characterized by five parameters consisting of the $x - y$ coordinates of the center point of the face region (c_x, c_y), the velocity in the x and y directions (v_x, v_y), and the height H_k of the face-bounded region. The width of the face-bounded region is always assumed to be 0.75 times the size of the calculated height. The transition matrix, Φ, which relates the current state to the predicted state after the time interval Δt is given as

$$\Phi = \begin{bmatrix} 1 & 0 & \Delta t & 0 & 0 \\ 0 & 1 & 0 & \Delta t & 0 \\ 0 & 0 & 1 & 0 & 0 \\ 0 & 0 & 0 & 1 & 0 \\ 0 & 0 & 0 & 0 & 1 \end{bmatrix}$$

The vector $\mathbf{z}_k \in \mathbb{R}^3$ represents the face position and height observed with the observation matrix

$$\mathbf{H} = \begin{bmatrix} 1 & 0 & \Delta t & 0 & 0 \\ 0 & 1 & 0 & \Delta t & 0 \\ 0 & 0 & 0 & 0 & 1 \end{bmatrix}$$

and $\mathbf{w}_k$ and $\mathbf{v}_k$ are the zero-mean, white, Gaussian random processes modeling the system noise. The whole filtering procedure consists of prediction and correction steps, which are carried out alternatively. The state in the next time step is predicted from the current state using

$$\begin{aligned} \mathbf{x}_{k+1|k} &= \Phi\mathbf{x}_{k|k} \\ \mathbf{z}_{k+1|k} &= \mathbf{H}\mathbf{x}_{k+1|k} \end{aligned}$$

Face detection is performed on the window of height $H_{k+1|k}$ and width $0.75H_{k+1|k}$ centered at a predicted position. Detection within the window instead of the whole image helps to reduce the detection time, which is important for real-time operations. The Kalman corrector is

$$\mathbf{x}_{k+1|k+1} = \mathbf{x}_{k+1|k} + K_{k+1}(\mathbf{z}_{k+1} - \mathbf{z}_{k+1|k})$$

where K_{k+1} is the Kalman gain, computed as

$$K_{k+1} = P_{k+1}H^T[HP_{k+1|K}H^T + R_{k+1}]^{-1}$$

The covariance matrix P is updated as follows

$$\begin{aligned} P_{k+1|k} &= \Phi P_{k|k}\Phi^T + Q_k \\ P_{k+1|k+1} &= [I - Kk + 1H_{k+1}]P_{k+1|k} \end{aligned}$$

where $Q_k = E[\mathbf{w}_k\mathbf{w}_k^T]$, $R_k = E[\mathbf{v}_k\mathbf{v}_k^T]$ and $P_{0|0} = E[\mathbf{x}_0\mathbf{x}_0^T]$. The face detector and the tracker are used simultaneously. The overall algorithm for face tracking is given as a flow chart in Fig. 3.

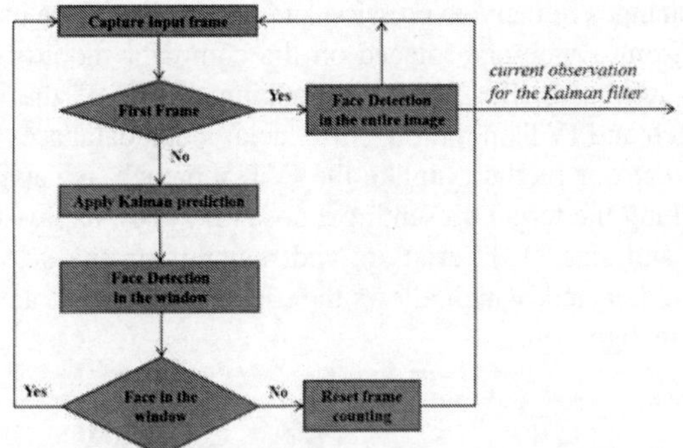

Fig. 3: Overall face tracking algorithm

7. Experiments

7.1 Face detection experiments

7.1.1 Experiment 1

To form an experimental dataset and evaluate the effectiveness of the proposed color face detection method in terms of face detection performance, a total of 7266 facial images from 980 subjects were collected from three publicly available face databases, CMU PIE [20], color FERET [21], [22], and IMM [23]. A total of 2847 face images of 68 subjects were collected from CMU PIE; for one subject, the images had different expressions and 21 lighting variations with "room lighting on" conditions. From Color FERET, a total of 4179 face images of 872 subjects were collected; for one subject, the images included five different pose variations. Specifically, the pose angles were in the range from -45^0 to $+45^0$. From IMM, a total of 240 face images of 40 subjects were collected; for one subject, the images include six different pose variations. Specifically, the pose angles were in the range from -30^0 to $+30^0$. The face images used in Experiment 1 were scaled down to their one-fourth size. Fig. 4 and 5 show some of the test images and SM results.

To evaluate the performance of the face detection algorithm, a number of detection rates and false alarms are used. The detection rate is defined as the ratio between the number of faces correctly detected and the actual number of faces, while a false alarm is a detection of the face where there is no face. Table 1 shows the results of the MS-RNN face-detection method on CMU PIE, color FERET, and IMM databases.

Fig. 4: Twelve of the 7266 images in the Experiment 1.

Fig. 5: Twelve of the 7266 skin map segmentation results in the Experiment 1.

Table 1: Experimental Results on CMU-PIE, color FERET, and IMM databases.

Database	Detection rate	False alarms
CMU-PIE	92.16%	175
color FERET	96.53%	16
IMM	98.65%	0

Table 1 shows that the proposed algorithm for face detection exhibits very good performance in detecting faces, which is also affected by scene condition variations, such as the presence of a complex background and uncontrolled illumination. However, the MS-RNN method is noted to be sensitive to the images where the background (neutral illumination) is turned off, mainly those obtained from

CMU-PIE database.

7.1.2 Experiment 2

This experiment used the CalTech [24] face database. A total of 450 frontal images of 27 people of different races and facial expressions were included. Each image was of 896×592 pixels. The experiment employed detection and false alarms to evaluate the face detection performance. Fig. 6 shows some detection results.

Fig. 6: Face detection results by the proposed method in the Experiment 2.

Table 2 shows the comparison of the results of the MS-RNN face detection method on CalTech databases with other fast face detection methods reported in [6], [7], which may be applied to real-time face tracking.

Specifically, the first method used for comparison extends the detection in gray-images method presented in [6] to detection in color images. The second method segments skin colors, in the HSV color space, using a self-organizing Takagi-Sugeno fuzzy network with support vector learning [7]. A fuzzy system is used, to eliminate the effects of illumination, to adaptively determine the fuzzy classifier segmentation threshold according to the illumination of an image. The proposed method showed the highest detection rate as well as the smallest number of false alarms, when compared with other methods.

Table 2: Experimental Results on CalTech database.

Method	Detection rate	False alarms
Texture + SVM [6]	95.7%	91
SOTFN-SV+IFAT [7]	95.7%	67
Proposed method	98.43%	20

7.2 Face tracking experiments

The proposed system was written in Visual C++ and implemented on a personal computer with an Intel Core i3 3.1 GHz CPU and Windows 7 operating system. The proposed detection system took 0.516 (s) for an image measuring 720×576 pixels. During the tracking process, the detection window size was 200×200 pixels, and the detection time was about 0.08 (s) if only the detection operation was conducted. The real-time tracking system uses a SONY CCD camera to capture images, and each image measured 720×576 pixels. At the start, a face was detected from the whole captured image, and subsequently, a face was detected within a predicted search region measuring 200×200 pixels.

7.2.1 Experiment 1

In this experiment, we tested the quality of the proposed face-tracking system on the standard IIT-NRC [25] facial video database compared with the Incremental Visual Tracker (IVT). This database contains short videos that show large changes in facial expression and orientation of the users taken from a web-cam placed on the computer monitor. In Fig. 7, we have illustrated the tracking results of the our approach and IVT on the IIT-NRC facial video database. We noted that our method, unlike the IVT approach, is capable of tracking the target presenting a pose (31, 206), expression (102), and size (13) variation, and maintaining the size of the face detected, which allows the use of the frames tracked in the recognition.

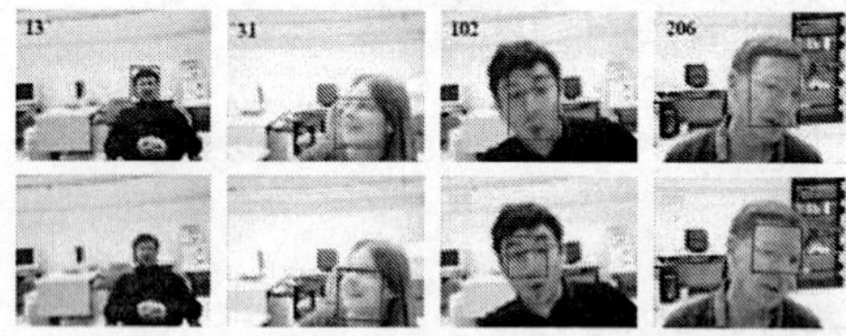

Fig. 7: Tracking results on IIT-NRC video face database: the upper row shows the results obtained with the proposed tracker, while the bottom row shows the results obtained by IVT.

7.2.2 Experiment 2

In this experiment, we tested the quality of the proposed face tracking system on a set of 500 video clips collected from YouTube. The frame size ranged from (320×240) to (240×180) pixels. Despite the heavy rate of noise in the video used, mostly due to the low resolution and high compression rate, our tracker successfully tracked 90% of the video clips. In Fig. 8, we have presented examples of well-tracked videos. The level of performance obtained by our tracker is more than satisfactory by taking into account the low quality and high variability in the data tested.

7.2.3 Experiment 3

Fig. 9 shows the tracking results for a succession of captured frames. These results show that, the proposed system can correctly track a subject under various complex motion and partial occlusion. By tracing the center point of the face detected in each frame, we obtained a motion

Fig. 8: Face Tracking results on YouTube video clips.

signature as shown in Fig. 10. Such motion signatures can be used to characterize human activities.

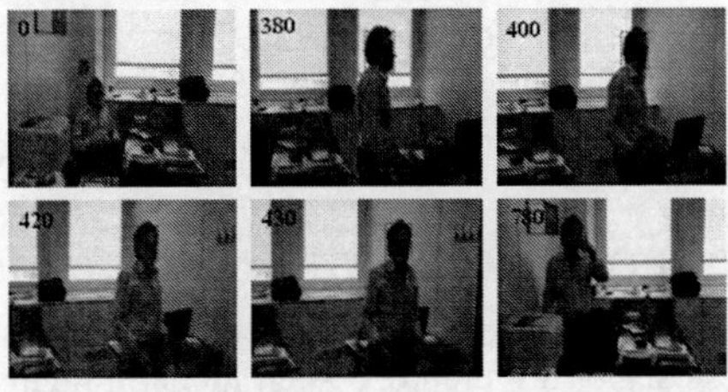

Fig. 9: Face tracking of a subject under various complex motion and partial occlusion.

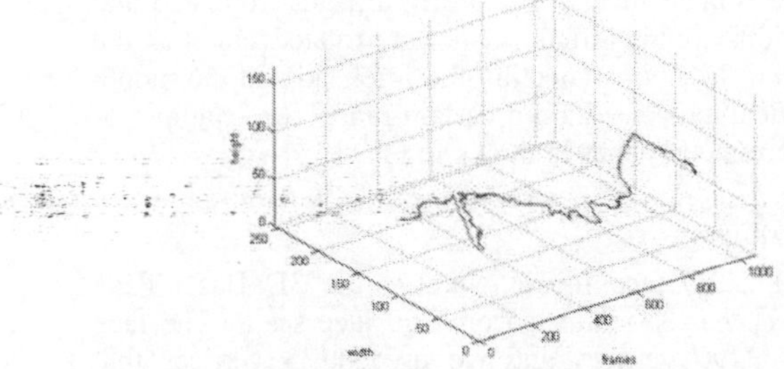

Fig. 10: The motion signature obtained by tracing the center point of the face detected in each frame.

8. Conclusions and future works

A new real-time face tracking system based on a face detection algorithm has been presented in this study. The fece detection method, based on rough fuzzy sets and on-line learning by NN, is applied to real-time face tracking using Kalman filter to predict the next face detection window and smooth the tracking trajectory. All our experiment and comparisons with other method demonstrate the performance of the proposed detection and tracking system. The ongoing work involves increasing the speed of our proposed system as well as adopting parallel processing provided by GPUs.

References

[1] Y.B. Sun, J.T. Kim, W.H. lee, "Extraction of face objects using skin color information," *Proc. IEEE Int'l Conf. Communications, Circuits and Systems and West Sino Expositions*, 2002, pp. 1136-1140.

[2] M. Soriano, B. Martinkauppi, S. Huovinen, M. Laaksonen, "Adaptive skin color modeling using the skin locus for selecting training pixels," *Pattern Recognition*, vol. 36, no. 3, 2003, pp. 681-690.

[3] P. Viola, M.J. Jones, "Robust real-time face detection," *Int'l J. Computer Vision*, vol. 57, no. 2, 2004, pp. 137-154.

[4] R. Lienhart, J. Maydt, "An extended set of Haar-like features for rapid object detection," *Proc. IEEE Int'l Conf. on Image Processing*, vol. 1, 2002, pp. 900-903.

[5] H. Rowley, S. Baluja, T. Kanade, "Neural network-based face detection," *IEEE Trans. Pattern Anal. Mach. Intell.*, vol. 20, no. 1, 1998, pp. 23-38.

[6] E. Osuna, R. Freund, and F. Girosi, "Training support vector machines: An application to face detection," *Proc. IEEE Int'l Conf. on Computer Vision and Pattern Recognition* (CVPR 97), pp. 130-136, 1997.

[7] C.F. Juang, S. W. Chang, "Fuzzy system-based real-time face tracking in a multi-subject environment with a pan-tilt-zoom camera", *Expert Systems with Applications*, vol. 37, no. 6, 2010, pp. 4526-4536.

[8] H.S. Kim, W.S. Kang, J.I. Shin, and S.H. Park, "Face detection using template matching and ellipse fitting," *IEICE Trans. Inf. Syst.*, vol.11, 2000, pp. 2008-2011.

[9] A. Petrosino, G. Salvi, "Rough fuzzy set based scale space transforms and their use in image analysis", *Int'l. J. Approximate Reasoning* vol. 41, 2006, pp. 212-228.

[10] Z. Pawlak, "Rough sets", *Int'l. J. Comput. Inform. Sci.*, vol. 11, no. 5, 1982, pp. 341-356.

[11] L.A. Zadeh, "Fuzzy sets", *Inform. Control* vol. 8, 1965, pp. 338-353.

[12] E.R. Caianiello, "A calculus of hierarchical systems," *Proc. Int'l. Conf. on Pattern Recognition*, Washington, DC, 1973, pp.1-5.

[13] D.E. Catlin, "Estimation, control, and the discrete Kalman filter," New York: Springer-Verlag, 1989.

[14] D. Dubois, H. Prade, "Rough fuzzy sets and fuzzy rough sets", *Int'l. Conf. on Fuzzy Sets in Informatics*, Moscow, September 20-23, 1993.

[15] E.R. Caianiello, A. Petrosino, "Neural networks, fuzziness and image processing", *Machine and Human Perception: Analogies and Divergencies*, V. Cantoni ed., Plenum Press, New York, 1994, pp. 355-370.

[16] M. Ceccarelli, A. Petrosino, "The orientation matching approach to circular object detection", *Proc. IEEE Int'l Conf. on Image Processing*, 2001, pp. 712-715.

[17] S. Lee, E. Lee, "Fuzzy neural networks", *Math. Biosci.*, vol. 23, 1975, pp. 151-177.

[18] P.K. Simpson, "Fuzzy min-max neural networks-Part I: Classification", *IEEE Trans. Neural Networks*, vol. 3, 1992, pp. 776-786.

[19] A. Ghosh, N.R. Pal, S.K. Pal, "Self-organization for object extraction and multilayer neural network and fuzziness measures", *IEEE Trans. Fuzzy Systems*, vol. 1, 1993, pp. 54-68.

[20] T. Sim and S. Baker, "The CMU pose illumination and expression database", *IEEE Trans. Pattern Anal. Mach. Intell.*, vol. 25, no. 12, 2003, pp. 1615-1617.

[21] P. J. Phillips, H. Wechsler, J. Huang, and P. Rauss, "The FERET database and evaluation procedure for face recognition algorithms," *Image and Vision Computing Journal*, vol. 16, no. 5, 1998, pp. 295-306.

[22] P. J. Phillips, H. Moon, S. A. Rizvi, and P. J. Rauss, "The FERET evaluation methodology for face recognition algorithms," *IEEE Trans. Pattern Anal. Mach. Intell.*, vol. 22, no. 10, 2000, pp. 1090-1104.

[23] M. B. Stegmann, B. K. Ersbøll, and R. Larsen, "FAME - A flexible appearance modeling environment", *IEEE Trans. Med. Imag.*, vol. 22, no. 10, 2003, pp. 1319-1331.

[24] Weber, Markus, "Face database collection of Markus Weber", [Online] 02 February 2006. Available: http://www.vision.caltech.edu/Image_Datasets/faces/.

[25] D. O. Gorodnichy, "Associative neural networks as means for low resolution video-based recognition", *Int'l Joint Conf. on Neural Networks* (IJCNN), 2005.

Pose-Invariant Face Recognition in Hyperspectral Images

Han Wang*
Department of Electrical Engineering and Computer Science
University of California, Irvine
Irvine, California 92697
Email: hwang5@uci.edu

Glenn Healey
Department of Electrical Engineering and Computer Science
University of California, Irvine
Irvine, California 92697
Email: ghealey@uci.edu

***Abstract*—Pose-invariant face recognition remains a challenging problem, especially when the pose change is large. Previous studies use either spatial or spectral information to address this problem. In this paper, we propose an algorithm that uses spatial and spectral information simultaneously to deal with large pose changes. We first learn 3D models from 2D images. We then use these 3D models to generate images in novel poses. Finally, we use spatial and spectral information to classify a test image. We demonstrate the effectiveness of the algorithm on a database of 200 subjects.**

Keywords—Face recognition, hyperspectral, Gabor filter, principal-component analysis (PCA), gradient descent

I. INTRODUCTION

The performance of face recognition systems degrades significantly in the presence of large pose variations due to the fact that image differences caused by pose changes are often large. Many algorithms have been proposed to address the problem. These methods can be divided into two categories: 2D techniques and 3D methods. The former category uses only 2D images while the latter uses 3D face models. PDM [1], AAM [2] and TFA [3] are representatives from the first category. 2D methods often require images of different poses which may not be available in practice. Studies also show that 2D methods can tolerate pose variation up to a certain limit ($\pm 45^\circ$) and beyond that the performance deteriorates dramatically [4]. Due to the fact that human heads are inherently 3D objects, 3D model-based methods are becoming popular. Representatives from this category include 3DMM [5] and systems proposed by Jiang et al. [6], Asthana et al. [7] and Prabhu et al. [8]. However, these methods have not provided results in the presence of large pose change (>60°). In this paper, we provide results on these pose changes as well. On the other hand, recent studies show that spectral discriminants also provide useful information and can be used for this purpose [9], [10], [11]. To make use of the flexibility of 3D models and spectral information, we propose an algorithm that learns personalized 3D models from 2D images and uses spatial and spectral information for recognition.

II. OVERVIEW OF THE ALGORITHM

The proposed face recognition algorithm consists of four stages. These stages are preprocessing, model training, feature extraction, and classification.

A. Preprocessing

Eye locations are first identified manually. Images are rotated such that the left eye and the right eye are at the same height in the rotated image. For profile images, forehead and mouth locations are identified. Images are rotated such that the angle between the line connecting the forehead and the mouth and the vertical axis is within a certain range. An example of original and rotated images is shown in Fig. 1.

B. Model Training

To learn a 3D face model, we use the 3D Basel Face Database [11] that is obtained from 200 face scans. The face model has 53490 vertices and we use 31133 vertices that comprise the face area. A face $S = (x_1, y_1, z_1, \ldots, x_n, y_n, z_n)^T$ is represented by n vertices where T is the transpose operation. It can also be represented using a basis according to

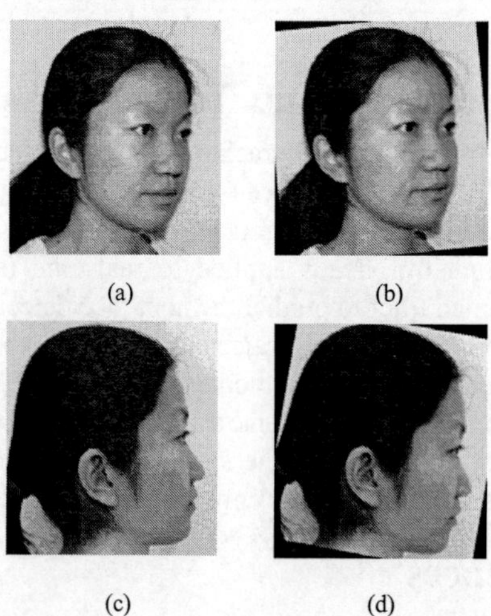

Fig. 1. (a) original 45° image (b) rotated 45° image (c) original 90° image (b) rotated 90° image

---
* For any inquiries, contact this author.

$$S = \overline{S} + P\alpha \quad (1)$$

where $\overline{s}$ is the mean shape, $P \in R^{3n \times m}$ is the shape basis and m is the number of eigenvectors, and $\alpha = (\alpha_1, \alpha_2, \ldots, \alpha_m)^T$ is the coefficient vector. In the study, we choose m = 50. We allow the face model to be scaled and translated according to

$$S^{'} = cS + T = c(\overline{S} + P\alpha) + T \quad (2)$$

where c is the scale ratio and T is the translation.

To learn the parameter vector (α, c, T), we use correspondences between the 3D model and the 2D image. We aim to find the parameter set that minimizes the sum of the squared error between the two sets of correspondences given by

$$(\alpha_0, c_0, T_0) = \min_{a,c,T} \sum_i ((c(\overline{S_i} + P_i\alpha) + T - S_i^{''})^2) \quad (3)$$

where i denotes the i_{th} correspondence and $S^{''}$ is the correspondence in the image.

We use steepest descent with random step size [13] to find the optimal parameters. In the study, gallery images are frontal images. Since frontal images do not have depth information, we also use correspondences in the probe image (a different pose). In the study, we use 65 correspondences in the frontal image and 22 correspondences in the 45° image and 26 correspondences in the 90° images. Most correspondences are anthropometric facial points [14] which can be identified uniquely, e.g., corner of the eye. Some correspondences are identified by using neighboring correspondences, e.g., the midpoint of the two neighboring correspondences. An example of the correspondences in the frontal, 45° and 90° images is shown in Fig. 2.

After the parameter set is estimated, we reconstruct a 3D face model according to (2). The correspondences in the 3D model often do not coincide with those in the frontal image. We add displacements to correspondences in the face model to make the two overlap. We interpolate displacements for non-correspondence vertices and add them to the model. Therefore, we learn a personalized face model given by

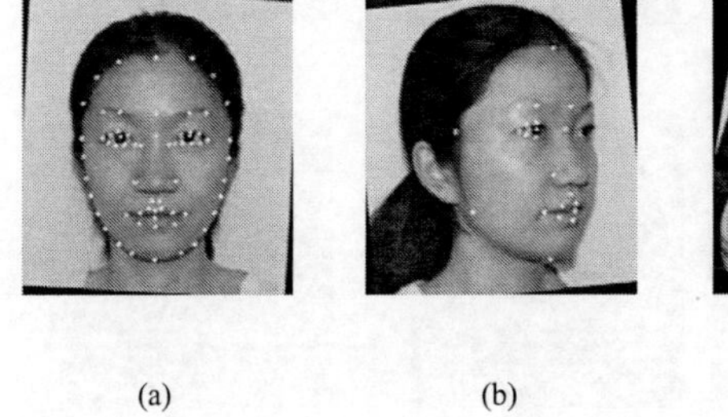

(a) (b) (c)

Fig. 2. Correspondences in (a) frontal image (b) 45° image (c) 90° image

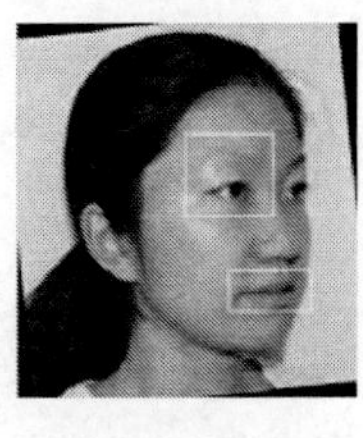

(a)

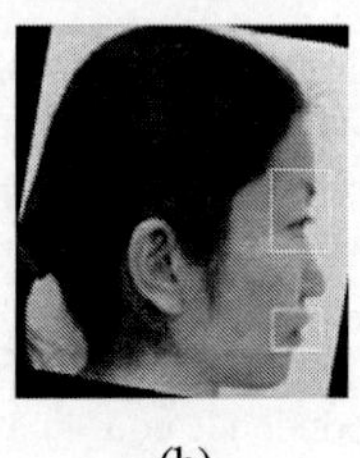

(b)

Fig. 3. Image regions selected in (a) 45° image (c) 90° image

$$S_d^{'} = c_0(\overline{S} + P\alpha_0) + T_0 + disp \quad (4)$$

where *disp* is the added displacement.

To learn texture information, we project the frontal image orthographically to the 3D model. For vertices that do not receive a texture assignment, their texture is interpolated.

C. Features

We use two types of features: spatial and spectral. Spatial features are extracted from 2D images. There are three kinds of spatial features: filtered images, correspondence PCA coefficients, and Gabor jets of correspondences.

For filtered image features, image regions centered around the eye and the mouth are used. An example of the image regions in 45° and 90° images is shown in Fig. 3 where white rectangles highlight the regions.

The image regions are filtered by Gabor filters. A Gabor filter is a sinusoidal function modulated by a Gaussian envelope given by

$$g(x,y) = a(x,y)c(x,y) \quad (5)$$

where

$$a(x,y) = \frac{1}{2\pi\sigma_x\sigma_y} e^{-0.5\left(\frac{x^2}{\sigma_x^2} + \frac{y^2}{\sigma_y^2}\right)} \quad (6)$$

is the Gaussian component and

$$c(x,y) = \exp(i(2\pi f(x\cos(\theta) + y\sin(\theta)))) \quad (7)$$

is the sinusoidal component. The standard deviations (σ_x, σ_y) define the size of the Gaussian envelope. f is the center frequency in the frequency domain and θ is the center frequency orientation in the frequency domain. The filtered image magnitude is given by

$$y(x,y) = |g(x,y) * I(x,y)| \quad (8)$$

where * denotes the convolution operation, || is the magnitude operation, and *I(x,y)* is the DC subtracted image region. To alleviate the effect of misalignment in images, a large scale is used, i.e., $x = 16$. We use $y = x/2$ and $f = 1/x$. Eight orientations are used, i.e., $\theta = [0,1/8,...,7/8]\pi$. This gives us 8 filtered images.

The second kind of spatial features are correspondence PCA coefficients. They are obtained by projecting correspondence coordinates *coor* to a basis given by

$$coor = \overline{coor} + B\beta + e \tag{9}$$

where β is the coefficient, B is a basis, $\overline{coor}$ is the mean coordinate, and e is an error term. The basis B is obtained by applying PCA to correspondence coordinates across images of the same pose. For example, a basis for 45° images is obtained by applying PCA to correspondence coordinates of all 45° images. In this study, the number of eigenvectors used captures 95% variation.

The third kind of spatial features are Gabor jets. They are obtained by applying Gabor filters at correspondences. A Gabor feature is defined as the magnitude of convolving a Gabor filter with an image point given by

$$y = | g(x,y) * I(x,y) | \tag{10}$$

where $g(x,y)$ is the Gabor filter and $I(x,y)$ is the DC subtracted image region centered around the point. The same Gabor filters used in extracting filtered image features are used to extract Gabor jet features. A Gabor jet is a vector $y = (y_1, y_2, \ldots, y_8)^T$ consisting of the Gabor features obtained by applying all Gabor filters to a correspondence.

Spectral features are represented by a 31-dimensional spectral mean vector extracted from a tissue sample. Three tissues are used. They are cheek, chin and hair. Sample locations are determined by moving away a fixed distance from a known location. For example, the left cheek sample in the frontal image is 60 pixels below the left eye and 15 pixels left of the left eye. Chin and hair samples are found similarly by using the mouth and forehead as references. We use size 11x11 for cheek and chin samples and 5x5 for hair sample. The spectral feature vector is obtained by averaging the reflectance of the pixels in the sample and normalizing the vector by its length.

$$\overline{R(\lambda)} = \frac{\frac{1}{n}\sum_{x,y} R(x,y,\lambda)}{|\frac{1}{n}\sum_{x,y} R(x,y,\lambda)|} \tag{11}$$

where $R(x,y,\lambda_K)$ is the reflectance at location (x,y) and wavelength λ and n is the number of pixels in the sample.

Fig. 4 (a) gives an example of the three tissue samples highlighted by the squares. The spectral vectors for the three samples are shown to the right.

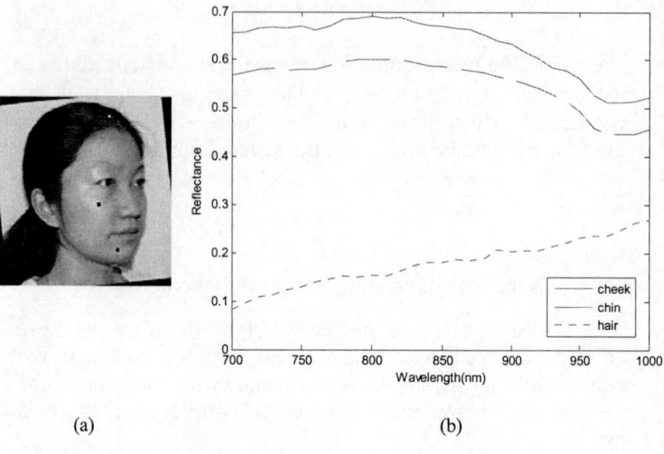

Fig. 4. (a) spectral samples (b) spectral mean

Spectral features have spatial variability depending on the location. To reduce the dependence on the location, we use a larger window to extract a set of spectral vectors. The window width and height is 3 times the size of the sample region and the spectral vector is extracted in regions every two pixels apart.

D. Classification

For each probe image, we use its correspondences and the correspondences of each gallery image to generate a 3D face model. We rotate the 3D model according to the pose of the probe. We then orthographically project the model to an image plane to generate a virtual image. An example of a frontal image, two rotated images and the virtual images of a subject is shown in Fig. 5.

The virtual image is then used as the face image of the subject used to generate the model. Spatial features are then extracted from the virtual image and the probe respectively. For filtered image features, we use the Euclidian distance to measure the similarity between the two filtered images given by

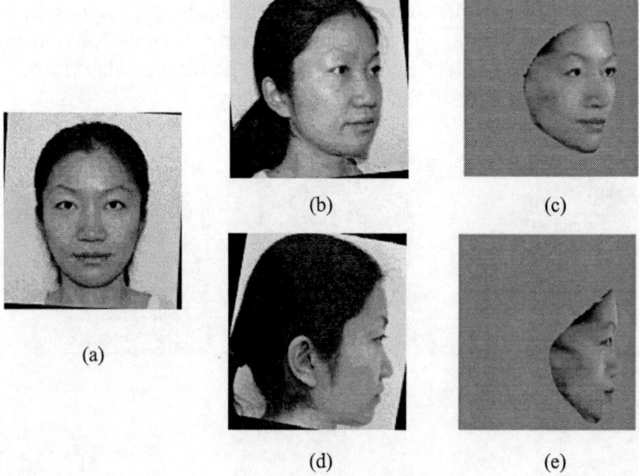

Fig. 5. (a) frontal image (b) 45° image (c) virtual 45° image (d) 90° image (e) virtual 90° image

$$d_I^t = \sum_j \frac{\sum_{x,y}(y_{v,j}^t(x,y) - y_{p,j}^t(x,y))^2}{n_j^t} \quad (12)$$

where $y_{v,j}(x,y)$ and $y_{p,j}(x,y)$ are the filtered virtual and probe images using filter j respectively, t represents the image region (eye or mouth), and n^t_j is the number of pixels in the region. To allow misalignment between $y_v(x,y)$ and $y_p(x,y)$, we allow one to be shifted between [-12,12] pixels with respect to the other and the one that minimizes (12) is chosen to define the distance.

For correspondence PCA features, we project correspondence coordinates in the virtual and probe images to the basis of the probe pose to obtain their coefficients according to (9). We use the Euclidian distance to measure the similarity between the two sets of coefficients given by

$$d_c = \sum_i (\beta_v(i) - \beta_p(i))^2 \quad (13)$$

where i denotes the i_{th} coefficient.

We also extract Gabor jet features from the virtual and probe images according to (10). We use the Euclidian distance to measure the similarity between two Gabor jets given by

$$d_g = \sum_{i,j} (y_v(i,j) - y_p(i,j))^2 \quad (14)$$

where i represents the i_{th} correspondence and j the j_{th} Gabor feature.

For spectral features, for each tissue type t, i.e., cheek, chin and hair, we extract a set of spectral vectors from the hyperspectral probe and the original hyperspectral gallery respectively. We use the Mahalanobis distance and the distance between the two sets of spectral vectors is defined as the smallest distance between the two sets given by

$$d_s^t = \min_{k\in[1,m],l\in[1,m]} [(\overline{R}_{g,k}^t - \overline{R}_{p,l}^t)^T \Sigma_t^{-1} (\overline{R}_{g,k}^t - \overline{R}_{p,l}^t)] \quad (15)$$

where g represents the gallery image and m is the number of spectral vectors in each set. Σ_t is the covariance matrix of the spectral vectors for tissue type t and is approximated by a diagonal matrix with elements corresponding to the variance of the spectral features in the database.

The total distance is a weighted average of all of the distance metrics given by

$$d = \sum_t c_I^t d_I^t + \sum_t c_S^t d_S^t + c_c d_c + c_g d_g \quad (16)$$

where the weights are the reciprocal of the standard deviation of the smallest distances of all subjects in each distance metric respectively.

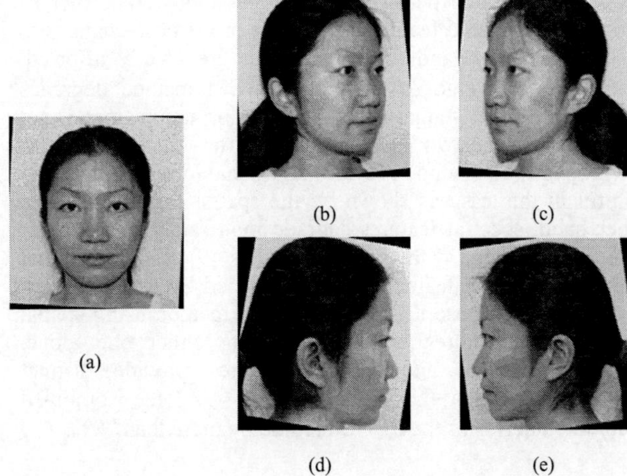

Fig. 6. Example of the five poses (a) frontal (b) left 45° image (c) right 45° image (d) left 90° image (e) right 90° image

III. EXPERIMENTS

We used a face database of 200 subjects for our experiments [9]. All images have 31 bands with center wavelengths separated by 0.01 μm over the near-infrared (NIR) (0.7 μm-1.0 μm). The spatial resolution is 494x468 pixels. We consider five images for each subject. Image fg is a frontal image, image fl1 is a left 45° image, image fr1 is a right 45° image, image fl2 is a left 90° image, and image fr2 is a right 90° image. An example of the five images is shown in Fig. 6. We use frontal images as the gallery and the other four images as probes. We use all subjects as test subjects. The experiment follows the closed universe model.

The classification rates using different features for the four poses are summarized in Table 1 where spatial means using all three spatial features. To compare with other algorithms, we used the EBGM method provided by the CSU Face Identification Evaluation System [15], [16], [17] and included the result in Table 1.

TABLE I. CLASSIFICATION RESULTS FOR THE DATABASE

Method \ Pose	45° left	45° right	90° left	90° right
Image	0.92	0.92	0.13	0.1
Coefficient	0.09	0.09	0.17	0.09
Gabor jet	0.37	0.47	0.14	0.05
Spatial	0.9	0.91	0.28	0.24
Spectral	0.85	0.78	0.69	0.66
Spectral+spatial	0.99	0.97	0.84	0.77
EBGM	0.87	0.85	0.02	0.03

When the probe pose is ±45°, the EBGM method, which only uses 2D information, gives more than 85% accuracy, suggesting that at this point spatial information in the frontal pose can still provide useful information. By using a 3D model, performance can be improved further as shown in the spatial features. When the probe pose changes to ±90°, both spatial and EBGM methods are greatly affected. With a pose change so large, the EBGM method degrades significantly. This suggests that frontal information alone is not enough when the two poses are very different. Nevertheless, the proposed 3D method provides additional information that is helpful in this case as shown by the spatial features. On the other hand, spectral features degrade moderately across pose. This is consistent with previous studies [9], [10], [11] that show that spectral features are less affected by pose changes. No matter what pose it is, the combined method using spatial and spectral features outperforms using either one alone, suggesting spatial and spectral features provide distinct information. When the probe pose is ±90°, the combined method outperforms the EBGB method by more than 70%.

The cumulative match score for the four poses is shown in Fig. 7 where rank N means the correct identity is within the top N candidates selected by the algorithm.

For the two 45° poses, the score of the combined method continues to improve as the rank increases. For the two 90° poses, the score picks up quickly and reaches 95% at rank 6 suggesting that the correct match is more similar to the probe than most candidates if it is misclassified in the first round.

Since frontal images provide a significant amount of information when the pose changes to ±45°, we simplified the algorithm for this case. To estimate the 3D model, we only use correspondences from the frontal image. In classification, only filtered image features are used. The classification results on the two 45° poses are shown in Table 2. For convenience, results obtained using the EBGM method are also included.

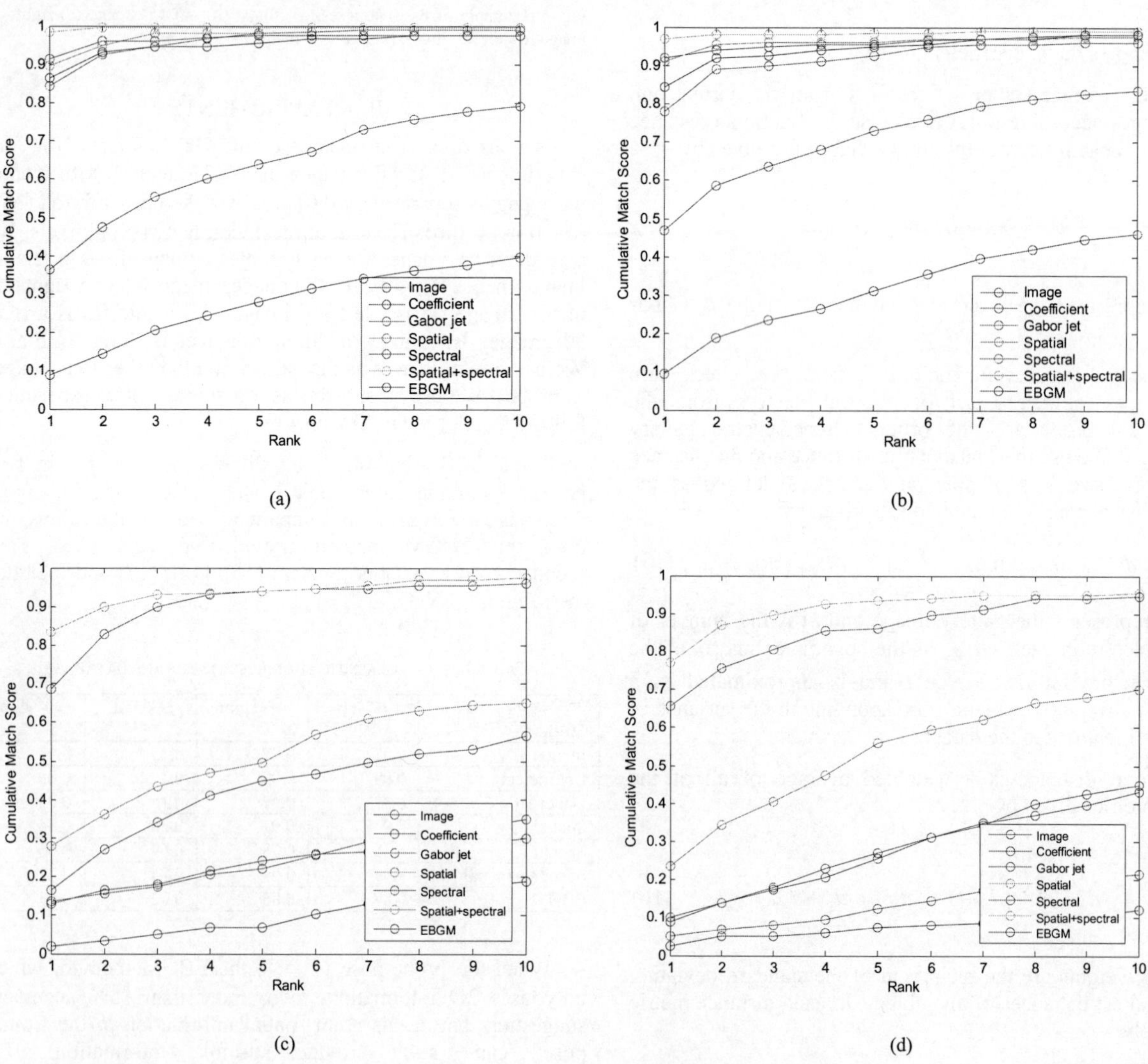

Fig. 7. Cumulative match score for (a) left 45° image (b) right 45° image (c) left 90° image (d) right 90° image

The result using filtered image features is comparable to the previous case where a personalized 3D model is used. It also outperforms the EBGM method by 5%, showing that a generic 3D model also helps in this case. The combined method is better than using either spatial or spectral features alone and outperforms the EBGM method by 10%. The cumulative match score using this approach is shown in Fig. 8.

TABLE II. CLASSIFICATION RESULTS FOR THE DATABASE

Method \ Pose	45° left	45° right
Image	0.93	0.93
Spectral+spatial	0.97	0.95
EBGM	0.87	0.85

The cumulative score is similar to the previous case suggesting that a generic 3D model is sufficient when the pose change is not larger than 45°.

IV. CONCLUSION AND FUTURE WORK

We have presented an algorithm for pose-invariant face recognition in hyperspectral images which uses both spatial and spectral information. We learned 3D face models from 2D images and used the models to generate virtual images at a different pose. Spatial features were extracted from the virtual images and were used with spectral features to recognize a test image. Compared to other related work, the proposed method provides a novel way to reconstruct 3D face models from 2D images and shows the effectiveness of using spatial and spectral information simultaneously. Future work could include using an advanced classifier to make greater use of the virtual images and integrating pose estimation into the framework.

V. ACKNOWLEDGEMENT

This research has been supported by an Army Research Office Grant.

REFERENCES

[1] D. Gonzalez-Jimenez and J. L. Alba-Castro, "Toward Pose-Invariant 2-D Face Recognition Through Point Distribution Models and Facial Symmetry," IEEE Transactions on Information Forensics and Security, vol. 2, no. 3, pp. 413–429, Sept.

[2] T. F. Cootes, G. J. Edwards, and C. J. Taylor, "Active appearance models," IEEE Transactions on Pattern Analysis and Machine Intelligence, vol. 23, no. 6, pp. 681–685, Jun.

[3] S. J. D. Prince, J. Warrell, J. H. Elder, and F. M. Felisberti, "Tied Factor Analysis for Face Recognition across Large Pose Differences," IEEE Transactions on Pattern Analysis and Machine Intelligence, vol. 30, no. 6, pp. 970–984, Jun. 2008.

[4] X. Zhang and Y. Gao, "Face recognition across pose: A review," Pattern Recogn., vol. 42, no. 11, pp. 2876–2896, Nov. 2009.

[5] V. Blanz and T. Vetter. Face recognition based on fitting a 3d morphable model. IEEE Trans. PAMI, 25(9):1063–1073, 2003.

[6] D. Jiang, Y. Hu, S. Yan, L. Zhang, H. Zhang, and W. Gao, "Efficient 3D reconstruction for face recognition," Pattern Recognition, vol. 38, no. 6, pp. 787–798, Jun. 2005.

[7] A. Asthana, T. K. Marks, M. J. Jones, K. H. Tieu, and M. Rohith, "Fully automatic pose-invariant face recognition via 3D pose normalization," 2011, pp. 937–944.

[8] U. Prabhu, J. Heo, and M. Savvides, "Unconstrained Pose-Invariant Face Recognition Using 3D Generic Elastic Models," IEEE Transactions on Pattern Analysis and Machine Intelligence, vol. 33, no. 10, pp. 1952 –1961, Oct. 2011.

[9] Z. Pan, G. Healey, M. Prasad, and B. Tromberg, "Face recognition in hyperspectral images," IEEE Transactions on Pattern Analysis and Machine Intelligence, vol. 25, no. 12, pp. 1552-1560, December 2003.

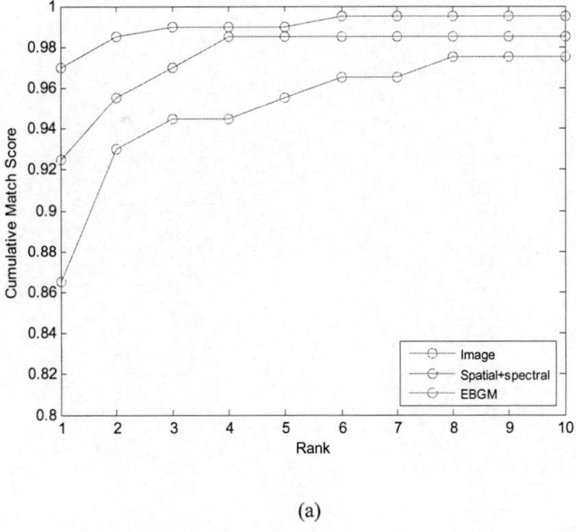

(a)

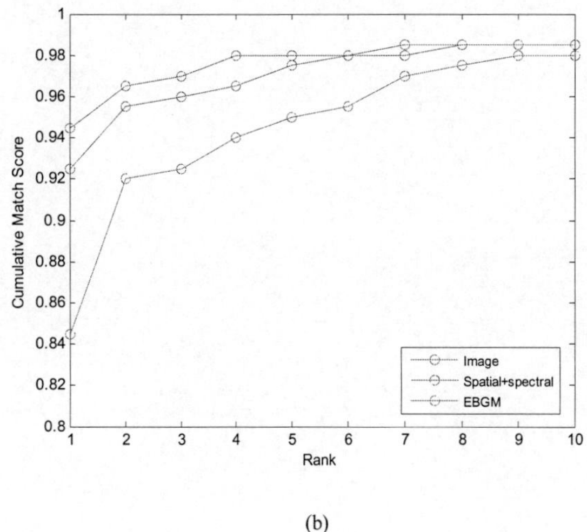

(b)

Fig. 8. Cumulative match score for (a) left 45° image (b) right 45° image

[10] Z. Pan, G. Healey, M. Prasad, and B. Tromberg, “Experiments on recognizing faces in hyperspectral images,” in Proceedings of SPIE, vol. 4725, pp. 168-176, 2002.

[11] S. A. Robila, “Toward Hyperspectral Face Recognition,” in Proceedings of SPIE, vol. 6812, 2008.

[12] P. Paysan, R. Knothe, B. Amberg, S. Romdhani, and T. Vetter, “A 3D Face Model for Pose and Illumination Invariant Face Recognition,” in Proceedings of the 2009 Sixth IEEE International Conference on Advanced Video and Signal Based Surveillance, Washington, DC, USA, 2009, pp. 296–301.

[13] M. Raydan and B. F. Svaiter, “Relaxed Steepest Descent and Cauchy-Barzilai-Borwein Method”, Computational Optimization and Applications, 21 (2002), pp. 155-167.

[14] L. G. Farkas, Anthropometric facial proportions in medicine. Thomas Books, 1987.

[15] J. R. Beveridge, D. S. Bolme, M. Teixeira, and B. Draper, “The CSU face identification evaluation system user's guide: version 5.0,” Tech. Rep., Computer Science Department, Colorado State University, Fort Collins, Colo, USA, May 2003.

[16] D. Bolme, J. R. Beveridge, M. Teixeira, and B. A. Draper, “The CSU face identification evaluation system: its purpose, features and structure,” in Proceedings of the 3rd International Conference on Computer Vision Systems (ICVS '03), vol. 2626 of Lecture Notes in Computer Science, pp. 304-313, April 2003.

[17] L. Wiskott, J. M. Fellous, and C. V. D. Malsburg, “Face recognition by elastic bunch graph matching,” IEEE Transactions on Pattern Analysis and Machine Intelligence, vol. 19, no. 7, July 1997.

Face Detection: Histogram of Oriented Gradients and Bag of Feature Method

L. R. Cerna, G. Cámara-Chávez, D. Menotti
Computer Science Department, Federal University of Ouro Preto
Ouro Preto, MG, Brazil

Abstract— *Face detection has been one of the most studied topics in computer vision literature; so many algorithms have been developed with different approaches to overcome some detection problems such as occlusion, illumination condition, scale, among others. Histograms of Oriented Gradients are an effective descriptor for object recognition and detection. These descriptors are powerful to detect faces with occlusions, pose and illumination changes because they are extracted in a regular grid. We calculate and vector quantizes into different codewords each descriptor and then we construct histograms of this codeword distribution that represent the face image. Finally, a set of experiments are presented to analyze the performance of this method.*

Keywords: Face Detection, Histogram of Oriented Gradients, descriptor, codeword, Bag of features.

1. Introduction

Actually, many applications and technologies inventions use computers because of their rapid increase of computational powers and the capability to interact with humans in a natural way, for example understanding what people says or reacting to them in a friendly manner, so through years they become more intelligent like humans. One technique that enable such natural human-computer interaction is face detection [17].

Face detection is a very important task to recognize a person by using a computer. Actually, many algorithms have been developed to make this detection task more easy but in real world scenario it is very difficult due to complex background, variations in scale, pose, color, illumination and among others. Because of its popularity many applications use it such as surveillance systems, digital camera, access control, human-computer interaction and so on.

How we can detect faces into a given arbitrary image? A possible solution is to segment this image into interest regions based on some homogeneity criterion, and then search and locate in all image regions where a face is. Methods in the literature have many restrictions because they do not vary pose and only work with frontal faces, constants lighting conditions, *etc*, (as seen in Figure 1) and when we evaluate with faces in real world scenarios their performance decrease and do not present good generalization and accuracy.

Fig. 1: Example of face images with huge variations in pose, facial expression, color, lighting conditions, *etc*.

There have been hundreds of face detection approaches in the literature. In order to simplify our study, we can group them into four categories: knowledge-based methods, feature invariant approaches, template matching methods and appearance-based methods [17].

The publication of Viola-Jones work increased the progress of the face detection area [15]. This framework presents problems when detects faces in complex backgrounds. Moreover, the processing time to extract and select features is very long due to the feature dimensions and the training time is very slow, demanding a great computer effort. On the other hand, the detection time is very fast since it uses a set of strong features selected.

Histograms of Oriented Gradient (HOG) are descriptors rotationally invariant which have been used in optimization problems as well as in computer vision [13], [6]. In our case, we apply in the face detection problem.

In this paper, we explore the representational power of HOG descriptors for face detection with Bag of features. We propose a simple but powerful approach to detect faces: (1) extract HOG descriptors using a regular grid, (2) vector quantization into different codewords each descriptor, (3) apply a support vector machine to learn a model for classifying an image as face or non-face based on codeword histograms.

The remainder of this paper is organized as follows. In Section 2, we present our proposed face detection method. Details of implementation are described in Section 3, and in Section 4, we present a set experiments. Finally the conclusion is presented in Section 5.

2. Face Detection Method

Histograms of Oriented Gradients are generally used in computer vision, pattern recognition and image processing to detect and recognize visual objects (i.e. faces). We propose to use HOG descriptors because we need a robust feature set to discriminate and find faces under difficult illumination backgrounds, wide range of poses, *etc*, by using feature sets that overcome the existing ones for face detection.

HOG is reminiscent of edge orientation histogram, SIFT descriptor and shape context. They are computed on a dense grid of cells that overlap local contrast histogram normalizations of image gradient orientations to improve the detector performance [5]. So that, this feature set performs very well for other shape based object classes (i.e. face detection) because of the distribution of local intensity gradients, even not precising any knowledge of the corresponding gradient [4].

To extract HOG descriptors, first count the occurrences of edge orientations in a local neighborhood of an image. This means the image is divided into small connected regions, called cells (*e.g.*, size 9) and the histogram of edge orientations is computed for each one. Depending on whether the gradient is unsigned or signed, the histogram channels are spread over $0° - 180°$ or $0° - 360°$.

To compensate the illumination, histogram counts are normalized by accumulating a measure of local histogram energy over the connected regions, then use the results obtained to normalize all cells in the block (*e.g.*, size 2) and finally, the combination of these histograms represents the HOG descriptor (see Figure 2).

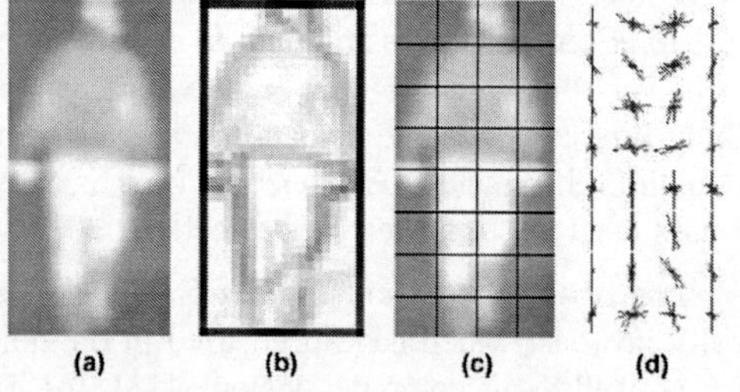

Fig. 2: Images from the various stages of generating a Histogram of Oriented Gradients feature vector. (a) Original pedestrian image, scaled to 20x40 pixels, (b) gradient image, (c) image divided into cells of 5x5 pixels, resulting in 4x8 cells, (d) resulting HOG descriptor for the image showing the gradient orientation histograms in each cell [11].

To make invariant the Hog descriptor in scale and rotation, extract descriptors from salient points by using a rotation normalization in the scale space of the image [5]. The steps are:

- Scale-space extrema detection: intends to achieve scale invariance.
- Orientation assignment: finds the dominant gradient orientation.
- Descriptor extraction.

Figure 3 shows an example patch with their corresponding HOGs.

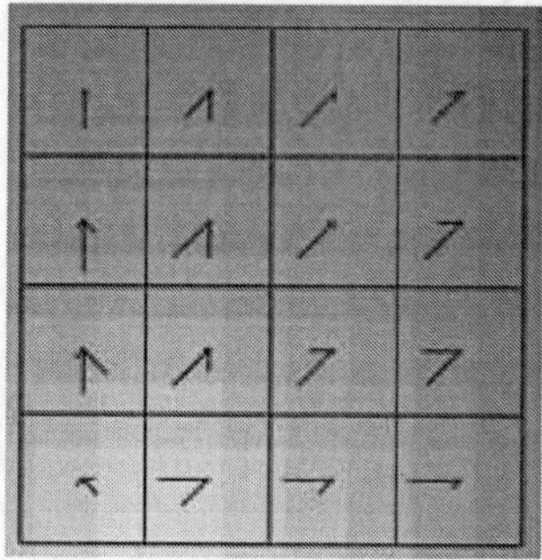

Fig. 3: Example HOG descriptors, patch size=8x8. Each cell of the patch shows the orientation of the gradients.

Orientation histograms have been used in many other methods, so they work really well when they are combined with local spatial histogramming and normalization in Lowe's Scale Invariant Feature Transformation approach [10]. In the case of Shape Context, it studies the cell and block shapes; initially used edge pixel counts without the orientation histogramming.

Advantages of HOG/SIFT representation are: it works with local shapes because it captures edge structure with a controllable degree of invariance to local geometric and photometric transformations (i.e. if translations or rotations are much smaller than the local spatial or orientation bin size, they are little different).

2.1 Bag of Features

Actually, Bag of words method overcomes the other methods for object detection. It represents an image as an orderless collection of local features [7] (i.e. in face representations local features can be an eye, ear, mouth, etc).

However, in face detection, object images belong to the same category (face images), histograms of orderless local features from the whole face do not have large enough between class variations [9].

In Bag of Words [7], orderless local features are extracted from images of different categories (face or non-face) as candidates for basic elements, *i.e.*, "words". Feature descriptors are represented like numerical vectors. By clustering methods, they convert numerical vectors to "codewords" (cluster center) to produce a "codebook". The number of total clusters is the codebook size. So each feature in an image is mapped to a codeword through the clustering process and they are used to represent the histogram (see Figure 4).

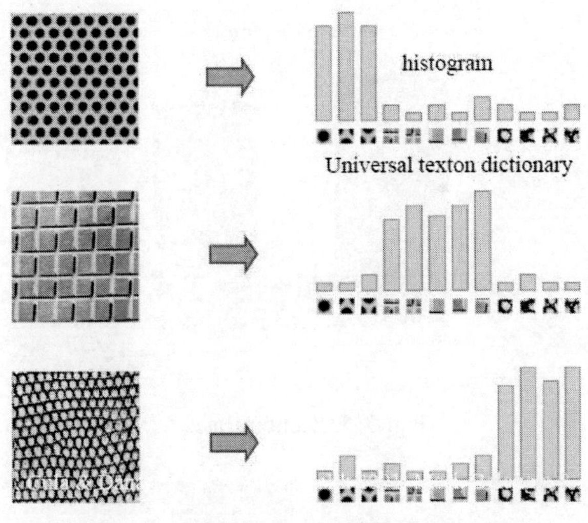

Fig. 4: Bag of features

In our work, we first extract the HOG descriptor of each image (face and non-face) and then we apply the clustering process to these features to obtain clusters with different sizes and each cluster center is the codeword that we used to construct histograms based on the frequency of their appearance in the image. The class of each feature is chosen using the minimum distance to the cluster center. And therefore we build groups of features in each cluster. Finally, we used these histograms to train our SVM classifier to detect faces in an input image. Figure 5, shows our model to extract HOG features and to construct histograms based on codewords.

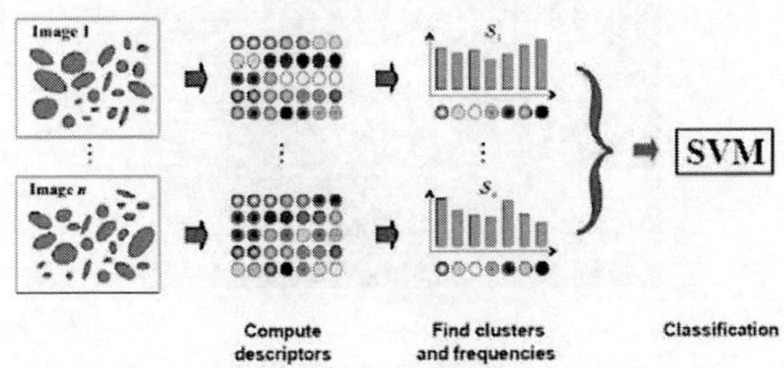

Fig. 5: Proposed Model for Face Detection

3. Implementation

This section describes the implementation of our method. This discussion includes details about the structure of training and building the detector.

3.1 Training dataset

The face training set consists of 2385 faces and 7025 non-faces images/patches of 50×50 pixels. The faces were extracted from two different face databases:

- AT&T Database contains ten different images for each of 40 distinct subjects, the images were taken at different times, varying the lighting and facial expressions. All the images were taken against a dark homogeneous background with the subjects in an upright frontal position [1].
- FEI Face Recognition Database is a Brazilian face database that contains a set of face images taken at the Artificial Intelligence Laboratory of FEI in São Bernardo do Campo, São Paulo, Brazil. There are 14 images for each of 200 individuals, adding up 2800 images. All images are colorful and taken against a white homogeneous background in an upright frontal position with profile rotation up to 180 degrees. [14].

We formed our database by choosing some faces of different datasets because we use frontal faces, faces with profile rotation and faces with illumination changes. Non-faces were extracted from images available in [16]. These non-faces have different sizes so we cut each image into sub images in a base resolution of 50×50pixels. From this process we obtained 7025 non-face images.

To evaluate our algorithms, we used the Label Faces on Wild Dataset that contains 2845 grayscale and color images with differents sizes, a wide range of difficulties including occlusions, difficult poses, and low resolution and out-of-focus faces, [8].

3.2 SVM Training

For training our models we use the Support Vector Machines algorithm [3], [12] since we need to learn a model to discriminate faces from non-faces samples. The linear kernel was chosen due to its capability to work with high dimensional features. We use the Libsvm library in Matlab for training our algorithms [2]. In contrast to the Viola-Jones algorithm which takes days for training the cascade, the training time was 2 to 4 minutes depending on the amount of training data (images features).

3.3 Classification and Detection

For classifying faces and non-faces we used the feature vector obtained by the histograms of the codewords. Our face detection method receive an input image, extract the feature vector of each candidate image subwindow and then classify as face or non-face by the trained model (see Figure 7).

4. Face Detection Experiments

This section describes experiments for validating the proposed face detector method. The SVM model is built using the entire training set described inSection 3;

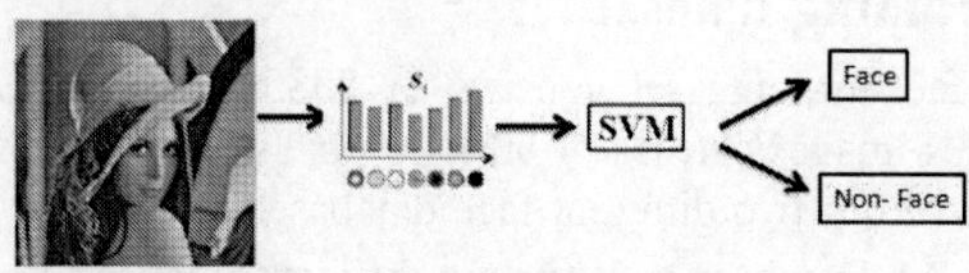

Fig. 6: Face Detection Method

First, we presented a set of experiments over the Training Dataset:

We use the standard image databases available on the internet described in section 3. So we have 2385 faces and 7025 non-faces samples to train. We divide the training database (faces+non-faces) because we only train with 30%.

We train our classifier with different codebook size because we wanted to see which one presents better results in our training dataset. First, we train our classifier with a codebook size equal to 10, the Accuracy over 6588 test samples was 99.71% and over 2822 train samples and the Accuracy was 100%.

Target Class	**Output Class**	
	Faces	Non-Faces
Faces	711	4
Non-Faces	4	2103

Table 1: Training Dataset Confusion Matrix, k=10.

We train our classifier with a codebook size equal to 100, the Accuracy over 1911 test samples was 84.51% and over 7499 train samples and the Accuracy was 85.71%.

Target Class	**Output Class**	
	Faces	Non-Faces
Faces	307	170
Non-Faces	0	1434

Table 2: Training Dataset Confusion Matrix, k=100.

For testing our method we used Label Faces on Wild Dataset. False Positive, True Positive and Accuracy are presented below. In this case, we annotated faces per images because when we will pass the detector it will return one rectangle per face and then we will use it to obtain detecion rates.

Figure 8 and Figure 9 presents the face detection of a random image selected.

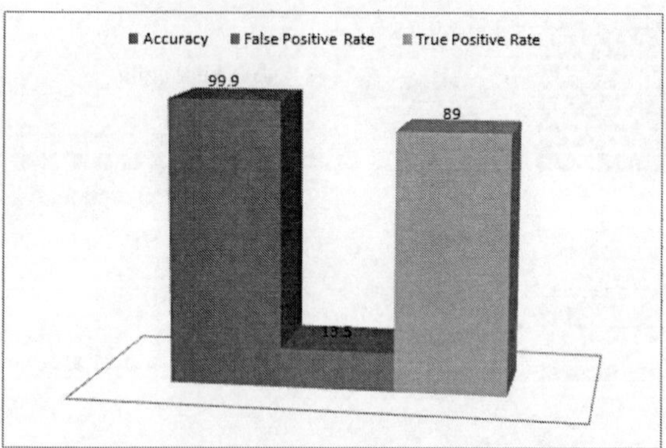

Fig. 7: Detection Rate

Fig. 8: Face Detection example 1

Fig. 9: Face Detection example 2

5. Conclusion

In this paper, we proposed, implemented and tested our Face Detection Method by using the SVM classifier. From experiments, we concluded that we can improve our results by using the Elastic Bunch Graph Matching Method to extract the most important parts in the face (eyes, nose, etc) and from them we can obtain HOG descriptors without using the entire image, so we reduce the number of operations. Moreover, we plan to perform more tests on other databases in order to verify how robust is the proposed method.

References

[1] A. L. Cambridge. The database of faces. http://www.cl.cam.ac.uk/research/dtg/attarchive/facedatabase.html, Apr. 2002.

[2] C.-C. Chang and C.-J. Lin. Libsvm : a library for support vector machines. *ACM Transactions on Intelligent Systems and Technology*, 2:1–27, 2011.
[3] C. Cortes and V. N. Vapnik. Support-vector networks. *Machine Learning*, 20(3):273–297, 1995.
[4] N. Dalal and B. Triggs. Histograms of oriented gradients for human detection. In *Computer Vision and Pattern Recognition, 2005. CVPR 2005. IEEE Computer Society Conference on*, volume 1, pages 886–893. IEEE, 2005.
[5] O. Déniz, G. Bueno, J. Salido, and F. De la Torre. Face recognition using histograms of oriented gradients. *Pattern Recognition Letters*, 32(12):1598–1603, 2011.
[6] P. Dollár, S. Belongie, and P. Perona. The Fastest Pedestrian Detector in the West. 2010.
[7] L. Fei-Fei and P. Perona. A bayesian hierarchical model for learning natural scene categories. In *Computer Vision and Pattern Recognition, 2005. CVPR 2005. IEEE Computer Society Conference on*, volume 2, pages 524–531. IEEE, 2005.
[8] V. Jain and E. Learned-Miller. Fddb: A benchmark for face detection in unconstrained settings. *University of Massachusetts, Amherst*, 2010.
[9] Z. Li, J.-i. Imai, and M. Kaneko. Robust face recognition using block-based bag of words. In *Pattern Recognition (ICPR), 2010 20th International Conference on*, pages 1285–1288. IEEE, 2010.
[10] D. G. Lowe. Distinctive image features from scale-invariant keypoints. *International Journal of Computer Vision*, 60(2):91–110, 2004.
[11] R. O'Malley, E. Jones, and M. Glavin. Detection of pedestrians in far-infrared automotive night vision using region-growing and clothing distortion compensation. *Infrared Physics & Technology*, 53(6):439–449, 2010.
[12] B. Schölkopf and A. J. Smola. *Learning with Kernels*. MIT Press, 2002.
[13] W. Schwartz, A. Kembhavi, D. Harwood, and L. Davis. Human Detection Using Partial Least Squares Analysis. 2009.
[14] C. L. Thomaz. Fei face database. http://fei.edu.br/ cet/facedatabase.html, 2012.
[15] P. Viola and M. Jones. Robust real-time face detection. *International journal of computer vision*, 57(2):137–154, 2004.
[16] J. Wu, S. C. Brubaker, M. D. Mullin, and J. M. Rehg. Fast and robust face, rare event detection. http://c2inet.sce.ntu.edu.sg/Jianxin/RareEvent/rare$_e vent.htm$, 2008.
[17] C. Zhang and Z. Zhang. A survey of recent advances in face detection. Technical report, Tech. rep., Microsoft Research, 2010.

Predicting Gaze Direction from Head Pose Yaw and Pitch

David O. Johnson[1] **and Raymond H. Cuijpers**[2]
[1,2]Human-Technology Interaction, Eindhoven University of Technology, Eindhoven, NL

Abstract - *Socially assistive robots (SARs) must be able to interpret non-verbal communication from a human. A person's gaze direction informs the observer where the visual attention is directed to. Therefore it is useful if a robot can interpret the gaze direction, so that it can assess whether a person is looking at it or some object in the environment. Gazing is a combination of head and eye movement, but detecting eye orientation from a distance is difficult in real life environments. Instead a robot can measure the head pose and infer the gaze direction. In this paper, we show that both the yaw and pitch of a human's gaze can be inferred from the measured yaw and pitch of the human's head pose with simple linear equations.*

Keywords: human robot interaction, gaze direction, head pose estimation

1 Introduction

Elderly people need more support due to their declining capabilities and age-related illnesses. Today that support is provided by younger caregivers. However, the ratio of younger caregivers to elderly people is decreasing in all developed countries. Worldwide, in 2010 there were fewer than nine persons of working-age per elderly person of 65 or older. By 2050 this ratio is expected to decrease to fewer than four working-age persons per elderly person [3]. This will lead to a problem of increasing demand for care and a shortage of caregivers [17].

Socially assistive robots (SARs) are one solution to this problem. SARs can provide reminders and instruction such as the nursing robot Pearl [14] and the Korean robotic language teacher EngKey [10]. They can also provide social support. Social support typically aims at reducing social isolation and enhancing well-being in the form of social interaction with users [5]. Humans use verbal and non-verbal communication. Thus, it is important for a SAR to be able to interpret non-verbal communication from a human. Gaze, or the direction in which the human is looking, is one form of non-verbal communication. Humans use gaze, with and without hand gestures, to point to an object. Humans also use gaze for turn-taking during conversations [7]. Gaze can also be used in navigation to position the robot so it is in the line of sight of the human when it is approaching. Gaze can also be used to determine if the human is paying attention to what the robot is saying.

Gazing is a combination of head and eye movement. The direction the head is looking, or head pose, can be measured by looking at the face [18][19][24]. The direction the eyes are looking is more difficult to determine (see Yamazoe et al. for a thorough discussion of appearance-based and model-based gaze estimation methods [23]). The goal of this research is to determine the gaze of the human (i.e., where the human is looking at) solely from the head pose (i.e., the direction of the head).

Many studies have modeled the relationship between head and eye movement in gazing [9][15][20][26]. But, these models are more suited to creating the behavior in the robot, than determining the gaze from head pose. Additionally as illustrated in Figure 1, these models only consider the yaw (i.e., left and right direction) of the gaze and not the pitch (i.e., up and down direction) or roll (i.e., tilt).

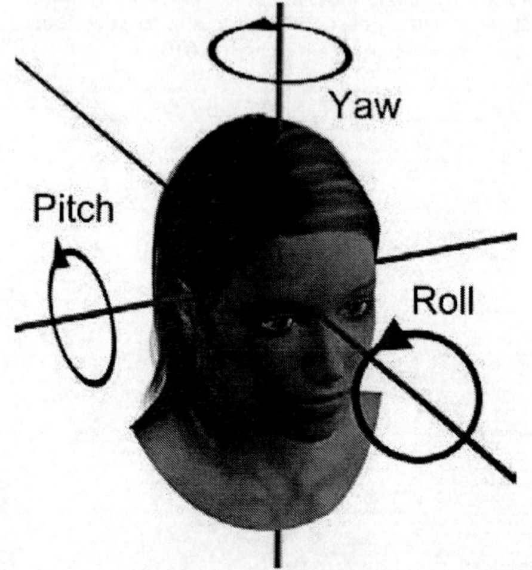

Figure 1. Head pose yaw, pitch, and roll.

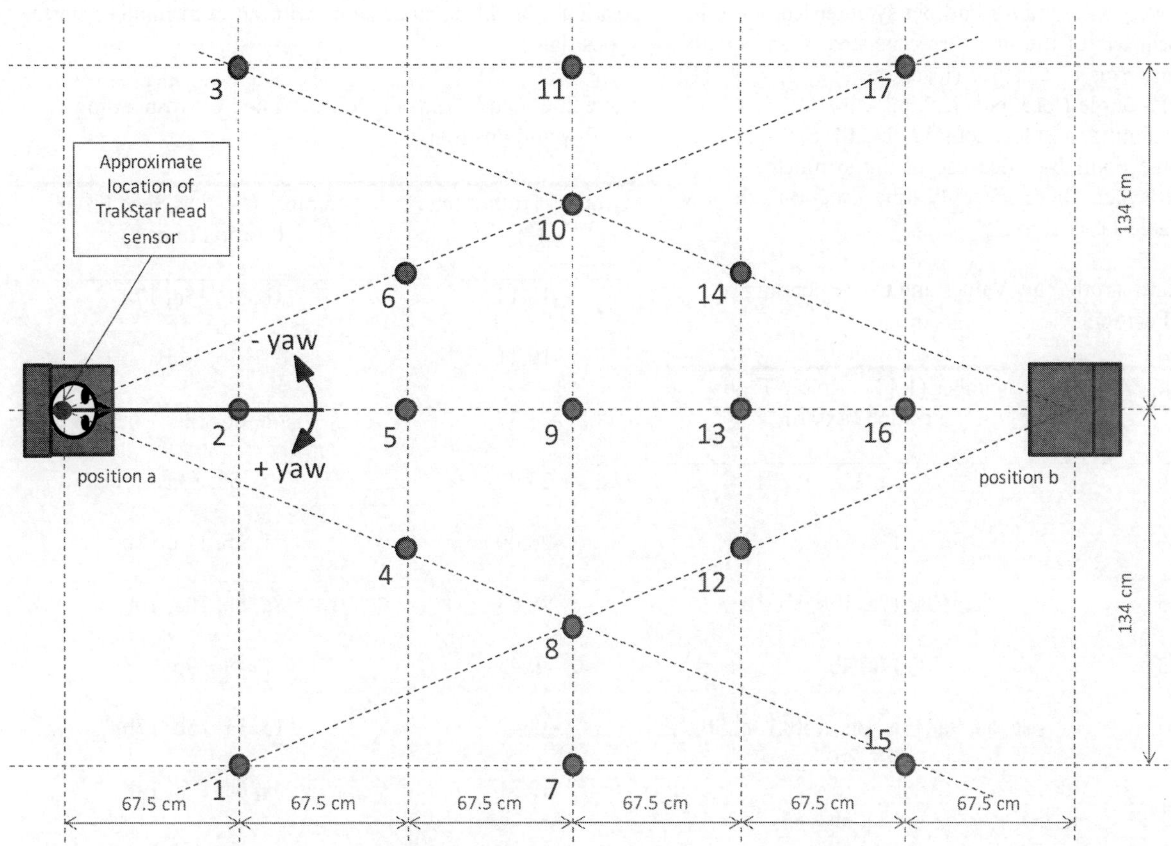

Figure 2. Overhead view of experimental set-up. The blue disks denote object locations on the ground floor. The locations consist of an equally spaced grid in terms of distance (locations 1, 2, 3, 7, 9, 11, 15, 16, 17) and angle (locations 4, 5, 6, 8, 9, 10, 15, 16, 17 from vantage point a, and locations 12, 13, 14, 8, 9, 10, 1, 2, 3 from vantage point b).

In this paper, we investigated the relationship between the yaw and pitch of a human's gaze and the yaw and pitch of the human's head pose. In an experiment we measured head orientations when participants looked at known object locations from two vantage points. The relative position of objects was chosen such that the viewer's gaze elevation, angle, and azimuth were systematically varied. With a linear model, which turns out to be sufficient, we relate the measured head pose to the ground truth of the gaze direction. From this relation the actual gaze direction can be inferred from the measured head pose.

2 Method

2.1 Design

The experiment was set up in a living room environment as illustrated in Figures 2 and 3.

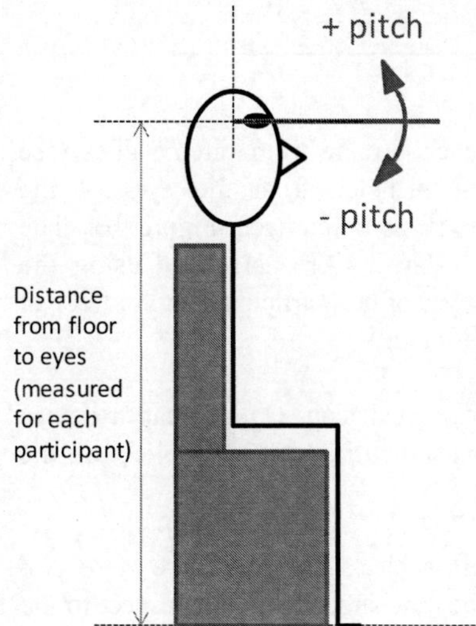

Figure 3. Side view of experimental set-up.

Two chairs were placed opposite from each other, at a distance of 405 cm. One chair was labeled 'position a' and the other chair was labeled 'position b'. In between the two chairs, there were 17 numbers laid out symmetrically on the floor. The locations of the numbers consisted of an equally spaced grid in terms of distance (locations 1, 2, 3, 7, 9, 11, 15, 16, 17) and angle (locations 4, 5, 6, 8, 9, 10, 15, 16, 17 from vantage point a, and locations 12, 13, 14, 8, 9, 10, 1, 2, 3 from vantage point b). Because of the symmetry of the experimental layout, there are only nine ground-truth yaw values (see Table 1).

Table 1. Ground-Truth Yaw Values and Corresponding Number and Position

Ground-Truth Yaw (°)	Number (1-17) As Seen From Position (a or b)
-63.26	3a, 15b
-33.49	11a, 7b
-21.65	6a, 10a, 17a, 12b, 8b, 1b
-11.23	14a, 4b
0.00	2a, 5a, 9a, 13a, 16a, 16b, 13b, 9b, 5b, 2b
11.23	12a, 6b
21.65	4a, 8a, 15a, 14b, 10b, 3b
33.49	7a, 11b
63.26	1a, 17b

Also, there are only eleven ground-truth pitch values (see Table 2), if a constant distance from the eyes of the participant to the floor is assumed (see Figure 3). The ground-truth values in Table 2 were calculated using the mean distance from the eyes of the participant to the floor of 118.9 cm (standard deviation 2.9).

The participants wore a baseball cap. On this cap a device was attached which measured the yaw and pitch of the participants head.

This study used a within-subjects design. There were two independent variables: the yaw and pitch, with respect to the participant, of the location where we asked the participant to look. The dependent variables were the yaw and pitch of the participant's head when he or she was looking at the specified location. The measurements were counterbalanced with respect to the starting position, meaning that the starting position was varied across the participants. Participants with an odd participant number started at position a, and the participants with an even number started at position b.

Table 2. Ground-Truth Pitch Values and Corresponding Number and Position

Ground-Truth Pitch (°)	Number (1-7) As Seen From Position (a or b)
-18.13	1b, 3b, 15a, 17a
-19.41	2b, 16a
-23.37	4b, 6b, 12a, 14a
-23.77	5b, 13a
-26.09	71, 7b, 11a, 11b
-28.63	8a, 8b, 10a, 10b
-30.43	9a, 9b
-38.40	1a, 3a, 15b, 17b
-39.31	4a, 6a, 12b, 14b
-41.38	5a, 13b
-60.42	2a, 16b

2.2 Design

There were 7 participants (6 males, 1 female), whose ages varied from 20 to 23 (mean age 21.6, standard deviation 1.0). Six of the participants received course credit for participating in the experiment and one was paid 5 euros for participating. All the participants were told that the experiment was not about reaction speed. Other than that, no information was provided about the purpose of the experiment.

2.3 Apparatus

The yaw and pitch of the participant's head were measured using the trakSTAR manufactured by the Ascension Technology Corporation. The trakSTAR is a high-accuracy electromagnetic tracking device for short-range motion tracking applications [1]. The participants were told to look at one of the 17 numbers on the floor with a computer voice through a speaker. Before the experiment, the participants were told to press a hand-held button when they were looking at the number. When the button was pushed, the yaw and pitch measured by the trakSTAR were recorded by the computer.

2.4 Procedure

The experiment was done in weeks 38 and 39 of 2012 during work hours (8:30-18:00). The participants were first given an eye test. After the eye test the participants were introduced to the experimental setup, which is shown in Figures 2 and 3. Half of the participants were seated in position a; the other half were seated in position b. The experimenter measured the distance from the ground to the eyes of the participant. The participant put on a baseball cap with the trakSTAR sensor on top of it. Then the experimenter explained the experiment.

The computer played pre-recorded messages, "Look at number x" with x being a number ranging from one to seventeen. The participant then had to find the number on the ground and look at it. When the participant was looking at the number he or she had to press a hand-held button which they were given before the experiment. Then, the next number was played until all fifty-one trials were completed. Each of the seventeen positions was measured three times in a random order.

After the first fifty-one trials the participant was asked to change seats and the experiment was repeated from the other vantage point. When the second session ended the participant was asked to take off the baseball cap. Participants were debriefed at the end and remarks were noted.

3 Results

Figure 4 shows the mean of the trakSTAR yaw measurements plotted as a function of the ground-truth yaw values. Regression analysis ($R^2 = 0.98$) shows a linear relation between the yaw of the head pose (trakSTAR yaw) and the participant's gaze (ground-truth yaw). We found a slope of 0.38 ± 0.02 ($t[7] = 21.40$, $p < 0.001$) and an intercept of 1.11 ± 0.64 ($t[7] = 1.75$, $p = 0.124$). The data are thus best described by the following equation:

$$y = 0.38x + 1.11 \quad (1)$$

where:

$$x = \text{yaw of measured head pose} \quad (2)$$

$$y = \text{yaw of gaze} \quad (3)$$

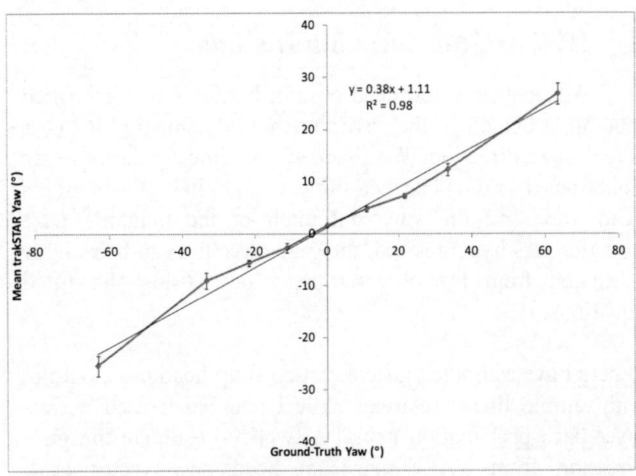

Figure 4. Mean trakStar Yaw (°) plotted as a function of Ground-Truth Yaw (°). Error bars denote standard errors of the sample mean.

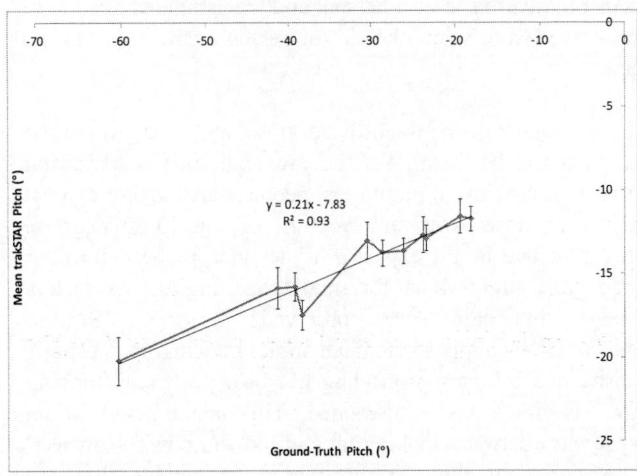

Figure 5. Mean trakStar Pitch (°) plotted as a function of Ground-Truth Pitch (°). Error bars denote standard errors of the sample mean.

Figure 5 shows the mean of the trakSTAR pitch measurements plotted as a function of the ground-truth pitch values. Regression analysis ($R^2 = 0.93$) shows the following linear relation between the pitch of the head pose (trakSTAR pitch) and the participant's gaze (ground-truth pitch). We found a slope of 0.21 ± 0.02 ($t[9] = 11.23$, $p < 0.001$) and an intercept of -7.83 ± 0.63 ($t[9] = -12.51$, $p < 0.001$). The data are thus best described by the following equation:

$$y = 0.21x - 7.83 \quad (4)$$

where:

$$x = \text{pitch of measured head pose} \quad (5)$$

$$y = \text{pitch of gaze} \quad (6)$$

4 Discussion and conclusions

We measured the head pose of human observers when looking at objects in the environment and compared it to the actual gaze direction. We found simple linear relations (see Equations 1 and 4) between the yaw and pitch of a human's head pose and the yaw and pitch of the human's gaze direction. As hypothesized, the gaze direction can be reliably estimated from the observed head pose using the fitted equations.

Others have estimated gaze direction from head pose, but not with simple linear relations. Yücel and Salah used a two-layer back-propagation neural network to estimate the gaze direction from a 3-dimensional head pose vector [25]. However, they did not check if there was a linear relation between the gaze direction and the head pose vector. Stiefelhagen et al., used an assumption to implicitly estimate the gaze direction from the head pose [16]. They assumed the focus of attention to be a person, and the estimated head pose was corrected to select the closest person as the target of the gaze.

The relationship between head pose and gaze direction turned out to be linear. For the yaw angle this is somewhat surprising considering that most people start looking against their own noses with an eye turn of say 40-60 degrees. Therefore one might expect a higher gain of head turn for large gaze angles than for small gaze angles. No such a change in gain was observed, however. Similar considerations apply to the pitch angle. Looking up is usually constrained by ones protruding eye brows whereas looking down is much less constrained. This could result in an asymmetry between looking up and looking down. However, from our data there is no reason to believe that the relationship between pitch of head pose and pitch of gaze direction is non-linear.

In real environments, objects may be large and cover a substantial part of the visual field like when admiring a new car of a friend, say. In such situations it is to be expected that many different locations within the interior of the object are being fixated. Our simple model does not say anything about how people perform gaze fixations within an object, nor how a scene of objects is scanned [6][13][21]. However, it seems reasonable to expect that the center of gravity of fixations within an object will adhere to the same simple relationships as we observed.

Previous research has established that humans estimate the gaze direction of another person from head pose and the features of the person's eyes [4][8][11][22]. Thus, it would seem logical that a robot should also use both head pose and eye features to estimate gaze direction. However, humans do not think in linear equations as easily as robots do, so it is also plausible that if the relationship between head pose and gaze is a simple linear relationship, as we have shown here, then a robot only needs to determine head pose to estimate gaze direction.

To summarize, we have shown that both the yaw and pitch of a human's *gaze* can be inferred from the measured yaw and pitch of the human's *head pose* with simple linear equations. Thus by measuring the human's head pose from its video stream, the robot can estimate where the human is gazing. Knowing where the human is gazing, will help the robot determine what object the human is pointing at, whether the human is paying attention to the robot, when it is the robot's turn in a conversation, and the direction to approach a human so it will be in the human's line of sight.

5 Acknowledgements

The research leading to these results is part of the KSERA project (http://www.ksera-project.eu) and has received funding from the European Commission under the 7th Framework Programme (FP7) for Research and Technological Development under grant agreement n2010-248085.

We would also like to thank Jan Roelof de Pijper, Ellen Hoefsloot, Milou de Louw, and Martijn van Vlijmen for their contributions to this work.

6 References

[1] Ascension Technology Cooperation (2011). 3D Guidance trakSTAR 2TM Installation and Operation Guide.

[2] Breazeal C, Kidd C, Thomaz A, Hoffman G, and Berlin M (2005). Effects of nonverbal communication on efficiency and robustness in human-robot teamwork. In Proceedings of the IEEE/RSJ International Conference on Intelligent Robots and Systems (IROS) (Edmonton, Alberta, Canada, August 2-6, 2005), 708-713.

[3] Bremner, J., Frost, A., Haub, C., Mather, M., Ringheim, K., & Zuehlke, E. (2010). World population highlights: Key finding from prbs 2010 world population data sheet. Population Bulletin, 65(2).

[4] Cline, M. G. (1967). The Perception of Where a Person Is Looking. The American Journal of Psychology, 80(1), 41-50

[5] Feil-Seifer, D. & Mataric, M. (2005). Defining socially assistive robotics. In proceedings of the Rehabilitation robotics, 2005. icorr 2005. 9th international conference on (p. 465 - 468). http://dx.doi.org/ 10.1109/ICORR.2005.1501143

[6] Hardiess, G., Gillner, S., and Mallot, H. A. (2008). Head and eye movements and the role of memory limitations in a visual search paradigm. Journal of Vision, 8(1):7, 1–13, doi:10.1167/8.1.7

[7] Kendon, A. (1967). Some functions of gaze-direction in social interaction. Acta psychologica, 26(1), 22.

[8] Langton, S. R. H. (2000). The mutual influence of gaze and head orientation in the analysis of social attention direction. The Quarterly Journal of Experimental Psychology, 53A (3), 825-845.

[9] Laurutis VP, Robinson DA (1986) The vestibulo-ocular reex during human saccadic eye movements. J Physiol 373: 209–233.

[10] Lee, S., Hyungjong, N., Jonghoon, L., Kyusong, L., Gary Geunbae, L., Seongdae, S., & Munsang, K. (2011). On the effectiveness of robot-assisted language learning. ReCALL, 23(01), 25-58. http://dx.doi.org/10.1017/S0958344010000273

[11] Lobmaier, J. S., Fischer, M. H., and Schwaninger, A. (2006). Objects Capture Perceived Gaze Direction. Experimental Psychology 2006, 53(2), 117–122. DOI 10.1027/1618-3169.53.2.117

[12] Lockerd A and Breazeal C (2004). Tutelage and Socially Guided Robot Learning. MIT Media Lab, Cambridge, MA, USA, 2004.

[13] Nguyen, A., Chandran, V., and Sridharan, S. (2006). Gaze tracking for region of interest coding in JPEG 2000. Signal Processing: Image Communication, 21(5), 359-377.

[14] Pineau, J., Montemerlo, M., Pollack, M., Roy, N., & Thrun, S. (2003). Towards robotic assistants in nursing homes: Challenges and results. Robotics and Autonomous Systems, 42(3-4), 271–281. Retrieved from http://linkinghub.elsevier.com/retrieve/pii/S0921889002003810

[15] Saeb S, Weber C, Triesch J (2011) Learning the Optimal Control of Coordinated Eye and Head Movements. PLoS Comput Biol 7(11): e1002253. doi:10.1371/journal.pcbi.1002253

[16] Stiefelhagen, R., Yang, J., & Waibel, A. (1999). Modeling focus of attention for meeting indexing. In Proc. Seventh acm int. conf. on multimedia, 1:3–10.

[17] Tapus, A., Mataric, M. J., & Scassellati, B. (2007). The grand challenges in socially assistive robotics. Robotics and Automation Magazine, 14(1), 1-7, http://dx.doi.org/10.1109/MRA.2007.339605.

[18] van der Pol, D., Cuijpers, R.H., & Juola, J.F. (2010). Head Pose Estimation for Real-Time Low Resolution Video. In proceedings of the European Conference on Cognitive Ergonomics, August 25-27, 2010, Delft, The Netherlands.

[19] van der Pol, D., Cuijpers. R.H., and Juola, J.F. (2011). Head pose estimation for a domestic robot. In proceedings of the 6th international conference on Human-robot interaction, March 6-9, 2011, Lausanne, Switzerland.

[20] Van Gisbergen JAM, Robinson DA, Gielen S (1981) A quantitative analysis of generation of saccadic eye movements by burst neurons. J Neurophysiol 45:417–442.

[21] Veneri G, Rosini F, Federighi P, Federico A, Rufa A. (2012). Evaluating gaze control on a multi-target sequencing task: the distribution of fixations is evidence of exploration optimisation. Comput Biol Med., 42(2), 235-44. doi: 10.1016/j.compbiomed.2011.11.013.

[22] Wilson, H. R., Wilkinson, F., Lin, L., and Castillo, M. (2000). Perception of head orientation. Vision Research, 40, 459–472.

[23] Yamazoe, H., Utsumi, A., Yonezawa, T., and Abe, S (2008). Remote Gaze Estimation with a Single Camera Based on Facial-Feature Tracking, In Proceedings of Eye Tracking Research & Applications Symposium (ETRA2008), pp.245--250.

[24] Yan, W., Torta, E., van der Pol, D., Meins, N., Weber, C., Cuijpers, R. H., and Wermter, S. (2013). Learning Robot Vision for Assisted Living. In J. Garcia-Rodriguez, & M. Cazorla Quevedo (Eds.), Robotic Vision: Technologies for Machine Learning and Vision Applications (pp. 257-280). Hershey, PA: Information Science Reference. doi:10.4018/978-1-4666-2672-0.ch015.

[25] Yücel, Z., & Salah, A. A. (2009). Head pose and neural network based gaze direction estimation for joint attention modeling in embodied agents. In Proc. Annual Meeting of Cognitive Science Society.

[26] Zee DS, Optican LM, Cook JD, Robinson DA, Engel WK (1976) Slow saccades in spinocerebellar degeneration. Arch Neurol 33: 243–251.

Automatic Method of Gender Dependent Age-Group Classification

Sae Hwang[1] and Emre Celebi[2]
[1] Department of Computer Science, University of Illinois at Springfield, Springfield, IL 62703, USA
[2] Department of Computer Science, Louisiana State University in Shreveport, Shreveport, LA 71115, USA

Abstract - *In this paper, we propose an automatic age-group classification algorithm based on gender information. The proposed method detects a face region, and then it identifies eyes and lips. Using the detected eyes and lips, four regions of interest are selected from a face to extract texture features. Unlike previous efforts which try to estimate the age-group of the facial image directly, our method uses two step classification. First, the gender of the facial image is estimated. Based on the result of the gender classification, the age-group of the facial image is estimated. The experimental results show that the accuracy of age-group classification can increase about 16% in the accuracy when gender information is considered. Overall, our proposed method can achieve about 89% accuracy in age-group classification.*

Keywords: Age-group classification, Gender classification, Face detection, Local Gabor binary pattern, Support vector machines

1 Introduction

Human face is the source of important perceptible information [1]. Personal identity, facial expression, race, gender, age and pose are the most important human characteristics revealed by facial attributes. Among them, age has its special characteristics and facial age estimation has many applications in our real world life e.g. security control and surveillance, age based HCI (human-computer interaction), biometrics, parental control and face retrieval over large scale facial image dataset [2, 3].

There have been many researches focus on the development of human-age estimation. According to a literature survey on recent research about age estimation, the design approaches can be divided into two main categories, the age estimation (in years) and age-group determination. In the age estimation in years, Yun et al. [4] used the database of human faces containing detailed age information to verify their proposed method. The spatial transformation of feature point was employed to express several age patterns with corresponding different ages. Each input facial image will be compared with age patterns to obtain the age estimation result.

In the estimation of the age group using facial data, the first research is the work by Kwon and Lobo [5]. They categorized gray scale images of the face into one of three age groups: babies, young adults and senior adults. They used anthropometric model of the face, the science of measuring sizes and proportions on human faces, in their study. They computed six ratios of distances between primary features of the face and separated babies from other two groups. Then, energy functions and snake lets were used to locate the wrinkles on the face. The computed wrinkle indexes were used to distinguish young adults from senior adults. The identification rate for the first group is below 68%. Lin et al. [6] used human facial features to distinguish the faces of young children or adults. First, the eyes detection module is used to find the actual eyes location and then the locations of the nose and mouth are determined. The distance between eyes and nose and the distance between two eyes are utilized as characteristic values. These two distances are transferred to a ratio to indicate the relationship in the adult and child region by practical observations. Their recognition rate was 75.9% and 71 % for child and adults respectively. Iga et al. [7] extracted features of Gabor wavelet transformation (GWT), textures (spots, wrinkles and flab), geometric arrangement, color, and hair information for age estimation. For each estimation process, SVM classifiers with one or a few kinds of those features are created and trained. Estimation results are obtained by voting of results of the classifiers, the range of age estimation is divided into 5 classes with 10 years old range.

Recently, there are some researches estimating human age and its gender at the same time [8, 9]. However, there are two main problems in these studies. First, they require a manual procedure to extract some ratio based global features such as the distance between lips to the nose tip, the distance between nose tip to the line joining two eyes, the distance between lips to the line joining two eyes, eccentricity of the face, ratio of dimension, width of lips. To extract these features, they need to identify some important regions such as eyes, noise, mouth, moustache, etc. manually.

Second problem is that gender classification and age-group classification are performed independently. However, the accuracies of humans' age estimation are affected by their gender. To address these two problems, we propose an automatic age-group classification algorithm based on gender information.

The rest of the paper is organized as follows: section 2 describes the proposed method in details, our data set and the experimental results are discussed in section 3 and conclusions are shown in section 4.

2 Proposed method

In this section, the procedure of the proposed method is described. The proposed method consists of four main stages. The first stage is detection of the facial image. The second stage is detection of the eyes and lips on the detected facial image. The next stage is feature extraction at the regions of interest (ROIs) which is identified based on the detected eyes and lips from the previous stage. The last stage is age-group classification and it consists of two steps of classification: gender classification and gender dependent age-group classification. First a facial image is classified into two gender groups: Male and Female. Based on the result of the first step, the same facial image is classified into three different age groups: Child, Adult and Old. Figure 1 shows the procedure of the proposed age-group classification system.

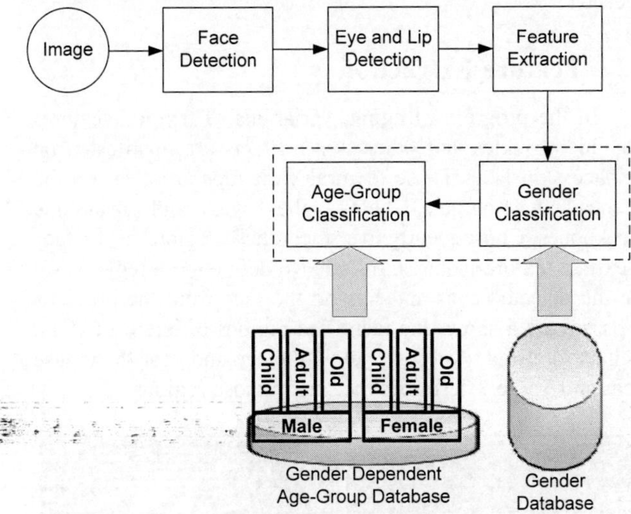

Figure 1: Procedure of Proposed Age-Group Classification

2.1 Face Detection

The first stage of the proposed age-group classification system is to detect the human face in the image frame. First, the skin color is utilized to segment possible human face area in a test image. The skin color may vary due to different lighting. To have a robust detection, the color space is adopted to define the range of skin colors. Based on the information of skin color from trained images, the skin color regions (Bskin) can be obtained as follows:

$$B^{skin} = \begin{cases} 1 & T_1^{C_b} \le C_b(x,y) \le T_2^{C_b}, \quad T_1^{C_r} \le C_r(x,y) \le T_2^{C_r} \\ 0 & \text{otherwise} \end{cases}$$

Figure 2 (a) shows the distribution of skin samples from the database in the C_b-C_r colour plane. The threshold values $T_1^{C_b} = 90$, $T_2^{C_b} = 112$, $T_1^{C_r} = 142$, and $T_2^{C_b} = 160$ are selected based on the skin color distribution and Figure 2 (c) shows the binary map of detected skin color regions (B^{skin}). The morphology closing procedure is then performed to reduce the noise in the image frame. Finally, an attentional cascade method [10] is used to verify whether the detected region is indeed a human face. Figure 2 (d) shows the detected face based on our face detection method.

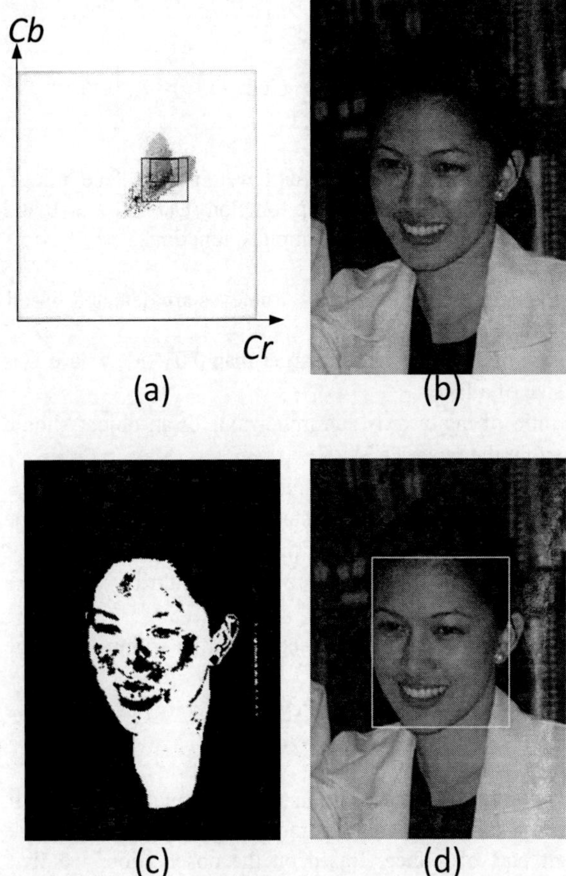

Figure 2: (a) Distribution of skin samples from the database in the C_r-C_b color plane, (b) Original image, (c) Binary map of skin color regions and (d) Face detection result

2.2 Eye and Lip Detection

The shape of an eye approaches a circle and the intensity value of central zone is lower than that outside the central zone in the circle. Based on the above information, we first use gray-level morphological operators to find some candidates of eyes. The output L_M of the gray-level morphological operation can be expressed as follows:

$$L_M(x,y) = \frac{Y(x,y) \oplus g(x,y)}{Y(x,y) \Theta g(x,y) + 1}$$

where $Y(x,y)$ denotes the intensity component in YC_bC_r color space; $\oplus$ is the dilation operator; Θ is the erosion operator; $g(x,y)$ represents the structure element and the size of $g(x,y)$ is 5×7 pixels representing an ellipse-like shape. By applying an adoptive threshold (T^*) to L_M, the binary map B^E for eye candidates is generated as follows:

$$B^E(x,y) = \begin{cases} 1 & \text{if } L_M(x,y) > T^* \\ 0 & \text{otherwise} \end{cases}$$

and

$$T^* = \arg_T \delta\left(\left(\frac{1}{H\times W}\times\sum_{x=0}^{H}\sum_{y=0}^{W} U(L_M(x,y)-T)\right)-0.1\right)$$

H and W represent the height and weight of a face image, respectively. $U(x)$ is the unit step function ($U(x)$=1 for x>0 and $U(x)$=0 for $x\leq 0$) and $\delta(x)$ is the impulse function.

Using the detected regions in B^E, true eyes are detected based on the following rules:

1) The size of an object should larger than $0.01\times N^2$, where N is the size of a face
2) The ratio of major axis and minor axis of an object should be within the range [1 2].
3) The distance of two objects should be larger than $0.6\times N$.
4) The angle between the horizontal line and the connected line of two eyes should be smaller than 45°.
5) The ratio of the sizes of two objects should be within the range [0.33 3].
6) The compactness of each object should be within the range [1 3].

Figure 3 (a) shows the detected eyes (red color) using the eye detection method described above.

A lip can be detected based on its edge information because it is observed that a lip contains more edge information in the low half part of a face. Based on the observation, we first perform Canny edge detection to obtain an edge map. The size of the search window is defined as follows:

$$B\_Width = 0.8 \cdot L_E \text{ and } B\_Height = 0.3 \cdot L_E$$

where L_E represents the distance of two eyes. For each pixel on the perpendicular bisector of the connected line of two eyes, the number of edge points is computed within a search window. The lip exists at the position where the number of edge points is the maximum value. Figure 3 (b) shows the illustration of our lip detection method.

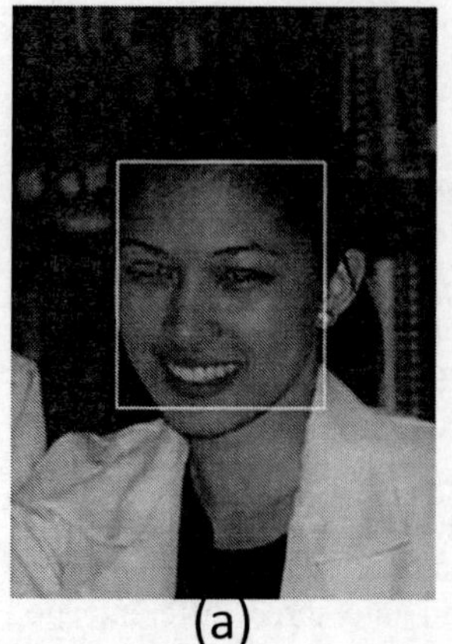

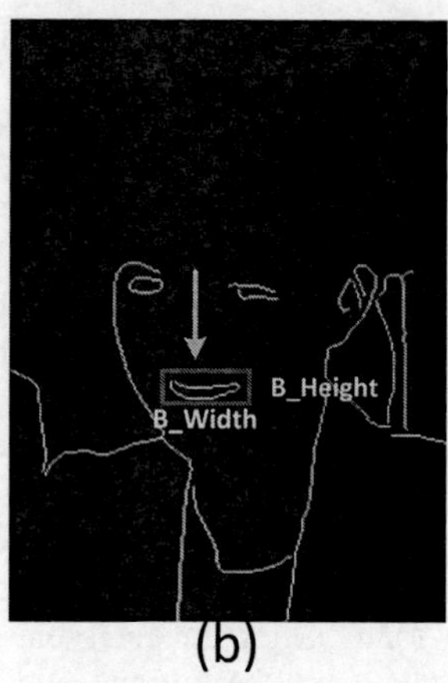

Figure 3: (a) Eye detection result in red color, (b) Illustration of lip detection

2.3 Feature Extraction

In the progress of aging, variations of textural features like fine wrinkles and other skin artifacts are manifested on the face skin [11]. These textural variations are clear on the forehead, eye-corners, below the eyes and near the cheekbones. Consequently, we select these regions of the face to extract texture features. In order to define these regions, we use the detected eyes and lips on the face from the previous steps. Figure 4 shows the identified regions of interest (ROIs) such as forehead, eyebrow, below the eye and near the mouse areas and Table 1 describes the size of those regions.

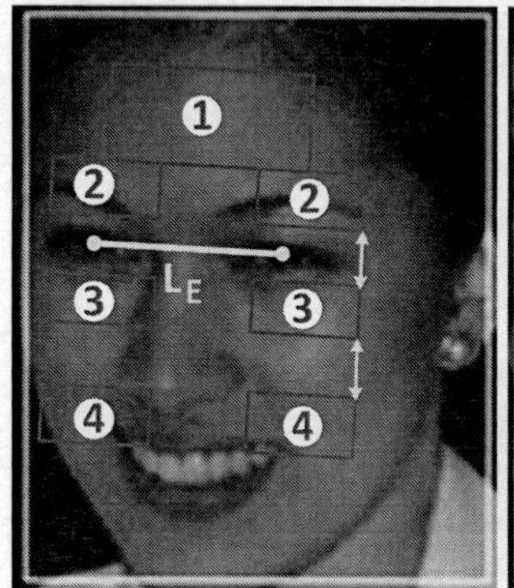

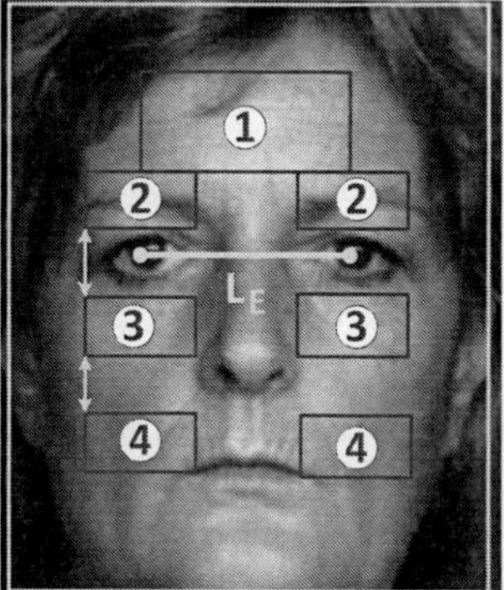

Figure 4: Identified regions of interest (ROIs) to extract features

Table 1: Size of regions of interest (ROIs)

Region	Weight	Height
1	L_E	½* L_E
2	½* L_E	¼* L_E
3	½* L_E	¼* L_E
4	½* L_E	¼* L_E

➢ L_E represents the distance between two eyes

2.3.1 Gabor filter

Gabor filters have been widely used in image processing over the past two decades. Gabor wavelet kernels have many common properties with mammalian visual cortical cells [12]. These properties are orientation selectivity, spatial localization and spatial frequency characterization. In this sense, Gabor filters offer the best simultaneous localization of spatial and frequency information.

A 2-D Gabor filter is an oriented complex sinusoidal grating modulated by a 2-D Gaussian function, which is given by the following:

$$h(x,y) = g(x,y)\exp(2\pi j(Ux+Vy)) = h_R(x,y) + jh_I(x,y)$$

where (U,V) is a spatial frequency, $g(x,y)$ is the Gaussian function with scale parameter σ and $h_R(x,y)$, $h_I(x,y)$ are the real and imaginary parts of $h(x,y)$ respectively.

$$g(x,y) = \frac{1}{2\pi\sigma^2}\exp\left(-\frac{x^2+y^2}{2\sigma^2}\right)$$

The Gabor filter is a bandpass filter centered on frequency (U,V) with bandwidth determined by σ. The parameters of a Gabor filter are represented by the spatial frequency U,V and scale σ. In general, a radial frequency $F\ (F = \sqrt{U^2+V^2})$, orientation θ ($\theta = \tan^{-1}(V/U)$) and σ are used instead in polar coordinates. The Gabor filtered output of an image $i(x,y)$ is obtained by the convolution of the image with the Gabor function $h(x,y)$ with adjustable parameters (f, θ, σ). We use f={0, 2, 4, 8, 16, 32, 64}, θ ={ 0, $\pi/6$, $\pi/3$, $\pi/2$, $2\pi/3$, $5\pi/6$}, and σ=4 in our experiments.

2.3.2 Local Gabor Binary Pattern

Local binary pattern is a nonparametric descriptor, which efficiently summarizes the local structures of images. The original LBP operator was introduced by Ojala [13] for texture description. The operator labels the pixels of an image with decimal numbers. First the values of each pixel around the center pixel are thresholded with the center pixel value. A binary number is extracted and a decimal value is calculated. An example of the basic LBP operator is shown in Figure 5.

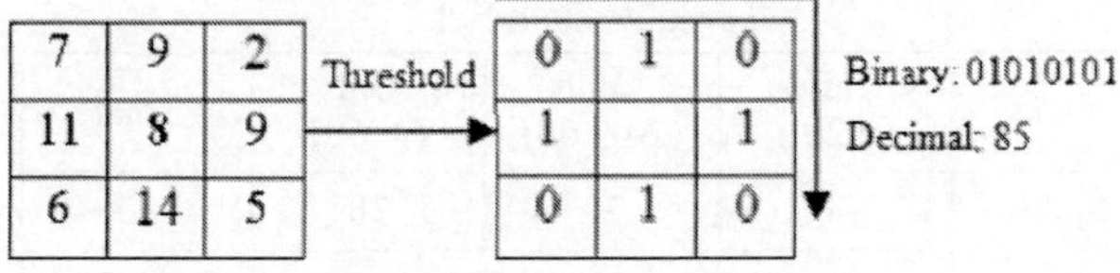

Figure 5: Example of LBP operator

Given a pixel at (x_c, y_c), the resulting LBP can be expressed in decimal form as follows:

$$LBP(x_c, y_c) = \sum_{p=0}^{p-1} s(i_p - i_c)2^p$$

where i_c and i_p are, respectively, gray-level values of the central pixel and P surrounding pixels in the neighborhood, and function $s(x)$ is defined as

$$s(x) = \begin{cases} 1, & \text{if } x \geq 0 \\ 0, & \text{if } x < 0 \end{cases}$$

To deal with the texture at different scales, the operator was later generalized to use neighborhoods of different sizes [14]. A Local Binary Pattern is called uniform if it contains at most two bitwise transitions from 0 to 1 or vice versa when the binary string is considered circular. Here we adopt a LBP operator $LBP^{u2}_{P,R}$. The subscript represents using the operator in a neighborhood of P sampling points on a circle of radius R and the superscript $u2$ stands for using uniform patterns and labeling all remaining patterns with a single label.

2.3.3 Local Binary Pattern

The combination of Gabor and LBP enhances the power of the spatial histogram, and exploits multi-resolution and multi-orientation Gabor decomposition. LGBP is impressively insensitive to appearance variations due to lighting and misalignment [15].

To extract LGBP features, in first step the images are convolved with the multi-scale and multi-orientation Gabor filters. The output of the first step is Gabor map pictures (GMPs). In the second step, each GMP is converted to Local Gabor Binary Pattern (LGBP) map by applying Local Binary Pattern (LBP) operator to a GMP and a histogram is computed for each region.

Finally the LGBP histograms of all the LGBP Maps are concatenated to form the final feature vector. The framework of LGBP approach is shown in figure 6.

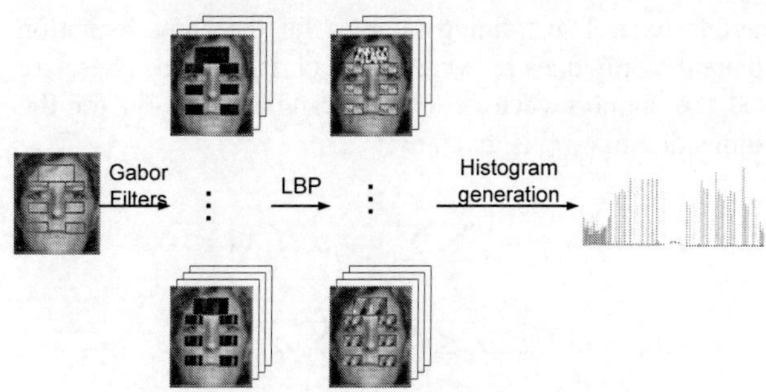

Figure 6: Process of LGBP features extraction

2.4 Support vector machines

Support vector machines (SVMs) have recently drawn considerable attention in the machine learning community due to their solid theoretical foundation and excellent practical performance. They are kernel-based learning algorithms derived from the statistical learning theory [16, 17]. SVMs have several advantages over the other classifiers such as decision trees and neural networks. The support vector training mainly involves optimization of a convex cost function. Therefore, there is no risk of getting stuck at local minima as in the case of backpropagation neural networks. Most learning algorithms implement the empirical risk minimization (ERM) principle which minimizes the error on the training data. On the other hand, SVMs are based on the structural risk minimization (SRM) principle which minimizes the upper bound on the generalization error. Therefore, SVMs are less prone to overfitting when compared to algorithms that implement the ERM principle such as backpropagation neural net-works. Another advantage of SVMs is that they provide a unified framework in which different learning machine architectures (e.g., RBF networks, feedforward neural networks) can be generated through an appropriate choice of kernel.

Consider a set of n training data points $\{\mathbf{x}_i, y_i\} \in \mathbf{R}^d \times \{-1, +1\}$, $i = 1, \ldots, n$, where **R** is a hyperplane, $\mathbf{x}_i$ represents a point in d-dimensional space and y_i is a two-class label. Suppose we have a hyperplane that separates the positive samples from the negative ones. Then the points **x** on the hyperplane satisfy $\mathbf{w} \bullet \mathbf{x} + b = 0$, where **w** is the normal to the hyperplane, $|b|/\|\mathbf{w}\|$ is the perpendicular distance from the hyperplane to the origin, and $\|\mathbf{w}\|$ is the Euclidean norm of **w**. If we take two such hyperplanes between the positive and negative samples, the support vector algorithm's task is to maximize the distance (margin) between them. In order to maximize the margin, $\|\mathbf{w}\|^2$ is minimized subject to the following constraints:

$$y_i(\mathbf{w} \bullet \mathbf{x} + b) \geq 1 - \xi_1, \qquad \xi_1 \geq 0 \quad \forall_i$$

ξ_1, $i = 1, \ldots, n$ are positive slack variables for non-linearly separable data. The training samples for the above equation hold are the only ones relevant for the classification. These are called the support vectors. The Lagrangian function for the minimization of $\|\mathbf{w}\|^2$ is given by:

$$L_k = \sum_{i=1}^{n} \alpha_i - \frac{1}{2} \sum_{i=1}^{n} \sum_{j=1}^{n} y_i y_j \alpha_i \alpha_j K(\mathbf{x}_i, \mathbf{x}_j)$$

$$\text{subject to } 0 \leq \alpha_i \leq C \text{ and } \sum_{i=1}^{n} \alpha_i y_i = 0$$

C is a penalty parameter to control the trade-off between the model complexity and the empirical risk, and K is a kernel function. This formulation allows us to deal with extremely high (theoretically infinite) dimensional mappings without having to do the associated computation. Some commonly used kernels are:

- Linear: $K(\mathbf{x}_i, \mathbf{x}_j) = \mathbf{x}_i^{\mathrm{T}} \cdot \mathbf{x}_j$
- Polynomial: $K(\mathbf{x}_i, \mathbf{x}_j) = (\gamma \mathbf{x}_i^{\mathrm{T}} \cdot \mathbf{x}_j + r)^d, \quad \gamma > 0$
- Radial basis function (RBF):

$$K(\mathbf{x}_i, \mathbf{x}_j) = \exp\left(\frac{-\gamma \| \mathbf{x}_j - \mathbf{x}_j \|^2}{2\sigma^2} \right), \quad \gamma > 0$$

- Sigmoid:

$$K(\mathbf{x}_i, \mathbf{x}_j) = \mathrm{Tanh}(\gamma \mathbf{x}_i^{\mathrm{T}} \cdot \mathbf{x}_j + r), \quad \gamma > 0$$

In this study, the radial basis function (RBF) was adopted for various reasons [18]. Firstly, the linear kernel cannot handle nonlinearly separable classification tasks, and in any case, is a special case of the RBF kernel. Secondly, the computation of the RBF kernel is more stable than that of the polynomial kernel, which introduces values of zero or infinity in certain cases. Thirdly, the sigmoid kernel is only valid (i.e. satisfies Mercer's conditions) for certain parameters. Finally, the RBF kernel has fewer hyper parameters (γ) which need to be determined when compared to the polynomial (γ, r, d) and sigmoid kernels (γ, r).

3 Experimental Results

To evaluate the proposed method, we made our data set from two face database: FACES [19] and FG-NET [20]. FACES database consists of 2052 color images of 171 subjects with two sets of six facial expressions per subject such as neutral, happy, angry, fearful, sad and disgusted. The age range of FACE database is between 19 and 80. FG-NET database consists of 1002 color and gray scale images of 82 subjects with 12 images per subject on average and age range between 0 and 69 years.

Because we need all color images and age range between 0 and 80 years, we select 468 color images of 117 subjects with 4 images per subject from FACES database for the adult and the old age groups and we select 252 color images of 63 subjects with 4 images per subject from FG-NET database for the young and the old age groups. Total number of images is 720 (=180*4). Table 2 describes our data set in details

Table 2: Data Set

	Child (<20)	Adult ($20 \sim 60$)	Old (>60)	Total
Male	30	30	30	90
Female	30	30	30	90
Total	60	60	60	180

First, Table 3 shows the experimental results of our gender classification based on three different texture features. In our experiment, we can achieve about 89% accuracy with Gabor

Filters, about 84% with LBP and about 94% with LGBP for the gender classification.

Table 3: Accuracy of Gender Classification

Features	Accuracy (%)
Gabor	89.44
LBP	83.88
LGBP	94.44

Table 4 shows the accuracy of age-group classification based on LGBP because it generates the highest accuracy in gender classification. The column of "Without Gender" shows the accuracy when gender classification is not applied and the column of "With Gender" shows the accuracy when gender classification is applied before classifying facial images into different age groups. By considering gender information, we can increase about 22% for 'Child', about 9% for 'Adult' and about 23% for 'Old' in the accuracy. Overall, we can increase about 16% in the accuracy by achieving about 89% accuracy in age-group classification with the consideration of gender information.

Table 4: Accuracy of Age-Group Classification

	Accuracy (%)	
	Without Gender	**With Gender**
Child	66.67	**88.33**
Adult	88.33	**91.67**
Old	63.33	**86.67**
Overall	72.78	**88.89**

4 Conclusions

In this paper, an automatic system of gender dependent age-group classification is proposed. Unlike previous efforts which try to estimate the age-group of the input image directly, our method uses two step classification. First, the gender of the input image is estimated. Based on the result of the gender classification, the age-group of the input image is estimated. The experimental results show that the accuracy of age-group classification can increase about 16% in the accuracy when gender information is considered. Overall, our proposed method can achieve about 89% accuracy in age-group classification

5 References

[1] L.A. Zebrowitz, *Reading Faces: Window to the Soul?*, Westview Press,1997.

[2] Yun Fu,Guodong Guo and Thomas S. Huang, "Age Synthesis and Estimation via Faces: A Survey", *IEEE Trans. on Pattern Analysis and Machine Intelligence*, vol. 32, no. 11, 2010.

[3] F. Gao and H. Ai, "Face Age Classification on Consumer Images with Gabor Feature and Fuzzy LDA Method," *Proceedings of IEEE International Conference on Advances in Biometrics*, pp. 132-141, 2009

[4] F. Yun, X. Ye and T. S. Huang, "Estimating Human Age by Manifold Analysis of Face Pictures and Regression on Aging Features," *Proc. of 2007 IEEE International Conference on Multimedia and Expo*, 2007, pp. 1383-1386.

[5] Y. Kwon and N. Lobo, "Age Classification from Facial Images," *Computer Vision and Image Understanding*, vol. 74, no. 1, pp.1-21, 1999

[6] S. Lin-Lin and 1. Zhen, "Modelling geiometric features for face based age classification," *Proc. of 2008 International Conference on Machine Learning and Cybernetics*, 2008, pp. 2927-2931.

[7] R. Iga, K. Izumi, H. Hayashi, G. Fukano and T. Ohtani., "A Gender and Age Estimation System from Face Iimages," *Proc. of SICE Annual Conference*, 2003, pp. 756-761.

[8] Ramesha K, Srikanth N, K B Raja, Venugopal K R and L M Patnaik, "Advanced Biometric Identification on Face, Gender and Age Recognition", 2009 International Conference on Advances in Recent Technologies in Communication and Computing, 2009, pp. 23-27

[9] Vahid Karimi and Ashkan Tashk, "Age and Gender Estimation by Using Hybrid Facial Features", *20th Telecommunications forum TELFOR* 2012

[10] P. Viola and M. Jones, "Rapid Object Detection Using a Boosted Cascade of Simple Features," *Proc. IEEE Con! on Computer Vision and Pattern Recognition*, England, 2001, pp. 511-518

[11] N.Ramanathana, R.Chellappa, and S. Biswas, "Computational methods for Modeling Facial Aging: A Survey", *J. Visual Languages and Computing*, vol. 20, no.3, pp.131-144, 2009.

[12] M. A. Webster and R. L. De Valois, "Relationship between Spatial-Frequency and Orientation Tuning of Striate-Cortex Cells," *J Opt Soc Am A*, vol. 2, 1124–1132, 1985.

[13] T. Ojala, M Pietikinen, and D. Harwood, "A comparative study of texture measures with classification based on featured distribution," *Pattern Recognition*, vol. 29, pp. 51-59, 1996.

[14] T. Ojala, M. Pietikainen, and T. Maenpaa, "Multi-resolution gray-scale and rotation invariant texture classification with local binary patterns," *IEEE Trans. Pattern Analysis and Machine Intelligence*, vol. 24, pp.971-987, Jul. 2002.

[15] W. Zhang, S. Shan, W. Gao, X. Chen, H. Zhang, "Local gabor binary pattern histogram sequence (lgbphs): a non-statistical model for face representation," *Proc. 2005 IEEE Int. Conf. Comput. Vis.*, pp. 786-791.

[16] V. Vapnik, Statistical learning theory, *Wiley*, 1998.

[17] CJC. Burges, A tutorial on support vector machines for pattern recognition, *Data Mining Knowledge Discovery*, vol. 2, no. 2, pp. 121–167, 1998.
[18] SS. Keerthi and C-J. Lin, Asymptotic behaviors of support vector machines with Gaussian kernel, *Neural Computation*, vol. 15, no. 7, pp. 1667–1689, 2003.
[19] Natalie C. Ebner, Michaela Riediger, and Ulman Lindenberger, "FACES—A database of facial expressions in young, middle-aged, and older women and men: Development and validation", *Behavior Research Methods* 2010, 42 (1), 351-362
[20] FG-NET, "The FG-NET aging database." [Online]. Available: http://www.fgnet.rsunit.com

Ensemble of Patterns of Oriented Edge Magnitudes Descriptors For Face Recognition

Loris Nanni,[1] Alessandra Lumini,[2] Sheryl Brahnam,[3] Mauro Migliardi[1]

[1]DEI, University of Padua, viale Gradenigo 6, Padua, Italy. {loris.nanni, mauro.migliardi}@unipd.it;
[2]DEI, Università di Bologna, Via Venezia 52, 47521 Cesena, Italy. alessandra.lumini@unibo.it;
[3]Computer Information Systems, Missouri State University, 901 S. National, Springfield, MO 65804, USA. sbrahnam@missouristate.edu

Abstract

In this work we propose an ensemble of descriptors for face recognition. Starting from the base patterns of the oriented edge magnitudes (POEM) descriptor, we developed different ensembles by varying the preprocessing techniques, the parameters for extracting the accumulated magnitude images (AM), and the parameters of the local binary patterns (LBP) applied to AM. Our best proposed ensemble works well regardless of whether dimensionality reduction by principal component analysis (PCA) is performed or not before the matching step. We validate our approach using the FERET datasets and the Labeled Faces in the Wild (LFW) dataset. We obtain very high performance rates in both datasets. To the best of our knowledge, we obtain one of the highest performances reported in the literature on the FERET datasets. We want to stress that our ensemble obtains these results without combining different texture descriptors and without any supervised approach or transform. Finally, two cloud use cases are proposed.
The MATLAB source of our best approach will be freely available: http://www.dei.unipd.it/wdyn/?IDsezione=3314&IDgruppo_pass=124

Keywords: Face recognition; ensemble of descriptors; patterns of oriented edge magnitudes; local binary patterns.

1 Introduction

The problem of face recognition has been considered since the very beginning of computer vision. In the last two decades it has been extensively studied due to the large number of government and commercial applications that require the development of robust and reliable systems. In general, there are three main categories of applications for face recognition: 1) face verification, which authenticates a person's identity by comparing his or her face with a corresponding template; 2) face identification, which recognizes a person's face by comparing it with a dataset of faces; and 3) face tagging, which is a particular case of face identification.

Different techniques have been proposed in the literature for face recognition, including Principal Component Analysis (PCA), Discriminant Analysis, Local Binary Patterns (LBP), neural networks, Elastic Template Matching, Algebraic moments, and many other ad hoc descriptors and classifiers. Existing face recognition techniques have be classified into four types [1], based on the way they define the face: 1) *appearance based approaches*, which use global texture features (including Eigenfaces [2] and other linear transformation approaches); 2) *model based approaches,* which work on the shape and the texture of the face, along with 3D depth information; 3) *geometry or template based approaches*, which compare the input image with a set of templates constructed either by using statistical tools or by analyzing local facial features and their geometric relationships (including Elastic Bunch Graph Matching algorithms [3]); and 4) *techniques using Neural Networks,* which are often used in combination with Gabor Filters [4].

For many applications, face recognition performance has reached a satisfactory level under the frontal pose and optimal lighting conditions. Performance degrades, however, with pose and lighting variations and in uncontrolled environments.

To deal with these problems, researches have focused their studies on the design of robust face descriptors that are not only discriminative but also insensitive to pose variations, changes in facial expression, and lighting conditions. For example, Pinto et al. [5] use V1-like and Gabor filters for face representation. Cao el al. [6] propose a method to encode the local micro-structures of a face into a set of more uniformly distributed discrete codes. In [7] and [8] a novel descriptor, called the Patterns of Oriented Edge Magnitudes (POEM) is proposed. POEM is an oriented spatial multi-resolution descriptor that captures rich information (self-similarity structure) about the original image. Other encouraging results in difficult conditions have been obtained in [9] using a sparse representation to select a feature for person-specific verification. The last two works aim to solve one of the most difficult problems in face recognition: descriptors gaining high recognition performance are usually computationally intensive, while low-complexity methods often do not perform reliably enough.

We start our study from one of the most efficient and high performing descriptors recently proposed in the literature: the POEM **[7]**. In this work we try to boost the performance of POEM, not by combining it with other texture descriptors (as in **[8]**), but by building an ensemble based on the variation of its parameters and of the enhancement approaches used before the feature extraction step. The most interesting finding is that building an ensemble in this easy way boosts the performance obtained by POEM. Another contribution of this paper is the definition of some variants of the POEM descriptor using dense LBP **[10]**, instead of LBP, for representing the AM images and for filtering the enhanced image by Gabor filters **[11]** before the POEM extraction step.

2 Ensemble of POEM Descriptors

2.1 The POEM Descriptor

The poem descriptor is based on the idea of characterizing the local face appearance and shape by the distribution of local intensity gradients, or edge directions.

The POEM feature extraction consists of three steps (see [12] for mathematical details):

1. Gradient computation and orientation quantization: first the gradient image is computed, then orientation of each pixel is discretized over 0-π (unsigned representation) or 0-2π (signed representation) (we use the unsigned representation).
2. Magnitude accumulation: a local histogram of orientations over all pixels within a local image patch (cell) is calculated to incorporate information from neighboring pixels.
3. Self-similarity calculation: the accumulated magnitudes are encoded across different directions using the self-similarity LBP-based operator within a larger patch (block). The final POEM descriptor at each pixel is the concatenation of all unidirectional POEMs at different orientations.

2.2 Designing an Ensemble of POEM Variants

In this work, we build our ensemble as follows:

- We propose to enhance the image using different methods, for each method a different POEM descriptor is extracted and used to train a classifier; the preprocessing techniques used in this work are detailed in section 2.3;
- The POEM descriptor depends on a high number of parameters that should be fine-tuned to the application: a) the number of orientations discretized, b) the size of the cell, c) the size of the block, and d) the number of neighbors considered in LBP. Instead of using a single set of optimized parameters, several descriptors are extracted using different sets of parameters, as reported in table 1. These sets of parameters have been proven to work quite well in several different datasets without ad hoc optimization (see [12]).

Number of orientations	cell size	Block size	LBP Neighbors
3	7	5	8
4	7	5	8
3	7	6	8
7	7	5	8
3	4	5	8
3	6	5	8
3	8	5	8
3	7	5	6
3	7	5	9
3	7	5	12

Table 1. Set of parameters used for building an ensemble

2.3 Prepressing Techniques

Image enhancement has advanced greatly in face recognition, especially when dealing with the problem of illumination changes. In this work we examined the following approaches:

- Adaptive single scale retinex (AR): The adaptive single scale retinex algorithm [13] is a variant of the retinex technique, which aims at improving poor scene detail and color reproduction in dark areas of the image. This method gained the best performance in our experiments;
- Anisotropic smoothing (AS): Introduced by Gross and Brajovic in [14], the algorithm computes the estimate of the illumination field and then compensates for it according to some aspects of human visual perception with the aim of enhancing the local contrast of the image;
- Difference of Gaussians (DG): This is a filtering-based normalization technique that relies on the difference of a Gaussians filter to produce a normalized image. This is accomplished by applying a bandpass filter to the input image (note: the log transform is applied to the image [15] before the filter is used);
- Gabor filtering (GF): The last preprocessing method used in this work is not an enhancement technique *per se* but rather a filter. Before the feature extraction step, the input image is filtered by a bank of Gabor filters (using the same Gabor's settings as in [3]).

.

3 Experimental Results

3.1 Datasets

We test our proposed ensembles using the FERET [11] and LFW [13] benchmark databases. The FERET database images are divided into five datasets: Fa, Fb, Fc, Dup1, and Dup2. Fa is the training set, and the other sets are used for testing. Fb contains pictures taken on the same day as the Fa pictures and with the same camera and illumination conditions. Fc contains pictures taken on the same day as the Fa pictures, but with different cameras and with different illumination conditions. Dup1 and Dup2 contain pictures taken on different days than the Fa pictures were taken, but within a year for Dup1 and longer than one year for Dup2. In our experiments, the FERET gray images are aligned using the true eyes position and cropped to 110 × 110 pixels.

The LFW [13] database contains 13233 images of celebrities. It is very challenging since it includes great variations in terms of lighting, pose, age, and even image quality. Two views of the database are provided. View 1, which is used for model selection only, contains a training set of 2200 face pairs and a testing set of 1000 face pairs. View 2 is for performance reporting, and is made up of 10 non-overlapping sets of 600 matches that can be used for 10-fold cross-validation of algorithms and parameters developed on View 1. In our experiments, the LFW gray images are aligned automatically according to the procedure described in [8] and cropped to 110 × 110 pixels.

3.2 Results

We test our ensembles on both databases using their official testing protocols. The performance indicator is the accuracy for the problem of person identification using the FERET dataset. For the LFW dataset, the classification accuracy of each match between two faces is either genuine or impostor (see [13] for more details). In Table 2, we provide a detailed description of the methods compared in our experiments, according to the following parameters:

- Preprocessing procedure: no preprocessing (NO), Adaptive single scale retinex (AR), Anisotropic smoothing (AS), Difference of Gaussians (DG), Gabor filtering (GF). Gabor filtering is applied both to original (NO) or enhanced image, according to the settings used in [3] (4 scales and 4 directions);
- Self-similarity calculation (SSC): LPB or Dense LBP (DLBP) [10] are used for the self-similarity calculation step of POEM;
- Dimensionality reduction and distance measure (DD): city block distance (CBD) is used to compare high dimensional POEM descriptors (in the original code, the chi-square distance (CS) is used), while angle distance (AD) is used when the descriptor is reduced to a lower space by PCA. In this work, we vary from [14] by using the same dimensionality parameter (D=500) and the same projection space (trained on FERET training set) for all the experiments (for both FERET and LFW). Moreover, when PCA is applied the square root normalization is performed before the matching, as in [14];
- Stand-alone/ensemble (SE): ensemble approaches are obtained by perturbing POEM parameters (see Section 2.2) or by perturbing the preprocessing techniques (see Section 2.3). The scores are fused by sum rule. We define: SA, stand-alone method; Ep, the perturbation of POEM parameters; Ee, perturbation of the preprocessing techniques; and E, the perturbation of both preprocessing techniques and the POEM parameters.

In Table 3, we report the accuracy obtained by our approaches on both databases. It should be noted that in order to test the robustness of our approach the same PCA projection matrix calculated in the FERET training set is used in LFW. Moreover, due to computational issues, only a subset of the proposed approaches (the most interesting ones) are tested on LFW.

By examining Table 3, the following conclusions can be drawn:

- Our ensembles are similar in performance to each other, and they outperform [14] in the FERET dataset without any strong optimization (i.e., by using the same parameter settings for the four FERET datasets and the LFW dataset);
- In LFW, the authors of [14] claim the highest results using an ad hoc projection matrix. In contrast, we use the projection matrix for PCA that is constructed using training images of the FERET dataset;
- It is clear that our idea for designing classifiers boosts the performance of the base POEM descriptor in both datasets (please note that $\boldsymbol{POEM_{LBP}^{PCA}(ar)}$ is based on the original code shared by [14]);
- Dense LBP obtains the same performance when the PCA projection is performed but outperforms LBP when the projection is not performed;
- Almost all the proposed ensembles outperform the stand-alone versions;
- Due to lack of space, we report comparisons only with already proposed POEM systems {Vu, 2012 #3994} [14]; it is clear that our system obtains good results without tuning the system for a given dataset (the same approach is used for both datasets). In [8] [12] [14] several state-of-the-arts approaches are compared. Our system obtains performance similar to the best approach tested in the FERET dataset (only two methods outperform our system: they obtain an average accuracy of 96.9% and 97.7% in the FERET dataset);
- The proposed system works well on the LFW dataset but not as well as other approaches. However, POEM has significantly lower complexity with respect other competing systems, which offsets this performance difference to some degree.

Name	Preprocessing	SSC	DD	SE	Description
$POEM_{LBP}^{CS}$	-	LBP	CS	SA	POEM descriptor (source code from [12])
$POEM_{LBP}$	-	LBP	CBD	SA	The method above using CBD
$POEM_{LBP}^{PCA}$	-	LBP	PCA+AD	SA	code of [14] with fixed PCA dimension (500)
$POEM_{LBP}^{PCA}(ar)$	AR	LBP	PCA+AD	SA	The method above using preprocessing
$POEM_{LBP}(ar)$	AR	LBP	CBD	SA	The method above without PCA
$POEM_{DLBP}^{PCA}$	-	DLBP	PCA+AD	SA	Use of DenseLBP
$E\_P_{LBP}^{PCA}(ar)$	AR	LBP	PCA+AD	Ep	Perturbation of POEM parameters
$E\_P_{LBP}(ar)$	AR	LBP	CBD	Ep	Perturbation of POEM parameters
$E\_P_{LBP}^{PCA}(\cdot)$	(AR, AS, DG)	LBP	PCA+AD	Ee	Perturbation of enhancement
$E\_P_{LBP}(\cdot)$	(AR, AS, DG)	LBP	CBD	Ee	Perturbation of enhancement
$E\_P_{LBP}^{PCA}(e)$	(AR, AS, DG)	LBP	PCA+AD	E	Perturbation of enhancement and parameters
$E\_P_{LBP}(e)$	(AR, AS, DG)	LBP	CBD	E	Perturbation of enhancement and parameters
$E\_P_{DLBP}^{PCA}(\cdot)$	(AR, AS, DG)	DLBP	PCA+AD	Ee	Perturbation of enhancement
$E\_P_{DLBP}(\cdot)$	(AR, AS, DG)	DLBP	CBD	Ee	Perturbation of enhancement
$E\_P_{DLBP}^{PCA}(gf)$	(AR, AS, DG)+GF	DLBP	PCA+AD	Ee	Perturbation of enhancement and of GF
$E\_P_{DLBP}(gf)$	(AR, AS, DG)+GF	DLBP	CBD	Ee	Perturbation of enhancement and of GF

Table 2. Compared approaches.

	FERET Datasets					LFW Dataset
Method	**Fb**	**Fc**	**Dup1**	**Dup2**	***Average***	
$POEM_{LBP}^{CS}$	95.2	95.9	77.1	77.4	86.4	74.3
$POEM_{LBP}$	95.7	96.4	77.0	79.5	87.1	74.3
$POEM_{LBP}^{PCA}$	98.5	97.9	87.8	82.9	91.7	-
$POEM_{LBP}^{PCA}(ar)$	98.5	**100**	90.4	89.3	94.5	74.9
$POEM_{LBP}(ar)$	94.1	98.5	77.3	78.6	87.1	-
$E\_P_{LBP}^{PCA}(ar)$	98.6	**100**	91.3	90.6	95.1	75.2
$E\_P_{LBP}(ar)$	94.4	98.0	78.4	79.1	87.4	-
$E\_P_{LBP}^{PCA}(\cdot)$	98.7	**100**	94.6	93.6	**96.7**	**76.9**
$E\_P_{LBP}(\cdot)$	95.2	99.0	81.9	82.5	89.6	-
$E\_P_{LBP}^{PCA}(e)$	98.9	**100**	94.3	93.6	**96.7**	76.8
$E\_P_{LBP}(e)$	95.2	99.0	81.4	81.2	89.2	-
$POEM_{DLBP}^{PCA}$	98.7	99.0	88.1	83.8	92.4	-
$E\_P_{DLBP}^{PCA}(\cdot)$	**98.8**	**100**	94.2	**94.0**	96.7	76.6
$E\_P_{DLBP}(\cdot)$	95.1	99.5	84.2	85.5	91.0	-
$E\_P_{DLBP}^{PCA}(gf)$	98.7	**100**	**94.7**	93.6	**96.7**	-
$E\_P_{DLBP}(gf)$	95.1	99.5	83.8	85.0	90.8	-
POEM [12]	98.1	99.0	79.6	79.1	88.9	75.4
POEM+PCA [14]	99.6	99.5	88.8	85.0	93.2	82.7

Table 3. Accuracy obtained by the methods proposed in this paper in FERET and LFW databases.

4 Two Use Cases

We now present two use cases based on smartphone-plus-cloud infrastructure. In the first case, we consider a face tagging service available to private smartphone users. The recent diffusion of smartphones has provided an unbounded source of photos that continues to grow daily. Many of these pictures end up inside social networks where they might automatically be tagged by the social network system. What we propose is a mechanism for automated face tagging where the results are delivered directly to the smartphone for user filtering before social sharing. This mechanism could be further enhanced to allow automated sharing of specific photos with selectable sets of friends tagged. In figure 1 we show the general architecture of the system.

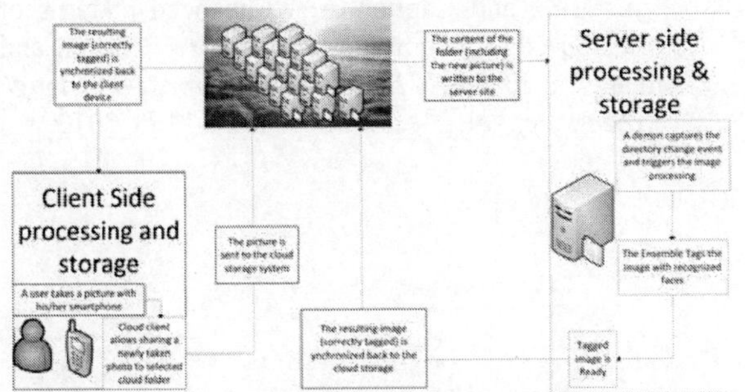

Figure 1 The general architecture of the system.

Several cloud storage providers have developed smartphone apps that allow both the direct uploading of photos taken by devices to personal cloud storage and the sharing of photos with other users. We suggest configuring the system so that when a photo is shared with a service provider the user would automatically trigger the processing of the photo by the server side face tagging application. To be more specific, each user would share a folder in the cloud with the face tagging service provider. A photo that needed to be processed would be uploaded to that shared folder using the cloud application, and then it would be synchronized to the server side folder by the cloud system. The appearance of this new photo would trigger the face tagging application that would in turn process it and generate results. These results would be written in the same directory so that the cloud application could automatically store it back into the cloud and synchronize it back to the smartphone. The mechanism for synchronization back to the smartphone might be provided by the app itself, or it might require the development of a special add-on leveraging the cloud API.

In our proof of concept experiments, we have tested an android app for the commercial cloud storage provider Syncplicity.[1] This app provides push notifications and automated sync-back for selected folders. Other solutions, such as Dropbox,[2] could be used, but they fail to provide automated sync-back to the smartphone. However, they have APIs that allow developing dedicated add-ons for such tasks.

Both solutions described above are based on cloud servers that are out of the control of both the smartphone user and the face tagging service provider since they are based on commercial cloud storage solutions. It is also possible to adopt a different approach leveraging the open source software provided by the OwnCloud project.[3] This project is dedicated to the development of an open source cloud server and clients for several desktop operating systems, such as Microsoft Windows, Linux, MacOS, and mobile operating systems, such as iOS and Android.

By leveraging this software, it would be possible for a face-tagging service provider to control the cloud storage. The absence of a third party storing the data would be especially relevant in the scenario of a security system. As an example, consider our second use case of a video surveillance system. Security cameras would scan choke-points in the area to be monitored in order to get clearer pictures of the people present. Both for privacy and for security reasons, it would not be possible to store these pictures on a public cloud; they would have to be sent to a private cloud hosted inside the premises of the face recognition server. In order to provide this level of security, an open source cloud solution, such as the above mentioned OwnCloud, could be used. Once the photographs have reached the face recognition server, they would be compared to a database of known persons of interest. In the case of a positive match, the system would push the picture and, possibly, a text file with a brief description of the subject to the smartphones of all the security agents on the premises.

5 Conclusion

In this paper, we have shown that it is possible to improve the performance of a single descriptor (POEM) by building an ensemble obtained by perturbing some steps in the face recognition process. In particular, our experiments show that the most reliable approach for building an ensemble is to perturb the enhancement method.

The main novelties our proposed system are the following: 1) our experiments show that it is possible to improve considerably a stand-alone descriptor by changing its parameters; 2) we also show that another easy way to boost the performance of a pattern recognition system is to use different enhancement techniques, and 3) some variants of the base POEM are proposed (e.g., using different

[1] EMC, Syncplicity, www.syncplicity.com, last retrieved on February the 13th 2013

[2] The Dropbox tour, www.dropbox.com/tour, last retrieved on February the 13th 2013

[3] OwnCloud, owncloud.org, last retrieved on February the 13th 2013

descriptors applied to AM or to filter the image by Gabor filters before the AM extraction) and are shown to enhance performance. Finally, two cloud use cases are outlined.

The main drawback of the proposed system is the increase computation time with respect to stand-alone methods. For example, considering $\boldsymbol{E\_P_{LBP}^{PCA}}(\cdot)$, the time for the enhancement and the feature extraction processes is ~1 second, while the matching time is ~ 0.00013 seconds (Intel i5 - 3.3GhZ - 8GRAM - parallelized Matlab code).

Suggestions for future experiments would include a) testing other feature transformations before the matching step, b) combining our proposed POEM-based approach with other descriptors, and c) testing other texture descriptors, instead of LBP, for representing the AM images of POEM.

References

[1] Muruganantham, S., and Jebarajan, T., “A comprehensive review of significant researches on face recognition based on various conditions,” *International Journal of Computer Theory and Engineering,* vol. 4, no. 1, pp. 7-15, 2012.

[2] Turk, M. A., and Pentland, A. P., “Eigenfaces for recognition,” *Journal of Cognitive Neuroscience,* vol. 3, no. 1, pp. 71-86, 1991.

[3] Zhang, B., Shan, S., Chen, X., and Gao, W., “Histogram of gabor phase patterns (HGPP): A novel object representation approach for face recognition,” *IEEE Transactions of Image Processing,* vol. 16, no. 1, pp. 57-68, 2007.

[4] Bhuiyan, A.-A., and Liu, C. H., “On face recognition using gabor filters,” in World Academy of Science, Engineering and Technology, 2007, pp. 51-56.

[5] Pinto, N., DiCarlo, J., and Cox, D., “How far can you get with a modern face recognition test set using only simple features?,” in CVPR’09, 2009.

[6] Cao, Z., Yin, Q., Tang, X., and Sun, J., “Face recognition with learning-based descriptor,” pp. 2707-2714, 2010.

[7] Vu, N.-S., and Caplier, A., “Face recognition with patterns of oriented edge magnitudes,” in ECCV, 2010.

[8] Vu, N.-S., “Exploring patterns of gradient orientations and magnitudes for face recognition,” *IEEE Transactions on Information Forensics and Security,* vol. 8, no. 2, pp. 295-304 2013.

[9] Liang, Y., Liao, S., Wang, L., and Zou, B., “Exploring regularized feature selection for person specific face verification,” in ICCV, 2011.

[10] Ylioinas, J., Hadid, A., Guo, Y., and Pietikäinen, M., “Efficient image appearance description using dense sampling based local binary patterns,” in Asian Conference on Computer Vision, 2012.

[11] Phillips, J., Moon, H., Rizvi, S. A., and Rauss, P. J., “The feret evaluation methodology for face-recognition algorithms,” *IEEE Transactions of Pattern Analysis and Machine Intelligence,* vol. 22, pp. 1090-1104, 2000.

[12] Vu, N.-S., Dee, H. M., and Caplier, A., “Face recognition using the POEM descriptor,” *Pattern Recognition Letters,* vol. 45, no. 7, pp. 2478-2488, 2012.

[13] Huang, G. B., Ramesh, M., Berg, T., and Learned-Miller, E., *Labeled faces in the wild: a database for studying face recognition in unconstrained environments*, vol. Technical Report 07-49, University of Massachusetts, Amherst, 2007.

[14] Vu, N.-S., and Caplier, A., “Enhanced patterns of oriented edge magnitudes for face recognition and image matching,” *IEEE Transactions on Image Processing,* vol. 21, no. 3, pp. 1352-1365, 2012.

An Indexing Method for Efficient Model-Based Search

Pat Jangyodsuk[1],Vassilis Athitsos[1]
[1]Computer Science and Engineering Department
University of Texas at Arlington
Arlington, Texas USA

Abstract—*Large databases of patterns, such as faces, body poses, fingerprints, or gestures, are becoming increasingly widespread, thanks to advances in computer technology. In this paper we focus on the problem of efficient search in such databases, when using model-based search. In model-based search, the user submits as a query a classifier, that has been trained to recognize the type of patterns that the user wants to retrieve. While model-based search can lead to good retrieval accuracy, the efficiency of model-based search can be inadequate if we need to apply the query classifier to every single database pattern. We propose a method for improving the efficiency of model-based search. The proposed method assumes that classifiers have been trained using JointBoost, and operates by defining an embedding, which maps both classifiers and database patterns into a common vector space. Using this embedding, the problem of finding the database patterns maximizing the response of the query classifier is reduced to a nearest neighbor search problem in a vector space. This reduction allows the use of standard vector indexing method to speed up the search. In our experiments, we show that the proposed embedding, together with a simple PCA-based indexing scheme, significantly improve the efficiency of model-based search, as measured on a database of face images constructed from the public FRGC-2 dataset.*

Keywords. Model-based search, indexing, face retrieval

1. Introduction

Current technology has made it quite feasible to create large databases of patterns, such as faces [9], body poses [11], [12], fingerprints, or gestures [4]. Identifying relevant content in such databases can have a variety of real-world uses, such as identifying photographs of a missing person in surveillance camera recordings, or locating occurrences of a specific sign (or sequence of signs) in a database of sign language videos. One common way of searching for content of interest is search-by-example, also known as similarity-based search: the user submits as a query an example of the type of patterns they want to retrieve (e.g., a photograph of the person for which they want to locate additional photographs). Another way to do search is search-by-model (for which we also use the term model-based search), where the user submits as a query a classifier trained to recognize the specific patterns of interest (e.g., a classifier trained to recognize the person whose photographs the user wants to retrieve).

For search-by-example, a large number of similarity-based indexing methods have been proposed to make this type of search more efficient, and capable of scaling to large databases. Reviews of indexing methods for efficient similarity-based search include [2], [6], [7]. However, for search-by-model, we are not aware of any method designed to speed up brute-force search, which involves applying the classifier submitted by the user to all database images. In this paper, we propose such a method, for the specific case where classifiers are constructed using JointBoost [14], which is a variant of AdaBoost [10]. As shown in [14], JointBoost can improve classification accuracy, compared to standard boosting methods, in multiclass problems with relatively few training examples per class, by forcing classifiers trained for different classes to share training information.

As a specific motivating application and case study, we use the topic of finding faces of a specific person in a database of face images. Such a database can be created fairly easily using modern technology, by running a crawler to download a large number of of images from the web, and running a standard face detector, e.g., [16], to identify the location of frontal views of faces. Similarly, such large databases can be compiled by law enforcement agencies, using pictures from surveillance cameras, so as to identify missing persons or criminal suspects.

In such a large database of face images, a key operation is to retrieve images of a specific individual. In principle, a classifier can be constructed on the fly, by providing some training photographs of the person of interest and applying a standard machine learning method, such as boosting or support vector machines [1], [10], [15]. The simplest way to do model-based search would involve applying this classifier to every single face image in the database. This brute-force approach takes time linear to the size of the database and would have difficulty scaling to very large databases. For example, databases of face images compiled by a web search engine or a large-scale surveillance camera network can easily reach sizes of millions or billions of face images.

Support for large database sizes can be provided if, instead of search-by-model we use search-by-example, and submit, as a query, a single mugshot of the person of interest. In that case, hash-based indexing methods such as Locality Sensitive Hashing (LSH) [5] can be applied and have provably sublinear time complexity. However, we argue that model-based search has the potential, at least in some applications, to be far more accurate than similarity-based search, as it is quite plausible that a query classifier, trained to recognize objects of a specific class, contains more information than a single query pattern from that class. Thus, we believe it is of interest to study the problem of designing efficient alternatives to brute force for the search-by-model paradigm, and we propose such an efficient alternative in this paper.

The proposed method uses an embedding formulation proposed in [13], which maps both database patterns X and JointBoost classifiers H to a common vector space. In [13], such an embedding was used for efficient classification of a single pattern X in a domain with a large number of classes. In our case, we have a different problem than in [13]. Instead of doing multiclass recognition of a single pattern X, meaning that we look for the classifier H_y that maximizes $H_y(X)$ for a specific X, we do model-based search, meaning that we look for patterns X maximizing $H_y(X)$ for a specific classifier H_y. We adapt the basic ideas from [13] to define an embedding that is appropriate for this problem. The embedding we propose reduces model-based search to nearest-neighbor search in a vector space. This reduction allows us to use tools from the arsenal of similarity-based indexing methods to speed up model-based search. More specifically, in this paper we combine the proposed embedding with a simple vector indexing scheme, based on PCA, to improve the efficiency of model-based search.

In our experiments we use a database of 19,965 face images, from the public FRGC-2 dataset [9]. Compared to brute-force model-based search, the proposed method obtains speed-ups of over an order of magnitude, with relatively small losses in retrieval accuracy. While our case study is limited to a database of faces, the proposed formulation is general, and can be applied to speed up search-by-model in databases of different types of patterns.

2. Using JointBoost in Model-Based Search

Let $\mathbb{X}$ be a space of patterns, and $\mathbb{Y}$ be a finite set of class labels. Every pattern $X \in \mathbb{X}$ has a class label $L(X) \in \mathbb{Y}$. In JointBoost [14], for each class $y \in \mathbb{Y}$ a boosted classifier $H_y : \mathbb{X} \to \mathbb{R}$ is trained to discriminate between patterns of class y and all other patterns. Classifier H_y is of the following form:

$$H_y = \sum_{m=1}^{d} \alpha_{y,m} h_m + k_y \ , \tag{1}$$

where each h_m is a weak classifier with weight $\alpha_{y,m}$, and k_y is a class-specific constant that gives a way to encode a prior bias for each class y [14].

The key difference of JointBoost from other boosting methods is that all classifiers H_y share the same weak classifiers h_m. The only thing differentiating the different classifiers is the weights $\alpha_{y,m}$ assigned to each weak classifier h_m. Forcing strong classifiers to share the same weak classifiers was shown in [14] to improve classification accuracy when limited training data are available for each class. The intuition behind this behavior is that, in JointBoost, weak classifiers are chosen to jointly optimize performance in multiple one-vs.-all classifiers, and thus the choice of weak classifiers is supported by more data. In contrast, in a standard boosting approach, each one-vs.-all classifier H_y would be trained in isolation. When training each H_y in isolation, while weak classifiers chosen for each H_y could potentially be better suited for recognizing class y (thus increasing accuracy), limited training data for class y may lead to overfitting (thus decreasing accuracy).

Higher (more positive) responses $H_y(X)$ indicate higher confidence that the true class label $L(X)$ of pattern X is y. In the typical JointBoost application, which is multiclass recognition, to classify a pattern $X \in \mathbb{X}$, we evaluate $H_y(X)$ for all $y \in \mathbb{Y}$, and classify X as belonging to the class y for which $H_y(X)$ is maximized.

In our problem, which is model-based search, JointBoost can be used to train classifiers recognizing specific classes of patterns, such as specific persons if we are searching a database of face images. The user provides as a query a classifier H_y, trained to recognize objects of class y. In the simplest (but inefficient) approach, the system applies H_y to every single database pattern X, and ranks patterns in decreasing order of the response $H_y(X)$. The user then can inspect the top K results, where K is a number determined either by the user or by the system (the system can have a threshold such that only responses above that threshold are shown to the user).

The classical formulation of JointBoost assumes that all classifiers are trained at the same time. This may be problematic in search-by-model applications, where we may not know in advance all possible classes that the user may search for. However, it is easy to adapt JointBoost to a situation where some classifier H_y is trained later, after the main training has occurred. In that case, the pool of weak classifiers h_m can remain the same pool that was chosen in the main training. To train the new classifier, the system can simply compute optimized weights $\alpha_{y,m}$ for that new classifier. This allows new classifiers to be built as needed.

In principle, for our application, a non-technical user can simply provide as a query a set of training examples for class y. The system, in a manner transparent to the user, can then train a classifier H_y on the fly, using those training examples as positives, and a large pool of other examples as negatives. Then, the system can submit H_y as the query classifier, on behalf of the user.

3. A Joint Embedding of JointBoost Classifiers and Patterns

In this section we propose an embedding V that maps both database patterns and JointBoost classifiers to a common vector space, and more specifically to points on the surface of a hypersphere. Using this mapping, the search for the database patterns X that maximize the response $H_y(X)$ of the query classifier H_y is reduced to the problem of finding the nearest neighbors of $V(H_y)$ among the embeddings $V(X)$ of all database patterns. The embedding is an adaptation of (but not identical to) the embedding proposed in [13], and in the following description we borrow heavily from [13].

In particular, we will map both JointBoost classifiers and database patterns into a $(d+2)$-dimensional vector space, where d is the number of weak classifiers that are used to define the JointBoost classifiers. We denote by $V(X)$ and $V(H_y)$ respectively the vectors corresponding to database pattern X and JointBoost classifier H_y. In defining this mapping, we will explicitly ensure that all resulting vectors have the same norm.

We begin by defining the vector $V(X)$ corresponding to each pattern X in space $\mathbb{X}$:

$$V(X) = (h_1(X), \ldots, h_d(X), 1, c_X) \; , \tag{2}$$

where h_m are the weak classifiers used in Equation 1, and c_X is a value calculated for each X, that ensures that all $V(X)$ have the same Euclidean norm.

Quantity c_X can be determined as follows: first, we need to identify what the maximum norm of any $V(X)$ would be if we set all c_X to zero, for all patterns X in our database $\mathbb{U}$:

$$N_{\max} = \sqrt{\max_{X \in \mathbb{U}}[(\sum_{m=1}^{d} h_m(X)^2) + 1]} \; . \tag{3}$$

Then, we define c_X as:

$$c_X = \sqrt{N_{\max}^2 - [(\sum_{m=1}^{d} h_m(X)^2) + 1]} \; . \tag{4}$$

By defining c_X this way, it can easily be verified that the Euclidean norm of every $V(X)$ is equal to $N_{\max}$.

Now we can define the vectors corresponding to JointBoost classifiers H_y. In particular, given a classifier H_y, we define an auxiliary vector $V_{\text{orig}}(H_y)$, and the vector of interest $V(H_y)$, as follows:

$$V_{\text{orig}}(H_y) = (\alpha_{y,1}, \ldots, \alpha_{y,d}, k_y, 0) \tag{5}$$

$$V(H_y) = \frac{N_{\max} V_{\text{orig}}(H_y)}{\|V_{\text{orig}}(H_y)\|} \tag{6}$$

In the above equations, $\alpha_{y,m}$ and k_y are the weights and class-bias terms used in Equation 1, and $\|V\|$ denotes the Euclidean norm of V.

Using these definitions, it is easy to verify that for any classifier H_y and pattern X it holds that:

$$H_y(X) = V_{\text{orig}}(H_y) \cdot V(X), \tag{7}$$

where $V_1 \cdot V_2$ denotes the dot product between vectors V_1 and V_2. We note that the $(d+2)$-th coordinate of $V(X)$, which is set to c_X, does not influence $V_{\text{orig}}(H_y) \cdot V(X)$, since the $(d+2)$-th coordinate of each $V_{\text{orig}}(H_y)$ is set to zero.

In model-based search, given a query classifier H_y, the system needs to return to the user the top K database patterns X that maximize $H_y(X)$ (for some given value of K). Equation 7 shows that finding the patterns X maximizing $H_y(X)$ is the same as finding the patterns X maximizing $V_{\text{orig}}(H_y) \cdot V(X)$. It readily follows that maximizing $V_{\text{orig}}(H_y) \cdot V(X)$ is the same as maximizing $V(H_y) \cdot V(X)$, since the dot products of $V(H_y)$ with each $V(X)$ are simply scaled versions of $V_{\text{orig}}(H_y) \cdot V(X)$, where the scaling value $N_{\max}/\|V_{\text{orig}}\|$ does not depend on X.

We will now take one additional step, to show that maximizing the dot product between $V(H_y)$ and $V(X)$ is the same as minimizing the Euclidean distance between $V(H_y)$ and $V(X)$. That can be easily shown, by using the fact that both $V(X)$ and $V(H_y)$ are vectors of norm $N_{\max}$, because the dot product and the Euclidean distance for vectors of norm $N_{\max}$ are related as follows:

$$\|V(X) - V(H_y)\|^2 = 2N_{\max}^2 - 2(V(X) \cdot V(H_y)) \; . \tag{8}$$

As shown in [13], the above equation can be easily derived as follows:

$$\|V(X) - V(H_y)\|^2 = \tag{9}$$

$$= (V(X) - V(H_y)) \cdot (V(X) - V(H_y)) \tag{10}$$

$$= (V(X) \cdot V(X)) + (V(H_y) \cdot V(H_y)) - 2(V(X) \cdot V(H_y)) \tag{11}$$

$$= 2N_{\max}^2 - 2(V(X) \cdot V(H_y)) \; , \tag{12}$$

using the fact that $V(X) \cdot V(X) = V(H_y) \cdot V(H_y) = N_{\max}^2$.

This result means that, given a query classifier H_y, finding the top K database patterns X that maximize $H_y(X)$ is reduced to finding the K nearest neighbor of $V(H_y)$ among all vectors $V(X)$ corresponding to database patterns X. The next section describes how to use that fact for speeding up model-based search.

The main difference of the embedding definition in this section from [13] stems from the fact that, in our problem, our goal is to find the patterns X maximizing the response $H_y(X)$ of a given classifier $H_y(X)$, as opposed to finding, in [13], the classifier H_y (among many classifiers) maximizing $H_y(X)$ for a given X. Due to the different goal in this paper, we have inserted value c_X as the value in the last dimension of $V(X)$ in Equation 2, and we have used value 0 for the last dimension of $V_{\text{orig}}(H_y)$, whereas the values used for those last dimensions are different (and, loosely speaking, switched) in [13].

4. Using the Embedding for Efficient Model-Based Search

So far we have established that, given a query classifier H_y, to find the top K database patterns X maximizing $H_y(X)$, it suffices to find the K nearest neighbors of $V(H_y)$ among all vectors $V(X)$ obtained from database patterns X. The importance of this reduction is that it allows use of any of several vector indexing methods to speed up the search, such as, e.g., the methods in [2], [5], [6].

In our experiments, we have been able to obtain significant speed-ups via a simple approach based on principal component analysis (PCA) [8]. Since the set of vectors $V(X)$ is computed off-line, we can use those vectors for an additional off-line step, where PCA is used to identify the principal components of those vectors and the corresponding projection matrix Φ. Given a query classifier H_y, its vector $V(H_y)$ can be projected to $\Phi(V(H_y))$ online, and then $\Phi(V(H_y))$ can be compared to the projections $\Phi(V(X))$ of the vectors corresponding to database patterns X.

PCA can easily be used within a filter-and-refine retrieval framework [7], as follows:

- **Input:** A query classifier H_y, and its vector representation $V(H_y)$.
- **Filter step:** Compute the projection $\Phi(V(H_y))$ to the lower-dimensional space, and rank database objects X in increasing order of the distance between $\Phi(V(X))$ and $\Phi(V(H_y))$.
- **(optional) Refine step:** Rerank the p highest ranked patterns X (where p is a system parameter), in decreasing order of $H_y(X)$. Beyond the top p patterns, the rest of the ranking computed by the filter step is not changed. In our experiments, $p = 0$, and thus no refine step is performed.
- **Output:** Return the K highest ranking patterns to the user. The number K of results to be returned is not something that we address in this paper, this number can be determined by the user or by the system.

As long as $d' \ll d$ (where d' is the number of dimensions of $\Phi(V(X))$, and d is the number of weak classifiers), the filter step is significantly faster than simply applying H_y to all database patterns X. At the refine step (if we opt to perform that step) we do apply H_y on some patterns X, but, typically p is much smaller than the number of all patterns in the database.

In our experiments, we set $p = 0$, meaning that we did not use a refine step at all, as we obtained sufficiently good results using just the rankings from the filter step.

5. Experiments

5.1 Dataset

As a case study, we conducted experiments on a large database of face images, that we constructed using the FRGC-2 public face dataset [9]. The dataset consists of 36,817 face images from 535 classes (i.e., 535 distinct persons). The image resolution that we used is 100 $\times$ 100. The actual database that we used contained 19,965 images. The remaining 16,852 images were used as training set, to train the JointBoost classifiers,

2,130 images from the training set were also used as a test set for the similarity-based search method described in Section 5.4, that we used as one of the baseline methods. We should note that, for that method, no training was needed. We ensured that each set (training, database, test) contains at least one sample from every class. Beyond that constraint, images were sampled randomly. Images were cropped to get only the facial region, and normalized to mean 0 and standard deviation 1 to remove influences of brightness and contrast.

5.2 JointBoost Implementation

We applied PCA [8] to the 16,852 training images, and we kept the top 200 components as input for JointBoost training. To avoid confusion, this PCA operation is NOT related to the PCA operation discussed in Section 4. Rather, this PCA operation is simply a feature extraction preprocessing step, before we apply JointBoost. In training JointBoost classifiers, the system formed weak classifiers h_m simply by choosing, for each h_m, a PCA dimension (out of the 200 dimensions we kept) and a threshold value. So, essentially each weak classifier was a decision stump.

JointBoost selected a total of 2,345 unique weak classifiers (thus, $d = 2,345$ in Equation 1).

5.3 Indexing Implementation

As described in Section 3, the number of dimensions of the vectors that we map classifiers and patterns to is $d+2$, where d is the number of weak classifiers in Equation 1. Therefore, the total number of dimensions is 2,347.

As we discuss in Section 4, we use PCA as the basis of our indexing method. The PCA projection matrix was trained from the embeddings $V(X)$ obtained from all 19,965 database images. We used the indexing method described in Section 4, without a refine step. Thus, the only parameter we needed to set was the number d' of PCA dimensions to use for the filter step. We show results with d' values 100, 200, and 500.

5.4 Baseline Methods

In our experiments, we compare (based on accuracy and efficiency) the proposed method with the following baseline methods:

- **Brute-force model-based search.** Here, we simply apply classifier H_y to every single database pattern X. The goal of this paper has been to propose a significantly more efficient alternative for this baseline method, without sacrificing too much in accuracy. Thus, it is important to examine the accuracy and efficiency trade-offs that our method achieves compared to brute force.
- **Brute-force similarity-based search.** Since similarity-based search is a common alternative to model-based search, we evaluated the accuracy of a similarity-based search method that used the Euclidean distance to compare a query image to database images. For this baseline method, we used as queries the 2,130 images that we designated as test set (and which were not part of the database).
- **Truncated JointBoost classifiers.** If we want to speed up model-based search using JointBoost classifiers (or any other boosted classifiers, for that matter), a very simple approach is to simply choose fewer weak classifiers (thus, use a smaller d in Equation 1). This is what we use in this baseline method. This method trades accuracy for efficiency (larger d means higher accuracy and longer running time), and its speed is quite similar to our method, as long as the number of weak classifiers used

in this baseline method is equal to the number of PCA dimensions that we use in our method.

We should note that, for our method, for brute-force model-based search, and for truncated JointBoost classifiers, as queries we used the 535 classifiers trained by JointBoost to recognize each of the 535 classes in the FRGC-2 dataset.

5.5 Measuring Precision and Recall

We use precision and recall as measures of accuracy. For a given number K of results presented to the user for a query, precision is the percentage out of the top K results that are actually correct, and recall is the fraction of correct results ranked as top K over the total number of correct results.

To compute precision and recall for a specific query, we first need to determine K, i.e., how many results to return for that query. We use the simple approach of using the same K for all queries. For each specific method, after fixing K, we computed the precision value and the recall value obtained for each query. We averaged those values over all queries, to obtain the precision value and the recall value for the entire set of queries, for that value of K. By varying K, we obviously obtain different precision/recall values for each method, ranging from recall 0 to recall 1. We plot these values to generate a traditional precision-vs.-recall curve, as shown on Figure 1.

5.6 Results

Figure 1 shows precision versus recall plots for our method (with 100, 200, and 500 PCA dimensions used) as well as for the baseline methods. Table 1 shows the speed-up obtained by different methods, compared to brute-force model-based search (which, by definition, has a speed-up of 1).

As shown on Figure 1, model-based search clearly outperforms the similarity-based search alternative in terms of accuracy. For example, for a recall rate of 0.4, similarity-based search obtains a precision under 0.05, whereas model-based search obtains a precision over 0.85. This result shows that, in this dataset, model-based search using a generic machine learning method (JointBoost) does much better than similarity-based search using a generic similarity measure (Euclidean Distance). This result motivates the need for methods, such as the method proposed in this paper, to speed up model-based search. We should note that better results may be obtainable in similarity-based search as well, using more sophisticated similarity measures, e.g., [3], [17]. Still, we considered it important to establish that our model-based search implementation, at the very least, is much more accurate than a simple implementation of similarity-based search. We should also note that similarity-based search could probably be made even more efficient by using some indexing method, but given its very low accuracy we did not explore that direction.

Figure 1 and Table 1 also show that our method obtains significant speed-ups over brute-force search with rather small losses in accuracy. For example, our method when using 200 PCA dimensions obtains a precision vs. recall curve rather close to that of brute-force search, while attaining a speed-up of a factor of 17.6, which is more than an order of magnitude. We note that, when using only 100 PCA dimensions, the accuracy of our method deteriorates noticeably.

Table 1
THE SPEED-UP FACTOR, COMPARED TO BRUTE-FORCE MODEL-BASED SEARCH, ATTAINED BY DIFFERENT METHODS.

Method	Speed up factor
Model-based search, brute force	1
Our method, 500 PCA dimensions	6.317
Our method, 200 PCA dimensions	17.573
Our method, 100 PCA dimensions	31.491
Truncated JointBoost, 500 dimensions	6.415
Truncated JointBoost, 200 dimensions	18.458
Truncated JointBoost, 100 dimensions	31.690
Similarity-based search, brute-force	11.785

Finally, we observe in Figure 1 that our method obtains much better accuracy-vs.-efficiency trade-offs compared to using truncated JointBoost classifiers. In terms of speed-up factors, our method with d' PCA dimensions obtains, as expected, roughly the same speed-up as truncated JointBoost classifiers using only d' weak classifiers, as shown on Table 1. However, for the same d' of 100, 200, or 500, our method obtains significantly better precision-vs-recall curves. This result further highlights the benefits of the proposed method, by showing that our method works better than the simple ad hoc solution of improving efficiency using fewer weak classifiers.

In summary, model-based search was far more accurate than similarity-based search, which was, on the other hand, far more efficient. This result motivates the need for methods, such as our own, to improve the efficiency of model-based search. Our method, using the proposed embedding and 200 PCA dimensions, obtained accuracy rather similar to that of brute-force model-based search, with a speed-up factor of 17.6.

6. Conclusions

We have proposed a novel indexing method for speeding up model-based search in databases of patterns. We have motivated our approach by showing that, in our case study, model-based search obtained much better accuracy than a simple similarity-based search implementation. Our proposed indexing method is based on an embedding that maps both classifiers and database patterns into a common vector space. Using that embedding, the task of finding the database patterns that maximize the response of the query classifier is reduced to finding nearest neighbors in a vector space. This reduction allows various general-purpose vector indexing methods to be used to speed up the search.

In our experiments on the public FRGC-2 dataset of face images, we have shown that the proposed embedding, combined with a rather simple PCA-based indexing scheme, provides significant speed-ups with only small losses in accuracy, compared to brute-force model-based search. In future work, we plan to explore more sophisticated vector indexing methods, to measure the extent to which they can further improve

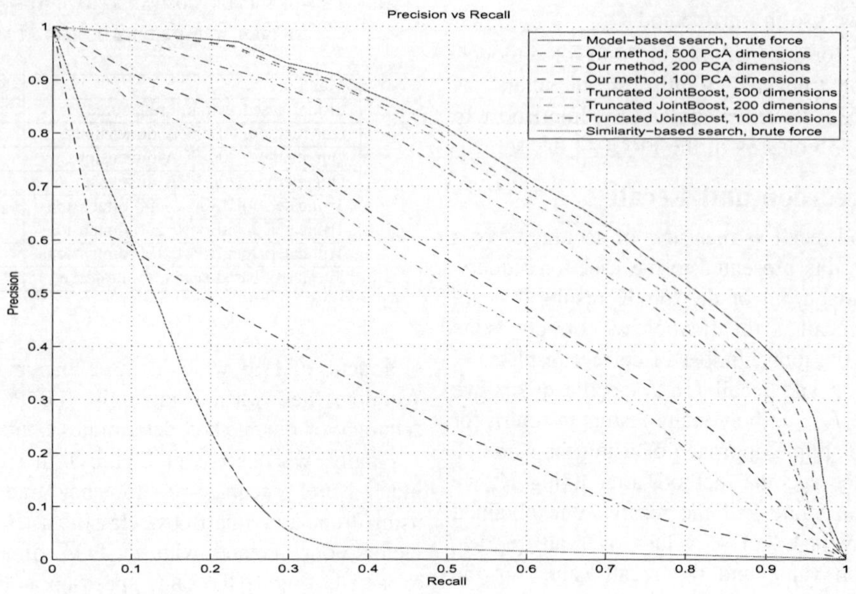

Fig. 1
THE PRECISION VS. RECALL CURVES FOR OUR METHOD WITH DIFFERENT NUMBERS OF PCA DIMENSIONS USED, AS WELL AS FOR BRUTE-FORCE MODEL-BASED SEARCH, BRUTE-FORCE SIMILARITY-BASED SEARCH, AND THREE TRUNCATED JOINTBOOST CLASSIFIERS.

efficiency. Also, as the proposed method specifically targets cases where classifiers are trained via JointBoost, we are interested in exploring the problem of designing indexing methods for more general types of classifiers, including, for example, support vector machines.

References

[1] E. L. Allwein, R. E. Schapire, and Y. Singer. Reducing multiclass to binary: a unifying approach for margin classifiers. *Journal of Machine Learning Research*, 1:113–141, 2000.

[2] C. Böhm, S. Berchtold, and D. A. Keim. Searching in high-dimensional spaces: Index structures for improving the performance of multimedia databases. *ACM Computing Surveys*, 33(3):322–373, 2001.

[3] C. Domeniconi, J. Peng, and D. Gunopulos. Locally adaptive metric nearest-neighbor classification. *IEEE Transactions on Pattern Analysis and Machine Intelligence*, 24(9):1281–1285, 2002.

[4] P. Dreuw, C. Neidle, V. Athitsos, S. Sclaroff, and H. Ney. Benchmark databases for video-based automatic sign language recognition. In *International Conference on Language Resources and Evaluation*, 2008.

[5] A. Gionis, P. Indyk, and R. Motwani. Similarity search in high dimensions via hashing. In *International Conference on Very Large Databases (VLDB)*, pages 518–529, 1999.

[6] G. R. Hjaltason and H. Samet. Index-driven similarity search in metric spaces. *ACM Transactions on Database Systems (TODS)*, 28(4):517–580, 2003.

[7] G.R. Hjaltason and H. Samet. Properties of embedding methods for similarity searching in metric spaces. *IEEE Transactions on Pattern Analysis and Machine Intelligence (PAMI)*, 25(5):530–549, 2003.

[8] I.T. Jolliffe. *Principal Component Analysis*. Springer-Verlag, 1986.

[9] P. J. Phillips, P. J. Flynn, T. Scruggs, K. W. Bowyer, J. Chang, K. Hoffman, J. Marques, J. Min, and W. Worek. Overview of the face recognition grand challenge. In *IEEE Conference on Computer Vision and Pattern Recognition (CVPR)*, pages 947–954, 2005.

[10] R.E. Schapire and Y. Singer. Improved boosting algorithms using confidence-rated predictions. *Machine Learning*, 37(3):297–336, 1999.

[11] G. Shakhnarovich, P. Viola, and T. Darrell. Fast pose estimation with parameter-sensitive hashing. In *IEEE International Conference on Computer Vision (ICCV)*, pages 750–757, 2003.

[12] J. Shotton, A. W. Fitzgibbon, M. Cook, T. Sharp, M. Finocchio, R. Moore, A. Kipman, and A. Blake. Real-time human pose recognition in parts from single depth images. In *IEEE Conference on Computer Vision and Pattern Recognition (CVPR)*, pages 1297–1304, 2011.

[13] A. Stefan, V. Athitsos, Q. Yuan, and S. Sclaroff. Reducing jointboost-based multiclass classification to proximity search. In *IEEE Conference on Computer Vision and Pattern Recognition (CVPR)*, 2009.

[14] A. Torralba, K. P. Murphy, and W. T. Freeman. Sharing visual features for multiclass and multiview object detection. *IEEE Transactions on Pattern Analysis and Machine Intelligence (PAMI)*, 29(5):854–869, 2007.

[15] Vladimir N. Vapnik. *The nature of statistical learning theory*. Springer-Verlag New York, Inc., 1995.

[16] P. Viola and M. Jones. Rapid object detection using a boosted cascade of simple features. In *IEEE Conference on Computer Vision and Pattern Recognition (CVPR)*, volume 1, pages 511–518, 2001.

[17] Laurenz Wiskott, Jean-Marc Fellous, Norbert Krüger, and Christoph von der Malsburg. Face recognition by elastic bunch graph matching. *IEEE Transactions on Pattern Analysis and Machine Intelligence*, 19(7):775–779, 1997.

Facial Expression Recognition Based on Significant Face Components Using Steerable Pyramid Transform

Ayşegül UÇAR
Fırat University, Mechatronics Engineering Department, Elazig, Turkey, e-mail: agulucar@ieee.org

Abstract – *Facial expression recognition is a challenging problem in many areas such as computer vision and human-computer interaction. To extract an effective facial features and then to classify them are the best important points of facial expression recognition process. In this article, a new automatic facial expression recognition algorithm is proposed in order to further enhance the recognition performance in terms of these two points. First, it is detected the some specific components of face, such as the mouth, eyes, eyebrows, and nose by Viola-Jones algorithm. Secondly it is extracted features by applying local Steerable Pyramid Transform (SPT) to each of facial component images. Thirdly it is used Support Vector Machines (SVM) classifiers for facial expression verification. Finally the classifier outputs are combined by decision fusion. The experiments on the Japanese Female Facial Expression (JAFFE) database and the Cohn-Kanade database show that the proposed Component based - Facial Expression Recognition (CFER) algorithm improves facial expression recognition performance compared to an algorithm combining SPT and Principal Component Analysis (PCA) using whole face images to the results in the literature.*

Keywords: Facial Expression Recognition, Steerable Pyramid Transform, SVM.

1 Introduction

Facial expression recognition is currently an active research topic and challenging due to its important in several real-world applications such as border security, forensic, virtual reality, and robotics in areas of human-computer interaction and computer vision [1-4]. Recently considerable research efforts relating to especially the facial expression recognition with high correctness have been increased the applications of facial expression recognition. In the Facial Action Coding System (FACS) in [5], the basic facial expressions were semantically coded as happiness, sadness, fear, anger, disgust, and surprise. However the expressions present a wide variation with respect to the individuals. Hence to assign to one to from six basic categories a facial expression relating to a person and to recognize that person from the images including different facial expressions are challenging problem [6-7].

A number of facial expression algorithms have been proposed. They could be classified into two categories: 1) Feature-based methods use the shape and location information of significant regions appearing the face geometry as the feature vector [8-9]. These methods provide the good intuitive results with high performance thanks to physical points but they need to accurate and reliable detection of face points. 2) Appearance-based methods extract facial features by applying a set of filters to whole face or a part of face and obtain high dimension data. The methods are firstly followed by some dimension reducing algorithms such as Principal Component Analysis (PCA), Linear Discriminant Analysis (LDA), and locality preserving and then the classifying algorithms such as Support Vector Machines (SVMs) and neural networks [10-11]. Appearance-based methods are capable of representing with a powerful subspace of overall space but they require large memory usage with respect to feature-based ones.

In recent years, a lot of methods have been successfully applied for facial expression recognition, including optical flow [12-13], Gabor wavelets [14-15], Local Binary Patterns [11], Zernike moments [6], and image ratio features [16]. The above studies have presented that there have still need to many researches in order to improve facial expression recognition performance. In this paper, Steerable Pyramid Transform (SPT) algorithm is used as an effective feature extractor in facial expression recognition.

The aim of this paper is to partially combine the advantages of feature based methods and appearance-based methods. In this paper, the Component based - Facial Expression Recognition (CFER) algorithm is proposed. The CFER algorithm consists of the following steps: i) Viola Jones algorithm is used to detect the face in the images and then the specific component regions relating to the cropped face image, ii) the each component image is preprocessed in order to provide more illumination invariant, iii) SPT algorithm is applied for extracting the local features relating to each facial component image, iv) the SVM classifiers are separately applied to each component image, v) the classifier results are combined.

Feature extraction step and classifying step are of great important in facial expression recognition. In this paper, the feature set is extracted firstly by applying SPT to the partitioned specific regions and then by computing some statistical features relating to each local portion. SVM classifiers that are ones of the best classifiers in the literature are used to classify facial expressions. When the proposed component based algorithm is compared to one using whole image, it presents more robustness to illumination and orientation and has higher recognition performance. In addition, since good physical points are detected and less feature numbers are determined, the proposed CFER algorithm does not need to any dimension reduction method. Moreover, CFER can be used in the forensic applications concerning occluded or partial face images.

The remainder of this paper is organized as follows. In Section 2, the SPT is introduced. In Section 3, it is given a short review about SVMs. In Section 4, the proposed CFER algorithm is described. In Section 5, the results from experiments are comparatively discussed with results in the literature. In Section 6, the conclusions are summarized.

2 Steerable Pyramid Transform

The Steerable Pyramid is a linear multi-resolution image decomposition method [17]. In SPT, an image is subdivided into a collection of subbands localized at different scales and orientations. The transform is invariant from translation and rotation.

Fig. 1 shows the operating logic of SPT. Input image is initially decomposed into the subbands of high-pass and low-pass using a high-pass filter $H_0(w)$ and a band lowpass filter $L_0(w)$. The lowpass subband is then decomposed into K-oriented portions using the bandpass filters $B_k(w)$ (k=0,1,...,K-1) and into a lowpass subband L_1 [17]. The process is done recursively by down and up subsampling the lower lowpass subband by a multiplier of 2 along the rows and columns.

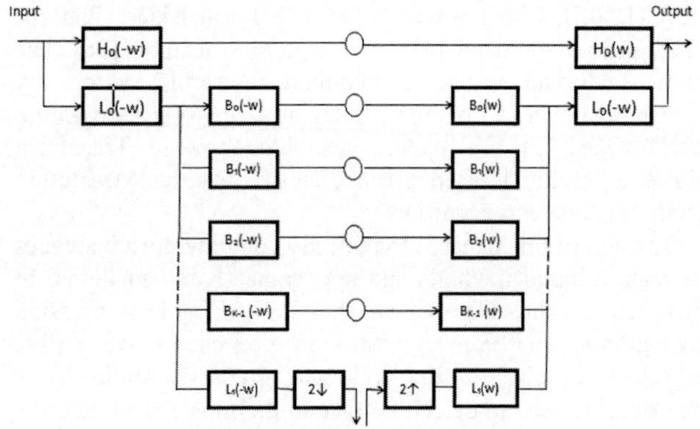

Fig. 1 Block diagram of pyramid decomposition [12]

Fourier domain formulations of the lowpass filters and highpass filters are defined as:

$$L_0(r,\theta) = L\left(\frac{r}{2},\theta\right), \tag{1}$$

$$H_0(r,\theta) = H\left(\frac{r}{2},\theta\right), \tag{2}$$

where r and θ are the polar frequency coordinates.

$$L(r,\theta) = \begin{cases} 2\cos\left(\frac{\pi}{2}\log_2\left(\frac{4r}{\pi}\right)\right), & \frac{\pi}{4} < r < \frac{\pi}{2} \\ 2 & r \geq \frac{\pi}{4} \\ 0 & r \leq \frac{\pi}{2} \end{cases} \tag{3}$$

$$B_k(r,\theta) = H(r)G_k(\theta), \; k \in [0, K-1] \tag{4}$$

where $B_k(r,\theta)$ is the K directional bandpass filters used in iterative steps with radial and angular parts:

$$H(r) = \begin{cases} \cos\left(\frac{\pi}{2}\log_2\left(\frac{2r}{\pi}\right)\right), & \frac{\pi}{4} < r < \frac{\pi}{2} \\ 1 & r \geq \frac{\pi}{2} \\ 0 & r \leq \frac{\pi}{4} \end{cases} \tag{5}$$

$$G_k(\theta) = \frac{(K-1)!}{\sqrt{K[2(K-1)]!}}\left[2\cos\left(\theta - \frac{\pi k}{K}\right)\right]^{K-1}. \tag{6}$$

Fig. 2 shows all filtered images at 3 scales consisting of 128x128, 64x64, and 32x32 and 4 orientation subbands consisting of -π /4, 0, π /4, and π /2 on a cropped original image of Cohn-Kanade database.

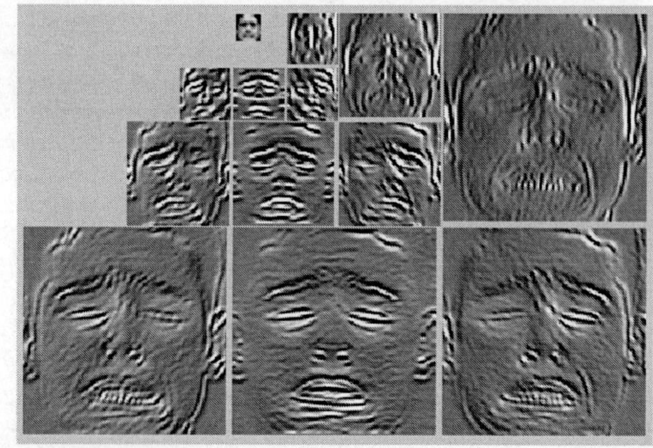

Fig. 2 Steerable pyramid transform (K=4 and J=3) on a cropped original image of Cohn-Kanade database

3 A Short Review for Support Vector Machines

For a training set of L points of the form $(x^1,y^1),\ldots,(x^L,y^L), x \in \mathcal{R}^n, y \in \{-1,1\}$, SVMs define a nonlinear mapping $\varphi(x)$ from input space to a higher dimensional feature space. When the input data is mapped to feature space, the two training classes may linearly separable in the feature space by the optimal discriminant function defined by

$$\ell(x) = w^T\varphi(x) + b \tag{7}$$

where $w \in \mathcal{R}^n$ is a weight vector and $b \in \mathcal{R}$ is a bias [18-19]. The optimal discriminant function is determined by using maximizing the margin and by minimizing the misclassification error. The margin is defined as the distance between the discriminant function and the samples nearest to the hyperplane [19]. SVM classifier solves the following primal optimization:

$$min_{w,b,\xi} \quad L_{primal}(w,\xi_i) = C\sum_{i=1}^{L}\xi_i + \frac{1}{2}\|w\|^2 \tag{8}$$

$$\text{subject to } y^i[w^T\varphi(x^i) + b] \geq 1 - \xi_i$$

The first term in Eq. (8) penalizes the sum of absolute errors ξ_i. The slack variables allow some points to be misclassified. The second term compels the margin to maximum. C is a trade-off constant between maximum margin and classification error. A higher C value provides a larger penalty for classification error.

By eliminating all primal variables in Eq. (8) and introducing Lagrange multipliers λ_i's, the dual quadratic optimization problem is constructed as the following one

$$max_\lambda L_{dual}(\lambda) = -\frac{1}{2}\sum_{i,j=1}^{L} \lambda_i \lambda_j y^i y^j K(x^i, x^j) + \sum_{i=1}^{L} \lambda_i \quad (9)$$

$$\text{subject to } \sum_{i=1}^{L} y^i \lambda_i = 0, \quad 0 \leq \lambda_i \leq C, \ i = 1, \dots, L$$

where $K(x^i, x^j)$ is called as the kernel function are presented in the form of inner product of $\varphi(x^i)^T \varphi(x^j)$.

The discriminant function is easily defined

$$l(x) = sign(\sum_{SVs} y^i \lambda_i K(x^i, x^j) + b) \quad (10)$$

where the Support Vectors (SVs) are defined as the data points x^i corresponding to $\lambda_i > 0$.

4 Proposed Facial Expression Recognition Algorithm

In this section, it is presented the proposed CFER algorithm. The block schema of the proposed CFER algorithm is given in Fig. 3. The CFER algorithm is applied at seven folds:

(1) Detected the face region in image by using Viola Jones algorithm,
(2) Preprocessing each image by histogram equalization in order to provide further illumination invariance [20],
(3) Determined the two face regions relating to eye pairs and nose by using Viola Jones algorithm [21] and extended the regions to cover the regions of eyebrow and mouth,
(4) Selected the significant face regions such as mount, nose, eye, and eyebrow on the obtained region in previous stage. The selection is standardized for all images without any manual process. Each specific region is partitioned to local regions [22],
(5) Extracted the representative feature set by applying SPT to each face component image,
(6) Apply SVM classifiers to the qualified coefficients,
(7) Verify the facial expression recognition by a weighted majority voting rule to the classifier output.

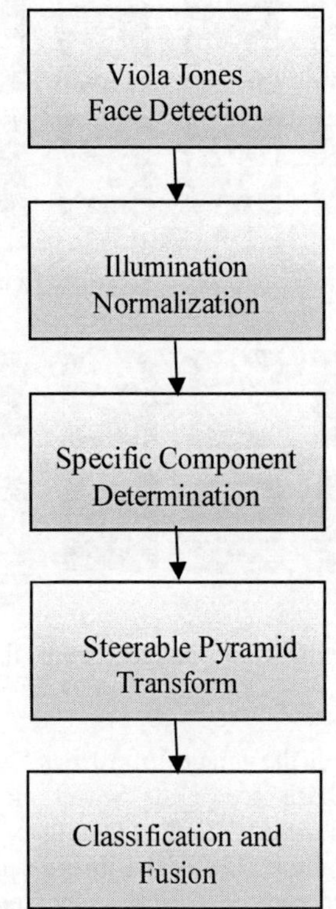

Fig. 3. The block schema of the proposed CFER algorithm

5 Experimental Results

To validate the accuracy of the proposed algorithm, it was used the Japanese Female Facial Expression database (JAFFE) [23] and the Cohn-Kanade database [24].

The JAFFE database consists of 213 grayscale facial expression images obtained from 10 female [23]. There are seven different facial expressions, such as happy, angry, disgust, fear, sadness, and surprise in addition to one neutral face expression. Each subject has two to four different images for each expression. Each image has the resolution of 256 x 256 pixels. Fig. 4. shows some images comprising seven basic facial expressions from the JAFFE database.

Cohn-Kanade database is one of the most comprehensive benchmarks for facial expression databases [24]. The database consists of 3911 images from 138 subjects ranged in age from 18 to 30 years. Sixty five percent is female, 15 percent is African-American and 3 percent is Asian or Latino. Fig. 5. shows some images comprising seven basic facial expressions from the Cohn-Kanade database. All image sequences have the resolution of 640 x 480 or 640 x 490 pixels.

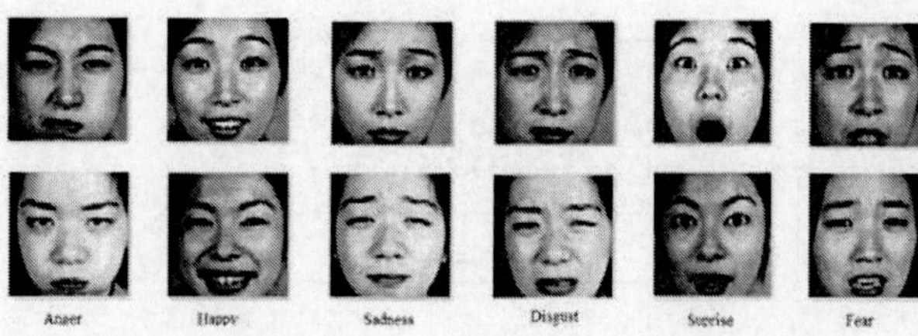

Fig. 4. Facial expression images from the JAFFE database

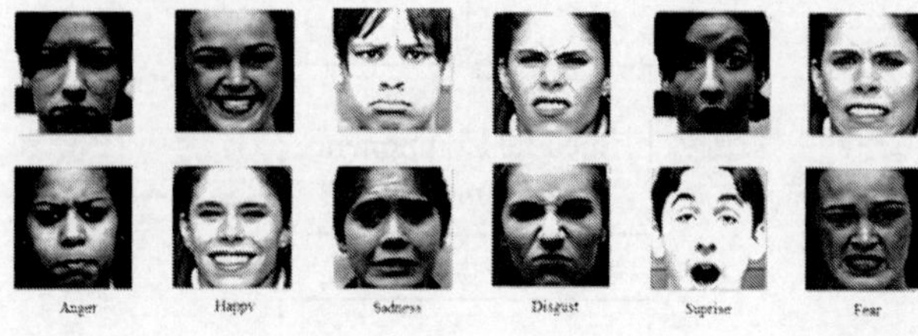

Fig. 5. Facial expression images from the Cohn-Kanade database

In this paper, all the images of 10 basic expressions from the JAFFE database are used. Seven class classification problem was constructed including neutral expression. For the Cohn-Kanade database, 258 of the image sequences given in [25] were selected such that each image sequence has eight images. Eight images were chosen from the last peak images of each image sequence. The image sequences consist of 2020 images (176 Anger, 264 Disgust, 256 Fear, 624 Happy, 324 Sadness, and 376 Surprise). To evaluate the generalization performance to all subjects in the experiments, it was adopted a 10-fold cross-validation testing scheme. It was partitioned the dataset randomly into ten groups of roughly equal numbers of subjects. Nine groups were used as the training data to train classifiers, while the remaining group was used as the test data. The above process was repeated ten times for each group in turn to be omitted from the training process. It was reported the average recognition results on the test sets.

The images of 10 subjects in the JAFFE database are classified into 10 sets, each of which includes images of one subject. Similarly, all images in the Cohn-Kanade database are classified into 10 similar sets and all images of one subject are included in the same set.

In the first stage of the CFER algorithm, the faces in the images were detected by using Viola Jones algorithm. Secondly all the images were cropped with respect to the determined face locations and scaled to 128×128 pixels resolution. Thirdly the eye and nose regions of face were detected by Viola Jones algorithm. The left hand side of Fig. 6 shows these two regions. The specific regions relating to eyebrow, eye, nose, and mouth were then determined. The regions relating to eyebrow, eye, nose, and mouth have resolutions 20x100, 15x100, 25x60, and 40x60, respectively. This pixel resolution was generalized for all databases. The right hand side of Fig. 6 shows these four regions. All component images were decomposed using SPT at 3 scales (128x128, 64x64, and 32x32) and 4 orientation subbands ($-\pi/4$, 0, $\pi/4$, and $\pi/2$) for each specific component. Local regions were constructed by an efficient pixel number of 5x5. In experiments, only all subbands relating to the first scale were used since the results of the first scale were better than the others. Three statistical features such as mean, entropy, and variance of each local image part were extracted. It was extracted the regions relating to eyebrow, eye, nose, and mouth are extracted the features of 60, 30, 36, and 72, respectively. Since the feature number was not large, there was no need to any additional dimension reduction algorithm. Fig. 7 shows the best important steps applying local SPT of CFER algorithm on a Cohn Kanade subject.

In this paper, it was used SVM classifiers in [18]. All features were classified by four SVM classifiers. The kernel and regularization parameters of SVM are determined by 10-fold cross validation scanning the chosen parameter range. The obtained results are fused by the weighed majority voting rule. The weights of constructed classifiers for each subband are determined by dividing itself correctness to the obtained total correctness.

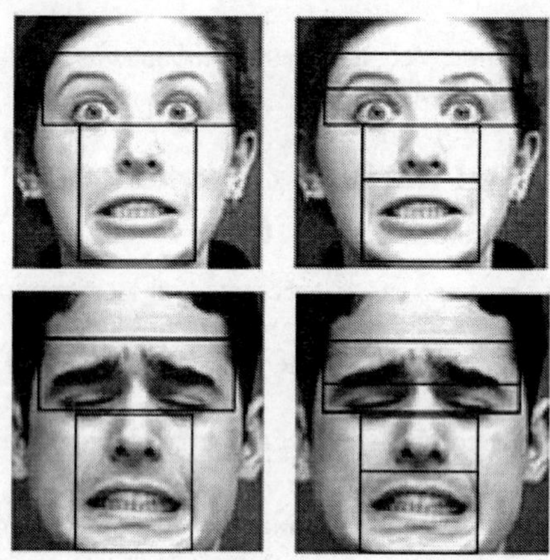

Fig. 6. The specific regions of a cropped face: Two components on the left hand side and all components on the right hand side

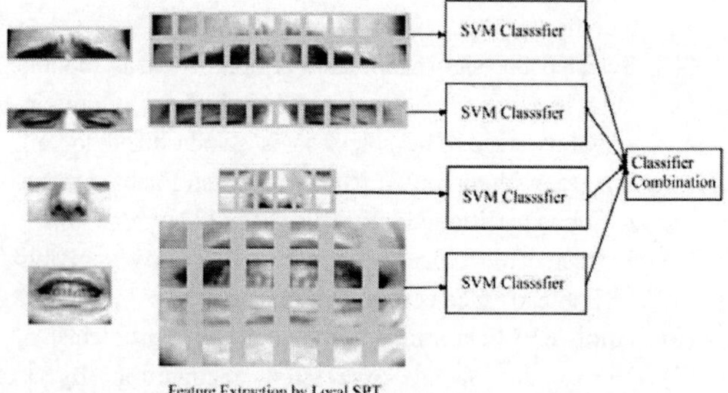

Fig. 7. Application of CFER algorithm on a image from the Cohn-Kanade database

Table 1and 2 show the performances of CFER algorithm on the JAFEE database and Cohn-Kanade database. Tables include the results of an algorithm applying SPT and PCA to whole image also. It is used the feature sets with 50 components by PCA. All results in Tables 1and 2 show that the performance can be increased up to around at least 5% by using CFER algorithm compared to the other. Table 3 shows that the proposed approach outperforms all of seven benchmarked approaches in [11, 15, 25-29] when both the JAFFE database and Cohn-Kanade database. In the literature, the selection of the training and testing sets and the number of facial expressions presents a wide of variation. For example [27] uses every two images from the peak frame, [11] gives the results based on five-fold cross validations and five expressions, and [15] uses leave-one-subject-out with seven facial expressions. It is difficult to make a right comparison with them. However the results of this paper appear satisfying.

Table 1. Recognition rates of CFER algorithm for the JAFFE database

Regions	Anger	Happy	Sadness	Disgust	Surprise	Fear	Neutral
Eyebrows	87.45	96.00	89.76	91.11	95.09	92.78	90.89
Eyes	88.88	92.24	91.00	91.23	89.05	82.22	86.90
Nose	89.12	88.80	78.00	88.23	91.92	98.12	96.56
Mouth	89.43	100	90.13	92.12	94.01	94.67	95.80
Fused	91.70	100	91.75	95.67	98.54	100	97.80
Whole Image	83.34	95.12	89.56	90.43	88.12	93.34	92.23

Table 2. Recognition rates of CFER algorithm for the Cohn-Kanade database

Regions	Anger	Happy	Sadness	Disgust	Surprise	Fear
Eyebrows	90.32	92.02	88.56	90.45	89.56	90.56
Eyes	82.54	98.01	87.56	89.23	94.75	89.80
Nose	88.54	95.00	89.02	91.12	94.75	91.54
Mouth	88.75	99.56	86.75	90.12	94.75	92.02
Fused	92.45	100	89.89	92.76	96.67	94.03
Whole Image	85.45	92.23	81.75	79.56	89.43	89.01

Table 3. Comparison with state-of-the-art performance of CFER

	JAFFE	Cohn-Kanade
CFER	95.42	96.22
[26]	88.13	-
[27]	92.93	94.48
[28]	91.00	-
[29]	83.84	95.87
[25]	89.13	
[11]	81.00	95.10
[15]	89.50	91.51

6 Conclusions

This paper presents a new facial expression recognition based on local SPT and histogram equalization. The important steps of this algorithm are to determine the specific facial regions and to compute the statistical features such as entropy, mean, and variance using local SPT and then to fuse the outputs of SVM classifiers applying to the features of each local patch. The recognition performances obtained on JAFEE and Cohn-Kanade databases have been shown to significantly better those in the literature and local SPT algorithm applied to whole face. Furthermore, the results shows that the proposed algorithm is robust to occlusion or missing information thanks to component based representations. The feature plan is to prove that the algorithm has the pose invariant property on the different datasets and to extent it to 3D facial expression.

Acknowledgements:

This paper was supported by the Firat University Scientific Research Projects Foundation (No. MF.12.33).

7 References

[1] K. Anderson and P. W. McOwan "A real-time automated system for recognition of human facial expressions", *IEEE Trans. Syst., Man, Cybern. B, Cybern.*, vol. 36, no. 1, pp.96 -105 2006

[2] I. Cohn, N. Sebe, L. Chen, A. Garg, and T. S. Huang "Facial expression recognition from video sequences:

Temporal and static modeling", *Comput. Vis. Image Underst.*, vol. 91, no. 1/2, pp.160 -187 2003

[3] Y. Zhang and Q. Ji "Facial expression understanding in image sequences using dynamic and active visual information fusion", *Proc. IEEE Int. Conf. Comput. Vis.*, vol. 2, pp.113 -118 2003

[4] Y. L. Tian, T. Kanade, and J. F. Cohn *Handbook of Face Recognition*, Eds: S. Z. Li and A. K. Jain, pp.247 -276 2005 :Springer-Verlag

[5] P. Ekman and W. V. Friesen "Constant across cultures in the face and emotion", *J. Pers. Soc. Psychol.*, vol. 17, no. 2, pp.124 -129 1971

[6] S. M. Lajevardi and Z. M. Hussain "Higher order orthogonal moments for invariant facial expression recognition" *Digit. Signal Process.*, vol. 20, no. 6, pp.1771 -1779 2010

[7] A. Uçar "Color Face recognition based on curvelet transform", *Proc. Int. Conf. Image Processing, Computer Vision and Pattern Recognition-IPCV'12,* pp. 561-566, Las Vegas USA, 2012

[8] G. Donato, M. Bartlett, J. Hager, P. Ekman, and T. Sejnowski "Classifying facial actions", *IEEE Trans. Pattern Anal. Mach. Intell.*, vol. 21, no. 10, pp.974 -989 1999

[9] Y. Tian, T. Kanade, and J. Cohn "Recognizing action units for facial expression analysis", *IEEE Trans. Pattern Anal. Mach. Intell.,* vol. 23, no.2, pp. 1 -9 2001

[10] W. Zhen and T. S. Huang, "Capturing subtle facial motions in 3d face tracking", *Proc. Ninth IEEE Int. Conf. Computer Vision,* pp. 1343-1350 2003

[11] C. Shan, S. Gong, and P. W. McOwan "Facial expression recognition based on Local Binary Patterns: A comprehensive study", *Image Vis. Comput.*, vol. 27, no. 6, pp.803 -816 2009

[12] Y. Yacoob and L. Davis "Recognizing human facial expression from long image sequences using optical flow", *IEEE Trans. Pattern Anal. Mach. Intell.*, vol.16, pp. 636 -642 1996

[13] I. Essa and A. Pentland "Coding analysis, interpretation, and recognition of facial expressions", *IEEE Trans. Pattern Anal. Mach. Intell.*, vol. 19, pp.757 -763 1997

[14] J. Goldfeather and V. Interrante "A novel cubic-order algorithm for approximating principal direction vectors", *ACM Trans. on Graphics*, vol. 23, pp.45 -63 2004

[15] W. Gu, C. Xiang, Y.V. Venkatesh, D. Huang, and H. Lin "Facial expression recognition using radial encoding of local Gabor features and classifier synthesis", *Pattern Recognit.*, vol. 45, no.1, pp. 80 -91 2012

[16] M. Song, D. Tao, Z. Liu, X. Li, and M. Zhou "Image ratio features for facial expression recognition application", *IEEE Trans. Syst., Man, Cybern. B, Cybern,* vol. 40, no. 3, pp.779 -788 2010

[17] E. P. Simoncelli, W. T. Freeman, E. H. Adelson, and D. J. Heeger "Shiftable multiscale transforms", *IEEE Trans. Inf. Theory,* vol. 38, no. 2, pp.587 -607 1992

[18] C.-C. Chang and C-J. Lin "LIBSVM: A library for support vector machines", *ACM Trans. Intelligent Systems and Techn.*, vol. 2, no. 3, pp. 1-27 2011

[19] A. Uçar, Y. Demir, and C. Güzeliş "A penalty function method for designing efficient robust classifiers with input-space optimal separating surfaces", *Turk. J. Elec. Eng. & Comp. Sci.,* isbn: doi:elk-1301-190, 2013

[20] S. M. Pizer, E. P. Amburn, J. D. Austin, R. Cromartie, A. Geselowitz, T. Greer, B. H. Romeny, J. B. Zimmerman, and K. Zuiderveld "Adaptive histogram equalization and its variations", *Comp. Vis. Graph. Image Process.*, vol. 39, no. 3, pp.355 -368 1987

[21] P. Viola and M. Jones "Robust Real-Time Face Detection", *Int. J. Computer Vision*, vol. 57, no. 2, pp.137 -154 2004

[22] M. E .Aroussi, M.E. Hassouni, S. Ghouzali, M. Rziza, and S. Aboutajdine "Local appearance based face recognition method using block based steerable pyramid transform", *Signal Process.*, vol. 91, no.1, pp.38-50 2011

[23] M. Lyons, S. Akamatsu, M. Kamachi, and J. Gyoba "Coding facial expressions with gabor wavelets", *Proc. IEEE Third Int. Conf. Automatic Face and Gesture Recognition*, pp. 200 -205 1998

[24] T. Kanade, J.F. Cohn, and T. Yingli "Comprehensive Database for Facial Expression Analysis", *Proc. IEEE Fourth Int. Conf. Automatic Face and Gesture Recognition*, pp. 46 -53 2000

[25] J. M. Buenaposada, E. Munoz, and L. Baumela "Recognising facial expressions in video sequences", *Pattern Anal. and Appl.*, vol. 11, no.1, pp. 101-116 2008

[26] T. Danisman, I. M.Bilasco, J. Martinet, and C. Djeraba "Intelligent pixels of interest selection with application to facial expression recognition using multilayer perceptron", *Signal Process.,* vol. 93, no. 6, pp.1547 - 1556 2013

[27] L. Zhang and D. Tjondronegoro "Facial expression recognition using facial movement features", *IEEE Trans. Affective Compt. Syst., Man, Cybern. B, Cybern.,* vol. 2, no. 4, pp.219 -229 2011

[28] G. Guo and C. Dyer "Learning from examples in the small sample case: Face expression recognition", IEEE *Trans. Syst., Man, Cybern. B, Cybern.,* vol. 35, no. 3, pp.477 -488 2005

[29] J. Wong and S. Cho "A face emotion tree structure representation with probabilistic recursive neural network modeling", *Neural Comput. Appl.,* vol. 19, no. 1, pp.33 -54 2010

Efficient Sparse Representation Classification Using Adaptive Clustering

Soheil Shafiee, Farhad Kamangar, Vassilis Athitsos, and Junzhou Huang
Department of Computer Science and Engineering, University of Texas at Arlington, Arlington, TX, USA

Abstract— *This paper is presenting a method for an efficient face recognition algorithm based on sparse representation classification (SRC) using an adaptive K-means clustering. In the context of face recognition, SRC is implemented based on the assumption that a face image from a particular subject can be represented as a linear combination of other face images from the same subject. SRC uses a set of extracted features from the original face images as columns of a training matrix. This training matrix is used to form an under-determined system of linear equations. An unknown face image can be classified by finding the sparse solution of this linear system using an l^1-norm optimization which has a quadratic time complexity. In practice using all the training face images for a large population increases computational and memory requirements which may not be feasible to be used in mobile devices. The proposed method reduces the size of the training matrix by using adaptive K-means clustering along with SRC method which lowers computational requirements of the overall recognition system. Experimental results on a face dataset with 14,794 training face images from 100 classes show that the new proposed method reduces the running time of the classification algorithm compared to SRC method while preserving the accuracy.*

Keywords: Sparse Representation, Adaptive Clustering, Face Recognition

1. Introduction

Face recognition is one of the most challenging real-world applications in computer vision and over the past few decades, several methods and algorithms have been proposed to solve this problem. The face recognition techniques could be broadly divided into two main groups, i.e. geometric feature-based and template matching approaches. The main idea in the geometric feature-based methods is to extract and record the relative position and salient properties of distinctive face features such as eyes, mouth corners, chin, and nose. The geometrical features are then used to create labeled graphs and structural models which can be used to discriminate between different classes (individuals) [1],[2].

The template matching algorithms, in their simplest forms, present the image of each face as a vector of intensity values in a multi-dimensional space. An unknown face is then compared to a set of known classes by using a metric, such as Euclidean distance. There are, of course, variations and sophisticated approaches to improve the speed and accuracy of the simple template matching algorithms.

Methods such as Eigen faces [3], Fisher faces [4] and Laplacian faces [5], reduce the dimensionality of the space by transforming face images into a coordinate system which provides more compact support. In [6], it is shown that any face can be represented in terms of its largest Eigen vectors called Eigen faces. Later, this approach was used in a face recognition algorithm [3]. Fisher linear discriminant was also used to extract face features [4]. Another well-known method is Laplacian faces, which uses Locality preserving projections to extract face features [5].

In [7], Wright et al. presented a new approach called Sparse Representation based Classification (SRC). This classification method works based on the emerging theory of compressive sensing (CS) and sparse signal representation [8], [9]. In SRC, face recognition problem is mapped into an under-determined system of equations which is solved using l^1-norm minimization. The sparse solution determines the class of the unknown face image. This method is shown to achieve high recognition accuracy compared to other dimensionality reduction methods, such as Eigen faces, Fisher faces and Laplacian faces [7].

SRC uses the entire training dataset to recognize each unknown face image. This implies that the speed of the recognition task at run time is directly affected by the number of training images. Given the high recognition accuracy of SRC, it becomes important to reduce the time and memory requirements of SRC. Improvements in time and memory efficiency can help make SRC a more practical solution for portable devices, and can also significantly decrease the computational load of SRC running on more powerful hardware.

The time complexity of SRC is quadratic to the number of training samples [10], and thus reducing the number of training samples by a relatively modest factor can have a significant effect on running time. Instead of using all samples, or using a random selection of samples, as proposed in [7], our method explicitly identifies an efficient representation of training samples. We achieve this by replacing the original training samples with cluster centers which are identified by using K-means clustering. The proposed approach also determines the number of clusters per class adaptively in order to optimize the runtime efficiency. As shown in the experiments, our method achieves significantly better tradeoffs of accuracy vs. efficiency compared to the method introduced in [7].

The rest of this paper is organized as follows:. In section 2 we briefly review compressive sensing theory and SRC method, In section 3 details of the proposed method based on K-means clustering is introduced. Finally the used face dataset and our experiment details are described in section 4.

2. Sparse Representation based Classification

2.1 Compressive Sensing Theory

The system of linear equations $\mathbf{y} = A\mathbf{x}$, where $A \in R^{m\times n}$ is an m by n matrix, is called an under-determined system if $m < n$. In this system, the measurement vector $\mathbf{y}$, is a column vector with m entries, and $\mathbf{x}$ which is a column vector with n entries is the vector to be recovered. The solution $\widehat{\mathbf{x}}$ to this equation is not unique and the sparsest solution to this equation can be obtained by solving the following optimization problem:

$$\widehat{\mathbf{x}}_0 = \arg\min \|\mathbf{x}\|_0 \text{ subject to } A\mathbf{x} = \mathbf{y}\,, \tag{1}$$

where $\|.\|_0$ denotes the l^0-norm, which counts the number of non-zero elements in vector $\mathbf{x}$. Finding the solution for $\mathbf{x}$, using (1) is an NP-hard problem because all the subsets of the entries for $\mathbf{x}$ should be considered [11].

Based on the theory of compressive sensing, if the solution $\widehat{\mathbf{x}}_0$ is sparse while satisfying certain constraints [8], the solution of the optimization problem (1) is equal to the solution of the following l^1-norm minimization problem:

$$\widehat{\mathbf{x}}_1 = \arg\min \|\mathbf{x}\|_1 \text{ subject to } A\mathbf{x} = \mathbf{y}\,. \tag{2}$$

In fact, vector $\widehat{\mathbf{x}}_1$ should not necessarily be sparse to be recovered by (2). It may be sparse in some domain (other than $\widehat{\mathbf{x}}_1$'s original domain) [12]. For instance, vector $\widehat{\mathbf{x}}_1$, could be a general non-sparse signal which has a sparse representation in frequency or Wavelet domain.

In practice, due to the existence of noise in measurements, the solution to $\mathbf{y} = A\mathbf{x}$ is not exact. In other words, the system of linear equations, $\mathbf{y} = A\mathbf{x}$ should be modified as $\mathbf{y} = A\mathbf{x} + \mathbf{n}$, where $\mathbf{n}$ is an n dimensional noise vector. In this case, the optimization problem (2) may be reformulated as follows:

$$\widehat{\mathbf{x}}_1 = \arg\min \|\mathbf{x}\|_1 \text{ subject to } \|A\mathbf{x} - \mathbf{y}\|_2 \le \epsilon\,, \tag{3}$$

where, $\epsilon > \|\mathbf{n}\|_2$, i.e. ϵ is larger than the energy of the noise.

2.2 Face Recognition Formulation based on Sparse Representation

The idea of face recognition in the context of sparse representation is to set up a system of linear equations, $\mathbf{y} = A\mathbf{x}$, where A is the training matrix, $\mathbf{y}$ is the unknown face image and $\mathbf{x}$ is the sparse representation of the unknown face as a linear combination of the training faces. Each training face image is an m dimensional vector $\mathbf{v}$ where $m = height \times width$. Assuming there are K_i training images from subject i in the dataset, the vectorized version of these face images from subject i, $\mathbf{v}_{i,1}, \mathbf{v}_{i,2}, \dots, \mathbf{v}_{i,K_i} \in \mathbb{R}^m$ span a face subspace where $\mathbf{v}_{i,q}$ is the qth training face vector in class i [13]. In an ideal situation, a test image j of the subject i, $\mathbf{y}_i^j \in \mathbb{R}^m$ could be represented as a linear combination of training images as follows:

$$\mathbf{y}_i^j = \mathbf{x}_{i1}^j \mathbf{v}_{i,1} + \mathbf{x}_{i2}^j \mathbf{v}_{i,2} + \dots + \mathbf{x}_{ik}^j \mathbf{v}_{i,K_i}\,, \tag{4}$$

where $\mathbf{x}_i^j \in \mathbb{R}$ are the coefficients and $[\mathbf{v}_{i,1}, \mathbf{v}_{i,2}, \dots, \mathbf{v}_{i,K_i}]$, is an $m \times K_i$ matrix whose columns represent vectorized training images from subject i. Considering all $n = K_1 + K_2 + \dots + K_s$ training images from all s subjects, the entire training set could be represented by the matrix $A \in \mathbb{R}^{m\times n}$ where

$$A = [\mathbf{v}_{1,1}, \mathbf{v}_{1,2}, \dots, \mathbf{v}_{1,K_1}, \mathbf{v}_{2,1}, \dots, \mathbf{v}_{2,K_2}, \dots, \mathbf{v}_{s,K_s}]\,. \tag{5}$$

The linear system shown in (4) can be represented in matrix form as

$$\mathbf{y} = A\mathbf{x}\,. \tag{6}$$

where $\mathbf{x} = [\mathbf{x}_{11}, \dots, \mathbf{x}_{1K_1}, \mathbf{x}_{21}, \dots, \mathbf{x}_{2K_2}, \dots, \mathbf{x}_{s1}, \dots, \mathbf{x}_{sK_s}]^T$.

The solution to equation (6) for an ideal test image $\mathbf{y}_i^j$, will be $\mathbf{z}_i^j$ which is a sparse vector whose entries are mostly zero except for the ones corresponding to i^{th} subject:

$$\mathbf{z}_i^j = [0, 0, \dots, 0, \mathbf{x}_{i1}, \dots, \mathbf{x}_{iK_i}, 0, 0, \dots, 0]^T\,. \tag{7}$$

If $m < n$, i.e. the number of pixels for each image is smaller than the total number of training images, equation (6) represents an under-determined system. Assuming that the face images from one subject represent a subspace with a lower dimension than m [13], it is possible to recover $\mathbf{x}$ by solving l^1-norm minimization problem (2). Having the recovered vector, $\mathbf{x}$, it is possible to find the class of the given test image. This classification method is called Sparse Representation-based Classification (SRC) [7].

In real applications, due to the existence of measurement noise, both training and test face images are noisy and it may not be possible to represent a test face image only as a linear combination of training images which belong to the same class. To address this problem, the constraint on the l^1-norm minimization problem is changed to consider the noise effect, as described in section 2.1, equation (3).

Another consideration in the SRC algorithm is the dimensionality of face images. if the dimensions of training face images are large, then it is necessary to have a large number of training samples for equation (6) to be under-determined. For example, if the resolution of the training images is 100×100, then matrix A will have 10^4 rows which implies that the number of training face images must be greater than 10^4.

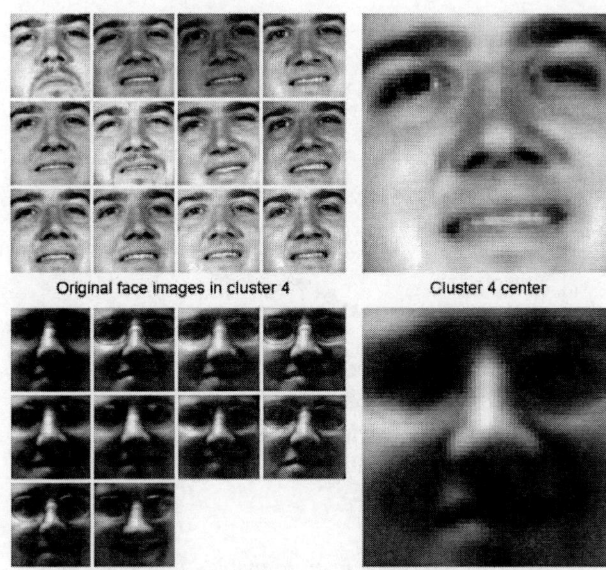

Fig. 1: Two examples of clusters formed for a face class, top: 12 face images (top left) form cluster 4 which is represented by its center (top right), bottom: 10 face images (bottom left) form cluster 6 which is represented by its center (bottom right).

In order to lower the number of rows in matrix A, it is possible to reduce the dimensionality of the original images, m, by using a set of d extracted features where $d \ll m$. Many of the feature extraction algorithms consist of linear transformations which may be represented as a matrix multiplication. In this case, the equation (6) could be rewritten as follows:

$$\widehat{\mathbf{y}} = R\mathbf{y} = RA\mathbf{x} = \widehat{A}\mathbf{x}, \tag{8}$$

where $\widehat{\mathbf{y}} \in \mathbb{R}^d$ represents the extracted feature vector of the original unknown image $\mathbf{y}$, and $R \in \mathbb{R}^{d\times m}$ with $d \ll m$, is a feature extraction matrix. $\widehat{A} \in \mathbb{R}^{d\times n}$ represents the training matrix with reduced dimensionality. Using equation (8), fewer training face images are needed to form an under-determined system of linear equations. Using $\widehat{A}$ as the training matrix, equation (3) can be reformulated as:

$$\widehat{\mathbf{x}}_1 = \arg\min \|\mathbf{x}\|_1 \text{ subject to } \left\|\widehat{A}\mathbf{x} - \widehat{\mathbf{y}}\right\|_2 \leq \epsilon. \tag{9}$$

Different dimensionality reduction matrices such as random projection, down-sampling, Eigen, Fisher, and Laplacian, are studied in [7]. In this paper we utilize three of the proposed methods: random projection, down-sampling, and Eigen features. Random projection algorithm employs a normal distribution function to randomly select a normalized subset of the original face images as features. Down-sampling method uses a bi-cubic algorithm to down-sample the original face images. The Eigen algorithm calculates the Eigen vectors of the original dataset to form the matrix R and uses this matrix to reduce the dimensionality of matrix A. The size of R matrices which were calculated for the three methods in this work are 100×3600.

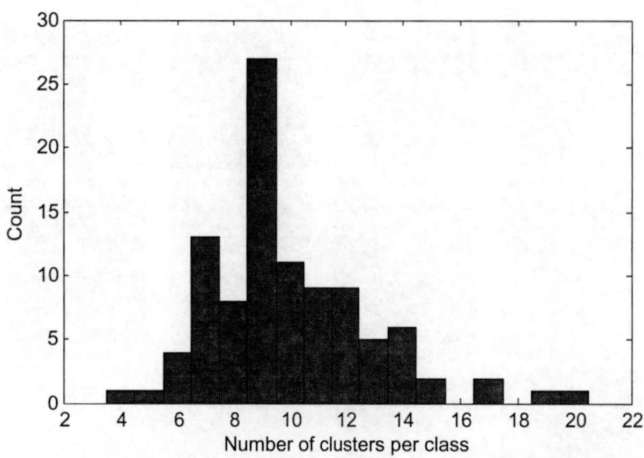

Fig. 2: Histogram of number of clusters for 100 classes based on adaptive clustering method ($Q_{max} = 20$ and τ=0.42167).

3. Sparse Representation-based Face Recognition using Adaptive Clustering

The computational complexity of the SRC method is quadratic [10] because it is based on l^1-norm solution of (9). This implies that if the number of training images is doubled, the time required for solving (9) will be quadrupled.

In this section we describe a method to reduce the number of columns in matrix A by using K-means clustering. As described in section 2.2, faces from one subject form a subspace of the original m dimensional space. Considering that many training face samples might contain similar information, using all the samples to represent a sub-space is inefficient. In this case, it would be more efficient to characterize each class by a more representative and smaller set of image vectors. A commonly used method to represent a group of samples by a smaller number of representatives is K-means clustering.

K-means clustering [14], [15] has been widely used in pattern recognition and machine learning applications and is a method to partition a dataset into k groups. K-means selects k cluster centers in data domain which are a more compact representation of the original data set.

In the proposed approach, the centers of the clusters are selected to form the columns of the matrix A. Fig. 1 shows two examples of sample face clusters for the same class along with the computed cluster representatives. Each sample is a 60×60 face image.

The number of clusters for each class is adaptively selected based on the variability of the training images for that

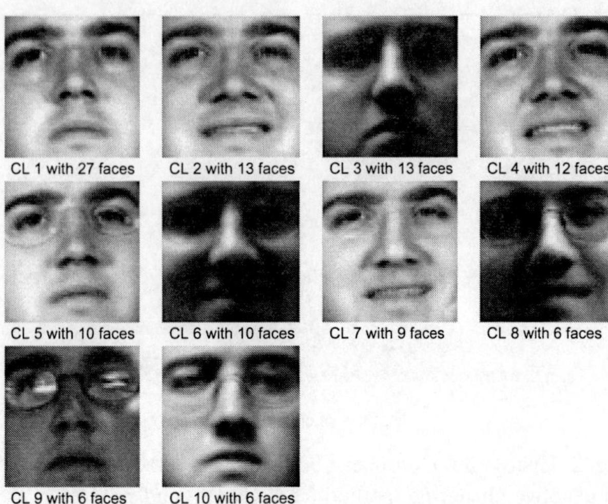

Fig. 3: Images of 10 cluster centers for one of the training classes with 112 face images. Number of face images are also shown for each cluster.

class. The variability of a cluster is defined as the maximum within-cluster sums of point-to-centroid distance measure

$$MaxDist_i = \max_j \left[\sqrt{\sum_{l=1}^{N_j^i} \left(u_l^{i,j} - C_j^i\right)^2} \right], \quad (10)$$

where, N_j^i is the number of samples in cluster j of class i and $u_l^{i,j}$ is the lth sample in j^{th} cluster of class i. C_j^i represents cluster center of the jth cluster in class i.

Consider a dataset with 100 classes and 15000 total number of training face images. The size of the matrix A for this dataset will be 3600×15000, assuming that each face is a 60×60 image. If a matrix of size 100×3600 is used for feature extraction, then the final size of the matrix $\widehat{A}$ for the original SRC will be 100×15000 (Equation (8) in section 2.2). In comparison, if the average number of clusters per class is selected to be 10, the size of the matrix $\widehat{A}$ for the proposed method will be 100×1000. Although the size of the matrix $\widehat{A}$ for the original SRC may be reduced by selecting a random subset of the training dataset, but the random selection of the images is not necessarily a good representative of each class in the dataset.

In practice, the number of clusters for class i, Q_i, is constrained by a predetermined maximum number of clusters, Q_{max}. Q_i, starts from one and is incremented as long as $Q_i < Q_{max}$ and $MaxDist_i$ is smaller than a fixed predetermined threshold, τ. Applying this approach on the training dataset will result in different number of clusters for each class. Classification based on this method is called K-SRC in this paper. The two parameters Q_{max} and τ allow the system to control the number of columns in the training matrix A. This adjusting feature enables efficiency versus accuracy tradeoff.

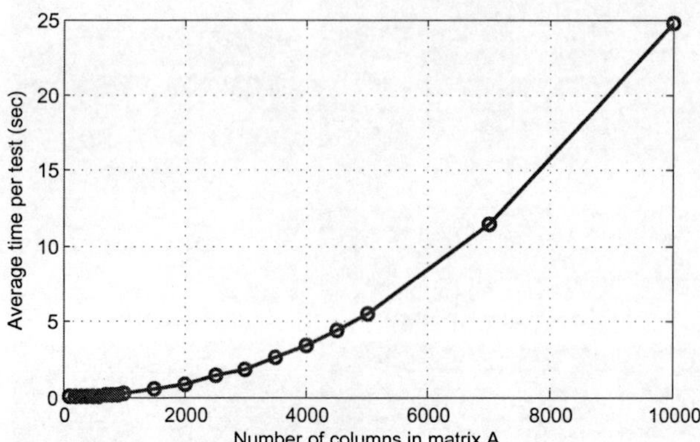

Fig. 4: Average time per test in SRC is super-linear to the number of columns in matrix A.

Fig. 2 shows the histogram of number of clusters for 100 classes based on adaptive clustering method. In this experiment, 100 classes are randomly selected from the face dataset. Total number of training samples for all classes is 14794 face images and each training sample is a cropped to a 60×60 gray face image, i.e. a 3600 dimensional vector. Adaptive clustering parameters Q_{max} and τ are selected such that after clustering the average number of clusters for each class is equal to 10 ($Q_{max} = 20$ and τ =0.42167). As a result, the total number of training samples in this experiment is 1000 which forms a 3600×1000 training matrix A. Changing τ will change the average number of clusters per class which results in a different number of columns in training matrix A. Our experiments in section 4 show how the size of training matrix A varies by increasing the threshold τ. Fig. 3 shows the formed cluster centers for one of the face classes in the training dataset. This class has a total number of 112 training samples. K-means algorithm with τ=0.42167 and $Q_{max} = 20$ was applied to this class and as a result, a total number of 10 clusters are formed. Each cluster is formed by different number of face samples which is also shown.

3.1 Results

The relationship between the running time and size of the training matrix for SRC algorithm is shown in Fig. 4. The average running time for both SRC and the proposed method is the same because they are both using the same process to solve the l^1−norm minimization problem, which is quadratic to the number of columns in the training matrix. It should be noted that at a same computational complexity, K-SRC achieves higher recognition rates than the original SRC, as shown by the experiments in section 4.

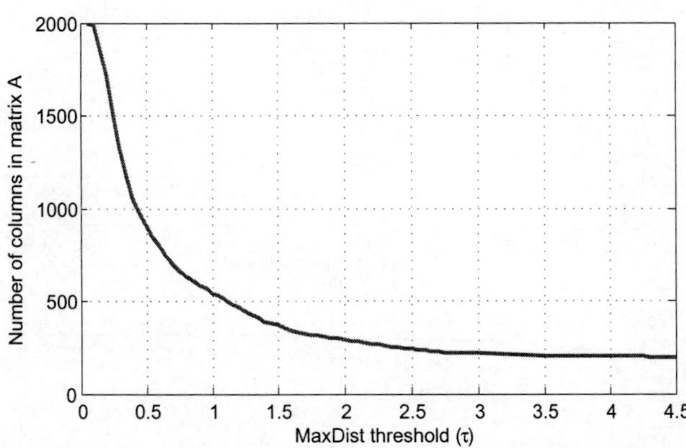

Fig. 5: The relationship between τ and number of columns in matrix A.

4. Experiments

4.1 The Face Dataset

The face dataset used in this work consists of 2D face images from the FRGC-2 dataset [16]. This dataset contains 36817 face images from 535 subjects (i.e., 535 classes). Among these classes, 100 classes were randomly selected for the experiments. Total number of training images is 14794 and the test dataset consists of 400 face images (4 test images per class) which are different from face images in the training set. The original resolution of the face images was either 1704×2272 or 1200×1600. All images were converted to gray images, normalized and cropped to 60 by 60 pixels.

The first set of experiments were conducted to evaluate the effect of the $MaxDist$ threshold, τ, on the number of columns in matrix A, which controls the tradeoff between running time and recognition accuracy. Fig. 5 shows how the number of columns in matrix A is affected by increasing the parameter τ. Parameter Q_{max} was set to 20 in this experiment. As it can be seen in this figure, when τ is increased from 0.05 to 4, the number of columns in matrix A decreases from 2000 to 204.

Face recognition performance for the original method (SRC) and new proposed method (K-SRC) is measured and compared with different number of columns in matrix A. Recognition accuracy simulations are done for 3 different methods introduced in [7] i.e. random projections, Eigen features, and down-sampling. Feature extraction matrix R is selected to have 100 rows in all simulations. Primal-dual algorithm introduced in [17] was used to solve the optimization problem (9).

In order to compare the recognition accuracy for the two methods (SRC and K-SRC), clustering parameters (Q_{max} and τ) are tuned to achieve some pre-determined total number of clusters (200, 300, ...) for K-SRC experiments. Then a similar number of training face images were randomly selected from the whole training dataset to from the training matrix A and the original SRC method was conducted on this set. With this scheme, it is possible to compare the recognition rate of both methods having similar computational load.

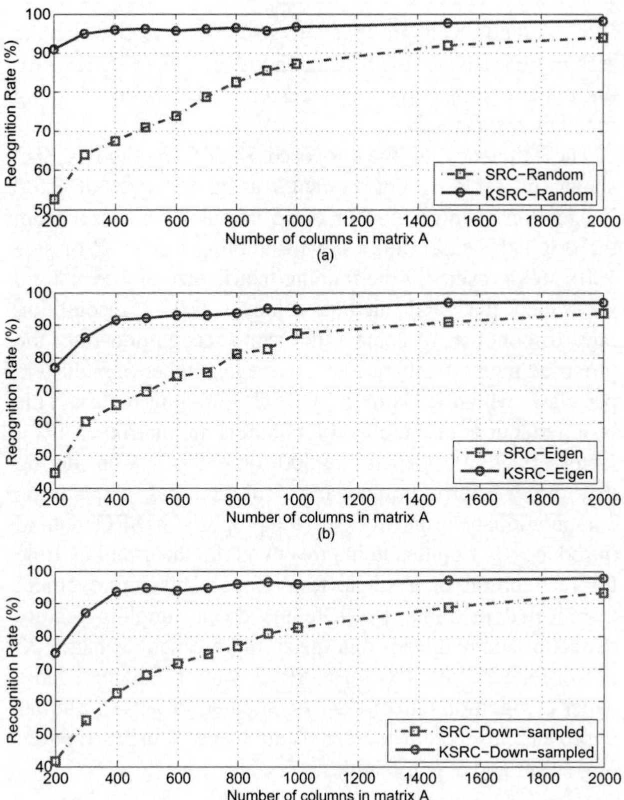

Fig. 6: Recognition rate for K-SRC (*blue solid line*) and original SRC (*red dashed line*) method using different sizes of matrix A, (a): Random projection, (b): Eigen features and (c): Down-sampling

Fig. 6 shows the recognition rates for different sizes of training matrices using random projection, Eigen features, and down-sampling. It can be seen that for the same number of columns in the training matrix, the proposed method has higher recognition rate compared to the original SRC method. For instance, using random projection for the K-SRC method with a 100×1000 A matrix (an average of 10 clusters per class), recognition accuracy is $\%95.75$ which is higher than the $\%85.5$ accuracy for the original SRC method with the same size of matrix A (10 training sample per class).

Fig. 7 shows the recognition rate of both SRC and K-SRC versus the average running time per test. Examination of Fig. 7 indicates that for the same average time per test, the K-SRC outperforms the SRC method in all the three feature extraction methods. For example , at the 100 msec average time per test, the recognition rates of the K-

SRC method are approximately %96, %93, %95 while the recognition rates for the SRC method are %76, %75, %70 for the random projection, Eigen features, and down-sampling methods respectively.

The efficiency of the proposed K-SRC method is also shown in Table 1. For example, using a subset of 3500 images (an average number of 35 samples per class) from the original dataset and a down-sampling matrix R of size 100×3600, results in the training matrix size of 100×3500 for which the SRC method achieves %94.2 recognition rate. In contrast, to achieve the same recognition rate, the proposed method only needs an average number of 5 clusters per class, which leads to a 100×500 training matrix. This is a reduction of number of columns in matrix A by a factor of 7 (3500 for SRC to 500 for K-SRC). Considering that the l^1−norm minimization solution has a quadratic computational complexity [10], the proposed K-SRC method introduces a significant improvement in the running time for recognition of a single test image. This improvement is reflected in Table 1, where the down-sampling feature extraction method leads to a speed improvement of factor 33 (2.64s for SRC to 0.08s for K-SRC) while achieving even a better recognition rate of %94.7 compared to %94.2. Similar improvements could be seen from Table 1 using random projection and Eigen features.

5. Conclusion

In this paper, we proposed an efficient method based on sparse representation classification (SRC) for face recognition application. In this approach, instead of using the original face images, clusters of training face images are used to form the training matrix. An adaptive K-means method is implemented to form the training data clusters. Adjusting the parameters of the adaptive clustering algorithm allows for a controlled trade off between speed and accuracy of the recognition process. Three different feature extraction algorithms were used in the experiments and results were compared with the original SRC algorithm. We have tested our method on a face dataset with 14794 training face images from 100 classes. Results show that the proposed approach reduces the running time and memory requirements of the recognition task while preserving the classification accuracy in comparison with the original SRC method. The experiments show that the proposed method can speed up the recognition process time up to 40 times when compared to the SRC algorithm. This improvements makes the new approach more feasible for implementation on mobile and other devices with low processing resources.

Table 1: Recognition rate, running time per test and number of columns in matrix A for K-SRC and SRC methods for classifications of faces from 100 subjects using random, Eigen and down-sampling features.

Method	K-SRC			SRC		
	Acc(%)	Time(s)	A Col.	Acc(%)	Time(s)	A Col.
Random	95.0	0.03	300	94.0	0.81	2000
Eigen	95.0	0.18	900	94.2	1.33	2500
Down-Sampling	94.7	0.08	500	94.2	2.64	3500

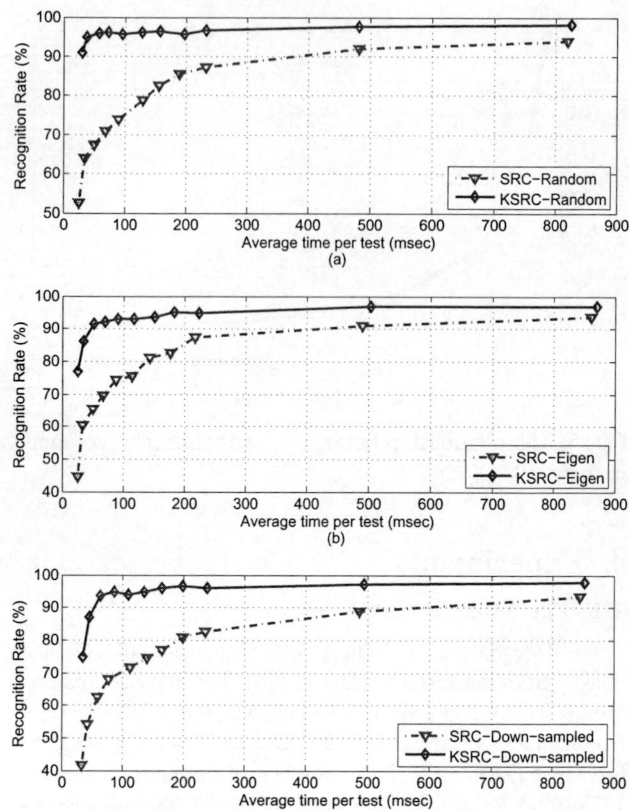

Fig. 7: Recognition rate for K-SRC (*blue solid line*) and original SRC (*red dashed line*) method versus the average execution time for each test, (a): Random projection, (b): Eigen features and (c): Down-sampling

References

[1] R. Jafri and H. R. Arabnia, "A survey of face recognition techniques," *Journal of Information Processing Systems*, vol. 5, no. 2, pp. 41–68, 2009.

[2] S. Chitra and G. Balakrishnan, "A survey of face recognition on feature extraction process of dimensionality reduction techniques," *Journal of Theoretical and Applied Information Technology*, vol. 36, no. 1, pp. 92–100, 2005.

[3] M. Turk and A. Pentland, "Eigenfaces for recognition," *IEEE International Conference on Computer Vision and Pattern Recognition*, 1991.

[4] P. Belhumeur, J. Hespanda, and D. Kriegman, "Eigenfaces versus fisherfaces: Recognition using class specific linear projection," *IEEE Transaction on Pattern Analysis and Machine Intelligence*, vol. 19, no. 7, pp. 711–720, 1997.

[5] X. He, S. Yan, Y. Hu, P. Niyogi, and H. Zhang, "Face recognition using laplacianfaces," *IEEE Transaction on Pattern Analysis and Machine Intelligence*, vol. 27, no. 3, pp. 328–340, 2005.

[6] M. Kirby and L. Sirovich, "Application of the karhunen-loeve procedure for the characterization of human faces," *IEEE Transactions on Pattern Analysis and Machine Intelligence*, vol. 12, no. 1, pp. 103–108, 1990.

[7] J. Wright, A. Yang, A. Ganesh, and S. Sastry, "Robust face recognition via sparse representation," *IEEE Transaction on Pattern Analysis and Machine Intelligence*, vol. 31, no. 2, pp. 210–227, 2009.

[8] D. Donoho, "Compressed sensing," *IEEE Transactions on Information Theory*, vol. 52, no. 4, pp. 1289–1306, 2006.

[9] E. Candes, "Compressive sampling," *International Congress of Mathematics*, 2006.

[10] D. Donoho and Y. Tsaig, "Fast solution of l1-norm minimization problems when the solution may be sparse," *Available Online: http://dsp.rice.edu/sites/dsp.rice.edu/files/cs/FastL1.pdf*, 2006.

[11] E. Amaldi and V. Kann, "On the approximability of minimizing nonzero variables or unsatisfied relations in linear systems," *Theoretical Computer Science*, 1998.

[12] R. Baraniuk, "Compressive sensing," *IEEE Signal Processing Magazine*, vol. 24, no. 4, pp. 118–121, 2007.

[13] R. Basri and D. Jacobs, "Lambertian reflectance and linear subspaces," *IEEE Transactions on Pattern Analysis and Machine Intelligence*, vol. 25, no. 2, pp. 218–233, 2003.

[14] J. B. MacQueen, "Some methods for classification and analysis of multivariate observations," *Proceedings of 5-th Berkeley Symposium on Mathematical Statistics and Probability*, 1967.

[15] R. Xu and D. Wunsch, "Survey of clustering algorithms," *IEEE Transactions on Neural Networks*, vol. 16, no. 3, pp. 645–678, 2005.

[16] P. Phillips, P. Flynn, T. Scruggs, and K. Bow, "Overview of the face recognition grand challenge," *IEEE Conference on Computer Vision and Pattern Recognition*, 2005.

[17] E. Candes and J. Romberg, "L1-magic : Recovery of sparse signals via convex programming," *Available Online: http://users.ece.gatech.edu / justin/l1magic/downloads/l1magic.pdf*, 2005.

AAM-based Facial Image Beautification

Alexander Limonov, Dowan Kim, Jinsung Lee, Kilsoo Jung, and Jongsul Min
DMC R&D Center, Multimedia Research Team
Samsung Electronics, Suwon, Republic of Korea

Abstract – *In this paper, we present a new image processing system for human frontal face beautification. The proposed method is largely divided into two steps: facial feature detection and 2D mesh warping. In particular, after obtaining facial features from an AAM-based facial tracker, we modify their positions in automatic and manual modes. Then, changed features are used to generate the output face image via mesh warping. Our system was tested on multiple real facial images. Experimental results show that the proposed method demonstrates the ability to beautify the face while keeping it look natural.*

Keywords: image processing, face detection;

1 Introduction

Since development of photography, people continuously have tried to improve the result and got more beautiful faces by applying various retouching and deblemishing techniques. In the era of digital photography, many methods of facial image beautification were developed.

We can classify facial image beautification techniques into three categories. The first category is based on image filtering techniques, where image filters are applied to the whole image or some parts of the image for improving skin color and removing blemishes [1]. The second one pertains to the 2D image warping [2], where facial features are moved to slightly different locations based on some judgment. The last one utilizes image synthesis techniques where some parts of image are synthesized or extracted from another image and blended with existing one [3]. Of course, it is possible to sequentially apply a number of different methods.

The proposed method belongs to the second category and is based on 2D mesh warping. The goal of our work is to provide users with ability to automatically beautify facial image in "1-click", while keeping their faces look natural.

2 Algorithm description

For the input image, we calculate facial features position and orientation by the active appearance model (AAM)-based facial tracker [4]. Based on AAM feature points, we define a 2D mesh on the image. Fig.1 shows an example of AAM feature points for the facial image on the right and corresponding 2D mesh on the left.

In the mesh we define a subset of mesh points corresponding to each facial feature. Then, we define parameters that control movement of certain mesh points to control the size of particular face features, such as eyes, mouth, nose, and chin. Each parameter identifies change amount for relative facial feature size.

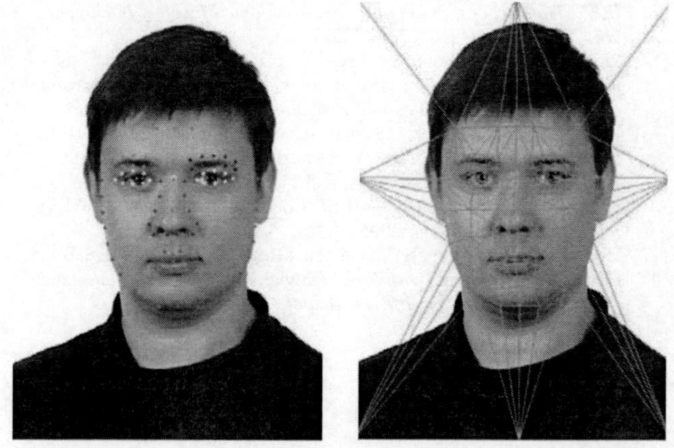

Fig.1. Right: AAM feature points, Left: 2D mesh model

Parameters can be set either manually by a user or determined by comparison of user facial features with reference facial data, where reference facial image also can be selected by the user. If the second mode is selected, parameters are set in the way that size of user's facial features becomes similar to the reference.

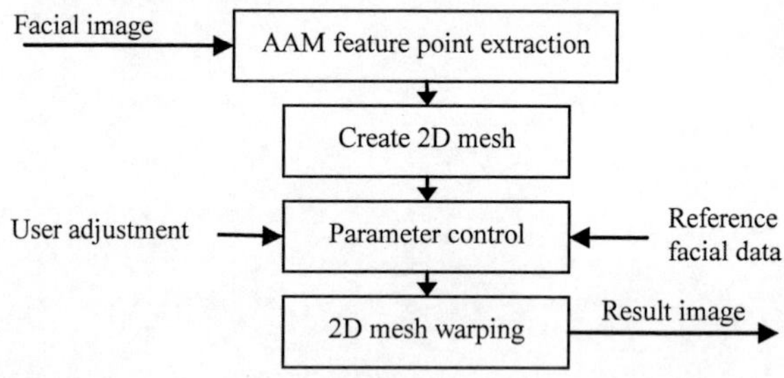

Fig.2. Facial image beautification algorithm flow chart

After all parameters are defined, we perform a 2D mesh warping operator to obtain the output image. Fig. 2 presents the algorithm data flow for the proposed facial beautification system.

Fig.3. Right: Input image, Left: Result image

In our system we implement following control parameters: mouth width and lip thickness, eye size, nose width and length, eyebrow position and chin shape. Moreover, we add a function to control a smile expression by moving mouth corners up or down. In order to avoid artifacts and keep image look natural, we apply limitation to control parameters so mesh points are not change position dramatically. Limits were derived experimentally for each parameter by subjective evaluation of image change noticeability and naturalness.

After image warping, we need to solve two major difficulties: background distortion and eyeglass distortion. In order to reduce such effects, we apply following concealment methods. In particular, we extract rectangular area around the user face and blend it with original input image. It may result in slightly blur image in the blending area, but make background distortion much less visible. For eyeglass distortion reduction, we utilize a method described in [5], where mesh points near to eyeglass frame are preserved.

3 Experimental result

We have tested our algorithm on a bunch of images taken by a commercial digital camera, web camera, and downloaded from internet. All images have a variety of resolutions and different head positions. Fig.3. shows result of our proposed algorithm for various head positions and facial expressions. In the majority of cases, our method works fine, as shown in Fig. 3, even when head is slanted or turned up or down. For the best result, we recommend to use frontal facial images with X or Y rotation angle limit of $\pm 15^{\circ}$. In some images, facial features were not able to be detected due to blur or low contrast or false detected, but the ration of such images in our database is relatively low.

4 Conclusion

In this paper, we have implemented a facial image beautification algorithm. The proposed method is robust even when AAM feature points are not detected very precisely. We believe that beauty standards may vary from person to person, so our algorithm provides a user-friendly control mechanism on the warping parameters, so everybody can get a satisfied result. We expect that our algorithm will be adopted in the photo-editing software in PC or mobile devices.

5 References

[1] Arakawa, K.; Nomoto, K.; "A system for beautifying face images using interactive evolutionary computing," Intelligent Signal Processing and Communication Systems, 2005. ISPACS 2005. Proceedings of 2005 International Symposium on , vol., no., pp. 9- 12, 13-16 Dec. 2005

[2] Tommer Leyvand, Daniel Cohen-Or, Gideon Dror, and Dani Lischinski. 2006. Digital face beautification. In ACM SIGGRAPH 2006 Sketches (SIGGRAPH '06). ACM, New York, NY, USA, , Article 169 .

[3] Rabi, S.A.; Aarabi, P.; "Face Fusion: An Automatic Method For Virtual Plastic Surgery," Information Fusion, 2006 9th International Conference on , vol., no., pp.1-7, 10-13 July 2006

[4] T. F. Cootes, G. J. Edwards, and C. J. Taylor. Active appearance models. IEEE TPAMI, 23(6):681–685. (2001)

[5] Dowan Kim, Sungjin Kim, Ying Huang, Jianfa Zou, JunJun Xiong and Jongsul Min; AAM-based Face Reorientation Using a Single Camera", ICCE 2013

Face recognition from one image per person with an enlarged training set

Jinghua Wang[1], Jane You[1], Qin Li[2], and Zhenhua Guo[3]
[1]Department of Computing, The Hong Kong Polytechnic University, Kowloon, Hong Kong
[2]Shenzhen University, Shenzhen, China
[3]Tsinghua University Shenzhen Graduate School, Shenzhen, China

Abstract - ***In some large-scale face recognition task, the training set only contains one image per person. This situation is referred to as one sample problem. The one sample problem is one of the open problems in the face recognition. This paper investigates principal component analysis, Fisher linear discriminant analysis, and locality preserving projections and shows why they cannot perform well in one sample problem. Based on the analysis, this paper proposes to enlarge the training set based on the inter-class relationship. This paper also extends LDA and LPP to extract features from the enlarged training set. The experimental results show the effectiveness of the proposed method.***

Keywords: face recognition; one image per person; one sample image problem; feature extraction

1 Introduction

Face recognition from one image per person (also referred to as one sample problem) is an important sub-area and recently attracts increasing attention [1]. One sample problem is particularly significant in some large scale identification problems, such as passport card identification, driver license identification, and law enforcement.

The most popular face recognition methods are subspace-based methods, including principal component analysis (PCA) [2], Fisher linear discriminant analysis (LDA) [3], locality preserving projections (LPP) [4], and so on. The subspace-based methods first seek a set of projection vectors and then project the original image onto these projection vectors. Their performances degrade significantly as the number of training images decreases. The task of face recognition from one image per person is an extreme situation where we have the fewest training images. Many popular subspace-based feature extraction methods [2-4] cannot achieve high classification accuracy in one sample problem.

Researchers have proposed methods to deal with one sample problem. The extensions of PCA [5-6] fade out the unimportant features in a preprocessing procedure before performing PCA. Wang et al. [7] solve one sample problem based on the assumption that human being exhibits similar intra-class variation. There are also some methods [8-10] that can enlarge the training set and turn the one sample problem into multiple samples problem. The methods [5-10] do not present the reasons that make one sample problem difficult.

In this paper, we analyze why face recognition is difficult from two different viewpoints. The first viewpoint is the principal of the popular feature extraction methods. We study the principals of PCA, LDA, and LPP and show why they cannot perform well or applicable to one sample problem. Secondly, we analyze why one sample problem itself is difficult. For the first time, we ascribe the difficulty of one sample problem to four reasons: 1. the training set is small; 2. one sample is not representative; 3. the intra-class variation is unknown or underestimated; and 4. the inter-class variation is overestimated.

Our analysis leads us to solve the one sample problem by enlarging the training set based on the inter-class relationship. By synthesizing many samples, our method not only turns the one sample problem into a multiple samples problem, but also can rectify the underestimated intra-class variation and the overestimated inter-class variation. In the enlarged training set, the synthesized images for one individual are independent from each other. This enhances the representative of the training set. We propose extensions of both LDA and LPP for feature extraction from the enlarged training set. These two extensions treat the real images and the synthesized images differently, and suitable for use on the enlarged training set. The experimental results show that the feature extraction methods achieve higher classification accuracy on the enlarged training set.

Section 2 analyzes why one sample problem is difficult. Section 3 proposes a new method to enlarge the training set based on inter-class relationship. Section 4 presents extensions of both LDA and LPP for the feature extraction on the enlarged training set. Section 5 performs experiments to evaluate the proposed method. Section 6 concludes this paper.

2 Why is one sample problem difficult?

In one sample problem, LDA degenerates to PCA. Both of them fail to capture the major identification difference when the testing face images are captured under different conditions [11]. This is justified experimental results in [1]. In one sample problem, the local structure is rarely useful for classification as the neighbor face images associate with different individuals. Thus, LPP which heavily relies on the local structure cannot perform well. Different from [1, 5], the rest will analyzes from a new viewpoint: why is one sample problem itself difficult?

Firstly, face recognition is essentially a SSS problem and the dilemma between the high dimension and the small sample size is even more serious in one sample problem.

Secondly, one image is not sufficiently representative. Face images of the same individual are different if captured under different conditions. One image is far from enough to represent the face images of one individual. Researchers found ways to predict one image from the others [12]. In the training stage of multiple samples problem, not only the available face images but also the predictable ones are useful. From a single image, however, it is difficult to predict novel images. In other words, the synthesized images are less reliable in one sample problem.

Thirdly, one sample problem deprives the opportunity to minimize the intra-class distance, as the intra-class variation is unavailable. So, the intra-class variation is large with high probability in the feature space and unfavorably affects the following classification procedure. Additionally, the intra-class variation is not available to train classifiers [13].

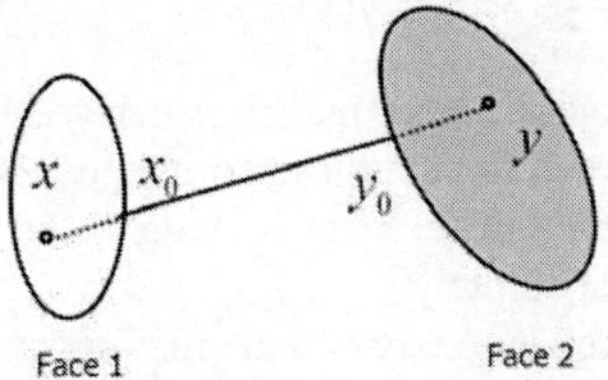

Figure 1 The overestimated inter-class variation. The two ellipses represent two clusters respectively formed by two different faces. x and y are two training images. x_0 and y_0 are two latent images.

Fourthly, the inter-class variation is overestimated in one sample problem. Assume the face images of two individuals respectively form a cluster, as shown in figure 1. In figure 1, the two ellipses represent two clusters respectively formed by the images of face 1 and face 2. Though the difference $y-x$ is considered as an inter-class variation in one sample problem, it $y-x$ is consists of three sections: two intra-class variations (x_0-x , $y-y_0$) and the real inter-class variation (y_0-x_0).When feature extraction methods maximize such an overestimated inter-class, they exaggerated the intra-class variations at the same time. This degrades the performance of the classification procedure.

3 Proposed method

3.1 Basic idea

In face space, images of the same individual are different and represented by different points. We assume that the images of one individual cluster together in this paper, as shown in figure 1. Regarding the image x from face 1 and y from face 2 as two points, we can use a line segment to joint them. This line segment consists of a series of points, each of which represents a latent image. This line segment can be represented by the following formula

$$z=\lambda x+(1-\lambda)y \quad where \ 0\le\lambda\le1 \tag{1}$$

Note that, it is not necessarily that all of these points are real images. The points in the middle of this line segment are far from both of the real images and they are not real images in most cases. However, the ones near to the end points can be considered as variations of the real images. In figure 2, we randomly choose two face images and synthesize nine novel images using (1) by setting the parameter $\lambda=0.1$, 0.2 … 0.9. The synthesized images are quite similar to y when λ equals 0.1 or 0.2, and similar to x when λ equals 0.8 or 0.9. We can take some of synthesized face images as variations of the real face images, and use them to enlarge the training dataset.

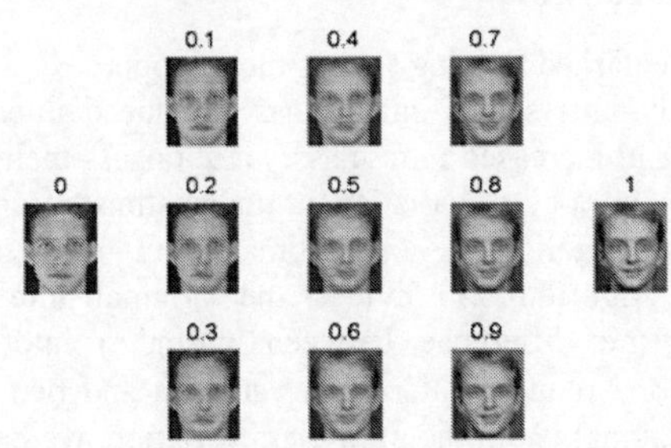

Figure 2 Weighted combinations of two face images. The numbers above the images are the parameter λ in equation (1)

3.2 Image Synthesis

We use the following algorithm for face image synthesis:

Algorithm 1

For each real image x , the following two steps synthesize its variations:

Step 1: among all the real images, find k nearest neighbors of x and denote them as $y_i(1\le i\le k)$, where y_1 is the nearest neighbor;

Step 2: synthesize images using $z_i = \lambda_i x + (1-\lambda_i) y_i$, where $1 \le i \le k$ and $1 - d(x, y_1)/(3 * d(x, y_i)) < \lambda_i \le 1$.

The above algorithm enlarges the training set. This training set has two properties.

Firstly, a image $z_i = \lambda_i x + (1-\lambda_i) y_i$ synthesized in step 2 is nearer to x than to any real face image different from x.

Proof:

Suppose y_1 is the nearest neighbor of x among all the real images, then we have the following formula

$$d^2(x, z_i) = (1-\lambda_i)^2 d^2(x, y_i) < \frac{1}{9} d^2(x, y_1)$$

(2)

Thus,

$$d(x, z_i) < \frac{1}{3} d(x, y_1) \quad (3)$$

Suppose y_k is a real image different from x, then

$$\begin{aligned} &d(y_k, z_i) > d(y_k, x) - d(x, z_i) \\ &\ge d(x, y_1) - d(x, z_i) > \frac{2}{3} d(x, y_1) \end{aligned} \quad (4)$$

Based on (3) and (4), we know that the synthesized image z_i is nearer to the real image it associating with than to the other real images.

Secondly, if z_i is a variation of x and z_j is a variation of y_j, then z_i is nearer to x than to z_j, i.e. $d(z_i, z_j) > d(x, z_i)$.

3.3 Discussion

The enlarged training set has three properties.

Firstly, this set of images has a reduced inter-class variation and increased intra-class variation. As mentioned above, the intra-class variation is underestimated and the inter-class variation is overestimated in one sample problem. Algorithm 1 divides the original inter-class variation (the difference between x and) into three portions (one reduced inter-class variation and two intra-class variations). With the intra-class variation, we have an opportunity to minimize it in the feature extraction procedure.

Secondly, the local structure is useful for classification in the enlarged training set. It is proved that the synthesized samples are nearer to the real face images belonging to the same individual than the real face images of the others. In other words, each image must have a neighbor that share the same class label with it. Because of this, the feature extraction method that keeps the local structure will generate a small intra-class variation in the feature space. Thus, the local structure is useful for classification.

Thirdly, the enlarged training set captures the variations x_i along different directions. Step 2 synthesizes images based on an image and its several neighbors, which are normally along different directions. This enriches the variations of the training set and enhances its representation. Also, the synthesized images are independent if they are synthesized based on different pairs of real images.

4 Extensions of LDA and LPP

The d dimensional vector $x_i\,(i = 1, 2, ..., c)$ represents the image from the i th individual. The j th synthesized image for the i th individual is represented by $z_j^i\,(1 \le i \le c; 1 \le j \le n_i)$. Thus, the training set consists $n_i + 1$ samples for the i th class, including one real image and n_i synthesized images. The following proposes extensions of LDA and LPP for dimension reduction.

4.1 LDA Extension

We take the real image as the mean of the i th class, and compute the intra-class scatter matrix as follows

$$S_w^* = \sum_{i=1}^{c} \sum_{j=1}^{n_i} (z_j^i - x_i)(z_j^i - x_i)^T \quad (5)$$

The inter-class matrix S_b is derived based on the y differences between the images. Due to the overestimated the inter-class variations, the inter-class scatter matrix is not accurately estimated. We newly define the inter-class scatter matrix as follows

$$S_b^* = \sum_{i_1 \ne i_2} \sum_{j=1}^{n_{i_1}} \sum_{k=1}^{n_{i_2}} (z_j^{i_1} - z_k^{i_2})(z_j^{i_1} - z_k^{i_2})^T \quad (6)$$

This inter-class scatter matrix is derived based on the differences between the synthesized images. Based on our discussion, such differences model the inter-class variations more accurately.

The feature extractors that maximize the Fisher criterion are the eigenvectors of the following generalized eigen-equation problem corresponding to the maximum eigenvalues

$$S_b^* \alpha = \lambda S_w^* \alpha \quad (7)$$

4.2 LPP Extension

LPP tries to learn a subspace that preserves the local structure of the image space. In this paper, we propose the following extension of LPP for one sample problem

$$\min \sum_{i=1}^{c} \sum_{j=1}^{n_i} (\alpha^T z_j^i - \alpha^T x_i)^2 S_j^i \quad (8)$$

We define S as follows

$$S_j^i = \begin{cases} \exp\left(-\|z_j^i - x_i\|^2 / t\right) \\ 0 \end{cases} \quad (9)$$

where the positive t defines the radius of the local neighborhood. In (8), we only consider the intra-class relationship between the real images and their synthesized variations. The physical meaning of (8) is as follows: the representations of the synthesized images z_j^i are expected to be neighbors of that of the real image in the feature space.

The projection vectors are the eigenvectors of the following generalized eigenvalue problem corresponding to the minimum eigenvalue

$$\left(ZDZ^T - 2ZEX + XFX\right)\alpha = \lambda\left(ZDZ^T + XFX\right)\alpha \qquad (10)$$

5 Conclusions

The Yale database [14] contains totally 165 images, 11 images from each of 15 individuals. The images have variations in lighting conditions facial expressions, and occlusion. To test the robust of the proposed method, we conduct no preprocessing on the images.

A subset of the FERET database [15] consists of 400 images from 200 individuals. Each person has two images (fa and fb) which are obtained at different times and with different facial expressions. The images are cropped to the size of 128 by 128.

In both Yale and FERET, we use the first image of each individual for training and the rest images for testing.

Besides the conventional PCA, LDA, and LPP, we compare our methods with other three methods [5, 10, 16] which are proposed to solve the one sample problem. The parameters of these three methods are set the same as those in [5, 10, 16], respectively. Additionally, we also compare our method with a LPP-based method which is referred to as projection-combined locality preserving projection (PCLPP). PCLPP first enriches the face images using the method in [5] then implements the LPP method on the enriched images. The methods performed on the enlarged training set are referred to as PCA on the enlarged training set (PCAoE), LDA on the enlarged training set (LDAoE), and LPP on the enlarged training set (LPPoE).

TABLE 1 THE PARAMETERS ON THE THREE DATABASES

database	Yale	FERET
Number of individual	15	200
k	7	21

Two important parameters in algorithm are: the number of neighbors k and the parameter λ. Table 1 presents the value of k in these three databases. We set the parameter λ_i as

$$\lambda_i = 1 - 0.9\times d(x, y_1)/(3*d(x, y_i)) \qquad (11)$$

where y_i is the i th nearest neighbor of x. Based on (11), $\lambda_1 = 0.7$ and λ_i increases as the i increases. Thus, the parameter is always larger than 0.7.

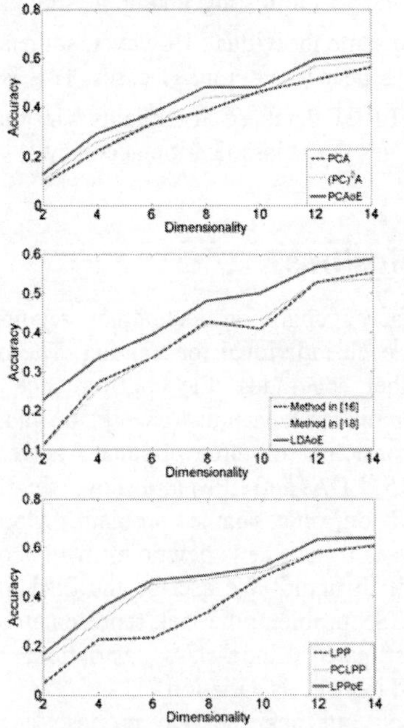

Figure 3 the experimental results on Yale database

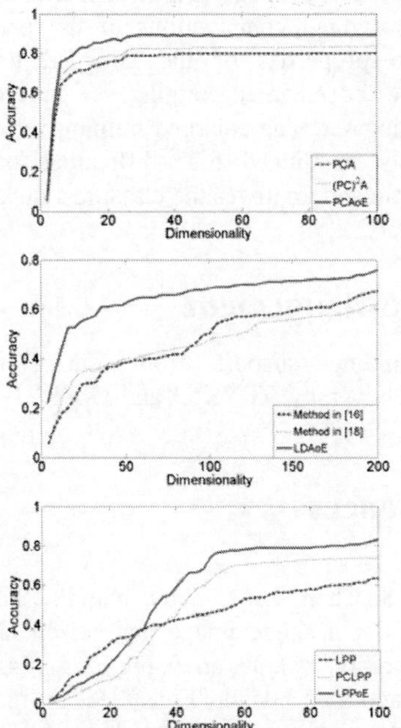

Figure 4 The experimental results on FERET database

The figures 3-4 plot the classification accuracy versus the number of feature extractors. These methods achieve the highest classification accuracy when performed on the enlarged training set. The enlarged training set improves the highest accuracy by larger than 3% for all of the three methods on the Yale. The improvement on the FERET is more significant. LPPoE improves LPP and PCLPP larger than 10%. In our experiment, a real training image x is not necessarily near to the testing image y, though x and y associates the same individual. However, some synthesized image for x is near to y in many cases. This is especially true on the FERET database. It explains why the proposed method achieves high classification accuracy.

6 Conclusions

Most face recognition techniques require multiple images from each individual for training. The one sample problem either degrades the performance of these techniques or makes them fail to work. In this paper, we analyze the principal of three popular feature extraction methods (PCA, LDA, and LPP) and show why they cannot perform well on one sample problem. Moreover, we present analyses from a new viewpoint: why is one sample problem itself difficult? We ascribe the difficulty to four reasons: the SSS problem; the lack representative samples; the underestimated intra-class variation; and the overestimated inter-class variation.`

Based on our analysis, we propose a method to synthesize images and enlarge the training set for face recognition from one image per person. The synthesized images are weighted combinations of the pairs of real images. Two properties of the enlarged training set proclaim that the enlarged training set can replace the original training set. The enlarged training set overcomes the previously mentioned four difficulties of the one sample problem and improves the classification accuracy in our experiments.

7 Acknowledgement

The funding support from the Hong Kong Polytechnic University (G-YK53 and G-YK77) is greatly appreciated.

8 References

[1] X. Tan, S. Chen, Z.-H. Zhou, and F. Zhang, "Face recognition from a single image per person: A survey," Pattern Recognition, vol. 39, no. 9, pp. 1725-1745, 2006.

[2] M. Turk and A. Pentland, "Eigenfaces for recognition," J. Cognitive Neuroscience, vol. 3, no. 1, pp. 71-86, 1991.

[3] P. N. Belhumeur, J. P. Hespanha, and D. J. Kriegman, "Eigenfaces vs. Fisherfaces: recognition using class specific linear projection," Pattern Analysis and Machine Intelligence, IEEE Transactions on, vol. 19, no. 7, pp. 711-720, 1997.

[4] X. He, S. Yan, Y. Hu, P. Niyogi, and H.-J. Zhang, "Face recognition using Laplacianfaces," Pattern Analysis and Machine Intelligence, IEEE Transactions on, vol. 27, no. 3, pp. 328-340, 2005.

[5] J. Wu and Z.-H. Zhou, "Face recognition with one training image per person," Pattern Recognition Letters, vol. 23, no. 14, pp. 1711-19, 2002.

[6] S. Chen, D. Zhang, and Z.-H. Zhou, "Enhanced (PC)2A for face recognition with one training image per person," Pattern Recognition Letters, vol. 25, no. 10, pp. 1173-1181, 2004.

[7] J. Wang, K. N. Plataniotis, and A. N. Venetsanopoulos, "Selecting discriminant eigenfaces for face recognition," Pattern Recognition Letters, vol. 26, no. 10, pp. 1470-1482, 2005.

[8] P. Niyogi, F. Girosi, and T. Poggio, "Incorporating prior information in machine learning by creating virtual examples," Proceedings of the IEEE, vol. 86, no. 11, pp. 2196-2209, 1998.

[9] F. De la Torre, R. Gross, S. Baker, and B. V. K. Vijaya Kumar, "Representational oriented component analysis (ROCA) for face recognition with one sample image per training class," in Computer Vision and Pattern Recognition, 2005. CVPR 2005. IEEE Computer Society Conference on, vol. 2, pp. 266-273 vol. 2, 20-25 June 2005.

[10]D. Zhang, S. Chen, and Z.-H. Zhou, "A new face recognition method based on SVD perturbation for single example image per person," Applied Mathematics and Computation, vol. 163, no. 2, pp. 895-907, 2005.

[11]X. Wang and X. Tang, "A unified framework for subspace face recognition," IEEE Transactions on Pattern Analysis and Machine Intelligence, vol. 26, no. 9, pp. 1222-1228, 2004.

[12]A. M. Martinez, "Recognizing imprecisely localized, partially occluded, and expression variant faces from a single sample per class," Pattern Analysis and Machine Intelligence, IEEE Transactions on, vol. 24, no. 6, pp. 748-763, 2002.

[13]S. Z. Li and J. Lu, "Face recognition using the nearest feature line method," Neural Networks, IEEE Transactions on, vol. 10, no. 2, pp. 439-443, 1999.

[14]A. S. Georghiades, P. N. Belhumeur, and D. J. Kriegman, "From few to many: illumination cone models for face recognition under variable lighting and pose," Pattern Analysis and Machine Intelligence, IEEE Transactions on, vol. 23, no. 6, pp. 643-660, 2001.

[15]P. J. Phillips, M. Hyeonjoon, P. Rauss, and S. A. Rizvi, "The FERET evaluation methodology for face-recognition algorithms," in Computer Vision and Pattern Recognition, 1997. Proceedings., 1997 IEEE Computer Society Conference on, vol. pp. 137-143, 17-19 Jun 1997.

[16]S. Chen, J. Liu, and Z.-H. Zhou, "Making FLDA applicable to face recognition with one sample per person," Pattern Recognition, vol. 37, no. 7, pp. 1553-1555, 2004.

Enhancing Faces Recognition by Image Feature Weights Learning Approach

Ying-Kuei Yang, Wei-Li Fang, Omar Bani Fayyad and Jung-Kuei Pan
Dept. of Electrical Engineering, National Taiwan Uni. of Sci. & Technology, Taipei, Taiwan
Email: yingkyang@yahoo.com

Abstract - *Most of 2DPCA-enhanced approaches improve face recognition rate while at the expense of computation load. In this paper, an approach is proposed to greatly improve face recognition rate with slightly increased computation load. In this approach, the 2DPCA is applied against a face image to extract important image features for selection. A weight is then assigned to each of selected image features according to the feature's importance to face recognition. The least mean square (LMS) algorithm is further applied to optimize the feature weights based on the recognition error rate during learning process in order to improve face recognition performance. The experiments have been conducted against ORL face image database to make performance comparisons among several better-known approaches, and the experimental results have demonstrated that the proposed approach not only has excellent face recognition rate of 99% but also requires only slightly higher computation load than 2DPCA, making the approach more practical to real face recognition applications..*

Keywords: face recognition, feature extraction, principle component analysis, least mean square, weight assignment, steepest decent algorithm.

1 Introduction

Face recognition in image processing has been significantly important because it can be applied in human life efficaciously. Research areas include building/store access control, suspect identification, security and surveillance [1]-[11].

Seceral algorithms have been proposed in face recognition. The best ones should be those that try not only to reduce computation cost but also to increase recognition rate [12][13]. Based on this viewpoint, principal component analysis (PCA) [14] has become a popular feature extraction algorithm in recent decades.

After PCA was proposed, Yang *et al.* [12] proposed the so-called two-dimensional principal component (2DPCA) algorithm aiming for better feature extraction of face images. The 2DPCA has achieved the goal of increasing recognition rate and reducing computation cost simultaneously [12]. Because 2DPCA has such good performance, various face recognition algorithms based on 2DPCA had been proposed and enhanced. For instance, the approach of "Two-directional two-dimensional PCA ($(2D)^2$PCA)" proposed by Zhang *et al.* [16] is to process a face image from transverse and longitudinal axis respectively and then perform the recognition by analyzing their shortest dimension. Low computation cost is the advantage of this approach. Unfortunately, its improvement on recognition rate is not ubiquitous in relatively large scale of training samples [15]. Sanguansat *et al.* [17] proposed the approach of "Two-dimensional principal component combined two-dimensional Linear discriminant analysis (2DPCA&2DLDA)" [17] to face recognition applications. Although this approach solves the small sample size problem, its computation cost is high due to the composition of 2DPCA and 2DLDA. Meng *et al.* [18] proposed the combination of 2DPCA with self-defined volume measure to perform feature extraction by 2DPCA first and then conduct classification by computing the distances of matrix volumes. This approach is more suitable to process applications with high dimensional data. Wang *et al.* [19] proposed "probabilistic two-dimensional principal component analysis" that combines 2DPCA with Gaussian distribution concept to mitigate the noise influence in face image recognition. Kim *et al.* [20] proposed "fusion method based on bidirectional 2DPCA" that reduces dimensions of both row and column vectors before performing face recognition procedure. It does increase recognition rate, but at the expense of high computation cost [21].

Aforesaid face recognition algorithms all have pros and cons. The algorithm "2DPCA" is especially designed for face image data, so the recognition performance is better than using traditional PCA. In this paper, an approach is proposed hoping to achieve the goal of increasing the recognition rate while not at expense of computation cost in face image recognition. This approach incorporates weights in projected feature vectors of 2DPCA and uses least mean square (LMS) algorithm to optimize the weights based on the recognition error rate during learning process in order to achieve better face recognition performance.

2 The least mean square-two dimensional principal component analysis

2.1 Two-dimensional principal component analysis (2DPCA)

The 2DPCA approach by Yang *et al.* [12] in 2004 is proposed particularly for two dimensional image data. Suppose there is an image data set Z={$\mathbf{A}_1$, $\mathbf{A}_2$,..., $\mathbf{A}_N$ } with N images, and the dimension of every image is $n \times n$. The covariance matrix of the image data set is computed by Eq. (1) and the average value of the data set is computed by Eq. (2).

$$\mathbf{R} = \frac{1}{N}\sum_{i=1}^{N}(\mathbf{A}_i - \overline{\mathbf{A}})(\mathbf{A}_i - \overline{\mathbf{A}})^T \quad (1)$$

$$\overline{\mathbf{A}} = \frac{1}{N}\sum_{i=1}^{N}\mathbf{A}_i \quad (2)$$

where $\mathbf{A}_i$ is an image in the data set, $\mathbf{R}$ is covariance matrix, and $\overline{\mathbf{A}}$ is data average.

After eigen-decomposition is performed for covariance matrix, k eigenvectors corresponding to the k biggest eigenvalues are selected. These eigenvectors are the projection vectors of the original image data set and the features of the image can therefore be extracted from those projection vectors as shown in Eq. (3).

$$\mathbf{Y}_i = \mathbf{A}\,\mathbf{X}_i \quad i=1,2,\ldots,k \quad (3)$$

where $\mathbf{Y}_i$ are projected feature vectors, $\mathbf{X}_i$ means eigenvectors. Suppose there are k biggest eigenvalues being selected, then a feature vector set $\mathbf{B}$=[$\mathbf{Y}_1$,$\mathbf{Y}_2$,...,$\mathbf{Y}_k$] in descending order of eigenvalues can be obtained and these projected feature vectors are the resultant principal components of an original image data $\mathbf{A}$ by 2DPCA.

Because 2DPCA processes a 2-dimensional face image directly, it can get better result of feature extraction. On the contrary, the conventional PCA needs to transform an image into one-dimensional data and therefore loses some feature information. Consequently, the recognition rate by 2DPCA is better than conventional PCA for 2-dimensional face images.

2.2 Least mean square algorithm (LMS)

Least mean square (LMS) is an adaptive filter algorithm in signal process [22], and it is applied in many engineering fields. Its input signals $\boldsymbol{u}(n)$ are computed by transversal adaptive filter to result in the output $y(n)$. The desired signal is $d(n)$ and $e(n)$ is the difference between actual output y(n) and desired output $d(n)$. After training by iteration process, $e(n)$ becomes smaller and smaller meaning the adaptive filter is closer to the ideal state.

The main essence of LMS is to make the error rate $e(n)$ as smaller value as possible. Hence, the cost function is defined as the expected value of squaring error rate, as shown in Eq. (4).

$$J(n) = E[e^2(n)] \quad (4)$$

In Eq. (4), the square operation is needed to avoid the problem caused by different sign characteristics because the error rate could be a either positive or negative value. The steepest decent algorithm[22] is then performed against the cost function to make the resultant error rate as small as possible. This operation process is shown as Eq. (5).

$$\hat{\mathbf{w}}(n+1) = \hat{\mathbf{w}}(n) + \mu\mathbf{u}(n)e(n) \quad (5)$$

Eq. (5) represents the process of adjusting weights by iteration operation. The symbol μ is step size. The learning process is repeated until the error rate has reached a pre-set satisfactory value.

2.3 The integration of least mean square with two-dimensional principal component analysis

The feature extraction algorithm 2DPCA has good performance in face recognition. Important features that are represented by projected feature vectors are selected during the process of eigen-decomposition. One projected feature vector represents one extracted feature. The projected feature vector that corresponds to the biggest eigenvalue represents the most important feature; the one that corresponds to second biggest eigenvalue represents the second important feature; and so on. After eigen-decomposition, the projected feature vectors are arranged in a row in the descending order of feature importance.

For 2DPCA and most of its extensions, every projected feature vector has equal weight. This is not a good idea in terms of improving recognition performance since the importance of each projected feature vector, meaning each feature, is different. Rather, the weight assigned to a projected feature vector should be related to the importance of the feature to that a projected feature vector corresponds. That is, the projected feature vector corresponding to the biggest eigenvalue should have highest weight during the process of face recognition.

Although methods have been proposed to assign different weights to projected feature vectors, most of them decide these weights based on trial-and-error process which is not only time-consuming but inefficient. In this paper, an approach is proposed by integrating least mean square with two-dimensional principal component analysis in order to efficiently obtain proper weight for each of selected features hoping to improve face recognition performance. The proposed approach uses LMS to dynamically adjust the weights of projected feature vectors associated with image features. Weights are adjusted based on the feedback of error rate calculated by each iteration.

Fig. 1 shows the proposed system structure based on the concept of an adaptive filter. In Fig. 1, $\boldsymbol{u}(n)$ is the projected feature vectors generated by 2DPCA, and is multiplied by weight matrix to get the output $y(n)$ through the transversal adaptive filter. The error rate e(n) is then calculated by nearest neighbor rule (NNR) and then further used by LMS inside the weight-control mechanism to dynamically adjust the weights of projected feature vectors. The weight matrix is initially set as $\hat{\mathbf{w}}(n)_{N\times m\times d}$ that has dimension N×m×d and value 1 in all matrix elements, where *n* means *n*-th iteration starting from initial value 1. The N means data amount and m×d is the dimension of every data.

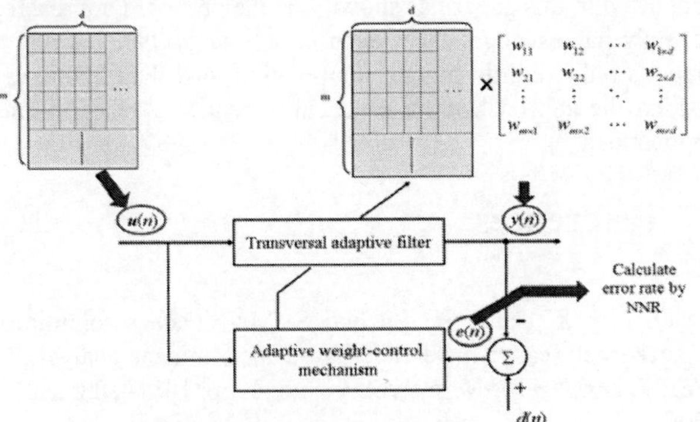

Fig 1: The system structure

To simplify the computation, the error rate of face recognition system is calculated by the nearest neighbor rule that is based on Euclidean distance shown in Eq. (6).

$$d = \|\mathbf{V} - \mathbf{P}\|_2 \quad (6)$$

The symbols **V** and **P** are vectors, and d is Euclidean distance. The operation of Eq. (6) computes the norm of **V-P**. Suppose **V**=(v_1, v_2, v_3) and **P**=(p_1, p_2, p_3), the norm of the two vectors is obtained as Eq. (7).

$$\|\mathbf{V} - \mathbf{P}\|_2 = \sqrt{(v_1 - p_1)^2 + (v_2 - p_2)^2 + (v_3 - p_3)^2} \quad (7)$$

After calculating the error rate by NNR, it is used by LMS iteration to adjust the feature weights as shown in Eq. (5). A threshold value is set for the error rate to avoid infinite iteration.

The face recognition rate is calculated as below. Suppose there are N face images, represented as $\mathbf{B}_1$, $\mathbf{B}_2$,..., $\mathbf{B}_N$, and each image is represented by a projected feature vector, such as [$\mathbf{Y}_1^1$, $\mathbf{Y}_2^1$,..., $\mathbf{Y}_d^1$] for $\mathbf{B}_1$ with m×d dimension. The classes of these N images are already known. Suppose a class-unknown image $\mathbf{T}_k$=[$\mathbf{T}_1$, $\mathbf{T}_2$,..., $\mathbf{T}_d$] is to be recognized against these N face images. The computation process is shown in Eq. (7).

$$d(\mathbf{B},\mathbf{T}) = \sum_{k=1}^{d} \|\mathbf{B}_k - \mathbf{T}_k\|_2 \quad (8)$$

where d is the calculated distance by NNR between the two images. The class of $\mathbf{T}_k$ is classified as the class of $\mathbf{B}_k$ if these two have minimum distance *d* in Eq. (8). The face recognition rate can therefore be obtained after classifying all N face images.

3 Experiments and analysis

The ORL database [23] is a well-known face image database and is used in this paper for experiments. There are 40 individual faces in ORL database. Each individual face has 10 different images making totally 400 face images in the database. The images were taken with a tolerance of some tilting and rotation of the face for up to 20 degrees [12][23]. In ORL database, all images are grayscale with dimension of 112×92. The pixel value range is 0~255.

Among the 10 different images of each individual face, 5 face images are selected as training data and the rest of 5 face images are used as testing data, making totally 200 images for training data and 200 images for testing data.

Fig 2 shows the error rate values during the first 300 LMS iterations respectively in the conducted experiment. In Fig. 2, the lowest error rate takes place at around 52th LMS iteration. It can also be observed in Fig 2 that the error rate is stabilized at certain value after around 135th LMS iteration, which means the feature weights have been learned to be the most appropriate values.

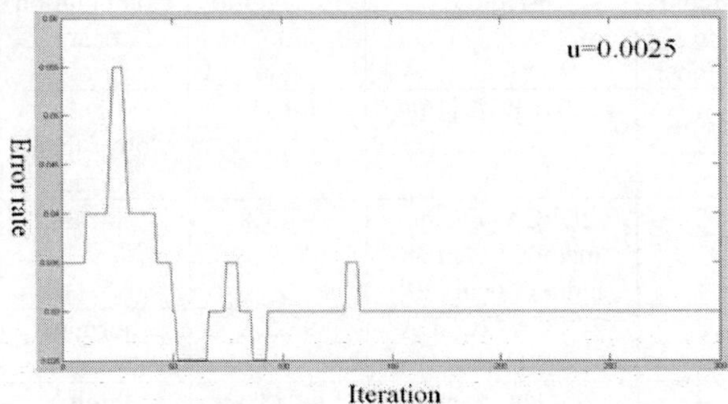

Fig. 2: Error rate during LMS iterations (300 times)

To see the improvement on face recognition during the LMS learning procedure, the face recognition rate is performed after each LMS iteration. The experimental result is shown in Fig. 3. The face recognition rate reaches the best value of 99% starting from around 52th LMS iteration in Fig. 3, which coincides with Fig. 2 that shows the lowest error rate takes places at 52th LMS iteration. Since then, the face recognition rate maintains at value 99% as the feature weights have been adjusted to appropriate values by the LMS learning procedure at this moment.

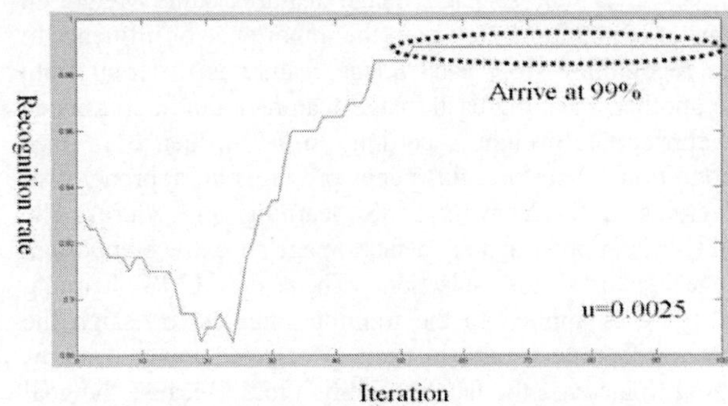

Fig. 3: Face recognition rate during LMS iterations

In Table 1, the experimental result of the proposed LMS-2DPCA in this paper is compared against some other methods which are enhancements from 2DPCA. The experiments are conducted against ORL database for all the methods indicated in Table 1. The table shows that the proposed approach has the best face recognition rate of 99% while the computation load is only normal. Although method 1 [16] has slightly lower computation load than the proposed approach, its face recognition rate is much lower. The good recognition performance of the proposed approach comes from the good adjustment to the image feature weights by LMS learning procedure. The normal computation load is contributed by the LMS' simple algorithm, making the whole computation cost is only slightly more than pure 2DPCA

Table 1: Performance comparison between the proposed approach and other methods

Method number	Method	Recognition rate	Computation cost
1	$(2D)^2$PCA [16]	90.5%	slighly lower than normal
2	2DPCA+Fusion method based on bidirectional [20]	92.5%	normal
3	2DPCA+2DLDA [17]	93.5%	normal
4	2DPCA+Kernel [24]	94.58%	high
5	2DPCA+Feature fusion approach [25]	98.1%	very high
6	**Proposed approach**	99%	normal

4 Conclusions

The 2DPCA is a good approach for 2-dimensional face image recognition. Although enhanced approaches based on 2DPCA have been proposed, most are either too time-consuming or no much improvement to face recognition. The 2DPCA treats all selected image features same weight in terms of recognition. However, the importance or influence to face recognition from each image feature is different from one another, meaning each image feature should be assigned an appropriate weight according to its influence to face recognition. Therefore, this paper proposes an approach that integrates 2DPCA with LMS learning procedure. The 2DPCA is applied against a face image to extract important image features for selection. Then the LMS learning procedure is applied to the training samples to assign the most appropriate weight to each of selected image features hoping to increase the face recognition rate. Because the goal is to make the face recognition error rate as small as possible, the image feature weights are adjusted based on the feedback of face recognition error amount by LMS iterations. Due to the simple algorithm, the additional computation cost required to run LMS learning procedure is only to a small extent of slightly more than pure 2DPCA. The experiments conducted in this paper has shown that the proposed approach not only has excellent face recognition rate of 99% but also requires only slightly higher computation load than 2DPCA, making the approach more practical to real face recognition applications.

5 References

[1] Q. Liu, X. Tang, H. Lu and S. Ma, "Face recognition using kernel scatter-difference-based discriminant analysis," *IEEE Trans. Neural Netw.*, vol. 17, no. 4, pp. 1081–1085, Jul. 2006.

[2] W. Zheng, X. Zhou, C. Zou and L. Zhao, "Facial expression recognition using kernel canonical correlation analysis (KCCA)," *IEEE Trans. Neural Netw.*, vol. 17, no. 1, pp. 233–238, Jan. 2006.

[3] X. Tan, S. Chen, Z. H. Zhou and F. Zhang, "Recognizing partially occluded, expression variant faces from single training image per person with SOM and soft k-NN ensemble," *IEEE Trans. Neural Netw.*, vol. 16, no. 4, pp. 875–886, Jul. 2005.

[4] P. Melin, O. Mendoza and O. Castillo, "Face recognition with an improved interval type-2 fuzzy logic Sugeno integral and modular neural networks," *IEEE Trans. Syst., Man, Cybern. A, Syst., Humans*, vol. 41, no. 5, pp. 1001–1012, Sep. 2011.

[5] N. Sudha, A. R. Mohan and P. K. Meher, "A self-configurable systolic architecture for face recognition system based on principal component neural network," *IEEE Trans. Circuits Syst. Video Technol.*, vol. 21, no. 8, pp. 1071–1084, Aug. 2011.

[6] W. W. W. Zou and P. C. Yuen, "Very low resolution face recognition problem," *IEEE Trans. Image Process.*, vol. 21, no. 1, pp. 327–340, Jan. 2012.

[7] N. S. Vu and A. Caplier, "Enhanced patterns of oriented edge magnitudes for face recognition and image matching," *IEEE Trans. Image Process.*, vol. 21, no. 3, pp. 1352–1365, Mar. 2012.

[8] J. Y. Choi, Y. M. Ro and K. N. Plataniotis, "Color local texture features for
color face recognition," *IEEE Trans. Image Process.*, vol. 21, no. 3, pp. 1366–1380, Mar. 2012.

[9] H. Chen, Y. Y. Tang, B. Fang and J. Wen, "Illumination invariant face recognition using FABEMD decomposition with detail measure weight," *IJPRAI*, vol. 25, pp. 1261- 1273, 2011.

[10] H. Yu, J. J. Zhang and X. Yang, "Tensor-based feature representation with application to multimodal face recognition," *IJPRAI* , vol. 25, pp. 1197-1217, 2011.

[11] G. Chiachia, A. N. Marana, T. Ruf and A. C. Ernst, "Histograms: A simple feature extraction and matching

approach for face recognition," *IJPRAI*, vol. 25, pp. 1337-1348, 2011.

[12] J. Yang, D. Zhang, A. F. Frangi and J. Y. Yang, "Two-dimensional PCA: A new approach to appearance-based face representation and recognition," *IEEE Trans. Pattern Analysis and Machine Intelligence.*, vol. 26, no. 1, pp. 131-137, Jan. 2004.

[13] J. Lu, X. Yuan and T. Yahagi, "A method of face recognition based on fuzzy c-means clustering and associated sub-NNs," *IEEE Trans. Neural Netw.*, vol. 18, no. 1, Jan. 2007

[14] L. Sirovich and M. Kirby, "Low-dimensional procedure for characterization of human faces," *J. Optical Soc. Am.*, vol. 4, pp. 519-524, 1987.

[15] W. H. Yang and D. Q. Dai, "Two-dimensional maximum margin feature extraction for face recognition," *IEEE Trans. Syst., Man, Cybern. B, Cybern.*, vol. 39, no. 4, pp. 1002-1012, Aug. 2009.

[16] D. Zhang and Z. H. Zhoua, "$(2D)^2$PCA: Two-directional two-dimensional PCA for efficient face representation and recognition," *Neurocomputing*, vol. 69, pp. 224–231, Jun. 2005.

[17] P. Sanguansat, W. Asdornwised, S. Jitapunkul and S. Marukatat, "Tow-dimensional linear discriminant analysis of principle component vectors for face recognition," *ICASSP 2006*, pp. 345-348, May. 2006.

[18] J. Meng and W. Zhang, "Volume measure in 2DPCA-based face recognition," *Pattern Recognition Lett.*, vol. 28, pp. 1203–1208, Jan. 2007.

[19] H. Wang, S. Chen, Z. Hu and B. Luo, "Probabilistic two-dimensional principal component analysis and its mixture model for face recognition," *Springer Neural Comput & Applic*, vol. 17, pp. 541–547, 2008.

[20] Y. G. Kim, Y. J. Song, U. D. Chang, D. W. Kim, T. S. Yun and J. H. Ahn, "Face recognition using a fusion method based on bidirectional 2DPCA," *Applied Mathematics and Computation.*, vol. 205, pp. 601–607, 2008.

[21] Y. Qi and J. Zhang, "$(2D)^2$PCALDA: An efficient approach for face recognition," *Applied Mathematics and Computation.*, vol. 213, no. 1, pp. 1-7, Jul. 2009.

[22] S. Haykin, *Adaptive Filter Theory*, 4rd Edition, Prentice-Hall, 2001.

[23] "The ORL face database", http://www.cl.cam.ac.uk/research/dtg/attarchive/facedatabase.htm

[24] N. Sun, H. X. Wang, Z. H. Ji, C. R. Zou and L. Zhao, "An efficient algorithm for kernel two-dimensional principal component analysis," *Neural Comput & Applic.*, 17, pp. 59-64, 2008.

[25] Y. Xu, D. Zhang, J. Yang and J. Y. Yang, "An approach for directly extracting features from matrix data and its application in face recognition," *Neurocomputing*, 71, pp. 1857-1865, Feb, 2008.

SESSION

SEGMENTATION ALGORITHMS AND APPLICATIONS

Chair(s)

TBA

Integration of Domain Specific Information in the Form of Color Homogeneity into MRF Based Image Segmentation

Özge Öztimur Karadağ, Fatoş T. Yarman Vural
Department of Computer Engineering, Middle East Technical University, 06531 Ankara, Turkey
oztimur@ceng.metu.edu.tr, vural@ceng.metu.edu.tr

Abstract— *We propose a Markov Random Field based image segmentation method which integrates domain specific information into MRF energy. The proposed segmentation method assumes that there is no labeled training set, but some priori general information referred as domain specific information about the dataset, is available. Domain specific information is received from a domain expert and formalized by a mathematical representation. The type of information and its representation depends on the content of the image dataset to be segmented. The proposed method, combines top-down and bottom-up segmentation approaches by associating the domain specific information into the MRF energy function in an unsupervised framework. Due to the inclusion of domain specific information, this approach can be considered as a first step to semantic image segmentation under an unsupervised MRF model. The proposed system is compared with the state of the art unsupervised image segmentation methods quantitatively via two evaluation metrics; consistency error and probabilistic rand index and satisfactory results are obtained.*

Keywords: MRF based image segmentation, domain specific information

1. Introduction

In the last decade, majority of the studies in the literature handle image segmentation and object recognition tasks simultaneously [?]. In these studies, top-down and bottom-up approaches are employed cooperatively and segmentation is enriched by information gathered from recognition or detection tasks. For this purpose, Markov Random Fields are employed in majority of the studies since they provide a neat framework for incorporation of information in various forms.

A group of MRF based methods employs a supervised approach to image segmentation problem by utilizing labeled datasets. They construct complicated energy functions which include various image features and relations among image parts. At the output, they provide labels for all image pixels. A second group of studies, takes an unsupervised approach and construct a relatively simpler energy function. The major difference between these two approaches is the availability of image labels. In most of the real life problems, labeling the images is not practical or possible. On the other hand, depending on the application domain one may extract a set of domain specific information which can be employed to guide the segmentation process. Remote sensing applications are good examples of such data sets, where one seeks a group of objects in a highly cluttered background. For instance, if the goal is to detect the airplanes or airports in a remotely sensed image, the unsupervised segmentation algorithms are quite naive to extract the airport regions or airplanes with a complete segmentation method. Similarly, supervised segmentation approaches require large amount of labeled data. Even if the sufficient labeled data is available, due to the large within class variances, supervised segmentation algorithms fail to extract the targeted objects. However, if one can employ a priori domain specific information into the segmentation method, it is more likely that the object of interest is extracted in whole regions. For example, it is well known that runways consists of two parallel lines and airports are constructed in a planar regions. This information is easily formalized by a mathematical model and can be employed in the segmetation algorithm. Similarly, in an image database of animals, we know that zebras have stripes, but we may not have a labeled set of zebras. In this study, this type of information about the problem domain is referred as *domain specific information*, and it can be represented in a wide range of mathematical forms, such as, a set of relations among the certain image parts, or basic image features such as color, texture or shape. For example, prior information indicating that *'image dataset to be processed consists of textured image parts'* is a kind of domain specific information.

2. Related Work

Markov Random Fields are first proposed as an image processing method by Geman and Geman [3] in 1984. They fomulate image segmentation in Markov Framework and showed that this problem can be modeled as a Gibbs Distribution. Majority of the studies in the literature employ a double clique model by employing first two terms of *equation 1*.

$$E(x) = \sum_{i \in S} \psi_i(x_i) + \sum_{i \in S, j \in N_i} \psi_{ij}(x_i, x_j) + \sum_{c \in C} \psi_c(x_c) \quad (1)$$

Here, S is the set of all image pixels corresponding to sites, N is a neighborhood system and x_i denotes the labelling of pixel i. In this equation, the first term, referred as unary potential, is generally defined as the negative log likelihood of a label being assigned to pixel i. In this part, it is assumed that the features follow Gaussian distribution and various features are utilized for this term [5], [4] whose formula is given in *equation 2*.

$$\psi_i(x_i) = \sum_{i \in S} \ln(\sqrt{2\pi}\sigma_{x_i}) + \frac{(i-\mu_{x_i})^2}{2(\sigma_{x_i})^2} \quad (2)$$

The second term, referred as pairwise potential or double clique, models the relations between neighboring image pixels or superpixels. It is a smoothness term which is usually modeled via Potts model. It takes zero if same label is assigned to two neighboring sites, otherwise it takes one or some positive value ï£ijβ as in *equation 3*.

$$\psi_{ij}(x_i, x_j) = \begin{cases} 0 & \text{if } x_i = x_j \\ 1 & \text{otherwise} \end{cases} \quad (3)$$

Various versions of Potts model are encountered in the literature. One direct modification is contrast sensitive Potts model [4], where the function takes a value, based on the level of difference between two neighboring sites.

The third term of Equation 1 is higher order potential, which is used in some studies for modeling high level dependencies in image. For this term, Kohli et. al. introduce region consistency potential which measures the level of consensus in labelings of pixels belonging to same superpixel group[4], [6].

Energy of MRF system is minimized usually by Simulated Annealing or Iterated Conditional Modes. Due to its stochastic nature, simulated annealing converges slowly. For this reason, Besag [7] proposed Iterated Conditional Modes for minimizing MRF energy, which is a deterministic algorithm based on the idea of optimizing local energy iteratively. On the other hand, graph cut based energy minimization methods propose fast approximate solutions for MRF based image segmentation [2].

3. MRF Based Segmentation Augmented with Domain Specific Information

3.1 Motivation

Our goal is to propose an MRF based image segmentation system which can be employed in applications where labels are not present, but some priori information about the given problem domain is available. This information, referred as domain specific information, may be represented in various forms and may be employed via different techniques. In this study, we consider the application areas where this type of expert information is available and assume that this information can be represented by some mathematical tools, such as low level image features, spatial relationships among the object of interest, general structure of background clutter.

The novelty of this study is the incorporation of high level information into segmentation process in an unsupervised framework. This is possible only if expert knowledge about given problem is available. If this is the case, then the system initially detects certain image parts via object detection, shape detection or obtain an initial labeling for the image using certain low level image features which is specified by domain expert. This initial labeling is later utilized in MRF based segmentation.

3.2 System Architecture and Energy Function

Initially, image is oversegmented by Mean Shift segmentation to obtain superpixels. Set of superpixels are represented as Equation 4 where N is the number of superpixels. For each superpixel, its Cie-Lab color features are estimated as the mean value of L, a, b channels separately, and each superpixel is represented by a three dimensional color feature. After that, a fine segmentation is obtained by Mean Shift. For this purpose, minimum region area parameter of Mean Shift segmentation is adjusted such that the number of regions is equal to a predefined number of regions K. This fine segmentation is represented as Equation 5 and for each region p_k with label ξ, mean and covariance of L, a, b values are estimated.

$$S_0 = \{s_i\}_{i=1}^{N} \quad (4)$$

$$S_1 = \{\{p_k, \xi\} | p_k = \cup s_j, \forall s_j \in p_k, \xi \in [1, K]\}_{k=1}^{M} \quad (5)$$

Domain specific information may be in various forms, it may be related to low level image features or it may be related to objects, object parts or shapes in the image. Regardless of its form, domain specific information is presented through predicates. Predicates are defined on superpixels as in Equation 6. In this equation, superpixels are clustered based on a certain property $\wp$ defined by the predicate P. This property may be related to color, texture or shape features of the superpixel or it may be related to the response of the superpixel for a specific object detector. In this way, superpixels are grouped to obtain **Domain Specific Map** as defined in Equation 7. In this equation, m_t is a set of superpixels satisfying predicate P_c which are assigned the same label ℓ. Available domain information may be presented through a set of predicates instead of a single predicate. In that case, for each piece of domain specific information a predicate is defined and a corresponding Domain Specific Map, DSM_c, is obtained. For example if domain expert states that image consists of homogenous regions then a domain specific map may be constructed as thresholding of the color histogram of that image. In this case, predicate is defined by a single property which states that superpixels with similar color values belong to the same region. In another domain, expert may provide

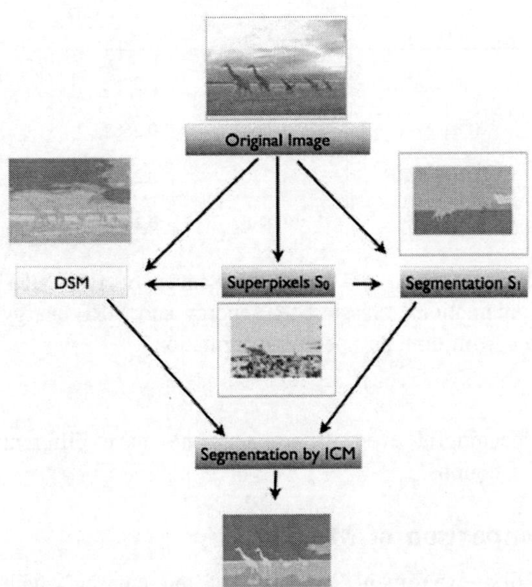

Fig. 1: System Architecture: For a given image, superpixels S_0 is obtained. A segmentation with K regions is obtained and mapped to S_0 to obtain S_1. Domain specific information is utilized on S_0 to obtain Domain Specific Map DSM. Information gathered from S_0, S_1 and DSM is employed on MRF energy in Equation 8 which is minimized by ICM.

information about objects in the imge, in which case object detector is employed and the output of the object detector indicating which superpixels belong to the stated object is utilized as domain specific map.

$$P_c(\cup s_i) = \begin{cases} TRUE & \text{if } \forall s_i \text{ satisfies property } \wp \\ FALSE & otherwise \end{cases} \tag{6}$$

$$DSM_c = \{\{m_t, \ell\} = \cup s_i | P_c(\cup s_i) = TRUE, \forall s_i \in m_t\}_{t=1}^{T} \tag{7}$$

After all the information from S_0, S_1 and DSM is gathered as shown in Figure 1, a random labeling L is assigned to superpixels which is iteratively updated by Iterated Conditional Modes in order to minimize MRF energy provided in *Equation 8*. In this equation, first term is constructed using CIELab color features and classical unary potentail as in *Equation 2*. Here, s_i is superpixel and l_i is its label in L. Second term is a smoothness term, which integrates domain specific information through *Equation 9*. Here, ψ functions are Potts models in two different labelings, L and DSM, l_i and l_j are the labels of superpixel s_i and s_j at L while ℓ_i and ℓ_j are the labels of that superpixels at DSM. The idea is that, while assigning a value to the second term by means of Potts model, the system does not only take into account the current segmentation L, but it also considers the domain specific map DSM.

$$E(x) = \sum_{s_i \in S_0} \psi_{s_i}(s_i, l_i) + \sum_{s_j \in S_0, s_i \in N_j} \phi(l_i, l_j, \ell_i, \ell_j) \tag{8}$$

$$\phi(l_i, l_j, \ell_i, \ell_j) = \phi(\psi_{ij}(l_i, l_j) \cap \psi_{ij}(\ell_i, \ell_j)) = \begin{cases} 0 & \text{if } l_i = l_j \wedge \ell_i = \ell_j \\ 1 & \text{otherwise} \end{cases} \tag{9}$$

ICM is run with R restarts and the segmentation result with minimum energy is selected among these R runs of ICM. Steos of the proposed system is provided in Algorithm 1.

Algorithm 1 Steps of DS-MRF

```
obtain S_0 by Mean Shift
estimate features for each superpixel μ
obtain S_1 by Mean Shift
for each label ξ_j do
    estimate model parameters (μ,Σ) from S_1
end for
obtain S_2 by Mean Shift
for each predicate P_c do
    obtain (DSM)_c
end for
DSM = ⋃(DSM)_c
for t from 1 to R do
    initialize a random labeling L
    for each superpixel s_i in S_0 do
        for each label l_j do
            estimate local MRF energy of s_i for l_j by Equation 8
        end for
        select label l* that minimizes the energy
    end for
end for
select configuration L* with the minimum energy
```

4. Experiments

The proposed system is run on Berkeley Segmentation Dataset [8] which is widely used for segmentation evaluation. The dataset consists of 300 images each of which have five to seven groundtruth segmentations. The dataset contains images from various domains; people, animals, scene etc. Although the images do not have a common property or they do not belong to same domain, it is assumed that color features are distinctive for the given dataset. In other words, domain specific information is assumed as 'Images in the dataset have homogenous regions' and for each image, distinctive color is selected among R, G, B channels by Karhunen Loeve Transform and thredholding based segmentation is applied, whose result is further utilized as DSM.

4.1 Segmentation Evaluation

4.1.1 Consistency Error

Given two segmentations masks of an image, consistency error measures the level of consistency among them. For each pixel p_i, segment S_1 containing this pixel in the first segmentation and the segment S_2 containing this pixel in the second segmentation are compared. Either there is a refinement relation between two segments, or there are overlapping pixels in two segments. Consistency between two segments are measured with *equation 10*.

$$E(S_1, S_2, p_i) = \frac{|R(S_1, p_i) \setminus R(S_2, p_i)|}{R(S_1, p_i)} \quad (10)$$

Here "\" is set difference operator which is non-symmetric. Using this local error measure, two error measures are defined first one is Global Consistency Error (GCE), which is provided in *equation 11*, and second measure is Local Consistency Error(LCE), which is given in *equation 12*.

$$GCE(S_1, S_2) = \frac{1}{n} min\left\{\sum_i E(S_1, S_2, p_i), \sum_i E(S_2, S_1, p_i)\right\} \quad (11)$$

$$LCE(S_1, S_2) = \frac{1}{n} \sum_i \{min\,\{E(S_1, S_2, p_i), E(S_2, S_2, p_i)\}\,. \quad (12)$$

GCE and LCE take values in the range [0,1] where values close to 0 indicates high segmentation performance. There are only two misleading cases; first one occurs if image has only one region, in which case consistency error return 0 and the other one occurs if there are N regions, where all pixels are assigned to different regions, in which case again consistency error is 0. In other words, if there is a refinement relation between two regions then consistency error is $zero$. Consistency errors are informative if two segmentations have approximately the same number of regions.

4.1.2 Probabilistic Rand Index

Probabilistic Rand Index (PRI) takes pixels in pairs and measures the ratio of compatibly labeled pixels in segmentations S_{test} and ground truth segmentations S_k with *equation 13*.

$$PR(S_{test}, \{S_k\}) = \frac{1}{\binom{N}{2}} \sum_{i<j} [c_{ij} p_{ij} + (1 - c_{ij})(1 - p_{ij})] \quad (13)$$

Here, N is the number of pixels in image, c_{ij} is the event of a pair of pixels i and j having the same label in image S_{test} and p_{ij} is the ground truth probability of two pixels having the same label estimated over all ground truth segmentations of the image. PRI takes values in the interval [0,1], where values close to 1 indicates high segmentation performance.

Method	PRI	GCE
N-Cut	0.5313	0.2052
Mean Shift	0.5649	0.2682
Classic MRF	0.7769	0.2353
DS-MRF	**0.8582**	**0.1884**

Table 1: Comparison of the Performances of two MRF based segmentations; classic MRF energy and MRF energy augmented with domain specific information

PRI is meaningful even if two segments have different number of regions.

4.2 Comparison of Methods

As a first experiment, a subset of the dataset which conforms with the provided domain specific information is selected. For this purpose 100 images which have homogenous regions are selected among 300 images. These images are selected both by visual inspection and by considering segmentation performance of the proposed system. In this experiment, proposed system is compared with three systems from the literature. First system is NCut Segmentation [13], second system is Mean Shift Segmentation [11] and the third system is the MRF based segmentation with a classic MRF energy which have Potts model for pairwise potential. Contribution of domain specific information is clearly presented by the comparison of these four systems via PRI and GCE as given in Table 1.

In the second experimental setup, proposed system is compared with three state of the art image processing methods over the whole dataset of 300 images; Mean Shift Segmentation [11], Normalized Cut Segmentation [13] and Efficient Graph Based Segmentation [15]. Publicly available systems [12], [14], [16] are utilized for implementation of the algorithms. Parameters of algorithms are selected based on the study of Pantofaru et al. [10], [9]. Number of regions is set as 5 for each algorithm. Spatial bandwidth parameter for Mean Shift segmentation is set as $h_s = 7$ while range bandwidth parameter is set as $h_r = \{3, 7, 11, 15, 19, 23\}$. Merge threshold criteria of Efficient Graph Based Segmentation is set as $k = \{5, 25, 50, 100\}$. Segmentation performance of these methods are compared via PRI and GCE as provided in *Table 2*. Parameters maximizing PRI and minimizing GCE are selected for each algorithm. Although the initial assumption on domain specific information is not true for all images in the dataset, MRF augmented with domain specific information (DS-MRF) obtained segmentation results that are competitive with state of the art unsupervised segmentation methods. Here, GCE is not as informative as PRI since number of regions varies among ground truth segmentation and the segmentation result.

Method	PRI	GCE
Mean Shift [11]	0.7477	0.2592
N-Cut [13], [14]	0.6836	0.3092
EGS [15], [16]	0.5756	0.0844
DS-MRF	**0.7415**	**0.2930**

Table 2: Comparison of the Performances of Suggested Domain Specific Segmentation Method with Mean Shift, N-cut and EGS methods

In Table 2 performance of two methods Mean Shift and DS-MRF are very close. DS-MRF is advantegous in terms of its robustness to parameters. In this experiment, S_0 and S_1 segmentations are obtained by Mean Shift by setting spatial and range bandwidth as 2 and changing the value of minimum region area. Hence, DS-MRF start with a random labeling and by employing a partially valid domain specific information, it obtains a segmentation with a similar accuracy as Mean Shift. Here, domain specific information is considered as partially valid since the assumption of color homogeneity is not true for all images and all regions.

Although the actual contribution of the proposed system is demostrated in the first experiment which is run on a smaller set of images that conform with the specified domain information, second experiment points out that DS-MRF is competitive with state of the art segmentation systems even if domain specific information is partially valid.

4.3 Segmentation Examples

In this study, it is assumed that color information is distinctive features of the given dataset. This assumption is true for a part of the dataset while it is not true for the rest of the dataset. In this section we provide results, indicating the effect of incorpotation of domain specific information into segmentation process. Segmentation results with high segmentation performance are provided at Table 3, while segmentations with low PRI are provided at Table 4. Considering the domain specific information regarding color features, the system obtains meaningful segmentations for images which have distinctive color information as provided in Table 3. While the system obtains unrealiable segmentations for images whose color information is not informative, as shown in Table 4.

Provided that a discriminating color channel is detected among R, G and B channels, an accurate segmentation is obtained. The required color information can be realized through visual inspection of these images. On the other hand, if image does not have discriminating color information then meaningful segmentation is not obtained by DS-MRF. Nevertheless, other systems whose results are also provided at Table 4 do not perform better than DS-MRF for those images.

Table 3: Images with high segmentation accuracy: First row is the original images and the following rows are the segmentation results for DS-MRF, Mean Shift, EG and N-Cut respectively.

5. Conclusion and Future Work

In this study, an unsupervised MRF based image segmentation system is proposed and competitive results with state of the art segmentation methods is obtained. The contribution of this study is to embed the domain specific information into the MRF energy function in a simple but effective way. Although the domain information assumed in the experiments is not true for all images, competitive results are obtained for overall dataset. And high segmentation accuracy is obtained for a selected set of images with provided domain specific property.

Throughout the experiments in this study, it is assumed that only one specification is available and it is related to color homogeneity, hence only one domain specific segmentation is obtained and incorporated into the MRF energy. Although the domain specific information assumed in this study is represented through simple predicates, more complex domain specific information may be available. Moreover, a set of domain specific information may be available in which case for each piece of information a distinct map need to be obtained and integrated to MRF energy.

This study can be considered as a first step to unsupervised

Table 4: Images with low segmentation accuracy: First row is the original images and the following rows are the segmentation results for DS-MRF, Mean Shift, EG and N-Cut respectively.

semantic segmentation systems where semantic information is introduced via the energy function without a training phase. In this preliminary study, the domain specific information is modeled by the color band thresholding. However, depending on the problem domain more sophisticated models can be incorporated in the energy function.

References

[1] Simon Fear. (2005). Publication quality tables in LaTeX. [Online]. Available: http://www.ctan.org/tex-archive/macros/latex/contrib/booktabs/booktabs.pdf

[2] Boykov, Y.; Veksler, O.; Zabih, R., "Fast approximate energy minimization via graph cuts," Pattern Analysis and Machine Intelligence, IEEE Transactions on , vol.23, no.11, pp.1222,1239, Nov 2001

[3] Geman S.,Geman D., Stochastic Relaxation, Gibbs Distributions, and the Bayesian Restoration of Images. IEEE Transactions on Pattern Analysis and Machine Intelligence, Vol. PAMI-6(6):721-741, November 1984

[4] Kohli, P.; Ladicky, L.; Torr, P.; , "Robust higher order potentials for enforcing label consistency," Computer Vision and Pattern Recognition, 2008. CVPR 2008. IEEE Conference on , vol., no., pp.1-8, 23-28 June 2008

[5] Zoltan Kato, Ting Chuen Pong, and John Chung Mong Lee. Color Image Segmentation and Parameter Estimation in a Markovian Framework. Pattern Recognition Letters, 22(3-4):309–321, March 2001.

[6] LadickyÌĄ, L.; Russell, C.; Kohli, P.; Torr, P.H.S.; , "Associative hierarchical CRFs for object class image segmentation," Computer Vision, 2009 IEEE 12th International Conference on , vol., no., pp.739-746, Sept. 29 2009-Oct. 2 2009

[7] Besag, J. "Spatial Interaction and the Statistical Analysis of Lattice Systems", Journal of the Royal Statistical Society, (1974) Series B, 36 (2), 192âĂŞ236.

[8] Martin, David R. and Fowlkes, Charless and Tal, Doron and Malik, Jitendra, A Database of Human Segmented Natural Images and its Application to Evaluating Segmentation Algorithms and Measuring Ecological Statistics, 2001, Technical Report, EECS Department University of California, Berkeley,

[9] Unnikrishnan, Ranjith and Pantofaru, Caroline and Hebert, Martial. Toward Objective Evaluation of Image Segmentation Algorithms. In IEEE Trans. Pattern Anal. Mach. Intell., (29) 6: 929-944, Year 2007.

[10] C. Pantofaru and M. Hebert, A Comparison of Image Segmentation Algorithms, The Robotics Institute, Carnegie Mellon University, Number CMU-RI-TR-05-40, 2005.

[11] D. Comaniciu, P. Meer, Mean Shift: A Robust Approach Toward Feature Space Analysis, IEEE Transactions on Pattern Analysis and Machine Intelligence Volume 24 Issue 5, May 2002, Page 603-619

[12] C. Christoudias, B. Georgescu, P. Meer: "Synergism in low-level vision." 16th International Conference on Pattern Recognition, Quebec City, Canada, August 2002, vol. IV, 150-155.

[13] Jianbo Shi, Jitendra Malik, "Normalized Cuts and Image Segmentation," IEEE Transactions on Pattern Analysis and Machine Intelligence, vol. 22, no. 8, pp. 888-905, Aug. 2000

[14] Timothee Cour, Stella Yu, Jianbo Shi, Normalized Cut Segmentation Code, Copyright 2004 University of Pennsylvania, Computer and Information Science Department

[15] Pedro F. Felzenswalb and Daniel P. Huttenlocher, Efficient Graph-Based Image Segmentation, International Journal of Computer Vision, Volume 59, Number 2, Septenber 2004

[16] Su Dongcai, Efficient Graph Based Image Segmentation Code, http://www.mathworks.com/matlabcentral/fileexchange/29299-efficient-graph-based-image-segmentation

BYY Harmony Learning of t Mixtures and Its Application to Unsupervised Image Segmentation

Chenglin Liu, Zhijie Ren, and Jinwen Ma
Department of Information Science, School of Mathematical Sciences
Peking University, Beijing, 100871, China
Email:jwma@math.pku.edu.cn

Abstract—*Bayesian Ying-Yang(BYY) harmony learning system and theory is a new kind of statistical learning approach. It has shown great advantages of parameter learning and model selection on finite mixture modeling. In this paper, we extend the BYY learning system to multivariate t mixtures and propose a gradient BYY harmony learning algorithm for t mixtures. Via optimizing the harmony function, this algorithm can determine the number of actual components during the parameter learning. Simulation experiments demonstrate that the algorithm is accurate and stable for model selection and parameter estimation. It is also robust to initializations, and suitable for model selection on high dimensional and multi-class datasets. Moreover, it is successfully applied to unsupervised image segmentation and exhibits a better segmentation performance in comparison with some typical existing algorithms.*

Keywords: Bayesian Ying-Yang (BYY) harmony learning, Multivariate t mixture, Parameter estimation, model selection, Image segmentation.

1. Introduction

Finite mixture model is a powerful tool for statistical data modeling. It has been widely applied to pattern recognition, signal processing and image analysis [1]. In finite mixture model, data are viewed as arising from a linear mixture of two or more populations or components with certain mixing proportions. Two major problems of finite mixture modeling are model selection and parameter learning. Actually, model selection is to determine the number of components in the mixture, while parameter learning tries to iteratively estimate the parameters of the component distributions as well as the mixing proportions. In order to determine a proper component number, a common way is to find the optimal component number via a certain selection criterion among a list of candidate component numbers. However, this method requires the numerous repeated parameter learning processes and needs a large computational cost.

In the light of the Bayesian Ying-Yang (BYY) harmony learning system and theory [2], a new learning mechanism has been developed to tackle such a finite mixture modeling problem with automatically model selection during the parameter learning. In fact, the modeling problem of Gaussian mixture has been solved with a BI-directional architecture of the BYY learning system for finite mixture [3]. Moreover, the conjugate, adaptive, and fixed-point learning algorithms [4]-[6] were further proposed to improve the efficiency of maximizing the harmony function. All of these methods can automatically allocate an appropriate number of Gaussianss to a given dataset, with the mixing proportions of the extra Gaussians attenuating to zero. Methodically, this BYY harmony learning approach can be further applied to any types of non-Gaussian mixtures and has been implemented on Poisson mixture [7] and Weibull mixture [8].

In this paper, we extend the BYY harmony learning mechanism to multivariate t mixtures. Under a BI-architecture of the BYY learning system for multivariate t mixtures, a (batch-way) gradient learning algorithm is proposed to achieve the parameter learning and automated model selection. Simulation experiments are performed to demonstrate performance of the gradient BYY learning algorithm. Moreover, this approach is successfully applied to unsupervised image segmentation.

2. Methods

In this section, we firstly describe the form of t distribution as well as t mixture. Then, we introduce the BI-architecture of the BYY learning system and derive the gradient BYY harmony learning algorithm for multivariate t mixtures.

2.1 Multivariate t Mixture

In statistics, a multivariate t distribution is a multivariate generalization of Student's t distribution. For the case of d dimensionality, if y and U are independent and distributed as $\mathcal{N}(0, \Sigma)$ and χ^2_ν, respectively, Σ is a $d \times d$ matrix and $\nu > 0$, let $x = y\sqrt{\nu/U} + \mu$, then x is subject to a multivariate t distribution with parameters $\{\Sigma, \mu, \nu\}$ and has the following density function:

$$f(x) = \frac{\Gamma(\frac{\nu+d}{2})|\Sigma|^{-\frac{1}{2}}}{(\pi\nu)^{\frac{d}{2}}\Gamma(\frac{\nu}{2})[1+\nu^{-1}\delta(x,\mu,\Sigma)]^{\frac{\nu+d}{2}}}, \quad (1)$$

where $\delta(x, \mu, \Sigma) = (x-\mu)^T\Sigma^{-1}(x-\mu)$.

A finite mixture distribution is defined as a probabilistic model with two or more component distributions mixed linearly in certain proportions, which can be expressed by

$$q(x|\Theta_k) = \sum_{j=1}^{k} \alpha_j q(x|\theta_j), \tag{2}$$

where $q(x|\theta_j)$ denotes component probability distribution with parameter θ_j, k denotes the number of components in the mixture, x denotes the variable, and $\alpha_j \geq 0$ denotes the proportion of the component with the constraint that $\sum_{j=1}^{k} \alpha_j = 1$. All parameters in the mixture model can be denoted as a set $\Theta_k = \{\alpha_j, \theta_j\}_{j=1}^{k}$.

If all $q(x|\theta_j)$ in Eq.(2) are multivariate t distributions, the finite mixture becomes a multivariate t mixture (t mixture) expressed as follows:

$$q(x|\Psi) = \sum_{j=1}^{k} \alpha_j q(x|\theta_j) = \sum_{j=1}^{k} \alpha_j f(x|\mu_j, \Sigma_j, \nu_j), \tag{3}$$

where Ψ is the set of all parameters and $\Psi = (\alpha_1, \ldots, \alpha_k, \theta_1, \ldots, \Theta_k)$, $\theta_j = \{\mu_j, \Sigma_j, \nu_j\}$.

2.2 Gradient BYY Harmony Learning Algorithm

We consider an observation $x \in \mathcal{X} \subset \mathcal{R}^n$ and its inner representation $y \in \mathcal{Y} \subset \mathcal{R}^m$. The BYY learning system tries to describe the relationship of these two parts via two types of Bayesian decomposition of the joint density: $p(x, y) = p(x)p(y|x)$ and $q(x, y) = q(y)q(x|y)$, which are called Yang machine and Ying machine, respectively [3], [5].

The goal of harmony learning on a BYY system is to extract the hidden probabilistic structure of x with the help of y by specifying all aspects of $p(y|x)$, $p(x)$, $q(x|y)$ and $q(y)$ together. The harmony learning principle is implemented by maximizing the functional:

$$H(p \parallel q) = \int p(y|x)p(x) \ln[q(x|y)q(y)]dxdy. \tag{4}$$

If both $p(y|x)$ and $q(x|y)$ are parametric, i.e, from a family of probability densities with parameter θ, the BYY learning system is said to have a BI-directional architecture (BI-architecture). Given sample set $D_x = \{x_t\}_{t=1}^{N}$, the following specific BI-architecture is utilized in the BYY learning system. The inner representation y is discrete, $\mathcal{Y} = \{1, 2, \ldots, k\}$; the observation $x \in \mathcal{R}^d$ is generated from a t mixture distribution. On the Ying space, we let $q(y = j) = \alpha_j \geq 0$ with $\sum_{j=1}^{k} \alpha_j = 1$. On the Yang space, we assume that $p(x)$ is a blind d-dimensional t mixture from which a set of sample data D_x is generated. Moreover, in the Ying path, we let each $q(x|y = j) = q(x|\theta_j)$ be a d-dimensional t distribution with parameter θ_j consisting of all its parameters. On the other hand, the Yang path can be constructed under the Bayesian principle by the following parametric form:

$$p(y = j|x) = \frac{\alpha_j q(x|\theta_j)}{q(x|\Theta_k)}, \qquad q(x|\Theta_k) = \sum_{j=1}^{k} \alpha_j q(x|\theta_j), \tag{5}$$

where $\Theta_k = \{\alpha_j, \theta_j\}_{j=1}^{k}$ and $q(x|\Theta_k)$ is just a t mixture model that will approximate the true t mixture $p(x)$.

With all these component densities into Eq.(4) and based on the given sample data set D_x, we get an estimate of $H(p\|q)$ by

$$J(\Theta_k) = \frac{1}{N} \sum_{t=1}^{N} \sum_{j=1}^{k} \frac{\alpha_j q(x_t|\theta_j)}{\sum_{i=1}^{k} \alpha_i q(x_t|\theta_i)} \ln[\alpha_j q(x_t|\theta_j)], \tag{6}$$

where $q(x_t|\theta_j)$ is a d-dimensional t distribution with parameters $\theta_j = \{\mu_j, \Sigma_j, \nu_j\}$. In the following, we will estimate the parameters and determine the proper component number k. According to the BYY harmony learning principle, maximizing the harmony function $J(\Theta_k)$ for t mixture can lead to automatic model selection with parameter learning. This allows the maximizing or learning process to match the estimate mixture to the actual distribution. As long as the initial value k is larger than the actual component number k^*, it can force the mixing proportions of the other $k - k^*$ extra components to attenuate to zero. To implement this, we will construct a gradient BYY learning algorithm to maximize the harmony function $J(\Theta_k)$ in the following.

For convenience, we define $U_j(x) = \alpha_j q(x|\theta_j)$ for $j = 1, 2, \ldots, k$. The harmony function $J(\Theta_k)$ is represented as

$$J(\Theta_k) = \frac{1}{N} \sum_{t=1}^{N} J_t(\Theta_k) = \frac{1}{N} \sum_{t=1}^{N} \sum_{j=1}^{k} \frac{U_j(x_t)}{\sum_{i=1}^{k} U_i(x_t)} \ln U_j(x_t). \tag{7}$$

Moreover, a so-called softmax representation is utilized to get rid of the constraints on α_j:

$$\alpha_j = \frac{e^{\beta_j}}{\sum_{i=1}^{k} e^{\beta_j}}, j = 1, \ldots, k, \tag{8}$$

where $-\infty < \beta_1, \ldots, \beta_k < +\infty$. Then, we obtain the partial derivatives of $J(\Theta_k)$ with respect to β_j and $\theta_j = \{\mu_j, \Sigma_j, \nu_j\}$ at sample point x_t as:

$$\frac{\partial J_t(\Theta_k)}{\partial \beta_j} = \frac{1}{q(x_t|\Theta_k)} \sum_{i=1}^{k} [1 - \sum_{l=1}^{k} (p(l|x_t) - \delta_{il}) \ln U_l(x_t)] \cdot (\delta_{ij} - \alpha_j) U_i(x_t), \tag{9}$$

$$\frac{\partial J_t(\Theta_k)}{\partial \theta_j} = \frac{1}{q(x_t|\Theta_k)} [1 - \sum_{l=1}^{k} (p(l|x_t) - \delta_{jl}) \ln U_l(x_t)] \cdot \alpha_j \frac{\partial q(x_t|\theta_j)}{\partial \theta_j}, \tag{10}$$

where δ_{ij} is the Kronecker function.

Letting

$$\lambda_i(t) = 1 - \sum_{l=1}^{k}(p(l|x_t) - \delta_{il}) \ln U_l(x_t), i = 1, \ldots, k, \quad (11)$$

and according to Eqs.(9)-(10), we have the following gradient BYY harmony learning rules to the dataset $D_x = \{x_t\}_{t=1}^N$:

$$\Delta\beta_j = \frac{\eta}{N}\sum_{t=1}^{N}\frac{1}{q(x_t|\Theta_k)}\sum_{i=1}^{k}\lambda_i(t)(\delta_{ij} - \alpha_j)U_i(x_t), \quad (12)$$

$$\Delta\theta_j = \frac{\eta}{N}\sum_{t=1}^{N} p(j|x_t)\lambda_j(t)\frac{\partial \ln q(x_t|\theta_j)}{\partial\theta_j}, \quad (13)$$

where $\eta > 0$ denotes the learning rate. Here, η starts from a reasonable initial value and then reduces to zero according to the following rules:

$$\eta^{new} = \begin{cases} 1.05 \times \eta^{old}, & J(\Theta^{new}) - J(\Theta^{old}) > 0; \\ 0.7 \times \eta^{old}, & \text{else.} \end{cases} \quad (14)$$

Based on Eq.(3) and $q(x_t|\theta_j) = q(x_t|\mu_j, \Sigma_j, \nu_j)$, we have the partial derivatives of the logarithm of t density function with respect to μ_j, Σ_j and ν_j in the following forms:

$$\frac{\partial \ln q(x_t|\mu_j, \Sigma_j, \nu_j)}{\partial\mu_j} = \frac{(\nu_j + d)\Sigma_j^{-1}(x_t - \mu_j)}{\nu_j + \delta(x_t, \mu_j, \Sigma_j)}, \quad (15)$$

$$\frac{\partial \ln q(x_t|\mu_j, \Sigma_j, \nu_j)}{\partial\Sigma_j} = -\frac{1}{2}[I_d - \frac{\Sigma_j^{-1}(x_t - \mu_j)(x_t - \mu_j)^T}{\nu_j + \delta(x_t, \mu_j, \Sigma_j)}]\Sigma_j^{-1} \quad (16)$$

$$\begin{aligned}\frac{\partial \ln q(x_t|\mu_j, \Sigma_j, \nu_j)}{\partial\nu_j} &= \frac{1}{2}\{\Psi(\frac{\nu_j + d}{2}) - \frac{d}{\nu_j} - \Psi(\frac{\nu_j}{2}) \\ &- \ln[1 + \nu_j^{-1}\delta(x_t, \mu_j, \Sigma_j)] \\ &+ \frac{(\nu_j + d)\delta(x_t, \mu_j, \Sigma_j)}{\nu_j(\nu_j + \delta(x_t, \mu_j, \Sigma_j))}\},\end{aligned} \quad (17)$$

where $\Psi(z) = \frac{\partial \ln\Gamma(z)}{\partial z}$, I_d is a d-dimensional identity matrix. Substituting $\frac{\partial \ln q(x_t|\theta_j)}{\partial\theta_j}$ in Eq.(13) with Eq.(15), we can obtain the gradient BYY harmony learning rule of μ_j. To guarantee Σ_j be positive definite after each iteration, we set $\Sigma_j = B_j B_j^T$, where B_j is a nonsingular square matrix [4]. The rule of B_j is as follows:

$$\begin{aligned}\Delta vec B_j =& \frac{\eta}{2N}\sum_{i=1}^{N}[p(j|x_t)\lambda_j(t)\frac{\partial(B_j B_j^T)}{\partial B_j} \\ & vec\{-[I_n - \frac{\Sigma_j^{-1}(x_t - \mu_j)(x_t - \mu_j)^T}{\nu_j + \delta(x_t, \mu_j, \Sigma_j)}]\Sigma_j^{-1}\}],\end{aligned} \quad (18)$$

where $vec(M)$ denotes the vector obtained by stacking the column vector of the matrix M. Detailed expression of $\frac{\partial(B_j B_j^T)}{\partial B_j}$ can be found in [4].

Similarly, we utilize the transformation: $\nu_j = v_j^2$, $-\infty < v_j < \infty$ to guarantee $\nu_j > 0$. The learning rule of v_j is given as follows:

$$\begin{aligned}\Delta v_j =& \frac{\eta}{N}\sum_{t=1}^{N} p(j|x_t)\lambda_j(t)\{\Psi(\frac{\nu_j + d}{2}) - \frac{d}{\nu_j} \\ &- \ln[1 + \nu_j^{-1}\delta(x_t, \mu_j, \Sigma_j)] \\ &- \Psi(\frac{\nu_j}{2}) + \frac{(\nu_j + d)\delta(x_t, \mu_j, \Sigma_j)}{\nu_j(\nu_j + \delta(x_t, \mu_j, \Sigma_j))}\}v_j.\end{aligned} \quad (19)$$

In each iteration, β_j, μ_j, B_j and v_j are updated according to the rule $\Phi_j^{new} = \Phi_j^{old} + \Delta\Phi_j, \Phi \in \{\beta, \mu, B, v\}$. The iteration will stop when it meet the stop criterion $|\Delta J| = |J(\Theta_k^{new}) - J(\Theta_k^{old})| < Threshold$.

3. Results

In this section, various simulation experiments are conducted to test the proposed gradient BYY harmony learning algorithm for t mixtures. Moreover, it is successfully applied to color image segmentation.

3.1 Simulation Experiments

In order to demonstrate the performance of the proposed algorithm on both model selection and parameter estimation, various simulation experiments are conducted on datasets with different sizes, component distributions, and degrees of overlap among the components. In addition, simulation experiments are also conducted on high dimensional and multi-class datasets.

3.1.1 Parameter Initialization

In the following simulation experiments, we set the initial learning rate $\eta_0 = 0.5$. Stop criterion threshold is set as $\Delta J < 5 \times 10^{-7}$. All mixing proportions should be larger than 0.05, that is, if $\alpha_j < 0.05$, the j-th component will be deleted directly and $k = k - 1$. Accordingly, the parameters of the other components will be modified. The initial values of $\{\beta_j\}_{j=1}^k$ are set to be equal or close, which makes the proposed algorithm converge efficiently. Moreover, B_j is initialized as identity matrix, v_j is set to be 1, and μ_j is initialed randomly via choosing one sample data as its initialization. In fact, we can give a better initialization for μ_j in terms of characteristics of the dataset in practical applications.

3.1.2 Stability and Robustness of the Proposed Algorithm on Model Selection

The aim of these simulation experiments is to demonstrate the stability of the proposed algorithm in parameter learning, the suitability in various data conditions, and the robustness to the initial parameters. Four 2D synthetic datasets S1-S4 are generated for the t mixtures with different conditions. The parameters of these t mixtures are listed in Table 1. A random selected data set of each type is shown in Fig.3(($\mathcal{S}_1$)-($\mathcal{S}_4$)).

Table 1: The parameters of the four 2D t mixtures $\mathcal{S}_1 - \mathcal{S}_4$, where N_j is the number of sample points for component j.

Set	j	μ_{j1}	μ_{j2}	σ^j_{11}	σ^j_{12}	σ^j_{22}	ν_j	α_j	N_j
$\mathcal{S}_1$	1	0	-3.0	0.50	0	0.50	3	0.25	400
	2	-3.0	0	0.50	0	0.50	3.5	0.25	400
	3	0	3.0	0.50	0	0.50	4	0.25	400
	4	3.0	0	0.50	0	0.50	4.5	0.25	400
$\mathcal{S}_2$	1	0	-3.0	0.45	-0.25	0.55	3	0.34	544
	2	-3.0	0	0.65	0.20	0.25	3.5	0.28	448
	3	0	3.0	1	0.10	0.35	4	0.22	352
	4	3.0	0	0.30	0.15	0.80	4.5	0.16	256
$\mathcal{S}_3$	1	2.5	0	0.20	-0.20	0.50	3	0.50	600
	2	0	2.5	0.40	0.10	0.20	3.5	0.30	360
	3	-1.5	-1.5	0.80	-0.20	0.30	4	0.20	240
$\mathcal{S}_4$	1	0	-3.0	0.28	-0.20	0.32	3	0.16	32
	2	-3.0	0	0.34	0.20	0.22	3.5	0.22	44
	3	0	3.0	0.50	0.04	0.12	4	0.28	56
	4	3.0	0	0.10	0.05	0.50	4.5	0.34	68

According to Table 1, $\mathcal{S}_1 - \mathcal{S}_4$ cover four different conditions. $\mathcal{S}_1$ is composed of four components with the same mixing proportion. The distributions of the four components are of the same variance but different means. $\mathcal{S}_2$ consists of four components with different proportions, and both the variances and the means are different among these distributions. $\mathcal{S}_3$ is composed of only three components, and $\mathcal{S}_4$ only includes 200 samples, which is a representation of small data set. The freedom degrees of the t distributions are different.

To determine the robustness to the proposed algorithm to the initial component number k, the following experiments adopt a set of k of values $\{k^*, 2k^*, 3k^*, 4k^*\}$ as the initial component number, where k^* was the actual component number. The proposed algorithm is conducted on each of the four synthetic datasets. The performances of the parameter learning are evaluated by relative square errors of each parameter μ, Σ, ν, α. For parameter $\{w_j\}_{j=1}^{k^*}$, let its actual value be $\{w_j^*\}_{j=1}^{k^*}$ and its estimation be $\{\hat{w}_j\}_{j=1}^{k^*}$, the relative square error of estimation Δw is defined as:

$$\Delta w = \sum_{j=1}^{k} \frac{|\hat{w}_j - w_j^*|^2}{|w_j^*|^2}. \quad (20)$$

The distribution of the relative square errors of the proposed algorithm on each dataset with different initial values is shown in Fig.1, where the rows denote $\mathcal{S}_1$-$\mathcal{S}_4$, respectively, the columns denote the different numbers of k, and the elments denote the corresponding relative square errors. Clearly, Fig.1 shows that the proposed algorithm can obtain accurate estimations of the parameters μ, Σ, α. The estimation of freedom degree ν is not as good as the others. This may be caused by the fact that the freedom degree of t distribution mainly reflects the tails of this distribution, which cannot be simulated well in synthetic data sets. In addition, the average relative square errors are consistent among the four datasets, which means that the proposed algorithm is suitable for various conditions. In $\mathcal{S}_4$, the relative square errors have large deviations, which indicates

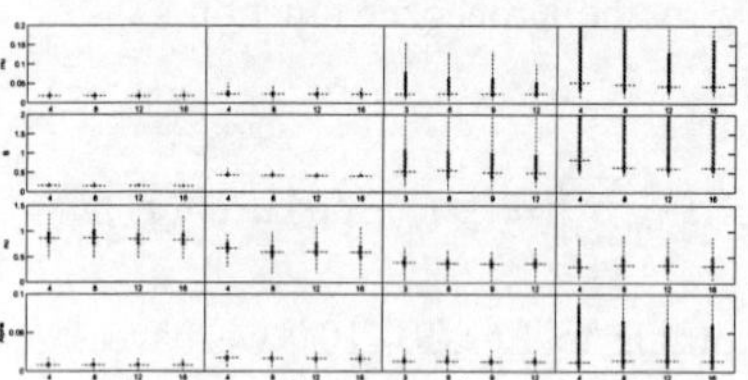

Fig. 1: The distributions of the relative square errors of parameter learning via the proposed algorithm on four datasets.

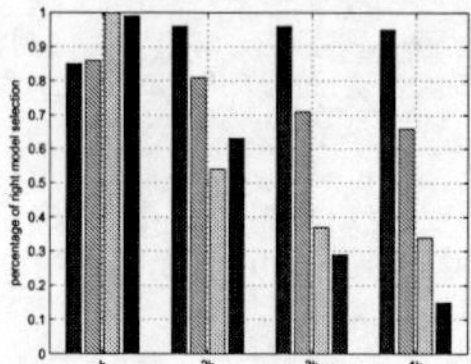

Fig. 2: The percentages of correct model selection of the proposed algorithm on four datasets.

that small data size may affect the stability of the algorithm. Moreover, the performance of the model selection is quite good, as shown in Fig.2. Actually, when $k \in [k^*, 3k^*]$, the proposed algorithm is robust to initializations, and can achieve correct model selection by attenuating the proportions of extra components to approximate zeros. However, when $k^* > 3k$, the proposed algorithm has more chance to choose a wrong component number. Therefore, we suggest the initialization of k satisfy $k^* < k < 3k^*$.

3.1.3 Influence of Overlap on 2D Model Selection

We further conduct the simulation experiments to evaluate the influence of overlap among the actual components on the performance of the proposed algorithm. Suppose that the size of two components are n1 and n2, respectively, and the total size of data set is n. Let $\alpha 1 = n1/n$ and $\alpha 2 = n2/n$, then the overlap between these two components can be computed via the following formula:

$$D^{12} = \frac{1}{n} \sum_{t=1}^{n} h_1(x_t) h_2(x_t), \quad (21)$$

where

$$h_j(x_t) = \frac{\alpha_j p(x_t|j)}{\alpha_1 p(x_t|1) + \alpha_2 p(x_t|2)}, \quad j = 1, 2. \quad (22)$$

In order to estimate the influence of the overlap degree on our model select method, we conduct simulation experiments on 16 datasets, including 4 previous datasets from $\mathcal{S}_1 - \mathcal{S}_4$, and 12 new datasets $\mathcal{S}_5 - \mathcal{S}_{16}$ generated from various t mixtures with different overlap degrees, as shown in Fig.3.

As compared to the previous 4 datasets $\mathcal{S}_1 - \mathcal{S}_4$, the overlap degrees of 12 new datasets $\mathcal{S}_5 - \mathcal{S}_{16}$ are relatively higher.

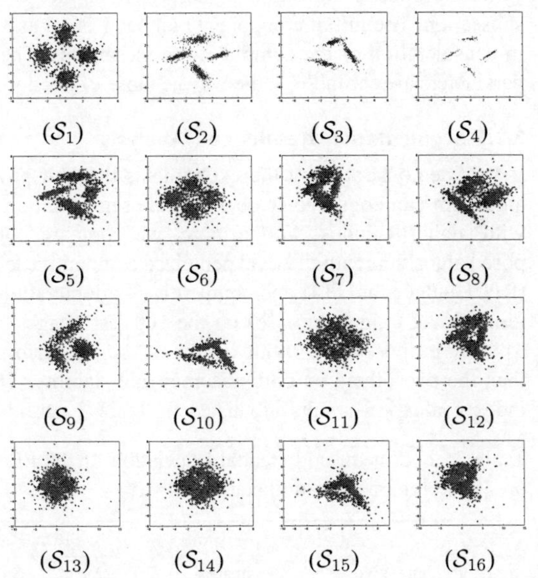

Fig. 3: Sixteen 2D t mixture datasets with different overlap degrees.

Table 2: The square errors of parameter estimation on 2D t mixture datasets $\mathcal{S}_1 - \mathcal{S}_{16}$ via the proposed algorithm.

Set	Overlap	$\Delta\mu$	$\Delta\Sigma$	$\Delta\alpha$
$\mathcal{S}_1$	0.0094	0.0073	0.1175	0.0017
$\mathcal{S}_2$	0.0098	0.0091	0.1337	0.0049
$\mathcal{S}_3$	0.0080	0.0059	0.1209	0.0016
$\mathcal{S}_4$	0.0015	0.0147	0.4303	0.0003
$\mathcal{S}_5$	0.0273	0.01829	0.16736	0.00571
$\mathcal{S}_6$	0.0354	0.00342	0.00897	0.00077
$\mathcal{S}_7$	0.0359	0.03360	0.05123	0.01989
$\mathcal{S}_8$	0.0369	0.01767	0.02113	0.01401
$\mathcal{S}_9$	0.0379	0.01910	0.02949	0.00689
$\mathcal{S}_{10}$	0.0430	0.01624	0.07575	0.01651
$\mathcal{S}_{11}$	0.0446	0.01577	0.02796	0.00108
$\mathcal{S}_{12}$	0.0561	0.06997	0.15257	0.04840
$\mathcal{S}_{13}$	0.0593	0.02853	0.19283	0.02649
$\mathcal{S}_{14}$	0.0761	0.11421	0.51857	0.55011
$\mathcal{S}_{15}$	0.0766	8.00712	1.25522	1.26347
$\mathcal{S}_{16}$	0.0784	3.07942	1.00916	0.16659

We implement the proposed algorithm on these 16 data sets. The initial value k is set as 7 for four-component datasets and 6 for three-component datasets. Table 2 lists the overlap degrees of each dataset, as well as the corresponding relative square errors of parameter μ, σ, α, respectively. Here, the overlap degree of a dataset is defined as the maximum overlap degree between any two components. According to Table 2, the increase of the overlap degree do not affect the proposed algorithm on model selection very much. However, it affects the parameter estimation. These and further experiments shows that the proposed algorithm has a good performance when the maximum of overlap degree is lower than 0.06. But the proposed algorithm hardly converges with correct model selection when the overlap degree is larger than 0.08. Moreover, when the overlap degree is in $[0.06, 0.08]$, the proposed algorithm can determine the correct component number, but has a larger error on parameter estimation, such as $\mathcal{S}_{14} - \mathcal{S}_{16}$ shown in Table 2.

3.1.4 High-Dimensional and Multi-Class Model Selection

Furthermore, we perform this algorithm on two 3D t mixture datasets, as shown in Fig.4. The mixing proportions of $\mathcal{S}_{17}$ are equal, but those of $\mathcal{S}_{18}$ are different.

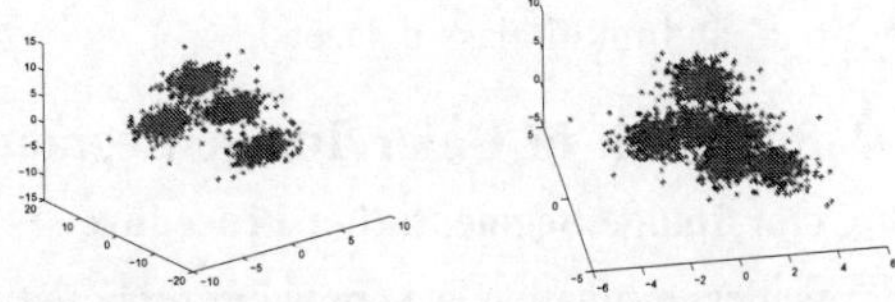

Fig. 4: Two 3D t mixture synthetic datasets. (a). DataSet $\mathcal{S}_{17}$ with $k^* = 4$ and mixed proportions $[0.25, 0.25, 0.25, 0.25]$; (b). DataSets $\mathcal{S}_{18}$ with $k^* = 6$ and mixed proportions $[0.2, 0.133, 0.2, 0.133, 0.167, 0.167]$.

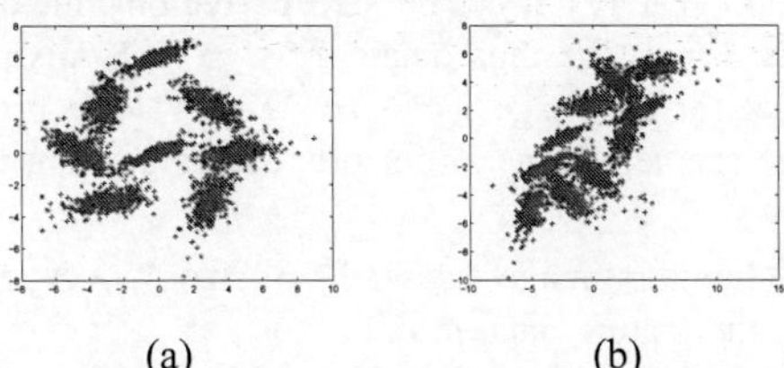

(a) (b)

Fig. 5: Multi-class t mixture datasets. (a). Dataset $\mathcal{S}_{19}$ with eight components and mixed proportions [0.125,0.125,0.125,0.125,0.125,0.125,0.125,0.125]; (b). Dataset $\mathcal{S}_{20}$ with ten components and mixed proportions [0.12,0.08,0.10,0.08,0.12,0.12,0.08,0.10,0.11,0.09].

The estimated proportions on the two datasets are [0.2483,0.2536,0.2489,0.2492] and [0.2004,0.1328,0.1990,0.1333,0.1667,0.1677], respectively. Thus, the proposed algorithm works well for higher dimensional datasets. In fact, in the following application of color image segmentation, we will extract eight features of an image as feature vector, that is, we will implement the proposed algorithm on eight-dimensional t mixture datasets. Finally, we conduct the proposed algorithm on multi-class t mixture datasets. Fig.5 gives two 2D multi-class t mixture datasets with eight components and ten components, respectively. The experimental results show that our proposed algorithm has a good performance on automatic model selection. It can make k components converge to the k^* actual components. When $k^* > 20$, by lowering the threshold α_j, the proposed algorithm can still realize correct model selection.

3.1.5 Summary of Simulation Experiments

In summary, our proposed gradient BYY learning algorithm can make model selection automatically during parameter learning on a dataset under different conditions and initializations. Generally, it can lead to correct model selection and acurrate parameter estimation. The stability of parameter learning is deteriorated only when the data size is too small. When $k \in [k^*, 3k*)$, it can converge to the true t mixture in most cases. In addition, the further experiments demonstrate that the overlap degree can affect its performance. However, this effect is inevitable when the data are too compact. Moreover, it is suitable for high-dimensional and multi-class datasets.

3.2 Application to Color Image Segmentation

3.2.1 Color Image Segmentation Procedure

For practical evaluation, we apply our proposed algorithm for t mixtures to unsupervised segmentation of color images. Here, we adopt three color features $L^*U^*V^*$ in $L^*u^*v^*$ color space [9], [10], three textural features HL, LH, HH using Discrete Cosine Transform (DCT) technique [11], and position features i, j. The size of region unit or patch is set as 3×3. We thus obtain $M \times N \times 8$ mixture feature dataset for an image I of size $M \times N$. The procedure of image segmentation via our proposed algorithm is given as follows:

1. Input an image dataset S_I of size $M \times N$, and extract the feature dataset.
2. Perform the proposed algorithm and produce the t-mixture model based on the dataset.
3. Calculate the posterior probability of the image pixel eigenvector with respect to all the components, and assign the pixel to the component with the maximum posterior probability. Each final component owns a class of pixels for segmentation. Calculate the mean RGB value of each class, and make it as the color values after segmentation.

3.2.2 Database and Evaluation Method

Three hundred color images and their corresponding figure-ground labels are downloaded from Berkeley Segmentation Database [12]. These images are divided into three groups in our application experiments, that is, the first 100 as training images, the last 100 as training images, and the middle 100 as test images. The Probability Rand (PR) index [13] is adopted to evaluate the segmentation performances. The PR index ranges from zero to one. A higher score means that the segmented image is more similar to the hand-labeled one. The statistics of the PR index reflect the accuracy and stability level of segmentation performance. The performance of color image segmentation by our proposed algorithm is described in the following subsection. The initial component number k is set as $10, 8, 6$ in consideration of the complexity of the images. The other parameters are set in the same way as those of Section 3.1.1.

3.2.3 Segmentation Results and Analysis

It is demonstrated by the experiments that our proposed algorithm can consistently obtain stable segmentation result with high PR index. Furthermore, we compare our proposed algorithm with the rival penalized competitive learning (RPCL) algorithm [14] and competitive agglomeration clustering (CAC) algorithm [15] on the 100 test images (group 3). Our proposed algorithm exhibits a better performance than the two others on both accuracy and stability. The PR index evaluation results are listed in Table 3. In addition,

Table 3: The mean and standard deviation of the PR index on 300 color image segmentation.

			PR Index	
Algorithm	No.	Images	Mean	Std
BYY	1	first 100 training images	0.737	0.111
BYY	2	last 100 training images	0.732	0.103
BYY	3	100 test images	0.737	0.108
RPCL	3	100 test images	0.727	0.132
CAC	3	100 test images	0.732	0.154

we count the number of images with different PR indexes. The performance of our proposed algorithm is very stable. Among the 300 color image segmentation results, 71% images have good segmentation results, with the PR index larger than 0.7. Only 4% images have very bad segmentation results, with the PR index less than 0.5. Those images often contain very confusing backgrounds, which introduce lots of noise to the image segmentation. The statistics of PR indexes of the 300 images segmentation is described in Fig.6, and some of the segmented images are shown in Fig.7.

3.2.4 Comparison with Generalized competitive Clustering Algorithm

The Generalized competitive clustering (GCC) algorithm is an unsupervised clustering method. It is derived from Fuzzy-C-Means algorithm, and can also carry out automatic model selection. In [16], the GCC algorithm was applied to color image segmentation, and presented the original and segmented images on her home page. In this section, we perform our proposed algorithm on these original images, and compare the segmentation results between these two algorithms.

As shown in Fig.8, even though the two algorithms can separate the objects from the backgrounds, the GCC algorithm generated the segments with relatively fuzzy boundaries, while our algorithm gives a clear boundaries. This may

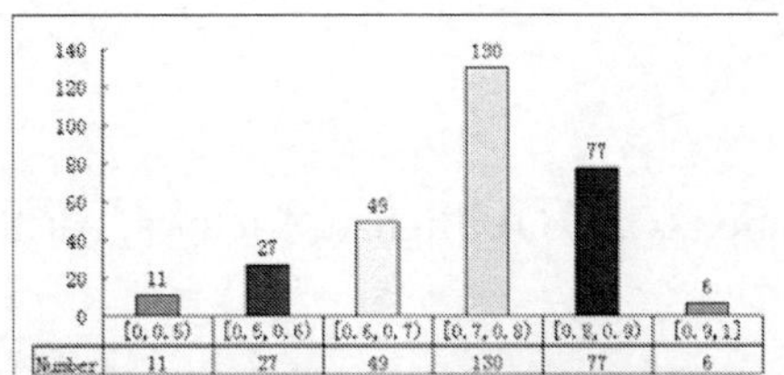

Fig. 6: Image numbers of different segmentation levels

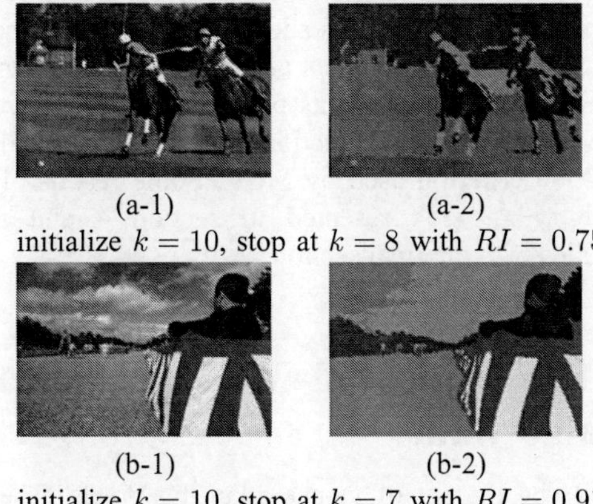

(a-1) (a-2)
initialize $k = 10$, stop at $k = 8$ with $RI = 0.75$

(b-1) (b-2)
initialize $k = 10$, stop at $k = 7$ with $RI = 0.91$

Fig. 7: Color image segmentation by the gradient BYY learning algorithm

(a) original image (b) GCC image (c) BYY image

Fig. 8: The comparison of the proposed algorithm and GCC algorithm on color image segmentation.

be caused bt the fact that the GCC algorithm detected object and background based on local histogram. In contrast, the proposed algorithm is based on t-mixture model, and takes consideration of various features of the images, including color, texture and position features. In summary, our algorithm have a better segmentation performance for boundary detection.

4. Conclusions

We have extended the BYY harmony learning mancinism to the learning of multivariate t mixtures and established a gradient BYY harmony learning algorithm which can make model selection automatically during parameter estimating. It is demonstrated by the simulation experiments that the proposed algorithm is effective and stable on both model selection and parameter estimation. It is robust to initializations if properly setting. Although the overlap degree may affect the learning performance, it is acceptable in the general case. In addition, the proposed algorithm is suitable for high-dimensional and multi-class datasets. Moreover, the proposed algorithm is successfully applied to unsupervised image segmentation.

Acknowledgment

This work was supported by the Natural Science Foundation of China for Grant 61171138.

References

[1] D.M. Titterington,Statistical analysis of finite mixture distribution,*John Wiley&Sons*,New York,1985.

[2] L.Xu, Ying-Yang machine: a Bayesian-Kullback scheme for unified learnings and new results on vector quantization, *Proceedings of 1995 International Conference on Neural Infromation Processing (ICONIP'95)*, vol.2, pp.977-988.

[3] J.Ma, T.Wang and L.Xu, A gradient BYY harmony learning rule on Gaussian mixture with automated model selection, *Neurocomputing*, 56(2004), pp.481-487.

[4] J.Ma, B.Gao, Y.Wang and Q.Cheng, Conjugate and natural gradient rules for BYY harmony learning on Gaussian mixture with automated model selection, *International Journal of Pattern Recognition and Artificial Intelligence* 19(5)(2005),pp.701-713.

[5] J.Ma and L.Wang, BYY harmony learning on finite mixture: adaptive gradient implementation and a floating RPCL mechanism, *Neural Processing Letters*, 24(1)(2006), pp.19-40.

[6] J.Ma and X.He, A fast fixed-point BYY harmony learning algorithm on Gaussian mixture with automated model selection, *Pattern Recognition Letters*, 29(6)(2008), pp.701-711.

[7] J.Ma, J.Liu and Z.Ren, Parameter estimation of Poisson mixture with automated model selection through BYY harmony learning, *Pattern Recognition*, vol.42, 2009, pp.2659-2670.

[8] Z.Ren and J.Ma, BYY Harmony Learning on Weibull Mixture with Automated Model Selection, *Lecture Notes in Computer Science*, vol.5263, 2008, pp.589-599.

[9] R.W.Hunt, The Basis in Human Eye Physiology of Three-Component Color Models, *in: Measuring color(3rd ed.)*, pp.39-46, Fountain Press, England, 1998.

[10] R.W.Hunt, Chromaticity Coordinates, *in: Measuring color(3rd ed.)*, pp.54-57, Fountain Press, England, 1998.

[11] S.Chen and B.Luo, Robust t-mixture modelling with SMEM algorithm, *Proceeding of the Third Internationa Conference on Machine Learning and Cybernetics*, Shanghai, August, 2004, pp.26-29.

[12] D.Martin,C.Fowlkes,D.Tal and J.Malik, A Database of Human Segmented Natural Images and Its Application to Evaluating Segmentation Algorithms and Measuring Ecological Statistics, *Proc.Int'l Conf. computer Vision*, 2005.

[13] R.Unnikrishnan, C.Pantofaru and M.Hebert, Toward Objective Evaluation of Image Segmentation Algorithms, *IEEE Transactions on Pattern Analysis and Machine Intelligence*, 29(6)(2007), pp.929-944.

[14] L.Xu, A.Krzyzak and E.Oja, Rival penelized competitive learning for clustering analysis, RBF net and curve detection. *IEEE Trans. Neural Netw*,4(4)(2006),pp.636-648.

[15] H.Frigui and R.Krishnapuram, Clustering by competitive agglomeration, *Pattern Recognition*,30(7)(1997),pp.1109-1119.

[16] N.Boujemaa, Generalized competitive clustering for image segmentation, *Proceeding of 19th International Conference of the North American Fuzzy Information Processing Society*,Atlanta, USA, 2000,pp.133-137.

Image Segmentation Using the MCV Image Labeling Algorithm

John Mashford
Commonwealth Scientific and Industrial Research Organisation (CSIRO), Highett, Victoria, Australia

Abstract - *This paper describes an improved version of the MCV image labeling algorithm. The algorithm is a hierarchical algorithm commencing with a partition made up of single pixel regions and merging regions or subsets of regions using a Markov random field (MRF) image model. The output can be a simple segmentation partition or a sequence of partitions which can provide useful information to higher level vision systems. In the case of an autoregressive Gaussian MRF the evaluation of sub-images for homogeneity is computationally inexpensive and may be effected by a hardwired feed-forward neural network. The merge operation of the algorithm is massively parallelizable.*

Keywords: image segmentation, concurrent vision, Markov random fields, vector valued pixels, MCV algorithm

1 Introduction

The concurrent vision approach formulated by Mashford *et al.* in [1,2] is based on the idea that segmentation and classification can be carried out concurrently using a hierarchical algorithm which generates a multiresolution partition tree. A particular instance of this approach utilizing Markov random fields (MRFs) to define a criterion for region homogeneity was described by Mashford in [3] and called Markov concurrent vision (MCV). MRFs have been used for many years in computer vision applications [4,5,6]. Dawoud and Netchaev [6] proposed a merge-based algorithm using MRFs for segmentation commencing with a partition obtained by watershed algorithm over-segmentation and using the Canny edge detector to guide the merge process. Alpert *et al.* [7] and Sharon *et al.* [8] describe an approach which utilizes hierarchical aggregation from a partition formed from single-pixel regions as in [1]. Approaches to concurrent segmentation and classification are described in [9,10].

The present paper describes a modification and improvement of the MCV algorithm, which may be called sequential MCV, or simply MCV. The improved algorithm is faster and more effective than the original MCV algorithm.

The MCV algorithm outputs a sequence of partitions (or superpixel sets (Zhang et al., 2011)) which may be useful to higher level vision systems because of their dynamic multiresolution scene representation and also because their structure, which is more elaborate than a simple segmentation, allows incremental processing of video sequences. It provides greater functionality for higher-level vision systems and provides a natural framework for generating high-level object representations at all scales and for implementing the content-based scalability requirement of the MPEG video standard.

The second section of this paper describes the (sequential) MCV algorithm, while Section 3 describes the MRF image evaluation criterion used by MCV. Some results of applying the algorithm are presented in section 4 and the paper concludes with the final section.

2 The sequential MCV image labeling algorithm

Let V be the set of values taken by pixels. Therefore an image can be considered as a map $\omega : X \rightarrow V$ where $X = \{1, \ldots, m\} \times \{1, \ldots, n\}$ is the image lattice. For grey-scale images $V = \{0, \ldots, d\text{-}1\}$ for some $d \geq 2$ (e.g. d = 256) while for color images $V = \{(v_1,v_2,v_3) : 0 \leq v_1, v_2, v_3 \leq d\text{-}1\}$, for some $d \geq 2$, is the set of RGB triples. More generally V may be a set of vectors of multispectral components or feature vectors.

Suppose that we have a connected window $W \subset \mathbf{Z}^2$ (where **Z** denotes the integers) containing the origin (such as a rectangle or disc centred at the origin), and an evaluation procedure $E : \Omega(R) \rightarrow \{0,1\}$ for all regions $R \subset W$ where $\Omega(R)$ is the set of all images on R ($\Omega(R) = \{\zeta : R \rightarrow V\}$). $E(\zeta) = 1$ if ζ is acceptable $E(\zeta) = 0$ otherwise. Define a point x to be a boundary point of a region R if

$$(x + W_0) \cap R \neq \phi \text{ and } (x + W_0) \setminus R \neq \phi, \quad (1)$$

where W_0 is some fundamental neighborhood of the origin such as the 8-neighbourhood. We also suppose that we have a permutation π_{pixels} of the pixels in the image lattice X and also a second window $\Psi \subset \mathbf{Z}^2$. The simplest example of such a permutation is obtained by carrying out raster scan on X, while a more useful permutation is a random permutation.

The MCV algorithm operates on a number of levels from level = 1 to level = max_level. At each level the pixels in X are selected sequentially according to π_{pixels}. If a selected pixel x bounds one or more regions in the evolving partition Π then the image ω in the window $(x + W) \cap X$ is evaluated for homogeneity. If $E(\omega|_{(x + W) \cap X}) = 1$ then Π is updated using the following procedure. Compute the region

$$S = \bigcup \{R \cap (x + \Psi) : R \in \Pi, R \cap (x + W_0) \neq \emptyset\}, \quad (2)$$

and update

$$\Pi := \{f(R) : R \in \Pi\}, \quad (3)$$

where

$$f(R) = R \cup S, \text{ if } x \in R, \text{ or, } R \sim S, \text{ if } x \notin R.$$

We consider a class of vision systems described by specifying

1. a sequence $W_1 \subset W_2 \subset \ldots \subset W_{n\_levels} \subset \mathbf{Z}^2$ of evaluation windows
2. a sequence $\Psi_1 \subset \Psi_2 \subset \ldots \subset \Psi_{n\_levels} \subset \mathbf{Z}^2$ of merge windows
3. evaluation functions $E_i : \Omega(R) \to \{0,1\}$ for all $R \subset W_i$ and $i = 1, \ldots,$ n_levels

The vision system operates by the following algorithm

1. initialize $\Pi_1 = \{\{x\} : x \in X\}$
2. for i = 1 to n_levels

   for j = 1 to mn

   (a) if π_pixels(j) is a boundary pixel evaluate ω in the window $(\pi\_pixels(j) + W_i) \cap X$

   (b) if it is homogeneous update Π according to the procedure described above

It is natural for the window sizes to increase as the region sizes increase. In order to apply this algorithm it is necessary to have specified windows W_0, and W_i and Ψ_i for $i = 1, \ldots,$ max_level, and evaluation maps E_i for $i = 1, \ldots,$ max_level.

3 Markov image evaluation

We are given some window W and a region $R \subset W$ (R will usually be equal to W but may be a proper subset of W if the point at which the window is located is sufficiently close to the edge of the image). We want to be able to evaluate images $\omega : R \to V$. The approach taken in MCV for image evaluation is that we assess images with respect to a Markov random field (MRF) image model. Let $\{G_x\}$ be a neighborhood system on R. Then an MRF on R with respect to $\{G_x\}$ is an (ergodic) stochastic process $\{\Phi_x\}$ with state space $\Omega(R)$ such that

$$P(\Phi = \omega) > 0, \forall \omega \in \Omega(R), \quad (4)$$

$P(\Phi_x = \omega_x \mid \Phi_y = \omega_y, y \neq x) = P(\Phi_x = \omega_x \mid \Phi_y = \omega_y, y \in G_x), \forall \omega \in \Omega(R)$.

If $\{\Phi_x\}$ is an MRF then, by the Hammersley-Clifford theorem there are potential functions $V_C : \Omega(C) \to \mathbf{R}$ for all $C \in \Lambda$ where Λ is the set of all cliques in $G = \{G_x\}$, such that the equilibrium distribution on $\Omega(R)$ (joint distribution) associated with $\{\Phi_x\}$ is given by

$$\pi(\omega) = \frac{1}{Z(T)} \exp(-U(\omega)/T), \quad (5)$$

where $U(\omega)$ for $\omega \in \Omega(R)$ is given by

$$U(\omega) = \sum_{C \in \Lambda} V_C(\omega|_C), \quad (6)$$

$T > 0$ is a constant and $Z(T) > 0$ is a normalizing constant given by

$$Z(T) = \sum_{\omega \in \Omega(R)} \exp(-U(\omega)/T). \quad (7)$$

T is called the temperature, $U : \Omega(R) \to \mathbf{R}$ is called the energy function and $Z : (0,\infty) \to (0,\infty)$ is called the partition function. The probability measure π is the Boltzmann distribution associated with the energy function U and therefore a stochastic process with equilibrium distribution π can be obtained using the Metropolis algorithm.

An image $\omega \in \Omega(R)$ can be evaluated, or assessed, by computing $\pi(\omega)$. If $\pi(\omega)$ is high then the image ω is likely to be produced by the MRF process while if $\pi(\omega)$ is low then the image ω is unlikely to be produced by the MRF process. If we choose a threshold $\tau \in [0,1]$ then we can define an evaluation map $E : \Omega(R) \to \{0,1\}$ by $E(\omega) = 1$ if $\pi(\omega) \geq \tau$, 0 otherwise.

It is straightforward to show that for all $\tau \geq 0$, there exists a $\rho \in \mathbf{R}$ such that for all $\omega \in \Omega(R)$ $\pi(\omega) \geq \tau \Leftrightarrow U(\omega) \leq \rho$. It is natural to take $\tau = \langle \pi \rangle$, where $\langle \pi \rangle$ denotes the expected value of $\pi(\omega)$ for $\omega \in \Omega(R)$ according to the MRF $\{\Phi_x\}$. Thus image evaluation can be carried out, for some $T > 0$, if we have specified an energy function $U : \Omega(R) \to \mathbf{R}$ and have determined an energy threshold $\rho = \rho(T)$. It is natural to use an autoregressive stochastic process for evaluating sub-images for homogeneity. Suppose that we have weights $\theta_x : G_x \to [0,1]$ with

$$\sum_{y \in G_x} \theta_x(y) = 1, \forall x \in R, \quad (8)$$

e.g. $\theta_x(y) = |G_x|^{-1}, \forall x \in R, y \in G_x$,

Then there is associated an autoregressive stochastic process for which we can write

$$\omega(x) = \sum_{y \in G_x} \theta_x(y)\omega(y) + \varepsilon(x), \quad (9)$$

where $\varepsilon(x)$ is a stochastic error term. If V is a set of vectors, $V \subset \mathbf{R}^b$, then an energy function $U : \Omega(R) \to \mathbf{R}$ associated with such an autoregressive process is

$$U(\omega) = \sum_{x \in R} d(\omega(x), \sum_{y \in G_x} \theta_x(y)\omega(y))^2, \tag{10}$$

where $d : \mathbf{R}^b \times \mathbf{R}^b \to [0,\infty)$ is a metric on $\mathbf{R}^b$ such as

$$d(u,v) = (\sum_{i=1}^{b} (v_i - u_i)^2)^{1/2}. \tag{11}$$

U defines an energy function in the sense defined above with respect to the neighbourhood system $G^{(2)}$ defined by

$$(\forall x, y \in R)\ ((x,y) \in G^{(2)} \Leftrightarrow (\exists z \in R)\ ((x, z) \in G, (z, y) \in G)). \tag{12}$$

The equilibrium distribution can be written as

$$\pi(\omega) = \frac{1}{Z(T)} \exp(-\sum_{x \in R} d(\omega(x), \sum_{y \in G_x} \theta_x(y)\omega(y))^2/T). \tag{13}$$

This is Gaussian in the vector of deviations from the weighted sum of neighboring values. Therefore the MRF associated with U is called an autoregressive Gaussian Markov random field (GMRF).

Suppose that G is a neighborhood system on $\mathbf{Z}^2$. Then a sequence $\{W_i\}$ of windows can be defined in a natural way by $W_i = G^{(i)}$ where $G^{(i)}$ are the neighborhood systems for $\mathbf{Z}^2$ defined recursively by

$$G^{(1)} = G,\ (x,y) \in G^{(i+1)} \Leftrightarrow (\exists z)\ ((x, z) \in G, (z, y) \in G^{(i)}). \tag{14}$$

In other words the $G^{(i)}$ are obtained by successive dilations with respect to the structuring element G starting from $W_1 = G$. This sequence of windows can be placed to form a multiresolution pyramid.

An image $\omega_{i+1} : W_{i+1} \to V$ can be viewed at a lower resolution on W_i as the image $\omega_i : W_i \to V$ defined by

$$\omega_i(x) = \sum_{y \in G_x} \theta_x(y)\omega_{i+1}(y). \tag{15}$$

An approach to evaluating an image $\omega_i : W_i \to V$ is to lower the resolution by i-1 steps to obtain an image $\omega_1 : W_1 \to V$ and then to evaluate ω_1 using Markov image evaluation. This form of image evaluation can be implemented as a feed-forward neural network by constructing a pyramidal neural network with connections from nodes $y \in G_x$ in W_{i+1} to x in W_i and giving each such connection a weight $\theta_x(y)$. Two more layers and a threshold unit can be used to effect the image evaluation of the lowest resolution image.

The output of the MCV system is a multiresolution sequence of partitions. After being processed to determine additional structures such as feature vectors and classifications for the regions in the partition sequence structure it may be passed to high level vision systems.

4 Some results of testing the MCV algorithm

For the experiments presented below the window Ψ_i was taken to be a square of side length $2r_i + 1$ where $r_i = 2^{i+1}$ pixels for i = 1, …, max_level. A random permutation of the pixels in the image lattice can be computed offline and read from a file by the algorithm if it is to operate on images of known fixed size, otherwise raster scan can be used. The algorithm was found to be more efficient when a random permutation was used. Typically a good segmentation is achieved using max_levels = 9 with a random permutation as opposed to requiring max_levels = 11 if raster scan is used.

The image presented in Fig. 2 is the result of segmenting the image shown in Fig. 1 using the MCV algorithm. The 27 largest "blobs" found are shown. The different objects identified are shown in different colors. It can be seen that the road and the sky are clearly identified. The large tree on the left hand side of the image is also identified, however its shadow is included as part of the identified object. The larger of the trees on the right hand side of the image is clearly identified and parts of the other trees on the right hand side are also identified. Other results are shown in Figs. 3-6.

5 Conclusions

The (sequential) MCV image labeling algorithm has been described. It is a hierarchical algorithm which may generate a

Fig. 1. Image from Google Street View

Fig. 2. Segmented image using MCV (objects identified) for image of Fig. 1

simple segmentation partition or a multiresolution sequence of partitions. It utilizes an MRF image model in order to evaluate sub-images for homogeneity. In the case of a Gaussian MRF this can be effected by a hardwired feed-forward neural network. The algorithm executes very rapidly on the Berkely segmentation benchmark dataset images and the merge operation of the algorithm is massively parallelizable.

Acknowledgements

The work described in this paper was funded by CSIRO CLW Division and other past divisions. The author would like to thank Chiang Liu for suggesting that I look at MRFs, Mike Rahilly for developing the image decoding and display programs and Felix Lipkin for providing the Google images. The author would also like to thank Steve Pahos, Vicki Tutungi, Jenny Stauber and Stewart Burn for supporting this work and Donavan Marney and Paul Davis for very helpful comments.

Fig. 3. Google Earth image

References

[1] Mashford, J.S. "A method for the development of parallel concurrent machine vision systems", Proc. ICCIMA'98 (International Conference on Computational Intelligence and Multimedia Applications 1998), World Scientific, pp. 378-383, Feb 1998.

[2] Mashford, J., Dai, W., Drogemuller, R. and Marksjö, B., "Image classifier and scene understanding systems of multi-agent teams", Proc. 2000 IEEE International Conference on Systems, Man and Cybernetics, Nashville, Tennessee, USA, pp. 1460-1465, Oct 2000.

[3] Mashford, J.S., "A neural Markovian concurrent vision system for object identification and tracking", Proc. of the 2004 International Conference on Computational Intelligence for Modelling, Control and Automation, Gold Coast, Australia, 2004.

[4] Li, S. Z., "Markov Random Field modelling in image analysis", Springer, London, 2001.

[5] Zhang, Y., Hartley, R., Mashford, J. and Burn, S., "Superpixels via Pseudo-Boolean Optimization", Proc. IEEE International Conference on Computer Vision, Barcelona, Spain, 1387-1394, Nov 2011.

[6] Dawoud, A. and Netchaev, A., "Preserving objects in Markov Random Fields region growing image segmentation", Pattern Analysis and Applications 15, 155-161, 2012.

[7] Alpert, S., Galun, M., Brandt, A. and Basri, R., "Image segmentation by probabilistic bottom-up aggregation and cue integration", IEEE Transactions on Pattern Analysis and Machine Intelligence 34(2), 315-327, Feb 2012.

[8] Sharon, E., Galun, M. Sharon, D., Basri, R. and Brandt, A., "Hierarchy and adaptivity in segmenting visual scenes", Nature 442, 810-813, Aug 2006.

[9] Cao, L. and Li, F.-F., "Spatially coherent latent topic model for concurrent segmentation and classification of objects and scenes", Proc. IEEE International Conference on Computer Vision, Rio de Janeiro, Brazil, 1080-1087, 2007.

[10] Kokkinos, I. and Maragos, P., "Synergy between object recognition and image segmentation using the expectation-maximization algorithm", IEEE Transactions on Pattern Analysis and Machine Intelligence 31(8), 1486-1501, Aug 2009.

Fig. 4. MCV segmentation of image of Fig. 3

Fig. 5. Berkeley segmentation benchmark dataset car image

Fig. 6. MCV segmentation of image in Fig. 5

Automatic Segmentation and Classification of Multiple Coronal Mass Ejections from Coronagraph Images

M. Jacobs[1], **L. Chang**[1], **and A. Pulkkinen**[2]
[1]Electrical Engineering/Computer Science Dept., The Catholic University of America, Washington, D.C., USA.
[2]NASA Goddard Space Flight Center, Greenbelt, Maryland, USA.

Abstract - *Solar weather and, specifically, Coronal Mass Ejections (CMEs) can have major impacts on the Earth by affecting electronics and even the astronauts in space. This has created a high interest in the study of CMEs in an effort to detect, track and forecast events in order to provide time for proper preparation. Automatic methods were recently proposed that segment CME images and estimate CME parameters such as their heliocentric location and velocity. This program, however, cannot handle multiple CMEs occurring within the same coronagraph image frame. In this paper, we address the issue of multiple CMEs events and propose a two-step clustering algorithm to handle it. The proposed algorithm has been tested and visually validated using 15 selected multiple CME events. The result shows that the proposed method successfully processes images containing multiple CMEs, and properly estimates the parameters for each individual CME within the image.*

Keywords: Image Segmentation; Space Weather; Multiple Coronal Mass Ejection, Pattern Recognition, Astrophysics

1 Introduction

Space weather can have major affects on the Earth. These affects range from benign auroras, electrical interference, damage of electrical equipment, to even increased radiation exposure at high altitudes. One type of space weather phenomena is Coronal Mass Ejections (CMEs), eruptions from the sun that launch streams of high energy particles into space and, sometimes at Earth. Due to the danger of these high energy particles, research has been conducted to provide a forecasting and tracking application for CMEs.

The National Aeronautics and Space Administration (NASA), the European Space Agency (ESA), and other nations' space programs have launched several missions specifically to observe these solar phenomena. The majority of these observations, however, only allow for two dimensional imaging and analysis. Three dimensional information must be extrapolated from a series of images of a given CME. One of the earliest models used for this purpose was the concept of conic approximation of CMEs. This cone model was originally introduced by Howard [1]. It has since been refined and used to extract three dimensional measurements from two dimensional images, including the solar longitude and latitude, velocity, and opening half angle of CME events [2], as seen in Figure 1. This technique was validated by comparing the extracted measurements to those observed by Earth-stationed instruments [3].

Until recently, all such analysis was done manually. Scientists visually identified CME mass in a series of consecutive coronagraph images and then used the difference between consecutive images to extract parameters of the CME . While those manual methods were feasible, they were "very subjective and time consuming [4]."

Pulkkinen et al [4] introduced an automatic pipeline called "CONED" that processed manually selected coronagraph images and extracted the CME parameters using the cone model. An outline of Pulkkinen's method is given in Figure 2 that will be explained in more details in the Method

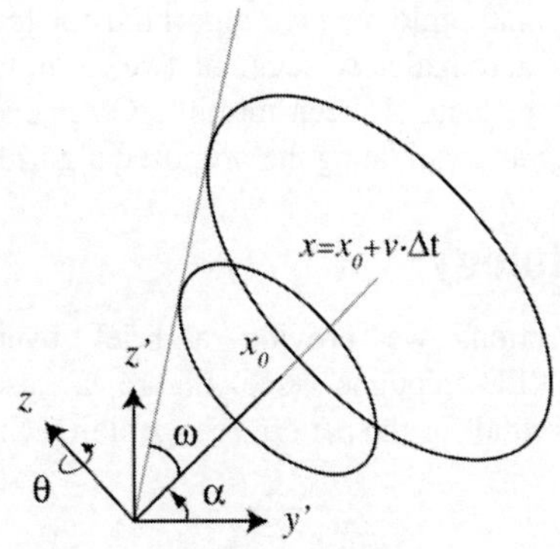

Figure 1 The Cone Model: "The plane (y', z') refers to the plane of sky (x'-axis points toward the observer, i.e. toward the reader). Angle α defines the direction of the propagation of the CME in the (y', z') plane, which will ultimately relate to the heliocentric latitude and longitude of the CME. ω is the opening half-angle of the cone, x_0 the initial distance of the cone front in the rotated coordinates (x, y, z) and v is the velocity of the cone front propagation. Δt indicates the time interval during which the cone front propagates from x_0 to x."[4].

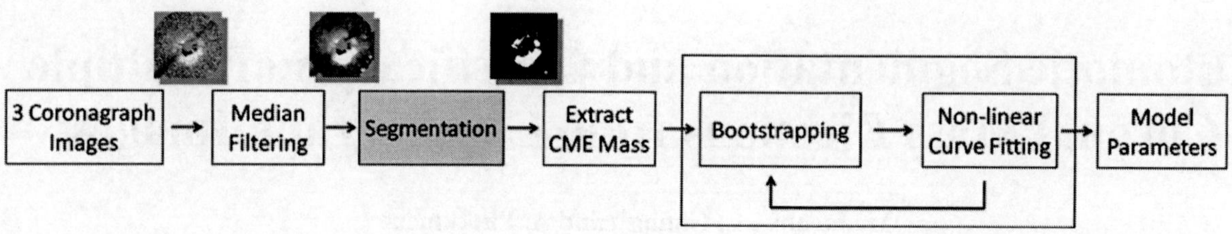

Figure 2 CONED Program: Automatic Pipeline for CME Processing

section.

While Pulkkinen's method was a success, it suffered from several shortcomings. Some of these shortcomings have already been addressed in our recent work [5]. However, an outstanding issue is the inability to handle cases where multiple CMEs occur in a single coronagraph image. The segmented points are mistakenly considered as a single CME, resulting in computation errors in model parameter estimations.

While multiple CMEs occur less frequently than single CMEs, they pose no less of a threat. This is particularly true in the rare case of multiple CMEs headed toward the Earth. A robust tracking and forcasting system must be able to capture every Earth-directed event even if a second event occurred in an overlapping time frame. A method of handling multiple CMEs is needed in order to provide adequate data for CME forecasting and predicting services.

To the best of our knowledge, this is the first paper to attempt to address the multiple CME events by using an automatic approach. We propose a two-step clustering algorithm combining a hard threshold [4], the active contour [6] and a single link agglomerative algorithm for hierarchical clustering [7] to automatically segment two or more CMEs, and to differentiate them. Fifteen multiple CME events were selected to testing and validating the proposed algorithm.

2 Methodology

In this section, we provide a brief overview of Pulkkinen's CONED pipeline, (see Figure 2) as well as necessary background for the pattern recognition techniques to be used.

2.1 Data

The data used in parameter extractions are white light difference coronagraph images taken by NASA and ESA's Solar and Hemispheric Observatory (SOHO) [8], specifically the Large Angle and Spectrometric Coronagraph (LASCO) C3 instrument [9]. The images are eight-bit unsigned integer grayscale images. The main goal is to identify the pixels in the image that contain the CME mass. However, in cases where two or more CMEs are present, an additional step is required to separate the mass of the two CMEs into two separate data sets. Later stages of the CONED program can only process the mass of a single CME, so each data point collected must be classified into the proper CME set. Note that it is assumed that the input image contains one or more CMEs. It is left for another system to identify coronagraph images that contains CME(s), which can then be processed through the CONED system presented here.

2.2 Pre-processing

In order to identify CME mass for use in parameter extraction, the CONED program must convert the grayscale to a binary image, where a "one" represents CME mass and a "zero" represents all other pixels. The main attribute used to segment the CME mass from the background is intensity or brightness. This is the key feature which separates the energetic CME(s) from the relatively empty background of space. Any algorithms used needs to be able to segment out regions containing spikes in intensity. However, due to the noisiness of the coronagraph difference images, a median filter is applied, adjusting each pixel's intensity to the median of its local area, contained in a 45 by 45 pixel box. This prevents random bright pixels in the background from being mistaken for part of the CME, which are usually large structures.

2.3 Segmentation

The next step in the CONED pipeline is to segment the image into CME and non-CME pixels. Below we will discuss the method originally used by Pulkkinen [4], methods presented by [5], and the new methods to be tested to segment and differentiate multiple CMEs.

2.3.1 Hard Threshold Method

In [4], an ad-hoc thresholding value at the 56th percentile intensity was used for segmentation. Due to the images' format, the values of intensities ranged from zero to 255. Thus, this threshold would always segment at 142.8. Pixels brighter than this are considered part of the CME and all others are disregarded. This method was developed via trial and error and suffered from over segmentation [5], however it was validated on data set of 14 images for which the 56th percentile was found to segment an adequate amount of CME mass [4].

2.3.2 Dynamic Methods

In [5], several dynamic methods were applied to the problem and were found to be more effective than the hard threshold method.

Otsu's method, originally proposed by Otsu [10] showed promise, though it was observed that it could not adapt to the wide range of situations presented in coronagraph images [5]. The algorithm is designed to find a threshold of segmentation that creates logical groups, specifically seeking to minimize the variance within each group. Otsu's method was tested on 14 CME events and it was successful in a majority of the events, but not all.

The K-means algorithm [11] proved to be the most promising of the new methods, adapting to all 14 single CME events presented in [5]. This method uses an iterative scheme to slowly fit the data into K clusters, where K is some integer, using an objective function. The objective function seeks to minimize the sum of the differences between each point in the cluster and the cluster's centroid or median. Though, it could theoretically work using random starting centroids, its performance can be vastly improved with good estimations of the starting centroids.

When moving to tackle the two CME cases, one intuitive approach was to use K-means with K=3. Theoretically, this could allow the separation of regions into the first and second CMEs and the background. However, early testing showed that this method was suffering from two problems. First, not all of the CME mass was being segmented, and second, the two CMEs were not being properly differentiated. Both of these problems were found to stem from the same issue: the dynamic range of CME intensity.

Both [4] and [5] had successfully used intensity as a discriminating factor between the CME and the background. However, their objective was meant to segment one, self-similar object. Multiple CMEs, however, can have random relative brightness. Sometimes they are similarly bright, other times one CME may be brighter than the other. While CMEs are all bright compared to the background, some CMEs are brighter than others. This was causing segmentation errors. In cases where one CME was brighter that the other, the K-means algorithm would not segment the weaker CME entirely. On the other hand, if they shared similar intensity, then the algorithm could not distinguish between the two. Therefore, K-means was deemed inadequate for the task of multiple CME segmentation and differentiation. A more competent technique was needed to capture both CMEs in one segmentation.

2.3.3 Threshold and Active Contouring

The active contour algorithm proposed by Chan and Vese in 2001 [6] has been used intensively in image segmentation such as medical imaging [12] and solar imaging [13]. Given a starting point (i.e., initial contours), the active contour algorithm iteratively adjusts the edge in order to conform to the region edge in the image. It does this using an optimizing energy function, which seeks to minimize the sum of the integral of the square difference between each point of a region and its region's mean. This is modeled as an outward force exerted by the region of interest and an inward force from the background.

While promising, active contouring requires an initial guess, one that would guarantee it be close to the actual CME. Due to its rapidness and consistent ability to capture most of a CME, the original CONED threshold method [4] was considered a good candidate. Active contour could then take care of any over- or under-segmentation suffered by the threshold. Thus a rough, hard threshold at the 56th percentile intensity was used as a starting point for active contouring.

2.4 Hierarchical Clustering

In cases containing only one CME, the image processing would be complete. The segmented CME data would pass directly to the parameter extraction phase, discussed in the next section. However, if this was done when two or more CMEs are present in the image, then the segmented data would be treated as a single CME for parameters extraction. This would result in the parameters extracted being erroneous. In order to compute accurate results for each CME, the data points must be differentiated into individual CMEs, so that parameters can be calculated one CME at a time. An additional step of clustering was deemed necessary to achieve this separation.

As stated earlier in subsection 2.3.2, intensity is no longer an effective discriminating feature to be used in clustering, as the relative intensity difference between the two CMEs is completely random. Clustering is instead performed based on two other new features: location, specifically the (x,y) coordinate of the data pixels, and the polar coordinates (r,θ).

An agglomerative hierarchical clustering algorithm using a single link is employed to accomplish this [7]. The algorithm starts by letting each data point, in this case, each pixel, be its own cluster. It then compares the clusters based on the provided features, and combines the two most similar clusters into one cluster. This process repeats until the target number of clusters is reached. Because of this, the algorithm can, theoretically, handle any number of CMEs, however the number of CMEs needs to be pre-determined, or a criteria (i.e., a cost function) needs to be defined to determine the optimal number of clusters. Once the clustering is complete, data points within the same cluster are processed as a single CME.

2.5 Parameter Extraction

Once the image is segmented and/or classified, a bootstrap algorithm begins 1000 iterations. For each iteration, 300 CME mass points (i.e., pixels) are selected. Their location in the image is used to estimate their three-dimensional location in space. Nonlinear curve fitting is then used to fit the cone model parameters to the data. The parameters include heliocentric longitude and latitude (the coordinates where the CME originated on the surface of the sun), the velocity of the mass, and the opening half angle of the cone estimation of the CME (see Figure 1.) The median result of the 1000 iterations is returned as the final result.

3 Results

In order to validate our approach, a data set of 15 events, with two to four images each, containing multiple CMEs was compiled (see Table 1). The new CONED system will be required to segment and differentiate the CME images. The accuracy of the segmentation and the correctness of the classification are visually examined by domain experts.

When examined visually, the CME images were segmented well in all 15 selected cases using the active contour method with the hard threshold as the initial guess. In addition, what is more important and impressive is that, in all 15 multiple CME events, the hierarchical clustering successfully classified multiple CMEs in an image. As examples, figures 3 and 4 show the classification results where two CMEs are partially overlapping angle-wise and are correctly separated. Figure 4 is particular interesting as it is an event where both CMEs are Earth-directed.

The 15 CME events were clearly segmented and differentiated which allowed the calculation of CME parameters for each individual event. Table 2 lists the calculated parameters for each CME in all 15 events. These results represent a major advancement in space weather prediction. For the first time, CME parameters have been calculated for multiple CMEs captured in, and automatically segmented and differentiated from the same set of images.

4 Discussion

The visual inspection by the domain experts has shown promising result on handling the multiple CME events using the proposed method. In order to fully validate our approach, we plan to demonstrate that the generated CME parameter results can be used for CME forecasting; that is, predicting the arrival time of CMEs aimed at Earth.

Preparations are currently underway to perform this validation using CME simulation software [14]. The simulation uses the CME model parameters generated by the CONED program as a starting point to model the CME's path from the Sun to the Earth. The simulation will return the time and date of the modeled CME's arrival at Earth. This result will be compared to the CME's actual arrival time as observed by Earth-based and Earth-orbiting based

Table 1 – Timestamps of Multiple CME Images [Format = yyyymmddhhmmss]

Event Number	Image 1	Image 2	Image 3	Image 4
1	20000423031800	20000423041800	20000423051800	
2	20000423134200	20000423141800	20000423144200	
3	20010531064200	20010531074200	20010531081800	
4	20011025164200	20011025171800	20011025174200	
5	20020927171800	20020927181800	20020927194200	
6	20120602050600	20120602054200	20120602061800	
7	20120608073000	20120608090600	20120608093000	
8	20120626005400	20120626013000		
9	20120702090600	20120702091800	20120702095400	
10	20120702180600	20120702190600	20120702200600	20120702215400
11	20120708165400	20120708170600	20120708171800	
12	20120708165400	20120708170600	20120708171800	
13	20120708193000	20120708201800	20120708203000	20120708204200
14	20120731135400	20120731143000	20120731150600	
15	20120817194200	20120817203000		

Table 2 - Calculated CME Parameters. Units in degrees for latitude, longitude, and opening half angle; km/s for velocity.

	Timecode	#	Latitude	Longitude	Opening Half Angle	Velocity
1	20000423031800	1	-1	2	44	964
		2	28	-6	19	465
2	20000423134200	1	33	-7	17	724
		2	-1	14	52	1734
3	20010531064200	1	-3	-29	29	1044
		2	-10	14	22	1061
4	20011025164200	1	-8	4	55	1625
		2	20	1	42	837
5	20020927161800	1	-26	-12	11	1008
		2	-24	12	24	509
		3	18	-32	26	618
6	20120602050600	1	0	30	47	849
		2	0	0	57	1669
7	20120608073000	1	16	-7	31	562
		2	-21	2	27	510
8	2012062600540	1	9	-24	19	792
		2	-12	-22	34	633
9	20120702090600	1	-5	-22	42	1551
		2	-5	15	44	1022
10	2012070218060	1	-25	4	11	443
		2	18	-4	33	701
11	20120704144200	1	25	5	16	759
		2	-34	13	14	654
12	20120708165400	1	22	34	88	915
		2	0	0	45	1000
13	20120708193000	1	-14	26	26	1244
		2	-10	5	59	1232
14	20120731135400	1	-9	21	20	583
		2	12	-9	38	890
15	20120817194200	1	9	17	38	1157
		2	24	-22	25	1300

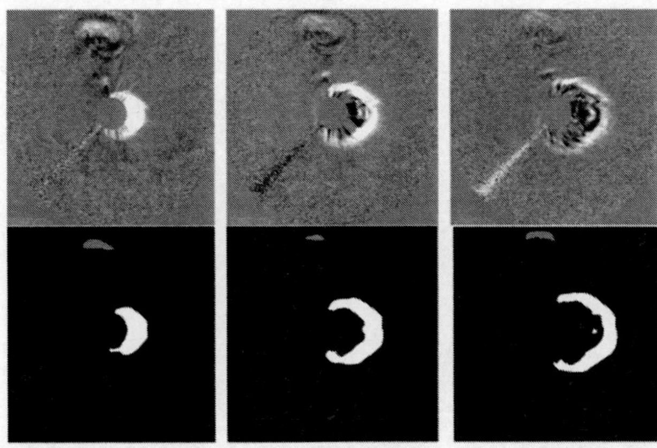

Figure 3. The first row shows the original coronagraph images, and the second row is the segmentation and classification results using the proposed method with event number 2 (see Table 1). Both CMEs are successfully differentiated.

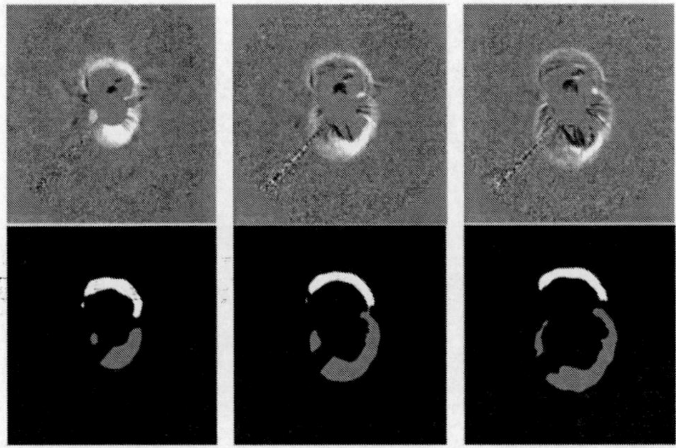

Figure 4. The first row shows the original coronagraph images, and the second row is the segmentation and classification results using the proposed method with event number 4 (see Table 1). Both CMEs are successfully differentiated.

instruments, such as the Advanced Composition Explorer (ACE) satellite [15].

It should be noted, however that all 15 events used in this paper are not comprised of "halo" CMEs; that is, CMEs directed at the Earth. The majority of the data set consists of instances where only one or none of the CMEs are Earth directed. This is due to the relative rarity, and the difficulty of combing through CME databases for ideal events. Thus, for these cases, visual examination must suffice for validation. Only cases that contain at least one halo CME can be used for simulation validation. It is our hope that a data set of more halo CMEs can be found before testing via simulation.

5 Conclusion & Future Work

This paper has presented the first successful method for the segmentation and differentiation of multiple CMEs. Our experiment has demonstrated the capability of our improved CONED algorithm to segment and differentiate a variety of multiple CME cases sufficiently enough to satisfy domain experts, as well as, generate legitimate CME parameters.

Much work still remains before CONED can be used as a fully featured CME processing pipeline. For example, an additional pre-processing strategy must be constructed to automatically detect if a given coronagraph image contains a CME. Also, thought must be given toward how to automatically detect the number of CMEs and whether this is done before segmentation or during clustering.

With the introduction of the new segmentation method for multiple CMEs, research is also planned to test its performance on single CMEs, comparing its performance to the methods used in [5].

6 Acknowledgement

SOHO LASCO data obtained via http://cdaw.gsfc.nasa.gov/CME_list/. This CME catalog is generated and maintained at the CDAW Data Center by NASA and The Catholic University of America in cooperation with the Naval Research Laboratory. SOHO is a project of international cooperation between ESA and NASA.

7 References

[1] R. A. Howard, D. J, Michels, N. R. Sheeley, Jr. and M. J. Koomen, "The Observation of a Coronal Transient Directed at Earth." The Astrophysical Journal, Vol. 263, p. L101- L104, 1982.

[2] X. P. Zhao, S. P. Plunkett, W. Liu, “Determination of geometrical and kinematical properties of halo coronal mass ejections using the cone model.” Journal of Geophysical Research, Vol. 107, No. A8, doi: 10.1029/2001JA009143, 2002.

[3] A. Taktakishvili, M. Kuznetsova, P. MacNeice, M. Hesse, L. Rastatter, A. Pulkinnen, A. Chulaki and D. Odstrcil, "Validation of the coronal mass ejection predictions at the Earth orbit estimated by ENLIL Heliosphere cone model." Space Weather, Vol. 7, 2009.

[4] A. Pulkkinen, T. Oates and A. Taktakishvili, "Automatic Determination of the Conic Coronal Mass Ejection Model Parameters." Solar Physics, Vol. 261, No. 1, pp. 115-126, 2009.

[5] M. Jacobs, A. Pulkkinen and L. Chang, "Improving Coronal Mass Ejection Segmentation Using Pattern Recognition Techniques," Proceedings of the 2012 International Conference on Image Processing, Computer Vision, and Pattern Recognition (IPCV'12), vol. II, pp. 975-980, 2012.

[6] T. F. Chan, L. A. Vese, "Active Contours Without Edges," IEEE Transactions on Image Processing, vol. 10, pp. 266-277, 2001.

[7] F. Murtagh, "A Survey of Recent Advances in Hierarchical Clustering Algorithms," The Computer Journal, vol. 26, pp. 354-359, 1983.

[8] V. Domingo, B. Fleck and A. I. Poland, "The SOHO Mission: An Overview," Solar Physics, vol. 162, pp. 1-37, 1995.

[9] G. E. Brueckner, et al. "The Large Angle Spectroscopic Coronagraph (LASCO)." Solar Physics, vol. 162, pp. 357-402, 1995.

[10] N. Otsu, "A Threshold Selection Method from Gray-Level Histograms." IEEE Transactions on Systems, Man, and Cybernetics, Vol. 9, p. 62-66, doi: 10.1109/TSMC.1979.4310076, 1979.

[11] S. P. Lloyd, "Least Squared Quantization in PCM." IEEE Transactions on Information Theory, Vol. IT-28, p. 129-137. doi: 10.1109/TIT.1982.1056489 1982.

[12] B. V. Dhandra and R. Hegadi, "Active Contours without Edges and Curvature Analysis for Endoscopic Image Classification," International Journal of Computer Science and Security, vol. 1, pp 19-32, 2007.

[13] C. D. Gill, L. Fletcher and S. Marshall, "Using active contours for semi-automated tracking of UV and EUV solar flare ribbons," Solar Physics, vol. 262, no. 2, pp. 355-371., 2010.

[14] D. Odstrcil, P. Riley, and X. P. Zhao, "Numerical Simulation of the 12 May 1997 Interplanetary CME Event." Journal of Geophysical Research, vol. 109, A02116, 2004.

[15] E.C. Stone, A.M. Frandsen, R.A. Mewaldt, E.R. Christian, D. Margolies, J.F. Ormes, and F. Snow. "The Advanced Composition Explorer." Space Science Reviews, vol. 86, pp. 1-22, 1998.

A New Multi-phase Soft Segmentation with Adaptive Variants

Hongyuan Wang[1], Fuhua Chen[2]
[1]School of Information Science & Engineering, Changzhou University, Changzhou, Jiangsu, China
[2]Dept. of Natural Science & Mathematics, West Liberty University, West Liberty, WV, USA

Abstract—*In this paper, we proposed a multiphase soft segmentation model for nearly piecewise constant images based on stochastic principle, where pixel intensities are modeled as random variables with mixed Gaussian distribution. The novelty of this paper mainly lies in using adaptive variants. Unlike some existing models where the mean of each phase is modeled as a constant and the variances for different phases are assumed to be the same, the mean for each phase in the Gaussian distribution in this paper is modeled as a product of a constant and a bias field, and different phases are assumed to have different variances, which makes the model more flexible. In addition, we developed a bi-direction projected primal dual hybrid gradient (PDHG) algorithm for iterations of membership functions.*

Keywords: Soft segmentation, multiphase segmentation, mixed Gaussian distribution, Primal-dual hybrid gradient (PDHG) algorithm, projection to simplex

1. Introduction

Soft segmentation is more flexible than hard segmentation. There have been many soft segmentation methods [8], [14], [15], [16], [17], [19]. Early soft segmentations are mostly based on Fuzzy C-mean (FCM) method which is originally very sensitive to noise. The model is then extended to different forms in order to make the model robust to noise [2], [11], [17].

Another class of soft segmentations is based on stochastic approaches [9], [10], [14], [19]. J. Shen proposed a general multiphase stochastic variational fuzzy segmentation model combining stochastic principle and Modica-Mortola's phase-transition theory [19]. The intensity of images was modeled as a mixed Gaussian distribution. The model assumed that membership functions should be either close to 1 or close to 0, which simplified the model but limited its application. For example, it's not reasonable to apply the model to partial volume segmentation since in that case the membership functions are usually neither close to 1 nor close to 0 at the boundary of different matters. Bias correction is an important mean in soft segmentation to deal with intensity inhomogeneity [1], [13], [17], [21]. For example, Wells et al proposed an expectation-maximization (EM) algorithm to solve the bias correction problem and the tissue classification problem [21].

In this paper, we proposed a stochastic variational model for multi-phase soft segmentation in the presence of noise and intensity inhomogeneity, where the image intensity at each point is modeled as a mixed Gaussian distribution with means and variances to be optimized. Different from J. Shen's work [19], our model does not set the assumption that membership functions must be close to either 1 or 0. So, our model are more suitable for soft segmentation and application to partial volume analysis. Since our model is developed based on the assumption that the image intensity is a mixed Gaussian distribution with possibly different variances for different phases, it is also different from [14], [17] in that our model adaptively corrects bias of intensities and removes noise by finding optimized mean and variances. It is demonstrated by experiments that our model is not only robust to noise, but also powerful in bias correction. The model can be implemented very fast using a bi-direction projected PDHG algorithm. The rest of the paper is organized as follows. The new model is developed in Section 2. The numerical implementation scheme is presented in Section 3. In Section 4, we show some experiment results and also give some explanation and analysis. Both synthetic images and authentic images are used. Finally, we summarize the paper with a short conclusion.

2. Model Development

Let $I(x)$ be a 2-D image defined on an open bounded domain Ω containing K phases. Let w be phase label variable (i.e., $w(x) \in \{1, \cdots, K\}$ for all $x \in \Omega$). At each pixel x, both $w(x)$ and $I(x)$ are viewed as random variables indexed by x. The probability that x belongs to the i-th phase is represented by the ownership functions $p_i(x)$, $1 \leq i \leq K$. If we denote the probability density function (PDF) of the random variable $I(x)$ given that x belongs to the i-th phase by $Prob(I(x)|w(x) = i)$, then the PDF of $I(x)$ is a mixed distribution given by

$$\sum_{i=1}^{K} Prob(I(x)|w(x) = i) p_i(x). \quad (1)$$

Suppose in further that $Prob(I(x)|w(x) = i)$ is a Gaussian PDF for each $i = 1, ..., K$ and all random variables $\{I(x) : x \in \Omega\}$ are independent. Then the likelihood (joint PDF) is

$$\prod_{x \in \Omega} \sum_{i=1}^{K} g(I|u_i(x), \sigma_i) p_i(x). \quad (2)$$

where

$$g(x|\mu,\sigma) = \frac{1}{(\sqrt{2\pi}\sigma)} exp(-\frac{(x-\mu)^2}{2\sigma^2}). \quad (3)$$

The negative log-likelihood is

$$E[I|P,U,\sigma] = -\int_\Omega log\left(\sum_{i=1}^{K} g(I|u_i(x),\sigma_i)p_i(x)\right) \quad (4)$$

where $P = [p_1, p_2, ..., p_K]$, $U = [u_1, u_2, ..., u_K]$, and $\sigma = [\sigma_1, \sigma_2 ..., \sigma_K]$. When each $u_i(x)$ is chosen to be a constant c_i respectively and $\sigma_i = \sigma$ for all i ($i = 1, 2, ..., K$), where σ is a fixed constant, then the model is deduced to a piecewise constant model. In paper ([14], [17]), $u_i(x)$ is constructed as the product of a constant c_i and a full field bias function $b(x)$ which is assumed to be close to 1. Now we assume $u_i(x) = c_i b(x)$ in (4) and let $c = (c_1, c_2, ..., c_K)$, which leads to the following energy functional $E_F(p,b,c,\sigma)$

$$E_F(p,b,c,\sigma) = \lambda\int_\Omega -log[\sum_{i=1}^{K} \frac{1}{\sqrt{2\pi}\sigma_i} exp(-\frac{(I(x)-b(x)c_i)^2}{2\sigma_i^2})p_i]dx. \quad (5)$$

By adding the L^2-norm of ∇b and the total variation of $p_i(x)$ to $E_F(p,b,c,\sigma)$ as regularity terms for bias field $b(x)$ and membership functions $p_i(x)$ respectively, we get the following energy functional $E_{FR}(p,b,c,\sigma)$ with Gaussian mixture and bias correction.

$$\begin{aligned} E_{FR}(p,b,c,\sigma) &= \lambda\int_\Omega -log[\sum_{i=1}^{K} \frac{1}{\sqrt{2\pi}\sigma_i} exp(-\frac{(I(x)-b(x)c_i)^2}{2\sigma_i^2})p_i]dx \\ &+\mu\int_\Omega |\nabla b|^2 dx + \sum_{i=1}^{K}\int_\Omega |\nabla p_i| dx \\ &\triangleq -\lambda\int_\Omega log(\sum_{i=1}^{K} f_i(x)p_i(x))dx \\ &+\mu\int_\Omega |\nabla b|^2 dx + \sum_{i=1}^{K}\int_\Omega |\nabla p_i| dx \end{aligned} \quad (6)$$

Remark. We want to mention that our model is not the first time to use Gaussian distribution. On the contrary, the Gaussian distribution has been introduced to many segmentation models, such as graph cut [4] and soft Mumford-Shah model [19]. The difference between the proposed model and the previous models is that those previous models all assume different Gaussian distributions have a same variance and usually fixed. However, in our model, we assume different Gaussian distributions have different variances which increases the flexibility.

3. Numerical Implementation

Note that the energy functional is convex with respect to all its variables except for variances. For fixed variances, global minimization can be achieved for any initialization. The Euler-Lagrange equations of variances, means and bias are as follows.

$$-\lambda\int_\Omega \frac{f_i p_i((I-bc_i)^2-\sigma_i^2)}{2\sigma_i^4\sum_{i=1}^{K} f_i p_i}dx = 0 \quad (7)$$

$$-\frac{\lambda}{\sigma_i^2}\int_\Omega \frac{f_i p_i (I-bc_i)b}{\sum f_i p_i}dx = 0 \quad (8)$$

$$-\lambda\frac{f_i p_i}{\sum_{i=1}^{K} f_i p_i}\frac{(I-bc_i)c_i}{\sigma_i^2} - \Delta b = 0 \quad (9)$$

Correspondingly, we use the following iteration schemes:

$$\sigma_i^{(n+1)} = \sigma_i^{(n)} + t_\sigma\lambda\left[\int_\Omega \frac{f_i p_i((I-bc_i)^2-\sigma_i^2)}{2\sigma_i^4\sum_{i=1}^{K} f_i p_i}dx\right]^{(n)} \quad (10)$$

$$c_i^{(n+1)} = c_i^{(n)} + t_c\left[\frac{\lambda}{\sigma_i^2}\int_\Omega \frac{f_i p_i (I-bc_i)b}{\sum f_i p_i}dx\right]^{(n)} \quad (11)$$

$$b^{(n+1)} = b^{(n)} + t_b\left[\lambda\frac{f_i p_i}{\sum_{i=1}^{K} f_i p_i}\frac{(I-bc_i)c_i}{\sigma_i^2} + \Delta b\right]^{(n)} \quad (12)$$

The challenge in the implementation is the optimization of membership functions $p_i(x)$ because of the constraints

$$1 \geq p_i(x) \geq 0 \ and \ \sum_{i=1}^{K} p_i(x) = 1 \quad (13)$$

which requires $p = (p_1, p_2, ..., p_K)$ lies in the simplex Δ_{K-1}. There have been two ways to deal with the simplex constraint. One is to use Lagrangian multiplier method (or augmented Lagrangian multiplier method) for $\sum_{i=1}^{K} p_i(x) = 1$, and add an exact penalty term for each $0 \leq p_i(x) \leq 1$ (see [3], [6] and [20]). The drawback of Lagrangian multiplier method is its low convergence rate. The so-called *exact penalty term* is exact only under some constraint and is not differentiable at end points, and must be replaced by a smoothed version for approximation which finally hurts the exactness. Another way to deal with the simplex constraint is to use the Euler-Lagrangian equation of the unconstraint problem for iterations and then project each iteration result to the simplex Δ_{K-1} [19]. The drawback of this method is that no general analytic expression can be written for all dimensions. For different dimensions, the projection functions are different, and need to be written in a different way. Especially, when the dimension is greater than three, the projection function becomes complicated, which leads to a low efficiency in both coding and implementation. In this paper, we give a novel way of projection using dual method. The projection can be expressed uniformly for all dimensions, and the analytic property is guaranteed due to dual theory.

Dual method has been extensively studied to deal with total variation which is not differentiable at points where the first order variation is zero. One of the popular example is Chambolle dual method [7]. Recently, M. Zhu and T. F. Chan developed a new algorithm combining the gradient decent method and dual method, called primal dual hybrid gradient method (PDHG) (see [22] for details). The method integrates the advantages of both gradient method and dual method, and thus faster than using either method. It is proved to be faster than using dual method only and its modified iteration form is guaranteed to converge when step size satisfies some condition (see [5], [12] and [18]). In our application, we adopted the ideal of PDHG and apply it to our model with constraint on simplex Δ_{K-1}.

3.1 Optimize membership functions using PDHG

By the principle of PDHG, to minimize (6) with respect to membership functions p_i $(i = 1, ..., K)$ under constraint (13), it is equivalent to solve the following discrete min-max problem

$$\max_{q \in X^K} \min_{p \in \Delta_{K-1}} -\langle p, Dq \rangle - H(p) \tag{14}$$

where $p = (p_1, ..., p_K)$, $q = (q_1, ..., q_K)$ and

$$\begin{aligned} H(p) =& \lambda \sum_{i,j=1}^{m,n} log \langle f(i,j), p(i,j) \rangle \\ =& \lambda \sum_{i,j=1}^{m,n} log \sum_{k=1}^{K} f_k(i,j) p_k(i,j). \end{aligned} \tag{15}$$

The descent direction for $min_{p \in R^K} \langle p, Dq \rangle + H(p)$ is $Dq + \nabla_p H(p)$. So, the evolution of membership p (primal step) is

$$p^{(n+1)} = P_{\Delta_{K-1}}(p^{(n)} + \tau_n(Dq^{(n)} + \nabla H(p^{(n)}))) \tag{16}$$

where $P_{\Delta_{K-1}}(v)$ is the projection to the simplex defined by

$$P_{\Delta_{K-1}}(x) \triangleq min_{z \in \Delta_{K-1}} \|z - x\| \tag{17}$$

for $\forall x \in R^K$, where $\| \cdot \|$ denotes the Euclidean distance. We will see a novelty method for the projection to simplex in the next section.

Since the first variation of (14) with respect to q_i is Dp_i, the dual step is

$$q_i^{(n+1)} = P_{X^K}(q_i^{(n)} + \theta^{(n)} Dp_i^{(n)}) \tag{18}$$

where P_{X^K} is the projection to space T defined by

$$[P_{X^K}(x)]_l = \frac{x_l}{max\{\|x\|_2, 1\}}. \tag{19}$$

where l denotes the number of component of a vector.

Therefore, the bi-direction projected PDHG algorithm for minimizing energy functional (6) is given by

$$\begin{cases} p^{(n+1)} = P_{\Delta_{K-1}}(p^{(n)} + \tau_n(Dq^{(n)} + \nabla H(p^{(n)}))) \\ q^{(n+1)} = P_{X^K}(q^{(n)} + \lambda \nabla p^{(n)}) \end{cases} \tag{20}$$

.

4. Experiment and Discussion

Since the main difference between our model and other Gaussian-distribution based model lies in the variable variants, we especially show the difference between variants varied and variants fixed. Since our model can be viewed as an extension of J. Shen's paper [19], we present many experimental results based on a comparison with J. Shen's model.

The first experiment aims at testing robustness to noise. In Fig.1, the original image contains obviously three phases. We added a mixed Gaussian noise with zero mean and an overall variance 0.03. First, we applied Shen's model. We choose $\lambda_1 = 5$, and stop iterations using criterion $max_{1 \le i \le 3}\{|c(i)_{new} - c(i)_{old}|\} < 0.001$, where $c(i)_{old}$ denotes the old mean before each iteration, and $c(i)_{new}$ denotes the new mean after each iteration (the same for the rest experiments). Then we applied our model (6) to the image. Obviously, the result of the new model is much better.

Explanation and analysis: This big difference comes from the difference of the fitting terms in two models. Note that in Shen's model, to make the fitting term small enough, the image intensity at each point must be very close to the mean of its phase. Thus it is sensitive to noise. Comparatively, in Model (6), the effect of isolated noise to the energy functional can be counteracted by the variances appeared in the denominators of the fitting term. So the new model is more robust to noise.

The second experiment aims at comparing robustness to bias. In Fig.2, the first line is the original biased image and its ground truth of all three membership functions. The second line and the third line show the soft segmentations obtained using Shen's model and the proposed model, respectively. Obviously, the proposed model gives more precise result compared with the ground truth since there is no bias in the segmentation.

Our third experiment aims to give a comparison between variances fixed and variances updated in the new model. For all the five lines, from left to right are the original image, three membership functions and hard segmentation, respectively. From the first line to the fourth line are the results with variances fixed. For example, we set $\sigma_i^2 = 0.005$ for all $(1 \le i \le 3)$ in the first line, and we set $\sigma_i^2 = 0.010$ for all $(1 \le i \le 3)$ in the second line, and so on. However, the last line is the result where variances are updated,

Fig. 1: Experiment 1: Robustness to noise. The first line: segmentation using Shen's model. The second line: segmentation using the proposed model. For each line, from left to right are original image, three membership functions and hard segmentation after thresholding.

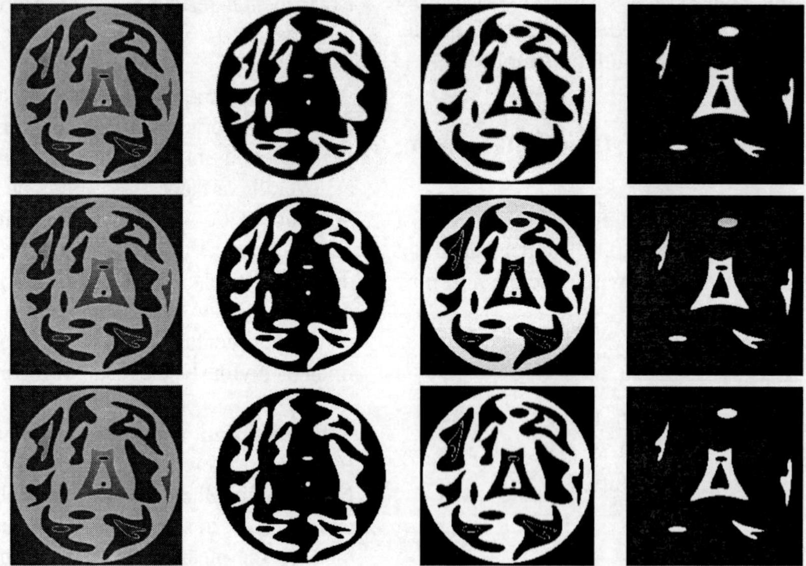

Fig. 2: Experiment 3: Robustness to bias. In the first line, from left to right are original image, and three ground truth membership functions. In the second line and the third line, from left to right are original image and soft segmentations (three membership functions) The second row is the soft segmentation using Shen's model, and the third line is the soft segmentation using the proposed model

and we obtained the final variances for the three phases, which are $\sigma_1 = 0.0069, \sigma_2 = 0.0193$, and $\sigma_3 = 0.0135$, respectively. Obviously, the last row gives the best result. This experiment shows that updating variances is better than fixing variances and assuming all of them are equal. Since Shen's model is a special case when all variances are fixed and the same, this experiment shows that the proposed model outperforms Shen's model.

Finally, we test our model using real images. In Fig.4, the liver is not very clear due to the existence of bias. Using Shen's model leads to a wrong result where a big part of the liver was incorrectly classified to background as shown in the first line. This can be easily seen from the hard segmentation. However, using the proposed model can get much better result as shown in the second line. This is because the fitting term in the model contains bias, as well as variance. By calculating the variances of the three phases, they are $0.013, 0.011$ and 0.002, respectively. This fact also proves that it is reasonable to assume that different phases may have different variances as in our model.

As we mentioned at the beginning of the paper, one of the most important application of soft segmentation is partial volume segmentation of MRI brain images. Fig.5 gives a comparison in MRI brain image soft segmentation. There is a big difference between the soft segmentations (the membership functions). By using MAP-AFCM model, most pixels are classified to be partial volume, i.e., its intensity is neither close to 1, nor close to 0 (In the figure, brightness of intensity means close to 1, darkness means close to 0, and intensity between brightness and darkness means partial volume). However, this is not true because it is well known that partial volume of MRI brain image should appear mostly

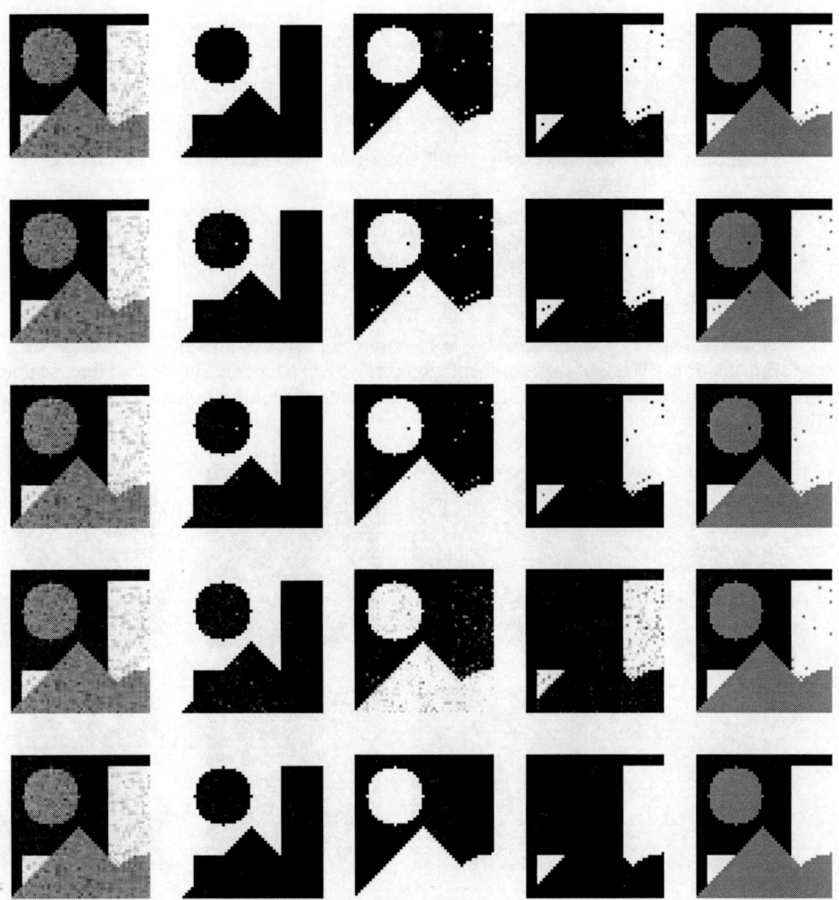

Fig. 3: Comparison between variances fixed and updated. In every row, the first three graphs are membership functions and the forth is the hard segmentation after thresholding. Row 1: result with $\sigma = 0.005$, Row 2: result with $\sigma = 0.010$, Row 3: result with $\sigma = 0.015$, Row 4: result with $\sigma = 0.020$, Row 5: result with σ updated.

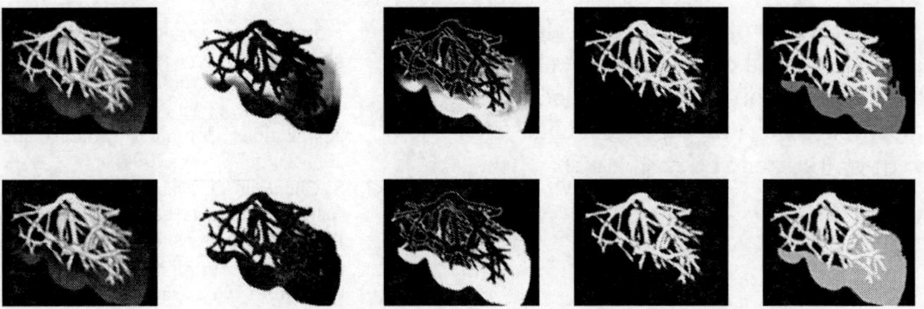

Fig. 4: MRI liver segmentation. The first line: segmentation using Shen's model. The second line: segmentation using the proposed model. From left to right: original image, three membership functions and hard segmentations, respectively.

often at the boundary of different tissues. Comparatively, using the proposed model can get more reasonable results, where the partial volume only appears at the boundary of different tissues.

We also present some natural images for comparison. In Fig.6, the left image is the original image, and the middle one and the right one are hard segmentations after thresholding using Shen's model and the proposed model, respectively. In Fig.7, the first column is the original image. We present all membership functions and hard segmentations for readers to compare. For all three examples, the results using our model are all better than using Shen's model.

5. Conclusion

In this paper, we proposed a stochastic variational model for multiphase soft segmentation based on Gaussian mixture. Compared with previously associated models, the proposed model is more robust to noise and bias. For implementation,

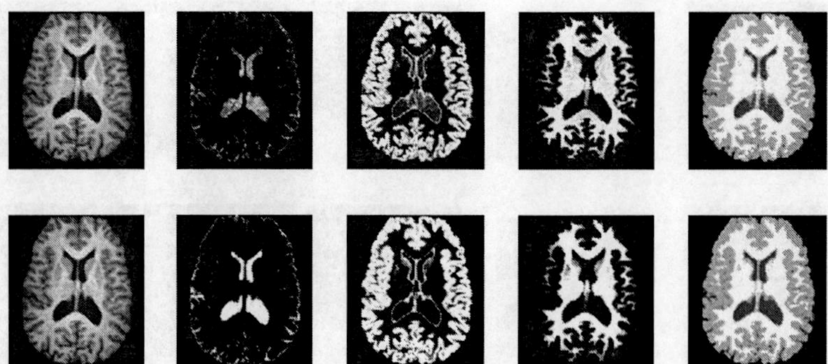

Fig. 5: MRI brain image segmentations. The first line: segmentation using Shen's model. The second line: segmentation using the proposed model. From left to right: original image, three membership functions (white matter, gray matter and CSF (cerebrospinal fluid)) and hard segmentations, respectively.

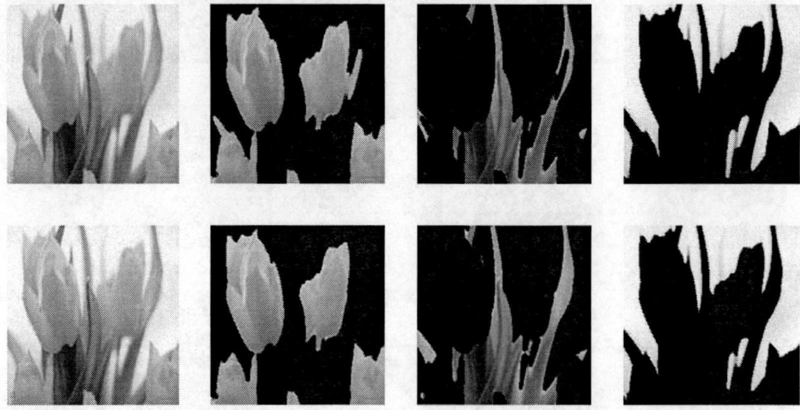

Fig. 6: Natural image segmentation after thresholding. From left to right: original image and three phases of hard segmentations. Line 1: Shen's model. Line 2: proposed model.

we developed a bi-direction projected PDHG algorithm, which is easy to carry out. Several experiments are presented to demonstrate the efficiency of our new model. Please address any questions related to this paper to Fuhua Chen by Email (fuhua.chen@westliberty.edu).

References

[1] M. N. Ahmed, S. M. Yamany, N. Mohamed, A. A. Farag, and T. Moriarty. A modified fuzzy C-means algorithm for bias field estimation and segmentation of MRI data, IEEE Trans. Med. Imag., vol.21, pp.193-199, 2002.

[2] J.C. Bezdek. A convergence theorem for the fuzzy ISODATA clustering algorithm. IEEE Trans. on Pattern Anal. Machine Intell., vol.2, pp. 1-8, 1980.

[3] X. Bresson, S. Esedoglu, P. Vandergheynst, J.-P. Thiran, and S. Osher. Fast global minimization of the active contour/ snake model. Jour. of Math. Imaging and Vision, vol. 28, pp. 151-167, 2007.

[4] Y. Boykov and G. Funka-Lea. Graph Cuts and Efficient N-D Image Segmentation. International Journal of Computer Vision (IJCV), vol.70(2), pp.109-131, 2006.

[5] Ethan S. Brown, Tony F. Chan, and Xavier Bresson, A Convex Relaxation Method for a Class of Vector-valued Minimization Problems with Applications to Mumford-Shah Segmentation. UCLA CAM Report, cam10-43, 2010.

[6] T. F. Chan, S. Esedoglu, and M. Nikolova, Algorithms for finding global minimizers of image segmentation and denoising models, SIAM J. Appl. Math. vol.66, pp. 1632-1648, 2006.

[7] A. Chambolle. An Algorithm for Total Variation Minimization and Applications. Journal of Mathematical Imaging and Vision, vol. 20(1-2), pp. 89-97, 2004.

[8] S. Chen and D. Zhang. Robust image segmentation using fcm with spatial constraints based on new kernel-induced distance measure. IEEE Transactions on Systems Man and Cybernetics, vol.34(4), pp.1907 - 1916, 2004.

[9] F. Chen, Y. Chen and H. D. Tagare. An improvement of sine-sinc model based on logrithm of likelihood. Proc. of IPCV - 08, vol.1, pp.222 - 227, 2008.

[10] A. Dempster, N. Laird, D. Rubin. Maximum likelihood from incomplete data via the EM algorithm. Journal Royal Statis. Society B, vol. 39, pp. 1 -8, 1977.

[11] J. C. Dunn. A fuzzy relative of the ISODATA process and its use in detecting compact well-separated clusters. Jounal of Cybernetics, vol.3, pp.32-57, 1973.

[12] Ernie Esser, Xiaoqun Zhang and Tony Chan. A General Framework for a Class of First Order Primal-Dual Algorithms for TV Minimization, Cam report cam09-67, August 2009.

[13] C. Li, R. Huang, Z. Ding, C. Gatenby, D. Metaxas, A variational level set approach to segmentation and bias correction of images with intensity inhomogeneity, MICCAI 2008, Part II, LNCS 5242, pp. 1083-1091, 2008.

[14] X. Li, L. Li, H. Lu and Z. Liang. Partial Volume Segmentation of Brain Magnetic Resonance Images Based on Maximum a Posteriori

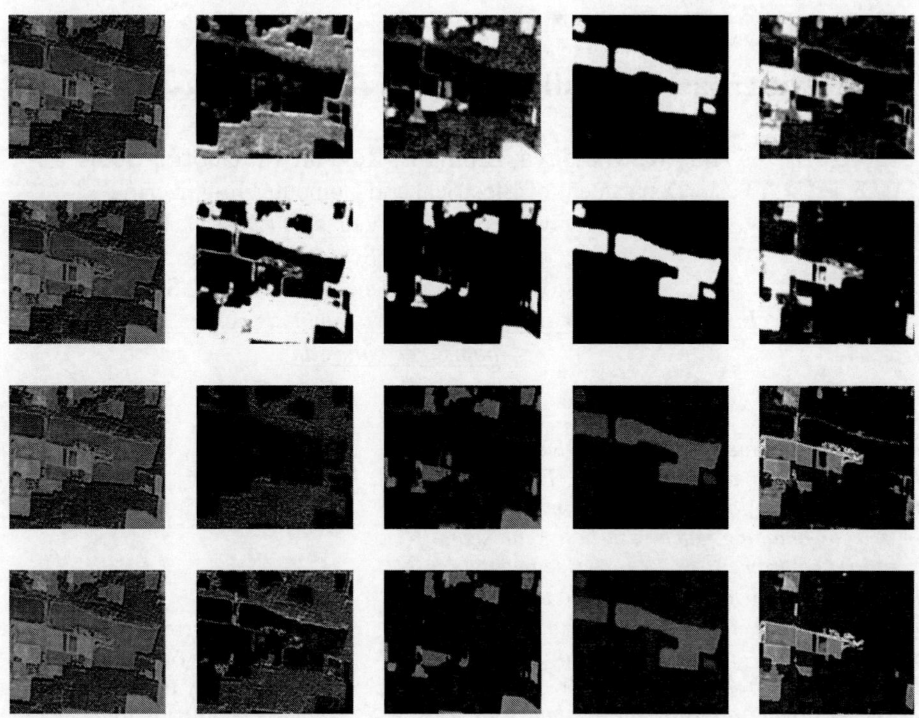

Fig. 7: Natural image segmentation after thresholding. Line 1: membership functions using Shen's model. Line 2: membership functions using the proposed model. Line 3: hard segmentations using Shen's model. Line 4: hard segmentations using the proposed model.

Probability. Med.Physis, 32(7), pp. 2337-2345, 2005.

[15] B. Mory and R. Ardon. Fuzzy region competition: A convex two-phase segmentation framework. In International Conference on Scale-Space and Variational Methods in Computer Vision, Proceedings, pp. 214 - 226, 2007.

[16] B. Mory, R.Ardon and J.P. Thiran. Variational Segmentation using Fuzzy Region Competition and Local Non-Parametric Probability Density Functions , ICCV, pp.1-8, 2007.

[17] D. L. Pham and J. L. Prince. An adaptive fuzzy C-means algorithm for the image segmentation in the presence of intensity inhomogeneities, Pattern Recognit. Lett., vol.20, pp. 57 -68, 1998.

[18] T. Pock, A. Chambolle, H. Bischof, and D. Cremers. An algorithm for minimizing the mumford-shah functional. In IEEE Conference on Computer Vision (ICCV), 2009.

[19] Shen.J. A Stochastic Variational Model for Soft Mumford-Shah Segmentation. International Journal of Biomedical Imaging. Volume 2006, cam05-54, 2006.

[20] Hiriart-Urruty, J.-B.; Lemarechal, C. Convex analysis and minimization algorithms. Grundlehren der mathematischen Wissenschaften pp. 305-306. Springer-Verlag, New York, 1993.

[21] W. Wells, E. Grimson, R. Kikinis, F. Jolesz, Adaptive segmentation of MRI data, IEEE Trans. Med. Imag., vol.15, pp. 429 - 442, 1996.

[22] M. Zhu and T. Chan, An Efficient Primal-Dual Hybrid Gradient Algorithm For Total Variation Image Restoration. CAM report, cam08-34, 2008.

FLAD-Feature Based Locally Adaptive Diffusion Based Image Denoising

Ajay K. Mandava, Emma E. Regentova, George Bebis*
Department of Electrical and Computer Engineering
University of Nevada, Las Vegas, NV 89154, USA
*Department of Computer Science & Engineering
University of Nevada, Reno, NV 89557, USA
Email: mandavaa@unlv.nevada.edu, emma.regentova@unlv.edu, bebis@cse.unr.edu

Abstract- *A novel patch based adaptive diffusion method is presented for image denoising. This is done with the purpose of locally and feature adaptive diffusion and for attaining patch-wise best peak signal to noise ratio. Our framework uses over-segmentation method to segment the image in to sensible regions and then diffusion of each segment/region to obtain the near-optimal solution and iterates to a lesser-segmented region/patches until a best PSNR value is attained. In performing diffusion the method uses the inverse difference moment (IDM) which is a robust feature in determining the amount of local intensity variation in the presence of noise. The experiments show that the proposed method delivers high denoising performance, both in terms of objective metric and the visual quality.*

Keywords: Diffusion, Patch, Region, Over-segmentation.

1. Introduction

Nonlinear anisotropic diffusion has drawn considerable attention over the past decade and has experienced significant developments as it gracefully diffuses the noise in the intra-region while inhibiting inter-region smoothing. Introduced first by Perona and Malik (PM diffusion) [1] the diffusion process is mathematically described by the following equation:

$$\frac{\partial}{\partial t} I(x,y,t) = \nabla \bullet (c(x,y,t)\nabla I) \qquad (1),$$

where I(x,y,t) is the image, t is the iteration step and $c(x,y,t)$ is the diffusion function monotonically decreasing of the magnitude of the image gradient. Two diffusivity functions proposed are:

$$c_1(x,y,t) = \exp\left(-\left(\frac{|\nabla I(x,y,t)|}{\lambda}\right)^2\right) \qquad (2)$$

and

$$c_2(x,y,t) = \frac{1}{1+\left(\frac{|\nabla I(x,y,t)|}{\lambda}\right)^2} \qquad (3),$$

where λ is referred to as a diffusion constant. Depending on the choice of the diffusivity function, equation (1) covers a variety of filters. The discrete diffusion structure is translated into the following form:

$$I_{i,j}^{n+1} = I_{i,j}^{n} + (\nabla t) \bullet \begin{bmatrix} c_N(\nabla_N I_{i,j}^n) \bullet \nabla_N I_{i,j}^n + c_S(\nabla_S I_{i,j}^n) \bullet \nabla_S I_{i,j}^n + \\ c_E(\nabla_E I_{i,j}^n) \bullet \nabla_E I_{i,j}^n + c_W(\nabla_W I_{i,j}^n) \bullet \nabla_W I_{i,j}^n \end{bmatrix} \qquad (4),$$

Subscripts N, S, E and W (North, South, East and West) describe the direction of the local gradient, and the local gradient is calculated using nearest-neighbor differences as

$$\nabla_N I_{i,j} = I_{i-1,j} - I_{i,j};\ \nabla_S I_{i,j} = I_{i+1,j} - I_{i,j}$$
$$\nabla_E I_{i,j} = I_{i,j+1} - I_{i,j}; \nabla_W I_{i,j} = I_{i,j-1} - I_{i,j} \qquad (5).$$

Generally, the effectiveness of the anisotropic diffusion is determined by (a) the efficiency of the edge detection operator to distinguish between noise and edges; (b) the accuracy of an "edge-stopping" function to promote or inhibit diffusion; and (c) the adaptability of a convergence condition to terminate the diffusion process automatically. The model in [1] has several practical and theoretical limits. It needs a reliable estimate of image gradients because with the increase of the noise level, the effectiveness of the gradient calculation degrades and deteriorates the performance of the method. Secondly, the equal number of iterations in the diffusion of all the pixels in the image leads to blurring of textures and fine edges.

Several authors have independently proposed modifications to the model to overcome the above problem. Catte et al. [2] used a smoothed gradient of the image, rather than the true gradient. The smoothing operator removes some of the noise which might have deceived the original PM filter. In this case, the scale parameter σ is fixed. In [3] authors have proposed the inhomogeneous anisotropic diffusion which includes a separate multiscale edge detection part to control the diffusion.

Yu et al. [4] proposed a method wherein the SUSAN edge detector is incorporated into the model. Noise insensitivity and structure preservation properties of SUSAN guides the diffusion process in an effective manner. Li et al. [5] proposed a context adaptive anisotropic diffusion via weighted diffusivity function by jointly exploiting contextual information (i.e. calculation of gray level variance) and spatial gradient. Chao and Tsai [6] proposed a diffusion model which incorporates both the local gradient and the gray-level variance to preserve edges and fine details while effectively removing noise. When the level of noise is high; noisy pixels in the image generally involve larger magnitudes of gray level variance and gradients than those of actual edges and fine details. Thus, the method is becoming inefficient quite soon. Wang et al. [7] proposed a local variance controlled scheme wherein spatial gradient and contextual discontinuity of a pixel are jointly employed to control the evolution. However, a solution to estimating the contextual discontinuity leads to an exhaustive search procedure, which causes algorithm to be too computationally expensive. Zhang et al. [8] presented a Laplacian pyramid-based nonlinear diffusion (LPND) method where Laplacian pyramid was utilized as a multiscale analysis tool to decompose an image into subbands, and then anisotropic diffusion with different diffusion flux is used to suppress noise in each subband. LPND tries to introduce sparsity and multiresolution properties of multiscale analysis into anisotropic diffusion. Another approach to context-based diffusion was researched in [9], where we proposed SWCD method. The multi-scale stationary wavelet analysis of the local neighborhood across the scales provides the edge information partially free of noise and thus makes possible the tunable diffusion. As a result, and due to the shift invariance property of stationary wavelet transform the PSNR has been improved compared to Shih's diffusion [10] which was performed on wavelet coefficients without consideration of the structural content of the local neighborhood.

State-of-the art denoising techniques all rely on patches, either for dictionary learning [11,12], collaborative denoising of blocks of similar patches [13] or for non-local sparse models [14]. Regularization with non-local patch-based weights has shown improvements on classical regularization involving only local neighborhoods [15, 16, 17]. The shape and size of patches should adapt to anisotropic behaviour of natural images [18, 19]. In spite of the high performance of the patch-based denoising techniques they generally produce artifacts even at a comparatively moderate noise levels. In addition, the size of the patch has a significant impact on the PSNR even for the similar or identical contents.

All above considerations suggest an approach which incorporates adaptation to the image local structure within optimally sized patches. Unlike block-transform based methods such as BM3D [15] which perform with a pre-determined optimum block size and clustering-based denoising methods such as KLLD [14] which uses a predetermined optimum number of classes, our method searches for an optimum patch size through iterative diffusion starting with a small patch size, that is a large number of patches and proceeds with a smaller number of patches, that is large patches until a best PSNR is attained and no further improvement is possible. To initialize the algorithm we use superpixel segmentation [20]. Each superpixel is diffused to the best PSNR, and then the process iterates on larger superpixels. In our pursuit of determining the local gradient and thus an amount of diffusion we use the inverse difference moment (IDM) feature [23]. We demonstrate that the feature is robust in determining the amount of local intensity variation in the presence of noise. Overall the diffusion process converges to PSNR levels known by the state-of-the-art methods with a minimum visible blocking/patching artifacts. The method is called feature based locally adaptive diffusion (FLAD) method.

The rest of the paper is organized as follows: Section 2 provides a theoretical background and introduces the method and implementation details. Section 3 presents results of the experiment; thereafter we conclude.

2. Feature Based Locally Adaptive Diffusion (FLAD)

2.1 Superpixel Segmentation

As it was pointed out earlier in this paper, we need the image to be over-segmented first. For this purpose we use superpixel segmentation. A single parameter of the method- k is a desired number of approximately equally-sized superpixels. The procedure begins with an initialization step where k initial cluster centers C_i are sampled on a regular grid spaced S pixels apart. To produce roughly equally sized superpixels, the grid interval is $S = \sqrt{N/k}$. The centers are moved to seed locations corresponding to the lowest gradient position in a 3x3 neighborhood, and thus avoid centering a superpixel on an edge. This reduces the chance of seeding a superpixel with a noisy pixel. Next, in the assignment step, each pixel i is associated with the nearest cluster center whose search region overlaps its location. A distance measure D, determines the nearest cluster center for each pixel. Since the expected spatial extent of a superpixel is a region of an approximate size SxS, the search for similar pixels is carried in a region of size $2Sx2S$ around the superpixel center. Once each pixel has been associated to the nearest cluster center, an update step adjusts the cluster centers to be the mean vector of all the pixels belonging to the cluster. The $L2$ norm is used to compute a residual error E between center locations of the new and the previous clusters. The assignment and update steps can be repeated iteratively until convergence. Experimentally, twenty iterations are sufficient for most images, and therefore throughout the rest of the paper we use this value.

2.2. Modified Diffusion

Mentioned above the normalized inverse difference moment (IDM) feature is visualized in Fig.1. The feature captures texture details in both coarse and fine structures. IDM will get small contributions from homogenous region and larger values in non-homogenous regions. Ranging between 0 and 1; the feature being 0 has an indication of a pixel being a part of a homogenous neighborhood. The value being 1 indicates that the pixel is a part of texture or an object boundary.
The diffusivity function of Eq.2 is modified to the following:

$$c_p = \exp\left(-\left(\frac{IDM(I)}{\lambda}\right)^2\right), p = N,S,W,E$$
,

where

$$IDM = 1 - \sum_{i=0}^{G-1}\sum_{j=0}^{G-1}\frac{1}{1+(i-j)^2}P(i,j)$$

Given an MxN neighborhood containing G gray levels

from 0 to G-1, let f(m,n) be the intensity at sample m, line

n of the neighborhood.

Then

$$P(i,j\,|\,\Delta x,\Delta y) = W\cdot Q(i,j\,|\,\Delta x,\Delta y),$$

Where

$$W = \frac{1}{(M-\Delta x)(N-\Delta y)};$$

$$Q(i,j\,|\,\Delta x,\Delta y) = \sum_{n=1}^{N-\Delta y}\sum_{m=1}^{M-\Delta x} A$$

and

$$A = \begin{cases} 1, iff\,(m,n) = i \quad and \quad f(m+\Delta x, n+\Delta y) = j \\ 0, elsewhere \end{cases}$$

For calculation we use 9x9 window centered at pixel(i,j).

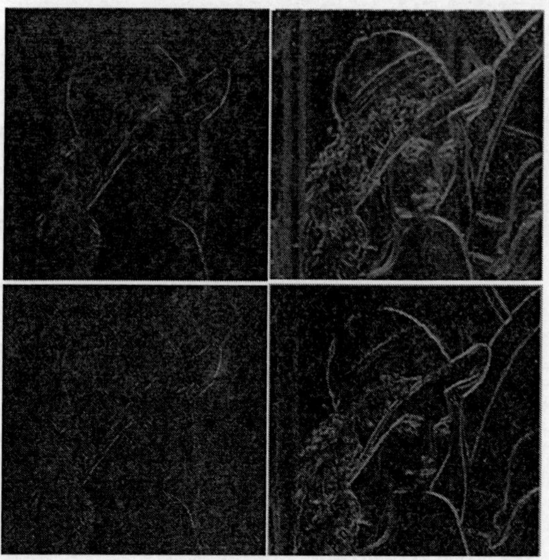

Fig.1 1st column: Gradient image for additive white Gaussian noise level σ =20, 40 for "Lena"; 2nd column: Inverse difference moment for additive white Gaussian noise level σ =20, 40

2.3 FLAD Algorithm

Let us denote I - input image, k – number of regions, m – number of merging steps, *Var* –intensity variance and n – number of diffusion steps. The method performs according to the following steps:

1. *Initialize m=0, α = 1.1, λ =10. Segment image into k (k≠1) regions.*
2. *Initialize n=0. Calculate PSNR for each region of initial partition, i.e.,* $[PSNR_k^{(0)}]_0$.
3. *Iteration step: Diffuse image pixel* $I_{i,j}$ *using Eq.(4).*
4. *For* $\forall R_i$: *if* $[PSNR_k^{(n+1)}]_m > [PSNR_k^{(n)}]_m$, *Goto Step 3; else Goto Step 6.*
5. *While* $R_m \neq I$, *for* $\forall$ *Ri ~ Rj, if* $Var(R_j) \leq \alpha * Var(R_i)$, *then* $R_i \cup R_j$; *m=m+1; update k;, Goto Step 2, else Repeat Step 5 with α = α+0.1.*
6. *Stop.*

3. Experimental Results

We now test the proposed method on the benchmark images corrupted by additive white Gaussian noise. Initial number of superpixel segments is set to 'k' = MxN/patch size; where MxN is the size of the image and the patch size is usually set globally (between 5x5 and 19x19). In our work, we calculate the bounds with the patch size of 8x8 for low noise levels i.e. σ≤40 and a larger patch size such as 11x11 for high noise levels i.e. σ>40. The diffusion constant $\lambda = 10$ in the evaluation of benchmark images with σ=10, 20, 30, 50 and 100 of the additive white Gaussian noise. Table I provides PSNR values by

Table I. PSNR of the proposed method.

Image/Noise, σ	**FLAD**				
	10	**20**	**30**	**50**	**100**
Lena	35.56	32.61	30.85	28.59	25.56
House	35.94	32.93	31.11	28.68	25.12
Peppers	34.48	31.05	29.03	26.56	23.18
Cameraman	33.99	30.18	28.24	25.89	23.08

Fig.2. First row: "Lena" image and Lena with additive white Gaussian noise level σ =100; Second row: results by BM3D and FLAD

Table II. PSNR comparison of different anisotropic diffusion methods for "Lena".

Method/ σ	**10**	**15**	**20**
Noisy	28.15	24.62	22.14
PM [1]	32.70	30.71	29.37
Catte [2]	33.27	31.39	30.09
Li [5]	34.28	32.41	31.15
GSZ FAB [21]	32.49	29.86	28.29
LVCFAB [7]	31.90	28.21	26.67
RAAD [22]	34.33	32.53	31.24
FLAD	**35.56**	**33.86**	**32.61**

Fig.3. First Column: "Lena" image with additive white Gaussian noise level σ =20 and 50; Second Column: corresponding results by FLAD

the proposed method for benchmark images. Second, the proposed FLAD algorithm is compared to six diffusion based methods which are considered as the state-of- the-art techniques in diffusion based denoising, which are FAB based diffusion, GSZ FAB [21], LVCFAB [7], and RAAD [22]. The improvement by FLAD for the given noise levels is ranging from 1.3 dB for low noise to 1.59dB for noise level with σ=100. Finally, the comparison to BM3D is due, and it shows that the performance of FLAD is 0.35 dB lower compared to that of the BM3D for noise level σ=10 and 0.39 dB lower for noise level σ=100. Fig.2 shows that lesser or no blocking/ringing artifacts are introduced by FLAD compared to those in BM3D denoised images. The denoising performance of the FLAD is further illustrated in Fig.3, where we show fragments of a few noisy (σ=20 and 50) test images and fragments of the corresponding denoised ones. The denoised images show high visual quality in the areas of smooth intensity transition and lesser or no ringing around contours of extended objects.

4. Conclusion

We have presented a novel FLAD algorithm for image denoising. The high performance of the method is attained due to the following properties: a) patch-based optimization of PSNR through iterative diffusion; b) agglomeration of patches and repetitive iteration of the process; c) modification of the diffusion function. The method has attained a highest performance in the class of advanced diffusion based methods and outperforms its counterpart by reducing visible blocking and ringing artifacts inherent to block- and transform-based methods.

Acknowledgement

This material is based upon work supported by NASA EPSCoR under Cooperative Agreement No. NNX10AR89A.

References:

1. P. Perona and J. Malik, “Scale-space and edge detection using anisotropic diffusion,” IEEE Transactions on Pattern Analysis and Machine Intelligence, vol. 12, no. 7, pp. 629–639, 1990.
2. F. Catté, P.-L. Lions, J.-M. Morel, and T. Coll, “Image selective smoothing and edge detection by nonlinear diffusion,” SIAM Journal on Numerical Analysis, vol. 29, no. 1, pp. 182–193, 1992.
3. V. B. Surya Prasath and Arindama Singh, “Well-Posed Inhomogeneous Nonlinear Diffusion Scheme for Digital Image Denoising,” Journal of Applied Mathematics, vol. 2010, Article ID 763847, 14 pages, 2010. doi:10.1155/2010/763847
4. Jinhua Yu, Jinglu Tan, Yuanyuan Wang. Ultrasound speckle reduction by a SUSAN-controlled anisotropic diffusion method. Pattern Recognition, 2010: 3083-3092.
5. H. C. Li, P. Z. Fan, and M. K. Khan, “Context-Adaptive Anisotropic Diffusion for Image Denoising,” IET Electronics Letters, vol.48, no.14, pp.827-829, 2012.
6. Shin-Min Chao, Du-Ming Tsai: An improved anisotropic diffusion model for detail- and edge-preserving smoothing. Pattern Recognition Letters 31(13): 2012-2023 (2010).
7. Y. Wang, L. Zhang, P. Li. Local Variance-Controlled Forward-and-Backward Diffusion for Image Enhancement and Noise Reduction. IEEE Transactions on Image Processing, 2007: pp.1854-1864.
8. Zhang Fan, Mo Yoo Yang, Mong Koh Liang, and Kim Yongmin, "Nonlinear Diffusion in Laplacian Pyramid Domain for Ultrasonic Speckle Reduction," IEEE Trans. Med. Imaging. 26, 200-211 (2007).
9. Ajay K. Mandava and Emma E. Regentova, “Image denoising based on adaptive nonlinear diffusion in wavelet domain”, J. Electron. Imaging 20, 033016 (Sep 14, 2011)
10. Shih, A.C.-C., Liao, H.-Y.M., Lu, C.-S.: A New Iterated Two-Band Diffusion Equation: Theory and Its Applications. IEEE Transactions on Image Processing (2003) DOI: 10.1109/TIP. 2003.809017.
11. M. Aharon, M. Elad and A. M. Bruckstein, “The K-SVD: An Algorithm for Designing of Overcomplete Dictionaries for Sparse Representation,” IEEE Transactions on Signal Processing, Vol. 54, No. 11, 2006.
12. P. Chatterjee and P. Milanfar, Clustering-based Denoising with Locally Learned Dictionaries (K-LLD), IEEE Transactions on Image Processing, vol. 18, num. 7, July 2009, pp. 1438-1451
13. K. Dabov, A. Foi, V. Katkovnik, and K. Egiazarian, “Image denoising by sparse 3D transform-domain collaborative filtering,” *IEEE Trans. Image Process.*, vol. 16, no. 8, pp. 2080-2095, August 2007.
14. J. Mairal, F. Bach, J. Ponce, G. Sapiro, and A. Zisserman, "Non-Local Sparse Models for Image Restoration," *Proc. of ICCV*, September-October 2009.
15. Gilboa, G., Osher, S.: Nonlocal operators with applications to image processing. Multiscale Model. Simul. **7**(3), 1005-1028 (2008).
16. Peyre, G., "Image Processing with Non-Local Spectral Bases" SIAM *Journal on* Multiscale. Modeling and Simulation 7, 2 *(2008) 703-730.*
17. X. Zhang, M. Burger, X. Bresson, and S. Osher, "Bregmanized Nonlocal Regularization for

Deconvolution and Sparse Reconstruction", SIAM Journal on Imaging Sciences, 3(3), 253-276, 2010

18. K. Dabov, A. Foi, V. Katkovnik, and K. Egiazarian, “A nonlocal and shape-adaptive transform-domain collaborative filtering”, Proc. Int. Workshop on Local and Non-Local Approx. in Image Process., LNLA 2008, Lausanne, Switzerland, August 2008.
19. Charles-Alban Deledalle, Vincent Duval and Joseph Salmon, *Non-Local Methods with Shape-Adaptive Patches (NLM-SAP)*, Journal of Mathematical Imaging and Vision, pp. 1-18, 2011
20. Achanta, R.; Shaji, A.; Smith, K.; Lucchi, A.; Fua, P.; Süsstrunk, S.; , "SLIC Superpixels Compared to State-of-the-Art Superpixel Methods," *Pattern Analysis and Machine Intelligence, IEEE Transactions on* , vol.34, no.11, pp.2274-2282, Nov. 2012
21. G. Gilboa, N. Sochen, and Y. Y. Zeevi, “Forward-and-backward diffusion processes for adaptive image enhancement and denoising,” *IEEE Trans. Image Process.* **11**(7), 689–703 (2002).
22. Y. Wang , R. Niu , L. Zhang and H. Shen "Region-based adaptive anisotropic diffusion for image enhancement and denoising", *Opt. Eng.* 49(11), 117007 (2010).
23. Cooper, G.R.J., “The Antialiased Textural Analysis of Aeromagnetic Data”, Computers & Geosciences v.35, p.586-591 (2009).

Segmentation of Online Handwritten Word by Estimating the Busy Zone of the Image

Rajib Ghosh
National Institute of Technology Patna
Computer Science and Engineering Department
Patna-800005, India

Abstract- *To take care of variability involved in the writing style of different individuals a novel approach has been proposed in this article to segment unconstrained handwritten Bangla words into characters. Online handwriting recognition refers to the problem of interpretation of handwriting input captured as a stream of pen positions using a digitizer or other pen position sensor. For online recognition of word the proper segmentation of word into basic strokes is very much important. For word segmentation, at first the busy zone of the whole word is calculated and then an estimated headline is imagined just above the starting point of the busy zone. Remove all the pixels crossing the estimated headline by checking their distance. Finally the segmentation is done. The system has been tested on 5500 Bangla word data and obtained around 94.9% of correct segmentation on word data from the proposed system.*

Keywords: Online, handwriting, segmentation, busy zone, headline

1 Introduction

With the development of digitizing tablets and micro computers, online handwriting recognition has become an area of active research since the 1960s. This became a need because machines are getting smaller in size and keyboards are becoming more difficult to use in these smaller device. Moreover, online handwriting recognition provides a dynamic means of communication with computers through a pen like stylus, as it is natural writing instrument and this seems to be an easier way of entering data into computers. However, wide variation of human writing style makes online handwriting recognition a challenging pattern recognition problem.

Work on online character recognition started gaining momentum about forty years ago. Numerous approaches have been proposed in the literature and the existing approaches can be grouped into three classes namely, (i) structural analysis methods where each character is classified by its stroke structures, (ii) statistical approaches where various features extracted from character strokes are matched against a set of templates using statistical tools and (iii) motor function models that explicitly use trajectory information where the time evaluation of the pen co-ordinates plays an important role. But work on online word recognition is in its nascent stage. For online word recognition first the adjacent combined characters must be segmented into individual characters or basic strokes. Then each character or basic strokes can be individually recognized. Some work is already there on online character recognition.

But work on online bangla word recognition is almost nil. Consequently, work on segmentation of Bengali online word is also nil. Many techniques are available for online recognition of English, Arabic, Japanese and Chinese characters but there are only a few pieces of work [4-7] available towards Indian characters although India is a multi-lingual and multi-script country. Also for online word recognition very few works are there in Indian languages. For example, in Tamil language [4] some works are there. Some works are available in English, Japanese and in Chinese [1-3]. But in Bengali no work is there on online word recognition as well as word segmentation. In this paper we propose a system for segmentation of online Bengali word. Segmentation of Bengali word is very difficult with compared to English because of its shape variability of the characters as well as larger number of character classes. See Figure-1 where examples of four Bangla characters are shown to get an idea of handwriting variability.

Figure 1. Examples of some Bengali online characters. First three columns show samples of handwritten characters and last column shows samples of a numeral.

There are twelve scripts in India and in most of these scripts the number of alphabets (basic and compound characters) is more than 250, which makes keyboard design and subsequent data entry a difficult job. Hence, online recognition of such scripts has a commercial demand. Although a number of studies have been done for online recognition of a few printed Indian scripts like Devnagari, Bengali, Gurumukhi, Oriya, etc. with commercial level accuracy, but to the best of our knowledge no system is commercially available for online word recognition of Bengali script. In this paper a scheme has been proposed for segmentation of online Bengali handwritten word into basic strokes by using the busy zone concept. Here we first compute the histogram of the words for computing the busy zone of the word. Then an estimated headline is imagined just above the starting point of the busy zone. Then calculate the distance of all the pixels of each stroke from the starting of the stroke. Then Segment the strokes at those pixels that are within the range of ±20 of the headline and whose total distance from the beginning and end of the stroke is greater than 25% of the length of that stroke. In my last paper on online bangla word segmentation [9] a scheme was proposed where segmentation was done by extracting different basic features of online Bengali handwriting.

The rest of the paper is organized as follows. In Section 2 we discuss about the Bengali language and data collection. Section 3 details the Segmentation method. The experimental results are discussed in Section 4. Finally, conclusion of the paper is given in Section 5.

2 Bangla Script and Online Data Collection

Bangla, the second most popular language in India and the fifth most popular language in the world, is an ancient Indo-Aryans language. About 200 million people in the eastern part of Indian subcontinent speak in this language. Bangla script alphabets are used in texts of Bangla, Assamese and Manipuri languages. Also, Bangla is the national language of Bangladesh. The alphabet of the modern Bangla script consists of 11 vowels and 40 consonants. These characters are called as basic characters. Writing style in Bangla is from left to right and the concept of upper/lower case is absent in this script. It can be seen that most of the characters of Bangla have a horizontal line (Matra) at the upper part. From a statistical analysis we notice that the probability that a Bangla word will have horizontal line is 0.994.

In Bangla script a vowel following a consonant takes a modified shape. Depending on the vowel, its modified shape is placed at the left, right, both left and right, or bottom of the consonant. These modified shapes are called modified characters. A consonant or a vowel following a consonant sometimes takes a compound orthographic shape, which we call as compound character. Compound characters can be combinations of two consonants as well as a consonant and a vowel. Compounding of three or four characters also exists in Bangla. There are about 280 compound characters in Bangla. Main difficulty of Bangla character recognition is shape similarity, stroke size and the order variation of different strokes. By stroke we mean the set of points obtained between a pen down and pen up. From the statistical analysis on our dataset we found that the minimum (maximum) number of stroke used to write a Bangla character is 1 (4). The average number of stroke per character is 2.2. We have also seen that the characters 'এ', 'ও' and '৭' are mostly written by single stroke whereas the character 'উ' is written by almost all writer by 4 strokes. It also found that the characters ','ঔ','ত','ন' etc, are always written by 2 strokes.

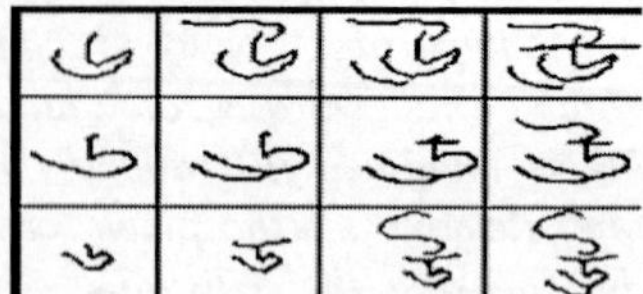

Figure2. Example of different stroke order for a character having four strokes

To illustrate this stoke order variation in Bangla script, Figure-2 shows a Bangla character that contains four different strokes. The left-most column shows the first stroke and this stroke is same for all the three samples of three different writers. Stroke- order varies from the second column onwards and the final (complete) character is shown in the right-most columns. From the 2nd column of Figure-3, it can be noted that the three samples have different shape. This is because of stroke order variation of the writers. For upper sample of the second column of Figure-3, the writer has given the upper stroke as second stroke. For middle sample of the second column the writer has given the lower stroke as second stroke. For lower sample, the writer has given the middle stroke as second stroke. Similar situation also occurs in 3rd column for Figure-2. Matra is a very common feature in Bangla and its length varies from writer to writer. It is seen that the presence or absence of Matra is the main difference between two characters. For example the character 'ত' is a basic character which has Matra but '৩' is a Bangla numeral and it does not have Matra.

For online data collection, the sampling rate of the signal is considered fixed for all the samples of all the classes of character. Thus the number of points M in the series of co-ordinates samples of all the classes of character. Thus the number of points M in the series of co-ordinates for a particular sample is not fixed and depends on the time taken to write the sample on the pad. As the number of points in actual trace of the characters are generally large and varies greatly due to high variation in writing speed, a fixed lesser number of points, regularly spaced in time are selected for further processing. The digitizer output is represented in the format of $p_i \in R^2 \times \{0,1\}$; $i = 1{:}M$, where p_i is the pen position having x-coordinate (x_i) and y-coordinate (y_i) and M is the total number of sample points. Let (p_i) and (p_j) be two consecutive pen points. We retain both of these two consecutive pen points (p_i) and (p_j) if the following condition is satisfied:

$$x^2 + y^2 > m^2 \;.........\; \text{(i)}$$

where $x = x_i - x_j$ and $y = y_i - y_j$. The parameter m is empirically chosen. We have set m equal to zero in Equation (i) to removes all consecutive repeated points.

Analyzing a total of 15000 Bangla characters we found that, for writing Bangla characters, the number of sample points (M) varies from 14 (for the character ড) to 176 (for the character ক্ষ) points. The average number of sample points in a Bangla character is 72. We also computed the average number of sample points in each character class. We noted that the character class (ঈ) has the maximum number of sample points and its average value is 113. The character class 'চ' has the minimum number (46) of sample points.

For data collection we have taken the Wacom Tablet and three datasheets (Figure-3) of words as interfaces covering all Bengali alphabets and vowel & consonant modifiers.

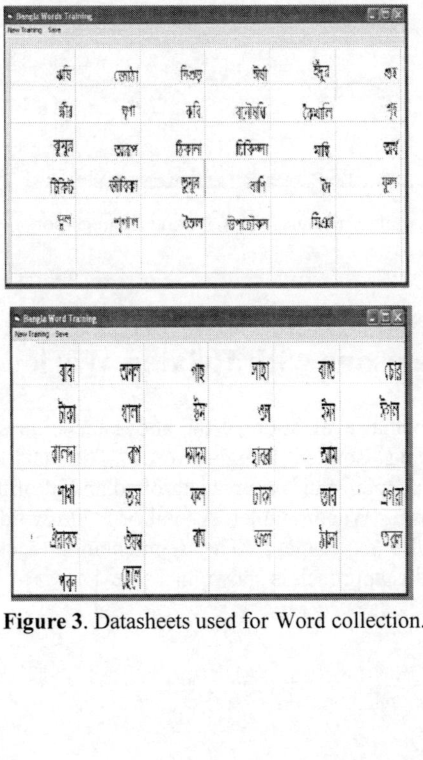

Figure 3. Datasheets used for Word collection.

3 Related Work

In bengali very few works are there on online handwritten document. Most of the works available on Bengali handwritten word segmentation are in offline. Although some works are available on online handwritten document in other languages. Here some of the works [5-7] available on segmentation of words into characters in Bengali online handwriting are discussed below:–

Online handwriting recognition refers to the problem of interpretation of Handwriting input captured as a stream of pen positions using a digitizer or other pen position sensor. For online recognition of word the segmentation of word into basic strokes is needed. The approach discussed in [5] is based on estimations of the positions of the headline and busy zone of the input word sample. Here after computing the busy zone, segmentation points are obtained along the trajectory of the pen movement where the pen-tip after travelling through the busy zone crosses/touches the headline(say,at point s1) and after some more time it again enters the busy zone(say at point s2) without lifting the pen-tip from the writing surface. Segmentation points include (i) mid points between s1 and s2 and (ii) endpoints of each constituent strokes save for the last stroke. For word segmentation, in [6] at first the word image is divided into two different zones. The upper zone is taken as the 1/3rd of the height of the total image. Now, based on the concept of downside movement of stroke in this upper zone each word is segmented into a combination of basic strokes. The segmentation is done at a pixel where the slope of six consecutive pixels satisfies certain angular value. The logic of segmentation in the system proposed in [7] is as follows: It is known that in Bengali handwriting the movement of each stroke is generally downside. By keeping this concept in mind it has been seen that in a downside movement of a stroke the point from where that downside movement starts at that point we have to split that stroke. This should be done only in the upper zone i.e. first 33% portion of the total height of the image. In the remaining 67% of the image, segmentation is not required. Generally people write any word in a manner where more than one alphabet is joined with one another. This joining is generally found in the upper 1/3rd portion of the image (exception in few cases). Different features of bangla characters are checked for this process such as i) Each pixel's distance from the start and end of the stroke, ii) The width of the stroke up to the pixel in question from the start and end of the stroke etc. Then some ratio has been taken between each pixel's distance and total stroke distance. Also the width of the stroke up to the pixel in question is also considered. After checking all these features the decision is taken about the segmenting point.

4 Segmentation

After collecting the different words using the datasheets shown in the Figure-3 the segmentation is started. For online recognition of word the proper segmentation of word into basic strokes is very much important.

4.1 Busy Zone Calculation Technique

Busy Zone of a word is the region of the word where a maximum portion of its characters lie. The busy zone is calculated using the following steps. First, we calculate the horizontal histogram from the topmost part of the entire word i.e. calculate no. of pixels in each row starting from the first row. In this way go downward and if the difference between the no. of pixels of any two rows is >=4 then mark that position. This is the start of the busy zone. Similarly, calculate the horizontal histogram from the bottommost part of the word i.e. calculate no. of pixels in each row starting from the last row. In this way go upward and if the difference between the no. of pixels of any two rows is >=4 then mark that position. This is the end of the busy zone. Figure-4 Shows the busy zone of one collected word.

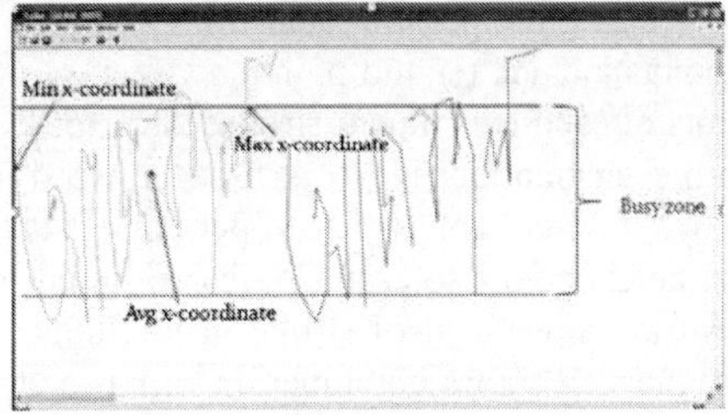

Figure 4. One word showing busy zone

4.2 Proposed approach

In this paper the proposed approach for segmentation is as follows:

1) Consider the busy zone of the whole word.
2) Find the minimum Y-coordinate (busy start) inside busy zone.
3) Imagine an estimated headline which is just above the starting point of the busy zone which is located at (busy start-1).
4) Calculate the distance of all the pixels of each stroke from the starting of the stroke.

   I.e. the distance of (x2, y2) from (x1, y1) is

$$Distance = \sqrt{(x1 - x2)^2 + (y1 - y2)^2}$$

5) Calculate the total_distance of all the pixels.
   i.e. total_distance=total_distance+distance
   (Where total_distance is initialize to 0, and when a new stoke starts the total_distance is again initialized to 0)
6) Segment the strokes at those pixels that are within the range of ±20 of the headline and whose total distance from the beginning and end of the stroke is greater than 25% of the length of that stroke.

By this approach the segmentation is done on all the words covering all the vowel and consonant modifiers and also covering all the alphabets in Bengali language. For example, Figure-5a and Figure-5b shows two instances of online handwritten word in joined manner. Figure-6.a and 6.b shows the images of Figure-5.a and 5.b after segmentation. Here after segmentation we will get the word in combination of basic strokes and / or characters. Here the first word is shown as combination of alphabets and vowel modifier আ kar and the second word is the combination of alphabet, vowel modifier আ kar and consonant modifier. Third word is the combination of alphabets and vowel modifiersএ kar.

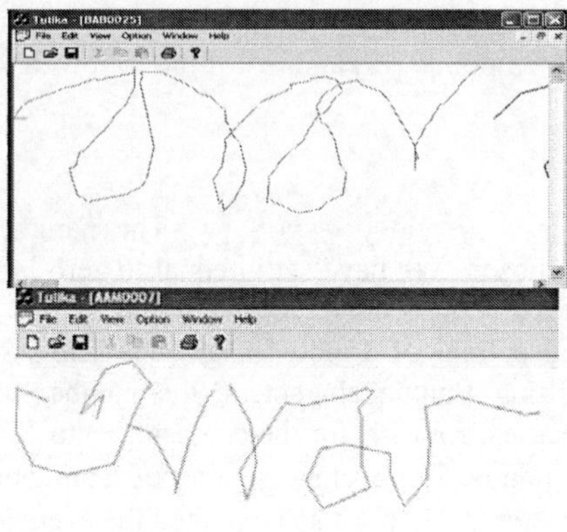

Figure 5a. Two Examples of online handwritten word written in joined manner before segmentation.

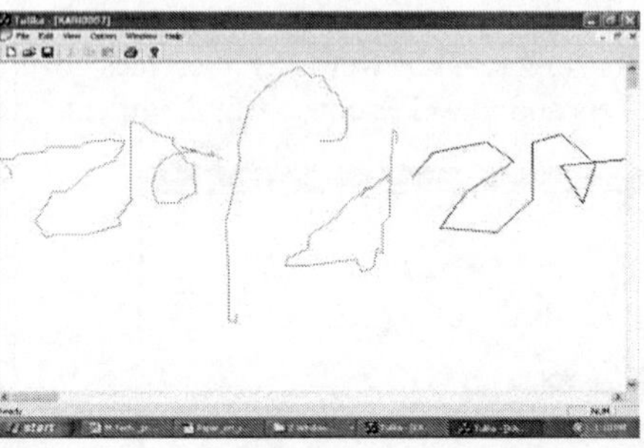

Figure 5b. Another Bangla Word before segmentation

5 Results and Experimental Comparisons with Related Work

The experimental evaluation of the above techniques was carried out using isolated Bangla words. The data were collected from people of different background and of different age group by using Wacom tablet. A total of 5,500 words are collected for the experiment. The segmentation accuracy obtained from this approach is shown in Table-1.

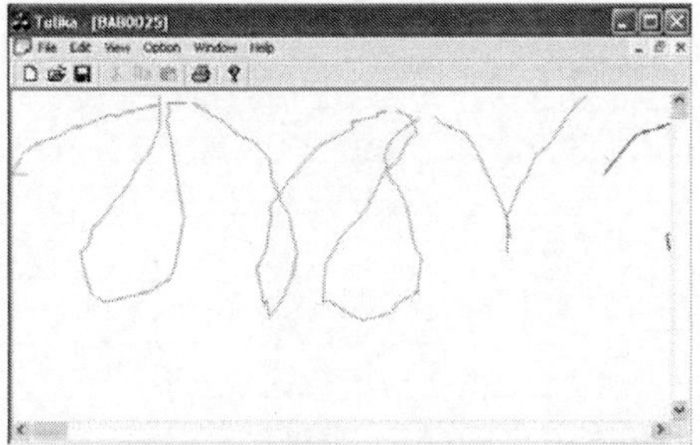

Figure 6.a. After segmentation shown in Figure-6.a

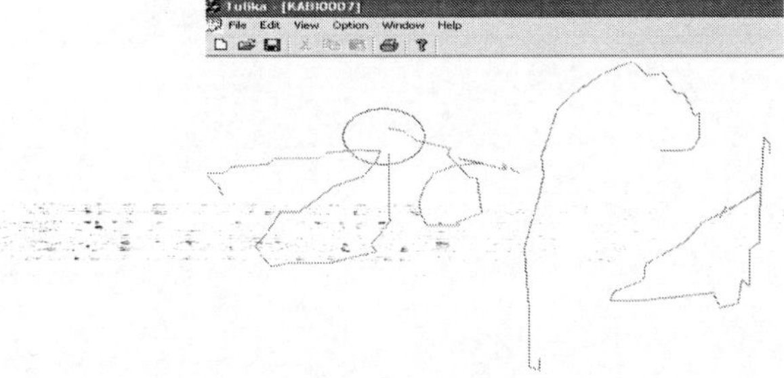

Figure 6.b. After segmentation shown in Figure-6.b

From the experiments it has been noted that the overall recognition accuracy of the proposed scheme is 94.9% for Bangla words considering the exact splitting of all joined basic strokes in a word into individual basic strokes. This result is better comparing to the approach mentioned in [7] where the correct segmentation result was 94% where in both the cases the no. of samples used for testing are same i.e. 5500 word data . This is even better than the approach discussed in [6] where the correct segmentation result was 81.13%. This comparison is shown in Table-2. In some words all joined basic strokes can't be splitted using this proposed scheme, only some joined basic strokes are splitted into individual strokes whereas the other joined basic strokes remain as it is. These cases we can say as partly segmentation. In the result of Table-1 correct segmentation rate does not include the partly segmentation cases. Most of the error occurs due to the differences of angles in vowel modifier's strokes when it is jointly written with any consonant alphabet.

6 Conclusion

This paper presents a scheme for the segmentation of Bengali online handwritten word. Using this technique different Bengali online handwritten word can be segmented into basic characters / strokes. This result will be helpful for recognizing Bengali words as the work for recognition of Bengali characters is already there. If the words written in joined fashion of basic strokes, then our proposed scheme can segment it as the combination of basic strokes which can be easily recognized by the character recognition scheme of online Bengali character using quadratic classifier. We tested the proposed system on 5500 data and got the encouraging result. Not much work has been done towards the online recognition of Indian scripts in general and Bangla in particular. So this work will be helpful for the research towards online recognition of other Indian scripts as well as for bangla in the level of word, text and so on. In fact the work for online recognition of Bengali handwritten word is going on by us and hopes that work can be completed successfully by taking the help of the current proposed work.

TABLE 1. Segmentation results on Bangla Word

Data	Correct Segmentation rate	Error rate
Word	94.9%	5.1%

TABLE 2: Experimental Comparisons with related works

Method	Data	Correct Segmentation rate	Error rate
Proposed	Word	94.9%	5.1%
Approach used in [7]	Word	94%	6%
Approach used in [6]	Word	81.13%	18.87%

7 References

[1] Wei Zhao, Jia-Feng Liu , Xiang-Long Tang, "Online handwritten English word recognition based on cascade connection of character HMMs", Proceedings of the First International Conference on Machine Learning and Cybernetics, vol.4, Beijing, 4-5 November 2002, pp. 1758- 1761.

[2] Xiang-Dong Zhou, Jin-Lun Yu, Cheng-Lin Liu, Nagasaki, T., Marukawa, K., "Online Handwritten Japanese Character String Recognition Incorporating Geometric Context", 9th IEEE International Conference on Document Analysis and Recognition, vol.1, Curitiba, Brazil, 23-26 September 2007, pp.48 – 52.

[3] Zhengbin Yao, Xiaoqing Ding, Changsong Liu, "On-line handwritten Chinese word recognition based on lexicon", 18th IEEE International Conference on Pattern Recognition, vol. 2 , Hong Kong, 20 – 24 August 2006, pp. 320 – 323.

[4] Bharath A., S. Madhvanath , "Hidden Markov Models for Online Handwritten Tamil Word Recognition", 9th IEEE International Conference on Document Analysis and Recognition , vol 1, Curitiba, Brazil , 23-26 September 2007, pp. 506-510.

[5] U.Bhattacharya, A.Nigam, Y.S.Rawat, S.K.Parui, "An Analytic scheme for online handwritten bangla cursive word recognition", Proceedings of the International Conference on Frontiers in Handwriting Recognition (ICFHR 2008), pp. 320 - 325, Montreal, Canada,19-21 August, 2008.

[6] Rajib Ghosh, Debnath Bhattacharyya, Samir Kumar Bandyopadhyay, " Segmentation of Online Bangla Handwritten Word", 2009 IEEE International Advance Computing Conference (IACC 2009), Patiala, India, 6-7 March 2009, pp. 777-782.

[7] Rajib Ghosh, "Segmentation of Unconstrained Online Bangla Handwritten Word by Extracting Basic Features", 2010 IEEE International Conference on Advances in Communication, Network, and Computing (CNC 2010), Calicut, Kerala, 4-5 October 2010, pp. 296-298.

An Adaptive and Fast Valley Emphasis Multilevel Otsu Thresholding Algorithm

Jianwu Long[1,2], **Xuanjing Shen**[1,2], **Haipeng Chen**[1,2,*], **He Zhang**[1,2]
[1]College of Computer Science and Technology, Jilin University, Changchun, Jilin, China
[2]Key Laboratory of Symbolic Computation and Knowledge Engineering, Ministry of Education, Jilin University, Changchun, Jilin, China

Abstract - *The multilevel thresholding problem is a challenge task due to the fact that the computation is usually very time-consuming for obtaining the optimal multilevel thresholds. Though the state-of-the-art multilevel thresholding algorithms applied various meta-heuristic techniques or acceleration strategies, they still directly searched the optimal thresholds in the whole histogram only for the fixed thresholds number given by the user. Considering that the optimal thresholds usually locate at the valleys of the histogram, we propose an adaptive and fast valley emphasis multilevel Otsu thresholding algorithm (AFVEO). We constrain the searching space in locations of all valleys of the histogram, and it can greatly reduce the iterations required for computing the between-class variance due to the fact that the number of valleys is much fewer than the size of the histogram. And most important we can obtain the optimal multilevel thresholds for different thresholds number without fixed one given by the user. The experimental results indicate that the proposed method is more efficient than traditional Otsu method, recursive Otsu method, valley emphasis Otsu method and neighborhood valley emphasis Otsu method.*

Keywords: Image segmentation, Multilevel thresholding, Otsu algorithm, Valley emphasis algorithm

1 Introduction

Automatic thresholding is one of the most popular image segmentation techniques and widely used in the field of image processing, computer vision and pattern recognition. Recently there are many thresholding algorithms [1], among them Otsu algorithm [2] is a powerful tool and widely used in many applications such as document image segmentation and recognition [3-4], automatic visual inspection of defects [5], etc. Otsu is a very simple and efficient thresholding algorithm, which aims at solving the bi-level threhsolding problem. Xu et al. found an inherent character that Otsu threshold is equal to the mean of the average intensities of two groups divided by this threshold [6].

When Otsu method is extended to multilevel thresholding, it is a challenge task due to the fact that the computation is very time-consuming. The multilevel thresholding algorithms have been studied widely in recently years. To reduce the computational complexity required for calculating the zero- and first-order cumulative moments and the between-class variance, Liao et al. proposed a recursive Otsu method [7]. But the searching space is the whole histogram and the number of iterations is very huge for a large thresholds number. Huang et al. presented a two-stage Otsu optimization approach by quantizing the histogram into smaller classes but this acceleration strategy loses much local details [8]. Swarm intelligence optimization is another scheme for the multilevel thresholding problem [9-13] such as the genetic algorithm, particle swarm optimization, ant colony, bacterial foraging algorithm, artificial bee colony algorithm, etc. Ng noticed that the objective of automatic thresholding is to find the valleys in the histogram and proposed a valley emphasis method [5]. Due to Ng's approach only considered the valley point information, Fan et al. presented an improved version named neighborhood valley emphasis algorithm which made full use of the neighborhood information for each threshold [14]. The above two approaches are very efficient when the thresholds number l is very small ($l < 5$) otherwise the computation is still expensive.

In order to overcome these problems we constrain the searching space in those valleys of the histogram. And in this paper we propose an adaptive and fast valley emphasis multilevel Otsu thresholding algorithm named AFVEO. Compared with the traditional Otsu method, the recursive Otsu method, the valley emphasis Otsu method and the neighborhood valley emphasis Otsu method, the proposed scheme is much more efficient and accurate.

The rest of this paper is organized as follows: Section 2 will briefly review four classic multilevel thresholding algorithms of the Otsu's family, including the traditional Otsu method (Otsu, 1979) [2], the recursive Otsu method (Liao et al., 2001) [7], the valley emphasis Otsu method (Ng, 2006) [5] and the neighborhood valley emphasis Otsu method (Fan and Lei, 2012) [14]. Section 3 then describes the details of the proposed AFVEO algorithm. The experimental results are illustrated in section 4. Finally section 5 will list the conclusions of this work.

2 Review of the Otsu methods

2.1 Traditional Otsu method

Assume each pixel of a given gray image is represented in L levels. The number of pixels with gray level i is denoted by n_i and i is ranged from 0 to L-1. The total number of all pixels can be expressed as $N=\sum_{i=0}^{L-1} n_i$. For a given pixel at level i, the corresponding occurrence probability can be easily computed by $p_i = n_i/N$ satisfying $p_i \geq 0$ and $\sum_{i=0}^{L-1} p_i = 1$.

If a gray image is divided into $l+1$ groups { C_1, C_2, ..., C_{l+1} } by l thresholds with gray values { t_1, t_2, ..., t_l }, where group C_1 contains gray levels [0, 1, ..., t_1], C_2 contains gray levels [t_1+1, ..., t_2], ..., and C_{l+1} contains gray levels [t_l+1, ..., $L-1$], then the class probability (or called zero-order cumulative moment) and the class total mean (or called first-order cumulative moment) for group C_k can be calculated as:

$$\omega_k = \sum_{i \in C_k} p_i \tag{1}$$

$$\mu_k = \frac{1}{\omega_k} \sum_{i \in C_k} i p_i \tag{2}$$

For simplicity, Eq.(2) is usually reformulated as:

$$\mu_k = \frac{\mu(k)}{\omega_k} \tag{3}$$

and,

$$\mu(k) = \sum_{i \in C_k} i p_i \tag{4}$$

Otsu (1979) selects the optimal thresholds { t_1^*, t_2^*, ..., t_l^* } by maximizing the following between-class variance σ_B^2:

$$\{t_1^*, t_2^*, \cdots, t_l^*\} = \underset{0 \le t_1 < t_2 < \cdots < t_l < L}{\arg\max} \{\sigma_B^2(t_1, t_2, \cdots, t_l)\} \tag{5}$$

where

$$\sigma_B^2 = \sum_{k=1}^{l+1} \omega_k (\mu_k - \mu_T)^2 \tag{6}$$

And in Eq.(6) μ_T is the total mean of the whole image and computed as follows:

$$\mu_T = \sum_{i=0}^{L-1} i p_i \tag{7}$$

2.2 Recursive Otsu method

During the iteration process, the traditional Otsu algorithm needs repeatedly calculating the zero- and first-order cumulative moments and the between-class variance and is very time-consuming to obtain the optimal thresholds. For reducing the huge computational complexity, Liao et al. (2001) proposed a modified version called recursive Otsu method. In this algorithm, an improved and efficient between-class variance $\sigma_B'^2$ is reformulated as follows:

$$\sigma_B'^2 = \sum_{k=1}^{l+1} \frac{(\mu(k))^2}{\omega_k} \tag{8}$$

And most important all the values of $\sigma_B'^2$ are pre-computed and stored in a so called H-table, thus the only thing during the searching process is to look up this H-table and do some simple summation:

$$\sigma_B'^2(t_1, t_2, \cdots, t_l) = H(0, t_1) + H(t_1+1, t_2) + \cdots + H(t_l+1, L-1) \tag{9}$$

where the H-table is calculated as:

$$\begin{cases} H(0,t_1) = \dfrac{(S(0,t_1))^2}{P(0,t_1)} \\ \vdots \\ H(t_k+1, t_{k+1}) = \dfrac{(S(t_k+1, t_{k+1}))^2}{P(t_k+1, t_{k+1})} \\ \vdots \\ H(t_l+1, L-1) = \dfrac{(S(t_l+1, L-1))^2}{P(t_l+1, L-1)} \end{cases} \tag{10}$$

with

$$P(u,v) = \sum_{i=u}^{v} p_i \tag{11}$$

$$S(u,v) = \sum_{i=u}^{v} i p_i \tag{12}$$

2.3 Valley emphasis Otsu method

Ng (2006) found that the objective of the automatic Otsu thresholding algorithm is to find the valleys in the histogram and all of them usually have small probability of occurrence, and thus proposed a valley emphasis Otsu method. The optimal thresholds { t_1^*, t_2^*, ..., t_l^* } are selected by the following criterion:

$$\{t_1^*, t_2^*, \cdots, t_l^*\} = \underset{0 \le t_1 < t_2 < \cdots < t_l < L}{\arg\max} \left\{ \left(1 - \sum_{j=1}^{l} p_{t_j}\right) \left(\sum_{k=1}^{l+1} \frac{(\mu(k))^2}{\omega_k} \right) \right\} \tag{13}$$

The only difference from the recursive Otsu method is the application of the weight $1-\sum_{j=1}^{l} p_{t_j}$ which ensures the optimal thresholds always locating at the valleys or the bottom rim of the histogram.

2.4 Neighborhood valley emphasis method

Ng's approach only considers the valley point information and fails in the case that the variance of the background is very different from that of the foreground especially for the bi-level thresholding problem. For this reason Fan et al. (2012) proposed an extended version based on the valley emphasis Otsu method named neighborhood valley emphasis Otsu method which made full use of the neighborhood information for each threshold. The neighborhood gray value $\overline{p}_i$ of the gray-level i is defined as:

$$\overline{p}_i = \sum_{j=-m}^{m} p_{i+j} \tag{14}$$

where m is the half neighborhood window size. We can clearly find that Ng's method is a special case of this algorithm if $m=0$ is set. With a different weight from Ng's method, the optimal thresholds { t_1^*, t_2^*, ..., t_l^* } of this new version are computed as:

$$\{t_1^*, t_2^*, \cdots, t_l^*\} = \underset{0 \le t_1 < t_2 < \cdots < t_l < L}{\arg\max} \left\{ \left(1 - \sum_{j=1}^{l} \bar{p}_{t_j}\right)\left(\sum_{k=1}^{l+1} \frac{(\mu(k))^2}{\omega_k}\right) \right\} \quad (15)$$

3 Proposed algorithm

All of the above mentioned algorithms mainly are applied to those simple multilevel thresholding problems with small thresholds number l (usually $l < 5$), otherwise they will become very time-consuming due to the key reason that a large number of iterations are required for calculating the between-class variance. For a fixed thresholds number l the total number of exhaustive search is C_L^l, which is a complex combination optimization problem for a gray image with the gray level $L = 256$. The other disadvantage of the four algorithms is that a fixed thresholds number l must be given by the user in advance. It is not straightforward to select the optimal number in practical applications. Thus we must check different level and obtain the optimal number l^* by maximizing the objective function. And then we can correctly extract the globally optimal thresholds { t_1^*, t_2^*, …, $t_{l^*}^*$ }.

In the valley emphasis method Ng noticed that the objective of thresholding is to find the valleys in the histogram, but he only applied this information to the objective function. In order to overcome this drawback we constrain the searching space in those valleys of the histogram not in the whole histogram. With this observation in mind, in this paper we propose an adaptive and fast valley emphasis multilevel Otsu thresholding algorithm, named AFVEO. The detail of our algorithm is described as follows:

Step1. Calculating the normalized histogram $h(i)$ of a given gray level image where gray level i ranges from 0 to $L-1$ and $L = 256$.

Step2. Smoothing the histogram to reduce the noise, and the new histogram is obtained by:

$$p_i = \frac{1}{2r+1}\sum_{j=-r}^{r} h(i+j) \quad (16)$$

where r is the half window size and $r = 2$ is suggested in this paper.

Step3. Removing all non-valleys that satisfy one of the following criterions:

$$p_{i-1} < p_i < p_{i+1} \quad (17)$$

$$p_{i-1} > p_i > p_{i+1} \quad (18)$$

$$p_{i-1} \le p_i \ge p_{i+1} \quad (19)$$

$$|p_i - p_{i-1}| \le \varepsilon \,\&\&\, |p_{i+1} - p_i| \le \varepsilon \quad (20)$$

Eqs.(17)~(20) illustrate monotonically increasing, monotonically decreasing, local peaks and invariant area, respectively. In this work the error $\varepsilon = 1.0\times10^{-5}$ is suggested. After all non-valleys are removed we can identify all the valleys denoted by $V(i)$ and the size of it is given by L'.

Step4. Calculating the neighborhood gray value $\bar{p}_i$ only for gray level $i \in V(i)$ using Eq.(14) and $m = 1$ is suggested in this paper.

Step5. Calculating the H-table only for gray level $i \in V(i)$ using Eq.(10).

Step6. For different thresholds number l ranging from 1 to $l_{\max}$, we select the optimal value l^* and the corresponding optimal thresholds { t_1^*, t_2^*, …, $t_{l^*}^*$ } in the domain of valleys $V(i)$ by maximizing the following objective function:

$$\{t_1^*, t_2^*, \cdots, t_{l^*}^*\} = \underset{0 \le t_1 < t_2 < \cdots < t_l < L}{\arg\max} \left\{ \left(1 - \sum_{j=1}^{l} p_{t_j}\right) \sigma_B'^2 \right\} \quad (21)$$

where $\sigma_B'^2$ is calculated by Eq.(9).

From extensive experiments we find that the optimal thresholds number l^* satisfies $l^* < 10$, thus in this paper $l_{\max} = 9$ is suggested. As the same as the traditional Otsu method (Otsu), the recursive Otsu method (ROtsu), the valley emphasis Otsu method (VEO) and the neighborhood valley emphasis Otsu method (NVEO), the total number of iterations of the AFVEO method is still $C_{L'}^l$. From the experiments we also find that there are only a few valleys in the histogram, that is to say $L' \ll L$, at last we can hugely reduce the iterations.

We will give an example to demonstrate the efficiency of the AFVEO method as follows. Fig.1 displays a gray image #55067 from BSD500 [15] and its histogram. Using the AFVEO method we identified $L' = 14$ valleys and marked red line in Fig.1(b). But for any gray images the size of their histogram is always $L = 256$. Table.1 shows the comparison of the iterations in different searching space. Due to $L' \ll L$ we can find that the iterations emphasizing valleys are greatly smaller than that of using histogram as the thresholds number l is increasing.

Table.2 gives the comparison of the running times for the five methods. From the table we can find that when $l = 1$ the original Otsu method is faster than the ROtsu, the VEO and the NVEO because it doesn't pre-create the H-table, but as the number l becomes larger, the H-table is very important. Unfortunately, the ROtsu, the VEO and the NVEO still work very poor especially when $l \ge 5$ is satisfied. And fortunately our algorithm is always efficient for different thresholds number even if the value $l = 9$ is set, so that we can readily determine the optimal thresholds number l^* and the corresponding thresholds.

(a) #55067 (b) smoothed histogram and valleys (red line marked)

Fig.1 Image #55067 and its histogram and valleys

Table.1 Comparison of the iterations in different searching space

Thresholds number	$l=1$	$l=2$	$l=3$	$l=4$	$l=5$	$l=6$	$l=7$	$l=8$	$l=9$
Histogram $L=256$	256	32640	2763520	174792640	8809549056	368532802176	—	—	—
Valleys $L'=14$	14	91	364	1001	2002	3003	3432	3003	2002

Table.2 Comparison of the running times for the five methods (unit: ms)

Thresholds number	$l=1$	$l=2$	$l=3$	$l=4$	$l=5$	$l=6$	$l=7$	$l=8$	$l=9$
Otsu	0.378	1.178	88.228	6765.98	409600.0	—	—	—	—
ROtsu, VEO, NVEO	0.865	1.302	50.775	3901.68	232528.0	12271004.0	—	—	—
AFVEO	0.375	0.376	0.384	0.509	0.658	0.872	1.568	0.866	0.617

4 Experimental results

Experiments are tested on PC with Microsoft Visual C++ 2008, Intel Xeon 3.10 GHz CPU and 2G memory. The testing images mainly come from the collection of the author (for experiment 1 including Rectangle, Coin and Wheel) and the BSD500 [15] (for experiment 2 including #86016, #118035, #241004 and #55067). To evaluate the efficiency and accuracy of the presented AFVEO method, the results are compared with those of the traditional Otsu method (Otsu), recursive Otsu method (ROtsu), valley emphasis Otsu method (VEO) and neighborhood valley emphasis Otsu method (NVEO). In our method, the optimal thresholds number l^* is identified automatically ranging from 1 to 9 and also the corresponding optimal thresholds. For the Otsu, ROtsu, VEO and NVEO methods, the fixed number l^* is set for fairness.

Fig.2 demonstrates the experimental results of our method including the optimal thresholds drawing in histogram, segmentation results and contour images. Fig.3 displays results of the other four methods. From experiment 1 we can find that the thresholding results have the same visual quality for the five algorithms. But in experiment 2 illustrated by Figs.4~5 the results of our method have the better visual quality and thresholding accuracy. And Table.3 gives the different optimal thresholds.

The comparison of the running times for the five algorithms is displayed in Table.4. It should be emphasized that the running times of our method contain the total times for different number l ranging from 1 to 9. From the comparison we can find that the implementation efficiency of our method is much better than the other four methods. Table.5 gives the objective function values of the proposed AFVEO method and the globally optimal resolutions exist and are unique in the range [1, 9].

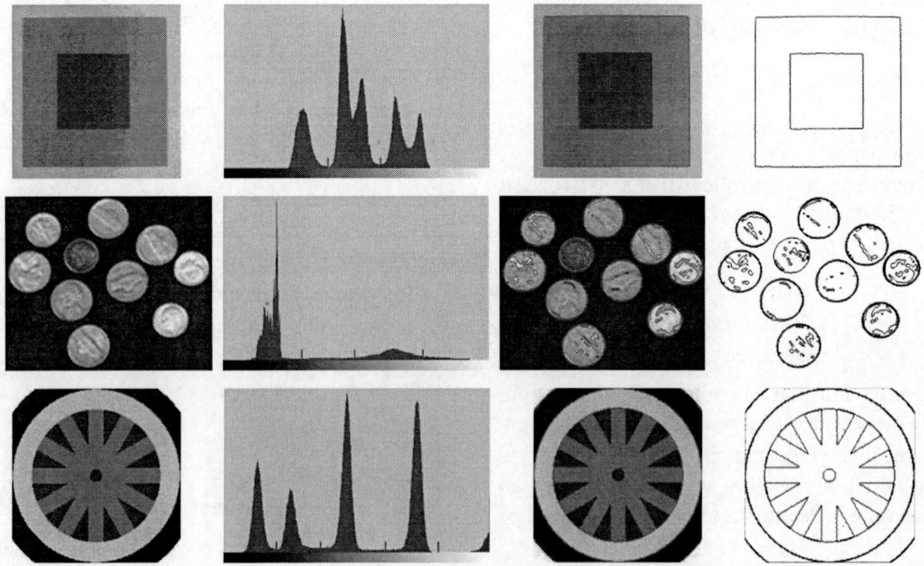

(a) Original images (b) Histogram and optimal thresholds (c) Segmentation results (d) Contour images

Fig.2 Experiment 1 of our method (row 1: Rectangle, row 2: Coin, row 3: Wheel)

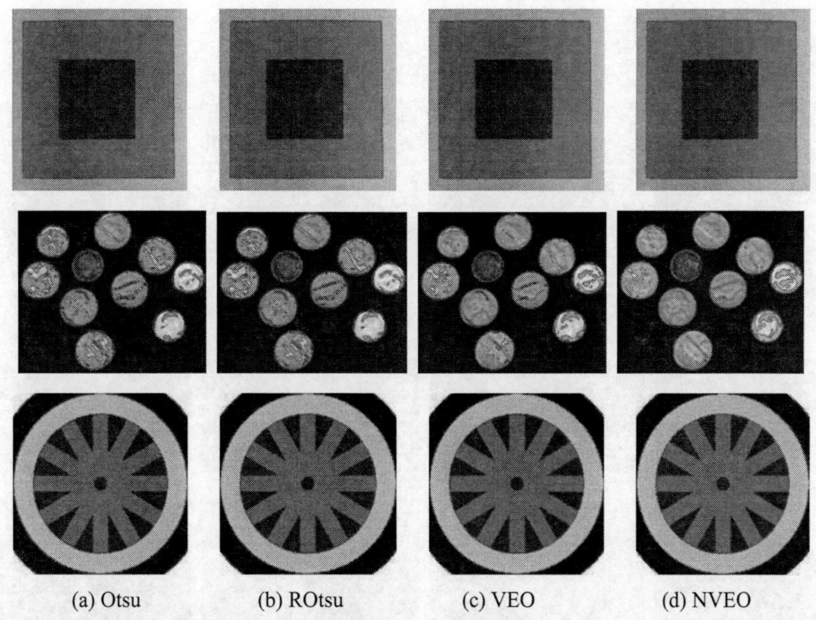

(a) Otsu (b) ROtsu (c) VEO (d) NVEO

Fig.3 Experiment 1 of the Otsu method, ROtsu method, VEO method and NVEO method

Fig.4 Experiment 2 of our method: the first row shows original images (#86016, #118035, #241004, #55067 respectively); the second row shows corresponding histograms and optimal thresholds; the third row shows corresponding segmentation results

Table.3 Comparison of the optimal thresholds for the five methods

Images	Optimal number l^* and thresholds of our method		Optimal thresholds with fixed level l^*			
	l^*	Optimal thresholds	Otsu	ROtsu	VEO	NVEO
Rectangle	2	100-151	99-148	99-148	99-151	99-150
Coin	3	76-127-192	77-134-181	77-134-181	77-129-193	76-118-204
Wheel	4	51-93-156-206	50-92-151-218	82-151-218-255	82-149-220-255	84-156-207-255
#86016	1	116	129	129	118	116
#118035	3	55-143-201	99-135-203	99-135-203	56-132-201	0-143-200
#241004	4	92-159-195-234	57-96-155-219	90-155-219-255	94-161-235-255	92-163-234-255
#55067	6	45-80-111-136 -177-191	42-80-105-136 -178-207	42-80-105-136 -178-207	47-80-105-136-179-187	0-1-2-53-136-188

(a) Otsu (b) ROtsu (c) VEO (d) NVEO

Fig.5 Experiment 2 of the Otsu method, ROtsu method, VEO method and NVEO method

Table.4 Comparison of the running times for the five methods (unit: ms)

Images	AFVEO	Otsu	ROtsu	VEO	NVEO
Rectangle	6.648	3.182	3.483	3.605	3.503
Coin	111.909	91.876	54.502	66.776	68.916
Wheel	1026.48	6824.14	4043.24	5112.62	5139.51
#86016	7.117	1.612	2.097	2.193	2.041
#118035	515.795	89.739	53.639	69.526	67.526
#241004	21.261	6827.93	4022.1	5348.05	5125.84
#55067	6.722	1.94882×10^7	1.24711×10^7	1.65269×10^7	1.50075×10^7

Table.5 #Valleys and objective function values of our method for different images

Images	#Valleys	Objective function values								
		l=1	l=2	l=3	l=4	l=5	l=6	l=7	l=8	l=9
Rectangle	4	17241.9	**17508.2**	17326.8	—	—	—	—	—	—
Coin	23	10358.8	10437.3	**10469.4**	10466.5	10462.9	10457.2	10448.8	10435.1	10412.9
Wheel	29	17225.2	17980.7	18120.3	**18180.1**	18178.8	18177.5	18176	18174.3	18172.6
#86016	13	**24694.4**	24692	24590.2	24477.6	24298.5	24098.8	23897.5	23686.5	23456.6
#118035	27	28986.3	29071.9	**29072.7**	29070.8	29068.5	29044.3	29017.4	28988.7	28960
#241004	19	20022.2	20841.8	21127	**21134.5**	21132.3	21129.8	21118.3	21105.6	21085.7
#55067	14	18387.6	19051.7	19297.3	19370.3	19371.9	**19372.5**	19367	19359.5	19349.8

5 Conclusions

In this work we propose an adaptive and fast valley emphasis multilevel Otsu thresholding algorithm, named AFVEO algorithm. The idea of our method is from the observation that the optimal thresholds locate at valleys of the histogram. Constraining the searching space in these valleys we greatly reduce the computational complexity required for calculating the zero- and first-order cumulative moments and between-class variance. The extensive experimental results demonstrate that our method is very efficient and accurate compared with the traditional Otsu method, recursive Otsu method, valley emphasis Otsu method and neighborhood valley emphasis Otsu method. In the future work we can apply the AFVEO algorithm to color images segmentation due to the perfect effectiveness and efficiency.

Acknowledgements

The research has been supported by National Natural Science Grant (No. 60973090), Natural Science Grant of Jilin Province (No. 201115025), the Opening Project of Key Laboratory Ministry of Education (No. 450060481223) and the Graduate Innovation Fund of Jilin University (No. 20121104).

References

[1] Sezgin M and Sankur B. Survey over image thresholding techniques and quantitative performance evaluation. Journal of Electronic Imaging, Vol.13, No.1, P146-168 2004.

[2] Otsu N. A threshold selection method from gray-level histograms. IEEE Transactions on Systems, Man and Cybernetics, Vol.9, No.1, P. 62-66, 1979.

[3] Chou CH, Lin WH and Chang F. A binarization method with learning-build rules for document images produced by cameras. Pattern Recognition, Vol.43, No.4, P. 1518-1530 , 2010.

[4] Pai YT, Chang YF and Ruan SJ. Adaptive Thresholding Algorithm: Efficient Computation Technique Based on Intelligent Block Detection for Degraded Document Images. Pattern Recognition, Vol.43, No.9, P.3177-3187, 2010.

[5] Ng HF. Automatic thresholding for defect detection. Pattern Recognition Letters, Vol.27, No.14, P.1644-1649, 2006.

[6] Xu XY, Xu SZ, Jin LH, et al. Characteristic analysis of Otsu threshold and its applications. Pattern Recognition Letters, Vol.32, No.7, P.956-961, 2011.

[7] Liao PS, Chew TS and Chung, PC. A fast algorithm for multilevel thresholding. Journal of Information Science and Engineering, Vol.17, No.5, P.713-727, 2001.

[8] Huang DY and Wang CH. Optimal multi-level thresholding using a two-stage Otsu optimization approach. Pattern Recognition Letters, Vol.30, No.3, P.275-284, 2009.

[9] Hammouche K and Diaf M, Siarry P. A comparative study of various meta-heuristic techniques applied to the multilevel thresholding problem. Engineering Applications of Artificial Intelligence, Vol.23, No.5, P.676-688, 2010.

[10] Sathya PD and Kayalvizhi R. Modified bacterial foraging algorithm based multilevel thresholding for image segmentation. Engineering Applications of Artificial Intelligence, Vol.24, No.4, P.595-615, 2011.

[11] Sathya PD and Kayalvizhi R. Optimal multilevel thresholding using bacterial foraging algorithm. Expert Systems with Applications, Vol.38, No.12, P.15549-15564, 2011.

[12] Horng MH. A multilevel image thresholding using the honey bee mating optimization. Applied Mathematics and Computation, Vol.215, No.9, P.3302-3310, 2010.

[13] Horng MH. Multilevel thresholding selection based on the artificial bee colony algorithm for image segmentation. Expert Systems with Applications, Vol.38, No.11, P.13785-13791, 2011.

[14] Fan JL and Lei B. A modified valley-emphasis method for automatic thresholding. Pattern Recognition Letters, Vol.33, No.6, P.703-708, 2012.

[15] Arbelaez P, Maire M, Fowlkes C, et al. Contour Detection and Hierarchical Image Segmentation. IEEE Transactions on Pattern Analysis and Machine Intelligence, Vol.33, No.5, P.898-916, 2011.

SESSION

TEXTURE ANALYSIS

Chair(s)

TBA

Reducing the Complexity of Multi-Dimensional LBP Texture Features using Genetic Optimisation

Niraj Doshi and Gerald Schaefer
Department of Computer Science
Loughborough University, U.K.
n.doshi@lboro.ac.uk, gerald.schaefer@ieee.org

Abstract— *Texture analysis and classification have received significant research interest and have been shown to be essential in many computer vision systems and applications. Local binary patterns (LBP) form a simple yet powerful texture descriptor characterising local neighbourhood properties, which, due to its effectiveness and robustness, is widely employed. LBP information can be gathered at multiple scales to improve the performance of the descriptor. While in conventional LBP this information is recorded, in form of a histogram, separately for each of the scales, it was shown that a multi-dimensional (MD) feature representation removes some ambiguity and leads to better texture classification. However, the generated MD-LBP histograms result in relatively large feature descriptors which limit their practical use. In this paper, we show that a feature selection stage based on a genetic algorithm can be successfully applied to reduce the dimensionality of MD-LBP features while maintaining effective texture classification.*

Keywords: Texture, local binary patterns, LBP, MD-LBP, feature selection, genetic algorithm.

1. Introduction

Texture analysis and classification form an important part of many computer vision tasks including content-based image retrieval, face analysis, medical image analysis, multimedia content classification and annotation. While various powerful texture descriptors have been developed, changes in orientation, scale, illumination and other confounding imaging factors still present challenges.

Local binary patterns (LBP), first introduced in [1], represents a relatively simple yet powerful texture descriptor describing the relationship of a pixel to its immediate neighbourhood. Later work [2] extended that concept to varying neighbourhoods, to make the method greyscale and rotation invariant and to emphasise "uniform" texture patterns.

LBP descriptors are obtained at pixel locations and summarised into histograms which then serve as texture descriptors. For multi-scale LBP, the information is obtained at multiple radii and the resulting histograms are concatenated into a feature vector. Although this gives improved texture recognition, it was shown in [3] that it also leads to a loss of information and added ambiguity. A multi-dimensional LBP (MD-LBP) histogram was thus proposed to preserve the relationships between scales and was shown to lead to further improved texture classification performance.

Although MD-LBP allows for better texture classification, it results in relatively large feature descriptors which limit its usefulness. For example, while the original uniform rotation invariant LBP descriptor calculated at three scales leads to a feature length of 30, an MD-LBP histogram with the same parameters has a total of 1000 bins. In this paper, we show that through application of a feature selection stage based on a genetic algorithm (GA) the dimensionality of MD-LBP features can be drastically reduced while maintaining good texture classification performance. We demonstrate this based on experiments on the Outex dataset.

2. LBP texture features

Local binary patterns (LBP) are simple yet effective texture descriptors. The original LBP variant [1] operates on a per-pixel basis, and describes the 8-neighbourhood pattern of a pixel in binary form. If

$$B = \begin{pmatrix} g_8 & g_1 & g_2 \\ g_7 & g_{(0,0)} & g_3 \\ g_6 & g_5 & g_4 \end{pmatrix} \tag{1}$$

is the 3×3 grayscale block of a pixel at location $(0,0)$ and its 8-neighbourhood, then the neighbouring pixels are set to 0 and 1 by thresholding them with the centre pixel value. The value of the central pixel is subtracted from each neighbour

$$LBP_1 = \begin{pmatrix} g_8 - g_c & g_1 - g_c & g_2 - g_c \\ g_7 - g_c & & g_3 - g_c \\ g_6 - g_c & g_5 - g_c & g_4 - g_c \end{pmatrix} \tag{2}$$

where $g_c = g_{(0,0)}$ for convenience, and the binary code is then generated by applying the thresholding function

$$s(x) = \begin{cases} 1 & \text{for } x \geq 0 \\ 0 & \text{for } x < 0 \end{cases} \tag{3}$$

at each location which results in

$$LBP_2 = \begin{pmatrix} s(g_8 - g_c) & s(g_1 - g_c) & s(g_2 - g_c) \\ s(g_7 - g_c) & & s(g_3 - g_c) \\ s(g_6 - g_c) & s(g_5 - g_c) & s(g_4 - g_c) \end{pmatrix} \tag{4}$$

Finally, the LBP pattern is obtained by

$$LBP = \sum_{p=1}^{8} s(g_p - g_c)2^{p-1} \tag{5}$$

The 256 possible patterns resulting from the above procedure are used to build a histogram, which serves as a texture descriptor for the image.

2.1 Circular LBP

In the above procedure, the 8-neighbourhood of each pixel is utilised. Clearly, four of these neighbours are at a different distance ($\sqrt{2}$) than the other four. To compensate this, a circular neighbourhood can be defined [2] where locations that do not fall exactly at the centre of a pixel are obtained through interpolation.

A neighbourhood is defined by R and P where R defines the distance of the neighbours to the centre, while P gives the number of samples at that distance that are employed as neighbours. If g_c is at $(0, 0)$, then the co-ordinates of the neighbouring pixels g_p, $p = 1, 2, \dots, P$, are given by $(-R\sin(2\pi p/P))$, $(R\cos(2\pi p/P))$.

2.2 Rotation invariant LBP

It has been shown [2] that rotation invariance is relatively simple to address in LBP. If a texture is rotated, essentially the patterns (that is the 0s and 1s around the centre pixel) rotate with respect to the centre.

Rotation invariant LBP codes, $LBP^{ri}_{P,R}$, can be generated through shift operations on the bit sequence so as to arrive at a sequence with a maximal number of leading 0s, i.e.

$$LBP^{ri}_{P,R} = \min\{ROR(LBP_{P,R}, i) \mid i = 0, 1, \dots, P-1\} \tag{6}$$

where $ROR(x, i)$ performs a circular bit-wise right shift by i bits.

2.3 Uniform LBP

Certain binary patterns are fundamental properties of texture and sometimes their frequency exceeds 90%. These patterns are called uniform [2], leading to $LBP^{u}_{P,R}$, and are defined by a uniformity measure which corresponds to the number of spatial transitions (i.e., changes from 0 to 1 and vice versa). Patterns with a uniformity measure of 2 are given by

$$LBP^{u2}_{P,R} = \begin{cases} \sum_{p=0}^{P-1} s(g_p - g_c) & \text{if } U(LBP_{P,R}) \leq 2 \\ P+1 & \text{otherwise} \end{cases} \tag{7}$$

where

$$U(LBP_{P,R}) = |s(g_p - g_c) - s(g_0 - g_c)| + \sum_{p=1}^{P-1} |s(g_p - g_c) - s(g_{p-1} - g_c)| \tag{8}$$

Clearly, rotation invariance, leading to $LBP^{riu2}_{P,R}$, can be achieved in the same way as above. For eight neighbours there are nine rotation invariant uniform LBP codes, two without any 0-1 changes (i.e., one with all 0s and one with all 1s) and the remaining seven with $1, \dots, 7$ ones in sequence. It has been shown [2] that focussing on these uniform patterns while aggregating all other (i.e., non-uniform) patterns into one group leads to improved texture descriptors. While LBP generates 256 patterns for an 8-neighbourhood, and LBP^{ri} generates 36 patterns, LBP^{riu2} results in 10 pattern classes for the same neighbourhood.

2.4 Multi-scale LBP

By defining several radii around a pixel, multiple concentric neighbourhood LBP codes can be extracted. While in principle any radius is feasible, attention is often restricted to the sets $r = \{1, 3\}$ and $r = \{1, 3, 5\}$. Also, while in general any number of neighbours could be defined, we found in our experiments that choosing 8 neighbours at all distances does not compromise accuracy while also corresponding to those directions (horizontal, vertical, and plus/minus 45 degrees) to which the human visual system is most sensitive to.

2.5 Multi-dimensional LBP

Multi-scale LBP is performed by concatenating the LBP features from each radii into a one-dimensional feature vector. In [3], it was shown that this results in a loss of information between different scales and added ambiguity. This is illustrated in Fig. 1 where an "image" consisting of the two samples on the top will lead to exactly the same LBP descriptor as the two samples on the bottom. Both resulting LBP histograms will have one entry each for bins (00001111) and (00111111) for both radii.

A multi-dimensional histogram is hence used to preserve relations between different radii. At each pixel, LBP codes at different scales are extracted, while the combination of these codes identifies the histogram bin that

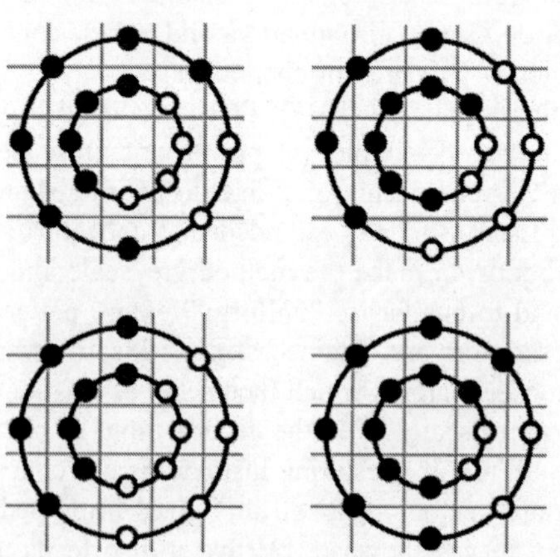

Fig. 1: Multi-scale LBP example.

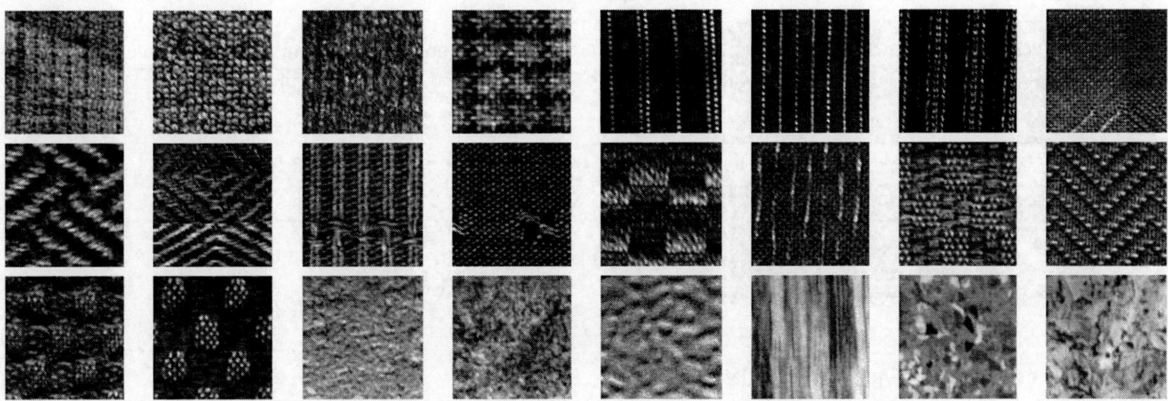

Fig. 2: Sample images of the 24 texture classes.

is incremented. For the example in Fig. 1, this gives a histogram with one entry for bin $(00001111, 00111111)$ and one entry for bin $(00111111, 00001111)$ for the top "image", while for the example at the bottom a histogram with one entry for $(00001111, 00001111)$ and one entry for $(00111111, 00111111)$ is obtained; i.e. two distinct histograms and hence two distinguishable texture descriptors are generated. MD-LBP has been shown to allow for improved texture classification in comparison to the original LBP variants [3].

3. Feature selection for MD-LBP

MD-LBP retains the relationships between scales, but at the cost of relatively large feature descriptors resulting in higher memory requirements and reduced processing speed. In this paper, we address this problem by applying a feature selection technique to reduce the length of MD-LBP descriptors.

In particular, we employ a feature selection algorithm that employs a genetic algorithm (GA) for selecting an optimal set of MD-LBP histogram bins, based on the technique presented in [4].

If we have M features of which we want to select N, then the resulting combinatorial optimisation problem has $\frac{M!}{2(M-N)!}$ possible solutions. Clearly, and especially for larger values of M, an exhaustive search is not feasible, and we consequently use a GA to search for a good feature set. The GA fitness function $\Phi = V - P$ is based on the principle of maximum relevance and minimum redundancy, where V, the relevance of a set with N features, is defined as

$$V = \frac{1}{N} \sum_{i=1}^{N} I(yh_i; y), \tag{9}$$

where $I(yh_i; y)$ is the mutual information of features and labels, and P is the redundancy between those features given by

$$P = \frac{1}{N^2} \sum_{i=1}^{N} \sum_{j=1}^{N} I(yh_i; yh_j), \tag{10}$$

where $I(yh_i; yh_j)$ is the mutual information between output features.

In the GA, each individual corresponds to a feature set of size N. The GA starts by randomly initialising a populating of N_{pop} (200 times the desired feature length in our implementation) individuals. Then, for each generated feature set V and P are calculated and the fitness Φ is recorded.

During each iteration, parents are randomly selected based on an asymmetric distribution function defined as

$$\text{Parent}_j = \text{round}(N_{pop}(e^{a\vartheta_j} - 1)/(e^a - 1)), \tag{11}$$

where $j = (1, 2)$ represents the parent number, a is set to 6 and ϑ_j is a random number with uniform distribution.

From the two parents, an offspring is generated by randomly selecting features from the two parents and ensuring that no duplicate features are selected. Selection and crossover is repeated until a full new population has been generated.

As stopping criterion, the uniformity of the population is used, expressed as the difference between the average and maximum of Φ. The algorithm terminates if this falls below a threshold (0.002) or if the maximum number of iterations (80) is reached. The individual of highest fitness then gives the selected features.

4. Experimental results

In our experiments, we performed texture classification on two databases from the Outex test suite [5]. Fig. 2 shows a sample image for each of the 24 classes used in both test suites; as can be seen the dataset is not simple as several texture classes are rather similar. As classifier, we employ standard support vector machines (SVMs) [6]. Since we have

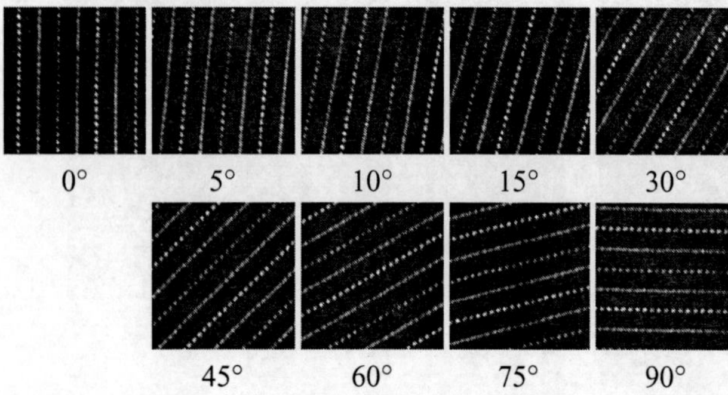

Fig. 3: Sample texture from the Outex_TC_10 dataset under different rotations.

more than two classes, we employ a one-against-one multi-class SVM [7] where for each SVM, we use a linear kernel and optimise the cost parameter $C \in [-1.1; 3.1]$ using a cross validation approach [8].

Our first experiment, performed on the Outex TC10 database, is designed to investigate a useful range of feature lengths to be used for our approach. The TC10 dataset is built from 24 texture classes captured at 9 rotation angles under the same illumination (see Fig. 3 for an example), with 20 samples of each class. The classifier is trained on 20 samples (at angle 0°) in each texture class, that is on 480 (24 × 20) images. Testing is performed on the other 8 angles, i.e. on 3840 (24 × 20 × 8) images.

We used $MD\text{-}LBP^{riu2}_{R=1,3}$ which gives $10 \times 10 = 100$ features and perform feature selection to extract 5 to 99 features. The results of these (and a curve fitting to a polynomial) are given in Fig. 4. From there, we observe that accuracy increases sharply up to about 30 features which we can hence consider as an indicator for minimum feature length. In the following, we thus perform GA feature selection based on 20, 30 and 40% of the total features for all experiments.

Table 1 gives classification results on the TC10 dataset.

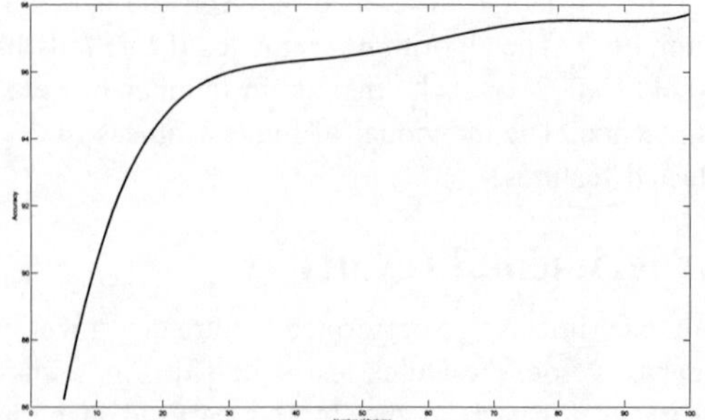

Fig. 4: feature length vs. classification accuracy for Outex TC10 dataset and $MD\text{-}LBP^{riu2}_{R=1,3}$

Table 1: Texture classification results on Outex TC10 dataset.

	no. of features	accuracy
$LBP^{riu2}_{R=1,3}$	20	95.81
$MD\text{-}LBP^{riu2}_{R=1,3}$	100	97.58
$GA\text{-}MD\text{-}LBP^{riu2}_{R=1,3}$	20	94.92
	30	95.32
	40	96.30
$LBP^{riu2}_{R=1,3,5}$	30	94.61
$MD\text{-}LBP^{riu2}_{R=1,3,5}$	1000	95.34
$GA\text{-}MD\text{-}LBP^{riu2}_{R=1,3,5}$	200	94.71
	300	95.21
	400	95.26

Table 2: Texture classification results on Outex TC12 dataset.

	no. of features	accuracy
$LBP^{riu2}_{R=1,3}$	20	85.35
$MD\text{-}LBP^{riu2}_{R=1,3}$	100	90.76
$GA\text{-}MD\text{-}LBP^{riu2}_{R=1,3}$	20	86.10
	30	88.43
	40	88.68
$LBP^{riu2}_{R=1,3,5}$	30	86.18
$MD\text{-}LBP^{riu2}_{R=1,3,5}$	1000	91.96
$GA\text{-}MD\text{-}LBP^{riu2}_{R=1,3,5}$	200	91.70
	300	91.76
	400	91.73

We can see that for $MD\text{-}LBP^{riu2}_{R=1,3}$ and selecting only 40% of the features, we obtain better classification performance compared to standard multi-scale LBP, although we don't quite match the performance of MD-LBP. For $MD\text{-}LBP^{riu2}_{R=1,3,5}$ and again selecting 40% of features, we again outperform conventional LBP and obtain results within a small margin (0.07%) of MD-LBP despite discarding 60% of its features.

The Outex TC12 database allows to evaluate texture classification across different illuminations. A classifier is trained on the same image set as TC10, but is tested on a total of 8640 images of the same textures under different rotations and captured under different light sources. Fig. 5 shows some samples from this dataset.

Classification results on this dataset are given in Table 2.

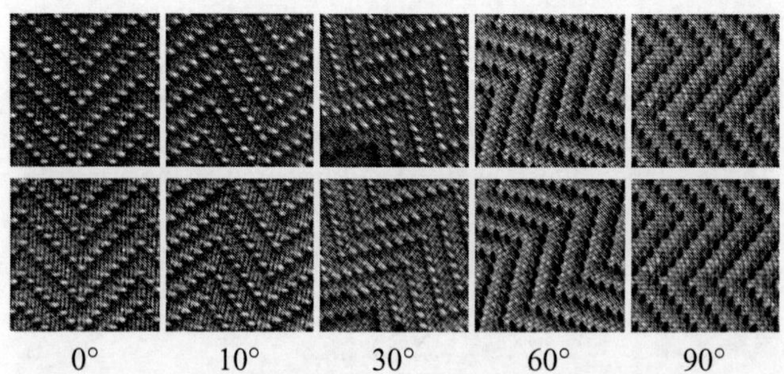

Fig. 5: Sample texture from the Outex_TC_12 dataset under different rotations and different illumination (top row "horizon", bottom row "tl84").

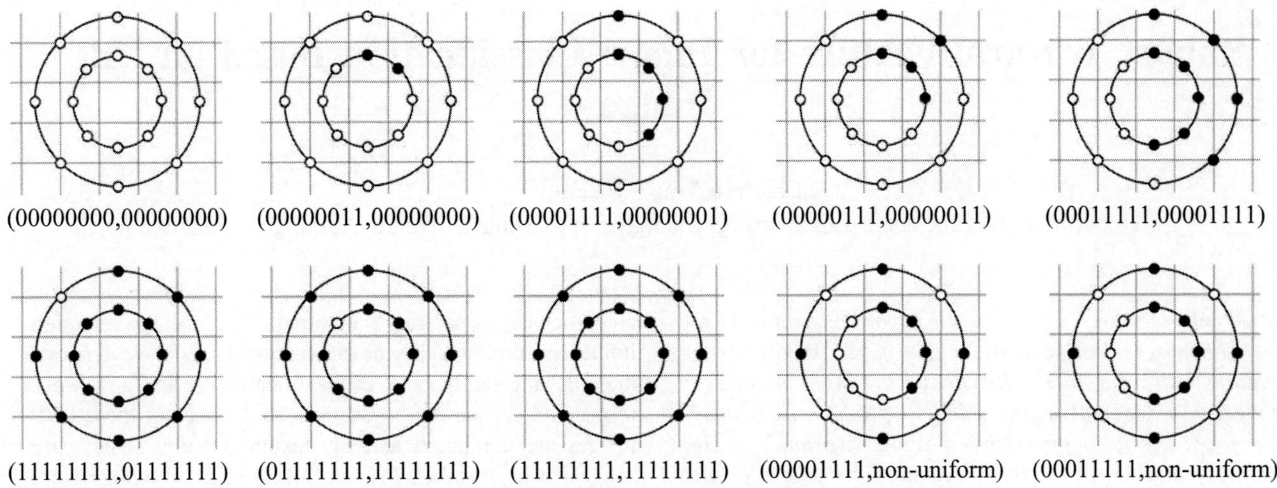

Fig. 6: Discriminative $MD\text{-}LBP^{riu2}_{R=1,3}$ patterns.

From there it is apparent that the results are similar to those obtained for TC10. That is, good texture classification based on a reduced MD-LBP feature set is possible, in particular for $MD\text{-}LBP^{riu2}_{R=1,3,5}$ where even when using only 20% of the features the results are almost the same as for full MD-LBP histograms.

Overall, it is clear that through application of the employed GA-based feature selection method, we are able to significantly reduce the dimensionality of MD-LBP features while maintaining good classification performance, in particular when calculating and integrating texture descriptors at three different radii.

We also inspected the features that were selected. For $MD\text{-}LBP^{riu2}_{R=1,3}$, a set of 10 features were selected in all experiments for both databases. These textures, which are depicted in Fig. 6 should hence give an indication of the most discriminative MD-LBP histogram bins.

5. Conclusions

Texture analysis and classification play an important role in many computer vision applications. Local binary patterns (LBP) is known as a powerful texture descriptor, especially when calculated at different scales. While this information from different LBP radii can be integrated into a single – MD-LBP – texture histogram, this also leads to relatively large feature vectors. In this paper, we have shown that through application of a feature selection algorithm, formulated as an optimisation problem and implemented using a genetic algorithm, a significant reduction of feature dimensionality is possible while maintaining good classification accuracy.

References

[1] T. Ojala, M. PietikÃd'inen, and D. Harwood, "A comparative study of texture measures with classification based on featured distributions," *Pattern Recognition*, vol. 29, no. 1, pp. 51 – 59, 1996.

[2] T. Ojala, M. Pietikainen, and T. Maenpaa, "Multiresolution gray-scale and rotation invariant texture classification with local binary patterns," *IEEE Transactions on Pattern Analysis and Machine Intelligence*, vol. 24, pp. 971–987, 2002.

[3] G. Schaefer and N. Doshi, "Multi-dimensional local binary pattern descriptors for improved texture analysis," in *21st Int. Conference on Pattern Recognition*, 2012, pp. 2500–2503.

[4] O. Ludwig and U. Nunes, "Novel maximum-margin training algorithms for supervised neural networks," *IEEE Transactions on Neural Networks*, vol. 21, no. 6, pp. 972–984, 2010.

[5] T. Ojala, T. Maenpaa, M. Pietikainen, J. Viertola, J. Kyllonen, and S. Huovinen, "Outex - new framework for empirical evaluation of texture analysis algorithms." in *16th Int. Conference on Pattern Recognition*, 2002, pp. 1:701 – 706.

[6] C. Cortes and V. Vapnik, "Support-vector networks," *Machine Learning*, vol. 20, pp. 273–297, 1995.

[7] C.-W. Hsu and C.-J. Lin, "A comparison of methods for multiclass support vector machines," *IEEE Transactions on Neural Networks*, vol. 13, no. 2, pp. 415–425, 2002.

[8] C.-C. Chang and C.-J. Lin, "LIBSVM: A library for support vector machines," *ACM Transactions on Intelligent Systems and Technology*, vol. 2, pp. 27:1–27:27, 2011.

Robust Textural Feature for Image Classification Based on LBP Image

Hanxu.You[1], **Jie.Zhu**[1]
[1]Department of Electronic Engineering, Shanghai Jiao Tong University, Shanghai, China

Abstract— *Texture of image is an important feature in the area of image classification. In this paper, robust texture features extracted from LBP image are used to classify images. New weight masks using to produce LBP image are proposed to improve the rotation invariance of the texture features. An octagon neighborhood shape is also applied in calculating co-occurrence matrices of LBP image since it takes into account all directions. As the distance is increasing, the angular resolution is improved. The SVM is used to classify the 8 kinds of different texture images with these features extracted from LBP image. Experimental results show that the proposed method is effective to meet requirements of image classification applications.*

Keywords: LBP Image, Weighting Mask, Rotation Invariance, Texture Feature, Image Classification

1. Introduction

Texture classification is a major field of development for various vision applications. Texture of image is an abstract term encompassing both random and deterministic variations of surface height. Characterizing the appearance of real world textured surfaces, which is a fundamental problem in computer vision and computer graphs, is to detect defects on texture field and sort these surfaces into different categories [1].

The approaches of mathematical modeling are grouped into structural, statistical and signal theoretic methods [2]. Structural methods, which are used in industrial quality control, are based on deterministic arrangement of textural elements. Statistical methods characterize the textures by a few statistical features. Most relevant textures descriptors like co-occurrence matrices [3][4] and Markov random fields [5]. Signal theoretic approaches focus on periodic pattern resulting in peaks in the spatial frequency domain, for instance, wavelet transformation [6], Gabor filtering [7] and Spectral Histograms [8] With the improvement the color texture feature, most of these approaches, used to defined for grey-level images, have extend to classify color images [9][10][11]. Local Binary Patterns (LBP) image, which is been proposed in 1996 by Ojala, is proved to improves the classification quality significantly [12][13][14].

Because of the well-performed LBP images, in this paper, we concentrate on the weight mask of local binary value based on pixel value of images. Two new weight masks are proposed in section 3 in order to reduce the direction influence introduced by the conventional mask. We generate the LBP images in both conventional ways and new ways respectively. Then the co-occurrence matrices of these LBP images are computed and the texture features, which are suggested by Haralick [4], are followed to be extract from them. A circle or regular square and octagon neighborhood shape strategy is tested in section 4. The selection of these features, extracted from different LBP images, improve the quality of image classification due to the low sensitivity of image angle. In the end, the Support Vector Machine (SVM) is used to classify the images with the features descriptors extracted by the former steps.

After introducing the method of generating LBP image, two new weight masks of local binary value are proposed in the second section of this paper. Then the well-known Haralick features are demonstrate in the next section (Section 3), a strategy of spatial dependence neighborhood shape is also implemented next to this demonstration. Results and conclusion of this paper are arranged in the last two sections (Section 4, Section 5).

2. LBP Image Generation

The attempts to extract textural features are normally concerned on image's spatial pixel values itself such as grey level images, RGB color space images and other images. Ojala [12] initially proposed the LBP method to describe textures present in grey level in 1996, and then LBP was introduced to calculate color texture by Maenpaa and Pietikainen in 2004, a new LBP image which is based on a vectorial analysis of colors are proposed by Porebski etc. in 2008. In this section, we firstly explain how LBP image are computed from original texture images. Then two kinds of weight masks are introduced to complete the whole procedure.

2.1 Image's Pixel Value

During the image processing, the image in its digital form is usually related to two factors, position and value, while being stored in the computer.

We suppose L_H and L_W are height and width of image in the spatial domains. (x, y) is represent the position of a pixel of image where $x \in (1, 2, 3, ..., L_H)$ and $y \in (1, 2, 3, ..., L_W)$, and $V_{x,y}$ is the Value of the pixel which is located at (x, y). That's to say, in grey scaled images, $V_{x,y}$ is obtained easily and usually limited to 0 to 255 as the gray value. While in the color space image, the value of pixels is usually represented by a vector, $S = (C_1, C_2, C_3)$, such as $S = (R, G, B)$ in RGB space. In order to obtain a total order of these vectors, Porebski choose to use the partial order relation. The Euclidean distance between the vector S and origin point $(0, 0, 0)$ are used to represent value in color space according to formula (1):

$$V_{x,y} = \sqrt{(C_1)^2 + (C_2)^2 + (C_3)^2} \quad (1)$$

$V_{x,y}$ is calculated as the reference of the pixels order. It means that the color $S^1 = (C_1^1, C_2^1, C_3^1)$ precedes or is not bigger than the color $S^2 = (C_1^2, C_2^2, C_3^2)$ if there is $\sqrt{(C_1^1)^2 + (C_2^1)^2 + (C_3^1)^2} \leq \sqrt{(C_1^2)^2 + (C_2^2)^2 + (C_3^2)^2}$. This rule can be expanded to most kinds of color space image.

2.2 Local Binary Pattern Image

Local binary pattern (LBP), firstly was proposed by Ojala in gray scaled images, and then was extended to color space images. The scalar LBP images extracted in color images are complicated.

The vectorial LBP images are introduced by Porebski in 2008. Instead of comparing the color components of pixels, the value of pixels, which is defined in section 2.1, are compared to calculate the LBP. The LBP is generated as follows:

Let $V_{x,y}$ represent the value or measurement of the pixel located at (x, y), and $V_{x',y'}$ is a neighbor value of this interest pixel, the neighborhood model is the frequently-used 8-neighbor model.

- Step 1: For each pixel (x, y) where $x \in (1, 2, 3, ..., L_H)$ and $y \in (1, 2, 3, ..., L_W)$, $V_{x,y}$ is obtained firstly.
- Step 2: Let$V_{x,y}$ be the threshold of LBP in the position of (x, y). If $|V_{x,y} - V_{x',y'}| \leq \mathcal{T}$, where $\mathcal{T}$ is a threshold to guarantee that the difference between center pixel and its neighbor is big enough. Then $T(x', y') = 0$, or else let $T(x', y') = 1$,where $T(\bullet)$ is the temporary neighbor binary value of pixel (x, y), and (x', y') is belong to (x, y) 's eight-neighborhood. Here we set Threshold belong to $30 - 10^2$.
- Step 3: neighbors are then weighted with the weight masks proposed in next sub-section. And then the weighted values are finally summed up to produce the LBP image.

Figure 1 illustrates our approach steps to obtain the LBP images.

2.3 Weight Masks

As showed in the Figure 1, the common mask which was proposed by Maenpaa and Pietikainen would causes inequality where the neighbors below the center are weighted more than the ones upside the center. Two new weight

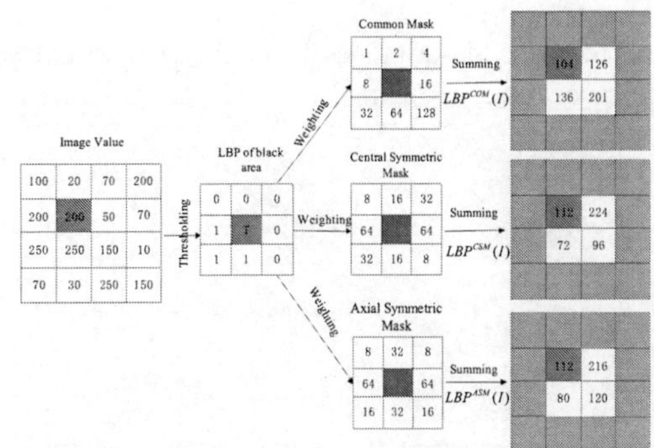

Fig. 1: Steps to obtain the LBP image and three different masks.

masks, considering the equality of the 8 neighbors, named Central Symmetric Mask (CSM) and Axial Symmetric Mask (ASM), are proposed in this paper. Due to the symmetrical characteristic of masks, it's acceptable to argue that the proposed masks can reduce the sensitivity of rotation from original images to some extent.

The three kinds of LBP images which are generated from original images through different masks are sent to produce Haralick features which are extracted from co-occurrence matrices.

3. Haralick Textures Features

Co-occurrence matrices, introduced by Haralick in 1973 [3], are classical statistical descriptors which takes the two important factors, image values and spatial interaction between pixels, into consideration.

Two elements, the angel or shape of neighborhood and the distance between neighbor and center pixel, are noteworthy. As the co-occurrence matrices are so sensitive to the differences of spatial resolution that different neighborhoods are fully concerned to computer the matrices. Figure 2 shows the strategy tested in our paper. An approximate circle or regular octagon neighborhood shape is applied in calculating co-occurrence matrices. Different spatial city-block distance d to compute the co-occurrence matrices for image classification of the BarkTex database[9], $d = 1, 5$ is improved to obtain the best performance of classification. Because of the octagon characteristics,d as the distance is increasing, the angular resolution is improved. When $d = 2$, angular resolution is 45%; When $d = 3$, angular resolution is 22.5%; When $d = 4$, angular resolution is 11.25%; In this paper, 4 different distances 2,3,4,5 are chose to produce co-occurrence matrices of the LBP image. Even though the co-occurrence matrices contain information about textural characteristics of the image, considering the large amount information, it's hard to identify which specific textural characteristic is represented by each of these textures[3]. 14 textural features which Haralick proposed to preserver the relevance of these descriptors, denoted $f_1 to f_{14}$, extracted from the co-occurrence matrices.

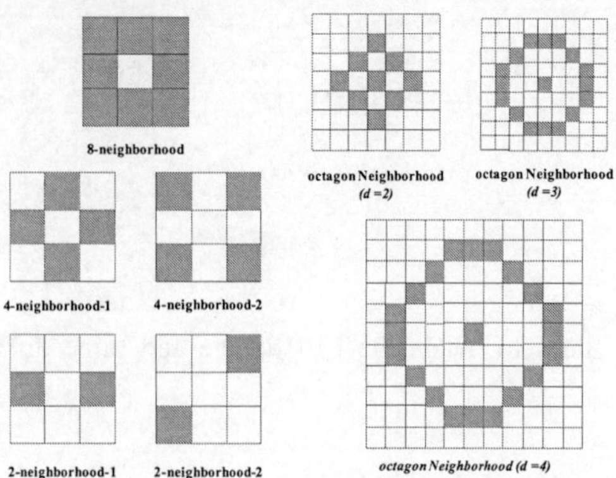

Fig. 2: Examples of neighborhood shapes and distances of neighbors.

As illustrated in Figure 1, we can obtain three kinds of LBP of original images, $LBP^{COM}(I)$, $LBP^{CSM}(I)$ and $LBP^{ASM}(I)$. Then for each kind LBP image, different co-occurrence matrices are obtained in the experiment part with different distances. All fourteen texture features are extracted from each co-occurrence matrices. Numeral experiments are tested in next part, and results are all compared in tables.

4. Experimental Results

4.1 Data Set Description

In order to show the performance of our approach for image classification, experimental results are achieved with the VisTex (color images)[15] and The Ponce Group (gray-level images)[16] database.

Images both in color and grey-level are tested in the experiments. The texture samples are equally divided into 8 categories (Bark in color (Type 1), Fabric (Type 2), Grass (Type 3), Flowers (Type 4), Bark in gray (Type 5), Fur (Type 6), Brick (Type 7), and Wood (Type 8)). Each kind of textures includes 64 training samples and 64 test samples as the training set and test set respectively with the size of 128×128. Besides, more interference factors like scalar and rotation are introduced into the last 4 kinds of textures (Type5, Type6, Type7, and Type8) to test the performance of our approaches.

All tests are run under Windows 7 and MATLAB v7.11.0 (2010b) on PC with Intel core2 Duo at 2.66GHz and 4.00GB of memory.

A simplified block diagram of image classification system is illustrated in Figure 3.

Figure 4 shows three textures and their three LBP images.

4.2 Classification Method

Support Vector Machine (SVM) is a new technology of machine learning, like multi-layer neural networks, which is

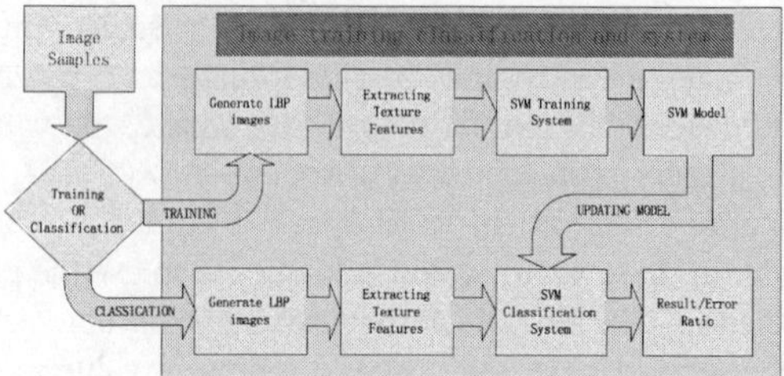

Fig. 3: A simplified block diagram of image classification system.

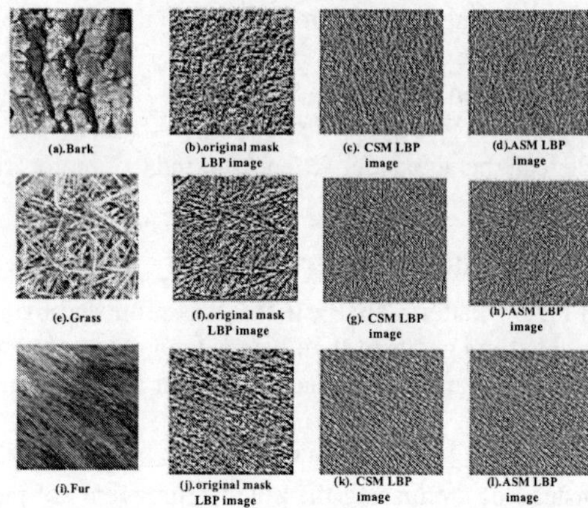

Fig. 4: textures and LBP images.

based on the concept of structural risk minimization (SRM). SVM was introduced into image classification [17][18] and received good results. The implementation of the SVM is based on the widely used SVM library called LIBSVM in this paper.

4.3 Experimental Results

To test that to obtain the robust texture features vector will not increase the time cost, an operation is carried out. The time cost is illustrated in Table 1.

Table 1: Time cost of computing features vector.

Sequence/ Distance	$d = 2$	$d = 3$	$d = 4$	$d = 5$
1	1.751925	1.755383	1.708932	1.878904
2	1.879645	1.825026	1.774709	1.763861
3	1.739955	1.729976	1.782761	1.733156
4	1.752363	1.737408	1.783557	1.750227
5	1.763010	1.758705	1.749044	1.743555
6	1.778565	1.716347	1.714817	1.764844
7	1.734292	1.733589	1.750750	1.767403
8	1.766934	1.819703	1.862923	1.828158
9	1.753156	1.765795	1.711614	1.735633
10	1.762095	1.742296	1.7368564	1.754747

According to the Table 1, though as the distance is increasing, more neighbors are selected to compute the co-occurrence matrices of samples, the running time does not

Table 2: Result of textures classification.

	Bark1	Fabric	Grass	Flower	Bark2	Fur	Brick	Wood	TOTAL/Accuracy
Bark1	64	0	0	0	0	0	0	0	64/100%
Fabric	1	60	0	3	0	0	0	0	64/93.75%
Grass	0	0	64	0	0	0	0	0	64/100%
Flower	0	1	0	61	2	0	0	0	64/95.31%
Bark2	1	0	0	0	58	3	2	0	64/90.63%
Fur	0	0	1	6	4	52	0	1	64/81.25%
Brick	0	0	0	0	12	2	50	0	64/78.13%
Wood	0	1	0	4	1	2	0	56	64/87.50%
TOTAL	66	62	65	74	77	59	52	57	512/90.08%

Table 3: Accuracy classification rate of textures.

	Conventional Method	CSM Only	ASM Only
$d = 2$	88.09%	86.98%	87.30%
$d = 3$	84.18%	83.01%	84.18%
$d = 4$	82.03%	81.45%	80.06%
$d = 5$	80.66%	81.64%	84.18%

Table 4: Best accuracy rate of each texture and the introduced strategy.

	Best Accuracy	Weighting Mask	Neighborhood Distance
Bark1	100%	Conventional	2
Fabric	100%	Conventional	3,4
Grass	100%	Conventional	3,4
Flower	100%	ASM	2
Bark2	93.75%	ASM	2
Fur	82.81%	ASM	2
Brick	78.13%	Conventional /CSM/ASM	3/(2,3)/5
Wood	93.75%	ASM	5

change much. When $d = 2$, 9 neighbors are selected, and the average running time $t = 1.7640$; When $d = 3$, 16 neighbors are selected, and the average running time $t = 1.7571$; When d = 4, 20 neighbors are selected, and the average running time $t = 1.7607$; When $d = 5$, 28 neighbors are selected, and the average running time $t = 1.7723$. The average running time result shows that an octagon neighborhood shape will not increase the operation time cost, but will obtain benefits of high angular resolution. It fully meets the requirement of image classification application.

Then, three masks are tested with different neighborhood distance respectively. Table 3 shows the result of each mask strategy. As shows in Table 3, common method is more sensitive with the distance, and ASM method is more stable than the other two. The average classification rate is 87%.

Table 4 shows the best result of each texture classification. All textures are correctly classified with high accuracy expect Brick texture. Common method perform better than proposed method in common ways, proposed method is more stable in the scale and rotation condition than common method.

All situation and factors are taken into account in the end, and a synthesize method are introduced. The table for the classification of the test textures is given in Table 2. The overall accuracy of classifier is found to be 90.08%. Details about assigned and true categories are listed in the table. This result, compared with 88.09% classification accuracy achieved using conventional method, shows that a significant improvement and stability of texture classification are obtained.

5. Conclusions

The originality of this work is that two new weighting mask are proposed in extracting LBP image from original image. Performance of all three masks are compared experimentally, result shows that stability of classification is much improved by our proposed method. An octagon neighborhood shape is selected to extracted co-occurrence matrices from LBP image. Result shows that octagon is available in achieving co-occurrence matrices. Finally, a synthesize method, considering the stability of ASM method, is tested in the end. Experimental results, achieved with the 8 texture from two texture database, show an accuracy of 90.08% is obtained by using the most suitable mask method and distance.

The perspectives of this work are firstly to find an efficient algorithm of selecting the textures features which are extracted from the co-occurrence matrices. And in the stage of classification with SVM, a better kernel function or parameter sets of the SVM which is selected to classify the features is to be found to improve the speed and accuracy of the classification.

References

[1] X. Xie, "A review of recent advances in surface defect detection using texture analysis techniques," *Electronic Letters on Computer Vision and Image Analysis.*, vol. 7, no. 7, pp. 1-22, 2008.

[2] T. R. Reed, J. M. H and D. Buf, "A review of recent texture segmentation and feature extraction techniques," *CVGIP: Image Understanding.*, vol. 57 no. 3, pp. 359-372, 1993.

[3] R. Haralick, K. Shanmugan and I. Dinstein."Textural features for image classification," *IEEE Transactions on Systems, Man and Cybernetics.*, vol.smc-3, no. 6, pp. 610-621, 1973.

[4] R. Haralick, "Statistical and structural approaches to texture," *Proceedings of the IEEE.*, vol. 67, no. 5, pp. 786ÍC804, 1979.

[5] Lei Wang and Jun Liu, "Texture classification using multi-resolution Markov random field models," *Pattern Recognition Letter.*, vol. 20, no. 2, pp. 171-182, 1999.

[6] G. Van de Wouwer, P. Scheunders, S. Livens and D. Van Dyck, "Wavelet correlation signatures for color texture characterization" *Pattern Recognition Letters.*, vol. 32, pp. 443-451, 1999.

[7] A. K. Jain and F. Farrokhnia, "Un-supervised texture segmentation using Gabor filters," *Pattern Recognition.*, vol. 24, no. 12, pp. 1167-1186, 1999.

[8] X. Liu and D.L. Wang, "Texture Classification Using Spectral Histograms," *IEEE transactions on image processing.*, vol. 12, no. 6, pp. 661-670, Jun. 2003.

[9] C. Palm, "Color texture classification by integrative co-occurrence matrices," *Pattern Recognition.*,vol. 37, no. 5, pp. 965-976, 2004.

[10] Q. Xu, J. Yang and S. Ding, "Color texture analysis using the wavelet-based hidden Markov model," *Pattern Recognition Letters.*, vol. 26, no. 11, pp. 1710-1719, Aug. 2005.

[11] Y. Mei and D. Androutsos, "Color Texture Retrieval Using Wavelet Decomposition in the Independent Components Color Space," *In Proceeding of the IEEE International Conference on Image Processing (ICIP'08).*, Canada, pp. 1379-1382, 2008.

[12] T. Ojala, M. Pietikainen, and D. Harwood, "A comparative study of texture measures with classification based on feature distributions," *Pattern Recognition Letters.*, vol. 29, no. 1, pp. 51ÍC59, 1996.

[13] T. Maenpaa and M. Pietikainen, "Classification with color and texture jointly or separately?"*Pattern Recognition.*, vol. 37, no.8, pp. 629-1640, 2004.

[14] Porebski, N. Vandenbroucke, and L. Macaire, "Haralick feature extraction from LBP images for color texture classification," *Image Processing Theory, Tools and Applications (IPTAąŕ08).*, Sousse, Tunisia, pp. 1-8, 2008

[15] http://vismod.media.mit.edu/vismod/imagery/VisionTexture/vistex.html

[16] Svetlana Lazebnik, Cordelia Schmid, and Jean Ponce, "A Sparse Texture Representation Using Local Affine Regions," *IEEE Transactions on Pattern Analysis and Machine Intelligence.*, vol. 27, no. 8, pp. 1265-1278, Aug. 2005.

[17] K. I. Kim, K. Jung, S. H. Park, and H. J. Kim, "Support Vector Machines for Texture Classification,"*IEEE Transaction on Pattern Analysis and Machine Intelligence.*, vol. 24, no. 11, pp. 1542-1550, Nov. 2002.

[18] B. Demir and S. Erturk, "Improving SVM classification accuracy using a hierarchical approach for hyperspectral images," *IEEE International Conference on Image Processing (ICIP'09).*, pp. 2849-2852, 2009.

Illumination and Rotation Invariant Texture Representation

Xiangyan Zeng, Masoud Naghedolfeizi, Sanjeev Arora,
Nabil Yousif, Ramana Gosukonda, Dawit Aberra
Department of Mathematics and Computer Science, Fort Valley State University, Fort Valley, GA, USA

Abstract—*In this paper, we propose a new feature for texture representation that is based on pixel patterns and is independent of the variance of illumination and rotation. A gray scale image is transformed into a pattern map in which edges and lines used to characterize the texture information are classified by pattern matching. The Gabor filters can enhance edge features, however, are not effective in edge pattern classification. We extract the pattern templates from image patches by Principal Component Analysis (PCA). Based on the pattern maps, the feature vector is comprised of a sorted histogram. The calculation of the features is simple and computationally efficient compared with other illumination and rotation invariant texture schemes*

Keywords: texture representation, pattern matching, principal component analysis (PCA), PCA pattern histogram

1. Introduction

Texture analysis is important for many research topics of computer vision and pattern recognition. Two main categories of techniques are texture classification and texture segmentation, which have applications in content-based image retrieval, surface inspection, remote sensing and medical image analysis. In the real world problems, textures occur irregularly at arbitrary resolutions and orientations with possibly varied illumination. Therefore, an effective texture measure should be resolution, gray-scale and rotation invariant. For texture segmentation problems, low computational complexity is another important consideration.

In the last two decades, many algorithms have been proposed for texture analysis. The research work can be categorized into three lines, including statistical analysis[1], filtering including wavelet transform [2][3], and local pattern methods[4][5]. Some have incorporated at least one property of resolution, gray-scale and rotation invariance. For instance, methods based on local patterns generally construct the features from the pattern of a small neighborhood (3x3 or 5x5) instead of pixel gray scale values and naturally remove the illumination variance influence. An up-to-date successful representative is the methods based on the local binary pattern (LBP). These methods obtain the feature vector from the histogram of binary patterns representing comparison of pixels gray scales in a circular local neighborhood. Rotation invariance is achieved by either circularly shifting the circles or performing a global match of the histograms.

In this paper, we extend a method that was proposed in [6] for texture representation that is very simple to calculate and free of the influence of illumination and rotation. A gray scale image is first transformed into a pattern map in which edges and background pixels are classified by pattern matching which is implemented by convolution. Fast Fourier transform can speed up this operation. Then, the feature vector is obtained from the sorted histogram of the pattern map within the texture window. The local spatial feature is extracted through pattern matching and structural rotation effect is removed by sorting the histogram. The statistics of this one map is much simpler than the up-to-date rotation invariant texture features.

To get a pattern map, we need to design a set of pattern templates and assign a pixel to a pattern that matches the neighbor region best. Gabor filter bank can extract texture features, however, it is demonstrated by our experiments that Gabor filters [7] are not effective as the pattern templates in the case that the textures are irregular and non-periodic. A natural way to get the templates is to analyze the image coding process and utilize the basis functions. We apply PCA to nature scene patches and use the basis functions as templates for pattern matching. The differences between these PCA basis functions and those of gradient operators are in that: instead of being designed by mathematics, they are obtained from the statistical analysis and represent the neighbor relationship of real images. As we will see in the following sections, pattern maps obtained by using PCA basis functions generally reflect edge and line features rather well. Hence PCA basis functions are good candidates for templates in pattern matching.

This paper is organized as follows. Section 2 briefly describes the background of texture representation using local binary patterns. In section 3, a texture feature based on pattern maps is proposed for texture representation. In section 4, experimental results are presented to demonstrate the effectiveness of the new method. Section 5 gives the conclusion.

2. Texture Feature Extraction by Local Binary Pattern (LBP)

2.1 Illumination invariant LBP

LBP is a texture descriptor for gray scale images. In the following discussion of LBP, we assume that a local neighborhood is centered on pixel g_c. The P pixels in the neighborhood form a clockwise circular chain with a radius R and are indexed as $(g_0, g_1, \dots, g_{P-1})$. LBP feature is illumination invariant. For each pixel g_c , the gray scale value is first transformed into a binary chain through thresholding:

$$(s(g_0 - g_c), s(g_1 - g_c), \dots, s(g_{P-1} - g_c)) \tag{1}$$

where

$$s(x) = \begin{cases} 1 & x > 0 \\ 0 & x < 0 \end{cases} \tag{2}$$

And the LBP feature of the pixel is obtained by multiplying each binary value with a binomial factor:

$$LBP_{P,R} = \sum_{p=0}^{P-1} s(g_p - g_c)2^p \tag{3}$$

After identifying the LBP pattern of each pixel, a $N \times M$ texture image is represented by the histogram:

$$H(k) = \sum_{i=0}^{N}\sum_{j=0}^{M} f(LBP_{P,R}(i,j),k), \quad k \in [0,K] \tag{4}$$

where

$$f(x,y) = \begin{cases} 1 & x = y \\ 0 & otherwise \end{cases} \tag{5}$$

and $K = 2^P$ is the maximum LBP pattern value. $H(k)$ quantifies the frequency of individual patterns corresponding to certain micro-features and represents the spatial structure of textures in the image.

2.2 Rotation invariant LBP

The LBP feature was modified to achieve rotation invariance.

$$LBP^{ri}_{P,R} = min\{ROR(LBP_{P,R}, i), i = 0, 1, \dots, P-1\} \tag{6}$$

where $ROR(x,i)$ performs a circular bit-wise right shift i times on the P bits of x.

2.3 Uniform patterns in LBP

The pattern value range in the above LBP is very wide. It has shown that LBP with the full range of patterns does not provide good discrimination[4]. It has been noticed that certain patterns are fundamental properties of textures. They are the "uniform" patterns which have very few (≤ 2) 0/1 bitwise transitions. For patterns of 8 bits, 00001000 has 2 bitwise transitions and is a uniform pattern, while 00101000 is not because it has 4 transitions. The number of "uniform" patterns is very manageable. For instance, 8 bits only have 9 distinct "uniform" patterns: 00000000, 00000001, 00000011, 00000111, 00001111, 00011111, 00111111, 01111111, and 11111111. These patterns can be represented by the numbers of '1's regardless of their locations. Therefore, the binomial factor in Equ. (3) is not needed. The new LBP descriptor that only uses the "uniform" patterns and is rotation invariant is defined as:

$$LBP^{uri}_{P,R} = \begin{cases} \sum_{p=0}^{P-1} s(g_p - g_c) & U(LBP_{P,R}) \leq 2 \\ P+1 & otherwise \end{cases} \tag{7}$$

where the U value of an LBP pattern is defined as the number of 0/1 bitwise transitions in that pattern

$$\begin{aligned} U(LBP_{P,R}) = & |s(g_0 - g_c) - s(g_{P-1} - g_c)| \\ & + \textstyle\sum_{p=1}^{P-1} |s(g_p - g_c) - s(g_{p-1} - gc)| \end{aligned} \tag{8}$$

"Uniform" patterns resemble flat areas and edges of varying curvature in images. "Nonuniform" patterns generally have much low frequency and will be grouped into one bin in the histogram.

3. A New Feature for Texture Representation

3.1 Texture feature extraction by pattern matching

In this section, we propose a new template pattern feature extraction method. The idea is also representing image textures by the frequency of certain patterns. However, the patterns are solid instead of consisting of only rim pixels as in LBP. Pattern labels are obtained through a template matching process.

A gray scale image is first transformed into a pattern map in which edges and background pixels are classified by pattern matching. Given a gray scale image **X**, convolution is performed with a set of K pattern templates of size $S \times S$ $\{\mathbf{w}_i, \quad i = 1, \dots, K\}$,

$$\mathbf{C}_i = \mathbf{w}_i * \mathbf{X} \tag{9}$$

The pattern label of a pixel (i,j) is obtained:

$$\mathbf{PL}(i,j) = k \tag{10}$$

where

$$\mathbf{C}_k(i,j) = max\{\mathbf{C}_l(i,j), \quad l = 1, \dots, K\} \tag{11}$$

The value of a pixel in the pattern map PL is the pattern label of its neighborhood in the original gray scale image **X**. After identifying the pattern of each pixel, a $N \times M$ texture image is represented by the histogram of patterns:

$$His(k) = \sum_{i=1}^{N}\sum_{j=1}^{M} f(PL(i,j),k), \quad k \in [1,K] \tag{12}$$

where

$$f(x,y) = \begin{cases} 1 & x = y \\ 0 & otherwise \end{cases} \tag{13}$$

Fig. 1: 348×348 nature scene images

Fig. 2: Sixteen 4×4 PCA basis functions

3.2 Rotation invariant texture feature

The above feature is easily modified to achieve rotation invariance. Pixels assigned to the same pattern will be assigned to another but still the same pattern after rotation. Based on this observation, a sorted histogram is rotation invariant.

$$SORT\left(His\left(k\right)\right), \quad k \in [1, K] \tag{14}$$

3.3 Pattern templates obtained by principal component analysis

Pattern templates represent the spatial features in an image and reflect that how a pixel is related to its neighboring pixels. A common method in statistics for analyzing inter-relations between variables is principal component analysis (PCA). Imagine that each image has been formed by a linear combination of basis functions that are the same for all images. The basis functions obtained from principal component analysis of a series of image patches represent the general relationship among neighboring pixels. Hancock has conducted principal component analysis of natural images and found that the basis functions resemble the derivatives of Gaussian operators [8]. In our work, PCA basis functions are used as the templates in the pattern matching process. We randomly choose 15000 4×4 block samples from two 348×348 nature images shown in Fig. 1 and obtain sixteen basis functions shown in Fig. 2. An important question concerns the selection of templates. Since PCA basis functions are sorted in order of decreasing variances, the templates of lower spatial frequencies account for the main part of the variance and are located in the front. It is logical to select the first several PCA templates which represent the most dominant relationships. The first basis is a Gaussian operator and is excluded in pattern matching.

4. Experimental Results

To demonstrate the effectiveness of the new texture feature extraction algorithm, we conducted simulation experiments of texture segmentation and compare the results with those of rotation invariant LBP. In the texture classification phase, different similarity measures have been used in the literature. In the segmentation circumstance, we use K-means which is a simple and efficient way to cluster data. In all the cases, we assume the number of cluster is known a priori.

Two images of 512×512 shown in Fig. 3 were tested in the experiment. The first image has five small scale textures which are relatively regular, while the second image has large scale textures. Both images contain a center portion which is a rotated texture. We selected the first 10 PCA templates except the Gaussian filter to transform the gray scale images into pattern maps. Template matching was performed using PCA basis functions and the pattern maps are shown in Fig. 4. Even though the value range of PCA pattern maps is much smaller than that of the original gray scale images, the structure of the textures are visually clear. The illumination variance in the fourth quadrant of image1 was removed in the corresponding PCA pattern map as shown in Fig. 4 (a). Based on the PCA pattern maps, the feature defined in Section 3.2 was determined within a $N \times M$ neighborhood window of each pixel, and the K-means algorithm was used for clustering the feature vectors into 4 classes. To focus on the spatial structure characteristics in texture classification/segmentation, we discarded the contrast (i.e. gray-scale variance) used in other related works [4][5]. We also segmented the images using rotation invariant $LBP_{8,1}$, and $LBP_{16,2}$. The segmentation results of the two images using the three texture descriptors are shown in Fig. 5 and 6, in which white dotted lines are displayed to show the boundaries between textures. Most misclassified pixels are near the boundaries of textures, which can be alleviated by more sophisticated classification methods.

As shown in the results, $LBP_{8,1}$ was very effective in discriminating small scale textures but not large scale textures. For the second image with larger scale textures, $LBP_{16,2}$ was used to achieve reasonable segmentation result. With the similar classification performance, the texture feature of LBP methods was much more computationally intensive. This is due to the complicated pixel-based operations for obtaining the pattern labels. In the meantime, the template matching in the proposed method is basically a convolution process, which is very fast and the computation time does not increase

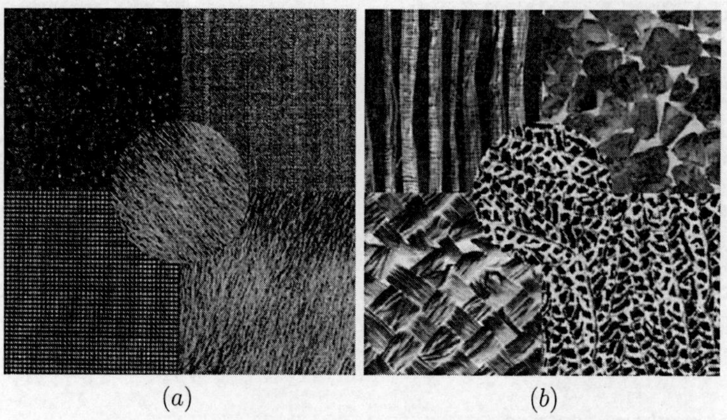

(a) (b)

Fig. 3: Original texture images (a) image1, (b) image2

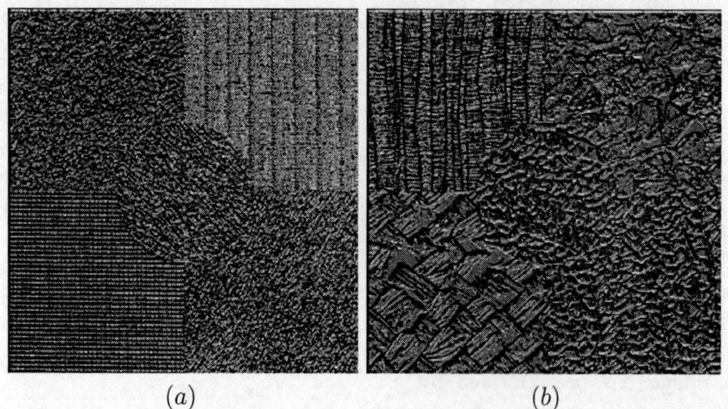

(a) (b)

Fig. 4: PCA maps of (a) image1, (b) image2

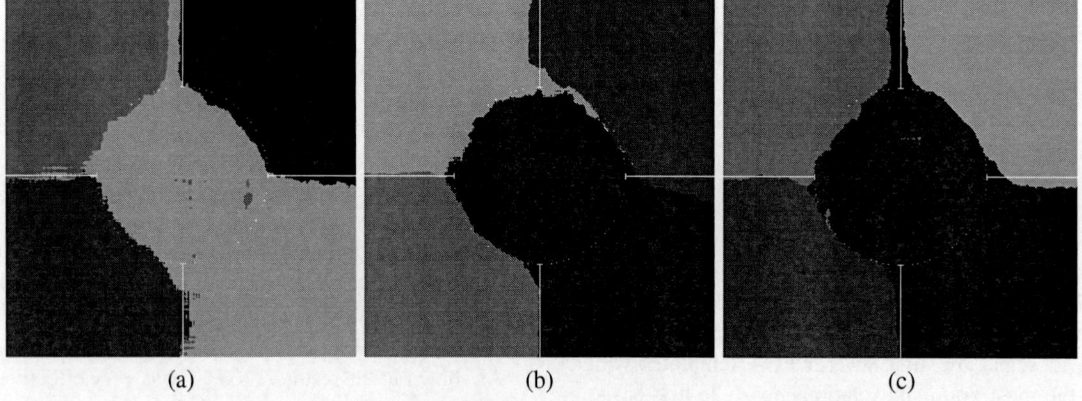

(a) (b) (c)

Fig. 5: Segmentation results of image1 with a texture window of 60×60. (a) the proposed feature, (b) $LBP_{8,1}$, (c) $LBP_{16,2}$

significantly with a different template size. The computation time of the three texture features for an image of 512×512 is shown in Table 1, which includes three different feature window sizes.

The feature window size affected the segmentation accuracy as it does in other segmentation approaches. In this experiment, we compared the performance of the three texture descriptors using 60×60, 80×80, and 100×100

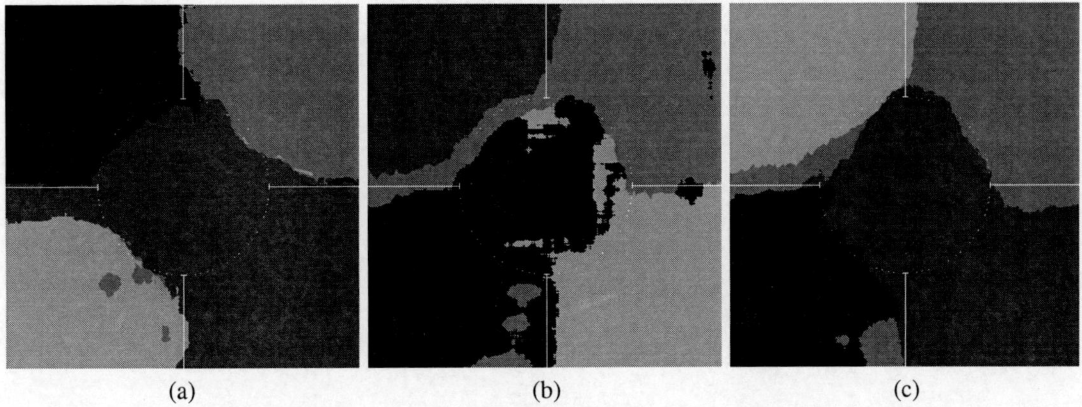

(a) (b) (c)

Fig. 6: Segmentation results of image2 with a texture window of 100 × 100. (a) the proposed feature, (b) $LBP_{8,1}$, (c) $LBP_{16,2}$

windows. The results are shown in Table 2 and 3. It is noted that smaller windows give better results for small scale textures in the first image, and larger windows yield better results for large scale textures in the second image.

5. Conclusion

Illumination and rotation invariance are highly desired for texture analysis in real world problems. Most approaches achieve these properties at the cost of intensive computation. This paper proposed a method that is simple yet effective in discriminating texture images. Using PCA basis functions of nature images as pattern templates can extract edges which are important components of textures. Sorting the histogram of pattern labels provides invariance to rotation. Compared to LBP methods whose computational cost dramatically increase with the neighborhood size, the proposed method is computational efficient for pattern templates of different sizes. The proposed texture feature can be used for texture segmentation and classification. The simulation experiments in texture segmentation indicated that it may be complementary to LBP in discriminating large and irregular textures. A future research direction is to combine both to achieve the best performance.

Table 1: Computation time (sec.) for an 512×512 image.

Feature window size	Proposed feature	$LBP_{8,1}$	$LBP_{16,2}$
60 × 60	3.83	25.64	30.61
80 × 80	6.63	44.6	54.38
100 × 100	9.99	67.3	82.26

Table 2: Classification error of Image1 (%) .

Feature window size	Proposed feature	$LBP_{8,1}$	$LBP_{16,2}$
60 × 60	4.28	3.98	3.75
80 × 80	5.45	4.08	4.89
100 × 100	7.11	4.29	6.06

Table 3: Classification error of Image2 (%) .

Feature window size	Proposed feature	$LBP_{8,1}$	$LBP_{16,2}$
60 × 60	11.91	21.27	11.29
80 × 80	7.59	22.24	9.66
100 × 100	7.29	21.96	8.83

References

[1] J. Mao and A.K. Jain, "Texture classification and segmentation using multiresolution simultaneous autoregressive models," *Pattern Recognition*, vol. 25, no. 2, pp.173–188, 1992.

[2] M. Unser, "Texture classification and segmentation using wavelet frames," *IEEE Trans. Image Processing*, vol. 4, pp.1549-1560, 1995.

[3] D. Dunn, W.E. Higgins and J. Wakeley, "Texture segmentation using 2-D gabor elementary function," *IEEE Trans. PAMI*, vol. 16, no. 2, pp,13-149, 1994.

[4] T. Ojala, M. Pietikain, and T. Maenpaa, "Multiresolution gray-scale and rotation invariant texture classification with local binary patterns," *IEEE Trans. PAMI*, vol. 24, no. 7, pp. 971-987, 2002.

[5] Z. Guo, L. Zhang, and D. Zhang, "Rotation invariant texture classification using LBP variance with global matching," *Pattern Recognition*,vol. 43, pp.706-719, 2010.

[6] X.-Y. Zeng, Y.-W. Chen, Z. Nakao and H.-Q. Lu, "Texture representation based on pattern map," *Signal Processing*, vol. 84, no. 3, pp. 589-599, 2004.

[7] X.-Y. Zeng, Y.-W. Chen, and Z. Nakao, "Texture Segmentation Based on Pattern Maps Obtained by Independent Component Analysis," *Proc. of 8th Int. Conf. on Neural Information Processing (ICONIP)*, pp. 1058-1061, 2001.

[8] P.J.B. Hancock, R. J Baddeley and L. S Smith, "The principal components of natural images," *Network*, vol. 3, pp. 61-73, 1992.

SESSION

SIGNAL PROCESSING AND APPLICATIONS - INCLUDING, VOICE, MUSIC, AND OTHERS

Chair(s)

TBA

An Approach to Classifying Four-Part Music

Gregory Doerfler, Robert Beck
Department of Computing Sciences
Villanova University, Villanova PA 19085
gdoerf01@villanova.edu

Abstract - *Four-Part Classifier (FPC) is a system for classifying four-part music based on the known classifications of training pieces. Classification is performed using metrics that consider both chord structure and chord movement and techniques that score the metrics in different ways. While in principle classifiers are free to be anything of musical interest, this paper focuses on classification by composer. FPC was trained with music from three composers – J. S. Bach, John Bacchus Dykes, and Henry Thomas Smart – and then tasked with classifying test pieces written by the same composers. Using all two-or-more composer combinations (Bach and Dykes; Bach and Smart; Dykes and Smart; and Bach, Dykes, and Smart), FPC correctly identified the composer with well above 50% accuracy. In the cases of Bach and Dykes, and Bach and Smart, training piece data clustered around five metrics – four of them chord inversion percentages and the other one secondary chord percentages – suggesting these to be the most decisive metrics. The significance of these five metrics was supported by the substantial improvement in the Euclidean distance classification when only they were used.*

Keywords: Four-Part Music, Classification, Metrics, Clustering

1 Introduction

The Four-Part Classifier system (FPC) began as an experiment in randomly generating four-part music that would abide by traditional four-part writing rules. The essential rules were quickly coded along with the beginnings of a program for producing valid chord sequences. But as the program evolved, it was moved in a new direction – one that could reuse the rules already written. The idea of creating a classification system which could be trained with music by known composers and tested with other music by the same composers became the driving force behind the development of this tool.

1.1 Related Work

While computer classification of music is nothing new, research is lacking in the domain of classifying *four-part* music. As for four-part-specific music systems, the 1986 CHORAL system created by Kemal Ebcioglu [5] comes closest to FPC's precursor program geared toward composition. Ebcioglu's system harmonizes four-part chorales in the style of J. S. Bach via first order predicate calculus. Newer research by Eric Nichols et al. [1] most closely matches the mature version of FPC but is not four-part-specific. Like FPC, their system operates in high dimensional space (FPC will be shown to be 19-space) but parameterizes the musical chord *sequences* of *popular* music. FPC does not consider the order of chords in its analysis but focuses instead on chord structure and the movements between parts.

1.2 Explanation of Musical Terms

In order for FPC to be understood in the steps that follow, a basic level of musical knowledge is required.

There are 12 pitches in a chromatic scale from which are derived 12 major keys. The names of each key range from A to G and include some intermediate steps between letters such as Bb or F#. Most important to the listener, the key serves as a musical "anchor" for the ear. All pitches can be understood in relation to the syllable *do* (pronounced "doh"), and all chords in relation to the I chord (the tonic). Both *do* and the I chord are defined by the key.

Although each key contains 12 pitches (or steps), only seven of them make up the diatonic scale (figure 1) – the scale used most often in western music (*do, re, mi, fa, sol, la, ti, do*). From bottom to top, the distances between the notes of the diatonic scale follow the pattern "whole step, whole step, half step, whole step, whole step, whole step, half step." Whether traversing the diatonic scale requires multiple sharps or flats is determined by the key signature at the beginning of the piece.

Fig. 1. Diatonic scale in C

From these seven diatonic notes, seven diatonic chords are possible. In four-part music, each chord is made up of four voices: soprano, alto, tenor, and bass. The arrangement of these voices produces chords in specific positions and inversions. For the sake of simplicity, the exact procedure for determining chord names and numbers has been omitted.

Notes differ not only by pitch but by duration. The shortest duration FPC handles is the eighth note followed by the quarter note, the dotted quarter note, the half note, the dotted half note, and lastly the whole note. The time signature dictates the number of beats in a measure and what type of note constitutes one beat. For example, in 3/4 time, there are three beats in a measure and a quarter note gets one beat. Since FPC only considers music in 3/4 or 4/4 time, a quarter note always gets one beat.

Finally, harmonic rhythm describes the shortest regular chord duration between chord changes. For example, in 4/4 a quarter-note-level harmonic rhythm means that chords change at most every beat. Harmonic rhythm is one of the most important components of traditional four-part analysis, its reliability crucial to correctly identifying chords and chord changes. For this project, only music with quarter-note-level harmonic rhythms was chosen, removing the need to identify harmonic rhythms programmatically.

2 Collecting the Pieces – Training and Test Pieces

A collection of four-part MusicXML files was created for use as training and test data by the FPC system. Four-part pieces were collected from websites in two different formats: PDF and MusicXML – with the PDFs later converted to MusicXML. A few hymns were entered by hand in Finale 2011, a music notation program capable of exporting to MusicXML.

2.1 Downloading and Converting Files

The two main websites used were Hymnary.org and JSBChorales.net. Hymnary.org is a searchable database of hymns, many of which are offered for download in PDF and MusicXML formats. For the purpose of this project, Hymnary's PDF files were found to be preferable to the compressed, heavily-formatted MusicXML files that proved difficult to touch-up. A few of the hymns entered by hand were taken from scans Hymnary made available on the site when it had information on a particular hymn but no character-containing electronic documents (e.g., native PDFs). The other site, JSBChorales.org, offers a collection of Bach chorales entirely in MusicXML format. These MusicXML files were found to be suitable.

XML and PDF files were downloaded from these sites and renamed using the format "title – classifier.pdf" or "title – classifier.xml" where "title" is the hymntune or other unique, harmonization-specific name of the composition and "classifier" is the composer. This naming convention was maintained throughout the project. Individually, the PDF files from Hymnary were converted to MusicXML using a software program called PDFtoMusic Pro. PDFtoMusic Pro is not a text-recognition program, so it can only extract data from PDFs created by music notation software, which all of them were. The free trial version of PDFtoMusic Pro converts only the first page of PDF files, which fortunately created no issue since all but a few of the downloaded hymns were single page documents. The XML files PDFtoMusic Pro produced carried the .mxl file extension and were compressed.

2.2 Formatting the MusicXML

Before the XML files could be used, it was necessary to adjust their formatting and, in the case of the .mxl variety, remove their compression. This was done with Finale. Once open in Finale, lyrics, chord charts, and any extraneous or visually interfering markings were removed manually. If the piece was written in open staff, as was the case with every Bach chorale, a piano reduction (two staves) was created in its place. Measures with pick-up notes were deleted and if beats had been borrowed from the last measure, they were added back. For these reinstated beats, the last chord of the piece was extended.

Any time two layers exist in the same staff of the same measure, FPC expects them to start and finish out the measure together. However, publishers and editors do not like to see note stems split multiple times in a single measure because one beat required it and so tend to add or drop layers mid-measure strictly for appearance (figure 2). When this happened, measures were adjusted by hand (figure 3).

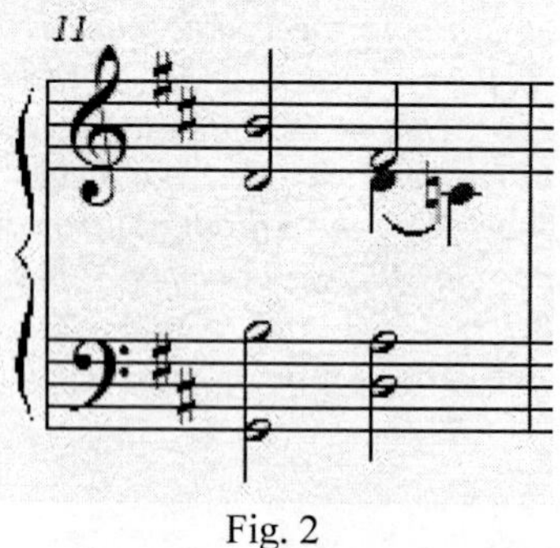

Fig. 2

Fig. 3

If two parts in the same staff double a note in unison but the staff did not use two layers to do it (figure 4), the parts were rewritten for that measure (figure 5). Any rests present were replaced with the corresponding note(s) of the previous chord.

Fig. 4

Fig. 5

Lastly, all measures were copied and pasted into a new Finale document to remove any hidden formatting. The files were then exported with the same naming convention as before and saved in a specific training piece or test piece directory for use by FPC.

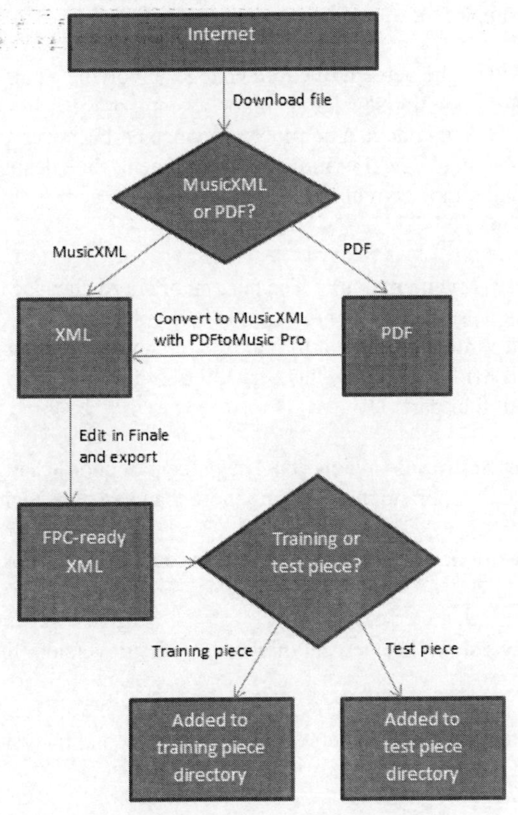

Fig. 6. Flow chart for collecting pieces

The next few sections describe how FPC works in general. Section 6 returns to the specific way FPC was used in this experiment.

3 Parsing MusicXML – Training and Test Pieces

By clicking the "Load Training XML" or "Load Test XML" button, the user kicks-off step 1 of the data-loading process: Parsing the XML.

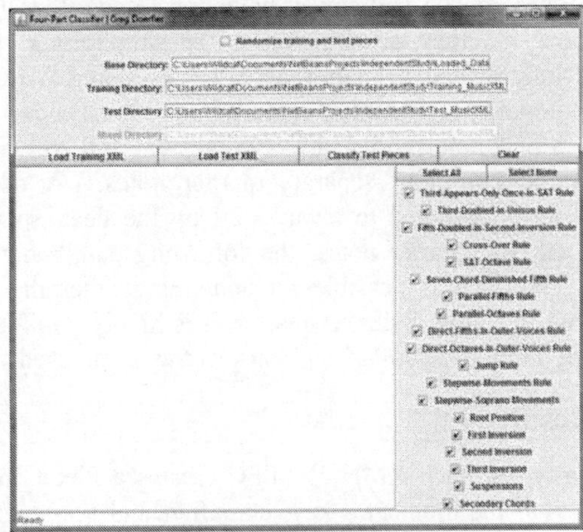

Fig. 7. FPC upon launch

3.1 Reading in Key and Divisions

First, FPC parses the key from each file, then the divisions. The number of divisions is an integer value defining quarter note duration for the document. All other note types (half, eighth…etc.) are deduced from this integer and recognized throughout the document. If a quarter note is found to be two, a half note is four.

3.2 Reading in Notes

MusicXML organizes notes by layers within staves within measures. In other words, layer 1 of staff 1 of measure 1 comes before layer 2 of staff 1 of measure 1, which precedes layer 1 of staff 2 of measure 1, and so on. Last is layer 2 of staff 2 of the final measure. If a staff contains only one layer in a particular measure, the lower note of the two-note cluster (alto for staff 1, bass for staff 2) is read before the upper note (soprano or tenor respectively). Since a measure might contain a staff with one layer and another with two, FPC was carefully designed to handle all possible combinations.

A note's pitch consists of a step and an octave (e.g., Bb and 3). A hash map is used to relate pitches to integers (e.g., "Bb3"→18), and these integers are used to represent each voice of a four-part Chord object.

3.3 Handling Note Values

In 3/4 and 4/4 time, a quarter-note-level harmonic rhythm means that chords change at most each beat.

Therefore the chord produced by the arrangement of soprano, alto, tenor, and bass voices at the start of each beat carries through to the end of the beat. This also means shorter notes moving between beats cannot command chords of their own. Quarter notes, which span a whole beat, are then the ideal notes to capture as long as they fall on the beat, which they always did. Likewise, eighth notes that fall on the beat are taken to be structurally important to the chord, so their durations are doubled to a full beat and their pitches captured whereas those that fall between beats are assumed to be passing tones, upper and lower neighbors, and other non-chord tones, so they are ignored. For simplicity's sake, anything longer than a quarter note is considered a repeat quarter note and sees its pitch captured more than once. For instance, a half note is treated as two separate quarter notes and a whole note four separate quarter notes. A dotted quarter note is assumed to always fall on the beat, so it is captured as two quarter notes; the following eighth note is ignored. While it is possible for something other than an eighth note to follow a dotted quarter, it is highly unlikely in 3/4 or 4/4, and it did not happen in any of the music used.

3.4 Results

Finally, for each XML file, FPC creates a Piece object comprising at the moment a key, classifier, and sequence of Chords. For each piece, it also produces a CSV file with the same information. The CSV files serve purely as logs.

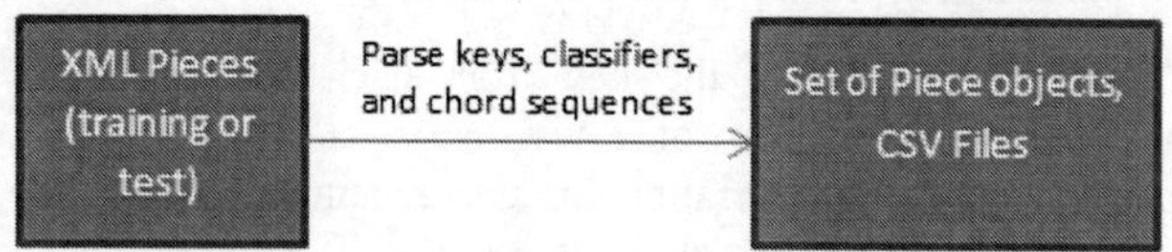

Fig. 8. Flow chart for creating Piece objects

4 Collecting Piece Statistics

After the XML has been parsed, FPC moves immediately to the next step: Collecting Piece Statistics.

4.1 Metrics

Statistics are collected for each piece via 19 Boolean tests on each chord or chord change. These Boolean tests produce the following metrics:

ThirdAppearsOnlyOnceInSATRule: The percent of chords whose third appears only once in the upper three voices. In classical writing, it is preferable that the third appear just once in the upper three voices.

ThirdNotDoubledInUnisonRule: The percent of chords whose third is not doubled in unison. Doubling the third in unison is usually avoided unless necessary.

FifthDoubledInSecondInversionRule: The percent of second-inversion chords whose fifth is doubled. It is preferable that the fifth be doubled in second inversion.

CrossOverRule: The percent of chords not containing overlapping parts. It is preferable that voices do not cross over. Doubling in unison is fine.

SATOctaveRule: The percent of chords whose soprano and alto pitches as well as alto and tenor pitches differ by not more than an octave. This is a fairly strict rule in classical, four-part writing. The distance between the bass and tenor does not matter and may be great.

SevenChordDiminishedFifthRule: The percent of vii° chords with a fifth. While the fifths of other chords are often omitted, the diminished fifth of a vii° chord adds an important quality and its presence is a strict requirement in classical writing.

ParallelFifthsRule: The percent of chord changes free of parallel fifths. This is a strict rule of classical writing.

ParallelOctavesRule: The percent of chord changes free of parallel octaves. This is also a strict rule.

DirectFifthsInOuterVoicesRule: The percent of chord changes free of direct fifths in the outer voices. This is a fairly important rule in classical writing.

DirectOctavesInOuterVoicesRule: The percent of chord changes free of direct octaves in the outer voices. This also is a fairly important rule.

JumpRule: The percent of chord changes involving a part jumping by a major seventh, a minor seventh, or the tri-tone. Jumping the tri-tone in a non-melodic voice part is never acceptable in classical writing, but from time to time, leaps by major and minor sevenths and even tri-tones are permissible if in the soprano.

StepwiseMovementsRule: The percent of chord changes in which at least one voice moves by no more than a major second. While this is not a formal rule of classical writing per se, good writing generally has very few chord changes in which all four parts leap.

StepwiseSopranoMovements: The percent of chord changes in which the soprano moves by no more than a major second.

RootPosition: The percent of chords in root position (root in bass).

FirstInversion: The percent of chords in first inversion (third in bass).

SecondInversion: The percent of chords in second inversion (fifth in bass).

ThirdInversion: The percent of chords in third inversion (seventh in bass).

Suspensions: The percent of chord changes involving a suspended note that resolves to a chord tone.

SecondaryChords: The percent of chords that are secondary dominants – chords borrowed from other keys that act as launch pads to chords that *do* belong in the key (diatonic chords). FPC handles all "V-of" chords (i.e., V/ii, Viii, V/IV, V/V, V/vi) and all "V^7-of" chords except V7/IV. "V^7-of" chords are simply recorded as "V-of" chords since they perform the same function.

After all 19 metrics are computed per piece, a TXT file is produced for backup.

Set of Piece objects (training or test)

For each piece, run all 19 tests on every chord or chord change and calculate average percent passing. Store percentages as metric values.

Set of updated Piece objects with 19 metric values, TXT files

Fig. 9. Flow chart for collecting Piece statistics

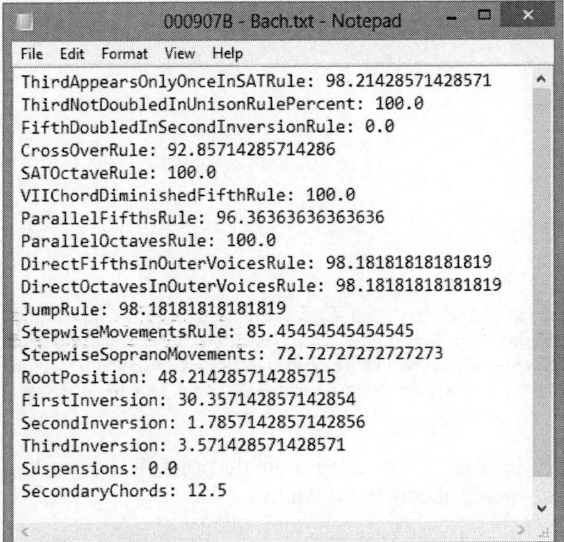
000907B - Bach.txt - Notepad

File Edit Format View Help

```
ThirdAppearsOnlyOnceInSATRule: 98.21428571428571
ThirdNotDoubledInUnisonRulePercent: 100.0
FifthDoubledInSecondInversionRule: 0.0
CrossOverRule: 92.85714285714286
SATOctaveRule: 100.0
VIIChordDiminishedFifthRule: 100.0
ParallelFifthsRule: 96.36363636363636
ParallelOctavesRule: 100.0
DirectFifthsInOuterVoicesRule: 98.18181818181819
DirectOctavesInOuterVoicesRule: 98.18181818181819
JumpRule: 98.18181818181819
StepwiseMovementsRule: 85.45454545454545
StepwiseSopranoMovements: 72.72727272727273
RootPosition: 48.214285714285715
FirstInversion: 30.357142857142854
SecondInversion: 1.7857142857142856
ThirdInversion: 3.571428571428571
Suspensions: 0.0
SecondaryChords: 12.5
```

Fig. 10. Sample TXT file for a Bach chorale containing 19 metric values (percentages)

5 Collecting Classifier Statistics – Training Pieces Only

The previous two steps – Parsing the XML and Collecting Piece Statistics – apply to the loading of both training and test data. Step 3, however, applies to training data only. If the user has clicked "Load Training XML," FPC now begins the final step before it is ready to start classifying test pieces: Collecting Classifier Statistics.

In the sections that follow, "classifier" with a lowercase "c" refers to the Piece object's string field while "Classifier" with a capital "C" refers to the Classifier object.

5.1 Approach

For each training piece belonging to the same classifier, a Classifier object is created. The mean and standard deviation are computed for each metric from all the pieces of the classifier and then stored in the Classifier object. For any piece, metrics outside three standard deviations of the mean are thrown out, and the means and standard deviations recalculated. Again, the whole piece is not thrown out, just the piece's individual metric(s). FPC updates each Classifier object with the new mean(s) and standard deviation(s) and then produces TXT files with the same information. Figure 11 provides an example to illustrate the process.

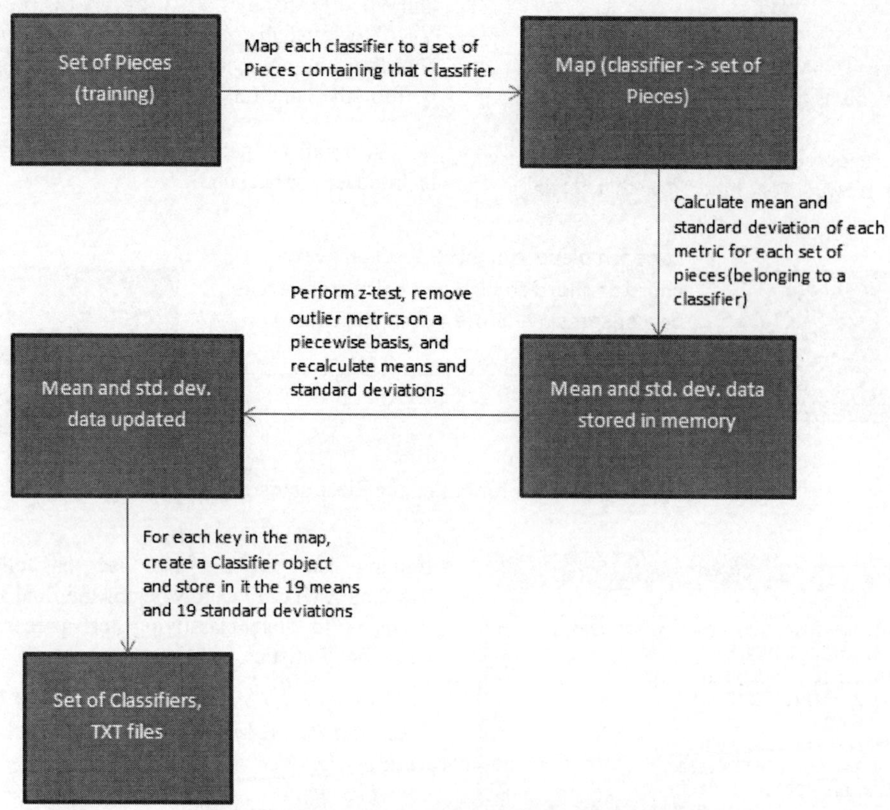

Fig. 11. Flow chart for collecting Classifier statistics.

Example: Pieces 1-10 belong to Classifier A, Pieces 11-20 to Classifier B, and Pieces 21-30 to Classifier C. The mean for metric X from Pieces 1-10 is calculated to be 15 (as in 15%) and the standard deviation is 5 (as in 5 percentage points). If Piece 10's metric X is 31, which is greater than 15 + 3 * 5 (z-test upper-bound), it is an outlier. Piece 10's metric X is therefore discarded and the mean and standard deviation for metric X are recomputed using Pieces 1-9. Classifier A then receives the new mean and standard deviation for metric X, and a TXT file is written. These steps are repeated for Classifiers B and C.

6 Classifying Test Pieces

Three techniques were used to classify test pieces from metric data: Unweighted Points, Weighted Points, and Euclidean Distance.

6.1 Classification Techniques

Unweighted Points is the simplest technique. It treats each metric equally, assigning a single point to a Classifier each time one of its metrics best matches the test piece. The classifier with the most points at the end is declared the winner and is chosen as the classification for the test piece.

Weighted Points was an original approach. It works similarly to Unweighted Points except metrics can be worth different amounts of points. First it calculates metric differences from the Classifiers: For each metric, it finds the Classifier with the highest value and the one with the lowest value. It subtracts the lowest value from the highest value, and the difference becomes the number of "points" that metric is worth. Then, like Unweighted Points, it looks to see which Classifier is closest to the test piece for each particular metric, only instead of assigning a single point, it assigns however many points the metric is worth.

Euclidean Distance is a standard technique for calculating distances in high-dimensional space. Here it focuses on one Classifier at a time, taking the square root of the sums of each metric difference (between test piece and classifier) squared. This is illustrated by the following formula where p is the classifier, q is the test piece, and there are n metrics.

$$d(p,q) = \sqrt{(p_1 - q_1)^2 + (p_2 - q_2)^2 + \dots + (p_n - q_n)^2}$$

Euclidean distance is calculated for each classifier, and the classifier with the smallest distance from the test piece is chosen as the classification.

6.2 User Interface

A row of four buttons allows the user to load training XML, load test XML, classify test pieces, and clear results. Above these buttons sit textboxes displaying the paths to files FPC will read or write on the user's machine during use. At the very top of the UI is a checkbox allowing FPC to select the training and test pieces from the collection *randomly*. Randomizing training and test pieces requires XML to be loaded each time a trial is run (since Classifiers will likely contain different data). Therefore, checking this box disables the "Load Training XML" and "Load Test XML" buttons, moving their combined functionality into the "Classify Test Pieces" button. Below the row of buttons is an information area, which displays the results of each step including test piece classification. To the right of the information area can be found a panel of checkboxes, which gives the user control over the metrics. Metrics can be turned on or off to see which combinations produce the most accurate results. At the very bottom of FPC sits a status bar that reflects program state.

6.3 Classification Steps

When the user clicks "Classify Test Pieces," test piece data from the TXT files created in step 2 (collecting piece statistics) is read and loaded into memory. It is true that if the user has performed steps in the normal order and loaded training XML before test XML, the test piece data would still be in memory, and reading from file would not be necessary. However, due to the sharing of Piece objects between training pieces and test pieces, if steps were done out of order, the Piece objects, if still in memory, might contain training data instead of test data. And because each TXT file is small, reading in the data proves a reliable way to ensure good system state if, for example, the user were to load training and test data, exit the program, and launch FPC again hoping to start classifying test pieces immediately without reloading. Here, reading from files is the simplest solution.

Next, if the Classifiers are not already in memory, the data is read in from the Classifier TXT files produced in step 3 (collecting classifier statistics). For each test piece, its metric values are compared with those of each Classifier. Each classification technique then scores the metrics and handles the results in its own, unique way.

6.4 Testing the Classification Techniques

Four-part music was selected comprising three composers: J. S. Bach, John Bacchus Dykes, and Henry Thomas Smart. Dykes and Smart were 19th century English hymnists while Bach was an early 18th century German composer. Dykes and Smart were chosen for their similarities with one another while Bach was chosen for his differences from them.

Using all 19 metrics, 20 trials were run per composer combination: (1) Bach vs. Dykes, (2) Bach vs. Smart, (3) Dykes vs. Smart, and (4) Bach vs. Dykes vs. Smart. The averages were then computed for each classification technique. Later, 20 more trials were run for Bach vs. Dykes using a subset of metrics thought most important.

Forty-five pieces in all were used – 15 per composer – and randomization was employed on each trial so that training pieces and test pieces could be different each time.

6.5 Classifying From Among Two Composers

For all three evaluation techniques, the averages of each trial, when classifying among two composers, came out well above 50% – the value expected from a two-composer coin toss. In fact, no individual trial fell below 50%.

Bach vs. Dykes – All Metrics

Technique	Correctness
Unweighted Points	82.5%
Weighted Points	86.8%
Euclidean Distance	71.5%

Bach vs. Smart – All Metrics

Technique	Correctness
Unweighted Points	92.1%
Weighted Points	89.3%
Euclidean Distance	69.3%

Dykes vs. Smart – All Metrics

Technique	Correctness
Unweighted Points	74%
Weighted Points	82.9%
Euclidean Distance	69.3%

The best technique overall was Weighted Points, demonstrating the strongest performance in two out of the three classifications.

6.6 Classifying From Among Three Composers

For all three evaluation techniques, the averages of each trial, when classifying among three composers, came out well above 33.3% - the value expected from random, three-way guessing. In fact, no individual trial dipped below 33.3%. The technique that worked best was Unweighted Points followed by Weighted Points at a close second.

Back vs. Dykes vs. Smart – All Metrics

Technique	Correctness
Unweighted Points	71%
Weighted Points	68.1%
Euclidean Distance	57.1%

6.7 Using Selective Metrics

If all 45 pieces were to be used to train the system, the resulting classifier data would represent what data from a randomized trial would look like on average. In this case, one can see that Bach's chord inversion statistics are far different from those of Dykes and Smart. Bach also relies more heavily on secondary:

Classifier Data from 45 Test Pieces

Five Classifiers	Bach	Dykes	Smart
Root Position	65.7%	62%	61.1%

First Inversion	22.1%	20%	22.02%
Second Inversion	2%	10.72%	10%
Third Inversion	1.1%	.6%	1.9%
Secondary Chords	11.5%	4.4%	3.9%

To test if FPC could even more accurately distinguish between Bach and either of the others, twenty additional trials were run for Bach and Dykes using only root position, first inversion, second inversion, third inversion, and secondary chords metrics.

Bach vs. Dykes – Five Metrics

Technique	Correctness
Unweighted Points	80.7%
Weighted Points	88.6%
Euclidean Distance	89.3%

Although Unweighted Points was 1.8 percentage points less accurate, Weighted Points improved by 1.8 percentage points, and Euclidean Distance was a surprising 17.8 percentage points more accurate. Whereas before, Euclidean Distance performed worst, here, it actually performed best. Using only these five metrics likely removed considerable amounts of "noisy" data, which suggests Euclidean Distance performs best with low noise.

7 Conclusions

It has been shown how FPC uses metrics based on chord structure and chord movement as input for three classification techniques. Furthermore, it has been demonstrated that conducting multiple randomized trials with test pieces of known classification allows the accuracy of FPC's guesswork to be easily measured.

The analyzed results from multiple trials indicate FPC is even more reliable than originally expected. Root position, first inversion, second inversion, third inversion, and secondary chords metrics have proven, at least in one case, to be the most important factors in distinguishing composer writing styles. A logical direction for future work would be to test FPC's performance classifying four-part music by time period instead of composer.

8 References

[1] Eric Nichols, Dan Morris, and Sumit Basu. 2009. Data-driven exploration of musical chord sequences. In *Proceedings of the 14th international conference on Intelligent user interfaces* (IUI '09). ACM, New York, NY, USA, 227-236. DOI=10.1145/1502650.1502683 http://doi.acm.org/10.1145/1502650.1502683

[2] Roberto De Prisco, Gianluca Zaccagnino, and Rocco Zaccagnino. 2010. EvoBassComposer: a multi-objective genetic algorithm for 4-voice compositions. In *Proceedings of the 12th annual conference on Genetic and evolutionary computation* (GECCO '10). ACM, New York, NY, USA, 817-818. DOI=10.1145/1830483.1830627 http://doi.acm.org/10.1145/1830483.1830627

[3] Torsten Anders and Eduardo R. Miranda. 2011. Constraint programming systems for modeling music theories and composition. *ACM Comput. Surv.* 43, 4, Article 30 (October 2011), 38 pages. DOI=10.1145/1978802.1978809 http://doi.acm.org/10.1145/1978802.1978809

[4] Michael Edwards. 2011. Algorithmic composition: computational thinking in music. *Commun. ACM* 54, 7 (July 2011), 58-67. DOI=10.1145/1965724.1965742 http://doi.acm.org/10.1145/1965724.1965742

[5] Kemal Ebcioglu. 1986. An Expert System for Chorale Harmonization. In *AAAI-86 Proceedings.* 784-788 http://www.aaaipress.org/Papers/AAAI/1986/AAAI86-130.pdf

Adaptive Smoothing and Wavelet Denoising for an Enhanced Speech Recognition System

Sonia Sunny[1], David Peter S[2], and K Poulose Jacob[3]
[1]Dept. of Computer Science, Cochin University of Science & Technology, Kochi, Kerala, India
[2] School of Engineering, Cochin University of Science & Technology, Kochi, Kerala, India
[3]Dept. of Computer Science, Cochin University of Science & Technology, Kochi, Kerala, India

Abstract - *Signals are corrupted by additive noise and removing noise from speech signals is one of the major challenges of an automatic speech recognition problem. In this paper, a speech recognition system is developed for recognizing speaker independent isolated words in Malayalam. Voice signals are sampled directly from the microphone and the background noise are reduced using wavelet denoising method based on Soft Thresholding (ST). Features are extracted using Discrete Wavelet Transforms (DWT). The extracted features are classified using Artificial Neural Networks (ANN), which produced a recognition accuracy of 88.5%. In this paper, a new algorithm named Adaptive Smoothing Soft Thresholding (ASST) is proposed for smoothing the signals by reducing sudden spikes in the signal. When the signal after smoothing is used for recognition, the Signal to Noise Ratio (SNR) is improved and a better recognition accuracy of 91.3% is obtained.*

Keywords: Speech Enhancement; Discrete Wavelet Transforms; Soft Thresholding; Adaptive Smoothing; Artificial Neural Networks

1 Introduction

Recovering data from noise is an important area of research since it affects the recognition accuracy of a speech recognition system. Speech enhancement and noise suppression are of great importance because reducing the amount of noise is one of the main criteria for developing a good speech recognition system. The original signal should be recovered from noisy data retaining the important properties of the original signal [1]. Traditional denoising schemes are based on linear methods, where the most common choice is the Wiener filtering. Recently, nonlinear methods, especially those based on wavelets have become increasingly popular [2]. Degradation of signals by noise is a key problem in signal processing. Now a days, signal denoising has become an intensive field of study because of the increasing applications of speech enhancement in the areas like digital mobile, radio telephony systems, pay phones in noisy environments, teleconferencing systems, hearing aids etc. The most widely used method for measuring the performance of a speech recognition system is calculating the recognition accuracy. Though many parameters affect the accuracy of the speech recognition system, the presence of background or additive noise is one of the key factors.

Additive noise is a severe problem that greatly degrades the quality, clarity and intelligibility of the speech signals. In order to solve this, it is necessary to enhance the corrupted signal through an appropriate speech enhancement algorithm. Based on the nature and properties of the noise sources, noise can be classified into many types. Additive noises like background noise, impulse noise, speaker interfering noise and non additive noises like speaker stress, non-linearities of microphones etc. affect the quality of the speech produced. In this work, we have used wavelet denoising based on soft thresholding because it is proven that noise can be significantly reduced without reducing the edge sharpness. In soft thresholding, a threshold is estimated as a limit between the wavelet coefficients of the noise and those of the target signal [3]. But simple threshold can suppress the noise only up to an extent. So here a new algorithm is proposed in order to smoothen the signal so that the magnitude of the sudden spikes in the signal are reduced. This in turn generates a signal which is smoother than the original signal. DWT and ANN are used for feature extraction and classification respectively.

The paper is organised as follows. Section 2 describes the statement of the problem. The Malayalam database used in the work is described in section 3. Section 4 gives a brief description of the architecture of the work which includes the pre-processing steps, feature extraction technique and the classification method. Section 5 presents the detailed analysis of the experiments done and the results obtained. Conclusions are given in the last section.

2 Statement of the Problem

The main goal of noise suppression is to improve the quality and intelligibility of the speech corrupted by background noise and to make speech recognition system more robust to input noise. This can be achieved using speech enhancement algorithms [4]. Since speech enhancement is an intermediate stage in the implementation of a speech recognition system which in turn improves the recognition accuracy, research in this area is of great importance. Here, wavelet denoising is employed which is considered a non-parametric method [5]. In this work, we have used two methods. One using soft thresholding and the other using a new algorithm to smoothen the edges of the signal followed by the application of soft thresholding. Comparison is done in terms of SNR, spectrograms of the signals and waveform plots for ST and ASST. Feature extraction is done using DWT and classification is performed using the Multi Layer Perceptron architecture of ANN.

3 Words database

Ten isolated words from Malayalam language are chosen to create the database. 1000 speakers of age between 6 and 70 are selected to record the words. Each speaker utters 10 words. Thus the database consists of a total of 10000 utterances of the spoken words. This gives a moderate size for our study. We have recorded the speech from 400 male speakers, 400 female speakers and 200 children for creating the database. Male, female and voice of children differ in pitch, frequency, phonetics and many other factors. The samples stored in the database are recorded by using a high quality studio-recording microphone at a sampling rate of 8 KHz (4 KHz band limited). The spoken words, words in English, their International Phonetic Alphabet (IPA) format and translation in English are shown in Table 1.

Table 1. Words Stored in the Database and their IPA Format

Words in Malayalam	Words in English	IPA format	English translation
ഓണം	Onam	/O:nΛm/	Onam
ചിരി	Chiri	/tʃiri/	Smile
വീട്	Veedu	/vi:də/	House
കുട്ടി	Kutti	/kuţi/	Child
മരം	Maram	/mΛrΛm/	Tree
മയിൽ	Mayil	/mΛjil/	Peacock
ലോകം	Lokam	/lokΛm/	World
മൗനം	Mounam	/maunəm/	Silence
വെള്ളം	Vellam	/vellΛm/	Water
അമ്മ	Amma	/ΛmmΛ/	Mother

4 System Architecture

In this paper, the speech recognition process is divided into three phases. In the first phase called pre-processing stage, the speech signals recorded are denoised using wavelets. The denoised signals are then given to the feature extraction stage where the relevant features are extracted. Finally, the extracted features are given for pattern classification. The different phases of this work are given below.

4.1 Pre-processing using wavelet Denoising

The speech signals are degraded by background noise. So pre-processing of speech signals is considered to be a crucial step in the development of a speech recognition system. There are different types of speech enhancement algorithms available like filtering techniques, spectral restoration techniques, model-based methods and wavelet based methods. Now more works are being done using wavelet denoising. Choice of the wavelet plays an important role in denoising. In this work, we have used the Daubechies wavelets which are the most popular wavelets that are found to be efficient in signal processing. In order to select an optimal wavelet function, the objective is to minimize reconstructed error variance and to maximize SNR. Wavelets with more vanishing moments are selected since it provides better reconstruction quality and introduce less distortion into processed speech. The speech signals are decomposed using DWT since it provides a time-frequency representation of the signal. Analysis and reconstruction of signals are done by the multi resolution filter banks and special wavelet filters of DWT [6].

4.1.1 Denoising using Soft Thresholding (ST)

The two popular thresholding functions used in denoising the signals using wavelets are the hard and the soft thresholding functions [7]. Hard thresholding sets to zero any element whose absolute value is lower than the threshold. Soft thresholding is an extension of hard thresholding. The elements whose absolute values are lower than the threshold are first set to zero and then shrinks the nonzero coefficients towards 0. Hard and soft thresholding can be defined as

$$X_{Hard} = \begin{cases} X & if \quad |X| > \tau \\ 0 & if \quad |X| \leq \tau \end{cases} \quad (1)$$

$$X_{Soft} = \begin{cases} sign(X)\ (|X| - |\tau|) & if \quad |X| > \tau \\ 0 & if \quad |X| \leq \tau \end{cases} \quad (2)$$

Where X represents the wavelet coefficients and ι is the threshold value. In this paper, soft thresholding is used for wavelet denoising. There are different ways to calculate the Threshold value. In this work, the threshold used is the universal threshold developed by by Donoho and Jonstone [8] which is defined as

$$\tau = \sigma\sqrt{2\log(N)} \quad (3)$$

Where σ is the standard deviation and N is the length of the signal. Standard deviation σ can be calculated as σ = MAD/0.6745, where MAD is the median of the absolute value of the wavelet coefficients. We assume that Additive White Gaussian Noise (AWGN) is added. Then, any signal y(t) can be represented by the summation of the original x(t) and the noise n(t) as [9] [10].

$$y(t) = x(t) + n(t) \quad (4)$$

The outline of the de-noising algorithm can be represented using the following steps.

- Choose a wavelet and a level N. Compute the wavelet decomposition of the signal at level N.
- For each level from 1 to N, select a threshold and apply soft thresholding to the detail coefficients.
- Compute wavelet reconstruction based on the original approximation coefficients of level N and the modified detail coefficients of levels from 1 to N.

4.1.2 Denoising using Proposed Adaptive Smoothing Soft Thresholding Method (ASST)

Different wavelet denoising algorithms for speech signals were developed by modifying the standard threshold values available [11][12] and by combining different thresholding techniques [13]. Here, a new idea is developed to smoothen the signal before applying thresholding. Speech signals are often contaminated by sudden, abrupt noise that are represented in the form of spikes or troughs. The spikes/troughs distort the calculations and produce erroneous results. Elimination of such sudden variations has always been a challenging problem. In ordinary thresholding, only the top/bottom portions of a spike are cut out. But the steep gradient in the waveform will exist which actually accentuates the distortion. Attenuating a distortion without actually affecting the original waveform is of prime importance. In the proposed ASST method, previous values are compared with future values to determine the general trend of the signal and thereby facilitating suppression of random troughs. If this sudden spikes are reduced by smoothing, then automatically more noise components can be reduced and the original signal can be captured in its fullness. When this smoothened signal is given for denoising using ST, we get better results in terms of SNR value.

In the proposed ASST, the sign of the present value of the sample and the next value are compared. Yi is compared with Yi + 1. If both the values are in the same direction and in an increasing trend, the samples are reproduced in total and amplified by a smoothening factor less than 1, say 0.5 which decrease when the trend continues. When there is a reversal in trend, the factor that is added is kept high to capture the reversal in total. If Y_i and Y_{i+1} are in opposite directions, or in other words if there is a sign change in magnitude, we apply a dominant factor limiting the fall. If the trend continues, the signal is again reproduced in total plus the factor.

4.2 Feature Extraction using DWT

The denoised signals obtained after preprocessing are then applied to the feature extraction phase to extract the features. This is the initial signal processing front end that converts speech signal into a more compact and convenient mode called feature vectors. The main advantage of the wavelet transforms is that it has a varying window size, being broad at low frequencies and narrow at high frequencies, thus leading to an optimal time–frequency resolution in all frequency ranges [14]. In DWT, the original signal passes through a low-pass filter and a high-pass filter and emerges as two signals, called approximation coefficients and detail coefficients. In speech signals, low frequency components are of greater importance than high frequency signals as the low frequency components characterize a signal more than its high frequency components [15]. DWT provides sufficient information both for analysis and synthesis and reduce the computation time. DWT is defined by

$$W(j,K) = \sum_j \sum_k X(k) 2^{-j/2} \psi(2^{-j} n - k) \quad (5)$$

Where Ψ (t) is the basic analyzing function called the mother wavelet. The successive high pass and low pass filtering of the signal is given by

$$Y_{high}[k] = \sum_n x[n] g[2k - n] \quad (6)$$

$$Y_{low}[k] = \sum_n x[n] h[2k - n] \quad (7)$$

Where Y_{high} (detail coefficients) and Y_{low} (approximation coefficients) are the outputs of the high pass and low pass filters obtained by sub sampling by 2. The filtering is continued until the desired level is reached according to Mallat algorithm [16].

4.3 Classification using ANN

During classification stage, the input data is trained using information relating to known patterns and then they are tested using the test data set. Since neural networks are good at pattern recognition, we have also adopted this method for classification. The ability of Neural Networks to deal with uncertain, fuzzy, or insufficient data makes it an efficient pattern recognizer [17]. In this work, we use the MLP architecture, which consists of an input layer, one hidden layer and an output layer. In most networks, the principle of learning a network is based on minimizing the gradient of error [18]. Here, the input is presented to the network and moves through the weights and nonlinear activation functions towards the output layer, and the error is corrected in a backward direction using the error back propagation correction algorithm.

MLP is a supervised learning network as well as a fully connected network. The main problem here is to classify the speech sample feature vectors into several speech classes. The number of nodes in the input layer equals the feature dimension whereas number of nodes in output layer is same as the number of words in the database. Usually, only one hidden layer is enough for efficient classification. The number of nodes in the hidden layer is adjusted empirically for superior performance of the system. An activation function is applied to the net input to calculate the output response of a neuron. The network used in this work uses the sigmoid activation function where the output varies continuously but not linearly as the input changes.

5 Experiments and Results

During pre-processing, different daubechies wavelets of orders db8, db12, db20 and db22 along with a noise of 5db are used for evaluating the performance of the proposed algorithm. The performance evaluation is calculated in terms of SNR value, spectrograms and waveform plots.

5.1 Evaluation using SNR

The table given below shows the comparison of SNR values using ST alone and using ASST. From the results it is clear that better results are obtained using db20.

Input SNR (db)	Wavelet used	Using ST	Using ASST
5	Db8	5.543	6.975
5	Db12	5.921	7.018
5	Db20	6.483	7.873
5	Db22	6.292	7.481

5.2 Evaluation using Spectrogram

Figure given below shows the spectrogram of the original signal, noisy signal, reconstructed signal using ST and reconstructed signal using ASST using db20.

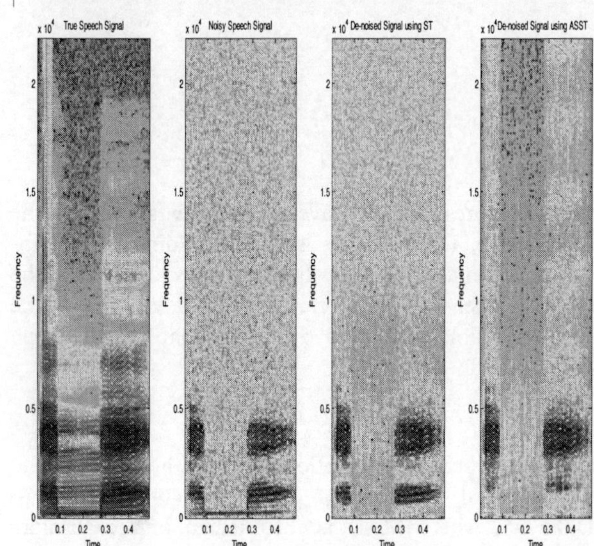

Fig. 1. Comparison of spectrograms

5.3 Evaluation using Waveform Plots

Figure given below shows the waveform plot of the original signal, noisy signal, reconstructed signal using ST and reconstructed signal using ASST using db20.

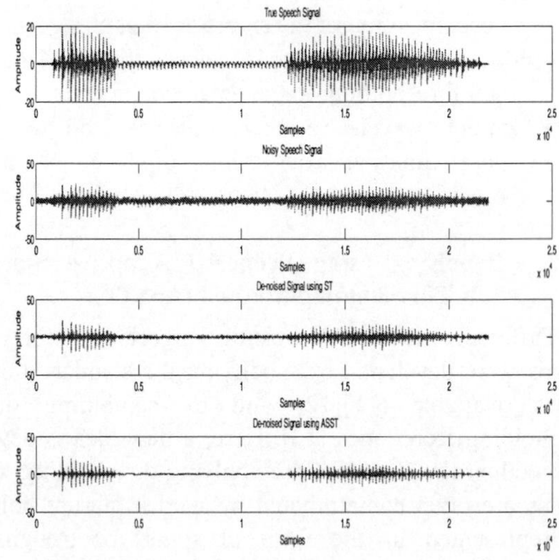

Fig .2. Comparison of waveform plots

The denoised signal after smoothing and soft thresholding are given to DWT where the features are extracted. 12 features are obtained using decomposition upto 8 levels. The original signal and the approximation and detail coefficients of word Amma at the 8th level is given below.

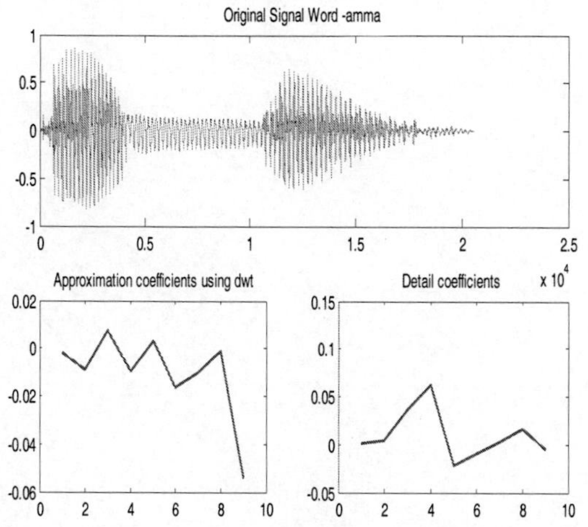

Fig. 3. Decomposition of word Amma at 8th level using DWT

The feature vectors obtained are given to MLP for classification. Here we have divided the database into three. 70% of the data is used for training, 15% for validation and 15% for testing. The classification results obtained by using ST alone and ASST are shown in table 2.

Table 2. Comparison of classification results

Pre-processing Method	Recognition accuracy %
Soft Thresholding	88.5
Adaptive Smoothing Soft Thresholding	91.3

6 Conclusion and Future Work

In this paper, a speech recognition system with improved performance is developed for recognizing isolated words in Malayalam using wavelet denoising based on soft thresholding and a new algorithm ASST for smoothing the signals. This algorithm enhances the performance of the speech recognition system by removing the sudden spikes which contain noise. When this algorithm is used along with soft thresholding, better results are obtained by an increase in the SNR value. All the 10000 samples from the database are used for evaluation. All the data gave an improvement in the results. From the results, it is clear that, smoothing the signal before applying any threshold method gives better results. The main advantage of adaptive smoothing of the signals is that, it can be applied along with any speech enhancement method. Different speech enhancement techniques can be used with ASST and the performance of these can be analyzed as an extension of this work.

7 References

[1] Byung-Jun Yoon, P. P. Vaidyanathan. "Wavelet-based denoising by customized thresholding"; IEEE International Conference on Acoustics, Speech and Signal Processing, Vol. No. 2, 925-928, May 2004.

[2] Weaver, J.B., Yansun, X., Healy, D. M. Jr., Cromwell, L.D. "Filtering noise from images with wavelet transforms"; Magnetic Resonance in Medicine, Vol. No. 21, Issue No. 2, 288-295, October 1991.

[3] Mohammed Bahoura, Jean Rouat. "Wavelet speech enhancement based on time–scale adaptation"; Speech Communication, Vol. No. 48, Issue No. 12, 1620–1637, December 2006.

[4] Hadhami Issaoui, Aïcha Bouzid, Noureddine Ellouze. "Comparison between Soft and Hard Thresholding on Selected Intrinsic Mode Selection"; IEEE conference on Sciences of Electronics, Technologies of Information and telecommunications, 1-5, March 2012.

[5] Slavy G. Mihov, Ratcho M. Ivanov, Angel N. Popov. "Denoising Speech Signals by Wavelet Transform"; Annual Journal Of Electronics, 712-715, 2009.

[6] Mahesh S. Chavan, Manjusha N.Chavan, M.S.Gaikwad. "Studies on Implementation of Wavelet for Denoising Speech Signal"; International Journal of Computer Applications, Vol. No. 3, Issue No.2, 1-7, 2010.

[7] S. Kadambe, P. Srinivasan. "Application of adaptive wavelets for speech"; Optical Engineering, Vol. No. 33, Issue No. 7, 2204-2211, July 1994.

[8] D.L. Donoho. "De-noising by soft thresholding"; IEEE transactions on information theory, Vol. No. 41, Issue No. 3, 613-627, May 1995.

[9] Yasser Ghanbari, Mohammad Reza Karami. "A new approach for speech enhancement based on the adaptive thresholding of the wavelet packets"; Speech Communication, Vol. No. 48, Issue No. 8, 927-940, August 2006.

[10] Tie Cai, Xing Wu. "Wavelet-Based De-Noising of Speech Using Adaptive Decomposition"; IEEE International conference on industrial technology, 1-5, April 2008.

[11] Rajeev Aggarwal, Jai Karan Singh, Vijay Kumar Gupta, Sanjay Rathore, Mukesh Tiwari, Anubhuti Khare. "Noise Reduction of Speech Signal using Wavelet Transform with Modified Universal Threshold"; International Journal of Computer Applications, Vol. No. 20, Issue No.5, 14-19, 2011.

[12] Saeed Ayat. " A New Method for Threshold Selection in Speech Enhancement by Wavelet Thresholding "; Proc. of 2011 International Conference on Computer Communication and Management, Vol. No. 5 IACSIT Press, Singapore, 451-455, 2011.

[13] Puneet Arora, Mohit Bansal. "Comparative Analysis of Advanced Thresholding Methods for Speech-Signal Denoising"; International Journal of Computer Applications, Vol. No. 59, Issue No.16, 28-32, 2012.

[14] Matko Saric, Luki Bilicic, Hrvoje Dujmic. "White Noise Reduction of Audio Signal Using Wavelets Transform With Modified Universal Threshold"; WSEAS transactions on information science and applications, Vol. No. 2, Issue No. 2, 279-283, 2005.

[15] Elif Derya Ubeyil. "Combined Neural Network model employing wavelet coefficients for ECG signals classification"; Digital signal Processing, Vol. No. 19, Issue No. 2, 297-308, March 2009.

[16] S .G. Mallat. "A Theory for Multiresolution Signal Decomposition: The Wavelet Representation"; IEEE Transactions on Pattern Analysis And Machine Intelligence, Vol. No. 11, Issue No. 7, 674-693, July 1989.

[17] Freeman J. A, Skapura D. M. "Neural Networks Algorithm, Application and Programming Techniques"; Pearson Education, 2006.

[18] Anil K. Jain, Robert P.W. Duin, Jianchang Mao. "Statistical Pattern Recognition: A Review "; IEEE Transactions on Pattern Analysis and Machine Intelligence, Vol. No. 22, Issue No. 1, 4-37, January 2000.

The ZCPA Based on the Gammachirp Filter Bank Used for Speaker Independent Recognition

X. Zhang, X. Liu, L. Huang, and Z. Wang
College of Information Engineering, Taiyuan University of Technology, Taiyuan, Shanxi, China

Abstract - *This paper presents the method of speech feature extraction based on the gammachirp filter bank that was used to extract Zero Crossing Peak Amplitude (ZCPA) feature, which worked as the input of the radial basis function (RBF) network. The gammachirp filter was implemented through a combination of a gammatone filter and an IIR asymmetric filter, which largely reduced the computational cost compared with the FIR method. The experiments were carried on the Korean isolate words in the speaker-independent recognition system. The results show that in case of taking no account of sound intensity, chirp factors can lead to different recognition results. When the chirp factor is 4, the result is better than that in other conditions.*

Keywords: Gammachirp filter; feature extraction; Zero Crossing Peak Amplitude (ZCPA); speech recognition

1 Introduction

The speech is the acoustic manifestation of linguistic information. Articulatory phonetics, acoustic phonetics, and auditory phonetics are three branches in modern linguistics [1]. The articulatory phonetics mainly studies the speech production mechanism. The acoustic phonetics focuses on analyzing speech by using acoustic methods. While the auditory phonetics is doing the research about physiological properties of speech perception, namely the acquirement of voice in human hearing process, the comprehension of speech in our brain, the storage and comparison of speech information in brain. Therefore, auditory phonetics could be implemented by using a speech recognition system.

The perception of speech in cochlear is always one of the hot topics in the auditory system research. The cochlear is generally taken as a set of band pass filter bank, where each band has sharp selectivity. This means that there is a frequency corresponding to every place in membrane. When the pure tone signal of this eigen frequency simulates cochlear, the corresponding place in membrane will reach the crest.

The common auditory filters include the resonant filter [2][3], the roex function filter[4], the gammatone filter [5], and the gammachirp filter [6]. The resonant filter is based on the characteristic of frequency selectivity of the basement membrane. The filter fully considers the sharp frequency selectivity, but ignores the characteristic of active feedback and nonlinearity of basement membrane. The roex filter was firstly used in masking experiment, which was used to fit human ear in identifying the specific signal frequency threshold in noisy environment. The roex function curve is slowly widened on the left side as the stimulus intensity increased, which is in line with cochlear asymmetric and level-dependent characteristics. However, on the right side, the slope of the curve is almost unchanged, which is different from the filter properties of cochlear. The gammatone filter has simple parameters, lower order and simple time-domain function, but it cannot realize the characteristic of asymmetric frequency response and level-dependent. The gammachirp auditory filter is an extension of the popular gammatone filter; it has an additional frequency-modulation term to produce an asymmetric amplitude spectrum.

In recent years, the gammachirp filter was successfully applied in many areas. The filter was combined with wavelet packet in the audio coding [7], and in the formant estimated [8] by Noureddine Ellouze. Lotfi Salhi applied the filter in the analysis of the speech signal by combining it with the wavelet transform [9]. The other researchers used the gammachirp filter for simulating basement membrane of the human ear, and got good results [10]. In addition, the gammachirp filter was successfully used in speaker recognition as the front-end feature extraction filter [11]. In this paper, the definition and implementation of the gammachirp filter are briefly introduced in the section 2 and 3. Section 4 presents the experiment results, and section 5 gives the conclusion.

2 Definition

The gammachirp filter was derived by Irino and Patterson in 1997. The complex impulse response of the gammachirp is given by the following:

$$g_c(t) = at^{n-1}\exp(-2\pi bERB(f_r)t)\exp(j2\pi f_r t + jc\ln t + j\phi)u(t)$$
$$u(t) = \begin{cases} 1, t \geq 0 \\ 0, t < 0 \end{cases}$$
$$ERB(f_r) = 24.7 + 0.108 f_r \tag{1}$$

where the time $t > 0$, a is the amplitude, n and b are parameters defining the envelope of the gamma distribution, $n = 4, b = 1.109$, f_r is the asymmetrical frequency, c is a parameter for the frequency modulation or the chirp rate, ϕ is the initial phase. The initial phase have limited impact on the power spectra, it is generally taken as zero. $\ln t$ is a natural logarithm of time, and $ERB(f_r)$ is the equivalent rectangular bandwidth of the auditory filter at f_r. Parameter c is chirp factor, which is linear with sound level P_s [12][13]. When $c = 0$, the chirp term, $c\ln t$, vanishes and equation (1) represents the complex impulse response of the gammatone filter that has the envelope of a gamma distribution function and its carrier is a sinusoid at frequency f_r. Accordingly, the gammachirp is an extension of the gammatone with a frequency modulation term. The Fourier transform of the gammachirp in Eq.(1) is derived as follows:

$$G_C(f) = \frac{a\Gamma(n+jc)e^{j\phi}}{\{2\pi bERB(f_r) + j2\pi(f - f_r)\}^{n+jc}}$$
$$= \frac{a\Gamma(n+jc)e^{j\phi}}{\left\{2\pi\sqrt{\bar{b}^2 + (f - f_r)^2} \cdot e^{j\theta}\right\}^{n+jc}} \tag{2}$$
$$\theta = \arctan\frac{f - f_r}{\bar{b}}$$
$$\bar{b} = bERB(f_r)$$

Simplify (2), then we get the following:

$$G_C(f) = \bar{a} \cdot \frac{1}{\left\{2\pi\sqrt{\bar{b}^2 + (f - f_r)^2}\right\}^n \cdot e^{jn\theta}} \cdot \frac{1}{\left\{2\pi\sqrt{\bar{b}^2 + (f - f_r)^2}\right\}^{jc} \cdot e^{-c\theta}}$$
$$\bar{a} = a\Gamma(n+jc)e^{j\phi} \tag{3}$$

where the first term $\bar{a}$ is a constant. The second term is known as the Fourier spectrum of the gammatone, $G_T(f)$. The third term represents an asymmetric function, $H_A(f)$, which will be described in details in next subsection. If we normalize the amplitude, the frequency response of the gammachirp can be represented as follows:

$$G_C(f) = G_T(f) \cdot H_A(f) \tag{4}$$

The amplitude spectrum is:

$$|G_C(f)| = |G_T(f)| \cdot |H_A(f)| \tag{5}$$

3 Implementation

As shown in Eq.(4), a gammachirp filter can be implemented by cascading a gammatone filter and an asymmetric filter. Since efficient implementations of the gammatone are already known [14,15], this section concentrates on an approximation filter for the asymmetric function. The well-known IIR Butterworth and Chebyshev filters can not satisfy the filter. Consequently, a new asymmetric compensation filter $H_C(f)$ can be designed as follows:

$$H_A(f) \approx H_C(z), z = e^{j2\pi f/f_s}$$
$$H_C(z) = \prod_{k=1}^{4} H_{Ck}(z) \tag{6}$$
$$H_{Ck}(z) = \frac{(1 - r_k e^{j\varphi_k} z^{-1})(1 - r_k e^{-j\varphi_k} z^{-1})}{(1 - r_k e^{j\phi_k} z^{-1})(1 - r_k e^{-j\phi_k} z^{-1})}$$

where the parameters of Eq.(6) are:

$$r_k = \exp\{-k.p_1.2\pi bERB(f_r)/f_s\}$$
$$\phi_k = 2\pi\{f_r + p_0^{k-1}.p_2.c.bERB(f_r)\}/f_s$$
$$\varphi_k = 2\pi\{f_r - p_0^{k-1}.p_2.c.bERB(f_r)\}/f_s \tag{7}$$
$$p_0 = 2, p_1 = 1.35 - 0.19|c|$$
$$p_2 = 0.29 - 0.004|c|$$

here, f_s is the sampling frequency. Figure 1 shows the frequency response of asymmetric compensation filter in different chirp factors. Figure 2 shows the frequency response of the gammachirp filter in $c = 4$, $f_r = 1931.1$ .Hz。

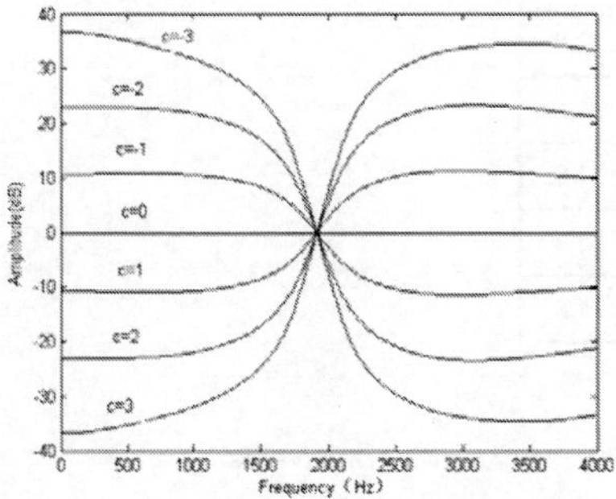

Figure 1. The Frequency Response of Asymmetric Compensation Filter with Different Chirp Factors

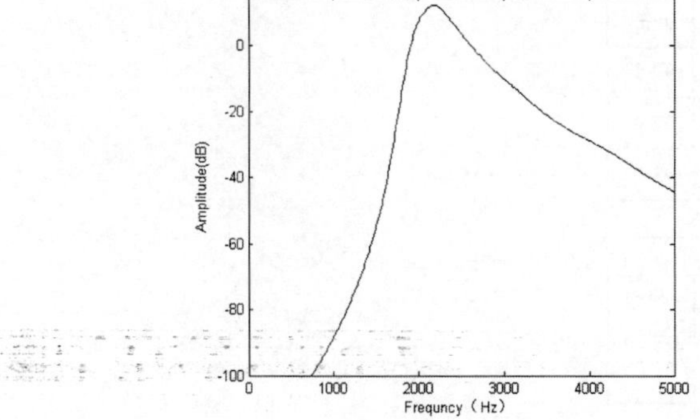

Figure 2. The Frequency Response of Gammachirp Filter in $c = 4$, $f_r = 1931.1$ Hz

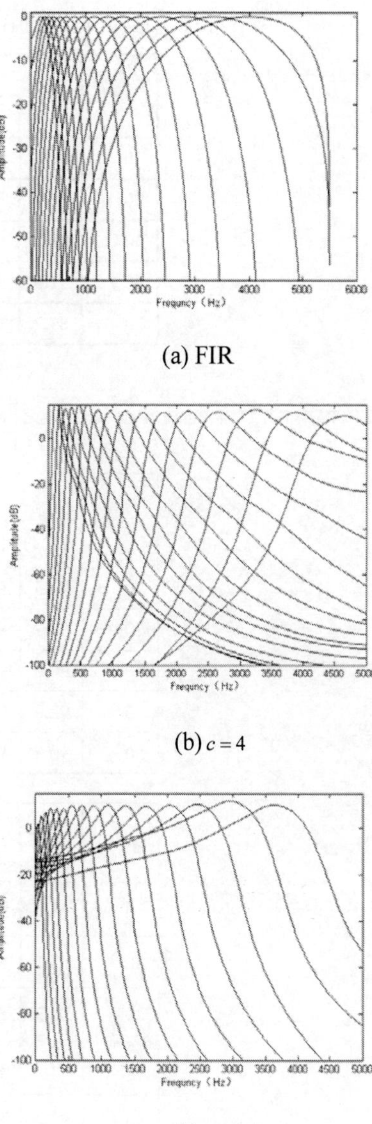

(a) FIR

(b) $c = 4$

(c) $c = -4$

Figure 3. The Frequency Response of the Gammachirp and FIR filter

4 Experiment

Traditional ZCPA system uses FIR filter to analog the characteristic of cochlear. In this paper, the gammachirp filter bank was used in the process of feature extracting. Without considering the level-dependent property of gammachirp filter, the recognition results were obtained by changing the value of chirp factor. Figure 3 shows the frequency response of the gammachirp filter and FIR filter.

The experiments were carried on the Korean isolate words in speaker-independent recognition system. The corpus include 50, 40, 30, 20, 10 Korean words made by 16 male speakers under different signal-to-noise rations (SNRs: 15dB, 20dB, 25dB, 30dB and clean). Each word was spoken 3 times. The utterances were sampled at 11025 Hz sampling rate with 16-bits resolution. 9 persons were used as training set, and the rest 7 as testing set. The ZCPA feature was the input of RBF network. Table I shows the results of the FIR filter in different SNRs.

TABLE I. THE RESULTS OF FIR FILTER IN DIFFERENT SNRS(%)

words	SNRs（dB）				
	15	20	25	30	clean
10	87.1	90.5	90.5	91.4	92.9
20	89.8	92.1	93.3	93.1	94.5
30	92.1	93.2	93.0	94.3	94.0
40	91.9	93.7	94.3	94.0	94.4
50	89.7	91.7	93.4	93.3	94.3

TABLE II. THE RESULTS OF GAMMACHIRP FILTER IN DIFFERENT CHIRP FACTORS AND SNR(%)

(a) $c = -4$

words	SNRs（dB）				
	15	20	25	30	clean
10	94.3	95.2	95.7	94.8	95.2
20	90.7	92.1	92.6	91.4	92.6
30	90.6	91.9	92.5	91.6	92.9
40	92.0	92.1	93.1	92.7	92.9
50	90.8	92.0	92.1	92.3	93.0

(b) $c = 0$

words	SNRs（dB）				
	15	20	25	30	clean
10	84.3	89.0	89.0	88.1	91.0
20	88.1	90.5	92.2	91.9	93.7
30	88.3	89.6	92.1	91.9	93.7
40	87.7	89.6	92.1	91.9	93.6
50	85.4	88.8	91.0	92.1	93.8

(c) $c = 4$

words	SNRs（dB）				
	15	20	25	30	clean
10	91.4	92.9	96.2	95.2	95.2
20	92.4	92.6	94.0	94.0	94.5
30	90.6	92.5	93.8	93.7	95.1
40	90.4	93.2	94.6	94.0	95.1
50	89.0	92.6	94.1	94.2	95.6

TABLE III. THE AVERAGE RESULTS OF FEATURES IN DIFFERENT SNR(%)

Filter	SNRs (dB)				
	15	20	25	30	clean
$c=-4$	91.7	92.7	93.2	92.6	93.3
$c=0$	85.4	88.8	91.0	92.1	93.8
$c=4$	90.8	92.8	94.5	94.2	95.1
FIR	90.1	92.2	93.0	93.2	94.0

By changing the value of the chirp factor, different gammachirp filter bank was obtained. The filter banks were used as the front-end filter for extracting ZCPA which was taken as the input of RBF network. The results of different chirp factors were shown in Table II. Table III shows the average recognition rates of different filter in different SNR.

From the above results, we can find the following facts.

(1) Table II shows that the gammachirp filter banks have the better performance than gammatone filter bank from 15dB to clean. 0.4% at least in 25dB 20 words and more than 10% in 15dB 10 words.

(2) Furthermore, the gammachirp filter in $c=4$ have better results compared with the case of $c=-4$. In addition to the case of 15dB the highest result 94.3% occurs in $c=-4$, the maximum results under other SNR is in $c=4$ condition.

(3) In Table III, we can see that between gammachirp filter in the case of $c=4$ and FIR filter, the former filter has the better performance in the clean condition. It is also the same trend in 30dB, 25dB and 20dB conditions. In 15dB, the case of $c=-4$ has better performance.

The explanation of the above results is as follows. The cochlear is considered to be band pass filter bank, and one of the properties is that the frequency response of the single filter is asymmetrical. While the frequency response of gammachirp filter is asymmetrical, the frequency response of FIR filter banks used in traditional ZCPA is symmetrical about the center frequency. The gammatone filter has the same reason. However, the FIR filter is designed channel by channel, which provides more accuracy in the design than that of gammatone filter. This explains why the FIR has the better recognition results than that the gammatone filter.

TABLE IV. THE AVERAGE RESULTS OF DIFFERENT GAMMACHIRP FILTER BANKS IN DIFFERENT SNR(%)

filter	SNRs (%)				
	15	20	25	30	clean
$c=-4$	91.7	92.7	93.2	92.6	93.3
$c=-2$	87.0	89.7	92.6	94.1	94.3
$c=2$	83.0	86.8	89.6	90.5	92.6
$c=4$	90.8	92.8	94.5	94.2	95.1

In paper [18], the experiments were carried on the gammachirp filter in the condition of $c=-2$ and $c=2$. The results show that the system has fine performance when $c=-2$. Table IV displays the average results for the different gammachirp filter banks with different SNRs.

The property of cochlear that is considered as filter bank is that the slope of the curve at low frequencies is more flat than that at high frequencies. That is when the chirp factor is negative, the filter has good performance. But from the above data, we can see that the gammachirp filter in $c=4$ works better than that in the other chirp factors, while the chirp factor is 2, the filter has the poorest performance. When the chirp factors are -2 and -4, the filter didn't have excellent performance. In reference [17], they had the same conclusion that the gammachirp filter in positive chirp factor gave satisfactory results.

5 Conclusions

In this paper, the gammachirp filter was used in the front-end ZCPA feature extracting process. The experiment results were obtained under the different chirp factors without considering the level of the sound pressure. The results show that the value of the chirp factor has significant impact on the property of the filter. However, the chirp factor is not the sole element that can influence the results, and the number of channels and the sound intensity of the input signal can also have impact on the results.

Acknowledgment

This project was sponsored by the International Technology Cooperation Plan of Shanxi Province (Grant No.2011081047), and the Returned Overseas Personnel Merit-funded Projects of Shanxi Province (Grant No. [2013] 68).

References

[1] Cheng qing Zong. Statistical natural language processing. Tsinghua University Press, pp.1-10, 2008.

[2] Lyon RF, Mead C. An analog electronic cochlear. IEEE Trans. Acoustics, Speech, and Signal Processing, vol.36, No.7. p p.1119-1134, 1988.

[3] Lyon RF. A computational model of filtering, detection, and compression in the cochlear. Proceedings of IEEE - ICASSP, 82:pp.1282-1285, 1982.

[4] Patterson RD, Moore BCJ. Auditory filters and excitation patterns as represonations of frequency resolution..Frequency selectivity in hearing, pp.123-177, 1986.

[5] Johannesma P. The pre-response stimulus ensemble of neurons in the cochlear nucleus. IPO Symposium on Hearing Theory, pp.58-69, 1972.

[6] Irino T, Patterson RD. A time-domain, level-dependent auditory filter: the gammachirp. Acoust Soc Am, 101:pp.412-419, 1997.

[7] Samar K, Kaïs O, Noureddine E. Realization of a psychoacoustic model for MPEG 1 using Gammachirp wavelete transform. Turkey: EUSIPCO, pp.120-123, 2005.

[8] Kaïs O, Zied L, Noureddine E. Formant estimation using Gammachirp filterbank. In Eurospeech, pp.2471-2474, 2001.

[9] Lotfi S. Design and implementation of the cochlear filter model based on wavelet transform as part of speech signals analysis..Research Journal of Applied Sciences, vol.2,No.4. pp. 512-521, 2007,.

[10] Yan Luo, Shouguo Zhao. Simulation of the human ear basilar membrane filter..Beijing Jiaotong University, pp.34-47, 2009.

[11] Yue Wang Zhihong Qin. Study on speech feature extraction algorithm in speaker recognition system. Jilin University, pp.63-75, 2009.

[12] Irino T, Unoki M. A time-varying, analysis/synthesis auditory filterbank using the Gammachirp. IEEE Int. Conf. Acoust. Speech Signal Processing (ICASSP-98), pp.3653-3656, 1998.

[13] Irino T, Unoki M. Analysis/Synthesis auditory filterbank based on Gammachirp. Computational Models of Auditory Function S. Greenberg and M. Slaney (Eds.) IOS Press, pp.397-406, 1999.

[14] Lixia Huang, Xueying Zhang Xueyan Liu. Different channels in Gammatone filter bank based on ZCPA for speaker-independent recognition task. ACPIM. International Asia Conference on Optical Instrument and Measurement, pp.74-77, 2010.

[15] Immerseel LV, Peeters S. Digital implementation of linear gammatone filters: comparison of design methods..Acoustics Research Letters Online (ARLO), vol.4,No.3, pp.59-64, 2003.

[16] [Kim DS, Lee SY, Kil RM. Auditory processing of speech signal for robust speech recognition in real-world noisy environments..IEEE Trans. Speech and Audio Proc, vol.7,No.2, pp.55-69, 1999.

[17] Khalil Abid, Kais Ouni, Nouredinne Ellouze.The effect chirp term in audio compression using a gammachirp wavelet. Network Infrastructure and Digital Content, 2009. IC-NID. IEEE International Conference on. 2009, pp.774 – 778, 2009

[18] Xueyan Liu, Xueying Zhang, Lixia Huang. Gammachirp filter bank applied in speech feature extraction.[OL]. Chinese scientific and technological papers online 2011-11-09. http://www.paper.edu.cn/index.php/default/releasepaper/content/201111-158.

An Improved Method for Estimating the a Priori Probability of Speech Absence for Enhancement of Speech

Aboubakar Nasser Samatin Njikam[1], and Huan Zhao[1]
[1]School of Information Science and Engineering, Hunan University, Changsha, Hunan, China

Abstract - *The efficiency of many noise suppression filters relied on an accurate estimation of their parameters such as the power spectral density of the noise (PSD) and the a priori speech absence probability (SAP). This work addresses the problem of estimation of the a priori SAP. The proposed method relied on the conditional probabilities of the noisy speech magnitude, assuming that speech is absent or present and by dynamically computed parameters of the a priori SAP using two factors: a smoothing-update factor and a factor related to the kth spectral component. The smoothing-update factor, which is based on a decision made in frequency band whether speech is present or absent, is computed by recursively averaging past spectral values of the a priori SAP. The factor related to the kth spectral component is computed using the a priori signal-to-noise ratio (SNR). The efficiency of the proposed algorithm over competitive ones, both in terms of background noise suppression and speech distortion, is assessed by the use of an objective measure namely average segmental signal-to-noise ratio (segSNR) plus a study of speech spectrograms.*

Keywords: Signal and speech processing, Enhancement techniques, Speech Absence Probability

1 Introduction

The optimally modified log-spectral amplitude estimator (OM-LSA) [1] was proposed to minimize the mean-square error of the log-spectra for speech signals under signal presence uncertainty. The algorithm is very efficient for noise suppression and improvement of quality of speech if its required parameters such as the a priori signal-to-noise ratio (SNR) and the a priori speech absence probability (SAP) are correctly-estimate. This paper focuses on the estimation of the a priori speech absence probability. A priori SAP refers to a probability that a speech is not present with respect to a frame and a frequency bin resulting from an input signal [2]. Several algorithms for estimating and updating the a priori sap have been proposed.

In [3] two methods for estimating the a priori of SAP were proposed. The first method, which is based on comparing the conditional probabilities of the noisy speech magnitude, assuming that speech is present or absent, can be considered as hard-decision approach. The second method proposed in [3] for estimating the a priori SAP is known as a soft-decision approach. Unlike the hard decision method which classifies input signal into speech presence or speech absence, the soft decision method is directly design to represent the probability that the input signal is from a speech absence state. The preceding two methods for estimating the a priori SAP were incorporated into an MMSE estimator and have shown to yield about 2-3 dB SNR improvement over the estimator that used a fixed a priori SAP [4, 5, 6].

In [6], Malah et Al. proposed a different method based on the a posteriori SNR. The decision on speech absence was based on a comparison of the estimated a posteriori SNR against a threshold. Its main drawbacks are the misclassification of voice activity causes unwanted artifacts [7, 8, 9].

Cohen in [1, 10] presented a technique for the computation of the a priori SAP estimator essentially based on three factors. In his work, a soft decision made on each frame whether speech is present or not and calculation of local and global factors of the a priori SNR are used as a parameters. This technique has shown to yield better performance in terms of objective segmental SNR measure over the pre-cited methods. But as in [6], undesired artifacts are introduces due to the misclassification of the speech activity.

In this paper an effective estimator for the a priori SAP is proposed. Next, after a brief description of the OM-LSA estimator, a detail description of the proposed estimator is presented. The technique is evaluated using an objective measure namely average segmental signal-to-noise ratio (segSNR) plus a study of speech spectrograms.

2 Description of the Optimally Modified Log-Spectral Amplitude

We assumed a clean signal x to be corrupted by uncorrelated additive background noise signal n. Considering short-time Fourier Transform (STFT)

$$Y_k(l) = X_k(l) + N_k(l)$$

where l stands for the frame index and k for the frequency band index.

Under the following two hypotheses:

$H_k^0(l)$: Speech absent

$H_k^1(l)$: Speech present

and based on a complex Gaussian assumption [5, 7] the conditional probabilities of the noisy speech magnitude are computed as below:

$$p(Y_k(l) \mid H_k^0(l)) = \frac{1}{\pi\lambda_k^n(l)} \exp\left\{-\frac{|Y_k(l)|^2}{\lambda_k^n(l)}\right\}$$
$$p(Y_k(l) \mid H_k^1(l)) = \frac{1}{\pi(\lambda_k^x(l) + \lambda_k^n(l))} \cdot \exp\left\{-\frac{|Y_k(l)|^2}{\lambda_k^x(l) + \lambda_k^n(l)}\right\} \quad (1)$$

where $\lambda_k^x(l) \triangleq E\left[|X_k(l)|^2 | H_k^1(l)\right]$ and $\lambda_k^n(l) \triangleq E\left[|N_k(l)|^2\right]$ respectively, indicate the variance of the clean speech and the variance of noise.

Therefore, the probability that speech is present denotes by $p_k(l) = p(H_k^1(l) \mid Y_k(l))$ is derived from Bayes formula [5]:

$$p_k(l) = \left\{1 + \frac{P(H_k^0(l))}{1 - P(H_k^0(l))}(1 + \xi_k(l))\exp(-v_k(l))\right\}^{-1} \quad (2)$$

in which $\xi_k(l) \triangleq \lambda_k^x(l) / \lambda_k^n(l)$ and $\gamma_k(l) \triangleq |Y_k(l)|^2 / \lambda_k^d(l)$ represent the a priori SNR and the a posteriori SNR, respectively. And $v_k(l) \triangleq \gamma_k(l)\xi_k(l) / (1 + \xi_k(l))$.

Let $L = |X|$ be the spectral speech amplitude. Its optimal estimate L'[7], considering statistically independent assumption of spectral components [6], is given by:

$$L_k'(l) = \exp\{E[\log L_k(l) \mid Y_k(l)]\} \triangleq G_k(l) \mid Y_k(l) \mid \quad (3)$$

Assuming Gaussian statistical model, we get

$$\begin{aligned} &E[\log L_k(l) \mid Y_k(l)] \\ &= E[\log L_k(l) \mid Y_k(l), H_k^1(l)]p_k(l) \\ &+ E[\log L_k(l) \mid Y_k(l), H_k^0(l)](1 - p_k(l)) \end{aligned} \quad (4)$$

Hence the following assumption can be made:

In absence of speech, a minimum gain G_{min} determined by a subjective criteria, is used:

$$\exp\left\{E[\log L_k(l) \mid Y_k(l), H_k^0(l)]\right\} = G_{min} \cdot |Y_k(l)| \quad (5)$$

In presence of speech, the conditional gain function given by

$$\exp\{E[\log L_k(l) \mid Y_k(l), H_k^1(l)]\} = G_k(l) \cdot |Y_k(l)| \quad (6)$$

is derived in [6] to be

$$G_k(l) = \frac{\xi_k(l)}{1 + \xi_k(l)} \exp\left(\frac{1}{2}\int_{v_k(l)}^{\infty} \frac{e^{-t}}{t} dt\right) \quad (7)$$

Therefore, Substituting (5) and (6) into (3), the gain function for the OM-LSA estimator is obtained by

$$G(k,l) = \{G_{H_1}(k,l)\}^{p(k,l)} \cdot G_{min}^{1-p(k,l)} \quad (8)$$

In the above scheme, the OM-LSA is modified by considering the uncertainty of speech in real environment, which requires the computation of speech absence probability (SAP). In the next section, we present an improved method for tracking the a priori SAP.

3 The Proposed A Priori SAP Estimation Method

Two factors $\alpha_k(l)$ and c_k are involved in the computation of the a priori SAP estimator, where $\alpha_k(l)$ represents a dynamic smoothing update factor which describes the speech absence probability of the current frame, and c_k a factor related to the *kth* spectral component.

3.1 Computation of a Dynamic Smoothing Update Factor

The process of computed the dynamic smoothing update factor is described below:

Assuming the two following hypotheses

$H_k^0(l)$: Speech absent

$H_k^1(l)$: Speech present

and based on Gaussian statistical model assumption [5, 7] the conditional probabilities of the observed signal are as follows:

$$p(Y_k \mid H_k^0) = \frac{2Y_k}{\lambda_k^n} \exp(\gamma_k) \tag{9}$$

$$p(Y_k \mid H_k^1) = \frac{2Y_k}{\lambda_k^n} \exp\left(-\frac{Y_k^2 + X_k^2}{\lambda_k^n}\right) I_0\left(\frac{2X_k Y_k}{\lambda_k^n}\right) \tag{10}$$

where $I_0(\cdot)$ represents the zero-order modified Bessel function.

Using the conditional probabilities from (9) and (10), a binary decision in frequency band k is given by

if $p(Y_k \mid H_k^1) > p(Y_k \mid H_k^0)$ then

$b_k = 0$ speech presence

else (11)

$b_k = 1$ speech absence

end

However, since X_k is unknown, the approximation $\xi_k \approx X_k^2 / \lambda_k^n$ is used instead. Hence,

$$p(Y_k \mid H_k^1) = \frac{2Y_k}{\lambda_k^n} \exp\left(-\gamma_k - \xi_k\right) I_0\left(2\sqrt{\gamma_k \xi_k}\right) \tag{12}$$

Therefore, the preceding condition (11) can be simplified and expressed in terms of γ_k and ξ_k as follows:

if $\exp(-\xi_k) I_0\left(2\sqrt{\gamma_k \xi_k}\right) > 1$ then

$b_k = 0$ speech presence

else (13)

$b_k = 1$ speech absence

end

From the above scheme, a dynamic smoothing update factor for frame l is derived by

$$\alpha_k(l) = \sin\left(1 - \beta * q_k(l-1) * b_k\right) \tag{14}$$

where β is a constant. The sinus function is used in order to track accurately and faster the a priori SAP. In the conventional method, the value of $\alpha_k(l)$ is fixed. The tracking speed of the a priori SAP is therefore constant.

3.2 Computation of the *kth* Spectral Component Factor

The *kth* spectral component factor is computed as follows

$$c_k = \sin(\delta^{\xi_k}) \tag{15}$$

where δ is a constant, and ξ_k is a prior SNR. The sinus function here is used to prevent clipping of speech onset or weak component while the a priori SNR is very helpful for eliminating musical noise.

3.3 Update of the a Priori SAP estimate

After computing the dynamic smoothing update factor and the *kth* spectral component factor, the a priori SAP estimate denoted as $q_k(l)$ is updated as follows

$$q_k(l) = (1 - \alpha_k(l)) + c_k * q_k(l-1) * \alpha_k(l) \tag{16}$$

The overall algorithm for estimating the a priori SAP can therefore be summarized as follows:

1. Using the conditional probabilities from equation (9) and (10), make a binary decision for frequency bin according to (13).
2. Compute the dynamic smoothing update factor using (14).

Table 1: segSNR scores for various estimators

Noise	Method	0dB	5dB	10dB	15dB	Noise	Method	0 dB	5 dB	10dB	15dB
White	Hard	0.956	3.242	5.709	8.043	Street	Hard	-0.73	1.255	4.110	6.373
	Soft	0.863	3.160	5.635	7.998		Soft	-0.74	1.319	4.131	6.403
	Malah et Al	0.867	3.188	5.595	7.996		Malah et Al	-0.82	1.141	4.062	6.372
	Cohen	1.065	3.399	5.909	8.162		Cohen	-0.62	1.242	4.102	6.424
	Proposed Method	**1.234**	**3.465**	**5.913**	**8.204**		Proposed Method	**-0.59**	**1.420**	**4.231**	**6.453**
Babble	Hard	-1.43	0.812	3.591	6.153	Car	Hard	-0.12	2.127	4.661	7.291
	Soft	-1.43	0.781	3.637	6.181		Soft	-0.19	2.066	4.586	7.266
	Malah et Al	-1.59	0.643	3.534	6.054		Malah et Al	-0.35	2.013	4.560	7.245
	Cohen	-1.40	0.839	3.686	6.163		Cohen	0.014	2.280	4.715	7.400
	Proposed Method	**-1.37**	**0.853**	**3.689**	**6.195**		Proposed Method	**0.158**	**2.368**	**4.845**	**7.453**

3. Compute the kth spectral component factor using (15).

4. Update the a priori SAP estimate using (16).

4 Performance Evaluation

For evaluation purposes, we select the state-of-the-art approaches for comparison, including hard-decision [3], soft-decision [3], Malah et al [4] and Cohen [1, 10]. Furthermore, we integrate the different a priori SAP methods into the OM-LSA estimator [1].

Speech data, segmented into 20-ms frames using a Hamming window with 75% overlap is used for analysis. A total of 15 utterances speech corrupted by babble, car, street and white noise at SNR level ranges from 0dB to 15dB, is taken from NOIZEUS database [13] which contains IEEE sentences corrupted by real-world noise from AURORA database [14].

An objective measure namely segmental SNR is chosen for evaluation. The segmental SNR measure is known as the best measure in terms of background noise distortion and takes into account residual noise [15]. Higher segSNR values indicate that the enhanced speech is more similar to the clean speech. Moreover, a visual study of speech spectrograms is done to complement the evaluation.

By analysis the segSNR scores obtained by various a priori SAP estimators reported in table 1, the first conclusion we can draw is, the proposed estimator gained the higher values in terms of segSNR measure (bold scores) over the other estimators for every types of noise and at different SNR input. On the other hand the proposed method is more efficient in residual noise suppression and speech distortion minimization than conventional estimators. The advantage of the proposed estimator is more significant for Car noise and at low input SNR levels for all types of noise. This is partially due to the reliable decision made by the proposed estimator when it comes to classify speech between speech present and speech absent, but also to its capacity to effectively track the SAP at each frequency band even at low SNR inputs. The estimator proposed by Cohen also gained good results compare to the other ones. This leads us to choose that estimator in order to conduct our study of speech spectrograms.

Figure 1 shows the enhanced speech obtained using the Cohen estimator (panel c) and the proposed estimator (panel d). Speech spectrograms of the clean speech and noisy speech (corrupted by street noise at 5dB SNR input level) are given respectively in panel (a) and panel (b). Visual inspection of speech spectrograms show that while the proposed estimator and the estimator proposed by Cohen slightly perform the same in terms of background noise suppression, the proposed algorithm does perform better in minimizing speech distortions introduced during the enhanced process (see arrows). This confirms results obtained in table 1.

5 Conclusions

This work proposed an improved method for estimating the a priori speech absence probability for speech enhancement by dynamically computed its parameters. The

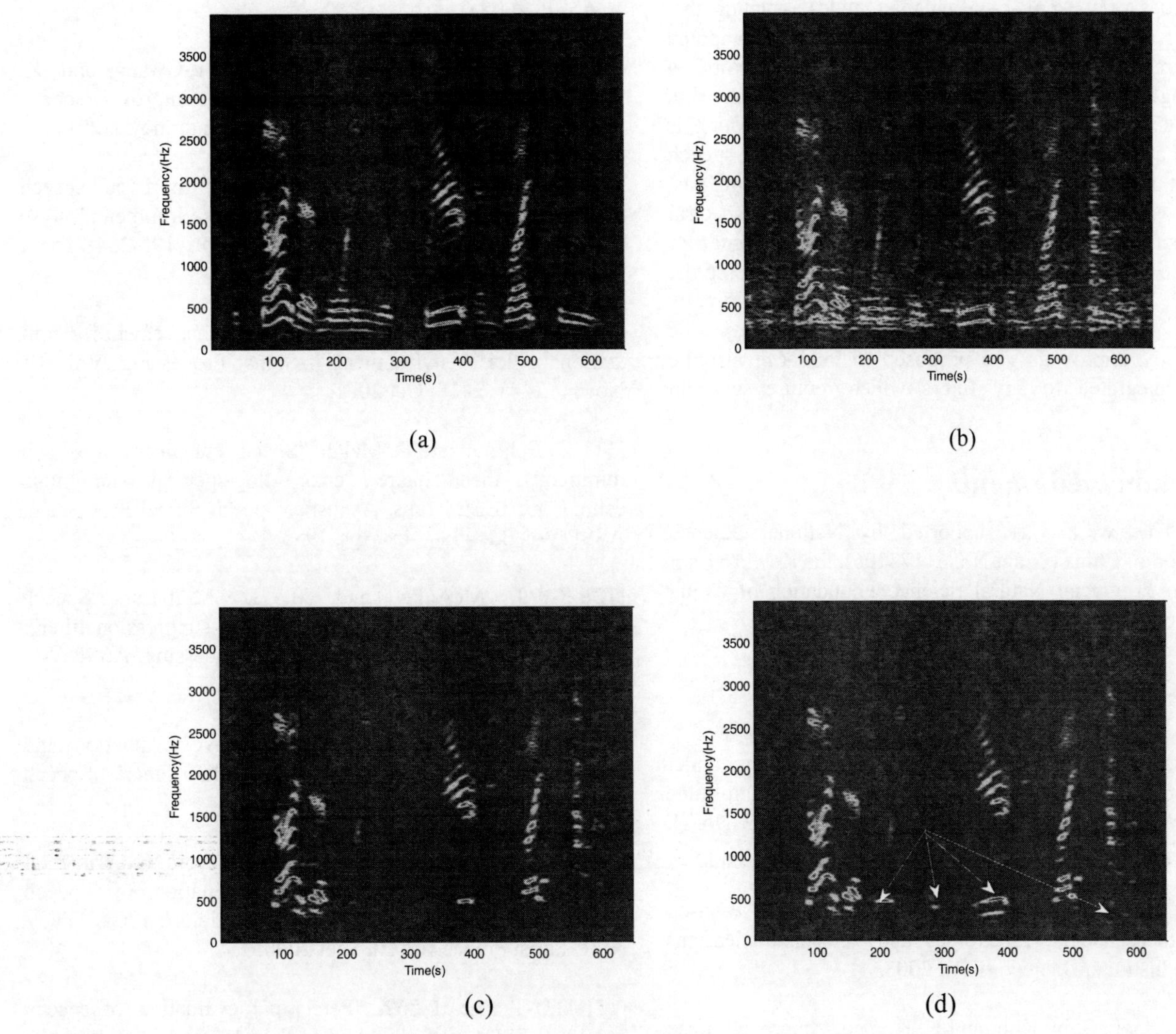

Figure 1: Speech spectrograms: (a) Clean speech, (b) Speech corrupted by street noise at 5dB, (c) Enhanced speech: Cohen estimator, (d) Enhanced speech: Proposed estimator. Arrows indicate the speech preserved during the enhancement process performed by the proposed method, while they are distorted during the enhancement process using the Cohen estimator.

proposed estimator is based on comparing the conditional probabilities of the noisy speech magnitude, assuming that speech is absent or present and by dynamically computed parameters of the a priori SAP using two factors: a smoothing-update factor and a factor related to the kth spectral component. The smoothing-update factor which is based on a decision made in frequency band whether speech is present or absent is computed by recursively averaging past spectral values of the a priori SAP. The kth spectral component factor is computed using the a priori signal-to-noise ratio (SNR). In this paper, we showed that by using the proposed estimator, the performance of the optimally modified log-spectral estimator (OM-LSA) can be significantly improved. The proposed method can also be directly integrated to any filters which require such an estimate.

6 Acknowledgment

This work was supported by National Science Foundation of China (Grant No. 61173106), the Key Program of Hunan Provincial Natural Science Foundation of China (Grant No.10JJ2046).

7 References

[1] Israel Cohen. "Optimal speech enhancement under signal presence uncertainty using log-spectral amplitude estimator"; IEEE Signal processing letters, Vol. 1.9 No. 4, 113-116, 2002.

[2] Song Joo Lee. "Method for estimation priori SAP based on statistical model"; Electronics and Telecommunications Research Institute, Daejeon (KR), 2008.

[3] I. Y. Soon, S. N. Koh, and C. K. Yeo. "Improved noise suppression filter using self-adaptive estimator of probability of speech absence"; Signal Processing, Vol. 75, 151–159, 1999.

[4] Y. Ephraim and D. Malah. "Speech enhancement using a minimum mean-square error short-time spectral amplitude estimator"; IEEE Trans. Acoustic. Speech Signal Processing, ASSP Vol. 32 No. 6, 1109–1121, 1984.

[5] N. S. Kim and J.-H. Chang. "Spectral enhancement based on global soft decision"; IEEE Signal Processing Letters, Vol. 7 No. 5, 108-110, 2000.

[6] D. Malah, R. V. Cox, and A. J. Accardi. "Tracking speech-presence uncertainty to improve speech enhancement in non-stationary noise environments"; in Proc. Int. Conf. Acoustics, Speech, Signal Processing, 789–792, 1999.

[7] C. Min-Seok and K. Hong-Goo. "An improved estimation of a priori speech absence probability for speech enhancement: in perspective of speech perception"; IEEE ICASSP, 2005.

[8] C. Jae-Hun, C. Joon-Hyuk, J. Yu-Gwang and K. NamSoo. "Speech enhancement based on improved speech presence uncertainty tracking technique"; Inter.noise, 2011.

[9] S. Young-ho and L. Sang-min. "Improved speech absence probability estimation based on environmental noise classification"; J. Cent. South Univ., Vol. 19, 2548-2553, 2012.

[10] I. Cohen and B. Berdugo. "Speech enhancement for non-stationary noise environments"; Signal Processing, Vol. 81, No. 11, 2403–2418, Oct 2001.

[11] Y. Ephraim and D. Malah. "Speech enhancement using a minimum mean-square error log-spectral amplitude estimator"; IEEE Trans. Acoustic. Speech Signal Processing, ASSP Vol. 33, 443–445, Apr. 1985.

[12] R. J. McAulay and M. L. Malpass. "Speech enhancement using a soft decision noise suppression filter"; IEEE Trans. Acoustic. Speech Signal Processing, ASSP Vol. 28, 137–145, Apr. 1980.

[13] Hu, Y. and Loizou, P. "Subjective evaluation and comparison of speech enhancement algorithms"; Speech Communication, Vol. 49, 588-601, 2007.

[14] H. Hirsch, and D. Pearce "The Aurora Experimental Framework for the Performance Evaluation of Speech Recognition Systems under Noisy Conditions"; ISCA ITRW ASR, Paris, France, 18-20, Sept 2000.

[15] ITU-T Rec. P.862. "Perceptual evaluation of speech quality (PESQ), and objective method for end-to-end speech quality assessment of narrowband telephone networks and speech codecs", 2000.

SESSION

POSTERS AND SHORT PAPERS

Chair(s)

TBA

Efficient Motion Vector Composition for H.264/AVC to SVC Video Transcoding

Yung-Hsiang Tang[1], Gwo-Long Li[2], and Mei-Juan Chen[1]
[1]Dept. of Electrical Engineering, National Dong Hwa University, Hualien, Taiwan
[2] Dept. of Video Coding Core Technology, Industrial Technology Research Institute, Hsinchu, Taiwan

Abstract - *To reduce the transcoding overhead between H.264/AVC and Scalable Video Coding, this paper proposes an efficient motion vector composition algorithm combined with adaptive search range decision. In our proposal, the decoded motion vectors of H.264/AVC are reused to derive the motion vectors in compliance with the hierarchical B prediction structure of Scalable Video Coding. Furthermore, the decoded motion vector and residual information are also considered to decide the search range for refining the composed motion vectors so that the composite motion vectors can be as accurate as possible. Simulation results demonstrate that our proposed transcoding algorithm can achieve better rate distortion performance and higher transcoding time reduction compared to previous work.*

Keywords: Transcoding, H.264/AVC, SVC, Motion Vector.

1 Introduction

H.264/AVC to Scalable Video Coding (SVC)[1] transcoding is one of the interesting topics since it can convert H.264/AVC bitstream to SVC bitstream for satisfying the application heterogeneities. However, the decoding and re-encoding process consumes lots of computational complexity especially for the motion estimation. In order to reduce computational complexity of transcoding, the method proposed in [2] uses the decoded motion vectors of H.264/AVC to reduce search range for accelerating the motion estimation process. However, the computational complexity would be high if the reference picture far from the current picture. The method proposed in [3] calculates the forward motion vectors of hierarchal B prediction structure by linear translation but lacks of composing backward motion vectors. This paper proposes an efficient motion vector composition algorithm to derive both of forward and backward motion vectors for SVC in compliance with hierarchical B prediction structure. In addition, a computational complexity reduced motion vector refinement algorithm is also proposed to further improve the accuracy of composed motion vectors.

2 Proposed Algorithm

Fig. 1 shows the flowchart of proposed algorithm for H.264/AVC to SVC video transcoding. Our proposed algorithm is mainly composed by two phases. The first phase is the motion vector composition which is used to generate the absent motion vectors just following the hierarchical B prediction structure. The second phase is the motion vector refinement which is used to refine the composed motion vectors so that the transcoding results can be as better as possible.

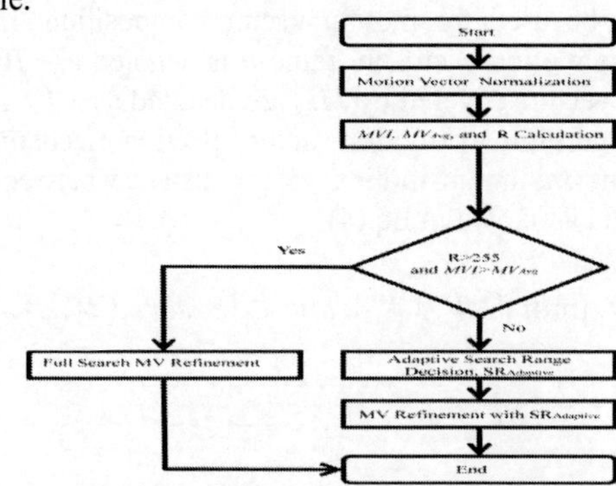

Fig. 1 Flowchart of proposed algorithm

2.1 Motion Vector Composition

To support temporal scalability, the prediction structure of H.264/AVC has to be changed first to satisfy the hierarchical B prediction structure of SVC. Fig. 2 shows the prediction architecture of H.264/AVC and SVC on the upper and bottom parts, respectively. It should be noticed that only the prediction structure of IPPP is treated in this paper. As shown in Fig. 2, we can find that only the motion vectors pointing to previous frame can be obtained from the decoded H.264/AVC bitstream. Therefore, the main goal of the proposed motion vector composition algorithm is to compose the motion vectors pointing to any reference frame with any frame distance as SVC prediction structure shown. Therefore, based on the smooth moving property between successive frames, the composite motion vectors for SVC can be calculated by

$$MV_n^F = \sum_{i=0}^{\frac{G}{2^l}-1} MV_{n-i}^f \quad (1)$$

MV_n^f and MV_n^F are the H.264/AVC decoded forward motion vectors and SVC forward motion vectors, respectively. G and l are the group of picture (GOP) size and the temporal layer index. However, for the backward motion vectors, H.264/AVC decoded motion vectors with IPPP prediction structure don't contain the motion vectors in backward direction. The proposed motion vector composition algorithm reuses the forward motion vectors decoded from H.264/AVC to compose the backward motion vectors of SVC as shown in following equations.

$$MV_n^b = -MV_n^f \quad (2)$$

$$MV_n^B = \sum_{i=0}^{\frac{G}{2^l}-1} MV_{n+i}^b \quad (3)$$

Although Eq.(1) to Eq.(3) can be used to compose the corresponding motion vectors both in forward and backward directions to satisfy the prediction structure of SVC, the problem will be faced during the motion vectors selection process due to the variable block size issue as shown in Fig. 3. When composing the corresponding motion vectors, our proposed algorithm needs to pick one motion vector from reference frame in order to derive the composed motion vectors. However, for the motion vector in frame *n* pointing to previous frame *n-1*, it might cover several blocks which have their own motion vectors. Therefore, our proposed algorithm needs to decide which motion vector will be selected to be used for motion vector composition. In our notation, the motion vector in frame *n* is denoted as MV_t and the motion vectors covered by MV_t are denoted as MV_c. In our proposed algorithm, the motion vector selection mechanism is based on the minimum motion vector distance between the MV_c and MV_t as shown in Eq.(4).

$$MV_n^f = MV_c \,|min\, ||MV_t\text{-}MV_c||,\ MV_c \in \{covered\ MVs\} \quad (4)$$

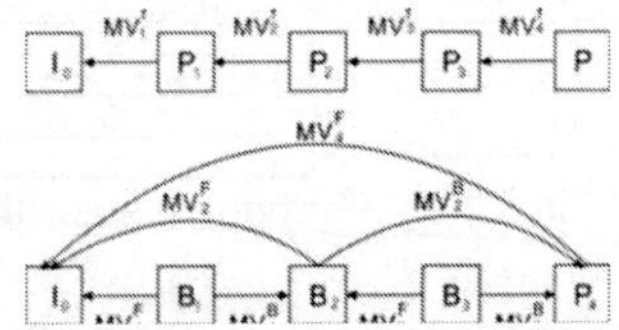

Fig. 2 The prediction structure of H.264/AVC on the upper part and SVC on the bottom part

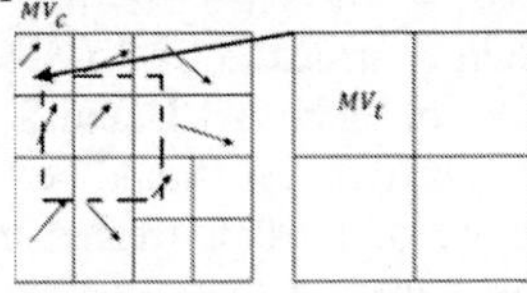

Fig. 3 The relationship between MV_t and MV_c

2.2 Motion Vector Refinement

In the proposed motion vector composition algorithm, the absent motion vectors will be composed to derive the motion vectors required for supporting temporal scalability in SVC. However, the composed motion vectors could not be the best motion vectors for SVC. Therefore, a motion vector refinement algorithm is further proposed to improve the accuracy of composed motion vectors. Fig. 1 exhibits the detailed operations of our proposed motion vector refinement algorithm. In our proposal, the motion vector intensity (MVI), averaged motion vector (MV_{Avg}), and the sum of absolute residuals (R) are calculated to determine the motion behavior of the current macroblock. If both conditions of R>=255 and MVI>MV_{Avg} are satisfied, the full search motion vector refinement process will be applied to refine the composed motion vectors around the motion vector predictor (MVP) of the current macroblock. Otherwise, a new search range shown in below will be decided to refine the composed motion vectors so that the overhead of motion vector refinement can be lighten when compared to full search motion vector refinement.

$$SR_{Adaptive} = \begin{cases} ||MVP - MV_n^F||, forward \\ ||MVP - MV_n^B||, backward \end{cases} \quad (5)$$

For spatial scalability, the motion vectors composed by our proposed algorithm in base layer will be directly used in spatial enhancement layer by simply using the upsampling mechanism.

3 Simulation Results

The proposed algorithm is evaluated by test sequences (200 frames for each sequence) with CIF and 4CIF resolutions for GOP with 8 frames compressed by the H.264/AVC reference software JM 18.0 and JSVM 9.18. Table 1 shows the comparison for the proposed algorithm with previous work [2]. From this table, we can find that our proposed algorithm can achieve better rate distortion performance as well as coding time reduction. On average, our proposed algorithm can further reduce the coding time 6.92% on average when compared to [2].

Table 1 Performance comparison for base layer of SVC

Sequence	BD-PSNR(dB)		BD-bitrate(%)		TS(%)	
	[2]	Pro.	[2]	Pro.	[2]	Pro.
Akiyo	-0.06	-0.04	1.61	1.16	80.58	82.15
Container	-0.12	-0.03	4.91	1.36	82.12	80.42
Foreman	-0.05	-0.05	1.23	1.41	46.51	55.35
Stefan	-0.24	-0.03	4.74	0.63	34.43	48.73
Harbour	-0.01	-0.02	0.34	0.64	64.56	78.78
Crew	-0.03	-0.03	0.96	0.98	57.02	54.70
Soccer	-0.04	-0.03	1.37	1.10	27.11	40.67
Average	-0.08	-0.03	2.17	1.04	56.05	62.97

4 Conclusions

This paper proposes a fast H.264/AVC to SVC transcoding algorithm by using the motion vector composition approach. In addition, a low computational complexity motion vector refinement algorithm is also proposed to further improve the accuracy of composite motion vectors. Through the proposed algorithm, the transcoding time can have better saving with high rate-distortion performance compared to previous work [2].

5 References

[1] ITU-T and ISO/IEC JTC 1: Advanced Video Coding for Generic Audiovisual Services. ITU-T Rec. H.264/AVC and ISO/IEC 14496-10, March 2009.

[2] R. Garrido Cantos, J. De Cock, J. L. Martínez, S. Van Leuven and P. Cuenca, "Motion-based temporal transcoding from H.264/AVC-to-SVC in baseline profile," *IEEE Transactions on Consumer Electronics*, vol. 57, no. 1, pp. 239-246, February 2011.

[3] H. Al-Muscati & F. Labeau, "Temporal transcoding of H.264/AVC video to the scalable format," *in Proceedings of 2nd International Conference on Image Processing Theory Tools and Applications*, pp. 138-143, July 2010.

An overview on the application of machine vision in soccer robots

Alina Trifan[1], António J. R. Neves[1], and Bernardo Cunha[1]
[1]ATRI, DETI / IEETA, University of Aveiro, 3810–193 Aveiro, Portugal

Abstract—*Robotic vision joins research challenges arrising from two different research areas: machine vision, as well as robotics. For soccer player robots, the aspects of full autonomy and real-time reaction are probably the most important ones that must be considered when developing a vision system. This paper presents an overview on the state of the art implementations and algorithms used in vision systems for robots playing soccer in the RoboCup competitions.*

1. Introduction

Just like humans, robots can "sense" the surrounding world by means of different sensors, but usually, the vision system is their main sensorial element since it is capable to provide a great amount of information such as spatial, temporal and morphological.

In robotic soccer, the environment is always changing, the ball and the robots are always moving, most of the time in an unpredictable way. The vision system is responsible for capturing all these fast changing scenes, processing them and taking valid decisions in the smallest possible amount of time, thus allowing real-time reactions.

This paper is structured in 6 sections, as follows: Section 2 gives an overview on the RoboCup initiative with emphasis on the RoboCup Soccer Leagues. Section 3 focuses on the most recent implementations of vision systems used in the Middle Size League. In Section 4 the Standard Platform League is detailed in terms of most common and novel approaches for implementing the vision systems of the robots. Section 5 focuses on the Humanoid League. Finally, Section 6 concludes the paper.

2. The RoboCup initiative

RoboCup is an international initiative that fosters research in robotics and artificial intelligence, on multi-robot systems in particular, through competitions like RoboCup Robot Soccer, RoboCup Rescue, RoboCup@Home and RoboCupJunior. The main focus of the RoboCup competitions is the game of soccer, where the research goals concern cooperative multi-robot and multi-agent systems in dynamic adversarial environments.

The RoboCup Robot Soccer competition is divided into the following leagues: Middle Size League (MSL), Standard Platform League (SPL), Humanoids League (HL), Small Size League (SSL) and Simulation League, which will not be detailed in this paper.

3. The Middle Size League

In the context of RoboCup, the Middle Size League (MSL) is one of the most challenging. In this league, each team is composed of up to 6 robots with a maximum size of $50cm \times 50cm$ width, $80cm$ height and a maximum weight of $40Kg$, playing in a field of $18m \times 12m$.

Many teams are currently taking their first steps in 3D ball information retrieving [1], [2], while also developing vision systems capable of detecting balls without a specific color [1], [3]. There are also some teams moving their vision systems algorithms to VHDL based algorithms taking advantage of the FPGA's versatility [1]. Even so, for now, the great majority of the teams base their image analysis in color search using radial sensors [4], [5], [6].

4. The Standard Platform League

In the Standard Platform League, all teams compete using the same robotic platforms, therefore all efforts are focused on software developments. Currently, the standard robotic platform is the NAO robot, designed by Aldebaran.These robots come equipped with 2 video cameras, however stereo vision is yet not allowed. In this league, robots play in teams of up to 4 players, on a field with a length of $6m$ and a width of $4m$. The ball used is an orange hockey ball.

For the color segmentation of the image, most teams choose the approach of scan lines. That is, the image is scanned either horizontally, vertically, or in both directions [7], [8] while looking for one of the colors of interest. Other approach is to segment images in regions of interest, to whom probabilities are assigned [9]. The information about a color of interest segmented is validated in most cases if there is a given threshold of green color in the proximity of the color of interest previously segmented [7], [8], [10].

Different approaches instead of simple color segmentation as a first step in processing the image are proposed in [11], [12], [13]. In [11] the vision system is mostly based on pattern recognition. The ball recognition algorithm is based on detecting a circle and filtering undesired noise. Regarding goal perception, scan lines segmentation combined with fuzzy logic detection have been used. [13] propose a vision module based on Reinforcement Learning with Decision Trees Algorithms.

5. The Humanoid League

In the Humanoid League, the soccer players are autonomous robots with a body imitating the human body.

There are three size classes in this league: KidSize (the height of the robots is between 30 and 60cm, TeenSize(100-120cm) and AdultSize(130cm). In the KidSize soccer competition teams of three, highly dynamic autonomous robots compete with each other. Since 2010 the TeenSize soccer competition features teams of two autonomous robots competing with each other. In AdultSize soccer, a striker robot plays against a goal keeper robot first and then the same robots play with exchanged roles against each other.

The vision systems of the teams participating in this league are based on standard webcams [14], [15], [16]. Similar to the approaches presented in the SPL Section, the teams focus on color segmentation and extraction of certain measurements of the segmented color blobs in order to decide if a region of a given color is an object of interest or not [14], [17]. In [18] they estimate the distance and angle to each feature by removing radial lens distortion and by inverting the projective mapping from field to image plane. All teams mention the use of a look-up-table in order to replace computational operations when labelling the colors of interest, with array operations [18], [19], [20].

In [21], [22], [23], [24], [25] the same algorithms based on scan lines, color segmentation followed by different thresholding methods or computation of several relevant measurements are presented. The only main differences can be found in the choice of the color space used for processing the image.

6. Conclusions

This paper presented an overview of the currently methodologies used for the implementation of the vision systems used in different types of soccer robots. Although similar in certain aspects, the implementations presented differ in many aspects, from image acquisition, using different color spaces, image segmentation based on different types of information, to the choice of algorithms used for the detection of tracking of the objects of interest.

7. Acknowledgements

This work was developed in the Institute of Electronic and Telematic Engineering of University of Aveiro and was partially funded by FEDER through the Operational Program Competitiveness Factors - COMPETE and by National Funds through FCT - Foundation for Science and Technology in the context of the project FCOMP-01-0124-FEDER-022682 (FCT reference PEst-C/EEI/UI0127/2011).

References

[1] Kanters, F., Hoogendijk, R., Janssen, R., Meessen, K., Best, J., Bruijnen, D., Naus, G., Aangenent, W., van der Berg, R., van de Loo, H., Heldes, G., Vugts, R., Harkema, G., van Brakel, P., Bukkums, B., Soetens, R., Merry, R., can de Molengraft, M.: Tech United Eindhoven Team Description, RoboCup 2011, Istanbul, Turkey (2011)

[2] Kappeler, U.P., Zweigle, O., Rajaie, H., Hausserman, K., Tamke, A., Koch, A., Eckstein, B., Aichele, F., DiMarco, D., Berthelot, A., Walter, T., Levi, P.: RFC Stuttgart Team Description, RoboCup 2011, Istanbul, Turkey (2011)

[3] Neves, A.J.R., Pinho, A.J., Martins, D.A., B.Cunha: An efficient omnidirectional vision system for soccer robots: From calibration to object detection. Mechatronics Journal (2010)

[4] Huang, M., Ge, X., Hui, S., Wang, X., Chen, S., Xu, X., Zhang, W., Lu, Y., Liu, X., Zhao, L., Wang, M., Zhu, Z., Wang, C., Huang, B., Ma, L., Qin, B., Zhou, F., Wang, C.: Water Team Description, RoboCup 2011, Istanbul, Turkey (2011)

[5] Lu, H., Zeng, Z., Dong, X., Xiong, D., Tang, S.: Nubot Team Description, RoboCup 2011, Istanbul, Turkey (2011)

[6] Nassiraei, A., Ishida, S., Shinpuku, N., Hayashi, M., Hirao, N., Fujimoto, K., Fukuda, K., Takanaka, K., Godler, I., Ishii, K., Miyamoto, H.: Hibikino-Musashi Team Description, RoboCup 2011, Istanbul, Turkey (2011)

[7] Trifan, A., Neves, A., Lau, N., Cunha, B.: A modular real-time vision system for humanoid robots. In: Proceedings of IS&T/SPIE Electronic Imaging 2012. ((in press, 2012))

[8] Rofer, T., Laue, T., Graf, C., Kastner, T., Fabisch, A., Thedieck, C.: B-Human Team Description, RoboCup 2011, Istanbul, Turkey (2011)

[9] leader@austrian kangaroos.com: Austrian Kangaroos Team Description, RoboCup 2011, Istanbul, Turkey (2011)

[10] TJArk.office@gmail.com: TJArk Team Description, RoboCup 2011, Istanbul, Turkey (2011)

[11] Hashemi, E., Ghiasvand, O.A., Jadidi, M.G., Karimi, A., Hashemifard, R., Lashgarian, M., Shafiei, M., Mashhadt, S., Zarei, K., Faraji, F., Harandi, M.A.Z., Mousavi, E.: MRL Team Description, RoboCup 2011, Istanbul, Turkey (2011)

[12] Akin, H.L., Mericli, T., Ozukur, E., Kavaklioglu, C., Gokce, B.: Cerberus Team Description, RoboCup 2011, Istanbul, Turkey (2010)

[13] Barrett, S., Genter, K., Hausknecht, M., Hester, T., Khandelwal, P., Lee, J., Tian, A., Quinlan, M., Sridharan, M., Stone, P.: TT-UT Austin Villa Team Description, RoboCup 2011, Istanbul, Turkey (2011)

[14] Han, J., Hopkins, M., Lahr, D., Orekhov, V., Hong, D.: CHARLI Team Description Paper, RoboCup 2011, Istanbul, Turkey (2011)

[15] Zhang, L., Zhou, C., Song, Z., Buck, N., Han, X., Yang, T., Loan, N., Hock, T., Calderon, C., Yue, P.: Robo-Erectus Sr-2011 Team Description, RoboCup 2011, Istanbul, Turkey (2011)

[16] Zhao, M., Liu, Y., Cheng, H., Cheng, L., Xu, C., Liu, X.: Tsinghua Hephaestus Team Description, RoboCup 2011, Istanbul, Turkey (2011)

[17] Acosta-Calderon, C., Mohan, R., Zhou, C., Hu, L., Yue, P.: A modular architecture for humanoid soccer robots with distributed behavior control. International Journal of Humanoid Robotics **5**(3) (2008) 397–416

[18] Behnke, S., Missura, M.: NimbRo Team Description Papaer, RoboCup 2011, Istanbul, Turkey (2011)

[19] Maneerwarn, T., Kawinkhreue, X., Butsonga, A., Kaewlek, N.: KMUTT Kickers Team Description, RoboCup 2011, Istanbul, Turkey (2011)

[20] Gupta, A., Agrawal, T., Srivastava, A., Deepak, G., Seth, D.: AcYut4 Team Description, RoboCup 2011, Istanbul, Turkey (2011)

[21] Friedman, M., Kohlbrecher, S., Petersen, K., Sholz, D., Thomas, D., Wojtusch, J., von Stryk, O.: Darmstadt Dribblers Team Description, RoboCup 2011, Istanbul, Turkey (2011)

[22] Seifert, D., Moballegh, H., Heinrich, S., Otte, S., Mielke, S., Schmude, N., Weissgerber, T., Wurfel, K., Jonschowski, R., Kulick, J., Frolich, M., Streckenbach, J., Lubitz, G., Geyso, N., Schubert, M., Yuo, F., Puhlmann, S., Victoria, O., Freitag, L., Rojas, R.: FUmanoids Team Description Paper, RoboCup 2011, Istanbul, Turkey (2011)

[23] Salehi, M., Lotfi, B., Alamirpour, P. nd Parsa, S.: MRL Team Description, RoboCup 2011, Istanbul, Turkey (2011)

[24] Ng, B., Calderon, C., Zhou, C.: Robo-Erectus Jr-2011 Team Description, RoboCup 2011, Istanbul, Turkey (2011)

[25] Pesek, T., Lee, B., McGill, S., Yi, S., Lee, D.: DARwIn Team Description, RoboCup 2011, Istanbul, Turkey (2011)

Automated coronary artery segmentation and calcified/non-calcified plaque measurement

Pei-Kai Hung[1], Chun-You Liu[1], Chia-Yun Hsu[1], Chao-Yu Huang[1], Wen-Jeng Lee[2], Tzung-Dau Wang[3] and Chung-Ming Chen[1,*]

[1]Institute of biomedical engineering, National Taiwan university, Taipei, Taiwan
[2]Department of Medical Imaging, National Taiwan university hospital, Taipei, Taiwan
[3]Department of Internal Medicine, National Taiwan university hospital, Taipei, Taiwan

Abstract - *Construction of reasonable coronary artery trees and quantitative analysis on vulnerable plaque are essential in the diagnosis of coronary artery disease. An automated algorithm is proposed for both coronary artery tree reconstruction and plaque detection in this study. Discrete wavelet transform (DWT) is introduced to prevent leakage from region growing and enhance the discrimination between coronary artery tree and surrounding tissues. Automated quantitative analysis of both calcified and non-calcified plaques is achieved. To derive an accurate volume estimate of a calcified plaque, the calcified plaque is identified from the coronary artery tree reconstructed from the CT image with contrast agent and its volume is derived from the CT image without contrast agent. The proposed method has been tested on eight sets of MSCT scan images with reasonable results.*

Keywords: discrete wavelet transform; vascular segmentation; quantitative analysis;

1 Introduction

Atherosclerosis is a chronic inflammatory response in the wall of coronary arteries where there are accumulations of fatty materials such as cholesterol. Conventionally, atherosclerosis is usually diagnosed by using the multi-slice computed tomography (MSCT). However, extraction of coronary artery trees and vulnerable plaque highly depends on manual operations with subjective decisions, which frequently results in inappropriate and inconsistent diagnosis. Assessments of coronary artery disease require accurate approaches for both vessel segmentation and plaque detection. Although various commercial toolkits provide solutions of vascular segmentation and plaque detection, human intervention is usually required. Moreover, the quantitative analysis supported for both of the coronary segments and vulnerable plaques is generally limited.

Region growing usually serves as a common approach to reconstructing a coronary artery tree. While region growing performs reasonably well in high-contrast vessel segments, it can easily leak from the low-contrast segments or those with weak edges. To avoid leakage, shape constraints of coronary vessels are incorporated in various approaches, such as the level-set techniques [1]. Although these constraints may limit the shape of vessels, they may cause difficulties in segmenting small vessels. With complicated pre-processing steps, some other approaches, like vessel-modeling, are introduced [2].

To achieve an effective vessel tracking, in this paper, region growing scheme is applied and its output is extended via a wavelet transform that smoothes coronary segments and trims unexpected leakages. By detecting the vessel segments with a specific spectrum of intensity, plaques with specific histogram can be collected individually. Agatston score, a measurement of coronary calcification, can only be calculated in MSCT images without imaging contrast agents. However, extraction of coronary tree with these images is impossible. In this study, we reconstruct the coronary artery trees in the CT images with contrast agent and acquire the positions of each calcified plaque. Position information is further applied to search the plaques from the CT images without contrast agent. After the plaques and their correlation between the CT images with and without contrast agents are assured, quantitative assessments of these calcified plaques can then be conducted. The analysis on non-calcified plaque is performed by detecting the increments generated during the wavelet transform.

2 Material and Method

2.1 Region growing scheme

Region growing scheme collects voxels according to a calculated scores rather than local intensity in this study. The calculated score is composed of two independent parameters, vessel-like intensity and contrast against the neighborhood. After the initial coronary artery tree is obtained, the output is denoted as T1, where there may still be leakages.

2.2 Wavelet transform

To obtain a better reconstruction of coronary artegry tree, a discrete wavelet transform (DWT) is performed [8]. DWT generates highest-, middle-, and lowest-frequency information of the coronary artery tree. By using the highest-frequency parts, which indicates the location of adventitia, a modified coronary tree T2 is derived where most leakages are trimmed.

2.3 Registration of calcified plaque

The calcified plaques are identified by detecting the high intensity part of T2. The detected plaques are sorted according to their distances from the root of the coronary artery tree. In the MSCT images of the same subject without contrast agent, calcified plaques are first detected by using their intensity and compared with the sorted plaques of the CT images with contrast agent. After their correlation is confirmed, the Agatston score is computed.

2.4 Detection of non-calcified plaque

T1 ∩ T2 may be considered as the lumen volume without leakages and T2 describes the volume within vessel wall. The difference regions between T1 ∩ T2 and T2, may be considered as the candidate regions of the non-calcified plaques. The final non-calcified plaques are determined by taking into account the partial volume effect and prior knowledge of coronary artery anatomy.

3 Result

Eight sets of MSCT scan images are examined and coronary artery trees are compared with physicians' solutions (manually built in GE system). The results show that the proposed algorithm generate reasonable coronary artery tree, most branches can be found (Fig.1.) and no leakage remains. Assessments of most calcified and non-calcified plaques are also achieved in this study (Fig.2.).

4 Discussion

Integration of wavelet transform and region growing scheme prevents the occurrence of leakage and facilitates inclusion or exclusion of voxels around plaques. It is because this scheme approximates the border between coronary segment and surrounding tissue where the highest-frequency part of DWT is found.

The correspondence of the calcified plaques in MSCT scans with and without contrast agent is sometimes difficult to establish because the number of plaques in both types of images may be different due to the contrast agent effect. This difficulty has been overcome in this study by grouping neighboring calcified plaques and calculating the correlation between lesions rather than plaques.

5 Conclusion

A new reconstruction algorithm for coronary artery trees has been proposed in this paper. It not only provides the tree morphology but also the candidate non-calcified plaques. By simultaneously taking into account the CT images with and without contrast agents, an automatic approach has been developed to derive a more accurate estimate of the sizes of the calcified plaques, which may provide a more effective risk assessment of for coronary artery diseases.

6 References

[1] Manniesing, R., Velthuis, B.K., van Leeuwen, M.S., van der Schaaf, I.C., van Laar, P.J., Niessen, W.J., 2006. Level set based cerebral vasculature segmentation and diameter quantification in CT angiography. Medical Image Analysis 10 (2), 200–214.

[2] Frangi, A.F., Niessen, W.J., Vincken, K.L., Viergever, M.A., 1998. Multiscale vessel enhancement filtering. In: Medical Image Computing and Computer-assisted Intervention (MICCAI'98), 1998, pp. 130–137.

[3] Burrus C.S., Gopinath R.A., and Gao H., Introduction to Wavelet Theory and Its Application. New Jersey: Prentice-Hall 1998.

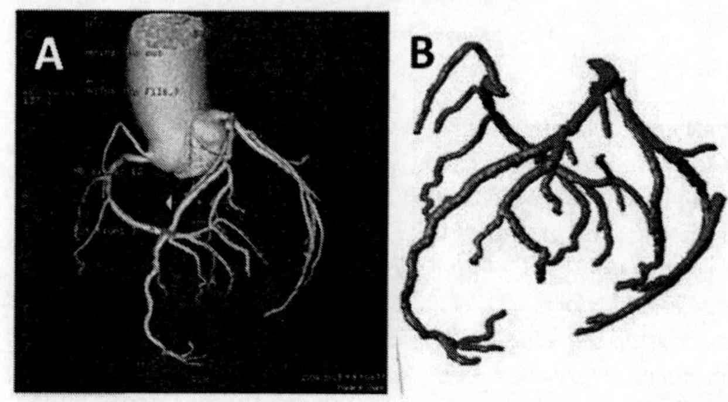

Fig. 1. Coronary tree delineated by (A) GE system (with human intervention) and (B) the proposed method.

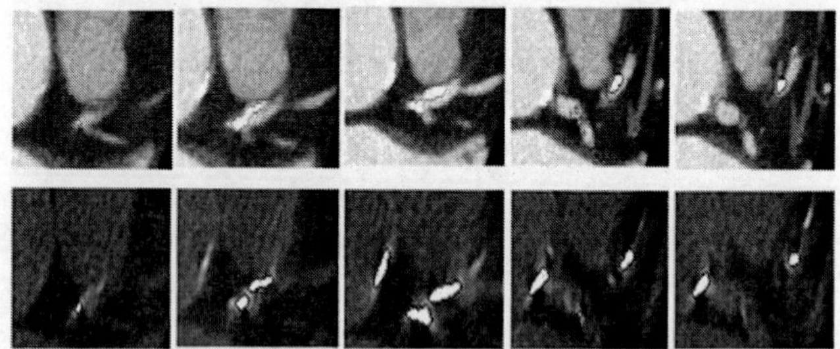

Fig. 2. A portion of CT images with (upper row) and without (lower row) contrast agent of the same subject, where the calcified plaques are enclosed by blue contours and the vessels are enclosed by the red contours (upper row only).

Quantitative assessment of female pattern hair loss

Pei-Kai Hung[1], Chun-You Liu[1], Chia-Yun Hsu[1], Chien-Wei Kung[1], Ren-Yeu Tsai[2], Sung-Jan Lin[1] and Chung-Ming Chen[1,*]

[1]Institute of biomedical engineering, National Taiwan university, Taipei, Taiwan

[2] Department of Dermatology and Skin Laser Center, Taipei Municipal Wan-Fang Hospital, Taipei Medical University, Taipei, Taiwan

Abstract - *Conventional diagnosis of female pattern hair loss is based on visual inspection of the images exhibiting baldness scalp. However, different medical doctors may come up with different severity grading due to the inherently subjective decision process. In this study, the appearance of baldness area is summarized into a quantitative descriptor, i.e., baldness width, by applying a level-set scheme and the principal component analysis. This descriptor is extracted to estimate the baldness severity and its diagnostic accuracy (82.9%) is validated by using the leave-one-out cross-validation method. It is expected that by monitoring the changes in baldness width, both prognosis and follow-up study of female pattern hair loss treatment can be reasonably assessed.*

Keywords: female pattern hair loss; baldness width; quantitative analysis;

1 Introduction

Female pattern hair loss (FPHL) is a common term for the decrease in central scalp hair density that occurs in many females. Typical features of FPHL are miniaturizations of affected hairs and decreases in central scalp (vertex, mid and frontal), bitemporal and parietal regions [1]. In FPHL patients, the baldness area, where poor hair coverage is found, is exhibited around the midline scalp. In clinical practice, the severity of FPHL is graded by visually inspecting the baldness area, including the exposed scalp and nearby non-vellus hair, which are fine, short, brittle, and may be the same color with pale skin or scalp,. By measuring the baldness area, the conventional grading method for severity of the FPHL is based on the Ludwig or Savin scales [2, 3]. Another important clue, hair loss at midline scalp, was discovered and applied in Olsen's work [4]. It is also revealed that midline hair loss in "Christmas tree" pattern is unique for FPHL.

Although the Ludwig and Savin scales are widely accepted, there are still two unavoidable defects: (1) cameras may capture FPHL images with different photographical conditions, such as exposure rate, and (2) every single grading simply depends on the physician's subjective decision. As a result, one single image may easily have diagnostic discrepancy among physicians. And, one camera operates in standard circumstance but captures images with different photography contrast and brightness. Therefore, normalization for all FPHL images is required to prevent inconsistent diagnosis of the FPHL images.

To build up an objective scaling of FPHL, in this paper, we propose a baldness width measure to characterize the baldness area. The goal of this study is to develop a lookup table that objectively describes and classifies the severity of FPHL in the hope of achieving adequate consistency and accuracy, both for diagnoses and follow-up assessments of treatment response.

2 Material and Method

2.1 Paitent and Sampled Images

This study performs a retrospective analysis of 44 subjects, each with 4 to 7 photos amounting to 245 images in total. These 44 subjects, who suffer from FPHL, have been classified into stages I-2, I-3, I-4, II-1, and II-2 on Savin scale based on the consensus gradings of two experienced medical doctors. Note that stage I-1 represents "normal".

2.2 Image acquisition, normalization and segmentation

For the assessment of hair loss, photos that clearly exhibit the midline scalp are taken by Nikon BM5. The camera configurations are aperture F-22, shutter speed 1/6400 sec., ISO 200, auto white-balance, 300 dpi and 3008*2000 in resolution. The flashlight of camera is fully charged before taking a new photo. For better distinctions between hair and normal scalp, a gray-scale transformation scheme, Hermite spline, is applied to regulate the exposure value for each photo.

To delineate the contour of the baldness area from the region of interest (ROI), the Chan and Vese level set method is employed (Fig.1.) [5]. The level set scheme is to generate and optimize a reasonable contour that maintains the homogenous intensity inside and outside the contour. The mean intensities inside and outside the contour are denoted as m1 and m2. With an arbitrarily given initial contour, the level set scheme will minimize the energy function as defined in Eq. (1):

$$E(c, m1, m2) = u * length(c) + v * area(inside(c)) + \lambda_1 * F1 + \lambda_2 * F2 \quad (1)$$

where

$$F1 = \int_{inside(c)} |I(x, y) - m1|^2 \, dxdy \quad (2)$$

$$F2 = \int_{outside(c)} |I(x, y) - m2|^2 \, dxdy \quad (3)$$

In these equations, $I(x, y)$ is the color depth of pixel (x, y). *length*(*c*) the circumference and *area*(*inside*(*c*)) the area inside the contour, where u, v, λ_1 and λ_2 are weighting factors. Minimization of energy function E results in a reasonable *contour*(c) that characterizes the baldness area.

2.3 Feature extraction

Based on the demarcated baldness area, we propose to characterize the severity of FPHL by the width of the baldness area regardless of its irregular contour and fragments. The width of the baldness area is defined as the length of the minor axis of the equivalent ellipse of the baldness area. The equivalent ellipse of the baldness is an ellipse with the same size and center of mass as the baldness area. The equivalent ellipse is derived by using the principal component analysis (PCA) is employed [6].

3 Result

Two-hundred and forty-five images from 44 subjects have been tested in this study. All images are pre-processed by using the Hermite spline to regulate the exposure values before delineation of the baldness areas. With the transformed images, the widths of the baldness areas of all 245 images are derived automatically. As an examples, Fig. 1 demonstrates the results for a subject of stage I-3, in which (A) is the image after Hermite spline, (B) the zero-level set, and (C) the baldness area derived from the zero-level set (green contour) and its equivalent ellipse (red contour). The width of the baldness area is then defined as the length of the minor axis of the equivalent ellipse.

Based on the widths of the baldness areas of the 245 images, a five-class Gaussian Bayes classifier may be constructed for classification of each image into a baldness stage according to Savin scale. Table 1 lists the means and standard deviations computed from the 245 images for these five classes. The effectiveness of using the width of baldness area to characterize FPHL has been validated by the leave-one-out cross-validation method, in which a five-class Gaussian Bayes classifier is constructed for each set of training data (244 images). With the Savin scale as the standard, the classification accuracy is 82.9% for the 245 images used in this study.

4 Discussion

The proposed baldness descriptor, i.e., the width of the baldness area, is shown to be promising for characterization of the severity of the FPHL. Based on the leave-one-out cross-validation method, the accuracy rate is about 82.9% when using Savin scale as the standard. The classification performance may be further improved if second descriptor, such as a descriptor characterizing the condition of the baldness area, is included and a more sophisticated classifier, e.g., SVM or neural network, is employed.

5 Conclusion

In this paper, we present an automated approach to classifying the severity of the FPHL. A baldness descriptor, i.e., the width of the baldness area, has been proposed to characterize the severity of the FPHL. By using 245 images, the proposed descriptor may achieve an accuracy of 82.9% using the leave-one-out cross-validation method.

6 References

[1] Olsen EA. Current and novel methods for assessing efficacy of hair growth promoters in pattern hair loss. Journal of the American Academy of Dermatology. 2003 Feb; 48(2):253-62.

[2] Ludwig E. Classification of the types of androgenetic alopecia (common baldness) occurring in the female sex. The British journal of dermatology. 1977 Sep; 97(3):247-54.

[3] Savin R. A method for visually describing and quantitating hair loss in male pattern baldness. J Invest Dermatol. 1992; 98:604.

[4] Olsen EA. The midline part: an important physical clue to the clinical diagnosis of androgenetic alopecia in women. Journal of the American Academy of Dermatology. 1999 Jan; 40(1):106-9.

[5] Chan TF, Vese LA. Active contours without edges. Image Processing, IEEE Transactions on. 2001; 10(2):266-77.

[6] Jolliffe I. Principal component analysis: Springer Verlag; 2002.

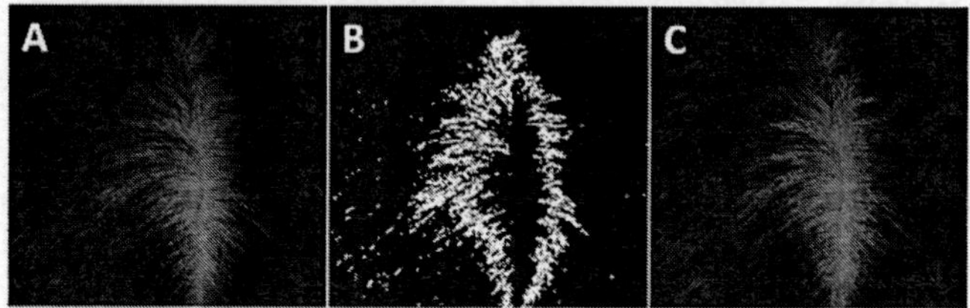

Fig.1. (A) An image transformed by Hermite spline showing a baldness area of stage I-3, (B) the zero-level set derived by using the Chan and Vese level set method (C) the baldness area derived from the zero-level set (green contour) and its equivalent ellipse (red contour)

Table-1. The model parameters of the 5-class Gaussian Bayes classifier for the widths of the baldness areas (computed from all 245 images) in correspondence to the severity of FPHL defined by Savin scale. (unit: pixel)

Savin scale	I-2	I-3	I-4	II-1	II-2
Mean	28.187	41.183	61.188	79.686	98.127
S.D.	2.822	5.090	7.537	6.552	4.889

Hand Detection in Depth Images Using Features of Depth Difference

Sung-Il Joo[1], Sun-Hee Weon[1], Ji-Man Hong[2], and Hyung-Il Choi[1]
[1]Department of Global Media, Soongsil University, Seoul, South Korea
[2]Department of Computer, Soongsil University, Seoul, South Korea

Abstract - *This paper proposes a method of using depth information to detect the hand region in real-time using the feature of depth difference. In order to ensure stable and speedy detection of the hand region even under conditions of lighting changes in the test environment, this study uses only features based on depth information, and proposes a method of detecting the hand region by means of the Adaboost classifier. Firstly, in order to extract features using only depth information, we calculate the difference between the depth value at the center of the input image and the depth value within the segmented block, and to ensure that hand regions of all sizes will be detected, we use the central depth value and the secondary linear model to predict the size of the hand region. Secondly, the Adaboost classifier is applied to implement training and recognition by extracting features from the hand region.*

Keywords: Hand Detection, Depth Image, Cascade, Adaboost, Gesture Recognition.

1 Introduction

The gesture interface is a subject that has been researched for a long time in the field of computer vision, and is a leading example of intelligent interface technology that maximizes users' convenience and intuitive access. Gesture recognition can be broadly classified into two types: researchers have developed the technology of detecting hands to recognize a static posture and the technology of recognizing dynamic gestures using the hand's movement trajectory. The research that relies on color information[1,2] are currently dominant, and recently there has also been active research into combining color and depth information[3] as well as using only depth information[4]. But these researches has some seriously problems that it is sensitive to changes in lighting, which results in low efficiency. In response, to solve the problems described above, this paper proposes a feature that uses only depth information to ensure that detection can be performed stably and quickly without being affected by lighting conditions in the test environment.

2 The Feature of Depth Difference

The purpose of this paper is to propose a feature from a depth image that is capable of quickly detecting the hand region using Adaboost. The leading example of techniques using Adaboost is face detection. Since faces have regular internal features such the eyes, nose and mouth, Haar-like features have been used. The hand region, however, does not include any clear features and a depth image only provides information regarding the hand's shape. We therefore propose the use of an extremely simple and efficient feature for tracking and detecting multiple hand regions

Table 1. The algorithm for feature extraction

Input :
I is input image.
N_x and N_y is number of block.

Initialize :
$step_x = I_w / 2N_x, step_y = I_h / 2N_y$
$block_w = I_w / N_x, block_h = I_h / N_y$
$End_x = 2N_x - 1, End_y = 2N_y - 1$

```
i=0
For x=0, ... End_x
   For y=0, ... End_y
      roi = Rect(x × step_x, y × step_y, block_w, block_h)
      Fv[i] = Depth_c − Area(roi)/(roi_w × roi_h)
      i=i+1
   end
end
```

Output :
The feature value array *Fv*.

[Table 1] is the feature extraction algorithm, which uses the input image I and N_x, N_y representing the number of sub-blocks intended to segment the image, to perform segmentation and extract the feature. I_w and I_h indicates the width and height of the input image, $step_x$ and $step_y$ indicate the displacement of sub-blocks for obtaining the feature, and $block_w$ and $block_h$ indicate the horizontal and vertical size of the sub-block. $Depth_c$ is the center depth value of the input image, while End_x and End_y are the horizontal and vertical numbers of the sub-blocks that are to be extracted from the input image.

Eq. (1) expresses the region's radius r according to depth value using a second order linear model, and y is the column vector consisting of the radius r of the region obtained from each training data as shown in Eq. (2). Also, P is the n*3 matrix generated using the depth value extracted from the center of the hand region. In Eq. (1), $\alpha = [\alpha_1 \quad \alpha_2 \quad \alpha_3]^T$.

Consequently, we were able to use the α obtained through Eq. (2) to calculate the region's radius corresponding to the depth value.

$$y = P\alpha \tag{1}$$

$$\alpha = (P^T P)^{-1} P^T y \,, \qquad P = \begin{bmatrix} 1 & x_1 & x_1^2 \\ 1 & x_2 & x_2^2 \\ \vdots & \vdots & \vdots \\ 1 & x_n & x_n^2 \end{bmatrix}, \; y = \begin{bmatrix} r_1 \\ r_2 \\ \vdots \\ r_n \end{bmatrix} \tag{2}$$

[Figure 1] shows the example of the proposed feature. Once given the input image and the training image, the feature is extracted from the given region until $N_x = 1, N_y = 1$ becomes $N_x = m, N_y = m$. For this paper, the test was performed with m set as 10. Using the proposed feature and the second order linear model, we can predict the size from the input image according to the depth value of the hand region which is the target of training, and thereby collect the training image. It is then possible to extract the proposed feature from the collected training image and use Adaboost to perform training and recognition in order to detect the hand region quickly and simply.

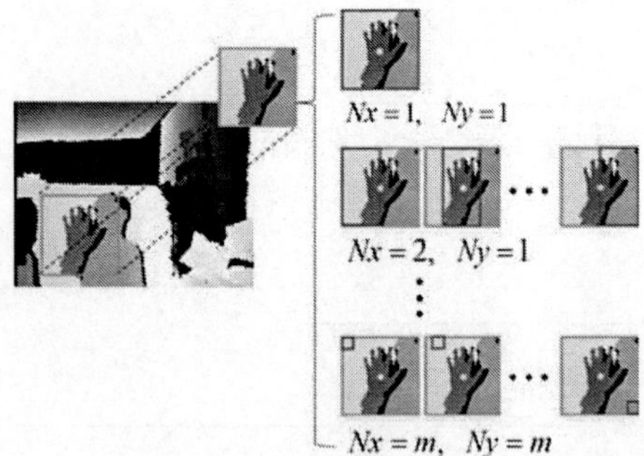

Figure 1. The example of the proposed feature

3 Experiment result

The test image used in this paper is the 320*240 size depth image obtained using Microsoft's Kinect, which was used as the input device. In the actual training, a total of 201 positive images were used, along with 12,967 negative images.

[Figure 2] presents the resulting test image from hand detection performed on an image input from the Kinect camera in real-time. The green quadrangle is the result of merging the detected hand regions. (A) and (B) in [Figure 2] means that the hand region was perfectly detected. However, in (C), although the left hand was completely detected, the right hand failed to be detected. This is because the hand shape exceeded the range permitted by the classifier. (D) show another example of erroneous detection in the case of the elbow, but this result can be adequately improved by collecting a wider variety of negative training sample images in the training stage. It should also be noted that it took approximately only 10 *ms* to locate the hand region in a single frame. We therefore anticipate that this method has much potential for application in real-time multiple hand region tracking systems. This paper has thus proposed a hand region detection method that will serve as the basis for gesture recognition, which should be followed by further research on multiple hand region tracking and recognition.

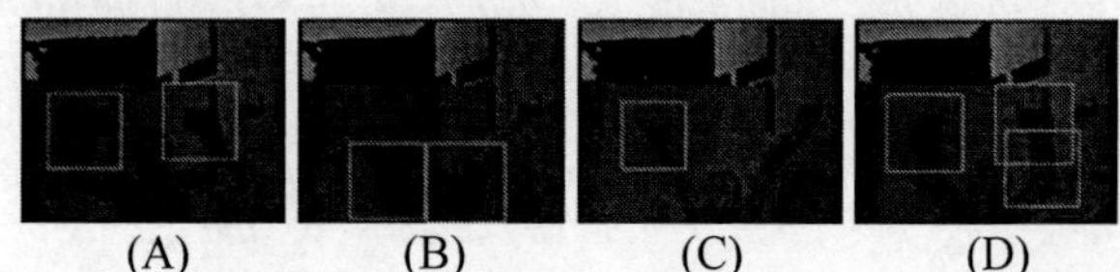

(A) (B) (C) (D)

Figure 2. Result of hand detection in real time

4 Conclusions

This paper has proposed a method that enables us to speedily and accurately detect the hand region using only depth information in lighting conditions. The proposed method also proved to be very quick and efficient when using Adaboost to detect the hand region. We therefore anticipate that this method has much potential for application in real-time multiple hand region tracking systems.

5 Ackowledgement

This research was supported by the Seoul R&BD Program(SS110013).

6 References

[1] H. I. Suk, B. H. Sin, "Dynamic Bayesian Network based Two-Hand Gesture Recognition", Journal of KIISE : Software and Applications, Vol. 35, No. 4, 2008.

[2] M. K. Bhuyan, D. R. Neog, M. K. Kar, "Fingertip Detection for Hand Pose Recognition", International Journal on Computer Science and Engineering (IJCSE), Vol. 4, No. 3, pp.501-511, 2012.

[3] P. Trindade, J. Lobo, J. P. Barreto, "Hand gesture recognition using color and depth images enhanced with hand angular pose data", Proc. of the 2012 IEEE International Conf. on Multisensor Fusion and Integration for Intelligent Systems (MFI), pp.71-76, 2012.

[4] P. Suryanarayan, "Dynamic Hand Pose Recognition using Depth Data", Proc. of the 2010 20th International Conf. on Pattern Recognition (ICPR), pp.3105-3108, 2010.

PET image analysis using Parametric Response Map for Mild Cognitive Impairment

Seung Hak Lee[1], Jong Hun Kim[1], Seong Jin Son[1], and Hyunjin Park[1*]
[1]School of Electronic and Electrical Engineering, Sungkyunkwan University, Korea

Abstract - *Longitudinal neuroimaging provides important information to find changes related to advance of Mild Cognitive Impairment (MCI) and Alzheimer's Disease (AD). Finding changes from normal/MCI state to AD state is crucial to apply optimal treatment options depending on the progression of AD. Using PET has been widely accepted to track such changes. A novel image analysis method called parametric response map (PRM) was proposed. Here, we applied PRM to longitudinal PET images to distinguish between healthy control (HC) and converting mild cognitive impairment (cMCI) patients. cMCI patients refers to patients who converted from HC to MCI. We considered five HC and five cMCI. Our approach of using PRM yielded promising performance of distinguishing between HC and cMCI patients.*

Keywords: Image Analysis, Parametric Response Map, Alzheimer's Disease, Mild Cognitive Impairment.

This work was supported by the NRF Korea grants 2012R1A2A2A01005939 and 20100023233. *Hyunjin Park is the corresponding author.

1 Introduction

AD is an important disease with global implications. Many AD patients start out as Healthy Control (HC) and progresses a mild demented state called MCI. Unfortunately many of these patients convert to AD and treatment options are very limited at the final stages of AD. It is important to find conversion from HC to MCI as early as possible for better treatment of AD. Here, we focus on distinguishing Healthy Control (HC) and converting Mild Cognitive Impairment (cMCI). We consider longitudinal image data that contains many time points per patient. Analyzing longitudinal image data is necessary to obtain information to assess changes from HC to cMCI patients. Many imaging techniques, including magnetic resonance imaging (MRI) and positron emission tomography (PET), have been used to distinguish between HC and cMCI patients. Here, we study using fluorodeoxyglucose (^{18}F, FDG) PET for HC and cMCI patient groups. PET images alone do not provide information to distinguish between HC and cMCI patients. Complex post processing procedures need to be applied to extract information from raw PET images and then statistical inference to distinguish between HC and cMCI can be made. The software package called statistical parametric mapping (SPM) is widely adopted for post-processing of PET images [1]. A novel image analysis method called PRM has been proposed [2]. The PRM approach has been shown to more sensitive at detecting changes of treatment response than conventional approaches based on summary statistics measured over region of interest (ROI). The PRM approach spatially aligns longitudinal images before and after treatment and then classifies voxels within a given ROI into three classes; unchanged, increased, and decreased in intensity. The volume fractions of three classes with respect to the total volume of ROI were different between responding and non-responding patients. Thus, the PRM approach can distinguish between responding and non-responding patients. Here, we apply the PRM approach to longitudinal PET images. We consider two groups. One group consists of HC patients. The other group consists of patients who converted from HC to MCI, which is referred to as the cMCI group. We wanted to explore whether the PRM approach could be used as a quantification tool to distinguish between HC and cMCI groups. We wanted to see if the PRM approach can be extended to quantifying differences related to progression from normal to MCI.

2 Material and Methods

2.1 Human Subjects and PET imaging

The longitudinal PET images came from a brain image data base called Alzheimer's Disease Neuroimaging Initiative (ADNI). Each patient had between three and six PET images from different time points. Five subjects belonged to HC group and five subjects belonged to cMCI group according to the following criterion. Our HC condition was specified as follows; MMSE scores between 28 and 30 and had CDR score of 0. Our cMCI condition was specified as follows; MMSE scores between 25 and 30 and had CDR scores between 0 and 0.5. Patients in the HC group were aged between 62 and 85. Patients in the cMCI group changed from our HC condition to MCI condition and were aged between 66 and 89. We considered pre-processed PET images with following steps. 1) The raw PET images contained six five-minute frames and each frame was spatially aligned (i.e., registered) to the first frame and then averaged improve image quality. 2) Then the image was re-oriented to the standard Talairach space and resampled to a 160x160x96 grid having 1.5mm cubic voxels. 3) Finally, the images were smoothed using an 8 mm full width half maximum (FWHM) filter.

2.2 Automatic ROI specification

The PRM analysis requires a ROI to be specified. We adopt an automatic method to propagate ROI defined on other images on to our PET images. A well-known atlas where 72 sub-cortical ROIs are labeled is available [3]. We registered (i.e., spatially aligned) this atlas and our PET images using an automatic registration algorithm based on mutual information and thin-plate splines [2] and then transferred the ROI information onto the PET image. We considered only hippocampus and para-hippocampus of both left and right hemispheres as our ROIs because hippocampus and para-hippocampus are considered as the primary ROI to be affected by progression of MCI and AD.

2.3 Parametric Response Map (PRM) analysis

The PRM analysis requires serially acquired images to be spatially aligned first, which is taken care of by the pre-processing steps of ADNI database. We considered between three and six longitudinal PET images. Assuming there are N time points available, N-1 PRM analyses are possible. The first would be between image of time 1 and time 2. The second would be between image of time 1 and time 3 and so on. The image of time 1 would be the baseline image with the earliest acquisition date. Individual voxels within the ROI were classified based on the extent of change observed in voxel intensity measured. Voxels which experienced gain in value greater than a pre-determined threshold were designated red, decreased by more than the threshold were designated blue, and otherwise designated green indicating no significant change. The volume fractions of three classes with respect to the total volume of ROIs were computed for PRM+ (red voxels denoting increased SUV), PRM− (blue voxels denoting decreased SUV), and PRM0 (green voxels denoting unchanged SUV). The pre-determined threshold was determined from region of normal brain region where 90% of intensity values fell into a range between (mean - threshold) and (mean + threshold). The determined threshold was set at 0.09.

3 Results

We report PRM+ and PRM- statistics for three types of PRM analysis, HC group, cMCI group before the MCI conversion, cMCI group after the MCI conversion in Table 1. We observed no significant difference (p-value > 0.05) between HC and cMCI group before MCI converting group for both PRM+ and PRM- as expected. We observed significant difference between HC and cMCI group after MCI conversion only for PRM- not PRM+. Out of four possible comparisons, results of three comparisons were as expected. Our results are preliminary findings with only five subjects in two groups (i.e. HC and cMCI). We expect to gain more statistical power as we collect more PET image data. The scatter plot of PRM analysis is given in Fig. 1 and there were noticeable differences in the scatter plot of PRM analysis between HC and converting MCI (after conversion). Even with limited subjects available we believe the PRM analysis has a great potential to detect changes from HC to MCI.

Table 1. PRM ANALYSIS RESULTS

	cMCI group before conversion Mean (std)	HC group Mean (std)	cMCI group after conversion Mean (std)
PRM- (blue)	0.02 (0.02)	0.008 (0.01)	0.05 (0.06)
	p-value = 0.27		p-value = 0.03
RPM+ (red)	0.005 (0.007)	0.01 (0.02)	0.02 (0.04)
	p-value = 0.29		p-value = 0.49

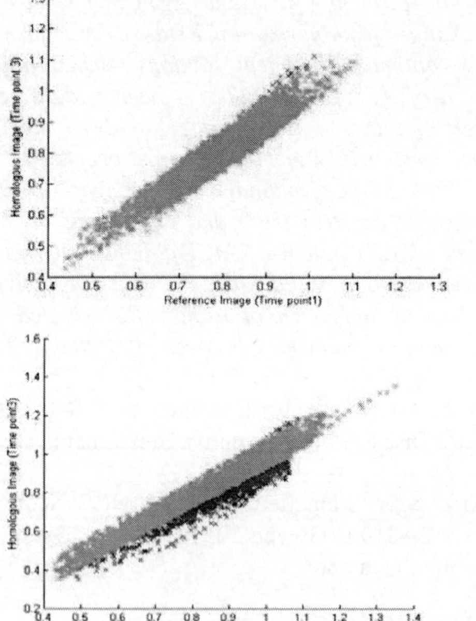

Fig. 1. The top figure is the scatter plot of PRM analysis for one Healthy Control patient. The bottom figure is the scatter plot of PRM analysis for one converting MCI patient (after conversion). Red dots denote voxel where PET intensity has increased, blue dots denotes voxels where intensity has decreased, and the green dots denote voxels where PET intensity remained relatively unchanged.

4 References

[1] K.J. Friston et al., "Statistical Parametric Maps in Functional Imaging: A General Linear Approach," Hum Brain Mapp, vol. 2, p.189-210, 1995.

[2] C.J. Galbán et al., "The parametric response map is an imaging biomarker for early cancer treatment outcome," Nature medicine, vol. 15, no. 5, pp. 572–6, 2009.

[3] N. Tzourio-Mazoyer et al., "Automated anatomical labelling of activations in spm using a macroscopic anatomical parcellation of the MNI MRI single subject brain," Neuroimage, vol. 15, pp.273-289, 2002

SESSION

LATE BREAKING PAPERS: IMAGE PROCESSING AND COMPUTER VISION APPLICATIONS

Chair(s)

Prof. Hamid Arabnia
University of Georgia

IMAGE REGISTRATION UNDER LARGER VIEW VARIATION USING 2EC FEATURES

Parvaneh Saeedi and Mao Mao

School of Engineering Science, Simon Fraser University, Burnaby, BC, Canada

ABSTRACT

This paper presents a fully automatic method for detecting and matching feature correspondences between aerial images of suburban regions with larger view variations. Primary features are defined by line segments and their intersections. These lines are constrained to correspond to the boundaries of rooftops. Potential match candidates are obtained by comparing features over two images, while accounting for geometrical transformation that are expected due to large view variations. Outliers are then identified and removed using an iterative method that relies of error minimization via least squares and epipolar constraint.

Index Terms— Geometrical feature matching, match correspondences, feature grouping, image registration

1. INTRODUCTION

Establishing match correspondences between two or more images is a challenging task especially under conditions such as oblique views, illumination changes, and large view variations. Most cutting-edge matching approaches extract affine-invariant regions and assess their similarities using geometrical or intensity-based properties. These methods perform well only for images with shorter baselines or small affine transformations. When establishing match correspondences in aerial images of suburban areas, the difficulties of the matching lie in: 1) significant visual dissimilarities that is due to point of view variation. 2) partial similarity of the background regions of physical scene features. 3) existence of repetitive pieces similar in shape, size, color and pattern in the construction of suburban areas. This paper presents an approach for creating robust features and matching them in complex suburban environments under large viewpoint variations.

2. RELATED WORK

The problem of wide baseline matching has been studied for many years. A wide variety of approaches involve detection of distinctive features and viewpoint invariant descriptors. Discrete points are among the most popular features used in the applications of computer vision. Among these features are SIFT [1], Mikolajczyk's interest points [2], Harris-Affine [3], and Hessian-Affine [4] features. One common trait of all the above features is the drop in the features' repeatability as the viewpoint differences increase [5]. Moreover, all of these methods assume that the local areas associated with features are planar, which might be a valid assumption for specific scenes.

Lines are also used as features for image registration. Schmid *et al.* [6] developed an approach using intensity values on the two sides of line segments. Wang *et al.* [7] introduced a segment grouping method based on spatial proximity and relative saliency, and a new descriptor based on configuration of line segment pairs. Goedeme [8] reported a system for navigation in horizontal direction using geometrical, color, and intensity invariant information of line segments. Since there are plenty of straight lines in indoor environments, methods that use lines as features are more utilized for indoor scenes. Using line segments as features has some drawback of its own. For example, the end points of line segments may not be very stable and will change locations as the viewing angle changes.

There are also some works that utilize combination of interest points and lines or edges. Tell *et al.* [9] created line segments between two Harris points as features. Kingsbury [10] proposed a matching system using SIFT descriptors and a pair-wise relationship descriptor between them. Eric [11] presented a descriptor by combining SIFT descriptor with a global context vector. Some methods have utilized straight lines and planar surfaces as features. In order to establish correspondences between images of building facades, Lee [12] utilized quadrilateral shapes (4 line segments and their intersections). He showed that his method finds a good number of true correspondences between two images of building facades even under up to 50 degrees viewing angle differences. It, however, required a dominant plane, i.e. a building facade, that limited its application's domain. Ding [13] proposed a method to map oblique aerial images onto LiDAR data using 2DOC feature, which were created based on orthogonal vanishing point pairs. The number of true 2DOC was significantly influenced by the type of buildings and urban environments. For large and simple building shapes, such as those in downtown district, the method worked well. However, for complex building structures like campus and residential areas, it failed up to 50% of the times. Wang [14] reported 3CS features to map oblique aerial images onto 3D LiDAR data. Each 3CS feature contained three line segments, which were connected based on their endpoints proximity. When registering two aerial images, 3CS feature could not be used directly, since the repeatability of such features in both images is too low.

In this paper, we introduce a new feature (2EC) for automatically establishing match correspondences between two oblique aerial images under a large projective transformation. The proposed method utilizes two straight lines and their intersections as a feature, which could correspond to a vertex and two connecting edges of a building's rooftop.

3. PROPOSED METHOD

This section describes details of the proposed method in the order they are executed.

3.1. Straight line extraction

The objective of this step is to extract a set of straight-line segments from the image. The algorithm implemented to achieve this goal is the Burns line detector [15], which utilizes both the gradient magnitude and orientation.

3.2. Line linking

The objective of this step is to link collinear line segments that are separated by very small gaps. Following algorithm describes linking process:

1. Sort the lines by a horizontal sweep across the image.
2. Use a divide-and-conquer method to find nearby lines.
3. Test each pair of nearby lines by checking conditions on lateral distances, lengths, slope difference, and overlap and underlap ratios, and decide if two lines should be linked. Details of these conditions can be seen in our previous work [16].

3.3. Edge map

Edge image is used as a map for extension of a line and its potential intersections. The original image is processed by canny edge detector, followed by dilation with a square structuring element of 3×3 pixels. In aerial images, smaller blobs usually correspond to protuberant objects or textures on the surface of rooftops, that could mislead us when extending lines. Thus, they are removed before the succeeding steps. Therefore, isolated blobs that are smaller than (1 square feet) or 400 pixels are removed from the edge map image.

3.4. 2EC Feature extraction

1. Line extension: Here we adjust the detected line segments according to the image edge map such that most of the corresponding edges to a rooftop is utilized. The extension of a line should not be too long as it could incorrectly represent multiple edges along the same direction and at close proximity. The line extension procedure has the following 3 steps:
   - All partial lines (less than 80% edge evidence) are deleted.
   - To cover breakage in the line segments corresponding to a building rooftop edge, each line segment is extended until there is no longer any overlap with the edge map.
   - The end points of each line segments should be in very close proximity of rooftop vertices. A maximum distance of 20 pixels is tolerated.
2. Line merge: In urban environments, often several parallel lines are located very closely together representing the same building edge. Therefore, it is necessary to merge such lines to form one long line that represent the building edge uniquely. Three criteria are used to merge two line segments:
   - Parallel or almost parallel: maximum difference 5°.
   - Maximum lateral line distance: 2 pixels.
   - Include some overlap.

   The merging process is carried out iteratively until no line segments can be merged together.
3. Line intersection: Using all the remaining lines (after extending and merging procedures), we compute the intersections of each line with all other lines. We record those intersections landed on actual line segments.
4. End point redefinition: To define the features robustly, the end points of each line should be checked and redefined if necessary. For this, Harris corners are detected and all corners with maximum 2 pixels lateral distance from the each line are found and projected onto that line. The two left- and right-most corners are considered as the end points of each line.
5. Removal of unstable lines: We classify three cases as unstable lines and remove them from our process. 1) Lines with no endpoints. 2) Lines with one of their end points too close to their intersection corner. 3) Short lines (25 pixels or less).

Fig. 1: Sample 2EC features extracted in two aerial images.

Figure 1 shows features corresponding to a rooftop. Images used in this work are from Pictometry dataset (typical size of 2672×4008 pixels). In this figure, red circles present the location of center points of 2EC features. Yellow line segments are the lines attached to the center points and blue stars are the end points of 2EC features.

3.5. Transforming features from one image to another

Here, we consider two assumptions: 1) the distance of the camera is much higher than the height of each building, and 2) the ground region corresponding to each input image is flat. Based on these two assumptions, each feature from the first image can be transformed onto the second image using the following procedure:

First, we transfer the image coordinates of features in I_1 into a coordinate system that located at the center of camera 1, C_1 (Figure 2). After this transformation the X axis will be along the North and Y axis along the East directions.

$$\begin{bmatrix} x_w \\ y_w \\ z_w \end{bmatrix} = R(yaw_1, pitch_1, roll_1) \begin{bmatrix} (u - p_{x_1}) \times d_{x_1} \\ (v - p_{y_1}) \times d_{y_1} \\ f_1 \end{bmatrix} \quad (1)$$

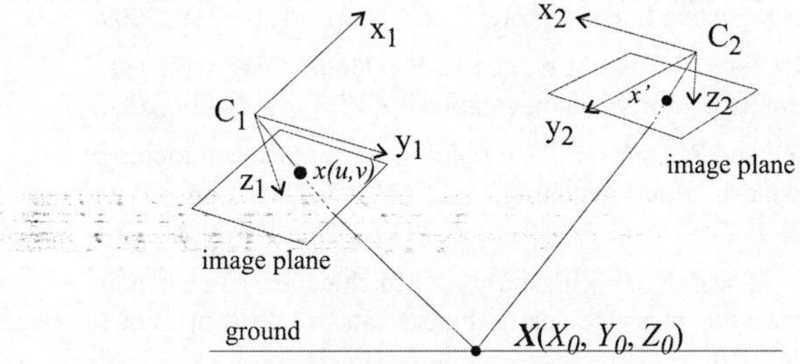

Fig. 2: Camera geometries.

The values of yaw_1, $pitch_1$,and $roll_1$ are provided in the metadata of I_1 and $(p_{x_1}, p_{y_1})^T$ are the coordinates of the principal point in I_1. d_{x1} and d_{y1} represent the conversion from image to world metric, and f_1 is the focal length of the first camera. $R(\alpha, \beta, \gamma)$ is defined by:

$$R(\alpha,\beta,\gamma) = \begin{bmatrix} \cos(\alpha) & -\sin(\alpha) & 0 \\ \sin(\alpha) & \cos(\alpha) & 0 \\ 0 & 0 & 1 \end{bmatrix} \begin{bmatrix} \cos(\beta) & 0 & \sin(\beta) \\ 0 & 1 & 0 \\ -\sin(\beta) & 0 & \cos(\beta) \end{bmatrix} \begin{bmatrix} 1 & 0 & 0 \\ 0 & \cos(\gamma) & -\sin(\gamma) \\ 0 & \sin(\gamma) & \cos(\gamma) \end{bmatrix} \quad (2)$$

The relationship between $(x_w, y_w, z_w)^T$ and it's projection on the ground surface, $X(X_0, Y_0, Z_0)^T$, is defined by:

$$\frac{x_w}{X_0} = \frac{y_w}{Y_0} = \frac{z_w}{Z_0} \quad (3)$$

Z_0 is the altitude of the camera 1 (from the metadata). X can be projected onto I_2 using the camera matrix P_2 [17]:

$$x' = P_2 X \quad , \quad P_2 = K_2 \left[R_2^{-1} \;\; -R_2^{-1} t_2 \right] \quad (4)$$

here, K_2 is the calibration matrix computed using the internal camera parameters [17]:

$$K_2 = \begin{bmatrix} f_2/d_{x_2} & 0 & p_{x2} \\ 0 & f_2/d_{y_2} & p_{y2} \\ 0 & 0 & 1 \end{bmatrix} \quad (5)$$

R_2 is the orientation of the camera 2 with respect to the world coordinate system centered at C_1. It is computed by:

$$R_2 = R^{-1}(lon_1, -lat_1 - 90, 0) \times R(lon_2, -lat_2 - 90, 0) \times R(yaw_2, pitch_2, roll_2) \quad (6)$$

where lat_1, lon_1, lat_2 and lon_2 are the latitudes and longitudes of the two cameras, and t_2 is the coordinate of the camera 2 in the world coordinate system. It is computed by:

$$t_2 = R^{-1}(lon_1, -lat_1 - 90, 0)(C_{cam_2} - C_{cam_1}) \quad (7)$$

C_{cam_1} and C_{cam_1} represent the 3D Cartesian coordinate with respect to ECEF (Earth-Centered, Earth-Fixed) coordinate system, and they are computed using the longitudes and latitudes of the two cameras [18].

3.6. Creating the search space

For every feature in I_1, we establish a search neighborhood in I_2, where its match most likely exists. For this, first, we transform the center point of the feature to I_2 (as in Section 3.5). we create a square neighborhood of size 1001×1001 pixels, centered at the transformed center. Then, we compute the epipolar line of the transformed center using the estimated fundamental matrix and create a tube of width 150 pixels along that line. Finally, we define the intersection of the above two regions as the search space.

3.7. Establishing match correspondence candidates

Given the a transformed feature descriptor defined by its center and two line segments, we examine all the features in the second image that fully or partially fall into the search space created in the previous section. We allow $\%10$ variation in length and 5° variation in the orientation of the corresponding lines. We find all features with the above characteristics and we calculate the correlation between the image areas that are defined by the parallelogram created by these features. Instead of using the intensity images, we use the gradient images (Sobel based). The candidate with the highest score is then chosen as the true match correspondence.

3.8. Optimizing the match correspondence establishment

Given a set of corresponding features between a pair of images, the problem of establishing match correspondences becomes the problem of optimizing a 3D transformation that projects features from one image coordinate system onto the another.

Using the first set of match candidates, we compute a projective matrix $\mathbf{p}$. With this transformation, features from I_1 are mapped to I_2: $x' = \mathbf{p}x$. The residual error in both coordinates ($E = \sqrt{E_u{}^2 + E_v{}^2}$) between the transformed points and their corresponding matches in I_2 are calculated next. For a feature to be considered an outlier, it must have a large residual error. In each iteration, the maximum allowed residual error is modified by incorporating statistical distribution of the residual error for all matches. Any feature with error larger than $\bar{E} + K\sigma(E)$ is removed. K is decreasing by the number of iterations: $\{3, 2.5, 2, 1.5\}$. Maximum 5 iterations are allowed with no removal in the first iteration. The process stops earlier if the maximum error residual of a cycle is less than 30 pixels, or if the number of matches falls below 20.

4. EXPERIMENTAL RESULTS

In this section we assess the stability and distinctiveness of 2EC features and compare it with SIFT, SURF and ASIFT features. For this, we have chosen 15 pairs of aerial Pictometry images that can be grouped in three classes. Every pair of images in these sets include about 90, 180 or 270° yaw rotations, some scale and pitch variations (up to 15°), as well as planar transformations up to 500 pixels in x and y directions. Figure 3 shows a sample pair that include 90° of yaw rotation.

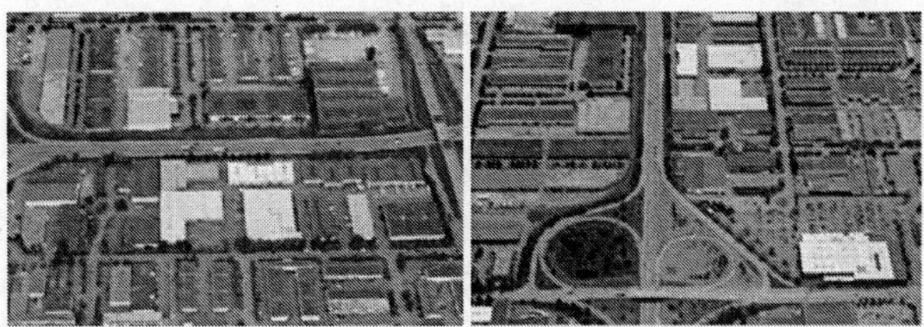

Fig. 3: Example of an aerial image pair with 90° yaw rotation.

Table 1: Mean accuracy of the matching using 4 different features in 15 pairs of oblique aerial images.

Image set no.	Mean yaw difference [^{o}]	SIFT [%]	SURF [%]	ASIFT [%]	2EC [%]
1-5	90	85.70	83.31	82.96	96.39
6-10	180	75.29	81.67	70.00	96.23
11-15	270	93.20	56.51	47.79	96.27

Table 1 represents the mean accuracy of the matching process using the proposed features and compares its performance with SIFT, ASIFT and SURF features. As shown in this table, our proposed features are more suitable for establishing match correspondences in oblique aerial imagery.

5. CONCLUSION

In this paper, we introduced a new type of image features that can be used for image registration, 3D reconstruction, or other applications of computer vision. We show the performance of our proposed features in establishing correspondences in oblique aerial images with large projective transformation. The proposed feature can be identified uniquely by maintaining geometrical relationships between its different constructing elements.

6. REFERENCES

[1] D.G. Lowe, "Distinctive image features from scale-invariant keypoints," *IJCV*, vol. 60, no. 2, pp. 91–110, 2004.

[2] K. Mikolajczyk and C. Schmid, "Indexing based on scale invariant interest points," *ICCV*, pp. 525–531, 2001.

[3] K. Mikolajczyk and C. Schmid, "An affine invariant interest point detector," in *ECCV*. 2002, pp. 128–142, Springer-Verlag.

[4] K. Mikolajczyk and C. Schmid, "Scale & affine invariant interest point detectors," *IJCV*, vol. 60, no. 1, pp. 63–86, 2004.

[5] K. Mikolajczyk, T. Tuytelaars, C. Schmid, A. Zisserman, J. Matas, F. Schaffalitzky, T. Kadir, and L. Van Gool, "A comparison of affine region detectors," *IJCV*, vol. 65, no. 1-2, pp. 43–72, 2005.

[6] C. Schmid and A. Zisserman, "Automatic line matching across views," *CVPR*, pp. 666–671, 1997.

[7] L. Wang, U. Neumann, and S. You, "Wide-baseline image matching using line signatures," *ICCV*, pp. 1311–1318, 2009.

[8] T. Goedem, T. Tuytelaars, and L. Van Gool, "Fast wide baseline matching for visual navigation," *CVPR*, pp. 24–29, 2004.

[9] D. Tell and S. Carlsson, "Combining appearance and topology for wide baseline matching," *ECCV*, vol. 2350, pp. 68–81, 2002.

[10] E.S. Ng and N.G. Kingsbury, "Matching of interest point groups with pairwise spatial constraints," *ICIP*, pp. 2693–2696, 2010.

[11] E.N. Mortensen, H. Deng, and L.G. Shapiro, "A sift descriptor with global context," *CVPR*, pp. 184–190, 2005.

[12] J.A. Lee, K.C. Yow, and A.Y.S. Chia, "Robust matching of building facades under large viewpoint changes," *ICCV*, pp. 1258–1264, 2009.

[13] M. Ding, K. Lyngbaek, and A. Zakhor, "Automatic registration of aerial imagery with untextured 3d lidar models," *CVPR*, 2008.

[14] L. Wang and U. Neumann, "A robust approach for automatic registration of aerial images with untextured aerial lidar data," *CVPR*, pp. 2623–2630, 2009.

[15] J.B. Burns, A.R. Hanson, and E.M. Riseman, "Extracting straight lines," *IEEE TPAMI*, vol. 8, no. 4, pp. 425–455, 1986.

[16] M. Izadi and P. Saeedi, "Three-dimensional polygonal building model estimation from single satellite images," *IEEE TGARS*, vol. 50, no. 6, pp. 2254–2272, 2012.

[17] R. Hartley and A. Zisserman, *Multiple View Geometry in Computer Vision*, Cambridge University Press, 2 edition, 2003.

[18] National Imagery and Mapping Agency, "Department of defense world geodetic system 1984: its definition and relationships with local geodetic systems," Tech. Rep., 2000.

Onboard Hover Control of a Quadrotor using Template Matching and Optic Flow

Ping Li[1], **Matthew Garratt**[2], **Andrew Lambert**[3], **Mark Pickering**[4] **and James Mitchell**[4]
School of Engineering and Information Technology, University of New South Wales, Canberra, Australia

Abstract—*Autonomous hover control of a low-cost Micro Air Vehicle (MAV) is considered in this paper. To avoid the long-term drift during hover, the 'snapshot' idea is practiced, where an image of the ground under the MAV is stored as the reference image, and the following images are directly compared with this reference image for estimating horizontal position. For hover control, the measured position is used in conjunction with the speed estimated from frame-to-frame image motion. All computations are performed onboard the vehicle and controller parameters are roughly tuned in the experiments. Flight tests carried out both indoors and outdoors prove the effectiveness of the proposed method for the hover control of a MAV.*

Keywords: Visual hover control, Micro aerial vehicle, snapshot, long-term drift.

1. Introduction

Much work has been devoted to the control of Micro Aerial Vehicles (MAV) using vision. Visual sensors are small, light-weight and have a large field of view and low power consumption, making them an ideal choice for platforms with limited payload. Visual means can act as a good complement to, if not replace, other navigation sensors for improving their positioning accuracy and reliability.

The relative movement of a MAV to the environment can be inferred from the frame-to-frame image motion known as optic flow (OF). Using a ventral camera and assuming altitude is available, horizontal velocity can be computed from OF and fed back to provide a speed damping effect during hover [1], [2]. If horizontal speed is provided by other sensors, OF can be utilized to estimate height for maintaining terrain-clearance [3]. OF is also used in other aspects like landing [2] and obstacle avoidance [4], [5], by exploiting the divergent flow pattern.

A big challenge for MAVs is that altitude (scale) information of the vehicle should be determined during flight. GPS signal coverage is easily lost in a confined space. A laser range finder is too heavy and power-demanding for MAV. Stereo vision can be used [6], however a minimum baseline is required that makes miniaturization difficult. Besides, the computational cost using two cameras is expected to be much more than that using just one camera. An approach in [7] makes an attempt to estimate height by doing texture analysis on a downward-looking camera. This method is proven to work only at low altitude environments with rich texture. With a monocular camera installed on their Pelican quadrotor, altitude is estimated [8] by combining Simultaneous Localization and Mapping (SLAM) algorithm with Inertial Measurement Unit (IMU). It is found in their experiments that the map is lost from time to time, and it takes a long time for the algorithm to recover. A short hovering period has to be inserted every few seconds to adjust the map with the gravity vector.

With only speed control using OF, the vehicle still drifts away over time in hovering because there is no absolute position feedback. A simple and unique pattern of known geometry is painted on the ground in [9] so that the MAV can identify the pattern to estimate altitude and horizontal position at the same time for hover control. This technique limits the operation of the vehicle to artificial environments while we target natural landscapes. Using a global map, the SLAM algorithm has the ability to correct for long-term drift [8], [10]. However, to store and update the map, SLAM is very time and memory consuming, usually requiring a powerful processing unit that is not available on a low-cost MAV.

The idea of visual snapshot is proposed in [11], where during hover, an image of the ground is captured and stored as the reference (snapshot) image, against which the following images are compared to calculate the absolute snapshot displacement for providing position feedback. In this paper, onboard hover control using both optic flow and snapshot algorithms is successfully implemented on an AR Drone version 1.0 quadrotor, which is a very cost-effective platform. Actual height is measured by the onboard ultrasonic sensor. A number of flight tests in both indoor and outdoor environments shows that the proposed approach can effectively prevent long-term drift against external disturbances.

2. Quadrotor Platform

2.1 Hardware and Software

The AR Drone 1.0 shown in Fig. 1 is a small battery-powered quadrotor. The four rotors, driven through brushless motors, control thrust by changing the Revolutions Per Minute (RPM) of each rotor. Onboard sensors are: (a) an ultrasonic sensor which has a range up to 6 m updating at 25Hz; (b) Bosch BMA150 3-axis accelerometers; (c) a

2-axis IDG500 gyroscope measuring pitch and roll rate, a single-axis EPSON XV3700 gyroscope for yaw rate [12]. As one of the mainboards, the navigation board has a 16-bit 40MHz PIC micro-controller that samples the inertial sensors at 200Hz. Another mainboard is the motherboard which features a 468MHz ARM9 processor, a 128MB RAM running at 200MHz and also a Wi-Fi chip. Multiple threads are managed by a BusyBox v1.14.0 version of the Linux operating system.

Fig. 1: Parrot ARDrone 1.0 with indoor hull and a laptop as the ground station.

The drone has two cameras: one is downward-looking with a 45°×35° field of view providing a color image of 176×144 pixels; the other is forward-looking with a 75°×60° field of view providing a color image of 640×480 pixels. The two cameras are connected to the ARM9 processor which encodes and sends the data from the cameras to a ground station through Wi-Fi link.

The downward-looking camera is of particular interest to us for the hover control. We have previously tried to use a laptop to process images transmitted from the drone and then send back command to control the hover. It is found that the hover performance is not so satisfactory, especially in outdoor environments where there is wind disturbance. Part of the reason may be the low frame rate available. The ventral camera is able to capture images at 60 fps but due to the imposed Wi-Fi limitation, a client can only receive images at 15 fps, which will bring more latency into the control system. The control signal also has to be sent through Wi-Fi, causing a delay in the drone's response. Therefore, we have chosen to perform the visual control onboard. This is achieved by building on an open source C program found in the personal blog of Hugo Perquin[1] that enables developers to have direct access to the onboard sensors and motors. One can modify the code, cross compile it into ARM executable files, open a *telnet* session to the drone and FTP those files to the drone's */data/video* folder as other folders ask for *sudo* access. Then, one can enter

[1]http://blog.perquin.com/blog/ar-drone-program-elf-replacement

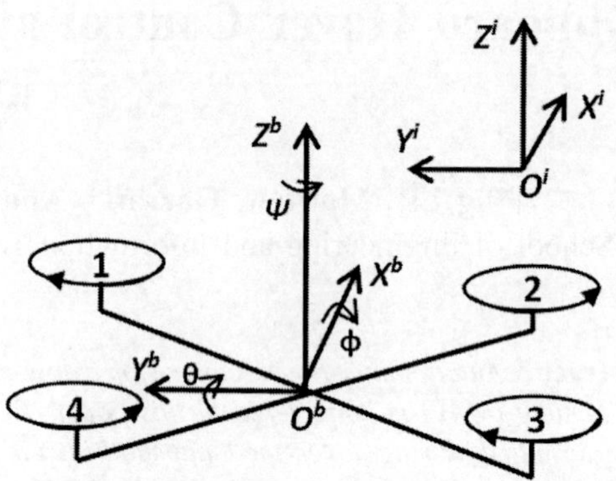

Fig. 2: The defined coordinate system for AR Drone.

that directory and run the program onboard containing their own algorithms instead of the original Parrot AR Drone program. A user interface called *Open Flight* written in $C\#$ is also included in the custom program that can send commands to the drone and log navigation data to a ground station. Starting from Perquin's program, image processing, sensor fusion and control algorithms have been added for our project.

2.2 Vehicle Dynamics and Control Structure

The definition of the coordinate system for the Drone is shown in Fig. 2. Generally, two coordinate systems are made use of to describe the motion of a MAV. One is the body coordinate system ($O^b - Z^bX^bY^b$) and the other is the inertial (world) coordinate system ($O^i - Z^iX^iY^i$). A quadrotor is an under-actuated system in that it has four independent rotors and six degree of freedom. The vertical motion is controlled by letting the four rotors change the rotating speed at the same time. Pitch (θ) angle can be adjusted through increasing (decreasing) the speed of rotor 3 and rotor 4 while decreasing (increasing) the speed of rotor 1 and rotor 2 by the same amount. Rolling (ϕ) and yawing (ψ) are regulated in a similar manner. The horizontal motion is realized by making the vehicle change its roll angle or pitch angle first. Therefore, a cascaded (inner-outer loop) structure [17] is often adopted, where the outer loop regulates the speed and position by sending attitude command to the inner loop. The inner loop will seek to manipulate a difference in the speed of the rotors for tracking the desired angle.

After the discussion above, the control commands sent to the four motors can be simply defined as:

$$r_1 = T_{total}/(cos(\phi) \cdot cos(\theta)) + \tau_\phi - \tau_\theta + \tau_\psi \quad (1)$$

$$r_2 = T_{total}/(cos(\phi) \cdot cos(\theta)) - \tau_\phi - \tau_\theta - \tau_\psi \quad (2)$$

$$r_3 = T_{total}/(cos(\phi) \cdot cos(\theta)) - \tau_\phi + \tau_\theta + \tau_\psi \quad (3)$$

$$r_4 = T_{total}/(cos(\phi) \cdot cos(\theta)) + \tau_\phi + \tau_\theta - \tau_\psi \quad (4)$$

where the commands τ_ϕ and τ_θ are the output of PID controller in the inner loop for the drone to reach the desired attitude. Note that AR Drone 1.0 does not have a magnetometer. Perquin's program uses a PI controller to control yaw. The yawing motion appears to be small in flight, so at the moment, we have not tried to make any change. T_{total} is composed of two parts: one is the trim value (T_{trim}) during hover and the other is output of a PD controller regulating height. A PI controller is utilized in the control of the horizontal speed to provide speed damping effect and bound the speed in hovering to a small value. A P controller is then used to control horizontal position based on the position estimation from snapshot displacement. The controller structure is shown in Fig. 3 with the control parameters roughly tuned in the experiments. In the figure, p, q, r are respectively the pitch rate, roll rate and yaw rate, $V_x, V_y, V_z, P_x, P_y, P_z$ are the estimated speed and position. θ_d, ϕ_d are the desired attitude command set by the outer loop.

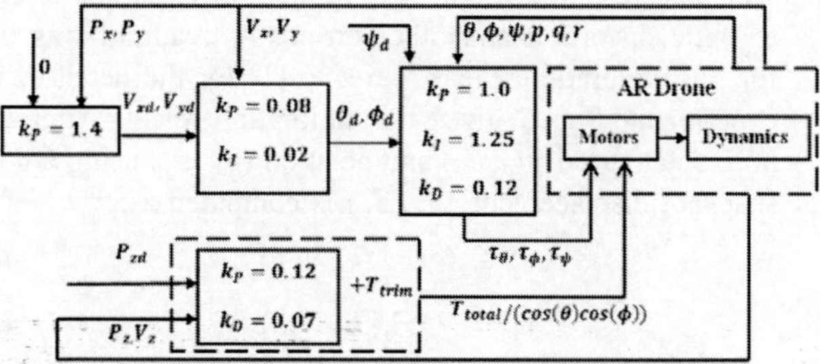

Fig. 3: Controller structure for hover control of the quadrotor with the controller parameters roughly tuned in the experiments.

3. Image Processing

For the frame-to-frame optical flow calculation, the Image Interpolation Algorithm (I^2A) [13] was used because it is robust to noise, fast to implement and able to give sub-pixel accuracy. For a better accuracy, an average filter is usually applied to images before using I^2A. Because only part of the image is needed in the motion estimation, filtering is thus only performed on the region of interest to save time. However, I^2A is not chosen for calculating snapshot displacement, as it is found to be very sensitive to illumination change. This creates a problem for the snapshot computation since lighting conditions may vary over time due to moving cloud interfering with the sunlight or self-shadowing of the vehicle. The Incremental Sign Correlation (ISC) [14] was demonstrated to be robust against illumination variation and chosen for the computation of snapshot displacement in this work. ISC is essentially a binary template matching algorithm that derives a binary image from the intensity image:

$$I_b(i,j) = \begin{cases} 1 & \text{if } I(i,j+1) > I(i,j), \\ 0 & \text{otherwise.} \end{cases} \quad (5)$$

where $I(i,j)$ is the intensity value, $I_b(i,j)$ is the binary value. When comparing two templates after the binary transformation, the Number of Non-Matching Points (NNMP) is used as the similarity measure. For binary template matching, logical operations can replace arithmetic operations, making the algorithm much faster than normal template matching, especially in hardware implementation. In order to further speed up the computation, the binary image was preprocessed in this way [15] that a location (i,j) in the new image I_B stores an integer, which encodes the bits from (i,j) to $(i,j+n)$ in the original binary image. This technique is explained in Fig. 4, for example, $I_B(i,j)$ is 11 if the bits from (i,j) to $(i,j+n)$ in the binary image is '1011' with n being 4. A Look up Table (LUT) with a size of $2^n \times 2^n$ can be constructed beforehand, from which one can directly know the number of different bits that two integers have. In this way, when computing the NNMP for two templates of 8 bits (see Fig. 4) with n being 4, only 2 look-up-table operations and 1 addition are required for this technique while direct comparison needs 8 XOR operations and 7 additions. With the template size unchanged, a choice of a large n seems to reduce the number of operations afterwards, but also consumes more memory and time in storing the coded image and a large LUT size. n is set to be 8 in the paper. Partial Distortion Search (PDS) [16] is also employed to reduce execution time. The idea is to terminate the calculation for a search point if the accumulated NNMP is larger than the minimum NNMP computed at that moment.

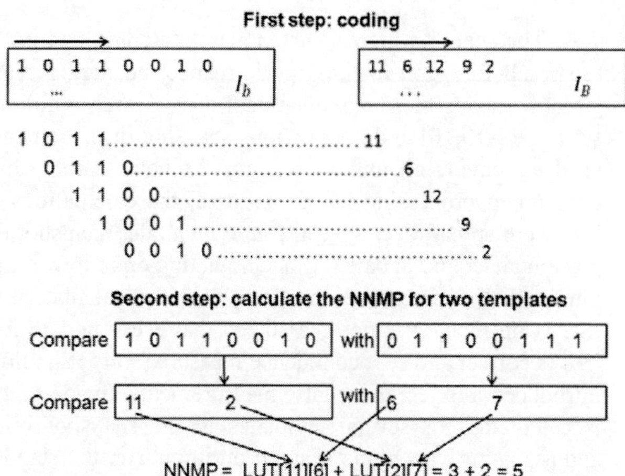

Fig. 4: The binary image is processed in a way that 4 successive bits are coded to an integer and stored in a new image. When calculating the NNMP for two binary templates, a look up table can help reduce the computation.

In our implementation, optic flow is calculated at 60

fps. The search window for template matching can not be too small for good tracking performance, but larger search window means more computational cost. Search window is set to be [-10,10] and the previous snapshot displacement is used to provide an initial guess for the next search. Given the limited processing power onboard, the calculations for ISC were spread over several frame intervals. Snapshot displacement can be updated by accumulating optic flow during intermediate frames and corrected once the calculation for ISC is finished. It is not guaranteed that every update from ISC is correct and so a confidence measure ($conf$) should be introduced to reject those false measurements. Image motion is calculated for several templates in the snapshot image and assuming yaw angle is small during hover, the standard deviation of the motion vectors for those templates can indicate the reliability of that measurement. The confidence measure is computed as:

$$conf = \sqrt{\frac{\sum_i (x_i - \bar{x})^2}{m}} + \sqrt{\frac{\sum_i (y_i - \bar{y})^2}{m}} \tag{6}$$

where m represents number of templates, x_i, y_i are the image displacement calculated with ISC in the X and Y direction for each template, and $\bar{x}, \bar{y}$ are the mean displacement for these templates. If the confidence measure is below a threshold, the result is used to correct for snapshot displacement and predict the next search, otherwise, the accumulation of optic flow is trusted. Sometimes with repeated pattern such as bricks or tiles, the algorithm may falsely track a similar region. This can be avoided by ruling out a sharp jump in the estimation. If the confidence measure remains beyond the threshold for a certain period of time, another snapshot image is taken as the new reference image.

4. Pose Estimation

4.1 Attitude

A simple complementary filter was used to estimate pitch and roll angle from the inertial sensors output:

$$\theta_n^- = \theta_{n-1}^+ + p \cdot dt \tag{7}$$

$$\theta_n^+ = k \cdot \theta_a + (1-k) \cdot \theta_{n-1}^- \tag{8}$$

$$\phi_n^- = \phi_{n-1}^+ + q \cdot dt \tag{9}$$

$$\phi_n^+ = k \cdot \phi_a + (1-k) \cdot \phi_{n-1}^- \tag{10}$$

where equation (7) and (9) predict pitch angle and roll angle with pitch rate p and roll rate q while equation (8) and (10) corrects the estimation by accelerometer measurement ($\phi_a = atan(a_y/a_z)$, $\theta_a = atan(-a_x/a_z)$, a_x, a_y, a_z are the accelerometer output with the unit being g). k is set at 0.015 in the subsequent experiments.

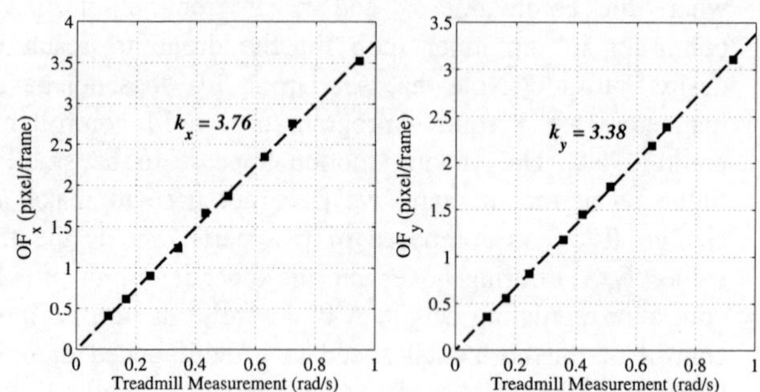

Fig. 5: Calibration for optic flow scale factor

4.2 Speed and Position

Optic flow in the X and Y direction, denoted as OF_x and OF_y, is measured in $pixel/frame$, before it can be used in the estimation of horizontal speed, the scale factor (k_x, k_y) that convert it to $radian/s$ should be found. The scale factor can be extracted according to the camera geometry (field of view and resolution), but it is prudent to re-calibrate it due to optic distortion and other errors. A treadmill was used for this calibration. Please refer to [1] for the detail of this experiment. Fig. 5 gives the calibration result. After that, horizontal speed (v_x, v_y) and position (p_x, p_y) using OF and snapshot displacement (S_x, S_y) is computed as:

$$v_x = (OF_x/k_x + p) \cdot P_z \tag{11}$$

$$v_y = (OF_y/k_y - q) \cdot P_z \tag{12}$$

$$p_x = (S_x/k_x + \theta) \cdot P_z \tag{13}$$

$$p_y = (S_y/k_y - \phi) \cdot P_z \tag{14}$$

where pitch rate and roll rate should be subtracted from the measured OF, and pitch angle and roll angle are subtracted from the snapshot displacement. Speed calculated from optic flow in equation (11) and (12) does not suffer from long-term drift but is very noisy. Speed integrated from acceleration is smooth but drifts over time. So once again these two are combined in the same way that pitch and roll angle are estimated, as in equation (7) to (10). Likewise, horizontal position during hover can be predicted using speed measurement and corrected with the position estimation from snapshot displacement. Perquin's program estimated vertical speed by linear regression based on height measurement from the ultrasonic sensor. Similar to the horizontal speed and position estimation, vertical acceleration can be incorporated to have a smoother vertical speed and height estimation. When pitch angle and roll angle are small, the actual accelerations (A_x, A_y, A_z) in the X^i, Y^i and Z^i direction can be approximated by [17]:

$$A_x = g \cdot (\theta + a_x) \tag{15}$$

$$A_y = g \cdot (-\phi + a_y) \tag{16}$$

$$A_z = g \cdot (a_z - 1) \tag{17}$$

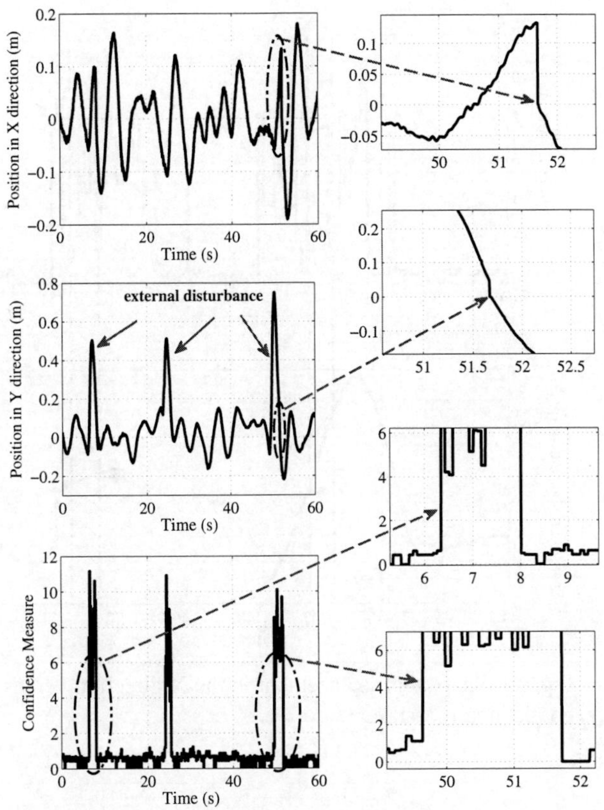

Fig. 6: Horizontal position and confidence measure during an indoor hover under external disturbance.

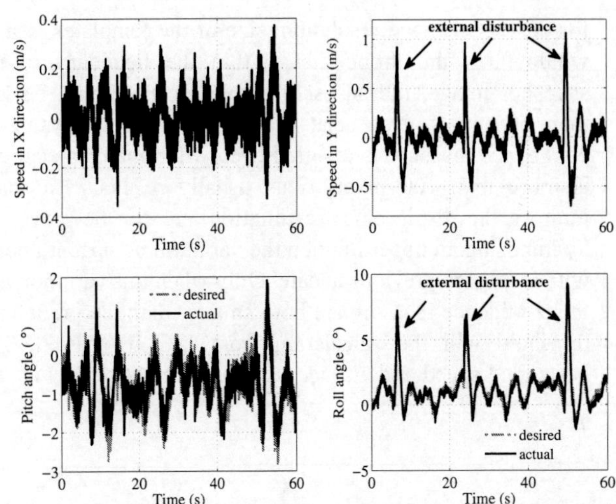

Fig. 7: Horizontal speed, pitch and roll response during an indoor hover under external disturbance

5. Flight Tests

A number of flight tests were conducted both indoors and outdoors. During hovering in an indoor environment, the drone was disturbed (mainly in the Y direction) by hand three times. Once it is pushed away from the visual anchor point, the confidence measure becomes very large (Fig. 6), and during this time the snapshot displacement is only updated using accumulation of OF. It is noted that for the first two disturbances, the drone is able to come back and lock onto the reference image. For the third case with larger perturbation, the drone failed to make its way back to the original hovering point but remains very close. In the experiment, if the confidence measure stays larger than 2 for 2 seconds, a new snapshot image will be taken. As seen from the zoomed figures pointed to by the dashed arrows in Fig. 6, for the first two disturbances the confidence measure remains larger than 2 for less than 2 seconds, but for the third case, this period is longer than 2 seconds, thus another reference image is captured and position estimation is reset to 0 for another round of tracking. If the tolerance period is raised (for example 3 seconds) for the confidence measure larger than 2, the vehicle may be able to find 'home' again. It seems that the use of a longer tolerance period is able to handle stronger perturbation, however, the integration of OF may have drifted so much that the vehicle can not go back. In fact, this tolerance period reflects how much the integration of OF is trusted. It should be mentioned that we have not tried to determine the optimal value for this tolerance period. The horizontal speed estimation and attitude response are displayed in Fig. 7. The desired attitude angle set by the outer loop are tracked very well by the inner loop.

Fig. 8: AR Drone flying outdoors over a repeated pattern.

Fig. 9 gives the horizontal position estimation and confidence measure during hovering outdoors as shown in Fig. 8. The confidence measure goes beyond the threshold more frequently than in the indoor environments. That means new snapshot images are taken more frequently. Despite that, the drone is observed to stay in the vicinity of the original hovering point. The vehicle is flying over an repetitive pattern (Fig. 8) in this experiment, when blown away by wind gust, it is possible to track a new region having similar templates to those in the snapshot image. Because for our case (image resolution, size of the templates, search window), if the drone flies within the boundary of the snapshot image, the snapshot displacement should be less than 50 pixels. Note that in Fig. 10, a small value in confidence measure is reported even when the displacement is more than 100 pixels. This usually results in a sharp jump in the displacement estimation and can be prevented by imposing an upper limit on the variation of current update with respect to previous update. Only when this variation and the confidence measure are both smaller than the predefined threshold will the calculation from ISC be trusted. The horizontal speed and attitude response are shown in Fig. 11.

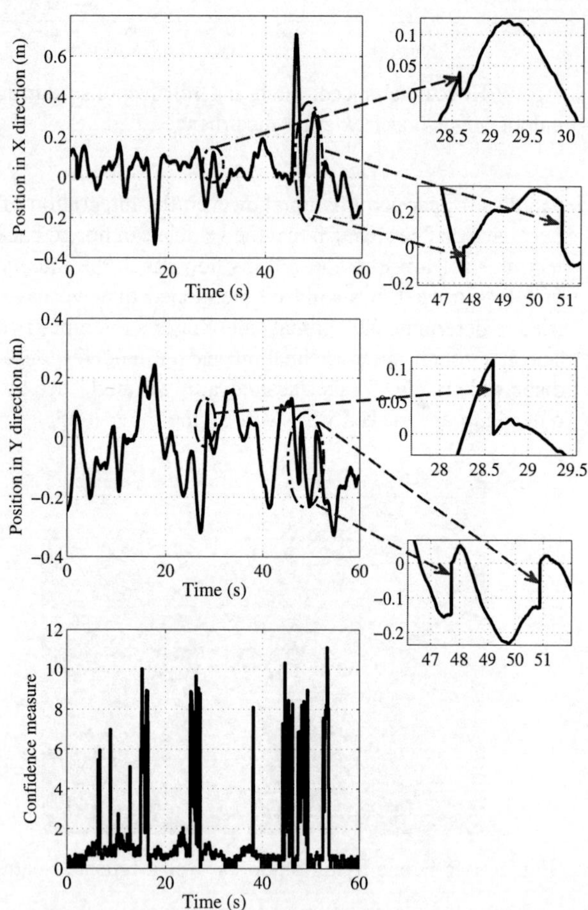

Fig. 9: Horizontal position and confidence measure during an outdoor hover with wind disturbance.

6. Conclusion

In this paper, the snapshot idea [11] is proven to be very effective in eliminating the long-term drift of a rotorcraft in hover. Based on an open source program, onboard implementation of visual algorithms, sensor fusion and controller design are successfully achieved. Flight tests demonstrate the proposed method work satisfactorily both indoors and outdoors even with repeated pattern and light wind disturbance. Although not proven in flight, the ISC algorithm has the ability to deal with illumination change. However, the limitation of the platform should also be mentioned. A strong wind gust can easily drive the drone away from the scene where snapshot image is captured. In fact, even moderate but non-constant wind is difficult enough to deal with. A varying

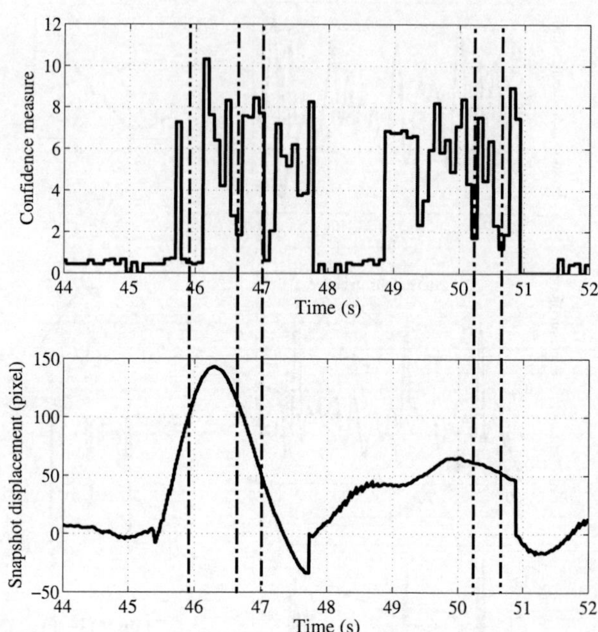

Fig. 10: Snapshot displacement in the X direction versus the confidence measure.

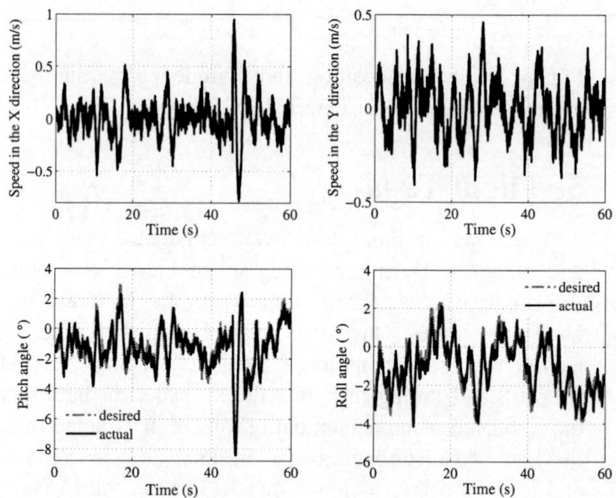

Fig. 11: Horizontal speed, pitch and roll response during an outdoor hover with wind disturbance.

wind condition will lead to a big variation in the attitude, which is the only way that an AR Drone can resist external disturbance. This is very likely to make the drone lose the visual anchor point (may be the reason why the confidence measure goes over the threshold more frequently outdoors than indoors) due to the small field of view of the downward-looking camera. In a dim-light condition, the image quality will get worse and degrades the results. For a good hovering performance under a wider range of circumstances, a better camera with larger field of view is preferred, or the rotors themselves can tilt [19] so that external disturbance can be counteracted without causing much change in the attitude of the vehicle.

Future work on this platform will focus on: (a) optimizing the controller parameters; (b) optimizing the combination of snapshot measurement with the integration of OF; (c) exploiting the distribution of motion vectors [18] for the purely visual control of height [11] and yaw angle as well as horizontal positions.

References

[1] M. Garratt and J. Chahl, "An Optic Flow Damped Hover Controller for an Autonomous Helicopter," in *22nd International UAV Systems Conference*, Bristol, April 2007.

[2] B. Hérissé, F. Russotto, T. Hamel and R. Mahony, "Hovering flight and vertical landing control of a VTOL Unmanned Aerial Vehicle using Optical Flow," in *International Conference on Intelligent Robots and Systems*, France, pp. 801–806, 2008.

[3] M. Garratt and J. Chahl, "Vision-Based Terrain Following for an Unmanned Rotorcraft," *Journal of Field Robotics.*, vol. 25, no. 4–5, pp. 284–301, 2008.

[4] S. Hrabar, G. Sukhatme, P. Corke and K. Usher, "Combined optic-flow and stereo-based navigation of urban canyons for a UAV," in *International Conference on Intelligent Robots and System*, Canada, pp. 3309–3316, 2005.

[5] J. Zufferey and D. Floreano, "Fly-Inspired Visual Steering of an Ultralight Indoor Aircraft," *IEEE Transactions on Robotics.*, vol. 22, no. 1, pp. 137–146, 2006.

[6] P. Corke, "An Inertial and Visual Sensing System for a Small Autonomous Helicopter," *Journal of Robotic Systems.*, vol. 21, no. 2, pp. 43–51, 2004.

[7] A. Cherian, J. Andersh, V. Morellas and N. Papanikolopoulos, "Autonomous altitude estimation of a UAV using a single onboard camera," in *International Conference on Intelligent Robots and System*, pp. 3900–3905, 2009.

[8] S. Weiss, D. Scaramuzzaand and R. Siegwart, "Monocular SLAM Based Navigation for Autonomous Micro Helicopters in GPS-Denied Environments," *Journal of Field Robotics.*, vol. 28, no. 6, pp. 854–874, 2011.

[9] S. Lange, N. Sunderhauf and P. Protzel, "A vision based onboard approach for landing and position control of an autonomous multirotor UAV in GPS-denied environments," in *International Conference on Advanced Robotics*, 2009.

[10] J. Engel, J. Sturm and D. Cremers, "Accurate Figure Flying with a Quadrocopter Using Onboard Visual and Inertial Sensing," in *Proc. of the Workshop on Visual Control of Mobile Robots (ViCoMoR) at the IEEE/RJS International Conference on Intelligent Robot Systems (IROS)*, 2012.

[11] M. Garratt, A. Lambert and H. Teimoori, "Design of a 3D snapshot based visual flight control system using a single camera in hover," *Auton Robot.*, September 2012.

[12] P. J. Bristeau, F. Callou, D. Vissière and N. Petit, "The Navigation and Control technology inside the AR. Drone micro-UAV," in *18th IFAC World Congress*, vol. 18, no. 1, Milano, Italy, pp. 1477–1484, 2011.

[13] Srinivasan. M, "An image interpolation technique for the computation of optic flow and egomotion," *Biological Cybernetics.*, vol. 71, no. 5, pp. 401–415, 1994.

[14] S. Kanekoa, I. Muraseb and S. Igarashia, "Robust image registration by increment sign correlation," *Pattern Recognition.*, vol. 35, pp. 2223–2234, 2002.

[15] Y. K. Wang and G. F. Tu, "Fast Binary Block Matching Motion Estimation using Efficient One-Bit Transform," *Department of Electrical Engineering, the Graduate School of Academia Sinica*, Beijing, China.

[16] O. Urhan, "Constrained one-bit transform-based motion estimation using predictive hexagonal pattern," *Journal of Electronic Imaging.*, vol. 16, no. 3, p. 033019, 2007.

[17] Y. Sun, "Modeling, identification and control of a quad-rotor drone using low-resolution sensing," *Master thesis, University of Illinois at Urbana-Champaign*, 2012.

[18] A. Hung, M. Pickering and M. A. Garratt, "Fast image registration using a multi-pass image interpolation approach," in *7th International Conference on Information Technology and Applications*, Sydney, Australia, pp. 21–24, Nov. 2011.

[19] S. K. Phang, C. X. Cai, B. M. Chen and T. H. Lee, "Design and Mathematical Modeling of a 4-Standard-Propeller (4SP) Quadrotor," in *Proceedings of the 10th World Congress on Intelligent Control and Automation*, Beijing, China, pp. 3270–3275, July. 2012.

A Fully Automatic Ship Localization Algorithm for Complex Backgrounds

Irene Camino García, Udo Zölzer
Faculty of Electrical Engineering, Helmut Schmidt University, Hamburg, Germany

Abstract— *Object localization is often necessary in order to accomplish further tasks, such as identification or classification. Maritime security or coastal surveillance are applications of high interest to maritime authorities. The images employed to perform these activities depend on their specific requirements. When the characteristics of the naval environment are visible, as in short range images, the background complexity increases greatly. Due to water reflections, the gray distribution might be very disperse throughout the image. Waves produce a large amount of edges, unusual in other contexts. Specially in wakes in the direction of the ship, waves might have even stronger edges than the ship. Furthermore, patterns of color or brightness are difficult to be found. In this case, user interaction has been proposed. This paper presents a fully automatic ship localization algorithm, valid also for complex backgrounds.*

Keywords: Ship Localization; Hough Transform; Edge Detection; Complex Backgrounds

1. Introduction

Maritime security or coastal surveillance are applications of great interest to maritime authorities nowadays. The images employed to perform these activities depend on their specific requirements. Remote sensing imagery has been widely employed because of its long operating distance and wide monitoring range. However, sometimes short range images are preferred due to their higher detail.

These activities imply ship identification and often feature extraction. These features may also be useful for further classification. For a reliable result, the ship location in the image must be obtained first.

In remote sensing images, ships usually have opposite gray values of the sea region. Furthermore, the gray distribution of the background is barely spread. This may facilitate the ship localization as noted by [1]. Simple shape analysis [2], histogram based segmentation [3] and filtering by local gradient analysis [4] are enough to extract the ship candidate. In contrast, if the gray distribution of the sea region is very disperse user interaction is needed [5]. This paper presents a fully automatic ship localization technique that overcomes the difficulties of complex backgrounds.

Short range naval images entail serious impediments for proper ship localization since the characteristics of this adverse environment are more visible. Due to the reflection effects the gray distribution varies highly, which might also lead to the existence of regions in the water. The incidence of light modifies not only the background intensity but also the color.

Besides, the number of edges produced by waves is particularly high. This rarely occurs in other scenarios. The waves might have stronger edges than the ship itself, specially in wakes in the direction of the ship.

In order to develop the proposed technique, we take into account the fact that most of the edges are randomly generated due to their nature (waves, clouds, ...). However, despite of this variety of edges, those that contribute to give the semantic sense of ship are, in fact, straight lines. By establishing the constraints to consider a set of points as line, we are able to reject most of these random edge points, thus taking advantage of these unfavorable characteristics.

The Hough Transform (HT), first described by [6], allows to accomplish this approach. It consists of different steps, and each of them has been deeply analyzed in terms of performance or robustness, but also improved by new contributions.

Different constraints have been suggested for the voting process, as the related to the quantization of the parameters [7]. The use of edge information in the voting process has also been frequently employed in literature. Thus, conditions can be established with respect to the gradient direction [8], [9]. Edge points can be restricted due to their magnitude gradient [10], [11], [12], too. However, since ships share some geometric characteristics the approach presented in this paper uses the geometry of their shapes instead. This leads to higher accuracy since short lines are now detected. Otherwise it is unlikely that they significantly contribute in the voting process, as noted by [11]. Besides, the enhancement of strong edges that belong to the background is avoided.

This paper is structured as follows. Section 2 briefly describes the HT, including the non-maximal suppression and the voting process. A preliminary localization approach is explained in Section 3 and the evaluation is discussed. A shape processing step that achieves a high reduction in undesired edge points is considered later in Section 4 as well as the final evaluation. Final conclusions and further considerations are drawn in Section 5.

Fig. 1: Examples of the images employed.

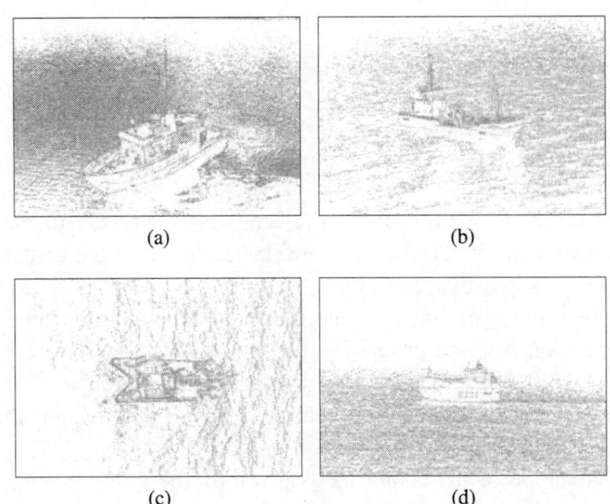

Fig. 2: Binary edge images obtained by means of the Canny operator.

2. The Hough Transform

The Standard Hough Transform (SHT), suggested by [13], employs the so-called normal parametrization. Following that notation, the edge points (x, y) standing in the picture plane are transformed into points (θ, ρ) in the parameter plane given by

$$x \cos\theta + y \sin\theta = \rho. \quad (1)$$

Collinear edge points share the values of the parameters θ, that describes the angle of its normal, and ρ, its algebraic distance from origin. The HT is performed by counting the mapping of collinear edge points for each point of the parameter space. The parameter space is represented by an accumulative array. The SHT keeps this count by incrementing the cells of this array in one unit accordingly. This increment is the vote, denoted by v. The longer the line, the higher the value contained in its respective cell is, if no gaps exist.

The resolution of the parameter plane depends on the quantization of ρ and the sampling rate of θ. Although the computational complexity is increased, the choice of finer quantization leads to better results. The quantization effects on the detection performance of the HT are dealt by [8] and [7].

Additional conditions might be imposed on the edge points and therefore many voting strategies can be implemented. Such constraints can lead to the enhancement of the edge points that fulfill certain requisites over the rest. Alternatively they can be restrictive with the edge points when considered collinear. These conditions can be combined to obtain both effects depending on the desired result. Different weighting functions might also be selected (linear, Gaussian, ...) to set the value of the vote.

The non-maximal suppression step yields as the quantization of the parameter space. After θ and ρ are computed by an edge detector, they have to be rounded to proceed to increment the respective cell accordingly. The rounding of the parameters leads to errors that might make the surrounding cells receive a significant number of votes. A regular procedure is to suppress these cells to prevent them from being selected as maxima. Additionally it is necessary to define the minimum value $v_{T_{min}}$ that a cell must contain to be selected.

3. Preliminary Localization

The localization approach follows several steps. First, the ship centerline is estimated in order to make the algorithm independent of bearing and elevation changes. A set of feature angles is defined for the enhancement of meaningful lines, i.e. those that determine the ship. Further processing is carried out on the results to achieve higher accuracy. A convex hull algorithm calculates the extreme points that mark the ship location.

The resolution of the images employed (see Fig. 1) is 3456×2304 and 3056×2296. The Canny operator [14] was chosen to detect the edges in the images, as in Fig. 2.

3.1 Ship Centerline Extraction

The ship centerline is defined by [1] as the line connecting the point of the bow through the center of the stern (see Fig. 3). In order to retrieve its slope θ_{cl}, the SHT is applied to make the most of the elongated nature of vessels. Therefore, the vote is set to $v = 1$ and $v_{T_{min}}$ must be set to a high enough value. Only $l_{T_{max}}$ lines are selected, as long as they fulfill the previous limitation. If the sea is a high-textured surface, the number of waves that may interfere in the extraction is avoided or at least limited.

The resolution of the parameter space is $360 \times (2 \cdot D + 1)$, with D the diagonal of the image. After picking a line, an

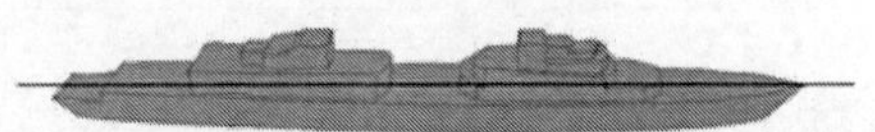

Fig. 3: Centerline sketch.

area of $(2 \cdot w + 1) \times (2 \cdot w + 1)$ cells is suppressed in the parameter space. The cell of the selected line is at the center and w is a positive constant.

Then, the resulting lines are clustered depending on their orientation θ. Each group j is composed of l_j lines, where $j = 0, \ldots, n-1$ and n is the number of groups. The line i of the group j fulfills that $\theta_{i,j} \in [\theta_{0,j}, \theta_{0,j} + \varphi]$ with $i = 0, \ldots, l_j - 1$ and $\theta_{0,j} + \varphi < \theta_{0,j+1}$.

The slope of the centerline is given by the group $\hat{\jmath}$ with

$$\hat{\jmath} = \arg\max_{j} l_j. \tag{2}$$

In case the centerline is not unique, the condition that applies is

$$\hat{\jmath} = \arg\max_{j} \sum_{i=0}^{l_j - 1} v_{T_{i,j}}, \tag{3}$$

where $v_{T_{i,j}}$ is the total value of votes of the line i that belongs to group j. The centerline takes the value of the average orientation of the lines of the selected group $\hat{\jmath}$, as given by

$$\theta_{cl} = \frac{\sum_{i=0}^{l_{\hat{\jmath}}-1} \theta_{i,\hat{\jmath}}}{l_{\hat{\jmath}}}. \tag{4}$$

The clustering allows to discard lines whose orientation might interfere. The selection of groups with many but short lines is avoided by setting $v_{T_{min}}$. By averaging the slopes, any possible deviation with respect to the real centerline is reduced. Lines with the same slope are weighted as many times as they appear, and consequently their influence is higher. The influence of long lines and the precision of θ_{cl} can be controlled by φ.

3.2 Feature Angles Enhancement

The feature angles correspond to the common features that all vessels share, i.e. horizontal lines for decks (θ_d), diagonals for keels (θ_k) and verticals for masts (θ_m). Their orientations are assumed to lie within certain ranges. They are fitted with respect to the centerline.

The feature angles enhancement is performed by a modified HT. It is able to detect lines regardless of their number of points and the strength of their gradient. For this goal, the non-maximal suppression remains the same, as well as $v_{T_{min}}$. There is no restriction regarding $l_{T_{max}}$ though. However, the vote of the lines whose orientations correspond to the feature angles is

$$v = \left\lfloor \frac{v_{T_{min}}}{s_{min}} \right\rfloor + 1. \tag{5}$$

This value guarantees that these lines reach the minimum value $v_{T_{min}}$ for being selected as long as they consist of the minimum number of points of a segment s_{min}. Otherwise they would be eliminated during the following segment processing. The value contained in the selected cells no longer represents the number of collinear edge points that voted for the line.

3.3 Segment Processing

One of the properties of the HT is the accumulation of points as part of lines even though there might be gaps in between. Therefore, a line is often divided into multiple segments and isolated points. Taking this property into account, a set of parameters can be defined for removing them. This idea has been employed earlier by [12], although the number of points of a line is taken under consideration. Here, line segments are employed instead. Obtaining more accurate results is possible then by choosing the

- minimum number of points s_{min} allowed to be part of a segment and the
- maximum allowed length of gaps denoted by g_{max}.

Line segments are allowed, in turn, to be broken due to gaps of shorter length than g_{max}. However, if the segment does not reach s_{min} all its points are eliminated.

The more edge points remain after the feature angles enhancement, the more probable disturbances are. Consequently it becomes more difficult to discriminate the desired edge points among them. The ratio of selected edge points to resolution gives a measure of the background complexity. However, to be consistent with the fact that some lines could only be selected by applying (5), constraints for θ_d need to be stricter. Therefore the background complexity is better classified according to

$$c_1 = \frac{N_d}{r} \times 1000, \tag{6}$$

with r as the number of pixels of the image and N_d the number of edge points of the lines enhanced by θ_d. And also according to

$$c_2 = \frac{N}{r} \times 1000, \tag{7}$$

where N is the total number of edge points after the feature angles enhancement, i.e $N = N_d + N_k + N_m$.

Different values of the constraints s_{min} and g_{max} may be set according to the classification of the background complexity. The value of s_{min} that computes (5) is the most restrictive. This procedure allows this approach to perform well also when the background is complex.

The convenience of the previous steps was already shown in [15]. However, the aim of this contribution is the ship localization. The ship location is defined by the convex hull of the ship. Therefore, the Graham's scan algorithm [16] is employed.

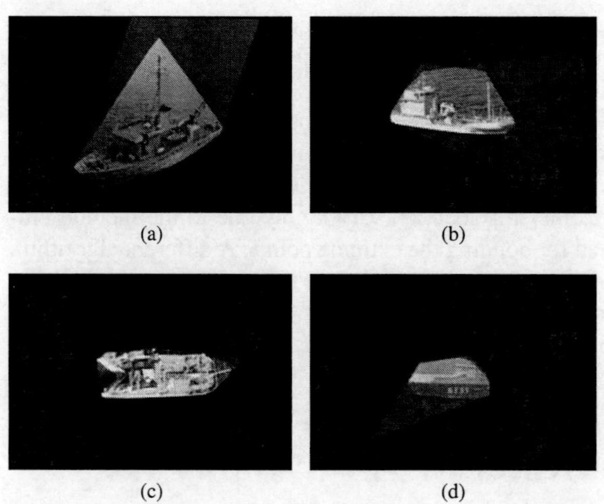

(a) (b) (c) (d)

Fig. 4: Results after segment processing, where red channel prevails in erroneously retrieved pixels, blue in erroneously rejected pixels and the correctly retrieved pixels remain.

For that, gaps in between the multiple segments of a line are not taken into consideration. Therefore, they compose a single segment that might mark the ship location. The Graham's scan algorithm is applied to their endpoints and calculates the extreme points of the convex hull.

3.4 Evaluation

The evaluation of the algorithm is accomplished on a dataset of 51 images. These images contain different models of ships under different illumination conditions. Furthermore, there are no constraints regarding the elevation or bearing. No simulated data is employed.

In order to assess the localization quality, the undesired edge points are manually removed from the binary edge image. The edge points corresponding to the ship remain in the resulting image. The Graham's scan algorithm is applied to them for obtaining the real ship location.

Both results are compared to give the evaluation, as it can be seen in Fig. 4. Pixels whose red channel prevails are the erroneously retrieved pixels and belong to the ship location under evaluation. On the contrary, pixels whose blue channel prevails are the erroneously rejected pixels and belong to the real ship location. The correctly retrieved pixels remain and they are shared by both ship locations.

The precision, or the fraction of pixels that were correctly retrieved by this algorithm is on average 82.88%. And the recall, defined as the fraction of correctly retrieved pixels of the real location, is on average 81.66%.

The precision is lower as it could be since the spurious segments make the ship location result in a larger area, when they remain. The recall is unrelated to the erroneously retrieved pixels. However, the extension of the ship location due to these spurious segments might affect the recall. The ship location might be composed of correctly retrieved pixels that would not be actually retrieved if the spurious segments were correctly rejected.

4. Shape Based Processing

As the preliminary evaluation shows, more accurate localization can be achieved. For that goal, the spurious segments should be eliminated.

Spurious segments are at a certain distance of the ship. In order to prune a segment candidate, a threshold d_{max} can be imposed to its distance d_c to the center of the image. The image is splitted into quadrants in order to take into consideration the eventual symmetry of the ships. The following procedure is iteratively performed for each of them.

Their elongated shapes should also be considered. Therefore, the maximum difference of segment angles $\Delta\theta$ is calculated, as well as the average distance of segments d. An adaptive threshold is proposed

$$d_{max} = f(d) \times d, \tag{8}$$

where $f(d)$ is a weighting function dependent on d. If $\Delta\theta$ is larger than $\Delta\theta_{max}$, where $\Delta\theta_{max}$ is set by the user, the threshold d_{max} can be calculated by

$$f(d) = \log_{0.4}(d) + 8.5. \tag{9}$$

Otherwise, the deviation of d may be high and a more permissive function applies,

$$f(d) = \log_{0.6}(d) + 14.7. \tag{10}$$

Both weighting functions are graphically shown in Fig. 5.

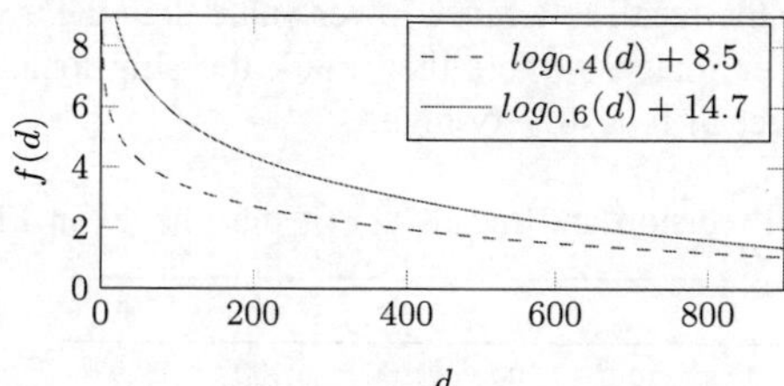

Fig. 5: Weighting functions.

The Graham's scan algorithm is applied to the endpoints of the remaining segments.

4.1 Evaluation

By accomplishing the same procedure described in 3.4, the average precision is 98.03% and the average recall, 77.14%. The effect of the shape based processing can be observed in Fig. 6.

As expected, the elimination of the spurious segments leads to a very precise ship location. The recall decreases as the precision increases, confirming the effect of the spurious

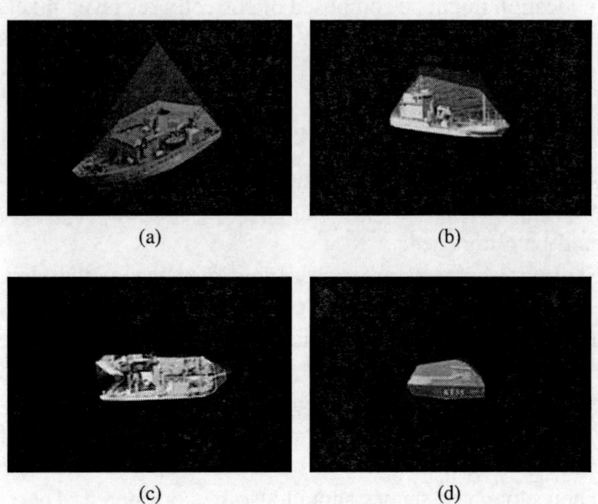

Fig. 6: Ship localization results, where red channel prevails in erroneously retrieved pixels, blue in erroneously rejected pixels and the correctly retrieved pixels remain.

segments. This loss is very small though, in comparison with the increase in precision.

The recall considers the desired edge pixels that were erroneously rejected. By inspecting the results it can be concluded that most of the erroneously rejected pixels correspond to areas marked by antennas. As they stand above, the area selected by the convexity algorithm increases much if the ship location is marked by their endpoints. This can be demonstrated in Fig. 6a. It can be seen that the ship location is accurate, as the corresponding precision shown in Table 1 also proves. But the endpoints of the antenna are missing and it reduces the recall to a much lower value than the average. In the other images, where they mark the ship location as well, the recall is also very high.

Table 1: Precision and recall (%) of the images in Fig. 6.

	6a	6b	6c	6d
precision	100	100	100	99.93
recall	64.81	81.19	93.12	92.22

5. Conclusions

By avoiding the enhancement of strong edges accurate ship localization is achieved, as short segments are extracted as well. Their extraction is necessary for higher precision, for example, in the bow or stern part. They can be extracted due to the voting process based on the features angles here developed. Some other approaches would fail as previously mentioned.

The algorithm could be improved in terms of performance since it makes use of the HT twice, perhaps a more accurate procedure to calculate the ship centerline could be employed. The extraction of the three main ship axes, not only the centerline, could be employed for a more complete feature angles enhancement.

The characterization of spurious segments by logarithmic functions improves the precision, that it is very high now. It is shown that missing low relevant elements as antennas makes the ship location vary highly due to the method employed for bonding the extreme points. A different algorithm, as active contour models, could be of interest to prevent it and obtain better recall. Yet, this ship localization has high recall and very high precision. Furthermore, no prior knowledge of the ship is required by the algorithm and user interaction is also avoided.

References

[1] S. Musman, D. Kerr, and C. Bachmann, "Automatic recognition of ISAR ship images ," *Transactions on Aerospace and Electronic Systems*, vol. 32, no. 4, pp. 1392 – 1404, 1996.

[2] C. Zhu, H. Zhou, R. Wang, and J. Guo, "A novel hierarchical method of ship detection from spaceborne optical image based on shape and texture features," *Transactions on Geoscience and Remote Sensing*, vol. 48, no. 9, pp. 149 – 155, 2010.

[3] J. Xu, K. Fu, and X. Sun, "An invariant Generalized Hough Transform based method of inshore ships detection." IEEE, 2011.

[4] L. Ma, J. Guo, Y. Wang, Y. Tian, and Y. Yang, "Ship detection by salient convex boundaries," in *3rd International Congress on Image and Signal Processing (CISP2010)*, vol. 1. IEEE, 2010, pp. 202 – 205.

[5] C. Kao, S. Hsieh, and C. Peng, "Study of feature-based image capturing and recognition algorithm," in *International Conference on Control, Automation and Systems (ICCAS)*. IEEE, 2010, pp. 1855 – 1861.

[6] P. V. C. Hough, "Methods and means for recognizing complex patterns." US Patent 3069654, 1962.

[7] J. Princen, J. Illingworth, and J. Kittler, "A hierarchical approach to line extraction based on the Hough transform," *Computer Vision, Graphics, and Image Processing*, vol. 52, pp. 57 – 77, 1990.

[8] T. M. van Veen and F. C. A. Groen, "Discretization errors in the Hough transform," *Pattern Recognition*, vol. 14, pp. 137 – 145, 1980.

[9] V. Kyrki and H. Kälviäinen, "Combination of local and global line extraction," *Real-Time Imaging*, vol. 6, no. 2, pp. 79 – 91, 2000.

[10] S. Guo, Y. Kong, Q. Tang, and F. Zhang, "Probabilistic Hough transform for line detection utilizing surround suppression," in *Proceedings of the 7th International Conference on Machine Learning and Cybernetics*, vol. 5. IEEE, 2008, pp. 2993 – 2998.

[11] F. O'Gorman and M. B. Clowes, "Finding picture edges through collinearity of feature points," *Transactions on Computers*, vol. C - 25, pp. 449 – 456, 1976.

[12] B. Keck, C. Ruwwe, and U. Zölzer, "Hough transform with weighting edge maps," in *Fifth IASTED International Conference on Visualization, Imaging, Image Processing (VIIP)*, 2005.

[13] R. O. Duda and P. E. Hart, "Use of the Hough transformation to detect lines and curves in pictures," *Comm. ACM*, vol. 15, pp. 11–15, 1972.

[14] J. Canny, "A computational approach to edge detection," in *Transactions on Pattern Analysis and Machine Intelligence*. IEEE, 1986, pp. 679–698.

[15] I. Camino-García and U. Zölzer, "Hough Transform based ship segmentation using centerline extraction and feature angles," in *International Conference on Signal Image Technology and Internet Based Systems (SITIS)*. IEEE, 2012, pp. 149 – 154.

[16] R. L. Graham, "An efficient algorithm for determining the convex hull of a finite planar set," *Inf. Process. Lett.*, vol. 1, no. 4, pp. 132–133, 1972.

Comparing Hand-Gesture and Finger-Touch Interfacing to Navigate Bulk Image-Sequence Data

V. Du Preez, E.P.Clarkson, S. Innes, D.Q. Quach and K.A. Hawick
Computer Science, Massey University, North Shore 102-904, Auckland, New Zealand
email: {dupreezvictor, dara.quach, elliot.clarkson}@gmail.com
redmansteve2@hotmail.co.uk, k.a.hawick@massey.ac.nz
Tel: +64 9 414 0800 Fax: +64 9 441 8181

June 2013

ABSTRACT

Modern interface devices such as depth field cameras and touch sensitive screen offer new scope for navigation large and complex image data sets. Image sequences from movies or simulations can be treated as hyper-bricks of navigable data. We have implemented an image navigation interface framework that supports a compatible set of both depth-field hand gestures and touch-screen finger movements. We report on how these two apparently disparate interfaces can be combined in a unifying software architecture and explore the human computer interaction space of suitable gestural and touch idioms and metaphors suitable for rapid interactive navigation and rendering of a sequence of images from a simulation, from photographic stills, or frames of a movie. We compare the two sorts of interaction and discuss a descriptive vocabulary for these and suggest some directions for development and use in other bulk data navigation interfaces.

KEY WORDS
image data navigation; gestures; touch screen; HCI.

1 Introduction

Improvements in and cheaper costs of image capture devices are making the problem of navigating and manipulating large sequences of image data more common. Simulations too, often generate large quantities of image data. Interacting with regular hyper-bricks of data in real interactive time is quite computationally feasible using modern processing technologies if one can find the right interaction metaphors to allow a user to express appropriate navigational commands. In this paper we investigate the interaction technologies such as depth field cameras and touch screens so that users can interact with image sequence data using both gestures and multi-finger touches.

Human-Computer Interaction is a relatively mature discipline [1] and many of the key guiding principles have

Figure 1: One of the authors (DQQ) demonstrating the prototype system using gestural interfaces that are detected by a Kinect depth-field camera, and used to direct the operations of a simulation model.

been well studied [2–4]. However, the widespread availability of new interface devices is leading to hitherto unexplored interaction mechanisms. The multi-touch capability of tablet computers [5] is a particularly interesting area that is still being explored by new communities of users for various disciplines.

The Kinect depth-field camera [6] is another commodity-priced device that has attracted a lot of attention as an enabler of innovative HCI modes for gaming applications [7–9], but also for applications including geospatial navigation [10], handicap and visual impairment support [11–13], and also interactive learning [14].

Widely available devices like the Kinect make possible a range of human interaction possibilities. The Kinect itself is a well integrated set of sensors [15] including cameras, orientation devices and sound capabilities. These systems and their software frameworks support detection of specific devices like paddles [16] or wands, but more interesting - and indeed natural, is for the user to use gestures [17–21] to interact with a sequence or brick or images or simulation model.

Gestural interfaces are not new [22] although with the very rapid product commoditization of touch sensitive tablet computing the research and textbook literature on multi-touch and gestural systems has not yet caught up and there are surprisingly few accounts of multi-touch applications and associated experiences [23].

In this present paper we are particularly interested in enabling different devices to support image navigation, with sets of either r hand gestures or screen touches having an intuitive relationship with one another. Figure 1 shows ...

HCI experiments and applications [24] have been widely reported in the literature for tablet computing [25] on data entry [26], database interaction [27], interactive training [28, 29] and simulation interaction [30, 31]. Software development work is also reported on HCI frameworks that will further enable these applications [32].

Much recently reported research has focused on interacting with 3D objects [33, 34]. Our present paper focuses on the human user as a 3D entity [35] that must be recognized and the detected [36] human activities [37] used as feedback into any interesting running simulation. Human detection [38] requires tracking the whole skeletal body [39, 40] as well as specifics such as head and hands [41]. There appears to be a wealth of work to be done in the field of HCI in appropriately categorising and naming appropriate 3D gestures so that suitable simulation driving libraries can be formulated. As we discuss in this paper, it is not necessarily feasible or indeed desirable to solely use gestures and a hybrid approach using some mix of gestural and speech/sounds [42] may be more natural for an image sequence navigator.

Our article is structured as follows: In Section 2 we describe the client-server architecture of our software combining interpretation of Kinect gestures or touch screen interactions. We present a set of photos explaining the set of hand gestures and multi finger clicks that e developed to express image sequence navigation in Section 3. In Section 4 we discus s some of the implications for this sort of device agnostic architecture and offer some conclusions and areas for further investigation in Section 5.

2 Method

Rather than modifying existing simulations to support gesture-based input, a plug-in application was developed which would interpret gesture information sent over the network and convert this to simulated key-presses on the host operating system. Java was chosen as the language for the server for platform independent testing. To interface with the server, separate software was written for

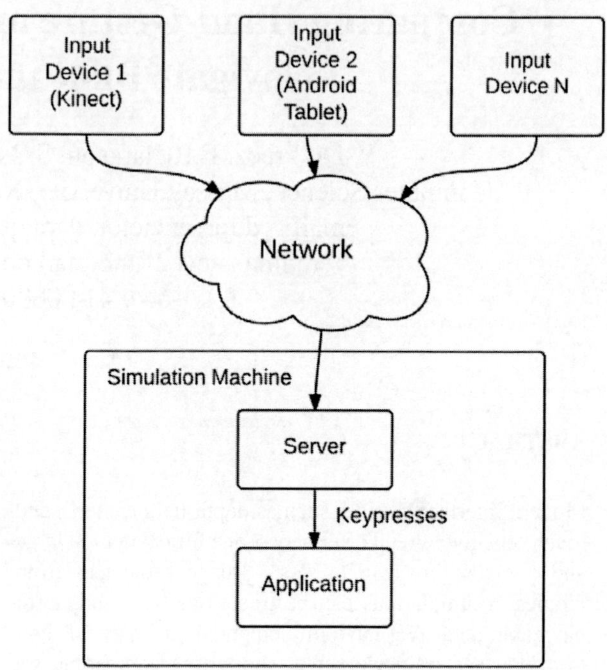

Figure 2: Architecture

each input device to decode gesture input. This recognition software can be on the input device itself (In the case of an Android tablet), on the host machine (in the case of the Kinect), or anywhere on the reachable network, provided it has fast access to the raw data provided by the input device. When gestures are recognised, a short string describing the detected gesture is sent over the network to the server application. These loosely coupled systems communicating over a network allows existing simulation software to quickly and easily make use of gesture input, often without any modification to the source code.

While this approach is flexible and easy to both implement and use, it is limited in that it can only offer as much control as the target program provides with hot-keys. This means that gestures such as rotation must be done iteratively; simulations will not be able to respond in real-time to the rotational degree of the gesture without modifications to the target simulation.

2.1 Input Device - Android

The Android API has large support for gestures, it being the main way to interact with most Android devices, and was very easy to implement. Gesture listeners, which cater for most generic gesture inputs, have been a part of the API since its creation. There is still some modification needed in order to recreate more specific gestures, such as fling left and fling right, but these were easy to build on top of the provided interface methods which cover a lot of the more common gestures.

Figure 3: Gesture to Key-press server, ready to turn gestures from the network into key-presses on the host machine.

Swipe Left Wait for a touch event to be placed and record the position. If the finger is raised in a different position on the screen with a lesser x dimension than the down even was recorded having then a swipe left has occurred.

Swipe Right Wait for a touch event to be placed and record the position. If the finger is raised in a different position on the screen with a greater x dimension than the down even was recorded having then a swipe right has occurred.

Pinch When 2 fingers are placed on the screen their positions and the distance between them is recorded. When the fingers are lifted off of the screen take the positions of each and find their distance apart from each other. If the second recorded distance is less than the first it is a pinch gesture

Spread When 2 fingers are placed on the screen their positions and the distance between them is recorded. When the fingers are lifted off of the screen take the positions of each and find their distance apart from each other. If the second recorded distance is greater than the first it is a spread gesture

Touch If a touch down event is recorded followed very quickly by an off touch event with very similar positions then a touch gesture has occurred.

Long Touch If a touch down event is recorded followed by an off touch event after 2 seconds and these two events have similar recorded positions then a long touch gesture has occurred.

2.2 Input Device - Kinect

The Kinect is made for tracking general body movements rather than fine manipulators. This restricts the variety of gestures the device is capable of accurately reporting. It is important to keep this in mind when designing gestures to be recognised by this device, using broad and deliberate motions to account for the lack of accuracy. We used the skeletal tracking to invoke these gestures using joints that represent major points in the skeleton body. This allowed us to track regions in the recognition with some positioning using x and y coordinates.

We achieved a gesture vocabulary that does not detect unwanted gestures. This makes it difficult to implement gestures that are consistent and reliable. We therefore implemented a rule-set that subtlety detects the required gesture. Figure 5 show how the implemented zoom-in gesture, similar to Android's pinch-to-zoom gesture is performed by bringing both hands above the neck and spreading them apart at a greater distance than the users shoulder width. Once the gesture has been performed the software idles until a new gesture is recognised.

3 Experimental Simulation Results

The system was tested on three applications, with two separate input devices. The server was run on a Mac host machine, and loaded with configurations of hot-keys for VLC media player, Xee image viewer, and Animaux, an agent based simulator running the Ising model. Figure 6 displays the gestures used and how they were mapped to

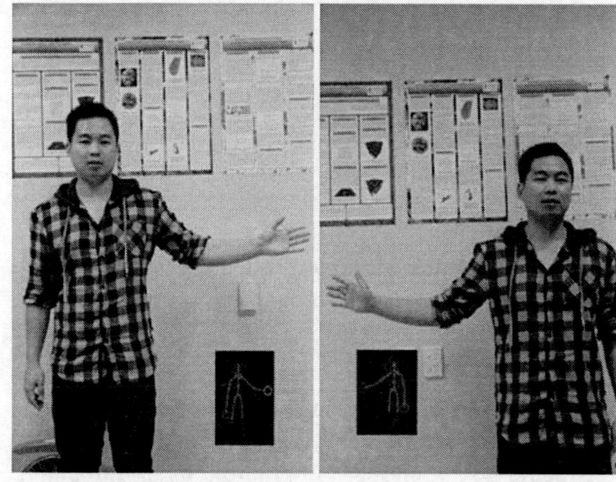

Figure 4 Kinect implemented gesture, showing the swipe of the motion gesture with the left and right hands on a video or image application.

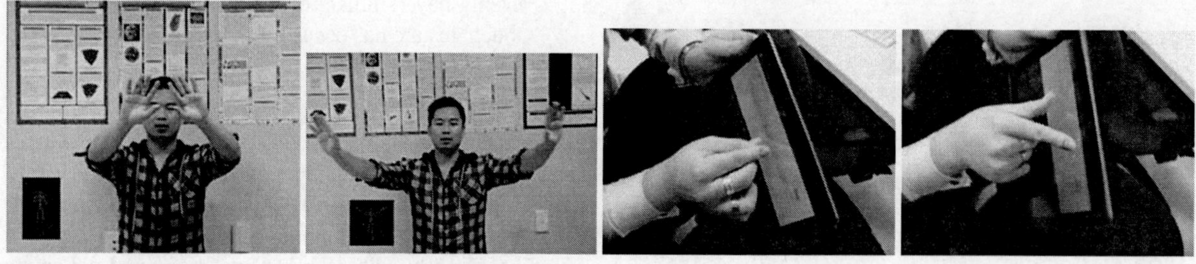

Figure 5 Performing the 'zoom in' gesture with the Kinect alongside its homomorphic equivalent on the Android tablet.

Kinect Gesture	Android Gesture	VLC	Xee	Ising Model
Swipe Left		Medium Forwards Jump	Next Image	Increase Critical Coupling
Swipe Right		Medium Backwards Jump	Previous Image	Decrease Critical Coupling
Pinch		-	Zoom Out	-
Spread		-	Zoom In	-
Hand Raise	Tap	Pause/Play	-	Next Iteration
Long Hand Raise	Long Tap	Stop	-	Run Simulation

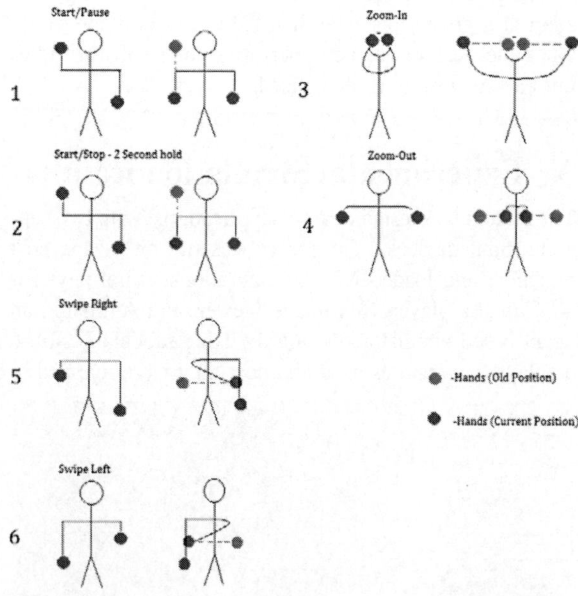

Figure 7: Diagrams illustrating all the gestures implemented in to Kinect gesture recognition.

different applications.

All combinations of device and application follow a similar format. A typical example with Xee and the Android tablet could go as follows: An Android tablet running a custom App for gesture recognition and network communication connects to the server. A 'fling left' gesture, when made on the Android tablet, would send a string describing the gesture just made to the server. The server, having previously been configured with Xee's keyboard shortcut for 'next image', uses Java's `Robot` class to send these key-presses to the active window. Xee will then change to display the next image.

3.1 Simulations Software

The system exhibited positive results when tested with advanced agent-based simulation software running the Ising model, making it appropriate for displaying the model to an audience or for allowing observers to interact with the model in an intuitive way. The existing software interface had a number of problems. It was crowded with intimidating elements, and the key combinations were model specific and occasionally esoteric. In comparison, the gesture overlay remained simple to operate provided it was configured correctly, completely bypassing the traditional methods of control. Configurations specific for particular models could be loaded and mapped to familiar gestures that reflect the action taken on the model.

A users existing knowledge can be transferred from even non-scientific applications. Knowing that performing a 'hand raise' gesture on the Kinect triggered a pause/play command in a media player can be directly applied to the agent-based simulation model, with the implication that the same gesture in the agent-based simulator would result in some kind of temporal manipulation (a 'next iteration' command for the Ising model.)

It was even possible to define a gesture to switch configurations on the gesture server, making it easier still to interact with complex models. Although introducing modes into an already complex system would result in a poor user experience, [43] it makes sense to switch configuration to match the model displayed in the simulation software if it changes. This allows users to perform the same familiar set of gestures and have it map to the control configuration suited for that model.

Hiding the interface and providing a standard set of interaction gestures means that non-scientists can interact with and manipulate models without having to have a deep understanding of the parameters that modify their behavior. This encourages exploration and investigation into what would otherwise be an intimidating concept to someone unfamiliar with complex systems.

3.2 Input Devices

While the two input devices tested are able to share many concepts such as the same motion to execute gestures (Further discussed in section 4.1), they also differ significantly in other areas. It is quite simple for an Android device to detect the start and end of a gesture, as these events correlate with the introduction and removal of fingers from the touch-screen. The Kinect is harder to work with in this regard, as the points of interest for gestures are almost always visible. The requirement for a voice command to initiate a gesture was briefly considered, but this was ultimately rejected in favour of comparing the location of interest points in relation to others. For example, a 'swipe left' gesture would only start when the left hand was below the waist, and the right hand between the waist and shoulders, and further away from the body than the right shoulder. This means transition from one device to the other is a more natural process, as there are no additional steps required; If the user is relaxed and acting in a sensible manner, a gesture on one device occupies the same logical space as on another. Gestures become more device-agnostic and universal, which means less to remember for the user.

An interesting observation is that both devices tested have some kind of processing capability. The Kinect outputs skeletal data which requires only minimal processing to convert into a useful gesture, and Android devices are completely capable of doing all gesture processing themselves and simply passing along a message indicating a gesture has been detected to the server. This may not always be the case, for example if the host machine is engaged in processing gestures from a web-cam. However, when it is the case, this lightens the load on the host machine, meaning its CPU resources are free to run more intensive simulation software. This could be important in interfacing with real-time simulations.

4 Discussion

Gestural computer interfacing is still in a relatively early stage of development and there is great scope for identifying and naming standard gestures for more widespread use in applications. Some of the touch and gestural notions like "pinch to zoom" have now become widely accepted and understood. Other named intuitive gestures will likely emerge from ongoing work in this area.

4.1 Homomorphic Gestures

Some gestures have a very clear method of execution across various devices. A 'pinch' gesture, for example, can be intuitively executed on the Kinect by bringing both hands together. The same gesture can be executed on Android by pinching the fingers together on the touch surface. These gestures can be considered homomorphic. Homomorphism is a desirable trait because such gestures facilitate information transfer - Skills learned on one platform become obvious and intuitive on another. The system architecture supports this paradigm by easily linking these gestures to the same action on the host machine, easily bringing together the motion with the desired intent.

4.2 Representing Continuous Data

Some gestures are well suited for delivering continuous output - That is, a continuously changing stream of data, which could be interpreted from the height of a hand, or the distance between fingers, for example. This is desirable because the rich data it provides would be suitable for modifying parameters of simulations in real time. However, there are some difficulties in transparently conveying the information to a simulation application. The implemented hot-key-based approach is only really suitable for discrete information packets, and a continuous stream would have to be represented as a plethora of key-presses. Something like a constantly changing floating point value is difficult to represent at all with this system.

In order for a program to receive continuous information in an input device agnostic manner, the program could listen for information on a stream input such as the `stdin` file descriptor, which could be provided either by a server listening for streams of gesture data over the network, or being piped in from a program which talks directly with an input device, bypassing the network entirely.

A potential problem with continuous data gestures is the requirement for some kind of termination of the gesture. For example, an intuitive end of a rotation gesture using a touch device is to simply remove ones hand form the touch surface. This stops the continuous stream of data, and the final value of any variable bound to that data can be set as the last value received. However, for the Kinect, the situation is slightly less obvious - There is no clear way to abruptly end a gesture such as hand elevation. Lowering ones hand out of the active gesture area is impossible without unwanted modification of gesture data. To remedy this, a further signal must be given to the device without modification of the interest point the Kinect is monitoring. This could be done with a voice command, or the movement of another, non-tracked interest point. However, this introduces the problem that performing this gesture is quite different between devices, which could make the process less intuitive.

5 Conclusions

We implemented gestures on the Kinect based of conventional touch-device gestures, we saw how these gestures relate and if there are some commonalities. We have shown that the Kinect could be used in the same manner as you would a touch-device, using only hand based gestures. The software developed shows that this could replace conventional key-bindings and change the way humans interact with computers. Hardware such as the Kinect shows that this could easily be achieved.

This will allow users to interact with computer applications as they would a touch-device. However the technology has some limitations, such as no finger recognition which restricts the amount of gestures that can be implemented. These gestures work very well with all the applications as a navigation tool for streams of data in picture and video software. The Kinect works well for the implemented gestures and shown very accurate and reliable data however only a small number of gestures could be implemented due to restrictions within the device.

Considering there is no set gesture vocabulary describing how humans should interact with these applications, we believe the gestures implemented show how ease of use is similar to accustomed finger gestures. Since these finger gestures such pinch to zoom are conventional for all touch devices these gestures we implemented should have the same effect with HCI.

We believe these gestures will become more generalised for humans to interact with a more similar technology. This will likely be available in standard user applications. We have shown that these uses could support video, imaging and simulation applications as a manipulation tool. The implemented gesture methods mechanics that could be much deeper refined, allowing scope to investigate a higher hierarchy of gestures using different devices and more complex gestures.

New technology such as the Leap Motion and Kinect 2.0 could allow whole new spectrum of gestures for human computer interaction. Increased precision and performance in finger recognition should allow these gestures used in touch devices to be more generalised.

References

[1] Dix, A., Finlay, J., Abowd, G., Beale, R.: Human-Computer Interaction. Prentice Hall (1993)

[2] Scogings, C.J.: The Integration of Task and Dialogue Modelling in the Early Stages of User Interface Design. PhD thesis, Massey University (2003)

[3] Diaper, D., Stanton, N., eds.: The Handbook of Task Analysis for Human-Computer Interaction. IEA (2004)

[4] Scogings, C., Philips, C.: Linking Task and Dialogue Modeling: Toward an Integrated Software Engineering Method. In: The Handbook of Task Analysis for Human-Computer Interaction. IEA (2004) 551–568

[5] Coulter, R.: Tablet computing is here to stay, and will force changes in laptops and phones. Mansueto Ventures (2011)

[6] McEwan, T.: Being kinected. ITNow **53** (2011) 6–7

[7] Nacke, L.E., Kalyn, M., Lough, C., Mandryk, R.L.: Biofeedback game design: Using direct and indirect physiological control to enhance game interaction. In: Proc. Computer Human Interaction (CHI 2011), Vancouver, BC, Canada (2011) 103–112

[8] Staiano, A.E., Calvert, S.L.: The promise of exergames as tools to measure physical health. Entertainment Computing **2** (2011) 17–21

[9] Turner, J., Browning, D.: Workshop on hci and game interfaces: A long romance. In: Proc. OZCHI 2010 : Design, Interaction, Participation, Brisbane, Queensland, Australia, Queensland University of Technology (2010)

[10] Boulos, M.N.K., Blanchard, B.J., Walker, C., Montero, J., Tripathy, A., Gutierrez-Osuna, R.: Web gis in practice x: a microsoft kinect natural user interface for google earth navigation. Int. J. Health Geograpics **10** (2011) 45

[11] Chang, Y.J., Chen, S.F., Huang, J.D.: A kinect-based system for physical rehabilitation: A pilot study for young adults with motor disabilities. Research in Developmental Disabilities **32** (2011) 2566–2570

[12] Cameirao, M.S., Badia, S.B., Oller, E.D., Verschure, P.F.M.J.: Virtual reality based rehabilitation and game technology. J. NeuroEngineering and Rehabilitation **7** (2010) 48

[13] Zollner, M., Huber, S., Jetter, H.C., Reiterer, H.: Navi - a proof-of-concept of a mobile navigational aid for visually impaired based on the microsoft kinect. In: Proc. 13th IFIP TC 13 Int. Conf. on Human-Computer Interaction (INTERACT'11), Lisbon, Portugal (2011)

[14] DePriest, D., Barilovits, K.: Live: Xbox kinect virtul realities to learning games. In: Proc. 16th Annual Technology, Colleges and Community Online Conference (TCC'11). Number ISSN 1937-1659, University of Hawaii (2011) 48–54

[15] Martynov, I., Kamarainen, J.K., Lensu, L.: Projector calibration by inverse camera calibration. In: Scandinavian Conf. on Image Analysis (SCIA2011). Number 6688 in LNCS, Ystad Saltsjobad, Sweden, Springer (2011) 536–544

[16] Rambone, F.: Table tennis paddle detection library for microsoft kinect. Master's thesis, Universita della Svizzeira Italiana, Faculty of Informatics (2011)

[17] Tang, M.: Recognizing hand gestures with microsoft?s kinect. Technical report, Stanford University, Dept. Electrical Engineering (2011)

[18] Deshayes, R., Mens, T.: Statechart modelling of interactive gesture-based applications. In: Proc. First International Workshop on Combining Design and Engineering of Interactive Systems through Models and Tools (ComDeisMoto),, Lisbon, Portugal (2011) INTERACT 2011, 13th IFIP TC13 Conf. on HCI.

[19] Doliotis, P., Stefan, A., McMurrough, C., Eckhard, D., Athitsos, V.: Comparing gesture recognition accuracy using color and depth information. In: Proc. Conference on Pervasive Technologies Related to Assistive Environments (PETRA), Crete, Greece (2011)

[20] Schwaller, M., Lalanne, D., Khaled, O.A.: Pygmi?creation and evaluation of a portable gestural interface. In: Proc. 6th Nordic Conf. on Himan Computer Interaction (NordiCHI 2010), Reykjavik, Iceland (2010) 773–776

[21] Ulribe, A., Alves, S., Rosario, J.M., Fiho, H.F., Perez-Gutierrez, B.: Mobile robotic teleoperation using gesture-based human interfaces. In: Robotics Symposium, 2011 IEEE IX Latin American and IEEE Colombian Conference on Automatic Control and Industry Applications (LARC), Bogota, Volombia (2011) 1–6

[22] Kortum, P.: HCI Beyond the GUI - Design for Hapric, Speech, Olfactory and other Nontraditional Interfaces. Morgan Kaufmann (2008)

[23] Rautaray, S.S., Kumar, A., Agrawal, A.: Human computer interaction with hand gestures in virtual environment. In: Proc. First Indo-Japan Conf. on Perception and Machine Intelligence (PerMin 2012). Number 7143 in LNCS, Kolkata, India, Springer (2012) 106–113

[24] Capra, R., Golovchinsky, G., Kules, B., Russell, D., Smith, C.L., Tunkelang, D., White, R.W.: Hcir 2011: The fifth international workshop on human-computer interaction and information retrieval. ACM SIGIR Forum **45** (2011) 102–107

[25] Preez, V.D., Pearce, B., Hawick, K.A., McMullen, T.H.: Human-computer interaction on touch screen tablets for highly interactive computational simulations. In: Proc. International Conference on Human-Computer Interaction, Baltimore, USA., IASTED (2012) 258–265

[26] Castellucci, S.J., MacKenzie, I.S.: Gathering text entry metrics on android devices. In: Proc. Computer Human Interactions (CHI2011), Vancouver, BC, Canada (2011) 1507–1512

[27] Buchanan, N.: An examination of electronic tablet based menus for the restaurant industry. Master's thesis, University of Delaware (2011)

[28] Johnson, M.G.B., Hawick, K.A.: Teaching computational science and simulations using interactive depth-of-field technologies. In: Proc. Int. Conf on Frontiers in Education: Computer Science and Computer Engineering (FECS'12), Las Vegas, USA, CSREA (2012) 339–345 a.

[29] MacDonald, J.E., Foster, E.M., Divina, J.M., Donnelly, D.W.: Mobile Interactive Training: Tablets, Readers, and Phones? Oh, My! In: Proc. Interservice/Industry Training, Simulation and Education Conference (I/ITSEC 2011). Number 11038, Orlando, Florida, USA (2011) 1–9

[30] Preez, V.D., Pearce, B., Hawick, K.A., McMullen, T.H.: Software engineering a family of complex systems simulation model apps on android tablets. In: Proc. Int. Conf. on Software Engineering Research and Practice (SERP'12), Las Vegas, USA, SERP12-authors.pdf, CSREA (2012) 215–221

[31] Pearce, B.T., Hawick, K.A.: Interactive simulation and visualisation of falling sand pictures on tablet computers. In: Proc. 10th International Conference on Modeling, Simulation and Visualization Methods)MSV'13). Number CSTN-196, Las Vegas, USA, WorldComp (2013) MSV2341

[32] Ali, S.I., Jain, S., Lal, B., Sharma, N.: A framework for modeling and designing of intelligent and adaptive interfaces for human computer interaction. Int. J. Applied Information Systems **1** (2012) 20–25

[33] Krainin, M., Henry, P., Ren, X., Fox, D.: Manipulator and object tracking for in-hand 3d object modeling. Int. J. Robotics Research **Online** (2011) 1–17

[34] Steinicke, F., Benko, H., Daiber, F., Keefe, D., de la Riviere, J.B., eds.: Proc. Special Interest Group Touching the 3rd Dimension (T3D). CHI 2011, Vancouver, BC, Canada, ACM (2011) ISBN 978-1-4503-0268-5/11/05.

[35] Schouten, B.A.M., Tieben, R., Ven, A., Schouten, D.W.: Human Behavior Analysis in Ambient Gaming and Playful Interaction. In: Computer Anaylsis of Human Behavior. Springer (2011) 387–403

[36] Luber, M., Spinello, L., Arras, K.O.: Learning to detect and track people in rgbd data. In: Proc. Workshop on Advanced Reasoning with Depth Cameras, Robotics Science and Systems (RSS), University of Souther California (2011)

[37] Sung, J., Ponce, C., Selman, B., Saxena, A.: Human activity detection from rgbd images. In: Proc. AAAI Workshop on Plan, Activity and Intent Recognition (PAIR 2011), San Francisco, USA (2011) 47–55

[38] Xia, L., Chen, C.C., Aggarwal, J.K.: Human detection using depth information by kinect. In: Proc. 2011 IEEE Comp. Soc. Conf. on Computer Vision and Pattern Recognition Workshops (CVPRW), Colorado Springs, Colorado, USA (2011) 15–22

[39] Suma, E.A., Lange, B., Rizzo, A.S., Krum, D.M., Bola, M.: Faast: The flexible action and articulated skeleton toolkit. In: Proc. IEEE Virtual Reality, Singapore (2011) 247–248 ISBN 978-1-4577-0038-5/11.

[40] Kar, A.: Skeletal tracking using microsoft kinect. Methodology **1** (2010) 1–11

[41] Garstka, J., Peters, G.: View-dependent 3d projection using depth-image-based head tracking. In: Proc. 8th IEEE Int. Workshop on Projector-Camera Sytems, Colorado Springs, USA. (2011) 52–58

[42] Molenaar, G.: Sonic gesture. Master's thesis, University of Amsterdam (2010)

[43] Andre, A., Degani, A.: Do You Know What Mode You're In? An Analysis of Mode Error in Everyday Things. In: 2nd Conference on Automation Technology and Human Performance. (1996)

An Improved Parallel Eight Direction Prewitt Edge Detection Algorithm

Mohammed Mohamed[1], and Gita Alaghband[2]
[1]Computer Science and Engineering, University of Colorado Denver, Denver, Colorado, USA
[2]Computer Science and Engineering, University of Colorado Denver, Denver, Colorado, USA

Abstract - *Detection algorithms are at the center of the recognition process in computer vision and image processing. This paper presents our design and implementation of efficient sequential and parallel edge detection algorithms that are capable of producing high quality results while performing at a rapid speed. The parallel version, derived from our efficient sequential algorithm, is designed for the new shared memory MIMD multicore platforms. The improved median filter is capable of suppressing impulse noise and other noises more effectively than the original. A global thresholding method augments our design to dynamically find a suitable thresholding value. In order to measure the quality and execution time, we test images with different sizes along with the original Prewitt and Canny edge detection algorithm already in Matlab, to show the possibility of using our design within different applications. The paper will demonstrate the ability to process extremely large images useful for biomedical image processing.*

Keywords: Parallel image processing, multicore MIMD, Prewitt edge detection, smoothing

1 Introduction

Edge detection is one of the most usable operations within the computer vision and the image processing fields. Detection algorithms are central for image analysis and recognition applications [1, 2]. Edge detection essentially looks for pixels in an image where a sharp change in intensity is taking place [3]. Having an efficient recognition algorithm in terms of quality and execution time can expedite the move towards real-time recognition applications. Our long-term goal is to eventually have an optimized high quality parallel algorithm capable of detecting efficiently. While the best known industry standard algorithm is Canny, it is shown to have high computational complexity [4]. We use the well-known Prewitt edge detection algorithm for its simplicity and computational efficiency. However, Prewitt's drawback is its sensitivity to noise making it unsuitable for most common image processing applications [4, 5, 6, 7]. Prewitt as well as Sobel edge detection algorithms offer the capability to detect edges with certain orientations [4, 8]. Prewitt edge detection algorithm as defined by Granzales, Woods and Edds is a discrete differentiation operator with the goal to calculate the gradient of the image intensity function, where the convolution operation is done on each pixel in both horizontal and vertical directions (0 and 90 degrees) [5]. This gradient edge detection algorithm looks for maximum and minimum derivatives of the image [3]. In order to detect edges in both horizontal and vertical directions, the input image is masked with two matrices (windows) each of size 3 by 3 (Figures 1.a.).

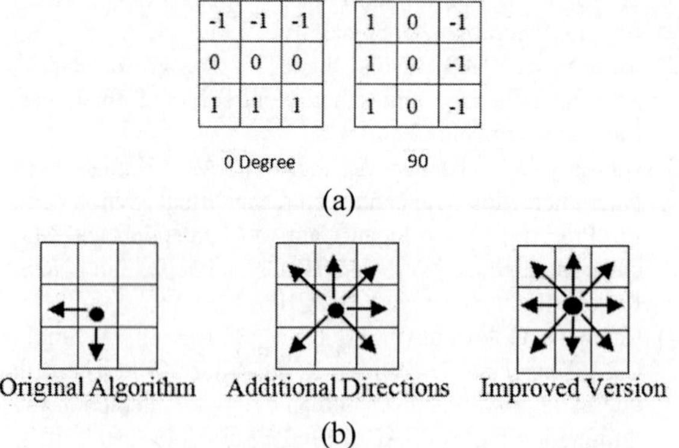

Figure 1: Bidirectional Prewitt edge detection algorithm vs. the improved version. (a) Windows used with original algorithm. (b) Directions of the detected edges.

Masking the input image with the windows in Figure 1(a), results in two intermediate templates (candidates). This means for each pixel there are at most two candidates to choose from. The strategy of election is to elect the pixel which has maximum intensity value (sharper changing) to represent that pixel within its final destination. However, limiting the algorithm to choose between only two candidates is not sufficient to produce accurate results. It is possible to use all possible eight directions as shown in Figure 1(b) and be able to detect edges from all eight candidates. An improved version of the original bidirectional algorithm that handles eight directions was proposed in 2008 by Ci and Chen [9]. The Pseudocode corresponding to the bidirectional Prewitt edge detection is represented in Figure 2. Adding more directions to the original algorithm improves the quality of the original Prewitt algorithm. Additional improvements such as incorporating thresholding and implicit smoothing techniques were suggested by Lei, Dewei, Xiaoyu, and Hui by 2011 [6].

A significant contribution of their work is the ability to use an implicit smoothing technique to enable the algorithm to work on noisy images. This was particularly important as the Prewitt edge detection algorithm is known to be sensitive to noise and therefore may not generate satisfactory results in the presence of noise. The implicit smoothing technique used in [6] calculates the gradient magnitude of the eight directions as the basis to find the final magnitude to reduce the effect of noise. Our experiments show that the gradient based implicit smoothing approach will not be very effective when the image is impacted with high noise percentage. In our work, we propose to use an explicit smoothing technique that can be applied to noisy images as a prefix step to the Prewitt edge detection algorithm [9]. Our results show an improvement in the quality and overall execution time even when we include the prefix smoothing step. In this paper we present an efficient parallel eight directions Prewitt edge detection augmented with explicit smoothing and iterative thresholding functionality capable of producing fast and accurate results.

The Pseudocode of the eight directions edge detection is very similar to the bidirectional presented in Figure 2 with additional 6 windows to convolve the image with a total of eight windows proposed in [6].

```
/* Where f(x,y) is the input image, k1(x,y)and  k2(x,y)are the two mask windows in
direction 0" and 90" respectively and  g(x,y) is the output image */
I[imgHeight, imgWidth]  := imRead(image);
                    /* imgHeight: image's height, imgWidth: image's width. */
k1[maskHeight,mWidth] := imRead(Mask);
                   /* maskHeight: mask's height, maskWidth: mask's width. */
k2[maskHeight,mWidth] := imRead(Mask);
                   /* maskHeight: mask's height, maskWidth: mask's width. */
h := (maskHeight-1)/2 ;
w := (maskWidth-1)/2 ;
for y := 0 until  imgHeight do
   for x := 0 until imgWidth do
     {  sum  = 0 ;  sum1 = 0 ;  sum2 = 0 ; /* initialization */
   for i := -h until h do
      for j := -w until w do
        { sum1 + = k1(j,i)*I(x-j,y-i) ; /*convolution in the first direct*/
          sum2 + = k2(j,i)*I(x-j,y-i); /* convolution in the second direct*/
           sum = max(sum1, sum2) } /* select the max intensity */
      g(x,y) = sum;   }                /* result image */
```

Figure 2: Original two directions Prewitt edge detection's Pseudocode.

Section 2 describes the design of the augmented parallel eight directions Prewitt algorithm. Section 3 covers the experimental results and analysis. Section 4 summarizes the paper and conclusions.

2 Augmented parallel eight direction Prewitt edge detection algorithm

The original bidirectional Prewitt algorithm is known for its good computational complexity but noise sensitivity; lack of an affective smoothing mechanism has mostly disqualified its usage. Analytical studies conducted in [7] indicate that Prewitt edge detection algorithm cannot be used along with practical images that are often corrupted with impulse noise as well as Gaussian and Poisson noises. Majority of images are often inflicted by varying degree of noise caused by transmission channels and camera sensors [7]. Furthermore, Prewitt algorithm does not incorporate a thresholding mechanism in order to produce binary images. Most object detection applications rely on background subtraction. The presence of only two values in the resulting binary image, one representing the object and the other representing the background, is desirable in object detection applications [10]. We have augmented our parallel algorithm with both smoothing and thresholding mechanisms. In this section we will first discuss our choices for smoothing and thresholding strategies and then present the description of complete parallel application.

2.1 Selecting an appropriate filter to use as prefix step to eight direction Prewitt

The stand-alone Prewitt algorithm does not incorporate any mechanisms to deal with noisy images. The Canny edge detection algorithm uses Gaussian filter or Blurring as a prefix smoothing mechanism [3, 5] to address the noise issue. Blurring can destroy some real edges during the process of noise suppression. Bilateral is known to be a better choice because it has less negative impact on real edges than Blurring. To select a suitable smoothing method, we conducted several experiments using Blurring, Median Blurring, Gaussian, Bilateral, Median filtering and an improved version of Median filter. Our improved Median filter, added as a prior step to localization in the eight direction Prewitt algorithm, shows the best results for suppressing impulse noises such as Salt and Pepper and at the same time is able to suppress other types of noises such as Gaussian and Poisson. Median filter is a nonlinear filter used to remove impulse noise with the least negative impact on the real edges [5, 11, 12]. This filter starts arranging all the pixels within the range of the specified window in ascending order to choose the median value. This approach helps keep some real values unchanged as opposed to the blurring technique that takes the average of all pixels within that neighborhood. The main idea behind our improved Median filter is to allow the window size be variable and not fixed as in the standard Median for the sake of not only better noise suppression capability but also operations reduction [12]. Larger window sizes can be used effectively in processing images with higher noise percentage using the same mechanism of Median filter. In the current version, we provide the users full control to judge the intensity of the noise in order to determine the desired window size. We recommend to start with a window of size 3x3, considered to be the standard case (level 1). If the resulting output reflects detection of false edges, users can increase the size of the window to 5x5(level 2), 7x7(level 3), 9x9(level 4), or double 9x9 (level 5) respectively. Double 9x9 stands for re-smoothing the results of level 4 with 9x9 window size. Our results demonstrate clear detection of edges in the presence of noise when smoothing is enabled. The experimental results are presented in the results section, Table 1 and Figure 6.

2.2 Dynamic Iterative Thresholding

Thresholding is desirable in many applications; we have added this functionality to the algorithm to be used when needed. There are many thresholding techniques available ranging from visual judgment using trial and error to reliance on global or local methods [5, 13, 14]. In this work we have selected to add the basic global thresholding method due to its computational simplicity, acceptable quality and applicability to a variety of applications [5]. The technique works iteratively to find the thresholding value as described in Figure 3.

Step 1: Start with initial guess for the thresholding value T.
/* For faster convergence, choose initial T to be the average of all intensities of the assigned work [5] */
Step 2: For each pixel, marked as group 1 (G_1) or group 2 (G_2):
 a. if img[i,j] > T, img[i,j] ε G_1
 b. else img[i,j] ε G_2
Step 3: For each group, find the average of intensities Av_1 and Av_2 respectively.
Step 4: Find the new threshold value: $T_{new} = (Av_1 + Av_2)/2$.
Step 5: Stop if $|T_{new} - T| \leq$ tolerant value; Otherwise $T = T_{new}$ and repeat the process from step 2.

Figure 3: The procedure of the Basic Global Thresholding.

2.3 Parallel application

Adding a smoothing mechanism with variable window sizes, six additional directions to the localization step and a global thresholding mechanism adds computational complexity to the original bidirectional Prewitt algorithm. These additional computations affect the overall performance. A parallel version of the proposed algorithm for the new shared memory MIMD multicore platforms is designed and implemented in order to speed up the computation. The parallel algorithm is designed and implemented using C/C++ as a base language and two open source libraries OpenMP and the open computer vision library (OpenCV) to overcome complexities added to the original algorithm. OpenCV library supports hundreds of optimized image processing algorithms mainly designed for real time applications contributing to the field of computer vision specifically [13, 15]. These libraries lend themselves well to parallel processing [13, 16]. One of the main challenges working on shared memory multiprocessors is the work distribution [1, 17]. Work, for good distribution, can be divided into rows, columns or blocks. Using appropriate mechanisms for data partitioning not only provides an independent chunk of data that can be processed concurrently but also will add flexibility in tuning the algorithm to run more efficiently on different architectural platforms to enhance data locality that in turn reduces the number of time-consuming cache misses. Work distribution starts by allowing each of the processors to copy its assigned private data to its local memory. To gain efficiency, it is desired to decrease the number of times needed to copy data from slower shared memory to local memory at each computational unit. The algorithm starts dividing the image into a number of equal sized tiles (sub-images). Parallel processes will work independently on different sub-images using a self-scheduling technique for work distribution. Each processor applies smoothing, localization, and iterative thresholding before writing the processed data to its final location as shown in Figure 4.

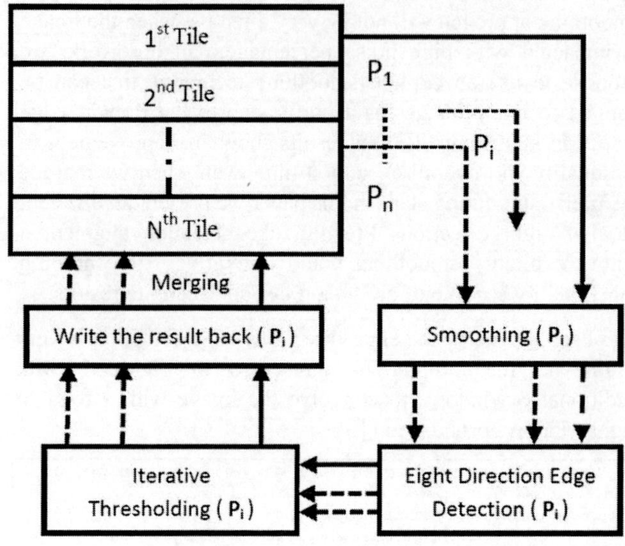

Figure 4: Processing life cycle.

As seen in Figure 4, the parallelism is applied at the highest possible level in which all work, in between the time of loading the main image up until merging sub-images, is done in parallel. We are presenting only partitioning into rows only. Yet our implementation supports all three partitioning methods (rows, columns, and blocks). The original input image is defined as an object (Region Of Interest, ROI) in the OpenCV library resulting in the need for some synchronization when the final result is written back to this object. This is a requirement enforced by OpenCV to guarantee data integrity, therefore, each processor will write the data to its original region of interest atomically. It is best to choose self-scheduling instead of pre-scheduling for good work balance. This will prevent the problem of having some processors idle while the others have excess work due to varying amount work required in each region of the image. It is important to note that sub-images are completely treated individually and are processed within the iterative thresholding mechanism separately. This strategy, according to our experiments, can result in better detection where more real edges are detected. Self-scheduling will overcome the difference in time required by applying the iterative thresholding mechanism on the assigned data as the number of computations may vary depending on the data itself.

Procedure of the proposed algorithm:

1) **Initialization**
   a) Input Image
   b) User specifies the following options:
      i) Partitioning Method: rows, columns, or blocks (due to the space constrain, we will demonstrate row partitioning only)
      ii) Number of desired sub images, [numOfSubImage];
      iii) Number of processes, [numOfProcl];
      iv) Enabled or disabled: Smoothing technique, Thresholding. [toSmooth],[toThreshold];
      v) Noise level of the image (visual guess): 1 very low – 5 very high. [levelOfNoise];
2) **Partitioning data**
   a) Divide into the sub work as specified by the user's chosen mechanism of partitioning.
   b) Divide the work among the assigned processors. Processes will self-schedule to obtain the next available work
3) **On each of the sub works (if any) do the following:**
   a) De-noising
      i) If smoothing is enabled :
         (1) Apply improved median filter with specific window size on the image.
         (2) The size of the window depends on the visual guess specified by the user at 1.b.v. (Noise Level)
   b) Localization
      Eight-direction Prewitt (as described in Section 1)
   c) Thresholding
      i) If thresholding is enabled then apply the basic iterative global thresholding (as described in Section 2.2, Figure 3)
   d) Merging data
      i) Merge the processed sub work to its final destination.
   e) Return processed image

Pseudocode of partitioning into rows (our implementation supports rows, columns and blocks partitioning mechanisms). The Pseudocode conventions are taken from [17]:

```
procedure parmain(initialization as specified in step 1)
   Img [imgHeight,imgWidth] := imRead[imgName];   /* Loading the image */
   workLoad := imgHeight/numOfSubImage;
   shared img, destImage, numOfSubImage, levelOfNoise, numOfProc, toThreshold,toSmooth, workLoad, imgWidth, imgHeight;
   private i, subImg,x,y;
   Self-Scheduled forall i := 0 until numOfSubImage  /* Dynamic Scheduling of parallel processes */
   begin   /* partitioning data into sub-images each having the same imgWidth but with specific height*/
     x := 0;
     y := i * workLoad;           /* We are giving an example of partitioning into rows */
     subImage := Rectangle( Img, Rect(x, y, imgWidth, imgHeight/numOfSubImage)); /* copy specified rect to subImage */
     if (toSmooth) then           /* De-noising: if smoothing is enabled */
        subImage := Smoothing (subImage,LevelOfNoise);
     end        /* Localization: Eighth direction Prewitt */
     subImage := eightDirections (subImage);
     if (Thresholding) then      /* Thresholding:  if thresholding is enabled */
        subImage := iterativeThresholding (subImage);
     end
     critical work;        /* Merging Data: /* Writing Data to its final destination*/
        mergeSubImage (destImage, subImage, Rect (x, y, imgWidth, imgHeight /numOfSubImage ));
     end critical;
        Release(subImage);
   end
   Return (destImage);       /* Return Processed image*/
End Procedure
```

Figure 5: Pseudocode of the proposed algorithm.

3 Experimental results and analysis

To compare the quality of the proposed Improved Median filter that uses variable-sized windows with the standard Median that uses a fixed window of size 3x3, we use the well-known Peak Signal-to-Noise Ratio PSNR (dB) [2]. The results are shown in Table 1 in which the test image (Lena see, Figure 6) is corrupted with varying degrees of impulse noise. As shown in Table 1, the improved Median filter generates significantly higher quality output than the standard in every case. The comparison of various window sizes and various noise levels and types can be seen from the first (input image indicating noise type and level) and forth (Median filter and the corresponding window size) columns of Figure 6. Each row of the figure represents application of different algorithms to the input image in column 1. To visually demonstrate the quality of the resulting image, using PSNR measurement, the output of the Canny (industry standard) is shown in Figure 6.

"Standard Canny" refers to the default run with Matlab 7.10.0 (R2010a) without any tuning (Column 2) while "best Canny" is the best results (Column 3) that can be produced by tuning the supported parameters.

From Figure 6 in the following page, we can see the capability of the proposed algorithm to suppress Salt & Pepper noise even when the image is impacted with very high noise percentage. Furthermore, the algorithm is able to suppress different types of noise with less impact on the real edges than the bidirectional Prewitt implemented with Matlab.

Table 1: Comparison of quality between standard Median filter and our proposed one using PSNR applied on Lena impacted with different percentage of impulse noise

Image: Lena 512 x 512, (see Figure 6 for image)				
Impulse Noise Percentage	Standard Median filter PSNR(dB)	Improved Median filter		
		PSNR (dB)	Window size	Noise level
10	33.5798	33.5798	3x3	level 1
20	29.5107	30.2259	5x5	level 2
30	24.1262	29.3523	5x5	level 2
40	19.1859	27.8228	5x5	level 2
50	15.3806	26.646	7x7	level 3
60	12.4786	25.2654	9x9	level 4
70	10.098	23.2942	Double 9x9	level 5

In order to provide a fair comparison of the efficiency of our algorithms and implementation choices, we compare the sequential execution times of our proposed method with the existing implementations of bidirectional Prewitt and Canny algorithms with Matlab that are already in-use in Table 2. Table 2 shows the results of all tests-cases run sequentially on the same platform. As mentioned in the previous section, our algorithms are implemented using C/C++ as the base language with OpenCV.

Table 2: Sequential run of the presented algorithm vs. the bidirectional Prewitt and Canny edge detections implemented within Matlab

Image Details		Intel I Core ™ i7-3720QM CPU @ 2.60 GHz, 16 GB RAM, 64-bit Windows 7, L1 D :4 x 32 Kbytes 8-way set associative, L1 I :4 x 32 Kbytes, 8-way set associative L2 : 4 x 256 Kbytes 8-way set, associative, L3 : 6 Mbytes 12-way set associative			
Image	Size	Proposed 8 Direction Prewitt by itself	Proposed: Smoothing (level1) & 8 Direction Prewitt & Iterative Thresholding	Matlab Bidirectional Prewitt	Matlab Canny Edge detection
15315 x 11624	169 MB	2.456 sec	3.51 sec	8.719067 sec	55.23517 sec
2250 x 2250	14.4 MB	0.063 sec	0.171 sec	0.8991 sec	2.411595 sec
1536 x 2048	5.91 MB	0.047 sec	0.109 sec	0.263233 sec	1.494402 sec
512 x 512	768 KB	0.0145 sec	0.016 sec	0.137101 sec	0.334044 sec
256 x 256	192 KB	0.001 sec	0.0025 sec	0.026171 sec	0.2432 sec

As shown in Table 2, our sequential implementation outperforms bidirectional Prewitt and Canny edge detections. It is important to note that in the table, execution times reported for our implementation include smoothing (with different levels), localization and the iterative thresholding technique. From observing Table 2 (running on Intel i7) processing an image of dimension 512 x 512 takes 16 ms resulting in 62.5 fps (Frames per Second) with level 1 smoothing [43 ms (23.2 fps) when it is smoothed with level 5]. Obviously higher noise percentage requires more computations for good suppression. However, we are able to accelerate the previous runs using 4 processors, running on the same platform, to 6 ms at 166 fps for level 1 smoothing [and 11 ms at 90.9 fps for level 5]. Having shown how efficient the algorithm works on images of small dimensions, we present the execution times of our parallel implementation working on larger images using two different multiple core platforms as its shows in Table 3 and Table 4 respectively. Due to space constraints a subset of the general cases are presented. The two multicore platforms used for our experiments are a 12-core AMD with Opteron module (Table 3) and a 64-core AMD with Bulldozer module (Table 4). The organizations of the two processors are quite different. The Opteron consists of two chips each with 6 cores each. Each Opteron core has its own private first level instruction and data caches of 64 KB size each and a private unified L2 cache of 512 KB. Every 6 core/chip share 6 MB of L3 cache. On the other hand, the 64-core AMD with Bulldozer consists of eight Bulldozer modules on one chip (16 cores). A Bulldozer module consists of two integer execution cores that share a first level instruction cache of 64 KB and a floating point unit. Each core has a private first level data cache of 16 KB. The two cores within one Bulldozer module share a unified L2 cache (2 MB). Every four modules share 16 MB of L3 cache.

The L1 data cache in Opteron is four times larger than the Bulldozer's L1 data cache. The idea of partitioning the image into a number of equal sized tiles helps enhance the locality of data. The main difference between Opteron and Bulldozer is that more resources are shared within the Bulldozer module. For instance, when we process relatively large images (29649 x 22008) using 32 cores, running on the Bulldozer, the best results are achieved when the parallel task is distributed such that each task is executed on every other core. This means the 32 Bulldozer modules, one active core per module, will be working compared to the case in which only 16 Bulldozer modules, two active cores per unit, are used. Using more Bulldozer units not only provides larger L3 cache, a total of total 128 MB on the four chips, but also allows each core to use the entire shared L2 cache as a dedicated second level cache and have exclusive use of the single floating point unit that is shared by the two integer cores. Although the communication is costly especially if the cores do not have shared cache space, i.e., the cost of one core accessing cache memory located on different chips, having a better data locality (when larger caches are used) enhances the overall performance of the application. This statement will not apply to all applications, but in our design we aimed to divide the input image to independent tiles in order to decrease the amount of communication required at the same time increases the locality of data gained from using larger cache space.

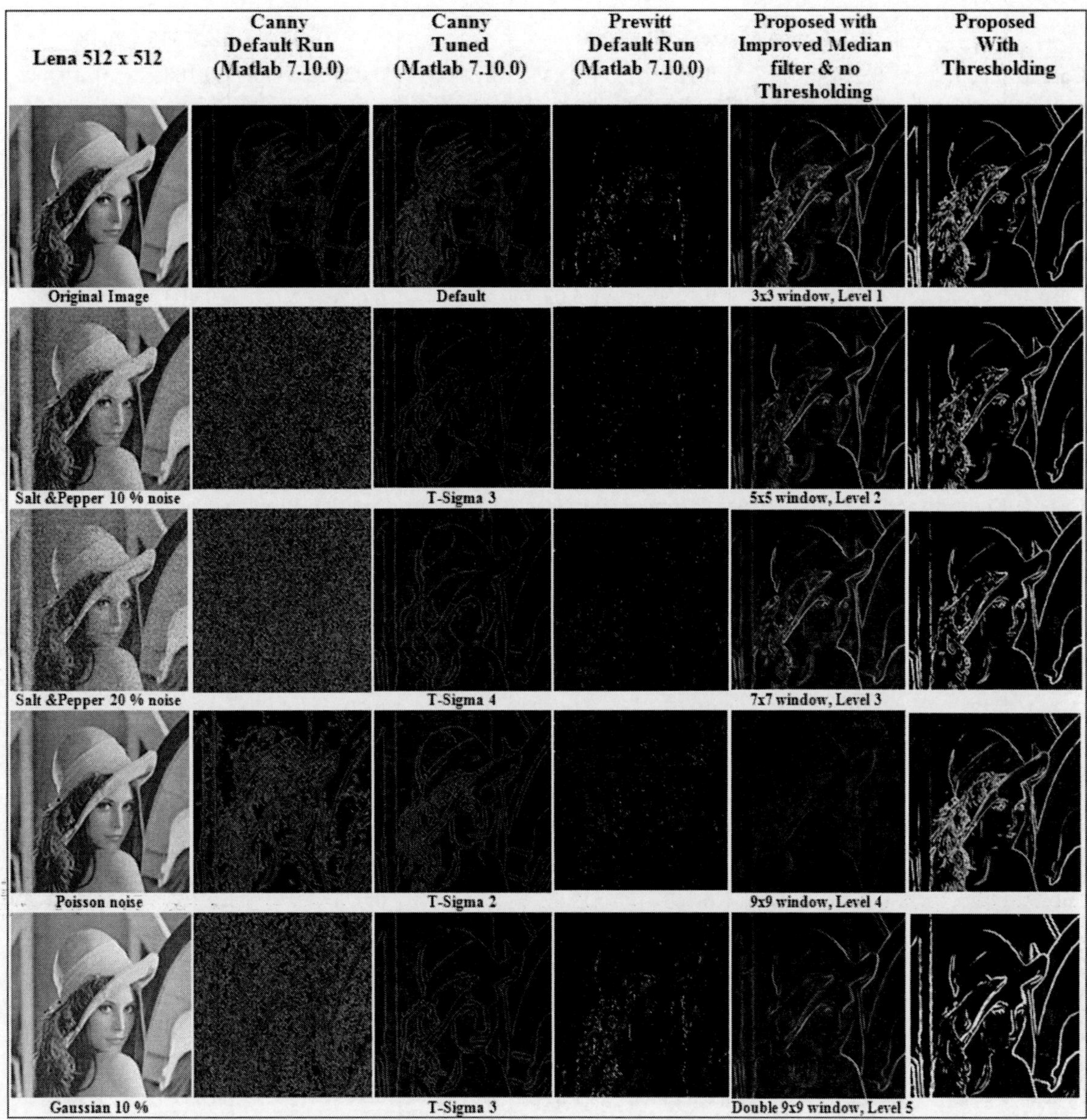

Figure 6: Output of Canny (industry standard) and bidirectional Prewitt vs. our proposed work

Table 3: Execution time for the proposed algorithm running on 12-core compute nodes

Case 1: Eight direction Prewitt, Case 2: Smoothing (level 1) & Eight direction Prewitt, Case 3: Smoothing (level 1) & Eight direction Prewitt & thresholding, Case 4: Smoothing (level 5) & Eight direction Prewitt & thresholding								
		Image of size 29649 x 22008				**Image of size 15315 x 11624**		
	N cores	**Best execution time T_N (sec)**	**Sequential T_1 (sec)**	**Speed up**	**Number of cores**	**Best execution time T_N (sec)**	**Sequential T_1 (sec)**	**Speed up**
Case 1	12	2.890	22.850	7.91	12	0.803	6.021	7.50
Case 2	12	3.145	23.798	7.57	12	0.843	6.534	7.75
Case 3	12	4.521	33.532	7.42	12	1.381	8.854	6.41
Case 4	12	13.015	143.52	11.03	12	3.724	39.45	10.59

		Image of size 2250 x 2250				Image of size 1536 x 2048		
Case 1	12	0.028	0.180	6.43	8	0.024	0.108	4.50
Case 2	12	0.032	0.189	5.91	8	0.026	0.114	4.38
Case 3	12	0.067	0.491	7.33	12	0.051	0.305	5.98
Case 4	12	0.147	1.589	10.81	12	0.130	1.016	7.82
		Image of size 2048 x 2048				**Image of size 2704 x 4064**		
Case 1	8	0.031	0.147	4.74	8	0.069	0.374	5.42
Case 2	8	0.031	0.156	5.03	8	0.075	0.403	5.39
Case 3	12	0.051	0.372	7.29	12	0.160	1.297	8.11
Case 4	12	0.132	1.201	9.10	12	0.348	3.959	11.38
12-core compute node (shared memory multi-processor, processor @ 2.2 Ghz of AMD (Opteron) type, 6x64 KB L1 instruction cache per processor, 6x64 KB L1 data cache per processor, 6x512 KB L2 per processor, 6MB L3 per processor, 24 GB RAM, 64-bit Linux version 2.6.18.								

Table 4: Execution time for the proposed algorithm running on 64-core compute nodes

Case 1: Eight direction Prewitt, Case 2: Smoothing (level 1) & Eight direction Prewitt, Case 3: Smoothing (level 1) & Eight direction Prewitt & thresholding, Case 4: Smoothing (level 5) & Eight direction Prewitt & thresholding								
		Image of size 29649 x 22008				**Image of size 15315 x 11624**		
	N cores	**Best execution time T_N (sec)**	**Sequential T_1 (sec)**	**Speed up**	**Number of cores**	**Best execution time T_N (sec)**	**Sequential T_1 (sec)**	**Speed up**
Case 1	28	1.35	19.07	14.13	28	0.39	5.22	13.38
Case 2	32	1.35	19.89	14.73	24	0.42	5.46	13.00
Case 3	32	1.86	28.14	15.13	32	0.65	7.64	11.75
Case 4	44	4.35	115.56	26.57	40	1.32	31.41	23.80
		Image of size 2250 x 2250				**Image of size 1536 x 2048**		
Case 1	12	0.027	0.155	5.74	12	0.019	0.096	5.05
Case 2	12	0.029	0.163	5.62	12	0.023	0.102	4.43
Case 3	16	0.051	0.460	9.02	16	0.040	0.284	7.10
Case 4	24	0.094	1.461	15.54	24	0.073	0.979	13.41
		Image of size 2048 x 2048				**Image of size 2704 x 4064**		
Case 1	12	0.023	0.126	5.48	16	0.040	0.324	8.10
Case 2	12	0.025	0.139	5.56	16	0.043	0.342	7.95
Case 3	12	0.043	0.336	7.81	24	0.117	1.135	9.70
Case 4	24	0.092	1.067	11.60	32	0.184	3.364	18.28
64-core compute node (shared memory multi-processor, processor @ 2.2 Ghz of AMD (Bulldozer) type, 1x64 KB L1 instruction cache per module which contains two execution cores, 2x16 KB L1 data cache per module, 1x2 MB L2 per module, 16 MB L3 shared by four modules (located on the same chip), 128 GB RAM, 64-bit Linux version 2.6.18.								

4 Conclusion

A parallel edge detection application based on eight direction Prewitt edge detection algorithm is designed and implemented to work on different multicore platforms efficiently. Different functionalities are added to the original Prewitt such as smoothing and a global thresholding mechanism. In order to suppress noise more efficiently, an improved Median filter that enables the application to work effectively on noisy images is added. This method not only strengthens the original algorithm by allowing it to work on noisy images more effectively but also lets it compete with the industry standard detection algorithm Canny. Our algorithm when run sequentially, with all added functionality and complexity included, outperforms the default runs of both Prewitt and Canny already implemented in Matlab. Our parallel implementation of the algorithm uses C/C++ as the base language with two open source libraries OpenCV and OpenMP. Different experiments show improved performance gained from processing different size images especially when the complexity of the problem increases. Variety of tuning mechanisms have been added throughout the design to allow flexibility of work distribution to enhance the overall performance. The parallel implementation of this application is tested on two new shared memory MIMD multicore platforms namely Opteron and Bulldozer. Finally this implementation can effectively be used within the applications of image processing that relies on fast and accurate edge detection.

5 References

[1] Prajapati, H.B.; Vij, S.K.; , "Analytical Study of parallel and distributed image processing," *Image Information Processing (ICIIP), 2011 International Conference on* , vol., no., pp.1-6, 3-5 Nov. 2011 doi: 10.1109/ICIIP.2011.6108870.

[2] Srivastava, G.K.; Verma, R.; Mahrishi, R.; Rajesh, S.; , "A novel wavelet edge detection algorithm for noisy images," *Ultra Modern Telecommunications & Workshops, 2009. ICUMT '09. International Conference on* , vol., no., pp.1-8, 12-14 Oct. 2009.

[3] Joshi, S.R.; Koju, R.; , "Study and comparison of edge detection algorithms," *Internet (AH-ICI), 2012 Third Asian Himalayas International Conference on* , vol., no., pp.1-5, 23-25 Nov. 2012 doi: 10.1109/AHICI.2012.6408439.

[4] Jun-Feng Xiong; Bin Fang; , "Edge detection in noisy image using kernel regression," *Wavelet Analysis and Pattern Recognition (ICWAPR), 2012 International Conference*, no., pp.45-52, 15-17 July 2012 doi: 10.1109/ICWAPR.2012.6294753.

[5] Gonzalez, R.C., Woods, R. E. & Eddins, S. L. (2010). *Digital Image Processing Using MATLAB*. (2nd ed.). Gatesmark, LLC.

[6] Lei Yang; Dewei Zhao; Xiaoyu Wu; Hui Li; Jun Zhai; , "An improved Prewitt algorithm for edge detection based on noised image," *Image and Signal Processing (CISP), 2011 4th International Congress on* , vol.3, no., pp.1197-1200, 15-17 Oct. 2011 doi: 10.1109/CISP.2011.6100495.

[7] Raman Maini; J.S Sohal; "Performance evaluation of Prewitt edge detection algorithm for noisy image," GVIP journal volume 6, issue 3, 2006.

[8] Qingwei Liao; Jingxin Hong; Meiqun Jiang; , "A comparison of edge detection algorithm using for driver fatigue detection system," *Industrial Mechatronics and Automation (ICIMA), 2010 2nd International Conference on* , vol.1, no., pp.80-83, 30-31 May 2010 doi: 10.1109/ICINDMA.2010.5538090.

[9] X L. Ci and G. G. Chen, Analysis and Research of Image Edge Detection Methods, Journal of Infrared, pp. 20-23, Jul 2008.

[10] Osman, M.K.; Mashor, M.Y.; Jaafar, H., "Performance comparison of clustering and thresholding algorithms for tuberculosis bacilli segmentation," *Computer, Information and Telecommunication Systems (CITS), 2012 International Conference on* , vol., no., pp.1,5, 14-16 May 2012
doi: 10.1109/CITS.2012.6220378.

[11] Liu Jing; Xinli Liu; Guofu Yin, "The research and implementation of the method of pretreating the face images based on OpenCV machine visual library," *Electronic and Mechanical Engineering and Information Technology (EMEIT), 2011 International Conference on* , vol.5, no., pp.2719,2721, 12-14 Aug. 2011 doi: 10.1109/EMEIT.2011.6023595.

[12] Kumar, P.S.; Srinivasan, K.; Rajaram, M., "Performance evaluation of statistical based median filter to remove salt and pepper noise," *Computing Communication and Networking Technologies (ICCCNT), 2010 International Conference on* , vol., no., pp.1,6, 29-31 July 2010 doi: 0.1109/ICCCNT.2010.5591652.

[13] Bradiski, G. & Kaebler, E. (2008). Learning OpenCV. O'Reilly Media, CA.

[14] Ningbo Zhu; Gang Wang; Gaobo Yang; Weiming Dai, "A Fast 2D Otsu Thresholding Algorithm Based on Improved Histogram," *Pattern Recognition, 2009. CCPR 2009. Chinese Conference on* , vol., no., pp.1,5, 4-6 Nov. 2009 doi: 10.1109/CCPR.2009.5344078.

[15] Culjak, I.; Abram, D.; Pribanic, T.; Dzapo, H.; Cifrek, M., "A brief introduction to OpenCV," *MIPRO, 2012 Proceedings of the 35th International Convention* , vol., no., pp.1725,1730, 21-25 May 2012.

[16] Matuska, S.; Hudec, R.; Benco, M.; , "The comparison of CPU time consumption for image processing algorithm in Matlab and OpenCV," *ELECTRO, 2012* , vol., no., pp.75-78, 21-22 May 2012.

[17] Jordan, H. F. & Alaghband, G. (2003). *Fundamentals Of Parallel Processing,* Upper Saddle River, NJ: Pearson.

LBP-based Hierarchical Sparse Patch Learning for Face Recognition

Yue Zhao[1]**, and Jianbo Su**[1]
[1]Department of Automation, Shanghai Jiao Tong University,
and Key Laboratory of System Control and Information Processing,
Ministry of Education, Shanghai, 200240, China

Abstract—*Local Binary Pattern (LBP) features and its variants are computed on the patches with the fixed positions and a fixed size in images, while the limited variety of the size and position cannot accurately measure the nature of face image. In this paper, we propose a new learning method, Hierarchical Sparse Patch Learning (HSPL), to select face patches with different positions and sizes for face recognition. HSPL employs a sparse learning model to hierarchically select patches at two levels: in level 1 the optimal patch candidates are figured out, while in level 2 the optimal patches from the candidates are obtained. LBP features are extracted from the optimal patches to recognize faces. Experimental results show that the proposed method is more efficient and achieves higher recognition rate than the other two compared methods.*

Keywords: Feature Description, Face Recognition, Patch Selection, LBP, Sparse Learning

1. Introduction

Face feature description plays an essential role for face recognition[1]. In recent years, many face feature description algorithms have been proposed, including Eigenface [2], Fisherface [3], Local Binary Pattern (LBP) [4] and Elastic Bunch Graph Matching [5]. Among them, LBP and its variants [4], [6], [7], [8], [9] are the most widely used face feature descriptors, which divide the face image into patches with the fixed positions and a fixed size to extract LBP features [10]. However, the way that LBP and its variants adopted for patch generation leads to limited variety of the size and position of the obtained features. In order to solve this problem, Zhang *et al.* [11] scan the face image with a scalable sub-window, and over 7000 sub-patches are obtained. Then they use Adaboost learning algorithm to select an optimal subset of local patches and extract LBP features from these patches.

By shifting and scaling a sub-window, abundant patches with different positions and sizes could be generated with Zhang's method [11]. The features extracted from these patches yield a more complete and agile description of the face image. Unfortunately, there are two problems of the application of Adaboost learning algorithm in Zhang's method. Firstly, the training process and the test process are not accordant. The training process of Adaboost is iterative, and each cycle selects only one patch. For any two patches generated in the neighboring cycles, the former is preferable to the latter for face recognition. But in the test process, all the patches are treated equally, which leads to inferior combination of selected patches for recognition. Secondly, the method is inefficient, since the optimal patch should be selected via comparisons among all patches in each cycle.

In order to attenuate these two problems, this paper proposes a new learning method, Hierarchical Sparse Patch Learning (HSPL), to select adaptive face patches, and then to recognize faces. Firstly, it proposes a feature transformation to generate within- and between-class distance vectors, and constructs a sparse learning model based on them, which can automatically select adaptive patches. Based on the sparse learning model, HSPL hierarchically select patches at two levels: in level 1 patch candidates are obtained by automatical parameter setting, while in level 2 the optimal patches from the candidates are reached.

The rest of this paper is organized as follows. The proposed method is presented in Section 2. In Section 3, some experiments are performed to evaluate the performance of the proposed method, followed by conclusions in Section 4.

2. Hierarchical Sparse Patch Learning

2.1 Sparse Learning Model for Adaptive Patch Selection

2.1.1 Within- and Between-class Distance Vectors Generation

Given any two face images I and $\tilde{I}$, if we shift and scale a sub-window on them, respectively, we can get N adaptive patches for each image with different positions and sizes [11]. $I = [T_1, \ldots, T_j, \ldots, T_N]$ and $\tilde{I} = [\tilde{T}_1, \ldots, \tilde{T}_j, \ldots, \tilde{T}_N]$, where T_j and $\tilde{T}_j$ are any one patch from I and $\tilde{I}$. After extracted LBP features [4] from T_j and $\tilde{T}_j$, two histogram feature vectors are obtained as $T_j = [t_1, \ldots, t_k, \ldots, t_l]$ and $\tilde{T}_j = [\tilde{t}_1, \ldots, \tilde{t}_k, \ldots, \tilde{t}_l]$, where T_j and $\tilde{T}_j$ are both a $1 \times l$ histogram feature vector. t_k and $\tilde{t}_k$ are the kth element of T_j and $\tilde{T}_j$ respectively.

The χ^2 distance d_j between two patches T_j and $\tilde{T_j}$ is formulated as:

$$\begin{aligned} d_j &= \chi^2(T_j, \tilde{T_j}) \\ &= \sum_{k=1}^{l} \frac{(t_k - \tilde{t}_k)^2}{t_k + \tilde{t}_k}. \end{aligned} \quad (1)$$

The χ^2 distance d_j between two patches T_j and $\tilde{T_j}$ is defined as:

$$\begin{aligned} D_i &= f(I, \tilde{I}) \\ &= [d_1, \ldots, d_j, \ldots, d_N] \\ &= [\chi^2(T_1, \tilde{T_1}), \ldots, \chi^2(T_j, \tilde{T_j}), \ldots, \chi^2(T_N, \tilde{T_N})], \end{aligned} \quad (2)$$

where D_i is the χ^2 distance vector of the ith couple of images I and $\tilde{I}$.

If I and $\tilde{I}$ are both from the same class, i.e., an identical person, D_i is considered as a within-class distance vector, otherwise as a between-class distance vector. It is easy to know that the number of within-class distance vectors is often greater than the one of the between-class. In this way, we transfer the original training samples from multiple classes to a set of within- and between-class distance vectors, which paves the way for the following sparse learning model.

2.1.2 Sparse Learning Model Construction

Let $W \in R^{V \times N}$ be the distance matrix consisted of V within- or between-class distance vectors, and $Y = [y_1, \ldots, y_i, \ldots, y_V]^{\mathrm{T}}$, where y_i is the label of the ith distance vector (namely, the ith row vector in W). label 0 and 1 are assigned to the within- or between-class distance vectors, respectively. The sparse linear regression of Y based on W has been verified in [12], then the face patches selection problem is formulated as the following linear system:

$$\begin{cases} Y = W\eta, \\ W = \begin{bmatrix} W^+ \\ W^- \end{bmatrix}, \end{cases} \quad (3)$$

where $\eta = [\eta_1, \ldots, \eta_j, \ldots, \eta_N]^{\mathrm{T}}$ is the selection indicator vector, W^+ and W^- are the subsets of corresponding within- and between-class distance vectors. The greater elements of η mean that the corresponding pathes are more discriminative for classification, and vice versa.

As mentioned in Subsection 2.1.1, the number of within-class distance vectors is greater than the number of between-class ones, we use Bootstrap[12] to resample on the set of between-class distance vectors for balancing the numbers of the within- and between-class distance vectors in W. Fig. 1 illustrates the idea of sparse learning model for face patches selection.

As the number of the patches is much larger than the number of the distance vectors (namely, $V > N$), it leads to an ununique solution of η in (3). A regularization term, lasso [13], [14], is introduced to (3) to solve this problem, and then a sparse minimization problem is obtained:

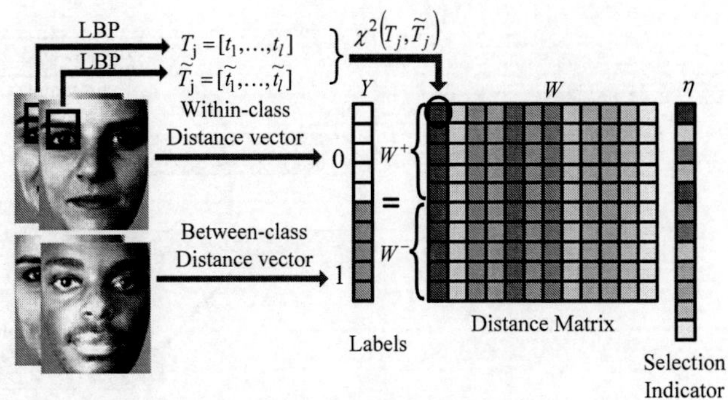

Fig. 1: A visual expression of the sparse learning model method for face patches selection.

$$\underset{X \in \mathbb{R}^N}{\arg\min} \|Y - W\eta\|_2^2 + \lambda\|\eta\|_1, \quad (4)$$

where $\lambda > 0$ is a complexity parameter which controls the amount of shrinkage: the larger the value of λ is, the greater the amount of shrinkage could be.

The method presented in [15] is used to solve the optimal solution η (4). In fact, a lot of elements of η are zeros. Hence, the patches corresponding to these zeros have no contribution to classification, which can thus be ignored. Similarly, negative elements of η are meaningless, and the corresponding patches are also ignored. At last, only the patches corresponding to the positive elements of η are reserved. This result indicates that by applying lasso to the problem (3), it encourages the sparsity simultaneously, which efficiently eliminate the redundancy of the patches.

By sorting the elements of η, we can gain a reasonable number of patches to achieve satisfactory face recognition performance. However, there is a limitation of the sparse learning model. Generally, the large number of patches leads to high dimensional data, which can not be computed by a common computer. In the following subsection, a hierarchical sparse learning scheme for adaptive patches selection is presented to overcome this problem.

2.2 Hierarchical Scheme for HSPL

2.2.1 Scheme Description

Hierarchical Sparse Patch Learning is exhibited in Fig.2 with two levels, which are explained below.

Level 1: Parallel Learning for Selecting Optimal Patch Candidates

If a training set is obtained from a face image dataset, we use the method in [11] to generate the adaptive patches with different positions and sizes to construct the patch set H. Generally, distance matrix W generated by H is too large to be processed with a common computer. Thus, we use the subset of H to generate W. We resample with replacement on H for m times, and the sampling rate

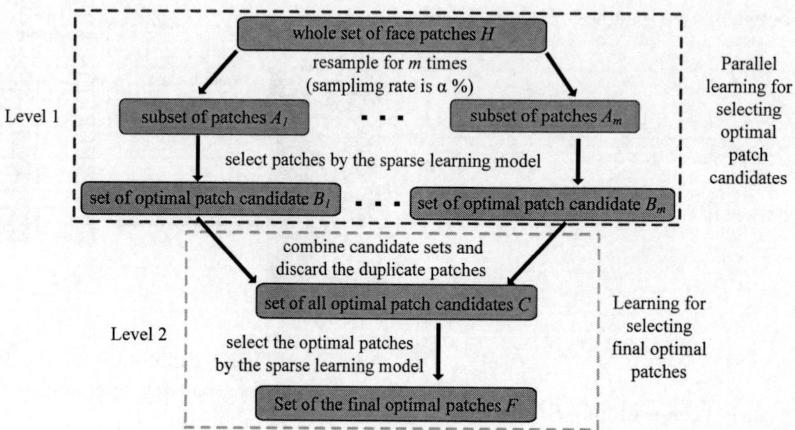

Fig. 2: Hierarchical Sparse Patch Learning.

is α. The range of α is $(0, \varepsilon]$, where ε, the upper limit of α, is determined by N (the number of H) and the memory capacity of the computer. α is presented to control the dimension of W, which can ensure W has a suitable dimension to be computed with a common computer. With the resampling way, m patch subsets are generated, which are $\{A_1, A_2, \cdots, A_m\}$. For each patch subset, we adopt the sparse learning model to select the patches, and the patches corresponding to the positive elements of the selection indicator vector η compose an optimal patch candidate set. Lastly, we obtain m optimal patch candidate sets, and suppose they are $\{B_1, B_2, \cdots, B_m\}$. As the patch subsets are produced by resampling with replacement, the optimal patch candidate sets have a lot of duplicate patches. It should be noted that the learning process in level 1 can be performed in parallel to improve computational efficiency.

Level 2: Learning for Selecting Final Optimal Patches

As mentioned above, in level 1 many duplicate patches are preserved in the optimal patch candidate sets. In level 2, we first combine all the optimal patch candidate sets and delete the duplicate patches, and then we get a whole optimal patch candidate set C. Lastly, we employ the sparse learning model (4) to generate a selection indicator vector η for all the patches in C. According to η, we can sort the patches in C to get the final optimal patches set F.

Then we extract LBP features from the patches in F for face recognition.

2.2.2 Parameter Selection

There are five parameters adopted in this scheme: N, ε, δ, α and m. N is the number of all the patches generated by shifting and scaling a sub-window on face images. It can be selected freely so long it is large enough. ε is the upper limit of the sampling rate α, and is determined by the memory capacity of the computer and N. To ensure a satisfactory δ, ($\delta \geq 0.95$ in our paper), m should be as little as possible and α should be as larger as possible. The optimization objective can be expressed as:

$$\begin{aligned} \min_{\alpha,m,\delta} \quad & \frac{m}{\alpha} \\ s.t. \quad & 0 < \alpha \leq \varepsilon, \\ & 1-(1-\alpha^2)^m = \delta, \\ & \delta \geq 0.95. \end{aligned} \tag{5}$$

By solving the optimization problem (5), we can get the values of parameters α, m and δ.

The relationship between α, m and δ are indicated by Fig. 3. Here, we first fixed one parameter, and then observe the change of the remaining two parameters. The conclusions drawn from Fig. 3 are as follows.

(a) When resampling times m is fixed, by comparing points A, B and C, we find that the rate of patches compared δ increases with growth of the sampling rate α.

(b) when δ has been assigned a certain value, m increases greatly with the reducing of α,which is indicated by points A, D and E.

(c) More importantly, for each α, δ increases fast with the growth of m at the beginning, but dose not increase obviously when m is larger than a certain value.

3. Experiments

In this section, we compare the proposed method with two methods LBP [4] and Boosting LBP [11] on FERET [16] face database. All images are normalized and cropped to 130×150 pixels and all the methods take Nearest Neighbors algorithm as the classification model.

3.1 Data Description and Parameter Setting

FERET database has totally 14,051 gray-scale images to represent 1,199 individuals, which contains variations in lighting, facial expressions, time, and ages. The subsets of fb (1,195 images), fc (194 images) and dupI (722 images) are

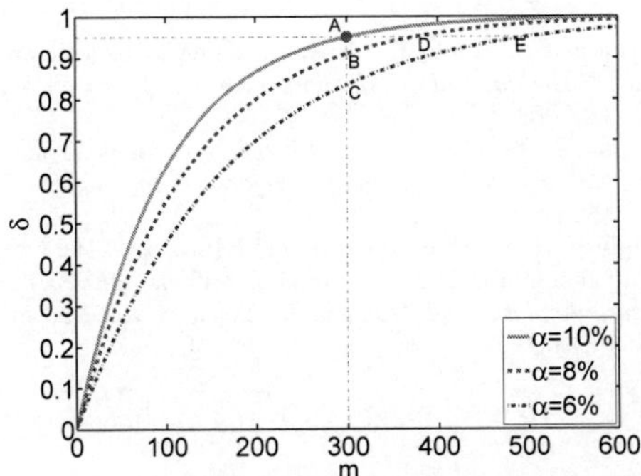

Fig. 3: The rate of patches comparedδ vs. sampling times m with different sampling rate α.

Table 1: Values of parameters for the proposed method

Parameter	N	α	m	ε	δ
Value	99280	10%	300	10%	0.95

selected as probe sets, and fa (1,196 images) as the gallery set. The standard FERET training set (736 images) and subfc training set (194 images) [4] compose the whole training set, which generates 551 positive samples and 658445 negative samples to construct the sparsing learning model in Section 2.1.2.

In our experiments, there are 99280 face patches generated for the whole patch set H, namely $N = 99280$. In terms of N and the memory capacity of our computer, the value of ϵ is determined to be $\epsilon = 10\%$. The remaining parameters α, m and δ are obtained by solving the optimization problem (5). All the parameter values can be seen in Table 1.

3.2 Results

In order to choose a reasonable number of final selected patches. We have drawn the recognition rate curves v.s. different patch numbers on three subsets of FERET database as shown in Fig. 4. From this figure, we can see that when the number of final selected patches is greater than 90, the recognition rate increases very slowly. To balance the performance and the time complexity, the reasonable number of the final patches is about 90. The proposed method finally select 92 optimal patches for face recognition.

Fig. 5 illustrates the positions and sizes of these 92 selected patches. It shows that the selected patches focus on the regions of eyes, nose and mouth, which can afford more discriminative features.

The comparison results of the three methods are presented in Table 2. Two groups of experiments have been performed in our paper. The first group of experiments are employed to compare two methods: the proposed method (with adaptive patches selection) and LBP (without adaptive patches selection)[4]. From the second and the forth rows of Table 2, we can see that the face recognition rate of

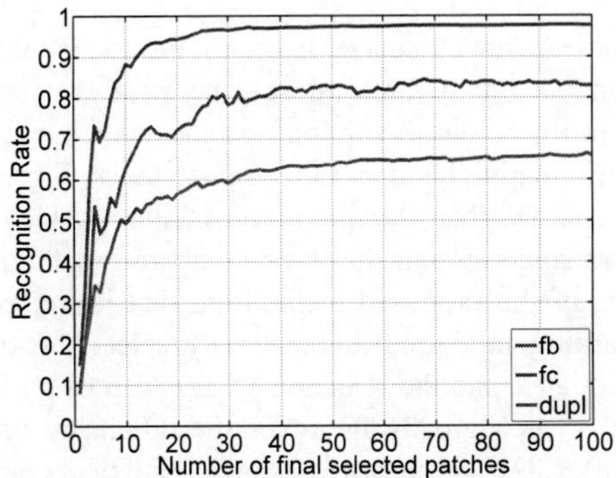

Fig. 4: The recognition results of 1-NN classifier on different number of the selected patches

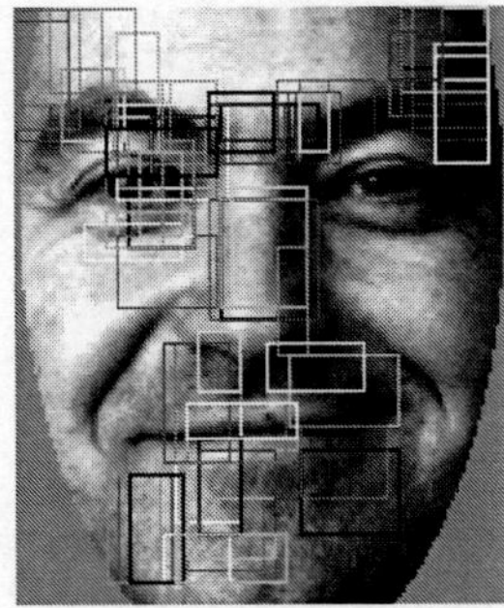

Fig. 5: The final selected patches of the proposed method

the method with adaptive patches selection is higher than the method without adaptive patches selection on all the three subsets. The second group of experiments are used to compare two methods both using the adaptive patches selection approach: the proposed method and Boosting LBP [11]. The results in the third and forth rows in Table 2 show that the recognition rate of the proposed method is higher than that of Boosting LBP, which indicates the performance of the proposed method is better than Boosting LBP. In a word, the performance of the proposed method is the best among the three methods.

4. Conclusions

This paper presents a new learning method, Hierarchical Sparse Patch Learning (HSPL), to efficiently and automatically select adaptive patches based on LBP for face

Table 2: Comparison results of different methods on FERET database.

method	Recognition rate (%)		
	fb	fc	dupI
LBP[4]	96.8	79.3	65.7
Boosting LBP [11]	97.2	69.6	**68.1**
Proposed	**97.7**	**83.5**	66.2

recognition. A novel sparse learning model is exhibited firstly, and then a hierarchical scheme with two levels is proposed to figure out the optimal patches which can afford more discriminative features to recognize faces. Experimental results show that the proposed method achieves the best performance among the three compared methods. The advantages of the proposed method are that it employs the sparse learning model to automatically select the optimal patch candidates, and the selection process can be performed in parallel, which greatly improves the efficiency of patch selection; Besides that, it proposes an automatical parameter selection method by solving an optimization problem, which ensures the satisfactory face recognition results for the proposed method.

Acknowledgment

This work is partially financially supported by the Key Project of National Natural Science Foundation of China (NSFC) under grant 60935001.

References

[1] N.S. Vu and A. Caplier, "Enhanced patterns of oriented edge magnitudes for face recognition and image matching," *IEEE Transactions on Image Processing*, vol. 21, no. 3, pp. 1352–1365, 2012.

[2] M. Turk and A. Pentland, "Eigenfaces for recognition," *Journal of cognitive neuroscience*, vol. 3, no. 1, pp. 71–86, 1991.

[3] P.N. Belhumeur, J.P. Hespanha, and D.J. Kriegman, "Eigenfaces vs. fisherfaces: recognition using class specific linear projection," *IEEE Transactions on Pattern Analysis and Machine Intelligence*, vol. 19, no. 7, pp. 711–720, 1997.

[4] T. Ahonen, A. Hadid, and M. Pietikainen, "Face description with local binary patterns: application to face recognition," *IEEE Transactions on Pattern Analysis and Machine Intelligence*, vol. 28, no. 12, pp. 2037–2041, 2006.

[5] L. Wiskott, J.M. Fellous, N. Kuiger, and C. von der Malsburg, "Face recognition by elastic bunch graph matching," *IEEE Transactions on Pattern Analysis and Machine Intelligence*, vol. 19, no. 7, pp. 775–779, 1997.

[6] Z. Guo, L. Zhang, D. Zhang, and X. Mou, "Hierarchical multiscale lbp for face and palmprint recognition," in *IEEE International Conference on Image Processing*, 2010, pp. 26–29.

[7] X. Li, W. Hu, Z. Zhang, and H. Wang, "Heat kernel based local binary pattern for face representation," *IEEE Signal Processing Letters*, vol. 17, no. 3, pp. 308–311, 2010.

[8] A. Petpon and S. Srisuk, "Face recognition with local line binary pattern," in *The 5th International Conference on Image and Graphics*. IEEE, 2009, pp. 533–539.

[9] W. Zhang, S. Shan, W. Gao, X. Chen, and H. Zhang, "Local gabor binary pattern histogram sequence (lgbphs): a novel non-statistical model for face representation and recognition," in *IEEE International Conference on Computer Vision*, 2005, pp. 786–791.

[10] C.T. Chiu and C.J. Wu, "Texture classification based low order local binary pattern for face recognition," in *IEEE International Conference on Image Processin*. IEEE, 2011, pp. 3017–3020.

[11] G. Zhang, X. Huang, S. Li, Y. Wang, and X. Wu, "Boosting local binary pattern (lbp) - based face recognition," *Advances in biometric person authentication*, vol. 3338, pp. 179–186, 2005.

[12] J. Friedman, T. Hastie, and R. Tibshirani, *The elements of statistical learning*, Springer Series in Statistics, 2001.

[13] R. Tibshirani, "Regression shrinkage and selection via the lasso," *Journal of the Royal Statistical Society. Series B (Methodological)*, pp. 267–288, 1996.

[14] I. Guyon and A. Elisseeff, "An introduction to variable and feature selection," *The Journal of Machine Learning Research*, vol. 3, pp. 1157–1182, 2003.

[15] J. Liu and J. Ye, "Efficient euclidean projections in linear time," in *The 26th Annual International Conference on Machine Learning*. ACM, 2009, pp. 657–664.

[16] P.J. Phillips, H. Moon, S.A. Rizvi, and P.J. Rauss, "The feret evaluation methodology for face-recognition algorithms," *IEEE Transactions on Pattern Analysis and Machine Intelligence*, vol. 22, no. 10, pp. 1090–1104, 2000.

A New Level Set Method for Biomedical Image Segmentation

Yide Ma, Weiying Xie, Zhaobin Wang, and Wen Li
School of Information Sci. Eng, Lanzhou University, Lanzhou, China

Abstract - *This paper presents a new biomedical image segmentation method that applies an edge-based level set method. According to low contrast in biomedical images, we mainly make focus on introducing the Laplace operator in external energy of level set method for accurately detecting object edge. A preliminary evaluation of the proposed method mainly performs on gallstone detection and extraction, mammographic image segmentation, iris inner location and polysaccharides extraction. Finally, the comparison experimental results demonstrate that our proposed approach potentially performs better than the representative level set method for biomedical image segmentation in terms of sensitivity, accuracy and specificity, with same initial contours.*

Keywords: Biomedical Image Segmentation; Level Set Method; External Energy.

1 Introduction

Osher and Sethian first introduced level set method in 1988 [1]. In the past two decades, level set methods have seen the rapid development in many aspects within the image processing and computer vision field, such as Global Optimization, Etching, Deposition, and Lithography Development and so on [2], especially in image segmentation. In fact, image segmentation is one of the fundamental and significant tasks in image processing and computer vision. Among the applications in image processing, level set method has great potential for developing image segmentation algorithm. There are large amounts of algorithms and techniques that have been developed to solve image segmentation problems, Malladi *et al.* [3] introduced shape modeling with front propagation based on level set method to implement image segmentation. Typically, an image segmentation study applying level set approach has been performed independently by Caselles *et al.* [4]. They presented geodesic active contour models based on curve evolution, geometric flows and level set method [3,4]. The fundamental principle of level set method is to represent a contour as the zero level set of a higher dimensional function, usually called a level set function (LSF), and to formulate the motion of the contour as the evolution of the level set function based on a partial differential equation (PDE). It is crucial to keep the evolving level set function as an approximate signed distance function non-periodically during the evolution, especially in a neighborhood around the zero level set. However, this process needs re-initialization, which is an absolutely necessary step to realize level set function to a signed distance function during the evolution. Re-initialization scheme has been extensively used as a numerical remedy for maintaining stable curve evolution and ensuring desirable results. So far, the re-initialization process is quite complicated in computation and has stable side effects. Moreover, the level set function can develop shocks. To avoid these problems, it is necessary to re-initialize level set function periodically, but when to apply the re-initialization and how to make re-initialization achieve periodically during the curve evolution are still serious problems as mentioned in [5]. These problems also remain in [3,4]. Li *et al.* [6] presented a new variational level set method to force the level set function to close to a signed distance function and eliminate the re-initialization procedure. Li's scheme obtained good results for medical image segmentation. Furthermore, a significant research effort has been devoted to the design of effective images segmentation methods based on Li's model over in recent years. The techniques based on Li's scheme and C-V model for SAR image segmentation implied in [7]. Lately, Li *et al.* [8] introduced a distance regularized level set evolution (DRLSE) by incorporating a double-well potential function used in the geodesic active contour model [4]. By contrast, the DRLSE is more efficient than conventional level set formulations applying to image segmentation. Ni et al. [9] proposed an advanced variational formulation based on DRLSE, named ADRLSE (advanced distance regularized level set evolution), that forces the level set function to be close to a signed distance function. The proposed method merges DRLSE equations and a signed pressure force function in [10].

However, most of biomedical images are often poor in contrast. Therefore, we improved the external energy of level set method based on Li's model so as to urge the zero level set to be much closed to the region to be segmented, the experimental results and comparisons show that we improved method outperforms.

The following part of this paper is divided into five sections. Section II overviews the level set method which gives a brief description of the traditional and variational level set method. Section III proposes the new algorithm for medical image segmentation. Section IV achieves the numerical implementation of our proposed method. Section V shows the experimental result by applying our approach to medical images. In the last section, a conclusion is made and some issues for further research are suggested.

2 Traditional level set model

To dates, level set method has been rapidly developed. Since the variational level set model is a modified version of the conventional level set model, we review the conventional level set model briefly and then provided improvements on it for practical application.

2.1 Overview of traditional level set model

Actually, level set method is mapping from higher dimensional to lower dimensional. This method is able to express curves of complex topology and to handle topological changes automatically, i.e. naturally splitting and merging. Also, the level set method can efficiently perform numerical computations involving curves and surfaces on a fixed Cartesian grid. The level set method is based on curve evolution theory which can be expressed as follows:

$$\frac{\partial C}{\partial t} = FN \tag{1}$$

Where, N, the inward normal vector to the curve C, can be represented as $N = -\nabla\phi/\nabla\phi$. F represents the speed function that controls the evolution of the curve C. The level set method supposes that the curve C are represented by the zero level set of a level set function $\phi(t,x,y)$.

$$C(t) = \{(x, y)|\phi(t, x, y) = 0\} \tag{2}$$

Level set equation, the curve evolution equation of the level set function ϕ, can be written in the following general form, i.e. partial differential equation (PDE):

$$\frac{\partial \phi}{\partial t} = F|\nabla\phi| \tag{3}$$

Applying to the image segmentation, the speed function F mainly relies on the image data and the level set function ϕ. Although level set method has desirable advantages being applied to a wide range, there exists problem that the level set function can develop sharp or flat shocks during the evolution. In term of this difficulty, a general numerical scheme known as re-initialization [1,10] is used periodically during the evolution.

$$\frac{\partial \phi}{\partial t} = sign(\phi)(1-|\nabla\phi|) \tag{4}$$

The re-initialization scheme considers level set function as a signed distance function to remain stable during the evolution process. However, this scheme may cause the zero level set away from the expected position [1], so this numerical scheme should be avoided.

2.2 Level set model without re-initialization

Li *et al.* [6] presented a new variational level set method to force the level set function to close to a signed distance function and completely eliminate the need of the re-initialization procedure. This variational formulation is associated with a penalty term that penalizes the deviation of the level set function from a signed distance function. The penalty term which plays a key role in the variational formulation is as follows:

$$P(\phi) = \int_\Omega \frac{1}{2}(|\nabla\phi| - 1)^2\, dxdy \tag{5}$$

Naturally, it makes function ϕ satisfying $|\nabla\phi| = 1$ closed to the signed distance function. The penalty term eliminates the need for re-initialization and allows the use of a simpler and more efficient numerical scheme in the implementation than those used for conventional level set formulations.

The edge indicator function g can move the zero level set to the object boundaries in image segmentation, it defines as:

$$g = \frac{1}{1+|\nabla G_\sigma * I|^2} \tag{6}$$

Here, I represents an image. G_σ, the Gaussian kernel with standard deviation σ, is used to smooth the image to reduce noise. The energy functional is defined as:

$$E = mE_{\text{int}} + E_{ext} = mP(\phi) + \lambda L_g(\phi) + \alpha A_g(\phi) \tag{7}$$

It's just the co-activation of the internal and external energies that make the zero level set curve C matching the boundaries well and reach a perfect effect of image segmentation. Where, m is a parameter controlling the penalization effect of the internal energy. The energy functional $L_g(\phi)$ computes the line integral of the function g along the zero level contour of ϕ. The energy functional $A_g(\phi)$ computes a weighted area of the region inside the zero level set. λ is the coefficient of the energy functional $L_g(\phi)$, and α is the coefficient of the energy functional $A_g(\phi)$. For images with weak object boundaries, the value of α should be chosen small to avoid the active contour passing through the object boundaries. $L_g(\phi)$ and $A_g(\phi)$ are defined by

$$L_g(\phi) = \int_\Omega g\delta(\phi)|\nabla\phi|dx \tag{8}$$

$$A_g(\phi) = \int_\Omega gH(-\phi)dx \tag{9}$$

Where, δ and H are the Dirac delta function and the Heaviside function, respectively. In most level set methods, the Heaviside function H and the Dirac delta function δ are approximated by the following functions:

$$H_\xi(x) = \begin{cases} \frac{1}{2}\left(1+\frac{x}{\xi}+\frac{1}{\pi}\sin\left(\frac{\pi x}{\xi}\right)\right), & |x| \le \xi \\ 1, & x > \xi \\ 0, & x < -\xi \end{cases} \tag{10}$$

$$\delta_\xi(x)=\begin{cases}\frac{1}{2\xi}\left[1+\cos\left(\frac{\pi x}{\xi}\right)\right], & |x|\le\xi\\ 0, & |x|>\xi\end{cases} \tag{11}$$

δ_ξ is the derivative of H_ξ, i.e. $H'_\xi=\delta_\xi$. By calculus of variations, the Gateaux derivative of the functional E in can be written as:

$$\frac{\partial\phi}{\partial t}=-\frac{\partial E}{\partial\phi}=m\left[\Delta\phi-div\left(\frac{\nabla\phi}{|\nabla\phi|}\right)\right]+\lambda\delta(\phi)div\left(g\frac{\nabla\phi}{|\nabla\phi|}\right)+\nu g\delta(\phi) \tag{12}$$

3 Improved level set model

In order to deal with intensity inhomogeneities in medical image segmentation, we formulate our method based on the detection of lesions and to locate suspicious regions in medical images for more detail examination by the attending physicians, in which intensity inhomogeneity is attributed to a component of an image. Since, several medical image databases are too big, it costs too much computational time. To take these two factors into account, we make our efforts on proposing new efficient level set method applied to medical images segmentation. Actually, our purpose is to remove blurring and highlight edge from medical images. Therefore, the Laplace operator is used, which could make the bright spot becoming much brighter than the surrounded pixels in the image. As is well known, Laplace operator, one of the edge detection operators, has nothing to do with the direction of an edge. This operator is also one of the simplest sharpening filters, whose response to isolated pixel is stronger than the response to the edge or line. It is noted that the Laplace operator is a second order differential operator in the n dimensional Euclidean space, applied to biomedical image $I(x,y)$ is defined as:

$$\Delta I(x,y)=\nabla^2 I(x,y)=\frac{\partial^2 I(x,y)}{\partial x^2}+\frac{\partial^2 I(x,y)}{\partial y^2}$$
$$=I_{xx}+I_{yy} \tag{13}$$

Here, Δ is the Laplace operator. The equation (13) can be implemented in discretized form as the following finite difference equation:

$$\Delta I=\left(I_{i+1,j}+I_{i-1,j}+I_{i,j+1}+I_{i,j-1}\right)-4I_{i,j} \tag{14}$$

Which illustrates that the gradient of pixel $I_{i,j}$ only relates to the four adjacent pixels in an image, i.e. $I_{i+1,j}$, $I_{i-1,j}$, $I_{i,j+1}$ and $I_{i,j-1}$, but is independent of $I_{i+1,j+1}$, $I_{i-1,j-1}$, $I_{i-1,j+1}$ and $I_{i+1,j-1}$ which are usually on the edge of an image. We apply quadric-direction Laplace operator defined as follow:

$$\Delta I(x,y)=I_{xx}+I_{yy}+I_{\theta\theta}+I_{\varphi\varphi} \tag{15}$$

This equation is discretized as follows:

$$\Delta I=[I_{i+1,j}+I_{i-1,j}+I_{i,j+1}+I_{i,j-1}+I_{i+1,j+1}$$
$$+I_{i-1,j-1}+I_{i+1,j-1}+I_{i-1,j+1}]-8I_{i,j} \tag{16}$$

Fig.1 and Fig.2 express quadric-direction Laplace operator and its template form, respectively. Let $J=\Delta I$, I is the true image, which measures an intrinsic physical property of the mammography being imaged, is therefore assumed to be piecewise (approximately) constant. So we redefined the edge indicator function by

$$f=\frac{1}{1+|\nabla G_\sigma * J|}=\frac{1}{1+|\nabla G_\sigma *(\Delta I)|} \tag{17}$$

Where, G_σ is also a Gaussian kernel with standard deviation σ with same function in equation (6). Because the gray scale of mass region in mammographic image is higher than the region surrounded, this function f usually takes smaller values at object boundaries than at other locations. As the application of Laplace operator, the bright mass becoming much brighter than the surrounded pixels in the image. So the edge detection function f is easier to become smaller.

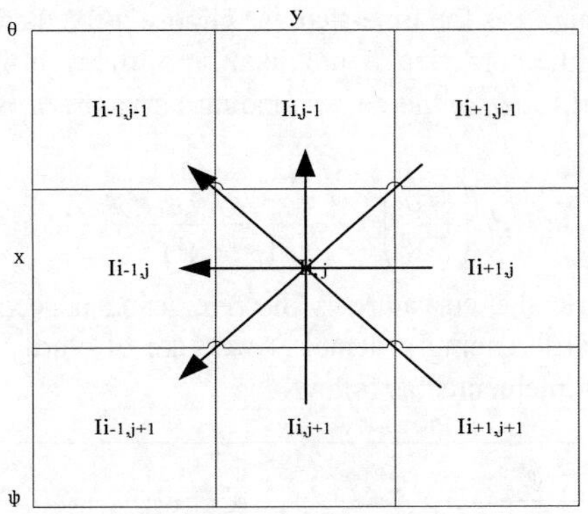

Fig. 1. The quadric-direction Laplace operator

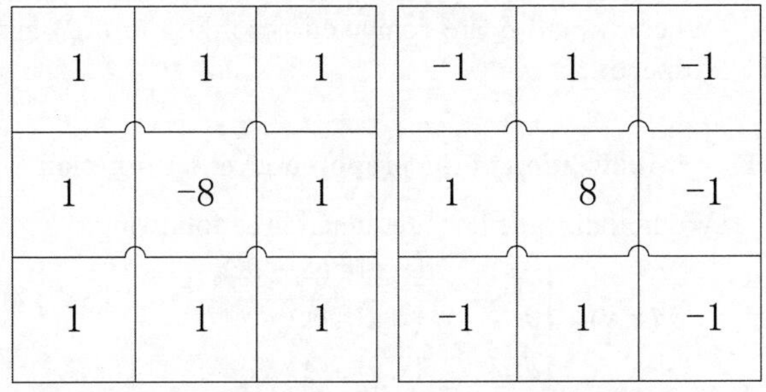

1	1	1
1	-8	1
1	1	1

-1	1	-1
1	8	-1
-1	1	-1

Fig. 2. The template of quadric-direction Laplace operator

The line integral of the function f along the zero level contour of ϕ and the weighted area of the region inside the zero level set are defined by

$$L_f(\phi)=\int_\Omega f\delta(\phi)|\nabla\phi|dx \tag{18}$$

$$A_f(\phi)=\int_\Omega fH(-\phi)dx \tag{19}$$

For the special case f=1, the energy functional $L_f(\phi)$ is minimized and $A_f(\phi)$ is exactly the area of the region inside Ω. The steepest descent process for minimization of the functional E can be written as the following gradient flow:

$$\frac{\partial\phi}{\partial t}=-\frac{\partial E}{\partial\phi}=m\left[\Delta\phi-div\left(\frac{\nabla\phi}{|\nabla\phi|}\right)\right]+\lambda\delta(\phi)div\left(f\frac{\nabla\phi}{|\nabla\phi|}\right)+\nu f\delta(\phi) \tag{20}$$

The function ϕ minimizes this functional to satisfy the Euler-Lagrange equation.

4 Update the proposed level set function

The partial differential equation in the continuous domain defined in Eq.(20) can be solved by a finite difference method in numerical scheme. All the spatial partial derivatives are approximated by the central difference and the temporal partial derivative is approximated by the forward difference. Then, the numerical scheme of the gradient flow mentioned above using the forward difference can be simply written as follows:

$$\frac{\partial\phi}{\partial t}=\frac{\phi_{i,j}^{k+1}-\phi_{i,j}^{k}}{\tau}=L(\phi_{i,j}^{k}) \quad (21)$$

Where τ is the time-step, we choose a fixed step size τ. $L(\phi_{i,j}^{k})$ is the numerical approximation of the right-hand side in (17). In $L(\phi_{i,j}^{k})$, the corresponding curvature κ is defined as:

$$\kappa=div\left(\frac{\nabla\phi}{|\nabla\phi|}\right)=\frac{\phi_{xx}\phi_y^2-2\phi_{xy}\phi_x\phi_y+\phi_{yy}\phi_x^2}{\left(\phi_x^2+\phi_y^2\right)^{3/2}} \quad (22)$$

Here, the curvature is discrete using a second-order central differencing scheme. For a sake of clarity, Eq.(20) can be implemented as follows:

$$\frac{\partial\phi}{\partial t}=\frac{\phi_{i,j}^{k+1}-\phi_{i,j}^{k}}{\tau}=L(\phi_{i,j}^{k})=m\left(\phi_{i+1,j}^{n}+\phi_{i-1,j}^{n}+\phi_{i,j+1}^{n}+\phi_{i,j-1}^{n}-4\phi_{i,j}^{n}-\kappa\right)$$
$$+\lambda\delta_{\xi}\left(\phi_{i,j}^{n}\right)f\kappa+vf\delta_{\xi}\left(\phi_{i,j}^{n}\right) \quad (23)$$

Where, κ and δ_{ξ} are computed according to (19) and (11), respectively.

4.1 Initialization of the proposed level set function

We initialize the level set function as following:

$$\phi_0(x,y)=\begin{cases}-d, & (x,y)\in\Omega_0-\partial\Omega_0\\ 0, & (x,y)\in\partial\Omega_0\\ d, & (x,y)\in\Omega-\Omega_0\end{cases} \quad (24)$$

It is a binary step function defined above that can be generated efficiently. Where Ω is an image domain, Ω_0 is a sub-region of the image domain, and $\partial\Omega_0$ is the boundary of Ω, and (x, y) is any pixel of the image. What is needed at the very beginning is a list of the coordinates of all required grid points together with their initial level set values. As previously mentioned in [5], if the regions of interest can be obtained in some way, then we can use these roughly obtained regions as the region Ω_0 to construct the initial level set function ϕ_0. Moreover, if the initial subset Ω_0 is close to the region to be segmented thus, not only a small number of iterations are needed to move the zero level set from the boundary of to the desired object boundary, but also the segmentation result is more efficient.

We propose to use a binary step function in (21) as the initial LSF, as it can be generated extremely efficiently. Thus, only a small number of iterations are needed to move zero level set from the boundary of Ω_0 to the desired object boundary.

The level set function evolves from a binary step function to an approximate signed distance function on a signed distance band (SDB). Because its values vary from $-d$ to d across the band at the rate of $|\nabla\phi|=1$ when the function ϕ becomes a signed distance function in the SDB. This means that the width of the SDB is approximately $2d$. Therefore, the width of the SDB is controlled by the constant d. In fact, the image domain is discrete grid, and the SDB should have at least one grid point on each side of the zero level set. In this context, the initial value of d is usually set as 2 mentioned in [8], d is chosen from the range $d\geq 1$ unless otherwise specified. In summary, the initial LSF in (32) can be defined again:

$$\phi_0(x,y)=\begin{cases}-2, & (x,y)\in\Omega_0-\partial\Omega_0\\ 0, & (x,y)\in\partial\Omega_0\\ 2, & (x,y)\in\Omega-\Omega_0\end{cases} \quad (25)$$

Where, Ω_0 can be obtained by thresholding or other efficient methods.

5 Experimental results

There are a variety of parameters, such as m, λ, v and the time-step τ. As well-known that the level set function will speed faster if the time-step is a relatively large. Nevertheless, the larger time step leads to steeply evolution. As many experimental results shown, it is better to set the evolution time-step as 5.0. The coefficient m as the weight value of internal energy, makes the level set function close to the signed distance function. Stability can be enforced using the CFL conditions, which means the numerical wave speed must be at least as fast as the physical wave speed [4]. In order to maintain level set evolution, the condition $m\tau\leq 0.25$ must be satisfied, which is the requirement of CFL conditions. The time step τ is already 5.0, so m is fixed as 0.04. Additionally, λ and v, the coefficients of external energy, are usually set as 5.0 and 0, respectively.

On the choice of medical ultrasound image, the study samples are the typical gallstone features and non-multiple lesions images. The actual gallbladder ultrasound images selected in this paper come from local hospital that is a subset of ultrasound images with typical characteristics from the hospital of Lanzhou. Gallstone is a high incidence of gallbladder disease, especially in the northwest of China. This is a publicly available and real dataset. The experimental results of gallstones extraction show in the first column of Fig.3. The first column shows multiple gallstones at the bottom of gallbladder and the new moon-shaped gallstone, respectively. The mammographic images segmentation results are shown in second column. The dataset used for evaluation of the proposed approaches for mammograms segmentation are selected from the Mini Mammographic image analysis database (MIAS) in United Kingdom (Suckling *et al.*, 1994). The images were stored in a format that is easy to read the images, PGM file format and of size 1024*1024 pixels. We applied the proposed method to all abnormal of MIAS dataset. Here, we show the segmentation results of two lesions in Fig.3. The first is one of the spiculated masses, and the second one represents other ill-defined masses. No matter taking into sensitivity of detection and actuality of segmentation, our proposed method performs better result. Iris inner boundary location is shown in the third column.

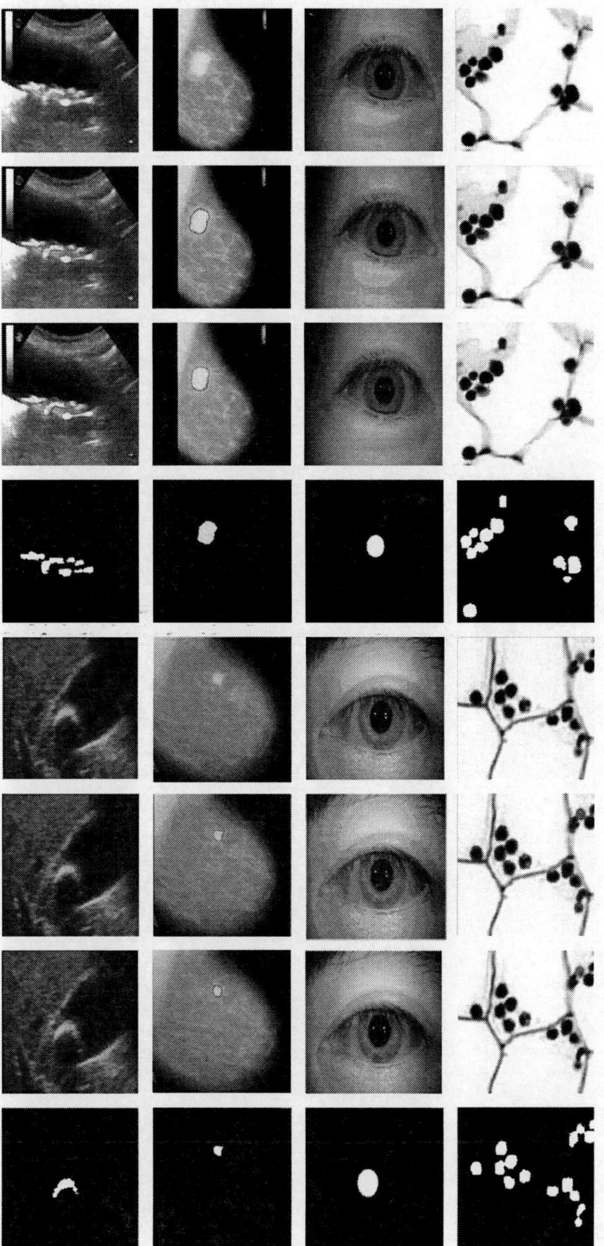

Fig. 3. Segmentation results of several medical images. The first column shows the results of gallstones in ultrasound images. Images in the second column show the segmentation results of mammograms. The third column shows the results of iris inner boundary location, and the last column shows the results of polysaccharides segmentation.

Furthermore, the binary images obtained after morphologic processing. Moreover, there are also two efficiency algorithm for iris image location in [11,12]. The last column shows examples of biological images polysaccharides of plant. In terms of different number of polysaccharides in each image, we all can accurately get them with our proposed method. After morphologic processing, we can clearly obtain 12 polysaccharides in the first picture and 15 in the next picture.

In Fig.3, all the experiments with red line are the results with our proposed method. Respectively, the blue line is the results with Li's model. Compared to Li's model, our proposed algorithm not only has better performance to detect the edge of each gallstone ultrasound image, mammograms, iris inner location and polysaccharides segmentation, but also accurately segment and extract.

TABLE I shows the detection results of different lesions. Se^a, Se^b represents the sensitivity of our method and Li's method [8], respectively.

TABLE I. DETECTION RESULTS FOR DIFFERENT LESIONS

Class of Lesions	Amount of Images	Our method		Li's method [8]	
		Images	Se^a (%)	*Images*	Se^b (%)
CIRC	23	19	82.6	15	65.2
SPIC	19	15	78.9	11	57.9
MISC	14	12	85.7	8	57.1
ARCH	19	14	73.7	9	47.3
ASYM	15	12	80	8	53.3

Although Li's model is much better at separating the main objects in the original images into meaningful regions with more natural shape, all the segmentation results are ineffective due to the low contrast in biomedical images.

6 Conclusions

In this paper, we have presented a novel automatic algorithm based on level set method for medical image segmentation. The main contribution of this work lies in that we introduce the Laplace operator in energy functional of level set method. Comparative experiments on biomedical image segmentation show that our method can achieve accurate segmentation results with same initial contours. In the future, we will apply our model to segment other types of images.

7 Acknowledgment

The authors would like to thank the reviewers for their comments that have helped improve this paper. This paper is jointly supported by National Natural Science Foundation of China (No. 61175012 & 61201421), Natural Science Foundation of Gansu Province (No. 1208RJ-ZA265), Specialized Research Fund for the Doctoral Program of Higher Education of China (No.2011021111-

0026), the Fundamental Research Funds for the Central Universities of China (No.lzujbky-2010-220, No.lzujbky-2012-38, No.lzujbky-2012-46, No.lzujbky-2013-k06), and chunhui plan cooperation research funds of the Ministry of education in China (No.Z2010084).

8 References

[1] S. Osher and J. Sethian, “Fronts propagating with curvature-dependent speed: Algorithms based on Hamilton-Jacobi formulations,” J. Comput. Phys., vol. 79, no. 1, pp. 12-49, Nov. 1988.

[2] S. Osher and R. Fedkiw, Level Set Methods and Dynamic Implicit Surfaces, Springer-Verlag, New York, 2002.

[3] R. Malladi, J. A. Sethian, and B. C. Vemuri, “Shape modeling with front propagation: A level set approach,” IEEE Trans. Pattern Anal. Mach. Intell., vol. 17, no. 2, pp. 158-175, Feb. 1995.

[4] V. Caselles, R. Kimmel, and G. Sapiro, “Geodesic active contours,” Int. J. Comput. Vis., vol. 22, no. 1, pp. 61-79, Feb. 1997.

[5] V. Caselles, F. Catte, T. Coll, and F. Dibos, “A geometric model for active contours in image processing”, Numer. Math., vol. 66, pp. 1-31, 1993.

[6] C. Li, C. Xu, C. Gui, and M. D. Fox, “Level set evolution without re-initialization: A new variational formulation,” in Proc. IEEE Conf. Comput. Vis. Pattern Recog., San Diego, CA, Jun. 2005, pp. 430-436.

[7] LU Min, HE Zhiguo, SU Yi, “An active contour model for SAR image segmentation,” IET international Radar Conference, pp. 1-5, 2009.

[8] C. Li, C. Xu, C. Gui, and M. D. Fox,” Distance regularized level set evolution and its application to image segmentation,” IEEE Trans. Imag. Proc., vol. 19, pp. 3243-3254, 2010.

[9] Ni Aijuan, Wei Gaofeng, Tian Feng, Qin Xiaoli, Yang Jian, Sun Qiuming, Xie Xinwu, “An advanced variational level set evolution for image segmentation,” International Symposium on Information Technology in Medicine and Education. pp. 732-736, 2012.

[10] J. Sethian, Level Set Methods and Fast Marching Methods. Cambridge, U.K.: Cambridge Univ. Press, 1999.

[11] Yan Li, Wen Li, Yide Ma, “Accurate Iris Location Based on Region of Interest,” IEEE International Conference on Biomedical Engineering and Biotechnology (iCBEB 2012), Macau, China, 2012.

[12] G. Xu, Z. Zhang, Y. Ma. Automatic Iris Segmentation Based on Local Areas[C]. The 18th International Conference on Pattern Recognition (ICPR 2006), Hong Kong, 2006, 505-508.

Edge Detection In X-ray Computed Tomography Images Using Weibull Distribution

Wafaa Kamel Al-Jibory , Ali El-Zaart
Department of Mathematics and Computer Science
Faculty of Science, Beirut Arab University, Beirut –Lebanon
waf_jibory@yahoo.com, dr_elzaart@yahoo.com

Abstract- *Computed Tomography (CT scan) is a medical imaging procedure that utilizes computer-processed X-rays to produce tomography images or 'slices' of specific areas of the body. These cross-sectional images are used for diagnostic and therapeutic purposes in various medical disciplines. Image processing uses for detecting for objects of CT images. Edge detection; which is a method of determining the discontinuities gray level images, is a very important initial step in Image processing. Many classical edge detectors have been developed over time. Some of the well-known edge detection operators based on the first derivative of the image are Roberts, Prewitt, Sobel which are traditionally implemented by convolving the image with masks. Also Gaussian distribution has been used to build masks for the first and second derivative. However, this distribution has a limit to only symmetric shape. This paper will use to construct the masks. The Weibull distribution which was more general than Gaussian because it has symmetric and asymmetric shape. The constructed masks are applied to images and we obtained good results.*

Keywords : Edge detection; Image processing;
Weibull Distribution; Gradient; CT Scan images.

1. Introduction

A CT scan is a construction of Computed Tomography scan. It is also known as a CAT (Computer Axial Tomography) scans. CT scanner is a special kind of X-ray machine, which combines many x-ray images instead of just one with the assistance computer. It employs the process of generating a 2-dimensional image with assistance of the computer. In some cases a 3-dimensional image can also be formed by taking many pictures of the same region from varying angles. Density and the Strength of the X-ray beams help in providing a cross-section of the body. CT scan [10] helps in inspecting the interiors of the body , differentiating normal and abnormal structures, and providing the necessary treatment. In recent times, it has become a necessary in locating tumors and giving suitable treatment by radiotherapy. CT scanner can be used now to picture of part of the body, including brain, lungs, kidney, liver and spine [2],[17]. An edge is usually a step change in intensity of the image (CT image). It corresponds to the boundary between two regions or a set of points in the image where luminous intensity changes very sharply[10]. Determination of, whether pixel is an edge point or not, bases on how much its local neighbours respond to a certain edge detector [13]. Over the years, many methods have been proposed for detecting edges in images. Some of the earlier methods, such as the Sobel and Prewitt detectors [11], used local gradient operators [12] to obtain spatial filter masks. The procedure is to compute the sum of products of the mask coefficients with the intensity values in the region encompassed by the mask [3]. Also the Canny edge detector which depends on the Gaussian distribution in obtaining the operators for the gradient and Laplacian masks is a well-known edge detector [9]. In this paper we propose method that will use Weibull Distribution instead of Gaussian distribution to obtain edge detection operators. The advantage of this method is that Gaussian distribution has limitation to only symmetric shape but Weibull Distribution has symmetric and asymmetric shape.

The rest of this paper is organized as follows. Section 2 introduces Gradient Edge Detection. Section 3 explains the Most famous Edge Detector. Gradient of Weibull Edge Detector is displayed in Section 4. Experimental result is shown in Section 5. Finally this paper presents conclusion and future work in Section 6.

2. Gradient Edge Detection

Gradient is a vector has certain magnitude and direction. In image processing, the gradient is the change in gray level with direction. This can be calculated by taking the difference in value of neighbouring pixels

Where ∇f is first order derivative of $f(x,y)$ define as:

$$\nabla^2 f(x,y) = \frac{\partial^2 f(x,y)}{\partial x^2} + \frac{\partial^2 f(x,y)}{\partial y^2} \quad (1)$$

The magnitude of this vector, denoted magn(f), Where

$$\text{magn}(\nabla f) = \sqrt{\left(\left(\frac{\partial f}{\partial x}\right)^2 + \left(\frac{\partial f}{\partial y}\right)^2\right)} \quad (2)$$

$$= \sqrt{\left(G_x^{\ 2} + G_y^{\ 2}\right)}$$

The direction of the gradient vector, denoted dir(f), Where

$$\text{dir}(\nabla f) = \tan^{-1}(G_y / G_x) \quad (3)$$

The magnitude of gradient provides information about the strength of the edge and the direction of gradient is always perpendicular to the direction of the edge.

3. The famous Edge Detector

Before introducing the proposed algorithm, this section reviews some of the main edge detection methods, such as the Sobel method and Gradient of Gaussian edge detector.

3.1. The Sobel Edge Detector

The Sobel method [3] utilizes two masks, S_x and S_y, which are shown in fig. 1, to do convolution on the gray image and then obtain the edge intensities G_x and G_y in the vertical and horizontal directions, respectively. The edge intensity of the mask center is defined as $|G_x|+|G_y|$. If the edge intensity of each pixel is larger than an appropriate threshold T, then the pixel will be regarded as an edge point. Unfortunately, the edge line detected by Sobel method is usually thicker than the actual edge [16].

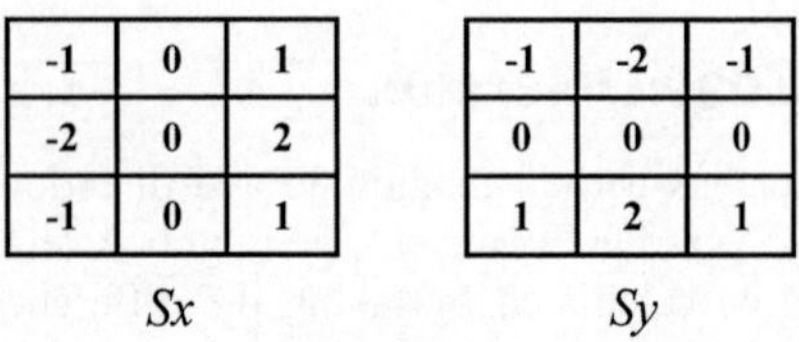

-1	0	1
-2	0	2
-1	0	1

Sx

-1	-2	-1
0	0	0
1	2	1

Sy

Figure 1. Two convolution masks in Sobel method.

3.2. The Gradient of Gaussian edge detector

An edge detection operator can reduce noise by smoothing the image, but this adds uncertainly to the location of the edge: or the operator can have greater sensitivity to the presence of edges, but this will increase the sensitivity of the operator to noise. The type of liner operator that provides the best compromise between noise immunity and localization, while retaining the advantages of Gaussian filtering is the first derivative of a Gaussian. This operator corresponds to smooth an image with Gaussian function and then computing the gradient. The gradient can be numerically approximated by using the standard finite-difference approximation for the first partial derivative in the x and y directions. The operator that is the combination of a Gaussian smoothing filter and a gradient approximation is not rotationally symmetric. The operator is symmetric along the edge and antisymmetric perpendicular to the edge (along the line of the gradient). This means that the operator is sensitive to the edge in the direction of steepest change, but it is insensitive to the edge and acts as a smoothing operator in the direction along the line

4. Gradient Of Weibull Edge Detector

The Gaussian distribution is the most popularly used as a model in the field of pattern recognition. It is used to build masks for the first and second derivative. However, it has limit to only symmetric shape. We will propose new method that uses Weibull Distribution which is more general than Gaussian because it has symmetric and asymmetric shape.

In this section the characteristic of 1D Weibull distribution will be explained and how calculate 2D Weibull distribution from 1D. The 1D Weibull distributions have the probability density function is given by:

$$1DW(x;\alpha,\beta) = \begin{cases} \alpha\beta x^{\beta-2} e^{-\alpha x^{\beta}} (\beta - 1 - \alpha\beta x^{\beta}) & x > 0 \\ 0 & \text{elsewhere} \end{cases} \quad (4)$$

The distribution can be skewed to the right as shown in Fig .3 or can be skewed to the left as shown in Fig.4. [8].

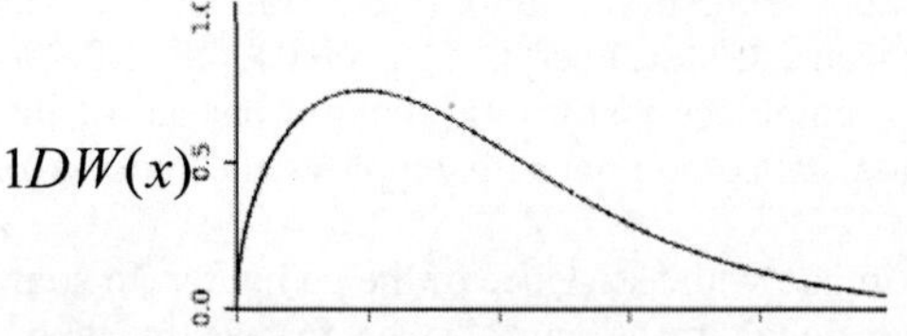

Figure 3. Probability density function of the Weibull distribution (alpha=1, beta=2)

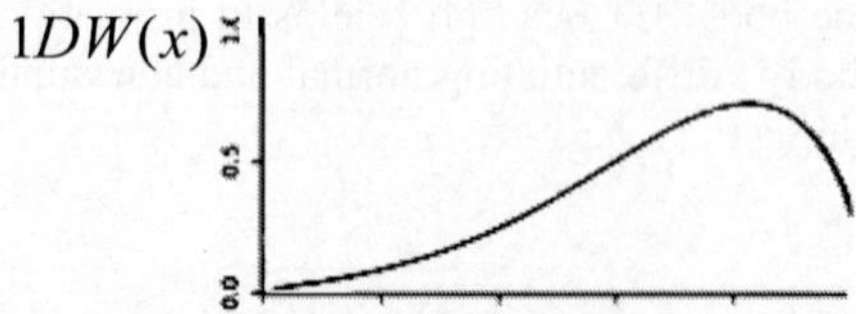

Figure 4. Probability density function of the Weibull distribution (alpha=1, beta=3)

The 2D Weibull distribution can be calculated by multiplying: $1DW(x;\alpha,\beta)$ and $1DW(y;\alpha,\beta)$ where f is"Eq. (4)" given by:

$$2DW(x,y;\alpha,\beta) = 1DW((x;\alpha,\beta)\times 1DW(y;\alpha,\beta) \quad (5)$$

$$= \begin{cases} \alpha^2\beta^2 x^{\beta-1} y^{\beta-1} e^{-\alpha(x^\beta+y^\beta)} \\ 0 \end{cases}$$

In the following section we will explain how perform smoothing using 2D Weibull Distribution then we will explain the applying of edge detection using the gradient of the 2D Weibull Distribution. After that we will present the edge detection using the Laplacian of 2D Weibull Distribution.

4.1. Smoothing Using 2D Weibull Distribution

We can construct smoothing filter from 2D Weibull Distribution. The method is to create general 3x3 mask from 2D Weibull Distribution as show bellow:

$2DW(x-d,y-d)$	$2DW(x-d,y)$	$2DW(x-d,y+d)$
$2DW(x,y-d)$	$2Dw(x,y)$	$2DW(x,y+d)$
$2DW(x+d,y-d)$	$2DW(x+d,y)$	$2DW(x+d,y+d)$

For 5x5 mask the left corner would be $2DW(x-2d,y-2d)$ and for 7x7 would be $2DW(x-3d,y-3d)$ also for 9x9 $2DW(x-4d,y-4d)$ and so on. The sum of all values of the mask must be 1 because it is smooth mask. The value d is incremental and the best value of incremental we can determine through the experiment.

4.2. Edge Detection using the Gradient of the 2D Weibull Distribution

The gradient mask of $2DW(x,y)$ can be constructed by obtaining the first partial derivative of x, y for $2DW(x,y)$. The first x derivative for $2DW(x,y)$ is given by:

$$= \begin{cases} \alpha^2\beta^2 x^{\beta-2} y^{\beta-1} e^{-\alpha(x^\beta+y^\beta)}(\beta-1-\alpha\beta x^\beta) & x>0, y=0 \\ 0 & \text{Elsewhere} \end{cases} \quad (6)$$

The first y derivative for $2DW(x,y)$ is given by:

$$= \begin{cases} \alpha^2\beta^2 y^{\beta-2} x^{\beta-1} e^{-\alpha(x^\beta+y^\beta)}(\beta-1-\alpha\beta y^\beta) & x>0, y=0 \\ 0 & \text{Elsewhere} \end{cases} \quad (7)$$

Using the first x derivative for $2DW(x,y)$ we can construct M_x mask:

$M_x 2DW$ $(x-incx, y-incy)$	$M_x 2DW$ $(x-incx, y)$	$M_x 2DW$ $(x-incx, y+incy)$
$M_x 2DW$ $(x, y-incy)$	$M_x 2DW(x,y)$	$M_x 2DW$ $(x, y+incy)$
$M_x 2DW$ $(x+incx, y-incy)$	$M_x 2DW$ $(x+incx, y)$	$M_x 2DW$ $(x+incx, y+incy)$

Using the first y derivative for $2DW(x,y)$ we can construct M_y mask:

$M_y 2DW$ $(x-incx, y-incy)$	$M_y 2DW$ $(x-incx, y)$	$M_y 2DW$ $(x-incx, y+incy)$
$M_y 2DW$ $(x, y-incy)$	$M_y 2DW(x,y)$	$M_y 2DW$ $(x, y+incy)$
$M_y 2DW$ $(x+incx, y-incy)$	$M_y 2DW$ $(x+incx, y)$	$M_y 2DW$ $(x+incx, y+incy)$

It is needed to calculate two increments one for x and the other for y.

The sum of the gradient mask should be zero. So after constructing the masks, they should be normalized. The positive values are added then divided by their sum to obtain 1 and the negative values are computed in the same way to obtain −1.

The obtained masks at alpha = 1, beta =2 are as follows:

0.6951	**1.5025**	**0.9850**
0	**0**	**0**
-0.3538	**-0.7648**	**-0.5014**

M_x

0.6951	**0**	**-0.3538**
1.5025	**0**	**-0.7648**
0.9850	**0**	**-0.5014**

M_y

After normalization we got these results:

0.2184	**0.4721**	**0.3095**
0	**0**	**0**
-0.2184	**-0.4721**	**-0.3095**

M_x

0.2184	**0**	**- 0.2184**
0.4721	**0**	**- 0.4721**
0.3095	**0**	**-0.3095**

M_y

The obtained masks at alpha = 1, beta =3 are as follows:

0.1550	1.2799	0.9149
0.1785	1.4738	1.0535
-0.2606	- 2.1526	-1.5388

0.1550	0.1785	-0.2606
1.2799	1.4738	-2.1526
0.9149	1.0535	-1.5388

After normalization we got these results:

0.0307	0.2532	0.1810
0.0353	0.2915	0.2084
-0.0660	-0.5447	-0.3894

0.0307	0.0353	-0.0660
0.2532	0.2915	-0.5447
0.1810	0.2084	-0.3894

5. EXPERIMENTAL RESULTS

We present in this section our experimental results of using Weibull Distribution in detecting edges using Gradient of this distribution and compare this result with Sobel.

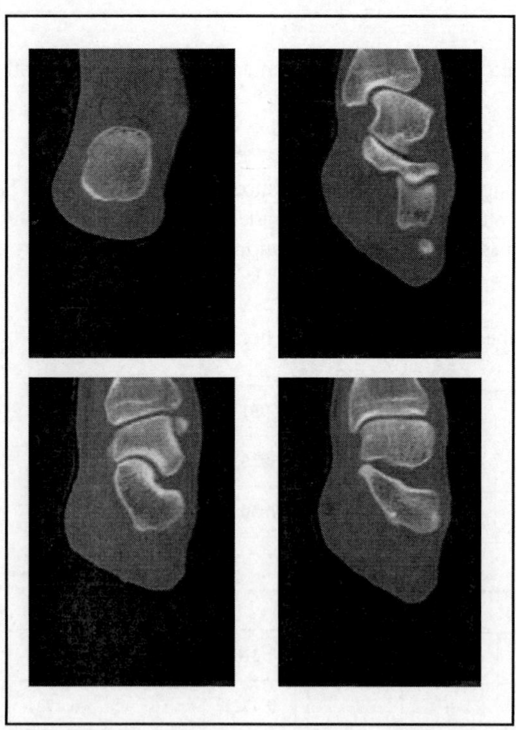

Figure 4. Original Images used in edge detection

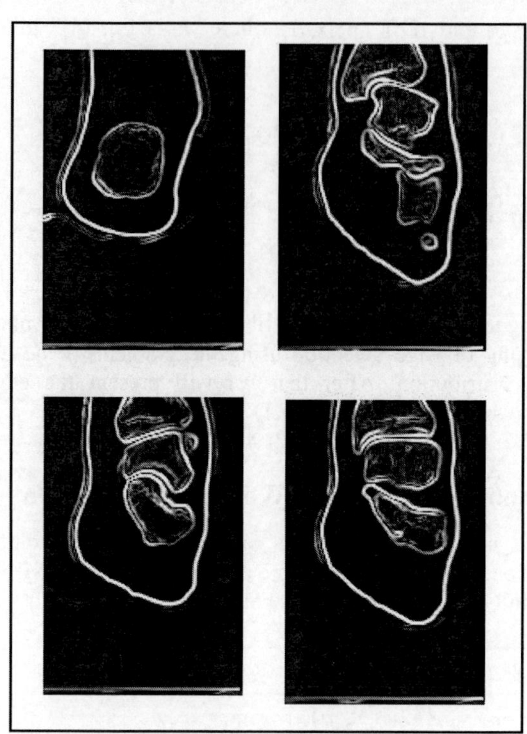

Figure 5. Sobel Results

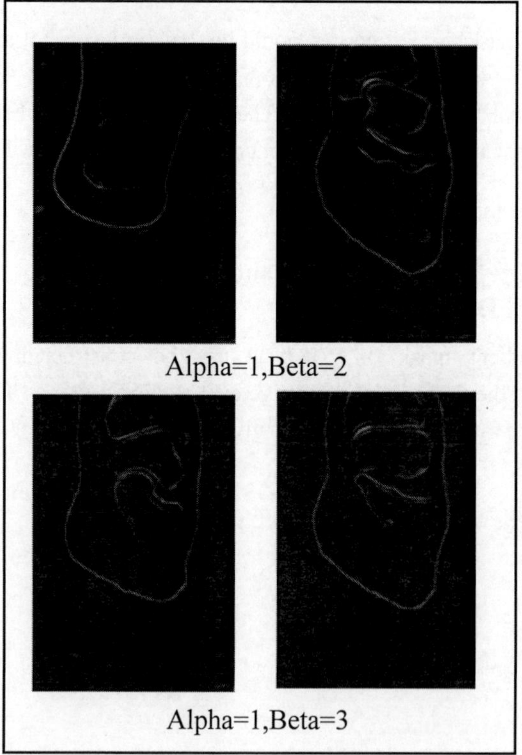

Figure 6. Results of the new Gradient detector of weibull of size 3x3

From Fig.5 and Fig.6 it can be notice that the Weibull distribution is better than the gradient of Gaussian method it produces thinner edges and less sensitive to noise. This is because the Gaussian distribution has limit to only symmetric shape but Weibull distribution has symmetric and asymmetric shape.

6. Conclusion and Future Work

Smoothing is a prior step in every edge detection process to suppress as much noise as possible. Edge detection using first derivative depend on Gaussian works well when the image contains sharp intensity transitions and low noise, while Edge detection using LOG make better localization, especially when the edges are not very sharp. We proposed new method that uses Weibull Distribution instead of Gaussian distribution to build masks for the first and second derivative and for smoothing image.

7. Acknowledgment

We thank the Dr. Toufic El Arwadi for his help on the mathematical calculation.

8. References

[1] Jong Kook Kim, Jeong Mi Park, Koun Sik Song, and Hyun Wook Park" Adaptive Mammographic Image Enhancement Using First Derivative and Local Statistics" IEEE Transactions on medical imaging, Vol.16,No.5,October 1997.

[2] M.GOMATHI Dr.P.Thangaraj , "A Computer Aided Diagnosis System For Detection Of Lung Cancer Nodules Using Extreme Learning Machine", International Journal of Engineering Science and

[3] Technology Vol. 2(10), 2010 [3] R. Gonzalez and R.Woods, "Digital image processing," 3rd Edition, Prentice Hall, New York, 2008, pp. 695.

[4] Trucco and Alessandro Verri." Introductory Techniques for 3-D Computer Vision" Prentice Hall, New York ,1998. Chapter 4.2.

[5] Chung-Chia Kang,Wen-JuneWang, "Anovel edge detection method based on the maximizing objective function," Taiwan, April 2007.

[6] John Canny. "A Computational Approach to Edge Detection Edge Detection".IEEE Transactions on Pattern Analysis and machine intelligence, Vol. PAMI-8, NO. 6, November 1986.

[7] Nick T. Thomopoulos, Arvid C. Johnson." Tables And Characteristics of the Standardized Lognormal Distribution", Proceedings of the Decision Sciences Institute, 2003, pp. 1031-1036.

[8]Sebahattin KIRTA, Derya DISPINARY, "Effect of Ranking Selection on the Weibull Modulus Estimation", Gazi University Journal of Science, 2012.

[9] Eiahl Al-Owaisheq, Areeb Al-Owaisheq and Ali El-Zaart, "A New Edge Detector Using 2D Beta Distribution". Proceedings of the 3rd IEEE International Conference on Information & Communication Technologies : from Theory to Application. April, 9-11, 2008, Syria.

[10] Zhi-Hua Zhou, Yuan Jiang, Yu-Bin Yang, Shi-Fu Chen, "Lung Cancer Cell Identification Based on Artificial Neural Network Ensembles", Artificial Ingelligence in Medicine, 2002, vol.24, no.1, pp.25-36.

[11] Richard J. Qian and Thomas S. Huang, "Optimal edge detection in two-dimensional images," Proc. Image Understanding Workshop, 1994, pp. 1581–1588.

[12] Mitra Basu, "Gaussian-Based Edge-Detection Methods A Survey," IEEE Transactions on systems, man, and cybernetics part C: applications and reviews, vol. 32, no. 3, August 2002.

[13] R. Gurcan, Isin Erer and Sedef Kent, "An Edge Detection Method Using 2-D Autoregressive Lattice Prediction Filters for Remotely Sensed Images," Istanbul Technical University Maslak, İstanbul, Turkey 2004.

[14] Hanna Chidiac and Djemel Ziou, "Classification of Image Edges," Universit´e de Sherbrooke, Sherbrooke (Qc), Canada, J1K 2R1.

[15] B. G. Schunck, "Edge detection with Gaussian filters at multiple scales," in Proc. IEEE Comp. Soc. Work. Comp. Vis., 1987.

[16] L.R. Liang, C.G. Looney, Competitive fuzzy edge detection, Appl. Soft Comput. J. 3 (2003) 123–137.

[17] Nikita Pandey and Sayani Nandy " A Novel Approach of Cancerous Cells Detection from Lungs CT Scan Images" International Journal of Advanced Research in Computer Science and Software Engineering. Volume 2, Issue 8, August 2012.

Wafaa Kamil S. Al-jibory: Currently he is a master student in Beirut Arab University, Department of Mathematics and Computer Science, Beirut, Lebanon (BAU). He has published proceedings in the areas of image processing and computer vision.

Ali El-Zaart was a senior software developer at Department of Research and Development, Semiconductor Insight, Ottawa, Canada during 2000-2001. From 2001 to 2004, he was an assistant professor at the Department of Biomedical Technology, College of Applied Medical Sciences, King Saud University. From 2004-2010 he was an assistant professor at the Department of Computer Science, College of computer and information Sciences, King Saud University. In 2010, he promoted to associate professor at the same department. Currently, his is an associate professor at the department of Mathematics and Computer Science, Faculty of Sciences; Beirut Arab University. He has published numerous articles and proceedings in the areas of image processing, remote sensing, and computer vision. He received a B.Sc. in computer science from the Lebanese University; Beirut, Lebanon in 1990, M.Sc. degree in computer science from the University of Sherbrooke, Sherbrooke, Canada in 1996, and Ph.D. degree in computer science from the University of Sherbrooke, Sherbrooke, Canada in 2001. His research interests include image processing, pattern recognition, remote sensing, and computer vision.

AN AUTOMATIC MODEL-BASED APPROACH FOR MEASURING THE ZONA PELLUCIDA THICKNESS IN DAY FIVE HUMAN BLASTOCYSTS

Dianna Yee[1], *Parvaneh Saeedi*[1] *and Jon Havelock*[2]

1. School of Engineering Science, Simon Fraser University, Burnaby, BC, Canada
2. Pacific Centre for Reproductive Medicine, Burnaby, BC, Canada

ABSTRACT

As technology for human In-Vitro Fertilization (IVF) advances, techniques in analyzing the quality and optimal time for embryo transfer are also growing in sophistication. This paper focuses on an automatic method for gauging the blastocyst development stage based on the measured thickness of the Zona Pellucida (ZP) in digital embryo images of Hoffman Modulation Contrast (HMC) microscopes. Ellipsoidal models are used to capture the ZP boundaries found via edge maps. Comparison of the acquired results with that of the state of the art indicates the efficiency and accuracy of the proposed method.

Index Terms— Human in-vitro fertilization, Image Processing, Zona Pellucida, Blastocyst Grading, Ellipse-Fitting.

1. INTRODUCTION

IVF is a process by which a females egg cells are fertilized outside the body. In IVF, women's ovaries are hyper-stimulated to create multiple ovarian follicles. The female egg cells are then retrieved from the follicles, fertilized and cultured for 1-5 days in controlled environmental conditions, after which one or more embryos are transferred to the patients uterus. Multiple embryos are generated in this process since not all embryos have implantation potential. These embryos are inspected while under development and only those with top-quality are transferred to the uterus. Morphological evaluation of embryo candidates for transfer is an invasive methods that characterize the biological properties of embryos based on individual characteristics of nucleus, ZP, blastomeres, and blastocysts.

The Gardner blastocyst grading system [1] is popularly employed to grade blastocyst embryos by assigning 3 separate quality scores based on the blastocyst development stage (scored from 1 to 6), and the quality of the inner cell mass (ICM), and trophectoderm (TE) (both graded from A to C). The algorithm in this paper focuses on an automated method for measuring the blastocyst development stage.

2. RELATED WORK

In the past 10 years, a limited number of research programs are presented for automatic analysis of human embryo microscopic images at different growth stages [2]. Some studies have tried to establish links between the thickness and morphology of the human ZP and embryo quality, and pregnancy rates [3]. Based on such criteria, active contours are most commonly used to identify the inner and outer boundaries of ZP automatically. Pedersen *et. al.* [4] used level sets by [5] to model embryos boundaries. Morales [6] presented a system using edge detection and active contours to highlight ZP contours. Karlsson *et. al.* [7, 8] described an automatic variational segmentation system for the outer and inner curves of embryos. Although this method reported some success in identifying the inner and outer circumferences, it failed to address disturbances due to poor quality images or nearby fragmented cellular clusters. Karlsson states that such noises naturally have curves to their shape and cause the segmentation method to fail. Recently a semi-automatic method was presented by Santos *et. al.* [9] that used an automated ellipse-model fitting of the ZP but grading assigned mainly based on the segmented area of the TE and ICM. They reported an accuracy of 67%,

The approach presented here is a fully automatic method that also uses an ellipse model but takes an iterative approach to refine the segmented results. The main contribution of this paper is proposing a simple yet intuitive method for automatically detecting ellipsoidal shapes in HMC microscopic images for ZP thickness estimation. The proposed method relies on edge detection and their relative spatial orientations to formulate a proper ellipse model. The image intensity values and gradients are used to refine the model. This algorithm assumes one blastocyst in each image and is intended to be robust, making it applicable to images with cellular noise.

3. PROPOSED METHOD

The proposed method in this paper includes five processes that are performed in a sequential order. Details of each process are presented in this section.

3.1. Create Initial Circular Model for Blastocyst

Initially, a simple circular model is used as a rough estimate of the center of mass and radius of the blastocyst. Dilating the edges detected with Canny and evaluating the convex hull of prominent connected edges, a circular mask forms the initial model. This allows for a priori information when extracting the inner ZP boundary. Treating the convex hull as an object, O, made up of N pixels, the center of O at is given by:

$$< x_c, y_v >= \lfloor \frac{1}{N} \sum_i N < x_i, y_i > \rfloor \quad (1)$$

If $S_{perimeter}$ denotes the set of pixels along the perimeter of O containing pixels p_i, which satisfies

$$S_{perimeter} = \{p_i | p_i \in O - erorded(O)\} \quad (2)$$

The pixel locations of the perimeter $< p_{i,x}, p_{i,y} >$ relative to the calculated center of O is a distance, r_i apart

$$r_i = \sqrt{(p_{i,x} - x_c)^2 + (p_{i,y} - y_c)^2} \quad (3)$$

The approximate radius of the circle is given by the average of all the radial distances calculated.

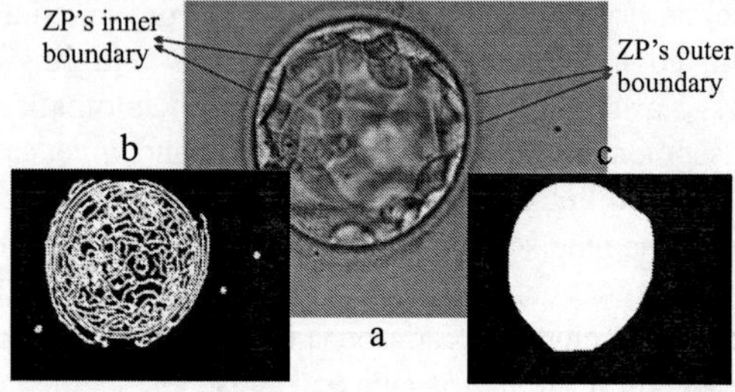

Fig. 1: a. HMC image of day-5 blastocyst. b. Dilated edges. c. Convex hull for the initial circle model

3.2. Inner Boundary ZP Detection

As seen in Figure 1.a, the inner ZP boundary is a prominent feature in the image classified by a strong and dark boundary. Considering the conic equation of an ellipse,

$$F(x, y) = A.X + f = 0 \quad (4)$$

where $A = [a\, b\, c\, d\, e]$ and $X = [x^2\, xy\, y^2\, x\, y]$. Let A_c denote the estimated vector of the parameters of A, and X denotes a matrix form of all the measured locations $< x, y >$. The linear least squares fitting [10] is used to minimize algebraic distance of the cost function:

$$Cost(A) = (A_c.X + f)'.(A_c.X + f) \quad (5)$$

and estimate an ellipse model. The quality of the fitted ellipse improves when the points measured are distributed along the entire perimeter of the ellipse, indicating a strong edge. Consider the Fourier series expansion of a 1D signal

$$F(x) = \sum_n A_n cos(n\omega x + \phi_n) \quad (6)$$

where ω is a constant and ϕ_n is the phase offset. The phase congruency of the signal is:

$$PC(x) = \max_{\theta \in [0, 2\pi]} \frac{\sum_n A_n cos(n\omega x + \phi_n - \theta)}{\epsilon + \sum_n A_n(x)} \quad (7)$$

here ϵ is added to prevent division by zero. The energy of the signal is given by:

$$E(x) = \sqrt{F(x)^2 + H(x)^2} \quad (8)$$

where $H(x)$ is the Hilbert transform of $F(x)$. $E(x)$ is proportional to the phase congruency:

$$pc(x) = \frac{E(x)}{\epsilon + \sum_n A_n(x)} \quad (9)$$

The phase congruency of a signal ranges in [0, 1], where 1 correlates to a strong edge feature where the Fourier components are maximally in phase. To apply phase congruency to a 2D signal, one has to consider the local energy over several orientations. In this application, 6 orientations were chosen. Using a Gabor filter on each orientation when calculating phase congruency, edge features are extracted. For each orientation θ, the phase congruency is calculated. The orientation with the highest energy is then assigned as the prominent orientation of each pixel location. As seen in Figure 2.a, the orient of the image is shown in six distinct colors. The edges along the inner ZP have a strong coherence in orientation that separates the perimeter into twelve distinct intervals.

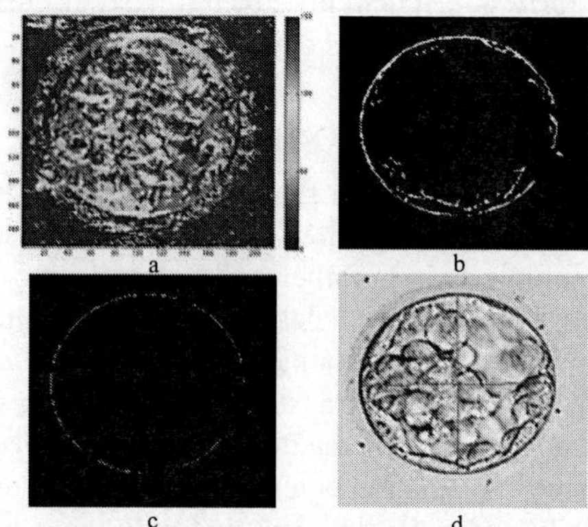

Fig. 2: a. Gabor filtered phase congruency at 30° increments. b. Strong edge candidates. c. Filtered edge candidates along the convex hull. d. Fitted ellipse on inner ZP boundary.

Treating the image as a 2D signal and using the relationship between signal energy and phase congruency, the strong edges relating to the inner ZP boundary can be distinguished from the outer ZP via thresholding the phase congruency image and also evaluating the strength of the edge by considering the area of the connected edge piece in each orientation.

Using the radius and center of the initial circle model, invalid candidates such as far away fragmented cellular clusters are removed (Figure 2.b). The edge candidates that coincide the outer perimeter of the convex hull of all the edges, as seen in Figure 2.c, are fitted with an ellipse as seen in Figure 2.d.

3.3. Outer Boundary ZP Detection

The previous method for the inner ZP detection fails for outer ZP as coherence in the orientation of the edges detected around the outer ZP is not as strong and is susceptible to noise. In addition, outer ZP boundary is more similar in intensity and texture granularity to the background. After removing the background of image, $T(I) = I - mean(I)$, the intensities around the outer ZP boundary can be seen with a greater contrast. Applying a threshold to the phase congruency of the image in union with the edges detected with Canny detector on $T(I)$, a binary image denoting pixels of significant edge potential is generated. Since the outer ZP is susceptible to low pixel intensity noise or the edges of fragmented cellular clusters, watershed segmentation is performed on the dilated mask to find erroneous regions with low pixel intensities. Super-imposing the convex hull of the inner ZP ellipse found and a dilated mask of the thresholded phase congruency image and edge detection of the transformed image, the distance transform of the complement is manipulated to yield basins for the watershed segmentation as seen in Figure 3.a. The mean intensity of these segmented regions is used to remove regions of low intensity, Figure 3.b. The remaining edge candidates, Figure 3.c, are used for ellipse fitting in subsequent steps.

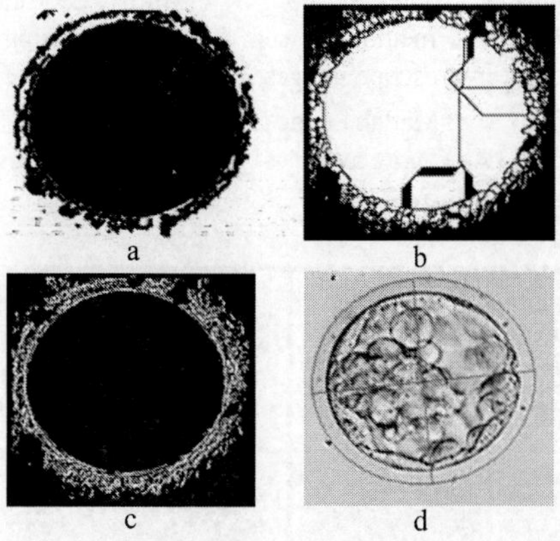

Fig. 3: a. Input for Watershed segmentation. b. Dilated phase congruency edge map segmented via Watershed. c. Strong edge candidates. d. Fitted ellipse on outer ZP boundary.

A similar approach for removing weak candidates based on the radial distance from the origin of the inner ZP model is applied. The modelled inner ZP boundary found can be abstracted by two parameters, r_o, the origin of the ellipse, and a function of radial distance between the ellipse boundary and r_o, $r(\theta)$, where θ is the angle between the radial vector and x-axis. The radial distance between a pixel location and r_o can be represented by $d(s_i, r_o)$ where s_i is the specific pixel location. Let S be the set of all strong candidates which satisfies the following constraint:

$$S = \{s_i | s_i \in (d(s_i, r_o) < (1+\alpha) d(r(\theta), r_o)) \cap (mean(edge_i(s_i)) > \beta mean(I))\} \quad (10)$$

where $mean(edge_i(s_i))$ is the mean pixel intensity of the connected region containing s_i and $\alpha = 0.4$ and $\beta = 0.5$ are chosen constants for thresholding. The fitted ellipse is shown in Figure 3.d.

3.4. Refinement of Boundaries Detected

In cases where there lies a deviant cellular cluster that may skew the fitted ellipse model, refinement is required. As seen in Figure 4.a, the skewing of fitted ellipse leads to an inaccurate model. Since the inner boundary of ZP generally includes dark edge points, the fitted ellipse should fall on pixels of lower intensities while the fitted ellipse of the outer ZP should fall on pixels with higher intensities. In the example in Figure 4.b, the red locations refer to inaccurate locations found in the initial inner ZP candidate in Figure 4.a as these pixel intensity values are suspiciously high compared to the other boundary points of the fitted ellipse. To refine the initial model, an automatic thresholding histogram approach is used that refines edge candidates of the fitted model to ignore such deviate noise. Figure 4.c shows the refined model.

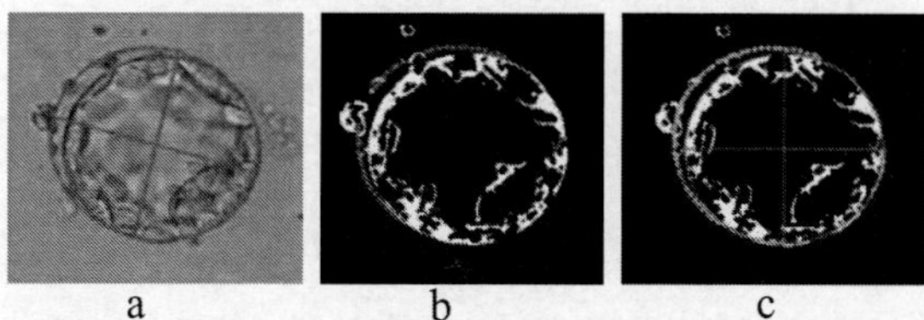

Fig. 4: a. Initial ellipse model. b. Inaccurate sampled model points shown in red. c. Ignored sample points in ellipse fitting shown in green, new ellipse model shown in continuous red.

3.5. Verification of Ellipse Models

In the case that a poor candidate is generated, edges along the modeled ellipse are not strongly developed. Here, the magnitude and orientation of the gradient of the ellipse models are used to evaluate the validity of the identified candidate.

Considering the parametric formula for an ellipse with major and minor axes a, b, centered at (X_c, Y_c) with angle between the X-axis and the major axis of the ellipse of θ,

$$\begin{aligned} X(t) &= X_c + acos(t)cos(\theta) - bsin(t)sin(\theta) \\ Y(t) &= Y_c + acos(t)sin(\theta) - bsin(t)cos(\theta) \end{aligned} \quad (11)$$

where t is in $[0 - 2\pi]$ and its respective tangential vector is $< X'(t), Y'(t) >$. Let $< dx, dy >$ be the gradient vector of a pixel location at $< X(t), Y(t) >$, the angle between the image gradient and tangential vectors at the ellipse candidates, Φ, is given by

$$cos(\Phi) = < \frac{X'(t)}{|X'(t)|}, \frac{Y'(t)}{|Y'(t)|} > . < dx, dy > \quad (12)$$

Φ should ideally be $\pi/2$ to indicate a strong edge. The deviation of Φ from $\pi/2$ and the magnitude of the gradient of the ellipse edge can indicate the validity of the edge detected. Choosing a limitation of $|cos\Phi| > \frac{1}{\sqrt{3}}$, we eliminate edges that make an angle less than 30° with the gradient vector. The choice of 30° parallels our choice of having 30° interval Gabor filters to distinguish between dissimilar edges.

4. EXPERIMENTAL RESULTS

We have tested our algorithm for a set of 20 images that also been manually graded by an expert.

4.1. ZP Detection

As mentioned earlier, the inner ZP candidates generated tend to be more accurate as the outer ZP boundary is more susceptible to image noise and cellular disturbances. The average running time of the algorithm written in Matlab, on a system with a 2.3 GHz Intel Core i7 processor, 16 GB 1600 MHz RAM and 250 GB SSD, is about 12 seconds. Figure 5 displays the final detected ZPs the input images.

4.2. Comparison with the Ground Truth

Comparing the areas within the ZP boundaries that were manually segmented, M, and automatically segmented, A, we define a metric of the error for our segmentation by:

$$ZP_{err} = (M \cap A) \cup \sim (M \cap A)^c \quad (13)$$

The above error denotes regions that the automated method missed or wrongfully included. This error is normalized using the area of the manually segmented boundaries:

$$ZP_{Nerr} = ZP_{err}/area(M) \quad (14)$$

The average normalized error for ZPs' outer and inner boundaries and their thickness for 20 test cases are shown in Table 1.

Table 1: Mean error results for 20 test cases.

Mean ZP outer boundary error [%]	Mean ZP inner boundary error [%]	Mean ZP thickness error [%]
2.9	7.6	6.9

5. CONCLUSION

Ellipse modeling for the ZP can be successful but one needs to take into account of probable environmental noise due to fragmented cellular clusters. Iteration refining based on histogram thresholding on valid image intensities and gradient magnitude and orientation can help correct such errors to provide more consistent automatically acquired results.

6. REFERENCES

[1] D. Gardner, J. Stevens, C. Sheehan, and W. Schoolcraft, "Analysis of blastocyst morphology," *Human preimplantation embryo selection*, pp. 79–87, 2007.

[2] Kay Elder, *human embryo preimplantation selection*, Informa UK Ltd, 2007.

[3] A. Gabrielsen, S. Lindenberg, and K. Petersen, "The impact of the zona pellucida thickness variation of human embryos on pregnancy outcome in relation to suboptimal embryo development. a prospective randomized controlled study.," *Hum Reprod*, vol. 16, no. 10, pp. 2166–70, 2001.

[4] U. Pedersen, O. Olsen, and N. Olsen, "A multiphase variational level set approach for modelling human embryos," in *IEEE workshop on Variational Geometric and Level Set Methods in C. V.*, 2003, pp. 25–32.

[5] H. Zhao, T. Chan, B. Merriman, and S. Osher, "A variational level set approach to multiphase motion," *Journal of Computational Physics*, vol. 127, no. 1, pp. 179–195, 1996.

[6] D. Morales, E. Bengoetxea, and P. Larraaga, "Automatic segmentation of zona pellucida in human embryo images applying an active contour model," *MIUA*, pp. 209–213, 2008.

[7] A. Karlsson, N. Chr. Overgaard, and A. Heyden, "A two-step area based method for automatic tight segmentation of zona pellucida in hmc images of human embryos.," in *Scale-Space*, 2005, vol. 3459 of *Lect. Notes in Comp. Sci.*, pp. 503–514.

[8] A. Karlsson, N. Chr. Overgaard, and A. Heyden, "Automatic segmentation of zona pellucida in hmc images of human embryos," in *ICPR*, 2004, vol. 3, pp. 518–521.

[9] E. Filho, J. Noble, M. Poli, T. Griffiths, G. Emerson, and D. Wells, "A method for semi-automatic grading of human blastocyst microscope images.," *Hum Reprod*, 2012.

[10] O. Gal, "Matlab code for ellipse fitting," 2003, `http://www.mathworks.com-/matlabcentral/fileexchange/3215-fitellipse`.

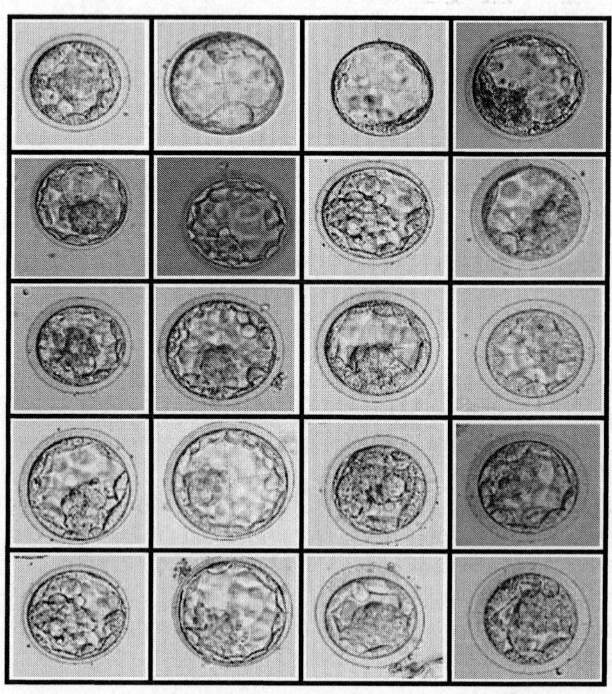

Fig. 5: Final estimated ZPs models superimposed in red.

MRI Abdominal Organ Tissue Identification using Statistical Distance in Color Space

Arend Castelein[1], Terrance Weeden[2], Xiuping Tao[3], H. Keith Brown[2], Yong Wei[1]

1. Department of Computer Science, University of North Georgia, Dahlonega, GA 30597, USA
2. Department of Clinical Anatomy, Philadelphia College of Osteopathic Medicine-Georgia, Suwanee, GA 30024, USA
3. Department of Chemistry, Winston Salem State University, Winston Salem, NC 27110, USA

Submitted to: IPCV'13: The 2013 International Conference on Image Processing, Computer Vision and Pattern Recognition

Abstract

Magnetic resonance imaging (MRI) is a powerful medical imaging technique to provide detailed images of soft abdomen organ tissues. An automatic organ tissue identification algorithm is useful for physicians to perform initial reading and interpret MRI images. The algorithm presented in the paper uses the distance in color space between centers of organ tissues to identify abdominal organs in MRI images. Experimental results show the algorithm is effective in the RGB, LAB and AB color spaces.

Key words: organ identification, MRI, image processing.

1. Introduction

Magnetic resonance imaging (MRI) is a powerful medical imaging technique to provide detailed images of soft abdomen organ tissues. Manual organ tissue identification by medical dosimetrist is time consuming. To become a dosimetrist requires special training. Hence, developing an automatic organ tissue identification algorithm is useful for physicians to perform initial reading and interpret MRI images.

Segmentation and identification of abdominal organs, such as kidney, liver, spleen, pancreas and stomach, from CT and MRI images, has been attracting a fair amount of research. Lee et al. [1] use a neural network that takes advantage of shape analysis, image contextual constraint, and between-slice relationship to extract disconnected regions from CT images. Fujimoto et al. [2] extract and recognize abdominal organs from CT images using 3D mathematical morphology. To overcome the problem of intensity inhomogeneity in MRI images, the parametric method for bias field estimation is used by Li et al. [3] The fuzzy version of k-means clustering (fuzzy c-means, FCM) is widely adopted for vector quantization and data compression [4][5].

This work uses color fusion MRI methodology to extract color images from longitudinal relaxation time T_1 and transverse relaxation time T_2 images. A previously established standardized acquisition and image processing protocol is used to produce color MRI images of a variety of abdominal tissues of human subjects. We assume that pixels for each tissue object in an MRI image have similar property, whilst pixels in different organ tissues are different in color space. Therefore, identifying an organ tissue in an MRI image becomes the problem of finding the closest set of pixels of a known tissue in the color space.

In this work, abdominal MRI images are first segmented using fuzzy c-means clustering in the $l*a*b$ color space [5]. A physician can choose a region of interest of an unknown abdominal organ in the segmented image. Statistical distances between the centers of known abdominal organ tissues and the region of interest of an unknown organ are used to identify which organ it belongs to. T-test is performed to further verify the results. Experiments show that the algorithm yields very satisfactory results. Results obtained from data in various color spaces are explored as well.

The remainder of the paper is as follows. Section 2 describes the statistical distance-based organ identification algorithm. Section 3 discusses the experimental data preparation and results. Section 4 concludes the paper with an outline for future work.

2. Statistical Distance-based Organ Identification

The different organs or tissues have different combinations of biophysical parameters that are mapped in MR images. When each of the parameter maps are assigned color masks and then fused into a single full color image, tissues with different biophysical parameters are displayed as different in color. Tissues with very similar biophysical parameters appear as very similar in color.

We assume that color is a constant property for each tissue object in an MRI image. Therefore identifying organ in an abdominal MRI image becomes the problem of finding the shortest distance between the center of a known abdominal organ tissues and the region of interest of the unknown organ.

The algorithm is designed to identify different organs from an MRI image based on the color center of that image. The color center of a region of interest is defined as follows:

$$C_j = \frac{1}{n}\sum_{i=1}^{n} i_j \qquad (2.1)$$

where C_j represents the center of color channel j (for example red, green or blue in RGB space) and n is the number of pixels in the region.

The distance for each pixel from the center of color channel C_j is calculated as follows

$$d_i = \sqrt{\sum_{j=1}^{m} (i_j - C_j)^2} \qquad (2.2)$$

where d_i is the Euclidian distance from center of the color space for pixel i and m is the number of channels in the color space. The mean of the distances is then calculated as follows

$$\bar{d} = \frac{1}{n}\sum_{i=1}^{n} d_i \qquad (2.3)$$

where n is the number of pixels in the region of interest. And then the standard deviation σ is calculated as shown here

$$\sigma = \sqrt{\frac{1}{n}\sum_{i=1}^{n}(d_i - \bar{d})^2} \quad (2.4)$$

This process is repeated for all the sets up images representing different organs.

After an unknown organ in an image, represented as u, is selected the probable organ identity is determined through the following process. The center of the color space C_u and the number of pixels in the image n are found as they were in the predefined data. Then it iterates through the following process for each known organ k. It starts by calculating the Euclidian distance between the center for the unknown image region and the center for known organ k.

$$d_{uk} = \sqrt{\sum_{j=1}^{m}(C_{uj} - C_{kj})^2} \quad (2.5)$$

m represents the number of color channels in the image. d_{uk} represents the distance between the centers of unknown image region u and known organ k. This distance is then converted into a t-score using the following equation

$$t_{uk} = \frac{d_{uk}}{\sigma_k / \sqrt{n}} \quad (2.6)$$

where t_{uk} represents the t-score for image region u compared to known organ k.

Basing the identity of the image region solely upon its distance from the organs color center can cause problems. In the graph below [6] notice that the center of the image, represented by the red line, is closer to organ B yet according to the frequency diagram the prospect of the organ adhering to organ A is more likely.

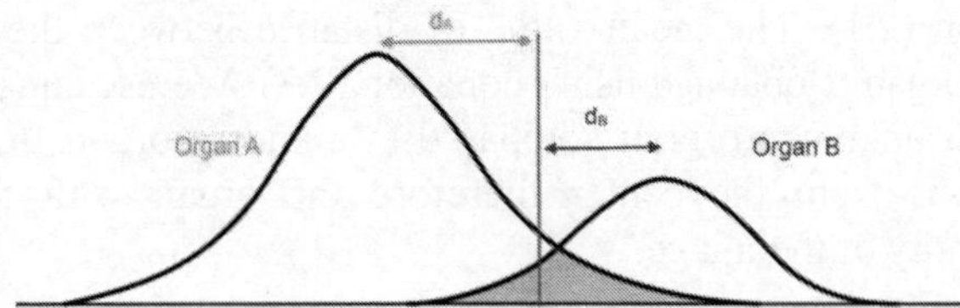

Fig 2.1 Centers of Organ Image and Color Distributions

Using t-distribution takes this problem into account by defining the distance in terms of how many standard deviations it is away from the organ.

3. Experimental Results

Images used in experiment are extracted from longitudinal relaxation time T_1 and transverse relaxation time T_2 MRI images. The ColorMRI[tm] methodology generates full color images from the plurality of gray tone images acquired by magnetic resonance imaging. The gray tone images are essentially mappings of biophysical/nuclear magnetic resonance parameters such as longitudinal relaxation time T_1, transverse relaxation time T_2, proton density (PD), magnetic susceptibility, gadolinium contrast media enhancement, etc. Assignment of color masks to each biophysical parameter image and subsequent fusion of the color masked images results in a full color image in which the unique color of each pixel in the RGB color space represents the combination of unique biophysical parameters of the tissue represented by that pixel.

Following is an example of an abdominal color MRI of labeled regions of interest. Liver, pancreas and kidney are labeled. Hepatic tissue (liver) is located on the far left side of the image. Renal tissue is found adjacent to the liver. Pancreatic tissue is located toward the center of the image.

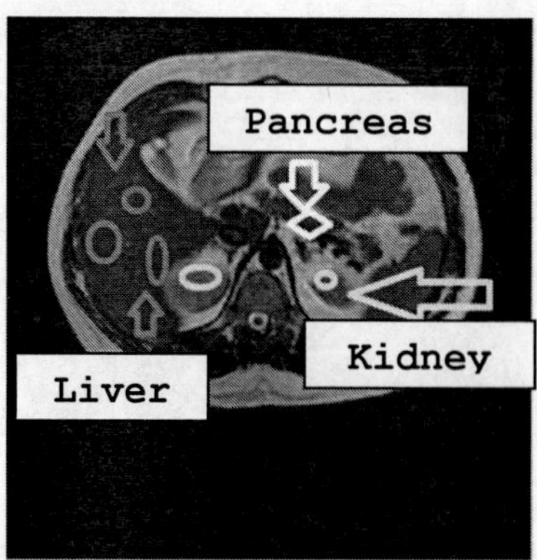

Fig. 3.1 An Abdominal Color MRI of Labeled Region of Interest

In the experiments, MRI images are separated into two groups. The training data set contains 80% of the whole set. The rest 20% are for the testing data set. From both the training and testing data set, images are first segmented using fuzz c-means clustering described in [5]. The regions of interest (ROI) of various abdominal organs are manually selected. The center of each ROI is calculated using equation (2.1). The mean value of distance between the ROI of an unknown organ and every known organ is obtained using equation (2.3). We use equation (2.5) to calculate the t-score for ROI of an unknown orgran compared to a known organ. A low t-score indicates fewer standard deviations from the center therefore the organ with the lowest t-score is determined to be the identity of the image.

Table 3.1 shows the centers and standard deviations of organs in the training data set in the RBG, LAB and AB color space respectively.

Name of Organ	Centers in RGB	Centers in LAB	Centers in AB	Standard Deviation in RGB	Standard Deviation in LAB	Standard Deviation in AB
Kidney	[114,87,114]	[104,143,117]	[143, 117]	6.63	3.77	3.51
Liver	[97,53,49]	[71, 147, 140]	[147, 140]	6.05	3.59	2.01
Muscle	[78,31,41]	[49, 151, 132]	[151, 132]	8.94	5.49	2.45
Pancreas	[107, 66, 59]	[83, 146, 140]	[146, 140]	8.7	5.23	1.5
Spleen	[114, 71, 94]	[91, 150, 122]	[150, 122]	4.68	2.8	1.68
Stomach	[143,174,213]	[178,124,104]	[124, 104]	10.19	5.3	4.49

Table 3.1 Centers and Standard Deviations of Known Organs of Training Data in RGB, LAB and AB Color Space

Accuracy (%)	**Kidney**	**Liver**	**Muscle**	**Pancreas**	**Spleen**	**Stomach**
In *RGB*	100	100	100	100	100	100
In *LAB*	100	100	100	100	100	100
In *AB*	100	100	67	75	100	100
Using t-score in *RGB*	100	100	100	100	100	100
Using t-score in *LAB*	100	100	100	100	100	100
Using t-score in *AB*	67	100	100	25	100	100

Table 3.2 Organ/Tissue Identification Results

Results of organ identification are listed in Table 3.2. It is demonstrated that the statistical distance-based identification algorithm yields very satisfactory results in both the *RGB* and *LAB* color spaces. The behavior of the algorithm in the *AB* space deserves a discussion.

In the *RGB* color space, differences among colors perceived by the human eye as being of the same entity are not mirrored by similar distances between the points representing those colors in the color spaces. The problem is reduced in the CIE *LAB* color space [7]. In the CIE *LAB* space, L represents the brightness, i.e. intensity. From the results shown in Table 3.2, it is noted that color intensities play an important role in distinguishing tissues.

Organ Name	**Distance in RGB Space**	**Distance in LAB Space**	**Distance in AB Space**
Kidney	61.6	31.9	25.7
Liver	20.1	13.8	**2.9**
Muscle	49.9	37.1	11.0
Pancreas	**5.2**	**3.4**	3.2
Spleen	38.9	21.7	20.6
Stomach	193.6	103.5	44.5

Table 3.3 Distances of a ROI of Pancreas from Other Organs

In our experiments, ROIs of pancreas are mis-identified as liver tissue in the *AB* space. Table 3.3 shows the distances of it from known organs. This is due to the histological differences between the two organs even though both are glandular organs. Hepatic tissue has a more extensive blood supply than the pancreas, allowing it to store iron, synthesize proteins, and house many mitochondria that contain cytochrome c. The presence of ferritin and cytochrome c has an effect on the imaging of the liver in that it lowers the signal of the waves that are recorded by the MRI scanner. This is evidenced by the brightness values of liver and pancreas listed in Table 3.1. Liver and pancreas tissue brightness values in the *LAB* space are 71 and 83 respectively. In the mean time, their *AB* components are similar, [147,140] and [[146,140] for liver and pancreas respectively.

4. Conclusions

In this paper, we use the statistical distance-based algorithm to identify abdominal organ in MRI images. Experimental results show that distance between centers of regions of interest of organ tissues can effectively distinguish tissues. Developing an automatic organ tissue identification algorithm is useful for physicians to perform initial reading and interpret MRI images. In the future, the algorithm will be further tested on more MRI data, and will be extended to identify other human tissues.

References

[1] Chien-Cheng Lee, and Pau-Choo Chung, “Recognizing abdominal organs in CT images using contextual neural networks and fuzzy rules,” in Proc. 22nd Annu. Int. Conf. of the IEEE Engineering in Medicine and Biology Society, Chicago, IL, July 23-28, 2000.

[2] Hideyuki Fujimoto, Lixu Gu, and Toyohisa Kaneko, “Recognition of abdominal organs using 3D mathematical morphology,” Trans. Inst. Electron. Inf. Commun. Eng. D-II, no. 5, pp. 843-850, May 2001.

[3] Chunming Li, ChenyangXu, Adam W. Anderson, and John C. Gore, "MRI Tissue Classification and Bias Field Estimation Based on Coherent Local Intensity Clustering: A Unified Energy Minimization Framework", J.L. Prince, D.L. Pham, and K.J. Myers (Eds.): IPMI 2009, LNCS 5636, pp. 288–299, Springer, 2009.

[4] Alan Wee-Chung Liew, and Hong Yan, “An adaptive spatial fuzzy clustering algorithm for 3-D MR image segmentation.” IEEE Trans. Med. Imag. 22(9), 1063–1075 (2003).

[5] Yong Wei, H. Keith Brown, Xiuping Tao, Samuel Moore, Dongshen Che, "Brain MRI Image Segmentation using Fuzzy C-Means Clustering", Proc. IPCV 2010, Las Vegas, Nevada, USA, July 12-15, 2010.

[6] Oswald Sonntag, Quality in the analytical phase, Biochemia Medica 20(2):147-53, 2010.

[7] L. Lucchese and S.K. Mitra, Color image segmentation: A state-of-the-art survey, *Image Process. Vis. Pattern Recog. Proc.*, Indian Nat. Sci. Acad. (INSA-A), v67 i2, 2001, pp. 207-221.

A Practical TDMA Protocol for Underwater Acoustic Networks Based on Relative Clock

Jiarong Zhang, Can Wang, and Gang Qiao
National Laboratory of Underwater Acoustic Technology, Harbin Engineering University,
Harbin, Heilongjiang Province, P.R. China

Abstract - *This paper proposes a practical TDMA protocol for underwater acoustic networks which are characterized by long propagation delays and limited energy. The protocol saves transmission energy by avoiding collisions while maximizing throughput. It is based on the relative clock by mapping the network schedule to every node's local clock and taking local clock to arrange work schedule. Node synchronization is not needed and clock offset is modified during data transmitting. This protocol achieves a throughput several times higher than that of the CSMA, while offering similar savings in energy. Although CS-ALOHA offers a similar throughput, it wastes much more power on collisions.*

Keywords: underwater acoustic networks; relative clock; TDMA

1 Introduction

As electromagnetic waves propagate poorly in sea water, acoustics provides the most obvious medium to enable underwater communications [1-3]. Underwater acoustic networks (UAN) have grate application values in marine research, natural disaster warning, underwater vehicles navigation, offshore defense and et al [4]. Underwater acoustic channel is challenging due to limited bandwidth, extended multipath, refractive properties of the medium, severe fading, rapid time-variation and large Doppler shifts [5-6]. Communication techniques originally developed for terrestrial wired and wireless channels need significant modifications to suit underwater channels [7-9]. Even worse, acoustic modem, key facility for UAN is energy limited and hard to recharge. Energy efficient protocols are critical needed for prolonging the UAN lifetime. Although CSMA (Carrier Sense Multiple Access) can reduce the collision energy waste as much as possible by hand-shaking mechanism, it also increases end-to-end delay during hand-shaking procedures since the propagation delay is very long. TDMA (Time Division Multiple Access) assign fixed time slot to every node to avoid collision, as well as reduce time wasting in channel reservation. But, in originally developed TDMA, strict clock synchronization is needed, while this is next to impossible in UAN. This fact has been recognized recently by several authors, and some possible TDMA protocols for underwater acoustic channel are proposed [10-11], but it needs the synchronization signal to be broadcasted periodically.

Corresponding author: Gang Qiao, qiaogang@hrbeu.edu.cn.

Here, we propose under the name of Relative Clock based Time Division Multiple Access (RC-TDMA) a practical protocol for centralized UAN. In this protocol, clock synchronization is not needed, network schedule is mapped to the node's local clock line and its individual work schedule is arranged according to signal arrival time and received network schedule, clock offset caused by quartz accuracy, position change or some other reasons will be modified during the data transmitting course.

The rest of this paper is organized as follows: Section 2 we detail the design of our RC-TDMA protocol. The performance of RC-TDMA is studied via extensive simulations in Section 3. In Section 4, we conducted a Lake Trail to validate the practicability of protocol. We conclude with directions for future work in Section 5.

2 Protocol description

Network topologies of UAN are usually divided into two categories: centralized and distributed. In centralized UAN, TDMA protocol is an ideal choice for avoiding collision and shortening end-to-end delay. The RC-TDMA protocol we proposed in this paper is based on the centralized topology, which can be illustrated as Fig.1 shows, consists of one gateway node (O) and some other sub-nodes (such as A, B, C), positions of these nodes are fixed.

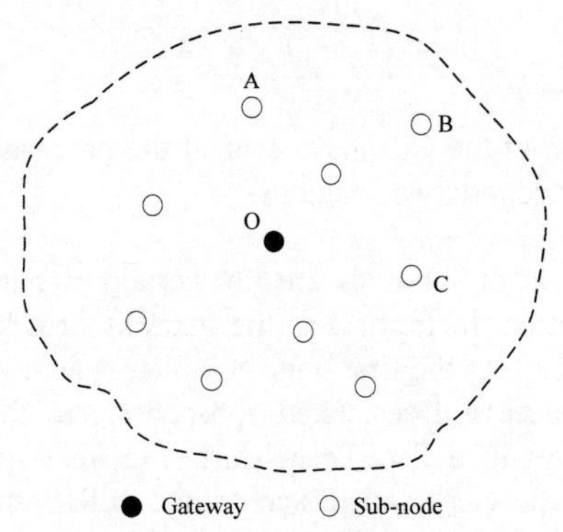

Fig.1 Network topology.

The basic considerations of RC-TDMA are using the local clock to arrange individual work schedule without any complex synchronization, make the nodes transmitting data in parallel according to their propagation delays to improve throughput, and modify the clock offset during data transmitting to avoiding collision. Work progress of RC-TDMA can be divided into three portions: schedule registration, schedule mapping and data transmitting, clock offset modifying.

2.1 Schedule registration

Schedule registration needs two steps: delay estimation and schedule arrangement. Propagation delay estimation is used to arrange schedule in staggered. We do not concern the propagation delay between the sub-nodes, only the gateway to sub-nodes propagation delays are needed. Fig.2 shows the main course of estimating the propagation delays between gateway and sub-nodes.

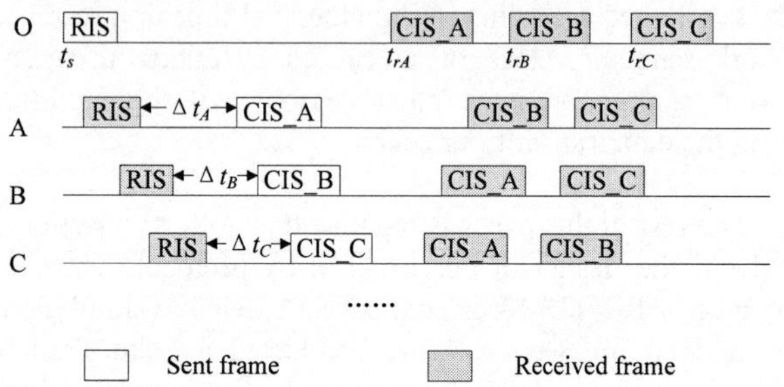

Fig.2 Flow chart of propagation delay estimation.

Let's take gateway O and sub-nod A to illustrating the propagation delay estimation procedure. On network initializing, O broadcasts the Require Initialize Signal (RIS) to A and records the send time t_s. After RIS arrived, A chooses a random interval time to send back the Clear Initialize Signal (CIS), which contains the interval Δt_A from RIS arrived to CIS sent. Arrive time t_{rA} of CIS from A will be recorded by O at the moment of CIS arrived, and the propagation delay between gateway O and sub-node A can be depicted as:

$$T_{pdA} = t_{rA} - t_s - \Delta t_A \tag{1}$$

Collision of the CIS may occur at the gateway, for this problem, we propose two solutions:

If the IDs of sub-nods are not certain, we use multi-stage registration. In first stage, the gateway broadcasts RIS to all sub-nodes. As the first stage complete, gateway records the IDs of successful registered sub-nodes and the corresponding delays in a list. Then, starts the next stage registration with the successful IDs contained in RIS, the corresponding sub-nodes keep silence. After this stage complete, new successful IDs and corresponding delays will be add to the list. This course will be repeated until no sub-node responses the RIS, which considered as the end of initialization.

If the IDs of sub-nodes are confirmed, we use polling registration. Gateway sends RIS to sub-nodes one by one and adds the succeeded IDs and corresponding delays to list sequentially until the last sub-node has been requested.

After all propagation delays have been obtained, the gateway arranges the schedule in interleaved to make the sub-nodes working in parallel according to the delays. For example, the receive time-window on gateway for sub-node A and B are respectively (0,10) s and (10,20) s as Fig.3 shows, propagation delay of sub-node B is 10 s longer than that of B, thus A and B can transmit data simultaneously without collision.

Fig.3 Receive time rectangle on gateway clock line.

Network schedule is as Fig.4 shows, each row filled with sub-node ID and its corresponding parameters including the working period T, working time-window T_{wi}, propagation delay T_{pdi} and sending time modified value t_{mi}. After schedule arrangement has been finished, the gateway dispatches it to all sub-nods.

ID_1	T	T_{w1}	T_{pd1}	t_{m1}
ID_2	T	T_{w2}	T_{pd2}	t_{m2}
ID_3	T	T_{w3}	T_{pd3}	t_{m3}

......

Fig.4 Network schedule information.

2.2 Schedule mapping and data transmitting

On receiving the schedule, each sub-nodes mark the arrival moment as the clock line start point, and find its corresponding parameters from the schedule, then, the data sending time t_{is} can be expressed as:

$$t_{is} = t_{ir} + t_{mi} + kT \tag{2}$$

Sub-nodes send data in their working windows, and keep a T_{di} length monitoring for acknowledgement (ACK) from gateway. If AKC is received, next send time will be modified according to the information from ACK, otherwise, the sub-node go to sleep and wake up automatically at next working period. This course can be illustrated as Fig.5 shows.

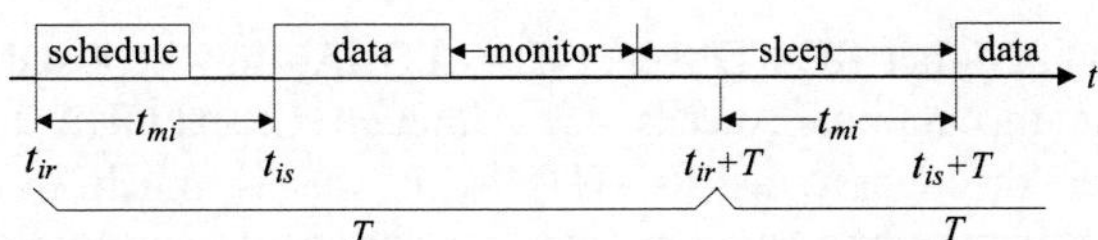

Fig.5 Mapping schedule to local clock line.

2.3 Clock offset modifying

Clock offset may occur caused by quartz accuracy or node position change drifted by flows. This need to be modified immediately or data collision would occur at gateway. Receive time-windows for each sub-nodes are created at the schedule registration stage on gateway' local clock line, guard interval (T_g) are also made between the adjacent time-windows allows the data arrival time has some offsets. If the offset exceeds the critical, ACK would be sent to the corresponding sub-node with the modified value contained. Fig.6 shows the receive time-windows setting.

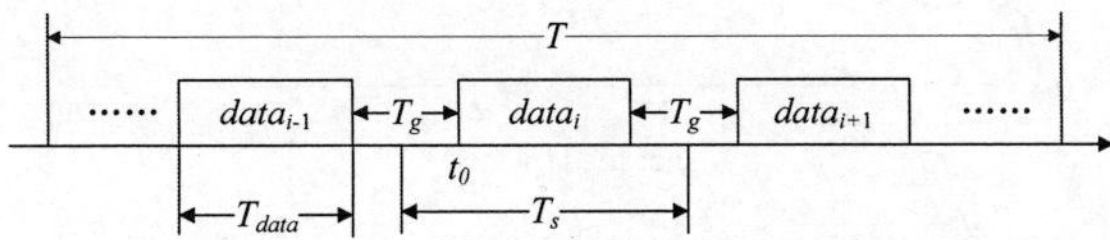

Fig.6 Receiving time-window setting on gateway's clock line.

Now, we take $data_i$ as an example to detail the clock offset modification. Let's assume that the data duration is T_{data}, and its arranged arrival time is t_0, T_s is the safe time that means if the data has been received completely in T_s, collision will not occur. T_s can be expressed as:

$$t_0 - \frac{1}{2}T_g < T_s < t_0 + T_{data} + \frac{1}{2}T_g \tag{3}$$

If $data_i$'s arrival time t_{ri} is in (t_0-0.5T_g, t_0+0.5T_g), then collision will not occur, gateway sends nothing, otherwise, ACK will be sent to sub-node i including modifying value Δt_m, which can be expressed as:

$$\Delta t_m = t_{ri} - t_0 \tag{4}$$

The sub-node i modifies its send time on receiving the ACK. If Δt_m>0, that means the arrival time for $data_i$ is lagged, and its next send time needs Δt_m earlier. In contrast, if Δt_m<0, sub-node i needs leg its send time Δt_m later.

3 Performance analyzing and simulating

To assess the protocol performance, we define the end-to-end delay as the duration of a packet generated to receive successfully, and the throughput as the total successful received packet numbers per second.

3.1 Performance analyzing

The end-to-end delay can be expressed as:

$$\begin{cases} T_{e2e} = \frac{L_{data}}{R} + T_{pd} + t_d + mT \\ m = [\frac{N_{load}}{C}] \end{cases} \tag{5}$$

Where, L_{data}, L_{ack}, means the frame length of data and ACK, R means the transmission rate, t_d means the waiting time for a sending course in a work-window, N_{load} means the net load of UAN and C means the sending capacity in a work-window, T and T_{pd} has the same meaning as defined before, [] means rounding a number to its nearest integer. As equation (5) shows, end-to-end delay (T_{e2e}) for RC-TDMA relates to the net load, work-window and sending capacity in each work-windows.

Throughput can be expressed as:

$$N_{thrpt} = \frac{[T-(N-1)T_g]\cdot R\cdot(1-p_n)}{L_{data}\cdot T} \tag{6}$$

Where, N is the sub-node numbers, p_n is the packets missing rate, T, R, T_g has the same meaning as defined before. The throughput will be affected by the guard interval length T_g and the packets missing rate p_n which depends on the channel conditions.

Now, we investigate the energy consumption of the RC-TDMA protocol for transmitting a packet. Assume that the modem has three states: sending, receiving and sleeping. As the energy consumption in sleeping state is extremely lower than the other two, we just consider the send and receive energy consumption. For one packet transmitting, include sending and receiving, energy consumption can be expressed as:

$$\begin{cases} E = (P_{snd}T_{snd} + P_{rcv}T_{rcv}) \\ T_{snd} = T_{rcv} = \frac{L_{data} + L_{ack}}{R} \end{cases} \tag{7}$$

Where, P_{snd} and P_{rcv} is the send power and receive power. In RC-TDMA protocol, there is neither hand-shaking energy wasting as in CSMA, nor collision energy wasting as in ALOHA.

3.2 Simulation results

Simulations were run in OMNeT++ 4.0, gateway was deployed in the center of the simulation region and the sub-nodes are distributed around the gateway randomly, other parameters are shown in Tab.1.

Tab.1 Simulation parameters

parameter	value
simulation region	1.5 km × 1.5 km
gateway numbers	1
sub-node numbers	10
max transmitting range	1 km
send power	80 mw
receive power	10 mw
control packet length	64 bits
data packet length	512 bits
transmission rate	4800 bps

The performance of the protocol was compared to that of CSMA, including Carrier Sensing ALOHA (CS-ALOHA) as a bench mark. In CS-ALOHA, nodes transmit packets whenever they see the channel idle, and therefore do not waste time on hand-shaking. CSMA is a previously proposed protocol for the underwater environment, based on RTS/CTS hand-shaking, nodes use RTS/CTS to reserve the channel to transmit data.

Fig.7 illustrates the results of T_{e2e} for these three protocols. As we can see, RC-TDMA delay depends on the T as equation (5) shows. In low net load, shorter T gets shorter T_{e2e}, while it is in contrast in high net load. Select a propel T can make the T_{e2e} of RC-TDMA shorter than CSMA and CS-ALOHA in any net load.

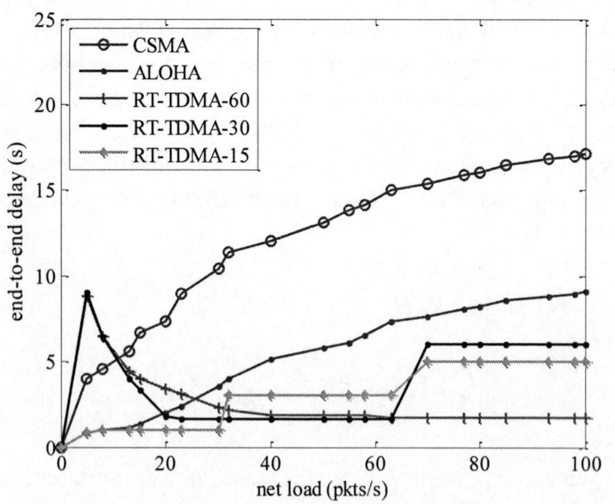

Fig.7 T_{e2e} of different protocols.

Fig.8-9 shows the results of throughput and energy consumption of these three protocols. As we can see, RC-TDMA and CS-ALOHA has a higher throughput than that of CSMA. In simulation, when the net load exceeds 60, CSMA throughput degrades as the load increases, which is not the case with either RC-TDMA or CS-ALOHA, they kept stable as the throughput exceeds 40. Although CS-ALOHA has similar throughput as RC-TDMA, it wastes much more energy for sending same amount packets. Additionally, RC-TDMA energy consumption does not vary as throughput changes.

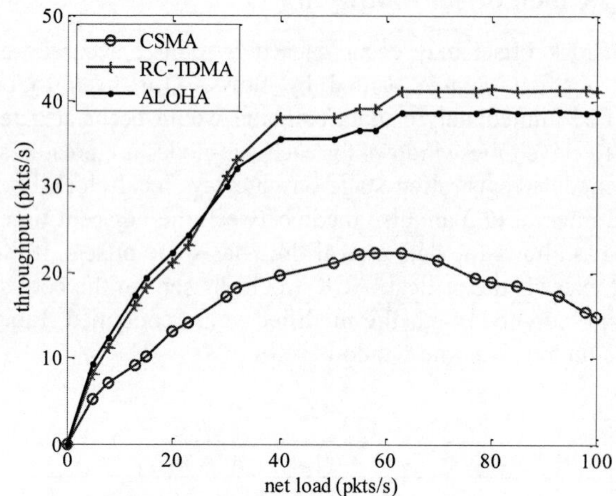

Fig.8 Throughput of different protocols.

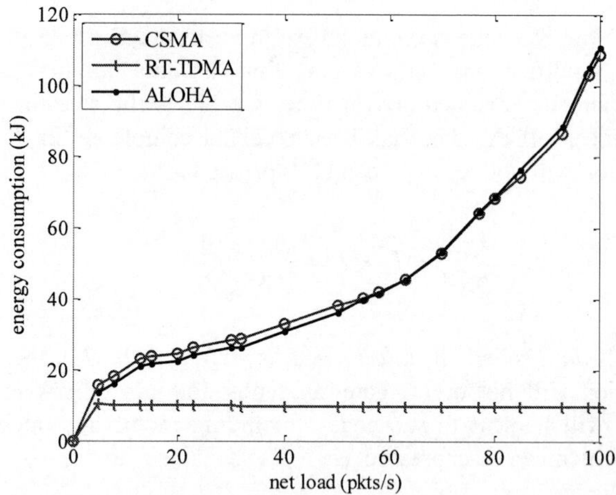

Fig.9 Energy consumption of different protocols.

4 Lake Trail results

In order to validate the practicability of this protocol, we conducted a Lake Trail in April 2013 at Qiandao Lake in Zhejiang province, China. Experiment region and nodes distribution schematic is shown in Fig.10, as well as the nodes pictures we used in this experiment. Depth of the experiment region is about 30-50 meters, the gateway is deployed near the ship and the 5 sub-nodes were randomly deployed around the gateway in range of 0.5-3 km. Nodes were deployed about 20 m below the surface with cement block and float. We used FSK to transmit control packets and OFDM to transmit data packets, frequency band is in 6-10 kHz. In schedule registration procedure we use polling registration, it cost about 5 minutes to complete the initialization, then the network start working automatically.

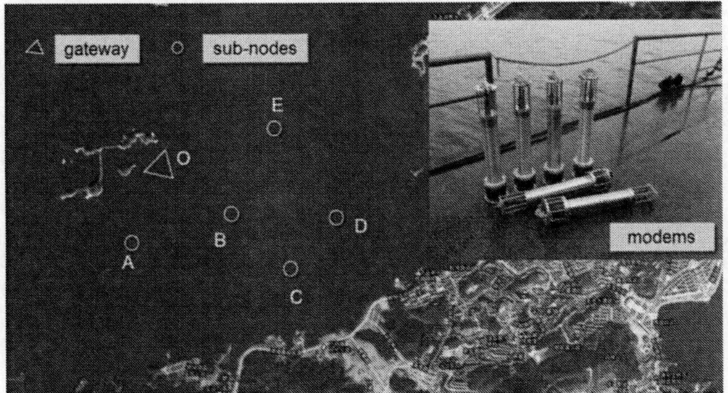

Fig.10 Lake Trail schematic and modem pictures.

The actual distance (obtained from GPS) of each sub-nodes to gateway and the measured propagation delay (including the modulate/demodulate time) are shown in Tab.2, as well as the t_{mi} (arranged by gateway while T=60, T_g=2).

Tab.2 Actual distance and measured T_{e2e}

node	Distance (km)	T_{e2e} (s)	t_{mi} (s)
A	1.56	4.61	7.39
B	0.65	3.99	0
C	2.51	5.23	30.77
D	2.89	5.48	42.52
E	2.01	4.92	19.08

The test was last almost 8 hours, statistics of each sub-node sending packets, modifying times and the gateway successfully received packets for each sub-nodes are shown in Tab.3.

Tab.3 Statistics of the test

node	Snd(pkts)	Rcv(pkts)	Modify(times)
A	1232	1205	109
B	1179	1130	113
C	1355	1341	98
D	1530	1525	76
E	1425	1403	89

Lake Trail results are well demonstrated that the protocol is practical and easy to be implemented, although no clock synchronize was made and no synchronization signal was periodically broadcasted, the network can work well without collision and modify the clock offset automatically during data transmitting.

5 Conclusions

In this paper, we proposed a practical TDMA protocol for UAN based on relative clock, this protocol do not need neither clock synchronization nor synchronize signal broadcasting periodically. It maps the network schedule to local clock line, and arrange individual work schedule according the schedule arrival time and its corresponding information in the network schedule. Gateway makes the sub-nodes work in parallel according their propagation delays and fixes the clock offset during data transmission. Simulation results show that it can achieve a throughput several times higher than that of the CSMA, while offering similar savings in energy. Although CS-ALOHA offers a similar throughput, it wastes much more power on collisions. The Lake Trail well validate that the proposed protocol is practical and easy to be implemented.

In future work, we will investigate the problem of old node missing or new node incoming, as well as its application in distributed network.

6 Acknowledgement

This paper is funded by the International Exchange Program of Harbin Engineering University for Innovation-oriented Talents Cultivation, and is supported in part by the National Natural Science Foundation of China under Grants No. 11274079, and the National High Technology Research and Development Program of China under Grant No. 2009 AA093601-2.

7 References

[1] Mandar Chitre, Shiraz Shahabudeen, and Milica Stojanovic. "Underwater acoustic communications and networking: Recent advances and future challenges"; Marine Technology Society Journal, Vol. 42, Issue 1, 103-116, Spr 2008.

[2] Jiarong Zhang, Gang Qiao, and Can Wang. "An intelligent management platform for underwater acoustic modem"; Proceedings of 2012 5th International Symposium on Computational Intelligence and Design, 2012, 93-96.

[3] Ethem M. Sozer, Milica Stojanovic, and John G. Proakis. "Underwater Acoustic Networks"; IEEE journal of oceanic engineering, Vol. 25, Issue 1, 72-83, Jan 2000.

[4] Milica Stojanovic. "Design and Capacity Analysis of Cellular-Type Underwater Acoustic Networks". IEEE journal of oceanic engineering, Vol. 33, Issue 2, 171-181 Apr 2008.

[5] Xiaoka Xu, Gang Qiao, Jun Su, and Pengtao Hu. "Study on turbo code for multicarrier underwater acoustic communication"; Proceedings of 2008 International Confe-

rence on Wireless Communications, Networking and Mobile Computing, 2008, 1-4.

[6] John G. Proakis, Ethem M. Sozer, Joseph A. Rice, and Milica Stojanovic. “Shallow Water Acoustic Networks”; IEEE Communications Magazine, Vol. 39, Issue 11, 114-119, Nov 2001.

[7] Ian F. Akyildiz, Dario Pompili, and Tommaso Melodia. “Underwater acoustic sensor networks: Research challenges”; Ad Hoc Networks, Vol. 3, Issue 3, 257-279, May 2005.

[8] Milica Stojanovic. “Recent Advances in High-Speed Under water Acoustic Communications”; IEEE journal of oceanic engineering, Vol. 21, Issue, 2, 125-135, Apr 1996.

[9] L. Magagnia, M. Sergio, and M. Nicolini. “A smart node architecture for underwater monitoring of sensor networks”; Sensors and Actuators A: Physical, Vol. 130-131, 290-296, Aug 2006.

[10] Zhong Zhou, Zheng Peng, Jun-Hong Cui, and Zhijie Shi. “Effcient Multipath Communication for Time-Critical Applications in Underwater Acoustic Sensor Networks”; IEEE/ACM transactions on networking, Vol. 19, Issue 1, 28-41, Feb 2011.

[11] Albert F. Harris, Milica Stojanovic, and Michele Zorzi. “Idle-time energy savings through wake-up modes in underwater acoustic networks”; Ad Hoc Networks, Vol. 7, Issue 4, 770-777, Jun 2009.

MINIMAL HAAR TRANSFORM FOR FPGA

Jordan Miller , Huda Al-Ghaib, and Reza Adhami
Electrical and Computer Engineering Department
The University of Alabama in Huntsville
Huntsville, AL, USA

ABSTRACT

There exist many options for hardware based image compression. The current image compression products exist as IP Cores for FPGAs and ASICs, and as fixed function ICs. These products support various image compression standards, but they all have a common downside of high cost. This paper presents an image compression implementation using the Haar wavelet transform that is practical for implementation in a mid-grade, relatively inexpensive FPGA. The design uses the discrete Haar wavelet transform for the image transformation. The proposed design was evaluated using four metrics: Design size, Signal-to-Noise Ratio (SNR) of the compressed image, Root Mean Square Error (RMS_{ERR}) of the compressed image, and a subjective analysis of the compressed image quality. The design cost was analyzed using the Xilinx ISE tool set. The SNR and RMS_{ERR} were analyzed using MATLAB. The measured results of the proposed design were compared to the JPEG and JPEG2000 image compression standards.

Keywords: Haar transform, wavelet transform, image compression, video compression.

1. INTRODUCTION

Image compression is quickly becoming a major part of our lives. Image compression is used in televisions, cell phones, cameras, etc. To accomplish the image compression task in a timely manner, for video, products must use some form of hardware based processing. This hardware based processing can be part of an applications processor, an IP Core for FPGAs or ASICs, or a dedicated IC. The downside to each of these options is the cost; royalties, fees, and parts cos. In order to prove a low cost option this paper presents an image compression design for FPGAs that provides quality compression at a low cost. To evaluate these design goals two software tools will be use:

i. The Xilinx ISE Design Suite [4] will be used to analyze the design size, which is directly related to the cost to implement.
ii. MATLAB [5] will be used to analyze the image compression quality of the design.

The proposed design was compared to two existing image compression standards, JPEG and JPEG2000 using the metrics of implementation cost; SNR, RMS_{ERR}, and a subjective analysis of quality.

2. DISCRETE HAAR WAVELET TRANSFORM

The Discrete Haar Wavelet Transform (DHWT) is good for a simple image compression implementation. The DHWT is implemented uses an averaging and differencing technique.

$$X = [a_1, a_2, a_3, \ldots a_n] \text{ } where \text{ } n = 2^m \quad (1)$$

First, take the average of the pairs of elements in X and the differences of each odd element and the corresponding average as shown in (2).

$$X_1 = [\frac{a_1+a_2}{2}, \ldots \frac{a_{\frac{n-1}{2}}+a_{\frac{n}{2}}}{2}, a_1 - \frac{a_1+a_2}{2}, \ldots a_{n-1} - \frac{a_{\left(\frac{n-1}{2}\right)}+a_{\frac{n}{2}}}{2}] \quad (2)$$

Next, repeat the first step, on the first half of the array X_1 and copy the second half of X_1 to create X_2. Repeat this process up to m times, using progressively smaller pieces of the previous array. Each averaging step is referred to as a transform level.

A. 2D Discrete Haar Wavelet Transform

To use the DHWT on an image the transform must be converted into a 2-dimensional matrix. The matrices for the first three steps of the DHWT are (3), (4), and (5). Each matrix represents a step, or a level, of transformation as described above.

$$A_1 = \begin{bmatrix} 0.5 & 0 & 0 & 0 & 0.5 & 0 & 0 & 0 \\ 0.5 & 0 & 0 & 0 & -0.5 & 0 & 0 & 0 \\ 0 & 0.5 & 0 & 0 & 0 & 0.5 & 0 & 0 \\ 0 & 0.5 & 0 & 0 & 0 & -0.5 & 0 & 0 \\ 0 & 0 & 0.5 & 0 & 0 & 0 & 0.5 & 0 \\ 0 & 0 & 0.5 & 0 & 0 & 0 & -0.5 & 0 \\ 0 & 0 & 0 & 0.5 & 0 & 0 & 0 & 0.5 \\ 0 & 0 & 0 & 0.5 & 0 & 0 & 0 & -0.5 \end{bmatrix} \quad (3)$$

$$A_2 = \begin{bmatrix} 0.5 & 0 & 0.5 & 0 & 0 & 0 & 0 & 0 \\ 0.5 & 0 & -0.5 & 0 & 0 & 0 & 0 & 0 \\ 0 & 0.5 & 0 & 0.5 & 0 & 0 & 0 & 0 \\ 0 & 0.5 & 0 & -0.5 & 0 & 0 & 0 & 0 \\ 0 & 0 & 0 & 0 & 1 & 0 & 0 & 0 \\ 0 & 0 & 0 & 0 & 0 & 1 & 0 & 0 \\ 0 & 0 & 0 & 0 & 0 & 0 & 1 & 0 \\ 0 & 0 & 0 & 0 & 0 & 0 & 0 & 1 \end{bmatrix} \quad (4)$$

$$A_3 = \begin{bmatrix} 0.5 & 0.5 & 0 & 0 & 0 & 0 & 0 & 0 \\ 0.5 & -0.5 & 0 & 0 & 0 & 0 & 0 & 0 \\ 0 & 0 & 1 & 0 & 0 & 0 & 0 & 0 \\ 0 & 0 & 0 & 1 & 0 & 0 & 0 & 0 \\ 0 & 0 & 0 & 0 & 1 & 0 & 0 & 0 \\ 0 & 0 & 0 & 0 & 0 & 1 & 0 & 0 \\ 0 & 0 & 0 & 0 & 0 & 0 & 1 & 0 \\ 0 & 0 & 0 & 0 & 0 & 0 & 0 & 1 \end{bmatrix} \quad (5)$$

Since A_1, A_2, and A_3, are matrices of the same dimension they can be multiplied together to create a single matrix that does three transformation steps.

$$W = A_1 A_2 A_3 \quad (6)$$

The matrix W is then defined as

$$W = \begin{bmatrix} 0.125 & 0.125 & 0.25 & 0 & 0.5 & 0 & 0 & 0 \\ 0.125 & 0.125 & 0.25 & 0 & -0.5 & 0 & 0 & 0 \\ 0.125 & 0.125 & -0.25 & 0 & 0 & 0.5 & 0 & 0 \\ 0.125 & 0.125 & -0.25 & 0 & 0 & -0.5 & 0 & 0 \\ 0.125 & -0.125 & 0 & 0.25 & 0 & 0 & 0.5 & 0 \\ 0.125 & -0.125 & 0 & 0.25 & 0 & 0 & -0.5 & 0 \\ 0.125 & -0.125 & 0 & -0.25 & 0 & 0 & 0 & 0.5 \\ 0.125 & -0.125 & 0 & 0.25 & 0 & 0 & 0 & -0.5 \end{bmatrix}$$

(7)

This matrix, W, is used to transform the rows of an 8x8 image block using the equation

$$X_R = XW \quad (8)$$

Where X is the image block to be transformed and X_R is the result of the transformation of the rows. To transform the columns of the image block the matrix is transposed and pre-multiplied with the row results.

$$X_{RC} = W^T X_R \quad (9)$$

X_{RC} is the result of the 2-Dimensional DHWT of the image block. To do the inverse transform of the image block the W matrix must be inverted resulting in the equations

$$X_R = W^{-1^T} X_{RC} \quad (10)$$

$$X = X_R W^{-1} \quad (11)$$

B. DHWT Implementation Features

The nature of the DHWT is important to the implementation of a simple image compression algorithm. As can be seen from the definition of W above the only values in the matrix are; 0, 0.5, 0.25, and 0.125. Each of these values can be substituted with a binary shift of; 0, 1, 2, and 3 respectively. This substitution is a key feature in using the DHWT to implement a simple image compression algorithm. Unlike other standard Wavelet Transforms such as Le Gall's 5/3 and CDF-9/7 the DHWT does not require any multiplication [5]. Since the DHWT requires no multiplications fixed point arithmetic could be used, resulting in the capability for lossless compression and increased processing speed.

3.DHWT Design Approach

The image compression algorithm was designed to fit in a system with other image processing blocks. In such systems the normal method of sourcing and sinking data is as a stream of pixels from the upper left corner of the image to the lower right corner. In order to support the compression of live video the image compression algorithm is capable of processing each image in a real time.

A. Design Criteria

The design criteria included compressing live videos at a resolution up to 1080p and a frame rate of 60 Hz (1080p60). The maximum pixel rate required to support 1080p60 is 148MHz. Image data was processed in the 4:2:2, YCbCr, color space. This is similar to the 4:4:4, RBG, color space. In the 4:2:2 color space only two pixels are displayed at a time, YCb or YCr. The use of the 4:2:2 color space allowed for the processing resources to be reduced by only requiring the processing of two color components at a time, as opposed to three that would be required for 4:4:4.

B. Image Capture

In the JPEG2000 standard, image compression is done on the entire image or large blocks of the image, referred to as tiles. In the JPEG standard, image compression is done on 8x8 blocks of an image. In order to reduce the required amount of data to process at once the proposed design used an 8x8 block approach.

The design stored the image in external memory and retrieved sequential 8x8 blocks, starting at the upper left corner of the image. These blocks were stored in local memory for processing by the DHWT.

The decision to use 8x8 blocks for processing allowed for the entire block to be held in local memory which facilitated low latency processing of the data. If the block size were increased, such as in JPEG2000, the amount of data needed to be stored locally would be too much, and require a different image compression algorithm.

C. Image Compression

Once a block of data was stored locally, the image compression could begin. The compression was a two stage processes. The first stage implements (8) and the second stage implements (9), with the intermediate and final results stored locally. Both (8) and (9) are 8x8 matrix multiplications; using straight matrix multiplication this would require eight multiplications for each pixel in the result with 64 pixels in each result, that would be 512 multiplications per processing step.

Trying to process all 512 multiplications in parallel proved to require a large amount of resources, driving up the cost of the FPGA and decreasing the maximum processing speed. In order to efficiently process the matrix multiplications a different matrix multiplication implementation was used. The parallel model described by Campbell and Khatri [6] was used. This method of matrix multiplication requires only 64 multiplications per cycle and splits the processing of the matrix into eight pipeline stages. This resulted in a smaller and faster design.

Due to the nature of the coefficients in the DHWT matrices the multiplications could be implemented as simple and fast shift registers. Since the DHWT coefficients were not being used for multiplication the coefficients could be represented using fewer bits to reduce the design size.

After each processing stage the resulting data was three bits larger. This increase in data size was required to maintain the data integrity until the final stage where quantization occurs.

In the final stage of compression the data was quantized to restore the data size back to eight bits. This was accomplished by setting all results that fall within a given threshold to zero. By setting these values to zero the number of consecutive zeros was increased as well as the overall number of zeros. After the data had been_threshold the second step of quantization could occur. In this step unnecessary data precision is removed. This is done by truncating all of the data at the decimal point and returning that data to eight bits. These two steps allow the data stream after encoding to be even smaller.

D. Image Transmission

After the data was compressed and truncated it would passed to a Huffman coding module (not part of the proposed design) [7]. This module would perform the run-length coding, and zig-zag processing of each image block. Data sourced by this module would be fully compressed and ready for transmission.

4. Results and Analysis

The proposed design was evaluated on four criteria; design size/cost, SNR, RMS_{ERR}, and a Subjective Analysis. The design size was evaluated using the Xilinx ISE Design Suite; and the SNR, RMS_{ERR} and subjective analysis were evaluated using MATLAB. For the quantitative and subjective analysis two images were used; a low frequency image, Peppers, and a high frequency image, Baboon. The results of the proposed design are compared with current implementations and standards.

A. Design Cost

The target FPGA for this implementation was the Xilinx Spartan6-LX45 [8]. The proposed design was compared against JPEG2000 compliant cores from Cast Inc. and JPEG compliant cores from Barco-Silex. A comparison of the image compression cores are shown in Table 1.

The proposed design was also compared against the Analog Devices ADV212, JPEG2000 Video Codec. In order to support higher resolution multiple video codecs were required. The proposed design is compared with the Analog Devices Codec in Table 2.

Table 1: FPGA Cost

	Algorithm	FPGA	Max Clock	Cost
Proposed	DHWT	XC6SLX45	150 MHz	$52
Cast Inc.	JPEG2000	XC6SLX150	66 MHz	$158
Cast Inc.	JPEG2000	XC5VLX155	190 MHz	$2,287
Barco-Silex	JPEG	XC5VLX30	135 MHz	$240
Barco-Silex	JPEG	XC6SLX45	90 MHz	$52

Table 2: Core and Codec

	Algorithm	IC	Max Clock	Cost
Proposed	DHWT	XC6SLX45	150 MHz	$52
Analog	JPEG2000	ADV212	74.25 MHz	$35
Analog	JPEG2000	ADV212	2 x 74.25 MHz	$70
Analog	JPEG2000	ADV212	4 x 74.25 MHz	$140

All of these alternates to the proposed design implement the full feature set of the standards. It is clear that the proposed design is very cost effective if a standards compliant compression is not required.

B. Signal to Noise Ratio (SNR)

The Signal to Noise Ratio (SNR) is one form of objective analysis used to measure the quality of the image compression. Specifically the SNR is used to measure the level of noise in the signal; in this case the SNR is measuring the noise resulting from the lossy compression of the image.

For the SNR analysis of the test images were processed using the DHWT, and the JPEG and JPEG2000 compression standards. The equation defined in (12) was used to compute the SNR of the processed images[9]. Where f is the original image and $\hat{f}$ is the test image after decompression.

$$SNR = \frac{\sum_{x=0}^{M-1}\sum_{y=0}^{N-1}\hat{f}(x,y)^2}{\sum_{x=0}^{M-1}\sum_{y=0}^{N-1}\left[\hat{f}(x,y)-f(x,y)\right]^2} \tag{12}$$

Table 3 and 4 show the results of the analysis of the Peppers and Baboon images, Figure 1 and 2, using the JPEG, JPEG2000, and DHWT. From the table is can be seen that the DHWT performs as well as, or better than JPEG, but worse than JPEG2000.

Figure 1: Peppers

Figure 2: Baboon

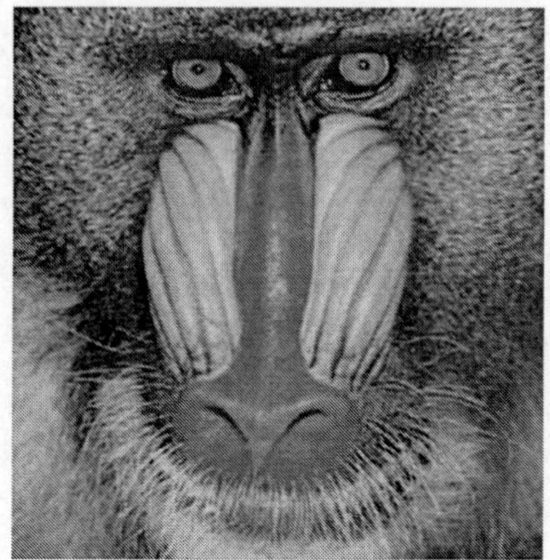

Table 3: SNR of Peppers Image

Peppers			
Compression Ratio	SNR (JPEG)	SNR (JPEG2000)	SNR (DHWT)
7.5	21.56	67.53	56.70
10	18.42	48.45	30.75
12.5	15.33	37.98	17.43
15	13.17	31.95	12.01

Table 4: SNR of Baboon Image

Baboon			
Compression Ratio	SNR (JPEG)	SNR (JPEG2000)	SNR (DHWT)
7.5	2.40	3.05	2.43
10	2.25	2.64	2.22
12.5	2.18	2.42	2.15
15	2.12	2.34	2.12

C. Root Mean Square Error (RMS_{ERR})

The Root Mean Square Error (RMS_{ERR}) is the second form of objective analysis used to measure the quality of the image compression. Specifically the RMS_{ERR} is used to measure the difference between a processed signal and the original; in this case the RMS_{ERR} is measuring the difference resulting from the lossy compression of the image.

For the RMS_{ERR} analysis of the test images were processed using the DHWT, and the JPEG and JPEG2000 compression standards. The equation defined in (13) was used to compute the SNR of the processed images [9]. Where f is the original image and $\hat{f}$ is the test image after decompression.

$$RMS_{ERR} = \sqrt{\frac{1}{MN}\sum_{x=0}^{M-1}\sum_{y=0}^{N-1}\left[\hat{f}(x,y) - f(x,y)\right]^2} \tag{13}$$

Table 5 and 6 show the results of the analysis of the Peppers and Baboon Images using the JPEG, JPEG2000, and DHWT. It is clear that the DHWT performs as well as, or better than JPEG until the compression ratio reaches 15:1, but is consistently worse than JPEG2000.

Table 5: RMS_{ERR} of Peppers Image

Peppers			
Compression Ratio	RMS_{ERR} (JPEG)	RMS_{ERR} (JPEG2000)	RMS_{ERR} (DHWT)
7.5	1.99	1.12	1.22
10	2.15	1.32	1.66
12.5	2.35	1.50	2.21
15	2.54	1.63	2.66

Table 6: RMS_{ERR} of Baboon Image

Baboon			
Compression Ratio	RMS_{ERR} (JPEG)	RMS_{ERR} (JPEG2000)	RMS_{ERR} (DHWT)
7.5	5.95	5.28	5.91
10	6.15	5.67	6.19
12.5	6.24	5.92	6.28
15	6.33	6.03	6.33

5. CONCLUSION

This paper has introduced and discussed image compression and the importance of its usage. The Discrete Haar Wavelet Transform was introduced as a low cost alternative to the JPEG and JPEG2000 image compression standards. The DHWT is much less expensive to implement than existing IP Core and ASIC solutions. At a compression ratio of 7.5:1 the DHWT provides good visual quality compression, but at higher compression ratios the quality of the DHWT compression deteriorates. This design could be enhanced by added inter-block processing to the compression, this would allow for better compression quality by reducing the nominal range of values that needed to be compressed.

6. References

[1] Analog Devices, Inc., "ADV212: JPEG 2000 Video Codec", http://www.analog.com/en/audiovideo-products/video-compression/adv212/products/product.html, 2012, Accessed: 10 June 12.

[2] Cast-Inc., "Cast JPEG2K-E Core – Xilinx FPGA Results", http://www.cast-inc.com/ip-cores/images/jpeg2k-e/jpeg2k-e-xilinx.htm, Accessed: 9 June 2012.

[3] BarcoSilex, "BA116 - Factsheet", http://www.barco-silex.com/sites/default/files/doc/BA116JPEGE_FS.pdf, 8 February 2011, Accessed: 16 July 2012.

[4] Adhami, Reza, "Lecture 13: 2-D Data Compression," Class notes for EE748, Department of Electrical and Computer Engineering, University of Alabama Huntsville, Apr. 20, 2011.

[5] Pande, A.; Zambreno, J.; , "Design and analysis of efficient reconfigurable wavelet filters," *Electro/Information Technology, 2008. EIT 2008. IEEE International Conference on*, vol., no., pp.327-332, 18-20 May 2008 doi: 10.1109/EIT.2008.4554323

[6] S. J. Campbell, S. P. Khatri, (2006) "Resource and Delay Efficient Matrix Multiplication using Newer FPGA Devices," Texas A&M Univ., TX. [Online], Available: http://www.ece.tamu.edu/~sunil/ projects-web/papers/mmult.pdf

[7] Xilinx Inc., "Variable Length Coding", http://www.xilinx.com/support/documentation/application_notes/xapp621.pdf, 31 January 2005, Accessed: 1 July 2012.

[8] Xilinx, Inc., "Spartan-6 Family Overview", http://www.xilinx.com/support/documentation/data_sheets/ds160.pdf, 25 October 2012, Accessed: 1 July 12.

[9] R. Gonzalez and R. Woods, "Image Compression," in *Digital Image Processing*, 3rd ed. Upper Saddle River: Pearson, 2008, pp. 525-626.

Improvised formulation of Scale Invariance for use of Geometric Moment Invariant functions in Real Time Image Processing

Vazeerudeen Abdul Hameed & Siti Mariyam Shamsuddin
Soft Computing Research Group
Faculty of Computer Science and Research Group
Universiti Teknologi Malaysia, Skudai, Johor Bahru
vazeerudeen@gmail.com & mariyam@utm.my

Abstract—*This paper presents a detailed study of the scale invariant nature of the geometric moment invariant functions for real time object recognition. The conventional formulation of the image scaling transform has been analyzed and proven to represent incomplete information. Derivations and experimental study shows that conventional formulation of scale invariance in some moment invariant functions causes poor discrimination when used for object recognition. Therefore a new method of accomplishing scale invariance in moment invariant functions has been proposed to accomplish better object recognition in real time. This is done by modifying the formulation of moment invariant functions to accommodate scaling without loss of information. The correctness of the proposed scale invariance formulations has been proven with suitable derivations. Performance improvement as accomplished in the proposed scale invariance formulations has been tested with sample evaluations.*

Keywords— invariance, moments, object recognition, scaling

1 Introduction

Real time image processing largely involves object recognition that has been accomplished by several techniques such as edge detection and matching, grey scale matching, geometric hashing, SIFT (Scale Invariant Feature Transform) and ASIFT (Affine Scale Invariant Feature Transform) transforms etc [1][2][3]. Object recognition via moment invariants has been proving to be successful over the various alternatives, which is evitable from the plethora of applications addressed using moment invariant functions [4][5][6]. This is due to the fact that image moments are invariant to several factors such as image rotation, scaling, translation, horizontal and vertical skew.

Moment invariants have a long time history that dates back to the theory of algebraic invariants that was studied and explained by David Hilbert, a German mathematician [7]. The moment M_{pq} of an image $f(x,y)$ is defined as

$$M_{pq} = \iint_D P_{pq}(x,y) f(x,y) dxdy \quad (1)$$

In (1), $r = p + q$ is the order of the moment and $p \geq 0, q \geq 0$. P_{pq} is a polynomial basis function. The polynomial basis function could be an orthogonal function or a non–orthogonal function.

Hu identified seven moment invariant functions made from non-orthogonal functions defined as in (2) [8]. These seven moment invariant functions which were inherently invariant to rotation and translation have been widely applied for several real time applications as evitable in Section 5 below. The geometric invariants were further extended in the works of Flusser and Suk in [9] to accomplish skew and stretch invariant moments. Although such an extensive contribution of moment invariants have been made available, their utilization in real time has suffered drawbacks as explained in Section 5.

$$m_{pq} = \sum_{x=1}^{n}\sum_{y=1}^{m} x^p y^q f(x,y) \quad (2)$$

2 Analysis of scaling transform

Certain transforms such as rotation and translation, cause a relocation of pixels in an image but do not cause a change in the information content of the image. However image scaling shall be considered to be a transformation causing proliferation of pixels during up scaling and loss of pixels when downscaling. Therefore, unlike the other transformations, scaling introduces change in the information content of an image. Downscaling causes loss of information while up scaling causes introduction of new information. Therefore a one to one relationship between a given image and its up scaled or downscaled form does not exist. On the contrary, a one to many relationship between them is found. This characteristic of scaling transform can be clearly understood from the following example.

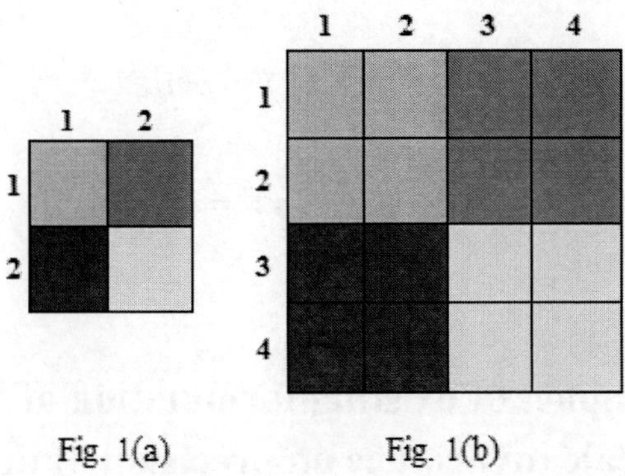

Fig. 1(a) Fig. 1(b)

The image in Fig.1(a) containing four pixels has been scaled by a scaling factor of $\alpha = 2$ to create the image in Fig.1(b). Conventionally, scaling has been understood to be accomplished by (3) where (x, y) and (x', y') are co-ordinates of the input image and scaled image respectively.

$$x' = \alpha x \\ y' = \alpha y \tag{3}$$

For the given images in Fig.1(a) and Fig.1(b) we find that (3) must be true for $\alpha = 2$. The pixels (1,1), (1,2), (2,1), (2,2) in Fig.1(a) have been relocated to (2,2), (2,4), (4,2), (4,4) in Fig.1(b) due to scaling, which explains the correctness of (3). However, in Fig. 1(b) there also remain certain other pixels such as (1,1), (1,2), (2,1), (1,3) and many others whose relationship with the pixels in Fig. 1(a) are not explained by the (3). Therefore we understand that the co-ordinate transformation represented in (3) does not completely express the process of scaling. This is an important reason for the approximate and poor discriminative invariance achieved by geometric moment invariants to scaling. Hence we could infer that a complete representation of the image scaling transform would help us to achieve better accurate invariance with moment invariant functions.

3 Proposed formulation for Image scaling

Image scaling could be alternatively represented completely with the help of (4) where $m = n = \alpha$ is the scaling factor by which the image undergoes scaling. It is worth noting that when $m \neq n$ the image is said to have undergone stretching.

$$\begin{aligned} f(x', y') = f(x, y) * J_{mn}, \quad & m = n = \alpha, \\ x = 1, 2, \ldots width(f(x, y)), & \\ y = 1, 2, \ldots height(f(x, y)) & \end{aligned} \tag{4}$$

Equation (4) performs two dimensional convolution with a unit matrix J_{mn} over every single pixel of a two dimensional digital image $f(x, y)$. The above equation explains image magnification or enlargement due to scaling.

Similarly deterministic de-convolution of the pixels in an image could represent image scaling to accomplish image reduction. The images in Fig.1(a) and Fig.1(b) could be tested to verify the correctness of (4). Consider the image in Fig.1(a). It has been scaled by $\alpha = 2$ to obtain Fig.1(b). Let the amplitudes of the pixels (1,1) ,(1,2), (2,1) and (2,2) be 10, 15, 20 and 5 respectively. Convolving these pixels with a unit matrix $J_{2,2}$ produces the following result in (5).

$$\begin{bmatrix} 10 * J_{2,2} & 15 * J_{2,2} \\ 20 * J_{2,2} & 5 * J_{2,2} \end{bmatrix} = \begin{bmatrix} 10 & 10 & 15 & 15 \\ 10 & 10 & 15 & 15 \\ 20 & 20 & 5 & 5 \\ 20 & 20 & 5 & 5 \end{bmatrix} . \tag{5}$$

While the L.H.S (Left Hand Side) of (5) represents the image in Fig.1(a), and the R.H.S (Right Hand Side) of the equation represents image in Fig.1(b). Hence we find that the formulation in (4) represents the process of scaling without loss of data. This formulation of image scaling shall be used in latter sections to achieve scale invariance in geometric moment invariant functions.

4 Existing formulation of scale invariance in geometric moment invariants

The moment invariant functions were conventionally made invariant to scaling with the help of the function in (6) where μ_{pq} and μ_{00} are the central moments of order $p + q$ and zero respectively [8].

$$n_{pq} = \frac{\mu_{pq}}{\mu_{00}^{(p+q+2)/2}} \tag{6}$$

This method of enabling the geometric moment invariant functions to scale invariance have been widely used as observed in [4-6], [9]. Scaling or similitude transformation was explained for co-efficient of algebraic forms by Hu in [8] where the scaling transform was represented as in (3). Further Hu explained the derivation of (6) from (3) in [8].

The derivation of the scale invariance shall be viewed in the perspective of digital images in order to understand its performance in scale invariant object recognition. The following derivation helps us to understand the impact of approximation in achieving (6). Consider the moment function in (7) where $f(x, y)$ is a two dimensional image function of size m x n.

$$\mu_{pq} = \sum_{x=1}^{n} \sum_{y=1}^{m} x^{pq} f(x, y) \tag{7}$$

Consider the Johann Faulhaber's formula for summation of series given as in (8) where Bi is Bernouli's number.

$$\sum_{x=1}^{n} x^p = 1^p + 2^p + ... + n^p = \frac{1}{p+1} \sum_{i=0}^{p} (-1)^{i\ (p+1)} C_i B_i n^{p+1-i} \quad (8)$$

Let the image $f(x,y)$ considered in (7) above be composed of all pixels of a constant amplitude ρ. The moment function for the image would now be

$$\mu_{pq} = \sum_{x=1}^{n} x^p [\sum_{y=1}^{m} (y)^q (\rho)] = \sum_{x=1}^{n} x^p \rho \sum_{y=1}^{m} (y)^q$$

From Faulhaber's formula in (8) the moment function can further be extended as follows.

$$\mu_{pq} = \sum_{x=1}^{n} x^p \rho \sum_{y=1}^{m} (y)^q$$

$$= \frac{\rho}{(p+1)(q+1)} \sum_{j=0}^{p} (-1)^{j\ p+1} C_j B_j n^{p+1-j} \cdot \sum_{i=0}^{q} (-1)^{i\ q+1} C_i B_i m^{q+1-i}$$

When the image $f(x,y)$ has been scaled by α times to form the image $F(\alpha x, \alpha y)$, we find that

$$\mu'_{pq} = \sum_{x=1}^{\alpha n} x^p \rho \sum_{y=1}^{\alpha m} (y)^q =$$

$$\frac{\rho}{(p+1)(q+1)} \sum_{j=0}^{p} [(-1)^{j\ p+1} C_j B_j (n)^{p+1-j}] \alpha^{p+1-j} \cdot \sum_{i=0}^{q} [(-1)^{i\ q+1} C_i B_i (m)^{q+1-i}] \alpha^{q+1-i}$$

where α^{q+1-i} and α^{p+1-j} are not constants and therefore cannot be eliminated in the summation. This elimination of scaling factor α is essential in order to accomplish the formulation (6) above. Hence only by approximating i, j to be zero, we may accomplish equation (6). This forces us to identify an improved formulation to achieve invariance to scaling. However for $p = q = 0$, we find that

$$\mu_{00} = \sum_{x=1}^{n} x^0 \rho \sum_{y=1}^{m} (y)^0 = mn\rho$$

$$\mu'_{00} = \sum_{x=1}^{\alpha n} x^0 \rho \sum_{y=1}^{\alpha m} (y)^0 = \alpha^2 mn\rho \quad (9)$$

$$\mu'_{00} = \alpha^2 \mu_{00}$$

5 Impact of existing formulation of scale invariance on precision of the moments

The moment invariant functions are commonly known to have some disadvantages. The need for very high degree of precision is a commonly reported problem [10]. As shown in (6) scale invariance was achieved by dividing the moment functions μ_{pq} by $\mu_{00}^{\frac{p+q+2}{2}}$. As the order of the moment invariant functions $(p+q)$ increases for a given image, the need for precision also increases simultaneously. In other words the larger the order of the moments the smaller is their magnitude.

As explained in [10-13] we know that higher order moment invariant functions are of great need for several reasons. Circularly symmetric objects can be better discriminated with the help of higher order moment invariant functions as in [10]. Authors in [10] have also elaborated on the need for higher order moment invariant functions. Authors in [9] have contributed completely independent affine moment invariants of highest order twelve from an extensive research. However this graph based method also suffered from high computational complexity which was addressed and reduced in [14].Despite such extensive research, we find from the above analysis that although we may have very high order moment invariant functions we need extremely large precision measures to utilize them effectively. The need for very high precision is also evitable from the experimental results shown in Section 7 of this paper. The following Table I, presents an evaluation of the work done using the existing moment invariant formulations and the difficulties faced in the research. It is evident from this study that the discriminatory ability of the Hu moment invariants had been poor due to which researchers had to modify the Hu moment invariants or combine other technologies such as SVMs (Support Vector Machines) to achieve better results. However in this process, the computational complexity of the Hu moment invariants also increased.

TABLE I: Appraisal of current research that uses Hu moment invariants

Reference	Important observations	Corrective measures
HaiFeng Zhang et. al. [15]	The Hu moments I1 to I7 were evaluated over the boundary of shapes to reduce computational complexity. However this approach reduced discriminatory ability due to minimal information from image boundaries.	The reduction in discriminatory ability is attributed to extremely small values obtained from the division factor in (6). This can be overcome from the formulation in (4).

Xiuxin Chen et. al. [4]	The authors were successful at discriminating the objects using a region based formulation of Hu moment invariants. However the experimental results have a large deviation in the measures for a given object for the first three Hu moment invariants which explained a compromise on the rotational invariance of the formulation.	The large deviation is caused from the increase in the order of the moments (p+q). As the order of the moments increases, the magnitude decreases as per the formulation in (4). This form of deviation can be overcome from convolution based formulation as in (4).
Fu Yan et. al. [16]	SAR image recognition was accomplished using Hu moment invariants. However heavily trained SVM was required as evitable in the experiment. The seven Hu moments have been computed without any justification of choice which increases the computational complexity.	The use of SVM could be alleviated and proper choice of Hu moment invariants could have been made. However huge discrepancy in the moments introduced by the scaling factor in (4) makes it difficult to choose the invariants.
Sheela et. al. [17]	The computational complexity is too large due to heavy pre processing and repeated estimation of Hu moment invariants at several iris sub regions. SVM has been used which requires adequate training to achieve good performance.	As explained above the use of SVM and its repeated training could be eliminated only if the consistency of the invariants could be preserved. Use of (6) to substitute (4) could achieve scale invariance with consistent measure of invariants.

6 Proposed formulation of Scale invariance and its impact on the precision of the moment invariant functions

Fundamentally we know that the moment invariant functions have been mainly used for uniquely identifying objects or in other words to perform object recognition. Object recognition in real time involves comparison of an existing image of an object with a newly obtained sample. The following derivation utilizes this real time nature of object recognition to improve scale invariance of moment invariants.

Consider a source image A. Let A be the scaled by a factor of α to obtain image B. From (9) above we can clearly estimate the scaling factor as shown in (10) below.

$$\mu_{00}^{B} = \alpha^{2}\mu_{00}^{A}$$
$$\alpha = \sqrt{\frac{\mu_{00}^{B}}{\mu_{00}^{A}}} \tag{10}$$

α from the formulation (10) could assume the following possibilities.

$\alpha > 1$ implies that the image B is larger in size that the image A.

$\alpha = 1$ implies that both the images A and B are of equal size.

$\alpha < 1$ implies that the image B is smaller in size that the image A.

Case $\alpha \geq 1$

The moment M_{pq} for the image B which is larger than or equal to in size of image A could be evaluated as in (11)

$$M_{pq} = \sum_{x}\sum_{y} x^{p} y^{q} G[f(m,n)], \quad k = \alpha,$$
$$\{m \in (kx-(k-1),...,kx),$$
$$n \in (ky-(k-1),...,ky)\} \tag{11}$$

The operator G in the above equation could be any of the aggregate functions such as maximum, minimum, median, mode, average etc.

Case $\alpha < 1$

The moment M_{pq} for the image B which is smaller in size than that of image A could be evaluated as in (12)

$$M_{pq} = \sum_{m}\sum_{n} m^{p} n^{q} f(x,y), \quad k = \frac{1}{\alpha},$$
$$\{m \in (kx-(k-1),...,kx),$$
$$n \in (ky-(k-1),...,ky)\} \tag{12}$$

These formulations were tested for correctness and performance as in the following Section 7.

7 Experimental Results and Analysis

The commonly reported disadvantage of moment invariants was their inability to distinguish circularly symmetric objects [11]. Therefore an experimental setup similar to that followed by authors in [11] was used to evaluate the performance of the proposed scale invariance formulations in this paper. A circle and an octagon of radius 98 pixels, as shown in Fig.(2) were used in the experiment. It is important to note that the images are circularly symmetric and contain very minimal features in them. The images were subjected to evaluation of the seven Hu moment invariants [8] and seventeen graph based invariants [9]. As shown in Table II, the original image of circle and octagon was scaled by factors of α=1/4, 1/3, 1/2, 1 (original size), 2, 3, 4. The moment invariant functions were evaluated over the scaled images using the existing formulations as in (6) and the proposed scale invariance formulations in (11) and (12). Table II presents measures of selected Hu moment invariants namely I_1, I_2, I_5, I_6 and graph based invariants I_{G1}, I_{G2}, I_{G6} and I_{G7}.

The following sections explain the performance appraisal of the existing and proposed scale invariance formulations as displayed in Table II based on two criteria namely Scale invariance and Discriminatory ability.

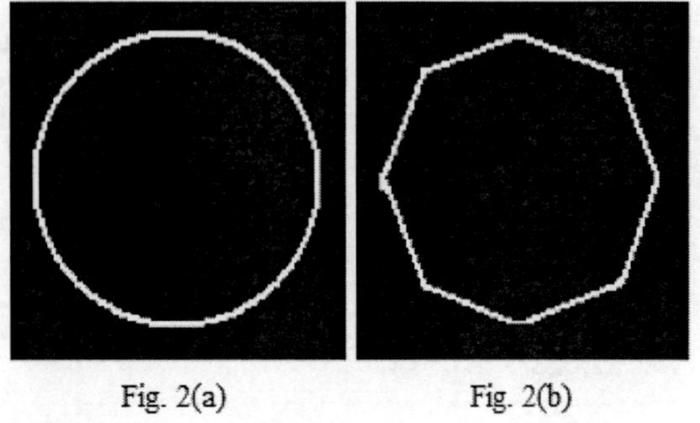

Fig. 2(a) Fig. 2(b)

7.1. Scale invariance

Consider the measure of invariant I_1 in Table I. The percentage standard deviation in the measure of I_1 for the circle and octagon according to existing formulation were 0.000211 0.000258 respectively. These measures for the proposed scale invariance formulations were 0.000178 and 0.000217 respectively. These values are found in the row %SD of Table II for invariant I_1.The deviation in the measures of the invariants, %SD, is very negligible for the existing and proposed scale invariance formulations. This characteristic was also observed in the case of all other invariants as in Table II. Moreover the %SD measure for the proposed scale invariance formulation is smaller than the existing formulation in all the invariants as presented in Table I. Therefore this proves that the proposed formulations are clearly better invariant to scaling than the existing formulations. This performance improvement can be attributed to the complete representation of scaling transform as proposed in (4) as against the approximate existing formulation in (3).

7.2. Discriminatory Ability

Consider the measure of invariant I_1 in Table I. The average measure of I1 for circle and octagon for existing scale invariance formulation was 0.0147 and 0.0145 respectively as shown in AVG row of Table II for invariant I_1. The measures are too similar to each other which explain the poor discriminatory ability of this invariant according to existing formulation. The percentage difference between the AVG measures is only 1.006% as shown in %DIFF row of the Table II for I_1. However the average measure, AVG of the same invariant I1 for the circle and octagon according to proposed scale invariance formulations was 5.94E+09 and 4.87E+09 respectively. These values are clear enough to discriminate the objects. The percentage difference, %DIFF has increased to 19.78%. Therefore with modified formulation the discriminatory ability has increased significantly for invariant I_1. Similar behavior was also found for the invariants I_2, I_{G1}, I_{G6} and I_{G7}.

However, the invariants I_5, I_6 and I_{G2} have equal or lesser discriminatory ability in proposed scale invariance formulation than the existing formulation which is evitable from the percentage difference, %DIFF measures presented in Table II. From this we understand that the existing formulations have good discriminatory ability only for some invariants but the proposed scale invariance formulation has better discriminatory ability for all the invariants.

Another important observation is this study over all the 24 invariants was that the existing formulation of scale invariance had extremely low discriminatory ability for the moment invariants composed of purely even orders as in the case of I_1, I_2, I_{G1}, I_{G6} and I_{G7}. However the proposed scale invariance formulation of scale invariance had reasonably good degree of discriminatory ability for all forms of moment invariants.

TABLE II: Measure of invariants over the images in Fig.(2) for existing and proposed scale invariance formulations for different scaling factors

	$I_1 = n_{20} + n_{02}$				$I_2 = (n_{20} - n_{02})^2 + (2n_{11})^2$			
	EXISTING FORMULATION		PROPOSED FORMULATION		EXISTING FORMULATION		PROPOSED FORMULATION	
α	Circle	Octagon	Circle	Octagon	Circle	Octagon	Circle	Octagon
0.25	0.0147	0.0145	5.94E+09	4.87E+09	2.25E-07	4.94E-08	3.67E+16	5.52E+15
0.33	0.0147	0.0145	5.94E+09	4.87E+09	2.25E-07	4.94E-08	3.67E+16	5.53E+15
0.5	0.0147	0.0145	5.94E+09	4.87E+09	2.25E-07	4.94E-08	3.67E+16	5.53E+15
1	0.0147	0.0145	5.94E+09	4.87E+09	2.25E-07	4.94E-08	3.67E+16	5.53E+15
2	0.0147	0.0145	5.94E+09	4.87E+09	2.25E-07	4.94E-08	3.67E+16	5.53E+15
3	0.0147	0.0145	5.94E+09	4.87E+09	2.25E-07	4.94E-08	3.67E+16	5.53E+15
4	0.0147	0.0145	5.94E+09	4.87E+09	2.25E-07	4.94E-08	3.67E+16	5.53E+15

AVG	0.0147	0.0145	5.94E+09	4.87E+09	2.25E-07	4.94E-08	3.67E+16	5.53E+15
%DIFF	1.005973		19.77842		127.96		147.61	
%SD	0.000211	0.000258	0.000178	0.000217	0.001255	0.001329	0.000723	0.00126

$I_5=(\eta_{30}-3\eta_{12})(\eta_{30}+\eta_{12})[(\eta_{30}+\eta_{12})^2-3(\eta_{21}+\eta_{03})^2]+(3\eta_{21}-\eta_{03})(\eta_{21}+\eta_{03})[3(\eta_{30}+\eta_{12})^2-(\eta_{21}+\eta_{03})^2]$					$I_6=(\eta_{20}-\eta_{02})[(\eta_{30}+\eta_{12})^2-(\eta_{21}+\eta_{03})^2]+4\eta_{11}(\eta_{30}+\eta_{12})(\eta_{21}+\eta_{03})$			
	EXISTING FORMULATION		PROPOSED FORMULATION		EXISTING FORMULATION		PROPOSED FORMULATION	
α	Circle	Octagon	Circle	Octagon	Circle	Octagon	Circle	Octagon
0.25	-6.70E-23	4.49E-19	-7.2E+35	1.88E+39	3.66E-15	9.35E-14	1.53E+26	2.02E+27
0.33	-6.70E-23	4.49E-19	-7.2E+35	1.88E+39	3.66E-15	9.35E-14	1.53E+26	2.02E+27
0.5	-6.70E-23	4.49E-19	-7.2E+35	1.88E+39	3.66E-15	9.35E-14	1.53E+26	2.02E+27
1	-6.70E-23	4.49E-19	-7.2E+35	1.88E+39	3.66E-15	9.35E-14	1.53E+26	2.02E+27
2	-6.70E-23	4.49E-19	-7.2E+35	1.88E+39	3.66E-15	9.35E-14	1.53E+26	2.02E+27
3	-6.70E-23	4.49E-19	-7.2E+35	1.88E+39	3.66E-15	9.35E-14	1.53E+26	2.02E+27
4	-6.70E-23	4.49E-19	-7.2E+35	1.88E+39	3.66E-15	9.35E-14	1.53E+26	2.02E+27
AVG	-6.7E-23	4.49E-19	-7.2E+35	1.88E+39	3.66E-15	9.35E-14	1.53E+26	2.02E+27
%DIFF	200.0597		200.1533		184.9191		171.8332	
%SD	-0.00071	0.001068	-0.00065	0.001305	0.001015	0.001221	0.000701	0.001021

$I_{G1}=n_{20}n_{02}-n_{11}^2$					$I_{G6}=n_{40}n_{04}-4n_{31}n_{13}+3n_{22}^2$			
	EXISTING FORMULATION		PROPOSED FORMULATION		EXISTING FORMULATION		PROPOSED FORMULATION	
α	Circle	Octagon	Circle	Octagon	Circle	Octagon	Circle	Octagon
0.25	5.41E-05	5.30E-05	8.82E+18	5.93E+18	0.000217	0.000213	5.56E+13	4.12E+13
0.33	5.41E-05	5.30E-05	8.82E+18	5.93E+18	0.000217	0.000213	5.56E+13	4.12E+13
0.5	5.41E-05	5.30E-05	8.82E+18	5.93E+18	0.000217	0.000213	5.56E+13	4.12E+13
1	5.41E-05	5.30E-05	8.82E+18	5.93E+18	0.000217	0.000213	5.56E+13	4.12E+13
2	5.41E-05	5.30E-05	8.82E+18	5.93E+18	0.000217	0.000213	5.56E+13	4.12E+13
3	5.41E-05	5.30E-05	8.82E+18	5.93E+18	0.000217	0.000213	5.56E+13	4.12E+13
4	5.41E-05	5.30E-05	8.82E+18	5.93E+18	0.000217	0.000213	5.56E+13	4.12E+13
AVG	5.41E-05	5.3E-05	8.82E+18	5.93E+18	0.000217	0.000213	5.56E+13	4.12E+13
%DIFF	1.931296		39.09621		1.665939		29.70031	
%SD	0.000421	0.000516	0.000355	0.000435	0.000752	0.000901	0.000655	0.000774

$I_{G2}=-n_{30}^2n_{03}^2+6n_{30}n_{21}n_{12}n_{03}-4n_{30}n_{12}^3-4n_{21}^3n_{03}+3n_{21}^2n_{12}^2$					$I_{G7}=n_{40}n_{22}n_{04}-n_{40}n_{13}^2-n_{31}^2n_{04}+2n_{31}n_{22}n_{13}-n_{22}^3$			
	EXISTING FORMULATION		PROPOSED FORMULATION		EXISTING FORMULATION		PROPOSED FORMULATION	
α	Circle	Octagon	Circle	Octagon	Circle	Octagon	Circle	Octagon
0.25	-1.68E-23	-5.80E-20	-1.8E+35	-2.4E+38	1.59E-13	1.52E-13	-2.17E+43	-1.39E+43
0.33	-1.68E-23	-5.80E-20	-1.8E+35	-2.4E+38	1.59E-13	1.52E-13	-2.17E+43	-1.39E+43
0.5	-1.68E-23	-5.80E-20	-1.8E+35	-2.4E+38	1.59E-13	1.52E-13	-2.17E+43	-1.39E+43
1	-1.68E-23	-5.80E-20	-1.8E+35	-2.4E+38	1.59E-13	1.52E-13	-2.17E+43	-1.39E+43
2	-1.68E-23	-5.80E-20	-1.8E+35	-2.4E+38	1.59E-13	1.52E-13	-2.17E+43	-1.39E+43
3	-1.68E-23	-5.80E-20	-1.8E+35	-2.4E+38	1.59E-13	1.52E-13	-2.17E+43	-1.39E+43
4	-1.68E-23	-5.80E-20	-1.8E+35	-2.4E+38	1.59E-13	1.52E-13	-2.17E+43	-1.39E+43
AVG	-1.7E-23	-5.8E-20	-1.8E+35	-2.4E+38	1.59E-13	1.52E-13	-2.2E+43	-1.4E+43
%DIFF	199.8843		199.7035		4.456949		43.76871	
%SD	-0.00071	-0.00267	-0.00066	-0.00263	0.00225	0.0027	-0.00023	-0.00027

8 Conclusion

The existing formulation of scale invariance of moment invariant functions was found to be less suitable for effective object recognition in real time due to mathematical approximations. The formulations were hence revised in order to meet the real time requirements of digital images. The mathematical correctness of the formulations was verified with appropriate derivations. However experiments were conducted to understand the robustness of the proposed scale invariance formulations to real time image processing. We know that a good formulation should be able to distinguish between images containing minimal information. Therefore, the experiments presented in this paper use two circularly symmetric objects with very minimal information in them. It was found from the experiments that the proposed scale invariance formulations were uniformly good at discriminating the images for all invariants. While the existing formulation had good discriminatory ability for some invariants, they had very poor discriminatory ability for other invariants. Through derivations and experiments it could be seen that the proposed formulation of scale invariance in moment invariant functions is more adapted and suitable for real time image processing.

Therefore this research has contributed a successful scale invariance formulation that increases the discriminatory ability and scale invariance of all the existing invariants with no increase in computational complexity. Hence this accomplishment ensures better utilization of moment invariants in real time digital image processing for object recognition and classification.

9 Acknowledgment

Authors would like to thank Universiti Teknologi Malaysia (UTM) for the support in Research and Development, and Soft Computing Research Group (SCRG) for the inspiration in making this study a success. This work is supported by The Ministry of Higher Education (MOHE) under Long Term Research Grant Scheme (LRGS/TD/2011/UTM/ICT/03-4L805).

10 References

[1] K. Mikolajczyk, C.Schmid, “A Performance Evaluation of Local Descriptors”, Pattern Analysis and Machine Intelligence, IEEE Transactions on, Vol. 27, pp. 1615 – 1630,2005

[2] J.-M. Morel and G. Yu, "ASIFT: A New Framework for Fully Affine Invariant Image Comparison," SIAM Journal on Imaging Sciences, vol. 2, pp. 438-469, 2009.

[3] Wong Yee Leng, Siti Mariyam Shamsuddin, “Writer Identification for Chinese Handwriting” International Journal of Advances in Soft Computing and Its Applications, , ISSN 2074-8523,Vol. 2, 2010

[4] Xiuxin Chen, Shiang.Wei, Suxia Xing ; Kebin Jia , “An effective image shape feature detection and description method”, Mechatronic Science, Electric Engineering and Computer (MEC), 2011 International Conference on, pp. 1957 – 1960, Aug. 2011

[5] Gao Fei and Wang Kehong, “The research of classification method of arc welding pool image based on invariant moments” Power Engineering and Automation Conference (PEAM), 2011 IEEE, Vol. 3, pp.73 - 76 , Sept. 2011

[6] Hongbo Mu and Dawei Qi, 2009, “Pattern Recognition of Wood Defects Types Based on Hu Invariant Moments”, Image and Signal Processing, 2009 CISP’09 2nd International Congress, Tianjin, p. 1-5 doi: 10.1109/CISP.2009.5303866

[7] D. Hilbert, “Theory of Algebraic Invariants,” Cambridge, U.K.: Cambridge Univ. Press, 1993.

[8] M.K.Hu, “Visual pattern recognition by moment invariants,” IRE Transactions on Information Theory, Vol. IT-8, pp. 179-187, Feb. 1962

[9] Suk. T and J. Flusser, 2010 “Affine moment invariants generated by graph method,” Pattern Recognition, 2010

[10] Suk. T and J. Flusser, “On the independence of rotation moment invariants,” Pattern Recognition, vol. 33, pp. 1405 – 1410, 2000.

[11] Flusser. J and T. Suk, 2006, "Rotation Moment Invariants for Recognition of Symmetric Objects", IEEE Trans. Image Proc., vol. 15, pp. 3784–3790, 2006.

[12] Flusser. J, T. Suk and B. Zitová. Moments and Moment Invariants in Pattern Recognition © 2009 John Wiley & Sons, Ltd. ISBN: 978-0-470-69987-4.

[13] Shamsuddin. S. M., M. N. Sulaiman & M. Darus, 2002, “Invarianceness of Higher Order Centralised Scaled-invariants Undergo Basic Transformations”, International Journal of Computer Mathematics, vol. 79, pp. 39-48, 2002.

[14] Hameed V.A, Shamsuddin S.M, “Faster Computation of Non Zero Invariants from Graph Based Method”, Communications in Computer and Information Science, Springer, ICIC, 272-279 (2012).

[15] H.F. Zhang, X. Zhang, “Shape recognition using a moment algorithm,” Multimedia Technology (ICMT), International Conference on, 3226-3229 (2011)

[16] Fu Yan, Wang Mei, Zhang Chunqin, “SAR Image Target Recognition Based on Hu Invariant Moments and SVM,” in Proceedings of Fifth International Conference on Information Assurance and Security, IEEE Trans, 585-588 (2009).

[17] Sheela, S.V., P.A. Vijaya, “Non-linear Classification for Iris patterns,” in Proceedings of the Multimedia Computing and Systems (ICMCS), International Conference Ouarzazate, Morocco, 1-5 (2011)

Fuzzy Attributed Skeleton Graphs for Visual Hand Posture Classification

M.Davydov and I.Nikolski
Information Systems and Networks department, Lviv Polytechnic National University, Lviv, Ukraine

Abstract—*A method for constructing a fuzzy attributed skeleton graph with the use of dominant boundary points is proposed, giving emphasis to obtaining a stable fuzzy graph from an object skeleton. The problem arose because skeletons could be changed a lot due to some small shape modifications caused by thresholding procedures. The major contribution of this paper is the use of dominant boundary points to calculate the weight of fuzzy vertices. Our approach is focused on eliminating differences in skeleton graphs caused by the computation methods based on thresholding. The performance of proposed method is evaluated on a database of handshapes.*

Keywords: Fuzzy attributed skeleton graphs; Fuzzy graph match; Graph edit distance; Hand posture recognition.

1. Introduction

The invariance of compact shape representation to image translation, scaling, rotation, noise, and small deformations is important for many computer vision applications such as handshape classification or recognition. Topological skeleton is one of such representations that was studied for a long time. Well-known skeletonization methods such as the medial axis transform [1], Zhang Suen thinning [2], morphological skeleton [3] suffer from boundary noise and can be drastically affected by rotation and small shape transformation. Methods that work with predefined skeleton structures require a database of predefined skeletons for a large number of possible object deformations [4].

The skeleton itself has no sufficient information to reconstruct the shape of the original object. Attributed graphs are more compact and reliable for shape comparison. The constructed attributed graphs can be efficiently compared using a graph edit distance (GED) [5], [6].

The procedure for converting a skeleton into an attributed graph is critical for minimizing in-class distances and maximizing distances between classes. However, the existing shape skeletonization methods do not provide any certainty factors with regard to skeleton branches. The decision to add a branch to a skeleton graph is made by comparing some computed values with a threshold value. If no decision is made at all, the resulting skeleton will highly depend on the shape orientation and boundary noise. When the threshold is passed, a branch is added to the graph resulting in its significant change. So, the constructed skeleton graph depends on the procedure of making decisions and the predefined thresholds. The well-known skeletonization methods that are based on contour partitioning with discrete curve evolution [7], skeleton strength maps [8], particle filters [9] suffer from a threshold-passing problem. Although these methods were developed to produce skeletons stable to boundary noise.

In order to solve this problem a fuzzy attributed graph is used. Thresholding procedures are converted into weighting functions and the obtained weights are assigned to graph vertices and edges. This leads to the reduction in distance between skeleton graphs built for shapes of the same class. The idea of weighting is similar to the idea of significance in shock grammars [10], but it can be used in a wider variety of methods based on attributed skeleton graphs.

2. Problem statement

Let C be a set of shapes from a particular subject area and $E \subset C \times C$ be an equivalence relation on C implied by subject area experts.

The problem of shape classification using a fuzzy attributed skeleton graph representation can be formulated as a problem of defining a skeletonization procedure $S : C \to G$, implementing a distance function $d : G \times G \to \mathbb{R}$ and finding a threshold value $t \in \mathbb{R}$ in such a way that

$$\forall c_1, c_2 \in C : d(S(c_1), S(c_2)) \leq t \Leftrightarrow c_1 \sim_E c_2 \qquad (1)$$

The exact solution of the problem is not always possible due to possible incorrectness of the equivalence relation and the shape roughness that is caused by the image noise. The false positive (FPR) and negative (FNR) rates can be evaluated over a testing set T to find solution candidates (S, d, t):

$$FPR(S, d, t, T) = P(d(S(c_i), S(c_j)) \leq t | \neg(c_i \sim_E c_j) \wedge c_i, c_j \in T), \qquad (2)$$

$$FNR(S, d, t, T) = P(d(S(c_i), S(c_j)) > t | c_i \sim_E c_j \wedge c_i, c_j \in T). \qquad (3)$$

The false positive and negative rates are used to calculate a common error rate that is a maximum of the above error rates:

$$ER(S,d,t,T) = max(FPR(S,d,t,T), FNR(S,d,t,T)). \quad (4)$$

Thus, the requirement (1) can be relaxed by reducing a problem of finding strict solutions to an error minimization problem

$$ER(S,d,t,T) \underset{S,d,t}{\to} min \quad (5)$$

where sub-optimal solutions can always be found.

3. The proposed solution

The proper choice of the skeletonization method, skeleton graph construction procedure, and the graph distance function is a task that requires keeping the balance between quality and speed, especially in real-time applications.

The main factors that affect the skeletonization algorithm selection are their execution speed, robustness, and the possibility to obtain weighting criteria for skeleton vertices. The Zhang Suen parallel thinning algorithm with dominant points detection on the boundary [11] was selected due to its parallel nature and simple dominant points weighting procedure.

Although there are several graph matching approaches based on invariants [12], tensors [13], genetic algorithms [14], and probabilistic approaches [15], the graph edit distance is an approach that is proved to be error-tolerant to noise and distortion in many of successful applications [16]. The graph edit distance is defined as the cost of the least expensive sequence of edit operations that are needed to transform one graph into another.

The outline of the proposed method is as follows:

1) trace shape boundary and assign weights to dominant points;
2) perform skeletonization while preserving dominant boundary points;
3) convert skeleton to fuzzy attributed skeleton graph;
4) compare obtained skeleton graphs with GED.

3.1 Assigning weights to boundary dominant points and skeletonization

In order to determine the boundary dominant points the sharpness of external corners is estimated over the boundary $\mathbf{c} = c_1 c_2 ... c_n$. This is done by evaluating $G_1(k)$, $G_s(k)$, and $F(k)$ functions:

$$G_1(k) = [(\mathbf{c}_k - \mathbf{c}_{k-1modn}) \times (\mathbf{c}_{k+1modn} - \mathbf{c}_k)]_z$$
$$G_s(k) = [(\mathbf{c}_k - \mathbf{c}_{k-smodn}) \times (\mathbf{c}_{k+smodn} - \mathbf{c}_k)]_z$$
$$F(k) = \begin{cases} 0, G_1(k) < 0 \lor G_s(k) < 0 \\ \dfrac{(\mathbf{c}_{k-smodn} - \mathbf{c}_k) \cdot (\mathbf{c}_{k+smodn} - \mathbf{c}_k)}{\|\mathbf{c}_{k-smodn} - \mathbf{c}_k\| \, \|\mathbf{c}_{k+smodn} - \mathbf{c}_k\|}, \\ \qquad G_1(k) \geq 0 \land G_s(k) \geq 0, \end{cases} \quad (6)$$

where k is a current boundary pixel and s is a step used to eliminate the influence of the boundary noise. The geometrical meaning of the function $F(k)$ is depicted in Fig. 1.

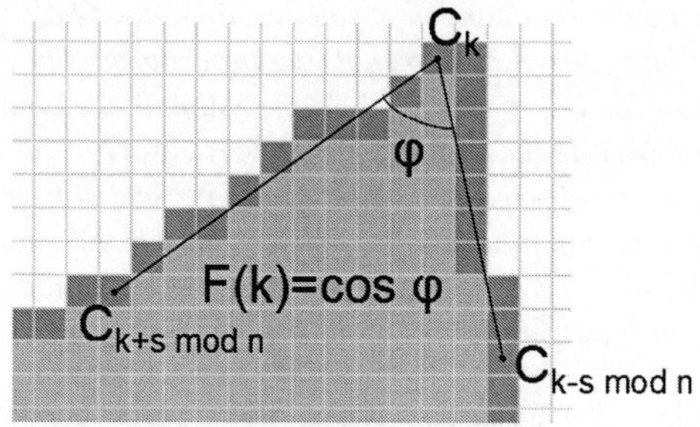

Fig. 1: Geometrical meaning of function $F(k)$. In this example, $s = 10$.

Dominant boundary points are detected as local maxima of function $F(k)$. If pixel k is a local maximum of function $F(k)$ than a vertex of skeleton graph is created at this pixel and its weight is calculated as $w(k) = min((F(k) - \cos\Phi) \cdot \alpha, 1)$, where $\cos\Phi$ is a threshold value and α is a weighting coefficient. A lot of digital curvature measurement approaches [17] can be adopted for detection of dominant boundary points as well.

Skeletonization is done by utilizing the modified Zhang Suen parallel thinning algorithm while preserving the dominant points. Figure 2 shows the skeletons with (Fig. 2(a)) and without (Fig. 2(b)) the dominant boundary points having been preserved. Position of skeleton vertices is easier to predict when dominant boundary points are used.

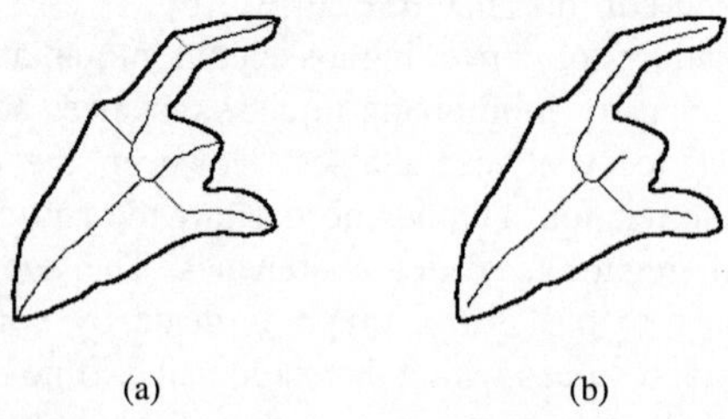

Fig. 2: Skeletons with (a) and without (b) the dominant boundary points having been preserved.

3.2 Converting skeleton to a skeleton graph

After the skeletonization is performed, the next step is to convert the skeleton to a skeleton graph. It can be done by means of a simple tracing approach during which all skeleton pixels are traced and vertices are created where several skeleton branches intersect. Unfortunately, this approach tends to skip important shape information (Fig. 3).

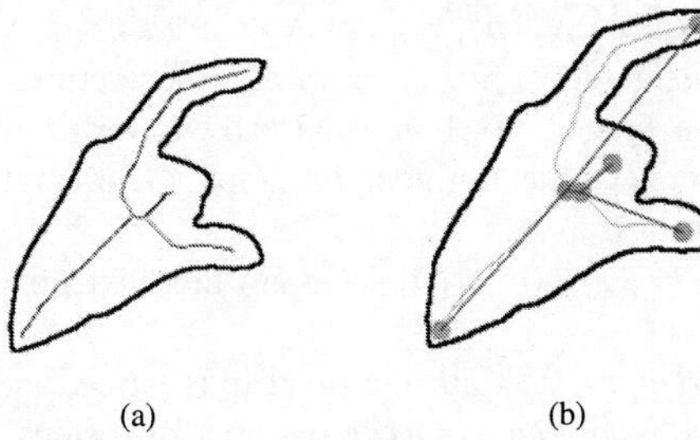

Fig. 3: Image skeleton (a) and the skeleton graph obtained by means of the simple tracing method (b).

In order to overcome this drawback of the simple tracing approach, a one-pass curve division algorithm is proposed. The main idea behind this algorithm is to evaluate the area $S(i)$ that is swept by the vector directed from the beginning of curve A to the current point P_i (Fig. 4). The size of area $S(i)$ is limited, and it should be split when it reaches its limit $S_L(i)$:

$$S_L(i) = k_1\|AP_i\| + k_2, \quad (7)$$

where coefficients k_1 and k_2 are used to adjust division sensibility to small curve variations. Values $k_1 = 1/8$ and $k_2 = 20$ were found to be suitable for converting handshape skeletons used in the conducted experiments.

Once the area passes the threshold value, a vertex is created at the last suitable ("good") point. This point is determined while tracing inequality

$$S(i) < S_L(i)/3 \quad (8)$$

and it usually resides near the center of the split segment (Fig. 4).

The weight of the vertex created by curve subdivision is set to a small value because its position can be changed due to small curve variations.

Before a formal description of *SkeletonGraph(M,V,UseSubdivision)* algorithm is given, we should introduce some notations. The input skeleton S is represented as a matrix $M = \{m_{ij}\}_{w\times h}$, $1 \leq i \leq w, 1 \leq j \leq h$, where w, h are the width and height of the matrix respectively, $m_{ij} \in \{0,1\}$ are its elements. The skeleton is represented by matrix elements equal to one. Let $M[p] = m_{ij}$ denote a pixel

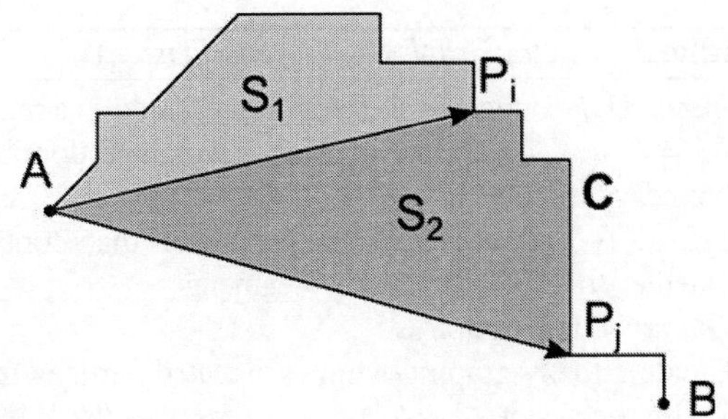

Fig. 4: Breaking the curve **C** during the one-pass tracing procedure. Here $S(i) = S_1$, $S(j) = S_1 + S_2$. P_i is determined to be the last suitable breaking point where inequality $S(i) < S_L(i)/3$ holds.

at coordinate $p = (i,j)$. Let $D_M(p)$ denote a set of neighbors of p where every matrix element is equal to one $\forall p_i \in D_M(p) : M[p_i] = 1$. Neighboring pixels should not be neighbors of each other $\forall p_i, p_j \in D_M(p) : p_i \notin D_M(p_j)$. The input skeleton should be D_M-connected and every pixel along its branches should have exactly 2 neighbors. A pixel with only one neighbor is a leaf vertex of a skeleton. The second input of the algorithm is a list of weighted dominant boundary points. Each point is represented as a pair (p, w) – a pixel coordinate and weight. In case where dominant points are not used or there isn't any point available, the second parameter is set to any leaf vertex of the skeleton or, if there are no leaf vertices, to any skeleton pixel. *UseSubdivision* parameter controls whether to subdivide curved segments or not.

Modification of graph G is done by means of $Add(G,p,w)$, $Contains(G,p)$, and $Join(G,p_1,p_2)$ functions. Function $Add(G,p,w)$ adds a vertex at coordinate p with a weight w to a graph G, function $Contains(G,p)$ verifies whether the graph G contains the vertex at coordinate p, and function $Join(G,p_1,p_2)$ joins vertices at coordinates p_1 and p_2.

SkeletonGraph algorithm traces skeleton segments and connects their endpoints in graph G. Tracing of segments is performed by using *TraceSegment* algorithm that can subdivide segments if $UseSubdivision = true$. *TraceSegment* affects both matrix M and graph G. Matrix M is modified to mark all passed segment pixels with zero values. They are erased from the matrix in order not to trace loops twice. New vertices are added to the graph G and connected if needed.

Both algorithm are given below (Algorithm 1 and 2).

The complexity of *SkeletonGraph* algorithm is $O(n)$ where n is the number of input skeleton pixels (i.e., the number of non-zero elements in matrix M). This is because all pixels are visited only once and the number of pixel neighbors is limited to 4 or 8.

Figure 5 shows the result of converting a skeleton into a skeleton graph with (Fig. 5(b)) and without (Fig. 5(c)) the use of segment subdivision.

Algorithm 1 *SkeletonGraph(M,V,UseSubdivision)*

Input: D_M-connected skeleton, represented as a matrix $M = \{m_{ij}\}_{w \times h}$, array of $N \geq 1$ weighted dominant boundary points $V = \langle v_k \rangle, v_k = (p_k, w_k), k = 1, 2, ..., N$, *UseSubdivision* parameter that controls whether to subdivide curved segments.
Output: Fuzzy graph G.

1. Create a fuzzy graph G with N isolated vertices from V, an open set $O = \{p_1, p_2, \ldots, p_N\}$ with N seed pixels from V, and a closed set $C = \emptyset$.
2. Take any seed pixel $p \in O$ and obtain its neighbors $D = D_M(p)$.
3. Remove the pixel p from the open set O and add it to the closed set C.
4. Perform steps 4.1-4.2 for all pixels $q \in D$.

4.1. If $M[q] = 1$, then $q_{end} = TraceSegment(p, q, UseSubdivision)$. Trace the segment, starting from pixel q, mark it with zeroes in matrix M, add the created vertices to graph G and obtain a segment endpoint q_{end}. The condition $M[q] = 1$ is essential to prevent loops from being traced two times.

4.2. If $q_{end} \notin C \wedge q_{end} \notin O$, add q_{end} to O.

5. If the set O is empty, return G, else go to step 2.

Obtaining a skeleton graph for a shape involves execution of skeletonization and applying *SkeletonGraph* algorithm. Two options to obtain a skeleton for a shape (with and without the use of boundary dominant points) and two options to convert a skeleton into a skeleton graph (with and without segment subdivision) have been studied. Overall 4 options depicted in Fig. 6(a)-(d) have been studied to convert a shape into a skeleton graph. These options yield to different calculation times and recognition rates as discussed in section 4.

3.3 Calculating edit distance between fuzzy attributed graphs

Let fuzzy attributed graph G be an ordered tuple $\langle V, E, A, B, \sigma, \mu, \alpha, \beta \rangle$ where V is a set of vertices, $E \subseteq V \times V$ is a set of edges, A, B are metric spaces for vertex and edge attributes respectively, $\sigma : V \to [0, 1]$ and $\mu : E \to [0, 1]$ are vertex and edge membership functions, $\alpha : V \to A$ and $\beta : E \to B$ are vertex and edge attribute assignment functions.

This definition of a fuzzy attributed graph is slightly different from the definition of a fuzzy attributed graph given in [18], where the fuzziness of attributes is explicitly defined.

An edit distance between fuzzy attributed graphs is defined by a set of editing operations and their cost functions. Bunke and Jiang [19] the costs for substitution, insertion, and deletion of vertices (c_{vs}, c_{vi}, c_{vd}) and edges (c_{es}, c_{ei}, c_{ed}) respectively. Ambauen et al. [20] propose to extend

Algorithm 2 *TraceSegment(p,q,UseSubdivision)*

Input: Pixel p that is a segment vertex, pixel q is the first pixel along the segment, *UseSubdivision* indicates whether to use segment subdivision.
Output: Segment endpoint q_{end}.

1. Let $S_A := 0$, $g := p$, $r := p$. Initialize the sweeping area S_A, "good" subdivision point g that is used in the segment subdivision process, and the reference vertex r.
2. If $|D_M(q) \setminus \{p\}| \neq 1 \vee Contains(G, q)$, then $Connect(G, q, r)$, $q_{end} := q$, and then return. If pixel q is a branch pixel or is already a vertex of graph G, connect the segment in graph G and return the endpoint q_{end}.
3. $q_{new} := (D_M(q) \setminus \{p\})$. Obtain the next pixel of the segment.
4. Set $M[q] := 0$. Mark the pixel q as passed.
5. If $UseSubdivision = true$ then perform steps 5.1-5.3, otherwise proceed to step 6.

5.1. $S_A := S_A + \frac{1}{2} \|\overline{pq} \times \overline{qq_{new}}\|$. Update the sweeping area.

5.2. If $|S_A| < \frac{1}{3} k_1 \|\overline{TP}\| + k_2$, then $g := q$. If the "good" point condition (8) is met then save the "good" point.

5.3. If $|S_A| \geq k_1 \|\overline{TP}\| + k_2 \wedge g \neq r$ then $Add(G, g, 0.1)$, $Connect(G, r, g)$, $r := g$, $S_A := 0$. If the sweeping area S_A overcomes the limit (7) then add a new vertex to graph G, connect it to the previous vertex r, reassign the previous vertex to g and initialize the sweeping area with zero.

6. Set $q := q_{new}$, go to step 2 (proceed to the next segment pixel).

the set of editing operations with vertex splitting and vertex merging operations that was useful in applications where the nodes of the considered graphs represent regions extracted by some segmentation procedure. For skeleton graphs, it is more natural to extend the list of editing operations with edge subdivision and vertex smoothing.

The subdivision of some edge e with endpoints $\{u, v\}$ yields a graph containing one new vertex w and two new edges (u, w) and $\{w, v\}$ replacing edge e.

The smoothing of the vertex w with two incident edges $\{v, w\}$ and $\{w, u\}$ is an operation that produces a new graph by deleting vertex w altogether with the incident edges and adding a new edge $\{v, u\}$. The vertex smoothing is allowed only if there is no $\{v, u\}$ edge in the original graph.

The proposed list of graph editing operations and their costs are presented in Table 1.

Calculating the edit distance between graphs G_1 and G_2 involves finding the shortest path between them in a state space generated by graph G_1 and all possible editing operations. Reisen et al. [21], propose to use A* search algorithm with heuristic estimate based on Munkres' algorithm [22] to

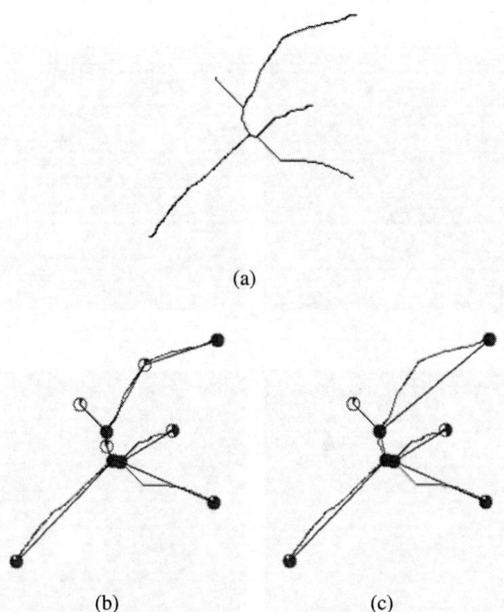

Fig. 5: Skeleton (a) and its skeleton graphs obtained by means of *SkeletonGraph* algorithm with *UseSubdivision=True* (b) and *UseSubdivision=false* (c). Vertex shading indicates its weight.

effectively compute the graph edit distances. However, they have no computation performance benefits on small graphs, so we used only first two steps of the Hungarian algorithm to reduce the maximum number of operations required to compute the estimate from $O(n^3)$ to $O(n^2)$.

4. Results

The developed algorithm was tested on a database of Ukrainian sign language alphabet handshapes. The database contains 165 images split into 33 classes, 5 images in each class.

Every image was processed by means of a skin-detection algorithm, smoothed, thresholded, and converted to a fuzzy graph by using 4 possible alternatives described in Section 3.2. The attributes of vertexes were calculated by using formula $\alpha(v) = (p(v) - \overline{p})/\sigma$, where $p(v)$ is the coordinate of the vertex's pixel, $\overline{p} = \frac{1}{n}\sum_i p(v_i)$, $\sigma = \sqrt{\frac{1}{n}\sum_i \|p(v_i) - \overline{p}\|^2}$. The edges had no attributes at all, and the leaves' edges weights were set to the corresponding vertex weights.

Although there is a lot of cost parameters in edit distance metric, the only parameter that affected the result significantly was c_{vs}, because it directly changed the ratio between the vertex attribute distance and the cost of all other operations. This result could be expected because this property of GED weights had been studied before in [23]. So we set $c_{vi} = c_{vd} = c_{ei} = c_{ed} = c_{es} = 1.0$, $c_{subd} =$

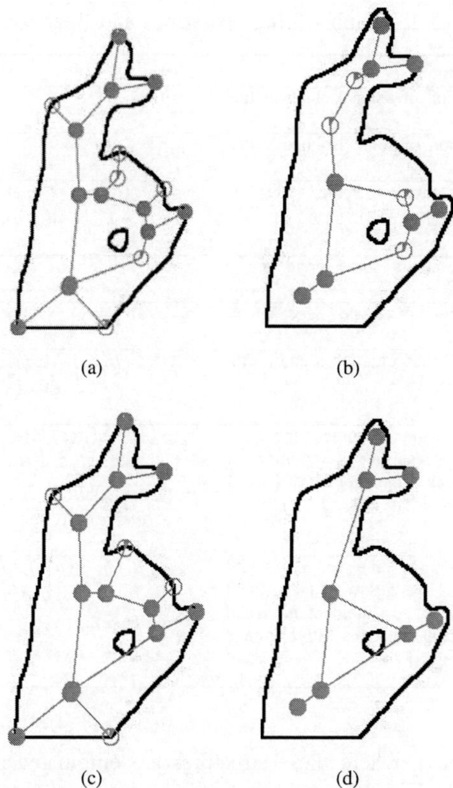

Fig. 6: Skeleton graphs of a shape, obtained with (a), (c) and without (b), (d) the use of dominant boundary points. Segment subdivision was used in (a) and (b).

$c_{smooth} = 0.9$ and calculated the parameter c_{vs} and the threshold t by minimizing expression (5):

$$ER(S, d, t, T) \underset{c_{vs},t}{\rightarrow} min. \tag{9}$$

The obtained minimal error rate and average edit distance calculation time for each of the studied skeleton graph construction methods are shown in Table 2. The corresponding thresholded graph comparison matrices are depicted in Figure 7. The calculation time was estimated on a computer with quad-core Intel Core i5-2400 CPU @ 3.10 GHz processor.

Although the method that uses boundary points and subdivisions to construct a fuzzy attributed graph exhibits the lowest error rate, it has the slowest calculation time because it creates a skeleton graph with more vertices than others algorithms.

The study of bad cases shows that most of graph edit distance problems were caused by graph structure modification illustrated in Figure 8. This graph modification is difficult to overcome by means of graph editing operations and requires either vertex splitting and merging operations or some special approach such as the one used in bone

Table 1: Graph editing operations and their costs

#	Operation	Cost
1	Insertion of some isolated vertex v	$c_{vi}\sigma(v)$
2	Deletion of some isolated vertex v	$c_{vd}\sigma(v)$
3	Substitution of some vertex v_1 with vertex v_2	$c_{vs}max(\sigma(v_1), \sigma(v_2)) \cdot d(\alpha(v_1), \alpha(v_2))$
4	Insertion of some edge $e = \{v, u\}$	$c_{ei}\mu(e)$
5	Deletion of some edge $e = \{v, u\}$	$c_{ed}\mu(e)$
6	Substitution of some edge e_1 with edge e_2	$c_{es}max(\mu(e_1), \mu(e_2)) \cdot d(\beta(e_1), \beta(e_2))$
7	Subdivision of some edge $e = \{u, v\}$ resulting in addition of vertex w with edges $e_1 = \{u, w\}$ and $e_2 = \{w, v\}$	$c_{subd}\,(max(\mu(e), \mu(e_1)) \cdot d(\beta(e), \beta(e_1)) + max(\mu(e), \mu(e_2)) \cdot d(\beta(e), \beta(e_2)) + c_{vi}\sigma(w)$
8	Smoothing some vertex w with regards to edges $e_1 = \{u, w\}$ and $e_2 = \{w, v\}$ incident to it and replacing the edges with one edge $e = \{u, v\}$	$c_{smooth}\,(max(\mu(e), \mu(e_1)) \cdot d(\beta(e), \beta(e_1)) + max(\mu(e), \mu(e_2)) \cdot d(\beta(e), \beta(e_2)) + c_{vd}\sigma(w)$

graphs [24], where these structures are eliminated as part of the graph simplification procedure. An example of such problem (i.e. hand postures of the same class had GED larger that the threshold) is depicted in Figure 9.

Table 2: Calculation time and minimal error rate obtained for methods studied.

#	Skeleton graph construction method		Average GED calculation time (ms)	Error rate (%)
	Dominant boundary points	*UseSubdividion*		
1	Used	true	2.4	7.9
2	Not used	true	0.14	10.3
3	Used	false	0.53	10.9
4	Not used	false	0.09	11.7

5. Conclusions

Shape representation based on the fuzzy attributed skeleton graph was studied for hand posture classification. This representation is compact and contains additional information about the object itself as well as certainty factors for graph edges and vertices. The procedure for converting skeletons to graphs was implemented and its parameters were studied. It was shown that the use of segment subdivision and vertex weighting procedure reduces the classification error. The cost of this error reduction is an increase in computation time, especially when fuzzy graphs are used.

The future research aims to eliminate GED problems that arise due to special vertex layout and to improve heuristic functions that can reduce computation time. The rate of

Fig. 7: Thresholded 165x165 graph comparison matrices for methods 1-4 from Table 2. The best result is the one with white squares diagonally and black filling in the rest of the area.

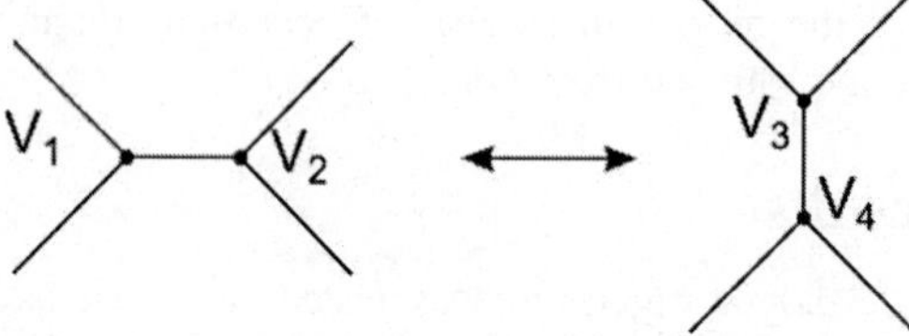

Fig. 8: Graph modification that causes large graph edit distance.

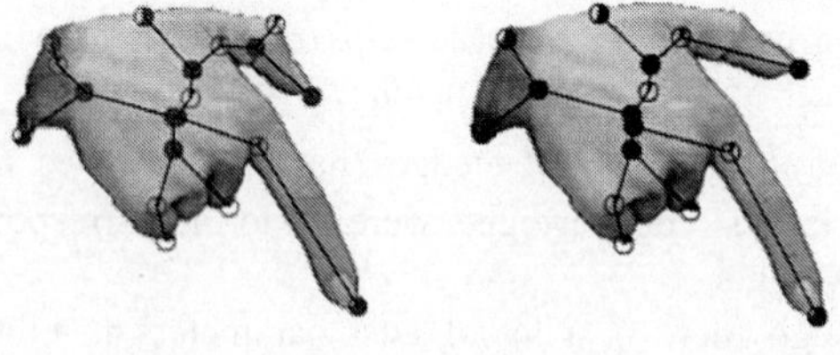

Fig. 9: Hand postures of the same class that were not recognized to be equivalent because of the structure illustrated in Fig. 8.

hand posture classification can also be increased by selecting several representatives of each shape class and providing appropriate thresholds for them.

Visual hand posture recognition obviously requires more information than the shape contour can provide, thus we believe that there is a large scope for improvement via use of hand illumination in the process of building skeleton graphs. We intend to explore this idea in the future.

References

[1] H. Blum, "Biological shape and visual science," *Journal of Theoretical Biology*, vol. 38, pp. 205–287, 1973.

[2] T. Y. Zhang, C. Y. Suen, "A fast parallel algorithm for thinning digital patterns," *ACM: Commun ACM.*, vol. 27, no. 3, pp. 236–239, Mar. 1984.

[3] J. Goutsias and D. Schonfeld, "Morphological representation of discrete and binary images," *Signal Processing, IEEE Transactions on.*, vol. 39, no. 6, pp. 1369–1379, 1991.

[4] M. van Eede, D. Macrini, A. Telea, C. Sminchisescu, and S. S. Dickinson, "Canonical Skeletons for Shape Matching," in *Proc. ICPR'06*, vol. 02, 2006, pp. 64–69.

[5] H. Bunke, "Inexact graph matching for structural pattern recognition," *Pattern Recognition Letters*, vol. 01, no. 4, pp. 245–253, May 1983.

[6] J. Rocha and T. Pavlidis, "A shape analysis model with applications to a character recognition system," *Pattern Analysis and Machine Intelligence, IEEE Trans. on*, vol. 16, no. 4, pp. 393–404, Apr. 1994.

[7] X. Bai, L. J. Latecki, and W.-Y. Liu, "Skeleton Pruning by Contour Partitioning with Discrete Curve Evolution," *Pattern Analysis and Machine Intelligence, IEEE Trans. on*, vol. 29, no. 3, pp. 449–462, Mar. 2007.

[8] L. J. Latecki, L. Quan-nan, B. Xiang, and L. Wen-yu, "Skeletonization using SSM of the Distance Transform," *ICIP'2007. IEEE International Conference on.* vol. 5, 16-19 Oct. 2007, pp. 349–352.

[9] X. Bai, X. Yang, L. Latecki, Y. Xu, and W. Liu, "Computing Stable Skeletons with Particle Filters," *PRICAI 2008: Trends in Artificial Intelligence*, ser. Lecture Notes in Computer Science, eds. T. Ho, Z. Zhou, vol. 5351, 2008, pp. 30–41.

[10] K. Siddiqi, B. B. Kimia, "A shock grammar for recognition," in *Proc. CVPR'96, IEEE Computer Society Conf. on*, 18-20 Jun. 1996, pp. 507–513.

[11] T. P. Nguyen and I. Debled-Rennesson, "Fast and robust dominant points detection on digital curves," in *Image Processing (ICIP), 2009 16th IEEE International Conference on*, 7-10 Nov. 2009, pp. 953–956.

[12] X. Bai, L. J. Latecki, "Path Similarity Skeleton Graph Matching," *IEEE Trans. Pattern Anal. Mach. Intell.*, vol. 30, 7 Jul. 2008, pp. 1282–1292.

[13] O. Duchenne, F. Bach, I.-S. Kweon, J. Ponce, "Tensor-Based Algorithm for High-Order Graph Matching," *IEEE Trans. Pattern Anal. Mach. Intell.* vol. 33, 12 Dec. 2011, pp. 2383–2395.

[14] M. Krcmar, A. P. Dhawan, "Application of genetic algorithms in graph matching," *Neural Networks, 1994. IEEE World Congress on Computational Intelligence., 1994 IEEE International Conference on*, vol. 6. 27 Jun - 2 Jul 1994, pp.3872–3876.

[15] R. Zass and A. Shashua, "Probabilistic graph and hypergraph matching," *Computer Vision and Pattern Recognition, 2008. CVPR 2008. IEEE Conference on*, 23-28 June 2008, pp. 1–8.

[16] Xinbo Gao, Bing Xiao, Dacheng Tao, Xuelong Li, "A survey of graph edit distance," *Pattern Anal. Appl. 13*, 1 Jan. 2010, pp. 113–129.

[17] M. Worring and A. W. M. Smeulders, "Digital Curvature Estimation," *Elsevier: CVGIP: Image Understanding*, vol. 58, Issue 3, pp. 366–382, Nov. 1993.

[18] A. Perchant and I. Bloch, "A new definition for fuzzy attributed graph homomorphism with application to structural shape recognition in brain imaging," in *Proc. IMTC'99*, vol. 3, 1999, pp.1801–1806.

[19] H. Bunke and X. Jiang, "Graph matching and similarity," in *Intelligent Systems and Interfaces. International Series in Intelligent Technologies*, vol. 15, pp. 281–304, 2000.

[20] R. Ambauen, S. Fischer, and H. Bunke "Graph Edit Distance with Node Splitting and Merging, and Its Application to Diatom Identification," in *Graph Based Representations in Pattern Recognition. Lecture Notes in Computer Science,* vol. 2726, pp. 95–106, 2003.

[21] K. Riesen and H. Bunke, "Approximate graph edit distance computation by means of bipartite graph matching," *Elsevier: Image and Vision Computing*, vol. 27, no. 7, pp. 950–959, 4 June 2009.

[22] J. Munkres, "Algorithms for the assignment and transportation problems," in *Journal of the Society for Industrial and Applied Mathematics*, vol. 5, pp. 32–38, Mar. 1957.

[23] H. Bunke, "Error Correcting Graph Matching: On the Influence of the Underlying Cost Function," *IEEE Trans. Pattern Anal. Mach. Intell.*, vol. 21, 9 Sep. 1999, pp. 917–922.

[24] D. Macrini, K. Siddiqi, and S. Dickinson, "From skeletons to bone graphs: Medial abstraction for object recognition", in *IEEE Conference on Computer Vision and Pattern Recognition, 2008, CVPR 2008*, 23-28 June 2008, pp.1–8.

"Judgments on Video Applications for Required Contents" - using Evidential Reasoning (ER) Algorithm

Rashed Mustafa [1,2,3,4] **and Dingju Zhu** [1, 2, 4,5,*]

[1] Laboratory for Smart Computing and Information Science, Shenzhen Institutes of Advanced Technology, Chinese Academy of Sciences, Shenzhen, China

[2] University of Chinese Academy of Sciences, Beijing, China

[3] Department of Computer Science and Engineering, University of Chittagong, Bangladesh

[4] Shenzhen Public Platform for Triple-play Video Transcoding Center, Shenzhen, China

[5] School of Computer Science, South China normal University, Guangzhou, China

Abstract *- Searching desired videos is now challenging due to scattered collection of large amounts of videos all over the world. It is very difficult to find appropriate video applications for different video contents required by different users from repositories. This paper contributes prioritizing videos using Multi criteria Decision Analysis Approach (MCDA) which is denoted as Evidential Reasoning Method (ER). In this research a simple case study presented over some classification of videos where particular object/person need to be identified. It has been shown that the approach best-prioritized shot-Stock videos for selecting particular object/person and ER approach is more efficient than Analytic Hierarchical Process (AHP).*

Keywords: ER, AHP, MCDA, eigenvector, pair wise matrix, Belief Rule Base (BRB)

1 Introduction

Analytic Hierarchical process (AHP) [2, 3, 4, 5] and Evidential Reasoning (ER) [15] is one of the ubiquitous approaches to solve Multi-Criteria Decision Problem (MCDP) [18, 23]. It is to be noted that, selection of videos is a multi-criteria decision problem since it has wide spread categories. This are basically in two classes: i) content oriented and ii) content less videos [6, 7]. The evidential reasoning approach (ER) is an evidence-based multi-criteria decision analysis (MCDA) method for dealing with difficulties having both quantitative and qualitative criteria under various uncertainties including ignorance, vagueness and randomness [18]. It has been used to support various decision analysis, assessment and evaluation activities such as environmental impact assessment [19], organizational self-assessment [23], weather prediction [22], image quality enhancement [21] etc. based on a range of quality models. Unlike AHP (aggregating average scores), [4] the ER employs an evidential reasoning algorithm developed on the basis of decision theory and the evidence contribution rule of Dempster-Shafer theory to aggregate belief degrees [16, 17, 19].

The rest of the paper organized as follows: in section 2 Evidential Reasoning Approach (ER) introduced for judging video categories, section 3 illustrates methodology for selection of videos using ER, in section 4 a brief analysis is elucidated for prioritized videos and finally conclusion part is described in section 5.

2. Evidential Reasoning (ER) Approach for Video Judgments

In this section we demonstrate ER approach to judgments on video categories. Choosing a desired video may have the following four evaluation grades: $\{H_1, H_2, H_3, H_4\}$={Slightly Preferred, Moderately Preferred, Preferred, Greatly Preferred}. Suppose there are M alternatives, Y_j (j=1,....M), to choose from N attributes, and X_i (i=1,...,N) to consider. Using four evaluation grades, the assessment of an alternative Y_1 on an attribute X_1, denoted by $S(X_1(Y_1))$ can be represented by the following belief structure:

$$S(X_1(Y_1)) = \{\beta_{1,1}, H_1, \beta_{2,1}, H_2, \beta_{3,1}, H_3, \beta_{4,1}, H_4\} \quad (1)$$

Where $1 >= \beta_{n,1} >= 0$ (n=1,...4) denotes the degree of belief that the attribute X_1 of the alternative Y_1 assessed to the evaluation grade H_n.

Just as equation (1) the second $S(X_2(Y_1))$ is given by

$$S(X_2(Y_1)) = \{\beta_{1,2}, H_1, \beta_{2,2}, H_2, \beta_{3,2}, H_3, \beta_{4,2}, H_4\} \quad (2)$$

The two assessments $S(X_1(Y_1))$ and $S(X_2(Y_1))$ can be aggregated to generate a combined assessment

---

* Corresponding author: Dingju Zhu. Address: Shenzhen Institutes of Advanced Technology, Chinese Academy of Sciences-518055, Shenzhen China. Email: dj.zhu@siat.ac.cn. Tel: +86-13316588865.

$S(X_1(Y_1)) \oplus S(X_2(Y_1))$

Let, $m_{n,1} = \omega_1\beta_{n,1}$ (n=1,…,4) and $m_{H,1} = 1-\omega_1$

$\sum_{n=1}^{4}\beta_{n,1} = 1-\omega_1$ and $m_{n,2} = \omega_2\beta_{n,2}$ (n=1,…,4) and

$$m_{H,2} = 1-\omega_2 \sum_{n=1}^{4}\beta_{n,2} = 1-\omega_2 \quad \text{.........................(3)}$$

Where each $m_{n,j}$, (j = 1, 2) is referred to as basic probability mass and each $m_{H,j}$, (j =1,2) is the remaining belief for attribute j unassigned to any of the Hn (n = 1, 2, 3, 4).

The weights of the attributes are given by ω_i (i=1..2) where ω_i is the relative weight of the ith basic attribute $0<=\omega_i<=1$. ω_i can be calculated by the following equations [20]

$$\omega_i = \alpha \frac{\omega_i}{\max_i\{\omega_i, i=1..2\}} \quad \text{...(4)}$$

$$\text{Here, } \alpha = \prod_{i=1}^{2}\left(1-\alpha\frac{\omega_i}{\max_i\{\omega_i, i=1..2\}}\right) <= \delta \quad \text{........(5)}$$

Here δ represents a small constant considering the degree of approximation for aggregation.

The ER algorithm is used to aggregate the basic probability masses to generate combined probability masses, denoted by m_n (*n*=1, …, 4) and m_H using the following equations [20]:

$m_n = z(m_{n,1}m_{n,2} + m_{H,1}m_{n,2} + m_{n,1}m_{H,2})$, (n=1…4)…………..(6)

$m_H = z(m_{H,1}m_{H,2})$ ……………………………………….(7)

$$\text{Where, } z=\left(1-\sum_{t=1}^{4}\sum_{\substack{n=1\\n\neq t}}^{4} m_{t,1}m_{n,2}\right)^{-1} \quad \text{..........................(8)}$$

The combined degrees of belief $\beta_n = \dfrac{m_n}{1-m_H}$ (n=1…4)…(9)

The combined assessment for the alternative Y_1 can then be represented as follows:

$S(Y_1) = \{(H_1, \beta_1), (H_2, \beta_2), (H_3, \beta_3), (H_4, \beta_4)\}$. …………..(10)

An average score for Y_1, denoted by $u(Y_1)$, can also be provided as the weighted average of the scores (utilities) of the evaluation grades with the belief degrees as weights, or $u(Y_1) = \sum_{i=1}^{4} u(H_i)\beta_i$ …………………… (11)

In (11) u (H_i) is the utility of the i-th evaluation grade H_i. If evaluation grades are assume to be equidistantly distributed in the utility space, for example, the utilities of the evaluation grades can be given as follows:

$u(H_1)$ = u (Slightly preferred) = 0.25.

$u(H_2$ = u (Moderately preferred) = 0.50.

$u(H_3)$ = u (Preferred) = 0.75.

$u(H_4)$ = u (Greatly preferred) = 1.00.

3. Methodology

Assessing Multi-criteria Decision problem; AHP utilized a pair wise judgment matrix. In which every value of that matrix can take one dimensional judgment value [section 2]. In contrast with this phenomenon Evidential Reasoning (ER) approach considers extended judgment matrix and every value of that matrix can take multidimensional value based on different evaluation grade and belief degree [section 2].

3.1 ER Based Approach

ER algorithm is briefly described in section 2. In this section an experimental framework using Evidential Reasoning (ER) for video judgments will be discussed. ER used an extended judgments matrix. This extended matrix for the case study of this paper is presented in the following table:

Table 1: Extended Judgment Matrix for Evidential Reasoning

Selection Decision	VOD (Y_1)	Shot-stock (Y_2)	Research (Y_3)	Document (Y_4)	I-video (Y_5)
Compositional (X_1)	S (X_1 (Y_1))	S (X_1 (Y_2))	S (X_1 (Y_3))	S (X_1 (Y_4))	S (X_1 (Y_5))
Bibliographic (X_2)	S (X_2 (Y_1))	S (X_2 (Y_2))	S (X_2 (Y_3))	S (X_2 (Y_4))	S (X_2 (Y_5))
Structural (X_3)	S (X_3 (Y_1))	S (X_3 (Y_2))	S (X_3 (Y_3))	S (X_3 (Y_4))	S (X_3 (Y_5))
Sensory Content (X_4)	S (X_4 (Y_1))	S (X_4 (Y_2))	S (X_4 (Y_3))	S (X_4 (Y_4))	S (X_4 (Y_5))
Topic Content (X_5)	S (X_5 (Y_1))	S (X_5 (Y_2))	S (X_5 (Y_3))	S (X_5 (Y_4))	S (X_5 (Y_5))

Table 2: Relative Importance of Video Data Types in Different Video Alternatives [1]

Selection Decision	VOD (Y_1)	Shot-stock (Y_2)	Research (Y_3)	Document (Y_4)	I-video (Y_5)
Compositional (X_1)	No	No	High	Low	High
Bibliographic (X_2)	High	Medium	High	Medium	High
Structural (X_3)	Low	No	High	Medium/High	High
Sensory Content (X_4)	No	High	High	High	Medium
Topic Content (X_5)	Low	Medium	High	High	High

We assumed that in table 2 [1], no importance means 90 percent of slightly preferred (H1) and 10 percent of moderately preferred (H2), low importance means 75 percent of slightly preferred (H1) and 25 percent of moderately preferred (H2), medium importance means 25 percent of moderately preferred (H2) and 75 percent of preferred (H3), and high importance means 10 percent of preferred (H3) and 90 percent of greatly preferred (H4).

3.1.1 Calculating Scores for VOD

Using equation (1) in section 3 and table 10, belief functions for VOD (Y_1) is:
S (X_1 (Y_1)) = {H_1, 0.9, H_2, 0.1, H_3, 0, H_4, 0}
[Compositional data is slightly preferred]
S (X_2 (Y_1)) = {H_1, 0, H_2, 0, H_3, 0.1, H_4, 0.9}
[Bibliographic data is greatly preferred]
S (X_3 (Y_1)) = {H_1, 0.75, H_2, 0.25, H_3, 0, H_4, 0}
[Structural data is moderately preferred]
S (X_4 (Y_1)) = {H_1, 0.9, H_2, 0.1, H_3, 0, H_4, 0}
[Sensory content data is slightly preferred]
S (X_5 (Y_1)) = {H_1, 0.75, H_2, 0.25, H_3, 0, H_4, 0} [Topic content data is moderately preferred]
Aggregating first two assessments

S (X_1 (Y_2) ⊕ S (X_2 (Y_2)
$\beta_{1,1} = 0.9$; $\beta_{2,1} = 0.1$; $\beta_{3,1} = 0$; $\beta_{4,1} = 0$;
$\beta_{1,2} = 0$; $\beta_{2,2} = 0$; $\beta_{3,2} = 0.1$; $\beta_{4,2} = 0.9$;
S (X_1 (Y_1))= 0.9*0.25+0.1*0.1=0.275
S (X_2 (Y_1))= 0.1*0.75+0.9*1=0.975
So S (X_2 (Y_1)) is 3.55 times important than S (X_1 (Y_1))
The weights ω_1 and ω_2 are normalized as follows [Equation 4, 5]
$\omega_2 = \omega_1/3.55$
Hence $(1-\alpha)(1-\alpha/3.55)=0.05$ and $\alpha=0.9322$, so $\omega_2 = 0.9322$ and $\omega_1 = 0.2626$
Now probability masses for these two assessments are [equations 6, 7]:
$m_{1,1} = 0.2363$; $m_{2,1} = 0.02626$; $m_{3,1} = 0$; $m_{4,1} = 0$;
$m_{H,1} = 0.7374$
$m_{1,2} = 0$; $m_{2,2} = 0$; $m_{3,2} = 0.09322$; $m_{4,2} = 0.839$
$m_{H,2} = 0.0678$

The combined probability masses are [equations 6, 7]:
$m_1 = (z)(m_{1,1}\, m_{1,2} + m_{1,1}\, m_{H,2} + m_{H,1}\, m_{1,2})$
z=1.3241 (Equation 8]
So, $m_1 = 0.0212$
$m_2 = (z)(m_{2,1}\, m_{2,2} + m_{2,1}\, m_{H,2} + m_{H,1}\, m_{2,2})=0.00236$
$m_3 = (z)(m_{3,1}\, m_{3,2} + m_{3,1}\, m_{H,2} + m_{H,1}\, m_{3,2})=0.091$
$m_4 = (z)(m_{4,1}\, m_{4,2} + m_{4,1}\, m_{H,2} + m_{H,1}\, m_{4,2})=0.8192$
$m_H = 0.0662$

Hence the combined assessment for these two attributes is:
$S (X_1 (Y_1)) \oplus S (X_2 (Y_1)) = \{H_1, 0.0227, H_2, 0.00252, H_3, 0.0974, H_4, 0.8773\}$

Linear aggregation for the third assessments
$[S (X_1 (Y_1) \oplus S (X_2 (Y_1)] \rightarrow A \oplus [S (X_3 (Y_1)] \rightarrow B$
$\beta_{1,1} = 0.0227; \beta_{2,1} = 0.00252; \beta_{3,1} = 0.0974; \beta_{4,1} = 0.8773;$
$\beta_{1,2} = 0.75; \beta_{2,2} = 0.25; \beta_{3,2} = 0; \beta_{4,2} = 0;$
A is 3 times important than B

The weights ω_1 and ω_2 are normalized as follows
$\omega_1 = 3\omega_2$
Hence $(1-\alpha)(1-\alpha/3)=0.05$ and $\alpha=0.9276$, so $\omega_2 = 0.3092$ and $\omega_1 = 0.9276$

Now probability masses for these two assessments are:
$m_{1,1} = 0.021; m_{2,1} = 0.00234 ; m_{3,1} = 0.0903; m_{4,1} = 0.8138;$
$m_{H,1} = 0.07256$
$m_{1,2} = 0.2319 ; m_{2,2} = 0.0773; m_{3,2} = 0; m_{4,2} = 0$
$m_{H,2} = 0.6908$

The combined probability masses are:
$m_1 = (z)(m_{1,1}\, m_{1,2} + m_{1,1}\, m_{H,2} + m_{H,1}\, m_{1,2})$
z=1.4
So, $m_1 = 0.035$
$m_2 = (z)(m_{2,1}\, m_{2,2} + m_{2,1}\, m_{H,2} + m_{H,1}\, m_{2,2})=0.0104$
$m_3 = (z)(m_{3,1}\, m_{3,2} + m_{3,1}\, m_{H,2} + m_{H,1}\, m_{3,2})=0.087$
$m_4 = (z)(m_{4,1}\, m_{4,2} + m_{4,1}\, m_{H,2} + m_{H,1}\, m_{4,2})=0.787$
$m_H = 0.08056$

Hence the combined assessment for these two attributes is:
$S (X_1 (Y_1)) \oplus S (X_2 (Y_1)) \oplus S (X_3 (Y_1)) = \{H_1, 0.03807, H_2, 0.0113, H_3, 0.0946, H_4, 0.856\}$

$[S (X_1 (Y_1) \oplus S (X_2 (Y_1) \oplus S (X_3 (Y_1)] \rightarrow A \oplus [S (X_4 (Y_1)] \rightarrow B$

$\beta_{1,1} = 0.03807; \beta_{2,1} = 0.0113; \beta_{3,1} = 0.0946; \beta_{4,1} = 0.856;$
$\beta_{1,2} = 0.9; \beta_{2,2} = 0.1; \beta_{3,2} = 0; \beta_{4,2} = 0;$
A is 3 times important than B

The weights ω_1 and ω_2 are normalized as follows
$\omega_1 = 3\omega_2$
Hence $(1-\alpha)(1-\alpha/3)=0.05$ and $\alpha=0.9276$, so $\omega_2 = 0.3092$ and $\omega_1 = 0.9276$
Now probability masses for these two assessments are:
$m_{1,1} = 0.0353 ; m_{2,1} = 0.0105; m_{3,1} = 0.0878; m_{4,1} = 0.794;$
$m_{H,1} = 0.0724$
$m_{1,2} = 0.2783; m_{2,2} = 0.0309; m_{3,2} = 0; m_{4,2} = 0$
$m_{H,2} = 0.6908$
The combined probability masses are:
$m_1 = (z)(m_{1,1}\, m_{1,2} + m_{1,1}\, m_{H,2} + m_{H,1}\, m_{1,2})$
z=1.4
So, $m_1 = 0.0761$
$m_2 = (z)(m_{2,1}\, m_{2,2} + m_{2,1}\, m_{H,2} + m_{H,1}\, m_{2,2})=0.0137$
$m_3 = (z)(m_{3,1}\, m_{3,2} + m_{3,1}\, m_{H,2} + m_{H,1}\, m_{3,2})=0.0849$
$m_4 = (z)(m_{4,1}\, m_{4,2} + m_{4,1}\, m_{H,2} + m_{H,1}\, m_{4,2})=0.7679$
$m_H = 0.0574$

Hence the combined assessment for these two attributes is:
$S (X_1 (Y_1)) \oplus S (X_2 (Y_1)) \oplus S (X_3 (Y_1)) \oplus S (X_4 (Y_1)) = \{H_1, 0.0807, H_2, 0.0145, H_3, 0.0901, H_4, 0.8147\}$
$[S (X_1 (Y_1) \oplus S (X_2 (Y_1) \oplus S (X_3 (Y_1) \oplus S (X_4 (Y_1)] \rightarrow \oplus [S (X_5 (Y_1)] \rightarrow B$

$\beta_{1,1} = 0.0807; \beta_{2,1} = 0.0145; \beta_{3,1} = 0.0901; \beta_{4,1} = 0.8147;$
$\beta_{1,2} = 0.75; \beta_{2,2} = 0.25; \beta_{3,2} = 0; \beta_{4,2} = 0;$

A is 3 times important than B
The weights ω_1 and ω_2 are normalized as follows
$\omega_1 = 3\omega_2$

Hence $(1-\alpha)(1-\alpha/3)=0.05$ and $\alpha=0.9276$, so $\omega_2 = 0.3092$ and $\omega_1 = 0.9276$
Now probability masses for these two assessments are:
$m_{1,1} = 0.075 ; m_{2,1} = 0.0135; m_{3,1} = 0.0836; m_{4,1} = 0.756;$
$m_{H,1} = 0.07218$
$m_{1,2} = 0.2319 ; m_{2,2} = 0.0773; m_{3,2} = 0; m_{4,2} = 0$
$m_{H,2} = 0.6908$

The combined probability masses are:
$m_1 = (z)(m_{1,1}\, m_{1,2} + m_{1,1}\, m_{H,2} + m_{H,1}\, m_{1,2})$
z=1.4
So, $m_1 = 0.12032$
$m_2 = (z)(m_{2,1}\, m_{2,2} + m_{2,1}\, m_{H,2} + m_{H,1}\, m_{2,2})=0.0223$
$m_3 = (z)(m_{3,1}\, m_{3,2} + m_{3,1}\, m_{H,2} + m_{H,1}\, m_{3,2})=0.0809$
$m_4 = (z)(m_{4,1}\, m_{4,2} + m_{4,1}\, m_{H,2} + m_{H,1}\, m_{4,2})=0.7311$
$m_H = 0.04534$

The aggregated assessment result [20] on five data types for VOD is:
$S (X_1 (Y_1) \oplus S (X_2 (Y_1) \oplus S (X_3 (Y_1) \oplus S (X_4 (Y_1) \oplus$

$S (X_5 (Y_1) = \{H_1, 0.126, H_2, 0.0234, H_3, 0.0847, H_4, 0.766\}$

Finally utility score for VOD = $u (Y_1) = 0.8727$
(Equation 11)

3.1.2 Calculation of Scores for Shot-stock video

Belief functions for Shot-stock video (Y_2) is:
$S (X_1 (Y_2)) = \{H_1, 0.9, H_2, 0.1, H_3, 0, H_4, 0\}$
[Compositional data is slightly preferred]

$S(X_2(Y_2)) = \{H_1, 0, H_2, 0.25, H_3, 0.75, H_4, 0\}$ [Bibliographic data is preferred]
$S(X_3(Y_2)) = \{H_1, 0.9, H_2, 0.1, H_3, 0, H_4, 0\}$ [Structural data is slightly preferred]
$S(X_4(Y_2)) = \{H_1, 0, H_2, 0, H_3, 0.1, H_4, 0.9\}$ [Sensory content data is greatly preferred]
$S(X_5(Y_2)) = \{H_1, 0, H_2, 0.25, H_3, 0.75, H_4, 0\}$ [Topic content data is preferred]

The combined assessment for these two attributes is:
$S(X_1(Y_2) \oplus S(X_2(Y_2) \oplus S(X_3(Y_2) \oplus S(X_4(Y_2) \oplus S(X_5(Y_2) = \{H_1, 0.01127, H_2, 0.092, H_3, 0.58, H_4, 0.483\}$
Scores for Shot-stock video, $u(Y_1) = 0.97$

3.1.3 Calculation of Scores for Research (Y_3)

Belief functions for research video (Y_3) is:
$S(X_1(Y_3)) = \{H_1, 0, H_2, 0, H_3, 0.1, H_4, 0.9\}$ [Compositional data is greatly preferred]
$S(X_2(Y_3)) = \{H_1, 0, H_2, 0, H_3, 0.1, H_4, 0.9\}$ [Bibliographic data is greatly preferred]
$S(X_3(Y_3)) = \{H_1, 0, H_2, 0, H_3, 0.1, H_4, 0.9\}$ [Structural data is greatly preferred]
$S(X_4(Y_3)) = \{H_1, 0, H_2, 0, H_3, 0.1, H_4, 0.9\}$ [Sensory content data is greatly preferred]
$S(X_5(Y_3)) = \{H_1, 0, H_2, 0, H_3, 0.1, H_4, 0.9\}$ [Topic content data is greatly preferred]

Similarly, it is shown that combined assessment for Research videos is:

$S(X_1(Y_3) \oplus S(X_2(Y_3) \oplus S(X_3(Y_3) \oplus S(X_4(Y_3) \oplus S(X_5(Y_3) = \{H_1, 0, H_2, 0, H_3, 0, H_4, 0\}$
Scores for Research video is, $u(Y_3) = 0.25$

3.1.4 Calculation of Scores for Document (Y_4)

Belief Functions for Document videos
$S(X_1(Y_4)) = \{H_1, 0, H_2, 0.75, H_3, 0.25, H_4, 0\}$ [Compositional data is moderately preferred]
$S(X_2(Y_4)) = \{H_1, 0, H_2, 0.25, H_3, 0.75, H_4, 0\}$ [Bibliographic data is preferred]
$S(X_3(Y_4)) = \{H_1, 0.75, H_2, 0.25, H_3, 0, H_4, 0\}$ [Structural data is moderately preferred]
$S(X_4(Y_4)) = \{H_1, 0, H_2, 0, H_3, 0.1, H_4, 0.9\}$ [Sensory content data is greatly preferred]
$S(X_5(Y_4)) = \{H_1, 0, H_2, 0, H_3, 0.1, H_4, 0.9\}$ [Topic content data is greatly preferred]

The combined assessment for these two attributes is:
$S(X_1(Y_4)) \oplus S(X_2(Y_4)) \oplus S(X_3(Y_4)) \oplus S(X_4(Y_4)) \oplus S(X_5(Y_4)) = \{H_1, 0.0023, H_2, 0.03, H_3, 0.207, H_4, 0.76\}$
Scores for document type video is, $u(Y_4) = 0.93$

3.1.5 Calculation of Scores for I-video (Y_5)

$S(X_1(Y_5)) = \{H_1, 0, H_2, 0, H_3, 0.1, H_4, 0.9\}$ [Compositional data is greatly preferred]
$S(X_2(Y_5)) = \{H_1, 0, H_2, 0, H_3, 0.1, H_4, 0.9\}$ [Bibliographic data is greatly preferred]
$S(X_3(Y_5)) = \{H_1, 0, H_2, 0, H_3, 0.1, H_4, 0.9\}$ [Structural data is greatly preferred]
$S(X_4(Y_5)) = \{H_1, 0, H_2, 0.25, H_3, 0.75, H_4, 0\}$ [Sensory content data is preferred]
$S(X_5(Y_5)) = \{H_1, 0, H_2, 0, H_3, 0.1, H_4, 0.9\}$ [Topic content data is greatly preferred]
Scores for I-Video is , $u(Y_5) = 0.96$

The overall scores of the video selection is:
$S(Y) = ((Y_1, 0.8277), (Y_2, \mathbf{0.97}), (Y_3, 0.25), (Y_4, 0.93), (Y_5, 0.96))$

Where $Y_1 \ldots Y_5$ denotes: VOD, Shot-stock, Research, Document and I-video respectively. The analysis of this result will be illustrated in section 4.

4. Results

Analytical approaches for ER presented in section 2. It is observed that approaches prioritized Shot-stock video for selecting particular person/object. The analysis is illustrated in the following consecutive subsections.

4.1 ER based Video Judgment

Figure 5 demonstrates overall video scores using Evidential Reasoning approach. It is shown that Shot-Stock video is the highest prioritized video, then I-video, document, VOD, research one by one. The result is same with AHP in highest but different in between research and I-video. Intelligent Decision System (IDS) [21] can also assess these results. ER generates more accurate results and can address uncertainties [14], vagueness and randomness [14]. It can also eliminate AHP's rank reversal problem [23]. The main focus of ER is supporting multi-valued or multidimensional attributes on any judgments, extending the decision matrix.

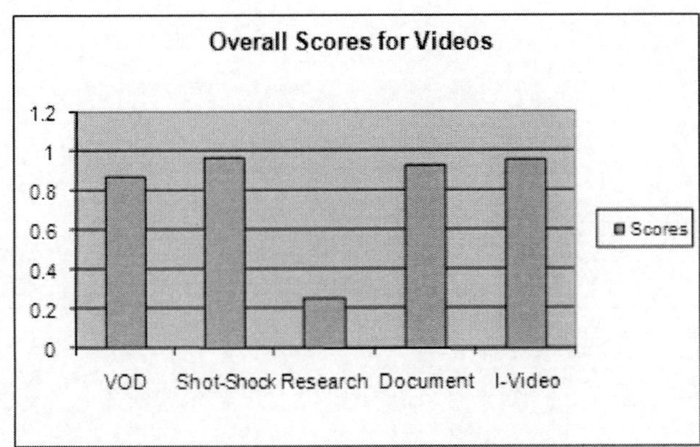

Figure 1: Overall Scores of Videos using ER

5. Conclusion

This research presented an ER based algorithm to select appropriate video prioritization. The method allows a good decision making scenario. Traditional system has lack of measuring the importance of video content and its selection criteria [11-13]. This paper demonstrated selection judgment of particular object/person from videos. It is shown that using the method the most appropriate type of video is Shot-Stock. The result is consistent with expert knowledge. To find particular objects and persons, shot-stock applications are used [9, 10], however obtaining the result through AHP be used to verify the existed expert knowledge is more convincing, and similarly can also be used to create new knowledge such as selection judgment of other things except existing knowledge such as the second, third, fourth, fifth appropriate type for judgment of particular object/person being document, research, I-Video, VOD and selection judgment of particular object/person [10] and selection judgment of interactive news[8] from videos. The main limitation of AHP is that, it doesn't support multidimensional attribute in decision matrix. Moreover AHP doesn't handle uncertainty [22] and vagueness. It has been shown from the experimental work that ER approach can address the problems raised by AHP. The system robustness will increase if belief rule [16] inferred the system.

Acknowledgements

This research was supported in part by Shenzhen Technical Project (grant no. HLE201104220082A) and National Natural Science Foundation of China (grant no. 61105133) and Shenzhen Public Technical Platform (grant no. CXC201005260003A)

References

[1] R. Hjelsvold, Roger Midtstraum and Olav Sandsta, Searching and Browsing A Shared Video Databases, http://home.online.no/~olmsan/publications/papers/mmdbms-chapter.pdf.

[2] T. Asahi, D. Turo, B. Shneiderman, Using treemaps to visualize the analytic hierarchy process, Information Systems Research 6(4), 1995, pp. 357-375.

[3] T. L. Saaty, Decision Making with Analytical Hierarchical Process, *Int. J. Services* Sciences,(2008), Vol. 1, No. 1

[4] T. L. Saaty *Theory and Applications of the Analytic Network Process*, Pittsburgh, PA, RWS Publications, 2005.

[5] A. Bakri, M. Bahari, A. A. Rahman, M. Y. Pathani, "Review Prioritization Methods in Analytic Hierarchy Process (AHP) ", *Jurnal Teknologi Maklumat, 2004.*

[6] J. R. Smith, S-F. Chang, VisualSEEk. " A Fully Automated Content-Based Image Query", System, ACM Multimedia Conference, Boston, MA, November, 1996.

[7] T.D.C. Little and D. Venkatesh. "Prospects for Interactive Video-on-Demand", IEEE Multimedia, 1(3):14-24, 1994.

[8] G. Miller, G. Baber, and M. Gilliland. "News On-Demand for Multimedia Networks", In Proceedings of ACM Multimedia 93, pages 383-392, Anaheim, CA, August, 1993

[9] Y. Ding and G. Fan, "Multi-channel Segmental Hidden Markov Models for Sports Video Mining", 2008.

[10] M. Fleischman, P. Decamp & D. Roy, "Mining Temporal Patterns of Movement for Video Content Classification", 2006.

[11] Y. Matsuo, M. Amano & K. Uehara, "Mining Video Editing Rules in Video Streams", MULTIMEDIA '02 Proceedings of the tenth ACM international conference on Multimedia, 2002.

[12] K. Shirahama, K. Ideno and K. Uehara, "Video Data Mining: Mining Semantic Patterns with temporal constraints from Movies", In Seventh IEEE International Symposium on Multimedia (ISM 2005), 12-14 December 2005, Irvine, CA, USA pages 598-604, IEEE Computer Society.

[13] S. Poullot, M. Crucianu & O. Buisson. "Scalable Mining of Large Video Databases Using Copy Detection", Proceeding of the 16th ACM international conference on Multimedia MM 08 Volume: pages, Publisher: ACM Press, 2008, Pages: 61-70.

[14] J. B. Yangs and D. L. Xu. "On The Evidential Reasoning Algorithm for Multiple Attribute Decision Analysis Under Uncertainty", IEEE transaction on systems, man and cybernetics- Part A: Systems and Humans, 2002, Vol. 32 No. 3.

[15] L. Xu & J. B. Yang. "Introduction to Multi-Criteria Decision Making and the Evidential Reasoning Approach", Working Paper No. 0106, Manchester School of Management University of Manchester Institute of Science and Technology PO Box 88 Manchester M60 1QD, ISBN: 1 86115 111 X, 2001.

[16] J. B. Yang, J. Liu, J. Wang, Belief Rule-Base Inference Methodology Using the Evidential Reasoning Approach RIMER", IEEE Transactions on Systems, Man and Cybernetics-Part A: Systems and Humans, 2006, Vol 36, No. 2.

[17] A. Taroun, and J. B. Yang, "Dempster-Shafer Theory of Evidence", Potential usage for decision making andrisk analysis in construction project management", *The Built & Human Environment Review, Volume 4, Special Issue 1, 2011.*

[18]https://phps.portals.mbs.ac.uk/JianBoYang/Research/tabid/1074/Default.aspx

[19] Y. M. Wang, J. B. Yang, D. L. Xu, "Environmental impact assessment using the evidential reasoning approach", European Journal of Operational Research 174 (2006), 1885–1913.

[20] D. Lingxu and J. B. Yang. "Intelligent Decision System for Self-Assessment", Published online in Wiley Inter Science (www.interscience.wiley.com), 2003 DOI: 10.1002/mcda.343.

[21] M. Zhang and S. S.Chen. "Evidential Reasoning in Image Understanding".

[22] B. Anrig, R. Haenni and N. Lehmann. "ABEL - A New Language for Assumption-Based Evidential Reasoning under Uncertainty", 1997.

[23] T.L. Saaty and L.G. Vargas. "The Legitimacy of Rank Reversal", Omega, 12(5), 513-516, 1984.

Cockpit noise enhancement for aircraft type recognition in short-wave speech communication

Donghu Nie[1],Xueyao Li[1], Gang Qiao [2]
[1]College of Computer Science and Technology, Harbin Engineering University, Harbin, Heilongjiang, China
[2]National Laboratory of Underwater Acoustic Technology, Harbin Engineering University, Harbin, Heilongjiang, China

Abstract - *Shortwave speech communications with aircraft cabin noise is a new strategy is used to identify the aircraft type. Speech in other areas is usually regarded as useful signal, but here was the most important interference to aircraft cabin noise signal. To assess speech noise interference, defines the SNR evaluation formula. In order to improve identification recognition rate, put forward a kind of adaptive model for enhancing cockpit noise and suppressing speech. To assess enhancement algorithm, energy spectrum level characteristics is extracted, and the binary classification tree based on support vector machine is designed. Experiment to estimate performance of the above methods was done, the average SNR improves by 22 db, the average recognition rate increases by about 35%. Experiments show that the speech suppression algorithm obtains the higher SNR gain and recognition rate gain. Despite the recognition rate is still low, but it provides the beneficial reference for subsequent research.*

Keywords: speech restrain; cockpit noise enhancement; short-wave speech communication; CZT; aircraft type recognition

1 Introduction

Aircraft type recognition based on short-wave speech communication could detect aircraft type information in large distance on condition of non-cooperation, which is a new aircraft type recognition method different from radar and image remote sensing. The basic thought of the technology is to identify aircraft type through the cockpit noise carried in short-wave speech communication, and it could work all-weather in a way that passively monitor. The effective distance can even reach tens of thousands of kilometers, and it also provides piecemeal type information of aircraft in unknown position. The information is so called information ash or information islet. It may be important intelligence when synthesized and become significant judge for decision makers to draft relevant strategy.

Sound signals of aircraft short-wave speech communication carry some information of cockpit reverberant field, such as engine noise, external pneumatic noise, fuselage vibration noise and so on[1]. Experienced person could recognize aircraft type from the noise it generates. While monitoring for long time does harm to one's health, for example, some noisy short-wave sound would lead to audition decline, it even makes people so boring that their work efficiency drops. The auditory fatigue may also lead to some important information ignored, or give people illusion so that they misjudge.

The former research on cockpit noise mainly focus on factors like noise control in cockpit[2], speech enhancement and detection of cockpit[3-4], noise source distinguish[5-6], and aircraft noise characters[7]. Cockpit noise is generally disposed as harmful noise, which is hardly utilized to identify targets for short-wave methods in long distance. In order to resolve the problem of aircraft type recognition through short-wave voice call that based mainly on manual work, the difficulties brought in by noncooperation correspondence, random interference in short-wave channel, speech noise interference ,unsteady and nonlinear factors of noise in cockpit must be overcome. The team author works for is doing relative research[8-10], e.g. Zhang xin-yu utilizes small wave decomposition and high-order cumulant to pick up the noise characters of 5 types of aircraft speech response intervals, who acquires elemental research findings, comparing the different classification effect between BT net and support vector machine (SVM), despite the situation is not studied that aircraft noise exists simultaneously as well as speech sound. There are no relevant reports except for this.

It contains cockpit noise when pilots use short-wave to communicate, so the noise may become target signals for aircraft type recognition. Nevertheless, the communication content is always very brief and the intervals between speech responses are so short that speech segment couldn't be picked out. Then the response interval can hardly be applied to recognize aircraft type as target signal. For this reason, the paper continues to research on the aircraft type recognition of non-speech segments between speech responses, besides, it also does some researches on the aircraft noise of 8 different types of speech segments. Contrary to traditional short-wave speech communication mainly enhancing speech and restraining background noise[11], the paper regards speech as interference noise and background noise as target signal, namely, it improves the performance of aircraft type recognition by studying the method of speech restrain and

Corresponding author: Donghu Nie， Email:niedonghu@hrbeu.edu.cn noise enhancement. Because of the complicated frequency spectrum and the unpredicted content of speech communication under non-cooperation circumstance, traditional speech handing methods could hardly restrain speech noise and enhance aircraft noise simultaneously. It most likely to filter the speech noise at the same time it destroys the aircraft noise. Accordingly, research on how to restrain speech interference and increase aircraft noise is a challenging task for aircraft type recognition.

Based on the analysis of cockpit noise, the paper provides a model to restrain speech and enhance noise, in addition, it evaluate the enhanced model using defined SNR equation. It extracts the feature of response noise and speech segments before and after being enhanced by CZT Transform, and finally acquires excepted effect, doing some tests for recognition through designed Binary classifier tree based on support vector machine, which lays foundation for later research.

2 Aircraft short-wave signal analysis

Signals of aircraft short-wave speech communication mainly consist of the radio communication in modulated frequency range between aircraft and the ground noise, cockpit background noise, and short-wave channel interference noise, which can be expressed with equation (1):

$$s = s_{plane} + n_{channel} + n_{speech} \tag{1}$$

Among, s represents for the recorded short-wave speech communication signal, s_{plane} represents for the cockpit noise signal, $n_{channel}$ stands for the short-wave channel interference noise, and n_{speech} stands for the short-wave speech communication noise. Generally speaking, most of the channel noise is weaken by demodulation and filtration, that is to say, $n_{channel} << n_{speech} + s_{plane}$, so the equation (1) can be redefined as the following equation (2):

$$s \approx s_{plane} + n_{speech} \tag{2}$$

The speech segment between pilots' speech responses in short-wave communication can be approximately regarded as cockpit background noise, which is called noise without speech segment and can be expressed as $x_{nonspeech}$.
Speech segment contains aircraft noise, and in theory the power spectrum density agrees with its contiguous non-speech segment, while most of them are covered by speech. Owing to the audiomasking effect, people can hardly detect the aircraft type by speech segment. Regard x_{speech} as speech segment signal and $x_{nonspeech}$ as reference, then equation (3) could roughly estimate the aircraft noise SNR (the speech is noise and the aircraft noise is signal).

$$SNR_{speech} \approx 10\log \frac{E\left\{\left|x_{nonspeech}\right|^2\right\}}{E\left\{\left|x_{speech}\right|^2\right\} - E\left\{\left|x_{nonspeech}\right|^2\right\}}$$

$$= 10\log \frac{\dfrac{\sum\left|x_{nonspeech}\right|^2}{M_{nonspeech}}}{\dfrac{\sum\left|x_{speech}\right|^2}{M_{speech}} - \dfrac{\sum\left|x_{nonspeech}\right|^2}{M_{nonspeech}}} \tag{3}$$

$$= 10\log \frac{M_{speech}\sum\left|x_{nonspeech}\right|^2}{M_{nonspeech}\sum\left|x_{speech}\right|^2 - M_{speech}\sum\left|x_{nonspeech}\right|^2}$$

Among SNR_{speech} stands for SNR of speech segment, and M_{speech} stands for the length of the speech segment while $M_{nonspeech}$ represents the length of non-speech segment, finally $E\{\bullet\}$ means to get the average.

3 Cockpit noise Enhancement model

The content of aircraft communication is always brief and in short intervals, it even has no pause and in more time, the speech and aircraft noise coexist, so it is necessary to research on how to recognize aircraft type by aircraft noise in speech segment. However, the SNR of speech segment is so low and aircraft noise is so seriously disturbed by strong speech signal, it can be hardly used for aircraft type recognition. The paper applies the feature of aircraft noise without any speech segment to set up a self-adapting aircraft noise enhanced model, which could restrain the speech interference at the same time destroy the cockpit noise as little as possible. Then it can used for aircraft type recognition.

According to equation (2), speech segment signal can be expressed as equation (4), that's to say, it equals to the sum of speech segment and non-speech segment in speech segment.

$$x_{speech} = n_{speech} + n_{plane} \tag{4}$$

Among, n_{speech} stands for the phonetic element of the speech segment and n_{plane} represents the noise ingredient. Theoretically, in circumstance of the same background noise, the cockpit noise component is identical with the power spectrum density of its contiguous non-speech segment, that's to say:

$$PSDx_{nonspeech}(e^{jw}) \approx PSDn_{nonspeech}(e^{jw}) \tag{5}$$

namely:

$$\frac{\left|X_{nonspeech}(e^{jw})\right|^2}{2\pi M_{nonspeech}} \approx \frac{\left|N_{plane}(e^{jw})\right|^2}{2\pi M_{speech}} \tag{6}$$

According to the above equations, non-speech segment is regarded as self-adapting filter to handle the speech segment, the cockpit noise inside will be enhanced then while the speech element will be restrained.

Regard equation (7) as the frequency response of the filter, namely:

$$H(e^{jw}) = X_{nonspeech}(e^{jw}) \tag{7}$$

So the filter can estimate the frequency spectrum for the cockpit noise in speech segment, namely:

$$\hat{N}_{plane}(e^{jw}) = H(e^{jw})X_{speech}(e^{jw})$$
$$= X_{nonspeech}(e^{jw})X_{speech}(e^{jw})$$
$$= X_{nonspeech}(e^{jw})(N_{speech}(e^{jw}) + N_{plane}(e^{jw})) \quad (8)$$
$$= X_{nonspeech}(e^{jw})N_{speech}(e^{jw}) + X_{nonspeech}(e^{jw})N_{plane}(e^{jw})$$

Define

$$Q = X_{nonspeech}(e^{jw})N_{speech}(e^{jw}) \quad (9)$$

and combine it with equation (6), it will be acquired as follows:

$$R = X_{nonspeech}(e^{jw})N_{plane}(e^{jw})$$
$$\approx X_{nonspeech}(e^{jw})\sqrt{\frac{M_{speech}\left|X_{nonspeech}(e^{jw})\right|^2}{M_{nonspeech}}} \quad (10)$$

If the length is the same between speech and non-speech segment, namely $M_{speech} = M_{nonspeech}$, then:

$$R \approx \left|X_{nonspeech}(e^{jw})\right|^2 \quad (11)$$

The equation (9) is the suppression to speech noise, and equation (10) is the enhancement to aircraft noise. So the ingredient of cockpit noise in speech segment can be estimated with equation (12):

$$\hat{n}_{plane} = IDFT(\hat{N}_{plane}(e^{jw}))$$
$$= \frac{1}{2\pi}\int_{-\infty}^{+\infty} X_{nonspeech}(e^{jw})X_{speech}(e^{jw})e^{jwn}d \quad (12)$$

According to the convolution theorem, the ingredient of cockpit noise in speech segment can also be evaluated with equation (13):

$$\hat{n}_{plane} = h * x_{speech} = x_{nonspeech} * x_{speech} \quad (13)$$

After filtering the speech segment and according to equation (8) as well as (10), equation (14) can be used to size up the SNR that cockpit noise is enhanced, namely:

$$\text{SNR}_{plane} = 10\log\frac{\int_{-\infty}^{+\infty}|R|^2\,dw}{\int_{-\infty}^{+\infty}|Q|^2\,dw}$$
$$\approx 10\log\frac{\int_{-\infty}^{+\infty}|R|^2\,dw}{\int_{-\infty}^{+\infty}(\left|\hat{N}_{plane}\right| - |R|)^2\,dw} \quad (14)$$

From the enhancement procedure above, it is indicated that non-speech segment lays the foundation of a successful algorithm. So without a non-speech segment the certain algorithm will be useless, while there is no need for the information of speech segment when there is non-speech segment. It is no purpose that the paper regards non-speech segment as self-adapting filter but to set up a more effective way to restrain speech and enhance cockpit noise through the research, which may provide foundation and reference for later research on filter model.

4 Analysis of Chirp Z Transform

4.1 Principles of CZT

Definition of discrete time signal x(n) is as follows:

$$X(z_r) = CZT[x(n)] = \sum_{n=0}^{\infty} x(n)z_r^{-n} = \sum_{n=0}^{\infty} x(n)A^{-n}W^{nr} \quad (15)$$

Among $z_r = AW^{-r}$, $A = A_0e^{j\theta_0}$, $W = W_0e^{-j\varphi_0}$, A_0 and W_0 are positive real number, so

$$z_r = A_0e^{j\theta_0}W_0^{-r}e^{-j\varphi_0 r} \quad (16)$$

$A_0, W_0, \theta_0, \varphi_0$ are defined as above, and only when $r = 0,1,\cdots,\infty$ the Z Transform of points $z_0, z_1, \cdots, z_\infty$ in Z plane can be calculated, which consist the path of the CZT. When $r = 0$, $z_0 = A_0e^{j\theta_0}$, the amplitude is A_0 and the argument is θ_0, and the Z Transform starts with them. When $r = M-1$, that's to say when $Q = z_{M-1}$, its polar coordinates are $Q = A_0e^{j\theta_0}W_0^{-(M-1)}e^{j(M-1)\varphi_0}$, which corresponds to the terminal point of the Z Transform.

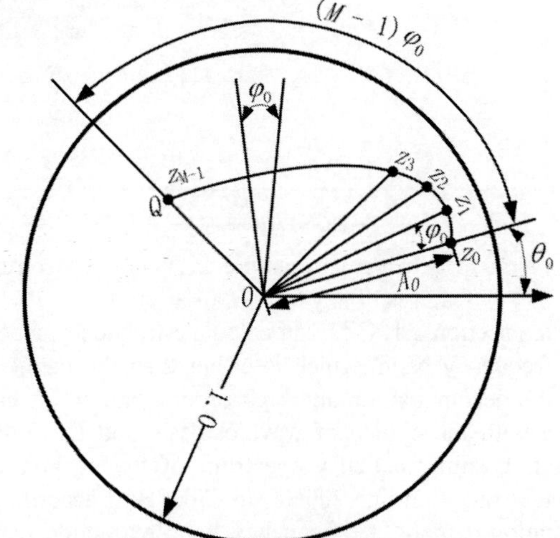

Fig.1 Transform path of CTZ

As fig.1 shows, transform path of CTZ is a helical line in z plane, and:

- ✧ When $A_0 > 1$, the helical line is outside the unit circle, otherwise it is inside the unit circle;
- ✧ When $W_0 > 1$, $A_0W_0^{-1} < A_0$ and the helical line rotates inward, otherwise it rotates outward;
- ✧ When $A_0 = W_0 = 1$, the transform path is a circular arc in a unit circle, and the number of the transform points M is not necessarily equals to the number of data points N;
- ✧ When $A_0 = W_0 = 1$ and $\theta_0 = 0, M = N$, CZT correspo-nds with DFT.

Accordingly, in order to get the signal's frequency spectrum, CZT in the unit circle should be realized, namely, $A_0 = W_0 = 1$. In the unit circle, given a random

θ_0 and ϕ_0 , an interestingfrequency separation and frequency resolution can be chosen.

4.2 Feature extraction

Including engine noise, fuselage vibration noise caused by chaos upper atmosphere, noise brought in by boundary layer pressure rise and fall, exhaust noise and system canal noise , the cockpit equals to a reverberant field, which provides important information for aircraft type recognition. Different type of aircraft has different mechanical structure, engine, fuselage trembling style. They lead to different noise feature and distribute diversely in the frequency band, so frequency band distribution can be an important character for aircraft type recognition.

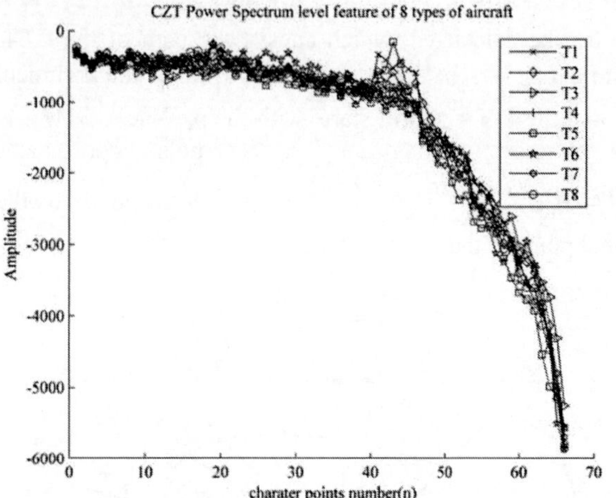

Fig 2.Non-speech segment sample CZT power spectrum features of any 8 types of aircraft

From section 3.1, CZT can calculate frequency spectrum in any frequency band, which is easier than the methods of mall wave decomposition and high-order cumulant, it has no business with the choice of wavelet basis and the order of cumulant. Useful frequency spectrum of the cockpit noise distributes range from 200Hz to 3000Hz, according to classification demands, 7 frequency band extraction features among are chosen respectively:

$$B=\{[2600\ 3000],\ [1500\ 2000],\ [1100\ 1400],\ [200\ 450],\ [1500\ 1950],\ [450\ 950],\ [1800\ 2600]\} \quad (17)$$

If fh_i and fl_i stand for the high and low boundary frequency of the $i(i$=0…6) frequency band respectively, the procedures of using CZT to extract power spectrum characteristic vector are as follows:

1) Apply CZT to calculate the frequency spectrum $X(z_i(r))$ of the i frequency band;
2) Calculate the power spectrum density fraction function of the i frequency band, namely:

$$PSL_i(r) = 10\log\frac{(X(z_i(r)))^2}{N(fh_i - fl_i)} \quad (18)$$

Among N indicates the number of CZT points;

3) Divide every frequency band $[fl_i, fh_i]$ into 1/18 octave, then the relevant frequency multiplication will be calculated, that is the length of characteristic vector, which is expressed as m:

$$m = \{3,7,6,21,6,19,6\} \quad (19)$$

Among m_i is the characteristic vector length of i frequency band. And if F_{ij} stands for the power spectrum density fraction sum of the i frequency band j octave, so:

$$F_{ij} = \sum_{r_{ij}}^{r_{ij+1}} PSL_i(r) \quad (20)$$

4) Construct characteristic vector using the equations above, then:

$$F_i = [F_{i1}, F_{i2}, \cdots, F_{ni}] \quad (21)$$

Figure 2 shows the any one characteristic vector of the 8 types of aircrafts. For easier observing, 7 frequency bands are drawn together. Outside the 7 frequency bands types of the aircraft frequency spectrums blend together and can't be distinguished. Every frequency band has its own characteristic vector length, so the Binary classifier tree based-on support vector machine was designed to recognize the 8 types of aircrafts. Each panel point $C_i(i$=0…6) of the classifier tree is a SVM, it is trained and tested by characteristic vector $F_i(i$=0…6) respectively. As figure 3 shows, SVM utilizes linear kernel function.

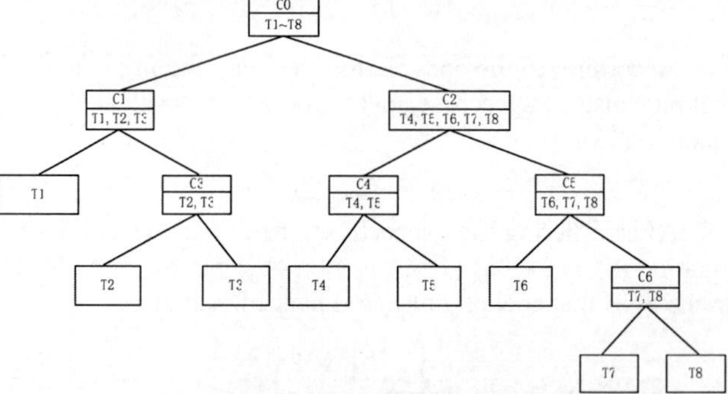

Fig.3 Design of binary classifier tree

The influence that change of factor likes aircraft' regime of flight, function mode of engine, flight height effects on the spectrum distribution isn't taken into account because this can be acquired through contents of speech communication or other info mediums, e.g. an aircraft is judged to land from the requirement of landing. Combined with the aircraft' regime of flight and recognized respectively, the influence that change of aircraft' flight regime brings can be lowed.

5 Experiment and analysis

5.1 Experimental data

Samples are the baseband signals that short-wave speech communication received, whose sampling frequency is 11.025kHz, and the speech communication is recorded in the scene. 8 types of aircrafts (T1~T8) speech and non-speech segments of the pilot answering intervals are chosen as target signals to test and recognize. Among them there are 40 samples in every non-speech segment classifier, whose length is 4096 points. Every 14 samples are selected as a training set to train each panel point of the binary classifier tree, while the remaining 26 samples as test. Besides, 20 samples of every speech segment classifier are selected for experiments of SNR estimate, aircraft noise enhancement and recognition, as well as their contiguous 20 non-speech segment samples. Among, the length of speech segment samples is 4096 points while the length of non-speech segment samples is between 1024 and 4096.

5.2 Cockpit noise enhancement experiment

According to equation (3) and (14) the mean SNR estimates of 8 types of speech segment cockpit noise are as chart 1 and chart 2 shows:

Tab.1 Mean SNR estimates of cockpit noise in speech segment

Aircraft type	T1	T2	T3	T4
Mean SNR(dB)	-19.50	-34.95	-17.74	-30.26
Aircraft type	T5	T6	T7	T8
Mean SNR(dB)	-8.17	-19.65	-31.13	-20.98

Tab.2 SNR estimates after cockpit noise is enhanced

Aircraft type	T1	T2	T3	T4
Mean SNR(dB)	0.63	1.55	0.87	1.45
Aircraft type	T5	T6	T7	T8
Mean SNR(dB)	0.93	1.11	1.48	0.60

Table 1 shows the mean SNR estimates of cockpit noise in speech segment, and table 2 indicates the SNR estimates after the cockpit noise is enhanced. Compared with Tab.1, its SNR improves a lot, which is raised up to over 0dB, the average gain is about 22dB.

Figure 4 describes a time domain waveform fore and after a speech segment sample passes a filter for non-speech segment. Phonetic element is weakened after enhancement, while cockpit noise is strengthened.

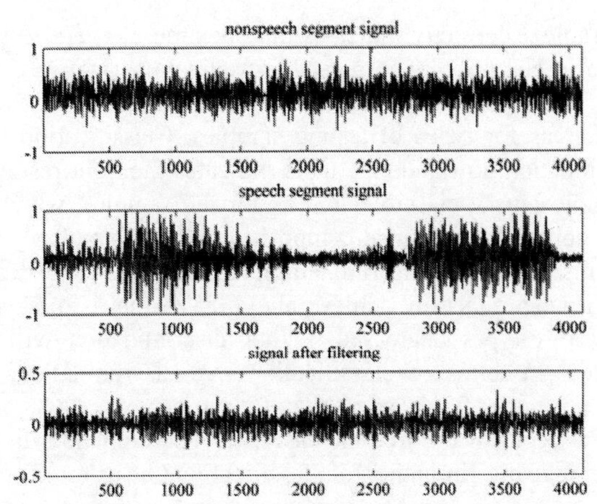

Fig.4 Cockpit noise enhancement of speech segment

5.3 Classifier recognition experiment

As Fig.2 shows, the procedure of train for classifier tree is followed. Firstly, divide the training samples of the 8 types of pilots answering interval noise into 2 groups, G01={T1,T2,T3} and G02={T4,T5,T6,T7,T8}. Extract characteristic vector F0 for every sample's0^{th} frequency band, regard 2 groups of samples as the 2 classes of SVM C0. Train C0 with the training samples is respectively 42 and 70.Then divide G01 into 2 subsets, G11={T1} and G12={T2,T3} by classifier C1, after that extract characteristic vector F1 in the 1th frequency band and train C1 with the training samples is respectively 14 and 28.For classifier C2, divide G02 into 2 subsets, G13={T4,T5} and G14={T6,T7,T8}, and then extract characteristic vector F2 in the 2th frequency band and train C2 with the training samples is respectively 28 and 42. As for classifier C3, divide G12 into 2 subsets, G21={T2} and G22={T3}, then extract characteristic vector F3 in the 3th frequency band and train C3 with the training samples is respectively 14and 14.As for classifier C4, divide G13 into 2 subsets, G23={T4} and G24={T5}, then extract characteristic vector F4 in the 4th frequency band and train C4 with the training samples is respectively 14 and 14.As for classifier C5, divide G14 into 2 subsets, G25={T6} and G26={T7,T8}, then extract characteristic vector F5 in the 5^{st}frequency band and train C5 with the training samples is respectively 14 and 28.As for classifier C6, divide G26 into 2 subsets, G31={T7} and G32={T8}, and the training number are respectively 14 and 14.Regard the remaining 26 samples of the sets as testing set and then test the classifier tree and classifiers of every layer, the outcomes can be acquired as the above table 3:

Tab.3 Classifications of non-speech segments (linear kernel function)

Classifier	Recognition rate on every node (%)								Mean recognition rate (%)
	T1	T2	T3	T4	T5	T6	T7	T8	
C0	75.00	0	10.00	100.0	85.00	100.0	95.00	100.0	65.00
C1	20.00	95.00	50.00						55.00
C2				40.00	70.00	90.00	70.00	75.00	69.00
C3		95.00	100.0						97.50
C4				60.00	35.00				47.50
C5						45.00	20.00	35.00	33.33
C6							35.00	80.00	57.50
Classifier recognition rate (%)	6.00	0	5.00	24.00	20.82	40.50	4.65	21.00	15.25

Table 3 correctly indicates the outcome of every testing sample is classified. The mean discrimination rightward the table shows the arithmetic mean discrimination of every classifier as for types of testing samples. Classification tree discrimination downside the table indicates the right result of the whole binary classifier tree as for the samples, which is the outcome of the vertical composition numbers multiplying. In terms of mean discrimination, discrimination of each classifier can generally achieve above 85%, that is to say, if the aircraft types decreased, higher discrimination will be achieved. In terms of classification tree discrimination, all others are under 90% except that T3 can achieve 100%, and with the depth of the tree increases, its discrimination drops. The average discrimination of classification tree as for all testing samples is 82.79%.

Extract character of the testing samples for 8 types of speech segments and then transform them to classification tree that has been trained by answer interval noise, namely the classification tree above, the classification results are as table 4 shows, no matter the mean discrimination or the classification tree discrimination is low, while someone individual is higher, such as C0 is for T4, T6, T8 and C3 is for T2, T3 all reach to above 95%, and this is caused by the either-or classification mode of SVM. In terms of the results, speech segments indeed contain some useful information for type recognition, but due to strong speech interference, its classification outcome is really bad and the total discrimination just reaches 15.25%.

Tab.4 Classification outcome of speech segments

Classifier	Recognition rate on every node (%)								Mean recognition rate (%)
	T1	T2	T3	T4	T5	T6	T7	T8	
C0	75.00	0	10.00	100.0	85.00	100.0	95.00	100.0	65.00
C1	20.00	95.00	50.00						55.00
C2				40.00	70.00	90.00	70.00	75.00	69.00
C3		95.00	100.0						97.50
C4				60.00	35.00				47.50
C5						45.00	20.00	35.00	33.33
C6							35.00	80.00	57.50
Classifier recognition rate (%)	6.00	0	5.00	24.00	20.82	40.50	4.65	21.00	15.25

Enhance the 8 types of speech segment samples in the light of the former algorithm, then extract the enhanced signal character and transform them to classification tree that has been trained by answer interval noise, the classification results are as table 5 shows. Compared with the unenhanced discrimination results of table 4, the total mean classification discrimination increases by 34.93%, so it's clear that enhancing algorithm really brings in gain. It is proved that the cockpit noise is relative stable in short time from the results of Tab.1 and Tab.2.

Tab.5 Classification results of the enhanced speech segment cockpit noise

Classifier	Recognition rate on every node (%)								Mean recognition rate (%)
	T1	T2	T3	T4	T5	T6	T7	T8	
C0	75.00	60.00	80.00	100.0	90.00	100.0	95.00	95.00	86.88
C1	80.00	95.00	95.00						90.00
C2				75.00	85.00	85.00	70.00	80.00	79.00
C3		65.00	85.00						75.00
C4				80.00	55.00				67.50
C5						75.00	65.00	80.00	73.33
C6							75.00	65.00	70.00
Classifier recognition rate (%)	60.00	37.05	64.60	60.00	42.06	63.75	32.42	39.52	50.18

In addition, every panel point of the classification tree is a SVM, so the choice of kernel function is of great influence to recognition results. The paper applies radical basis function, multinomial kernel function and multilayer perception function to experiments respectively, while the data of train and test is the same with Tab.3, the mean discriminations of classification tree are respective 74.74%, 74.93%, 56.69%, which are all lower than that of the linear kernel function, 82.79%. Experiments of Zhang xin-yu conclude that classification discrimination is the highest when radical basis function is used. It's the characteristic vector and different classifier structure that cause the different results, and her experiment types are 3 less than the paper, while not all the types of aircrafts are the same.

5.4 Results analysis

Above experimental results show that, power spectrum density features extracted by CZT can well indicate the substantive characteristics of the aircraft type, which is carried by the response intervals of pilot communicating. Combined with binary classifier tree based-on support vector machine, more satisfying results can be achieved, despite the un-ideal recognition for speech segment, which is leaded to by strong speech interference. After coped by noise enhancing model, speech segments bring in good gain for SNR and discrimination, however, discrimination is not so good as the SNR's raise, this is because the SNR after enhancement doesn't reach 2dB, and the interference is still large, which prevents the discrimination from improving.

According to the different characteristic distribution in every frequency band of different type of aircraft, samples are divided into 2 subsets, and each subset is divided into 2 subsets too, until subset has only one type, which is key to binary classifier tree based on SVM. It's known from the above experiments that the greater the depth of binary classifier tree is, the lower the discrimination is. For example, mean discrimination is always higher than that of classifier tree, this is because mean discrimination can be regarded as a binary classifier tree with depth of 1, while classifier tree discrimination as a binary classifier tree with depth more than 1. Binary classifier tree of the paper is designed based on 8 types of small sample aircraft type recognition. When new aircraft type or sample is added, the structure of tree must be redesigned according to the experiments. The extent should be increased so that the depth is lowed to improve classification performance.

6 Conclusions

The paper analyzes the physical characteristics of the aircraft speech communication signals of short-wave channel and raises a model to restrain speech and enhance cockpit noise, then defines an estimating equation of SNR, provides a feature extracting algorithm of power spectrum density that based on CZT. The results of experiment for recognition of pilot response intervals noise concludes that power spectrum density characteristics could well indicates aircraft type information carried by response intervals and gets satisfying recognition. Experiments of SNR evaluating and classification recognition fore and after enhancement of speech segment indicate that noise enhancing model brings in large SNR and recognition gain. These also simultaneously show that regarding neighboring non-speech segment as self-adoptive filter to cope with speech segment is effective to restrain speech and enhance cockpit noise, while the low total discrimination indicates that there is strong speech interference inside the enhanced signal. Experiments for SVM shows that different features fit different kernel function and can't be lumped together.

Research above lays foundation to further researches, except for study on speech response interval noise, methods to improve aircraft type recognition in speech segment should be detailed studied. When speech segments are manages in the way this paper puts forward, influence likes features of the speech itself and short-wave channel should be considered for further interference elimination of cockpit noise. In addition, except for improved binary classifier tree, recently popular Yin-yang theory may be tried.

7 References

[1] Zhang Rong,Qin Haoming. Investigation of Measurement and Analysis of the Cabin Noise of fuselage[J].Noise and Vibration Control.2009,6(s1):481-483.

[2] HU Ying,CHEN Kean,PAN Kai.Optimization Design about Plane Cabin Noise Based on Statistical Energy Analysis[J].Noise and Vibration Control.2007,4(2): 65- 68

[3] Gao Qian,Liu Mabao,Yue Kaixian.Speech Enhancement in Cockpit Using Arithmetic Joining Method[J].ACTA AERONAUTICA ET ASTRONAUTICA SINICA. 2009,30(7): 1203- 1207.

[4] LEI Ming,LI Xue-ren,LI Guo. Robust Speech Endpoint Detection in Airplane Cockpit Voice Background[J]. JOURNAL OF VIBRATION AND SHOCK.2008,27(10): 83- 886.

[5] Qiao Weiyang,Ulf Michel.Experimental Study on Airframe Noise with Improved Data Reduction Method of Microphone Array Measurements[J]. ACTA AERONAUTICA ET ASTRONAUTICA SINICA.2008, 29(3):527-533

[6] HSIAO F B,HAN S Y,HSIEH S C,et al.Sound source separation and identification for aircraft cockpit voice recorder[J].Journal of Aerospace computing, Information and Communication,2004(12):466-483.

[7] Qiao Weiyang,Xu Kaifu,Wu Zhaowei, Huang Wenchao,Qin Haoming.Noise Radiation of Large-scale Commercial Aircraft in Take-off and Landing[J].ACTA AERONAUTICA ET ASTRONAUTICA SINICA.2008,29(3):534-541.

[8] ZHANG Xin-yu,LI Xue-yao,ZHANG Ru-bo. Recognizing aircraft type using a support vector machine and a higher order cumulant[J]. JOURNAL OF HARBIN ENGINEERING UNIVERSITY.2010, 31(3):366-370.

[9] Xinyu Zhang, Xueyao Li,Rubo Zhang,Guanqun Liu.Aircraft type recognition based on short-wave communication[C].ICIA 2008,2008,6:1328-1332.

[10] Liu Feng,Li Xueyao,Liang Zhilan.Short-wave aviation communication signal analysis and aircraft classification[C].IMSCCS 2008,2008,10:114-118

[11] Nie Donghu, Li Xueyao, Zhang Rubo.Research of A Novel Weak Speech Stream Detection Algorithm[C]. Lecture Notes in Computer Science Series, vol.4222,2006,598-60 .

Acknowledge : supported by the Fundamental Research Funds for the Central Universities under Grant NO.HEUCF 100604

Educational effectiveness of using a Shared Virtual Immersive Environment for Teaching English as Second Language

Diego-Mauricio Torres-Arias, Helmuth Trefftz
Instituto NETSYS - Universidad EAFIT
Calle 15 No. 5 – 28, Montenegro, Quindío, Colombia - AA 3300, Medellín, Colombia.

ABSTRACT: In recent years, with the advent of the Web, the potential use of virtual environments for educational processes had undergone an exponential increase, moving quickly from the use of web tools to social networks, and from these to immersive virtual environments including Second Life. In relation to the teaching and learning processes, these metaverses, as they are called, are widely used for research and application of educational processes, especially in the area of languages learning. The purpose of this article is to describe the findings of applying an educational interaction based on English as Second Language through the use of Second Life, a shared immersive virtual environment.

Key words: shared virtual environments, metaverse, virtual reality, avatar, teaching English as a second language.

1. INTRODUCTION

In recent years, technological advances have been vital in the development of new paradigms of teaching in different areas of education. Bridging the classroom, the teacher and the student knowledge, has been the focus of such developments. An evolution has occured from the classroom to the web pages and hyperlinks, then the Web Quest, Wikis, forums, study groups, platforms like Moodle and Blackboard, networks and knowledge in the cloud and others. These paradigms have led teachers and students to handle high levels of complexity, to live in diversity of opinion based on personal knowledge provided from a network: "the model learning for the digital age" [1]. The next step in the evolutionary chain of virtual learning environments is the emergence of virtual environments, both immersive and semi-immersive. Some examples are Unity [17], OpenSimm [19] and Second Life [20], the latter being the first to appear as a sum of technologies encompassing not only 3D visualization and immersivity, but also as a technology integrator of chat, VoIP and real-time interaction through customizable avatars.

Universities and other education institutions have an active presence [2] on metaverses. An example is offered by a recent research focused on the sociological, psychological and economic advantages of using SecondLife as support for people with social challenges allowing them to overcome social anxieties and fears, and by examining the satisfaction of participating in collaborative sessions according to their gender [3]. In the case that concerns us, learning English as a second Language, projects, organizations and schools dedicated to the teaching of English already exist in Second Life. These institutions use traditional and constructivist philosophies and even create new paradigms as dogma or SLOODLE, among them find AVALON –[13] - and NIFLAR-[14] (experimental worlds for teaching English in 3D) and TEACH YOU TEACH ME (Island in buddy network [15]). In the area of educational projects there are several notorious examples: AvatarEnglish.com learning school. Edunation II and III, which houses special islands different schools, and institutions of education paths of great global significance, such as the Technological Institute of the Americas (ITLA), Harvard, Massachusetts Institute of Technology (MIT) and Stanford University, as well as Colombian Andes University. These facts indicate that the implementation of these new technologies in the field of teaching and learning "is not so much a technological problem, as a social challenge that requires an educational solution" [5].

The purpose of the project that is described in this article is to evaluate the level of absorption of information learned through a remote and immersive 3D environment such as SecondLife (SL), in juxtaposition with classical learning process in the classroom. The idea is to provide information on which decisions can be made effectively and justify (or not) spending on virtual education centers, islands (in this context, an island is a virtual portion of territory which is sold by SecondLife client to an entity).

2. RELATED WORK

The School of Science at the University of Denver, has reproduced their campus in Secondlife under the name of "Science School". According to Jeffrey Corbin, the university makes experiments that would be dangerous in real life [7].

A growing number of research groups, institutes and universities such as the University of the Andes, Uniminuto,

EAFIT (in Colombia), Cornell University (in the U.S.), Universidad Carlos III (in Spain), among others, incorporate immersive worlds to generate a new way of learning and doing science. Some of these efforts and innovative works, are registered by conventional experimental techniques such as observation, in which students practicing "leave the notes of the experiments" [7].

The ILR (Institute for Labor Relationships) at Cornell University performed research exercises in second life about unusual themes and used formal numerical methods for the interpretation of the data, a clear example is the experiment called "Living Large: The Powerful overestimate Their Own Height Study 3" [6], in which they explored the correlation of the perception of an individual power and her avatar's height in Second Life.

3. Why use a virtual immersive environment as teaching and learning tool?.

Virtual worlds or metaverses are simulated spaces of social interaction on the web that aims to mimic the real world in their geographical, sociographic, economic and communication, but overcoming the limitations of the real physical world. These virtual worlds can simulate real-world laws or have their own rules. In virtual worlds inhabitants are represented by avatars.

Because of its interesting features, technologies like virtual reality simulation environments and immersive virtual environments make a strong appearance in the concept of imitation of real worlds. The Multi-User Dungeon experiment [9] directed by. Philip Rosedale, in which an alternate universe, populated by avatars, with a real and independent economy in which the rules were created by users, is described. From this point of view, Second Life is part of Web 2.0, a social networking becoming 3D [10]. Second Life is divided geographically into Sims, which are virtual pieces of virtual land of 65,000 m2, which are divided, in turn, into different levels (N4, N5, etc ...) depending on the web server that hosts them, and the time delay and network traffic that is supported . At the same time, access to Second Life is divided by zones according to their contents: PG is for all ages, M (Mature) contains moderate content, and A (Adult) includes fully adult content. To access the two latter types of content the user must be authorized.

Second Life has more than 7 million users worldwide, and generates a revenue of about 1.7 million per day in businesses such as advertising, sale of islands, and schools of different areas, including foreign language teaching and especially English [11].

Several instituions use the system for teaching English as Second Language. Events such as SLanguages 2009 conference and the second life for European Day of Languages [12], a second life for European Day of Languages: Langauges treasure hunt event in Virtual World, have taken place. Organizations or users involved in the business have looked for measurements of the effectiveness of the platform or the methods used for the teaching of second languages (English, French, Spanish or other languages). As far as we know, there are no comparisons of the effectiveness of education systems within SecondLife with reference to other type systems methodologies such as Moodle, Blackboard, Sloodle (integration of Second Life and Moodle in learning procesees) [4], and the Traditional teaching classroom,

4. Explanation Of The Research Model To Be Applied

The focus of this document is to compare the learning effectiveness of two groups of students (using pretest and post-test data) when they are exposed to two different learning environments: one using Second Life and the other using a traditional methodology.

To launch the pilot phase it was necessary to divide in a random way the chosen course into two groups: experimental group (who in this case received English foreign language class through the SecondLife platform) and control group (who continued to attend class sessions under the traditional method teaching). Both groups received lessons on the same topic but in different environments and with different methodology.

This experimental model allowed us to create a baseline of knowledge of the subject to be measured in both the experimental and the control group, this through an initial testing (pre-test) level of skill in handling the issue to explain to both groups.

First, the group was sepparated and a pre-test was applied in order to determine the base line. Then, the experimental group received an introduction to the SecondLife platform, which included: account creation, avatar customization, explanation of the tools that the platform SecondLife offered to move, transport, communication and data capture. Students in the experimental group were told not exchange information about the platform with a control group members, the same was made with control group members.

After the two groups received instruction on the same English language topics (each group using a different methodology), a final assessment (post-test) tool was used in order to capture data that indicated the final level reached. The results of the pre- and post-test were compared, both for the experimental and the control groups. The results were also discriminated by gender.

5. Instruments And Techniques

The following instruments and techniques were handled with the purpose of getting relevant data suitable for this research project.

5.1 Pretest

The pretest was about the use of "Present Simple" tense. In particular, about the students' knowledge about the conjugation of verbs in third person, and also allowed us to place the student in the A1 level (up 2.2 points) or A2 level (greater than 2.2 points). This pretest.

The pretest was based in five dimensions: a) application in the context of third person inflection (fill in blanks in order to know if they knew when to apply the third person), b) answering the questions according to the reading comprehension and grammar and structure using the right inflection. c) management of inflection according to the termination of the verb (Fill in blanks in order to check students' knowledge of the rules that compose the third person). d) selecting the best question or phrase according to the grammatical structure of it and the correct use of inflection (for checking the students' ability to reject wrong structures among some sentences illustrated). e) paragraph writing (free writing production using the simple present, especially their understanding of the third person and it was assessed by a gridding). This pretest showed the following results:

Of the sample of 26 students surveyed 24 are in A2 level of the common European framework, only 2 are in A1 level.

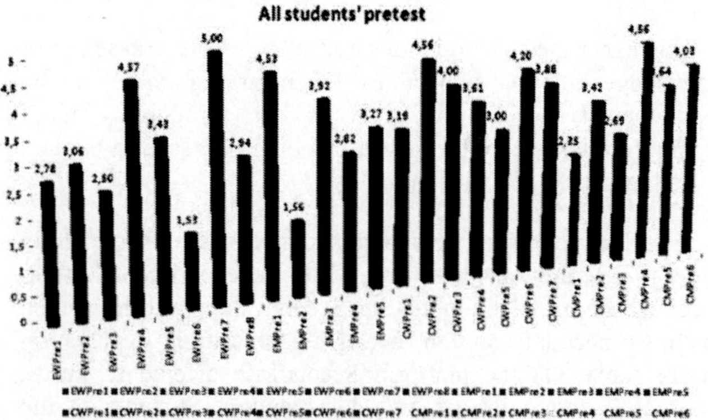

Graph1: All Student's Pretest

5.2 Post-Test

The post-test sought students' final knowledge about Present Simple, especially in the application of the third person. This post-test was composed by five elements similar to the pretest. The first one, as in the pretest, the students needed to fill some blanks with some verbs, however, there were less blanks than the pretest. The second one was a short text to check students' both reading comprehension and the grammatical structure to answer some questions of that text. The third one, showed students' understanding of the third person rules. The fourth one was a multiple-choice task of answers and sentences to determine the students' capacity to identify the right sentence. And the fifth one showed the students' writing production level for using the simple present, and especially, for applying the third person when necessary.

6 User Experience Evaluation

A survey, composed of 10 questions, was presented to the students in order to determine how they felt about the interaction with the Second Life platform, their favorite tools, communication between classmates and professor, points of view about the requested places and activities, the avatars which represented them and how they felt when they had to use English on the platform.

7. Introduction To Second Life

Prior to the implementation of the teaching sessions, one or more sessions of introduction to the use of immersive virtual platform were conducted, according to the needs of the experimental group. The purpose of these sessions were to ensure the proper handling Second Life as a learning platform. The following steps took place:

a. Download the installer (Second Life Viewer latest version).
b. How to the install the product.
c. How the product runs.
d. How to log into the Second Life platform.
e. How to create and to personalize the avatar.
f. How to move within the platform (walk, run, fly, teleport).
g. How to use gestures and objects.
h. How to interact with others (chat, I.P. Voice, invitations).

8. Implementing the Teaching Sessions.

A learning path can be described as the way forward for particular knowledge. For this purpose, a blog with four pages, each of which had a specific function within the route, was created. The four pages were:

Page 1: Presentation of the theme of language to develop with the corresponding grammar. Page 2: Presentation of a character-based or context in which to develop the theme. Page 3: Traversing the path of learning and activities during the same within the 3D world - chosen environments and Page 4: Links with the thematic evaluation.

In the first screen, the student had access to the theme of language study with the tips needed to understand its application from the grammatical point of view. The second screen or character introduced a context with the application of grammatical aspects of the language. The third screen offered a journey through different parts of the metaverse in order to meet specific missions (activities) through which the student applied the learned grammar, learned more about the characters or themes raised and exposed his handling of the subject studied. The fourth and final screen contained a number of links that could be used to test student learning.

9. MEASURING THE RESULTS OF THE PROCESS.

The table1 shows the analisys and comparison values for every student in the pretest and post-test in the experimental women's group and their corresponded quantity and percentage of improvement. The real names of the students who were involved in this research were changed by codes in order to protect real identity.

TESTER NAME	PRETEST EXPERIMENTAL WOMEN'S GROUP FINAL SCORE	POST-TEST EXPERIMENTAL WOMEN'S GROUP FINAL SCORE	IMPROVEMENT	PERCENTAGE IMPROVEMENT %	
EWPre1/EWPost1	2,78	4,45	1,67	0,33	
EWPre2/EWPost2	3,06	4,71	1,65	0,33	
EWPre3/EWPost3	2,50	3,57	1,07	0,21	
EWPre4/EWPost4	4,57	4,80	0,23	0,05	
EWPre5/EWPost5	3,43	4,95	1,52	0,30	
EWPre6/EWPost6	1,53	4,41	2,88	0,58	
EWPre7/EWPost7	5,00	4,75	-0,25	-0,05	
EWPre8/EWPost8	2,94	4,36	1,42	0,28	
	3,23	4,5	1,27	0,25	AVERAGE

Table 1: Contrast Experimental Women Pretest/Post-test

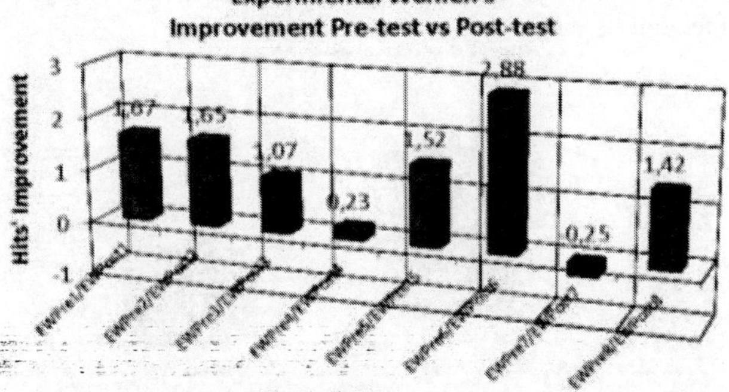

Graph 2: Contrast Pretest/Post-test Experimental Women's Hits' Improvement

According to the graph2 there was one significant improvement between first score and the last one, it means that the topic was taught with effectiveness and students (Experimental women) showed us a significant difference that was a range between 21% and 58% in the majority of the cases.

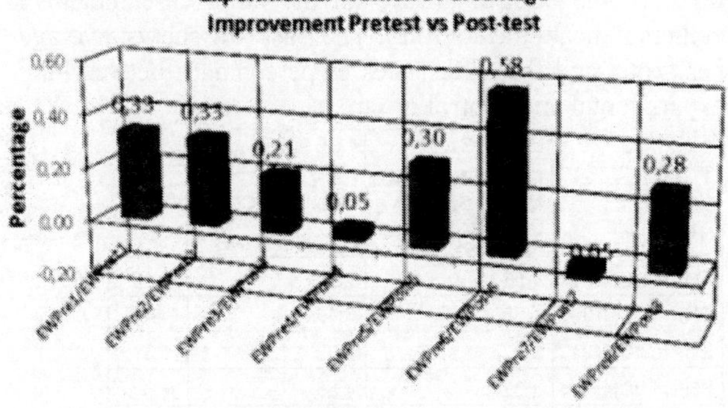

Graph 3: Contrast Pretest/Post-test Experimental Women's Percentage Improvement

Table2 and graphs 4 and 5 show the comparative values for every student in the pretest and post-test in the experimental men's group and their corresponded quantity and percentage of improvement.

TESTER NAME	PRETEST EXPERIMENTAL MEN'S GROUP FINAL SCORE	POST-TEST EXPERIMENTAL MEN'S GROUP FINAL SCORE	IMPROVEMENT	PERCENTAGE IMPROVEMENT %	
EMPre1/EMPost1	4,53	4,55	0,02	0,004	
EMPre2/EMPost2	1,56	2,11	0,55	0,110	
EMPre3/EMPost3	3,92	4,85	0,93	0,186	
EMPre4/EMPost4	2,82	3,08	0,26	0,052	
EMPre5/EMPost5	3,27	4,83	1,56	0,312	
	3,22	3,88	0,66	0,13	AVERAGE

Table 2: Contrast Experimental Men Pretest/Post-test

The experimental men's group offered different level of improvement between pretest and post-test hits. It was ranked between 5% and 31%, with only one exception, that is described in the graphs 4 and 5:

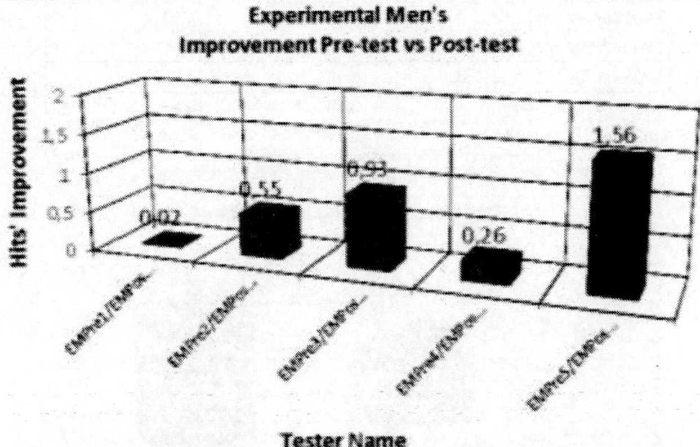

Graph 4: Contrast Pretest/Post-test Experimental Men's Hits' Improvement

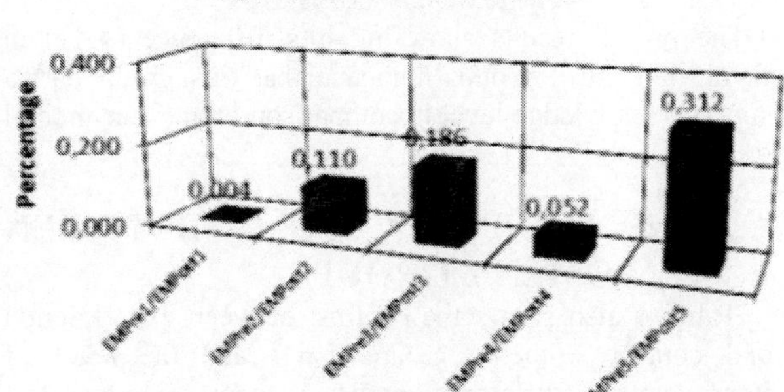

Graph 5: Contrast Pretest/Post-test Experimental Men's Percentage Improvement

10. OVERALL ANALISYS (CONTRAST PRETEST – POST-TEST) BY GENRES

This Analysis intends to show the overall improvement obtained by the students in both groups (Experimental and Control).

10.1 Pretest Between Women's Groups

Table 3 shows the contrast between experimental and control women's groups results and the level of improvement (difference between them). In the last column, the positive numbers indicate that the cipher is in favor of the control group; on the other case, negative ciphers indicate the contrary. The Last row shows: average per group and the differences of percentages between the experimental and control group.

TESTER NAME	PRETEST EXPERIMENTAL WOMEN'S GROUP FINAL SCORE	PRETEST CONTROL WOMEN'S GROUP FINAL SCORE	
EWPre1/CWPre1	2,78	3,19	0,41
EWPre2/CWPre2	3,06	4,56	1,5
EWPre3/CWPre3	2,50	4,00	1,5
EWPre4/CWPre4	4,57	3,61	-0,96
EWPre5/CWPre5	3,43	3,00	-0,43
EWPre6/CWPre6	1,53	4,20	2,67
EWPre7/CWPre7	5,00	3,88	-1,12
EWPre8/	2,94	3,78	0,84
	3,23	**3,78**	**4,41**
	0,55	**0,11**	

Table 3: Contrast women's Pretest

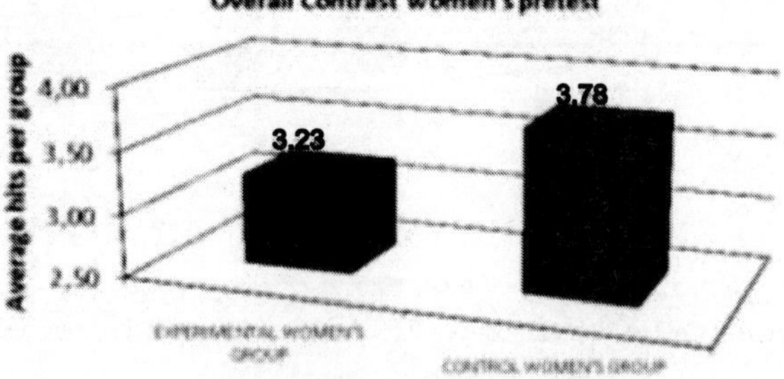

Graph 6: Overall contrast women's pretest

The pretest results show big hits difference (4.41) in favor of control group; it means that this group had a superior knowledge level in comparison with experimental group.

10.2 POST-TEST BETWEEN WOMEN'S GROUPS

Table 4 also shows the contrast between experimental and control women's group results and the level of improvement (difference between them). In the last column, the positive numbers indicate that the cipher is in favor of the control group; on the other case, negative ciphers indicate the contrary. The Last row shows: average per group and the differences of percentages between the experimental and control group.

TESTER NAME	POST-TEST EXPERIMENTAL WOMEN'S GROUP FINAL SCORE	POST-TEST CONTROL WOMEN'S GROUP FINAL SCORE	
EWPost1/CWPost1	4,45	4,25	-0,2
EWPost2/CWPost2	4,71	4,86	0,15
EWPost3/CWPost3	3,57	4,64	1,07
EWPost4/CWPost4	4,80	4,20	-0,6
EWPost5/CWPost5	4,95	4,40	-0,55
EWPost6/CWPost6	4,41	4,84	0,43
EWPost7/CWPost7	4,75	4,16	-0,59
EWPost8/	4,36	4,48	0,12
	4,5	**4,48**	**-0,17**
	0,02	**0,0043**	

Table 4: Contrast women's Post-test

The post-test results showed a little difference (0.17) in hits in favor of experimental group; it means that this group had a superior knowledge level in comparison with control group; in other words, the virtual immersive environment was more effective than traditional teaching method.

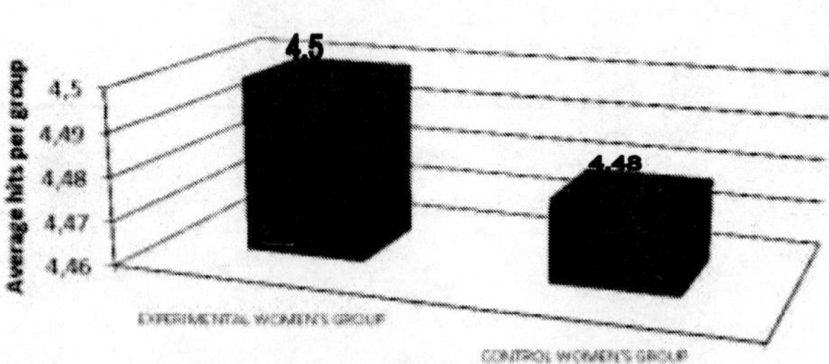

Graph 7: Overall Contrast Women's Post-test

10.3 Pretest Between Men's Groups

Table 5 as well as the women's groups in the tables and graphs above, shows the contrast between experimental and control men's groups results and the level of improvement (difference between them). In the last column, the positive numbers indicate that the cipher is in favor of the control group; on the other case, negative ciphers indicate the contrary. The Last row shows: average per group and the differences of percentages between the experimental and control group.

TESTER NAME	PRETEST EXPERIMENTAL MEN'S GROUP FINAL SCORE	PRETEST CONTROL MEN'S GROUP FINAL SCORE	
EMPre1/CMPre1	4,53	2,35	-2,18
EMPre2/CMPre2	1,56	3,42	1,86
EMPre3/CMPre3	3,92	2,69	-1,23
EMPre4/CMPre4	2,82	4,56	1,74
EMPre5/CMPre5	3,27	3,64	0,37
/CMPre6	3,22	4,03	0,81
	3,22	**3,45**	**1,37**
	0,23	**0,05**	

Table 5: Contrast experimental/control Men's pretest

The pretest results show 1.37 as difference in favor of control men's group; it means that this group had a superior knowledge level in comparison with experimental group in the use of the proposed thematic as is shown in the graph8:

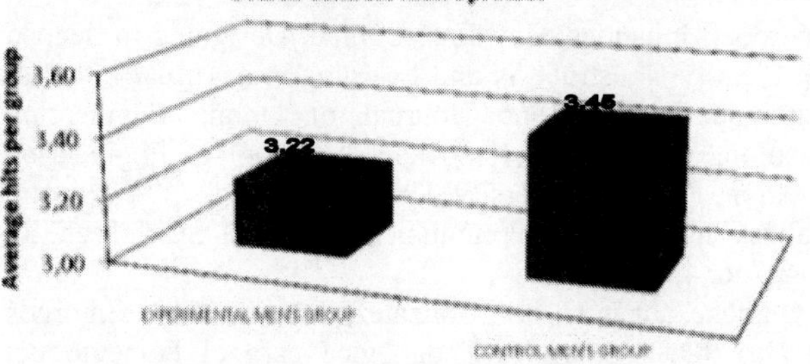

Graph8: Overall Contrast Men's Pretest

10.4 Post-Test Between Men's Groups

The contrast between experimental and control men's groups results and the level of improvement (difference) between them in the post-test stage is shows in table 6. In last column can find positive numbers when difference benefit control group or negative if it is at the contrary. Last row show us: average per group and sum (experimental group minus control group) of hits for winner group (negative value for experimental and positive value for control).

TESTER NAME	POST-TEST EXPERIMENTAL MEN'S GROUP FINAL SCORE	POST-TEST CONTROL MEN'S GROUP FINAL SCORE	
EMPre1/EMPost1	4,55	3,33	-1,22
EMPre2/EMPost2	2,11	4,90	2,79
EMPre3/EMPost3	4,85	3,95	-0,9
EMPre4/EMPost4	3,08	4,85	1,77
EMPre5/EMPost5	4,83	4,14	-0,69
/EMPost6	3,88	4,46	0,58
	3,88	4,27	2,33
	0,39	0,078	

Table 6: Contrast experimental/control Men's post-test

The post-test results show a hits difference in favor of control men's group of 2.33; it means that this group had a superior knowledge level in comparison with experimental group in the use of the proposed thematic.

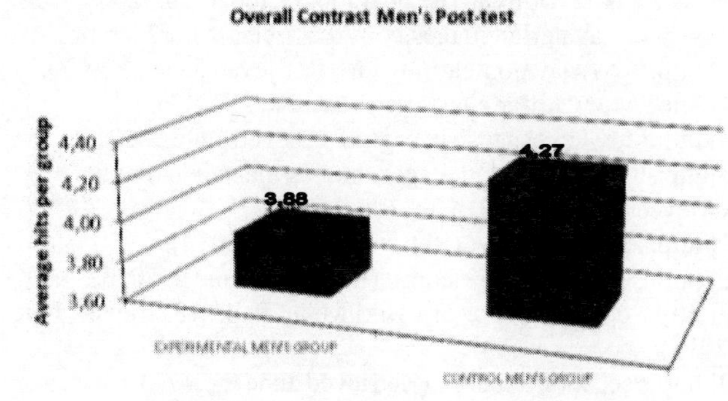

Graph 9: Overall Contrast men's Post-test

In this case, the virtual immersive environment was less effective than the traditional teaching method.

In conclusion, we can see that in both cases the women reached results with higher levels than men. Both groups (experimental and control) and in both genres (women and men) obtained a significant improvement of hits between in the pretest and post-test. In contrast to the men's genre (who got better results in traditional teaching method), for women the use of the immersive environment on the Second Life Platform was more effective.

10.5 General Overalls

In general, data shows that, when contrasting the final results between the experimental and control groups, both methods (traditional and virtual) presented an improvement in the quantity of hits. Moreover, both methods offer (in a scale from one to five) as result a high level of effectiveness and they were practically equal. As you can see, the following overall charts and graphs:

EXPERIMENTAL GROUP	CONTROL GROUP	IMPROVEMENT	PERCENTAJE IMPROVEMENT DIFFERENCE %
3,22	3,63	0,40	0,08

Table 7: Overall contrast experimental/control group pretest

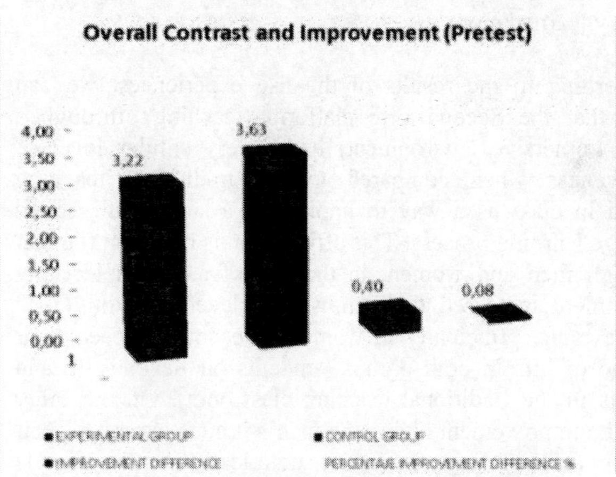

Graph 10: Overall Contrast and Improvement (Pretest)

EXPERIMENT GROUP	CONTROL GROUP	IMPROVEMENT	PERCENTAJE IMPROVEMENT DIFFERENCE %
4,26	4,22	0,12	0,02

Table 8: Overall contrast experimental/control group post-test

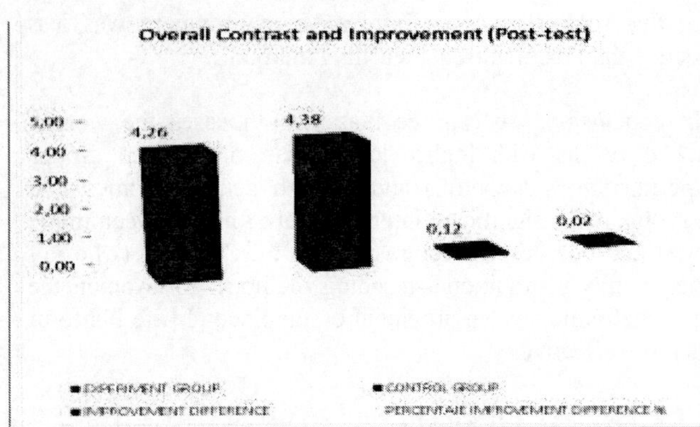

Graph 11: Overall Contrast and Improvement (Post-test)

11. CONCLUSIONS

For the majority of students in level A2 (european common framework) in the department of modern language of University of Quindio, the virtual immersive environments were unknown, either for pedagogical purposes or any other type of virtual interaction.

The majority of students that participated in this research expressed that they prefered traditional teaching-learning processes in classroom, instead of Second language learning. In addition, those processes generated in them the impression that they learned more.

According to the results of the use experiences, we can affirm that the Second Life platform (teaching through a virtual immersive environment) has a very similar level of effectiveness when compared to the traditional teaching method in class as a way to implement a successful second language learning process. This affirmation is based on the fact that both men and women, in the use of a virtual learning environment increased their knowledge level regarding to a specific topic, principally in women who could exceed their baseline of hits in both groups (students on SecondLife and students in the traditional teaching classroom). On the other hand, the improvement hits in the men's groups exceeded their baseline as the women's, but it was less than the female groups.

Second Life platform shows us a superior percentage difference in relation to the traditional class attendance average; it was 0.8 % more effective than the traditional method, it means that in fact one virtual immersive environment is more useful and operative for the teaching and learning process in a second language because the learning is more practical and enriching, and it is focused on a specific learning into a specific context.

REFERENCES

[1] Siemens, George. 2007. Conectivismo: Una teoría de aprendizaje para la era digital. Traducción: Diego E. Leal Fonseca.

[2] Baker, S. C., Wentz, R. K., and Woods, M. M. 2009. Using Virtual Worlds in Education: Second Life® as an Educational Tool. Teaching of Psychology. Volumen 36, No. 1. ISSN-0098-6283.

[3] Strobel, Johannes, Hawkins, Conrad. Designing in Second Life: Identity Construction and Learning in a Virtual Informal Environment. Apr. 1965. Journal of Online Engineering Education, Vol. 1, No. 1, Article 2. School of Engineering Education, Purdue University, USA.R. W. Lucky, "Automatic equalization for digital communication," Bell Syst. Tech. J., vol. 44, no. 4, pp. 547–588.

[4] Quinche, Juan C., L. González, Franci. 2011. Entornos Virtuales 3D, Alternativa Pedagógica para el Fomento del Aprendizaje Colaborativo y Gestión del Conocimiento en Uniminuto. Corporación Universitaria Minuto de Dios, Bogotá-Colombia.

[5] Garrison, D.R., Anderson,T. 2005. El e-learning en el siglo XXI: Investigación y práctica. Octaedro Barcelona España.

[6] Duguid, M. M. & Goncalo, J. A. (2011). Living large: The powerful overestimate their own height [Electronic version]. Retrieved [08-06-2012], from Cornell University, ILR School site: http://digitalcommons.ilr.cornell.edu/articles/456/.

[7] Grupo Avatar. "Hacemos experimentos que en la vida real resultarían peligrosos". En: Second Life. [en línea]. (2008). [Consultado 8 jun. 2012]. Disponible en http://blog.pucp.edu.pe/item/23389/hacemos-experimentos-que-en-la-vida-real-resultarian-peligrosos#more

[8] Jairo, (June 17, 2009). Historia y características de los mundos virtuales. En Technolives. Recuperado February 18, 2011 from http://www.tecnolives.com/historia-y-caracteristicas-de-los-mundos-virtuales.

[9] Wagner James Au. . (2008). The making of second life: notes from the new world. 1st edition. ISBN: 976-0-06-135320-8. Harper Collins publishers.

[10] Pakula. J. (February10 2011). ¿Qué es Second Life?: un metaverso. En Second Life data. recuperado February 20, 2011 from http://secondlifedata.wordpress.com/category/second-life-historia/

[11] Vickers, Howard. (2007): Language Teaching Gains Second Life: Virtual Worlds Offer New Methods to Teach Languages. La Paz Bolivia. recuperado October 23, 2009 from <http://www.avatarlanguages.com/pressreleases/pr1_en.php>.

[12] Vickers, Howard. (2007): A Second Life for European Day of Languages: Language Treasure Hunt Event in Virtual World. La Paz Bolivia. recuperado October 23, 2009 from <http://www.avatarlanguages.com/pressreleases/pr2_en.php>.

[13] http://www.avalonlearning.eu. (Retrieved June 2, 2013).

[14] http://www.niflar.eu. (Retrieved June 2, 2013).

[15] http://tuwien.esnaustria.org/. (Retrieved June 2, 2013).

[16]http://www.avatarlanguages.com/es/mapadelsitio.php. (Retrieved June 2, 2013).

[17] http://unity3d.com/. (Retrieved June 2, 2013).

[18] http://www.vastpark.com/. (Retrieved June 2, 2013).

[19] http://opensimulator.org/wiki/Main_Page. (Retrieved June 2, 2013).

[20] http://secondlife.com/. (Retrieved June 2, 2013).

An Investigation into Content Based Video processing in Cloud Computing Paradigm

Rashed Mustafa [1,2,3,4] **and Dingju Zhu** [1,2,4,5,*]
[1] Laboratory for Smart Computing and Information Science, Shenzhen Institutes of Advanced Technology, Chinese Academy of Sciences, Shenzhen, China
[2] University of Chinese Academy of Sciences, Beijing, China
[3] Department of Computer Science and Engineering, University of Chittagong, Bangladesh
[4] Shenzhen Public Platform for Triple-play Video Transcoding Center, Shenzhen, China
[5] School of Computer Science, South China normal University, Guangzhou, China

Abstract - *Finding Obscenity from videos is a crucial issue due to social and ethical reasons of using online resources. Dating back to two decades the research on this ground has been started. Most of the works are based on image based skin color detection which is not a suitable method for finding obscenity from videos. The reason for this is that, there are many skin like pixels such as beach photos, human skin like animal, skin colored painting that enables false positive (FPR) and false negative rate (FNR). Moreover frame checking time is also a performance factor. In addition all works performed well on some particular set of data. In this paper some aspects of finding obscenity from videos is described delineating strength, weakness and possible extensions of prior works. Introducing some new features and incorporation of multiple classifiers and transfer learning will lead the work more robust. In addition traditional multimedia cloud computing has been investigated in this paper following some extensions.*

Keywords: Content Based Video Processing (CBVP), Transfer Learning (TL), Multimedia Cloud Computing (MCC)

1 Introduction

Due to huge development on Information and Communication Technology, there is an enormous number of online resource monitoring cells all over the world. In spite of those security systems, it doesn't check content based video appropriately. This is a threat for the Internet users while using computers in office or in front of family members or children. Moreover malicious content contradicts social and ethical issues. Hence content based video processing especially for identifying obscenity has now been a challenging research

area. It has been almost two decades when Forsyth [1] published the first paper in this issue on "Finding Naked People". After that a large numbers of works have been accomplished by different scholars all over the world. Text based protection system has been used in early 2000 for screening malicious contents from the Internet [2, 3]. This system is not working for those sites having malicious contents but non objectionable site name. In support of this

Drawback, we can find millions of sites that contain objectionable videos.

The remaining parts of this article can be categorized according to the following ways: section 2 briefly describes literature review; different skin detection methods summarized in section 3, in section 4 some open research issues are proposed and finally a comprehensive discussion is presented in section 5.

2 Literature Review

There are extensive literatures on obscenity detection from videos but in this paper some significant works has taken into consideration. Those papers mainly focused on large connected skin regions, erotogenic organs, and feature descriptors following some different classifiers.

The following figure demonstrates number of significant works published since 1996 to till now. It has been observed that in 2010 most of the papers published due to significant improvement of machine learning tools.

* Corresponding author: Dingju Zhu. Address: Shenzhen Institutes of Advanced Technology, Chinese Academy of Sciences-518055, Shenzhen China. Email: dj.zhu@siat.ac.cn. Tel: +86-13316588865.

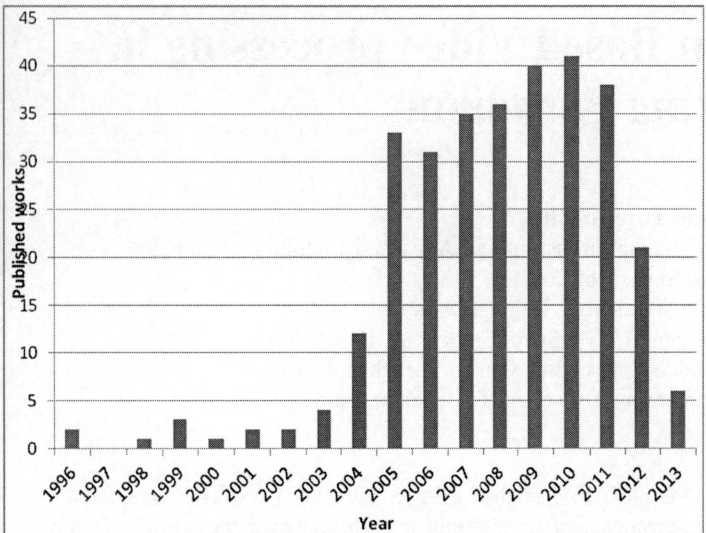

Figure 1 : Published works (1996-2013) on content based pornography detection

To the best of our knowledge, only a few papers for detecting obscene videos have emerged.

In recent, Lee et al [4] proposed the hierarchical system for detecting obscene videos which consists of three phases called the Early Detection, the Real-time Detection, and the Posterior Detection. In early detection textual information collected from video frames, in the second phase frame by frame checking using image processing tool. Then, the authors encrypt the textual data through a hash function where the result is used as a signature that identifies the video. The SVM trained by the sample images in the database decides the obsceneness of the frames. The last phase, Posterior Detection, is performed based on group of frame (GoF) features. Color histogram of each frame in the hue-saturation-value (HSV) space has been calculated using 256 bins and use the averaged histogram as the feature vector for the GoF. The SVM is employed for the detection as well.

A three step method for identifying obscene videos was employed in [5, 6]. In the first step, tensors and motion vectors were utilized to extract key frames. Then, a cube based colour model was employed for skin detection. Finally suspected videos were recognized by the proposed algorithm.

Rea N et al (2006) [7] proposed a multi stage approach for content based obscene detection in videos. In this method, visual motion information and periodicity in the audio stream were utilized to detect obscene videos.

In [8], an adaptive skin detection algorithm was suggested for content based video classification. The algorithm first detected the face area and calculated the skin parameters using the detected face area. Then, using a statistical approach, skin regions were detected.

According to the method of Qian W et al (2005 [9]; extracting video frames, motion vectors were calculated and employed to segment video frames to frames with global or local motions. For local motion, skin regions were extracted and edge moments were utilized to classify each key frame as an objectionable or a benign frame. The method suffers from using the spatial information of only key frames. The method also needs a general database for matching of moment.

In [10], key technologies for obscene video recognition in the compressed video domain were illustrated. The algorithm extracted skin regions and detected key frames in the compressed domain. In this approach key frames were extracted applying a threshold to the number of skin pixels. Finally a decision tree was utilized to classify key frames.

Lee H et al (2006) [11] proposed two models of features for objectionable video classification. The first model utilized features based on single frame information and the second feature model was based on the group of frames. The features of the two models were classified using two SVM classifiers. The authors extended their work [12] to a multilevel hierarchical system, which utilized very similar features for detecting objectionable videos. The method included three phases, which were executed sequentially. In the first phase, initial detection was performed based on hash signatures prior to a video being downloaded or played. In the second phase, single frame based features were utilized for the detection followed by a third phase where the detection was completed by features based on the group of frames reflecting the overall characteristics of the video. Both algorithms sampled frames periodically to avoid the computational overhead for finding the key frames of a video. This method will not work for the classification of video episodes with different categories in the same video file.

There is another method where motion vectors were extracted from MPEG video stream and smoothed using a median filtering [13]. Then the periodicity of motion vectors was extracted and, based on the motion features, obscene videos were detected. The method uses only motion information for classification. Therefore, the algorithm cannot recognize objectionable videos with global motions or videos with no considerable motion.

Choi et al [14] proposed the X Multimedia Analysis System (XMAS) for the recognition of obscene video frames. The system provided a method for the recognition of obscene videos based on multiple models and multiclass SVM. The system sampled video frames at a rate of 1 frame/second and used MPEG - 7 visual descriptors for feature extraction. The method used only spatial features and its functionality was restricted to MPEG - 7 files. Most of the existing methods for obscene video recognition use only the information of key frames or spatial information for video classification. Additionally, they generally cannot differentiate between normal videos with a high volume of skin region and obscene videos.

It has been observed from extensive reviewing the literature that, there are two fundamental concepts in detecting obscenity. i) Skin detection and ii) Color spaces. It will be delineated shortly in section 3.

3 Skin Detection

Skin detection is a bit challenging task due to large variations in appearance, color and shape, occlusion, intensity, location of light source etc [2, 3]. Noise can appear as speckles of skin like color, and many other objects for example wood, cooper and some clothes that are often confused as skin [15]. The noise can also be occurred by illumination that is the change of light source distribution and the illumination level (indoor, outdoor, highlights, shadows, non-white-lights) produces a change in the color. Illumination for the same person can be differed using different camera. Human skin color can be varied from person to person due to ethnicity. As for example skin color for the people of Asian differs with African, Caucasian and Hispanic groups. Some other factors such as age, sex, body parts, makeup, hairstyle, costumes, background colors, shadows, motion etc also affects the skin color appearance [16]. In general, human skin is characterized by a combination of red and melanin (yellow and brown) and there is somewhat a range of hue for skin and saturation that represent skin-like pixels.

Forsyth DA, et. al (1996) [1] demonstrates an automatic system for telling whether there are naked people present in the image [17] tried to detect adult images by considering color, texture and geometrical features of an image. Jedynak B et al (2003) [18] proposed a statistical model for skin detection. Zeng et al (2004) [19] proposed an intelligent adult image detector, called Image Guarder, which can automatically analyze the image content, efficiently recognize adult images. [20] Articulated a work on pixel-based skin detection for pornography filtering. In connection of this work later Hedieh S et al (2007) [21] proposed a similar work on a Boosted Skin Detection Method based on Pixel and Block information. In this work the authors implemented boosted pixel-based skin detector architecture.

3.1. Color Spaces

Low level image processing is requires for identifying obscenity from video. One of the major preprocessing tasks is selecting color space and model. The choice of color space can be considered as the primary step in skin-color classification. The RGB color space is the default color space for most available image formats. Any other color space can be obtained from a linear or non-linear transformation from

RGB. The color space transformation is assumed to decrease the overlap between skin and non-skin pixels thereby aiding skin-pixel classification and to provide robust parameters against varying illumination conditions. It has been observed that skin colors differ more in intensity than in chrominance [22]. Hence, it has been a common practice to drop the luminance component for skin classification. Several color spaces have been proposed and used for skin detection. In this section, we review the most widely used color spaces for skin detection and their properties. The following are widely used color model [22, 23, 24 and 25]:

i) Normalized RGB
ii) HSI
iii) HSV
iv) HSL (Fleck HSV)
v) TSL
vi) YCbCr
vii) YES, YUV, YIQ

3.2 Experimental Results on Skin Detection

In order to proper justification we tested several skin detection methods. For simplicity we used a sample video of 7 minutes duration as input then extracted all key frames. It is to be noted that our system considered 25 Frame per seconds (FPS) and there are total 10,500 frames of which 447 key frames were extracted. Summary of the results are as follows:

Table 1 : Comparative Evaluation

Method	Identified Key Frames as Objectionable	Accuracy		
		TPR	FPR	FNR
Rehg and Jones skin color mixture of Gaussian model [32]	29	96.2%	12.1%	8.2%
Big skin detection for adult image identification [17]	19	84.3%	13.2%	20.4%
Skin Map [33]	27	94.3%	9.2%	7.1%

It has been observed that Rehg and Jones [32] method is the best among the three methods but it has quiet large FPR. According to the integrity, Skin map [33] method proved to be the best skin detection method because it has low FPR and

FNR. This is to be noted that if any key frame of a video denoted as objectionable then there is high probability having obscenity in subsequent frames. Based on this ground truth we can bypass significant frame check.

4 Open Research Issues

In this section some emerging open research issues related to this paper will be discussed.

4.1 Choice of Classifiers and Feature Selection

Video is consists of frames, group of frames can form shots and semantically meaningful shots can be considered as scene. Hence the primary steps of any video processing are video segmentation which can be made either by frame, shot or scene level segmentation. Researchers need to pay attention for temporal behaviour of video content. For example similarities between frames, hard cuts, camera movement, audios etc are the key points of content based video processing. In order to achieve obscenity most of the researchers followed shot and cut detection, shot duration, motion capture, audios, illumination rate etc for identifying obscenity. In addition some image processing can also be utilized for accuracy. There are some problems such as partly nude, non obscene but sexual exposure etc. To reduce false detection researchers are paying more attention on video contents but in that case performance of the system degrades. In this situation cloud based system can make the system more robust. But the problem is to cope video processing into the cloud computing system. Substantial development requires achieving this goal.

Hybrid classifiers (SVM and Adaboost) can be use for better performance. Sometimes censored videos may also be useful for education purposes or may be categorized according to age and culture. These things will be done perfectly by incorporation of knowledge base [34 and 35]. Necessary steps could be done, training the stored database and auto updateable database. In addition unsupervised transfer learning [26] can be applicable instead of traditional supervised classification because it is impossible to classify specific nude picture using a predefined set of dataset. Since there are more and more different kinds of objectionable pictures, the traditional machine learning algorithm maybe perform inefficient to find new type of nude picture based on the old training datasets. In this situation transfer learning can be applicable to assist the discovery procedure.

4.2 Multimedia Cloud Computing

Multimedia cloud computing becoming a popular research topic due to wide spread information sharing and up gradation of network bandwidth. There are many works has been accomplished in cloud computing handling multimedia (Audio, video, image) but very little works in processing content based multimedia. [27, 28, 29 and 30]. Still now there are only three methods to process contents of images in cloud computing. i) HIPI (Hadoop Image Processing Interface [30]) ii) Hadoop SEQENCE files [30] and iii) BIGS [28].

Sequence files perform better than standard applications for small files, but must be read serially and take a very long time to generate [30]. HIPI Image Bundle have similar speeds to Sequence files, do not have to be read serially, and can be generated with a MapReduce program [30]. Additionally, HIPI Image Bundles are more customizable and are mutable, unlike Sequence files.

For instance, HIPI has the ability to only read the header of an image file using HIPI Image Bundles, which would be considerably more difficult with other file types. Those three methods of handling images in Hadoop can process images based on some ground truth and image statistics. No work efficiently process video according to appropriate machine learning scenario. In [31] the use of parallel SVM in Hadoop has been elucidated but still there in need rigorous analysis. In this perspective, scholars can think about how to fit machine learning strategies in Cloud Computing architecture.

5 Discussions and Conclusions

Most of the existing works are based on skin color region detection which can't perfectly recognize whether a video contain obscenity in general sense. The reason for this is that, there are many skins like pixels such as beach photos, human skin like animal's fur, skin colored painting etc which enable false positive rate. In addition all existing works perform well on particular set of video dataset. It has been observed that, in spite of successfully applying skin color segmentation and geometrical structure of human body, eventually it was failed to detect naked body perfectly due to absence of machine learning tools [1]. On the other hand, using skin color segmentation and machine learning tools improve detection rate. Here choice of appropriate color models, skin detection algorithms and classifiers are the factors of performance. The performance of pornography detection has been dramatically changed using human body parts specifically erotogenic parts. In this case choice of proper color model, skin segmentation algorithms, classifiers and human erotogenic body parts are the factors.

In all cases a specific dataset has been applied for test images and hence the detection could not satisfy for all types of arbitrary nude images. Because there are huge amount of nude images available in their different pose, angle, illumination condition, partial occlusion, highly and partially exposed form. In this case unsupervised transfer learning could be a solution because it creates new data sets from already learned old datasets and thus would perform well on random unlabelled nude picture identification.

There are some common trends in every detection algorithms taking consideration of accuracy and performance. These two things are inversely proportional. To minimize this challenges parallel and distributed systems can be applicable. If we consider accuracy of obscenity detection then should pay attention for substantial improvement of existing image based obscenity detection or if we consider a suitable existing method and want to improve the performance of the system then we should pay attention for applying parallel and distributed system. A cloud computing system can be utilized in this perspective. Content based image processing in the cloud is still an open research issue. The reason for this is that in cloud computing paradigm only text based data can be recognizable and there is no such built in tool to handle byte oriented image data [Mohamed H. Almeer (2012)]. Some scholars indicated to handle this problem using Hadoop SEQUENCE file [Hadoop (2013)]. But this technique also not had been proved yet. Recently there are two tools has been deployed to process large-scale image such as HIPI [30] and BIGS [28]. These two techniques devoted to process some special images for example remote sensing and medical images. It is not sure whether it can work on objectionable images or not. There is another problem of processing images in distributed environment. Image or frame can't be split during the processing phase because it affects the quality of the original video frame during merging [27]. If those issues could be resolved then the performance of the CBPD (Content based pornography detection) will increase significantly.

Acknowledgements

This research was supported in part by Shenzhen Technical Project (grant no. HLE201104220082A) and National Natural Science Foundation of China (grant no. 61105133) and Shenzhen Public Technical Platform (grant no. CXC201005260003A)

References

[1] Forsyth DA, Fleek M, and Bregler C. "Finding naked people", In Proc. of 4th European Conference on Computer Vision, pp. 593–602, 1996.

[2] Kjeldsen R and Kender J. "Finding Skin in Color Images ", Proc. Second International Conference on Automatic Face and Gesture Recognition, pp. 312-317, 1996.

[3] Yogarajah P, Condell J, Curran K and et al. "A dynamic threshold approach for skin segmentation in color images ", In Proc. IEEE International Conference on Image Processing, pp.2225-2228, 2010.

[4] Jae-Ho Lee. "Automatic Video Management System Using Face Recognition and MPEG-7 Visual Descriptors", ETRI Journal, vol. 27, p.806-809, 2005.

[5] B.S. Manjunath, Philippe Salembier, and Thomas Sikora. " Introduction to MPEG- 7 ", John Wiley & Sons, LTD, 2002.

[6] Qian W, Wei - Ming H, Tie - Niu T. "Detecting Objectionable Videos ", Acta Automatica Sinica 31(2): 280 - 286, 2005.

[7] Rea N, Lacey G, Lambe C, Dahyot R (2006): Multimodal Periodicity Analysis for Illicit Content Detection in Videos. In: 3rd European Conference on In Visual Media Production (CVMP). pp. 106 - 114.

[8] Khan R, Stottinger J, Kampel M. "An adaptive Multiple Model Approach for FastContent based Skin Detection in Online Videos ", In: Proc. of the First ACM Workshop on Analysis and Retrieval of Events/actions and Workflows in Video Streams. pp 89-95,2008.

[9] Kim C.Y, Kwon O.J, Kim W.G, Choi S.R. "Automatic System for Filtering Obscene Video ", In: 10th International Conference on Advanced Communication Technology pp.1435 - 1438, 2008.

[10] Shiwei Z, Li Z, Suyu W, Lunsun S. "Research on Key Technologies of Pornographic Image/video Recognition in Compressed Domain", Journal of Electronic 26(5): 687 - 691, 2009.

[11] Lee H, Lee S, Nam T. "Implementation of High Performance Objectionable Video Classification System", In: 8th International Conference on Advanced Communication Technology pp. 959 - 962, 2006.

[12] Lee S, Shim W, Kim S. "Hierarchical System for Objectionable Video Detection", IEEE Transactions on Consumer Electronics 55 (2): 677–684, 2009.

[13] Zhiyi Q, Yanmin L, Ying L, Kang J, Yong C. "A Method for Reciprocating Motion Detection in Porn Video Based on Motion Features", In: 2nd IEEE International Conference on Broadband Network & Multimedia Technology pp. 183 - 187, 2009.

[14] Choi B, Kim J, Ryou J. "Retrieval of Illegal and Objectionable Multimedia", In: IEEE 4th International Conference on Networked Computing and Advanced Information Management pp. 645 - 64, 2008.

[15] Wong KW, Lam KM and Siu WC. "A robust scheme for live detection of human faces in color images", Signal Process. Image Commun. 18 (2), 103–114, 2003.

[16] Kakumanu P, Makrogiannis S, Bourbakis N. "A survey of skin-color modeling and detection methods", Pattern Recognition 40 (3) 1106–112, 2007.

[17] Yin H, Xu X, Ye L. "Big skin detection for adult image identification", Workshop on digital media and digital content management, Jiaxing University, China, 2011.

[18] Jedynak B, Zheng H, Aoudi M. "Statistical models for skin detection", IEEE Workshop on Statistical Analysis in

Computer Vision, in conjunction with CVPR Madison, Wisconsin, June 16–22, 2003.

[19] Zheng QF, Zhang MJ, Wang WQ. "Shape-based Adult Image Detection", ICIG, pp 150-153, 2004.

[20] Abadpour A and Kasaei S. "Pixel-Based Skin Detection for Pornography Filtering", Iranian Journal of Electrical & Electronic Engineering, 2005.

[21] Hedieh S., Najafi M, and Kasaei S. "A Boosted Skin Detection Method Based on Pixel and Block Information", Proceedings of the 5th International Symposium on Image and Signal Processing and Analysis 2007, 27-29, page(s) 146-151.

[22] Vezhnevets V, Sazonov V, Andreeva A. "A survey on pixel-based skin color detection techniques", GRAPHICON, pp. 85–92, 2003.

[23] Zarit BD, Super JB, Quek FKH. "Comparison of five color models in skin pixel classification", International Conference on Computer Vision, ICCV99.

[24] Wu H, Chen, Yachida QM. "Face detection from color images using a fuzzy pattern matching method", IEEE Trans. Pattern Anal. Mach. Intell. 21 (6), 557–563, 1999.

[25] Yang MH, Ahuja N. "Gaussian Mixture model for human skin color and its application in image and video databases", Proceedings of SPIE: Conference on Storage and Retrieval for Image and Video Databases, vol. 3656, pp. 458–466, 1999.

[26] Pan SJ and Yang Q. "A Survey on Transfer Learning", IEEE Transactions on Knowledge and Data Engineering, VOL. 22, NO. 10, 2010.

[27] Mohamed H. Almeer. "Cloud Hadoop Map Reduce For Remote Sensing Image Analysis", Journal of Emerging Trends in Computing and Information Sciences, vol 3 no 4, 2012.

[28] Ramos-Pollan R, Gonzalez FA, Caicedo JC, Cruz-Roa A, Camargo JE, Vanegas JA, Perez SA, Bermeo JD, Otalora JS, Rozo PK, Arevalo JE. "BIGS: A framework for large-scale image processing and analysis over distributed and heterogeneous computing resources"," e-science, pp.1-8, IEEE 8th International Conference on E-Science, 2012.

[29] Pereira, R. et al. "An Architecture for Distributed High Performance Video Processing in the Cloud", Proc. of IEEE 3rd International Conference on Cloud Computing (CLOUD), pp. 482-489, 2010.

[30] Chris S, Liu L, Sean A, and Jason L. "HIPI: A hadoop image processing interface for image-based map reduces tasks", B.S. Thesis. *University of Virginia, Department of Computer Science, 2011.*

[31] SVM. Available at http://www.quora.com/Support-Vector-Machines/What-is-the-best-way-to-implement-an-SVM-using-Hadoop (accessed at 05-19-2013).

[32] Michael J. Jones , James M. Rehg. "Statistical color models with application to skin detection", International Journal of Computer Vision, v.46 n.1, p.81-96, 2002.

[33] Phung S.L, Bouzerdoum A, Chai D. "A Novel Skin Color Model in YCbCr Color Space and its Application to Human Face Detection". In: IEEE International Conference on Image Processing (ICIP2002), pp. 289–292, 2002.

[34] Mustafa R. Zhu Dingju. "A New Approach to Judgments of Video Applications for Required Contents"-12th International Congress on Computer Science, Computer Engineering and Applied Computing (World Comp 2012)

[35] Mustafa Rashed, Zhu Dingju. "A Knowledge based system for Mining Association rule for video Judgments", IEEE ICT & KE, Bangkok, Thailand, 2012.

SESSION

VISION AND IMAGING ALGORITHMS AND APPLICATIONS

Chair(s)

Prof. Hamid Arabnia
University of Georgia

Robust Model for Vehicle Type Identification in Video Traffic Surveillance

Rensso Mora Colque[1] **and Guillermo Camara Chavez**[2]
[1]Computer Science Department, Universidad Catolica San Pablo, Arequipa, Peru
[2]Computer Science Department, Ouro Preto, Minas-Gerais, Brazil

Abstract— *Vehicle classification is an inherently difficult problem. Most of researches for vehicle type recognition use images where there are only one vehicle in restricted conditions. In traffic surveillance videos have many different conditions, which increase the degree of difficulty in recognizing the type of vehicle. Thus, the various restrictions in the conventional models make them limited, creating the need of sophisticated models that combine segmentation techniques that allow to extract the information needed to recognize a vehicle within a complex scenario. This work presents a model for vehicle type recognition in traffic surveillance videos. The main obstacle in this kind of videos is the great quantity of information and the constantly variations in the scene. This work presents a model based on local features.*

Our proposed method is divided into two stages. In first stage, the moving objects are segmented using frame difference techniques, the background image is progressively generated by a heuristic function. In the second stage, each segment(image region with one or more vehicles) is processed, a local descritor is used for feature extraction and this information is organized in a visual vocabulary. A SVM classifier is used for recognizing occlusions and the type of vehicle. We introduce a very simple method to remove occlusions, this method is based on intensity level reduction.

Keywords: Background image; frame difference; temporal intensity histogram; reward and penalty function

1. Introduction

Video Based Surveillance System(VBSS) is a branch of Intelligent Transportation Systems (ITS) that have been widely explored in the last years. New models for ITS require more information about the vehicular traffic. Nowadays, robust systems join different resources to manage the information at public transportation or predict some traffic situations. Vehicle type could add very useful information for control systems, for example: vehicles in forbidden lanes, plate number, the quantity of trucks in determinate avenue, vehicle classifications, etc. Also the vehicle type can be used as statistical information in traffic predictions, for example, the number of trucks coming in determinate area may generate a traffic jam in next blocks or in street intersections. Despite of many investigations in the area [1], like vehicle counting [2], vehicle speed detection[3], vehicle tracking [4]; vehicle type recognition is not a trivial task and in most cases, it englobes many processes. However, this would be useful, because other kind of knowledge like: speed, position, count, trajectory, etc. can be deduced from initial vehicle segmentation in the video surveillance. An important clue in video monitoring is the target object, where most of information in video traffic sequences corresponds to vehicles. Then, the accurate detection of vehicles is the key in any VBSS.

Literature presents studies about vehicle type recognition, a particularity in most of these researches is that the images contain a single vehicle that occupies almost the entire image [5] [6] [7]. In video traffic surveillance, these models cannot be suitable because exist many restrictions about the environment and the vision area of the camera. There are some characteristics in video traffic sequences that differentiate them from other kind of vehicle recognition. ***The camera position***, that commonly is over six meters over the floor [8]. In outdoors scenes ***the lighting*** is an important factor, because it can produce false object movement, or decrease the illumination of regions in the scene and consequently removes representative features of interest objects (vehicles). Another factor is the ***weather***, that can introduce noise in the sequences. There are also other factors that difficult the vehicle recognition like video encryption, camera vibration, occlusion between the cars, etc. All of them can produce many distortions like: shadows, increase or decrease the appearance of colors, reflection and occlusion. These factors make difficult the vehicle type recognition, especially for vehicle segmentation and feature extraction.

a) Related works: Kagesawa *et.al.* [9] propose a method based on local-feature (eigen-windows) configuration, it employs infra-red images. This model uses B-snake technique to segment the vehicles. A problem with this work is that it needs many vehicle examples in different angles. Yiguang *et.al.* [10] propose a method that uses a hybrid neural network to identify the type based on head face vehicle's dimensions. This method has many restrictions like: different vehicle's dimensions, different types of head faces and the images have to be captured at a specific position. Ambardecar [11] introduces a method that identifies the vehicle type using 3D models. This method requires many 3D models and also it has many camera restrictions. In literature, many methods of vehicle type recognition contain certain restrictions that can not be applied in the case of video surveillance or traffic in real-time solutions. Furthermore, in surveillance videos the environment conditions are so changeable that many models with certain restrictions may not apply.

This paper describes a method for vehicle type (motorcycles, cars and buses) classification in video traffic sequences. Our model aims to be adaptive to the conditions attached to city traffic, as well as being adaptable to different climatic conditions of the environment. We use frame difference to segment moving objects, then representative features are extracted using Scale-invariant feature transform (SIFT) [12]. Segmented image features are organized in a visual dictionary. Then a classification process is divided in two recognition steps. A first step recognize the occlusions in the segments. For this stage, we introduce an occlusion removal technique. Finally, vehicle types are identified in the last step.

Our proposed method segments the vehicles from video surveillance where the quality of the images are low and the feature extraction results in a difficult task. This occurs because, the vehicle images usually are tiny and have low resolution. For occlusion removal, our model introduces a novel and simple method to divide the occluded vehicles and then performs the vehicle recognition. Another important outline is that the proposed method can identify the vehicle type from different vision points.

This paper is organized in the following sequence: in Section 2, we present our proposed approach, which is composed by moving object segmentation, feature extraction and vehicle type recognition. In Section 3, is described the moving object segmentation. Feature extraction and Visual vocabulary is described in Section 4. The final vehicle type recognition is shown in Section 5. In Section 6 the experimental results are explained and discussed. Finally, in Section 7 the conclusion are exposed.

2. Our Proposed Method

In Fig. 1, we present a diagram of our model. This model is based on local-features, it segments moving objects using frame difference technique [13], then features are extracted from segmented images using the SIFT descriptor [12]. The extracted features of the moving segments lacks of global information. Our model builds a visual vocabulary in order to join representative features in clusters [14]. Thus, the features are organized using the semantic information of the segments. Each image contains a feature vector builded using the visual vocabulary [15], for final vehicle type classification, the model uses two Support vector machines (SVM) [16], the first discriminates the occlusions an the second recognizes the vehicle type. In case of occlusions, our model performs an occlusion removal technique and extracts already the feature vector for the new divided segments.

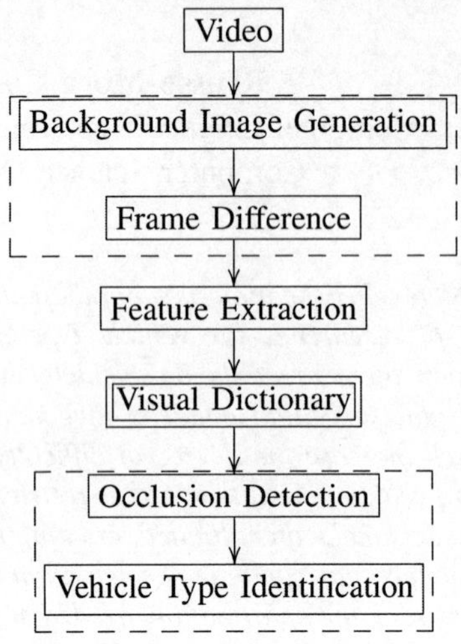

Fig. 1: Our proposed model.

3. Segmentation

Background subtraction is a commonly used technique for segmenting out objects of interest (vehicles) in a scene [17]. Due to constantly changing conditions, some specific background image generation techniques exist for outdoor scenes [18]. Once the background image is generated, the moving object segment is remarked using a binary mask builded by the diference between the observed frame and the generated background image.

3.1 Background Image Generation

Mora and Camara [19] proposed a method for progressive background image generation; it uses a heuristic function to update the information about the static segments. This method regenerates progressively the background image. This technique uses the changes in the partial background image that corresponds to changes between two consecutive generation frames, and a heuristic function that updates the temporal histogram of each pixel. The heuristic function rewards and penalizes the intensities that present a considerable change between generations, it uses a neighborhood criteria and adaptive variables that allow the method to react quickly to changes in the scene also these variables can be set for different traffic conditions.

This method is divided in three parts: partial background generation, histogram update and background register.

3.1.1 Partial Background

In this initial step, an image, called partial background, that contains the static segments between two generations is builded using the Eq. 1.

$$Pb_i(p) = \begin{cases} \frac{f_i(p)+f_{i-1}(p)}{2} & if\ |f_i(p) - f_{i-1}(p)| < \gamma \\ -1 & otherwise \end{cases} . \quad (1)$$

where, f_i and f_{i-1} are two consecutive frames. The resulted image Pb contains the information about the static segments in recent time, this step aims to be more adaptive for eventual changes in the background image.

3.1.2 Histogram Update

Each pixel in the image has a histogram in which intensity behavior of pixel is represented by scalar values. These histograms are modified by a reward and penalty function.

Basically, the values in the histogram are modified when considerably variations in the pixel intensity occurs. It means, if the difference between the value of the partial background with the last generated background image is bigger than a threshold, then this pixel intensity suffers a variation in its group (background/foreground). The modifications in the histograms are done using a neighborhood scheme, the idea is to increment or to decrement a group of intensities. Thus, if a determinate evaluated intensity bin has to be modified, it and its neighbor intensities will suffer a modification using normal distribution centered in the evaluated intensity bin. All these modifications are resume in two rules:

- Reward the intensity (bin and its neighborhood), that remains in two consecutive background generation.
- Reward the incoming intensity, and penalize the last growing intensity.

Note, that the first rule is accomplished when pixel intensity has not significant variation, in the other hand, second rule is applied when pixel intensity suffers a big variation.

In each generation all the histograms are updated.

3.1.3 Background Generation

The background image H is recalculated from the updated histograms. For each pixel in the image, the method looks for the highest cumulative value, the bin position of this value corresponds to the background intensity that will be set in the histogram table or background image.

3.2 Moving Objects Segmentation

Once the background image was generated, the vehicles can be segmented from the frame. Commonly, a binary mask of moving objects is generated by the difference between the current frame and the background. In most cases, this image contains noise and it is necessary to filter the resulting image. But in gray scale, some background intensities are similar to the foreground. For example, in some tests the windshields are too similar with the track intensities, these region is consider as background leaving dark spots in the region corresponding to a vehicle. In 2, we can see a frame difference between background image and the current frame, it is clear that some pixels in vehicles are similar to the background intensities. Morphological operators are used to eliminate noise, the result is a binary mask with black spaces inside region that correspond to a vehicle. To avoid this hides intensities of the binary mask, our method also uses another frame difference, this time between two consecutive frames. First, we explain the equation that builds the binary masks using next equation:

$$B = \begin{cases} 1 & if\ |I_1 - I_2| < \kappa \\ 0 & otherwise \end{cases} , \quad (2)$$

where I_1 and I_2 are images, depending on the case I_2 can be a previous frame or the background image, κ is a threshold.

Thus, we define B_{ff} and B_{fb} as the resulted binary mask between two consecutive frames (the current frame and the previous frame) and the binary mask between the current frame and the background, respectively. The final segment mask Fr is the union result $B_{ff} \cup B_{fb}$. The image Fr is filtered by morphological operators. The builded binary mask is used to segment the vehicles, applying a size criteria, where small objects are unconsidered and vehicles are extracted as small images.

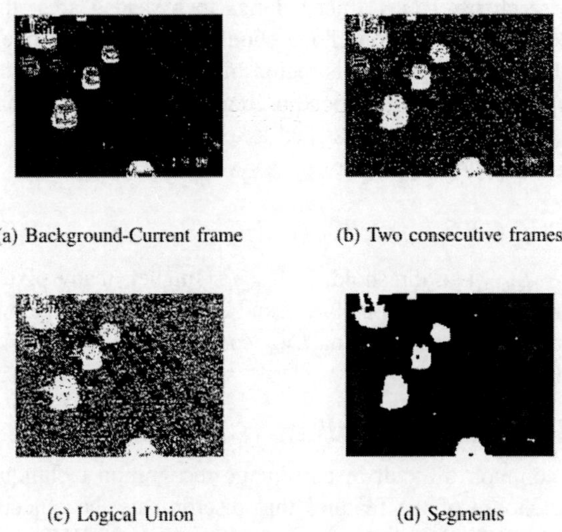

(a) Background-Current frame (b) Two consecutive frames

(c) Logical Union (d) Segments

Fig. 2: Background Image Generation

3.3 Shadow Removal

Due to light conditions cars project shadows that can occlude other vehicle or cause a false effect of movement. In this work, we use the method proposed by Jakes *et.al.* [20] for shadow removal. This method estimates the pixels considered as shadows using normalized cross-correlation to detect shadow pixel candidates, since it can identify scaled versions of the same signal.

Thus we have, $Bg(i,j)$ a generated background image, and $f(i,j)$ is a frame from vÃdeo sequence. For each pixel (i,j) such that $Sg(i,j) = 1$ (that must be part of moving objects), we define a template matrix Tij with dimensions $(2N+1)\times(2N+1)$, where $T_{ij}(n,m) = I(i+n, j+m)$, for $-N \leq n \leq N$ e $-M \leq m \leq M$, this template corresponds to the neighborhood pixel (i,j).

Then a CNC between the template T_{ij} and the background image Bg in pixel (i,j) is given by:

$$CNC(i,j) = \frac{ER(i,j)}{E_B(i,j)E_{T_{ij}}}, \quad (3)$$

where,

$$ER = \sum_{n=-N}^{N} \sum_{m=-N}^{N} B(i+n, j+m)T_{ij}(n,m), \quad (4)$$

$$E_B(i,j) = \sqrt{\sum_{n=-N}^{N} \sum_{m=-N}^{N} B(i+n, j+m)^2}, \quad (5)$$

$$E_{T_{ij}} = \sqrt{\sum_{n=-N}^{N} \sum_{m=-N}^{N} T_{ij}(n,m)^2}. \quad (6)$$

For each pixel (i,j) that belongs to a shaded area, the CNC Tij in the neighborhood should be large (near one), and the energy E_{Tij} in this region must be smaller than the energy $E_B(i,j)$ of corresponding region in the background. Thus, a pixel (i,j) is classified as part of the shadow if it meets the following relation:

$$CNC(i,j) \geq L_{cnc} \text{ e } E_{Tij} < E_B(i,j), \quad (7)$$

where, L_{cnc} is a threshold. If L_{cnc} is smaller, many pixels belonging to the moving object can be considered as shadow. Otherwise, a large value of L_{cnc} can disregard the area of the shadow.

4. Feature Extraction

A common difficult in any image recognition technique is the choose of the features that discriminate the objects. We use SIFT descriptor for feature extraction. SIFT is a well know descriptor in the literature, a main advantage of this method is its invariance conditions (scale, rotation, translation and partially to occlusions). Vehicles in traffic videos suffer these transformations.

The SIFT descriptor uses a gradient histogram as attribute for each characteristic point. Where an image has different number of characteristic points. When spatial local features are extracted, they only provide a very local and unstructured representation of the video clips. One way to give a more meaningful representation is to use the bag of features (BoF) approach [15]. Using BoF requires the construction of a visual vocabulary.

4.1 Visual Vocabulary and Feature Histograms

Visual Vocabulary [15] is a set of feature clusters, where each word of this vocabulary is a set of characteristic that belongs a cluster. We create our visual vocabulary using descriptors previously extracted from segmented images of cars, motorcycles and buses. In this step, we use the LBG non-supervised clustering algorithm [14] to generate z centroids.

The feature histogram of an image is formed by a vector of size z (the same number of centroids). The algorithm calculates the Euclidean distance of a descriptor with all the centroids, the centroid with minimal distance updates the same position in the cluster histogram, increasing this bin in a unit.

5. Vehicle Type Recognition

Our model uses Support vector machines (SVM) [21] to classify the vehicle type. The SVM is a binary classifier, novel improvements [22] introduce enhancements in the algorithm that allows it to classify more than two classes. In this work, we use three groups: cars, motorcycles and buses. Our model uses two classifiers, the first was trained to recognize segments with occlusion, the second was trained to recognize the vehicle type.

The method builds two visual vocabularies. The first is divided in two groups: occluded and not occluded. A second vocabulary contains the information about the cars, motorcycles and buses. An initial step in the recognition process is to determine if the moving segment, extracted in the previous step, contains only one vehicle, in occlusion case the method performs a second segmentation.

5.1 Occlusion Segmentation

Depending of the camera position a vehicle may occlude partially or totally by other, increasing the difficult to segment the cars. In some videos, the camera position avoids the apparition of occlusion, but in many cases, especially in low angle cameras the occlusion is always present.

We propose a simple method to split the segments with occlusions into segments with small size and with only one vehicle inside. The proposed method reduces the intensity levels to eliminate some details that join the occluded cars. First, we assume that vehicles usually have a region that covers almost all the vehicle, this region has an uniform color, usually perceived colors of windshield and tires are different to chassis. It is clear, that exist many regions with different colors, for that the method reduces the intensities in just four intensities in order to decrease the details. In this reduction, the vehicles are clear or dark. We define four intensity clusters, the first intensity (black) represents of background. Actually, the other three segments are the intensities that we use to separate the vehicles. The K-means algorithm [23] is used to the intensity quantization. After define the intensities, small color segments are dismissed these segments are not enough representative. Thus, the representative color of the vehicles are used to divide them, in the case of vehicles with same color, the method uses characteristics like the brightness to separate the vehicles. The remained color segments still have noise, thus , morphological operators are used to filter them. A binary mask is created that represents the separated vehicles. In 3 is showed the process, the classifier detects the occlusion in the image. First, the method reduces the number of intensities (in order to eliminate details), after that, color regions are filtered with morphological operators. Finally, a binary mask is generated, where each segment receives a label.

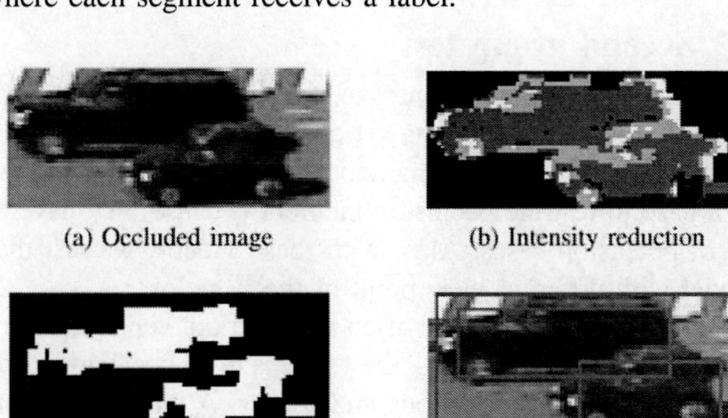

(a) Occluded image (b) Intensity reduction

(c) Binary mask (d) Separated vehicles

Fig. 3: Intensity Segment Reduction

5.2 Type recognition

Once the vehicles are segmented, their features are extracted and processed for the final vehicle type recognition using the second classifier.

The image set contains all the vehicles (cars, motorcycles and buses) and

6. Experiments

Our model is divided in two parts: the moving object segmentation and vehicle recognition. The first part is tested with different videos [24][25], basically to test the background generation algorithm. In second part, we use two main groups of videos to test the framework. The first one, is composed by our own videos, these videos are very noisy. The second group is a long time duration video of a street intersection [26], these videos have heavy traffic flow and many occlusions.

6.1 First group test

Several datasets have been proposed for evaluating vehicle detection algorithms. However, these datasets mostly consist of images of vehicles restricted to frontal/rear and side poses, which in our opinion, is insufficient for capturing the entire degree of variation in the appearance of cars in surveillance videos due to changes in pose, viewpoint, illumination and scale. We create our own ground truth to train our classification method. We use 400 images of different vehicles (200 cars,100 motorcycles,100 buses). The occlusion classifier was trained with 200 that contain occlusion cases and the whole set as examples of images with no occlusion.

In Figure 4, can be appreciated an observed frame and the generated background image from the same video. This sequence contains many noises, such as: constantly lighting variation, vibrations, poor camera encryption, etc. We use the following parameters for the generator background function for all video sequences: $v1 = 1$, $v2 = .1$ and $v3 = .9$, these variables represents the multipliers of m_1, m_2 and m_3 of the background generation algorithm.

(a) Current frame

(b) Background image

Fig. 4: Background image generation.

The model uses a determinate region of the scene for observation (ROI; region of interest). Depending on the size of a vehicle, this one may appears many times in the ROI. Each time a vehicle appears, it passes for a type recognition process. In Fig. 5, it can be appreciated an example of a ROI in an observed frame (the darker region at the bottom of the image).

Fig. 5: Observation region.

We track each vehicle using a spatial-temporal criteria, where in two consecutive frames, a region in the image only contains a one vehicle [27]. This technique allows the method to count and track each vehicle. The transition of a vehicle from the beginning of the ROI at the end, corresponds to many frames, in each frame a vehicle receives a label. When vehicle outcome of the scene, its type (car, motorcycle, bus) is defined using a voting criteria using its previous assigned labels. In Fig, 6, we appreciate an image of the ROI where a vehicle is tracked.

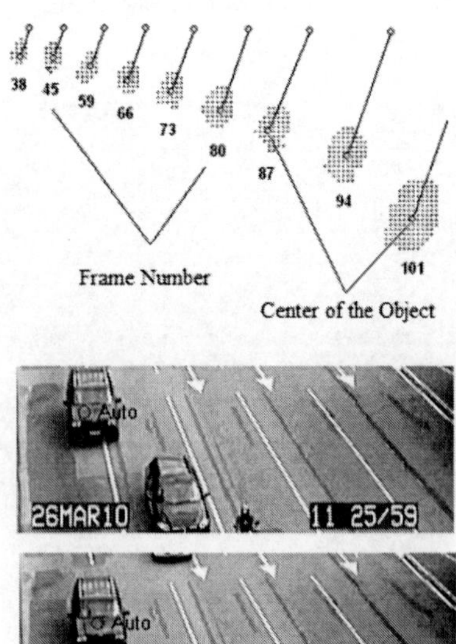

Fig. 6: Vehicle tracking.

In Table 1, is shown the confusion matrix for our own set of videos composed of four videos. We also made a vehicle trajectory recognition [28], and using a voting model we define the vehicle type. The total accuracy in these tests was 83.33%. We also do other tests using SURF [29] descriptor, but the general recognition decreased by 5% in almost all cases.

Table 1: Confusion matrix

	Cars	Motorcycles	Buses
Cars	89,58	10,42	0,00
Motorcycles	0,00	75,00	25,00
Buses	21,43	14,29	64,29

6.2 Second group test

In the second experiment, we use the MIT traffic video data set [26]. The MIT data set consists of 20 videos of an avenue intersection, with many occlusion cases. We use this data base to test the occlusion method, because they have a lot of occlusion cases. Also, with these videos, we test the model with different view point of the vehicles.

Due to the characteristic of an intersection, vehicles come from many directions. Thus, the vehicles in an occlusion may appear in different directions and senses. A single segment with occlusion can contain from two to five cars. In this case, we just recognize the vehicles and their types, we can not use the trajectory algorithm used in the first experiment. The challenge in this second experiment is the occlusion removal step since the vehicles are constantly occluded by others. The classifier detects the occlusions with 96% of accuracy, our model achieves to separate 80% of the occlusions, separating into their constitutive elements. Finally, the vehicle type accuracy was of 85%. It is important to notice that our model recognize a vehicle from different directions, i.e., we can recognize a vehicle by the front, side, rear and other views.

7. Conclusions and Discussions

This paper presents a local feature based model for vehicle type recognition. The presented model fits in many traffic situations and different weather conditions and also does not need camera calibration.

The background model uses partial background images, which are robust to camera vibrations, camera movements (pan, zoom, tilt, track) and illuminance changes. The heuristic function allows the method to react faster when a background pixel suffers a change in its intensity. In segmentation step, the moving object mask is builded using more than one frame diference. Actually, most of methods just use the difference between the observed frame and background image. Adding the two consecutive frame difference, a big amount of noise can be eliminated. Using local features, we can obtain a good representation of the vehicles, and the visual vocabulary helps to organize these knowledge for a later recognition stage. The final step is supported by SVM, that is a well known and powerful classifier.

It is important to outline, our video data set is from surveillance camera, these sequences contains much noise and a low quality encryption. The classifiers using for test were trained with a tiny set of vehicle images, nevertheless, the accuracy of the multi-view vehicle type recognition obtained is promising. Also, the proposed method introduce a technique for occlusion removal, it uses a very simple operations. Therefore, there is a lack in the divide occlusion method, especially in case of big vehicles (trucks) with different colors.

Finally, our model is capable to detect and classify vehicles requiring minimal scene-specific knowledge.

8. Acknowledgments

The authors are grateful to CNPq and CAPES, Brazilian research funding agencies, for the financial support to this work.

References

[1] V. Kastrinaki, M. Zervakis, and K. Kalaitzakis, "A survey of video processing techniques for traffic applications," *Image and Vision Computing*, vol. 21, pp. 359–381, 2003.

[2] B. Tamersoy and J. Aggarwal, "Counting vehicles in highway surveillance videos," in *Pattern Recognition (ICPR), 2010 20th International Conference on*, aug. 2010, pp. 3631 –3635.

[3] W. Zhu and M. Barth, "Vehicle trajectory-based road type and congestion recognition using wavelet analysis," in *Intelligent Transportation Systems Conference, 2006. ITSC '06. IEEE*, sept. 2006, pp. 879 –884.

[4] J. Kato, T. Watanabe, S. Joga, Y. Liu, and H. Hase, "An hmm/mrf-based stochastic framework for robust vehicle tracking," *Intelligent Transportation Systems, IEEE Transactions on*, vol. 5, no. 3, pp. 142 – 154, sept. 2004.

[5] X. Clady, P. Negri, M. Milgram, and R. Poulenard, "Multi-class vehicle type recognition system," in *Proceedings of the 3rd IAPR workshop on Artificial Neural Networks in Pattern Recognition*, ser. ANNPR '08. Berlin, Heidelberg: Springer-Verlag, 2008, pp. 228–239.

[6] S. Rahati, R. Moravejian, E. Mohamad, and F. Mohamad, "Vehicle recognition using contourlet transform and svm," in *Information Technology: New Generations, 2008. ITNG 2008. Fifth International Conference on*, april 2008, pp. 894 –898.

[7] Y. Du and Y. Feng, "Vehicle detection from video sequence based on gabor filter," in *Electronic Measurement Instruments, 2009. ICEMI '09. 9th International Conference on*, aug. 2009, pp. 2–375 –2–379.

[8] N. Kanhere and S. Birchfield, "Real-time incremental segmentation and tracking of vehicles at low camera angles using stable features," *Intelligent Transportation Systems, IEEE Transactions on*, vol. 9, no. 1, pp. 148 –160, march 2008.

[9] M. Kagesawa, A. Nakamura, K. Ikeuchi, and H. Saito, "Local-feature based vehicle class recognition in infra-red images using imap parallel vision board," in *Intelligent Transportation Systems, 2000. Proceedings. 2000 IEEE*, 2000, pp. 334 –339.

[10] Y. Liu, Z. You, L. Cao, and X. Jiang, "Vehicle detection with projection histogram and type recognition using hybrid neural networks," in *Networking, Sensing and Control, 2004 IEEE International Conference on*, vol. 1, march 2004, pp. 393 – 398 Vol.1.

[11] A. A. Ambardekar, "Efficient vehicle tracking and classification for an automated traffic surveillance system," Master's thesis, University of Nevada, December 2007.

[12] D. G. Lowe, "Object recognition from local scale-invariant features," in *Proceedings of the International Conference on Computer Vision-Volume 2 - Volume 2*, ser. ICCV '99. Washington, DC, USA: IEEE Computer Society, 1999, pp. 1150–. [Online]. Available: http://dl.acm.org/citation.cfm?id=850924.851523

[13] R. Radke, S. Andra, O. Al-Kofahi, and B. Roysam, "Image change detection algorithms: a systematic survey," *Image Processing, IEEE Transactions on*, vol. 14, no. 3, pp. 294 –307, march 2005.

[14] Y. Linde, A. Buzo, and R. Gray, "An algorithm for vector quantizer design," *Communications, IEEE Transactions on*, vol. 28, no. 1, pp. 84 – 95, jan 1980.

[15] L. Wu, S. Hoi, and N. Yu, "Semantics-preserving bag-of-words models and applications," *Image Processing, IEEE Transactions on*, vol. 19, no. 7, pp. 1908 –1920, july 2010.

[16] E. Osuna, R. Freund, and F. Girosit, "Training support vector machines: an application to face detection," in *Computer Vision and Pattern Recognition, 1997. Proceedings., 1997 IEEE Computer Society Conference on*, jun 1997, pp. 130 –136.

[17] M. Piccardi, "Background subtraction techniques: a review," in *Systems, Man and Cybernetics, 2004 IEEE International Conference on*, vol. 4, oct. 2004, pp. 3099 – 3104 vol.4.

[18] N. S. Naraghi, "A comparative study of background estimation algorithms," Master's thesis, Eastern Mediterranean University, September 2009.

[19] R. V. H. Mora-Colque and G. Cámara-Chávez, "Progressive background image generation of surveillance traffic videos based on a temporal histogram ruled by a reward penalty function," in *Sibgrapi 2011 (XXIV Conference on Graphics, Patterns and Images)*, T. Lewiner and R. Torres, Eds. Maceió, AL: IEEE Computer Society Conference Publishing Services, august 2011.

[20] J. Jacques, C. Jung, and S. Musse, "Background subtraction and shadow detection in grayscale video sequences," in *Computer Graphics and Image Processing, 2005. SIBGRAPI 2005. 18th Brazilian Symposium on*, oct 2005, pp. 189 – 196.

[21] V. Vapnik, "An overview of statistical learning theory," *Neural Networks, IEEE Transactions on*, vol. 10, no. 5, pp. 988 –999, sep 1999.

[22] C.-W. Hsu and C.-J. Lin, "A comparison of methods for multiclass support vector machines," *Neural Networks, IEEE Transactions on*, vol. 13, no. 2, pp. 415 –425, mar 2002.

[23] R. C. Gonzalez and R. E. Woods, *Digital Image Processing*, 2nd ed. Boston, MA, USA: Addison-Wesley Longman Publishing Co., Inc., 2001.

[24] K. Institute. (2011) Video data set.

[25] A. Video and S. based Surveillance. (2007) Video data set 2. Www.eecs.qmul.ac.uk/ andrea/avss2007_d.html.

[26] X. M. X. Wang and E. Grimson. (2009) Video data set using in unsupervised activity perception in crowded and complicated scenes using hierarchical bayesian models. Http://www.ee.cuhk.edu.hk/ xgwang/MITtraffic.html. [Online]. Available: http://www.ee.cuhk.edu.hk/ xgwang/MITtraffic.html

[27] E. Dallalzadeh and D. S. Guru, "Feature-based tracking approach for detection of moving vehicle in traffic videos," in *Proceedings of the First International Conference on Intelligent Interactive Technologies and Multimedia*, ser. IITM '10. New York, NY, USA: ACM, 2010, pp. 254–260.

[28] E. Atkociunas, R. Blake, A. Juozapavicius, and M. Kazimianec, "Image processing in road traffic analysis," *Nonlinear Analysis, Modelling and Control, Vol. 10, No 4*, pp. 315–332, 2005.

[29] H. Bay, T. Tuytelaars, and L. V. Gool, "Surf: Speeded up robust features," in *In ECCV*, 2006, pp. 404–417.

Hyperspectral Compression using Specialized Spectral Sensitivity Functions

Kaveh Heidary

Department of Electrical Engineering and Computer Science, Alabama A&M University
PO Box 702 Normal AL 35762 USA, kaveh.heidary@aamu.edu

Abstract

Synthetic-color is the use of technology to emulate the basic means by which animals acquire and use spectral information. It begins with sensing of the scene using multiple broad and overlapping spectral sensitivity functions analogous with cone cells of the human vision system. In this paper we develop an algorithm to obtain a set of near-optimal application-specific spectral sensitivity functions for synthetic-color systems. The user-designed sensitivity functions result in concurrent good intra-class packing and interclass integrity in the synthetic-color space for reflectance classes with known statistics. This method leads to improved color discrimination and results in more robust spectral classifiers.

Keywords Synthetic-Color, Spectral Compression, Classification

I. Introduction

A hyperspectral image (HSI) is comprised of a data cube with three axes: two spatial and one spectral. Some aspects of HSI processing may involve locating and classifying targets of interest by utilizing their spectral and spatial characteristics. Data compression is a vital element of any HSI system in which processing speed is an important consideration. The implicit assumption is that the processing can be done with COTS hardware or its military equivalent.

The process described here involves compressing the data cube along the spectral axis by linearly combining the entire set of spectral planes. This converts the 3D HSI data cube to a corresponding 2D array which constitutes a spatial map. The weight coefficients used in the linear combination represent the spectral sensitivity function best suited for recognizing the target either against all possible other image content or against known clutter and other target types. Here, the process of discrimination and segmentation of images involves two or more broad and overlapping spectral sensitivity functions, akin to the cone cell sensitivities of animal vision systems [1-4]. Compressing the HSI with each one of a limited set of spectral sensitivity functions leads to a set of few spatial maps compared to the hundreds in the original data cube. The resultant set of spatial maps (monochromatic images) constitutes a single synthetic-color image. Using three spectral sensitivity functions, for example, leads to a compressed image, similar in terms of computational requirements to a color RGB image.

$$A(x,y) = \int_{\lambda_{min}}^{\lambda_{max}} S_A(\lambda) I(x,y,\lambda) d\lambda \, , B(x,y) = \int_{\lambda_{min}}^{\lambda_{max}} S_B(\lambda) I(x,y,\lambda) d\lambda \, , C(x,y) = \int_{\lambda_{min}}^{\lambda_{max}} S_C(\lambda) I(x,y,\lambda) d\lambda \quad (1).$$

Where, x, y, λ denote spatial and spectral variables, $I(x,y,\lambda)$ represents the HSI, $S_A(\lambda), S_B(\lambda), S_C(\lambda)$ are spectral sensitivity functions, and $A(x,y), B(x,y), C(x,y)$ are the spatial maps associated with the resultant tri-color synthetic image. The radiation intensity along the xy-direction is proportional to the spectral characteristic and intensity of incident light at xy and the spectral reflectance of the surface at that location. In (1) we have used three spectral sensitivities in order to compress the HSI to the ABC synthetic-color image. The radiance function at each pixel has been projected to a vector in the ABC space. Designing an effective compression mechanism involves computation of an appropriate set of spectral sensitivity functions. The number of required spectral sensitivity functions and the form of each function are application dependent.

In some applications two or more surface classes with known spectral reflectance functions must be distinguishable from each other and from all other unknown surfaces [5,6]. It is noted that spectral intensity emanated from a particular surface class has a great deal of volatility owing to multitude of factors such as surface irregularities including roughness and surface orientation with respect to the sensor and source, uncertainties in the incident light due to variable excitation including spectral and intensity conditions, and shadowing effects. The spectral intensity function for any surface class is, in general, a random process, and the objective is to design spectral sensitivities that lead to concurrent maximum intra-class packing and inter-class integrity in the compressed space. In other applications, several surface classes with stochastic reflectance characteristics may represent background, and one must be able to distinguish, in the compressed space, between background-class surfaces and any other surface. This will allow the image processing system to operate on the compressed image for classification and removal of clutter (background), followed by other operations such as shape recognition including determination of target identity, position, scale, and orientation.

We seek to design broad and overlapping spectral sensitivity functions such that projection of the HSI data preserves the salient spectral diversity among various target classes of interest, while it maintains robust separation between targets and expected background and noise.

II. Background

In order to illustrate the principle of spectral sensitivity design, one needs to generate simulated reflectance functions that can be systematically varied in order to offer any desired level of difficulty. Generating class-specific sets of simulated reflectance functions with arbitrarily large populations allows detailed examination of the effects of various spectral sensitivity parameters on system performance. Reflectance classes are comprised of simulated reflectance functions obtained from a user prescribed function space. A parametric function generator was developed, whereby arbitrarily large sets of simulated reflectance functions can be synthesized. Assigning a set of function parameters is tantamount to choosing a reflectance class. This prompts the function generator to create a user-specified number of reflectance functions with arbitrary, albeit user-controlled, intra-class variability as shown below.

$$\bar{\Gamma}(\lambda) = \sum_{m=1}^{M}\left[\frac{U_m}{1+e^{-\alpha_m(\lambda-\lambda 1_m)}} + \frac{V_m}{1+e^{\beta_m(\lambda-\lambda 2_m)}}\right], \quad \Gamma(\lambda) = \frac{\bar{\Gamma}(\lambda)}{max(\bar{\Gamma}(\lambda))} \qquad (2).$$

Where, $\bar{\Gamma}, \Gamma$ are raw and normalized reflectance functions, respectively, and λ is the wavelength. Each one of the component functions in (2) is monotonic in [0-1]. The parameters $\lambda 1_m$, $\lambda 2_m$ represent inflection points, α_m, β_m determine steepness, U_m, V_m are weights, and M represents the number of basis functions constituting the reflectance. The selection of a set of parameters leads to one synthesized reflectance function, which can be viewed as the prototype of a reflectance class. Likewise, selecting a second set of parameters leads to a reflectance function representing the prototype of the second reflectance class. In order to generate manifold reflectance functions associated with the same reflectance class, the parameters (U_m, V_m, α_m, β_m, $\lambda 1_m$, $\lambda 2_m$) are chosen from normal probability distribution functions with user prescribed means and variances. Selection of the set of mean values for the distribution functions is tantamount to specifying a certain class. The reflectance function parameters are chosen from the following Gaussian distributions.

$$\lambda 1_m \sim N(\lambda 10_m, \sigma_{\lambda_1}^2), \lambda 2_m \sim N(\lambda 20_m, \sigma_{\lambda_2}^2), U_m \sim N(1, \sigma_A^2), V_m \sim N(1, \sigma_B^2), \alpha_m \sim N(\alpha_0, \sigma_\alpha^2), \beta_m \sim N(\beta_0, \sigma_\beta^2) \quad (3).$$

Where, the break point means $\lambda 10_m, \lambda 20_m$ for $1 \le m \le M$ are selected from $\lambda_{min} \le \lambda \le \lambda_{max}$ $(i.e. \lambda_{min} = 350nm, \lambda_{max} = 700nm)$, and the typical values for standard deviations and other parameters are: $\sigma_{\lambda 1} = \sigma_{\lambda 2} = 1nm$, $\sigma_A = \sigma_B = 0.05$, $\sigma_\alpha = \sigma_\beta = 0.01$, $\alpha_0 = \beta_0 = 0.05$. The σ values are used to control intra-class variability of reflectance functions. A set of reflectance functions containing a user-specified number of elements and representing a particular surface-class is obtained from the generating function in (2). A single set of break-point means is chosen and subsequent random perturbation of this set, and random generation of other parameters as shown in (3) give rise to the reflectance function set. In the following example we chose parameter values M=3, λ10= [400 500 600], λ20= [380 510 660], σ= [0.03 0.02 0.01 0.04 0.02 0.04], where elements of σ are the standard deviations of the probability distributions of (3). A large set (N=1000) of spectral reflectance functions representing the Class-one surfaces were generated and six randomly chosen samples are plotted in Figure 1, where each function is normalized with respect to maximum reflectance. In order to generate the Class-two reflectance functions, parameter values M=4, λ10= [430 530 550 630], λ20= [300 450 500 585] and the same σ values as Class-one were used. Plots of six randomly chosen samples of one-thousand generated Class-two reflectance functions are also shown in Figure 1. It is noted that for any one of the two surface classes, reflectance at a certain wavelength is not normally distributed.

We used two spectral sensitivity functions, A and B, to reduce each reflectance function to a 2D vector by projecting the reflectance onto the AB synthetic-color space using (1). Projecting every pixel of the HSI onto the AB-space leads to the respective compressed synthetic-color image. Figure 2 shows the spectral sensitivities, where two equal-width Gaussians are used for A and B functions, respectively. It is noted that areas under the two sensitivities are equal, which implies equal sensor responses to white light, and they are normalized such that white light is projected to (255,255) in the AB space. The plots in the bottom-row of Figure 2 show projections of one-hundred samples from each surface class in the synthetic-color space.

Inspecting samples of the reflectance functions in Figure 1 reveals a great deal of intra-class volatility. One also notes some characteristic differences between reflectance functions of the two classes. This example illustrates that the degree of inter-class separation of the two surface classes, in the 2D synthetic-color space, is determined by the widths and means-separation of the two Gaussian sensitivities as demonstrated by the plots of Figure 2.

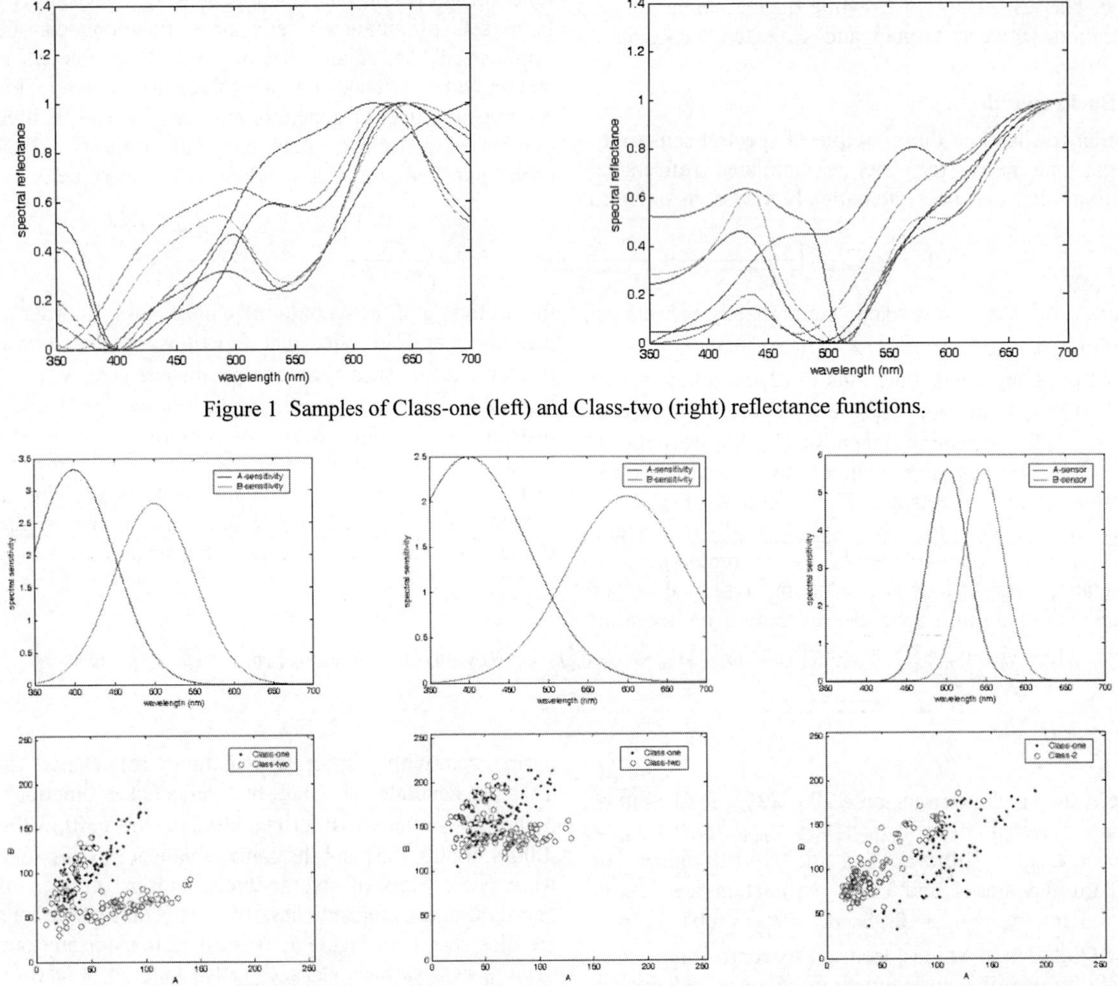

Figure 1 Samples of Class-one (left) and Class-two (right) reflectance functions.

Figure 2 The top-row plots show two spectral sensitivity functions corresponding to the AB synthetic-color system for three cases. The bottom-row plots show the projections of Class-one and Class-two surfaces in the compressed AB synthetic-color space using the corresponding sensitivities in the top-row.

III. Optimization of spectral sensitivity functions

In Section II it was shown that choosing a set of spectral sensitivity functions maps a surface class to a corresponding set of vectors in the synthetic-color space. It was also shown that the choice of spectral sensitivities greatly impacts how two different surface classes are related in the compressed space vis-à-vis the mutual relationship between synthetic-color clouds associated with color vectors of the two classes. In order to assess the utility of the spectral sensitivity functions a quality metric must be devised. A set of spectral sensitivities are used for compressing the HSI inputs and transforming them to the respective synthetic-color images at the output. The discussion here is limited to problems where the objective is to assure that two surface classes with distinct but very similar reflectance characteristics remain separated and distinguishable from each other in the synthetic-color space.

Each surface class in the synthetic-color space is characterized by one prototype synthetic-color vector, a covariance matrix, and a radius. An arbitrary vector in the synthetic-color space is labeled with a particular surface-class, i.e. class-k, if its Mahalanobis distance with respect to that class is less than or equal to the respective class radius.

$$d\left(\vec{W},\vec{V}_0^{(k)}\right) = \sqrt{\left(\vec{W},\vec{V}_0^{(k)}\right)\Sigma^{(k)^{-1}}\left(\vec{W},\vec{V}_0^{(k)}\right)^T} \;\; ; \; d\left(\vec{W},\vec{V}_0^{(k)}\right) \le R^{(k)} \Rightarrow \vec{W} \in \{class-k\} \quad (4).$$

Where, $\vec{W}$ denotes a synthetic-color vector, $\vec{V}_0^{(k)}, \Sigma^{(k)}, R^{(k)}$ represent the surface-class-k prototype vector, covariance matrix, and radius, respectively. Superscripts T and -1 denote, respectively, matrix transpose and inversion, and $d\left(\vec{W},\vec{V}_0^{(k)}\right)$ is the distance between the color-vector and class-k. Given a set of labeled reflectance functions, associated with known samples of two surface classes, and a set of N spectral sensitivities, the following process is used to compute the quality-factor Q of the compression process. The reflectance functions of each class are mapped to the N-dimensional synthetic-color space as follows.

$$W_{m,n}^{(k)} = \int_{\lambda_{min}}^{\lambda_{max}} S_n(\lambda) I_m^{(k)}(\lambda) d\lambda \;,\; \vec{W}_m^{(k)} = \left\{W_{m,n}^{(k)}\right\} \;\; ; \; 1 \le k \le 2, \; 1 \le n \le N, \; 1 \le m \le M^{(k)} \quad (5).$$

Where $S_n(\lambda)$ denotes one of N spectral sensitivity functions, $I_m^{(k)}(\lambda)$ is the spectral intensity at the sensor due to an arbitrary class-k surface, k denotes one of two surface classes, $M^{(k)}$ is the number of training samples for surface class-k, and $[\lambda_{min}, \lambda_{max}]$ denotes the range of wavelengths over which the sensor is responsive. Here and henceforth light intensity and spectral reflectance terms are used interchangeably. In (5) $\vec{W}_m^{(k)}$ denotes a vector in the synthetic-color space representing sample-m of class-k surface. Each surface class is represented by a set of vectors in the synthetic-color space.

A user-specified percentage γ of the surface samples from each class are considered outliers. Typical values for γ are between zero and five. The two sets of vectors for classes one and two in (5), are used to compute initial estimates of the prototype-vector, covariance matrix, and radius for each class as follows.

$$\vec{V}_0^{\prime(k)} = \frac{1}{M^{(k)}}\sum_{m=1}^{M^{(k)}} \vec{W}_m^{(k)} \;,\; \Sigma'^{(k)} = cov\left(\left\{\vec{W}_m^{(k)}\right\}\right) \;,\; R'^{(k)} = \max_m\left(d\left(\vec{V}_0^{\prime(k)},\vec{W}_m^{(k)}\right)\right) \; ; \; 1 \le k \le 2, 1 \le m \le M^{(k)} \quad (6).$$

Where $\vec{V}_0^{\prime(k)}, \Sigma'^{(k)}, R'^{(k)}$ denote the initial estimates of, respectively, prototype vector, covariance matrix, and radius for the class-k surfaces. When outlier percentage is zero, the prototype-covariance-radius parameters are equal to their initial estimates given in (6). For γ values other than zero, however, these parameters are adjusted as follows. the vector-prototype distances for each class are computed as follows.

$$r_m^{(k)} = d\left(\vec{V}_0^{\prime(k)},\vec{W}_m^{(k)}\right) \;\; ; \; 1 \le k \le 2 \;,\; 1 \le m \le M^{(k)} \quad (7).$$

The distances of (7) are sorted, and the largest $round(0.01\gamma M^{(k)})$ are eliminated from each set of synthetic-color vectors. The remaining vectors constitute non-outlier vectors for the respective classes. Equation (6) is then applied to the non-outlier sets to compute the sought after parameters. Given an unlabeled synthetic-color vector, its distance with respect to each prototype vector is computed using (4). If the distance is less than the radius of a particular class, it is labeled accordingly, otherwise it remains unclassified.

For the two-class problem considered here, three parameters related to the quality of the set of spectral sensitivities, utilized for compression of the HSI data cubes to synthetic-color images, are defined as follows. The angle between two classes of synthetic-color vectors is defined as the angle between the respective prototype vectors.

$$\alpha_{i,j} = \frac{\vec{V}_0^{(i)} \cdot \vec{V}_0^{(j)}}{\left\|\vec{V}_0^{(i)}\right\| \left\|\vec{V}_0^{(j)}\right\|} \;,\; \left\|\vec{V}_0^{(i)}\right\| = \sqrt{\sum_{n=1}^{N}\left(V_{0,n}^{(i)}\right)^2} \;\; ; \;\; 1 \le i,j \le 2 \quad (8).$$

Equation (4) is used to compute the distance between all non-outlier class-two vectors and the class-one prototype $\vec{V}_0^{(1)}$. The number of vectors for which this distance is greater than the class-one radius $R^{(1)}$ is denoted as $\bar{M}^{(2)}$. Likewise, distances between non-outlier class-one vectors and the class-two prototype are computed, and the number of vectors for which the computed distance is greater than the class-two radius is denoted as $\bar{M}^{(1)}$. Zero-quality is defined as follows.

$$Q_0 = \frac{\bar{M}^{(1)} + \bar{M}^{(2)}}{(1-0.01\gamma)(M^{(1)} + M^{(2)})} \quad (9).$$

For cases where the synthetic-color vectors for classes one and two are completely separated and form two clearly divided clouds Q_0=1. On the other hand, when projected reflectance functions form two clouds that are intermingled in the synthetic-color space, the respective Q_0 is less than one. It is noted that a set of spectral sensitivity functions that result in the Q_0 value close to unity does not guaranty good surface classification. In cases where class-one and class-two prototype vectors lie on the same radial line passing through the coordinate center of the synthetic-color system, changes in the incident light intensity can lead to misclassification of surface classes. In order to better account for the separation of data clouds in the synthetic-color space and the angle between respective prototype color vectors, the quality factor Q is defined as follows.

$$Q = \sin(\alpha)Q_0 \qquad (10).$$

Where α and Q_0 are given in (8) and (9), respectively. A near-optimal spectral compression system is designed by setting the number of spectral sensitivities, which determines the dimensionality of the synthetic-color space, and choosing the shape of each sensitivity function in order to maximize Q in (10).

IV. Simulations

The following example involves two surface classes whose reflectance functions are generated by (2-3). The parameters of the underlying random processes from which the reflectance functions for surface classes one and two are spawned are set as follows. The standard deviations are set at $[\sigma_{\lambda 1}\ \sigma_{\lambda 2}\ \sigma^{(1)}\ \sigma^{(2)}\ \sigma_{\alpha}\ \sigma_{\beta}]$ = [0.020 0.010 0.025 0.030 0.025 0.040], two sets of break points for class-one are chosen to be $\lambda 1_m$= [380 500 530], $\lambda 2_m$= [400 420 640], and two sets of class-two break points are set at $\lambda 1_m$= [300 400 450 640] and $\lambda 2_m$= [340 400 420 700]. One-thousand reflectance functions from each class were generated. Five randomly selected samples of the reflectance functions from each class are plotted in Figure 3, in order to show that both surfaces exhibit considerable intra-class variability. A difficult example has been deliberately chosen to illustrate the efficacy of the spectral compression method described here. In order to simplify the bi-color compression mechanism design problem, we set the two sensitivity means at 466.67nm and 583.33nm and assume they are of equal width. The percent-outlier parameter is set to γ=5. The sensitivity widths (standard deviations of Gaussians) were varied from 11.67nm to 93.33nm, and the quality factors Q, Q_0 and angle α were computed using (8-10), and are plotted in Figure 3. It is noted that best performance, namely greatest Q, is achieved for σ=11.67nm. The synthetic-color class prototype vectors are also shown in Figure 3. Table 1 lists the prototype vectors, covariance matrices, and radii for both classes. It is seen that the class-one classifier is almost circular owing to the small value of off-diagonal terms in comparison to the diagonal terms of its covariance matrix. The class-two classifier, on the other hand, resembles a tilted ellipse as evident from relatively large value of the off-diagonal term.

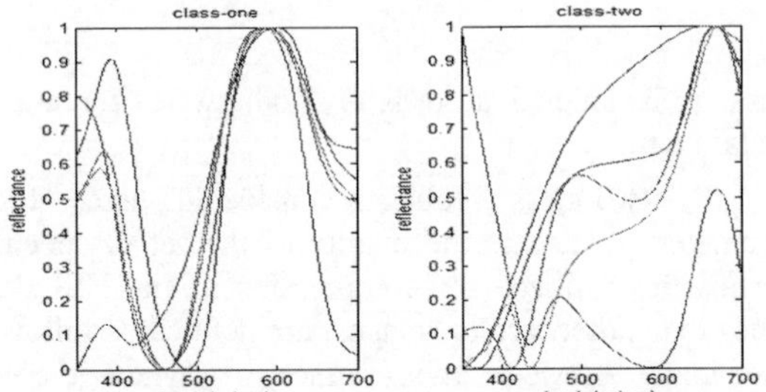

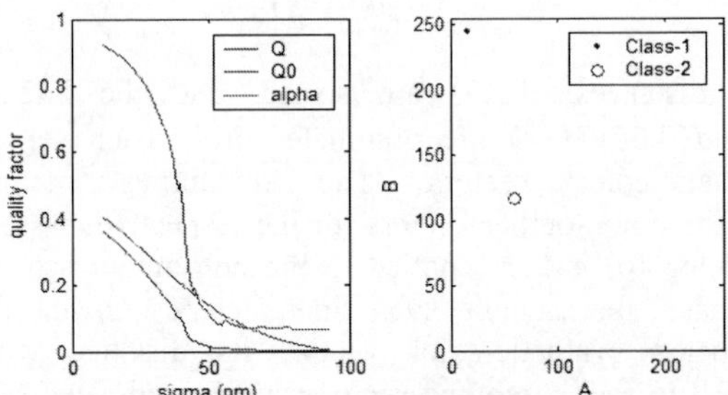

Figure 3 The left two plots show samples of reflectance functions for two surface classes. Third plot from the left shows quality factors Q, Q_0, and separation angle α versus spectral sensitivity function width σ. The plot on the right shows prototype vectors in the bi-color AB synthetic color space.

Table 1 computed classifier for the 2D projection problem

	Class-one	Class-two
Prototype	$\vec{V}_0^{(1)}$=[15.9 244.7]	$\vec{V}_0^{(2)}$=[59 116.4]
Covariance	$\Sigma^{(1)} = \begin{bmatrix} 369.7 & -27.3 \\ -27.3 & 305.5 \end{bmatrix}$	$\Sigma^{(2)} = \begin{bmatrix} 1632.3 & 1212.9 \\ 1212.9 & 2141.6 \end{bmatrix}$
Radius	$R^{(1)}$=5.73	$R^{(2)}$=2.87

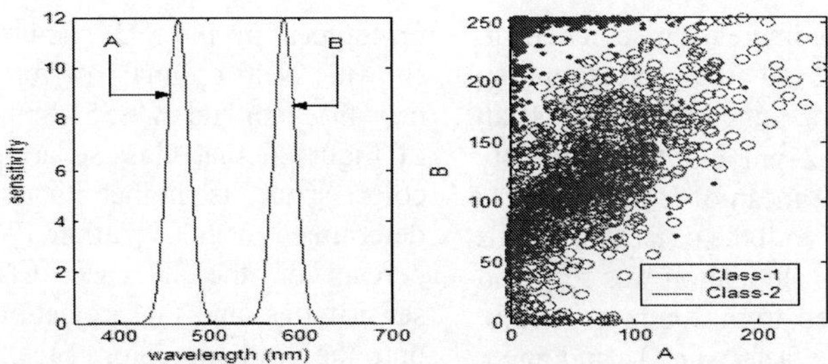

Figure 4 Near-optimal spectral sensitivities for a two-channel sensor (left) and synthetic-color vectors for surface classes-one and two (right).

Considered next is a different 2D spectral compression system applied to the same sets of reflectance functions. Here, the standard deviations of two Gaussian sensitivities are set to 20nm. The two means are placed symmetrically at two sides of the center of the spectral band. Means separation was varied from 20nm to 100nm. Table 2 lists characteristics of the near-optimal classifier. Figure 5 shows plots of the quality factor parameters and the prototype vectors in the synthetic-color space, as well as the sensitivity functions that result in highest Q-factor, and the reflectance function projections in the synthetic-color space. It is seen that two sensitivities with equal widths σ=20nm, and means at 502nm and 548nm result in better than seventy-percent separation of classes in the synthetic-color space.

Table 2 computed classifier for the 2D projection problem

	Class-one	Class-two
Prototype	$\vec{V}_0^{(1)}$=[114.3 125.9]	$\vec{V}_0^{(2)}$=[40.7 99.2]
Covariance	$\Sigma^{(1)} = \begin{bmatrix} 764.6 & 637.2 \\ 637.2 & 1575.6 \end{bmatrix}$	$\Sigma^{(2)} = \begin{bmatrix} 798.7 & 728.7 \\ 728.7 & 1098.7 \end{bmatrix}$
Radius	$R^{(1)}$=2.65	$R^{(2)}$=3.06

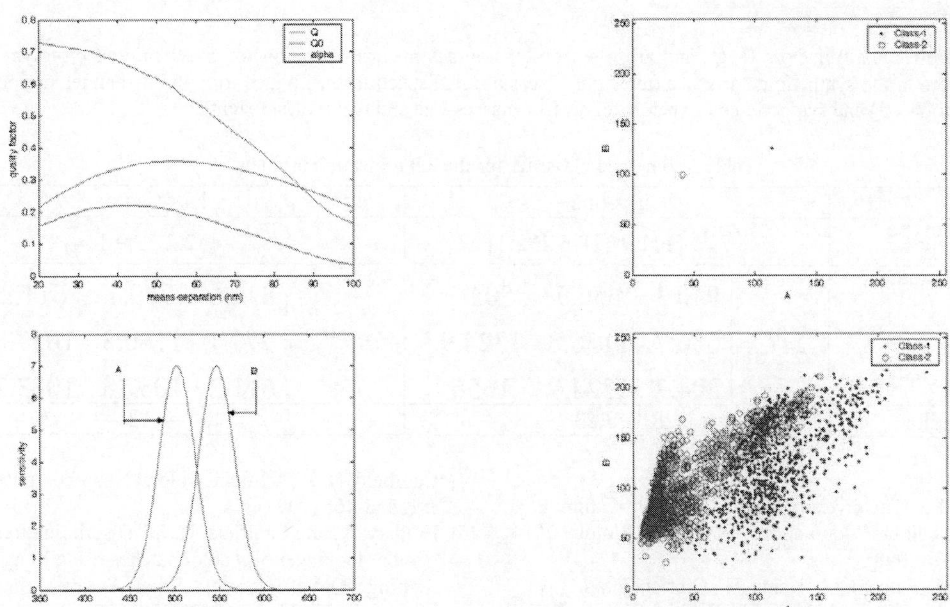

Figure 5 Quality factors Q, Q_0 and angle α (top-left) versus means separation for σ=20nm, and prototype vectors in the synthetic-color space (top-right). Near-optimal spectral sensitivities for a two-channel sensor (bottom-left) and synthetic-color vectors for surface classes-one and two (bottom-right).

Next, we consider a 3D compression mechanism utilized to convert the HSI to the corresponding synthetic-color image. We assume three Gaussian sensitivities of equal width σ=20nm and means equally separated from each other. The mean of B-sensitivity is fixed at mid-band m_B=525nm, with the other two means placed at two sides of m_B. The simulation was repeated as means-separation was varied from 20nm to 100nm. Figure 6 shows plots of quality factors Q, Q_0, and angle α as functions of means-separation. The class prototypes in the 3D synthetic-color space are also shown. Near-optimal performance is achieved for m_A=495.2nm and m_C=554.8nm. It is seen from the plots of Figure 6 that class-separation in the 3D synthetic-color space is higher than eighty-five percent, as determined from Equation (9), compared to seventy-percent for the 2D case. Also plotted are the ABC sensitivities, and the projections of two surface classes onto the synthetic-color space. The classifier parameters are tabulated in Table 3.

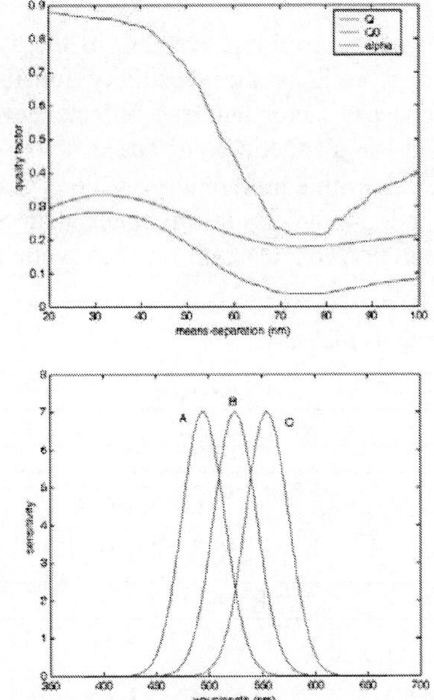

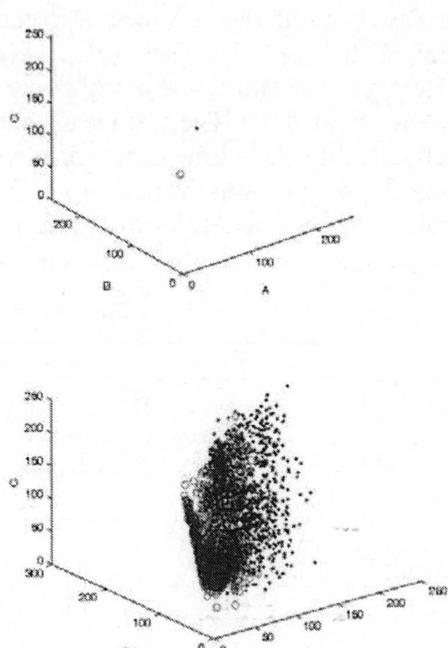

Figure 6 Quality factors Q, Q_0 and angle α (top-left) versus means separation for σ=20nm, and prototype vectors in the synthetic-color space (top-right). Near-optimal spectral sensitivities for a three-channel sensor (bottom-left) and synthetic-color vectors for surface classes-one and two (bottom-right).

Table 3 computed classifier for the 3D projection problem

	Class-one	Class-two
Prototype	$\vec{V}_0^{(1)}$=[111.9 118.6 132.1]	$\vec{V}_0^{(2)}$=[42.2 59.9 114]
Covariance	$\Sigma^{(1)} = \begin{bmatrix} 940.3 & 656.7 & 504.7 \\ 656.7 & 1156.8 & 1324.9 \\ 504.7 & 1324.9 & 1656 \end{bmatrix}$	$\Sigma^{(2)} = \begin{bmatrix} 824.6 & 779.1 & 611.2 \\ 779.1 & 1160.3 & 1057.8 \\ 611.2 & 1057.8 & 1083.2 \end{bmatrix}$
Radius	$R^{(1)}$=3.23	$R^{(2)}$=3.12

V. References

[1] Parker, A.R., "The diversity and implications of animal structural colours," Journal of Experimental Biology 201, 2343-2347 (1998).

[2] Cencini, M., Falconi, M., Kantz, H., Olbrich, E. and Vulpiani, A., "Chaos or Noise: Difficulties of a Distinction," Physical Review E 62, 427-437 (2000).

[3] Jacobs, G.H. Comparative Color Vision, Academic Press, New York (1981).

[4] Caulfield, H. J. 'Artificial Color," Neurocomputing, Vol. 51, 463-465 (2003).

[5] Heidary, K. and Caulfield, H. J., "Discrimination among similar looking, noisy color patches using Margin Setting," Optics Express, Journal of Optical Society of America, Vol. 15, No. 1, 62-75 (2007).

[6] Heidary, K. and Caulfield, H. J., "Color classification using margin-setting with ellipsoids," Signal, Image and Video Processing, 1-18, DOI 10.1007/s11760-012-0349-6 (2012).

Semantic Visual Decomposition Modelling for Improving Object Detection in Complex Scene Images

Ge Qin
Department of Computing
University of Surrey
United Kingdom
g.qin@surrey.ac.uk

Bogdan Vrusias
Department of Computing
University of Surrey
United Kingdom
b.vrusias@surrey.ac.uk

Abstract — **We propose a systematic method for constructing a compositional model for recognising object instances in images of real life subjects. The model is trained on a set of visual examples of contained in a given image, in order to capture the visual characteristics of the contained objects, and to derive spatial relationships between the internal key sub-components of each object instance. The recognition method focuses on extracting visual similarities at the component level in three feature spaces: histogram of boundary distribution, intensity histogram, and histogram of oriented gradient (HOG). Principle Component Analysis (PCA) is used for the component selection and feature weighting. The proposed recognition method is not only capable of improving the accuracy of popular object detection algorithms, but also offers a systematic way of generating detection models.**

Keywords — Contextual object recognition, semantic object modelling, visual object decomposition.

I. INTRODUCTION

Visual recognition has been one of the most popular research areas in computer vision for the last half of the century. The research community nowadays focuses on semantically understanding the objects and its surrounding environment, beyond the visual appearance. Human beings are naturally capable of identifying both visual and semantic similarities for a given set of images. On one hand, we are able to extract similarities in shape, colour, texture or patterns in other photometric domains; on the other hand, we are also capable of interpreting the contextual information beyond the visual appearances and associate objects or scenes based on their semantic similarities. Such combination of visual and semantic analysis gives us the flexibility to select which information, visual or semantic, to use in order to achieve a particular recognition.

It is unquestionable that better visual processing techniques provide better object recognition result and further simplify the semantics derivation. Improving the performances of classic image processing techniques [1, 2] have direct impacts on the performance of object recognition. Compared with the classic content-based information retrieval (CBIR) systems [3, 4], the research interests have been gradually moved from specific context-based object retrieval towards generic knowledge-based scene understanding [5, 6], focusing on visual analysis over images using queries relating to the visual features and compositions of visual features.

Compositional based recognition is considered as a commonly accepted way of exploiting prior knowledge around the detecting model in the form of parts and the relationship between them [7, 8]. Borenstein [9] proposed a recognition system to extract a cow or a runner from its natural background by combining visual similarity driven bottom up segmentation stitching with knowledge driven top down splitting. Although the recognition only works on simple data, i.e. single object that is visually distinctive from the background, it provides a way to systematically recognise small visually descriptive pieces; group the pieces to form semantically descriptive objects guided by a model template. It can be considered as the very first initial step to derive high-level object knowledge by analysing low-level visual descriptions.

Oliva and Torralba's research reveals that statistical structure within the processing images plays a key fundamental role in generic scene understanding [10, 11]. Boutell's [12, 13] work in natural scene recognition analyses the trend of the spatial colour moment and uses it as a semantic feature to recognise outdoor scenes. He also developed a generative model to monitor pair-wise spatial relationship between semantic objects appeared in one scene instance. Currently, most scene understanding is performed on long distance natural landscape scenes. Such scene domain is advantageous as the semantic features are monolithic and normally applicable to the whole image. Furthermore, segmentation on long distance scene images usually outputs fewer regions, which simplifies the spatial relationship analysis between those regions. However, this scene understanding approach is difficult to be applied to recognition of structured object in indoor or closed scenes, which contain more detailed semantics relationships within an object or between objects.

The present work attempts to improve the recognition performance based on existing image processing techniques, by the addition of systematically extracted semantic information of the objects detected in the image. An object model is trained in a supervised fashion [14, 15] and the visually distinctive features, within each key component forming the detecting object, are extracted and weighed accordingly. As shown in Figure 1, the recognition process is split into two stages: *Hypothesis Generation* and *Hypothesis Validation*. Hypothesis Generation produces image patches that have overall similarities when comparing against the object model; and Hypothesis Validation examines the visual appearances and spatial relationship of the components inside the generated hypothesis to determine if sufficient details are extracted to announce the object recognition. Unlike other similar research that focuses mainly on natural landscape scenes, the presented work focuses mainly on street scenes with structural objects, where semantic relationships are embedded within the image details and are more consistent than general landscape themes.

II. MODEL CONSTRUCTION

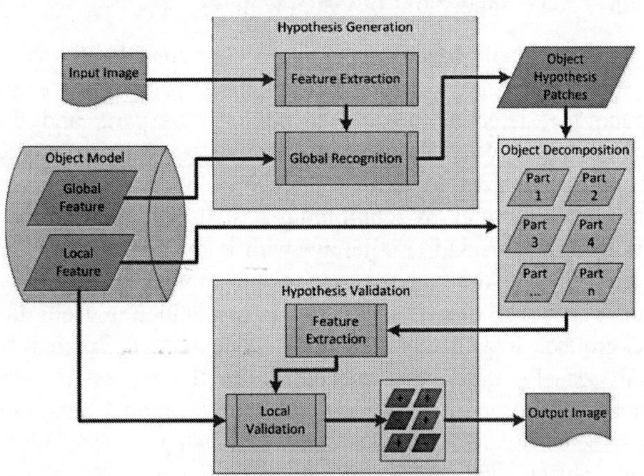

Fig. 1. Object recognition proposal.

Many cutting edge compositional based recognition methods focus on building a codebook containing a large amount of discriminative local features to describe the detecting object. In this work, instead of attempting to directly recognise a complicated structural object from processing arbitrary local features, we propose an intermediate stage to fuse the low-level visual information into components with basic semantic information. The overall recognition of an object depends on the successful recognition of several key sub-components of the object, which makes the recognition less dependent on the overall set of visual appearances of the detecting object.

The object model, $O:\{\omega,\varphi_N^n\}$, consists the information at two feature levels: global level features and local level features. For global feature, ω captures the boundary distribution of the entire object; for local features, φ_N^n records visual patterns of the components within an object, for every component n in the collection of components N. For a particular component φ_N^i within the object, we represent the component using three visual feature descriptors, including boundary distribution (ε), histogram of oriented gradient (θ), and intensity histogram (γ). The model is constructed in a supervised approach, where the detecting object and its inner-components are labelled in the training samples. The feature map for each component is built in an un-supervised way, in which visual similarities among the training samples over a specific feature space are extracted; and the feature map only records the most distinctive features shared among most of the training samples.

A. Object Decomposition

Object decomposition focuses on decomposing the targeted contextual objects into visually simple but semantically meaningful components. Such compositional approach enables us to construct a hierarchical knowledge model for the detecting object, which contains the visual semantic (i.e. visual grammar) about the detecting objects. In this work, the decomposition rule is derived from modelling the labelled intercity street scene image samples from MIT LabelME dataset [16].

B. Feature Extraction

Shape is a robust feature against photometric variations. In this work, PB boundary detector [17] is used to extract boundary in the processing image. From the output of the PB boundary detection, we are able to accumulate the boundaries map to compute the histogram map of boundary distribution and use it to monitor the similarities of boundary orientation shared among individual object instances. Every point in the histogram map of boundary distribution is assigned with a value indicating the likelihood of detecting a boundary point at that location [14][14]. The map is used as the global level feature descriptor to generate recognition hypotheses; and it is also used as one of the local level descriptors to validate the previously generated hypotheses.

The Histogram of Oriented Gradient (HOG) is another commonly used descriptor, which captures local feature appearances by analysing the intensity gradients distribution of the targeted areas of interest [18]. HOG is able to generate a good performance in capturing strong directional feature at localised regions. Following Felzenszwalkb's approach [19] we apply filter kernels $[-1\ \ 0\ \ 1]$ and $[-1\ \ 0\ \ 1]^T$ over an 8×8 sub-region in the targeting gray-scale image using a sliding window approach. The gradient magnitude for each pixel is summarised into a one dimensional 9-bin histogram, each of which records the intensity of the gradient at that specific direction. Further normalisation is carried out to adjust the gradient histogram vector according to its surrounding windows. Finally, we accumulate the HOG distributions for all samples for a given component to derive the similarity in the oriented gradient for that component.

The intensity distribution is tracked and monitored using gray-scale intensity histograms in a 32-bin feature vector. Due to the unstable intensity distribution at the global object level, the intensity analysis is only applied at the component level. The intensity similarity is calculated between the image patch and the model; then multiplied by the customised weighting to compute the recognition confidence for the component, which consequently contributes to the overall object recognition score.

C. Component Selection

Since an object's sub-components are defined by the manual annotations provided in the sample image dataset, each component has its own distinctiveness and it therefore contributes differently towards the object recognition process. Principle Component Analysis (PCA) is used to extract a set of key principle components that dominate the object recognition. As explained in previous chapter, we take into consideration of three features for every component, i.e. boundary distribution, intensity distribution and histogram of oriented gradient (HOG), together with three of its relational information, i.e. occurrence frequency, relative location, and relative size.

During the encoding process, each component is converted into a 55-bit feature vector (9-bit for boundary distribution, 32-bit for intensity histogram, 9-bit for HOG distribution, 1-bit for occurrence, 2-bit for relative location, and 2-bit for relative size). For each element $i \subseteq I$ in the feature vector, we calculate the difference between the element value $v(n_i)$, against its mean value $\overline{v(n_i)}$; then normalise the difference by dividing it with 2 standard deviation $\sigma(n)$. We discard elements that reside outside the 2 standard deviation, to cover 95% of the sample data. The relevance score for each component C is then calculated by averaging the individual normalised distances for each element in the feature vector, as shown in (1).

$$C = \frac{\sum_{n=1}^{N}(1-V(n))}{N} : 0 \le V(n) \le 1 \quad (1)$$

Every vehicle sample is converted into a N-element vector $\{C_1, C_2, \dots, C_N\}$, each of which represents the relevance score of a component. To balance the performance with the computation overhead, we decided to only select the top 6 components, which accumulatively contribute towards the recognition of the 77% of the samples, i.e. wheel, rim, window, tail light, head light, windshield.

D. Component Recognition

To achieve recognition for a targeted component, a set of similarity measures are performed over different feature spaces between the component candidate and the feature maps stored in the model. For each feature space, we convert the extracted feature into a 1-D vector space and measure its correlation against the mean vector.

The boundary map of a given sample is divided into 8-by-8 pixel windows. Within each window, we compute the overall score for that window by dividing the total intensity energy with the total number of edge points in that window to generate a 1-D vector with $N \times M$ elements. Similarly, for the histogram of oriented gradient (HOG), every window is represented in a 9-bin 1-D vector, each bin represent a direction. For colour intensity, we convert the intensity distribution for each of the R*G*B band into a 32-bin array.

For each feature for any given component, a mean vector is computed across the complete sample set. The normalised Euclidean distance metric, i.e. Mahalanobis distance D_M, shown in (2), is calculated between every sample δ_n against the mean vector $\bar{\delta}$ to measure how close the sample is against the centroid of the entire sample set. Then we compute the standard deviation of the Mahalanobis distances to represent the variation spread between individual samples to the mean and reverse standard deviation stated to convert it into a value between 0 to 1, as shown in (3), and use it as the weighting score in the processed feature space for that component.

$$D_M(\mathrm{n}) = \sqrt{(\delta_\mathrm{n} - \bar{\delta})^\mathrm{T} \mathrm{S}^{-1} (\delta_\mathrm{n} - \bar{\delta})} \quad (2)$$

$$W = \left| 1 - \sqrt{\frac{1}{N} \sum_{n=1}^{N} \left(D_M(\mathrm{n}) - \overline{D_M}\right)} \right| \quad (3)$$

Successful recognition of an individual component contributes towards the recognition of the whole object. Assessment over the semantic relationship is also carried out between the component candidate and other identified components. Figure 2 shows the spatial relationship between filtered key individual components within the detecting object. The relative size matrix for each component is also monitored to ensure the recognitions for each individual component are consistent towards to the whole contextual object recognition. This mutual spatial map together with the relative size restriction significantly reduces the searching domain for the remaining components when one component is identified, therefore improve the detection efficiency significantly.

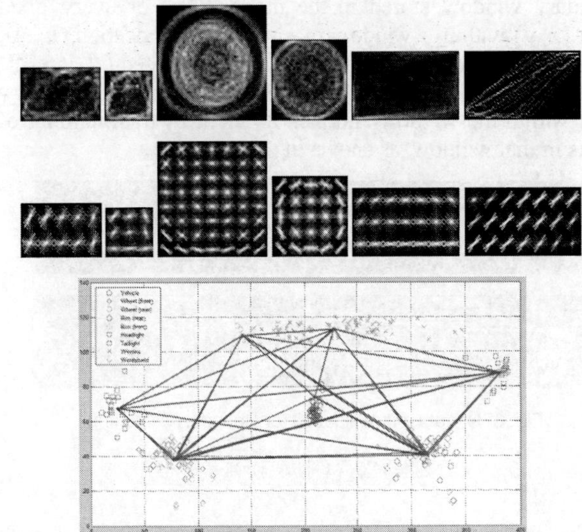

Fig. 2. Boundary & HOG distribution for each Component (Headlight, Taillight, Wheel, Rim, Window, Shield).

III. Object Recognition

The object recognition process is divided into two stages: an approximation process, Hypothesis Generation, is first applied to quickly restrict the searching areas; then a more comprehensive matching, Hypothesis Validation, is performed to verify the generated hypotheses by recognising each component and examine their inter-spatial relationships.

Thresholding is applied to determine when recognition in a specific feature space is achieved. Standard deviation is computed between feature maps from individual samples and feature means stored in the object model. Thresholds are set dynamically, depending on whether the recognition is applied to the global object level, or local component level. For the hypothesis generation at a global object level, we set the threshold to be within 3 standard deviations away from the mean value to ensure we include the maximum number of true positive hypotheses. Whereas for the hypothesis validation, we set the threshold for each component at each feature space to be within 1 standard deviation from the mean, in order to filter out as many false positive hypotheses as possible, and therefore increase the recognition accuracy.

A. Hypothesis Generation

For the hypothesis generation, the exhausted sliding window searching is applied over a set of scales, scanning through the whole image to generate potential object hypotheses. The set of scales are pre-defined covering from 5% to 50% of the size of the processing image.

Boundary detection is first applied to each processing image patch P, to extract its boundary map B_P, as shown in Figure 3. Each candidate window, shown in top row, is compared against the boundary distribution map of the global object stored in the object model, shown in bottom row. The boundary map B_P is then segmented into 8x8 pixel windows, and each window B_P^n is compared against the corresponding boundary window stored in the model B_M^n. For every pixel point (x, y) within a window of size $X \times Y$ at location (h, w), we measure the difference of the intensity between B_P^n and B_M^n, by summing up the boundary intensity difference for every point within the window and then divide it by total number of points in that window, as shown in (4).

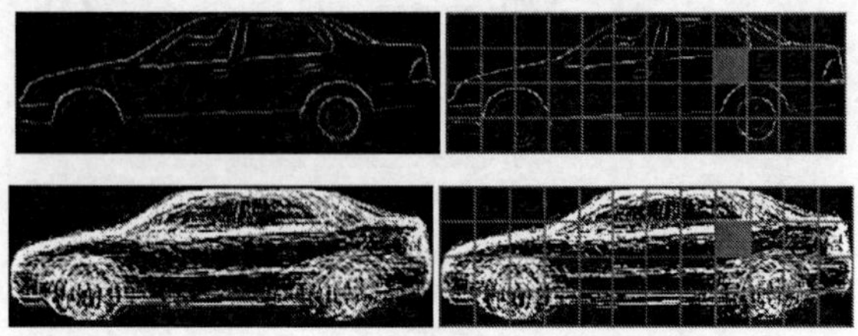

Fig. 3. Hypothesis Validation for Boundary Matching.

$$\beta(h, w) = \frac{\sum_{x=1}^{X}\sum_{y=1}^{Y} 1 - \left| \|B_S(x,y)\| - \overline{B_M(x,y)} \right|}{X \times Y} \quad (4)$$

The processing sample is converted into a 1-D vector, each element in the vector represents the boundary intensity difference for a corresponding window at location (h, w). A mean boundary vector β_M is extracted in the same way from the model's boundary histogram map. The boundary distribution matching ω for the object is calculated using Mahalanobis distance between β_P and β_M, shown in (5). Every sample that pass the pre-defined matching threshold is considered to be a potential object candidates. Thus a set of candidates $H: \{h_1, h_2, \ldots, h_m\}$ output from the hypothesis generation is collected and passed into the hypothesis validation process to verify the recognition.

$$\omega = \sqrt{(\beta_S - \beta_M)^T S^{-1} (\beta_S - \beta_M)} \quad (5)$$

B. Hypothesis Validation

Hypothesis generation provides a set of locations, where there are potentially high probabilities of being identified as object instances. For all the hypotheses that passed the threshold during the hypothesis generation process, they are treated as potential object candidates, and decomposed into sub-regions according to the object model for further validation. Hypothesis validation examines the corresponding sub-regions of the extracted hypotheses and attempt to validate the hypotheses by identifying its essential sub-components according to the object model. The component recognition result is then consolidated together to validate the recognition of the whole object. The recognition at local component level is carried out in three feature spaces, boundary distribution (ε), histogram of oriented gradient (θ), and intensity histogram (i).

For the validation of boundary distribution ε_i for each component, it is similar like the boundary distribution matching at the global object level. For any particular component i, we divide the boundary map B_{S_i} into 4×4 pixel windows and calculate the boundary distribution $\beta_i(h, w)$ for each window at location (h, w). We then compute the boundary distribution matching ε_i between the processing image region B_{S_i} and model B_{M_i}, in the form of Mahalanobis distance (6).

$$\varepsilon_i = \sqrt{\left(\beta_{S_i} - \beta_{M_i}\right)^T S^{-1} \left(\beta_{S_i} - \beta_{M_i}\right)} \quad (6)$$

For the histogram of oriented gradient θ, we compute HOG feature for every 8×8 pixel window for each component i to generate a HOG map G. Within each window, we use the direction with the highest gradient intensity to represent the gradient of the window, shown in (7); and the HOG matching between sample ϑ_{S_i} and model ϑ_{M_i} is calculated in Mahalanobis distance shown in (8).

For intensity histogram γ, we convert the gray scale intensity map of the process image into a 32-bit histogram μ_{S_i} and compute the Mahalanobis distance between the processing image μ_{S_i} and the histogram in model μ_{M_i}, shown in (9).

The final recognition for each component is the sum of the matching result from all three feature spaces multiplied by its corresponding weighting W, shown in (10). Object hypotheses with validation scores that pass the threshold are considered to be the correct hypotheses.

$$\vartheta_i\left(G(h, w)\right) = \max\left(G(h, w) \times [1^{-1}, 0, 1]\right) \quad (7)$$

$$\theta_i = \sqrt{\left(\vartheta_{S_i} - \vartheta_{M_i}\right)^T S^{-1} \left(\vartheta_{S_i} - \vartheta_{M_i}\right)} \quad (8)$$

$$\gamma_i = \sqrt{\left(\mu_{S_i} - \mu_{M_i}\right)^T S^{-1} \left(\mu_{S_i} - \mu_{M_i}\right)} \quad (9)$$

$$Score = \sum_{n=1}^{N}(\varepsilon_i \times W(\varepsilon_i) + \theta_i \times W(\theta_i) + \gamma_i \times W_n(i)) \quad (10)$$

IV. Experiment

We compare the performance of the proposed method of semantic visual decomposition modelling (SVDM) against popular existing recognition methods: contour template matching (CTM) [15], top-down and bottom-up segment merging/splitting (TDBU) [9], and part-based deformable models (PBDM) **Error! Reference source not found.**.

A. Dataset

The training samples for model construction are extracted from street scene images in MIT LabelME dataset [16], an online dataset allowing customised annotations at component level. Object model is built on 40 training samples selected containing sufficient visual details for each annotated component. The recognition performance is evaluated using the MIT StreetScene dataset. The MIT StreetScene dataset contains professionally labelled and verified annotations at a contextual object level. We compared the recognition results against state-of-the-art methods and also against the manually annotation benchmark provided within MIT StreetScene dataset.

B. Contour Template Matching (CTM)

Contour template matching is a simple but classic recognition method based on matching the boundary orientation of an object candidate with the contour model. The distances between the centre point O and the intersection point m at a particular angle are measured between the object candidate and the contour model, stated in (11). Two intersection points are considered to be a matching pair if their distance differences within a pre-defined threshold and an object instance contain sufficient matching pairs identified to support the hypothesis.

$$Dis(O,m) = \sqrt{(O_x - m_x)^2 + (O_y - m_y)^2} \quad (11)$$

In this work, we set to examine the contour matching with different numbers of distance pairs between the candidate window and the vehicle model; different thresholds in distance variation and different threshold for the number of matching. In general, the method has fast execution; however, the recognition is easily tempered by noise regions. For instance, foliage regions are often matched with any shape due to the large amount of evenly distributed noise edges generated due to the illumination changes. Increasing the number of distance pairs and thresholds is able to improve the recognition accuracy. The consequence is that the computation complexity also increases proportionally to the number of pairs involved in the recognition.

C. Top-Down and Bottom-Up Matching (TDBU)

Combination of top-down and bottom-up (TDBU) is a recognition method using template matching guided by the segmentation maps from the two extreme directions. Going through the coarse segmentation maps in a top-down approach is able to restrict the searching areas for the detecting object. Once the locations of the potential object hypothesis are identified, a bottom-up approach is applied to look into the hypothesis locations to validate the hypotheses by merging or splitting the segments in those locations with the guidance of the detailed segmentation maps.

The targeted image is firstly over-segmented, and individual segments are recursively merged base on the colour and texture saliency against the adjacent segments. A hierarchy of segment maps can be generated from the merging order, with few distinctive segments on the top of the hierarch and over-segmented regions at the bottom. Going through the hierarchy from top to bottom, a set of hypotheses can be generated by matching the overlapping area between the template and the grouped segments in the hypothesis location.

The main drawback of the TDBU method is that it does not cope well in recognising objects with complicated background. Since its performance is heavily influenced by the initial over-segmentation. In other words, the detecting object cannot be recognised if it cannot be separated from the surrounding segments in the merging decision tree. Furthermore, TDBU turns to be computational intensive when processing complicated real life images, in which the detecting objects are small comparing the background. The situation is worsened when the detecting objects is visually indistinguishable from the background areas.

D. Part-Based Deformable Modelling (PBDM)

The part-based deformable modelling method described in this paper is based on the work of Felzenszwalb [25] based on histogram of oriented gradient (HOG). Like other codebook based approaches, the parts-based deformable model is constructed using a loosely supervised approach by training the object model using labelled object samples; however, leaving the recognizable inner parts of the object to deform in a unsupervised way. Template model used by Felzenszwalkb is shown in Figure 15. Hypotheses are generated through a coarse matching at the root level and the hypotheses are further reinforced by a deformable parts matching, aiming to capture the detailed patterns that are not visible at the coarse level.

PBDM performs the recognition at two levels. A quick object detection is carried out in a sliding window approach at coarse root level; then recognition for its deformable parts at a refined level. The object recognition result is the summation of the recognition score for each deformable part, computed by comparing the HOG feature map θ extracted for each image patch $P(x,y)$ against the object model M at scale $w \times h$. M_0 is the coarse level object model and M_i^N are the individual deformable parts in the object model.

In HOG vehicle model, the most distinctive features is concentrated around the wheel regions, while the other vehicles regions can be described as horizontal HOG features. Matching this HOG model against image patches is sufficient to robustly separate the vehicle instances from the rest regions even in such a challenging dataset with complicated background. However the recognition performance reduces when processing images containing horizontal representation in the HOG feature space. Furthermore, Fellzenszwalb's method only requires marking the whole training samples with bounding boxes; and leave objects' inner components to "self-deform" based on visual integrity. Those inner parts are only grouped based on visual similarity. They encapsulate limited semantic information and thus cannot be used to assist in filtering out semantics false position hypotheses.

E. Semantic Visual Decomposition Modelling (SVDM)

SVDM extracts and analyses features in the forms of the histogram of boundary, histogram of oriented gradient and intensity histogram. Instead of generating the inner components using an unsupervised deformable approach, SVDM encapsulates both the visual appearances and the spatial relationships of the inner components into the object model based on object annotations provided with the training dataset. In the recognition process, template matching is performed for each component, examining boundary, HOG, and intensity histogram at the specific locations based on the spatial map stored within the object model.

Template matching is applied across the whole image using a sliding window approach to generate object hypotheses. Figure 4 (a) is a processing image sample, we analyse it through the hypotheses generation to output a hypotheses map recording where each hypothesis is located and its similarity matching, showing as the intensity in the map, against the object model, shown in Figure 4 (b). For each object hypothesis generated, recursive matching is applied to identify the components that form the object to validate the hypothesis, as shown in Figure 4 (c) to (g). The final recognition result is the combination of hypothesis generation result at the object level with the hypothesis validation result at the component level, shown in Figure 4 (h). Comparing with the PBDM, with a more restricted validation process deployed during the recognition, the SVDM approach is able to filter out false positives that are generated during the hypothesis generation process.

The SVDM also experiences the side effect that troubles many component based recognition methods, but unlike other, the proposed method can recover from the effect of low thresholds since the validation stage can eliminate most of the false positives. Another type of misrecognitions (false positives) can be generated when recognitions at component level over-rules the recognition at the vehicle level. For example, the wheels and wheel rims from two different vehicles are extracted at their expected locations are matching with high confidence to form a vehicle object. So the SVDM starts to generate misrecognition by stitching components from different objects that match the recognition model. This can be eliminated by increasing the threshold in the hypothesis generation stage to minimise the number of candidate objects to be considered, and therefore restricting the object-level matching to allow for too many false positive objects.

F. Method Evaluation

Headings For the performance comparison across the different methods we used a subset from the MIT StreetScene dataset by randomly selecting 80 images containing 150 vehicle instances from the side view and mixing them together with 80 randomly selected street images with no vehicle present. The number of vehicle instances and the location for each vehicle instance is not restricted in the image set. The manual annotation of this subset of StreetScene images is considered by the research community as ground truth for recognition performance evaluation.

To evaluate the performance of the recognition, we consider a vehicle instance to be identified correctly if the recognition result has an intersection ratio that is greater 90% with the manual annotation provided in the MIT StreetScene dataset. With the recognition validation at component level, thresholding is applied to determine if a key component is identified. As explained previously, the threshold is set to be the mean plus 1 standard deviation. Based on the results obtained from the experiments, the proposed SVDM method (see Figure 5 and Table I) outperformed both CTM and TDBU methods, and it is also able to deliver a matching performance against the PBDM method based on HOG feature. Like the

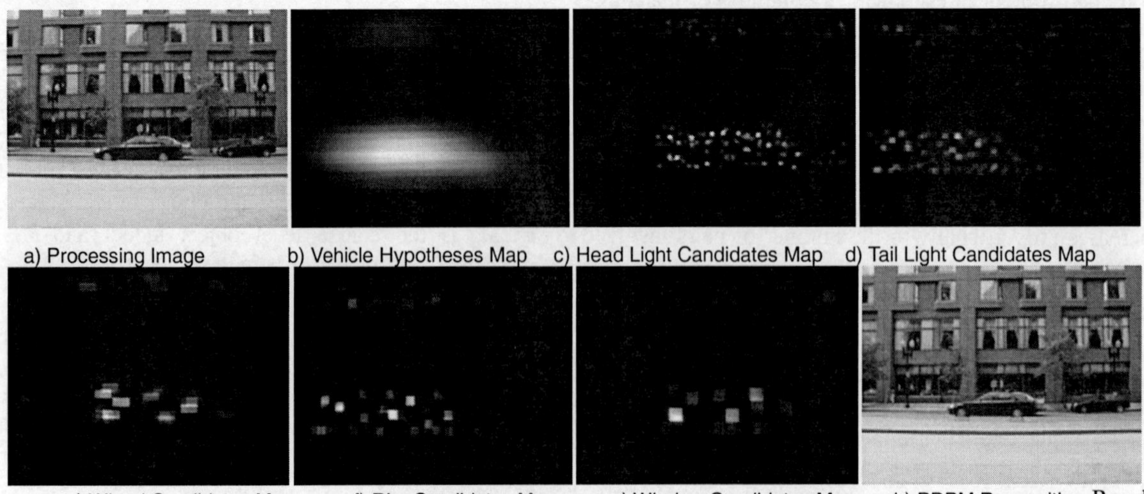

Fig. 4. Semantic Virtual Decomposition Modelling (SVDM) process for validating the hypothesis.

PBDM method, SVDM has a high recall (97% and 95% respectively) and therefore retrieves most objects from the scene, but the proposed PBDM method has slightly better precision (61% against 59% for the PBDM) and therefore a higher F-measure, at 0.74, which is the highest against all other methods overall.

In general, the proposed method works well with vehicle recognition due to its highly structural representation. With a tight threshold, the proposed SVDM is able to generate more accurate recognition result comparing to the PBDM method. However, when a loose threshold is applied, the SVDM does not handle as well as the PDBM method and it is easier to confuse vehicle instances with background patches that share similar visual patterns.

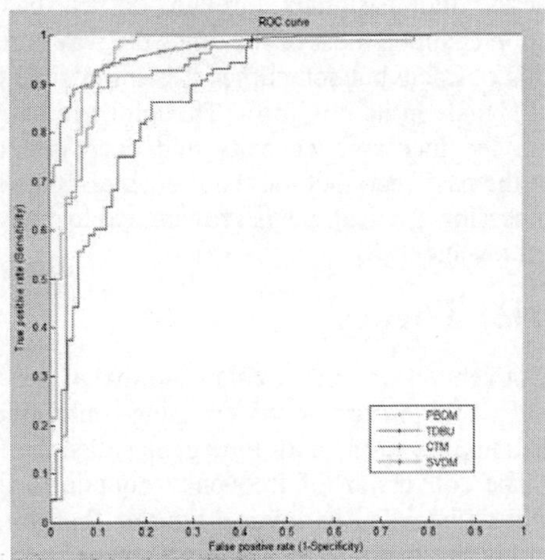

Fig. 5. Performance Comparison.

TABLE I. RECOGNITION RESULT COMPARISON

Method	Recognition Performance		
	Precision	Recall	F-measure
CTM	42%	88%	0.5686
TDBU	62%	73%	0.6705
PBDM	59%	97%	0.7337
SVDM	61%	95%	0.7429

V. ACKNOWLEDGMENT

In conclusion, we proposed a method to automatically construct object models by analysing visual and semantic spatial characteristics of each object's compositional inner-parts. The proposed method is built on the boundary and Histogram of Oriented Gradient (HOG) features. Comparison is carried out against existing benchmark recognition methods such as CTM, TDBU, and PBDM over the same dataset. The proposed SVDM method is able to generate an improvement in the recognition accuracy comparing with those popular detection methods, with the added benefit of having an automatic way of generating models for object detection.

Further work will be focused in extending the SVDM to monitor objects from multiple classes. For example, SVDM can be extended to monitor scene recognition by using statistical analysis focusing mainly on the co-occurrence and spatial relationships between objects of difference classes instead of visual appearances of inner object components. Other features can also be considered for the object recognition, so that more false positives can be discarded.

REFERENCES

[1] J. Harel, C. Koch, et al, "Graph-based visual saliency", *Proceedings of Neural Information Processing Systems*, pp. 545-552, 2006

[2] S. Bileschi and L. Wolf, "A Unified System For Object Detection, Texture Recognition, and Context Analysis Based on the Standard Model Feature Set", *British Machine Vision Conference*, 2005.

[3] J.R. Smith, F.F. Chang, "VisualSEEK: a fully automated content-based image query system", *Proceedings of ACM Multimedia*, pp. 87-88, 1997.

[4] Y. Rui, T.S. Huang, et al, "Relevance feedback: a power tool in interactive content-based image retrieval", *IEEE transaction in Circuits Systems Video Technol. Vol.8 (5)*, pp. 644-655, 1998.

[5] J. Vogel, and B. Schiele, "Semantic Modeling of Natural Scenes for Content-Based Image Retrieval", *Journal of Computer Vision*, Vol.72, pp. 133-157, 2007.

[6] L. Li, R. Socher, et al, "Towards Total Scene Understanding: Classification, Annotation and Segmentation in an Automatic Framework", *the Joint VCL-ViSU workshop*, 2009.

[7] Oliva, A. and Torralba, A. "Modeling the Shape of the Scene: A Holistic Representation of the Spatial Envelope", *International Journal of Computer Vision*, vol.42, vol.3, pp.145-175, 2001.

[8] M. A. Grudin, "On internal representations in face recognition systems", *Pattern Recognition*, vol.33 (7), pp. 1161-1177, 2000.

[9] E. Borenstein, J. Malik, et al, "Combining Top-down and Bottom-up Segmentation", *IEEE Conf. on Computer Vision and Pattern Recognition*, 2004.

[10] A. Oliva and A. Torralba, "Modeling the shape of the scene: A holistic representation of the spatial envelop", *International Journal of Computer Vision*, pp. 145-175, *2001.*

[11] A. Torralba. "Comtextual priming for object detection", *Internatioal Journal of Computer Vision*, pp. 169-191, 2003.

[12] M. Boutell, A. Choudhury, Jiebo Luo, and C. M. Brown, "Using Semantic Features for Scene Classification: how Good do they Need to Be?", IEEE Intl. Conf. on Multimedia and Expo, pp. 785-788, 2006.

[13] M. R. Boutell, J. Luo, C. M. Brown, "Scene Parsing Using Region-Based Generative Models" IEEE Transactions on Multimedia, vol.9(1), pp. 136-146, December2006

[14] G. Qin and B. Vrusias, "Adaptable Models and Semantic Filtering for Object Recognition in Street Images", *Int. Conf. on Signal and Image Processing Applications*, 2009.

[15] G. Qin, B. Vrusias, and L. Gilliam, "Background Filtering for Improving of Object Detection in Images", *International Conference on Pattern Recognition*, 2010.

[16] B. C. Russel, and A. Torralba, "LabelME: a database and web-based tool for image annotation", *International Journal of Computer Vision*, vol.77, pp.157-173, 2008.

[17] David Martin, Charless Fowlkes, and Jitendra Malik, "Learning to detect natural image boundaries using local brightness, color, and texture cues", *IEEE Trans. PAMI*, vol 26, pp. 530–549, 2004.

[18] Dalal, N, "Histograms of oriented gradients for human detection", *Computer Vision Pattern Recognition, IEEE Computer Society, 2005.*

[19] Felzenszwalb, P. F., Girshick, R. B., et al. "*Object detection with discriminatively trained part-based models", IEEE transactions on pattern analysis and machine intelligence,*vol.32, pp. 1627-1645, 2010.

Image Compression, Comparison between Discrete Cosine Transform and Fast Fourier Transform and the problems associated with DCT

Imdad Ali Ismaili [1], Sander Ali Khowaja [2], Waseem Javed Soomro [3]
[1]Institute of Information and Communication Technology, University of Sindh, Jamshoro, Sindh, Pakistan
[2]Institute of Information and Communication Technology, University of Sindh, Jamshoro, Sindh, Pakistan

Abstract - The research article focuses on the Image Compression techniques such as. Discrete Cosine Transform (DCT) and Fast Fourier Transform (FFT). These techniques are chosen because of their vast use in image processing field, JPEG (Joint Photographic Experts Group) is one of the examples of compression technique which uses DCT. The Research compares the two compression techniques based on DCT and FFT and compare their results using MATLAB software, Graphical User Interface (GUI). These results are based on two compression techniques with different rates of compression i.e. Compression rates are 90%, 60%, 30% and 5%. The technique allows compressing any picture format to JPG format. The result shows that DCT is better technique than FFT; however the compression results are same as that of 30% compression to 5% compression reflecting not significant change in visual results excepting the file size varying to small fraction. The compression technique works fine with the images having little noise but the compression technique due to its lossy nature don't work very well in medical images such as CT, X-ray etc.

Keywords: *Image Compression, JPEG, Discrete Cosine Transform, Fast Fourier Transform, Image Processing*

1 Introduction

As we can analyze that demand for multimedia data through the mobile network and conveniently accessing the concerned data through mobile services is growing day by day. In order to make the multimedia data usage efficient and insidious it is essential that the data representation and techniques for encoding the data at different platforms or in all applications should follow the same standard. In all multimedia data categories image data has got the highest preference because of its usage and lion's share in terms of the bandwidth consumption for multimedia communication. Due to this it is very necessary as well as a challenge for the researchers to develop efficient methods for image compression for effective and efficient use of bandwidth.

In spite of many disadvantages of analog representation of signals compared to digital counterpart, they need smaller number of bits for storage and transmission. For example, a low-resolution television quality color video of 36 frames/sec where each frame comprises of 800 x 600 pixels need more than 240 Mbps for storage, so the digitized color video for the duration of 1 hour will almost require 96 Gbps for storage. Similarly, the requirement for the HDTV will be much higher than the calculations mentioned above; this increases the bandwidth requirement of the channel which is very costly. This is the challenging part for the researchers to transmit theses digital signals through limited bandwidth communication channel, most of the times the way is found to overcome this obstacle but sometimes it is impossible to send these digital signals in its raw form. Though there has been a revolution in the increased capacity and decreased cost of storage over the past years but the requirement of data storage and data processing applications is growing explosively to out space this achievement.[8]

2 Fourier Theory

Conversion of Time domain or spatial description i.e. pixel by pixel description of an image into frequency domain which applies to the entire image is called the Fourier Transform. The conversion of frequency domain to the real space description is called its inverse Fourier Transform. We can easily study the function as it is represented as the series of sum of Sines and Cosines but it has a disadvantage of very complex computation. [4]

3 Discrete Fourier Transform

The Discrete Fourier Transform (DFT) is the study of Fourier analysis of finite-domain discrete time signals. The DFT is central to many kinds of signal processing, including the analysis of compression of video and sound information. DFT requires large number of multiplications and additions for the calculation. For example a 8-point DFT, there are 8 complex multiplications and 7 complex additions, that's why DFT is computed efficiently using a Fast Fourier Transform (FFT) algorithm. [4]

4 Fast Fourier Transform

To find the N-DFT of a given sequence, we only need to compute the N/2 complex coefficients, while the second N/2 complex coefficients can be achieved by manipulating the data from the first calculation. Hence N-point DFT requires N2 additions. But with Decimation in Time algorithms, it requires computing two times N/2-point DFT. Therefore, number of additions required is

$$2\left(\frac{N}{2}\right)^2 = 2\left(\frac{N^2}{4}\right) = \frac{N^2}{2} \quad (1)$$

Therefore, the complexity is halved. This is how FFT uses Decimation in Time algorithm to reduce the computational time for DFT computation. So, we can say that FFT is a faster version of DFT.

Most of the information is contained in low frequency components as they are associated with the pattern in the image. Details in the image are provided by high frequency components, but they are very susceptible to noise which causes spurious effects, it is easier to remove the noise in frequency domain by just applying the masks to the image within the frequency domain. Many filters in image processing are based on FFT.

5 Discrete Cosine Transform

The transformation of two-dimensional matrix of pixel values into an equivalent matrix of spatial frequency components can be carried out using a mathematical technique known as the discrete cosine transform (DCT). The transformation operation itself is lossless, apart from some small rounding errors in mathematics but once the equivalent matrix of spatial frequency components, known as coefficients, has been derived then any threshold can be dropped. It is only at this point that the operation becomes lossy.

6 Methodology

One of the most popular standards used for compression is JPEG standard. It is also known as baseline mode or lossy sequential mode which is based on DCT and is adequate for most compression applications, the input and output images are limited to eight bits, while the quantized DCT coefficient values are restricted to 11 bits. The DCT is a mathematical function that transforms image data from the spatial (pixel by pixel processing) to the frequency domain. For an M x N image, the spatial domain represents the color value of each pixel. The frequency domain considers the image data as 2-dimensional waveform and represents the wave form in terms of its frequency components.

7 Image Processing

Image processing is the field in which an image is processed to extract some of the information or features embedded in it. These features or information can be fetched by processing photographs or video frames. Digital Image processing refers to the processing applied on to the digital image which contains finite number of elements at a particular location and value and are referred as Pixel or Picture elements. Pixel is said to be the smallest element in the image. Monochrome images varies in intensity from black to white and the color image stores 3 numbers for each pixel which are red, green and blue.

8 JPEG Algorithm

Discrete Cosine Transform is the real transform which makes it more attractive then Fourier Transform. The DCT has excellent energy compaction properties. For a typical image, most of the visually significant information is present in just a few coefficients of the DCT. For this reason, the DCT is often used in image compression applications. DCT is defined for 1-D as well as 2-D signals as shown in below equations 1 & 4 respectively.

$$C(u) = a(u)\sum_{x=0}^{N-1} f(x)\cos\left[\frac{(2x+1)u\pi}{2N}\right], u = 0,1,\ldots,N \quad (2)$$

Whereas

$$a(u) = \left\{\sqrt{\frac{1}{N}} \quad for\ u = 0\right. \quad (3)$$

$$a(u) = \left\{\sqrt{\frac{2}{N}} \quad for\ u = 1,\ldots,N-1\right.$$

(4)

$$C(u,v) = a(u)a(v)\sum_{x=0}^{N-1}\sum_{y=0}^{N-1} f(x,y)Cos\left[\frac{(2x+1)u\pi}{2N}\right]Cos\left[\frac{(2y+1)v\pi}{2N}\right] \quad (5)$$

$$f(x,y) = \sum_{u=0}^{N-1}\sum_{v=0}^{N-1} a(u)a(v)C(u,v)\,Cos\left[\frac{(2x+1)u\pi}{2N}\right]Cos\left[\frac{(2y+1)v\pi}{2N}\right] \quad (6)$$

Where as a(u) is defined as above in equation (3) & (4) and u,v=0,1,.....,N-1

9 Quantization

In theory, providing the forward DCT is computed to a high precision using say, floating point arithmetic, there is a very little loss of information during the DCT phase. Although in practice small losses occur owing to use of fixed point arithmetic, the main source of information loss occurs during the quantization and entropy encoding stages, where the compression takes place.

The sensitivity of the eye varies with spatial frequency, which implies that the amplitude threshold below which the eye will detect a particular spatial frequency also varies. In practice, therefore, the threshold values used vary for each of the 64 DCT coefficients. These are held in a 2-dimensional matrix known as the quantization table with the threshold value to be used with a particular DCT coefficient in the corresponding position in the matrix, so the threshold value is important and in practice it is compromise between the level of compression that is required and the resulting amount of information loss that is acceptable.

$$\begin{bmatrix} 10 & 10 & 15 & 20 & 25 & 30 & 35 & 40 \\ 10 & 15 & 20 & 25 & 30 & 35 & 40 & 50 \\ 15 & 20 & 25 & 30 & 35 & 40 & 50 & 60 \\ 20 & 25 & 30 & 35 & 40 & 50 & 60 & 70 \\ 25 & 30 & 35 & 40 & 50 & 60 & 70 & 80 \\ 30 & 35 & 40 & 50 & 60 & 70 & 80 & 90 \\ 35 & 40 & 50 & 60 & 70 & 80 & 90 & 100 \\ 40 & 50 & 60 & 70 & 80 & 90 & 100 & 110 \end{bmatrix} \quad (7)$$

10 Need for Compression

The importance of these compression techniques are discussed above. However there are always preferences to these applications. Bandwidth availability is not the same everywhere, sometimes it is very difficult to arrange the internet facility or establish a communication network in an area where the infrastructure is not meeting our needs. By allowing such rates of compression we are giving flexibility as to what extent they can bear the loss of information. These areas may include Flood affected areas, areas which are recently struck by a storm etc.

11 Applications

Following are the applications in which these compression techniques can be used.

1. E-Health Systems
2. Telemedicine
3. Video Conferencing
4. Monitoring and Surveillance

These are the major applications where these compression techniques can be used and the need for using is a compulsion because remote areas have limited resources, bandwidth limitation is one of the limited resources which need more financial requirements.

12 Tools

To show the results for this compression technique MATLAB i.e. Matrix Laboratory is used. Reason for using this tool is that MATLAB is very popular nowadays in every educational institution and is very sophisticated in use of simulation and design purposes. Results of this research paper uses MATLAB Guide (Graphical user interface) so that is should be user friendly.

13 Results

Results are shown below in the following figures using DCT and FFT Respectively.

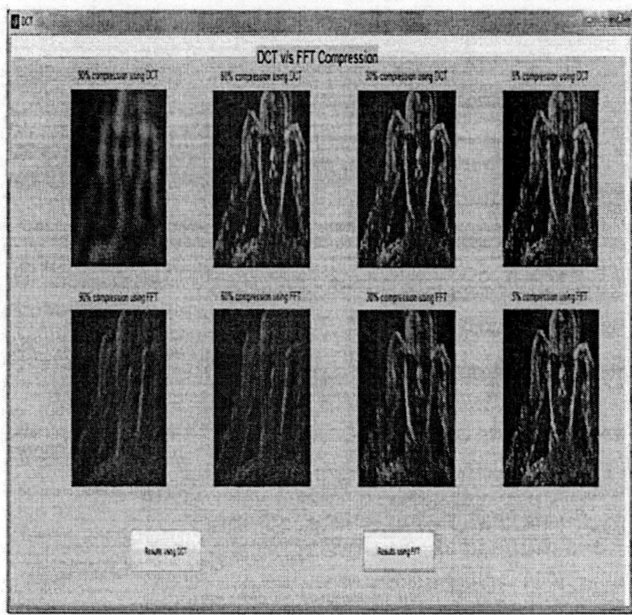

Fig. 1 Image Compression using DCT and FFT

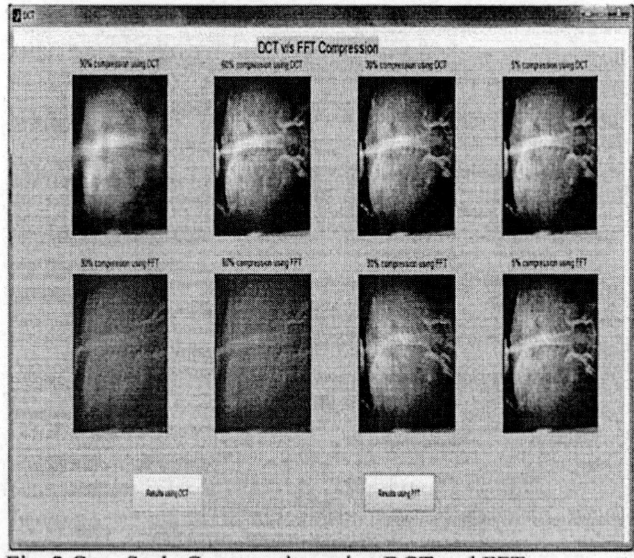

Fig. 2 Gray Scale Compression using DCT and FFT

TABLE I

Shows the comparison for both techniques with respect to the file size

S. No	Color Type	Technique	Compression Rate	Original Size	Compressed Size
1	RGB	DCT	90%	10KB	1.8KB
2	RGB	DCT	60%	10KB	2.94KB
3	RGB	DCT	30%	10KB	3.26KB
4	RGB	DCT	5%	10KB	3.27KB
5	RGB	FFT	90%	10KB	1.77KB
6	RGB	FFT	60%	10KB	2.23KB
7	RGB	FFT	30%	10KB	2.97KB
8	RGB	FFT	5%	10KB	3.21KB
9	Grayscale	DCT	90%	12KB	1.70KB
10	Grayscale	DCT	60%	12KB	2.24KB
11	Grayscale	DCT	30%	12KB	2.32KB
12	Grayscale	DCT	5%	12KB	2.33KB
13	Grayscale	FFT	90%	12KB	1.67KB
14	Grayscale	FFT	60%	12KB	1.87KB
15	Grayscale	FFT	30%	12KB	2.16KB
16	Grayscale	FFT	5%	12KB	2.28KB

14 Conclusion

This paper shows the results for JPEG Compression using FFT and DCT implemented in MATLAB Graphical User Interface (GUIDE). This interface has been tested on all types of images but one of the main problems associated with the compression techniques is the blocking technique which breaks the image into block of 8 x 8, 16 x 16 or bigger. The higher the compression ratio is applied these blocks start to become visible which is also said the blocking effect. It can be tolerated in the normal image but in medical imaging loss of information at this extent have no forbearance. So our future work is to develop an algorithm for compressing the medical images minimal losses or no losses as well as the encryption technique which can be implied to the images.

15 References

[1] Gonzales Rafael C., Woods Richard E. & Eddins Steven L. [Digital Image Processing]

[2] Ahmed, N., Natarajan,T., and Rao, K.R. "Discrete Cosine Transform", IEEE Trans. Computers, 90-93, Jan1974

[3] Rao, K.R. and Yip,P. " Discrete Cosine Transform: Algorithms, Advantages, Applications" Academic Press, Boston, 1990

[4] Martucci, S.A. "Symmetric convolution and the discrete sine and cosine transforms", IEEE Trans. Signal Processing SP-42, 1038-1051(1994).

[5] An anonymous FTP site for more JPEG documentation is : ftp.uu.net/graphics/jpeg/.

[6] Feig,E., Winograd,S., "Fast algorithms for the discrete cosine transform", IEEE Transactions on Signal Processing 40 (9), 2174-2193 (1992).

[7] Halsall Fred, [Multimedia Communication], Pearson Publications

[8] Acharya, Tinku and Ray, Ajoy K., [Image Processing, Principles and Applications], Wiley Publications

[9] Chowdhry,Z.M., Ismaili,I.A. and Baloch,A.K. "Compression Algorithm for Low and High Spatial Frequency Images" Mehran University Research Journal of Engineering & Technology, Vol.23, No.3, (July 2004)

Pseudo 2D Hidden Markov Model Based Face Recognition System Using Singular Values Decomposition Coefficients

Mukundhan Srinivasan
Department of Electronics & Communication Engineering
Alpha College of Engineering
Chennai, TN India
mukundhan@ieee.org

Sabarigirish Vijayakumar
Retail Domain
Tata Consultancy Services (TCS)
Chennai, TN India
sabarigirish@ieee.org

Abstract— **A new Face Recognition (FR) system based on Singular Values Decomposition (SVD) and pseudo 2D Hidden Markov Model (P2D-HMM) is proposed in this paper. The state sequence of the pseudo 2D HMM are modeled independently which gives superior results when compared to regular 2D HMMs. As a novel point presented here, we have maintained a limited number of quantized Singular Values Decomposition (SVD) coefficients as features vectors describing blocks of face images. This makes the FR system more robust and less complex. Experiments are carried out to evaluate the proposed approach on the Olivetti Research Laboratory (ORL) face database. In order to reduce the computational complexity and the process memory consumption the images are resized to a specific dimension in the JPEG format. The system achieves a recognition rate of 99.5% which is much better than the recognition rates of the previous HMM approaches.**

Keywords— Face Recognition (FR), Singular Values Decomposition (SVD), pseudo 2D Hidden Markov Model (P2D-HMM)

I. INTRODUCTION

Face Recognition has been an prominent area of research in the image processing and pattern recognition domains. Over the past two decades, numerous FR researches and studies have been carried out in the field of Computer Vision (CV) [1]. FR has many real-time applications like biometrics, surveillance, security access control, Human Computer Interaction (HCI), robotic vision, video indexing and smart environments. These applications demand robust, accurate, efficient, fast and easily trainable Face Recognition (FR) systems. Research and studies in attempt to achieve these goals has led to rapid development of cheap and yet so very competent FR system that has ultimately commercialized the system.

Face Recognition from static images and dynamic sequences is an active research area with numerous applications as stated above. An excellent attempt to survey FR is given in [1]. Despite many achievements, however, external parameters such as pose variation, discrepancy in illumination, facial expression, gender recognition and twins' recognition are still a paradox. A human face is a very complex object with features varying over the time domain and thus a FR system must operate under many varying parameters. In order to avoid these problems, a perspective based approach was initiated and developed [2]. This approach was carried out in two stages; the first process was to calculate the face images' orientation and alignment and the second step was to recognize these faces using a dataset of corresponding images.

The success of HMM in speech processing and recognition was well noted. The HMM when proposed in [3] had a very similar approach by nature. The architecture proposed in [3] was extended and refined by Nefian's work in [4]. In spite of implementing DCT as observational vectors the system had some flaws with respect to the effect of illumination, expression and pose. In this paper, we propose an advanced FR system that is based on Pseudo 2D Hidden Markov Model (P2D-HMM) and SVDs as feature vectors. It is evident that this proposed method is stable and suitable for providing solution to face recognition problems due to the two-dimensional wrapping capabilities of P2D-HMM. A major point of novelty of our approach is the fact that the FR system proposed works directly on JPEG standards without any necessity of decompressing the images before recognition. We consider this as a practical advantage over the other face recognition systems.

II. RELATED LITERARY WORK

There are several face recognition methods. Some common face recognition methods are Geometrical Feature Matching [5], Eigen faces method [6,7], Bunch Graph Matching (BGM) [8], Neural Networks (NN) [9,10], Support Vector Machines (SVM) [11], Elastic Matching [7] and Hidden Markov Models (HMM) [4]. We briefly review some of the notable approaches.

The first approach, proposed by Kanade [5] in the 70's, were based on geometrical features. Geometrical Feature Matching techniques are based on the extraction of a set of geometrical features forming the picture of a face. Their system achieved 75% recognition rate on a database of twenty persons, using two images per person; one for training and the other for test. In summary, geometrical feature matching techniques do not provide a high degree of accuracy and also are rather time-consuming. The other approach, one of the well-known face recognition algorithms, is Eigen faces method [6,7]. This method uses the Principal Component Analysis (PCA) to project faces into a low dimensional space. This method showed to be not very robust versus the variations of face orientation.

In [6], the authors reported 90.5% correct recognition on ORL database. In summary, eigen faces method is a fast, simple and practical method. However, it generally does not

Affiliation:
Both the authors Mukundhan Srinivasan and Sabarigirish Vijayakumar are *IEEE Members*.

provide invariance over changes in scale and lighting conditions. Neural Networks is one of the approaches which have been used in many pattern recognition tasks. The attractiveness of using neural networks could be due to their ability in nonlinear mapping. The paper [10] used Probabilistic Decision- Based Neural Network (PDBNN) for face recognition which had been capable to recognize up to 200 people and could achieve up to 96% correct recognition rate. In general, neural network approaches encounter problems when the number of face classes increases. The last approach is the stochastic modeling of non-stationary vector time series based on Hidden Markov Models (HMM) which has been widely used in recent years.

III. THE METHODOLOGY

A. *HMM for Training and Classificaion*

The proposed FR approach is based on pseudo two-dimensional Hidden Markov Model (P2D-HMM). The Hidden-Markov Models are a set of statistical models used to represent and characterize the statistical properties of a signal [12].

Every HM model consists of two correlated processes layers: (*i*) an underlying unobservable Markov chain with finite number of states, their transition probability matrix and an initial state probability distribution matrix and (*ii*) a set of probability density function (PDFs) that are associated with each individual state.

After each iteration, a transition to another state depending on the transition probability matrix is carried out and a vector is

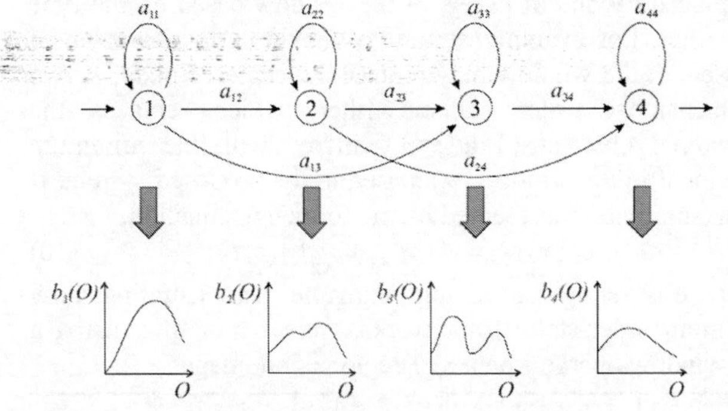

Figure 1. 1D-HMM with four states PDFs.

created depending on a probability density function (PDF) which is assigned to each state. Figure 1 shows a 1D-HMM with four states and assigned PDFs. We first describe the 1D-HMM and then extend the P2D-HMM from this.

1) *1D Hidden Markov Model*

The fundamental elements to build a HMM are listed below:

Layer (*i*)

- N = $|S|$ is the number of states in the model, where $S = \{s_1, s_2, \dots, s_N\}$ is a set of all possible states. The state model at any arbitrary time t is given by $q_t \in S, 1 \leq t \leq T$, where T is the length of the observation sequence.
- M = $|V|$ is the number of different observations vector symbols, where $V = \{v_1, v_2, \dots, v_N\}$ is a set of all possible feature vectors v_i. The feature vector at any arbitrary time t is given $o_t \in V$.
- A', the state transition probability matrix is given by $A = \{ai, j\}$ where

$$a_{i,j} = P[q_t = S_j | q_{t-1} = S_i]\ 1 \leq i, j \leq N \quad (1)$$

With the constraints, $0 \leq a_{i,j} \leq 1$, and

$$\sum_{j=1}^{N} a_{i,j} = 1, 1 \leq i \leq N \quad (2)$$

- 'B', the observational vector probability matrix is given by $B = \{b_j(k)\}$, where

$$b_j(k) = P[O_t = v_k | q_t = S_j],\ 1 \leq j \leq N; 1 \leq k \leq M \quad (3)$$

- '∏', the initial state distribution, i.e. $\prod = \{\mu_i\}$ where

$$\pi_i = P[q_1 = S_i], 1 \leq i \leq N \quad (4)$$

Expressing the corresponding matrix 'A', 'B', '∏' in a canonical form, we have:

$$\lambda = (A, B, \prod) \quad (5)$$

It must be mentioned that, this above representation corresponds to a discrete hidden model, wherein the observations are discrete vectors chosen from a finite set $V = \{v_1, v_2, \dots, v_N\}$.

Layer *(ii)*

The most general characterization of the probability function (pdf) is a finite mixture of the form as below:

$$b_i = \sum_{k=1}^{M} c_{ik} N(O, \mu_{ik}, U_{ik}),\ 1 \leq i \leq N \quad (6)$$

where c_{ik} is a set of coefficients for the kth mixture in the state *i*. Generally the function $N(O, \mu_{ik}, U_{ik})$ is said to be a Gaussian PDF with mean and covariance matrix μ_{ik} and U_{ik} respectively.

This probability can be effectively calculated by the Forward-Backward Algorithm.

2) *Pseduo 2D Hidden Markov Model*

An extension of 1D-HMM to work on two-dimensional vectors are Pseudo 2D-HMM [13,14]. When compared to a

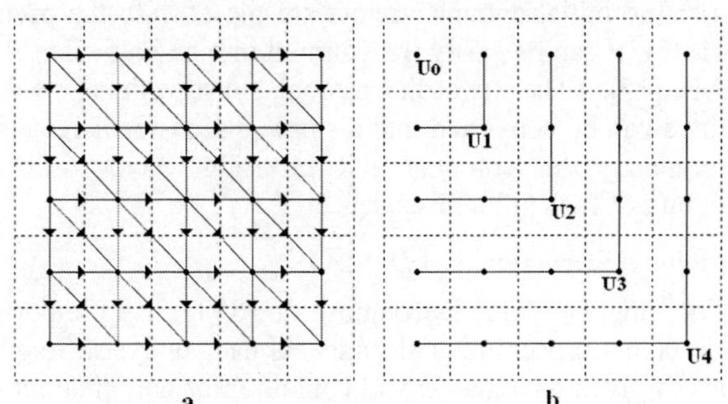

Figure 2. (a) State transition diagram for 2D-HMM (b) decomposed sub-state sequence.

2D-HMM the sate sequences in the columns are independently modeled of the state sequence of the neighboring columns. The state sequence transition diagram for a 2D-HMM is shown in figure 2.

Pseudo 2D-HMMs are nested 1D-HMMs. A superior HMM models the sequence of columns in an image. The super states have 1D-HMM to model the rows inside the columns. Figure 3 shows a pseudo 2D-HMM with four super states containing three states of 1D-HMM in each super state.

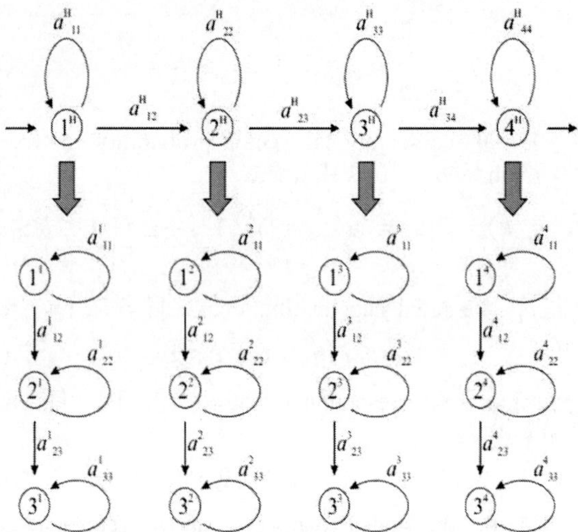

Figure 3. Pseudo 2D-Hidden Markov Model.

The shown P2DHMM has linear structure which implies that only self-transition and transitions to the corresponding super states are possible. The joint probability over all possible states sequence is:

$$P(O|\lambda) = \sum_{q\in Q^X} \pi^H_{q1} P_{q1}(x) \prod_{x=2}^{X} a^H_{qx} P_{qx}(x) \quad (7)$$

$$P_i(x) = \sum_{q\in Q^X} \pi^i_{q1} b_{q1}(O_{x1}) \prod_{y=2}^{Y} a^i_{q_{y-1}q_y} b_{q1}(O_{xy}) \quad (8)$$

and can be calculated by two nested Forward-Backward Algorithms.

After the initial column vectors are placed into the pseudo 2D-HMM, it can be easily transformed into an equivalent 1D-HMM [15]. The two-dimensional observational vector obtained can be converted into a single dimensional sequence by scanning the columns and inserting vector and the beginning of each column sequence.

B. Feature Extraction – SVD

The Singular Value Decomposition (SVD) is an important tool in signal processing and statistical data analysis. Singular values of given data matrix will contain information about the noise levels, the energy, the rank of the matrix, etc. As singular vectors of a matrix are the span bases of the matrix, and orthogonally normal, they can exhibit some features of the patterns embedded in the signal. SVD provides a new way for extracting algebraic features from an image vector. A singular value decomposition of an $m\times n$ matrix X is any function of the form:

$$X = U\Sigma V^T \quad (9)$$

where $U(m\times n)$ and $V(m\times n)$ are orthogonal matrix, and $\Sigma(m\times n)$ is a diagonal matrix of singular values with components $\sigma_{ij} = 0, i \neq j$ and $\sigma_{ij} > 0$.

Moreover, it can be proved that there exists non unique matrices U and V such that $\sigma_1 \geq \sigma_2 \geq \cdots \geq 0$. The columns of the orthogonal matrices U and V are called the left and right singular vector respectively. These matrices are mutually orthogonal [16].

The main theoretical property of SVD relevant to face image recognition is its stability on face image. Singular values represent algebraic properties of an image [17]. So because of these reasons and some experimental results, we find out that SVD is a robust feature extraction technique for face images.

Many FR systems commonly use preprocessing to improve the performance. In this proposed system we implement a order static filter which directly affects the speed and recognition rate.

1) Filtering

The order-static filters are non-linear filter that work on the spatial domain. Their operations are as follows; a sliding window moves from left to right and top to down with steps of size one pixel, at each situation the centered pixel is replaced by one of pixels of the window based on the type of filter. For example minimum, maximum and median of pixels of the window may replace the centered pixel. A two dimensional order statistic filter, which replaces the centered element of a 3×3 window with the minimum element in the window, was used in the proposed system. It can simply be represented by the following equation.

$$f(x,y) = Min_{(s,t)\in S_{xy}}\{g(s,t)\} \quad (10)$$

Figure 4 shows a simple example demonstrating how minimum order-static filter works. Here a min filter using a 3×3 window operates on a 3×3 region of an image.

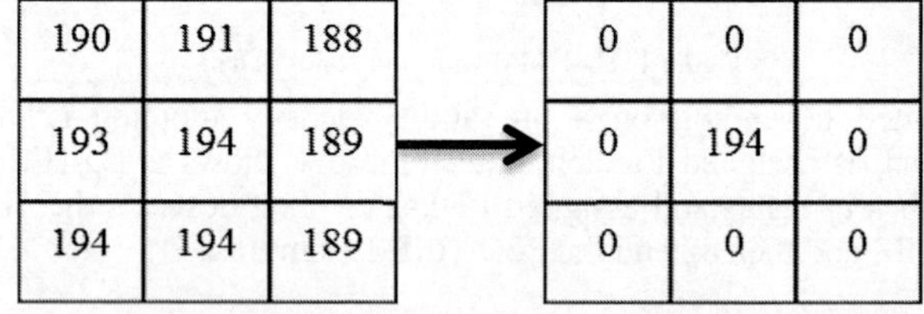

190	191	188
193	194	189
194	194	189

→

0	0	0
0	194	0
0	0	0

Figure 4. Operation of minimum order static filter

It is evident that this filter has smoothening effect and reduces the information of the image.

2) Quantization

SVD coefficients are continuous values. These coefficients built the observation vector. As we propose to implement a discrete HMM, these continuous values need to be quantized. This is carried out by the process of rounding off, truncation, or by other nonlinear process.

Consider a vector $X = \{x_1, x_2 \dots x_3\}$ as the continuous components. Suppose X needs to be quantized into D levels. Thus the difference between any two successive values will be:

$$\Delta_i = \frac{x_{max} - x_{min}}{D} \quad (11)$$

Once the value of Δ_i is known it can be replaced with the quantized values as:

$$x_{quantized} = \frac{x_i - x_{min}}{\Delta_i} \quad (12)$$

Thus all components of X will be quantized.

C. Classification

The next step is the statistical classification base on the HMM. A HMM is trained for every subject in the database using the Baum-Welch (BW) Algorithm is used to determine the probability of each face image with the test image.

We use, for recognition purposes the Viterbi Algorithm since it is faster than the Forward-Backward algorithm. It also allows automatic segmentation of the face images. This is shown in figure 5.

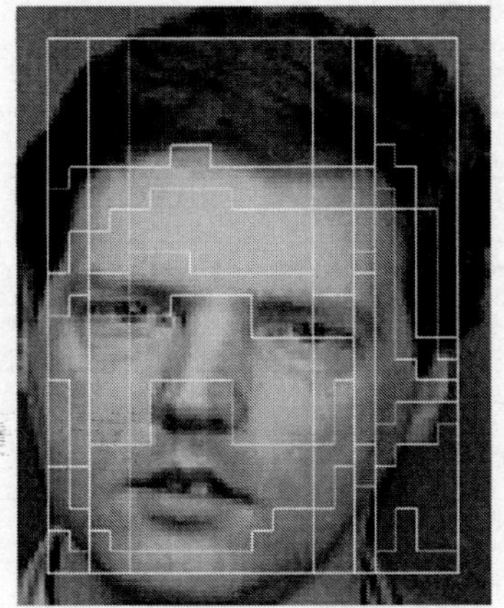

Figure 5. Segmentation of the Human Face.

The image to be recognized is matched with the person whose face model has the highest probability on the tested image.

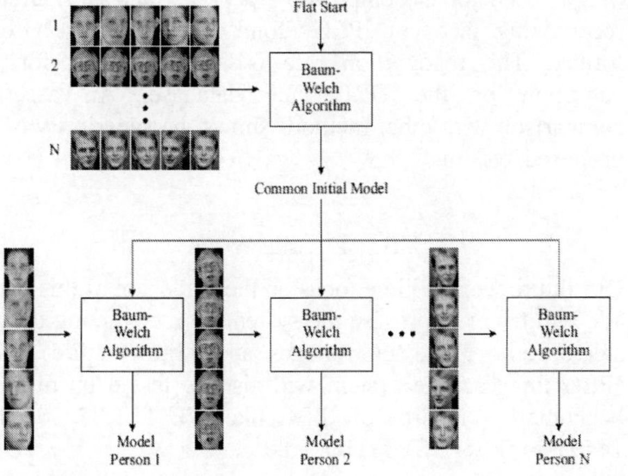

Figure 6. Training Process.

The BW algorithm is used to train the HMM for each person gives the HMM parameters corresponding to a maximum likelihood function depending on the initial model parameters as in [17]. Thus, it is vital to have good initial model for the HMM. We train a general model common to all subjects and then model them individually. The common model is refined to the face model of a subject in particular. Figure 6 shows this process.

D. Recognition

The recognition system works as the algorithm described in figure 7. After extracting the observational vectors from the training phase, the probability of the observational vector is computed.

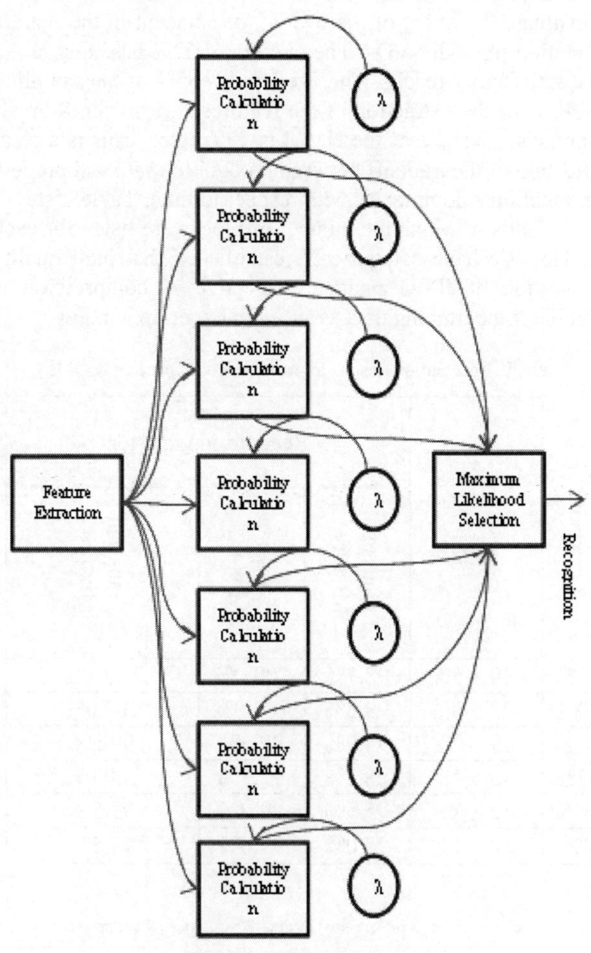

Figure 7. Recognition Process.

IV. Experimental Results

The proposed recognition system is tested against the ORL face database. This database contains 40 face images of 10 test subjects captured in different poses, expressions and illumination conditions. The images are resized to 64×64 resolution to reduce the complexity. The first five images of each subject is used to train the model and the next set of five images is used for testing the FR system.

The FR system is tested on different quadratic sizes with linear structures and one to three Gaussian components for the PFDs. As the number of states increases the computational time also increases. Table 1 shows recognition rates for the testing parameters.

TABLE I. Recognition Results for various states and components

States (m×n)	Component 1	Component 2	Component 3
2×2	81.0%	99.5%	100.0%
4×4	97.0%	100.0%	100.0%
6×6	98.5%	100.0%	100.0%
8×8	100.0%	100.0%	100.0%

An experiment was carried out with different block in order to evaluate the effect of the overlap of adjacent in the feature extraction through SVDs. The overlap of 62% has emerged to give satisfactory results. The overlap of ~65% of the sampling window for the extraction of the features varies from 0 pixels to 6pixels. The size of the HMM is 7×7 states. This is a clear indication of the tradeoff between recognition rate and process computational complexity with respect to time. Table 2 shows these results in which the number of blocks are listed for each overlap. We have categorically established that high quality recognition of JPEG image irrespective of compression is possible if the training data as sufficient overlap window.

TABLE II. Recognition Results for various Block Overlaps & GMs

Overlap (%)	Blocks (M×N)	Recognition rate for		
		1 Gaussian Mixture	2 Gaussian Mixture	3 Gaussian Mixture
65%	40 × 50	98.7%	100.0%	100.0%
50%	27 × 35	99.5%	100.0%	100.0%
35%	19 × 23	98.0%	99.5%	99.5%
27%	15 × 18	98.2%	99.5%	100.0%
10%	12 × 15	95.5%	99.0%	99.5%
0%	10 × 13	93.0%	99.0%	99.5%

V. JUXTAPOSITION WITH EXISTING SYSTEMS

The below Table 3, shows a comparison of the different FR systems tested on the ORL database. The recognition rate of our proposed system is clearly higher than the other systems on this database.

The proposed algorithm is developed in MATLAB environment using an Intel Core i7 processor @ 3.40 GHz.

The first ever P2D-HMM was presented in [15] with a recognition rate of 94.5%. The major point of difference is that our approach is that the use of SVD coefficients for feature extraction instead of gray values or DCTs. In addition to this, the column of the image vector is modeled independently i.e. as super states while in [15] the row are modeled as super states. The modeling of columns has an advantage over the rows because variation in pose of the face image can be tackled by columns.

TABLE III. Comparative results on ORLDB

Method (Learning algorithm + Feature Extraction)	**Percentage of Error (%)**	**Reference**
Sliding HMM + Grey tone	13%	[18]
Eigenface	~10%	[6]
Pseudo 2D HMM + Gray tone	5%	[15]
EBGM	<20%	[7]
PDNN	5%	[10]
Continuous n-tuple classifier	~3%	[19]
Up-Down HMM + DCT`	16%	[20]
Correlation matching	15%	[21]
Ergodic HMM + DCT	>0.5%	[22]
P2D HMM + DCT	0-0.1%	[23]
SVM + PCA	3%	[11]
ICA	15%	[24]
Gabor filter + rank	~9%	[25]
Markov Random Fields	13%	[26]
Pseudo 2D-HMM + SVD	<0.5%	This paper.

VI. CONCLUSION

In this paper, a Face Recognition system is described based on Pseudo 2D-Hidden Markov Model (P2D-HMM) and Singular Vector Decomposition (SVD) which is capable of recognizing faces in JPEG (Joint Picture Expert Group) format. The recognition rate is nearly perfect for test condition of the ORL face database. An assertive comparison with other methods shows the superiority of the proposed system.

VII. FUTURE WORK

Our future work will be focus on the extension of this paper. We will try to improvise the system by recognizing derived stereoscopic 3D JPEG images and Mutli-Picture format JPEG images. The system will also be tested on different benchmark standards of JPEG like ITU-T T.87, ISO/IEC 14495-1 (JPEG-LS), ITU-T T.801

REFERENCE

[1] R. Chellapa, C. Wilson, S. Sirohey, Human and machine recognition of faces: a survey, Proc. IEEE 83.

[2] A. Pentland, B. Moghadam, T. Starner and M. Truk, " View based and modular eignspaces for face recognition," in Proceedings on IEEE Computer Society Conference on Computer Vision and Pattern Recognition, pp. 84-90, 1994.

[3] F. Samaria and S. Young. HMM-based architecture for face identification. Image and Vision Computing,12(1994)8, 537–543.

[4] A. Nefian and M. Hayes. An embedded HMM-based approach for face detection and recognition. IEEE Int. Conf. on Acoustics, Speech and Signal Processing, Phoenix, AZ, 1999, 3553–3556.

[5] Kanade T. "Picture Processing by Computer Complex and Recognition of Human Faces," Technical report, Dept. Information Science, Kyoto Univ., 1973.

[6] Turk M. and Pentland A., "Eigenfaces for Recognition," J. Cognitive Neuroscience, Vol. 3, No. 1, pp. 71-86, 1991.

[7] Zhang J., Yan Y., and Lades M. Face recognition: eigenface, Proceedings of the IEEE, Vol. 85, No. 9, elastic matching and neural nets. September 1997.

[8] Wiskott L., Fellous J.-M., Krüger N., and Vondder malsburg C.. "Face Recognition by Elastic Bunch Graph Matching" IEEE Transaction on Pattern Analysis and Machine Intelligence, Vol 19, No 7, pp. 775-779, July 1997.

[9] Lawrence S., Giles C.L., Tsoi A. C., and Back A.D., "Face Recognition: A Convolutional Neural-Network Approach," IEEE Trans. Neural Networks, Vol. 8, pp. 98-113, 1997.

[10] Lin S., Kung S., and Lin L.. "Face Recognition/Detection by Probabilistic Decision- Based Neural Network" IEEE Trans. Neural Networks, Vol 8, No 1 pp. 114–131, January 1997.

[11] Guo G., Li S. Z., , and Kapluk C.. "Face recognition by support vector machines," Image and Vision Computing, Vol. 19, No. 9-10, pp. 631–638, 2001.

[12] L Rabiner and B. Young, "Funadamentals of Speech recognition. Englewood Cliffs, NJ: Prentice-Hall, 1993.

[13] O. E. Agazzi and S.S. Kuo Pseudo Two-Dimensional Hidden Markov Model for Document Recognition, AT&T Technical Journal 72 (5) (Oct 1993) 60-72.

[14] E. Levin and R. Pieraccini, Dynamic Planar Wraping for Optical Character Recognition, Proc. IEEE Int. Conf. on Acoustics, Speech and Signal Procewssing (ICASSP), San Francisco, Califonia, March 1992, pp 149-152.

[15] F. Samaria, Face Recogniton using Hidden Markov Model, PhD thesis, Engineering Department, Cmabridge University, October 1994.

[16] Hong Z., "Algebraic feature extraction of image for recognition," Pattern Recognition, Vol. 24, No. 4, pp. 211-219, 1991.

[17] L Rabiner, A utorial on Hidden Markov Model and Selected Applications in Speech Processing, Proc. Of the IEEE 77 (2) Oct 1993.

[18] Samaria F. and Harter A.. "Parameterization of a Stochastic Model For Human Face Identification," In Proceedings of IEEE Workshop on Applications of Computer Vision, Sarasota, Florida, December 1994.

[19] Lucas S. M., "Face recognition with the continuous n-tuple classifier," In Proceedings of British Machine Vision Conference, September 1997.

[20] Nefian A. V. and Hayes M. H.. "Hidden Markov Models for Face Recognition," In Proceedings IEEE International Conference on Acoustics, Speech and Signal roccessing (ICASSP), pp. 2721–2724, Seattle, May 1998.

[21] Lam K. M. and Yan H., "An analytic-to-holistic approach for face recognition on a single frontal view," IEEE Transactions on Pattern Analysis and Machine Intelligence, Vol. 20, No. 7, pp. 673–686, 1998.

[22] Kohir V. V. and Desai U. B., "Face recognition using DCTHMM approach," In Workshop on Advances in Facial Image Analysis and Recognition Technology (AFIART), Freiburg, Germany, June 1998.

[23] Eickeler S., Mller S., and Rigoll G., "Recognition of jpeg compressed face images based on statistical methods," Image and Vision Computing, Vol. 18, No. 3, pp. 279–287, 2000.

[24] Yuen P. C. and Lai J. H., "Face representation using independent component analysis," Pattern Recognition, Vol. 35, No. 6, pp. 1247–1257, 2002.

[25] Ayinde O. and Yang Y., "Face recognition approach based on rank correlation of gabor filtered images," Pattern Recognition, Vol. 35, No. 6, pp. 1275–1289, 2002.

[26] Huang R., Pavlovic V. and Metaxas D. N., "A Hybrid Face Recognition Method using Markov Random Fields," IEEE, 0-7695-2128-2, 2004.

[27] A. P. Dempster, N. M. Laird, and D. B. Rubin, "Maximum likelihood from incomplete data via the em algorithm," Journal of the Royal Statistical Society: Series B, vol. 39, no. 1, pp. 1–38, 1977.

[28] L. E. Baum, T. Petrie, G. Soules, and N. Weiss, "A maximization technique occurring in the statistical analysis of probabilistic functions of markov chains," Ann. Math. Stat., vol. 1, pp. 164–171, 1970.

[29] Mukundhan Srinivasan and Vijayanarayanan.A "Independent Component Analysis of Edge Information for Face Recognition under Variation of Pose and Illumination," in Proceedings of Fourth International Conference on Computational Intelligence, Modelling and Simulation(CimSIM2012), pp226-231, Sept. 2012.

[30] Bicego M., Castellani U., and Murino V., "Using Hidden Markov Models and Wavelets for face recognition," In Proceedings IEEE International Conference on Image Analysis and Processing (ICIAP), 0-7698-1948-2, 2003.

Improved Region of Interest for Infrared Images Using Rayleigh Contrast-Limited Adaptive Histogram Equalization

S. Erturk

Kocaeli University Laboratory of Image and Signal processing (KULIS)

41380 Kocaeli, TR

Abstract—**This paper presents an improved approach for region of interest (ROI) extraction in infrared (IR) images using Contrast-Limited Adaptive Histogram Equalization (CLAHE). Previous approaches use global image enhancement to increase the accuracy for ROI extraction in IR images. It is shown in this paper that the performance can be increased significantly using a local enhancement approach. CLAHE is used for this purpose in this paper to facilitate local image enhancement in an efficient way. It is shown that the proposed approach improves the ROI extraction performance.**

I. INTRODUCTION

Detection and tracking of targets in infrared (IR) images is an important task particularly for defence and security applications. However detecting targets in infrared images can be challenging because of changing environmental conditions, sensor noise and low signal-to-noise ratio imaging [1].

The region of interest (ROI) in the infrared image basically comprises image parts that potentially include any target of interest. In practice, the target of interest can be stationary or moving. In terms of application and utilization the ROI extraction process can be categorized into two approaches: human detected region of interest (hROI) which makes use of a human operator to identify ROIs, and algorithmically (or automatically) detected region of interest (aROI) which does not require user intervention and obtains the ROI automatically according to image characteristics through image processing [2]. This paper proposes a novel approach for the second case.

In case of video and moving targets it is possible to use optical flow [3], background difference [4,5] or frame difference for ROI extraction and potential target detection. However, these approaches are likely to fail in case of stationary targets. Furthermore in some applications it might not be possible to use a series of images from the same scenery, which might for example be the case if the infrared camera is mounted on a moving platform.

In cases of stationary targets or changing scenery, segmentation and threshold based approaches are typically in order to detect potential targets and extract ROI. In [6], the ROI extraction is accomplished using an intensity threshold that is adaptively obtained as

$$TH = \max\{I\} - \text{Intensity Margin} \quad (1)$$

where the intensity margin can be adjusted according to image characteristics to determine correct and false detection rates. In [7] it is noted that the ability of previous approaches to obtain an appropriate threshold value changes significantly across different scenes. Therefore an approach to consistently define a suitable threshold value has been developed in [7] and the ROI threshold is obtained as

$$TH = \arg\min_{\mathrm{TH}} \{\textstyle\sum_{i=1}^{TH} H(I_{ad}) \geq k \times A\} \quad (2)$$

where $H(I_{ad})$ shows the histogram of the smoothed intensity adjusted image, A is the total area of the histogram and k is a variable that can be used to adjust correct detection and false detection rates.

This paper proposes to improve the approach presented in [7] using a local enhancement approach. Contrast-Limited Adaptive Histogram Equalization (CLAHE) is utilized for this purpose in the threshold detection process. It is shown that the proposed approach significantly improves the ROI extraction performance.

II. Contrast-Limited Adaptive Histogram Equalization (CLAHE) of IR Images

Ordinary image histogram equalization (HE) uses the information derived from the entire (global) image histogram to transform all pixels of the image. HE is a successful enhancement approach if the distribution of pixel values is similar throughout the image. However, when the image contains regions that are significantly lighter or darker than most of the image, which is the typical case in IR images, the contrast in those regions is not sufficiently enhanced [8].

For infrared images that typically contain regions (typically targets) that are lighter than the overall image, local or adaptive histogram equalization (AHE) that uses local information to obtain a transformation function from the neighbourhood pixels is required for successful enhancement. The local neighbourhood used in AHE is usually referred to as image tile. Hence, AHE operates on image parts (usually referred to as image tiles), rather than the entire image. For each pixel, a window around that pixel to cover the neighbourhood region, as shown in Fig.1, is utilized to obtain the transformation function of that pixel. In this way, the enhancement is performed in a local approach. This approach is applied to all pixels in the image. The transformation function is obtained just as in regular histogram equalization and the difference in AHE is only that a local image part is utilized in the enhancement process. The window size, or neighbourhood size, is a variable parameter that can be adopted according to image resolution, content and desired effect. To reduce computational load it is possible to divide the image into non-overlapping blocks (tiles) and apply AHE to each individual tile separately. In this case usually interpolation across block (tile) boundaries is utilized to avoid discontinuities.

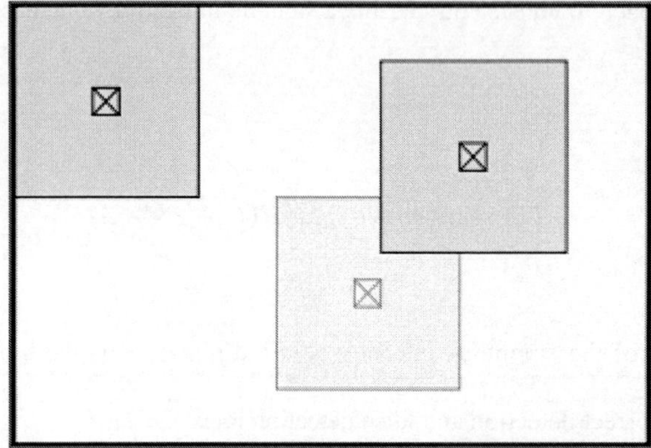

Fig.1. Neighbourhood window in AHE [12].

An important practical limitation of AHE is that image regions that are fairly homogenous can cause amplification of noise because in this case a narrow range of pixel values are mapped to the entire visualization range. Contrast limited AHE (CLAHE) was developed to prevent this over-amplification of noise in homogenous regions [9]. In histogram equalization the transformation function is obtained using the cumulative distribution function (CDF) of pixel values. The contrast amplification is given by the slope of the transformation function that is proportional to the slope of the CDF. CLAHE limits the amplification amount thereby avoiding undesired results in locally homogenous regions of the image. This is accomplished by clipping the histogram at a pre-defined fixed or adaptive value before computing the CDF to limit the slope of the CDF and hence limiting the slope of the transformation function. Uniform regions in an image tile will cause high peaks in the histogram in the corresponding pixel values. Originally, in CLAHE the part of the histogram that is above a certain level (clip limit) is redistributed among all histogram bins, as shown in Fig. 2, and because high values in the histogram are avoided through this approach, the slope of the CDF and in turn the slope of the transformation function will be limited.

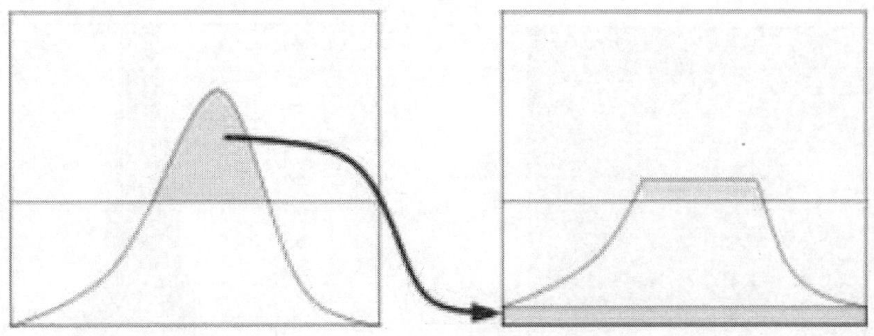

Fig2. Clipping of histogram in CLAHE [12].

In some applications, as in infrared imaging, a uniform re-distribution is not preferred because it distributes the corresponding values evenly into the entire dynamic range without discriminating between background and foreground and thereby also amplifies noise to some extent [10]. In order to overcome this problem it is possible to utilize non-uniform distribution functions. The Rayleigh function is one of the popular non-uniform distribution functions used for this purpose, enabling the image contrast to be enhanced without saturating uniform and high intensity areas [10] The Rayleigh distribution facilitates superior distribution of intensities so that good background and target (ROI) separation can be accomplished. Note that some other non-uniform distributions such as Gaussian and exponential are also available for this purpose.

Rayleigh contrast-limited adaptive histogram equalization (RCLAHE) can be divided into the following steps [10]:

Step 1: Divide image into tiles into non-overlapping regions (tiles)

Step 2: For each tile construct the histogram and clip the histogram by the input clip value.

Step 3: Transform intensity values after histogram clipping into the Rayleigh distribution. This can be defined mathematically in the form of

$$g = g_{min} + \left[2 \propto^2 \ln\left(\frac{1}{1-P(f)}\right)\right]^{1/2} \tag{3}$$

where g_{min} is the minimum pixel values, $\propto$ is the Rayleigh distribution parameter, $P(f)$ shows the CDF and g is the computed pixel value. Note that a higher Rayleigh parameter ($\propto$) value results in increased contrast enhancement while increasing saturation and noise amplification.

Step 4: Use interpolation (usually bilinear) of the mapping of each pixel of neighbouring tiles to avoid discontinuity.

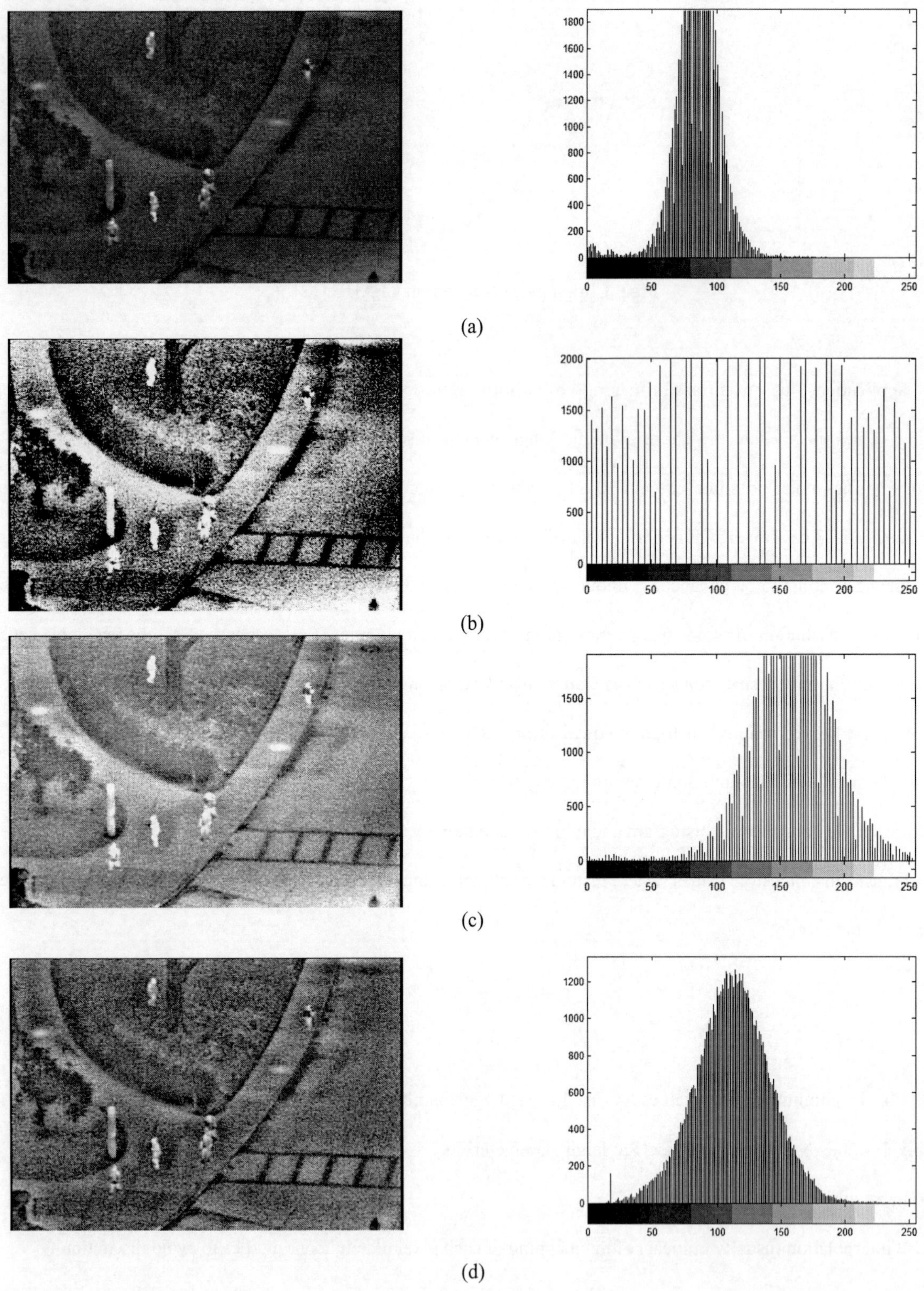

Fig. 3. (a) Sample IR image and histogram (b) Global HE result and histogram (c) Intensity adjusted result and histogram (d) RCLAHE result and histogram

Fig 3 shows a sample IR image together with the global HE result, the intensity adjusted result and the RCLAHE result together with the corresponding histograms. It is observed the RCLAHE provides superior enhancement in that the contrast in enhanced without over-saturation and over-amplification of noise.

In the proposed ROI extraction approach for infrared images the suitable threshold value of [7] has been adopted so that the ROI threshold is obtained as

$$TH = \arg\min_{\mathrm{TH}} \{\textstyle\sum_{i=1}^{TH} H(I_{RCLAHE}) \geq k \times A\} \quad (4)$$

where $H(I_{RCLAHE})$ shows the histogram of the Rayleight Contrast-Limited Adaptive Histogram Equalization Image, A is the total area of the histogram and k is a variable that can be used to adjust correct detection and false detection rates.

The utilization of RCLAHE as pre-process in the ROI extraction for infrared images enables superior performance by improving correct detection vs. false detection rates, as is shown in the experimental results section.

III. Experimental results

For comparison purposes the threshold detection approaches presented in [6] and [7] for ROI extraction in infrared images are utilized. To provide quantitative results, the OTCBVS Benchmark Dataset Collection [11] is used. Experimental results will be provided for Dataset 01: OSU Thermal Pedestrian Database, with 9 sequences (sequence 3 is excluded because it is in inverted form) having a total of 883 targets. Fig.4 shows the Receiver Operating Characteristic (ROC) curves for the approaches presented in [6] and [7]. The correct detection rate is the ratio of the number of correctly included targets in the ROI to the number of total targets present. The false detection rate is the ratio of the number of incorrectly included regions in the ROI (i.e. regions that are actually not targets) to the number of total targets present.

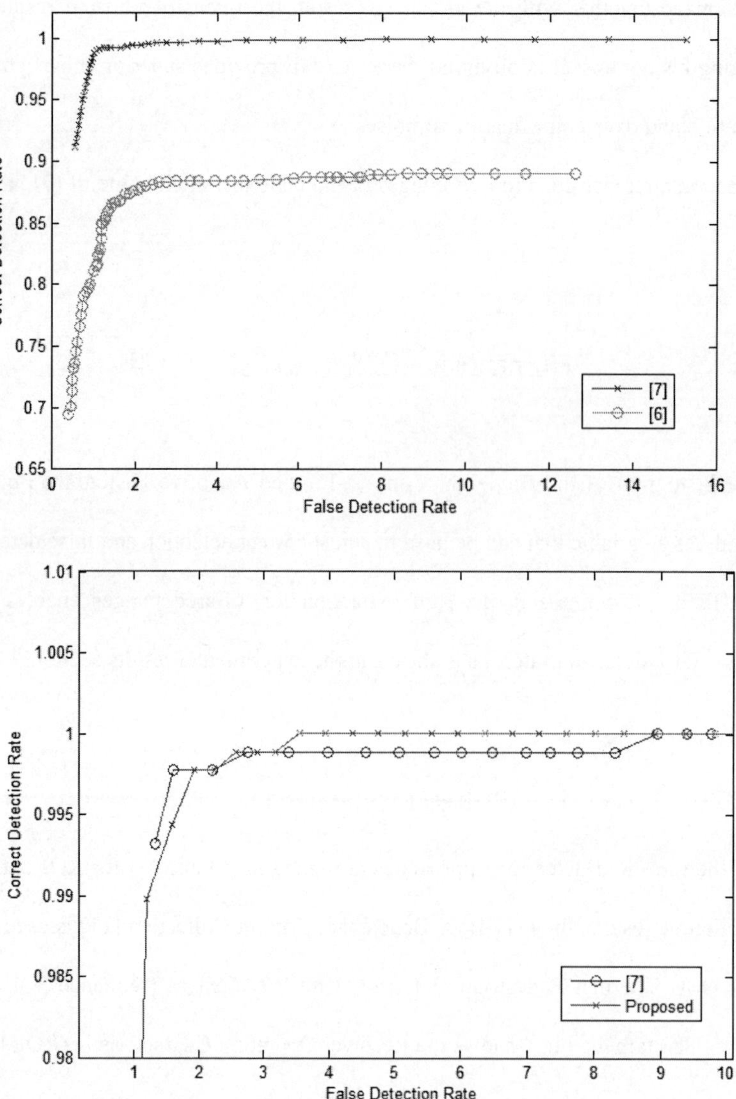

Fig 4. ROC curves for proposed approach, [6], and [7].

In the overall performance it is observed that the proposed approach as well as the method presented in [7] provides consistent threshold values for ROI extraction, which is not valid for the approach presented in [6]. An important point is the case in which all targets are correctly included in the ROI, i.e. the correct detection rate is unity. It is observed that the proposed approach provides lower false alarms in this case compared to the approach presented in [7]. For the 9 sequences used in the experimental results, in the case where all 883 targets are successfully included in the ROI extracted by the methods, the proposed approach provides only 3141 regions without target, while the approach presented in [7] provides 7901 regions without target. This is a significant reduction in ROIs that do not include any target, demonstrating that the proposed RCLAHE based approach provides superior performance.

IV. Conclusion

A novel approach for ROI extraction and potential target detection in IR images based RCLAHE is presented in this paper. Rayleigh Contrast Limited Adaptive Histogram Equalization is used to provide local enhancement of infrared images, improving the ROI detection accuracy. This information is used to obtain the final ROI of the infrared image. The process can be used as pre-processing in combination with other approaches to improve accuracy in future work.

Acknowledgment

This work has been partly supported by the Turkish State Planning Agency project number DPT 2011K120330 and the Scientific and Technological Research Council of Turkey (TUBITAK) as TEYDEB project number 7091014.

References

[1] Z. Shaoa, X. Zhua, Jun Liub, "Morphology infrared image target detection algorithm optimized by genetic theory", The International Archives of the Photogrammetry, Remote Sensing and Spatial Information Sciences. Vol. XXXVII. Part B4. Beijing, pp.1299-1304, 2008.

[2] C.M. Privitera, L.W. Stark, "Algorithms for defining visual regions-of-interest: comparison with eye fixations," IEEE Transactions on Pattern Analysis and Machine Intelligence. vol. 9, pp. 970-982, Dec. 2000.

[3] B. J. Fleet and D. Beauchemin, "Performance of optical flow-techniques," International Journal of Computer Vision. vol.1, pp. 42-77, December 1994.

[4] K. Toyarea, J. Krumm, B. Brumitt and B. Meyers, "Wallflower: Principles and practice of background maintenance", International Conference on Computer Vision, pp. 255-261, Sep. 1999.

[5] H.C. Kefeli, O. Urhan, S. Ertürk, "Double stage video object segmentation by means of background registration using adaptive thresholding", IEEE Signal Processing and Communications Applications Conference (SIU'2005), pp.80-83, May 2005.

[6] Y. Fang, K. Yamada, Y. Ninomiya, B.K.P. Horn, I. Masaki, "A shape-independent method for pedestrian detection with far-infrared images", IEEE Transactions on Vehicular Technology, Vol.53, No. 6, pp. 1679-1697, Nov. 2004.

[7] R. O'Malley, M. Glavin, E. Jones, "An Efficient Region of Interest Generation Technique for Far-Infrared Pedestrian Detection", International Conference on Consumer Electronics, ICCE, Jan. 2008.

[8] S. M. Pizer, E. P. Amburn, J. D. Austin, et al., "Adaptive Histogram Equalization and Its Variations". Computer Vision, Graphics, and Image Processing Vol. 39, pp. 355¬-368, 1987.

[9] K. Zuiderveld, "Contrast Limited Adaptive Histogram Equalization"., P. Heckbert: Graphics Gems IV, Academic Press 1994, ISBN 0-12-336155-9.

[10] Siavash Yousefi, Jia Qin, Zhongwei Zhi, Ruikang K. Wang, "Uniform enhancement of optical micro-angiography images using Rayleigh contrast-limited adaptive histogram equalization", Quantiative Imaging in Medicine and Surgery, Vol. 3, No 1, Feb 2013.

[11] IEEE OTCBVS WS Series Bench, J. Davis, M. Keck, "A two-stage approach to person detection in thermal imagery," Proc. Workshop on Applications of Computer Vision, Jan. 2005.

[12] http://en.wikipedia.org/wiki/Adaptive_histogram_equalization

Expert System Design for Cotton Harvesting Using Shape and Fractal Features

Mahua Bhattacharya[1*], Medhabi Verma[1], Vivek Shukla[1], S.S. Kohli[2], P Rajan[3]

1. Dept. of Information Communication Technology
Indian Institute of Information Technology and Management
Gwalior 474010 , India

2. Department of Science & Technology
Ministry of Science & Technology
New Mehrauli Road, New Delhi, India

3. CSIR CMERI Centre of Excellence for Farm Machinery,
Gill Road, Ludhiana, India

*corresponding author: bmahua@hotmail.com

Abstract— In present work authors have proposed methods based on machine vision for cotton boll plucking systems. We have used shape based features and also have used fractal features to study the level of maturity of the cotton boll to take a computer controlled decision to drive a electromechanical system. This will finally provide an expert system to find the decision regarding the maturity of the cotton boll. Based on this decision an electro mechanical system will be designed to perform the task of cotton boll picking.

Keywords- Cotton harvesting; image processing; shape based feature; fratcal; machine vision

I. INTRODUCTION

Agriculture is one of the biggest sectors in India. Cotton continues to occupy an important place as the premier crop of commerce in our country. Cotton boll & seed are important & critical link in the chain of agricultural activities as it contains in itself the blue print for the agrarian prosperity in incipient form [1]. Cotton picking is labour intensive job as it requires huge amount human labour for cotton picking which can be reduced by developing computer based automatic cotton plucking systems.

Over the past, many automatic cotton picking harvesting devices have been developed, which fall generally into three categories: mechanical harvesters, and vacuum harvesters. Their shortcoming depends on tendency of picking up dirt, broken branches, weed seeds, finely divided foreign material, maintenance and time taken for operation. Such solution will also provide the scope to reduce the losses and damage, by making the practice precise, which may occur during cotton harvesting. In this respect we may refer that the techniques of image processing and AI based methodologies in automation of agricultural products are well proven worldwide.

In present work, we propose a computer vision module for cotton harvesting equipment which could carry out automatic detection and harvesting of the ripe cotton bolls. Use of such techniques will require adequate control of autonomous harvesting operation.

Machine Vision also has great application on the cultivation of cotton [2]. Machine vision is a continuously growing area of the research dealing with processing and analysing of image data. It plays a key role in the development of intelligent systems [3]. In this paper, we are discussing about the machine vision part of the cotton harvesting system for which we have utilized shape based feature in conjunction with fractal features of the cotton boll. The techniques help is in better analysis of results to find the maturity level of the cotton ball for plucking.

The aim of the work is to develop an electromechanical device consisting of nozzle/ECV and vacuum source, a camera, one computer with dedicated software installed, and an electronic controller. The system will be initiated in proper time as per the output of the image analysis and recognition process. The image processing software will analyze the images / pictures and will provide the necessary decision when the target will be ready to be picked up. At the same time the objective will be to develop the system which will differentiate the mature crop feature (cotton) from an immature or a premature one by analyzing the different image features based on shape, contour, color, intensity and texture. Final goal is to design a PC controlled expert system implementing image processing and soft computing approaches. This will be cost effective, efficient, and will reduce the damages related to the picking of matured cotton bolls.

As a first attempt we intend to design and development a more *efficient mechanized software tool for picking cotton buds* by introducing the computerization and implementation of computer vision based techniques in the picking process.

II. MOTIVATION

Production of cotton is one of the most labor intensive industry, therefore such type of mechanized systems are quite helpful in reducing labor cost & overall production cost. The analysis of the cotton harvesting system has done in [4] which include pattern recognition for cotton harvesting for image acquisition where two CCD cameras are used.

When the cotton buds are fully matured bolls these are overlapped and the image data are partially lost or incomplete. To precisely identify the hidden cotton in the natural environment, firstly the images are segmented by R-B channel in RGB colour model to reduce the computational complexity as suggested in [5]. Shape and boundary based features have been used for classification of patterns as described in [6], [7]. In present work, we have suggested methods based on *shape and fractal based features* to find the stages of cotton buds towards maturity. This information as a decision from the computerized system in the form of electrical pulses / signals will be used to drive the electromechanical system for the plucking process. This automation is required for a speedy and efficient cotton plucking process which may reduce the cost and wastage and other environmental hazards appearing in the various stages of harvesting.

II Methodology Development using Computer Vision Based Technique

The methodology development for mechanization of efficient picking process will be based on image processing and soft computing based tools. The techniques will provide the computer controlled decision in the process to pick up when these are fully matured.

A small camera will perform the image acquisition. The system will be initiated in proper time as per the output of the image analysis and recognition process. This will analyze the images / pictures and will provide the necessary decision by actuating the sensor when cotton boll will be ready for picking.

Steps for Image Analysis:

Image acquisition: Image acquisition is the creation of digital images, typically from a physical scene. The *acquisition* of images (producing the input image in the first place) is referred to as imaging. A database of images of both premature and mature stages have to be acquired to identify characteristics extracting features which will act as a knowledge base for decision making systems.

Image analysis: Image analysis is the extraction of meaningful information from images; mainly from digital images by means of digital image processing techniques. Digital Image Analysis is when a computer or electrical device automatically studies an image to obtain useful information from it.

Pre-processing: Real world data are generally Incomplete: lacking attribute values, lacking certain attributes of interest, or containing only aggregate data; Noisy: containing errors or outliers. This may involve image pre-processing steps to enhance suspicious structures in the image. Pre-processing commonly comprises a series of sequential operations, including atmospheric correction or normalization, image registration, geometric correction, and masking.

Segmentation: Image segmentation is the process of partitioning a digital image into multiple segments. The segmentation is based on measurements taken from the image and might be *grey level*, *colour*, *texture*, *depth* or *motion*. The goal of segmentation is to simplify or change the representation of an image into something that is more meaningful and easier to analyze. Image segmentation is typically used to locate objects and boundaries (lines, curves, etc.) in images. More precisely, image segmentation is the process of assigning a label to every pixel in an image such that pixels with the same label share certain visual characteristics. The result of image segmentation is a set of segments that collectively cover the entire image, or a set of contours extracted from the image. Each of the pixels in a region is similar with respect to some characteristic or computed property, such as color, intensity, or texture. Adjacent regions are significantly different with respect to the same characteristic.

Feature extraction: After that we will be extracting important information and features from image. Basically transforming the input data into the set of features is called feature extraction. Various algorithms may be used to detect and isolate various desired portions or shapes (features) of a digitized image. Features extraction will include extracting features as shapes, contours, colours, textures, intensity levels, homogeneity, edge, corners, shapes, blobs, ridges etc.

Classification recognition: Once the features are decided, they are used for classification. This requires development of a fuzzy neural based classifier which may be further refined using genetic algorithms or optimization algorithms .

Development of decision making model: Classification will be followed by development of decision making model that will guide sensor.

The images of cotton buds have been acquired from the field and have been converted into digital form using camera / sensors which are mounted on the machine. Here the acquired image is cleaned from noise, converted into grayscale image from a RGB image. The process converts the input image in grayscale format, and then converts this grayscale image to binary by thresholding. The output binary image has values of 0 (black) for all pixels in the input image with luminance less than level 1 (white).

Boundary extraction of binary image contains only the perimeter pixels of objects in the input image for which principle of connectivity is used. A pixel is part of the perimeter, if it is nonzero and it is connected to at least one zero-valued pixel [8].

A. *Fractal analysis of feature*

Most works on the fractal analysis were performed in terms of evaluation of the fractal dimension [9]. Fourier transform is a powerful tool of image analysis. The fractal dimension analysis may be used on the images after using Fourier transform. The fractal dimensions of details in different direction can be calculated by computing the slope of the graph between frequency and power spectral density.

$$S(x) \propto x^{-a} \qquad (1)$$

$$a = 8 + 2D \qquad (2)$$

Where D is the fractal dimension

Power spectral density of 2D of an $M_x \times M_y$ image can be calculated with 2D FFT, the equation follows as:

$$f(u,v) = \sum_{x=0}^{M_x-1}\sum_{y=0}^{M_y-1} z(x,y)e^{-j2\pi\left(\frac{ux}{M_x}+vy/M_y\right)} \qquad (3)$$

$$u \in \{0, M_{x-1}, 0M_{y-1}\}, \quad v \in \{0, M_{x-1}, 0M_{y-1}\}$$

Where Z(x,y) is the grey value of image which corresponds to the height function of the 2D topological surface where u and v are frequency variables therefore 2D PSD can be calculated as follows

$$S(k) = |F(u.v)|^2 \qquad (4)$$

By plotting the graph between logarithmic values of frequency and magnitude we can compute the fractal dimension

B. *Extraction of shape based feature*

When the input data to an algorithm is too large to be processed and also to be redundant, the input data will be transformed into a reduced representation set of features called feature vector. Transforming the input data into the set of features is called feature extraction. If the features extracted are carefully chosen it is expected that the features set will extract the relevant information from the input data in order to perform the desired task using this reduced representation instead of the full size input.

A set of features has been computed for each required area identified as buds. The features are like area, mean, standard deviation, variance, skew, entropy, energy, mod, median, RMS. The formulae for every feature are described below: for each of the formulae: *T* is the total number of pixels, *g* an index value of image *I*, *K* the total number of grey levels , *j* the grey level value , *I*(*g*) the grey level value of pixel *g* in image *I*, *N*(*j*) the number of pixels with grey level *j* in image *I*, *P*(*I*(*g*)) the probability of grey level value *I*(*g*) occurring in image *I*, *P*(*g*) = *N*(*I*(*g*))/*T*, and *P*(*j*) is the probability of grey level value *j* occurring in image *I*, *P*(*j*) = *N*(*j*)/*T*.

Notations of the features are as:

1. $average\ graylevel = \frac{1}{T}\sum_{g=0}^{T-1} I(g)$ (5)
2. $energy = \sum_{j=0}^{K-1}[P(j)]^2$ (6)
3. $entropy = -\sum_{j=0}^{K-1} P(j)\log_2[P(j)]$ (7)
4. $variance(\sigma^2) = \sum_{g=0}^{T-1}(j - AvgGrey)^2$ (8)
5. $SD(\sigma) = \sqrt{\sum_{g=0}^{T-1}(j - AvgGrey)^2}$ (9)
6. $skew = \frac{1}{\sigma_j^3}\sum_{j=0}^{K-1}(j - AvgGrey)^3$ (10)
7. $rms\ value = \sqrt{\frac{1}{T}\sum_{g=0}^{T-1} I(g)^2}$ (11)
8. $Mode = max(N(j))$ (12)

III. RESULTS

Experiments done over a set of different images of cotton buds which include both premature and mature cotton buds. Figure 1 shows the cotton buds at different stages of maturity, extracted boundary of the cotton buds, and plots of the slope and variation of the intercept which has been computed using fractal analysis.

Table 1 is gives us detailed information about the shape based features of the cotton bolls in terms of various parameters such as area, mean, variance, skew etc. At present we are demonstrating for nine such cases as results where data 1 to data 4 represent premature cotton bolls and data 5 to data 9 are the cotton buds of mature stage. (fig.1)

Table 1

Data	Area	mean	SD	RMS	Variance	Skew	Entropy	Median	Mode
1	6721	123.5	77.43	147.2	5995	35.5	7.74	131	254
2	4590	158.6	74.1	175.7	5491	-339.9	7.47	170	254
3	7234	100.1	68.9	122.1	4748	366.7	7.47	106	254
4	2551	111.7	63.9	128.8	4091	256.8	7.8	105	254
5	4923	145.3	89.3	171.6	7979	-107	7.35	203	214
6	3541	124.6	63.1	129.8	4647	250.3	7.71	143	214
7	6805	171.8	67.5	184.6	4569	-673.7	7.35	172	254
8	4642	177.8	66.4	189.9	4416	-831.7	7.41	205	254
9	7163	112.7	69	147.7	4531	-614.2	7.31	187	254

IV. CONCLUSION

Form the fractal analysis of the image of both premature and mature cotton bolls, we have observed that variation of intercept and slope is much higher for mature buds compared to premature cotton buds. We also see that crossover point for *standard deviation* (SD) parameter from premature to mature stage is around 63.5 and general tendency of other parameters is of increase or decrease of value over a period of maturity.

As an introduction of such technique to Indian agriculture we are proposing image processing and soft computing based tools for the analysis of the images of cotton bolls which are exactly in the mature form to be picked up. It has been thought that a vision based expert system will be able to control the mechanism of the picking envisaging more suitable approaches for optimum and economic harvesting. As a first attempt we intend to design and develop an *electro-mechanical device assisted by dedicated image processing software for picking cotton bolls.* This concept will be demonstrated at Lab level followed by limited field testing. And it will pave a way towards development of a full scale prototype.

REFERENCES

[1] Jamuna KS, Karpagavalli S, Vijaya M S Revathi P, Gokilavani S, Madhiya E "Classification of Seed Cotton Yield based on theGrowth stages of Cotton crop using MachineLearning Techniques" 2010 International Conference on Advances in Computer Engineering.

[2] Sankar, D. Thomas, T. "Analysis of mammograms using fractal features " India Nature & Biologically Inspired Computing, 2009. NaBIC 2009. World Congress on Issue Date: 9-11 Dec. 2009

[3] Weixin Wang, Duanyang Qu,Benxue Ma,Yage Wang "Cotton Top Feature Identification based on Machine Vision&Image Processing" Computer Science and Automation Engineering (CSAE), 2011 IEEE International Conference on 10//06/ 2011

[4] Matti Pietikainen, Juha Roning, "Machine vision and intelligent systems" INFOTECH OULU Annual Report 2002,pp. 32-40.

[5] Mulan Wang, Jieding Wei, Jianning Yuanl, KaiyunXu "A Research for Intelligent Cotton Picking Robot Based on Machine Vision" Proceedings of the 2008 IEEE International

Conference on Information and Automation June 20 -23, 2008, Zhangjiajie, China.

[6] Mulan Wang Kun Liu "Image Recognition Technology in Intelligent Cotton Harvesting Machine" 2011 International Conference of Information Technology, Computer Engineering and Management Sciences.

[7] Arpita Das and Mahua Bhattacharya," GA Based Neuro Fuzzy Techniques for Breast Cancer Identification ",International Machine Vision and Image Processing Conference, ,IEEE Computer Society, pp136 - 141. 2008.

Acknowledgements

Authors like to acknowledge the support given by Department of Science & Technology, Ministry of Science & Technology, Govt. of India for the collaborative national research program entitled : *Vision Based Expert System for Picking of Cotton.*

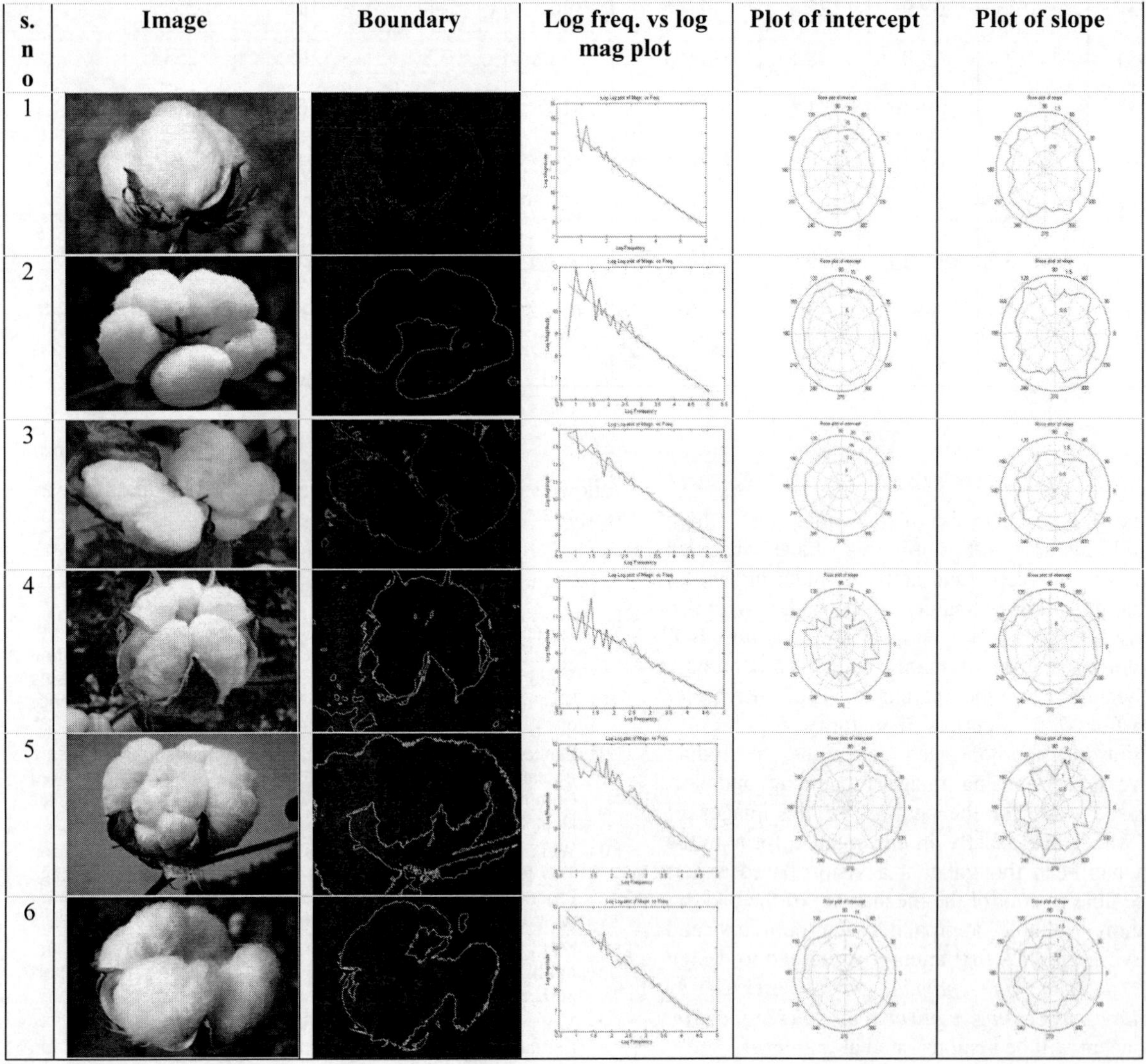

Fig.1 : Images of cotton buds at various stages with boundaries and plot of intercept and slope

Depth Based Dual Component Dynamic Gesture Recognition

Helman Stern, Kiril Smilansky, Sigal Berman

Department of Industrial Engineering and Management, Deutsche Telekom Labs at BGU
Ben-Gurion University of the Negev, Beer-Sheva, 84105, Israel
helman@bgu.ac.il, kirilsm@gmail.com, sigalbe@bgu.ac.il
The 2013 International Conference, IPCV'13

Abstract – *In this paper we describe several approaches for recognition of gestures that include simultaneous arm motion and hand configuration variations. Based on compound (dual component) gestures selected from the ASL we developed methods for recognizing such gestures from Kinect sensor videos. The method consists of hand segmentation from depth images followed by feature extraction based on block partitioning of the hand image. When combined with trajectory features a single-stage classifier is obtained. A second method which classifies arm movement and hand configuration in two-stages is also developed. These two methods are compared to a moment based classifier from the literature. Using a database of 11 subjects for training and testing the average classification accuracy of the one-stage classifier was the highest (95.5%) and that of the moment based classifier was the lowest (20.9%). The two-stage classifier obtained an average classification accuracy of 61.1%.*

Keywords: Gesture recognition, human-machine interaction, dynamic motion gestures, sign language

1. Introduction

Gesture recognition systems (GRS) offer a natural and intuitive way for interaction with machines and electronic devices such as computers and robots. GRS can both enhance user experience and offer improved operational capabilities more suitable for the requirements of modern technological devices. The vocabulary of many GRSs include either dynamic gestures, where meaning is conveyed in the arm/hand movement, or static gestures where meaning is based on arm/ hand pose. Compound gestures, in which meaning is conveyed in both motion and pose, can enrich the gesture vocabulary and are frequently found in sign languages (SL).

The difficulty of designing a classifier for SLs is not only because of their multimodal nature (face expression, head pose and nodding, body part proximity, torso movements) but also the myriad variations of motion signing itself (two handed signs, complex hand configuration changes combined with arm motion, arm pose, cyclic movements, etc. One such sign structure is that of gestures composed of a number of different components such as; hand configuration, hand orientation, change of hand location (due to arm movements), etc. Thus, in this paper we study a class of dual component signings which are part of the ASL. Also, because of the recent surge in the availability of depth enabled video cameras which reduce the amount of classification and image processing requirements, we have selected this as our source of gesture signal input.

We consider dual component gestures comprised of an arm component and a hand component. As each component with regard to motion can be either static or dynamic, of the four possible cases we are only interested in those with at least one dynamic component. Following Ong and Ranganath [1] classification schemes can be divided into those that use a single classification stage and those that classify components of a gesture and then integrate them for final gesture classification.

We provide a new taxonomy for gestures, highlighting the different types of meaning conveying components and possibilities for "compound gestures". Gestures from American Sign Language (ASL) are then used to demonstrate the taxonomy and ground the research within a realistic recognition problem. A recognition algorithm suitable for compound gestures was developed. Recognition is based on both block partition values of hand configuration and hand trajectory angles. Two classification methods were developed; (i) a one-stage classifier based on using a single vector of all features (configuration and motion) and (ii) a two-stage classifier based on a separate classification of the hand configuration component and the arm motion component, followed by a concatenative stage where the recognized components are recombined into a final gesture. In addition, a moment based method from the literature, Agrawal and Chaudhuri [2], was tested for comparative purposes.

In the following section we provide a short background on gesture recognition systems and signing gestures. In section 3 we propose our taxonomy and gesture set. Following the introduction of the architecture for classifying dual component gestures in section 4, the method of segmentation of each component from a depth map and feature extraction is discussed. Our proposed algorithms for dual component gesture classification and the moment-based method are covered in section 5. Experimental testing of the algorithms and a discussion of the results are the subjects of section 6 and 7, respectively. Final conclusions appear in section 8.

2. Background and related literature

2.1 Gesture recognition system architecture

The architecture of the hand gesture recognition system is depicted in Fig. 1. A continuous video is captured by a sensor (camera) mounted in front of the viewer who is gesturing with his/her hand. The frames of the video are separated, and sent to a tracker which locates the hand in each image. The tracking algorithm calculates a centroidal position of the hand. A sequence of centroids constitutes a gesture trajectory which is then extracted from the video stream.

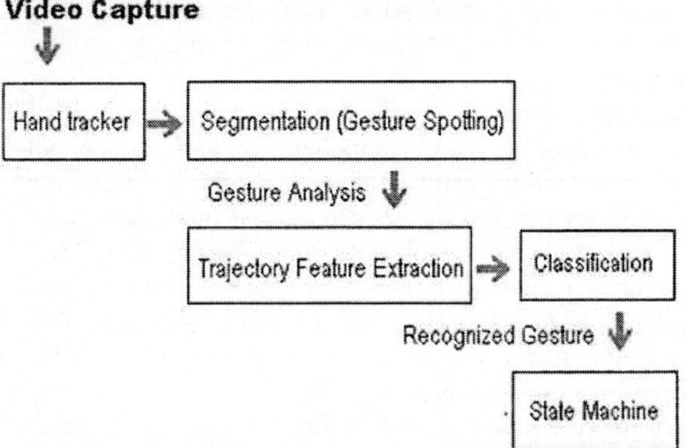

Figure 1. Architecture for a gesture recognition system

This trajectory is processed and its descriptive features are extracted. These features are then fed into the classification module, which recognizes the particular gesture. When a gesture is recognized its representative command is sent to a state machine, which can take the form of a controllable physical or virtual object.

2.2 Motion gesture classification

For motion gesture classification dynamic time warping (DTW) and hidden Markov models (HMM) are most often used. HMM is a generative classification method, quantifying the probability that an input vector could have been generated from a model constructed for each gesture based on the training set. In contrast DTW is a discriminative classification method directly comparing the input vector to template vectors of each gesture. The longest common subsequence (LCS) algorithm follows the same idea as DTW, using a distance function as a similarity measure between a temporal test sequence and a pattern Frolova, et al [3].

2.3 SL gesture recognition

Survey papers on SL recognition are scarce. However, we did find two. The first, by Havasi and Szabo [4] describes a semi-automatic construction of a sign database, and gives a summary of technical and linguistic issues of the signing effort. The second by Ong and Ranganath [1] reviews SL data capture, feature extraction and classification and the integration of non-manual (hand) signs with hand sign gestures. Mitra and Acharya [5] divide SLs into three major types; (i) finger-spelling, (ii) word level sign vocabulary, and (iii) non-manual features. Finger spelling is used for characters, word level signs are used for most of the communication, and non-manual features are facial expressions, positions of tongue, mouth, and body. An integration of motion gesture recognition and posture recognition is presented in Rashid, et al. [6]. Depth information and orientation features are classified by HMM and support vector machines. Rokade, et al. [7]. proposed using gesture trajectory features and key frames, followed by DTW for recognizing ASL gestures. Agrawal and Chaudhuri [2] used spatial moments up to the second order as features and principle component analysis (PCA) for classifying between gestures that were characterized both by hand motion and hand configuration.

3. Gesture vocabulary and taxonomy

Ten gestures are selected from the ASL vocabulary (Table 1) to ground the research within a realistic recognition problem. The gestures were chosen such that they will emphasize the importance of recognizing both arm/hand trajectory and hand configuration.

A two-layered gesture taxonomy for hand-pose trajectory combinations is shown in Fig. 2. The selected ASL gestures were placed in the taxonomy tree of Fig. 2 according to their static/dynamic component properties. A hand pose-trajectory is considered as a two-component gesture: (a) hand configuration, and (b) hand location(s). Each may be either static or dynamic. The hand location component may be either (i) a static hand location (no arm movement during a gesture period) or (ii) a dynamic hand trajectory (arm movement). The hand component may be either (i) a static hand configuration (no hand configuration change during a gesture period) or (ii) a dynamic hand configuration (hand configuration change during the gesture period). It is clear that a dynamic gesture is defined as having at least one dynamic component.

Table 1. Ten ASL gestures used for testing (X – Horizontial , Y - Vertical, Z – toward the camera)

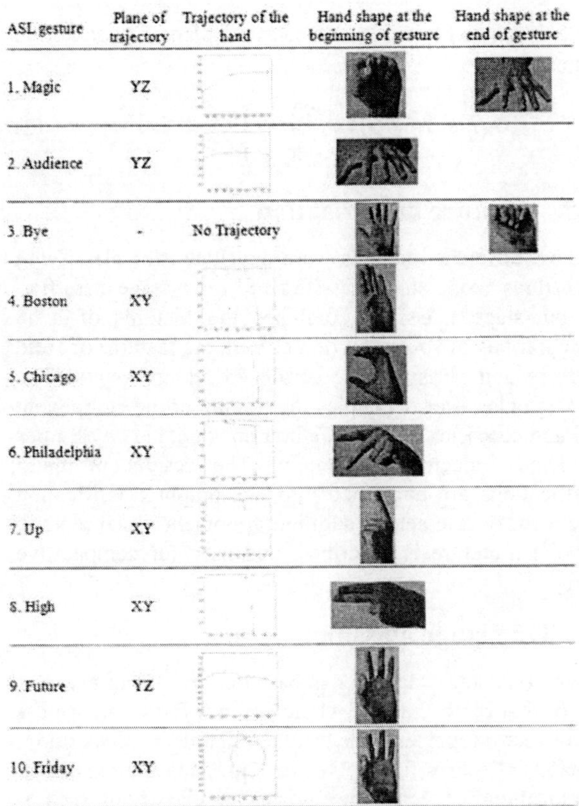

ASL gesture	Plane of trajectory	Trajectory of the hand	Hand shape at the beginning of gesture	Hand shape at the end of gesture
1. Magic	YZ			
2. Audience	YZ			
3. Bye	-	No Trajectory		
4. Boston	XY			
5. Chicago	XY			
6. Philadelphia	XY			
7. Up	XY			
8. High	XY			
9. Future	YZ			
10. Friday	XY			

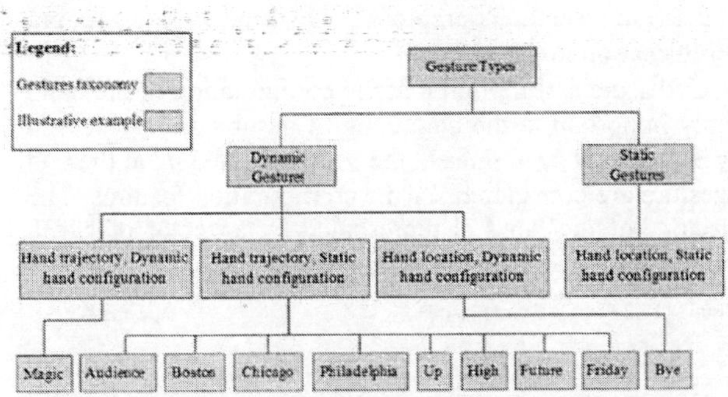

Figure 2. Gesture taxonomy based on static/dynamic combinations

4. Compound gesture classification

The architecture of the developed recognition method is depicted in Fig. 3. The first stage, hand segmentation, is based on a depth map and the hand centroid location in each frame. For each frame, the hand region is segmented and features of the hand configuration are extracted. Additional features of hand trajectory during the gesture are also extracted. The features are then used for classifying the gesture into one of the gesture classes in vocabulary. Two different classifiers were developed: a one-stage classifier, which classifies the gestures using a single vector of all features, and a two stage classifier, which first separately classifies configuration features and motion features and then classifies the gesture using the results of the first stage. This chapter is organized according to the architecture stages.

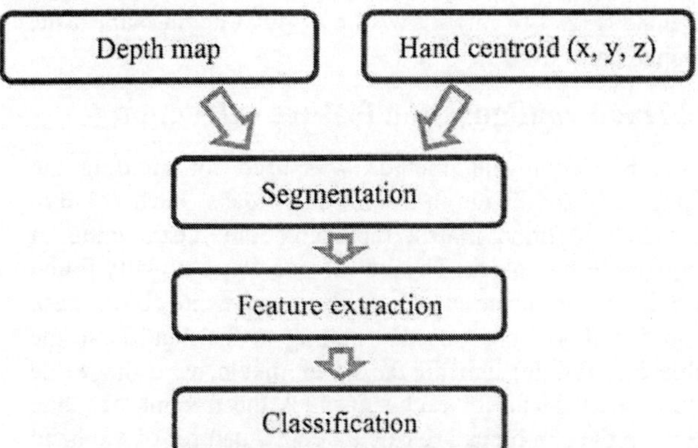

Figure 3. Gesture classification system diagram

4.1 Hand segmentation

The purpose of this stage, as shown in Fig. 4, is to segment the hand from the rest of the depth map, for each frame in the gesture video. The target of this process is to segment the hand as tightly as possible without losing regions of the hand itself. The output of the segmentation is a scaled intensity image in which pixels that belong to the hand have a scaled value above one and all the other pixels have a value of zero (black).

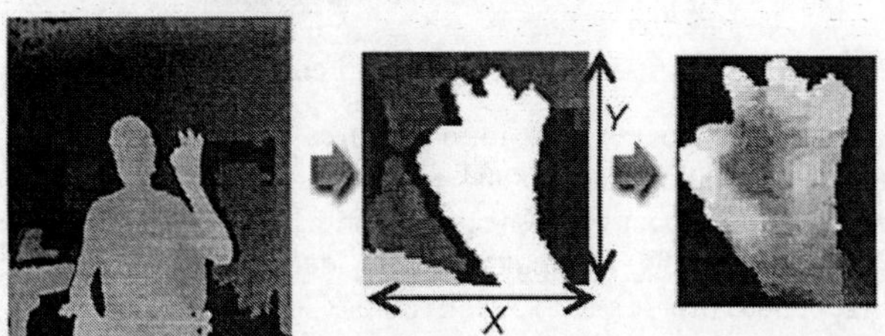

Figure 4. Hand segmentation. Left: Depth map with overlaid hand centroid marked by a red X sign; Middle: segmented hand region; Right: A tight bound about the segmented hand.

The segmentation starts with cropping the hand region of interest (ROI) using the pinhole camera model which determines the hand ROI dimensions *X, Y* (in pixels) based on the distance ***Z*** between the hand and the camera (obtained by the depth map). Hand ROI dimensions are computed using the basic equations of perspective projections:

$$Y = F_y \frac{H_h}{Z} \quad ; \quad X = F_x \frac{H_w}{Z} \qquad (1)$$

Where F_x and F_y are the camera's focal length in the horizontal and vertical axis, respectively. The hand width H_w and height H_h are based on average dimensions as reported in Pheasant, and Haslegrave [8]. The hand centroid

[x (pixels), y (pixels), z (mm)] is acquired from the hand tracker and the hand ROI is centered about it as shown in Fig. 4 (middle). Finally, a bounding box is created around the hand. Fig. 4 (right) shows the original depth map of the cropped hand ROI.

4.2 Hand configuration feature extraction

A block partition method was used for dividing the segmented hand image into *NxM* sub-blocks. Each value in the block partition matrix represents the mean value of pixels in the sub-block. The matrix size was optimally found by a direct parameter as 8x5. A black and white (BW) mask is produced where pixels that belong to the hand have the value one (white) and all the other pixels have the value zero (black). Then, for each sub-block the fraction of white pixels in the sub-block are calculated as features of the hand configuration. Fig. 5 shows a block partition in which each cell of the 8x5 matrix on the right side represents the mean value of the matching sub block of the BW mask on the left side.

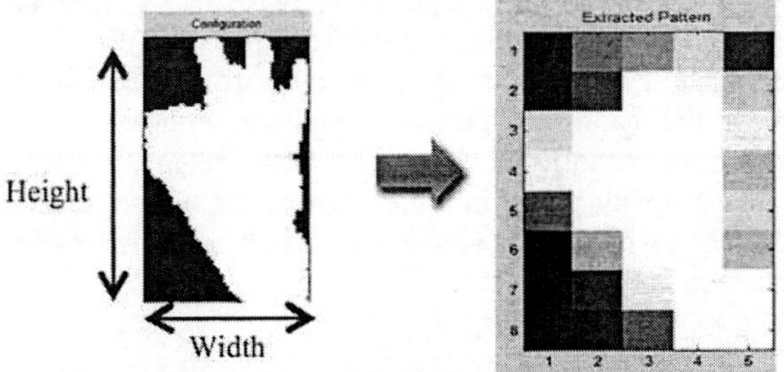

Figure 5. Block partition of hand configuration

The *NxM* block white ratio features representing the hand configuration are extracted from each segmented frame and the aspect ratio [height / width] of the bounding box is additionally computed and added to the feature vector. Therefore for a 8x5 cell matrix the length of the configuration feature vector is 41.

4.3 Hand trajectory feature extraction

For a gesture video of n frames a sequence of n hand centroids [x (pixels), y (pixels), z (mm)] are acquired from the hand tracker. Because all the gestures in our database are in fact 2D (XY plane or YZ plane), the plane with the maximum motion in it is chosen and the sequence of points is projected on that plane. This is a common phenomenon where dynamic gestures are planar even when the gesture vocabulary is embedded in 3D space. Each sample trajectory is of different length varying from 12 to 78 frames, depending on the time it took the subject to perform the gesture, therefore we normalize the length of the trajectory. The trajectory is resampled into n=39 points and transformed into a vector of n-1=38 absolute angles of the hand motion direction. The computation of each absolute angle is done using eq. 2 where x and y are the coordinates of the hand centroids in the selected plane of maximum motion.

$$\theta_i = \tan^{-1}\left(\frac{y_i - y_{i-1}}{x_i - x_{i-1}}\right) \qquad (2)$$

5. Gesture classification

Two different methods were developed for classifying the gestures, a one-stage classifier and a two-stage classifier. The one-stage classifier combines the features of hand configurations of some key frames with the features of hand trajectory and classifies the combined feature vector. The two-stage classifier decouples the gesture at the component level and classifies hand configurations of some key frames and hand trajectory separately. The results of these classifications are combined into one output classification using a fuzzy rule set. In addition a moment based method from the literature is described, and used for comparative testing.

5.1 One-stage classifier

The one-stage classifier is based on one feature vector (Fig. 6) that represents the whole gesture. For each frame a feature vector represents the hand configuration. In addition, the hand trajectory feature vector represents the change in hand location between frames. Instead of classifying each of those channels of information separately, a classification of a full feature vector is employed which takes into account all information in the gesture.

Under the assumption that the configuration of the hand is only important at the beginning of gesture and at the end of gesture, only $n1$ frames at the beginning and $n2$ at the end of gesture are considered for the configuration features. The trajectory of the hand is represented by a vector of N=38 absolute angles of the hand motion direction.

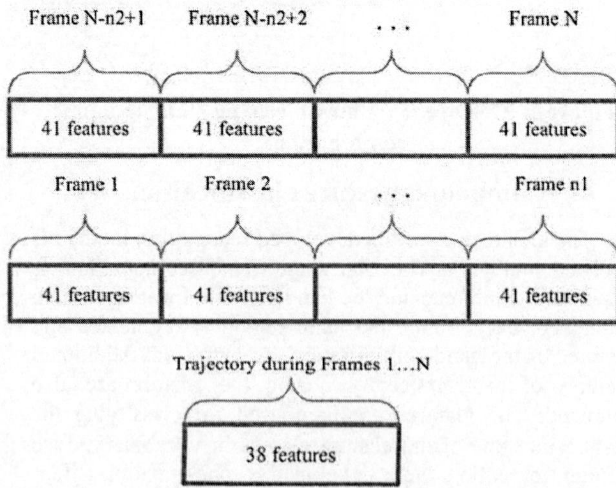

Figure 6. Classification features. Top: End configuration features; Middle: Beginning configuration features;

Bottom: Hand trajectory features

The feature vectors for the hand configuration and motion trajectory were combined into a single feature vector after using PCA. The combined feature vectors (one for each test gesture) were used to train and test the K-nearest-neighbor (KNN) classifier using a Euclidean distance measure.

5.2 Two-stage classifier

In the first stage, the hand configuration and motion trajectory are decoupled and fuzzy membership of each are derived. This is initiated with the hand configurations in *n1* first and *n2* last frames of the gesture, which are subsequently, combined into two membership vectors using a fuzzy rule base (one for the hand configuration at the beginning of the gesture and one for the end). Another membership vector for hand trajectory is computed based on HMM classifier.

In the second stage, a fuzzy rule base is used for combining the three different membership vectors. The result is a single membership vector, with different degrees of belonging to each of the gestures in the gesture vocabulary. Finally a defuzzification phase is executed, where the gesture is classified into the gesture class with the highest degree of membership.

5.3 Moment based classifier

The moment based classifier suggested by Agrawal and Chaudhuri [2] was used to provide a comparison to our one and two-stage algorithms. One of the main differences between Agrawal and Chaudhuri's method and ours is they do not use block partition features, but instead use a set of moments calculated from a BW hand image. These moments are concatenated over all frames of the gesture video and classified by a PCA classifier in a one stage procedure.

6. Experiments

The two classifiers which were developed, and the moment based classifier suggested by Agrawal and Chaudhuri [2], were implemented using Matlab™ (Mathworks, USA). In all implementations, the PrimeSense sensor and OpenNI[1] were used to acquire depth image videos and track the hand centroid. This section starts with the description of the database used for testing the developed algorithms. The database consists of samples of the ten gesture ASL vocabulary which were recorded using the PrimeSense sensor. We then describe the classification evaluation process. Three experiments were performed: testing the one-stage, two-stage and the moment based classifiers, with a comparison made between them.

6.1 Gesture training and testing data base

The evaluation of the classification methods was done using the ten ASL gesture vocabulary shown in Table 1. Gestures of 11 subjects aged 25 to 46 (10 male, 9 female) were recorded. Each subject provided 5 samples of each of the 10 gesture types. A leave one subject out cross validation experiment was performed. Accordingly, a total of eleven experiments were conducted with 50 samples per gesture used for training in each experiment and 5 samples per gesture for testing.

6.2 One –stage classifier evaluation

Before the evaluation the values of several important feature and classifier parameters were determined by a direct search method. Recall that, for our composite gestures the hand component was extracted only at the start and end of the gesture trajectory, where different hand configurations were expected to have occurred. Thus, the number of frames at the start and end of the gesture from which the hand component is extracted are two parameters that need to be determined. Two other feature parameters are the number of rows and number of columns of the optimal block partition of the hand image. For the KNN classifier we also determined the optimal number nearest neighbors and the number of clusters. The final parameters and the range over which they were optimized are shown in Table 2. It should be noted that the number of clusters *N* for the KNN represent the number of forms used to represent each of the gestures. In effect, we used a constraint to insure an equal number of forms for each gesture (to allow for the natural variability of a gesture due different user's motion behavior. Since this resulted in 4 forms for each gesture, the final number of clusters used for the 10 gesture KNN was 40. The parameter evaluation was based on the accuracies of the classifier using a gesture test set for each candidate parameter set.

The trajectory of the hand was represented by a vector of 38 absolute directional hand motion angles (Fig.6 and eq 2), after reforming all gestures to a common length. The hand configure component feature vector is of length $(n1+n2)$ x no blocks (8X5) + 1 (aspect ratio). So for the $n1=6$ start frames the start hand feature length is 246, and for the $n2=1$ end frame the end hand feature length is 41. For the start and end hand component vectors we used PCA to reduce the dimensionality to 30 and 11, respectively (based on first eigenvalues that explain 85% of the variance).

The hand trajectory feature vector was added to the reduced hand configuration vectors resulting in a full 79 feature vector of the gesture. These vectors are used for training and testing the classifier.

Table 2. Parameters for optimization

Param	Description	Min	Max	Optimum
M	Number of rows for the block partition	3	20	8

[1] http://www.openni.org/

N	Number of columns for the block partition	3	20	5
k	Number of nearest neighbors for classification	1	6	1
$n1$	Number of frames at the beginning of gesture	1	10	6
$n2$	Number of frames at the end of gesture	1	10	1
N	Number of clusters for K-means	1	10	4

6.3 Two –stage classifier evaluation

Nine possible hand configuration classes were specified, according to the hand shapes at the beginning and end of the ASL gestures. A training set of feature vectors was constructed for each configuration class, based on the $n1$ first and $n2$ last frames of the gesture training set.

For each frame, membership values of hand configuration were computed using KNN. A cosine amplitude, r_{ij}, was used as a similarity measure between the tested feature vector i and a training feature vector j (eq. 2).

$$r_{ij} = \frac{|\sum_{k=1}^{m} F_{ik}F_{jk}|}{\sqrt{(\sum_{k=1}^{m} F_{ik}{}^2)(\sum_{k=1}^{m} F_{jk}{}^2)}} \quad (2)$$

Where m is the feature vector length and F_{ik} is the k-th feature of vector i. The cosine amplitude r_{ij} can get a value between zero (for perpendicular vectors) and one (for parallel vectors). Then, the membership value $M_i(C)$ of frame i for configuration class C is the mean value of k highest measures between the tested feature vector and the training feature vectors belong to that configuration class (eq. 3).

$$M_i(C) = \text{mean}_{(j|j\in C, r_{ij}\in E(C))}\{r_{ij}\} \quad (3)$$

Where C is the configuration class and $E(C)$ is the set of k highest measures of the class.

Membership vectors were computed for the hand configurations, one for the beginning of the gesture and one for the end. A Fuzzy rule base was used for combining the first $n1$=**6** frames into one membership vector and the last $n2$=**1** frames into second membership vector, respectively.

The membership value for each configuration class for the start and end of the gesture was the maximum membership value of the first six frames and the membership value of the last frame, respectively (eq. 4).

$$M_{start}(C) = \max_{(i\in 1..6)}\{M_i(C)\} \quad (4)$$
$$M_{end}(C) = M_N(C)$$

Six possible hand trajectory classes were specified. Because paths in the YZ plane differed considerable from the paths in the XY plane the plane of motion is not considered during the classification.

The HMM algorithm used for trajectory classification, Frolova, et al. [3]. contained eight states, which were the eight possible motion directions. The output was a log-likelihood vector of the dataset which was used as the membership vector of the trajectory, $M_{traj}(T)$, where T is a possible trajectory.

Ten fuzzy rules combined the results of the trajectory and hand configuration classifications. For example: "If the configuration at the start is *closed fist* **and** at the end is *hand stretched forward* **and** the trajectory is *forward* then the ASL gesture is ***Magic***". Where the **and** directive is translated into a minimum function and the membership value for each gesture is given in eq. 5.

$$M(G) = \min\{M_{start}(Cstart(G)) \quad (5)$$
$$M_{end}(Cend(G)), M_{traj}(T(G))\}$$

Where $Cstart(G), Cend(G)$ and $T(G)$ are the configurations of the start and end of gesture class G and the trajectory of gesture class G, respectively. Finally, a test gesture was classified to the gesture class with the highest membership value.

6.4 Moment based classifier evaluation

Agrawal and Chaudhuri's method, unlike ours, uses a set of spatial moments up to the second order calculated from a BW hand image to represent the hand configuration. were. For each nth frame, the feature vector is:

f(n)=[A(n) Cx(n) Cy(n) Cxx(n) Cxy(n) Cyy(n)] (6)

where, Cxx(n), Cxy(n) and Cyy(n) are the second order spatial moments of the hand region, Cx(n) and Cy(n) are the first order moments and A(n) is the zero order moment. For the whole gesture, each moment creates a trajectory, thus six feature trajectories represent the gesture, characterized both by the motion of the hand in space and the changing configuration of the hand throughout the gesture. After Using PCA for dimensionality reduction the test data are presented to a PCA classifier.

7. Results and discussion

According to the 95% confidence intervals (Table 3), the one-stage classifier gave significantly better results than the other two classifiers. The average classification accuracy of the one-stage classifier was the highest (95.45%) and that of the moment based classifier was the lowest (20.91%). The two-stage classifier obtained an average classification accuracy of 61.09%.

Table 3 Comparative classification accuracies

	One-stage Classifier	Two-stage Classifier	Moment Classifier
Ave. accuracy	95.45%	61.09%	20.91%
Confidence interval (%) (95.0%)	[92.2,98.7]	[51.4,70.8]	[17.6,24.2]

With the two-stage classifier, many (53%) of the "Magic" (1) gestures were classified as "Audience" (2). The trajectories were correctly classified, however the configurations are not what causes the misclassification. Fig. 7 shows examples of the misclassified configurations. The left image, for the "Magic" gesture, shows an intermediate phase between the closed fist configuration and the open hand stretched forward and therefore cannot be recognized. The center and right images show the "C" and "P" configurations twisted towards the camera causing a deformed view and therefore cannot be recognized.

Figure 7. Misclassified configurations

With the moment-based classifier, many of the gestures were classified as "Magic" (1) or "Audience" (2). Because those gestures are performed towards the camera the area of the hand region is changing through the gesture therefore scaling by the area in the first frame becomes insufficient. For the one-stage classifier the most confused gestures were "Chicago" (5) and "Philadelphia" (6), who share the same hand trajectory, but have different hand configurations which occasionally look alike after the block partition is performed. Fig. 8 shows an example of the hand configurations.

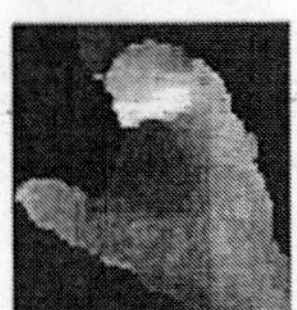 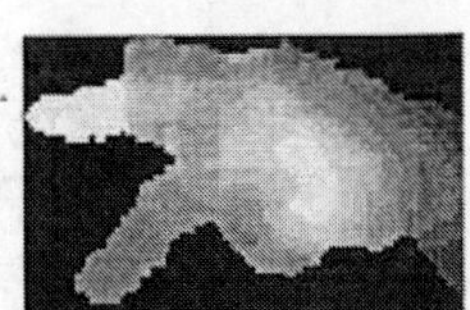

Figure 8. ASL "C" compared to "P"

As an additional observation, there are interactions between the different motion modalities within the compound gesture performed by the users. Even when the text-book hand-configurations are identical in two gestures with different trajectories, the configurations actually performed may differ. Especially when taking into account the dynamic evolvement of the configuration, as the person performing the gesture is moving his/her hand while constructing the configuration. Therefore the component classifier of a particular hand configuration class over all types of gestures containing it is trained on all variations of the hand class, even those effected or distorted by particular trajectory paths.

8. Conclusions

Two different methods were developed for classifying sign language gestures; a one-stage classifier and a two-stage classifier. The one-stage classifier combines the features of hand configurations of some key frames with the features of hand trajectory and classifies the combined feature vector. The two-stage classifier decouples the gesture at the component level and classifies hand configurations, of key frames and hand trajectory separately. The results of these classifications are combined into one output classification using a fuzzy rule set. In addition a moment based method from the literature is described, and used for comparative testing

The classification methods were tested using ten ASL gestures. The vocabularies were arranged according to a new dynamic taxonomy of gesture constructs. Gestures were captured using a PrimeSense 3D sensor and were executed by 11 subjects. The average percent classification accuracy of the one-stage classifier was the highest ,95.45, that of the moment based classifier was the lowest 20.91. The two-stage classifier obtained an average classification accuracy of 61.09. In the future, we intend to add face and body part detection which will allow the integration of non-manual components into the gesture definitions.

Acknowledgements

This research was partially supported by Deutsche Telekom AG. We acknowledge the help of Dr. Darya Frolova, Noam Geffen, Tom Godo, Eti Almog, Omri Mendels, Merav Shmueli, and Shani Talmor.

References

[1] S. C. W. Ong, S. Ranganath, "Automatic Sign Language Analysis: A Survey and the Future beyond Lexical Meaning"; IEEE Trans. On Pattern Analysis and Machine Intelligence, Vol.27, No. 6, pp. 873-891, 2005.

[2] T. Agrawal, S. Chaudhuri, ,"Gesture Recognition Using Position and Appearance Features," Paper presented at the Image Processing, 2003. ICIP 2003, Conf. Proceedings, Vol.3, No. 2, II, pp.109-12, 2003.

[3] D. Frolova, H. Stern, S. Berman, "Most probable longest common subsequence for recognition of gesture character input.," IEEE Transactions on Systems, Man, and Cybernetics, Part B: Cybernetics, Vol. 42, Issue 3, pp. 277-290, 2013

[4] L. Havasi, H.M. Szabo, "A Motion Capture System for Sign Language Synthesis: Overview and Related Issues," in Proceedings of Computer as a Tool, EUROCON 2005 Vol.1 , pp. 445-448, 2005.

[5] S. Mitra, T Acharya, " Gesture Recognition: A survey," IEEE Trans, on Systems Man, and Cybernetics-Part C: Applic. & Reviews, Vol.37, No. 3, pp. 311-324, 2007

[6] O. Rashid, A. Al-Hamadi, B. Michaelis, "A framework for the integration of gesture and posture recognition using HMM and SVM," Paper presented at ICIS, Vol. 4, pp. 572-577, 2009

[7] U. S. Rokade, D. Doye, M. Kokare, "Hand gesture recognition using object based key frame selection," Paper at Digital Image Processing, pp. 288-291, 2009

[8] S. Pheasant, C. M. Haslegrave, "Bodyspace: Anthropometry, ergonomics, and the design of work," Boca Raton: CRC Press, 2000

Acoustic signal processing via neural network towards motion capture systems

E. Volná, M. Kotyrba, R. Jarušek
Department of informatics and computers, University of Ostrava, Ostrava, Czech Republic

Abstract - *The aim of this article is to outline possibilities of sound and its physical properties during shooting of moving objects. Attention was devoted to the specific location of a fixed point in the space and time. We present two proposed methods that are based on neural networks. We also proposed appropriate topologies of the systems that depend on the required accuracy, acoustic properties and selected sound technologies. At first, we identified a distance between an active transmitter and a receiver on the basis of sound pulses transmitted from transmitters in the defined domain. After that a neural network uses obtained distances between transmitters and a receiver as its inputs to determine an actual position of the receiver in space. We developed two models, which outcomes are compared in conclusion.*

Keywords: Acoustic signal processing, neural networks, motion capture system, Fourier transform.

1 Sound waves processing

When sound impacts on the solid barrier, it causes its reflection or bending which depend on the ratio between the size of the barrier and the wavelength of sound. If the dimension of the barrier is bigger than the wave length of the sound, the sound is reflected according to the rule: *"The angle of reflection equals the angle of incidence"* and this phenomenon can be simply viewed as the problem of propagation of light rays. Value of intensity (residual energy) of reflected sound signal is defined by the physical properties of the material and it is different for different sound frequencies. Generally speaking, for the lower frequency absorption coefficient is smaller, with increasing frequency coefficient of absorption is increasing. We write (1):

$$a = \frac{i_0 - i}{i_0} \quad (1)$$

where:
a - sound absorption coefficient at reflection
i - intensity of the reflected waves
i_0 - intensity of the incident wave

Fig. 1 shows the sound pulse as a rectangular signal, which is generated from the sum of odd harmonics frequencies with a prescribed amplitude. Additionally, it is very easy generated and its transmission over sinusoidal signal is multiple. Just these sound waves form the basis of motion capture systems that are aims of this article.

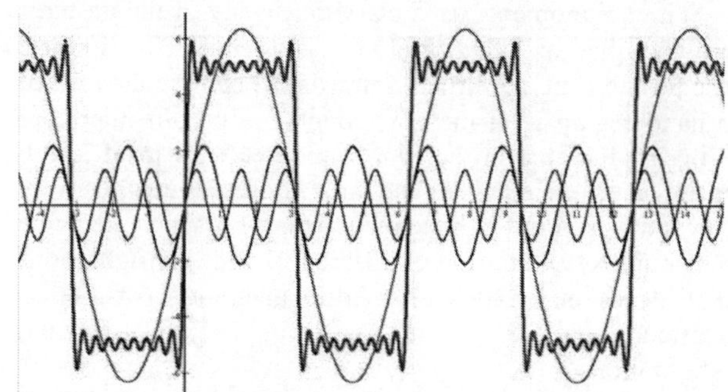

Figure 1: A sound pulse as a rectangular signal [11]

2 Acoustic motion capture systems

Capturing motion or motion tracking (MoCap) is used to provide a digital recording using the markers. Currently, there are several techniques for tracking. Computer software which is provided to the motion capturing record positions, angles, velocity, acceleration, and pulse points in the real time. For now, an unused option of the Motion Capture is a system for determining the positions of points in the space which uses the physical properties of audible sound. Since the speed of sound propagation in the environment is constant, it's possible to calculate an audio signal's absolute distance according to the degree of its delay. If this happens for at least three transmitters, receivers can determine the position of the spatial coordinates via triangulation. Several motion capture technologies have been proposed in the last two decades. The advantages and disadvantages of the dominant approaches are argued in several excellent surveys [3, 5].

Acoustic systems use the time-of-flight of an audio signal to compute the marker locations. Most current systems are not portable and handle only a small number of markers. With the Bat system [13], an ultrasonic pulse emitter is worn by a user, while multiple receivers are placed at fixed locations in the environment. A system by Hazas and Ward [4] extends ultrasonic capabilities by using broadband signals; Vallidis [9] alleviates occlusion problems with a spread-spectrum approach; Olson and colleagues [7] are able to track receivers without known emitter locations. The Cricket location system [8] fills the environment with a number of ultrasonic beacons that send pulses along with RF signals at random times in order to minimize possible signal interference. This allows multiple receivers to be localized independently. A similar system is presented by Randell and Muller [10], in which the beacons emit pulses in succession using a central controller. Lastly, the WearTrack system [3], developed for augmented reality applications, uses one ultrasonic beacon placed on the user's finger and three fixed detectors placed on the head-mounted display. This system can track the location of the finger with respect to the display, based on time-of-flight measurements.

3 Acoustic motion capture systems based on neural networks

We present two proposed MoCaps that are based on neural networks, e.g. their appropriate topologies that depend on the required accuracy, acoustic properties and selected sound technologies. At first, we identified a distance between an active transmitter and a receiver on the basis of sound pulses transmitted in the defined domain. After that a neural network uses obtained distances between transmitters and a receiver as its inputs to determine an actual position of the receiver in space.

3.1 System design

The article introduces experimental study of an audible MoCap system developed via neural networks. Designing a measurement system has been defined the following initial requirements [12]:

- Active area (domain), where the captured objects move, has to be so large to be able to cover the range of moving objects.
- Active area should not restrict the moving objects.
- The system accuracy must be constant throughout the active area.
- The system must be able to adapt to environmental changes (e.g. change in temperature).
- The system must be able to detect measurement errors and correct them.
- The output of the system must be data that should be acceptable in other systems (e.g. 3D programs).
- The system should be able to work in real time.
- The whole system, including technology, should be applicable in any environment.

According to the initial requirements, we proposed two system topologies containing five or three transmitters positioned around the space. All transmitters were put into a horizontal plane so that the plane split the space into two half-space, namely the half-space above the floor and half-space under the floor. We introduced a coordinate system into the half space above the floor, see Fig. 2,3. Our proposed system is based on speakers that generate a signal that is recorded sensor. Gradually we emit an acoustic pulse from different transmitters into the microphone. As the space is defined with microphone placement transmitters, we are sure that one sound pulse leaves the room with a microphone even before then second transmitter in turn sends its pulse. Thus, in the area one pulse is only in the current time.

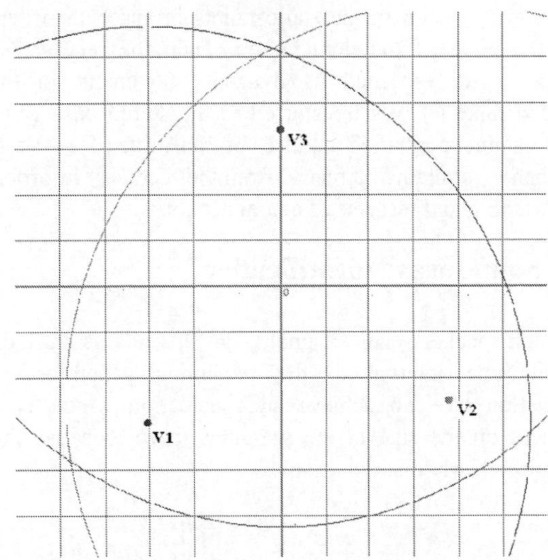

Figure 2: A coordinate system 3 transmitters' positions (V1 - V3).

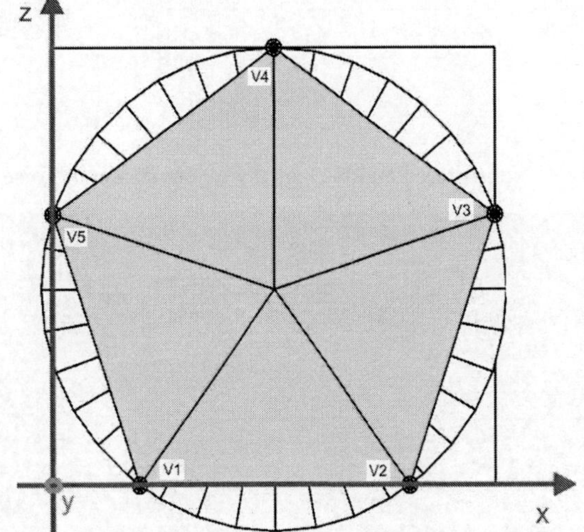

Figure 3: A coordinate system 5 transmitters' positions (V1 - V5).

We had to fulfill the following conditions of sound parameters in order to system worked well [6]:

- The system used sound waves at a frequency of 4410 Hz.
- Sound pulse, used as a measurement medium and it is radiated by any transmitter, must leave the domain before any other transmitter starts sending its impulses. This is the most important condition for the proper system functioning.

- Sound pulse must be adequately long to receive it the satisfaction in receiver and process it.
- Sound pulse must be adequately short not to overload space domain by reflections from walls or objects in the room.

There were made measurements in domains shown in Fig. 2,3 where we changed the receiver position for each measurement and we obtained 33 audio records. Initially, receiver was placed in the static points in space in order to cover the edge of the domain too. Then the receiver was moving so we recorded its dynamic movement in time. Recorded material was transferred to the stereo base (where the left channel contained impulses of transmitted V1 - V5 and right channel contained a record from the receiver) in order to create training and test sets of neural networks.

3.2 Sound wave identification

Each speaker sends a signal (Fig. 5), which is shifted by optional time interval to the remaining generators. By optimization we can achieve such detection which is not dependent on the size of the scanning space, because these signals are clearly distinguishable.

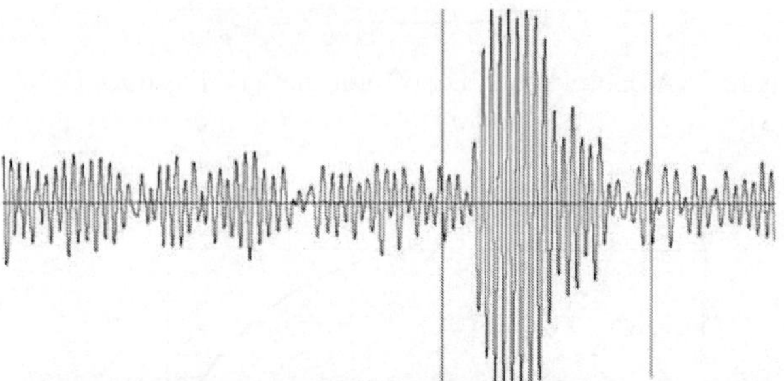

Figure 4: Non-filtered audible signal with environment noise

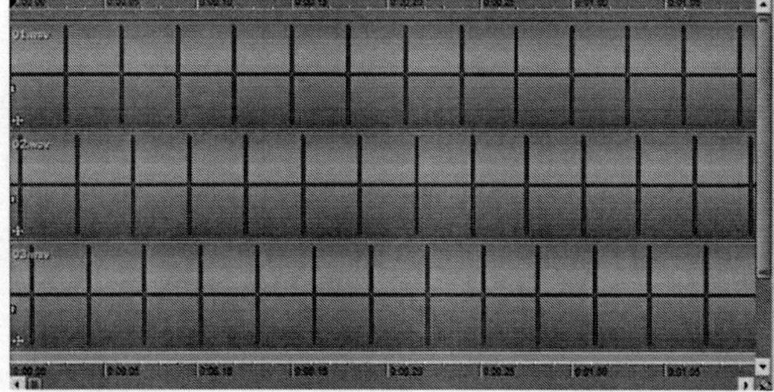

Figure 5: Shift of the individual audio signals from each speakers

To the filtered sound sample scanned by the receiver and to the detection the sound pulse's onset we use the Fourier transformation, specifically FFT - Fast Fourier Transform [1]. At 4410 Hz sample rate (set to sound card) and the number of samples 1024 (2^{10} - necessary for FFT) scanned sample is then processed by the transformation matrix and there is selected only zone with frequency of the sound pulse (4410Hz). A band remains unchanged, while the other zones are reset. Then we perform the inverse FFT and after that we get a filtered sample (Fig. 4). In such a filtered sample we simply find the maximum, which then determines the onset of the sound pulse in the sample.

This neural network is able to find the beginning of the sound pulse of transmitter and transform this information into a numerical value expressing the distance between the transmitter and receiver. We used a multilayer neural network with one hidden layer that was adapted by backpropagation algorithm [2]. Input data of the training set included fixed range of values of one sample with the length of one (main) sequence, which contained 882 patterns. Number of patterns in the training set was 1744. Neural network architecture is the following: 88 units in input layer, 120 units in hidden layer, 44 units in output layer.

Input vector of the training set included 88 values from the interval <0, 1>. Values present standard maximal and minimal subsequence values of 20 samples from the main sequence, e.g. pairs of maximum from positive numbers and minimum from negative numbers. The last two samples from the main sequence were omitted. Output vector of the training set included 44 values from the set {0, 1}. If we divide the main sequence into 44 parts (each part includes 20 samples), then the part, which contains a front edge flag of the pulse equals 1 and all other values remain this value.

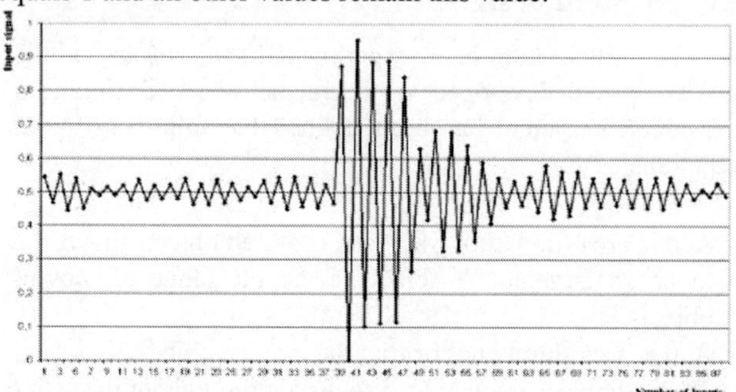

Figure 6: Non-filtered audible signal with environment noise

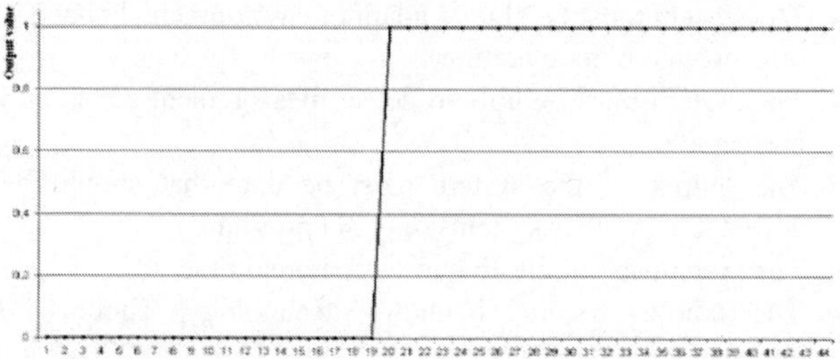

Figure 7: Visualization of the output training vector

Choice of format of input data (input vector) was an important moment, see Fig. 6. We preferred maximal and minimal values of subsequences, because their average values did not give desired results. Similarly, the format of output data (output vector) was proposed as a no decreasing function with the skip point in front edge flag of the pulse (Fig. 7). Fig. 8 shows calculation of random sequences that form the test set.

The proposed network was able to recognize from input data the pulse signal with an accuracy of 20 samples (e.g. $20 * 0,\overline{7}\,\text{cm} \doteq 15,4\,\text{cm}$), which is higher than the level of our desired accuracy.

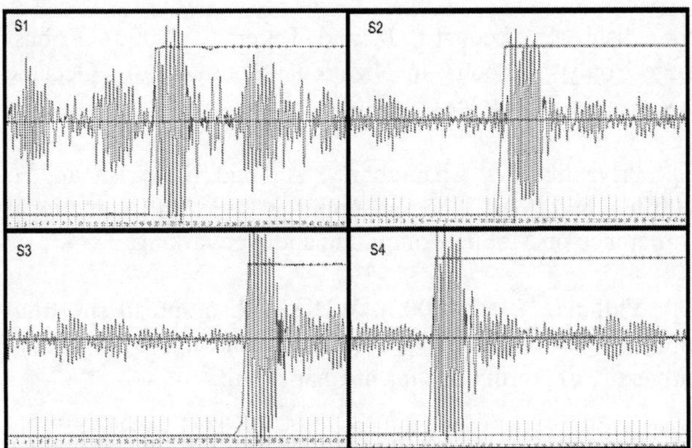

Figure 8: Test sequences (S1 - S4)

3.3 Coordinates generation

In our experimental study, we used a multilayer neural network with one hidden layer that was adapted by backpropagation algorithm [2] for the task of calculating the coordinates of points in space.

The philosophy of the application is simple. The distance between the individual transmitter and receiver is calculated from given coordinates of three or five transmitters and randomly generated three-dimensional coordinates of fictional receiver, which is located in the domain Fig. 2, 3. We must transform these values to the coordinates (x, y, z). Both data represent a training set which are used during a neural network adaptation. Each training pattern consists of three or five input components (the distance from three transmitters to a receiver) and three output components (x, y, and z coordinates in space). The actual distance is then determined by Euclidean distance calculations.

Experimental setting – 3 transmitters' positions

The neural network was adapted by set of 3000 training vectors, whose uniformly cover the all domain space (Fig. 2, 3). The suggested parameters of our experimental work are the following:

- Input layer: 3 units
- Hidden layer: 6 units
- Output layer: 3 units
- Activate function: a sigmoid
- Learning rate: 0,3

Experimental setting – 5 transmitters' positions

The neural network was adapted by set of 4000 training vectors, whose uniformly cover the all domain space (Fig. 2). The suggested parameters of our experimental work are the following:

- Input layer: 5 units
- Hidden layer: 12 units
- Output layer: 3 units
- Activate function: a sigmoid
- Learning rate: 0,3

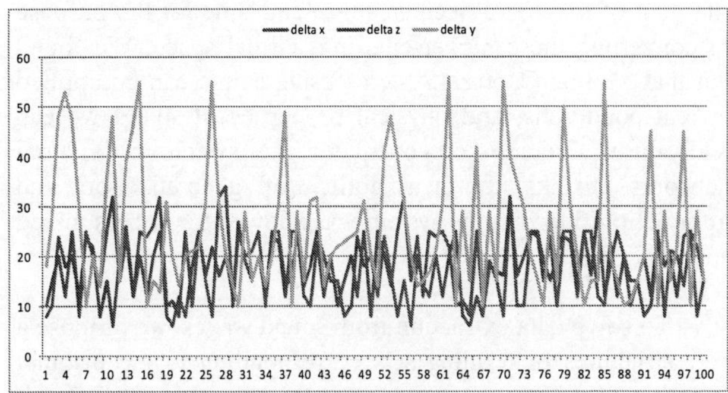

Figure 9: Measurement results - neural network error in cm (axes x: 100 test sequences). 3 transmitters' positions

3.4 Coordinates generation

In test phase, we used the adapted neural network for real data which were obtained from an audio sample. Of course it is necessary to normalize this data and because of it we determine the maximum distance at which the receiver (microphone) can occur. Distances are normalized to the interval <0, 1>.

Test set includes 100 patterns. Measurement results were shown in Fig. 9 (3 transmitters' positions) and Fig. 10 (5 transmitters' positions). Both experimental results are very similar. We are able to summarize them as follows:

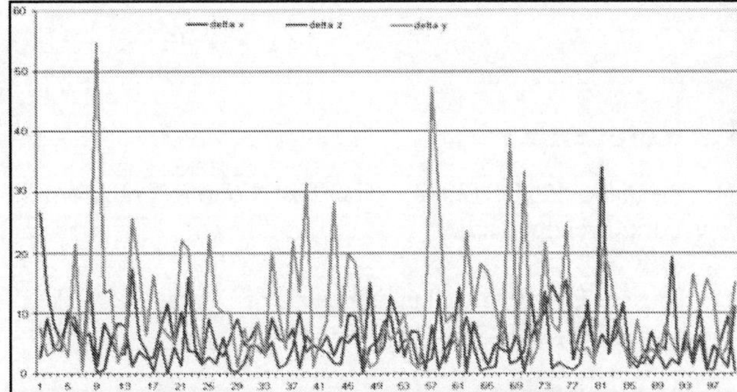

Figure 10: Measurement results - neural network error in cm (axes x: 100 test sequences). 5 transmitters' positions

- Calculating accuracy of *horizontal* coordinates (x, z) was, on average, 2,5 cm.

- Calculating accuracy of the *vertical* coordinate (y) was, on average, 5,5 cm. This reality was due to real disposition of transmitters, where the change about 1 cm in height indicated minimal changing of distance from transmitters. In the case that the vertical coordinate was close to zero, the network error was increased in the calculation.

4 Conclusion

The objective of the paper helps to outline the possibilities of using sound and its physical properties during shooting of moving objects in space and time for the purpose of converting these movements into virtual space. We found out that Motion Capture Systems using sound can be applied in real conditions, and physical properties of sound we can really use. Crucial component of the system are neural networks, thanks to their ability of generalization and information filtering, the system was allowed to process mixed and noisy data.

To solve data extraction from sound waves, we propose a new structures of training sets corresponding to the original structure that means it is used to separate all difficult recognizing patterns from the training data set, therefore the main emphasis of this paper is focused on the fact, how to properly design training set for given neural networks. This work deals with determining of receivers' positions in space and time. The proposed systems also solve specific moving objects. Here, the limiting factor is only a number of transmitters, the domain size and average acoustics properties in room. Number of receivers can be in this configuration theoretically unlimited, we have to provide sufficient computing power. We developed two models with 3 or 5 transmitters. Both models were compared and we received very similar experimental outcomes. As the vertical coordinate was close to zero, both models' errors were greater than in horizontal direction. For this reason, we are going to develop 3D MoCap system, which could be able to reduce inaccuracies in vertical direction too.

5 References

[1] Brigham, E. O. (2002). The Fast Fourier Transform. New York: Prentice-Hall.

[2] Fausett, L., (1994),: "Fundamentals of Neural Network". 1st ed. Prentice Hall, ISBN: 0-13-334186-0.

[3] Hazas, M., and Ward, A. (2002). A novel broadband ultrasonic location system. In International Conference on Ubiquitous Computing, 264–280.

[4] Hightower, J., and Borriello, G. (2001). Location systems for ubiquitous computing. Computer 34, 8 (Aug.), 57–66.

[5] Huber, D., M., Runstein, R., E. (2005) Modern Recording Techniques. Sixth edition, Focal Press. ISBN: 0240806255.

[6] Olson, E., Leonard, J., and Teller, S. (2006). Robust range only beacon localization. Journal of Oceanic Engineering 31, 4 (Oct.), 949–958.

[7] Priyantha, N., Chakraborty, A., and Balakrishnan, H. (2009). The cricket location-support system. In International Conference on Mobile Computing and Networking, 32–43.

[8] Vallidis, N. M. (2002). WHISPER: a spread spectrum approach to occlusion in acoustic tracking. PhD thesis, University of North Carolina at Chapel Hill.

[9] Randell, C., and Muller, H. L. (2001). Low cost indoor positioning system. In International Conference on Ubiquitous Computing, 42–48.

[10] Volná, E., Jarušek, R., Kotyrba, M., Janošek, M. and Kocian, V. (2011). Data extraction from sound waves towards neural network training set. In R. Matoušek (ed.): Proceedings of the 17th International Conference on Soft Computing, Mendel 2011, Brno, Czech Republic, pp. 177-184. ISBN 978-80-214-4302-0, ISSN 1803-3814.

[11] Volná, E., Jarušek, R., Kotyrba, M. and Rucký, D. (2013) „Dynamical Motion Capture System Involving via Neural Networks". In Banerjee, S. and Erçetin, Ş.Ş. (eds.) The proceedings of Symposium of Chaos, Complexity and Leadership, ICCLS2012 (Springer Complexity series) – in press.

[12] Ward, A., Jones, A., and Hopper, A. (1997). A new location technique for the active office. Personal Communications 4, 5 (Oct.), 42–47.

[13] Welch, G., and Foxlin, E. (2002). Motion tracking: no silver bullet, but a respectable arsenal. Computer Graphics and Applications 22, 6 (Nov./Dec.), 24–38.